EXEGETICAL DICTIONARY
OF THE
NEW
TESTAMENT

VOLUME 2

ἐξ – ὀψώνιον

edited by
Horst Balz and
Gerhard Schneider

WILLIAM B. EERDMANS PUBLISHING COMPANY
GRAND RAPIDS, MICHIGAN

Originally published as
Exegetisches Wörterbuch zum Neuen Testament
Band II, Lieferungen 1-11
Copyright © 1981 by
Verlag W. Kohlhammer GmbH, Stuttgart, Germany

English translation copyright © 1991 by
William B. Eerdmans Publishing Company
255 Jefferson Ave. SE, Grand Rapids, Michigan 49503
All rights reserved

Printed in the United States of America

Reprinted 2000

Library of Congress Cataloging-in-Publication Data

Exegetical dictionary of the New Testament.

   Translation of: Exegetisches Wörterbuch zum Neuen Testament.
   Includes bibliographical references.
   Contents: v. 1. Aarōn-Henōch — v. 2. Ex-Opsōnion.
   1. Bible. N.T. — Dictionaries — Greek.
2. Bible. N.T. — Criticism, interpretation, etc.
3. Greek language, Biblical — Dictionaries —
English. I. Balz, Horst Robert. II. Schneider, Gerhard, 1926-
BS2312.E913 1990   225.4'8'03   90-35682
ISBN 0-8028-2808-6 (v.2)

EXEGETICAL DICTIONARY

OF THE

NEW TESTAMENT

CONTENTS

EDITORS' FOREWORD

The first volume of the *Exegetisches Wörterbuch zum Neuen Testament (EWNT)* appeared in 1980. Thanks to the dependable cooperation of authors and publisher, the editorial work was able to move forward in such a way that the second and third German volumes appeared just two and three years after the first, bringing the work to completion with its treatment of the whole vocabulary of the New Testament. Our thanks are due not just to W. Kohlhammer Verlag, but especially to numerous colleagues, who did not shrink from the tiresome and time-consuming work on the articles in the dictionary. They have also contributed to the fact that *EWNT* promises to become a standard and complete resource for exegesis. Now, with the progress of the English-language edition, the work is beginning to reach an ever-widening audience.

The principles and goals set forth in the Foreword to the first volume have been maintained in all three volumes, above all in regard to the extent of the individual contributions. Reviews of the work have endorsed the intention of *EWNT* and the manner in which that intention has been carried out — and have pointed out the necessity of such a tool for students, church workers, and scholars. The reviews have been favorable especially with regard to the clarity and the informativeness of the articles, the extensive bibliographies, and the treatment of the whole vocabulary of the New Testament including all names and the most important textual variants. They have also mentioned positively the transliteration of all Greek keywords in the article headings.

This affirmation of our planning and of the execution of this project gives us secure hope that the *Exegetical Dictionary of the New Testament* will also prove itself in practical use.

Bochum, October 1981/November 1991

Horst Balz
Gerhard Schneider

Our special thanks go to the translators of this volume of the *Exegetical Dictionary of the New Testament*. James W. Thompson translated the material through the article on μεταμορφόω. John W. Medendorp translated the balance of the articles, beginning with μετάνοια/μετανοέω. Our thanks also go to Professors Balz and Schneider for updating the bibliographies in this volume to include works published through 1990.

The Publishers

INTRODUCTION

The *Exegetical Dictionary of the New Testament (EDNT)* is a guide to the forms, meaning, and usage of every word in the text of the third edition of *The Greek New Testament (UBSGNT)*, which is equivalent to the text of the twenty-sixth edition of the Nestle-Aland *Novum Testamentum Graece (NTG)* and the text followed in the *Vollständige Konkordanz zum griechischen Neuen Testament (VKGNT;* see abbreviations list for full publication data on these works). Words in the most important textual variants in *UBSGNT* and *NTG* are also included, and the authors of *EDNT* articles have been granted the freedom to depart from the basic text of these two editions where they have deemed it appropriate.

The *heading* of each *EDNT* article, along with identifying the word to be discussed, supplies the following information:

- The gender of common nouns is identified by inclusion of the nominative singular article.
- The declension of nouns is identified by inclusion of the genitive singular ending.
- Whether an adjective has one, two, or three sets of endings (corresponding to the three genders) is specified by a boldface number.[1]
- The word is transliterated.
- The meaning of the word is indicated by one or more English translations (sometimes divided according to verb voice or adjectival or substantival use of an adjective).[2]
- An asterisk (*) appears at the end of the heading line if all New Testament occurrences of a word are at least mentioned in the body of the article.

A group of words related by form and meaning is sometimes treated in one article with multiple heading lines. In that case, a cross reference (→) is placed at each word's normal alphabetical location.

> καλέω   *kaleō*   call, invite; appoint
> κλῆσις, εως, ἡ   *klēsis*   call (noun), summons
> κλητός, 3   *klētos*   called
>
> κλῆσις, εως, ἡ   *klēsis*   call (noun), summons
> → καλέω.
>
> κλητός, 3   *klētos*   called
> → καλέω.

The *body* of a shorter article normally mentions all New Testament occurrences of a word, grouped, if appropriate, according to different usages and different kinds of contexts in which the word is found, and discusses the more interesting, difficult, or controversial occurrences. Shorter articles also often include

---

1. **1:** third declension adjectives in which the three genders have the same forms; **2:** adjectives in which masculine and feminine forms are identical, including second declension adjectives in -ος, -ον and third declension adjectives in -ης, -ες and -ων, -ον; **3:** adjectives in which the three genders have different forms, including first and second declension adjectives in -ος, -η/-α, -ον and -ούς, -ῆ/-ᾶ, -οῦν, first and third declension adjectives in -υς, -εια, -υ and those formed like πᾶς, πᾶσα, πᾶν, and a few adjectives which combine declensional patterns in ways not listed here.

2. The headings of articles are usually not a complete guide to meaning, since in some cases only a selection of documented meanings is included and since the bodies of articles discuss the meanings of words as they appear in context in different usages.

some bibliography listing discussions in reference works, journal articles, monographs, and commentaries of New Testament usage of the word and of passages in which the word plays a decisive role.

More is provided for more significant words—actually many of the words in the New Testament, including both words of great frequency and words that express significant New Testament concepts. *Longer articles* are usually divided into numbered sections, sometimes with lettered subsections, and often include an outline listing the sections and subsections. An extended bibliography, which emphasizes recent works, usually precedes the body of a longer article.

Κηφᾶς, ᾶ *Kēphas* Cephas*

1. Occurrences in the NT — 2. Origin and meaning — 3. John 1:42 — 4. 1 Cor 15:5 — 5. Paul (1 Corinthians, Galatians)

Lit.: C. K. BARRETT, "Cephas and Corinth," *idem, Essays on Paul* (1982) 28-39. — R. E. BROWN, K. P. DONFRIED, and J. REUMANN, ed., *Peter in the NT* (1973). — O. CULLMANN, *Peter: Disciple–Apostle–Martyr* (²1962). — *idem, TDNT* 95-112. — J. A. FITZMYER, "Aramaic *Kepha'* and Peter's Name," FS Black (1979) 121-32. — P. LAMPE, "Das Spiel mit dem Petrusnamen–Matt. XVI.18," *NTS* 25 (1978/79) 227-45. — R. PESCH, *Simon-Petrus. Geschichte und geschichtliche Bedeutung des ersten Jüngers Jesu Christi* (1980). — For further bibliography → πέτρα, → Πέτρος, see Brown, et al., 169-77; *TWNT* X, 1230-32.

The body of a longer article generally proceeds from a statistical summary of the word's New Testament occurrences, through discussion of the word's range of meanings and of the variety of usages in which it is found in the New Testament, to treatment of the exegetical and theological significance of the word in the different blocks of New Testament literature. Included where relevant is treatment of the background of New Testament usage of the word in classical Greek, the Septuagint, post-Old Testament Judaism, and Hellenistic literature. For names of persons and places, consideration is given to the historical background of the person's or place's significance in the New Testament. Where one of these longer *EDNT* articles touches on matters of significant disagreement among scholars, the author of the article summarizes and enters into the discussion.

Both shorter and longer articles include cross-references (→) to other articles where further treatment of words or exegetical problems under discussion are touched on. An English index will appear in Volume 3.

CONTRIBUTORS

Franz Annen, Chur, Switzerland
Horst Balz, Bochum, Germany
Gerhard Barth, Wuppertal, Germany
† Hans-Werner Bartsch, Frankfurt am Main,
   Germany
Johannes B. Bauer, Graz, Austria
Jörg Baumgarten, Cologne, Germany
Wolfgang Beilner, Salzburg, Austria
Hans Dieter Betz, Chicago, USA
Otto Betz, Tübingen, Germany
Johannes Beutler, Frankfurt am Main, Germany
Werner Bieder, Basel, Switzerland
Udo Borse, Bonn, Germany
Gijs Bouwman, Tilburg, Netherlands
Ingo Broer, Siegen, Germany
Jan-Adolf Bühner, Tübingen, Germany
Rolf Dabelstein, Uetersen, Germany
Gerhard Dautzenberg, Gießen, Germany
Jost Eckert, Trier, Germany
Winfried Elliger, Tübingen, Germany
Herbert Fendrich, Essen, Germany
Peter Fiedler, Freiburg, Germany
Gottfried Fitzer, Vienna, Austria
Joseph Fitzmyer, Washington, D.C., USA
Hubert Frankemölle, Paderborn, Germany
Johannes Friedrich, Jerusalem, Israel
Heinz Giesen, Hennef, Germany
Horst Goldstein, Lilienthal, Germany
Wolfgang Hackenberg, Witten, Germany
Josef Hainz, Frankfurt am Main, Germany
Lars Hartman, Uppsala, Sweden
Günter Haufe, Greifswald, Germany
Roman Heiligenthal, Freiburg, Germany
Otfried Hofius, Tübingen, Germany
Harm W. Hollander, Haarlem, Netherlands
Traugott Holtz, Halle, Germany
Axel Horstmann, Hamburg, Germany
Hans Hübner, Göttingen, Germany
Ulrich Kellermann, Mülheim, Germany
Karl Kertelge, Münster, Germany
Walter Kirchschläger, Lucerne, Switzerland

Heribert Kleine, Bochum, Germany
Wilhelm Köhler, Wuppertal, Germany
†Helmut Krämer, Bethel, Germany
Heinrich Kraft, Kiel, Germany
Reinhard Kratz, Bensheim, Germany
Jacob Kremer, Vienna, Austria
Armin Kretzer, Würzburg, Germany
Horst Kuhli, Königstein, Germany
Heinz-Wolfgang Kuhn, Munich, Germany
Jan Lambrecht, Louvain, Belgium
Peter Lampe, Richmond, Virginia, USA
Edvin Larsson, Oslo, Norway
Michael Lattke, Brisbane, Australia
Simon Légasse, Toulouse, France
Ragnar Leivestad, Aas, Norway
Meinrad Limbeck, Stuttgart, Germany
Robert Mahoney, Saarbrücken, Germany
Otto Merk, Erlangen, Germany
Helmut Merkel, Osnabrück, Germany
Helmut Merklein, Bonn, Germany
Otto Michel, Tübingen, Germany
Hans-Jürgen van der Minde, Göttingen, Germany
Christoph Müller, Bern, Switzerland
Paul-Gerd Müller, Trier, Germany
Gottfried Nebe, Bochum, Germany
Poul Nepper-Christensen, Aarhus, Denmark
Kurt Niederwimmer, Vienna, Austria
Johannes M. Nützel, Münster, Germany
Peter von der Osten-Sacken, Berlin, Germany
Hermann Patsch, Munich, Germany
Henning Paulsen, Hamburg, Germany
Sigfred Pedersen, Rønde, Denmark
†Carl-Heinz Peisker, Mühlheim, Germany
Rolf Peppermüller, Bonn, Germany
Rudolf Pesch, Munich, Germany
Wilhelm Pesch, Mainz, Germany
Gerd Petzke, Kelkheim, Germany
Josef Pfammatter, Chur, Switzerland
Eckhard Plümacher, Berlin, Germany
Wolfgang Pöhlmann, Lüneburg, Germany
Wiard Popkes, Hamburg, Germany

CONTRIBUTORS

Karl-Heinz Pridik, Wuppertal, Germany
Walter Radl, Augsburg, Germany
Mathias Rissi, Stonington, Maine, USA
Hubert Ritt, Regensburg, Germany
Hans-Joachim Ritz, Schwelm, Germany
Joachim Rohde, Berlin, Germany
Jürgen Roloff, Erlangen, Germany
Eugen Ruckstuhl, Lucerne, Switzerland
Alexander Sand, Bochum, Germany
Dieter Sänger, Flensburg, Germany
Wolfgang Schenk, Eppstein, Germany
Gerhard Schneider, Bochum, Germany
Ulrich Schoenborn, Wetter-Mellnau, Germany
Luise Schottroff, Kassel, Germany
Tim Schramm, Hamburg, Germany
Friedrich Schröger, Passau, Germany

Benedikt Schwank, Beuron, Germany, and
    Jerusalem, Israel
Georg Strecker, Göttingen, Germany
August Strobel, Jerusalem, Israel
Hartwig Thyen, Heidelberg, Germany
Wolfgang Trilling, Leipzig, Germany
Peter Trummer, Graz, Austria
Franz Georg Untergassmair, Osnabrück, Germany
Martin Völkel, Dortmund, Germany
Nikolaus Walter, Jena, Germany
Joachim Wanke, Erfurt, Germany
Peter Weigandt, Kassel, Germany
Alfons Weiser, Vallendar, Germany
Michael Wolter, Bayreuth, Germany
Hans-Theo Wrege, Schleswig, Germany
Dieter Zeller, Mainz, Germany
Josef Zmijewski, Fulda, Germany

Unsigned articles have been written by the editors, those on pp. 1-21, 94-214, 283 (κέρας)-354, and 446 (μύρον)-533 by Gerhard Schneider and those on pp. 23-93, 214-283 (κεράννυμι), 356-446 (μυρίος), and 534-555 by Horst Balz.

ABBREVIATIONS

1. The Bible and Other Ancient Literature

a. Old Testament

Gen	Genesis	Cant	Canticles
Exod	Exodus	Isa	Isaiah
Lev	Leviticus	Jer	Jeremiah
Num	Numbers	Lam	Lamentations
Deut	Deuteronomy	Ezek	Ezekiel
Josh	Joshua	Dan	Daniel
Judg	Judges	Hos	Hosea
Ruth	Ruth	Joel	Joel
1–2 Sam	1–2 Samuel	Amos	Amos
1–2 Kgs	1–2 Kings	Obad	Obadiah
1–2 Chr	1–2 Chronicles	Jonah	Jonah
Ezra	Ezra	Mic	Micah
Neh	Nehemiah	Nah	Nahum
Esth	Esther	Hab	Habakkuk
Job	Job	Zeph	Zephaniah
Ps(s)	Psalm(s)	Hag	Haggai
Prov	Proverbs	Zech	Zechariah
Eccl	Ecclesiastes	Mal	Malachi

b. Apocrypha and Septuagint

1–4 Kgdms	1–4 Kingdoms	1–4 Macc	1–4 Maccabees
Add Esth	Additions to Esther	Pr Azar	Prayer of Azariah
Bar	Baruch	Pr Man	Prayer of Manasseh
Bel	Bel and the Dragon	Sir	Sirach (Ecclesiasticus)
1–2 Esdr	1–2 Esdras	Sus	Susanna
4 Ezra	4 Ezra	Tob	Tobit
Jdt	Judith	Wis	Wisdom of Solomon
Ep Jer	Epistle of Jeremiah		

c. New Testament

Matt	Matthew	1–2 Thess	1–2 Thessalonians
Mark	Mark	1–2 Tim	1–2 Timothy
Luke	Luke	Titus	Titus
John	John	Phlm	Philemon
Acts	Acts	Heb	Hebrews
Rom	Romans	Jas	James
1–2 Cor	1–2 Corinthians	1–2 Pet	1–2 Peter
Gal	Galatians	1–3 John	1–3 John
Eph	Ephesians	Jude	Jude
Phil	Philippians	Rev	Revelation
Col	Colossians		

ABBREVIATIONS

d. Pseudepigrapha and Early Church Writings

Acts Pet.	Acts of Peter	Eph.	Ephesians
Acts Pet. and Andr.	Acts of Peter and Andrew	Magn.	Magnesians
Acts Phil.	Acts of Philip	Phld.	Philadelphians
Acts Thom.	Acts of Thomas	Pol.	Polycarp
Apoc. Abr.	Apocalypse of Abraham	Rom.	Romans
Apoc. Mos.	Apocalypse of Moses	Smyrn.	Smyrnaeans
Apoc. Pet.	Apocalypse of Peter	Trall.	Trallians
Asc. Isa.	Ascension of Isaiah	Irenaeus	
Augustine		Haer.	Adversus Haereses
Civ. D.	De Civitate Dei	Jos. As.	Joseph and Aseneth
Con. Adult.	De Coniugiis Adulterinis	Jub.	Jubilees
2–3 Bar.	Syriac, Greek Apocalypse of Baruch	Justin	
Barn.	Barnabas	Apol.	Apologia
Bib. Ant.	Pseudo-Philo Biblical Antiquities	Dial.	Dialogue with Trypho
1–2 Clem.	1–2 Clement	Mart. Isa.	Martyrdom of Isaiah
Clement of Alexandria		Mart. Pol.	Martyrdom of Polycarp
Paed.	Paedagogus	Odes Sol.	Odes of Solomon
Prot.	Protrepticus	Origen	
Quis Div. Salv.	Quis Dives Salvetur	Cels.	Contra Celsum
Strom.	Stromata	Pol.	Polycarp
Did.	Didache	Phil.	Epistle to the Philippians
Diog.	Epistle to Diognetus	Ps.-Clem. Hom.	Pseudo-Clementine Homilies
1–3 Enoch	Ethiopic, Slavonic, Hebrew Enoch	Ps.-Clem. Rec.	Pseudo-Clementine Recognitions
Ep. Arist.	Epistle of Aristeas	Pss. Sol.	Psalms of Solomon
Epiphanius		Sib. Or.	Sibylline Oracles
Anc.	Ancoratus	T. Abr.	Testament of Abraham
Haer.	Haereses	T. Job	Testament of Job
Eusebius		T. Mos.	Testament ("Assumption") of Moses
HE	Historia Ecclesiastica	T. Sol.	Testament of Solomon
Gk. Apoc. Ezra	Greek Apocalypse of Ezra	T. 12 Patr.	Testaments of the Twelve Patriarchs
Gos. Eb.	Gospel of the Ebionites	T. Ash.	Testament of Asher
Gos. Eg.	Gospel of the Egyptians	T. Benj.	Testament of Benjamin
Gos. Heb.	Gospel of the Hebrews	T. Dan	Testament of Dan
Gos. Mary	Gospel of Mary	T. Gad	Testament of Gad
Gos. Naass.	Gospel of the Naassenes	T. Iss.	Testament of Issachar
Gos. Naz.	Gospel of the Nazarenes	T. Jos.	Testament of Joseph
Gos. Pet.	Gospel of Peter	T. Jud.	Testament of Judah
Gos. Thom.	Gospel of Thomas	T. Levi	Testament of Levi
Gos. Truth	Gospel of Truth	T. Naph.	Testament of Naphtali
Herm.	Shepherd of Hermas	T. Reu.	Testament of Reuben
Man.	Mandates	T. Sim.	Testament of Simeon
Sim.	Similitudes	T. Zeb.	Testament of Zebulun
Vis.	Visions	Tertullian	
Hippolytus		Apol.	Apologia
Haer.	Refutatio Omnium Haeresium	Praescr. Haer.	De Praescriptione Haereticorum
Philos.	Philosophumena	Vit. Proph.	Lives of the Prophets (Vitae Prophetarum)
Ign.	Ignatius		

e. Qumran and Related Texts

The standard abbreviations are used (see J. A. Fitzmyer, *The Dead Sea Scrolls: Major Publications and Tools for Study* [Sources for Biblical Study 8, ²1977]).

f. Rabbinic Literature

m.	Mishnah	b.	Babylonian Talmud
t.	Tosefta	y.	Jerusalem Talmud

'Abot	'Abot	Nazir	Nazir
'Arak.	'Arakin	Ned.	Nedarim
'Abod. Zar.	'Aboda Zara	Neg.	Nega'im
B. Bat.	Baba Batra	Nez.	Neziqin
Bek.	Bekorot	Nid.	Niddah
Ber.	Berakot	Ohol.	Oholot
Beṣa	Beṣa (= Yom Ṭob)	'Or.	'Orla
Bik.	Bikkurim	Para	Para
B. Meṣ.	Baba Meṣi'a	Pe'a	Pe'a
B. Qam.	Baba Qamma	Pesaḥ.	Pesaḥim
Dem.	Demai	Qinnim	Qinnim
'Erub.	'Erubin	Qidd.	Qiddušin
'Ed.	'Eduyyot	Qod.	Qodašin
Giṭ.	Giṭṭin	Roš Haš.	Roš Haššana
Ḥag.	Ḥagiga	Sanh.	Sanhedrin
Ḥal.	Ḥalla	Šabb.	Šabbat
Hor.	Horayot	Šeb.	Šebi'it
Ḥul.	Ḥullin	Šebu.	Šebu'ot
Kelim	Kelim	Šeqal.	Šeqalim
Ker.	Keritot	Soṭa	Soṭa
Ketub.	Ketubot	Sukk.	Sukka
Kil.	Kil'ayim	Ta'an.	Ta'anit
Ma'aś.	Ma'aśerot	Tamid	Tamid
Mak.	Makkot	Tem.	Temura
Makš.	Makširin (= Mašqin)	Ter.	Terumot
Meg.	Megilla	Ṭohar.	Ṭoharot
Me'il.	Me'ila	Ṭ. Yom	Ṭebul Yom
Menaḥ.	Menaḥot	'Uq.	'Uqṣin
Mid.	Middot	Yad.	Yadayim
Miqw.	Miqwa'ot	Yebam.	Yebamot
Mo'ed	Mo'ed	Yoma	Yoma (= Kippurim)
Mo'ed Qaṭ.	Mo'ed Qaṭan	Zabim	Zabim
Ma'aś. Š.	Ma'aśer Šeni	Zebaḥ.	Zebaḥim
Našim	Našim	Zer.	Zera'im

Bar.	Baraita	Pesiq. R.	Pesiqta Rabbati
Mek.	Mekilta	Pesiq. Rab. Kah.	Pesiqta de Rab Kahana
Midr. Qoh.	Midrash Qoheleth	Rab.	Rabbah
Pesiq.	Pesiqta		

g. Targums

Tg. Esth I, II	First or Second Targum of Esther	Tg. Onq.	Targum Onqelos

h. Other Ancient Authors and Writings

Aelian		Aristophanes	
NA	De Natura Animalium	Av.	Aves
Aeschylus		Lys.	Lysistrata
A.	Agamemnon	Ra.	Ranae
Ch.	Choephori	Aristotle	
Pers.	Persae	Cael.	De Caelo
Pr.	Prometheus Vinctus	Cat.	Categoriae
Th.	Septem contra Thebas	EN	Ethica Nicomachea
Appian		Fr.	Fragmenta
BC	Bella Civilia	GA	De Generatione Animalium
Rom. Hist.	Romanae Historiae	Metaph.	Metaphysica
Apuleius		Pol.	Politica
Met.	Metamorphoses	Rh.	Rhetorica
		Sens.	De Sensu

ABBREVIATIONS

Arrian
    An.   *Anabasis*
Cicero
    Verr.   *In Verrem*
    Corp. Herm.   *Corpus Hermeticum*
Demosthenes
    Or.   *Orationes*
Epictetus
    Diss.   *Dissertationes*
    Ench.   *Enchiridion*
Euripides
    Ba.   *Bacchae*
    El.   *Electra*
    Fr.   *Fragmenta*
    Hipp.   *Hippolytus*
    Ion   *Ion*
    Ph.   *Phoenissae*
    Tr.   *Trodes*
Hesiod
    Op.   *Opera et Dies*
    Th.   *Theogonia*
Homer
    Il.   *Iliad*
    Od.   *Odyssey*
Horace
    Ep.   *Epistulae*
    Sat.   *Satirae*
Iamblichus
    VP   *De Vita Pythagorica*
Josephus
    Ant.   *Antiquitates Judaicae*
    Ap.   *Contra Apionem*
    B.J.   *De Bello Judaico*
    Vita   *Vita Josephi*
Lucian
    Abd.   *Abdicatus*
    Am.   *Amores*
    Apol.   *Apologia*
    DMeretr.   *Dialogi Meretricii*
    Herm.   *Hermotimus*
    JTr.   *Juppiter Tragoedus*
    Tim.   *Timon*
    Tox.   *Toxaris*
Nonnus
    D.   *Dionysiaca*
Philo
    Abr.   *De Abrahamo*
    Aet.   *De Aeternitate Mundi*
    Agr.   *De Agricultura*
    All.   *Legum Allegoriae*
    Cher.   *De Cherubim*
    Conf.   *De Confusione Linguarum*
    Congr.   *De Congressu Eruditionis Gratia*
    Decal.   *De Decalogo*
    Det.   *Quod Deterius Potiori insidiari soleat*
    Ebr.   *De Ebrietate*
    Exsec.   *Exsecrationibus*
    Flacc.   *In Flaccum*
    Fug.   *De Fuga et Inventione*
    Gig.   *De Gigantibus*
    Her.   *Quis Rerum Divinarum Heres Sit*
    Imm.   *Quod Deus Sit Immutabilis*

    Jos.   *De Josepho*
    Leg. Gai.   *Legatio ad Gaium*
    Migr.   *De Migratione Abrahami*
    Mut.   *De Mutatione Nominum*
    Omn. Prob.   *Quod Omnis Probus Liber Sit*
      Lib.
    Op.   *De Opificione Mundi*
    Plant.   *De Plantatione*
    Praem.   *De Praemiis et Poenis*
    Post.   *De Posteritate Caini*
    Sacr.   *De Sacrificiis Abelis et Caini*
    Sobr.   *De Sobrietate*
    Som.   *De Somniis*
    Spec. Leg.   *De Specialibus Legibus*
    Virt.   *De Virtutibus*
    Vit. Mos.   *De Vita Mosis*
Philostratus
    VA   *Vita Apollonii*
Pindar
    I.   *Isthmian Odes*
    P.   *Pythia*
Plato
    Ap.   *Apologia*
    Cra.   *Cratylus*
    Criti.   *Critias*
    Ep.   *Epistulae*
    Euth.   *Euthydemus*
    Euthphr.   *Euthyphro*
    Grg.   *Gorgias*
    La.   *Laches*
    Lg.   *Leges*
    Men.   *Meno*
    Phd.   *Phaedo*
    Phdr.   *Phaedrus*
    Phlb.   *Philebus*
    Plt.   *Politicus*
    Prt.   *Protagoras*
    R.   *Republic*
    Smp.   *Symposium*
    Tht.   *Theaetetus*
    Ti.   *Timaeus*
Pliny
    HN   *Historia Naturalis*
Plutarch
    Alc.   *Alcibiades*
    Alex. Fort.   *De Alexandri Fortuna Aut Virtute*
    Ant.   *Antonius*
    Caes.   *Caesar*
    Cons. ad Apoll.   *Consolatio ad Apollonium*
    De Cup. Div.   *De Cupiditate Divitiarum*
    Demetr.   *Demetrius*
    Fab.   *Fabius Maximus*
    Is.   *Isis and Osiris*
    Luc.   *Lucullus*
    Lyc.   *Lycurgus*
    Num.   *Numa*
    Pomp.   *Pompeius*
    Praec. Con.   *Praecepta Coniugalia*
    Quaest. Conv.   *Quaestiones Convivales*
    Quaest. Rom.   *Quaestiones Romanae*
    Sol.   *Solon*
    Thes.   *Theseus*

Ps.-Plato	Pseudo-Plato	Suetonius	
Ax.	*Axiochus*	*Caes.*	*De Vita Caesarum*
Seneca		Tacitus	
Ep.	*Epistulae Morales*	*Ann.*	*Annales*
Prov.	*De Providentia*	*Hist.*	*Historiae*
QN	*Quaestiones Naturales*	Virgil	
Sophocles		*Aen.*	*Aeneid*
Aj.	*Ajax*	Xenophon	
Ant.	*Antigone*	*Ages.*	*Agesilaus*
El.	*Electra*	*An.*	*Anabasis*
OC	*Oedipus Coloneus*	*Cyr.*	*Institutio Cyri (Cyropaedia)*
OT	*Oedipus Tyrannus*	*HG*	*Historia Graeca (Hellenica)*
Ph.	*Philoctetes*	*Hier.*	*Hiero*
Tr.	*Trachiniae*	*Mem.*	*Memorabilia*
		Oec.	*Oeconomicus*

i. Inscriptions, Fragments, Papyri, and Anthologies

ÄgU	Ägyptische Urkunden aus den Staatlichen Museen zu Berlin, Griechische Urkunden I-XI (1895-1970)
CIG	*Corpus Inscriptionum Graecarum* I-IV (ed. A. Boeckh, et al.; 1828-77)
CIJ	*Corpus Inscriptionum Judaicarum* I-II (1936, 1952)
CIL	*Corpus Inscriptionum Latinarum* I-XVI (1862-1943, ²1893-)
CPJ	*Corpus Papyrorum Judaicarum* (1957ff.)
IG	*Inscriptiones Graecae* (1873-1939)
NHC	*Nag Hammadi Codices*
OGIS	*Orientis Graeci Inscriptiones Selectae* I-II (ed. W. Dittenberger; 1903, 1905, reprint 1960)
Pap. Fayûm	*Fayûm Towns and the Papyri*, ed. B. P. Grenfell, A. S. Hunt, and D. Hogarth (1900)
Pap. London	*Greek Papyri in the British Museum* I-II (ed. F. G. Kenyon; 1893, 1898), III (ed. F. G. Kenyon and H. I. Bell; 1907), IV-V (ed. H. I. Bell; 1910, 1917)
Pap. Mich.	*Papyri in the University of Michigan Collection* I-VIII (1931-51)
Pap. Oxy.	*The Oxyrhynchus Papyri* I-XLI (ed. B. P. Grenfell, A. S. Hunt, et al.; 1898-1972)
Pap. Ryl.	*Catalogue of the Greek Papyri in the John Rylands Library at Manchester* I-IV (1911-52)
Pap. Tebt.	*The Tebtunis Papyri* I-III (ed. B. P. Grenfell, A. S. Hunt, et al.; 1902-38)
PGM	*Papyri Graecae Magicae. Die griechischen Zauberpapyri* (ed. K. Preisendanz, et al.; ²1973, 1974)
Preisigke, *Sammelbuch*	F. Preisigke, F. Bilabel, and E. Kiessling, *Sammelbuch griechischer Urkunden aus Ägypten* I-XI (1915-73)
SIG	*Sylloge Inscriptionum Graecarum* I-IV (ed. W. Dittenberger; ³1915-24, reprinted 1960)

2. Modern Writings

Commentaries on biblical books are identified by the abbreviations for the names of the biblical books (p. xi above) in italics.

AAWLM.G	Abhandlungen der Akademie der Wissenschaften und der Literatur in Mainz. Geistes- und sozialwissenschaftliche Klasse
AB	Anchor Bible
ABAW	Abhandlungen der bayerischen Akademie der Wissenschaften
Abel, *Géographie*	F.-M. Abel, *Géographie de la Palestine* I-II (1933-38)
Abel, *Grammaire*	F.-M. Abel, *Grammaire du Grec biblique* (1927)
Abel, *Histoire*	F.-M. Abel, *Histoire de la Palestine depuis la conquête d'Alexandre jusqu'à l'invasion arabe* I-II (1952)
ABR	*Australian Biblical Review*
AJA	*American Journal of Archaeology*
ALBO	Analecta Lovaniensia Biblica et Orientalia
ALUOS	*Annual of Leeds University Oriental Society*
AnBib	Analecta Biblica
ANRW	*Aufstieg und Niedergang der römischen Welt*
ANVAO.HF	Avhandlinger i norske videnskaps-akademie i Oslo. Historisk-filosofisk klasse
ARW	*Archiv für Religionswissenschaft*
AsSeign	*Assemblées du Seigneur*
ASNU	Acta seminarii Neotestamentici Upsaliensis

ABBREVIATIONS

ASTI	*Annual of the Swedish Theological Institute*
ATANT	Abhandlungen zur Theologie des Alten und Neuen Testaments
ATR	*Anglican Theological Review*
AV	Authorized (King James) Version
AzT	Arbeiten zur Theologie
BA	*Biblical Archaeologist*
BAGD	W. Bauer, W. F. Arndt, F. W. Gingrich, and F. Danker, *A Greek-English Lexicon of the NT and Other Early Christian Literature* (²1979)
BBB	Bonner biblische Beiträge
BDF	F. Blass, A. Debrunner, and R. W. Funk, *A Greek Grammar of the NT and Other Early Christian Literature* (1961)
Benoit, *Exégèse* I-III	P. Benoit, *Exégèse et Théologie* I-III (1961-68)
BeO	*Bibbia e oriente*
Beginnings	*The Beginnings of Christianity*, Part I: *The Acts of the Apostles* (ed. F. J. Foakes-Jackson and K. Lake; 1920-33)
BETL	Bibliotheca ephemeridum theologicarum Lovaniensium
BEvT	Beiträge zur evangelischen Theologie
Beyer, *Syntax*	K. Beyer, *Semitische Syntax im NT* I/1 (1962)
BFCT	Beiträge zur Förderung christlicher Theologie
BHH	*Biblisch-historisches Handwörterbuch* I-III (single pagination; ed. B. Reicke and L. Rost; 1962-66)
BHT	Beiträge zur Historischen Theologie
Bib	*Biblica*
BibLeb	*Bibel und Leben*
BibS(N)	Biblische Studien (Neukirchen)
Billerbeck	(H. Strack and) P. Billerbeck, *Kommentar zum NT aus Talmud und Midrasch* I-IV (1922-28)
BK	*Bibel und Kirche*
BKAT	Biblischer Kommentar: Altes Testament
BL	*Bibel-Lexikon*, ed. H. Haag (²1968)
Black, *Approach*	M. Black, *An Aramaic Approach to the Gospels and Acts* (³1967)
BNTC	Black's NT Commentaries
Bornkamm, *Aufsätze*	G. Bornkamm, *Gesammelte Aufsätze*. I: *Das Ende des Gesetzes. Paulusstudien*; II: *Studien zu Antike und Urchristentum*; III-IV: *Geschichte und Glauben* (1952-1971)
Bousset/Gressmann	W. Bousset, *Die Religion des Judentums im späthellenistischen Zeitalter* (ed. H. Gressmann; ⁴1966 = ³1926)
Braun, *Qumran*	H. Braun, *Qumran und das NT* I-II (1966)
BRL	*Biblisches Reallexikon* (ed. K. Galling; ²1977)
BSac	*Bibliotheca Sacra*
BT	*The Bible Translator*
BTB	*Biblical Theology Bulletin*
BTS	*Bible et Terre Sainte*
BU	Biblische Untersuchungen
Bultmann, *Glauben*	R. Bultmann, *Glauben und Verstehen. Gesammelte Aufsätze* I-IV (1933-65)
Bultmann, *History*	R. Bultmann, *History of the Synoptic Tradition* (1963)
Bultmann, *Theology*	R. Bultmann, *Theology of the NT* I-II (1951, 1955)
BWANT	Beiträge zur Wissenschaft vom Alten und Neuen Testament
ByZ	*Byzantinische Zeitschrift*
BZ	*Biblische Zeitschrift*
BZAW	Beihefte zur *Zeitschrift für die alttestamentliche Wissenschaft*
BZNW	Beihefte zur *Zeitschrift für die neutestamentliche Wissenschaft*
CB	*Cultura bíblica*
CBG	*Collationes Brugenses et Gandavenses*
CB.NT	Coniectanea biblica, NT Series
CBQ	*Catholic Biblical Quarterly*
Chantraine, *Dictionnaire*	P. Chantraine, *Dictionnaire étymologique de la langue grecque* (1968-)
Colloquium	*Colloquium: Australia and New Zealand Theological Review*
Compendia	Compendia Rerum Judaicarum ad Novum Testamentum
Conzelmann, *Theology*	H. Conzelmann, *An Outline of the Theology of the NT* (1969)
ConNT	Coniectanea neotestamentica
Cremer/Kögel	H. Cremer and J. Kögel, *Biblisch-theologisches Wörterbuch des neutestamentlichen Griechisch* (¹¹1923)
CTM	Calwer Theologische Monographien
CurTM	*Currents in Theology and Mission*

DACL	Dictionnaire d'archéologie chrétienne et de liturgie I-XV (ed. Cabrol, Lelercq, et al.; 1903-53)
Dalman, *Arbeit*	G. Dalman, *Arbeit und Sitte in Palästina* I-VII (1928-42, reprinted 1964)
Dalman, *Worte*	G. Dalman, *Die Worte Jesu* ([2]1930)
DB	*Dictionnaire de la Bible* I-IV (ed. F. Vigoroux; 1895-1912)
DBSup	*Dictionnaire de la Bible, Supplément* (1928-)
DBT	*Dictionary of Biblical Theology* (ed. X. Léon-Dufour; 1967, [2]1972)
Deissmann, *Light*	A. Deissmann, *Light from the Ancient East* ([2]1927)
Dibelius, *Botschaft*	M. Dibelius, *Botschaft und Geschichte. Gesammelte Studien* I-II (1953, 1956)
Dibelius, *Tradition*	M. Dibelius, *From Tradition to Gospel* (n.d.)
Diels, *Fragmente*	H. Diels and W. Kranz, *Die Fragmente der Vorsokratiker* ([11]1964)
DJD	Discoveries in the Judean Desert
DNTT	*New International Dictionary of NT Theology* I-III (ed. C. Brown; 1975-78)
DSp	*Dictionnaire de spiritualité, ascétique et mystique* (1932ff.)
DTh	*Deutsche Theologie*
Dupont, *Béatitudes*	J. Dupont, *Les Béatitudes* I-III (1969, 1973)
EAEHL	*Encyclopedia of Archaeological Excavations in the Holy Land* I-IV (ed. M. Avi-Yonah and E. Stern; 1975-78)
EBD	*Eerdmans Bible Dictionary* (ed. A. Myers; 1987)
ÉBib	Études Bibliques
EdF	Erträge der Forschung
EE	*Estudios Ecclesiasticos*
EHS	Europäische Hochschulschriften
Eichrodt, *Theology*	W. Eichrodt, *Theology of the OT* I-II (1961, 1967)
EKKNT	Evangelisch-katholischer Kommentar zum NT
EKKNT (V)	EKKNT Vorarbeiten
EKL	*Evangelisches Kirchenlexikon* Iff. (ed. E. Fahlbusch; [2]1961ff.)
EL	*Ephemerides Liturgicae*
EncJud	*Encyclopaedia Judaica* I-XVI (1971-72)
EPM	*Evangelische Predigtmeditationen*
ERE	*Encyclopedia of Religion and Ethics* I-XII (ed. J. Hastings; 1908-26)
ErJb	*Eranos-Jahrbuch*
EstBib	*Estudios biblicos*
EstFr	*Estudios Franciscanos*
ETL	*Ephemerides theologicae Lovanienses*
ETS	Erfurter theologische Schriften
ETSt	Erfurter theologische Studien
EuA	*Erbe und Auftrag*
EvQ	*Evangelical Quarterly*
EvT	*Evangelische Theologie*
ExpTim	*Expository Times*
EWG	J. B. Hofmann, *Etymologisches Wörterbuch des Griechischen* (reprinted 1950)
FARG	Forschungen zur Anthropologie und Religionsgeschichte
Frisk, *Wörterbuch*	H. Frisk, *Griechisches etymologisches Wörterbuch* I-III (1960-72)
FRLANT	Forschungen zur Religion und Literatur des Alten und Neuen Testaments
FS	Festschrift
FS Bardtke	*Bibel und Qumran* (FS H. Bardtke; 1968)
FS Black (1969)	*Neotestamentica et Semitica* (FS M. Black; 1969)
FS Black (1979)	*Text and Interpretation* (FS M. Black; 1979)
FS Bornkamm	*Kirche* (FS G. Bornkamm; 1980)
FS Braun	*Neues Testament und christliche Existenz* (FS H. Braun; 1973)
FS Bruce	*Apostolic History and the Gospel* (FS F. F. Bruce; 1970)
FS Bultmann (1954)	*Neutestamentliche Studien* (FS R. Bultmann; 1954)
FS Bultmann (1964)	*Zeit und Geschichte* (FS R. Bultmann; 1964)
FS Conzelmann	*Jesus Christus in Historie und Theologie* (FS H. Conzelmann; 1975)
FS Cullmann (1962)	*Neotestamentica et Patristica* (FS O. Cullmann; 1962)
FS Cullmann (1967)	*Oikonomia. Heilsgeschichte als Thema der Theologie* (FS O. Cullmann; 1967)
FS Cullmann (1972)	*Neues Testament und Geschichte* (FS O. Cullmann; 1972)
FS Dahl	*God's Christ and His People* (FS N. A. Dahl; 1977)
FS Daube	*Donum Gentilicium* (FS D. Daube; 1978)
FS Davies	*Jews, Greeks, and Christians* (FS W. D. Davies; 1976)
FS de Zwaan	*Studia Paulinum in honorem Johannis de Zwaan* (1953)
FS Dodd	*The Background of the NT and Its Eschatology* (FS C. H. Dodd; 1954)

ABBREVIATIONS

FS Friedrich	*Das Wort und die Wörter* (FS G. Friedrich; 1973)
FS Goguel	*Aux sources de la tradition chrétienne* (FS M. Goguel; 1950)
FS Greeven	*Studien zum Text und zur Ethik des NT* (FS H. Greeven; 1986)
FS Haenchen	*Apophoreta* (FS E. Haenchen; 1964)
FS Jeremias (1960)	*Judentum, Urchristentum, Kirche* (FS J. Jeremias; 1960)
FS Jeremias (1970)	*Der Ruf Jesu und die Antwort der Gemeinde* (FS J. Jeremias; 1970)
FS Käsemann	*Rechtfertigung* (FS E. Käsemann; 1976)
FS Kilpatrick	*Studies in NT Language and Text* (FS G. D. Kilpatrick; 1976)
FS Kuhn	*Tradition und Glaube. Das frühe Christentum in seiner Umwelt* (FS K. G. Kuhn; 1971)
FS Kümmel	*Jesus und Paulus* (FS W. G. Kümmel; 1975)
FS Michel	*Abraham unser Vater. Juden und Christen im Gespräch über die Bibel* (FS O. Michel; 1963)
FS Moule	*Christ and Spirit in the NT* (FS C. F. D. Moule; 1973)
FS Mussner	*Kontinuität und Einheit* (FS F. Mussner; 1981)
FS Rengstorf	*Theokratia* II (FS K. H. Rengstorf; 1973)
FS Rigaux	*Mélanges Bibliques en hommage au B. Rigaux* (1970)
FS Schelkle	*Wort Gottes in der Zeit* (FS K. H. Schelkle; 1973)
FS Schlier	*Die Zeit Jesu* (FS H. Schlier; 1970)
FS Schmid (1963)	*Neutestamentliche Aufsätze* (FS J. Schmid; 1963)
FS Schmid (1973)	*Orientierung an Jesus* (FS J. Schmid; 1973)
FS Schnackenburg	*Neues Testament und Kirche* (FS R. Schnackenburg; 1974)
FS Schürmann	*Die Kirche des Anfangs* (FS H. Schürmann; 1977)
FS Smith	*Christianity, Judaism, and Other Greco-Roman Cults* I-IV (FS M. Smith; 1975)
FS Stählin	*Verborum Veritas* (FS G. Stählin; 1970)
FS Vögtle	*Jesus und der Menschensohn* (FS A. Vögtle; 1975)
FS Wikenhauser	*Synoptische Studien* (FS A. Wikenhauser; 1953)
FS Wikgren	*Studies in the NT and Early Christian Literature* (FS A. P. Wikgren; 1972)
FS Zimmerman	*Begegnung mit dem Wort* (FS H. Zimmerman; 1980)
FTS	Frankfurter theologische Studien
Fuchs, *Aufsätze*	E. Fuchs, *Gesammelte Aufsätze* I-III (1959-65)
FV	*Foi et Vie*
FzB	Forschungen zur Bibel
GCS	Die griechischen christlichen Schriftsteller
Glotta	*Glotta. Zeitschrift für die griechische und lateinische Sprache*
Goppelt, *Theology*	L. Goppelt, *Theology of the NT* I, II (1981, 1982)
GPM	*Göttinger Predigtmeditationen*
Haenchen I-II	E. Haenchen, *Gesammelte Aufsätze*. I: *Gott und Mensch* (1965); II: *Die Bibel und wir* (1968)
Hahn, *Titles*	F. Hahn, *The Titles of Jesus in Christology* (1969)
Hatch/Redpath	E. Hatch and H. A. Redpath, *A Concordance to the Septuagint* I-III (1897-1906)
Helbing, *Grammatik*	R. Helbing, *Grammatik der Septuaginta. Laut- und Wortlehre* (1907)
Hengel, *Judaism*	M. Hengel, *Judaism and Hellenism* I-II (1974)
Hennecke/ Schneemelcher	E. Hennecke, *New Testament Apocrypha* I-II (ed. W. Schneemelcher and [English translation] R. McL. Wilson; 1963, 1965)
Hermeneia	Hermeneia—A Critical and Historical Commentary on the Bible
HJ	*Historisches Jahrbuch der Görres-Gesellschaft*
HKNT	Handkommentar zum NT
HNT	Handbuch zum NT
HNTC	Harper's NT Commentaries
HSCP	*Harvard Studies in Classical Philology*
HTG	*Handbuch theologischer Grundbegriffe* I-II (ed. H. Fries; 1962, 1963)
HTKNT	Herders theologischer Kommentar zum NT
HTR	*Harvard Theological Review*
HUCA	*Hebrew Union College Annual*
HUT	Hermeneutische Untersuchungen zur Theologie
HWP	*Historisches Wörterbuch der Philosophie* (1971-)
ICC	International Critical Commentary
IDB	*Interpreter's Dictionary of the Bible* I-IV (ed. G. A. Buttrick, et al.; 1962)
IDBSup	*Interpreter's Dictionary of the Bible, Supplementary Volume* (ed. K. Crim; 1976)
IEJ	*Israel Exploration Journal*
IKZ	*Internationale kirchliche Zeitschrift*
Int	*Interpretation*
ITQ	*Irish Theological Quarterly*
JAC	Jahrbuch für Antike und Christentum

JBL	*Journal of Biblical Literature*
Jeremias, *Parables*	J. Jeremias, *The Parables of Jesus* (^{2}1972)
Jeremias, *Theology*	J. Jeremias, *NT Theology* (1971)
JETS	*Journal of the Evangelical Theological Society*
JHS	*Journal of Hellenic Studies*
JNES	*Journal of Near Eastern Studies*
Johannessohn, *Präpositionen*	M. Johannessohn, *Der Gebrauch der Präpositionen in der Septuaginta* (1926)
JPOS	*Journal of the Palestine Oriental Society*
JQR	*Jewish Quarterly Review*
JR	*Journal of Religion*
JSHRZ	*Jüdische Schriften aus hellenistisch-römischer Zeit* I-V (ed. W. G. Kümmel; 1973-)
JSJ	*Journal for the Study of Judaism*
JSNT	*Journal for the Study of the NT*
JSOT	*Journal for the Study of the OT*
JSS	*Journal of Semitic Studies*
JTC	*Journal for Theology and the Church*
JTS	*Journal of Theological Studies*
Judaica	*Judaica. Beiträge zum Verständnis des jüdischen Schicksals in Vergangenheit und Gegenwart*
Jülicher I-II	A. Jülicher, *Die Gleichnisreden Jesu* I-II (1910)
Kairos	*Kairos. Zeitschrift für Religionswissenschaft und Theologie*
Käsemann, *Versuche*	E. Käsemann, *Exegetische Versuche und Besinnungen* I-II (^{4}1965, ^{3}1968)
KBANT	Kommentare und Beiträge zum Alten und Neuen Testament
KBL$^{2, 3}$	L. Koehler and W. Baumgartner, *Lexicon in Veteris Testamenti Libros* (^{2}1958); *Hebräisches und Aramäisches Lexikon zum AT* (^{3}1974-)
KD	*Kerygma und Dogma*
KEK	Kritisch-exegetischer Kommentar über das NT
KKTS	Konfessionskundliche und Kontroverstheologische Studien
KlT	Kleine Texte
KNT	Kommentar zum NT
Kopp, *Places*	C. Kopp, *The Holy Places of the Gospels* (1963)
KP	*Der Kleine Pauly. Lexikon der Antike* I-V (ed. von Ziegler and Sontheimer; 1964-75)
KQT	*Konkordanz zu den Qumrantexten* (ed. K. G. Kuhn; 1960)
Kühner, *Grammatik*	R. Kühner, *Ausführliche Grammatik der griechischen Sprache* I by F. Blass, II by B. Gerth (1890-1904)
Kümmel I, II	W. G. Kümmel, *Heilsgeschehen und Geschichte* I-II (1965, 1978)
Kümmel, *Introduction*	W. G. Kümmel, *Introduction to the NT* (^{2}1975)
Kuss I-III	O. Kuss, *Auslegung und Verkündigung* I-III (1963-71)
LAW	*Lexikon der Alten Welt* (ed. C. Andresen, H. Erbse, et al.; 1965)
LD	Lectio Divina
LebZeug	*Lebendiges Zeugnis*
Leipoldt/Grundmann	*Umwelt des Urchristentums* I-III (ed. J. Leipoldt and W. Grundmann; I: ^{2}1967, II: ^{3}1972, III: 1966)
Levy I-IV	J. Levy, *Wörterbuch über die Talmudim und Midraschim* (^{2}1924 = 1963)
Lewy, *Fremdwörter*	H. Lewy, *Die semitischen Fremdwörter im Griechischen* (1895 = 1970)
LingBibl	*Linguistica Biblica*
LSJ	H. G. Liddell, R. Scott, H. S. Jones, and R. McKenzie, *A Greek-English Lexicon* (^{9}1940)
LTK	*Lexikon für Theologie und Kirche* I-XI (ed. J. Höfer and K. Rahner; ^{2}1957-67)
Maier/Schreiner	*Literatur und Religion des Frühjudentums. Eine Einführung* (ed. J. Maier and J. Schreiner; 1973)
Mayser, *Grammatik*	E. Mayser, *Grammatik der griechischen Papyri aus der Ptolemäerzeit* I-II (1906, 1934)
MH	*Museum Helveticum*
Moore, *Judaism*	G. F. Moore, *Judaism in the First Centuries of the Christian Era* I-III (1927, 1930)
Morgenthaler, *Statistik*	R. Morgenthaler, *Statistik des neutestamentlichen Wortschatzes* (1958)
Moule, *Idiom-Book*	C. F. D. Moule, *An Idiom-Book of NT Greek* (^{2}1959)
Moulton, *Grammar*	*A Grammar of NT Greek:* I by J. H. Moulton (^{2}1908), II by W. F. Howard (1963), III, IV by N. Turner (1963, 1976)
Moulton/Milligan	J. H. Moulton and G. Milligan, *The Vocabulary of the Greek Testament, Illustrated from the Papyri and Other Non-literary Sources* (1930)
MTS	Münchener theologische Studien
MTSt	Marburger theologische Studien
MTZ	*Münchener theologische Zeitschrift*
MySal	*Mysterium Salutis*
Nägeli, *Wortschatz*	T. Nägeli, *Der Wortschatz des Apostels Paulus* (1905)

ABBREVIATIONS

NedTTs	*Nederlandse theologisch tijdschrift*
Neot	*Neotestamentica*
N.F.	Neue Folge
NICNT	The New International Commentary on the NT
NIGTC	New International Greek Testament Commentary
Nilsson, *Geschichte*	M. P. Nilsson, *Geschichte der griechischen Religion. II: Die hellenistische und römische Zeit* ([2]1961)
NKZ	*Neue Kirchliche Zeitschrift*
NorTT	*Norsk Teologisk Tidsskrift*
NovT	*Novum Testamentum*
NovTSup	Novum Testamentum Supplements
NRT	*La nouvelle revue théologique*
NTAbh	Neutestamentliche Abhandlungen
NTD	Das Neue Testament Deutsch
NTG	*Novum Testamentum Graece* (ed. E. Nestle and K. Aland; [25]1963; ed. K. Aland, M. Black, C. M. Martini, B. M. Metzger, and A. Wikgren; [26]1979)
NTL	NT Library
NTS	*New Testament Studies*
NTTS	NT Tools and Studies
OBO	Orbis Biblicus et Orientalis
OCD	*The Oxford Classical Dictionary* (ed. H. G. L. Hammond and H. H. Scullard; [2]1970)
OLZ	*Orientalische Literaturzeitung*
OPTAT	*OPTAT: Occasional Papers in Translation and Text Linguistics*
OTL	OT Library
ÖTK	Ökumenischer Taschenbuch-Kommentar
OTS	*Oudtestamentische Studiën*
Pape, *Wörterbuch*	W. Pape, *Griechisch-deutsches Wörterbuch* I-II ([6]1914)
Passow I-II	F. Passow, *Handwörterbuch der griechischen Sprache* I-II ([5]1841, 1857)
PEQ	*Palestine Exploration Quarterly*
PG	J.-P. Migne, *Patrologiae cursus completus. Series Graeca* (1857-1936)
PGL	G. W. H. Lampe, *A Patristic Greek Lexicon* ([4]1976)
PL	J.-P. Migne, *Patrologiae cursus completus. Series Latina* (1841-64)
Preisigke, *Wörterbuch*	F. Preisigke, *Wörterbuch der griechischen Papyrusurkunden* I-III (1925-31), Supplement I (1971)
Prümm, *Handbuch*	K. Prümm, *Religionsgeschichtliches Handbuch für den Raum der altchristlichen Umwelt* (1943 = 1954)
PW	(A.) *Paulys Real-Encyclopädie der classischen Altertumswissenschaft* (ed. G. Wissowa and W. Kroll; 1893-)
QD	Quaestiones Disputatae
RAC	*Reallexikon für Antike und Christentum* (ed. T. Klauser; 1941-)
Radermacher, *Grammatik*	L. Radermacher, *Neutestamentliche Grammatik* ([2]1925)
RB	*Revue Biblique*
RE	*Realencyclopädie für protestantische Theologie und Kirche* I-XXIV ([3]1896-1913)
RechBib	Recherches bibliques
Reicke, *NT Era*	B. Reicke, *The NT Era* (1968)
REJ	*Revue des études Juives*
RevistBib	*Revista bíblica*
RevQ	*Revue de Qumran*
RGG	*Die Religion in Geschichte und Gegenwart* I-VI (ed. K. Galling, et al.; [3]1957-62)
RHPR	*Revue d'histoire et de philosophie religieuses*
RHR	*Revue d l'histoire des religions*
RIDA	*Revue internationale des droits de l'antiquité*
Ristow/Matthiae	*Der historische Jesus und der kerygmatische Christus* (ed. H. Ristow and K. Matthiae; [3]1964)
RivB	*Rivista Biblica*
RMP	*Rheinisches Museum für Philologie*
RNT	Regensburger Neues Testament
Robertson, *Grammar*	A. T. Robertson, *A Grammar of the Greek NT in the Light of Historical Research* ([4]1934)
RQ	*Römische Quartalschrift für christliche Altertumswissenschaft und Kirchengeschichte*
RSPT	*Revue des sciences philosophiques et théologiques*
RSR	*Recherches de science religieuse*
RSV	Revised Standard Version
RTL	*Revue théologique de Louvain*
RTM	*Revista di Teologia Morale*

RTP	*Revue de théologie et de philosophie*
SacVb	*Sacramentum Verbi* (= *Encyclopedia of Biblical Theology;* ed. J. B. Bauer; ³1967)
SANT	Studien zum Alten und Neuen Testament
SBFLA	*Studii biblici franciscani liber annuus*
SBLMS	Society of Biblical Literature Monograph Series
SBLSCS	Society of Biblical Literature Septuagint and Cognate Studies
SBS	Stuttgarter Bibelstudien
SBT	Studies in Biblical Theology
SBU	Symbolae Biblicae Upsalienses
ScEc	*Sciences Ecclésiastiques*
ScEs	*Science et esprit*
Schelkle, *Theology*	K. H. Schelkle, *Theology of the NT* I-IV (1971-78)
Schlier I-III	H. Schlier, *Exegetische Aufsätze und Vorträge* I-III (1956-71)
Schmidt, *Synonymik*	J. H. H. Schmidt, *Synonymik der griechischen Sprache* I-IV (1876-86, reprinted 1967-69)
Schnackenburg I-II	R. Schnackenburg, *Christian Existence in the NT* (1968, 1969)
Schnackenburg, *Botschaft*	R. Schnackenburg, *Die sittliche Botschaft des NT* (²1962)
SCHNT	Studia ad Corpus Hellenisticum Novi Testamenti
Schürmann I-III	H. Schürmann, *Traditionsgeschichtliche Untersuchungen zu den synoptischen Evangelien* (1968-76)
Schulz, *Q*	S. Schulz, *Q. Die Spruchquelle der Evangelisten* (1972)
Schürer, *History*	E. Schürer, *The History of the Jewish People in the Age of Jesus Christ* I-III/1-2 (revised and ed. G. Vermes, F. Millar, and M. Black; 1973-87)
Schwyzer, *Grammatik*	E. Schwyzer, *Griechische Grammatik* I-IV (1939-71)
SDAW	*Sitzungsberichte der deutschen Akademie der Wissenschaft zu Berlin*
SdNT	Die Schriften des NT
SE	*Studia Evangelica* (= TU 73, 87, 88, etc.)
SEÅ	*Svensk exegetisk årsbok*
SGU	Studia Graeca Upsaliensia
SHAW	Sitzungsberichte der Heidelberger Akademie der Wissenschaften. Philosophisch-historische Klasse
SHR	Studies in the History of Religion
SHVL	Skrifter utgivna av k. humanistiska vetenskapssamfundet i Lund
SJT	*Scottish Journal of Theology*
SM	*Sacramentum Mundi: An Encyclopedia of Theology* I-IV (ed. K. Rahner, et al.; 1968-70)
SNT	Studien zum NT
SNTSMS	Society for NT Studies Monograph Series
SNTU	*Studien zum NT und seiner Umwelt*
SNVAO	Skrifter utgitt av det norske videnskaps-akademi i Oslo
SO	*Symbolae Osloenses*
Sophocles, *Lexicon*	E. A. Sophocles, *Greek Lexicon of the Roman and Byzantine Periods* I-II (³1888)
SPCIC	*Studiorum Paulinorum Congressus Internationalis Catholicus*
Spicq, *Notes*	C. Spicq, *Notes de lexicographie néo-testamentaire* I-II, Suppl. (1978-82)
SR	*Studies in Religion/Sciences religieuses*
SSA	Schriften der Sektion für Altertumswissenschaft (Deutsche Akademie der Wissenschaft zu Berlin)
ST	*Studia theologica*
StOr	*Studia Orientalia* (Societas orientalis Fennica)
SUNT	Studien zur Umwelt des NT
SvTK	*Svensk teologisk kvartalskrift*
TBeitr	*Theologische Beiträge*
TBl	*Theologische Blätter*
TBü	Theologische Bücherei
TCGNT	B. Metzger, *A Textual Commentary on the Greek NT* (1971)
TDNT	*Theological Dictionary of the NT* I-X (ed. G. Kittel and G. Friedrich; 1964-76)
TDOT	*Theological Dictionary of the OT* (ed. J. Botterweck and H. Ringgren; ²1974-)
TEH	Theologische Existenz heute
TF	Theologische Forschung
TGl	*Theologie und Glaube*
THAT	*Theologisches Handwörterbuch zum AT* I-II (ed. E. Jenni and C. Westermann; 1971, 1976)
ThDiss	Theologische Dissertationen (Basel)
ThGL	*Thesaurus Graecae Linguae ab H. Stephano constructus* I-IX (ed. Hase and Dindorf; 1831-65)
ThJb(L)	*Theologisches Jahrbuch* (Leipzig)
THKNT	Theologischer Handkommentar zum NT
Thrall, *Particles*	M. Thrall, *Greek Particles in the NT* (1962)

ABBREVIATIONS

TLZ	*Theologische Literaturzeitung*
TPQ	*Theologisch-Praktische Quartalschrift*
TQ	*Theologische Quartalschrift*
TRE	*Theologische Realenzyklopädie* (ed. G. Krause and G. Müller; 1976-)
Trench, *Synonyms*	R. C. Trench, *Synonyms of the NT* ([9]1880)
TRev	*Theologische Revue*
TRu	*Theologische Rundschau*
TS	*Theological Studies*
TSK	*Theologische Studien und Kritiken*
TT	*Teologisk Tidskrift*
TTK	*Tidsskrift for teologi og kirke*
TTS	*Trierer Theologische Studien*
TTZ	*Trierer Theologische Zeitschrift*
TU	Texte und Untersuchungen zur Geschichte der altchristlichen Literatur
TViat	*Theologia Viatorum*
TW	Theologie und Wirklichkeit
TWAT	*Theologisches Wörterbuch zum AT* I- (ed. G. J. Botterweck and H. Ringgren; 1970-)
TWNT	*Theologisches Wörterbuch zum NT* I-X (ed. G. Kittel and G. Friedrich; 1933-79)
TZ	*Theologische Zeitschrift*
UBSGNT	*The Greek NT* (ed. K. Aland, M. Black, C. M. Martini, B. M. Metzger, and A. Wikgren; [3]1975)
UNT	Untersuchungen zum NT
UTB	Uni-Taschenbücher
UUÅ	*Uppsala universitetsårsskrift*
VC	*Vigiliae Christianae*
VD	*Verbum Domini*
VF	*Verkündigung und Forschung*
VKGNT	*Vollständige Konkordanz zum griechischen NT* I-II (ed. K. Aland; 1978, 1983)
Volz, *Eschatologie*	P. Volz, *Die Eschatologie der jüdischen Gemeinde im neutestamentlichen Zeitalter* (1934)
Von Rad, *Theology*	G. von Rad, *OT Theology* I, II (1962, 1965)
VSal	Verbum Salutis
VT	*Vetus Testamentum*
WBB	*Wörterbuch zur biblischen Botschaft* (ed. X. Léon-Dufour; 1964, [2]1967)
Wettstein, *NT*	J. J. Wettstein, *Novum Testamentum Graecum* I-II (1751-52, reprinted 1962)
Wikenhauser, *Geschichtswert*	A. Wikenhauser, *Die Apostelgeschichte und ihr Geschichtswert* (1921)
Wikenhauser/Schmid	A. Wikenhauser and J. Schmid, *Einleitung in das NT* ([6]1973)
WMANT	Wissenschaftliche Monographien zum Alten und Neuen Testament
WPKG	*Wissenschaft und Praxis in Kirche und Gesellschaft*
WTJ	*Westminster Theological Journal*
WuD	*Wort und Dienst. Jahrbuch der Kirchlichen Schule Bethel*
WUNT	Wissenschaftliche Untersuchungen zum NT
ZAW	*Zeitschrift für die Alttestamentliche Wissenschaft*
ZBK	Zürcher Bibelkommentare
ZDMG	*Zeitschrift der deutschen morgenländischen Gesellschaft*
ZDPV	*Zeitschrift des deutschen Palästina-Vereins*
ZdZ	*Zeichen der Zeit*
ZEE	*Zeitschrift für evangelische Ethik*
Zerwick, *Biblical Greek*	M. Zerwick, *Biblical Greek* (1963)
ZKG	*Zeitschrift für Kirchengeschichte*
ZKT	*Zeitschrift für katholische Theologie*
ZM	*Zeitschrift für Missionswissenschaft*
ZNW	*Zeitschrift für die neutestamentliche Wissenschaft*
Zorell, *Lexikon*	F. Zorell, *Novi Testamenti Lexicon Graecum* ([2]1931)
ZRGG	*Zeitschrift für Religions und Geistesgeschichte*
ZST	*Zeitschrift für systematische Theologie*
ZTK	*Zeitschrift für Theologie und Kirche*
ZWT	*Zeitschrift für wissenschaftliche Theologie*

3. General

Sigla in textual notes are from the twenty-fifth and twenty-sixth editions of *NTG*.

acc.	accusative	masc.	masculine
act.	active (voice)	mid.	middle
adj(s).	adjective(s), adjectival(ly)	mm.	millimeter(s)
adv(s).	adverb(s), adverbial(ly)	ms(s).	manuscript(s)
aor.	aorist	MT	Masoretic Text
Aram.	Aramaic	neut.	neuter
art.	(definite) article	nom.	nominative
AT	Altes Testament, Ancien Testament	NT	New Testament, Neues Testament, Nouveau Testament
ch(s).	chapter(s)		
conj.	conjunction	obj.	object, objective
dat.	dative	opt.	optative
def. art.	definite article	OT	Old Testament
dir. obj.	direct object	p(p).	page(s)
diss.	dissertation	par.	parallel
ed.	edition, edited, editor(s)	partc.	participle
Eng.	English	pass.	passive
esp.	especially	pf.	perfect
fem.	feminine	pl.	plural
fig.	figurative(ly)	plupf.	pluperfect
frag.	fragment	pred.	predicate
fut.	future	prep(s).	preposition(s), prepositional
g.	gram(s)	pres.	present
gen.	genitive	pron.	pronoun
Germ.	German	Q	Hypothetical source of material common to Matthew and Luke but not found in Mark
Gk.	Greek		
Heb.	Hebrew		
impf.	imperfect	rel.	relative
imv(s).	imperative(s)	sg.	singular
ind.	indicative	subj.	subject, subjective
inf(s).	infinitive(s)	subjunc.	subjunctive
intrans.	intransitive(ly)	subst.	substantive, substantivally
km.	kilometer(s)	tr.	translated, translation
κτλ.	etc. (Greek)	TR	Textus Receptus
L	Material in Luke not found in Matthew or Mark	trans.	transitive(ly)
		t.t.	technical term
l(l).	line number(s)	v(v).	verse(s)
Lat.	Latin	vb(s).	verb(s)
LXX	Septuagint	Vg.	Vulgate
M	Material in Matthew not found in Mark or Luke	v.l.	variant reading
		voc.	vocative
m.	meter(s)		

TRANSLITERATION SCHEME

Greek

α	*a*	η	*ē*	ϱ	*r*	
ᾳ	*ą*	ῃ	*ę̄*	ῥ	*rh*	
β	*b*	θ	*th*	σ, ς	*s*	
γ	*g*	ι	*i*	τ	*t*	
γγ	*ng*	κ	*k*	υ	*y (u in diphthongs)*	
γκ	*nk*	λ	*l*	φ	*ph*	
γξ	*nx*	μ	*m*	χ	*ch*	
γχ	*nch*	ν	*n*	ψ	*ps*	
δ	*d*	ξ	*x*	ω	*ō*	
ε	*e*	ο	*o*	ῳ	*ǭ*	
ζ	*z*	π	*p*	ʽ	*h*	

Hebrew and Aramaic

Consonants

א	*ʼ*	ח	*ḥ*	פ	*p̱*
ב	*ḇ*	ט	*ṭ*	פּ	*p*
בּ	*b*	י	*y*	צ	*ṣ*
ג	*ḡ*	כ	*k*	ק	*q*
גּ	*g*	כּ	*k*	ר	*r*
ד	*ḏ*	ל	*l*	שׂ	*ś*
דּ	*d*	מ, ם	*m*	שׁ	*š*
ה	*h*	נ, ן	*n*	ת	*ṯ*
ו	*w*	ס	*s*	תּ	*t*
ז	*z*	ע	*ʽ*	

Vowels

_	*a*	◌ֻ	*u*	◌ְ (vocal)	*e*
◌ָ	*ā, o*	הָ	*â*		*ᵃ*
◌ֶ	*e*	יֵ	*ê*		*ĕ*
◌ֵ	*ē*	יִ	*î*		*ᵒ*
◌ִ	*i*	וֹ	*ô*	
◌ֹ	*ō*	וּ	*û*	

ἕξ

→ ἐκ.

ἕξ   hex   six*

Mark 9:2 par. Matt 17:1: "after *six* days." Luke 4:25 (*six* months); 13:14 (*six* days [work days]); John 2:6 (*six* stone water jugs); 12:1 (*six* days before the Passover); Acts 11:12 (*six* brothers); 18:11 (*six* months); Jas 5:17 (*six* months); Rev 4:8 (*six* wings). Other numbers which include ἕξ: John 2:20 (46 years); Acts 27:37 (in the ship were 276 people); Rev 13:18 (the number 666; see H. Kraft, *Rev* [HNT]).

ἐξαγγέλλω   exangellō   proclaim*

The compound appears in the LXX; Philo *Plant.* 128; *T. Jos.* 5:2, 3 and elsewhere, in the NT in 1 Pet 2:9 ("so that *you may proclaim* τὰς ἀρετάς") and in the shorter ending of Mark (πάντα τὰ παρηγγελμένα); cf. J. Schniewind, *TDNT* I, 69.

ἐξαγοράζω   exagorazō   redeem, buy up*

Lit.: F. BÜCHSEL, *TDNT* I, 126-28. — DEISSMANN, *Light* 360-67. — W. ELERT, "Redemptio ab hostibus," *TLZ* 72 (1947) 265-70. — S. LYONNET, "L'emploi paulinien de ἐξαγοράζειν au sens de 'redimere' est-il attesté dans la littérature grecque?" *Bib* 42 (1961) 85-89. — E. PAX, "Der Loskauf. Zur Geschichte eines neutestamentlichen Begriffes," *Antonianum* 37 (1962) 239-78. — For further bibliography see *TWNT* X, 956.

Ἐξαγοράζω is used twice to demand the *buying up* of the time (Eph 5:16; Col 4:5); this imperative use of the vb., ἐξαγοράζετε τὸν καιρόν, is derived from the wisdom tradition. In contrast to Dan 2:8 LXX this does not mean "gain time for oneself," but rather *buy up* the time in taking advantage of all the possibilities at hand, esp. with the double connotation of καιρός as limited period of time (1 Cor 7:29) and as decisive moment (e.g., Rom 13:11): the time given by God until the end of the world and the opportunity that is offered which is not to be left unused. Thus Col 4:5 is determined by the missionary motivation and objective of winning those who remain outside, while the more general exhortation in Eph 5:16, which is probably derived from Col 4:5, is based on the dangerous, Satanic end time (cf. 6:12f., 16).

Paul uses ἐξαγοράζω in Gal 3:13 and 4:5 to designate the universal redemptive act of Christ: with his vicarious death Christ has redeemed us from the law (4:5) and from the death-producing curse (3:13), which is the enslaving burden on humanity. Thus ἡμᾶς in 3:13 and 4:5 must include Jews as well as Gentile Christians, for the law for Paul has universal validity. Moreover, he equates enslavement under the law (4:5) with enslavement under the world powers (4:3, 8ff.). With this language Paul alludes to redemption of slaves, but not to Greek sacral

manumission. For Paul the decisive fact is that Christ, not a man, appears as purchaser, and together the obligations and commitments to the old master are severed. Furthermore, the one who is redeemed has no need to contribute a ransom of his own. Indeed, he cannot, for the representative death of Christ is at the same time the price and the method of the redemption (cf. esp. Pax 274ff.; Deissmann's thesis, *Light* 323, that Paul is dependent on Greek sacral manumission, can thus be refuted). Paul does not say to whom the price is paid. This purchase through Christ has universal validity and is the end result of the adoption of humanity by God (4:5) and thus the gift of the Spirit (3:14b; 4:6). Thus the promised blessing to Abraham becomes finally a reality for the peoples of the world (3:14a).

R. Dabelstein

ἐξάγω   exagō   lead out, bring out*

Out of a land, Acts 7:36, 40; 13:17; Heb 8:9; out of a prison, Acts 5:19; 12:17; 16:37, 39; *lead* sheep out of the pen, John 10:3; with an indication of direction: Mark 15:20 (with ἵνα); Luke 24:50 (Bethany); Acts 21:38 (wilderness, cf. Exod 16:3).

ἐξαιρέω   exaireō   take out, pull out*

Matt 5:29; 18:9, from the eye: "*pluck it out.*" Other occurrences in the mid., *remove, deliver from something:* Acts 7:10, 34; 12:11; 23:27; Gal 1:4; *select/set apart, save:* Acts 26:17. M. Buscemi, "*Exaireomai,* verbo di liberazione," *SBFLA* 29 (1979) 293-314; Spicq, *Notes* Suppl., 276-79.

ἐξαίρω   exairō   take away, remove*

1 Cor 5:13: "*remove* the evil from your midst"; 5:2 Koine al: "so that he might be *removed* from your midst."

ἐξαιτέομαι   exaiteomai   ask for, request*

Luke 22:31: "Satan *has asked for* you, in order to sift you . . ."; cf. *T. Benj.* 3:3. G. Stählin, *TDNT* I, 194.

ἐξαίφνης   exaiphnēs   unexpectedly, suddenly*

Mark 13:36: "so that he (the lord of the house) does not come *unexpectedly* and find you sleeping." In connection with heavenly appearances, Luke 2:13; Acts 9:3; 22:6. Luke 9:39 (cf. par. Mark): "and *suddenly* he cries."

ἐξακολουθέω   exakoloutheō   come after

→ ἀκολουθέω 5.

ἑξακόσιοι, 3   hexakosioi   six hundred*

Rev 13:18, of the number of the beast: "It is a human

number; and its number is *six hundred* sixty-six." → ἕξ. 14:20: "Blood flowed from the wine press . . . for one thousand *six hundred* stadia (σταδίων χιλίων ἑξακοσίων).

ἐξαλείφω   *exaleiphō* wipe off, erase*

Acts 3:19: "so that your sins *are blotted out*" (cf. Ps 108:14 LXX; 3 Macc 2:19; *1 Enoch* [Greek] 10:20). Col 2:14: "He *abolished* the bond against us." Rev 3:5, of the erasing of the name from the book of life; 7:17 and 21:4: God *will wipe away* every tear from their eyes."

ἐξάλλομαι   *exallomai* leap*

Acts 3:8: the man born lame *leaped.*

ἐξανάστασις, εως, ἡ   *exanastasis* resurrection → ἀνάστασις.

ἐξανατέλλω   *exanatellō* spring up, sprout*

Of the rapid sprouting of the seed, Mark 4:5 par. Matt 13:5.

ἐξανίστημι   *exanistēmi* raise up, stand up* → ἀνάστασις.

ἐξαπατάω   *exapataō* deceive, lead astray*

In Rom 7:11 "sin" is the subject; it *deceived* "me" διὰ τῆς ἐντολῆς (perhaps: *enticed;* cf. 2 Cor 11:3). Of the serpent's deception of Eve, 2 Cor 11:3 (it *enticed* her; cf. Herodotus ii.114); 1 Tim 2:14. In Rom 16:18 Paul warns of some who "*deceive* the hearts of the simpleminded" with pretty words. 1 Cor 3:18: ἑαυτὸν ἐξαπατάω, *deceive oneself.* 2 Thess 2:3: "No one *should deceive* you." A. Oepke, *TDNT* I, 384.

ἐξάπινα   *exapina* suddenly*

Mark 9:8: "*suddenly* . . . they did not see anyone."

ἐξαπορέομαι   *exaporeomai* fall completely into embarrassment, despair*

With the gen. of that about which it occurs: 2 Cor 1:8 (τοῦ ζῆν, "of life"). Absolute in 4:8: οὐκ ἐξαπορούμενοι, *not despairing.*

ἐξαποστέλλω   *exapostellō* send out, send away*

1. Occurrences in the NT — 2. "Send" — 3. "Send away" — 4. Gal 4:4, 6

Lit.: J. BLANK, *Paulus und Jesus* (1968) 258-79. — I. HERMANN, *Kyrios und Pneuma* (1961) 94-97. — W. KRAMER, *Christ, Lord, Son of God* (1966) 111-15. — D. MÜLLER, *DNTT* I, 126-

37. — K. H. RENGSTORF, *TDNT* I, 406. — E. SCHWEIZER, *TDNT* VIII, 374-76, 383f. — *idem*, "Zur Herkunft der Präexistenzvorstellung bei Paulus," *idem, Neotestamentica* (1963) 105-9. — *idem*, "Aufnahme und Korrektur jüdischer Sophiatheologie im NT," *Neotestamentica* 110-21. — *idem*, "Zum religionsgeschichtlichen Hintergrund der 'Sendungsformel' Gal 4.4f, Rom 8.3f, Joh 3.16f, 1 Joh 4.9," *idem, Beiträge zur Theologie des NT* (1970) 83-95.

1. Of the 12 occurrences in the NT, 10 are in the Lukan writings (3 in Luke; 7 in Acts). Ἐξαποστέλλω is thus a favorite word of Luke's, who also uses → ἀποστέλλω and → ἀπόστολος. The other two occurrences are in Gal 4:4, 6. The vb. is also found in Luke 24:49 v.l. and in the "shorter" Markan ending. Because στέλλω has another meaning and the prep. ἀπό in ἀποστέλλω often has little weight, it is possible that in Luke 1:53; 20:10, 11; Acts 9:30; 11:22; 17:14; 22:21; and perhaps also Gal 4:4, 6 the prep. ἐκ (= from, away) is used to strengthen ἀπό. Otherwise the vb. ἐξαποστέλλω—as is usually the case in koine—is scarcely different in meaning from ἀποστέλλω.

2. In a few passages in Acts ἐξαποστέλλω means *send to another place.* According to 7:12 Jacob sends his sons to Egypt; according to 9:30 the brothers in Jerusalem send Paul to Tarsus, and according to 11:22 Barnabas is sent to Antioch; in 17:14 the disciples in Berea send Paul "on a journey to the sea." In 7:12 and 11:22 those who are sent have a task; according to 9:30 and 17:14 Paul, who is "sent away," escapes the danger.

Twice Christ is the subject of ἐξαποστέλλω. In the trance in the temple Paul learns (Acts 22:21) that Jesus "*will send* him far away to the Gentiles" (the v.l. in D has pres. tense), and the resurrected one announces (Luke 24:49) that he *sends* (ἐξαποστέλλω according to *NTG*[25]; 𝔭[75] ℵ* C Koine A D read ἀποστέλλω) the promise of the Father (= the promised Spirit) to the disciples.

In other passages God is the subj. of ἐξαποστέλλω: in Acts 12:11 Peter says that he knows that God has *sent* an angel to liberate him; in 13:26 the vb. stands in the pass., and God is the logical subj.: "The word (= the kerygma, the news of the salvation which has appeared in Jesus) *is sent* to us."

3. In Luke 1:53 God is the sender; the meaning of ἐξαποστέλλω is here *send away:* God has "*sent* the rich *away* empty." As in 1:53 Luke constructs ἐξαποστέλλω with a double acc. in the parable of the wicked tenants in 20:10, 11. Each time the second acc. is formed with κενός. In 20:10 ("the tenants beat him and *sent* him *away* empty-handed") he takes over Mark 12:3, where ἀπέστειλεν κενόν appears; 20:11 repeats the preceding verse with only minor variations.

4. Gal 4:4, 6 can be compared with Acts 12:11. As God sent his angel (from heaven), he sends his Son and the Spirit of his Son from himself. However, the two

Galatians passages are weightier in content. They belong to the unit 4:1-7: Christians are no longer slaves but sons and heirs through the sending of the Son. Apparently in Gal 4:6 Paul repeats the vb. in reference to the Spirit under the influence of 4:4 (in Rom 8:15 and Gal 3:14 the expression "receive [λαμβάνω] the Spirit" appears). However, it is noteworthy that the same vb. is used in Luke 24:49 (v.l.) with reference to the sending of the Spirit. The train of thought in Gal 4:6 is: "That (probably declarative, not causal "because") you are sons (pres.)," is indicated in the proof: "God *has sent* (aor.) the Spirit of his son into our hearts, who cries (pres.): Abba, Father" (→ ἀββά 3). The two present tenses indicate a permanent situation and a possibility for Christians. The aor. refers to what has happened (at baptism). One may ask whether the sending of the Spirit is the result or the basis of the sonship. As in Gal 4:6, Rom 8:15 also has κράζω and ἀββὰ ὁ πατήρ; cf. also υἱοθεσία in Rom 8:15 and Gal 4:5, υἱοὶ (θεοῦ) in Rom 8:14 and Gal 4:6, κληρονόμος in Rom 8:17 and Gal 4:7; cf. also δουλεία in Rom 8:15 with δοῦλος in Gal 4:6. These parallels indicate not only that we have a typical Pauline thought here, but probably also that Paul is taking up a traditional formula; cf. the Abba cry *and* the association of sonship and the possession of the Spirit (see Wis 9:10-17, "where the vb. ἐξαποστέλλω, which is elsewhere never used by Paul, appears," Schweizer, *Beiträge* 92).

According to 4:4 God "*sent* his Son." Here the aor. refers to the past, once-for-all fact of the incarnation. A comparison of Gal 4:4f.; Rom 8:3f.; John 3:16f.; and 1 John 4:9 permits the conclusion that a firmly fixed pre-Pauline form of proclamation existed. It included first the sending formula, in which God is the one who sends his Son, and then the purpose clause, which expresses the salvific meaning of the sending. It is uncertain whether this schema originally used a particular vb. along with the stereotyped association of "the Father–his Son." If so, ἐξαποστέλλω, ἀποστέλλω, and πέμπω (or δίδωμι) are possibilities. Presumably already at the pre-Pauline stage and certainly in Paul (and John) the sending formula is associated with a preexistence christology: the heavenly, preexistent Son of God becomes man; Gal 4:4 emphasizes also that he becomes a Jew. The two parallel and equal purpose clauses of 4:5 express the soteriology of Paul. Thus the stress lies on it.   J. Lambrecht

ἐξαρπάζω *exarpazō* take away forcibly → ἁρπάζω 4.

ἐξαρτίζω *exartizō* finish, complete, equip*

Acts 21:5: ἐξαρτίσαι τὰς ἡμέρας, "the days *ended*." 2 Tim 3:17, "*equipped* for every good work." Spicq, *Notes* I, 253-55.

ἐξαστράπτω *exastraptō* flash, gleam*

Luke 9:29, in the fig. sense of the bright *gleaming* garment of Jesus at the transfiguration (cf. par. Mark 9:3, where στίλβω, "shine," is used); cf. Luke 24:4 (different from par. Mark).

ἐξαυτῆς *exautēs* immediately, at once*

Derived from ἐξ αὐτῆς τῆς ὥρας (cf. Philo *Mut.* 142). Mark 6:25; Acts 10:33; 11:11; 21:32; 23:30; Phil 2:23.

ἐξεγείρω *exegeirō* raise, awaken*

1 Cor 6:14: "God will . . . also *raise* us." Rom 9:17, citing Exod 9:16: "You I *have raised up/allowed to appear* for this purpose"; on the origin of the passage cited, in which ἐξεγείρω does not appear (see however Zech 11:16 LXX), cf. H. Schlier, *Rom* (HTKNT) on 9:17. A. Oepke, *TDNT* II, 338.

ἔξειμι *exeimi* go out*

Acts 13:42; 17:15. In the sense of *depart*, 20:7. With ἐπί, 27:43: "he ordered them . . . *to get to* land."

ἐξελέγχω *exelenchō* convict, punish

Jude 15 TR (in place of ἐλέγχω): "The Lord came, . . . to *convict/punish* because of their works."

ἐξέλκω *exelkō* carry away, sweep away*

Jas 1:14: "*swept away* and enticed by his own desires" (ἐξελκόμενος καὶ δελεαζόμενος).

ἐξέραμα, ατος, τό *exerama* vomit*

2 Pet 2:22, in the saying about the dog that returns to its own *vomit* (cf. Prov 26:11).

ἐξεραυνάω *exeraunaō* inquire, investigate*

Ἐξεραυνάω is Hellenistic for ἐξερευνάω (BDF §30.4). 1 Pet 1:10: The prophets "searched and *inquired* concerning (περί) this σωτηρία." G. Delling, *TDNT* II, 655-57.

ἐξέρχομαι *exerchomai* come out

1. Occurrences in the NT — 2. Semitic influence — 3. The Jesus tradition — 4. Demons

Lit.: J.-A. BÜHNER, "Zu Form, Tradition und Bedeutung der ἦλθον-Sprüche," *Das Institutum Judaicum der Universität Tübingen 1971/72* 45-68. — E. JENNI, *THAT* I, 755-61. — L. KÖHLER, K. L. SCHMIDT, and A. DEBRUNNER, "Hebr. *jāṣā'* und Mk 8:11," *TZ* 3 (1947) 471-73. — J. SCHNEIDER, *TDNT* II, 678-80. — For further bibliography see *TWNT* X, 1086.

1. Of the 214 occurrences (excluding Mark 16:20; John 8:9), more than three-fourths appear in the Evangelists (38 in Mark, 43 in Matthew, 44 in Luke and 29 in Acts, 28 in John) and 1–3 John (4); also Revelation (14), Hebrews (5), and James (1).

As a vb. of self-movement signifying change of place from one point of origin, ἐξέρχομαι most commonly relates to a living thing, but it also is used with respect to things associated with the main subject (blood, John 19:34; Rev 14:20; lightning, Matt 24:27; thoughts, Matt 15:18f.; blasphemy and praise, Jas 3:10; a cry, Rev 16:17; 19:5). It is, of course, used most in narrative contexts (so also 2 Cor 2:13; 8:17; Phil 4:15). It is more specific in relation to the simple form, a complement to εἰσέρχομαι (the two are connected in John 10:19; Acts 1:21, *associate with*) and προσέρχομαι, and a synonym of ἀπέρχομαι and ἐκπορεύομαι.

2. The *ca.* 750 occurrences in the LXX are, for the most part, translations of the qal of *yṣ'* (785 occurrences according to Jenni). Thus it is used less often for the leaving of a place (so Matt 5:26 par., *get out;* Acts 16:19, hope that has *vanished;* 1 John 2:19, *gone out* from the community) than to emphasize the appearance at a particular place (Acts 28:3, *coming out* of the serpent). Five NT occurrences are in OT citations: Matt 2:6 (*come from;* cf. Heb 7:5, *descended from* Abraham); Acts 7:3f., 7 (Abraham's departure; cf. Heb 11:8 bis), Rom 10:14 (the *spreading* of a report; cf. 1 Thess 1:8; 1 Cor 14:36; Mark 1:28 par.; John 21:23; also Luke 2:1, an edict *goes out*), 2 Cor 6:14 (*separate oneself;* cf. Rev 18:4 and 3:12, *be separated*). Heb 3:16 recalls the *Exodus* from Egypt. The idiom in 1 Cor 5:10, "*leave* the world" (= die; BAGD s.v.)., also has a Semitic background.

Where the vb. appears in a text without a partitive gen. and a corresponding prep., the prep. in the compound has a semitizing character. Thus the point of origin is not emphasized in such a way that it would stand in the foreground. Ἐξέρχομαι in these cases means *come* (Köhler: 1 Sam 17:4; Zech 5:5, and elsewhere): of enemies, Mark 3:6, 21 (in the latter with a complementary infinitive); 8:11 (Schmidt, against G. Wohlenberg, *Mark* [KNT] ad loc.: "came out of their hiding place"), of false teachers, 1 John 4:1; 2 John 7; of Satan, Rev 20:7; of angels of judgment, Matt 13:49; 9 times in Revelation for visionary *appearances:* of horses in 6:2 (with final partc. and ἵνα; 4 times of angels (each time after a preceding impf. of the simple form), 14:15, 17f.; 15:6; of locusts, 9:3; of a sword, 19:21.

Where the vb. has a final complement describing a task, a messenger's account of his mission is present as a variation of the final ἦλθον sayings (Dan 9:23). Here ἐξέρχομαι means *appear as a messenger* (Bühner): Mark 1:38 (and thus v. 35 is also intended); then Mark 4:3 is

an allegorizing form of the messenger's account of himself. Such a report is present where the following account is primarily about the activity of proclamation, either indirectly or directly: Jesus, Mark 2:13; his emissaries, 6:12; healed men, Mark 1:45; 2:12 (making 1:28 concrete!); Matt 9:31f. (as expansion of 9:28), wandering prophets, 3 John 7 (with final ὑπέρ). This form is present further in the Johannine syntagma, which appears six times, of first person aor. + partitive gen. + gen. referring to God as content of the messenger's account of himself (8:42, parallel to the simple form, cf. 3:2; 13:3; 16:27f.; 17:8) and reception by those who are his (16:30; cf. v. 27 and 17:8) in the framework of the Johannine sending-christology (cf. 8:42; 17:8, complementary to ἀποστέλλω). Here there is no final determination, while the reciprocal return to God gives the personal claim a new determination (13:3; 16:28).

3. In Mark the compound is frequently used and appears (except in 7:29f.) always in the aor., the normal tense for narratives. It is used *ca.* 20 times in pericope introductions and transitions and serves to join activities, 13 times in the preparatory form of the conjunctive partc. Typical of Mark is also the pleonastic repetition of the prep. of the compound to indicate the point of origin (10 times, also ἀπό only in 11:12, ἐκεῖθεν in 6:1; 9:30, ἔξω in 14:68), while the complementary indication of direction appears only 7 times (εἰς, 1:28; 8:27; 11:11; 14:26, 28; παρά, 2:13; ἐπί for the personal adversary in 14:48). The most frequent subject is Jesus (1:35, 38; 2:13; 5:2; 6:1, 34; 7:31; and [concluding with] 8:27!); also in the pl. with his followers (1:29; 6:54; 9:30; 11:11; 14:26).

In contrast the usage in Q is grammatically and functionally more comprehensive, but it remains within the framework of the primary meaning (13 times: Luke 7:24-26 par.; 9:5 par.; 11:24 bis par.; 12:59 par.; 14:23 par.; also 11:14; 14:18; 17:27; and Matt 24:26f.).

For Matthew increased use of the conjunctive partc. is characteristic (19 times, of which 3 are in the pres.: 8:28; 9:32; 27:32). Pleonastic ἐκ is limited to 5 occurrences, and ἀπό is used in 12:43 (Q); 15:22; 17:18; 21:4 (redactional). The direction of the action is named in the normal proportion mentioned above. Jesus is the subject only 5 times, and only from 13:1 (14:14; 15:21; 21:17; 24:1; only 26:30 has him accompanied by others).

Luke uses the conjunctive partc. only 12 times (pres. in Luke 9:6; 21:37 and 10 times in Acts). In place of the pleonastic prep. (only Acts 7:4; 17:33; 22:18) ἀπό (Luke 13 times, Acts 3 times) is characteristic. The prep. of direction is used in the normal proportion mentioned above (Luke 8 times, Acts 5 times). Jesus is the subject only 8 times, but is addressed in the imv. in Luke 5:8 and 13:31.

The conjunctive partc. is entirely absent in narrative

contexts in John. The frequency of the vb. within the Easter week narrative is striking (13 occurrences from 12:13 to 21:3 in contrast to 7 occurrences from 1:43 to 11:44). Absolute usage is characteristic in these 20 occurrences (9 times: 11:31, 44; 13:30f.; 18:1, 4, 16; 20:3; 21:3).

4. In Mark the second significant complex of usage (9 times) is in four exorcisms (1:25f.; 5:8, 13; 7:29f.; 9:25f., 29), where the three Markan imvs. appear, which demand that the demons *leave*.

Matthew has reduced the passages referring to demons to four passages (only 8:32 and 17:18 are from Mark), despite the Q additions (12:43f.).

In contrast, the demons in Luke are most often the subject (12 times in the Gospel: 4:35 bis, 36, 41; 8:2, 29, 33, 35, 38; 11:14, 24 bis; Acts 8:7; 16:18). Typical is the Lukan complementary usage θεραπεύω ἀπό (Luke 8:2), which indicates that Luke viewed all sickness as demonic: From Jesus the victorious healing power went out continually (impf. 6:19 as doublet to 8:46), *driving out the powers of destruction.*

                                   W. Schenk

ἔξεστιν   *exestin*   it is permitted, it is possible*
ἐξόν   *exon*   it is permitted, it is possible (partc.)*

1. Occurrences in the NT and general usage — 2. Semantic associations in the NT — 3. 1 Cor 6:12; 10:23

Lit.: H. CONZELMANN, *1 Cor* (Hermeneia, 1975) 108-9. — J. DUPONT, *Gnosis* (1949) 291-308. — E. FASCHER, *1 Cor* (THKNT) I (1975) 174f. — W. FOERSTER, *TDNT* II, 560f. — E. GÜTTGEMANNS, *Der leidende Apostel und sein Herr* (FRLANT 90, 1966) 226-28. — E. LOHSE, "Jesu Worte über den Sabbat," FS Jeremias (1960) 79-89. — W. SCHMITHALS, *Gnosticism in Corinth* (1971) 230-34.

1. The impersonal vb. ἔξεστιν occurs 28 times in the NT (Matthew has 8, Mark has 6, Luke has 5, John has 2, Acts has 3, and 1 Corinthians has 4). The neut. partc. ἐξόν appears 3 times (Acts 2:19; 2 Cor 12:4 without a copula, cf. BDF §§127.2; 424: "perhaps the nominative absolute"; Matt 12:4: οὐκ ἐξὸν ἦν). Both forms are normally followed by an inf. (except Mark 2:24; Luke 6:2; 1 Cor 6:12; 10:23) and are basically the same in meaning. In 14 of the total of 31 passages a negative appears with ἔξεστιν/ἐξόν to signify a prohibition or something that is impossible (2 Cor 12:4).

῎Εξεστιν appears outside the NT to indicate what is permitted or forbidden according to law or the divine will, e.g., a marriage, Aeschylus *Prom.* 648; Xenophon *An.* vii.1.21; of a cultic prohibition, Herodotus i.183. The Stoa can speak of the → ἐξουσία of man over himself (Diogenes Laertius vii.121; Epictetus *Ench.* xiv.2); a formulation comparable to 1 Cor 6:12; 10:23 is not present there (Dupont 305). The LXX uses the negative with ἔξεστιν/ἐξόν in the later writings for general prohibitions (2 Esdr 4:14; Esth 4:2; 1 Macc 14:44) and especially to designate what

is forbidden in the Jewish law (3 Macc. 1:11; 4 Macc 5:18; cf. Josephus *Ant.* xx.268). Rabbinic usage of *rᵉšûṭ* for what is permitted or forbidden is comparable.

2. Frequently in the Gospels ἔξεστιν is used for regulations of the Jewish law, negatively, for work forbidden on the sabbath, e.g., plucking grain (τί ποιοῦσιν τοῖς σάββασιν ὃ οὐκ ἔξεστιν;), Mark 2:24 par. Matt 12:2/Luke 6:2; bearing of a pallet, John 5:10. The question in Mark 3:4 (par. Matt 12:10, [12]/Luke 6:9; cf. 14:3), ἔξεστιν τοῖς σάββασιν ἀγαθὸν ποιῆσαι ἢ κακοποιῆσαι . . . ; is likewise formulated in a juridical way: *Is it permitted?* In connection with the situation described, it becomes a fundamental question, which at the same time exposes the inquirer, who can only react with silence: If your sabbath law permits the destruction of life (either by hindering the healing of a sick person or, more probably, by lying in wait for Jesus as he is destined for destruction), but forbids the saving of life (through healing), any sabbath concession contradicts the essential intent of the sabbath. The meaning of the question is thus: "*Is it within one's legal rights* on the sabbath . . . ?"

The cultic prohibition of eating the showbread is referred to in Mark 2:26 par. Matt 12:4/Luke 6:4 (cf. Lev 24:9; 1 Sam 21:7); the prohibition of marriage of relatives (in connection with adultery) is found in Mark 6:18 par. Matt 14:4 (cf. Lev 18:16; Deut 25:5f.); the right to divorce is mentioned in Mark 10:2 par. Matt 19:3 (cf. Deut 24:1). Matt 27:6 (cf. Deut 23:18) mentions the prohibition of bringing "impure money" into the temple.

The question of the Pharisees and Herodians about the payment of taxes, which was intended to entrap Jesus (Mark 12:14 par. Matt 22:17/Luke 20:22) was directed toward what is right with God, and was intended to bring Jesus into conflict with Roman law. Roman law is alluded to in John 18:31; Acts 16:21; 22:25 (cf. also the question of "ecclesiastical law," οὐκ ἐξόν ἐστιν, in Ign. *Smyrn.* 8:2). General usage of the right of the owner is mentioned in Matt 20:15 ("Am I not *allowed* to . . . ?"). A rhetorical formula is ἐξὸν εἰπεῖν μετὰ παρρησίας, "I *may* speak to you confidently . . ." (Acts 2:29). Paul speaks to the tribune with the "politeness" of the prisoner: "*May* I say something to you?" (21:37).

In 2 Cor 12:4 ἃ οὐκ ἐξὸν ἀνθρώπῳ λαλῆσαι refers to the "inexpressible words" (ἄρρητα ῥήματα) that Paul heard in his vision and "which no one *is able* to utter." The translation "may not" (cf. R. Bultmann, *2 Cor* [Eng. tr., 1985] 222) understands the statement against the background of the secret formulas of the mysteries. However, Paul emphasizes that an ἄνθρωπος, who (still) belongs to the earth, can participate in the heavenly phenomenon, but is not able to speak the "heavenly language" (cf. also K. G. Kuhn, *TDNT* II, 561n.1). This interpretation corresponds to the fact that Paul distances himself twice (vv. 2f.) in his person from the ecstatic experience as "event" and places the accent totally on the participation in the heavenly world granted by God (cf. also Philo *Her.* 259, 266; *Jos. As.* 14:3; *1 Enoch* 71:11, where Enoch can join in the heavenly praise of God only after his transformation).

3. Paul uses the phrase πάντα (μοι) ἔξεστιν 4 times, in 1 Cor 6:12a, b; 10:23 (twice, without μοί). He limits the phrase each time with an additional clause: ἀλλ' οὐ πάντα συμφέρει (reminiscent of the Stoa) in 6:12a and 10:23a, ἀλλ' οὐκ ἐγὼ ἐξουσιασθήσομαι ὑπό τινος in 6:12b, and ἀλλ' οὐ πάντα οἰκοδομεῖ in 10:23b. Inasmuch as Paul elsewhere never describes the freedom of Christians with the legally determined formula πάντα (μοι) ἔξεστιν, which could be understood against the background of the superior consciousness (ἐξουσία) of the Stoic or Gnostic consciousness of authority (Schmithals, Güttgemanns), in all probability he cites a Corinthian slogan or at least a saying which the Corinthians have made their own. The saying certainly did not derive from Paul himself (against H. Lietzmann and W. G. Kümmel, *1–2 Cor* [HNT, [4]1949] ad loc.). Rather, the Pauline message of freedom had been developed into the self-confident morality of the pneumatics under the influence of Gnostic-dualistic consciousness (cf. W. Schrage, *ZNW* 67 [1976] 214-34, esp. 217-20). For the pneumatic all earthly things are "adiaphora," matters that do not affect his essential life.

The first limitation (6:12a/10:23a) has no theological accent, and can be explained from the framework of Cynic-Stoic ethics (cf. Conzelmann). Probably it is not a component of the Corinthian speech. Paul appeals to the widespread knowledge of the danger of libertinism perverting freedom and presents his better knowledge as a reminder to the Corinthians (cf. 7:35; 2 Cor 8:10; 12:1). The second limitation indicates the connection to the theme under discussion: the wordplay ἔξεστιν/ἐξουσιασ-θήσομαι in 6:12b brings into view πορνεία as a threatening danger (cf. vv. 15-20). Οὐκ οἰκοδομεῖ in 10:23b is further elaborated in v. 24 and points to the larger context, particularly to the consideration of "another person's conscience" and the commitment to the salvation of everyone (cf. vv. 29, 32f.). In order to maintain in the translation the inadequacy of the citation for expressing Paul's view of freedom, it is best to accent the legal aspect of ἔξεστιν: "Everything *is permitted* (for me)/I am *at liberty*" (cf. Fascher, Conzelmann, Schmithals 231f.).   H. Balz

ἐξετάζω *exetazō* investigate, find out*

Imv. ἐξετάσατε is used in Matt 2:8 with περί: "*investigate* diligently concerning the child," and in 10:11: "*Find out/inquire* who in it is worthy." John 21:12: "None of the disciples dared to *inquire*."

ἐξηγέομαι *exēgeomai* tell, relate, report*

1. Occurrences in the NT — 2. Luke-Acts — 3. John 1:18

Lit.: C. K. BARRETT, *John* (1978) 170. — F. BÜCHSEL, *TDNT* II, 908. — R. SCHNACKENBURG, *John* (Eng. tr.) I (1967) 274. — SPICQ, *Notes* I, 256-58.

1. Except for John 1:18 ἐξηγέομαι appears in the NT only 5 times in the Lukan double work (cf. the almost synonymous → διηγέομαι): Luke 24:35; Acts 10:8; 15:12, 14; 21:19 (also *Herm. Vis.* iv.2.5; *1 Clem.* 49:2; *Gos. Pet.* 11:45). The vb. means (*descriptively*) elaborate, explain, report. In John 1:18 the meaning *reveal* (divine mysteries) is present (cf. Plato *R.* iv.427c; v.469a; see also Sir 43:31: ἐκδιηγέομαι); according to BAGD s.v., ἐξηγέομαι is often a "t.t. for the activity of priests and soothsayers who impart information or reveal divine secrets; also used w[ith] ref[erence] to divine beings themselves"; references in BAGD (see also R. Bultmann, *John* [Eng. tr., 1971] 83; Barrett).

2. The subjects of the vb. in Luke-Acts (following the sequence of the passages in → 1) are the Emmaus disciples, Cornelius, Barnabas and Paul, Simeon, and Paul. The content of the reports in Acts is the experience of the act of God, which the narrator understands as evidence that the Gentile mission is God's (revealed) will and assignment. In Luke 24:35 the two Emmaus disciples *report* to the Jerusalem congregation "what happened on the road and how he [Jesus] made himself known to them in the breaking of bread." In all instances the author himself has previously narrated what the speaker reports as his testimony. Thus (cf. the use of → διηγέομαι in Luke 8:39; 9:10; Acts 9:27; 12:17) Luke indicates how he wants his "report" (διήγησις, Luke 1:1) to be understood and where the origins of his report are to be found.

3. John 1:18b emphasizes (polemically) the exclusive (cf. 18a) role of the divine logos as revealer. He is called "(the) only God" or (according to Θ Koine it vg) "the only Son." The "only" one *has brought* (ἐξηγήσατο) to the earth the once-for-all (aor.) *revelation* which he received from his direct experience of God. The invisible God has now been revealed through Jesus Christ in his "glory," "grace and truth" (vv. 14, 17). → μονογενής 5.
                                                            G. Schneider

ἐξήκοντα *hexēkonta* sixty*

Mark 4:8, 20 par. Matt 13:8, 23, of the *sixty*fold yield of the seed. 1 Tim 5:9 in the requirement that the widow should be "not less than *sixty* years old." Other NT numbers with *sixty*: Rev 11:3 and 12:6 (1260 days); 13:18 (the number of the beast: 666). Luke 24:13: "to a village *sixty* [p[75] A B D, etc.] stadia [*ca.* 11 km.] from Jerusalem" (on the variant reading ἑκατὸν ἑξήκοντα "one hundred sixty" [*ca.* 30 km.] in א K* Θ Π, etc., which fits the location of → Ἐμμαοῦς [Emmaus/Nikopolis], see J. Wanke, *Die Emmauserzählung* [1973] 37-39).

ἐξῆς *hexēs*   next (in a sequence) (adv.)*

Lit.: H. SCHÜRMANN, *Luke* (HTKNT) I (1969) 399, 569. — M. VÖLKEL, "Exegetische Erwägungen zum Verständnis des Begriffs καθεξῆς im lk Prolog," *NTS* 20 (1973/74) 289-99, esp. 295.

In the NT ἐξῆς (like the derivative → καθεξῆς) appears only in the Lukan double work (5 times). Outside the NT ἐξῆς is attested from Homer on—on the nonliterary attestation, see Moulton/Milligan s.v. It appears also in Hellenistic Judaism (LXX, Philo, Josephus, *T. 12 Patr.*). The NT uses the adv. only in a temporal sense, normally in (redactional) introductory verses of a section (Luke 7:11; 9:37; Acts 21:1). Except in Luke 7:11 (ἐν τῷ ἑξῆς) the simple dat., τῇ ἑξῆς (ἡμέρᾳ) (cf. BDF 200.1), is used to indicate a temporal relationship. In most instances the pertinent noun must be supplied (as in *Ep. Arist.* 262; Josephus *B.J.* ii.430; Pap. Oxy. no. 1063, l. 6), as in Luke 7:11: ἐν τῷ ἑξῆς (χρόνῳ), *subsequently/in the ensuing time*, or in Acts 21:1; 25:17; 27:18 (also Luke 7:11 א* C D W; cf. Schürmann 569n.113): τῇ ἑξῆς (ἡμέρᾳ), *on the following day*. The full phrase is in Luke 9:37 (τῇ ἑξῆς ἡμέρᾳ, so also *SIG* no. 1170, l. 24; Josephus *Ant.* iv.302) and indicates that the phrase is to be completed in this way elsewhere (i.e., ἑξῆς is not to be substantivized; cf. BDF §241.2).

Both ἑξῆς passages in Luke speak of the temporal sequence of Jesus' journeys (to Nain; from the Mount of Transfiguration), while the three passages in Acts speak of Paul's journeys (first-person "we" reports in 21:1 and 27:18; the report of Festus before Agrippa II in 25:17). ἑξῆς has a function similar to the Lukan → καθεξῆς.

                            G. Schneider

ἐξηχέω *exēcheō*   trans.: cause to resound; pass.: be caused to resound, ring out*

1 Thess 1:8: "The word of the Lord *has sounded forth* from you not only in Macedonia and Achaia."

ἕξις, εως, ἡ   *hexis*   exercise, practice*

Heb 5:14, of the sense organs, "which are trained *by practice* (διὰ τὴν ἕξιν)."

ἐξίστημι *existēmi*   confuse; intrans.: lose one's senses, be outside oneself*

1. Intrans. with a weakened meaning — 2. Trans. — 3. 2 Cor 5:13 and Mark 3:21

Lit.: G. HARTMANN, "Mk 3,20f," *BZ* 11 (1913) 249-79. — J. LAMBRECHT, "The Relatives of Jesus in Mark," *NovT* 16 (1974) 241-58, esp. 244-46. — W. MUNDLE, *DNTT* I, 526-30. — A. OEPKE, *TDNT* II, 459f. — H.-H. SCHROEDER, *Eltern und Kinder in der Verkündigung Jesu* (1972) 110-24. — J. E. STEINMUELLER, "Jesus and the οἱ παρ' αὐτοῦ (Mk. 3:20-21)," *CBQ* 4 (1942) 355-59. — H. WANSBROUGH, "Mark 3:21—Was Jesus out of His Mind?" *NTS* 18 (1971/72) 233-35. — D. WENHAM, "The Meaning of Mark III.21," *NTS* 21 (1974/75) 295-300. — A. WIMMER, "Apostolos quosdam exiisse, ut Jesum domum ducerent (Marcus 3:20 sq)," *VD* 31 (1953) 131-43.

The vb. ἐξίστημι (including related forms ἐξιστάνω and ἐξιστάω) appears in the NT 17 times. Three meanings can be distinguished.

1. The most frequent meaning is a weakened meaning in the intrans.: a mental condition of being *outside oneself* or of *astonishment* because of amazement or fear. Mark uses the vb. 3 times, Luke 8 times (2 times in the Gospel, 6 times in Acts) in this sense. Matthew writes in 12:23, "The whole crowd *was astonished*." Inasmuch as he uses θαυμάζω in the parallel text 9:33 (as does Luke in 11:14; probably already in Q), ἐξίσταντο in Matt 12:23 is apparently written under the influence of Mark 3:21, but with a different meaning. As in Matt 12:23, those who are present (the disciples, the people) are astonished after a miracle of Jesus in Mark 2:12; 6:51; and 5:42 par. Luke 8:56. In Luke 2:47 the amazement is the result of a remarkable appearance of the young Jesus in the temple.

In Acts also ἐξίστημι appears in connection with a wonderful event brought about by God: 2:7, 12 (miracle of languages at Pentecost); 9:21 (preaching of Paul); 10:45 (gift of the Spirit to the Gentiles); and 12:16 (liberation of Peter from prison). According to 8:13 Simon Magus is astonished by the miracles which Philip performs.

2. It is striking that directly before Acts 8:13 the same vb. ἐξίστημι is used twice trans.: Simon Magus *astonished* the people with his magical practices (8:9, 11). In Luke 24:22 the disciples say: "Some women from our company *shocked* us." In these three passages ἐξίστημι means "*confuse someone, confound, drive outside oneself*" (in a weakened sense).

3. Two NT passages remain, to which a stronger meaning must be attributed. In 2 Cor 5:13 Paul writes, "For if *we are in ecstasy* (ἐξέστημεν), it is for God; if we are in our right minds (σωφρονοῦμεν), it is for you." Paul probably alludes to his extraordinry "ecstatic" experiences (→ ἔκστασις 1); cf. 2 Cor 12:1-6. With the contrast between the aor. and the pres. that follows, he indicates that the ecstatic condition for him was temporary and not common. With the contrast of "for God—for you" he expresses himself in a somewhat critical and polemical position with respect to the apostolic value of these extraordinary gifts.

In Mark 3:21 the relatives of Jesus come out to seize him, "for they said, 'He *has lost his senses*'" (i.e., he is not in his right mind; ἐξέστη is a "timeless aorist," V. Taylor, *Mark* [1963] ad loc.). While 2 Cor 2:13 has a positive connotation, a negative sense is present here. Mark himself brings the conviction of the relatives into association with the opinion of the scribes, according to whom Jesus is possessed (v. 22). Mark 3:20f. appears to have been composed by Mark himself (probably on the basis of Q texts, cf. Luke 11:14; Matt 9:32-34; 12:22-23). Mark continues after the interruption in 3:22-30 with the pericope of the "true relatives" (3:31-35).

The numerous old and new attempts to avoid the apparent meaning of the astonishing saying by the relatives (Mary!) are not convincing, e.g., saying that οἱ παρ' αὐτοῦ (v. 21a) were the disciples, that ἔλεγον (v. 21b) might be an impersonal vb. ("it was" [= the people] said), that the subj. of ἔλεγον was the people (see v. 20, ὄχλος), or that ἐξέστη could be understood to mean only that he (Jesus!) *was astonished*.　　　　　　　　J. Lambrecht

ἐξισχύω　*exischyō*　be able*

Eph 3:18: "so that you *may be able* to comprehend. . . ."

ἔξοδος, ου, ἡ　*exodos*　departure

Lit.: BAGD s.v. — E. JENNI, *THAT* I, 755-61. — LSJ s.v. — W. MICHAELIS, *TDNT* V, 103-9. — MOULTON/MILLIGAN s.v. — *PGL* s.v. — PREISIGKE, *Wörterbuch* with Suppl. I, s.v.

1. The noun ἔξοδος appears in literary contexts from Sophocles and Herodotus on. It also appears in papyrus documents and frequently in the LXX (Preisigke mentions more than 80 papyrus passages; there are more than 70 in the LXX). The basic meaning is a) (verbal): act of leaving, b) (spatial): place from which or through which one leaves. Its opposite is → εἴσοδος, "entrance." For the numerous special meanings from the commercial, juristic, and military background, cf. Michaelis 104f.

2. In the NT ἔξοδος occurs 3 times. a) The earliest in time is Heb 11:22, which refers to Gen 50:24, where Joseph predicted before his death that God would lead the children of Israel into the land of promise. For this event, the *Exodus* from Egypt, ἔξοδος is, already in the LXX, a t.t. (see the heading of the book of Exodus in the LXX; cf. Michaelis 104; Jenni 760). b) In Luke 9:31 and 2 Pet 1:15 ἔξοδος is used to mean *departure from life* (= death). This meaning is found also in Hellenistic Jewish literature (cf. Josephus *Ant.* iv.189; Wis 3:2; 7:6; Philo, *Virt.* 77; *T. Naph.* 1:1), in Arrian (Epictetus *Diss.* iv.4.38), and in Christian writers (Justin *Dial.* 105:5, cf. 105:3: ἔξοδος τοῦ βίου; Irenaeus *Haer.* iii.1 = Eusebius *HE* v.1.36, 2.3, 8.3; Canon 13 of the Council of Nicea

[*Conciliorum Oecumenicorum Decreta,* 1962, 11]; Pap. London 77 [sixth century A.D.]; cf. also Clement of Alexandria *Strom.* iii.9). In a later time the meaning "future destiny" is found (*Herm. Vis.* iii.4.3).

　　　　　　　　　　　　　　　　　　R. Peppermüller

ἐξολεθρεύω　*exolethreuō*　root out *

Acts 3:23, citing Lev 23:29 LXX: everyone who does not listen to that prophet "*will be rooted out* from the people." J. Schneider, *TDNT* V, 171; C. M. Martini, *Bib* 50 (1969) 1-14.

ἐξομολογέω　*exomologeō*　confess, praise*

1. Occurrences and meaning — 2. Confession of sins — 3. Praise

Lit.: G. BORNKAMM, "Lobpreis, Bekenntnis und Opfer," *idem, Aufsätze* III, 122-39. — D. FÜRST, *DNTT* I, 344-48. — O. HOFIUS, *Der Christushymnus Phil 2,6-11* (1976) 18-55. — R. J. LEDOGAR, "Verbs of Praise in the LXX Translation of the Hebrew Canon," *Bib* 48 (1967) 29-56. — O. MICHEL, *TDNT* V, 199-220 (bibliography). — C. WESTERMANN, *THAT* I, 674-82.

1. The vb. ἐξομολογέω appears 10 times in the NT. The act., which is also rare in Greek outside the NT, appears only once: In Luke 22:6 it is used in a secular sense and has there the meaning which is most often associated with the simple form → ὁμολογέω—*promise, give a pledge* or *agree, consent*. The other 9 occurrences, all mid., have a theological meaning indebted to religious usage in the LXX (*ca.* 110 occurrences), which has received a specific shape from the Hebrew vb. *yādâ.*

The root *ydh* includes in the MT—and then also in the Qumran and rabbinic texts—the two nuances of "praise God" (normally in the hiphil *hôdâ*) and "confess sins before God" (thus the hithpael *hiṭwaddâ*). The striking double meaning is to be explained by the fact that both praise and confession of sins refer back to one preceding—saving and judging—demonstration of God's power. Thus they express the answer with which people publicly recognize Yahweh and give him the honor (see Bornkamm; Westermann; Von Rad, *Theology* I, 356-70).

The LXX renders *hiṭwaddâ*, "confess sins," with ἐξομολογέομαι only in Dan 9:4, 20. Corresponding to the MT the vb. in v. 20 is associated with the acc. obj. τὰς ἁμαρτίας. However, in v. 4 it is used in the absolute (= "make a confession of sins"). The same usage is found frequently in Hellenistic Jewish literature (τὰς ἁμαρτίας: *Jos. As.* 11:11; 12:3; Josephus *Ant.* viii.129; absolute: *Jos. As.* 14:1; Josephus *B.J.* v.415; *Apoc. Mos.* 25:3 [act.]). It is comparatively close in meaning to the secular "openly acknowledge/confess something" (Sus 14; Josephus *B.J.* i.625; Plutarch *Num.* 16.3; *Ant.* 59.5; Lucian *Herm.* 75).

In contrast to the use of the word in secular Greek, in the LXX ἐξομολογέομαι takes on a totally new sense, as the vb. is used commonly to translate *hôdâ*, "praise," and appears along with such terms as → ψάλλω, "sing praises," and → αἰνέω, "praise" (see Pss 17:50; 34:18; 56:10; 99:4). Analogous to the Hebrew construction *hôdâ lᵉ*, the corresponding obj. (God or the name of God) appears in the dat. Michel 205 describes the use of the vb. in the sense of "praise" correctly as a "lexical Hebraism." The original meaning "recognize/acknowledge" still remains, inasmuch as ἐξομολογέω, like its Hebrew equivalent, expresses the fact that in praise the public acknowledgement and testimony of the saving power of God takes place (cf. Ledogar 40f.). In dependence on the LXX ἐξομολογέω, "praise," is found in *Pss. Sol.* 10:5; 15:2; 16:5; *T. Job* 40:2; and Philo *All.* i.80 (cf. 82); ii.95 (cf. 96); iii.26.

Corresponding to the usage of the LXX, ἐξομολογέομαι means also in the NT and other early Christian literature: a) *confess sins* (Mark 1:5 par. Matt 3:6; Jas 5:16; *Herm. Vis.* i.1.3 and often; cf. *Did.* 4:14; 14:1), *make a confession of sins* (absolute: Acts 19:18; Rom 14:11; *1 Clem.* 52:1f.; *2 Clem.* 8:3); b) *praise* (Matt 11:25 par. Luke 10:21; Rom 15:9 [citing Ps 17:50 LXX]; *1 Clem.* 61:3; *Herm. Man.* x.3.2) or *confess in praise* (so Phil 2:11, where confession is associated with the aspect of praise [cf. 2 Macc 7:37]).

2. Through a public confession of sin penitent Jews declared their repentance at the baptism of John (Mark 1:5 par.; cf. 1QS 1:24ff.; CD 20:28ff.) and newly converted Christians declared their rejection of superstitious practices before the Church (Acts 19:18). Jas 5:16 speaks of a confession of sin by one of the members of the Christian community. Whether this is exclusively for the case of sickness mentioned in 5:14f. or is like *Did.* 4:14; 14:1— a confession which everyone in the Church should make before each other—cannot be decided with certainty.

In the context of Rom 14:10b-12 Paul interprets the Scripture citation in v. 11 from Isa 45:23b LXX (A Q אcorr) as a reference to the final judgment. Therefore he finds in ἐξομολογέομαι in v. 11b a reference to the eschatological confession of sin that every person must make before the judgment seat of God (Michel 215; Hofius 50n.113; otherwise, e.g., Käsemann, *Rom* [Eng. tr.] ad loc.).

3. The decision of God to open himself and his salvation in Jesus' activity esp. to the poor and lowly is the subject of the thanksgiving in Matt 11:25f. par. The introductory formula ἐξομολογοῦμαί σοι, ὅτι, "I *praise* you, that," corresponds to the phrase '*ôḏe̅ā kî* in the OT psalms (Pss 86:12f.; 118:21; 138:1f., and elsewhere; cf. Sir 51:1f.; *Pss. Sol.* 16:5) and in the songs of Qumran (1QH 2:20, 31; 3:19, 37, and elsewhere).

The pre-Pauline Christ hymn in Phil 2:6-11 speaks in vv. 10f.—taking up the oath of God in Isa 45:23b LXX (A Q אcorr)—of the universal homage, including proskynesis and acclamation, to be given at the final consummation to the crucified and exalted Christ, who is the Lord of the world: every creature in heaven, on earth, and under the earth will *confess:* "Jesus Christ is Lord" (v. 11). And thus they will join in the cry heard in worship in which the Church already confesses Jesus as → κύριος

(Rom 10:9; 1 Cor 12:3). The background for this saying is the richly attested expectation, found in the OT and in ancient Judaism, of a universal homage to Yahweh, the king of the world (see Hofius 41ff.). The widely held interpretation, which sees in 2:10f. a description of the subjection of the godless powers and their acclamation of Christ—understood as a judicial act—at his exaltation, is hardly tenable (see Hofius 18ff.).   O. Hofius

ἐξόν *exon* possible, permitted

Partc. of → ἔξεστιν.

ἐξορκίζω *exorkizō* adjure, cause to swear*

Matt 26:63 (cf. Mark): ἐξορκίζω σε κατὰ τοῦ θεοῦ, "*I adjure you* by (the living) God." J. Schneider, *TDNT* V, 464f.

ἐξορκιστής, οῦ, ὁ *exorkistēs* exorcist*

Acts 19:13, of the traveling Jewish exorcists (cf. also the description of exorcism in that environment in Josephus *Ant.* viii.42-49). J. Schneider, *TDNT* V, 464f.

ἐξορύσσω *exoryssō* dig up, (of eyes) tear out*

Mark 2:4, of the "digging out" of the (clay) roof, in order to let down the pallet with the lame man. Gal 4:15, of the Galatians who, at that time, would have—if possible—*torn out* their eyes for Paul.

ἐξουδενέω *exoudeneō* treat with contempt*

Mark 9:12, of the Son of man, "that he will suffer much and *be treated with contempt.*"

ἐξουθενέω (-όω) *exoutheneō (-oō)* have a low opinion of, scorn, reject contemptuously*

Luke 18:9; 23:11; Acts 4:11; Rom 14:3, 10; 1 Cor 1:28; 6:4; 16:11; 2 Cor 10:10; Gal 4:14; 1 Thess 5:20; Mark 9:12 v.l.

ἐξουσία, ας, ἡ *exousia* freedom; ability; power; authority

1. Occurrences and meanings in the NT — 2. a) God's ἐξουσία — b) The ἐξουσία of Jesus — c) The ἐξουσία of the Church — d) Supraterrestrial powers — e) Authority to command — f) Domain — 3. Romans 13 — 4. 1 Cor 11:10

Lit.: P. AMIET, "Exousia im NT," *IKZ* 61 (1971) 233-42. — O. BETZ and C. BLENDINGER, *DNTT* II, 601-16 (bibliography). — W. FOERSTER, *TDNT* II, 560-75 (bibliography). — W. GRUND-MANN, *Der Begriff der Kraft in der neutestamentlichen*

Gedankenwelt (BWANT 4, 8, 1932). — J. Lange, *Das Erscheinen des Auferstandenen im Evangelium nach Mattäus* (FzB 11,
1973). — K. Prümm, *Diakonia Pneumatos. Der 2. Korinther-
brief als Zugang zur apostolischen Botschaft* II (1962), ch. 8,
excursuses III and IV. — H. Schlier, *Principalities and Powers
in the NT* (1961). — For further bibliography see *TWNT* X,
1080f.

On Romans 13: M. Borg, "A New Context for Romans
XIII," *NTS* 19 (1972/73) 205-18. — U. Duchrow, *Christenheit
und Weltverantwortung. Traditionsgeschichte und systematische
Struktur der Zweireichelehre* (1970). — J. Friedrich, W. Pöhlmann, and P. Stuhlmacher, "Zur historischen Situation und Intention von Röm 13,1-7," *ZTK* 73 (1976) 131-66 (bibliography).
— E. Käsemann, *Rom* (Eng. tr., 1980) (bibliography). —
F. Neugebauer, "Zur Auslegung von Röm 13,1-7," *KD* 8 (1962)
151-72. — A. Strobel, "Zum Verständnis von Rm 13," *ZNW*
47 (1956) 67-93.

On 1 Cor 11:10: G. Dautzenberg, *Urchristliche Prophetie*
(1975) 265-69. — G. D. Fee, *1 Cor* (NICNT, 1987) (bibliography pp. 492f., nn. 3, 7). — A. Feuillet, "Le signe de puissance
sur la tête de la femme," *NRT* 95 (1973) 945-54. — J. A.
Fitzmyer, "A Feature of Qumran Angelology and the Angels of
1 Cor XI:10," *NTS* 4 (1957/58) 48-58. — M. D. Hooker,
"Authority on Her Head," *NTS* 10 (1963/64) 410-16. —
A. Jaubert, "Le voile des femmes (1 Cor XI.2-16)," *NTS* 18
(1971/72) 419-30.

1. Ἐξουσία occurs in both secular Greek and in the LXX—
in the latter not as frequently as the related term δύναμις (about
50 occurrences in contrast to *ca.* 400 of δύναμις; on the distinction between the two see below)—and most often translates
Heb. *memšālâ*. In the LXX ἐξουσία can mean the "unrestricted
sovereignty of God." However, this meaning must be determined
from the context as it in no way is inherent in the term itself
(Foerster 565).

Ἐξουσία occurs in the NT 102 times, most frequently
in Revelation (21 occurrences) and Luke (16 occurrences). The term includes a very wide range of meaning,
from *authority* to the "rulers and functionaries of the spirit
world" (BAGD s.v. 4cβ). Its nuances cannot always be
rendered precisely, esp. the transition between the first
three meanings given in BAGD: 1. freedom, right;
2. ability, power; 3. authority, warrant. These meanings
are fluid because right and authority cross over to each
other, authority presupposes power/ability (cf., e.g., Acts
8:19 and numerous texts in Revelation), and the first
meaning encompasses the third. Ἐξουσία is associated
with the following categories: God, Jesus/Son of Man,
disciples/Church, human beings, and Satan, and is used
abstractly for earthly and supraterrestrial powers.

2. a) The power of God, which makes the eschatological determination concerning humankind, is above every
other power (Luke 12:5). There is no appeal to a higher
norm against God's authority. Thus his right and creative
freedom are compared with the power of a potter who
can form from clay whatever he wishes (Rom 9:21). This
divine perfect power is not only affirmed in argument,
but is also confessed doxologically (Jude 25).

However, God allows his Son to participate in his
authority, and has given to him the power to exercise
judgment (John 5:27; this may also be the meaning of
John 17:2, cf. R. Schnackenburg, *John* [Eng. tr., 1982]
III, 171), but to the Church he has given the authority to
forgive sins (Matt 9:8). Over against the tense imminent
expectation Luke indicates that God's authority alone
determines the time of the parousia (Acts 1:8).

b) The life of Jesus is characterized by ἐξουσία in
numerous ways: his teaching is distinguished by its
authority before the scribes, as Mark affirms, but Matthew demonstrates, with the Sermon on the Mount (Matt
7:29 par.; Mark 1:27), because the ἐξουσία of Jesus indicates for Matthew "that Jesus recognizes the will of God,
which is laid down in the Torah and fully establishes its
force" (Lange 32). The opponents of Jesus ask him both
about the right (authority) of forgiving sins which in
Judaism is reserved to God alone (Matt 9:6 par.) and
about his right to cleanse the temple (Matt 21:23f. par.;
21:27 par.). Jesus gives the disciples a share in his authority to cast out demons (Mark 3:15; 6:7 par.).

The Johannine Jesus has the power and the freedom
to give his life and to take it up again (John 10:18). The
political power comes to know that its power over Jesus'
body was granted by God (19:10f.), a fact which is also
true in Luke 4:6 for the devil. As the resurrected one all
power in heaven and on earth has been given to him (Matt
28:18; cf. also Rev 12:10), so that it concerns "his being
entrusted with the eschaton, in which the salvation and
judgment of the world come in Jesus" (Lange 166f.).

A unique feature of Luke's usage is that Luke
frequently places ἐξουσία and δύναμις next to each other
(4:36; 9:1; cf. also 10:19). Thus Luke hardly has the
intention of bringing the power of Jesus (and his disciples) into a special relationship to the πνεῦμα (so
H. Schürmann, *Luke* [HTKNT] 246n.177, 500), as both
terms are used practically as synonyms (cf. H. Conzelmann, *The Theology of St. Luke* [1960] 182). That the
difference between ἐξουσία and the stem δυνα- should not
be too strongly emphasized can be seen from Luke 12:5
and Rom 9:21.

Ἐξουσία is used of the earthly Jesus in his superiority
over demons and scribes and in his participation in the
power of God. It is used for the resurrected one in his
comprehensive position of power. However, one cannot
say that ἐξουσία used in connection with Jesus has the
character of divine power from the very beginning because of its background in the LXX usage (so Foerster
568f.; cf. R. Bultmann, *John* [Eng. tr., 1971] 57n.5). The
authority of Jesus is not characterized normally as something that is transferred from God (cf. of course Matt
28:18 and John 5:27).

c) The right and power of the disciples appears in
various contexts: it is portrayed in the image of the

miraculous power (ability) to walk on serpents and scorpions, and in the power over the might of the enemy (Luke 10:19), "the subjection of the malicious and dangerous powers of the evil one" (G. Baumbach, *Das Verständnis des Bösen* [1963] 181). Altogether different is John 1:12, where believers receive "the *capacity* to become children of God from the Logos" (Schnackenburg, *John* I [1968], 261). In Acts 8:19 the authority/ability of the disciples to bestow the Spirit is addressed, while 9:14; 26:10, 12 refer to the authority given by the chief priests to Paul for the arrest of Jewish apostates.

The apostolic right to live from the gospel and to take along a wife on the missionary journeys is mentioned in 1 Cor 9:4-6, 12, 18; 2 Thess 3:9. This is an authority given to the apostles from the Lord for building up the Church (2 Cor 10:8; 13:10). Although Paul explicitly says in the latter passage that he will use stern measures and his right is evidently assumed, Prümm exaggerates when he writes that "the witness in itself is sufficient to prove the jurisdictional ecclesiastical office at the highest level of his right which is, except for the primacy, a divinely ordained institution" (139).

Christian freedom, which is limited by the consideration of other people (1 Cor 8:9), and freedom of the will (7:37) are both designated ἐξουσία. The context emphasizes in both passages that ἐξουσία is granted to the disciples; they do not receive it from their own authority, but from the authority of God and Jesus, and must act accordingly.

d) The NT use of ἐξουσία for supraterrestrial powers is new, i.e., attested neither in the LXX nor in Hellenistic Greek (cf., to be sure, 2 Macc 3:24 and Foerster 571). Because this usage it is difficult to recognize with certainty, it is disputed whether the ἐξουσίαι, esp. in the Pauline literature (frequently with ἀρχαί), are supraterrestrial powers (Eph 1:21; 6:12; 1 Cor 15:24; Col 1:16; 2:15; 1 Pet 3:22; cf. also Eph 2:2) and whether they are to be seen as hostile toward God in every instance or are in individual passages (e.g., Eph 3:10 and Col 2:10) good (angelic) powers sent by God (cf. Schlier 14f.n.13; Foerster 573f.). This question is of secondary significance, for the emphasis of the statement is on the place of the exalted one above all powers (cf. Neugebauer 169f.).

e) The authority of a ruler to command is designated in Matt 8:9 par.; Luke 19:17; 20:20; Rev 17:12 with ἐξουσία.

f) In Luke 4:6 and 23:7 ἐξουσία means the *territorial domain* (of Herod). In Col 1:13 (cf. also Acts 26:18) this meaning is transferred to Satan. In Eph 2:2 the "ruler of the power of the air" is meant in the phrase τὸν ἄρχοντα τῆς ἐξουσίας τοῦ ἀέρος (so J. Gnilka, *Eph* [HTKNT] ad loc.).

3. O. Cullmann has suggested that ἐξουσίαι ὑπερ-έχουσαι carries a double meaning in Rom 13:1: here along with the state are the "invisible angelic powers and authorities" (*The State in the New Testament* [1956] 66). The state is understood as the executive power of those invisible powers. Strobel and Neugebauer, among others, have opposed this view for significant reasons (cf. esp. the difference in usage between Paul and the deutero-Pauline letters and the suggestion by Strobel that only one of the passages that Cullmann uses as proof is Pauline in the full sense), so that earthly powers alone are mentioned in Rom 13:1-7. Which of the two views is correct?

Contrary to the widespread view, often assumed without discussion, the passage does not speak simply and absolutely of the state, but rather of the state in its various manifestations or the functions that it bears, as pl. ἐξουσίαι and ἄρχοντες evidently indicate. When ἐξουσία appears in the sg. in Rom 13:1b, that is not because the state is under discussion, but because all of the functions of the exercise of power are, according to Paul, traced back to God. The closer characterization of these powers as ὑπερέχουσαι could scarcely refer to them merely as "those who bear rule" (so G. Delling, *TDNT* VIII, 524), but rather to the superior character of those who bear such a function (cf. Strobel 79).

In the discussion of the most recent years the question has been asked to what extent Rom 13:1-7 is specifically Christian and to what extent it has been shaped by Jewish tradition. Neugebauer in particular and Duchrow following him have rejected the frequently represented view (texts in Käsemann 354f.) that in the idea of unconditional submission to the powers there is a widespread (Hellenistic) Jewish commonplace, even if they concede "that the concept of a divinely given rule as such, apart from its definite employment with respect to the ruler and the ruled, could have been been found by Paul in Hellenistic Judaism" (Duchrow 155; cf. Neugebauer 158). This view, that probably the *basis* for the parenesis but not the parenesis itself, was already present in the Jewish tradition (cf. Sir 4:27 [Hebrew]) is to be considered. This is also the case with respect to the first question, for which one normally looks to the context (cf. finally Friedrich, Pöhlmann, and Stuhlmacher 148ff.).

4. A satisfactory explanation for the difficult passage 1 Cor 11:10 and for the use of ἐξουσία in it has not yet been found.

The difficulty is, on the one hand, that the argument in 11:4-9, which is resumed in v. 10, is not certain (cf. H. Conzelmann, *1 Cor* [Eng. tr., Hermeneia] 189). It is, on the other hand, that when the argument is resumed—perhaps because of the lack of clarity of the preceding material (cf. v. 16)—a new basis for the argument is introduced: "because of the angels" (cf. Fitzmyer 49f.). Even if the presence of angels in the cult of Qumran is attested (1QS^a 2:3-11), the arguments for the thesis that Paul's reasoning involves good angels given by God can in any case scarcely be accepted. For the reason for the article with ἀγγέλους, cf. Braun, *Qumran* I, 194. Hooker's argument that evil angels are nowhere found in the NT and thus do not fit the context of Christian worship is probably mistaken (cf. Braun) in the first place; in the second place it overlooks the fact that the reference to the angels in any interpretation goes beyond the context.

Because the apotropaic, or at least magical, protecting

effect of a head covering is attested (b. Šabb. 156b; cf. Billerbeck II, 403f.), the remaining understanding of ἐξ-ουσία in 1 Cor. 11:10, "have *power/strength* on the head" —as a symbolic interpretation of the veil—is perhaps to be preferred.   I. Broer

ἐξουσιάζω *exousiazō* have power (to do something or over someone)*

Lit.: W. FOERSTER, *TDNT* II, 560-75. — E. KÄHLER, *Die Frau in den paulinischen Briefen* (1960) (bibliography). — C. MAURER, "Ehe und Unzucht nach 1 Korinther 6,12–7,7," *WuD* 6 (1959) 159f. — W. SCHRAGE, "Zur Frontstellung der paulinischen Ehebewertung in 1 Kor 7,1-7," *ZNW* 67 (1976) 214-34 (bibliography). — For further bibliography → ἐξουσία.

This vb., derived from ἐξουσία, occurs only 4 times in the NT (the compound κατεξουσιάζω 2 times), and means "have ἐξουσία" with all of the meanings associated with ἐξουσία, esp. *ability*, right, permission (to act).

In 1 Cor 7:4 the construction with negatives preceding the vbs. in the otherwise chiastically constructed sentence is to be noted. The authority of people over their own bodies is denied. 1 Corinthians thus presupposes the equality of man and woman. Thus the distinct motif in v. 5 of reciprocal consideration may be expressed. The absence of any reference here to Paul's reservations against marriage coheres with their clear mention in the context—cf. 7:7ff. and possibly 7:1, if this is not a citation of Paul's opponents (so, e.g., H. Conzelmann, *1 Cor.* [Hermeneia, 1975] 117)—and with the fact that 7:3ff. thinks not only of those who are married at the present moment but also of those to be married (on the discussion, cf. Schrage 229n.60). (On the peculiarity of this situation in which the woman has at her disposal the body of the man, in relation to the history of religions, cf. Schrage 231n.68.) Whether Paul argues against sexual abstinence in general (so Schrage 217) or against the proclamation of libertine views of sexual intercourse (so Maurer 160) must remain undecided in this passage. In any case the apostle rejects the one-sided saying of the Corinthians (7:1) in an almost strangely modern way.

With the libertinistic slogan "all is lawful" in 1 Cor 6:12,which has been influenced by Gnosticism, like the saying in 7:1 (cf. E. Güttgemanns, *Der leidende Apostel und sein Herr* [1966], 226ff. [bibliography]), other Corinthian circles (than those cited in 7:1) justify fornication and participation in pagan cultic meals (cf. 6:13). Paul takes up this slogan (verbally) and then immediately shatters it with the following limitations. The freedom in which all things are permitted is in danger of being dominated by "something." Thus freedom is lost and becomes slavery. Freedom must therefore be oriented toward the συμφέρον or according to οἰκοδομεῖν (cf. 10:23). Even if the freedom slogan of the Corinthians fits formally into

both the Cynic-Stoic and Gnostic views, the juxtaposition of libertine and ascetic circles in the Corinthian church suggests the strong influence of Gnosticism (with Schrage 217ff., against Schmithals, *Gnosticism in Corinth* [1971] 389f.).

Finally, in Luke 22:25—a passage in which the assignment to a special tradition needs reexamination, despite the common view, the partc. οἱ ἐξουσιάζοντες is used to mean *rulers*.

ἐξοχή, ῆς, ἡ *exochē* preference, excellence

Κατ' ἐξοχήν, *par excellence* (Strabo i.2.10; Philo *All.* i.106; *SIG* 810.16 [A.D. 55]. Acts 25:23: ἄνδρες οἱ κατ' ἐξοχὴν τῆς πόλεως, "the *most prominent* men of the city."

ἐξυπνίζω *exypnizō* awaken*

John 11:11, metaphorically: "I am going in order to *awaken* him [Lazarus]." Cf. Job 14:12 LXX: the "awakening" of the dead.

ἔξυπνος, 2 *exypnos* awakened, awake*

Acts 16:27: ἔξυπνος γενόμενος, "when he [the jailer] *awoke*."

ἔξω *exō* out (from within), outside (adv. and improper prep.)*

1. Distribution and usage in the NT — 2. Answering the question "whither?" — a) As an adv. — b) As an improper prep. — 3. Answering the question "where?" — a) As an adv. — b) As an improper prep. — 4. Attributive — 5. Subst. (οἱ ἔξω)

Lit.: BAGD s.v. — J. BEHM, *TDNT* II, 575f. — BDF §§103, 184, 266. — LSJ s.v. — MAYSER, *Grammatik* II, 531f. — Preisigke, *Wörterbuch,* with Supplement, s.v. — SCHWYZER, *Grammatik* II, §§463, 538f. — For further bibliography see *TWNT* X, 1081.

1. Ἔξω as adv. and improper prep. is attested in Greek literature since Homer, and in papyrus documents since the third century before Christ. The LXX uses it with both functions. In the NT it appears 63 times (and as v.l. in Luke 8:54; 24:50; Acts 5:23b; Rev 11:2; 14:20). Attributive use of ἔξω (→ 4) is found in the Gospels and Acts only in Acts 26:11, and subst. use (→ 5) only in Mark 4:11. By comparison, ἔξω is used as merely an adverb of place outside the Gospels and Acts only in Hebrews, 1 John, and Revelation.

2. a) Ἔξω as an adv. in response to the question "whither?" appears as a rule after the vbs. βάλλειν, "throw," ἄγειν, "lead," and ἔρχεσθαι, "come," and its compounds (Mark 14:68; Matt 5:13/Luke 14:35; Matt 13:48; 26:75/Luke 22:62; Luke 8:54 v.l.; Luke 13:28;

24:50 v.l.; John 6:37; 9:34f.; 11:43 [where "come" is to be supplied in the elliptical phrase δεῦρο ἔξω]; 12:31; 15:6; 18:29; 19:4, 5, 13; Acts 9:40; 16:30; 1 John 4:18; Rev 3:12; 11:2). In all of these passages ἔξω can be translated *out*. In Acts 5:34 the expression ἔξω ποιῆσαι means "lead *out*."

b) With the gen. ἔξω in answer to the question "whither?" is used similarly (→ 2.a) after verbs of movement where the point of origin is indicated by the ablative gen.; in all passages the translation *out of* is suitable: Mark 5:10; 8:23; 11:19; 12:8/Matt 21:39/Luke 20:15; Matt 10:14 v.l.; 21:17; Luke 4:29; Acts 4:15; 7:58; 14:19; 16:13; 21:5, 30.

3. a) Ἔξω is used in response to the question "where?" with the meaning *outside (of), outside* (synonymous with → ἔξωθεν) in Mark 1:45; 3:31f. par. Matt 12:46f./Luke 8:20; Mark 11:4; Matt 26:69; Luke 1:10; 13:25; John 18:16; 20:11; Acts 5:23 v.l.; Rev 22:15.

b) As an improper prep. with the gen. ἔξω (synonymous with → ἔξωθεν) is found in Luke 13:33 ("*outside* Jerusalem"); Heb 13:11, 12, 13; Rev 14:20 v.l.

4. Ἔξω appears in the attributive position in Acts 26:11 ("in the *foreign* [= non-Jewish] cities") and 2 Cor 4:16 ("our *outer* person," i.e., the person as a transitory mortal in contrast to the inner person who is renewed). On the attributive use cf. ÄgU IV, 114: ἐν τοῖς ἔξω τόποις; Polybius 5.63.8.

5. οἱ ἔξω (synonymous with οἱ ἔξωθεν, 1 Tim 3:7), literally: "those who are *outside*," Mark 4:11, of the mass of people who do not belong to the disciples; 1 Cor 5:12f.; Col 4:5; 1 Thess 4:12: non-Christians, apparently, on the basis of the situation, Gentiles.

R. Peppermüller

ἔξωθεν *exōthen* from without, outside (adv.)*

Matt 23:27, 28; Mark 7:18; 2 Cor 7:5; 1 Pet 3:3 (adj.). As subst. with the art.: οἱ ἔξωθεν, *those who are outside* (1 Tim 3:7; → ἔξω 5); τὸ ἔξωθεν, *the outside* (Matt 23:25 par. Luke 11:39, 40). With gen. following: Mark 7:15; Rev 11:2a; 14:20. In the sense of *outside*: Rev 11:2b: "throw *out*."

ἐξωθέω *exōtheō* thrust out, drive out*

Acts 7:45, of the peoples "whom God *drove out* before the face of our fathers," i.e., before them; 27:29, as a nautical t.t.: *run aground on the shore, beach.*

ἐξώτερος, 3 *exōteros* outside, situated outside (adj.)*

Comparative adj. related to the adv. ἔξω (BDF §62); superlative in τὸ σκότος τὸ ἐξώτερον, "the darkness *farthest out*" (Matt 8:12; 22:13; 25:30).

ἔοικα *eoika* resemble*

Pres. 2nd perf. (of εἴκω), followed by the dat. in Jas 1:6 (the wave of the sea); 1:23 (a man).

ἑορτάζω *heortazō* celebrate a feast*

Of the Passover feast as an image of the Christian life, 1 Cor 5:8: "so *let us celebrate*" (cf. Philo *Sacr.* 111).

ἑορτή, ῆς, ἡ *heortē* feast*

Lit.: BAGD s.v. — BDF §200. — LSJ s.v. — *PGL* s.v. — PREISIGKE, *Wörterbuch,* with Supplement, s.v.

1. Ἑορτή is attested in Greek literature since Homer, in papyrus documents since the third century B.C., in the LXX frequently with the meaning, *feast/feast day*. In the NT ἑορτή appears 25 times (and in Luke 23:17; Acts 18:21 as v.l.).

2. a) In all Synoptic occurrences (Mark 14:2 par. Matt 26:5; Mark 15:6 par. Matt 27:15; Luke 2:41f.; 22:1; 23:17 v.l.) and in John (2:23; 4:45; 6:4; 11:56; 12:12, 20; 13:1, 29) ἑορτή is the designation for Passover (ἑορτὴ τοῦ πάσχα in Luke 2:41; John 13:1; ἡ ἑορτὴ τῶν ἀζύμων ἡ λεγομένη πάσχα in Luke 22:1; cf. Exod 23:15; 34:18, 25; Ezek 45:21 LXX). In Acts 18:21 v.l. Paul says that he must celebrate the coming feast in Jerusalem; ἑορτή is to be understood here, too, as the Passover.

c) Ἑορτὴ τῶν Ἰουδαίων in John 5:1 cannot be more precisely determined (consequently the additions in numerous mss.; the art. ἡ may make it refer to *the* feast of the Jews, Passover; so the addition in Λ: τῶν ἀζύμων; minuscule 131 adds, however, ἡ σκηνοπηγία).

d) In Col 2:16, ἐν μέρει ἑορτῆς, "regarding a *feast*," ἑορτή is used with the general meaning of a *feast* (juxtaposition of ἑορτή, νεομηνία, and σάββατα is found already in 1 Chr 23:31; Hos 2:11 LXX). It can thus be translated: "No one should judge you in food and drink or in matters involving a *feast* or a new moon or a Sabbath."

e) With preps.: Ἐν τῇ ἑορτῇ (Mark 14:2 par. Matt 26:5; John 2:23; 4:45; 7:11; 12:20, simple dat. only in Luke 2:41) responds to the question "when?" (cf. BDF §200). Κατὰ ἑορτήν (Mark 15:6 par. Matt 27:15; Luke 23:17 v.l.) is a general reference: "at each *feast*" (cf. BDF §224.3). Πρὸ τῆς ἑορτῆς (John 13:1), "before the *feast*." Εἰς τὴν ἑορτήν (John 4:45; 7:8, 10; 11:56; 12:12) indicates direction, "to the *feast*," in response to the question "where?" but in John 13:29 has the meaning "in consideration of/ for the *feast*."

R. Peppermüller

ἐπαγγελία, ας, ἡ *epangelia* pledge, promise (noun)**
ἐπαγγέλλομαι *epangellomai* promise (vb.); profess**
ἐπάγγελμα, ατος, τό *epangelma* promise (noun)*

1. Occurrences of the word group in the NT — 2. Mean-

ings — 3. Syntactic relationships — 4. Paul — 5. Hebrews — 6. Other writings — 7. Ἐπάγγελμα

Lit.: K. BERGER, "Abraham in den paulinischen Hauptbriefen," *MTZ* 17 (1966) 47-89. — R. BULTMANN, "Ursprung und Sinn der Typologie als Hermeneutischer Methode," *idem, Exegetica* (1967) 369-80 (= *TLZ* 75 [1950] 206-11). — J. ECKERT, *Die urchristliche Verkündigung im Streit zwischen Paulus und seinen Gegnern nach dem Galaterbrief* (BU 6, 1971) 79-86. — L. GOPPELT, *Typos: The Typological Interpretation of the OT in the NT* (Eng. tr., 1982) 136-52, 209-38. — E. GRÄSSER, *Der Glaube im Hebräerbrief* (MTSt 2, 1965). — S. H. HOOKE, *Promise and Fulfillment* (1963). — H. HÜBNER, *Law in Paul's Thought* (1984) 15-20, 51-60. — G. KLEIN, "Röm 4 und die Idee der Heilsgeschichte," *EvT* 23 (1963) 424-47. — S. LOERSCH, *LTK* X, 706. — O. MICHEL, *Heb* (KEK, ⁶1966) 192f. — C. ROSE, "Verheißung und Erfüllung. Zum Verständnis von ἐπαγγελία im Hebräerbrief," *BZ* 33 (1989) 60-80. — F. J. SCHIERSE, *Verheißung und Heilsvollendung* (1955). — J. SCHNIEWIND and G. FRIEDRICH, *TDNT* II, 576-86. — S. K. WILLIAMS, "Promise in Galatians: A Reading of Paul's Reading of Scripture," *JBL* 107 (1988) 709-20. — For further bibliography see *TWNT* X, 1081.

1. These three words appear primarily in the NT epistles. Ἐπαγγελία is found a total of 52 times, ἐπαγγέλλομαι 15 times, and ἐπάγγελμα 2 times (both in 2 Peter). While the Synoptics use the word group rarely (Mark has the vb. once, Luke-Acts has the vb. once [in Acts] and the noun ἐπαγγελία 9 times, of which 8 are in Acts; the word group does not appear in Matthew), it is used primarily in Paul (22 times). Hebrews also has ἐπαγγελία and ἐπαγγέλλομαι frequently (a total of 18 times). The rare occurrence in the Synoptic tradition and in the Johannine literature (2 occurrences, both in 1 John) is striking; also remarkable is the total absence of the word group in Revelation.

2. The three words are to be rendered almost exclusively with *promise, pledge.* Ἐπαγγελία and ἐπαγγέλλω are synonymous in secular Greek with the other stems formed with αγγελ- and mean *announcement/announce* (cf. LSJ s.v.). Where the word group is used in the LXX (17 times), it renders a variety of Hebrew words. Thus the unspecific sense is maintained here, as in secular Greek. The meaning *promise of salvation* originated first in Judaism, and later became a decisive feature for NT usage (cf. 2 Macc 2:17; *Pss. Sol.* 12:6; *T. Jos.* 20:1). Thus *2 Bar.* 57:2 speaks of the "promise of the future life"; 59:2 speaks of the "promise of the reward." These promises are associated with fulfillment of the law. The word group takes on a specific christological meaning with the origin and development of the concept of the gospel in Paul: The εὐαγγέλιον as the promise of salvation brings together the theological concepts of the *word of promise* and the *promised blessing.*

3. a) The one who gives the ἐπαγγελία is always God (except in Acts 23:21: The Jews who wish to kill Paul on the way to the Sanhedrin await the *agreement* of the tribune). The promise proceeds from God, who is its guarantor. Thus because of the firmly fixed form and the unmistakable age, the gen. of θεός does not need to appear. On the other hand the gen. appears when the person from whom the *promise* comes is emphasized (cf. Rom 4:20; 2 Cor 1:20) or when the promised blessing is of special importance for mankind (Heb 9:15; 1 Tim 4:8; 2 Pet 3:4, etc.). In order to emphasize the promised blessing, the gen. τῆς ἐπαγγελίας can be added to a noun to give a more exact determination ("as a kind of gen. of quality," BAGD s.v. 2.a; so Gal 4:28; Rom 9:8; Heb 11:9, and often). Uses with preps. occur in Gal 3:18b (δι᾽ ἐπαγγελίας); 4:23 (διὰ τῆς ἐπαγγελίας; δι᾽ ἐπαγγελίας is a variant reading assimilating to 3:18b); 3:18a (ἐξ ἐπαγγελίας); Eph 6:2 (ἐν ἐπαγγελίᾳ); κατ᾽ ἐπαγγελίαν (Gal 3:29; Acts 13:23; cf. also 1 Tim 1:1 ℵ).

b) The promise is addressed to people, most commonly specific individuals who are chosen by God. Abraham is the most frequent addressee (Gal 3:18; Rom 4:13; Heb 6:12-17; Acts 7:17), then Isaac and Jacob (Heb 11:9), the patriarchs (Rom 15:8; Acts 26:6f.), Sarah (Heb 11:11), the prophets (Heb 11:32f., in connection with the "heroes" of the OT), and finally the Israelites (Rom 9:4). According to Eph 2:12 the Gentiles were excluded from the *promise.* The addressees who are mentioned are "types" in the context of the idea of promise and point toward Christians, who as believers are the essential recipients and bearers of the *promise* (Gal 3:22; 2 Cor 7:1; Acts 2:39). Thus the idea of fulfillment accompanies the concept of promise: The *promises* made in the OT are interpreted in the NT as (finally or provisionally) fulfilled. According to Gal 3:16 Christ himself is the recipient of the *promise.* He is the "true" descendant, i.e., the voice of the Scripture speaks here in reference to "the only" (ἐφ᾽ ἑνός; cf. F. Mussner, *Gal* [HTKNT] 236-40).

c) The content of the *promise* is the messianic salvation, which is expressed in various images derived from the OT, especially in Heb (11:9, land; 4:1, sabbath rest; 6:14f., descendants; 9:15, eternal inheritance). Despite the strong commitment to the OT, Hebrews also associates the promises of God with the messianic salvation as it has dawned in Jesus Christ.

4. a) In Gal 3:13-18 Paul shows that in Christ the blessings of Abraham have come to believers and that the law cannot annul the *promise,* which holds the inheritance within it. In the context of the theme which is central for Paul, "law and faith" (3:1-5, 12), he proclaims his soteriological "program": "Christ has redeemed us from the curse of the law. . ." (3:13) and thus the *promise* originally made is now realized in the pneuma and received in faith (v. 14; the variant reading εὐλογία instead of ἐπαγγελία in v. 14b is a later assimilation to

v. 14a, cf. H. Schlier, *Gal* [KEK] 140f.n.2). This basic idea is, in relation to the *promise* given to Abraham, elaborated in vv. 16 (pl.), 17, 18 (2 occurrences), 21 (pl.), and 22 and concluded in 3:29. Paul clarifies these soteriological statements ("To give a human example," v. 15): a testament that is legally valid cannot be annulled: thus the *promises* have the character of a διαθήκη (v. 15; cf. Berger 54). The *promises* made to Abraham (cf. Gen 12:2f., 7; 13:15f.; 15:4-6; 17:1-8) are the blessing that Abraham received. However, for Paul the decisive definition of the *promise* is not determined by this, but it is rather given to "the seed" (sg.! v. 16). This seed is Christ. In him the *promise* is fulfilled. Thus the law, which came in the interim, changes nothing. Law and *promise* are mutually exclusive (v. 18), for the promise consists in the demonstration of grace (χαρίζομαι, v. 18).

b) While Gal 3:13-18 treats the subject of faith and *promise,* Romans 4 considers the problem of "the way of salvation for Jews and Christians" (cf. Berger 48). Paul again (Rom 4:13-25) takes up the thought of the *promise* to Abraham. However, Abraham is now as the recipient of the promise a type for all believers, Jews as well as Gentiles (cf. vv. 17a, 18). In an "exegetical midrash" (O. Michel, *Rom* [KEK, [13]1966] 114) Paul interprets the precept of 3:21 that one is justified by faith without works of the law (cf. 1:16f.). Abraham received the promise, not on the basis of works of the law (as opposed to the rabbinic tradition; cf. Billerbeck III, 204-6), but on the basis of righteousness by faith: 4:13, 17. Against all appearances (vv. 20f.) Abraham believed and became—as recipient of the promise (Gen 15:7 and 18:18) —father (Rom 4:17) of all who believe in the one who was put to death and raised for our justification (v. 25). Παντὶ τῷ σπέρματι (v. 16) means here all "who aspire to attain the promise not on the basis of the law alone (v. 14), but on the basis of the faith of Abraham" (U. Wilckens, *Rom* [EKKNT] I, 271).

c) In a summary statement Paul takes up the subject of the *promise* again in Romans 9 (cf. vv. 4, 8, 9). Paul sees the "mystery of Israel" (H. Schlier, *Röm* [HTKNT] 228) in the fact that the Israelites or the patriarchs have the promises (v. 4, pl.), but that only a portion of them in reality are in possession of this promise of salvation. Again the reference is made to the example of Abraham in order to show that not all Israelites really belong to "spiritual" Israel. It is not natural descent, but rather the fact of being "called" (v. 7b), or "reckoned" (v. 8b), that opens access to the promise and constitutes the real Israel. Gen 18:10, 14 is the historical presupposition of the λόγος τῆς ἐπαγγελίας (Rom 9:9), in which the freedom of the will of God is in no way limited in the sense of an unrestricted promise for the Jews alone.

5. Heb 4:1 speaks of the *promise* of entering into the rest of God. However—and this is a modification of the idea of the promise—the fulfillment is yet to come. Because the promise has not yet been finally realized, the Church should be concerned that no one remain behind ("seem to have remained behind"). The author refers to the judgment of God in Ps 94:11 LXX ("I have sworn in my wrath, They shall never enter into my rest!"; cf. Deut 12:9). Of course the psalm does not speak of a *promise* (cf. Heb 3:11, where the text again is cited without a reference to the subject of "promise"). The content of the statement is decisive in describing the security in God which is yet to be realized; the author has a unique use of ἐπαγγελία. Inasmuch as εὐαγγέλιον does not appear in Hebrews, ἐπαγγελία takes on the meaning of "gospel," which is more precisely described in 4:2 as λόγος τῆς ἀκοῆς. God, the ἐπαγγειλάμενος (6:13; 10:23; 11:11), reveals himself in the word of promise, through which the Church is directed to the future. The OT promises are fulfilled in Christ, but not yet in believers. While it is said of those of the old covenant, "They all died in faith without receiving *the promises* . . ." (11:13), the faith of Christians is "confident expectation in what is hoped for" (cf. Grässer 126-36). What Abraham, Isaac, and Jacob received as promise (11:8, 9) remains unfulfilled. The same thing can be said of the many other witnesses of OT history (11:11-38): the fulfillment was denied to them also (v. 39). The believers of the new covenant must first arrive: 11:39f. To be sure, the "recognition in praise is in no way denied" to the conduct of the OT witnesses (H. Strathmann, *Heb* [NTD] 146), but for the sake of those who believe in Christ the fulfillment has been delayed.

6. The association of ἐπαγγελία and ζωή in the Pastoral Epistles is noteworthy. Pious conduct alone is useful because it has the promise of the present and the coming life (1 Tim 4:8). Similarly Paul introduces himself in the prescript of 2 Timothy: He is an "apostle of Jesus Christ through the will of God according to the *promise* of life in Christ Jesus" (1:1). If the content of the promise is limited more generally to "eternal life," it remains nonetheless decisive for the present and future life of the Church, for God is here the guarantor of this promise (Tit 1:2).

Although in 2 Pet 2:19 the vb. has the general meaning of *promise* (the false teachers *promise* freedom, but in reality they are slaves of corruption), ἐπαγγελία in 3:1-13 has a theological sense. Scoffers ask, "Where is the *promise* of his coming?" (3:4). The announcement of the imminent parousia has not been fulfilled. Ἐπαγγελία is here separated from the stream of OT tradition. The Church has, since Christ, developed a new understanding of *promise.* It is now used fully in association with the early Church's announcement of the parousia, the delay of the parousia, and those who scoff at the parousia (cf.

K. H. Schelkle, *1–2 Pet* [HTKNT] 224f., 227). The Church answers the scoffers: "The Lord does not delay the *promise*" (3:9). God stands by his word. He does not take back his promise.

7. In secular Greek the relatively rare **ἐπάγγελμα** (cf. LSJ s.v.) means *promise, confession.* The word does not appear in the LXX. In the NT it appears only in 2 Pet 1:4 and 3:13. In both passages the noun has the same meaning as ἐπαγγελία. Against the false teachers and scoffers (3:4) the greatness of the *promises* is emphasized (1:4). The content of the promise is the new heavens (pl.) and new earth (3:13). In dependence on Isa 65:17; 66:22 LXX the goal of the promise is more precisely described under the image of the new heaven and new earth. Through the new creation God will reveal himself as the righteous one. The author of 2 Peter moves within the future expectation of Judaism (cf. Rev 21:1) without slipping into incredible or mythological statements. His conviction is decisive: The present is the time of testing. "The individual must prepare for the end with a holy and pious life in order that he can participate in the new creation in which full righteousness will rule (v. 11)" (G. Schneider, *Neuschöpfung oder Wiederkehr?* [1961] 72f.).   A. Sand

ἐπαγγέλλομαι *epangellomai* promise; profess
→ ἐπαγγελία

ἐπάγγελμα, ατος, τό *epangelma* promise
→ ἐπαγγελία 1, 7.

ἐπάγω *epagō* bring (something) on (someone)*

Acts 5:28: "*bring* the blood of this man on us"; 2 Pet 2:1: "*bring on* destruction"; 2:5: "*brought* the flood *upon* the world."

ἐπαγωνίζομαι *epagōnizomai* fight
→ ἀγών 1, 5.

ἐπαθροίζω *epathroizō* assemble in addition*

Luke 11:29, pass. partc.: "as the people *had gathered even more.*"

Ἐπαίνετος, ου *Epainetos* Epaenetus*

Name in the list of greetings in Rom 16:5. Ἐπαίνετος is called by Paul ἀπαρχὴ τῆς Ἀσίας, "firstfruits of Asia" (for Christ), and is thus "the first convert in western Asia Minor, of which Ephesus is the center." E. Käsemann, *Rom* (Eng. tr.) ad loc.; cf. also 1 Cor 16:15.

ἐπαινέω *epaineō* praise, approve, sanction
→ ἔπαινος.

ἔπαινος, ου, ὁ *epainos* praise, recognition (noun)*
ἐπαινέω *epaineō* praise (vb.), approve, sanction*

Lit.: A. FRIDRICHSEN, "Der wahre Jude und sein Lob. Röm 2,28f.," *Symbolae Arctoae* 1 (1922) 39–49. — H. PREISKER, *TDNT* II, 586–88. — A. STROBEL, "Zum Verständnis von Rm 13," *ZNW* 47 (1956) 67–93, esp. 79f. — W. C. VAN UNNIK, "Lob und Strafe durch die Obrigkeit. Hellenistisches zu Röm 13,3–4," FS Kümmel 334–43. — For further bibliography → αἰνέω; see also *TWNT* X, 1081.

1. The vb. ἐπαινέω appears in the NT 6 times, of which 5 are in Paul. While the simple form → αἰνέω is used in the NT exclusively for praise given to God, the compound has the religious meaning "*praise* God" only in Rom 15:11 (citing Ps 116:1 LXX). In the remaining NT passages it is used of humans and their conduct, corresponding to common Greek usage (→ 2.a). According to the parable in Luke 16:8a Jesus *praises* the decisive and clever activity of the dishonest steward (see Jeremias, *Parables* 45ff., 181f.; G. Schneider, *Luke* [ÖTK] 330ff. [bibliography]; H. Weder, *Die Gleichnisse Jesu als Metaphern* [1978] 262ff.). In Paul ἐπαινέω is found— except for the citation in Rom 15:11—only in the instructions in 1 Corinthians 11 (vv. 2, 17, 22 bis). If the vb. in vv. 2 and 22 is to be translated *praise,* the meaning in v. 17 would evidently be *approve/sanction* (cf. Sophocles *El.* 591; Aristophanes *Lys.* 70; Josephus *Ant.* xiv.293, 341; BAGD s.v.). Vv. 17 and 22 both have the phrase οὐκ ἐπαινῶ, a litotes: "*I cannot approve*" = "I must strongly object" (v. 17); "*I cannot praise you*" = "I must strongly disapprove" (v. 22).

2. Of the 11 NT occurrences of the subst. ἔπαινος 9 are in the Pauline Epistles (of which 3 are in Ephesians) and 2 in 1 Peter.

a) In 2 Cor 8:18 Paul speaks of the *praise* that one of his coworkers receives in the churches for his work in the spread of the gospel (cf. Sir 31:11 [Heb.]; 39:10; 44:8, 15).

The practice of the Roman authorities of commending worthy citizens through a public record or through inscriptions (see Strobel), and the maxim of the Hellenistic ethic of the state, according to which the commendation of the upright and punishment of the unworthy belongs among the basic duties of the authorities (see van Unnik), form the background to the statements in Rom 13:3(f.) and 1 Pet 2:14. In both passages ἔπαινος is of course used in a formal way: It means "the civil recognition and thus the legal protection that everyone can expect who conducts himself properly" (L. Goppelt, *1 Pet* [KEK] 185).

In the catalog of virtues in Phil 4:8, which is indebted to Hellenistic moral philosophy, ἔπαινος designates the *object of praise.* Under consideration are the values and conduct that receive approval and recognition according to the general ethical judgment.

b) In three passages, the subject is *praise* granted to humans by God. In each case the final judgment is in view. With this praise the true Jew (Rom 2:29 [cf. vv. 7, 10]), the proclaimer of the gospel (1 Cor 4:5), and the Christian whose faith has been tested in suffering (1 Pet 1:7) receive recognition through God's saving judgment.

c) In the introductory blessing in Eph 1:3-14, the saving action of God in Christ occurs "to the *praise* of his glory" (vv. 12, 14) or "to the *praise* of the glory of his grace" (v. 6). In this designation two aspects may be connected with each other (cf. Rom 15:7b): God himself is glorified in his salvific work (see H. Schlier, *Eph* [1957] ad loc.), and this finds its echo in the praise with which the Church glorifies God and his saving grace. That the redemptive work of glorification serves the praise of God is also expressed in the doxology of Phil 1:11.   O. Hofius

ἐπαίρω *epairō* lift up*

Lit.: BAGD s.v. — J. JEREMIAS, *TDNT* I, 185f. — KÜHNER, *Grammatik* II/2, 663 (index). — MOULTON/MILLIGAN s.v. — PREISIGKE, *Wörterbuch* s.v.

1. Most of the 19 NT occurrences are in the Lukan double work (6 in the Gospel, 5 in Acts); 4 are in John. The other occurrences are in Matt 17:8; 2 Cor 10:5; 11:20; and 1 Tim 2:8. Act. forms followed by an acc. are most common (16 times), normally to designate human (sense) organs or body parts. An exception is found in Acts 27:40: *lift/hoist* the foresail (E. Haenchen, *Acts* [Eng. tr., 1971] 696, 708) or *haul before* (the wind) (Conzelmann, *Acts* [Eng. tr., Hermeneia, 1987] 220).

2. a) The expression "*lift the eyes*" is commonly connected with a vb. of seeing: *look up* (and *see, notice*): Matt 17:8; Luke 16:23; John 4:35; 6:5 (see W. Michaelis, *TDNT* V, 377). In other passages it is constructed with εἰς in order to indicate who is looked at or the direction of the following statement: Jesus *lifted his eyes* on his disciples, who are addressed in the Sermon on the Plain (the disciples including the multitude of people as well as the apostles, cf. vv. 13, 17): Luke 6:20. In prayer Jesus *lifted up his eyes* to heaven (John 17:1; cf. 11:41). In his humility and shame, the tax collector who prayed did not dare *look up* to heaven (Luke 18:13; see BAGD).

b) The phrase "*raise the voice*" is found in the Lukan writings before an outcry or address and means *call, speak loudly.* In Luke 11:27 a woman *calls* in order to get a hearing "from among the crowd" (so H. J. Vogels, *NT graece et latine* [1955] and others), or "a woman in the crowd" raised her voice (so, e.g., J. Ernst, Luke [RNT] 377, with *NTG* and others). According to Acts 2:14 Peter *raised his voice* in order to get the attention of those present (after the miracle of Pentecost, cf. vv.

12f.). Loud cries of the crowds declare surprised amazement (14:11) or angry indignation (22:22; cf. 21:36).

c) The appearance of the Son of Man on a cloud is the signal for Christians to "*lift their heads*" in order to look forward confidently to the coming redemption (see W. Grundmann, *Luke* [THKNT] 385); others (e.g., B. J. Zmijewski, *Die Eschatologiereden des Lukasevangelium* [1972] 232): in order to demonstrate pride and joy (Luke 21:28).

d) "*Lifting* the hands" is a gesture of prayer (1 Tim 2:8). The disciples respond to the final blessing that Jesus gives with lifted hands, and to his reception into heaven by kneeling (Luke 24:50-52). Echoes of OT blessings (Lev 9:22-24; Sir 50:20f.) are unmistakable (Grundmann, 453f.).

e) Judas' betrayal of Jesus resembles the perfidy of a man who "*lifts his heel*" (John 13:18) over his table companion in order to trample on him (a free citation of Ps 40:10 LXX; of those who are confined to the sickbed, cf. 40:4, 9; see R. Schnackenburg, *John* [Eng. tr.] III [1982], 25).

3. a) The use of the pass. in the report of the ascension of Jesus suggests a supernatural cause: he was *taken up* (by the power of God, Acts 1:2, 11; → ἀναλαμβάνω).

b) Paul uses ἐπαίρω pass. and fig. in the argument with his opponents who *rise up* (militantly) against the knowledge of God (2 Cor 10:5) and *are overbearing* with respect to the Corinthians (11:20).   U. Borse

ἐπαισχύνομαι *epaischynomai* be ashamed
→ αἰσχύνομαι 4.

ἐπαιτέω *epaiteō* beg*

Luke 16:3: "I am ashamed to *beg*"; 18:35: "a blind man sat on the roadside and *begged* (ἐπαιτῶν)."

ἐπακολουθέω *epakoloutheō* come after
→ ἀκολουθέω 5.

ἐπακούω *epakouō* hear, answer*

2 Cor 6:2: "I have *listened* to you" (Isa 49:8 LXX). G. Kittel, *TDNT* I, 222; J. Barr, "The Meaning of ἐπακούω and Cognates in the LXX," *JTS* 31 (1980) 67-72; Spicq, *Notes* Suppl., 236-38.

ἐπακροάομαι *epakroaomai* listen to*

Acts 16:25: "the prisoners *listened* to them [αὐτῶν: Paul and Silas]."

ἐπάν *epan* as soon as, when*

With the conjunction δέ: Matt 2:8: "*As soon as* you

have found"; Luke 11:22: *"when* he overcomes him"; 11:34: *"when* it [the eye] is evil."

ἐπάναγκες *epanankes* out of compulsion, of necessity*

Acts 15:28: τὰ ἐπάναγκες, *the necessary things,* in reference to the duties laid down in the "apostolic decree" (v. 29).

ἐπανάγω *epanagō* go up, return*

Of *setting out* with a boat (from land), Luke 5:3f. Of the *return* of Jesus into the city, Matt 21:18.

ἐπαναμιμνῄσκω *epanamimnēskō* remind again (of something)*
→ ἀνάμνησις.

ἐπαναπαύομαι *epanapauomai* rest, take a rest*

Luke 10:6: "your peace *will rest* on him." Rom 2:17: *"rely on/rest on* the law (νόμῳ)." O. Bauernfeind, *TDNT* I, 351.

ἐπανέρχομαι *epanerchomai* return*

Luke 10:35: "at my *return*"; 19:15: "at his *return*"— in both cases ἐν τῷ with acc. + inf. used temporally.

ἐπανίστημι *epanistēmi* stand, rise up*

Mark 13:12 par. Matt 10:21: "children *will rise up* against their parents" (cf. Mic 7:6 LXX).

ἐπανόρθωσις, εως, ἡ *epanorthōsis* restoration, correction*

2 Tim 3:16, of the Scripture: "profitable . . . for *correction,* for training in righteousness." H. Preisker, *TDNT* V, 450; Spicq, *Notes* I, 259f.

ἐπάνω *epanō* on; over (adv., improper prep.)*

Lit.: ABEL, *Grammaire* §44w. — BAGD s.v. — BAUER, *Wörterbuch* s.v. — BDF (index s.v.) — LSJ s.v. — MAYSER, *Grammatik* I/3, 279; II/1, 375; II/2, 601. — MOULTON, *Grammar* I, 99; II, 522 (index); III, 407 (index). — MOULTON/MILLIGAN s.v. — PREISIGKE, *Wörterbuch* s.v. — RADERMACHER, *Grammatik* 144.

1. The NT has 19 (+ 1) occurrences (1 in Mark, 8 in Matthew [+ 21:7 v.l.], 5 in Luke, 2 in John, 1 in 1 Corinthians, 2 in Revelation). Ἐπάνω is a composite adv. used most often (16 times) as an improper prep. (with gen.). The boundary between adv. and prep. is often fluid (BDF §203), e.g., Luke 11:44, walk *over* (i.e., *over* the graves; adv., see BDF §215); 10:19 (prep.; → 2.a).

2. As prep. with spatial meanings:

a) *On:* sit *on* animal(s): Matt 21:7 (or *on* the garments that were lying there? see E. Klostermann, *Matt* [HNT] 165); Rev 6:8; *on* the throne of God: Matt 23:22; *on* a stone: 28:2; be set *on* a mountain: 5:14; *on* the altar: 23:18, 20; tread *on* snakes and scorpions: Luke 10:19.

b) *Over, above:* the star *over* the place where the child was: Matt 2:9; Jesus bent *over* Simon's mother-in-law, who was ill (or, as in, e.g., W. Grundmann, *Luke* [THKNT] 124f., he went *up* to her head): Luke 4:39; the inscription (tablet) *above (over)* the head of the crucified one: Matt 27:37; the abyss *over* the fallen dragon is closed and sealed: Rev 20:2f.

3. As prep. with a fig. meaning: have precedence *over,* have authority *over* cities: Luke 19:17, 19; he who comes from above (from heaven) is *above* all people, including John the Baptist: John 3:31a (c).

4. As adv., a colloquialism in place of πλείων (BDF §185.4): *over* (a number): sell for *more than* 300 denarii: Mark 14:5; Christ appeared to *more than* 500 brothers: 1 Cor 15:6.

                                   U. Borse

ἐπάρατος, 2 *eparatos* cursed*

John 7:49: "But the crowd, who do not know the law, are *cursed.*" Billerbeck II, 494-519; F. Büchsel, *TDNT* I, 451; R. Schnackenburg, *John* (Eng. tr.) II (1979), ad loc.

ἐπαρκέω *eparkeō* assist, help*

1 Tim 5:10 (the afflicted); 5:16a, b (widows).

ἐπαρχεία, ας, ἡ *eparcheia* eparchy, province*

Acts 23:34: Paul is asked, "From what *province* are you?" and the governor learns "that he comes from Cilicia"; 25:1: "now when Festus had come into the *province. . . .*"

ἐπάρχειος, 2 *eparcheios* belonging to an eparchy

Acts 25:1 p74 ℵ* A: τῇ ἐπαρχείῳ (to be completed with: χώρᾳ), in place of τῇ ἐπαρχείᾳ, "in the province"; see E. Haenchen, *Acts* (Eng. tr., 1971) ad loc.

ἔπαυλις, εως, ἡ *epaulis* farm, estate*

Acts 1:20, in the (adapted) citation of Ps 68:26 LXX: "His *habitation* will become desolate," in reference to the fate of Judas (vv. 18f.).

ἐπαύριον *epaurion* in the morning*

In the NT always in τῇ ἐπαύριον (to be completed with ἡμέρᾳ), *on the next day* (Matt 27:62; Mark 11:12; John

1:29, 35, 43; 6:22; 12:12; Acts 10:9, 23, 24; 14:20; 20:7; 21:8; 22:30; 23:32; 25:6, 23).

Ἐπαφρᾶς, ᾶ *Epaphras* Epaphras*

The name (perhaps an abbreviated form of Ἐπαφρόδιτος) of a Christian from Colossae (Col 4:12) who was the founder of the church there (1:7). In Phlm 23 he gives his greeting as a fellow prisoner of Paul. E. Lohse, *Col and Phlm* (Eng. tr., Hermeneia, 1971) on Col. 1:7 and 4:12f.; W. D. Thomas, "Epaphras," *ExpTim* 95 (1983/84) 217f.

ἐπαφρίζω *epaphrizō* splash*

Jude 13, metaphorically of waves "which *toss up* their shamelessness [like foam]."

Ἐπαφρόδιτος, ου *Epaphroditos* Epaphroditus*

A coworker of Paul. Phil 2:25: "my brother and fellow worker and fellow soldier, and your messenger and minister to my need" (cf. also 4:18). Paul wants to send Epaphroditus to Philippi (2:25-30). J. Gnilka, *Phil* [HTKNT] 161-64.

ἐπεγείρω *epegeirō* stir up*

Acts 13:50, of "the Jews" in Antioch of Pisidia, who incited the population of the city and *stirred up* a persecution against Paul and Barnabas; 14:2, likewise of Jews, here in Iconium, who "*stirred up* and embittered the minds of the Gentiles against the brethren."

ἐπεί *epei* because; otherwise*

Lit.: ABEL, *Grammaire* 381 (index). — BAGD s.v. — BDF §§455f. — KÜHNER, *Grammatik* II/2, 663 (index). — LSJ s.v. — Mayser, *Grammatik* II/1, 272; II/2, 601 (index); II/3, 237 (index). — MOULTON/MILLIGAN s.v. — RADERMACHER, *Grammatik* 236 (index).

1. The connecting word ἐπεί is found 26 times in the NT. It is distributed among the Gospels (1 in Mark, 3 in Matthew, 1 in Luke, 2 in John), Paul (3 in Romans, 5 in 1 Corinthians, 2 in 2 Corinthians), and Hebrews (9 occurrences). It also appears in textual variants in Luke 7:1 and Rom 11:6. The conjunction is most often used causally, to express an opposite view (*otherwise,* 3 times in Paul), temporally only in the variant reading (TR, in place of ἐπειδή) ἐπεὶ δέ, *after,* in Luke 7:1 (see BAGD; BDF §455,1).

2. In affirmative statements:
a) Completely causal: *because, since,* followed by the pres. (Matt 27:6; Luke 1:34; 1 Cor 14:12; 2 Cor 11:18; 13:3; Heb 4:6 [→ b]; 5:2; 9:17), with the impf., "*since it

was the day of preparation*" (Mark 15:42; John 19:31; also Matt 21:46; John 13:29; Heb 6:13), with the aor. (Matt 18:32; Heb 11:11), with the pf. (Heb 2:14 [→ b]; 5:11).
b) With οὖν, as a conclusion from an OT citation: *since therefore* (Heb 2:14; 4:6).
c) Indicating a possible reason: *for otherwise* (BDF §§358.1; 456.3; Rom 11:6a [v.l. in v. 6b], 22; Heb 9:26).
d) Strengthened by ἄρα, giving an absurd reason: "*otherwise* you would have to go out of the world" (1 Cor 5:10); "*otherwise* your children would be unclean, but as it is they are holy" (7:14).

3. In interrogative sentences:
a) In opposition, regularly with the future, *otherwise, but then* (sometimes, e.g., in BAGD, taken as causal: *for otherwise,* → 2.c): 1 Cor 14:6: "*otherwise* how can the outsider say the Amen [if you pray with the spirit]?"; 15:29: "*otherwise* what do they do [i.e., in the dispute about the resurrection, cf. v. 29b] who baptize for the dead?"; Rom 3:6: "*but then* how could [i.e., if our unrighteousness shows his righteousness, v. 5a; followed by explanation in v. 7, as in 1 Cor 15:29] God judge the world?" Here, however, the false conclusion is already answered by μὴ γένοιτο, "far be it (i.e., an unrighteousness of God)," to which, according to some, ἐπεί corresponds: "How *otherwise* [if God were unrighteous] could God judge the world?" (e.g., H. Schlier, *Rom* [HTKNT] 95)
b) Of the possible reason in a contrary-to-fact question: Heb 10:2: "*otherwise* [cf. BDF §360.2] would they not have ceased being offered?"   U. Borse

ἐπειδή *epeidē* after, because (conj.)*

Temporal conjunction, *after:* Luke 7:1. Used causally in other NT occurrences: *since then, because* (Luke 11:6; Acts 13:46; 14:12; 15:24; 1 Cor 1:22; 14:16; Phil 2:26; also Matt 21:46 C Koine W, etc.); ἐπειδὴ γάρ, *for since* (1 Cor 1:21; 15:21).

ἐπειδήπερ *epeidēper* inasmuch as (conj.)*

Luke 1:1, causal: "*Inasmuch as* many have sought . . ." (cf. Thucydides vi.18.13; Dionysius of Halicarnassus ii.72; Josephus *B.J.* i.17; cf. BDF §456.3).

ἐπεῖδον *epeidon* look at

2nd aor. of → ἐφοράω.

ἔπειμι *epeimi* draw near, approach, follow*

In the NT (only in Acts) only the partc., always fem.: τῇ ἐπιούσῃ (ἡμέρᾳ), *on the following day* (Acts 7:26;

16:11; 20:15; 21:18), (νυκτί) *in the following night* (23:11).

ἐπείπερ *epeiper* since indeed (conj.)

Rom 3:30 Koine D* G pm: ἐπείπερ εἷς ὁ θεός, "*since indeed* God is one."

ἐπεισαγωγή, ῆς, ἡ *epeisagōgē* introduction*

Heb 7:19: "there is the *introduction* of a better hope."

ἐπεισέρχομαι *epeiserchomai* fall upon suddenly, force one's way*

Luke 21:35: "The last day *comes over* all inhabitants of the earth." In the sense of a sudden and violent invasion, 1 Macc 16:16; Josephus *Ant.* xi.265.

ἔπειτα *epeita* thereupon, then*

1. The adv. ἔπειτα apears 16 times in the NT, of which 10 occurrences are in Paul (6 in 1 Corinthians, 3 in Galatians, 1 in 1 Thessalonians, also as v.l., e.g., in 1 Cor 15:5, 7 in place of εἶτα, cf. also 12:28 TR εἶτα in place of ἔπειτα). It appears consistently in sequences and enumerations. Along with the function of indicating relationship in subject matter, it is also used to indicate temporal relationship.

2. The simple sequential relationship is found in Luke 16:7 (ἔλεγεν τῷ πρώτῳ, v. 5): ἔπειτα ἑτέρῳ, "*then* to the next one," and in the "autobiographical" summary in Gal 1:13ff., where Paul relates separate periods with the aid of ἔπειτα = *then, after that* (v. 18: ἔπειτα μετὰ ἔτη τρία; v. 21: ἔπειτα, i.e., after the 15 days in Jerusalem; 2:1: ἔπειτα διὰ δεκατεσσάρων ἐτῶν). Similarly John 11:7: ἔπειτα μετὰ τοῦτο (pleonastic, cf. BDF §484; continuation from τότε, v. 6), "*then* finally" (= after the two-day stay); Jas 4:14, in the play on words ὀλίγον φαινομένη, ἔπειτα καὶ ἀφανιζομένη, "it appears for a brief time and *then* it disappears."

Ἔπειτα is used to connect subsequent elements in series (temporally or in subject matter); thus after πρῶτον, δεύτερον, and τρίτον, ἔπειτα appears twice with the fourth and fifth (last) member in 1 Cor 12:28: *then.* In 1 Cor 15:6 ἔπειτα, *then, thereupon,* continues the traditional series of witnesses (cf. ὤφθη Κηφᾷ, εἶτα τοῖς δώδεκα, v. 5); likewise v. 7, *after that,* in which εἶτα indicates the end of the traditional material (v. 7b), and Paul adds himself with ἔσχατον δέ as the temporal and actual conclusion of the series of eyewitnesses (v. 8). Taken as a whole, the sequence in vv. 5-8 is temporal (cf. esp. v. 8), but among the individual parts of the list the emphasis may lie on various witnesses and groups of witnesses, and not on the temporal sequence.

3. Ἔπειτα has an unambiguously temporal significance in the series ἀπαρχή—ἔπειτα—εἶτα in 1 Cor 15:23(f.) and in πρῶτον—ἔπειτα, "first—*then*" (15:46; 1 Thess 4:(16),17; Heb 7:27). In Heb 7:2 ἔπειτα is used within a sequence of subject matter: πρῶτον—ἔπειτα δὲ καί, "first, and *then*" (cf. Jas 3:17).

                                           H. Balz

ἐπέκεινα *epekeina* beyond (adv.)*

Acts 7:43, citing Amos 5:27 (there ἐπέκεινα Δαμασκοῦ): "I will remove you *beyond* Babylon." The alteration of the Amos passage is the consequence of indicating that the prediction has been fulfilled (by the Babylonian exile); see T. Holtz, *Untersuchungen über die alttestamentlichen Zitate bei Lukas* (1968) 18.

ἐπεκτείνομαι *epekteinomai* stretch out, reach*

Phil 3:13: "I *strain forward* to what lies ahead," i.e., toward the goal lying in front of Paul.

ἐπενδύομαι *ependyomai* put on*
→ ἐνδύω.

ἐπενδύτης, ου, ὁ *ependytēs* outer garment*

John 21:7: Peter put on the *outer garment* which he had put down for work.

ἐπέρχομαι *eperchomai* come to, come over (someone)*

Lit.: J. SCHNEIDER, *TDNT* II, 680.

This compound of ἔρχομαι is a favorite word of Luke. Outside of Luke's Gospel (3 occurrences) and Acts (4 occurrences) it appears only in Eph 2:7 and Jas 5:1 (also Luke 21:35 v.l.). The neutral meaning *come to* appears in Acts 14:19: Jews from Antioch and Iconium *came there.*

The meaning *come over (someone)* (ἐπί with acc., Luke 1:35; 21:35 v.l.; Acts 1:8; 8:24; 13:40) appears frequently in the negative sense (Luke 11:22: "when one who is stronger than he *comes over* him and defeats him") relating to events that bring with them destruction, esp. condemnation in the coming judgment (Luke 21:26 [absolute τὰ ἐπερχόμενα; cf. LXX; *Herm. Sim.* ix.5.5], v. 35 v.l.; Acts 8:24; 13:40; Jas 5:1).

Eph 2:7 ("to show the abundant wealth of his grace in the *coming* ages") refers to "the *coming* ages," not in a threatening sense, but rather as a neutral temporal term (J. Gnilka, *Eph* [HTKNT] 121); cf., however, "the coming age," *Herm. Vis.* iv.3.5; also iii.9.5 (coming judgment); iv.1.1; *Sim.* vii.4 (coming distress).

Two corresponding Lukan passages (in personal address to the recipient of the promise) speak of the "Holy

Spirit," who will *come upon* Mary (Luke 1:35) or the apostles (Acts 1:8) (ἐπὶ σέ, ἐφ' ὑμᾶς; → ἐπισκιάζω 4).

G. Schneider

ἐπερωτάω *eperōtaō* ask

Lit.: H. GREEVEN, *TDNT* II, 687-89. — For further bibliography see *TWNT* X, 1086f.

1. This compound (56 NT occurrences) is more frequent than the simple form → ἐρωτάω, as was the case already in the LXX (there *ca.* 85 occurrences, the simple form *ca.* 70 occurrences; the textual tradition alternates between the two). With the exception of Rom 10:20 (a citation and the only occurrence referring to God); 1 Cor 14:35 (probably a post-Pauline gloss); and John 9:23; 18:7, the vb. is limited to the Synoptic Gospels. It is never derived from Q. It is frequent in Mark (25 occurrences); Matthew takes it over from him 5 times and in dependence on Markan usage uses it redactionally 3 times; Luke (17 occurrences + Acts 5:27; 23:34) takes it over from Mark 7 times and in 8:9 exchanges the Markan simple form for the compound.

2. The vb. designates a one-sentence utterance that calls upon the one addressed to give information, a decision, or confirmation about a situation corresponding to the assumed competence of the one addressed. Thus in Mark it introduces a direct question 21 times (and 2 times an indirect question), which in the narrative amount to answers: The narrative function of personal conversation is for him an important stylistic feature in bringing in evaluative discussions within the narrative contexts. Hence the two reports of non-questions (9:32; 12:34) receive their special function.

In Matthew the vb. always has an adversarial connotation, of judicial investigation. The first occurrence, in 12:10, introduces this aspect unmistakably; it is also to be heard in 16:1 (against BAGD s.v.; Greeven 687: not "request") and is retained in 17:10 in order to emphasize that the disciples report the opinion of the adversary. The simple form also has this meaning in Matthew.

W. Schenk

ἐπερώτημα, ατος, τό *eperōtēma* promise*

Lit.: S. AALEN, "Oversettelsen av ordet ἐπερώτημα i dapstedet 1 Pet 3,21," *TTK* 43 (1972) 161-75. — H. GREEVEN, *TDNT* II, 688f. — R. E. NIXON, "The Meaning of 'Baptism' in 1 Petr 3,21," *SE* IV (1968) 437-41. — G. C. RICHARDS, "1 Peter 3,21," *JTS* 31 (1930) 195; 32 (1931) 77. — SPICQ, *Notes* I, 261f.

This NT hapax legomenon in 1 Pet 3:21 is most often interpreted in its context as "an *appeal* to God for a clear conscience" (BAGD s.v.; Greeven; cf. the commentaries of H. Windisch/H. Preisker, E. Schweizer, F. W. Beare, K. H. Schelkle, W. Schrage, and J. B. Bauer, ad loc.).

This interpretation is given because the word cannot have the classical meaning *question* (*Herm. Man.* xi.2). Since this common interpretation is not attested, but is deduced from the context contrary to the use of the compound, one should think rather of a *vow* ("pledge to God," LSJ s.v.; Richards; B. Reicke, *The Disobedient Spirits and Christian Baptism* [1946] 181f.; G. R. Beasley-Murray, *Baptism in the NT* [1963] 260f.; Kuss I, 144n.95, 147; J. B. Souček, *GPM* 16 [1961/62] 237f.; commentaries by Selwyn and Best).

The word is attested since the second century A.D. as a t.t. for any question concerning a treaty (Moulton/Milligan 231f.; Preisigke, *Wörterbuch* I, 527f.). A latinism in a letter from Rome near the end of the first century is to be taken similarly: The *stipulatio* ("promise" as an obligation established by official interrogation) is ancient Roman legal practice as part of a legal obligation, as the book title of the *Stipulatio Aquiliana* (first century B.C.) indicates. The narrower meaning "treaty" is not to be taken too strictly, inasmuch as the comprehensive legal practice of the *stipulatio* began to degenerate into a mere treaty in the first century (F. Schulz, *Geschichte der römischen Rechtswissenschaft* [1961] 372).

Inasmuch as the context in 1 Peter suggests that βάπτισμα, as in Mark 10:38f., refers to suffering in persecution (Nixon), the interpretation of this suffering in persecution as an obligation and a *promise* before God, proceeding from the desire to obey God (subj. or obj. gen.), is to be preferred.

W. Schenk

ἐπέχω *epechō* hold firm; intrans.: pay attention to; stay*

Phil 2:16: "*hold fast* the word of life." In the sense of *fix attention, observe,* Luke 14:7; Acts 3:5; 1 Tim 4:16. Acts 19:22: Paul "*stayed* in Asia for a while."

ἐπηρεάζω *epēreazō* threaten, abuse, slander*

Luke 6:28: "pray for those who *abuse* you" (par. Matt 5:44 Koine D W Θ, etc). 1 Pet 3:16 (as in Luke 6:28 the pl. partc. οἱ ἐπηρεάζοντες): "those who *slander* your good conduct in Christ."

ἐπί *epi* with gen.: on, at the time of, over; with dat.: on, while, over; with acc.: while, over

1. Occurrences in the NT — 2. With gen. — a) Local — b) Temporal — c) Fig. — 3. With dat. — a) Local — b) Temporal — c) Fig. — 4. With acc. — a) Local — b) Temporal — c) Fig. — d) In fixed phrases

Lit.: On preps. in general → ἀνά. BAGD s.v. — BDF §§233-35. — E. FERGUSON, " 'When You Come Together': Ἐπὶ τὸ αὐτό in Early Christian Literature," *Restoration Quarterly* 16 (1973) 202-8. — M. J. HARRIS, *DNTT* III, 1193-96. — JOHANNESSOHN, *Präpositionen* 305-24. — KÜHNER, *Grammatik* II/1, 495-505. — MAYSER, *Grammatik* II/2, 462-82. — MOULE, *Idiom-Book* 49f. — MOULTON, *Grammar* III, 271f. — RADERMACHER, *Gram-*

matik 137-46. — P. F. REGARD, *Contribution à l'Étude des Prépositions dans la langue du NT* (1919) 417-66. — SCHWYZER, *Grammatik* II, 465-73.

1. In koine Greek prep. phrases appear more frequently in place of the simple cases than in classical; compound vbs. increase over against simple forms. Preps. thus take on some expansion and shift of significance. Some blurring of the lines of meaning between the cases occurs, and use with the acc. becomes more prominent.

Ἐπί appears in the NT 891 times and is rather uniformly distributed in all of the NT literature (though less frequent in John). It is fourth in frequency among preps. in the NT (after ἐν, εἰς, and ἐκ). It is most often found with the acc. and least often with the dat. (Morgenthaler, *Statistik* 160), but is, among preps. found with three cases, the one most evenly spread among the cases. Blurring of meaning among the cases is also most common with ἐπί. As a verbal prefix ἐπι- is the second most frequent (after συν-) of the preps. Its basic meaning is *on* (Kühner 495; Schwyzer 465); further meanings are *at, near, to; during; because* (Frisk, *Wörterbuch* I, 535).

2. With gen.:

a) Local: *On, close by, at* (answering the question "where?"): Matt 6:19, *on* the earth; Acts 5:23, *at* the doors. *To, onto* (answering the question "to what place?"): Mark 4:26, *onto* the earth; John 6:21, *into* the boat; Luke 22:40, *to* the place. *Before* (with persons): Acts 25:9, *before* me (as the judge; A. Schalit, *ASTI* 6 [1968] 106-13).

b) Temporal: *At the time of, during, in:* Matt 1:11, *at the time* of the Babylonian captivity; Mark 2:26, *at the time* of the high priest Abiathar (i.e., when Abiathar was high priest); Acts 11:28, *during the reign of* Claudius; Rom 1:10, *during/in* my prayers; Jude 18, *in* the last time; 1 Pet 1:20, *at* the end of the times.

c) Fig.: Of sovereignty or oversight *over:* Rom 9:5, ὁ ὢν ἐπὶ πάντων θεός, God who is *over* all; Rev 20:6, ἐπὶ τούτων οὐκ ἔχει ἐξουσίαν, he has no power *over* these; Matt 24:45, ὃν κατέστησεν ὁ κύριος ἐπὶ τῆς οἰκετείας αὐτοῦ, whom the Lord has set *over* his household. Speak *about:* Gal 3:16, οὐ λέγει ἐπὶ πολλῶν, ἀλλ' ἐφ' ἑνός. It does not refer *to* many, but *to* one. Do *to:* John 6:2, τὰ σημεῖα ἃ ἐποίει ἐπὶ τῶν ἀσθενούντων, the signs he did *on* those who were sick. *On the basis of:* 2 Tim 5:19, ἐπὶ δύο ἢ τριῶν μαρτύρων, *on the basis of* (the statements of) two or three witnesses. *In accordance with:* Mark 12:14 and often, ἐπ' ἀληθείας, *in accordance with* the truth (= truly, in truth).

3. With dat.:

a) Local: *on, in, over, close by, at* (answering the question "where?"): Matt 14:8, *on* a platter; Acts 3:11, *in* the hall; Eph 1:10, τὰ ἐπὶ τοῖς οὐρανοῖς, what is *in* the heavens; Matt 24:33, *at* the door. *To* (answering the ques-

tion "to what place?"): Acts 11:19, *in the direction of* Stephen.

b) Temporal: *During, in, at the time of:* Eph 4:26, *during* your anger; John 4:27, ἐπὶ τούτῳ, *during* this; 2 Cor 1:4, *at the time of* all our affliction; Heb 9:26, *at* the end of the times.

c) Fig.: Of sovereignty or oversight *over:* Matt 24:47, ἐπὶ πᾶσιν τοῖς ὑπάρχουσιν αὐτοῦ καταστήσει αὐτόν, he will set him *over* his entire possession. Believe *in:* Luke 24:25. Hope, trust *in:* Rom 15:12; Luke 11:22. Rejoice, be amazed, be angry *over:* Matt 18:13; Luke 4:22; Rev 12:17. Do *to:* Acts 5:35. Write *about:* John 12:16. Give testimony *about:* Heb 11:4. Give thanks *for:* 1 Cor 1:4. *In addition, besides:* Luke 3:20, *in addition* to all; 2 Cor 7:13. Adversarial, *against:* Luke 12:53, father *against* son. *On the basis of, by:* Matt 4:4, live *by* bread; Acts 3:16, *on the basis of* faith; 2:26, *on the basis of* hope; Heb 10:28, *on the basis of* two or three witnesses. Ἐφ' ᾧ (= ἐπὶ τούτῳ ὅτι), *because:* Rom 5:12. Of purpose, goal, or result: *to:* Gal 5:13, you were called *to* freedom; Eph 2:10, created for good works. Of manner, mode: *with:* 2 Cor 9:6, *with* full hands, abundant; Matt 18:5 and often, ἐπὶ τῷ ὀνόματί μου, *in* my name (*by using/calling* my name); ἐπὶ τῷ ὀνόματί (τινος), receive, baptize, teach, do a miracle, come preach, speak *in* the name [of someone]; Luke 1:59, ἐκάλουν αὐτὸ ἐπὶ τῷ ὀνόματι τοῦ πατρὸς αὐτοῦ, they named him *after* his father.

4. With acc.:

a) Local: *Over, on, near, against* (answering the question "to what place?"): Acts 7:11, *over* all Egypt; Matt 13:5, *on* the ground; 17:6, *on* their faces; Luke 24:1, *to* the grave; John 19:33, *near/alongside* Jesus; Luke 15:4, go *after* the lost one; 14:31, ἐρχομένῳ ἐπ' αὐτόν, who marched *against* him. *On, over, at, by* (answering the question "where?"): John 12:15, sit *on* the foal of an ass; Rev 7:15, ἐπ' αὐτούς, *over* them; Jas 5:14, pray *over* him; Luke 17:35 and often, ἐπὶ τὸ αὐτό, *at* the same place/ together; 2 Thess 1:10, ἐφ' ὑμᾶς, *with* you; Rev 3:20, *at* the door.

b) Temporal: *At* (answering the question "when?"): Luke 10:35, ἐπὶ τὴν αὔριον, *on* the following day; Acts 3:1, ἐπὶ τὴν ὥραν τῆς προσευχῆς, *at* the hour of prayer. *During, throughout, for* (answering the question "[for] how long?"): Acts 13:31, *for* many days; Luke 4:25, *throughout* three years; 18:4, ἐπὶ χρόνον, *for* a while; Rom 7:1 and often, ἐφ' ὅσον (χρόνον), *as long* as.

c) Fig.: Of sovereignty or oversight *over:* Luke 1:33, he will rule *over* the house of Jacob; 12:14, who made me a judge *over* you? Matt 25:21, you were faithful *over* a little. *Besides, in addition:* Phil 2:27, λύπην ἐπὶ λύπην, grief *upon* grief. Of power or action, *at, over, on:* Luke 3:2, the word of God came *on* John; Matt 10:13, your peace should come *upon* it; 2 Cor 12:9, so that the power of Christ may rest *on* me. Turning *to, toward:* Luke 1:17, the hearts of the fathers turn *to* the children. Believe *in:* Acts 9:42. Trust, hope *in:* Matt 27:43; 1 Pet 1:13. Complain, cry *over:* Rev 1:7; Luke 23:28. Write *about:* Mark 9:13, as it is written *about* him. Do *to:* Acts 4:22, the man *on* whom the miracle was performed. Hostile expressions or acts *against, toward:* 1 Cor 7:36, act dishonorably *against/toward* his maiden; Mark 10:11, he commits adultery *against* her; 2 Cor 10:2, ἐπί τινας, *toward* certain people. *For, because of:* Acts 4:21, all praise God *because of (for)* what has taken place; Mark 15:24, as they cast lots *for* them. Of purpose, goal, or result, *to:* Matt 3:7, ἐπὶ τὸ βάπτισμα, *for* baptism; Luke 23:48, ἐπὶ τὴν θεωρίαν ταύτην, *to* this sight; Heb 12:10, ἐπὶ τὸ συμφέρον, *for* our good; Luke 4:43, ἐπὶ τοῦτο, *for this purpose;* Matt 26:50, ἐφ’ ὅ, *for* what purpose?

d) Fixed phrases: Acts 28:6, ἐπὶ πολύ, *for a long time;* 20:9, ἐπὶ πλεῖον, *for a long time;* 24:4, ἐπὶ πλεῖον, *for a longer time;* 2 Tim 3:9, ἐπὶ πλεῖον, very far; Acts 4:17, μὴ ἐπὶ πλεῖον, no further; 10:16, ἐπὶ τρίς, three times; Matt 25:40, ἐφ’ ὅσον, as much as; Rom 11:13, ἐφ’ ὅσον, inasmuch as.   W. Köhler

ἐπιβαίνω *epibainō* climb up, go up, go in*

In the NT only in Matthew and Acts: ἐπιβεβηκὼς ἐπὶ ὄνον, "*riding* on an ass" (Matt 21:5, citing Zech 9:9; cf. 1 Kgdms 25:20). Of *boarding* a ship (Acts 21:2; 27:2; 21:6 TR). With indication of place: *enter, move to:* εἰς τὴν ᾽Ασίαν (20:18); εἰς Ἰεροσόλυμα (21:4); τῇ ἐπαρχείᾳ, "to the province" (25:1).

ἐπιβάλλω *epiballō* lay on, put on; throw oneself (on something); throw, fall to*

There are 18 occurrences in the NT. Most frequently the vb. occurs in the phrase, "*lay* hands *on* someone" (with ἐπί: Matt 26:50 par. Mark 14:46 TR; Luke 20:19; 21:12; John 7:30; 7:44; Acts 5:18; 21:27; with dat.: Mark 14:46; Acts 4:3; with inf.: κακῶσαι, 12:1). Also: "*put* one's hands to the plow" (Luke 9:62); "*put* a patch (ἐπίβλημα) *on*" (Matt 9:16 par. Luke 5:36); "*lay* garments *on*" (Mark 11:7); "*lay* a noose on someone's neck" (1 Cor 7:35). It is used intrans. of waves, which *beat on* or *into* a boat (Mark 4:37). Τὸ ἐπιβάλλον μέρος τῆς οὐσίας means "the part of the property which *falls to* (someone)" (Luke 15:12; also frequent in the papyri: see Mayser, *Grammatik* II/1, 84).

᾽Επιβαλὼν ἔκλαιεν (Mark 14:72) probably means "he *began* to weep" (cf. the v.l. ἤρξατο κλαίειν D Θ 565 it vg syr, etc.; 1 Esdr 9:20; Diogenes Laertius vi.27; BDF §308). It is also suggested that the partc. be translated "he veiled his head" or "he considered the words of Jesus" (cf. Diodorus Siculus xx.43.6; Marcus Antoninus x.30, ἐπιβάλλων τούτῳ [τὸν νοῦν], "considering this"). But

these two suggestions make it necessary either to understand some elided obj. (perhaps τὸ ἱμάτιον) or to understand the partc. as a duplication of v. 72b (καὶ ἀνεμνήσθη). See G. M. Lee, *Bib* 53 (1972) 411f.   H. Balz

ἐπιβαρέω *epibareō* burden, oppress*

1 Thess 2:9; 2 Thess 3:8, in the phrase πρὸς τὸ μὴ ἐπιβαρῆσαί τινα ὑμῶν, "that a *burden may not fall* on any one of you." Ἵνα μὴ ἐπιβαρῶ (2 Cor 2:5) elaborates on the preceding ἀπὸ μέρους, which qualifies the following πάντας ὑμᾶς. The injury inflicted on the apostle has not affected Paul personally, but "to a (greater) measure" (namely, the majority, cf. v. 6), the whole church. The parenthetical ἵνα μὴ ἐπιβαρῶ underscores therefore the qualifying function of ἀπὸ μέρους: "that (it) not *weigh* [too heavily]," or "in order not *to burden* [him] [even more]." Often another meaning not attested elsewhere for ἐπιβαρέω, "pile together a great burden of words/say too much," is assumed; cf. BAGD s.v. From the context, this meaning is not necessary.

ἐπιβιβάζω *epibibazō* let (someone) climb, put (someone on something)*

Luke 10:34: "he *set him on* his own animal"; 19:35; Acts 23:24.

ἐπιβλέπω *epiblepō* look at, care for*

Luke 1:48 (citing 1 Kgdms 1:11): "you *have cared for* the lowly estate of your maidservant"; similarly with a personal dir. obj., Luke 9:38; with a negative association, Jas 2:3: "you *pay attention* to. . . ."

ἐπίβλημα, ατος, τό *epiblēma* patch*

Mark 2:21 par. Matt 9:16/Luke 5:36 (bis).

ἐπιβοάω *epiboaō* call, cry out (loudly)

Acts 25:24 C Koine E pl: ἐπιβοῶντες in place of βοῶντες.

ἐπιβουλή, ῆς, ἡ *epiboulē* plan, plot*

In the NT only in Acts, of *plots* by the Jews against Paul: 9:24; 20:3, 19; 23:30.

ἐπιγαμβρεύω *epigambreuō* become related by marriage, marry as brother-in-law*

Of levirate marriage, Matt 22:24 (cf. Deut 25:5 Aquila; Gen 38:8 v.l.; Mark 12:19/Luke 20:28): "his [oldest] brother should *marry* his wife" (against Lev 18:16; 20:21). E. Lövestam, *BHH* 1746f.

ἐπίγειος, 2 *epigeios* earthly*

1. Occurrences and meanings — 2. John 3:12 — 3. Paul — 4. Jas 3:15

Lit.: BAGD s.v. — R. JEWETT, *Paul's Anthropological Terms* (1971) 201-304. — H. SASSE, *TDNT* I, 680f. — For further bibliography see *TWNT* X, 1023.

1. This adj. occurs in Greek and Hellenistic literature, but not in the LXX. In the NT (7 occurrences) it has various nuances: spatial *(earthly);* conceptually defining (of events that take place on the earth), describing humans and powers on the earth, and—in connection with other adjs.—defining and qualifying. In the background stands the distinction: *"earthly-heavenly."*

2. John 3:12(f.) stands alone: Actions that take place *on earth* such as baptism and the giving of the Spirit are declared to Nicodemus, but events "in heaven" remain veiled. Only the Son of Man has access to them, as he alone has the right to ascent, just as he also descended. (On the distinction *"earthly-heavenly"* cf. Wis 9:16; 2 Esdr 4:8, 21; Ign. *Trall.* 5:2). We have here a revelatory statement colored by the wisdom tradition, which accents the right of the Son of Man. The statement is intended as an intensifier.

3. a) Paul distinguishes between *earthly* and heavenly bodies in 1 Cor 15:40f. (bis), corresponding to the glory of the heavenly and *earthly* celestial bodies. In the comparison and analogy he depends on the guarantee of "body" and "radiance." He represents an older apocalyptic tradition of the "transfigured" body in the heavenly world and attempts to assure this conceptual possibility —even necessity—in the Hellenistic discussion.

b) Even more graphic is the attempt in 2 Cor 5:1ff. to speak of the *earthly* "tabernacle," of this "tent" in contrast to the "building from God." The adjective *earthly* stands here in contrast to "not made with hands" and "eternal." Here Paul is interpreting an older apocalyptic tradition.

c) The hymn in Phil 2:5-11 concludes with the praise by the heavenly, *earthly,* and subterranean powers (v. 10) and their acclamation: Κύριος Ἰησοῦς Χριστός; the three cosmic dimensions unite in the eschatological acknowledgement of sovereignty.

d) Phil 3:19 seems to be polemical and pointed against enthusiasts who glorify the "belly" and "shame," and thus surrender the heavenly for the *earthly.* In this case the heavenly and future salvation is lost.

4. According to Jas 3:15 there is a wisdom that comes down from above, but also its opposite, which is *earthly,* psychic, and demonic; it expresses itself in passion and contentiousness. The false wisdom lacks the power to overcome its earthly origin.

In later Gnosticism (e.g., *Gospel of Truth* [Nag Hammadi

Codex I, columns 22, 30f., 40f.]) the idea of substance determining the "heavenly" and the "earthly" is strengthened.

O. Michel

ἐπιγίνομαι *epiginomai* come on, enter*

Acts 28:13: "*as* the south wind *came up.*" 27:27 A pc vg, of the onset of night.

ἐπιγινώσκω *epiginōskō* know, observe*

1. Occurrences and meaning — 2. a) Matthew and Mark — b) In the Lukan literature — c) Elsewhere in the NT

Lit.: R. BULTMANN, *TDNT* I, 689-719. — E. D. SCHMITZ, *DNTT* II, 390-409.

1. The vb. ἐπιγινώσκω occurs in the NT 44 times (γινώσκω occurs 221 times); it is esp. frequent in Luke (7 occurrences) and in Acts (13 occurrences), but does not appear in the Johannine literature. It means: a) *know accurately, completely;* b) *recognize;* c) *acknowledge.* In addition it can carry a meaning largely congruent with that of the simple form → γινώσκω (1).

2. a) As a rule ἐπιγινώσκω is used by Matthew and Mark without a theological interest. The following meanings are found: *know* (Matt 7:16, 20; 14:35; 17:12; Mark 6:54), *observe* (Mark 2:8; 5:30; 6:33) and *recognize* (Matt 17:12). It does have a theological meaning in Matt 11:27 (the parallel in Luke 10:22 has the simple form): The relationship of the Son to the Father and that of the Father to the Son is the basis and content of the revelation. *Know* means here (as in the OT and Jewish tradition) not primarily an intellectual event, but rather acceptance of the electing love of the Father (election, knowledge of God, and revelation are also connected with each other frequently in the Qumran literature: cf. 1QS 4:22 and often).

b) In the Lukan literature also ἐπιγινώσκω is used in an almost exclusively general way, thus, e.g., with the meanings *know* (Luke 24:16, 31; Acts 3:10; 4:13; 27:39), *observe* (Luke 1:22; 5:22; Acts 19:34), *learn* (Luke 7:37; 23:7; Acts 9:30; 12:14; 22:24, 29; 23:28; 24:8, 11; 28:1), *understand* (Acts 25:10), and *know exactly, fully* (Luke 1:4). In the Emmaus story ἐπιγινώσκω refers not only to (deeper) recognition, but also to *seeing* or *discovering* the resurrected one (Luke 24:16, 31).

c) Ἐπιγινώσκω appears 10 times in Paul (it is esp. frequent in 1 and 2 Corinthians); it also appears in Col 1:6; 1 Tim 4:3; and 2 Pet 2:21. The phrase δικαίωμα τοῦ θεοῦ ἐπιγνόντες in Rom 1:32 refers, as in v. 28 (→ ἐπίγνωσις 2.a), not to a theoretical knowledge of God, but rather to obedient recognition of the will of God (cf. vv. 19, 21). Ἐπιγινώσκω has no special theological meaning in 1 Cor 16:18 *(recognize)* and 1 Cor 14:37; 2 Cor 1:13f. *(know, understand)* (cf. 2 Cor 6:9). In 1 Cor 13:12

the full knowledge of God is the content of the eschatological promise; in 2 Cor 13:5 there is a reference to a knowledge about Jesus Christ. Col 1:6 speaks of knowledge of the grace of God ἐν ἀληθείᾳ. The combination of → ἐπίγνωσις (2.b) and → ἀλήθεια takes on greater significance in the Pastorals; to be a Christian means to preserve the ἐπίγνωσις ἀληθείας.   W. Hackenberg

ἐπίγνωσις, εως, ἡ *epignōsis* knowledge*

1. Occurrences in the NT and meaning — 2. a) The Pauline literature — b) The deutero-Pauline literature — c) Hebrews and 2 Peter

Lit.: R. BULTMANN, *TDNT* I, 689-719. — M. DIBELIUS, "Ἐπίγνωσις ἀληθείας," *Neutestamentliche Studien für G. Heinrici* (1914) (= Dibelius, *Botschaft* II, 1-13). — E. D. SCHMITZ, *DNTT* II, 392-406. — K. SULLIVAN, "Epignosis in the Epistles of Paul," *Studiorum Paulinorum Congressus internationalis catholicus* II (1963), 405-16.

1. The noun ἐπίγνωσις appears 20 times in the NT (γνῶσις appears 29 times); it does not appear in the Johannine literature (neither does γνῶσις). Ἐπίγνωσις appears frequently in the Pauline and deutero-Pauline literature (15 times), but not in the Gospels or in Acts. It means *knowledge* (cognition; see BAGD s.v.; cf. also → γινώσκω 3.c).

2. a) In the authentic Pauline letters ἐπίγνωσις appears 5 times (Rom 1:28; 3:20; 10:2; Phil 1:9; Phlm 6). It is used consistently in the OT sense, i.e., *knowledge* as recognition of (the will of) God that is effective in the conduct of the one who knows God. Intellectual understanding and existential recognition belong together. Thus Rom 1:28 is not concerned primarily with theoretical knowledge of God (on the part of the Gentiles), but with preservation or rejection of the correct knowledge of the will of God (ποιεῖν τὰ μὴ καθήκοντα). The same is true in the intercession in the letter to Philemon: Faith is demonstrated in ἐπίγνωσις παντὸς ἀγαθοῦ (v. 6; τὸ ἀγαθόν means the will of God). Likewise ἐπίγνωσις appears within an intercession in Phil 1:9.

b) The connection between knowing God and the proof in right conduct is also apparent in Col 1:9f.: ἐπίγνωσις is directed to the θέλημα θεοῦ. The "bearing of fruit and growth" in right conduct is brought forth ἐν τῇ ἐπιγνώσει τοῦ θεοῦ (1:10; cf. Eph 1:17; Phil 1:9). Col 3:10 also concerns the ethical direction. This combination of knowledge of the divine will with the demand to follow him in right conduct is determined by the OT presuppositions. In Col 2:2 (in the argument against the Colossian heresy) the discussion concerns the ἐπίγνωσις τοῦ μυστηρίου τοῦ θεοῦ, Χριστοῦ (cf. 1:26f.), which, as in 1:9, is directed to knowledge of the divine will. In Eph 4:13 the Son of God is the content of the knowlege.

In the Pastorals the phrase ἐπίγνωσις τῆς ἀληθείας (cf. Dibelius) is used almost as a t.t. describing conversion to the Christian faith (1 Tim 2:4; 2 Tim 2:25; 3:7; Titus 1:1; cf. also Heb 10:26; 2 Pet 1:3 [→ c]; *2 Clem.* 3:1; on the terminological connection of → ἐπιγινώσκω and → ἀλήθεια, cf. Col 1:6). Ἀλήθεια designates here the "correct teaching"; and ἐπίγνωσις has "quite clearly an intellectual, semidogmatic stress" (Schmitz 405).

c) In 2 Pet 2:20 ἐπίγνωσις is perhaps a slogan of the (Gnostic) opponents against whom the author writes. As in Heb 10:26, so in 2 Pet 1:2f., ἐπίγνωσις is used in an almost technical sense for the call to the Christian faith. Yet this knowledge must also be demonstrated in righteous conduct (2 Pet 1:8; 2:20f.; cf. Rom 1:28).

W. Hackenberg

ἐπιγραφή, ῆς, ἡ *epigraphē* inscription*

Of the *inscription* on the Roman silver denarius (→ δηνάριον), which is brought to Jesus so that he may answer the question about the head tax (with εἰκών; Mark 12:16 par. Matt 22:20/Luke 20:24). The obverse of the most frequently used denarius at the time of Jesus had the head of Tiberius and the inscription: *Ti(berius) Caesar Divi Aug(usti) F(ilius) Augustus;* on the reverse, with the image of Livia, the mother of Caesar, it read: *Pontif(ex) Maxim(us)* (see illustrations, *BHH* 1983f.; *ISBE* III, plate 35; *EBD* 729; see also B. Kanael, *BHH* 2242; E. Stauffer, *Christ and the Caesars* [1955] 112-37; W. Schrage, *Die Christen und der Staat im NT* [1971] 33f.).

In Mark 15:26 par. Luke 23:38 the subject is the *inscription* on the cross of Jesus, the so-called *titulus,* a tablet coated with white gypsum and written on with black letters, in which, according to Roman custom, the basis of Jesus' condemnation to death was stated: ὁ βασιλεὺς τῶν Ἰουδαίων (Mark; Luke adds οὗτος; John 19:19f. speaks of a τίτλος written in three languages; cf. Luke 23:38 v.l.) G. Delling, *BHH* 1005; *BL* 993; E. Bammel, "The *Titulus,*" *Jesus and the Politics of His Day* (ed. E. Bammel and C. F. D. Moule; 1984) 353-64.

H. Balz

ἐπιγράφω *epigraphō* write on, provide an inscription, inscribe*

In the lit. sense, Mark 15:26: ἦν ἡ → ἐπιγραφὴ . . . ἐπιγεγραμμένη, "an inscription . . . was *written*"; with ἐν, Acts 17:23: "an altar on which was *the inscription*"; Rev 21:12: "*inscribed* names"; fig. with ἐπὶ in OT citations: Heb 8:10 (Exod 19:6); 10:16 (cf. Jer 38:33 LXX), of God, who *will inscribe* his laws on hearts/in minds.

ἐπιδείκνυμι *epideiknymi* show, exhibit, prove*

Matt 16:1: *show* (a sign from heaven); 22:19 (par.

Luke 20:24 TR): *let me see;* Matt 24:1; Luke 24:40 TR: *show;* Luke 17:14: *show, present* oneself (to the priests). The mid. in Acts 9:39 has the meaning *show on oneself, exhibit.* Fig. in Acts 18:28: *prove* (from the Scriptures); Heb 6:17: *show, explain;* → δείχνυμι.

ἐπιδέχομαι *epidechomai* receive as a guest, accept*

3 John 10: *welcome* the brethren (into his house). V. 9 fig.: "Diotrephes does not *recognize* us [i.e., our authority]."

ἐπιδημέω *epidēmeō* live/be present as a stranger*

Of Jews from Rome in Jerusalem, Acts 2:10; of foreigners in Athens, 17:21; cf. 18:27 D.

ἐπιδιατάσσομαι *epidiatassomai* prescribe in addition, add a codicil*

Gal 3:15, in reference to a legally valid testament, which no one will *change with a codicil.*

ἐπιδίδωμι *epididōmi* give up, hand over*

Give a stone (Matt 7:9 par. Luke 11:11a v.l.), a serpent (Matt 7:10 par. Luke 11:11b), a scorpion (Luke 11:12), a piece of fish (24:42; pass. 4:17). The resurrected one *handed* both disciples in Emmaus the bread (24:30). *Deliver* a letter (Acts 15:30). With an obj., τὸ πλοῖον, Acts 27:15: "we *surrendered* it [the ship to the wind] and were driven."

ἐπιδιορθόω *epidiorthoō* set right (fully/in addition)*

Titus 1:5, with obj. τὰ λείποντα: "so that *you fully set right* what is lacking."

ἐπιδύω *epidyō* go down, set (upon)*

Eph 4:26: "Let not the sun *go down* on your wrath" (μὴ ἐπιδυέτω ἐπὶ . . .).

ἐπιείκεια, ας, ἡ *epieikeia* forbearance, gentleness → ἐπιειχής.

ἐπιειχής, 2 *epieikēs* gentle, kind*
ἐπιείκεια, ας, ἡ *epieikeia* forbearance, gentleness*

Lit.: F. D'AGOSTINO, "Il tema dell' epieikeia nella s. Scrittura," *RTM* 5 (1973) 385-406. — K. DUCHATELEZ, "L'epieikeia' dans l'antiquité grecque, païenne et chrétienne," *Communio* 12 (1979) 203-31. — A. VON HARNACK, " 'Sanftmut, Huld und Demut' in der alten Kirche," *Festgabe für J. Kaftan* (1920) 113-29. — R. LEIVESTAD, " 'The Meekness and Gentleness of Christ,' II Cor. X.1," *NTS* 12 (1965/66) 156-64. — A. DI MARINO,

"L'epieikeia cristiana," *Divus Thomas,* third series, 29 (1952) 396-424. — H. PREISKER, *TDNT* II, 588-90. — C. SCPICO, "Bénignité, Mansuétude, Douceur, Clémence," *RB* 54 (1947) 321-39.

1. The adj. appears 5 times in the NT, all in the Epistles. The noun appears twice (Acts 24:4; 2 Cor 10:1).

2. Two different meanings are possible, both of which are found first in the LXX.

a) In the LXX the two words are used for the gentleness or forbearance of God (1 Kgdms 12:22; Ps 85:5; Wis 12:18; Bar 2:27; Dan 3:42; 4:27; 8:12; 2 Macc 2:22; 10:4), of a king (Esth 3:13; 8:12; 2 Macc 11:27; 3 Macc 3:15; 7:6), and of a prophet (2 Kgdms 6:3). Common to these passages is the "benevolence of the sovereign" (Harnack).

In the NT the word group is used only twice in this way (with Leivestad 158). In Acts 24:4 the Jewish accuser addresses the governor, Felix, mentioning his *kindness* in order to win him for the accusation. 1 Pet 2:18 demands of slaves not only to be submissive to the good and *gentle,* but also to the "overbearing."

b) Wis 2:19 understands ἐπιείκεια in the sense of the humble, patient firmness of the righteous one who stands on the side of the poor (2:10), is called son of God (1:16) in the midst of the scorn of the godless (2:13, 16, 18), and willingly takes on himself unrighteousness and mistreatment by trusting in God.

In 2 Cor 10:1 Paul defends himself against the accusation that he is "weak" (ταπεινός), appealing to the πραΰτης καὶ ἐπιείκεια τοῦ Χριστοῦ. In v. 10 he takes up ταπεινός again, with ἀσθενής. The apostle can make a virtue of this word because he knows that God's power is revealed in human weakness. His opponents do not understand that it is weakness about which Paul can boast (11:30; 12:9; 13:3). In his weakness he follows his Lord. This understanding is confirmed with πραΰτης, which defines ἐπιείκεια more precisely. The ἐπιείκεια of Christ is thus not a royal majesty (against Preisker, Harnack). The other texts fit here: According to Phil 4:5 the Christians should make known to all their *forbearance* (τὸ ἐπιεικές), which lives from the joy in the Lord, who is near. According to 1 Tim 3:3 the bishop should not only be ἐπιειχής with respect to his position of authority, but in his private life, as the other virtues show, in which the ἐπιείκεια is imbedded. In Titus 3:2 this meaning is so clear that it is conceded even by Preisker (590). This is also the case of the "wisdom from above" (Jas 3:17), where in the context ἐπιειχής is in no way "given the attributes of rule" (Preisker 586).

H. Giesen

ἐπιειχία, ας, ἡ *epieikia* forbearance, gentleness

Alternative form of ἐπιείκεια (→ ἐπιειχής).

ἐπιζητέω *epizēteō* seek after, strive after, demand*

13 occurrences in the NT, occasionally strengthening the simple form → ζητέω: *(eagerly) seek after* someone (Luke 4:42; Acts 12:19), *be on the lookout* (for future salvation; Heb 11:14; 13:14), *strive for* (Matt 6:32 par. Luke 12:30; Rom 11:7; Phil 4:17 bis), *wish/demand* (Acts 13:7, with inf.; 19:39), ἐπιζητέω σημεῖον, "*demand a sign*" (Matt 12:39 par. Luke 11:29 v.l.; Matt 16:4 par. Mark 8:12 v.l.).

ἐπιθανάτιος, 2 *epithanatios* sentenced to death, condemned to death*

1 Cor 4:9, in a depiction of the apostles: ὡς ἐπιθανατίους.

ἐπίθεσις, εως, ἡ *epithesis* laying on*

In the NT always in the fixed phrase ἐπίθεσις τῶν χειρῶν, *laying on of hands:* Acts 8:18; 1 Tim 4:14; 2 Tim 1:6; Heb 6:2. *BL* 663 (bibliography); J. Coppens, *BHH* 632-36 (bibliography); D. Daube, "The Laying On of Hands," *The NT and Rabbinic Judaism* (1956) 224ff.; Spicq, *Notes* I, 268f.; D. W. Wead, *ISBE* II, 611f. (bibliography).

ἐπιθυμέω *epithymeō* desire, strive for
→ ἐπιθυμία.

ἐπιθυμητής, οῦ, ὁ *epithymētēs* one who desires
→ ἐπιθυμία.

ἐπιθυμία, ας, ἡ *epithymia* desire, longing
ἐπιθυμέω *epithymeō* desire (vb.), strive for
ἐπιθυμητής, οῦ, ὁ *epithymētēs* one who desires*

1. Occurrences in the NT — 2. Meaning — 3. Usage and synonyms — 4. a) Paul and James: The sequence desire —sin—death — b) 1 John 2:15-17: ἐπιθυμία and κόσμος

Lit.: G. BORNKAMM, "Sin, Law and Death," *Early Christian Experience* (1969) 87-104. — F. BÜCHSEL, *TDNT* III, 167-72. — M. DIBELIUS and H. GREEVEN, *Jas* (Hermeneia, 1976) 90-99. — E. GERSTENBERGER, *THAT* I, 74-76. — idem, *THAT* I, 579-81. — H. HÜBNER, *Law in Paul's Thought* (1984) 69-78. — E. KÄSEMANN, *Rom* (Eng. tr., 1980) 191-99. — S. LYONNET, " 'Tu ne convoiteras pas' (Rom 7,7)," FS Cullmann (1962) 157-165. — idem, "Quaestiones ad Rom 7,7-13," *VD* 40 (1962) 163-83. — G. MAYER, *TDOT* I, 134-37. — J. B. METZ, *LTK* II, 108-12. — W. Metzger, "Die neōterikai epithymiai in 2 Tim 2,22," *TZ* 33 (1977) 129-36. — F. MUSSNER, *Jas* (HTKNT, [2]1967) 84-97. — H. SCHLIER, *Rom* (HTKNT, 1977) 220-27. — H. SCHÖNWEISS, *DNTT* I, 456-58. — G. WALLIS, *TDOT* IV, 452-62. — P. WILPERT, *RAC* II, 62-78. — For further bibliography see *TWNT* X, 1111.

1. The vb. ἐπιθυμέω appears 7 times in the Synoptics and Acts (of which 5 are in Luke and 1 in Acts), 4 times in Paul, and once each in 1 Timothy, Hebrews, James, 1 Peter, and Revelation. The noun is more concentrated in the letters: 34 times vs. only once each in Mark, Luke, John, and Acts. 10 occurrences are in Paul (5 in Romans alone), and 9 in the deutero-Pauline literature.

2. Ἐπιθυμέω and ἐπιθυμία are derived from → θυμός, first "spirit, courage, wrath, sense" (Frisk, *Wörterbuch* I, 693), then also "passion, passionate desire," in which the formation of the word is based on the motif of desire and striving in θυμός. As in the LXX, where ἐπιθυμέω is most often used in an ethically neutral sense to designate humankind in its need (e.g., Gen 31:30; Deut 14:26), in the NT in most references (11 of 16) it has the ambivalent sense, *desire, strive for, long to have/do/be* something. Only in five instances is the word used for *(forbidden) desire*. Of these Rom 7:7; 13:9 cite the commandment of the Decalogue (Exod 20:17/Deut 5:21). 1 Cor 10:6 alludes to Num 11:4, 34. Although Matt 5:28 sharpens the commandment of the Decalogue in Exod 20:13/Deut 5:17 (LXX), the formulation is aided by Exod 20:17/Deut 5:21. Where ἐπιθυμέω in the LXX is used with this negative sense, it is normally a tr. of the qal of *ḥāmaḏ*. The formulation in Rom 7:7; 13:9, which cites the prohibition of desiring the wife of one's neighbor or the property of another without the acc. obj. and thus radicalizes the commandment, already existed in Jewish tradition, as 4 Macc 2:6 demonstrates: μὴ ἐπιθυμεῖν εἴρηκεν ἡμᾶς ὁ νόμος.

This development is apparent in the NT use of the noun ἐπιθυμία. Following Jewish thought (see *Apoc. Mos.* 19:3: "For ἐπιθυμία is the beginning [κεφαλή] of every sin"; on the rabbinic idea of the evil impulse, the *yēṣer hārā'*, see Moore, *Judaism* I, 479-83 and Levy II, 258f.), ἐπιθυμία is used almost exclusively in the NT—contrary to the LXX—in the negative sense: *(evil) desire,* for Paul and James an important (→ 4.a) theological t.t. (W. D. Davies, *Paul and Rabbinic Judaism* [[4]1980] 23ff. incorrectly relates the the rabbinic *yēṣer hārā'* doctrine to Romans 7 because he interprets Romans 7 autobiographically.)

Because σάρξ is not an anthropological term, but is instead strictly a theological term for the individual locus of the transsubjective power of sin (→ ἁμαρτία), the close relationship between ἐπιθυμία and σάρξ should not mislead one into interpreting ἐπιθυμία as primarily sexual desire. Of course ἐπιθυμία is also used of the misuse of sexual desire.

Sometimes the vb. ἐπιθυμέω takes on the character of something esp. urgent, e.g., Luke 22:15, ἐπιθυμίᾳ ἐπεθύμησα, *I have desired longingly* (cf. Gen 31:30). Ἐπιθυμητής in 1 Cor 10:6 refers to godless desire, thus the evil ἐπιθυμία of mankind.

3. Both vb. and noun are often found in contexts of related or synonymous concepts, e.g., in 1 Tim 3:1 with ὀρέγομαι ("strive for"), in Rev 9:6 with ζητέω ("strive for"), in Titus 3:3; Jas 4:1f. with ἡδονή ("[evil] desire"), in Gal 5:24 with πάθημα ("passion"), and in 1 Thess 4:5 ἐν πάθει ἐπιθυμίας, "in passion *desire.*"

Ἐπιθυμέω appears with the acc. obj. of the person (Matt 5:28, the woman as object of sexual desire), with a gen. obj. (e.g., Acts 20:33), and with the inf. (e.g., Matt 13:17; Luke 15:16, 21f.). Of particular significance among descriptive genitives found with ἐπιθυμία is σαρκός ("fleshly *desires,*" Gal 5:16; Eph 2:3; 2 Pet 2:18 [cf. K. H. Schelkle, *1 and 2 Pet* [HTKNT] 216 n.1]; 1 John 2:16; see also 1 Pet 2:11: τῶν σαρκικῶν ἐπιθυμιῶν; Rom 13:14; 2 Pet 2:10 [cf. Jude 7]: ἐπιθυμία in relationship to σάρξ).

Ἐπιθυμία is used in catalogs of vices in Col 3:5; Titus 3:3; 1 Pet 4:3; it is also found near or within the larger context of catalogs of vices in Rom 1:24; Gal 5:16; 1 Tim 6:9; 2 Tim 3:6; 1 Pet 4:2.

4. a) In both Rom 7:7ff. and Jas 1:13ff. ἐπιθυμία is used in the context of the temptation story of Genesis 3. In both passages the sequence is ἐπιθυμία–ἁμαρτία–θάνατος ("*desire*–sin–death"). Only in Rom 5:12 is the sequence ἁμαρτία–θάνατος found. In Jas 1:13ff. *desire,* sin, and death are quasi-personified powers, while in Rom 5:12 these powers are sin and death. In Rom 7:7 this is also the case at least for sin. Despite these points of correspondence between Paul and James the differences are considerable. The respective arguments indicate these differences:

In Rom 7:7-12 sin is described as a wily power that employs the law as a basis of operations (ἀφορμή) in order to cause the individual to sin. Of course Paul condenses this section into such a strong theological concentration that one can scarcely unravel the ideas that have been intertwined, and sometimes only assumed, not fully articulated. The concrete experience of sin in v. 7a occurs when the law says, "You shall not desire," and the individual recognizes himself as one who desires. However, there is no speculation concerning why the individual is fundamentally one who desires in an evil way.

From the context of 7:7-12 and from the entire complex of statements in Romans, ἐπιθυμία has a double connotation: πᾶσαν ἐπιθυμίαν in v. 8 means both the *antinomian* (from the allusion to Genesis 3 in vv. 8ff.) and the *nomistically* (Rom 10:3) understood ἐπιθυμία (Bornkamm 90; Schlier 223: "All manner of desire [is] . . . included in unrighteousness and self-righteousness"). That the individual does not have the freedom to live without desire is indicated unambiguously in the relationship between Rom 7:7ff. and 5:12ff.: Every person before and out of Christ is brought to sinful desire by sin, be-

cause it is a cosmic power, i.e., a power that determines all humanity. The blurred quality of Paul's argument in 7:7ff. is to be seen in the fact that v. 7a depicts primarily a noetic relationship between law and sin, while in v. 7b the noetic understanding turns into an ontic one: when the individual experiences himself as one who desires, desire comes into being (Hübner 76).

The one who desires in Romans 7 is estranged from himself. He believes, in his desiring, that he is aiming at life, yet in reality he desires death. He does not know what he is doing (v. 15). In the argument, this point is esp. the case for the individual who has nomistic desires. But this means that the person under law cannot understand fully the dreadfulness of sin and desire.

For Jas 1:13 the personification of ἐπιθυμία (v. 14) and the appeal to Genesis 3 (Mussner 89: a "psychological interpretation of the story of the fall") serves the practical intention of the saying in vv. 16-18 (Dibelius and Greeven 93): the author wants to repudiate the false idea that God is the source of temptation. Temptation occurs, instead, through one's own *desire* (v. 14). Where desire comes from is indicated just as little as Rom 5:12 says where sin originates. The sequence known from Paul of ἐπιθυμία–ἁμαρτία–θάνατος is described genealogically in Jas 1:15. Ἐπιθυμία appears "as a kind of harlot" (Mussner 88), who conceives sin through her harlotry; by whom she conceives is again not said. Sin in turn conceives death. Nevertheless in James everything is much more harmless than in Paul. Here the tempted one needs only to reject the temptress. Ἐπιθυμία is no longer discussed in connection with the Pauline dialectic of unavoidable fate and the deed for which one is responsible (Rom 5:12). James's teaching about desire, sin, and death is not integrated into a soteriological theology, as it is in Paul.

b) In 1 John 2:15-17 ἐπιθυμία is divided into the desire of the flesh, of the eyes, and of the pride of life and is an expression for an existence that receives its determination "of the world" (κόσμος) and is thus godless.

Probably R. Bultmann goes too far (*1–3 John* [Eng. tr., Hermeneia] 33) when he views the gen. describing ἐπιθυμία, "of the flesh," as "a power hostile to God." The three genitives of v. 16 are, as v. 17 suggests, characterizations of the "earthly-temporal" (R. Schnackenburg, *1–3 John* [HTKNT] 127-33): "We do not learn what the ultimate roots of ἐπιθυμία are" (Schnackenburg 128).

H. Hübner

ἐπικαθίζω *epikathizō* sit down on*

Matt 21:7, with ἐπάνω, "he *sat down* on them [the ass and the foal]."

ἐπικαλέω *epikaleō* name, call upon*

1. Occurrences in the NT — 2. Meaning — 3. Ἐπικαλέω [τὸ ὄνομα] + obj.

Lit.: R. BAUMANN, *Mitte und Norm des Christlichen* (NTAbh 5, 1968). — W. BOUSSET, *Kyrios Christos* (1970) 130ff., 149, 153. — BULTMANN, *Theology* I, 126-28. — L. COENEN, *DNTT* I, 271-76. — O. CULLMANN, "Alle, die den Namen unseres Herrn Jesus Christus anrufen," *idem, Vorträge und Aufsätze 1925-1962* (1966) 605-22. — J. DUPONT, "Nom de Jesus," *DBSup* VI, 514-41, esp. 520-25. — K. GALLING, "Die Ausrufung des Namens als Rechtsakt in Israel," *TLZ* 81 (1956) 65-70. — GOPPELT, *Theology* II, 79f. — HAHN, *Titles* 108f. — W. HEITMÜLLER, *Im Namen Jesu* (FRLANT 1-2, 1903). — A. KERRIGAN, "The 'Sensus Plenior' of Joel, III,1-5 in Act., II,14-36," *Sacra Pagina* (ed. J. Coppens, et al., BETL 12-13, 1959) II, 295-313. — W. KRAMER, *Christ, Lord, Son of God* (1966). — P.-É. LANGEVIN, " 'Ceux qui invoquent le nom du Seigneur' (1 Cor 1,2)," *ScEc* 19 (1967) 373-407; *ScEs* 20 (1968) 113-26; 21 (1969) 71-122. — LSJ s.v. — K. L. SCHMIDT, *TDNT* III, 496-501. — P. VIELHAUER, "Ein Weg zur neutestamentlichen Christologie?" *EvT* 25 (1965) 24-72, esp. 43-45. — U. WIKKERT, "Einheit und Eintracht der Kirche im Präskript des 1 Kor," *ZNW* 50 (1959) 73-82.

1. The frequent use of the simple vb. → καλέω in the NT (148 times) is to be contrasted to the less frequent occurrence of ἐπικαλέω (30 times). Luke has a special preference for ἐπικαλέω (Luke 22:3 v.l.; 20 times in Acts). Paul uses ἐπικαλέω 5 times (3 times in Romans, once each in 1 and 2 Corinthians); ἐπικαλέω appears once each in Matthew, 2 Timothy, Hebrews, James, and 1 Peter.

The basic meaning *name, give a name* appears predominantly in the passive forms of the vb. (→ 2.a), where ἐπικαλέω is equated with the simple form of the vb. (cf. ἐπικαλέω and καλέω in Acts 1:23). In the mid. voice ἐπικαλέω means *call upon, call to oneself* (→ 2.b). In connection with τὸ ὄνομα or a personal obj. ἐπικαλέω (predominantly mid.) means *call upon in confession* (→ 3).

2. a) The completion of a personal name with a surname is expressed with the pass. partc. of ἐπικαλέω in the attributive position (aor. ἐπικληθείς in Matt 10:3 v.l.; Acts 4:36; 12:25; pres. ἐπικαλούμενος in Luke 22:3 v.l.; in Acts 10:18; 11:13; 12:12; 15:22 v.l.) or with ind. pass. forms (aor. ἐπεκλήθη in Acts 1:23; pres. ἐπικαλεῖται in 10:5, 32). In Matt 10:25 ἐπικαλέω (aor. ind. act. trans.) is used in the identification of a proper name.

b) The appeal to God as witness in 2 Cor 1:23 is to be understood as a juridical expression (Ἐπικαλέω has this meaning already in classical Greek: cf. Herodotus ii.39; iii.8; Antipho i.30; Plato *Lg.* ii.664c). Ἐπικαλέω is used in the mid. voice to render the t.t. *appellatio* or *provocatio* in texts concerning the trial of Paul (Acts 25:11f., 21, 25; 26:32; 28:19; this meaning is present already in Demosthenes *Or.* xviii.127).

3. a) In connection with the generally Semitic expanded personal obj. (ἐπικαλέω τὸ ὄνομα [τοῦ] κυρίου) ἐπικαλέω is used in the mid. voice in a theological sense to refer to the confession of faith in the Church's acclamation, which always has as its content the "name," the proclaimed Lord himself.

From the context Rom 10:13 (πᾶς . . . ὃς ν ἐπικαλέσηται τὸ ὄνομα κυρίου σωθήσεται [Joel 3:5 LXX]) is to be interpreted as the invocation (v. 10b) of Jesus as Kyrios (cf. v. 9a), in which is the basis for the salvation of mankind. Ἐπικαλέω is here, as in v. 12b (αὐτόν refers to κύριος in v. 12a), used of the cry of *confession*. Here the OT background, in which calling on the name is the source of a relationship of possession (also in the sense of a legal claim), is to be considered (→ ὄνομα).

Also in an OT citation in Peter's speech in Acts 2:21 (Joel 3:5 LXX) the aspect of confession of faith in the Kyrios stands in the foreground: The words of Joel, which were originally intended in an eschatological sense, are drawn into the present time of salvation with the Spirit-filled proclamation (cf. vv. 16, 22-24). Ἐπικαλέω τὸ ὄνομα τοῦ κυρίου is already in 1 Cor 1:2 (pre-Pauline) a reference to all (on the basis of baptism, cf. v. 13) within the assembled congregation who confess Christ as Lord (H. Conzelmann, *1 Cor* [Eng. tr., Hermeneia] 23: "The Christians"). It stands here as a statement which is the basis of unity (with "all" also in *Herm. Sim.* ix.14.3; Josephus *B.J.* v.438, ἐπικαλέω τὸ ὄνομα τοῦ θεοῦ: "swear"). In Rom 10:14 this nuance of ἐπικαλέω is elucidated as (liturgical) acclamation by being related to → πιστεύω. In Acts 9:14, 21 ἐπικαλέω τὸ ὄνομα is connected with a pron. referring to Christ. This reference is suggested in 22:16; in Acts 7:59 the obj. is removed in favor of direct address.

2 Tim 2:22 (ἐπικαλέω τὸν κύριον) and 1 Pet 1:17 (ἐπικαλέω πατέρα) offer better Greek expressions for the same content; 1 Pet 1:17, in dependence on Rom 8:15; Gal 4:6 (→ ἀββα 3), is an example of the new gift of addressing God as Father.

b) The same meaning of ἐπικαλέω is present in a different kind of construction in Heb 11:16 ("God is confessed [= called upon] as God"); the inf. ἐπικαλεῖσθαι is to be regarded as pass. In Jas 2:7 (τὸ καλὸν ὄνομα τὸ ἐπικληθὲν ἐφ' ὑμᾶς) the aor. pass. partc. is used of transfer of ownership through calling on the name of Jesus in baptism (cf. 1 Cor 1:2; → βαπτίζω). The OT anchoring of this manner of thought is indicated in Acts 15:17 (= Amos 9:12 LXX; cf. Deut 28:10; Isa 43:7; Jer 14:9, etc.).

W. Kirchschläger

ἐπικάλυμμα, ατος, τό *epikalymma* cover (noun), pretext*

1 Pet 2:16, fig.: "freedom not as a *pretext* for evil."

ἐπικαλύπτω *epikalyptō* veil, cover (vb.)*

Rom 4:7, pass. (citing Ps 31:1 LXX), fig. with subj. αἱ ἁμαρτίαι.

ἐπικατάρατος, 2 *epikataratos* cursed*

Gal 3:10 (citing Deut 27:26), 13 (cf. Deut 21:23): ἐπικατάρατος πᾶς ὅς/ὁ . . . ; → καταράομαι.

ἐπίκειμαι *epikeimai* lie upon*

1. Literal — 2. Fig. — 3. As a theological expression

Lit.: F. BÜCHSEL, *TDNT* III, 655. — CREMER/KÖGEL 591. — MOULTON/MILLIGAN 240. — WETTSTEIN, *NT* I, 684, 814; II, 136.

1. John uses ἐπίκειμαι only in the lit. sense, in 11:38 of the tomb and in 21:9 of fish *lying on* a charcoal fire. From the usage of the vb. in 11:38 one can conclude that the structure of the tomb of Lazarus is to be visualized differently from that of the tomb of Jesus, for which a large stone blocked the horizontal access to the tomb. The tomb of Lazarus is to be visualized as a hole in the ground covered and sealed by a stone. This structure corresponds to the graves spoken of in Luke 11:44 and the tomb of Lazarus which is currently displayed (Kopp, *Places* 268f., 278-81). The iconographic tradition is, on the other hand, traced back to the Latin translation *monumentum*.

John 21:9 is marked by lively description. The scene is prematurely blended into the story of the catch of fish. As the disciples climb out of the boat, they first see (pres.!) a charcoal fire "lying there" (κειμένην); the v.l. καιομένην (burning) is probably intended as a corrective: the red-hot coals (cf. 18:18) would not be seen from the boat. Then they see the "fish" (ὀψάριον, lit. "cooked food," here probably fish, cf. modern Greek ψάρι, "fish") lying on the fire, and finally they see the bread.

2. In Luke-Acts ἐπίκειμαι is used fig. with the meaning *press upon* of a storm (Acts 27:20) and a crowd (Luke 5:1; 23:23). Thus it always concerns something menacing. According to Luke 5:1 the crowd seeks miraculous healing (cf. 6:19), while in 23:23 Jesus is rejected by the people (λαός!). Because 5:1 is apparently a Lukan creation, the verse is a counterpart to 23:23, just as the confession of Peter in 5:8 corresponds to the denial scene in 22:54-62.

3. Ἐπίκειμαι has a theological meaning in Paul. He uses the vb. in 1 Cor 9:16 to characterize his apostolic authority, which he experiences as a divine compulsion (→ ἀνάγκη 3), from which he cannot withdraw. "'Ανάγκη lies on me," one says of the destiny one is seized by (Homer *Il.* vi.458). The closest parallels are the OT prophets, for whom likewise the commission to proclaim is an inescapable destiny (Amos 3:8; Jer 1:6; 20:9).

Heb 9:10 says of OT legal regulations (δικαιώματα σαρκός) that they are *laid down* only for a fixed period. The word betrays a Christian interpretation of the law as a burden (cf. *Did.* 6:2f.).   G. Bouwman

ἐπικέλλω *epikellō* bring to shore, run aground*

Acts 27:41, with obj. τὴν ναῦν, as nautical t.t.

Ἐπικούρειος, ου, ὁ *Epikoureios* Epicurean*

In the NT only in Acts 17:18 (τινὲς . . . τῶν Ἐπικουρείων καὶ Στοϊκῶν φιλοσόφων . . .) as the designation of a philosophical school (cf. also Josephus *Ant.* x.277) traced back to Epicurus (341-270 B.C.). Along with the Stoics they are regarded by the author of Acts as the best-known philosophical view. Nothing in the context is said about their teaching; Luke probably thought of them as the representatives of materialism and atheism. C. Schneider, *BHH* 421; E. Haenchen, *Acts* (Eng. tr., 1971) ad loc.

ἐπικουρία, ας, ἡ *epikouria* help*

Acts 26:22: ἐπικουρίας . . . τῆς ἀπὸ τοῦ θεοῦ, "*help* . . . from God."

Ἐπικούριος, ου, ὁ *Epikourios* Epicurean → Ἐπικούρειος.

ἐπικρίνω *epikrinō* determine, decide*

Luke 23:24 (Mark 15:14 differs), of Pilate's judgment.

ἐπιλαμβάνομαι *epilambanomai* seize, grasp*

19 occurrences in the NT, of which 5 are in Luke and 7 in Acts; connected with the gen. or acc. of person or thing: *grasp* someone (e.g., for help or healing; Matt 14:31; Mark 8:23, τῆς χειρὸς τοῦ τυφλοῦ; Luke 9:47; 14:4; Acts 9:27; 17:19; 23:19; Heb 8:9, God as subject); *seize, lay hold of* someone (with hostile intent: Acts 16:19; 18:17; 21:30), in the sense of *capture* (21:33); *seize/snatch up* someone (Luke 23:26); fig.: "*catch* someone in a word" (lit. "*seize* on a word": 20:20 [λόγου], 26 [ῥήματος]); *grasp* something, in the sense of *acquire for oneself* (1 Tim 6:12, τῆς αἰωνίου ζωῆς; 6:19, τῆς ὄντως ζωῆς); *care about* (Heb 2:16 bis).

ἐπιλανθάνομαι *epilanthanomai* forget, neglect*

Forget (Mark 8:14 par. Matt 16:5; Jas 1:24), *be unconcerned about/neglect* (Phil 3:13, obj. τὰ . . . ὀπίσω); with negative: *be concerned about* (Heb 13:2, τῆς φιλοξενίας; v. 16, τῆς δὲ εὐποιΐας καὶ κοινωνίας); in reference to God's constant fidelity (Luke 12:6; Heb 6:10).

ἐπιλέγω *epilegō* name (in addition); select*

John 5:2, pass., in reference to the "Hebrew" name of the Pool of Bethesda (Bethzatha); Acts 15:40, mid.: "Paul *selected* Silas."

ἐπιλείπω *epileipō* leave, fail*

Heb 11:32: ἐπιλείψει με . . . ὁ χρόνος, "time *would fail* me."

ἐπιλείχω *epileichō* lick*

Luke 16:21, with obj. τὰ ἕλκη ("the sores").

ἐπιλησμονή, ῆς, ἡ *epilēsmonē* forgetfulness

Jas 1:25: ἀκροατὴς ἐπιλησμονῆς, "the hearer who (immediately) *forgets*."

ἐπίλοιπος, 2 *epiloipos* remaining*

1 Pet 4:2: τὸν ἐπίλοιπον . . . χρόνον, "the time (still) *remaining*"; subst. τὰ ἐπίλοιπα, "the rest," Luke 24:43 Koine, etc.

ἐπίλυσις, εως, ἡ *epilysis* analysis, interpretation*

2 Pet 1:20: ἰδία ἐπίλυσις, "one's own *interpretation*"

ἐπιλύω *epilyō* loosen; interpret; settle*

Mark 4:34, of the interpretation of a parable (cf. *Herm. Sim.* v.3.1f.); Acts 19:39, in reference to a decision in the regular assembly of the people.

ἐπιμαρτυρέω *epimartyreō* testify*

1 Pet 5:12: ἐπιμαρτυρῶν, used with παρακαλῶν.

ἐπιμέλεια, ας, ἡ *epimeleia* care, attention*

Acts 27:3: ἐπιμελείας τυχεῖν, "participate in the *care/ be cared for*." Spicq, *Notes* I, 270-76.

ἐπιμελέομαι *epimeleomai* care for*

With gen. of the person, Luke 10:34, 35: ". . . for him"; with the obj. ἐκκλησίας θεοῦ, 1 Tim 3:5. Spicq, *Notes* I, 69-71, 270-76.

ἐπιμελῶς *epimelōs* carefully, diligently*

In Luke 15:8 a woman seeks *diligently* until she finds a lost coin. Spicq, *Notes* I, 270-76.

ἐπιμένω *epimenō* remain, persist (in something)*

16 occurrences in the NT (including John 8:7, elsewhere not in the Gospels), of which 6 are in Acts within the travel reports. In half of the references ἐπιμένω is used in the literal sense of *remain* (at a specific place), normally with an indication of the duration of the stay (Acts 10:48; 21:4, 10; 28:12, 14; 1 Cor 16:7, 8; Gal 1:18). Phil

1:24: "*remaining/enduring* in the flesh" (τῇ σαρκί = in this life, cf. v. 22).

Elsewhere the fig. meaning is used: *persist* in something (with dat.)/*continue* to do something (with partc.): John 8:7: "they kept on questioning him"; Acts 12:16: "Peter *continued* knocking"; Rom 6:1: *continue in* (the realm of) sin; 11:22: *in* the kindness of God; v. 23: not *persist in* unbelief; Col 1:23: *abide in* faith; 1 Tim 4:16: ἐπίμενε αὐτοῖς, "*remain steadfastly in*" (attention to "yourself and your teaching," v. 16a).

ἐπινεύω *epineuō* nod, consent*

Acts 18:20: οὐκ ἐπένευσεν, Paul did not *consent*.

ἐπίνοια, ας, ἡ *epinoia* idea, intention*

Acts 8:22: ἡ ἐπίνοια τῆς καρδίας σου, used negatively of the (evil) *plan* of Simon Magus.

ἐπιορκέω *epiorkeō* swear falsely, break an oath*

In Matt 5:33 οὐκ ἐπιορκήσεις most likely means "*you shall* not *swear falsely/commit perjury*," conforming to the most common meaning of ἐπιορκέω (see LSJ s.v.). According to Chrysippus Stoicus ii.63 (*Fragmenta*, ed. H. von Arnim), who distinguishes, e.g., between ἐπιορκέω and ψευδορκέω, the translation "you shall not break an oath" would be possible; cf. also *Did.* 2:3. Matt 5:33 is probably formulated in conection with Lev 19:12 (perhaps also Exod 20:7); in Jewish tradition both perjury and empty oaths are sharply condemned. Where they are intentional, they are punished by scourging (cf. Billerbeck, I, 321-27; J. Schneider, *TDNT* V, 177-80.

ἐπίορκος, 2 *epiorkos* perjured*

1 Tim 1:10, subst. "perjurers," in a catalog of vices with ψεῦσται.

ἐπιοῦσα, ης, ἡ *epiousa* approaching

Partc. of → ἔπειμι.

ἐπιούσιος, 2 *epiousios* necessary (for existence), belonging to the day*

1. The problem — 2. Interpretations — 3. Differences between Matthew and Luke

Lit.: BAGD s.v. (bibliography). — H. BOURGOIN, "Ἐπιούσιος expliqué par la notion de préfixe vide," *Bib* 60 (1979) 91-96. — J. CARMIGNAC, *Recherches sur le "Notre Père"* (1969) 121-43, 214-20 (bibliography). — W. D. DAVIES and D. C. ALLISON, *Matt 1–7* (ICC, 1988) 607-9. — W. FOERSTER, *TDNT* II, 590-99. — P. GRELOT, "La quatrième demande du 'Pater' et son arrière-plan sémitique," *NTS* 25 (1978/79) 299-314. — JEREMIAS, *Theology* 199-201. — W. MUNDLE, *DNTT* I, 251f. — B. ORCHARD,

"The Meaning of the Ton Epiousion (Mt 6,11 = Lk 11,3)," *BTB* 3 (1973) 274-82. — J. STARCKY, "La quatrième demande du Pater," *HTR* 64 (1971) 401-9. — A. VÖGTLE, "Der 'eschatologische' Bezug der Wir-Bitten des Vaterunser," FS Kümmel, 344-62. — E. M. YAMAUCHI, "The 'Daily Bread' Motif in Antiquity," *WTJ* 28 (1965/66) 145-56. — For further bibliography see *TWNT* X, 1081f.

1. The translation of ἐπιούσιος creates special problems because the word occurs only in the Lord's Prayer (Matt 6:11; Luke 11:3) and because its attestation in Greek literature is doubtful and its derivation uncertain. The ancient translations and the interpretations of the Church Fathers differ already.

2. a) According to the dominant eschatological understanding of the first centuries and according to an interpretation of the translation in the *Gospel of the Hebrews* (*māhār* = "for tomorrow," apud Jerome *Commentary on Matthew* [on 6:11], *PL* XXVI, 44), ἄρτος ἐπιούσιος can mean "the bread *for tomorrow,*" i.e., "the bread *of the time of salvation,*" the "bread *of life.*" Thus ἐπιούσιος can be derived from ἰέναι or from εἶναι, though the second etymology is to be preferred. It must not be associated with a spiritualization and isolation of the eucharistic meal from the daily meal, inasmuch as one can assume that for the disciples every mealtime with Jesus was an anticipation of the eschatological meal: "Now, here and now, today, give us the bread of life, in the midst of our sorry existence" (Jeremias 201).

b) From Origen comes the suggestion that ἐπιούσιος is to be understood as ἐπὶ τὴν οὐσίαν, thus "the bread *necessary for existence.*" In this connection one may recall Prov 30:8 and esp. the manna of the OT people of God. This interpretation (apart from its hardly tenable etymological derivation) gains in weight when one considers ἐπιούσιος (together with σήμερον or καθ' ἡμέραν) as an attempt to do justice to the Hebrew of Exod 16:4 (*dᵉbar-yôm bᵉyômô*, "a day's portion for every day"; so Starcky). The translation "the (quantity of) bread *that we need*" can be derived from the logic of the entire Lord's Prayer: After the first three requests for the eschatological revelation of God's work of salvation, in the "we" requests Jesus focuses on the situation of the disciples; thus the bread request liberates them from anxiety for the coming day in favor of what is now really necessary (so Vögtle).

c) Similar is the derivation from ἐπιέναι, "coming": "give us this day the bread *that belongs (to it).*"

d) Some connect ἄρτος ἐπιούσιος with ἡ ἐπιοῦσα ἡμέρα (from ἔπειμι) and translate "the bread *for the coming day.*" In this view *the present day that is dawning* is intended; ἐπιούσιος is used to avoid using the same term twice: "give us today the bread *for today.*"

e) Ἐπιούσιος is also understood as a unique form, an adj. derived from the partc. of ἔπειμι, "coming." The

petition is, then, a request that the bread which is present not be poorly distributed on account of human sin, but that it *come to each one* (Orchard).

3. Matthew uses σήμερον and employs the aor. imv. of the vb. The request refers thus to the actual need "of this day." Luke adds καθ' ἡμέραν and formulates it in the pres., and thus he casts the request in a stronger catechetical direction: the disciple should turn to God "each day."

C. Müller

ἐπιπίπτω *epipiptō* fall upon*

1. This vb. appears 11 times in the NT, of which 8 occurrences are in Lukan material and one each are to be found in Mark (3:10), Romans (15:3), and Revelation (11:11). It appears in textual variants in John 13:25 (p⁶⁶ א* Koine D Θ, in place of ἀναπίπτω); Acts 8:39 (A); 10:10 (Koine E lat syr); 13:11 (p⁷⁴ C Koine E); 19:6 (D); 23:7 (B*).

2. The literal meaning *fall upon, throw oneself upon* someone, *rush at* someone (esp. with hostile intent; cf. Moulton/Milligan s.v.) appears with the dat. in Mark 3:10 (of the sick who *press upon* Jesus in order to be healed) and Acts 20:10 (of Paul, who *throws himself on* the dead youth in Troas). In all other passsages it appears with ἐπί with the acc. (Acts 8:16 with the dative), e.g., in the phrase "*fall upon* someone's neck" (in order to kiss him: Luke 15:20; Acts 20:37; cf. Gen 45:14; 46:29; Tob 7:6 א; 11:9, 13).

The vb. is used fig. of fear (φόβος) that *comes on/over* a person (Luke 1:12; Acts 19:17; Rev 11:11; cf. Josh 2:9; Jdt 2:28 and often; Job 4:13 and often) and of (unexpected) events or experiences that *fall upon* a person ("reproaches" in Rom 15:3 [Ps 68:10 LXX]); a trance in Acts 10:10 v.l. [cf. Gen 15:12 LXX; Dan 10:7 Theodotion); darkness in 13:11 v.l.).

Characteristic of Acts are references to the Holy Spirit *falling upon* (groups of) people (cf. Ezek 11:5): in 8:16, "it *had not fallen on* any of them [the Samaritans]; they were only baptized"; in 10:44, "it *fell upon* all who heard the word [the family of Cornelius]"; in 11:15, "it *fell on* them, as also on us at the beginning [i.e., at Pentecost]"; cf. the variants in 8:39; 19:6. On the Lukan distinction between water baptism and Spirit baptism, see S. Brown, *ATR* 59 (1977) 135-51.

G. Schneider

ἐπιπλήσσω *epiplēssō* reproach, snap at*

1 Tim 5:1 (with negative) with dat. πρεσβυτέρῳ, opposite of παρακαλέω.

ἐπιπόθεια, ας, ἡ *epipotheia* desire, longing

Alternative form of → ἐπιποθία.

ἐπιποθέω *epipotheō* desire, demand*

There are 9 occurrences in the NT, none in the Gospels or in Acts. The vb. is used in reference to congregations and congregational leaders with acc. (2 Cor 9:14; Phil 1:8; 2:26), with ἰδεῖν (Rom 1:11; 1 Thess 3:6; 2 Tim 1:4), with ἐπενδύσασθαι (2 Cor 5:2), and with γάλα as obj. (1 Pet 2:2).

Jas 4:5 is difficult: τὸ πνεῦμα is probably the subj. (not a supplied θεός) and ἐπιποθέω is absolute referring to *striving* against envy/jealousy (cf. 3:13–4:4; 4:6-12, where the "greater grace [4:6a] takes the place of "pride"). Another view is: "he [God] yearns jealously over the spirit . . ." (so RSV; cf. BAGD s.v.; M. Dibelius, *Jas* [Eng. tr., Hermeneia] ad loc.; W. Schrage, *Jas* [NTD] ad loc.; Spicq, *Notes* I, 277-79).

ἐπιπόθησις, εως, ἡ *epipothēsis* desire, longing*

2 Cor 7:7 (with gen. ὑμῶν), 11 (i.e., "*longing* for me [Paul]").

ἐπιπόθητος, 2 *epipothētos* longed for*

Phil 4:1: ἀδελφοὶ . . . ἀγαπητοὶ καὶ ἐπιπόθητοι in the introduction of the parenetic conclusion of the letter; cf. also Rom 15:23; *1 Clem.* 65:1.

ἐπιποθία, ας, ἡ *epipothia* desire, longing*

Rom 15:23: ἐπιποθία . . . τοῦ ἐλθεῖν πρὸς ὑμᾶς, of Paul's desire, which has lasted for years, to travel to Spain via Rome.

ἐπιπορεύομαι *epiporeuomai* go (to)*

Luke 8:4: τῶν . . . ἐπιπορευομένων πρὸς αὐτόν, of people *streaming* out of all the cities to Jesus.

ἐπιράπτω *epiraptō* sew on*

Mark 2:21: ἐπίβλημα . . . ἐπιράπτω ἐπὶ ἱμάτιον παλαιόν, *sew* a patch . . . on an old garment (TR ἐπιρράπτω). F. Hahn, *EvT* 31 (1971) 357-75.

ἐπιρίπτω *epiriptō* throw on, put on*

In the lit. sense *throw*, Luke 19:35 (ἐπιρίπτω τὰ ἱμάτια ἐπὶ τὸν πῶλον); fig., 1 Pet 5:7: *cast* cares on God (ἐπ' αὐτόν).

ἐπιρράπτω *epirraptō* sew on

Alternative form of → ἐπιράπτω.

ἐπιρρίπτω *epirriptō* throw on, put on

Alternative form of → ἐπιρίπτω.

ἐπίσημος, 2 *episēmos* excellent, distinguished; infamous*

Rom 16:7: *distinguished* among the apostles (ἐν τοῖς ἀποστόλοις); in the negative sense, Matt 27:16, of the *notorious* prisoner (Jesus) Barabbas.

ἐπισιτισμός, οῦ, ὁ *episitismos* provisions, supplies*

Luke 9:12: ἵνα . . . εὕρωσιν ἐπισιτισμόν, "in order to get *provisions.*"

ἐπισκέπτομαι *episkeptomai* look at; visit
ἐπισκοπέω *episkopeō* look at; pay attention to*

1. Occurrences in the NT — 2. Range of meaning — 3. Usage

Lit.: BAGD s.v. — H. W. BEYER, *TDNT* II, 599-605. — H. FÜRST, *Die göttliche Heimsuchung* (1965). — J. GNILKA, "Der Hymnus des Zacharias," *BZ* 6 (1962) 215-38. — W. C. ROBINSON, *Der Weg des Herrn* (1964) 50-59. — P. VIELHAUER, "Das Benedictus des Zacharias," *idem, Aufsätze zum NT* (1965) 28-46. — For further bibliography see *TWNT* X, 1082f.

1. Ἐπισκέπτομαι appears 11 times in the NT. More than half of these occurrences are in Luke-Acts (3 in Luke, 4 in Acts); there are also 2 in Matthew, 1 in Hebrews, and 1 in James. Ἐπισκοπέω occurs in Heb 12:15 and 1 Pet 5:2.

2. The NT occurrences, which have a pre-history in the LXX, have 4 different meanings. Most frequently ἐπισκέπτομαι means *visit*, with the related meaning *care for* someone (6 times). The vb. also means *seek out/look out (for)* (2 times) and, finally, with God as subj., *graciously visit* (3 times in the Lukan special material). Ἐπισκοπέω (pres. partc. in both occurrences) means *pay attention* (lest . . .).

3. a) In the logia about the judgment of the world in Matt 25:36, 43, the reference is to visiting the sick and the imprisoned in the sense of *care for*. According to the speech of Stephen Moses decided to *seek out* his people *in order to care for* them (Acts 7:23). Likewise Paul and Barnabas decided to visit the churches founded on the "first missionary journey" in order to find out how they were, thus to *care for* them. The phrase in the citation from Ps 8:5 LXX in Heb 2:6b, "and of the son of man, that you *care for* him," can be interpreted either as a reference to individual man or christologically in the sense of a Son of Man christology (cf. O. Michel, *Heb* [KEK⁷] 138). According to Jas 1:27 the characteristic of pure and undefiled worship is to *care for* widows and orphans in their affliction. This is the manifestation of the demand of vv. 22-25 to be doers and not hearers only.

b) The vb. is used in Acts 6:3; 15:14 with the meaning *seek out:* The apostles summon the members of the congregation to seek out seven men who are suitable to undertake the daily care of the Greek-speaking widows. The brother of the Lord refers in his speech at the Apostolic Council to the report of Peter describing how God had sought out a people from the Gentiles to win for his name.

c) In Heb 12:15 and 1 Pet 5:2 ἐπισκοπέω means *pay attention* or *take care lest:* "Pay attention, that no one fail to attain the grace of God" and "Tend the flock of God among you, of which you *have charge,* not by constraint but willingly, according to the will of God." Both passages are directed to leaders in the church.

d) Ἐπισκέπτομαι refers to God's *gracious visitation* only in Luke, of which 2 occurrences are in the Benedictus of Zechariah (1:68, 78): In the introduction of the song of praise there is a reference to the gracious visitation of the people in the salvation history of the past in order to prepare way for the redemption (v. 68, connected in v. 69 with the Davidic kingship). The conclusion (v. 78) promises God's visitation for the dawning time of fulfillment. The commentary in the choral response at the raising of the boy at Nain apparently understands this raising as the fulfillment of the prediction in the Benedictus of Zechariah: "God has *graciously visited* his people" (7:16). The addition of "for good" in a few mss. is meant to indicate that a gracious and not a chastising visitation is spoken of.

J. Rohde

ἐπισκευάζομαι *episkeuazomai* make preparations*

In the NT and early Christian literature only mid.: Acts 21:15: ἐπισκευασάμενοι, we *prepared* (for departure).

ἐπισκηνόω *episkēnoō* move in, take up residence*

2 Cor 12:9: "so that the power of Christ *may take up residence* in me."

ἐπισκιάζω *episkiazō* cast a shadow, overshadow*

1. Meanings and occurrences in the NT — 2. Peter's shadow in Acts 5:15 — 3. Mark 9:7 par. — 4. Luke 1:35

Lit.: W. BIEDER, "Der Petrusschatten, Apg 5,15," *TZ* 16 (1960) 407-9. — M. DIBELIUS, "Jungfrauensohn und Krippenkind," *idem, Botschaft* I, 1-78, esp. 18-22. — P. W. VAN DER HORST, "Peter's Shadow: The Religio-Historical Background of Acts V.15," *NTS* 23 (1976/77) 204-12. — C. MUGLER, *Dictionnaire historique de la terminologie optique des Grecs* (1964) 162f. — J. M. NÜTZEL, *Die Verklärungserzählung im Markusevangelium* (FzB 6, 1973) 141-44, 246-49. — L. SABOURIN, "The Biblical Cloud," *BTB* 4 (1974) 290-311. — H. SCHÜRMANN, *Luke* (HTKNT) I (1969), 52-56, 560f. — S. SCHULZ, *TDNT* VII, 399f.

1. The compound vb. ἐπισκιάζω is derived from → σκιά (shadow) and means *cast a shadow, overshadow.* In the NT it occurs 5 times: in the transfiguration story (Mark 9:7 par. Matt 17:5/Luke 9:34), in the narrative of the annunciation to Mary (Luke 1:35 [and Justin *Apol.* i.33.6 in dependence on Luke]), and in the report of the anticipated healing effect of Peter's shadow (Acts 5:15). Except in Matt 17:5 par. Luke 9:34, which have acc. (unlike Mark), the obj. of the overshadowing (persons in all 5 occurrences) is in the dat. The subj. in Mark 9:7 par. is the "cloud" (→ νεφέλη), in Luke 1:35 the "power of the most high," and in Acts 5:15 "the shadow" of Peter.

In secular Greek ἐπισκιάζω generally has no positive nuance. But in the LXX it does (for Heb *škn,* "come down": Exod 40:35 [of the "cloud" over the tabernacle; cf. MT *škn*/LXX σκιάζω in Num 9:18, 22; LXX καλύπτω in Exod 24:15]; Prov 18:11; cf. ἐπισκιάζω as a term for God's protection, Pss 90:4; 139:8). In Exod 40:34 the cloud is "the medium of the divine activity and possession" (Schulz); NT uses of ἐπισκιάζω are correspondingly positive. In Philo ἐπισκιάζω is "a kind of key word" (Schulz 402) used in a dualistic framework in a spiritual sense.

2. Whether the author of Acts takes up a tradition with the reference to the healing shadow of Peter (so E. Haenchen, *Acts* [Eng. tr., 1971] 245) cannot be determined with certainty. Probably he intended to do more than merely describe the expectation of the people (with Haenchen, *Acts* 243), for he took the motif here perhaps from Mark 6:56f. ("at least the fringe of [Jesus'] garment"). Correspondingly Acts 19:12 reports concerning Paul and the healing power of his "handkerchiefs and aprons." The healing power of Peter's shadow serves to concretize the healing power of the "apostles" (5:12); of course vv. 13f. indicate that v. 15 is to be understood as the activity of *believing* people, that the sick were even carried into the streets "so that, as Peter came by, at least (κἄν) his shadow might *fall on* some of them."

3. Mark 9:7 par. describes the *overshadowing* by the "cloud." When Matthew and Luke give the obj. (the three disciples) in the acc. (αὐτούς), perhaps a full covering of those present is in mind (cf. Luke 9:34b). Behind the motif is Exod 40:34f. LXX (νεφέλη—ἐπισκιάζω—σκηνή—Moses). The cloud is the sign of the presence of God, who (as in Exod 24:15f.; *Jub.* 1:2f.; cf. Sabourin) speaks from it. In this sense ἐπισκιάζω designates perhaps "the covering-concealing descent of the cloud" (R. Pesch, *Mark* [HTKNT] II, 76; cf. Isa 4:5f.).

4. Luke 1:34f. is primarily a creation of the Evangelist (G. Schneider, *BZ* 15 [1971] 255-59). The two parallel statements of the annunciation, "The Holy Spirit will come over (→ ἐπέρχομαι) you, and the power (δύναμις) of the most high will *overshadow*" (v. 35a), are not inspired by the (Markan) story of the transfiguration (→ 3), but rather by the baptismal scene (Mark 1:10f. par. Luke 3:22) and by the idea of the Holy Spirit as a divine δύναμις that "comes upon" someone (ἐπί with acc., Acts

1:8); cf. Ps 139:8, where God is addressed as the δύναμις τῆς σωτηρίας μου, whose protection *overshadows* the head of the one who is praying.

In view of the preceding question of the virgin (→ παρθένος) Mary (v. 34), the understanding of ἐπισκιάζειν as a "counterpart for human procreation" (Dibelius 19) or as a euphemism for the procreative act would seem apparent. But the lack of any real parallels in the literature of the time (against van der Horst 211f., who appeals to B. George, *Zu den altägyptischen Vorstellungen vom Schatten als Seele* [1970] 112f.) and esp. the theological context of the passage in Hellenistic Judaism (the work of God's Spirit in creation) and in the Lukan work (christology and universal soteriology) all indicate that this view is without foundation. Through the (ultimately mysterious) work of God's Spirit, according to v. 35b, the child of Mary is the "Son of God" in his origin and nature (cf. Schürmann 52f.).

                                           G. Schneider

ἐπισκοπέω *episkopeō* look at, pay attention
→ ἐπισκέπτομαι.

ἐπισκοπή, ῆς, ἡ *episkopē* visitation; office; office of overseer*

Lit.: A. ADAM, "Die Entstehung des Bischofsamtes," *WuD* 5 (1957) 104-13. — idem, *RGG* I, 1300-3. — C. K. BARRETT, *Church, Ministry, and Sacraments in the NT* (1985) (index). — H. W. BARTSCH, *Die Anfänge urchristlicher Rechtsbildungen* (1965). — BAGD s.v. — W. BAUER, *Orthodoxy and Heresy in Earliest Christianity* (1971). — H. W. BEYER, *TDNT* II, 606-22. — N. BROX, *Die Pastoralbriefe* (RNT, ⁴1969) 147-52. — H. VON CAMPENHAUSEN, *Ecclesiastical Authority and Spiritual Power in the Church of the First Three Centuries* (1969). — L. COENEN, *DNTT* I, 188-92 (bibliography 200-201). — M. DIBELIUS and H. CONZELMANN, *The Pastoral Epistles* (Hermeneia, 1972) 54-57. — J. ERNST, "Amt und Autorität im NT," *TGl* 58 (1968) 170-83. — G. FITZER, "Die Entwicklung des Vorsteheramtes im NT," *Pro Oriente* (1975) 91-109. — G. FRIEDRICH, "Geist und Amt," *WuD* 3 (1952) 61-85. — A. HARNACK, *RE* XX, 508-46. — E. KÄSEMANN, "Ministry and Community in the NT," idem, *Essays on NT Themes* (1964). — H. KARPP, *RAC* II, 394-407. — K. KERTELGE, *Gemeinde und Amt im NT* (1972). — J. MCKENZIE, "Amtsstrukturen im NT," Concilium 8 (1972) 239-45. — H.-J. MICHEL, *Die Abschiedsrede des Paulus an die Kirche Apg 20,17-38* (1973). — W. NAUCK, "Probleme frühchristlichen Amtsverständnisses," *ZNW* 48 (1957) 200-220. — J. ROHDE, *Urchristliche und frühkatholische Ämter* (1976). — H. SCHLIER, "Die Ordnung der Kirche nach den Past," Schlier I, 129-47. — R. SCHNACKENBURG, "Episkopos und Hirtenamt," *Episkopus* (FS M. Faulhaber, 1949) 66-88 (cf. idem, *The Church in the NT* [1965]). — E. SCHWEIZER, *Church Order in the NT* (1961). — K. STALDER, "Episkopos," *IKZ* 61 (1971) 200-232. — For further bibliography see *TWNT* X, 1082f.

1. Of the 4 occurrences in the NT, 2 are in Luke-Acts (Luke 19:44; Acts 1:20). The others are in 1 Tim 3:1 and 1 Pet 2:12 (also 1 Pet 5:6 v.l.).

2. a) Both Luke 19:44 and 1 Pet 2:12 have the sense that the vb. has in Luke 1:68, 78; 7:16: *gracious visitation*. Luke 19:44 stands within Jesus' lament over Jerusalem at his entry into the city and belongs to Luke's special material. Ignoring what could be understood as the political overtones of the Davidic kingship (cf. 19:38), Luke interprets Jesus' entry as a salvific visit, which serves the city πρὸς εἰρήνην (v. 42). Because the city does not recognize the entering king as bringer of salvation nor his coming as a gracious divine visitation, the result will be destruction in war.

In 1 Pet 2:12 the expression "day of *visitation*" from Isa 10:3 LXX is taken up and used within an exhortation concerning conduct among the Gentiles. It concerns the duty of Christians in the concrete relationships of life. Their good works should be the decisive witness of correct conduct, in order to lead the Gentiles to revise their judgment about Christians. Then they will see them not as evildoers and will be able to praise God at the day of visitation. What is intended is therefore a day of God's gracious act leading to conversion, not an eschatological day of judgment.

Ἐπισκοπή appears as a v.l. in 1 Pet 5:6, perhaps under the influence of 2:12: "Humble yourselves under the mighty hand of God, so that he may exalt you at the time of the *gracious visitation*," when the previous humiliation will be changed into exaltation.

b) In two other passages ἐπισκοπή refers to an *office*. In the pericope of the special election of Matthias to fill the apostolic circle to its original number, Peter cites Ps 108:8 LXX in his speech (Acts 1:20). The citation is derived from the personal lament of an individual who describes how he is falsely accused. The opponents then proclaim their goal that his office should be received by another. In the context of Peter's speech ἐπισκοπή means here the apostolic office, which Judas lost through his suicide and which then had to be handed over to another as a ministry (vv. 17, 25).

In 1 Tim 3:1 ἐπισκοπή has the meaning *office of overseer* or of *supervisor*. The word stands in the introductory verse of the list of qualifications for the Christian congregational overseer. It is improbable that the Pastorals, with this use of the term, already presuppose the existence of the monarchical episcopate. The impression is given that one does not, so to speak, automatically grow into this office through longer affiliation and testing, but rather that one can consciously strive for it.

                                         J. Rohde

ἐπίσκοπος, ου, ὁ *episkopos* bishop (overseer)*

Lit.: E. LOHSE, "Episkopos in den Pastoralbriefe," *Kirche und Bibel* (FS E. Schick, 1979) 225-31. — idem, "Die Entstehung des Bischofsamtes in der frühen Christenheit," *ZNW* 71 (1980) 58-73. — G. SCHÖLLGEN, "Monepiskopat und monarchischer Episkopat. Eine Bemerkung zur Terminologie," *ZNW* 77 (1986) 146-51. — B. E. THIERING, "*Mebaqqer* and *Episkopos* in the Light of the Temple Scroll," *JBL* 100 (1981) 59-74. — For further bibliography → ἐπισκοπή.

1. This noun appears 5 times in the NT. It refers to Christ in 1 Pet 2:25 and elsewhere to individuals who have a function or an office in the Christian community (Acts 20:28; Phil 1:1; 1 Tim 3:2; Titus 1:7).

2. In Greek, ἐπίσκοπος can be a designation for a variety of offices (Beyer 611-614). Frequently it refers to secular activities (Karpp 395ff.). A religious concept stands behind this term when it has the meaning "guardian, watchman, and protector." Even if the more precise definition of the office designated by ἐπίσκοπος is often difficult, it almost always relates to oversight or administration (J. Gnilka, *Phil* [HTKNT] 38). The question of the origin of the ἐπίσκοπος in the NT—whether from Greek associations, from temple overseers in Judaism, from synagogue overseers, or from the Qumran sect—receives differing answers in the scholarship (see Adam, Dibelius and Conzelmann, Nauck, Karpp).

In the NT ἐπίσκοπος appears in two passages in a close association with the image of the shepherd. According to 1 Pet 2:25 Christ is the shepherd and *overseer* of souls. This passage stands at the end of the slave parenesis, in which Christ has already been portrayed, with an allusion to Isaiah 53, as the model of suffering without retaliation. Of course vv. 24-25 no longer have the particular situation of the slave in view. Instead, the statements about redemption in the hymn from v. 22 refer to Christ and leave the exhortation to slaves in the background.

In Acts 20:28 the presbyters of the church are called the *overseers* who should tend the flock of God, i.e., the church (cf. Schnackenburg). Here apparently bishops and presbyters are equated: the presbyters who lead the local church at Ephesus are addressed as "bishops." Of course this speech does not reflect the organization of the Pauline mission churches, but presupposes rather the offices in Christian congregations at the time of the origin of Acts —at the end of the first century.

Likewise the Pastorals do not reflect the organization of the Christian churches in the last years of Paul's life, but that of the period when the deutero-Pauline writings came into existence—at the end of the first century. In both passages in the Pastorals ἐπίσκοπος appears in the sg. (1 Tim 3:2; Titus 1:7). At the same time both Titus 1:7 and Acts 20:28 equate presbyters and bishops, for in Titus 1:5 "Paul" has commissioned Titus to install elders in the cities of Crete. Then in the qualifications that follow, which are derived from the tradition, the requirements that an ἐπίσκοπος should bring to the office are given (likewise in the qualifications for the office from 1 Tim 3:2ff.). In both cases one is not to conclude from the sg. that already a single bishop is assumed as a monarchical leader at the head of the community. The sg. is rather to be understood generically (so, among others, Brox 148f. *contra* von Campenhausen 107).

In *1 Clem.* the identity of presbyters and bishops is still presupposed. The monarchical bishop appears first as the only leader of the local church first in Ignatius. It is not certain, however, whether Ignatius describes existing conditions or sets up ideal requirements that do not yet correspond to reality (Bauer 61f.).

The earliest NT passage in which the title of ἐπίσκοπος appears is Phil 1:1. Here the ἐπίσκοποι (pl.) and the διάκονοι (deacons) are addressed in the prologue of the letter along with the other members of the congregation. This is the only passage in the authentic letters of Paul in which function-bearers of the church are designated with terms later associated with offices. However, the ἐπίσκοποι and deacons of Philippians cannot be identified with those of the Pastorals. As in secular Greek, ἐπίσκοπος can also be the term for officers who have financial responsibilities. Consequently the thesis is sometimes represented (by Fitzer and Harnack among others) that the passage is concerned with people commissioned to collect the contribution for Paul, to whom the imprisoned apostle is thus especially grateful. However, only the end of the letter mentions the collection and there Paul offers his thanks to the whole congregation (4:10-19).

J. Rohde

ἐπισπάομαι *epispaomai* pull over the foreskin*

According to 1 Cor 7:18, one who was circumcised when he was called should not *pull over the foreskin* (μὴ ἐπισπάσθω). The medical t.t. occurs in this usage—for the concealment of circumcision—only here; cf. also 1 Macc 1:15, ἐποίησαν ἑαυτοῖς ἀκροβυστίας; Josephus *Ant.* xii.241, τὴν τῶν αἰδοίων περιτομὴν ἐπεκάλυψαν; *T. Mos.* 8:3; Billerbeck IV, 33f.

ἐπισπείρω *epispeirō* sow afterward*

Matt 13:25: ἐπέσπειρεν ζιζάνια ἀνὰ μέσον τοῦ σίτου, "*sow* weeds among the wheat."

ἐπίσταμαι *epistamai* understand, know, be acquainted with*

1. Occurrences in the NT — 2. Meaning — 3. Use as a rhetorical term

Lit.: A. W. ARGYLE, "The Greek of Luke and Acts," *NTS* 20 (1973/74) 441-45 (442). — G. KLEIN, "Der Synkretismus als theologisches Problem in der ältesten christlichen Apologetik," idem, *Rekonstruktion und Interpretation* (1969) 262-301 (277f.). — MOULTON/MILLIGAN 245. — ROBERTSON, *Grammar* 314. — B. SNELL, "Wie die Griechen lernten, was geistige Tätigkeit ist," *JHS* 93 (1973) 172-84 (183).

1. Ἐπίσταμαι appears most frequently in Acts (9 of 14 NT occurrences: 10:28; 15:7; 18:25; 19:15, 25; 20:18; 22:19; 24:10; 26:26). The vb. does not appear, however,

in Luke's Gospel at all (Argyle). This is partially to be explained by the fact that the particular rhetorical usage (→ 3) has no use in the Gospel. Besides, the following is to be considered: While Luke, in agreement with normal Christian usage, uses γινώσκω when the content of the proclamation is the obj., he uses ἐπίσταμαι always in a secular sense. This is to be seen from Acts 19:15, where the evil spirit says, "Jesus I know (γινώσκω) and *I know* of Paul (ἐπίσταμαι)." In the parallel to the only Markan occurrence of the vb. (Mark 14:68, used synonymously with οἶδα), Luke has omitted it (Luke 22:57; cf. also Matt 26:70), apparently because the use of this vb. with Jesus as the obj. seemed inappropriate. Further occurrences of ἐπίσταμαι (once each) are found in 1 Timothy, Hebrews, James, and Jude.

2. Ἐπίσταμαι refers primarily to practical capability rather than theoretical knowledge, while with οἶδα ("know," "have seen") theoretical knowledge is predominant (Snell; Zorell, *Lexicon* s.v.). In Jude 10 the two vbs. are used together: The godless "revile what they do not know (οἶδα), and in what they *understand* (ἐπίσταμαι) by instinct, as irrational animals, they are destroyed." The knowledge from experience indicated by ἐπίσταμαι stands in contrast to faith: Heb 11:8 interprets Abraham's departure from his homeland into the unknown as an act of faith. Philo (*Migr.* 9) derives the same conclusion from fut. δείξω in Gen 12:1. Jas 4:14 brings the basic insecurity of human existence into consciousness: even the next day is removed from our knowledge.

3. In the speeches of Acts ἐπίσταμαι is used esp. for rhetorical purposes. The formula, "you know . . ." (ἐπίστασθε), enables the speaker to mention what is already known (Acts 10:28; 15:7; 19:25; cf. 22:19; 26:26). The purpose is purely literary; e.g., the allusion to 10:1ff. in 15:7 cannot be understood by the hearers of Peter, but can by the readers of the book. In the farewell speech ἐπίσταμαι introduces the μνεία (the memory of the life of the speaker), which should lead to imitation (Acts 20:18; cf. v. 31). 1 Tim 6:4, where empty disputes are denounced, is derived from a rhetorical background.

G. Bouwman

ἐπίστασις, εως, ἡ   *epistasis*   pressure; attack (noun); mob*

In early Christian literature only in Acts 24:12 and 2 Cor 11:28 (both times v.l. → ἐπισύστασις). Acts 24:12: ἐπίστασιν . . . ὄχλου, "the *attack/riot* of the crowd" (cf. 2 Macc 6:3); 2 Cor 11:28: ἐπίστασίς μοι (on the dat. see BDF §202) ἡ καθ' ἡμέραν is best rendered "the daily *pressure* on me," esp. in view of vv. 28b, 29. The other possible meanings of ἐπίστασις, "attention, hindrance, resistance," are difficult to fit with the dat. μοι on the one

hand, and with the positive statement of v. 28b on the other hand.

ἐπιστάτης, ου, ὁ   *epistatēs*   master (voc. only)*

Lit.: O. GLOMBITZA, "Die Titel διδάσκαλος and ἐπιστάτης für Jesus bei Lukas," *ZNW* 49 (1958) 275-78. — A. OEPKE, *TDNT* II, 622f.

1. Ἐπιστάτης appears only in the voc. and only in Luke (5:5; 8:24, 45; 9:33, 49; 17:13), principally in miracle stories. With one exception (17:13) it is the disciples who address Jesus in this way. In the Synoptics the approximate equivalents are ῥαββί, κύριε, and διδάσκαλε (cf., e.g., Mark 4:38 par.; 9:5 par., 38 par.); the latter two are also used by Luke, while he avoids the common transliteration ῥαββί used by the other Evangelists.

2. No particular Hebrew or Aramaic word is known to be the basis for ἐπιστάτης, nor does the usage in secular Greek necessitate a particular translation. Ἐπιστάτης designates, e.g., an overseer over flocks, one who drives elephants, an Egyptian taskmaster (Exod 1:11; 5:14 LXX), a leader in an athletic society, the supervisor of a temple, a music teacher, or the governor of a city (cf. Oepke 623).

The etymology of the word (ἐπιστάτης = "one who stands over another") and the contexts in which he uses it indicate a nuance in meaning: While Luke uses κύριε of messianic dignity (e.g., 2:11; 5:12; 7:6; 9:61) and διδάσκαλε of Jesus' teaching authority (e.g., 10:25; 18:18; 20:21, 28, 39), ἐπιστάτης is used of Jesus in his authoritative position within a definite group, his disciples. This is supported by the fact that we find ἐπιστάτης almost exclusively in the mouth of the disciples, and the examples from secular Greek correspond to this. Ἐπιστάτης thus refers to Jesus' authority to instruct and to his special responsibility (cf. esp. Luke 8:24!) for the group of disciples that he has assembled. Luke 17:13 seems to exclude this interpretation, for Jesus is called upon here from a group that is independent of him and is asked for help. But the difficulty is removed by assuming what Luke wanted to express: When the group of lepers begs Jesus for help, it subjects itself *eo ipso* to his authority. Thus ἐπιστάτης is always best translated *master*.

W. Grimm

ἐπιστέλλω   *epistellō*   communicate by letter, instruct*

Acts 15:20; 21:25, in reference to the so-called Apostolic Decree: *instruct/lay on;* Heb 13:22: "for *I have written* to you briefly."

ἐπιστήμων, 2   *epistēmōn*   well informed, understanding*

Jas 3:13, with σοφός.

ἐπιστηρίζω *epistērizō* strengthen*

Only in Acts: 14:22 (τὰς ψυχάς); 15:32 (with τοὺς ἀδελφούς as obj.), 41 (τὰς ἐκκλησίας); 18:23 (πάντας τοὺς μαθητάς).

ἐπιστολή, ῆς, ἡ *epistolē* letter*

1. Terminology — 2. On the genre of NT letters — 3. Ἐπιστολή in NT statements

Lit.: D. E. AUNE, *The NT in Its Literary Environment* (1987) 158-225. — G. J. BAHR, "The Subscriptions in the Pauline Letters," *JBL* 87 (1968) 27-41. — K. BERGER, "Apostelbrief und apostolische Rede. Zum Formular frühchristlicher Briefe," *ZNW* 65 (1974) 190-231. — H. D. BETZ, "The Literary Composition and Function of Paul's Letter to the Galatians," *NTS* 21 (1974/75) 353-79. — H. BOERS, "The Form Critical Study of Paul's Letters. 1 Thessalonians as a Case Study," *NTS* 22 (1975/76) 140-58. — N. BROX, *Falsche Verfasserangaben. Zur Erklärung der frühchristlichen Pseudepigraphie* (1975). — G. J. CUMING, "Service-Endings in the Epistles," *NTS* 22 (1975/76) 110-13. — W. G. DOTY, "The Classification of Epistolary Literature," *CBQ* 31 (1969) 183-99. — E. FASCHER, *RGG* I, 1412-15 (bibliography). — G. FINKENRATH, *DNTT* I, 246-49. — J. A. FISCHER, "Pauline Literary Forms and Thought Patterns," *CBQ* 39 (1977) 209-23. — J. M. GIBBS, "Canon Cuming's 'Service-Endings in the Epistles'—A Rejoinder," *NTS* 24 (1977/78) 545-47. — U. B. MÜLLER, *Prophetie und Predigt im NT* (1975) 47-107. — K. H. RENGSTORF, *TDNT* VII, 593-95. — B. RIGAUX, *Paulus und seine Briefe. Der Stand der Forschung* (1964). — J. SCHNEIDER, *RAC* II, 564-85 (bibliography), esp. 574-76. — F. SCHNIDER and W. STENGER, *Studien zum Neutestamentlichen Briefformular* (NTTS 11, 1987). — S. K. STOWERS, *Letter Writing in Greco-Roman Antiquity* (1986).—A. SUHL, *Paulus und seine Briefe. Ein Beitrag zur paulinischen Chronologie* (1975). — K. THRAEDE, *Grundzüge griechisch-römischer Brieftopik* (1970). — J. L. WHITE, "Introductory Formulae in the Body of the Pauline Letter," *JBL* 90 (1971) 91-97.

1. Ἐπιστολή is "'what is transmitted by the messenger,' usually the 'letter'" (Rengstorf 593). The related vb. ἐπιστέλλω is used of "'transmitting a message or direction' either by word of mouth or more esp. in writing" (*ibid.*). Acts 15:20; 21:25; and Heb 13:22, where the vb. occurs, "bring out very clearly the authoritative and almost official nature of the primitive Christian epistle" (*ibid.*). The vb. διαστέλλομαι refers to a "categorical command"; Mark (5:43; 7:36 bis; 8:15; 9:9) reserves it for Jesus (*ibid.*, 591f.; cf. also Matt 16:20; Acts 15:24; Heb 12:20).

2. Because of the extraordinary theological and historical importance of the NT letters we cannot limit ourselves to those passages (→ 3) where the NT speaks explicitly of a *letter*. It remains true that "A monograph is needed on the early Chr[istian] epistle" (Rengstorf 594n.2). The NT letters are individually and in their totality an essential theological topic.

Within the collection of NT writings, the literary genre "letter" is abundantly documented in a variety of types. Thus 21 independent letters are included (of which 2, Hebrews and 1 John, are anonymous; lost letters are perhaps referred to in 1 Cor 5:9; Col 4:16) as well as texts of letters within the framework of Acts (15:23-29; 23:26-30).

The seven "letters" in Rev 2:1–3:22 are analogous. But they "all lack components of the letter formula," and represent "a different form of communication" (H. Kraft, *Rev* [HNT] 52). On the basis of Rev 1:1; 22:21 one can speak of a certain stylization of this document.

The NT letters characteristically vary the common protocol at their beginning (prescript and proemium) and end from what is found in other letters of the time. These letters take on their characteristic features from both the individual features and, to some extent, the total content. Paul was apparently decisive for the development of the typical NT letter formula. The extensive elaboration of the address and greeting in the proemium (including reference to the content of the letter: cf. Rom 1:1-7; 1 Cor 1:1f.; Gal 1:1-5) and the blessings and thanksgivings, which do not differ from the genre but are individually formed in content (they are lacking in Gal 1:6-9 [in keeping with the content of the letter] and are determined by the situation in 1 Cor 1:4-9; Phil 1:3-11), have become, like the final greetings and blessings, texts with a specific Christian proclamation because of their content. Hence liturgical usage could have been an analogous example for the creation of a form (cf. Rom 16:25-27; Eph 3:20f.; Jude 25).

The letters are, for the most part, occasional writings (so all of the authentic letters of Paul). They are directed to a specific community and are to be read publicly (Philemon, written to a house church, has certain limitations). The other NT letters are more likely teaching letters (Deissmann, *Light* 228-30 distinguishes too radically between letter and epistle). The boundaries between the two forms are fluid. The paramount significance of the extant NT letters arises from the fact that in the beginning (because of imminent expectation?) scarcely any programmatic writings came into existence.

In general only seven Pauline letters are today assumed to be authentic (Romans, 1 and 2 Corinthians, Galatians, Philippians, 1 Thessalonians, and Philemon). Scholarship is uncertain as to whether *all* of the remaining 14 independent letters are to be considered pseudonymous, but it is hardly disputable that at least some of them are pseudonymous. That pseudonymous literature was written is an important historical and theological indication of the impact in the early Christian Church of the authentic Pauline letters. Pseudonymous writing (one must also consider the work of secretaries: cf. Ephesians, 1–2 Timothy, and 1 Peter) gave recognition to the binding character of the recognized writings and thus placed pseudonymous writings in the "apostolic" authority. Among other things, the decline in the imminent expectation, that is, the process of Christian time, leads to thematic writing; the problem of tradition and church order can be seen. Even if a direct terminological connection between ἐπιστολή and ἀποστέλλειν is not demonstrable, one can nevertheless perceive an essential connection. "Apostolic" authority and "apostolic" service are claimed for the corresponding Christian letters. This is also decisive for the collection (perhaps also for the redactor, as in 2 Corinthians and Philippians).

Actual private letters are not present in the NT. In no instance have answers to letters been preserved. In the letters attributed to Paul references to coauthors (on a principle of collegiality?) appear. Analogies have been drawn between the NT letters and classical prophecy (cf. Rom 10:15 and Isa 52:7; Rom 1:1 and Isa 61:1). It has also been pointed out that Paul in 2 Cor 3:1-3 indicates that, for the author, the letters are letters of Christ (Rengstorf 594). Some NT letters presuppose questions which have been raised (1 Thess 4:13; 5:1; 1 Cor 7:1, 25; 8:1; and often) or involve debates that have recently arisen through preachers who have appeared in the midst of the congregations addressed (Galatians and 2 Corinthians). Romans takes the proclamation to a community that is unknown to Paul. At least the larger letters have apparently been dictated (cf. Rom 16:22; cf. also the final greeting in Paul's own hand: 1 Cor 16:21; Gal 6:11; Phlm 19; also Col 4:18; 2 Thess 3:17!). A determination of the form of the thematic letters of the NT according to precise characteristics of the genre cannot presently be done with sufficient objectivity.

3. Paul claims special validity for his letters. According to 1 Thess 5:27 he requests in a strikingly ceremonious way that his letter be read to all of the brethren (because of the missionary situation, or juxtaposition of Gentile and Jewish Christian churches, or a division that has occurred?). 1 Cor 1:2 and 2 Cor 1:1 presuppose the transmission of the letter from the church receiving the letter to others. Col 4:16 (deutero-Pauline) indicates that the letters of the apostle (or letters in his name) were exchanged in various churches.

2 Thessalonians (likewise presumably deutero-Pauline) gives a parallel list of "spirit(-revelation), word (of a living proclamation) and *letter* (as though) from us" as three qualifying types of proclamation (2:2; cf. prophets, teachers!). According to 2:15 one receives tradition through word or "our *letter*" (probably a reference to 1 Thessalonians). The word of the letter's author, according to 2 Thess 3:14, should be binding on the church; if anyone does not obey it, the church should break off fellowship with that person. In a final comment in 3:17 the writing is presented as authenticated with Paul's own hand and thus confirmed in its validity (though the problem of pseudonymity remains!).

2 Pet 3:1 also understands the letter as the reaffirmation of the teaching spoken by the holy prophets and apostles concerning the commandment of the Lord and Savior. This document knows a collection of Paul's letters (cf. K. H. Schelkle, *1–2 Pet* [HTKNT] 236f.), and offers the view that the sayings that Paul "has written to you according to the wisdom given to him" (on this development of the view of inspiration see Schelkle 236) were twisted with ruinous consequences (3:16).

Paul understood his letters as binding instructions (cf. 1 Cor 5:9, "not to associate with fornicators"). The letters serve the purposes of church order (2 Cor 7:8). The grief caused by one letter led to repentance (cf. 7:9). The power of Paul's letters (10:9), which was recognized also by his opponents (scarcely in an ironical way), is understood by the apostle himself as the means of his apostolic authority, whether through bodily presence or through letters (10:10f.). He was prepared to write letters of recommendation (which apparently carried considerable clout; cf. Philemon; Rom 16:1f.; 1 Cor 16:3 on a letter accompanying the collection to Jerusalem; cf. comments in the letters to churches: 1 Cor 4:17; 16:10f.; Phil 2:19-23; 2 Cor 8:22-24; cf. Col 4:7-9; Eph 6:21f.). Such letters appear also to have been falsified or misused (2 Cor 3:1).

Paul can also use *letter* in a fig. sense. Before God and in the presence of those who seek Paul's legitimation, the church in Corinth, which was founded (and tended) by Paul, is a letter of recommendation (2 Cor 3:2). One may conclude from 3:2f. (note the mixing of imagery) that Paul has seen the believers (their "heart") as an open possibility for God's Spirit to express himself in their person through his presence. However, the Christians have become a *letter* of Christ (v. 3) for the apostle's benefit, through which they came to faith. This can be known and read by all men (v. 2). Thus Christ expresses his efficacy and his confirmation for the apostle (v. 3). This letter is also binding (note the comparison "on stone tablets," an allusion to the Sinai event; also the contrast "heart of stone—heart of flesh," cf. Ezek 11:19; 36:26; Jer 31:33; Prov 7:3).

The legal effect of letters is indicated also in Acts 9:2; 22:5, where Paul receives them from the high priest and from the Sanhedrin so that he can proceed with his activity of persecuting (on the historical problem cf. E. Haenchen, *Acts* [Eng. tr., 1971] 320). The stylized letter in Acts 15:23-29 is a binding communication of a "legal" arrangement (conduct that will assure the table fellowship between Jewish Christians and Gentile Christians). Christians who have been certified transmit this letter (v. 30). The letter communicated and mentioned in Acts 23:25-30 is without theological significance, but is a witness to the literary gift of the author of Acts.

W. Beilner

ἐπιστομίζω *epistomizō* stop the mouth, bring to silence*

Titus 1:11: οὓς (the false teachers) δεῖ ἐπιστομίζειν. Spicq, *Notes* I, 280f.

ἐπιστρέφω *epistrephō* turn; intrans.: turn around, return

ἐπιστροφή, ῆς, ἡ *epistrophē* conversion*

1. Occurrences and meanings — 2. Contexts of usage

Lit.: P. AUBIN, *Le probleme de la 'conversion'* (1963). — W. BARCLAY, *Turning to God* (1963) 11-26. — G. BERTRAM, *TDNT* VII, 722-29. — H. CONZELMANN, *The Theology of St. Luke* 98-101. — R. MICHIELS, "La conception lucanienne de la conversion," *ETL* 41 (1965) 42-78.

1. The vb. ἐπιστρέφω appears in the NT 36 times. It is a preferred word of Luke (7 occurrences in Luke, 11 in Acts), but also appears with some frequency in the other two Synoptic Gospels (Mark 4 times, Matthew 4 times). 3 occurrences of the vb. are found in Paul (2 Cor 3:16; Gal 4:9; 1 Thess 1:9), and 2 each in James and Revelation. Further occurrences are in John 21:20; 1 Pet 2:25; and 2 Pet 2:22. Textual variants in Matt 9:22; Luke 2:20; John 12:40; and 2 Pet 2:21 are also to be considered. Ἐπιστροφή, *conversion*, appears in the NT only at Acts 15:3.

The trans. meaning of the vb., *turn*, is found only in Luke 1:16, 17 and Jas 5:19, 20. Elsewhere the vb. is intrans.: *turn around, return* (e.g., Matt 12:44; Mark 5:30; 8:33; 13:16; Luke 2:39; 8:55; John 21:20; Acts 15:36; 16:18; Rev 1:12; see BAGD s.v. 1.b.α.), esp. in a "moral" sense: *repent, be converted* (act. and mid.). The noun also has this meaning in Acts 15:3. Ἐπιστρέφω in a "moral" sense designates primarily the fulfillment of religious "conversion"; thus the vb. is used in a way similar to that of the LXX. Yet the usage is limited, for the vocabulary of conversion is often represented by μετανοέω and → μετάνοια, although in Lukan material ἐπιστρέφω predominates over μετανοέω (14 occurrences; μετάνοια appears 11 times).

2. Two occurrences of ἐπιστρέφω have a special feature. 2 Pet 2:22 (cf. Prov 26:11) condemns the libertine false teachers who have turned away from the traditional Christian ethic (ὑποστρέψαι, v. 21) and have *returned* (ἐπιστρέψας) to their shameless behavior. An analogous reproach was already formulated by Paul in Gal 4:9, there in reference to Gentile Christians who were tempted to *return* to the weak and beggarly domination of Jewish legal observance under the influence of the Judaizing preachers.

On the other side the annunciation by the angel in Luke 1:16b gives the (trans.) vb. a positive sense: the

Baptist will "*turn/convert* many of the Israelites to the Lord their God"; he will thus prepare for the eschaton. Similarly, the citation of Isa 6:9f., a *locus classicus* in the NT, is used in reference to Israel, always in view of Jewish unbelief. In the Synoptics the citation supports the answer to the question: Why does Jesus speak in parables? Mark 4:12 lets the last phrase (μήποτε ἐπιστρέψωσιν . . .), which is far removed from the dispute over the possibility of repentance, be understood in the sense of "perhaps they will *repent*." It occurs also in Matthew (13:15), who, in emphasizing the responsibility of Israel (cf. ὅτι, v. 13), can see here only the consequence of Israel's hardening. In the same way Acts 28:27 accents the development through which Israel henceforth is excluded from salvation in favor of the Gentiles (cf. v. 28). Even more severe is the formula in John 12:40 (στρέφω; TR: ἐπιστρέφω); it appears in a context (12:39, 40) that makes God the one who acts directly in the hardening— leaving out of account the preceding intentional rejection of the revelation.

In Acts the apostolic preaching invites a response of repentance and prepares the way for the Jews first (3:19, 26; 9:35), then (and esp.) for the Gentiles (11:21; 14:15; 15:3, 19; 26:18-20). The juxtaposition of μετανοέω and ἐπιστρέφω (3:19; 26:18-20) expresses in a twofold way that anyone who has changed his outlook on the old content of faith must still *turn/convert* (in the act of faith, 11:21) to the God who in Jesus Christ brings about salvation. Paul expresses this fact concretely in 1 Thess 1:9 (cf. Acts 14:15) in one of the two passages that use ἐπιστρέφω for entrance to Christianity. The other is in 2 Cor 3:16 in a Christian "midrash" on Exod 34:33-35: The veil with which Moses covered his face in order to cover the divine brightness represents the blinding of Israel, which is unable to observe in its holy Scriptures τὸ τέλος τοῦ καταργουμένου (v. 13); only turning (ἐὰν ἐπιστρέψῃ) to Kyrios Christ (cf. Hos 14:2f.; Joel 2:13; and often) takes away the obstacle (v. 16). The christological orientation is even clearer in 1 Pet 2:25. Here the author uses a classical motif (cf. Ezek 34:5; Zech 10:2; Isa 56:10f.; Ps 119:176; Matt 18:12f. par.) in order to express the turning of the Gentiles, the "lost sheep," to Christ the shepherd.

The parenesis in Jas 5:19 takes up the theme and encourages the members of the Church to *bring back* (ἐπιστρέφω in an active sense) those who have wandered away; whoever "*brings back* a sinner from his error will save his soul from death . . ." (5:20). Here the concern is to bring back brothers who have been led into error to an authentic Christian life. Likewise the passage involving Peter in Luke 22:32, καὶ σύ ποτε ἐπιστρέψας: he is invited, after his momentary failure (the denial), to draw power out of his Easter experience, which he will communicate to his brothers. Perhaps Luke 17:4 presupposes that reconciliation with the brother is the result of an inner "return" to Christ, which brings about ecclesiastical unity.

S. Légasse

ἐπιστροφή, ῆς, ἡ *epistrophē* conversion
→ ἐπιστρέφω.

ἐπισυνάγω *episynagō* gather, assemble*

Of the *gathering* of the "children of Jerusalem" (Matt 23:37a), which is compared to the *gathering* of the brood of a hen (v. 37b par. Luke 13:34); of the *summoning together* of the elect from the four winds (Mark 13:27 par. Matt 24:31); pass. of the *assembling* of a great crowd (Mark 1:33; Luke 12:1); of birds of prey (Luke 17:37).

ἐπισυναγωγή, ῆς, ἡ *episynagōgē* gathering, assembly*
→ συναγωγή.

ἐπισυντρέχω *episyntrechō* run together*

Mark 9:25, with subj. ὄχλος.

ἐπισύστασις, εως, ἡ *episystasis* riot, uproar*

In the NT only in Acts 24:2 Koine pm; 2 Cor 11:28 H I Koine pm in place of → ἐπίστασις.

ἐπισφαλής, 2 *episphalēs* uncertain, dangerous*

Acts 27:9, in reference to the *dangerous* sea journey (in autumn).

ἐπισχύω *epischyō* grow strong, press urgently*

Luke 23:5: ἐπίσχυον λέγοντες, "they said *even more urgently*" (as a strengthening of v. 2).

ἐπισωρεύω *episōreuō* pile up, accumulate*

2 Tim 4:3, with obj. διδασκάλους.

ἐπιταγή, ῆς, ἡ *epitagē* order, direction
→ ἐπιτάσσω 3.

ἐπιτάσσω *epitassō* command*
ἐπιταγή, ῆς, ἡ *epitagē* order, direction*

1. Occurrences in the NT — 2. Ἐπιτάσσω — 3. Ἐπιταγή

Lit.: O. BETZ, "Jesu heiliger Krieg," *NovT* 2 (1958) 116-37. — G. DELLING, *TDNT* VIII, 36. — H. KEE, "The Terminology of Mark's Exorcism Stories," *NTS* 14 (1967/68) 232-46.

1. Ἐπιτάσσω occurs 10 times in the NT, with 4 each in Mark and Luke and 1 each in Acts and Philemon.

Ἐπιταγή occurs 7 times in the NT, of which 4 are in Paul and 3 are in the Pastorals.

2. Ἐπιτάσσω appears in the NT in three linguistic contexts and designates:

a) Secular: the brief command of one of high rank on the basis of the authority given him (Mark 6:27: King Herod Antipas; Acts 23:2: the high priest Ananias) or an appropriate directive (Mark 6:39: Jesus at the feeding of the 5,000 in respect to the eating arrangements; Luke 14:22: the host referring to the invited guests).

b)—In contrast to powerless encouragement "in love" —the apostolic authority to transmit instructions to a believer as if to a subordinate (Phlm 8; cf. → διατάσσω in Paul).

c) Messianic: the forcible and powerful command of Jesus to the demons (Mark 1:27 par. Luke 4:36; Mark 9:25; Luke 8:31) or to the powers of nature conceived as demonic powers (Luke 8:25; cf. Ps 106:29 LXX and, on the subject, Pss 65:8; 89:10). This command leaves absolutely no freedom of action for the demons (Mark 1:27; Luke 8:25); the spoken word is effective promptly and precisely, just like the creative word (cf. Mark 9:25f.; Luke 8:31ff. with Gen 1:3, 9). A synonymous vb. is → ἐπιτιμάω ("reprimand, rebuke," Heb. *g'r*) seen in Mark 1:25, 27; 9:25; Luke 8:24, 25.

3. The noun ἐπιταγή has the following meanings in the NT:

a) The *concrete command* of God which corresponds to his will and plan for salvation in a definite point in time (Rom 16:26; 1 Tim 1:1; Titus 1:3; cf. Wis 18:15; 19:6). The full revelation of the salvation that was determined at the beginning occurs "now," κατ' ἐπιταγήν, through the call of the apostle (1 Tim 1:1; cf. Col 1:1; Eph 1:1), through the apostolic preaching (Titus 1:3), and through prophetic writings (Rom 16:26).

b) The trustworthy, transmitted and binding *concrete instruction* of Jesus, the messianic teacher (1 Cor 7:6; 7:25). It is clearly distinguished from the γνώμη ("opinion, counsel") of the apostle, which is indeed produced by the Spirit and secured by argument, but is not absolutely binding.

c) The *engagement of apostolic authority* in the proclamation of the true message of salvation (Titus 2:15; 2 Cor 8:8; cf. the vb. in Phlm 8). Ἐπιταγή means in Titus 2:15a more than "the impress of the pastoral word" (*contra* Delling 37). A proposed translation is: "Declare this [i.e., the central kerygma; cf. v. 14 with Mark 10:45!], exhort and instruct with the *full engagement of your apostolic authority*." The apostolic authority to make commands is assumed in 2 Cor 8:8; yet here it is evident that Paul cannot appeal to it in all situations, but instead often advances only his own γνώμη (v. 10).

W. Grimm

ἐπιτελέω *epiteleō* carry out, accomplish, bring to an end*

1. Occurrences in the NT and general meaning — 2. Individual occurrences — 3. Gal 3:3; 2 Cor 7:1; 1 Pet 5:9

Lit.: G. DELLING, *TDNT* VIII, 49-87.

1. In the NT ἐπιτελέω is used a total of 10 times: 7 times by Paul, 2 times in Hebrews, and in 1 Pet 5:9. Originally an intensified form of → τελέω, in the Hellenistic age ἐπιτελέω cannot often be distinguished in usage and content from τελέω. In both words the nuance of "conclusion, end, goal" (→ τέλος), depending on tense and context, can be operative as *direction* of the action or *goal that has been reached* or is *to be reached*, i.e., the end.

2. The following Pauline passages are not problematic: Rom 15:28, where the context places the weight on completion, settlement, conclusion; 2 Cor 8:6, 11a, where the contrast with προενάρχομαι (which appears twice in this context and is used nowhere else in the NT) emphasizes execution or completion (even if it does not involve reaching the end point as such); and 2 Cor 8:11b, where the readiness in desiring (ἡ προθυμία τοῦ θέλειν) is compared to τὸ ἐπιτέλεσαι (absolute), the *accomplishment, completion.* All four passages have the aor. of ἐπιτελέω (ἐπετέλεσα).

These four passages are all concerned with the collection of money for the church in Jerusalem. Ἐπιτελέω is also used in secular Greek with the meaning "pay something in accordance with an obligation"; however, this usage cannot with certainty be attested in the NT (perhaps, however, for τελέω). The meaning "pay" is out of the question in the first three passages; it is possible that it resonates in the fourth passage, however.

Also unproblematic is Phil 1:6, where, indeed, with the retention of the meaning *carry out, accomplish,* the accent is shifted more in the direction of *finish* (the fut. ind. is not limited to one mode of action).

In accordance with the linear aspect of the pres. tense system, the accent remains on the process of the completion or accomplishment itself in both occurrences in Hebrews (8:5; 9:6), where the first context—the building of the tabernacle—suggests the meaning *produce* or simply *make,* and the second, liturgical context demands more the nuance of *complete, execute.*

3. Despite the contrast with ἐναρξάμενοι (cf. Phil 1:6) in Gal 3:3, the linear verbal aspect of the pres. is dominant: For Paul it concerns the present conduct of the Galatians. Indeed, the pass. is possible here (BAGD s.v.: "will you be made complete in the flesh?"). However, the mid. is more probable: *"are you ending in this way?"* or *"do you want to carry through* in this way?").

In 2 Cor 7:1 it is unclear how Paul could demand that the Christians bring about or produce holiness. First, the

exact meaning of the infrequent word ἁγιωσύνη (→ ἅγιος 2) is uncertain. Here, in any case, it is associated with purification and fear of God. Secondly, the linear, uncompleted aspect of the pres. (cf. Luther 1545: *fortfahren mit der Heiligung* ["continue in sanctification"]) is not to be overlooked: it involves effort in any case. The parallels from *Ep. Arist.* 133, 166 (cited by BAGD s.v. 2), appear to make possible the tr. *"act in a holy way."*

Becausing of the lack of parallels it is uncertain in 1 Pet 5:9 whether the sufferings *"are accomplished* in the case of the brotherhood" or are *laid on* them (BAGD s.v. 4); the distinction is unimportant for the argument of the letter.

R. Mahoney

ἐπιτήδειος, 3 *epitēdeios* required, necessary*

Subst. in Jas 2:16: τὰ ἐπιτήδεια τοῦ σώματος.

ἐπιτίθημι *epitithēmi* act.: lay on; assign; mid.: attack; hand over*

There are 39 occurrences in the NT, predominantly in the Synoptic Gospels (7 in Matthew, 8 in Mark, 5 in Luke) and Acts (14 occurrences), with none in Paul. In most occurrences the vb. has the literal meaning *lay something on,* usually in the fixed phrase ἐπιτίθημι τὰς χεῖρας/τὴν χεῖρα with the dat., acc., or ἐπί (Matt 9:18; 19:13, 15; Mark 5:23; 6:5; 7:32; 8:23, 25; 16:18; Luke 4:40; 13:13; Acts 6:6; 8:17, 19; 9:12, 17; 13:3; 19:6; 28:8; 1 Tim 5:22). The dir. obj. can also be ἱμάτια (Matt 21:7), φορτία (23:4), στέφανον (*"place* a crown of thorns *on,* Matt 27:29; John 19:2; cf. ἐπέθηκαν ἐπάνω τῆς κεφαλῆς αὐτοῦ, *"place* over his head," Matt 27:37), πρόβατον (Luke 15:5), σταυρόν (23:26), πηλόν (ἐπὶ τοὺς ὀφθαλμούς, *"put* clay on the eyes," John 9:15), ζυγόν (Acts 15:10), βάρος (15:28 pass.), or φρυγάνων τι πλῆθος (28:3).

Fig. ἐπέθηκεν ὄνομα, *"assign* a name" (Mark 3:16, 17); πληγὰς ἐπιθέντες, *"give* blows" (Luke 10:30; Acts 16:23); absolute ἐάν τις ἐπιθῇ ἐπ᾽ αὐτά, *"if anyone adds (anything) to"* (Rev 22:18a; cf. Deut 4:2); ἐπιθήσει ὁ θεὸς ἐπ᾽ αὐτὸν τὰς πληγάς, *"God will lay on/add to* him the plagues" (Rev 22:18b, as a consequence of v. 18a).

Mid. *attack, touch* (Acts 18:10); *give to/equip* with something (28:10).

ἐπιτιμάω *epitimaō* overcome with a powerful word, rebuke

Lit.: G. A. BARTON, "The Use of ἐπιτιμᾶν in Mark 8:30 and 3:12," *JBL* 41 (1922) 233-36. — O. BÖCHER, *Christus Exorcista* (1972). — A. CAQUOT, *TDOT* III, 49-53. — H. C. KEE, "The Terminology of Mark's Exorcism Stories," *NTS* 14 (1967/68) 232-46. — G. LIEDKE, *THAT* I, 429-31. — R. PESCH, "Eine Lehre aus Macht," *Evangelienforschung* (ed. J. B. Bauer, 1968) 241-76. — H. PREISKER, *TDNT* II, 623-27. — L. SCHENKE, *Die Wundererzählungen des Markusevangeliums* (1974). — For further bibliography see *TWNT* X, 1083.

1. Outside the Synoptics (27 occurrences) ἐπιτιμάω is found only in 2 Tim 4:2 and Jude 9. Matthew has 6 occurrences, Mark has 9, and Luke has 12. In addition the vb. is found in textual variants in Matt 16:20 and Mark 10:14.

2. Ἐπιτιμάω is closely connected with Jesus' message and the reaction to it (a). Sometimes it is used of brotherly reproof (b). Once it is reserved for God himself in the struggle against heretics (c).

a) When Jesus breaks the power of the unclean spirit (Mark 1:25 par. Luke 4:35), which is the representative of evil powers (pl. in Mark 1:24, 27!), the sovereignty of God begins to make its way (cf. 1:14f. and esp. Matt 12:28 par.). The commanding word of Jesus overcomes the (demonic) force of the wind and of the waves (Mark 4:39 par.) and liberates the youth from his unclean spirit (Mark 9:25 par. Matt 17:18/Luke 9:42). According to Luke 4:39 Jesus, through his word, defeats Peter's mother-in-law's fever, which is also thought of as demonic.

When Jesus acts in this way, he demonstrates that he stands entirely on the side of God, who alone according to the OT (Ps 18:6 = 2 Sam 22:16; Ps 104:7, etc.) and Qumran literature (1QapGen 20:28; 1QM 14:9-11, etc.) has the right to overcome the godless powers. It is important that magical practices, which are known from Hellenistic exorcism stories, are foreign to the NT.

According to Mark 3:11f. Jesus orders the demons not to make known that he is the Son of God. Similarly Jesus charges his disciples not to speak to anyone about him (Mark 8:30 par. Matt 16:20 v.l./Luke 9:21), probably because his Messianic role could be misunderstood in political terms. When Jesus spoke of the suffering of the Son of Man (v. 31), Peter rebuked him (Mark 8:32). Jesus' rebuke of Peter moves close to the exorcism stories: The "Satan" in Peter is overcome, and Peter is brought back to discipleship (cf. 8:34-38). When the disciples rebuke those who want to bring children to Jesus (Mark 10:13 par.), this is scarcely a mere literary preparation for the following words of Jesus. The disciples seek to protect not Jesus, but themselves, from being disturbed, because they have not grasped that "to such" belongs the kingdom of God (vv. 15f.).

"Many" from the people, not the disciples (so R. Pesch, Mark [HTKNT] II, 172), seek to silence the blind man (Mark 10:48 par. Matt 20:31/Luke 18:39), not because the Son of David title "could be interpreted in national-political terms, and thus Jesus' mission claim could be reinterpreted" (Pesch), but because the crowd that followed Jesus from Jericho (v. 46) thought of the blind man as an intruder. Their rebukes could have blocked the way to discipleship (v. 50).

b) The presupposition for the brotherly rebuke (Luke 17:3b) is sin. Its goal is repentance before God and the brother's forgiveness. In 2 Tim 4:2 the task of rebuking

belongs to the bishops. According to Luke 23:40 one criminal rebukes the other in order to dissuade him from blasphemy against Jesus (v. 39), apparently with the goal of moving him toward faith in Christ (cf. vv. 41-43).

c) That according to Jude 8 false teachers even blaspheme the angelic powers (δόξαι) is the occasion for the author to recall (v. 9) the dispute of the archangel Michael with Satan over the body of Moses. Michael did not presume to pronounce a reviling judgment on Satan (→ ἐπιφέρω), but left the victory to God ("The Lord rebuke you," citing Zech 3:2 LXX). God will also overcome the false teachers (cf. vv. 10-15).   H. Giesen

ἐπιτιμία, ας, ἡ *epitimia* punishment*

2 Cor 2:6, as the *rebuke* by the majority of the church (not classical, but cf. Wis 3:10; papyri).

ἐπιτρέπω *epitrepō* permit*

1. Occurrences in the NT — 2. Range of meaning — 3. "If the Lord/God permits"

Lit.: MOULTON/MILLIGAN s.v.

1. Use of ἐπιτρέπω is distributed somewhat proportionally in the NT: Matthew has 2 occurrences, Mark has 2, Luke 4, John 1, Acts 5, 1 Corinthians 2, 1 Timothy 1, and Hebrews 1. Luke has doubled the Synoptic usage in the sayings on discipleship (Matt 8:21; Luke 9:59, 61) and in the story of the healing of the Gerasene demoniac (Mark 5:13; Luke 8:32 bis). This may cohere with the fact that the vb. expresses a relationship of superiority (→ 2) and is also used in Acts in this connection.

2. The subjs. of ἐπιτρέπω are normally persons who assume an official position. Pilate *permits* the body of Jesus to be taken from the cross (John 19:38). In the question about divorce the regulation of the Mosaic law that in the case of the divorce of a wife a letter of divorce be delivered is interpreted as permission: Moses *permitted* it (Mark 10:4 par. Matt 19:8). The demons request of Jesus that they be *allowed* to enter into the swine (Mark 5:13; Luke 8:32; cf. par. Mark). The permission, which Jesus gives, probably corresponds to the original request in Mark 5:10 that he not send them out of the land. The original schematic narrative style, which is normal in exorcism stories (cf. Mark 1:23-27), is given a fictional embellishment. The request for a concession is a fixed part of Jewish and Hellenistic miracle stories.

In Acts the Roman authorities are the ones esp. who conduct themselves properly toward Paul and *permit* him to give his defense speech (Acts 21:39, 40; 26:1), to look for his friends (27:3), and to live in his own rented quarters (28:16). In 26:1 the polite pass. formula "It is permitted for you" is used; cf. 28:16. In the *mulier taceat* verse (1 Cor 14:34; cf. 1 Tim 2:12) the impersonal pass. ἐπιτρέπεται refers to church order and thus to the post-Pauline origin of this passage (see H. Conzelmann, *1 Cor* [Eng. tr., Hermeneia] 246n.53).

3. The so-called *condicio Jacobea,* "if the Lord *permits* it" (Jas 4:15: ἐὰν ὁ κύριος θελήσῃ) is a well-known rhetorical phrase used to show the humility of the speaker. It occurs in connection with ἐπιτρέπω in 1 Cor 16:7; Heb 6:3; cf. Acts 18:21; 1 Cor 4:19. For nonbiblical occurrences see BAGD s.v.; G. Schrenk, *TDNT* III, 47n.32; F. Hauck, *James* (KNT) on 4:15.   G. Bouwman

ἐπιτροπεύω *epitropeuō* function as procurator

Luke 3:1 D: ἐπιτροπεύοντος (in place of ἡγεμονεύοντος), of the office of Pilate.

ἐπιτροπή, ῆς, ἡ *epitropē* commission, authority*

Acts 26:23, with ἐξουσία ("authority"), probably *commission* (of the chief priests).

ἐπίτροπος, ου, ὁ *epitropos* steward, overseer, guardian*

Matt 20:8, of the *overseer* in the vineyard; Luke 8:3 mentions Chuza, the wife of Herod's *steward,* who probably administered royal property (cf. ἐπίτροπος as a loanword in the rabbinic literature: Billerbeck II, 164); Gal 4:2: *guardian* (of an heir before the age of majority), with οἰκονόμοι. The meaning "governor" does not appear in the NT (see, however, Luke 3:1 D).

ἐπιτυγχάνω *epitynchanō* partake of, attain*

With gen. τῆς ἐπαγγελίας (Heb 6:15; cf. 11:33); with acc. (Rom 11:7 bis); with the obj. to be supplied from the previous clause (Jas 4:2).

ἐπιφαίνω *epiphainō* appear
→ ἐπιφάνεια 2.

ἐπιφάνεια, ας, ἡ *epiphaneia* appearance*

1. Occurrences and meaning — 2. Ἐπιφαίνω — 3. Ἐπιφανής

Lit.: F. BAUMGÄRTEL, "Das Offenbarungszeugnis des AT," *ZTK* 64 (1967) 393-422. — R. BULTMANN and D. LÜHRMANN, *TDNT* IX, 1-10. — A. COPPO, "Luci epifaniche nella terminologia dell'A. e del NT," *EL* 73 (1959) 310-34. — B. GÄRTNER, *DNTT* III, 317-20. — V. HASLER, "Epiphanie und Christologie in den Pastoralbriefen," *TZ* 33 (1977) 193-209. — E. JENNI, " 'Kommen' im theologischen Sprachgebrauch des AT," *Wort-Gebot-Glaube* (FS W. Eichrodt, 1970) 251-61. — J. JEREMIAS, *Theophanie. Die Geschichte einer alttestamentlichen Gattung* (1977). — J. KOENIG, "Aux origines des théophanies iahvistes,"

RHR 169 (1966) 1-36. — H. J. KRAUS, "Die ausgebliebene Endtheophanie. Eine Studie zu Jes 56-66," *ZAW* 78 (1966) 317-32. — J. K. KUNTZ, *The Self-Revelation of God* (1967). — D. L. LÜHRMANN, *Das Offenbarungsverständnis bei Paulus und in paulinischen Gemeinden* (1965). — idem, "Epiphaneia. Zur Bedeutungsgeschichte eines griechischen Wortes," FS Kuhn 185-99. -- C. MOHRMANN, *Epiphaneia* (1953). — E. PAX, *ΕΠΙΦΑΝΕΙΑ. Ein religionsgeschichtlicher Beitrag zur Biblischen Theologie* (1955). *Idem, RAC* V, 832-909. — *Idem, SacVb* 224-27. — R. PFISTER, PW Suppl. IV (1924), 277-323. — J. REINDL, *Das Angesicht Gottes im Sprachgebrauch des AT* (1970) 112f. — E. SCHNUTENHAUS, "Das Kommen und Erscheinen Gottes im AT," *ZAW* 76 (1964) 1-21. -- SPICQ, *Notes* I, 284-87. — D. WACHSMUTH, *KP* V, 1598-1601.

1. The noun ἐπιφάνεια is used 6 times in the NT and only in the later NT literature, in the Pastoral Epistles and in the similarly late pseudepigraphic 2 Thessalonians (from the Pauline school). Titus 2:13: "Waiting for the blessed hope and *appearing (adventum)* of the glory of our great God and Savior, Christ Jesus"; 1 Tim 6:14: "Blameless until the *appearing* of our Lord Jesus Christ"; 2 Tim 1:10: "Grace appeared now through the *appearing* of our Savior, Christ Jesus, who abolished death"; 4:1: "I bear witness before God . . . by his *appearing* and his kingdom"; 4:8: "All who love his *appearing*"; 2 Thess 2:8: The Lord will "destroy the antichrist at the *appearing* of his coming" (ἐπιφάνεια τῆς παρουσίας αὐτοῦ is to be understood pleophorically as a hendiadys).

All six occurrences refer to the anticipated second appearance of the resurrected and exalted Christ at the end of time, on the last day. At the same time the word suggests the kingdom of God, which has already arrived, and is manifested in the death and the conquering of death by Kyrios Christus.

The word in secular Greek already indicated the appearance of the saving deity and the experience of the saving act. But it also designated the cultic presence of the god-like ruler in the Hellenistic-Roman state cult. For the NT usage the OT theophanic motif of the coming of Yahweh into the world must be considered. The early Church saw in the incarnation of Jesus Christ as well as in his second advent in the final parousia the personal realization of the promised "coming of God." Thus "epiphany" can be at least partially synonymous with "parousia," as in 2 Thess 2:8. The LXX only rarely used this term for the appearances of God (2 Kgdms 7:23). Beginning with 2 Maccabees it appears more often (2:21; 3:24; 5:4, etc.). NT use of ἐπιφάνεια signifies that in the Christ-event God has appeared in the world and believers are summoned before the appearance of the judge of the world in decision, confession, and responsive action.

2. The vb. **ἐπιφαίνω,** *appear*,* occurs four times in the NT. In Acts 27:20 it means, in the context of the report of the shipwreck of Paul, that the sun and stars could not be seen because of the stormy weather. Here it has the technical-meteorological meaning of an observation of the weather. In the song of Zechariah (Luke 1:79, citing Isa 9:1; 42:70) God's illuminating appearance for those

who sit in darkness and the shadow of death is praised.
The birth of Jesus, the Son of David, is confessed to be
the light of the presence of God in the world. In Titus
2:11; 3:4 the vb. is used with a specifically christological
meaning (→ 1): "The grace of the savior God *has appeared* to all people"; "But when the goodness and loving
kindness of God our Savior *appeared*"; both times the
incarnation and the witness of the life of Jesus of Nazareth
in their universal soteriological consequence for all
people is envisioned.

The adj. **ἐπιφανής**, *shining forth**, is used in Acts 2:20
in the scriptural proof in Peter's Pentecost sermon (citing
Joel 3:4): "Before the coming of the great and *manifest* day
of the Lord." In the context of this reference to the parousia
the adj. means *impressive, fearful, evident, demonstrative,
manifest.* At the last day, with the return of the sovereign
Christ, the living power of the resurrected and exalted Lord
Christ will be apparent to the whole creation.

P.-G. Müller

ἐπιφανής, 2 *epiphanēs*   shining forth
→ ἐπιφάνεια 3.

ἐπιφαύσκω *epiphauskō*   light up, shine*

Eph 5:14: ἐπιφαύσει σοι ὁ Χριστός, "Christ *will shine*
on you," part of a citation not attested elsewhere, perhaps
from an early Christian hymn; see M. Dibelius, *Eph*
(HNT, ³1953) ad loc.

ἐπιφέρω *epipherō*   produce; bring forward; impose*

Rom 3:5: ὁ ἐπιφέρων τὴν ὀργήν, of God, "who *imposes*
the judgment of wrath"; Jude 9: κρίσιν ἐπενεγκεῖν
βλασφημίας, "to *impose* a judgment of blasphemy," i.e.,
condemnation of the devil (βλασφημίας, in view of the
sharp critique in v. 8, is not to be seen as obj. gen. ["judgment on the basis of blasphemy"]; elsewhere Acts 19:12
v.l.; 25:18 v.l.; Phil 1:17 v.l.

ἐπιφωνέω *epiphōneō*   cry loudly, call, shout*

Luke 23:21: but they *shouted out* (following προσε-
φώνησεν, v. 20); Acts 12:22: "but the people *broke out in
cheering*"; 21:34: "some *cried* one thing, some another";
22:24: "why they *cried* so loudly against him."

ἐπιφώσκω *epiphōskō*   shine; dawn*

Καὶ σάββατον ἐπέφωσκεν (Luke 23:54), according to
the context, refers to the *beginning* of the sabbath on the
evening of the day of preparation. The understanding of
Matt 28:1 is disputed: ὀψὲ δὲ σαββάτων, τῇ ἐπιφωσκούσῃ
εἰς μίαν σαββάτων. Because ὀψέ can mean "late" (as an
adv.; see BDF §164.4) or "after" (as an improper prep.),

ὀψὲ δὲ σαββάτων can mean the *beginning* of the first day
of the week, i.e., the evening of the sabbath (according
to the Jewish reckoning of the day; so, e.g., W. Grundmann, *Matt* [THKNT ad loc.]; E. Schweizer, *Matt* [Eng.
tr.] ad loc.; see esp. E. Lohmeyer, *Matt* [KEK] 404n.1).
However, it can also mean (according to Roman reckoning) the early morning of the first day of the week (cf.
Mark 16:1; Luke 24:1; John 20:1; see also Billerbeck I,
1051-53). The former is more probable; Matt 28:1ff. describes an event in the night after the sabbath; cf. also
v. 13.

ἐπιχειρέω *epicheireō*   take in hand, attempt*

Luke 1:1: "After many *have undertaken* . . . ," perhaps also, in the literary sense, more critical: "have attempted" (see G. Klein, "Lukas 1,1-4 als theologisches
Programm," FS Bultmann [1964] 193-216, esp. 195f.);
Acts 9:29; 19:13: *attempt.*

ἐπιχέω *epicheō*   pour on/over*

Luke 10:34: "he *poured* oil and wine *on* his wounds."

ἐπιχορηγέω *epichorēgeō*   grant; offer; support (vb.)*
ἐπιχορηγία, ας, ἡ *epichorēgia*   support (noun)*

1. Occurrences and meaning — 2. Paul — 3. Colossians
and Ephesians — 4. 2 Pet 1:5, 11

Lit.: BAGD s.v.

1. The noun, which appears twice in the NT, is formed
from the vb., which appears 5 times. The vb., intensified
by the ἐπί, is formed from χορηγέω, which itself appears
twice in the NT. In the Hellenistic age the Attic meaning
of χορηγέω, "to defray the cost for a chorus," fades into
the early fig. meaning, "bring forth money for something," then "deliver something, grant; furnish" (see LSJ
s.v.)

2. The undisputed Pauline passages are not
problematic: in 2 Cor 9:10 the vb. appears alongside
χορηγέω, where both mean *offer, make available,* or simply *give;* likewise Gal 3:5 (also here the continuous,
linear pres. should be noted). In Phil 1:19 ἐπιχορηγία is
support or simply *help.*

3. More difficult is the pres. pass. partc. in Col 2:19:
Proceeding from the head (= Christ), the entire body
(σῶμα) grows, ἐπιχορηγούμενον καὶ συμβιβαζόμενον (held
together) through joints and ligaments. On the one hand,
because of the functions of joints and ligaments that are
known to us and because of the parallelism (characteristic
of Colossians; cf. Kümmel, *Introduction* 240), ἐπιχορηγούμενον could mean *supported* in the structural, static

sense. On the other hand, the metaphor of growth and the idea of supporting by supplying associated with the word suggest the meaning *provided for,* i.e., with nourishment (cf. E. Schweizer, *Col* [Eng. tr.] ad loc.). Eph 4:16, which is dependent on Col 2:19, is even more difficult: The body produces its growth from the head (= Christ), held together by "every joint τῆς ἐπιχορηγίας." Here both the manner of *support*—whether structural or nutritional—and the function of the gen.—whether appositional (epexegetic), obj., or otherwise—are uncertain. It appears that the authors of Colossians and Ephesians accept a certain lack of clarity, a confusion of images, in order to set forth more clearly against the false teachers the absolute meaning of Christ, the head, for his body, the Church (see H. Conzelmann, *Eph-Col* [NTD] 109-11, 192-95).

4. The exact meaning of ἐπιχορηγήσατε in 2 Pet 1:5 and the material following in vv. 5-7 is difficult to understand (cf. BDF §493). 1:8f. appears to presuppose no particular relation to the previously listed virtues. Thus the meaning *add* for ἐπιχορηγήσατε is sufficient and suitable. The fut. pass. in 1:11 (ἐπιχορηγηθήσεται) is prompted more unconsciously than consciously by 1:5; the clause can simply be translated "entrance into the eternal kingdom *will be given* to you."   R. Mahoney

ἐπιχορηγία, ας, ἡ *epichorēgia* support
→ ἐπιχορηγέω.

ἐπιχρίω *epichriō* spread, cover*

John 9:6: ἐπέχρισεν τὸν πηλὸν ἐπὶ τοὺς ὀφθαλμούς (ἐπέθηκεν in B); 9:11: ἐπέχρισεν τοὺς ὀφθαλμούς.

ἐποικοδομέω *epoikodomeō* build up, build on something, construct
→ οἰκοδομή.

ἐποκέλλω *epokellō* be stranded, run aground*

Acts 27:41 Koine pl (in place of ἐπικέλλω).

ἐπονομάζω *eponomazō* call, give a name*

Rom 2:17 pass.: "If you *call* yourself a Jew."

ἐποπτεύω *epopteuō* look at, have before the eyes, observe*

In 1 Pet 2:12 the absolute partc. ἐποπτεύοντες demands completion with a supplied ἔργα, and ἐκ τῶν καλῶν ἔργων refers to δοξάσωσιν: "*When they behold* these [the good works]"; 3:2, referring to flawless conduct (of wives).

ἐπόπτης, ου, ὁ *epoptēs* observer, onlooker*

2 Pet 1:16, probably from the language of the mysteries (e.g., Plutarch *Alc.* 22.4; see BAGD s.v.; LSJ s.v.), fig.: ἐπόπται . . . τῆς . . . μεγαλειότητος, "*initiated witnesses* of the majesty [of God]."

ἔπος, ους, τό *epos* word*

Heb 7:9, in the common phrase ὡς ἔπος εἰπεῖν, "so to speak."

ἐπουράνιος, 2 *epouranios* heavenly

1. Occurrences and meaning — 2. Special uses in the NT — a) of God, Christ, and the powers — b) Apocalyptic usage — c) "Proceeding from heaven" — d) Heavenly salvation

Lit.: BAGD s.v. — H. BIETENHARD, *Die himmlische Welt im Urchristentum und Spätjudentum* (1951). — L. BRUN, "Jesus als Zeuge von irdischen und himmlischen Dingen. Joh 3,12-13," *SO* 8 (1929) 57-77. — R. BULTMANN, *John* (Eng. tr., 1971) 147-49. — B. GÄRTNER, *The Temple and the Community in Qumran and the NT* (1965) 88-99. — P. KATZ, *Philo's Bible* (1950) 141-46. — F. TORM, "Der Pluralis οὐρανοί," *ZNW* 33 (1934) 48-50. — H. TRAUB, *TDNT* V, 509-43.

1. This adj. appears from the time of Homer and is also found in Plato, Philo (*All.* iii.168), Josephus (*Ant.* i.69), and 3 Macc 6:28; 7:6. In the NT (19 occurrences) it has a variety of nuances as a substitute for a Hebrew prep. combination. In general, heaven and earth are spatially separated from each other. Despite their outward separation various thought forms (analogies, correlations, correspondences) establish a combination of the two realms. The coming of the kingdom of heaven in history brings with it a new knowledge of the heavenly realms; yet all apocalyptic awaits a final opening of the heavenly world and the new creation of heaven and earth.

2. a) In a prophetic warning concluding a parable of Jesus, Matt 18:35 speaks of the "Father in heaven" (οὐράνιος, v.l. ἐπουράνιος). The adj. occurs in a liturgical context also in *1 Clem.* 61:2 (voc. δέσποτα ἐπουράνιε). In the liturgical confessional statement in Eph 1:20; 2:6 Jesus Christ is said to be in *heaven* (pl. subst. ἐν τοῖς ἐπουρανίοις) after his exaltation. The powers and authorities in Phil 2:10; Eph 3:10; 6:12 are of a *heavenly* kind. However, they are involved in the battle between light and darkness partially as opposing powers, not as messengers. Heaven itself is divided into a variety of levels and realms; God's messengers stand in opposition to those of Satan (cf. the related adj. → πνευματικός, Eph 6:12).

b) That which is withdrawn from human eyes but has been described in earlier texts of Scripture is *apocalyptic*

(John 3:12; Heb 8:5; 9:23; 11:16; cf. Wis 9:16; 2 Esdr 4:1-21; Hippolytus *Haer.* v [a Naassene sermon]). 2 Tim 4:18 speaks in elevated language about the *"heavenly kingdom,"* Heb 12:22 of the *"heavenly* Jerusalem."

c) A further level is present where the adj. takes on the meaning *proceeding from heaven* and thus speaks of origin (= ἐξ οὐρανοῦ). Paul's placing the first and last man in correspondence in 1 Cor 15:45-49 belongs here (also used here is the adj. πνευματικός, v. 44). The Hellenistic relationship should not obscure the fact that a Hebrew basis is present: on the one hand the formation of mankind from the earth, and on the other hand the appearance of the Son of Man and the saints of the Most High (Dan 7:13-14; 7:18; Phil 3:21). With Easter the process of transformation begins; the Son of Man includes the transformation of the saints. Paul thinks in corporate terms (not mystically): As the earthly one was, so are those who are earthly, and as the heavenly one is, so are those who are *heavenly* (οἱ ἐπουράνιοι, v. 48). Thus *heavenly* is a quality that corresponds to the transformation. The train of thought is basically future-oriented (v. 49), but in correspondence to the Hebrew view of space and time it may include the present as well (T. Boman, *Hebrew Thought Compared with Greek* [1960], 147f.). Those who are *heavenly* (v. 48) correspond to the "saints" (Dan 7:21, 25; *1 Enoch* 48:4; 1QM 12:1-5). Thus Paul's apocalyptic is based on a definite Hebrew foundation.

d) If the heavenly world is the place where God lives, into which the believer, according to the apocalyptic view, can be removed, the inheritance of the pious that has been preserved is to be regarded also as present because one is certain of living in the reality of God (H. W. Kuhn, *Enderwartung und gegenwärtiges Heil* [1966] 183f.). Eph 1:3 is characteristic: God has blessed us with every kind of spiritual blessing which is kept in *heaven* (ἐν τοῖς ἐπουρανίοις). Reception of this blessing is probably associated with baptism. The phrase "partakers *of a heavenly* calling" (Heb 3:1) is to be connected with the baptismal act: the call comes from heaven, has the manner of heaven, and leads to life, which is determined by the apostolic instructions.

O. Michel

ἑπτά *hepta* seven
ἕβδομος, 3 *hebdomos* seventh

Lit.: BAGD s.v. (bibliography). — B. C. BIRCH, *ISBE* III, 559. — D. R. DAVIS, "The Relationship Between the Seals, Trumpets and Bowls in the Book of Revelation," *JETS* 16 (1973) 149-58. — G. REICHELT, *Das Buch mit den sieben Siegeln in der Apokalypse des Johannes* (Diss. Göttingen, 1975). — K. H. RENGSTORF, *TDNT* II, 627-35. — E. D. SCHMITZ, *DNTT* II, 690-92. — E. SCHWEIZER, "Die sieben Geister in der Apk," *idem, Neotestamentica* (1963) 190-202. — A. STROBEL, *BHH* 1785 (bibliography). — H. ZIMMERMANN, "Die Wahl der Sieben (Apg

6,1-6)," FS für J. Kardinal Frings (1960) 364-78. — For further bibliography see *TWNT* X, 1084.

1. Ἑπτά occurs 88 times in the NT, with most of the occurrences in Revelation (56), while outside the Synoptic Gospels (24 occurrences) and Acts (8 times) it appears only in Heb 11:30. Ἕβδομος is found 9 times, of which 5 are in Revelation.

2. The general oriental and esp. OT significance of the number seven as an expression of fullness and inclusiveness and its frequent usage as a typical number for an amount that is neither too small nor too large is present also in the NT (see Rengstorf 627-30), where it appears in various connections:

a) In most occurrences it is a round number for "little," with no deeper meaning (7 loaves, Matt 15:34; cf. 16:10; Mark 8:5, 20), or for "many" (7 baskets, Matt 15:37; cf. Mark 8:8).

b) Ἑπτὰ ἡμέραι stands for "a week" (Acts 20:6; 21:4, 8, 27; 28:14; Heb 11:30; see Josh 6:3f.); cf. *"seventh* day," Heb 4:4 (bis).

c) Ἑπτά serves to underline a great number and is also used to indicate frequency or power: ἑπτὰ ἕτερα πνεύματα (Matt 12:45 par. Luke 11:26, cf. ἑπτὰ δαιμόνια (of Mary Magdalene, Matt 16:9; Luke 8:2), ἑπτὰ υἱοί (Acts 19:14), ἑπτὰ ἀδελφοί (who stand under the commandment of levirate marriage, Matt 22:25, 26; Mark 12:20, 22, 23; Luke 29:31, 33; cf. Deut 25:5ff.).

d) In Revelation ἑπτά plays an important role as an expression for the totality and fullness of God and his eschatological acts (7 lampstands, 1:12, 13, 20; 2:1; 7 stars, 1:16, 20; 2:1; 3:1; the lamb with 7 horns and 7 eyes, 5:6; 7 angels, 8:2, 6; 11:15; 15:1, 6, 7; 16:1; 21:9; 7 trumpets, 8:2, 6; 7 thunders, 10:3, 4; 7 plagues, 15:1, 6; 7 bowls, 15:7; 16:1; 21:9). There is also the sweeping power of the godless powers (7 heads of the dragon, 12:3; 7 horns of the beast, 13:1, cf. 17:3, 7, 9, 11). The book with 7 seals (5:1, 5; 8:1) contains the fullness of the secrets of the eschaton. Some of the occurrences are based on texts or on facts; thus, e.g., 17:9 may refer to the 7 hills of Rome, the 7 thunders in 10:3f. may refer to the sevenfold φωνή θεοῦ of Ps 28:3-9 LXX, and the 7 lampstands may refer to the menorah of the Jerusalem temple. The 7 churches in Asia (1:4, 11, 20) represent the totality of Christians, who are addressed (cf. Muratorian Canon; Hennecke/Schneemelcher I, 44). E. Lohmeyer's attempt (*Rev* [HNT] 182ff.) to demonstrate that the number seven is a principle by which Revelation is composed has scarcely found agreement.

e) According to Acts 6:3 the "twelve" (→ δώδεκα) bring about the selection of *seven* men "to wait on tables." According to 21:8 this was a fixed group of "the seven" alongside "the twelve." The model might have been the governing bodies of Jewish communities consisting of seven men (Rengstorf 634; E. Haenchen, *Acts* [Eng. tr., 1971] ad loc.).   H. Balz

ἑπτάκις *heptakis* seven times*

In the NT only in the saying about forgiveness derived from Q. It is used to refer to a relatively large number. According to Matt 18:21, 22 it does not suffice to forgive "up to *seven times*" (ἕως ἑπτάκις), i.e., with limitations, but rather in a grotesquely increased way, "up to seventy-seven times," i.e., without limitation (→ ἑβδομηκοντάκις; D*: "seven times seventy times"). Luke 17:4 (bis) emphasizes that a brother who sins *seven times* in one day and who "turns to you *seven times* and repents," is to be forgiven every time, i.e., likewise without limit.

ἑπτακισχίλιοι, 3 *heptakischilioi* seven thousand*

Rom 11:4: κατέλιπον . . . ἑπτακισχιλίους ἄνδρας (cf. 1 Kgs 19:18), as a type for the "remnant" (v. 5).

ἑπταπλασίων, 2 *heptaplasiōn* sevenfold

Luke 18:30 D it syr^hmg in place of πολλαπλασίων.

Ἔραστος, ου *Erastos* Erastus*

1. The Greek name of a Christian in Corinth, identified as ὁ οἰκονόμος τῆς πόλεως, "the city treasurer," who sends greetings to the Roman church (Rom 16:23). G. Theissen, *The Social Setting of Pauline Christianity* (1982) 75-83, wants to equate this Erastus with an aedile (presumably named to that office at a later time) Erastus named in an inscription found in 1929. See below for further bibliography.

2. In Acts 19:22; 2 Tim 4:20 an Erastus appears as coworker of Paul on his missionary journeys. Since in both passages Corinth or Achaia plays a role, the same person could be intended as the one in Rom 16:23. H. J. Cadbury, *BHH* 422; *idem*, "Erastus of Corinth," *JBL* 50 (1931) 42-58; *BL* 405.

ἐραυνάω *eraunaō* inquire, investigate*

A late form of classical ἐρευνάω (BDF §30.4). John 5:39, of the (Jewish) *search* (for life) in the Scriptures; similarly 7:52 (absolute) of the (Jewish) *search* of the Scriptures; of God, Rom 8:27, ὁ ἐραυνῶν τὰς καρδίας, cf. Prov 20:27; Rev 2:23, ὁ ἐραυνῶν νεφροὺς καὶ καρδίας, in the sense of critical examination; of the Spirit in 1 Cor 2:10, πάντα ἐραυνᾷ, "he explores everything"; of the OT prophets, 1 Pet 1:11. G. Delling, *TDNT* II, 655-57.

ἐργάζομαι *ergazomai* work, accomplish, carry out
ἐργασία, ας, ἡ *ergasia* employment, profession; gain*
ἐργάτης, ου, ὁ *ergatēs* worker

1. Occurrences in the NT — 2. Meanings and semantic fields — 3. Ἐργασία — 4. ἐργάτης

Lit.: G. BERTRAM, *TDNT* 635-55. --- H. C. HAHN, *DNTT* III, 1147-59. — C. LINDHAGEN, *ΕΡΓΑΖΕΣΘΑΙ Apc* 18:17; *Hes* 48:18, 19. *Die Wurzel ΣΑΠ im NT und AT. Zwei Beiträge zur Lexikographie der griechischen Bibel* (UUÅ, 1950, no. 5). — For further bibliography see *TWNT* X, 1084f.

1. Ἐργάζομαι appears in the NT a total of 41 times, of which 17 are in the Pauline corpus. Ἐργασία is found 5 times in Luke-Acts and once in Ephesians. Ἐργάτης is limited primarily to Matthew and Luke (6 and 4 respectively of the total of 16 occurrences).

2. From the time of Homer ἐργάζομαι means *work, be active* (intrans.), *produce, bring about, carry out* (trans.). The general meaning *work* is also frequent in the NT (Luke 13:14; John 9:4b; Acts 18:3; 1 Cor 9:6; 2 Thess 3:10, 12). Paul *works* day and night for his sustenance (1 Thess 2:9; 2 Thess 3:8; cf. 1 Cor 4:12 on the strain of his work) and encourages the Church ἐργάζεσθαι ταῖς χερσίν as part of their Christian conduct (1 Thess 4:11). Matt 25:16 speaks of allowing "money to *work*." In John ἐργάζομαι receives a specific theological meaning: It expresses Jesus' claim to be equal to God (John 5:17; cf. 9:4), for, as revealer, he works as God *works*. The goal of God's activity is that people believe on the revealer who has been sent. Thus they *do* the works of God (John 6:28f.). The phrase ἔργα ἐργάζομαι is already frequent in the LXX (Exod 31:5; Num 8:15, etc.) and is attested frequently in the NT (Matt 26:10 par.; John 3:21; 9:4; Acts 13:41 citing Hab 1:5; 1 Cor 16:10).

In Paul ἐργάζομαι can take on the meaning *perform works* and thus become a subject within the field of justification by works or judgment according to works: In the phrase ἐξ ἔργων (Rom 4:2) the contrast between ἐργαζόμενος/μὴ ἐργαζόμενος develops the opposition faith/works (v. 5). In Romans 3 work is as closely associated with the law as faith is associated with Jesus Christ. In 2:10 reference is made to the eschatological judgment (cf. Matt 7:23, οἱ ἐργαζόμενοι τὴν ἀνομίαν; 2 John 8); τῷ ἐργαζομένῳ τὸ ἀγαθόν implies the concept of good works, which in the final judgment form the criterion for receiving the eschatological benefits of salvation.

The same usage of ἐργάζομαι (τὸ) ἀγαθόν is found also in *3 Bar.*: The phrase ὅσα ἐργάζονται ἀγαθά is used of weighing the works of the righteous (11:9), pictured here hypostatically. The concept of weighing good and bad works at the final judgment is derived from Egypt and is carried on into the Jewish-Christian realm (cf. *T. Abr.* [A] 12).

In Jas 1:20 ἐργάζομαι is used of *doing* the righteousness of God, which is the fulfillment of the divine demands (cf. K. Berger, *ZNW* 68 [1977] 266-75, against M. Dibelius and H. Greeven, *Jas* [Eng. tr., Hermeneia] 110, which has "produce"; cf. 2 Kgdms 8:15; *Pss. Sol.*

9:5, etc.). Even if one translates Jas 1:20 simply with *do*, in 2 Cor 7:10 it takes on the meaning of κατεργάζομαι, "bring about/produce," and becomes a t.t. for derivation and origin within a series (Herodotus vii.102; *T. Jos.* 10:1; Rom 4:15; Jas 1:3).

3. The meaning and usage of **ἐργασία** in the NT cannot be distinguished from usage in secular Greek. In a polemic against the Gentiles the full exercise of sexual debauchery is called ἐργασία ἀκαθαρσίας πάσης (Eph 4:19). Ἐργασία designates both the *gain* from the sale of one's product (Acts 16:16, 19; 19:24) and in general the *trade* in which one is involved (19:25). The clause δίδωμι ἐργασίαν, "make an *effort*" (Luke 12:58), is not attested elsewhere (on ἐργασία = *effort*, cf. Josephus *Ant.* iii.35).

4. In secular Greek **ἐργάτης** designates generally one who does something (Euripides *El.* 75), then esp. one who works for wages as part of an occupational group (farm workers: Philo *Agr.* 5; Josephus *B.J.* iv.557); then also slaves (Josephus *Ant.* xii.194). While ἐργάτης in Matt 10:10 par. Luke 10:7 is the *worker* in general who is worthy of his food or his payment, Matt 9:37f. par. Luke 10:2 refers to the *farm worker* and Matt 20:1f., 8 refers to the *worker* in the vineyard. In a sermon of judgment against the unsociable rich (so F. Mussner, *Jas* [HTKNT] 193), the accusation against the property owners becomes concrete in the fact that they hold back the pay of the *workers* (Jas 5:4).

Apostles and teachers can be described as *workers* in a fig. sense. In a heated polemic Paul calls false teachers and false apostles ἐργάται δόλιοι (2 Cor 11:3). Κακοὶ ἐργάται (Phil 3:2) does not refer to the works-righteousness of the opponents of Paul (against R. Bultmann, *Der Stil der paulinischen Predigt und die kynisch-stoische Diatribe* [1910] 105), but rather to their missionary activity. The noteworthy fact that Paul uses ἐργάτης only in a negative way is not continued in the Pastorals. In contrast to the false teachers Timothy is encouraged to become an ἐργάτης ἀνεπαίσχυντος (2 Tim 2:15; cf. *T. Benj.* 11:1β).

R. Heiligenthal

ἐργασία, ας, ἡ *ergasia* employment, profession; gain
→ ἐργάζομαι 3.

ἐργάτης, ου, ὁ *ergatēs* worker
→ ἐργάζομαι 4.

ἔργον, ου, τό *ergon* work, task

1. Occurrences in the NT — 2. Meaning and usage — 3. "Work" in John — 4. Judgment according to good and evil works — 5. "Faith and works" in Paul and James

Lit.: K. BERGER, "Der Streit des guten und des bösen Engels um die Seele," *JSJ* 4 (1973) 1-18. — G. BERTRAM, *TDNT* II, 635-55. — G. BORNKAMM, "Gesetz und Natur (Röm 2,14-16)," idem, *Aufsätze* II, 93-118. — C. BURCHARD, "Zu Jak 2,14-26," *ZNW* 71 (1980) 27-45. — K. P. DONFRIED, "Justification and Last Judgment in Paul," *ZNW* 67 (1976) 90-110. — G. EICHHOLZ, *Glaube und Werke bei Paulus und Jakobus* (1961). — C. W. FISHBURNE, "1 Cor III 10-15 and the Testament of Abraham," *NTS* 17 (1970/71) 109-15. — F. FLÜCKIGER, "Die Werke des Gesetzes bei den Heiden (nach Röm 2,14ff.)," *TZ* 8 (1952) 17-42. — H. C. HAHN, *DNTT* III, 1147-59. — R. HEILIGENTHAL, *Werke als Zeichen* (WUNT II/9, 1983). — H. HÜBNER, "Was heißt bei Paulus 'Werke des Gesetzes'?" *Glaube und Eschatologie* (FS W. G. Kümmel, 1985) 123-33. — J. A. KLEIST, " 'Ergon' in the Gospels," *CBQ* 6 (1944) 61-68. — O. KUSS, "Die Heiden und die Werke des Gesetzes," *MTZ* 5 (1954) 77-98. — E. LOHMEYER, "Gesetzeswerke," idem, *Probleme paulinischer Theologie* (1954) 33-74. — E. LOHSE, "Glaube und Werke—zur Theologie des Jakobusbriefs," *ZNW* 48 (1957) 1-22. — L. MATTERN, *Das Verständnis des Gerichtes bei Paulus* (1966) 141-92. — E. PETERSON, "ΕΡΓΟΝ in der Bedeutung 'Bau' bei Pls," *Bib* 22 (1941) 439-41. — J. RIEDL, *Das Heilswerk nach Johannes* (1973). — J. SCHMID and W. PESCH, *LTK* X, 1049-52. — E. SYNOFZIK, *Die Gerichts- und Vergeltungsaussagen bei Paulus* (1977). — W. C. VAN UNNIK, "The Teaching of Good Works in 1 Peter," *NTS* 1 (1954/55) 92-110. — R. WALKER, "Allein aus Werken. Zur Auslegung von Jak 2,14-26," *ZTK* 61 (1964) 155-92. — R. B. WARD, "The Works of Abraham. James 2,14-26," *HTR* 61 (1968) 283-90. — U. WILCKENS, *Rom* (EKKNT) I (1978) 127-31, 142-46. — idem, "Was heißt bei Paulus: 'Aus Werken des Gesetzes wird kein Mensch gerecht?' " idem, *Rechtfertigung als Freiheit. Paulusstudien* (1974) 77-109. — For further bibliography see *TWNT* X, 1084f.

1. The 169 instances of ἔργον in the NT are distributed rather evenly among the individual writings of the NT, although the limited number of occurrences in the Synoptics (10) is striking. In only 9 cases do gen. phrases with God, Christ, or Lord appear, while 15 of a total of 30 occurrences of "*good* works" are found in the Pastorals alone. The relationship of ἔργον and νόμος is typical for Paul (3 occurrences in Romans, 6 in Galatians); the association of ἔργον and λόγος is attested a total of 7 times.

2. In the NT ἔργον means, as in secular Greek (Aristophanes *Av.* 862; Xenophon *Mem.* ii.10.6; Epictetus *Diss.* i.16.21), *work, task.* This is the case in the phrase ἔργον τοῦ κυρίου (1 Cor 15:58; 16:10; Phil 2:30), where the gen. designates the one who commissions the work. The prep. phrase εἰς ἔργον refers in Acts 13:2; 14:26; 15:38 to the missionary task (cf. Phil 1:22; 1 Thess 5:13; 2 Tim 4:5). The coordination of ἔργον and λόγος (Xenophon *Hier.* 7.2; Epictetus *Diss.* i.29.56; iv.1.140; Sir 3:8; cf. 35:22; 4 Macc 5:38; Josephus *Ant.* xvii.220) encompasses the unity of human conduct (2 Cor 10:11; Col 3:17; 1 John 3:18, etc.) and in the formula δυνατὸς ἐν ἔργῳ καὶ λόγῳ (Luke 24:19; Acts 7:22) identifies prophetic power.

Frequently ἔργον is used of a deed done or being done: as a *work* of God (Heb 1:10; 4:3, 4, etc.), of Jesus (Matt 11:2; Acts 13:41; Rev 15:3; on John → 3, esp. of the miracles), and of humans, to designate the totality of their deeds. With the latter collective τὸ ἔργον appears for pl. ἔργα (Gal 6:4; Heb 6:10; Rev 22:12). In gen. phrases ἔργον can express the mode of relationship to a power or group (Rom 13:12; Gal 5:19; Eph 5:11; 1 John 3:8; cf. Rev 2:6; also Rom 2:15; 3:20; Gal 2:16; 3:2, 5, 10). Κατὰ τὰ ἔργα is a criterion for evaluation in judgment (→ 4).

Human work can be described as ἀγαθόν or καλόν (Matt 5:16; Acts 9:36; Rom 2:7, etc., esp. in the Pastorals), or as πονηρόν, νεκρόν, or ἄκαρπον, etc. (Col 1:21; Heb 6:1; 9:14; Eph 5:11).

3. John knows both the *work* of Jesus (4:34; 17:4) and the *works* of Jesus (5:20, 36; 9:3f.; 10:25, 32, 37f.; 14:10-12). The sg. underlines the unity of the work. The *work* of Jesus attests that he is the Christ (John 5:36; 10:25; cf. 7:7). As something given by God, it stands for the total revelatory work of Jesus (R. Bultmann *John* [Eng. tr., 1971] 265). The realization of the *work* commissioned by God (John 4:34; 5:36; 17:4; cf. 9:4) through the revealer is continued in the activity of the μείζονα ἔργα of the disciples (John 14:12; after the death of the charismatic one his works multiply and increase in his disciples: cf. *T. Job* 47ff.; Acts 2:22, 43). The ἔργα τοῦ Χριστοῦ also serve as a legitimizing proof in Matt 11:2-6.

4. The semantic field of "judgment according to *works*" is common to the NT and noncanonical literature (Sir 16:12ff.; 4 Ezra 7:34ff.; *1 Enoch* 63:8f., etc.). Along with the hypostatizing of *works* (1 Tim 5:24f.; Rev 14:13) and the idea of the "treasure of good *works*" (1 Tim 6:18; cf. Matt 6:20; Luke 12:33) the prep. phrase κατὰ τὰ ἔργα (Rom 2:6; 2 Cor 11:15; 1 Pet 1:17; Rev 2:23, etc.) esp. refers to judgment according to works. Except in Revelation the form this theme takes is characteristically parenetic; thus John 3:19-21, formulated in present-eschatological terms, comes as the conclusion of a sermon of Jesus. The theme of judgment by works can be used both to introduce (1 Pet 1:17) and conclude (1 Tim 5:24f.) individual pareneses. In addition the divine freedom can be set out against the background of rejection of judgment based on works: In Rom 9:11f. and 2 Tim 1:9 the divine freedom is realized where the individual is without any prior works. Rom 2:6-11 speaks of a judgment based on works within the framework of an eschatological sermon on repentance (cf. Pr Man 7ff.; *T. Zeb.* 9:6ff.; Wis 11:23; *Jub.* 5:17ff.); the statement refers intentionally to the equality of Jews and Gentiles before the judgment and is used to discredit human works. In 1 Cor 3:13ff. the reference is to the test of Christian works in the final judgment (on the meaning of ἔργον in the sense of "building," cf. Peterson). The hypos-

tatizing of the work here is useful in the distinction of person and work, inasmuch as Paul does not threaten his opponents with personal destruction in the judgment (v. 15). The interdependence of present conduct and future judgment according to works finds particular expression in the personal anticipation of the divine action of judging (in the testing of one's own work).

Works take on considerable significance in Pauline parenesis; one's relationship to the old or new aeon is seen in one's works (Rom 13:12; Gal 5:19ff., where the individual works are each listed in a catalog of vices; on the theme of recognizability according to works cf. Rev 2:19; 3:1, 8, 15). Περιπατεῖν ἐν πνεύματι is made concrete in doing the fruit of the Spirit (note the parallelism of ἔργα τῆς σαρκός and καρπὸς τοῦ πνεύματος in Gal 5:19, 22; cf. Rom 13:3; 1 Cor 9:1; 15:58; 2 Cor 9:8). In the Pastorals the eschatological association recedes more into the background. The theme of good works is very significant in the ethic of the community and therefore a part of a parenesis related to the community situation (1 Tim 2:10; 2 Tim 2:21, etc.).

5. The phrases ἐξ ἔργων νόμου and χωρὶς ἔργων νόμου (Rom 3:20, etc.) are used by Paul in his treatment of the replacement of the old way of salvation in the law by the new way of salvation in Jesus Christ. The expression ἐξ ἔργων νόμου can be abbreviated, on the one hand, by ἐξ ἔργων (Rom 4:2; cf. 9:32) and, on the other hand, by ἐκ νόμου (4:16, cf. v. 13). In this context ἔργα designates the mode of relationship to the law and is then used for the contrast to faith in Jesus Christ. (Ἔργον νόμου in 2:15 indicates the analogous manner in which the Gentile Christians adopted the way of the law. The sg. is explained by the fundamental nature of the statement.)

Paul derives the antithesis of grace and works from Alexandrian Jewish creation theology (Philo *All.* iii.77-79; cf. 2 Tim 1:9; Titus 3:5) and assigns *work* and grace to different "ages" (Rom 3:20, 21, 24). His separation of "faith and *works*" with reference to justification is innovative (cf. the parallel usage of "faith and *works* in 4 Ezra 7:34f.; *2 Bar.* 51:7; 1 Macc 2:51f., etc.). Because the human acceptance of the new way of salvation is indicated with πίστις and Χριστός according to an early Christian formula, and grace and works form a traditional antithesis (4 Ezra 8:32, 36), Paul can contrast the formula ἐκ πίστεως Χριστοῦ (Rom 3:26) with the newly formed phrase ἐξ ἔργων νόμου, where the concern is not with the contrast between faith and works in itself, but with the replacement of the old by the new way of salvation.

Rom 3:20-26 is prefigured in Gal 2:11-21, where Paul takes the ideas of the Galatians, coming from the debate with the Jewish Christians. In Romans he formulates a temporal sequence (the time of the law = the time of divine forbearance; the time of the revelation of the new way of salvation).

The argument in Jas 2:14-26 takes over the juxtaposition of πίστις and δικαιόω from the Abraham tradition and explains that faith and works necessarily belong together (2:26). An understanding of faith is presupposed which is related primarily to knowledge and recognition of the one God (in Hellenistic missionary Judaism: Philo *Op.* 170-72; *Virt.* 216; cf. Jas 2:19). The problem of defining the relationship of confession and ethics is here resolved through the emphasis on the interrelationship of faith and works (in Judaism faith and works belong together: see above). James's concern is to avoid the discrepancy between word and deed; faith demonstrates only through works that it is not dead (2:17, 26).

R. Heiligenthal

ἐρεθίζω *erethizō* irritate, spur on*

2 Cor 9:2: "Your zeal has *spurred on*"; Col 3:21, addressed to fathers: "*provoke* not your children."

ἐρείδω *ereidō* press, become fixed*

Acts 27:41, intrans.: "The bow [of the ship] became stuck."

ἐρεύγομαι *ereugomai* speak plainly*

Matt 13:35 ἐρεύξομαι κεκρυμμένα, "*speak plainly* what has been hidden" (cf. Ps 78:2).

ἐρευνάω *ereunaō* inquire, investigate

Alternative form of → ἐραυνάω.

ἐρημία, ας, ἡ *erēmia* desert
→ ἔρημος.

ἔρημος, 2 *erēmos* lonely, deserted
ἐρημία, ας, ἡ *erēmia* desert*

1. Occurrences in the NT — 2. Meanings — 3. Usage of the desert

Lit.: BAGD s.v. — O. BÖCHER, *DNTT* III, 1004-8. — H. CONZELMANN, *The Theology of St. Luke* (1960) 18-22. — V. FRITZ, *Israel in der Wüste* (1970). — R. W. FUNK, "The Wilderness," *JBL* 78 (1959) 205-14. — G. KITTEL, *TDNT* II, 657-60. — U. W. MAUSER, *Christ in the Wilderness* (1963). — C. C. McCOWN, "The Scene of John's Ministry and its Relation to the Purpose and Outcome of His Mission," *JBL* 59 (1940) 113-31. — W. SCHMAUCH, *Orte der Offenbarung und der Offenbarungsort im NT* (1956) 27-47. — S. TALMON, *IDBSup* 946-49. — For further bibliography see *TWNT* X, 1085f.

1. Of the 48 NT occurrences of ἔρημος 41 appear in the Gospels and Acts and 4 are pl. (adj. in Mark 1:45; subst. in Luke 1:80; 5:16 [cf. Mark 1:45; 8:29]). Ἐρημία appears only 4 times in the NT.

2. Except in Gal 4:27 (= "the desolate [i.e., childless] one") ἔρημος, which was in Attic still an adj. with three endings (Arrian *An.* iii.3.3; BAGD; cf. BDF §59.2), is used subst. with an ellipsis of γῆ or χώρα (BDF §241.1). It therefore refers to a lonely deserted place, a waterless and therefore uninhabited region, the *wilderness* (Matt 24:26), or the sterile *steppe,* useful only for grazing, the "grassland" (Luke 15:4; BAGD). As a geographic term it refers either to the wilderness of Judea (Matt 3:1; cf. John 11:54), i.e., the "stony, barren eastern declivity of the Judaean mountains toward the Dead Sea and lower Jordan Valley" (BAGD) and the "Araba" (= steppe, desert) of the Jordan Valley itself (Mark 1:4 par.; cf. Funk 214), or to the Arabian desert, i.e., the Sinai peninsula (Acts 7:30).

Ἐρημία denotes an uninhabited (Mark 8:4 par. Matt 15:33), therefore dangerous (2 Cor 11:26), inhospitable, and hostile (Heb 11:38) land.

Ἔρημος as an adj. can be used of a *deserted* road (Acts 8:26) or a house that is *abandoned* (Acts 1:20) or *desolate* (Matt 23:38). In 9 instances it is used to mean *lonely, secluded,* or *peaceful,* always in connection with τόπος (-οι) (e.g., Mark 6:31, 32, 35 par.).

3. At the beginning of the Gospels John appears as a preacher of repentance and a baptizer. It is in "the *desert*" that God's word encounters him (Luke 3:2) and that John carries on his work (Mark 1:4 par. Matt 3:1; Matt 11:7 par. Luke 7:24). "The desert in this context is not so much a geographical as a symbolical element, for it signifies the prophet" (Conzelmann 20n.3). He is "the voice of one crying/in the desert/prepare the way of the Lord" (Mark 1:3 par.; John 1:23 = Isa 40:3 LXX).

Against the MT and in contrast to 1QS 8:14, "in the desert" is always understood in the NT as modifying "the one crying," indeed with a reference to the LXX and rabbinic treatments (cf. Billerbeck I, 96f.; II, 154); however, the LXX text leaves the question open, as indicated above.

Jesus makes his beginning in the desert. After his baptism he is "driven out" (Mark 1:12) or "led out" (Matt 4:1) "from the Jordan (below sea level) into the highland" (BAGD 53) or "led by the Spirit into the desert/for forty days/tempted by the devil" (Luke 4:1f.; the tr. differs when ἐν is used in place of εἰς [BDF §218]; the impf. is used to describe [BDF §327], and the partc. specifies purpose or subsequent action [BDF §§339.2; 418.4]). The desert, on the one hand, mediates the nearness of God, while on the other hand it leads to the conflict with Satan. (On the difficulty of the OT origin of the motif of the 40 days cf. Kittel 658; H. Balz, *TDNT* VIII, 136-38.)

Messianic movements gather in the desert, such as the zealot groups described in Josephus *B.J.* ii.259, 261 (cf.

vi.351; vii.438) and Acts 21:38 (cf. Matt 24:26). The expectation of messianic salvation from the desert (cf. also Rev 12:6, 14) is connected to prophetic promises (Isa 40:3; Jer 31:2; Ezek 34:25; Hos 2:16; cf. Billerbeck I, 96f.). Also in the background is the historical experience of the wilderness wandering, in which Israel under the leadership of Moses experienced the nearness and faithfulness of God (Acts 13:18). Consequently in the NT Moses in the period of the wilderness can appear as a type of Jesus (Acts 3:22; 7:36-38; Heb 3:1-6), and the Church can be described as the people of God in the wilderness (Heb 3:7-11, 15-19; cf. 1 Cor 10:1-13).

As a place of God's gracious activity the wilderness is the residence of ascetics and prophets (cf. Luke 1:15, 80; 7:25 par.). But they also encounter dangers there. Besides its inhospitable nature (Heb 13:38), the desert is also the place of demons (Luke 8:29; cf. Matt 12:43 par.).

W. Radl

ἐρημόω *erēmoō* lay waste, destroy, lay bare*

Matt 12:25 par. Luke 11:17, of a kingdom *laid waste* by inner division (civil war); Rev 17:16, fig. of *stripping* (ἠρημωμένην ποιήσουσιν) a harlot (a reference to Rome); similarly 18:17: the wealth (of Rome) "*has been destroyed* in one hour"; 18:19 (ἡ πόλις).

ἐρήμωσις, εως, ἡ *erēmōsis* devastation, destruction*

Mark 13:14 par. Matt 24:15, in the apocalyptic phrase βδέλυγμα τῆς ἐρημώσεως, "abomination of *desolation*" (on the details → βδέλυγμα 3); the par. in Luke 21:20 refers instead to the *desolation* of Jerusalem. For bibliography see *TWNT* X, 1086.

ἐρίζω *erizō* quarrel*

Matt 12:19, of the παῖς: οὐκ ἐρίσει οὐδὲ κραυγάσει (cf. Isa 42:2), "he will not *quarrel* nor cry aloud." Spicq, *Notes* I, 288.

ἐριθεία, ας, ἡ *eritheia* self-interest, selfishness*

Lit.: F. BÜCHSEL, *TDNT* II, 660-61. — SPICQ, *Notes* I, 288-91.

1. The noun ἐριθεία is found 7 times in the NT, only in the Epistles, 5 times in Paul. 5 times it is sg., twice (2 Cor 12:20; Gal 5:20) it is pl.

2. The origin of this rare word, which is attested before the NT only in Aristotle *Pol.* v.3.1302b.4; 1303a.14, in the sense of selfish striving for advantage in a group, is obscure. Probably it is derived from ἐριθεύω, "be active as a laborer," and not from ἔρις.

a) In Phil 1:17 the proclaimers who are determined by *self-interest* are contrasted to those whose motivation is love (v. 16). Ἐριθεία can mean here only conduct

determined by selfishness. This is also the case in 2:3, where *self-interest* and "conceit" are contrasted with humility. Christians who act in this way are concerned with their own well-being, not that of others (cf. v. 4).

Rom 2:8 characterizes people who are determined by *selfishness* also as those who do not obey the truth, are compliant toward unrighteousness, and fall under judgment because they in their stubbornness and impenitent hearts store up for themselves wrath for the day of judgment (v. 5). However, one who patiently carries out good work and strives for glory, honor, and immortality is given eternal life by God (v. 7), because such a person does the good (v. 10), unlike those who are selfish. The context gives ἐριθεία an eschatological coloring.

Jas 3:14, 16 mentions ἐριθεία together with ζῆλος. One who has jealousy and *selfishness*, not party spirit (so F. Mussner, *Jas* [HTKNT] 169, 171; similarly M. Dibelius and H. Greeven, *Jas* [Eng. tr., Hermeneia], on 3:14), in his heart should not boast and (καὶ *consecutivum;* cf. BDF §442.2 on Jas 4:17) thus lie against the truth. Disorder and every evil deed are the consequences of jealousy and *selfishness* (v. 16). Such conduct is the characteristic of false wisdom, which is earthly, unspiritual, and demonic (v. 15). Here the word is evidently eschatologically determined.

b) The effects of self-centered conduct are probably intended in the pl. of ἐριθεία in Gal 5:20 and 2 Cor 12:20. Intrigues could be in mind here.

H. Giesen

ἔριον, ου, τό *erion* wool*

Heb 9:19: ἐρίου κοκκίνου, "red *wool*"; Rev 1:14: ἔριον λευκόν with ὡς χιών, "white *wool*, like snow" (cf. Dan 7:9).

ἔρις, ιδος, ἡ *eris* dispute, quarrel*

Lit.: SPICQ, *Notes* I, 290f. — A. VÖGTLE, *Die Tugend- und Lasterkataloge im NT* (1936) s.v. — S. WIBBING, *Die Tugend- und Lasterkataloge im NT* (1959) 81-108, esp. 96f.

1. Ἔρις occurs in the NT only in Paul (7 times) and in the Pastorals (2 times). The pl. form is ἔριδες in 1 Cor 1:11, but ἔρεις in Titus 3:9. The acc. sg. in Phil 1:15 is ἔριν (so also Titus 3:9 v.l.); see BDF §47.3.

2. Ἔρις is always used of *disputes* that endanger the Church:

a) Paul learns from Chloe's people about *quarrels* (1 Cor 1:11), i.e., factions in the church, which are traced back to an attachment of individuals to a specific apostle or teacher or to Christ (v. 12). 1 Cor 3:3, where ἔρις is paired with ζῆλος, likewise means factions in the church (v. 4). According to Phil 1:15 there are not only those who proclaim Christ out of goodwill (εὐδοκία), but also those who do so "from envy and *strife*." The context (vv. 16-18) suggests that the concern here is with the danger to the unity and the peace of the Church.

b) Ἔρις belongs to the fixed content of the Pauline vice catalogs. Gal 5:20 mentions ἔρις among the "works of the flesh." In Rom 1:29 it is numbered among the deeds of unrighteousness that are characteristic of the time before faith in Christ. Such activity has an unmistakable destructive effect in society. In Rom 13:13 and 2 Cor 12:20 ἔρις appears in a rhetorical duplication with ζῆλος (cf. already 1 Cor 3:3). In both cases there is a concern over strife and jealousy that threaten the harmony of the church.

c) In the Pastorals the vice catalogs serve in the struggle against heretics. Jealousy and contentiousness are nourished by the false teachers. One who does not possess the words of Jesus and the teaching of the Church, yet claims to possess the truth, can act only out of base motives and cause destruction (1 Tim 6:4). The overseer of the church should protect against *contentiousness* and wrangling over the law, which do not benefit (Titus 3:9). After a second warning he should exclude the sectarian from the church.   H. Giesen

ἐρίφιον, ου, τό *eriphion* kid, goat*

Diminutive of → ἔριφος. Matt 25:33: ἐρίφια ("to the left") in contrast to πρόβατα ("to the right"); cf. ἔριφος in v. 32 with the same significance.

ἔριφος, ου, ὁ *eriphos* goat*

Matt 25:32, in contrast to πρόβατα; v. 33, assimilated to → ἐρίφιον; Luke 15:29.

Ἑρμᾶς, ᾶ *Hermas* Hermas*

1. A Roman Christian greeted in Rom 16:14.

2. The author of "The Shepherd" (*ca.* A.D. 150; cf. *Herm. Vis.* 1.1.4, etc.), a brother of the Roman bishop Pius. He has no relationship to the Hermas of the NT according to the Muratorian Canon. K. Aland, *BHH* 694f.

ἑρμηνεία, ας, ἡ *hermēneia* interpretation, translation
→ ἑρμηνεύω 4.

ἑρμηνεύω *hermēneuō* interpret, translate*
διερμηνευτής, οῦ, ὁ *diermēneutēs* interpreter, translator*
διερμηνεύω *diermēneuō* translate, interpret, explain*
ἑρμηνεία, ας, ἡ *hermēneia* interpretation, translation*
μεθερμηνεύω *methermēneuō* translate*

1. Basic meaning — 2. "Translate" (into Greek) — 3. "Interpret" (the Scriptures) — 4. "Interpretation" of glossolalia — 5. Δυσερμήνευτος (Heb 5:11)

Lit.: J. Behm, *TDNT* II, 661-66. — A. C. Thiselton, *DNTT* I, 679-84. — H. Weder, "Die Gabe der *hermēneia* (1. Kor 12 und 14)," *Wirkungen hermeneutischer Theologie* (FS G. Ebeling, 1983) 99-112. — For further bibliography see *DNTT* I, 584; *TWNT* X 1086.

1. The basic meaning of the word stem ἑρμηνευ- is: *provide an expression* of something (interpret, explain, make intelligible), *give expression* to one's own (or another's) thoughts. Derived from the latter is the nuance, known in the history of religions but not used in the NT, "bring the thoughts of God (or a god) to expression, speak in ecstasy" (so in Plato and esp. also in Philo; texts in Behm 663). Likewise derived is the usual meaning *translate, interpret* (from one language into another) an existing utterance, whether oral or written.

Between the simple verb and the compounds with δι- and μεθ- there is scarcely any difference in meaning; consequently the textual tradition fluctuates between the simple and compound forms (Luke 24:27; John 1:38). In μεθερμηνεύω the prefix emphasizes the nuance of mediation (from one language to another); the meaning of the compound is limited entirely to *translate*.

2. Ἑρμηνεύω (also δι- and esp. μεθερμηνεύω) is used most frequently where foreign words, usually Hebrew or Aramaic, are translated for the Greek-speaking reader. The introductory phrase is most often ὅ/τοῦτ' ἐστιν μεθερμηνευόμενον; it can also be reduced to a mere ὅ/τοῦτ' ἐστιν. In particular it is used of:

a) Terminology such as rabbi = "teacher" (John 1:38) or Messiah = Christ (John 1:41; cf. 4:25).

b) Personal names such as Barnabas = "Son of Exhortation" (Acts 4:36) and Tabitha = "gazelle" (9:36); in 13:8 it appears that Luke wants to translate the name Elymas with ὁ μάγος, "magician" (on the philological problem, see E. Haenchen, *Acts* [Eng. tr., 1971] 398; BAGD 253).

c) A colloquial nickname such as that of the disciple Simon: Cephas/Petros = "rock" (John 1:42, though it was not there but in Matt 16:18 that the connection is first made; → Πέτρος).

d) The symbolic name Immanuel for the Messiah, which is rendered with the phrase "God (is) with us" (Matt 1:23, → Ἐμμανουήλ). The name Melchizedek is translated in Heb 7:2 for the sake of a theological statement: he is "king of righteousness" and also, it is noted, "king of Salem," which is itself translated "king of peace." Thus Hebrews introduces the interpretation of Melchizedek as the prototype, indeed as the preincarnation of Jesus, the eschatological bearer of salvation.

Such translations of biblical names for the purpose of theological interpretation is common in Hellenistic Judaism. The OT itself derived specific meanings from many names, and it appears that a type of etymological-allegorical dictionary of names existed in Alexandrian Judaism. The Hebrew names of the patriarchs and others were interpreted in Greek (under the influence of the Stoic interest in etymology). Philo, who himself knew no Hebrew, appears to have used such lists. The translations of names play an important role in his allegorical interpretation of OT figures. In addition, both translations in Heb 7:2 are known to him (*All.* iii.79). The translation of the name Melchizedek is also found in Josephus (*Ant.* i.180; *B.J.* vi.438).

e) Individual topographical names are also translated: Γολγοθά = "place of the skull" (Mark 15:22); the NT does not work out any implications from this name, but it later had effects in passion iconography and meditation: the cross of Jesus stands at the place where Adam's skull is buried and the death of Christ creates redemption for Adamic humanity. Also Σιλωάμ = "sent" (John 9:7, without apparent interpretation). The addition of the translation is by no means associated with a particular intent in all cases; it reflects merely the fact that early Christian tradition, originating in the Semitic-speaking realm, was transferred to the common speech of late antiquity during the course of the Gentile mission.

f) This is especially the case in the bilingual rendering of a few Aramaic phrases. Thus in Mark 5:41 Jesus' call to the deceased girl is given in Aramaic and Greek: Ταλιθα κουμ, "Girl . . . arise" (similarly 7:34: Εφφαθα, "be opened"). Both are given probably because of the idea of the magical effect of the original formula as such (Bultmann, *History* 221f.). (Luke and Matthew omit respectively the Aramaic words [Luke 8:54] and the call itself [Matt 9:25].) In Mark 15:34, however, a historicizing motif is the basis for giving in Aramaic Jesus' last utterance from the cross (identical to the "cry of dereliction" in v. 37), which is based on Ps 22:1(2) (cf. E. Schweizer, *Mark* [Eng. tr., 1970] ad loc.). The translation then allows it to be understood by the reader.

Nowhere in the NT is a consciousness by the authors of a difficulty in translation evident, although in view of the interpretation of many OT passages it could have been introduced. In contrast one may compare the grandson and translator of Jesus Sirach, who articulates clearly a consciousness of the problem (Sirach Prologue ll. 15-26), while Philo on the other hand accepts the Greek text of the Bible entirely as it is given, and indeed regards it as inspired and thus doubtlessly identical in meaning to the original (*Vit. Mos.* ii.37-40).

3. In Luke 24:27 (cf. also Acts 16:16 D) διερμηνεύειν (or the uncompounded form in Luke 24:27 D) means *interpret, explain, bring to expression* what is hidden. Essentially synonymous is διανοίγειν in v. 32: it refers to an "opening" of what has previously been closed. The resurrected one himself opens for the disciples a completely new understanding of the OT: The Scriptures, from Moses to "all of the prophets," refer to him, particularly to his suffering and his exaltation (v. 26). The work of Jesus, especially his death (crucifixion as the accursed death spoken of in Deut 21:23), does not harmonize with Jewish messianic expectation (vv. 19-21).

Now a new christological interpretation of the OT opens the possibility of recognizing and proclaiming Jesus as the Messiah sent by God. It is widely recognized that Luke himself expresses a central concern here (cf. J. Wanke, *Die Emmauserzählung* [1973] 85-95, 118-20).

4. Finally the word group appears with διερμηνεύω, (δι-)ἑρμηνευτής, and ἑρμηνεία in 1 Corinthians 12 and 14 in connection with speaking in tongues. Paul demands that tongue speakers express themselves in the assembly only when an ἑρμηνευτής is present and able to *translate* and make intelligible to the congregation what has been said in the tongues. Paul appears to perceive glossolalia (which he has practiced) as a type of foreign language that can to some extent be translated word for word. His consideration of "so many different languages in the world" (14:10) appears to suggest this view (O. Betz, *TDNT* IX, 295). In any case translation, like glossolalia itself, is a gift of the Spirit (12:10). It is the capacity to grasp what moves the one who speaks in tongues and to render it into normal speech. The one who speaks in tongues can also be the translator of his own glossolalia (14:5c, 13; v. 27 can also be understood in this way). However, without an additional gift, he is not able to translate. He must rather pray (v. 13). Because everyone by no means has the gift (12:30), tongue speakers (three at most!) should first ascertain whether an interpreter is present in the congregation before they begin to speak in tongues (14:27f.). → γλῶσσα 6.

Paul explains clearly the reason for such limitations: glossolalia without interpretation is indeed able to praise God, but it speaks only for itself and for God (14:2, 4a, 28b), while the church experiences no "edification," strengthening, or challenge (14:4f., οἰκοδομή). Apparently there was cause to counteract the overflowing of glossolalia in the Corinthian church assembly; those who were not so gifted became seccond-class and superfluous.

It is important that Paul does not—like Plato and Philo— use ἑρμηνεία and διερμηνεύειν for the articulation of divine mysteries on the basis of a special revelation (not even in 1 Cor 14:2!). Instead he refers to making intelligible a specific kind of human speech that is otherwise unintelligible to the listeners. Inasmuch as Paul regards the tongue speaker as a responsible subject of his speech, it is probably not suitable to speak of a "language of angels."

5. **Δυσερμήνευτος***, *difficult to explain* or *difficult to interpret, difficult to make intelligible.* The latter meaning is the one in mind in Heb 5:11 (the only NT occurrence; O. Michel, *Heb* [KEK] 234). A very serious warning is given in the tone of an accusation, which climaxes in the main statement—to which Luther took exception— that those who have once placed their lives under the gospel and have then fallen away will have no possibility of a second repentance. This warning is introduced with "Therefore we have many things to say (to you), and this (the many things) is *difficult to make intelligible.*" In view

of the receptive capacity of the hearers or readers, which has not increased since the time they became Christians (in the meantime they should have been in a position to be teachers, v. 12!), but has decreased, they have become —so the author complains—νωθροί ("indolent, dull") in understanding.

Here something like a "hermeneutical" problem resonates: the problem of mediating between the content of the gospel and the hearers, who are not disposed toward this content by their own presuppositions. However, this situation does not issue in a call for mediating spokesmen; instead, a charge is made against the readers, from whom one could have expected more in the capacity to understand spiritual things. It indicates also that the conflict lies not only on the level of the capacity for noetic understanding, but (also) on the existential level (cf. the juxtaposition of "understanding" and "right [mature] conduct," 1QS 5:23f. [Michel 234]).   N. Walter

ἑρμηνία, ας, ἡ *hermēnia* interpretation, translation

Alternative form of ἑρμηνεία.

Ἑρμῆς, οῦ *Hermēs* Hermes*

1. A Greek god (the good companion, the helper of wanderers and merchants—but also of thieves—and the mediator between gods and humans). In Lystra the crowd addresses Barnabas as Zeus and Paul as Hermes, "because he was the chief speaker" (Acts 14:12).

2. A Roman Christian greeted in Rom 16:14.

Ἑρμογένης, ους *Hermogenēs* Hermogenes*

A Christian from Asia who, among others, turned away from "Paul" (2 Tim 1:15).

ἑρπετόν, οῦ, τό *herpeton* reptile*

As a designation of an unclean animal (cf. Lev 11:10ff., 20, 23; esp. vv. 29ff.) alongside τετράποδα and πετεινά in Acts 10:12; 11:6; in a series of types of animals, which can be subdued by humans, Jas 3:7. J. Feliks, *BHH* 1005.

ἐρυθρός, 3 *erythros* red*

Acts 7:36; Heb 11:29, of the "*Red* Sea" (cf. Exod 14:9ff.).

ἔρχομαι *erchomai* come, go

1. Meaning — 2. Usage in the LXX — 3. General usage in the NT — 4. Special usage in the NT — a) The Synoptic tradition — b) The Johannine literature

Lit.: E. ARENS, *The ΗΛΘΟΝ-Sayings in the Synoptic Tradition* (OBO 10, 1976). — J. BECKER, *Johannes der Täufer und Jesus von Nazareth* (BibS[N] 63, 1972) 66-104. — J.-A. BÜH-

NER, *Der Gesandte und sein Weg im vierten Evangelium* (WUNT 2, 1977) 138-54. — BULTMANN, *History*, 153-56, 411f. — O. CAMPONOVO, *Untersuchung zu den 'Ich bin gekommen'-Worten bei den Synopt.* (Diss. Fribourg, 1975). — E. FASCHER, "Jesus der Lehrer," idem, *Sokrates und Christus* (1959) 134-74, esp. 139-56. — A. HARNACK, "'Ich bin gekommen'; Die ausdrücklichen Selbstzeugnisse Jesu über den Zweck seiner Sendung und seines Kommens," *ZTK* 22 (1912) 1-30. — E. KÄSEMANN, "The Problem of the Historical Jesus," idem, *Essays on NT Themes* (1964) 15-47. — idem, "The Beginnings of Christian Theology," *NT Questions for Today* (1969) 82-104. — W. G. KÜMMEL, *Promise and Fulfillment* (1957) 25-36, 105-21. — H. PATSCH, *Abendmahl und historischer Jesus* (CTM A/1, 1972) 108-15, 170-80. — N. PERRIN, *Rediscovering the Teaching of Jesus* (1967) 54-82. — J. SCHNEIDER, *TDNT* II, 666-84; II, 926-28. — SCHULZ, *Q* 258-60. — G. THEISSEN, *Sociology of Early Palestinian Christianity* (1978) 10f. — For further bibliography see *TWNT* X, 1086.

1. The vb. ἔρχομαι, attested since Homer, means *come* and *go*. It is used with respect to persons, the time, things, and events and is further defined with such prep. prefixes as ἀπό, εἰς, ἐξ, and πρός. The significant (fig. or cultic) use of the word in biblical literature for the spiritual coming of God (or a god) has its analogies in ancient prayer texts, magical papyri, and hymns: with the fixed formulas ἔρχου, ἐλθέ (μοι), εἴσελθε, etc., a person begs for the epiphany of the deity (Schneider 666 gives many texts).

2. In the LXX ἔρχομαι stands as an equivalent normally for *bw'* (and sporadically for 34 other Hebrew words), primarily with the literal-local meaning: Animals *come* to drink, Gen 30:38; Abraham goes to Canaan, 12:5; Joseph to his brothers, 37:19. In the fig. sense it can refer to times or generations that come and go (2 Chr 21:19; Ps 70:18; Eccl 1:4, etc.), or to misfortune, suffering, and death that *come* upon persons (e.g., Pss 43:18; 54:16). The psalmist complains that fear and trembling have *come* upon him (Ps 54:6: φόβος καὶ τρόμος ἦλθεν ἐπ' ἐμέ); he requests that his entreaty *come* before God (Ps 101:2), that God's mercy *come* over him, that God himself rush to his aid (Pss 118:41; 79:3). According to 1 Kgdms 9:16 Israel's cry for help has *come* to God (ἦλθε βοὴ αὐτῶν πρός μέ), like the cry over Sodom and Gomorrah (Gen 18:21).

In the eschatological sayings of the OT ἔρχομαι or the synonym ἥκω is firmly anchored as a t.t. Faith anticipates judgment and salvation: God *comes* to judge the earth (Pss 95:13; 97:9); his day (or the days of the Lord) will *come* and will be dreadful (Joel 3:4; Zech 14:1; Mal 3:22; Hos 9:7). But God also *comes* to save his people and *comes* with power . . . , μετὰ ἰσχύος ἔρχεται (Isa 40:10f.; cf. also 35:4; 59:20; Ps 49:2; Zech 14:5ff.; and esp. Isa 61:1ff.). Then the people will *come* to Zion (Isa 60:5f.; Jer 16:19; Hag 2:7). Yahweh himself *comes* and assembles them: ἔρχομαι συναγαγεῖν πάντα τὰ ἔθνη . . . (Isa 66:18).

Hope for salvation is expressed also in terms of messianic expectation. The Messiah is the *coming one* in the absolute sense, "he who *comes* in the name of the Lord" (Ps 117:26); "see, your king *comes* to you"—ἰδοὺ ὁ βασιλεύς σου ἔρχεται σοι (Zech 9:9). It is also said of the Son of Man in the primary passage, Dan 7:13, that he *comes* on the clouds of heaven (ἤρχετο or ἐρχόμενος ἦν).

3. NT usage corresponds (generally) to usage in secular Greek and the LXX. Most of the 631 NT occurrences (besides *ca.* 760 of the various compounds) mean *come* or *go* in the literal-local sense: people *come* to the Jordan for baptism, the sick who seek help *come* to Jesus (Matt 2:1f.; 3:7; 8:2, etc.), the festal pilgrims *go* a day's journey (ἦλθον ἡμέρας ὁδόν), Jesus *goes* to Capernaum or *comes* into the house of Peter or into his city (Luke 2:44; Matt 4:13; 8:14; 9:1, etc.).

The NT also uses the vb. fig. as it was used in speech of the time: rivers of water *pour (come)*, Satan *comes* (Matt 7:25, 27; Mark 4:15), days will *come*, occasions for vexation and apostasy *come* (cf. Matt 9:15; Luke 17:22; 21:6; 23:29; Matt 17:1; 18:7), the hour *comes*, so also the wrath or the judgment (cf. Mark 14:4; John 4:21, 23; Eph 5:6; Col 3:6; Rev 3:10; cf. Acts 2:20; Rev 3:3; 16:15). Paul marks the turning point of salvation with the use of ἔϱχομαι: the law has *come;* until faith *came* we were subjected to it; it was valid until the seed *came*, to whom the promise was given; with Christ the fullness of time *has come* (Rom 7:9; Gal 3:19, 23ff.; 4:4). The vb. is also used of the *coming* aeon (ὁ αἰὼν ὁ ἐϱχόμενος = ὁ μέλλων, Mark 10:30; Luke 18:30; cf. Eph 2:7). Luke speaks once of the *coming* sabbath (Acts 13:44).

A few expressions also attested outside the NT deserve mention: Mark 5:26: εἰς τὸ χεῖϱον ἐλθεῖν, "become (continually) worse," here of the condition of the woman with the issue of blood; Luke 15:17: εἰς ἑαυτὸν ἐλθεῖν, "he *came* to himself"; Acts 19:27: εἰς ἀπελεγμὸν ἐλθεῖν, "*come* into disrepute"; in 2 Cor 12:1 Paul makes the transition to a new point with ἐλθεῖν εἴς τι, "*come* to speak about something."

4. a) In the center of both Jesus' proclamation and early Christian preaching are those statements that speak of the coming of God's sovereignty, of the coming of Jesus, and of the coming of people to Jesus. Central to the content of Jesus' message is God's sovereignty (→ βασιλεία τοῦ θεοῦ). The references are both present and future. Jesus announces the imminence of God's sovereignty; he reckons in faith with its arrival in the near future and prays: "Your kingdom/sovereignty *come*" (Matt 6:10 par. Luke 11:2). The disciples are promised that they will not taste death until they see God's sovereignty *come* in power (Mark 9:1; cf. also 13:28; Matt 10:23; cf. Kümmel, 25ff.). An urgent imminent expectation is expressed in this saying, which Jesus shares with John the Baptist and the community of Qumran. Such a (time-conditioned) hope has not been fulfilled; as an unfulfilled promise it entered into the treasury of faith of the Christian Church.

The message of Jesus is not thus discredited, for its unmistakable characteristic lies not in the futuristic, but rather in the present kingdom of God statements. Jesus, in contrast to his own time and to the irritation of many of his contemporaries, affirms the presence of God's sovereignty already in what he says and

does. Here his self-understanding and self-consciousness are evident in a striking way (Luke 11:20 par. Matt 12:28 in connection with Luke 10:18; Mark 3:27 par.; Matt 11:12; Luke 16:16; and esp. Luke 17:20f.; cf. also Kümmel 109ff.; 43f.; Käsemann, "Problem" 43f.; Perrin 63ff.).

In the futuristic sayings about the (imminent) coming of the kingdom of God it is affirmed that God is not yet "all in all"; in the present sayings it is emphasized that the sovereignty of God is also already present: the boundary between present and future has already been torn; Jesus proclaims his time as an integrated part of the time of salvation, as the "fully valid beginning of the total future" (Becker 82). His eschatology can be appropriately described as "eschatology in the process of being realized."

Perrin has suggested that Jesus, in contrast to Jewish and early Christian terminology, "regularly uses the verb 'to come' in connection with the Kingdom" and avoids other verbs (58). *Come* is suitable, corresponding to the dialectic of present and future, to express the relationship of doing and allowing, of activity and passivity for the arrival of the sovereignty of God.

In a series of "'I'-sayings" (Bultmann 150ff.) Jesus speaks comprehensively of the purpose of his coming: Luke 12:49: "I *have come* (ἦλθον) to cast fire upon the earth"; cf. Matt 5:17; 10:34; Mark 2:17 par. Matt 9:13/Luke 5:32 (and cf. Mark 1:38 par. Luke 4:43; the Markan εἰς τοῦτο γὰϱ ἐξῆλθον is taken up by Luke with ἐπὶ τοῦτο ἀπεστάλην; further ἀπεστάλην sayings are in Matt 10:40; 15:24; Luke 10:16; Mark 9:37; → ἀποστέλλω). Closely related to the ἦλθον sayings are a few sayings, transposed from the first into the third person sg., that characterize the sending of Jesus with the use of the titular ὁ υἱὸς τοῦ ἀνθϱώπου (Mark 10:45 par. Matt 20:28; Luke 19:10 [cf. the v.l. of Matt 18:11 and Luke 9:56a]; 7:33f. par. Matt 11:18f.).

In critical scholarship sayings that begin with *I have come* or *I have not come* are widely considered church formations "because with this terminology they seem only to gather up the significance of the appearance of Jesus as a whole" (Bultmann 156); they allow "the voice of the exalted Lord to be heard through the mouth of a prophet" (Käsemann, "Beginning" 97). Such an (all-inclusive) evaluation is scarcely correct. It is undoubtedly true that not all of the ἦλθον sayings are authentic as we now have them. Early Christian tradition thoroughly shaped and formed them (e.g., by the reception of the Son of Man christology). It formed variants, making use of authentic sayings of Jesus at its disposal to serve as a "point of departure." Thus Luke 7:33f. par. (without the Son of Man title) is totally unquestioned; likewise Luke 12:49; 12:51 par.; Mark 2:17; and the essential basis of Mark 10:45. The latter passage is, in the history-of-religions environment, characteristic of the "work" of Jesus and not derived from post-Easter theology (Patsch 170ff.). The ἦλθον sayings give information about Jesus' self-understanding, as do Mark 2:27; 7:15; and the "Amen, I say to you" of the antitheses, which also depict Jesus' consciousness of being sent. He has come as the savior of sinners, as a "ransom for the many."

The question of the Baptist, "Are you the one who is to come (σὺ εἶ ὁ ἐρχόμενος), or must we wait for another?" is answered positively with a reference to the prophetic promises being fulfilled in Jesus (cf. Isa 29:18f.; 35:5f.; 61:1); Jesus is the coming one of the promise; the Church confesses him as the one who has come; the self-consciousness of Jesus brings to expression here, analogous to the content of the ἦλθον sayings of the (certainly authentic) macarism: "And blessed is the one who takes no offense in me" (Luke 7:18-23 par. Matt 11:2-6).

The coming of people to Jesus is described in various ways with the use of ἔρχομαι. In a general and unspecific way it can mean that the crowd, Pharisees and scribes among others, *come* to Jesus (e.g., Mark 2:13; 3:8; 7:1, etc.); such a coming has another dimension where the healing power of Jesus is experienced (cf. Mark 5:33; Matt 8:2; 9:18; 15:25) or his meaning is recognized: the wise men from the East *have come* to worship the newborn king (Matt 2:2). The disciples also have *come* to Jesus; they have given up home, family, and possessions and—as "wanderers" like Jesus (cf. Theissen 10f.)—they have accepted discipleship for themselves; cf. Mark 1:18, 20; 8:34 par. (ἔρχεσθαι ὀπίσω μου is synonymous here with ἀκολουθεῖν); 10:28f.; Luke 6:47.

b) In John and the Johannine letters ἔρχομαι has come to be used in christological statements in a striking way. John 5:43; 7:28; 8:14, 42; 9:39; 10:10; 12:47; 13:3; 16:28; 18:37 say of the Johannine Christ that he has come from God; as the one sent by God he is the Messiah. He comes not in his own name, but in the name of the Father. His coming means life and light for the dark and dead world. He has come to save the cosmos; he does this because he witnesses to the truth. Ἔρχομαι is also used of the return of the Johannine Christ (14:3; 21:22f.). The time between his first and second comings is "bridged" by the coming (15:26; 16:7) and the presence (14:16, 26; cf. 1 John 2:1) of the Paraclete. Docetic christology denies the confessional statement that "Jesus Christ *has come* in the flesh" (. . . ἐν σαρκὶ ἐληλυθώς, 1 John 4:2; 2 John 7).

The specific Johannine reference to "the coming of the hour" deserves special mention. It is used, on the one hand, for the time of salvation that approaches in Jesus (John 4:21, 23; 5:25: . . . ἔρχεται ὥρα καὶ νῦν ἐστιν) and also for Jesus' hour of suffering and death, which in Johannine theology is the hour of his glorification: 7:30 and 8:20 affirm that Jesus' hour has not yet come, while Jesus says or knows in 12:23; 17:1; and 13:1 that "the hour *has come* when the Son of Man will be glorified."

T. Schramm

ἐρῶ *erō* I will say

Fut. of → λέγω, → εἶπον (see BDF §101 s.v. λέγειν).

ἐρωτάω *erōtaō* ask, request

1. Occurrences and usage in the NT — 2. *Ask* — 3. *Request*

Lit.: G. T. D. ANGEL, *DNTT* II, 879-81. — H. N. BREAM, " 'No Need to Be Asked Questions': A Study of John 16:30," FS R. T. Stamm (1969) 49-74. — H. GREEVEN, *TDNT* II, 685-89. — For further bibliography see *TWNT* X, 1086f.

1. In the LXX the vb., like its compound → ἐπερωτάω, has only the meaning *ask*, while "request" is expressed with αἰτέω. The presence of both meanings with the one word in the NT may be explained as the result of Hellenistic secular usage (Deissmann, *Light* 168, n. 2, 181, n. 12 to p. 179) as well as the influence of the ambiguous Heb. *š'l* ("ask, request") and the similarly ambiguous Lat. *rogare*. Of the 63 NT occurrences, 27 (leaving out John 8:7) have the meaning *ask* and 36 have the meaning *request*.

2. The meaning *ask* is limited to the Gospels, but is never found in Q. Mark has it only twice (4:10 for an indirect question, 8:5 for a direct question), alongside the more frequent word → ἐπερωτάω. Three times Matthew reduces it from the compound in the Markan text (16:13; 19:17; 21:24) and gives it the same function of introducing a disputed question that the compound has. In Luke the simple form (6 occurrences + Acts 1:6) is used 4 times in place of the Markan compound (9:45; 20:3; 22:68; 23:3), and in 19:31 it appears precisely as a hyponym for εἶπον in Mark. It is frequent only in John (15 occurrences), where the usage corresponds to that of the compound. Special accents are to be seen in two passages:

Luke 14:32 uses redactionally the LXX version of the common Hebrew greeting formula "inquire about the condition of someone" (G. Gerlemann, *THAT* II, 842). Thus the simple form with the mere acc. here does not mean "request" (against BAGD s.v.; Greeven). Instead, the total syntactical construction refers to the act of "submission" (E. Klostermann, *Luke* [HNT, ²1929] ad loc.): the greeting as such depicts a ritualized act of diminishing aggression.

John 16:23 is christologically important: In the time of the post-Easter presence of Jesus as the Paraclete (16:13), it is no longer necessary to *consult* Jesus. This is confirmed in anticipation by the disciples (Bream): Everyone (not only the disciples) is freed from the dubious pressure of *consulting* Jesus through the oracles of false prophets (cf. *Herm. Man.* xi.2-5; R. E. Brown, *John* [AB] ad loc.).

3. The preferred meaning *request* is seen in Luke (9 occurrences + 6 in Acts) and John (12 occurrences + 1 John 5:16; 2 John 5), while the only Markan passage, 7:26, is also taken over and transferred to Matt 15:23. In Phil 4:3; 1 Thess 4:1; 5:12; 2 Thess 2:1 epistolary exhor-

tations are introduced in an explicitly performative way (first person ind. pres.: "with these words"—cf. also Luke 14:18f.; 16:27; 2 John 5; synonymous to → παρακαλέω in Phil 4:2; 1 Thess 4:1; Luke 7:3f.; 8:37 [cf. Mark 5:17]; in Luke 8:31 παρακαλέω is taken up and then replaced in 8:38 by another synonym, → δέομαι). In John 16:26 and 1 John 5:16 αἰτέω is used synonymously.

With this meaning, the word is used as a circumlocution for a friendly request to do something, most often in indirect speech. In Luke this is normally done with the inf. (Luke 5:3; 8:37; Acts 3:3; 10:48; 16:39; 18:20; 23:18; cf. also John 4:40; 1 Thess 5:12; 2 Thess 2:1) or ὅπως (Luke 7:3; 11:37; Acts 23:20), in John most often with ἵνα (4:47; 17:15, 20; 19:31, 38; 2 John 5; cf. also Mark 7:26; Luke 7:36; 16:27; 1 Thess 4:1). Less frequent is direct discourse with a direct imv. (Matt 15:23; Luke 14:18f.; Phil 4:3; John 4:31; or the polite request in John 12:21).

In John the vb. is used of Jesus' prayer: Jesus speaks in advance of his prayer for those who belong to him (14:16), and then the prayer itself is recorded (17:9 [bis], 15, 20). But after Easter such an *intercession* is no longer regarded as necessary (16:26). Also in 1 John 5:16 the vb. is used of the Church's prayer of request.

W. Schenk

ἐσθής, ῆτος, ἡ *esthēs* clothing, garment*

Luke 23:11, of the splendid (white) *garment* placed on Jesus by Herod Antipas (cf. A. Oepke, *TDNT* IV, 17), apparently to ridicule him as "messianic" king (see also W. Grundmann, *Luke* [THKNT] ad loc.; G. Schneider, *Luke* [ÖTK] ad loc.); cf. also Acts 12:21: ἐσθὴς βασιλική, of the *royal robes* of King Herod Agrippa I; in Jas 2:2, 3 ἐσθὴς λαμπρά is used of the "splendid *garment*" of the rich man in contrast to the "shabby *garment*" (ἐσθὴς ῥυπαρά) of the poor man (v. 2b); in Luke 24:4 (ἐσθὴς ἀστράπτουσα, "dazzling *apparel*") and Acts 1:10 (ἐν ἐσθήσεσι λευκαῖς, "in white *garments*") the word indicates the heavenly origin of both men; on the dat. ending -ήσεσιν (Acts 1:10; Luke 24:4 C Koine Θ) in place of -ῆσιν, see BDF §47.4.

ἐσθίω, ἔσθω *esthiō, esthō* (2nd aor.: ἔφαγον *ephagon*) eat*

1. Occurrences in the NT — 2. Forms — 3. Meaning — 4. Usage

Lit.: J. Behm, *TDNT* II, 689-95. — G. Braumann, *DNTT* II, 271-73. — G. Gerleman, *THAT* I, 138-42. — M. Ottosson, *TDOT* I, 236-42. — R. Smend, "Essen und Trinken—ein Stück Weltlichkeit des AT," *Beiträge zur alttestamentlichen Theologie* (FS W. Zimmerli, 1977) 446-59. — For further bibliography see *TWNT* X, 1087.

1. The vb. occurs 158 times in the NT and is concentrated in Matthew (24 occurrences), Mark (27), Luke (33), John (15), Acts (7), Romans (13, all in ch. 14), 1 Corinthians (27, most in chs. 8–11), and Revelation (6). It appears also in 2 Thess 3:8, 10, 12; Heb 10:27; 13:10; Jas 5:3.

a) Ἐσθίω is often used in parallelism with πίνω (Matt 6:25, 31; 11:18, 19; 24:49; 26:26; Mark 2:16; Luke 5:30, 33; 7:33, 34; 10:7; 12:19, 29, 45; 13:26; 17:8, 27, 28; 22:30; John 6:53; Acts 9:9; 23:12, 21; 1 Cor 9:4; 10:7, 31; 11:22, 26, 27, 28, 29; 15:32; Rom 14:21; see also Smend, 446-59). In a few cases it is completed with the pass. of χορτάζω, "be full" (Mark 6:42 par.; 8:8; Matt 15:37; John 6:26).

b) Frequent objs. are ἄρτος (Mark 3:20; 7:5; Matt 15:2; Luke 7:33; 14:1, 5; John 6:23; 1 Cor 11:26f.; 2 Thess 3:8, 12) and its pl. (Mark 2:26 par.; 6:44; 7:2; with the prep. ἐκ, John 6:26, 50, 51; 1 Cor 11:28). Other objs. are τὸ πάσχα (Mark 14:12 par.; 14:14 par.; Luke 22:15, 16; John 18:28), σάρξ (John 6:52f.) and its pl. (Jas 5:3; Rev 17:16; 19:18), καρπός (Mark 11:14; 1 Cor 9:7), κρέας (1 Cor 8:13; Rom 14:21), and τὸ μάννα (John 6:31, 49).

Ἐσθίω is used with the preps. ἐκ, παρά, and μετά. Μετά is used of eating with others (e.g., "with my disciples," Mark 14:14; Luke 22:11; in reference to the betrayer, Mark 14:18; in reference to a Pharisee's invitation, Luke 7:36).

c) Subjects of ἐσθίειν (φαγεῖν) in the NT are primarily human beings: Only rarely is it used of animals (Mark 7:28 par. Matt 15:27; Luke 15:16; Rev 17:16; 19:18). It is used also of destructive elements (Jas 5:3: rust; Heb 10:27: fire).

2. In accord with Greek tense usage, the pres. ἐσθίω is used primarily to describe a continuous, linear activity, while the 2nd aor. ἔφαγον is used of punctiliar action (BDF §318). The future φάγομαι is formed from the aorist (BDF §74.2). The two defective vbs. are frequently used as equivalents (cf. Rom 14:2). The form ἔσθω at times underlies the partc. (ἔσθων in text variants in Mark 1:6; Luke 7:33, 34; 10:7) and also stands behind ἔσθητε (Luke 22:30; cf. Num 15:19; BDF §101 s.v.).

3. Ἐσθίω designates the basic human act of receiving nourishment and means *eat, feed oneself.* Alongside these simple meanings, the vb. can be translated to reflect its social element as *have a meal, dine.* In the Pharisaic charges ἐσθίω takes on a negative aspect like Germ. *schlemmen* (Eng. feast, gorge). Fig. usage in John is to be noted. The meaning *devour, consume* is used with respect to animals and the destructive elements of rust and fire (→ 1.c).

4. a) In the Gospels ἐσθίω is used of the simple food intake of John the Baptist (Mark 1:6), whose ascetic life is contrasted to the way of life of Jesus (Matt 11:8 par. Luke 7:33f.), whose meals with "tax collectors and sin-

ners" are criticized (in Mark 2:16; Matt 9:11; Luke 5:30 the disciples are included in the charge; cf. Luke 15:2). The disciples themselves are compared with the disciples of the Baptist, who fast (Luke 5:33; Mark 2:18; and Matt 9:14 formulate it as a contrasting pair: fast—do not fast), and are rebuked by the Pharisees and scribes for not holding to the Jewish tradition in matters of eating (Mark 7:5; Matt 15:2).

In two parallel sayings in the Lukan mission speech (Luke 10:7, 8) *eating* what is at hand and offered to those who are sent out is considered compensation and payment for their activity (cf. 1 Cor 9:4, 13; 2 Thess 3:8). Without a concrete subj. the impf. ἤσθιον in Luke 17:27, 28, which is best translated *one ate,* appears with other words that belong to the "worldly" sphere of activity and that signify the lack of concern characteristic of humanity.

The vb. also appears in the Synoptic reports of the Last Supper in Jesus' reference to the betrayer, "*who eats with me*" (Mark 14:18), and in reference to the Last Supper event itself (partc. in v. 22 par. Matt 26:26) and as an eschatological preview of the "*eating* and drinking at my table in my kingdom" (Luke 22:30). In Mark 7:28 par. Matt 15:27 ἐσθίω is used of dogs, a figure for Gentiles, who also want to participate in the messianic salvation. In Luke 15:16 it is used of the pigs in the parable of the lost son.

In the Pauline corpus ἐσθίω occurs in connection with the question about the permissibility of eating meat offered to idols (1 Cor 8:7, 10; 10:18, 25, 27, 28, 31). It is also used in the argument over whether the proclaimer and benefactor in spiritual matters can lay claim to material gifts as remuneration; Paul did not lay claim to these gifts (1 Cor 9:13; cf. 9:4; Luke 10:5-8; 2 Thess 3:8). Ἐσθίω also appears in connection with the dispute over eucharistic practice (1 Cor 11:26, 27, 28, 29). The Romans were also moved by a dispute over *eating* that was similar to the dispute in Corinth. The dispute in Rome concerned whether or not a vegetarian diet should be followed (Rom 14:2, 3, 6, 20).

The exhortation in 2 Thess 3:10, 12 apparently involves those who misunderstand the reality to which work belongs because of their eschatological expectation. Ἐσθίω is figuratively used of the fire that will *devour/consume* the sinner in Heb 10:27.

b) Aor. ἔφαγον is more commonly used in the NT than ἐσθίω as an expression for an action taking place at a particular point in time.

In the opening and concluding statements of the section in Matt 6:25 par. Luke 12:22 and Matt 6:31 par. Luke 12:29 (Q), Jesus warns against anxiety concerning food. In a defense against Pharisaic charges Jesus refers to the example of David, who, along with his followers, *ate* the showbread in the temple (Mark 2:26 par.). The activity of proclaiming often does not leave Jesus and his dis-

ciples the time to eat (3:20; 6:31). On the other hand, concern directed to the hearers who have endured a long time leads to the question of what they shall *eat* (6:36; 8:1). In the miracle of the feeding Jesus demonstrates in the giving of bread and fish that he is the giver of life (6:37 par.; 6:42 par.; 6:44 [φαγόντες] par. Matt 14:21 [ἐσθίοντες]; Mark 8:1, 2 par. Matt 15:32; Mark 8:8 par. Matt 15:37; cf. John 6:5, 23). In the healing of the daughter of the synagogue leader (Mark 5:35-43), Jesus also shows that he is the one who provides. After the recovery of the sick child and her return to normal human life, Jesus gives the command to give the girl something to *eat* (v. 43). Φαγεῖν τὸ πάσχα (Mark 14:12 par.; 14:14 par.; Luke 22:15, 16; John 18:18) refers primarily to the eating of the lamb (cf. 2 Esdr 6:20-21).

In addition to the usage which he holds in common with Mark, Matthew has ἔφαγον in other passages. In relation to the question of purity and impurity Matthew adds, in accordance with his more precise description of Jewish purity laws (Matt 15:2), a clarifying clause declaring unmistakably that "*eating* with unwashed hands does not defile a man" (15:20). A decisive criterion at the final judgment is earthly conduct, particularly readiness to give the hungry something *to eat* (25:35, 42). In Matthew's Last Supper account the imv. φάγετε (without par.) probably appears as a strengthening of the imv. λάβετε (26:26).

Luke 4:2 emphasizes (over against the simple statement in the Matthean temptation story that Jesus fasted) the absoluteness of Jesus' fasting with the double denial: "and he *ate* nothing at all." Frequently Luke uses the term in meal situations: at banquets where Jesus is a participant (7:36; 14:1, 15), and on the occasion of the return of the son (15:23). Eating can thus have a function of indicating mutuality. Elsewhere eating in and of itself can be a sign of folly, as in the parable of the foolish farmer (12:19), and of thoughtlessness (13:26; cf. 17:27). The unworthy servant brings food and drink to his master and can then sit down to eat (17:8). Jesus' eating before the eyes of his disciples after the resurrection attests to the reality of the resurrected one and to the unity of Jesus' existence before and after his death (24:43).

In John the same word is used on various levels. The fig. use (4:32; 6:50, 51) corresponds to the literal usage (4:31, 33; 6:26, 31, 49, 52, 58). Within the eucharistic speech, of course, the activity of eating becomes understandable (6:52, 53) only as a sacramental-real event. Thus ἔφαγον is replaced by the even stronger equivalent τρώγω (bite, chew, 6:54, 56, 57, 58).

In Acts ἔφαγον appears in three contexts. At the end of the first part of the narrative of Paul's call it signifies the situation between conversion and commissioning as a time of self-denial (9:9). In a revelatory experience regarding those things which are, in the Jewish sense, clean and unclean, the command is given to Peter to kill and *eat* (10:13). He refuses because of his belief that the stipulations regarding food were still binding (10:14; 11:7). Finally, the phrase "neither to *eat* or drink" is found twice in oaths by Paul's opponents for the period of time until they have killed him (23:12, 21).

Paul uses ἔφαγον and the present form ἐσθίω in responding to the question of whether it is permissible to eat meat that has been offered to idols (1 Cor 8:8, 13). In 9:4 he defends himself against charges concerning his apostolic office (cf. 9:1f.) which deny his authority to accept food and drink for his proclamation. Nevertheless he has from the beginning refused this right (cf. 9:12b), as 2 Thess 3:8 likewise indicates. In the OT material used parenetically here (1 Cor 10:1-5), Paul can concede to the people of God in the wilderness *food* analogous to the eucharist (v. 3). At the same time he warns the Christian Church—again with an OT model—that a fateful chasm exists between the possession of the sacrament and life. The activity of eating, drinking, and dancing, introduced from the Scripture citation, are seen not simply as purely this-worldly acts, but are rather to be understood from the OT background as idolatry (cf. Exod 32:6). "*Eat* the Lord's Supper" (1 Cor 11:20) has a structural similarity to the phrase "*eat* the Passover" (cf. *Did.* 9:5; Heb 13:10). What is spoken of here is a meal eaten to satisfy hunger, which led to disregard of the brother (1 Cor 11:21), as well as the eucharist itself. A brotherly admonition in 11:33 concludes the discussion of the grievances: "come together *to eat*" probably refers to the entire celebration, as does the introductory phrase "*to eat* the Lord's Supper" (v. 20). The summons, "let us *eat* and drink" (15:32), is for Paul the unavoidable and necessary consequence for one who does not reckon with the resurrection of the dead and for whom an imminent death is final.

In Rom 14:2 Paul uses φαγεῖν and ἐσθίειν alongside each other, which suggests a certain interchangeability. In the context of the dispute between the "strong" and the "weak" concerning the eating of meat, Paul makes two demands: First, one's own action is to be in harmony with his brother, i.e., when the brother is offended, one should not *eat* meat (14:21); secondly, one should listen to one's own conscience, which makes itself known in the form of διακρίνειν, i.e., in misgiving and doubt (14:23).

Heb 13:10 alludes to the eucharist (cf. 1 Cor 11:20), in which those who belong to the OT order have no part. In Jas 5:3 the image of the *consuming* or *devouring* fire is spoken to the rich as a warning.

In Revelation ἔφαγον is used metaphorically in two passages. "*Eating* of the tree of life" (2:7) is a fig. eschatological promise of eternal life. The background is the tree of life in Paradise (cf. Gen 3:22). The idea of "*consuming* the little book" (10:10) comes from the OT

call narrative in Ezek 2:8–3:3 and signifies here also the commission to proclaim salvation and damnation. As in Jas 5:3, ἔφαγον is to be rendered *devour, consume,* and refers to the judging and punishing activity done in 17:16 by the beast to the harlot (Babylon-Rome) and in 19:18 by the birds of prey to the hostile powers of the antichrist. The OT background for the first image is Ezek 23:25ff. (καταφαγεῖν) and Dan 7:7 (ἐσθίειν). Ezek 39:17-20 is the background for the second image (φαγεῖν). The reference to "*eating* meat offered to idols" refers to concrete situations in the church (2:14, 20). The text suggests that the reference is to libertinistic false teachings that have seduced the church (2:15, Nicolaitans; 2:20, false prophets).

H.-J. van der Minde

Ἐσλί *Hesli* Esli*

An ancestor of Joseph named in the genealogy of Jesus (Luke 3:25).

ἔσοπτρον, ου, τό *esoptron* mirror*

Lit.: BAGD s.v. (bibliography). — H. CONZELMANN, *1 Cor* (Eng. tr., Hermeneia) ad loc. — SPICQ, *Notes* I, 292-95. — L. T. JOHNSON, "The Mirror of Remembrance (James 1:22-25)," *CBQ* 50 (1988) 632-45. — G. KITTEL, *TDNT* I, 180.

Jas 1:23, in the literal sense: κατανοοῦντι τὸ πρόσωπον . . . ἐν ἐσόπτρῳ. Here the ephemeral nature of the image in the mirror is accented (v. 24). 1 Cor 13:12, fig.: "we see [God] now through a *mirror* only in an obscure way" (because direct sight is not yet possible).

ἑσπέρα, ας, ἡ *hespera* evening*

Luke 24:29: πρὸς ἑσπέραν ἐστίν, "it is toward *evening*"; Acts 4:3; 28:23: ἀπὸ πρωὶ ἕως ἑσπέρας.

ἑσπερινός, 3 *hesperinos* of the evening*

Of the first, or "evening," watch of the night (Luke 12:38 D λ it).

Ἑσρώμ *Hesrōm* Hezron*

One of the ancestors in the genealogy of Jesus (Matt 1:3; Luke 3:33; cf. 1 Chr 2:5 [v.l.], 9; Ruth 4:18f., Ἑσρών, v.l. in v. 18, Ἑσρώμ).

ἑσσόομαι *hessoomai* be weaker, be inferior*

2 Cor 12:13: ὃ ἡσσώθητε . . . (v.l. ἡττήθητε), "in what way *were you the loser* in comparison to the other churches. . . ?"

ἔσχατος, 3 *eschatos* latter; last

1. Occurrences in the NT — 2. Colloquial usage — 3. The reward of the disciples — 4. Dispute among the

disciples — 5. Different eschatological meanings in Paul — 6. As an eschatological t.t. in post-Pauline literature — 7. The "last day" in John — 8. The self-understanding of the revealer in Revelation

Lit.: J. BAUMGARTEN, *Paulus und die Apokalyptik* (WMANT 44, 1975) 99-110. — E. GRÄSSER, *Hebr 1,1-4* (EKKNT [V] 3, 1971) 55-91. — G. KITTEL, *TDNT* II, 697f. — H.-G. LINK, *DNTT* II, 55-59. — U. LUZ, *Das Geschichtsverständnis des Paulus* (BEvT 49, 1968) 332-58. — W. C. VAN UNNIK, "Der Ausdruck ἕως ἐσχάτου τῆς γῆς (Apg 1,8) und sein alttestamentlicher Hintergrund," *idem, Sparsa Collecta* I (1973), 386-401. — For further bibliography see *TWNT* X, 1087.

1. This adj. appears 52 times in the NT: 10 in Matthew, 5 in Mark, 6 in Luke, 7 in John, 3 in Acts, 5 in Paul (all in 1 Corinthians), 6 in Revelation, and elsewhere in 2 Tim 3:1; Heb 1:2; Jas 5:3; 1 Pet 1:5, 20; 2 Pet 2:20; 3:3; 1 John 2:18 (bis); and Jude 18. The adv. ἐσχάτως appears only in Mark 5:23.

2. In much of the NT ἔσχατος appears with various colloquial associations: The vineyard owner sends his son to the tenants as *last in a series* (= finally, Mark 12:6); the servants are not the only ones killed, for the heir is also. When the Sadducees ask Jesus about the resurrection, they report that after the death of the seven brothers, "the wife died as the *last* of all" (Mark 12:22); Matthew and Luke use ὕστερον instead of ἔσχατος, as does Matt 21:37 (ὕστερον, which is more frequent than ἔσχατος in Matthew, designates a temporal sequence in the sense of "later, subsequently" rather than the irrevocable end, which is expressed with ἔσχατος). This sense ("last") is also to be seen in the reference to the *last* day (the seventh or eighth) as the high point of the seven-day Feast of Tabernacles (John 7:37). Payment of the *last* (remaining) penny represents the total liquidation of debt in the course of a legal dispute as a necessary element of reconciliation before coming to worship (Matt 5:26 par. Luke 12:59).

Τὰ ἔσχατα is used comparatively (pl. except in Matt 27:64): At the return of the unclean spirits "*later* (τὰ ἔσχατα) it will be worse for the man than before" (Matt 12:45 par. Luke 11:26). In the eyes of the chief priests and Pharisees the resurrection is, in comparison with the life of Jesus, "the *last* fraud," which is greater than the first (Matt 27:64). Likewise, to return to a life entangled with the world—after the liberation from it through the knowledge of Jesus Christ—is regarded as worse than the original entanglement (2 Pet 2:20). Before the charges against the church of Thyatira, there is praise of the trend to growth: "your *latter* works are more [more numerous, greater] than the first" (Rev 2:19).

In a geographic indication of the horizon of service, Acts takes literally the promise to Isaiah (49:6) and applies it to Paul and Barnabas: "to the *end* of the earth" (13:47; cf. 1:8). Only once is ἔσχατος used adv. in the sense of "lying *at the last gasp/at the point of death*" (of the daughter of Jairus, Mark 5:23).

3. The saying, "the *last* will be first and the first will be *last*" (or inverted: Mark 10:31 par. Matt 19:30) is originally a "free logion" referring to the "reversal of earthly relationships" (Bultmann, *History* 177; Link 57: "How quickly man's fortunes change overnight"), and is used secondarily in various contexts with varying perspectives (Luke 13:22ff.: many-few; 14:7ff.: exaltation-humiliation): Jesus' saying about reward (Mark 10:28-31) promises a hundredfold gain in the present time —with persecutions, of course—and eternal life in the coming age. In order to safeguard against an improper certainty of salvation, Jesus (or Mark?) must have added the first-last logion as a final warning. It is noteworthy that Luke has omitted it (18:28-30). Matthew's expanded version, however, limits the reward to eternal life in the kingdom of heaven by means of Peter's explicit question (τί ἄρα ἔσται ἡμῖν; 19:27) and the saying in 19:28. Thus though the promise to the many (19:30) originally referred to the rich (since the unit 19:28-30 is originally formulated as the second addendum to the pericope of the rich young man) it is extended to all disciples by means of the context (vv. 25, 27ff.; cf. G. Bornkamm, G. Barth, and H. J. Held, *Tradition and Interpretation in Matthew* [NTL, 1963] 120n.2, 236). The saying thus takes on an eschatological-parenetic function.

This logion-answer to Peter's question is also added by Matthew to the explanation of the parable of the workers in the vineyard (20:1-15): The "advantage" of those who have worked twelve hours is removed first in the sequence of the recipients of the reward (20:8: from the *last* to the first, according to Jülicher II, 462, "a device of the narrator"), and then esp. in the amount of the payment (one denarius for each). This calls forth the protest of the now "disadvantaged": "these *last* have worked [only] one hour" (v. 12). The generosity of the vineyard owner corresponds to the envy of the workers: "I choose to give to the *last* as much as I give to you" (v. 14). As a summary Matthew then adds the sentence from 19:30—corresponding to the reversal seen in the parable. Thus the parable determines the interpretation of the logion: It is not the reversal of earthly relationships but God's goodness that is determinative for the kingdom of heaven, and this goodness guarantees the reward without distinction in the coming kingdom.

4. This logion (→ 3) is taken up by Q and then by Luke in the framework of the question (Luke 13:22ff.): Who will be able to sit at table in the kingdom of God? Many will want to come into the kingdom of God, but only a few will enter the narrow door. Those who believe that they have their secure place will have to vacate their

seat: The *last* will be the first and the first will be the *last* (13:30).

Parallel to the anxiety about a place in the kingdom of God is the dispute among the disciples over status (Mark 9:33ff. par. Matt 18:1ff./Luke 9:46ff.): Who gives status to whom? Jesus answers: "If anyone wants to be first, he will be the *last* of all," which means "servant of all" (Mark 9:35). In Matthew and Luke the eschatological dimension of the question is absent (although Luke 9:48 has the addition: small-great). In Matthew the question is subordinated to and answered by the reference to repentance and becoming like children—of course primarily with a view to entry into the kingdom of God.

The parable of the places at the table in Luke 14:7ff. moves in a similar direction: One who sits at a place reserved for those of higher rank is in danger of being banned from the table at the end (v. 9). It is better to take the *last* place so that one may be invited by the host to take a higher place and thus to be honored, as in the saying: "Everyone who exalts himself will be humbled, and one who humbles himself will be exalted" (Luke 14:11; cf. Mark 9:35; Matt 18:4). This rule for table manners is "the introduction to an 'eschatological warning,' which looks forward to the heavenly banquet, and is a call to renounce self-righteous pretensions and to self-abasement before God" (Jeremias, *Parables* 193).

5. In Paul ἔσχατος appears twice as an eschatological term: a) Within the framework of his apostolic self-understanding and b) within the horizon of the eschatological "timetable":

a) In contrast to the self-understanding of the Corinthian opponents Paul represents the thesis that God has set forth the apostles as the least, like those who are condemned to death, as a spectacle before the world, as the foolish, weak, and despised—for Christ's sake (1 Cor 4:9f.). Paul understands himself as standing in the succession of the apostles; at the same time the succession of witnesses to Easter is concluded with him (15:3-10). He takes up the pre-Pauline confessional statement (probably up to v. 5) and extends the line of Easter witnesses up to himself: "But *last of all* he appeared . . . also to me" (v. 8). Thus he designates himself as irrevocably the last in a series but at the same time disqualifies himself (cf. 4:13) as one who does not belong precisely in the series, but nevertheless stands at the end (15:8: "miscarriage"; v. 9: "the least of the apostles").

b) The eschatological "timetable" in 1 Cor 15:20-28 (cf. Luz 332-58; Baumgarten 99-110 [and the literature cited there] for the following) speaks of the destruction of death as that of the "*last* enemy" (v. 26). Just as death has come into the world through one man (Adam), so this power is subject to destruction before God comes into his unlimited sovereignty: Death is a personal reality which is the last in a series of hostile powers. As the last enemy it has an antithetical relation to Christ, the first in a succession. As the first one through his resurrection has already taken the power by anticipation, so at the end the power must finally be snatched from death. In the Adam-Christ typology in vv. 44ff. Paul can make the corresponding designation of Christ as the ὁ ἔσχατος Ἀδάμ (v. 45): Christ is not the "second," but rather the *last* Adam. He stands for the reality of the resurrection of the dead and God's unlimited claim to sovereignty. In order to carry this through, death is placed with "the reality to be destroyed by Christ, which Paul describes in v. 24 in a traditional way with the words ἀρχή, ἐξουσία, and δύναμις" (Baumgartner 104). The one who carries out the conquest of the hostile powers is Christ. The destruction of death is thus the last act of the rule of Christ, before he delivers the rule that has been delegated to him for a while back to God (the construction becomes clear when v. 24b is subordinated and considered prior to the first clause; cf. Baumgarten 102f.), who then has unrestricted rule (v. 28).

With the reference to the "*last* trumpet" as the eschatological signal in 1 Cor 15:52, which appears within a small apocalyptic excursus (on the trumpet of God, see 1 Thess 4:16; cf. Matt 24:31; *Did.* 16:6; 4 Ezra 6:23), Paul marks the point in time of the eschatological transformation of Christians who are alive at the parousia and of the resurrection of the dead. Paul is not thinking here of the "*last*" in a series (i.e., of seven trumpets, as in Rev 8:2; 11:15; cf. *Sib. Or.* iv.173f.); he intends rather the trumpets *of the end time,* even if the pre-Pauline tradition presupposed a series. The accent lies here on the futurity and suddenness of the eschatological change.

6. In Peter's Pentecost sermon (Acts 2:17) the citation of Joel 3 inherits a decisively eschatological focus from the vocabulary of late Israelite and early Christian apocalyptic. "It will happen in the *last* days, says God. . . ." Here an eschatological t.t. for the end time is employed (cf. 1 Thess 5:1: χρόνοι and καιροί as synonyms). This t.t. is used also in the introduction of the eschatological vice catalog in 2 Tim 3:11 in an undetermined forewarning about the days which come as "evil times," the time before the parousia, kingdom, and judgment (cf. 4:1, 8, 18), a time when faith is tested. James uses the eschatological t.t. in the context of the parousia and judgment, of course in a weakened sense within the framework of an accusation against the rich: "You have laid up treasures for the *last* days" (5:3).

The reference to the end time in the proemium of 1 Peter has an unambiguous future-eschatological meaning: The author strengthens the churches in view of the "inheritance . . . kept in heaven" for those who are "guarded by faith for a salvation to be revealed at the *last* time" (1:5).

Jude 18 takes up an apocryphal "apostolic word" in a warning against the seductive false teachers: "At the end of time (ἐπ' ἐσχάτου τοῦ χρόνου) there will be scoffers. . . ." The author sees the prediction as fulfilled in his time; with this "citation" he pursues not an eschatological, but rather an apologetic intention. This warning against scoffers occurs in a definite eschatological context in 2 Peter: The author sees himself and the Church exposed to scoffers, who use the delay of the parousia to raise the doubting and scoffing question: "Where is the promise of his parousia?" (3:4). However, the author sees even the appearance of these scoffers as a sign of the end time (3:3), which is the time before the cosmic transformation at the day of the Lord (cf. vv. 4b and 10:13) and the coming of which is guaranteed by the appearance of the scoffers. However, the end is delayed by God himself.

In Heb 1:2; 1 Pet 1:20; and 1 John 2:18 (bis) ἔσχατος is used in the framework of a (future-)eschatological conception, but with a christological or present-eschatological sense:

The historical perspective of the exordium of Hebrews —in accordance with the basic theme of correspondence, distinction, and superiority—contrasts God's speaking to the fathers through the prophets and God's speaking to us in Jesus Christ. However, this speaking is not simply one stage on a time line, for in Jesus Christ the *last* time ("in these *last* days," v. 2; more detail on the reception and interpretation of this traditional formula is given in Grässer 77f.) has arrived: "the time in which a new, incomparable chance is granted" (Grässer 78). Thus the content is close to Gal 4:4 ("the fullness of time") and 1 Pet 1:20.

In 1 Pet 1:20, in the midst of a christological excursus (vv. 18-21), the author of 1 Peter falls back on eschatological terminology. Just as Christ was already chosen in advance before the foundation of the world, so also was he "revealed at the *end* of the times (ἐπ' ἐσχάτων τῶν χρόνων) for your sake." The end time is thus unambiguously determined by the cross and resurrection of Christ.

1 John knows the concept of the "*last* hour" (2:18 bis; cf. the eschatological appeal for watchfulness with its apocalyptic form in Rom 13:11). The last hour is for the tradition of 1 John shaped by the appearance of the antichrist (cf. 2 Thess 2). Because the present is marked by the appearance of "many antichrists," it is clear that it is now the "*last*" hour before the coming of the parousia. Consequently the Church's task is to abide in Christ (1 John 2:28).

7. John's Gospel takes up an eschatological concept from the OT, the fixed t.t. "at the *last* day" (ἐν τῇ ἐσχάτῃ ἡμέρᾳ), which is closely associated with the "day of Yahweh" traditions (more detail in E. Jenni, *THAT* I, 707-26; G. von Rad and G. Delling, *TDNT* II, 943-53; Baumgarten 64f.). John (according to R. Bultmann, *John* [Eng. tr.,

1971] ad loc.: the ecclesiastical redaction of John!) uses this term stereotypically (except in 7:37; → 2) in the futuristic-eschatological sense: in the figurative discourse on the bread of life (ch. 6) the t.t. designates the *time of the resurrection* of those who see the Son and believe in him (v. 40). The one who accomplishes the resurrection for them is Jesus himself. The point in time is the future, but more exact reflection is not given.

In the conversation between Mary and Jesus over the deceased Lazarus, John presents the grieving sister as a witness to the traditional belief in the resurrection: "He will arise at the resurrection on the *last* day" (11:24). Jesus says, by contrast: "I am the resurrection and the life. Whoever believes in me will live, even if he dies; and everyone who lives and believes in me, will never die" (11:25f.).

John 12:48 takes over the OT idea of a judgment at the last day, but gives this traditional idea a specific interpretation: Jesus' word qualifies the believer eschatologically already on the basis of acceptance or rejection of the word. In that respect the judgment is already anticipated. One encounters God himself in the encounter with the revealer, and the judgment takes place. Here God's will is dominant as the will to salvation ("eternal life").

8. The revealer like a son of man (Rev 1:13) makes himself known to John: "Fear not. I am the first and the *last* and the living one, and I was dead, and behold, I am alive for evermore, and I have the keys of death and Hades" (vv. 17f.; cf. 2:8). This self-understanding of the revealer evidently takes up the Isaiah tradition (but with ὁ ἔσχατος substituted for μετὰ ταῦτα in Isa 44:6 LXX and for εἰς τὸν αἰῶνα in Isa 48:12 LXX). In contrast to the word of judgment in Isaiah the question of God's uniqueness does not stand in the foreground. However, the old salvific assurance "fear not" is adopted. The content concerns the comprehensive view of the revealer as the one who is Lord over beginning and end, creation and consummation, and death and life. What was characteristic of Yahweh and is characteristic of God (cf. Rev 22:13 with 1:8) now belongs to the ruler: unlimited power. He is the one who was before the entire world and time and the one who will be in all eternity. As "the firstborn of the dead" (1:5) he possesses the power of the keys of death: he opens it for those who receive eternal life and attain the resurrection, and he closes it for those who are rejected. Such authority has been ratified through the cross and resurrection (cf. 1:8; 2:8).

The climax of the revealer's self-description is the announcement of his imminent coming in judgment (22:12f.): "I am the Alpha and the Omega, the first and the *last*, the beginning and the end." With him comes the redemption that is analogous to creation. But his power remains derivative from the one who says: "I am the

Alpha and the Omega . . . , who is and who was and who comes, the Almighty One" (1:8).

In the framework of the vision of the seven bowls ἔσχατος appears as the characteristic of the seven *last* plagues (15:1; 21:9). The story of God's wrath is outlined here in analogy to the Exodus, but as part of the eschatology of Revelation: The "plagues" are adopted into the eschatology but are reduced to the eschatological number seven. The numerically *last* become the eschatologically relevant in view of the completion of the wrath of God.

J. Baumgarten

ἐσχάτως *eschatōs* finally*

Mark 5:23: ἐσχάτως ἔχει, "my daughter is *near the end* [i.e., death]."

ἔσω *esō* within, inside (adv.)
ἔσωθεν *esōthen* from within; within (adv.)
ἐσώτερος, 3 *esōteros* inner

1. Local sense — 2. Use with other adverbs of place — 3. Sociological sense — 4. Ethical contexts — 5. "Outer" vs. "inner" — 6. The ἔσω ἄνθρωπος

Lit.: J. BEHM, *TDNT* II, 698f. — BDF §§103; 104.2; 184. — MAYSER, *Grammatik* I/3, 122; II/2, 528.

1. a) In the local sense ἔσω in response to the question "where?" corresponds to the prep. ἐν: *within, inside,* with a certain emphasis: *in a (closed) room* (John 20:26 [cf. v. 19!]; Acts 5:23 [and 5:22 D]). The innermost room of a building is signified by ἐσώτερος, with an emphasis on inaccessibility or security: Acts 16:24: "the *inner* prison": Heb 6:19, "the *inner* area behind the curtain" = the holy of holies of the [heavenly] temple.

b) Where it is used to indicate direction of movement, ἔσω strengthens or replaces the prep. εἰς: Mark 14:54 par. Matt 26:58: Peter follows "right *into the inner part* of the building"; Mark 15:16: Jesus is led "further *inside* the palace" (see BAGD s.v.).

c) Ἔσωθεν, *from within,* answers the question "whence?" (Luke 11:7, the friend disturbed at night).

2. Ἔσωθεν is also used with other advs. of place with -θεν (κυκλόθεν, ὄπισθεν, also ἔξωθεν in v.l.) to mean *from all sides, everywhere, through and through.* In Rev 4:8 creatures (→ θηρίον) around God's throne are described as full of eyes κυκλόθεν (in accord with Ezek 1:18) καὶ ἔσωθεν, "all around and *within*" (= through and through); similarly Rev 4:6: ἔμπροσθεν καὶ ὄπισθεν; thus they represent the omnipresence of God, before whom nothing remains hidden.

The sealed scroll (→ βιβλίον 3) is described in Rev 5:1 as written "*on the inner* and back side." Generally only the front side of a parchment roll was written on,

and it was *inside* when the scroll was rolled). A special form of "double document," as if the scroll's special feature were that the content is in force and a copy of the text could be read at any time without breaking the seal (cf. Deissmann, *Light* 35, et al.), is not in mind (H. Kraft, *Rev* [HNT] 105), since the seer and the whole cosmos are in tension over who will be able to see the contents of the scroll (vv. 2-4). The phrase indicates, rather, the distressing profusion of eschatological events in the plan of God, which can scarcely be contained on the scroll. The plan will be made known and set in motion only after the opening of one of the seals by the victorious lamb, who alone is qualified to open it (6:1-17; 8:1).

3. In a sociological sense the contrast between οἱ ἔσω and οἱ → ἔξω designates the demarcation between a "group" to which one belongs (here: the Christian community) and the (outside) world (1 Cor 5:12; 𝔓⁴⁶ reads οἱ ἔσωθεν).

4. In the logion in Matt 23:25 (Q), which originally concerned the ritual purity of objects, ἔσωθεν takes on an ethical focus. The Pharisees keep cups and plates clean on the outside (or "outwardly"), but "*within* they [the vessels!] are full of that which comes from extortion and rapacity"; Matthew continues (v. 26): "You blind Pharisees, take care that what is in the cup (τὸ → ἐντός 1) is clean [i.e., probably: acquired honestly], so that the outside may also be clean." Those who are addressed are thus responsible for the (ritual) purity of the utensil. Later (vv. 27f.) Matthew uses the outer-inner contrast directly in reference to persons: "*within* you are full of hypocrisy and iniquity."

Luke (11:39) has already modified the Q saying in this sense: "but *inside* you are full of extortion and wickedness." What follows, which is probably shaped by Luke (11:40), says: "You fools, has not the same one who created the outside also created the *inside?*" i.e., the purity that is *within* is (at least!) as important before God as outer, ritual purity.

The transition to the ethical is also present in the fig. use of the phrase in the saying about wolves in sheep's clothing (Matt 7:15). Their outward appearance—their "clothing"—suggests that they are prophets, while in truth (ἔσωθεν) they act as tempters in the Church.

5. The change in Luke 11:39 from Matt 23:25 (= Q; → 4) corresponds to the spiritualization of the outer/inner contrast that lies behind Mark 7:21, 23 (without par. in Luke; par. Matt 15:19f. without this word group). There it is said that it is not impure things (ritual or physical) entering through the mouth into the stomach of a person that causes impurity, but rather that which comes "*from within,* out of the heart" of the person. The heart as the "inner self" of a person is seen here as the location of

(evil!) wishes, desires, and pursuits (Mark 7:21f.). In comparison to them ritual impurity is insignificant (Matt 15:20b makes this explicit).

That "Hellenistic" anthropology is employed in the words of Mark 7:20-23 (cf. Bultmann, *History* 48, 166) does not mean that the core of Mark 7:1-23—which is the logion in v. 15— and thus the statement in 7:20-23 do not go back to Jesus, but rather to Hellenistic Judaism. What is decisive is whether vv. 20-23 are an adequate consequence of v. 15 or not (on the debate, cf. on the one side K. Berger, *Die Gesetzesauslegung Jesu* I [1972], 462-507 and on the other W. G. Kümmel in FS Friedrich 35-46; H. Hübner, *NTS* 22 [1975] 319-45).

The contrast between outer and inner is described in another way when Paul says that in Macedonia he endured "fighting without, *fear within*" (2 Cor 7:5). In a specific situation attacks from other persons and inner unrest (over the condition of the church in Corinth) came together, torturing and obstructing him. *Within* is here—without ethical connotation—what happens in the "soul" of the person.

6. The ἔσω ἄνθρωπος of Rom 7:22 is—like the → ἐγώ of vv. 7-25 in general—an abstractly conceived entity. The "*inner person*" is what the individual should be, in distinction from what he actually is. According to a person's essential determination by God he should find his joy in the law (according to Psalm 119). In fact he is dominated by the strivings of the σάρξ and is hostile to God's will.

The contrast between the inner and outer man in 2 Cor 4:16 is different. Here Paul speaks of his existence as an apostle of Jesus Christ. As such he is outwardly shaped by his participation in the crucified existence of his Lord: By suffering, which is like that of Christ, his outward person is destroyed; by contrast the "*inner* person" is "renewed" day by day—lifted up and strengthened in the hope of being glorified with him, a hope that comes through the resurrection of Jesus Christ (4:17; cf. 3:18; Rom 8:17). Here the contrast is between the visible and the invisible in the existence of the Christian (cf. v. 18), but not between the unreal and the real, in that the presently suffering σῶμα of the person is for Paul not just an unessential "outward cover" of his existence. (On the relationship to Hellenistic anthropology, cf. R. Bultmann, *2 Cor* [Eng. tr.] 124-26.)

Eph 3:16 can also be understood analogously to 2 Cor 4:16: For the reader the power of the Holy Spirit is requested for the strengthening of the "*inner person*." But the opposite term, the "outer," does not appear here; there is no reason to see here a Gnostic negative evaluation of the outward/bodily (as does J. Gnilka, *Eph* [HTKNT] 183; see, in contrast, H. Schlier, *Eph* 168-70, who thinks of the "pneumatic" person implanted in baptism). Corresponding to the ἔσω ἄνθρωπος apparently are the "hearts" of the readers; the center of the person is intended.

N. Walter

ἔσωθεν *esōthen* from within; within (adv.)
→ ἔσω.

ἐσώτερος, 3 *esōteros* inner
→ ἔσω.

ἑταῖρος, ου, ὁ *hetairos* companion, friend*

Matt 20:13; 22:12; 26:50; cf. 11:16 v.l. in place of ἑτέροις. Spicq, *Notes* I, 296-98.

ἑτερόγλωσσος, 2 *heteroglōssos* speaking a foreign language
→ γλῶσσα 5, 6.

ἑτεροδιδασκαλέω *heterodidaskaleō* spread a different teaching
→ διδασκαλία 4.

ἑτεροζυγέω *heterozygeō* go together (with another animal) under an unsuitable yoke/pull a strange rope*

2 Cor 6:14, in a warning against fellowship with ἄπιστοι. Spicq, *Notes* I, 299f.

ἕτερος, 3 *heteros* other

1. Occurrences and relation to ἄλλος — 2. Range of meaning — 3. Disputed passages — a) Acts 2:4 — b) Rom 13:8 — c) Gal 1:6f. — d) Gal 1:19

Lit.: S. AALEN, *BHH* 2249f. — F. C. BAUR, "Kritische Übersicht über die neuesten, das γλώσσαις λαλεῖν in der ersten christlichen Kirche betreffenden Untersuchungen," *TSK* 12 (1838) 618-702. — H. W. BEYER, *TDNT* II, 702-4. — BDF §§64.6; 247.3; 306; 480.3. — J. K. ELLIOTT, "The Use of ἕτερος in the NT," *ZNW* 60 (1969) 140f. — W. GUTBROD, *TDNT* IV, 1036-91. — K. HAACKER, "Das Pfingstwunder als exegetisches Problem," FS Stählin 125-31. — G. HOWARD, "Was James an Apostle? A Reflection on a New Proposal for Gal i 19," *NovT* 19 (1977) 63f. — W. MARXSEN, "Der ἕτερος νόμος von Röm 13,8," *TZ* 11 (1955) 230-37. — F. SELTER and C. BROWN, *DNTT* II, 739-42. — L. P. TRUDINGER, "ΕΤΕΡΟΝ ΔΕ ΤΩΝ ΑΠΟΣΤΟΛΩΝ ΟΥΚ ΕΙΔΟΝ, ΕΙ ΜΗ ΙΑΚΩΒΟΝ. A Note on Galatians i 19," *NovT* 17 (1975) 200-202. — For further bibliography see *TWNT* X, 1087.

1. Of the 100 occurrences in the NT (including ἑτέρως in Phil 3:15), 50 appear in Luke-Acts, 10 in Matthew, 9 in Romans, and 11 in 1 Corinthians. The frequency in Luke-Acts is at the expense of → ἄλλος. The avoidance of ἕτερος in favor of ἄλλος in Mark (the exception in 16:12 is secondary on text-critical grounds), John (except in 19:37), and Revelation is noteworthy and is explicable stylistically only on the basis of the postclassical interchangeability of ἕτερος and ἄλλος. Only in Luke-Acts is the frequency of ἕτερος partially explicable on the basis

of the original meaning *the other of two.* Luke has a strong liking for contrasting pairs and dramatic contrasts (→ 2). The later text tradition of the NT attempted to restore the classical use of ἕτερος under an Atticizing influence, which in individual instances is an argument for the less classical reading (Elliott).

2. Approximately half of the occurrences have the connotation of something *additional: a further* or *additional instances of a type.* So, among others, in connection with πολλοί (cf. Matt 15:30; Luke 3:18; 8:3; 22:65; Acts 2:40; 15:35), in enumerations (cf. Matt 16:14; Luke 8:6-8; 9:59, 61; Rom 13:9; 1 Cor 12:9f.; Heb 11:36), and in the time reference τῇ ἑτέρᾳ (ἡμέρᾳ) (Acts 20:15; 27:3). The generic term can thus remain unexpressed, so that apparently dissimilar objects are connected (cf. Matt 8:21; Luke 22:58; 23:32). The connection lies here in the similar action, so that an adverbial tr., *furthermore, additionally,* or *besides,* may be suggested. Frequently ἕτερος links a second Scripture citation to the first (John 19:37; Acts 13:35; Heb 5:6), in which case the old dual sense of ἕτερος remains in effect (cf. Deut 19:15?). This preservation of the old sense is often to be assumed elsewhere, particularly where it is used with → πρῶτος (cf. Matt 21:30; Luke 16:7; with a third member: Luke 14:19f.; 19:20; 20:11) or in contrast to → εἷς; there it concerns most often contrasting positions (except in Luke 5:7), types of behavior, or fates (cf. Matt 6:24 par.; Luke 7:41; 17:34f.; 18:10; 23:40; Acts 23:6; 1 Cor 4:6).

The adversative use, in which ἕτερος points to a pertinent alternative, extends from the simple affirmation of distinction in identity (Matt 11:3 par. Luke 7:19 v.l.; Mark 16:12; Luke 9:29; Acts 8:34; 1 Cor 15:40; 2 Cor 8:8; Jas 2:25; of change of location: Luke 9:56; Acts 12:17) to the connotation of "strangeness" (Acts 2:4; 1 Cor 14:21; Jude 7) and the connotation of hostile opposition (Rom 7:23; 2 Cor 11:4; Gal 1:6) or personal rivalry (Matt 6:24 par.; Luke 16:18; Acts 4:12; 12:7; Rom 7:3). Passages that speak of *another* as a replacement or successor also have an adversative association (Acts 1:20; 7:18; Rom 7:4; Heb 7:11, 13, 15).

Passages in which ἕτερος, synonymous with ὁ → πλησίον, designates the *neighbor* have special weight. In such instances it sometimes refers to the abstract concept of the neighbor (so Rom 2:1; 13:8, → 3.b; 1 Cor 10:24; Gal 6:4; Phil 2:4; Jas 4:12 v.l.); this is not, however, always the case: it can also be used of particular persons or types of persons that one has contact with, as defined by the context (Rom 2:21; 1 Cor 6:1; 10:29; 14:17). Thus the dignity and interest of the fellow human is either set alongside one's own personhood and interest (designated with forms of → ἑαυτοῦ and → ἴδιος; so Rom 2:1, 21) or given priority to oneself (so 1 Cor 10:24, 29; 14:17; uncertain: Phil 2:4); Gal 6:4f. emphasizes that neither can substitute for the other.

3. The meaning of ἕτερος is disputed in the following passages:

a) Λαλεῖν ἑτέραις γλώσσαις in Acts 2:4 was frequently interpreted until F. C. Baur as "speech in unfamiliar expressions" (or something similar), in order to avoid the idea of a miracle of language. But that such a miracle of language is in mind is, nonetheless, assured (cf. Aalen) by vv. 4, 8 (despite v. 13): the Galilean disciples speak in languages which are *strange to them* but are recognized (ἕτερος/ἴδιος) by groups of listeners as *their own.* The scoffing ἕτεροι of v. 13 are not to be ascribed to another stratum (so the widespread view). Their reaction is, rather, to be explained from the predominance of unintelligibility for each individual listener (the text refers not to a miracle of hearing, but a miracle of speaking). The scene as a whole corresponds to 1 Cor 14:21-23 and does not contradict 1 Cor 14:7f. (cf. Haacker).

b) Gutbrod, Marxsen, and F. Leenhardt (*Rom* [Eng. tr., 1961] ad loc.) understand ἕτερος in Rom 13:8, in reliance on older interpreters, as an attribute of νόμος, with differing consequences with respect to content. In response to this one may reply that ἀγαπάω elsewhere in Paul never appears without an obj., while ὁ ἕτερος can be used in place of ὁ πλησίον (→ 2); cf. O. Michel, *Rom* (KEK, ⁵1978) 409, n. 5. → Νόμος without the art. is also attested elsewhere.

c) It is apparent from the context of Gal 1:6f. that the ἕτερον εὐαγγέλιον is a proclamation *of a different kind* and a message in competition with the proclamation of Paul. Interpretation of the rel. clause ὃ οὐκ ἔστιν ἄλλο varies, however. The frequent tr., "there is no other (gospel)" (RSV: "Not that there is another gospel; NIV: "which is no gospel at all"), does not do justice to the clause. If one links the clause to εὐαγγέλιον, then he says about this "other gospel": "it is in reality no *further,* additional gospel for one to choose"; i.e., it does not deserve the name "gospel." Ἄλλος and ἕτερος are here, as in Acts 4:12, not interchangeable; ἄλλος bears an additive connotation, while ἕτερος has an adversative nuance. The essential concern in Gal 1:6f. is not some false teaching, but rather the structure of the proclamation as gospel and its legalistic falsification.

d) Trudinger proposes to translate Gal 1:19: "I did not see anyone other than the apostles, except for James," or more briefly, "Except for the apostles, I saw only James." Thus the problem of the apparent identification of James as an apostle is solved. Howard correctly rejects this translation, inasmuch as the texts cited by Trudinger are not appropriate for the linguistic usage in Gal 1:19. Moreover, a comparable comparative gen. construction is attested only for the neut. noun ἕτερον ("something other than"; cf. Plato *Prt.* 333a).

K. Haacker

ἑτέρως *heterōs* differently, otherwise*

Phil 3:15: εἴ τι ἑτέρως φρονεῖτε, "if in anything you are *otherwise* minded."

ἔτι *eti* still, yet

There are 93 occurrences in the NT, of which the most frequent usage is in Revelation (22 occurrences), Luke (16), and Heb (13; cf. also BDF §459.4; 474.3).

In temporal statements ἔτι denotes the continuation of a condition or of an action: *still/even now* or (negative) "no *longer*," e.g., very frequently in the phrase ἔτι αὐτοῦ λαλοῦντος, "while he was *still* speaking (Matt 12:46; Mark 5:35, etc.); εἰ ἔτι ἀνθρώποις ἤρεσκον, "if I *still* wanted to please humans" (Gal 1:10; cf. 5:11); in reference to the future: πῶς ἔτι, "how *from now on*" (Rom 6:2); ἔτι ἐκ κοιλίας μητρός αὐτοῦ, "*even (= already)* in the mother's womb" (Luke 1:15); repeatedly in John in the phrase ἔτι μικρὸν (χρόνον), "*yet* a little while" (cf. BDF §127.2; John 7:33; 12:35; 13:33; 14:19); negative ἀλλ' οὐδὲ ἔτι νῦν, "but even now not *yet*" (1 Cor 3:2); οὐ μὴ ἔτι, "no *more*" (Heb 8:12; 10:17; Rev 3:12; 18:21, 22 ter, 23 bis); τί ἔτι, "why/*still*" (Mark 5:35; Matt 26:25).

In other contexts ἔτι means *still/further/besides* or (negative) "no *more*," e.g., εἰς οὐδὲν . . . ἔτι εἰ μή, "no *longer* except" (Matt 5:13); ἔτι ἕνα ἢ δύο, "one or two *others/more*" (18:16); ἔτι τε καί, "and *besides/in addition*" (Luke 14:26; Acts 21:28); ἔτι ἅπαξ, "once *more*" (Heb 12:26); in drawing conclusions in a question: τί οὖν ἔτι, "why therefore *still?*" (Rom 9:19; cf. 3:7; Gal 5:11).

ἑτοιμάζω *hetoimazō* prepare*

1. Occurrences in the NT — 2. Constructions — 3. Meaning

Lit.: BAGD, s.v. — W. GRUNDMANN, *TDNT* II, 702-4. — S. SOLLE, *DNTT* III, 116-18.

1. Ἑτοιμάζω appears in the NT a total of 40 times, most frequently in the Synoptics and esp. in Luke (14 occurrences) and in Revelation (7 occurrences).

A further occurrence is in Mark 15:1 v.l. (ἑτοιμάσαντες, ℵ C L 892 in place of ποιήσαντες, A B K W, etc.). R. Pesch (*Mark* [HTKNT] II, 455, n. a) regards it as original and has the text speak of drafting rather than passing a resolution; he also considers parallel influence from Matt 27:1 v.l. (ἐποίησαν D a c f). Against this position is E. Lohmeyer (*Mark* [KEK] 334), who decides in favor of the better attestation of ποιήσαντες, and *TCGNT* 117, according to which the ambiguous συμβούλιον ποιεῖν, which can refer to the assembly as such (council) or its resolution (counsel), has been deliberately clarified by mss. that have ἑτοιμάσαντες in the sense of the latter.

2. Normally ἑτοιμάζω has an acc. obj. In Mark 14:15 and Luke 9:52 it has only the dat. obj. and designates the preparation of the meal or of lodging for someone (τινί). It is used absolutely in Luke 12:47; 22:9, 12.

At the beginning of the conversation about the preparation of the Passover meal the Synoptics differ in the syntactic construction: Mark 14:12 has no obj. and has a ἵνα clause following; Matt 26:17 has a dat. obj. (σοι) followed by an inf. In both cases this comes in a question from the disciples. Luke 22:8 has dat. and acc. objs. (ἡμῖν τὸ πάσχα) and a ἵνα clause following. Here the vb. appears as the commission from Jesus, who takes the initiative.

For what purpose the angels are prepared is indicated with a ἵνα clause in Rev 8:6 and in 9:15, where there is a subst. with εἰς (cf. 9:7; 2 Tim 2:21). On ἀπό (in place of ὑπό) with the pass. in Rev 12:6 cf. BDF §210.2.

3. The actions designated by ἑτοιμάζω in the NT rarely involve specific ethical stance. The objs. of ἑτοιμάζω are seldom persons. In most cases they are inanimate objects, and the vb. refers normally not to their preparation in the sense of change, but rather to their production— "making" rather than "preparation." Thus it corresponds to Heb. *kûn*, which the LXX normally renders with ἑτοιμάζω.

Thus ἑτοιμάζω in the material realm designates, besides *equipping* a horse for battle (Rev 9:7) and *furnishing (adorning)* the New Jerusalem (21:2), *preparing* a meal (Mark 14:12, 15, 16 par.; Matt 22:4; Luke 12:47; 17:8), the *preparing* ointment (Luke 23:56; 24:1), *accumulating* or *storing* goods (12:20); also *preparing* of a way (Rev 16:12), *preparing* lodging (Phlm 22; Luke 9:52: *preparing* quarters), *building* a city (Heb 11:16), *building* residences (John 14:2, 3) and a secure place (Rev 12:6), *building* the heavenly kingdom as well as the fiery hell (Matt 25:34, 41), preparing the salvation in Jesus (Luke 2:31) and the blessedness hidden in God (1 Cor 2:9), and finally *determining* the order of seating in the kingdom of Jesus (Mark 10:40 par.; the divine pass. in Mark is explained in Matthew and in later Markan mss.). The compound προετοιμάζω in Rom 9:23 and Eph 2:10 expresses the idea of *preparation beforehand* to glory or to good works. In Mark 15:1 v.l. ἑτοιμάζω refers to *drawing up* a resolution.

Where ἑτοιμάζω is used of persons: Soldiers are *made available* and therefore should report for duty (Acts 23:23); the bride has *made herself ready* (Rev 19:7), just as the angels *stand ready* (9:15; cf. 8:6).

In 2 Tim 2:21 ἑτοιμάζω has an ethical and religious significance ("*ready* for every good work"), which is esp. present in Luke 1:17, where a messianic task is described: *making ready* a "*prepared*" (BAGD) people through the task of bringing about repentance (cf. v. 16). The citation from Isa 40:3 (Mark 1:3 par.), used in all of the Synoptics, aims also in this direction. The *preparation* of the way of the Lord (cf. Luke 1:76) means nothing other than the repentance of Israel.

W. Radl

ἐτοιμασία, ας, ἡ *hetoimasia* readiness, preparedness

→ ἕτοιμος.

ἕτοιμος, 3 *hetoimos* ready, prepared*
ἐτοιμασία, ας, ἡ *hetoimasia* readiness, preparedness*
ἐτοίμως *hetoimos* readily*

1. Occurrences in the NT — 2. Grammatical details — 3. Range of meaning — 4. Ἕτοιμος in the sayings of Jesus

Lit.: BAGD s.v. — W. GRUNDMANN, *TDNT* II, 704-6. — S. SOLLE, *DNTT* III, 116-18.

1. The adj. ἕτοιμος occurs in the NT 17 times, 8 of which are in the Synoptic Gospels. In the authentic Pauline letters it appears only in 2 Corinthians, there 3 times, along with 1 appearance of the adv. The latter is found a total of 3 times, each time in the phrase ἐτοίμως ἔχω. The subst. is found only in Eph 6:15.

2. The adj. with three endings (cf. 2 Cor 9:5; 1 Pet 1:5) betrays in the NT, as Matt 25:10 shows, a tendency toward two endings (BDF §59.2). Readiness is usually expressed with ἕτοιμός εἰμι. With persons ἐτοίμως ἔχω is also found (Acts 21:13; 2 Cor 12:14; 1 Pet 4:5), as is ἐν ἑτοίμῳ ἔχω (2 Cor 10:6). The purpose for which one is ready is in these cases expressed with an inf. An inf. follows ἕτοιμος also in Luke 22:33, a declined form with τοῦ in Acts 23:15, a final form in 1 Pet 1:5. Ἕτοιμος πρός τι appears in Titus 3:1 and 1 Pet 3:15.

3. Ἕτοιμος refers:

a) To things: The money for the collection for Jerusalem is to *be ready* (2 Cor 9:5). Paul does not want to win fame for τὰ ἕτοιμα, "on a field that has already been cultivated" (10:16). A furnished (with cushions?) upper room is *prepared* (Mark 14:15). A wedding celebration is *prepared* (Matt 22:8); everything is *ready* (v. 4), so that immediately the call to the dinner is made: "the meal is *ready*" (ἤδη ἕτοιμά ἐστιν: Luke 14:17; cf. BAGD). Jesus says of his unbelieving relatives that their time (καιρός) is *there,* always *at their disposal* (7:6). 1 Pet 1:5 speaks of the salvation that is *ready* to be revealed (BAGD).

b) To persons: Christians should be *ready* for every good work (Titus 3:1) and ready to give an answer to everyone who asks for a reason (1 Pet 3:15; cf. Eph 6:15: ἐτοιμασία, *readiness* [to battle] for the gospel). Jesus also summons one to be *ready* for the coming of the Son of Man, to be *prepared* for him (Matt 24:44 par. Luke 12:40; cf. Matt 25:10). Peter and Paul are likewise *ready* for prison and death with Jesus or for him (Luke 22:33; Acts 21:13). Paul is *ready* to go to Corinth (2 Cor 12:14) and to punish all disobedience (10:6). A group of conspirators

in Jerusalem is *ready;* they have *decided* to kill Paul (Acts 23:15, 21).

c) To God: He is *ready* for the judgment (1 Pet 4:5).

4. Where ἕτοιμος appears in sayings of Jesus it refers to eschatological readiness:

a) The Synoptic parables contain the imperative to be ready, but it is expressed in a variety of ways. According to Matt 22:1-14 (par.?) the meal is ready (vv. 4, 8), in contrast to those who are invited. The reference to the wrath of the host clarifies Jesus' exhortation to be ready and to decide now. In Matt 24:42-44 par. and 25:1-13 those who are affected are ready (or not ready) with respect to a coming event; thus a demand for watchfulness is given to the listeners. Here two proclamation situations and perspectives are indicated. In the first case Jesus speaks out of the consciousness that the kingdom of God is already present (Luke 14:17; → 3); one must now decide concerning it. In the second the Church lives in expectation of the coming parousia. Now one must be ready for the coming decision.

b) John 7:6 is not meant positively; for if the καιρός is always there, "thus in truth it is never there" because "the world is completely ignorant of the moment of authentic decision" (R. Bultmann, *John* [Eng. tr.] 293). "The always available worldly existence never arrives at the true existence" (R. Schnackenburg, *John* I [Eng. tr.], 217).

W. Radl

ἐτοίμως *hetoimōs* readily
→ ἕτοιμος.

ἔτος, ους, τό *etos* year

There are 49 occurrences in the NT, of which 15 are in Luke and 11 are in Acts. The following constructions are important: ἦν . . . ἐτῶν δώδεκα, "she was twelve years old" (Mark 5:42; cf. Acts 4:22); χήρα ἕως ἐτῶν . . . , "a widow to the age of eighty-four *years*" (Luke 2:37); κατ᾽ ἔτος, "annually" (2:41); ἐγένετο ἐτῶν . . . , "he was twelve *years* old" (2:42; cf. 8:42); ἐπὶ ἔτη . . . , "for three and one-half *years*" (half of the frequently occurring period of seven years, 4:25; cf. Acts 19:10); ἀπὸ ἐτῶν . . . , "for twelve *years*" (Luke 8:43; cf. Rom 15:23); . . . ἔτη ἔχων, "who had thirty-eight years behind him" (John 5:5); ἐξ ἐτῶν . . . , "for eight *years*" (Acts 9:33; cf. 24:10); ὡς ἔτεσιν . . . , "for about four hundred fifty *years*" (13:20); δι᾽ ἐτῶν πλειόνων, "now after some *years*" (24:17; cf. Gal 2:1); otherwise μετὰ ἔτη τρία, "three *years* later" (1:18; cf. 3:17); μὴ ἔλαττον ἐτῶν . . . γεγονυῖα, "not under the age of sixty *years*" (1 Tim 5:9).

The following phrases with numbers are also to be mentioned: three years (as a typical time period, Luke 13:7); twelve years, e.g., of the issue of blood (Matt 9:20; Mark 5:25, 42; Luke 8:43), Jesus' age (2:42; cf. also

8:42); "about thirty *years* old," ὡσεὶ ἐτῶν τριάκοντα, of Jesus at the beginning of his ministry (3:23); forty years, as a general period of time (a generation, see H. Balz, *TDNT* VIII, 135-39; Acts 7:30, 36, 42; 13:21; cf. 4:22); forty-six years as the time for building the (Herodian) temple (John 2:20); sixty years, in association with the selection of widows (the age of transition to old age, 1 Tim 5:9); four hundred years (Acts 7:6); four hundred thirty years (Gal 3:17); one thousand years (2 Pet 3:8 bis and in Rev 20:2, 3, 4, 5, 6, 7 for the thousand-year messianic reign before the end; cf. *1 Enoch* 91:12ff.; *4 Ezra* 7:28f.; *2 Bar.* 29:3ff.).

εὖ *eu* well (adv.)*

Absolute: Matt 25:21, 23 (Luke 19:17 v.l.): "very good!/excellent!"; εὖ ποιέω, "do *good*" (Mark 14:7); εὖ πράξετε (Acts 15:29) can mean "it will be for your *well-being*" (cf. Philo *Virt.* 170; 2 Macc 9:19) or (more probably) "you will do *right*" (cf. Philo *Mut.* 197; Ign. *Eph.* 4:2; *Smyrn.* 11:3; so also the understanding of D Ir Tert and the Vg [*bene agetis*] and of the Coptic and Armenian translations; cf. also E. Haenchen, *Acts* [Eng. tr., 1971] ad loc.); ἵνα εὖ σοι γένηται, "so that it will be *well* with you" (Eph 6:3).

Εὖα, ας *Heua* Eve*

2 Cor 11:3, referring to the temptation of Eve by the serpent (cf. Gen 3:1ff.); 1 Tim 2:13: Ἀδὰμ . . . πρῶτος ἐπλάσθη, εἶτα Εὖα (with reference to Gen 2:21ff.) as the basis for the subordination of the woman.

εὐαγγελίζω *euangelizō* proclaim*

1. Occurrences in the NT — 2. Meaning — 3. Nontechnical usage — 4. Εὐαγγελίζω as a t.t. for "proclaim the Christian message" — 5. Εὐαγγελιστής

Lit.: → εὐαγγέλιον.

1. Εὐαγγελίζω appears 54 times in the NT. Almost half of the occurrences are in Luke-Acts, 10 in Luke (besides 1:28 v.l.), 15 in Acts (plus Acts 16:17 D*). In Paul εὐαγγελίζω appears 19 times; elsewhere in the NT it appears twice each in Ephesians, Hebrews, and Revelation, 3 times in 1 Peter, and once in Matthew.

2. The act. appears only in Rev 10:7; 14:6; Acts 16:17 D*; it belongs to later Greek (BAGD s.v.) and has the same meaning as the frequently attested mid. form: *proclaim/bring a good report.* The pass. appears 8 times: *be proclaimed/receive a (good) report.* The technical (→ 3) and nontechnical senses are to be distinguished. Only the latter presupposes a christological acc. obj. (Ἰησοῦν, etc.) and is a t.t. for *proclaim the message of Christ* (→ 4).

3. Besides the seldom-attested secular meaning (= *inform;* e.g., 1 Thess 3:6, however, in connection with πίστιν and ἀγάπην) the nontechnical use covers a wide theological spectrum. Subjs. of εὐαγγελίζω in Luke include angels (1:19, 28 v.l.; 2:10), John the Baptist (3:18), Jesus (4:18, 43; 7:22, etc.), and disciples of Jesus (9:6). The objs. of the proclamation also vary: χαρὰν μεγάλην (2:10), βασιλείαν (4:43; 8:1; pass.: 16:16; with περί: Acts 8:12), πίστιν (Gal 1:23), εἰρήνην (in OT citations: Acts 10:36; Rom 10:15, etc.), and ἐπαγγελίαν (Acts 13:32). In connection with prophetic proclamation εὐαγγελίζω can take on the meaning *announce/promise;* thus Rev 10:7 (of the fulfillment of secrets that God has announced to his prophets); esp. in Hebrews in the pass.: the OT people of God "received the promise" that they will indeed enter into the rest, but because of disobedience they have not experienced the fulfillment; correspondingly the Christian people of God stand under the promise (4:2, 6).

The nontechnical use is anticipated in the OT (cf. Isa 52:7 and Nah 2:1 to Acts 10:36; Rom 10:15; Isa 61:1 to Matt 11:5 par. Luke 4:18; 7:22) and can be rendered *announce (eschatological) salvation* (contrary to the reference in *NTG* at Eph 2:17 the vb. εὐαγγελίζω is not found in Isa 57:19 LXX; also εὐαγγέλιον εὐαγγελίζειν [Rev 14:6; mid.: 2 Cor 11:7 pass.; Gal 1:11] is not in the OT). This narrow textual basis does not justify deriving εὐαγγελίζω solely from the OT and Jewish tradition. Indeed, Judaism after the OT attests a similar usage when the partc. *mᵉḇaśśēr* ("the eschatological message of joy") appears, apparently in dependence on Isa 52:7; Nah 2:1 (1QH 18:14; 11QMelchizedek 16); however a corresponding εὐαγγελιζόμενος for Jesus appears in the NT only in two redactional, i.e., late, passages of Luke (8:1; 20:1). Moreover, Hellenistic literature knows εὐαγγελίζω in the religious sense: According to Philo the recovery or the coronation of the emperor (*Leg. Gai.* 18, 231) is the object of εὐαγγελίζω. In Philostratus (*VA* i.28; viii.27) the arrival of a beneficent θεῖος ἀνήρ is the object of εὐαγγελίζω. In the NT εὐαγγελίζω stands not only within the OT and Jewish sphere of influence, but also within that of the Greek and Hellenistic linguistic world.

4. For the technical christological-soteriological meaning the characteristic acc. objs. are Ἰησοῦν (Acts 8:35; 17:18 + τὴν ἀνάστασιν), Χριστὸν Ἰησοῦν (5:42; cf. Eph 3:8), and κύριον Ἰησοῦν (Acts 11:20; cf. Gal 1:16: αὐτόν = υἱὸν θεοῦ). They designate the salvific meaning of the Christ-event. Because the Christ-event, understood in this way, is represented in the proclamation in which Christ is the content, the acc. of εὐαγγελίζω can also be → εὐαγγέλιον or λόγον (Acts 8:4; cf. 15:35; 1 Pet 1:25) instead of the personal obj. Such interchangeable usage is assumed where εὐαγγελίζω is used absolutely (*proclaim the gospel:* Luke 9:6; Acts 14:7; 1 Cor 1:17, etc.; cf. also 1 Pet 4:6: pass. with dat. [preaching in Hades to the dead]). This connection confirms the thesis that the earliest Christian tradition of the vb. and the noun was closely connected with christological formulas in the Hellenistic churches (1 Cor 15:1f.; Rom 1:15 → εὐαγγέλιον 3, 5).

It is unlikely that Jesus used a Hebrew or Aramaic equivalent for εὐαγγελίζω in his proclamation. The only reference worthy of mention, Matt 11:5 par., is dependent and derived from the citation of Isa 61:1. In the Q context, it involves the preaching of the earthly Son of Man, who announces "the good news" to the poor.

In Pauline usage εὐαγγελίζω refers to the total task of the apostle in proclamation (with βαπτίζειν: 1 Cor 1:17). Its content can be seen in the respective epistolary contexts. It is addressed to the Gentiles (Gal 4:13; 2 Cor 10:16; Eph 3:8, etc.). One cannot distinguish between missionary preaching and preaching addressed to the Church (cf. Rom 1:15 with 15:20; Gal 1:16, 23). Paul apparently distinguishes his proclamation from that of his opponents when he, in his commission from God, proclaims the Christ-event in its manifestation of grace and judgment (Gal 1:8ff.; cf. 1 Cor 9:16, 18).

In Acts εὐαγγελίζω is a t.t. for the preaching of the Jerusalem apostles (5:42; 8:25) and the early Christian missionaries (8:4, 35, 40; 11:20, → 5), esp. Paul and his companions (13:32; 14:7, 15, 21; 16:10; 17:18).

In 1 Peter the εὐαγγελισάμενοι are the preachers who, in contrast to the OT prophets, who prophesied only concerning future grace, proclaimed the gospel "in the Holy Spirit" to the later Christian generation (1:12).

5. **Εὐαγγελιστής**, *proclaimer**, is rare in Greek literature (*IG* XII1, 675, 6: the priestly proclaimer of oracles) and occurs only 3 times in the NT. Acts 21:8: Philip, a member of the group of seven (cf. 6:5), missionary in Samaria (8:4ff.), is εὐαγγελιστής in Caesarea. 2 Tim 4:5: Timothy, the apostolic pupil of Paul (cf. 1 Thess 3:2; Phil 2:19ff.) is instructed to "do the work of an εὐαγγελιστής," i.e., carry out the ministry of a Christian *preacher*. Eph 4:11: the εὐαγγελισταί are listed after the apostles and prophets, but before the pastors and teachers, among the workers in the Church. In all three occurrences, therefore, the εὐαγγελισταί are placed after the apostles and are not primarily missionaries, but instead serve the Church through the proclamation of the gospel. A clearly demarcated church office is not apparent. Since Hippolytus *De Antichristo* 56; Tertullian *Adversus Praxean* 21, 23 the authors of the NT Gospels have been called εὐαγγελισταί.

G. Strecker

εὐαγγέλιον, ου, τό *euangelion* gospel*

1. Occurrences in the NT — 2. Meaning — 3. Pre-NT tradition — 4. Derivation in the history of religions — 5. The εὐαγγέλιον as the message concerning Christ

Lit.: U. BECKER, *DNTT* II, 107-14. — P. BLÄSER, *HTG* I, 355-63. — N. A. DAHL, "Hva betyr εὐαγγέλιον i det Nye Testamente?," *SvTK* 36 (1960) 152-60. — D. DORMEYER, "Die Kompositionsmetapher 'Evangelium Jesu Christi, des Sohnes Gottes' Mk 1,1. Ihre theologische und literarische Aufgabe in der Jesus-Biographie des Mk," *NTS* 33 (1987) 452-68. — J. A. FITZMYER,

"The Gospel in the Theology of Paul," *Int* 33 (1979) 339-50. — H. FRANKEMÖLLE, *Evangelium. Begriff und Gattung* (1988). — G. FRIEDRICH, *TDNT* II, 707-37. — GOPPELT, *Theology* II, 107-17. — J. HUBY and X. LÉON-DUFOUR, *L'Evangile et les Evangiles* (VSal 11, 1954). — H. KOESTER, "From the Kerygma-Gospel to Written Gospels," *NTS* 35 (1989) 361-81. — U. LUCK, "Inwiefern ist die Botschaft von Jesus Christus 'Evangelium'?" *ZTK* 77 (1980) 24-41. — R. P. MARTIN, *ISBE* II, 529-32. — O. MICHEL, *RAC* VI, 1107-60. — E. MOLLAND, *Das paulinische Euangelion. Das Wort und die Sache* (ANVAO.HF, 1934, no. 3) (cf. O. Michel, *TLZ* 60 [1935] 141f.). — H. SCHLIER, "Εὐαγγέλιον im Römerbrief," FS Schelkle 127-42. — W. SCHMAUCH, *EKL* I, 1213-16. — J. SCHMID, *LTK* III, 1255-59. — *idem*, *SacVb* 328-32. — R. SCHNACKENBURG, " 'Das Evangelium' im Verständnis des ältesten Evangelisten," FS Schmid (1973) 309-24. — W. SCHNEEMELCHER, "Gospel," Hennecke/Schneemelcher I, 71-75. — J. SCHNIEWIND, *Euangelion. Ursprung und erste Gestalt des Begriffs Evangelium* (BFCT II/13, 25, 1927, 1931) 185-96. — SPICQ, *Notes* Suppl., 299-305. — G. STRECKER, "Literarkritische Überlegungen zum εὐαγγέλιον-Begriff im Markusevangelium," FS Cullmann (1972) 91-104.— *idem*, "Das Evangelium Jesu Christi," FS Conzelmann 503-48. — P. STUHLMACHER, ed., *The Gospel and the Gospels* (1990). — *idem, Das paulinische Evangelium. I. Vorgeschichte* (FRLANT 95, 1968).— H. WEDER, " 'Evangelium Jesu Christi' (Mk 1,1) und 'Evangelium Gottes' (Mk 1,14)," *Die Mitte des NT* (FS E. Schweizer, 1983) 399-411. — Wikenhauser/Schmid 203-7. — For further bibliography see *DNTT* II, 114f.; *TWNT* X, 1087f.

1. Most of the 76 occurrences in the NT are in the Pauline letters (48 in the genuine letters, 8 in the deutero-Paulines). Only 12 are in the Gospels (Matthew has 4, Mark has 8). The word does not appear in Luke's Gospel, the Johannine literature, Titus, Hebrews, 2 Peter, James, or Jude. In the Gospels εὐαγγέλιον is used both absolutely (Mark 1:15, etc.) and with the gen. (Matt 4:23, etc.: τῆς βασιλείας, → 5). Both Mark and Paul found εὐαγγέλιον used absolutely and with the gen. phrase τοῦ θεοῦ or τοῦ Χριστοῦ in the Hellenistic Christian tradition prior to them. No distinction is made, as the subj. gen. and the obj. gen. cannot actually be separated.

2. In contrast to the usage in the OT and Jewish and secular Greek literature ("news of victory" or "recompense for a good report"; → 4) εὐαγγέλιον in the NT denotes the news that concerns God or comes from God. Along with the unrestricted usage (Rev 14:6; presupposed in Matthew, → 5) εὐαγγέλιον is a t.t. for the *message about Christ* (so also in the absolute τὸ εὐαγγέλιον); this is widely understood as "joyful tidings"—a tr. that nevertheless does not fit all of the occurrences, since the content of the εὐαγγέλιον can be not only "grace," but also "judgment" (Rom 2:16; Rev 14:6f., etc.). Possibly through the influence of the secondary superscriptions of the Gospels (e.g., εὐαγγέλιον κατὰ Μάρκον), εὐαγγέλιον became a term for the Gospels (Irenaeus *Haer.* iv.20.6; Clement of Alexandria *Strom.* i.136.1).

3. The term εὐαγγέλιον or its Hebrew or Aramaic equivalent was probably not a part of the proclamation of the historical Jesus. The word is also not attested in the collection of logia (Q). Inasmuch as the attempt to assume an old tradition in Rev 14:6 is not convincing (→ 5), the NT use of εὐαγγέλιον is not to be traced back to the Palestinian Jewish Christian community. This conclusion suggests that the early Christian usage came from pre-Pauline tradition (1 Thess 1:1ff.; 1 Cor 15:1ff.; Rom 1:1ff.), for Paul assumes that the term, which he uses absolutely, is known both in the churches founded by him and in the other churches.

1 Thess 1:9b-10 is a pre-Pauline confessional unit of tradition that probably belonged originally to the Christian baptismal tradition. The the content of the parallelism is characteristic for the Hellenistic Christian sphere (repentance to the "living and true God" and expectation of the Son of God). The combination of the soteriologically-christologically accented tradition with the term εὐαγγέλιον (v. 5) makes it probable that already before Paul monotheistic and christological sayings were combined with εὐαγγέλιον in the early Hellenistic Christian churches. This does not permit the derivation of the word from the monotheistic missionary preaching of the Hellenistic synagogue.

In 1 Cor 15:1ff. a traditional unit is present, particularly in vv. 3-5. The pre-Pauline composition is suggested by the un-Pauline phrases and the metric structure (fourfold ὅτι). One may assume that the tradition ended with v. 5a (ὤφθη Κηφᾷ) and that vv. 5b-7 are a Pauline addition out of existing, probably oral, tradition connected to the preceding with εἶτα or ἔπειτα, the Pauline formulas used in series. The confession has no unambiguous setting and is (in this version) to be ascribed to the Hellenistic Church.

The εὐαγγέλιον passages (1 Cor 15:1-2) have been connected with the confession by Paul in dependence on the Hellenistic Christian Church-tradition. Hence it follows that, as in 1 Thessalonians 1, the christological accent, i.e., the connection with the atoning death and resurrection of Christ, was transmitted as an essential content of the pre-Pauline εὐαγγέλιον tradition.

In Rom 1:1 also εὐαγγέλιον (vv. 1, 9) is connected with a pre-Pauline confession. Un-Pauline language, participial constructions, parallelism, and the two-stage christology indicate that vv. 3b-4a are a traditional piece completed by Paul with an eye to specificity (κατὰ σάρκα and κατὰ πνεῦμα ἁγιωσύνης). In the Pauline context the formula cited has the function of identifying the "gospel" of Paul with the "faith" of the Roman church. Apart from the question whether Paul received this confessional formula in connection with the word εὐαγγέλιον, what was said above is confirmed: For the pre-Pauline Hellenistic Christian mission churches the

christological interpretation of εὐαγγέλιον is to be assumed.

Although the instances of εὐαγγέλιον in Mark are to be attributed to the redaction (→ 5), the usage reflects pre-Markan tradition. As a comparison with Paul indicates, usage both with gen. θεοῦ (1:14) or Ἰησοῦ Χριστοῦ (1:1) and absolutely (1:15; 8:35; 10:29; 13:10; 14:9) are traditional. In pre-Markan usage, no distinction was made in content. The consistent christological reference confirms that the pre-Pauline/pre-Markan conception was christologically centered. A specific association of the pre-Markan christological elements (apocalyptic?) cannot be identified.

4. In accordance with secular usage of εὐαγγέλιον, the Hebrew noun $b^e\bar{s}\hat{o}r\hat{a}$ means "compensation for a message of victory" (2 Sam 4:10; 18:22) or "message of victory" (2 Sam 18:20, 25, 27; 2 Kgs 7:9). In the LXX εὐαγγέλιον appears with the same meaning, but only in the pl. (2 Kgdms 4:10); there is also the fem. ἡ εὐαγγελία ("good tidings," 2 Kgdms 18:20-27; 4 Kgdms 7:19). The distance between the OT-Jewish tradition and NT use of εὐαγγέλιον is considerable, particularly in view of the fact that the Hebrew and Greek nouns appear in neither the MT nor the LXX with a theological meaning.

Greek and Hellenistic uses of the word correspond partially to the secular usage of the LXX (e.g., Homer Od. xiv.152: "reward for good tidings"). However, a religious meaning in the Hellenistic tradition is at least attested by the Jewish writers Philo and Josephus. While Philo uses the vb. (→ εὐαγγελίζω 3), the noun is found in Josephus B.J. ii.420 (= "good news") and iv.618, where the elevation of Vespasian as Caesar is referred to. The combination of εὐαγγέλιον with the cult of Caesar and the offering of sacrifices is known to the world of Josephus, and thus the religious-technical, sacral meaning is also known. This is confirmed in B.J. iv.656 (the proclamation of Caesar).

Hellenistic inscriptions also attest the religious sense: In connection with ruler worship an ancient inscription from the 4th cent. B.C. indicates that a salvific meaning is associated with εὐαγγέλια (OGIS I, 13, 20). Of special importance is the inscription from Priene (OGIS II, 458), in which εὐαγγέλια denotes both the announcement of the coming redemption accompanying the appearance of the emperor (ll. 37f.) and the good tidings of the redemptive event (ll. 40f.). Despite the rhetorical style it is clear that εὐαγγέλια both here and in other Hellenistic texts (cf. Deissmann, Light 366f.), as well as in Josephus, designates redemptive events that affect the lives of the inhabitants of the Empire.

The primary basis of NT use of εὐαγγέλιον is probably to be found in the circle of the Hellenistic ruler cult. Although the NT does not explicitly distance itself from the terminology of the Hellenistic ruler cult or the Roman Caesar cult, this separation is made in content, for the singular εὐαγγέλιον distinguishes the Christ-event as a unique eschatological fact from all εὐαγγέλια in the non-Christian world.

An unequivocal OT-Jewish or Hellenistic-Greek source of the εὐαγγέλιον has not been established. The NT proclamation of the εὐαγγέλιον can take on both OT-Jewish and Hellenistic-Greek traditional elements. Thus the primary dependence of the noun on Greek-Hellenistic tradition is evident. By this means the new thing expressed by the Christian proclamation can be articulated in an intelligible way in its own environment.

5. a) In 1 Thessalonians, Paul's earliest letter, εὐαγγέλιον is, on the one hand, a *nomen actionis* for the preaching task that resulted in the founding of the church (1:5). Here the realization of the preaching task is designated as an expression of ἀγάπη (2:8; cf. 3:2). On the other hand, it represents the content of the "gospel"—clearly in combination with λαλέω (2:2) and κηρύσσω (2:9)—that has been entrusted to the apostle for proclamation. This content has a monotheistic-christological aspect, as he includes the confession of the salvific meaning of the cross and resurrection of Jesus Christ (cf. 1:8-10 with 4:14). Εὐαγγέλιον is a spirit-empowered word which also produces pneumatic deeds; for it manifests the election of the person (1:4), which was made at the beginning, as a call to salvation (2:12). The ἐν κυρίῳ/Χριστῷ sayings of 1 Thessalonians reflect the tension between the "already" and the "not yet" contained in the εὐαγγέλιον concept. The soteriological content of the Pauline proclamation is determined by the apocalyptic context (cf. the future-forensic meaning of παρουσία in 2:19; 3:13; 4:15; 5:23); the eschatological salvation is experienced by anticipation in the gift of the Spirit (1:5; 4:8; 5:19).

The exegetical problems of Galatians, esp. of the important passages 1:6 and 2:7, cannot be elaborated on here (see bibliography above; → ἕτερος 3). Even if an unequivocal reconstruction of the traditional unit in 2:7f. is not possible, it nevertheless concerns a tradition that was transmitted in Hellenistic churches, which suggests in this connection that the proclamation of the apostle was called εὐαγγέλιον. In 1:6f. Paul identifies the one gospel, which is the standard for the legitimation of Christian proclamation, with the εὐαγγέλιον τοῦ Χριστοῦ. The gen. is to be understood as neither exclusively obj. (cf. 1:16) nor exclusively subj. (cf. 1:12). Rather, he characterizes the εὐαγγέλιον as authorized by the exalted Lord. The subject of the Pauline gospel (1:7; 2:2) is the Christ-event, likewise faith as the acceptance of the proclamation (cf. 1:23). Unlike 1 Thessalonians, in Galatians Paul develops his gospel as the message of justification. As the content of the gospel, the Christ-event is the overcoming of human righteousness based on law and the founding of a life based on the χάρις θεοῦ (1:11; 2:19-21). The "truth of the gospel" is experienced as the justification of the sinner (2:5, 14).

In 1 and 2 Corinthinas εὐαγγέλιον is used throughout for the proclamation of Paul (1 Cor 4:15; 9:12ff.; 2 Cor 2:12; 4:3f.; 8:18; 10:14). 1 Cor 15:1ff. characterizes the content of the εὐαγγέλιον as the kerygma of the death and resurrection of Jesus Christ (cf. 2 Cor 9:13), while other occurrences are subordinated (9:12ff.) to the parenetic-ethical purpose of 1 Corinthians. In 2 Corinthians, where there is a comparison with the opponents, the person and mandate of Paul are basically in view (11:1ff.). Because

the εὐαγγέλιον is preached, eschatological acceptance of those who believe and rejection of those who do not occurs (4:3).

Romans pursues further the relationship developed in Galatians between, on the one hand, εὐαγγέλιον as Paul's proclamation (1:9) or the Christian message in general (10:16; 11:28) and, on the other hand, the event of justification. The content of the Pauline proclamation, the righteousness of God revealing itself to faith, is based on the kerygma of Christ (1:3f.; cf. 15:19). The εὐαγγέλιον has a horizon in salvation history (1:1f.; the situation is different in the late un-Pauline concluding doxology [16:25-27], in which the εὐαγγέλιον is compared with the revelation of a mystery kept secret for ages [v. 25]). It is, furthermore, the basis for the universal perspective of the Pauline preaching; for the εὐαγγέλιον is a δύναμις, through which God's righteousness becomes a saving reality for every believer (1:16f.). However, the message of justification is not the only subject of the gospel, for the proclamation of judgment according to works (2:16) also belongs to Paul's message. While it may not be unequivocally certain whether the ethical instruction of the apostle also belongs to the content of εὐαγγέλιον, the unity of "indicative" and "imperative" of the Christ-event is certain for Paul (cf. Gal 5:25), and the εὐαγγέλιον is a general norm for the conduct of the Church (15:16; cf. Gal 2:14; Phil 1:27).

The two prison epistles, Philippians and Philemon, indicate the comprehensive perspective of the Pauline εὐαγγέλιον concept. Εὐαγγέλιον is here interpreted primarily through the situation of Paul's imprisonment (Phil 1:7, 16). The gospel is a power establishing partnership between the apostle and the Church (1:5; 2:22; 4:3, 15; Phlm 13). His suffering serves the expansion of the gospel (Phil 1:12). In addition the gospel provides the norm for the Church's conduct and safeguards the unity of the faith (1:27).

b) In the probably deutero-Pauline Colossians the word εὐαγγέλιον appears only at the margin of the essential emphasis of the letter—the confession of the presence of the salvation that has been and is being produced in Christ—and is coordinated with ἐλπίς in the triad of "faith, love, and hope." As the content of the proclamation by the local church and the worldwide Church, the gospel opens the way to the eschatological future (1:5). This emphasis is underlined by the second occurrence of the word: along with "faith," the "hope of the gospel" is reckoned among the foundation stones on which the Church is built (1:23). Thus it is clear to the author that such a hope in the reality of Christ is securely founded (cf. 1:27).

The occurrences of εὐαγγέλιον in Ephesians interpret the parallel passages in Colossians. Corresponding to Col 1:5 εὐαγγέλιον in Eph 1:13f. articulates the object of hope: The ἀρραβὼν τῆς κληρονομίας, the first installment toward the "redemption of the possession," is promised to the Church through the gospel. In 3:6 (cf. Col 1:23) εὐαγγέλιον determines the content of the mystery of Christ: It mediates also to the Gentiles participation in the promise. By the insertion of τοῦ εὐαγγελίου in Eph 6:19—in place of τοῦ Χριστοῦ in Col 4:3—the mystery of Christ is identified with the mystery of the gospel, which the apostle is commissioned to proclaim (a probably correct reading in 𝔓⁴⁶ B G Tertullian Ambrosiaster does not have τοῦ εὐαγγελίου, which is apparently a secondary assimilation to Col 4:3). The proclamation of the εὐαγγέλιον is incumbent not only on the apostle, but also on the Church; it stands under the demand to stand for the εὐαγγέλιον τῆς εἰρήνης (Eph 6:15, citing Isa 52:7).

The concern of 2 Thessalonians to confront a Christian-apocalyptic enthusiasm and thus to claim the authority of Paul is reflected not only in the apocalyptic sections of the letter, but also in its use of εὐαγγέλιον. With the impending final judgment, which brings appropriate justice on the persecutors of the Church, the judgment is completed on those who are disobedient to the "gospel of our Lord Jesus Christ" (1:8; cf. 1 Pet 4:17). According to 2:14 the apostle's proclamation, which is described as the εὐαγγέλιον, results in the calling of the Church. Here the will of God as the one who elects is manifest and is the basis for expecting the δόξα of the exalted Lord, Jesus Christ. The reference to the exalted one (cf. 1:8f., 12; 2:13f., 16; 3:3, 5, 16) and the author's authoritative proclamation of the gospel serve the preservation of the faith.

c) In the post-Pauline letters of 1 and 2 Timothy εὐαγγέλιον is associated with the post-apostolic image of Paul. As a teacher of the Church Paul lays the basis for correct teaching (cf. 1 Tim 1:10). Taking up the Pauline tradition, 1 Tim 1:11 uses liturgical language to designate the apostle's mission of proclamation as εὐαγγέλιον τῆς δόξης τοῦ μακαρίου θεοῦ. The heavenly δόξα is here, as in 2 Cor 4:4-6 and Col 1:27, the content of the gospel. However, the ethical context (1 Tim 1:3-10) indicates that the post-Pauline proclamation of the gospel at the same time leads to a position which corresponds to the demands of Church order.

Just as the Pastorals reflect Paul's situation of suffering, so 2 Tim 1:10 sets forth in a liturgical participial style the meaning of the εὐαγγέλιον in the presence of suffering and death. The "gospel" overcomes death and reveals "life and immortality." The apostolic pupil must be ready to suffer for the gospel according to Paul's model. In this way the power of God is demonstrated (1:7f.), just as it is said in Rom 1:16 to be identical with the εὐαγγέλιον. If such suffering is experienced "for the sake of the elect" (2:10), the Church as a whole is summoned to bear suffering and death (2:8) κατὰ τὸ εὐαγγέλιον μου (so also Rom 2:16; 16:25). The basis for the persistence in suffering

lies in the kerygma of Christ, the citation of which in 2 Tim 2:8, 11 relies directly or indirectly on the two-stage christological formula of Rom 1:3f.

d) Except for the secondary passage in Mark 16:15 a total of 7 occurrences of εὐαγγέλιον in Mark (1:1, 14f.; 8:35; 10:29; 13:10; 14:9) belong to redactional material. They are thus to be interpreted primarily in connection with the literary context of the Second Gospel. The close connection between εὐαγγέλιον and the person of Christ indicates also for Mark that the term is derived from the christological tradition of the Hellenistic Church (cf. esp. 1:1; 14:9). In the pre-Markan tradition εὐαγγέλιον is completed by the obj. gen. τοῦ Χριστοῦ. The Evangelist Mark has, however, used the gen. in the subj. sense, whereby Jesus has become the proclaimer of the gospel (cf. 1:14f.). Thus 1:1 is to be understood primarily in the subj. sense. In 13:10 and 14:9 the subj. use cannot be excluded. The terms in 8:35 and 10:29 can involve both the Church's proclamation of Christ and Christ's preaching.

Mark turns from the preaching about Christ to the preaching of Christ in order to orient the Church toward the image of the Son of God and Son of Man who was active in the past. However, Mark has oriented εὐαγγέλιον not only historically, but also apocalyptically. Jesus' proclamation of the gospel is not only the "fulfillment of the time," but the future reign of God is announced as well (1:15: ἤγγικεν = future oriented). The occurrence of the word in 8:35 is likewise apocalyptically oriented: One's response to Jesus is equivalent to one's response to the gospel and determines one's acceptance or rejection at the judgment. In any case εὐαγγέλιον here has also the character of the message of the approach of the reign of God proclaimed by Jesus.

If Mark does not distinguish terminologically between the gospel of Jesus and the post-Easter gospel, he nevertheless shows that the Church's proclamation of the Gospel (13:10; 14:9) relies on the word of Jesus. This includes the demand for taking up the cross (8:34). Thus the cross of Jesus is not exclusively an interpretive criterion of the εὐαγγέλιον, but rather the tangible reality of the overarching motif of the hiddenness of the revealer, which finds a partial resolution at Easter and finally points toward the parousia (9:1, 9, etc.). Correspondingly in 10:29 the persecuted disciples are promised an eschatological future, and in 13:10 the εὐαγγέλιον is itself an apocalyptic event, part of the "woes of the end time" (13:8). The "gospel of Jesus Christ," which in Mark is portrayed in the life of Jesus as part of the framework of salvation history, is promised to Jews and Gentiles after the cross and resurrection and is realized in the persecution of the Church as the anticipation and announcement of the coming reign of God.

Matthew takes over most of the Markan εὐαγγέλιον passages. The exceptions are motivated by the subject matter (Mark 1:1 is eliminated because of Matt's genealogy and birth stories, while Mark 8:35 and 10:29 are eliminated on the basis of the prominence given to the person of Christ in Matthew; Mark 1:14f. basically appears in Matthew 4:23 and 9:35). Matthew never uses εὐαγγέλιον absolutely, but always in combination with τοῦτο (24:14; 26:13) or τῆς βασιλείας (4:23; 9:35; 24:14). This indicates that Matthew has found an unrestricted use of the concept and thus reflects a pre-NT (Greek-Hellenistic) usage. The content of εὐαγγέλιον is more closely related to the proclamation of Jesus than in Mark (and is frequently used with κηρύσσω). Gen. τῆς βασιλείας has an obj. sense. Thus one cannot distinguish between the proclamation and teaching of Jesus. Εὐαγγέλιον is an ethical demand of Jesus and eschatological instruction by the Kyrios and is directed to the Church and the world (cf. 28:18-20).

The word is not found in Luke. The two occurrences in Acts refer to the proclamation of the apostles among the Gentiles (15:7; 20:24). This modification to a t.t. does not suggest that the word can be used for the preaching of Jesus, particularly in view of the fact that the apostolic proclamation in Acts is not a repetition of the preaching of Jesus, but rather is determined basically by the salvation event in the cross and resurrection of Jesus Christ.

e) In the only occurrence in 1 Peter (4:17) εὐαγγέλιον τοῦ θεοῦ signifies the early Christian apocalyptic content of the message of Christ, in that it is placed in the parenesis regarding the Church's suffering in persecution: Whereas those who suffer as Christians receive the promise, those who are disobedient to the εὐαγγέλιον will receive punishment in the judgment. Contrary to 1 Cor 11:32 (cf. 2 Thess 1:8), the concept of the judgment on the unbelievers has become an independent motif; εὐαγγέλιον has become here a component of a tradition-historically secondary reflection that interprets the OT wisdom tradition of Proverbs (1 Pet 4:18; Prov 11:31).

The only occurrence of the noun in Revelation (14:6) is, like the use of the vb. (10:7; → εὐαγγελίζω 3), to be attributed to the final redactor of Revelation on the basis of language and composition. Thus the passage is not an appropriate starting point for the reconstruction of the earliest Christian tradition history. In addition the content of the passage is widely separated from the early Christian apocalyptic tradition. The "eternal gospel," which the "other angels" proclaim, is addressed to all peoples and languages. Its content is an unrestricted call to repentance, which is connected to an announcement of the judgment (v. 7). Fundamental to the passage, however, as in the rest of the NT, is the christological objective: the εὐαγγέλιον is the message of Christ, which is oriented toward the coming Kyrios, who will speak judgment and exercise grace (cf. 22:20f.).   G. Strecker

εὐαγγελιστής, οῦ, ὁ *euaggelistēs* proclaimer → εὐαγγελίζω 5.

εὐαρεστέω *euaresteō* please (vb.); pass.: take delight in*

Only in Hebrews: 11:5, of Enoch, who *pleased* God by his faith; 11:6; 13:16, of the sacrifices by which God *is pleased* (pass.). F. Luciani, "Uso e significato del verbo *euaresteō* in Filone Alessandrino," *Verifiche* 6 (1977) 275-97, 557-88.

εὐάρεστος, 2 *euarestos* pleasing, pleasant*

There are 9 occurrences in the NT, of which 5 are in Paul. The word is widespread in koine, but rare in the LXX (only in Wis 4:10; 9:10). In the NT it is used almost exclusively of deeds that are *pleasing* to God or Christ: Rom 12:1: εὐάρεστον τῷ θεῷ, of the living and holy sacrifices of the bodies of believers (cf. δόκιμος τοῖς ἀνθρώποις, 14:18); further Phil 4:18; 2 Cor 5:9 (εὐάρεστοι αὐτῷ); Eph 5:10; Col 3:20 (εὐάρεστον ἐν κυρίῳ); Heb 13:21 (εὐάρεστον ἐνώπιον αὐτοῦ); absolute τὸ ἀγαθὸν καὶ εὐάρεστον καὶ τέλειον as content of the will of God, Rom 12:2. According to Titus 2:9 slaves are to conduct themselves in a way that is *pleasing* to their masters. Εὐάρεστον is a comprehensive fundamental term in parenetic language involving the believer's task of examining the will of God in one's particular situation. W. Foerster, *TDNT* I, 456f.; H. Bietenhard, *DNTT* II, 814-17.

εὐαρέστως *euarestōs* in a pleasing manner*

Heb 12:28: λατρεύωμεν εὐαρέστως τῷ θεῷ, i.e., "with reverence and awe."

Εὔβουλος, ου *Euboulos* Eubulus*

A Christian who, according to 2 Tim 4:21, is among those who send greetings to Timothy.

εὖγε *euge* well done! superb!*

An interjection, Luke 19:17 (v.l. → εὖ).

εὐγενής, 2 *eugenēs* of noble birth, of high rank*

Luke 19:12, of a *man of high rank*. The context suggests a "nobleman" or "prince," at any rate a claimant to the throne (the passage alludes to Herod Archelaus's journey to Rome; cf. Josephus *Ant.* xvii.11). 1 Cor 1:26, with σοφοί and δυνατοί, of *noble* in the social sense (cf. also 4:10; Origen *Cels.* ii.79; see G. Theissen, *The Social Setting of Pauline Christianity* [1982] 70-73); Acts 17:11, of the Jews of Beroea, who were *more high-minded* (ἦσαν εὐγενέστεροι) than those of Thessalonica. Spicq, *Notes* I, 301-4.

εὐδία, ας, ἡ *eudia* fair weather

Matt 16:2 C D Koine L W, etc. Spicq, *Notes* I, 305f.

εὐδοχέω *eudokeō* be pleased, select, decide*

1. Occurrences and meanings — 2. Theological usage — a) Christological — b) Soteriological — c) Prophetic-apostolic

Lit.: S. LÉGASSE, *Jésus et l'enfant* (1969) 180-82. — O. MÜNDERLEIN, "Die Erwählung durch das Pleroma. Bemerkungen zu Kol 1,19," *NTS* 8 (1961-62) 264-76, esp. 266-71. — G. SCHRENK, *TDNT* II, 738-42.

1. The vb. appears in the NT 21 times, of which 9 are in the authentic Pauline letters. Matthew and Hebrews have 3 occurrences each; Luke has 2. Other occurrences are in Mark 1:11; Col 1:19; 2 Thess 2:12; and 2 Pet 1:17. The vb. does not appear in the Johannine literature. The subj. of εὐδοχέω is normally God; in only 7 instances is it a human being.

NT use of εὐδοχέω, a vb. of the will, is shaped by the influence of the LXX. The meanings alternate between *want, decide,* and *choose.* The occurrences with a human subject have no particular theological content (Rom 15:26, 27; 2 Cor 5:8; 12:10; 1 Thess 2:8; 3:1; 2 Thess 2:12).

2. The 14 occurrences in which God is the subj. are distributed between usages that have a christological, soteriological, or prophetic-apostolic accent:

a) The first type occurs in the heavenly voice at the baptism of Jesus (Mark 1:11 par. Matt 3:17/Luke 3:22; *Gospel of the Hebrews* in Epiphanius *Haer* 30.17), where the influence of Isa 42:1 is apparent. In Matt 17:5 and 2 Pet 1:17 the statement at the transfiguration is assimilated to the voice at the baptism (cf. Mark 9:7 par. Luke 9:35). The same christological perspective is seen in Matt 12:18-21 (v. 18: ὃν εὐδόχησεν ἡ ψυχή μου), where Isa 42:1-4 is cited. In these examples the idea of the divine election predominates in view of the singular and transcendent designation of Christ, the only Son (the ἀγαπητός). The same christological view is seen in Col 1:19 (cf. Ps 67:17 LXX); according to the most probable interpretation the "fulness" (→ πλήρωμα) of the saving riches that dwell in Christ (so that he may mediate them to humankind; cf. 2:9-11; Eph 1:23) refers to the free and absolute decree of God.

b) This decree confirms even more clearly its independence from any human convention when Paul says in 1 Cor 1:21 that the salvation of believers rests on a divine decision, which includes the "foolish" message of the cross. The salvation is—in the realization of the same decree— assured to the "little flock" of the poor, who are under God's protection (Luke 12:32). However, this aspect has a negative counterpart: The mass of Israelites, because of their own sin, did not obtain what God had provided, and only a minority came into the delight of the divine plan. Correspondingly, Heb 10:38 (citing Hab 2:4 LXX) emphasizes that the individual without faith places a hindrance in the way of God's plan and can thus be destroyed (v. 39). Thus the writer shows that the absoluteness of the divine will does not exclude human freedom. Thus the sacrifices of the old covenant could—in a corresponding way— "paralyze" the plan of salvation without the obedience of the "heart" (10:6, 8); only Christ could bring it to fulfillment through his obedience (vv. 7, 9).

c) Finally Paul sees in his call to be a messianic prophet the object of an unconditioned and purely gracious (διὰ τῆς χάριτος αὐτοῦ) decree of God regarding Paul himself (Gal 1:15; cf. 1 Cor 9:17-18).

S. Légasse

εὐδοχία, ας, ἡ *eudokia* pleasure, will, decree*

1. Occurrences and general meaning — 2. The epistles — 3. Matt 11:26 par. Luke 10:21 (Q) — 4. Luke 2:14

Lit.: BAGD s.v. — P.-R. BERGER, "Lk 2,14: ἄνθρωποι εὐδοχίας. Die auf Gottes Weisung mit Wohlgefallen beschenkten Menschen," *ZNW* 74 (1983) 129-44. — *idem,* "Menschen ohne 'Gottes Wohlgefallen' Lk 2,14?" *ZNW* 76 (1985) 119-22. — G. SCHRENK, *TDNT* II, 738-51. — G. SCHWARZ, "'... ἄνθρωποι εὐδοχίας'? (Lk 2,14)," *ZNW* 75 (1984) 136f. — For further bibliography see *TWNT* X, 1088f.

1. Εὐδοχία is probably a Hellenistic Jewish form from → εὐδοχέω and appears almost exclusively in Jewish or Christian literature. The most important background for NT use (9 occurrences) is the LXX (28 occurrences in the *Psalms of Solomon,* 8 in Psalms, and 16 in Sirach): Most frequently εὐδοχία is the tr. of Heb. *rāṣôn* (which is, however, most often represented by other Greek words), "good pleasure, will," and is usually employed in references to the εὐδοχία of God. When it is used of persons, it is sometimes used of an evil will.

2. In Rom 10:1 Paul speaks of the εὐδοχία of his own heart for the Jews. Although the frequent tr. *wish* from → εὐδοχέω is indeed possible, the use of the subst. elsewhere suggests a stronger content: so Schrenk 746: "the will of the heart" or (according to Harnack) "loving will." According to Phil 1:15, some who preach Christ δι' εὐδοχίαν do so out of love, according to v. 16. Others, by contrast, do so out of envy and rivalry. Here also εὐδοχία is more than a weak feeling; it is *goodwill.* According to Phil 2:13 God produces "both the will and the work ὑπὲρ τῆς εὐδοχίας": With "for, in the interest of" as the meaning of ὑπέρ (BDF §231), either God's εὐδοχία (he acts from his own decree because it pleases him) or that of people (above and beyond goodwill; cf. BAGD s.v. εὐδοχία and s.v. ὑπέρ 1.e) might be intended. If Paul's previous usage

speaks for the second possibility, the general background makes the first more probable (→ 4, on Luke 2:14).

The Paul of 2 Thessalonians prays in 1:11 that God might complete or fill the Thessalonians with "every εὐδοκίαν ἀγαθωσύνης [of the good] and every work of faith" in power. Here also it is possible that εὐδοκία refers to the goodness of God (perhaps: that God's *good pleasure* should be realized; so Schrenk 746); but in this case the context (cf. also 1 Thess 1:3) makes the thought of human εὐδοκία more probable. However, the force of the gen., the relationship to the good, is uncertain. The gen. is either subj. (the *will* that comes from the good or uprightness; so BAGD) or obj. (perhaps *decision* for the good; so G. Friedrich, *1-2 Thess* [NTD] ad loc.).

In Eph 1:5, 9 εὐδοκία is unambiguously used for the free *will* and *decision* of God (κατὰ τὴν εὐδοκίαν . . . αὐτοῦ, in v. 5 with προορίσας, in v. 9 with ἣν προέθετο).

3. In Matt 11:26 par. Luke 10:21 (Q) also εὐδοκία is God's sovereign *decree* (Schrenk 747; cf. BAGD s.v. ἔμπροσθεν 2.d), corresponding to ᾧ ἐὰν βούληται in the following verse (see P. Hoffmann, *Studien zur Theologie der Logienquelle* [1972] 109).

4. In Luke 2:14 the variant reading εὐδοκία (nom.) — e.g., Koine — is not to be rejected from the outset (*TCGNT* ad loc.). However, the gen. εὐδοκίας is probably original (B* ℵ* A D). Again it is possible to understand the gen. in the sense of human εὐδοκία, of course not in the sense of a meritorious achievement, but rather that God, with the peace that he gives, also provides the opening for it. Most probably, however, the gen. points to God's free decision (Schrenk 748-50); this interpretation is now supported by the parallel "sons of good pleasure" from Qumran (1QH 4:32f.; 11:9); see C.-H. Hunzinger, *ZNW* 44 (1952-53) 85-90; 49 (1958) 129f.; J. A. Fitzmyer, *TS* 19 (1958) 225-27; R. Deichgräber, *ZNW* 51 (1960) 132; J. Jeremias, *ZNW* 28 (1929) 13-20. The message of the angels is thus the proclamation of the gift of God's peace to people of divine *good pleasure* (Schrenk 750; H. Schürmann, *Luke* [HTKNT] I, ad loc.; cf. G. Schwarz, *BZ* 15 (1971) 260-64, who prefers to eliminate εὐδοκία on the basis of a tr. into Aramaic).

R. Mahoney

εὐεργεσία, ας, ἡ   *euergesia*   benefit, good deed
→ εὐεργετέω.

εὐεργετέω   *euergeteō*   do good*
εὐεργεσία, ας, ἡ   *euergesia*   benefit, good deed*
εὐεργέτης, ου, ὁ   *euergetēs*   benefactor*

1. Occurrences in the NT and meanings — 2. The word group in Hellenism — 3. Theological range of the word group in Luke-Acts

Lit.: G. BERTRAM, *TDNT* II, 654f. — H. BOLKESTEIN, *Wohltätigkeit und Armenpflege im vorchristlichen Altertum* (1939) 95-102, index s.v. — U. BUSSE, *Die Wunder des Propheten Jesus* (FzB 24, 1977) 434-37. — F. W. DANKER, *Benefactor: Epigraphic Study of a Graeco-Roman and NT Semantic Field* (1982; see also *idem, Luke* [Proclamation, 1976] 6-17). — DEISSMANN, *Light* 253. — B. KÖTTING, *RAC* VI, 848-60. — A. D. NOCK, "Soter and Euergetes," *The Joy of Study*, FS F. C. Grant (1951) 127-48. — J. OEHLER, *PW* VI, 978-81. — H. SCHÜRMANN, *Jesu Abschiedsrede* (NTAbh 20/5, 1957) 70-73. — E. SKARD, *Zwei religiös-politische Begriffe: Euergetes-Concordia* (1932). — Spicq, *Notes* I, 307-13.

1. The word group has its focal point in Luke-Acts, where each of the three words is used once. In the rest of the NT only εὐεργεσία appears again (1 Tim 6:2).

The latter abstract noun designates *doing right* in general, but particularly *a good deed* as a single act or in general (Homer *Od.* xxii.235, 374; Herodotus iii.47, 67; iv.165; v.11; Xenophon *An.* vii.7.47; Plato *Grg.* 513e; the LXX connects the word with God, who worked wonders at the exodus from Egypt: Ps 77:11; Wis 16:11, 24). In 1 Timothy it is used for believing masters, whom the slaves should serve, "because those who devote themselves to *kindness* are faithful and beloved (by God)." Acts 4:9 speaks of the *good deed* done to a sick man (ἀνθρώπου ἀσθενοῦς). Later Christian occurrences are in *1 Clem.* 19:2; 21:1; 38:3; *Diog.* 8:11; 9:5.

The vb. means *do good, give charity, show kindness* (in the LXX and elsewhere again of the wonder-working activity of God at the exodus: Wis 11:5, 13; 16:2). It appears absolutely in Acts 10:38 in Peter's speech to Cornelius as the term characterizing the work of Jesus, "who went about and *did good* (διῆλθεν εὐεργετῶν) and healed all. . . ." In other early Christian literature the vb. appears in *1 Clem.* 20:11; *Diog.* 10:6; Ign. *Rom.* 5:1.

The noun εὐεργέτης is used of the one who does good deeds, the *benefactor*. It is used in Luke 22:25 in a saying of Jesus to the disciples (probably redactional; see Schürmann 72): The worldly rulers "are called *benefactors*" (→ 2). The admonition in v. 26 is addressed to the disciples: "But not so with you. Rather the greatest among you should be as the least, and the leader as the one who serves."

2. Εὐεργέτης is attested frequently in Hellenism as a titular predicate of rulers and other prominent persons (philosophers, discoverers, physicians; Herodotus viii.85; Xenophon *HG* vi.1.4; Plato *Grg.* 506c; also in inscriptions: see *SIG* index s.v.; Moulton/Milligan 260f.; LSJ s.v.; also on coins: see Deissmann 253f. and papyri. In Jewish literature this title is used in the same way (Add Esth 8:12n. [RSV 16:13]; 2 Macc 4:2; 3 Macc 3:19; Philo *Omn. Prob. Lib.* 118; *Flacc.* 81; Josephus *B.J.* iii.459). The double pred. σωτὴρ καὶ εὐεργέτης is frequent (Pap. London [II] 177, 24; a Spartan inscription cited in Moulton/Milligan 261 [of Hadrian]; *IG* XII/1, 978 [of Trajan]; Add Esth 8:12n.; Josephus *B.J.* iii.459). This versatile usage (seen as well with the other words in the word group) is associated with the cul-

ture-optimism of the Hellenistic world. Various men (rarely the gods; see Nilsson, *Geschichte* 183) are "hailed as benefactors because of their contributions to the development of the human race" (Bertram 654). The Augustan renaissance in particular made the (probably already much used) title a basic term in religion and politics (Skard). The emperors were considered divine saviors and benefactors of humanity because they made the culture possible with the *pax romana* (cf. Bertram 654; A. Alföldi, *MH* 11 [1954] 145-51).

3. Although the occurrences of the three words in Luke-Acts are not clearly coordinated with each other, the three passages have their own theological profile. In Acts 10:38 the activity of Jesus is described by the two partcs. εὐεργετῶν and ἰώμενος. Jesus' beneficence is essentially the healing activity for "all who were under the control of the devil"; it is done in the Holy Spirit, in "power" and with God's help.

Correspondingly the healing of the lame man in front of the temple (3:1-10) preceding 4:9 (also here in the mouth of Peter) is described as εὐεργεσία done for a sick man. Because of this (ἐπί with the dat.) the apostles are examined for unlawful conduct. The examiners wanted to know "through whom was this one healed" (σέσωται)." Here not only the normal parallels "savior and benefactor" (→ 2) are taken up (cf. also Luke 6:9: ἀγαθοποιῆσαι with σῶσαι), but it is made clear that the apostles are not the essential benefactors. Behind their healing act stands Jesus, whom the Jewish authorities have crucified (Acts 4:10)—with two κακοῦργοι (Luke 23:32, 33, 39 [different from par. Mark]). Nevertheless the title "benefactor" is not used of Jesus (*1 Clem.* 23:1; 59:3 speaks of God as benefactor; on this see Acts 14:17: God as ἀγαθουργῶν).

The true benefactor of mankind forbids his disciples from calling themselves εὐεργέται (Luke 22:25f.). The formulation presupposes that worldly bearers of the title in reality exercise sovereignty and power over the people. However, one who is greatest in the community of Jesus (i.e., a Church leader?) should distinguish himself (cf. also 6:33, 35: ἀγαθοποιέω, cf. Busse) by serving according to the model of Jesus (v. 27) and should not strive for recognition and titles (cf. Matt 23:6-12).

G. Schneider

εὐεργέτης, ου, ὁ *euergetēs* benefactor
→ εὐεργετέω.

εὔθετος, 2 *euthetos* fit, suitable*

Luke 9:62: not *fit* for the kingdom of God; 14:35, of salt, which is *fit* neither for the land nor the dunghill; Heb 6:7: βοτάνη εὔθετον, "*useful* vegetation."

εὐθέως *eutheōs* immediately*
→ εὐθύς.

εὐθυδρομέω *euthydromeō* go directly*

Acts 16:11, with εἰς; 21:1, absolute.

εὐθυμέω *euthymeō* be of good cheer*

In the NT only intrans.: Acts 27:22, 25; Jas 5:13 (in contrast to κακοπαθέω). Spicq, *Notes* I, 314-17.

εὔθυμος, 2 *euthymos* confident, cheerful*

Acts 27:36: εὔθυμοι δὲ γενόμενοι. Spicq, *Notes* I, 314-17.

εὐθύμως *euthymōs* cheerfully*

Acts 24:10: εὐθύμως τὰ περὶ ἐμαυτοῦ ἀπολογοῦμαι, "I make my defense *gladly*." Spicq, *Notes* I, 314-17.

εὐθύνω *euthynō* make straight; guide*

John 1:23: εὐθύνατε τὴν ὁδὸν κυρίου (cf. Isa 40:3); Jas 3:4, pres. partc. ὁ εὐθύνων, "the *pilot.*"

εὐθύς, 3 *euthys* straight (adj.)*
εὐθύς, εὐθέως *euthys, eutheōs* immediately (adv.)

1. Occurrences in the NT — 2. Meanings — 3. Εὐθύς in miracle stories

Lit.: K. BERGER, *Exegese des NT* (UTB 658, 1977) 22f. — D. DAUBE, *The Sudden in the Scriptures* (1964) 46-72. — R. PESCH, *Mark* [HTKNT] I (1976) 18f., 89. — E. J. PRYKE, *Redactional Style in the Marcan Gospel* (SNTSMS 33, 1978) 87-96. — G. RUDBERG, "ΕΥΘΥΣ," ConNT 9 (1944) 42-46. — L. RYDBECK, *Fachprosa, vermeintliche Volkssprache und NT* (SGU 5, 1967) 167-76. — D. TABACHOVITZ, *Die Septuaginta und das NT* (Skrifter utgivna av Svenska Institutet i Athen 8⁰ IV, 1956) 29-35. — G. THEISSEN, *Urchristliche Wundergeschichten* (SNT 8, 1974) 199f.

1. As an adj. εὐθύς appears 8 times in the NT and, with the exception of Acts 9:11 (the "*straight* street" in Damascus), is always used metaphorically.

As an adv. εὐθύς appears 87 times in the NT (36 times in the form εὐθέως, 51 times in the form εὐθύς). It is a temporal adv. and appears almost exclusively in narrative texts (miracles, figurative language, parables) and is used there to show connections and relations among sections of text. The striking frequency in Mark (42 times; 26 times in the construction καὶ εὐθύς) is only partly attributable to the Markan redactor; εὐθύς was already present in the pre-Markan tradition. Of 18 occurrences in Matthew, 14 have a direct par. in Mark (the others are in Matt 14:31; 24:29; 25:15; 27:48). Luke has εὐθύς 7 times, but only once from Mark (Luke 5:13). In the Markan material he often deletes it or replaces it with παραχρῆμα (Luke 5:25; 8:44, 55; 18:43; 22:60). The other Lukan references are in Q material (6:49; 12:36, 54) and in Lukan special material (14:5; 17:7). An exception is 21:9 (added in Markan material). John uses εὐθύς 6 times. Of the 10 occurrences in Acts, 5 belong in the context of miracles or visions (Acts 9:18, 34; 10:16; 12:10; 16:10). The other occurrences (Gal 1:16; Jas 1:24; Rev 4:2) confirm the rule that εὐθύς is limited to narrative and figurative language. A single exception is 3 John 14 (epistolary style).

2. In the citation of Isa 40:3f. LXX (Mark 1:3 par. Matt 3:3; Luke 3:4f.) the adj. designates the way of Yahweh in the wilderness. In Acts 13:10 (cf. Ezek 33:17 LXX; Hos 14:10; Pr Azar 4; Sir 39:24) it designates the "straight ways" of God for humankind. The way of the pious, the conduct demanded by God, is designated as straight (2 Pet 2:15; cf. 1 Kgdms 12:23; Prov 2:13, 16; 20:11 LXX; Isa 26:7; Wis 10:10). The metaphor of the way makes possible the image of the "heart that is right" (Acts 8:21; 4 Kgdms 10:15; Ps 77:37 LXX, etc.).

The temporal meaning of the adv. never has the connotation of the unexpected or sudden that is associated with ἄφνω or ἐξαίφνης, but rather indicates, as with ἐξαυτῆς, a temporal or logical result (forthwith, at once; Mark 14:72; John 19:34, etc.). Thus εὐθύς often has the function of showing the (temporal) connection of narrative units. Thus it is found esp. at the beginning (Mark 1:12, 21, 29; 6:45; 14:43; 15:1; Acts 9:20) or end (Mark 1:28; 4:29; 5:43; 8:10; Acts 10:16; 12:10; 16:10) of textual units. In Mark εὐθύς is an important compositional element of the narrative.

3. In the Synoptic miracle stories and those in John and Acts one finds a uniform use of εὐθύς. In healing and deliverance miracle stories (Mark 1:42 par.; 2:12; 5:29, 42; 7:35; 10:52 par.; John 5:9; Acts 9:18, 34) εὐθύς designates the point where the miracle begins or is recognized (Matt 14:31; Mark 6:50; John 6:21). Healings are proceeded by a word or a gesture of the miracle worker, so that the suddenness of the event (Theissen 199) is not stressed, but rather the combination of the word (gesture) and the miracle, which is perceived as a consequence.

Use of → παραχρῆμα is related. In 15 of 18 occurrences in the NT—in healing miracles (Luke 1:64; 4:39; 5:25; 8:44, 47, 55; 13:13; 18:43; Acts 3:7), miracles of punishment (Matt 21:19f.; Acts 5:10; 12:23; 13:11), and in a miracle of the opening of a door (Acts 16:26)—it designates the moment when the miracle occurs or is recognized.   W. Pöhlmann

εὐθύς, εὐθέως euthys, eutheōs immediately (adv.) → εὐθύς (adj.)

εὐθύτης, ητος, ἡ euthytēs straightness; uprightness, justice*

Heb 1:8: ἡ ῥάβδος τῆς εὐθύτητος, "the righteous scepter" (citing Ps 44:7 LXX).

εὐκαιρέω eukaireō have time, have opportunity, be occupied*

Mark 6:31: "they had no time to eat"; Acts 17:21, of the Athenians, who "were occupied with nothing other than . . ."; 1 Cor 16:12: ὅταν εὐκαιρήσῃ, "as soon as he finds the opportunity." Spicq, Notes I, 318-20.

εὐκαιρία, ας, ἡ eukairia favorable opportunity*

Matt 26:16 par. Luke 22:6: Judas sought a favorable opportunity to deliver over Jesus. Spicq, Notes I, 318f.

εὔκαιρος, 2 eukairos suitable, well-timed*

Mark 6:21: ἡμέρας εὐκαίρου, "a suitable day"; Heb 4:16: εὔκαιρον βοήθειαν, "help at the right time." Spicq, Notes I, 319.

εὐκαίρως eukairōs at an appropriate opportunity*

Mark 14:11, of Judas (cf. Matt 26:16 par. Luke 22:6 [εὐκαιρία]); 2 Tim 4:2, asyndeton with ἀκαίρως, "whether at an appropriate or inconvenient time." A. J. Malherbe, " 'In Season and out of Season': 2 Timothy 4:2," JBL 103 (1984) 235-43; Spicq, Notes I, 320.

εὔκοπος, 2 eukopos easy*

In the NT only in the comparative and always in the construction (τί) εὐκοπώτερόν ἐστιν, "which is easier" (Mark 2:9 par. Matt 9:5/Luke 5:23; Mark 10:25 par. Matt 19:24/Luke 18:25; Luke 16:17).

εὐλάβεια, ας, ἡ eulabeia fear, fear of God, piety*

In Heb 12:28 εὐλάβεια (with δέος) most likely means fear/awe (cf. v. 29).

Heb 5:7 is very much disputed: Εἰσακουσθεὶς ἀπὸ τῆς εὐλαβείας can be rendered "(Christ) was heard because of his fear of God/piety" (cf. BAGD s.v. [bibliography]; BDF §210.2 [bibliography]; O. Michel, Heb [KEK] ad loc.; G. Friedrich, "Das Lied vom Hohenpriester im Zusammenhang von Hebr 4,14–5,10," idem, Auf das Wort kommt es an. Gesammelte Aufsätze [1978] 279-99, esp. 289f., etc.; → ἀπό 4.b). Because Christ's (human) fear is stressed in the context, others translate "he was heard from his anxiety" (cf. A. Strobel, Heb [NTD] ad loc.) or "he heard and was freed from his anxiety" (U. Wilckens, Das NT [²1971] ad loc.), or conjecture an οὐκ before εἰσακουσθείς (following A. von Harnack; cf. R. Bultmann, TDNT II, 753; for discussion cf. esp. Michel ad loc.). Corresponding to the relation of the fixed Christ/high priest sayings in 4:14ff. Christ was not spared weakness and the fear of death (cf. 4:15; 5:2, 7a; the tradition of Mark 14:36 par. and esp. Luke 22:43f.

likewise; also Ps 116:3ff.), but was spared defeat by the power of death (θάνατος, Heb 5:7; cf. Friedrich 188f.). Thus εὐλάβεια in v. 7 involves a "once-for-all" (cf. 4:15) *devotion to God* or *piety*. Because of this he was heard by God and as τελειωθείς was made the basis of salvation and true high priest for all obedient persons (vv. 9f.). See also E. Grässer, *Heb* (EKKNT) I, 302-5.   H. Balz

εὐλαβέομαι *eulabeomai* take heed; be reverent*

Heb 11:7, of Noah, who built the ark *in reverence* (εὐλαβηθείς) for the divine instruction and thus proved his faith (Vg. *metuens*); Acts 23:10 TR in place of φοβηθείς.

εὐλαβής, 2 *eulabēs* pious, reverent*

In the NT always with ἀνήρ, ἄνδρες, or ἄνθρωπος: Luke 2:35, of Simeon (with δίκαιος); Acts 2:5, of *pious* Jews from the Diaspora who live in Jerusalem; 8:2, of the men who buried Stephen; 22:12, of Ananias (εὐλαβής κατὰ τὸν νόμον).

εὐλογέω *eulogeō* praise, commend, extol; bless; say the prayer (at the meal)*

1. Occurrences and meaning — 2. Praise of God and blessing — 3. Table benediction — 4. Εὐλογητός — 5. Εὐλογία

Lit.: W. BEYER, *TDNT* II, 754-63. — BILLERBECK I, 685-87; IV, 627-34. — R. DEICHGRÄBER, *Gotteshymnus und Christushymnus in der frühen Christenheit* (1967). — L. GOPPELT, *1 Pet* (KEK, 1978) 90-92, 225-29. — H.-G. LINK, *DNTT* I, 206-15. — J. MATEOS, *Filologia Neotestamentaria* I (1988) 5-25 (on εὐλογία). — H. PATSCH, "Abendmahlsterminologie außerhalb der Einsetzungsberichte," *ZNW* 62 (1971) 210-31. — J. SCHARBERT, "Die Geschichte der bārûk-Formel," *BZ* 17 (1973) 1-28. — idem, *LTK* IX, 590-92 (bibliography). — W. SCHENK, *Der Segen im NT* (1967). — R. SCHNACKENBURG, "Die große Eulogie Eph 1,3-14," *BZ* 21 (1977) 67-87. — A. STUIBER, *RAC* VI, 900-928. — C. WESTERMANN, *Der Segen in der Bibel und im Handeln der Kirche* (1968). — For further bibliography see *TWNT* X, 1089f.

1. The word group from the stem εὐλογ- appears primarily in the Synoptics, Paul, and Hebrews. There are 41 occurrences of the vb., 8 of the adj. εὐλογητός, and 16 of the noun εὐλογία (→ 4, 5). Because of its biblical-Semitizing background it appears only rarely in the later parts of the NT, in some parts not at all. The noun is found only in the Epistles.

The restriction of the meaning in contrast to secular usage ("speak well") reflects the LXX background, where the stem represents Heb. *brk*, "bless." Absolute εὐλογέω has (as a Semitism) the special meaning *say the table blessing*. Only here is the word group synonymous and interchangeable with the group from the stem εὐχαρ-. The

Hellenizing completion of the vb. with an obj. (Mark 8:7; Luke 9:16; cf. 1 Cor 10:16) could allow the meaning *consecrate* (BAGD s.v.). However, in our literature this meaning is not probable.

2. God's saving deeds call forth thankful praise (Luke 1:64; 2:28; 24:53; cf. Jas 3:9). Paul demands that praise of God in ecstatic speech remain intelligible for outsiders (1 Cor 14:16).

In a conscious biblicistic way Luke and Hebrews have the meaning *bless* when they provide a scenic depiction of the final blessing (Luke 2:34; 24:50) or refer to the fathers and the ancestral blessing (Heb 7:1, 6, 7; 11:20f.). While the Abrahamic blessing (Gen 22:16-18; 18:18; 12:3) is seen in Heb 6:14 as a challenge to exercise patient endurance, in Peter's speech in Acts it serves as the basis for the sending of Jesus to the Jews (3:26); Paul, however, bases his doctrine of justification on the example of Abraham's faith, which was blessed by God (Gal 3:9). The giver of the blessing is ultimately always God, who blesses his own people here (Eph 1:3) and in the final judgment (Matt 25:34). This is also apparent in the use of the divine passive of the cry of homage, "*blessed be (by God)*," addressed to Mary and the fruit of her womb (Luke 1:42), to Jesus as he arrives in Jerusalem (Mark 11:9 par. Matt 21:9/Luke 19:38/John 12:13; Matt 23:39 par. Luke 13:35 [Q]; cf. Ps 117:26 LXX), and to the kingdom of God that arrives through him (Mark 11:10).

With "*Bless* those who curse you" (Luke 6:28a) as the third line, the commandment to love one's enemies is filled out in the Sermon on the Plain as a four-line saying. This addition, which concretizes Jesus' demand and reflects the Church's situation, is—as a free traditional saying—used parenetically by Paul and 1 Peter (Rom 12:14; 1 Cor 4:12; 1 Pet 3:9; cf. *Did.* 1:3).

3. In accordance with the Jewish regulation (*b. Ber.* 35a) Jesus says the blessing before the meal when he feeds the 5,000 (Mark 6:41/Luke 9:16) or 4,000 (Mark 8:7) hungry people and when he eats with the Emmaus disciples (Luke 24:30). These texts stand in connection with the Last Supper reports in the history of tradition. In both cases Jesus says the blessing (Mark 14:22 par. Matt 26:26) before he breaks the bread, in the same way as the father in the Jewish household. On the occasion of his argument over eating meat sacrificed to idols (1 Cor 10:14ff.), Paul, in consciously liturgical language, recalls the cup of blessing, "which we *bless*" (v. 16; *not* "which we consecrate"). The frequent use of → εὐχαριστέω is characteristic of these texts and betrays the development of liturgical-sacramental terminology. It is present either as a parallel tradition (feeding: Mark 8:6 par. Matt 15:36; Last Supper: Luke 22:19/1 Cor 11:24, cf. Justin *Apol.* i.66.3) or as a textual variation (Mark 8:6, 7; Mark 14:22, 23 par. Matt 26:26, 27). This coexistence of the two terms,

which appears elsewhere (1 Cor 14:16f.; Josephus *Ant.* viii.111; *Corp. Herm.* i.26.6, 27.2), does not permit conjecture either about a difference in meaning or a gradual replacement of one vb. by the other.

4. **Εὐλογητός**, *blessed, praised**, is a tr. of Heb. *bārû*. It belongs to a doxological type of expression that is derived from an OT and Jewish traditional form of prayer. In the NT it always refers to God. The Benedictus of Zechariah (Luke 1:68) takes up the doxological conclusion of the books of Psalms (Pss 41:14; 72:18; 89:53; 106:48). God is praised as Creator (Rom 1:25) and Father of our Lord Jesus Christ (2 Cor 11:31; so also in the blessing formula in the epistolary proemium: 2 Cor 1:3; Eph 1:3; 1 Pet 1:3). Thus Rom 9:5 is to be understood in an analogous way. The title "Son of the *blessed*" in the question of the high priest (Mark 14:61) avoids the name of God in a Jewish manner.

5. Only Rom 16:18 reminds one of the secular Greek meaning of **εὐλογία*** — "fine speaking" (and there it is intended negatively). In Rev 5:12, 13; 7:12 the collecting of synonymous terms in doxologies give εὐλογία the meaning *praise*.

Elsewhere the meaning is consistently *blessing*. The giver of the blessing is God (or Christ; Heb 6:7; Gal 3:14), even where the blessing is pronounced by a person (Heb 12:17: ancestral blessing, cf. 11:20f.). The opposite is— as in Gen 27:12, 29, etc.—curse (Jas 3:10). Because Christians are called to inherit the blessing of God, the *ius talionis* is excluded for them (1 Pet 3:9; parenesis in dependence on Luke 6:28). Paul calls the collection for the Jerusalem church a *blessing,* which includes the OT sense of generosity, abundance in gifts and proceeds (2 Cor 9:5 bis, 6 bis; cf. Rom 15:29). The antithesis of blessing and curse is interpreted christologically within the doctrine of justification in Galatians 3: Through his death on the cross, Christ has become a curse, so that Gentiles can also have a part in the blessing to Abraham, which consists of the gift of the Spirit through faith (3:14; cf. 3:8f.). In the eulogy in the hymnic introduction to the letter, Eph 1:3 uses the root εὐλογ-, with its various nuances in meaning, to praise God that believers who have received the blessing of God (in baptism) live as members of the body of Christ in his heavenly kingdom. In 1 Cor 10:16 Paul interprets the "cup of *blessing*" (Heb. *kôs šel bᵉrāâ*) of the Lord's Supper as "sharing" in the blood of Christ, i.e., real participation in the death of Christ. Paul received the interpretation of the cup('s contents) as the blood in the Last Supper tradition (11:25); he interprets it as the saving death of Christ (cf. Rom 3:25; 5:9). → ποτήριον.   H. Patsch

εὐλογητός, 3 *eulogētos* blessed, praised
→ εὐλογέω 1, 4.

εὐλογία, ας, ἡ *eulogia* praise; blessing; fine speaking
→ εὐλογέω 1, 5.

εὐμετάδοτος, 2 *eumetadotos* generous**

1 Tim 6:18, with κοινωνικούς in an admonition to the rich. Spicq, *Notes* I, 321f.

Εὐνίκη, ης *Eunikē* Eunice**

The mother of Timothy (2 Tim 1:5), to whom she is a model of "sincere faith," whom she instructed in the "holy Scriptures" (3:16), and whose father was a Greek Gentile (cf. Acts 16:1, where Eunice is described as a γυνὴ Ἰουδαία πιστή, which is hardly compatible with her [unlawful] marrage to a Gentile; see Billerbeck II, 741).

εὐνοέω *eunoeō* be favorably inclined, be well disposed**

Matt 5:25: ἴσθι εὐνοῶν . . . ταχύ, in reference to the opponent in a trial, *make friends again/come to an understanding.*

εὔνοια, ας, ἡ *eunoia* goodwill, affection**

Eph 6:7, of Christian slaves: μετ' εὐνοίας δουλεύοντες, serving with *goodwill;* 1 Cor 7:3 v.l.: ὀφειλομένην εὔνοιαν, in place of ὀφειλήν.

εὐνουχίζω *eunouchizō* castrate, emasculate
→ εὐνοῦχος.

εὐνοῦχος, ου, ὁ *eunouchos* eunuch, castrated man**
εὐνουχίζω *eunouchizō* castrate, emasculate**

1. Occurrences in the NT — 2. The social and religious environment — 3. Matt 19:12 — 4. Acts 8:27ff.

Lit.: J. BLINZLER, " 'Zur Ehe unfähig . . .' Auslegung von Mt 19,12," idem, *Aus der Welt und Umwelt des NT. Gesammelte Aufsätze* I (1969) 20-40. — D. G. BURKE, *ISBE* II, 200-202. — L. H. GRAY, *ERE* V, 579-84. — H. HITZIG, PW II/2, 1772f. — A. HUG, PW Suppl. III, 449-55. — J. JEREMIAS, *Jerusalem in the Time of Jesus* (1969) index s.v. — A. D. NOCK, "Eunuchs in Ancient Religion," *ARW* 23 (1925) 25-33. — A. SAND, *Reich Gottes und Eheverzicht im Evangelium nach Matthäus* (1983). — J. SCHNEIDER, *TDNT* II, 765-68. — For further bibliography see *TWNT* X, 1090.

1. This word group appears in the NT in only two passages, in Matt 19:12 (εὐνουχίζω twice, εὐνοῦχος 3 times) and Acts 8 (εὐνοῦχος, vv. 27, 34, 36, 38, and 39).

2. The social and religious background of the word group has a number of differing aspects:

a) In all of ancient society eunuchs were as a whole among the most despised and scorned of human groups. Usually they were deliberately mutilated slaves (see texts on social status esp. in Gray 582f.). The custom of mutilating apparently came from the Orient and found entry into Rome at the end of the Republican era (Hug 449-51). In Judaism eunuchs were among the classes deprived of rights: They could not have a place or a voice in the Sanhedrin or in criminal court (Jeremias 343).

b) Esp. in the Orient, and later in Rome, as also, e.g., at the Herodian court, a minority of eunuchs rose to high and influential positions in family and government. *Eunuch* could thus be a synonym for "high official" (on this and the problem of etymology, cf. Gray 579).

c) It is uncertain to which group the prohibition of castration by Domitian (Suetonius *Caes.* iii.84; Dio Cassius lxvii.2) and his successors (cf. Hitzig) was aimed. The reasons that have been given are moral excesses, excessive influence, and the greed of the slave dealers (texts in Hug 551f.).

d) Self-castration of male priests was practiced in the fertility cults of Asia Minor (Artemis, Atargatis, Cybele, etc.). The purpose of this custom was ritual purity and dedication of the priest's entire life to the revered deity (Nock). These priests were despised and scorned outside the cult.

3. Knowledge of the social and religious background is absolutely necessary for understanding Matt 19:12. The saying in v. 12 is combined by Matthew with the pericope on divorce (19:1-9 par. Mark 10:2-12) by means of a question from the disciples (v. 10) and an introduction to the saying (v. 11). As a result vv. 10-12 take on the form, perhaps initiated by Mark 10:10, of supplementary instruction to the disciples. The text names three kinds of *eunuchs:* a) those mutilated naturally, b) those mutilated by human action, and c) those who have mutilated themselves for the sake of the kingdom of heaven. The understanding of the last of these is disputed.

The following considerations can be given in favor of a literal, i.e., nonmetaphorical understanding: 1) the context, inasmuch as c) is not set apart from examples a) and b), which are certainly literal; 2) the framework, which emphasizes the exacting demand of the saying; and 3) the social and history-of-religions background, which does not exclude self-castration.

The following considerations can be given against the literal understanding and for a fig. understanding: 1) Little is known about a custom of self-castration in the Christian tradition, which was, in fact, explicitly forbidden (cf. *Apostolic Constitutions* viii.47.21-24). 2) A fig. use of the word group is known (Philostratus *VA* vi.42; Clement of Alexandria *Strom.* iii.7.59). 3) Less significant is that the majority of interpreters have always understood this passage in a fig. way.

A final decision appears to be impossible. Our difficulty of conceiving of such a radical demand should not exclude the possibility that in the circle of an extreme and thoroughgoing wandering radicalism—in a tradition of thoroughgoing renunciation of marriage and family

and solidarity with those who were fully disenfranchised —such a practice was widespread. After all, a fig. understanding of the text, even if it is essentially weakened, points in the same direction.

4. In Acts 8:27ff. a *eunuch* is mentioned who has apparently moved up to a high position in the government (→ 2.b). Inasmuch as δυνάστης is likewise mentioned as a term for his position (v. 27), *eunuch* is probably to be understood literally.

G. Petzke

Εὐοδία, ας *Euodia* Euodia*

A Christian woman in Philippi who is admonished, along with Syntyche, τὸ αὐτὸ φρονεῖν (Phil 4:2). According to v. 3 both have together with Paul "struggled for the gospel."

εὐοδόω *euodoō* be on a good path, succeed, go well*

In the NT only pass. and fig.: Rom 1:10: εἴ πως ἤδη ποτὲ εὐοδωθήσομαι, "whether I will finally *succeed*"; 1 Cor 16:2: ὅ τι ἐὰν εὐοδῶται, "as much as he *may prosper*" (not "as much as he makes a profit"); 3 John 2 (bis): *be in good health, go well* (with ὑγιαίνω).

εὐπάρεδρος, 2 *euparedros* steadfast, faithful*

1 Cor 7:35, subst. with εὔσχημον: "so that you may remain without distraction proper and *faithful* to the Lord." Not attested before Paul.

εὐπειθής, 2 *eupeithēs* obedient, compliant*

Jas 3:17, of the "higher wisdom": *compliant* (with ἁγνή, εἰρηνική, ἐπιεικής, etc.). Spicq, *Notes* I, 323f.

εὐπερίστατος, 2 *euperistatos* easily entangled, made captive*

Heb 12:1, of ἁμαρτία (p[46] εὐπερίσπαστος). Spicq, *Notes* I, 325f.

εὐποιΐα, ας, ἡ *eupoiïa* charity, good deed*

Heb 13:16, with κοινωνία. Spicq, *Notes* I, 327.

εὐπορέω *euporeō* be financially able*

Acts 11:29 mid.: καθὼς εὐπορεῖτό τις, "everyone as he *is able*." Spicq, *Notes* I, 328f.

εὐπορία, ας, ἡ *euporia* wealth, abundance, comfortable livelihood*

Acts 19:25: ἡ εὐπορία ἐστιν ἐκ, "our *livelihood* depends on . . ." Spicq, *Notes* I, 328f.

εὐπρέπεια, ας, ἡ *euprepeia* beauty, ornament*

Jas 1:11: ἡ εὐπρέπεια τοῦ προσώπου, of the *beauty* of the flower of the grass (cf. Isa 40:7). Spicq, *Notes* I, 330.

εὐπρόσδεκτος, 2 *euprosdektos* pleasant, welcome, favorable*

With reference to God: *pleasing* "sacrifices," Rom 15:16 (προσφορὰ τῶν ἐθνῶν εὐπρόσδεκτος); 1 Pet 2:5 (πνευματικὰς θυσίας εὐπροσδέκτους τῷ θεῷ). With reference to humans: Rom 15:31 (διακονία . . . εὐπρόσδεκτος τοῖς ἁγίοις); 2 Cor 8:12, of readiness for the collection (present in Corinth), which is *welcome* insofar as it is based on what one has, not on what he does not have. Paul does not assure the donors that they will not be overstrained (against R. Bultmann, *2 Cor* ad loc.), but instead challenges them to act in accordance with what they have prepared. 1 Cor 6:2: καιρὸς εὐπρόσδεκτος in the citation of Isa 49:8: καιρὸς δεκτός (v. 2a). Paul interprets his text through the reformulation: "Now is the *favorable/welcome* time." Spicq, *Notes* I, 331f.

εὐπρόσεδρος, 2 *euprosedros* steadfast*

1 Cor 7:35 TR in place of → εὐπάρεδρος.

εὐπροσωπέω *euprosōpeō* look good*

Gal 6:12: εὐπροσωπῆσαι ἐν σαρκί, "(want to) *make a good impression before humans.*"

εὐρακύλων, ωνος, ὁ *eurakylōn* northeast wind*

Acts 27:14 as t.t. of seagoing language (formed from εὖρος, "southeast wind," and Lat. *aquilo,* "north wind"; cf. BDF §5).

εὑρίσκω *heuriskō* find*

1. Linguistic structure — 2. General narrative style — 3. As a key word of a theology of revelation — 4. Official language — 5. Derivatives

Lit.: O. Betz, *Offenbarung und Schriftforschung in der Qumransekte* (1960) 15-40. — R. Bultmann, *Jesus and the Word* (1958²). — F. Christ, *Jesus Sophia* (1970) 100-19. — R. Pesch, "Über die Autorität Jesu," FS Schürmann, 25-55.—G. Schneider, *Die Passion Jesu nach den drei älteren Evangelien* (1973) 55-64, 102f. — P. Vielhauer, "'Ανάπαυσις, zum gnostischen Hintergrund des Thomas-Evangeliums," FS Haenchen 281-99. — B. T. Viviano, *Study as Worship* (1978) 66-71. — H.-T. Wrege, "Jesusgeschichte und Jüngergeschick nach Joh 12,20-33 und Hebr 5,7-10," FS Jeremias (1970) 259-88. — For further bibliography see *TWNT* X, 1090.

1. "Seek" (ζητέω) and "find" appear frequently as complementary vbs. The unique experience is to find without seeking (so possibly Luke 4:17). But to seek without finding is senseless (Cant 3:2; 5:6; cf. Hos 2:9 [love]; Lam 1:19 [food]; Rev 9:6 [death]; cf. the parables of destiny in Matt 12:43-45 par.; Luke 13:6-9, cf. Mark 11:12-14 par.). At the same time seeking is not synonymous with finding; as interpreted religiously the alternative "find/not find" is a question of the presence of God or the hardening of the person (see, however, Philo *All.* iii.47).

While the wide usage of εὑρίσκω (176 occurrences in the NT) leads to a correspondingly broad meaning (see H. Preisker, *TDNT* II, 769f.), the corresponding vb. ("seek") is often made concrete by various expressions within the context—or is to be assumed, as in the frequent Semitizing pass. constructions (e.g., Luke 9:36 par.; Acts 8:40; Phil 2:7; Rev 12:8; 16:20; 20:11).

2. In general narrative style the first part of the double predicate is usually a vb. of movement (the opposite sequence in Matt 13:44, 46?; Luke 5:18f.? John 12:14; Acts 21:2; 27:6; Rev 10:15?). In particular it describes how one moves somewhere (Gk. ἔρχομαι/πορεύομαι/γίνομαι, etc.) or where one encounters someone or something (Acts 9:32f.; 13:6; 18:1f.; 19:1; 28:13f.; 2 Cor 2:12; cf. negative Heb 11:5) or learns that something has happened (Mark 7:30; 14:37, 40 par.; Luke 7:10; 8:35; 24:1-5, 22-24, 33; John 11:17; Acts 5:10, 22f.; 10:27). The conditional association between the two vbs. can have the character of a promise, so that the movement of the person in obedience to a sign or command that has been given implies that he will find what he is seeking (Mark 11:2, 4 par.; 14:16 par.; Matt 17:27; Luke 2:12; John 21:6).

In many of the occurrences the inner connection between the two vbs. can be weakened, so that the "finding" appears to be by chance (Matt 18:28; 27:32; John 2:14; 5:14; 9:35; Acts 17:23?). On the other hand, the element of "seeking" involved in the journey can be developed and expanded with ζητέω or corresponding words (Luke 2:44-46; cf. Matt 2:8; Luke 11:24f. par.; 13:6f. par.; John 6:24ff.; cf. Mark 1:36f.; Acts 11:25f.; cf. 9:1f.; 2 Tim 1:17). The connection can also be stressed in a stylistic manner within the material of the parable when the vb. of movement expresses intensive seeking by itself (Matt 20:6; 22:9f.). The seeking-finding motif is the essential motif in a few NT parables, esp. Matt 13:45f. (with roots in the OT, e.g., Prov 2:4; 3:13ff.; 8:9ff.); 18:12f. par.; Luke 15:8f. In the rabbinic literature cf. *Mek.* 14:5, etc.; in Philo, however, fig. material is introduced to illustrate a sudden and surprising finding (*Imm.* 91-93).

3. This basic structure of usage of the vb. characterizes in particular a group of prominent sayings involving a theology of revelation. This is the case with Matt 7:7, 8 par. Luke 11:9, 10, where with 3 general sayings

("proverbs") there is the formulation "one who seeks finds." As the preceding saying ("everyone who asks receives") expresses "beggar wisdom" (K. H. Rengstorf, FS Köberle [1958] 28f.) this saying expresses "finder wisdom" (cf. also Billerbeck I, 458; on the meaning of *dāraš/pāraš* in the theology of revelation in the Qumran literature see, e.g., 1QS 8:11-16; 9:13-20; CD 6:19; 15:10; on the Greek tradition, see, e.g., Epictetus *Diss.* i.28.20; iv.1.51; on the Gnostic tradition, see *Gos. Thom.* 1 [cf. *Gos. Truth* 17:3f.], 2 [cf. Pap. Oxy. 654, 5-9; Clement of Alexandria *Strom.* v.14.96], 92, 94 [cf. Matt 7:7f. par.]; Irenaeus *Haer.* ii.17; ii.46.2; Tertullian *Praesc. Haer.* 10; 43.1; *Pistis Sophia* 184.11; 250.4; 347.15). This idea appears in combination with the creation as a source of religious knowledge (Acts 17:27); see B. Gärtner, *The Areopagus Speech and Natural Revelation* (1955) 144-69; cf. also Philo *Abr.* 87.

In the NT context the confident expectation of the presence of God ("find") is primarily associated with the common life of the Church, because it has its basis and its actual life in God's acts through Jesus Christ; so Matt 18:20 (cf. *Mek.* 20:24; W. Grundmann, *Matt* [THKNT] ad loc.); this certainty of the presence of God serves as a motivation for common prayer (18:19). In other words, we have here the same correspondence between God's eschatological reality in this world and the eschatological attitude of mankind, defined through prayer (= seek) as in the earlier stratum of tradition in Matt 7:7-8/Luke 11:9-10. Despite the imperative form of the saying the guarantee for this hearing of prayer lies not with the person who "seeks," but rather with the object that "is sought and found," i.e., by God (cf. the parables in Matt 7:9-11 par.). According to the biblical view, otherwise God would not be God, but rather an idol (cf. Matt 6:7f., 32).

For OT examples, one may note Deut 4:29, where Yahweh alone is the one who is to be sought. He alone is the one who allows himself to be found (4:7; cf. also 1 Kgs 18:20-39; Jer 29:12-14 LXX with the corresponding chain of sayings attached to the prayer). In the wisdom literature it is wisdom that wants to be sought and can be found (Prov 16:8 LXX; Wis 1:1f.; 6:12).

Although the two verses in Matthew and Luke have been transmitted in a fully identical form, the context is different. At the same time, however, the eschatological existence of the individual is defined in both cases by prayer, including the Lord's Prayer (in Luke as part of a catechesis on prayer, 11:1-13). In the Sermon on the Mount, which has as its consistent major theme the conditions and demands of the kingdom of God in this world, existence is characterized in general by the demand "Seek first the kingdom and its righteousness. . . ." (Matt 6:33). And the assurance that the kingdom of God, "together with everything else," will be given (parallel argumentation on an eschatological level in Rom 8:31f.) is based on the concept of God (Matt 5:45; 6:26-30). The same

trust in prayer, which is conditioned by God, is the basis for the chain of sayings in 7:7-8.

Matt 11:28-29 is Matthean special material, but 11:25-27 is parallel to Luke 10:21f. Here the imv. takes on a personal-christological foundation: "Come to me. . . ." Jesus himself is the guarantee for the presence of God as eschatological reality.

The expression "find rest" stands in connection with the OT tradition with its roots in the hope of the wilderness generation for a firm, secure residence in the promised land (cf. Deut 3:20; 12:9f.; 25:19; Josh 1:13, 15; 1 Kgs 8:56; Ps 95:11: Christian interpretation in Heb 3:7–4:11; see O. Hofius, *Katapausis* [1970] 53-58). This hope was individualized and spiritualized in the wisdom literature (esp. Wis 8:16; Sir 6:27f.; 51:26f.) and is found in connection with central Gnostic conceptions (*Odes Sol.* 26:12f.; *Gos. Thom.* 51, 60; *Gos. Truth* 40:30ff.; 42:18ff.).

Noteworthy is the specific content of the christological motivation of Matt 11:29 ("I am meek and humble of heart"; lacking in *Gos. Thom.* 90), which binds the composition in 11:25-30 both to the Sermon on the Mount, with its introductory beatitudes, and to the farewell discourse in 28:18-20 (cf. 11:27 and 28:18). In the latter Christ's command to go out is connected, in the Jesus tradition, which became fixed in Matthew (μανθάνω/διδάσκω), with the promise of the presence of Jesus as the one who has been given authority (cf. *1 Clem.* 16:17; *Odes Sol.* 42:5-8; cf. also H. D. Betz, "The Logion of the Easy Yoke [Matt 11:28-30]," *JBL* 86 [1967] 23f.).

Another christologically based statement regarding existence can be attributed to the same theological context: "Whoever finds his life will lose it, and whoever loses his life for my sake will find it." This expression is found in the commissioning of the Twelve in Matt 10:39, as well as in the call to discipleship in 16:25, which is related to Jesus' announcement of his death in response to the disciples' confession of his messiahship at Caesarea Philippi (v. 25a, *find* = "save," as in 8:35; Luke 9:24; cf. 17:33; John 12:25; for comparative materials from late antiquity see H. Braun, *Gesammelte Studien zum NT und seiner Umwelt* I [³1971], 136-58; J. B. Brauer, "Wer sein Leben retten will . . . [Mk 8:3 Parr.]," FS Schmid [1963], 7-10).

In the NT the idea of "finding one's life" through "losing one's life" cannot be related to asceticism (*Gos. Thom.* 110), martyrdom (*Gos. Thom.* 58), military experiences, or wisdom, nor is it related to the highest, albeit self-denying, moral achievement, but rather to "denying oneself" by taking the cross upon oneself, that is, by becoming a disciple of Jesus. Therefore the paradox of these alternatives has a truly diametrical character. The alternative becomes an expression of the radicalized eschatological contrast also known from a series of statements on the kingdom of God (Mark 10:14, 24, 31, 45; cf. John 13:12-15) and represents a reevaluation that is preserved on the existential-sociological level in Luke

15:24, 32 ("lost, but found"; cf. 19:10) and in Paul (Phil 3:7-9: ". . . I consider all things loss . . . that I may be found in [Christ]").

The expression also contains a tension between the eschatological present (lose) and the eschatological future (find), which corresponds to the eschatology of the earliest Jesus tradition (e.g., Luke 12:8-9) as well as to its christology (note the sequence of Mark 8:34-38).

This earliest eschatology and christology can also be seen in Matt 7:13-23, although this material appears to be preserved in its more primitive form in Luke (vv. 13-14; cf. Luke 13:24). The eschatological expression "narrow gate"/"narrow path" (cf. J. Jeremias, *TDNT* VI, 922f.) retains its christological explanation (cf. *Herm. Sim.* ix.12.1,5-6; *Ps.-Clem. Hom.* 3:52; or John 10:9!) in Matt 7:21-23 (note the [original?] Lukan sequence at 13:24 and 25f.), where finding the entrance into the kingdom of God depends on whether one has acted according to the will of the Father as it is presented in the interpretation of Jesus (e.g., in the Sermon on the Mount). If a person does not in this way confess Jesus (and thereby the Father), neither will Jesus confess that person before the Father in heaven at the final judgment (Matt 7:23; 10:32, ὁμολογέω).

The form of the revelation-theological concept of hardening, which is expressed in the negative formulation of the double predicate (seek, but not find), has its roots in the OT, as do the other allusions to hardening (Hos 5:6; Amos 8:12; Prov 1:28; 14:6; cf. Heb 12:17). And as with the other hardening traditions (cf. *Gos. Thom.* 59, 92), it has been transferred from a setting in the circle of disciples during the life of Jesus to a setting in the early Church or to concern with Jews who believed in Christ and Jews who denied Christ (John 1:38f., 41, 43, 45; 7:34-36; cf. Isa 55:6) or with Israel's rejection of Jesus and the (primarily) Gentile Christian Church (Rom 10:20 [cf. Isa 65:1]; cf. Luke 13:24).

4. In forensic language εὑρίσκω relates the conclusion of an investigation into the facts of a charge (αἰτία) or of a dispute (ζήτησις/ζήτημα; cf. Acts 23:28f.; 24:20, etc.). In the account of the trial of Jesus the term is used in the following ways: a) In the description of the Sanhedrin's actions it is used to make clear that the desire of the Jewish authorities to have Jesus executed did not stem from the several accusations confirmed by eyewitnesses, such as his statements against the temple, but rather, from Jesus' insistence, whether direct or indirect, that he held a unique eschatological position (Mark 14:55-64 par.; Matt 26:59-66). b) In connection with the events that took place before the Roman govenor Pilate it is used (3 times in Luke, as well as in John) to make clear that from Pilate's perspective as governor there was nothing to corroborate the charge of fomenting rebellion, which

could justify an execution. It is explicitly indicated that it was the accusation of the Jews to which Pilate ultimately acceded (Luke 23:2, 4, 14, 22, 24-25; cf. Acts 3:13 in contrast with 13:28; John 18:38; 19:4, 6, 16). Paul also was found to have done nothing worthy of death (Acts 25:25; 26:31, 32; cf. 24:12, 18; referring to the Jews, 23:9 in contrast with 24:5; 25:7).

Another form of "official" language is found in the expression "*find* favor in your sight/before you," referring to (among other things) the granting of a request (or prayer) by a higher "authority" or the completely unexpected kindness experienced from above. As a Semitism, it is found frequently in the LXX (e.g., Gen 30:27; 33:8, 10, 15; 34:11; 39:4; 47:25, 29; 50:4; Ruth 2:2, 13; 1 Kgdms 16:22; 2 Kgdms 14:22). In regard to humans' relation to God see esp. Gen 6:8 (Noah); 18:13 (Abraham); 19:19 (Lot); Exod 33:13, 16 (Moses), etc. In the NT this expression is found in Luke 1:30 (Mary); Acts 7:46 (David); 2 Tim 1:18; Heb 4:16.

5. The vb. εὑρίσκω is very often used in the second basic sense, where its (possibly originally derived) content is more or less clearly related to → 4. As an expression of knowledge or experience εὑρίσκω means *find, find out, think, know* (pass.: *be evident = be*): Matt 1:18; 8:10 par.; 24:46 par.; Mark 13:36 par. Luke 12:37f.; Luke 6:7; 17:18; 18:8; 19:48; Acts 4:21; 5:39; 12:19; 13:22; 17:6; 19:19; 27:28; Rom 7:10, 21; 1 Cor 4:2; 15:15; 2 Cor 5:3; 9:4; 11:12; 12:20; Gal 2:17; 1 Pet 1:7; 2:22; 2 Pet 3:14; 2 John 4; Rev 2:2; 3:2; 5:4; 14:5; 18:14-24; 20:15. In the sense of *receive, obtain, gain, acquire*: Luke 9:12; John 10:9; Acts 7:11; Rom 4:1; Heb 9:12.   S. Pedersen

εὐροκλύδων *euroklydōn* (probably) southeast wind

In Acts 27:14 this noun is used in place of εὐρακύλων in the Koine text. There are various possible meanings: "southeast wind, which stirs up the waves" or "wind that stirs up broad waves," also generally "hurricane" (cf. BAGD s.v., LSJ s.v. Εὐρυκλύδων). Since the word is found only here, it is possible that the copyist was seeking to reconcile v. 14 to v. 13 (νότος, "south/southwest wind") by replacing -ακύλων ("north wind") with a more general word.

εὐρύχωρος, 2 *eurychōros* wide, broad*

In Matt 7:13 parallel with πλατεῖα ἡ πύλη (cf. *TCGNT* ad loc.), for "broad is the road (εὐρύχωρος ὁδός) that leads to destruction."

εὐσέβεια, ας, ἡ *eusebeia* reverence, piety, religion*
εὐσεβέω *eusebeō* revere, show reverence toward*
εὐσεβής, 2 *eusebēs* respectful (of order), pious*
εὐσεβῶς *eusebōs* piously*

1. Occurrences in the NT — 2. Semantic field — 3. The Pastorals — 4. 2 Peter

Lit.: N. BROX, *Die Pastoralbriefe* (RNT, 1969) 124f., 171-77. — W. FOERSTER, *TDNT* VII, 175-85. — W. GÜNTHER, *DNTT* II, 91-95 — D. KAUFMANN-BÜHLER, *RAC* VI, 985-1052. — S. T. Mott, "Greek Ethics and Christian Conversion," *NovT* 20 (1978) 22-48, esp. 22-30.

1. With the exception of Acts 3:12, the noun is found only in the Pastorals (10 times) and 2 Peter (4 times). The adj. is found in Acts 10:2, 7 and 2 Pet 2:9 and the adv. in 2 Tim 3:12 and Titus 2:12. The vb. appears in Acts 17:23 and 1 Tim 5:4.

2. In accordance with secular usage, εὐσεβ- indicates respect for existing values or value structures, as, e.g., when 1 Tim 5:4 addresses the obligation of children and grandchildren to support their (grand)mothers. Likewise, the characterization of Cornelius and his soldier as εὐσεβής (Acts 10:2,7) must be understood in this broader sense. This no doubt entails something of the predication "God-fearing"; v. 22 replaces εὐσεβής with "righteous" (cf. 2 Pet 2:9, with the antonym ἄδικοι). Its specific application to the religious sphere is manifest in Acts 17:23 in reference to the people of Athens; correspondingly, εὐσέβεια is applied by Peter to himself and John in Acts 3:12. The proximity of broad and narrow usage can be explained by the fact that social structures were derived from the religious realm or by the conviction that those structures were thought to be guaranteed by the divine. Reverence is then an especially appropriate response to the numinous; here the religious life itself is in view (cf. also 1 Tim 2:10, θεοσέβεια).

3. The Pastorals manifest the range of Hellenistic usage of the word group. In line with 1 Tim 5:4, Titus 2:12 can be cited: the life of the Christian is determined (with understandable sacrifice of ἀνδρείως) by the cardinal virtues (cf. Aeschylus *Th.* 610). The context makes it clear that this humanistic ideal only gains meaning and fulfillment in the light of God's redemptive acts (a corresponding sentiment on the Jewish side is found already in Philo). Similarly, 1 Tim 2:2 places the manner of life sought "in all *reverence* and honor" in the service of God's universal redemptive purposes. That does not simply imply that a peaceful "bourgeois" manner of life is to be expected for the Christian, as is expressly stated in 2 Tim 3:12. Here the εὐσεβῶς ζῆν is explicitly qualified as "in Christ Jesus." This christological characterization is brought to bear in the remaining εὐσέβεια passages as well. The setting of the Pastorals lays out thereby an understanding of religion as a whole (cf., e.g., 4 Macc 9:29f.). Thus also in the description of Paul in Titus 1:1: His apostolate is bound up with the "knowledge of the truth," which is accessible to believers. The false teachers,

however, do not attain the "teaching" that is anchored in this knowledge (1 Tim 6:3), one of the "sound" expressions of which is presented as a "mystery of godliness" in the hymn to Christ in 3:16. Moreover, the false teachers (with their false γνῶσις) display only the appearance of religion, while denying its reality (2 Tim 3:5). The context makes clear the link between an improper manner of life and false teaching. The blasphemy, selfishness, and greed first mentioned here are also denounced in 1 Tim 6:5 (cf. 6:9f.). In contrast to this, the Church office-holder is admonished to practice his piety with "contentment" (vv. 6-10). This manner of life, which has as its goal the fundamental christological values (6:11, εὐσέβεια is here one of them), must of course be practiced (by every Christian; 4:7). When it is practiced, real benefit is derived from it, since true piety holds the promise of life, both in this present world and in the world to come (4:8; cf. 6:6, 12-16).

4. 2 Pet 1:3 characterizes human existence horizontally and vertically as "life and piety." By way of contrast, the context permits εὐσέβεια in the list in 1:6f. to be understood concretely as "compassion" (Kaufmann-Bühler 1032, with reference to Augustine *Civ. D.* i.3). Finally, individual acts of a "pious life" are intended in 3:11 (for the pl. cf. Josephus *Ant.* xviii.127).

P. Fiedler

εὐσεβέω *eusebeō* revere, show reverence toward
→ εὐσέβεια.

εὐσεβής, 2 *eusebēs* respectful (of order), pious
→ εὐσέβεια.

εὐσεβῶς *eusebōs* piously
→ εὐσέβεια.

εὔσημος, 2 *eusēmos* easily recognizable, clear*

1 Cor 14:9: ἐὰν μὴ εὔσημον λόγον δῶτε, "if you do not speak an intelligible word [because speaking in tongues]. . . ."

εὔσπλαγχνος, 2 *eusplanchnos* compassionate, tender-hearted*

In the list of virtues in Eph 4:32 with χρηστοί and χαριζόμενοι ἑαυτοῖς; 1 Pet 3:8, with φιλάδελφοι and ταπεινόφρονες. Cf. Pol. *Phil.* 5:2; 6:1.

εὐσχημόνως *euschēmonōs* properly
→ εὐσχήμων.

εὐσχημοσύνη, ης, ἡ *euschēmosynē* propriety, decency
→ εὐσχήμων.

εὐσχήμων, 2 *euschēmōn* esteemed, respectable*
εὐσχημόνως *euschēmonōs* decently, seemly*
εὐσχημοσύνη, ης, ἡ *euschēmosynē* propriety, decorum*

Lit.: G. DAUTZENBERG, *Urchristliche Prophetie* (1975) 278-84. — H. GREEVEN, *TDNT* II, 770-72. — For further bibliography → ἀσχημοσύνη.

The noun (1 Cor 12:23) and adv. (3 occurrences) occur only in Paul, the adj. (1 Cor 12:24; subst. in 7:35) also in Mark (15:43) and Acts (13:50; 17:12).

The Mark and Acts passages refer to persons: Joseph of Arimathea, a member of the Sanhedrin, and ("God-fearing") Gentile women (and men, since Acts 17:12 refers also to "men") who are both opponents and converts of the Christian missionaries; the common tr., *noble, eminent,* is supported here by the parallel term πρῶτοι in Acts 13:50. It is noteworthy that Matt 27:57, in contrast to Mark, gives the material basis ("rich"), while Luke has "good and just" (Luke 23:50). Apparently for Luke εὐσχήμων was already established in the sense that it bears in Acts. This narrowing of the term in the direction that it has in secular usage assumes a meaning that also involves the inner attitude, including the intention: Whatever is respected should also be "respectable"; i.e., it can also be *seemly, proper;* conversely what is respectable should expect respect.

In Paul this nuance is especially present in 1 Thess 4:12 through the focus on "those outside [the Christian Church]." In "conduct becoming [for the Christian]" (Rom 13:13) should the "Lord Jesus Christ" be effective (v. 14). 1 Cor 7:35 refers to the apostle's instructions concerning marriage and virginity; these "rules of conduct"—for Christians with their imminent expectation—are intended to serve undivided devotion to the Lord. With the image of the body εὐσχημοσύνη stands parallel to τιμή in 12:23f.: We treat particular parts of the body with more "honor" than others, according to the arrangement of the Creator; thus their lack of "esteem" in comparison to the others is remedied and harmony among the members is preserved. The general statement in 14:40 (parallels in Dautzenberg 279) summarizes the "congregational rule" in vv. 26ff.; he refers to the ideal Jewish Christian worship service, which is also attested for the mystery cults. P. Fiedler

εὐτόνως *eutonōs* powerfully, intensely, energetically*

Luke 23:10: εὐτόνως κατηγοροῦντες, "as they *vehemently* accused him; Acts 18:28: εὐτόνως . . . διακατηλέγχετο, "he *powerfully/energetically* confuted them."

εὐτραπελία, ας, ἡ *eutrapelia* joking, idle/imprudent talk*

This noun was used literally and positively in the sense of "cleverness, humor." But in early Christian literature it is always negative: Eph 5:4, with αἰσχρότης and μωρολογία. P. W. van der Horst, "Is Wittiness Unchristian? A Note on εὐτραπελία in Eph. V 4," *Miscellanea Neotestamentica* (NovTSup 48, ed. T. Baarda, W. C. van Unnik, and A. F. J. Klijn) II (1978), 163-77.

Εὔτυχος, ου *Eutychos* Eutychus*

According to Acts 10:9 a νεανίας ὀνόματι Εὔτυχος went to sleep during Paul's evening sermon at Troas and fell from the third floor window; cf. also 20:4 D. F. F. Bruce, *BHH* 449; *BL* 444; E. Haenchen, *Acts* (Eng. tr., 1971) ad loc. (bibliography).

εὐφημία, ας, ἡ *euphēmia* honor, fame, praise*

2 Cor 6:8, with δυσφημία: "in slander and *praise.*"

εὔφημος *euphēmos* pleasing, praiseworthy, well-sounding*

Phil 4:8: εὔφημα, after προσφιλῆ and before ἀρετή and ἔπαινος, most likely: *pleasing.*

εὐφορέω *euphoreō* bear good fruit, have a good yield*

Luke 12:16, of the land of the rich farmer.

εὐφραίνω *euphrainō* rejoice*

1. Occurrences and usage — 2. OT context — 3. NT context — 4. Εὐφροσύνη

Lit.: R. BULTMANN, *TDNT* II, 772-75. — H. CONZELMANN, *TDNT* IX, 359-76. — F. DEBUYST, "Das Fest als Zeichen und Vorwegnahme der endgültigen Gemeinschaft," *Concilium* (1968) 646-57. — B. REICKE, *Diakonie, Festfreude und Zelos* (1951) 167-229. — A. B. DU TOIT, *Der Aspekt der Freude im urchristlichen Abendmahl* (1965). — H. WINDISCH, *Die Frömmigkeit Philos* (1909) 55-60.

1. Εὐφραίνω appears in the NT 14 times, 6 times in Luke (in parables), twice in Acts, 3 times in Paul, 3 times in Revelation. Of these 5 to 7 are in OT citations or allusions. The act. appears only in 2 Cor 2:2. Εὐφραίνω is used parallel to → χαίρω (Luke 15:32; 2 Cor 2:2f.; Rev 11:10) and → ἀγαλλιάομαι (Acts 2:26); in the LXX the parallelism is with the preceding word (e.g., Hab 1:15; Zeph 3:14), esp. in the poetic texts (*parallelismus membrorum:* 1 Kgdms 1:20; Ps 20:1, etc.).

The vb. is used in contexts of relationship. Jubilant joy presupposes the experience of the realization of community. Where the relationship is denied or is in conflict, the vb. takes on a negative connotation (Deut 28:63; 2 Kgdms 1:20; Pss 29:2 LXX; 34:15 LXX; Isa 65:13).

Paul brings out this linguistic structure in his question: "Who is there to *make me glad* but the one whom I have pained?" (2 Cor 2:2). The chief sin in one's relationship to God is denial of God as the cause for joy; cf. the interpretation of the joy over the golden calf of Exod 32:1-6 (see Hos 9:1) in Acts 7:40-42: ". . . they *rejoiced* in the works of their hands" (cf. 1 Cor 10:7).

2. In the OT this rejoicing in relationship is primarily connected to the experience of the presence and help of God (LXX Pss 9:3; 30:8; 39:17f.; 68:33; 2 Chr 6:41; Zech 10:7, etc.), i.e., to the cult as the experience actualizing and confirming the relationship to God, who has intervened to redeem and again redeems (e.g., Pss 42:4; 84:7; 91:5ff.). This intervention that establishes relationship is aimed at the individual (Pss 20:7 [the king]; 33:3, etc.) as well as the people.

3. In Acts 2:26 the vb. expresses a jubilant, joyous confession that God's redeeming presence is connected with Jesus *sui generis*. This was the case not only in his earthly activity (v. 22), but also in his death on the cross (vv. 23ff.). Jesus' death and resurrection become a testimony to the totality and universality of the joy in relationship, manifested, on the one hand, by the unity of the eucharistic community (2:46: . . . μετελάμβανον τροφῆς ἐν ἀγαλλιάσει καὶ ἀφελότητι καρδίας) and, on the other hand, by the character of the eschatological outpouring of the Spirit as its destroys boundaries (cf. the citation of Joel in 2:17-21).

The universality of this joy as it creates unity is made precise in Rom 15:10 in a radical reinterpretation of Deut 32:43 LXX: Gentiles should *rejoice* over God's presence in Christ together with Jews (cf. v. 13). In Gal 4:25-27 the OT invitation to the barren one to rejoice over God's marvelous creative intervention (Isa 54:1ff.) is utilized in a corresponding reinterpretation of the expectations associated with the city of Jerusalem (cf. among other passages Isa 65:17ff.; see F. Mussner, *Gal* [HTKNT] ad loc.). Consequently the heavenly Jerusalem becomes the eschatological city of joy. In Revelation also, where the challenge to joy and jubilation is made in the decisive phases of the apocalyptic description, OT texts are used with a varying reinterpretation (11:10; 12:12; 18:20). Rev 11:10 indicates that the joy at the victory over the evil powers can be embodied in the exchange of gifts at the table fellowship (cf. Esth 9:19, 22).

In OT wisdom literature εὐφραίνω can express joy in other relationships, e.g., general togetherness at eating and drinking (among others Eccl 5:18; 10:19), joy over a marriage partner (Sir 26:2), or over children (Prov 10:1; 17:21; 23:24f.). Luke 15:29 corresponds to this. The father's invitation to the older brother to participate in the joyous feast that he has abundantly prepared when the younger son returns (Luke 15:22-24, 32) includes in its religious interpretation also God's jubilant joy (cf. 15:7, 10) when a person returns to a relationship that God has kept unconditionally open, while the individual has attempted to live from his own possibilities. Wherever life is lived by the strength of the possibilities of God, joy is a duty (v. 32: ἔδει), a joy of repentance, which is known from Deut 30:9 (among other texts) and Philo *Som.* ii.172-78.

It is this relationship to God which is lacking in the man described in Luke 12:16-19 (cf. Eccl 3:12; Jas 4:13ff.). Therefore the rich farmer is called a fool (cf. Ps 14:1; Luke 12:20f.; Matt 6:19-21). Another form of false joy is the refusal of table fellowship with others, with those who are destitute (Luke 16:19-21). In this case no future fellowship is possible (Luke 16:24f.; cf. Matt 10:42; see also E. W. Seng, *NovT* 20 [1978] 136-55).

4. Εὐφροσύνη, *gladness, joy**, occurs only in Acts 2:28 (cf. 2:26, → 3) and 14:17, where it is emphasized that the concrete joy in creation, whose symbol was the joy of harvest (Isa 9:3, etc.), belongs in one's relationship to God, who is the giver of life and thus also the source of joy.

S. Pedersen

Εὐφράτης, ου *Euphratēs* Euphrates*

Rev 9:14; 16:12, in the phrase ὁ ποταμὸς ὁ μέγας Εὐφράτης in the sixth vision of the trumpets, of the angels of destruction at the *Euphrates River*, and in the sixth vision of the bowls of the drying up of the *Euphrates*, so that the way was prepared for the rulers of the east. L. Delekat, *BHH* 448; *BL* 444.

εὐφροσύνη, ης, ἡ *euphrosynē* gladness, joy → εὐφραίνω 4.

εὐχαριστέω *eucharisteō* be thankful, thank; give thanks (at a meal); say the eucharistic prayer*

1. Occurrences and meaning — 2. Proemium and parenesis — 3. Table blessing and eucharist

Lit.: H. CONZELMANN, *TDNT* IX, 407-15. — H.-H. ESSER, *DNTT* III, 817-19. — E. LOHSE, *Col and Phlm* (Eng. tr., Hermeneia, 1971) 14-22, 32-34. — H. PATSCH, "Abendmahlsterminologie außerhalb der Einsetzungsberichte," *ZNW* 62 (1971) 210-31. — J. M. ROBINSON, "Die Hodajot-Formel in Gebet und Hymnus des Frühchristentums," FS Haenchen 194-235. — A. STUIBER, *RAC* VI, 900-928.

1. The vb., which in the LXX appears first in the Apocrypha, and is then seen in Hellenistic Jewish literature, appears 38 times in the NT, esp. in Paul and the Gospels. It designates (with few exceptions: Luke 17:16; Rom 16:4) thanks rendered to God, who is explicitly named as a dat. obj. or is to be inferred from the context. The special meaning, unique to the NT, *say the table benediction*, is a Semitism (and here interchangeable with → εὐλογέω). Absolute εὐχαριστέω refers to the liturgical

language of the Lord's Supper and was a t.t. in the post-Pauline period for the eucharistic prayer.

2. When Paul and his imitators insert a fixed formula of thanksgiving, the style corresponds to that of the Hellenistic letter. In the briefer variants the author thanks God and gives the basis for the thanksgiving in a ὅτι clause, which normally involves the addressees: the gift of grace in the church (1 Cor 1:4), their faith (Rom 1:8), faith and love (2 Thess 1:3); cf., outside the introduction of the letter, acceptance of the word of God (1 Thess 2:13) and election (2 Thess 2:13). In as many as three participial clauses the longer form adds the occasion for the thanksgiving: works of faith (1 Thess 1:2ff.), participation in the gospel (Phil 1:3ff.), faith and love (Phlm 4ff.; Col 1:3ff.; Eph 1:15ff.). Also in reference to himself Paul can express thanksgiving to God within a theological argument (1 Cor 1:14; 14:18; cf. Acts 28:15). In contrast, the Gentiles do not thank God, although they acknowledge him (Rom 1:21). Thanksgiving is a parenetic obligation (2 Cor 1:11; Eph 5:20; Col 1:12; 3:17; 1 Thess 5:18). The doxology of the elders before God (Rev 11:17ff.; cf. Did. 9:2, 3; 10:2f., 4ff.) indicates the Jewish background of the NT formulations (Pss 134–136; Jdt 8:25; 1QH 2:20, 31, etc.). Paul apparently thinks of the liturgical place of such prayers of thanksgiving when he demands a form of personal thanksgiving in the worship service which is intelligible (1 Cor 14:17). On personal prayer of thanksgiving, see, on the one hand, the prayer of the Pharisee (Luke 18:11) and, on the other hand, the prayer of Jesus at the raising of Lazarus (John 11:41).

3. In conformity with the Jewish practice (b. Ber. 35a) Paul says the table benediction before a meal (Acts 27:35). This custom was common in the Christian communities; thus the apostle can refer to it within an argument (Rom 14:6). This prayer is also under consideration in 1 Cor 10:30 when, during the debate on eating meat offered to idols, Paul raises the rhetorical question of why he is denounced for that for which he gives thanks.

In the Last Supper accounts Jesus expresses thanksgiving over the bread (Luke 22:19 par. 1 Cor 11:24) or over the cup of blessing (Mark 14:23 par. Matt 26:27; cf. Luke 22:17). Here, as in the passages about the feeding of the four thousand (Mark 8:6: prayer over the bread; par. Matt 15:36: over bread and fish) or five thousand (John 6:11, 23: bread) the common use of → εὐλογέω is noteworthy. The characteristic stereotype of the feeding terminology betrays the conserving influence of the Lord's Supper liturgy. Εὐχαριστέω without an obj. takes on here (as later in Did. 9:1; 10:1, 7) the special meaning *say the eucharistic prayer.*   H. Patsch

εὐχαριστία, ας, ἡ *eucharistia* prayer of thanksgiving, thanksgiving, prayer of praise (at a meal); eucharist*

Lit.: J.-P. AUDET, "Literary Forms and Contents of a Normal εὐχαριστία in the First Century," *SE* I (1959) 643-62. — H. SCHLIER, *Eph* (⁶1968) 234. — For further bibliography → εὐχαριστέω.

1. The noun, like the vb., has no direct equivalent in the OT. However, it is known in Hellenistic Jewish literature. It appears 15 times in the NT, esp. in Paul; it does not appear in the gospel tradition. With one exception (Acts 24:3) God is the recipient of the thanksgiving. In the Apostolic Fathers εὐχαριστία is a t.t. for the Lord's Supper.

2. For Paul the thanksgiving has a basic meaning. He desires to "render a *thanksgiving*" (1 Thess 3:9, as it were a spiritual *tôdâ,* cf. Pss 50:14; 107:22, etc., where Aquila, in contrast to the LXX, also has εὐχαριστία) to God as a response to the joy that the church in Thessalonica has given him, but he summons himself to repeated thanksgivings in worship and in private life. In connection with his argument concerning speaking in tongues (→ εὐλογέω 2) he demands that the uninitiated must be able to say a knowledgeable "Amen" to the *thanksgiving and praise* to God (1 Cor 14:16). The thanksgiving in worship may also be the subject of 2 Cor 4:15 and 9:11f. (on the occasion of the collection for the poor in Jerusalem. Alongside supplications, prayers, and intercessions for those in authority, *thanksgiving* also has its place (1 Tim 2:1). The demand for thanksgiving is a basic element of parenesis (Eph 5:4; Phil 4:6; Col 2:7; 4:2). "Thanksgiving is the essential and favorite means of Christian expression" (Schlier).

With an appeal to God's creation Paul rejects ascetic food laws, insofar as food is enjoyed with thanksgiving, i.e., with the benediction at the table (1 Tim 4:3, 4; → εὐλογέω 3, 5). *Thanksgiving* belongs to the doxology of the heavenly being before the throne of God (Rev 4:9; 7:12).

3. Because of the interchangeability of the stems εὐχαριστ- and εὐλογ- in reference to the table benediction and because of the identification of εὐχαριστία with the eucharist tradition from the end of the 1st cent. (cf. Did. 9:1, 5), εὐχαριστία takes on the meaning *Lord's Supper* (Ign. Eph. 13:1; Phld. 4; Smyrn. 8:1; cf. Justin Apol. i.65f.). In 1 Cor 10:16 G pc syᵖ τὸ ποτήριον τῆς εὐλογίας (which has become unintelligible) is replaced by τὸ ποτήριον τῆς εὐχαριστίας, "cup of the Eucharist."

        H. Patsch

εὐχάριστος, 2 *eucharistos* thankful*

Col 3:15: καὶ εὐχάριστοι γίνεσθε, "and be *thankful.*"

εὐχή, ῆς, ἡ *euchē* prayer, vow → εὔχομαι 3.

εὔχομαι *euchomai* pray, request; wish*
εὐχή, ης, ἡ *euchē* prayer; vow*

1. Occurrences in the NT, synonyms, and meanings —
2. Εὔχομαι — 3. Εὐχή

Lit.: A. CITRON, *Semantische Untersuchung zu σπένδεσθαι-
σπένδειν-εὔχεσθαι* (1965) 73-101, 116-20. — G. DELLING, *BHH*
1288f. — J. HERRMANN and H. GREEVEN, *TDNT* II, 775-808, esp.
775-78, 800-808. — H. SCHÖNWEISS, *DNTT* II, 855-64. — For
further bibliography see *TWNT* X, 1091-93.

1. In contrast to the compounds προσεύχομαι (85 NT
occurrences) and προσευχή (37 occurrences), the simple
forms εὔχομαι and εὐχή occur only 7 and 3 times respectively in the NT; neither appears in the Gospels, and the
noun does not appear in Paul. Thus the simple forms, which
are attested since Homer for the general appeal to the deity,
is supplanted by the compound in the LXX and even more
noticeably in the NT. Other NT expressions for "pray,
request" include αἰτέω (70 occurrences), βοάω (12), δέομαι
(22) ἐρωτάω (63), κράζω (56), γονυπετέω (4), εὐλογέω (42),
εὐχαριστέω (38), and προσκυνέω (60). While in classical
Greek and in the LXX εὔχομαι can mean "vow, pledge"
along with the meanings "pray, request" (e.g., Num 11:2,
"pray" [πρός κυρίον]; 30:3: εὔχομαι εὐχήν, "take a vow")
and the secular meaning "wish" almost totally disappears
in the LXX (only in Jer 22:27; εὐχή, "wish," appears neither
in the LXX nor in the NT), in the NT the meanings for the
vb. are *pray, request, wish*. The noun has the meanings *vow*
and *prayer*.

2. a) **Εὔχομαι** in the NT is used with the dat. (Acts
26:29), with πρός (2 Cor 13:7), with ὑπέρ (Jas 5:16), with
a dependent inf. (with acc.: Acts 26:29; 27:29; Rom 9:3;
2 Cor 13:7; 3 John 2), and with an acc. obj. (2 Cor 13:9).
The exact content of εὔχομαι is disputed in the interpretation of individual passages.

b) The meaning *wish* can only be accepted with
certainty where God is not named as the addressee:
ηὔχοντο ἡμέραν γενέσθαι, "*they wished* for day to come,"
i.e., *they yearned* for the day" (Acts 27:29). The impf.
ηὐχόμην expresses a (an unfulfilled) wish: "for *I
wished* . . ." (Rom 9:3; cf. ἤθελον in Gal 4:20; see BDF
§359.2). It does not involve Paul's offer of self-sacrifice,
but, expressed in literary terms, his deep grief (cf. v. 2)
over his brothers κατά σάρκα. 3 John 2 (περὶ πάντων
εὔχομαι . . . ," *I desire* that in everything it will go well
with you . . .") is closely associated with the customary
form known elsewhere in ancient private letters: πρό
πάντων εὔχομαι (cf. Pap. Oxy. II, 292; see Greeven 776).
The shift in content is significant: the concern for well-
being and health is not foremost for the writer of 3 John,
but he can assume the "spiritual welfare" of the addressees (v. 2b).

c) In 2 Cor 13:7, 9 Paul *prays* to God that the Corinthians do nothing evil (εὐχόμεθα δὲ πρὸς τὸν θεὸν μὴ ποιῆσαι
ὑμᾶς κακὸν μηδέν, v. 7), and he prays that they be "set
right" with God (τοῦτο καὶ εὐχόμεθα, τὴν ὑμῶν κατάρτησιν,

v. 9). With this request to God Paul does not desire to
provide proof of his apostleship (cf. v. 3); rather, he
desires for the sake of the Church and the truth to reply
to the possible charge that he is "untested" (v. 7c) when
the Church does good through God's help and is no
longer dependent on the proof of the testing of the apostle
(at his future visit in Corinth, vv. 2f.). The (intercessory)
prayer of Paul here is thus an appeal to God for help and
preservation. It is thus an expression of the weakness of
believers who have their strength in Christ; to that extent
it also has the character of an admonition to the Church.

Jas 5:16 also speaks of intercessory prayer (εὔχεσθε
[προσεύχεσθε A pc, προσεύχεσθαι B; cf. also vv. 13, 14, 17,
18] ὑπὲρ ἀλλήλων), now for healing of the sick (cf. εὐχὴ τῆς
πίστεως, v. 15; δέησις, v. 16b). Prayer in faith, and not
anointing with oil alone (cf. vv. 14f.), brings about
healing. Εὐξαίμην ν τῷ θεῷ in Acts 26:29 (potential opt. with ἄν is
rare in the NT and occurs only in Luke and in Acts; only in
Acts 26:29 does it appear in a main clause) is probably to
be rendered "*I want to ask* God" (dat. only here in the NT,
in the LXX frequently with the meaning "pledge, vow").
In principle, corresponding to the literary-rhetorical connection, the tr. "*I wished*" would be possible (cf. BDF
§385.1); τῷ θεῷ is, however, to be considered as a dat. dir.
obj., not as a dat. of advantage or ethical dat.

3. **Εὐχή** (προσευχή P al) apears in the sense of (intercessory) prayer for the sick in Jas 5:15 (→ 2).

In Acts 18:18 and 21:23 εὐχή means *oath* (cf. the usage
of the LXX, → 1). The author thinks both times of the
Nazirite vow and refers expressly to the cutting of the
hair (κειράμενος . . . τὴν κεφαλήν, 18:18; ἵνα ξυρήσονται
τὴν κεφαλήν, 21:23; see Num 6:1-21, esp. vv. 5, 9, 11f.,
18f.). 18:18 is problematic because cutting the hair took
place not at the beginning of the vow, but at the end. In
addition, it usually coincided with the fulfillment of the
vow in the Jerusalem temple. In a foreign country the
undertaking of a vow was possible, but not its conclusion
and scarcely the shaving of the Nazirite (see also Billerbeck II, 749-51; certainly a special rule for impurity in
conformity with Num 6:11 is not under consideration).
In 21:23 Paul is to release four men from the Nazirite
vow (εὐχὴν ἔχοντες ἐφ' ἑαυτῶν, cf. Num 6:7; cf. also
Josephus *Ant.* xix.294), in the course of which he likewise
takes the vow on himself (v. 24; cf. v. 26; → ἁγνός 3),
unless (which is improbable) the reference is to the levitical purification from uncleanness (e.g., after a period of
time in a foreign land) within seven days. (Would such
an impurity not have affected the four men? So Billerbeck
II, 757-61; G. Stählin, *Acts* [NTD] ad loc.). The Lukan
portrayal can be only partially brought into agreement
with the rabbinic regulations (see E. Haenchen, *Acts*
[Eng. tr.] ad loc.), i.e., the εὐχή as it affects the four men,
but not the apparent seven-day Nazirite vow of Paul.

H. Balz

εὔχϱηστος, 2 *euchrēstos* useful, serviceable*

2 Tim 2:21, of a vessel that is *useful* to its owner (εὔχϱηστον τῷ δεσπότῃ); 4:11, of Mark: ἔστιν . . . μοι εὔχϱηστος εἰς διακονίαν; cf. Phlm 11 on Onesimus.

εὐψυχέω *eupsycheō* be of good courage, be calm*

Phil 2:19: ἵνα . . . εὐψυχῶ γνοὺς τὰ πεϱὶ ὑμῶν; cf. *Herm. Vis.* i.3.2. Spicq, *Notes* I, 337f.

Εὐωδία, ας *Euodia* Euodia*

Variant spelling of → Εὐοδία.

εὐωδία, ας, ἡ *euōdia* pleasant odor*
ὀσμή, ῆς, ἡ *osmē* scent, aroma*

1. Occurrences in the NT and meanings — 2. Fig. use of ὀσμὴ εὐωδίας — 3. 2 Cor 2:14-16

Lit.: R. BULTMANN, *2 Cor* (Eng. tr., 1985) 62-67. — G. DELLING, *TDNT* V, 493-95. — O. FLENDER and C. BROWN, *DNTT* III, 599-601. — S. HAFEMANN, *Suffering and the Spirit* (WUNT 19, 1986), esp. 43-51. — E. LOHMEYER, *Vom göttlichen Wohlgeruch* (SHAW 10/9, 1919). — A. STUMPFF, *TDNT* II, 808-10. — For further bibliography see *TWNT* X, 1093.

1. Εὐωδία occurs 3 times in the NT, twice (Phil 4:18; Eph 5:2) in the gen. construction ὀσμὴ εὐωδίας, and once in 2 Cor 2:15 in direct proximity to and, to some extent, parallel to ὀσμή (vv. 14, 16). Both terms are fig. in these passages. Ὀσμή is also used literally in John 12:3: "The house was filled with the *aroma* of the oil (→ μύϱον)."

2. The phrase ὀσμὴ εὐωδίας is the LXX tr. of Heb. *rêᵃḥ nîḥōᵃḥ*, "pleasing odor" (Gen 8:21; Lev 1:9, 13, 17, etc.). Already the LXX, by thus twice using the stem ὀδ- in its rendering, has given up the ancient concept of sacrifice (food for the deity by means of the fragrance; cf. F. Stolz, *THAT* II, 46). The gen. phrase appears with reference to spiritual (→ λογικός) worship in *T. Levi* 3:6 (of the heavenly worship), Sir 39:14 (of the praise of God by the pious), 1QS 8:9; 9:4f. (of the prayer of the Qumran community), and *Barn.* 2:10 (of the praise of the Creator).

Paul uses the phrase in Phil 4:18 along with other sacrificial expressions to characterize the gifts with which the Philippians had supported him as a spiritual sacrifice given to God: "I have a surplus, since I received your gifts from Epaphroditus, a *pleasing fragrance,* an acceptable sacrifice (→ θυσία), pleasing to God (→ εὐάϱεστος)."

In Eph 5:2 ("Walk in love, as Christ also loved us and gave himself for us as a gift and sacrifice to God as a *fragrant offering*") the phrase is used to interpret the self-giving of Christ with the terms of sacrificial language. One may assume, however, that the appeal for imitation of Christ is not limited to the example of → ἀγάπη given by him (3. c). If the memory of his self-

sacrifice "for us" is indebted to the traditional christological formula and the saving sacrifice can be imitated only in a limited way, the characterization of this offering as a "gift and sacrifice . . ." is probably not to be considered just an example of the plerophoric style of Ephesians. Instead it may be parenetically motivated, with Christ placed before the eyes of the addressees as the example and model of the spiritual worship to which they have been called. It is disputed whether τῷ θεῷ is attracted to θυσίαν or to εἰς ὀσμὴν εὐωδίας. The LXX knows the expression εἰς ὀσμὴν εὐωδίας τῷ κυϱίῳ (Lev 2:12; 6:14; Dan 4:37a). But Exod 29:18 has τῷ κυϱίῳ before εἰς ὀσμὴν εὐωδίας in a predication of sacrifice. The flow of language seems to point in this direction in Eph 5:2.

3. The origin and meaning of the fragrance metaphor in 2 Cor 2:14-16 are decided upon in varied ways:

Ὀσμὴν τῆς γνώσεως αὐτοῦ (v. 14) is: "*fragrance,* which consists in his knowledge" (gen. of apposition, BDF §167.2). Under the assumption that → θϱιαμβεύω alludes to the Roman practice of the triumphal procession, the image of the fragrance is associated to that frame of reference, so that Paul would be portraying himself as an incense bearer in this triumphal procession (so W. Bousset *2 Cor* [SdNT] 179; C. F. G. Heinrici, *2 Cor* [KEK] 104).

However, both the presence of the image of the triumphal procession and the derivation of the image of the fragrance from this association of images are disputable (Stumpff 809; Bultmann 63f.; H. Lietzmann and W. Kümmel, *1–2 Cor* [HNT] 108). As the continuation in 2:15f. shows, the phrase is linked to the symbolic language of the "divine fragrance" (Lohmeyer; Delling 495; Bultmann 63-67), which was familiar in antiquity, in order to set forth the almost material and local (ἐν παντὶ τόπῳ) presence and the life-giving power of the knowledge of God offered through the proclamation.

The idea of the "divine fragrance" presupposes a characteristic material understanding of fragrance as the bearer of energy for life and death (Job 14:9: Aristotle *Sens.* 5 p445a 17; Plato *Ti.* 66e). Fragrance can be understood as a sign of divine presence and divine life (Euripides *Hipp.* 1392; Plutarch *Is.* 15). In the OT and Jewish realm, the symbolism of fragrance has not entered into statements about God but is used in sayings about wisdom (Sir 24:15), righteousness (Sir 39:13f.; *2 Bar.* 67:6), and paradise (*3 Bar.* 25:3-6; 32:3f.).

In connection with v. 14a, Paul wants to say with the metaphor of the "*fragrance* of his knowledge," that God brings his knowledge everywhere into public view (→ φανεϱόω) through his apostles, that it is present and calls forth a decision.

With Χϱιστοῦ εὐωδία ἐσμὲν τῷ θεῷ, "We are the *aroma* of Christ for God" (v. 15), the image of the fragrance is taken up with εὐωδία and transferred to the apostles. The LXX phrase ὀσμὴ εὐωδίας (→ 2) and the qualification "for God" have given occasion to the interpretation that Paul is here and in v. 14 dependent on the symbolism of sacrifice: according to v. 14 the fragrance of the sacrifice would rise to God (Lietzmann and Kümmel 108). According to v. 15, the apostolic existence is compared to a sacrifice (cf. Phil 2:17; Lietzmann and Kümmel, ad loc.). This assumption runs counter to the complex of statements in 2:15b, 16 that are aimed at the effect of the apostle among other people. The metaphorical usage of the saying would not be understood under the assumption of a wider reference with the imagery (Stumpff 809f.; H. Windisch, 2 Cor [KEK] 98). The derivation of the saying "We are the *aroma* of Christ" from the idea that Χριστός may come from → χρίω, "anoint," that ointment has a fragrance and that the apostle in a special way is anointed (cf. 2 Cor 1:21), thus carrying forward the aroma of Christ (Windisch, ad loc.), is likewise, by itself, not justified by the context (Stumpff 810). Instead the metaphor illustrating the "knowledge of God" in v. 14 is consistently transferred in v. 15 to those who, as apostles, spread the knowledge. The knowledge of God is directly personalized in them (M. A. Chevalier, *Esprit de Dieu, paroles d'hommes* [1966] 104). When Paul in v. 15b calls the objects of the *aroma* "those who are being saved and those who are perishing," the division into two opposite groups militates against the metaphor of the *aroma*. It is also not to be explained from ancient symbolism (Bultmann 67f.). Instead Paul thinks of the effect of his preaching. The decision regarding it determines one's participation in the final salvation, and thus the two groups, the σωζόμενοι and the ἀπολλύμενοι, arise through the preaching, i.e., through the apostles as "*aroma* of Christ."

The apposition, "to one a *fragrance* from death to death, to the other a *fragrance* from life to life" (v. 16a), gives an effective conclusion to the saying in v. 15. Εὐωδία again alternates with ὀσμή (cf. the parallel usage of both expressions in Sir 24:15).

The prepositions ἐκ . . . εἰς, "from . . . to," present difficulties. If one takes them literally, the *fragrance* would have not only a double effect ("to"), but also, as the contrast indicates, two differing origins and qualities. This would be conceivable for the positive part of the parallel with εὐωδία in v. 15; but how could the *fragrance* have the quality of death? One must then derive both statements from the death and resurrection of Jesus, so that the apostles seem to one to be the scent of a corpse, while to the other they seem to be a breath of life. Such a christological basis is improbable, however. It has scarcely any support in the text, but must rather be supplied; the meaning "scent of a corpse" would be fully outside the scope of the imagery of the *fragrance*, which is decisive from v. 15 to v. 16. It would be extremely problematic in the context of Pauline theology. It is more probable that Paul thinks of the situation of the proclaimer and his effect, as earlier in v. 15.

In a rhetorically effective way (chiasmus in 2:15b-16a) Paul brings the statement about his apostolic preaching to a close with the help of the metaphor of the fra-

grance, as he uses the prep. arrangement "from . . . to" as a unifying stylistic figure (cf. Rom 1:17; 2 Cor 3:18; 4:17) by which he strengthens and emphasizes impressively the terms "death" and "life," which describe the effect of the proclamation (cf. BAGD s.v.; Bultmann 67). Jewish traditions about the dual effect of the Torah for harm or benefit (Philo *Mut.* 202) or as a "medicine of life" and "medicine of death" (*b. Taʿan.* 7a *Bar.*, in Billerbeck III, 498) are comparable.

                                     G. Dautzenberg

εὐώνυμος, 2   *euōnymos*   on the left, left*

There are 9 occurrences of this adj. in the NT, 5 in Matthew, 2 in Mark, and the others in Acts 21:3 and Rev 10:2. Except in Acts 21:3, it is found contrasted with "right," usually in the phrase ἐξ εὐωνύμων (see also BDF §141.2). So Mark 10:37 (v.l.), 40 par. Matt 20:21, 23 of the places of honor "at the right and at the *left* of Jesus; Mark 15:27 par. Matt 27:38: two λῃσταί were executed at the "right and *left*" of Jesus; here also places of honor may be in mind, but in a taunting sense (cf. R. Pesch, *Mark* [HTKNT] II, 485f.). At the final judgment the goats will stand *at the left* of the Son of Man (Matt 25:33), and those ἐξ εὐωνύμων will be condemned (v. 41). Rev 10:2, of the *left* foot of an angel; Acts 21:3: "when we left Cyprus *on the left* (εὐώνυμον)."

ἔφαγον   *ephagon*   eat

2nd aor. of → ἐσθίω, ἔσθω.

ἐφάλλομαι   *ephallomai*   leap upon*

Acts 19:16, of a possessed man who *leaped upon* the Jewish exorcists: ἐφαλόμενος . . . ἐπ᾽ αὐτούς (ἐφαλλόμενος ℘41 Koine E pl).

ἐφάπαξ   *ephapax*   at one time, once for all*

Ἐφάπαξ, like ἅπαξ, is used most in Hebrews (3 of 5 NT occurrences): 7:27, of the final reconciliation through Christ, who sacrificed himself *once for all* (τοῦτο γὰρ ἐποίησεν ἐφάπαξ ἑαυτὸν ἀνενέγκας, in contrast to the "daily" sacrifices of the high priests; on the problem, see O. Michel, *Heb* [KEK] ad loc.); cf. 9:12 (εἰσῆλθεν ἐφάπαξ εἰς τὰ ἅγια); 10:10, of the sanctification of believers through the *once-for-all* sacrifice of the body of Jesus Christ; see further → ἅπαξ 3.

Paul, who uses ἅπαξ only in the numerical sense, uses ἐφάπαξ in Rom 6:10 of the once-for-all and thus permanent (for believers) change from the death of Christ for sins to the life for God (τῇ ἁμαρτίᾳ ἀπέθανεν ἐφάπαξ; cf. 1 Pet 3:18). The christophany before more than 500 brothers *at once* (1 Cor 15:6; this meaning only here in the NT) is not otherwise mentioned (see H. F. von Campenhausen, *Der*

Ablauf der Osterereignisse und das leere Grab [SHAW 1952/24, ³1966] 13-15; J. Kremer, *Das älteste Zeugnis von der Auferstehung Christi* [1966] 71-74).

Ἐφεσῖνος, 3 *Ephesinos* Ephesian

Rev 2:1 TR: τῆς Ἐφεσίνης ἐκκλησίας, in place of ἐν Ἐφέσῳ.

Ἐφέσιος *Ephesios* Ephesian*

Acts 19:28, 34: μεγάλη ἡ → Ἄρτεμις Ἐφεσίων (a common form of acclamation, see E. Haenchen, *Acts* [Eng. tr.] ad loc.); 19:35: "Men *of Ephesus* (ἄνδρες Ἐφέσιοι)" and as designation of the city (Ἐφεσίων πόλις); 21:29: Trophimus *"from Ephesus"* (τὸν Ἐφέσιον).

Ἔφεσος *Ephesos* Ephesus*

Lit.: BAGD s.v. — D. BOYD, *IDBSup* 269-71. — W. M. CALDER and J. M. COOK, *OCD* 387. — W. ELLIGER, *Ephesos* (1985). — E. HAENCHEN, *Acts* (Eng. tr., 1971) 549-57. — B. JOANNIDIS, *BHH* 418f. — E. LESSING and W. OBERLEITNER, *Ephesos* (1978). — F. MILTNER, *Ephesos, Stadt der Artemis und des Johannes* (1958). — E. PEREIRA, *Ephesus: Climax of Universalism in Luke-Acts* (1983). — E. SCHÄFER, *LAW* 821-23. — L. BÜRCHNER, *PW* V, 2773-2822. — *BL* 402. — For further bibliography see BAGD, Haenchen, Joannidis, *BL*.

A rich commercial city on the west (Aegean Sea) coast of Asia Minor at the mouth of the Caÿster River. From 133 B.C. it was the capital of the province of Asia and seat of the proconsul. Ephesus was famous for its culture and its cult (esp. the temple of Artemis, destroyed in 356 B.C. and later rebuilt; → Ἄρτεμις).

Ephesus is mentioned in Acts at the end of the "second missionary journey" (18:19, 21) and at both the beginning and end of the "third missionary journey" (18:24; 19:1, 17, 26; 20:16, 17). It was a center of Pauline activity. Paul himself speaks of Ephesus only in 1 Corinthians, which was written there (15:32; 16:8); otherwise see Eph 1:1 ℵᶜ A B³ D al (cf. *TCGNT* ad loc.); 1 Tim 1:3; 2 Tim 1:18; 4:12; Rev 1:11; 2:1. According to the Pastorals Ephesus was the home church of Timothy. Among the seven churches of the circular letters in Revelation, Ephesus is listed first.

ἐφευρετής, οῦ, ὁ *epheuretēs* inventor*

Rom 1:30, in a catalog of vices: ἐφευρετὰς κακῶς, those who either *"devise* evil" (cf. 2 Macc 7:31) or "seek evil" or "allow it to be sought" (see H. Schlier, *Rom* [HTKNT] 65).

ἐφημερία, ας, ἡ *ephēmeria* order of priests*

Luke 1:5, 8: the *order of priests*, i.e., the "weekly division" to which Zechariah belonged (see Billerbeck II,

55-68, 71; W. Grundmann, *Luke* [THKNT] ad loc.; Schürer, *History* II, 245-50).

ἐφήμερος, 2 *ephēmeros* daily*

Jas 2:15, of the *"daily* food requirement" (ἐφημέρη τροφή).

ἐφικνέομαι *ephikneomai* reach, come to*

In the course of his defense in 2 Cor 10:13, 14 Paul emphasizes that the standard set by God for his judgment is the jurisdiction of his own mission: ἐφίκεσθαι ἄχρι καὶ ὑμῶν, *"that we reach* even to you" (v. 13; the inf. interprets the preceding μέτρου [on the attraction of the rel., cf. BDF §294], but refers back to καυχησόμεθα); in v. 14, οὐ γὰρ ὡς μὴ ἐφικνούμενοι εἰς ὑμᾶς is either to be rendered with "not as such who do not *come* to you [as missionaries, as is the case with the opponents]" or more generally as referring to the missionary jurisdiction of Paul: "for not as such who cannot *come* to you." See also R. Bultmann, *2 Cor* [Eng. tr.] ad loc.

ἐφίστημι *ephistēmi* approach, press forward; stand by, be at hand*

There are 21 occurrences in the NT, all in Luke-Acts except for 1 Thess 5:3; 2 Tim 4:2, 4 (7 in Luke, 11 in Acts). *Approach,* with dat. (Luke 2:9; 24:4; Acts 4:1; 23:11), with ἐπί (Acts 10:17; 11:11), with ἐπάνω αὐτῆς, "he *came to* her head/to her at the head of the bed" (possibly also "bent over her," Luke 4:39), absolute (2:38; 10:40; 20:1; Acts 6:12; 12:7; 22:13; 23:27); in an ominous sense, *draw near/come upon* someone, with ἐπί (Luke 21:34; 1 Thess 5:3); *attack,* with dat. (Acts 17:5); elsewhere "approach" in the sense of *be ready/be at hand* (2 Tim 4:2); *be (directly) impending* (4:6). In Acts 28:2 διὰ τὸν ὑετὸν τὸν ἐφεστῶτα can be understood as referring to rain that was beginning or "imminent," perhaps even "delayed."

ἐφνίδιος, 2 *ephnidios* suddenly

Alternative form of → αἰφνίδιος.

ἐφοράω *ephoraō* look at, gaze at*

Luke 1:25, absolute with inf.: "he *looked upon* me, to take away"; Acts 4:29, with ἐπί: *"look upon* their threats."

Ἐφραίμ *Ephraim* Ephraim*

According to John 11:54 Jesus leaves the immediate vicinity of Jerusalem and goes to a city called Ephraim near the wilderness. It can no longer be identified with certainty. Perhaps a city (Aphairema, 1 Macc 11:34?) in the old tribal territory of Ephraim is in mind. G. Dalman, *Orte und Wege Jesu* (1924) 231-35; BAGD s.v.; J. A. Soggin, *BHH* 421 (2); R. Bultmann, *John* [Eng. tr., 1971] ad loc.; W. Ewing and R. J. Hughes, *ISBE* II, 119 (2); B. Schwank, "Efraim in Joh 11,54," *L'Évangile de Jean* (ed. M. de Jonge; 1977) 377-83.

ἐφφαθα *ephphatha* be opened (imv.)*

In Mark 7:34, a Greek rendering (εφφεθα in אֵ³ D [W] latt sa) of the imv. hithpael of Aram. *p*ᵉ*taḥ* (with regressive assimilation of *t* to *p*), "open." The Evangelist provides the tr.: διανοίχθητι. The command is addressed to the whole person, not just to the diseased organ. On the linguistic problem, cf. G. Dalman, *Grammatik des jüdisch-palästinischen Aramäisch* (²1905 = 1960) 278n.1, who assumes a fem. pl.; Billerbeck II, 17f.; J. A. Emerton, *JTS* 18 (1967) 427-31; M. Black, FS Rigaux 57-62; I. Rabinowitz, *ZNW* 53 (1962) 229-38; *idem, JSS* 16 (1971) 151-56; S. Morag, *JSS* 17 (1972) 198-202; *TRE* III, 602-10, esp. 606.

ἐχθές *echthes* yesterday (adv.)*

John 4:52; Acts 7:28: the preceding day (v.l. in both texts χθές); Heb 13:8, in the acclamatory formula Ἰησοῦς Χριστός ἐχθές (v.l. χθές) καὶ σήμερον ὁ αὐτὸς καὶ εἰς τοὺς αἰῶνας: the past time of the believing community (cf. v. 7); see also F. V. Filson, *"Yesterday"; A Study of Hebrews in the Light of Chapter 13* (SBT II/4, 1967); O. Michel, *Heb* [KEK] ad loc.

ἔχθρα, ας, ἡ *echthra* hostility
→ ἐχθρός.

ἐχθρός, οῦ, ὁ *echthros* enemy*
ἔχθρα, ας, ἡ *echthra* hostility*

1. Occurrences in the NT — 2. Eschatological-apocalyptic sayings — 3. The enemies of God — 4. Dualistic and polemical sayings — 5. The personal enemy — 6. The enemy of the church

Lit.: H. BIETENHARD, *DNTT* I, 553-55. — W. FOERSTER, *TDNT* II, 811-15. — A. S. GEYSER, *BHH* 467f. — X. LÉON-DUFOUR, *Dictionary of the NT* (1980) 176f. — O. LINTON, "St. Matthew 5:43," *ST* 18 (1964) 66-79. — D. LÜHRMANN, "Liebet eure Feinde (Lk 6,27-36/Mt 5,39-48)," *ZTK* 69 (1972) 412-38. — G. MOLIN, "Mt 5,43 und das Schrifttum von Qumran," FS Bardtke 150-52. — F. NEUGEBAUER, "Die dargebotene Wange und Jesu Gebot der Feindesliebe. Erwägungen zu Lk 6,27-36/Mt 5,38-48," *TLZ* 110 (1985) 865-76. — J. A. SANDERS, *IDB* II, 101. — J. SAUER, "Traditionsgeschichtliche Erwägungen zu den synoptischen und paulinischen Aussagen über Feindesliebe und Wiedervergeltungsverzicht," *ZNW* 76 (1985) 1-28. — J. SCHARBERT, *SacVb* 220-24. — *idem, BL* 474f. — L. SCHOTTROFF, "Non-Violence and the Love of One's Enemies," *Essays on the Love*

Commandment (1978) 9-39. — O. J. F. SEITZ, "Love Your Enemies," *NTS* 16 (1969-70) 39-54. — M. SMITH, "Mt 5.43: 'Hate Thine Enemy,' " *HTR* 45 (1952) 70-73. — G. STRECKER, "Die Antithesen der Bergpredigt," *ZNW* 69 (1978) 36-72, esp. 65-69. — For further bibliography see *DNTT* I, 557; *SacVb* 224; *TWNT* X, 1093f.

1. Ἐχθρός appears 32 times and ἔχθρα 6 times in the NT. Neither appears in the Johannine literature. Ἐχθρός is always used as a masc. subst. except possibly in Matt 13:28 (BAGD s.v.).

2. NT usage is strongly influenced by the OT and Jewish tradition. In addition to Luke 1:71, 74 (hope for the liberation of Israel from its *enemies* [Ps 105:9f.]; cf. *Pss. Sol.* 17:45) and Luke 19:43 (a prophetic threatening word; see H. Ringgren, *TDOT* I, 214f.; E. Jenni, *THAT* I, 121f.) , eschatological-apocalyptic sayings are found in citations of Ps 110:1. While the *enemies* in Mark 12:36 par.; Acts 2:35; Heb 1:13; 10:13 are not specified, in an anti-enthusiast argument in 1 Cor 15:25f. (so also Heb 10:12f.!) they are the demonic powers (v. 24) who must be destroyed by the exalted and enthroned Christ (see H. Conzelmann, *1 Cor* [Eng. tr., Hermeneia] 272; cf. K. Berger, *Die Auferstehung des Propheten und die Erhöhung des Menschensohnes* [1976] 251); the subjection of the last enemy, death, makes eschatological life possible. Luke 19:27 allegorizes the vengeance of a claimant to the throne on his enemies (on the historical background, cf. Josephus *B.J.* ii.80ff., 111) as the destruction of the enemies by the Christ who was persecuted by them, but who now is enthroned and has returned for the final judgment (cf. *1 Enoch* [Greek] 1:1).

The description of the destruction of the *enemies* of the two witnesses in Rev 11:5 "through fire which pours from their mouth" refers to the OT prophetic tradition (2 Kgs 1:10; cf. Luke 9:54 A C D W Θ Koine; Jer 5:14). Here is an expression of their divine mission. This is indicated also in Luke 10:19: The authority of the messengers sent from God gives them power over the opponent. The context in both Revelation and Luke indicates that the ἐχθροί are those characterized by the vb. → ἀδικέω [3]). This legitimacy of God's messengers underlines also the emphasis on the role of the *enemies* as eyewitnesses of the exaltation of the witnesses in Rev 11:12 (cf. *T. Mos.* 10:10) in agreement with v. 9.

3. In the semantic field of the admission of the Gentiles to salvation, the Pauline and deutero-Pauline letters speak of them (and sinners in general) as *enemies* of God and of his people *ante Christum*. The opposite term is καταλλαγή/→ καταλλάσσω (nonbiblical: Herodotus i.61; vii.145; Aristotle *Rh.* 1367b.17; Plato *R.* viii.566e; Philo *Virt.* 118; Josephus *Ant.* xvi.267, etc.): Rom 5:10; Eph 2:14, 16; Col 1:21. Conversely the Jews are κατὰ τὸ εὐαγγέλιον, thus *post Christum*, the *enemies* of God.

Eph 2:14, 16 indicate that one cannot separate *hostility* to God and to his people. Taking up Isa 57:19, the author shows that the hostility between Gentiles and Jews, which is created by the law (v. 14), is abolished only when the hostility of *both* to God is removed and *both have become* one new person. This idea is also formulated in Rom 5:10.

4. *"Hostility* against God," in the context of the dualism of flesh and Spirit in relation to God (Rom 8:7f.), is the practice of striving after the σάρξ, inasmuch as it is incapable of obedience to the law of God, which stands on the side of πνεῦμα (7:14). An analogous reference is Gal 5:20, where ἔχθραι are numbered among the works of the σάρξ, which stand in opposition to the fruits of the πνεῦμα.

With the frequent contrasting pairs φίλος/φιλία and ἐχθρός/ἔχθρα in Jas 4:4, the Johannine-sounding (cf. 1 John 2:15f.; 4:5) *dualism of God and the world* is formulated, which is the linguistic expression (cf. the context) of a sectarian ethic (cf. also Jas 1:27). The polemical statements in Phil 3:18 and Acts 13:10 are likewise each constructed with an obj. gen.: The *"enemies* of the cross of Christ" in Phil 3:18 are the opponents of the Pauline gospel, which has its polemical center in the cross (see H. W. Kuhn, *ZTK* 72 [1975] 40f.).

Acts 13:10 ("*enemy* of all righteousness") takes up a term of Jewish adversarial reproach: cf. 4 Macc 9:15 (τῆς οὐρανίου δίκης ἐχθρέ); *Apoc. Abr.* 14:7 ("Enmity for you is a righteous act"); *Apoc. Pet.* (E. Bratke, *ZWT* 36/1 [1893] 483).

5. The personal *enemy* is in view in Matt 10:36 (cf. Epictetus *Diss.* ii.22.7); 13:25, 28 (in v. 39 interpreted by Matthew as the devil); Luke 23:12; Rom 12:20 (citing Prov 25:21). Cf. the early Jewish reception and interpretation of Exod 23:5, which calls for overcoming hostility (A. Nissen, *Gott und der Nächste im antiken Judentum* [1974] 304ff.): Philo *Virt.* 116ff.; 4 Macc 2:14; pseudo-Phocylides 140ff. (also Nissen 308n.956, 313; Billerbeck III, 302).

Matt 5:43 also belongs within this connection (see Linton; Seitz; Billerbeck I, 364-68): Matthew associates the OT commandment to love one's neighbor with the command to love one's enemies (see also Philo *Virt.* 116ff.; Sir 27:18; 29:5f.). Matt 5:43c is not a reflection on an OT and Jewish "command to hate," as in, e.g., 1QS 1:10 (Foerster 814; Seitz 49; see Braun, *Qumran* I, 17; cf. Molin), but is intended rather to enhance rhetorically the antithesis to 5:44 and is to be explained from that background (cf. G. Strecker, *Der Weg der Gerechtigkeit* [1971] 24n.5 [p. 25]).

The command to love one's enemies (Matt 5:44 par. Luke 6:27, 35; on the history of the tradition, see Lührmann) already in Q refers to the conduct of the Church toward its enemies (see Matt 5:44b), which is distinguished by the overcoming of simple reciprocity of love, as practiced by the tax collectors and Gentiles (Matthew)

or the sinners (Luke). For Jesus himself it doubtless has to do with the simple call to "love your enemies" (Lührmann 425f.), which is is directed to the wandering charismatics traveling with him and which comes to expression in its distinctive ethical radicalism. Against Hengel (*Was Jesus a Revolutionist?* [1971] 26ff.; for a critique, cf. Schottroff, 203f.), an anti-Zealot view is hardly in mind, for it is not the Romans, but the enemies of Jesus' followers who are in view.

6. According to 2 Thess 3:14 the Church should avoid one who is not discerning, but not exclude him, i.e., regard him as an "enemy" (according to Matt 18:17 as "a Gentile and a tax collector"), but warn him as a "brother" (enemy and brother are contrasted also in Epictetus *Diss.* ii.10.13). Gal 4:16 is also to be understood in this sense: Paul assumes that the Galatians, because of his ἀληθεύειν, no longer regard him as a brother, but as an *enemy*, i.e., as no longer belonging to the community.

M. Wolter

ἔχιδνα, ης, ἡ   *echidna*   poisonous snake*

Literal in Acts 28:3. Fig. in the rebuke γεννήματα ἐχιδνῶν, "brood of *vipers*" (Matt 3:7 par. Luke 3:7; Matt 12:34; 23:33). W. Foerster, *TDNT* II, 815.

ἔχω   *echō*   have

1. Occurrences in the NT — 2. Meanings — 3. Usage — 4. *Have* as a theologically significant term

Lit.: G. AGRELL, *Work, Toil and Sustenance* (1976) 68-152. — W. BIENERT, *Die Arbeit nach der Lehre der Bibel* (1954) 185-408. — H. F. VON CAMPENHAUSEN, "The Christians and Social Life according to the NT," *Tradition and Life in the Church*, (1968) 141-59. — G. DAUTZENBERG, "Der Verzicht auf das apostolische Unterhaltsrecht," *Bib* 50 (1969) 212-32. — H. J. DEGENHARDT, *Lukas—Evangelist der Armen* (1965). — D. J. DOUGHTY, "The Presence and Future of Salvation in Corinth," *ZNW* 66 (1975) 61-90. — J. EICHLER, *DNTT* I, 635-39. — E. ELLWEIN, *Heilsgegenwart und Heilszukunft im NT* (1964). — H. HANSE, *TDNT* II, 816-27. — M. HENGEL, *Property and Riches in the Early Church* (1974). — I. SOISALON-SOININEN, "Der Gebrauch des Verbes ἔχειν in der Septuaginta," *VT* 28 (1978) 92-99. — G. THEISSEN, "Wanderradikalismus," *ZTK* 70 (1973) 245-71. — *idem, The Social Setting of Pauline Christianity* (1982) 27-67. — For further bibliography see *TWNT* X, 1094.

1. This vb. is used more than 700 times in the NT, esp. in the Gospels (Matthew 75 times, Mark 72 times, Luke 78 times, John 88 times), which is related to their lively narrative style. Among the NT writings the Johannine literature is particularly prominent (thus 1 John about 28 times, Revelation about 101 times). The use of ἔχω diminishes especially where the epistolary literature demonstrates an argumentative style. But this does not mean that the word has little theological significance.

2. The vb. has a great breadth of meaning: *have, keep, possess;* aor.: *acquire, take possession;* intrans.: *be, be situated* (BAGD s.v.). The word designates any form of combining two entities, including those of a personal, material, and metaphorical kind. Aristotle involved himself exhaustively with the meaning of the word and introduced it into his categories (*Metaph.* iv.23.1023a; cf. *Cat.* 15.15b). Ἔχω has no direct Hebrew equivalent. The relationship expressed in the Greek vb. is rendered in Hebrew in other ways (other expressions, preps., dat., etc.). The consequence is that the LXX renders more than 50 different expressions with ἔχω. NT usage agrees with the range of meanings found in classical and Hellenistic Greek (Hanse 816f.). The theological content must nevertheless be elaborated on with consideration to the underlying presuppositions found in the Hebrew OT.

3. The subj. of ἔχω in the NT can be Christ, other supra-earthly beings, i.e., angels and demons, individual Christians, or the Church. Normally, however, Christ and the transcendent powers appear as objs. of ἔχω. Other objs. of the vb. are personal qualities or spiritual gifts, i.e., fearlessness, peace with God, access to grace, etc. In many instances the vb. indicates a having in which the objects are family, friends, enemies, or material things. In the following discussion, the focus is on the numerous instances in which the vb. has theological significance. ·

4. As indicated (→ 3), Christ can be the subj. of the having. Rev 1:18 is noteworthy, as here Christ, the Son of Man, is the one who *possesses* the key of death and of Hades. Belonging to this motif are the Johannine statements that the Son *has* the life in himself (John 5:26) and that he *has* the power to lay down his life and to take it again (10:18). Even during his earthly life Jesus, as the Son of Man, has the power to forgive sins (Mark 2:10 par.). The saying in Rev 3:1 (cf. 1:4; 4:5; 5:6), that Christ *has* the seven spirits of God, is unusual. It probably means that he has sovereignty over these powers (and with it a portion of the sovereignty of God). Christ's victory over death means finally victory over the authority of the devil, who until now *has had* unlimited power over death (Heb 2:14).

Other beings take the position of the subj. In Rev 7:2 an angel *has* the seal of the living God; the seven angels before God's throne *have* seven trumpets (8:6); the beast *has* ten horns and seven heads (13:1), etc.

Most statements with ἔχω are formulated from the human perspective. The people of God or the individual members of the people of God *have* various objs. Appearing rarely and sounding peculiar are references to, among others, "*having* God." But they can be easily understood against the background of OT assumptions (despite the lack of a Hebrew equivalent for ἔχω in the OT). At the center of the OT message is the conviction

that God has made Israel his own possession and himself the God of this people. He is the obj. of this *having.* Israel *has* him as its God (Pss 32:12; 143:15 LXX; cf. Hos 2:21-25); he is the inheritance of the Levites (Deut 10:9; 18:2; Num 18:20; Ezek 44:28), because they have no property in the land. He is the refuge of the individual (Pss 17:3; 26:1 LXX). These sayings obviously include no idea of acquiring or possessing of God in the literal sense. They are, rather, an expression of the close association between Yahweh and his people.

Very similar are NT sayings for *having* God (even if they are formulated from christological assumptions). Esp. significant are the expressions in the Johannine literature. In 1 John 2:23 the concern is with "not *having*" or *having* the Father, which is intimately associated with one's relationship to the Son. "Fellowship" with the Father—indeed, through the Son—stands here, as also in 2 John 9 (probably in a polemic against docetic tendencies), in the foreground.

The other NT references to "having God" are less striking. Rom 1:28 speaks of *having* God ἐν ἐπιγνώσει. Here the concern is with the role of knowledge as a means of fellowship with God (cf. 1:21), not with "possessing" God. In Col 4:1, the author reminds earthly lords (household masters, slaveholders) that they *have* a Lord in heaven, who keeps watch over the interest of the weak. Here ἔχω is not an expression for a form of fellowship, but rather its function is a reminder that there is a God who watches over righteousness. The Jews *have* God as Father (John 8:41). The significance here is thus the fatherhood, not the having.

As already indicated, most statements regarding having a divine being are concentrated on Christ. In 1 John 5:12 it is said that one who *has* the Son *has* life. God has given us eternal life in his Son (5:11). Here the Son is thus connected exclusively with life (ζωή), the central salvific concept of the Johannine literature. He is the bearer of life because of his unique relationship to the Father (1 John 2:23; 2 John 9; cf. John 10:30, 38; 14:20). In 1 John 2:1f. his salvific role is described with other terms: "we *have* a helper (παράκλητος) with the Father," who himself is the expiation (ἱλασμός) for our sins and for the sins of the world. Here also Christ is the only bearer of salvation. To *have* him, i.e., to have fellowship with him, means to have a part in the reconciliation which he has accomplished (cf. John 13:8).

Sayings of a similar structure appear also in Hebrews. According to 4:14-16 we *have* a great high priest, who (through his exaltation) has passed through the heavens. He can have sympathy with our weaknesses because he has been tempted in the same way that we are. Thus we can with confidence approach his throne of grace. In 8:1 the concept of the exaltation is given further elaboration: We *have* such a high priest, who has sat down at the right hand of the throne of the majesty in the heavens. The priestly service that he carries out is chiefly one of intercession (cf. 8:6; 10:21), a function that he can carry out because of the sacrifice that he has made (9:14).

Less frequent are references to *having* the Spirit. This probably is the result of the fact that the Christian is baptized into the body of Christ through the Spirit (1 Cor 12:13) and is thus within the sphere of the Spirit. Thus it is less natural to speak of an (individual) possession of the Spirit. However, a few examples can be given. Rom 8:9 speaks of one *having* (or not *having*) the Spirit. The context indicates, however, that the Spirit could as easily have been the subj. (the passage speaks of dwelling; cf. also 1 Cor 6:19). Possession of the Spirit includes an existence within a pneumatic fellowship, in which the subject-object relationship cannot be sharply defined. Anyone who stands outside this sphere does not belong to Christ. As the Spirit belongs to the gifts of the last age, the sayings take on a distinct eschatological shape (which then provides a foundation for ethical exhortations: Rom 8:11ff.). According to Rom 8:23 we *have* the Spirit as the firstfruits (ἀπαρχὴ τοῦ πνεύματος, gen. of apposition), which consists in the Spirit; cf. 2 Cor 1:22; 5:5, where the Spirit is described as the deposit or pledge (ἀρραβῶν) of the coming glory. Paul's statement in 2 Cor 4:13ff. (cf. the context) that he *has* the Spirit of faith (πνεῦμα τῆς πίστεως) is eschatologically oriented. His statement in 1 Cor 7:40, in which he remarks (ironically?) that he *has* the Spirit of God (so that he can offer advice in Christian conduct), has another accent. *Having* the Father, the Son, and the Spirit is consequently synonymous with an incorporation into the community with God. This involves at the same time "having" salvation and everything associated with it.

In the Johannine literature one finds numerous statements to the effect that one who *has* the Son, *has* eternal life (John 3:15f.; 3:36; 5:24, 26; 6:40, 54; 1 John 5:12; cf. John 8:21; 1 John 3:15). That one possesses salvation in the present is indicated most strongly in the Johannine literature, but is not unknown in the other writings of the NT. Related, but not so strongly accented, perspectives are found also in Paul. One can recall the Spirit as the firstfruits (Rom 8:23; cf. 2 Cor 1:22; 5:5). Rom 5:1 speaks of the peace (εἰρήνη) that those who are justified *have* (ind.) with God, and of access (προσαγωγή, cf. 2:18) to grace, a formulation indicating that salvation is something that Christians *have* or actually possess. The same is true of the freedom (ἐλευθερία) that Christians *have* (freedom from νόμος, Gal 2:4); cf. also Eph 1:7 and Col 1:14, where redemption (ἀπολύτρωσις) is described as the possession of Christians. Possession of peace, of access to grace, of freedom, etc., are not a final *having*. Final salvation lies in the future. A good example of this orientation toward the future is 2 Cor 5:1 (cf. Phil 1:23) and

the statements about the hope (ἐλπίς) of Christians (Rom 15:4; 1 Thess 4:13; cf. Eph 2:12; see also the use of → σωτηρία).

In connection with his apostolate Paul speaks often of *having:* He *has* confidence (2 Cor 3:4); through hope he *has* boldness (3:2); in his ministry he *has* a part in God's mercy (4:1). He and his coworkers *have* a treasure in breakable jars, so that the power of God appears more clearly (4:7).

Other NT passages speak of *having* salvation and the blessings of salvation. Christians *have* hope of the resurrection (Acts 24:15; cf. 1 Thess 4:13). They *have* a good conscience (Acts 24:16; Heb 10:2; 1 Pet 3:16; cf. 1 Tim 1:9; Heb 13:18), a reward (Matt 5:46; 6:1), a treasure in heaven (Matt 19:21 par.), which is synonymous with eternal life (Matt 19:16, etc.).

The use of ἔχω in the NT indicates that Christianity can be characterized positively as a "religion of having" (Hanse 826). A negative counterpart is seen in the texts that speak of a demonic *having*. However, the issue is never raised in terms of a human possession. This *having* is a possession by the demons (cf. Matt 11:18 par.; Luke 7:33; 8:27; see also Mark 5:15; 7:25; 9:17; Luke 4:33; 13:11; Acts 8:7; 16:16; 19:13). Jesus is accused of having Beelzebul (Mark 3:22 par.), which in John 7:20; 8:48f., 52 (cf. 10:20) is given a military connotation and is rendered graphically with "be crazy."

E. Larsson

ἕως *heōs* as long as, while, until, up to

1. Occurrences in the NT — 2. Origin and range of meaning — 3. Usage and significant instances in the NT — a) Matthew — b) Luke-Acts — c) Paul — d) Summary

Lit.: BAGD s.v. — BDF §216. — JEREMIAS, *Theology* 46f. — MOULTON, *Grammar* III, 110f., 276.

1. Ἕως appears 146 times in the NT, with a preponderance in Matthew (49 occurrences) and Luke-Acts (50). The limited use in the Epistles (e.g., of Paul) and the later NT witnesses is striking (e.g., 10 occurrences in John).

2. Ἕως is known in both secular and koine Greek. In the former use as a conj. surpasses the prep. use (Homer, Plato), which becomes known after the end of the 4th cent. B.C. (Schwyzer, *Grammatik* II, 550f.). a) According to the evidence of classical literature (Plato, Xenophon), ἕως in the *temporal* sense can indicate both the simultaneity of two actions (*as long as/while*) and the goal and/or end point of an action *(until)*. Whether the meaning is inclusive or exclusive *(until and subsequently* vs. *up to that point and no further)* and whether ind., opt., or subjunc. (normally with ἄν) follows depend on the respective conditions and circumstances of the goal that is striven for. b) As a prep. with the gen. *(up to)* ἕως can have a temporal or spatial sense, but is also used of measure or extent.

The koine appears to have a similar direction, frequently in the papyri (Mayser, *Grammatik* II/2, 522-26); ἕως appears here often in alternation with μέχρι as a temporal conj. It is also used (fig.) to describe the measure and degree of an action (indicating either the minimum or the maximum), more rarely as a local particle.

This existing range of meaning determines also NT usage. Here ἕως appears as a conj. in the temporal as well as the final sense (more frequently combined with οὗ, as in Matt 14:22, or ὅτου, as in Luke 12:50), as an adv., and as an improper prep. with the gen. The particles μέχρι and ἄχρι are synonyms, while the advs. ἄνω, κάτω, ἔσω, ἔξω, and ἄρτι are used to intensify the word (BDF §216.3).

3. A survey of the central passages of the NT literature provides an impression of the variety of possibilities for usage and can establish and illustrate the major emphases:

a) The occurrences in Matthew, which, at least in part, presuppose Mark, but in most cases alter or expand it, give prominence to the *temporal* (conj. as prep.) aspect in which the beginning (ἀπό) and end (ἕως) of a period of time are signified; e.g., 1:17 and 23:35, where the connecting links and interval of a generation are set forth as significant. It is also seen when only the goal is envisioned in an inclusive or exclusive sense: inclusive, e.g., 1:25 (*until* Mary gave birth to her son [and afterward]); 5:18 (*until* heaven and earth pass away [and afterward]). On the other hand, ἕως is used to exclude in 11:12f. (all of the prophets . . . prophesied *up to the time of* John (in contrast to Luke 16:16: μέχρι Ἰωάννου); "We have a different evaluation of John, and indeed a different view of the history of salvation, depending on whether ἕως / μέχρι are understood inclusively or exclusively. According to Luke who understands μέχρι *inclusively,* the Baptist still belongs to the period of the law and the prophets. . . . According to Matthew . . . John the Baptist is already a part of the new aeon. . . ." (Jeremias 47)

Also worthy of mention is the prophetic-future character of ἕως in sayings that include an announcement of salvation (Matt 26:29 from Mark 14:25; similarly Matt 17:9) or a prophecy of doom (23:39; 24:34), often with οὐ μή, the subjunc., and ἄν (16:28 from Mark 9:1). Here the prophetic genus and manner of expression of the LXX

provide the basis (cf. Isa 55:10, 11; Jer 23:20), where no direct Heb. equivalent for ἕως is given (Hatch/Redpath 592f.). Passages with an eschatological-judging element also point in this direction: Matt 13:30 (*until* the time of the harvest; cf. also 18:30, 34: the period of time for the rectification); positive: 28:20 (*until* the end of the world). A temporal limitation (*up to/as many as*) is found in 18:21f., while 17:17 (from Mark 9:19: How long . . . ?) reflects a degree of (emotional) accent. The sayings in 14:22 (cf. Mark 6:45) and 26:36 (cf. 18:30, 34; strengthened with οὗ) reflect finality. The local sense occurs in 26:58 (from Mark 14:54).

b) In the Lukan tradition (including Acts) prep. use is much in evidence, in the temporal sense in Luke 1:80; Acts 1:22; 7:45; with the local meaning in Luke 2:15; 4:42; 22:51, esp. frequent in Acts, e.g., 1:8; 9:38; 11:19; here also used to demarcate ("from . . . to"), e.g., Acts 8:10; 28:23. Use as a conj., with the accent at the conclusion of the clause, is picked up from Luke 12:50 and 13:8 and taken over in the parable in 15:4, 8 (in rhetorical questions). Ἕως appears in a cultic-prophetic context only in Luke (22:16, 18). The (final) inf. used as a noun after ἕως is attested in Acts 8:40.

c) The Pauline letters (esp. 1 and 2 Corinthians) have ἕως as a prep. and as a conj., without any new emphases. Of the later literature, John is worthy of mention, as it often connects ἕως with ἄρτι to speak of the present situation (2:10; 5:17; 16:24), to indicate duration (12:35, 36), or to indicate the goal (21:22, 23). In an eschatological context ἕως appears in James and 2 Peter, similarly Rev 6:10f. and 20:5.

d) In summary one may observe: Ἕως can indicate both the continuity and the finality of an action. It can be used for what is continuing, for what is already concluded, and also for the future time period. In individual cases it can indicate a local limitation as well as a limitation of degree and measure. However, it can also take on a significance for salvation history or a prophetic sense, and it can also be significant in judicial-eschatological sayings.   A. Kretzer

Z ζ

Ζαβουλών *Zaboulōn* Zebulun*

The name of one of the twelve patriarchs (Gen 30:20) and thus of an Israelite tribe (Acts 7:8). The tribal area of Zebulun is mentioned in Matt 4:13, 15 (Isa. 9:1) with that of Naphtali.

Ζακχαῖος, ου *Zakchaios* Zachaeus*

An → ἀρχιτελώνης at whose home Jesus was a guest (Luke 19:2, 5, 8). G. Schneider, *Luke* (ÖTK) II, on 19:1-10 (bibliography).

Ζάρα *Zara* Zerah*

A personal name in Matt. 1:3 (cf. 1 Chr 2:4).

Ζαχαρίας, ου *Zacharias* Zechariah*

A common personal name (OT, Aristeas, Josephus), in the NT for two men: 1. The father of John the Baptist (Luke 1:5, 12, 13, 18, 21, 40, 59, 67; 3:2). 2. A man who was murdered (Luke 11:51; Matt 23:35, according to the latter "the son of → Βαραχίας (Barachiah)."

ζάω *zaō* live
→ ζῶ.

Ζεβεδαῖος, ου *Zebedaios* Zebedee*

A personal name, in the NT of the father of the apostles John and James (Mark 1:19, 20 par. Matt 4:21 bis/ Luke 5:10; 3:17 par. Matt 10:2; 10:35 par. Matt 20:20; Matt 26:37 [cf. Mark 14:33]; 27:56 [cf. Mark 15:40]: "the mother of the sons of Zebedee"; John 21:2, οἱ τοῦ Ζεβεδαίου, with the corresponding sg. ὁ τοῦ Ζεβεδαίου in Mark 1:19 par. Matt 4:21a; 3:17 par. Matt 10:2).

ζεστός, 3 *zestos* hot*

Rev 3:15 (bis), in a rebuke to the church at Laodicea, which (like water?) is neither cold (ψυχρός) nor *hot*, but lukewarm (χλιαρός) and therefore (as unpalatable) is spit out. A. Oepke, *TDNT* II, 876f.; H. Kraft, *Rev* (HNT) ad loc.

ζεῦγος, ους, τό *zeugos* yoke, pair*

Luke 14:19: ζεῦγος βοῶν, "a *yoke* of oxen"; 2:24: ζεῦγος τρυγόνων, "a *pair* of turtledoves" (cf. Lev 5:11; 12:8 LXX) as a sacrifice brought by the poor.

ζευκτηρία, ας, ἡ *zeuktēria* rope, binding*

In the NT only in Acts 27:40 (pl.): ἀνέντες τὰς ζευκτηρίας τῶν πηδαλίων, "while they loosened the *bindings* (guy-ropes) of the steering rudders." As long as one was at anchor, both rudders were tied (cf. E. Haenchen, *Acts* [Eng. tr., 1971] 708).

Ζεύς, Διός *Zeus* Zeus*

The Greek (of Indo-European origin) name of the "father" of the gods (see K. Schauenburg, *LAW* 3333-36), in the NT only in Acts 14:12, 13: The crowd in Lystra (after a healing miracle) calls Barnabas *Zeus* (acc. Δία) and Paul Hermes, and the priest of (the temple of) *Zeus* prepares a sacrifice. See E. Haenchen, *Acts* (Eng. tr.) 426f. Perhaps the identification of both preachers is to be explained by the saga of Philemon and Baucis (Ovid *Metamorphoses* viii.611-724). A. B. Cook, *Zeus*, 3 vols. (1914-40); M. P. Nilsson, et al., *OCD* 1146f.; Prümm, *Handbuch* (index s.v.); Nilsson, *Geschichte* II (index s.v.); H. Schwabl, *PW* Suppl. X/A (1972) 253-376; Suppl. XV (1978) 993-1411, 1441-81; E. Simon, *PW* Suppl. XV, 1411-41 (archaeological).

ζέω *zeō* cook, boil*

In the NT only fig., pres. partc. with dat. of cause τῷ πνεύματι. Rom 12:11, of a summons to be τῷ πνεύματι ζέοντες, "*aflame* in the Spirit" (H. Schlier, *Rom* [HTKNT] ad loc.: of the Holy Spirit, who grants zeal). Acts 18:25, of Apollos, who "spoke *ardently* in the Spirit (so E. Haenchen, *Acts* [Eng. tr.] ad loc.; BAGD s.v. understands ζέων of emotions: "burning zeal") and taught accurately about Jesus." A. Oepke, *TDNT* II, 875f.

ζηλεύω *zēleuō* be eager, zealous*

In the NT only in Rev 3:19b (absolute) in the summons to the church at Laodicea: ζήλευε οὖν καὶ μετανόησον.

ζῆλος, ου, ὁ *zēlos* zeal*
ζῆλος, ους, τό *zēlos* zeal*
ζηλόω *zēloō* strive, be zealous*

1. Occurrences in the NT — 2. Meaning — 3. Lines of tradition — 4. John — 5. Acts — 6. Paul — 7. Hebrews and James

Lit.: H. C. HAHN, *DNTT* III, 1166-68. — M. HENGEL, *The Zealots* (1989). — G. SAUER, *THAT* II, 647-50. — A. STUMPFF, *TDNT* II, 877f. — S. WIBBING, *Die Tugend- und Lasterkataloge im NT* (1959) 77-108. — For further bibliography see *DNTT* III, 1169f.; *TWNT* X, 1096f.

1. Ζῆλος (16 NT occurrences) and ζηλόω (11 occurrences) appear in the NT predominantly in Paul (18 times, not in the Pastorals), also in John (once), Acts (4 times), Hebrews (once), and James (3 times). The word is almost totally absent in the Jesus tradition, in reference to Jesus as well as his opponents; it is rare likewise in the literature that is under stronger Greek influence, suggesting that a Jewish influence in its usage exists.

2. Ζῆλος (with the same meaning whether with ὁ or τό) and ζηλόω designate a passionate commitment to a person or cause (Stumpff 876). The motivation can vary: commitment to the highest values, fascination, contact with sacred sentiments, injured honor, rivalry or envy, contentiousness, and irritability. Correspondingly differentiated is the evaluation of the term between positive, neutral, and negative connotations. The respective standpoint plays a considerable role.

3. In the NT four lines of tradition can be seen:
a) The OT and Jewish "holy zeal" (cf. Hengel 146-228: John 2:17; Rom 10:2; 2 Cor 11:2; Phil 3:6; Heb 10:27).
b) Hostility occasioned by ill will (Acts 5:17; 7:9; 13:45; 17:5), in which stubbornness, anger, and (except for 7:9) religious duty can all play a role.
c) "Jealousy" in the vice catalogs (Rom 13:13; 2 Cor 12:20; Gal 5:20; Jas 3:14, 16; 4:2; similarly 1 Cor 3:3; 13:4). Here a fixed tradition is present (e.g., Sir. 40:4; 1QS 4:10; cf. H. Schlier, *Gal* [KEK] on 5:20), esp. in combination with, e.g., ἔρις. Jealousy is here "the kind of zeal which does not try to help others but rather to harm them" (Stumpff 882).

d) The desire to attain goals or to be devoted to someone (1 Cor 12:31; 14:1, 39; 2 Cor 7:7, 11; 9:2; Gal 4:17 bis, 18).

4. According to John 2:17 the cleansing of the temple by Jesus reminds the disciples of Ps 69:10. Jesus' zeal includes both reverence and holy wrath; his being "consumed" by zeal is intended more objectively than inwardly: it "causes his death" (R. Schnackenburg *John* [Eng. tr.] ad loc.).

5. In all occurrences in Acts (5:17; 7:9; 13:45; 17:5) the rage of the Jews or their ancestors toward their opposition (Christians or Joseph) reacts to new attainments in prestige. The rage is thus derived directly from envy; the tr. "passionate agitation" is inadequate. According to the view of Luke a general lack of discernment is involved (7:51ff.; 13:45f.). Apparently Luke also wants to characterize a "typical Jewish fervor," where no positive self-understanding is evident (otherwise 21:20; Gal 1:14).

6. Paul uses ζῆλος and ζηλόω with various meanings:
a) Jealousy as a typical expression for "fleshly" conduct in contrast to the Spirit or to love (Rom 13:13; 1 Cor 3:3; 13:4; 2 Cor 12:20; Gal 5:20). Here the term describes a hostile attitude toward other people.
b) False pious zeal (κατὰ ζῆλος . . . , κατὰ δικαιοσύνην), according to Phil 3:6, leads to intolerant persecution (cf. Gal 1:13f.). Ζῆλος θεοῦ appears twice. In Rom 10:2 Paul acknowledges that Israel has a *zeal for God* (obj. gen.), although "not according to correct insight." Paul respects earnest striving (cf. Acts 22:3).
c) According to 2 Cor 11:2 Paul is the father of the bride who is *eager* (H. Windisch, *2 Cor* [KEK] ad loc.) to present the Church as a pure bride to Christ. Θεοῦ ζῆλος (qualitative gen., with R. Bultmann, *2 Cor* [Eng. tr., 1985] ad loc.; other possibilities are gen. of origin or author, subj. gen.) alludes to the "holy zeal" of Yahweh (cf. Sauer 649). Inasmuch as Paul is not watchful in his own interest, one may speak indirectly, if at all, of "jealousy"; preferably: "I watch over your exclusive relationship to Christ as would be appropriate for God himself" (cf. Hengel 177f.: vicariously jealous for God).
d) According to 1 Cor 12:31; 14:1, 39, the Christian should strive for charismata, pneumatica, and esp. προφητεύειν (likewise 14:12), presumably through prayer (14:13). Paul praises another activity in 2 Cor 9:2: *enthusiasm* for the collection.
e) 2 Cor 7:7, 11 and Gal 4:17f. speak of "wooing" (F. Mussner, *Gal* [HTKNT] ad loc.). In 2 Cor 7:7, 11 ζῆλος appears together with other evidences of the Church's desire to purify its relationship to God. Gal 4:17f. is different: the opponents' appeal for the affection of the Galatians (categories of interhuman relationships, cf. 4:15, 19). Paul also favors being sought after for what

is good; here, however, there is an οὐ καλῶς, for the Church would then be "shut out" from Paul (ἐκκλεῖσαι refers to the relation of Paul to the Church: so E. Güttgemanns, *Der leidende Apostel und sein Herr* [1966] 183; Mussner [see Mussner for other views]).

7. Heb 10:27 refers to Isa 26:11 LXX: for the deliberate sinner only judgment and a consuming *"fury of fire"* remain (an image describing the person of God as judge: A. Strobel, *Heb* [NTD] ad loc.). Jas 3:13–4:3 contrasts peaceable wisdom with combativeness (including ζῆλος, 3:14, 16; 4:2, twice with ἐριθεία, "baseness"; F. Büchsel, *TDNT* II, 660); it comes "from below" (3:15), from the ἡδοναί (4:1, 3).   W. Popkes

ζηλόω *zēloō* strive, be zealous*
→ ζῆλος.

ζηλωτής, οῦ, ὁ *zēlōtēs* zealot, fanatic*

1. Occurrences in the NT — 2. Meanings — 3. Luke 6:15; Acts 1:13

Lit.: BAGD s.v. — M. HENGEL, *The Zealots* (1989). — R. A. HORSLEY, "The Zealots: Their Origin, Relationships and Importance in the Jewish Revolt," *NovT* 28 (1986) 159-92. — H. MERKEL, *IDBSup* 979-82. — D. M. RHOADS, *Israel in Revolution 6-74 C.E.* (1976). — A. STUMPFF, *TDNT* II, 882-88. — For further bibliography see *TWNT* X, 1096f.

1. The *nomen auctoris* ζηλωτής (from the vb. ζηλόω [→ ζῆλος]) appears 8 times in the NT. In 6 occurrences a gen. follows and gives the subject or person to which the zealous involvement is directed.

2. In 1 Cor 14:12 Paul states that the Corinthians strive zealously for spirits (= spiritual gifts); he summons them to strive to build up the Church.

In looking back at his pre-Christian life Paul describes himself as one with "particular *zeal* for the law that had been passed on by the fathers" (Gal 1:14). Similarly he emphasizes his earlier Pharisaic-legalistic orientation in Phil 3:5. Thus he underlines the miracle of the revelation that called him, as one who was unprepared, to be the missionary for the gospel free of law. According to Acts 22:3 Paul calls himself, upon being falsely accused by the Jews of defiling the temple, one who is *"zealous* for God." This recalls his own testimony; yet the break caused by his encounter with Christ is not apparent. "Unlike the historical Paul (Phil 3:4-11), the Lukan Paul does not reject his earlier zeal for the Law, he only condemns the false conclusions that he once drew from it" (H. Conzelmann, *Acts* [Eng. tr., Hermeneia] 186; cf. K. Löning, *Die Saulustradition in der Apostelgeschichte* [1973] 165-69).

According to Acts 21:20 ten thousand Jews who were zealous for the law became believers. Despite the exaggerated number the strict law observance of the early Jerusalem Church at the time of James (cf. M. Hengel, *ZTK* 72 [1975] 198f.) is reflected here.

In 1 Pet 3:13 the Christians who are discriminated against and threatened by the pagans are asked: "Who will do you evil when you are *zealous* for what is good?" Despite the language, which is reminiscent of Hellenistic moral philosophy, the author has a specifically Christian content in mind (cf. 3:8f., 16). It is not entirely clear whether the idea is that zeal for the good can keep evil at a distance (so W. Schrage, *1 Pet* [NTD] 99, with reference to 2:14; L. Goppelt, *1 Pet* [KEK] 233) or only that "evil cannot ultimately affect Christians" (N. Brox, *1 Pet* [EKKNT] 157).

At the end of Titus 2:11-14, which is strongly affected by concepts of Hellenistic piety and moral philosophy, the purpose of Jesus' sacrificial death is formulated as: He has "given himself to redeem us from all unrighteousness and to purify for himself a people of his own who are *zealous* for good works" (v. 14). Despite the greater weight given to "good works" in the Pastorals (1 Tim 2:10, etc.; Titus 2:7; 3:8, 14), the soteriological statement remains the foundation for the ethical imperative (cf. O. Merk, *ZNW* 66 [1975] 91-102).

3. Absolute ὁ ζηλωτής appears as a designation for a disciple of Jesus, Simon, in Luke 6:15 and Acts 1:13. The Synoptic parallels read ὁ Καναναῖος (Mark 3:18; Matt 10:3), the Aramaic equivalent for ὁ ζηλωτής (Hengel 69f.).

Absolute οἱ ζηλωταί is found in Josephus, *B.J.* iv.196; v.250 for the resistance fighters against the Roman occupation forces. They probably gave themselves this name in connection with Phinehas (Numbers 25) and Elijah (1 Kgs 19:9ff.). The Zealot movement was called into being by Judas the Galilean and Zadok the Pharisee when Judea was transformed into a Roman province in A.D. 6. The primary impulse was the uncompromising intensification of the first command of the Decalogue: No one but God is to be revered as "king" or "lord," and thus no stranger may rule over Israel. Payment of taxes to the Roman Caesar meant recognition of foreign rule and was thus apostasy from Yahweh. The Zealots were also distinguished by strict observance of the sabbath, intensification of the cultic commands for purity, and the demand of circumcision for Gentiles. For the liberation of Israel one must work together with God: One should proceed with force against both Gentile and Jewish lawbreakers. The movement ended with the conquest of Jerusalem in A.D. 70 and the suicide of the defenders of the Masada fortress in A.D. 73. The attempt to make Jesus himself a Zealot on the basis of the Zealot origin of one of his disciples contradicts essential parts of his proclamation and is thus mistaken (cf. Hengel 377-79; H. Merkel, *BK* 26 [1971] 44-47; J. P. M. Sweet, "The Zealots and Jesus," *Jesus and the Politics of His Day* [ed. E. Bammel and C. F. D. Moule; 1984] 1-9).   H. Merkel

ζημία, ας, ἡ *zēmia* disadvantage, loss*

Phil 3:7, 8: ζημίαν ἡγοῦμαι, "I count [something] as *loss"* (Xenophon *Mem.* ii.3.2, 4.3; Epictetus *Diss.*

ii.10.15; iii.26.25); Acts 27:10, 21, with ὕβρις: "with injury and much *loss*" (v. 10, in the announcement of Paul; v. 21 of the "injury and the *loss*" because of the storm). A. Stumpff, *TDNT* II, 888-92; B. Siede, *DNTT* III, 136f.; Spicq, *Notes* I, 339-42.

ζημιόω *zēmioō* inflict injury; pass.: suffer injury, suffer damage*

Only the pass. appears in the NT. It appears with κερδαίνω in Mark 8:36 (ζημιωθῆναι τὴν ψυχὴν αὐτοῦ) par. Matt 16:26 (cf. Luke 9:25, ἑαυτὸν δὲ ἀπολέσας ἢ ζημιωθείς); Phil 3:8 (τὰ πάντα ἐζημιώθην). In Mark 8:36 par. it involves loss of the "life" for which one can gain nothing in return; see G. Dautzenberg, *Sein Leben bewahren* (1966) 68-82. In Phil 3:8 (→ ζημία) Paul declares his willingness to "*suffer every loss* in order to gain Christ"; see J. Gnilka, *Phil* (HTKNT) 191-95.

1 Cor 3:15 speaks of the (material) *loss* one *suffers* (in BAGD s.v. 2, however, it is translated *be punished*) when one's "work" is burned up. 2 Cor 7:9: "so that you *suffered* no *loss* (ζημιωθῆτε) through us" (RSV). A. Stumpff, *TDNT* II, 888-92; B. Siede, *DNTT* III, 136f.; Spicq, *Notes* I, 339-42.

Ζηνᾶς *Zēnas* Zenas*

Personal name of a Christian "lawyer" (νομικός), Titus 3:13.

ζητέω *zēteō* seek
ζήτημα, ατος, τό *zētēma* dispute, point of controversy*

1. Occurrences in the NT — 2. Meaning — 3. Ζητέω — 4. Ζήτημα

Lit.: H. GREEVEN, *TDNT* II, 892-96. — H. G. Link, *DNTT* III, 530-32. — For further bibliography see *TWNT* X, 1097f.

1. Ζητέω appears 117 times in the NT, of which 83 are in the Gospels (Matthew has 14, Mark 10, Luke 25, and John 34). The vb. appears 20 times in the Pauline corpus, once in Hebrews, twice in 1 Peter, and once in Revelation. Ζήτημα appears only in Acts (15:2; 18:15; 23:29; 25:19; 26:3).

2. The vb. means *seek, search for, investigate, study, consider* (in agreement with its use in secular Greek literature), *strive for* something. In the LXX it is found *ca.* 400 times and normally stands for Heb. piel of *bqš*. Ζήτημα (literally *what is sought*) is found in the NT only with the meaning *point of controversy*.

3. a) **Ζητέω** is sometimes used in the NT for seeking in a nonreligious sense: Mary and Joseph *seek* the boy Jesus (Luke 2:45, 48f.), Jesus *is sought* by his family

(Mark 3:32 par.), the messengers of Cornelius *seek* Peter (Acts 10:19, 21; cf. also 13:11; 27:30). This nonreligious seeking can take hostile forms: Herod *seeks* the child Jesus in order to kill him (Matt 2:13; cf. 2:20). Hostile seeking is indicated clearly in the attempts of Jesus' opponents to catch him with a question and to kill him (Mark 11:18 par.; 12:12 par.; 14:1 par.). The same is true of the plan of Judas to find a suitable moment to betray Jesus (Mark 14:11 par.). Among the numerous Johannine sayings which belong here are esp. 7:19ff.; 8:40; 10:39, etc. The LXX has a nonreligious use of ζητέω in similar connections, e.g., Gen 37:16; Exod 2:15; 1 Kgdms 24:10; 25:29; 26:20; Isa 11:21; Ps 34:4.

b) In religious use the subj. can be God (or Christ) as well as a human person. In both cases the relationship of God and human is given, and the concern is with God's preservation and protection.

In John 4:23 God (the Father) seeks those who will pray to him in Spirit and in truth. Here ζητέω has the significance of *want, require*. The owners of the vineyard in Luke 13:6f. *expect* fruit from the fig tree. This seeking includes at the same time a demand or expectation. Luke 12:48 is similar: to whom much is given much *is required* (God is the logical subj. of the pass. construction). In 1 Cor 4:2 also God is the subj. of ζητεῖται.

A different use of ζητέω appears in John 7:18, where Jesus says that he *seeks* the honor of the one who has sent him (i.e., God). In 8:50 it is God himself who *seeks* his honor, i.e., the realization of his will in the Son. Here ζητέω is associated with κρίνω ("judge"), i.e., with the thought of the judgment on those who do not look after the possibility of salvation in Christ. Ζητέω in connection with God is thus frequently an expression for God's claim. However, the meaning of God's ζητεῖν is not yet exhausted in this aspect, as Luke 13:6ff. indicates. In the parable of the lost sheep (Matt 18:12ff.; cf. Luke 15:3ff.) God's loving search stands in the foreground. This is also true of the programmatic saying about the mission of the Son of Man to seek and save the lost (Luke 19:10). God's earnest seeking after the lost is indicated briefly but impressively in the parable of the lost coin (Luke 15:8ff.). The report of the call of Saul (Acts 9:11) stands within the same point of view.

By way of exception, the devil can also appear as the adversary of God (and of humans) and as the subj. of ζητέω. Thus Christians should be encouraged to exercise watchfulness, so that they are not overcome by him (1 Pet 5:8).

Humans can normally be the subj. of ζητέω in the religious sense. Their seeking can be mistaken and can consist in the demand for signs (Mark 8:11 par.), in striving to save one's own life (Luke 17:33), in seeking after Jesus as a one who gives material support (John 6:26), in the establishment of one's own righteousness (Rom 10:3), in the desire for (human) wisdom (1 Cor 1:22), in seeking after one's own advantage (Phil 2:21), or in striving after one's own honor (John 7:18a; 1 Thess 2:6). In contrast to this false direction, the correct ζητεῖν of humans is identified as seeking for salvation. The disciples are encouraged programmatically to *seek* first the kingdom of God and his righteousness, and then everything will be added to them (Matt 6:33; Luke 12:31). Intensive seeking, that which involves the whole person, is spoken of in the teaching of Jesus: The parable of the merchant and the pearl (Matt 13:45) elaborates on this total engagement, which is necessary to attain what one is striving for (the kingdom of heaven). The seriousness of this striving is underlined in the fact that many want to enter through the narrow gate of salvation when it is not possible for them (Luke 13:24). The Zacchaeus narrative (Luke 19:1ff.) is an example of correct seeking (cf. vv. 3ff.), and the saying of Jesus illuminates this seeking from the side of God (v. 10).

The Pauline corpus speaks of seeking after the things that belong to Christian existence. The addressees are exhorted, either directly or indirectly, to seek glory, honor, and immortality (Rom 2:7) and the benefit of the many, i.e., their salvation (1 Cor 10:33b), to pursue the edification of the community (1 Cor 14:12), and to seek what is above, where Christ is (Col 3:1; cf. 1 Pet 3:1).

Neither friends nor enemies can follow Christ where he is going (i.e., to the Father), and they will thus *seek* him in vain (John 8:21; 13:33). This is a situation which, for the disciples, is only temporary and will later change (16:20ff.). One notes that all reports of the resurrection in the Gospels use ζητέω (Matt 28:5; Mark 16:6; Luke 24:5; John 20:15). This seeking of the crucified one leads the seekers to the resurrected one.

4. **Ζήτημα** is used to designate a subject under dispute. A good example is Acts 15:2: Paul and his coworkers are sent to Jerusalem to get clarity over a point of dispute about which there is a difference of opinion (ζήτησις, v. 2a), i.e., the question of circumcision of Gentile Christians (cf. the other occurrences in 18:15; 23:29; 25:19; 26:3).   E. Larsson

ζήτημα, ατος, τό *zētēma* dispute, point of controversy
→ ζητέω.

ζήτησις, εως, ἡ *zētēsis* investigation, dispute, debate*

Lit.: → ζητέω.

1. Ζήτησις appears 7 times in the NT (John 3:25; Acts 15:2, 7; 25:20; 1 Tim 6:4; 2 Tim 2:23; Titus 3:9). The LXX does not use the word. The basic meaning is what one would expect from the relation to ζητέω: *investiga-*

tion, but this meaning is seldom what is intended in the NT. The word also means *discussion, dispute, debate,* which is what is most thought of in the NT: the discussion or debate resulting from a religious or cultural ζητεῖν.

2. In 1 Tim 6:4 ζήτησις is used in connection with false teachers, who are described as arrogant and without knowledge. This indicates that they have an unhealthy craving for *arguments* (ζητήσεις) and disputes about words (λογομαχίας). This leads in turn to unfortunate relationships within the congregation, e.g., to envy, dissension, slander, etc. In this section of 1 Timothy there is no doubt about the meaning of the word, as the parallelism with λογομαχία indicates.

In Acts 15:2 the word is used likewise with the meaning of *debate.* In 15:7 also and in John 3:25 ζήτησις takes on the meaning *dispute.* The meaning of ζήτησις in Acts 25:20 is more difficult to determine. In v. 19 Festus says that the accusation against Paul has been caused by "controversies" (ζητήματα) of the Jewish religion; when he refers to this in v. 20 as ἀπορούμενος . . . ζήτησιν, he may mean that he believes that he is not qualified to conduct an investigation in these questions.

In 2 Tim 2:23 Timothy is encouraged by the author to have nothing to do with stupid and senseless ζητήσεις. Here ζήτησις, viewed by itself, points to "unnecessary investigations," but the context indicates unambiguously that stupid and unnecessary *discussions* are meant. The same is true of the admonition in Titus 3:9: Here also the tr. "investigation" is possible, but the context speaks for the meaning *debate.*   E. Larsson

ζιζάνιον, ου, τό *zizanion* darnel; pl.: weeds

In the NT only pl., Matt 13:25, 26, 27, 29, 30, 36, 38, 40 (in the parable of the *weeds* among the wheat, 13:24-30 [cf. *Gos. Thom.* 57], and its interpretation, vv. 36-43). The word is probably of Semitic origin (Lewy, *Fremdwörter* 52) and refers most probably to darnel (*lolium temulentum;* Billerbeck I, 667; BAGD s.v. [bibliography]; Jeremias, *Parables* 224f.), which looks like wheat during the early stages of its growth. On the parable see Jeremias, *Parables* 81-85, 224f.; *idem,* FS Cullmann (1962) 59-63.

Ζοροβαβέλ *Zorobabel* Zerubbabel*

Personal name in Matt 1:12, 13; Luke 3:27, the son of Σαλαθιήλ (Shealtiel); according to Matt 1:13 father of Ἀβιούδ (Abiud), according to Luke 3:27, of Ῥησά (Rhesa). Zerubbabel was a descendant of David (1 Chr 3:19) and governor of Judea under Persian sovereignty (Hag 1:1, 14; 2:2). A. Petitjean, *ETL* 42 (1966) 40-71; G. Sauer, FS L. Rost (BZAW 105) 199-207; H. G. M. Williamson, *ISBE* IV, 1193f. (bibliography); *LTK* X, 1355f.; *BL* 1927 (bibliography).

ζόφος, ου, ὁ *zophos* darkness, gloom*

Heb 12:18, between γνόφος and θύελλα, "darkness, *gloom,* and a tempest," as phenomena of the theophany (cf. Deut 4:11 LXX, where σκότος appears in the triad instead of ζόφος). The noun is used in particular of the *gloom* of the underworld (cf. Homer *Od.* xx.356: ὑπὸ ζόφον) and the underworld itself (cf. Homer *Il.* xv.191; xxi.56; *Od.* xi.57): ὁ ζόφος τοῦ σκότους, "*the gloom* of the darkness/the darkest *hell* (2 Pet 2:17; Jude 13). The σειραὶ ζόφου (2 Pet 2:4) are the shackles of *hell.* The fallen angels, according to Jude 6, are "kept by eternal chains in *darkness* (ὑπὸ ζόφον: covered by darkness)."

ζυγός, οῦ, ὁ *zygos* yoke; pair of scales*

1. Occurrences — 2. As a metonym for lack of freedom — 3. Christological usage

Lit.: J. B. BAUER, "Das milde Joch und die Ruhe. Mt 11,28-30," *TZ* 17 (1961) 99-106. — G. BERTRAM and K. H. RENGSTORF, *TDNT* II, 896-901. — H. D. BETZ, "The Logion of the Easy Yoke and of Rest," *JBL* 86 (1967) 10-24. — BILLERBECK I, 608-10. — A. VAN DEN BORN, *BL* 850f., 1863. — F. CHRIST, *Jesus Sophia* (1970) 100-119. — H. FRANKEMÖLLE, *Jahwebund und Kirche Christi* (1974) 98f. — A. FRIDRICHSEN, "Eine unbeachtete Parallele zum Heilandsruf Mt 11,28ff.," FS Wikenhauser 83-85. — R. HENTSCHKE, *BHH* 869. — H.-G. LINK and C. BROWN, *DNTT* III, 1160-65. — D. LOTZE, "Aspekte der Sklaverei im Altertum," *ZdZ* 17 (1963) 330-38. — E. SCHWEIZER, *Mt und seine Gemeinde* (1974) 54-57. — R. SMEND, *BHH* 2121f. — G. STRECKER, *Der Weg der Gerechtigkeit* (1962) 172-75. — M. J. SUGGS, *Christology and Law in Matthew's Gospel* (1970) 62-97. — For further bibliography see *DNTT* III, 1165; *TWNT* X, 1098.

1. This noun is used 6 times in the NT and has the meaning *pair of scales* only in Rev 6:5 (metonymy for rising prices, v. 6), while in the remaining passages the meaning "yoke" appears, always in the fig. sense. In the LXX the *ca.* 75 references are distributed rather equally between the two meanings. The semantic reference of the Greek expression is based on the crossbeam of the scales or the pole used as a yoke for beasts of burden (cf. 3 Macc 4:9: beams between the planks of the ship).

2. The adj. prep. phrase ὑπὸ ζυγόν in the one-sided rule for slaves in 1 Tim 6:1 has the common sociological meaning *subject, dependent:* ζυγός belongs traditionally in the Greek semantic field of the → δουλεία (Sophocles *Aj.* 944; Plato *Ep.* 8.354d; 1 Macc 8:17f., 31). When Acts 15:10 rejects the idea of placing Mosaic laws as a yoke on the Gentile Christians, it is to be noted that Luke has in mind not a theological concept of the law, but rather a sociological concept ("Jewish customs"). On the other hand, in Gal 5:1 the yoke characteristic of slavery, in which a relapse is threatened, is described theologically by the antonym of the "free service" created by Christ (W. Schenk, *EPM* 4 [1975/76] 328-33, apud Lotze). The

yoke is confidence in one's own actions arising from lack of trust in God's pledge of unconditional love.

3. "My yoke" (Matt 11:29f.) as a positive metaphor for being taken into service by wisdom itself, which gives rest (Sir 51:26f.), appears in Jesus' "call of the Savior" (probably a new redactional form; a treatment of tradition only if *Gos. Thom.* 90 is independent of Matthew). There it specifies the Matthean content of the revelatory statement in vv. 25-27 (from Q). Direct synonyms and parallels are → μανθάνω and φορτίον ("duty") in the anti-Pharisaic sense of Matthew (23:4): ζυγός belongs to the terminology of the Matthean understanding of discipleship, in which one follows Jesus' interpretation of the law rather than that of the Pharisees. A suprenym of the Matthean word group is → θέλημα as the "will" of the Father.   W. Schenk

ζύμη, ης, ἡ *zymē* leaven (noun), yeast*
ἄζυμος, 2 *azymos* unleavened*
ζυμόω *zymoō* ferment, leaven (vb.)*

1. Occurrences in the NT and meaning — 2. Grouping of NT occurrences — 3. The Synoptics and Acts — 4. Paul

Lit.: G. BEER, *Pesachim* (1912). — J. JEREMIAS, *The Eucharistic Words of Jesus* (²1966) 55-62. — *idem*, *TDNT* V, 896-904, esp. 899f. — O. MICHEL, *RAC* I, 1056-62. — A. NEGOITA and C. DANIEL, "L'énigme du levain," *NovT* 9 (1967) 306-14. — H. WEDER, *Die Gleichnisse Jesu als Metaphern* (1978) 128-38. — H. WINDISCH, *TDNT* II, 902-6. — For further bibliography see *TWNT* X, 1098.

1. The word stem ζυμ- appears in the NT only in the Synoptics, Acts, and Paul. Ζύμη appears 13 times, ζυμόω 4 times, and ἄζυμος 9 times. These words are used of baking and as such are unambiguous; metaphorically they suggest power of penetration or negative influence.

2. In content and the tradition history, the occurrences can be divided into three groups: a) References to the Jewish Feast of Unleavened Bread, τὰ ἄζυμα ("festal pl.": Mark 14:1 par.; 14:12 par.; Acts 12:3; 20:6; 1 Cor 5:7f.). The feast (see esp. Exod 12f.) had been connected with the Passover for a long time (consequently the overlapping in naming and enumeration; see Mark 14:1, 12; Luke 22:1). On the meanings of the unleavened bread itself (Exodus bread, bread of misery, etc., eschatological meanings also) see Jeremias, *Eucharistic Words*. b) Figurative sayings and maxims, "(a little) leaven leavens the whole lump," among others (Matt 13:33 par.; 1 Cor 5:6; Gal 5:9; cf. Plutarch *Quaest. Rom.* 109; *Quaest. Conv.* iii.10.3; BAGD s.v.; H. Schlier, *Gal* [KEK] 170). c) The special formulation "leaven of the Pharisees . . .": Mark 8:15 par.; Matt 16:11f.

3. a) The Synoptics mention the Feast of Unleavened Bread in the dating of the Passion week. However, the

interest is on the Passover, not on the Unleavened Bread, and no interpretation of it is given. Acts refers twice to the "days of unleavened bread." The time reference in 12:3 is more noteworthy than in 20:6; the combination with the Passover (12:4) is reminiscent of the Passion of Jesus (H. Conzelmann, *Acts* [Hermeneia] ad loc.; cf. A. Strobel, *NTS* 4 [1957/58] 210-15).

b) The parable in Matt 13:33 par. emphasizes the penetrating power of leaven and the disproportion between the leaven and the extraordinary amount of meal. It is uncertain whether concealment is accented and a "shock effect" (leaven as a negative symbol) is intended (so Weder 133f. and R. W. Funk, *Interpretation* 25 [1975] 161f.; Windisch 905 understands the symbol in a positive way and refers to Matt 5:11). Jesus wants to set forth the certainty of the coming of the kingdom. Matthew emphasizes that God's kingdom penetrates the world (E. Schweizer, *Matt* [Eng tr.] ad loc.); in the Lukan context it is said that the kingdom of God cannot be hindered by Israel's resistance. *Gos. Thom.* 96 is totally different; here the Gnostic forms his existence (see Weder 137f.).

c) The original meaning of Mark 8:15 par. is uncertain (Negoita and Daniel assume a confusion of Aramaic words: speech instead of leaven). Is ζύμη neutral (in the sense of "influence") or negative (cf. Windisch 906)? Does "of Herod" refer to political ambitions (E. Lohmeyer, *Mark* [KEK] ad loc.; R. Pesch, *Mark* [HTKNT] ad loc.; according to E. Stauffer, FS O. Eissfeldt [1959], 172, the activity of spies is in mind)? Mark uses the saying as an unresolved riddle; in combination with 3:6; 12:13 he most likely means hostile, alarming intrigues (otherwise Pesch: demand for a sign; W. Grundmann, *Mark* [THKNT] ad loc.: hindrance to faith). Matthew (16:12) is unambiguous: teaching of the Pharisees and Sadducees (who fit here; cf. V. Taylor, *Mark* [1952] 365, about a possible connection to the opponents of Paul in Gal 2:4). Luke thinks similarly; he refers to the hubris typical of the Pharisees.

4. In 1 Cor 5:6; Gal 5:9 the saying is negatively determined by the context. Galatians refers more to false teaching than to false teachers (see F. Mussner, *Gal* [HTKNT] ad loc.): a small deviation from the truth (v. 7, specifically in the matter of circumcision, vv. 2, 11) has fatal consequences. Similarly, 1 Cor 5:6 refers to the toleration of ethical misconduct. Then in vv. 7f. a spiritualizing "statement for the feast of the ἄζυμα = πάσχα" (Windisch 905; on the tradition, cf. Jeremias, *Eucharistic Words;* whether in connection with 16:8 inferences can be drawn about the actual Jewish or even Christian festival is disputed; cf. A. Schlatter, *Paulus, der Bote Jesu* [⁴1969] ad loc.; H. Conzelmann, *1 Cor* [Hermeneia] ad loc.). The Church should be shaped entirely by the new quality, i.e., here sincerity and truth. On the basis of the death of Christ,

the Church is the pure festal community (the ind. comes first) and should correspondingly keep itself pure (the image changes: the Church "has" or "is leaven").

W. Popkes

ζυμόω *zymoō* ferment, leaven
→ ζύμη.

ζῶ *zō* live
ζωή, ῆς, ἡ *zōē* life

1. Occurrences in the NT — 2. General concepts — 3. Paul — a) Basic ideas — b) Life under the dominion of death — c) The liberated life — 4. John — a) The concepts connected with ζωή — b) The christological and soteriological content of "life" — 5. Luke-Acts

Lit.: BAGD s.v. ζωή. — G. BERTRAM, R. BULTMANN, and G. VON RAD, *TDNT* II, 832-75. — I. BROER, "Auferstehung und ewiges Leben im Johannesevangelium," *"Auf Hoffnung hin sind wir erlöst" (Röm 8,24)* (SBS 128, ed. I. Broer and J. Werbick; 1987) 67-94. — R. BULTMANN, *TDNT* III, 7-25. — G. DAUTZENBERG, *TRE* XX, 526-30. — P. HOFFMANN, *Die Toten in Christus* (NTAbh N.F. 2, 1969). — J. D. KILPATRICK, "Atticism and the Future of ζῆν," *NovT* 25 (1983) 146-51. — G. KLEIN, "Aspekte ewigen Lebens im NT," *ZTK* 82 (1985) 48-70. — J. A. L. LEE, "The Future of ζῆν in Late Greek," *NovT* 22 (1980) 289-98. — H.-G. LINK, *DNTT* II, 476-84. — C. F. D. MOULE, "The Meaning of 'Life' in the Gospel and Epistles of St. John," *Theology* 78 (1975) 114-25. — F. MUSSNER, *ZQH. Die Anschauung vom 'Leben' im vierten Evangelium unter Berücksichtigung der Johannesbriefe* (MTS 1.5, 1952). — G. RICHTER, "Die Deutung des Kreuzestodes Jesu in der Leidensgeschichte des Johannesevangelium," *idem, Studien zum Johannesevangelium* (1977) 58-73. — R. SCHNACKENBURG, "Life and Death according to John," *idem, John* II (Eng. tr., 1979) 352-61. — L. SCHOTTROFF, *Der Glaubende und die feindliche Welt* (WMANT 37, 1970) 115-296. — G. STRECKER, *1-3 John* (KEK) 66-70, 288f. — H. THYEN, "Aus der Literatur zum Johannesevangelium," *TRu* 43 (1978) 328-59. — U. WILCKENS, *Die Missionsreden der Apostelgeschichte* (1974) 137-78. — For further bibliography see BAGD s.v. ζωή; *DNTT* II, 483f.; *TWNT* X, 1094-96.

1. Ζῶ occurs 140 times, esp. in the Pauline corpus (particularly Romans, with 23 occurrences), John (17 occurrences), and Revelation (13 occurrences). It occurs rarely in the Synoptics (Matthew has 6, Mark 3, and Luke 9) and in the Johannine letters (1 occurrence in 1 John). Ζωή (a total of 135 occurrences) is similarly distributed. However, 1 John has 13 occurrences.

2. As in other ancient religions, "life" is used in early Christianity to characterize salvation. Common to the OT, Judaism, and Christianity is the term "living God" (cf. W. Stenger, *TTZ* 87 [1978] 61-69). In each context there is a specific nuance to this term, e.g., that he is the (one) living God in contrast to the dead idols, i.e., the other gods (e.g., 1 Thess 1:9). As in apocalyptic Judaism,

which awaited a resurrection, NT Christianity hopes for ζωὴ αἰώνιος, "eternal *life,*" after the resurrection of the dead, the life of the coming aeon (the pre-Markan usage in Mark 10:17, 30 is typical). This term is found in almost all NT writings.

Matthew makes use of this apocalyptic idea. He uses the noun ζωή, along with βασιλεία τῶν οὐρανῶν or χαρά, etc., as an expression for eschatological salvation, which in his Gospel is vividly and emphatically set over against eternal punishment. In Matthew this eschatology primarily serves ethics. The reward promised to right actions is (eternal) life.

Concepts such as the tree of life, the book of life, and the water of life are widely attested in ancient religions (a wealth of material from the history of religions is found in R. Bultmann, *John* [Eng. tr., 1971] on 4:10; 15:1; W. Bousset, *Rev* [KEK] on 2:10; 3:5). In the NT, John makes metaphorical use of these myths (→ 4), but they appear esp. in the apocalyptic mythology of Revelation. Here the salvation in the future world, which the seer sees, means that one is registered in the book of *life* (13:8; cf. 3:5; 17:8; 20:12, 15; 21:27), that one can drink of the water of *life* (22:17; cf. 21:6; 7:17; 22:1) and can eat of the tree of *life* (2:7; cf. 22:2, 14, 19), and that one will wear the crown of *life,* the crown of victory of the martyrs (2:10).

A characteristic statement of the kerygma of the NT, which appears in many areas of the NT (esp. Paul, Revelation, Luke, and to a certain extent John), is that Christ, as the resurrected or exalted one, is the living one who promises life.

3. a) "Life" and "death" are terms used by Paul to express central soteriological categories similar to ἐλευθερία, εἰρήνη, δικαιοσύνη or δουλεία, ἁμαρτία, etc. For the concept of "life," physical death plays only an incidental role. The sting of death is sin (1 Cor 15:56), not the fear of death. The spirit of δουλεία εἰς φόβον (Rom 8:15) does not afflict the unredeemed person with the fear of death (Bultmann 17; H. Schlier, *Rom* [HTKNT] ad loc.), but with the fear of God's judgment (K. Barth, *Rom* [1954] ad loc.; O. Michel, *Rom* [KEK] ad loc.; E. Käsemann, *Rom* [Eng. tr., 1980] ad loc.). The fact that human life is mortal and transitory (φθορά, Rom 8:21; θνητὸν σῶμα, 6:12; 8:11) means primarily that it is a life enslaved by sin, from which Christ has liberated (6:12-14) and will liberate (8:11, 21). The decisive fact for the end of the dominion of death is the resurrection of Christ (and the baptism of the believer), not physical death.

When Paul speaks nonmetaphorically of death as the end of physical life, he understands life and death together as the totality of physical existence. The end of life is a constituent part of life. The end result of life can be characterized either by salvation or condemnation. The

individual can live or die to the Lord (Rom 14:7f.; Phil 1:21; 2 Cor 5:9) or to sin (Rom 6:2). Death and life are also used in this nonmetaphorical sense in Rom 8:39: Paul wants to enumerate the totality of the entire creation, which is not able to make the love of God ineffective.

For Paul, however, metaphorical use of the words "life" and "death" stands in the foreground for soteriological matters. When he speaks of death, he normally means slavery to sin, which lies behind the believer, the living death, from which he has been liberated (e.g., Rom 8:2, 6, 13). The boundary between metaphorical and nonmetaphorical use is not to be drawn strictly. In Rom 5:12, e.g., both are addressed at the same time (→ b).

b) For Paul no one can serve two masters: one either serves and lives to death and sin or lives to the Lord (Rom 6:16; 14:8) in a liberated existence. The life under the dominion of death has its origin in the power of ἁμαρτία. Mythologically expressed, death has its cause in Adam's fall (5:12-14; cf. 1 Cor 15:20-22) or in the confrontation with the law of God (Rom 7:9). Paul does not think here of the logic of a myth that narrates the story of humanity, but rather of the logic of the relationship of dominion. Death is a king whose power is derived from ἁμαρτία (5:12-14, 17). It is the instrument of dominion for ἁμαρτία (5:21), its "wages," with which it pays its slaves (6:22f.). The fact that all must die has its cause in sin (5:12). This far-reaching death is only superficially the transitoriness of everything living, for actually collective death is more: the enslavement of the whole creation, which is sold under sin (see only 8:19-22; 7:14). Since Adam the creation moans: "Who will redeem me from the body of death?" (7:24).

The terror of death is, however, not the necessity of dying, but rather the inability to realize life. This inability, of which Paul speaks with horror, comes as the inability to fulfill the will of God, the Torah, fully (Rom 8:7f.). The Torah is meant to give life (7:10, 12), but the individual is a helpless slave of sin, its puppet, who does lawlessness and unrighteousness (see, e.g., 6:12-14, 19; 8:7). Life under sin and death is a pursuit of life, which always produces only death (7:16, 22). In the presence of the liberation through Christ the dominion of sin becomes apparent. It becomes apparent to the believer what lies behind him, that this is his past which has confronted him.

With this radical interpretation of sin's power for death Paul stands alone, both within the NT and within comparable religious traditions in antiquity. In particular, the comparison with Gnostic texts is appropriate. There the power of death does not reach the essential "I" of the individual (see Schottroff 115-69). Because Paul sees the power of sin over the *entire* person as so radically effective, the concept of an immortal soul is not only un-Pauline, but even anti-Pauline.

c) Paul, who thinks of the power of sin in such radical terms, also understands life, the salvation that Christ makes possible, in a total and comprehensive sense: The *total* person, the person as σῶμα, is liberated (see only Rom 6:12-14), and *all* people are the objects of the divine saving activity (see 5:18). Life is unlimited existence, ζωή αἰώνιος (6:22f., etc.), ἀνάστασις νεκρῶν (1 Cor 15:21, etc.). Paul thinks apocalyptically. The resurrection of the dead has its beginning, its cause, its irrefutable realization in the resurrection of Christ (Christ is πρωτότοκος ἐν πολλοῖς ἀδελφοῖς, Rom 8:29; cf. ἀπαρχή, 1 Cor 15:20, 23). Present and (apocalyptically conceived) future in Paul cannot be separated temporally or materially. We are ὡσεὶ ἐκ νεκρῶν ζῶντες (Rom 6:13), we have died to sin through baptism (6:2, 11), and live in the hope of the resurrection of the dead (on hope, see esp. 8:24f.). We live and will live (present ζωή: 6:4, 11; 8:2, 6, 10; future ζωή: 1:17; 2:7; 5:17f., 21; 8:11, 13), we are liberated and will be liberated (6:18, 22; 8:21). Expressed pointedly: Paul could formulate 8:11 also in the present.

Even in regard to the future hope Paul does not think of a describable eschatological myth or of a colorful image of the new life; he thinks rather of power relationships: Christ is the κύριος, and the redeemed person is his δοῦλος. Paul has incidentally a certain difficulty in describing the new life also as slavery—now under the dominion of Christ (Rom 6:19; 8:15), because he associates δουλεία with the social reality in which the slave is not the son (8:15) and does not belong to those who have been freed (6:19). The slaves of Christ are free and have the Spirit of sonship. Paul has a theological reason for describing the liberated existence as δουλεία (although, as one can see, he employs the language of δουλεία very consciously in the context of the reality of his society): The universal power of ἁμαρτία stands in opposition to the universal power of Christ. Moreover, Paul employs the language of slavery under Christ where individual believers want to understand their freedom as dominion over other people (14:4).

In concrete terms, the freedom of the slaves of Christ is to be seen under three aspects: the fulfillment of the will of God (the Torah), the life in hope, and the victory over the actual tribulations (persecutions) as members of the Church of Christ. Anyone who lives in Christ can fulfill the law. The νόμος τοῦ πνεύματος τῆς ζωῆς (Rom 8:2) liberates from the νόμος of sin and death (Paul uses νόμος here as an expanded term for attachment to a sphere of power as in 7:1-6, 21-23) and enables one to fulfill the νόμος τοῦ θεοῦ. This means that life in the Spirit (Gal 5:25) or (περιπατεῖν) ἐν καινότητι ζωῆς (Rom 6:4) or—as Käsemann says—"worship [in] everyday life" ("Worship and Everyday Life," *NT Questions of Today* [1969] 188-95) in its daily humility is the beginning of the future, of the resurrection of the dead. The very concrete efforts of Paul toward the shaping of one's existence in this sense are to be seen in the entire Pauline corpus and are to be seen as steps toward the realization of the new life. Because we live to the Lord, we are not in a position to judge or despise our brother (14:3, 4).

Both the individual fate of Paul and frequently the life of the Pauline churches are influenced by θλῖψις: from hostility from the populace (see only 1 Thess 2:14), from the threat of death (see, e.g., μάχαιρα, Rom 8:35) and poverty (on this sense of θλῖψις, see 2 Cor 8:13) and the various lists of sufferings, e.g., Rom 8:35). When Paul speaks of θλῖψις, he means esp. these concrete experiences of suffering and less frequently suffering in a general sense (*contra* Bultmann, *Theology* I, 349-51). The believer stands under the dominion of Christ in the (almost spatially understood) love of God, from which nothing can separate him (8:35, 39).

The new life is thus presently experienced in the practice of community life, which is required in Romans 14 and 15, in the power to resist in the presence of sufferings, and in the hope that sees in this daily worship the beginning of the resurrection of the dead for the entire creation.

4. a) John speaks of "life" in the following connections:

Death and Life. Anyone who receives the revelatory word of Jesus "has passed from death into life" (5:24). That person will not see or taste death forever (8:51f.; cf. 11:26). The concept is taken from the event of physical death. The believer lives beyond physical death. Of course the transcending of death does not mean immortality. Thus the life beyond death could only be misunderstood (8:52). John uses the words "death" and "life" here in a double sense: only in a subordinate way is physical death intended. One who hears the word of the revealer transcends the more comprehensive death of separation from God. The two miracles of life in John (4:46-53; 11:1-44) reveal Jesus as a remarkable miracle worker who can heal the sick child of the βασιλικός from a distance and bring about the resurrection of Lazarus, who had been dead for three days. The narratives are concentrated totally on the portrayal of Jesus as a giver of life (also 4:46-53; although the sick child is not dead, it is made alive). Jesus can restore physical life, but that is not the real miracle. The real miracle is that he gives true life to anyone who believes. In contrast to this life, the physical life that is restored in both miracles is of only secondary importance (see 11:25f.). John uses physical death and its conquest as a means for elucidating what true life is. Human mortality is not the plight from which faith proceeds, and immortality is not the true life spoken of in John.

Light and Life: Jesus the giver of life gives the light of life (8:12), is the light of the world (8:12), gives light and life (1:4) to the creation. The image of the morning of creation is evoked. The darkness of chaos is ended by Christ, the giver of life. The creation makes clear what it means that Jesus is the light and the life. Light and life are interchangeable terms, as in Gnosticism (history-of-religions material is found esp. in R. Bultmann, *John* [Eng. tr., 1971]; R. Schnackenburg, *John* [Eng. tr.], both on 1:4).

Eternal Life and Condemnation. The life that Jesus gives is eternal life. Whoever has eternal life will not be lost in eternity (3:15f.; 10:28; 3:36; 5:24; 6:40, 47) and will not come into judgment. Ἀπολλύομαι here designates, as elsewhere in the NT (see only 1 Cor 1:18), eternal destruction. Here apocalyptic concepts are taken up and given a new interpretation in a characteristic Johannine way. The eschatological judgment takes place now for the person who does not believe in Jesus as the revealer of God (see only 3:18). The forceful future-eschatological sayings such as 5:27b-29 must be understood as subsequent additions. The reinterpretation of apocalyptic expectations is esp. massive (perhaps even polemical) where the *resurrection of the dead* is interpreted as the present time of faith (see esp. 11:24-26; 5:21, 25). Where Jesus belongs and is believed in, the resurrection of the dead already takes place. The νεκροί —i.e., for John, those who do not have the true life— hear the voice of the Son of God, and when they really hear (i.e., accept his word), they will live (5:25). The apocalyptic image is clear, but in John it is an *image* for something else.

Living Water and Bread of Life: Jesus is the bread of life (6:35, 48) and gives the bread of life (6:51) and the water of life (4:10; 7:38; see F. Hahn, FS Dahl 51-70). John here alludes to mythological concepts (see the above-mentioned collection of materials—however, not with the intent to contrast the Jesus revelation critically with these myths. He uses the mythological material as an image or as a metaphor. For him the contrast to bread that one can eat and the actual water in the well (see 4:10-15; 6:26f.) is important: They are always confused by humans with the true bread and water.

Sacramental Means of Life. In a post-Johannine unit (or better, the "eucharistic reinterpretation"; see Thyen 337), the bread of life speech of 6:51b-58, the bread of life is understood totally differently than in the preceding section. It is the σάρξ and the blood of Jesus which will give fellowship with Jesus (v. 56), i.e., life (v. 53, ζωὴ ἐν ἑαυτοῖς), eternal life, and resurrection at the last day (vv. 54, 58) to the one who eats (τρώγω is meant drastically: "crunch") and drinks. Life is thus mediated here in an exclusively sacramental way.

b) Jesus himself *is* the life (11:25; 14:6) in the sense that he *gives* the life. Thus John can without any problem bring together the bread, which Jesus is, and that which he gives

(→ a). Jesus gives life as he reveals himself. He says who he is and what he has heard from the Father. John uses—as indicated—a multitude of conceptual materials in order to express this concept of life. The fact that Jesus is and gives life is dependent not primarily (as for Paul) on his resurrection or exaltation, but rather on his origin from above, from God (see only 3:11-17). Because of the promise of a reunion with Jesus in the context, the formulation ἐγὼ ζῶ καὶ ὑμεῖς ζήσετε in 14:19 can refer to the Easter experience. However, it is the peculiarity of John that the christological statement ἐγὼ ζῶ . . . does not depend specifically on Easter. It is true ἐν ἀρχῇ (1:1). The life that Jesus gives draws its vividness only from images and concepts used metaphorically (→ a) and from the so-called misunderstandings, which are intended to clarify what the true life is. It is not immortality or the final future resurrection of the dead (→ a). The raising of Lazarus is only a resource for understanding the true life. The true life, which Jesus gives, is a definitive "eternal" life, and the the believer will "never" see death (8:51f.). It is present life (ἔχειν, e.g., 3:15f., 36), but it anticipates an unlimited future (4:14; 6:27; 12:25). If one seeks the concrete realization of this life, one must think of the role of brotherly love in John and of the concrete experiences of the Johannine church, which are most ascertainable in the story of the Passion of Jesus. Conduct in the true life is not described in greater detail.

5. Luke speaks of life in a strongly theological sense esp. in two connections, that of the resurrection and that of correct conduct.

Jesus has been raised from the dead by God (on the interest of Luke in the resurrection of Christ as a deed of God, see esp. Wilckens 137-50). This resurrection means for Luke that the σάρξ of Jesus is not decayed (Acts 2:27, 31; 13:35; cf. Ps 16:10). The disciples could grasp him (Luke 24:36-43). The life of the resurrected one means, most importantly, that he again has a physical life, like that of Tabitha or Eutychus after they were miraculously raised from the dead (Acts 9:41; 20:12). His resurrection also has an eschatological meaning. It shows that Jesus will judge the living and the dead, the entire οἰκουμένη (10:42; 17:30f.). He is the first who has risen from the dead (26:23). He is the ἀρχηγὸς τῆς ζωῆς (3:15; cf. 5:31), i.e., the first resurrected one, not the originator of life (H. Conzelmann, *The Theology of St. Luke* [1960] 206). The just and the unjust will rise (24:15), and the just then await eternal life (see Luke 18:30 [from Mark]). For Luke Paul is esp. eloquent on this matter in connection with his trial (Acts 23:6; 24:16; 26:6, 7; cf. 18:10). With respect to the resurrection of Jesus and the expectation of the resurrection of the dead, it is esp. important for Luke that people orient themselves in their practical conduct toward this future life. One can, like the Jews who killed Jesus, judge oneself and prove oneself unworthy of eternal life (13:46). The way to life is μετάνοια, forgiveness of sins (11:18; 13:38 after 13:32-37) and the fulfillment of the Torah (see esp. Luke 10:25-31; 16:27-31). One who turns to life *and* lives according to the Torah, will attain to eternal life. Luke sees two major emphases: mercy and the proper relationship with life-threatening possessions (see Luke 12:15 and the story of the rich ἄρχων in 18:18-30).

Luke 15:11-32 uses "death" and "life" in a metaphorical sense (vv. 24, 32), which, however, is included in the former. μετάνοια and the forgiveness of sins are the step from death to life. For Luke the message of Christ is thus the message of life (Acts 5:20). For him nothing is so grotesque as to exchange the ἀρχηγὸς τῆς ζωῆς for a murderer (3:15) or to seek the living among the dead (Luke 24:5). One can see the ethical stress in Luke at key formulations such as Luke 10:28 and Acts 11:18. "Do this and you will live!" (in reference to the Torah), God has given μετάνοια εἰς ζωήν. It is not sin and death, as in Paul, that has humankind in its grip, but rather concrete foes of life. Luke mentions wealth and covetousness esp. frequently (Luke 12:15 is a representative statement; see L. Schottroff and W. Stegemann, *Jesus von Nazareth, Hoffnung der Armen* [1978] 89ff.). L. Schottroff

ζωγρέω *zōgreō* capture (alive)*

In the NT only fig. Luke 5:10 in the word of Jesus to Simon Peter (Mark 1:17 differs): "From now on you will *catch* (ἔσῃ ζωγρῶν) people" (fig. use of ζωγρέω in connection with the catch of fish also in Aristaenetus *Ep.* 2.23). 2 Tim 2:25 admonishes the addressees to reject the rebellious and again to bring them to repentance "from the snare of the devil, after being *snared* by him (ἐζωγρημένοι ὑπ' αὐτοῦ) for his will [= fulfillment of his will]." Spicq, *Notes* I, 343-45.

ζωή, ῆς, ἡ *zōē* life
→ ζῶ.

ζώνη, ης, ἡ *zōnē* belt, girdle*

In the NT the noun is used of the leather *belt* of John the Baptist (Mark 1:6 par. Matt 3:4; cf. 4 Kgdms 1:8 = Josephus *Ant.* ix.22), of Paul's *belt* (Acts 21:11a, b), which Agabus uses for a prophetic sign, and of the golden *belt* of the Son of Man (Rev 1:13) and the golden *belts* of the angels (15:6). One's *belt* serves also for the safekeeping of money (Mark 6:8 par. Matt 10:9). A. Oepke, *TDNT* V, 302-8; F. Selter, *DNTT* III, 120-21.

ζώννυμι, ζωννύω *zōnnymi, zōnnyō* gird*

John 21:18a, b: "*you girded* yourself . . . another *will gird* you" (fig. prophecy of death, perhaps with a double

meaning of ζώννυμι ["shackle"]; R. Schnackenburg, *John* III [Eng. tr., 1982] 366f.); Acts 12:8 mid. (cf. Josephus *B.J.* ii.129), *gird oneself,* in the word of the angel to Peter in prison: "*Gird yourself* and fasten your sandals." A. Oepke, *TDNT* V, 302-8; F. Selter, *DNTT* III, 120-21.

ζῳογονέω *zōogoneō* make alive, preserve alive*

Lit.: E. SCHWEIZER, *TDNT* IX, 635-58, esp. 637f. — SPICQ, *Notes* I, 346f. — For further bibliography → ζῶ.

Ζῳογονέω can mean: *make alive* (as in 1 Tim 6:13) or *preserve alive* (Acts 7:19). Because of the eschatological context and esp. because of 21:19, Luke 17:33 is to be translated with the act.: On the day of the Son of Man the same courage in the face of death is demanded as in the situation of persecution (9:24). One who does not look back, as did Lot's wife (see 17:32), and wants to save his life *will attain* life *(be made alive)*.
L. Schottroff

ζῷον, ου, τό *zōon* living being, animal*

1. Occurrences in the NT and general usage — 2. Hebrews, 2 Peter, and Jude — 3. Revelation

Lit.: R. BULTMANN, *TDNT* II, 832-43, 873. — For further bibliography see *TWNT* X, 1094-96.

1. Ζῷον, with 23 occurrences in the NT, of which 20 are in Revelation, belongs to the same word stem as ζωή and characterizes every being that has a spirit (cf. Bultmann 833f. [texts]): *living creature.* The word can be used of humans as well as animals, but is most often used of animals, which can be characterized more precisely with ἄλογον (e.g., Plato *Prt.* 321b). It is also used of heavenly creatures (cf. Bultmann 833, 873).

2. In Heb 13:11 sacrificial animals burned outside the camp are called ζῷα. 2 Pet 2:12 and Jude 10 refer to ζῷα ἄλογα; in these texts, between which there is probably a literary dependence, the false teachers are compared to "unreasonable *beasts.*"

3. In Revelation ζῷον refers exclusively to the four heavenly *creatures* who surround the heavenly throne in the vision of the seer (4:6): They resemble a lion, an ox, a creature with a human face, and an eagle (v. 7: 4 occurrences); they have wings and are full of eyes around and within (v. 8); they praise God (vv. 8f.; 5:8, 14; 19:4); the individual creatures can exercise functions of service, such as opening the first four seals (6:1, 3, 5, 7) and giving the seven bowls (15:7). Further references to the four creatures are in 5:6, 11; 6:6; 7:11; 14:3.

The author of Revelation has derived the concept of the four heavenly creatures from a tradition that is to be seen, e.g., in Ezekiel 1. In general it is assumed that this tradition is influenced by ancient Babylonian astrology (cf. the commentaries on Rev 4:6ff.), in which the creature with the human face is intended to designate a scorpion. The four creatures originally represent the entire circle of the signs of the zodiac and also the four elements of the world (thus the eagle appears in the place of aquarius). In Revelation the origin of the creatures has been obscured; they are the highest class of angels, whose chief function consists in the praise and service of God. The comparison of these four creatures with the four Evangelists has been known since Irenaeus *Haer.* iii.11.8.   G. Petzke

ζῳοποιέω *zōopoieō*   make alive, give life to*

Lit.: → ζῶ.

Ζῳοποιέω is used in the NT in an exclusively soteriological sense (on the concept of life → ζῶ 1). The subj. of ζῳοποιεῖν is God (John 5:21; Rom 4:17; 8:11) or Christ (John 5:21; 6:63; 1 Cor 15:22, 45). Ζῳοποιέω is understood primarily as the raising of the dead (parallel to ἐγείρω, John 5:21; see also, however, Rom 4:17; 8:11; 1 Cor 15:22, 45; see also 1 Pet 3:18).

But the word also retains an association with the creation: In Rom 4:17 the justification of the godless is seen as the resurrection of the dead and as *creatio ex nihilo.* The universal dimension of hope in Paul is made clear in this statement. A new creation has begun. 1 Cor 15:35-45 is comparable: Between the sowing and the plant lies death. The life of the plant is new life (v. 36). The first Adam was ψυχὴ ζῶσα, i.e., representative of a creation that serves ἁμαρτία. The last Adam begins a new creation: Christ makes alive (πνεῦμα ζῳοποιοῦν, 15:45). Ζῳοποιέω refers to the present and future of the life made possible by Christ.

For Paul the νόμος cannot *make alive* (Gal 3:21), for this can be done only by the promise (cf. 2 Cor 3:6). The law is, indeed, given εἰς ζωήν (Rom 7:10), but the liberation through Christ is required to bring the life-intention of the law to realization.

The interpretation of John 6:63 is dependent on the entire understanding of John and esp. on 1:14. Is the σάρξ of Jesus a paradoxical, scandalous revelation (so R. Bultmann, *John* [Eng. tr., 1971] ad loc.) or "the place of the breakthrough" (Käsemann, *Versuche* II, 34)? The *life-giving* Spirit is Jesus, the Revealer who is speaking.

L. Schottroff

H η

ἤ *ē* or; or also; than (participle)

1. Disjunctive — a) Exclusive — b) Nonexclusive — c) In questions — 2. Comparative — a) After a comparative form — b) Without a preceding comparative form

Lit.: BAGD s.v. — BDF §§185, 245f., 298, 446, 448. — LSJ s.v. — MAYSER, *Grammatik* II/2, 140, 142, 516; II/3, 53, 138-40. — MOULTON, *Grammar* III, 216, 334. SCHWYZER, *Grammatik* II, 564f.

1. The particle ἤ is attested from the time of Homer in literary and nonliterary texts. In the NT there are 344 occurrences.

a) Ἤ, *or,* and ἤ-ἤ / ἤτοι-ἤ, *either-or,* coordinate two or more mutually exclusive terms or statements (Lat. *aut*). E.g., Mark 11:30 par. Matt 21:25/Luke 20:4: "from heaven *or* from people?"; John 9:2: "this one *or* his parents?"; Rev 3:15: "cold *or* hot." Ἤ-ἤ in the NT appears only in Q passages (Matt 6:24 par. Luke 16:13; Matt 12:33); ἤτοι-ἤ only in Rom 6:16.

b) More frequently disjunctive ἤ is used nonexclusively to link terms that are related or complementary: *or* in the sense of *or also* (Lat. *vel*). Consequently the alternation of καί and ἤ in a few mss. (cf. Matt 20:23; Mark 3:33; Luke 12:29; Acts 2:45; 10:14; 17:21, 27; 1 Cor 5:10; Eph 5:4; Col 2:16; 1 Tim 2:9; also Luke 11:11). E.g., Matt 5:18: "an iota *or* a dot"; 6:25, 31: "What we should eat *or* drink *or* put on?"; 7:16; 10:11, 14, 19, 37; 12:25; Luke 12:29 (all from Q); Mark 4:17 par. Matt 13:21: "tribulation *or* persecution"; John 7:48; Acts 1:7; Rom 1:21; 4:13; Jas 4:13; 1 Pet 1:18; Rev 14:9. The combination ἤ-καί, *or also/or even,* appears in Matt 7:10; Luke 11:11f.; 12:41; 18:11; Rom 2:15; 4:9; 14:10; 1 Cor 5:10 v.l.; 9:8; 16:6; 2 Cor 1:13b. Three or more terms can be placed in sequence by ἤ (Acts 20:33; 1 Cor 5:10 v.l.; 1 Tim 2:9 v.l. [3 occurrences]; Luke 18:29; 1 Cor 14:6; Col 2:16; Rev 13:16f. [4 occurrences]; 1 Cor 5:11 [5 occurrences]; Rom 8:35 [6 occurrences]; Matt 19:29 [depending on the reading, as many as 8 occurrences]).

Ἤ is frequently used with indefinite numbers (John 2:6; 6:19; Acts 25:6; 1 Cor 14:27; 1 Tim 5:19; Heb 10:28).

Where a disjunctive statement (or rhetorical question) is stated negatively, ἤ can be translated *(neither-)nor* (e.g., Mark 4:21; 7:12; Matt 5:18; 7:16; 10:19; John 8:14; Acts 1:7; Rom 1:21; 1 Cor 1:13; Gal 3:15; Phil 3:12; Rev 13:17).

c) Ἤ is used frequently to introduce rhetorical questions to which a negative answer is expected (Matt 7:9: "*Or* is there one among you . . . ?"; 12:5: "*Or* have you not read . . . ?"; cf. 20:15; 26:53; Luke 13:4; Rom 3:29; 6:5; 7:1; 9:21; 11:2; 1 Cor 6:9, 16, 19; 9:8; 10:22; 2 Cor 11:7; 13:5; Jas 4:5; a double question in 1 Cor 14:36). Questions associated with a preceding question are connected by ἤ, often in combination with interrogative τίς, τί, or πῶς (Matt 7:4; 16:26; Mark 4:30; 8:37; 11:28; Luke 12:11; 14:31; 20:2; John 4:27; 9:21; Rom 3:1; 10:7; 11:34f.; 1 Cor 7:16; 9:6f.; 2 Cor 6:14f.). In double questions the second part is normally introduced with ἤ, while the first stands without a particle (Matt 9:5 par. Mark 2:9/Luke 5:23; 1 Cor 4:21; Gal 1:10; only in John 7:17 do we have πότερον . . . ἤ).

2. a) Ἤ is also used as a particle of comparison after comparatives (e.g., Matt 10:15 par. Luke 10:12; Matt 11:22, 24 par. Luke 16:17 [from Q], Matt 19:24 par. Mark 10:25/Luke 18:25: "easier . . . *than*"; Rom 13:11; 1 Cor 7:9; 14:5; 1 Pet 3:17; 2 Pet 2:21; 1 John 4:4). Esp. frequent is the construction μᾶλλον ἤ, "more, rather *than*" (Matt 18:13; John 3:19; 12:43 [μᾶλλον ἤπερ]; Acts 4:19; 5:29; 20:35; 27:11; Gal 4:27; 1 Tim 1:4; 2 Tim 3:4; Heb 11:25). Also seen are comparative forms of πολύς with ἤ (Matt 26:53 v.l.; Luke 9:13; John 4:1; Acts 24:11 v.l.) and comparative ἤ after πρίν, "before" (Matt 1:18; Mark 14:30; Luke 2:26; 22:34 v.l.; Acts 2:20 v.l.; 7:2; 25:16).

b) The positive with a comparative meaning can stand in place of the comparative, e.g., καλόν ἐστιν . . . ἤ, "it is better . . . *than*" (Matt 18:8f. par. Mark 9:43, 47; 1 Cor 9:15); ἔξεστιν . . . ἤ, "it is lawful . . . rather *than*" (Mark 3:4 par. Luke 6:9); χαρὰ ἔσται . . . ἤ, "there will be more joy . . . *than*" (Luke 15:7); λυσιτελεῖ . . . ἤ, "it would be better for him . . . *than*" (Luke 17:2); θέλω . . . ἤ, "I would rather . . . *than*" (1 Cor 14:19).

In John 13:10 v.l. and Acts 24:21 ἤ has the meaning of εἰ μή, *except/then it would be;* likewise ἀλλ' . . . ἤ, *"unless, except for,"* in Luke 12:51; 1 Cor 3:5 v.l.; 2 Cor 1:13 (cf. BDF §448.8).   R. Peppermüller

ἤ   *ē*   truly

Heb 6:14 TR reads ἦ μήν, "truly." This adv. usage is attested from the time of Homer (e.g., Josephus *Ant.* xv.368; xvii.72). Εἰ μήν is to be read in Heb 6:14 (with 𝔭⁴⁶ ℵ A B C D). BAGD s.v.; H. Conzelmann, *1 Cor* (Hermeneia) ad loc., considers whether ἦ is to be read in 1 Cor 9:10, 15.

ἡγεμονεύω   *hēgemoneuō*   be ruler/commander
→ ἡγεμών.

ἡγεμονία, ας, ἡ   *hēgemonia*   supreme command, government
→ ἡγεμών 5.

ἡγεμών, όνος, ὁ   *hēgemōn*   prince, governor*
ἡγεμονεύω   *hēgemoneuō*   be ruler/commander*
ἡγεμονία, ας, ἡ   *hēgemonia*   supreme command, government*

1. Matt 2:6 — 2. The Roman governor of Judea as ἡγεμών — 3. Other "rulers" — 4. The vb. in Luke 2:2 (Quirinius) — 5. Ἡγεμονία (of Tiberius)

Lit.: BAGD s.v. — H. DIECKMANN, "Das fünfzehnte Jahr des Caesar Tiberius," *Bib* 6 (1925) 63-67. — I. H. EYBERS, "The Roman Administration of Judea Between A.D. 6 and 41," *Theologia Evangelica* 3 (1970) 131-46. — LEIPOLDT/GRUNDMANN I (1975), 155-67. — *KP* IV 1049, 1151, 1199-1201. — H.-G. PFLAUM, PW XXIII/1 (1957) 1240-79. — REICKE, *NT Era* 134-37, 227-52. — SCHÜRER, *History* I, 357-470. — M. STERN, "The Province of Judea," *The Jewish People in the First Century* (ed. S. Safrai and M. Stern; Compendia I/1, 1974) 308-76. — G. ÜRÖGDI, PW Suppl. X (1965) 667-70. — A. WIKENHAUSER, *LTK* VIII, 789f.
On the governorship of Pilate and its emphasis in the Matthean Passion story: J. BLINZLER, *Der Prozeß Jesu* (1969) 266. — N. A. DAHL, "Die Passionsgeschichte bei Mt," *NTS* 2 (1955/56) 17-32. — J. F. QUINN, "The Pilate Sequence in the Gospel of Matthew," *The Dunwoodie Review* 10 (1970) 154-77. — P. WINTER, *On the Trial of Jesus* (1961), esp. 51-61.
On the citation in Matt 2:6: J.-M. VAN CANGH, "La Bible de Matthieu: Les citations d'accomplissement," *RTL* 6 (1972) 205-11. — E. LOHMEYER and W. SCHMAUCH, *Matt* (KEK, 1967) 23. — E. NELLESSEN, *Das Kind und seine Mutter* (SBS 39, 1969) 35-49. — W. ROTHFUCHS, *Die Erfüllungszitate des Matthäusevangeliums* (1969) 60f., 126f. — K. STENDAHL, *The School of St. Matthew and its Use of the OT* (ASNU 20, ²1968) 99-101.
On the Governorship of Quirinius: R. E. BROWN, *The Birth of the Messiah* (1977) 547-56 (bibliography). — J. ERNST, *Luke* (RNT, 1977) 101-4. — H. W. HOEHNER, "Chronological Aspects

of the Life of Christ," *BSac* 130 (1973) 338-51. — H. U. INSTINSKY, *Das Jahr der Geburt Christi* (1957). — W. LODDER, *Die Schätzung des Quirinius bei Flavius Josephus* (1930). — H. R. MOEHRING, "The Census in Luke as an Apologetic Device," FS Wikgren 144-60. — G. SCHNEIDER, *Luke* (ÖTK, 1977) 64-69. — SCHÜRER, *History* I, 399-427 (bibliography). — A. VÖGTLE, *Was Weihnachten bedeutet* (²1977) 41-56.

1. The general meaning of ἡγεμών, *prince, ruler,* is present in the redactionally adapted citation of Matt 2:6. As the birthplace of the Messiah, Bethlehem is addressed as "by no means least among the *rulers* of Judah." In the Hebrew text of Mic 5:1 the reference is to the "regions of Judah" (*beʾalpê yehûdâ*). In contrast to this local meaning, the LXX has the collective "among the thousands of Judah" (ἐν χιλιάσιν Ἰούδα). Matthew's citation agrees with neither. As with many changes within this citation, what we have is apparently a "messianic reinterpretation" (Nellessen 42), which Matthew has taken up.

2. The office of the Roman governor of Judea is referred to with ἡγεμών in Matt 27:2, 11a, b, 14, 15, 21, 27; 28:14; Luke 20:20 (Pilate); Acts 23:24, 26, 33; 24:1, 10 (Felix); 26:30 (Festus). The exercise of this office is referred to with ἡγεμονεύω in Luke 3:1. The prevailing and official title of the governor of the Roman province was in fact ἐπίτροπος and at times ἔπαρχος. But ἡγεμών appears as a designation of the governor of Judea also in Josephus *Ant.* xviii.55. The occurrences of ἡγεμών as a designation of the governor of Judea are limited to the redactional stratum of the Matthean Passion and resurrection texts (Matt 27–28), the Lukan account of the question about paying taxes to Caesar (Luke 20), the "synchronism" of the appearance of the Baptist (the vb. in Luke 3:1), and the Lukan information about the governorships of Felix and Festus, under whom Paul was taken prisoner and placed on trial (Acts 23–24, 26). The title in the passages named designates an office with appropriate political power, judicial function, and power of military force.

3. Originally in the persecution passage of Mark 13:9 "the Roman procurators of Judea" were intended (R. Pesch, *Mark* [HTKNT] II, 284); but Mark goes beyond this and thinks of *rulers* in various regions, as do the Synoptic parallels in Matt 10:18; Luke 21:12. In addition the obedience parenesis of 1 Pet 2:14 has in view Caesar's *governors* as authorities in the various provinces.

4. The vb. in Luke 2:2 is used of the administrative office of the Roman legate of Syria, → Κυρήνιος (Quirinius). Because a period of office for Quirinius cannot be established in the time period presupposed by Luke, some have attempted to understand ἡγεμονεύω in a more general way, perhaps as the chief authority for the

Orient (Ernst 103). However, apart from the absence of unambiguous references, Josephus *Ant.* xv.345 argues for understanding the vb. as a reference to the actual exercise of office by the legate (H. Schürmann, *Luke* [HTKNT] 99-101; Vögtle 49f.).

5. Ἡγεμονία appears in the NT only in Luke 3:1, where it designates the *period of the rule* of the emperor Tiberius (14 B.C.–A.D. 37). This information serves the intention of the Evangelist in emphasizing the worldwide significance of Jesus, the one who brings salvation, whose way the Baptist prepares.

A. Weiser

ἡγέομαι *hēgeomai* lead, rule; believe, think, consider

Lit.: F. BÜCHSEL, *TDNT* II, 907-9. — E. GRÄSSER, "Die gemeindevorsteher im Hebräerbrief," *Vom Amt des Laien in Kirche und Theologie* (FS G. Krause, 1982) 67-84. — E. HAENCHEN, *Acts* (Eng. tr., 1971) 426. — P. HOFFMANN and V. EID, *Jesus von Nazareth und eine christliche Moral* (1975) 186ff. — E. KÄSEMANN, *Rom* (Eng. tr., 1980) 346. — O. MICHEL, *Rom* (KEK, [5]1977) 302f. — R. SCHNACKENBURG, *John* I (Eng. tr., 1968), 279. — SPICQ, *Notes* I, 348-52. — For further bibliography see *TWNT* X, 1098.

1. Ἡγέομαι with the meaning *lead, rule,* attested since Homer, appears in the NT and other early Christian literature only in the pres. partc. ὁ ἡγούμενος for "men in any leading position" (BAGD s.v.). It is used of the eschatological king and good shepherd who leads the people of God (in a combination of citations from Mic 5:1, 3 and 2 Kgdms 5:2 in Matt 2:6) and of Joseph as "regent" over Egypt (Acts 7:10).

It is also used of church functionaries. Judas Barsabbas and Silas, together with Paul and Barnabas, are sent as delegates of the Apostolic Council to Antioch and are "*leading* men among the brethren" (ἄνδρες ἡγούμενοι . . . , Acts 15:22). The author of Hebrews mentions church *leaders* in a greeting (πάντες οἱ ἡγούμενοι, 13:24). He distinguishes them from the ἅγιοι, the "normal" church members, mentioning the leaders first. Thus he indicates that for him a hierarchically structured church is in view; since they are leaders of the church responsible to God as "watchers over souls," obedience is due to the ἡγούμενοι (13:17). To those who have died (a martyr's death?) a good remembrance is due as those worthy of imitation (13:7). The paradoxical hierarchy that Jesus had held up as a model and had recommended to the disciples is here and elsewhere in the NT modified in favor of an "early catholic" appreciation of office, even if it is not given up. Already Luke 22:24-27 (including the Lukan variation on the Synoptic parallel in v. 26: καὶ ὁ ἡγούμενος ὡς ὁ διακονῶν) makes of Jesus' demand for the renunciation of power "an instruction for the proper use of position and power in the Church" (Hoffmann and Eid 227).

According to Acts 14:11 in Lystra Barnabas and Paul were considered gods in human form: Barnabas is "identified" as Zeus, Paul as Hermes, "because he was the *chief* speaker" (ἐπειδὴ αὐτὸς ἦν ὁ ἡγούμενος τοῦ λόγου). This usage, while unique in the NT, is not without Greek parallels (see BAGD s.v.; Haenchen).

2. In addition to Acts 26:2 (Paul *considers* himself fortunate to be able to defend himself before King Agrippa), ἡγέομαι appears in the NT with the meaning *believe, think, consider* elsewhere only in the Epistles (19 occurrences). It is followed by an inf. in the fixed expression "*consider* necessary/right, that . . ." (ἀναγκαῖον/δίκαιον ἡγέομαι, 2 Cor 9:5; Phil 2:25; 2 Pet 1:13) or with a double acc. (e.g., Phil 3:7, what was gain for Paul before Christ, he *has regarded* as loss for the sake of Christ: ταῦτα ἥγημαι . . . ζημίαν; 2:6, Christ, who was in the form of God, has not *counted* it as spoil, i.e., did not grasp eagerly to be like God: οὐχ ἁρπαγμὸν ἡγήσατο τὸ εἶναι ἴσα θεῷ).

Paul formulates 1 Thess 5:13 in an unusual but unambiguous way: the church "should hold the κοπιῶντες and προϊστάμενοι particularly in honor (ἡγεῖσθαι ὑπερεκπερισσοῦ . . . "; with the adv. ἡγεῖσθαι is intensified *in bonam partem*). Similarly Phil 2:3: *count* one another higher than yourselves (ἀλλήλους ἡγούμενοι ὑπερέχοντας ἑαυτῶν); Rom 12:10 says the same, with the comparative attested only here (τῇ τιμῇ ἀλλήλους προηγούμενοι), thus not (with Luther) "precede, beat one to it," but rather *prefer, regard more highly* (cf. Käsemann 346; Michel 303).

T. Schramm

ἡδέως *hēdeōs* gladly*

The adv. of ἡδύς (pleasant, sweet) appears in the NT in connection with ἀκούω (Mark 6:20; 12:37) and ἀνέχομαι (2 Cor 11:19). The comparative ἥδιον, *rather,* does not appear in the NT (see, however, *1 Clem.* 2:1; 62:3). The superlative ἥδιστα, *very gladly* (with καυχάομαι or δαπανάω), appears in the NT in 2 Cor 12:9, 15; cf. Acts 13:8 D. Spicq, *Notes* I, 353f.

ἤδη *ēdē* already; now

Lit.: BAGD s.v. — LSJ s.v. — PREISIGKE, *Wörterbuch* s.v. (including Suppl.). — SCHWYZER, *Grammatik* II, 563.

1. Ἤδη is attested in literature from the time of Homer and in papyrus documents and the LXX. It appears frequently and designates temporal or logical proximity.

2. Ἤδη appears in the NT 62 times (not in 2 Corinthians, Galatians, Ephesians, Colossians, 1 Thessalonians, Titus, Philemon, Hebrews, James, 1 Peter, 2–3 John, Jude, or Revelation). It is used absolutely (e.g., Matt 3:10 par.) or connected with a time reference (e.g., Matt 15:32; not in the Epistles). It can appear in main clauses

(e.g., Matt 3:10 par.), subordinate clauses (introduced by ὅταν, e.g., Matt 24:32 par., or ὅτι, e.g., Luke 14:17), inf. clauses (e.g., Mark 4:37), partc. clauses (e.g., John 19:33, esp. gen. absolute, as in Mark 6:35, no examples in the Epistles). In almost all passages ἤδη is to to be translated *already*, e.g., Matt 3:10 par.: "the axe lies *already* at the root. . . ." The tr. *now* fits in 2 Tim 4:6: "For I am *now* being offered. . . ."

In John 4:35 the punctuation is decisive for the tr. of ἤδη: If ἤδη concludes the statement, it means: "Look at the fields, that they are *already* white unto harvest. The reaper receives wages. . . ." If, however, ἤδη introduces the following statement, it means: "Look at the fields, that they are white unto harvest. The reaper *now* receives wages. . . ."

In a few passages ἤδη is not temporal. Rather, it indicates that something results from the preceding circumstances ("logical proximity," see BAGD); so Matt 5:28; John 3:18: "he who does not believe is condemned *already*"; 1 Cor 6:7.

The phrase ἤδη ποτέ means *"now so far," "at last finally"* (Phil 4:10); εἴ πως ἤδη ποτέ means "whether I somehow *finally* have success . . ." (Rom 1:10).

R. Peppermüller

ἡδονή, ῆς, ἡ *hēdonē* desire, pleasure, enjoyment*

Lit.: E. BEYREUTHER, *DNTT* I, 458-61. — V. CATHREIN, *Lust und Freude* (1931). — J. DUPONT, "La parabole du semeur dans la version de Luc," FS Haenchen 97-108. — B. GERHARDSSON, "The Parable of the Sower and its Interpretation," *NTS* 14 (1967/68) 165-93. — B. REICKE, *Diakonie, Festfreude und Zelos in Verbindung mit der urchristlichen Agapenfeier* (1951). G. STÄHLIN, *TDNT* II, 909-26. — A. VÖGTLE, *Die Tugend- und Lasterkataloge im NT* (1936), index s.v. — P. ZINGG, *Das Wachsen der Kirche* (1974) 93. — For further bibliography see *TWNT* X, 1098.

Originally ἡδονή meant the *feeling of desire* perceived through the sense of taste. Through the widening of the concept ἡδονή became a term for desire of the senses (Herodotus) as well as of the spirit (Plato, Aristotle). However, already in antiquity a narrowing of the concept took place through the distinction between the higher and lower ἡδονή. This led in Hellenism to the meaning "sensual joy, sexual pleasure," and to the ethically negative evaluation by the Cynics, Stoics, and popular philosophy. This narrowing and negative evaluation of ἡδονή is reflected in all five occurrences in the NT.

In the post-Easter interpretation of the parable of the sower, Luke has altered the Markan text (Luke 8:14), when he places among "the seductive powers of everyday life" (J. Ernst, *Luke* [RNT] 269) "the *pleasures* of life," which choke those who have recently come to faith. All 4 occurrences in the Epistles are in parenesis and stand under the influence of Hellenistic popular philosophy. In a catalog of vices Titus 3:3 characterizes pre- and anti-Christian conduct as "enslaved to every *lust*." Jas 4:1 sees

in the *lusts* that war within the members the cause of outward disputes and warns against prayer in which the one who prays intends to waste everything in *pleasures* (ἐν ταῖς ἡδοναῖς ὑμῶν, v. 3). 2 Pet 2:13 says of false teachers that they consider revelry in the daytime the sum of *pleasure*.

A. Weiser

ἡδύοσμον, ου, τό *hēdyosmon* mint*

Matt 23:23 par. Luke 11:42: ἀποδεκατοῦτε τὸ ἡδύοσμον, "you tithe *mint*." Billerbeck I, 932f. (no explicit witness for the tithing of mint is known!).

ἦθος, ους, τό *ēthos* custom, practice, habit

The noun (known as early as Hesiod and Herodotus) appears in the NT only in 1 Cor 15:33 (pl.): ἤθη χρηστά, "good *morals*" (in a proverb; cf. BAGD s.v.). Ἦθος is also used in Acts 16:21 v.l.; 26:3 v.l. in place of ἔθος for Jewish laws; it appears also in *1 Clem.* 1:2 (the ἦθος of hospitality); 21:7 (of chastity). H.-H. Esser, *DNTT* II, 436f.

ἥκω *hēkō* have come, be present

Lit.: J. JEREMIAS, *Jesus' Promise to the Nations* (1958) 51ff. — O. MICHEL, *Heb* (KEK, [7]1975) 335ff., 355ff., esp. 362-66. — R. SCHNACKENBURG, *John* I (Eng. tr., 1968) 327-31. — J. SCHNEIDER, *TDNT* II, 926f. — SCHULZ, *Q* 271-77, 323-30 (bibliography).

1. Ἥκω, pres. in form, indicates result *(have come/be present)*. In Hellenistic literature it could also be inflected as pf. (BDF §101 s.v.). It is used this way frequently in the LXX, but only once in the NT (Mark 8:3).

2. Ἥκω occurs predominantly in cultic-sacramental and theological contexts. "It denotes the coming of the deity to man, primarily to those participating in the cult" or "the coming of men, of cultic participants, to the deity" (Schneider 927, with many references). Usage in the LXX and early Christian literature corresponds *mutatis mutandis* to the general usage.

In the NT there are, in addition to Mark 8:3, only a few other occurrences of the simple secular-local use of ἥκω: The lost son *has come* (home, Luke 15:27); Jesus *has come* from Judea to Galilee (John 4:47: ἥκω and ἔρχομαι used interchangeably); the representatives of the Jews from Rome *have come* to Paul in his residence to hear what he thinks (Acts 28:23 v.l.).

The other occurrences are distinguished in various ways by references to the eschatological coming of humankind or of the Lord (or of his judgment) to salvation or destruction: Jesus expects and threatens that innumerable (Gentiles) *will come* from east and west to gain a part in the kingdom, while "the sons of the kingdom" fall to judgment (Matt 8:11 par. Luke 13:28f.; cf.

Jeremias; Schulz 323ff.). The days (of judgment) *will come* on Jerusalem, plagues *will come* on Babylon, "all of this" *will come* on this generation (Luke 19:43; Rev 18:8; Matt 23:26), but only after the proclamation of the gospel in all the world, only after the eschatological tribulation does the end *come:* καὶ τότε ἥξει τὸ τέλος (24:14). The Lord *comes* unexpectedly (in judgment) also for his disciples; his day or he himself *comes* like a thief (Matt 24:50 par. Luke 12:46 [cf. Schulz 271ff.]; 2 Pet 3:10; Rev 3:3).

John and Hebrews use ἥκω in characteristic christological statements: John 2:4: "My hour *has* not yet *come*"; 6:37: "Everything which my Father gives me *will come* (ἥξει) to me, and whoever *comes* to me (τὸν ἐρχόμενον), I will not cast out"; 8:42; cf. 1 John 5:20: "I proceeded from God and I *have come* to you" (ἐκ τοῦ θεοῦ ἐξῆλθον καὶ ἥκω). The readiness of Christ for a once-for-all sacrifice is underlined by the author of Hebrews by a citation from Ps 39:8 LXX: ἰδοὺ ἥκω, "Behold, *I come* to do your will" (10:7, 9); he portrays the certainty of Christian hope with the words of the prophet Habakkuk (2:3): ὁ ἐρχόμενος ἥξει καὶ οὐ χρονίσει, "the coming one *will come,* and shall not tarry" (10:37).   T. Schramm

ηλι   *ēli*   my God*

Transliteration of Heb. 'ēlî (Ps 22:2) in Matt 27:46 (bis). Matthew's source had → ελωι (from Aramaic; Mark 15:34). The form ηλι is also found (as a secondary corrective) in Mark 15:34 D.

Ἠλί   *Ēli*   Eli*

Transliteration of the personal name 'ēlî (so, e.g., 1 Kgdms 1:3; 2:12, 20, 22; 3 Kgdms 2:27) appearing in Luke 3:23 as the name of Joseph's father.

Ἠλίας, ου   *Ēlias*   Elijah*

1. Occurrences in the NT — 2. Elijah in the OT and in early Judaism — 3. Illustrative references to Elijah — 4. Functions of Elijah in the NT

Lit.: R. BAUCKHAM, "The Martyrdom of Enoch and Elijah: Jewish or Christian?" *JBL* 95 (1976) 447-58. — K. BERGER, *Die Auferstehung des Propheten und die Erhöhung des Menschensohnes* (SUNT 13, 1976) 9-149, 228-35. — H. BIETENHARD, *DNTT* I, 543-45. — Billerbeck IV, 764-798. — M. BLACK, "The 'Two Witnesses' of Rev. 11:3f. in Jewish and Christian Apocalyptic Tradition," FS Daube 227-37. — P. DABECK, "Siehe, es erschienen Moses und Elias (Mt 17,3)," *Bib* 23 (1942) 175-89. — *Élie le prophète* (Études Carmélitaines, 1956), esp. M.-É. BOISMARD, "Élie dans le NT," I, 116-28; M.-J. STIASSNY, "Le prophète Élie dans le Judaisme," II, 199-255. — G. FOHRER, *Elia* (ATANT 31, 1957). — G. FRIEDRICH, "Lk 9,51 und die Entrückungschristologie des Lukas," FS Schmid (1973) 43-77. — J. GNILKA, " 'Mein Gott, mein Gott, warum hast du mich verlas-

sen?' (Mk 15,34 par.)," *BZ* 3 (1959) 294-97. — HAHN, *Titles* 354-56, 365-72. — R. A. HAMMER, "Elijah and Jesus: A Quest for Identity," *Judaism* 19 (1970) 207-18. — G. HENTSCHEL, *Die Elijaerzählungen. Zum Verhältnis von historischem Geschehen und geschichtlichen Erfahrung* (1977). — J. JEREMIAS, *TDNT* II, 928-41. — P. JOUON, "Le costume d'Élie et celui de Jean Baptiste," *Bib* 16 (1935) 74-81. — W. C. KAISER, "The Promise of the Arrival of Elijah in Malachi and the Gospels," *Grace Theological Journal* 3 (1982) 221-33. — C. A. KELLER, "Wer war Elia?" *TZ* 16 (1960) 298-313. — G. MOLIN, "Der Prophet Elijahu und sein Weiterleben in den Hoffnungen des Judentums und der Christenheit," *Judaica* 8 (1952) 65-94. — P. M. K. MORRIS, "Elijah and Jesus in Mark's Gospel," *Trivium* (1966) 121-33. — J. M. NÜTZEL, "Elija- und Elischa-Traditionen im NT," *BK* 41 (1986) 146-53. — idem, *Die Verklärungserzählung im Markusevangelium* (FzB 6, 1973) 102-22. — R. PESCH, "Zur Entstehung des Glaubens an die Auferstehung," *TQ* 153 (1973) 200-228, 270-83. — I. DE LA POTTERIE, "L'onction du Christ," *NRT* 80 (1958) 225-52, esp. 226-29. — M. REHM, "Eli, Eli, lamma sabachtani," *BZ* 2 (1958) 275-78. — J. A. T. ROBINSON, "Elijah, John and Jesus: An Essay in Detection," *NTS* 4 (1957/58) 263-81 = idem, *Twelve NT Studies* (1962) 28-52. — H. SEEBASS and N. OSWALD, *TRE* IX, 498-504. — M. E. THRALL, "Elijah and Moses in Mark's Account of the Transfiguration," *NTS* 16 (1969/70) 305-17. — U. WILCKENS, *Resurrection* (1978) 105-9. — T. L. WILKINSON, "The Role of Elijah in the NT," *Vox Reformata* 10 (1968) 1-10. — D. ZELLER, "Elija und Elischa im Frühjudentum," *BK* 41 (1986) 154-60. — For further bibliography see *DNTT* I, 545; *TWNT* X, 1098f.

1. The name Ἠλίας appears in the NT 29 times besides the v.l. in Luke 9:54. It appears 25 times in the Synoptic Gospels (9 in Matthew, 9 in Mark, 7 in Luke) and in John 1:21, 25; Rom 11:2; and Jas 5:17. In the treatment of the word one must also consider the many allusions to the figure of Elijah. In the Gospels Elijah is mentioned in connection with the identity of both John the Baptist and Jesus; he appears together with Moses on the Mount of Transfiguration; and the people who hear the cry of the crucified Jesus interpret it: "See, he is calling for Elijah" (Mark 15:35).

2. In order to understand the meaning of Elijah in the NT, it is necessary to recall both the information from 1 Kings 17–2 Kings 2 and the corresponding traditions in early Judaism (including Mal 3:1, 23-24 and Sir 48:1-12). In Judaism Elijah was viewed as the helper in time of need and was called upon as such. Intense concern was given to his return. Often he is a messianic figure; at other times he is the predecessor of the Messiah. He will allay wrath, effect peace, and restore the tribes of Jacob (cf. Sir 48:10). In other expectations he is the one who announces the time of salvation, struggles against the antichrist, and anoints the Messiah (see Billerbeck, Fohrer, Jeremias 928-34, Keller, Molin, Stiassny).

3. Three events from the life of Elijah are mentioned in the NT to illustrate specific situations:
a) The narrative of the long drought in Israel (1 Kgs 17–18) is mentioned in Luke 4:25-26: "There were many widows in Israel in the time of Elijah when the heaven

was shut up for three years and six months, and when there came a great famine over the whole land; and Elijah was sent to none of them, but rather to Zarephath, in the land of Sidon, to a widow." In this way Jesus illustrates, although in an overdrawn way, the saying: "No prophet is acceptable in his own country" (4:24). In Luke this is a reference to the coming Gentile mission. According to Jas 5:17-18 Elijah was a righteous man and nevertheless merely human like us. His earnest prayer "that it not rain" (1 Kgs 17:1 is not a prayer) and that it rain again after three years and six months (cf. 1 Kgs 18:42; for the change from "three" to "three and one-half years" cf. Dan 7:25; Rev 12:14, etc.—also Luke 4:25), is for us a model of prayer (vv. 13-15).

b) Paul refers in Rom 11:2-4 to 1 Kgs 19:1-18 (the flight of Elijah: "the 7,000 who have not bowed the knee to Baal" are a proof that a remnant remains also "in this time"; a defeatism like that of Elijah is not justified). Probably there is also a literary connection between Luke 22:43 and 1 Kgs 19:5-8: the motif of the strengthening angel.

c) In Luke 9:54 James and John want to call down fire from heaven to destroy the inhospitable Samaritans; there is here an apparent reference to 2 Kgs 1:9-12 (cf. Sir 48:3). A widespread variant (A C D among others; according to *TCGNT* "a gloss derived from some extraneous source, written or oral") is added: ὡς καὶ Ἠλίας ἐποίησεν ("as Elijah also has done").

Heb 11:35, 37 refers to the figure of Elijah also without mentioning his name. According to Origen (and others) 1 Cor 2:9 is derived from a Jewish Elijah apocalypse; according to Epiphanius Eph 5:14 was also taken from "Elijah." This suggestion "is most unlikely" (Jeremias 930).

4. a) It is evident that in Mark 15:34-36 Elijah is regarded as a helper in time of need. The crucified Jesus calls: ελωι, ελωι . . . (v. 34). A few of those standing nearby apparently misunderstand this intentionally: "He calls for Elijah. Will Elijah come to take him down?" (vv. 35f.). It is not certain whether the bystanders were thinking that if Elijah did not intervene and help, then Jesus would not be the Messiah. Matthew writes in 27:46-49: ηλι, ηλι (v. 46), which comes closer to the name of Elijah (of which the abbreviated form is Eli), and does not indicate a deliberate misunderstanding by the hearers (Ἠλίαν φωνεῖ, v. 47; cf. v. 49). Matthew also alters the Markan "take down" to the stronger "rescue" (σώσων, v. 49). Luke omits this episode. → ελωι.

b) During the transfiguration of Jesus on the mountain (Mark 9:2-8 par. Matt 17:1-8/Luke 9:28-36) Elijah and Moses appear and talk with Jesus (Ἠλίας: Mark 9:4, 5 par. Matt 17:3, 4; Luke 9:30, 33). The meaning and function of these two figures have been been understood in

various ways. R. Pesch, *Mark* (HTKNT) II, 74f., gives this opinion: "That Elijah and Moses speak with Jesus . . . indicates that Jesus belongs to their world. . . . Against the multitude of speculation in the history of interpretation one may affirm that the appearance of Elijah and Moses for the benefit of the disciples has nothing directly to do with the eschatological return of the two figures. What is presupposed is merely their elevation and *their metamorphosis* into a heavenly existence, from which they can appear." Nevertheless their appearance seems to stand also in connection with their eschatological function: Before the end these personages, taken up into heaven and kept there, must appear again.

In Mark 9:3 Elijah appears (in contrast to the chronological order) first (otherwise in v. 4); the attention of Mark is directed, as also in 9:11, 12, 13 (par. Matt 17:10, 11, 12), particularly to Elijah. This is "corrected" in Matthew and Luke. Luke adds the content of the conversation in 9:31: It involved Jesus' imminent ἔξοδος in Jerusalem (Luke 9:28-36 stands between the two Passion predictions in 9:22, 44).

c) In the conversation after the transfiguration (Mark 9:9-13 par. Matt 17:9-13) the view of the scribes (and of contemporary Judaism) is cited by the three disciples: Elijah must come. Jesus affirms this: Elijah will come and "restore everything" (cf. Mal 3:23-24); but he adds: Elijah has already come and has suffered. Only Matt 17:13 elaborates further: "The disciples understood that he was speaking about John the Baptist"; cf. 11:14: "He (= the Baptist) is Elijah, who is to come." The text in Q already referred to the Baptist (Matt 11:10 par. Luke 7:27; cf. Mark 1:2) with reference to the Elijah who is to return according to Mal 3:23-24. Probably the clothing of the Baptist (Mark 1:6 par. Matt 3:4) suggested the reference to Elijah (cf. 2 Kgs 1:8). The saying of the Baptist himself, which is probably not historical, that he is not Elijah (John 1:21; see also v. 25) indicates the degree to which the people looked forward to Elijah's return. This is indicated also in Mark 6:15 par. Luke 9:8 and Mark 8:28 par. Matt 16:14/Luke 9:19, where the opinion of the people that Elijah has appeared in Jesus is mentioned.

Luke omits the particular reference to the clothing of the Baptist as well as the conversation after the transfiguration. He seems to want to avoid an explicit identification of the Baptist with Elijah. Luke 1:17 says only (with a reference to Sir 48:10-11; Mal 3:23-24) that John goes before God "in the power of Elijah." Apparently for Luke Elijah is rather the type of the "prophetic" Jesus. Luke characterizes the public life of Jesus with material from the Elijah tradition (often also in contrast to it): see 4:25-26; 7:11-17 (cf. 1 Kgs 17:8-24); 9:8, 10 (opinions about Jesus), 30, 33, 51 (? ἀνάλημψις; cf. 2 Kgs 2:11; 1 Macc 2:58; Sir 48:1), 54, 62 (cf. 1 Kgs 19:20); see de la Potterie 226-29.

d) In Rev 11:3-13 the two witnesses are described with elements of (Moses and) Elijah: fire (v. 5; cf. 2 Kgs 1:10) and drought (v. 6; cf. 1 Kgs 17:1). The author of Revelation probably wants to express with these "two witnesses" not individuals, but rather a collective: the persecuted and witnessing Christian community of his time. Can it be assumed that he is here dependent on a pre-Christian Jewish tradition, according to which Enoch and Elijah return before the end, appear as prophets of repentance, become involved in a battle with the antichrist and are killed, are raised after three and one-half days, go into heaven, then return once more and kill the antichrist (see Jeremias 940-41, Berger, Black, but also Bauckham and J. M. Nützel, *BZ* 20 [1976] 59-94)? Do Mark 6:15 and 8:28 also point to this tradition, which is to be found in a variety of forms in various (often later) apocalyptic writings and in Christian writings (see Berger)? These data about the martyrdom and resurrection of the eschatological prophet are expressed in the discussion over the origin of the Easter faith (see Bauckham, Berger, Nützel, Pesch *[Entstehung]*, Wilckens). Earlier literature on Revelation 11 includes: W. Bousset, *The Antichrist Legend* (1896) 203-17; D. Haugg, *Die zwei Zeugen* (1936); J. Munck, *Petrus und Paulus in der Offenbarung Johannis. Ein Beitrag zur Auslegung der Apokalypse* (1950) 81-120.   J. Lambrecht

ἡλικία, ας, ἡ *hēlikia* age; period of life; era; bodily stature*

Lit.: J. R. BUISMANN, Ἡλικία, *NedTTs* 19 (1930) 139-45. — M. DIBELIUS and H. GREEVEN, *Col, Eph, Phlm* (HNT, ³1953) 82. — J. GNILKA, *Eph* (HTKNT, 1971) 214f. — W. GRUNDMANN, *Luke* (THKNT, ²1961) 97. — JEREMIAS, *Parables* 171. — J. E. RENIÉ, "Et Jesus proficiebat sapientia et aetate et gratia apud Deum et homines," *Studia Anselmiana* 27/28 (1951) 340-50. — J. SCHNEIDER, *TDNT* II, 941-43. — H. SCHÜRMANN, *Luke* I (HTKNT, 1969) 134-38. — G. STÄHLIN, *TDNT* VI, 703-19, esp. 712f.

1. This noun, attested from the time of Homer, has the meanings in classical Greek of: a) "age, period of life" (often specified as youthful [e.g., Homer *Il.* xvi.808; 4 Macc 8:2, 10, 20] or advanced [e.g., Homer *Il.* xxii.419] or the "age of ability/responsibility/maturity"; cf. εἰς ἡλικίαν ἔρχεσθαι, "enter into adulthood" [Diodorus Siculus xviii.57.2]; ἡλικίαν ἔχειν, "be of age" [Plato *Euth.* 306d]); b) "era, (the) generation (now living)" (e.g., Demosthenes *Or.* 60.11); and c) "bodily stature, growth," originally probably as a sign of a definite age (e.g., Herodotus iii.16; Plato *Euth.* 271b, etc.; in the LXX in Sir 26:17: "Like the shining lamp on the holy lampstand, so is a beautiful face on a stately figure [ἐπὶ ἡλικίᾳ στασίμῃ]").

2. In the NT ἡλικία appears with the meanings *age* and *bodily stature*. Which is intended is clear, on the one hand, in John 9:21, 23 (the parents of the man born blind avoid an apparently dangerous answer with the statement: ἡλικίαν ἔχει, i.e., "he has the *age [of majority]*/is an adult

[he can answer for himself]") and Heb 11:1 (Sarah is pregnant παρὰ καιρὸν ἡλικίας, "past the time of *age* for childbearing") and, on the other hand, in Luke 19:3 (Zacchaeus climbed a sycamore tree to see Jesus, ὅτι τῇ ἡλικίᾳ μικρὸς ἦν, "because he was small *of stature*").

In the other occurrences ἡλικία has been assigned sometimes one, sometimes the other meaning, in Eph 4:13 to be sure only in view of the metaphorical usage: "We will all reach the unity of faith, . . . the perfect man, the measure of the *stature* of the fullness of Christ" or "the measure of the *age of complete maturity* of Christ" (εἰς μέτρον ἡλικίας τοῦ πληρώματος τοῦ Χριστοῦ). The context suggests the spatial conception (cf. Dibelius/Greeven), but does not exclude the temporal meaning.

In Luke 2:52, however, the reference is certainly to age (*contra* Schürmann, et al.), as in the "parallels" (*SIG* II, 708, 18, cited by Stählin, 713f.; BAGD s.v., et al.): Jesus increased in wisdom and age (προέχοπτεν ἐν τῇ σοφίᾳ καὶ ἡλικίᾳ) and in χάρις with God and people.

The idea of age, which is not determined by stature, is also the concern in the eschatological logia tradition, according to which no one is able to add to his or her *length of life* by a single cubit (= a brief period: cf. Jeremias 171) by anxiety (Matt 6:27 par. Luke 12:25; cf. also the shorter variant traditions of the same meaning in Pap. Oxy. 655 fragment Ib [Hennecke/Schneemelcher I, 111; not in *Gos. Thom.* 36]).   T. Schramm

ἡλίκος, 3 *hēlikos* how large, how small*

Col 2:1: ἡλίκον ἀγῶνα ἔχω, "what great labor I have," i.e., "how hard I labor"; Jas 3:5, in wordplay: ἡλίκον πῦρ ἡλίκην ὕλην ἀνάπτει, "what a *small* fire, what a *great* forest it sets ablaze." The contrasting meaning of ἡλίκος *(how small, how large)* "is rather charming, and in addition it is corroborated by parallels" (M. Dibelius and H. Greeven, *Jas* [Hermeneia] 191). The contrast between a small cause and a great effect here, as in v. 4, represents "the tongue" and the disastrous results of its misuse.

ἥλιος, ου, ὁ *hēlios* sun*

1. The sun in its natural function — 2. "Rays" like the sun — 3. Apocalyptic conceptions — 4. The influence of the sun cult

Lit.: S. AALEN, *Die Begriffe "Licht" und "Finsternis" im AT, im Spätjudentum und im Rabbinismus* (SNVAO II/1, 1951), index s.v. — D. A. HAGNER, *DNTT* III, 730-33. — T. HARTMANN, *THAT* II, 987-99. — J. MAIER, "Die Sonne im religiösen Denken des antiken Judentums," *ANRW* II/19/1 (1979) 346-412.

1. Ἥλιος appears 32 times in the NT, 13 times in Revelation. A significant number of the occurrences have the natural function of the sun in view: In Matt 5:45 the sun is said to be subject to God's creative activity. Also

mentioned are the sun's rising and setting as an indicator of time (Mark 1:32 par. Luke 4:40; Mark 16:2; cf. Eph 4:26; see Plutarch *De Fraterno Amore* 17 [488c]; Deut 24:15) and of geographic direction (Rev 7:2; 16:12), as something seen (Acts 13:11; cf. Eccl 7:11), and as a reference point for sailors (Acts 27:20), and the experience of its scorching heat (Mark 4:6 par. Matt 13:6; Jas 1:11; Rev 7:16; cf. also 16:8; Ps 121:6; Isa 25:4; 49:10; Jer 17:8; Hartmann 990). 1 Cor 15:41 is also intended as a reference to nature. The comparison in the christophany of Acts 26:13 is oriented to the natural appearance of the sun as the strongest source of light (cf. Aalen 80-86 on OT references). The idea that the sun (and moon) will no longer be necessary in the age to come (Rev 21:23; 22:5; cf. *Sib. Or.* v.480-83) is based on the functions of the heavenly bodies as sources of light and dividers of time. As such it belongs to the realm of this world and its history, which will cease with God's reality.

2. Special significance is given to comparison of one's appearance or countenance with the rays of the sun. This comparison is used of the righteous people of the end time (Matt 13:43), of Jesus at the transfiguration (17:2), of the one like a Son of Man (Rev 1:16), and of the revealing angel (10:1). This thought has a broad Jewish history, which goes back to Judg 5:31 (cf. Dan 12:3) with 4 Ezra 7:97 (cf. *1 Enoch* 38:4; 39:7; 104:2); *2 Enoch* 1:5 (also 66:7); *Jos. As.* 18:9 (see also 6:2); and the rabbinic references in Billerbeck II, 790 and A. Schlatter, *Matt* (1929) 446, 527. This breadth of usage is illuminating. The radiance of the sun is a sign of glory, which the redeemed righteous ones, the angels (cf. *2 Bar.* 51:10; *1 Enoch* 51:4f.), and Christ share.

3. In the apocalyptic description of the end the damage to and destruction of the sun play a role. This expectation is taken over from the OT and Jewish tradition (on the OT see Hartmann 998; on Jewish tradition *T. Mos.* 10:5; *Sib. Or.* iii.801; v.346-48). Mark 13:24 par. Matt 24:29 alludes to Isa 13:10. Acts 2:20 belongs to the citation of Joel 3:1-5. The same passage stands behind Rev 6:12. However, Rev 8:12; 9:2 have no direct background. The darkening of the sun is a cosmic sign that gives a threatening signal for the end. The treatment of the motif in Luke is noteworthy: in Luke 21:25 it is modified from what is in Mark and Matthew; in 23:45 it is connected with the crucifixion; in Acts 2:20 it is included in the interpretation of the Pentecost event. The eschatological meaning of the Christ-event is thus emphasized.

Whether a special tradition lies behind the designation of the angel's position in Rev 19:17 (ἐν τῷ ἡλίῳ) cannot be determined; perhaps it signifies the highest point in the firmament.

4. The NT gives no indication of influence from the veneration of the sun, either in statements against that worship or in references to it: The sun cult is apparently not a concern of the NT authors. Rev 12:1 takes up the image of the *regina caeli*, but interprets it within the history of salvation. The total usage of the word indicates the Bible's astonishingly objective description of nature.

T. Holtz

ἧλος, ου, ὁ *hēlos* nail*

In the NT only in John 20:25 (bis), of the nails used to crucify Jesus: ὁ τύπος τῶν ἥλων, "the mark/impression of the *nails*" (v. 25a); ὁ τόπος τῶν ἥλων, "the place of the *nails*" (v. 25b). Thomas says that he will believe that the Lord has appeared (and has been raised) when he can see and handle the marks made by the crucifixion. See J. W. Hewitt, "The Use of Nails in Crucifixion," *HTR* 25 (1932) 29-45; J. Blinzler, *Der Prozeß Jesu* (1969) 377-79.

ἡμεῖς *hēmeis* we

Lit.: BAGD s.v. ἐγώ. — BDF §§277.1; 280; 284. — H. J. CADBURY, " 'We' and 'I' Passages in Luke-Acts," *NTS* 3 (1956/57) 128-32. — M. CARREZ, "Le 'Nous' en 2 Corinthiens," *NTS* 26 (1979/80) 474-86. — E. VON DOBSCHÜTZ, "Wir und Ich bei Paulus," *ZST* 10 (1932/33) 251-77. — E. HAENCHEN, " 'We' in Acts and the Itinerary," *JTC* 1 (1965) 65-99. — A. VON HARNACK, "Das 'Wir' in den johanneischen Schriften," *SDAW* (1923) 96-113. — U. HOLZMEISTER, "De 'plurali categoriae' in Novo Testamento et a patribus adhibito," *Bib* 14 (1933) 68-95. — J. J. KIJNE, "We, Us and Our in I and II Corinthians," *NovT* 8 (1966) 171-79. — E. PLÜMACHER, "Wirklichkeitserfahrung und Geschichtsschreibung bei Lukas. Erwägungen zu den Wir-Stücken der Apg," *ZNW* 68 (1977) 2-22. — RADERMACHER, *Grammatik* 72-74. — R. SCHNACKENBURG, *1-3 John* (HTKNT, ⁵1975) 49-65 (on 1 John 1:1-4). — H. SCHÜRMANN, *Luke* I (HTKNT, 1969) 1-8 (on 1:1f.). — E. STAUFFER, *TDNT* II, 354-58.

1. The first person pl. personal pron. appears frequently in the NT (864 occurrences in all cases), but not half as frequently as the corresponding pron. of the second person, ὑμεῖς (1,847 occurrences). This confirms the character of the NT as "address." While ἡμεῖς appears most often in the gen. case (ἡμῶν), ὑμεῖς most often appears in the dat. (ὑμῖν) and the gen. (ὑμῶν). Ἡμεῖς appears in the NT writings (in all cases) in the following order of frequency: Acts (126), 2 Corinthians (108), Luke (69), Romans (59), 1 John (56), 1 Corinthians (54), Matthew (49), John (49), 1 Thessalonians (48), and Hebrews (31).

2. Nom. ἡμεῖς, like other first and second person personal prons., is "employed according to the standards of good style as in classical Greek for contrast or other emphasis" (BDF §277.1), e.g., Luke 23:41; 1 Cor 1:23; 2:12. For the emphatic usage of ἡμεῖς the esp. frequent combinations καὶ ἡμεῖς (Matt 6:12; Luke 3:14; 2 Cor 1:6,

etc.: about 36 occurrences) and ἡμεῖς δέ (Luke 24:21; Acts 6:4; 1 Cor 2:12, etc.: about 20 occurrences) are symptomatic. Less frequent are ἡμεῖς γάρ (only in Paul: 2 Cor 6:16; Gal 5:5; Phil 3:3), ἡμεῖς οὖν (3 John 8), and ἡμεῖς πάντες or πάντες ἡμεῖς (John 1:16; Acts 2:32; 10:33; 1 Cor 12:13; 2 Cor 3:18; Eph 2:3). The contrast ἡμεῖς vs. ὑμεῖς is characteristic of Pauline style (1 Cor 4:10; 2 Cor 4:12; 6:12; 13:9).

Use of ἡμεῖς in place of ἐγώ is frequent among Greek writers and was also widespread in common speech. The writer (or speaker) used it to establish or emphasize a relationship with his readers (or hearers); on the literary pl. *(pluralis sociativus)* see BDF §280. The author of Acts uses ἡμεῖς in the so-called "we" passages (Acts 20:6, 13; 21:7, 12) to emphasize both his relationship as the narrator to Paul as well as his character as eyewitness. In the Pauline letters *we* is frequently not the individual author ("literary" pl., e.g., Gal 1:8), but rather the church or Paul and his coworkers (cf. also 1 John 1:4; cf. Schnackenburg 52). An ecclesiological *we* is present in Luke 1:1f. (Schürmann 8 on v. 2; Schürmann understands ἐν ἡμῖν in v. 1 as an "eschatological" *we*); similarly John 1:14; 1 John 2:1b, 2, 3, 5, 18b, etc. The author of Hebrews appears to use the sg. and pl. without distinction (BDF §280).

3. Gen. ἡμῶν appears with a large variety of preps, most frequently with ἐξ (Luke 24:22; Acts 15:24; 2 Cor 4:7; 7:9; 8:7; 1 John 2:19 [four times]), then with μετά (μεθ') (Matt 1:23; Luke 9:49; 24:29; 2 Thess 1:7; 5 times in 1–2 John), περί (1 Thess 1:9; 5:25; Col 4:3; 2 Thess 3:1; Titus 2:8; Heb 11:40; 13:18), ὑπέρ (Mark 9:40; 11 times in Paul; Eph 5:2; Titus 2:14; Heb 6:20; 9:24; 1 John 3:16), and 12 other preps.

Gen. ἡμῶν is also governed by vbs. (Mark 12:7; Luke 20:14; Acts 7:40; 24:4; 2 Cor 8:4; 1 John 4:6 bis; 5:14, 15) and appears with substantives (Matt 20:33; John 11:48; Acts 16:20; 6 times in Paul; 2 Thess 2:1; 2 Pet 3:15; 1 John 3:20; Jude 3; on this use of the gen., see BDF §284; Kühner, *Grammatik* II/1, 619f.). Ἡμῶν also appears in the gen. absolute clauses (BDF §§417; 423), esp. frequently in Acts (16:16; 20:7; 21:7; 26:14; 27:18, 27) and in Paul (Rom 5:6, 8; 2 Cor 4:18; 7:5), elsewhere only in Matt 28:13 (M) and Heb 10:26. Noteworthy are the phrases (εἷς) ἔκαστος ἡμῶν (Acts 17:27; Rom 14:12; 15:2; Eph 4:7) and τὰ περὶ ἡμῶν (Acts 28:15; Eph 6:22; Col 4:8).

4. Dat. ἡμῖν appears esp. with the prep. ἐν (Luke 1:1; 7:16; 24:32; John 1:14; 17:21; Acts 1:17; 2:29; 6 times in Paul; Eph 3:20; 2 Tim 1:14; Heb 13:21; Jas 4:5; 1 John 1:8, 10; 3:24; 4:12 bis, 13, 16; 2 John 2), but also with σύν (only 5 times, all in Luke-Acts) and παρά (Matt 22:25). The simple dat. occurs in Paul, primarily with vbs. of giving in reference to God's salvific gifts to Christians (Rom 5:5; 8:32; 12:6; 1 Cor 2:12; 15:57; 2 Cor 5:5,

18; 10:13; cf. 1 Cor 1:18, 30; 2:10; 8:6. On the question (of the demoniac) τί ἡμῖν καὶ σοί; "What (is between) *us* and you?" (Mark 1:24 par. Luke 4:34; Matt 8:29 differs from Mark), in which a "repelling formula" is involved, see R. Pesch, *Mark* (HTKNT) I, 122.

5. Acc. ἡμᾶς appears with the preps. ἐπί (10 times, of which 5 are in Luke-Acts, none in Paul), πρός (9 times, all in Mark, Matthew, and Luke-Acts except for 1 Thess 3:6), εἰς (9 times, of which 5 are in Paul), and διά (only in Paul: δι' ἡμᾶς, Rom 4:24; 1 Cor 9:10 bis).

G. Schneider

ἡμέρα, ας, ἡ   *hēmera*   day

1. Occurrences in the NT — 2. Meanings — 3. Usage

Lit.: P. AUVREY and X. LÉON-DUFOUR, *WBB* 642-47. — O. CULLMANN, *Christ and Time* (1964). — G. DELLING, *Das Zeitverständnis des NT* (1940). — S. J. DEVRIES, *Yesterday, Today and Tomorrow: Time and History in the OT* (1975). — E. JENNI, *THAT* I, 707-26. — K. LEHMANN, *Auferweckt am dritten Tag nach der Schrift* (1968). — U. LUZ, *Das Geschichtsverständnis des Paulus* (1968) 310-17. — J. NELIS, *BL* 1700-1704. — G. VON RAD and G. DELLING, *TDNT* II, 943-53. — For further bibliography see JENNI; LEHMANN; *TWNT* X, 1099f.

1. The noun appears in the NT *(UBSGNT)* 389 times, in all the NT documents except 2 and 3 John. Because of its literary form, Acts uses it most (94 times), while the Pauline letters have a relatively limited usage (45 occurrences in the Pauline corpus without the Pastorals). The NT has no derivatives (cf. Pape, *Wörterbuch* s.v.).

In the Gospels and Acts there are narrative phrases such as "in those *days*" (Mark 1:9; 8:1; Luke 2:1; Acts 9:37; frequent in the LXX, cf. Judg 18:1; 19:1; 1 Kgdms 3:1; 28:1; cf. Beyer, *Syntax* 32), in Luke-Acts also (cf. the distinction in Schürmann, *Luke* [HTKNT] I, 65n.162) "in these *days* (Luke 1:39; 6:12; Acts 1:15; 6:1; cf. BDF §§291.3; 459.3) and "before these *days*" = before this time (Acts 5:36; 21:38). The adv. acc. (τὸ) καθ' ἡμέραν, *daily*, is common (Mark 14:49; Luke 16:19; 19:47; 2 Cor 11:28; Mayser, *Grammatik* II/2, 436; BDF §160). Also common are the temporal acc. and gen. νυκτὰ καὶ ἡμέραν (Mark 4:27; Luke 2:37; Acts 20:31) and νυκτὸς καὶ ἡμέρας (Mark 5:5; Luke 18:7; Acts 9:24; 1 Thess 2:9; 3:10; 1 Tim 5:5), *day and night*, dat. ἡμέρᾳ καὶ ἡμέρᾳ, *day by day* (2 Cor 4:16, following Heb. *yôm wayôm*, Esth 2:11; 3:4; cf. Jenni 716), and many other combinations (cf. BAGD s.v. 2).

2. The noun appears with numerous meanings, a result of the variety of meanings in OT Hebrew usage: a) a unit of time consisting of twenty-four hours, b) the time of sunlight, c) time itself or a period of time, particularly the time of one's life or activity, or d) a particular day:

a) The astronomical unit of time incorporates the night and stands in a cycle of hours, days, months, and years

(Rev 9:15; Mark 13:22; Matt 25:13; cf. Gal 4:10). It is used to indicate a definite day, but in the NT never one that can be dated (Luke 23:12), or to designate a length of time in a sequence of days (three days, Mark 8:2; six days, Mark 9:2; two days, Mark 14:1; the following day, Luke 9:37 [but cf. 𝔭⁴⁵], etc.), often combined with a traditional symbolic or proverbial sense (forty days, Acts 4:22; 7:23, 30, 36; 13:18, 21; forty days, Mark 1:13; Luke 4:2; "forty days and nights," Matt 4:2). (On the number three in connection with the resurrection, → 3.a; on the beginning of the day in Hebrew, see Jenni 710.)

b. 1) *Day* as the designation for the time of brightness, of (sun)light in contrast to the night occurs frequently in the literal sense, e.g., in the phrases "at daybreak" (Luke 4:42; 6:13, etc.; cf. 2 Pet 1:19), "in the middle of the day" = at noon (ἡμέρας μέσης, Acts 26:13), "the burden [heat] of the day" (Matt 20:12), "the day is wearing away" = it is becoming evening (Luke 9:12; 24:29), "by day/in the daytime" (Luke 21:37; Rev 21:25: gen. of time, with or without the art. as in classical; cf. BDF §186.2, 3), and "throughout the day" (Acts 5:42) and generally to designate the workday (Matt 20:2, 6). 2 Pet 2:13 chastises those who lead a gluttonous life in the daytime. According to John 11:9 the day has twelve hours; one who walks in the day does not stumble.

2) These passages form a transition to the fig. sense: *day* as the realm of light, of brightness, from which the life of the Christian should be determined. Behind this usage stands the general human and particularly religious relationship between light (day) = good, darkness (night) = evil (cf. esp. on Qumran, F. Nötscher, *Zur theologischen Terminologie der Qumran-Texte* [BBB 10, 1946] 92-133). The Johannine Jesus puts himself in the pl. with his disciples: "We must do the works of the one who sent me (!), as long as it is *day*" (John 9:4). In the "night," which for Jesus comes with the Passion, but for the disciples means any hindrance to their work, no one can work (cf. R. Schnackenburg, *John* II [Eng. tr., 1979] 241f.; cf. 1 John 2:8-11, "be in the light" = love one's brother). The parenesis in 1 Thess 5:1-11 is based on the nearness of "the *day* of the Lord" (v. 2, cf. v. 4; → 3.b). As "sons of the light and of the *day,*" those who are not "of the night and darkness," Christians are summoned to watchfulness and sobriety (vv. 5-8; cf. Rom 13:12f.). Ὑιοὶ ἡμέρας is not attested elsewhere in biblical Greek, or in the Qumran literature. Ὑιοὶ (or τέκνα, Eph 5:8) φωτός is not found in the LXX (J. E. Frame, *Thess* [ICC] 185), yet is frequently represented in the Qumran literature (cf. *KQT* 33-35).

c) Ἡμέρα as *time, period of time,* etc., in a variety of usage, is based on the OT (cf. Jenni 711-14, 717-22) and is specifically connected to the characteristics of the Semitic perception of time (cf. Delling 48-54). Yet it is also known in classical (Sophocles *Aj.* 131) and koine Greek

(LSJ s.v.; BAGD s.v. 4). In the NT we see 1) a more neutral and, in a certain way, 2) a more defined sense of "time," but clear boundaries are not drawn between the two.

1) "In the *days* [of Herod]" (Luke 1:5; Matt 2:1 without art.) refers to the period of Herod's rule; in reference to John the Baptist it means the time of his activity (Matt 11:12). "Our days," i.e., "our lifetime" in general, is mentioned in Luke 1:75; the same meaning appears specifically with reference to Noah (Luke 17:26a par.; 1 Pet 3:20), Lot (Luke 17:28a), Elijah (Luke 4:25), and David (Acts 7:45). That he was "without beginning of life" (μήτε ἀρχὴν ἡμερῶν . . . ἔχων) is said of Melchizedek in Heb 7:3. Heb 5:7 speaks of "the *days* of his flesh," i.e., the time of the earthly-human existence of the Son of God.

2) In Acts 15:7 Peter looks back to "the ancient *times*" of the early Church (cf. Heb 10:32; otherwise Matt 23:30; Acts 5:37), which are already seen as exemplary and normative. This usage of "days" refers less frequently to the past than to the (eschatological) future (as in Mark 2:20) and is sometimes used for the announcement of an event that is already taking place: "in the last *days*" (ἐν ταῖς ἐσχάταις ἡμέραις)—i.e., *now*—the promise of the Spirit is fulfilled (Acts 2:17, 18; cf. Jas 5:3; Heb 1:2). In the later NT period negative references are made to the present "evil *days*" (Eph 5:16; cf. 2 Pet 3:3). At other times "days" is used to point to the future—the end of the days, the last days, the days of judgment, which will come (Mark 13:17, 19, etc. par.; 2 Tim 3:1; Luke 21:22, ἡμέραι ἐκδικήσεως; cf. Rev 10:7). "The *days* of the Son of Man" are mentioned in Luke 17:22 (cf. v. 24; "the days of the Messiah" is a fixed rabbinic expression: Billerbeck IV, 799-976). The promise of the exalted one, on the other hand, that he will be with the disciples "all *days* until the end of the world" (= forever), is determined by duration (Matt 28:20; cf. εἰς ἡμέραν αἰῶνος, "until the *day* of eternity" = the day [of God], which is eternity, 2 Pet 3:18; cf. Sir 18:10).

d) Particular days are generally emphasized because they have been set aside for a specific purpose (Luke 1:80; Acts 12:21; 21:26; 28:23; John 12:7; 1 Cor 4:3: the day of judgment, as in secular Greek; cf. G. Delling, *TDNT* II, 950) or have been esp. marked off, as with feast days and days of celebration such as the sabbath (Luke 4:16; 13:14b, 16; John 19:31; Acts 13:14), the *day* of Pentecost (Acts 2:1; 20:16), "the *day* of unleavened (bread)" = Passover (Luke 22:7; pl. in Acts 12:3; 20:6). "The *day* of the Lord" (κυριακὴ ἡμέρα), when the prophet was called (Rev 1:10), is disputed: Is it "the day of Yahweh" = the "last day," experienced in a visionary way, i.e., the Christian Easter (C. W. Dugmore, FS Cullmann [1962] 272-81), or (more probably, with most interpreters) the Christian Sunday (W. Stott, *NTS* 12 [1965-66]

70-75; critical response to both: K. A. Strand, *NTS* 13 [1966/67] 174-81)?

Observance of *"days,* months, [festival] times, and years," probably derived from Jewish calendar piety, is condemned in Gal 4:10 as a relapse into legalism (4:8-11; cf. F. Mussner, *Gal* [HTKNT] 297-304). Similar practices, connected with demands for ascetic continence, are known in Col 2:16ff.; Rom 14:5f. (history-of-religions material is in H. Schlier, *Rom* [HTKNT] 403-6).

3. In addition to the semantic fields already mentioned, of special significance are use of ἡμέρα in regard to a) "the third *day,*" in connection with the kerygma of the resurrection, and b) the future-eschatological *day* of the end.

a) The numerical datum "on the third *day*" belongs to the foundation of the witness to the resurrection in the NT (1 Cor 15:4; Luke 24:7, 21, 46; Acts 10:40; cf. the Passion predictions in Mark 8:31 par.; 9:31 par.; 10:34 par.; Matt 12:40). The alternation between dat. "on the third *day*" (Paul, Luke, Matthew; cf., however, Matt 27:63), and the prep. phrase "after three *days*" (Mark; cf. also "in three *days,* John 2:19f.) denotes no material difference, but has instead a linguistic basis (Delling, *TDNT* II, 949; VIII, 220). The origin of the statement is widely disputed. Derivations from the mystery religions ("dying and rising gods"), from targumic and midrashic traditions ("the third day" as a turning to salvation; see Lehmann), or from an idiomatic term for a small unit of time) are less probable. Rather, the reference to Hos 6:2 as a Christian "proof from Scripture" (cf. P. Hoffmann, *TRE* IV, 482f.) and perhaps the historical reference to the discovery of the empty tomb (Mark 16:2; the dawning day would be counted as a whole: cf. Delling, *TDNT* II, 950f.; so among others U. Wilckens, *Resurrection* [1978] 10f.) are more probable.

b) The center of gravity in NT use of ἡμέρα is in references to the eschatological *day* of the end, the day of judgment and redemption. This usage is derived from the OT and Jewish tradition of "the day of Yahweh" (Jenni; Volz, *Eschatologie* 163ff.; K.-D. Schunck, *VT* 14 [1964] 319-30).

1) The Synoptic tradition, most often the logia source (Q), speaks of "that *day*" or "those *days.*" It refers in this way to the day of judgment (Luke 10:12; ἐν ἡμέρα κρίσεως in Matt 10:15; 11:22, 24; 12:36 [M]) and esp. to "the *day* of the Son of Man," as in Luke 17:22-37, which can be labelled the "logia apocalypse." There "the appearance" of the Son of Man and the warning against false security are sharply formulated (cf. vv. 22, 24, 26, 27, 28, 30, 31; Schulz, *Q* 277-87). The uncertainty of this *day* or the "hour" (of the parousia) is addressed in the parable of the faithful and evil servants (Luke 12:42-46 par.; cf. 12:39f.). In Mark the occurrences are found in

his apocalypse (13:17 par., v. 20 par. [v. 24 par.], v. 32 par.: the uncertainty "of this *day*") and refer to day(s) of apocalyptic horror. Jesus can, however, look toward the banquet in the kingdom of God in a positive way (14:25 par.). Matthew and Luke develop this usage found in their sources (Matt 7:22; 24:42; 25:13; Luke 21:6, 22, 34; 23:29).

Authentic Jesus tradition is to be found in only a few instances (and is particularly found in Mark 14:25 par.), as individual logia appear almost exclusively in association with the apocalyptically oriented theologies of Mark and Q. The OT and Jewish usage has apparently been carried on in a significant way in a Christian framework.

2) Outside the Synoptics the topos of the *day* appears predominantly in parenetic contexts and church usage that has already become traditional (Luz 313f.). Only Paul, in all the NT, speaks of the parousia *of Christ as "the day* of the Lord" (1 Cor 1:8; 5:5; 2 Cor 1:14; 1 Thess 5:2; in the Pauline tradition: 2 Thess 2:2); cf. "the *day* of (Jesus) Christ" (in the NT only in Phil 1:6, 10; 2:16). Paul knows also the absolute ἡμέρα (1 Cor 3:13; 1 Thess 5:4; cf. Rom 2:16; Heb 10:25; 2 Pet 1:19). But "*day* of the Lord" in 2 Pet 3:10, 12 (cf. Acts 2:20 in the citation of Joel 3:4 LXX) refers to God.

The idea of judgment stands in the foreground and becomes explicit in formulations such as "*day* of wrath" (Rom 2:5; cf. Rev 6:16f.), "*day* of judgment" (2 Pet 2:9; 3:7; Jude 6; 1 John 4:17), "evil *day*" (Eph 6:13), "in that *day*" (2 Thess 1:10; 1 Tim 1:12, etc.), and probably also in "*day* of visitation" (1 Pet 2:12). The saving aspect of the *day* is, however, mentioned: "*day* of salvation" (2 Cor 6:2), "of redemption" (Eph 4:30).

3) In John's Gospel three characteristics, which appear in combination with the shape of traditional eschatology, are noteworthy. First is the expression, which is unique in the NT (and in apocalyptic literature), "*the* last day" (ἡ ἐσχάτη ἡμέρα). In 11:24 it is perhaps derived from the Evangelist, who gives it a new interpretation in vv. 25f. But it is probably inserted redactionally in other passages to correct a radical-present understanding of Johannine eschatology (6:39, 40, 44, 54; 12:48).

Secondly, the early Christian expression "that *day,*" which is normally given a future meaning (→ 3.b.1) is given a new interpretation. In the Johannine farewell discourse it refers to the day of the new present fellowship with the exalted Lord, in which the participants now "know" him and thus no longer "ask" anything (14:20; 16:23, 26; on the whole matter see R. Schnackenburg, *John* II [Eng. tr., 1979], 426-37).

Thirdly, "my *day,*" which Abraham saw and rejoiced in (John 8:56; cf. *T. Levi* 14:5, 14), is probably the day of the Messiah, i.e., the time of his revelation to Israel (cf. John 9:4; 11:9; → καιρός, ὥρα).   W. Trilling

ἡμέτερος, 3 *hēmeteros* our, ours*

Ἡμέτερος normally appears with a noun, as in Acts 2:11 (our languages); 24:6 v.l. (our law); 26:5 (our religion); Rom 15:4 (our instruction); 2 Tim 4:15 (our words); 1 John 1:3 (our fellowship); 2:2 (our sins). Τὸ ἡμέτερον in Luke 16:12 v.l. is "what is *ours*" (according to v. 11 the true riches). Οἱ ἡμέτεροι in Titus 3:14 are *our people* (so also *Mart. Pol.* 9:1), i.e., the Christians.

ἡμιθανής, 2 *hēmithanēs* half dead*

Luke 10:30: "they left him lying *half dead*." The adj. is also attested in, among other places, 4 Macc 4:11.

ἥμισυς, 3 *hēmisys* half (adj. and subst.)

Ἥμισυς used adjectivally takes its gender and number in combination with a noun, as in τὰ ἡμίση (neut. pl.) τῶν ὑπαρχόντων, Luke 19:8 D² Ψ. The better-attested text (א B, etc.) has τὰ ἡμίσια τῶν ὑπαρχόντων, "*half* of my goods." Τὸ ἥμισυ, *half*, also appears in the other NT passages: Mark 6:23 ("up to *half* of my kingdom"); Rev 11:9, 11 ("three days and a *half*" = three and a *half* days); 12:14 (ἥμισυ καιροῦ, "a *half* of a time" = a half time, as in Dan 12:7 LXX).

ἡμιώριον, ου, τό *hēmiōrion* half hour*

Rev 8:1 of the stillness in heaven, which lasted "about *half an hour*" (ὡς ἡμιώριον). The form ἡμίωρον also appears (A C pc); cf. Kühner, *Grammatik* I/2, 323.

ἡνίκα *hēnika* when, at the time that*

The temporal particle ἡνίκα appears in 2 Cor 3:15 in connection with ἄν and the pres. subjunc. *(whenever)*, in 3:16 with ἐάν and the aor. subjunc. *(as soon as)*: "Whenever Moses is read, a veil lies on their hearts" (v. 15) until today; "*as soon as*" Israel turns to the Lord, however, "the veil will be removed" (v. 16); on the context, see S. Schulz, *ZNW* 49 (1958) 1-30; W. C. van Unnik, *Sparsa collecta* I (1973), 194-210. BDF §455.1.

ἤπερ *ēper* than*

In John 12:43 ἤπερ appears after μᾶλλον (so also Tob 14:4 א): "they loved honor among people more *than* honor with God."

ἤπιος, 3 *ēpios* gentle, friendly*

1 Thess 2:7 v.l. (A Koine, etc.): "we were *kind/gentle* (ἤπιοι) among you"; 𝔭⁶⁵ B C D*, etc., read νήπιοι (childlike). 2 Tim 2:24: ἤπιος πρός τινα ("*friendly* to someone"), "a servant of the Lord . . . should be *kind* to all"

(opposite: μάχεσθαι); D G* here νήπιον. On both passages see *TCGNT* 629f.; Spicq, *Notes* I, 355-57.

Ἤρ *Ēr* Er*

A personal name in Luke 3:28, the father of Elmadam (Gen 38:3; Philo *Post.* 180).

ἤρεμος, 2 *ēremos* quiet*

1 Tim 2:2: "so that we may lead *a quiet* and tranquil life (ἤρεμον καὶ ἡσύχιον βίον) in all piety." This is desired as the outcome (ἵνα) of intercessory prayer for civil authority (v. 1); cf. N. Brox, *Die Pastoralbriefe* (RNT) 123-25.

Ἡρῴδης, ου *Hērǭdēs* Herod*

1. Herod I — Herod Antipas — 3. Agrippa I

Lit.: General: F. M. Abel, "Exils et tombeaux des Herodes," *RB* 53 (1946) 56-74. — G. Baumbach, *TRE* XV, 159-62. — A. H. M. Jones, *The Herods of Judea* (1938; ²1967). — W. Otto, PW Suppl. II, 1-191. — S. Perowne, *The Later Herods* (1958). — S. Sandmel, *IDB* II, 585-94. On Herod I: Abel, *Histoire* I, 324-406. — S. Applebaum, *EncJud* VIII, 375-85. — E. Bammel, "Die Rechtsstellung des Herodes," *ZDPV* 84 (1968) 73-79. — B. Bayer, *Encyclopaedia Judaica* (Berlin/Charlottenburg, 1928-34) VIII, 375-87. — S. G. F. Bandon, "Herod the Great," *History Today* 12 (1962) 234-42. — M. Grant, *Herod the Great* (1971). — S. Perowne, *The Life and Times of Herod the Great* (1956). — B. Reicke, "Herodes der Grosse," *Reformatio* 9 (1960) 24-34. — idem, *NT Era* 84-107. — idem, *BHH* 696-700. — S. Sandmel, *Herod: Profile of a Tyrant* (1967). — A. Schalit, *König Herodes* (1969) (basic). — Schürer, *History* I, 287-329. — M. Stern, "The Reign of Herod and the Herodian Dynasty," *The Jewish People in the First Century* I (Compendia Rerum Iudaicarum ad Novum Testamentum I/1, ed. S. Safrai and M. Stern, 1974) 216-82(-307). On Matthew 2: R. E. Brown, *The Birth of the Messiah* (1977) 165-230. — P. Gaechter, "Die Magierperikope," *ZKT* 90 (1968) 257-95. — M. Hengel and H. Merkel, "Die Magier aus dem Osten," FS Schmid (1973) 139-69. — A. Vögtle, "Das Schicksal des Messiaskindes," *ThJb(L)* (1968) 126-59. — idem, *Messias und Gottessohn* (1971). — idem, "Die matthäische Kindheitsgeschichte," *L'Évangile selon Matthieu* (BETL 29, ed. M. Didier, 1972) 153-58 (-183). On Herod Antipas: Abel, *Histoire* I, 440-43. — J. Blinzler, *Herodes Antipas und Jesus Christus* (1947). — idem, *Der Prozeß Jesu* (1969) 284-300. — F. F. Bruce, "Herod Antipas, Tetrarch of Galilee and Peraea," *ALUOS* 5 (1963-65) 6-23. — M. Dibelius, "Herodes und Pilatus," *ZNW* 16 (1915) 113-26. — V. E. Harlow, *The Destroyer of Jesus* (1954). — H. W. Hoehner, *Herod Antipas* (1972) (bibliography). — Reicke, *NT Era* 124-26. — Schürer, *History* I, 340-53. — J. B. Tyson, "Jesus and Herod Antipas," *JBL* 79 (1960) 239-46. — For further bibliography → Ἡρῳδιάς.

1. Herod I (born *ca.* 73 B.C., reigned 37-4 B.C.) was son of the Idumean Antipater and his Nabatean wife, Cypros (cf. Josephus *Ant.* xiv.158–xvii.199; *B.J.* i.180-673). He was governor of Galilee

and fled to Rome after the fall of the Parthians and the seizure of power by the Hasmonean Antigonus (40-37 B.C.). In Rome Herod became client king *(rex socius et amicus populi Romani)* of the Jewish land, including Idumea, Galilee, and Samaria (leased by Cleopatra), upon his request and at the instigation of Antony, in place of the unreliable Hasmonean dynasty.

Herod is mentioned in the NT only in Matthew 2 (vv. 1, 3, 7, 12f., 15f., 19, 22); Luke 1:5; and Acts 23:35. Luke 1:5 dates the birth of John the Baptist to "the days of Herod," which are synchronized with the time of the birth of Jesus (2:1) and according to Luke occurred in the years between the Syrian *apographe* around 7-6 and the death of Herod in 4 B.C.

In the legendary childhood story in Matthew 2, a dramatic novella in the style of the Jewish birth haggadah, Herod appears in connection with a Moses typology (according to the Jewish maxim, "as with the first redeemer, so with the last") in the role of the pharaoh disturbed by astrologers who secures his rule through a threatened murder of children.

This characterization of Herod is historically accurate: He secured his conquered kingdom by overthrowing the Sanhedrin (executing the Sadducean priestly aristocracy and taking control of the office of high priest) and by exterminating the Hasmonean royal house, which was bound to him through marriage. He was driven by innate distrust and constant fear of a rival claimant. He was stirred up by the provocative scorn of his (actually beloved!) wife, Mariamne, and the influences of his mother and sister, Salome, to execute Aristobulus III (brother-in-law and high priest, 36 B.C.), Hyrcanus II (former high priest, 31 B.C.), Mariamne (29 B.C.), Alexandra (mother-in-law, 28 B.C.), Alexander and Aristobulus (sons of Mariamne, 7 B.C.), Kostobar, and the sons of Baba. Finally, insane fear of losing his power and of being murdered seized the king, who had at his disposal a system of informers to trace and defeat any resistance, as the many changes of his will and the execution of his son Antipater a few days before his own agonizing death in Jericho (of intestinal cancer?) indicate.

Herod considered himself a Hellenist. His building projects (e.g., the refounding of Samaria as Sebaste and of Strato's Tower as Caesarea with monumental buildings and temples for the Cult of Caesar; Herodium; the country seat at Jericho; fortresses at Hyrcania, the Alexandrium, Machaerus, and Masada) and his efforts on behalf of Hellenistic culture outside Palestine were connected with his self-understanding as the Jewish emissary for the redeeming *pax Romana.*

Acts 23:35 refers to the palace at Caesarea. Mark 13:1; Matt 24:1f.; Luke 21:5 refer to Herod's rebuilding of the temple in Jerusalem, which began in 20 B.C., without mentioning his name. The theater, amphitheater, hippodrome, Antonia Fortress, and palace of Herod in Jerusalem are not mentioned (cf., however, on both Mark 15:16 par.; John 19:13).

2. Ἡρῴδης is also a NT designation for Antipas, son of Herod I and Malthace.

Antipas (cf. Josephus *Ant.* xvii.20, 188, 224-49, 318-20; xviii.27, 36-38, 101-26, 136, 148-50, 240-56; *B.J.* i.562, 646,

664-68; ii.20-38, 80-100, 167f., 178-83; *OGIS* 416f.; Dio Cassian 59.20f.) was raised in Rome and promoted Hellenistic culture (the building of Sepphoris, Livias, and Tiberias) in a long, peaceful reign (4 B.C.–A.D. 39) as tetrarch of Galilee and Perea, a title bestowed by Rome. He demonstrated a pro-Jewish attitude, particularly in his aloofness from the procurator Pilate (cf. Luke 13:1; 23:12; Philo *Leg. Gai.* 299-304).

Love for his second wife Herodias and her thirst for power brought about his downfall under Aretas IV, the father of Antipas's discarded first wife. When Antipas appealed for the royal crown from Gaius, he was thwarted by his brother-in-law Agrippa I (→ 3; → Ἀγρίππας) and by the accusation that he had been involved in a conspiracy against Tiberius with the Parthians. In A.D. 39 he was banned to Lugdunum (Lyon), where he and Herodias died. His domain, along with the tetrarchy of Philip, fell to Agrippa I.

Antipas is correctly called tetrarch in the NT (Matt 14:1; Luke 3:1, 19; 9:7), but is also incorrectly given the title of king (Mark 6:14, 22, 25-27; Matt 14:9). The Synoptics make him, along with his second wife Herodias, responsible for the murder of the prophet John the Baptist (Mark 6:14-29; Matt 14:1-12; Luke 3:19f.); Josephus *Ant.* xviii.116-19 indicates that anti-Zealot calculation lay behind this action.

Again according to the Synoptics, Antipas persecuted Jesus. In Matt 14:1, 12 (leaving aside Mark 6:7-13) Antipas's threat follows the refusal of faith in Jesus' homeland. Mark 8:15 warns against the incessant destructive hostility of Antipas, who responds to the faith with persecution (cf. 3:6; 6:14-29). Luke profiles the figure of the opponent of Jesus: 3:1 arranges Jesus' appearance in its historical framework. 3:19 marks a unit within salvation history: with the death of the Baptist the time of the law and the prophets comes to an end (16:16) and the proclamation of the gospel begins, to which Antipas responds negatively, in contrast to the people in the surrounding area (8:3; Acts 13:1). He is inquisitive (Luke 9:7-9; 23:8); he has the cunning treachery of a weakling (13:31-33); he acts with contemptuous scorn (23:6-12) and with deadly hostility together with Pilate (Acts 4:25-27; cf. Ps 2:1f.). The pre-Lukan tradition in Luke 23:6-12 (conjectured from reports such as 9:9; Philo *Leg. Gai.* 300; Josephus *Ant.* xviii.122?) already reflects the tendency to make Antipas and Pilate witnesses to the innocence and the unpolitical nature of the messiahship of Jesus.

3. Ἡρῴδης is also used in Acts 12:1, 6, 11, 19, 21 as the popular name of Agrippa I; → Ἀγρίππας.

                                     U. Kellermann

Ἡρῳδιανοί, ῶν, οἱ *Hērōdianoi* Herodians*

1. Occurrences in the NT — 2. Designation of a Jewish group — 3. Opponents of Jesus, esp. in Mark

Lit.: B. W. BACON, "Pharisees and Herodians in Mark," *JBL* 39 (1920) 102-12. — W. J. BENNET, "The Herodians of Mark's Gospel," *NovT* 17 (1975) 9-14. — E. BICKERMAN, "Les

Hérodiens," *RB* 47 (1938) 184-97. — C. DANIEL, "Les 'Hérodiens' du NT sont-ils des Esséniens?" *RevQ* 7 (1970) 397-402. — H. W. HOEHNER, *Herod Antipas* (1972) 331-42. — P. JOÜON, "Les 'Hérodiens' de l'Évangile," *RSR* 28 (1938) 585-88. — W. OTTO, PW Suppl. II, 200-202. — B. REICKE, *BHH* 703. — H. H. ROWLEY, "The Herodians in the Gospels," *JTS* 41 (1940) 14-27. — S. SANDMEL, *IDB* II, 594f. — A. SCHALIT, *König Herodes* (1969) 378-81. — K. WEISS, *TDNT* IX, 35-39, esp. 39. — P. WINTER, *On the Trial of Jesus* (1961) 128f.

1. The Herodians are mentioned in the NT always in association with the Pharisees (Mark 3:6; 8:15 𝔭45 W Θ, etc.; 12:13). Matthew (except in 22:16) and Luke replace Ἡρῳδιανοί with other Jewish groups. Ἡρωδεῖοι in Josephus *B.J.* i.319 is the Grecized form of the Latin.

2. Mark 12:13, where Jewish groups are listed, refers with "Herodians" to a group of partisans of Herod Antipas (→ Ἡρῴδης 2), who as friends of the Romans (invective) or royalists (so Hoehner) played the same role in Galilee as the Sadducees in Jerusalem (cf. Matt 16:6 with Mark 8:15). Such groups existed already at the time of Herod I (→ Ἡρῴδης 1; cf. Josephus *Ant.* xiv.450; xv.2; *B.J.* i.319); they bestowed messianic admiration on him because of the success of his reign and the consequent integration of his domain into the world peace of Octavian (Schalit 412ff.), which was understood as redemption (cf. the early Christian writers, Bickerman, Rowley, Schalit), and attempted to convince public opinion of the legitimacy of the usurper.

3. In Mark the Herodians seek to make an attempt on Jesus' life. Their association with the Pharisees (12:13), even as emissaries of the Sanhedrin, has been interpreted as a projection back from the time of Agrippa I, who was friendly with the Pharisees (→ Ἡρῴδης 3), or, according to Winter, Agrippa II, or as opportunistic loyalty to Rome among Pharisees after the fall of Sejanus in A.D. 31 (so Reicke). In the redactional (!) Markan passage opponents and friends of Rome and representatives of Jerusalem and Galilee come together, that in itself a contradiction of how things were, in order to confront Jesus with the Zealot question (12:13). The naming of the Herodians is significant (cf. 8:15) in itself, as Antipas persecuted Jesus and had the jurisdiction over capital crimes.

U. Kellermann

Ἡρῳδιάς, άδος *Hērōdias* Herodias*

1. Occurrences in the NT — 2. Biography according to Josephus — 3. Mark 6:17-19 par.

Lit.: F. M. ABEL, "Exils et tombeaux des Hérodes," *RB* 53 (1946) 56-74, esp. 71-73. — H. CROUZEL, "Le lieu d'exil d'Hérode Antipas et d'Hérodiade selon Flavius Josèphe," *Studia Patristica* X (TU 107, 1970) 275-80. — J. GNILKA, "Das Martyrium Johannes des Täufers (Mk 6,17-29)," FS Schmid (1973) 78-92. — H. W. HOEHNER, *Herod Antipas* (1972) 110-71, 257-

63. — W. LILLIE, "Salome or Herodias?" *ExpTim* 65 (1953/54) 250f. — W. OTTO, PW Suppl. II, 202-5. — I. DE LA POTTERIE, "Mors Joannis Baptistae (Mc 6,17-29)," *VD* 44 (1966) 142-51. — B. REICKE, *BHH* 703f. — Reicke, *NT Era* 124-26. — S. SANDMEL, *IDB* II, 595. — SCHÜRER, I, 340-53. — M. STERN, "The Reign of Herod and the Herodian Dynasty," *The Jewish People in the First Century* (Compendia Rerum Iudaicarum ad Novum Testamentum I/1, ed. S. Safrai/M. Stern; 1974) 216-307, esp. 284-89. — For further bibliography → Ἡρῴδης 2.

1. Herodias is mentioned in the NT only in Matt 14:3, 6; Mark 6:17, 19, 22; Luke 3:19.

2. According to Josephus (*B.J.* i.552, 557; ii.182; *Ant.* xvii.12-14; xviii.109-19, 136, 148, 240-55) Herodias was the granddaughter of Herod I and the daughter of Aristobulus, who was executed in 7 B.C., and Bernice. She married Herod's son Herod Boethus, who lived in Rome and was excluded from the throne succession. There his half-brother Antipas (→ Ἡρῴδης 2) fell in love with the heiress to the Hasmonean-Herodian love of power, who was dissatisfied with the political passivity of her husband. The victim of the deceit, the wife of Antipas, fled to her father, the Nabatean king Aretas IV, whose victory in the campaign of vengeance could be prevented only by the Romans. When Gaius named the brother of Herodias, Agrippa I (→ Ἡρῴδης 3), king over the tetrarchy of Philip, Herodias urged her husband also to seek the title of king from Rome. Because of the intrigue of Agrippa, Antipas was removed from office and banished to Lugdunum (Lyon in Gaul) in A.D. 39, to which Herodias voluntarily accompanied him.

3. In the legendary novella in Mark 6:17-29 (par. Matt 14:3-12), which has been embellished with Jewish and Hellenistic motifs and which goes back to a brief martyr report from the disciples of the Baptist (Gnilka), Herodias is a second Jezebel (1 Kgs 19:2) who persecutes the Baptist with hatred because he reproached her husband for his forbidden marriage with his sister-in-law. Despite the protective custody of Antipas and his influence on him, John the Baptist succumbed to the vengeance of Herodias (in Tiberias?). Even if Josephus, who places John's death at Machaerus, does not describe this intrigue, it is historically possible. If it is not historical, the relationship between the death of the Baptist and the marital history of Antipas (cf. Josephus *Ant.* xviii.109-19) provided the basis for the development of the tradition. Mark 6:17 (Matt 14:3) confuses Boethus, for whom the alternative name Philip is not known, with the tetrarch Philip, whom Salome, the daughter of Herodias, married.

U. Kellermann

Ἡρῳδίον, ωνος *Hērōdiōn* Herodion*

A Jewish Christian and συγγενής of Paul, whom Paul greets in Rom 16:11.

Ἡσαΐας, ου *Ēsaias* Isaiah*

An important OT prophet, under whose name the largest prophetic book in the Scripture was disseminated (cf. 1QIsaᵃ, 1QIsaᵇ, 4QpIsaᵃ⁻ᵈ; see also *Asc. Isa., Mart. Isa.*). All 22 NT occurrences of his name are references to the book of Isaiah, whether they refer to the book itself (Luke 4:17; γέγραπται, Mark 1:2; Luke 3:4; ἀναγίνωσκω, Acts 8:28, 30) or to him as speaking in his writing (λέγει, Rom 10:16, 20; 15:12; κράζει, 9:27) or as the speaker (τὸ ῥηθὲν διὰ Ἠσαΐου, Matt 4:14; 8:17; 12:17; 13:35 v.l.; cf. 3:3; 13:14; 15:7; Mark 7:6; John 1:23; 12:38, 39, 41; Acts 28:25 [the Holy Spirit spoke through Isaiah]; Rom 9:29). *DBSup* VI, 647-729; C. R. North, *IDB* II, 731-44; N. W. Porteous, *RGG* III, 600f.; W. Werbeck, *RGG* III, 601-11; J. Ziegler, *LTK* V, 779-82; *BL* 779-86; O. Kaiser, *BHH* 850-57; J. M. Ward, *IDBSup* 456-61.

Ἠσαῦ   *Ēsau*   Esau*

The older twin brother of the patriarch Jacob (Gen 25:25f.). Rom 9:13 says (citing Mal 1:2f.) that God "hated" Esau and "loved" Jacob. Heb 11:20 mentions the blessing of Isaac on his sons Jacob and Esau (Gen 27:27-41). 12:16 says Esau had his mind on lower things (βέβηλος), because he disregarded his birthright (Gen 25:33f.). H. Odeberg, *TDNT* II, 953f.; V. Maag, *TZ* 13 (1957) 418-29.

ἥσσων, 2   *hēssōn*   less, weaker*

A comparative adj., also seen as ἥττων, with no corresponding positive. 1 Cor 11:17: εἰς τὸ ἧσσον συνέρχεσθε, "you come together for the *worse*" (i.e., it is worse at your assemblies); 2 Cor 12:15: ἧσσον ἀγαπῶμαι, "am I loved *in a smaller measure?*" (ἧσσον as adv. = *less*).

ἡσυχάζω   *hēsychazō*   conduct oneself quietly, be silent
→ ἡσυχία.

ἡσυχία, ας, ἡ   *hēsychia*   rest, stillness, silence*
ἡσυχάζω   *hēsychazō*   conduct oneself quietly, be silent*
ἡσύχιος, 2   *hēsychios*   quiet, tranquil*

1. Occurrences in the NT — 2. Meanings — 3. Usage

Lit.: B. REICKE, *BHH* 1624f. — G. SCHELBERT, *BL* 1494f. — SPICQ, *Notes* I, 358-64.

1. The noun occurs 4 times in the NT, the vb. 5 times, the adj. twice. Codex D has the noun and the vb. one more time each (Acts 21:40; 22:2). Of the 11 occurrences, 5 are in Luke-Acts alone, 3 are in 1 Timothy, and 1 Thessalonians, 2 Thessalonians, and 1 Peter have 1 each.

The noun is used with μετά (2 Thess 3:12), with ἐν (1 Tim 2:11, 12 with adj. meaning), and with παρέχειν (Acts 22:2 with a verbal meaning); in Acts 21:40 D it is parallel to σιγή ("silence"). The vb. appears in the NT only in the intrans. act., in Luke-Acts only in the 1st aor. (4 times; as a dental stem it is formed without the dental: ἡσύχασα),

in 1 Thess 4:11 in the pres. inf. The adj. is used in 1 Tim 2:2 with the noun βίος; in 1 Pet 3:4 with πραΰς and the noun πνεῦμα. As an adj. formed with -ος it has two endings.

2. The primary meanings in Greek literature, "rest, peace, tranquility," are those present in the NT. Jesus is left alone/in peace by his adversaries (Luke 14:4 [L]). Peter leaves the other apostles silenced in the discussion of the Gentile mission (Acts 11:18); Paul is left in peace after the well-intended attempt to persuade him not to go to Jerusalem (Acts 21:14). The word group can imply more than silence, involving unusual attention (Acts 22:2) or assurance in eschatological expectations (1 Thess 4:11; 2 Thess 3:2), which make one free for daily work. The request for quietness in worship (1 Tim 2:11, 12) does not forbid questioning or speaking in general, but rather speaking that creates a disturbance. Finally, a well-balanced quietness is designated as a virtue of wives (1 Pet 3:4); order and peace are considered a condition worth striving for (1 Tim 2:2; cf. the sabbath rest as a gift [see Luke 23:56] and ἡσυχία as a t.t. for πλήρωμα, the fullness of being among the Christian Gnostics; see G. Bornkamm, *TDNT* IV, 824n.162).

3. The word group is always used of people, e.g., in the parenesis directed to wives, who are influenced by visible things (cosmetics, fashion)—not by the invisible—and by unbridled emancipation; of men who are influenced by eschatological fanaticism; of wives who are faithful in keeping the sabbath; of the opponents of Jesus who have been silenced; of groups of individuals; and of the Church, in which the concern is to have and to keep the peace.

C. H. Peisker

ἡσύχιος, 2   *hēsychios*   quiet, tranquil
→ ἡσυχία.

ἤτοι   *ētoi*   either*

Ἤτοι–ἤ, "*either*-or": Rom 6:16: "as slaves, *either* of sin unto death or of obedience unto righteousness."

ἡττάομαι   *hēttaomai*   succumb, be overcome*

In the NT only pass.: be defeated, succumb. 2 Cor 12:13 v.l. (A Koine pl, in place of ἐσσόομαι): ἡττώθητε ὑπὲρ τὰς λοιπὰς ἐκκλησίας, "be inferior to the other churches"; 2 Pet 2:19, 20: "by whatever one *is overcome*, he has become its slave" (v. 19), "when they *succumb* to them [the defilements of the world] . . ." (v. 20).

ἥττημα, ατος, τό   *hēttēma*   defeat*

Rom 11:12: τὸ ἥττημα αὐτῶν: the *defeat* of the Jews means wealth for the Gentile peoples; 1 Cor 6:7: "That is already a *defeat* for you, that you have lawsuits with one another."

ἥττων, 2 *hēttōn* less, weaker
→ ἥσσων.

ἠχέω *ēcheō* resound, roar*

1 Cor 13:1: "*resounding* brass (χαλκὸς ἠχῶν) or clanging cymbal"; cf. Herodotus iv.200; Plato *Prt.* 329a. Of the roaring/raging of the sea, Luke 21:25 TR; cf. Ps 45:4 LXX; Jer 5:22 LXX. J. Schneider, *TDNT* II, 954f.

ἦχος, ου, ὁ *ēchos* clang, noise, call*

Luke 4:37, of the *reports* concerning Jesus (ἦχος περὶ αὐτοῦ); Acts 2:2: a *sound* from heaven came "like the rushing of a roaring, mighty wind" (the Pentecost miracle); Heb 12:19, of the *sound* of the trumpet.

ἦχος, ους, τό *ēchos* clang, noise*

Neut. ἦχος is found in Luke 21:25: ἐν ἀπορίᾳ ἤχους θαλάσσης, "in perplexity because of the *roaring* of the sea" (→ ἠχέω), and possibly also in Luke 4:37; Acts 2:2 (→ ἦχος, ου).

ἠχώ, οῦς, ἡ *ēchō* sound

This noun appears in the NT only in Luke 21:25 in the Westcott/Hort edition (ἐν ἀπορίᾳ ἠχοῦς; → ἦχος, ους). It also appears in, e.g., Job 4:13; Wis 17:18.

Θ θ

θα *tha* (come!)
→ μαϱανα θα.

Θαδδαῖος, ου *Thaddaios* Thaddeus*

A disciple of Jesus in the "list of apostles" between "James the son of Alphaeus" and "Simon the Cananaean" (Mark 3:18 par. Matt 10:3). D reads in both passages Λεββαῖος instead of Θαδδαῖος; cf. Dalman, *Worte* 40, who assumes that the same person was called in Semitic *libay* and in Gk. Θευδᾶς (from which *taday*/Θαδδαῖος arose).

θάλασσα, ης, ἡ *thalassa* sea, lake

1. "The (unspecified) sea" — 2. Specific referents — 3. Narratives set at the sea. — 4. "Sea and land" — 5. The "evil sea" — 6. Fig.-symbolic usage — 7. In comparisons

Lit.: BAGD s.v. — DALMAN, *Arbeit* VI, 343-70. — O. EISSFELDT, "Gott und das Meer in der Bibel," *idem, Kleine Schriften* III (1966) 256-64. — E. HILGERT, *The Ship and Other Related Symbols in the NT* (1962). — R. KRATZ, *Rettungswunder. Motiv-, traditions- und formkritische Aufarbeitung einer biblischen Gattung* (1979). — E. STRUTHERS MALBON, "The Jesus of Mark and the Sea of Galilee," *JBL* 103 (1984) 363-77. — G. THEISSEN, " 'Meer' und 'See' in den Evangelien," *SNTU* 10 (1985) 5-25. — For further bibliography see Kratz; → ὕδωρ, → λίμνη.

1. Θάλασσα is used of "the (unspecified) sea," most often in sayings where the subject is "faith" (Mark 9:42 par. Matt 18:6/Luke 17:1f.; Mark 11:23 par. Matt 21:21; cf. Luke 17:6).

2. As a geographic term θάλασσα is used: a) rarely of the "Red *Sea*" (Acts 7:36; Heb 11:29), b) in isolated cases of the Mediterranean Sea (Acts 10:6, 32; 17:14; 27:30, 38, 40; 28:4; Rev 18:17, 19 [originally in reference to Tyre—Ezek 26f.—here in reference to Babylon = Rome]), and c) most often of the "*Sea* of Galilee" (the Lake of Gennesaret), both with some specific designation (Mark 1:16; 7:31; Matt 15:29 [θάλασσα τῆς Γαλιλαίας]; John 6:1 [θάλασσα τῆς Γαλιλαίας τῆς Τιβεριάδος]; 21:1 [θάλασσα τῆς Τιβεριάδος]) and indirectly, as determined

by place designations, continuous itinerary, or context (Mark 2:13; 3:7; 4:1, 39, 41; 5:1, 13, 21; 6:47, 48, 49; Matt 4:15 [citing Isa 8:23–9:1, there the area at the Mediterranean Sea]; 8:24, 26, 27, 32; 13:1; 14:24, 25, 26; 17:27; John 6:16, 17, 18, 19, 22, 25; 21:7).

The "pre-Markan collection of miracle stories" is especially noteworthy. Here various individual narratives are brought together redactionally representing the most important subgenres of miracle stories within a missions-theological and christological standpoint (OT background, motif of surpassing greatness: Jesus is more than . . .). They are coordinated and arranged concentrically within a unified geographic framework: All the stories take place at or on the "Sea of Galilee" (Mark 3:7; 4:1; 4:39, 41; 5:1, 13; 5:21; 6:47ff.). The Sitz im Leben may be the Gentile mission carried on by Galilean Jewish Christian-Hellenistic circles, which were oriented by OT as well as Hellenistic thought. The Evangelist Mark has split the collection (3:7-12; 4:1; 4:35-39, 41; 5:1-20; 5:21-43; 6:32-44; 6:45-52; 6:53-56; cf. R. Pesch, *Mark* [HTKNT] I, 277-81, etc.).

In John the Sea of Galilee, called the "Sea of Tiberias," appears only in the signs source, which reflects a certain relationship with the pre-Markan miracle collection, and in the supplementary ch. 21, which demonstrates apparent reminiscence of ch. 6.

Luke consistently uses λίμνη (Γεννησαρέτ).

3. Θάλασσα obviously appears in the narratives associated with a setting at the sea (Mark 1:16-20 par. Matt 4:18-22 [the call of the fishermen to be disciples]; Mark 4:35-41 par. Matt 8:23-27 [the stilling of the storm]; Mark 5:13 par. Matt 8:32 [the herd of swine driven into the sea]; Mark 6:45-52 par. Matt 14:22-33 [Jesus walking on the sea]; Matt 13:47-50 [the parable of the net]; Matt 17:27 [the coin in the fish's mouth]; John 6:16-25 [Jesus walking on the sea]; 21:1-23 [the appearance at the Sea of Tiberias]; Acts 27–28 [Paul's journey to Rome and shipwreck]; Rev 18:17, 19 [cf. Ezek 26f.]).

4. The combination "sea and land" is common (Matt 23:15 [+ ξηρά]; Rev 7:1, 2, 3; 10:2, 5, 8 [+ γῆ]). Most

often the sea is mentioned as a realm of creation together with heaven and earth as a term for the entire cosmos (Acts 4:24; 14:15; Rev 5:13; 7:1ff.; 10:6; 12:12; 14:7; 21:1; cf. Exod 20:11; Ps 146:6; Jonah 1:9).

5. Even the modern person, with a background of technical progress, encounters the power of the sea, the dynamic energy of the water, with a certain awe and uneasiness. The ancient person, imprisoned in mythic thought, saw in the water the unpredictable, mostly destructive, chaotic element even more. The ancient world, ruled by gods and demons, was believed to be ruled most of all by evil deities of the sea. The sea storm and its effects were considered an expression of divine wrath and punishment. In the ancient oriental myths of creation a good god of light and heaven battles and defeats the evil, dark deity who embodies the sea chaos, the chaos dragon (Marduk-Tiamat, Baal-Yam). But the threat of chaos remains continually present. In the OT use of this tradition, the final conquest of the mythical monster Rahab, Leviathan, the dragon, the primal sea is ascribed to Yahweh, the God of creation. His superiority is demonstrated in his power to call forth and calm the sea and his mastery over the floods. The increasing concern with demons in Jewish apocalyptic and late antiquity gives life to the concept of the "evil sea."

The NT "miracle stories of rescue," such as Mark 4:35-41 par. and Mark 6:45-52 par., become intelligible against this background. Jesus demonstrates in the stilling of the storm episode, for which the Jonah story provides a basis both in structure and content, that he is the one who surpasses the OT and Hellenistic wonder workers; he acts as Yahweh himself when he threatens the demonic elements (→ ἐπιτιμάω) and brings them to silence. In the story of Jesus' walking on the water, in which the rescue miracle is dominated by motifs of epiphany, he has fully entered the role of the OT God.

The NT rescue miracle stories have apparently both missionary-theological and didactic-parenetic purposes. In Matthew the narratives involve primarily the disciples (= the Church). The central dialogue involves the problem of discipleship in faith ("little faith," 8:26; 14:31).

The demonic understanding of the water is to be seen also in Mark 5:13; the legion of demons is sent into the "impure" herd of swine, which runs into the sea and drowns: the demons have returned to their own primal element.

The thinking of Jewish apocalyptic has its direct continuation within the NT in Revelation. The sea is viewed as the realm of the devil and of the demons (Rev 12:12), as the abyss from which the beast—the type of the antichrist—arises (11:7; 13:1) as the embodiment of Babylon, i.e., Rome (18:21). The sea is annihilated in the judgment (8:8ff.; 20:13; 21:1), in which the power of Satan and of death is broken.

6. Fig.-symbolic usage is present when the capacity to walk on the water is promised to the unshakable believer. The prototype of such usage is the Reed Sea miracle of the Exodus (so Heb 11:29), and the distinct narrative form is seen in the motif of the preservation of faith in the midst of temptation in the story of Peter's walking on the water (Matt 14:28-31). The doubter, however, will—as it is figuratively expressed—sink into the water; at times he is compared to the unpredictable elements (Jas 1:6; Jude 13). The fate of "being sunk" is threatened to those who give occasion for offense (cf. the usage of σκάνδαλον; Mark 9:42 par. Matt 18:6/Luke 17:1f.).

7. Finally, θάλασσα appears in comparisons such as "as numerous as the sand of the *sea*" (Rom 9:27; Heb 11:12; Rev 20:8; cf. Gen 22:17; Isa 10:22; Hos 2:1) and metaphors such as "*sea* of glass" (Rev 4:6; 15:2).

R. Kratz

θάλπω *thalpō* warm (vb.); care for*

The fig. sense *bestow great care on,* of the mother with her children, 1 Thess 2:7. Of the wife whom the husband should *cherish* as "his own flesh," Eph 5:29. Spicq, *Notes* I, 365f.

Θαμάρ *Thamar* Tamar*

The daughter-in-law of Judah and mother of Perez and Zerah (Gen 38:6, 27-30). In the NT only in Matt 1:3. G. Kittel, *TDNT* III, 1-3; H. Stegemann, FS Kuhn 246-76; for further literature see *TWNT* X, 1100.

θαμβέω *thambeō* be alarmed*
θάμβος, ους, τό / ον, ὁ *thambos* astonishment, fear, terror*

1. Occurrences and meaning — 2. In reaction to theophany — 3. In reaction to healing — 4. In reaction to authoritative teaching — 5. In reaction to divine working

Lit.: G. BERTRAM, *TDNT* III, 4-7. — O. BETZ and W. GRIMM, *Wesen und Wirklichkeit der Wunder Jesu* (1977) 51f., 77-92, 105. — JÖRG JEREMIAS, *Theophanie* (1965). — W. MUNDLE, *DNTT* II, 620-26. — R. OTTO, *The Idea of the Holy* (²1950), esp. 13-19. — G. THEISSEN, *Urchristliche Wundergeschichten* (SNT 8, 1974) 78-80, 102-6.

1. Θαμβέω appears 3 times in the NT (all trans. and pass.), θάμβος likewise 3 times. The vb. and noun are related to the Indo-European root *dhabh*, "strike, be struck," and refer to the absolute terror pressed upon a person in the context of divine revelation. It indicates a sudden bewilderment and total shock. The compound → ἐκθαμβέω is intensive.

Θαμβέω and θάμβος alternate with the relatively synonymous φοβέομαι, τρέμω (τρόμος), ἐξίσταμαι (ἔκστασις), and ταράσσομαι. It renders no specific OT Hebrew term, but is used rather for a variety of Heb. vbs. such as *bāhal* niphal, *bāʿaṭ* niphal and piel, *ḥāpaz* qal and niphal, *ḥārad, pāḥad* qal and piel, and *rāgaz*, which denote either a movement caused by fear or the emotional state in itself (Bertram 5). The OT theophany tradition is the essential theological foundation for NT usage of θαμβέω/θάμβος. The stem is used in a similar way in classical Greek; cf. Polybius xx.10.9: ἔκθαμβοι γεγονότες ἔστασαν ἄφωνοι πάντες, οἱονεὶ παραλελυμένοι καὶ τοῖς σώμασι καὶ ταῖς ψυχαῖς διὰ τὸ παράδοξον τῶν ἀπαντωμένων. Illustrative also is Plutarch fragment 178 (ed. F. H. Sandbach, *Moralia* VII [1967] 107): In death one must go through τὰ δεινὰ πάντα, φρίκη καὶ τρόμος καὶ ἱδρὼς καὶ θάμβος and then enter into the sphere of φῶς τι θαυμάσιον.

2. According to Luke 5:9 the first "appearance" of Jesus before Peter results in a θάμβος in connection with a miracle, i.e., the terror experienced in the presence of the revelation of the Holy One (cf. Exod 3:5-6; Isa 6:1ff.). This indicates that Peter's call to be a fisher for people occurs in a way that is as compelling as that of the OT prophets. Peter comes to know Jesus at once as the "holy one of God" who, like Moses, reflects the radiance of God for a limited period of time (cf. Exod 34:29-35).

Exod 34:29ff. also explains Mark 9:15 (against Bertram 6n.13): As Jesus returns from the Mount of Transfiguration, the people are *greatly amazed* (ἐξεθαμβήθησαν)—apparently by the radiance of his glory. The "miracle of the radiance" in Mark 16:5, 6 is similar: The women at the empty tomb *were fearful* in the presence of the young man in radiant apparel. Corresponding to the event of the theophany the fear is taken away from them: "Do not be afraid" (μὴ ἐκθαμβεῖσθε).

3. The reaction of the bystanders to an exorcism is described in Mark 1:27 par. Luke 4:36 with θαμβέω/θάμβος: Fear in the presence of a theophany is intended, as is indicated by the flashing and by the bewildered knowledge of the "holy God" (Mark 1:24) and of his unique authority (v. 27). Acts 3:10, 11 also has theophanic elements: The onlookers were filled with θάμβος (here "reverential enthusiasm") and ἔκστασις; the entire people ran together with the apostles "in reverential astonishment" (ἔκθαμβοι; D θαμβηθέντες).

4. In view of Mark 1:27 (the authoritative teaching that evokes amazement) it seems appropriate to understand θαμβέω in 10:24 as amazement in the presence of the holiness of God that has come near in the teaching of Jesus.

5. In whatever way the syntactical problem of Mark 10:32 is solved (by distinction between "followers" in the narrower sense and unnamed people who accompany them?), θαμβέω refers here to the fear of those who recognize God at work (in salvation history!) in the story of the suffering of the Messiah, which is now becoming clear. The emotional duress of Jesus in Gethsemane (Mark 14:33) is also an expression of deep perplexity: direct experience of the divine will in what is now happening.

On the theological problem associated with the word group θαμβέω one may ask: Is Bertram correct (6-7) when he sees in the astonishment or fear responding to a theophany only a "preparatory stage in the Christian possession of salvation," an "attitude" of those who are without? Does it not designate rather moments of the highest certainty, namely that of being overwhelmed by God to the deepest levels of human existence (so Betz and Grimm 77-103)?

W. Grimm

θάμβος, ους, τό / ου, ὁ *thambos* astonishment, fear, terror
→ θαμβέω.

θανάσιμος, 2 *thanasimos* deadly*

In the secondary Markan ending, Mark 16:18: "when they drink something *deadly*, it will not harm them"; Ign. *Trall.* 6:2, of *deadly* poison (so also Philo, Josephus).

θανατηφόρος, 2 *thanatēphoros* death-bringing*

Jas 3:8, of the tongue, which is "a restless evil full of *death-bringing* poison" (cf. Ign. *Trall.* 11:1: καρπὸς θανατηφόρος).

θάνατος, ου, ὁ *thanatos* death*
ἀποθνῄσκω *apothnēskō* die*

1. Occurrences in the NT — 2. Paul — 3. The Synoptics and Acts — 4. The Johannine literature — 5. The later NT writings — 6. Ἀθανασία

Lit.: L. R. BAILEY, *Biblical Perspectives on Death* (1979). — C. C. BLACK II, "Pauline Perspectives on Death in Romans 5-8," *JBL* 103 (1984) 413-33. — H. BRAUN, "Das 'Stirb und Werde' in der Antike und im NT," idem, *Gesammelte Studien zum NT und seiner Umwelt* (³1971) 136-58. — R. BULTMANN, *TDNT* III, 7-25. — W. DIEZINGER, "Unter Toten freigeworden. Eine Untersuchung zu Röm III-VIII," *NovT* 5 (1962) 268-98. — L. FAZEKAŠ, "Taufe als Tod in Röm 6,3ff.," *TZ* 22 (1966) 305-18. — A. FEUILLET, "La règne de la mort et la règne de la vie (Rom. V,12-21)," *RB* 77 (1970) 481-521. — J. GEWIESS, "Das Abbild des Todes Christi (Röm 6,5)," *HJ* 77 (1958) 339-46. — M. GOTHEIM, "Die Todsünden," *ARW* 10 (1907) 416-84. — J. HERKENRATH, "'Sünde zum Tode,'" *Aus Theologie und Philosophie* (FS F. Tillmann; 1950) 119-38. — R. MARTIN-ACHARD, *BHH* 1999-2002. — H. SCHLIER, "Der Tod im urchristlichen Denken," Schlier IV, 101-16. — W. SCHMITHALS, *DNTT* I, 430-41. — E. SCHWEIZER, "Dying and Rising with Christ," *NTS* 14 (1967/68) 1-14. — R. SCROGGS, "Romans VI,7," *NTS* 10 (1963/64) 104-8. — E. STOMMEL, "Das 'Abbild seines Todes' in Röm 6,5 und der Taufritus," *RQ* 50 (1955) 1-21. — L. WÄCHTER, *Der Tod im AT* (1967). — idem, "Spekulationen über den Tod im rabbinischen Judentum," *Kairos* 20 (1978) 81-97. — For further bibliography see *DNTT* I, 446f.; *TWNT* X, 1100-1103.

1. Θάνατος appears 20 times in the Synoptics, 8 times in Acts, 32 times in the Johannine literature (8 in John,

6 in 1 John, 18 in Revelation), 47 times in Paul (22 in Romans, all in chs. 1–8, 8 in 1 Corinthians, 9 in 2 Corinthians, 6 in Philippians, 1 each in Colossians and 2 Timothy), 10 times in Hebrews, and twice in James. Ἀποθνῄσκω is found 23 times in the Synoptics, 4 times in Acts, 32 times in the Johannine literature (26 in John, 6 in Revelation), 37 times in Paul (19 in Romans, 7 in 1 Corinthians, 4 in 2 Corinthians, 2 each in Galatians, Colossians, and 1 Thessalonians, and 1 in Philippians), 7 times in Hebrews, and once in Jude.

2. According to Paul, *death* has entered the world as a personified power, has penetrated to all humanity like an epidemic (Rom 5:12), and has incited all to sin (1 Cor 15:56). Thus from the fall of Adam and as a result of the fall death has established a domain of sovereignty (15:21; Rom 5:14, 17), in which in its turn sin came to power (5:21) among humankind, who deserved the judgment of death through their conduct (1:32) and had to *die* (1 Cor 15:22). All have behaved as slaves of sin (Rom 6:16f.), who in their activities ran toward death as the end of their deeds (6:16, 21). Thus the sinful person uses the good divine commandment in such a way that the power of sin results in futile deeds (7:12). Thus it not only "leads to *death*" (7:10) apart from repentance and salvation and "produces *death*." Such a person carries out "the law of *death*" (8:2), so that the demands present in his intention and striving as "flesh" always produce *death* (8:6). Following the Psalmist, Paul asks, as representative of the groaning creation (8:23), about the one who redeems (7:24) from the "last enemy" (1 Cor 15:26). The question comes out of the experience of "this" reality of death, which takes shape in the bodily existence standing in need of redemption. Thus death's sphere of power is unfolded in a chronological line toward a final time, in which—in new imagery for death—death is paid as wages earned for service to sin (Rom 6:21) or stands before the eyes as a granary, to which the harvest is brought in as husks (7:5).

In christological reflection Paul employs the confessional formula that Jesus has *died* and has been raised (1 Thess 4:14); Jesus' death and resurrection was already interpreted soteriologically ("for us," 5:10). Christ *died* (Rom 8:34) for sinners (5:8), for the weak and ungodly (5:6), for enemies (5:10). Christ's action was thus not called forth by the law of sympathy, according to which a righteous man may call forth admiration and imitation and only a "good" man could be ready to die (5:7). Instead Christ, with his constant readiness to commend his love, has not only kept a person alive by dying; he has liberated us "once for all" (6:10) from the power of sin, a power that he himself has experienced (2 Cor 5:21; Rom 6:10). As the resurrected one he has now eluded the power of death and thus *dies* "no more" (6:9). Paul re-

gards human hostility toward God as brought to an end through the death of Christ (Rom 5:10; cf. Col 1:22).

This is a universal event: Christ is the one who has "*died* for all" (2 Cor 5:14). His death has the result that those for whom he died are the multitude of those who are conscious of the fact that "Christ *died* for the remission of our sins" (1 Cor 15:3). Paul sees two aspects of this: On the one hand, he has in view the universal movement of all people in the fate shared with Adam, so that they inexorably run to meet death ("in Adam all *died*," 15:22). Indeed, they have already been marked with the hand of death ("through the fall of the one the many have died," Rom 5:15). On the other hand, Paul recognizes the universal destiny of all people to experience the end of hostility toward God ("Therefore all *died*," 2 Cor 5:14), as a consequence of which all can make use of the lifetime remaining to them (cf. 1 Pet 4:2!) "for him who *died* for their sake and was buried" (2 Cor 5:15). But this one does precisely by granting an opening to the brother who causes one's Christian life to have a different form, the brother "for whom" or "for whose sake" "Christ *died*" (Rom 14:15; 1 Cor 8:11). In this way they "proclaim the Lord's *death*" in the Lord's Supper in unity of brotherhood (11:26). If the goal of Christ's death and resurrection is lordship over the dead and the living (Rom 14:9), then his death is not to be understood as an egoistic act, but rather as a sacrifice to the Lord (14:7f.).

Anticipation of the experience of death in the words "but I *died*" (Rom 7:10) is to be understood as a fruit of the new life. The concern in Romans 7 is neither a biographical nor a psychologically descriptive I. It is rather the confession of one who has found his new I beyond death in Christ. This person no longer lives as I, but as one who through the struggle within his members (7:23) has found his life in faith in the Son of God (Gal 2:20).

If Paul has put death's power behind him ("*Death*, where is your sting?" 1 Cor 15:55) in faith in the Son of God, he places himself in opposition, on the one hand, to materialistic hedonists who indulge their pleasures in the awareness that tomorrow they will die (15:32). He opposes in a more sweeping way those "who live according to the flesh" (Rom 8:13), who now, as a consequence of their rejection of the gospel, hasten the process of decay ("fragrance from *death* to *death*," 2 Cor 2:16). On the other hand, he also opposes Gnostic enthusiasts who interpret the anticipation of eschatological salvation in such a way that they regard the dying within one's ministry as irrelevant. Paul emphasizes to them the "daily *dying*" (1 Cor 15:31). This daily experience in ministry (2 Cor 4:12; 6:9), which has already caused Paul to receive the "judgment of *death*" (1:9) in a time of acute danger, is for Paul brought about by God, who gives the apostle over to death in order that he may experience the life of Jesus through death (4:11). From such a danger of *death* (or "from such dangers of death," *de tantis periculis,* 2 Cor 1:10 Vg; cf. 11:23) he has experienced the redeeming God (1:10).

Rom 6:2 is to be seen within this context. According to 6:11 those who are baptized regard themselves as "dead." They have died to the power of sin in such a way that, on the basis of the death of Christ, they can be called to the path that leads "from the world of the dead" (6:13), which is equal to "entrance" into the realm of salvation. Paul thus knows a triumphant "we have death behind us" and a sober "we die daily" in meeting life's experience. Thus he expects of Christians that they know how to concern themselves with *death* as hopeful victors (1 Cor 3:22; 15:55). Therefore *death* cannot separate one from the love of God in Jesus Christ (Rom 8:38), who is able to credit the apostle who has "been won" for missionary service through death with an ultimate win, in which the martyr himself has a portion (Phil 1:21; 3:10f.). Paul thus responds to both materialistic hedonism and spiritual fanaticism.

How, where, and when have we *died* with Christ" (Rom 6:8)? One can look neither to the historical crucifixion by itself nor to the historical event of baptism by itself. Instead, with σύν (v. 8) one sees an indication of the pilgrimage of faith ("we believe that we will also live with him"), in which the crucifixion and baptism both have their specific places. Paul recalls *death* at baptism (6:4) in order to remind those who have been baptized that they are to acknowledge from now on the death of the old person, who has been crucified with Christ (6:6, 11). We find the key to understanding 6:5 when we observe Paul's emphasis on the proximity and the distance to the *death* of Christ: Where Christians are spoken of as having "grown together" or having been "united" with Christ once for all, the close relationship with Christ is emphasized—without leading to the thought of mystical dying with Christ in baptism. But where Paul speaks of Christians being united with Christ in the "likeness" of his death, Paul emphasizes that Christ died a unique (atoning) death. Paul needed to emphasize both sides in order to avoid either introducing those who had been baptized into a historicizing view of the death of Christ or enticing them into a mystical emotion-laden idea of union. He desired rather to summon them to the historical path of the new life, in which by faith they put to death the evil deeds of the body (→ θανατόω, Rom 8:13).

Through the death of Christ they are as free from subjection to the law in order to serve God (Rom 7:6) as a wife is free of her deceased husband (7:2f.). This life in the freedom of service to God, which is diametrically opposite to the "service of *death*" (2 Cor 3:7), has been accomplished so that the believer "*has died* to the law through the law" (Gal 2:19) because his Lord, in whom he believes, "was under the law" (4:4). This freedom in

service is so important for Paul that, without his apostolic "boast," it would be left for him only to die (1 Cor 9:15). In order not to diminish the effect of the death of Jesus, the believer must regard himself as one who has been purchased from the power and the curse of the law (Gal 2:21; 3:13). He is thus so much oriented to the resurrection (Rom 6:5) that he dares to use the image of the *dying* grain of seed for the subject of "being made alive." Thus Paul is not interested in an automatic process of animation (cf. *1 Clem.* 24:5), nor in an idea of continuity as such, which the v.l. ζωογονεῖται could suggest (A 89 108 Epiphanius Chrysostom^codd; cf. R. Bultmann, *TDNT* II, 874f.) and which is important to him elsewhere. He is interested rather in the eschatological new creation, an event that will occur with the destruction of death (1 Cor 15:26, 54; cf. 2 Tim 1:10).

In Colossians the theological course apparent in Romans is made precise in relation to the new context: "You have *died* with Christ to the elemental spirits [astral powers]" (Col 2:20). One may ask if "reflective attention" to the meaning of the astral powers leads unconditionally to religious veneration of them (so E. Lohmeyer, *Col, Phlm* [KEK, ⁴1959] 104). "Separation" from (ἀπό) the στοιχεῖα means in practical terms a life freed from rituals and rules (2:21f.) under the dominion of Christ (3:1f.), who will use the "elements" of the world in a transforming action without allowing his liberated children to fall under the sovereignty of the powers.

The statements about death in Philippians are characterized by Paul's ability to see both the completeness of the obedience of Christ "unto *death*" (2:8) and the continuity of the commitment of the ailing Epaphroditus when he was near death (2:27, 30). He thus demonstrates how the one who follows Christ may be "like Christ in his *death*" (3:10), even if Christ is set apart from him in his "*death* on the cross" (2:8).

3. a) In the Synoptic Gospels θάνατος is used of judgment, which for Jesus in Gethsemane, who, unlike Jonah (Jonah 4:9; cf. H. W. Wolff, *Obad, Jonah* [Eng. tr., 1986] 172f.) already experienced the sorrow of death (Mark 14:34; Matt 26:38), led to the punishment of death (F. Büchsel, *TDNT* III, 941f.). It is used similarly in the Passion predictions (Mark 10:33; Matt 20:18), in the Passion narrative (Mark 14:64; Matt 26:66), and in the report of the disciples on the road to Emmaus (Luke 24:20). In Luke Pilate emphasizes the innocence of Jesus, who has committed nothing "worthy of *death*" (Luke 23:15, 22). It is emphasized similarly in the judgment scene before Felix and Festus that Paul has done nothing "worthy of *death*" (Acts 23:29; 25:25; 26:31; cf. 13:28; 25:11; 28:18), even if he once had persecuted Christians "unto *death*" (Acts 22:4). The comment about the readiness of Peter to walk with Jesus the way "to *death*" (Luke

22:33; Mark in 14:31 has [under Pauline influence? cf. Matt 26:35] συναποθνήσκω) resembles another context where Paul's readiness to die steps aside (Acts 21:13a; 25:11) and serves to emphasize the once-for-all death of Jesus, in whose service persons are "handed over to *death*" by their own family members (cf. Mark 13:12; Matt 10:21; → παραδίδωμι).

b) Matthew has Jesus work among his own people, who live "in the land and shadow of *death*" (Matt 4:16; cf. Luke 1:79): death (see Isa 9:2; H. Wildberger, *Isa* [BKAT] on 25:8a; C. Barth, *Die Errettung vom Tode in den individuellen Klage- und Dankliedern des AT* [1947] 53-67) is, on the one hand, the dark realm for the living (S. Schulz, *TDNT* VII, 397) and, on the other hand, the end point of human existence, that which casts its shadow. Those who succumb to it include the demons that enter the swine (Matt 8:32), the men who died without children in the fictitious story told by the Sadducees (Mark 12:19-22; Matt 22:24, 27; Luke 20:28, 29, 31, 32, 36), the rich man and the poor man in the parable (Luke 16:22), even the man Jesus (Mark 15:44), and Tabitha after her illness (Acts 9:37). It is also punishment (cf. Exod 21:17) for those who speak evil of their parents (Mark 7:10; Matt 15:4; cf. C. Schneider, *TDNT* III, 468).

If death casts its shadow, life casts its light: While the multitude sees the epileptic boy already in the realm of death (Mark 9:26, → νεκρός), Jesus takes care that he "arises." Accordingly God takes the *death* of Abraham's father as the occasion for the son to set out to settle in the land of promise (Acts 7:4). Finally, God has caused Jesus himself to rise from the dead after he has loosed the "pangs of *death*" (2:24). Behind this expression stands the messianic expression, applied here to Jesus, that the "womb" of death has released the redeemer in the midst of pain from the captivity in which it had held him. Pain, imprisonment, and motifs of liberation overflow into one another (cf. G. Bertram, *TDNT* IX, 673f.; W. Bieder, *Die Vorstellung von der Höllenfahrt Jesu Christi* [1949] 64-66). Jesus responds to the message that the daughter of Jairus is not only lying at the point of *death* (Luke 8:42), but has finally (cf. Luke 8:53) *died* (Mark 5:35) with the statement that "the girl is sleeping" (→ καθεύδω, Mark 5:39; Matt 9:24; Luke 8:52) in order to attest to death as a reality that is temporally limited. That they will "not taste *death*," i.e., not experience it, is the promise given to the elect who will experience the parousia of the Son of Man and thus the final coming of the kingdom of God (Mark 9:1; Matt 16:28; Luke 9:27).

4. a) The person who believes in Jesus, according to John's Gospel, will not surrender to the fate of death (11:26) and is not content with preservation from death (11:21, 32, 37). He has instead passed from the sphere of death, in which dying occurs as a matter of course (6:49,

58; 8:52f.), is expected (4:47, 49), or is indeed pronounced as a promise of destruction of unloving (1 John 3:14b) sinners (John 8:21, 24; cf. Prov 24:9 LXX; Ezek 18:24). The believer has passed into the sphere of life (John 5:24), where love exists (1 John 3:14). Thus the believer will not "see" death (as a hostile power?), i.e., not experience it (John 8:51f.). Indeed, since he eats bread from heaven, he will "not *die*" (6:50; 11:26; 21:23a). This does not preclude the fact that men such as Lazarus (11:14, 25) or the disciple whom Jesus loved (21:23) must *die*. However, this death is temporary and can therefore be described as sleep (11:11). Lazarus's illness was not meant to end in death (11:4). John emphasizes that Jesus, whom the Jews wanted to execute for blasphemy (19:7), and the martyr Peter have died a special death (12:33; 18:32; 21:19). Jesus died, as Caiaphas, the prophet "without knowing or wishing" it (R. Bultmann, *John*, on 11:51), said, "not only for the people" (→ λαός, 11:50; 18:14) but also to gather the scattered children of God (11:51). His death does not lead to private glorification (→ δοξάζω), but to the "great fruit" in the gathering of those who are in the Diaspora (John 12:24).

b) Even though the "sin unto death" is originally sin that merits the bodily punishment of death (*Jub.* 21:22), the sin mentioned in 1 John 5:16 is not a sin that directly brings about death. It is rather an offense in which the wrongdoer aligns himself by his deed with the futility of death (πρὸς θάνατον) and thus already experiences death as an annihilating power by anticipation in the doing of the evil deed. 1 John does not say that this sin can be "seen" in the brother. However, he warns against this actually existing sin without minimizing the zeal for intercession.

c) In Revelation dying is a part of the judgment imposed by God: the living creatures in the sea (8:9; 16:3) and many people have to die (8:11). The agony of dying is so great that "the natural desire" to die (F. Büchsel, *TDNT* III, 170)— unlike the experience of Paul in Phil 1:23—springs up in those who wish to be spared from further judgments in life before their final death takes away their agony of life (9:6). Θάνατος denotes the realm of the dead (20:13), to which Christ has the key (1:18). It is the "end of life," to which the Christian, as a combatant in the arena, maintains faithfulness (2:10) in the surrender of his self-love (12:11). It is the name of the rider who brings pestilence (6:8a) and then of the pestilence itself (2:23; 6:8b; 18:8; cf. Jer 15:2; Job 27:15), which death, because of its divine authority, allows to come upon humankind. When the "mortal wound" of the beast (13:3, → θηρίον) is healed, it is attested that the power of the antichrist, which is manifested politically in the hostile acts against Christians by the Roman Empire, came to life again after a crisis.

Those who "*die* in the Lord" (14:13) "have come to the end of all hardship *in extremis* in a full and total life decision for Christ" (W. Bieder, *TZ* 10 [1954] 22). In 3:2 the church at Sardis is seen from two perspectives: On the one hand it is spiritually dead (→ νεκρός); on the other hand, as it still has time for repentance, what "remains" is at the point of death. The "second *death*" (20:6, 14; 21:8) is to be understood as the eschatological depravity, which will in turn fall prey to destruction and thus lose its "power" (20:6). If the "second death" is prepared for the rebellious in the time of persecution, the finality of the condemnation of lost sinners is not yet decided, for even this second death itself will come to an end. The time of death is limited. It will "be no more" in any form (21:4).

5. a) According to Hebrews, Jesus could not be saved from death (5:7), but had to go through the suffering of death (2:9) and thus taste death for everyone. Thus he had a fellowship with those who spend their lives in the "fear of *death*" (2:15) or who must die "once," as with Jacob (11:21), perhaps in the midst of blessings (9:27; cf. 11:13), or who must suffer death by the sword (11:37). His death brings about the "redemption" from those sins committed under the first covenant (→ ἀπολύτρωσις, 9:15), which in weighty cases led to the result that the sinner had to *die* upon the testimony of witnesses (10:28). His death brought his testament into effect (9:16). The blood of Jesus thus speaks better than the blood of Abel because the Abel who *died* (11:4), who was regarded as a righteous man and as a judge (*T. Abr.* 11), but who called out for God's avenging justice, could not bring redemption. While the OT priests and levites in their service would face the inexorable boundary of death (Heb 7:8, 23), Enoch, in contrast to Simeon (Luke 2:26), did not experience death, but was taken up (Heb 11:5, → μετατίθημι).

b) James sees death as the offspring of sin (1:15) in a way that is to be contrasted to Paul's view (Rom 6:21; 7:5). The person who brings others to repentance (→ ἐπιστρέφω) can contribute to the sinner's redemption from death, which is seen as a dangerous, life-threatening realm.

c) The "twice-*dead* trees" (Jude 12) are false teachers, who were once as Gentiles far from God and spiritually dead and now demonstrate that they have fallen once more into spiritual death through their heretical behavior at the agape feast.

d) In the confessional fragment in 1 Pet 3:18 the death of Christ "for the remission of sin" is emphasized in its once-for-all significance (→ ἅπαξ 3).

6. Ἀθανασία, *immortality.** Since the mortal has to put on *immortality* (1 Cor 15:53, 54), it is clear to Paul that immortality is nothing inherent in the person or his soul. The NT thus does not indicate that the Lord's Supper is a medicine of immortality (φάρμακον ἀθανασίας, Ign.

Eph. 20:2). Rather, a line of demarcation is drawn between the claims of immortality by the Caesar and God who "alone has *immortality*" (1 Tim 6:16).

W. Bieder

θανατόω   *thanatoō*   kill*

Θανατόω is used of the killing of Jesus (Mark 14:55; Matt 26:59; 27:1; 1 Pet 3:18) and his disciples (Matt 10:21; Luke 21:16).

According to Paul the Roman Christians were redeemed (1 Cor 7:23) by the body of Christ (→ σῶμα) for the resurrected Lord (cf. Rom 14:8). They have *put to death* the old person, which is a loss to the power of the law (Rom 7:4; cf. the context, vv. 1-4). As people who have been made alive, they must put to death evil deeds through the Spirit, i.e., destroy and eliminate by root and branch (8:13) the deeds that one can do (8:12), even though dead (7:10). Thus those who "*are put to death* every day" (8:36; cf. Ps 44:23) are called to an active involvement that allows them to withstand the power of evil in concrete terms. In the midst of tests and chastisements they are paradoxically "not *surrendered to death*" (cf. G. Bertram, *TDNT* V, 624n.178), but as those who are "dying" they are called to remain in life (2 Cor 6:9; Ps 118:8).

W. Bieder

θάπτω   *thaptō*   bury*

1. Occurrences in the NT — 2. 1 Cor 15:4 — 3. Matt 8:21f. par. Luke — 4. Other passages

Lit.: BILLERBECK IV/1, 578-92 (burial of the dead). — M. HENGEL, *The Charismatic Leader and His Followers* (1981) 3-15 (on Matt 8:21f. par. Luke). — H. G. KLEMM, "Das Wort von der Selbstbestattung der Toten," *NTS* 16 (1969/70) 60-75. — J. KREMER, *Das älteste Zeugnis von der Auferstehung Christi* (SBS 17, 1966) 36-39 (on 1 Cor 15:4). — J. NELIS, *BL* 182-85. — R. DE VAUX, *Ancient Israel* (1961) 56-61 (death and burial).

1. The vb. θάπτω appears rarely in the NT, but is common in the LXX, most often for *qābar*. Of 11 NT occurrences, 7 are in Luke-Acts, 3 in Matthew (including Q Matt 8:21, 22 par. Luke 9:59, 60), and 1 in 1 Cor 15:4. The 3 pass. occurrences (all 2nd aor. ἐτάφη) follow the widespread report schema of the OT: "He/she died and was buried" (Luke 16:22; Acts 2:29; 1 Cor 15:4; cf. Gen 35:8, 19; Num 20:1; Deut 10:6; Judg 10:2, 5; 12:7, 10, 12, 15, etc., frequently with the location of the grave named). While θάπτω is usually used literally, the Pauline corpus uses figuratively the compound → συνθάπτω (Rom 6:4; Col 2:12, both pass. and both referring to baptism), which does not appear elsewhere in the NT.

The noun → τάφος (burial, grave) appears 6 times in Matthew and elsewhere in the NT only in Rom 3:13 (fig., in a citation). Also related are ἐνταφιάζω (Matt 26:12; John 19:40) and the noun ἐνταφιασμός (Mark 14:8; John 12:7).

2. In the ancient formula that Paul cites in 1 Cor 15:3b-5, ἐτάφη (v. 4) in reference to Christ stands in second place among the four finite vbs. (after ἀπέθανεν and before ἐγήγερται and ὤφθη). The strictly symmetric arrangement of the formula indicates that "he *was buried*" (ἐτάφη) is coordinated with the reference to death (ἀπέθανεν; → 1). Like the fourth vb. (ὤφθη), ἐτάφη emphasizes the factual nature of the preceding statement, i.e., the death (Kremer 37). A correspondence, now antithetical, probably also exists between ἐτάφη and ὤφθη: The concealment of the one who was buried corresponds antithetically to the open proclamation of the resurrected one. One cannot prove conclusively that the formula with ἐτάφη looks back to the discovery of the "empty tomb" (cf. Mark 16:1-8).

3. In Matt 8:21f. par. Luke 9:59 (Q) a would-be disciple says to Jesus that he wants first to be permitted *to bury* (θάψαι) his father. Jesus responds: "Let the dead *bury* (θάψαι) their own dead." In Matthew the answer precedes the command to "follow me." In Luke the (redactional) addition is made: "But as for you, go and proclaim the kingdom of God." Jesus' refusal to permit the burial of the father places the demand for immediate discipleship (→ ἀκολουθέω 4) above an urgent duty of law and custom and calls for a break with custom and family (Hengel 8-15). When Jesus says that one should let the dead bury their own dead, he probably thinks of a life that no longer stands under the power of death. However, he scarcely intends to describe those who do not follow him as "spiritually dead" (against Hengel 8f.; Klemm). Cf. G. Schneider, *Luke* [ÖTK] I, 230-32.

4. Matt 14:12 (cf. Mark 6:29) reports at the end of the narrative of the murder of John the Baptist that his disciples took the body (τὸ πτῶμα) and buried it. Whether "the body" or (the person of) John is understood as the object of the burial cannot be determined on text-critical grounds (B ℵ * read αὐτόν, C Koine D W have—as Mark 6:29 does—αὐτό).

Luke 16:22 (L) follows this schema: He (the rich man) died and was buried (→ 1). Perhaps the contrast is between his burial (appropriate to his class) and his misery in the realm of the dead (v. 23)—and the fate of the poor man (v. 22a does not have ἐτάφη).

Acts 2:29 says (in Peter's Pentecost sermon) about David "that he died and *was buried* and his tomb (μνῆμα) is among us to this day." The presence of David's tomb in Jerusalem is intended to prove that the previously cited "Davidic" prophecy (Ps 15:8-11 LXX) does not refer to David, but to the resurrection of Jesus, who was not "left in Hades" (v. 31).

In Acts 5:6, 9, 10 θάπτω is used of the burial of Ananias and his wife Sapphira. In vv. 6, 10 the acc. obj. is to be supplied accordingly.

                           G. Schneider

Θάρα   *Thara*   Terah*

The father of Abraham (Luke 3:34 [Gen 11:27-32]).

θαρρέω   *tharreō*   be courageous*

This vb. appears 5 times in 2 Corinthians (5:6, 8; 7:16; 10:1, 2) and in Heb 13:6. 2 Cor 5:6, 8; Heb 13:6: *have good courage/be confident;* 2 Cor 7:16: θαρρέω ἔν τινι, *have confidence* in someone; 10:1: θαρρέω εἴς τινα, *be courageous* toward someone. W. Grundmann, *TDNT* III, 25-27; *TWNT* X, 1103 (bibliography); W. Mundle, *DNTT* I, 327f.; Spicq, *Notes* I, 367-71.

θαρσέω   *tharseō*   be courageous*

In the NT only in the Gospels and Acts. Θαρσέω is probably an older alternative form of θαρρέω. Mark 6:50 par. Matt 14:27: θαρσεῖτε, with the linking (and supporting reason) "It is I, fear not"; Mark 10:49; Matt 9:2 (cf. Mark 12:5); 9:22 par. Luke 8:48 v.l. (cf. Mark 5:34); Acts 23:11: imv. θάρσει; John 16:33; imv. pl. θαρσεῖτε (with "I have overcome the world"). W. Grundmann, *TDNT* III, 25-27; *TWNT* X, 1103 (bibliography); W. Mundle, *DNTT* I, 327f.; Spicq, *Notes* I, 367-71.

θάρσος, ους, τό   *tharsos*   courage*

Acts 28:15: θάρσον λαμβάνω, "take *courage*" (cf. Josephus *Ant.* ix.55). Spicq, *Notes* I, 371.

θαῦμα, ατος, τό   *thauma*   that which is marvelous, miracle; amazement*

In the objective sense of that which causes amazement, 2 Cor 11:14. Rev 17:6, on the other hand: *amazement* (ἐθαύμασα . . . θαῦμα μέγα). G. Bertram, *TDNT* III, 27-42; → θαυμάζω.

θαυμάζω   *thaumazō*   be amazed, be astonished

1. Occurrences in the NT — 2. Meaning — 3. Usage — 4. Miracle stories — 5. The individual Gospels

Lit.: G. BERTRAM, *TDNT* III, 27-42. — G. MINETTE DE TIL-LESSE, *Le secret messianique dans l'évangile de Marc* (LD 47, 1968) 264-78. — W. MUNDLE, *DNTT* II, 621-26. — K. TAGAWA, *Miracles et Évangile. La pensée personnelle de l'Évangéliste Marc* (1966) 92-122. — G. THEISSEN, *Urchristliche Wundergeschichten* (1974) 78-80. — For further bibliography see *TWNT* X, 1103.

1. Θαυμάζω appears in the NT a total of 43 times, most (30) in the Gospels. Luke has the most with 13, Matthew

has 7, Mark 4, John 6, Acts 5, and Revelation 4. Paul uses the vb. only in Gal 1:6 (and 2 Thess 1:10). It occurs also in 1 John 3:16 and Jude 16. The compound ἐκ-θαυμάζω *(marvel greatly)* appears only in Mark 12:17.

2. Θαυμάζω is related by root to θεάομαι ("see") and denotes the amazement that is awakened through sight. It can most often be translated with *be amazed, be astonished* and has several nuances, depending on context. It can refer to a bewildered, questioning astonishment (Luke 24:12; John 3:7) or surprise (Mark 15:44; Luke 1:63) and can also include fear (Luke 8:25). In other instances it involves a joyful (Luke 24:41) or impressed (Matt 9:33) astonishment. Reverence and even adoration can be meant (Rev 13:3; 2 Thess 1:10), as can the opposite, an alienated (Luke 11:38) or rejecting (John 5:20) astonishment. That θαυμάζω in both secular Greek and the LXX often refers to the reaction of people to the presence and action of a deity is to be noted in the interpretation of numerous NT passages.

3. In regard to the subjects to whom astonishment is ascribed, it is noteworthy that in the Gospels it most often refers to a group of people, esp. an indeterminate crowd described as πάντες, οἱ ὄχλοι, οἱ ἄνθρωποι, etc. Less often are the disciples or opponents of Jesus the ones who are astonished.

Θαυμάζω can be used transitively, but more frequently is intrans. The basis for the astonishment can be stated with the preps. ἐπί, διά, ἐν, περί or with a dependent clause introduced by ὅτι or εἰ.

With regard to content, the astonishment in the Gospels is almost always directed to Jesus, his life, and his works (→ 4, 5). Outside the Gospels 2 Thess 1:10 is noteworthy: There it is the Lord that is *marveled at.* In Rev 13:3; 17:6, 7, 8 apocalyptic figures (the beast and the great harlot Babylon) are also objects of astonishment. 13:3 uses the aor. pass. with the act. meaning, which is frequent in later Greek but appears only here in the NT.

The phrase θαυμάζοντες πρόσωπα in Jude 16 also deserves attention. This formula appears in the LXX frequently for Heb. *nāśā' pānîm* and means "have regard for the appearance of a person" (cf. Jas 2:1, προσωπολημψία).

4. The motif of astonishment or fear has its place (not always, of course) in the miracle stories both in the Synoptics and in Jewish and Hellenistic miracle literature (cf. Tagawa 92-94; Theissen 79). Not only is it used of the emotional reaction of the witnesses to the miracle, but it is also a literary means of drawing the reader's attention to the significance of the event described and to the revelation of the divine mystery. The Synoptics also use, along with θαυμάζω (Mark 5:20; Matt 8:27 par. Luke 8:25; Matt 9:33 par. Luke 11:14; 15:31; 21:20),

θαμβεῖσθαι, ἐξίστασθαι, ἐκπλήσσεσθαι, φοβεῖσθαι, etc., with no clear preference.

5. In general, θαυμάζω takes on its own consistent profile in the individual Gospels. For Mark the entire activity of Jesus is accompanied by the astonishment of the disciples and the crowds, especially in the first part of the Gospel up to the confession of Peter (8:27-30). Thus Mark uses θαυμάζω only rarely (5:20; 15:5, 44), and ἐκθαυμάζω once (12:17).

In Matthew, θαυμάζω is predominant among the other vbs. of astonishment, especially in connection with the miracles of Jesus (Matt 8:27; 9:33; 15:31; 21:20). Characteristic of Matthew is the fact that he is normally concerned to interpret the astonishment (λέγοντες, 8:27; 9:33; 21:20; βλέποντας, 15:31). Consequently the attitude of astonishment has a positive evaluation (9:33; 15:31).

Θαυμάζω appears most frequently in Luke. From the birth of Jesus (2:18, 33) to his resurrection (24:12, 41) his life and work evoke astonishment. There is astonishment at his preaching in Nazareth (4:22), at individual miracles (8:25; 11:14), and in response to his entire work (9:43). Astonishment in Luke is positively interpreted as "an awesome sense of astonishment at the divine" (Bertram 39), which is manifest in Jesus. However, it is not yet identical with authentic faith (cf. esp. 4:22; 9:43).

The usage of the Fourth Gospel is different. In John 3:7 and 5:28 (cf. also 1 John 3:13) θαυμάζω stands in a rhetorical expression also known from rabbinic and Hellenistic literature (R. Schnackenburg, *John* I [Eng. tr., 1968] 373). In the Fourth Gospel, like the other Gospels, Jesus is the object of astonishment. However, except in 4:27 (disciples) not his followers, but the Jews are the ones who are astonished (5:20, 28; 7:15, 21). Θαυμάζω is thus "a term for the impact made by the works of Jesus" (Bertram 40).

F. Annen

θαυμάσιος, 3 *thaumasios* wonderful
→ θαυμαστός.

θαυμαστός, 3 *thaumastos* wonderful, astonishing*
θαυμάσιος, 3 *thaumasios* wonderful*

1. Occurrences in the NT — 2. Meaning — 3. Usage

Lit.: G. BERTRAM, *TDNT* III, 27-42. — C. F. D. MOULE, "The Vocabulary of Miracle," idem, ed., *Miracles* (1965) 235-38. — W. MUNDLE, *DNTT* II, 621-25.

1. Θαυμάσιος appears in the NT only in Matt 21:15. Θαυμαστός is also rare (Mark 12:11 par. Matt 21:42; John 9:30; 1 Pet 2:9; Rev 15:1, 3; 2 Cor 11:14 v.l.).

2. In Hellenistic Greek, there is no difference in meaning between the adj. θαυμάσιος and the verbal adj. θαυμαστός (Bertram 27). In John 9:30 τὸ θαυμαστόν

means *the astonishing thing*. Elsewhere in the NT it is to be translated *wonderful* (in the sense of a "wonder").

3. In the LXX, esp. in the Psalms, both adjectives are frequently used of God's marvelous deeds. They also appear in the NT with this meaning (except in John 9:30), including in the Psalm citations in Matt 21:42 par. Mark 12:11 and Rev 15:3. In 1 Pet 2:9 the reference is to the *wonderful* light of God. Rev 15:1 speaks of a *wonderful* sign in heaven. It is significant that the wonders of Jesus are called θαυμάσια only once (Matt 21:15); the NT prefers δυνάμεις and σημεῖα for Jesus' miracles.

F. Annen

θεά, ᾶς, ἡ *thea* goddess*

Acts 19:27 (+ v. 35 v.l.), of Artemis: ἡ μεγάλη θεά, *"the great goddess"* (cf. H. Conzelmann, *Acts* [Hermeneia] 165).

θεάομαι *theaomai* see, behold, look at; consider*

1. NT occurrences — 2. Meaning — 3. Usage

Lit.: R. BULTMANN, *John* (Eng. tr., 1971), esp. 69 nn. 2, 4. — F. HAHN, "Sehen und Glauben im Johannesevangelium," FS Cullmann (1972) 125-48. — K. LAMMERS, *Hören, Sehen und Glauben im NT* (1966), esp. 83-106. — J. MÁNEK, *BHH* 1688f. — W. MICHAELIS, *TDNT* V, 315-82. — H. WENZ, "Sehen und Glauben bei Joh," *TZ* 17 (1961) 17-25. — For further bibliography see *TWNT* X, 1204.

1. This vb. appears 22 times in the NT, 9 times in the Synoptics (4 times in Matt, twice in the inauthentic ending of Mark, 3 times in Luke), 3 times in Acts, once in Paul, 6 times in John, and 3 times in 1 John. The defective vb. appears in the NT only in the pf. and 1st aor. mid. and pass. Pres. and impf. are replaced by θεωρέω. Θεάομαι appears with an acc. obj., often with a complementary partc. or ὅτι. The dat. with the pass. corresponds to ὑπό τινος.

2. Θεάομαι in the NT always signifies the act of seeing with the eyes, as with the other vbs. of seeing (e.g., ὁράω, εἶδον, βλέπω, ὀπτάνομαι, θεωρέω). Nevertheless, it is not a perfect synonym for the other vbs. of seeing; nor is it a t.t. for seeing the resurrected one, seeing glory, or for the seeing that leads to faith.

The etymology of the vb. indicates its particular connotation: it is derived from θέα ("view, appearance"; cf. θέατρον, "theater"; θεατής, "spectator"), and in Homer it is used in solemn, elevated language for astonished, lingering, admiring, reflective observation. This significance can be perceived in the NT, where the vb. regularly connotes intensive, thorough, lingering, astonished, reflective, comprehending observation.

Thus Paul intends not only to see the Roman church, but also to tarry there (Rom 15:24). The Pharisees want

to be admired (Matt 23:5; cf. 6:1). The disciples want to observe closely Christ, who has died (Luke 23:55) and has been raised (Mark 16:11, 14; Acts 1:11). Jesus wants to observe carefully those who are called (Luke 5:27; John 1:38). One observes things, persons, and activities carefully and reflectively (John 4:35; 6:5; Matt 11:7 par. Luke 7:24; 22:11; Acts 21:27; 22:9; 1 John 4:12) and can go beyond reflective observation to an awareness of matters that are not perceptible to the senses (John 1:14, 32; 11:45; 1 John 1:1; 4:14).

Thus the vb. is used of a specific seeing with the bodily eyes (cf. 1 John 1:1: eyes and hands), i.e., in some circumstances, connected to a impression beyond the senses, i.e., to the event of revelation.

3. Θεάομαι refers in most cases to normal perception of earthly persons, things, processes, and activities (e.g., people, disciples, a church, guests, Jesus, a reed, a tomb, fields, light, the process of maturing), but also to what is perceived by unusual perception (e.g., Christ, God, Spirit, glory, resurrection, discipleship).

In the majority of Johannine occurrences (John 1:14, 32; 11:45; 1 John 1:1; 4:14) recognition of Jesus' glory and decision for faith in him follows the seeing of him, his person, and his works.

C. H. Peisker

θεατρίζω *theatrizō* exhibit, place on display*

Heb 10:33: θεατριζόμενοι, *put on display.* G. Kittel, *TDNT* III, 42f.

θέατρον, ου, τό *theatron* theater; play, spectacle*

Acts 19:29, 31, of the amphitheater in Ephesus. With its almost 25,000 seats (F. Rehkopf, *BHH* 1966; *BL* 1736), it could contain the great mass of people incited by Demetrius against Paul and his companions. It is referred to in other texts as a place for public assembly (Deissmann, *Light* 113). In 1 Cor 4:9 Paul uses the word of a spectacle, in order to say, in contrast to the Stoic image of the heroic struggle of the wise man as a worthy spectacle for gods and men (cf. Seneca *Prov.* ii.9; *Ep.* 64.4-6), that God has placed the apostles on public display like men condemned to death: Those who see them believe that they are watching only a wretched spectacle, but they are in reality witnesses of the true struggle of the missionaries of Christ in the world. G. Kittel, *TDNT* III, 42f.; H. Conzelmann, *1 Cor* [Hermeneia] ad loc. (bibliography).

H. Balz

θεῖον, ου, τό *theion* sulphur*

Luke 17:29 (cf. Gen 19:24 LXX): πῦρ καὶ θεῖον, "fire and *sulphur.*" The same combination (at times with καπνός, "smoke") is in Rev 9:17, 18; 14:10; 19:20; 20:10; 21:8.

θεῖος, 3 *theios* divine*

θειότης, ητος, ἡ *theiotēs* divinity*

Lit.: BAGD s.v. — E. Käsemann, *Romans* (Eng. tr., 1980) 36-41. — H. Kleinknecht, *TDNT* III, 122f. — H. Köster, *TDNT* IX, 251-77, esp. 255, 275. — LSJ s.v. — H. Lietzmann, *Rom* (HNT, ⁵1971) 31f. — For further bibliography → θεός.

The concept represented by these words is typical for religious Hellenism, including Hellenistic Judaism, but is represented in the NT only in isolated instances. Lukan theology adopts positively neut. τὸ θεῖον, the *Deity* (Acts 17:29; cf. v. 27 v.l.). Paul also takes up θειότης once in a positive way from Hellenistic philosophy (Rom 1:20; cf. Col 2:9). This is also the case in 2 Pet 1:3, 4, where redemption is described as "participation in the *divine* nature."

H. D. Betz

θειότης, ητος, ἡ *theiotēs* divinity
→ θεῖος.

θειώδης, 2 *theiōdēs* sulphurous*

In the NT only in Rev 9:17 (→ θεῖον), of riders with "*sulphurous* armor."

θέλημα, ατος, τό *thelēma* will (noun)

1. NT occurrences — 2. Meaning — 3. Usage — 4. The Gospels — 5. The Pauline literature — 6. The late apostolic letters

Lit.: H. Frankemölle,*Jahwebund und Kirche Christi* (1974) 275-79 (on Matthew). — E. Käsemann, *Rom* (Eng. tr., 1980). — S. Pancaro, *The Law in the Fourth Gospel* (1975) 368-79. — H. Schlier,*Rom* (HTKNT, 1977). — W. Schrage, *Die konkreten Einzelgebote in der paulinischen Paränese* (1961) 163-73. — G. Schrenk, *TDNT* III, 52-62. — For further bibliography see *TWNT* X, 1103f.

1. Θέλημα occurs in the NT 62 times, of which 60 are sg. and 2 are pl. (Acts 13:22 [citing Isa 44:28 LXX]; Eph 2:3).

2. Θέλημα can represent both (objectively) what is willed and (subjectively) the act of willing. In John 1:13; 1 Cor 7:37 θέλημα refers specifically to male sexual *desire*.

3. In most NT occurrences of θέλημα God's will is spoken of. Twice it is used of the will of the exalted Christ (Acts 21:14; Eph 5:17), once of that of the devil (2 Tim 2:26), and 12 times of human will, most often in contrast to God's will.

4. Among the four Gospels Matthew and John speak more often of the *will* of God (Mark only in 3:35; Luke only in 22:42).

For Matthew the will of God is always "the *will* of the Father" in heaven (→ πατήρ; 6:9f.; 7:21; 12:50; 18:14;

21:31; 26:42). Thus 7:21-23 leaves no doubt that for Matthew—as for Judaism—the will of God is identical with the Torah (→ νόμος): Those who do not do the will of God work lawlessness (→ ἀνομία). Now, however, the law of God reveals the essential goal of God's will as love of God and neighbor (cf. 22:34-40; 24:12). Thus loss of "one of the little ones" cannot be the divine will (18:14; on the use of θέλημα ἔμπροσθεν τοῦ πατρὸς ὑμῶν cf. Dalman, *Worte* 173). The submission of Jesus to God's will is mentioned only in connection with the Gethsemane narrative (Matt 26:42; Luke 22:42).

But in John's Gospel Jesus refers directly to "the *will* of the one who sent me" as the basis and content of his entire life (4:34; cf. 5:30; 6:38). The Father wills the life of those whom he has given to the Son (6:39), and the Son fulfills his will when he raises all those who see him and believe in him at the last day (6:40). In this respect the Johannine Christ embodies the Torah, which likewise has as its goal the life of people (cf. already Deut 28:1-14; 30:15-20). Because the Father's will is the basis for all that the Son says and does, the truth of the Son's teaching is revealed only to the one who likewise is committed to the will of God (7:17).

5. In the Pauline literature also θέλημα is used most often of God's will (the exceptions are 1 Cor 7:37; 16:12; Eph 2:3), which is spoken of from various perspectives:

a) Rom 2:18; 12:2; Col 1:9; 4:12; 1 Thess 4:3; 5:18 refer to the divine will as it presses the person toward acts of obedience; only Rom 2:18, which speaks to Jews, identifies this will with the Torah. God's will is, according to 1 Thess 4:3, the sanctification of the person (ἁγιασμός), according to 5:18, constant thanksgiving. According to Rom 12:2, God's will is "that which is good, well pleasing and perfect," knowledge of which is possible only for one whose mind has been continually renewed through the divine Spirit given in baptism (Käsemann 323-27; Schlier 358-62). In Col 1:9; 4:12 also, knowledge of the divine will is related to the wisdom and insight (σοφία, σύνεσις) given by the Spirit; i.e., it is not connected to a growing knowledge of a document, the Torah, but to growth in the knowledge of God.

b) God's will can also shape the form of one's life: Thus Jesus' sacrifice of his life is based on "the *will* of our God and Father" (Gal 1:4). Thus Paul is called to be an apostle "through God's *will*" (2 Cor 1:1; cf. Col 1:1; Eph 1:1; 2 Tim 1:1), and thus the advance of his apostolate is determined by God's will (Rom 1:10; 15:32). However, the extraordinary commitment of the Macedonians in the collection for the Jerusalem church is rooted in God's loving will (cf. 2 Cor 8:1, 5).

c) The subject of the opening blessing in Ephesians is the divine (saving) will that determines the entire human and cosmic history: God's benevolent (→

εὐδοκία) will, which is now (through the ministry of the apostle, 3:1-11) made known (1:9) and which has the purpose of summing up everything in Jesus Christ (1:9f.), is the true basis for the fact that "those who believe in Christ Jesus" (1:1) have become God's children and have attained to God (1:5, 11).

6. In the late apostolic writings there is no doubt of the fundamental and decisive power of the divine will, esp. in view of Jesus' Passion (Heb 10:7, 9f.) and suffering (1 Pet 3:17; 4:19). It is always the will of the "faithful Creator" (1 Pet 4:19; cf. Rev 4:11), he who intends good toward humankind (1 John 5:14; cf. Heb 10:10) and who equips each person with what is needed to fulfill his will, i.e., "that which is pleasing before him through Jesus Christ" (Heb 13:21). M. Limbeck

θέλησις, εως, ἡ *thelēsis* willing, will*

Heb 2:4: "according to his [God's] *will*." G. Schrenk, *TDNT* III, 62.

θέλω *thelō* will, be willing; want, desire

1. Occurrences in the NT and meaning — 2. Usage — 3. The Gospels. — 4. Paul's letters — 5. The non-Pauline letters

Lit.: H. RIESENFELD, "Zum Gebrach von ΘΕΛΩ im NT," *Arbeiten und Mitteilungen aus dem neutestamentlichen Seminar zu Uppsala* 1 (1936) 1-8. — G. SCHRENK, *TDNT* III, 44-52. — For further bibliography see *TWNT* X, 1103f.

1. Θέλω appears 209 times in the NT. Most often it signifies *willing*—whether in the sense of wish (Matt 20:21; 1 Cor 4:21; Gal 4:20, etc.), decision and intention (Luke 13:31; John 6:67; Gal 1:7; 1 Thess 2:18, etc.), or command (Matt 18:23; Luke 1:62; Rev 11:6). Under the influence of LXX usage, which uses θέλω as a tr. of *hāpēs bᵉ*, "have a liking for," θέλω can also mean *have a liking for, love* (Mark 12:38; Matt 9:13/12:7 [citing Hos 6:6 LXX]; 27:43 [citing Ps 21:9 LXX]; Luke 20:46; Heb 10:5, 8 [citing Ps 39:7 LXX]; Col 2:18). Θέλω appears in the weakened sense of *want* in Acts 2:12; 17:20. In 2 Pet 3:15 it has the unusual meaning of *affirm something* in opposition to the actual fact.

2. The subjects of θέλω can be God (Matt 9:13; 12:7; 27:43; Rom 9:16, 18, etc.), the exalted Christ (1 Cor 4:19), and the devil (Luke 4:6), but in most cases θέλω is used of human willing.

3. According to the consistent witness of the NT writings the basic and controlling function of the will of God is to be found in the realization of human and cosmic salvation (→ θέλημα). Nevertheless the human will is not insignificant. This can be seen especially in the Synop-

tics, in which several features are noteworthy: a) Θέλω is used of God's will in only three or four instances (Matt 9:13/12:7 [citing Hos 6:6 LXX]; 20:14, 15; and indirectly Mark 14:36 par. Matt 26:39). b) Jesus speaks of his own will at most just 5 times (Mark 1:41 par. Matt 8:3/Luke 5:13; Mark 14:36 par. Matt 26:39; Matt 23:37 par. Luke 13:34; Matt 15:32; Luke 12:49). c) Once what is spoken of is the will of the devil (Luke 4:6). d) In all other instances θέλω refers to human volition.

When one disregards theologically irrelevant passages (Matt 2:18; 5:40, 42; Mark 6:22; Luke 5:39; 8:20, among others), it is further noteworthy that human volition is spoken of in two connections: 1) in connection with healings, in which it is specified that the individual must *want* to be healed (Mark 1:40f. par. Matt 8:2f.; Luke 5:12f.; Mark 10:51 par. Matt 20:32; Luke 18:41; Matt 15:28), and 2) in connection with discipleship to Jesus, both where Jesus formulates the conditions of discipleship (Mark 8:34f. par. Matt 16:24f.; Luke 9:23f.; Mark 10:35f., 43f. par. Matt 20:21, 26f.; Matt 7:12 par. Luke 6:31; Mark 9:35; Matt 19:17, 21; Luke 14:28) and where he seeks in the parables to win people to specific patterns of conduct (Matt 13:28; 18:30; 21:29; 22:3; Luke 15:28; 19:14, 27). The life of following Jesus is dependent on the will of the individual. Thus the call to discipleship in the word of Jesus occurs as inquiry and invitation, not as a "must."

John also knows of human will (cf. 5:21; 6:67; 7:17; 15:7). But for John the individual is so totally "determined from outside" (8:44; 17:24; 21:18, 22f.) that there is no interest in the individual's will.

Mark and John place statements about Jesus' will in the service of christology: Jesus' lordship is revealed in the capacity to act from his own will (Mark 3:13; 6:48; 7:24; 9:30; John 1:43; 5:21; 6:11; 7:1; 17:24).

4. If in only a few passages in the proclamation of Jesus he speaks of his own will (→ 3), this reserve changes in a striking way in the Epistles of Paul: of the 53 occurrences of θέλω in Romans, 1 Corinthians, 2 Corinthians, Galatians, 1 Thessalonians, and Philemon, 25 are first person sg. (including Romans 7) and 2 first person pl. as a circumlocution for the sg.

Paul is conscious that it is God who acts on the human will and brings about its accomplishment (Phil 2:13; cf. Rom 9:16, 18). Yet this does not prevent him from *wishing* that "all were as I" (1 Cor 7:7; cf. 14:18f.)—and this is in no way limited to the question of marriage or singleness. It is esp. his knowledge that he wishes to become the knowledge of his addressees ("*I do* not *want* to leave you in ignorance": Rom 1:13; 11:25; 1 Cor 10:1; 11:3; 12:1; 2 Cor 1:8; 1 Thess 4:13) and to shape the conduct of their lives (cf. Rom 16:19; 1 Cor 7:32; 10:20; 14:5; 2 Cor 12:20). Wherever Paul, as in Corinth or Galatia, comes into contact with an "alien will," his passionate opposition and resistance are awakened (2 Cor 11:12; Gal 1:7; 4:9, 17-21; 6:12f.).

5. The (not) willing of the addressees is the concern in the non-Pauline letters (of 23 occurrences in these letters θέλω is first person sg. twice [Col 2:1; 3 John 13] and first person pl. once [Heb 13:18]). The norm is Scripture (cf. Heb 12:17; Jas 2:20-26; 1 Pet 3:8-12) or the saving work of Christ (cf. 1 Tim 1:4-7; 2:1-4; 1 Pet 3:17f.; Rev 2:21).   M. Limbeck

θεμέλιον, ου, τό *themelion* foundation, basis*
θεμέλιος, ου, ὁ *themelios* foundation, basis*
θεμελιόω *themelioō* found, establish*

1. Usage and occurrences — 2. Literal usage — 3. Fig. usage

Lit.: A. FRIDRICHSEN, "Themelios, 1 Kor 3,11," *TZ* 2 (1946) 316f. — P. L. HAMMER, "Canon and Theological Variety in the Pauline Tradition," *ZNW* 67 (1976) 84-86. — H. MUSZYNSKI, *Fundament, Bild und Metapher in den Handschriften aus Qumran. Studie zur Vorgeschichte des neutestamentlichen Begriffs ΘΕΜΕΛΙΟΣ* (AnBib 61, 1975). — K. L. SCHMIDT, *TDNT* III, 63f. — For further bibliography see *TWNT* X, 1104.

1. Θεμέλιον, -ος is attested in secular Greek (first in Homer) in both literal and fig. usage. It is a subst. adj. in which the masc. form (understanding λίθος) is more frequent. In most NT passages, however, because the endings are the same, whether it is masc. or neut. cannot be determined with certainty. The LXX uses θεμέλιον, -ος only in the literal sense, though one cannot dismiss the possibility that passages such as Isa 28:16; 54:11 have influenced NT usage and usage in Jewish literature (including Qumran). The use of the vb. coincides with that of the adj. The adj. form appears in the NT 16 times and the vb. 5 times. On the fig. use, which appears only in the epistolary literature, cf. → οἰκοδομή and → ἑδραίωμα.

2. In the Gospels both subst. and vb. are always literal. In the parable of the house on the rock (Matt 7:21-27 par. Luke 6:46-49), which concludes the Sermon on the Mount and illustrates metaphorically the contrast between (only) hearing and (also) doing, Luke uses the subst. adj. twice of the *foundation of the house* (6:48f.). Matthew speaks of the *founding* of the house on the rock (Matt 7:25; Luke 6:48 v.l., apparently under the influence of Matthew). In the same way θεμέλιος in Luke 14:29 is used (in a metaphor of building a tower) of the *foundation* of a tower. In Acts 16:26 the *foundations* of the prison are called θεμέλια.

In Heb 11:10 and Rev 21:14, 19 (bis) θεμέλιος is used of the *foundations* of the heavenly city and the twelve (so Rev 21:14) *foundation stones* of the heavenly city, which (so 21:14b) is erected on the basis of the apostles.

Here is seen the common apocalyptic concept of the unshakable foundations of the heavenly city established by God. In Heb 1:10, Ps 101:26 LXX is cited: God *created* the earth.

3. The fig. use is limited to the epistolary literature and has its emphasis in the Pauline and post-Pauline tradition. As in contemporary Judaism (e.g., 1QS 7:17; 8:4ff.) and Greek literature (e.g., Epictetus *Diss.* ii.15.8) θεμέλιον, -ος is used metaphorically of the building of the community and its teaching ("system of instruction").

In relation to this image of the building up of the Church, Paul does not want to build on the *foundation* of another (Rom 15:20). Here the "foundation" is the work of other missionaries. In 1 Cor 3:10-12 (ter) Paul likens himself to a "skilled master builder," who lays the right *foundation,* the only one that can be laid, namely Jesus Christ. This statement is a response to the variety of parties that call on their respective leaders. In Eph 2:20 this thought has been essentially changed, for now the apostles and prophets determine the *foundation.* Also different is the related metaphor in 2 Tim 2:19: As the context indicates, the *foundation* is now the Church itself (cf. Hammer on the development of this metaphor).

In 1 Tim 6:19 θεμέλιον is used of the *foundation* for the future that one can gather through good works. In Heb 6:1 it is the *foundational* teaching. According to Eph 3:17 the addressees are *grounded* in love; according to Col 1:23 they continue, firmly *grounded* in faith; according to 1 Pet 5:10 God *establishes* the believers: In all three passages the vb. is used in reference to persons.   G. Petzke

θεμέλιος, ου, ὁ *themelios* foundation, basis
→ θεμέλιον.

θεμελιόω *themelioō* found, establish
→ θεμέλιον.

θεοδίδακτος, 2 *theodidaktos* instructed by God*

1 Thess 4:9: "you are yourselves *taught by God* to love one another." Cf. *Barn.* 21:6: "Βε θεοδίδακτοι" (= let yourselves be taught by God). E. Stauffer, *TDNT* III, 121; Spicq, *Notes* I, 372-74.

θεομαχέω *theomacheō* fight against God

Acts 23:9 Koine joins to the anacoluthon "But if a spirit or an angel spoke to him—?" the request μὴ θεομαχῶμεν: ". . . *let us* not *resist God*" (probably in dependence on 5:39, → θεομάχος). O. Bauernfeind, *TDNT* IV, 528.

θεομάχος, 2 *theomachos* fighting against God*

Acts 5:39: "You might even be found *opposing God*," in the counsel of Gamaliel. Luke is hardly directly dependent on Euripides *Ba.* 45, 325, 1255 (θεομαχέω). A. Vögeli, *TZ* 9 (1953) 415-38; O. Bauernfeind, *TDNT* IV, 528; H. Conzelmann, *Acts* (Hermeneia) ad loc.

θεόπνευστος, 2 *theopneustos* inspired by God*

In 2 Tim 3:16 θεόπνευστος is attributive and refers to πᾶσα γραφή ("every Scripture" or statement of Scripture): "Every Scripture *inspired* by God is also profitable (καὶ ὠφέλιμος) for teaching/instruction." E. Schweizer, *TDNT* VI, 453f.; C. Brown, *DNTT* III, 491f.; A. Piñero, *Filologia Neotestamentaria* 1 (1988) 143-53.

θεός, οῦ, ὁ (ἡ) *theos* God, god (goddess)

1. General usage — 2. The Jewish and Hellenistic background of NT usage — 3. The NT understanding of "God" — 4. NT teaching concerning God — a) Jesus — b) The Synoptics — c) John — d) Paul — e) The rest of the NT — 5. Other deities — 6. Divine men — 7. Polemical usage

Lit.: On 1: BAGD s.v. — CHANTRAINE, *Dictionnaire* 429f. — C. DEMKE, *TRE* XIII, 645-52. — FRISK, *Wörterbuch* I, 662f., III, 104. — K. GOLDAMMER, et al., *RGG* II, 1701-17. — H. KLEINKNECHT, *TDNT* III, 65-121 (bibliography). — LSJ s.v. — H. RINGGREN, *TDOT* I, 267-84. — W. SCHMAUCH, *BHH* 585-89.
On 2: H. D. BETZ, *Lukian von Samosata und das NT* (TU 76, 1961) 23-59, index s.v. θεῖος, θεός, Gottmensch. — idem, ed., *Plutarch's Ethical Writings and Early Christian Literature* (SCHNT 4, 1978), index s.v. θεῖος, θεός, God(s). — idem, ed., *Plutarch's Theological Writings and Early Christian Literature* (SCHNT 3, 1975), index s.v. θεῖον, θεός, God(s). — W. BURKERT, *Griechische Religion der archaischen und klassischen Epoche* (1977) 406-8. — NILSSON, *Geschichte* 569-78. — H. STEGEMANN, "Religionsgeschichtliche Erwägungen zu den Gottesbezeichnungen in den Qumrantexten," *Qumran, sa piété, sa théologie et son milieu* (ed. M. Delcor; 1978) 195-217. — G. WIDENGREN, *Religionsphänomenologie* (1969) 46-129.
On 3: G. EBELING, *Dogmatik des christlichen Glaubens* I: *Der Glaube an Gott den Schöpfer der Welt* (1979) 158-91.
On 4: H. D. BETZ, *Gal* (Hermeneia, 1979) 213-19. — idem, "Jesus as Divine Man," *Jesus and the Historian* (FS E. C. Colwell, 1968) 114-33. — BULTMANN, *Theology.* — CONZELMANN, *Theology,* index s.v. God. — J. COPPENS, ed., *La Notion biblique de Dieu: Le Dieu de la Bible et le Dieu des philosophes* (1976). — C. DEMKE, "'Ein Gott und viele Herren,'" *EvT* 36 (1976) 473-84. — C. H. HOLLADAY, *Theios Aner in Hellenistic Judaism: A Critique of the Use of this Category in NT Christology* (1977). — G. REIM, "Jesus as God in the Fourth Gospel: The OT Background," *NTS* 30 (1984) 158-60. — J. SCHLOSSER, *Le Dieu de Jésus* (LD 129, 1987). — W. SCHRAGE, "Theologie und Christologie bei Paulus und Jesus auf dem Hintergrund der modernen Gottesfrage," *EvT* 36 (1976) 121-54. — C. SPICQ, *Dieu et l'homme selon le NT* (1961) 13-100. — W. STENGER, "Die Got-

tesbezeichnung 'lebendiger Gott' im NT," *TTZ* 87 (1978) 61-69. — D. L. TIEDE, *The Charismatic Figure as Miracle Worker* (1972). — For further bibliography see Coppens, Holladay, and Tiede.

1. In the NT (ὁ) θεός is used frequently as the common term for the deity. The nom. appears with or without the def. art. In the other cases as well the art. can be absent without any apparent difference in meaning. Thus (ὁ) θεός has become a fixed term (see BDF §§254.1; 268.2; BAGD). Ἡ θεός (Artemis) appears in Acts 19:37 (→ θεά, → Ἄρτεμις). The Jewish practice of avoiding the divine name through circumlocution is found also in the NT (see Matt 5:33-37; cf. BDF §130.1; Billerbeck I, 330ff.; H. Bietenhard, *TDNT* V, 252ff.), but is not systematically followed through. One reason for this is that θεός is not actually a name of God but rather a title (see Kleinknecht 65ff.; Burkert 406ff.). The etymological derivation of θεός is still uncertain (see Frisk, Chantraine).

2. The NT concept of θεός is linked to the Jewish doctrine of God in the Hellenistic period. The tetragram is avoided in the NT as in Jewish writings (see L. M. Pákozdy, *BHH* 1956). The NT also takes over Jewish monotheism (→ εἷς, → μόνος) and the struggle against polytheism, so that it has recourse to the Hellenistic critique of religion (Gal 4:8f.; 1 Cor 8:4-6; 10:10; Rom 1:18-23; Acts 7:40; 8:9ff.; 12:22; 14:11ff.; 17:18ff.; 19:23ff.). The one who is revered in the NT is called "the only true *God*" (John 17:3; also 3:33; Rom 3:4; 1 John 5:20) and the "living *God*" (Matt 16:16; 26:63; John 6:57; Acts 14:15; 2 Cor 3:3; 6:16; 1 Thess 1:9; cf. Rev 1:8).

On the other hand the NT interpretation of God and his work is the basis for the separation of Judaism and Christianity. The NT development is indicated in the expansion of the predicates for God through christological and soteriological formulas (cf. Rom 15:6; 2 Cor 2:17; 11:31; Gal 1:1, 3f.; Eph 3:2, etc.). The separation from the Jewish understanding goes hand in hand with a convergence with the Hellenistic-philosophical understanding. The theologically unique feature in the NT doctrine of God consists in the development of christology and soteriology.

3. The existence of God is presupposed in the NT, as in all of antiquity. However, θεός does not essentially designate the existence of God, but rather his presence, his epiphany. In the cult the individual calls on God and experiences his presence (see 1 Cor 14:24f.). This experience can be of an enthusiastic type and can be expressed in compelling astonishment, in fear and joy. The appropriate reactions to this experience are thanksgiving, doxology, and prostration (cf. Luke 17:15f.; 18:9ff.; John 11:41; Rom 1:8ff.; 7:25; 16:25ff.; Gal 1:5, etc.).

Characteristic of the NT understanding of God is the relationship between the transcendence and immanence.

On the one hand God is "in heaven" (Matt 6:9f. par.; 7:11; 11:25) and strictly distinguishable from everything that is of this world. On the other hand, however, he is present (Matt 6:1-18; Rev 1:8) and omniscient (Matt 6:8, 32; Acts 1:24; 15:8). John 4:24 gives a programmatic formulation: "*God* is Spirit, and those who worship him must worship him in Spirit and in truth." It is thus "idolatry" to want to limit his presence to temples or statues (John 4:20ff.; Acts 7:48; 17:24; Rom 2:22; 1 Cor 8:4; 10:7, 19; 12:2).

As a rule all of the terms for God drawn from human language and the human conceptual world are to be regarded only as metaphors. Thus all attributes of God must be considered metaphors (→ κύριος, → πατήρ, → ὕψιστος, etc.). Also metaphorical are all gen. phrases such as βασιλεία τοῦ θεοῦ, δύναμις τοῦ θεοῦ, πνεῦμα τοῦ θεοῦ, υἱὸς τοῦ θεοῦ, etc. (see BAGD s.v.). Attempts to define God are thus exceptional (cf. Acts 14:15ff.; 17:23ff.; Rom 15:33; 1 Cor 14:33; 2 Cor 1:3; 13:11; 1 Thess 5:23; 1 Pet 5:10): God is Spirit (John 4:24), light (1 John 1:5), love (4:7f., 16).

4. Although instruction concerning God stands in the center of the NT proclamation, this teaching never appears as an isolated subject or speculative theistic system. Instruction about God occurs instead when the topic is the individual, i.e., the individual's relationship to God, to his fellow human, and to the world. Christology and soteriology are both aspects of teaching about God. It is characteristic not only of the NT, but of antiquity in general, that sayings about θεός can be made only within the framework of human self-understanding and the human experience of life. Bultmann's judgment on Pauline theology is thus undoubtedly correct and also holds true of all instruction concerning God: "Every assertion about God is simultaneously an assertion about man and vice versa. For this reason and in this sense Paul's theology is, at the same time, anthropology" (Bultmann, *Theology* I, 191).

a) Jesus' teaching about God stands in close association with the Judaism of his time, but within the various teachings about God in the Jewish theology of this period Jesus occupies a distinct place. The characteristic feature neither may be described simply as "Christian," nor be contrasted to Judaism as non-Jewish. It is true that Jesus' teaching about God is sharply profiled and polemical, especially against the Pharisees. But it does not go beyond Jewish thought, but instead is concentrated on central statements of the Jewish doctrinal tradition. The question of which commandment is "first" is answered by Jesus in total agreement with orthodoxy and its use of the *šᵉmaʿ yiśrāēl* of Deut 6:4: "Hear, O Israel, the Lord our *God* is the only Lord" (Mark 12:28-34).

For Jesus it is not a matter of dispute whether the Torah is be fulfilled, but only what is to be considered fulfillment of the Torah in God's eyes. In the Torah God demands the whole person (Mark 12:33), not merely respect for isolated prescriptions taken literally (see the antitheses of the Sermon on the Mount in Matt 5:21-48 as well as the hermeneutical principles in 5:17-20).

Jesus' proclamation of the imminence of God stands in close association with this idea. The primary term for this is "the kingdom of God," by which God's presence is interpreted as the βασιλεία; i.e., this originally apocalyptic term is taken from the distance of the other world and placed within "imminent expectation": "the time is fulfilled, and the kingdom of God is at hand" (Mark 1:15). To declare this imminence of God anew is the overall significance of Jesus' preaching (esp. the parables) and deeds.

God's imminence is expressed in prayer in the address "Father" (Matt 6:9-13; Luke 11:2-4; → ἀββά, → πατήρ). As certain as it may be that this address is present in Jewish tradition and common in antiquity (see H. Ringgren, *TDOT* I, 1-19; G. Schrenk, *TDNT* V, 951-59; G. Quell, *TDNT* V, 965-69), the uniform use of this address in the Jesus tradition indicates that it was typical of his teaching about God. Calling God "Father" implies a relationship of trust between God and humankind, which on the human level is analogous only to the relationship between a child and his or her father. The father's role is seen in his care and kindness (Matt 6:9-13 par.; Matt 5:45; 6:25-33) and in his mercy and readiness to forgive (Matt 6:12 par.; 6:14 par.; Luke 15:1-10, 11-32; 18:9-14, etc.). Answering to this on the human side is "sonship," an old eschatological expectation (cf. Matt 5:9; Rom 8:19; 2 Cor 6:18) that has, like the kingdom of God, come near (Matt 5:45, 48; cf. Gal 3:26-28; 4:4-7; 1 Thess 5:5). Jesus' crucifixion represents the extreme crisis of belief in the Father (cf. Mark 14:32-36 par.; Luke 23:34, 46). But according to the theology of Mark, in Jesus' cry of dereliction, "My God, my God, why have you forsaken me?" (Mark 15:34), his sonship is manifested: "Truly, this man was the Son of God!" (v. 39).

b) In the Synoptic Gospels there is little interest in the development of teaching concerning God. More to the point, the the Son of God christology is implicitly a doctrine of God (see Mark 1:9-11, 14f., 24; 3:11; 4:11f.; 8:27ff.; 14:61ff. par.; Matt 4:1ff., 13ff.; 11:25ff.; 16:13ff.; 28:16ff.; Luke 2:10ff.; 24:19ff., 25ff., 44ff.; Acts 1:3ff., etc.).

c) On the other hand John develops the teaching concerning God further, in harmony with his christology and soteriology. The christologies of the Johannine sources are brought together and subsumed under the logos christology (see the Johannine hymn in 1:1ff.). Jesus is the absolutely divine revealer, the preexistent logos, the creator of everything, who took on human form and appeared as "divine man." But his creation rejected him; to the few disciples who recognized and accepted him he promised the kingdom of God (cf. 3:3, 5; 18:36). The title "Son of God" is reserved for Jesus (1:18, 34, 49; 3:16ff., etc.; 20:31). The Father sent him (3:17, 28, 34; 5:36, 38; 6:29, 57; 10:36; 17:18ff.; 20:21), which was a deed of love (3:16, 35; 10:17; 14:21ff.; 15:9; 17:24, 26). In him God has shown his δόξα (1:14; 2:11; 8:54; 13:31f.; 14:13; 17:1ff.; 21:19).

As the perfect revealer Jesus is himself θεός (1:1b; 20:28). In this title, which appears here first in the NT, (cf., however, Phil 2:6; cf. also → εἰκών) the older predicative meaning of θεός shines through. Of course a distinction is made between the Father and the Son: the Son has "come from" the Father (3:2; 8:42; 13:3; 16:27ff.; 17:8) and has taken on human form (1:14) to reveal the knowledge of God (3:1ff., 17ff.; 10:14f., 38; 17:3ff.) and to return then to the Father (3:8; 7:33; 8:14, 21f.; 13:3, 33, 36; 16:5, 10, 17). The Father and the Son are, nonetheless, one (10:30, 38; 14:7ff.; 17:11, 21ff.) in that which constitutes the nature of God: in → ἀγάπη (3:16; 10:14ff.; 13:1ff.; 14:21ff.; 15:9ff.; 17:23ff.). Because God is ἀγάπη (1 John 4:7ff.; 5:1ff.), Jesus is, as the one who perfectly portrays it (3:16-21; 4:34; 5:36; 17:4, 23; 19:28, 30), θεός.

d) In the authentic Pauline Epistles the traditional Christian teaching about God is changed only slightly. The numerous uses of θεός stands in essential contrast to Paul's slight interest in the doctrine of God in the narrower sense. But Paul does establish a few noteworthy accents. With all of the weight on christology, Paul holds firmly to monotheism (→ εἷς 3): behind everything is the saving will of God (Gal 1:4; 1 Cor 1:1; 2 Cor 1:1; 8:5; Rom 1:10; 12:2; 15:32; → θέλημα 5). God is the source of all χάρις (Rom 1:7; 3:24; 5:15ff.; 1 Cor 15:10) and the goal of redemption (1 Cor 15:20-29). Great significance is placed on the final judgment and of the required → δικαιοσύνη (Gal 2:15-21; 5:5; Rom 1:16f.; 3:21ff.; 8:3ff.). The doctrine of God's wrath is strongly shaped by this presupposition (Rom 1:18ff.; → ὀργή). In the same connection the apostle expresses a sharp critique against the contemporary decadence in the realm of religion (Rom 1:18-24) and morality (vv. 25-32). This critique is strongly influenced by Hellenistic philosophy. The ultimate goal for Paul and his gospel is the proper worship of God (Rom 12:1-2; Gal 4:8-10).

e) The teaching concerning God in the deutero-Pauline letters and the Pastorals is limited to the transmission of teaching formulas (see, e.g., Eph 2:4-10; 4:5f.). Evident is assimilation to the language and thought forms of the mysteries (Eph 3:1-19; 4:24; Col 3:1-4, 12-17) and of ordinary Hellenistic piety (see the summary of the Christian τέλος in 1 Tim 1:5-11). Little remains to be said of Hebrews, 1 and 2 Peter, Jude, and Revelation; one notices only that in these writings the

language of Diaspora Judaism, including apocalyptic, stands in the foreground.

5. Non-Christian deities are referred as θεός only in polemical contexts (Acts 7:40, 43; 19:37; 2 Thess 2:4), with the exception of the reference to the "unknown God" (Acts 17:23). Terms such as οἱ λεγόμενοι θεοί (1 Cor 8:5) and οἱ φύσει μὴ ὄντες θεοί (Gal 4:8) are to be understood against the background of Hellenistic philosophy of religion (see Betz, *Galatians* 213ff.).

6. The use of θεός in reference to humans is predominantly rejected as "pagan" (Acts 3:12; 10:26; 12:22ff.; 14:11ff.; 28:6). Christology plays a special role. While the gospel traditions exhibit forms of a θεῖος-ἀνήρ christology (see Betz, *Jesus*), John first speaks of Jesus as θεός (→ 4.c). But this christology must be justified against the charge that a man is being deified (John 10:29ff.).

7. Θεός is given a negative value when it is affirmed of opponents in Phil 3:19 that their *god* is the belly. This critique is probably originally a proverb, and is perhaps anti-Epicurean (cf. Billerbeck III, 622; Lohmeyer, *Phil, Col, Phlm* [KEK] 154f.). Indeed, the devil can be called ὁ θεὸς τοῦ αἰῶνος τούτου (2 Cor 4:4).   H. D. Betz

θεός, οῦ, ἡ   *theos*   goddess*

In Acts 19:37 the town clerk (v. 35) says that Paul and his companions "are neither temple robbers nor do they blaspheme against our *goddess* [Artemis]."

θεοσέβεια, ας, ἡ   *theosebeia*   reverence for God, religion*

1 Tim 2:10 in parenesis directed to women, who should "profess *religion* through good works." In addition to *2 Clem.* 20:4, the noun appears esp. in *Diog.* (1:1; 3:3; 4:5, 6; 6:4). G. Bertram, *TDNT* III, 123-28; *TWNT* X, 1109 (bibliography); Spicq, *Notes* I, 375-78.

θεοσεβής, 2   *theosebēs*   pious, God-fearing*

John 9:31: "If anyone is a *worshiper of God* and does his [God's] will, God listens to him." G. Bertram, *TDNT* III, 123-28; *TWNT* X, 1109 (bibliography); Spicq, *Notes* I, 375-78.

θεοστυγής, 2   *theostygēs*   hating God*

Before the NT this adj. is attested only in the pass. meaning *hated by God* (e.g., Euripides *Tr.* 1213) or *God-forsaken*. In the catalog of vices in Rom 1:30 the active meaning *hating God* is seen (so clearly *Ps.-Clem. Hom.* 1:12; cf. the subst. θεοστυγία, "hatred of God," *1 Clem.* 35:5).

θεότης, ητος, ἡ *theotēs* deity*

Lit.: H. S. NASH, Θειότης–Θεότης, Rom I.20; Col. II.9," *JBL* 18 (1899) 1-34. — E. SCHWEIZER, *Col* (Eng. tr., 1982) 137f. — E. STAUFFER, *TDNT* III, 119.

The abstract noun θεότης, derived from θεός, appears in the NT only in Col 2:9: In Christ lives πᾶν τὸ → πλήρωμα τῆς θεότητος σωματικῶς. The noun θεότης is not found, e.g., in the LXX or Josephus, but is attested in other Hellenistic literature (Plutarch, Lucian, Proclus; cf. also *Corp. Herm.* 12:1; 13:7a). Θεότης means (in contrast to θειότης, "divinity, divine quality") "deity, the rank of God." In early Church literature (already in *Herm. Man.* x.1.4; xi.5.10, 14) θεότης takes on new importance and is frequently used (see *PGL* s.v. [637-39]).

The meaning of the Colossians passage is not entirely clear. It can mean: In Christ *the deity* lives (not only partially, but) in its totality (cf. Bornkamm, *Aufsätze* I, 144f.). In light of 1:19 (in Christ lives πᾶν τὸ πλήρωμα), however, the gen. τῆς θεότητος appears to be epexegetical: In Christ the entire fullness, i.e., *the deity*, lives bodily/actually (cf. J. Ernst, *Col* [RNT] 198-200). The actualizing extension of 1:19 (Schweizer 137) gives additional explanation of the term πλήρωμα with respect to its essential content (Ernst 199). In Christ lives "not just the divine nature in itself, but also together with the resurrection body the beginning of the redeemed creation" (Ernst 200).

G. Schneider

Θεόφιλος, ου *Theophilos* Theophilus*

Lit.: H. J. CADBURY, *Beginnings* II, 507f. — idem, *The Book of Acts in History* (1955) 113. — E. HAENCHEN, *Acts* (Eng. tr., 1971) 136. — K. LAKE and H. J. CADBURY, *Beginnings* IV, 2. — H. SCHÜRMANN, *Luke* (HTKNT, 1969) 13f. — B. H. STREETER, *The Four Gospels* (1936) 539. — A. VÖGTLE, "Was hatte die Widmung des lukanischen Doppelwerks an Theophilos zu bedeuten?" *idem, Das Evangelium und die Evangelien* (1971) 31-42. — A. WIKENHAUSER, *LTK* X, 87.

1. The Greek name Θεόφιλος appears from the third century B.C. Because of the neutral theophoric element, Jews frequently bore the name (Cadbury, *Book*).

2. Theophilus, to whom Luke addressed his Gospel and Acts, was instructed in Christian teaching, according to Luke 1:4. One cannot determine whether a Greek or Jewish origin is signified by the name. The address κράτιστε (Luke 1:3; omitted in Acts 1:1) can designate members of the senatorial or equestrian (*vir egregius* or *clarissimus*) rank. But in Luke 1:3 it is not titular, but instead an honorific address ("most excellent Theophilus"). One cannot therefore conclude anything about the Christian faith among the leading ranks. Clear indicators for this can be found around A.D. 200 (Tertullian *Apol.* 37.4). Theophilus is not addressed as a man of

position and rank, but rather as a Christian to whom respect is given. He is thus a historical figure; the name is not a symbol for all who love God (so the fathers after Origen). He is likewise not a pseudonym for a clandestine Christian from the Roman imperial court (T. Flavius Clemens, consul in A.D. 95—so Streeter). The dedication to Theophilus does not signify that this is a private letter, but emphasizes instead the claim of the author to portray the apostolic kerygma in its worldwide significance.

W. Pöhlmann

θεραπεία, ας, ἡ *therapeia* service, healing, servanthood
→ θεραπεύω 7.

θεραπεύω *therapeuō* heal, make well

1. Basic meaning and occurrences in the NT — 2. Types of healings — 3. The relationship of healing to Jesus' proclamation — 4. The manner of the healings — 5. Healings by the apostles — 6. In nonmessianic contexts — 7. Θεραπεία

Lit.: O. BETZ, *TRE* XIV, 763-68. — O. BETZ and W. GRIMM, *Wesen und Wirklichkeit der Wunder Jesu* (1977) 30-66. — H. W. BEYER, *TDNT* III, 128-31. — J. A. COMBER, "The Verb *therapeuō* in Matthew's Gospel," *JBL* 97 (1978) 431-34. — R. and M. HENGEL, "Die Heilungen Jesu und medizinisches Denken," *Medicus Viator* (Festgabe R. Siebeck, 1959) 331-61. — B. LINDARS, "Elijah, Elisha and the Gospel Miracles," *Miracles* (ed. C. F. D. Moule; [2]1966) 62-79. — A. NOLAN, *Jesus Before Christianity* (1977) 30-66. — K. SEYBOLD and U. MÜLLER, *Krankheit und Heilung* (1978). — A. SUHL, *Die Wunder Jesu, Ereignis und Überlieferung* (1968), esp. 7-23. — G. THEISSEN, *Urchristliche Wundergeschichten* (1974) 98-101. — For further bibliography see *TWNT* X, 1109.

1. The vb. appears 43 times in the NT, esp. in Matt (16 times) and Luke-Acts (Gospel 14 times, Acts 5 times); there are 5 occurrences in Mark, 1 in John, and 2 in Revelation. The detailed accounts in the Gospels demonstrate that θεραπεύω is not used in the Jesus tradition of a therapeutic process in the modern sense, but rather of the effect of the healing deed of Jesus. NT usage is thus linked to the last stage of the linguistic development in the Greek-speaking world, where θεραπεύω can mean "serve" and then also—in view of the service of physicians—"serve a sick person," "give medical treatment." From there it is a small step to the effective sense "make well" (e.g., Plato *Grg.* 513d; see Beyer 128f.). Because of the eschatological significance and the presence of the miraculous (→ 3) in the healings of Jesus, the appropriate tr. is *heal (miraculously)* or *make whole*, i.e., restore a person to health.

The vb. appears occasionally in the words of Jesus (Matt 8:7; Luke 14:3), but most often in narrative comments, very frequently in summaries and redactional notes (Mark 1:34; 3:10; 6:5, 13; Matt 4:23f.; 8:16; 12:22; 14:14; 15:30; 19:2; 21:14; Luke 4:40; 5:15; 6:18; 7:21; 8:2).

2. Θεραπεύω is used of both exorcistic activities (Matt 4:24; 12:22; 17:16; Luke 6:18; 8:2) and the removal of bodily ailments such as blindness and lameness (e.g., John 5:10). This is one reason, among others, that Jesus' healings and exorcisms of demons are not to be sharply distinguished.

3. The acts of healing are not described as interruptions of causal connections within natural law, but rather as manifestations of the kingdom of God in the struggle of the powers (cf. esp. Matt 11:2-6; 12:28). Thus they are repeatedly called δυνάμεις (Matt 11:20ff.; 14:2; Mark 6:2, 5, 14; 9:39; Acts 2:22). They are mentioned alongside the proclamation of the gospel (Matt 4:23; 9:35). Jesus' θεραπεύειν is the saving of life and the restoration of the creation (Mark 3:2, 4, 5; cf. 8:25; Luke 13:13), the loosing of Satan's bonds (Luke 4:18; 13:16; cf. Mark 3:27; 7:35), and always an eschatological event, marked as such by Jesus' preference for healing on the sabbath (Mark 3:4; Luke 13:16; 14:3; John 5:9; 9:14): The eschaton is "sabbath" time (Isa 61:1f. and Luke 4:19; Matt 11:28). Jesus' conflict with the Pharisees regarding the sabbath reveals two different understandings of θεραπεύω: The Evangelists use the word of (eschatological, prophetically proclaimed [cf. Isa 26:19; 35:5ff.; 53:4; 61:1ff.]) saving event (Luke 13:13, 16; cf. John 5:9ff.; 9:14ff.); the Pharisees think of a secular medical activity, one forbidden on the sabbath (Luke 13:14; cf. John 5:9ff.; 9:14ff.).

4. Four aspects of the healing activity of Jesus are significant:

a) The motive: The initiative normally comes from the sick persons. Jesus heals from a passionate mercy, sometimes increased to a holy wrath because of the injured creature (Mark 1:41, 43; 3:5; 6:34; 7:34; 8:2; 9:19; John 11:33, 38).

b) The outward means: Very rarely is there "medical" involvement or "medicines" (Mark 7:33; 8:23), more frequently simply contact such as grasping the hand or touching with the hand (Mark 1:31; 5:23, 41; 6:5; 7:32; 8:23, 25; 9:27; Luke 4:40; 13:13; 14:4).

c) The force behind the healing: This is the unconditional, mountain-moving (volitional) faith of the sick person (Mark 6:5f.; 5:28f., 34; 10:52; Luke 17:19; cf. Mark 11:23; Matt 17:20) or of one who intercedes (Mark 2:3-5; 5:36; 7:25ff.; 9:23f.; Matt 8:5ff.; 15:28), which cooperates with the faith or concentrated will of Jesus (Mark 1:40ff.; 9:24; Matt 15:28).

d) Characteristic of Jesus is power as creator: The spoken word is enough by itself; it is "immediately" (εὐθύς, παραχρῆμα) turned to reality, in analogy to the creative word that overcame chaos (cf. Gen 1–2: Matt 8:8, 13; Mark 1:41f.; 2:11f.; 3:5; 7:34f.; Luke 13:12f.; cf. also the words of "struggle" in Mark 1:25f.; 5:8; 9:25f.).

5. The Twelve receive a part of the messianic authority: They are sent out in pairs to preach the basileia and to heal (Matt 10:1; Luke 9:1f.; 10:9; cf. Mark 3:15; 6:7). Successful healings are reported in Mark 6:13; Luke 9:6; 10:17, while an unsuccessful one is reported in Mark 9:18. The apostles' post-Easter preaching is accompanied by miraculous healings (θεραπεύω appears in Acts 4:14; 5:16; 8:7; cf. 3:1ff.; 8:7; 9:32ff.; 28:8f.). In contrast to Jesus' intention, these have come to be regarded as conclusive σημεῖα (4:16; 5:12).

6. In Acts 17:25 θεραπεύω is used (as already in Plato *Euthphr.* 13d) of cultic service that the creator of heaven and earth and the Father of Jesus Christ does not need. It is used in a nonmessianic sense of a temporary healing of the wound of the dragon, the antichrist (Rev 13:3).

7. The noun **θεραπεία**, *healing, service**, corresponds in meaning to the vb. in the Jesus narrative (Luke 9:11) and in Rev 22:2, where the reference is to the tree that provides *healing* for the nations. In the parable in Luke 12:42 it is used of *household servants*, for whose care a faithful steward is sought.

                                           W. Grimm

θεράπων, οντος, ὁ   *therapōn*   servant*

Heb 3:5, of Moses (as in Exod 4:10; Num 12:7; Wis 10:16, so also *1 Clem.* 4:12; 43:1; 51:3, 5; *Barn.* 14:4), who—in contrast to the "Son," Jesus Christ (v. 6)—is only a *servant*. H. W. Beyer, *TDNT* III, 132.

θερίζω   *therizō*   reap, harvest (vb.)*
θερισμός, οῦ, ὁ   *therismos*   harvest (noun)*

1. Occurrences and meaning — 2. Usage of θερίζω — 3. NT uses of θερίζω — 4. Θερισμός

Lit.: A. VAN DEN BORN, *BL* 432f. — DALMAN, *Arbeit* III, 1-66. — F. HAUCK, *TDNT* III, 132f. — F. MUSSNER, *Gal* (HTKNT, 1974) 403-7. — SCHULZ, *Q* 288-98. — A. WEISER, *Die Knechtsgleichnisse der synoptische Evangelien* (1971) 226-72. — For further bibliography see *TWNT* X, 1109.

1. The vb. appears 21 times in the NT and the noun 13 times. Paul does not use the noun, but uses the vb. 7 times. In the non-Pauline Epistles only James has the vb. (once). The remaining occurrences are distributed among the Synoptics, the Gospel of John, and Revelation: The vb. is used 3 times each in Matthew and Luke, 4 times in John, and 3 times in Revelation; the noun is used once

in Mark, 6 times in Matthew, 3 times in Luke, and once in Revelation.

The literal meaning, *harvest,* is present in Matt 6:26 (par. Luke 12:24) and John 4:36 (bis). The transition to the fig. sense is present already in John 4:36, where "reaping" is brought into association with "eternal life." James 5:4 refers to literal *reapers.* The noun is used in the literal sense in John 4:35 (bis).

2. Θερίζω frequently appears in connection with σπείρω, "sow" (Matt 6:26; 25:24, 26; Luke 12:24; 19:21, 22; John 4:36b, 37; 1 Cor 9:11; 2 Cor 9:6 bis; Gal 6:7, 8 bis). "Sowing and *reaping*" are the beginning and the end of a growth process. In proverbial usage (Gal 6:7b; Matt 25:24, 26; Luke 19:21, 22; John 4:37) a fig. expression from the OT (Ruth 2:3ff.; Prov 22:8; Job 4:8; Sir 7:3) is taken up and given a new interpretation. Apocalyptic traditions are taken up in Rev 14:15 (bis + θερισμός): The one who sits on the clouds is summoned to send the sickle and to *reap* "because the hour has come to *reap,* because the *harvest* of the earth has become ripe" (→ 3.e; cf. *Gk. Apoc. Ezra* 4:28ff.; *2 Bar.* 70:2ff.); the idea of judgment is associated with the images of sowing and reaping.

3. a) In 1 Cor 9:11 Paul distinguishes between sowing spiritual good and *reaping* material benefits (τὰ σαρκικά); the Christian missionaries have a claim on earthly support (Rom 15:27) after they have already sown spiritual benefits. The idea of judgment is expressed in Gal 6:7b-9. V. 7b introduces the idea with the statement: "Whatever a person sows, that will he also *reap.*" V. 8 gives the proof for the correctness of this statement on a theological level: The contrast between sowing and *reaping* becomes a soteriological contrast between → σάρξ and → πνεῦμα or between corruption and eternal life (cf. Rom 6:20-23). While 2 Cor 9:6 uses the contrast expressed in the statement to point to the correspondence between deed and recompense, the statement is radicalized in Gal 6:7b-9: The "eschatological future" (Mussner ad loc.) emphasizes that destruction and eternal life both grow out of the soil in which they were sown. But ethical motivation is not left out of account, as the use of θερίζω in v. 9 indicates. The relationship of sowing and *reaping* "provides a motive for human conduct in the present aeon" (Hauck 133). The indicative continues in the imperative as an appeal for the responsibility of the individual not to become weary in doing good.

b) Matt 25:24, 26 and Luke 19:21, 22 use the vb. twice each in the parable of the money held in trust. The evil servant, who did not manage his money, says out of fear and for his own justification that his master is hard (σκληρός; Matthean hapax) or severe (αὐστηρός; Lukan hapax); he *reaps* where he has not sown, he gathers where he has not scattered (Luke has altered and rearranged the

text: Schulz, *Q* 291, *contra* Weiser, who does not attribute the parable to the Q tradition). In v. 26 the servant's charge is affirmed by the master (cf. Jülicher II, 483) but in the form of a question: The master takes the servant at his word and thus justifies his act as judge.

c) John 4:36-38 stands in the context of missionary theology. He who *reaps* receives his wages already, which is defined more precisely as "fruit for eternal life" (v. 36a); for he who sows and he who *harvests* should rejoice together (cf. the joy of harvest in Isa 9:2; Ps 125:5f. LXX), i.e., the Father and the Son (R. Schnackenburg, *John* I [Eng. tr., 1968] 451). After the transitional saying in v. 37, v. 38 gives the concrete significance: In the future (cf. 20:21) the disciples are those who are sent by Jesus and who *reap* although they have not entered into the labor. "The task of the disciples then is only one of harvesting" (R. Bultmann, *John* [Eng. tr., 1971] 199).

d) In the judgment saying against the rich in Jas 5:1-6 landowners who withhold wages from the reapers are presented as examples. V. 4, which is formed in a synthetic parallelism, speaks in the second part of the outcry of the *reapers,* which has reached the ears of God (cf. Gen 4:10; Isa 5:9; *1 Enoch* 47:1; 97:5). The content of the saying has been shaped already in the OT (Sir 34:25f.; Deut 24:14f.; Lev 19:13, etc.) and expresses the view that God does justice to the disenfranchised and will requite the rich for their unrighteous conduct.

e) Rev 14:15, 16 announces the last judgment in the image of the harvest. The Son of Man (from 19:11-13 one is able to give concrete shape to the undefined saying of 14:14) has the harvest sickle (δρέπανον, in the NT only in Mark 4:29 and 7 times in Rev 14) in his hand in order to *harvest* the ripe crop. The image of the harvest is not described in greater detail. However, it suggests the eschatological gathering of the elect by the Son of Man (cf. Mark 4:29; 13:27; Matt 3:12; 9:37; 13:30). The *harvesting* of the lost is scarcely in view (so, among others, E. Lohse, *Rev* [NTD] 79).

4. **Θερισμός** is used literally in John 4:35. The missions-oriented saying (→ 3.c) is introduced by the affirmation that there are yet four months, and then is the *harvest (time).* Jesus corrects this position ("there is yet time enough"). The harvest (as eschatological event) is already at hand; for the fields are "glistening (white) for *harvest* (πρὸς θερισμόν)," i.e., the *harvest* must begin.

Mark 4:29 (in Mark only) uses the image of the *harvest* in a saying about God's activity in judgment. Here the parable of the seed growing secretly is concluded with a citation from Joel 4:13: When the seed bears its crop, the *harvest* time has arrived.

In Matt 13:30 (bis, M), 39 (M) the idea is: weeds and wheat will be separated from each other on the day of the *harvest.* Matthew uses the metaphorical saying in the context of the concrete situation of his Church: In the interpretation of the parable (Matt 13:36-43) the harvest is understood as the end of this aeon and thus as the conclusion of the Church's time of testing.

Matt 9:37f. and Luke 10:2 have adopted a Q logion according to which "the *harvest* is great, but the laborers are few . . ." (θερισμός 3 times in each Gospel: Matt 9:37, 38a, b; Luke 10:2b, c, d). The image from the daily life of Palestine refers to the necessity of gathering the ripe harvest, thus of having many harvest workers available. The logion expresses the fateful discrepancy between the urgency of the task and the limited number of workers on the day of harvest (cf. A. Polag, *Die Christologie der Logienquelle* [WMANT 45, 1977] 71).

Rev 14:15 has the phrase "the *harvest* of the earth": → 2, 3.e.   A. Sand

θερισμός, οῦ, ὁ *therismos* harvest
→ θερίζω 4.

θεριστής, οῦ, ὁ *theristēs* harvest worker, reaper, mower*

In the NT only in Matt 13:30, 39 of the reapers, who must first bind the weeds (v. 30). In the allegorical interpretation of the parable the θερισταί are the angels (v. 39), who gather "the sons of the evil one" (vv. 38, 41f.).

θερμαίνομαι *thermainomai* warm oneself*

Mark 14:54, 67, of Peter, who warmed himself at the fire (θερμαινόμενος, par. John 18:18b, 25). John 18:18a of the servants who made a charcoal fire at the court of the high priest and *"warmed* themselves." Jas 2:16, in speaking of those who refused the poor real help and sent them away with the words, *"Be warmed* and filled" (also of clothing in Hag 1:6; Job 31:20).

θέρμη, ης, ἡ *thermē* heat*

Acts 28:3, of a poisonous snake that came out of the burning twigs "on account of *the heat*" (ἀπὸ τῆς θέρμης) and bit Paul's hand.

θέρος, ους, τό *theros* summer*

In the parable of the fig tree (Mark 13:28 par. Matt 24:32/Luke 21:30): When the tree produces leaves, "you know that *summer* is near."

Θεσσαλονικεύς, έως, ὁ *Thessalonikeus* Thessalonian*

Residents of the city of → Θεσσαλονίκη (Thessalonica). In the salutations in 1 Thess 1:1 and 2 Thess 1:1: "to the ἐκκλησία Θεσσαλονικέων." Acts 20:4 names the

Thessalonians Aristarchus and Secundus as companions of Paul. 27:2 mentions Aristarchus again ("a Macedonian *from Thessalonica*") as a companion of Paul.

Θεσσαλονίκη, ης *Thessalonikē* Thessalonica*

A Macedonian city on the Thermaic Gulf founded around 315 B.C. north of the ancient city of Therme. Paul founded a Christian congregation in Thessalonica according to Acts 17:1-10a. V. 1 mentions a Jewish synagogue in which Paul preached for three weeks (v. 2). Those who came to faith included not only Jews, but also "God-fearing Greeks" (v. 4). An uproar against Paul and Silas was instigated from the Jewish side (vv. 5-10a); thus the Jews of Beroea were described as "nobler than those in Thessalonica" (17:11); 17:13 mentions "the Jews from Thessalonica." In Phil 4:16 Paul speaks of his stay in Thessalonica, during which the Philippians supported him. 2 Tim 4:10 says that Demas has abandoned Paul and gone to Thessalonica. On the history of the city and its church see E. Oberhummer, PW VI/1, 143-63; H. Leclercq, *DACL* XV/1, 624-713; B. Rigaux, *1-2 Thess* (ÉBib) 3-32; B. Reicke, *RGG* VI, 850f.; E. Meyer, *LAW* 3069; O. Volk, *LTK* X, 108-11; *KP* V, 761-63 (bibliography); W. Elliger, *Paulus in Griechenland* (1978) 78-116.

Θευδᾶς, ᾶ *Theudas* Theudas*

According to Acts 5:36 Gamaliel recalls the appearance of *Theudas* and his four hundred followers: "He was slain, and all who followed him were dispersed and came to nothing." According to Josephus *Ant.* xx.97-99 the revolt of the Jewish insurgent occurred in the time of the governor Cuspius Fadus (from A.D. 44), making the date given in Acts chronologically incorrect. Schürer, *History* I, 455f.; E. Haenchen, *Acts* (Eng. tr., 1971) 252, 257.

θεωρέω *theōreō* see, watch, view as a spectator

1. Occurrences in the NT — 2. Meanings — 3. In John

Lit.: R. BULTMANN, *John* (Eng. tr., 1971). — E. HAENCHEN, "Der Vater, der mich gesandt hat," Haenchen I, 68-77. — F. HAHN, "Sehen und Glauben im Johannesevangelium," FS Cullmann (1972), 125-41. — W. MICHAELIS, *TDNT* V, 315-70. — F. MUSSNER, *Die johanneische Sehweise und die Frage nach dem historischen Jesus* (1965). — H. SCHLIER, "Glauben, Erkennen, Lieben nach dem Johannesevangelium," Schlier II 279-93. — R. SCHNACKENBURG, *John* (Eng. tr., 1968-82). — H. WENZ, "Sehen und Glauben bei Johannes," *TZ* 17 (1961) 17-25.

1. Θεωρέω is found 58 times in the NT (including John 6:2, where ἐθεώρουν is to be read for the one occurrence of ἑώρων); it is found primarily in the Lukan writings (7 occurrences in Luke, 14 in Acts) and in John (24 occurrences). Paul does not use θεωρέω at all. The vb. is found primarily in the pres. and impf. The impf. replaces ἑώρων,

and in John the present replaces ὁράω. The possible interchange with βλέπω is insignificant, while the interchange with θεάομαι is often based on the subject matter. On the distinctions of basic meanings among the vbs. of seeing, cf. Michaelis, 316ff.

2. Θεωρέω shares in the variety of meanings found in the vbs. of seeing, from simple sense perception to inner comprehension of that which is not subject to sense perception. The basic meaning *observe/view as a spectator* is presupposed in the description of the crucifixion and burial of Jesus (Mark 15:40, 47 par. Matthew; Luke 23:35; however, cf. θεάομαι in v. 55 [!]; John 20:6). John 20:6 moves beyond the basic meaning of literal seeing of an object to the level of an indication that "points to the resurrection" (Schnackenburg III, 312).

Also to be mentioned in this regard is simple seeing of Jesus' signs (John 2:23; 6:2) and deeds (7:3), which is the basis for inadequate faith (cf., however, Bultmann 232 and → 3) or for making a false claim about Jesus (2:23f.; cf. 7:4f.).

Frequently, esp. in Acts, θεωρέω stands for *perceive/recognize* (John 4:19; 12:19; Acts 4:13; 17:22; 21:20; 27:10; 28:6; Heb 7:4). Although supernatural phenomena can also be the obj. of θεωρέω (Luke 10:18; John 20:12; Acts 7:56; 10:11), θεωρέω is not a t.t. for visionary seeing.

3. John 6:40 is especially significant for Johannine use of θεωρέω. Here physical seeing appears not to be intended, and θεωρέω seems to be simply a synonym for πιστεύω. But since 6:36 (ὁράω) suggests a negative possibility (*seeing* and not believing), a distinction is still to be made between θεωρέω and πιστεύω. Accordingly θεωρέω includes the objective possibility of faith in Jesus and is thus the expression of the *claim* of the revelation, which is intended for all.

To be distinguished from this is use of θεωρέω in Johannine passages in which the *possibility* of seeing—for a specific group, for the cosmos in 14:17, 19, for the disciples (!) in 16:10, or for a temporally fixed but limited period (16:16, 17, 19), again for the disciples—is excluded. In the first instance the inability to see is an expression of the total unbelief. This is obviously not the case for 16:10. That the disciples also no longer *see* is, as 16:7 already indicates, to be understood within the framework of 16:16f. There the limitation of the possibility of seeing refers to the time until the coming of the Spirit, in whose activity the revelation continues, not to the time until the parousia and probably not to the time between the Passion and resurrection of Jesus. Only here, therefore, in the time of the Spirit, can θεωρέω or οὐ θεωρέω mean the decision actually made between belief and unbelief.

From this perspective one is also to understand 12:45 (cf. 14:9f.). The verse itself does not cancel out 1:18, nor does it venture a statement about "the inner relationship between Father and Son" (Michaelis 363). Rather, it describes the quality of the event of revelation as one that is historical and thus basically accessible, also as something unique and irreplaceable.

In summary John may have introduced the concept of "seeing" at essential places in the Gospel because he wanted to express both the objective possibility of decision in response to the revelation and thus its comprehensive claim, and at the same time to give conceptual expression to the decision that is made.   M. Völkel

θεωρία, ας, ἡ   *theōria*   sight, spectacle*

Luke 23:48 (cf. Mark 15:39) mentions those "who came to this *sight* [the crucifixion of Jesus]." In 3 Macc 5:24 θεωρία appears in a similar context.

θήκη, ης, ἡ   *thēkē*   container, holder*

John 18:11: "Put your sword into its *sheath*." This meaning of θήκη is also found, e.g., in Josephus *Ant.* vii.284.

θηλάζω   *thēlazō*   give suck; suck*

In the absolute sense: αἱ θηλάζουσαι, in the the lament over *nursing mothers* (Mark 13:17 par. Matt 24:19/Luke 21:23); on the other hand the θηλάζοντες in Matt 21:16 (Ps 8:3 LXX) are *sucklings*. The blessing of the mother's womb and of the breasts "which you *have sucked*" (Luke 11:27) refers to Jesus' mother. On the other hand μαστοὶ οἳ οὐκ ἐθήλασαν (instead of ἔθρεψαν) in Luke 23:29 v.l. (Koine A W) are "Breasts that *have* not *given suck.*"

θῆλυς, 3   *thēlys*   female; subst.: female (animal), woman*

Lit.: BAGD s.v. — G. DAUTZENBERG, " 'Da ist nicht männlich und weiblich,' Zur Interpretation von Gal 3,28," *Kairos* 24 (1982) 181-206. — F. MUSSNER, *Gal* (HTKNT, 1974) 264f. with n. 94.

From the point of view of etymology, θῆλυς signifies "breast feeding" (related to θῆσθαι, from θηλή, mother's breast; cf. Lat. *felare*, "give suck," *filius*, "suckling"). It designates the female among animals, people, and gods. It is connected with ἄρσην in Gen 1:27, and is thus used of sexual differentiation and unity in human couples in Mark 10:6; Matt 19:4 (CD 4:21!). The difference has become meaningless at the level of salvation: Gal 3:28. On the basis of this statement *Gos. Eg.* (Clement of Alexandria *Strom.* iii.92; *2 Clem.* 12:2); *Gos. Thom.* 22; *Acts Thom.* 129; *Gos. Naass.* (Hippolytus *Haer.* v.7.15), the *Gospel of the Valentinians* (NHC I.4.132.21); and *Pistis Sophia* 143 derive the idea of the restoration of the androgynous primal human.

Θήλεια is often a synonym for γυνή (cf. Jdt 9:10; 13:15; 16:5 with Judg 9:54). In Rom 1:26f. θήλειαι is not used pejoratively but because the more common phrase γυναῖκες αὐτῶν could mean "their wives"; Paul mentions female homosexuality before male homosexuality (v. 27) because it, in contrast to male homosexuality, was also despised by Gentiles: According to Lucian *Am.* 28 ὁμιλίαι of men with men are εὐπρεπεῖς ("proper"). But female homosexuality was perceived as a punishment of God (Ovid *Metamorphoses* ix.724-29; cf. Rom 1:24, 26, 28; Seneca *Ep.* 95.21; Martial *Epigr.* i.90.7; Lucian *DMeretr.* 5; there is no depiction on ancient vases). Furthermore, male homosexuality was itself regarded as θήλεια νόσος (Herodotus i.105; Philo *Abr.* 136; *Spec. Leg.* i.325; iii.37; Clement of Alexandria *Prot.* ii.24.1).

J. B. Bauer

θήρα, ας, ἡ *thēra* net, trap*

Rom 11:9, in an (altered) citation of Ps 68:23 LXX: "Let their table become for them a snare and a *trap!*" (θήρα after παγίς, apparently corresponding to Ps 34:8 LXX).

θηρεύω *thēreuō* hunt*

Fig. in Luke 11:54, of the trap by Jesus' opponents, who want to "*catch* him in something he might say" in order to incriminate him (cf. Mark 12:13 par. Matt 22:15/ Luke 20:20). Plato *Grg.* 489b has the phrase ὀνόματα θηρεύων in the sense of "giving chase" to the words of another to see if they make a mistake.

θηριομαχέω *thēriomacheō* fight with wild beasts*

Lit.: BAGD s.v. (bibliography). — A. J. MALHERBE, "The Beasts of Ephesus (1 Cor 15:32)," *JBL* 87 (1968) 71-80.

In the NT only in 1 Cor 15:32: εἰ κατὰ ἄνθρωπον ἐθηριομάχησα ἐν Ἐφέσῳ. It is disputed whether Paul speaks (1) of an actual fight with a beast, or (2) metaphorically of the mortal dangers that he underwent in Ephesus (cf. 1 Cor. 4:9, ὡς ἐπιθανατίους, ὅτι θέατρον ἐγενήθημεν . . . ; so, e.g., H. Lietzmann and W. G. Kümmel, *1–2 Cor* [HNT] ad loc.), or (3) literally of a fight with a beast that has not occurred: "If I . . . should have had to fight with beasts . . ." (so, e.g., B. J. Weiss, *1 Cor* [KEK] ad loc.; J. Héring, *1 Cor* [Eng. tr.] 171f.; see also H. Conzelmann, *1 Cor* [Hermeneia] 277f. with n. 132).

General usage permits literal as well as fig. interpretation of the vb., e.g., in the letters of Ignatius, literal: *Eph.* 1:2 (ἐν Ῥώμῃ θηριομαχῆσαι); *Trall.* 10 (τί δὲ καὶ εὔχομαι θηριομαχῆσαι); cf. *Smyrn.* 4:2 (ἑαυτὸν . . . δέδωκα . . . πρὸς θηρία); fig.: *Rom.* 5:1 (μέχρι Ῥώμης θηριομαχῶ, where a division of soldiers is compared with ten leopards to whom the writer is "chained" during his transport from Syria to Rome; v. 2 speaks again in the lit. sense of a fight with beasts that Ignatius awaits). The image is wide-spread in the ancient agonistic motif (see Malherbe) and belongs to the context of the Cynics' critique of the exaggerated value of athletic achievements: The "battle" of the wise man is the true athletic struggle (cf. also 1 Cor 9:24-27; *1 Clem.* 5:1ff.; 6:1f.).

In 1 Cor 15:29 and 30-32a Paul raises two questions intended to show the ad absurdum nature of the Corinthian denial of the resurrection of the dead. These two questions refer to a Corinthian practice (baptism for the dead, v. 29) and to the apostolic existence of Paul (vv. 30-32a) and are constructed to be parallel to each other: τί clause, εἰ clause, τί clause (v. 31 is inserted as a solemn declaration). While the εἰ clause in v. 29 takes up an affirmation of the Corinthian opponents, v. 32a alludes to the life-threatening struggle of the apostle in Ephesus, which he has taken up of his own accord and for the sake of Christ: "If I, humanly speaking, appeared in Ephesus *as one who fights against wild beasts,* what do I gain [if there is no resurrection of the dead]?" (cf. also 2 Cor 1:8; 4:11; 6:4f.; 11:23ff.; important also in this connection is 1 Cor 16:8). An actual *damnatio ad bestias,* which was decreed only with capital offenses against persons of lower status, would at any rate stand in conflict with Acts 22:25-29, according to which Paul is said to have stood on his rights as a Roman citizen (cf. T. Mommsen, *Römisches Strafrecht* [1899] 925-28). Moreover, Paul would hardly have remained silent about such a condemnation in his catalogs of suffering.

H. Balz

θηρίον, ου, τό *thērion* animal, beast

1. Occurrences — 2. Meaning — 3. Usage

Lit.: O. BÖCHER, *Die Johannesapokalypse* (EdF 41, 1975). — M. É. BOISMARD, "L'Apocalypse de Jean," *Introduction critique au NT* IV: La tradition johannique (1977) 12-55. — W. FOERSTER, *TDNT* 133-35. — H. KRAFT, *Rev* (HNT, 1974). — W. PÖHLMANN, *Die heidnische, jüdische und christliche Opposition gegen Domitian. Studien zur neutestamentlichen Zeitgeschichte* (Diss. Erlangen, 1966). — E. SCHÜSSLER FIORENZA, "Religion und Politik in der Offenbarung des Johannes," *Biblische Randbemerkungen* (1974) 261-72. — For further bibliography see Böcher; Boismard; *TWNT* X, 1109f.

1. Of the 46 occurrences in the NT, 39 are in Revelation (→ 3.b), 1 in Mark, 3 in Acts, and 1 each in Titus, Hebrews, and James (→ 3.a).

2. In Revelation the bestial embodiment of the evil antichrist figure is dominant, but in the rest of the NT occurrences the focus is on the wild, untamed, and dangerous beast. In enumerations there is an indication of the influence of the style of the LXX, according to which θηρία is used of the wild beasts of the land.

3. a) According to Mark 1:13 Jesus, when he was tempted by Satan, was driven out to the dangers of the

wilderness among the *wild beasts*. Inasmuch as it is said that he was served by the angels, no fellowship with the beasts in the sense of a paradiselike situation could be intended.

There is in Peter's vision a fourfold enumeration (Acts 11:6): "Four-footed animals of the earth and *wild beasts*, reptiles, and birds of the heaven." Thus the variety of types of animals are described, and it is said that they can no longer be divided into clean and unclean as in Leviticus 11. In the enumeration in Acts 10:12 there is no reference to the "wild beasts." The Hebraic-sounding phrases presuppose, at least partially, some basic OT passages (see Gen 1:24; 6:11; esp. 7:14 LXX). In Acts 28:4 *beast* is used of a poisonous snake. In Titus 1:12 the Cretans are described as, among other things, "evil beasts." This description is given in a hexameter which, according to Clement of Alexandria (*Strom.* i.59.2), derives from the poet Epimenides.

Exod 19:13 (LXX) is cited in Heb 12:20. Here it is said that the holiness of the mountain of God is not to be profaned by a *wild beast*.

Jas 3:7 names types of animals that can be tamed: *wild beasts* and birds, reptiles, and sea creatures.

b) Revelation (except in 6:8) treats the *beast* as the embodiment of the antichrist's evil, introducing it suddenly and without preparation in 11:7. Coming from the deep, the beast contends with and kills the two prophets of the eschaton. In 13:1ff. it arises from the sea. In 13:11ff. a second *beast* comes forth from the land. Both are embodiments of the antichrist and of the lying prophet and symbolize the (political) demons of the eschaton (see Job 40:15ff., 25ff.). The chief figure of this sketch is always the "first *beast*" (13:12), who bears a mortal but healed wound (13:3), and who has received his authority from the dragon (= Satan; 13:4). An image is made of "the other *beast*" (14ff.) for the people to worship (13:14ff.). The beast has its "name" and its "number," 666, the interpretation of which demands wisdom. Its followers bear a special sign (16:2). It also possesses a throne (16:10), over which God's wrath is poured out. From its mouth comes impurity (16:13). It is seen as a "scarlet beast" (17:3), upon which Babylon the harlot (= Rome) sits, full of blasphemous names, seven heads (= hills) and ten horns (= partial dominions).

Revelation 17 in particular offers help in deciphering the mystery, for here it is said that the beast "was and is not and is to come" (17:9ff.). Accordingly, it concerns one of five anti-Christian Caesars, who has already ruled and will return as the eighth (*Nero redivivus?*). As the chief opponent of the *Christus victor* the beast will be overcome in the final battle and thrown into the fiery lake of judgment (19:20; 20:10).

Just as the beasts (= world kingdoms) in Daniel 7 stand in contrast to the kingdom of the one like the Son

of Man, so also in Revelation the beast stands in radical contrast to the portrayal of the lamb. In contrast to the lamb's readiness to suffer, the beast embodies the anti-Christian world power of the eschaton. The background of the period of Domitian is evident.

                 A. Strobel

θησαυρίζω *thēsaurizō* gather (treasures), store up*
→ θησαυρός.

θησαυρός, οῦ, ὁ *thēsauros* treasure chest; treasure*
ἀποθησαυρίζω *apothēsaurizō* store up*
θησαυρίζω *thēsaurizō* gather (treasures), store up*

1. Occurrences in the NT — 2. Meaning — 3. Usage — a) Positive usage in the literal sense — b) Criticism of the rich — c) Sayings about recompense — d) Wisdom traditions

Lit.: K. BERGER, "Materialien zu Form und Überlieferungsgeschichte neutestamentlicher Gleichnisse," *NovT* 15 (1973) 1-37. — J. DAUVILLIER, "La parabole du trésor et les droits orientaux," *RIDA* third series, 4 (1957) 107-15. — H.-J. DEGENHARDT, *Lukas—Evangelist der Armen* (1965) 78ff., 88-93. — J. D. M. DERRETT, "Law in the NT: The Treasure in the Field (Mt. XIII,44)," *ZNW* 54 (1963) 31-42. — J. DUPONT, "Les Paraboles du trésor et de la perle," *NTS* 14 (1967/68) 408-18. — J. EICHLER and C. BROWN, *DNTT* II, 829-36. — J. C. FENTON, "The Parables of the Treasure and the Pearl (Mt 13,44-46)," *ExpTim* 77 (1965/66) 178-80. — F. HAUCK, *TDNT* III, 136-38. — J. D. KINGSBURY, *The Parables of Jesus in Matthew 13* (1969) 110-17, 125-29. — K. KOCH, "Der Schatz im Himmel," *Leben angesichts des Todes* (FS H. Thielicke; 1968) 47-60. — B. KÜBLER, PW II/11, 7-13. — W. MAGASS, "Der Schatz im Acker," *LingBibl* 21-22 (1973) 2-18. — H. MERKLEIN, *Die Gottesherrschaft als Handlungprinzip* (1978) 64-69 (on Matt 13:44). — W. PESCH, "Zur Exegese von Mt 16,19-21 und Lk 12,33-34," *Bib* 41 (1960) 356-78. — H. RIESENFELD, "Vom Schätzesammeln und Sorgen—ein Thema urchristlicher Paränese," FS Cullmann (1962) 47-58. — SCHULZ, *Q* 142-45, 316-20. — D. ZELLER, *Die weisheitlichen Mahnsprüche bei den Synoptiker* (1977) 77-81 (on Matt 6:19-21). — *idem*, "Zu einer jüdischen Vorlage von Mt 13,52," *BZ* 20 (1976) 223-26 (bibliography). — L. ZIEHEN, PW II/11, 1-7. — For further bibliography see *TWNT* X, 1110.

1. The noun appears 17 times in the NT, θησαυρίζω 8 times, and the compound ἀποθησαυρίζω only in 1 Tim 6:19. The stem θησαυρ- is relatively frequent in the words of Jesus (the noun appears 7 times, the vb. 3 times, excluding parallels).

2. The noun sometimes refers to (originally? so Ziehen) *the place where something valuable is kept;* thus clearly in Matt 2:11: "they opened their *treasure chests*" —then also *what is kept*, the *treasure*. The vb. θησαυρίζω thus refers to the action of *bringing* something to a storehouse or of *gathering* a treasure. The obj. is acc.; the dat. is used of the person for whom it takes place.

NT terms related in meaning and found in the same contexts are τὰ ἀγαθά (Luke 12:18f.), τὰ κτήματα (Mark 10:22), ὁ πλοῦτος

(Rom 2:4; Col 2:2; Heb 11:26; Jas 5:2), τὰ ὑπάρχοντα/ἡ ὕπαρξις (Matt 19:21; Luke 12:33), and phrases such as πάντα ὅσα ἔχεις (Luke 18:22). With these terms only movable goods are in view. Parallel to θησαυρίζειν are ἑτοιμάζειν in Luke 12:20 and τηρεῖν in 2 Pet 3:7. The NT passages indicate what constituted treasure in antiquity: gold and silver coins (Jas 5:3; Matt 2:11), luxurious clothing (Jas 5:2b), which are damaged by moths (Matt 6:19f.), reserves of grain and food (Luke 12:16-21), which decay or are eaten by animals (Jas 5:2a; Matt 6:19f.), and expensive perfumes (Matt 2:11).

3. a) Where a capital economy was unknown, one had to assure the future by gathering money and material possessions. A few texts use θησαυρίζω in this connection in a positive sense. In 1 Cor 16:2 Paul recommends that each person in Corinth *save* what he can and put it aside to be collected weekly. A common treasury seems not to be assumed. In 2 Cor 12:14c he uses, in regard to his relationship with the Corinthian church, the generally recognized axiom (cf. Philo *Vit. Mos.* ii.245; Plutarch *De Cup. Div.* [*Moralia* 526]) that it is not the small children who must *save* for their parents, but the parents who must *save* for the children.

As a figure in parables θησαυρός represents that which is of surpassing value. The parable in Matt 13:44 (M) is intended to demonstrate, like the parallel in vv. 45f., that the attainment of the kingdom of heaven is by itself the reward for commitment that seems absurd to the world (cf. *T. Job* 18:6-8; cf. Berger 2-7).

The imagery presupposes that treasures were "concealed" from thieves and plunderers (cf. Isa 45:3 [*maṭmôn* parallel to '*ôṣār*]; 1 Macc 1:23; Josephus *Ant.* xii.250; *b. Pesaḥ.* 119a; Plato *R.* 548a). They were often buried in the ground (cf. Matt 25:18 [cf. Billerbeck I, 971f.]; 2 Enoch 51:2; Maximus Tyrius 15:5h). Discovering a forgotten treasure while plowing (*Lev. Rab.* 5 [108b]; see Billerbeck I, 674) or planting a tree (Philo *Imm.* 91) was considered a stroke of luck (Aristotle *EN* 1112a; Lucian *Tim.* 29f., 40f. in words ascribed to Pluto), about which one might dream (Lucian *Herm.* 71f.; Artemidorus *Oneirocriticus* 2.549). Inasmuch as the thing found belonged to the owner of the land according to Roman and Jewish law (cf. Kübler, Dauvillier, Derrett), a worker could acquire it for himself by buying the land (cf. Horace *Sat.* ii.6.10; *Midr. Cant.* 4:13 [116a]; and parallels in Billerbeck I, 674; cf. *Gos. Thom.* 109; Philostratus *VA* vi.39). In Matt 13:44 the legality of the act is not questioned.

b) In admonitions to the rich the NT uses this word group in a critical way and also in fig. senses in order to make plausible distribution of riches to the poor as a value. Matt 6:19-21 comes closer to the Q form of Jesus' saying than Luke 12:33f., where the practical consequence is expressed in a clearer and more radical way. The wisdom saying in Matt 6:19f. seeks to deter one from *gathering treasures,* using a common motif (cf. only Prov 23:4f.; Jas 1:10f.) to recall their transitoriness. The originally independent saying in v. 20 argues that *treasure* binds the heart to it (cf. Ps 62:11b; on later forms cf. Pesch 377).

The judgment sermon in Jas 5:1-6 has a more apocalyptic tone. To *amass treasures* in the last days (v. 3c) makes no sense, especially since they are acquired through injustice (vv. 4-6; cf. Prov 10:2; 21:6; Mic 6:10; *1 Enoch* 97:8f.). The rich go to destruction along with the treasures in which they have trusted (cf. *1 Enoch* 94:8; 93:3).

Death also proves the folly (→ ἀφροσύνη 3) of the one who *gathers reserves* (cf. Ps 38:7 LXX): This is the lesson that Luke 12:21 (cf. Dupont, *Beatitudes* III, 115-18) draws from the illustrative elaboration in 12:16-20. One should instead "be rich toward God," i.e., according to Matt 6:20, *hoard treasures* in heaven. By what means? The call to discipleship in Mark 10:21 says: If the rich man sells his possessions and gives to the poor (cf. Philo *Spec. Leg.* iv.74 against θησαυροφυλακεῖν) he will have *treasure* in heaven, which guarantees eternal life (v. 17).

Likewise later in 1 Tim 6:19: Through doing good (v. 18) the rich *lays up* (ἀποθησαυρίζω) a good foundation in order to attain eternal life. In Heb 11:26 the parenesis points not to giving of alms but to suffering, which Moses considered greater in riches than the fabled θησαυροί of the Egyptians. Also here that recompense is thought of (cf. 10:34: "better and abiding possession") makes possible such a paradoxical revaluation, in which faith becomes apparent.

c) The treasures in heaven are good works, which are in safekeeping with God and which he later gives to the one who does good. This idea bridges the gap between human activity and final reward.

It is associated with the OT view of the heavenly storeroom ('*ôṣ^erôt*) in which Yahweh stores rain and wind (cf. Deut 28:12; Pss 33:7; 135:7; Jer 10:13 = 51:16) and the weapons of his wrath, snow and hail, in order to bring them down on the day of punishment (Deut 32:34f.; Job 38:22f.; Jer 50:25; Sir 43:14; *1 Enoch* 17:3). According to 1QS 10:2; 1QH 1:12; 1QM 10:12 (cf. *Odes Sol.* 16:15) also kept there are light and darkness, i.e., the decisive mysteries of time, which have been communicated to the Qumran community. Philo refers esp. to Deut 28:12 and 32:34f.: In heaven there is a treasure of the good, God himself. He opens it to those who are his, but punishes the sinners on the day of vengeance with the treasure of evil, which is still temporarily bound (*All.* iii.105f.; *Imm.* 150; *Migr.* 121; *Her.* 76; *Fug.* 79).

The intertestamental wisdom literature encourages charity by saying that the money given is not lost, but will be replaced by God and bring about blessings in the midst of distress (cf. Tob 4:9; 12:8f.; Sir 3:4; 17:22f.; 29:10-12; *Pss. Sol.* 9:5). In apocalyptic literature the treasure of good deeds laid up in heaven will first be manifest in the final judgment (*1 Enoch* 38:2; 4 Ezra 6:5; 7:77; 8:33; *2 Bar.* 14:12; 24:1; *2 Enoch* 50:5). According to *t. Pe'a* 4:18 (24) King Monabaz distributed his treasures to the poor in order to gather treasures on high (see Billerbeck I, 430). Among the works of love the rabbis distinguish between interest, which one enjoys already in this world, and capital, which remains for the coming world (*b. Pe'a* 1:1; see Billerbeck I, 430). In the heavenly treasure house (Aram.

ginzā', gᵉnîz; see Billerbeck II, 268) treasures of life are kept prepared for the righteous (cf. Prov 2:7 LXX; *Exod. Rab.* 45 [101a; see Billerbeck III, 268]; *b. Ḥag.* 12b [Billerbeck III, 657]; *Memar Marqah* 4:9).

Just as one can "gather the fulfillment of commandments as treasures *(sîggēl)*" (a rabbinic phrase, see Billerbeck I, 431), so also one can gather condemnation by doing evil (Prov 1:18; 16:27 LXX). The sinner despises the wealth of God's goodness and *stores up* wrath, which is released on the day of wrath (Rom 2:5; cf. Philo *All.* iii.105f.). In 2 Pet 3:7 God is the concealed subj. (divine pass.) of θησαυρίζω; but here also the *storing up* serves to overcome the difference in time between the present and the certain judgment to come.

d) A final area of usage is dominated by the wisdom tradition. In most instances here θησαυρός is used metaphorically. In Q the figure in Matt 12:35 par. Luke 6:45a comments on the figures in Luke 6:43, 44a, b; it identifies the "fruits" as the conduct of the person. The saying in 6:45b, which perhaps circulated independently, is restricted here to the act of speaking. Both conduct in general and speaking in particular come from the *treasury* of the heart. This Luke develops by adding a subj. gen. from v. 45b. Because each person's θησαυρός has the same quality as the manifestations thereof, the θησαυρός cannot be simply the container (so Jülicher II, 121 *contra* most commentators, who assume that the gen. is appositional; so *T. Ash.* 1:9b: ὁ θησαυρὸς τοῦ διαβουλίου). The basis for what is expressed here may be the idea, attested in Philo, that through the exercise of the good in the soul a treasure of the καλόν is stored up (*Det.* 35, 43; *Ebr.* 200; *Conf.* 50, 69; *Gos. Thom.* 45b: treasure in his heart).

In the brief parable of Matt 13:52 (M) θησαυρός refers to the *storeroom* from which the master takes out both new and old (cf. Isocrates i.133: ὥσπερ ἐκ ταμείου). If this was used of the teacher of Torah in Jewish tradition (Zeller), the image is nonetheless suggested by the wisdom tradition, which compares observance of wisdom with a treasure (cf. Sir 20:30 = 41:14).

In Prov 2:4 striving for wisdom is likened to the search for treasure. Acquiring wisdom is better than acquiring gold and silver (Job 28:15-19; Prov 3:14f.; 8:10f., 19; 16:16; 20:15; Eccl 7:11f.; Wis 7:8f.; 8:5; cf. Sir 51:21; *T. Levi* 13:7). In Prov 21:20; Wis 7:13f. θησαυρός is a metaphor for wisdom (cf. Maximus Tyrius 15:5g; Philo *Cher.* 48; *Imm.* 92f.); in Isa 33:6; Ps. Menander 70 it is a metaphor for fear of God (cf. Tob 4:21; *b. Ber.* 33b; Billerbeck I, 430). The θησαυροί σοφίας (Sir 1:25; cf. Diodorus Siculus ix.10) can be understood as its inaccessible treasuries, according to Bar 3:15; elsewhere it is the good of accumulated insight (*2 Bar.* 44:14; Xenophon *Mem.* i.6.14; iv.2.9; Plato *Phlb.* 15e; Philo *Congr.* 127). When wisdom is identified with God's wisdom, with its unfathomable treasures prepared under his throne (*2 Bar.* 54:13; cf. *Memar Marqah* 3:1; Genizah left part 2:6), it can be made accessible only through revelation (cf. Bar 3:15-38; *1 Enoch* 46:3 through the Son of Man).

Does the kingdom of heaven appear in place of wisdom in Matt 13:44, particularly since the value of wisdom is sometimes compared with that of the pearl (Job 28:18; Prov 3:15; 8:11; cf. Matt 13:45f.)?

This metaphor may be in the background in 2 Cor 4:7. Θησαυρὸν τοῦτον refers to the gospel (vv. 3f.; so most) or to the διακονία τῆς δόξης (v. 1; so R. Bultmann, *2 Cor* [Eng. tr.] 112). Paul has it in an earthly vessel, as treasures were often held in clay jars. Jewish traditions similarly contrast wisdom (*b. Ta'an* 7a; see Billerbeck I, 861) or the Torah (*Sipre Deut* 11:22 §48 [84a]; see Billerbeck III, 516) with its insignificant human bearers. In Col 2:3 "*treasures* of wisdom and knowledge" appear alongside an analogous construction with πλοῦτος (v. 2). They are hidden in Christ, i.e., he is the only place where all knowledge is to be found (cf. 1:26f.). This is a comment against the "philosophy" of the false teachers (vv. 4, 8).

Also in gnosticizing writings (*Acts Pet.* 20; Silvanus [NHC vii.4] 107.1ff.) there are in Jesus, the wisdom, "hidden treasures." In Gnosticism the treasure motif plays a great role (cf. *Gos. Thom.* 76, 109 and the references in Hauck 138).

D. Zeller

Θιγγάνω *thinganō* touch*

Θιγγάνειν τινός, "*touch* something": Heb 12:20 ("if an animal *touch* the mountain"; cf. Exod 19:12 LXX); of hostile touching, Heb 11:28 ("that the destroyer of the firstborn might not *touch* them"). In Col 2:21 the negative imv. is used absolutely: "do not *touch*"; this involves perhaps "an intense caricature" of the legal demands (E. Lohse, *Col, Phlm* [Hermeneia] ad loc.).

Θλίβω *thlibō* press hard, afflict
→ θλῖψις.

Θλῖψις, εως, ἡ *thlipsis* affliction, hardship*
Θλίβω *thlibō* press hard, afflict*

1. Occurrences and general meaning — 2. NT usage

Lit.: B. AHERN, "The Fellowship of His Sufferings (Phil 3,10). A Study of St. Paul's Doctrine on Christian Suffering," *CBQ* 22 (1960) 1-32. — R. J. BAUCKHAM, "Colossians 1,24 Again: The Apocalyptic Motif," *EvQ* 47 (1975) 168-75. — N. BAUMERT, *Täglich sterben und auferstehen. Der Literalsinn von 2 Kor 4,12-5,10* (SANT 34, 1973). — J. CARMIGNAC, "La théologie de la souffrance dans les hymnes de Qumrân," *RevQ* 9 (1961) 365-86. -- M. CARREZ, *De la souffrance à la gloriére* (1964). — G. LE GRELLE, "La plénitude de la parole dans la pauvreté de la chair d'après Col 1,24," *NRT* 81 (1959) 232-50. — E. GÜTTGEMANNS, *Der leidende Apostel und sein Herr* (FRLANT 90, 1966). — E. KAMLAH, "Wie beurteilt Paulus sein Leiden?" *ZNW* (1963) 217-32. — A. J. MATTILL, "The Way of Tribulation," *JBL* 98 (1979) 531-46. — R. SCHIPPERS, *DNTT* II, 807-9. — H. SCHLIER, *TDNT* III, 139-48. — W. SCHRAGE, "Leid, Kreuz und Eschaton. Peristasenkataloge als Merkmal paulinischer theologia crucis," *EvT* 34 (1974) 141-75. — G. H. P.

THOMPSON, "Eph 3,13 and 2 Tim 2,10 in the Light of Col 1,24," *ExpTim* 71 (1959/60) 187-89. — For further bibliography see *TWNT* X, 1110.

1. Θλίβω has its basic meaning of *press, crush, rub, push* in the NT only in Mark 3:9 (similarly συνθλίβω, Mark 5:24, 31; ἀποθλίβω, Luke 8:45) and Matt 7:14 (squeeze together, i.e, *narrow*). Elsewhere (8 NT occurrences) it bears the fig. sense: *afflict*. The noun θλῖψις is always (45 NT occurrences) used in the fig. sense in the NT, often in connection with στενοχωρία, ἀνάγκη, διωγμός, πάθημα, and λύπη, and not always distinguished from them. It is used of *persecution, affliction* or the experience of *oppression*, (extreme) *affliction, need,* or (inner) *tribulation*.

Θλῖψις is used in a general way in 2 Cor 8:13; 1 Tim 5:10; Jas 1:27 of the tribulation of the poor, particularly the widow and orphan, in Acts 7:10 of the great misery of hunger, and in John 16:21 of birth pangs, probably not as an allusion to the apocalyptic motif of the messianic birth pangs.

The NT preference for θλῖψις in the fig. sense corresponds to the LXX, where θλῖψις (very often in the sg.) is used, like its Hebrew equivalents of 1) situations of extreme need or misery for the people of Israel (e.g., Exod 3:9; 4:31; 1 Macc 9:27)—in apocalyptic texts of eschatological affliction (e.g., Dan 12:1; Hab 3:16; Zeph 1:5; cf. 1QM 1:12)—and 2) the suffering of the individual righteous person, a central theme of Jewish apocalyptic taken over from the wisdom literature (e.g., Pss 33:20; 36:39; cf. 4 Ezra 7:89; *2 Bar.* 15:8; 48:50; 1QH 2:6-12; cf. Schlier 140-42; Carmignac 374ff.; Schrage 142-49). The particular significance of θλῖψις in the NT is shaped by this background.

2. a) In isolated cases within Jewish preaching of judgment θλῖψις designates a threatened *affliction* and *torment*, which comes as punishment (Rom 2:9; 2 Thess 1:6; Rev 2:22; cf. Carmignac 369). More frequently θλῖψις refers to the eschatological "(great) *affliction* as has not been since the beginning of the creation" (Mark 13:19 par. Matthew [Luke has ἀνάγκη] = Dan 12:1; cf. Mark 13:24 par. Matthew; likewise Rev 7:14). This θλῖψις is numbered among the "woes" (→ ὠδίν) that immediately precede the end and is occasioned by persecution. (In Matt 24:9 ["Then will they deliver you *to affliction*"] θλῖψις means *persecution* itself [cf. par. Mark 13:10]). In 1 Cor 7:28 ("they will have *affliction* in their flesh [= earthly life]") Paul takes up a motif of apocalyptic (cf. 7:26, 29) in order to reinforce the recommendation to remain unmarried (cf. Mark 13:17 par.; Luke 23:29; because of their concern for each other [1 Cor 7:32ff.] and their cares for the family, those who are married are more exposed to eschatological affliction).

In 1 Thess 3:3b the troubles (1:6)—in an apocalyptic sense—that originated with persecution are identified as the afflictions that necessarily accompany the apostolic proclamation and the life of Christians ("this is to be your lot"). As such they can be anticipated (3:4; John 16:33; Acts 20:23). That they are inescapable serves as comfort and encouragement in order "that no one be disturbed by these *afflictions*" (1 Thess 3:3a).

Paul may have understood the θλῖψις of persecution as eschatological θλῖψις (1 Thess 3:7; 2 Cor 1:8; 4:8; 8:2; Rom 8:35; Phil 4:14; cf. Schlier 144-46), which stands in a close relationship to the power of death (Rom 8:35f.; 2 Cor 1:8; 11:23; cf. Schlier 147f.). According to 2 Thess 1:4-7 the affliction of those who have carried on the persecution is a demonstration of God's righteous judgment, which has already begun. In Rev 2:9f. such affliction, which brings forth poverty, is characterized as that which is derived from the devil and lasts only a brief time (cf. 3:10).

b) The eschatological aspect is not the only one, however. The misery of persecuted Christians (Acts 11:19) was seen in the early Church in connection with the afflictions of the pious of the old covenant (cf. Acts 7:10; Heb 11:37) and thus as properly belonging to the Christian life (Acts 14:22; cf. E. Haenchen, *Acts* [Eng. tr., 1971] ad loc.; Heb 10:33).

Characteristic of the NT is the close connection between afflictions suffered by Christians and those suffered by Jesus Christ. What Paul writes holds true not only for him (Güttgemanns 323ff.), but for all Christians (Kamlah 231; Schrage 159, with reference to 2 Cor 1:4, 6 and the paradigmatic significance of Paul's suffering according to 1 Thess 1:6-7; 2:14-15; Phlm 1, 29f.), if the apostle knows that he himself is affected to a definite extent (2 Cor 1:5).

These afflictions are not limited to persecution (cf. Mark 4:17 par. Matt 13:21: "affliction *or* persecution for the sake of the word"). According to Phil 1:17 the opponents of Paul cause *affliction* in addition to his chains. In 2 Cor 7:4f. the θλίψεις are more precisely defined as "fightings without, fears within." Pl. θλίψεις in 2 Cor 6:4f. is defined by the enumerated afflictions (cf. 12:10) in the related peristasis catalog. "Much *affliction* and anguish of heart" (2:4) is the sorrow that the apostle experiences in response to events in Corinth.

All afflictions have a positive meaning. Therefore, one need not be ashamed because of them, but may rather boast ("for we know that *affliction* produces endurance, endurance produces character . . . ," Rom 5:3). Affliction requires endurance (12:12), and this in turn gives the possibility for character (δοκιμή, cf. 1 Pet 1:7), i.e., it allows those who are afflicted to learn that they are among those who have hope for a share in God's glory (Rom 5:2; cf. 15:4; Jas 1:2). Paul can even write: "This slight momentary *affliction* produces an eternal weight of glory beyond all comparison" (2 Cor 4:17); i.e., the future glory is not merely not to be compared to the momentary affliction (cf. Rom 8:18), but rather the affliction itself produces the surpassing greatness of the glory (cf. R. Bultmann, *2 Cor* [Eng. tr., 1985] ad loc.; untenable is Baumert's [129-34] connection of καθ᾽ ὑπερβολήν with ἐλαφρόν ["affliction that is insignificant beyond all measure"]).

In addition to the meaning for one's own future, afflictions also have a meaning for others: From the comfort that he has experienced in affliction, Paul can comfort others who are afflicted (2 Cor 1:4). Indeed, affliction occurs "for your comfort and salvation" (1:6; cf. Eph 3:13: "for your glory"; also 2 Tim 2:10). Paul does not say explicitly how this happens, but it is apparently connected with the fact that these afflictions, which are experienced as "the sufferings (→ πάθημα) of Christ" (2 Cor 1:5; cf. 4:10: → νέκρωσις; Gal 6:17: τὰ στίγματα)—for Christ's sake and in association with Christ (Rom 8:17: συμπάσχω; Phil 3:10; Rev 1:9: → κοινωνία; cf. 1 Cor 12:26f.)—are the means by which the life mediated through Christ is granted (cf. 2 Cor 4:10-12).

c) Col 1:24 speaks in a singular way of the θλίψεις τοῦ Χριστοῦ, *afflictions of Christ,* of which the apostle "replaces" (ἀνταναπληρῶ) what is lacking (ὑστερήματα). This he does in his earthly existence ("in my flesh"), which is surrendered to death. Are the "afflictions of Christ," like the suffering "in my flesh" (v. 24a), Paul's own afflictions (suffered for the sake of Christ, in imitation of Christ, or in the fellowship of sufferings with Christ) or the afflictions of another (Jesus, the Church described as "Christ," or Christ understood in the manner of a "corporate personality" [cf. 1 Cor 12:12])? The answer depends on the interpretation of the entire sentence and of the Pauline or deutero-Pauline theology of suffering. (The interpretation that refers to the "messianic woes" [most recently Bauckham] fails, among other reasons, because of the late composition of Colossians.) Unless an expression conditioned by the opponents is used, the unusual statement is best explained as indicating that the apostle, as proclaimer of the gospel, represents the position of Christ. In his suffering brought about by his apostolic commitment he brings to completion Christ's work, which is connected with affliction in this world (on the various interpretations, cf. J. Ernst, *Col* [RNT]; E. Schweizer, *Col* [Eng. tr., 1982] ad loc. with bibliography).

Because the affliction experienced in fellowship with Christ and in his service looks toward the future glory and the salvation of others, the believer can experience not only comfort in it, but can also experience joy because of the Holy Spirit (1 Thess 1:3; 2 Cor 7:4; 8:2; Col 1:24; 1 Pet 1:6-9; 4:13; Jas 1:2-4). (On the connection of θλῖψις with future [not present] joy in apocalyptic, cf. Schrage 145f. [bibliography].)

                                            J. Kremer

θνῄσκω *thnēskō* die*
θνητός, 3 *thnētos* mortal*

   Lit.: → θάνατος.

Θνῄσκω is used literally 8 times in the NT: *die* (Matt 2:20; Mark 15:44; Luke 7:12; 8:49; John 11:44; 19:[21 TR]33; Acts 14:19; 25:19) and once in fig.: In 1 Tim 5:6 the widow who lives a self-indulgent life is said to be *spiritually dead,* either in view of the true life with God or because she is *inutilis* (Calvin) for the Church.

While the LXX uses ὁ θνητός subst. of the "mortal person" (Job 30:23; Prov 3:13; 20:24) and the Apostolic Fathers follow this usage (*1 Clem.* 39:2; *Diog.* 9:2), the NT uses θνητός as an adj. with σάρξ or σῶμα or in neut. sg. τὸ θνητόν. The *"mortal* flesh" (2 Cor 4:11) and the *"mortal* body" (Rom 8:11) are important for Paul in attesting the awakening power of God on the mortal person at the present time. From this he concludes that "sin should not rule in the *mortal* body" (Rom 6:12). Thus for Paul the process of dying as such is not important: He sees *mortality* already "swallowed up by life" (καταπίνω) in the sense that no room is left for meditations on death (2 Cor 5:4). This does not hinder Paul from recognizing the actuality of death: it is "this *mortality*" which must put on immortality (1 Cor 15:53f.).

                                           W. Bieder

θνητός, 3 *thnētos* mortal
→ θνῄσκω.

θορυβάζω *thorybazō* disturb; pass.: be disturbed
→ θόρυβος.

θορυβέω *thorybeō* set in turmoil; pass.: get excited
→ θόρυβος.

θόρυβος, ου, ὁ *thorybos* noise, turmoil, riot*
θορυβάζω *thorybazō* disturb; pass.: be disturbed*
θορυβέω *thorybeō* set in turmoil; pass.: get excited*

1. Occurrences in the NT — 2. Meanings — 3. Usage

   Lit.: BAGD s.v. — Frisk, *Wörterbuch* I, 678. — Passow I, 1422.

1. The noun appears 7 times in the NT (twice each in Matthew and Mark, 3 times in Acts). Of the two vbs., θορυβέω appears more frequently and in the same writings as the noun (once each in Matthew, Mark, and Acts). Θορυβάζω appears only in Luke 10:41 (L). Mark 5:39 and Matt 9:23 (θορυβέω) stand in a relationship of literary dependence, as do Mark 14:2 and Matt 26:5 (θόρυβος). The word group is more frequently represented in Luke-Acts (6 occurrences); Mark and Matthew each have 3 occurrences.

2. Θόρυβος has the general meaning *noise, sound* (Mark 5:38; Acts 21:34; *Mart. Pol.* 8:3; 9:1), but designates also *confusion, turmoil, uproar,* esp. in noisy crowds of people (Mark 14:2 par. Matt 26:5; Matt 27:24; Acts 20:1; 24:18); Passow: "esp. the confused chaotic noise and shrieking of many people and the resulting unrest, disorder, consternation, confusion, esp. that noise of an assembly of people." Θορυβέω means in the act. *set in turmoil* (Acts 17:5), in the pass. *become/be disturbed* (Mark 5:39; Matt 9:23; Acts 20:10). Θορυβάζω, *disturb* (cf. *1 Enoch* [Greek] 14:8; Dositheus *Ars grammatica* 71:16), appears in the pass. in Luke 10:41: θορυβάζῃ, you *are troubled* (περί τι: "because of something"). Terms related in linguistic history with the word group are Lat. *turbare* and *turbulare,* French *troubler* and *trouble,* Eng. *trouble,* and Germ. *Trubel.*

3. In the story of Jairus's daughter Jesus sees, as he comes to the house of the synagogue ruler, "the θόρυβος and people weeping and crying loudly" (Mark 5:38). He asks: "Why *are you perplexed* (τί θορυβεῖσθε) and why do you weep? The child is not dead, but is sleeping" (v. 39). Jesus' question indicates that the perplexity and the wailing are inappropriate and corresponds to Paul's imv. in Acts 20:10: "Do not *be alarmed* (μὴ θορυβεῖσθε), for his soul is in him." The Matthean Jairus story (Matt 9:23) speaks of "flute players and the *noisy* crowd." Whether the tr. in these contexts should be *noise* or *confusion* remains uncertain; probably both aspects are intended (→ 2).

In the Passion story the reference is to *uproar/tumult:* Jesus should not be killed during the Passover festival so that no *riot* occur among the people (Mark 14:2 par. Matt 26:5). Matt 27:24 speaks in a redactional expansion of the text of Pilate's realization that "the *riot* had become stronger" (in reference to the Barabbas scene), of Barabbas's subsequent release, and of Jesus' scourging and delivery to be crucified (v. 26).

In Acts various riots are mentioned (cf. also συγχύννω, "stir up," 21:27, 31). In 17:5 the Jews in Thessalonica *set the city in an uproar* against Paul and Silas. 20:1 refers to the *riot* in Ephesus (19:23-40; cf. also v. 29: σύγχυσις, v. 40: στάσις). 21:34 mentions the *riot* at the temple when Paul was arrested and that the tribune could not determine anything with certainty. In 24:18 Paul says at his defense that he was at the temple "with no crowd or *disturbance*" (cf. 21:27-34; see E. Haenchen, *Acts* [Eng. tr., 1971] ad loc.).

Θορυβάζω is a NT hapax in Luke 10:41 (Koine A Γ Δ Π al read τυρβάζω, "confuse"), where Jesus reproaches Martha: "you *are anxious* and *troubled* because of many things" (μεριμνᾷς καὶ θορυβάζῃ περὶ πολλά). V. 42 emphasizes that only "one thing is necessary," hearing Jesus' word (v. 39). See G. Schneider, *Luke* (ÖTK) I, ad loc.

                       G. Schneider

θραύω *thrauō* shatter*

In the NT only in Luke 4:18: The pf. pass. partc. τεθραυσμένοι, *broken,* is derived (as in *Barn.* 3:3) from Isa 58:6 LXX.

θρέμμα, ατος, τό *thremma* domesticated animal*

John 4:12 (at Jacob's well) recalls Jacob and "his sons and his *animals,*" who drank from the well.

θρηνέω *thrēneō* mourn, lament*

Matt 11:17 par. Luke 7:32: ἐθρηνήσαμεν, in Jesus' saying about the children at play: "*We sang dirges* and you did not mourn [i.e., weep]"; F. Mussner, *Bib* 40 (1959) 599-612; O. Linton, *NTS* 22 (1975-76) 159-79; D. Zeller, *ZNW* 68 (1977) 252-57. The vb. appears in Luke 23:27 (referring to wailing women) alongside κόπτομαι (as in Matt 11:17) and in John 16:20 with κλαίω (as in Luke 7:32). G. Stählin, *TDNT* III, 148-55.

θρῆνος, ου, ὁ *thrēnos* dirge

Matt 2:18 C Koine D W: θρῆνος καὶ κλαυθμός, "*wailing* and weeping." Θρῆνος is added secondarily in dependence on Jer 38:15 LXX. G. Stählin, III, 148-55.

θρησκεία, ας, ἡ *thrēskeia* religion, cult, piety*

1. Basic meaning and usage — 2. NT usage — 3. The NT attitude toward the cultic

Lit.: BAGD s.v. — W. CARR, "Two Notes on Colossians," *JTS* 24 (1973) 492-500. — M. DIBELIUS, *Col, Eph, Phlm* (HNT, 1953) 35, 38-40. — M. DIBELIUS and H. GREEVEN, *Jas* (Hermeneia, 1976) 120-23. — F. O. FRANCIS, "Humility and Angelic Worship in Col 2:18," *ST* 16 (1962) 109-34. — E. LOHSE, *Col, Phlm* (Hermeneia, 1971) 96-98, 117-19. — F. MUSSNER, *Jas* (HTKNT, 1967) 110-14. — K. L. SCHMIDT, *TDNT* III, 155-59. — E. SCHWEIZER, *Col* (Eng. tr., 1982) 159f. — SPICQ, *Notes* I, 379-83. — For further bibliography see *TWNT* X, 1110.

1. This word, which is difficult to explain etymologically (cf. Frisk, *Wörterbuch* 682), denotes in its basic meaning holy service, thus religion and its practice, "with particular emphasis on the zealousness of such practice" (Schmidt 156). The object of religious observance is often found with θρησκεία in the obj. gen.: τοῦ θεοῦ (Herodianus Historicus iv.8.7; Josephus *Ant.* i.222; xii.271; *Corp. Herm.* xii.23), τοῦ ὑψίστου (*1 Clem.* 45:7), τῶν ἀγγέλων (Col 2:18), τοῦ Ἀπόλλωνος (Gallio inscription [*SIG* 801]), τῶν ἀνωνύμων εἰδώλων (Wis 14:27), τῶν θεῶν (Philo *Spec. Leg.* i.315); ἡ περὶ αὐτὸν θρησκεία appears in Josephus *Ant.* i.223f. To distinguish between one "religion" and another θρησκεία is defined more precisely with an adj., pron., or gen. of possession: πάτριος (Josephus *Ant.* xix.282; cf. xx.13: τὰ πάτρια θρησκεύειν),

ἡμετέρα (Acts 26:5), Ἰουδαίων (4 Macc 5:6), τῆσδε τῆς (5:13), ἡμῶν (1 Clem. 62:1).

2. Just as θρησκεία appears only 5 times in the LXX, of which 2 are in 4 Macc 5:7, 13, it appears rarely in the NT also (4 times). In each NT document where it appears it has a different meaning:

a) In Acts 26:5 θρησκεία, as in 4 Maccabees 5, where it appears in the words of the pagan Antiochus, is used of the Jewish *religion*. In the speech before Agrippa the Jew, who is "familiar with all Jewish customs and controversies" (v. 3), and Festus the Roman, Paul says: "I have lived according to the strictest party of our *religion*."

b) In Col 2:18 θρησκεία τῶν ἀγγέλων is *(cultic) worship* of angels, *service* to angels, or the angel *cult*. It does not refer to a heavenly service of worship by angels (subj. gen.), but to a human activity (obj. gen.).

This conclusion is indicated by the resumption of the thought of v. 18 in v. 23, where such a "self-chosen cult," such a "self-made religion" (BAGD 218) is rejected. Schweizer 159 interprets the "angels" according to the traditional understanding of the Bible. The angels are associated closely with God (and Christ) (Luke 9:26; 1 Thess 3:13; 1 Tim 5:21; Rev 3:5; 18:4), perhaps also with the Spirit of God (cf. Acts 8:26 with 29, 39), so that, as Rev 19:10 indicates, such angel worship suggests itself. The context in Colossians 2, however, conflicts with this interpretation. In vv. 8 and 20 the "world elements" (cf. Gal 4:3, 9) stand in polemical opposition to Christ. Their cult is rejected in v. 23 with the terms of v. 18.

c) Θρησκεία appears twice, one immediately after the other, in Jas 1:26, 27, a structure made rhetorically effective through this chiastic arrangement and the asyndetic connection. Examples of false or true *piety* are given.

3. The infrequent use of θρησκεία in the NT corresponds to that of other cultic terms such as θεραπεία, λατρεία, ἐπιμέλεια, λειτουργία, and ἱερουργία (cf. in detail Schmidt 158). The cause and consequence of this fact are identical: Christianity fundamentally required no special cultic approach.   W. Radl

θρησκός, 2 *thrēskos* religious*

Jas 1:26: "If anyone thinks he is *religious,* and does not bridle his tongue . . . , his religion (θρησκεία) is in vain." K. L. Schmidt, *TDNT* III, 155-59; Spicq, *Notes* I, 382f.

θριαμβεύω *thriambeuō* make known*

1. Occurrences in the NT and meaning — 2. 2 Cor 2:14 — 3. Col 2:15

Lit.: BAGD s.v. — G. DELLING, *TDNT* III, 159f. — R. B. EGAN, "Lexical Evidence on Two Pauline Passages," *NovT* 19 (1977) 34-62. — S. J. HAFEMANN, *Suffering and the Spirit* (WUNT 19, 1986) 18-39. — P. MARSHALL, "A Metaphor of Social Shame: ΘΡΙΑΜΒΕΥΕΙΝ in 2 Cor. 2:14," *NovT* 25 (1983)

302-17. — H. S. VERSNEL, *Triumphus* (1970) 3-24. — L. WILLIAMSON, "Led in Triumph," *Int* 22 (1968) 317-32. — For further bibliography see Hafemann; *TWNT* X, 1110.

1. Θριαμβεύω appears in the NT only in 2 Cor 2:14 and Col 2:15. It is widely assumed that in both passages the vb. carries the same meaning as Lat. *triumpho,* "celebrate a triumphal procession over." Such usage is attested otherwise in Greek literature (Plutarch), but the use of θριαμβεύω in both NT passages scarcely fits in with the paradigms known from antiquity. Therefore, that it means *make known* in its NT occurrences is proposed below.

2. If θριαμβεύω in 2 Cor 2:14 were alluding to the image of the triumphal procession, the passage would be about a triumphal procession of God through the world, in which (a) Paul or the apostles are led along as defeated enemies (Delling 160; Williamson 325f.). If one takes the analogy to the Roman triumphal processions—there are no others—less rigorously, it could also mean that (b) God leads Paul or the apostles in the triumphal procession in the same way that a general would his officers and soldiers (LSJ 806; for a weakened allusion to the image of the triumphal procession, H. Lietzmann and W. G. Kümmel, *1–2 Cor* [HNT] 108, 198; R. Bultmann, *2 Cor* [Eng. tr., 1985] 63). The image of the triumphal procession also provides the background for the translation (c): "allow to triumph": God grants the triumph, and the apostles are the victors (so the translations of Luther, the Zürcher Bibel, F. Tillmann, and older commentaries; see BAGD; cf. BDF §§148.1; 309.1).

Considerations against these interpretations are: a) they fit poorly in the context, in which Paul refers not to his victory through God, but rather to his role as mediator (→ εὐωδία); there are no uses of the term in Greek literature corresponding to b) and c) (Williamson 322); in c) the role of the apostle is overrated. Moreover, the Greeks used θριαμβεύω to describe actual triumphal processions; there are no texts indicating a fig. use of the term in NT times.

Despite the long translation and interpretive tradition the meaning *make known,* which is independent of Lat. *triumphus,* is preferable (for this sense of the word see Moulton/Milligan 293, referring to ÄgU IV, 1061, l. 19; it is also attested in Ctesias *Persica* 13 and 58, where it is incorrectly classified by BAGD; cf. Williamson 320-22; cf. also the basic considerations on θριαμβεύω in Versnel 24). The idea that God "always" *makes* the apostles *known* has a parallel in the same section of 2 Corinthians (6:9; cf. 1 Cor 4:9) and forms a good background to 2:14b: Because God makes the apostles known, he can spread "the fragrance of the knowledge of him" through them. The "in Christ" that follows θριαμβεύοντι ἡμᾶς should express the idea that God makes them known in their relationship to Christ as proclaimers of the gospel of Christ (cf. F. Neugebauer, *In Christus* [1961] 80).

3. The complex statement in Col 2:15 describes the subjection of the powers (ἀρχαί, ἐξουσίαι): God has "stripped" (ἀπεκδύομαι), i.e., disarmed them; he has "placed them on display" (→ δειγματίζω). The description

is concluded by the participial construction θριαμβεύσας αὐτοὺς ἐν αὐτῷ. One possible understanding is that both preceding statements fit into the idea of a triumphal processional, which is here condensed. In this case God would have the defeated powers marching behind Christ "in the same way as the Roman emperor made prisoners of war march behind the one whose triumph it was" (E. Schweizer, *Col* [Eng tr., 1982] 151; cf. E. Lohse, *Col, Phlm* [Hermeneia] 112). But the position of θριαμβεύσας at the end of the sentence is noteworthy, and one must ask whether θριαμβεύω is sufficient to understand the way of Jesus to the cross as a triumphal processional of God (so Delling 160).

A second possible understanding sees θριαμβεύω in a more general sense as "conquer" (BAGD). Texts for this usage can be found only for Lat. *triumpho*.

Another possible view is to understand θριαμβεύω as "make known," perhaps in the pejorative sense of "expose" (Ctesias *Persica* 13.15: expose/make someone known to be a false ruler) or "mock" (*Vita Euripidis* 137.89 according to Delling 160n.2). In this case the partc. θριαμβεύσας would be an alternative repetition and summary of the ideas expressed with "disarmed" and "place on display," and the concluding ἐν αὐτῷ would be a reminder that God has publicly exposed the powers through the Christ event.   G. Dautzenberg

θρίξ, τριχός, ἡ   *thrix*   hair*

This noun is used primarily in reference to human hair (12 times in the NT). Mark 1:6 par. Matt 3:4 speak of the garment of the Baptist made of camel's *hair,* Rev 9:8a of the long *hair* of the apocalyptic locusts ("like women's hair," v. 8a). The expression *"the hairs* of your head" appears in Matt 10:30 par. Luke 12:7 ("they are numbered"). In Luke 7:38 the sinful woman dries the feet of Jesus "with the *hairs* of her head" (cf. v. 44; see the parallels in John 11:2; 12:3). Matt 5:36; Luke 21:18; Acts 27:34 speak of a single *hair* in emphasizing God's protecting care for the most trifling object. 1 Pet 3:3 contrasts outward adornment "by braiding *the hair"* with "the hidden person of the heart" (v. 4). Rev 1:14 says of the Son of Man: "his head and his *hair* were white as wool" (cf. Dan 7:9 Theod.).

θροέω   *throeō*   be frightened*

Mark 13:7 par. Matt 24:6: μὴ θροεῖσθε, "Do not *be alarmed."* The pass. carries the same sense also in 2 Thess 2:2.

θρόμβος, ου, ὁ   *thrombos*   drops*

Luke 22:44: "his [Jesus'] sweat became like *drops* of blood falling on the ground."

θρόνος, ου, ὁ   *thronos*   throne, seat of power

1. Occurrences in the NT — 2. Linguistic considerations — 3. NT usage

Lit.: E. BAMMEL, "Versuch zu Col 1,15-20," *ZNW* 52 (1962) 88-95. — H. BIETENHARD, *Die himmlische Welt im Urchristentum und Spätjudentum* (WUNT 2, 1951) 53-73. — BILLERBECK I, 974-79. — C. BLENDINGER, *DNTT* II, 611-15. — O. HOFIUS, *Der Vorhang vor dem Thron Gottes* (WUNT 14, 1972). — K. P. JÖRNS, *Das hymnische Evangelium* (SNT 5, 1971). — J. MAIER, *Vom Kultus zur Gnosis* (Kairos. Religionswissenschaftliche Studien 1, 1964) 61-86, 95-106. — L. MOWRY, "Revelation 4-5 and Early Christian Liturgical Usage," *JBL* 71 (1952) 75-84. — H. P. MÜLLER, *Formgeschichtliche Untersuchungen zu Apc 4f.* (Diss. Heidelberg, 1962) 1-14, 195-201. — W. W. READER, *Die Stadt Gottes in der Johannesapokalypse* (Diss. Göttingen, 1971) 138-41. — O. SCHMITZ, *TDNT* III, 160-67. — G. SCHOLEM, *Major Trends in Jewish Mysticism* (Eng. tr., ³1954) 40-79, 356-58. — For further bibliography see *TWNT* X, 1110f.

1. Θρόνος appears in the NT *ca.* 60 times, three-fourths of which are in Revelation. Most of the remaining occurrences are in Matthew (5:34; 19:28 bis; 23:22; 25:31) and the Lukan writings (Luke 1:32, 52; 22:30; Acts 2:30; 7:49); the others are in Col 1:16; Heb 1:8; 4:16; 8:1; 12:2.

2. Θρόνος is related linguistically to θρᾶνος ("bench, stool") and θρῆνυς ("footstool") and means, according to the definition of Athenaeus vi.192e, the ἐλευθέριος καθέδρα σὺν ὑποποδίῳ. Whereas θρόνος is originally a designation for a good and esp. a higher chair for honored guests (Homer *Od.* i.130; viii.65f.), it was later used for the seat of the king or the seats of the gods and became in the pl. a circumlocution for royal power and dominion (Aeschylus *Ch.* 565, 969; *Pr.* 912; Sophocles *OT* 237; *OC* 426).

3. Corresponding to the range of meanings already observable in the Greek world, the NT authors or the traditions on which they rely combine a variety of ideas with the θρόνος concept.

a) Most frequently it is *God* who sits on a throne (Heb 8:1; 12:2; Rev 1:4; 3:21; 4:2f., 9f.; 5:1; 7:10, 15; 11:16; 19:4; 21:5, etc.) in heaven (cf. 1 Kgs 22:19; Ps 11:4; 103:19, etc.). For John the seer the phrase ὁ καθήμενος ἐπὶ τοῦ θρόνου (e.g., 4:9f.; 5:1; 6:16; 7:10; 21:5) serves as a traditional t.t. for God (cf. 1 Kgdms 4:4; 4 Kgdms 19:15; Ps 79:2 LXX; Isa 37:16) in his function as ruler and judge.

Rev 4:2-8 gives the only NT description of the divine throne and its surroundings: Around it are a rainbow (v. 3), and from it go forth lightning, voices, and thunder (v. 5). Twenty-four elders sit on twenty-four thrones around him (v. 4). Seven spirits, i.e., God's subservient throne angels (cf. 8:2 and E. Schweizer, "Die sieben Geister in der Apokalypse," *idem, Neotestamentica* [1963] 198f.; *contra* Bietenhard 60f.) stand as torches before it (v. 5). Four living creatures (ζῷα) with the appearance respectively of a lion, an ox, a person, and an eagle praise God with the words, "holy, holy, holy" (v. 8b). These together complete the divine area around the throne. God himself, who sits on the throne, is not described. Only the radiance proceeding from him is mentioned (v. 3a).

The tradition history of the background of this throne scene is found in the realm of the OT and Judaism, even if its roots go back to ancient oriental throne symbolism. To sit on a throne —in the LXX θρόνος is almost always a tr. of Heb. *kissē'*, see Hatch/Redpath I, 655f.— in the OT is the prerogative of the king (Gen 41:40; 2 Sam 14:9) or of other highly placed persons (Exod 11:5; 12:29; 1 Kgs 2:19; Neh 3:7 LXX). Special significance and dignity are given to the *throne of David*. Not only is the promise of God's saving presence to Israel connected with it (2 Sam 7:12-16; Ps 89:5, 30, 37, etc.), it is also a synonym for power and dominion (2 Sam 3:10; Jer 22:30; Ps 132:11-18), just as is the case sometimes for the throne in general (Isa 14:13).

In particular Yahweh's claim to dominion is manifested in the fact that he sits on a *throne* in heaven (cf. the "enthronement Psalms," 47:9; 89:15; 93:2; 97:2. In other passages the temple, the temple mount (Jer 14:21; 17:21), or Jerusalem (3:17) is the place of Yahweh's throne, associated here with the mythological conception of the mountain of God (cf. Isa 14:13). If Isa 66:1 stands alone in the OT with the words, "Heaven is my throne and earth is my footstool," the subject is not at all unique in showing the OT concept of Yahweh's throne (cf. C. Westermann, *Isa 40–66* [OTL] 412f.).

The decisive elements for the throne scene in Revelation 4 come from Ezekiel's vision of the throne-chariots and the "vision of the heavenly throne" in Isaiah 6 (H. Wildberger, *Isa* [BKAT] I, 236), as the common individual features demonstrate. On the other hand the major differences are not to be overlooked. Isaiah's vision takes place in the *Jerusalem temple:* Yahweh is enthroned at the place of the ark in the most holy place (on the discussion of the ark of the covenant as the place of Yahweh's throne cf. Maier 61-86). But John the apocalyptist sees the *heavenly world* "in the Spirit," and his vision has cosmic dimensions. Different from Ezekiel 1–2 is that God's throne in Revelation 4–5 is not a moving object but a firmly fixed *throne*.

An entire succession of speculations in ancient Judaism was esp. dependent on Ezekiel 1. These belong to the circle of rabbinic esotericism and to what is known as merkabah mysticism (Scholem, Billerbeck). Inasmuch as the most important thing in heaven is God's throne, these speculations have relied principally on it. Rabbinic texts say that the throne of God in the highest heaven is separated from the rest by a curtain (*pargôd*), so that no can look at the glory of God illicitly. Only especially selected ones may go through the curtain (see Hofius 4-12).

b) The remaining NT passages in which θρόνος appears absolutely or connected with a gen. that defines the noun more precisely, presuppose OT throne concepts and/or elaborate on them. Matt 5:34f. takes up Isa 66:1 as a basis for the absolute prohibition of oaths. Matt 23:16-22 is different: While here the reference is likewise to heaven as the θρόνος τοῦ θεοῦ (v. 22), the possibility of the oath by heaven, however, is presupposed as customary and permitted. Acts 7:49 (Lukan redaction making use of a spiritualizing cultic motif?) cites Isa

66:1f. with polemical intent and criticizes the temple structure in general: God does not dwell in a work of human hands (χειροποίητος), for "heaven is my throne, and the earth is the footstool for my feet."

The OT promise regarding David's throne plays a major role in the NT, where it is taken up and interpreted christologically. In the annunciation to Mary by Gabriel the θρόνος Δαυίδ is conferred on Jesus (Luke 1:32) in words that certainly allude to 2 Sam 7:12-16. The κληθήσεται of v. 32 may be understood adoptionistically (cf. Pss 2:7; 89:27-30). The fulfillment of Nathan's prophecy in Jesus Christ is also expressed in Acts 2:30 (cf. vv. 29, 30f.). Christ is *the* legitimate descendant of David's throne. This θρόνος is not limited to earthly power, but is in heaven and includes the claim to universal sovereignty (vv. 34b, 35, citing Ps 109:1 LXX).

The incomparable dignity and power of the exalted Lord is emphasized in a special way in Heb 1:8a, where Ps 45:7 is applied to Christ. The passage promises an eternal throne actualized from the Nathan promise. According to 4:16 and 8:1 Christ sits on the "throne of grace" (4:16) or "at the right hand of the throne of the majesty" (8:1, referring again to Ps 110:1) as the heavenly high priest. Grace (χάρις) and majesty (μεγαλοσύνη) are circumlocutions for God himself or for his activity (gen. of quality), so that here Christ as exalted one shares in the sovereignty of God. 12:2 elaborates in a similar way: The one who was obedient in suffering is now exalted and enthroned in power and majesty.

Comparable formulations, but in an apocalyptic context, are found in Revelation, esp. ch. 5. A lamb (ἀρνίον), looking as if it had been slain (5:6), takes a sealed book from the hand of one "who sits on the throne" (5:7; → a). When he takes the scroll the lamb is proclaimed king of the eschaton and is praised by those assembled in the heavenly throne room (5:8-14; cf. 7:9f., 17; 22:3). Here the heavenly enthronement of the one who suffered and was crucified on earth is expressed as a victory over all his enemies. Unique for the NT is that Rev 2:13 also has Satan sitting on a throne (cf. 13:2; 16:10). Here there is apparently a characterization of the sovereign power of the adversary, which is, of course, temporally limited.

Matthew has two sayings of the Lord according to which the Son of Man appears in the new world of God (so → παλιγγενεσία in 19:28 is to be understood) or at his parousia (25:31) on the θρόνος δόξης αὐτοῦ as judge, to sit together with the twelve disciples, who likewise sit on thrones (19:28b par. Luke 22:30) to judge the twelve tribes of Israel (on the use of the title Son of Man in these passages, cf. C. Colpe, *TDNT* VIII, 447f.). Again the image of the θρόνος or θρόνοι is used to express the sovereign power that the enthroned are able to exercise. Matt 19:28b implies the eschatological-apocalyptic restitution of the twelve tribes of Israel. Luke 1:52 ("he [God] puts down the mighty from their thrones and exalts the lowly") indicates that the birth of Jesus the Messiah is the beginning of the rule of God, who ends the misery of Israel and of the poor and brings the final equilibrium (L. Schottroff, *EvT* 38 [1978] 300-306).

c) A peculiar feature in the use of θρόνος, not found elsewhere in the NT, is present in Col 1:16. Through juxtaposition with κυριότητες, ἀρχαί, and ἐξουσίαι, the θρόνοι are seen to be an allusion to the Colossian false teaching. Thus the θρόνοι, like the other three terms in the list, represent *angelic powers,* which are significant in the Colossian speculation about angels (cf. *2 Enoch* 20:1 [A]; *T. Levi* 3:8; *contra* Bammel 90-93).

D. Sanger

Θυάτ(ε)ιρα, ων, τά   *Thyat(e)ira*   Thyatira*

Lit.: BAGD s.v. — A. VAN DEN BORN, *BL* 1750. — W. H. BUCKLER, "Monuments de Thyatire," *Revue de philologie* 37 (1913) 289-331. — D. H. FRENCH, "Prehistoric Sites in Northwest Anatolia," *Anatolian Studies* 19 (1969) 41-98. — F. HAHN, "Die Sendschreiben der Johannesapokalypse," FS Kuhn 357-94. — J. KEIL, PW VI/1 (1936) 657-59. — H. KRAFT, *Rev* (HNT, 1974) 67-74. — E. LOHMEYER, *Rev* (HNT, [3]1970) 27-31, 40-43. — D. MAGIE, *Roman Rule in Asia Minor* (1950) 123, 977f. — O. F. A. MEINARDUS, "The Christian Remains of the Seven Churches of the Apocalypse," *BA* 37 (1974) 69-82. — M. J. MELLINK, "Archaeology in Asia Minor," *AJA* 74 (1970) 157-78, 77 (1973) 169-93, 79 (1975) 201-22. — E. OLSHAUSEN, *KP* V, 804. — W. M. RAMSAY, *The Letters to the Seven Churches of Asia* (1904, [2]1963). — L. ROBERT, *Villes d'Asie Mineure* ([2]1962) 269. — G. SCHILLE, *Anfänge der Kirche* (1966) 43-53. — A. SUHL, *Paulus und seine Briefe* (SNT 11, 1975) 189-91. — A. WIKENHAUSER, *LTK* X, 176f. — WIKENHAUSER, *Geschichtswert* 410f.

1. The ancient city of Thyatira, in Lydia on the Lycus, on the road from Pergamum to Sardis, is today called Akhisar. Settled in the pre-Hellenistic period, it became a military colony under Seleucus I in 281 B.C. and developed into a significant commercial and industrial city. The handicraft of those who were dyers of purple and their association are frequently attested in literary works and in inscriptions. In 129 B.C. Thyatira came under Roman rule.

2. Θυάτ(ε)ιρα is mentioned in the NT in Acts 16:14 and 3 times in Revelation. According to Acts 16:14 Lydia, a dealer in purple from Thyatira, hears the preaching of Paul, is baptized (v. 15), and invites him and his companions into her house. The idea that the account is a legend about the founding of the church in Thyatira, which Luke has shifted to Philippi (Schille 50-53), cannot be assumed (Suhl 189-91). Rev 1:11 mentions the church of Thyatira among the seven churches addressed. The letter to "the angel of the church at Thyatira" (2:18) praises the Christian conduct of the church, but charges it with tolerating the false prophetess Jezebel (→ Ἰεζάβελ)

and speaks to the genuine part of the church (2:24) to encourage it to remain firm in what it has.

A. Weiser

θυγάτηρ, τρός, ἡ   *thygatēr*   daughter*

1. Occurrences — 2. Literal — 3. Fig.

Lit.: BILLERBECK I, 586f. — J. JEREMIAS, *Jerusalem in the Time of Jesus* (Eng. tr., 1969) 359-76. — P. KETTER, *Christus und die Frauen* (1949-50). — J. LEIPOLDT, *Die Frau in der antiken Welt und im Urchristentum* (1962). — E. LÖVESTAM, *BHH* 1999. — H. VORLÄNDER, *DNTT* III, 1055f. — G. WALLIS, *BHH* 1999.

1. Θυγάτηρ occurs 28 times in the NT. Most of the occurrences are in the Synoptic Gospels (8 in Matthew, 5 in Mark, 9 in Luke) and in Acts (3). It also appears in John 12:15; 2 Cor 6:18; and Heb 11:24.

2. Θυγάτηρ is usually used in the NT of a *daughter* in relation to her father (Matt 9:18; 10:37; Mark 5:35; Luke 2:36; 8:42, 49; Acts 7:21; 21:9; Heb 11:24) or mother (Matt 10:35; 14:6; 15:22, 28; Mark 6:22; 7:26, 29; Luke 12:53 bis), independent of how old the daughter is. One is probably to conclude that the reference is to a girl who is not yet at the age for marriage (under twelve and one-half years) in Matt 9:18 par. (the *daughter* of the head of the synagogue) and Mark 7:26, 29 par. (the *daughter* of the Syro-Phoenician woman), whereas the *daughter* of Herodias (Mark 6:22 par.) would have already reached this age. The 84-year-old prophetess Anna (the number probably indicates her age, not her years of being a widow [G. Schneider, *Luke* [ÖTK] I, 72] is called the *daughter* of Penuel (Luke 2:36). Here the relationship as daughter has precedence over the attachment to the deceased husband. The designation *daughter* of Pharaoh (Acts 7:21; Heb 11:24), which is taken from the Moses tradition (Exod 2:5-10), includes another accent: It does not describe a father-child relationship in the literal sense, but suggests the status of the daughter corresponding to the royal dignity of the king.

The occurrence of θυγάτηρ in the predominant Palestinian tradition appears against the background of a strongly patriarchal social order. Thus the θυγάτηρ had—corresponding to the social position of the woman—a *status minoris.* A distinction was made among girls between the q^etanāh (minor, up to twelve years old) and the na^{·a}rah (virgin, twelve to twelve and one-half years). Until a girl came to be of marriagable age, she was subordinate in every respect to the authority of the father, which was then transferred to her husband. Marriages were arranged for girls by their fathers. This *patria potestas* was so extensive that the father could even sell his (under-age) daughter into slavery. Legal affairs of the daughter were ineffective without the agreement of the father. The bride price paid by the bridegroom also belonged to the father. Within this juridically unprotected position of the daughter in relation to the father one could view the daughter as a commercial object, and this situation was certainly widespread. Of course it was especially widespread among the lower social levels, where the productivity of the daughter and the expected bride price were of decisive economic meaning (numerous references in Jeremias).

With reference to the firmly decreed social order a Q logion, in dependence on Mic 7:6, prophesies in Matt 10:35 par. Luke 12:53 (bis) the breakup of the familial bond: mothers will be set against their *daughters* (and *daughters* against their mothers in Luke). Here the apocalyptic idea of the disturbance of the order of human life in the course of the eschatological affliction is presupposed. The rule in Q that disciples not place love for *daughter* (among others) above love for Jesus (Matt 10:37) also belongs within this framework. It was originally intended to show the radical alternative between family relations and the discipleship Jesus demanded (cf. Luke 14:26). Leaving "father and mother, son and *daughter*"—here Matthew may be giving the parallelism that is in Q—is for Q an expression of eschatological consciousness, which anticipates in the following of Jesus the Son of Man the collapse of human community.

3. Θυγάτηρ has a fig. meaning as a Semitic idiom to designate a woman or a collective portrayed as a woman ("daughters of Zion") without involving a bodily parent-child relationship. Jesus says to a person he is healing: "My *daughter,* your faith has made you well" (Mark 5:34 par. Matt 9:22/Luke 8:48). On the other hand, θυγάτηρ in Luke 1:5 ("his [i.e., Zechariah's] wife was from the *daughters* of Aaron") and 13:16 ("*daughters* of Abraham") is used in a genealogical sense in one case to refer to ancestry from the priestly tribe and in the other case to indicate membership in the elect people. In 2 Cor 6:18 θυγάτηρ is used in a figure from adoption. The passage appears within the framework of a non-Pauline insertion (2 Cor 6:14–7:1) and stands in connection with a group of OT citations. The statement that God will be Father to the "sons and *daughters*" (i.e., all Israel) takes up the idea of election as an image of intimate community (cf. Jer 32:38). The same designation is found in Acts 2:17 (citing Joel 3:1-5 LXX), but now in reference to succeeding generations. The "*daughters* of Zion" appear similarly as a personified figure (Matt 21:5; John 12:15, in dependence on Zech 9:9), in reference to Jerusalem and its inhabitants.   H.-J. Ritz

θυγάτριον, ου, τό *thygatrion* little daughter*

Jairus speaks in Mark 5:23 of his *little daughter* (τὸ θυγάτριόν μου; not in the Matthean and Lukan parallels); 7:25: θυγάτριον αὐτῆς (not in the Matthean parallel), of the *little daughter* of the Syro-Phoenician woman.

θύελλα, ης, ἡ *thyella* storm, whirlwind*

Heb 12:18, in the "inventory" of the theophany (Deut 4:11; 5:22): θύελλα with → ζόφος.

θύϊνος, 3 *thyinos* from the citron tree*

Rev 18:12, among the valuable objects of the merchants, which no one buys (v. 11): πᾶν ξύλον θύϊνον, "all kinds of wood *from the citron tree*" (= scented wood).

θυμίαμα, ατος, τό *thymiama* incense; incense offering*

This noun appears only in Luke 1:10f. and 4 times in Revelation. Luke 1:10: "at the hour of *incense offering*" (cf. H. Schürmann, *Luke* [HTKNT] I, 31); v. 11: the angel of the Lord stands "at the right side of the *incense offering* (= altar of incense, Exod 30:1, 27; 2 Macc 2:5)." Revelation has only the pl. in the sense of *incense* (5:8; 8:3, 4; 18:13).

θυμιατήριον, ου, τό *thymiatērion* altar of incense*

Heb 9:4, of the golden θυμιατήριον in the most holy place; θυμιατήριον in this sense appears also in Philo *Her.* 226; *Vit. Mos.* ii.94; Josephus *B.J.* v.218; *Ant.* iii.147, 198.

θυμιάω *thymiaō* make an incense offering*

Luke 1:9, of Zechariah: ἔλαχε τοῦ θυμιᾶσαι (1st aor. inf.), "it fell his lot *to make the incense offering*"; → θυμίαμα.

θυμομαχέω *thymomacheō* be very angry*

Acts 12:20: Herod (Agrippa I) was *very angry* (θυμομαχῶν) at the inhabitants of Tyre and Sidon. The vb. appears also in Polybius ix.40.4; xxvii.8.4; Plutarch *Demetr.* 22.

θυμόομαι *thymoomai* (pass.) become angry*

Matt 2:16, of Herod: ἐθυμώθη λίαν, "he became very angry." Absolute use of θυμόομαι is found also in Polybius v.16.4; *T. Dan* 4:4. H. Schönweiss, *DNTT* I, 105f.

θυμός, οῦ, ὁ *thymos* anger, wrath*

1. Occurrences in the NT — 2. Meaning — 3. Usage

Lit.: F. BÜCHSEL, *TDNT* III, 167f. — A. T. HANSON, *The Wrath of the Lamb* (1957) 50, 62, 65, 86f., 159-80, 206-9. — H. SCHÖNWEISS, *DNTT* I, 105f. — For further bibliography see *TWNT* X, 1111.

1. Of the 18 occurrences in the NT 10 are found in Revelation, 2 in the Lukan literature, and 6 in the Epistles.

2. The original meaning of the word is "what is moved or moves." From that beginning it became the "life principle" or the "life power." In secular Greek it involves an

entire gradation of meanings: "desire, impulse, passion, courage, disposition, reflection." However, in later usage (in the prose writers, Plato, Thucydides, and others) θυμός means primarily "courage, anger, wrath." Jewish and NT usage is dependent on the later secular Greek usage. While in the LXX the original distinction between θυμός as emotion and → ὀργή as expression of emotion is almost totally lost, in later Judaism and in the NT an undeniable hesitation exists in associating θυμός—contrary to ὀργή—with God (in the NT only in Rom 2:8 and in Revelation), probably because of the primarily emotional connotations of the word θυμός.

3. In the Lukan literature and in the Epistles (except for Rom 2:8) θυμός is used of humans. In Luke 4:28 and Acts 19:28 it denotes *anger* as the reaction of a group of people to an unacceptable speech. In Heb 11:27 it is used of the king's *anger*. In the other 4 occurrences (2 Cor 12:20; Gal 5:20; Eph 4:31; Col 3:8) θυμός appears in catalogs of vices. In Eph 4:31 and Col 3:8 it is found next to ὀργή with no demonstrable distinction. In 2 Cor 12:20 and Gal 5:20 it appears in the pl. *(outbreaks of wrath)* in a formal group including ἔρις, ζῆλος, θυμοί, and ἐριθεῖαι.

In Rom 2:8 θυμός refers, together with ὀργή, to the divine wrath of the final judgment. The combination as a designation of God's wrath is certainly taken from the OT (cf., e.g., Deut 9:19; Ps 2:5; Hos 13:11). In Revelation θυμός is used in one instance of the devil's *wrath* (12:12) and in the other instances of the divine *wrath*, which is poured out over humanity as wine of wrath (as a horrible plague) (see 14:8, 10, 19; 15:7; 16:1, 19; 18:3; 19:15; cf. 15:1). This concept of the wine of wrath and cup of wrath is from the OT (Isa 51:17, 22; Jer 25:15ff.; Ps 75:9, etc.). The expression θυμός τῆς ὀργῆς (16:19; 19:15) is from the OT (see, e.g., Num 14:34; Deut 13:17; Ps 69:24). The "wine" or the "wine of wrath" (certainly not "poisonous wine" or "wine of passion") of Babylon the harlot, from which the peoples have drunk (17:2 and 14:8; 18:3; cf. Jer 51:7f.), refers on the one hand to the sins of the peoples; on the other hand it is actually identical with the wine of God's wrath.

H. W. Hollander

θύρα, ας, ἡ *thyra* door, gate, entrance*

1. Literal meaning — 2. Depictions of miracles involving the opening of a door — 3. Fig. use

Lit.: BAGD s.v. — DALMAN, *Arbeit* VII, 50-56; 67-74. — F. EBERT, PW VI/A/1 (1936) 737-42. — J. JEREMIAS, *TDNT* III, 173-80. — R. KRATZ, *Auferweckung als Befreiung. Eine Studie zur Passions- und Auferstehungstheologie des Matthäus* (1973). — idem, *Rettungswunder. Motiv-, traditions- und formkritische Aufarbeitung einer biblischen Gattung* (1979). — O. WEINREICH, "Gebet und Wunder," idem, *Religionsgeschichtliche Studien* (1968) 38-298.

1. In the lit. sense θύρα can indicate any kind of *door, gate,* or *entrance:* Mark 1:33; 2:2; 11:4; Matt 6:6; Luke 11:7 (of the house); John 10:1, 2 (of the sheep enclosure); 18:16; 20:19, 26; Acts 3:2 (the "Beautiful Gate" of the temple); 12:13 (of the entrance court); 21:30 (of the inner court of the temple); 5:19, 23; 12:6; 16:26 (of the prison); Mark 15:46; 16:3; Matt 27:60 (the entrance to the tomb). The vbs. ἀνοίγω and κλείω are most often found with "door." The closed door protects against importunity (Luke 11:7) and against persecution by opponents (John 20:19) and preserves seclusion (Matt 6:6).

2. In Acts 5:19, 23; 12:6; 16:26 (the *door* of a prison in each case) θύρα appears in the framework of a "miracle of a door-opening or miracle of liberation" (cf. Weinreich; Kratz, *Rettungswunder*). Associated motifs—secure locks, shackles, watchmen, appearance of an angel, earthquake, nocturnal liberation, and "automatic" door opening—belong to the narrative schema of the genre, which was common throughout antiquity. Miraculous liberations were esp. described in connection with the spread of the cult of Dionysus in accounts about the god or his followers (Euripides *Ba.*; Nonnus *D.*) and in the "lives" of the θεῖοι ἄνδρες (Philostratus *VA*; Artapanus on Moses). The "Sitz im Leben" of the genre of stories about miracles of the opening of doors and of liberation is the effort involved in the acceptance and missionary expansion of a new cult or religion. Thus the first three miracles of liberation involving Peter and Paul (with Silas) in Acts serve the purpose of legitimizing the missionaries and demonstrating that the true God is engaged on the side of the proclaimers and that his opponents will be put to shame (→ θεομάχος).

In Mark 15:46; 16:3; Matt 27:60 the related motifs signify the influence of miraculous elements of door openings and of deliverance stories on account of the tomb narrative: The resurrection of Jesus is "deliverance" from the tomb and from death through the "saving" intervention of God (cf. in detail Kratz, *Auferweckung; Rettungswunder*). The appearance of Jesus in a closed room in John 20:26 has another function: The resurrected one is no longer subject to the laws of this world.

3. Fig. use of θύρα is relatively frequent:

a) The spatial image of standing at the *door* is used of direct temporal proximity (Acts 5:9), most often with an eschatological aspect (Mark 13:29 par. Matt 24:33; Jas 5:9).

b) A *door* can also represent symbolically the reciprocal reconciliation of God and the individual: God is, without limit, "open." The individual "opens" himself entirely in faith and in the readiness to repent (Rev 3:7f., 20). God, in his grace, opens the door to faith for the Gentiles (Acts 14:27), and opens the door to successful work for the missionaries (1 Cor 16:9; 2 Cor 2:12; Col 4:3).

c) The gate that leads to eternal savation is narrow (Luke 13:24); so much greater is the danger (in the judgment) of being excluded for those who have come too late (Matt 25:10; Luke 13:25). Jesus, the judge and Son of Man, possesses the key to power (cf. Rev 3:7f.; cf. also Matt 16:13-20).

d) The imagery in John 10:7-9 is developed from the concretizing terminology (the shepherd goes to his sheep through the open door, the thief creeps in) in vv. 1f. Ἐγώ εἰμι ἡ θύρα τῶν προβάτων might first have the meaning "the door *to* the sheep," but then also (v. 7) "the door *for* the sheep." In any case this image of the door emphasizes the exclusive claim of Jesus as the one who brings salvation.

R. Kratz

θυρεός, οῦ, ὁ *thyreos* long shield*

Eph 6:16, metaphorically of the *"shield* of faith."
A. Oepke, *TDNT* V, 312-14.

θυρίς, ίδος, ἡ *thyris* window*

Acts 20:9, of the young man Eutychus, who sat at *the window opening* (ἐπὶ τῆς θυρίδος) and fell out when he went to sleep. In 2 Cor 11:33 Paul reports that he was "let down in a basket through a window (διὰ θυρίδος) in the city wall."

θυρωρός, οῦ, ὁ (ἡ) *thyrōros* doorkeeper*

Mark 13:34, of the task of the θυρωρός to watch the house; John 10:3, of the *doorkeeper* who opens the door for the true shepherd; 18:16, 17, of the *woman who kept the door,* allowed Peter into the court of the high priest, and asked him about his relationship to the disciples (v. 17, ἡ παιδίσκη ἡ θυρωρός).

θυσία, ας, ἡ *thysia* act of sacrificing; sacrifice, sacrificial meal*
θύω *thyō* sacrifice, slaughter, murder; mid.: offer a sacrifice, sacrifice for oneself*

1. Meanings and relationship to other sacrificial terminology, esp. in the OT — 2. Occurrences and references in the NT — 3. The Synoptics and Acts — 4. Paul and 1 Peter — 5. Ephesians and Hebrews

Lit.: BAGD s.v. — J. BEHM, *TDNT* III, 180-90. — J. CASABONA, *Récherches sur le Vocabulaire des Sacrifices en Grec* (1966). — E. E. CARPENTER, *ISBE* IV, 260-72. — O. CASEL, "Die Λογικὴ θυσία der antiken Mystik in christlich-liturgischer Umdeutung," *Jahrbuch für Liturgiewissenschaft* 4 (1924) 37-47. — M. DIBELIUS, "Die himmlische Kultus nach dem Hebräerbrief," *idem., Botschaft* II, 160-76. — W. FAUTH, *KP* IV, 307-10.

— D. GILL, "Thysia and *sᵉlāmîm:* Questions to R. Schmid's *Das Bundesopfer in Israel,*" *Bib* 47 (1966) 255-62. — R. HENTSCHKE, *RGG* IV, 1641-47. — H.-J. HERMISSON, *Sprache und Ritus im altisraelitischen Kult. Zur "Spiritualisierung" der Kultbegriffe im AT* (WMANT 19, 1965) 29-64. — E. KÄSEMANN, *Rom* (Eng. tr., 1980) 325-31. — K. KERTELGE, "Die 'reine Opfergabe'. Zum Verständnis des 'Opfers' im NT," *Freude am Gottesdienst* (FS J. G. Plöger, 1983) 347-60. — H. LIETZMANN, *Rom* (HNT, ⁵1971) 106-10. — J. MAIER, *Die Tempelrolle vom Toten Meer* (UTB 829, 1978) 29-39. — O. MICHEL, *TDNT* V, 202f. — R. RENDTORFF, *Studien zur Geschichte des Opfers im Alten Israel* (WMANT 24, 1967). — L. SABOURIN, *DBS* X, 1483-1545. — H. SCHLIER, *Rom* (HTKNT, 1977) 350-62. — T. R. SCHREINER, *ISBE* IV, 273-77. — P. STENGEL, *Opfergebräuche der Griechen* (1910; repr. 1972). — F. THIELE and C. BROWN, *DNTT* III, 417-36. — K. WEISS, *TDNT* IX, 65-68. — H.-D. WENDLAND, *RGG* IV, 1647-51. — H. WENSCHKEWITZ, *Die Spiritualisierung der Kultusbegriffe Tempel, Priester und Opfer im NT* (Angelos Beihefte 4, 1932). — R. B. WRIGHT, *Sacrifice in the Intertestamental Literature* (Diss. Hartford, 1966). — Y. YADIN, *Megillat hamMiqdaš. The Temple Scroll* I-III (1977). — R. K. YERKES, *Sacrifice in Greek and Roman Religions and Early Judaism* (1952). — L. ZIEHEN, PW XVIII, 579-627. — For further bibliography see *DNTT* III, 437f.; *ISBE* IV, 272f., 277; *RGG* IV, 1646f., 1651; *TDNT* III, 180; *TWNT* X, 1111-13.

1. While the act. forms of the vb. emphasize reverence for the deity (offering of thanksgiving), in the mid. forms the requests, goals, and needs of those who sacrifice stand in the foreground. The sacrifice that is referred to with θύω originated in the domestic family meal in which parts of the slaughtered animal were burned and offered to the goddess of the hearth. Thus the basic meaning of θύω would be "flare up" (of the fiery smoke; cf. θυμίαμα, θυμιατήριον, θυμιάω, θυμός, etc.). Already in the Homeric period the θυσία was a ritually regulated public cult meal in which portions were burned for the deity. This almost total analogy to the rite of the *šᵉlāmîm* sacrifice in Israel (cf. Rendtorff 119ff.) may not be totally coincidental, but instead rest on its dependence on the θυσία (Gill).

On the other hand, the oblation and sacrificial meal of the observant community, the sacrifices totally given to the deity— whether by an individual or by a cult community—were called ὁλοκαύτωμα and σφάγιον, "burnt offering" and "blood offering." Offering of such sacrifices was never spoken of in ancient times with θύω, but always with such vbs. as ἐντέμνω and particularly with → σφάζω and σφαγιάζομαι, just as the LXX normally renders *šāḥaṭ* ("slaughter") by σφάζω. In situations of suffering and danger σφάγια were regularly brought to the gods. Where σφάζω is not used for "sacrifice" (in the NT: Rev 5:6, 9, 12; 13:8; 6:9; 18:24), it means "slay mercilessly" (in the NT: 1 John 3:12; Rev 6:4; 13:3). The tragedians often called a defenselessly murdered person a σφάγιον.

This fixed linguistic convention came to be relaxed after the end of the Greek cult, so that the LXX can even render Heb. *šāḥaṭ* occasionally by θύω (Exod 12:21; Judg 12:6; 2 Chr 29:22, 24; 30:15, 17; 35:1, 6, 11; Isa 22:13; 66:3). But θύω appears more frequently in the LXX, 140 times (along with its "synonym" θυσιάζω, which appears 43 times in the LXX but not at all in the NT), as the tr. of Heb. *zābaḥ* ("slaughter, sacrifice"). This pattern of translation has its basis in the synthesis of two originally independent types of sacrifices, which had long since taken place: *zebaḥ* and *šᵉlāmîm* became *zebaḥ-šᵉlāmîm,* which is firmly connected with the "sacrificial meal" (cf. Rendtorff 149ff.).

Θυσία is frequent in the LXX (about 400 occurrences; θυσίασμα occurs 12 times). It is used for *zebaḥ* and 130 times for *minhâ*, which had in Israel long been fixed terms for the total sacrificial cult (Rendtorff 191f.). Where θυσία has no corresponding term in the Hebrew text (*ca.* 40 times), its meaning is to be determined from this development of usage.

2. The vb. appears in the NT 14 times. In Matt 22:4; Luke 15:23, 27, 30; Acts 10:13; 11:7 it has the non-religious meaning *slaughter*. In Mark 14:12; Luke 22:7; 1 Cor 5:7 it is used of the *slaughtering* of the Passover lamb. In John 10:10 θύω refers—as κλέπτω and ἀπόλλυμι indicate—to *murder*. Except for the Passover passages mentioned, whose associated sacrificial meaning is determined by the obj., the "Passover lamb," and not by θύω itself, θύω is used only in Acts 14:13, 18 and 1 Cor 10:20 in the technical sense of offering sacrifice, in both instances *pagan* sacrifices, so that a negative accent is given. When a sacrifice pleasing to God is spoken of, such vbs. as δίδωμι, προσφέρω, and ἀναφέρω (θυσίαν) are used. Of the 28 occurrences of the noun θυσία, half are in Hebrews (→ 5), 5 are in the Synoptics, 2 in Acts, 4 in Paul, and 1 in Ephesians.

3. In two instances Matthew, in his treatment of Markan material, has placed on the lips of Jesus the saying from Hos 6:6 (cf. 1 Sam 15:22; Isa 1:10ff.; Ps 40:7f.), "I desire mercy and not *sacrifice*": in the story of Jesus' eating with tax collectors (Matt 9:13) and in the story of the "gleaning" on the sabbath (12:7). As already in the OT and Jewish tradition of the saying, in both Matthean instances it does not involve a critique or a rejection of the sacrificial cult, but an injunction to give unconditional precedence to mercy. Thus Matthew (in 9:13) portrays Jesus' table fellowship with "tax collectors and sinners" as the "fulfillment" of the prophetic word, as is indicated by the reason given for his practice ("for I have not come . . ."). In 12:7 the saying from Hosea does not serve an abstract critique of "Pharisaic casuistry," but instead rebukes the concrete unmercifulness of those who, under the pretext of the sabbath commandment, close their eyes to the hunger of the poor. Nothing can be concluded from Matthew's use of Hos 6:6 about his view of sacrifice; cf. also Matt 5:23f.!

Mark 9:49 D pc it also throws no light on the question of sacrifice. And if Mark (12:33) has the scribe say that the fulfillment of the double commandment is more important than all burnt offerings and sacrifices (→ ὁλοκαύτωμα and θυσία), he is in harmony with the broad stream of Jewish tradition (cf. 1 Sam 15:20ff.; Ps 51:18f.; Billerbeck I, 499f.; Hermisson 143f.).

That Jesus' mother, in accordance with Lev 12:1ff., brings a pair of turtledoves as a burnt offering and sin offering, reflects both the piety and the poverty of Jesus'

parents. Only when the required "one-year-old sheep" is beyond one's means may such a substitute be offered (cf. the material in Billerbeck II, 123f.). Jewish sacrificial practice is also presupposed in Luke 13:1.

In Stephen's speech (Acts 7:41f.) the citation from Amos 5:25-27 LXX should not be interpreted as a critique of the Jewish sacrificial system by the "Hellenists." Instead, what is criticized (in contrast to the intention of Amos, who praises the period in the wilderness as a time without *sacrifice*) is that Israel did *not* sacrifice to God in the wilderness, but rather to idols!

4. Paul establishes the idea that the Lord's Supper unites the communicants with their Lord (→ σῶμα) by arguing that the Israelites who participated in the sacrificial meal were partners in the "sacrificial altar" (→ θυσιαστήριον 2) and thus in Yahweh as its Lord (1 Cor 10:18; cf. 8:4ff.; see also Lev 7:6, 15; Deut 18:1ff.). Only "in Christ," i.e., in the Church of Jews and Gentiles, and not "since Christ," has that been set aside. Thus the reference to "Israel according to the flesh" has no negative accent here (cf. Rom 9:5!), as if Paul wanted to contrast the the Church as "spiritual Israel" or "true Israel" to the "fleshly Israel." The point of the comparison with the sacrificial meal is not the sacrificial character of the meal, but rather its role in establishing fellowship. The idea of the Lord's Supper as a sacrifice has no foundation here. In contrast to the sacrifices of Israel (θυσίαι), which were required by the Torah and were pleasing to God, Paul gives pagan sacrifices the derogatory term εἰδωλόθυτα (1 Cor 10:19; 8:4ff.).

Rom 15:16 and the comparison of the apostle's ministry with that of the priests of Israel who lived from the portions of the sacrifices (1 Cor 9:13) indicate that Paul understood his work as a priestly service. Despite his basic rejection of such "sacrificial offerings," the Philippians alone were permitted to provide material support. He describes their gifts as "pleasing *sacrifices*" (Phil 4:18). Phil 2:17 is difficult and is probably also to be understood in this connection: θυσία here is hardly the Philippians' "sacrificial activity" in the form of their faithful practice; instead this practice itself is the *sacrifice* that the imprisoned apostle offers, possibly with the additional "drink offering" of his own martyr's blood (on the "drink offering," cf., e.g., Lev 23:37). In the environment of the addressees → σπένδω was almost always used of libation offerings; θυσία and → λειτουργία clearly indicate that the word has that sense here (cf. 2 Tim 4:6; for other suggested interpretations cf. O. Michel, *TDNT* VII, 535f.).

The summons of 1 Peter to its readers to offer pleasing "spiritual *sacrifices*" (2:5) should not be taken as a scriptural basis for a "general priesthood" in contrast to or as a termination of a specific priestly service. The reciprocally defined metaphors in the context (5:1-10) describe Christians as God's own possession. Correspondingly the image of the "spiritual *sacrifices*" describes the practice of their daily lives (cf. 1:15; 5:1) as they follow the suffering Christ (5:21; cf. N. Brox, *1 Pet* [EKKNT] 89ff.).

As a result, 1 Pet 2:5 (like the entire Epistle) stands entirely in the Pauline tradition and corresponds exactly to the demand in Rom 12:1f. to offer God one's own "bodily existence" as a "living, holy, and pleasing *sacrifice*" and one's "reasonable worship." As clearly and intentionally as the limits of the narrow cultic circle may be burst open here and extended to the entirety of secular existence, the passage cannot be understood as an explicit polemic against the cult.

5. While Paul describes the once-for-all and definitive atoning sacrifice of Christ with such terms as αἷμα and ἱλαστήριον, Eph 5:2 and Hebrews say that Christ gave himself as a θυσία. Thus Hebrews contrasts the heavenly high priesthood of Christ and his offering of himself as an antitype to the earthly priesthood and its sacrificial ministry. All human priests have been appointed to offer sacrifices and gifts for sins (5:1; 8:3), including their own sins and then the sins of the people (7:27). Yet all of their sacrifices, which they offer daily year after year (10:1), are not able to perfect them (10:1) in their "conscience" (9:9). Thus the Torah, as a mere "shadow," lacks the power of the future good things (10:1). In the earthly cult also sacrifices offered in "uprightness" (πίστις) of heart are superior to all others (11:4; cf. the Jewish tradition: "The Holy One, blessed be he, speaks to Israel: My sons, I accept from you no burnt offering, no sin offering, no guilt offering, and no meal offering, unless you bring about my good pleasure through prayer, entreaty, and uprightness of heart" [*Pesiq. R.* 198b]). Yet the true sacrifices are not brought to God in the earthly cult, but rather in the heavenly one (9:23). Through the unrepeatable sacrifice of his own body, Christ as the heavenly high priest has removed all sins once for all (9:26; 10:1ff.). If one now sins again in the knowledge of this truth, there remains no sacrifice that can bring about atonement (10:26; cf. 6:5f.). Only the "sacrifice of praise" (θυσία αἰνέσεως) of confession and the "sacrifice" of good works toward others (13:15f.) are "well pleasing" from now on.

The Qumran community sharply rejected the contemporary sacrificial ministry in the Jerusalem temple as a godless misrepresentation of the "true" cult revealed at Sinai by Yahweh, the calendar and form of which are described in the Temple Scroll. The community replaced it according to "the law for this age" by its own strictly ritualized community life, understood itself as a priesthood, and hoped for the imminent eschatological restitution of the temple cult.

After the destruction of the temple in the A.D. 70, alongside the Pharisaic hope for the renewal of the sacrificial service (cf. the seventeenth of the eighteen benedictions: ". . . Restore the service to the holy place in your temple; take delight in Israel's

sacrifice and prayer . . ." [cf. *m. Soṭa* 7:7]), there developed in priestly circles a cult mysticism that conceived of the previous earthly cult as a mere shadow of the heavenly original, which takes place before the cherub chariot of God (the *merkābā*). Thus these circles could accept relatively easily the end of the earthly temple. There is much to suggest that the spiritual home of the author of Hebrews is to be sought in such circles; for he seems to give a new interpretation of the preexistence christology of the Hellenistic Church and its sacrificial interpretation of the cross of Christ with the help of theologoumena from these circles (H.-M. Schenke, "Erwägungen zum Rätsel des Hebräerbriefs," FS Braun 421-37). In any case Hebrews is, in tone and content, anything other than a hostile anticultic polemic against a sacramental Christianity that wished to substitute its observance of the Lord's Supper for animal sacrifice (so G. Theissen, *Untersuchungen zum Hebräerbrief* [1969] 79-83).

         H. Thyen

θυσιαστήριον, ου, τό *thysiastērion* altar*

1. Occurrences in the NT and meaning — 2. Altars in general — 3. Burnt offerings — 4. The Altar of incense — 5. Revelation — 6. Hebrews 13:10

Lit.: S. AALEN, "Das Abendmahl als Opfermahl im NT," *NovT* 6 (1963) 128-52. — J. BEHM, *TDNT* III, 180-90. — K. GALLING, *Der Altar in den Kulturen des alten Orients* (1925). — H. J. KLAUCK, "Θυσιαστήριον—eine Berichtigung," *ZNW* 71 (1980) 274-77. — O. MICHEL, *Heb* (KEK, ⁶1966) 502f. — F. J. SCHIERSE, *Verheißung und Heilsvollendung* (1955) 190f. — For further bibliography see *TWNT* X, 1111-13.

1. This noun occurs 23 times in the NT, where it denotes the altar of Israel's God, as in the LXX (Lev 4:7, etc.). Βωμός is used of altars of foreign gods (Acts 17:23; cf. also 1 Macc 1:59).

2. In Rom 11:3 (citing 3 Kgdms 19:10) and Jas 2:21 (the altar of the sacrifice of Isaac) θυσιαστήριον is used of altars in general.

3. Numerous occurrences refer to the *altar of burnt offerings* in the Jerusalem temple. It was a square block of unhewn stone 25 m. on each side and 7.5 m. high with a ramp leading up to it (Josephus *B.J.* v.225; somewhat different is *m. Mid.* 3:1ff.). In the Herodian temple it stood in the forecourt of the Israelites. Matt 23:35 par. Luke 11:51 (Q?) refers to the last murder mentioned in the OT (2 Chr 24:20-22), which occurred in the forecourt of the temple between the temple entrance and the altar of incense. The Matthean special material in Matt 5:23, 24; 23:18, 19, 20 indicates that the temple cult, despite Jesus' critique of it, remained a definite reality for the life of Jewish Christianity before 70.

In 1 Cor 9:13 Paul draws an analogy from cultic law: "Those who are employed in the temple service have a share in the altar"; i.e., those priests who provide for the altar cult receive their support from the temple ministry.

In the same way Christian missionaries, who likewise provide a holy ministry, have the right to support by the churches. In 10:18 also the cultic sphere is mentioned in an analogy: The Israelite priests are "partners in the altar"; because they eat from the sacrifices, they are associated with the altar and the God of this altar. In the same way the participants in pagan cult meals are "partners of demons," i.e., they fall under the sphere of the power of demons, to whom these meals are devoted. Heb 7:13 concludes that because Jesus did not belong to the tribe of Levi, which alone was responsible for the service of the altar, but to the tribe of Judah, "from which no one has served at the altar," the levitical priesthood and consequently the temple cult has come to an end.

4. Luke 1:11 speaks of the *altar of incense* in the temple of Jerusalem. While Zechariah presses the incense against the coals, the angel appears to him "at the right side of the altar of incense," i.e., between it and the seven-branched lampstand.

5. Revelation speaks of the *altars of the heavenly sanctuary*. Indeed, what is mentioned is the heavenly altar of burnt offerings (6:9; 9:13; 11:1; 14:18; 16:7). The seer sees under it "the souls of those who had been slain" (6:9), i.e., the martyrs: The blood of the sacrificial animals was poured at the foot of the altar, and the soul, i.e., the life, is in the blood. Thus what is intended is: The martyrs are in direct proximity to God. If a voice goes out from this altar, "which stands before God," saying that a punishment will now be the fate of humanity (9:13), it is to be understood as an answer to the martyrs' prayers. 14:18, where an angel proceeds from the altar to give instructions for the harvesting of the grapes (a portrayal of judgment), and 16:7, where the altar itself speaks and confirms the judgments of God, are similar. In 8:3 (bis), 5 the smoke ascending from the altar represents the prayers of the saints. The instruction to the seer to measure the temple, the altar of burnt offerings and those who worship there, but not the court outside the temple (11:1), is to be interpreted in an ecclesiological context: The Church will be preserved in the general destruction.

6. The difficult passage in Heb 13:10 speaks of a *Christian altar*, probably in a fig.-metaphorical sense. In formal terms, it involves a sacral-legal determination of exclusion: Those who "serve the tent," i.e., those who belong to the previous order of purification, are "not permitted" to eat from the *altar* of Christ. The views offered by older scholarship—*altar* as metaphor for the atoning death of Jesus, from which the Church lives, or Christian Lord's Supper—are to be given up in favor of a combination of both motifs: The passage concerns exclusion from the eucharistic table fellowship, which is established by the sacrifice of Christ ("altar").

J. Roloff

θύω *thyō* sacrifice, slaughter, murder; mid.: offer a sacrifice, sacrifice for oneself
→ θυσία.

Θωμᾶς, ᾶ *Thōmas* Thomas*

1. In NT lists of the Twelve — 2. Occurrences in John — 3. Thomas's role in John

Lit.: W. Baier, *BL* 1743-45. — A. Dauer, "Zur Herkunft der Tomas-Perikope Joh 20,24-29," *Biblische Randbemerkungen* (Schülerfestschrift R. Schnackenburg; 1974) 56-76.— K. Staab, *LThK* X, 118f. — On the noncanonical literature, see Hennecke/Schneemelcher I, 278-307 *(Gos. Thom.)*, 307f. *(Thomas the Athlete)*, 388-401 *(Infancy Gospel of Thomas);* II, 425-531 *(Acts Thom.).*

1. The name Θωμᾶς appears in the NT outside John (→ 2, 3) only in the four lists of the Twelve (Mark 3:16b-19; Matt 10:2-4; Luke 6:14-16; Acts 1:13). The name is always in the middle group in these lists (Mark 3:18 par. Matt 10:3/Luke 6:15; Acts 1:13d), to which also Philip, Bartholomew, and Matthew belong. In Matthew and Luke he is paired with Matthew. In Matthew he is the first-mentioned of the two, in Luke, as in Mark, he is named after Matthew. In Acts he is paired with Philip before Bartholomew and Matthew.

2. The name of Θωμᾶς appears 7 times in John (11:16; 14:5, 20, 24, 26, 27, 28; 21:2; also 20:29 v.l.). In 14:5, 8f. he is connected with Philip. In 11:16; 30:24; 21:2 he is also called Didymus (→ Δίδυμος, "twin," a Greek tr. of the Aramaic name and a post-Easter designation).

3. In John 11:6 Thomas discloses that he does not grasp what Jesus has in mind. However, he expresses his intent not to leave Jesus in danger of death. The disciples' understanding is also the concern in 14:5. But to the Bible reader Thomas is esp. known from 20:24-29. In 20:24 he is—as elsewhere in the Jesus tradition only Judas is—introduced as "one of the Twelve" (cf. 6:66-71): In the same way that there was only one within the closest circles around Jesus who made possible the betrayal, so also Thomas is here distinguished from the other members of the group as the one who played the role of doubter of the resurrection. When he was overcome by the appearance of Jesus to him and the knowledge of his own heart, he too became an original mediator of the message of the resurrection. Yet everyone who believes without having seen stands above Thomas and the group of original witnesses (20:29).

In John 21:2 Thomas is named directly after Peter and before the sons of Zebedee, presumably an indication that he played an important role in the founding period of the

Johannine communities in that area. This is the presupposition for his frequent appearance in the Fourth Gospel. Here the memory of a disciple who had reputation and influence has been deposited. This does not mean, of course, that the Johannine texts in which he appears treat concrete events from his life. The literary structure of misunderstanding, which is often used in connection with his appearance, and his designation as representative of the disciples and the Twelve speak against this view.

E. Ruckstuhl

θώραξ, ακος, ὁ   *thōrax*   breastplate*

1 Thess 5:8: "Let us be sober, and put on the *breastplate* of faith and of love. . . ." Eph 6:14 stands in the biblical tradition: "equipped *with the breastplate* of righteousness" (Isa 59:17 LXX; Wis 5:18). Alongside this metaphorical usage of θώραξ, Revelation knows the literal meaning (both times pl.): 9:9: "they had scales like iron *breastplates*"; 9:17: "*breastplates* as of fire." A. Oepke, *TDNT* V, 308-10.

Ι ι

Ἰάϊρος, ου *Iaïros* Jairus*

A synagogue ruler (Mark 5:22 par. Luke 8:41). On the derivation of the Greek form of the name cf. BAGD s.v.; cf. also R. Pesch, *BZ* 14 (1970) 252-56.

Ἰακώβ *Iakōb* Jacob

Lit.: BAGD s.v. — A. VAN DEN BORN, *BL* 800-802. — H. ODEBERG, *TDNT* III, 191f. — A. WEISER, *RGG* III, 517-20. — For further bibliography see van den Born, Weiser.

The West Semitic name of the son of Isaac, the origin of which can be explained in more than one way (Gen 25:24-26; 27:36: folk etymology), appears regularly in the NT in an undeclined form. This form is to be contrasted to what is seen in, e.g., Josephus. It appears a total of 27 times in the NT, of which 5 are in the genealogies of Jesus (Matt 1:2 bis, 15f. [in 15f. not the patriarch but the father of Joseph of Nazareth]; Luke 3:34) and 5 are in a ceremonious expression for God: ὁ θεὸς ᾽Αβραὰμ καὶ ᾽Ισαὰκ καὶ ᾽Ιακώβ (Acts 3:13; 7:32; cf. Matt 22:32 par. Mark 12:26/Luke 20:37). This epithet for God is derived from Exod 3:6, 15, played a significant role thereafter, and made its way into pagan magic (texts in BAGD).

The identity of Jacob as the ancestor of the twelve tribes of Israel is unquestioned in the NT (cf. Acts 7:8 bis; John 4:12 [here emphatically from the mouth of Jews: ὁ πατὴρ ἡμῶν ᾽Ιακώβ]) and is the basis for the reference to the people of Israel as the οἶκος ᾽Ιακώβ or simply as ᾽Ιακώβ, which is also borrowed from the OT (Exod 19:3; Isa 2:5; Luke 1:33; Acts 7:46; Num 23:7; Isa 40:27; Rom 11:26 [citing Isa 59:20]). The early Jewish idea of Jacob dining together with the other ancestors and righteous people at the eschatological meal in the basileia (cf. Billerbeck IV, 1154-65; Schulz, *Q* 325) is found in the NT only in the logion in Matt 8:11f. par. Luke 13:28, which is derived from Q. This passage threatens the exclusion of the "sons of the kingdom" (Matthew) and the participation of the Gentiles at this meal. In Romans 9 Jacob, as the one who was preferred over Esau, functions

as an example of God's absolute freedom in his gracious election (9:10-13; v. 13: scriptural proof from Mal 1:3). In Hebrews 11 Jacob is one of a series of witnesses to faith that begins with Abel and culminates with Abraham (11:20, 21; cf. v. 9).

E. Plümacher

Ἰάκωβος, ου *Iakōbos* James*

1. The brother of the Lord — 2. The son of Zebedee — 3. The son of Alphaeus — 4. The relative of Mary — 5. The father of the apostle Judas

Lit.: K. ALAND, "Der Herrenbruder Jakobus und der Jakobusbrief," *TLZ* 69 (1944) 97-104. — K. BALTZER and H. KÖSTER, "Die Bezeichnung des Jakobus als ᾽ΩΒΛΙΑΣ," *ZNW* 46 (1955) 141f. — K. BEYSCHLAG, "Das Jakobusmartyrium und seine Verwandten in der frühchristlichen Literatur," *ZNW* 56 (1965) 149-78. — J. BLINZLER, "Rechtsgeschichtliches zur Hinrichtung des Zebedäiden Jakobus (Apg XII,2)," *NovT* 5 (1962) 191-206. — idem, *Die Brüder und Schwestern Jesu* (1967). — A. BÖHLIG, "Zum Martyrium des Jakobus," *NovT* 5 (1962) 207-13, revised in *idem, Mysterion und Wahrheit. Gesammelte Beiträge zur spätantiken Religionsgeschichte* (1968) 112-18. — idem, "Jacob as an Angel in Gnosticism and Manicheism," *Nag Hammadi and Gnosis* (ed. R. McL. Wilson; Nag Hammadi Studies 14, 1978) 122-30. — F. C. BURKITT, "Levi Son of Alphaeus," *JTS* 28 (1927) 273f. — H. VON CAMPENHAUSEN, "Die Nachfolge des Jakobus. Zur Frage eines urchristlichen 'Califats,'" *ZKG* 63 (1950/51) 133-44. — E. FASCHER, "Jerusalems Untergang in der urchristlichen und altkirchlichen Überlieferung," *TLZ* 89 (1964) 81-98. — W.-P. FUNK, *Die zweite Apokalypse des Jakobus aus Nag-Hammadi Codex V* (1976). — B. GUSTAFSSON, "Hegesippus' Sources and His Reliability," *Studia Patristica* III/1 (ed. F. L. Cross; 1961) 227-32. — M. HENGEL, "Jakobus der Herrenbruder —der erste 'Papst'?" *Glaube und Eschatologie* (FS W. G. Kümmel, 1985) 71-104 (on 1). — N. HYLDAHL, "Hegesipps Hypomnemata," *ST* 14 (1960) 70-113. — *idem,* "Die Versuchung auf der Zinne des Tempels (Matth. 4,5-7/Luke 4,9-12," *ST* 15 (1961) 113-27. — G. KITTEL, "Die Stellung des Jakobus zu Judentum und Heidenchristentum," *ZNW* 30 (1931) 145-57. — idem, "Der geschichtliche Ort des Jakobusbriefs," *ZNW* 41 (1942) 71-105. — H. KOCH, "Zur Jakobusfrage Gal. 1,19," *ZNW* 33 (1934) 204-9. — H. J. LAWLOR, "The Hypomnemata of Hegesippus," *idem, Eusebeiana* (1912) 1-107. — D. H. LITTLE, *The Death of James, the Brother of Jesus* (Diss. Rice University, 1971). — E. MEYER, *Ursprung und Anfänge des Christentums*

III: *Die Apostelgeschichte und die Anfänge des Christentums* (1923) 69-77, 174-77. — J. MUNCK, *Paul and the Salvation of Mankind* (1959). — L. OBERLINNER, *Historische Überlieferung und christologische Aussage. Zur Frage der "Brüder Jesu" in der Synopse* (1975). — W. PRATSCHER, *Der Herrenbruder Jakobus und die Jakobustradition* (FRLANT 139, 1987). — E. RUCKSTUHL, *TRE* XVI, 485-88 (on 1). — W. SCHMITHALS, *Paul and James* (SBT 46, 1965). — H. J. SCHOEPS, *Theologie und Geschichte des Judenchristentums* (1949). — idem, "Jacobus O DIKAIOS KAI WBLIAS. Neuer Lösungsvorschlag in einer schwierigen Frage," idem, *Aus frühchristlichen Zeit. Religionsgeschichtliche Untersuchungen* (1950) 120-25. — idem, "Die Pseudoklementinen und das Urchristentum," *ZRGG* 10 (1958) 3-15. — E. SCHWARTZ, "Zu Eusebius Kirchengeschichte," *ZNW* 4 (1903) 48-66. — idem, "Über den Tod der Söhne Zebedaei. Ein Beitrag zur Geschichte des Joh," idem, *Gesammelte Schriften* V (1963) 48-123. — E. STAUFFER, "Zum Kalifat des Jacobus," *ZRGG* 4 (1952) 193-214. — idem, "Petrus und Jakobus in Jerusalem," *Begegnung der Christen* (ed. M. Roesle and O. Cullmann; 1959) 361-72. — G. STRECKER, *Das Judenchristentum in den Pseudoklementinen* (TU 70, 1958) 137-254. — C. C. TORREY, "James the Just and His Name 'Oblias,' " *JBL* 63 (1944) 93-98. — T. ZAHN, *Forschungen zur Geschichte des neutestamentlichen Kanons und der altkirchlichen Literatur.* VI/2: *Brüder und Vettern Jesu* (1900) 225-364. — E. ZUCKSCHWERDT, "Das Naziräat des Herrenbruders Jakobus nach Hegesipp (Euseb. h.e. II, 23,5-6)," *ZNW* 68 (1977) 276-87.

1. James the "brother of the Lord" (Gal 1:19) is mentioned in Mark 6:3 par. Matt 13:55 as the first of the four brothers of Jesus (→ ἀδελφός 3, 4). During Jesus' lifetime, James reacted to Jesus' works with reservations (Mark 3:21, 31). 1 Cor 15:7 names him as a witness of an Easter epiphany. This is normally interpreted to mean that James became a believing disciple of Jesus only as a result of the appearance of the resurrected one. As brother of the Lord and witness to Easter he then possessed a special authority in the first communities (cf. also Acts 12:17). When Paul (around A.D. 35?) was in Jerusalem, he visited Cephas and James (Gal 1:18f.).

In the 40s James was one of the three "pillars" (Gal 2:9, → στῦλος), who concluded the agreement with Paul and Barnabas at the Jerusalem conference concerning the recognition of the Gentile mission (Gal 2:1-10; Acts 15, where James is mentioned in v. 13). The Jerusalem authorities were not "Judaizers," and neither was James. They had nothing to do with the "false brothers" (Gal 2:4). At the conference no conditions were laid on the Gentile mission, and circumcision was not required for Gentile Christians (Gal 2:3-6). Whereas nothing was required of Gentile Christians, James required (so it seems) of Jewish Christians observance of the ritual commandments of the law. He thus rejected (out of consideration for the food laws of the Jews; cf. F. Mussner, *Gal* [HTKNT] 140-42) table fellowship of Jewish and Gentile Christians (Gal 2:12). After the departure of Peter the leadership of the Jerusalem church seems to have devolved upon James. The episode in Gal 2:12f. demonstrates the extensive influence of James beyond Jerusalem. Paul visited him on his third trip to Jerusalem (Acts 21:18), apparently in order to deliver the collection of the Gentile churches.

According to Jewish Christian tradition James bore the honorific title ὁ δίκαιος ("the Just"; Hegesippus *Hypomnemata* v, apud Eusebius *HE* ii.23.4, 7, etc.; iv.22.4; Clement of Alexandria *Hypotyposes* vi, apud *HE* ii.1.3; vii, apud *HE* ii.1.4f.; *Gos. Heb.* 7; pseudo-Josephus, apud *HE* ii.23.20). The widespread occurrence of this tradition is also reflected in Gnostic texts (*Gos. Thom.* 11 (12); the first *Apocalypse of James* [NHC V.3] 32.2f.; cf. 6f.; the second *Apocalypse of James* [NHC V.4] 44.13f., 18; 59.22 (?); 60.12; 61.14). Hegesippus (Eusebius *HE* ii.23.7) also mentions another honorific title: ὠβλίας. Perhaps (as Torrey assumed, cf. also Baltzer and Köster) ΩΒΛΙΑΣ is an incorrect form of ΩΒΔΙΑΣ. The interpretation of it (περιοχὴ τοῦ λαοῦ) could then recall Obad 1 LXX (so Baltzer and Köster).

Josephus *Ant.* xx.200 reports that James was a victim of the persecution of the Jerusalem church by the high priest Ananus, who had James (and a few other members of the church) stoned during the vacancy between the death of Festus and the arrival of Albinus (A.D. 62?).

Legendary reports about the martyrdom of James are in Hegesippus *Hypomnemata* v, apud Eusebius *HE* ii.23.10-18 and (similar in many ways) the second *Apocalypse of James* 61.13ff. There is a brief note in Clement of Alexandria *Hypotyposes* vii (Eusebius *HE* ii.1.5). Perhaps *Ps.-Clem. Rec.* i.66-71 belongs here in a wider sense. These reports are related in individual motifs, but it is uncertain what the precise tradition-historical relationship is (cf. Funk 172-78, 194-98). Hegesippus, in a final statement of his report (Eusebius *HE* ii.23.18 to the end of the ch.), connects the martyrdom of James with the immediately following siege of Jerusalem. The assumption is that the city's fall was God's punishment for the execution of James. This view is found —of course with no direct temporal connection—also in pseudo-Josephus (Eusebius *HE* ii.23.20; this text was known already by Origen: *Cels.* i.47; cf. ii.13. *in Matt.* 10:17). However, no conclusion can be drawn from the entire hagiographically oriented observation in Hegesippus about the chronology of the martyrdom of James (as if a later assessment were necessary).

The Epistle of James probably derives from an unknown Christian who "placed his exhortatory writing under the authority of the former leader of the church in Jerusalem" (Kümmel, *Introduction* 291); cf. 1:1. In Jude 1 the author describes himself as brother of James.

In a later period James played a special role in the traditions and ideologies of various Jewish Christian groups. The legend in *Gos. Heb.* 7 makes him, as it appears, the first believing witness of the resurrection appearances. Hegesippus *Hypomnemata* v (Eusebius *HE* ii.23.4-18) deals with traditions from Jewish circles, which have a strong legendary coloring and give to James the highest reputation. On the extraordinary role of James in the Pseudo-Clementine literature (the legendary James portrait in the various strata of the literature is not uniform) cf. Strecker 137-45, 194-96, 235, 246-54, and *passim*. (The anti-Paulinism peculiar to the *Kerygma Petrou* cannot be claimed for the historical James!)

Gnostic groups also took possession of James (perhaps originally through the mediation of Jewish Christians who influenced Gnosticism; cf. *Gos. Thom.* 11 [12]). On the misuse of the figure of James in Gnosticism, cf. the first *Apocalypse of James* (*NHC* V.3), the second *Apocalypse of James* (*NHC* V.4), the Naassenes in Hippolytus *Haer.* v.7.1; x.9.3. The brother of the Lord is probably also intended with the James of the Gnostic *Apocryphon of James* (*NHC* I.2). Cf. also Hennecke/Schneemelcher II, index s.v.

2. James, the son of Zebedee and brother of John, a fisherman on the Lake of Gennesaret, was called to follow Jesus along with his brother (Mark 1:19f. par. Matt 4:21f.; cf. Mark 1:29 and Luke 5:10). He belonged to the group of the "Twelve" (Mark 3:17 par. Matt 10:2/Luke 6:14/Acts 1:13; → δώδεκα 4). According to Mark 3:17 Jesus gave him and his brother the sobriquet → Βοανηργές. Peter, James, and John play a special role as eyewitnesses in Mark 5:37 par. Luke 8:51 (the raising of Jairus's daughter); Mark 9:2 par. Matt 17:1/Luke 9:28 (the transfiguration); and Mark 14:33 (Gethsemane; cf. Matt 26:37). In Mark 13:3 Peter, James, John, and Andrew ask about the time and the signs of the eschatological events. The two sons of Zebedee are esp. prominent in Luke 9:54 and Mark 10:35ff. par. (cf. also 10:41 par.). Mark 10:39 predicts their martyrdom in a veiled way.

Acts 12:2 reports briefly the martyrdom of James: King Herod (Agrippa I) had him executed with the sword (A.D. 44?) in the course of a persecution of Christians.
On the problematic legal questions see Blinzler. James was, according to him, "most probably not prosecuted and condemned by King Agrippa himself, but by the Jerusalem Sanhedrin, of course with the full agreement and possibly the active cooperation of the king" (*NovT* 5 [1962] 205f.). On the means of the punishment (according to Sadducean law?) see *ibid.* 200-206. Clement of Alexandria offers a legendary report in *Hypotyposes* vii (Eusebius *HE* ii.9.2f.). On later traditions concerning James see Hennecke/Schneemelcher II, index s.v.

3. James, the son of Alphaeus (→ Ἀλφαῖος), was also a member of the Twelve (Mark 3:18 par. Matt 10:3/Luke 6:15/Acts 1:13). According to D Θ *f*[13] it Tatian, the tax collector who was called to discipleship was not named Levi, son of Alphaeus, but James, the son of Alphaeus (a later correction). Cf. Hennecke/Schneemelcher II, index s.v.

4. Mark 15:40 knows a James with the designation ὁ μικρός ("the little one" or "the younger one"); cf. O. Michel, *TDNT* IV, 650). The text names a Mary (his daughter or mother or wife) among the witnesses of the execution of Jesus.

Whether Μαρία ἡ Ἰακώβου τοῦ μικροῦ καὶ Ἰωσῆτος μήτηρ (see the variants) refers to one or two women is uncertain. If only one is intended, Mary was the mother of James the less and of his brother Joses. The parallel in Matt 27:56, Μαρία ἡ τοῦ Ἰακώβου καὶ Ἰωσὴφ μήτηρ (see the variants), appears to refer to only one person (cf. 27:61!) and makes Mary the mother of James alone. → Μαρία 4.

Μαρία ἡ τοῦ Ἰακώβου is mentioned again in Mark 16:1, this time as a witness of the empty tomb; cf. Luke 24:10.

5. James, the father (less probably: the brother) of the apostle Judas (not Iscariot), one of the Twelve, is mentioned in Luke 6:16; Acts 1:13. → Ἰούδας 7.

K. Niederwimmer

ἴαμα, ατος, τό *iama* healing
→ ἰάομαι 1, 4.

Ἰαμβρῆς *Iambrēs* Jambres*

2 Tim 3:8 mentions "Jannes and *Jambres*" as those who "resisted Moses." → Ἰάννης.

Ἰανναί *Iannai* Jannai*

Personal name in Luke 3:24, the father of Melchi.

Ἰάννης *Iannēs* Jannes*

In 2 Tim 3:8 "*Jannes* and Jambres" are mentioned as a negative example because they "resisted" (ἀντέστησαν) Moses. The reference is to the Egyptian magicians of Exod 7:8-25, who are said to have competed with Moses before Pharaoh. The names go back to Jewish tradition (Schürer III/2, 781-83; M. Dibelius and H. Conzelmann, *The Pastoral Epistles* [Hermeneia] ad loc.). The reading of many textual witnesses (G lat and others), "*Jannes* and Mambres (Μαμβρῆς)," corresponds to the fluctuation in the tradition. See Billerbeck III, 660-64; L. L. Grabbe, "The Jannes-Jambres Tradition in Targum Pseudo-Jonathan and Its Date," *JBL* 98 (1979) 393-401; H. Odeberg, *TDNT* III, 192f.; *TWNT* X, 1113f. (bibliography).

ἰάομαι *iaomai* heal, make well
ἴαμα, ατος, τό *iama* healing*
ἴασις, εως, ἡ *iasis* healing*

1. Occurrences in the NT — 2. The miracle stories — a) Usage and meaning — b) Healing and faith — c) Assessment of the healing miracles of Jesus — 3. Fig. sense — 4. Ἴαμα — 5. Ἴασις

Lit.: R. H. FULLER, *Interpreting the Miracles* (1963) 29-37. — H. VAN DER LOOS, *The Miracles of Jesus* (NovTSup 9, 1965) 293-336, 339ff. — A. OEPKE, *TDNT* III, 194-215. — A. RICHARDSON, *The Miracle Stories of the Gospels* (1942). — For further bibliography see *TWNT* X, 1114.

1. Ἰάομαι appears 26 times in the NT, esp. in Luke (11 occurrences), and 4 times in Matthew, 3 times in John,

4 times in Acts, and once each in Mark, Hebrews, 1 Peter, and James. Ἴαμα appears only in 1 Corinthians (3 occurrences). Ἴασις appears only in Luke-Acts, once in Luke and twice in Acts.

2. a) Ἰάομαι is used as an alternative to the more usual θεραπεύω in the sense of *make well* with no difference of meaning. But only ἰάομαι is used in the fig. sense, and it does not have the wider meaning "take care of, serve," as does θεραπεύω. While both vbs. can be used of healing either by a physician or by supernatural intervention, in the NT ἰάομαι appears, except in fig. usage, only in connection with miracles of healing. The same is true for ἴαμα and ἴασις (but not for → ἰατρός).

Ἰάομαι is thus used of extraordinary deeds done by individuals equipped with divine power (→ δύναμις). The dynamistic view is esp. evident where the mere touch of clothing brings about healing, as in the story of the woman with the issue of blood in Mark 5:25-34 par., in which it is said that Jesus noticed that power went out from him at the touch of his garment (cf. Mark 6:56; Luke 6:19; Acts 19:12). It is characteristic of Luke that he speaks of the power of the Lord to heal (5:17; cf. 6:19). Luke 5:17 can even give the impression that Jesus only occasionally possessed this power. This can hardly be Luke's meaning, for he elsewhere affirms that Jesus heals all the sick and the possessed on his way (9:11; Acts 10:38; cf. Luke 6:18). Jesus imparts the same power also to his disciples (Luke 9:1f.; 10:9, 17). The derivative nature of their ability is evident in the fact that the healing occurs through the name of Jesus (Acts 3:6, 12, 16; 4:30; 9:34).

b) Often healing appears to be dependent on the faith of the sick person or an intercessor (Mark 5:34 par.; 6:5f.; 10:52 par.; Matt 8:10; 15:28). This does not signify healing through faith; a psychosomatic explanation is misguided. (In a few cases the sick person is not present.) Faith is necessary because what is involved is not magic, but the reception of divine salvation. In the story of the young demoniac in Mark 9:14-29 par. it is noteworthy that the disciples who first attempted to cast out the evil spirit were censured because of their lack of faith. It appears to be the view of Jesus that everything is possible for one who believes (v. 23), for the prayer of a believer can accomplish everything (v. 29; cf. Matt 17:20).

c) The credibility of the stories must be examined individually. It is certain that healing the sick played a very significant role in the life of Jesus (in contrast to the Baptist: John 10:41). In the healings Jesus expresses his compassion (e.g., Luke 13:16), but in particular he demonstrates his divine authority (Mark 2:10, → ἐξουσία). A certain tension exists between the sharp rejection of miracles of legitimation (Mark 8:11 par.) and the significance of miracles as authenticating signs. The demand

for miracles is condemned as superstition, while faith is always accompanied by miracles. In part this appears to be the normal experience of all believers, and in part the miracles belong to the time of salvation. Jesus himself regarded the healing miracles as signs of the kingdom of God (Luke 7:22 [Q]; 11:20 [Q]). The miracles proclaim the arrival of the kingdom and the fall of Satan (Luke 10:18; cf. Acts 10:38).

3. Ἰάομαι is used in a fig. sense for the saving intervention of God in association with OT texts in Matt 13:15; John 12:40; Acts 28:27. In a similar way Isa 53:6 is related to 1 Pet 2:24. The general conception that sickness is the consequence of sin (e.g., John 9:2) lies behind this fig. usage. The imagery in Heb 12:13 is more ethical-parenetic: "so that the lame not be put out of joint, but rather be healed."

4. Ἴαμα appears in the construction χάρισμα ἰαμάτων in 1 Cor 12:9, 28, 30. The "gift of healing" is here a special capability of individual members of the congregation. One can conclude from Rom 15:19; 2 Cor 12:12 that these gifts belonged to the characteristic signs of an apostle.

5. Ἴασις is used only by Luke. In Luke 13:32 ἰάσεις ἀποτελῶ is only a circumlocution for ἰάομαι (literally "I perform *healings*"). Acts 4:22 speaks of signs of healing in connection with the healing of a lame beggar by the apostles, and 4:30 mentions ἴασις together with signs and wonders as the work of God's hand through the name of Jesus.

               R. Leivestad

Ἰάρετ *Iaret* Jared*

The name of Enoch's father: Luke 3:37 (cf. Gen 5:15, 18; 1 Chr 1:2; *1 Enoch* [Greek] 106:13, in all of which the form Ἰάρεδ also appears).

ἴασις, εως, ἡ *iasis* healing
→ ἰάομαι 1, 5.

ἴασπις, ιδος, ἡ *iaspis* jasper*

In antiquity the term jasper was not limited to the variety of quartz that bears the name today, but could designate any opaque stone (BAGD s.v.). In the NT ἴασπις appears only in Revelation: 21:18, 19; λίθος ἴασπις in 4:3; 21:11.

Ἰάσων, ονος *Iasōn* Jason*

A frequent personal name, which (as an authentic Greek name) was used among Jews as an alternative for Ἰησοῦς (BDF §53.2d). In the NT two different persons are called *Jason:* In Rom 16:21 Jason is a kinsman of Paul to whom greetings are sent. In Acts 17:5, 6, 7, 9 a man named Jason is the host of Paul and Silas in Thessalonica.

ἰατρός, οῦ, ὁ   iatros   physician*

Lit.: K. BETH, *RGG* III, 194-98. — F. GRABER and D. MÜLLER, *DNTT* II, 166-69. — H. GREEVEN, *Krankheit und Heilung nach dem NT* (Lebendige Wissenschaft 8, 1948). — R. HERZOG, *RAC* I, 720-25. — A. KÖBERLE, *RGG* I, 636f. — F. KUNDLEIN, *Der griechische Arzt im Zeitalter des Hellenismus* (1979). — D. LÜHRMANN, "Aber auch dem Arzt gib Raum (Sir 38,1-15)," *WuD* 15 (1979) 55-78. For further bibliography see *TWNT* X, 1114.

The NT has 7 occurrences of ἰατρός, one in Matthew, 2 in Mark, 3 in Luke, and 1 in Colossians. The noun is used only as a designation for the physician's profession and does not occur in the fig. sense or as a christological title. In Col 4:14 we learn that Luke, Paul's coworker, was a physician. (It was not considered unspiritual to use the services of a physician; cf. Luke 10:34; 1 Tim 5:33.) The view that the Lukan literature is characterized by medical terminology and ideas cannot be upheld. In Mark 5:26 and Luke 8:43 we hear of women who have consulted physicians without success and at great cost and pain. The intent is not to bring physicians into disrepute but to show the extent of the women's illnesses. Two proverbial phrases are placed on the lips of Jesus: Mark 2:17 par. Matt 9:12/Luke 5:31: "The strong (= healthy) do not need a *physician,* but rather the sick"; Luke 4:33: "*Physician,* heal yourself."

                           R. Leivestad

ἴδε   ide   behold

The original imv. ἰδέ became established as a particle. Consequently the form ἴδε is used when more than one person is addressed *(behold)* and when that which is to be observed is in the nom. instead of the acc. (BDF §§107; 144). The particle most often appears at the beginning of the clause (in the middle, however, in John 3:26) and is esp. frequent in John (15 occurrences), Mark (7), and Matthew (4); it also appears in Gal 5:2 (and John 19:5 v.l.; Rom 2:17 v.l.).

Mark, Matthew, and John use ἴδε only in discourse. Mark sometimes uses it in association with an interrogative (Mark 2:24; so also John 11:36) or a demonstrative (Mark 13:21 ὧδε and ἐκεῖ). Mark, Matthew, and Paul also use, in addition to ἴδε, → ἰδού. The latter is used more frequently, exclusively in Luke-Acts, James, and Revelation, but only 4 times in John. P. Fielder, *Die Formel 'und siehe' im NT* (1969), esp. 17-48; R. Van Otterloo, *OPTAT* 2 (1988) 34-64.

ἴδιος, 3   idios   one's own, peculiar to, belonging to an individual

1. Occurrences in the NT — 2. a) Adj. usage — b) Subst. usage — c) Adv. usage — 3. In John

Lit.: BAGD s.v. — R. BULTMANN, *John* (Eng. tr., 1971) 56f., 488f. — J. JERVELL, "Er kam in sein Eigentum," *ST* 10 (1956) 14-27.

1. Ἴδιος appears as an adj. 11 times in the Synoptic Gospels, 7 times in John, 12 times in Acts, 25 times in the Pauline letters, 21 times in the deutero-Pauline letters and Hebrews, and 10 times in the Catholic Epistles. The subst. τὸ ἴδιον appears in the sg. only in John 15:19; the pl. οἱ ἴδιοι is found twice in John and in Acts 4:23; 24:23; τὰ ἴδια appears in Luke 18:28; John 1:11 (→ 3); 8:44; 16:32; 19:27; Acts 21:6. Adv. κατ' ἰδίαν appears with reference to Jesus in the Synoptics 15 times and in Acts 23:19; Gal 2:2. Ἴδιος does not appear at all in Revelation.

2. a) NT usage is determined by LXX usage, which consistently translates the personal suffix as a possessive pron. with ἴδιος (e.g., Gen 47:18: ὑπολείπεται ἡμῖν . . . τὸ ἴδιον σῶμα καὶ ἡ γῆ ἡμῶν; likewise Deut 15:2; Job 2:11; 7:10, etc.). In the NT the adj., used as a possessive pron., has a more or less emphatic sense (Matt 9:1: ἦλθεν εἰς τὴν ἰδίαν πόλιν).

Characteristic for the usage are the various readings of Matt 13:57: B D Θ pc have (οὐκ ἔστιν προφήτης ἄτιμος εἰ μὴ) ἐν τῇ πατρίδι καὶ ἐν τῇ οἰκίᾳ αὐτοῦ; Koine W pl have ἐν τῇ πατρίδι αὐτοῦ; ℵ pc have ἐν τῇ ἰδίᾳ πατρίδι (= John 4:44); C has ἐν τῇ ἰδίᾳ πατρίδι αὐτοῦ. The text-critical decision is not as simple as is often assumed. The pleonasm of C can be disregarded as superfluous on the basis of B D pc, but John 4:44 is scarcely the occasion for the insertion of ἰδίᾳ. In any case the readings indicate how the word was understood.

In Matt 22:5 the adj. is a possessive pron., as in 22:14. The Synoptic parallels (Mark 13:34; Luke 19:13) read αὐτοῦ or ἑαυτοῦ instead of ἴδιος. In Matt 25:15 the adj. is used with an emphatic sense: ἑκάστῳ κατὰ τὴν ἰδίαν δύναμιν, "to each according to *his own* ability" (cf. Mark 15:20; Luke 2:3 v.l.; 6:41, 44). Although the word can have a special meaning in John (→ 3), its adj. use in 1:41; 4:44; 10:3, 12 is as in the Synoptics.

In the Pauline Epistles adj. usage (the opposite of ἀλλότριος) often has its own theological emphasis (Rom 8:32: [ὁ θεὸς] τοῦ ἰδίου υἱοῦ οὐκ ἐφείσατο; 10:3: τὴν ἰδίαν [δικαιοσύνην] ζητοῦντες στῆσαι; 14:4: τῷ ἰδίῳ κυρίῳ στήκει ἢ πίπτει). Paul emphasizes against anti-Semitic Gentile Christianity the abiding validity of the election of Israel in Rom 11:24: οὗτοι οἱ κατὰ φύσιν ἐγκεντρισθήσονται τῇ ἰδίᾳ ἐλαίᾳ. The individual reference is underscored by use with ἕκαστος (1 Cor 3:8: ἕκαστος δὲ τὸν ἴδιον μισθὸν λήμψεται ["the wages that are *due him*"] κατὰ τὸν ἴδιον κόπον ["corresponding to his *own* labor"]; similarly 1 Cor 7:7; 15:23, 38). However, an individualizing intention is not in evidence here, for the relationship of the individual to the community or to Israel is the main concern. Thus Paul can also use the expression in a negative sense (cf. 1 Cor 11:21).

Throughout the NT Epistles the predominant use is the simple usage with varying emphases, which corresponds to the usage outside the NT (1 Cor 4:12: κοπιῶμεν ἐργαζόμενοι ταῖς ἰδίαις χερσίν; Josephus *B.J.* vi.347: καὶ τὸν ναὸν ἰδίαις χερσὶν ἐνεπρήσατε). Ἴδιος is used of the relationship of the wife to her husband or vice versa in Acts 24:24; 1 Cor 7:2, 4; 14:35; Eph 5:22; Col 3:18 v.l.; Titus 2:5; 1 Pet 3:1, 5; with reference to the family or the household, cf. 1 Tim 3:4f., 12; 5:4. Only in Acts 4:32 does ἴδιος have the meaning "private property": καὶ οὐδὲ εἷς τι τῶν ὑπαρχόντων αὐτῷ ἔλεγεν ἴδιον εἶναι, ἀλλ' ἦν αὐτοῖς ἅπαντα κοινά (cf. the passages in secular Greek in BAGD s.v. 10.a.α). The opposite is what is held in common. Καιροῖς ἰδίοις (1 Tim 2:6; 6:15; Titus 1:3) refers to a point in salvation history, the time of God's promise, which is fulfilled καιρῷ ἰδίῳ, according to Gal 6:9.

b) The subst. οἱ ἴδιοι in 2 Macc 12:22; Josephus *B.J.* i.42 has the meaning "comrades in battle," while in Sir 11:34 the word is used of relatives. In the NT the first of these uses is seen in the "company" of faith in Acts 4:23; 24:23, while 1 Tim 5:8 is the only occurrence of the second. It is disputed whether the reference in Epictetus *Diss.* iii.8.7 to the "disciples of a philosopher" can be transferred to John 13:1 (so BAGD s.v. 3a).

Τὰ ἴδια with the meaning "home, homeland" is common in Greek literature. John 16:32; 19:27 is to be translated in this way; likewise Acts 21:6 (cf. 5:18; 14:18 v.l.). But in Luke 18:28 it designates possession in the widest sense: ἰδοὺ ἡμεῖς ἀφέντες τὰ ἴδια ἠκολουθήσαμέν σοι. Both the variety of textual readings and the Synoptic parallels (ἀφήκαμεν πάντα), which influenced the v.l. of ℵ Koine pm, indicate that the reference is to property, which understanding is then specifically suggested by the reference to house and family in Jesus' response. The tr. of 1 Thess 4:11 is difficult: πράσσειν τὰ ἴδια is best interpreted on the basis of the following ἐργάζεσθαι ταῖς ἰδίαις χερσίν as "to do *your own*" (= "to work with your hands"). The pl. in John 8:44 and the sg. τὸ ἴδιον in John 15:19 designate that which belongs to Satan or to the world.

c) Adv. use of κατ' ἰδίαν with the meaning it bears in the NT is attested in Josephus *B.J.* ii.199: (Πετρώνιος) τοὺς δυνατοὺς κατ' ἰδίαν καὶ τὸ πλῆθος ἐν κοινῷ συλλέγων. . . . In the same way it is said either that Jesus withdraws from the crowd to pray or that he takes his disciples aside (Matt 14:13, 23; 17:1, 19; 20:17; 24:3; Mark 4:34; 6:31f.; 7:33; 9:2, 28; 13:3; Luke 9:10; 10:23). In Acts 23:19 the phrase has the same meaning, while in Gal 2:2 it is used of the *separate* gathering of the δοκοῦντες with Paul. Adv. ἰδίᾳ occurs with the same meaning only in 1 Cor 12:11.

3. While the previously mentioned passages of John fit with the usage named, an emphatic meaning with a theological significance is to be found in John 5:18, 43; 7:18; 10:3f., 12. This is to been seen in the prologue, in which 1:11 is a disputed point in the interpretation: εἰς τὰ ἴδια ἦλθεν, καὶ οἱ ἴδιοι αὐτὸν οὐ παρέλαβον. While Bultmann (56f.) interprets τὰ ἴδια as the human world and οἱ ἴδιοι as humans, C. K. Barrett (*John* [1978] ad loc.) interprets both as God's own people. In support of Bultmann's interpretation is that in Exod 19:5; Deut 7:6 LXX ʿam seḡullâ is translated with λαὸς περιούσιος. Probably Bultmann's interpretation is correct for the pre-Christian hymn, while John understood τὰ ἴδια as God's own people and οἱ ἴδιοι as the Jews at the time of Jesus (so R. Schnackenburg, *John* I [Eng. tr., 1978] 258-60).

In John 13:1 οἱ ἴδιοι are the smaller circle around Jesus, formed after the events of 6:60-71. These have been given to Jesus by God, and are identical with οἱ ἐμοί in 10:14.

H.-W. Bartsch

ἰδιώτης, ου, ὁ *idiōtēs* layperson, uneducated person*

Lit.: BILLERBECK III, 454-56. — H. SCHLIER, *TDNT* III, 215-17. — SPICQ, *Notes* I, 384-86.

1. In Greek usage ἰδιώτης means both "private person" in contrast to public officials, and "stranger" in contrast to members of the group or local persons. Although the word does not appear in the LXX, it was taken over as a loanword with the same meaning in the rabbinic literature: heḏeyôṭ can thus designate a human being in contrast to the deity. The meaning is determined concretely by its context or by the contrast that is made. In the NT the Greek word appears 5 times, of which 3 are in 1 Corinthians 14 (vv. 16, 23, and 24).

2. In Acts 4:13 the apostles are called ἄνθρωποι ἀγράμματοι καὶ ἰδιῶται (Hippolytus *Philos.* ix.11.1 uses the same phrase): they are uneducated and are not scribes. Similarly, Paul calls himself ἰδιώτης τῷ λόγῳ in 2 Cor 11:6. His intent is not to describe himself as generally uneducated, but rather to emphasize οὐ τῇ γνώσει. Thus the phrase is to be translated "unversed in speaking" (cf. Hippolytus *Philos.* viii.18: ἰδιῶται τὴν γνῶσιν; similarly Justin *Apol.* i.39.3; in 60.11 parallel to βάρβαροι).

In 1 Corinthians 14 Paul uses the term in reference to untranslated glossolalia. It is disputed whether Paul is concerned about the church member who is incapable of glossolalia or the non-Christian outsider. In v. 16 ὁ ἀναπληρῶν τὸν τόπον τοῦ ἰδιώτου might refer to a church member whose status (cf. τόπον in Acts 1:25) leaves him ignorant of glossolalia. The meaning in 14:23 is also ambiguous: "When the whole church assembles and all speak in tongues, εἰσέλθωσιν δὲ ἰδιῶται ἢ ἄπιστοι, will they not say that you are mad? But if all prophesy, εἰσέλθη δέ τις ἄπιστος ἢ ἰδιώτης, he is convicted by all." Schlier (217) and Conzelmann (*1 Cor* [Hermeneia] 243) see no distinction between ἄπιστος and ἰδιώτης, while BAGD (s.v. 2), referring to the t.t. of religious associations, understands ἰδιώτης as a type of proselyte, a participant who is not fully a member. The parallel to βάρβαρος in Justin [see above] is also present in 1 Cor 14:11.

H.-W. Bartsch

ἰδού *idou* see, behold

Ἰδού is literally the aor. mid. imv. sg. (ἰδοῦ, from ὁράω), which is written as a demonstrative particle with the acute accent. The number of occurrences in the NT writings are (in order of frequency): Matthew 62, Luke 57, Revelation 26, Acts 23, Mark 7, James 6, John 4, Hebrews 4, Paul (only in 1–2 Corinthians, Galatians, Romans) 9, Jude, and 1 Pet 1 each.

Ἰδού serves, like Heb. *hinnēh*, to enliven the narrative, either to awaken attention (e.g., Luke 22:10; John 4:35; 1 Cor 15:51; 2 Cor 5:17; Jas 5:9; Jude 14; Rev 1:7; 9:12; 11:14), to introduce something new (e.g., after a gen. absolute in Matt 1:20; 2:1, 13, etc.: καὶ ἰδού; Matt 2:9; 3:16, etc., also Luke-Acts: ἰδού), in the middle of a speech (Matt 23:34; Acts 2:7; 13:11; 20:22, 25), to emphasize the importance of a subject (Matt 19:27; Mark 10:28; Luke 13:16; 15:29; 19:8, etc.), or as a summons to more careful consideration and observation (Matt 10:16; 11:8; 22:4; Mark 14:41; Luke 2:48; 7:25). In connection with a noun or finite vb. the meaning is *here/there is, here/there was, here/there comes/came* (Matt 3:17; 12:10; Luke 7:34; Acts 8:27, 36; John 19:5, in Revelation frequently εἶδον καὶ ἰδού [4:1; 6:2, 5, 8; 7:9; 14:1, 14]). BAGD s.v.; P. Fiedler, *Die Formel "und siehe" im NT* (1969); R. Van Otterloo, *OPTAT* 2 (1988) 34-64.

Ἰδουμαία, ας *Idoumaia* Idumea*

The mountainous territory south of Judea (= Edom). Mark 3:8 reports that the crowds following Jesus came not only from Galilee, but also from Judea (v. 7), "Jerusalem, Idumea, from beyond the Jordan, and from about Tyre and Sidon." On this list, cf. R. Pesch, *Mark* [HTKNT] I, 200 (the list is seen from Galilee). Abel, *Histoire* I, 261-64; L. Grollenburg, *LTK* V, 610f.

ἱδρώς, ῶτος, ὁ *hidrōs* sweat*

Luke 22:44, of the "blood"-*sweat* of Jesus (blood-sweat as a miraculous phenomenon is mentioned in Apollonius Rhodius iv.1284f.; Appian *BC* iv.4 §14). L. Brun, *ZNW* 32 (1933) 265-76; G. Schneider, *BZ* 20 (1976) 112-16; W. J. Larkin, *NTS* 25 (1978/79) 250-54.

Ἰεζάβελ *Iezabel* Jezebel*

The wife of King Ahab who supported the cult of Baal and persecuted the prophets (Elijah) of Yahweh (1 Kgs 16–2 Kgs 9). 2 Kgs 9:22 accuses her of harlotry and sorcery. Rev 2:20 uses Jezebel's name for a woman who called herself a "prophetess" and who was dangerous to the faith of the Church. Cf. H. Odeberg, *TDNT* III, 217f.; H. Kraft, *Rev* (HNT) ad loc.

Ἱεράπολις, εως *Hierapolis* Hierapolis*

A city in Phrygia on the Lycus River now called Pamukkale. Col 4:13 mentions it alongside Laodicea: Epaphras "has worked hard for you [the Colossians] and for those in Laodicea and Hierapolis." R. Fellmann, *LAW* 1295.

ἱερατεία, ας, ἡ *hierateia* priestly office, priestly service*

Luke 1:9: "According to the custom of the *priesthood*" the task of burning incense fell to Zechariah. Heb 7:5, of the OT *priestly office* (received by sons of Levi). G. Schrenk, *TDNT* III, 251; H. Seebass, *DNTT* II, 232-36; J. Baehr, *DNTT* III, 36.

ἱεράτευμα, ατος, τό *hierateuma* priesthood*

Lit.: J. BLINZLER, "ΙΕΡΑΤΕΥΜΑ. Zur Exegese von 1 Petr 2,5 u. 9," *Episcopus* (FS M. Cardinal Faulhaber, 1949) 49-65. — H. GOLDSTEIN, *Das Gemeindeverständnis des Ersten Petrusbriefs* (Diss. Marburg, 1973), esp. 46-115. — G. SCHRENK, *TDNT* III, 249-51.

1. The word is found in the LXX and the literature dependent upon it. The only NT occurrences are in 1 Pet 2:5, 9. In the interpretation of the pericope 1 Pet 2:4-10 one may assume: a) that vv. 6-8 reflect an early Christian tradition of christological statements based on OT λίθος passages; b) that vv. 9-10 likewise involve an early Christian reading of the OT that employs both a combination of prophetic citations and Exod 19:6 to indicate the identity of the new people of God; and c) that elements from 2:6-8, 9-10 are taken up in the introductory vv. 4-5, which appear to be a preexisting paraphrasing exposition (Goldstein 46-51).

2. In vv. 9-10 the combination of Hosea and Isaiah passages (Hos 1:6, 9; 2:1, 3, 15 [MT]; Isa 43:20f.), which is derived from tradition, is (in comparison to Rom 9:25-33) unique in its inclusion of the words βασίλειον ἱεράτευμα ἔθνος ἅγιον (Exod 19:6) in Isa 43:20. The insertion evidently signifies that the Church, as God's royal palace (LXX: βασίλειον—to be read as a subst.) finds itself in a direct relationship to God, which has not been previously known and that it, as a society of priests, does not have this relationship to God for itself. Instead, it is God's holy people in its ministry of testifying and missionary activity (Goldstein 64-82).

3. In the introductory thematic variation (vv. 4-5) the author inserts ἱεράτευμα ἅγιον from v. 9. Ἅγιον originally had the function of characterizing ἔθνος more precisely. The "holy *priesthood*" is described in greater detail in the following phrase by the final-attributive inf. "to offer spiritual sacrifices" (v. 5b). The four terms ἱεράτευμα, ἅγιος, θυσία, and πνευματικός interpret one another (Goldstein 83-115).   H. Goldstein

ἱερατεύω *hierateuō* perform priestly service*

The vb. is found in late Greek literature, the LXX, and Josephus (*Ant.* iii.189; xv.253); it does not appear in Philo. In the NT it appears only in Luke 1:8, where it is used of the priestly service of Zechariah. It also appears in *1 Clem.* 43:4 for the priestly ministry of the tribe of Levi and in Justin *Apol.* i.62.2 for pagan priestly activity. G. Schrenk, *TDNT* III, 248f.

Ἰερεμίας, ου *Ieremias* Jeremiah*

The prophet Jeremiah is explicitly cited five times in the NT (see *UBSGNT* 899), but only mentioned by name 3 times, all in Matthew, in 2:17 and 27:9 in the formula "Then was fulfilled what was spoken by the prophet Jeremiah, who said. . . ." Matt 16:14 (cf. Mark 8:28) mentions Jeremiah after John the Baptist and Elijah in the disciples' response to Jesus. Billerbeck I, 730; J. Jeremias, *TDNT* III, 218-21; C. Wolff, *Jeremia im Frühjudentum und Urchristentum* (TU 118, 1976); *TWNT* X, 1114 (bibliography).

ἱερεύς, έως, ὁ *hiereus* priest

1. Occurrences and significance — 2. The Synoptics and Acts — 3. Hebrews — 4. Revelation

Lit.: J. Baehr, *DNTT* III, 32-42. — P.-M. Beaude, *DBSup* X, 1170-1342. — Billerbeck I, 2-5; II, 55-68, 646-50. — Eichrodt, *Theology* I, 392-436. — E. Grässer, *Der Glaube im Hebräerbrief* (1965) 211-14. — J. Jeremias, *Jerusalem in the Time of Jesus* (1969) 147-207. — B. Kötting, "Die Aufnahme des Begriffs 'Hiereus' in den christlichen Sprachgebrauch," *Text —Wort—Glaube* (FS K. Aland, 1980) 112-20. — F. J. Schierse, *Verheißung und Heilsvollendung* (1955). — G. Schrenk, *TDNT* III, 257-65. — Schürer, *History* II, 237-308. — M. Stern, "Aspects of Jewish Society: The Priesthood and Other Classes," *The Jewish People in the First Century* (Compendia 1) II (1976) 561-630. — For further bibliography see Schürer, *History* II, 237f.; *TWNT* X, 1114-18.

1. The NT uses this noun 31 times, of which 14 are in Hebrews. Mark has it twice, Matthew 3 times, and Luke-Acts 8 times (5 in the Gospel, 3 in Acts). John has it only in 1:19, and Revelation has three occurrences. Its absence in Paul and the post-Pauline tradition and the rest of the NT Epistles other than Hebrews is striking. The

NT uses ἱερεύς of pagan *priests* (Acts 14:13), but esp. of Jewish *priests*. In christological terms Christ is the ἱερεύς who according to Heb 5:6; 7:17, 21 (v.l.) is *priest* "after the order of Melchizedek," or, according to 10:21, "the great *priest*." In Rev 1:6; 5:10; 20:6 Christians are called *priests* of God.

2. The commandment of Jesus to the lepers, "Show yourself to the *priests*" (Mark 1:44 par. Matt 8:4/Luke 5:14; cf. sg. in Luke 17:14 [L]), refers to the legal ordinance (Lev 13:19) according to which it was the task of the priest to take certain health-related measures to insure cultic impurity and, after the removal of the illness, to declare the restored purity. Jesus' command is not intended primarily to support priestly authority, but rather to demonstrate Jesus' authority (εἰς μαρτύριον αὐτοῖς).

In Mark 2:26 (par. Matt 12:4/Luke 6:4) Jesus refers to the example of David and his companions, who in an emergency situation ate the consecrated bread kept in the house of God (cf. 1 Sam 21:5, 7). The example serves as support for the saying that the sabbath commandment may not take precedence over care for people. Matt 12:5f. (M) sharpens the matter more with the suggestion that the priests regularly profane the sabbath, even if they are guiltless. Again Jesus' freedom toward the sabbath rule is emphasized. Here the appeal is made to the Scripture: Hos 6:6; cf. 1 Sam 15:22.

Clear criticism of the priesthood is found in Luke 10:31f.: The Samaritan, with his readiness to help, is superior to the *priest* and the levite (the combination *priests* and levites is found only in John 1:19). Only in Luke 1:5, 8 and Acts 6:7 do priests stand in a positive relationship to the event of salvation.

3. In the christological statements about the Son as intercessor in Hebrews, Christ's atoning death and exaltation are described with the image of the high priest (→ ἀρχιερεύς 4). The (historical) distinctions between the high priest and the levitical priesthood are not consistently maintained (cf. 5:6 with 5:10; 6:20; also 7:20 with 7:26, 27, 28, etc.). Christ is also called the *priest* after the order of Melchizedek (5:6, 10; 6:20; 7:1, 11, 15, 17) as well as "the perfect high priest" (Grässer 213). The high priest sayings of Hebrews take on their special christological force and significance against the background of the imperfect levitical priesthood (7:14, 20, 23; 8:4, etc.).

4. Rev 1:6; 5:10; 20:6 take up Exod 19:6 (though the LXX has ἱεράτευμα instead of ἱερεῖς). The priestly dignity granted to the Church is part of the royal dignity given to them by the Lord and his Christ. The priesthood that is granted here is by no means literal, not only because the temple has been destroyed, but also because in the new, heavenly Jerusalem there will be no temple and thus

no priestly temple service (21:22). Instead, God, as ruler of all, and the lamb will take over the function of the temple.   A. Sand

Ἰεριχώ *Ierichō* Jericho*

Lit.: J. R. BARTLETT, *Jericho* (1982). — K.-H. BERNHARDT, *TRE* XVI, 586-88. — *BRL* 152-57 (bibliography). — G. FOERSTER and G. BACCHI, *EAEHL* II, 550-74 (bibliography). — H. HAAG, *LTK* V, 896-98. — K. M. KENYON, *Digging Up Jericho* (1957). — idem, *Excavations at Jericho* (2 vols., 1960, 1965). — KOPP, *Places* 256-61. — E. SELLIN and C. WATZINGER, *Jericho* (1913).

An oasis city in the Jordanian lowland of Judea, at the time of Jesus a toll-collection point (Luke 19:1) on the much-traveled road to Jerusalem. This road led through desolate mountain terrain (Josephus *B.J.* iv.474) and was notoriously dangerous (Luke 10:30). Heb 10:30 refers to the conquest of Jericho under Joshua (Josh 6). Elsewhere in the NT Jericho is mentioned only in the Synoptics. Jesus' visit there is treated in Mark 10:46 (bis) par. Matt 20:29/Luke 18:35 (the healing of a blind man); Luke 19:1 (Zacchaeus). In the parable of the Good Samaritan a man goes "from Jerusalem down to Jericho" and falls in the hands of robbers (Luke 10:30).

ἱερόθυτον, ου, τό *hierothyton* meat offered in sacrifice
→ εἴδωλον 1, 2.

ἱερόν, οῦ, τό *hieron* sanctuary, temple*

1. Occurrences in the NT — 2. The temple building — 3. The temple as a cult site — 4. Jesus and the temple

Lit.: BAGD s.v. — X. LÉON DUFOUR, *Dictionary of the NT* (1980) 396f. — LSJ s.v. ἱερός III.2. — MAYSER, *Grammatik* II/1, 24; II/2, 606 (index); II/3, 240 (index). — MOUTON/MILLIGAN s.v. — F. MUSSNER, "Jesus und 'das Haus des Vaters' — Jesus als 'Tempel,' " *Freude am Gottesdienst* (FS J. G. Plöger, 1983) 267-75. — PREISIGKE, *Wörterbuch* I, 692; III, 259f. — G. SCHRENK, *TDNT* III, 230-47. — For further bibliography → ναός.

1. Τὸ ἱερόν, literally *the holy place, sanctuary,* occurs 71 times in the NT, 9 of them in Mark, 11 in Matthew, 14 in Luke, 25 in Acts, 11 in John, and 1 in Paul. In 1 Cor 9:13 ἱερόν is a general term for the cult: "Do you not know that those who are employed in the holy [i.e., the temple service, neut. pl. of the adj. ἱερός] eat from the holy [τὰ ἐκ τοῦ ἱεροῦ = the yield of the temple service; this second τά is a secondary reading *contra* H. Conzelmann, *1 Cor* [Hermeneia] 156n.2). Acts 19:27 concerns "the *temple* of Artemis" at Ephesus (→ ναός 2). All other occurrences refer to the *temple* in Jerusalem.

The word signifies the entire area of the temple, in contrast to ναός, which primarily (though not exclusively)

designates the temple building, → ναός 5.a). A clear distinction between ἱερόν (see Schrenk 234), ναός (see O. Michel, *TDNT* IV, 882-89), and τόπος (see H. Köster, *TDNT* VIII, 204) is not possible.

2. Jesus and the disciples know the temple as a remarkable and impressive building complex, which will nevertheless be destroyed (Mark 11:11; 13:1f. par. Matt 24:1f./Luke 21:5f.; 13:3). The "pinnacle of the *temple*" is a place where Jesus was tempted (Matt 4:5-7 par. Luke 4:9-12; see Schrenk 236). Jesus taught near the temple treasury (John 8:20; cf. Mark 12:41-44 par. Luke 21:1-4; see R. Schnackenburg, *John* II [1979], 195f.) and walked in Solomon's portico (John 10:23; cf. Acts 3:11; 5:12). Peter healed a lame man at the "Beautiful Gate" (Acts 3:2, 10; see Kopp, *Places* 290).

3. The temple as a cult site:

a) The ministries of the temple: The priests discharge the sabbath service (Matt 12:5). The "*temple* captain" performs the highest police power (Acts 4:1; 5:24 [26]). At their side stand the temple officers, who in Luke 22:(4)52 are called *[temple]* officers (στρατηγοὶ τοῦ ἱεροῦ; Schrenk 271; on whether this term is incorrect see W. Grundmann, *Luke* [THKNT] 389f., 414n.7).

b) The temple as a place of piety: People prayed at the temple (Luke 2:27-32, 37f. [and fasted]; 18:10; 24:53; Acts [2:46f.] 3:1, 8f.; 22:17; → c). Sacrifices were offered and vows fulfilled (Luke 2:22-24, 27; Acts 21:23-27; 24:17f.). Jesus viewed the activities of tradesmen as irreconcilable with the temple as a "house of prayer" (Mark 11:15-17 par. Matt 21:12f./Luke 19:45f./John 2:14-17; see Schrenk, 243; O. Michel, *TDNT* V, 121).

c) The temple as a place of revelation of Christ (see Schrenk 243): through Simeon and Anna (Luke 2:25-38; see Schrenk 245), in Jesus' insight and answers (2:46f.), in Jesus' miracles (Matt 21:14f.; cf. John 2:23), in the children's hosanna (Matt 21:15f.), in a miracle done by Peter (Acts 3:1-10, cf. 12f., 16; 4:9f.), and in a vision of Paul (Acts 22:17-21).

d) The temple as a site of teaching: Jesus teaches there (Mark 11:16f.; 12:35; 14:49 par. Matt 26:55; Matt 21:23; Luke 19:47; 20:1 [→ e]; 21:37f.; John 7:14, 28; 8:2 [cf. Luke 21:37f.]; 18:20), as do the apostles (Acts 5:20f., 25, 42; → e).

e) The temple as a place where the gospel is proclaimed: by Jesus (Luke 20:1) and by the apostles (Acts 5:42).

f) The temple as a place for meeting and conversation, including disputes (Mark 11:27f.; Luke 22:53; John 5:14; 10:23f.; 11:56).

g) The temple as a dangerous place: for Jesus (Mark 11:15, 18; John 8:59; 10:23, cf. vv. 31, 39; see also 11:7f.), for the apostles (Acts 4:1-3; 5:25f.), and for Paul (Acts 21:27-30; 24:6; 26:21).

h) Offenses against the temple: Paul is accused of having taught unfavorably concerning the temple (τόπος), of having begun disputes in the temple, of causing an uproar, and of having profaned the temple by taking a Gentile within its precincts (see Schrenk 233f., 246); he repudiates all these accusations (Acts 21:27-30; 24:5f., 12f., 18f.; 25:8).

4. For Jesus the temple is the house (→ οἶκος) of his Father (John 2:16; cf. Luke 2:49). He is greater than the temple (Schrenk 244) and claims the right to cleanse the temple, teach in it, perform miracles, and accept homage (→ 3.b-e). He does not answer the question concerning authority (according to John, a demand for a sign) raised by his opponents (Mark 11:27-33 par. Matt 21:23-27/Luke 20:1-8; not unambiguously John 2:18-21; → ναός 6.d).

                               U. Borse

ἱεροπρεπής, 2 *hieroprepēs* holy; reverent*

Titus 2:3, of the attitude of older women in the Church. G. Schrenk, *TDNT* III, 253f.; H. Seebass, *DNTT* II, 235; Spicq, *Notes* I, 387f.

ἱερός, 3 *hieros* holy*

Lit.: R. ASTING, *Heiligkeit im Urchristentum* (1930) 234-36. — J. T. HOOKER, *Hieros in Early Greek* (1980). G. SCHRENK, *TDNT* III, 221-30. — H. SEEBASS, *DNTT*, II, 232-36.

The infrequency of this adj. in the NT corresponds to the rare usage in the LXX, which renders Heb. *qōdeš* almost exclusively with ἅγιος, while ἱερός appears only in Josh 6:8 and Dan 1:2. The reason for this restraint is probably the "pagan and cultic sense" of ἱερός (Schrenk 226); for in Greek ἱερός is the holy in itself without any ethical connotation, that which has been dedicated to the gods. It is esp. used of sacrifices (τὰ ἱερά, almost always pl.).

In 1 Cor 9:13 Paul defends his claim to remuneration for his service (9:10f.) with the argument that in the OT (Deut 18:1-4; Num 18:1, 8, 9, 31) the priests received a specific portion of the sacrifices. Τὰ ἱερά has here the concrete meaning of the sacrificial gift, and by extension, whatever belongs to the temple (BAGD s.v.); θυσιαστήριον in v. 13 esp. brings to mind the OT sacrifices.

2 Tim 3:15 speaks—uniquely—of the *holy* Scriptures (τὰ ἱερὰ γράμματα); statements about the holiness of Scripture are elsewhere in the NT consciously avoided. What is intended are the OT writings, which teach about salvation in Jesus Christ through faith.

In the shorter inauthentic Markan ending it is reported (probably as a corrective to the saying in Mark 16:8) that Jesus commissioned the proclamation of eternal salvation through the men associated with Peter; this message (κήρυγμα) is called "*holy and imperishable.*" In Col 4:13 preference is to be given to the

name of the city Hierapolis (with Laodicea) rather than to the v.l. preferred by Westcott and Hort, Ἱερᾷ Πόλει.   A. Sand

Ἱεροσόλυμα *Hierosolyma* Jerusalem
Ἱερουσαλήμ *Ierousalēm* Jerusalem

1. Forms and occurrences in the NT — 2. OT and Judaism — 3. The Gospels and Acts — a) Mark — b) Matthew — c) Luke — d) Acts — e) John — 4. Other NT writings — a) Paul — b) Hebrews — c) Revelation

Lit.: M. BACHMANN, *Jerusalem und der Tempel. Die geographisch-theologischen Elemente in der lukanischen Sicht des jüdischen Kultzentrums* (1980). — O. BAR-YOSEF, B. MAZAR, et al., *EAEHL* II, 579-647. — R. BERGMEIER, "'Jerusalem, du hochgebaute Stadt,'" *ZNW* 75 (1984) 86-106. — O. BÖCHER, "Die heilige Stadt im Völkerkrieg," *Josephus-Studien* (ed. O. Betz, et al.; 1974) 55-76. — H. CONZELMANN, *The Theology of St. Luke* (1961) 73-94. — J. DERENBOURGH, *La distruzione di Gerusalemme del 70 nei suoi riflessi storico-letterari* (1971). — J. K. ELLIOTT, "Jerusalem in Acts and the Gospels," *NTS* 23 (1976-77) 462-69. — E. FASCHER, "Jerusalems Untergang in der urchristlichen und altkirchlichen Überlieferung," *TLZ* 89 (1964) 81-98. — G. FOHRER and E. LOHSE, *TDNT* VII, 292-338. — L. GASTON, *No Stone on Another* (1970). — D. GEORGI, *Die Geschichte der Kollekte des Paulus für Jerusalem* (1965), esp. 13-27. — idem, "Die Visionen vom himmlischen Jerusalem in Apk 21 und 22," FS Bornkamm 351-72. — *Gerusalemme. Atti della XXVI settimana Biblica* (1982). — C. H. GIBLIN, *The Destruction of Jerusalem according to Luke's Gospel* (AnBib 107, 1985). — B. HOLMBERG, *Paul and Power* (1978) 14-57. — J. JEREMIAS, "Die Einwohnerzahl Jerusalems zur Zeit Jesu," *ZDPV* 63 (1943) 24-31. — idem, *Jerusalem in the Time of Jesus* (1969). — idem, "ΙΕΡΟΥΣΑΛΗΜ/ΙΕΡΟΣΟΛΗΜΑ," *ZNW* 65 (1974) 273-76. — K. KENYON, *Royal Cities of the OT* (1971) 13-52. — H. VAN DER KWAAK, "Die Klage über Jerusalem (Matth. XXIII 37-39)," *NovT* 8 (1966) 156-70. — B. LIFSHITZ, "Jérusalem sous la domination romaine," *ANRW* II/8 (1977) 444-89. — E. LOHMEYER, *Galiläa und Jerusalem in den Evangelien* (1936) 41-46 (reprinted in *Das Lukasevangelium* [ed. G. Braumann; 1974] 7-12). — M. RISSI, *Die Zukunft der Welt. Eine exegetische Studie über Johannesoffenbarung 19,11–22,15* (1966) 48-59. — W. C. ROBINSON, *Der Weg des Herrn* (1964), esp. 30-43. — K. H. SCHELKLE, "Qumran und NT in ihrer Umwelt," *TQ* 139 (1959) 385-401. — W. SCHMAUCH, *Orte der Offenbarung und der Offenbarungsort im NT* (1956) 81-121. — G. SCHNEIDER, *Luke* (ÖTK, 1977) 389-91 (excursus). — J. SCHREINER, *Sion-Jerusalem, Jahwes Königssitz* (1963). — R. SCHÜTZ, "Ἱερουσαλημ und Ιεροσολυμα im NT," *ZNW* 11 (1910) 169-87. — H. SCHWIER, *Tempel und Tempelzerstörung. Untersuchungen zu den theologischen und ideologischen Faktoren im ersten jüdischen-römischen Krieg* (1989). — W. STÄHLIN, "Jerusalem hat Mauern und Tore," idem, *Wissen und Wahrheit* (1973) 85-94. — K. STENDAHL, "Quis et unde? An Analysis of Mt 1-2," FS Jeremias (1960) 94-105. — P. STUHLMACHER, "Die Stellung Jesu und des Paulus zu Jerusalem," *ZTK* 86 (1989) 140-56. — D. D. SYLVA, "Ierousalēm and Hierosoluma in Luke-Acts," *ZNW* 74 (1983) 2-21. — P. TRUMMER, "Die Bedeutung Jerusalems für die neutestamentliche Chronologie," *Memoria Jerusalem* (FS F. Sauer, 1977) 129-42. — L. H. VINCENT and A.-M. STÈVE, *Jérusalem de l'AT,*

3 vols. (1954-56). — P. WELTEN, J. K. ELLIOTT, et al., *TRE* XVI, 590-635. — J. C. DE YOUNG, *Jerusalem in the NT* (1960). — F. ZEHRER, "Gedanken zum Jerusalem-Motiv im Lukasevangelium," *Memoria Jerusalem* 117-27. — F. ZEILINGER, "Das himmlische Jerusalem," *Memoria Jerusalem* 143-65 (on Revelation and Hebrews).

1. In the NT Ἱερουσαλήμ and Ἱεροσόλυμα appear a total of 139 times. Most occurrences are in the Gospels and Acts (64 and 61). Both forms of the name are derived from the LXX, in which the books belonging to the Hebrew canon use the Hebraizing form Ἱερουσαλήμ, which is not used in secular Greek. In the Apocrypha the form (τὰ) Ἱεροσόλυμα, which also appears in the nonbiblical writers, is generally used.

Ἱερουσαλήμ often had an archaizing or festive ring, while Ἱεροσόλυμα had a more common and neutral ring. In Mark, Matthew, and John the Hellenistic form is the standard (an exception is Matt 23:37, where the festive form, derived from Q, fits well). In Luke and Acts it is more difficult to perceive a consistent usage, although in Luke Ἱερουσαλήμ predominates, making it consistent with the Evangelist's style of harmonizing with the Bible. In Acts 1–7, which treat the early Church, Ἱερουσαλήμ is used (except in 1:4). From ch. 8 on the usage is mixed without any perceptible consistency.

2. In OT history Jerusalem was the royal city of the Davidic kingdom and, after the division of the kingdom, as the location of the temple, a religious center. It was the place of revelation (Amos 1:2; Isa 2; Joel 3:13, etc.) and was selected by God (cf. Deut 12:5, etc.), the place where the people met their God in the temple cult. Thus the expectations of salvation during the Exile were esp. connected with Jerusalem (Ps 137; Jer 3:17; 31:38ff., etc.). According to the prophets the election by Yahweh stood in contrast to the apostasy of the city's inhabitants. The prophets proclaimed God's judgment on the city (Jer 6:22ff.; Ezek 4:1ff., etc.), a judgment to be executed by the Gentiles. But in faithfulness to his promises, Yahweh would again restore Jerusalem, and it would become the goal of the pilgrimage of the peoples (Isa 2:22ff.; Jer 3:17, etc.). It would even become a life-giving center of the world (Isa 24:23; Ezek 47:1ff., etc.).

In the early Jewish period Jews outside Jerusalem prayed facing Jerusalem (cf. Dan 6:11) and, when possible, went to the festivals. Diaspora Jews sent their gifts to the temple of their ἱερόπολις or μητρόπολις (Philo *Leg. Gai.* 225, 281; cf. Jerusalem as mother of all Israelites: 4 Ezra 10:7). God was expected to fulfill the various eschatological expectations of salvation in Jerusalem (Billerbeck IV, 883ff., 919ff.). These expectations were expressed with conceptions of a heavenly, preexistent Jerusalem. Thus the final salvation was portrayed as something radically new, given by God, and indeed as the elected and protected city of God's revelation and imminence.

At the time of Jesus, Jerusalem was a large city with *ca.* 25,000 inhabitants (Jeremias, *ZDPV*). Herod the Great had altered the city in a zealous building program. These alterations included the new construction of the temple. The highest Jewish authority, the Sanhedrin, met in Jerusalem. The priests and scribes of Jerusalem gave wide-ranging instructions concerning correct life and conduct for all Jews. At the time of the procurators (after A.D. 6) there was a Roman garrison at the Antonia fortress, while the procurators only occasionally went from Caesarea to Jerusalem, primarily during festivals. The tension between the Jewish theocracy and the Roman authority led to the Jewish war, which brought with it the siege and conquest of Jerusalem by Vespasian and Titus (A.D. 70). The city was destroyed and the temple was burned. The pious interpreted the destruction as divine punishment brought on by the sins of the inhabitants.

3. a) For Mark, Jerusalem, including esp. the theocracy, is the place of hostility and failure (3:22; 7:1ff.; more neutral, however, 1:5 and 3:8). In the third Passion prediction (10:32ff.) Jerusalem is prominent as the place of the Passion and resurrection. The representatives of the theocracy are made responsible for the dreadful judgment (v. 32). 11:1ff. describes the entry of the Messiah into the capital of the "kingdom of David" (v. 32), the city of the expected salvation. Here, however, is the beginning of the predicted suffering. The cleansing of the temple (11:15-17) and Jesus' instruction and claim to authority (11:17; 11:22–12:40) deepen the conflict with the Jerusalem authorities (11:18, 27; 12:12f., 38ff.) and have an effect in his later trial (14:55ff.; cf. vv. 1f., 10f., 49). In conformity to halakah (Billerbeck IV, 41f.) Jesus celebrates the Passover meal "in the city" (14:13, 16) with his disciples.

b) In Matthew the Markan perspective is further developed. Among the geographic names that play a role in the infancy narrative (Stendahl), Jerusalem is not the place of birth and of the youth of the Messiah, but only the place of hostility. It is not only the murderous Herod who is troubled at the words of the magi, but "with him all of Jerusalem" (2:3), the city that killed the prophets and those sent to it by God (23:37). In Jerusalem, the city of religious learning, the decisive conflict with the Pharisees and the scribes takes place (cf. 15:1), and "in the city" (28:11) the elders bribe the guards at the tomb who are the indirect witnesses of the resurrection.

In contrast to the Markan parallel, in Matthew the first Passion prediction (16:21) has the explicit statement that Jesus must go to Jerusalem in accordance with the divine will (δεῖ) in order to suffer (cf. 20:17ff.). Jesus thus shares the fate of the OT messengers of God (23:37 and v. 34). Thus he is described after his entry into the agitated city as "the prophet from Galilee." In the word of judgment in 23:37ff. Jerusalem stands for Israel, to which Jesus has made his appeal (cf. Isa 31:5), but which has nevertheless refused to accept the divine call (cf. Deut 1:32; Hos 11:2). Thus its "house," esp. the temple, is "left" (cf. 24:1), delivered to the enemies and withdrawn from divine protection (cf. Deut 32:10f.). The same topic is discussed in 21:33-46 and 22:7. The Matthean community probably thinks here of its associations with Jews and of the events of the Jewish war.

For Matthew, however, Jerusalem is also "the holy city" (cf. Isa 48:3; 52:1; Dan 9:24): Holiness rests on the temple, the dwelling of God who protects his own people; this lies behind the second temptation (4:5ff.). Jerusalem is also "the city of the great king" (5:35; cf. Ps 48:2), so that an oath by Jerusalem becomes an oath by God. In "the holy city" appear also the saints who have been raised (27:52f.), probably as a sign of the coming of the eschatological salvation through Jesus' death and resurrection; the temple and the cult have now played out their role (v. 51).

c) Even if Luke begins (1:5ff.) and ends (24:53) with the temple, he does not mention it explicitly until 2:22. As self-evident as it may be that the Passion takes place in Jerusalem (24:18), the Evangelist does not explicitly indicate this fact in the Passion narrative. (Only in the Passover meal does "the city" come briefly into view.)

But from Luke 9:31 on, Jerusalem is repeatedly mentioned as the place of the suffering; Jesus "goes" toward it of his own free will (9:51, 53; 13:22; 17:11; 18:31; 19:28) because "it cannot be that a prophet should die away from Jerusalem" (13:33). The Evangelist connects the (Q) lament over Jerusalem (13:34f.) to this saying, which is introduced in the report of Jesus' journey to Jerusalem, which began in 9:51. Jerusalem is portrayed not only as the place of Jesus' execution, but also as the executioner. Thus follows the hiddenness of the Messiah and the destruction. Jerusalem should see him as the coming one, in accordance with Ps 118:26, however (probably) as one who comes in judgment. At the end of the journey to Jerusalem (19:41-44), the same theme is sounded: Jerusalem does not recognize the time of its visitation and will thus be destroyed.

In Jesus' eschatological discourse reference is made (in place of the Markan abomination of desolation) to the destruction of Jerusalem (21:20), which is the recompense prophesied in Scripture (v. 22). After this punishment Jerusalem will "be trodden under foot by the Gentiles [Zech 12:3 LXX] until the times of the Gentiles [probably the period of Gentile rule over Jerusalem] are fulfilled." Also in 23:28ff. the fate of Jerusalem and its inhabitants is mentioned: If the execution of Jesus is horrible, even more horrible will be the plagues "on dry wood."

With the mention of Jerusalem in 2:22-38, 41-52 Luke may be gently indicating that "Jesus' appointed place is Jerusalem, and the way of Jesus will end in Jerusalem" (Schneider 390). Thus the temptation placed in Jerusalem (4:9) is shifted to the end of the report. In Jerusalem the temptations ended "for a time" (4:13; cf. 22:3, 28; Conzelmann 28, 75f.n.4). As the city of Jesus' suffering and death, Jerusalem is the place of his "exodus" (9:31) and of his "ascent" (9:51); it is there and in its environs that the appearances of the resurrected one are placed (24:13, 33f., 36). Thus Jerusalem becomes a center of salvation history, for "from Jerusalem" (24:47), according to the Scripture, the message should go out to all peoples.

d) This interpretation of Jerusalem is developed in Acts. "The word of the Lord" proceeds "from Jerusalem" (cf. Isa 2:3). There the apostles of the resurrected one are instructed about the kingdom of God (1:3), there they wait for (Luke 24:49; Acts 1:4f.) the Spirit and receive it (2:1ff.). Thus they are witnesses "in Jerusalem (2:14-20; 3:12-26; 4:8-12, 16, 33; 5:28-32, 42) and to the ends of the earth" (1:8). The world mission thus proceeds from Jerusalem, and the expanding Church has its center there. The Jerusalem apostles confirm the Samaritan mission and bring, so to speak, the Spirit to Samaria (8:14-25); in Jerusalem Paul, the Apostle to the Gentiles, begins his work first as persecutor (8:1, 3; 9:1ff.), then as a preacher (9:26-29). In Jerusalem Peter must first defend the baptism of Gentiles (11:2-18); from Jerusalem Barnabas is sent as an encourager to Antioch (11:22). From Jerusalem come prophets (11:27), to Jerusalem the Antiochians bring support through Saul and Barnabas (11:29f.; 12:25). Here the question of the relationship of Gentiles to the law is determined (15; 16:4). There Paul concludes the second "missionary journey" (18:22), and there he begins the third (18:23), in order to end it there according to the instruction of the Spirit in Jerusalem. From Jerusalem he is led, according to his witness, to Rome in order to bear witness there (23:11; 25–28). Jerusalem is also, however, as it was for Jesus (4:27; 13:27f.; cf. Luke 5:17, 21), the place of rejection of the word (22:18) and hostility against its witnesses (4:5; 5:17f.; 21:11ff.; 25) and against the faithful (8:1; 9:2, 13, 21; 22:5).

Jerusalem has a role in salvation history (Conzelmann 209ff.): The author and his readers can view the beginning period as the historical presupposition for their situation. They find themselves, so to speak, at "the end of the world"; their Church has been severed from the Jerusalem, the original site; the beginning period is over, but the present Church stands in continuity and historical unity with it and is thus "integrated into redemptive history" (Conzelmann 212).

e) In John Jerusalem is a showplace of the struggle between God and the world, between faith and unbelief in the presence of the work of the Son of God and the revelation of his glory. In their own situation the readers may recognize this struggle. In almost every instance where Ἰουδαῖοι appear in this struggle, it occurs in Jerusalem. Thus the faith awakened through signs in Jerusalem is lacking (2:23; 3:12; cf., however, 4:45), and there the Son encounters threats and unbelief from the world (5:16; 7:25, 30, 32; 8:59; 10:22-39; 11:46-57). After the Son has completed his work, the hour has come in which his body has become the place of the true cultus, the true encounter with God and the revelation (2:21f.; 4:20ff.).

4. a) Whereas the meaning of Jerusalem for the authors already discussed lies especially in the past, for Paul it is otherwise. Jerusalem is for him the center of the Church, the place from which the word of God, the gospel, goes out (cf. Isa 2:3; 1 Cor 14:36; Rom 15:19) and from which "spiritual things" have come to the Gentiles (Rom 15:27; 2 Cor 8f.). He is not indifferent as to whether he is recognized by those in Jerusalem as an apostle and indeed as the apostle to the Gentiles (Gal 1:18–2:21). It appears, however, that Paul to some extent regarded himself as one sent from Jerusalem and commissioned with the collection to the "poor" (Gal 2:10). His wish that his "ministry for Jerusalem be accepted by the saints" (Rom 15:26-31; cf. 1 Cor 16:1-4) must be seen in the light of the tension between his position as an apostle independent of Jerusalem (Gal 1:16f.) and his concluding task and its evaluation by Jerusalem.

In Gal 4:21-31 Paul argues against the demand for circumcision with the apocalyptic tradition of the heavenly Jerusalem, the Jerusalem above, which is contrasted to the present Jerusalem. The latter stands for Judaism, which is enslaved and zealous for the law, while the former is free and "our mother." The pres. tense is noteworthy: Salvation is already here. Despite the antipathy of the Judaizers Christianity will triumph: As the inhabitants are like children indebted to the mother city for life and protection, Christians now have a free life, preserved and protected by God.

b) The same tradition is present also in Hebrews. In Heb 12:22 the urgency of the exhortation is based on the fact that the Church has come to the city of the living God, the heavenly Jerusalem. Jerusalem stands here for the salvation that is not limited by the visible (cf. v. 11); the addressees find themselves already present in proximity to the sovereign and judging God, together with the festal assembly of angels and the Church of the firstborn (probably a designation of the Christian community). If the addressees are in a sense already in the divine world, living from it and obligated to it, they are nevertheless reminded in 13:14 that this eschatological salvation experience is a goal that is not already present, but is to be attained.

c) Jerusalem is mentioned in Rev 11:8 as the city "in which its Lord was also crucified." The eschatological witnesses share the fate of Jesus at this place of ungodliness and sin, which has fallen under judgment (11:2).

Revelation also has the tradition of the new, heavenly Jerusalem. In contrast to those who falsely claim to be Jews (3:9), the victors in the heavenly Jerusalem will be full citizens (3:12); indeed, the false Jews will bow down before the victors (3:9). In Revelation 21 the glory of the Jerusalem that descends at the end is described. In the metaphorical language some of the customary ideas associated with Jerusalem recur. This Jerusalem is actually "holy" (21:2), i.e., it and its people belong to the divine sphere; their close relationship with God and the lamb is expressed with the symbolism of the bride (cf. 19:7). The covenant promise of the presence of God among his people and of their relationship with him is fulfilled (21:3), and with his divine protection all tribulation, including death, has come to an end. In 21:10ff. the supraterrestrial glory of the city is painted in colors from Ezekiel 40–48.

L. Hartman

Ἱεροσολυμίτης, ου, ὁ *Hierosolymitēs* inhabitant of Jerusalem*

Pl. *inhabitants of Jerusalem* appears in Mark 1:5 (πάντες) and John 7:25 (τινες ἐκ τῶν). The noun is formed from the name of the city in the form → Ἱεροσόλυμα.

ἱεροσυλέω *hierosyleō* rob temples*

Rom 2:22, with κλέπτω (v. 21) and μοιχεύω as in Philo *Conf.* 163. G. Schrenk, *TDNT* III, 255f.; H. Seebass, *DNTT* II, 235; D. B. Garlington, "Ἱεροσυλεῖν and the Idolatry of Israel (Romans 2,22)," *NTS* 36 (1990) 142-51.

ἱερόσυλος, 2 *hierosylos* pertaining to a temple robber, subst.: temple robber*

Acts 19:37, in the subst. form ὁ ἱερόσυλος, *the temple robber.* However, a more general meaning (*behave irreverently* toward the sanctuary) is possible (BAGD s.v.). G. Schrenk, *TDNT* III, 256f.; H. Seebass, *DNTT* II, 235.

ἱερουργέω *hierourgeō* act as a priest*

Rom 15:16, with the obj. "the gospel": Paul *serves* the gospel *as priest* or *in a priestly manner.* G. Schrenk, *TDNT* III, 247f.; H. Seebass, *DNTT* II, 235.

Ἱερουσαλήμ *Ierousalēm* Jerusalem
→ Ἱεροσόλυμα.

ἱερωσύνη, ης, ἡ *hierōsynē* priesthood, priestly status*

In the NT only in Heb 7:11, 12, 24 (v. 14 v.l.), of the levitical *priesthood,* of the change in the *priesthood,* and of Jesus, who has the ἱερωσύνη "permanently." G. Schrenk, *TDNT* III, 247; H. Seebass, *DNTT* II, 233.

Ἰεσσαί *Iessai* Jesse*

The father of David (1 Kgdms 16:1, 10, etc.): Matt 1:5, 6; Luke 3:32; Acts 13:22; also Rom 15:12 in a citation of Isa 11:10 LXX (ἡ ῥίζα τοῦ Ἰεσσαί).

Ἰεφθάε   *Iephthae*   Jephthah*

Heb 11:32 mentions Ἰεφθάε (Judg 11:1–12:7) in the enumeration of "judges" and prophets before David and Samuel who "through faith conquered kingdoms" (v. 33).

Ἰεχονίας, ου   *Iechonias*   Jechoniah*

Matt 1:11, 12 mentions "Jechoniah and his brothers at the time of the deportation to Babylon" (v. 11). Jechoniah is the son of Joshua (v. 11) and father of Shealtiel (v. 12). According to 1 Chr 3:15f. King Jechoniah was the grandson of Josiah.

Ἰησοῦς, οῦ   *Iēsous*   Jesus

1. Occurrences in the NT — 2. Origin of the name — 3. Bearers of the name other than Jesus of Nazareth — 4. Jesus of Nazareth — a) Use of the name in the NT (overview) — b) The life of Jesus — c) Jesus in the Gospels and Acts — d) Jesus in the Pauline corpus — e) Jesus in the other NT writings

Lit. (esp. on 4): G. AULÉN, *Jesus in Contemporary Historical Research* (1976). — E. BAMMEL and C. F. D. MOULE, ed., *Jesus and the Politics of His Day* (1984). — C. K. BARRETT, *Jesus and the Gospel Tradition* (1967). — G. BAUMBACH, *Jesus von Nazareth im Lichte der jüdischen Gruppenbildung* (1971). — W. BEILNER, *Jesus ohne Retuschen* (1974). — J. BLANK, *Jesus von Nazareth* (1972). — J. BLINZER, *The Trial of Jesus* (1959). — G. BORNKAMM, *Jesus of Nazareth* (1960). — H. BRAUN, *Jesus of Nazareth: The Man and His Time* (1979). — R.-L. BRUCK-BERGER, *Die Geschichte Jesu* (1967). — R. BULTMANN, *Jesus and the Word* (²1958). — C. BURCHARD, *KP* II, 1344-54. — J. CABA, *El Jésus de los Evangelios* (1977). — H. CONZELMANN, *Jesus* (Eng. tr. of article in *RGG*, 1973). — DALMAN, *Worte.* — G. DEL-LING, "Geprägte Jesus-Tradition im Urchristentum," *Studien zum NT und zum hellenistischen Judentum* (1970) 160-75. — *idem,* "Der 'historische Jesus' und der kerygmatische Christus," *ibid.* 176-202. — M. DIBELIUS, *Jesus* (Eng. tr., ²1963). — J. DUPONT, ed., *Jésus aux origines de la christologie* (1975). — P. FIEDLER, *Jesus und die Sünder* (1976). — P. FIEDLER and L. OBERLINNER, "Jesus von Nazareth. Ein Literaturbericht," *BibLeb* 13 (1972) 52-74. — W. FOERSTER, *TDNT* III, 284-93. — J. DE FRAINE and H. HAAG, *BL* 833-43. — J. GNILKA, "Neue Jesus-Literatur," *TRev* 67 (1971) 249-58. — M. GOGUEL, *Jesus and the Origins of Christianity* (1933). — GOPPELT, *Theology* I. — M. GRANT, *Jesus* (1977). — E. GRÄSSER, "Der historische Jesus im Hebräerbrief," *ZNW* 56 (1965) 63-91. — *idem, Die Naherwartung Jesu* (1973). — *idem,* "Der Mensch Jesus als Thema der Theologie," FS Kümmel 129-50. — W. GRUNDMANN, *Die Geschichte Jesu Christi* (1961). — HAHN, *Titles* (index s.v.). — M. HENGEL, *Was Jesus a Revolutionist?* (1971). — H. W. HOEHNER, *Chronological Aspects of the Life of Christ* (1977). — T. HOLTZ, *Jesus von Nazaret* (1981). — JEREMIAS, *Parables.* — *idem, Theology.* — *idem, Jesus und seine Botschaft* (1976). — E. KÄSEMANN, "The Problem of the Historical Jesus," *Essays on NT Themes* (1964). — K. KERTELGE, ed., *Rückfrage nach Jesus* (1974). — J. KLAUSNER, *Jesus of Nazareth* (1929). — W. G. KÜMMEL, *Dreißig Jahre Jesusforschung (1950-1980)* (1985). — *idem,*

"Ein Jahrzehnt Jesusforschung (1965-1975)," *TRu* 40 (1975) 289-336; 41 (1976) 197-258, 295-363. — *idem,* "Jesusforschung seit 1951," *TRu* 31 (1965). — *idem, Promise and Fulfillment* (1961). — M. LEHMANN, *Synoptische Quellenanalyse und die Frage nach dem historischen Jesus* (1970). — X. LÉON-DUFOUR, *The Gospels and the Jesus of History* (1968). — H. LEROY, *Überlieferung und Deutung* (1978). — A. LINDEMANN, "Jesus in der Theologie des NT," FS Conzelmann 27-57. — U. LUZ, "Das Jesusbild der vormarkinischen Tradition," FS Conzelmann 347-74. — J. MAIER, *Jesus von Nazareth in der talmudischen Über-lieferung* (1978). — H. MERKLEIN, *Die Gottesherrschaft als Handlungsprinzip. Untersuchungen zur Ethik Jesu* (1978). — K. NIEDERWIMMER, *Jesus* (1968). — E. PERCY, *Die Botschaft Jesu* (1953). — N. PERRIN, *Jesus and the Language of the King-dom* (1976). — *idem, Rediscovering the Teaching of Jesus* (1967). — R. PESCH and A. ZWERGEL, *Kontinuität in Jesus* (1974). — W. PESCH, ed., *Jesus in den Evangelien* (1970). — P. POKORNÝ, "Der irdische Jesus im Johannesevangelium," *NTS* 30 (1984) 217-28. — J. W. PRYOR, "Paul's Use of *Iēsous*: A Clue for the Translation of Romans 3:26?" *Colloquium* 16 (1983) 31-44. — K. H. RENGSTORF, *DNTT* II, 330-32. — RISTOW/MAT-THIAE. — J. M. ROBINSON, *A New Quest of the Historical Jesus* (SBT 25, 1959). — J. ROLOFF, "Auf der Suche nach einem neuen Jesus-Bild," *TLZ* 98 (1973) 561-72. — *idem, Das Kerygma und der irdische Jesus* (1970). — A. SAND, "Jesus im Urteil jüdischer Autoren der Gegenwart (1930-1976)," *Catholica* 31 (1977) 29-38. — E. P. SANDERS, *Jesus and Judaism* (1985). — E. SCHILLE-BEECKX, *Jesus: An Experiment in Christology* (1979). — W. SCHMITHALS, "Paulus und der historische Jesus," *ZNW* 53 (1962) 145-60. — R. SCHNACKENBURG, *God's Rule and Kingdom* (1963). — G. SCHNEIDER, "Jesus-Bücher und Jesus-Forschung 1966-71," *TPQ* 120 (1972) 155-60. — K. SCHUBERT, *Jesus im Lichte der Religionsgeschichte des Judentums* (1973). — H. SCHÜRMANN, *Das Geheimnis Jesu* (1972). — E. SCHWEIZER, *TRE* XVI, 670-726. — G. N. STANTON, *Jesus of Nazareth in NT Preaching* (1974). — E. STAUFFER, *Jesus and His Story* (1960). — G. STRECKER, "Die historische und theologische Problematik der Jesusfrage," *EvT* 29 (1969) 453-76. — W. TRILLING, *Fragen zur Geschichtlichkeit Jesu* (³1969). — *idem, Die Botschaft Jesu* (1978). — É. TROCMÉ, *Jesus and His Contemporaries* (1973). — G. VERMES, *Jesus the Jew* (1973). — A. VÖGTLE, *LTK* V, 922-32. — *idem, SacVb* 419-37. — *idem,* "Jesus von Nazareth," *Ökumenische Kirchengeschichte* (ed. Kottje and Moeller; 1970) I, 3-24. — H. ZIMMERMANN, *Jesus Christus. Geschichte und Verkündigung* (1973). — For further bibliography see *DNTT* II, 343-46; *SacVb* 436f., 1019f.; *TWNT* X, 1118-20.

1. The name Jesus appears in the NT a total of 919 times, only 6 in reference to persons other than Jesus of Nazareth (→ 3). The name is most frequent in the Gospels (244 occurrences in John, 152 in Matthew, 88 in Luke, 82 in Mark); after that it appears most frequently in Acts (70 occurrences), Romans (37), 1 Corinthians (26), Philippians (22), and Ephesians (20), and then, in all other NT writings, less than 10 times in 2 Peter (9), Colossians (7), Philemon (6), Jude (6), Titus (4), James (2), 2 John (2), and 3 John (none).

2. The name Ἰησοῦς occurs frequently in the LXX and is there most often a rendering of *yᵉhôšûaʿ*/*yᵉhôšuaʿ* and the later form of the name, *yēšûaʿ* (see Hatch/Redpath III, 84). In addition

to Joshua the son of Nun (Exod 17:9f.; Num 11:28, etc.) Ἰησοῦς is used in the LXX of other persons, e.g., the high priest Joshua (Hag 1:1; Zech 3:1) and the levite Joshua (2 Chr 31:15). The LXX form is based on the postexilic shortened form of the name and makes it declinable with the attachment of final sigma in the nominative.

From the second century A.D. the name yēšûaʿ/Jesus disappears as a proper name in Judaism (the rabbinic literature returns to the old longer form of the name). But at the time of Jesus of Nazareth, it was still widespread (Foerster 285-87). The name meant originally "Yahweh helps/is salvation" (cf. the interpretation in Philo *Mut.* 121: σωτηρία κυρίου). The shorter form yēšûaʿ leaves the theophoric element no longer recognizable, but is reminiscent of the vb. yšʿ (cf. Sir 46:1: an interpretation of the name *Joshua*). Matt 1:21 indicates that the vb. yšʿ (→ σῴζω) was connected to the name Jesus (Foerster 289f.): "for he will save his people from their sins (σώσει)." Rabbinic Judaism regularly referred to Jesus of Nazareth, not with yēšûaʿ and even less with the otherwise recurring theophoric older name, but called him instead yēšû. This has been regarded as an intentional garbling of the name (Billerbeck I, 64; cf. G. Dalman, *Jesus-Jeschua* [1922, 1929, reprinted 1967] 6, 225). It lacks both the theophoric element and the vb. yšʿ, which signifies "salvation."

3. While in the NT 913 passages use the name Jesus for Jesus of Nazareth (Jesus Christ; → 4), in only 6 instances does it appear as the name of (4) other persons; cf. also the compound Βαριησοῦς (→ e).

a) In dependence on the form of the name in the LXX, Acts 7:45 and Heb 4:8 use Ἰησοῦς for *Joshua*, the son of Nun and successor of Moses, who led the Israelites to Canaan (→ 2). The first passage (from the speech of Stephen) recalls the bringing of the holy tabernacle "into the land of the nations"; the second denies the conclusion that Joshua had already "led the people of God into rest" (against Josh 22:4).

b) In Matt 27:16, 17 a few textual witnesses give the "infamous prisoner" → Βαραββᾶς (so ℵ A B, etc.) the double name *Jesus* Barabbas (Θ f¹ 700* syrˢ, ᵖᵃˡ Origen). On the preference for the reading with the double name, cf. *TCGNT* ad loc.

c) In the genealogy of Jesus in Luke 3:29 the son of Eliezer is given the name *Jesus* (RSV *Joshua*).

d) In Col 4:11 the third-named coworker of Paul, a "Jesus who is called Justus," is described as one who was "from the circumcision."

e) In the entourage of the proconsul of Cyprus there was, according to Acts 13:6, a Jewish sorcerer named → Βαριησοῦς (Barjesus = "son of Jesus").

4. a) In reference to *Jesus of Nazareth*, in the Gospels the name by itself, (ὁ) Ἰησοῦς (col. A in the chart below) predominates. But because of the frequency of the name Jesus had to be distinguished from other bearers of the name. Therefore, in the Gospels "Jesus of Nazareth" (and other such distinctions) was used (col. B). Outside the Gospels (except in Revelation) the name Jesus is usually associated with christological titles (col. C). Among these,

the combinations "Jesus Christ" (C1) and "Christ Jesus" (C2) stand out numerically. Other predicates are also found, sometimes with "Christ" (C3). The information given in this chart of frequencies is at some points only approximate, esp. because of uncertain textual traditions.

		A	B	C1	C2	C3	Total
(4.c)	Matt	141	3	1		5	150
	Mark	74	4			4	82
	Luke	81	3			3	87
	John	238	4	2			244
	Acts	31	5	9	4	20	69
(4.d)	Rom	2		7	12	16	37
	1 Cor	1		3	7	15	26
	2 Cor	7		2	1	9	19
	Gal	1		5	8	3	17
	Phil	1		4	12	5	22
	1 Thess	3			2	11	16
	Phlm				3	3	6
	Eph	1			10	8	20
	Col				3	3	6
	2 Thess					13	13
	1 Tim				10	4	14
	2 Tim			1	10	2	13
	Titus			1		3	4
(4.e)	Heb	5		3		5	13
	Jas					2	2
	1 Pet			8	1	1	10
	2 Pet			1		8	9
	1 John	5		2		5	12
	2 John			1		1	2
	3 John						0
	Jude			2		4	6
	Rev	9		3		2	14
		600	19	56	83	155	913

On A ([ὁ] Ἰησοῦς): Ἰησοῦς in the NT frequently has (corresponding to the classical use of personal names in general) no art. However, it can be used with the art. as a result of anaphora. "An untranslatable nuance of the language is often involved" (BDF §260). Use of the art. was viewed as colloquial (Mayser, *Grammatik* II/2, §§54f.). In the Synoptics (except in the voc.) Ἰησοῦς generally has the art. (e.g., Mark 1:24; Matt 26:69, 71). However, the art. is not used at the first mention of Jesus by that name in Matthew and Mark (Mark 1:9; Matt 1:16 [Luke 4:4 has the anaphoric art.]) or at the first appearance of the resurrected one in Matthew and Luke (Matt 28:9; Luke 24:15). Corresponding to classical usage, Luke uses the name without the art. relatively frequently (cf. F. Rehkopf, *Die lukanische Sonderquelle* [1959] 51-53). In John ὁ Ἰησοῦς and Ἰησοῦς are equally frequent (the art. does not appear, e.g., in the formulaic phrase ἀπεκρίθη Ἰησοῦς in John 3:3, 5, 10; 18:36, etc.; the anaphoric art., nevertheless, in, e.g., 18:37). The letters and Revelation (Acts also in part) usually omit the art. since no narrative anaphora is present (BDF §260.1); cf., however, Rom 8:11; 2 Cor 4:10f.; Gal 6:17, also the anaphoric art. in 1 Thess 4:14; Eph 4:21; 1 John 4:3, similarly Acts 1:1 in connection with the Third Gospel.

On B ("Jesus of Nazareth," etc.): In order to distinguish him from other bearers of the name, Jesus is designated by place of origin (only in the Gospels and Acts): Ἰησοῦς → Ναζαρηνός (Mark 1:24; Luke 4:34), Ἰησοῦς ὁ → Ναζαρηνός (Mark 10:47; 14:67; 16:6; Luke 24:19), Ἰησοῦς ὁ → Ναζωραῖος (Matt 26:71 [cf. 2:23; Luke 18:37; John 18:5, 7; 19:19; Acts 2:23 with additional predicates in 3:6; 4:10]; 6:14; 22:8; 26:9), Ἰησοῦς ὁ ἀπὸ Ναζαρέθ (Acts 10:38), Ἰησοῦς ὁ ἀπὸ Ναζαρέθ τῆς Γαλιλαίας (Matt 21:11; cf. Mark 1:9]), "Jesus the son of Joseph (John 6:42), from Nazareth" (John 1:45), Ἰησοῦς ὁ Γαλιλαῖος (Matt 26:69).

On C1 and C2 ("Jesus Christ" and "Christ Jesus" without additional predicates and not in ἐστίν statements such as John 20:31; 1 John 2:22; 5:1): While Ἰησοῦς Χριστός (C1) is in most cases understood as a double name, Paul's preferred phrase Χριστός Ἰησοῦς (C2; also in Ephesians, Colossians, and the Pastorals) has more the sound of the titular sense ("the Messiah Jesus"). Both doublets probably originated in (confessional) statements with the pred. nom. (Jesus [is] the Christ; Christ [is] Jesus). But in Pauline usage the idea of a double designation stands in the foreground, as the examples itemized in C3 demonstrate. The strangeness of the Christ title ("Messiah" = "anointed one") in the Gentile Christian churches probably required the transition to a double name, by which (ὁ) Χριστός became a name for Jesus (W. Grundmann, *TDNT* IX, 542). "By means of this commonly used name the unmistakable uniqueness of Jesus is emphasized" (*ibid.* 540). In the Pauline literature the double form is used "at significant points" (*ibid.* 541), e.g., in opening salutations and in the conclusions to individual sections.

On C3 ("Jesus Christ" and "Christ Jesus" with additional christological predicates, not including statements such as 1 Cor 8:6; Phil 2:11; 1 John 4:15; 5:5; because of the brevity of what follows the formulations will be noted without attention to their tradition history; see the articles on the different titles noted):

The most frequent detailed phrase (38 occurrences) is ὁ κύριος ἡμῶν Ἰησοῦς Χριστός, our Lord *Jesus* Christ (Acts 15:26; Rom 5:1, 11; 15:6, 30; 16:24; 1 Cor 1:2, 7, 8, 10; 15:57; 2 Cor 1:3; 8:9; Gal 6:14, 18; 1 Thess 1:3; 5:9, 23, 28; Eph 1:3, 17; 5:20; 6:24; Col 1:3; 2 Thess 2:1,

14, 16; 3:6, 18; 1 Tim 6:3, 14; Jas 2:1; 1 Pet 1:3; 2 Pet 1:8, 14, 16; Jude 17, 21). Next in frequency is ὁ κύριος ἡμῶν Ἰησοῦς, our Lord *Jesus* (Rom 16:20; 1 Cor 5:4 bis; 2 Cor 1:14; 1 Thess 2:19; 3:11, 13; 2 Thess 1:8, 12; Heb 13:20; Acts 20:21), and ὁ κύριος Ἰησοῦς, the Lord *Jesus* (Mark 16:19; Luke 24:3; Acts 1:21; 4:33; 8:16; 11:20; 15:11; 16:31; 19:5, 13, 17; 20:24, 35; 21:13; 1 Cor 11:23; 16:23; 2 Cor 4:14; 11:31; 1 Thess 2:15; 4:2; Phlm 5; Eph 1:15; 2 Thess 1:7; 2:8; Rev 22:21). Jesus is also called κύριος in related expressions: ὁ κύριος Ἰησοῦς Χριστός, the Lord *Jesus* Christ (Acts 11:17; 28:31; Rom 13:14; 1 Cor 6:11; 2 Cor 13:13; Phil 4:23; Phlm 25 (only Paul), Κύριος Ἰησοῦς, Lord *Jesus* (Acts 7:59; Rom 10:9; 14:14; 1 Cor 12:3; Phil 2:19; 1 Thess 4:1; Col 3:17; Rev 22:20), and κύριος Ἰησοῦς Χριστός, Lord *Jesus* Christ (Rom 1:7; 1 Cor 1:3; 2 Cor 1:2; Gal 1:3; Phil 1:2; 3:20; 1 Thess 1:1; Phlm 3; Eph 1:2; 6:23; 2 Thess 1:1, 2, 12; 3:12; Jas 1:1). The following "Lord Jesus" passages place the name Jesus first: Ἰησοῦς Χριστὸς ὁ κύριος ἡμῶν, *Jesus* Christ our Lord (Rom 1:4; 5:21; 7:25; Jude 25); the same phrase preceded by ὁ υἱὸς αὐτοῦ (1 Cor 1:9); Ἰησοῦς Χριστὸς κύριος, *Jesus* Christ, Lord (2 Cor 4:5); Ἰησοῦς ὁ κύριος ἡμῶν, *Jesus* our Lord (Rom 4:24; 1 Cor 9:1; 2 Pet 1:2); Χριστὸς Ἰησοῦς ὁ κύριος ἡμῶν, Christ *Jesus* our Lord (Rom 6:23; 8:39; 1 Cor 15:31; 1 Tim 1:2, 12; 2 Tim 1:2), and Χριστὸς Ἰησοῦς ὁ κύριός μου (Phil 3:8; see also ὁ Χριστὸς Ἰησοῦς ὁ κύριος [ἡμῶν] in Eph 3:11; Col 2:6).

In the Pastorals and 2 Peter "Jesus Christ" and "Christ Jesus" appear with the title → σωτήρ (2 Tim 1:10; Titus 1:4; 2:13; 3:6; 2 Pet 1:1, 11; 2:20; 3:18). While the Pastorals speak of Jesus as σωτήρ ἡμῶν, 2 Peter has σωτήρ Ἰησοῦς Χριστός. It is strikingly seldom that the name Jesus (Christ) is connected with the title Son of God (→ υἱός; Heb 4:14; 1 John 1:3, 7; 3:23; 5:20; 2 John 3). Further and partially unique formulations are found in Heb 3:1; 12:2, 24; 1 John 2:1; Jude 4.

The Synoptics confess Jesus as "Son of David" (Matt 1:1; Mark 10:47; Luke 18:38), "Son of God" (Mark 1:1), "Son of the most high God" (Mark 5:7; Luke 8:28), "king of the Jews" (Matt 27:37; cf. John 19:19). The phrase Ἰησοῦς ὁ λεγόμενος Χριστός occurs only in Matthew (1:16; 27:17, 22). In Acts 3:13; 4:27, 30 Jesus is called the → παῖς of God. One may compare also Matt 21:11 (Jesus as "prophet"), Mark 9:5 (→ ῥαββί as direct address), and Luke 17:13 (→ ἐπιστάτης as direct address).

b) The major sources for our knowledge of Jesus' life and teaching are the Synoptic Gospels; the other NT writings, including John, are considered of only secondary significance.

Within the Synoptic tradition "the smaller units," as the more ancient traditional material (in comparison with the redactional "framework" of the Gospels), take precedence. They are nevertheless to be evaluated critically with respect to their historical value because christological intentions were already present in the earliest tradition, of course in the form of narration about Jesus or actualizations of his preaching (on the criteria see F. Lentzen-Deis in Kertelge 78-117). The oldest Passion narrative and—in view of the proclamation of Jesus—the logia source (Q) take a certain precedence. Nonbiblical sources have only a tertiary significance. The apocryphal Jesus-tradition has little value as a source (see, in addition to Hennecke/Schneemelcher, esp. W. Bauer, *Das Leben Jesu im Zeitalter der neutestamentlichen Apokryphen* [1909]). The noncanonical sayings of Jesus (agrapha) are insignificant in illuminating the message of Jesus (cf. J. Jeremias, *Unbekannte Jesusworte*, [4]1965 [cf. Eng. tr. of [2]1951: *Unknown Sayings of Jesus* [1957], which lacks additional discussion by O. Hofius). The few non-Christian witnesses to Jesus can possibly confirm evidence in the Gospels, but can provide no new information (Tacitus *Ann.* xv.44; Suetonius *Caes.* v.25.4; Josephus *Ant.* xx.200; *b. Sanh.* 43a *Bar.*; cf. J. B. Aufhauser, *Antike Jesus-Zeugnisse* [1925]; Blinzler 22-49).

Jesus was born during the lifetime of Herod the Great, who died in 4 B.C. According to Matt 2:1, 5; Luke 2:4, 11 Jesus was born in Bethlehem, which is not historically certain—and grew up in Nazareth ("Jesus of Nazareth," → 4.a). After he had been baptized as an adult by John in the Jordan and after the end of John's activity (with his arrest), probably at the beginning of A.D. 28, Jesus began his public proclamation of the dawn of the awaited kingdom of God (→ βασιλεία τοῦ θεοῦ) in his own works. In connection with his message he granted to people (as an anticipation of God's final judgment) the forgiveness of their sins. At the same time he called all people to repentance (→ μετάνοια 4). Jesus saw true fulfillment of God's will (and of the Torah) in love for God and neighbor, including even one's enemies.

The call to repentance, which was made primarily in Galilee, was not generally accepted. Perhaps after a "Galilean crisis" (so F. Mussner, FS Schmid [1973] 238-52) a new task was given to the narrow circle of the Twelve (→ δώδεκα), Jesus' messengers for the gathering of all Israel. This narrower circle, which had been selected from the larger group of followers of his "disciples" (→ μαθητής; → ἀκολουθέω), were given the task of being the core of the community of disciples and the first (programmatic) bearers of the Jesus tradition (Mussner 247f.). Thus a new beginning was established.

On the way to Jerusalem Jesus became certain of his imminent violent death. Whether he understood or proclaimed this death already as an atoning death cannot be determined. The question can be answered positively for the "Last Supper" at the latest (H. Schürmann, *Jesu ureigener Tod* [1975] 16-96; R. Pesch, *Mark* [HTKNT] II, 354-77).

Jesus' messianic claim can be seen in a few of his characteristic statements and actions, even if his self-consciousness is not articulated with a title. Jesus' table fellowship with "tax collectors and sinners" and his provocative "sabbath violations" called forth opposition from his opponents, the Pharisees. His exorcisms and

healings, which stood in close connection with his proclamation, were for him actual signs of the dawning kingdom of God. Jesus' claim to authority is seen also in the call to discipleship (M. Hengel, *The Charismatic Leader and His Followers* [1981] 84-88). In Jerusalem his action at the temple (the "cleansing of the temple"), a "messianic" demonstration, led directly to the reaction of the (Sadducean) priesthood and the Sanhedrin. In the trial against Jesus the title Messiah (→ Χριστός) appears to be an interpretation of Jesus' claim concerning himself. He evidently accepted this title, even if Mark 14:61f. indicates that it did not define his authority exhaustively. The leading circles of the Sanhedrin were able to bring about his condemnation to death on the cross before Pilate, the Roman judge (→ σταυρός, → σταυρόω), by accusing him of being a messianic pretender. From the condemnation to death on a cross it can be concluded that Jesus "did nothing before Pilate to become free of this accusation, but not that he himself played the role of a revolutionary and political messianic pretender" (Vögtle, "Jesus von Nazareth" 20). He was crucified at the Passover festival, probably in the year 30, outside the gates of Jerusalem. It is disputed whether the day of his death fell on the fourteenth (so John) or the fifteenth (so the Synoptics) of Nisan in the year in question.

c) The predominance of the name Jesus in the Gospels and its use alone indicates that the authors of the Gospels intend to report concerning the "earthly" Jesus, the man "Jesus of Nazareth." Yet they point out clearly in varying ways at the beginnings of their Gospels that the same Jesus whose earthly works and death they report is the Christ of the Christian confession (Mark 1:1, 9, 11, 24; Matt 1:1, 16, 18, 21, 25; Luke 1:31-33, 35; 2:11, 21, 49; John 1:17f., 45). One can understand the Gospels as explications of the confessional statement "Jesus is the Christ." They assume that the resurrection of Jesus not only emphasizes his "messianic" status, but even serves as proof (Mark 16:6f.; Matt 28:5f.; Luke 24:3, 5f., 19, 26, 34; John 17:3; 20:31; 21:21).

The people use the name Jesus (of Nazareth) when they speak of him (Matt 21:11; Mark 10:47a; 14:67; Luke 24:19; John 1:45; 18:5, 7) or—with other vocatives—when they address him (Mark 1:24; 10:47b; Luke 17:13; 23:42). The overwhelming majority of the numerous (esp. in Matthew and John) occurrences of the name Jesus are in narrative texts in the Gospels. In Luke the name Jesus is less prominent; Luke uses ὁ → κύριος in narrative 16 times, of which 22:61 and 24:3 are different from Mark (cf. John 6:23; 20:2, 18, 20, 25).

Acts speaks of Jesus (without christological titles added) when it refers to the "life of Jesus" (e.g., 1:1, 14, 16; 10:38) or when non-Christians speak of him (4:18; 5:40; 17:7; 19:13, 15; 25:19). Yet Jesus makes himself known to Saul with this name (9:5; 22:8; 26:15); the angels use it at the ascension (1:11), and Stephen also uses it (7:55). The apostolic proclamation says essentially that Jesus is the Christ (17:3; 18:5, 28); thus "Jesus is proclaimed" (8:35; 9:20) or one teaches "about Jesus" (18:25; 28:23; cf. 5:42; 8:12; 11:20; 28:31). His death and resurrection are the essential features (2:22, 32, 36; 3:13, 20; 5:30; 10:38; 13:23, 33; 17:3; 18:5, 28). A characteristic phrase in Acts is "the name (→ ὄνομα) of Jesus (Christ)" (2:38; 3:6; 4:10, 18, 30; 5:40; 8:12; 9:27; 10:48; 16:18; 26:9). The phrase "the Lord Jesus" also appears frequently (→ a on C3).

d) Paul uses Ἰησοῦς alone esp. in 1 Thessalonians (1:10; 4:14 bis) and 2 Corinthians (4:5, 10 bis, 11 bis, 14; 11:4) and also in Rom 3:26; 8:11; 1 Cor 12:3; Gal 6:17; Phil 2:10. Thus it is apparent that he "is thinking especially of the historical Jesus" (Foerster 289), i.e., where the subject is Jesus' death and resurrection (1 Thess 1:10; 4:14a; Gal 6:17; 2 Cor 4:10a, b, 11a, b, 14; Rom 8:11). 1 Thess 1:10 and 4:14 refer to Jesus' parousia and the resurrection of "those who sleep." Of the phrases "in the name of Jesus" (Phil 2:10), → ἀνάθεμα Ἰησοῦς (1 Cor 12:3), and ὁ ἐκ πίστεως Ἰησοῦ (Rom 3:26), the latter two are probably Pauline in form: "Cursed is Jesus" is formulated as a contrast to κύριος Ἰησοῦς (cf. H. Conzelmann, 1 Cor [Hermeneia] ad loc.); in Rom 3:26 Ἰησοῦς is the object of faith, corresponding to Gal 2:16 and 3:22 (see H. Schlier, Rom [HTKNT] ad loc.). In 2 Cor 4:5 and 11:4 the prep. phrase "for Jesus' sake" appears (διά with acc.). The phrase διὰ τοῦ Ἰησοῦ is present in 1 Thess 4:14b; cf. the corresponding "through Jesus Christ" in Rom 1:8; 16:27; Gal 1:1; Phil 1:11; cf. Eph 1:5; Heb 13:21; 1 Pet 4:11. In contrast, use with → ἐν signifies "in Christ Jesus" (Rom 6:11; 8:1, 2, etc.).

In the deutero-Pauline letters and the Pastorals use of the simple name Jesus becomes insignificant (only Eph 4:21: "truth in Jesus"); the double form "Jesus Christ" appears without added predications only 3 times (Eph 1:5 with διά; 2 Tim 2:8, speaking of Jesus' resurrection; Titus 1:1: "apostle of Jesus Christ"). In the Pastorals Χριστός almost always appears first in the double form and never appears without Ἰησοῦς (see W. Grundmann, TDNT IX, 560-62).

e) In the remaining NT writings (ὁ) Ἰησοῦς appears alone in three books—several times in each (5 times each in Hebrews and 1 John, 9 times in Revelation). James, Jude, and 2 Peter have only the formulation Ἰησοῦς Χριστός, repeatedly connected to the κύριος title; Χριστός has become a name for Jesus (Grundmann 562f.).

Hebrews (see besides Grässer, "Des historischer Jesus," also O. Hofius, FS Jeremias [1970] 132-41; J. Roloff, FS Conzelmann 143-66) speaks of Jesus in connection with his earthly existence (2:9), his suffering and death (2:9; 10:19; 13:12), and his role as forerunner (6:20). He is the "surety of a better covenant" (7:22).

Against Gnostic (?) teachings 1 John formulates the confessional statement that Jesus is "the Christ" (5:1; negative in 2:22) and "Son of God" (4:15; 5:5); thus it becomes decisively important to "confess Jesus" (4:3; on the variant readings see TCGNT ad loc.; cf., however, also the counterarguments by R. Schnackenburg, 1–3 John [HTKNT] ad loc.).

Revelation has the expression ἡ → μαρτυρία Ἰησοῦ (1:9; 12:17; 19:10 bis; 20:4; cf. 17:6: pl. "the witnesses of Jesus"). The author was on the island of Patmos "for the sake of the word of God and the testimony of Jesus" (1:9); the concern is with the confessing witness for Jesus. The author endures "in Jesus" with the faithful (1:9), in "faith in Jesus" (14:12). The recipient of the revelation hears Jesus speak from heaven, "I, Jesus" (22:16).

G. Schneider

ἱκανός, 3 *hikanos* sufficient, qualified, large enough

1. Occurrences in the NT — 2. Meaning — 3. Usage and syntax — 4. 2 Cor 2:16–3:6 — 5. Confessional language — 6. Luke 22:38

Lit.: BAGD s.v. — G. BERTRAM, "ΙΚΑΝΟΣ in den griechischen Übersetzungen des AT als Wiedergabe von *schaddaj*," *ZAW* 70 (1958) 20-31. — O. CULLMANN, "Die Bedeutung der Zelotenbewegung für das NT," *idem, Vorträge und Aufsätze 1925-1962* (1966) 292-302, esp. 298. — FRISK, *Wörterbuch* I, 719f. — W. VON MEDING, *DNTT* III, 728-30. — K. H. RENGSTORF, *TDNT* III, 293-96. — H. SCHÜRMANN, *Jesu Abschiedsrede Lk 22,21-38* (1977) 132f. — V. TAYLOR, *The Passion Narrative of St. Luke* (1972) 66-68. — M. WEIPPERT, *THAT* 873-81. — For further bibliography see *TWNT* X, 1120.

1. Of the 39 NT uses of this adj. the largest number are found in Luke (9) and Acts (18). Matthew and Mark, on the other hand, have only 3 occurrences each, while Paul has 5 (in 1–2 Corinthians; also Rom 15:23 v.l.) and the Pastorals one (2 Tim 2:2).

2. The etymology, based on ἵκω (Frisk), suggests: a) a sufficient or generally great quantity: "enough, sufficient, sufficient many," or b) a suitable quality, in the sense of "good, useful" in relation to suitability or propriety.

3. The word is used frequently in Hellenistic literature and in the LXX and has a broad usage: The LXX (Ruth 1:20, 21) and esp. the later Greek translations use it—with questionable etymological derivation—as a tr. of the divine name *šaddai,* signifying the one who is sufficient in himself and provides full sufficiency (Bertram 31; Weippert 876). The NT uses ἱκανός both attributively and absolutely (Acts 12:12; 14:21; 19:19; 1 Cor 11:30) as a relative quantitative referent for people, disciples, words, time, etc. It also is used as a pred. (with inf., ἵνα, or πρός) of suitability for something. The nom. neut. form with ποιῆσαι (Mark 15:15) describes the will of Pilate to satisfy the people and to set Barabbas free. In combination

with λαβεῖν the adj. refers to acceptance of a security (Acts 17:9).

4. The word group ἱκανός, ἱκανότης, and ἱκανόω takes on special significance in the polemic of Paul in 2 Cor 2:16–3:6: Over against the self-commendation and the use of letters of recommendation by his opponents, Paul emphasizes that the capacity for thinking (judgment) and ministry comes "not from us; instead our *sufficiency* is from God, who has made us *sufficient* as ministers of a new covenant" (3:5f.).

5. A similar sense is evident also in the confessional language of the Gospels (Mark 1:7, etc.): In comparison to the Messiah, who comes from God, human capability is insufficient for the most insignificant things. Confession of one's own insufficiency, expressed with ἱκανός and → ἄξιος, "worthy," is spoken in praise of the coming one.

6. Jesus' answer, ἱκανόν ἐστιν, "it is *sufficient*" (Luke 22:38), has given occasion for misinterpretations. Here he repudiates the two swords that are presented and breaks off the conversation about the conduct of the disciples in the time of persecution. That the statement is not to be understood as sanctioning the use of weapons is indicated in the similar usage in Luke 22:51: "up to here and no further!" (Schürmann 133).   P. Trummer

ἱκανότης, ητος, ἡ *hikanotēs* competence, suitability*

2 Cor 3:5: "our *competence* is from God." K. H. Rengstorf, *TDNT* III, 293-96; W. von Meding, *DNTT* III, 728-30.

ἱκανόω *hikanoō* make competent*

2 Cor 3:6: "who *has made* us *competent* to be ministers of a new covenant"; Col 1:12, of God the Father, "who *has qualified* us to share in the inheritance of the saints in light." K. H. Rengstorf, *TDNT* III, 293-96; W. von Neding, *DNTT* III, 728-30.

ἱκετερία, ας, η *hiketeria* entreaty*

Heb 5:7, of Christ, who "in the days of his flesh brought prayers and *entreaties* (ἱκετερίας)" before God. F. Büchsel, *TDNT* III, 296f.

ἰκμάς, άδος, ἡ *ikmas* moisture*

Luke 8:6, of seed that withers "because it has no *moisture*" (cf. Mark 4:6: "because it has no roots").

Ἰκόνιον, ου *Ikonion* Iconium*

A city in Asia Minor visited by Paul and Barnabas (Acts 13:51; 14:1, 19, 21; 16:2). They had a successful mission there (14:1), but had to flee to Lycaonia (Lystra and Derbe; 14:5f.). Although Jews from Iconium agitated against Paul in Lystra as well (14:19), Paul returned to Iconium to "strengthen the souls of the disciples" (14:21f.). Acts 16:2 mentions the Christian congregation in Iconium with that of Lystra. 2 Tim 3:11 mentions (cf. Acts 14:2-6) among the persecutions that Paul suffered one in Iconium. The city is today named Konya; it was considered to be partly in Phrygia (Xenophon *An.* i.2.19; Pliny *HN* v.41; Acts 14:5f.), and partly in Lycaonia (Strabo xii.6.1). *KP* II, 1360; H. Conzelmann, *Acts* (Hermeneia) 107.

ἱλαρός, 3 *hilaros* cheerful, happy*

2 Cor 9:7: "God loves a *cheerful* giver" (cf. ἄνδρα ἱλαρὸν καὶ δότην, Prov 22:8a); here the meaning *friendly* also comes into view (Nägeli, *Wortschatz* 65f.). R. Bultmann, *TDNT* III, 297-99.

ἱλαρότης, ητος, ἡ *hilarotēs* cheerfulness, happiness, friendliness*

Rom 12:8: "he who does acts of mercy, [let him do so] with *cheerfulness* (ἐν ἱλαρότητι)." → ἱλαρός. R. Bultmann, *TDNT* III, 297-99.

ἱλάσκομαι *hilaskomai* be reconciled; expiate*

Lit.: F. BÜCHSEL, *TDNT* III, 301-18. — K. GRAYSTON, "Hilaskesthai and Related Words in the LXX," *NTS* 27 (1980/81) 640-56. — D. HILL, *Greek Words and Hebrew Meanings* (1967) 23-48. — H.-G. LINK and C. BROWN, *DNTT* III, 148-66. — J. E. LUNCEFORD, *A Historical and Exegetical Inquiry into the NT Meaning of the "ἱλάσκομαι" Cognates* (Diss. Baylor University, Waco, TX, 1979). — R. NICOLE, *EvQ* 49 (1977) 173-77. — For further bibliography see *DNTT* III, 174-76; *TWNT* X, 1120 (bibliography); → ἱλαστήριον.

Luke 18:13, with the pass. meaning *be reconciled* (with dat.): "*Be merciful* to me a sinner (ἱλάσθητί μοι τῷ ἁμαρτωλῷ)." Heb 2:17, of the service of Jesus the high priest: "in order to *expiate* the sins of the people (εἰς τὸ ἱλάσκεσθαι)."

ἱλασμός, οῦ, ὁ *hilasmos* expiation; propitiation → ἱλαστήριον 3.

ἱλαστήριον, ου, τό *hilastērion* that which expiates, expiatory gift; place of expiation*

1. Meaning, esp. in the LXX — 2. NT usage — 3. Ἱλασμός

Lit.: F. BÜCHSEL and J. HERRMANN, *TDNT* III, 301-23, esp. 319-23. — A. DEISSMANN, "ΙΛΑΣΤΗΡΙΟΣ und ΙΛΑΣΤΗΡΙΟΝ —eine lexikalische Studie," *ZNW* 4 (1903) 193-212. — C. H. DODD, *The Bible and the Greeks* (1935) 94f. — G. FITZER, "Der Ort der Versöhnung nach Paulus," *TZ* 22 (1966) 161-83. — L. GOPPELT, *Typos* (Eng. tr., 1982) 148f. — M. GÖRG, "Eine neue Deutung für *kâpporæt*," *ZAW* 89 (1977) 115-18. — E. KÄSEMANN, *Rom* (Eng. tr., 1980) 91-101. — E. LOHSE, *Märtyrer und Gottesknecht* (²1963) 149-54. — S. LYONNET and L. SABOURIN, *Sin, Redemption, and Sacrifice* (1970) 163-66. — T. W. MANSON, "ἱλαστήριον," *JTS* 46 (1945) 1-10. — L. MORALDI, "Sensus vocis ἱλαστήριον in R 3,25," *VD* 26 (1948) 257-76. — L. MORRIS, "The Meaning of ἱλαστήριον in Rom III,25," *NTS* 2 (1955-56) 33-34. — H. SCHLIER, *Rom* (HTKNT, 1977) 110f. — R. SCHNACKENBURG, *1-3 John* (HTKNT, ⁵1975) 92f. — P. STUHLMACHER, "Recent Exegesis on Romans 3:24-26," *idem, Reconciliation, Law, and Righteousness* (1986) 94-109. — U. WILCKENS, *Rom* (EKKNT) I (1978) 190-93. — For further bibliography see *DNTT* III, 174-76; *TWNT* X, 1120f.

1. This noun is subst. neut. of the adj. ἱλαστήριος, "for propitiation/pertaining to expiation" (Exod 25:16; 4 Macc 17:22; Josephus *Ant.* xvi.182). In Greek literature it was used of a gift of consecration or expiation brought to the deity, most frequently in the form of a consecrated stele (Dio Chrysostom xi.121; W. R. Paton and E. L. Hicks, *The Inscriptions of Cos* [1891] 81, 347). Only in a single reference on an Egyptian papyrus of the second century A.D. does the word have the meaning "propitiatory sacrifice" (Pap. Fayûm no. 313).

Ἱλαστήριον becomes a fixed term in the LXX, where it is the tr. of Heb. *kappōret.* The *kappōret,* according to Exod 25:17-22, was the most important cult object in the most holy place in the tabernacle and the temple. It was a gold plate placed on the ark of the covenant. On both sides of it were the cherubim, whose wings covered the abode of the invisible God. As such it was the place at which atonement was made for the entire community of Israel on the great Day of Atonement in accordance with God's ordinance. The high priest sprinkled the blood of a young bull on the *kappōret* (Lev 16). This technical use of ἱλαστήριον continued in the literature of Hellenistic Judaism (Philo *Cher.* 25; *Vit. Mos.* ii[iii].95ff.).

2. Ἱλαστήριον appears only twice in the NT. In Heb 9:5 the LXX language is taken up within the context of a description of the most holy place in the earthly sanctuary: above the ark of the covenant "were the cherubim of glory, which overshadowed the *mercy seat.*"

Less unambiguous is Rom 3:25, where ἱλαστήριον appears in connection with a pre-Pauline, apparently Jewish Christian tradition, in which the death of Christ is interpreted typologically on the basis of the ritual of atonement. His death is the eschatological expiatory event established by God, which transcends and at the same time abrogates the previous forms of atonement in the cult. Although the interpretation of ἱλαστήριον as the cultic *place of atonement,* the *kappōret,* is suggested by the conceptual framework, numerous recent exegetes have favored the tr.: "whom God has publicly set forth as an expiation (or expiatory sacrifice)" (Käsemann 91;

Schlier 102; Lohse 149-54). This interpretation is based on the fact that ἱλαστήριον here, in contrast to its usage in the LXX, is without the art. and that a comparison of Christ with the *kappōret* is not logical, since then Christ's blood would have to be sprinkled on the *kappōret,* which he himself was.

However, these arguments are by no means conclusive (so correctly Stuhlmacher 96ff.; Wilckens 191ff.). The absence of the art. is to be explained from the formal style, and the impression of a logical break turns out to be unfounded when one recognizes that the center of the typology is not the literal ritual of expiation by sprinkling of blood, but rather the establishment of a new *place* of expiation to surpass the former one: In the place of the *kappōret* concealed in the temple and the ritual of the rite of expiation associated with it, God has put forward Jesus to bring about expiation through "his blood," i.e., by giving his life. The crucified one has thus become the place where God himself has brought about expiation publicly and for all. Thus Good Friday has become the great Day of Atonement. Linguistic reasons also speak for this interpretation: The meaning "expiation" or "expiatory sacrifice" for ἱλαστήριον is scarcely attested. Therefore we can translate: "God has publicly set him forth as the *place of expiation* through faith in his blood."

3. Ἱλασμός, *atonement,* derived from the vb. → ἱλάσκομαι, is a noun of action, which generally describes the actions through which atonement is accomplished (so Plutarch *Fab.* xviii.3; *Sol.* xii.5; Philo *Plant.* 61; *Her.* 179; *Congr.* 89, 107). In the LXX it can also occasionally be used of expiatory sacrifice (Ezek 44:27; 2 Macc 3:33).

In the NT ἱλασμός appears only in 1 John 2:2; 4:10, both times in a formulaic phrase, which goes back to older tradition and which designated Christ as "*expiation* for our sins." The meaning becomes clear when one observes its proximity to Rom 3:25 in tradition history: Jesus Christ is the place established by God where the expiation made possible by him takes place. The consequence is that guilt is removed and the relationship to God is restored. In the background stands the idea, though it is weakened in comparison to Rom 3:25, of Good Friday as the great eschatological Day of Atonement (→ 2).   J. Roloff

ἵλεως, 2 *hileōs* gracious, benevolent*

The adj. ἵλεως is the only NT instance of the so-called Attic second declension (BDF §44.1), which appears otherwise to have disappeared from koine Greek. The referent of ἵλεως in the NT is always God: Heb 8:12: "I will be *gracious*" (cf. Jer 38:34 LXX). In Matt 16:22 Peter's words, ἵλεώς σοι, κύριε, are to be completed correspondingly: "[God be] *gracious* to you, Lord," i.e., may God prevent Jesus' Passion (so earlier editions of German predecessor of BDF; BDF §128.5, on the other hand, argues that ἵλεως does not mean "gracious" in Matt 16:22 and that a copula is not to be supplied in Peter's words). F. Büchsel, *TDNT* III, 300f.; *TWNT* X, 1120f. (bibliography); H.-G. Link and C. Brown, *DNTT* III, 148-60.

Ἰλλυρικόν, οὖ *Illyrikon* Illyricum*

In Rom 15:19 Paul says that he has spread the gospel "from Jerusalem and as far around as Illyricum." Since Dalmatia was referred to as *Illyris superior* and Pannonia as *Illyris inferior* (E. Meyer and B. Saria, *LAW* 1374f.), Paul must have visited one of these regions. The other NT letters and Acts know nothing of these visits. According to 2 Tim 4:10 Titus went to Dalmatia, apparently to continue the mission. BAGD s.v. suggests that Paul visited (southern) Illyricum from Macedonia. According to E. Käsemann, *Rom* (Eng. tr., 1980) ad loc., Jerusalem and Illyricum designate in Rom 15:19 "the limits of missionary activity."

ἱμάς, άντος, ὁ *himas* strap*

Mark 1:7, of a sandal *strap* (so also Luke 3:16 par. Mark; John 1:27). In Acts 22:25 τοῖς ἱμᾶσιν might be understood as instrumental dat. (Paul is tied up *with the thongs*), but is rather to be translated as an indication of purpose: Paul is stretched out *for the straps,* i.e., for scourging.

ἱματίζω *himatizō* clothe*

Mark 5:15 par. Luke 8:35, of the healed demoniac: The people see him sitting "*clothed* and in his right mind."

ἱμάτιον, ου, τό *himation* garment, cloak*

Lit.: BAGD s.v. — A. van den Born, *BL* 960-62. — G. Cornfeld, ed., *Pictorial Bible Encyclopedia* (1964) 221-27. — G. Fohrer, *BHH* 962-65. — E. Haulotte, *Symbolique du vêtement selon la Bible* (1966). — H. Weigelt, *DNTT* I, 316f. — U. Wilckens, *TDNT* VII, 687-91.

1. Ἱμάτιον appears 60 times in the NT (on the secondary fulfillment citation in Matt 27:35b cf. *TCGNT* 69), almost exclusively in narrative and in Revelation (in the letters only in Jas 5:2; 1 Pet 3:3 and in the citation in Heb 1:11, 12 [v. 12 subsequently added to Ps. 101:27 LXX]). 25 of these occurrences are sg. and 8 appear in connection with other words for clothing: χιτών (Matt 5:40 par. Luke 6:29; John 19:23; Acts 9:39), ἱματισμός (Luke 7:25; John 19:24), χλαμύς (Matt 27:31), and περιβόλαιον (Heb 1:12). In Revelation (cf. 6:11; 7:9, 13 with 3:5, 18; 4:4; also 7:14; 22:14 with 19:13) ἱμάτιον alternates with στολή. Luke (Luke 23:11; 24:4; Acts 1:10; 10:30; 12:21) uses ἐσθής of esp. striking clothing (Wilckens 690).

2. Ἱμάτιον is used of both *garments* in general (pl. *clothing*) and specifically the *outer garment,* i.e., the *mantle* or *cloak* with openings for the arms. *Outer garment* and undergarment are explicitly contrasted in Matt 5:40 par. Luke 6:29. Matthew speaks of a lawsuit and uses the sequence χιτών-ἱμάτιον. Luke, however, describes a robbery (see BAGD s.v., which gives examples from papyri that attest the frequent theft of cloaks in antiquity), using the opposite sequence. The outer garment is certainly intended where the reference is to the laying down of the cumbersome ἱμάτιον, as in the account of Stephen's stoning (Acts 7:58; 22:20); in the account of the leaping Bartimaeus, who apparently used his ἱμάτιον both as a bed and as a cloak (Mark 10:50; cf. R. Pesch, *Mark* [HTKNT] II, 173); and, despite the pl., in an account of footwashing (John 13:4, 12). The outer garment is also something that can be sold (Luke 22:36), that the woman with the issue of blood touches (Mark 5:27, 28, 30 par. Matt 9:20, 21/Luke 8:44), that the people of Jerusalem spread over the colt along the way (Mark 11:7, 8 par. Matt 21:7, 8/Luke 19:35, 36), that is grabbed as one escapes (Mark 13:16 par. Matt 24:18), or that is thrown over oneself (Acts 12:8). Whether the tearing of the ἱμάτια (Matt 26:65, of only *one* person) always involves just the outer garment (so BAGD s.v.) is doubtful (cf. van den Born 962).

3. The NT most often speaks of the ἱμάτιον in a routine way. It is either itself the subject or is used as a point of comparison: In the first case direct reports are given of what happens with garments: they are made (Acts 9:39), taken (Mark 13:16 par.), put on (Mark 15:20 par. Matt 27:31; Luke 8:27; John 13:12; Acts 12:8; 1 Pet 3:3), taken off (Mark 10:50; Acts 16:22), relinquished (Matt 5:40), taken away (Luke 6:29), inscribed with a name (Rev 19:16), guarded (16:15; Acts 7:58; 22:20), divided (Mark 15:24 par. Matt 27:35/Luke 23:34/John 19:23, 24), and sold for money (Luke 22:36). In the second case the garment serves generally as an image of transience (Heb 1:11, 12; cf. Jas 5:2); an old garment stands for the superseded old order (Mark 2:21 par. Matt 9:16 bis/Luke 5:36b), and the new garment for the valid order, which is to be preserved (Luke 5:36a). A white garment (Rev 3:5, 18; 4:4) symbolizes the faithful and a defiled garment (3:4) symbolizes apostasy; the victor (cf. Isa 63:2f.) is clad in a robe dipped in blood (19:13), and purple robes are worn by royalty (John 19:2, 5).

The NT also knows the garment as a concrete symbol. The condition and inner workings of a person are expressed by his or her appearance, which includes clothing. This is the case of the shining garments of the transfigured Jesus (Mark 9:3 par. Matt 17:2), of the power-filled cloak of the Savior (Mark 5:27, 28, 30 par.; 6:56 par. Matt 14:36), and of the "soft" clothing of the "indolent" aristocrats (Luke 7:25). It is also to be seen when people shake their garments with punitive disdain (Acts 18:6) or spread them in reverent excitement (Mark 11:7, 8 par.), tear them in painful concern (Matt 26:65; Acts 14:14), or angrily throw them in the air (22:23).

W. Radl

ἱματισμός, οῦ, ὁ *himatismos* clothing, apparel*

Luke 7:25: οἱ ἐν ἱματισμῷ ἐνδόξῳ, "those in gorgeous *apparel*"; 9:29 (cf. Mark 9:3: τὰ ἱμάτια), of the "radiant *apparel*" of the transfigured Christ. 1 Tim 2:9 of the "costly *attire* [of the women]"; John 19:24 (= Matt 27:35 v.l.): "they cast lots for my *clothing*" (Ps 21:19b LXX); Acts 20:33 in Paul's words: "I coveted no one's silver or gold or *clothing*."

ἵνα *hina* that, so that, in order that

1. Overview — 2. The logia source (Q) — 3. Mark — 4. Matthew — 5. Luke-Acts — 6. The Johannine literature — 7. The Epistles — 8. Revelation

Lit.: BAGD s.v. — BDF index s.v. (448). — D. S. DEER, "More About the Imperatival Hina," *BT* 24 (1973) 328f. — H. KRÄMER, "Zum sprachlichen Duktus in 2 K 10, V. 9 u. 12," FS Friedrich 97-100 (p. 98 on independent ἵνα clauses in general). — P. LAMPE, "Die markinische Deutung des Gleichnisses vom Sämann, Mk 4,10-12," *ZNW* 65 (1974) 140-50 (142f. on Mark as a whole). — I. LARSEN, "The Use of *Hina* in the NT, with Special Reference to the Gospel of John," *Notes on Translation* 2 (1988) 28-34. — G. M. LEE, "Three Notes on ἵνα," *Bib* 51 (1970) 239f. (on John 15:8, 13; Mark 4:12). — W. G. MORRICE, "The Imperatival ἵνα," *BT* 23 (1972) 326-30. — C. F. D. MOULE, *An Idiom-Book of NT Greek* (²1959), index s.v. — MOULTON, *Grammar* III, 94f., 100-106, 138f., etc.; IV, 23, 36, 73f., 92, etc. — F. NEIRYNCK, *The Minor Agreements of Matthew and Luke Against Mark* (1974) 217-19. — H. RIESENFELD, "Zu den johanneischen ἵνα-Sätzen," *ST* (1965) 213-20. — A. P. SALOM, "The Imperatival Use of ἵνα in the NT," *ABR* 6 (1958) 124-41. — E. STAUFFER, *TDNT* III, 323-33. — ZERWICK, *Biblical Greek*, esp. §§406-15, 425f., 428f. — For further bibliography see Moulton; Salom; Stauffer; *TWNT* X, 1122.

1. Use of ἵνα is an indicator of the linguistic level of a NT author. Besides a) the classical *final* usage *(in order that),* the following possibilities are seen in koine:

b) In *consecutive* usage *(so that)* ἵνα indicates logical consequence.

c) In the koine independent ἵνα clauses develop from classical independent ὅπως clauses, taking an *imperatival* meaning ("that he only" = "he should"; "that you [not]," etc.).

d) Ἵνα κτλ. appears in place of the inf. (or ὅπως) *in complementary or obj. clauses with vbs.,* esp. in vbs. of willing, striving, requesting, commanding, and causing (e.g., θέλω ἵνα; BDF §§388; 392).

e) Ἵνα κτλ. appears in place of the inf. *in subj. clauses with impersonal vbs.* (e.g., συμφέρει ἵνα).

f) Ἵνα κτλ. appears in place of the complementary inf. *with the adjectives* ἄξιος *and* ἱκανός.

g) *Epexegetical* ἵνα (in place of an inf.) elaborates on the content of a subst. (e.g., "this is the work of God, *that,*" John 6:29; ἡ ἐξουσία αὕτη ἵνα, "this power, *by which,*" Acts 8:19; Mark 11:28). The demonstrative can also be omitted (e.g., μισθὸς ἵνα, "reward, *that in,*" 1 Cor 9:18; ἐντολὴ ἵνα, "commandment *that*"; ἡ ὥρα ἵνα, etc.). Or the subst. can be omitted so that the demonstrative stands alone (τοῦτο ἵνα, "this, namely *that*").

h) A causal, temporal, or rel. ἵνα is sometimes proposed (cf. Zerwick 412ff., 425f., 428f.), but is nowhere compellingly attested in the NT.

i) A usage not common in classical Greek is where ἵνα is final, but the ἵνα clause appears in the fut.

j) *Elliptical* ἵνα occurs in ἵνα ἀλλ', with which some idea must be supplied: "but this has happened (happens) *so that*" (esp. in John: 15:25; 1:8 [add ἦλθεν]; 9:3 [add ἐγεννήθη τυφλός]; 11:52 [add ἀποθνήσκει]; 13:18 [add v. 18a: "I have not selected all of you"]; 14:31 [add "I will die because of the prince of the world"]; 1 John 2:19 [add "they have not remained with us"]; Mark 4:22b [add ἐγένετο ἀπόκρυφον]; 14:49 [add κρατεῖτέ με or in conformity with Matt 26:56]). In John 1:22; 9:36, supply "answered" before ἵνα. After ἵνα supply γένηται in Rom 4:16; 1 Cor 1:31; 2 Cor 8:13; εὐαγγελιζώμεθα, -ωνται in Gal 2:9.

2. Where it is clear that ἵνα appears in the logia source (Q) it is used in a vernacular, unclassical way (Matt 4:3 par. Luke 4:3: εἰπὲ ἵνα; Matt 7:12 par. Luke 6:31: θέλω ἵνα; Matt 8:8 par. Luke 7:6: ἱκανός ἵνα). One cannot determine with certainty whether other, esp. final, usages are from Q or from some other tradition or are redactional (Matt 7:1; Luke 14:23; 22:30 are redactional; Luke 11:50; 6:34 probably derive from Q-Luke; Matt 10:25 [impersonal ἀρκετόν with ἵνα subj. clause]; Luke 19:15; 12:36 cannot be placed with certainty).

3. In Mark final ἵνα appears only 33 times (of a total of 64 occurrences of ἵνα). Final ἵνα often appears after vbs. of sending (5 times) or giving (5 times), where in Attic Greek the inf. would be used; also after vbs. of movement (6 times).

With regard to non-final ἵνα: Mark has a preference for obj. clauses after vbs. of request and command (20 times!). Ἵνα is also used in obj. clauses after other vbs. (6:25; 9:30; 10:35; 10:37; 11:16), elliptically after ποιέω (10:51), as a complement with ἀγγαρεύω (15:21), in a subject clause with γέγραπται (9:12), imperatively (5:23a; 12:19), and epexegetically (11:28).

Some of the final ἵνα clauses in Mark can be interpreted otherwise, including 2:10 (imperatival; final would be ἵνα dependent on the supplement "I want to say to you") and 11:25 (consecutive). On 4:12 five other possibilities have been proposed: consecutive (C. H. Peisker, *ZNW* 59 [1968] 126f.), causal (E. Lohmeyer, *Mark* [KEK] ad loc.); rel., conforming to Aram. *dy*, "those who, seeing, see" (T. W. Manson, *The Teaching of Jesus* [1935] 76ff.); epexegetical to τὰ πάντα, "to them all is imparted in parables, namely that they," with the Isaiah citation rendering the content of the parable of the seed (Lampe 141). Jeremias (*Parables* 17) supplements with ἵνα πληρωθῇ. To interpret ἵνα in 4:22a as rel. is unnecessary: "nothing is hidden, unless it is *for the purpose of* being revealed."

4. Of the 39 occurrences in Matthew 16 are from Mark, 3 to 5 are from Q (see above), and 17:27 (final) is perhaps also traditional (M). Therefore, almost half of the occurrences are redactional. Redactional use is, for the most part, unclassical: ἵνα κτλ. is used as a complement or obj. clause with vbs. (26:4; 28:10; 27:20 is redactionally influenced by Mark 15:11), as a subj. clause with συμφέρει (5:29, 30; 18:6), epexegetically with θέλημα and εὐκαιρία (18:14; 26:16). In 23:26; 26:5 (redactional) we see final (or imperatival) use; in 18:16; 26:63 and in Matthew's typical formula ἵνα πληρωθῇ τὸ ῥηθέν (1:22; 2:15; 4:14; 12:17; 21:4) redactional final ἵνα introduces OT citations.

Omissions of Markan ἵνα clauses often result from Matthew's preference for direct speech over Markan indirect speech: Often the Markan ἵνα clauses are turned into imperatives (Mark 7:26; 9:9; 14:35; 6:8, 25; 5:23a). Final ἵνα clauses are transformed into infinitives (Mark 12:2; 14:12; 15:20) or paratactically changed to main clauses (Mark 5:23b; 14:10; 15:32; 6:41; 8:6).

5. a) Luke's Gospel has 46 occurrences of ἵνα, 14 from Mark and 3 to 9 from the Q tradition (see above).

b) In L the final sense appears in 14:10 (nonclassical with fut.), 29; 15:29; 16:4, 9, 24; 18:5; 19:4; it is characteristic of L to insert subordinate clauses into these ἵνα clauses ("so that when," 14:10; 16:4, 9; cf. 14:29). Epexegetical ἵνα follows τοῦτο in 1:43 (traditional). Obj. clauses are in 16:27; 10:40; 16:28. Δέομαι ἵνα in L material at 21:36; 22:32 is probably redactional.

c) The Lukan redaction can be seen in 4 nonclassical examples: obj. clauses in 7:36; 8:32; a subj. clause with impersonal λυσιτελεῖ in 17:2; and consecutive usage in 9:45. The classical final usage is found in 1:4; 8:12, 16; 11:33; and 20:14 (in place of Markan parataxis). Luke strives to use (though not consistently) the final sense as in classical Greek; this is indicated by his omission of Markan ἵνα: Nonclassical obj. clauses after vbs. are removed (Mark 14:35) or changed to inf. (Mark 5:18, 43; 8:30; cf. Mark 3:12 with Luke 4:41) or to imv. in direct speech (Mark 6:8; cf. Mark 15:11 with Luke 23:18). Final ἵνα and nonclassical ἀγγαρεύω ἵνα are changed into the Attic inf. of purpose after vbs. of giving (Mark 6:41; 15:21). The nonclassical imperatival ἵνα becomes παρακαλέω + inf. (Mark 5:23/Luke 8:41).

Epexegetical ἵνα is removed (Mark 11:28); cf. also the improvement in comparison to Mark 10:17; 4:21f. These changes in relation to Markan ἵνα clauses correspond to the total Lukan effort to write a more elevated classical language.

d) Of 15 occurrences in Acts 11 are final (but in 21:24 with the fut.). In contrast to most NT writings, ἵνα is not in Acts the preferred means of expressing purpose. Luke readily uses instead the more select ὅπως (10 times) and the Attic inf. of purpose after vbs. of giving and appointment (12:4; 16:4, etc.). The nonclassical obj. clause ἵνα κτλ. appears only in 19:4 (16:36 is more likely final). Epexegetical ἵνα with ἐξουσία, ἐντολή, and βουλή appears in 8:19; 17:15; 27:42. It is noteworthy that 11 of 15 occurrences in Acts are in (colloquial) direct speech.

6. The Johannine literature has a preference for ἵνα (145 occurrences in the Gospel, 26 in the Epistles), with one ἵνα clause sometimes following another (John 1:7; 15:16f.; 17:21-24, etc.). In contrast to Luke, John does not prefer equivalent inf. constructions; to express purpose he almost always uses ἵνα.

a) Final ἵνα appears *ca.* 105 times in the Gospel and 13 times in the letters, sometimes, however, with the nonclassical fut. Specific types are to be distinguished: 1) Final ἵνα often follows vbs. of movement, 9 times of Jesus: "I have come *in order that*"; (cf. John 6:15, 50; 10:10a; 11:11, 16, 19, 31, 55; 12:9, 20, etc.). 2) The same occurs in the Johannine sending formulas (John 3:17 bis; 1 John 4:9; John 1:19; 7:32, etc.). 3) Characteristic of John is the indication of the purpose of Jesus' speaking (5:34; 11:42; 13:19; 14:29; 15:11; 16:1, 4, 33; 17:13). In the same way the author speaks of the purpose of his own writing (20:31: here the fixed usage of the Johannine circle is present: γράφω ἵνα, 1 John 1:4; 2:1; 5:13; ἀπαγγέλλω ἵνα, 1 John 1:3; cf. 3:11; John 19:35). 4) Final ἵνα ἡ γραφή/ὁ λόγος πληρωθῇ is found 9 times and sometimes reflects a consecutive or imperatival sense. 5) Besides tr. as final, other alternatives are possible in some instances, including consecutive (John 3:21; 4:36; 6:7; 12:38, 40; 16:24) and imperatival (11:15; 12:7, 35; 14:31; 17:21b, 23a, 26, etc.). But in the unliterary occurrence in 5:7 the final meaning is still evident: "I have no one, *in order that* he may bring" (cf. *'ên l*ᵉ). 6) Specific goals in John are given formulaic dress with the final ἵνα-clause: the faith of Christians (John 1:7b; 6:30; 9:36; 11:15, 42; 13:19; 14:29; 19:35; 20:31; 1 John 5:13), their joy (John 15:11; 17:13; 16:24; 4:36; 1 John 1:4; 2 John 12), the unity of the Church (John 11:52; 17:11, 21, 22, 23a; 1 John 1:3), life (John 3:15; 5:40; 10:10b; 17:2; 20:31; 1 John 4:9, etc.), and the *doxa* of God and of Christ (John 11:4; 14:13; 17:1, 24; 5:23; cf. 12:23; 9:3). From the indicative of salvation follows ethics, expressed with the final clause (13:34, 15; 17:26; 15:2, 16).

b) Consecutive ἵνα appears in John 5:20; 9:2; 1 John 1:9 (→ a.5).

c) In 18 instances obj. clauses with ἵνα follow vbs. (among others John 8:56: "desired with delight"; 13:2: βάλλω εἰς τὴν καρδίαν ἵνα; 12:7: "leave her alone" [cf. Mark 11:16; → 3, but also possibly final or imperatival]; 17:21: ἐρωτάω ἵνα.

d) In John 16:7; 11:50 ἵνα introduces subj. clauses with συμφέρει, in 1:27, a complement to ἄξιος in 1:27.

e) In 27 Johannine occurrences ἵνα is epexegetical: 1) After nouns with the demonstrative pron.: "this is God's will, that" (John 6:39, 40; 15:12; 1 John 3:11, 23; 4:21; 5:3; 2 John 6a; John 6:29; 17:3). On Church catechesis as the setting of these formulaic phrases, see Riesenfeld. 2) The demonstrative can also be omitted (ἐντολὴ ἵνα, John 13:34; 11:57; ὥρα ἵνα, 13:1; 16:2, 32; 12:23; ἐμὸν βρῶμά ἐστιν ἵνα, 4:34; συνήθεια ἵνα, 18:39; χρείαν ἔχω ἵνα, 2:25; 16:30; 1 John 2:27; ἀγάπη ἵνα, 1 John 3:1, 3). Ἵνα is also epexegetical after independent demonstratives (John 15:8, 17; 15:13 [ταύτης, i.e., ἀγάπης]; 1 John 4:17; 3 John 4 [τούτων]).

7. About 83% of Paul's use of ἵνα is final, while in the deutero-Paulines Colossians and 2 Thessalonians the percentages are only 46% and 43%. The more theoretical the intellectual context, the more classical is Paul's use of ἵνα; the more familiar (e.g., in the greetings in 1 Corinthians 16; see below), the less classical it is. In Romans all 30 occurrences are final. In Galatians of a total of 17 occurrences only 2:10 is possibly imperatival; 5:17 probably has a consecutive sense. In 1 Corinthians 43 of the 57 occurrences are final (in 5:2 a consecutive or imperatival use is also possible). Nonclassical usages are epexegetical (16:12b: θέλημα ἵνα; 9:18) and imperatival (7:29; in 1:15 final is also possible). Obj. clauses with vbs. are found in 16:10, 12a, 16 (παρακαλέω ἵνα or imperatival); 1:10; 4:2; 14:1, 5a, 12, 13. A subj. clause with an impersonal expression appears in 4:3. In 2 Corinthians 37 of the 44 occurrences are final (of which 8:13 may also have an imperatival meaning). The sense is consecutive in 1:17, epexegetical in 11:12, imperatival in 8:7; 10:9 (Krämer 97: "that I not give the appearance"). Paul esp. likes the obj. clause with ἵνα after παρακαλέω (8:6; 9:5; 12:8; 3 times in 1 Corinthians; 1 Thess 4:1). 1 Thessalonians has 7 occurrences of ἵνα. In 5:4 it has a consecutive meaning, while the other 5 occurrences are final. Philippians has 12 occurrences. In 1:9 ἵνα appears to be epexegetical (τοῦτο ἵνα); in 2:2 imperatival or epexegetical with χαρά. Philemon has 4 occurrences, 3 of them final. In v. 19 ἵνα is imperatival ("not to mention," Krämer 98).

In 2 Thessalonians 3 of the 7 occurrences are final. In 1:11; 3:1, 2, 12 ἵνα introduces obj. clauses. Characteristic of Ephesians and Colossians are ἵνα-clauses after expressions of prayer (7 times, see below). In Colossians 6

of the 13 occurrences are final. Ἵνα introduces obj. clauses after vbs. of prayer (1:9; 4:3, 4, 12); the clauses can also be rendered as final. Other obj. clauses after βλέπω and ποιέω are in 4:16 (bis), 17. In Ephesians 22 of the 23 occurrences are final (in 6:3 with fut.). But 1:17; 6:19f. can also be epexegetical (προσευχαὶ ἵνα; δέησις ἵνα). In 5:33 ἵνα is imperatival. The Pastorals have 33 occurrences, nearly all final. The imperatival use is found only in 1 Tim 1:3 (Titus 2:4 is more likely final or consecutive). An obj. clause appears in 1 Tim 5:21.

Characteristic of the whole Pauline corpus are ἵνα clauses that indicate the meaning for the existence of the Christian of Christ's death (Rom 14:9; Gal 3:14; 4:5; 2 Cor 5:15, 21; 8:9; 1 Thess 5:10; Titus 2:14; Eph 5:26) and of the cross (Rom 6:4, 6; 8:17; 1 Cor 3:18; 2 Cor 4:7, 10, 11; 11:7; 12:7, 9; cf. Gal 2:19; 2 Cor 7:9; 11:16; 2 Tim 2:10). Cf. 1 Pet 1:7; 2:24; 3:18; 5:6.

Almost all uses of ἵνα in James (4 ocurrences), 1 and 2 Peter (15 occurrences), and Hebrews (20 occurrences) are final. Heb 13:17 is more likely final than imperatival (v. 17b is parenthetical). In 2 Pet 3:17 ἵνα μή appears in place of Attic ὅπως μή after φυλάσσομαι. In 1 Pet 4:6 a causal sense is proposed (Moulton, Grammar IV, 130); note, however, εἰς τοῦτο, which is parallel to the final ἵνα. Characteristic of Hebrews are 5 final ἵνα μή clauses: Christians should not become weary and stumble (3:13; 4:11; 6:12; 12:3, 13).

8. a) Of the 42 occurrences in Revelation 27 are final; 5 of these, however, can be interpreted as consecutive (6:2; 8:12; 11:6; 13:15a) or epexegetical (9:15: ὥρα ἵνα; if final, ἵνα would be dependent on ἐλύθησαν). In 16:15; 22:14 final ἵνα is dependent on τηρῶν or πλύνοντες; a causal interpretation of 22:14 (μακάριοι ἵνα) is unnecessary.

b) In other than final use, the nonclassical fut. in the ἵνα clause becomes more frequent (7 times). Consecutive use is found in 9:20 and 13:17 (καί v.l.); possibly also in 13:13 (cf. Matt 24:24; or ἵνα is epexegetical to σημεῖα: "namely, that/and indeed"). Along with epexegetical (21:23: χρεία ἵνα [prolepsis]) and imperatival (14:13) ἵνα, there are also obj. clauses after ποιέω (3:9; 13:12, 15b, 16) and subj. clauses with ἐρρέθη (6:11; 9:4). Typical of Revelation is the Semitizing ἐδόθη ("it was permitted"), with ἵνα κτλ. as a subj. clause (6:4; 9:5 bis; 19:8; cf. 13:15, etc. with inf.). Behind it stands yinnāṯēn with inf. (Esth 9:13).

P. Lampe

ἱνατί hinati why, for what reason*

The scriptio continua (for ἵνα τί) is derived from ἵνα τί γένηται, "in order that what may happen?" (BDF §12.3). It is attested in only three NT authors: Matthew (9:4 [not in the Markan parallel]; 27:46 = Ps 21:2 LXX), Luke (Luke 13:7 [L]; Acts 4:25; 7:26), and Paul (1 Cor 10:29).

Ἰόππη, ης   *Ioppē*   Joppa*

The seaport city *Joppa* (Heb. *yāp̄ô(')*, modern Jaffa), on the Palestinian coast (the Plain of Sharon), is mentioned in the NT only in Acts 9:36–11:18 (10 times there). On the history see Schürer, *History* II, 110-14; R. North, *LTK* V, 851f.; *BL* 806f. Here Tabitha was raised by Peter (Acts 9:36, 38, 42, 43) and Peter was called by Cornelius to Caesarea (10:5, 8, 23, 32; 11:13) and "saw a vision in a trance" (11:5; cf. 10:9-16).

Ἰορδάνης, ου   *Iordanēs*   Jordan*

The Jordan is the major river of Palestine. Its source is in the Anti-Lebanon Range, and from there it flows through the Lake of Gennesaret and into the Dead Sea. It is mentioned in the NT primarily in connection with the baptismal activity of John (Kopp, *Places* 99-112; Mark 1:5 par. Matt 3:5, 6; Luke 3:3; John 1:28; 3:26; 10:40 [according to John, "beyond the *Jordan*"]). Jesus was baptized in the Jordan (Mark 1:9; Matt 3:13; Luke 4:1). Among the crowds who followed Jesus and heard his preaching were some, among others, "from beyond the *Jordan*" (Mark 3:8 par. Matt 4:25). Jesus himself visited "the area beyond the *Jordan*" (Mark 10:1 par. Matt 19:1; cf. John 10:40), i.e., he went to Transjordan/Perea. Πέραν τοῦ Ἰορδάνου appears also in Matt 4:15 in the citation of Isa 8:23–9:1. Abel, *Géographie* I, 161-76, 423-29, 474-83; N. Glueck, *The River Jordan* (1954); K. H. Rengstorf, *TDNT* VI, 608-23; K. Höpf, *LTK* V, 1118f.; *BL* 879f.

ἰός, οῦ, ὁ   *ios*   poison; rust*

Rom 3:13c: *"venom* of a snake" (Pss 13:3; 139:4 LXX). *Poison* with a metaphorical meaning: Jas 3:8, of the tongue ("full of deadly *poison*"); 5:3, however, with the meaning *rust* (cf. *Diog.* 2:2). O. Michel, *TDNT* III, 334-36; H. Peucker, *BHH* 571.

Ἰουδαία, ας   *Ioudaia*   Judea*

1. Derivation of the name and occurrences in the NT — 2. Range of meaning — 3. Traditional phrases — 4. The Gospels, Acts, and Paul

Lit.: Y. AHARONI, *The Land of the Bible* (1967) 297-304, 336-65. — S. APPLEBAUM, "Judaea as a Roman Province: The Countryside as a Political and Economic Factor," *ANRW* II/8 (1977) 355-96. — idem, *Judaea in Hellenistic and Roman Times* (1989). — W. D. DAVIES, *The Gospel and the Land* (1974). — G. VON RAD, K. G. KUHN, and W. GUTBROD, *TDNT* III, 356-91.

1. The Hellenistic name ἡ Ἰουδαία (always with the art.) is an adj. derived from the Aramaic gentilic *yᵉhûḏay*, to which χώρα is to be suplied ("the *Jewish* land," Mark 1:5). The adj. is used in the NT as a subst. proper noun

and appears predominantly in the Gospels (8 occurrences in Matthew, 3 in Mark, 10 in Luke, 6 in John) and Acts (12 occurrences). There are 4 occurrences in Paul's letters and none in the rest of the NT.

2. a) Ἰουδαία designates the area of the former southern kingdom, which was primarily in the territory of the tribe of Judah (greater Judah from Beersheba to Mizpah, Joshua 15; cf. "the house of Judah," 1 Kgs 12:21, 23). After the fall of Jerusalem to Babylon it was placed first under Samaria, and then later established as a separate province (*mᵉḏînâ*) under the Persians (Ezra 2:1). After Herod the Great, Judea was governed by a Roman prefect and subject to the province of Syria (Josephus *Ant.* xviii.2; Luke 3:1: Pilate).

b) In a wider sense Ἰουδαία is used of the region of Palestine, the area inhabited by Jews, thus including Galilee and Perea along with Samaria, Idumea, and the coastland under the Hasmoneans, Herod the Great, Agrippa I, and the procurators of A.D. 44-66. From A.D. 70-150 Judea comprised a Roman province of its own (cf. *"Iudaea capta"* on the victory coins of Vespasian).

3. Traditional phrases are "the entire land of Judea" (Mark 1:5; cf. Acts 26:20; Deut 34:2; CD 4:3; 6:5), "the area of Judea" (Mark 10:1; Matt 19:1; cf. Ezek 48:8), "all the hill country of Judea" (Luke 1:65; cf. Josh 11:21; also Luke 1:39: "into the hill country, to a city of Judea"; cf. 2 Sam 2:1), "the wilderness of Judea" (Matt 3:1; cf. Judg 1:16; Ps 63:1), "the inhabitants of Judea" (Acts 11:29; cf. 2 Chr 30:25), "Bethlehem of Judea" (Matt 2:1, 5; cf. Judg 17:7; Ruth 1:2), "Jerusalem and (all) Judea" (Matt 3:5; 4:25; cf. Zech 14:21; 2 Kgs 24:20). A new combination in the NT is "Galilee, *Judea,* and Jerusalem" (Luke 5:17). On "the king of Judea" (Luke 1:5: Herod the Great), cf. 1 Kgs 15:17; on Archelaus as royal ruler (Matt 2:22) cf. Josephus *B.J.* i.668; on the rule of Pilate (Luke 3:1), cf. Josephus *Ant.* xviii.55.

4. a) (cf. 2.a) According to Matt 2:1, 5; Luke 2:4 Bethlehem in Judea was the birthplace of Jesus (cf. Mic 5:1). John the Baptist is more closely associated with Judea, since he was from "the hill country of Judea" (between the Shephelah and the Judean desert; Luke 1:65; cf. v. 39) and worked in the "wilderness of Judea" (Matt 3:1), to which people from Judea went out (Mark 1:5; Matt 3:5). The "wilderness of Judea" probably refers to the steppes of the hill country west of the Dead Sea; Matt 3:5, on the basis of Isa 40:3, includes also the desolate marl land on both sides of the Jordan. Although Jesus worked primarily in Galilee, according to Mark 3:7; Matt 4:25; Luke 5:17 people from Jerusalem and Judea came to him there. In these passages the demarcation of Judea from Galilee, Idumea, and Transjordan is clear.

In John Judea and Jerusalem are prominent as the area of Jesus' activity: he has baptized (3:22) in the "Jewish land," i.e., in the land of Judea. According to 4:43-45 Judea and Jerusalem must be considered the home area of Jesus in which no one shows honor to a prophet (despite 1:45f.; 7:1, 41f., *contra* Mark 6:4); the temple is indeed "the house of my Father" (2:16; cf. Luke 2:49). Judea is repeatedly Jesus' point of departure in journeys to Galilee (John 4:3, 47, 54; cf. 7:1; to the contrary in 11:7, cf. 7:3).

But according to Mark 10:1 Jesus came "into the area of Judea beyond the Jordan" after a long period of activity, which was now concluded (so also Matt 19:1); Perea, ruled by Herod, is thus here reckoned to Judea. In the apocalyptic discourse in Mark 13 Jesus offers the advice that at the high point of the distress "the inhabitants of Judea flee into the mountains" (v. 14 par. Matt 24:16/Luke 21:21). The final catastrophe will thus have its center in Judea, in which earlier under Antiochus IV (1 Macc 2:28) and later in the resistance against Rome the mountainous wasteland offered refuge.

b) (cf. 2.b) Luke uses "Judea," in the sense common in the Hellenistic-Roman world, for the land of the Jews, i.e., all Palestine (see H. Schürmann, *Luke* [HTKNT] I, 29n.12). This is seen esp. in the phrase "all Judea." Herod the Great was "king of Judea" (Luke 1:5; cf. Agrippa I, Acts 12:19). Jesus preached in the "synagogues of Judea," i.e., in all Palestine (Luke 4:44); people from "all Judea" came to him as word of the wonders of the great prophet spread (6:17; 7:17). Correspondingly it was said before Pilate that Jesus "stirs up the people, teaching throughout all Judea, from Galilee even to this place" (23:5).

This is also the usage in Acts: If Jesus' works began in Galilee and included all Judea (Acts 10:37), then later "the entire land of Judea, [including] Samaria and Galilee" was the object of the missionary efforts of the scattered Hellenists (8:1; 9:31); Paul was also a participant in this (26:20). The "brothers in Judea" appear in 11:1 at the side of the Jerusalem apostles as the core of the Church to whom the Gentiles were joined. Along with Jerusalem, the stronghold of the apostolic teaching and the point of origin of the mission (1:8; 15:1-32; in accordance with Isa 2:3), Judea was the point of origin of early Christian prophets (11:29; 21:10) and of Judaizing zealots (Acts 15:1). For Diaspora Jews Judea was the source of instruction (28:21). In the list of the Diaspora areas in 2:9 Judea is probably a later addition (cf. *TCGNT*).

c) Paul also considered Jerusalem a leading center for teaching (Gal 1:17f.; 2:1; Rom 15:19) and Judea a center for the life of the Church. Although he was personally not known to the "churches of Judea," he held forth the "churches of God which are in Judea" as a model of Gentile Christians who have endured persecutions by Jews (1 Thess 2:14; cf. the "disobedient [Jews] in Judea," Rom 15:31). Judea is also mentioned as the goal of Paul's journey on behalf of the collection (2 Cor 1:16); according to Acts 11:29 the "brothers in Judea" were already supported materially by the church in Antioch.   O. Betz

ἰουδαΐζω *ioudaïzō* live as a Jew*
Ἰουδαϊκῶς *Ioudaïkōs* in a Jewish manner, according to Jewish custom*
Ἰουδαϊσμός, οῦ, ὁ *Ioudaïsmos* Judaism, Jewish manner*

Lit.: W. GUTBROD, *TDNT* III, 382f. — M. HENGEL, *Judaism and Hellenism* (1974). — idem, *Between Jesus and Paul* (1983) 1-29. — idem, *Jews, Greeks, and Barbarians* (1980). — *PGL* 674f.

1. Ἰουδαΐζω and Ἰουδαϊκῶς are hapax legomena in the NT and appear together in Gal 2:14. Titus 1:14 has the adj. → Ἰουδαϊκός ("Jewish myths"). Ἰουδαϊσμός appears only in Gal 1:13f. in the phrase ἐν τῷ Ἰουδαϊσμῷ. These Hellenistic terms originated in the defense against the acute Hellenization of Judaism in the second century B.C. (cf. Ἰουδαϊσμός, 2 Macc 2:21; 8:1; 14:38). Paul uses them, as Ignatius of Antioch would later (the vb. in *Magn.* 10:3, the noun in *Magn.* 8:1; 10:3; *Phld.* 6:1), in the struggle for the freedom of Gentile Christians from the efforts of Judaizers.

2. In contrast to ἑλληνίζω, "have command of the Greek language," which is formally similar, ἰουδαΐζω refers to the practice of the Jewish religion and customs by Gentiles who are either sympathetic to Judaism or who have been converted to it. A related term is ἑβραΐζω.

a) The vb. appears in Esth 8:17 (LXX) together with περιτέμνομαι and represents *hityahēd*, "live as a Jew"; the Roman officer Metilius promised to "live as a Jew according to the law," even to be circumcised (ἰουδαΐζειν, Josephus *B.J.* ii.454); Gentiles in Syria who lived as Jews were called ἰουδαΐζοντες (*B.J.* ii.463). Ἰουδαϊκός, used elsewhere of Jewish origin, was also, like Ἰουδαϊσμός (*yahᵃdût*), used of Jewish life lived according to the law, which was oppposed to the Ἑλληνισμός and Ἑλληνικὸς βίος (2 Macc 4:10-15; 6:9; 11:24) propagated by Antiochus IV Epiphanes. Jewish orthopraxy was realized esp. in the practice of circumcision and the observance of the food laws (2 Macc 2:21; 8:1; 14:38; cf. 15:1, 5). King Antiochus attempted to "force" (ἀναγκάζειν) every Jew to renounce the Jewish way of life (Ἰουδαϊσμός) by eating unclean food (4 Macc 4:26).

b) Paul, on the other hand, repudiated Peter for "forcing" this Jewish way of life according to the law (ἀναγκάζεις . . . ἰουδαΐζειν, Gal 2:14) by withdrawing from table fellowship with Gentiles although he lived like a Gentile and "not like a Jew" (οὐκ Ἰουδαϊκῶς); such unstable conduct was a transgression of the law, which was again recognized as binding (2:18). Paul, however, distinguished himself before his call by his "conduct in

Judaism (ἐν τῷ Ἰουδαϊσμῷ)," in which he greatly surpassed his contemporaries (Gal 1:13f.). This expressed itself not only in his zeal for the traditions of the fathers (v. 14), but also in his persecution and destruction of "the Church of God" (1:13), i.e., in deluded acts of violence not unlike those once committed by Antiochus and his helpers.   O. Betz

Ἰουδαϊκός, 3 *Ioudaïkos* Jewish*

Titus 1:14 warns against "*Jewish* myths" (Ἰουδαϊκός probably refers to their derivation and associations) and "human instructions." W. Gutbrod, *TDNT* III, 382.

Ἰουδαϊκῶς *Ioudaïkōs* in a Jewish manner, according to Jewish custom
→ ἰουδαΐζω

Ἰουδαῖος, 3 *Ioudaios* Jewish; Jew

1. Frequency and distribution in the NT; associated terms — 2. Greek and Jewish usage — 3. The Synoptics — 4. Paul — 5. John — 6. Acts — 7. Revelation

Lit.: J. ASHTON, "The Identity and Function of the *Ioudaioi* in the Fourth Gospel," *NovT* 27 (1985) 40-75. — H. BAARLINK, "Zur Frage nach dem Antijudaismus im Markusevangelium," *ZNW* 70 (1979) 166-93. — E. BAMMEL, "Judenverfolgung und Naherwartung. Zur Eschatologie des 1 Thess," *ZTK* 56 (1959) 294-315. — C. K. BARRETT, *The Gospel of John and Judaism* (1975). — M. BARTH, *Jesus, Paulus und die Juden* (1968). — *idem, Israel and the Church* (1969). — W. BAUER, *John* (HNT, [3]1933) 31. — O. BETZ, "Israel bei Jesus und im NT," *Jüdisches Volk—gelobtes Land* (Abhandlungen zum christlichen-judischen Dialog 3, ed. W. P. Eckert, N. P. Levinson, and M. Stöhr; 1970) 275-89. — R. G. BRATCHER, "'The Jews' in the Gospel of John," *BT* 26 (1975) 401-9. — T. L. BUDESHEIM, "Jesus and the Disciples in Conflict with Judaism," *ZNW* 62 (1971) 190-209. — T. A. BURKILL, "Anti-Semitism in Mark's Gospel," *NovT* 3 (1959) 34-53. — J. M. CASABÓ SUQUÉ, "Los judíos en el evangelio de Juan y el antisemitismo," *RevistB* 35 (1973) 115-29. — D. M. CROSSAN, "Anti-Semitism and the Gospel," *TS* 26 (1956) 189-214. — G. J. CUMING, "The Jews in the Fourth Gospel," *ExpTim* 60 (1948/49) 291. — N. A. DAHL, *BHH* 905. — *idem,* "Kristus, jødene og verden etter Johannesevangeliet," *NorTT* 60 (1959) 189-203. — W. D. DAVIES, "Paul and the People of Israel," *NTS* 24 (1977/78) 4-39, revised in *idem, Jewish and Pauline Studies* (1984) 123-52, 341-56. — W. P. ECKERT, N. P. LEVINSON, and M. STÖHR, ed., *Antijudaismus im NT? Exegetische und systematische Beiträge* (Abhandlungen zum christlichen-judischen Dialog 2, 1967). — J. A. FITZMYER, "Anti-Semitism and the Cry of 'All the People' (Mt 27:25)," *TS* 26 (1965) 667-71. — F. FLÜCKIGER, "Zur Unterscheidung von Heiden und Juden in Röm 1,18–2,3," *TZ* 10 (1954) 154-58. — D. GONZALO MAESO, "Hebreo, Israelita, Judío. Breve disquisición filológica," *CB* 18 (1961) 3-14. — L. GOPPELT, *Christentum und Judentum im ersten und zweiten Jahrhundert* (BFCT II/55, 1954); partial Eng. tr.: *Jesus, Paul and Judaism: An Introduction to NT Theology* (1964). — E. GRÄSSER, "Die antijüdische

Polemik im Johannesevangelium," *idem, Text und Situation. Gesammelte Aufsätze zum NT* (1973) 50-69. — W. GUTBROD, *TDNT* III, 369-91. — E. HAENCHEN, "Judentum und Christentum in der Apg," Haenchen II, 338-74. — C. J. A. HICKLING, "Attitudes to Judaism in the Fourth Gospel," *L'Évangile de Jean* (BETL 44, ed. M. de Jonge; 1977) 347-54. — M. HINDERLICH, *Lukas und das Judentum. Eine Untersuchung des dritten Evangelium und der Apostelgeschichte nach ihrem Verhältnis zum Judentum* (Diss. London, 1958). — R. HUMMEL, *Die Auseinandersetzung zwischen Kirche und Judentum im Matthäusevangelium* (BEvT 33, [2]1966). — J. JERVELL, *Luke and the People of God* (1972). — J. JOSZ, "Die Juden im Johannesevangelium," *Judaica* 9 (1953) 129-42. — G. KLEIN, "Präliminarien zum Thema 'Paulus und die Juden,'" FS Käsemann 229-43. — R. KUGELMANN, "Hebrew, Israelite, and Jew in the NT," *Bridge* I (1955) 204-24. — K. G. KUHN, *TDNT* III, 360-69. — R. LEISTNER, *Antijudaismus im Johannesevangelium?* (TW 3, 1974). — M. LOWE, "Ἰουδαῖοι of the [NT] Apocrypha," *NovT* 23 (1981) 56-90. — *idem,* "Who Were the Ἰουδαῖοι?" *NovT* 18 (1976) 101-30. — W. LÜTGERT, "Die Juden im Johannesevangelium," *Neutestamentliche Studien* (FS G. Heinrici, 1914) 147-54. — *idem,* "Die Juden im NT," *Aus Schrift und Geschichte* (FS A. Schlatter, 1922) 137-48. — N. MANSSON, *Paulus och Judarna* (1947). — F. W. MARQUARDT, *Die Juden im Römerbrief* (1971); cf. G. KLEIN, *EvT* 34 (1974) 201-18. — R. MAYER, *DNTT* II, 304-16. — W. A. MEEKS, "'Am I a Jew?': Johannine Christianity and Judaism," FS Smith I, 163-86. — P. NOTHOMB, "Nouveau regard sur 'les Juifs' de Jean," *FV* 71 (1972) 65-69. — G. G. O'COLLINS, "Anti-Judaism in the Gospel," *TS* 26 (1965) 663-66. — A. OEPKE, *1 Thess* (NTD, [13]1972) 165-67. — P. VON DEN OSTEN-SACKEN, "Das paulinische Verständnis des Gesetzes im Spannungsfeld von Eschatologie und Geschichte," *EvT* 37 (1977) 549-87. — S. PANCARO, "The Relationship of the Church to Israel in the Gospel of St. John," *NTS* 21 (1974/75) 396-405. — F. PHILIPPI, *Paulus und das Judentum nach den Briefen und der Apostelgeschichte* (1916). — A. F. PUUKKO, "Paulus und das Judentum" *StOr* 2 (1928) 1-87. — F. QUIÉVREUX, "'Les Juifs' dans le quatrième Evangile," *FV* 57 (1958) 249-61. — G. VON RAD, *TDNT* III, 356-59. — B. REICKE, "Jesus och judarna enligt Markusevangeliet," *SEÅ* 17 (1952) 68-84. — M. RISSI, "Das Judenproblem im Lichte der Johannes-Apk," *TZ* 13 (1957) 241-59. — S. SANDMEL, *Anti-Semitism in the NT?* (1978). — L. H. SCHIFFMAN, *Who Was a Jew? Rabbinic and Halakhic Perspectives on the Jewish-Christian Schism* (1985). — H. SCHLIER, "Von den Juden. Röm 2,1-29," Schlier I, 38-47. — R. SCHNACKENBURG, *John* I (Eng. tr., 1968) 165-67. — T. L. SCHRAM, *The Use of "Ioudaios" in the Fourth Gospel* (Diss. Utrecht, 1974). — M. H. SHEPHERD, "The Jews in the Gospel of John. Another Level of Meaning," *ATR Supplement Series* 3 (1974) 95-112. — P. SZEFLER, "Zydzi w czartej Ewangelii," *Studia Polckie* 2 (1974) 17-41. — TRENCH, *Synonyms* 137ff. — E. VOLTERRA, "'Yhwdy' e 'rmy' nei papiri aramaici del V sec. provenienti dall' Egitto," *Rendiconti della Academia Nazionale dei Lincei* 18 (1963) 132-73. — U. VON WAHLDE, "The Johannine 'Jews': A Critical Survey," *NTS* 28 (1982) 33-60. — *idem,* "The Terms for Religious Authorities in the fourth Gospel: A Key to Literary Strata?" *JBL* 98 (1979) 231-53. — M. C. WHITE, *The Identity and Function of the Jews and Related Terms in the Fourth Gospel* (Diss. Emory University, Atlanta, 1972). — H. WINDISCH, *Paulus und das Judentum* (1935). — S. ZEITLIN, "The Names Hebrew, Jew, and Israel," *JQR* 43 (1952/53) 365-79. — D. Zeller, *Juden und*

Heiden in der Mission des Paulus. Studien zum Römerbrief (1973). — For further bibliography → Ἰσραήλ; see *TWNT* X, 1122-24.

1. With a total of 195 occurrences, Ἰουδαῖος is among the most frequently used words in the NT. In 9 occurrences it is used adjectivally (Mark 1:5; John 3:22; Acts 2:14; 10:28; 13:6; 19:14; 21:39; 22:3; 24:24); in all other instances it is substantival. The two uses of the word are semantically interchangeable, for on the one hand the adj. appears most often with an optional subst. (ἀνήρ/ἄνδρες, Acts 2:14; 10:28; 22:3; ἄνθρωπος, 21:39; γυνή, 24:24; γῆ, John 3:22; χώρα, Mark 1:5), and the pl. subst. is frequently attributive gen., which is close in meaning to the attributive adj. (cf. χώρα τῶν Ἰουδαίων, Acts 10:39, with τὴν Ἰουδαίαν γῆν, John 3:22).

The distribution among NT writings is very unequal. Acts and John have the most occurrences, with 79 and 71 respectively. The Synoptics use the word a total of 17 times (7 occurrences in Mark, 5 each in Matthew and Luke). In the Pauline corpus there are 26 occurrences, with the predominant usage in Romans (11 occurrences), 1 Corinthians (8), and Galatians (4), while 2 Corinthians, 1 Thessalonians, and Colossians each have 1 occurrence. There are 2 occurrences in Revelation. The distribution according to number shows a strong dominance of the pl. over the sg. (171 to 24), which is especially extreme in the Synoptics (16 pl., 1 sg.), while in Paul a more equal distribution of pl. and sg. is present (14 pl., 11 sg. [+ 1 in Colossians]). In fact, Romans has 3 occurrences of the pl. (3:9, 29; 9:24) over against 8 sg. (1:16; 2:9, 10, 17, 28, 29; 3:1; 10:12). Of the total of 171 occurrences of the pl., 42 are attributive gen., most frequently (18 times) in βασιλεὺς τῶν Ἰουδαίων, followed by συναγωγὴ τῶν Ἰουδαίων (4), ἑορτὴ τῶν Ἰουδαίων (3), and πάσχα τῶν Ἰουδαίων (2).

2. The form of Ἰουδαῖος, which first appears in Greek in Clearchus and Theophrastus, follows the usual model for words in the α stem with the suffix -αιος (for numerous examples see K. Zacher, *De nominibus Graecis in* αιος, αια, αιον [1877]; G. Sandsjoe, *Die Adjektive auf* -ΑΙΟΣ [Diss., 1918]; Schwyzer, *Grammatik* I, 467). The word form, against which the seldom used competing form Ἰουδέος (see Hatch/Redpath III, s.v.) could not succeed, stands, along with the other Greek names for Oriental peoples with the gentilic ending -αιος, under the influence of the ending -ai of the Aramaic root word yᵉhûḏāi (cf. G. Dalman, *Grammatik des jüdischen-palästinischen Aramäisch* [²1905] §36.1; A. Cowley, *Aramaic Papyri of the Fifth Century B.C.* [1923] 290 s.v.). The Aramaic origin of the ethnic designation is known in the earlier Greek witnesses: καλοῦνται . . . παρὰ Σύροις Ἰουδαῖοι (Clearchus apud Josephus *Ap.* i.179)).

The Hebrew tribal name yᵉhûḏâ is the basis of the gentilic form in both its Aramaic and Greek forms. It was derived from the name of the mountain ridge between Jerusalem and the Dead Sea (J. Hempel, *BHH* 898) and designated the tribe of Judah or its eponymous ancestor. After the division of the kingdom it was the name of the southern kingdom; in the Persian period it was used for the administrative area around Jerusalem (Neh 5:14). The word yᵉhûḏî, which is seldom used in the OT, designates members of the tribe of Judah (2 Kgs 16:16; Jer 32:12). In the postexilic period it designates also the members of the people of Israel without regard to tribal membership and place of residence. Thus Aram. yᵉhûḏāy is the normal self-designation of Jews in Elephantine (A. Cowley, index s.v.).

This was also the case in the Greek-speaking Diaspora: Jews identified themselves as Ἰουδαῖοι (see *CPJ*, index s.v.; *CIJ*, index s.v.; G. Mayer, *Index Philoneus* [1974] s.v.; A. Schalit, *Namenwörterbuch zu Flavius Josephus* [1968]). Other terms such as Ἰσραήλ and Ἰσραηλίτης were limited primarily to prayer formulations (e.g., 3 Macc 2:6, 10) and similar forms of religious speech (e.g., 3 Macc 6:32; 7:16, 23) or to descriptions of the preexilic period (on the activities of Joshua, cf. Schalit s.v. Ἰουδαῖος, Ἰσραήλ, Ἰσραηλίτης).

Usage among Jews in Palestine was very different (cf. Kuhn 361ff.; White 86ff.): In the books of the Apocrypha and Pseudepigrapha originating in Palestine Ἰουδαῖος either does not appear at all (Tobit, Sirach, Judith, *Psalms of Solomon*, 4 Ezra, *Testaments of the Twelve Patriarchs*, etc.) or it appears occasionally with the more commonly used Ἰσραήλ, limited to specific communication situations (so in 1 Maccabees in words of non-Jews [10:23; 11:50], in diplomatic correspondence with non-Jewish rulers [here in the mouth of both parties; see Kuhn, 362f.], and in self-designation in official documents, as in domestic usage [see Kuhn 361]). In the Qumran literature yᵉhûḏî/yᵉhûḏāi is not attested at all (on jᵉhûḏâ see *KQT* s.v.). In rabbinic literature it appears seldom, most often in the rendering of Gentile statements (e.g., j. *Šeb.* 35b; *Gen. Rab.* 11 on 2:3), while the limited attestation of usage as a self-designation among Jews (m. *Ned.* 11:12 [3 times]; b. *Meg.* 13a) probably indicates only imitation of "the usage of non-Jews or of the diaspora" (Kuhn 363).

3. Synoptic use of Ἰουδαῖος is remarkably similar to Palestinian Jewish usage (→ 2), for it does not appear there "as a proper name for the people to whom Jesus comes" (Gutbrod 375). Instead, the Synoptists differentiate either according to membership in a group or the position of the respective parties (ἀρχιερεύς, γραμματεύς, πρεσβύτερος, Σαδδουκαῖος, Φαρισαῖος, etc.) or they speak of → Ἰσραήλ when they have in mind the people as a totality. For the Synoptists, therefore, it is especially significant that their view of the Jewish environment (either from the tradition or from the historical Jesus) is never indicated with Ἰουδαῖος.

Of the 7 occurrences in Mark, 5 are found in βασιλεὺς τῶν Ἰουδαίων (15:2 par. Matt 27:11/Luke 23:3; Mark 15:9, 12; 15:18 par. Matt 27:29/Luke 23:37; Mark 15:26 par. Matt 27:37/Luke 23:38), a title reserved exclusively for Jesus. Its usage in Mark and Luke is limited to statements by non-Jews in the Passion story (Pilate: Mark 15:2, 9, 12; soldiers: v. 18 [the Pharisees and scribes say: ὁ βασιλεὺς Ἰσραήλ, v. 32]; the titulus: v. 26). Matthew has the title also in the question of the magi about the king of the *Jews* (2:2).

The remaining Synoptic occurrences involve "the *Jewish* land" (Judea; → Ἰουδαία: Mark 1:5), "the elders

of the *Jews*" (Luke 7:3: "rulers of the local community,"
cf. G. Schneider, *Luke* [ÖTK] I, 165), the characterization
of the city of Arimathea as "a city of *the Jews*" (Luke
23:51), a parenthetical explanation of the Jewish custom
of handwashing at meal times (Mark 7:3; cf. J. Gnilka,
Mark [EKKNT] I, 280f.), and a reference to Jews as those
who spread the accusation "until this day" (Matt 28:15)
that the disciples stole the body of Jesus.

4. a) Paul frequently describes humanity as divided
into Jews and non-Jews, with the latter most often called
"Greeks" (→ Ἕλλην; cf. 2 Macc 4:36; 11:2; 3 Macc 3:8,
etc.; a synonymous alternative is → ἔθνη [cf., e.g., 1 Cor
1:22]). Thus we see the collective sg. (cf. Kühner, *Grammatik* II/1, 14; Schwyzer, *Grammatik* II, 41f.) in Rom
1:16; 2:9f.; 10:12; Gal 3:28; (Col 3:11) and the pl. in Rom
3:9, 29; 9:24; 1 Cor 1:22-24; 10:32; 12:13.

That which distinguishes "the Jew(s)" is Israel's election and resulting privileges. In the Pauline definition of
the gospel as "the power of God . . . to salvation for
everyone who believes, for the Jew first and also for the
Greek" (Rom 1:16), this distinction is both presupposed
and relativized: Paul paradoxically connects the Jew's
priority (πρῶτον) with the equality of Jew and Gentile,
thus actually "making an actually worthless concession"
(so H. Lietzmann, *Rom* [HNT, ⁵1971] 30). Instead, he
"gives Judaism precedence for the sake of the continuity
of the plan of salvation" (E. Käsemann, *Rom* [Eng. tr.,
1980] 23). Rom 2:9f. makes a special point of this paradox in the view that the precedence of the Jew in accordance with his works, which is precedence in the experience of the tribulation of the condemned person (v. 9)
as well as the precedence in the acquisition of δόξα, τιμή,
and εἰρήνη (v. 10), is for the Jew in both cases only an
instance of "primus inter pares" (U. Wilckens, *Rom*
[EKKNT] I, 127).

Rom 2:28f. (direct address to the fictitious Jewish
conversation partner from 2:17) contrasts the visible *Jew*
(ὁ ἐν τῷ φανερῷ Ἰουδαῖος) and his physical circumcision
with "the *Jew* in secret" with his "circumcision of the
heart in the Spirit," in order to demonstrate that existence
as "true Jew" does not depend on outward matters, but
on the fulfillment of the law (v. 25), which even replaces
circumcision (v. 26). The objection, which asks what the
"advantage of the *Jew*" or "the value of circumcision"
are (3:1), is answered by the statement that the Jews have
been entrusted with the λόγια τοῦ θεοῦ (v. 2): "Israel is
and remains distinguished by the fact that God's promises
were entrusted to it" (Bornkamm, *Aufsätze* IV, 142).

In 1 Cor 1:22ff. the concern is not with the position
of Jews and Gentiles before God, but with their respective
responses to the revelation, for which *Jews* demand signs
and Greeks demand wisdom (v. 22). Christian preaching,
however, presents Christ as the crucified one, which, in

accord with the respective perceptions, is a stumbling
block to Jews and folly to the Greeks, while the crucified
Christ (v. 23) is "for those who have been called, both
Jews and Greeks, . . . God's power and God's wisdom."

b) The division of humanity into Jews and Gentiles
is, like sexual distinctions and distinctions in legal status,
removed in baptism. The distinctions are not eliminated,
but have lost any significance for salvation (Gal 3:28).
The same idea is present in Col 3:11 and 1 Cor 12:12 (on
the word choice, structure, and sequence cf. F. Mussner,
Gal [HTKNT] 264n.94). In other Pauline statements of
similar structure and intention the contrast of Jew and
Gentile does not appear but is described with alternative
terminology (Gal 6:15: circumcision vs. uncircumcision
[foreskin]).

The test of the unity based on baptism was table
fellowship with both groups (cf. Billerbeck IV, 374-78).
This was practiced in Antioch, with Peter participating,
but then it led to a conflict when emissaries from
Jerusalem objected to it (Gal 2:11ff.). Peter "drew back
and separated himself" (v. 12), "and with him other Jews
also acted insincerely" (v. 13), causing Paul to ask the
provocative question: "If you, though a *Jew*, live like a
Gentile and not like a Jew, how can you compel these
Gentiles to live like Jews?" (v. 14).

c) 1 Thess 2:14 makes the harassment of the local
congregation by their non-Christian countrymen (συμφυ-
λέτης must, in light of 1:9, refer primarily to Gentiles; cf.
E. von Dobschütz, *1 Thess* [KEK] 109f.; see Acts 17:5ff.
for another portrayal) parallel to the persecution of the
"Christian churches of God in Judea . . . by the Jews."
This is followed by sharp anti-Jewish invective in vv. 15f.
The passage's lack of concreteness, the authenticity of
which has been disputed (e.g., B. A. Pearson, *HTR* 64
[1971] 79-94), can be explained most easily by assuming
that Paul "takes up traditional Christian accusations and
traditional pagan charges against the Jews and completes
them with an eschatological perspective on obstacles to
the Pauline Gentile mission" (Kümmel I, 412; similarly
O. Michel, "Fragen zu 1 Thessalonicher 2,14-16. Antijüdische Polemik bei Paulus," Eckert, et al., 52ff.). One
indication, among others, of the manner of Jewish opposition to the mission is to be seen in Paul's reference
in the catalog of sufferings in 2 Cor 11:24 to the five
times he suffered the synagogue's punishment of beating
(the so-called 'arba'im [makkot]) (cf. Billerbeck III,
527ff.; H. Windisch, *2 Kor* 355f.).

5. In comparison with the Synoptics, John is noteworthy not only for its much more frequent use of
Ἰουδαῖος, but even more for the different manner of its
use of the word. John consistently abandons the differentiation of Jews into groups and positions and refers to
"the Jews" as a homogeneous body of individuals, whose

essential characteristic is portrayed in their hostility to Jesus and in their rejection of his mission. Just as they did with John the Baptist (1:19), they oppose Jesus from the very beginning (2:18) and continually seek his life (5:16, 18; 7:1; cf. v. 19; 8:22-24, 37-59; 10:31-39; 11:45-53; 19:7). Thus about half of the occurrences of Ἰουδαῖος are in descriptions of conflict situations between Jesus and "the Jews" or in similar texts with clear anti-Jewish tendencies (1:19; 2:18, 20; 3:25; 5:10, 16, 18; 6:41, 52; 7:1, 11, 13, 15; 8:22, 48, 52, 57; 9:18, 22; 10:24, 31, 33; 11:8, 54; 13:33; 18:12, 14, 31, 36; 19:7, 31, 38; 20:19). The identification of these "Jews" and the determination of their function in the Johannine polemic are by no means certain: While for some interpreters "the Jews" is nothing but a cipher for "the world" that is hostile to God (R. Bultmann, *John* [Eng. tr., 1971] 86; Conzelmann, *Theology* 328, etc.), others argue that one can see in them historical entities, either Jews who observe the law (Lütgert), "Judeans" (Lowe), or the representatives of the Jewish leadership circles (Leistner and others).

The long-recognized uneven usage in John conflicts with any one-dimensional explanation (cf. Gutbrod 378ff.; Grässer 52ff.; Leistner 142ff.; White 166ff.; Bratcher 401ff.), for along with the occurrences mentioned above in polemical contexts there is also a widely distributed neutral use of the word. Here "the Jews" are not regarded as antagonists, but the crowd of people apart from any appraisal (10:19; 11:19, 31, 33, 36, 45; 12:9, 11; 18:20, 38; 19:12, 14, 20, 21). "Jews" are mentioned sometimes in contrast to non-Jews (18:33, 35, 39; 19:3, 19, 21) and sometimes as people whose customs and instititions must be explained (2:6, 13; 3:1; 4:9; 5:1; 6:4; 7:2; 11:55; 19:40, 42). Where the transition to the negative use of the term is made cannot always be determined precisely. At any rate no pejorative connotation inheres in the isolated word Ἰουδαῖος, only in particular contexts. "The great number of such contexts tends to create a certain fixity of usage in this direction" (Gutbrod 378). The basic openness of the term can be seen in the fact that John also knows Ἰουδαῖοι who believe in Jesus (8:31; 11:45; 12:11) and that he has the Samaritan woman at the well call Jesus himself a *Jew* (4:9). That John does not deny Israel's role in salvation history is indicated in 4:22, even if he also "considers it a stage which has been left behind" (Schnackenburg, *John* I, 436).

The uneven use of Ἰουδαῖος scarcely argues for a differentiation of sources, and attempts to make it do so (e.g., White 326ff.) have not led to convincing results. These tensions in the use of the word arise from the Evangelist, in accordance with his dualistic perspective: He fills the ungodly cosmos with participants, but even though reality is portrayed with the use of paradigmatic figures, it is not reduced to mere symbolism.

6. The use of Ἰουδαῖος in Acts has much in common with John's (→ 5; Gutbrod 380), not only in the frequency of the word (→ 1), but also in an abundance of associations in content: Acts almost totally abandons the differentiation of groups seen in the Synoptics and uses Ἰουδαῖος as the normal term for all members of the Jewish people, whether in Palestine (10:22, 28, 39; 12:3, 11; 21:11, etc.) or in the Diaspora (9:22, 23; 11:19; 13:5, 6, 43, 45, 50; 14:1, 4, 5, 19; 16:1, 3, 20; 17:1, 5, 10, 13; 18:2, 4, 5, 12, 14, 19, 24, 28; 19:10, 13, 14, 17, 33, 34; 20:3, 19, 21, etc.). In contrast to John and the Synoptics, "Jew" appears here as a self-designation (21:39; 22:3) and as a form of address in communications among Jews (2:14). As in John the polemical content is not associated with the word itself (cf. the use in the purely constitutive sense in 13:6; 14:1; 18:4; 19:10, 17, etc.), but is determined by the context (e.g., 9:23; 12:3; 13:50, etc.). Christians can also be described as Jews, but this usage is normally restricted to instances where something particular is associated with the person's Jewish ancestry (16:1; 18:2) or where it is an indication of the person's subjection to the law (10:28, etc.). That proselytes are not included among the Ἰουδαῖοι is suggested by the juxtaposition of both groups in 2:11; 13:43 (here, however, προσηλύτων stands along with σεβομένων—either "a careless manner of expression" or a gloss; see Conzelmann, *Acts* [Hermeneia] 106; cf., however, 2:5, 11!). The attributive designation of Jewish institutions and officials as "synagogue of the *Jews*" (13:5; 14:1; 17:1, 10), "law of the *Jews*" (25:8), and πρεσβύτεροι (25:15; cf. Luke 7:3) and πρῶτοι τῶν Ἰουδαίων (25:8; 28:17) is hardly to be understood as simply a factual explanation for uninformed readers, but is an expression of the distance between the Church and Judaism at the time of the writing of Acts.

The Jews are in Acts instigators of anti-Christian agitation, and they oppose the Christian missionaries everywhere and attempt repeatedly to kill Paul (9:23, 29; 14:19, etc.). The constantly recurring disputes take place stereotypically according to the following sequence: "initial success of the Christian mission, attack by the Jews, further journey by the Christian missionaries" (Haenchen II, 61). The severity of the break with the Jews in the course of this conflict is emphasized three times in a special way through Paul's announcement that he will subsequently go only to the Gentiles (13:46; 18:6) and through the statement that salvation has gone to the Gentiles (28:28). The twofold repetition and the apparent failure to carry out this plan in 14:1; 19:8ff. indicate neither lack of seriousness nor a regional restriction of Paul's announcement, but correspond to the literary technique of the author (see Hanchen II, 371). Undoubtedly from 13:46 on, Paul completes his missionary attempts among the Jews only as an exercise in duty in order that their hardness of heart, which was willed by God (28:26f.), is plainly shown. The portrayal of repeated conflicts between Christian missionaries and Jews is historically correct in its essentials, although the Lukan historical construction is to be seen in the manner of these conflicts and in the indication that they were based on the irritation of the Jews brought about by the Christian preaching of the resurrection (E. Haenchen, *Acts* [Eng. tr., 1971] 115). Despite all the similarities in the place of the "Jews" in John and in Acts, one cannot speak of a consistent agreement between the two in their usage (against Lütgert, "Juden im NT" 146).

7. Twice Revelation speaks of ostensible *Jews,* those "who say they are Jews but are not, but are the synagogue of Satan" (2:9) and "who say they are *Jews,* and are not, but are lying" (3:9). Clearly for the author of Revelation "Jew" was an honorable name being usurped by illegitimate claimants. However, it is by no means certain whether the "pseudo-Jews" whom he attacks are adherents of the Jewish religion who slander Christians (Gutbrod 382; W. Bousset, *Rev* [KEK] 208f., 227f.; R. H. Charles, *Rev* [ICC] I, 56f., 88; J. Weiss and W. Heitmüller, *Rev* [SNT] 248, 252; E. Lohmeyer, *Rev* [HNT] 24, 35; E. Lohse, *Rev* [NTD] 26, 33) or "a syncretistic Christian group" (H. Kraft, *Rev* [HNT] 61).   H. Kuhli

Ἰουδαϊσμός, οῦ, ὁ *Ioudaïsmos* Judaism, Jewish manner
→ ἰουδαΐζω.

Ἰούδας, α *Ioudas* Judas*

1. The name and its significance — 2. Occurrences in the NT — 3. The son of Jacob — 4. The son of Joseph — 5. Judas the Galilean — 6. Judas Iscariot — 7. Judas the apostle — 8. The brother of Jesus — 9. Judas of Damascus — 10. Judas Barsabbas — 11. The author of Jude

Lit.: J. BLINZLER, *Die Brüder und Schwestern Jesu* (SBS 21, 1967) 124-29. — A. VAN DEN BORN, *BL* 889, 892. — J. ERNST, *Luke* (RNT, 1977) 209f. — J. GNILKA, *Mark* (EKKNT) I (1978) 136-43. — W. GRUNDMANN, *Mark* (THKNT, ⁶1973) 79f. — idem, *Luke* (THKNT, ⁶1971) 137f. — E. HAENCHEN, *Der Weg Jesu* (1966) 137f. — D. HAUGG, *Judas Iskarioth in den neutestamentlichen Berichten* (1930). — M. HENGEL, *The Zealots* (1988) 76-145. — H.-J. KLAUCK, *Judas—ein Jünger des Herrn* (1987). — R. MEDISCH, "Der historische Judas," *Theologie der Gegenwart in Auswahl* 31 (1988) 50-54. — J. NELIS, *BL* 893f. — R. PESCH, *Mark* (HTKNT) I (1976) 207ff. (bibliography). — H. SCHÜRMANN, *Luke* (HTKNT) I (1969) 317ff. — G. SCHWARZ, *Jesus und Judas* (BWANT 123, 1988). — W. VOGLER, *Judas Iskarioth* (Theologische Arbeiten 42, ²1985).

1. Heb. *yᵉhûḏâ* was written *y'wdh* in Qumran as a result of the weakening of intermediate *h* (cf. M. Baillet, "Les paroles des luminaires," *RB* 68 [1961] 195-250, here 205). It was from this form that Gk. Ἰούδα(ς) developed. The original meaning of the name is unknown. Gen 29:35 gives a popular etymology based on *ydh,* "praise." As the name of the tribe of Judah, which honored Judah, the fourth son of Jacob, as its ancestor, the proper name Judas served in the early postexilic period to emphasize purity of descent. In a later period, as Israel's past came to be placed in an ideal light, one wished the child with this name something of the glory of previous times. Thus Judas became a favorite name both in Palestine and in the Diaspora.

2. Ἰούδας appears 44 times in the NT and refers to 9 different individuals (→ 3-11).

3. Ἰούδας, the fourth son of Jacob, is mentioned 3 times in the genealogies of Jesus (Matt 1:2, 3; Luke 3:33). Ἰούδας designates the tribe or house of Judah, from which Jesus as Messiah descended (Matt 2:6 bis; Heb 7:14; Rev 5:5; 7:5). Heb 8:8 (citing Jer 38:31 LXX) refers to the new covenant that God makes with the house of Judah, while in Luke 1:39 Ἰούδας is used of the area of the tribe of Judah.

4. In Luke 3:30 an otherwise unknown Judas son of Joseph is mentioned in one of the preexilic lists of seven.

5. Judas the Galilean, referred to in Gamaliel's speech in Acts 5:37, declared open resistance against the Romans after the domain of → Ἀρχελάος became a Roman province and a census was carried out by Quirinius, the Roman governor of Syria. "He upbraided them as cowards for consenting to pay tribute to the Romans and tolerating masters, though they had God for their Lord" (Josephus *B.J.* ii.118). Even though the rebellion that he led failed quickly, Josephus describes him as the actual originator of the later Zealot movement (Hengel 76-145).

6. According to the unanimous witness of the Gospels Jesus was handed over to the Jewish authorities by one of the Twelve (→ δώδεκα) whose name was Judas (Mark 14:43; Matt 26:47; Luke 22:47; John 18:3). In the lists of the Twelve (Mark 3:16-19; Matt 10:2-4; Luke 6:14-16) this Judas, always mentioned last, bears the name Iscariot (→ Ἰσκαριώθ), as he does in Matt 26:14; Mark 14:10; Luke 22:3; John 6:71; 12:4; 13:2, 26, while in Matt 26:25, 47; 27:3; Mark 14:43; Luke 22:47, 48; John 13:29; 18:2, 3, 5; Acts 1:16, 25 the name Iscariot is not present.

7. The list of apostles in Luke 6:14-16 mentions a second Judas in place of Thaddeus (Mark 3:18; Matt 10:2). This Judas is distinguished from Judas Iscariot by the addition τοῦ Ἰακώβου (= son of James; cf. John 14:22). Unless a secondary fusion of names caused by the subsequent incorporation of Judas Iscariot into the circle of Twelve has occurred (so Haenchen), the most likely explanation for the mention of Judas son of James is that Luke is dependent on a special tradition. This view is also supported by the the correct tr. of *qan'ān* (Mark 3:18; Matt 10:4: ὁ Καναναῖος) with ὁ ζηλώτης (Luke 6:16; Acts 1:13), which can scarcely be attributed to Luke.

8. In Mark 6:3; Matt 13:55 a Judas is mentioned among the brothers (→ ἀδελφός 4) of Jesus. The later author of the Epistle of Jude refers to him (→ 11).

9. According to Acts 9:11 Saul lived "in the house of Judas" on Straight Street after his conversion.

10. In Acts 15:22, 27, 32 a Judas Barsabbas, not known elsewhere is numbered among the leading men (ἄνδρες ἡγούμενοι) of the Jerusalem church. With Silas he was called upon to bring the letter to Antioch that reported the decisions of the Apostolic Council.

11. The author of Jude calls himself Judas, servant of Jesus Christ, brother of James (Jude 1). Since James— without a more precise designation—could only refer to the James the brother of the Lord (cf. Jas 1:1; Gal 1:19; 2:9; 1 Cor 15:7), and since only one pair of brothers named James and Judas is known, i.e., James and Judas the brothers of Jesus (Mark 6:3; Matt 13:55, → 8), Jude is obviously supposed to be a brother of Jesus. Against this claim is that the letter is written in cultivated Greek, that the author cites the Greek version of *1 Enoch,* and that in vv. 3 and 17 the author looks back on the apostolic era as past (Kümmel, *Introduction* 427ff.).

M. Limbeck

Ἰουλία, ας   *Ioulia*   Julia*

Feminine name, in the NT only in Rom 16:15 for the recipient of a greeting. In 16:7 𝔭⁴⁶ vgˢ read Ἰουλία instead of → Ἰουνιᾶς/Ἰουνία.

Ἰούλιος, ου   *Ioulios*   Julius*

A frequent proper name of the period, in the NT of a centurion of Caesar's cohort (Acts 27:1, 3) to whom Paul was delivered (v. 1) in Caesarea for transfer to Rome. According to v. 3 Julius was kind to Paul and permitted him to visit his friends in Sidon.

Ἰουνιᾶς, ᾶ   *Iounias*   Junias*
Or: Ἰουνία, ας   *Iounia*   Junia*

This name, occurring in Rom 16:7, is not attested in the masc. form (*Junias;* perhaps a shortened form of *Junianus*). It may be that the feminine name *Junia* is meant, in which case Paul would be referring here to a Jewish Christian married couple, Andronicus and Junia, who are "of note among the apostles." V. Fàbrega, "War Junia(s), der hervorragende Apostel (Röm 16,7), eine Frau?" JAC 27/28 (1984/85) 47-64; P. Lampe, "Iunia/ Iunias: Sklavenherkunft in Kreise der vor-paulinischen Apostel," ZNW 76 (1985) 132-34; R. R. Schulz, "Rom. 16,7: Junia or Junias?" *ExpTim* 98 (1986/87) 108-10; U. Wilckens, *Rom* (EKKNT) III, 135f.

Ἰοῦστος, ου   *Ioustos*   Justus*

A frequent name ("the just one") of Jews and proselytes, in the NT of three persons: 1. Joseph Barsabbas (Acts 1:23; → Ἰωσήφ 8), 2. the Corinthian proselyte Titius (Acts 18:7; → Τίτιος), and 3. a Jewish Christian named Jesus (→ Ἰησοῦς 3.d), who was a coworker of Paul according to Col 4:11.

ἱππεύς, έως, ὁ   *hippeus*   horseman*

According to Acts 23:23, 32 "seventy *horsemen*" (and additional troops) accompanied Paul in order to bring him safely to Caesarea.

ἱππικός, 3   *hippikos*   pertaining to a horseman*

Rev 9:16: "The number of the troops *of cavalry* (τῶν στρατευμάτων τοῦ ἱππικοῦ)." Used subst. ἱππικός means cavalry (e.g., Herodotus vii.87), so that in Rev 9:16 what is meant is a large number of *horsemen.*

ἵππος, ου, ὁ   *hippos*   horse*

Lit.: J. S. CONSIDINE, "The Rider on the White Horse. Apocalypse 6:1-8," *CBQ* 6 (1944) 406-22. — E. DORNSEIFF, "Die apokalyptischen Reiter," *ZNW* 38 (1959) 196f. — H. FREHEN and H. HAAG, *BL* 1369f. — H. GERHOLD, *Die apokalyptischen Reiter (Apk 6,1-8)* (Diss. Vienna, 1972/73). — M.-L. HENRY, *BHH* 1438f. — H. KRAFT, *Rev* (HNT, 1974) 114-18. — O. MICHEL, *TDNT* III, 336-39. — A. STEIER, PW XIX/2, 1430-44. — J. WIESNER, *LAW* 1209-17, esp. 1212f. — For further bibliography see *TWNT* X, 1122.

1. In contrast to our culture, in which horses occupied a central place until the first decades of this century, horses appear in the Bible only in contexts of "war," "cavalry," and "king." They are also mentioned in the OT unhesitatingly in relation to God as the true king of Israel. In the NT ἵππος appears 17 times. Except in Jas 3:3, where it is used with "ship" as an example of great power and size which must nevertheless be restrained or "kept in rein," it appears only in Revelation. There it appears in relation to the battles that precede God's rule, but has itself no relation to the kingdom of God.

2. With the "horsemen of the apocalypse" (Rev 6:1-8) comes the beginning of the woes of the turn of the ages. The vision is self-contained and is not to be equated with that of the horseman of 19:11. The horsemen together depict neither plagues nor punishment, but war with its consequences, which are the first of the catastrophes in the collapse of the old world and its order.

The first horseman, on the "white *horse*" (v. 2), wears a crown, the sign of honor of the Roman conqueror and of victory over the enemy. His appearance means the end of the Augustan peace and the collapse of order. While the Roman Empire is the background here, the prophecy does not refer to it alone, but to the entire world. Thus the horseman is not identified with a specific people, and he carries the bow as a typical weapon for a horseman.

The second horseman on the "fiery red *horse*" (v. 4) represents bloodshed, which is closely connected with victory over the enemy and the battles associated with and preceding victory. The third horseman on the "black *horse*" (v. 5) represents famine and hunger. Grain becomes scarce because farmers are slain or driven away; olive trees and wine produce, even if no one tends them.

The fourth horsemen on the "pale *horse*" (v. 8), death, concludes the work of the three that have preceded him. Hades is associated with him, and no other instrument symbolizing his activity is mentioned; it corresponds to the crown, the sword, and the scales. The horse's color symbolizes the work of its rider. However, our perception at this point is strongly shaped by the vision of Revelation.

Horses appear also in the fifth (9:1-12) and sixth (9:13-21) visions of the trumpets. The blowing of the trumpet of the angel announces plagues which are supposed to bring humanity to repentance. The fifth trumpet vision is prompted by the eighth Egyptian plague (Exod 10:13ff.) and Joel's vision of the locusts (Joel 2). To the eyes of the prophet the swarm of locusts become a host of demons that torment humankind for five months. The locusts (vv. 7, 9), which are like horses, become beasts who increasingly reveal their origin out of the abyss. In the sixth vision of the trumpets a fiery host, led by four angels (= angels of the winds), torment humankind. Here the flames are described with the image of stallions (vv. 17 bis, 19). The plagues are occasioned by the divine command; the swarm of locusts and the fiery host are, however, powers hostile to God, who resist God and with their resistance set up a work that God has foreseen.

In Rev 14:14-20 the seer observes "the harvest of the earth" as a harvest of wheat (vv. 14-16) and as a harvest of grapes (vv. 17-20). The grape harvest signifies God's judgment, which takes place outside the holy city and is compared to a wine press; the flow of blood rises as high as a *horse's* bridle (v. 20). Whether bloodshed (as in *1 Enoch* 100:2-3) happens because the sinners kill one another or because they are beaten back by the city is not indicated. The vision of the rider on the "white *horse*" could give an answer (Rev 19:11, 19, 21; immediately after the first closing of the book); the heavenly armies, also arrayed in white linen, follow him (v. 14). As the one who executes the final judgment, he may be identified with the Messiah, even if he is not described as such. The first of the "apocalyptic riders" (see above) has served here as a paradigm for the author. The rider executes judgment on the nations who, together with their *horses,* are devoured by the birds of the heaven (v. 18). Since he (according to Isa 63:5) has no helper at his victory, his garment is sprinkled with blood. The blood is the blood of the enemy, a sign of his battle and victory. Centuries pass before the portrayal of the triumphant Christ as a rider on a horse becomes possible.

Horses (in the literal sense) appear finally in Rev 18:13; one can no longer sell or buy them in Babylon.

H. Kraft

ἶρις, ιδος, ἡ   *iris*   rainbow*

Rev 10:1: an angel "dressed with a cloud and with a *rainbow* on his head"; in 4:3 ἶρις is probably also (*contra* BAGD s.v. 2: a colored halo) a *rainbow:* "a *rainbow* around the throne [of God], in appearance like emerald." K. H. Rengstorf, *TDNT* III, 339-42.

Ἰσαάκ   *Isaak*   Isaac*

Lit.: R. ALBERTZ and M. BROCKE, *TRE* XVI, 292-301. — A. VAN DEN BORN, *BL* 778f. — R. KILIAN, *Isaaks Opferung. Zur Überlierferungsgeschichte von Gen 22* (1970). — H. KREMERS, *EKL* II ([1]1958) 392f. — H. ODEBERG, *TDNT* III, 191-93. — G. SCHMITT, *BHH* 775f. — A. WEISER, *RGG* III, 902f.

1. The name of Ἰσαάκ appears 20 times in the NT, 4 times in Matthew, once in Mark, 3 times in Luke, 4 times in Acts, 3 times in Paul's letters, 4 times in Hebrews (all in the series of paradigms in ch. 11), and once in James.

2. In contrast to → Ἀβραάμ, who appears as a single figure separate from the tradition of the patriarchs (Luke 16:22-31), Ἰσαάκ has no independent significance, but appears normally in genealogical contexts in association with the other patriarchs, esp. with Abraham. Rom 9:10 could be considered an exception, where Paul speaks in the context of salvation history of Ἰσαάκ "our father." This designation refers, however, to the sonship of Isaac under the promise. He can thus be called "father" because he, as the "seed" promised to Abraham, legitimates (cf. Gal 4:28) the faithful as "children of the promise" (v. 8). Isaac also has an indirect function of legitimation as a member of the ancestral line of Jesus (Matt 1:2 bis par. Luke 3:34). Acts 7:8 (bis), in dependence on Gen 17:10; 21:4, recalls the covenantal sign of circumcision established by God (διαθήκη περιτομῆς), which was given to Isaac.

The connection with the patriarchs culminates in the triadic predicate for God as "the God of Abraham, *Isaac,* and Jacob." In Acts 7:32 this is used in relation to the self-attestation of God before Moses (Exod 3:6), in Acts 3:13 in relation to the beginning of God's salvific action toward Israel, to which Jesus' glorification, as the completion of this saving action, is contrasted. This title for God is also mentioned as a theological proof of the resurrection and a refutation of the hypothetical story of the Sadducees, which is based on a situation not mentioned in the rule of levirate marriage (Mark 12:26 par. Matt 22:32/Luke 20:37; cf. Deut 25:5-10): On the basis of the understanding of God as the God of the living (cf. Pss 6:6; 115:17), it is concluded that the patriarchs did not remain in death, for otherwise God could not have been in relationship to them. This corresponds to the view of Abraham, *Isaac,* and Jacob as heavenly figures.

In accordance with this, Jesus' pronouncement of judgment (Matt 8:11f. par. Luke 13:28f.) grants the three patriarchs places in the table fellowship with the Gentiles, while the υἱοὶ τῆς βασιλείας (Matthew) come into the place of "darkness." Behind this view is the eschatological motif, given a transcendent modification and now directed against Israel, of the pilgrimage of the peoples to Zion (cf. Isa 2:2f.; Mic 4:1f., etc.). Luke offers an intensified version, as alongside the patriarchs the prophets also have table fellowship with the Gentiles and thus appear as signs against Israel. Moreover, the relationship between the heavenly realm and that of "darkness" is transparent (cf. Luke 16:22-31): Those who are excluded "see" Abraham, *Isaac,* and Jacob in fellowship with the Gentiles and rage with "weeping and gnashing of teeth." This conduct expresses their hostility to God, not their misery.

The references to Isaac in Hebrews 11 appear in the context of the author's view of salvation history and the eschatological understanding of "the Christian Church as the 'last generation' in a history of faith" (O. Michel, *Heb* [KEK] 370). The stereotyped usage of πίστει becomes the dominant motif, referring to the definition in v. 1. V. 9 mentions Isaac and Jacob (!) as sharing the same living circumstances of Abraham, so that together with him they live in a "strange land" (= Canaan). Their designation as "joint heirs of the same promise" refers to the promise of the land to Abraham (Gen 12:1; 26:3; 35:12). However, ἐπαγγελία in Heb 11:17 is used of the promise of descendants (Gen 12:2; 15:5) fulfilled in Isaac, to which Abraham held "in faith" when God demanded of him the sacrifice of the child (Gen 22:1f.). Heb 11:18 cites Gen 21:12 to confirm the conflict of faith that Abraham endured. In Heb 11:20 Isaac blesses Jacob and Esau "concerning future things" (περὶ μελλόντων). What is intended is probably that Isaac looked toward the saving plan of God.

Over against a Paulinism faulted with a one-sided emphasis on the indicative of justification by faith, Jas 2:21 counters with the thesis of justification by works in Abraham, who "actively" demonstrated his readiness to sacrifice Isaac.   H.-J. Ritz

ἰσάγγελος, 2 *isangelos* like an angel*

Luke 20:36 (cf. Mark 12:25), of the resurrected (of the eschaton), who neither marry nor are given in marriage. While Mark emphasizes the contrast to earthly existence ("but will be like angels" [who do not marry]), Luke says: "for they can no longer die, for they are *equal to angels* and are sons of God, being sons of the resurrection." Cf. G. Schneider, *Luke* (ÖTK) II, ad loc.; G. Kittel, *TDNT* I, 87.

Ἰσκαριώθ *Iskariōth* Iscariot*
Ἰσκαριώτης, ου *Iskariōtēs* Iscariot*

1. Occurrences in the NT — 2. The different forms — 3. Iscariot = the man of Kerioth — 4. Iscariot = Sicarius — 5. Iscariot = the false one — 6. Historicity — 7. The Gospels

Lit.: Y. ARBEITMANN, "The Suffix of Iscariot," *JBL* 99 (1980) 122-24. — P. BENOIT, "Der Tod des Judas," *idem, Exegese und Theologie* (1965) 167-81. — J. D. M. DERRETT, "The Iscariot, $m^e sîrâ$, and the Redemption," *idem, Studies in the NT* III (1982) 161-83. — B. GÄRTNER, *Die rätselhaften Termini Nazoräer und Iskariot* (1957). — H. L. GOLDSCHMIDT and M. LIMBECK, *Heilvoller Verrat?* (1976). — D. HAUGG, *Judas Iskarioth den neutestamentlichen Berichten* (1930). — M. HENGEL, *The Zealots* (1961) 46-53. — J. A. MORIN, "Les deux derniers des Douze: Simon le Zélote et Judas Iskariôth," *RB* 80 (1973) 332-58. — F. SCHULTHESS, "Zur Sprache der Evangelien," *ZNW* 21 (1922) 241-58. — D. P. SENIOR, *The Passion Narrative According to Matthew* (1975) 41-50, 343-97. — C. C. TORREY, "The Name 'Iscariot,' " *HTR* 36 (1943) 51-62. — *idem,* "Studies in the Aramaic of the First Century AD," *ZAW* 65 (1953) 228-47. — M. WILCOX, "The Judas Tradition in Acts I.15-26," *NTS* 19 (1972/73) 438-52.

1. Ἰσκαριώθ and Ἰσκαριώτης appear in the NT as a designation for the Judas who betrayed Jesus to the authorities (→ Ἰούδας 6, → παραδίδωμι).

2. Ἰσκαριώθ is the form found in Mark 3:19; 14:10; Luke 6:16 (+ Matt 10:4 C; Luke 22:47 D). Ἰσκαριώτης appears in Matt 10:4; 26:14; Luke 22:3; John 6:71; 12:4; 13:2, 26; 14:22 (+ Mark 3:19 A Koine; 14:10 A Koine; Luke 6:16 A Koine). It is striking that the initial letter I is lacking in codex C (Mark 3:19; Luke 6:16; John 6:71: Σκαριώθ; Matt 10:4; 26:14; Mark 14:10: Σκαριώτης; John 12:4; 12:2, 26; 14:22: ἀπὸ Καρυότου), in the early Latin tr. (*Scarioth* or *Scariotis*), and in Mark 14:10; Matt 26:14; John 6:71 in the old Syriac tr.

3. According to the most commonly held view Iscariot is to be interpreted as ᾿îš $q^e rîjôt$, "man of Kerioth," since a) a Jewish place named Kerioth is known from Josh 15:25, b) Heb. ᾿îš *ṭôb* is rendered in 2 Kgdms 10:6, 8 with Ιστωβ, and c) Ἰούδας Σίμωνος Ἰσκαριώτου (John 6:71; 13:26) is possible only if Ἰσκαριώτης involves a place of origin.

Against this interpretation are the following: a) ᾿îš is a Hebrew word and does not belong within the common Aramaic speech from which the designation Iscariot comes. b) In biblical usage ᾿îš can have a singular sense before a tribal name, but not before the name of a city (Schulthess 251; on Mishnaic usage see Schulthess 252; Torrey 54); if Iscariot designated the place of origin, ὁ ἀπό would be expected as a tr. for ᾿îš (cf. John 12:21; 21:2 and John 12:4; 13:2, 26; 14:22 D). c) If the name represented by Iscariot began with a long vowel, the omission in Σκαριώτης, etc., would be unintelligible. d) Ἰούδας Σίμωνος Ἰσκαριώτου can be understood as a mistranslation of *yᵉhûḏâ bar šim'ôn 'îšqarjā'* = Ἰούδας Σίμωνος Ἰσκαριώτης (so John 13:2) or an assimilation of the no longer understood Ἰσκαριώτης to Σίμωνος.

4. According to another interpretation Lat. *sicarius,* "assassin, bandit," the Roman designation for nationalistic Jewish extremists, is concealed in Iscariot.

Against this view is the following: a) The sicarii are known only from the time of Governor Festus on (from A.D. 52), not at the time of Jesus (Josephus *B.J.* ii.254-65; *Ant.* xx.186; Acts 21:38). b) The designation *sicarius/*σικάριος becomes the Jewish loan word *sîqār* (Levy III, 518). c) The first vowel in sicarius/σικάριος is long and could scarcely have been eliminated with the Aramaizing of the word (Torrey 58).

5. Starting from Aram. *šᵉqar* and *šiqray/šᵉqaryā',* "liar," which with the ending -a and with aleph prostheticum becomes *išqarya',* Iscariot can be taken as "*the liar, the* false one" (Torrey; Gärtner 42).

In favor of this interpretation are the following: a) It explains the use of the designation Iscariot from the common speech at the time of Jesus. b) It makes the loss of an unstressed initial vowel in later mss. intelligible. c) The charge of falsehood *(šeqer)* plays a significant role in the polemic of early Judaism (Goldschmidt and Limbeck 47f.). d) The Aramaic interpretation of Psalm 55, which in the Jewish tradition was interpreted against the background of Ahithophel, the archetypal traitor to the people and to friends, also gives—in contrast to the biblical text—the concept of falsehood *(šᵉqar)* a central significance (Gärtner 62-64).

6. The question of the historicity of Judas Iscariot can only be answered in the larger context of the historicity of the Twelve (δώδεκα; see Goldschmidt and Limbeck 49-53).

7. Even if all the Gospels agree in the portrayal of the deed of Iscariot, they nevertheless give differing accents in describing the person of Iscariot:

a) For Mark Iscariot is one of the Twelve (14:10, 20, 43; esp. noteworthy is 14:20, only in Mark) who sat with Jesus at table (ὁ ἐσθίων μετ' ἐμοῦ, only in Mark 14:18). In Iscariot the Church meets its own possibility.

b) Matthew interprets the deed and the fate of Iscariot with the aid of Zech 11:12f.: Through the deed of Iscariot, which was accepted by the Jewish authorities, a breach within the Jewish people took place, one like that which had taken place between Judea and Samaria. When the chief priests—in contrast to Deut 21:7f.—bought a plot of ground with the money from blood that was shed innocently, they laid this guilt on their people (Goldschmidt and Limbeck 60-74).

c) Luke sees in Iscariot an instrument of Satan (22:3). Only Luke calls Iscariot a traitor (6:16). Iscariot's fate is that which is meant for the ungodly (Acts 1:16-20; see Benoit).

d) For John Iscariot is likewise an instrument of Satan (6:70; 13:2) and also a thief (12:6). From the beginning Jesus stands at a distance from Iscariot (6:71). Jesus' death has no effect on Iscariot (13:10f.), since he is the son of perdition (17:12).

M. Limbeck

ἴσος, 3 *isos* equal*

1. General usage and occurrences in the NT — 2. As an expression of Christ's relationship to God — 3. Ἰσότης

Lit.: E. BEYREUTHER,*DNTT* II, 497-500. — J. GEWIESS, "Die Philipperbriefstelle 2,6b," FS Schmid (1963) 69-85. — E. KÄSEMANN, "Kritische Analyse von Phil. 2,5-11," idem, *Versuche* I, 51-96. — E. LOHMEYER, *Kyrios Jesus* (SHAW 1927/28, 4, 1928). — SPICQ, *Notes* Suppl., 351-59. — G. STÄHLIN, *TDNT* III, 343-55. — K. THRAEDE, *RAC* XI, 122-64. — For further bibliography see *TWNT* X, 1122.

1. Ἴσος appears in the NT 8 times, once each in Matthew, Luke, John, Acts, Philippians, and Revelation, and twice in Mark. It means esp. *equivalent,* but becomes indistinguishable from → ὅμοιος. When "sinners" loan money to each other, they do so in the expectation of receiving the *equivalent* in return (Luke 6:34). Workers murmur because the *same* pay is given to those who have not worked as long (Matt 20:12). According to Rev 21:16 the three dimensions of the new Jerusalem are the *same,* so that it has the form of perfection. When Peter preaches in Cornelius's house, God gives those who hear the *same* gift as he gives to Jews who come to faith in Christ, the Holy Spirit, and he opens to them access to the Church; in contrast to 1 Cor 12:4ff. the charisma is here identified with the Spirit itself, who is here individualized. Because the statements by the witnesses were not *consistent,* i.e., did not sound the *same* (cf. Stählin 345f.; *m. Sanh.* 5:4), the council, in accord with strict Jewish trial procedure, found insufficient evidence against Jesus (Mark 14:56, 59).

2. The two theologically significant uses of ἴσος place Jesus in relation to God. In John 5:18 the Jews condemn Jesus for his actions on the sabbath, saying that he made himself *equal* to God. What is meant is not the unity and oneness of Jesus with God, which is, however, the content of Jesus' answer in vv. 19ff., but that he placed himself in a position *equivalent* to God when he acted against God's commandment with his claims. The same meaning, "*on a par with* (i.e., *alongside*) God" is found in ἴσα θεῷ in Phil 2:6, which is thus not identical in meaning with the preceding affirmation, ἐν μορφῇ θεοῦ. Ἁρπαγμός is *res rapienda* (cf. Gewiess). The statement says, then, that Christ was (preexistently) in the reality of God, but did not place himself alongside God. To this corresponds

what follows, the statement of renunciation with οὐ–ἀλλά, which is likewise based in "Christ's own will" (Käsemann 72). A direct reference to Gen 3:5 is not apparent; what is apparent is the problem with Deut 6:4 posed for the Church that confesses Christ as Kyrios.

3. Ἰσότης, *equality, fairness** (cf. Philo *Her.* 141-206), is important in Hellenistic philosophy but is seldom used in the NT. Col 4:1 employs a fixed expression (common in the form δίκαιος καὶ ἴσος; cf. LSJ s.v. ἴσος 2, 3; Stählin, 347, 350ff.) to demand of masters that they grant to their slaves τὸ δίκαιον καὶ τὴν ἰσότητα, "justice and *equity.*" This is obviously not a reference to social equality. In 2 Cor 8:13, 14 Paul gives as a reason for the collection for Jerusalem (unlike Rom 15:27) the *balance* of scarcity and plenty which should exist among the churches (cf. R. Iori, *RivB* 36 (1988) 425-38).   T. Holtz

ἰσότης, ητος, ἡ *isotēs* equality, fairness
→ ἴσος 3.

ἰσότιμος, 2 *isotimos* equal in value, equal*

2 Pet 1:1 calls the addressees those who have obtained "a faith *of equal standing* [= the same] as we." G. Stählin, *TDNT* III, 349f.

ἰσόψυχος, 2 *isopsychos* of the same magnanimity, likewise excellent*

In the NT only in Phil 2:20: "For I have no one of the *same excellence* [as Timothy], who will genuinely care for your welfare." Ἰσόψυχος probably does not refer to identity of mind with Paul (*contra* E. Beyreuther, *DNTT* II, 499). P. Christou, *JBL* 70 (1951) 293-96; J. Gnilka, *Phil* (HTKNT) ad loc.

Ἰσραήλ *Israēl* Israel

1. Frequency and distribution in the NT — 2. As a personal name — 3. As the name of a people — a) The Synoptics — b) John — c) Acts — d) Paul — 4. Figurative use for the Church?

Lit.: M. BARTH, *Israel und die Kirche im Brief des Paulus an die Epheser* (1959); cf. *idem,* "Conversion and Conversation: Israel and the Church in Paul's Epistle to the Ephesians," *Int* 17 (1963) 3-24; *Israel and the Church* (1969), esp. 79-117. — O. BETZ, "Die heilsgeschichtliche Rolle Israels bei Paulus," *Theologische Beiträge* 9 (1978) 1-21. — *idem,* "Israel bei Jesus und im NT," *Jüdisches Volk—gelobtes Land* (Abhandlungen zum christlichen-jüdischen Dialog 3, ed. W. P. Eckert, N. P. Levinson, and M. Stöhr; 1970) 273-89. — BULTMANN, *Theology* I, 96-98. — CONZELMANN, *Theology* 248-52. — H. CONZELMANN, *The Theology of St. Luke* (1960) 145-49, 157-69. — N. A. DAHL, *Das Volk Gottes* (1941). — *idem,* "Der Name Israel. Zur Auslegung von Gal 6,16," *Judaica* 6 (1950) 161-70. — G. DEL-

LING, "Israels Geschichte und Jüngergeschehen nach Acta," FS Cullmann (1972) 187-97. — W. ELTESTER, "Israel im lukanischen Werk und die Nazarethperikope," *Jesus in Nazareth* (BZNW 40, ed. W. Eltester; 1972) 76-147. — A. GEORGE, "Israël dans l'oeuvre de Luc," *RB* (1968) 481-525. — L. GOPPELT, *Christentum und Judentum im ersten und zweiten Jahrhundert* (1954). — *idem, Typos: The Typological Interpretation of the OT in the New* (1982). — J. VAN GOUDOEVER, "The Place of Israel in Luke's Gospel," *NovT* 8 (1966) 111-23. — W. GUTBROD, *TDNT* III, 371f., 383-88. — J. HEMPEL, *BHH* 782-86. — F. HESSE, "Die Israelfrage in neueren Entwürfen biblischer Theologie," *KD* 27 (1981) 180-97. — H. HÜBNER, *TRE* XVI, 383-89. — J. JERVELL, *Luke and the People of God* (1972). — J. JOHNSTON, "The Church and Israel: Continuity and Discontinuity in the NT Doctrine of the Church," *JR* 34 (1954) 26-36. — E. KÄSEMANN, "Paul and Israel," *idem, NT Questions of Today* (1969) 183-88. — P. KERSTJENS, *Israël selon la chair.' L'arrière-fonds judéo-chrétien de la Première Épître aux Corinthiens et l'interpretation de 'Ισραήλ κατὰ σάρκα* (1 Cor 10,18) (Diss. Gregorian University, Rome, 1969/70). — O. KNOCH, "Die Stellung der Apostolischen Väter zu Israel und zum Judentum," FS Zimmerman, 347-78. — K. G. KUHN, *TDNT* III, 360-66. — N. LOHFINK, *Die Sammlung Israels. Eine Untersuchung zur lukanischen Ekklesiologie* (SANT 39, 1975). — L. DE LORENZI, ed., *Die Israelfrage nach Röm 9–11* (Colloquium Paulinum 4, 1978). — U. LUZ, *Das Geschichtsverständnis des Paulus* (BEvT 49, 1968). — F. W. MAIER, *Israel in der Heilsgeschichte nach Röm 9–11* (1929). — R. MAYER, *DNTT* II, 304-16 — D. J. MOO, "Israel and Paul in Romans 7,7-12," *NTS* 32 (1986) 122-35. — C. MÜLLER, *Gottes Gerechtigkeit und Gottes Volk. Eine Untersuchung zu Röm 9–11* (FRLANT 86, 1964). — J. MUNCK, *Christ and Israel* (1967). — F. MUSSNER, " 'Ganz Israel wird gerettet werden' (Röm 11,26)," *Kairos* 18 (1976) 241-55; cf. *idem, Tractate on the Jews: The Significance of Judaism for Christian Faith* (1984) 28-38. — A. OEPKE, *Das neue Gottesvolk in Schrifttum, Schauspiel, bildender Kunst und Weltgestaltung* (1950). — P. VON DER OSTEN-SACKEN, "Israel als Anfrage an die christliche Theologie," *Treue zur Thora* (FS G. Harder, 1977) 72-83. — J. PAINTER, "The Church and Israel in the Gospel of John: A Response," *NTS* 25 (1978/79) 103-12. — C. PLAG, *Israels Wege zum Heil. Eine Untersuchung zu Römer 9 bis 11* (1969). — M. RESE, "Israel und Kirche in Römer 9," *NTS* 34 (1988) 208-17. — *idem,* "Die Vorzüge Israels in Röm 9,4f. und Eph 2,12. Exegetische Anmerkungen zum Thema Kirche und Israel," *TZ* 31 (1975) 211-22. — P. RICHARDSON, *Israel in the Apostolic Church* (SNTSMS 10, 1969). — K. H. SCHELKLE, "Israel und Kirche im Anfang," *TQ* 163 (1983) 86-95. — *idem, Israel im NT* (1985). — *idem, Theology* IV, 163-94. — K. L. SCHMIDT, *Die Judenfrage im Lichte der Kapitel 9–11 des Römerbriefs* (1947). — R. SCHMITT, *Gottesgerechtigkeit—Heilsgeschichte— Israel in der Theologie des Paulus* (1984). — G. SCHNEIDER, *Luke* (ÖTK) II (1977) 424-26. — G. SCHRENK, "Was bedeutet 'Israel Gottes' (Gal 6,16)?" *Judaica* 5 (1949) 81-94. — *idem,* "Der Segenswunsch nach der Kampfepistel," *Judaica* 6 (1950) 170-90. — *idem, Die Weissagung über Israel im NT* (1951). — M. SIMON, *RGG* II, 946f. — *idem, Verus Israel* (Eng. tr., 1986). — G. STRECKER, *Das Land Israel in biblischer Zeit* (1983). — P. STUHLMACHER, "Zur Interpretation von Römer 11,25-32," *Probleme biblischer Theologie* (FS G. von Rad, 1971) 555-70. — R. C. TANNEHILL, "Israel in Luke-Acts: A Tragic Story," *JBL* 104 (1985) 69-85. — TRENCH, *Synonyms* 137ff. — W. TRILLING,

Das wahre Israel. Studien zur Theologie des Matthäusevangeliums (SANT 10, 1964). — I. WILLI-PLEIN, "Israel als Bezeichnung eines nachisraelitischen Gottesvolkes," *Judaica* 37 (1981) 70-75, 148-53. — S. ZEITLIN, "The Names Hebrew, Jew, and Israel," *JQR* 43 (1952/53) 365-79. — For further bibliography → Ἰουδαῖος; see *TWNT* X, 1122-24.

1. The indeclinable proper name Ἰσραήλ appears in the NT 68 times. Of this number, 2 occurrences are in Mark, 12 in Matthew, 12 in Luke, 4 in John, and 15 in Acts. The Pauline corpus has 17, of which two-thirds (11) are in Romans 9–11; 2 Corinthians has 2, and 1 Corinthians, Galatians, Ephesians, and Philippians each have 1. The other occurrences are in Hebrews (3 occurrences) and Revelation (3 occurrences).

2. The NT has no independent interest in the use of "Israel" as a personal name (so 34 times in Gen 32:29–50:25 over against 75 uses of "Jacob"); it occurs merely in the rendering of Hebrew words that associate the people Israel with the patriarch Jacob/Israel through descent. Already in the Hebrew explicit reference to the ancestor was largely lost and replaced by collective reference to the people.

The most frequent use in the NT is the description of the members of the people of Israel as "the sons [children] of *Israel*." B*e*nê yiśrā'*e*l appears 637 times in the MT and is mediated through the LXX to the NT (Luke 1:16; Acts 5:21; 7:23 [citation], 37; 9:15; 10:36 [citation]; Rom 9:27 [citation]; 2 Cor 3:7; Heb 11:22; Rev 2:14; 7:4; 21:12 [citation]). The members of the people of Israel can also be called "house (= family) of *Israel*" (146 times in the MT; Matt 10:6; 15:24; Acts 2:36; 7:42; Heb 8:8 [citation], 10 [citation]) with no conscious reference to the ancestor. This is also the case for the use of the geographic designation of Palestine as the land of *Israel,* which was standard among Palestinian Jews (in the NT only in Matt 2:20, 21).

That genealogy is in mind in the formulation οἱ ἐκ Ἰσραήλ (Rom 9:6) cannot be ruled out: "those who are descended from Israel (= Jacob)" (BAGD s.v.; A. Schlatter, *Gottes Gerechtigkeit* [1935] 297; O. Michel, *Rom* [KEK, ¹⁴1978] 231, et al.). However, Ἰσραήλ can also be understood here collectively with partitive ἐκ: "those who are members of the people of Israel by birth" (Gutbrod 383). That Phil 3:5 (ἐκ γένους Ἰσραήλ; cf. LXX Jdt 6:2; 3 Esdras 1:30 [= RSV 1 Esdr 1:32]) is to be understood primarily as referring to descent from the tribe of the patriarch on the basis of the parallel with φυλῆς Βενιαμίν is not compelling.

3. a) In the Synoptic Gospels Ἰσραήλ is used in a manner corresponding to the usage in Palestinian Judaism (→ Ἰουδαῖος 2), in which Israel is a designation of the Jewish people. In many instances the usage accents the religious aspect of membership in the people. Thus

reference is made to the God of Israel (Matt 15:31; Luke 1:68) and to the king of Israel (Matt 27:42; Mark 15:32). The Messiah is expected as a consolation for Israel (Luke 2:25), and the hope is for redemption through him (24:21). The work of Jesus takes place "in Israel" (Matt 8:10 par. Luke 7:9). Indeed, it is limited to "the lost sheep of the house of Israel": Matt 10:6; 15:24 (on this key saying in Matthew's theology derived from the missionary debate of the Palestinian Church [Bultmann, *History* 163] see Trilling 99-105). Despite the relatively equivalent religious content of the word Israel in Matthew and Luke, in some instances a great distinction exists between the religious conceptions of the two gospels with respect to the determination of the relationship of Christianity to Judaism: While Matthew associates Jesus' call to repentance to Israel and his announcement of the kingdom of God directly with the Church (Goppelt, *Theology* II, 229), according to Luke-Acts "the Church as the people of God exists in continuous development from Israel to the Gentiles" (Schneider 426). Along with the use of Ἰσραήλ for "the specific nature of this people as the people of God" (Gutbrod 385), there are also other widely distributed passages that use the term in a purely factual sense (e.g., Matt 2:20; 9:33; 10:23; Luke 1:80; 4:25, 27).

b) It is a generally recognized assumption that John consistently uses Ἰσραήλ in contrast to Ἰουδαῖος "in a much more uniform and fixed sense" (Gutbrod 385) for the people of God in contrast to the negative use of "Jews," those who stand as representatives for a world that is hostile to God. This is not without foundation when one observes in the four instances of the use of "Israel" that it is employed in either a positive or neutral sense. However, this view is not to be taken absolutely, since, except in John 1:31, Ἰσραήλ is used in fixed formulations (1:49; 12:13: king of Israel) or in formulations analogous to common word combinations (3:10: teacher of Israel).

c) The frequency of the ethnic designation Israel in the first part of Acts (14 occurrences in chs. 1–13 [1:6; 2:36; 4:10, 27; 5:21, 31; 7:23, 37, 42; 9:15; 10:36; 13:17, 23, 24]) in comparison with the single occurrence in the rest of the book (28:20) is to be explained neither in primary literary-critical terms, nor alone on the basis of the content of the book (so the alternatives in Gutbrod 386), but rather from the theological intent of the Lukan portrayal. For Luke "Israel, insofar as it refuses to believe, becomes the Jewish people" (Eltester 119). This fact is to be seen in the continuing process of the narrative of Acts wherein "the division of Israel at the preaching of the gospel" (Eltester 121; cf. Conzelmann, *Theology of St. Luke* 145f.) has the consequence that the portion of the Jewish people who come to faith realizes its existence as Israel, while the unbelieving portion gives up its function in salvation history and "becomes Judaism, with which Christianity, in the Lukan view, is concerned" (Eltester 121). The emphatic use of λαός both for Israel (Acts 21:28; 28:17, etc.) and for the Church (15:14; 18:10) indicates to what extent both entities converge for Luke (Conzelmann, *Theology of St. Luke* 163f. with n.1 on 164), although in Acts the two are not explicitly equated and "Israel" is never used as a designation for the Church and Christianity (cf. George 523; Richardson 161).

d) It is indisputable that Ἰσραήλ has in Paul a specific religious meaning in comparison with Ἰουδαῖος. This fact is especially apparent in the distribution of both words in Romans, where chs. 1–8 use Ἰουδαῖος exclusively and from ch. 9 on Ἰσραήλ is consistently used.

In the play on words, "not all from Israel are Israel" (Rom 9:6; the v.l. Ἰσραηλῖται D G vg, etc. is a gloss), Paul affirms that descent from the ancestor Israel or membership in the people by blood (→ 2) is not sufficient to make valid the claim to be Israel, for "Israel is constituted first of all by the promise" (Luz 35), which cannot be immanently continued nor bodily implanted, but must always be given and preserved (E. Käsemann, *Rom* [Eng. tr., 1980] 260ff.).

The citation of Isa 10:22f. appears in Rom 9:27f. after the promise to the Gentiles contained in the citation of Hos 2:1. It is there as a word of judgment—(only) a remnant (of Israel) will be saved. However, Paul affirms that the promise continues for Israel also, of course in a way different from the promise to the Gentiles, since it is limited only to a "remnant." Although the Gentiles, without striving for the righteousness (from the law), attained the righteousness (from faith; Rom 9:30), Israel erred in seeking this righteousness according to the law (9:31) and thus failed to attain the goal by the works of the law (11:7).

The situation of the "disobedient and rebellious people" Israel (Rom 10:21, citing Isa 65:2) is described by Paul as a "hardening in part" (→ πώρωσις ἀπὸ μέρους), "until the fullness of the Gentiles have come in" (11:25; 11:25-27 is an integral part of Romans and not a secondary insertion from an unknown Pauline letter, *contra* Plag 60). In this Pauline interpretation the Jewish traditions of Israel's restoration and the pilgrimage of the peoples to Zion have been transformed (E. Käsemann, *Rom* [Eng. tr., 1980] 309). The Semitic (BDF §275.4) πᾶς Ἰσραήλ (11:26) is to be understood collectively as the totality of the Israel that is now hardened (v. 25) and the remnant that is already coming to faith (11:1f.; Luz 292ff.). "For Paul the end of all history is not the coming to faith by the Gentiles in Rom 10:4ff., but rather the justification of both Gentiles and Jews" (Stuhlmacher 568).

4. Despite the early demonstrable Christian self-understanding as the legal successor of Israel, the NT exercises extraordinary reserve in using the designation Ἰσραήλ with respect to the Church or Christians. Thus when one observes the beginning of the usurpation of the name by Christians in the reference to the Israel according to the flesh (1 Cor 10:18), even this is not conclusive, for Ἰσραὴλ κατὰ σάρκα does not demand a correlative Ἰσραὴλ κατὰ πνεῦμα any more than numerous other κατὰ σάρκα phrases (Richardson 122n.5).

There is widespread agreement that the Pauline reference to the Israel of God (Gal 6:16) refers to Christians, either to Jewish Christians as distinguished from other Christians by the copula καί (Schrenk) or—by means of the epexegetical function of καί—to all Christians, as in the preceding discussion. Neither explanation is, however, totally satisfactory, for, on the one hand, nothing indicates a limitation of the saying to Jewish Christians (Dahl, et al., against Schrenk); on the other hand, it is evident that "addition of καὶ ἐπὶ τὸν Ἰσραὴλ τοῦ θεοῦ . . . (widens) the circle of addressees" (F. Mussner, *Gal* [HTKNT] 417). A possible explanation is offered in the extension of the greeting of peace (cf. H. Lietzmann and W. G. Kümmel, *1–2 Cor* [HNT, [5]1969] on 1 Cor 1:2b!) to "the total Israel of God, wherever they may be" (H. Schlier, *Gal* [KEK] 283). But one may not exclude the possibility that here the original Israel comes into view (D. Lührmann, *Gal* [ZBK] 102), either in its portion which does not yet believe, but will come to faith in the future—"an Israel (of God) within (all) Israel" (Richardson 82; similarly: E. D. Burton, *Gal* [ICC] 357f.)—or (more probably) the same as the πᾶς Ἰσραήλ of Rom 11:26 (Mussner, *Gal* 417n.61).

H. Kuhli

Ἰσραηλίτης, ου, ὁ   *Israēlitēs*   Israelite*

1. Occurrences in the NT, Jewish usage, word formation, and written forms — 2. Individual occurrences — 3. Relation to Ἰουδαῖος

Lit.: BAGD s.v. — D. Gonzalo Maeso, "Hebreo, Israelita, Judío. Breve disquisición filológica," *CB* 18 (1961) 3-14. — W. Gutbrod, *TDNT* III, 369-91, esp. 383-88. — R. Kugelmann, "Hebrew, Israelite, and Jew in the NT," *Bridge* 1 (1955) 204-22. — H. Kuhli, "Nathanael—'wahrer Israelit'? Zum angeblich attributiven Gebrauch von ἀληθῶς in Joh 1,47," *Biblische Notizen* 9 (1979) 11-19. — K. G. Kuhn, *TDNT* III, 359-69, esp. 359-65. — LSJ s.v. — R. Mayer, *DNTT* II, 304-16. — Trench, *Synonyms* 137ff. — M. C. White, *The Identity and Function of the Jews and Related Terms in the Fourth Gospel* (Diss. Emory University, Atlanta, 1972) 161f., 276-78. For further bibliography → Ἰουδαῖος, → Ἰσραήλ.

1. With a total of only 9 NT references, Ἰσραηλίτης has a rate of frequency in comparison with Ἰουδαῖος of 1 to 22. It is found 5 times with voc. ἄνδρες in four speeches and a cry of alarm in Acts (2:22; 3:12; 5:35; 13:16; 21:28). Besides that it appears once in John (1:47) and 3 times in Paul (Rom 9:4; 11:1; 2 Cor 11:22; the reading in D G vg, etc., in Rom 9:6 [Ἰσραηλῖται in place of Ἰσραήλ] is a gloss).

The relative infrequency of the word corresponds to the

reserve of contemporary Judaism in the use of it. It appeared as infrequently in daily use as the Hebrew equivalent *yiśrᵉēlî*. While Palestinian and Babylonian Jews used *yiśrā'ēl* of individual members of the people (for examples see Kuhn 362), Hellenistic Jews used 'Ιουδαῖοι, which was common in the Gentile world, and limited the designation 'Ισραήλ essentially to contexts involving religious speech (for examples → 'Ιουδαῖος, → 'Ισραήλ). Ωηερε 'Ισραηλίτης is used, however, a religious frame of reference is neither a necessary nor a sufficient condition. More decisive for the choice of the word than the distinction between the religious and nonreligious spheres is the change of epochs marked by the Exile, which led to the use of 'Ισραηλίτης in describing the preexilic period and 'Ιουδαῖοι for members of the people in the time of the second temple. Thus Josephus, when describing the ancient time, speaks predominantly of 'Ισραηλῖται (188 times in *Ant.* ii-xi); but then he uses 'Ιουδαῖοι predominantly from *Ant.* xi.6 onward and exclusively from xi.317 to the end of the *Antiquities*. 'Ισραηλίτης was thus reserved for a part of history that was now closed. Its use by a contemporary Jew must, therefore, have been an archaism limited to specific occasions and rhetorical formulas of address (cf. 4 Macc 18:1).

The formation of the Greek word with the suffix -ιτης corresponds to the formation of foreign names according to the pattern "Αβδηρα/'Αβδηρίτης (cf. Kühner, *Grammatik* I/2, 284; on the LXX see H. St.-J. Thackeray, *A Grammar of the OT in Greek* [1909] 171). There is not just one written form, and a single work can even use more than one (e.g., in D, 'Ισραηλεῖται in Acts 2:22; 5:35; 21:28; 'Ισραηλῖται in Acts 3:12; 13:16).

2. a) John 1:47 is most often translated "a true *Israelite*, in whom there is nothing false," so that Nathanael, who is characterized with these words, appears "in contrast to the 'Jews' as a representative of the true people of God" (J. Schneider, *John* [THKNT] 79; similarly Trench 142; R. Bultmann, *John* [Eng. tr., 1971] 104; R. Schnackenburg, *John* I [Eng. tr., 1968] 316; BAGD s.v.). The advocates of this interpretation understand ἀληθῶς as attributive, based on classical usage, but they overlook that in one group of texts cited (e.g., Ruth 3:12; Plutarch *Is.* 3.353c) no attributive use is present, while the remaining texts cited cannot be parallels to John 1:47 (e.g., Plato *Phd.* 109e; Josephus *Ant.* ix.256; *SIG* 834, 6) because the art. appears in them, which is an almost indispensable feature in attributive use of the adv. (cf. Kühner, *Grammatik* II/1, 594ff.; Radermacher, *Grammatik* 110; Mayser, *Grammatik* II/2, 168ff.). But the art. does not appear in the Nathanael passage (cf. Kuhli 13ff.). It is further to be noted that in John 1:47 the emphasis is not on 'Ισραηλίτης, but rather on the second half of the verse (White 161), so that ἀληθῶς does not characterize the authentic representative of God's people, but emphasizes rather the facticity of the whole saying: "Behold, [here comes] indeed an *Israelite*, who is without deceit."

b) Acts uses 'Ισραηλίτης only in connection with ἄνδρες as an address to hearers in conformity with traditional Greek rhetoric. It is so used in Peter's Pentecost sermon (2:22), his speech at Solomon's portico (3:12),

Gamaliel's speech to the Sanhedrin (5:35), Paul's speech at Pisidian Antioch (13:16), and in the cry for help against Paul's alleged desecration of the temple (21:28). The change of address within the same speech (2:14: ἄνδρες 'Ιουδαῖοι; 2:22: ἄνδρες 'Ισραηλῖται) indicates that no fundamental distinction exists between 'Ιουδαῖος and 'Ισραηλίτης, but perhaps an increase in familiarity is intended (cf. the third address ἀδελφοί, v. 29; E. Haenchen, *Acts* [Eng. tr., 1971] 179). Luke's preference for the address "Israelites" corresponds to his otherwise attested inclination to use archaic speech (cf. E. Plümacher, *Lukas als hellenistischer Schriftsteller* [SUNT 9, 1972] 72ff.).

c) In 2 Cor 11:22 Paul counters the appeal of his opponents to their participation in the privileges of the people of God with the statement that he also has fulfilled all of the qualifications as a Hebrew, *Israelite*, and seed of Abraham. A sharp conceptual distinction between the three predicates is scarcely possible; rather, Paul describes his full membership in the people of God redundantly, using the devices of enumeratio, rhetorical question, and epiphore.

In Rom 9:4 Paul states the reason for his participation in the fate of the Jewish people, which is described passionately in vv. 1-3, with the statement: "They are *Israelites*" (literally ". . . who are *Israelites*"). This designation, which was uncommonly used of contemporaries, evokes the blessings (v. 4b) that were given to the people in the past and reinforces the abiding validity of their place as the people of God.

In Rom 11:1 Paul concludes from the call that he himself has received as an *Israelite* from the tribe of Benjamin that God has not rejected his people (v. 2); this conclusion from the destiny of the individual to that of the people is "extremely bold" (Käsemann 299).

3. The distinctions between 'Ιουδαῖος and 'Ισραηλίτης are frequently exaggerated. At the same time, the words are not synonyms, but belong to differing levels of discourse. Unlike 'Ιουδαῖος, 'Ισραηλίτης is most often an expression of conscious solemnity. On the basis of this conclusion, which is valid for the NT as well as Jewish literature, the relationship of the two words can best be described as that of homoionyms since they are "interchangeable insofar as they refer to a single concept, but not in their nuances and evocative power" (S. Ullmann, *Grundzüge der Semantik* [1972] 102).   H. Kuhli

'Ισσαχάρ *Issachar* Issachar*

Indeclinable name of one of the twelve patriarchs (Gen 30:18) and of an Israelite tribe (49:14; Num 1:28f., etc.). Rev 7:7, of those designated from "all the tribes of the sons of Israel" (v. 4): "from the tribe of Issachar, twelve thousand."

ἵστημι, ἱστάνω *histēmi, histanō* stand; place

1. Occurrences in the NT and meanings — 2. Semantic fields — 3. Of Christian existence

Lit.: S. AMSLER, *THAT* II, 328-32, 635-41. — W. GRUND-MANN, "Stehen und Fallen in qumranischen und neutestamentlichen Schrifttum," *Qumran-Probleme* (SSA 42, ed. H. Bardtke; 1963) 147-66. — idem, *TDNT* VII, 636-53. — H. HÜBNER, *Law in Paul's Thought* (1984) 137-49. — R. PESCH, *Die Vision des Stephanus* (1966). — M. WOLTER, *Rechtfertigung und zukünftiges Heil* (1978) 121-23.

1. Ἵστημι (an alternative form is ἱστάνω) appears in the NT 154 times (*VKGNT* II, s.v.). The usage is predominant in narrative texts (Gospels, Acts, Revelation), while στήκω, which appears 10 times, occurs predominantly in the Epistles—esp. in Paul. In most cases ἵστημι has (on the tr. possibilities and the resulting special meanings cf. Grundmann, *TDNT* VII, 646-47; BAGD s.v.) generally a local meaning and is made concrete from information in the context. Ἵστημι is intrans. in the pf. and plupf., as is στήκω, which is formed from the pf. of ἵστημι, with the meaning *stand*, often similar in meaning to → εἰμί (Matt 13:2: "the crowd *stood* [par. Mark 4:1: "was"] at the shore"; 12:46 [par. Mark 3:31: στήκω; 16:28 par.; 27:47; Mark 11:5; Luke 5:1f.; 13:25; John 1:26; 18:5; Acts 12:14) and often specifying only bodily posture (e.g., at prayer: Matt 6:5; Mark 11:25; Luke 18:11 [13]; Acts 1:23; cf. also Jas 2:3).

In addition, ἵστημι serves to characterize the end of a movement: *stand still* (intrans.: Matt 2:9; 20:32 par.; Luke 7:14; Acts 9:7), *stop* (trans.: Acts 8:38). Luke 8:44 has ἵστημι with a medical meaning: her bleeding *ceased* (cf. Pap. Oxy. no. 1088, l. 21; Dioscurides, ed. M. Wellmann, I, 129; II, 178, of a nosebleed).

The characteristic contrast between ἵστημι and → πίπτω has the same semantic significance in differing contexts. Ἵστημι sometimes takes on the meaning *stand firm, resist* (Matt 12:25 par. Mark 3:24f. [cf. Luke 11:17, where πίπτω appears]; Matt 12:26 par. [cf. 1 Kgdms 13:14; Philo *Leg. Gai.* 117]; Rom 14:4; 1 Cor 10:12 [cf. v. 13, πειρασμός; *b. Sanh.* 89b; *m. 'Abot* 5:3: Abraham "stood firm," 'md, in temptations). The antithesis of ἵστημι and πίπτω is also present in Eph 6:11, 13.

Rev 6:17 (τίς δύναται σταθῆναι;) alludes to Joel 2:11, where a question with τίς follows the announcement of judgment (likewise Pss 75:8, 10 LXX; 147:6 LXX; Nah 1:5f.; cf. also Mal 3:2; Ps 129:3 LXX). In Rev 6:17; Pss 75:8 LXX; 147:6 LXX; Nah 1:6 these τίς questions refer to the previously mentioned wrath of God, so that here a fixed semantic field can be assumed.

2. In addition to this general usage, ἵστημι and στήκω appear in various specific associations and contexts. Ἵστημι appears relatively frequently, e.g., for *standing* before a judge or a court (Matt 27:11; Mark 13:9; Acts 4:7; 5:27; 22:30; 24:20; 25:10; 26:6; Rev 20:12). Ἵστημι has a cultic meaning where the subject is *standing* before or in the presence of God. This is esp. said of angels in the heavenly court (Rev 7:11; 8:2f.; cf. 2 Chr 18:18; Dan

7:10, etc.) and of messengers of God (Rev 11:4, citing Zech 4:3, 11-14; cf. K. Berger, *Die Auferstehung des Propheten und die Erhöhung des Menschensohnes* [1976] 265f. nn. 95, 97).

In the OT and the Qumran literature the priests and the cultic assembly "stand" before God (Lev 9:5; Deut 29:9; Josh 24:1; 1 Kgs 8:14; 2 Chr 29:11, etc.; 1QH 7:30f.; 11:13; cf. Amsler 331). The idea here is that of a spatial realm of holiness where Yahweh resides (cf. Wolter 108, 121f.). Luke 21:36 (cf. *1 Enoch* 62:8!); Jude 24; and Rev 7:9 employ this priestly (cf. Rev 7:15: "they serve") motif (e.g., Num 5:16) to describe the attainment of eschatological salvation, which was already thought of in Judaism as fellowship with the angels and thus as standing near God (cf. *1 Enoch* 60:2; Zech 3:7 LXX; 1QH 3:21f.; 11:13; 1QS 11:7-9, etc.; see H.-W. Kuhn, *Enderwartung und gegenwärtiges Heil* [1967] 66ff.; cf. also 4 Macc 17:18). Correspondingly there are those who must stand apart, including victims of defiling illnesses (Luke 17:12) and sinners (Luke 18:13; Rev 18:10, 15, 17). Such persons may not come before God or Christ, i.e., stand in the realm of holiness (cf. Exod 20:18-21).

The style of appearance descriptions is seen in Luke 6:8; Acts 26:16 (cf. 9:6); Rev 11:11 (citation of Ezek 37:10). According to Berger (*Auferstehung* 154, 189) the command "stand up" or "stand on your feet" balances "the difference in position between the one who appears and the visionary" and thus allows for mutual conversation (abundant extracanonical references in Berger 531-34; cf. also *Apoc. Abr.* 10:5, 15; *1 Enoch* [Greek] 14:25; *2 Bar.* 13:2). The manner of the appearance corresponds to this: The one who appears *stands* near the one to whom the appearance is made (Luke 1:11; 24:36; John 20:14, 19, 26; 21:4; Acts 10:30; 11:13; 16:9; worthy of mention also are Acts 1:10; 27:23 [→ παρίστημι]; Luke 2:9; 24:4; Acts 12:7; 23:11 [→ ἐφίστημι]; Luke 9:32 [→ συνίστημι]; cf. Philo *All.* iii.38; extracanonical texts in Berger 433n.21 and esp. in G. Lohfink, *Die Himmelfahrt Jesu* [1971] 199n.136).

Acts 7:55f. is striking, inasmuch as Stephen sees Jesus *standing* at the right hand of God, in contrast to Ps 110:1 and the way the scene is usually described in the NT. This has been repeatedly discussed (a critical survey of the literature is in Pesch 13-36). According to Pesch the Son of Man has risen here in judgment and at Stephen's accusation the judgment has fallen on Israel (55). Pesch associates Acts 7:55f. with Isa 3:13 and *T. Mos.* 10:3. *T. Mos.* 10:3 and the other texts mentioned by Berger (*Auferstehung* 629n.574) in support of Pesch's thesis belong to the general OT concept of Yahweh rising against his enemies to engage them in battle (cf., e.g., Pss 12:6; 68:2; Isa 33:10, etc.; *T. Mos.* 10:7; *1 Enoch* [Ethiopic and Greek] 100:4; for a critique see M. Hengel, *ZTK* 72 [1975] 194n.141), so that the reference remains vague and indirect, esp. since Acts 7:56 makes no reference to a possible judgment saying. Thus some factors suggest that in Acts 7:55f. also a vision form is present (cf. Lohfink, *Himmelfahrt* 199): ἵστημι describes, as in the other texts named, the manner of the appearance and has thus displaced καθήμενον.

In Mark 7:9 D W Θ al it sy^s/p; Rom 3:31; Heb 10:9; also Rom 10:3; 2 Tim 2:19, ἵστημι stands in opposition to vbs. with the connotation of "terminate, annul," and thus is used to express an arrangement that is valid. Matt 18:16; 2 Cor 13:1 (citing Deut 19:15) also use ἵστημι in this way: With two or three witnesses what is said has validity (cf. Billerbeck I, 790f.).

The meaning of Rom 3:31 is sharply disputed (cf. Hübner). It must be interpreted against the background of Mark 7:9 and a whole set of LXX passages in which ἵστημι refers to the law, as in Rom 3:31 (e.g., Deut 28:69; 1 Kgdms 15:11 A L+, 13; 4 Kgdms 23:3, 24; 2 Chr 35:19; 2 Esdr 15:13; 20:33; Jer 42:14, 16). It involves, in the first place, the *fulfillment* of the law (cf. esp. 1 Kgdms 15:11, where the same textual variation as in Mark 7:9 occurs: v.l. is τηρέω in each case). Rom 3:31 must, therefore, be interpreted in association with v. 27b (the contrast between the law of faith and the law of works). The law, as God's will attested in the OT (→ νόμος), is a law of faith and not of works and is thus fulfilled and made valid only through faith (v. 31).

Against Gnostic heretics (cf. v. 18) 2 Tim 2:19 emphasizes truth authoritatively founded and sealed by God, which is thus the only valid truth (on ἵστημι and θεμέλιος cf. Isa 51:16).

3. Paul esp. uses ἵστημι and στήκω of present Christian existence, either in affirmative statements, where ἵστημι is pf. with a pres. meaning (cf. BDF §341; Rom 5:2; 11:20; 14:4; 1 Cor 7:37; 15:1; 2 Cor 1:24), or in appeals (1 Cor 16:13; Gal 5:1; Eph 6:14; Phil 1:27; 4:1; Col 4:12; 1 Thess 3:8; 2 Thess 2:15; 1 Pet 5:12). He prefers the pf. of ἵστημι, using στήκω almost exclusively in appeals. Both vbs. are used absolutely or with ἐν with theological abstract nouns (with χάρις, Rom 5:2; 1 Pet 5:12; πίστις, Rom 11:20; 1 Cor 16:13; 2 Cor 1:24; εὐαγγέλιον, 1 Cor 15:1; πνεῦμα, Phil 1:27; κύριος, Phil 4:1; 1 Thess 3:8), and both vbs. closely approximate the Johannine → μένω (the LXX uses μένω and ἵστημι to render the same Hebrew vbs.) in being linked to Jewish sayings about standing/abiding in the law, in the covenant, etc. (1 Kgdms 26:19; 4 Kgdms 23:3; Sir 11:20; 43:10; T. Dan 5:4; T. Jos. 1:3; Bib. Ant. 9:4; cf. John 8:44). In the same way ἵστημι and στήκω are used absolutely (Rom 14:4; 1 Cor 10:12; Gal 5:1; Eph 6:14; Col 4:12; 2 Thess 2:15; cf. Exod 14:13 LXX) to describe in an almost codelike way Christian existence (which is tested, to be sure, cf. 1 Cor 10:12). Implicit is the contrast to "falling" (→ 1) or "wavering." This "standing" (and not wavering or falling) is a way of describing the existence of the pious in the Qumran community (1QH 4:31f., 36f.; 5:28f.; 7:7f., etc.) and of the Gnostics (cf. *Gos. Truth* 23:35ff.); in Philo this thought plays a great role (cf. Grundmann, *TDNT* III, 644; J. Pascher, *Η ΒΑΣΙΛΙΚΗ ΟΔΟΣ* [1931] 228ff.).

When it is combined with the idea of entrance (→ προσάγω/προσαγωγή) ἵστημι (Rom 5:2) has an originally cultic component (→ 2; cf. Heb 4:16; Wolter 107ff.), which is spiritualized through the understanding of the salvific event as transference into the salvific realm of grace (cf. Gal 1:6; 5:4). An analogy is found in Philo, who speaks of transference into the realm of σοφία (cf. Wolter 112, 125f.; E. Brandenburger, *Fleisch und Geist* [1968] 56f., 202f.).

M. Wolter

ἱστορέω *historeō* visit*

Lit.: F. BÜCHSEL, *TDNT* III, 391-96. — J. D. G. DUNN, "The Relationship between Paul and Jerusalem according to Galatians 1 and 2," *NTS* 28 (1982) 461-78 = *idem, Jesus, Paul, and the Law* (1990) 108-26. — *idem*, "Once More—Gal 1,18: ἱστορῆσαι Κηφᾶν: In Reply to Otfried Hofius," *ZNW* 76 (1985) 138f. = *Jesus, Paul, and the Law* 127f. — O. HOFIUS, "Gal 1,18: ἱστορῆσαι Κηφᾶν," *ZNW* 75 (1984) 73-85. — G. D. KILPATRICK, "Galatians 1.18 ΙΣΤΟΡΗΣΑΙ ΚΗΦΑΝ," *NT Essays: Studies in Memory of T. W. Manson* (1959) 144-49. — K. F. ULRICHS, "Grave verbum, ut de re magna. Nochmals Gal 1,18: ἱστορῆσαι Κηφᾶν," *ZNW* 81 (1990) 262-69.

This vb. denotes a visit for the purpose of (among other things) becoming acquainted (e.g., Plutarch *Thes.* 30.3; *Pomp.* 40.2; *Luc.* 2.9; Epictetus *Diss.* ii.14.28; iii.7.1; Josephus *B.J.* vi.81; *Ant.* i.203; *OGIS* no. 694). It is used in Gal 1:18 of the first visit of the newly converted Paul to Jerusalem, which took place "in order to *get acquainted* with Cephas." Thus Paul emphasizes that he had no previous contact with the earliest Church (cf. v. 17) and traveled to Jerusalem only to "get acquainted" with Peter (in a two-week visit). The vb. also appears as a v.l. in Acts 17:23 in Clement of Alexandria in place of ἀναθεωρέω, of the "visit" of Paul to Athens. D* reads here διϊστορέω. These variants are secondary, but they illuminate the understanding of ἱστορέω in Gal 1:18.

G. Schneider

ἰσχυρός, 3 *ischyros* strong, powerful*

Lit.: W. GRUNDMANN, *Der Begriff der Kraft in der neutestamentlichen Gedankenwelt* (1932). — *idem, TDNT* III, 397-402.

Ἰσχυρός appears 28 (or 29) times in the NT. It can be used of persons (Heb 11:34; 1 John 2:14; Rev 5:2; 6:15; 10:1; 18:8, 21; 19:18) or other subjects (Matt 14:30 B² C D K L W, etc.; Luke 15:14; Heb 5:7; 6:18; Rev 18:2, 10; 19:6). Characteristic of this word is use with other terms for strength and power (δύναμις, ἐνεργέω, κράτος, ἐνδυναμόω). Antithesis to weakness (ἀσθενής) is also significant. As the dense usage of ἰσχυρός in Revelation esp. indicates, use of this adj. is based on OT language. It has a close association with God: God is the *strong one* in the literal sense (Rev. 18:8). Such a connection between the divine sphere and strength (see also 1 John 2:14, where the strength of those addressed is based on their fidelity to God's word) as well as the dynamic aspect of power dominates the usage of both the Synoptic Gospels (a) and the Pauline tradition (b):

a) Mark 1:7 (cf. Matt 3:11; Luke 3:16—on the content also Acts 13:25) stands within the preaching of the Baptist, which is oriented to the future. Here the connection between Mark 1:7 and v. 8 could already be present in the tradition. John refers to a coming one (→ ἔρχομαι 4.a), who is *mightier* than he and will prove to be greater. Such superiority is based on the power of the baptism of the Spirit or fire. The identity of this coming, *mightier* one within the proclamation of the Baptist is disputed; suggestions include the Son of Man, God, the Messiah, the eschatological prophet, or an unknown eschatological figure. It is also unclear whether this coming one belongs within the context of salvation or judgment. The central fact appears nonetheless to be the emphasis on the superiority of this stronger one to the Baptist, which facilitated the early Christian reference to and identification of the stronger one with Jesus.

In Mark 3:27 (Matt 12:29; cf. Luke 11:21f.) an isolated fig. saying is present (this is indicated by the comparison of the Markan text with the tradition in Matthew and Luke), which has now been inserted into the compositional unit of 3:22-30. In Luke, who uses the image differently and possibly makes use of special traditions (cf. F. Katz, *Lukas 9,52–11,36. Beobachtungen zur Logienquelle und ihrer hellenistisch-judenchristlichen Redaktion* [Diss. Mainz, 1973]; Käsemann, *Versuche* I, 242-48), the influence of theological language is already apparent; the image remains. The original image, by contrast, speaks of the conquest of a strong man by a stronger, more powerful one, who invades his kingdom. In such a conquest the power of Jesus' works and thus the presence of the kingdom becomes apparent.

b) 1 Cor 1:25 and the other Pauline texts (the word appears only in 1–2 Corinthians) places ἰσχυρός in the context of the Pauline theology of the cross; the stylistic development of the text (cf. the transition in vv. 24, 25) is significant, but the proximity of ἰσχυρός to δύναμις/δυνατοί (vv. 24, 26) remains important. At the same time the antithesis to weakness is maintained (cf. also 2 Cor 10:10). Foolishness and the scandal of the cross prove to be σοφώτερον and ἰσχυρότερον than all sophia, and thus, because of their superiority, ultimately incompatible with it. In 1:27 Paul turns in diatribe style (v. 26!) *ad hominem* to the readers: Paul recalls their election and call by God, which is folly in human terms, because it was not oriented to human standards and claims, but rather annuls human claims and puts them to shame. 4:10 is related to this usage in 1:27; 4:9 ironically contrasts the weakness of the apostle and the strength of the congregation. The three antitheses of 4:10 define the self-consciousness of the

Corinthian church for Paul on the basis of the *theologia crucis*. Finally, 10:22 uses a rhetorical question to remind the Corinthians that God, who alone is mighty, demonstrates that their would-be strength is weakness (cf. 10:9).

H. Paulsen

ἰσχύς, ύος, ἡ *ischys* strength, power
→ ἰσχύω 3.

ἰσχύω *ischyō* be powerful, able

1. Occurrences and meaning — 2. Usage — 3. Ἰσχύς

Lit.: W. GRUNDMANN, *Der Begriff der Kraft in der neutestamentlichen Gedankenwelt* (1932). — idem, *TDNT* III, 402-6.

1. Ἰσχύω occurs 28 times in the NT; it means *be strong, be powerful; be capable of doing, be able*.

2. Along with the strikingly frequent, but less theologically accented use of ἰσχύω in the Lukan literature (Luke 6:48; 8:43; 13:24; 14:6, 29, 30; 16:3; 20:26; Acts 6:10; 15:10; 19:16, 20; 25:7; 27:16), Mark 2:17 is esp. to be noted (par. Matt 9:12; on the content cf. also Luke 5:31, where in the place of ἰσχύοντες the related ὑγιαίνοντες appears): In a wisdom saying it is said of the physician that he is present not for *the healthy,* but for the sick. In an abbreviated way this saying brings the scene of 2:13-16—Jesus' fellowship with tax collectors and sinners— to its essential focus. There is much to argue for this saying as an originally isolated saying from which 2:17b can be separated (esp. the parallels in tradition history). V. 17b expands the image with δίκαιοι/ἁμαρτωλοί and summarizes the mission of Jesus with the ἦλθον saying (cf. here E. Arens, *The ΗΛΘΟΝ-Sayings in the Synoptic Tradition: A Historico-critical Investigation* [1976]).

In Gal 5:6 ἰσχύω is used of the powerlessness and meaninglessness of ἀκροβυστία and περιτομή in relation to the power of faith, which is active in love (→ ἐνεργέω 2). Phil 4:13 orients the power of the apostle to the gift provided in Christ (→ ἐνδυναμόω 2). In Jas 5:16 ἰσχύω is used of the effective power of prayer, while in Acts 19:20 it is used in an almost technical way for the power of the missionary proclamation (cf. Heb 4:12; → ἐνεργέω 2).

3. For ἰσχύς, which appears in the NT 10 times with the meaning *power, strength,* the OT background, as also with ἰσχυρός and, in part, ἰσχύω, is to be observed. This is to be seen esp. in the citations in 2 Thess 1:9, where Isa 2:10 LXX is taken up and modified, and Mark 12:30, 33. Without this background the NT understanding of ἰσχύς would be unintelligible. Closely related are the "theological" sayings, which understand God as the only location of strength and all strength only as derived (so probably also 2 Pet 2:11 of the ἰσχύς of the angels), and the close contact, sometimes even interchangeability,

with other terms for strength and power such as κράτος, δύναμις, and ἐνέργεια (so in part the LXX).

Mark 12:30, 33 (cf. Luke 10:27; on the differences from Mark and Matthew cf. Bornkamm, *Aufsätze* III, 37-45) appears within the compositional unit 12:28-34, the debate over the question of the first and most important commandment. The answer is given by Jesus in a reference to Deut 6:4f.; the repetition of this answer in 12:33 by the scribe emphasizes again the importance of the double commandment of love. It is not coincidental that the LXX text of Deut 6:5 is altered here (cf. Bornkamm): ἰσχύς appears in the place of δύναμις. One cannot attribute a special meaning to such a variation, however. One must recall the closeness of the two terms in the LXX.

In a series of sayings related to the subject of ἰσχύς, Rev 5:12 employs the term with a doxological ἄξιος — acclamation with respect to God (on ἄξιος cf. W. C. van Unnik, "Worthy Is the Lamb. The Background of Apoc. 5," FS Rigaux 445-61). In Rev 7:12 this occurs in a related way (here of course within the framework of a doxological εἰς αἰῶνα acclamation), again in association with other expressions for power.

Such close contact with comparable terms is also seen in Eph 1:19 (ἐνέργεια); 6:10 (→ ἐνδυναμόω 2; cf. 3:16; Col 1:11). Traditional parenetic material is used in 1 Pet 4:11 (probably not without the influence of the Pauline understanding of charisma) to attribute the charisma of service in the congregation, the διακονεῖν, to that power which God has granted to believers. Here, not coincidentally, the verse concludes with a doxology.

H. Paulsen

ἴσως *isōs* perhaps, probably*

Luke 20:13 (cf. Mark 12:6): When he sends his "beloved son," the owner of the vineyard thinks ἴσως τοῦτον ἐντραπήσονται, *perhaps they will heed him*."

Ἰταλία, ας *Italia* Italy*

The name Ἰταλία appears in the NT only in Acts (18:2; 27:1, 6) and Hebrews (13:24). In connection with Paul's journey to Rome: εἰς τὴν Ἰταλίαν (Acts 27:1, 6). Correspondingly 18:2: Aquila had recently arrived "from Italy." According to v. 2b this means: from Rome. Heb 13:24: "Those from Italy greet you" (οἱ ἀπὸ τῆς Ἰταλίας). This greeting can be understood most easily to mean that the author writes from outside Italy and that "those from Italy" send greetings to their countrymen. According to C. Spicq, *Heb* [ÉBib] I, 261-65, the verse suggests a greeting *from* Italy, where the book was written; cf. O. Kuss, *Heb* [RNT] ad loc. On the name Italy, see B. Andreae, *LAW* 1418.

Ἰταλικός, 3 *Italikos* Italian*

Acts 10:1: ἡ σπεῖρα ἡ Ἰταλική, "the *Italian* cohort," to which Cornelius belonged. This was apparently an auxiliary unit made up of freedmen that was sent from Italy to Syria and is known to have been there in the first and second centuries A.D.; cf. E. Haenchen, *Acts* (Eng. tr., 1971) 346n.2.

Ἰτουραῖος, 3 *Itouraios* Ituraean*

Luke 3:1: Ἰτουραία χώρα, literally "the *Ituraean* land" (= Ituraea), in reference to the area belonging to the tetrarchy of Philip (at the Lebanon and the Anti-Lebanon; capital city: Chalcis). Schürer, *History* I, 561-73; W. Schottroff, "Die Iturärer," *ZDPV* 98 (1982) 125-52.

ἰχθύδιον, ου, τό *ichthydion* small fish*

Mark 8:7 par. Matt 15:34, before the multiplication of the loaves and fishes: The people had ἰχθύδια ὀλίγα (Matthew, ὀλίγα ἰχθύδια).

ἰχθύς, ύος, ὁ *ichthys* fish (noun)*

1. Occurrences; 1 Cor 15:39; the OT — 2. The tradition of the parables — 3. Miracle stories — 4. Narratives of resurrection and call

Lit.: DALMAN, *Arbeit* VI, 343-70. — J. DÖLGER, ΙΧΘΥΣ I-V (1910-43), esp. vol. I. — J. ENGMANN, *RAC* VII, 949-1097. — E. R. GOODENOUGH, *Jewish Symbols in the Greco-Roman Period* V (1956) 3-61. — R. M. GRANT, "One Hundred Fifty-three Large Fish," *HTR* 42 (1949) 273-75. — E. HILGERT, *The Ship and Related Symbols in the NT* (1962) 105-23. — U. H. J. KÖRTNER, "Das Fischmotiv im Speisungswunder," *ZNW* 75 (1984) 24-35. — J. MÁNEK, "Fishers of Men," *NovT* 2 (1958) 138-41. — R. MEYER, "Der Ring des Polykrates. Mt. 17,27 und die rabbinische Überlieferung," *OLZ* 40 (1937) 665-70. — R. PESCH, *Der reiche Fischfang* (1969). — I. SCHEFTELOWITZ, "Das Fischsymbol im Judentum und Christentum," *ARW* 14 (1911) 1-53, 321-92. — C. W. F. SMITH, "Fishers of Men," *HTR* 52 (1959) 187-203.

1. Ἰχθύς appears 20 times in the NT, 19 of those in the Gospels (5 times in Matthew, 4 in Mark, 7 in Luke, 3 in John), elsewhere only in 1 Cor 15:39. The latter is a saying based on OT creation traditions (Gen 1:26, 28; 9:2; Job 12:8; Ps 8:9; Hos 4:3; Ezek 38:20; Dan 2:38 LXX; cf. Zeph 1:3) that distinguishes the basic groupings of animals (and their flesh, σάρξ) as an image of the variety that will characterize the new creation (= the resurrection of the dead). In John 21 ἰχθύς occurs with → ὀψάριον (vv. 6, 8, 11/9, 10, 13).

Other fish motifs occur in the OT: on Solomon cf. 3 Kgdms 5:13. Catching fish with hooks or nets served as an image of surprising or unavoidable evil fate (Eccl 9:12; Jer 16:16; Ezek 12:13; 17:20; 29:4f.; 32:3; Hab 1:14f.; cf. 1QH 5:8, etc. [see O. Betz, *RevQ* 3 [1961] 53-59]); Mark 1:17 par.; Luke 5:10 has a positive connotation for the motif of catching fish (→ 4). In other contexts the number or size of fish is an expression of messianic abundance (Ezek 47:8-10; *Tg. Onq.* on Gen 49:16; *T. Zeb.* 5:5-6 [Zebulun the first fisherman; cf. Gen 49:13]; *Gen. Rab.* 13:16; cf. *Gos. Thom* 8).

2. Ἰχθύς designates *fish* as a common food.

Thus of the fish in the rivers (Exod 7:18, 21; Ps 104:29 LXX) or in the sea (Isa 50:2), which the Lord can allow to die out as a punishment, or which the wilderness generation can wish to return (Num 11:5). Nehemiah, who is faithful to the law, is angered that fish from Tyre are sold on the sabbath in Jerusalem (Neh 13:16), perhaps at the fish market, which gave to one of the city gates the name "fish gate" (Neh 3:3; cf. Zeph 1:10; 2 Chr 33:14).

Use of fish as food is confirmed by the many Jewish descriptions of catching fish (Josephus describes the Sea of Gennesareth as an esp. preferred place for catching fish: *B.J.* iii.508) and eating fish (see Billerbeck I, 683f.). A distinction is made between clean and unclean fish; only those with fins and scales were to be eaten (Lev 11:9-12 par.; cf. Matt 13:47f.); fish were not to be slaughtered ritually and their blood could be consumed.

This general usage is the basis for the image in Matt 7:10 (par. Luke 11:11); in Pliny also the fish is compared with the serpent (the winding movement: *HN* xi.73). The image of Jesus says that the beneficence of the creation —despite the evil conduct of people toward each other —is to be seen in the fact that a father does not make a fool of his hungry child and does not, e.g., give him a snake (similar to a fish) when he asks for a fish. This confirms the indisputable beneficence of the Creator toward the creation. On the other hand, in the legendary description in Matt 17:24-27 (M) there is a weakened form of a story known both to Herodotus (iii.42) and in a variety of Jewish forms (*b. Šabb.* 119a; *Pesiq. R.* 23, etc.).

3. In NT usage also (Mark 6:38, 41, 43 par.; Matt 15:36) ἰχθύς is to be understood concretely as food. Here it is to be eaten with bread: on the one hand, fish are included in the thanksgiving over the bread (Mark 6:41 par.; Matt 15:36—corresponding to *m. Ber.* 6:5, 7; cf. Mark 8:7); on the other hand they are not mentioned in the conversation following the miracle (Mark 8:14-21 par.).

In the version in John 6 concrete realism (v. 9: barley bread and cooked fish; Moulton/Milligan 470) and symbolic-christological interpretation appear alongside each other (vv. 26f., 32ff.). However, in the detailed Johannine interpretation the fish play no role (against R. H. Goodenough, *JBL* 64 [1945] 145-82), although the account is associated with the Jewish manna tradition and despite 1 Cor 10:2-4, where the manna and water traditions (Exod 16–17) are interpreted in parallel christological terms. The manna-rock tradition is even expanded in individual instances with the fish motif (esp. *Sifre* on Num 11:22; *b. Yoma* 75a).

4. John 21 includes three traditional elements, of which the first two become intertwined with each other (vv. 1-14): a) The resurrection tradition which, with its antidocetic intent—as in Luke 24:42—describes the resurrected one, on the one hand, as needing food, including fish; on the other hand, he is described as the one who has table fellowship with his disciples (Luke 24:28-32; Acts 1:41; 10:41); b) description of a miraculous catch of fish, a sign that manifests that the messianic era has come. Here John 21 has the same function as Luke 5:1-11; cf. the description of the number and size of the fish in both texts (21:6, 11/5:6-7; → 1). John 21 and Luke 5 also have in common that the coming of the messianic era should be proclaimed—indeed, on a universal level (the number of 153 fish expresses totality and universality).

S. Pedersen

ἴχνος, ους, τό   *ichnos*   footprint*

This noun appears in the fig. sense in the NT, with the idea of walking *in the steps* (τοῖς ἴχνεσιν) of another: 2 Cor 12:18 with περιπατέω, Rom 4:12 with στοιχέω: walk *"in the steps"*; 1 Pet 2:21 with ἐπακολουθέω, "follow the footprints (of Christ)." A. Stumpff, *TDNT* III, 402-06.

Ἰωαθάμ   *Iōatham*   Jotham*

Personal name in Matt 1:9 bis (Luke 3:23-31 D: Ἰωαθάν): the father of Ahaz (cf. 1 Chr 3:12f.).

Ἰωανάν   *Iōanan*   Joanan*

Personal name in Luke 3:27: the father of Joda (v. 26); cf. 2 Chr 17:15; 23:1.

Ἰωάννα, ας   *Iōanna*   Joanna*

Fem. personal name (on the form Ἰωάνα see BDF §40). Luke 8:3 mentions "Joanna, the wife of Chuza (→ Χουζᾶς), a steward of Herod [Antipas]" among the women who accompanied Jesus and supported him. She is mentioned also in 24:10 (with Mary Magdalene and "Mary the mother of James." She is thus a witness of the resurrection as well as a witness of the "earthly" works of Jesus. A. Hastings, *Prophet and Witness in Jerusalem* (1958) 38-49.

Ἰωάννης, ου   *Iōannes*   John

1. Meaning and occurrences in the NT — 2. John the Baptist — 3. The son of Zebedee — 4. The author of Revelation — 5. John Mark — 6. The father of Peter — 7. A member of the Sanhedrin

Lit.: On 2: K. ALAND, "Zur Vorgeschichte der christlichen Taufe," FS Cullmann (1972) 1-14. — M. BACHMANN, "Johannes

der Täufer bei Lukas: Nachzügler oder Vorläufer?" FS Rengstorf 123-55. — J. BECKER, *Johannes der Täufer und Jesus von Nazareth* (BibS[N] 63, 1972). — O. BÖCHER, "Johannes der Täufer in der neutestamentlichen Überlieferung," *Rechtfertigung, Realismus, Universalismus in biblischer Sicht* (FS A. Köberle; 1978) 45-68. — idem, *TRE* XVII, 172-81. — S. L. DAVIES, "John the Baptist and Essene Kashruth," *NTS* 29 (1983) 569-71. — A. VON DOBBELER, *Das Gericht und das Erbarmen Gottes. Die Botschaft Johannes des Täufers und ihre Rezeption bei den Johannesjüngern im Rahmen der Theologiegeschichte des Frühjudentums* (1989). — J. ERNST, *Johannes der Täufer* (BZNW 53, 1989). — C. H. KRAELING, *John the Baptist* (1951). — G. LINDESKOG, "Johannes der Täufer," *ASTI* 12 (1983) 55-83. — J. P. MEIER, "John the Baptist in Matthew's Gospel," *JBL* 99 (1980) 383-405. — J. MURPHY-O'CONNOR, "John the Baptist and Jesus," *NTS* 36 (1990) 359-74. — E. NODET, "Jésus et Jean-Baptiste selon Josèphe," *RB* 92 (1985) 321-48, 497-524. — K. RUDOLPH, *Die Mandäer* I (FRLANT 74, 1960) 66-80, 222-52. — W. SCHENK, "Gefangenschaft und Tod des Täufers. Erwägungen zur Chronologie und ihren Konsequenzen," *NTS* 29 (1983) 453-83. — J. THOMAS, *Le mouvement baptiste en Palestine et Syrie* (1935). — H. THYEN, "ΒΑΠΤΙΣΜΑ ΜΕΤΑΝΟΙΑΣ ΕΙΣ ΑΦΕΣΙΝ ΑΜΑΡΤΙΩΝ," *The Future of Our Religious Past* (ed. J. M. Robinson; 1971) 131-68. — P. VIELHAUER, "Das Benedictus des Zacharias," *ZTK* 49 (1952) 255-72. — idem, *RGG* 804-8 (bibliography). — W. WINK, *John the Baptist in the Gospel Tradition* (1968).
On 3: W. BAUER, Hennecke/Schneemelcher II, 51-56. — F.-M. BRAUN, *Jean le théologien et son évangile dans l'église ancienne* I (1959) 299-397. — R. E. BROWN, *John I-XII* (AB, 1966) lxxxvii-civ. — KÜMMEL, *Introduction* 234-46. — T. LORENZEN, *Der Lieblingsjünger im Johannesevangelium* (SBS 55, 1971). — R. SCHNACKENBURG, *John* I (Eng. tr., 1968) 75-104. — III (Eng. tr., 1982) 375-88 (bibliography). — E. SCHWARTZ, "Über den Tod der Söhne Zebedaei" (1904), idem, *Gesammelte Schriften* V (1963) 48-123. — H. THYEN, "Entwicklungen innerhalb der johanneischen Theologie und Kirche im Spiegel von Joh 21 und der Lieblingsjüngertexte des Evangeliums," *L'Évangile de Jean. Sources, rédaction, théologie* (BETL 44, ed. M. de Jonge; 1977) 259-99. — idem, "Aus der Literatur zum Johannesevangelium," *TRu* 42 (1977) 211-61 (bibliography). — P. VIELHAUER, *Geschichte der urchristlichen Literatur* (1975) 453-60.
On 4: H. KRAFT, *Rev* (HNT, 1974) 9-11 (bibliography). — KÜMMEL, *Introduction* 469-72 (bibliography).
On 5: W.-H. OLLROG, *Paulus und seine Mitarbeiter* (WMANT 50, 1979) 47-49.

1. Greek form of the Hebrew name *yôḥānān* (e.g., 2 Kgs 25:23; Jer 40:8ff.; Neh 12:22f.; an important bearer of the name in early postbiblical Judaism is Johanan ben Zakkai) or *yᵉhôḥānān* (e.g., Ezra 10:6; 1 Chr 26:3; Neh 6:18). The name has the typical form of a Semitic nominal sentence: "Yahweh is gracious." Its Greek form Ἰωάννης—on the orthography, cf. the literature cited in BAGD s.v.—is rare in pre-Christian literature (cf. 1 Macc 2:1f.; 9:36, 38; 13:53; 1 Esdr. 8:38; 9:29; *Ep. Arist.* 42, 49, 50; and often in Josephus), but is frequently attested in literature of the Christian era.

The name appears 135 times in the NT for six different persons; also as a v.l. in John 1:29 and Rev 21:2 and in the late superscript κατὰ Ἰωάννην of the Fourth Gospel.

2. The name of John the Baptist appears 91 times (exclusively in the Gospels and Acts [+ John 1:29 v.l.]).

Of historical value as a source for reconstructing the form and significance of the Baptist, besides the NT references, is the witness to his appearance and martyrdom in Josephus (*Ant.* xviii.116ff.). On the other hand the Baptist traditions in the "Slavic Josephus" (*B.J.* ii.110, 168) are without historical value. This is also the case for the Mandean reports about the Baptist, of which the tradition history belongs to the later strata of the Mandean literature and presupposes the Christian tradition in its apocryphal and legendary development (cf. Rudolph 66ff.).

Immediately after the martyrdom of the Baptist a sect of John was formed in which he was revered in almost messianic terms, making the movement a serious competitor to the early Christian movement. The reports about the Baptist in the NT are shaped by this situation. They are derived in part from the milieu of the Baptist sects (so, e.g., the birth story in Luke 1) and in part from Christian polemical rejection of claims for the Baptist. And in part they reflect accurately the extremely high evaluation of the Baptist by Jesus. With consideration of this complex character of our sources, one can reconstruct the following portrait of the Baptist and his impact:

Despite its legendary character and echo of the biblical story of Samuel, one may infer from the account of the Baptist in Luke 1 that he was the son of an old priestly family. A direct relationship between John and Essenism of the Qumran form could scarcely have existed. Certain analogies are due to the fact that we have here relics of the complex wealth of the Jewish religion in the first half of the first century.

The designation "the Baptist" (ὁ βαπτίζων, Mark 1:4; 6:14, 24) or ὁ βαπτιστής (Josephus *Ant.* xviii.116 in addition to Matthew and Luke; not present in John!) has no analogy and makes baptism the unmistakable distinguishing feature of John. As an eschatological sacrament of repentance it was a once-for-all and final offer of salvation from God to all Israel (βάπτισμα μετανοίας εἰς ἄφεσιν ἁμαρτιῶν, Mark 1:4 par.). Anyone who submitted to the saving "water baptism" of John would avoid the wrath of the judge of the world and escape the destruction of his imminent "baptism of fire." (This ancient correspondence between baptism of "water" and baptism of "fire" is still visible in Q [Matt 3:11 par. Luke 3:16f.]. Of course the distinction between Christian "baptism of the Spirit" and John's mere "baptism of water" has already been superimposed: cf. Mark 1:8; Acts 19:1ff.) The offer of baptism *to* Israel, the accomplishment of it by John, and its effect of forgiving sins distinguish the baptism of John from the earliest contemporary practice of proselyte baptism, in which one baptized oneself as a ritual cleansing and initiation from the Gentile world. John's baptism is likewise distinguished from the sacramental, but nevertheless continuously repeated baptism of the Mandeans and the washings of Qumran—likewise self-baptisms—by its eschatological once-for-allness and the decisive role of the "Baptist." It must be regarded against the background of the Palestinian-Syrian baptist movement (Thomas) as an "original creation" of John (Vielhauer); → βαπτίζω 2, → βαπτιστής.

As God's final messenger before the threatened catastrophe of baptism in fire, John took up the prophetic proclamation (cf. Matt 11:9 par.; 14:5; Mark 11:32 par.; Luke 1:76, etc.) of total reorientation of one's direction in life (→ μετάνοια). His appearance in the desert (Mark 1:3 par.; Matt 11:7 par.; John 1:23; cf. the function of Isa 40:3 also in 1QS 8:12ff.; 9:19), his manner of life, and his attire (Mark 1:6) explicitly emphasize this eschatological role. Perhaps John understood himself (cf. Mark 9:13) as the prophet Elijah of Mal 3:23f. who returns before the dreadful "day of Yahweh." At any rate his "disciples" understood him in this role; cf. the explicit Christian polemical rejection of this role in John 1:19ff.

In contrast to this understanding of John as the one who prepares the way for Yahweh, which leaves no room for another messianic figure in the interim (ἰσχυρότερος in Mark 1:7 is originally a circumlocution for the divine name), the unmistakable tendency of the Christian witness to the Baptist makes him the forerunner of Jesus the Messiah (Mark 1:7ff. par.; John 1:23). Indeed, his baptism becomes a diagnostic instrument for knowledge of Jesus (John 1:31ff.) and John himself becomes a "witness" to the exclusive revelation, preexistence, and sonship of Jesus (John 1:6ff., 15, 19ff., 29ff.; 3:27ff.; 5:31ff.). Parallel to this tendency is the transformation of the portrait of the baptizer in the wilderness into the preacher of repentance, which is most noticeable in the Lukan redaction of the Baptist passages: The preaching to the different occupations by John (Luke 3:10ff.) is actually a parenesis of the Third Evangelist to his church.

The messianic role of John and the threatening extent of the movement that he stirred up (cf. Matt 3:5) corresponds to his execution by the tetrarch Antipas in the fortress Machaerus in Perea (Josephus *Ant.* xviii.116ff.). The political motivation for his elimination given by Josephus is preferable as an explanation to the legendary description of the Baptist's death in Mark 6:17ff. par., which serves the purpose of placing the commission of the disciples in the shadow of martyrdom.

Jesus, who was impressed by the eschatological message of John and was undoubtedly baptized by him (a situation which, according to the witness of the Gospels, increasingly created difficulties for Christians with the competing Baptist sects), and who praised John as the "greatest of men" and as the one who was "more than a prophet" (Matt 11:7ff. par.), probably belonged to the inner circle of John's disciples until the death of the latter. At any rate only after John's martyrdom did Jesus begin his public work, for only under this circumstance could he be considered John-*redivivus* (Mark 6:14ff.; 8:28). It is also probable that Jesus' first disciples came from the

circle of the Baptist (John 1:35ff.). Thus John was actually, as Jesus' teacher, the one who prepared the way.

The literary place of the legend of Mark 6:17ff. makes it necessary to understand παραδοθῆναι of 1:14 as "imprison," rather than reading it with its simple meaning. The juxtaposition in the Synoptic Gospels of the imprisoned John and Jesus (cf. esp. Matt 11:2ff. par.), to say nothing of the simultaneous work of baptizing in the Fourth Gospel (3:22ff.; 4:1ff.), serves the Christians effectively in overcoming doubts from the Baptist about Jesus and thus in challenging the messianic claims made by the disciples of John. One may not, on the basis of the secondary corrective to the account of Jesus' baptismal activity, conclude its historicity. Such an important witness for Christian baptismal activity could not have eluded early Christian notice. The saying about the kingdom suffering violence (Matt 11:12 par.) also suggests that Jesus' public work began after John's death, for the statement probably derives from Jesus and looks back on the work of the Baptist as an era that has been closed.

Along with the negative witnesses to the Baptist in John 1:19ff., the Benedictus of Zechariah (Luke 1:67ff.; cf. Vielhauer) and possibly the material that lies behind John 1:1-12 are witnesses to a quasi-messianic veneration given to John by his followers.

3. John the son of Zebedee and brother of James is mentioned 30 times in the Synoptics, Acts, and Gal 2:9; also—without the name—in John 21:2.

After the martyrdom of his brother James under Herod's grandson, Agrippa I, around the year 43 (Acts 12:1f.), John appears along with James the brother of the Lord and Peter in Paul's report of the Apostolic Council. There John is a member of the triumvirate of στῦλοι who lead the Jerusalem church and are in charge of the negotiations with the people of Antioch (Gal 2:9; cf. Acts 15:7, 13, where John is of course not mentioned by name). One may conclude from the formulation in Acts 12:2 that John surpassed his brother in importance. At least he appears after the death of James and before the rise of the brother of the Lord to be the leading figure next to Peter. This is reflected in the narratives of Acts 3:1ff.; 4:13ff.; and 8:14ff. On the basis of this fixed constellation in the tradition, Luke identifies the two anonymous disciples of Mark 14:13 who were sent to prepare the Passover with Peter and John (22:8).

The name of the Galilean fisherman John is firmly anchored in the lists of the Twelve together with the name of his brother (Mark 3:13ff.; Luke 6:12ff.; Matt 10:1ff.; Acts 1:13). He belongs to the first who were called (Mark 1:16ff.; Matt 4:18ff.; Luke 5:1ff.; cf. John 21:1ff.). The Synoptics portray him, along with Peter and James, as one of the closest confidants of Jesus: at the withdrawal from the public eye into the stillness of the house (Mark 1:29), as witness of the raising of Jairus's daughter (Mark 5:37; Luke 8:51), at the Transfiguration (Mark 9:2ff. par.), at the eschatological discourse (Mark 13:3), and at Jesus' prayer in Gethsemane (Mark 14:32ff.; Matt 26:36ff.). John asks his master about the right of the strange exorcist (Mark 9:38; Luke 9:49), and with James he wants fire from heaven to be called down as a judgment on the Samaritan village that did not receive Jesus (Luke 9:54). At their request for the places of honor in the coming glory of Jesus at his right and left hand, the brothers are told that God alone can grant such a request, yet they must be near Jesus in his lowliness and, like him, suffer a martyr's death (Mark 10:35ff.).

Notwithstanding this announcement—it is probably a *vaticinium ex eventu*, so that the violent death of John apparently occurred even before the writing of Mark—the Synoptic portrait of John occasioned the early readers of the Fourth Gospel to identify the mysteriously anonymous figure, "the disciple whom Jesus loved" (John 13:21ff.; 19:25ff., 35; 20:2ff.; 21:1ff.; probably also 1:35ff., where the first one called remains anonymous, as well as 18:15f.), who according to John 21:24 wrote the Gospel, with John. The presence at the Last Supper of "the beloved disciple" in the circle of the Twelve (John 13:23; cf. Mark 14:17 par.; Luke 22:8) and the designation given to him indicate that he was one of Jesus' closest confidants.

Inasmuch as the true identity of the man, whose pupils posthumously (John 21:20ff.) placed him in the highly symbolic scenes of their Gospel with the honorific pseudonym "the disciple whom Jesus loved," would have been known in the Johannine school, the identification of him with John could have taken place only late and with considerable resistance. This identification becomes clear as the dominant ecclesiastical tradition in the Muratorian Canon (9ff.), which says that John was the author of John, Revelation, and 1–3 John. According to Eusebius *HE* iii.18.1, 20.8f., 23.3f.; v.8.4, 20.6, which relies on Irenaeus *Haer.* ii.22.5; iii.1.2, 3.4, John was exiled to Patmos under Domitian and there wrote Revelation. Until the time of Trajan he was active as the most esteemed authority in Ephesus, where he died of a natural death in old age after writing the Gospel (cf. Clement of Alexandria *Quis Div. Salv.* 42.2; *Acts of John, passim;* Tertullian *De anima* 50; further references in Bauer). This tradition was bitterly contested at the end of the second century by the Roman presbyter Gaius, who declared the Fourth Gospel a forgery by the Gnostic Cerinthus, and was opposed by the tradition of the Palestinian martyrdom of John (Mark 10:39; Papias apud Philip Sidetes [TU V/2, 170]; Syriac Martyrologium [KlT 2/8]), which has been almost totally omitted from consideration. Ignatius knows of no Ephesian stay by John, and the first commentator on John, Heracleon (in Clement of Alexandria *Strom.* iv.2.170), emphasizes that, of the Twelve, only Matthew, Philip, Thomas, and Levi died a natural death.

In no case can John have been written by the Galilean fisherman, according to Acts 4:13 an ἄνθρωπος ἀγράμματος, on both internal and external grounds. Instead the "elder John," who is mentioned by Papias (in Eusebius *HE* iii.39.3ff.) and clearly distinguished from the apostle John, could be identical with the "elder" of 2 John 1 and 3 John 1 and with the revered tradition bearer, the "disciple whom Jesus loved" in the Gospel, so that

the legend of the son of Zebedee was fostered by the sharing of the name.

The beloved disciple texts of John are literarily all secondary and unhistorical. Inasmuch as they reach their intended climax only in John 21, they derive from the author of this "epilogue," who is to be regarded as the editor and creator of the Gospel in the form in which it has been transmitted. In addition to authorizing the Johannine tradition, the Gospel in its present form fosters the veneration of an important personality of the Johannine circle, who died shortly before the editing of the Gospel, causing pain to the community (John 21:20ff.). This personality could be identical with the "elder" of the two shorter Johannine Epistles (cf. Thyen, "Entwicklungen").

4. John, the prophet and author of Revelation, is mentioned by name 4 times (Rev 1:1, 4, 9; 22:8 [+ 21:2 v.l.]). He calls himself "John servant of God" (1:1) and nowhere claims apostolic authority. He calls himself a prophet (cf. 22:9, though this might have been added by a later hand), and is distinguished from the apostles (18:20; 21:14). He writes his book under his own authority around A.D. 98. He is by no means identical with the author of John and/ or the Johannine Epistles.

5. John, who is called by the Latin name Mark, is mentioned 5 times in Acts (12:12, 25; 13:5, 13; 15:37) and as Μᾶρκος in Phlm 24; Col 4:10; 2 Tim 4:11; and 1 Pet 5:13. He was a Jewish Christian coworker of Paul and, according to Col 4:10, the nephew of Barnabas. → Μᾶρκος, → Βαρναβᾶς.

6. In John 1:42 (v.l. Ἰωνᾶ); 21:15, 16, 17 Simon is called son of John, but in Matt 16:17—as in John 1:42 Koine pl lat sy—Σίμων Βαριωνᾶ.

7. John, an otherwise unknown member of the Sanhedrin (D [it]: Ἰωνάθας), is mentioned in Acts 4:6.

H. Thyen

Ἰώβ   *Iōb*   Job*

The suffering righteous man whose story is told in the book of the same name. Jas 5:11 mentions him as an example of patient endurance; cf. *1 Clem.* 17:3; 26:3.

Ἰωβήδ   *Iōbēd*   Obed*

David's grandfather (Ruth 4:17; Matt 1:5 bis; Luke 3:32).

Ἰωβήλ   *Iōbēl*   Jobel

David's grandfather (→ Ἰωβήδ) according to Luke 3:32 B ℵ* sy^s. Cf. Ὠβήλ in D*.

Ἰωδά   *Iōda*   Joda*

A personal name in Luke 3:26 (cf. 1 Esdr 5:56 [RSV 5:58]): the son of Johanan (Ἰωανάν, v. 27).

Ἰωήλ *Iōēl* Joel*

An OT prophet and the book named for him. Acts 2:16 interprets the miracle of Pentecost as the fulfillment of "what was spoken by the prophet Joel" and cites Joel 3:1-5a LXX in vv. 17-21.

Ἰωνάμ *Iōnam* Jonam*

A personal name in Luke 3:30: the son of Eliakim and father of Joseph (→ Ἰωσήφ 2).

Ἰωνᾶς, ᾶ *Iōnas* Jonah*

Lit.: Y.-M. DUVAL, *Le livre de Jonas dans la littérature chrétienne grecque et latine* (1973). — R. A. EDWARDS, *The Sign of Jonah in the Theology of the Evangelists and Q* (SBT II/18, 1971). — J. JEREMIAS, *TDNT* III, 406-10. — G. SCHMITT, "Das Zeichen des Jona," *ZNW* 69 (1978) 123-29. — P. SEIDELIN, "Das Jonaszeichen," *ST* 5 (1951) 119-31. — M. SEKINE, *BHH* 881f. — A. VÖGTLE, "Der Spruch vom Jonaszeichen," FS Wikenhauser 230-77. — For further bibliography see *TWNT* X, 1124f.

Jonah (Heb. *yônâ*), a prophet of the time of Jeroboam II, is not the author of the biblical book of the same name, but is instead its "hero," about whom marvelous things are reported (in addition to the central event with the fish there are five other miracles). "The story of Jonah provided plenty of opportunity for fantastic embellishment" in Judaism (Jeremias 407).

Jonah's name appears in the NT only in the pericope regarding "the sign of Jonah" (Matt 12:38-40 par. Luke 11:29f., 32; Matt 16:4). Two events from Jonah's life are mentioned, his three days in the fish's belly and his preaching of repentance in Nineveh. Literary criticism shows that the demand for a sign was transmitted in two forms, as seen in Mark 8:11-13 par. Matt 16:1-4 as well as Luke 11:16, 29-32 par. Matt 12:38-42. According to Mark Jesus absolutely refused to give a sign from heaven; no mention is made of Jonah. In Matt 16:4 an addition is made to the Markan original (probably from Q; see below): "except the sign of *Jonah.*" Here the precise meaning of the sign of Jonah is not given. The logia source (Q) also knows a report about the demand for a sign. After the rebuke of "this generation" (Matthew adds the more intensive "adulterous"), both Luke 11:29 and Matt 12:39 agree in emphasizing that "no sign will be given except the sign of *Jonah.*"

In the added interpretations of the sign Matthew and Luke go different ways. Matthew connects Jonah's three-day stay in the fish's belly with the stay of the Son of Man (three days and three nights) "in the heart of the earth" (v. 40), and only then adds the reference to Jonah's preaching of repentance; in Matthew Jonah is not only a sign as preacher of repentance, but esp. as a reference to the death of the Son of Man. Luke, on the other hand, speaks (11:30-32) only of Jonah's preaching of repentance in order to affirm—as also in Matthew—that here,

in the person of Jesus, greater things take place. That both Matthew and Luke regard Jonah's preaching of repentance as the essential sign (→ σημεῖον) can be seen in the fact that Matthew explicitly mentions Jonah's prophetic activity (12:39: τοῦ προφήτου), and Luke speaks of Jonah's kerygma (11:32; cf. Matt 21:41). In making Jonah himself "a sign to the Ninevites" in Luke 11:30, the Evangelist is able to draw a parallel with the Son of Man, who will bring judgment at the parousia on the unbelievers who demand a sign (cf. the fut. in v. 30).

On the v.l. Ἰωνᾶ (John 1:42; 21:15, 16, 17) as the name of the father of the apostles Simon and Andrew, which the TR suggests, see *TCGNT* 201.

A. Sand

Ἰωράμ *Iōram* Joram*

Transliteration of the Hebrew name *yᵉhôrām*, a king in Jerusalem and son of Jehoshaphat (1 Kgs 22:51; 2 Chr 21:3ff.; Josephus *Ant.* ix.58). He appears in the genealogy of Jesus in Matt 1:8 (bis). A. Jepsen, *BHH* 884; *BL* 878.

Ἰωρίμ *Iōrim* Jorim*

A personal name in the genealogy of Jesus in Luke 3:29 that is not attested in the OT.

Ἰωσαφάτ *Iōsaphat* Jehoshaphat*

Transliteration of the Hebrew name *yᵉhôšāpāṭ*, a king in Jerusalem and son of Asaph (1 Kgs 15:24; 22:2ff.; 2 Chr 17:1ff.). He appears in Matt 1:8 (bis) in the genealogy of Jesus. A. Jepsen, *BHH* 886; *BL* 880.

Ἰωσείας *Iōseias* Josiah

Alternative form of → Ἰωσίας.

Ἰωσῆς, ῆ (ῆτος) *Iōsēs* Joses*

Ἰωσῆς is a Grecized, declinable form of the Hebrew name *yôsēp* (abbreviated *yôsēh;* cf. BDF §53.2). 1. Mark 6:3: a brother of Jesus, who in par. Matt 13:55 is called → Ἰωσήφ (5). 2. Mark 15:40, 47: the son of a Mary and brother of "James the Less"; in par. Matt 27:56 called → Ἰωσήφ (9) (v.l. Ἰωσῆς). 3. Acts 4:36 TR as name of → Ἰωσήφ (7) → Βαρναβᾶς. 4. Luke 3:29 TR in place of Ἰησοῦς (son of Eliezer).

Ἰωσήφ *Iōsēph* Joseph*

1. The patriarch — 2. The son of Jonam — 3. The son of Matthat — 4. The husband of Mary — 5. The brother of Jesus — 6. Joseph of Arimathea — 7. Joseph Barnabas — 8. Joseph Barsabbas — 9. The son of a Mary

Lit.: W. BAUER, *Das Leben Jesu im Zeitalter der neutestamentlichen Apokryphen* (1909), index s.v. (564). — J. BLINZLER,

LTK V, 1124 (on 6, 8), 1129f. (on 1, 4, 6) (much bibliography). — R. E. BROWN, *The Birth of the Messiah* (1977), index s.v. (on 4). — V. ERMONI, *DB* III, 1655-74 (on 1, 4). — K. GALLING and C. MAURER, *RGG* III, 859-61 (on 1, 4). — HENNECKE/ SCHNEEMELCHER, index s.v. (II, 835). — E. PLÜMACHER, *TRE* XVII, 245f. (on 4).

1. The patriarch Joseph (cf. Gen 30:22-24; 37; 39-50), the son of Jacob and Rachel, is mentioned 9 times by name in the NT. The name *yôsēp* means "May he [the Lord] add" (namely, more sons, cf. Gen 30:24). John 4:5 mentions the land that "Jacob gave to his son Joseph" (cf. Josh 24:32). In Stephen's speech in Acts 7 the name occurs 5 times (vv. 9, 13 bis, 14, 18); reference is made to the sale of Joseph into Egypt and his elevation to the regency by Pharaoh (vv. 9f.), his making himself known to his brothers and his origin becoming known to Pharaoh (v. 13), and his bringing his father and entire family to Egypt (vv. 14f.). At the beginning of a new section of the speech (vv. 17-19) the Exodus story is introduced with the reference to a new Egyptian king "who did not know Joseph" (v. 18; cf. Exod 1:8). In Heb 11:21 it is mentioned that at his death Jacob blessed "each of the sons of Joseph" by faith (Gen 48:17-20), in Heb 11:22 that by faith Joseph, at his death, made mention of "the Exodus of the sons of Israel and gave directions for [the burial of] his bones" (Gen 50:24-26; see O. Kuss, *Heb* [RNT]). At the end of the enumeration of the twelve thousand elect of each of the tribes of Israel, Rev 7:8 mentions the tribes of Joseph and Benjamin; on the list of the tribes, in which Dan is missing, see H. Kraft, *Rev* (HNT) 126f.

2. Joseph, the son of Jonam, Luke 3:30.

3. Joseph, the son of Matthat, Luke 3:24.

4. Joseph, "the husband of Mary" (Matt 1:16, 19f.), is mentioned by name 14 times (Matt 1:16, 18, 19, 20, 24; 2:13, 19; Luke 1:27; 2:4, 16; 3:23; 4:22; John 1:45; 6:42 + text variants in Matt 1:16; Luke 2:33, 43). Matthew 1–2 is primarily narrated from the perspective of Joseph, while Luke 1–2 places Mary in the foreground.

Matt 1:16 says that "Jacob begat Joseph"; then the schema of the "genealogy" (*a* begat *b*) is clearly interrupted in order to signal the different nature of the beginning of Jesus' life: At the naming of Joseph an appositional phrase is added: "the husband of Mary, of whom Jesus the Christ was born." When Mary was betrothed to Joseph, she was to be found pregnant "by the Holy Spirit" "before they had come together" (1:18). At first Joseph wanted to put Mary away quietly in order not to bring shame upon her (v. 19; on this alternative see Billerbeck I, 50-53). But an angel prompted him to marry her (v. 20). Joseph acted accordingly and took "his wife" to himself (v. 24), without having sexual relations with her (v. 25). 2:13 reports the angel's command to Joseph, to bring "the

child and his mother" to safety from Herod to Egypt, and of the fulfillment of these instructions (vv. 14, 15a). After Herod's death an angel commanded Joseph to return again "to the land of Israel" (vv. 19f.). Joseph followed the command, but did not go to Judea, because of → Ἀρχέλαος, but to Nazareth, where he took up residence (vv. 21-23a). In 13:55 the inhabitants of Nazareth ask: "Is this [Jesus] not the carpenter's son (→ τέκτων)?"— an uncertain reference to the occupation of Joseph, since in the Markan original (Mark 6:3) it is Jesus who is called a τέκτων.

Luke 1:27 begins with the statement that Mary was betrothed to Joseph "of the house of David" at the time of the angel's annunciation (cf. also v. 34 with Matt 1:18). In the birth story of 2:1-20 it is reported that Joseph (with his betrothed, who was pregnant), on the occasion of the taxation, went from Nazareth to Bethlehem "because he was from the house and lineage of David" (v. 4). The shepherds found "Mary and Joseph and the child" (v. 16) in Bethlehem. Luke emphasizes the Davidic lineage of Joseph (1:27; 2:4; cf. 3:23, 31), but at the same time that it was only the general supposition (ὡς ἐνομίζετο) that Jesus was Joseph's son (3:23; cf. Matt 1:16). Several textual variants intend to show that Joseph was not Jesus' real father (e.g., Luke 2:33 K X Δ Θ, etc.: Joseph, instead of "his father"; 2:43 C Koine A, etc.: "Joseph and his mother" instead of "his parents"). In the Nazareth pericope (Luke 4:22) the (critical) listeners ask regarding Jesus: "Is this not Joseph's son?" (par. Mark 6:3 has → Μαρία [2.c]; cf. Matt 13:55).

In John 1:45 Philip refers to Jesus as "the son of Joseph from Nazareth." In 6:42 "the Jews" ask, "Is this not Jesus, the son of Joseph, whose father and mother we know?" (cf. Luke 4:22; Matt 13:55) in order to reject Jesus' claim "that he came down from heaven." Jesus' critics think that they know Jesus' father and mother and yet know nothing of his real origin (cf. 7:27f.; see R. Schnackenburg, *John* II [Eng. tr., 1979] on 6:42).

5. Matt 13:55 mentions a Joseph among the brothers of Jesus with James, Simon, and Judas. The parallel in Mark 6:3, however, calls this brother Joses (according to the best mss.). This difference is to be explained as an assimilation of the Galilean pronunciation of the name Ἰωσή(ς) to the correct Hebrew form of the name (→ 1); see *TCGNT* ad loc.

6. The Passion narratives of the Gospels refer to "Joseph of Arimathea (→ Ἀριμαθαία)" (Mark 15:43, 45 par. Matt 27:57, 59/Luke 23:50; John 19:38; also *Gos. Pet.* 2:3; 6:23; see J. Blinzler, *Der Prozeß Jesu* [⁴1969] 391-97, 435-37; I. Broer, *Die Urgemeinde und das Grab Jesu* [1972], esp. 138-200). According to Mark 15:43 Joseph was "a respected member of the council"; according to Luke 23:50 he was "good and just." "He awaited

the kingdom of God" (Mark 15:43 par. Luke 23:51). Luke mentions that he did not agree with the council's decision and procedure against Jesus (v. 51). According to Matt 27:57 he was "rich," though he was a disciple of Jesus (John 19:38, "secretly, for fear of the Jews"). He requested from Pilate the body of Jesus for burial (Mark 15:43, 45 par. Matthew, Luke), took it from the cross, covered it in linen cloth, and buried it (Mark 15:46 par. Matthew/Luke; Mark, Matthew: in a stone grave; Luke: in a rock-hewn grave). According to John 19:39-42 Jesus was buried by both Nicodemus and Joseph (cf. Broer 230-49).

7. Acts 4:36: a Levite of Cypriot origin "who was given the name Barnabas by the apostles"; → Βαρναβᾶς.

8. Acts 1:23 names as "candidates for apostleship" both Matthias and a Joseph, "named Barsabbas"; → Βαρσαββᾶς.

9. Matt 27:56 mentions among the women at the cross of Jesus, besides Mary Magdalene (par. Mark 15:40) and the mother of the sons of Zebedee (Mark: Salome), also "Mary, the mother of James and Joseph" (Mark: "the mother of James the Less and of Joses"). Matthew has changed the Markan alternative form of the name "Joses" to "Joseph" (as also in Matt 13:55; → 5). Joseph/Joses is otherwise not known and is not identical with Joseph/Joses in Matt 13:55 (Mark 6:3).   G. Schneider

Ἰωσήχ *Iōsēch* Josech*

A personal name in the genealogy of Jesus in Luke 3:26 that is not attested in the OT.

Ἰωσίας, ου *Iōsias* Josiah*

Greek form of the Hebrew name *yōʾšîyāhû,* a king in Jerusalem (2 Kgs 21:24; 2 Chr 34:1; Josephus *Ant.* x.48). He is the son of Amon (Matt 1:10) and the father of Jeconiah (1:11) in the genealogy of Jesus. A. Jepsen, *BHH* 890, 893; *BL* 882.

ἰῶτα, τό *iōta* iota*
κεραία, ας, ἡ *keraia* small hook or stroke*

Lit.: G. BARTH, "Matthew's Understanding of the Law," G. Bornkamm, G. Barth, and H. J. Held, *Tradition and Interpretation in Matthew* (NTL, 1963) 58-164, esp. 64-73. — G. STRECKER, *Der Weg der Gerechtigkeit. Untersuchungen zur Theologie des Matthäus* (1974) 36-39. — G. SCHWARZ, "ἰῶτα ἓν ἢ μία κεραία (Mt 5,18)," *ZNW* 66 (1975) 268f. (bibliography). — For further bibliography → νόμος, → πληρόω.

1. Iota (I, ι) is the ninth letter of the Greek alphabet (as a numerical sign it represents 10, since originally the letter digamma preceded it). In the only mention of it in the NT (Matt 5:18) it is the Greek counterpart to the Heb. *yôḏ (y). Yôḏ* is in fact the smallest letter of the Hebrew alphabet (where it is the tenth letter and has the numerical value of 10).

2. Κεραία is derived from κέρας, "horn," and means elsewhere "stick, pole," but in the NT at Matt 5:18 par. Luke 16:17 *small hook or stroke.* This expression is most often interpreted as the ornamental line or decorative crown on Hebrew block script, rarely as the small stroke that allows one letter to be mistaken for another (e.g., ד and ה).

3. Matthew 5:18 is found in the context of three sayings about the law (vv. 17-19), which succinctly introduce the subject of the law in the Sermon on the Mount (through 7:12) and which are represented in turn in the following antitheses. Exegetes are not in agreement on either the setting of the individual sayings or whether they form an original unity or were later brought together; relative certainty can be gained only on the question of the present context in Matthew. "Law and prophets" (v. 17) in Matthew is often a brief formula for the binding commandments of God (7:12; 11:13; 22:40), which were to be fulfilled in all consistency. In v. 18 Matthew sharpens this commandment in a decisive way. The introductory amen-formula used here, which probably referred originally to the eschaton (cf. 24:34f.), refers now to the consistent fulfillment of the *whole* law until God's will is accomplished (the second ἕως introduces a final clause). The concern is thus (as v. 20 elaborates) with the fulfillment of righteousness; to fulfill righteousness means to be obedient to the will of the Father (cf. 3:15). God's will in the law, according to Matthew, is not found in the scribes' interpretation (23:2f., 13f.), but in Jesus' interpretation ("but I say to you"); Jesus is God's final "exegete" (cf. John 1:18). The law is not cancelled by Jesus, but is instead surpassed. As the progression of the Sermon on the Mount indicates, the ethic of Jesus is not a lax, diluted form of Jewish ethics, but an intensification (cf. v. 20) in fulfilling God's commandment and in the love of neighbor (5:43ff.; 7:12; 19:19; 22:29f.; also 9:13 and 12:7). Thus Matthew has given the framework that is developed in the following antitheses. The parallel saying in Luke 16:17—probably representing the Q tradition—is found in a relatively loose association in Luke.   R. Kratz

K κ

κἀγώ *kagō* and I, but I

Κἀγώ, derived from crasis of καὶ ἐγώ (cf. BDF §18), appears 84 times in the NT, with special frequency in John (30 occurrences, with none in 1–3 John), 1 Corinthians (10), and Matthew (9).

Like → καί, κἀγώ can be used as a coordinating or copulative conjunction: *and I* (e.g., Luke 2:48; linking clauses: John 10:27ff.); *and I* in the sense of *as I* expresses a mutual relationship between two statements (John 14:20; 15:5; Gal 6:14; Rev 2:6); *and I* can also express a result (Matt 11:28; John 15:4). In most cases κἀγώ is to be rendered *I too,* thus esp. in taking up a preceding "I" (e.g., Matt 2:8; 10:32f.; Luke 1:3; John 1:31, 33; Acts 8:19; Rev 3:10) or meaning *so I too* (John 10:15; 15:9), *I also* (2 Cor 11:22 ter), (as) *I too* (in comparison with others: 1 Cor 7:8, 40; 10:33; Phil 2:19), taking up emphatically a preceding λέγω ὑμῖν (Luke 11:9).

Adversative *but I* is found in Acts 10:28; Jas 2:18a; rhetorical τί ἔτι κἀγώ, "why . . . *am I still* . . . , in Rom 3:7 (cf. 1 Thess 3:5: "for this reason *I then also* . . .").

καθά *katha* just as*

Matt 27:10 (citing Exod 9:12 LXX): καθὰ συνέταξέν μοι κύριος. Cf. BDF §453.

καθαίρεσις, εως, ἡ *kathairesis* destruction, tearing down*

Literal: 2 Cor 10:4: πρὸς καθαίρεσιν ὀχυρωμάτων, "for the *destruction* of bulwarks"; fig.: 10:8; 13:10, εἰς οἰκοδομὴν καὶ οὐκ εἰς καθαίρεσιν (ὑμῶν).

καθαιρέω *kathaireō* take down, destroy*

1. Occurrences in the NT — 2. Meanings — 3. On Luke 1:52

Lit.: C. SCHNEIDER, *TDNT* III, 411-13.

1. Of the 9 occurrences in the NT, 6 are in the Lukan literature, 2 in Mark (cf. 15:46 par. Luke 23:53), and 1 in Paul.

2. The wide spectrum of meaning that αἱρέω has in classical and Hellenistic usage—from "take" to "grasp" to "kill," mid. "choose" (in the NT only mid., → αἱρέομαι)—is reflected in the NT use of καθαιρέω: *remove* Jesus from the cross (Mark 15:36, 46; Luke 23:53; Acts 13:29), *tear down* barns (Luke 12:18; here, as in LXX, e.g., Jer 49[42]:10, opposed to οἰκοδομέω), *overturn* rulers (Luke 1:52), *destroy* nations (Acts 13:19). In contrast to classical and Hellenistic syntax, καθαιρέω appears in Acts 19:27 with the gen. of separation: *suffer the loss of* the magnificence (BDF §180.1; see also BAGD s.v.). R. Bultmann translates 2 Cor 10:4 (v. 5 in Eng. versions) appropriately "thus we *destroy* sophisms" (*2 Cor* [original Germ.: KEK] 183f.; this not reflected in the Eng. tr. of the commentary).

3. According to the Magnificat (Luke 1:46ff.) the Christian "revaluation of all values" is symptomatically manifest in God's action toward Mary. The consequences of this action extend into the political dimension in God's overturning of powers (καθεῖλεν δυνάστας ἀπὸ θρόνων, v. 52; an OT motif: see the summary in E. Klostermann, *Luke* [HNT] 18f.) and the exaltation of the lowly. "Only a revelation from God—or better, the reality that comes with God's coming—can [in a hopeless political-social situation] create a remedy. This revolution will also be political . . ." (H. Schürmann, *Luke* [HTKNT] I, 76).

H. Hübner

καθαίρω *kathairō* purify, cleanse*

John 15:2, of the *cleansing* of the vine or of the branch (by cutting off the useless sprout); cf. R. Schnackenburg, *John* III (Eng. tr., 1982) ad loc.; fig.: Heb 10:2 TR.

καθάπερ *kathaper* just as, like*

There are 13 occurrences in the NT, all in Paul (12 occurrences) and Heb 4:2. 6 occurrences are in the phrase καὶ καθάπερ, "so also" (Rom 4:6; 2 Cor 1:14; 1 Thess 3:6, 12; 4:5; Heb 4:2); others introduce the image of the "body": καθάπερ γάρ (with οὕτως following), "for *as*"

(Rom 12:4; 1 Cor 12:12), and are used in the formulation of Scripture references: *as* (10:10; 2 Cor 3:13); also: *just as* (3:18; 8:11 [without a vb.]); *as also* (1 Thess 2:11). Καθάπερ appears as v.l. for καθώς with γέγραπται in Rom 3:4; 9:13; 10:15; 11:8.

καθάπτω *kathaptō* grasp, seize*

Acts 28:3, mid.: a serpent *fastened* onto Paul's hand (ἔχιδνα . . . καθῆψεν τῆς χειρὸς αὐτοῦ), so that it could be seen hanging onto his hand (v. 4); cf. BDF §310.1.

καθαρίζω *katharizō* purify, cleanse; make pure, declare pure
→ καθαρός.

καθαρισμός, οῦ, ὁ *katharismos* cleansing, rite of cleansing
→ καθαρός.

καθαρός, 2 *katharos* pure, clean; innocent; undefiled
ἀκαθαρσία, ας, ἡ *akatharsia* impurity; immorality
ἀκάθαρτος, 2 *akathartos* impure; shameless, licentious
καθαρίζω *katharizō* purify, cleanse; make pure; declare pure
καθαρισμός, οῦ, ὁ *katharismos* cleansing, rite of cleansing
καθαρότης, ητος, ἡ *katharotēs* purity*

1. Occurrences in the NT — 2. Clean and unclean OT and Jewish symbol system — 3. Clean and unclean in Hellenism — 4. The use of the word field in the NT — a) The synoptic tradition — b) Paul — c) The Pauline school — d) The Gentile mission and the "apostolic council" — e) Hebrews and John/1–3 John

Lit.: G. ANDRÉ and H. RINGGREN, *TDOT* V, 330-42. — BAGD s.v. — K. BERGER, *Die Gesetzauslegung Jesu* I (WMANT 40, 1972) 465-75. — H. BRAUN, *Spätjüdisch-häretischer und frühchristlicher Radikalismus* II (BHT 24/2, 1957) 62-73. — G. W. BUCHANAN, "The Role of Purity in the Structure of the Essene Sect," *RevQ* 4 (1963) 397-406. — M. DOUGLAS, *Purity and Danger. An Analysis of Concepts of Pollution and Taboo* (1966). — J. T. FORESTELL, *The Word of the Cross* (AnBib 57, 1974) 155-57. — W. H. GISPEN, "The Distinction Between Clean and Unclean," *OTS* 5 (1948) 190-96. — F. HAUCK, *TDNT* III, 413-31. — H.-J. HERMISSON, *Sprache und Ritus im altisraelitischen Kult* (WMANT 19, 1965) 84-99. — H. HUPPENBAUER, "*Ṭhr* und *ṭhrh* in der Sektenregel von Qumran," *TZ* 13 (1957) 350f. — W. KORNFELD, "Reine und unreine Tiere im AT," *Kairos* 7 (1965) 134-47. — G. VAN DER LEEUW, *Phänomenologie der Religion* (^{3}1970) 386-93. — B. A. LEVINE, *In the Presence of the Lord* (1974). — E. LOHSE, *RGG* V, 944. — F. MAASS, *THAT* I, 646-52, 664-67. — J. MAIER, *Die Tempelrolle vom Toten Meer* (UTB 829, 1978), esp. 50-53. — R. MEYER, *TDNT* III, 418-23.

— J. NEUSNER, *The Idea of Purity in Ancient Judaism* (1973). — J. H. NEYREY, "The Idea of Purity in Mark's Gospel," *Semeia* 35 (1986) 91-128. — W. PASCHEN, *Rein und Unrein. Untersuchung zur biblischen Wortgeschichte* (SANT 24, 1970). — F. PFISTER, PW Suppl. VI, 146-62. — W. PÖTSCHER, *KP* III, 164-66. — R. RENDTORFF, *Die Gesetze in der Priesterschrift* (FRLANT 62, 1954) 38-56. — idem, *RGG* V, 942-44, 947f. — H. RINGGREN, *TDOT* V, 287-96. — M. SMITH, "The Dead Sea Sect in Relation to Ancient Judaism," *NTS* 7 (1960/61) 347-60. — B. E. THIERING, "Inner and Outer Cleansing at Qumran as a Background to NT Baptism," *NTS* 26 (1979/80) 266-77. — L. M. WEBER, *LTK* VIII, 1144f. — Y. YADIN, *Megillat hamMiqdaš. The Temple Scroll* (Hebrew edition) I-III (1977). — J. K. ZINK, "Uncleanness and Sin," *VT* 17 (1967) 354-61. — For further bibliography see André and Ringgren; Maass; Pötscher; *TWNT* X, 1125.

1. The adj. καθαρός appears 27 times in the NT. It does not appear in Mark or, except in Rom 14:20, in the Pauline Epistles. Ἀκαθαρσία appears 10 times, in the Gospels only in Matt 23:27. Ἀκάθαρτος appears 32 times with special frequency in Mark (11 occurrences), Luke (6), Acts (5), and Revelation (5). The vb. καθαρίζω has 31 occurrences, of which Matthew and Luke each have 7, Mark and Hebrews each have 4, and Acts has 3. A few mss. have the Ionic form καθερίζω (see BDF §29.1), which was widespread in Hellenistic literature. Καθαρισμός appears 7 times in the NT and not at all in Matthew or Paul; in the NT it replaces the more common καθαρμός and κάθαρσις. Καθαρότης is found only in Heb 9:13. Belonging to the same field of meaning are → κοινός/κοινόω and → ἅγιος/ἁγιάζω.

2. The NT outlook on OT and Jewish purity laws is represented not only in uses of "pure" and "impure," but also in the larger context of the conduct of Jesus and the apostles (Luke 7:36ff.; Gal 2:11ff.; Acts 10–11, etc.). Their actions took place in accord with or in conflict with the laws and are intelligible only against this background. For this reason Mark had to preface his discussion of the problem (Mark 7) with an explanation for his non-Jewish readers (7:3f.).

The fundamental insight of the anthropologist C. Lévi-Strauss, according to which "a myth is made up of all its variants" (*Structural Anthropology* [1963] 213), is true of the dualistic system of purity and impurity in the Bible. It must be conceived as a "symbolic universe" that constitutes and establishes society, which shapes Israel's total conduct, actions, and expectations. The presence and functioning of such rules alone distinguishes a "society" from a mere accumulation of animate objects. Whereas elsewhere such values as "equality," "honor," and "justice" are dominant, in Israel the contrasting spheres of "pure" and "impure" stand at the top of the pyramid. Through agreement, negation, dominance, and negotiation they make differing social situations comparable to each other and thus structure the total social and physical universe of Israel as a "symbolic system" (Douglas 2-6).

Our classification of "cultic," "ritual," "religious," "moral," or "hygienic," which derives from a totally different hierarchy of values and interests, is therefore totally inappropriate for describing the biblical contrast "purity-impurity." Although he is not sufficiently consistent, Neusner attempts to reflect these insights when he largely avoids the categories of "cultic" and "ritual," since they often conceal rather than explain the concrete and often drastic consequences of "impurity." Moreover, they cause the contemporary reader to think in terms of the antonym "moral" and finally mislead one into inappropriate interpretive categories such as the "spiritualization" of the cultic (cf. Hermisson). Furthermore, interpreting the terms for "pure" and "impure" as simple metaphors for "good" and "evil" is either a tautology (Douglas 129ff.) or a transformation of Israel's social reality into an entirely different symbolic universe, whether consciously or unconsciously. Thus what is involved in Isa 6:1ff. or Psalm 51 is not a late "spiritualization" of originally "cultic" phenomena into the ethical, but rather the fossils from the early period, in which all transgressions produced impurity and all impurity was sin. Impurity is the consequence of the continuing attack of evil and demonic powers, which threaten Israel, its houses, its land, and its God. The house of the deity in Israel must esp. be protected against their throngs through blood rituals (Levine 67-77).

The priestly class, to whom we are indebted for their work in gathering and editing the largest portion of the biblical canon, attempted—with considerable success—to center almost all rules of purification around the temple and to associate them with its cult. Inasmuch as all taboos are thus subordinated to the will of God, their neutralization is attained. However, the rules of purification remaining outside the temple cult—such as lists of unclean animals, sexual taboos, etc., indicate that the concern is not with the "original meaning" of the purity rules, but rather with a process of selection determined by "priestly propaganda" (Neusner 120)—as effective as it may have been—which serves their exercise of power: the stabilization of the hierocracy, the continuation of male dominance, and the maintenance of the rules of the traditional marriage and family (Douglas 140ff.).

The literature cited above can be consulted on the mechanisms for selection in the ideal of purity held by Pharisees and Zealots, which are derived from entirely different interests from those of the OT; on the dominant role of purity in the Qumran community, in which the community itself replaced the temple in Jerusalem as the true sanctuary and the essential dualism of which hardly rests on foreign "influence," but on the ancient priestly understanding of "pure" and "impure" and the danger of defiling powers of darkness; on the transformation of the rules of purity by Philo as representative of Alexandrian Judaism; and on the rabbinic appropriation of the rules of purity after the destruction of the temple.

3. In the religious world of Greece from the time of Homer and in ancient Rome there was a comprehensive system of purification and rites of expiation (καθαρμοί and *lustrationes*). However, the contrast of pure and impure never played a dominant role here, especially since in Greece cult and state were always separate spheres and the Roman cult of the state, which was used as a political instrument, had lost its power of attraction and thus, for the mass of the population, the existential significance of its rites of lustration. In addition, all of the efforts of Augustus for religious reform and the restoration of the deteriorated temples were not able to effect any essential changes. This was due not only to the widespread religious skepticism, in which "pure" and "impure" had long been used commonly

for moral purity and personal integrity (cf. the Aristotelian theory of catharsis of body and soul under the effect of tragedy), but also to the rush to the rapidly growing mystery cults. Indeed, these cults, with their promise of "salvation," in contrast to the state religions, were shaped by more or less distinct systems of purification, and thus of an associated dualism of pure and impure. However, they stood in considerable tension with daily life in the Empire.

4. a) Most NT references to "pure/impure" are in Synoptic reports of purification from leprosy and exorcism of "unclean spirits." Leprosy was one of the most serious symptoms of impurity (cf. Lev 13–14; *m. Neg.*). A leper was "as one who is dead" (Num 12:12) and had to roam about outside the city walls in torn clothes, veiled beard, and streaming hair and cry, "Unclean, Unclean" (Lev 13:45f.). If purity was regained, it had to be affirmed by a priest and sealed by appropriate acts and sacrifices. It is within this framework that healed persons in the NT are required to show themselves to the priests and to offer the required sacrifices (Mark 1:44 par. Luke 5:14; Luke 17:14). Indeed, if Jesus' contact with leprosy is primarily a gesture transmitting purifying power (cf. also Mark 5:25ff.), it is nevertheless noteworthy, within this background, that the infecting power of impurity is overlooked and that no report is given of an associated "purification" of Jesus (Mark 1:40f. par.). Purification from leprosy, which earlier the wilderness prophet Elisha performed (Luke 4:27), was, along with raising the dead and exorcism, a messianic sign of the eschaton (Matt 11:5 par. Luke 7:22). The disciples were also sent out with authority to accomplish these signs (Matt 10:8).

Mark portrays Jesus' appearance as the Spirit-endowed Son of God (1:10f.) clearly and programmatically as the eschatological battle and victory of the "holy God" (1:24; 3:11) over Beelzebul, the prince of demons (3:22ff.), and all his "unclean spirits." Thus at Jesus' first public appearance in the synagogue of Capernaum the demon speaks for all his sinister associates in the moment when their time has come: ". . . you have come to destroy us!" (1:24 par. Luke 4:34; cf. Mark 3:11). Jesus gives his disciples a share in this authority over "unclean spirits" (Mark 6:7; Matt 10:1; cf. Acts 5:16; 8:7; see also Rev 16:13; 18:2). The evil suggestion of the scribes that Jesus serves Beelzebul and has an "unclean spirit" (Mark 3:22ff. par.; cf. Matt 9:32ff.), is "blasphemy" of the "Holy Spirit" that rests on him, and thus it is the "unforgivable sin" (Mark 3:22ff.). Through his expulsion of the "unclean spirits" (Mark 5:1ff. par.; 7:25; 9:25 par. Luke 9:42; cf. Matt 12:43-45 par. Luke 11:24-26) Jesus is in the process of plundering the goods of the conquered and imprisoned prince of demons.

When Jesus contrasts fearful observation of the purity laws, a mere "human ordinance," with keeping "God's command," which has been recklessly set aside, and proclaims as a messianic secret that nothing external is able to defile a person (Mark 7 par.), he actually declares "all foods clean" (7:19). Inasmuch, however, as he never denies that the evil thoughts and deeds coming from the heart actually defile, but instead teaches people to fear them, he remains, despite the radicality of his critique, on the level of the pure-impure system (cf. on Mark 7 Paschen 155ff.; see also Matt 23:25ff.; Luke 11:37ff.).

b) In early Christianity Paul is undoubtedly the most reflective representative of the insight that God, through Christ, the "new Adam" (Rom 5:12ff.), has bestowed his saving and purifying "righteousness" (Rom 3:21, etc.) on the Gentiles as impure sinners (Gal 2:15; cf. Rom 1:24; 6:19) in the fullness of time. Not only they alone, but also their children in marriages with unbelieving partners are sanctified and pure through faith (1 Cor 7:14). Whatever does not come from faith is impure and sinful (Rom 14:20; cf. Titus 1:15 [→ μιαίνω]).

c) In the Pauline school the mutual relationship of Jews and Gentiles (Gal 2:1ff.; Rom 1:16; 9–11), which is of saving significance, diminishes, and the Gentile Church, which Christ has redeemed from "lawlessness" through his sacrificial death, has usurped the place of the "purified people of God" (Titus 2:14; cf. Eph. 5:26). 2 Cor 6:14–7:1 is entirely outside the Pauline frame of reference. Inasmuch as it does not fit the context of 6:13 and 7:2, it is probably a marginal comment by a reader who stood close to the ideology of the Qumran community (cf. H. Braun, *TRu* 29 [1963] 221ff.).

d) Paul's insight at his call that God has acted eschatologically to declare the impure Gentiles pure "without the law" is also the dominant motif of the narrative of the programmatic opening of the Gentile mission by Peter (Acts 10–11). The "unclean animals" of the vision symbolize the Gentiles themselves and food that in Jewish eyes is "unclean" (11:3). In the report and in the manner of its repetition before those who were true to the law in Judea (11:4ff.), there is a reflection of the conflict over the acceptance of the uncircumcised into God's people and esp. a reflection of the conflict over table fellowship between Jews who held strictly to the purity laws and Gentile Christians. This conflict was also the reason that the Christians of Antioch responded to an intervention by Jewish Christians (Acts 15:1ff.) by sending a delegation to Jerusalem under the leadership of Paul and Barnabas. This led to the "Apostolic Council," which decisively confirmed (Acts 15 and Gal 2) the freedom of Gentile Christians from the law: "For God *has cleansed* their hearts by faith" (Acts 15:9).

Despite this unity in fundamentals, the problem continued in the practice of the churches (cf. only Gal 2:11ff.). The "Apostolic Decrees" (Acts 15:19f., 28f.; 21:25) are one attempt to find a compromise allowing for interaction and common life for both sides in the churches. Despite the report of Acts 15, Paul's words in Gal 2:1ff., esp. vv. 11ff., show that it is impossible that the "Apostolic Decrees" were concluded in the presence of Paul and the "Apostolic Council" (cf. also Acts 21:25). Neither in this nor in other matters did Paul concern himself with making decrees (cf. Philemon!). He concerned himself with insight and responsibility, and he appealed for respect for the path and conscience of the weaker brother (Rom 14:14ff.; cf. 1 Cor 8:7ff.). Unfortunately that problem was "disposed of" by the overwhelming Gentile Christian majority, by its usurpation of Israel's precedence in salvation (Rom 9:1ff.), and by the Christian view of the destruction of the temple as God's definitive judgment of rejection, a view that was unthinkable for Paul and fateful for both sides.

e) The ideas of purity in Hebrews and John (including 1–3 John) are deeply rooted in the Jewish heritage: Hebrews (→ θυσία 5) reinterprets the early Christian idea of the purifying expiatory offering with the help of Jewish merkabah speculation, in which the perfect cultic ministry of the angels occurs in the heavenly sanctuary. The role of Melchizedek (cf. 11QMelchizedek; Philo *All.* iii.79) as a high-priestly throne angel, here equated with Michael, probably belongs to this tradition. Christ, who is introduced immediately as exalted above all angels (Heb 1:4ff.), is installed in the heavenly sanctuary as high priest after the order of Melchizedek on the basis of his self-sacrifice. He now effects the definitive cleansing, which the earthly cult was capable of doing only in a preliminary and shadowy way (cf. 7:26ff.; 9:13ff.; 10:2, etc.).

The programmatic statement in John 1:17 is not an antithesis of "law" and "grace," but rather a description of the eschatological fulfillment and surpassing of the purification granted by the law. According to 2:1ff. the eschatological and definitive purification by the "Spirit of truth" desired by the Qumran community (1QS 4:20ff.; cf. Forestell 155ff.), symbolized in the inexhaustible quantity of the wine in contrast to the Jewish water rites (2:6), is present in the word and work of Jesus and effects the full purification and relationship to God among the disciples (13:1ff.; 15:3; cf. 3:25; 1 John 1:7ff.).

H. Thyen

καθαρότης, ητος, ἡ   *katharotēs*   purity
→ καθαρός.

καθέδρα, ας, ἡ   *kathedra*   seat, chair*

Lit.: BILLERBECK I, 909, 915f. — I. RENOV, "The Seat of Moses," *IEJ* 5 (1955) 262-67. — C. ROTHER, "The 'Chair of Moses' and its Survivals," *PEQ* 81 (1949) 100-11. — E. L. SUKENIK, *Ancient Synagogues in Palestine and Greece* (1934) 57-61.

Καθέδρα is found with its original meaning *seat, chair* in the pericope of the temple cleansing (Mark 11:15-19 par.). While Matthew follows the Markan original, so that both speak of the καθέδραι, the *seats* of the sellers of doves (Mark 11:15; Matt 21:12), Luke has omitted the saying about an actual physical action against the sellers and has left out Mark 11:15b, c, 16.

Another meaning is present in Matt 23:2. Here the καθέδρα Μωϋσέως is distinguished from other seats, which are to be understood as seats of honor (πρωτοκαθεδρίαι) for synagogue dignitaries (v. 6), which, as the context indicates, were places in the synagogue esp. desired by members particularly concerned about their reputation and prestige (cf. the πρωτοκλισία at the festal meals, v. 6). The καθέδρα Μωϋσέως belonged as a seat of honor to the permanent furniture of the synagogue. According to Matthew's report it was the official teaching chair for the scribes and Pharisees. In this statement Matthew explicitly emphasizes the teaching authority of these two religious groups: Their teaching is binding for the people. But Matthew emphasizes in ch. 23 (and not only in this chapter) that the practice of piety by these religious leaders stands in contradiction to the Torah of Moses and that they are not worthy of imitation. Thus he indicates that they are unworthy occupants of the καθέδρα of Moses, which declares the will of God in the synagogue.

                                          A. Sand

καθέζομαι *kathezomai* sit, sit down*

Of the 7 occurrences in the NT most have the meaning *sit*, e.g., as teacher "in the temple" (καθέζεσθαι ἐν τῷ ἱερῷ, Matt 26:55; Luke 2:46; cf. καθέζεσθαι ἐν τῷ συνεδρίῳ, "*sit* in the Sanhedrin," Acts 6:15; see also 20:9: καθέζεσθαι ἐπὶ τῆς θυρίδος); καθέσθαι ἐν τῷ οἴκῳ, "*remain* at home" (John 11:20); absolute *sit there* (20:12). The meaning *sit down* is seen only in John 4:6: ἐκαθέζετο οὕτως ἐπὶ τῇ πηγῇ, "*he sat down*, just as he was, at the well" (cf. also 6:3 v.l.).

καθείς *katheis* each one

In the NT only as v.l. in place of καθ᾽ εἷς in John 8:9; Rom 12:5.

καθεξῆς *kathexēs* in succession*

Lit.: J. Kürzinger, "Lk 1,3: . . . ἀκριβῶς καθεξῆς σοι γράψαι," *BZ* 18 (1974) 249-55. — F. Mussner, "Καθεξῆς im Lukasprolog," in FS Kümmel 253-55. — G. Schneider, "Zur Bedeutung von καθεξῆς im lukanischen Doppelwerk," *ZNW* 68 (1977) 128-31. — H. Schürmann, *Luke* (HTKNT) I (1969) 12f. — M. Völkel, "Exegetische Erwägungen zum Verständnis des Begriffs καθεξῆς im lukanischen Prolog," *NTS* 20 (1973/74) 289-99.

Καθεξῆς (likewise → ἑξῆς) appears only in Luke-Acts (5 occurrences). It represents temporal, spatial, or logical succession: *in order, in (the correct) order* (cf. BAGD s.v.). In Luke 1:3 καθεξῆς σοι γράψαι speaks of the determination of the author "to write *in order*" for the one to whom the book is dedicated." Here Luke probably refers esp. to (salvation-historically oriented) narrative according to the schema of "promise and fulfillment" (Schneider); to be done καθεξῆς narrative should be able, according to v. 4, to show the "reliability" of the "words" of instruction (cf. Acts 11:4).

In Luke 8:1 ἐν τῷ καθεξῆς means *in what follows* (cf. τὸ καθεξῆς, *Mart. Pol.* 22:3), *later on,* a redactional reference to the way of Jesus (cf. Luke 7:11; 9:37, → ἑξῆς) in the preaching of "the kingdom of God." "Samuel and *the successors*" (οἱ καθεξῆς, the prophets after Samuel, *the successors*) have *one by one in order* announced the "prophet like Moses" (Acts 3:24; cf. *T. Jud.* 25:1: a series of persons). According to Acts 11:4 Peter described *in order* the circumstances that led to Cornelius's baptism. The sequence of events demonstrated God's intention in favor of the Gentile mission. It is reported of Paul in 18:23 that "he went through the region of Galatia and Phrygia *in order*" (cf. → ἑξῆς of the way of Paul in Acts 21:1; 27:18).

                                        G. Schneider

καθερίζω *katherizō* cleanse, purify

Alternative form of → καθαρίζω.

καθεύδω *katheudō* sleep

1. Occurrences in the NT — 2. The Synoptic Gospels — 3. In parenesis

Lit.: K. M. Fischer, *Tendenz und Absicht des Epheserbriefes* (FRLANT 111, 1973) 140-46. — E. Fuchs, "Die Zukunft des Glaubens nach 1. Thess 5,1-11," *idem, Aufsätze* III, 334-63. — W. Harnisch, *Eschatologische Existenz. Ein exegetischer Beitrag zum Sachanliegen von 1. Thess 4,13–5,11* (FRLANT 110, 1973) 142-52. — P. Hoffmann, *Die Toten in Christus. Eine religionsgeschichtliche Untersuchung zur paulinischen Eschatologie* (NTAbh N.F. 2, 1966). — M. Lautenschlager, "Εἴτε γρηγορῶμεν εἴτε καθεύδωμεν. Zum Verhältnis von Heiligung und Heil in 1 Thess 5,10," *ZNW* 81 (1990) 39-59.

1. Καθεύδω appears 22 times in the NT. The only occurrences outside the Synoptics are in Eph 5:14; 1 Thess 5:6, 7, 10. In the NT literature καθεύδω, like → κοιμάομαι, designates *sleep* in both the natural sense and the fig. sense. However, it is not used euphemistically as a term for death (on 1 Thess 5:10 → 3).

2. Καθεύδω is used of natural sleep in Mark 4:27 (as in Matt 13:25; 25:5). The passage points to the imperturbability of the sower in the rhythm of waking and sleeping because he is certain of the harvest. The em-

phasis on Jesus' sleeping in the boat (Mark 4:38 par.) serves as a basic element of the motif of the rescue miracle and accents the disciples' lack of understanding (4:40). Sleep is criticized in the Synoptics (except for the implied criticism in the warning in 13:36) only in Mark 14:37. Jesus' admonition (14:38) goes beyond the concrete situation, as the term πειρασμός indicates. Mark 5:39 par. warrants special mention. There can be no doubt that the girl's actual death is presupposed (5:23, 35). Jesus refers to her death as sleep, but the customary euphemistic softening of the idea of death is not intended, but rather an indication that, because of his presence, her death is merely temporary (cf. Hoffmann 203). Consequently Jesus "treats" the girl as one who was sleeping (5:41).

3. In Eph 5:14 καθεύδω appears in what has been shown to be a hymn, although its exact origin cannot be determined. It is most likely a baptismal hymn. If the summons to the sleeper to wake up is associated with baptism, the reference to baptism is the basis for the admonition in v. 15, parallel to the analogous image of light (v. 8a) and the parenesis (v. 8b).

Paul employs καθεύδω in 1 Thess 5:6, 7 in connection with the ind. of salvation in v. 5, likewise in the framework of baptism. If v. 10 again takes up the ind. christologically, καθεύδω remains difficult: If it is true, as the majority of exegetes assume, that γρηγορέω ("be watchful") and καθεύδω are used here of the contrast between the living and the dead, then γρηγορέω and καθεύδω would, uniquely for Paul, refer to life and death, which is, in view of the Pauline terminology of 1 Thess 4:14f. and the hortatory use of γρηγορέω and καθεύδω (5:6), a difficult assumption to make. Thus 5:10 contains an essential paradox, perhaps an expression of a final precedence of the ind. (vv. 5, 9f.) over the imv. (vv. 6, 8).

M. Völkel

καθηγητής, οῦ, ὁ *kathēgētēs* teacher, leader, guide*

In the NT only in Matt 23:10 (bis), most likely in the sense of *master;* Jesus rejects any claim to leadership made by anyone in the Church, since he alone is the disciples' καθηγητής (cf. 23:8 v.l.). The word is used frequently in Hellenistic literature of the authority of teachers and of those whose actions are given as models (e.g., Plutarch *Alex. Fort.* ii.327f. [of Aristotle], etc.). In this respect Matt 23:10 is a development of v. 8. Spicq, *Notes* I, 389-91.

καθήκω *kathēkō* come to, approach, be fitting*

Impersonal οὐ καθῆκεν αὐτὸν ζῆν, "he *ought* not live" (Acts 22:22; on the impf. cf. BDF §358.2). In Stoic literature the neut. pres. partc. τὸ καθῆκον designates that

which is incumbent and appropriate, as a result of the claims of the human world and of one's own nature (cf. Diogenes Laertius vii.107ff.; Epictetus *Diss.* ii.17.31). The Pauline formulation ποιεῖν τὰ μὴ καθήκοντα in Rom 1:28 does not take up the philosophical expression directly, for which the negation would be τὸ παρὰ τὸ καθῆκον (H. Schlier, *TDNT* III, 439f.), but reflects more popular usage (cf. τὰ μὴ καθήκοντα, 2 Macc 6:4; 3 Macc 4:16). The concern in Rom 1:28 is thus with what is *not permitted/not fitting* before God. H. Schlier, *TDNT* III, 439f.; G. Bühring, *Untersuchungen zur Anwendung, Bedeutung und Vorgeschichte der stoischen 'numeri officii'* (Diss. Hamburg, 1960); *TWNT* X, 1126 (bibliography).

κάθημαι *kathēmai* sit; sit down; be enthroned

1. Occurrences in the NT — 2. Meanings and usage — 3. Psalm 110 and the tradition history of exaltation christology

Lit.: M. BLACK, "The Throne-Theophany, Prophetic Commission and the 'Son of Man': A Study in Tradition-History," *FS Davies* 57-73. — J. DUPONT, "Assis à la droite de Dieu. L'interprétation du Ps 110,1 dans le NT," *Resurrexit. Actes du symposion sur la résurrection de Jésus* (ed. E. Dhanis; 1974) 423-36. — idem, "Le logion des douze trônes (Mt 19,28; Lc 22,28-30)," *Bib* 45 (1964) 355-92. — T. F. GLASSON, " 'Plurality of Divine Powers' and the Quotations in Hebr 1,6ff.," *NTS* 12 (1965/66) 270-72. — HAHN, *Titles* 129-35. — D. M. HAY, *Glory at the Right Hand. Ps 110 in Early Christianity* (SBLMS 18, 1973). — M. HENGEL, *The Son of God: The Origin of Christology and the History of Jewish-Hellenistic Religion* (1976). — O. KEEL, *Jawhe-Visionen und Siegelkunst. Eine neue Deutung der Majestätsschilderungen in Jes 6, Ez 1 und 10 und Sach 4* (SBS 84 and 85, 1977). — idem, *Die Welt der altorientalischen Bildsymbolik und das AT. Am Beispiel der Psalmen* (1972). — R. KEMPTHORNE, "The Markan Text of Jesus' Answer to the High Priest (Mark XIV 62)," *NovT* 19 (1977) 197-208. — S. LÉGASSE, "Jésus devant le Sanhédrin. Recherche sur les traditions évangéliques," *RTL* 5 (1974) 170-97. — B. LINDARS, *NT Apologetic* (1961) 45-51. — O. LINTON, "The Trial of Jesus and the Interpretation of Psalm CX," *NTS* 7 (1960/61) 258-62. — W. R. G. LOADER, "Christ and the Right Hand. Ps CX,1 in the NT," *NTS* 24 (1977/78) 199-217. — E. LÖVESTAM, "Die Davidssohnfrage," *SEÅ* 27 (1962) 72-82. — G. LOHFINK, *Die Himmelfahrt Jesu. Untersuchungen zu den Himmelfahrts- und Erhöhungstexten bei Lukas* (SANT 26, 1971). — F. J. MOLONEY, "The Targum on Ps 8 and the NT," *Salesianum* 37 (1975) 326-36. — F. NEUGEBAUER, "Die Davidssohnfrage (Mk XII,35-37 parr.) und der Menschensohn," *NTS* 21 (1974/75) 81-108. — A. F. SEGAL, *Two Powers in Heaven: The Significance of the Rabbinic Reports about Binitarism, Ditheism and Dualism for the History of Early Christianity and Judaism* (Diss. Yale University, 1975). — O. J. F. SEITZ, "The Future Coming of the Son of Man: Three Midrashic Formulations in the Gospel of Mark," *SE* VI (1973) 478-94. — J. THEISOHN, *Der auserwählte Richter. Untersuchungen zum traditionsgeschichtlichen Ort der Menschensohngestalt der Bilderreden des äthHen* (SUNT 12, 1975). — J. W. THOMPSON, "The Structure and Purpose of the Catena in Heb 1:5-13," *CBQ* 38 (1976) 352-63. — W. THÜSING, "Erhöhungsvorstellung und Parusieerwartung in der ältesten nachösterlichen Christologie," *BZ* 11 (1967) 95-108, 205-22; 12 (1968) 54-80, 223-40. — For further bibliography see *TWNT* X, 1126.

1. The 92 occurrences in the NT are concentrated in the Gospels (47) and Revelation (33) as compared with Acts (7) and the Epistles (4). The use of the word for an event that is seen is favored by the literary form of narrative description.

2. Κάθημαι is to be understood within the context of the place of sitting at the time of the NT: People sat on the ground (children at play, Matt 11:16 par. Luke; beggars, the lame, and the blind at the side of the road, Mark 10:46 par. Matthew/Luke; John 9:8; Acts 3:10; Peter with the servants at the fire, Mark 14:54 par. Matthew/Luke; in the courtyard, Matt 26:69; the watchman at the cross, 27:36; cf. *BRL* 229). Sitting on the ground while watching (Mark 2:6) is common when a crowd of spectators comes together (Mark 3:32, 34); one sits for writing and associated activities (Mark 2:14 par. Matthew/Luke; Luke 16:6; John 2:14). The man who before was possessed sits peacefully on the ground "like a normal man" (Mark 5:15 par. Luke). People sit on the earth as a sign of grief or repentance (Luke 10:13; cf. Matt 4:16; on κάθημαι = *dwell*, cf. Heb. *yāšaḇ*, Luke 21:35). Jesus also sits down to teach (Matt 5:15; 13:1; Mark 9:35; John 8:2).

In a culture where sitting on the ground was common, an elevated sitting place had a special weight of authority: In the ancient orient the earthly king and the heavenly lord sit on thrones in accordance with the worldview and ideology (cf. Keel, *Jahwe-Visionen* 33f.; LXX use of κύριος καθήμενος ἐπὶ τῶν Χερουβίν [e.g., Ps 79:2]; on *sit down = be enthroned*, cf. Rev 18:7). In the NT the apocalyptic seer takes over the phrase ὁ καθήμενος ἐπὶ τῷ θρόνῳ to describe God in visual terms (Rev 4:2ff.; 5:7, 13; 6:16; 7:10, etc.; cf. Matt 23:22). The authoritative Roman court official sits on a βῆμα (Matt 27:19; Acts 25:6, 17; cf. Acts 23:3: the t.t. κάθησθαι κρίνων, "*sit to judge*").

In Revelation the twenty-four elders sit around God's throne on their own thrones wearing white robes of heavenly sanctity and glory and golden crowns (4:4). Despite this array, the emphasis is on their cultic function, not their function as rulers (11:16). These heavenly figures correspond to the earthly Church and its council of elders. Furthermore, the authority of the twelve disciples as rulers and judges over Israel corresponds to that of the Son of Man, who in earthly lowliness and homelessness promised to his disciples that they would sit on thrones with him in the future (Matt 19:28 par. Luke; Mark 10:41-45 par. Matthew/Luke). Here, where the subject is the enthronement of the Son of Man and participation in it, the martyr tradition, which is oriented in the contrast of "now" and "in the past," is superimposed on

the tradition of authority, which more strongly points to the present correspondence of "heavenly" and "earthly" (cf. Col 3:1; Eph 1:20; 2:6f.; Heb 12:2; Rev 3:21; → 3). If Jesus sits on a mountain to teach (Matt 5:1; 15:29; Mark 13:3 par. Matthew; John 6:3), the symbolism of the mountain as place of revelation and place of the deity (cf. the revelation to Moses in Exodus 20; Keel, *Bildsymbolik* 100-105) indicates the dignity of the teacher.

3. Of central meaning for the NT christology is the use of κάθημαι in the statement regarding the sitting of the heavenly Christ at God's right hand.

The linguistic form of this saying is derived from Ps 110:1 (cf. Hay). This psalm belongs entirely within the realm of OT royal theology, according to which the king is begotten/adopted by God, and his earthly throne is legitimized with his cosmic place of honor, his sitting at God's right hand (cf. Keel, *Bildsymbolik* 234ff. with illustration 342). Alongside the (more ancient tradition-historical? cf. Hay, 27-33) interpretation in terms of the descent of the Messiah from the house of David (cf. Mark 12:35-37; Acts 2:34-36) stands the Hasmonean interpretation, which begins in Ps 110:4 and says of the ruling Hasmonean that he is leader and high priest in eternity: εἶναι . . . ἡγούμενον καὶ ἀρχιερέα εἰς τὸν αἰῶνα (1 Macc 14:41; cf. Hay 24).

At the same time there is also the interpretation that becomes decisive for the NT, which associates enthronement and priestly dignity with a heavenly figure (cf. Hay 26f.) and sees the destiny of the righteous ones in Israel in heavenly-eschatological terms in the righteousness of God (cf. K. Berger, *Die Auferstehung des Propheten und die Erhöhung des Menschensohns* [1976] 40-42): Daniel 7 apparently assumes Psalm 110 (cf. the explicit connection in Mark 14:62 and *b. Sanh.* 38b; Hay 26; Berger, *Auferstehung* 404f.n.563; on the interpretation of Psalm 110 in the Enoch–Son of Man tradition in the similitudes in 1 Enoch, cf. Theisohn 94-99) and, like the entire Enoch literature (on the "sitting" of Metatron cf. *b. Ḥag.* 14b with *3 Enoch* 48C), establishes the Son of Man as the judge and high priest authorized by God. His heavenly authority for judgment and intercession is realized in the salvation of the righteous and "saints of the most high."

11QMelchizedek is also unintelligible without Ps 110:4— even if the psalm is not cited: Melchizedek demonstrates his authority to judge when he executes the eschatological Year of Jubilee as heavenly high priest. An allusion to the heavenly throne also appears in *T. Job* 33:3, 9: The Job who was afflicted on earth knows of a heavenly throne at God's right hand and of the splendor of God's kingdom, which rests on "the chariots of the Father"; for the interpretation of the fate of the suffering righteous one here reference is not made in Hellenistic-individualistic terms to the Son of Man figure, but is shaped by an early form of Merkabah mysticism (doctrine based on the throne chariots of Ezekiel 1).

The NT relies consistently on the apocalyptic-mystical interpretation of Psalm 110. In the reception of the psalm we have an entirely ancient interpretation of Jesus' fate (cf. Berger 124; against the interpretation given wide currency by Hahn, *Titles* 168ff., which assumes an antithesis between an imminent expectation and a later coordination of Christ and the heavenly world); it sees in his death and resurrection the transfer of the authority of the heavenly Son of Man to this righteous one. The oldest literary stratum in 1 Cor 15:25f. assumes a combination of Psalm 110 and the Son of Man passage in Ps 8:7 (brought together in an old collection of citations? on the Son of Man interpretation of Psalm 8 in the targum see Moloney): In the earthly destiny and the heavenly throne of the Son of Man–Adam (cf. Metatron as primal Adam in *3 Enoch* 48C) the righteousness and sovereignty of all the righteous (= believers) receives its basis.

Rom 8:34 describes the work of the one who sits at God's right hand as priestly intercession (Ps 110:4; cf. on Metatron as heavenly high priest: *3 Enoch* 15B; *Num. Rab.* 12:15); this interpretation is then found in Hebrews (8:1; 10:12: the heavenly high priest sits at God's right hand) and comes to full development in the Johannine teaching of the Son of Man–Paraclete: In his death on the cross the Son of Man ascends his heavenly throne and assumes his task of intercession as heavenly high priest in the form of the advocate. The doctrine of the exaltation of the the the Son of Man takes on a meaning from the time of Daniel 7 which includes the fate of the righteous.

This meaning is given expression in Acts 5:31 (ἀρχηγὸν καὶ σωτῆρα ὕψωσεν τῇ δεξιᾷ αὐτοῦ, "he has exalted him to his right hand as leader [of salvation] and savior"); Col 3:1; Eph 1:20; 2:6. We have here a baptismal mysticism that associates the believer's participation in the fate of the Son of Man–Christ in his heavenly existence; in the destiny of Christ as Son of Man, culminating in his exaltation, God brings about the eschatological humanity of the believer. From the heavenly throne of the one who sits at God's right hand a view is given, within this apocalyptic cult mysticism, to creation and preexistence (Heb 1:3; John 1:1ff.; cf. Hengel 66-76), to the position of the exalted one, who is raised above every heavenly creature (Heb 1:13), and to the eschatological defeat of the enemy (1 Cor 15:25), which is now visible.

The Christ who sits at God's right hand is enthroned as Son of Man and high priest (cf. Rev 5:13, etc.: the lamb with the enthroned one); thus the connection with the martyr-tradition is always to be observed: In Jesus' destiny the NT sees the archetype of the martyr who has been justified by God (Heb 12:2). As a reward for his victory the Christian martyr may join the true witness and sit on his throne (Rev 3:21; cf. *T. Job* 33:3) and may— esp. in the dying vision—receive from the gaze of the one who stands at God's right hand the certainty of being taken into the heavenly glory and holiness of the Son of Man (Acts 7:56). One may assume with some reason that this martyrological teaching associated with the doctrine of the Son of Man's exaltation has its beginning in NT tradition in Jesus' charismatic announcement of his destiny. Mark 14:62 par. Matthew/Luke is thus the oldest

occurrence; this is also supported by the originally anti-Davidic interpretation of Ps 110:1 in Mark 12:36 par. (cf. also the martyr tradition in Acts 2:34-36: God has made this one Christ whom you crucified). A clear extension of the originally unified notion of resurrection/exaltation becomes palpable in the narrative tradition that gives a chronological view of the appearances of the resurrected one in legendary-biographical form (Mark 16:19; Acts 1:3ff.).

               J.-A. Bühner

καθημερινός, 3 *kathēmerinos* daily*

Acts 6:1, of the "*daily* support" (ἐν τῇ διακονίᾳ τῇ καθημερινῇ), probably the feeding of the needy in the early Church; cf. E. Haenchen, *Acts* (Eng. tr., 1971) ad loc.; G. Schneider, *Acts* (HTKNT) I, 423f.

καθίζω *kathizō* sit down; cause to sit down*

1. Occurrences — 2. In ordinary private life — 3. In public and political life — 4. Religious and theological significance

Lit.: BAGD s.v. — J. BLINZLER, *Der Prozeß Jesu* (⁴1969) 346-56. — E. HAENCHEN, "Jesus vor Pilatus," *TLZ* 58 (1960) 93-102. — J. KREMER, *Pfingstbericht und Pfingstgeschehen* (SBS 63 and 64, 1973) 107-17. — S. MITTMANN, *BL* 1745-47. — I. DE LA POTTERIE, "Deux livres récents sur le procès de Jèsus," *Bib* 43 (1962) 87-93. — C. SCHNEIDER, *TDNT* III, 440-44. — B. SCHWANK, "Der königliche Richter: Jo 19,8-16a," *Sein und Sendung* 29 (1964) 196-208. — W. THÜSING, *Erhöhungsvorstellung und Parusieerwartung in der ältesten nachösterlichen Christologie* (SBS 42, 1969).

1. This vb. appears 46 times in the NT, most frequently in Matthew (8 occurrences), Mark (8), Luke (7), and Acts (9). It is used both trans./causatively and intrans.

2. In addition to the simple basic meaning (e.g., Matt 13:48; Mark 12:41; 14:32; Acts 8:31; 13:14; 16:13; 1 Cor 10:7), καθίζω can occasionally be rendered *ride* (Mark 11:2, 7 par. Luke 19:30), *stay* (Matt 26:36; Luke 24:49; Acts 18:11), and even *consider, calculate* (cf. Luke 14:28, 31). It is used frequently in speaking of teachers (Matt 23:2; Luke 4:20; cf. 16:6); according to rabbinic custom both teacher and pupils sit. Jesus sits when he preaches (Matt 5:1; Mark 9:35; Luke 5:3; John 8:2). Sitting is accompanied by no special dignity in this context, in contrast to the political realm.

3. Among both Jews and Gentiles public officials are spoken of as sitting (cf. 1 Cor 6:4), and possession of higher office is indicated by the posture of sitting. Thrones, however, were reserved for rulers (John 19:13; Acts 12:21; cf. also Acts 2:30; Exod 11:5; 12:29; 1 Kgs 1:17; 3:6, 8:25). The high-priestly and judicial offices (when they were not united under the regency) also had the dignity associated with sitting (cf. Acts 23:3; 25:6,

17). This special distinction was not given to lower administrative officials and governing bodies. For the pious believer, however, it is not the king who is enthroned, but God himself. The king is merely a visible representative.

4. The primitive religious idea expressed in the image of the enthroned God, which has Canaanite roots, is strongly represented in the OT (cf. 1 Sam 4:4; 2 Sam 6:2; 1 Kgs 22:19; 2 Kgs 19:15; 1 Chr 13:6; Pss 9:8; 11:4; 47:9; 80:2; 99:1; 103:19; Isa 6:1; 37:16; 66:1; Jer 3:17; 14:21; Ezek 1:26; 10:1; Dan 3:55, etc.). In the NT this highest human concept is used to express the inexpressible. "Sitting at the right hand" of the Father is an expression used of Jesus (Mark 16:19; Eph 1:20; Heb 1:3; 8:1; 10:12; 12:2; cf. also Mark 10:37, 40 par. Matt 20:21, 23, etc.). The seat on the right as a place of honor signifies both the final fulfillment of messiahship in terms of Psalm 110 (a royal psalm; Jesus is not merely the one who sits on David's throne, but also lord of the world) and Jesus' final recognition as Christ (W. Grundmann, *TDNT* II, 39). In the eschaton the messianic king is enthroned together with his Church (Rev 3:21; 20:4) and in the final judgment destroys (Matt 19:28; 25:31) the place where the antichrist is enthroned (2 Thess 2:4). In the miracle of Pentecost (Acts 2:3) Christ's power is already revealed and *sits* (ἐκάθισεν) in the form of tongues on everyone in the Church and opens the eschatological era for those who open their hearts to him (cf. E. Schweizer, *TDNT* VI, 406, 410).

                                      F. Schröger

καθίημι *kathiēmi* lower, let down*

Act. in Luke 5:19 (διὰ τῶν κεράμων; cf. par. Mark 2:4); Acts 9:25 (διὰ τοῦ τείχους; cf. 2 Cor 11:33 (διὰ θυρίδος . . . διὰ τοῦ τείχους). Pass. in Acts 10:11 (ἐπὶ τῆς γῆς); 11:5 (ἐκ τοῦ οὐρανοῦ).

καθίστημι, καθιστάνω *kathistēmi, kathistanō* conduct; appoint; bring about*

1. Meanings and occurrences in the NT — 2. In juristic contexts — 3. In NT soteriology and Christology

Lit.: L. C. ALLEN, "Is 53,11 and its Echoes," *Vox Evangelica: Biblical and Historical Essays* (ed. R. P. Martin; 1962) 24-28. — E. BRANDENBURGER, *Adam und Christus. Exegetisch-religionsgeschichtliche Untersuchung zu Röm 5,12-21* (WMANT 7, 1962) 161f. — O. CULLMANN, *The Christology of the NT* (NTL, ²1963) 170-74. — J. D. M. DERRETT, *Law in the NT* (1970). — *idem*, " 'Eating Up the Houses of Widows': Jesus's Comment on Lawyers?" *NovT* 14 (1972) 1-9. — J. DE FRAINE, *Adam und seine Nachkommen. Der Begriff der 'Korporativen Persönlichkeit' in der Heiligen Schrift* (1962) 134-36, 215. — O. MICHEL, *Heb* (KEK, ⁷1975) 137-42, 217. — F. MUSSNER, *Jas* (HTKNT, 1964) 162-65. — A. OEPKE, *TDNT* III, 444-47. — J. M. WEDDERBURN, *Adam and Christ. An Investigation into the Background of 1 Cor 15 and Rom 5:12-21* (Diss. Cambridge, 1970/71). — S. WIBBING, *DNTT* I, 471f.

1. This vb. appears 21 times in the NT. The meanings *conduct; install; bring about,* which are attested in koine and the LXX (cf. Oepke), belong also to the content of the word in the NT (καθιστάνω = *conduct* only in Acts 17:15), although in the NT a legal and theological qualification and nuance are to be observed.

2. In the parables in Matt 24:45-51 par. Luke and Matt 25:14-30 par. Luke Jesus presupposes Palestinian legal customs regarding household and property management: It is customary for the master of the house to give authority to trustworthy δοῦλοι (= "members of the household"; cf. Derrett, *Law* 19) over parts of his own property; thus according to Matt 24:45-51 he appoints a member of the household to watch over the household (in Luke 12:42 the one appointed is an οἰκονόμος; on the tasks of the "son of the house" cf. *b. Šeb.* 48b). Authority can be misused (on "eats and drinks" as a t.t. for misappropriation of goods cf. Derrett, "Eating" 4), but when it is used appropriately it can also be extended to a wider authority (Matt 24:47; on the origin of the expression and on the subject cf. Acts 7:10). In Matt 25:21, 23 καθίστημι is used of the partnership of the members of the household in the administration of the property for the purpose of earning a profit (cf. Derrett, *Law* 17-31). In Luke 12:14; Acts 7:27, 35 a person's authority to judge is rejected. In Acts 6:3; Titus 1:5 καθίστημι is used of installation in Church office. In Heb 5:1; 7:28; 8:3 it is used of the high priest's cultic and legal authority (cf. 3:1: the high priest as ἀπόστολος).

3. The juridical sense is also decisive for the understanding of καθίστημι in Jas 3:6; 4:4; 2 Pet 1:8; Rom 5:19. According to James that a person belongs to the κόσμος and possesses eschatological hostility toward God is demonstrated, indeed fulfilled, in human ἀδικία. According to 2 Pet 1:8 the confirmation of election and calling constitutes the eschatological judgment for the believer, so that one is not ineffective and unfruitful, but stands in the knowledge of the Lord.

In Rom 5:19 Paul refers to the eschatological judicial act of installation in the realm of righteousness or of sin: In Christ's all-encompassing obedience, which determines all destiny, God establishes his eschatological righteousness as a judicial verdict that will restore for the πολλοί—the believers, the members of Christ—the relationship to this righteousness. In retrospect, according to Paul, it becomes apparent—with the acceptance of the corporate ἄνθρωπος doctrine—that Adam's disobedience has established the unrighteousness of humankind. This judicial act of καθίστημι, which eschatologically determines and divides history, has a christological basis in that the person and destiny of Christ are both comprehended in the eschatological καθίστημι of God (cf. καθίστημι in the interpretations of Psalms 2, 8, and 110 in Heb 2:6-10; 5:1-10; 7:21-28). The eschatological legal expression in the word καθίστημι is derived in both Hebrews and Paul from the presupposed mystery of the fate and dignity of the Son of Man (cf. Michel 138; Cullmann 170-74).   J.-A. Bühner

καθό *katho* as; to the degree that, insofar as*

Rom 8:26: καθὸ δεῖ, *"as we ought";* in designating measurement: *to the extent that,* 2 Cor 8:12a; similarly v. 12b; 1 Pet 4:13.

καθόλου *katholou* completely, altogether*

Acts 4:18: τὸ καθόλου μὴ φθέγγεσθαι, "not to speak *at all."* Cf. BDF §399.3.

καθοπλίζω *kathoplizō* equip, fortify with arms; mid.: arm oneself*

Luke 11:21: ὁ ἰσχυρὸς καθωπλισμένος, "the strong man, *fully armed/with his weapons."*

καθοράω *kathoraō* consider, perceive*

Rom 1:20, in a wordplay: τὰ γὰρ ἀόρατα . . . νοούμενα καθορᾶται, since the beginning of creation one can grasp "[God's] invisible nature in his works and *have them before one's own eyes."* Perception of the world as God's work is a possibility made available also to the Gentiles, to whom the self-revealing God makes himself known. Καθοράω in the wordplay denotes physical perception and also "(in)sight" into God's essential nature through observation of his works. The concern is not only with "spiritual perception" (against W. Michaelis, *TDNT* V, 379-81; see also U. Wilckens, *Rom* [EKKNT] I, ad loc.).

καθότι *kathoti* because; insofar as*

With the meaning *because* in Luke 1:7; 19:9; Acts 2:24; 17:31; with the meaning *insofar as, to the same degree as* in Acts 2:45; 4:35 (both καθότι ἄν τις χρείαν εἶχεν)

καθώς *kathōs* as

1. Occurrences — 2. Meaning — 3. Major usage

Lit.: BAGD s.v. — J. A. FITZMYER, "The Use of Explicit OT Quotations in Qumran Literature and in the NT," in *Essays on the Semitic Background of the NT* (1971) 3-58, esp. 7-16. — B. M. METZGER, "The Formulas Introducing Quotations of Scripture in the NT and the Mishnah," *idem, Historical and Literary Studies* (1968) 52-63.

1. Καθώς is used *ca.* 280 times in the LXX and 180 times in the NT. It appears esp. frequently in the Johannine literature (31 times in John), though not at all in Revelation or in James or Jude. In the Pastorals καθώς appears only once, though it is commonly used in Paul's

letters (18 occurrences in Romans [including 9:13; 10:15, where B has καθάπερ, though καθώς has the about same level of textual attestation, e.g., 𝔭[46]], 19 in 1 Corinthians, 12 in 2 Corinthians, and 13 in 1 Thessalonians). Καθὼς καί, which bears the same meaning as καθώς alone, is esp. preferred in Ephesians and 1 Thessalonians (with each having 6 of the 15 NT uses of the combination). Καθὼς γέγραπται is found 23 times, of which 12 are in Romans (→ γραφή 3, 4).

2. Καθώς sometimes functions as a comparative particle (1 Thess 4:13; 1 John 3:12), but most often as a subordinating conj. (cf. BDF §453), where the most important function is also comparison. Καθώς can therefore be translated *(just) as* and *so far, just as* (4:33; Acts 11:29). It also has the causal meaning *insofar as* (Rom 1:28; cf. BAGD) and at least once (Acts 7:17) it has a temporal meaning *(as soon as).*

3. Although NT use of καθώς is very diverse, two major features are to be seen. One is in connection with the language of OT promise and NT fulfillment and the other in analogies involving God, Christ, and the disciples.

a) The first usage is attested in the Evangelists, Hebrews, and esp. in Paul. Καθώς serves either direct comparison with an event involving an OT person such as Jonah (Luke 11:30), Noah (17:26), Lot (17:28), Moses (John 3:14; Heb 8:5), Abraham (Gal 3:6), Cain (1 John 3:12), or "the fathers" (John 6:58) or serves as a part of various introductory formulas for OT citations. The most important introductory citation with καθώς is καθὼς γέγραπται (besides Romans also in Matt 26:24; Mark 1:2; 9:13; 14:21; Luke 2:23; Acts 7:42; 15:15; 1 Cor 1:31; 2:9; 2 Cor 8:15; 9:9; cf. John 6:31; 12:14). Καθώς is used in reference to the OT also in Luke 1:55, 70; 2:20; 5:14; John 1:23; 7:38; Acts 7:44, 48; Rom 9:29; 1 Cor 14:34; 2 Cor 6:16; Heb 3:7; 4:3, 7; 5:6. These formulas in the NT emphasize the agreement of the NT event and its proclamation with the word of God contained in the OT. In wording they have their points of correspondence already in the Hebrew OT, in the Qumran writings, and in the rabbinic literature.

b) In the subject God-Christ-disciples καθώς is used esp. in the Johannine literature (cf. Eph 4:32). Καθώς here describes the agreement between Father and Son (John 5:30; 8:28; 12:50; 14:31; 17:2) and between Jesus and his disciples (13:15, 34; 15:12; 17:14, 16; 1 John 2:6, 27; 3:3, 7, 23; 4:17; cf. 2 John 4:6) and in analogies involving both relationships (John 6:57; 10:15; 15:9, 10; 17:11, 18, 21, 22; 20:21; cf. 17:23).   W. Radl

καθώσπερ *kathōsper* just as*

Heb 5:4: καθώσπερ καί (TR καθάπερ καί), *"just as also /as also";* 2 Cor 3:18 v.l.

καί *kai* and; also; even

1. Occurrences in the NT — 2. Usage of καί — 3. Usage of καὶ . . . καί — 4. Καί = *also, even*

Lit.: BAGD s.v. — BEYER, *Syntax* 29-72. — BDF §442. — J. BLOMQVIST, *Das sogenannte kai adversativum* (SGU 13, 1979). — P. FIEDLER, *Die Formel "und siehe" im NT* (SANT 20, 1969) 9-26. — KÜHNER, *Grammatik* II/2, 253-56. — A. LAURENTIN, "*We' attah—Kai nun.* Formule caractéristique des textes juridiques et liturgiques (à propos de Jean 17,5)," *Bib* 45 (1964) 168-97, 413, 432. — MAYSER, *Grammatik* II/3, 140-45. — MORGENTHALER, *Statistik* 164ff. — A. VINCENT, "El valor atenuado de διό καί (= 'por eso en cierto modo') dentro y fuera del NT," *EstBib* 32 (1973) 57-76. — VKGNT II, ad loc.

1. Καί is used "much more commonly [in the NT] than in literary Gk." (BAGD). With 9,164 occurrences, it is, after ὁ, the most frequently occurring particle in the NT and three times more frequent than the next particle in frequency (δέ). Καί's percentage of the total number of words in the individual writings ranges generally from 4% to 7%. Outside of this range are Galatians with 3.3%, Matthew with 9.8%, and Revelation with 11.5%. In the Pauline letters καί represents only 3.3 to 4.7% of the total number of words in Romans, 1 Corinthians, 2 Corinthians, and Galatians. In the other letters, however, it represents about 5.5 to 7%; cf. also Luke (7.6%), Acts (6.2%), John (5.6%), and 1–3 John (6.1%).

2. Καί most often serves as a conj.—corresponding to *and*—to link similar parts of sentences or clauses. This coordination can also take place with πολλοί followed by an attributive: e.g., John 20:30: πολλὰ καὶ ἄλλα σημεῖα, "many other signs."

The unusually frequent use of καί to link statements in a narrative (e.g., Matt 7:25-27; 9:9-11; on Acts 13:17-22 cf. BDF §442), which is very different from classical Greek usage, is to be explained by the proximity to colloquial speech or the influence of Aramaic, or perhaps by the prevailing taste of the time. Even parenthetical material is sometimes introduced with καί (John 2:9; Rom 1:13; 2 Pet 1:18).

In regard to individual structures of words and sentences simple coordination with καί has in the NT clearly gained ground over other forms of coordination and subordination. Out of faithfulness to the style of the original it should be more strongly considered than is usual that there is a difference between the tendency and intention of a statement, which one can elucidate by interpreting and translating, and its linguistic form, which at many points in the NT would undoubtedly have appeared defective to the exacting reader of the Greek language—to the same degree as the tr. *and* seems to the careful reader of English. But there are still cases in which tr. of καί with *and* is misleading or inexplicable. For that reason in what follows the empirically ascertainable tendencies of

usage of καί are assembled and must be examined individually to see whether they are sufficiently rendered with *and* or to avoid misleading the reader must be translated with *and* along with another coordinating conj. or by some altogether different coordinating or subordinating conj.

a) Καί in place of a temporal conj.: e.g., Mark 15:25: "it was the third hour *and* . . . ," in the sense of "as . . ."; esp. with ἐγένετο with a time reference and καί following: e.g., Acts 5:7: "there was an interval of about three hours/ it was three hours *until* . . . ," i.e., "after three hours."

b) Καί in place of a rel. pron.: e.g., Mark 2:15: "there were many, *and* they followed him," i.e., ". . . who followed him."

c) Καί in place of a linking construction with ὅτι, a partc., or an inf. with acc.: e.g., Rev 6:12: "*and* I saw, *and* an earthquake took place," e.g., ". . . that an earthquake was occurring."

d) Καί with a result, equivalent to *and so/and then* (in place of a dependent clause with *that/so that*): e.g., Matt 5:15, 25; 8:9; particularly often with the fut. after an imv.: e.g., John 1:39: "come, *(and) so/then* you will see"; this is in accord with classical usage or—more probably—done under Semitic influence (cf. Beyer 252).

e) Καί with a purpose: e.g., Matt 26:53: "I can ask my Father *and* he will . . . ," in the sense of ". . . that/in order that he. . . ."

f) Καί with the main clause after a preceding dependent clause, "due primarily to Hebrew" (BDF §442.7): e.g., ὅτε . . . καί, "as . . . *then.*"

g) Καί connecting a pair of words in place of some other constructions: e.g., Acts 23:6: ἐλπὶς καὶ ἀνάστασις, "hope *for* resurrection"; Luke 6:48: ἔσκαψεν καὶ ἐβάθυνεν, "he dug *(and* thus made it) deep."

h) Καί linking a question "when the questioner takes up the word of another with astonishment" (Kühner 247): Mark 10:26: καὶ τίς in the sense of "who then"; cf. Luke 1:43; 10:29; John 9:36; 14:22.

i) Καί not for linking something new, but for deepening, explaining, or completing what has been said already, in the sense of *indeed/namely*, or in combination with οὗτος: e.g., Luke 8:41: "*indeed* he was . . ."; John 1:20: "he made a confession . . . , *indeed* he confessed. . . ."

j) Καί in an adversative relationship meaning *but/and yet* or *although:* e.g., Matt 5:29; 10:20. Matt 18:21 probably also belongs here: "How often shall my brother sin against me *and nevertheless* I forgive him?" (*contra* Blass and Debrunner, *Grammatik* [Germ. original, [14]1976] §442n.14).

As already in classical Greek (cf. Kühner 291), καί can stand instead of the usual οὐδέ/μηδέ, transferring a preceding negation to a second or third member: e.g., Matt 5:25; 7:6, etc.: μήποτε . . . καί; John 12:40: ἵνα μὴ . . . καὶ . . . καί; esp. Eph 5:3ff.

3. Καὶ . . . καί most often emphasizes the additional and the special character of the combination, as in (emphatic) *and* or *both . . . and* (e.g., Matt 8:27; 10:28). The special aspect can lie also in the contrast of terms or clauses, as in *on the one hand . . . on the other hand/and yet* (e.g., John 15:24; Acts 23:3); this is esp. clear where one of the pair has οὐ (καὶ οὐ . . . καί or καὶ . . . καὶ οὐ: e.g., John 17:25; Luke 5:36; οὔτε . . . καί appears in place of καὶ οὐ . . . καί in John 4:11 and 3 John 10).

4. Καί was originally an added adv., normally with a strengthening or intensifying function, corresponding to Eng. *also/even*. This usage continued and is esp. frequent before personal and demonstrative prons., often with crasis, e.g. κἀγώ and κἀκεῖνος. Other examples are Matt 5:46: οὐχὶ καί, "not even"; John 5:25: καὶ νῦν ἐστιν, "*and* is already here"; before comparatives in Matt 11:9; John 14:12; but also after interrogatives as an intensifier, e.g., 1 Cor 15:29: τί καί, "why *then*"; and after rel. prons. confirming the preceding thought: ὃς καί, "who *also*"; cf. Acts 1:11; 13:22.

In dependence on classical usage where numbers are involved, καί occasionally crosses over into an alternating function: e.g., 2 Cor 13:1, "of two, *even* (= up to/or) three witnesses"; without numbers also in Matt 12:37; 20:23, etc. J. Jeremias, *Unbekannte Jesusworte* (³1963) 55n.25, associates this function of καί with Semitic *wᵉ* = "respectively, or" (with examples).

Διὸ καί means "therefore *to a certain degree*" (cf. Vincent. On use of καί with other particles → s.v.

K.-H. Pridik

Καϊάφας, α *Kaïaphas* Caiaphas*

Lit.: E. BAMMEL, *RGG* III, 1091. — *idem*, "Die Bruderfolge im Hohenpriestertum der herodianisch-römischen Zeit," *ZDPV* 70 (1954) 147-53. — BILLERBECK I, 985. — D. R. CATCHPOLE, *The Trial of Jesus* (1971) 168-72. — A. DAUER, *Die Passionsgeschichte im Johannesevangelium* (1972) 66-99. — J. JEREMIAS, *Jerusalem in the Time of Jesus* (1969) 194-98. — S. J. KATZ, *Encyclopaedia Judaica* (1928-34) IX, 354f. — T. LOHMANN, *BHH* 918f. — REICKE, *NT Era* 143-45. — G. SCHRENK, *TDNT* III, 265-83, esp. 270f. — SCHÜRER, *History* II, 216, 230. — E. M. SMALLWOOD, "High Priests and Politics in Roman Palestine," *JTS* 13 (1962) 14-34. — E. STAUFFER, *Jerusalem und Rom* (1957) 67-70. — M. STERN, "The Province of Judea," *The Jewish People in the First Century* (Compendia 1, ed. S. Safrai and M. Stern) I (1974) 308-76, esp. 349f., 353. — A. WIKENHAUSER, *LTK* V, 1242. — P. WINTER, *On the Trial of Jesus* (1961) 31-43.

Joseph Caiaphas (Aram. *qaiiāpa'*, which can mean "interpreter, seer" or "inquisitor"; the NT uses only the surname [9 times]; also *m. Para* 3:5; *t. Yebam.* 1:1) was installed in the office of → ἀρχιερεύς (Josephus *Ant.* xviii.35) by the Roman procurator Valerius Gratus in A.D. 18. The office was, as a rule, conferred annually by the Romans. But as a skillful political tactician, Caiaphas was able through his subservience (and later apparently also through payments to Pilate) to hold the office nineteen years. His removal by the legate Vitellius in A.D. 37 (*Ant.* xviii.95) certainly had more than just a temporal connection with Pilate's removal from office.

As high priest Caiaphas presided over the → συνέδριον when it turned Jesus over to Pilate. However, while Mark speaks only of the ἀρχιερεύς (14:47, 53f., 60, 63, 66), Matt 26:3, 57 historicizes, appending the name. John does the same thing five times and thus has Caiaphas play the decisive role in a preliminary meeting with a diplomatic counsel based on considerations of expediency (11:49; 18:14), which may be a typical description of his character given in anecdotal form. But the interrogation of the imprisoned Jesus in John 18:19-24 is ascribed to the former high priest → Ἄννας (2), and Caiaphas is only briefly mentioned. When only v. 13 calls Annas the father-in-law of Caiaphas, this may represent nothing more than John's tendency to characterize types of associated groups through kinship.

Luke 3:2 and Acts 4:6 subordinate Caiaphas to Annas and falsely regard Annas as the official high priest (temporal ἐπί with gen. taken over from Mark 2:26) during the time of the Baptist's activity as well as the period of the early Church. These Lukan texts are perhaps dependent on the Johannine tradition. In Luke 22:50, 54 the anaphoric art. can only refer to Annas. Luke has entirely omitted the high priest from the trial of the Sanhedrin. A harmonizing attempt at an explanation, which suggests that a former high priest held the title and that the influence of Annas must have been great because one of his sons held the office before Caiaphas and four more after him, cannot solve the literary contradictions of the late postapostolic period.

The later references to Caiaphas in *Gos. Eb.* 3; *Gos. Naz.* 33; *Acts Pet.* 8; *Acts Thom.* 32; *Ps.-Clem. Rec.* i.44-71 are dependent on the Gospels.   W. Schenk

καίγε *kaige* at least; even; really

In the NT only as v.l.: Luke 19:42: *at least;* Acts 2:18: *and even;* 17:27: *really* (in Acts in place of καί γε).

Κάϊν *Kaïn* Cain*

Transliteration of the Hebrew name *qayin,* the son of Adam and Eve (Gen 4:1). According to Heb 11:4 Abel offered a better sacrifice than Cain; 1 John 3:12 mentions Cain as his younger brother's murderer; according to Jude 11 the life of the heretics and false teachers corresponds to "the way of Cain": Cain is represented as the epitome of the apostate. K. G. Kuhn, *TDNT* I, 6-8; → Ἄβελ.

Καϊνάμ *Kaïnam* Kenan*

A personal name appearing twice in Jesus' genealogy according to Luke, in 3:36 for the son of Arphaxad (only LXX: Gen 10:24; 11:12f.), in 3:37 as the transliteration of the Hebrew name *qênān*, son of Enosh (Gen 5:9).

καινός, 3 *kainos* new*
ἀνακαινίζω *anakainizō* renew*
ἀνακαινόω *anakainoō* renew*
ἀνακαίνωσις, εως, ἡ *anakainōsis* renewal*
καινότης, ητος, ἡ *kainotēs* newness; new nature*

1. Occurrences in the NT — 2. Meanings in common speech — 3. Wisdom sayings regarding Old and New — 4. The new covenant — 5. The new creation in Paul — 6. Καινότης — 7. The new person in Ephesians — 8. The eschatological new creation in Revelation — 9. The new commandment — 10. Compounds

Lit.: J. BAUMGARTEN, *Paulus und die Apokalyptik* (WMANT 44, 1975), esp. 163ff. — J. BEHM, *TDNT* III, 447-54. — H. HAARBECK, H.-G. LINK, and C. BROWN, *DNTT* II, 670-74. — F. HAHN, " 'Siehe, jetzt ist der Tag des Heils.' Neuschöpfung und Versöhnung nach 2. Kor. 5,14–6,2," *EvT* 33 (1973) 244-53. — R. A. HARRISVILLE, "The Concept of Newness in the NT," *JBL* 74 (1955) 69-79. — U. LUZ, "Der alte und der neue Bund bei Paulus und im Hebräerbrief," *EvT* 27 (1967) 316-36. — G. SCHNEIDER, "Die Idee der Neuschöpfung beim Apostel Paulus und ihr religionsgeschichtlicher Hintergrund," *TTZ* 68 (1959) 257-70. — idem, *Neuschöpfung oder Wiederkehr? Eine Untersuchung zum Geschichtsbild der Bibel* (1961). — H. SCHWANTES, *Schöpfung der Endzeit* (AzT I/12, 1963) 26-31. — E. STEGEMANN, "Alt und Neu bei Paulus und in den Deuteropaulinen (Kol-Eph)," *EvT* 37 (1977) 508-36. — P. STUHLMACHER, "Erwägungen zum ontologischen Charakter der καινὴ κτίσις bei Paulus," *EvT* 27 (1967) 1-35. — For further bibliography see *TWNT* X, 1126.

1. The adj. καινός appears 38 times in the NT: 5 times in Mark, 4 times in Matthew, 3 times in Luke, 8 times in Revelation, and in John 13:34; 19:41; Acts 17:19, 21; 1 Cor 11:25; 2 Cor 3:6; 5:17; Gal 6:15; Eph 2:15; 4:24; Heb 8:8, 13; 9:15; 1 John 2:7, 8; 2 John 5; and 2 Pet 3:13 (bis). The noun καινότης appears in Rom 6:4; 7:6.

2. The meaning *new* in the sense of *unused/recently made available* is seen in the texts concerning Jesus' burial: Joseph of Arimathea had prepared a *new* tomb in the rock, which he made available for Jesus' body (Matt 27:60; John 19:41). The powerful teaching of Jesus is described (Mark 1:27) as new in the sense of *previously unknown:* He leaves the impression of a new teacher of the law but with his power over demons he surpasses the capability of the scribes (vv. 21ff.). Also *previously unknown*, indeed *strange* to the Athenians, is Paul's "*new* teaching" at the Areopagus (Acts 17:19). Here there is no specific contrast to an old teaching; rather, the listeners demonstrate a special interest in new things (Acts 17:21: only use in the NT of the comparative).

In the inauthentic ending of Mark it is promised to the disciples who are sent out that special capabilities will be given to those who come to faith, among them, speaking in tongues, which is described as "speaking in *new* tongues" (Mark 16:17). This ability was analogous to early Christian glossolalia, but is given here the characteristic of newness.

At the conclusion of the parables in Matthew Jesus compares every scribe who is well instructed in matters relating to the kingdom to a master of the house "who takes out of his treasure what is new and what is old" (13:52). Tradition and new teaching are here placed alongside each other in a synthetic manner.

3. Jesus answers the question of the people (Mark 2:18; according to 9:14 it is asked by John's disciples) about why his disciples do not fast with two proverbial wisdom sayings: "No one sews a piece of unshrunk cloth on an old garment; if he does the patch tears away from it, the *new* from the old, and a worse tear is made" (Mark 2:21). Luke 5:36 takes over this figure and alters it by adjusting it to reality: Tearing the new patch is not the basic problem; it is rather the fact that the new and the old do not match. In Mark 2:22 and Luke 5:37-39 as in Matt 9:17 a related figure is that of new wine in old vs. new wineskins. In the antithesis "old-*new*" the wine is new (οἶνον νέον) and the wineskins are "old" (παλαιός) or *new* (καινός). Thus a bit of folk wisdom is taken up (cf. Josh 9:13): one puts new (= fresh) wine in *new* skins.

With this metaphor Jesus associates fasting, by means of the old garment and the old wineskins, with the past era. At the same time the incompatibility of the new and the old is established and metaphorically demonstrated by reference to two instances from ordinary life. The interpretation is to be made by the audience. Fasting is reserved for when Jesus is absent from his people (Matt 9:15; according to Mark 2:20, "on that day"). Thus fasting is an expression of sorrow in the time of the bridegroom's absence.

4. The oldest reference to the idea of the "*new* covenant" is found in the saying over the cup in the tradition of the Last Supper reported by Paul: "This cup is the *new* covenant in my blood" (1 Cor 11:25). Already the pre-Pauline tradition (for more detail on the layering of the text see G. Bornkamm, "Lord's Supper and Church in Paul," *idem, Early Christian Experience* [1969] 123-60) had interpreted the event of the cross as the ratification of a covenant in which the one who drinks from the cup is included in the covenant. There is thus an actualization of Jer 31:31 (LXX 38:31: διαθήκη καινή) within the horizon of the theology of the cross. Participation in the Lord's Supper is also a continuing proclamation of the

death of the Kyrios—until his return (11:26). In the time between the cross and Christ's return the Church's celebration of the meal establishes the brotherhood of the new covenant.

For Paul the meaning of the new covenant was not in that it annulled or replaced the Sinai covenant, but in that it brought it to full force with special dignity: From 2 Cor 3:6 ("he has made us competent to be ministers of the *new* covenant, not of the letter, but of the Spirit. . .") and from the t.t. *"new* covenant" it cannot be concluded that the "old" covenant is abrogated. Through the story of Jesus of Nazareth God demonstrates his covenant, which has not been cancelled. The history of the covenant experiences its eschatological expansion through inclusion of the peoples of the world in Israel's story of election and promise (Rom 9–11). In the event of the covenant that involves Israel and the peoples of the world God announces his gift to humankind. For Paul this *pro nobis* of God has taken on a new quality in Jesus Christ and finds its ultimate meaning in the cross. Corresponding to it is the one people of God, which is the Israel of God as a consequence of the call into God's liberating future, which is opened through the cross and resurrection.

The Synoptic Lord's Supper texts report the saying over the cup in varied ways: Mark 14:24 par. Matt 26:28 maintains the unity of the covenant ("the blood of the covenant"). Secondary textual variants also, like the cup saying in the Lukan version (Luke 2:20), have the t.t. *"new* covenant" (Marcion, however, eliminates καινή in Luke 22:20!). Mark and Matthew understand the Lord's Supper as the anticipation of the eschatological banquet: The full community with the founder is then given when he drinks the wine *anew* in the kingdom of God (Mark 14:25 par.). According to Mark and Matthew full fellowship with the Lord awaits the new table fellowship in the kingdom of God, while Luke already has the newness of the covenant, whose fulfillment in the kingdom of God lies yet in the future (Luke 22:16: the reference to the new drinking is omitted here entirely!).

Hebrews contrasts the new covenant with the old under a christological perspective: Christ as high priest is mediator of a better covenant (8:6: κρείττονός ἐστιν διαθήκης μεσίτης), which is "established on better promises." The author places himself fully in the tradition of Jeremiah 31 (Heb 8:8), which he sees fulfilled in Christ as high priest: Because the first covenant was not blameless, a second was needed (8:7). With the reference to the "new covenant" Jeremiah declared the first one obsolete (Heb 8:13: πεπαλαίωκεν). Just as the first part of the tent is a parable for the present time (9:9), the contents of the first covenant are oriented to the earthly world (9:1). And just as Christ, the high priest of the coming good things, "has entered through the greater and more perfect tent" (9:11) into the sanctuary and has brought about a once-

for-all, perfect sacrifice of redemption, he is the mediator of a new and better covenant: Through the death of Christ "the transgressions under the first covenant" receive expiation; at the same time "those who are called receive the promise of the eternal inheritance" (9:15) as an eschatological promise of the mediator of the new covenant.

5. The motif of the καινὴ κτίσις (like the phrase itself) appears in the NT only in 2 Cor 5:17 and Gal 6:15 (on the following, cf. Baumgarten 163-70 and the literature cited above). Deutero- and trito-Isaianic traditions (Isa 42:9; 43:19; 48:6; 65:17; 66:22) were taken up into late Israelite apocalyptic literature (*Jub.* 4:26; *1 Enoch* 72:1; *4 Ezra* 7:75; *2 Bar.* 32:6; 44:12; 1QS 4:25) and comprise the tradition from which Paul took over the motif—directly or indirectly.

Over against the obvious cosmological and futuristic-eschatological associations (so Stuhlmacher, et al.) the Pauline interpretation of this motif is determined by the context: reconciliation based on christology provides the major idea of 2 Cor 5:14-21; therefore, εἴ τις ἐν Χριστῷ, καινὴ κτίσις. The statement about the new creation is in the present (v. 17a) or perfect (v. 17b) tense, describing the individual member of the body of Christ. The major motifs are the presence and universality of salvation within the framework of the idea of God's reconciling work (Baumgarten 169f.). The inclusive statement about Jesus' vicarious atonement on the cross (v. 14c) implies that no power any longer belongs to the evil one (v. 17b). In relation to the crucified and resurrected one and his body—the Church—salvation as "new creation" is already a reality (cf. 1 Cor 10:11; 2 Cor 6:2). The reconciliation of the world—an anthropological, not cosmological-universal, concept (world = humankind)—is the concern of the God who acts to bring salvation. "The ministry of reconciliation" or of righteousness (2 Cor 3:9) and the preaching of "the word of reconciliation" as a consequence of the reconciliation at the cross are entrusted to the one who has been apprehended by the new creation. The promise of peace and mercy (Gal 6:16) is also given to that person.

6. The noun **καινότης**—as often where Semitic adjectives are represented—occurs in the NT only in Rom 6:4 and 7:6 (cf. on the following G. Bornkamm, "Baptism and New Life in Paul [Romans 6]," *Early Christian Experience* [1969] 71-86; E. Käsemann, *Rom* [Eng. tr., 1980] ad loc.): The newness of life stands in antithesis to pre-Christian life. Through baptism Christians are buried with Christ, i.e., transferred to him, as they also —on the basis of the resurrection of Christ—will walk in a new life. This possibility and reality of new life have already begun for Christians with Christ's resurrection, but nevertheless stand under the eschatological reservation of the not-yet. Thus the apostle distinguishes between

Jesus' resurrection, which has occurred already, and the expectation of the resurrection of believers in the future. In one's conduct and in the *nova oboedientia* (6:12-23) the resurrection is, however, already anticipated, and its power is already a present reality. "The freedom of Christians from the power of the Torah" (Käsemann 190) is involved.

The antithesis of καινότης and παλαιότης (Rom 7:6; cf. 2:29; 2 Cor 3:6) elucidates the resulting change of the aeons and is a summary of Romans 7 and 8: Service "in the *new life* of the Spirit, not [= no longer] in the old life of the letter" overcomes the power of the law in practical existence (for more detail see Käsemann 190f.; *idem*, The Spirit and the Letter," *idem, Perspectives on Paul* [1971] 138-66, esp. 146f.).

7. Ephesians uses the term *"new* person" in both christological (2:15) and anthropological (4:24) senses: In and through Christ a new person came into existence, in which both parts (of the people of God)—Jews and Gentiles—became a unity, and "the dividing wall of hostility" (2:14) was broken down. He overcame Jewish legalism, reconciled the hostility between Jew and Gentile, and created reconciliation with God through the cross. Christ brings peace as good news among humankind and at the same time brings peace with God through free "access in one Spirit to the Father" (2:18).

The parenesis corresponds to the christological perspective (4:17): The Church must put off the former Gentile conduct, the "old person," as a garment and put on the new person, "who is created in the likeness of God in true righteousness and holiness" (4:24). This alteration of the traditional figure of changing clothing (cf. 1 Cor 15:53; 2 Cor 5:2ff.; Gal 3:27; Rom 13:12, 14) is likewise a consequence of the renewal in the inner being through the Spirit (4:23; cf. also 2:1-10) as an act of the individual (4:25ff.).

8. The eschatological new creation spoken of in Revelation is—taking up elements of OT, late Israelite, and early Christian apocalyptic—anticipated theocentrically, universally, and in the imminent future. Central to this universal-cosmological eschatology is the statement of the enthroned world ruler: "Behold, I make all things *new*" (21:5). The temporal proximity of the imminent eruption of cosmological changes (1:1, 3; 3:11; 22:6, 7, 10, 12) is thus universal: These are described, within the framework of Revelation's three-level view of the world, as a *"new* heaven" and a *"new* earth" (21:1).

The figure of the new heaven and new earth (cf. Isa 65:17; 66:22), which is derived from the OT, can in fact be the expectation of the majority, as in the case of 2 Pet 3:13. The goal of this eschatological creation theology is the inner association of creation and salvation, redemption as the consummation of creation and the universal sovereignty of the world ruler, whose power reaches not only mankind but everything in creation (on the ethical consequences cf. E. Grässer, *WPKG* 68 [1979] 98-114, esp. 105). The conceptual framework is formed by the tradition of the "day of Yahweh," in which the coming of the Messiah stands at the center, a coming that proceeds with cosmic changes involving the destruction of the old elements through fire (2 Pet 3:10, 12), and (a) new heaven(s) and a new earth are created *ex nihilo* in a second act of creation in analogy to the first (Rev 21:1). The newness is understood especially as a reversal of earthly relationships (21:4; 2 Pet 3:13).

At the center of the vision is—again in dependence on the OT "day of the Lord" traditions and in association with the concept of the heavenly archetype—the expectation of the holy city, the *"new* Jerusalem," coming down from God out of the new heaven (Rev 3:12; 21:2; cf. 4 Ezra 7:26; 10:54; 13:36; rabbinic texts in Billerbeck III, 796), beautiful as a bride going to her wedding (the description of the new Jerusalem follows in Rev 21:9–22:5). The new Jerusalem also receives from God a *"new* name" (3:12; cf. Isa 62:2), as does the holy one (Rev 3:7, 12). Those who overcome and become citizens of the new heaven and new earth (2:17; 19:12), indeed the pillars in the temple (3:12), also receive new names.

In the eschatological praise *"new* songs" are sung before the lamb and before the throne (5:9; 14:3; cf. Pss 144:9; 147:7; 149:1): Before the opening of the book with the seven seals the four creatures and the twenty-four elders fall down before the lamb and sing a *"new* song of praise" (5:9f.) in honor of the lamb. In a similar scene —this time on Mount Zion—the 144,000 "firstborn" are distinguished by the fact that they can learn a *"new* song" and that they pay homage to the enthroned with their song (14:3).

9. At the beginning of the Johannine farewell discourse (numerous exegetes speak of a "postscript") Jesus formulates his bequest: "A *new* commandment I give to you" (John 13:34; cf. 15:12, 17). The content is of course not new. He commands neither love of neighbor (Lev 19:18) nor love of enemy (Matt 5:44) but brotherly love (cf. 1 Thess 4:9) in analogy to his love for his disciples (cf. → ἀγάπη 3.d). Love for one another will in the future be the distinguishing characteristic of discipleship (13:35). Jesus' friends should stand with him in a relationship analogous to his relationship to the Father (keeping the commandments and abiding in love): "If you keep my commandments, you will remain in my love" (15:10). Thus the *"new* commandment" is not new in the sense of being previously unknown or nonexistent, but is "the law of the eschatological community, for which the attribute 'new' denotes not an historical characteristic, but its essential nature. The command of love, which is grounded

in the love of the Revealer received by the disciples, is 'new' in so far as it is a phenomenon of the new world which Jesus has brought into being" (R. Bultmann, *John* [Eng. tr., 1971] 527).

1 and 2 John stand entirely in the light of John's Gospel, but do not allow the *new* of the commandment of brotherly love to remain isolated: Over against false teachers 1 John 2:7—and then also 2 John 5—clearly indicate that a new phenomenon of spiritual history is involved. In reality the old commandment is the matter of concern. It has existed from the beginning (cf. also 1 John 3:11) and its author is God himself (3:23; 4:21; 2 John 4). Nevertheless the commandment is new as "an eschatological reality" (R. Bultmann, *1–3 John* [Hermeneia, 1973] on 1 John 2:7). Against the background of darkness-light dualism in 1 John and the coordination of hatred for the brother with darkness and brotherly love with light, the new commandment—coordinated with the light—can renew and strengthen the old one (2:8-11).

10. The compound forms of the word do not, as a rule, have the theological profile of the adj. or of the noun. Ἀνακαινίζειν (εἰς μετάνοιαν) appears in the NT only in Heb 6:6, there with the sense of *renew, restore* (of those who have fallen away) or "*bring once more* to repentance." A second repentance, a repeated beginning leading to expiation, is not possible.

In 2 Cor 4:16 ἀνακαινόω refers—in antithesis to the destruction of the ἔξω ἄνθρωπος—to the daily renewal of the ἔσω ἄνθρωπος through the Spirit of God. Col 3:10 uses the same vb. of the new person, whom Christians have "put on" (→ 7) as those who are *renewed* to the knowledge of their likeness with the Creator.

Ἀνακαίνωσις appears only in Rom 12:2 and Titus 3:5. "Do not be conformed to this world but be transformed in renewed thinking" (Rom 12:2, the tr. in E. Käsemann, *Rom* [Eng. tr., 1980] ad loc.). Thus, as a consequence of baptism (cf. Gal 2:20), one lives "in terms of the new birth and with a new orientation" (*ibid.* 330); i.e., what is involved is the *renewal* of the power of critical judgment in view of the will of God. Titus 3:5 accents the existential reality of the salvation and *renewal* through the Holy Spirit that has taken place in baptism.

J. Baumgarten

καινότης, ητος, ἡ *kainotēs* newness
→ καινός.

καίπερ *kaiper* although, even if*

In the NT always followed by a partc. to form a concessive clause: Phil 3:4; Heb 5:8; 7:5; 12:17; 2 Pet 1:12; Rev 17:8 v.l.; see also BDF §425.1; F. Scheidweiler, *Hermes* 83 (1955) 220-30.

καιρός, οῦ, ὁ *kairos* time; period of time, moment; opportunity

1. Occurrences in the NT — 2. Related words and synonyms — 3. Paul — 4. The deutero-Paulines — 5. The Synoptics — 6. Acts — 7. John — 8. The Pastorals — 9. Hebrews — 10. 1 Peter — 11. Revelation

Lit.: J. BARR, *Biblical Words for Time* (SBT 33, 1962). — J. BAUMGARTEN, *Paulus und die Apokalyptik* (WMANT 44, 1975) 180-97, 209-13, 221ff. — G. DELLING, *TDNT* III, 455-65. — F. HAHN, " 'Siehe, jetzt ist der Tag des Heils'. Neuschöpfung und Versöhnung nach 2. Kor. 5,14– 6,2," *EvT* 33 (1973) 244-53. — H. C. HAHN, *DNTT* III, 833-39. — A. LINDEMANN, *Die Aufhebung der Zeit. Geschichtsverständnis und Eschatologie im Epheserbrief* (SNT, 1975). — U. LUZ, *Das Geschichtsverständnis des Paulus* (BEvT 49, 1968). — For further bibliography see Baumgarten 180n.1; *DNTT* III, 849f.; *TWNT* X, 1126f.

1. Καιρός appears 85 times in the NT: 5 times in Mark, 10 in Matthew, 13 in Luke, 3 in John, 9 in Acts, 17 in the undisputed Pauline letters, 6 in the deutero-Pauline letters 2 Thessalonians, Ephesians, and Colossians, 7 in the Pastorals, 4 each in Hebrews and 1 Peter, and 7 in Revelation (including 3 times in 12:14).

2. Καιρός in the sense of *point in time, moment, instant* is reflected in the derivatives εὐκαιρέω (Mark 6:31; Acts 17:21; 1 Cor 16:12), εὐκαιρία (Matt 26:16; Luke 22:6), εὔκαιρος (Mark 6:21; Heb 4:16), εὐκαίρως (Mark 6:31 v.l.; 14:11; 2 Tim 4:2), ἀκαίρως (2 Tim 4:2), and πρόσκαιρος (Mark 4:17; Matt 13:21; 2 Cor 4:18; Heb 11:25). More frequently καιρός itself appears in connection with "day" terminology (at that *time* = on that day) and in agreement with and distinction from χρόνος(-οι), αἰών(-ες) and, in John, ὥρα.

3. In Paul's letters (Rom 3:26; 5:6; 8:18; 9:9; 11:5; 12:11 v.l.; 13:11; 1 Cor 4:5; 7:5, 29; 2 Cor 6:2 bis; 8:14; Gal 4:10; 6:9, 10; 1 Thess 2:17; 5:1) καιρός belongs together with χρόνος and αἰών in the Pauline word field for "time." Καιρός and χρόνος are used partially as synonyms, esp. where the "statement of a specific duration of time of human life in the calendrical sense" (Baumgarten 187) is involved. But χρόνος designates a "period of time" in the linear sense, while καιρός frequently refers to "eschatologically filled time, time for decision." At the same time Paul takes over traditional formulas that speak of the aeons (ὁ αἰὼν οὗτος appears 7 times). In contrast to the deutero-Pauline letters (Eph 1:21; 2:7), Paul does not use the term "this aeon" for what stands over against "that aeon" or "the aeon to come" (see Baumgarten 181-89 for details). Paul avoids the demonstrative pron. when speaking of the *present time* (except in the citation of Gen 18:10, 14 in Rom 9:9) and says instead ὁ νῦν καιρός ("the now existing time": Rom 3:26; 8:18; 11:5; 2 Cor 8:14).

In Paul καιρός has a wide spectrum of meaning: In Rom 5:6 a past moment in time is spoken of. In Rom 9:9; 1 Cor 7:5; 1 Thess 2:17; and Gal 6:10 an indefinite *period of time* is referred to. Gal 4:10 refers to *beginnings of the seasons* (H. Schlier, *Gal* [HTKNT] ad loc.) or to *feasts* (Delling 461).

The special Pauline accent in the understanding of καιρός is where "the eschatological time that began with the sending of Christ" (W.-G. Kümmel in H. Lietzmann, *1-2 Cor* [HNT] 205) is indicated. In 2 Cor 5:14–6:2 Paul says that in the activity of "the word of reconciliation" the OT word from Isa 49:8 is fulfilled and made effective. Therefore the apostle explicitly emphasizes: "Behold, now is the acceptable *time*, behold, now is the day of salvation" (6:2; cf. F. Hahn 252f.).

1 Cor 7:29 offers a statement of early Christian prophecy: ὁ καιρὸς συνεσταλμένος ἐστίν. Καιρός refers to the time remaining until the parousia and the judgment. The time remaining is "condensed," "shortened," "pressed," thus "short." "Behind this statement stands the motif of the shortened final period of affliction before the divine judgment and/or the motif of the amputation of time" (Baumgarten 222). In a similar way the Church's knowledge of the time is illustrated through the "eschatological call to watchfulness." Salvation (σωτηρία) is nearer for the Church than it was previously when the Church came to faith: *Time* here is "extraordinarily relevant eschatological time," in that future-eschatological events are paraenetically anticipated. The connection of the future moment of judgment—which for the Church is oriented toward salvation—with eschatologically relevant time until the parousia, time rich in opportunity, is offered in Gal 6:9f. As long as time exists, every moment is "the decisive moment," in which sides must be taken (Rom 12:11 v.l.; cf. E. Käsemann, *Rom* 346).

For Paul, then, καιρός refers also to "the coming moment of judgment and/or parousia" (1 Cor 4:5; Gal 6:9; 1 Thess 5:1; cf. Gal 4:10, the only use of the pl., here synonymous with χρόνος). It is noteworthy that Paul does not use phrases like ὁ καιρὸς ἐγγύς (ἐστιν) or ἤγγικεν (→ 5).

Where Paul provides the basis for argument he consistently confirms that the καιρός of parousia and judgment limits the time of salvation, which has arrived in the Christ event, as a time of decision (cf. esp. 1 Cor 10:11). To that extent the present καιρός is also "the time of the worldwide body of Christ and of the Gentile mission" (Käsemann, *Versuche* I, 100). "The christologically and soteriologically filled present time [is] the middle and key of time, toward which history flows and from which it comes" (Baumgarten 193). Alongside the christological middle of time comes the (traditional) theocentric dimension: The future is the time of the work of God. The Pauline understanding of time culminates in the interpretation of "the future determined by the present" and "the present determined by the future": The future is thus a) time of the work of God, b) limited time, and c) time opened for the confirmation of the faith of the Church of Jesus Christ (see Baumgarten 195f.).

4. In the deutero-Pauline letters (2 Thess 2:6; Eph 1:10; 2:12; 5:16; 6:18; Col 4:5) some of the variants of meaning in the Pauline understanding of καιρός are taken over: 2 Thess 2:6 refers to the parousia as his (the Lord's) time on "the day of the Lord" (v. 2). The historical epoch of time before the Christ event is described in Ephesians as a time without hope and without God (2:12) for the Gentiles. Just as Gal 4:4 refers to the time when Jesus was sent as the πλήρωμα τοῦ χρόνου, Eph 1:10 uses πλήρωμα τῶν καιρῶν: The fullness of the eschatologically relevant time is given. This understanding corresponds to the idea of the present as a *time* of testing (Eph 5:16). "Buy up *the time*" (Col 4:5)—so the corresponding admonition to employ every possibility of using the remaining time. In comparison, the use of καιρός in Eph 6:18 is not specific: The author encourages the Church to pray "at all *times* in the Spirit," to be persistent in watchfulness and intercession.

5. In the Synoptics the general meaning *every time* appears rarely (Luke 21:36). More frequent is "at that *time*" in redactional transitions connecting the material that follows with what precedes without the connection being precise or historically reliable (Matt 11:25; 12:1; 14:1; cf. also Luke 13:1).

Καιρός is used also as a designation of "harvest *times*" (Matt 13:30: wheat; Mark 11:13: figs; Mark 12:2 par.; Matt 21:34, 41: fruit) and "*times* of the day" (Matt 24:45; Luke 12:42: "at the *right* time" = mealtime).

The proclamation of John the Baptist's birth (Luke 1:20) refers to an indefinite *moment* in the future. So also the reference to the moment when the devil renewed his temptation (Luke 4:13: ἄχρι καιροῦ). Thus the brevity of the time and the moment can be accented (Luke 8:13: seed without root).

A bridge to the eschatological meaning of καιρός is provided by texts in which a specific *period of time* is spoken of: The lament over Jerusalem is based on the fact that the city did not know the *time* of its "visitation" (Luke 19:44; cf. 1 Pet 2:12). In contrast to Mark 14:12ff. par., where the question of locale ("where is my guest lodging?") stands at the center, Matt 26:18 has: "The master says: my *time* is near (ὁ καιρός μου ἐγγύς ἐστιν)": a reference to the Passover meal as opening the *time* of Jesus' Passion.

Closely associated in tradition history is καιρός with eschatological expectations. In the context of encouragement to watchfulness Mark gives the reason: You do not know πότε ὁ καιρός ἐστιν (13:33), affirming the unknown, unforeseeable *moment* of Jesus' parousia. The Markan report (1:14f.) summarizes the proclamation of Jesus: The καιρός is fulfilled in the proclamation in Mark's time: "*Now* the βασιλεία τοῦ θεοῦ is immediately at the door. . . . It is obvious what the evangelist means by it: the Parousia" (W. Marxsen, *Mark the Evangelist* [1969] 133), an imminent but not yet occurring event, which demands "repentance" and "faith" in the gospel.

In Luke the eschatological time of persecution and horror prior to the actual time of salvation can be understood as an eschatological timetable (21:9: πρῶτον; vv. 10-28: τότε 4 times; cf. 1 Cor 15:20-28). As the καιροὶ ἐθνῶν they precede the essential kairos (21:24; cf. vv. 27f.: the parousia of the Son of Man and the ἀπολύτρωσις). The false prophets who appear during this time will proclaim that the καιρός (21:8; secondary addition of Luke, so Bultmann, *History* 327). Luke, however, affirms—in accord with his view of history—that the τέλος has not yet come. This background gives urgency to the demand for watchfulness (v. 36). Correspondingly Luke has Jesus ask the crowd why they do not know how to interpret "this *time*" (12:56) of conflict and hostility that Jesus brings and the signs of the time (cf. the textually uncertain addition in Matt 16:3).

The redactional final stage seen in Mark 10:30 par. has the detailed expansion of the hundredfold reward: ". . . now in this *time* houses and brothers . . . with persecutions and in the coming age eternal life." Behind this saying is undoubtedly the doctrine of the two ages. The present time, which is contrasted to the coming aeon, is described as "this *time*" of persecution and suffering. The reward of eternal life is reserved for the future world-age of the kingdom of God.

6. Acts 14:17 uses the pl. (καιροὺς καρποφόρους) in the sense of "fruitful *seasons of the year.* Καιρός is also used with the demonstrative pron. as a loose redactional link for indicating a *point in time* (12:1; 19:23) and to denote a *point in time* in the past (7:20: birth of Moses), an unknown future *time* (13:11: the lifting of the blindness of Barjesus) or a future *favorable moment* or *opportunity* (24:25). The theocentric determination of the καιροί as *historical epochs* for peoples and states is seen particularly in the Areopagus speech (17:26). The theocentric quality of the time characterizes the reservation given by the resurrected one: "It is not for you to know χρόνους ἢ καιρούς that the Father has placed in his own power" (1:7: on the synonyms χρόνοι and καιροί cf. Wis 8:8; Dan 2:21; 1 Thess 5:1). But the times are not simply ambivalent, but are oriented to salvation: times of refreshing (3:20: parousia) before the ἀποκατάστασις πάντων (3:21, unique in the NT).

7. In John καιρός appears infrequently. Jesus says to his brothers: "My *time* is not yet here, but your *time* is

always here" (7:6) and "My *time* has not yet been fulfilled" (v. 8). In the not-yet of the καιρός the not-yet of Jesus' suffering stands in the foreground. However, the imminent *time* of suffering will become at the same time the eschatologically filled time of the final revelation (a major motif in John is → ὥρα). "Your καιρός" is thus all times, while Jesus' works, which are eschatological acts, summon forth in each moment acts of decision and thus place one in the *time* of decision (see R. Bultmann, *John* [Eng. tr., 1971] 292f. for details). John 5:4 is a secondary gloss.

8. The occurrences of καιρός in the Pastoral Epistles are focussed on the eschatological meaning of καιροί (5 of 7 occurrences are pl.): The death of Jesus as ransom for all is the testimony for "proper *times*" (1 Tim 2:6: καιροῖς ἰδίοις) in the sense of an indefinite eschatological future: "a term referring to the history of salvation, a phrase which originally meant the time determined by God in the promises" (M. Dibelius and H. Conzelmann, *The Pastoral Epistles* [Hermeneia] 43; cf. 1 Cor 15:20, 23; Rom 8:23). Terminologically identical is the *moment* of the epiphany of Jesus Christ, which is indefinite as to its point in time, although its actual certainty is attested (1 Tim 6:15). Ἐν ὑστέραις καιροῖς (1 Tim 4:1) refers to the indefinite future during the time of the apostasy before the consummation (cf. 2 Tim 3:1: "troublesome times" [καιροὶ χαλεποί]). The warning that a *time* (sg.) will come when people will not endure sound teaching (2 Tim 4:3) also refers to the καιρός of the apostasy. Therefore Timothy should always (at opportune and inopportune times) stand up for the word. 2 Tim 4:6 refers to the *moment* of the death of the author of the epistle.

In the prescript of Titus (1:2f.) the author describes his theocentric view of time and history: the revelation of his word to his time (καιροῖς ἰδίοις) in the epoch of the activity of the apostle (ἐν κηρύγματι) corresponds to the protological promise (πρὸ χρόνων αἰωνίων) of eternal life. The time of revelation is at the same time the time of confirmation in the apostolic task.

9. According to Heb 9:9f. the two tents (or parts of the tent) symbolize the present time and future time (= the time of a better order). The author sees the Church as living in the tension between the two aeons. The present is the time of sacrifice, the future, the new aeon, is characterized by the adoration of God in the heavenly sanctuary (cf. O. Michel, *Heb* [KEK] ad loc.).

The remaining occurrences in Hebrews refer to the untimely "power of procreation" (Michel 396), which Abraham, with Sarah, received "despite their *time* of life" (11:11), and to the "*opportunity* to return" (Michel 400) to the earthly fatherland, which the patriarchs would have had if the idea had occurred to them (11:15).

10. In 1 Peter καιρός appears exclusively in the eschatologically defined sense: The author assumes that the Spirit of Christ was already present (and hidden) in the prophets as they looked into the future to the time of the suffering of Christ and the subsequent doxa (cf. 1:9), which was promised, expected, and examined by them, but was only revealed to the witnesses alive in the author's day (1:11f.). The hope of Christians thus rests on the salvation (σωτηρία) that is completely revealed in the eschaton (1:5: ἐν καιρῷ ἐσχάτῳ). The present stands under the seriousness of the beginning of God's judgment (τὸ κρίμα, only here in 1 Peter; κρίνειν, however, in 1:17; 2:23; 4:5f.). Its beginning in the present comprises the essential καιρός. It begins with the Church (4:17). Corresponding to this earnesness in the parenesis is present lowliness and humility. For the obedient God causes it to be followed by exaltation at the right time (5:6: ἐν καιρῷ; the v.l. ἐπισκοπῆς is probably a secondary addition in dependence on 2:12).

11. The consistent apocalyptic character of Revelation is verified by the use of καιρός. Thus Revelation takes up the motif of the three and one-half *times* (12:14: καιρὸν καὶ καιροὺς καὶ ἥμισυ καιροῦ, citation of Dan 12:7 LXX or 7:25 LXX/Θ? cf. also Rev 11:2; 12:6; further texts in Baumgarten 186n.33) and the image of the battle with the dragon, which continues only a "short *time*" (12:12) in the final drama. The essential eschatological framework is provided by the announcement at the beginning and the end: ὁ (γὰρ) καιρὸς ἐγγύς (ἐστιν) (1:3; 22:10): The eschatological *time* is near. Revelation offers the interpretation of this καιρός throughout the book. It is to be seen concretely in the doxology of the twenty-four elders (11:17f.): God's wrath will bring judgment (ὁ καιρὸς τῶν νεκρῶν) within the context of the world ruler's sovereignty and the conflict with the enflamed wrath of the peoples. The prophets, the saints, and those who fear God's name will receive a "reward," while the rest will be delivered over to destruction.   J. Baumgarten

Καῖσαρ, αρος, ὁ *Kaisar* Caesar, (Roman) emperor*

Lit.: BAGD s.v. — A. VAN DEN BORN, *BL* 907f. — K. CHRIST, *LTK* V, 635-38. — H. DESSAU, *Geschichte der römischen Kaiserzeit* (2 vols., 1924-30). — M. DIBELIUS, "Rom und die Christen im ersten Jahrhundert," *idem, Botschaft* II, 177-228. — O. ECK, *Urgemeinde und Imperium* (1940). — H. GRUNDMANN, *RGG* III, 1059f. — M. HENGEL, *Christ and Power* (1977). — G. HERZOG-HAUSER, PW Suppl. IV (1924) 806-53. — G. KITTEL, *Christus und Imperator* (1939). — LEIPOLDT/GRUNDMANN I, 13-67, 127-42. — E. LOHMEYER, *Christuskult und Kaiserkult* (1919). — A. VON PREMERSTEIN, *Vom Werden und Wesen des Prinzipats* (ABAW 15, 1937). — REICKE, *NT Era* 225-317. — A. ROSENBERG, PW IX (1914) 1139-54. — W. SCHRAGE, *Die Christen und

der Staat nach dem NT* (1971). — E. STAUFFER, *Christ and the Caesars* (1956). — H. VOLKMANN, *KP* II, 1110-12; IV, 1135-40.

On Luke 2:1; 3:1: H. DIECKMANN, "Kaisernamen und Kaiserbezeichnung bei Lukas," *ZTK* 43 (1919) 213-34. — idem, "Das fünfzehnte Jahr des Caesar Tiberius," *Bib* 6 (1925) 63-67. — H. FLENDER, *St. Luke, Theologian of Redemptive History* (1967) 57-59. — H. W. HOEHNER, "Chronological Aspects of the Life of Christ," *BSac* 130 (1973) 338-51. — H. U. INSTINSKY, *Das Jahr der Geburt Christi* (1957).

On John 19: E. BAMMEL, "Φίλος τοῦ Καίσαρος," *TLZ* 77 (1952) 205-10. — J. BLINZLER, *Der Prozeß Jesu* (⁴1969) 265, 337f. — A. DAUER, *Die Passionsgeschichte im Johannesevangelium* (SANT 30, 1972).

On Paul's Appeal to Caesar in Acts: H. J. CADBURY, "Roman Law and the Trial of Paul," *Beginnings* V, 297-338. — J. DAUVILLIER, "À propos de la venue de saint Paul à Rome," *Bulletin de Littérature Ecclésiastique* (Toulouse) 61 (1950) 3-26. — G. LOMBARDI, "Motivi giuridici dell' appello di Paolo a Cesare," *S. Paolo da Cesarea a Roma* (ed. B. Mariani; 1963) 9-20. — T. MOMMSEN, "Die Rechtsverhältnisse des Apostels Paulus," *ZNW* 2 (1901) 81-96. — W. RADL, *Paulus und Jesus im lukanischen Doppelwerk* (1975) 204-9, 325-45. — A. N. SHERWIN-WHITE, *Roman Society and Roman Law in the NT* (1963). — V. STOLLE, *Der Zeuge als Angeklagter* (BWANT 102, 1973) 40-55, 264-67.

Καῖσαρ appears 29 times in the NT. Except for Phil 4:22, it appears only in the Gospels (18 times) and Acts (10 times).

It appears 4 times in Mark, all in the pericope about paying taxes to Caesar (12:14, 16, 17 bis). The scene takes place at the time of Tiberius (A.D. 14-37). Jesus' answer recognizes the authority of the state, but relativizes this authority with the reference to the authority of God. Cf. R. Pesch, *Mark* [HTKNT] II, 224-29 (bibliography). Matthew and Luke take over the pericope with the 4 occurrences from Mark (Matt 22:17, 21 ter; Luke 20:22, 24, 25 bis). Luke makes a redactional reference to the scene when in 23:2 he concretizes the accusations that have been made against Jesus. He coordinates—likewise redactionally—the information about the birth of Jesus (2:1) with measures taken by the government of Caesar Augustus (30 B.C.-A.D. 14) and the appearance of the Baptist and Jesus (3:1) with the rule of Emperor Tiberius (A.D. 14-37) in order to express the worldwide meaning of the salvific events.

John uses Καῖσαρ 3 times, all in Jesus' trial before Pilate. Although the name is not given, Tiberius is the one who is meant. The Jews threaten Pilate when he considers setting Jesus free of the charge of being no "friend of *Caesar*" (19:12a); they play off the royal claim of Jesus against the authority of Caesar (19:12b) and intensify this conflict by saying that they recognize no king but Καῖσαρ (19:15), thus surrendering their own religious identity. "Friend of *Caesar*" probably designates goodwill, but is more likely a title (R. Schnackenburg, *John* III [Eng. tr., 1982] 262).

In Acts 17:7 Paul and his companions are charged by the Jews in Thessalonica with acting against Caesar's laws when they proclaim Jesus as messianic king. But Paul is not convicted. Luke thus indicates clearly that Christianity does not endanger the Roman state, and he lets Paul say explicitly before Festus in Caesarea in 25:8 that he has been guilty of nothing against the emperor. All of the other occurrences in Acts refer to Paul's appeal (→ ἐπικαλέω 2.b) to Caesar (25:10, 11, 12 bis, 21; 26:32; 27:24; 28:19). Nero was in office at this time (A.D. 54-68). Paul makes use of his right as a Roman citizen when he demands through *provocatio* (Stolle 266) to be judged directly before Caesar. For Luke it stands in the foreground that Paul was a witness to the gospel in Rome, the center of the world empire, and that this corresponds to the divine plan (27:24, δεῖ).

In Phil 4:22 Paul conveys greetings from a Christian group "of *Caesar's* household." This is probably a reference to slaves and freedmen in Ephesus at the time of Nero (J. Gnilka, *Phil* [HTKNT] 182).   A. Weiser

Καισάρεια, ας *Kaisareia* Caesarea*

1. Caesarea on the Sea (*Caesarea maritima*)

Lit.: M. AVI-YONAH, *EncJud* V, 6-13. — I. BENZINGER, PW III/1 (1897) 1291-94. — G. BÖING, *LTK* V, 1244. — A. FROVA, et al., *Scavi di Caesarea Maritima* (1965). — L. HAEFELI, *Caesarea am Meer* (NTAbh 10/5, 1923). — E. KUTSCH, *RGG* I, 1580f. — L. I. LEVINE, *Roman Caesarea* (1975). — B. LIFSHITZ, "Césarée de Palestine, son histoire et ses institutions," *ANRW* II/8 (1977) 490-518. — A. NEGEV, *EAEHL* I, 270-85 (bibliography on archaeology). — H. TREIDLER, *KP* III, 48f. — J. RINGEL, *Césarée de Palestine* (n.d.). — SCHÜRER, *History* II, 115-18.

A seaport city built by Herod the Great at Strato's Tower in honor of Caesar Augustus, Caesarea became the residence of the Roman procurator. After the death of Agrippa I (A.D. 44) it was the base for Roman troops. In the NT Caesarea is mentioned only in Acts, where its name appears 15 times: Philip went from Ashdod to Caesarea and proclaimed the gospel (8:40). In Caesarea (10:1, 24; 11:11) the first baptism of a Gentile took place as a result of divine instruction and arrangement. Luke depicts it as a programmatic event. Agrippa I dies in Caesarea during a public appearance (12:19; cf. Josephus *Ant.* xix.343-52). The remaining 10 occurrences concern Paul: When his life in Jerusalem is threatened, he flees beyond Caesarea to Tarsus (9:30). From the "second missionary journey" he returns to Antioch after going through Caesarea (18:22), where he visits the church. At the end of the "third missionary journey" he stays at Philip's house (21:8), where Agabus prophesies his imprisonment; then Christians from Caesarea accompany him to Jerusalem (v. 16). Acts 23:23, 33; 25:1, 4, 6, 13

mention Caesarea as the place where Paul was kept under Roman protective custody. Through the change of scene from Jerusalem to Caesarea Luke indicates the transition of the Pauline witness to Christ from the Jewish to the Gentile-Roman world, which has its goal in the imperial metropolis of Rome.

2. Caesarea Philippi

Lit.: M. AVI-YONAH, *EncJud* IV, 162f. — BAGD s.v. 1. — I. BENZINGER, PW III/1 (1897) 1290f. — A. VAN DEN BORN and W. BAIER, *BL* 281f. — KOPP, *Places* 231-35. — SCHÜRER, *History* II, 169-71.

A city at the northernmost source of the Jordan at the foot of the southern slope of Mt. Hermon. The settlement and region were originally called Πανιάς because of the sanctuary of Pan there. It was inhabited primarily by a non-Jewish population. Herod the Great erected a temple of Augustus there (Josephus *Ant.* xv.363; *B.J.* i.404) and his son Philip built a city there and named it Caesarea in honor of Caesar Tiberius. The city is thus called Καισάρεια ἡ Φιλίππου in Josephus and the NT. It is mentioned in Mark 8:27 and, in dependence on Mark, Matt 16:13 as the place near which Peter made the messianic confession concerning Jesus.   A. Weiser

καίτοι *kaitoi* although, and yet*

This conj. is used adversatively with a finite vb. in Acts 14:17 (v.l. καί τοι γε): *and yet;* cf. John 4:2 v.l.; Heb 4:3 with gen. absolute: *although;* cf. BDF §§425.1; 450.3.

καίτοιγε *kaitoige* although, to be sure*

In the NT only in the (redactional?) formulation of a parenthesis as a strengthening of καίτοι: John 4:2 (the only instance of γε in John): καίτοιγε Ἰησοῦς αὐτὸς οὐκ ἐβάπτιζεν, "*to be sure* Jesus himself did not baptize."

καίω *kaiō* kindle; burn; burn up*

There are 11 occurrences in the NT. Literal in Matt 5:15: *lighting* a lamp (the emphasis is not on the lighting but on the "burning" of the light); Luke 12:35, pass.: (continual) *burning;* λύχνοι καιόμενοι, "*burning* lamps"; cf. John 5:35; Rev 4:5: seven *burning* torches of fire; 8:8: a "fiery *burning* mountain" (πυρὶ καιόμενον); 8:10; 19:20: καιομένη ἐν θείῳ, "*burning* with sulphur" (cf. Gen 19:24); similarly Rev 21:8: καιομένη πυρὶ καὶ θείῳ; the phrase κεκαυμένῳ πυρί, "to a *blazing* fire," in Heb 12:18 is an allusion to Deut 4:11; 5:23. The pass. means *be burned down* in John 15:6 (of vines thrown into a fire); 1 Cor 13:3 v.l.: ἵνα καυθήσομαι, either voluntary martyrdom (execution by burning) or self-immolation as an ascetic achievement (see K. L. Schmidt, *TDNT* III, 464-67; BAGD s.v. 2; H. Conzelmann, *1 Cor* [Hermeneia] ad loc.). Fig. in Luke 24:32: "did not our hearts burn [within us]?" (καρδία . . . καιομένη).

κἀκεῖ *kakei* and there; there also*

Formed from καὶ ἐκεῖ through crasis. There are 10 occurrences in the NT: *and there* (Matt 5:23; 10:11; 28:10; Mark 1:35; 14:15 v.l.; John 11:54; Acts 14:7; 22:10; 25:20; 27:6); *there also* (Acts 17:13; Mark 1:38 v.l.).

κἀκεῖθεν *kakeithen* and from there, and then*

Formed by crasis from καὶ ἐκεῖθεν. There are 10 occurrences in the NT: of place (Mark 9:30; 10:1 v.l.; Luke 11:53; Acts 7:4; 14:26; 16:12; 20:15; 21:1; 27:4; 28:15); temporal: *and then* (Acts 13:21).

κἀκεῖνος, 3 *kakeinos* and/also that/this one

Formed from καὶ ἐκεῖνος by crasis. Expressing direct or immediate proximity: *and this (one)* (Matt 15:18; Mark 16:11, 13; John 7:29; 19:35 v.l.); after ταῦτα: *and that* (Matt 23:23 par. Luke 11:42); *this one also/he too* (Mark 12:4, 5; Luke 20:11; John 6:57; cf. 14:12: "*he* will *also* . . ."; 10:16; 17:24; 2 Tim 2:12; Heb 4:2; Matt 20:4 v.l.). To designate a greater distance: *and that* (Luke 11:7; 22:12; Acts 18:19); *that one also* (Acts 5:37; 15:11: "in the same way as *those also*"; Rom 11:23; 1 Cor 10:6).

κακία, ας, ἡ *kakia* wickedness, evil; burden*

1. Occurrences in the NT — 2. Matt 6:34 — 3. The concrete κακία of Simon Magus in Acts 8:22 — 4. Κακία as characteristic of non-Christian life

Lit.: → κακός.

1. The 11 occurrences of κακία in the NT are widely distributed; κακία is not a preferred word of any NT writing or group of writings. In the LXX it appears *ca.* 80 times as a tr. of *rāʿâ* and is not esp. frequent beyond that. Its NT usage does not reflect aspects of philosophical-ethical discussion (as in, e.g., Diogenes Laertius vii.92f.). Gnostic usage is in part very different (e.g., *Corp. Herm.* x.8: κακία δὲ ψυχῆς ἀγνωσία), in part very similar (e.g., *Corp. Herm.* vi.4: ὁ γὰρ κόσμος πλήρωμά ἐστι τῆς κακίας, ὁ δὲ θεὸς τοῦ ἀγαθοῦ).

2. Κακία was seldom used to mean "burden"; the instance in the Sermon on the Mount is unique in the NT. Matt 6:34 concludes the "didactic poem about anxiety" (W. Grundmann, *Matt* [THKNT] ad loc.) with a gnomic wisdom affirmation about one's daily *burden*.

3. Only in the disputed Simon Magus pericope does κακία refer to some specific action. It is historically clear from the Lukan narrative composition from what *evil*

Simon should turn away (Acts 8:22): He had wanted to purchase with money the power that the apostles had in transmitting the Holy pneuma by laying on of hands (v. 19).

4. As in Acts 8:22 κακία has a moral meaning in the remaining occurrences: It is (a) characteristic of non-Christian life. Inasmuch as no development can be seen from Paul to the deutero-Pauline letters and Pastorals to the Catholic Epistles, these occurrences can be brought together for examination. First κακία has—like its antonym ἀρετή—a very general and unspecific sense, which can be strengthened by πᾶσα (Rom 1:29; Eph 4:31; 1 Pet 2:1). This general sense is seen in 1 Cor 14:20; 1 Pet 2:16, where *wickedness* or *evil* (the tr. *burdens* should be avoided) refers to human, esp. Christian, wrong conduct, against which a warning is given in 1 Cor 5:8; Jas 1:21, where *wickedness* is mentioned alongside → πονηρία or ῥυπαρία, and in Rom 1:29; Col 3:8; Eph 4:31; Titus 3:3; 1 Pet 2:1, where κακία, *evil*, stands among other terms for morally reprehensible acts. As Rom 1:29 most clearly shows, human *evil* is a characteristic of existence before the justification sola gratia/sola fide, i.e., existence under God's wrath (cf. also 1 Cor 5:8; Titus 3:3). However, it is placed thematically under other concepts (as, e.g., → ἁμαρτία).

In every instance besides Rom 1:29 κακία is found in a parenetic context. The traditional combination with → ἀποτίθημι (*put off* in the fig. sense) in Col 3:8; Jas 1:21; 1 Pet 2:1 is noteworthy; these statements call for rejection of a behavior and are closely connected with contrasting positive exhortations: The axiomatic saying in 1 Pet 2:16 demonstrates "the effect of Pauline theology" (K. H. Schelkle, *1–2 Pet* [HTKNT] ad loc.). Christian (NT) existence and ethics are determined by ἐλευθερία; freedom as radical liberation from κακία leaves no room for evil to one's fellow human.

                                          M. Lattke

κακοήθεια, ας, ἡ *kakoētheia* malice; craftiness*

Rom 1:29, in the catalog of vices in vv. 29-31 with φθόνος, φόνος, ἔρις, and δόλος. The proximity to δόλος (immediately preceding) indicates that the meaning is understood best as *craftiness;* cf. Aristotle *Rh.* ii.13.1389b.20: ἔστι γὰρ κακοήθεια τὸ ἐπὶ τὸ χεῖρον ὑπολαμβάνειν πάντα; see also Philo *Som.* ii.192; Josephus *Ap.* i.222. Spicq, *Notes* I, 392f.

κακολογέω *kakologeō* speak evil of, revile*

Mark 7:10 par. Matt 15:4: ὁ κακολογῶν πατέρα ἢ μητέρα, in the rendering of the fourth commandment of the Decalogue and the OT law involving parents (citing Exod 21:16 LXX; cf. Prov 20:9a; see also Billerbeck I, 709-11); *speak evil* of Jesus (Mark 9:39), τὴν ὁδόν (Acts 19:9).

κακοπάθεια, ας, ἡ *kakopatheia* suffering; endurance of suffering, painful effort
Alternative form of → κακοπαθία.

κακοπαθέω *kakopatheō* suffer evil, endure suffering*

2 Tim 2:9; Jas 5:13: *endure evil;* 2 Tim 4:5; 2:3 v.l., of constant *endurance of* the *suffering* that necessarily comes to the proclaimer or the combatant for the sake of Christ. Spicq, *Notes* I, 394-96.

κακοπαθία, ας, ἡ *kakopathia* suffering; endurance of suffering, painful effort*

According to Jas 5:10 the prophets are a model of constant *endurance of suffering* and longsuffering (κακοπαθία καὶ μακροθυμία). The tr. "suffering, affliction" would likewise be possible (cf. Mal 1:13; 2 Macc 2:26f.; Jas 5:13), but the reference to the prophets (or Jewish martyrs) (cf. Matt 5:12; 23:29ff.; Heb 11:32ff.) and the association with μακροθυμία suggest rather readiness for suffering (cf. 4 Macc 9:8; Philo *Vit. Mos.* i.154). M. Dibelius and H. Greeven, *Jas* (Hermeneia) ad loc.; BAGD s.v.; Spicq, *Notes* I, 394-96.

κακοποιέω *kakopoieō* do evil, do wrong, cause harm*

There are 4 occurrences in the NT, always with the antonym → ἀγαθοποιέω or ἀγαθὸν ποιέω (Mark 3:4). The word is basically synonymous with κακὸν ποιέω/πράσσω (e.g., Matt 27:33; Acts 9:13; Rom 3:8; 13:4, etc.). Mark 3:4 par. Luke 6:9, in the narrative of the healing of a withered hand on the sabbath: To *do evil* (i.e., to spy on the healer or hinder the healing) cannot be the purpose of the sabbath; 1 Pet 3:17, in reference to wrong conduct in general; similarly 3 John 11. J. R. Michaels, *NTS* 13 (1966/67) 394-401.

κακοποιός, 2 *kakopoios* doing evil, criminal (adj.)*

In the NT only in 1 Pet (2:12, 14; 4:15; 3:16 v.l.; also John 18:30 v.l.), always subst.: *evildoer.* In 1 Pet 2:12, 14, it involves the contrast between doing good and doing evil, in v. 14 in a formulaic reference to the civil realm (cf. Rom 13:4), in v. 12 the charge against Christians as κακοποιοί. In 4:15 it appears in a catalog of vices with φονεύς, κλέπτης, and ἀλλοτριεπίσκοπος, probably in the general sense of *criminal, law breaker,* one who must rightly fear "suffering" from the authorities (cf. 3:16f.). In the situation of persecution reflected in 1 Peter, the word thus has a special meaning that goes beyond the general ethical connotation, inasmuch as Christians are indeed charged as κακοποιοί, reflecting the point of view

of society and the authorities (2:12; 3:16). J. B. Bauer, "Aut maleficus aut alieni speculator (1 Petr 4,15)," *BZ* 22 (1978) 109-15; L. Goppelt, *1 Pet* [KEK] 238f., 307f.

κακός, 3 *kakos* bad, evil*

1. Statistical and general information — 2. The Pauline letters — 3. The Gospels and Acts — 4. In other writings

Lit.: E. ACHILLES, *DNTT* I, 561-67. — J. BERNHART, *HTG* I, 184-97. — W. GRUNDMANN, *TDNT* III, 469-87. — H. HAAG, *Vor dem Bösen ratlos?* (1978). — G. HARDER, *TDNT* VI, 546-66. — W. OELMÜLLER, *Handbuch philosophischer Grundbegriffe, Studienausgabe* I (1973) 255-68. — For further bibliography → ἁμαρτία; see Haag, *DNTT* I, 567; *TDNT* X, 1127.

1. Almost half of the *ca.* 50 occurrences of κακός in the NT are in the Epistles of Paul, esp. Romans (15 occurrences). The rest are broadly distributed, as is the case with → κακία. Like the frequently used antonym → ἀγαθός, the adj. κακός is a word of common speech (as with corresponding words in other languages!) in which the tr. must vary (idiomatically) when the context or a special phrase requires it. Of the many compounds in Greek with κακός (cf. Pape, *Wörterbuch* I, 1299-1305; LSJ 861-64; *PGL* 694-96) only a few appear in the NT. Subst. use, esp. of neut. (τὸ κακόν, John 18:23; Rom 2:9; 7:21; 12:21 bis; 13:4 bis; 16:19; 1 Cor 13:5; 3 John 11; τὰ κακά, Luke 16:25; Rom 3:8; 1 Tim 6:10), is shaped by the same generality and indefiniteness seen in κακία. The NT is widely separated from the philosophical (cosmological or ethical) discussion of the problem Πόθεν τὰ κακά (Plotinus i.8 [51]; cf. also i.7 [54]: Περὶ τοῦ πρώτου ἀγαθοῦ).

2. Except in Col 3:5, where *evil* ἐπιθυμία are attacked in a catalog of vices, Pauline uses of κακός are all in the authentic Epistles. Κακός describes negatively ἐργάτης (Phil 3:2), ἔργον (Rom 13:3), and—in a citation from Menander—ὁμιλία (1 Cor 15:33, where χρηστός is the opposite of κακός). In Rom 14:20 κακός has the sense of *causing harm:* "It is *wrong* for one to eat" what is basically pure and "give offense" (opposite: καλόν; cf. BDF §223.3; BAGD s.v. διά). Elsewhere Paul uses only the neut. subst. with striking frequency, most often in the sg. Where he uses the pl. (Rom 1:30, in a vice catalog: → κακία; 3:8; 1 Cor 10:6), the sg. would likewise be possible (cf. LSJ 863 on the alteration in Plotinus, → 1); at any rate both τὸ κακόν and τὰ κακά can be translated *the evil.*

In ethical-parenetic texts Paul combines κακός with a vb. of doing, i.e., ποιέω (Rom 3:8; 13:4a; 2 Cor 13:7), κατεργάζομαι (Rom 2:9), or πράσσω (Rom 7:19; 13:4b). If the mention of κακός is noteworthy almost everywhere in the context, Rom 9:11 and 2 Cor 5:10 must also be mentioned. Here πράσσω ἀγαθόν or φαῦλον (the v.l. κακόν in both passages is well attested!) describes the sum of human conduct. The positive contrast to ἀγαθόν is also explicitly shown where Paul polemicizes against the law of recompense (Rom 12:17, 21; 1 Thess 5:15). The appeal in Rom 16:19 is strongly reminiscent of 1 Cor 14:20 (→ κακία 4). Evil is also incompatible with love (Rom 13:10; 1 Cor 13:5). Κακός in Rom 7:19 (opposite: ἀγαθόν) and 7:21 (opposite: καλόν) is of great theological significance. For Paul the origin of evil is sin (→ ἁμαρτία 4.a) as a historical-cosmic power. But sin is provoked by the law (→ νόμος).

3. Paronomasia like κακοὺς κακῶς ἀπολέσει in Matt 21:41, the parable of the wicked vinedressers, is very common (cf. BDF §488.1a; BAGD 785; Pape, Wörterbuch I, 1303). In the parable in Matt 24:45-51 par. Luke 12:42-46, which is derived from Q, only Matt 24:48 uses κακός in the eschatological disqualification of the servant's misconduct. Human wicked conduct, which is enumerated in a list as πάντα ταῦτα τὰ πονηρά, and which defiles people, originating from their inner person, is designated in its totality as διαλογισμοὶ οἱ κακοί, "evil thoughts" (Mark 7:21). Τὰ κακά is used in Luke 16:25 (cf. Acts 8:24 D) of the lifelong misery of Lazarus, in contrast to the luxurious good fortune (τὰ ἀγαθά) of the rich man. The occurrence of κακός in the Passion narrative is interesting. While in John 18:30 (cf. v. 23, → κακῶς) Jesus is accused by the Jews as an evildoer (κακὸν ποιῶν, yet note v. 1!), in the Synoptics Pilate asks (Matt 27:23/Mark 15:14/Luke 23:22) what Jesus has done that is criminal and worthy of condemnation (τί γὰρ κακὸν ἐποίησεν;).

Forensic use is also present in Acts 23:9, when the scribes as a party within the Sanhedrin cannot charge Paul with any evil. He had done (ἐποίησεν, 9:13) much evil to the saints in Jerusalem. Whereas κακὸν πάσχω (28:5) means suffer harm, in 16:28 πράσσω ἑαυτῷ κακόν refers to suicide.

4. The aphorism in 1 Tim 6:10, "the love of money is the root of all evil," is not specifically Christian (cf. M. Dibelius and H. Conzelmann, The Pastoral Epistles [Hermeneia] ad loc.). In Titus 1:12 the Cretans, among others, are characterized with a citation from Epimenides as beasts (κακὰ θηρία). The nature of the evils (κακά) done by Alexander according to 2 Tim 4:14 cannot be determined from the context. The reference in Rev 2:2 to the "evil creatures" is similarly vague, making any identification difficult (H. Kraft, Rev [HNT] ad loc.). Ps 34:13-17 is stamped by the contrast between good and evil; the citation in 1 Pet 3:10-12 is reminiscent of Paul's earlier exhortation (Rom 12:17; 1 Thess 5:15), in which he rejected the practice of returning evil for evil (1 Pet 3:9). 3 John 11 also speaks against evil and for the good. The expression διάκρισις καλοῦ καὶ κακοῦ in Heb 5:14 is

certainly dependent on Gen 2:17 (γινώσκειν καλὸν καὶ πονηρόν); here also the sum of human possibilities for behavior may be in mind (as in Rom 9:11 and 2 Cor 5:10, → 2). In Rev 16:2 κακός is pleonastic—with → πονηρός —included in a mixed citation from the LXX; a nuance in meaning is, however, scarcely noticeable. Among other characteristics Jas 3:8 calls the tongue "restless evil" (BAGD s.v.). In 1:13 the gen. pl. is to be understood as neut.: God cannot be tempted by evil.   M. Lattke

κακοῦργος, 2 kakourgos criminal (adj.); subst.: evildoer, criminal*

There are 4 occurrences in the NT, all subst.: Luke 23:32, 33, 39, of the two criminals crucified with Jesus; 2 Tim 2:9, of "Paul," who sits in prison "like a criminal." In contrast to → κακοποιός, κακοῦργος has an unambiguously criminal sense. Spicq, Notes I, 397-99.

κακουχέω kakoucheō torture, mistreat*

In the NT only as pass. partc.: Heb 11:37, with ὑστερούμενοι and θλιβόμενοι in the description of the suffering of the pious Jews; 13:3, of those who are illtreated (parallel to οἱ δέσμιοι), whose suffering everyone can sympathize with in his or her own σῶμα.

κακόω kakoō do evil, mistreat; make angry*

There are 6 occurrences in the NT: do evil (Acts 7:6, 19; 12:1; 18:10; 1 Pet 3:13, opposite ἀγαθοῦ ζηλωταί); make angry/provoke (Acts 14:2: ἐπήγειραν καὶ ἐκάκωσαν).

κακῶς kakōs badly, evilly*

1. The Synoptics — 2. With vbs. of speaking, John 18:23; Acts 23:5 — 3. Κακῶς αἰτέομαι, Jas 4:3

Lit.: → κακός.

1. This adv. appears in many idiomatic phrases (cf. Pape, Wörterbuch I, 1303; LSJ 863). In the Synoptics it appears most frequently (4 times each in Matthew and Mark, twice in Luke) in the expression κακῶς ἔχω, be sick (BAGD s.v.). Use of this expression in healing stories, as with other terms for sickness (Matt 4:24; Mark 1:32, 34 par. Matt 8:16; Mark 6:55 par. Matt 14:35; Luke 7:2), does not indicate any precise medical knowledge. In the wisdom "saying about the physician" (R. Pesch, Mark [HTKNT] I, ad loc.) in Mark 2:17 par. Matt 9:12/Luke 5:31, κακῶς ἔχοντες, like the antonym ἰσχύοντες, has a fig. meaning. Two other phrases are more concrete: Whereas the daughter of the Canaanite woman in Matt 15:22 is "severely possessed by a

demon" (κακῶς δαιμονίζεται), the epileptic in 17:15 "suffers *terribly*" (κακῶς πάσχει, though the original text may be κακῶς ἔχει—so ℵ B L Θ). On the paronomasia in Matt 21:41 → κακός 3.

2. Jesus' statement before Annas in John 18:23, εἰ κακῶς ἐλάλησα (opposite: εἰ δὲ καλῶς), is to be understood neither on the basis of κακόν in the same verse nor just from the narrow context, but on the basis of the entire Johannine accusation (at the trial). Κακῶς εἶπον in the ironically employed LXX citation (Exod 22:27) placed in Paul's mouth in his speech before the Sanhedrin in Acts 23:5 is more idiomatic. Like the parallel κακολογέω (*qālal* piel; otherwise translated κακῶς εἶπον or, most often, καταράομαι) it means *curse* and is the tr. of *'ārar* (elsewhere most often translated with καταράομαι or ἐπικατάρατος).

3. The meaning of "ask *badly*" in Jas 4:3 (on the synonymity of αἰτέομαι with αἰτέω cf. M. Dibelius, *Jas* [Hermeneia] ad loc.) is explained from the immediate context, where the fault in "not receiving" is blamed on "desires" (→ ἡδονή), which, according to 4:1, "are used in a pejorative sense" (F. Mussner, *Jas* [HTKNT] ad loc.). They become the cause (πόθεν!) of disputes within the Church(es).

M. Lattke

κάκωσις, εως, ἡ *kakōsis* mistreatment, affliction*

Acts 7:34 (citing Exod 3:7), of the *mistreatment* of the people of God in Egypt (with στεναγμός).

καλάμη, ης, ἡ *kalamē* stalk of grain, reed, straw*

1 Cor 3:12, with χόρτος and ξύλα as "building materials" that last only for a short time, an image for that which is worthless (opposite χρυσόν, ἄργυρον . . .) because it is only what remains after the harvesting of what is valuable (the grain; cf. Homer *Od.* xiv.214). Paul does not use the image to describe the usefulness of the building materials, but to show the descent from what is valuable and lasting to what has no value. See also Billerbeck III, 334f.

κάλαμος, ου, ὁ *kalamos* reed, stalk; reed pen*

There are 12 occurrences in the NT: the *reed* swaying in the wind (an image for instability, Matt 11:7 par. Luke 7:24; cf. 1 Kgs 14:15); κάλαμος συντετριμμένος, "a broken *reed*" (Matt 12:20; probably not a reference to the broken stalk as a sign of the judgment of death, but as an image for weakness, *contra* W. Zimmerli, *TDNT* V, 669; cf. Isa 42:3 LXX); *reed* (Mark 15:19 par. Matt 27:30; Mark 15:36 par. Matt 27:29); *reed pen* (3 John 13: διὰ

μέλανος καὶ καλάμου); *measuring reed* (Rev 11:1: κάλαμος ὅμοιος ῥάβδῳ; 21:15: μέτρον κάλαμον χρυσοῦν; v. 16; cf. Ezek 40:3).

καλέω *kaleō* call, invite; appoint
κλῆσις, εως, ἡ *klēsis* call (noun), summons
κλητός, 3 *klētos* called

1. Occurrences of the word group in the NT — 2. Meaning and usage — 3. Καλέω — a) Call, invite — b) Name, be named — c) Jesus as the one who calls — 4. Καλέω, κλῆσις, and κλητός as technical terms for the divine call — a) Paul — b) The deutero-Paulines — c) 1 Peter, 2 Peter/Jude — d) Hebrews and Revelation

Lit.: F. AGNEW, "Vocatio primorum discipulorum in traditione synoptica," *VD* 46 (1968) 129-47. — W. BIEDER, *Die Berufung im NT* (1961). — L. COENEN, *DNTT* I, 271-76. — I. DAUMOSER, *Berufung und Erwählung bei den Synoptikern* (1954). — H. GIESEN, "Berufung nach dem NT," *Theologie der Gegenwart* 23/2 (1980) 8-14. — P. GRELOT, "La vocation ministérielle au service de Dieu," RechBib VII (1965) 159-73. — W. W. KLEIN, "Paul's Use of *kalein*," *JETS* 27 (1984) 53-64. — R. PESCH, *Mark* (HTKNT) I (1976) 108-16, 162-70. — G. RICHTER, *Deutsches Wörterbuch zum NT* (1962) 97-101. — H. SCHLIER, *Der Brief an die Epheser. Ein Kommentar* (⁴1963) 82-84. — K. L. SCHMIDT, *TDNT* III, 487-96. — K. STENDAHL, "The Called and the Chosen: An Essay on Election," A. Fridrichsen, et al., *The Called and the Chosen* (1953) 63-80. — F. WAGNER, *TRE* V, 684-88. — D. WIEDERKEHR, *Die Theologie der Berufung in den Paulusbriefen* (1963). — H. ZIMMERMANN, *Neutestamentliche Methodenlehre* (⁶1978) 96-110. — For further bibliography see Daumoser; Pesch; *TWNT* X, 1127.

1. The vb. appears in almost every NT document. The occurrences are numerous in Matthew (17) and esp. in Luke-Acts (24), where compounds are also frequently used. In Paul and in the deutero-Pauline letters καλέω is found *ca.* 30 times, most often with a different meaning from what is seen in Luke (→ 2). Κλῆσις (*calling*) appears only in Paul's letters and literature influenced by Paul (9 times in the Pauline letters, once each in Hebrews and 2 Peter). Κλητός (*called*) is also used primarily in Paul (7 times + once each in Matthew, Jude, and Revelation).

2. In the NT καλέω has the following variants in meaning: a) with acc.: *call* someone, in the sense of *call to oneself, invite;* b) with the double acc.: *name*, pass.: *be named, have as a name* (καλούμενος = *named, by the name of*). The broad distribution of these meanings corresponds to usage outside the NT. c) Alongside the primary sense *call, invite,* καλέω also frequently has the fig. meaning *appoint,* under the influence of the LXX. This appears predominantly in Paul's letters and writings influenced by Paul, where the verbal subst. κλῆσις, *appointment,* and the adj. κλητός, *called,* appear.

Καλέω is used with κλῆσις in 1 Cor 7:20; Eph 4:1, 4; 2 Tim 1:9. The word group appears in the semantic field of ἐκλέγομαι/ἐκλεκτός in Matt 22:14; Rom 8:28; 2 Pet 1:10; Rev 17:14. The one calling is God or (rarely) Jesus Christ. Those called are Israel, individually elected ones, Jesus, individuals, or all believers of the new covenant. The goal of the call is the fulfillment of a salvation-historical role or the new salvation in Christ.

3. a) Καλέω appears without special theological significance in the sense of *call* or have someone called (e.g., Mark 3:31: Jesus' mother and brothers sent someone to call him; see also Matt 2:7; 20:8). This calling can have a sense of command (cf. Matt 25:14; Acts 4:18; 24:2). The fig. meaning of καλέω, *appoint,* is thus prepared for and is given where the call proceeds from God or Jesus Christ (→ 3.c, 4).

Sometimes καλέω appears with the meaning *invite* (cf. 1 Cor 10:27; Luke 7:39; John 2:2). In the parable of the seating places at the meal (Luke 14:7-11) those *invited* (κεκλημένοι) are challenged to demonstrate modesty. The demand that the poor, maimed, lame, and blind be invited corresponds to the intention of Jesus and the social view of Luke, as true love is to be seen in renunciation of earthly recompense (14:12-14).

The parable of the invitation to the great supper, according to the basic motif in the various traditions (Luke 14:15-24; Matt 22:1-14; *Gos. Thom.* 64), compares the fate of Jesus' proclamation of the kingdom of God to the invitation to the feast. Those first invited do not follow the call (Luke 14:16-20; Matt 22:3-5) and thus forfeit their invitation (Luke 14:24; cf. Matt 8:11); in their place the poor, sick, and sinners, who are despised by the pious in Israel, are now the ones admitted to the invitation (Luke 14:21b, 22; Matt 22:9). However, in the expansion of the parable in the story of the one without the festal garment (22:11-13) Matthew points out to believers in Jesus, those who understand themselves to be invited by God to the marriage feast of his Son, the necessity of ethical verification (cf. v. 10), for to them apply the words: "Many are *called* (κλητοί), but few are chosen" (v. 14; cf. 20:16 v.l.; → ἐκλεκτός 2).

The promised salvation of believers is expressed in the macarism of Rev 19:9, "Blessed are those who are *invited* to the marriage supper of the lamb."

b) As in classical Greek and the LXX, καλέω has also the meaning *name, give a name,* in which the pass. is predominant and the partc. καλούμενος introduces the name or epithet (cf. Luke 6:15: Simon, *called* Zealot"; Acts 15:37: "John *with the surname* Mark"; Acts 10:1: "a man in Caesarea *with the name* Cornelius," etc.).

The name (→ ὄνομα) can be significant, as esp. when the names are given in the narratives of the promise of the births of John the Baptist and Jesus, which correspond to OT tradition (cf. Luke 1:13, 21; Matt 1:21 with Gen 16:11; 17:19; also Isa 7:14). In accordance with the traditional schema of giving a name at the annunciation in which the future of the child is revealed (Gen 16:12; 17:19), it is said of Jesus' unique destiny in salvation history: "He will be great and *be called* Son of the Most High . . ." (Luke 1:32; cf. Isa 9:6f.; 2 Sam 7:14; according to Luke 1:76 John will *"be called* prophet of the Most High"). As the one begotten by the Holy Spirit Jesus *will be called* "holy" and "Son of God" (Luke 1:35).

In reply to the questions who the Messiah is and where he comes from, according to Mark 12:35-37a par. Luke 20:41-44/Matt 22:41-46, the designation of Christ as "Son of David" is not sufficient, for David, "in the Holy Spirit" (Mark), "calls" (Mark: λέγει, Luke/Matthew: καλεῖ) him "Lord" (κύριον) "in the book of Psalms" (Luke), i.e., Ps 110:1.

According to many biblical texts, how one is addressed is significant for one's place in salvation history. The characterization of believers from Jews and Gentiles in the citation in Rom 9:25f. indicates the close connection that often exists between the giving of the name and election. "I *will call* those who were not my people my people and the the one who was not beloved I *will call* beloved. And at the place where it was said to them: You are not my people, there they *will be called* sons of the living God" (Rom 9:26/Hos 2:23). According to the parable of the lost son (Luke 15:11-32), the one who confesses to his father that he is no longer worthy to *be called* his son (vv. 19, 21) escapes the forfeiture of the name because of his repentance and the love of his father.

The nature and place of the person before God can be expressed in the call and the name; cf. Matt 5:9: "Blessed are the peacemakers, for they *will be called* sons of God" (see also v. 19); 1 John 3:1: "Behold, what great love the Father has given us: we *are called* children of God, and so we are." The christological basis of eschatological salvation consists, according to Heb 2:11, in the fact that the Son of God "is not ashamed to *call* them brethren."

Paul expounds the grace of the divine call when he confesses: "I am the least of the apostles, unfit to *be called* an apostle because I persecuted the Church of God. Yet through the grace of God I am what I am . . ." (1 Cor 15:9f.), while Jas 2:23 emphasizes that Abraham's faith, which was demonstrated in works, was "reckoned for righteousness" (Gen 15:6) and that he *"was called* the friend of God" (cf. Isa 41:8; 2 Chr 20:7; *Jub.* 19:9; *Apoc. Abr.* 6:9; CD 3:2).

A unique form of expression is to be seen in the mysterious biblical names in Revelation. Jerusalem, the great city, "is spiritually *called* [i.e., with a deeper interpretation of the name] Sodom and Egypt" (11:8). Here the reference is either to sexual sin and idolatry (Jer

23:14; Ezek 16:46, 49) or to coming destruction (Joel 3:19). The mysterious statement that the place where the powers of darkness are brought together "*is called* Armageddon in Hebrew" (16:16), is intended to suggest the battleground at Megiddo (cf. Judg 5:19; 2 Kgs 23:29f.; Zech 12:11). The rider on the white horse, "who *is called* Faithful and True" (19:11)—the tr. of the Hebrew word "amen"—is to be understood as the returning and victorious Christ, whose "name" "*is also called:* the word of God" (v. 13).

c) The idea of a *call* has a more evident theological significance where it is introduced in the gospel narratives of the call of the disciples than it has in Luke 14:15-24 par.; Rom 8:25f.; Heb 2:11. In the pericope of the call of the disciples (Mark 1:16-20 par. Matt 4:18-22) καλέω occurs, however, only in the second scene: "and immediately he [Jesus] *called* them [James and John]" (Mark 1:20 par.). The content of the call is not given, but it appears in the first scene in the call of Simon and Andrew. Comparison with 1 Kgs 19:19-21 and Mark 2:14 indicates that the call narrative was a literary form, shaped here by the resurrection faith in Jesus the Lord and by the parenetic interests of those who passed on the tradition. Jesus is proclaimed as the one who calls disciples from their previous ties into discipleship and participation in the proclamation of the kingdom of God (cf. Luke 9:57-62 par. Matt 8:19-22) through the sovereign power of his divine word (cf. Isa 55:10f.). The one who is summoned follows the call without delay. What was historically more likely to be a difficult and gradual process of attachment to Jesus is here brought together into a decisive moment.

The pericope of the call of the tax collector Levi and of the table fellowship of Jesus with the tax collecters and sinners (Mark 2:13-17 par. Luke 5:27-32/Matt 9:9-13) concludes with the justification of Jesus' offensive conduct in the words of a saying of Jesus: "I have not come to *call* the righteous, but sinners" (Mark 2:17 par. Matt 9:13). Over against the Pharisaic practice of separation by the pious, who understood themselves as righteous (cf. Luke 18:9), Jesus defends his table fellowship with sinners as the initial realization of the sovereignty of God (cf. Luke 14:15-24 par.). Luke emphasizes more explicitly human activity when he speaks of the call of sinners "to repentance" (a Lukan addition, 5:32).

4. Καλέω as a designation of the sovereign divine summons in the theological sense of *call* is found in the NT predominantly in Paul and in the Pauline tradition and, together with κλῆσις, a t.t. from the Pauline vocabulary for the divine call, and the more widely distributed κλητός, reveals basic elements of the biblical-Christian understanding of existence and salvation.

a) In Gal 1:15f. Paul describes his call to apostleship, which coincided with the call to faith, in dependence on the OT stories of the call of the prophets, and emphasizes the following motifs: God's free, gracious decision (εὐδόκησεν), the election (separation) of the one who is called from the first moment of his existence (cf. Jer 1:5; Isa 49:1, 5), the call by God's grace (ἐκάλεσεν), the revealing of Jesus as the Son of God, and the role within salvation history (cf. Jer 1:5; Isa 49:6). The close relationship between the gift of the call and the role is indicated in Rom 1:1: "Paul, servant of Jesus Christ, *called* an apostle, separated for the gospel of God" (cf. 1 Cor 1:1).

According to the NT and Pauline understanding, the apostle is not the only one called. All who believe in Christ are *called* saints, those who are sanctified in Christ Jesus (1 Cor 1:2; cf. Rom 1:7). They are *called* (Rom 9:24; 1:5f.) as those who are "*called* by Jesus Christ" (Rom 1:6), "not only from the Jews, but also from the Gentiles." According to God's will they are his people (Rom 9:25f., → 3b).

Just as God's sovereign call ensues in the history of Israel when he, e.g., calls Jacob and not Esau (Rom 9:12f.) and does not revoke his "gifts" and his *call* (κλῆσις, Rom 11:29), according to Paul's apocalyptic hope, Christians are graciously elected by God, who "gives life to the dead and *calls* into existence things that do not exist" (Rom 4:17). In Rom 8:28-30 the apostle accents this calling of the elect to salvation in the most radical way and in a powerful optimistic view of salvation: "But we know that to those who love God, everything works together for the good, to those who are *called* (κλητοί) according to [his] purpose. For those whom he foreknew he also predestined to be conformed to the image of his Son, that he might be the firstborn among many brethren; and those whom he predestined he also *called,* and those whom he *called,* he also justified; and those whom he justified he also glorified." The "purpose" of God (→ πρόθεσις), his "foreknowledge" (προγινώσκω), and his "foreordination" (προορίζω) precede the call. To stand in the call of God means to be "justified" (→ δικαιόω) and to have a part in the glory of Christ (cf. 2 Cor 3:18; → δοξάζω) with the goal of being "conformed" to the image of the Son of God (cf. 2 Cor 4:4; → εἰκών). To a certain extent the sum of the Pauline statements about the call is contained in Rom 8:26-30. However, the radical statement of the apostle's theology of grace is given from the very first of his writings.

In 1 Thessalonians Paul reminds the members of the church of his exhortation "to walk worthy of God, who *calls* you into his kingdom and to glory" (2:12); Paul then gives the assurance, "He who *calls* you is faithful, and he will do it" (5:24; cf. 1 Cor 1:9). God stands by his salvific decree, and his call is not void (cf. Rom 8:28; Phil 1:6), even if adversities in the life of the believer call it into question. Of course those who are called out of the old world (cf. Gal 1:4) must lead a new life, for they are not called "to impurity, but to sanctification" (ἐν ἁγιασμῷ, 1 Thess 4:7).

Galatians also speaks of the danger to the one who is called when the apostle affirms in great dismay that the Galatians, in turning to the law as an apparently additional way of salvation, have fallen away "from the one who *called*" them "in grace" (ἐν χάριτι) to "another gospel" (1:6; cf. 5:8). It is difficult to determine whether ἐν χάριτι refers to the grace of the divine call (cf. 1:15) or the goal, the community of salvation in Christ (cf. 5:4; on ἐν with a possible final sense cf., besides 1 Thess 4:7 [see above], 1 Cor 7:15: "God *has called* us to peace [ἐν εἰρήνῃ]). With the appeal, "*You have been called* to freedom (ἐπ᾽ ἐλευθερίᾳ), brothers," Gal 5:13 accents the goal of the calling, but at the same time warns against both failing to carry to fruition the new possibilities for life and drawing false conclusions from the Christian freedom from the law.

The call of the believer from the old life to a new life is not connected in 1 Corinthians with interest in a social revolution, for in Paul "the form of this world is passing away" (7:31). He can place the values of this world so much in a penultimate place that he reminds the Corinthians, with regard to their *call* (κλῆσις), that not many wise, mighty, or prominent people "are elected" (1:26-29; → ἐκλέγομαι 3). In 7:17-34 he encourages them to maintain the status they had when they received the divine *call* by keeping the commandments and considering this their lot, given by God (v. 17). Neither the circumcised nor the uncircumcised should alter his place, but "everyone should remain in the *calling* in which he *was called* (ἐν τῇ κλήσει ᾗ ἐκλήθη)" (v. 20). Κλῆσις here, in contrast to the normal Pauline use of the word, hardly refers to the "calling," but rather to the condition in which (not into which) one was called. The admonition to the slave not to be anxious but to remain in his place points also in this direction: "For he *who was called* in the Lord as a slave (ὁ γὰρ ἐν κυρίῳ κληθεὶς δοῦλος) is a freedman of the Lord; likewise he *who was called* as a free person is a slave of Christ" (vv. 21f.). In Christ ethnic, social, and sexual status is "taken away" (Gal 3:28; 1 Cor 12:13) and thus has value no longer. Therefore, the one called in freedom can look dispassionately at the institutions of this world.

Believers, those who *"are called"* by God "into fellowship with his Son Jesus Christ" (1 Cor 1:9), must stand the test in order to attain "the prize of the upward *calling* (τῆς ἄνω κλήσεως) of God in Christ Jesus" (Phil 3:14). The call, which Paul indicates is his life goal, is seen here within the perspective of its future completion (on ἡ ἄνω κλῆσις cf. *2 Bar.* 4:15; Gal 4:26); it began with conversion to Christ and attains its goal in eternal fellowship with him.

b) Colossians emphasizes the unity in Christ (3:11) of believers from many backgrounds and admonishes the Christians to bring to realization the peace of Christ, to which they *have been called* "in one body," the Church (3:15; cf. 1 Cor 7:15). Even more suggestive is the reference in Ephesians to the future dimension of the calling: "One body and one Spirit, as you *were* also *called* in the hope of your *calling*" (4:4). The call is connected with relationship to the Church. The summons to walk "worthy of the *calling*" (4:1) and to grasp (1:18; cf. Wis 5:5; 1QH 3:20-22) the great goal prepared by God, the "hope of his *calling*" and the "riches of the glory of his inheritance among the saints," proceeds from it.

In 2 Thess 1:11 the testing of believers, those who are "*called* by the gospel" (2:14), is presupposed. At the same time God's support is considered necessary when the text says: "May our God make you worthy of the *calling*."

1 Tim 6:12 names, as the motivation for fighting the good fight of faith, eternal life as the goal to which God has *called* Christians in their baptism. The *call,* which is demonstrated in redemption, is, according to 2 Tim 1:9, based on the eternal holy will of God, "who redeemed us and *called* us with a holy *calling,* not according to our works, but according to his own purpose and grace, which was given to us in Christ Jesus ages ago. . . ."

c) 1 Peter speaks of the call in order to strengthen believers on the way of their lives as aliens (1:1; 2:11). In the context of the biblical sayings about the election of the new people of God, believers are reminded that God "*has called* them out of darkness into his marvelous light" (2:9). Their conduct must correspond to the one who *has called* them and is "holy" (1:15; cf. 2:5, 9). They must not return evil for evil, but on the contrary bless, because they have been *called* "to inherit a blessing" (3:9). It belongs to the nature of Christian existence to endure suffering in following Christ; for this purpose Christians have been *called* (2:20f.). However, the time of suffering is brief in comparison to the "eternal glory in Christ": "the God of all grace" will "restore, establish, strengthen, and settle" those who are called (5:10).

Jude 1:1 also speaks of the strengthening benevolence of God for *those who have been called* (κλητοί), characterizing them as "beloved in God the Father and kept for Jesus Christ." The gift of divine power that leads to eternal life and godliness is, according to 2 Pet 1:3, associated with the knowledge of the Lord Jesus, which he gives to those whom he has called; however, they must through their own effort "confirm their *calling* (κλῆσις) and election" (1:10).

d) Hebrews challenges the Christians to consider the future blessings: "Holy brothers, who share in the heavenly *call,* consider the apostle and [heavenly] high priest of our confession" (3:1). The reference is probably to the call that leads to heaven. As the one appointed by

God and, like Aaron, called to be high priest (5:4-6), through his death Christ has become "mediator of a new covenant," "so that *those who are called* (οἱ κεκλημένοι) receive the promise of eternal life" (9:15). Abraham is mentioned among many witnesses as a model of faith who, when he was *called*, was obedient only to God's word of promise (11:8).

Revelation is intended to strengthen the faith of those who are called in the situation of distress and temptation when it mentions as companions of the victorious lamb, the King of kings, "those who are *called* and chosen and faithful" (17:14, → ἐκλεκτός 5), and praises "*those who are called* (οἱ κεκλημένοι) to the marriage feast of the lamb" (19:9).   J. Eckert

καλλιέλαιος, ου, ἡ *kalliëlaios* cultivated olive tree*

Rom 11:24, over against the → ἀγριέλαιος; the same contrast appears also in (pseudo-) Aristotle *De Plantis* i.6.280b.40.

κάλλιον *kallion* better (adv.); very well*

The comparative of → καλῶς is used in Acts 25:10 in place of the superlative; cf. BDF §244.2.

καλοδιδάσκαλος, 2 *kalodidaskalos* teaching what is good*

Titus 2:3: The old women should be *teachers of what is good* (for the young women); elsewhere not attested.

Καλοὶ λιμένες *Kaloi limenes* Fair Havens*

An inlet open to the east on the south side of Crete near the city of Lasea and east of Cape Littinos; it is presently called Kali Liménes. The name means *good/ pretty harbor*. There Paul warned the crew of the ship that they should not continue the journey because of the approach of winter (Acts 27:8ff.). The name of the bay appears nowhere else in ancient literature, but καλός is found often as a term for a useful harbor (e.g., Diodorus Siculus iii.44.7; v.10.1). BAGD s.v.; L. Robert, *Hellenica* 11/12 (1961) 263-66; P. Bratsiotis, *BHH* 616; E. Haenchen, *Acts* (Eng. tr., 1971) ad loc.

καλοποιέω *kalopoieō* do good*

2 Thess 3:13, in an admonition to the whole church: μὴ ἐγκακήσητε καλοποιοῦντες, "do not be weary in *well-doing*"; cf. Gal 6:9.

καλός, 3 *kalos* beautiful; good

1. Occurrences in the NT, semantic field — 2. Basic

meanings — 3. Paul — 4. John — 5. The Pastorals and 1 Peter

Lit.: E. BEYREUTHER, *DNTT* II, 102-5. — N. BROX, *1 Pet* (EKKNT, 1979). — L. GOPPELT, *1 Pet* (KEK, 1978) 159-63. — E. GRASSI, *Die Theorie des Schönen in der Antike* (1962). — W. GRUNDMANN, *TDNT* III, 536-50. — C. W. REINES, "Beauty in the Bible and the Talmud," *Judaism* 24 (1975) 100-107. — P. ROSSANO, "L'ideale del bello (καλός) nell' etica di S. Paolo," *Studiorum Paulinorum Congressus* (AnBib 17/18, 1963) II, 373-82. — G. F. SNYDER, "The Tobspruch in the NT," *NTS* 23 (1976/77) 117-20. — C. SPICQ, *Théologie morale du NT* (1965) 146-53. — idem, *Les Épîtres Pastorales* II (⁴1969) 676-84. — H. J. STOEBE, *THAT* I, 652-64. — W. C. VAN UNNIK, "The Teaching of Good Works in 1 Peter," *NTS* 1 (1954/55) 92-110. — idem, "Die Rücksicht auf die Reaktion der Nicht-Christen als Motiv in der altchristlichen Paränese," FS Jeremias (1960) 221-34. — H. WANKEL, καλὸς καὶ ἀγαθός (Diss. Würzburg, 1961). — C. WESTERMANN, "Das Schöne im AT," *Beiträge zur alttestamentlichen Theologie* (FS W. Zimmerli, 1977) 479-97. — For further bibliography see *TWNT* X, 1131.

1. The 100 occurrences of καλός are distributed among 15 NT books. The word appears frequently in the Pastorals (24 times), but does not appear in Acts (except in 27:8: → Καλοὶ λιμένες), Colossians, Ephesians, 1–3 John, Revelation, and other writings.

In NT usage, καλός is almost synonymous with → ἀγαθός. Both words can be used in place of each other: cf. 1 Tim 2:10 with 5:10; Titus 1:16 with 2:7; Eph 2:10 with Heb 10:24: "*good* works"; Acts 23:1 with Heb 13:18: "*good* conscience"; Mark 3:4 with Matt 12:12: "do *good*." "In the first place one can say that ἀγαθός designates more the disposition and the resulting ethical value, while καλός describes more the appearance of the good in praiseworthy actions" (T. Zahn, *Matt* [KNT, ⁴1922] 206n.62). In the LXX καλός is principally an equivalent for *ṭôb*, "(ethically) good" (cf. Gen 2:9; 3:22; Deut 12:28, etc.), though ἀγαθός is much more frequently so used, and for *yāpeh*, "beautiful" (Gen 12:14; 2 Kgdms 14:27; Cant 1:8, etc.; cf. Westermann). In the NT, as in the OT, "the beautiful" in the sense of the Platonic or Hellenistic idea (cf. Grundmann 540-43; Grassi; Wankel) is never under consideration.

Καλοκἀγαθία is found in the NT only in Jas 5:10 v.l.; cf. Ign. *Eph.* 14:1 and also the (accidental?) combination in Luke 8:15 (unlike par. Mark 4:20): ἐν καρδίᾳ καλῇ καὶ ἀγαθῇ ἀκούσαντες τὸν λόγον (but → 5).

2. Καλός is to be translated *beautiful* in the sense of an aesthetic judgment only in Luke 21:5 (λίθοι καλοί). It predominantly designates what is *ethically good, noble, worth striving for.* Antonyms can be → κακός (cf. Rom 12:17; Heb 5:14) or → πονηρός (cf. 1 Thess 5:21f.). Distinctive concepts are: "*good* work" (Mark 14:6 par. Matt 26:10; John 10:33; 1 Tim 3:1), "*good* works" (Matt 5:16; John 10:32; 1 Tim 5:10, 25; 6:18; Titus 2:7, 14;

3:8, 14; Heb 10:24; 1 Pet 2:12), "*good* conduct" (Jas 3:13; 1 Pet 2:12), "*good* conscience" (Heb 13:18), and simply "the *good*" (only in Paul: 1 Thess 5:21; Gal 6:9; 2 Cor 13:7; Rom 7:18, 21). It is noteworthy that καλός is used most often to designate the ethical quality of conduct. Where persons are directly spoken of, ἀγαθός is used (cf. Mark 10:17; Matt 5:45; 12:35; 20:15, etc.). Even more frequent, of course, is → δίκαιος in the biblical sense, which indicates the difference from Greek ethics. Καλός is used of persons only in reference to specific vocations or offices (cf. John 10:11, 14: "*good* shepherd"; 1 Tim 4:6: "*good* servant"; 2 Tim 2:3: "*good* soldier"; 1 Pet 4:10: "*good* steward").

In a wider sense καλός can connote the (physical) perfection, suitability, or usefulness of an object, usually in metaphorical speech, and can be translated *useful, profitable, precious, flawless,* etc. (cf. Matt 3:10, of fruit; Mark 4:8, of the land; Matt 13:24, of seed; v. 45, of a pearl; v. 48, of fish, opposed to → σαπρός; Luke 6:38, of a measure; v. 43, of a tree, opposed to σαπρός; 8:15, of the heart; John 2:10, of wine).

To be noted separately is the formulaic use of καλός in the phrase καλόν (ἐστιν) (e.g., Mark 9:5: "it is *good* that we are here"). Yet this can also be understood to indicate that which is salutary and good before God (cf. Mark 7:27; 1 Cor 7:1, 8, 26; Heb 13:9; also Mark 9:42: "it is better for him," 43, 45, 47; cf. Snyder).

3. In Paul καλός diminishes in significance in comparison with ἀγαθός (→ ἀγαθός 4). In parenesis the apostle can encourage readers to "hold to the *good*" (1 Thess 5:21), to "take thought of the *good*" (Rom 12:17; 2 Cor 8:21), or simply to "do the *good*" (Gal 6:9; 2 Cor 13:7; cf. Jas 4:17 and → καλῶς ποιεῖν). A significant feature is the apostle's characterization of the Mosaic Torah as *good* (Rom 7:16; cf. 1 Tim 1:8). The apostle knows that the law is to be compared with the holy will of God, but only insofar as God's will demands realization by the individual and thus discloses our lost condition (cf. Rom 7:7-13; → νόμος).

4. In John 10:11, 14 ("the *good* shepherd") καλός has (here emphasizing the shepherd's sacrifice of his life) an absolute meaning, perhaps comparable to → ἀληθινός in 6:32 ("the true bread"); 15:1 ("the true vine"). Use of καλός in 10:11, 14 is presumably suggested by the image of the shepherd (cf. Billerbeck II, 536f.). Only in John (10:32f.) are the works of Jesus characterized as "*good* works." The Evangelist is referring to the revelatory signs of Jesus (→ σημεῖον), which are done with the authority of the Father. The Jews, however, think of "good works" in a narrower sense (= works of love and alms; on the Jewish background cf. Billerbeck IV/1, 536-58, 559-610; J. Jeremias, *Abba. Studien zur neutestamentlichen Theo-*

logie und Zeitgeschichte [1966] 109-14; A. Nissen, *Gott und der Nächste im antiken Judentum* [1974], esp. 267ff.).

5. The frequent use of καλός in the Pastorals signals an altered understanding of Christianity. Christianity moves close to "reasonable" and bourgeois conduct. As in Stoic ethics, καλός serves to designate what is good, excellent, orderly, and right (cf. Grundmann 550; Spicq, *Épîtres Pastorales;* Preisigke, *Wörterbuch* s.v.). Thus "*good* works" (1 Tim 5:10, 25; 6:18; Titus 2:7, 14; 3:8, 14; also 1 Pet 2:12; Heb 10:24) refers primarily to good social conduct on the part of Christians. In 1 Tim 5:10 the training of children and hospitality are considered among good works. Officeholders (Titus 2:7), the rich (1 Tim 6:18), and the entire people of God (Titus 2:14; 3:8, 14) are to excel in "good works." The bishop should have a "*good* reputation" among outsiders. The motif of consideration of the Gentile world comes more strongly into view (cf. also 1 Tim 3:3; Titus 3:8; van Unnik, "Rücksicht," 229f.).

1 Pet 2:12 admonishes (probably in dependence on Matt 5:16): "Lead a *good* life among the Gentiles in order that, when they slander you as criminals, they may see your good deeds and praise God on the day of judgment because of your *good* works" (cf. tr. in Brox; cf. van Unnik, "Teaching"). Exemplary social conduct should become a "daily witness" (Goppelt 162).

The use of καλός in these sources, which comes closer to the Greek understanding than earlier texts, does not conceal the fact that here also ethical conduct remains a consequence of the grace of God. The parenesis is finally anchored in the kerygma of Christ. Thus in it the cross, which powerfully stands in opposition to ancient concepts of "perfection" and "beauty," maintains its place.

J. Wanke

κάλυμμα, ατος, τo *kalymma* cover, veil*

Lit.: BAGD s.v. — R. BULTMANN, *2 Cor* (Eng. tr., 1985) 84-96. — J. CARMIGNAC, "II Corinthiens iii.6, 14 et le Début de la Formulation du Nouveau Testament," *NTS* 24 (1977/78) 384-86. — C. J. A. HICKLING, "The Sequence of Thought in II Corinthians, Chapter Three," *NTS* 21 (1974/75) 380-95. — A. OEPKE, *TDNT* III, 560f. — S. SCHULZ, "Die Decke des Moses," *ZNW* 49 (1958) 1-30. — For further bibliography see BAGD; Bultmann.

There are 4 occurrences in the NT, all in 2 Cor 3:13, 14, 15, and 16 in Paul's description of the glory of the ministry of the new covenant of the Spirit as that which excels and contrasts with the ministry of the law. The first occurrence is literal (v. 13), of the *cover* with which Moses veiled the radiance of his face, according to Exod 34:33-35, after his encounter with God at Sinai, and only when he did not stand before God or speak with the people in the name of God. According to Paul Moses did this to conceal (v. 7) from the Israelites the end of the transitory radiance. Paul then uses the word figuratively of the "*veil* at the reading of the old covenant" (κάλυμμα ἐπὶ τῇ ἀναγνώσει τῆς παλαίας διαθήκης μένει, v. 14) and "on the hearts" of the hearers (κάλυμμα ἐπὶ τὴν καρδίαν κεῖται, v. 15). Just as Moses removed the veil when he went before the Lord (Exod 34:34), so it will be taken from (the heart of) Israel when Israel turns to God (περιαιρεῖται τὸ κάλυμμα, v. 16). The veil of Moses depicts, on the one hand (in a surpassing way), the freedom of the new covenant of the apostle of Christ; on the other hand it depicts (as a type) the concealment of the glory of God and the blindness to this glory within the realm of the "old covenant."

H. Balz

καλύπτω *kalyptō* cover, conceal; pass.: be concealed*

1. Occurrences — 2. Literal usage — 3. Fig. usage

Lit.: W. MUNDLE, *DNTT* II, 212-14. — A. OEPKE, *TDNT* III, 556-92. — For further bibliography see *TWNT* X, 1131-33.

1. Καλύπτω is used in the NT 8 times, twice each in Matthew and Luke, and in 2 Cor 4:3 (bis); Jas 5:20; 1 Pet 4:8.

2. Used literally καλύπτω refers to a concrete subject or object that covers or is covered. In the account of the stilling of the storm, Matt 8:24 says that the waves swept up by the storm *covered* the small ship (i.e., engulfed it). Here καλύπτω is used of the theme of endangerment to life with reference to the Church's situation of persecution.

In Luke 23:28-31 Jesus, on the way to the cross, calls upon the women who are weeping to sing the funeral dirge, not for him, but for themselves and their children, because the time is coming when it will seem preferable to be unborn or dead. This announcement of judgment over Jerusalem is a retrospective view of the events of the year A.D. 70. In the saying in v. 30, which has probably been inserted secondarily, apparently in dependence on Hos 10:8 (see G. Schneider, *Luke* [ÖTK] ad loc.), καλύπτω is evidently originally a term for burial (Oepke 557).

The image in Luke 8:16, which develops the interpretation of the parable in vv. 10-15, illustrates a discipleship that bears fruit and shines forth. The basis for the image is the normal practice in which one does not *cover* with a vessel a light that has been kindled so that it is incapable of giving light.

3. Used fig. καλύπτω refers to a spiritual event. In Matt 10:26 καλύπτω appears in the context of Jesus' instructions to the disciples as they set out on a mission. The synonymous parallelism of the logion accents the

reference to hiddenness (κεκαλυμμένον with κρυπτόν): What is *concealed* will finally be revealed. The interpretation of the word results from the connection with vv. 26-33. The disciples are commissioned to testify to their faith (v. 27) and their readiness for martyrdom (vv. 28-31). The confession of the exalted Lord before "the heavenly Father" (v. 32) corresponds to their witness of faith, just as denial of him corresponds to those who neglect their mission (v. 33). Καλύπτω has in view the conduct of the disciples as emissaries of faith.

In 2 Cor 4:3 (bis) Paul uses the contrast "veiling-revelation" in his argument. The good news is *veiled* for those who do not accept it and are thus lost. Καλύπτω does not denote fate, but rather it presupposes human free will and freedom of choice.

Against the background of the Jewish concept of a heavenly record-keeping of good deeds and sins (cf. Sir 3:29f.; Tob 4:10), καλύπτω in 1 Pet 4:8 refers to the power of love to cover sins. The saying used in the parenesis here—that brotherly love "*covers* a multitude of sins"— is from Prov 10:12 and was perhaps an early Christian maxim (cf. *1 Clem.* 49:5; *2 Clem.* 16:4). It is to be understood "ambiguously" (L. Goppelt, *1 Pet* [KEK] 285): it speaks of both the one who demonstrates love and the one who receives it.

Πλῆθος ἁμαρτιῶν appears again with καλύπτω in Jas 5:20. Here it refers to the one who restores a sinner who has erred from the "way." Thus the ἁμαρτωλός is not to be seen as a heretic, but—corresponding to the ethical intent of James—as a member of the Church who has not conducted himself as a Christian.

H.-J. Ritz

καλῶς *kalōs* beautifully, well

Lit.: → καλός.

1. The adv. καλῶς appears 37 times in the NT. It does not appear, e.g., in Ephesians, Colossians, 1–2 Thessalonians, or Revelation. The most frequent usage is in Mark (6 occurrences).

Καλῶς most often designates the suitability or appropriateness of an action or a state of affairs (Mark 7:37: "he has done all things *well*"; Luke 6:48: "because it [the house] was *well* built"; Gal 5:7; 1 Cor 14:17; Jas 2:3: "sit *well* here"). Καλῶς ποιεῖν can mean (however → 2) "act/ behave *rightly, appropriately*" (1 Cor 7:37f.; Jas 2:8, 19) or "do *well*" (Acts 10:33; Phil 4:14). Particularly with vbs. of speaking, hearing, etc., καλῶς denotes correctness (e.g., Mark 7:6: "*Well* did Isaiah prophesy of your hypocrisy"; 12:28; Luke 20:39; Acts 25:10 [κάλλιον]; John 4:17; 8:48; 13:13; 18:23; cf. also Mark 12:32: *"Right!"*; Rom 11:20: *"That is true"*). In 1 Tim 3:13; 5:17 καλῶς links appropriate and exemplary leadership with "caring *well* for one's own house" (3:4, 12). The ironic uses of the word in Mark 7:9 ("excellently do you reject God's commandment") and 2 Cor 11:4 ("you submit to it *readily enough*") belong in this category.

2. Corresponding to the wider basic meaning of → καλός, "(morally) good, noble," καλῶς can also express a moral value judgment (cf. Gal 4:17: "they are jealous of you not *in a good way*"; Heb 13:18: "live *honorably*"). Καλῶς ποιεῖν then means: "do *good*" (Matt 12:12: "it is permitted to do *good* on the sabbath"; [par. → ἀγαθὸν ποιέω in Mark 3:4 and → ἀγαθοποιέω in Luke 6:9]; Luke 6:27: "do *good* to those who hate you" [ἀγαθοποιεῖν in v. 33]). In Mark 14:7 the rarely used εὖ (ποιεῖν) has the same meaning (see BDF §102.3).

J. Wanke

κἀμέ *kame* and me, me also
Acc. of → κἀγώ.

κάμηλος, ου, ὁ/ἡ *kamēlos* camel*

Lit.: G. AICHER, *Kamel und Nadelöhr* (1908). — E. BEST, "The Camel and the Needle's Eye (Mk 10:25)," *ExpTim* 82 (1970/71) 83-89. — O. BÖCHER, "Wölfe in Schafspelzen," *TZ* 24 (1968) 405-26, esp. 408-12. — DALMAN, *Arbeit* VI, 147-60. — J. D. M. DERRETT, "A Camel through the Eye of a Needle," *NTS* 32 (1986) 465-70. — J. FELIKS, *EncJud* V, 72f. — J. P. FREE, "Abraham's Camels," *JNES* 3 (1944) 187-93. — P. JOÜON, "Le costume d'Élie et celui de Jean Baptiste," *Bib* 16 (1935) 74-81. — R. LEHMANN and K. L. SCHMIDT, "Zum Gleichnis vom Kamel und Nadelöhr und Verwandtes," *TBl* 11 (1932) 336-440. — O. MICHEL, *TDNT* III, 592-94. — E. NESTLE, "Zum Mantel aus Kamelshaaren," *ZNW* 8 (1907) 238. — P. VIELHAUER, "Tracht und Speise Johannes des Täufers," *idem, Aufsätze zum NT* (1965) 47-54. — F. H. WEISSBACH, PW X/2, 1824-32. — H. WINDISCH, "Die Notiz über Tracht und Speise des Täufers Johannes," *ZNW* 32 (1933) 65-87. — For further bibliography see *TWNT* X, 1133.

1. Corresponding to the general culture and animal world of the Near East, the camel (of various kinds) appears in OT descriptions as far back as the patriarchal period and is attested into the second to fourth millennia in Egypt, Megiddo, etc. It was ridden and was a beast of burden (Gen 24:10-64; 31:17, 34; 37:25; 1 Sam 30:17; 1 Kgs 10:2 par.; 1 Chr 12:41; Isa 21:7; 30:6; Tob 9:2, 5; Jdt 2:17). Herds of camels are mentioned in descriptions of property and of noteworthy wealth (Gen 24:35; 30:43; 1 Chr 27:30; Job 1:3, 17; 42:12; 2 Esdr 2:67 par.; Tob 10:10). Thus camels can be given as a gesture (Gen 12:16; 32:7, 15), stolen as booty (1 Sam 15:3; 27:9; 1 Chr 5:21; 2 Chr 14:14; Jer 30:24, 27 LXX), struck by God's punishment (Exod 9:3; Zech 14:15), or used concretely of the "messianic fullness" (Isa 60:6).

Nevertheless the camel is unclean according to Jewish food regulations (Lev 11:4; Deut 14:7; see also Philo's interpretation of these passages in *Agr.* 131-45). This did not affect use of camel's hair and skin for clothing or tents. Those who led camels had a socially low rank (comparable, e.g., to shepherds).

2. Κάμηλος appears in the NT 6 times, all in the Gospels:

a) The appended biographical report in Mark 1:6 par. Matt 3:4 (not present in Luke or John) concerning John the Baptist's clothing (of camel's hair) and food (interpreted as "manna" in *Gos. Eb.* 2 [Hennecke/Schneemelcher I, 157]) is intended to be illustrative of his role as a desert prophet in association with the citation of Isa 40:3 (probably corresponding to the Baptist's self-understanding within salvation history). As such it can be regarded as a concretizing parallel to Matt 11:7ff. par. Luke 7:24ff., where desert life and "soft raiment" (as well as "cultivated" food) are viewed as opposites; in addition, the food that is mentioned is known from Bedouin life. Woolen clothing is a symbol of the "true" prophet (cf. Zech 13:4; *Mart. Isa.* 2:10; see also Heb 11:37); the references to it and to the "life in the house of a king" could serve also as underpinning for the general interpretation of the Baptist in the NT context as the "new" Elijah expected to come as messianic forerunner (cf. the tradition of the appearance and work of the OT Elijah in 2 Kgs 1:8 [see Josephus *Ant.* ix.22]; 1 Kgs 19:9-21; 2 Kgs 2:8, 13f.; and the expectation in Luke 1:15-17, 76-79).

b) In Mark 10:17-31 par., vv. 23-27 and 28-31 serve as a deepened instruction for the disciples after vv. 17-22. The primary (though any alternative would be false) fact of Jesus' demand in v. 21 is not, as a condition, to sell everything for the benefit of the poor, but to have one's treasure (i.e., one's heart) with God, that is, to stand with God in service for the benefit of those who are in need —rather than with mammon for one's own benefit (cf. Luke 16:19ff.; 1 Tim 6:17ff.). The question of inheriting eternal life is thus not a question of engagement with humankind (v. 17), but exclusively of God's goodness and the possibilities of God (vv. 18, 27; cf. Rom 4:16-22). For a person on the basis of his own possibilities—and the rich are here the poorest, against all human judgments (cf. v. 31)—to enter through the "narrow gate" of life (the "narrow way," Matt 7:13f.) would be equivalent to the largest animal (the camel) passing through the smallest opening (the eye of a needle; Mark 10:25 par. Matt 19:24/Luke 18:25).

Thus one should reject both the view that κάμηλος is to be read as κάμιλος ("cable"; see BDF §24)—although that view is actually not impossible—and the idea that the "needle's eye" was an actual historical (small) gate in the city wall of Jerusalem. The image of an elephant going through the eye of a needle is known from rabbinic literature (*b. Ber.* 55b; *b. B. Meṣ.* 38b), as is the image of the eye of the needle as the smallest opening (*Midr. Cant.* 5:2; *Pesiq. R.* 15). An apparent allusion to Mark 10:25 is seen in the Koran: "The unbelievers do not enter into paradise before a camel goes through the eye of a needle" (7:38).

The possibilities of the person correspond, however, to those of small children: "Accept" is one's only life possibility (Mark 10:15 par.). And this condition for "inheritance" of the kingdom of God is actualized as a demand for unconditional discipleship (v. 21c) to Jesus, who himself lived and died in the selfless service of his faith in God on behalf of those who were in need (10:41-45).

c) In accordance with this is Matt 23:24 (M): Those

who teach another way as the way of Jesus block the way both for themselves and for others (v. 13; cf. 15:9). When a blind man leads other blind persons to abandon the way of service to God for others (justice, mercy, faith, v. 23), he does not lead them on the way, but into the pit (15:13-14). Or in another image: in one's zeal to avoid eating a gnat (the smallest animal), he swallows a camel (the largest animal; cf. the contrast of louse and camel in *b. Šabb.* 12a, 107b).

S. Pedersen

κάμινος, ου, ἡ *kaminos* oven, furnace*

This noun is used literally in images in Revelation: 1:15: the fiery *furnace* (κάμινος πεπυρωμένη; cf. Dan 3:6: κάμινος τοῦ πυρὸς καιομένη; the *furnace*, Ezek 22:20); 9:2: ὡς καπνὸς καμίνου μεγάλης (cf. Exod 19:18). It is also used fig. of the fire of hell: Matt 13:42, 50: βαλοῦσιν αὐτοὺς εἰς τὴν κάμινον τοῦ πυρός (cf. 4 Ezra 7:36; Billerbeck I, 673).

καμμύω *kammyō* close (one's eyes)*

Matt 13:15; Acts 28:27: τοὺς ὀφθαλμοὺς αὐτῶν ἐκάμμυσαν (citing Isa 6:10 LXX), "they *shut* their eyes," an image for rejection of the message by the Jews. The vb., formed from the compound καταμύω, was treated in popular speech as in biblical Greek as a simple vb. (see BAGD s.v.; BDF §69.1).

κάμνω *kamnō* be exhausted, tire; be ill*

Heb 12:3: ἵνα μὴ κάμητε ταῖς ψυχαῖς ὑμῶν ἐκλυόμενοι, "so that you not *be weary* and fainthearted in your souls." The statement is determined by the preceding image of the race (vv. 1f.). Dat. ταῖς ψυχαῖς probably belongs to the vb. κάμνω and not to the following partc., which is here, as also in Gal 6:9 (cf. Heb 12:5 as citation from Prov 3:11), probably used in the absolute sense. On the phrase κάμνω ταῖς ψυχαῖς (τῇ ψυχῇ) cf. Job 10:1; *Herm. Man.* viii.10; Diodorus Siculus xx.96.3; see also BAGD s.v.; O. Michel, *Heb* [KEK] ad loc., who understand κάμνω in the absolute sense [cf. Josephus *Vita* 209; Rev 2:3 TR]). Jas 5:15, of the healing of a *sick person* (τὸν κάμνοντα) by the prayer of faith. Spicq, *Notes* I, 400-402.

κἀμοί *kamoi* and to me, to me also
Dat. of → κἀγώ.

κάμπτω *kamptō* bend, bow

In the NT with γόνυ/γόνατα, of "*bending* the knee" as a sign of reverence or submission. Trans. Rom 11:4: ... τῇ Βάαλ; Eph 3:13: ... πρὸς τὸν πατέρα; intrans. Rom 14:11: ἐμοὶ ..., citing Isa 45:23 LXX; Phil 2:10: ἐν τῷ ὀνόματι Ἰησοῦ ....

κἄν *kan* and if; even if (only); at least*

Κἄν occurs 17 times in the NT. It is formed through crasis from καὶ ἐάν and is used as a concessive or conditional conj. or as a particle (cf. BDF §§18; 374).

Conditional *and if:* Mark 16:18; Luke 12:38: κἄν ... κἄν, *whether ... whether;* 13:9a, as a hypothetical conj.: κἄν μὲν ... [sc. "so it is good"], εἰ δὲ μή γε (see BAGD s.v. 1; BDF §454.4); John 8:55; 1 Cor 13:3: κἄν ... καὶ ἐάν (cf. 13:2: καὶ ἐάν ... καὶ ἐάν); Jas 5:15; Matt 10:23 v.l. Concessive *even if, although:* Matt 21:21; 26:35; John 8:14; 10:38; 11:25; *even if only,* Heb 12:20. As particle *even if only:* Mark 5:28; *at least:* 6:56; Acts 5:15; 2 Cor 11:16.

Κανά *Kana* Cana*

Lit.: E. BAMMEL, *BHH* 926. — C. KOPP, *Das Kana des Evangeliums* (1940). — *idem, Places* 143-54. — R. M. MACKOWSKI, " 'Scholars' Qanah.' A Re-examination of the Evidence in Favor of Khirbet Qanah," *BZ* 23 (1979) 278-84. — R. RIESNER, "Fragen um 'Kana in Galiläa," *BK* 43 (1988) 69-71. — G. SCHILLE, *Anfänge der Kirche* (1966) 186f. — For further bibliography see Bammel; *BL* 913.

The place name Κανά (Heb. *qāneh,* "reed") is mentioned in the NT only in John 2:1, 11; 4:46 as the place where Jesus miraculously changed water into wine (4:46ff.) and healed the son of a royal official (according to v. 47 Cana was in the mountains above Capernaum) and in 21:2 as the home of Nathanael. Cana is described in all passages as Κανὰ τῆς Γαλιλαίας (cf. Josephus *Vita* 86), probably to distinguish it from the Cana near Tyre mentioned in Josh 19:28. The location of Cana is uncertain: Much can be said in favor of Khirbet Qânā, *ca.* 14 km. northeast of Nazareth (thus the older tradition; cf. Kopp, *Places* 143ff.). But since the beginning of the sixteenth century Kefr Kennā, *ca.* 9 km. northeast of Nazareth, has been suggested, probably because of its favorable location on the road to Tiberias.

Καναναῖος, ου, ὁ *Kananaios* Cananaean*

Surname of the second Simon in the Twelve (Mark 3:18 par. Matt 10:4). Inasmuch as Simon is called ὁ ζηλωτής in the parallels in Luke 6:15; Acts 1:13, the reference is not to Cana, but to the Aramaic equivalent to → ζηλωτής (3), "zealot." M. Hengel, *The Zealots* (1988) 69f.; *TRE* III, 606.

Κανανίτης, ου, ὁ *Kananitēs* man from Cana, Cananite*

V.l. and thus an independent interpretation of the TR for → Καναναῖος in Mark 3:18 par. Matt 10:4.

Κανδάκη, ης *Kandakē* Candace*

Acts 8:27 (... δυνάστης Κανδάκης βασιλίσσης Αἰθιόπων), as a Greek rendering of the common title of an Ethiopian queen (cf. Meroean *Ka[n]take* or *Ka[n]dakit;* Pliny *HN* vi.186: *regnare feminam Candacen, quod nomen multis iam annis ad reginas transiit;* see also Strabo xvii.1.54; Dio Cassian liv.5). The author of Acts probably saw the title as the name of the individual. BAGD s.v. (bibliography); J. N. Sevenster, *BHH* 930; *BL* 915 (bibliography); E. Haenchen, *Acts* (Eng. tr., 1971) ad loc.; G. Schneider, *Acts* (HTKNT) I, 499f.

κανών, ονος ὁ *kanōn* rule of conduct, standard*

Lit.: H. W. BEYER, *TDNT* III, 596-606. — H. Y. GAMBLE, *The NT Canon* (1985), esp. 15-18. — J. GUHRT, H.-G. LINK, and C. BROWN, *DNTT* III, 399-402. — B. M. METZGER, *The Canon of the NT* (1987), esp. 288-93. — K. PRÜMM, *Diakonia Pneumatos* I (1967) 587-93. — A. SAND, *Kanon* (Handbuch der Dogmengeschichte 1/3a, 1974). — For further bibliography see *DNTT* III, 404; *TWNT* X, 1133f.; Sand.

1. Κανών is found 4 times in the NT, all in Paul's letters (Gal 6:16; 2 Cor 10:13, 15, 16; cf. Phil 3:16 v.l.). As a loanword based on Semitic *qāneh*, it had the basic meaning "reed"; as a "straight" staff it took on the meaning "standard," "measure." The LXX uses κανών once in this sense of a total of 3 occurrences (4 Macc 7:21). But already here a change of meaning is to be seen: κανών becomes a *rule of conduct*, a standard for making judgments.

2. In the blessing in Gal 6:16 Paul summarizes what he has said concerning the opponents and their false teachings. "Peace and mercy" are wished for all who agree "with this *canon*" (i.e., that of Paul); for through the Spirit the Christian is a new creation (6:15). Κανών is thus the new standard for the believer.

In Phil 3:16 *NTG* and *UBSGNT* provide the text: "Only let us live up to what we have attained." A significant number of mss. have (in dependence on Gal 6:16?) changes of position and additions (φρονεῖν and κανών). In accordance with p[16, 46] ℵ A B, etc., *NTG* and *UBSGNT* do not take κανών into account. In the presumably secondary glosses κανών has the same meaning as in Gal 6:16: *standard* of Christian conduct.

3. In the difficult text 2 Cor 10:9-18 Paul gives his personal defense; he rejects the charge of his opponents, in which his apostolic authority with respect to the church is disputed. Paul appeals 3 times to the *standard* that has been granted to him (v. 13 in connection with → μέτρον). God himself has given him the *measure,* the *direction,* according to which he should go to Corinth in fulfillment of the apostolic authority with which he has been commissioned. This meaning in v. 13 is also present in 15b. Here κανών does not mean the geographical region (against Prümm, et al.). Instead, the apostle boasts that he cannot proceed beyond the limit given to him. V. 16 speaks of "another person's *standard.*" Even if in this verse one must consider "textual corruption" as a pos-

sibility (H. Windisch, *2 Cor* [KEK] 312), κανών still has here the same meaning as in vv. 13 and 15, but with a more negative emphasis: Paul rejects any boasting that rests on a strange *measure.*

                                          A. Sand

Καπερναούμ *Kapernaoum* Capernaum
Alternative form of → Καφαρναούμ.

καπηλεύω *kapēleuō* trade with; sell, offer for sale*

2 Cor 2:17: οὐ . . . καπηλεύοντες τὸν λόγον τοῦ θεοῦ. The vb. (from κάπηλος, "tradesman") plays a role in Greek polemic against the Sophists, which criticizes the marketing of spiritual and intellectual goods for profit and is concerned less with "adulteration" (Luther) than the gaining of a profit. BAGD s.v.; R. Bultmann, *2 Cor* [Eng. tr., 1985] ad loc.; S. Hafemann, *Suffering and the Spirit* (WUNT 2/19, 1986) 103-76; Spicq, *Notes* I, 403-6.

καπνός, ου, ὁ *kapnos* smoke*

Acts 2:19: ἀτμὶς καπνοῦ, "vapor *of smoke*" (citing Joel 3:3 LXX); 12 occurrences in Revelation: of the "rising" of smoke (cf. Exod 19:18; Isa 34:10): Rev 8:4; 9:2 (ter); 14:11; 19:3; with "fire" and "sulphur": 9:17, 18; in a citation of Isa 6:4: Rev 15:8; further: 9:3; 18:9, 18.

Καππαδοκία, ας *Kappadokia* Cappadocia*

A territory and Roman province in eastern Asia Minor mentioned in the list of peoples in Acts 2:9 as homeland of Diaspora Jews present in Jerusalem. 1 Pet 1:1 addresses Christians in Cappadocia and other places. W. Ruge, PW X, 1910-17; *BL* 925 (bibliography); R. Fellmann, *LAW* 1486f.

καρδία, ας, ἡ *kardia* heart

1. Occurrences and meaning — 2. Usage — 3. Paul — 4. The Synoptics — 5. John and the other late writings

Lit.: J. B. BAUER, "De 'cordis' notione biblica et judaica," *VD* 40 (1962) 27-32. — idem, *SacVb* 360-63. — F. BAUMGÄRTEL and J. BEHM, *TDNT* III, 605-14. — BULTMANN, *Theology,* 220-27 (on Paul). — G. DAUTZENBERG, *Sein Leben bewahren. Ψυχή in den Herrenworten der Evangelien* (SANT 14, 1966) 114-23. — A. M. DENIS, "L'Apôtre Paul, prophète 'messianique' des Gentiles. Étude Thématique de I Thess II,1-6," *ETL* 33 (1957) 245-318. — P. HOFFMANN, *HTG* 686-90. — J. JEREMIAS, "Die Muttersprache der Evangelisten Matthäus," *ZNW* 50 (1959) 270-74. — R. JEWETT, *Paul's Anthropological Terms* (1971) 305-33. — E. LERLE, "Καρδία als Bezeichnung für den Mageneingang," *ZNW* 76 (1985) 292-94. — F. H. VON MEYENFELDT, *Het hart* (leb, lebab) *in het Oude Testament* (1950). — H. RUSCHE, "Das menschliche Herz nach biblischem Verständnis," *BibLeb* 3 (1962) 201-6. — H. SCHLIER, "Das Menschenherz nach dem Apostel Paulus," idem III, 184-200. — T. SORG, *DNTT* II, 180-84. — W. D. STACEY, *The Pauline View of Man* (1956) 194-97. — For further bibliography see *DNTT* II, 184; *TWNT* X, 1134f.

1. Καρδία is found in all the NT writings except Titus, Philemon, 2–3 John, and Jude. The 157 occurrences are widely distributed to the extent that it is not esp. favored by any particular author (there is a certain predominance in Lukan writings: Luke has 22 occurrences, Acts has 21).

With regard to meaning, the NT is dependent on OT and Jewish usage. Καρδία is not regarded, as in the Greek understanding, as an organ in the physiological sense and the location of mental and spiritual feeling (Behm 608f.), but is the equivalent for Heb. lēḇ/lēḇāḇ. The LXX translated both terms consistently with καρδία (only seldom with διάνοια or ψυχή). Καρδία refers thus to the *inner person*, the seat of understanding, knowledge, and will, and takes on as well the meaning *conscience*. A new orientation appears in the NT where a pron. is used for the person, where the OT would prefer "heart" (cf. Matt 9:3; 16:7; 2 Cor 2:1, etc.); on the other hand, καρδία is used for the *I* of the person when the reference is to "the hidden person of the *heart*" (1 Pet 3:4).

2. The use of καρδία for a place of concealment makes it possible for a person to speak "in" his or her *heart* (Matt 24:48 par. Luke 12:45; Rom 10:6; Rev 18:7) or to bear something that has been experienced "in" his or her *heart* (Luke 1:66; 21:14; Acts 5:4). On the other hand, the power of faith comes ἐκ καρδίας (ὑπηκούσατε: Rom 6:17; cf. 1 Tim 1:5 [ἀγάπη ἐκ . . . καρδίας]; 2 Tim 2:22; 1 Pet 1:22; Acts 8:37 v.l.). In a fig. sense reference can be made to the *heart* of the earth (Matt 12:40; cf. Jonah 2:4; Ezek 27:4, 25f., etc.) or to the *heart* in contrast to something outward (2 Cor 5:12; 1 Thess 2:17). Circumlocutions with καρδία can replace a simple pron., though in all such cases it is stronger than the simple pron. (cf. Mark 2:6 with 2:8; also John 16:22; Col 4:8; Jas 5:5).

The theological meaning of καρδία is more significant than simple anthropological usage: The καρδία is the "place" of the person in which the encounter with God is realized in the positive or negative sense, in which religious life has its firm ground, and from which the ethical conduct of the person is determined. A peculiar instance is to be seen in the formulas of benediction in 1 Thess 3:11-13; 2 Thess 2:16-17; 3:5. In these texts the request is made to God in a hymnic way that he might establish, encourage, and strengthen the *hearts* of the believers.

3. a) In 1 Thessalonians Paul remains primarily within the traditional use of Jewish anthropological terminology (absent are such important Pauline anthropological terms as σάρξ, συνείδησις, πνεῦμα τοῦ ἀνθρώπου, etc.). Characteristic is the use of καρδία in texts that contain a defense of Paul against false statements about him. According to 1 Thess 2:4 God is the one "who tests our *hearts*," the guarantor that Paul's apostolic activity (cf. 2:1-12) is

legitimate and is unjustly challenged by his opponents (Jewish wandering prophets?). In v. 17 Paul expresses the wish to see the brothers again. Although he is absent in person, he is not absent "in *heart*." Bodily absence is unimportant. Only the spiritual bond, based on the καρδία, is important. Here Paul remains "more in the spirit of Hebraic psychology" than in 1 Cor 5:3, where a similar idea is present (cf. E. von Dobschütz, *1–2 Thess* [KEK] 120).

Gal 4:6 (the only occurrence of καρδία in Galatians) emphasizes that God "has sent the Spirit of his Son into our *hearts*." The two occurrences in Philippians (1:7f.; 4:7) combine Jewish with Greek concepts. In 1:7 καρδία stands with φρονεῖν and σπλάγχνα (v. 8); in 4:7 it appears with νοῦς and νόημα. The use of σπλάγχνα is striking. In the late writings of the LXX σπλάγχνα became interchangeable with καρδία (Prov 12:10; Wis 10:5; Sir 30:7, etc.); in Phil 1:8 it must remain uncertain whether σπλάγχνα is to be translated "heart," as in v. 7, or "love." However, in both passages no dichotomous or trichotomous understanding is present.

b) The 16 occurrences of καρδία in 1–2 Corinthians and the 15 in Romans likewise remain within Jewish usage: The person is always seen in his or her totality. From the heart come shameful desires (Rom 1:24). The human heart is hardened, unrepentant (2 Cor 3:14f.; Rom 2:5), and without understanding (Rom 1:21). Even when it is said of the Gentiles that they have a knowledge of what is good and right before God "in their *hearts*" (Rom 2:15), a pessimistic element is still predominant in the view of the human καρδία. This view follows the OT: "The heart is deceitful beyond measure and corrupt. Who can understand it?" (Jer 17:9). Therefore any repentance must be established in the heart (1 Cor 4:5). "The circumcision of the *heart*" is demanded (Rom 2:29). God lets his light shine in *hearts* (2 Cor 4:6), pours his love (Rom 5:5) and his Spirit into the *heart* (2 Cor 1:22; Gal 4:6f.). However, "this heart remains veiled. In its truth it appears finally at the appearance of Christ" (Schlier 200).

4. In the Synoptics as well the meaning of καρδία is determined essentially by the OT. In his preaching of the kingdom of God Jesus addresses the *heart* of humankind: The word of God is sown in the *heart* (Matt 13:19; Luke 8:12, 15). The decision for or against faith occurs in the *heart* (Mark 11:23; Matt 13:15b; Luke 24:25); in the *heart* one's stubbornness toward God is shown (Mark 3:5; 6:52; 8:17; Matt 13:15a). When one's actions no longer come from the heart and when thought, speech, and activity are divided, one is a hypocrite (Mark 7:1-23; Luke 12:1, 56). Matthew in particular sees a demonstration of hypocrisy in th character of the Pharisees (Matt 6:1-8, 16-24; 7:15-23). Over against this hypocrisy Jesus demands unity of *heart*, word, and deed (Matt 12:34;

Luke 6:45). "This emphatic summons to the heart in Jesus' preaching does not represent a spiritualism; it always presupposes the deed of the person, but intends to prevent hypocrisy and lies" (Hoffmann 688).

The question of the greatest commandment is answered by Jesus with a reference to Deut 6:5 (Mark 12:30, 32 par.; on the textual variants and problems of tradition history see Jeremias). Although none of the Gospels agrees exactly with the LXX tradition, they all agree with the LXX in saying that one should love God "with all the *heart*" and placing this demand emphatically at the beginning. The reliance of Jesus' message on the OT's view of humankind is again evident: The individual is obligated to love God from his innermost being, wholly, and with an undivided loyalty.

5. John 12:40 cites the statement about hardening in Isa 6:9f. (καρδία appears twice): The unbelief that is present in the *heart* is decisively made clear in Jesus. The betrayal of Jesus (13:2) comes from the heart of Judas. Perplexity (14:1, 27) and sorrow (16:6) occur in the heart (cf. 16:20, 22). But the hearts of the disciples will rejoice at "that day," i.e., at the day of the glorification of Jesus (16:22f.).

The four occurrences in 1 John (3:19, 20 bis, 21) give a witness that the human heart can itself be the accuser, but that God, because of his knowledge, is greater than the accusing heart and recognizes the works of brotherly love. In the heart one must prove oneself in obedience and perseverance (2 Thess 3:5; cf. Rom 6:17). The peace of Christ establishes its sovereignty in the heart (Col 3:15f.). God tests the depth of the heart because it is evil, unbelieving, and darkened (Heb 3:12; Eph 4:18). The late writings of the NT also remain on the foundation of the OT and of Judaism. Καρδία is—despite slight variations in accent—the center of the person, that which determines one's life and from which one must determine one's life.

A. Sand

καρδιογνώστης, ου, ὁ *kardiognōstēs* one who knows the heart*

This noun occurs only in Christian texts: Acts 1:24; 15:8, of God; cf. *Herm. Man.* iv.3.4. E. Haenchen, *Acts* (Eng. tr., 1971) ad loc.; J. B. Bauer, "Καρδιογρώστης, ein unbeachteter Aspekt (Apg 1,24; 15,8)," *BZ* 32 (1988) 114-17.

καρπός, ου, ὁ *karpos* fruit, grain
ἄκαρπος, 2 *akarpos* unfruitful*

1. Occurrences in the NT; literal and fig. usage — 2. Proverbial phrases — 3. Parables — 4. John — 5. Mission and parenesis in the epistles — 6. Fruit of the body; eschatological fruit

Lit.: F. HAUCK, *TDNT* III, 614-16. — R. HENSEL, *DNTT* I, 721-23. — A. LOZERON, *La Notion de Fruit dans le NT* (Diss. Lausanne, 1957). — E. OSSWALD, *BHH* 503. — For further bibliography see *TWNT* X, 1135.

1. The noun appears 66 times in the NT, esp. frequently in the Gospels (19 occurrences in Matthew, 5 in Mark, 12 in Luke, and 10 in John), and 9 times in Paul. The adj. appears 7 times.

Fruit in the OT is spoken of as the result of planting and growth, and is associated with trees, crops, and eating. Because of its association with the idea of deed and result, it is used in reference to human conduct (e.g., Pss 1:3; 58:12; Isa 3:10). In the concluding pareneses of the holiness law (Lev 26:4, 20) and of Deuteronomy (7:13; 28:18) the flourishing or destruction of fruit as a blessing or curse of God is made dependent on conduct with regard to the commandments.

In the NT also "fruit" shifts between literal (Luke 12:17; Acts 14:17 [adj.]; Jas 5:18) and fig. uses (Gal 5:22: "the *fruit* of the Spirit is love . . ."), in which the images recede in favor of references to those who are addressed (John 15:1ff. of the vine, grape, and fruit). Here different perspectives on judgment are in evidence (Matt 3:10 par. Luke 3:9: "Every tree which does not bring forth good *fruit* will be cut down and thrown into the fire"; John 15:2ff.; Luke 13:6ff.: fig tree without fruit; Mark 11:12ff.: cursing of the fig tree without fruit), without leaving the apparently literal level.

2. Proverbial phrases appear in 1 Cor 9:7 ("who plants a vineyard and does not enjoy its *fruit?*"); 2 Tim 2:6 (the "claim for support"); Mark 12:1ff. (the claim of the vineyard owner against the evil workers); Jas 5:7 ("the farmer awaits the precious *fruit*"). The tree-fruit material in the concluding parenesis of the Sermon on the Mount (Matt 7:16b par. Luke 6:44b; Matt 7:17f. par. Luke 6:43; Matt 7:16a par. Luke 6:44a) is accentuated in terms of the final judgment by Matthew himself by means of 7:21ff. The agreement between plants and *fruit* allows a conclusion about the plant or tree to be drawn from its *fruits,* i.e., a conclusion about the quality of the disciple's discipleship from the disciple's deeds. In this sense the *fruits* are relevant to the judgment. Matt 7:19 is a redactional citation from the Baptist tradition in Matt 3:10 par. Luke 3:9. The group of sayings in Matt 12:32-37 is totally different. "Fruit" is used not of acts, but of speech (cf. the independent par. in *Gos. Thom.* 44f.; H.-T. Wrege, *Die Gestalt des Evangeliums* [1978] 124ff.). In the present context fruit thus means speech as expression and result of the theological condition of the person (cf. Sir 27:6 LXX). Matthew gives redactional emphasis to the significance of the fruit as obedience to Jesus' instructions (cf. Matt 7:16a, 20); the accent is directed outwardly against Israel (21:41, 43). Already in the tradition (from Jesus?) Mark 12:1ff. places Jesus at the end of the series of those sent to demand the fruit of the vineyard from the

workers. Thus in the structure of the form of the gospel created by Mark, the last dispute introduced involves the earthly Jesus: the conflict breaks out over the fruits.

3. In the parable of the sower in Mark 4:2ff.; *Gos. Thom.* 9 the good earth brings forth extraordinary *fruit* (4:8), while the thorns have previously hindered any *fruit* (v. 7). The allegory refers to cares and wealth (4:19 par. Matt 13:22: ἄκαρπος). It associates fruitbearing with accepting the missionary word (v. 20: καρποφορέω, see Jeremias, *Parables* 77-79). In the parable of the seed growing secretly in 4:26ff. (no par.), v. 28 (καρποφορέω) emphasizes the independence of fruitbearing from the person and comes esp. near to sayings about the coming of the kingdom of God. V. 29 marks the coming of the kingdom of God as harvest in the image of the ripeness of the *fruit*. In the parable in Matt 13:24ff. (M) the ripening of the *fruit* (v. 26) designates the moment in which the weeds appear together with the wheat.

4. John 4:36 reflects the post-Easter mission which, as in the kingdom parables, is depicted as a harvest. It speaks of fruit for eternal life (R. Bultmann, *John* [Eng. tr., 1971] ad loc.).

The image of the vine, its branches, and its fruit in 15:1 proceeds from clear identifications (v. 1: "*I am the true vine and my Father is the vinedresser*"; v. 5: "*I am the vine, you are the branches*") that provide the basis for all the following admonitions. This is also emphasized in v. 16 with the election of the disciples by Christ for the purpose of bearing *fruit*. Branches that do not bear fruit will be destroyed (15:2a, 5b, 6), but those that bear *fruit* will be "purified" in order that they may be stimulated to bear more fruit. The reference is to one's deepening of his relationship to the revelatory word (15:3; see Bultmann ad loc.) and abiding "in me" (15:4ff.).

The fruit motif in John 12:24 is directly connected with the kerygma concerning Jesus' death ("Unless a grain of wheat falls into the earth and dies, it remains alone; but if it dies, it bears much *fruit*"). But in 12:24-26a a preliterary group of sayings about discipleship underlies the image (H.-T. Wrege, FS Jeremias [1970] 267-73), which is interpreted in the present context in terms of the death of the revealer; Jesus is thus the first who brings fruit with his death.

5. "*Fruit* of the work" in Phil 1:22 (cf. Isa 3:10; Jer 17:10; 32:19) refers to the missionary activity of Paul and is related to Rom 1:13. According to Col 1:6 the gospel brings fruit (καρποφορούμενον) into the whole world. In Rom 6:21f. *fruit* is understood as the conduct of one's life in the realm either of salvation or of damnation (cf. also Rom 7:4f.). In Phil 4:17; Rom 15:28 *fruit* is used of the gift of the church for Paul or Jerusalem (cf. the debate in E. Käsemann, *Rom* [Eng. tr., 1971] 396-401).

Descriptive genitives are found in Isa 10:12 (MT); Phil 1:11 ("*fruit* of righteousness"; cf. Prov 11:30; 13:2); Gal 5:22 ("*fruit* of the Spirit" in contrast to the works of the flesh, v. 19); Eph 5:9 ("*fruit* of the light"; 5:11 polemicizes against the "*unfruitful* works of darkness"); Heb 12:11 ("peaceful *fruit* of righteousness"); similarly Jas 3:18. The background in wisdom literature is evident in Jas 3:17 (cf. also Col 1:10), while the eschatological background is evident in the preaching of the Baptist in Matt 3:8 par. Luke 3:8.

Here also belong the texts with ἄκαρπος: Titus 3:14 focuses on practical needs; 2 Pet 1:8 concludes a list of virtues; Jude 12 is part of a rebuke against heretics. 1 Cor 14:14 has real weight: the understanding remains *fruitless* in the act of speaking in tongues.

6. Luke 1:42 ("*fruit* of the womb") and Acts 2:30 ("*fruit* of the loins"; cf. 2 Kgdms 7:12f.; Ps 131:11 LXX) belong to the common OT mode of expression about the fruit of the body. Heb 13:15 is likewise shaped by this background ("*fruit* of the lips"; cf. Ps 50:14, 23; Isa 57:19; 1QS 10:6, 8).

Using the idea of the correspondence of primal beginning and eschaton, Rev 22:2 associates the tree of Paradise in Gen 2:9 with Ezek 47:12 (see H. Kraft, *Rev* [HNT] 274). In the city of Jerusalem that comes down from heaven (21:10) the tree of life gives *fruit* each month (22:2; see also the fruit motif in 5 Ezra [2 Esdr] 2:18; 1QH 8:4ff.).

H.-T. Wrege

Κάρπος, ου *Karpos* Carpus*

An otherwise unknown Christian in Troas mentioned in a personal note in 2 Tim 4:13. P. Trummer, *BZ* 82 (1974) 193-207.

καρποφορέω *karpophoreō* bear fruit*

There are 8 occurrences in the NT. In the lit. sense of the earth, which "*bears fruit* of itself" (→ αὐτομάτη ἡ γῆ καρποφορεῖ, Mark 4:28). Fig. of the effect of the word in those who hear it and accept it and thus *bear fruit* abundantly (Mark 4:20 par. Matt 13:23/Luke 8:15). Similarly of the new life of those who have died to the law through the death of Christ and now "*bear fruit* to God" (ἵνα καρποφορήσωμεν τῷ θεῷ, dat. of advantage, Rom 7:4), while they previously under the realm of sin's power were impelled to "*bear fruit* to death" (εἰς τὸ καρποφορῆσαι τῷ θανάτῳ, v. 5; see also 4 Ezra 9:31); καρποφορέω here designates the total yield of human life. In Col 1:10 καρποφορέω is used in reference esp. to Christian conduct (ἐν παντὶ ἔργῳ ἀγαθῷ καρποφοροῦντες καὶ αὐξανόμενοι . . .); in 1:6 καρποφορέομαι mid. stands for the effect of the gospel, which "grows and *bears fruit* in all the world" (καρποφορούμενον καὶ αὐξανόμενον; on this combination cf. also v. 10 and Gen 1:22, 28; Mark 4:8; see also E. Lohse, *Col and Phlm* [Hermeneia] ad loc.). → καρπός 5.

καρποφόρος, 2 *karpophoros* fruitful, fruit bearing*

Acts 14:17: καιροὶ καρποφόροι, *"fruitful* times," with the gift of rain as a sign of God's beneficence; perhaps also in the sense of *"fruitful* seasons," i.e., "harvest times," which follow the rain as a time of germination and growth (cf. also Wis 7:18); → καιρός 6; see BAGD s.v. καιρός 1.

καρτερέω *kartereō* be strong, be steadfast, endure*

Heb 11:27, of Moses: τὸν γὰρ ἀόρατον ὡς ὁρῶν ἐκαρτέρησεν, either absolute: he *endured,* or (more likely)— in reference to the partc.—"he had the invisible as though it were *firmly* before his eyes." BAGD s.v.

κάρφος, ους, τό *karphos* splinter*

Matt 7:3, 4, 5 par. Luke 6:41, 42 (bis), in Jesus' figure of speech regarding the *splinter* and the "beam" (→ δοκός) to designate the small in contrast to the large.

κατά *kata* with gen.: down from; through; against; by; with acc.: through; during; by; according to

1. Occurrences in the NT — 2. With the gen. — a) Of place — b) Fig. use — 3. With the acc. — a) Of place — b) Of time — c) Fig. use — d) Periphrastic alternative to the simple gen.

Lit.: On preps. in general → ἀνά. — BAGD s.v. — BDF §§224f. — H. J. GENTHE, *Die spezifische Bedeutung von κατά mit dem Akkusativ in den theologischen Aussagen des Apostels Paulus* (1969). — JOHANNESSOHN, *Präpositionen* 245-59. — KÜHNER, *Grammatik* II/1, 475-80. — MAYSER, *Grammatik* II/2, 427-40. — C. F. D. MOULE, *An Idiom-Book of NT Greek* (²1958) 58-60, 88-92. — RADERMACHER, *Grammatik* 137-46. — P. F. REGARD, *Contribution à l'Étude des Prépositions dans la langue du NT* (1919) 466-90. — SCHWYZER, *Grammatik* II, 473-81.

1. Κατά appears in the NT 476 times and is eighth in frequency among preps. in the NT. Use with the acc. is more frequent than with the gen. As a prefix to vbs. κατα- is third in frequency (after συν- and ἐπι-). Κατά with the acc. and as a verbal prefix is typical of the Lukan and Pauline literature and Hebrews but rare in the Johannine literature and Revelation (Morgenthaler, *Statistik* 160).

Κατά with the gen. originally designates the point of origin or the goal of an action. Κατά with the acc. designates the area over which a movement extends. In both cases the basic meaning *down/downwards* is operative (Kühner 475). As with the other preps., κατά shows a tendency toward expansion and unclarity of meaning in

the Hellenistic period. Thus an unambiguous delimitation of the nuance is not possible in all cases. Moreover, it is clear in the use of κατά that prep. phrases appear increasingly in the place of the simple case (→ ἐπί 1).

2. With the gen.:
a) Of place: *down from* (Matt 8:32 par.: *"down from* the slope"; 1 Cor 11:4: κατὰ κεφαλῆς ἔχων (τι), "have something hanging *down* from the head/have something *on* the head"), *down into* (2 Cor 8:2: ἡ κατὰ βάθους πτωχεία, "the poverty *reaching into the depths* [i.e., deep, great poverty]"), *throughout, in* (Acts 9:42: "*throughout* all Joppa/*in* all Joppa"; Luke 23:5, etc.: "*in* the entire region"; 4:14: "*through* all the surrounding country").
b) Fig.: *against,* in a hostile sense, with vbs. of action, speaking, being able, being (Acts 14:2: "bring up *against* a brother"; Matt 5:11: "say every kind of evil *against* you"; 2 Cor 13:8: "we are not able to do anything *against* the truth"; Mark 9:40: "whoever is not *against* us"; Matt 5:23: "he has something *against* you [in his heart]"), (swear) *by* (Heb 6:13: "*by* himself"; v. 16: "*by* the hearers"; Matt 26:63: "*by* the living God").

3. With the acc.:
a) Of place: *throughout, over, in, at* (Luke 8:39: "*throughout* the entire city/*in* the entire city"; 15:14: "*throughout* that land"; Matt 24:7: κατὰ τόπους, "*at* [many] places"; Acts 11:1: "*throughout* Judea/*in* Judea"; 24:14: "everything that stands *in* the law"), *along, alongside* (Acts 27:5: τὸ πέλαγος τὸ κατὰ τὴν Κιλικίαν, "the sea *along* [the coast of] Cilicia"), *to, toward, up to* (Luke 10:32: "come *up to* the place; Acts 8:26: "*toward* the south"; Phil 3:14: "*toward* the goal"; Gal 2:11, etc.: κατὰ πρόσωπον, "*to* the face," "face to face," "personally," "in the face of," "before"; 2 Cor 10:7: τὰ κατὰ πρόσωπον, "what lies *before* the eyes"; Gal 3:1: κατ' ὀφθαλμούς, "*before* the eyes"), *for, by* (Rom 14:22: κατὰ σεαυτόν, "*for* yourself, *by* yourself"; Acts 28:16: μένειν καθ' ἑαυτόν, "stay alone *by* himself"; Mark 4:10: κατὰ μόνας, "*for* oneself alone"), distributive (Acts 2:46; 5:42: κατ' οἶκον, "house *to* house/*in* the [individual] houses"; 15:21, etc.: κατὰ πόλιν, "city *by* city/*in* [every] city").
b) Of time: *during* (Heb 1:10: κατ' ἀρχάς, "*in* the beginning"; Acts 12:1: κατ' ἐκεῖνον τὸν καιρόν, "*at* that time"; Rom 5:6: κατὰ καιρόν, "*at* that time/then"; Matt 1:20: κατ' ὄναρ, "*during* the dream"; Acts 16:25: "*about* midnight"), distributive (Luke 2:41: κατ' ἔτος, "year *by* year/annually"; similarly Heb 9:25, etc.: κατ' ἐνιαυτόν; Matt 26:55, etc.: κατ' ἡμέραν, "day *by* day/each *day*/ daily," often with πᾶσαν [Acts 17:17] or ἑκάστην [Heb 3:13]; 1 Cor 16:2: "*on each* first day of the week/*on each* Sunday"; Matt 27:15: "*at each* festival").
c) Fig.: 1) distributive (along with local and temporal distributive use, κατά is also used distributively in a fig. sense; here a clear distinction of nuances is not possible:

1 Cor 14:27: "*only* two or at most three"; v. 31: καθ' ἕνα πάντες, "everyone, one *after* the other"; John 21:25: καθ' ἕν, "one *after* the other/each detail"; alternatively Acts 21:19: καθ' ἓν ἕκαστον; Rev 4:8: ἓν καθ' ἕν, "one *like* the other/each"; Mark 14:19: εἷς καθ' εἷς [undeclined nom. —so BAGD 232—or κατά used as adv.—so BDF §224.3; cf. also Regard 488f.], "one *after* the other"; Rom 12:5: τὸ καθ' εἷς, "individually"/"individual"; Mark 6:40: "*by* hundred and *by* fifty"; Heb 9:5: κατὰ μέρος, "part *for* part/in part"; John 10:3: κατ' ὄνομα, "name *for* name/ each by name").

2) Final: *for the purpose of, for* (in some of these instances the tr. *according to* is also possible: John 2:6: "*for* the purification/*corresponding to* the regulations for purification"; 2 Cor 11:21: "*to* my shame"; Titus 1:1: ἀπόστολος κατὰ πίστιν ἐκλεκτῶν, "apostle *for* the faith of those who are elect/apostle, in order to lead the elect to faith" or "apostle, *corresponding to* the faith of those who are elect").

3) Of homogeneity, similarity, correspondence, manner: *according to, in accordance with, corresponding to, like* (Luke 2:22, etc.: "*according to* the law"; v. 39: πάντα τὰ κατὰ τὸν νόμον κυρίου, "everything [to be performed] *according to* the law of the Lord"; 1 Cor 15:3: "*according to* [the] Scripture[s]"; Acts 18:14: κατὰ λόγον, "*according to* order" or "*from* a rational point of view/*with* full right and authority"; Rom 8:27, etc.: κατὰ θεόν, "*according to* God's will"; Matt 16:27: "he will requite each one *according to* what he has done"; 2:16: κατὰ τὸν χρόνον, "*corresponding to* the time"; 9:29: "*corresponding to* your faith"; 25:15: "*corresponding to* his ability"; Gal 4:28: κατὰ Ἰσαάκ, "*like* Isaac"; Luke 6:23, etc.: κατὰ τὰ αὐτά, and Acts 14:1: κατ' τὸ αὐτό, "*in* the same *way*," "likewise"; 2 Thess 2:3: κατὰ μηδένα τρόπον, "*in* any way"; Mark 1:27: κατὰ ἐξουσίαν, "*with* authority"; 1 Cor 14:40: κατὰ τάξιν, "*in* order/*orderly*"; Rom 8:12, etc.: κατὰ σάρκα, "*according to* the flesh," but Rom 1:3, etc.: "*with regard to* the flesh"; Heb 3:3: καθ' ὅσον, "*as*").

4) Of reason: *on the basis of, because, from* (Eph 3:3, etc.: κατὰ ἀποκάλυψιν, "*on the basis of* revelation/ *through* revelation"; Acts 3:17: κατὰ ἄγνοιαν, "*from* ignorance"; Matt 19:3: κατὰ πᾶσαν αἰτίαν, "*for* any cause").

5) Of direction or relationship: *with respect to, in relation to* (Acts 24:22: τὰ καθ' ὑμᾶς, "what *concerns* you /your affairs"; Acts 17:22, etc.: κατὰ πάντα, "*in* every respect").

d) As an alternative for an attributive or possessive gen. (Acts 26:3: τὰ κατὰ Ἰουδαίους ἔθη, "the customs/laws of the Jews"; Heb 11:7: ἡ κατὰ πίστιν δικαιοσύνη, "the righteousness of faith"; 1 Tim 6:3: ἡ κατ' εὐσέβειαν διδασκαλία, "the religious teaching"; cf. also the superscriptions of the Gospels: κατὰ Μαθθαῖον, etc.; Rom 11:21: οἱ κατὰ φύσιν κλάδοι, "the natural branch"; Eph 6:5: οἱ κατὰ σάρκα κύριοι, "earthly masters"; Acts 17:28: οἱ καθ' ὑμᾶς ποιηταί, "your

poets"; Eph 1:15: ἡ καθ' ὑμᾶς πίστις, "your faith"; Acts 18:15: νόμος ὁ καθ' ὑμᾶς, "your law").

W. Köhler

καταβαίνω *katabainō* go down; come down

1. Occurrences in the NT — 2. Meanings — a) Geographic-spatial — b) Religious

Lit.: J. BLANK, *Krisis* (1964) 78f. — R. SCHNACKENBURG, *John* II (Eng. tr., 1979) 30-69. — G. SCHNEIDER, "Engel und Blutschweiss," *BZ* 20 (1976) 112-16. — J. SCHNEIDER, *TDNT* I, 518-23.

1. Καταβαίνω appears 81 times in the NT, 30 times in the Synoptics (11 in Matthew, 6 in Mark, 13 in Luke), 19 times in Acts. The word is also frequently found in John (17 times + John 5:4 v.l.) and Revelation (10 times), while it appears only rarely in the epistolary literature (Rom 10:7; 1 Thess 4:16; Eph 4:9, 10; Jas 1:17).

2. Depending on the standpoint of the speaker and the manner of the movement, καταβαίνω is to be translated *come down, go down,* or *climb down.* Its meaning is thus the opposite of that of → ἀναβαίνω. Two distinctive nuances can be distinguished:

a) In the Synoptics and Acts the geographic-spatial sense without any special religious quality is predominant (37 of the 49 occurrences). Thus, because of the high elevation of Jerusalem and the temple, one *goes down* or *comes down* from it (e.g., Mark 3:22; Luke 2:51; 10:30, 31; 18:14; Acts 8:15, 26; 24:1, 22; 25:6, 7). In the same way the language of Acts 18:22 ("he went down [from Ephesus] to Caesarea, went up, greeted the church, and *went down* to Antioch") suggests that Paul visited Jerusalem (cf. E. Haenchen, *Acts* [Eng. tr., 1971] 544).

According to Luke 6:17, after the calling of the Twelve Jesus went down from the mountain (cf. Matt 5:1) in order to teach the people at a level place, probably at the foot of the mountain. The narrative style suggests that one should read the scene in the light of the Sinai event (Exod 32–34; H. Schürmann, *Luke* [HTKNT] I, 311, 320). In Luke 22:44 the comparison "his sweat became like drops of blood *falling* on the ground" illustrates the earnestness of the prayer; it is not the description of an extraordinary phenomenon of ἀγωνία (i.e., hemohydrosis).

When the descent of natural events like storm (Luke 8:23), rain (Matt 7:25, 27), fire (Luke 9:54; Rev 13:13; 20:9), and hail (Rev 16:21) is described with καταβαίνω, the religious dimension (→ b) must also be considered. In particular the redactional κατέβη in Luke 8:23 is hardly concerned with the particular wind relationships at the Sea of Gennesaret (descending wind), but with the fact that the demonstration of power was given and intended by God.

b) Outside the Synoptics and Acts a specific religious

meaning of καταβαίνω is dominant (26 of 32 occurrences). This use of the word is based on the cosmology of the ancient Near East, according to which the world was divided vertically. Over the (flat) earth are the firmament, the water, and finally heaven (→ οὐρανός) as the location of God and heavenly beings; under the earth is the world of the dead (→ ἄβυσσος, → ᾅδης). Thus already in the LXX καταβαίνω appears often for the descent of God or of a heavenly being (texts in F. Mussner, *ZΩH* [1952] 54f.). Stephen says in Acts 7:34 that God came down to liberate his people from Egypt (cf. Exod 3:8 LXX). Jas 1:17 has the maxim that every good and every perfect gift "*comes down* (partc. καταβαῖνον with δώρημα) from the Father of [heavenly] lights." Angels also come down as messengers of God (Matt 28:2; Rev 10:1; 18:1; 20:1; on John 1:51 → ἀναβαίνω 4). In the reports of Jesus' baptism he sees the Spirit of God come down like a dove upon him (Mark 1:10 par. Matt 3:16). In Luke 3:22 this event is visible to all; in John 1:32, 33 the Baptist testifies to it.

In John it is primarily the Son of Man himself who has come down from heaven; as such he alone is able to ascend (John 3:13) into heaven. The Evangelist's formulation here is in sharp contrast to Gnosticism (Blank 79, *contra* R. Bultmann, *John* [Eng. tr., 1971] 149); use of καταβαίνω of the incarnation as the presupposition for redemption is also emphasized repeatedly in the "bread speech" of 6:22-59. Here Jesus refers to himself—directly (vv. 38, 42) or in the image of the bread of life (vv. 33, 41, 50, 51, 58)—as the one who has come down from heaven. The living bread, unlike the manna, brings eternal life, not exclusively for Israel, but for the world (v. 33).

In Eph 4:9, 10 a christological interpretation is given to Ps 68:19: The one who ascended can only be the one "who *has descended* to the lower parts of the earth." Here also καταβαίνω designates the incarnation of the preexistent Christ in a formulation related to the one in John 3:13.—In 1 Thess 4:6 καταβαίνω is used of the descent of the κύριος at the parousia. In Rev 3:12; 21:2, 10 it is used of the eschatological events: the new Jerusalem *comes down* from heaven.   H. Fendrich

καταβάλλω *kataballō* cast down; mid.: lay a foundation, establish*

Pass. in 2 Cor 4:9: "*cast down*, but not destroyed"; mid. in Heb 6:1: μὴ πάλιν θεμέλιον καταβαλλόμενοι, "without *laying* the foundation again."

καταβαρέω *katabareō* burden (vb.), weigh down*

2 Cor 12:16: ἐγὼ οὐ κατεβάρησα ὑμᾶς, "I was not *a burden* to you" ("by not receiving support from you"; cf. 11:9). Absolute in *Herm. Man.* ix.28.6.

καταβαρύνω *katabarynō* burden (vb.), weigh down*

Mark 14:40: "Their eyes *became heavy/were closing*" (καταβαρυνόμενοι; cf. Matt 26:43, βεβαρημένοι).

κατάβασις, εως, ἡ *katabasis* descent, slope, downward climb*

Luke 19:37, of the *road* that *goes down* the Mount of Olives.

καταβιβάζω *katabibazō* bring down, force someone to come down

Matt 11:23 v.l. par. Luke 10:15 v.l.: ἕως (τοῦ) ᾅδου καταβιβασθήσῃ (in place of καταβήσῃ).

καταβολή, ῆς, ἡ *katabolē* foundation*

Lit.: BLACK, *Approach* 83-89. — H.-H. ESSER, *DNTT* I, 376-78. — F. HAUCK, *TDNT* III, 620f. — O. HOFIUS, " 'Erwählt vor Grundlegung der Welt' (Eph 1,4)," *ZNW* 62 (1971) 123-28.

1. The subst. καταβολή, which in non-NT Greek has a relatively broad range of meaning (see LSJ s.v.), is found in the NT, except in Heb 11:11 (→ 3), only in the phrases πρὸ καταβολῆς κόσμου (John 17:24; Eph 1:4; 1 Pet 1:20) and ἀπὸ καταβολῆς κόσμου (Matt 13:35 [v.l. ἀπὸ καταβολῆς]; 25:34; Luke 11:50; Heb 4:3; 9:26; Rev 13:8; 17:8).

Both phrases are attested so far only in the NT and in texts dependent upon it. Esser is incorrect in saying (377) that ἀπὸ/ ἐκ καταβολῆς κόσμου was used by writers "from Polybius (2nd cent. B.C.) onwards"; it does, however, have analogies in Jewish literature (→ 2.b). NT influence is present when for *ab initio orbis terrarum* (*T. Mos.* 1:14) Gelasius *Historia Ecclesiastica* ii.17.17 has πρὸ καταβολῆς κόσμου.

2. Καταβολὴ κόσμου corresponds to κτίσις κόσμου in Rom 1:20 and means "*foundation/creation* of the world" (cf. the use of καταβολή in 2 Macc 2:29; Josephus *Ant.* xii.64 and of καταβάλλομαι in 2 Macc 2:13; *Ep. Arist.* 104).

a) Πρὸ καταβολῆς κόσμου, "before the *foundation* of the world," indicates absolute pretemporality and premundaneness. According to John 17:24 Christ is the Son beloved of the Father before the world and time, the one who possesses the divine → δόξα from eternity (cf. v. 5). 1 Peter expounds the eternal saving decree of God (cf. 1:1): Before the creation of the world Christ was chosen to redeem the lost by his atoning death (v. 19). This statement includes the idea of a pretemporal election of the redeemed in a way similar to Eph 1:4 (cf. 2 Tim 1:9f.).

The idea is already present in ancient Judaism: God has elected Israel "before the creation of the world" = *qôdem bᵉrîʾat ʿôlām*, etc. (so rabbinic literature, e.g., *Midr. Pss.* 10 §1; 74 §1; 93 §3) or πρὶν γενέσθαι τὰ πάντα (so Hellenistic Judaism: *Jos. As.* 8:9[11] [50:1 in Batiffol]).

b) Ἀπὸ καταβολῆς κόσμου is used simply to designate time in Matt 13:35; Luke 11:50; Heb 4:3; 9:26. It has in view the conclusion of the creative work of God: "since the *creation* of the world/since the [completion of the] *creation* of the world." In Matt 25:34 (the preexistence of the eschatological blessing) and Rev 13:8; 17:8 (predestination; cf. CD 2:7) it refers to a divine decision that took place at the *absolute beginning,* so that its meaning comes close to that of πρὸ καταβολῆς κόσμου.

The same sense can be found in the rabbinic literature in the phrases *min yômā' de'iṯbᵉrê 'almā',* "since the creation of the world" (*Tg. Cant.* 8:2); *mittᵉhillaṯ bᵉrîyāṯô šel 'ôlām,* "since the beginning of creation" (*Pesiq.* 21:5; *Midr. Esth.* 1:1; cf. *T. Mos.* 1:14, 17); and *miššēšeṯ yᵉmê bᵉrē'šîṯ,* "since the six days of creation" (*Mek.* on Exod 14:15).

3. The statement in Heb 11:11a is disputed both text-critically and exegetically (see esp. Black). Because the t.t. καταβολή σπέρματος designates only the male function in procreation (texts in Wettstein, *NT* ad loc.), Sarah cannot be the subject, but rather—as the context also demands (vv. 8-12)—only Abraham. With Black 86f. and *UBSGNT* the appropriate reading is: πίστει—καὶ αὐτὴ Σάρρα στεῖρα—δύναμιν εἰς καταβολὴν σπέρματος ἔλαβεν, "through faith—and although Sarah was herself barren—he [Abraham] received the power for *procreation.*"

O. Hofius

καταβραβεύω *katabrabeuō* deprive of the prize of victory, deprive of victory*

Col 2:18: "No one *may take away* [as umpire] *the prize of victory* (καταβραβευέτω)."

καταγγελεύς, έως, ὁ *katangeleus* proclaimer, herald*

Acts 17:18: ξένων δαιμονίων δοκεῖ καταγγελεὺς εἶναι, a judgment made by some Athenian philosophers with regard to Paul, which is certainly intended to be reminiscent of the accusation against Socrates. Cf. E. Haenchen, *Acts* [Eng. tr., 1971] ad loc.

καταγγέλλω *katangellō* proclaim*

1. Occurrences in the NT — 2. Acts — 3. The Pauline corpus

Lit.: J. SCHNIEWIND, *TDNT* I, 70f.

1. Acts has 11 occurrences, while the Pauline corpus has 7. There are only two occurrences in the LXX (2 Macc 8:36; 9:17), in the second of which the usage comes close to that of the NT ("*proclaim* God's power").

2. In Acts 13:5; 15:36; 17:17 καταγγέλλω has "word of God/of the Lord" as its obj. Καταγγέλλω is clearly a t.t. of Luke for missionary preaching (cf. 17:3 and 16:17).

The content of the preaching, even with all of the differing nuances of the speeches (cf. 4:2; 13:38; 17:23), is clearly unified in Jesus Christ (17:3) and God's saving actions in and through him (cf. also 8:14; 11:1). This is, however, also a question of perspective (16:17, 21).

As already in his Gospel, Luke uses different vbs. of proclamation in Acts: Instead of καταγγέλλω τὸν λόγον τοῦ θεοῦ/τοῦ κυρίου, he can also and without any noticeable difference in meaning use λαλέω τὸν λόγον τοῦ θεοῦ/ τοῦ κυρίου (cf. Acts 4:29, 31; 8:25; 16:32). Acts 15:35 is thus esp. instructive, insofar as here διδάσκω, εὐαγγελίζομαι, and καταγγέλλω are used in succession with τὸν λόγον τοῦ κυρίου as obj. Luke probably did not differentiate between these phrases, although he can consistently, as in Acts 4:2, designate the apostolic preaching in general with διδάσκω and can use καταγγέλλω for a special aspect, in consideration of the Sadducees who are present. 26:23 is included in this usage, while in 3:24 καταγγέλλω almost takes the meaning of προκαταγγέλλω: *promise, prophesy.*

3. Paul's usage in 1 Cor 9:14 comes close to that of Luke, although καταγγέλλω is used in a more open way and tends toward meaning "be active as messengers of faith." Paul, like Luke, can use other vbs. of proclamation alongside καταγγέλλω: In Phil 1:14-18 τὸν λόγον λαλέω, τὸν Χριστὸν κηρύσσω, and τὸν Χριστὸν καταγγέλλω (vv. 17, 18) are used in succession. As with Luke, Paul's concern is with missionary preaching, the content of which is simply Christ (or "Jesus Christ and him only as the crucified one," 1 Cor 2:1).

It is clear from 1 Cor 11:26 that the proclamation of the gospel happens not only through the word. Here the reference is not to the sacramental word accompanying the cultic act, but to eating the bread and drinking the cup because of their relationship to Jesus' death (cf. v. 23b) as the proclamation (of the saving meaning?) of his death. Rom 1:8 could be included in this usage of Paul's, insofar as the faith penetrating the world from the Roman church is now understood as gospel for all the world (cf. H. Schlier, *Rom* [HTKNT] 36). In Col 1:28 "the weight of the apostolic message, a message basic for the foundation of the church, is shifted onto the activity of providing advisory accompaniment" (Schweizer, *Col* [Eng. tr., 1982] 111).

I. Broer

καταγελάω *katagelaō* laugh at, deride*

Mark 5:40 par. Matt 9:24/Luke 8:53: καὶ κατεγέλων αὐτοῦ, scornful laughter at Jesus' words. K. H. Rengstorf, *TDNT* I, 658f.

καταγινώσκω *kataginōskō* condemn, accuse*

Pass. in Gal 2:11, of Cephas: ὅτι κατεγνωσμένος ἦν,

"for he was *condemned/placed in the wrong*," i.e., by his conduct in Antioch (less in view of a judgment of public opinion); cf. R. Bultmann, *TDNT* I, 714f.; BAGD s.v. Act. in 1 John 3:20, 21 with ἡ καρδία as subj.: "whenever our hearts *condemn* us"; cf. *T. Gad* 5:3; Sir 14:2.

κατάγνυμι *katagnymi* shatter, break*

Matt 12:20 (κάλαμον); John 19:31, 32, 33 (τὰ σκέλη): "*break* the legs," a practice known as *crurifragium,* which was meant to hasten the death of a crucified person. This was done to the two crucified with Jesus (vv. 31f.). But Jesus' bones (as with the Passover lamb) were not broken (v. 33; cf. v. 36; Exod 12:10, 46; Num 9:12). On the form, see BDF §§66.2; 101 s.v. ἀγνύναι.

καταγράφω *katagraphō* write; record; sketch, draw*

John 8:6, of Jesus: κατέγραψεν (v.l. ἔγραψεν) εἰς τὴν γῆν, probably a narrative detail intended to show Jesus' superiority over his questioners, thus: "he *painted* [something] on the ground with his finger"; cf. J. Becker, *John* (ÖTK) ad loc.

κατάγω *katagō* lead down, bring down*

Besides Luke 5:11 (καταγαγόντες τὰ πλοῖα ἐπὶ τὴν γῆν, "*bringing* the ship *to land* [from the sea]") and Rom 10:6 (Χριστὸν καταγαγεῖν, "*to bring* Christ *down* [from heaven]"), this vb. appears esp. frequently in Acts: 9:30: "*bring down* [from Jerusalem] to Caesarea"; 22:30; 23:15, 20, 28: all of bringing Paul down from the fortress Antonia to a lower level in Jerusalem. 27:3; 28:12; 21:3 v.l., pass., a t.t. in seafaring: *be brought to land/put in.*

καταγωνίζομαι *katagōnizomai* overcome, vanquish*

Heb 11:33: κατηγωνίσαντο βασιλείας, as the first example of the deeds of faith by judges, kings (David), and prophets of Israel (v. 32); → ἀγών 1, 2.

καταδέω *katadeō* bind up, bandage*

Luke 10:34, with obj. τὰ τραύματα: "*bind* the wounds."

κατάδηλος, 2 *katadēlos* very clearly, evident, open*

Heb 7:15: περισσότερον ἔτι κατάδηλον, "even more *clearly.*"

καταδικάζω *katadikazō* condemn*

Matt 12:7: τοὺς ἀναιτίους; Jas 5:6: τὸν δίκαιον (with ἐφονεύσατε); pass. in Matt 12:37: ἐκ τῶν λόγων σου

καταδικασθήσῃ (opposed to δικαιωθήσῃ); Luke 6:37b; absolute in 6:37a: "*judge* not."

καταδίκη, ης, ἡ *katadikē* condemnation*

Acts 25:15: αἰτούμενοι κατ' αὐτοῦ καταδίκην (because they demanded his [Paul's] *condemnation*)."

καταδιώκω *katadiōkō* run after, pursue*

Mark 1:36: κατεδίωξεν αὐτόν, "he *hurried after* him"; cf. also Ps 22:6 LXX; otherwise usually in a hostile sense.

καταδουλόω *katadouloō* enslave*

2 Cor 11:20: εἴ τις ὑμᾶς καταδουλοῖ, in reference to the presumptuous claims of the opponents; Gal 2:4, likewise fig., of the attempt to transform the freedom of faith back into slavery (to the law); → δουλεύω 1, 2, 5.

καταδυναστεύω *katadynasteuō* treat violently, suppress*

According to Jas 2:6 the rich *act violently* against the Christian community (καταδυναστεύουσιν ὑμῶν); cf. *Diog.* 10:5; pass. in Acts 10:38: Jesus healed "all who *were oppressed*" by the devil."

κατάθεμα, ατος, τό *katathema* accursed*

Rev 22:3, in the description of the eschatological condition of paradise: "And there will be no longer anything *accursed*" (cf. Zech 14:11 LXX: ἀνάθεμα), for the sin leading to God's anathema has been removed; cf. *Did.* 16:5. J. Behm, *TDNT* I, 355; G. Menestrina, "Κατάθεμα," *BeO* 21 (1979) 12.

καταθεματίζω *katathematizō* curse*

Matt 26:74, with ὀμνύειν, of Peter, who confirmed his denial of Jesus with self-imprecations and an oath; cf. the intensification from v. 70 to v. 72 to v. 74. J. Behm, *TDNT* I, 355f.

καταισχύνω *kataischynō* shame, make ashamed*

1. Occurrences in the NT — 2. Meaning — 3. Usage

Lit.: H. C. KEE, "The Linguistic Background of 'Shame' in the NT," *On Language, Culture, and Religion* (FS E. A. Nida, ed. M. Black and W. A. Smalley; 1974) 133-47. — M. WOLTER, *Rechtfertigung und zukünftiges Heil. Untersuchungen zu Römer 5,1-11* (BZNW 43, 1978) 150-53. — For further bibliography → αἰσχύνομαι; see *TWNT* X, 962.

1. This vb. is a compound from αἰσχύνω, is attested from Homer *Od.,* and is frequent in the LXX. It appears

13 times in the NT, 8 times ind., 5 times subjunc. Only one occurrence is in the Gospels (Luke 13:17).

2. It means concretely *violate* in the sense of *disfigure* (1 Cor 11:4f.), but consistently (7 times pass., 4 times act.) *shame, to bring to shame* (R. Bultmann, *TDNT* I, 188f.; BAGD s.v.). The subjective mid. meaning *be ashamed* (cf. Sophocles *Ph.* 1382; → αἰσχύνομαι 2, 4) is seen in Luke 13:17.

3. Except in Rom 5:5 (ἐλπίς), the subj. of καταισχύνω is a person (e.g., God in 1 Cor 1:27; Paul in 2 Cor 7:14) or a group of persons (e.g., the Corinthians in 1 Cor 11:22). The dir. obj. can be a group of persons (1 Cor 1:27; 11:22; cf., e.g., Plato *La.* 187a) or can be impersonal (1 Cor 1:27; 11:4f.; cf., e.g., Homer *Od.* xvi.293). An absolute causative use (cf. BAGD 3.a) with a negative is found in Rom 5:5. In 5 other instances, all pass., the vb. is connected with a negative.

Used as an antonym 4 times in Paul is καυχάομαι (see Wolter 151; K. Berger, *Exegese des NT* [1977] 145). Pass. καταισχύνω is synonymous with the simple vb. (cf. 2 Cor 10:8; Luke 13:17; Isa 45:16; see A. Fuchs, *Sprachliche Untersuchungen zu Mt und Lk* [1971] 184), and involves the objective idea *be confounded* (→ αἰσχύνομαι 3). When Paul boasts to Titus of the church at Corinth, he is not *put to shame* (2 Cor 7:14); when he boasts to the Macedonians of their goodwill in the collection, he does not want to *be put to shame,* along with the Corinthians (9:4). Act. usage is seen in Rom 5:5 (in reference to καυχώμεθα in v. 2 see esp. Wolter) and 1 Cor 1:27: God has *shamed* the wise and the strong, so that no one may boast before him.

In 1 Pet 3:16 it is said that the Gentiles who now revile Christians are to be placed in a situation where they will have to *be ashamed* (R. Bultmann, *TDNT* I, 190). In Luke 13:17 the opponents of Jesus are already in this situation. In Rom 9:33; 10:11; and 1 Pet 2:6 the citation of Isa 28:16 (pass. with negative) is to be interpreted correspondingly. In 1 Cor 11:22 the reference is to the *shaming* of the poor at the Lord's Supper. Vv. 4f. refer to the *dishonoring* of the head in the worship service with or without the head covering by man and woman. The most exact parallels are in Josephus *Ant.* xx.89 (cf. J. Weiss, *1 Cor* [KEK] ad loc.) and Babrius 82.8 (see Moulton/Milligan s.v.).

A. Horstmann

κατακαίω *katakaiō* burn; burn down*

As an image of judgment, Matt 3:12 par. Luke 3:17: τὸ ἄχυρον ("the chaff") κατακαύσει πυρὶ ἀσβέστῳ; cf. Matt 13:30, 40: τὰ ζιζάνια, "the weeds"; 1 Cor 3:15: εἴ τινος τὸ ἔργον κατακαήσεται . . . ; in an apocalyptic image of the end, Rev 8:7 (ter): one-third of the earth and the trees and all of the green grass; cf. 2 Pet 3:10 v.l.; of the fall

of the "whore of Babylon," Rev 17:16; 18:8; of the *burning* of the flesh of sacrificial animals outside the camp on the Day of Atonement, Heb 13:11 (citing Lev 16:27). According to Acts 19:19 the Ephesian converts publicly *burned* their magic books worth 50,000 drachma; on the burning of books in antiquity, cf. K. Lake and H. J. Cadbury, *Beginnings* IV, 243.

κατακαλύπτω *katakalyptō* veil*

Lit.: H. CONZELMANN, *1 Cor* (Hermeneia, 1975) on 11:3ff. — A. JAUBERT, "Le Voile des femmes (I Cor. xi.2-16)," *NTS* 18 (1971/72) 419-30. — A. OEPKE, *TDNT* III, 561-63. — G. SCHWARTZ, "ἐξουσίαν ἔχειν ἐπὶ τῆς κεφαλῆς? (1 Korinther 11,10)," *ZNW* 70 (1979) 249. — W. O. WALKER, "1 Corinthians 11:2-16 and Paul's Views Regarding Women," *JBL* 94 (1975) 94-110.

In the NT only mid.: 1 Cor 11:6 (bis), 7: women must *veil* themselves (v. 6) during the worship service (with a veil, v. 10), while men, the image of God, may not (in v. 7 τὴν κεφαλήν is probably acc. of relation; cf. Gen 38:15). Paul defends the obligation of the Corinthian women by appealing to oriental and Jewish custom, probably in consideration of the Jewish Christians in the Church. He also appeals to the order of creation and to the natural appearance of women, in order to keep dangers from them (v. 10) without, however, questioning the position of woman and man ἐν κυρίῳ (v. 11).

κατακαυχάομαι *katakauchaomai* boast, be overbearing*

Absolute in Rom 11:18b; Jas 3:14; with obj. gen. τῶν κλάδων in Rom 11:18a; with the meaning *triumph* in Jas 2:13 (κατακαυχᾶται ἔλεος κρίσεως).

κατάκειμαι *katakeimai* lie down, recline*

There are 12 occurrences in the NT. Of the sick: Mark 1:30 (κατέκειτο πυρέσσουσα, "she lay with a fever"); 2:4; Luke 5:25; John 5:3, 6; Acts 9:33; 28:8 (πυρετοῖς . . . συνεχόμενον κατακεῖσθαι). *Recline at table* (at a festive meal), regularly formulated as an absolute: Mark 2:15 par. Luke 5:29; Mark 14:3; Luke 3:37; ἐν εἰδωλείῳ κατακείμενον, "share in a temple meal": 1 Cor 8:10. → ἀνάκειμαι.

κατακλάω *kataklaō* break, shatter*

In the NT only of *breaking* of bread: Mark 6:41 (τοὺς ἄρτους) par. Luke 9:16, in both passages with εὐλόγησεν.

κατακλείω *katakleiō* close up, confine*

Luke 3:20 (ἐν φυλακῇ); Acts 26:10 (ἐν φυλακαῖς); cf. Jer 39:2.

κατακληροδοτέω *kataklērodoteō* divide by lot, distribute

Acts 13:19 TR: κατεκληροδότησεν (in place of κατεκληρονόμησεν).

κατακληρονομέω *kataklēronomeō* give as an inheritance*

Acts 13:19, of God, who *gave* Israel the land of the seven peoples in Canaan *as an inheritance* (cf. Deut 7:1): κατεκληρονόμησεν τὴν γῆν αὐτῶν.

κατακλίνω *kataklinō* cause to sit down, cause to lie down; pass.: lie down*

This vb. appears in the NT only in Luke's Gospel: Act. in 9:14: κατακλίνατε αὐτοὺς κλισίας, "*let them recline* in groups . . ."; 9:15. Pass. in 7:36: εἰσελθὼν . . . κατεκλίθη, "he went in . . . and *reclined at the table*"; 24:30; 14:8: μὴ κατακλιθῇς εἰς τὴν πρωτοκλισίαν, "do not *recline* at the place of honor."

κατακλύζω *kataklyzō* inundate, flood (vb.), overflow*

2 Pet 3:6 of the Genesis flood, through which the world of that time *was inundated* (ὕδατι κατακλυσθείς); cf. Ezek 13:11, 13.

κατακλυσμός, οῦ, ὁ *kataklysmos* flood (noun)*

In the NT only of the Genesis *flood* (cf. Josephus *Ant.* i.92f.): Matt 24:38; 24:39 par. Luke 17:27: ἦλθεν ὁ κατακλυσμός; 2 Pet 2:5: κατακλυσμὸν . . . ἐπάξας, "as he [God] let the *flood* erupt."

κατακολουθέω *katakoloutheō* follow
→ ἀκολουθέω 5.

κατακόπτω *katakoptō* strike, beat*

Mark 5:5, of the Gerasene demoniac: κατακόπτων ἑαυτὸν λίθοις, "he *struck* himself with stones" (cf. Billerbeck I, 491f.).

κατακρημνίζω *katakrēmnizō* fall down (from a height)*

Luke 4:29: ὥστε κατακρημνίσαι αὐτόν, "in order to *throw* him *off the cliff*"; cf. 2 Chr 25:12.

κατάκριμα, ατος, τό *katakrima* punishment
→ κατακρίνω.

κατακρίνω *katakrinō* condemn*
κατάκριμα, ατος, τό *katakrima* punishment*
κατάκρισις, εως, ἡ *katakrisis* condemnation*

1. Occurrences in the NT; meanings — 2. The condemnation of Jesus — 3. The wisdom-eschatological principle of judgment — 4. Paul

Lit.: H. R. BALZ, *Heilsvertrauen und Welterfahrung* (1971) 116-23. — E. BRANDENBURGER, *Adam und Christus* (1962) 219-47. — F. BÜCHSEL, *TDNT* III, 951f. — J. GNILKA, "Die Verhandlung vor dem Synhedrion und vor Pilatus nach Markus 14,53–15,5," EKKNT (V) 2 (1970) 5-21. — L. MATTERN, *Das Verständnis des Gerichts bei Paulus* (1966) 62-64, 91-102. — P. VON DER OSTEN-SACKEN, *Römer 8 als Beispiel paulinischer Soteriologie* (1975) 20-57, 165-75, 226-47, 312-14. — H. PAULSEN, *Überlieferung und Auslegung in Römer 8* (1975). — W. SCHENK, *Der Passionsbericht nach Markus* (1974) 229-43. — G. SCHNEIDER, "Gab es eine vorsynoptische Szene 'Jesus vor dem Synedrium'?" *NovT* 12 (1970) 22-39. — idem, *Die Passion Jesu nach den drei älteren Evangelien* (1973) 55-67. — E. SYNOFZIK, *Die Gerichts- und Vergeltungsaussagen bei Paulus* (1977). — U. WILCKENS, *Rom* (EKKNT) I (1978) 127-31, 142-46, 322-28.

1. The vb. κατακρίνω appears in the LXX only 4 or 5 times, representing Heb. *gazar* only in Esth 2:1. There are 15 occurrences in the NT (omitting the 3 in Mark 16:16; John 8:10f.), one-third of them in Paul (1 Cor 11:32; Rom 2:1; 8:3, 34; 14:23), who alone in the NT uses the Hellenistic neologism κατάκριμα (Rom 5:16, 18; 8:1 as *nomen resultantum* designating "the punishment following sentence," BAGD s.v.), which is not present in the LXX, and κατάκρισις (2 Cor 3:9 in the same sense, but in 7:3 as a *nomen actionis* without juridical connotation: "the giving of a negative judgment"). Paul thus has half of all the occurrences of this word group.

2. Mark uses the vb. in a juridical sense in his two related and obviously redactional occurrences (10:33; 14:64) for the *condemnation* (cf. Sus 53; Dan 4:37a LXX; Sus 41, 48, 53 Theodotion) of Jesus to death. The dat. of the punishment in 10:33 (as in Dan 4:37a LXX; Josephus *Ant.* x.124; 2 Pet 2:6; *SIG* II, 736, 160ff.) is evidently a Latinism [*damnare morte*]. Mark affirms that Jesus' condemnation was legal (V. Taylor, *Mark* [1952] ad loc.); this cannot with certainty be attributed to his tradition (Schenk; *contra* R. Pesch, *Mark* [HTKNT] ad loc.). Matthew has taken over both passages (20:18; 27:3, the latter giving a different reading from Mark 14:64). Luke eliminates them.

3. The wisdom-eschatological principle that the deeds of one person provide the standard for the conduct of others in order to demonstrate their unrighteousness and thus bring about their condemnation (Wis 4:16: "The righteous man who has died will condemn the ungodly who are living"; Josephus *Ant.* x.238; *Mek. Exod.* 12:1) appears in Q in Luke 11:31f. par. Matt 12:41f. and in Heb 11:7 (a simple form also in Rom 2:27). 2 Pet 2:6 lies within a sequence of historical examples of condemnation and destructive punishments. Because these prelimi-

nary examples of destruction will be recapitulated in the final judgment, they can serve at the present as an example and a warning.

4. In Pauline usage it is noteworthy that all of the passages in Romans are to be understood in their compositional relation to each other. They belong to the semantic field of the christologically determined justification by God. The comprehensive horizon of thought is not a principle of recompense, but rather the principle of correspondence of deed and condition, in which the word group has as its chief semantic component "surrender, hand over." Rom 2:1 proceeds from the empirically demonstrable fact that everyone "places the blame" on the other and does the same thing for which he blames others, and thus demonstrates the universal human fallen condition and inexcusability (as in 2 Sam 12). As a result of the resurrection of Jesus from the dead the decision of God against the sinner is to be expected neither from a postmortem nor a transhistorical judgment; nor does it remain open. Instead it lies in the death that separates from God and that is shared with Adam (Rom 5:16, 18; 2 Cor 3:9, cf. v. 7). On the basis of Jesus' resurrection, his death has now become the destruction of the power of sin, in which the final judgment on sin has now taken place, as Rom 8:3 formulates as a summary of the positive statements of 5:15ff. This judgment of death over the entire Adamic humanity and the absolute hopelessness accompanying it become a thing of the past for the individual when the resurrected one takes control of his life. The individual is certain of freedom from this judgment of death (Rom 8:1). Rom 8:34 summarizes this certainty in a traditional catechetical question-answer formulation in which the change of subj. between the questions and answers demonstrates the irrelevance of the question and points to the absurdity of there being anyone to accuse or condemn. The logical fut. demonstrates that the trial situation is a permanent event, and the powers of destruction are concretized historically.

1 Cor 11:32 distinguishes between the simple vb. (as educative refining judgment) and the compound vb., which is used for the total condemnation to which all of Adamic humanity is subject. The concern is not that judgment be anticipated and thereby lightened; rather, radically different judgments are thought of.

The vb. stands in Rom 14:23 in the framework of a wisdom conditional sentence and refers to the basic connection between deed and condition: "have no future." Thus an antithetical inversion of the macarism in v. 22b provides the conclusion to the concrete admonitions.

W. Schenk

κατάκρισις, εως, ἡ *katakrisis* condemnation → καταχρίνω.

κατακύπτω *katakyptō* bow down*

John 8:8: πάλιν κατακύψας, "he *bowed down* again" (cf. κάτω κύψας, v. 6).

κατακυριεύω *katakyrieuō* become lord, subjugate, rule*

Mark 10:42 par. Matt 20:25 of the despotism of princes over the people (κατακυριεύουσιν with κατεξουσιάζουσιν); cf. Ps 118:133 LXX of the rule of ἀνομία; Josh 24:33b (A) of foreign rule; 1 Pet 5:3: μηδ' ὡς κατακυριεύοντες τῶν κλήρων, in an admonition to the elders not to *rule over* those in the Church assigned to them, but to be models for them as shepherds; Acts 19:16: κατακυριεύσας ἀμφοτέρων, "he *overpowered* both" (with ἴσχυσεν κατ' αὐτῶν). W. Foerster, *TDNT* III, 1098; K. W. Clark, FS Kilpatrick 100-105.

κατακαλέω *katalaleō* speak ill/evil of, slander*

Jas 4:11 (ter) with objects ἀλλήλων, ἀδελφοῦ, and νόμου, the second and third with κρίνειν. Similarly 1 Pet 2:12: ἐν ᾧ καταλαλοῦσιν ὑμῶν ὡς κακοποιῶν; pass. in 3:16. Absolute ὁ καταλαλῶν, "the slanderer," in *Herm. Man.* ii.2 (ter).

κατακαλιά, ᾶς, ἡ *katalalia* slander, calumny*

In the NT only in vice catalogs: 2 Cor 12:20, after ἐριθεῖαι; 1 Pet 2:1: ἀποθέμενοι . . . φθόνους καὶ πάσας καταλαλιάς; cf. φεύγειν καταλαλιᾶς, *1 Clem.* 30:1.

κατάλαλος, 2 *katalalos* evil speaking, slanderous*

Rom 1:30, subst. in a vice catalog after ψιθυρισταί ("tale bearer"): *slanderer;* cf. *Herm. Sim.* vi.5.5.

καταλαμβάνω *katalambanō* grasp, catch; mid.: seize, lay hold of*

There are 15 occurrences in the NT, most pass. or act. The basic meaning *grasp* is found only in Paul: Rom 9:30: κατέλαβεν δικαιοσύνην; absolute in 1 Cor 9:24 (τὸ βραβεῖον is to be supplied from the context): "attain the prize of victory"; Phil 3:12a; pass. in v. 12b: κατελήμφθην ὑπὸ Χριστοῦ Ἰησοῦ; v. 13. In John 1:5 (ἡ σκοτία αὐτὸ οὐ κατέλαβεν [i.e., τὸ φῶς]) the meaning *comprehend, accept* enters in (cf. R. Schnackenburg, *John* I [Eng. tr., 1968] ad loc.; W. Nagel, *ZNW* 50 [1959] 132-37).

Lay hold of, fall upon: Mark 9:18 (with subj. πνεῦμα ἄλαλον); *surprise:* John 12:35 (σκοτία); 1 Thess 5:4 (ἡ ἡμέρα ὡς κλέπτης); *catch:* John 8:3 (ἐπὶ μοιχείᾳ); 8:4 (ἐπ' αὐτοφόρῳ μοιχευομένη).

The mid. appears with the meaning *realize, grasp, comprehend* in Acts 4:13; 10:34; 25:25; Eph 3:18. G. Delling, *TDNT* IV, 10; BAGD s.v.

καταλέγω *katalegō* select, enroll into a register*

1 Tim 5:9: pass. χήρα καταλεγέσθω, *"should be selected* as a widow. . . ."* This is related to the recognition of a special position of widows, which was apparently based on the church's selection; cf. also 5:3ff., 9bff. and the instruction to church leaders not to choose women under sixty years old (v. 11); so also G. Stählin, *TDNT* IX, 445-55. A regular "widows' list" is not in view.

κατάλειμμα, ατος, τό *kataleimma* remainder, remnant

Rom 9:27 v.l.: τὸ κατάλειμμα σωθήσεται (citing Isa 10:22 LXX), in place of ὑπόλειμμα.

καταλείπω *kataleipō* leave; leave behind; leave remaining*

There are 24 occurrences in the NT, used in references to objects, places, and persons: *Leave:* a place (Matt 4:13), a land (Heb 11:27), "the narrow way" (2 Pet 2:15), persons (Matt 16:4; 19:5 par. Mark 10:7 [cf. Eph 5:31]; Matt 21:17). *Leave behind* (Acts 18:19; 24:27; Titus 1:5 v.l.), at death (Mark 12:19, 21; Luke 20:31), by a change of office (Acts 25:14, pass.). *Abandon, let go* (Mark 14:52; Luke 5:28); *leave alone* (10:40; cf. BDF §392.1f; 15:4; pass. *be left alone* in John 8:9; *be left behind* in 1 Thess 3:1); *neglect* (Acts 6:2). *Leave remaining* (God as subj.: Rom 11:4; cf. 3 Kgdms 19:18). *Depart from* (Acts 21:3: "We *left* [Cyprus]"). Of the promise "still *remaining"* (ἐπαγγελίας καταλειπομένης): Heb 4:1.

καταλιθάζω *katalithazō* stone to death*

Luke 20:6 (cf. par. Mark/Matthew): "all people will *stone* us" (καταλιθάσει ἡμᾶς); the vb. appears only in Christian texts; cf. W. Michaelis, *TDNT* IV, 267f.

καταλλαγή, ῆς, ἡ *katallagē* reconciliation
→ καταλλάσσω.

καταλλάσσω *katallassō* reconcile*
ἀποκαταλλάσσω *apokatallassō* reconcile*
καταλλαγή, ῆς, ἡ *katallagē* reconciliation*

1. Occurrences in the NT — 2. Meanings outside the NT — 3. Paul — 4. Colossians — 5. Eph 2:16 — 6. The atonement sayings as interpretations of the word and way of Jesus

Lit.: C. BREYTENBACH, *Versöhnung. Eine Studie zur paulinischen Soteriologie* (1989). — F. BÜCHSEL, *TDNT* I, 251-59. — BULTMANN, *Theology* 285-87. — J. F. COLLANGE, *Énigmes de la deuxième épître de Paul aux Corinthiens* (SNTSMS 18, 1972) 266-80. — E. DINKLER, "Die Verkündigung als eschatologischsakramentales Geschehen. Auslegung von 2 Kor 5,14–6,2," FS

Schlier 169-89. — J. DUPONT, *La réconciliation dans la théologie de Saint Paul* (ALBO 2/32, 1953). — H.-J. FINDEIS, *Versöhnung—Apostolat—Kirche. Eine exegetisch-theologische und rezeptiongeschichtliche Studie zu den Versöhnungsaussagen des NT* (FzB 40, 1983). — J. A. FITZMYER, "Reconciliation in Pauline Theology," *No Famine in the Land* (FS J. L. McKenzie, ed. J. W. Flanagan and A. W. Robinson; 1975) 155-77. — V. P. FURNISH, "The Ministry of Reconciliation," *CurTM* 4 (1977) 204-18. — L. GOPPELT, "Versöhnung durch Christus," *idem, Christologie und Ethik* (1968) 147-64 (cf. *idem, Theology* II, 135-41). — F. HAHN, " 'Siehe, jetzt ist der Tag des Heils.' Neuschöpfung und Versöhnung nach 2 Kor 5,14–6,2," *EvT* 33 (1973) 244-53. — M. HENGEL, "Der Kreuzestod Jesu Christi als Gottes souveräne Erlösungstat. Exegese über 2 Kor 5,11-21," *Theologie und Kirche. Reichenau-Gespräch der Evangelischen Landessynode Württemberg* (²1967) 60-89. — O. HOFIUS, " 'Gott hat unter uns aufgerichtet das Wort von der Versöhnung' (2 Kor 5,19)," *ZNW* 71 (1980) 3-20. — *idem,* "Erwägungen zur Gestalt und Herkunft des paulinischen Versöhnungsgedankens," *ZTK* 77 (1980) 186-99. — H. HÜBNER, "Sühne und Versöhnung," *KD* 29 (1983) 284-305. — E. KÄSEMANN, "Some Thoughts on the Theme 'The Doctrine of Reconciliation in the NT,' " *The Future of our Religious Past* (ed. J. M. Robinson; 1971) 49-64. — D. LÜHRMANN, "Rechtfertigung und Versöhnung," *ZTK* 67 (1970) 437-52. — R. P. MARTIN, "NT Theology: A Proposal. The Theme of Reconciliation," *ExpTim* 91 (1979/80) 364-68. — *idem, Reconciliation: A Study of Paul's Theology* (1981). — H. MERKLEIN, *Christus und die Kirche. Die theologische Grundstruktur des Epheserbriefes nach 2,11-18* (SBS 66, 1966). — E. SCHWEIZER, "Versöhnung des Alls. Kol 1,20," FS Conzelmann 487-501. — P. STUHLMACHER, " 'He Is Our Peace' (Eph. 2:14). On the Exegesis and Significance of Ephesians 2:14-18," *idem, Reconciliation, Law, and Righteousness* (1986) 182-200. — H. VORLÄNDER and C. BROWN, *DNTT* III, 166-74. — K. WENGST, "Versöhnung und Befreiung. Ein Aspekt des Themas 'Schuld und Vergebung' im Lichte des Kolosserbriefes," *EvT* 36 (1976) 14-26. — M. WOLTER, *Rechtfertigung und zukünftiges Heil. Untersuchungen zu Römer 5,1-11* (BZNW 43, 1978) 35-89.

1. This word group appears in the NT only in the Pauline corpus. The vb. καταλλάσσω is used 6 times in the authentic Pauline Epistles; it is used once of human relationships (1 Cor 7:11) and 5 times of the God-human relationship (Rom 5:10 bis; 2 Cor 5:18, 19, 20). The noun καταλλαγή is found 4 times (Rom 5:11; 11:15; 2 Cor 5:18, 19). The compound with the double prep. ἀποκαταλλάσσω is attested only in Christian literature; the 3 NT occurrences are in Col 1:20, 22; Eph 2:16.

2. The word stem καταλλαγ-, a compound from → ἀλλάσσω, "change, alter," originally meant "exchange"; from Herodotus, Xenophon, Plato, etc., on it was used with the synonymous διαλλαγ- fig. for the "exchange" of hostility, anger, or war for friendship, love, or peace; it thus designates reconciliation in the human or political realm. An interesting special case is Plutarch's designation of Alexander the Great as "reconciler of everything," sent by God to unite humanity into a world state (*Alex. Fort.* i.329c; cf. Wolter 57f.). Texts for a special religious usage are almost totally nonexistent (Dupont 7-28; Wolter 39). But in Hellenistic Judaism we do see καταλλαγ- (and διαλλαγ-) used of the relationship of God to his people (2 Macc 1:5; 5:20; 7:33; 8:29). Here

the initiative for reconciliation with God proceeds from the human side. Thus Josephus can write that the deity allows himself to be easily reconciled by those who confess and repent (*B.J.* v.415), but he also knows that there are instances in which God does not allow himself to be reconciled (*Ant.* iii.315; vi.144-56). It is essential that reconciliation with God be effected by human initiative (prayer, repentance), but no cultic acts are presupposed.

The NT language of reconciliation is more dependent on the Hellenistic world (cf. Hengel, Hahn) and less on ancient Judaism (*contra* Wolter). O. Hofius (*ZTK* 77 [1980] 186-99) attempts to derive the Pauline idea of reconciliation from deutero-Isaiah, but, because of the absence of the word group, must take several detours in order to attempt to be convincing.

3. a) Paul uses the vb. of human relationships only in 1 Cor 7:11: When a woman separates from her husband, she should remain unmarried or be reconciled to her husband, i.e., resume the marital relationship. The same use of καταλλάσσω is found in ancient marriage documents from the Hellenistic era (Pap. Oxy. 104, 27; DJD II, 250). The other Pauline uses of the vb. and the noun refer to the God-human relationship.

b) 2 Cor 5:19a, b is probably to be regarded as pre-Pauline (so P. Stuhlmacher, *Gerechtigkeit Gottes bei Paulus* [²1966] 77n.2; Collange 270-72 [only 19a]; Furnish 210f., over against Käsemann 53, who considers vv. 19-21 a "pre-Pauline hymnic fragment"): "God *has reconciled* the world to himself through Christ, not counting their trespasses against them." Hellenistic Jewish Christianity probably originally expressed the universal meaning of the Christ-event with this formulaic expression: The Gentiles, as sinners and outsiders (cf. *Pss. Sol.* 1:1, 8; 2:1f.; 17:30; Gal 2:15), have access to salvation only through this act of God's grace. Earlier interpretations of the death of Jesus with their cultic linguistic and thought forms remained more within the horizon of strict Jewish Christianity.

c) Paul appeals to this tradition in 2 Cor 2:14–7:4 (probably a fragment of a separate letter; see Bornkamm, *Aufsätze* IV 162-94; Collange, 6-15, 318-20) in connection with a major dispute over the understanding of the apostolate. The opponents boast of their ecstatic experiences and miraculous powers. Jesus was for them a "second Moses" and was considered primarily a wonderworker (D. Georgi, *The Opponents of Paul in Second Corinthians* [1985] 229-38, 271-77). Paul, however, makes the death of Jesus in its saving and shaping power the norm for apostolic existence. This polemical context provides the background for understanding Paul's description of his office as a "ministry of *reconciliation*" (5:18). Here he also uses the designations "ministry of the Spirit" (3:6, 8) and "ministry of righteousness" (3:9) in order to "emphasize the inferiority of the Mosaic office, to which the opponents appeal, and the superior quality of his own office, which has been authorized by God." The description "characterizes the Pauline δι-

ακονία as determined and authorized by the objective reconciliation of God with humanity" (Wolter 81f.). In addition, Paul completes the formula in v. 19c with a statement about the simultaneous nature of the act of reconciliation and the initiation of the preaching of reconciliation (Dinkler 176f.); as "ambassador in place of Christ," he makes the appeal: "*Be reconciled* to God" (5:20). "Christ *is* therefore *Lord* of the world because God has reconciled the world through him, and he *becomes* its *Lord* when it becomes reconciled to him by the gospel and by faith" (Goppelt 158). The consequence of this reconciling act of God is that those who believe become the "righteousness of God" (5:21).

d) The language of reconciliation is taken up also in Rom 5:1-11, which concludes the train of thought that began in 1:18 (so U. Wilckens, *Rom* [EKKNT] I, 286f.; Wolter 201-16). The details of 2 Corinthians are expanded in fundamental ways: 1) Reconciliation is necessary because all humanity stands in a hopeless situation without salvation under the wrath of God (Rom 1:18–3:20). 2) Reconciliation results as the demonstration of God's love for sinners (5:8), the ungodly (v. 6), the weak (v. 6), and God's enemies (v. 9). "*The subject of reconciliation* for Paul is therefore *exclusively God;* it proceeds entirely from him, *and it is entirely his work*" (Hengel 74f.). 3) The actual basis of the reconciliation that has taken place is the atoning death of Jesus (5:6, 8, 9; cf. 3:21-26). 4) The individual must accept justification by faith (5:1); only so can one receive the reconciliation (v. 11). The human recipient remains entirely passive. 5) As those who have been reconciled, believers have the certainty of being saved at the final judgment (v. 10).

e) The last Pauline reference is Rom 11:15. As a premise for an argument from the lesser to the greater Paul says that the rejection by Israel means the reconciliation of the world. Already from 9:24 Paul has set forth the transition of the promise to the Gentiles; καταλλαγὴ κόσμου is to be understood as the consequence of the διακονία τῆς καταλλαγῆς of 2 Cor 5:18.

f) In considering these relationships, one cannot accept Käsemann's view that Paul has merely taken over the language of reconciliation and subordinated it to his view of justification. One must rather agree with Hengel, 83f., that in the oriental view the "variety of approaches" is characteristic, so that Paul lays stress on the saving significance of the death of Jesus by placing alongside each other the different categories of thought: reconciliation from the political-social realm, expiation from the cultic realm, justification from the forensic realm, and redemption from the area of human rights.

4. The 3 occurrences of ἀποκαταλλάσσω in Colossians likewise demand a distinction between tradition and redaction:

a) One can assume today that Col 1:15-20 employs an older Christ hymn (cf. P. Benoit, FS Smith I, 226-63 [bibliography]). Without prejudice to individual differences among the attempts to reconstruct the original hymn, two strophes are recognizable, which praise Christ as mediator of creation and redemption. "The cosmic christology in strophe 1 corresponds to a cosmic soteriology in strophe 2" (H. Hegermann, *Die Vorstellung vom Schöpfungsmittler im hellenistischen Judentum und Urchristentum* [1961] 101). It pleased the divine "fullness" to dwell in the resurrected one (v. 19), "and through him and unto him *to reconcile* all things" (v. 20a). This statement, which certainly derives from the hymn (cf. Hegermann; E. Schweizer, *Col* [Eng. tr., 1982] 79-81), is unique: Unlike the pre-Pauline tradition of 2 Cor 5:19a, b, it does not concern the reconciliation of the world of humanity to God, but instead involves the reconciliation between the parts of the universe. In the background of this statement stands "the feeling, widespread throughout the Hellenistic world, of living in a world that is breaking up, in which the struggle of everything against everything else characterizes the whole of nature" (Schweizer, *Col* 81; cf. *idem, Versöhnung*). These natural powers are now reconciled once for all.

b) The author of the Epistle (with E. Lohse, *Col and Phlm* [Hermeneia] 177-83, perhaps a pupil of Paul; cf. W. Marxsen, *Introduction to the NT* [Eng. tr., 1968] 184f.) interprets this cosmic soteriology in a radical way. No longer is it the universe that is the body of which the head is Christ; rather, the Church is the body (thoroughly substantiated by E. Käsemann, "A Primitive Christian Baptismal Liturgy," *Essays on NT Themes* [1964] 149-68: 150f.; also Schweizer, *Col* 58). In the tradition of Pauline soteriology the author of the Epistle describes the event more precisely as the establishment of peace through the blood of Christ's cross (v. 20b; Käsemann 152; Schweizer, *Col* 83f.). In vv. 21-23 the author finally applies the hymn directly to the readers, who were once "alienated" and "hostile," but through the death of Christ have been once for all reconciled to him. Now they must hold firm to this indicative of salvation "in faith" and in the "hope of the gospel." Thus the author guards against a fanatical leap from the reality of the world, a danger that the author of the hymn did not recognize.

5. The final NT statement about reconciliation appears in Eph 2:16. The narrow context in 2:14-18 employs traditional sayings, but is (with Merklein; Stuhlmacher; and Wolter 63-65, *contra* J. Gnilka, *Eph* [HTKNT] 147-52; A. Lindemann, *Die Aufhebung der Zeit* [1975] 152-59) not to be regarded as a hymn that has been adapted. The author of the Epistle himself interprets the work of Christ as that which has made "the two realms," namely the Jewish and Gentile world, "into one" (v. 14), and has

"destroyed the law with its commands" so that he "might create a new person" (v. 15) from the "two [kinds of] persons," the Jew and the Gentile, and thus "*reconcile* the two into one body with God through the cross" (v. 16). Reconciliation is, as in Colossians, the deed of Christ; thus the consequence of reconciliation with God is the reconciliation of the two groups that previously were hostile to each other. With "the comprehensiveness of this understanding of peace and reconciliation" (Stuhlmacher 189) the author of Ephesians has interpreted the Pauline tradition in an appropriate way.

But one may note a change in perspective over against Paul's view: Through Jesus' death on the cross, the Church is first created as realm of salvation; reconciliation is given through it. This "primacy of ecclesiology over soteriology" is characteristic of the author of Ephesians (Merklein 62-68).

6. To what extent are these statements about reconciliation an appropriate interpretation of the word and way of Jesus? One must see the "essential impulse" in the earthly Jesus (Goppelt 152; cf. also P. Stuhlmacher, "Jesus as Reconciler. Reflections on the Problem of Portraying Jesus within the Framework of a Biblical Theology of the NT," *idem, Reconciliation, Law, and Righteousness* [1986] 1-15):

a) In his parables (Luke 15:11-32; 18:10-14; Matt 18:23-35; 20:1-15), Jesus described God as the one who is "unconditionally benevolent," whose gift is not dependent on prior human achievements. "The offer of salvation as the center of the proclamation of Jesus to 'tax collectors and sinners' took place without regard for the religious and sociological distinctions sanctioned by the law" (J. Becker, FS Conzelmann 115). He proclaimed the reconciliation of all with God and in the table fellowship with the disenfranchised let that reconciliation become a social reality (cf. J. Roloff in *Gottesdienst und Öffentlichkeit* [ed. P. Cornehl and H.-E. Bahr; 1970] 88-117, esp. 96-99).

b) "The death of Jesus is scarcely motivated by anything other than by his collision course with the law" (Becker); Jesus consciously accepted the consequence of his actions. In this respect his death belonged to his own work of reconciliation. When the Antiochian tradition, on which Paul depended, and the Pauline school formulate their "preaching of reconciliation," this formulation occurs in essential continuity with the Jesus tradition, insofar as "the experience of God for Paul, exemplified in the cross and resurrection, was none other in its essential nature than what one could see in Jesus' view of God" (Becker 125). An overview of the narrative and theologically reflected traditions of early Christianity demonstrates that "reconciliation" is a central category for describing the Christ-event.

H. Merkel

κατάλοιπος, 2 *kataloipos* left, remaining*

Acts 15:17: οἱ κατάλοιποι τῶν ἀνθρώπων, "all other [Gentile] peoples" (citing Amos 9:12 LXX).

κατάλυμα, ατος, τό *katalyma* lodging, shelter*

Lit. (on Luke 2:7): P. BENOIT, "Non erat eis locus in diversorio (Lc 2,7)," FS Rigaux 173-86. — M. BYRNE, "No Room for the Inn," *Search* 5 (1982) 37-40. — W. GRUNDMANN, *Luke* (THKNT, 1961) on 2:7. — M. HENGEL, *TDNT* IX, 53-55 with n. 46. — E. PAX, " 'Denn sie fanden keinen Platz in der Herberge.' Jüdisches und frühchristliches Herbergswesen," *BibLeb* 6 (1965) 285-98.

This noun is derived from the special meaning of the compound → καταλύω (2), "rest, stop at." Luke 2:7, probably *lodging* in general (in which Jesus' parents could find no place); *guest room* would also be possible (cf. πανδοχεῖον, "lodging," 10:34). Luke emphasizes that Jesus' birth occurred outside ordinary human living quarters, whether in a stall or a cave. Mark 14:14 par. Luke 22:11: a *guest room* (in a house; cf. the context) in which Jesus ate the Passover with his disciples.

καταλύω *katalyō* dissolve, destroy; annul; rest*

1. occurrences in the NT — 2. Meanings — 3. Theological relevance

Lit.: G. BARTH, in G. Bornkamm, G. Barth, and H. J. Held, *Tradition and Interpretation in Matthew* (NTL, 1963) 58-105, 159-64. — F. BÜCHSEL, *TDNT* IV, 338. — H. HÜBNER, *Das Gesetz in der synoptischen Tradition* (1973) 15-39. — J. JEREMIAS, "Die Drei-Tage-Worte der Evangelien," FS Kuhn 221-29. — E. LINNEMANN, *Studien zur Passionsgeschichte* (1970) 109-35. — R. PESCH, *Mark* (HTKNT) II (1977) on 13:2 (bibliography). — G. STRECKER, *Der Weg der Gerechtigkeit* (FRLANT, ²1966) 137-47. — G. THEISSEN, "Die Tempelreinigung Jesu. Prophetie im Spannungsfeld von Stadt und Land," *TZ* 32 (1976) 144-58. — N. WALTER, "Tempelzerstörung und synoptische Apokalypse," *ZNW* 57 (1966) 38-49.

1. Of 17 occurrences of καταλύω in the NT, 14 are in the Synoptics and Acts and only 3 in Paul. Matthew takes over all 3 Markan occurrences and Luke only 1.

2. Καταλύω is a compound of → λύω (which appears in Matt 5:19 in the same context as καταλύω in v. 17; on the tension between vv. 17 and 19 see Strecker 145) and has the basic meaning *loosen, dissolve*. The range of meanings in the NT includes: *destroy* (the temple [ναός]: Mark 14:58/15:29 par. Matt 26:61/27:40; Acts 6:14; the missionary work [ἔργον]: Acts 5:38f.; see also Rom 14:20: ἔργον here = the work of building the Church [v. 19, οἰκοδομή]; see also Gal 2:18), *throw down* (building stones: Mark 13:2 par. Matt 24:2/Luke 21:6), *annul* (the law [νόμος]: Matt 5:17; cf. 2 Macc 2:22), *demolish* (our earthly dwelling, the body: 2 Cor 5:1; see R. Bultmann, *2 Cor* [Eng. tr., 1985] 131f.). Only in Luke (9:12; 19:7) does καταλύω mean *rest, lodge* (literally "unharness the pack animals"; cf. κατάλιμα, "lodgings").

3. The programmatic saying in Matt 5:17 is important for Matthew's total presentation and probably not (as W. Grundmann, *Matt* [THKNT] 44; Strecker 144 as-

sume) totally redactional (Bultmann, *History* 138, 155, 408 judges rightly [vv. 17-20 arise from the Church's debates regarding the law]; cf. Hübner 32ff.). It portrays Jesus as one who does not *annul* the law through partial modification, but rather fulfills (πληρῶσαι) it. The saying is thus the christological variant of Rom 3:31; → καταργέω 3. According to Barth (159) Matt 5:17 rejects antinomian tendencies within the Church; cf., however, the opposing view of Strecker 137n.4. The possibility that v. 17 rests on preredactional material containing the Jewish charge that Jesus abrogates the law is worthy of consideration.

The authenticity of the prophetic announcement of the temple's total destruction (Mark 13:2) is disputed (authentic: Pesch, Jeremias, Theissen; contrary views: J. Gnilka, *Mark* [EKKNT] II, Linnemann, Walter). But the arguments against authenticity fail in view of Jesus' critical attitude toward the cultic part of the Torah (cf. 7:15) with respect to its implications for the temple cult. Inasmuch as Mark 14:58 cannot be separated from the context of Jewish eschatological (according to *Tg. Isa* 53:5 even messianic) expectations, the saying has perhaps been misunderstood as a Jewish polemic ("false witness") from the Passion tradition behind Mark (but of course not in the form in Mark 14:58) after it had come into existence as a christological development of Mark 13:2 (see also John 2:19ff.: λύσατε . . .).

H. Hübner

καταμανθάνω *katamanthanō* observe, pay attention to, consider*

Matt 6:28: "*Consider* the lilies" (καταμάθετε . . . πῶς).

καταμαρτυρέω *katamartyreō* bear witness against*

Mark 14:60 par. Matt 26:62; Matt 27:13 par. Mark 15:4 TR (in place of κατηγορέω). This compound is often used in connection with "false" witness for the prosecution. H. Strathmann, *TDNT* IV, 508-10.

καταμένω *katamenō* stay, dwell*

Acts 1:13: ἦσαν καταμένοντες; 1 Cor 16:6 v.l. (in place of παραμένω).

καταμόνας *katamonas* alone (adv.)

An elliptical form to be completed with a fem. noun (see BDF §241.6): Mark 4:10 TR; Luke 9:18 TR (in place of κατὰ μόνας).

κατανάθεμα, ατος, τό *katanathema* accursed

Rev 22:3 TR (in place of κατάθεμα).

καταναθεματίζω *katanathematizō* curse

Matt 26:74 TR (in place of καταθεματίζω).

καταναλίσκω *katanaliskō* consume, eat up*

Heb 12:29: ὁ θεὸς . . . πῦρ καταναλίσκον, "a *consuming* fire" (citing Deut 4:24; 9:3 LXX).

καταναρκάω *katanarkaō* disable, be a burden*

In the NT only in a fig. sense in Paul's statement that he will not *be a burden* by exercising the right to support (2 Cor 11:9; 12:13, 14). It is taken in this sense by Vg. *(nulli onerosus fui/non gravavi/non ero gravis);* the Peshitta; Jerome *Epistula* 121.10.4, etc. (cf. also BAGD s.v.; LSJ s.v.). E. B. Allo (2 Cor [ÉBib, ²1956] 283) incorrectly derives the meaning "dazzle, talk (someone) into (doing something)" from medical use of the vb. for narcosis. See Spicq, *Notes* I, 412f.

κατανεύω *kataneuō* wave, signal*

Luke 5:7: "they *signaled* to their partners in the other boat" (followed by inf.; cf. BDF §400.7).

κατανοέω *katanoeō* notice, observe, consider*

There are 14 occurrences in the NT: *notice* (by observation: Acts 27:39 [an inlet]; by consideration: Matt 7:3 par. Luke 6:41 [the beam in one's own eye]; Luke 20:23 [their cunning]), *consider, pay attention to* (Luke 12:24 [the ravens]; 12:27 [the lilies]; Rom 4:19 [one's own dying body]), *focus one's eyes on* (Heb 3:1 [on Jesus]), *take heed* (10:24 [to one another]), *gaze at* (Jas 1:23, 24 [one's own face in the mirror]), absolute: *look closely* (Acts 7:31, 32; 11:6).

καταντάω *katantaō* reach, arrive at, come to*

There are 13 occurrences in the NT, of which 9 are in Acts. Most are in the literal sense of *arrive* at a place (with εἰς: Acts 16:1; 18:19, 24; 21:7; 25:13; 27:12; 28:13; with ἄντικρυς: 20:15). Others are fig. *reach/attain* to something (with εἰς: 26:7; Eph 4:13: εἰς τὴν ἑνότητα τῆς πίστεως; Phil 3:11: εἰς τὴν ἀνάστασιν τὴν ἐκ νεκρῶν). Of the encounter of people with something that *comes to* them (with εἰς: 1 Cor 10:11: τὰ τέλη τῶν αἰώνων; 14:36: ὁ λόγος τοῦ θεοῦ). O. Michel, *TDNT* III, 623-25; I. Peri, "Gelangen zur Vollkommenheit. Zur lateinischen Interpretation von καταντάω in Eph 4,13," *BZ* 23 (1979) 269-78; Spicq, *Notes* I, 414f.

κατάνυξις, εως, ἡ *katanyxis* piercing; stupor*

Rom 11:8, fig.: πνεῦμα κατανύξεως, "spirit of *stupor*" (citing Isa 29:10 LXX). H. Greeven, *TDNT* III, 626.

κατανύσσομαι *katanyssomai* be pierced; feel pain*

Acts 2:37, fig. (so in the LXX): κατενύγησαν τὴν καρδίαν, "they *were pierced* in [their] heart[s]" (citing Ps 108:16 LXX). H. Greeven, *TDNT* III, 626.

καταξιόω *kataxioō* consider worthy*

In the NT only pass.: with gen. of the thing: 2 Thess 1:5: καταξιωθῆναι . . . τῆς βασιλείας τοῦ θεοῦ; followed by the inf.: Luke 20:35; 21:36 v.l.; Acts 5:41; W. Foerster, *TDNT* I, 380.

καταπατέω *katapateō* crush/trample with the feet*

Fig. (of swine): Matt 7:6; pass. in Matt 5:13; Luke 8:5; in the sense of *"oppress* one another/*trample with the feet"*: Luke 12:1: ὥστε καταπατεῖν ἀλλήλους; fig. in Heb 10:29: *"despise* the Son of God/*trample with the feet."* H. Seesemann, *TDNT* V, 943-45.

κατάπαυσις, εως, ἡ *katapausis* rest (noun); resting place*

καταπαύω *katapauō* cause to rest; rest*

1. NT occurrences and usage — 2. Κατάπαυσις — 3. Καταπαύω

Lit.: O. BAUERNFEIND, *TDNT* III, 627f. — D. R. DARNELL, *Rebellion, Rest and the Word of God. An Exegetical Study of Hebrews 3,1–4,13* (Diss. Duke University, 1973). — J. FRANKOWSKI, "Requies, Bonum Promissum populi Dei in VT et in Judaismo (Hebr 3,7–4,11)," *VD* 43 (1965) 124-49, 225-40. — O. HOFIUS, *Katapausis. Die Vorstellung vom endzeitlichen Ruheort im Hebräerbrief* (1970). — E. KÄSEMANN, *The Wandering People of God* (1984) 58-75. — H. A. LOMBARD, "Katápausis in the Letter to the Hebrews," *Neot* 5 (1971) 60-71. — D. A. LOSADA, "La Reconciliación como 'Reposo,'" *RB* 36 (1974) 113-28. — G. THEISSEN, *Untersuchungen zum Hebräerbrief* (1969) 124-29. — H. ZIMMERMANN, *Das Bekenntnis der Hoffnung* (1977) 129-45. — For further bibliography see *TWNT* X, 1135.

1. Both noun and vb. appear in the NT only in Acts (once each) and in Heb 3:7–4:13 (the noun 8 times, the vb. 3 times). Except in Acts 14:18, where the vb. has the meaning *dissuade* someone from something (cf. Dan 11:18 Theodotion; *T. Job* 14:5), the two words have a religious usage in all NT occurrences.

2. The occurrences of κατάπαυσις are all derived from the LXX: Acts 7:49 cites Isa 66:1; Hebrews 3–4 cites Ps 94:11 LXX, sometimes word-for-word (3:11; 4:3b, 5) and sometimes paraphrasing (3:18; 4:1, 3a, 10, 11).

Religious uses of the noun in ancient Jewish writings are all derived from the LXX. *Jos. As* 8:9 (50:1f. Batiffol = 8:11 Philonenko) is derived from Ps 94:11, and *Jos. As.* 22:13 (73:19f. Batiffol = 22:9 Philonenko) is shaped by Isa 66:1.

The noun is always intrans. in the LXX, where it means, corresponding to the Hebrew equivalent, *m^enûhâ*, both "rest" (e.g., 3 Kgdms 8:56) and "place of rest" (Deut 12:9; Pss 94:11; 131:14, etc.). The latter, the local sense, is seen in Hebrews 3–4, in dependence on Ps 94:11 LXX. The author understands the κατάπαυσις mentioned in the Psalm to be the heavenly dwelling of God, which God has appointed as the eschatological *resting place* (cf. *Jos. As.* 8:9) for his people. Through God's word in Jesus Christ (1:2) the Christian community is given the reliable promise that they will enter into the κατάπαυσις at the day of salvation. The prerequisite for this is, of course, that they, unlike the wilderness generation (Num 14), hold unwaveringly to the word of promise in faith and obedience.

3. The vb. καταπαύω means *bring to the place of rest* in Heb 4:8 (trans., as in Exod 33:14 LXX, etc.), but in Heb 4:4, 10 it means *rest/repose* (intrans., as in the supporting passage, Gen 2:2 LXX). Heb 4:9 shows that the rest promised (v. 10) to God's people may not be understood in the sense of a quietistic ideal (→ σαββατισμός).
O. Hofius

καταπαύω *katapauō* cause to rest; rest → κατάπαυσις 3.

καταπέτασμα, ατος, τό *katapetasma* curtain*

1. The curtains in the (earthly) temple — 2. The curtain in the heavenly sanctuary (Hebrews)

Lit.: BILLERBECK, I, 1043ff. — O. HOFIUS, *Der Vorhang vor dem Thron Gottes* (1972). — S. LÉGASSE, "Les voiles du temples de Jérusalem," *RB* 87 (1980) 560-89. — R. PESCH, *Mark* (HTKNT) II (1977) 498f. — C. SCHNEIDER, *TDNT* III, 628-30. — For further bibliography see Pesch 502f.; *TWNT* X, 1135.

1. Καταπέτασμα appears 6 times in the NT (Mark 15:38 par.; Heb 6:19; 9:3; 10:20).
The OT reports concerning the tabernacle (→ σκηνή) mention a curtain (*māsāk*) at the entrance to the holy place (Exod 26:36f., etc.) and a curtain (*pārōket*) before the most holy place (26:31ff., etc.). In the LXX καταπέτασμα is used for both curtains. These two curtains had, according to Josephus, analogies in the outer and inner curtains of the Solomonic and Herodian temples (*Ant.* viii.75, 90; *B.J.* v.212, 219). In Philo *Spec. Leg.* i.231, 274 the outer curtain is called τὸ πρότερον καταπέτασμα. In Heb 9:3 the inner *curtain* (of the tabernacle) is called τὸ δεύτερον καταπέτασμα.
According to Mark 15:38 par. Matt 27:51/Luke 23:45 the καταπέτασμα τοῦ ναοῦ was split at the death of Jesus. Which of the two temple curtains is intended is disputed, as is the symbolic significance of this event. Inasmuch as only the *pārōket* had high cultic significance (see Lev 4:6, 17; 16:2, 11ff.), only it could have been intended. Among the suggested interpretations (a sign of Israel's judgment, an advance indication of Israel's destruction, a confirmation of Jesus' messianic identity), preference

is to be given to the soteriological interpretation: Through his vicarious death Jesus has opened access to God once for all, so that sin offerings will no longer be needed.

2. A widespread view, shared by the author of Hebrews (see 8:5), saw in the earthly sanctuary the copy of an actual heavenly original. In the heavenly sanctuary a *curtain,* corresponding to the *pārōket,* veils the dwelling of God with the throne of glory (see Hofius 4ff.). Heb 6:19 and 10:20 refer to this curtain, which in rabbinic esoteric texts is usually called *pargôd.* Τὸ ἐσώτερον τοῦ καταπετάσματος in Heb 6:19 (cf. Lev 16:2, 12, 15 LXX) designates the most holy place, which is called τὰ ἅγια in Heb 8:2; 9:8, 12, (24); 10:19.

The two statements in Heb 6:19f.; 10:19f. belong within the context of the doctrine of the self-offering of Jesus, the heavenly high priest, as it is developed in the typological interpretation of the ritual described in Leviticus 16. In connection with the προσφορὰ τοῦ σώματος at the cross (10:10), Jesus then entered into the heavenly most holy place in order to offer his shed blood (9:11ff., 24ff.). Through this atoning act Jesus has effected purification from sins (1:3; 9:14, 26; 10:1-18; 13:12) and at the same time received the high-priestly prerogative of entering through the curtain into the most holy place of God (10:19f.). Because Jesus is now seated at God's right hand as the eternal high priest and guarantor for the eschatological εἴσοδος of the faithful, this "object of hope" can be described as a "secure and steadfast anchor of the soul which enters into the [heavenly] most holy place" (6:19f.).
O. Hofius

καταπίνω *katapinō* drink down, devour, consume*

In the proper sense (though metaphorical): Matt 23:24: "*swallow* a camel"; 1 Pet 5:8: the devil, "like a lion . . . , seeks whom he can *devour*" (ζητῶν τινα καταπιεῖν); cf. Jer 28:34 LXX, as an image for total destruction; Rev 12:16 (cf. Num 16:30-33); pass.: *drown* (Heb 11:29). In Paul always fig. and pass.: *devour/fully consume:* 1 Cor 15:54: κατεπόθη ὁ θάνατος εἰς νῖκος, "death *is swallowed up* in victory" (cf. Isa 25:8; on the textual history, see H. Conzelmann, *1 Cor* [Hermeneia] ad loc.); similarly 2 Cor 5:4; of *being engulfed* in sorrow: 2:7 (cf. Philo *Gig.* 13). L. Goppelt, *TDNT* VI, 158f.

καταπίπτω *katapiptō* fall down; fall*

Luke 8:6; Acts 26:14: "We all *fell down* on the earth"; 28:6: *"fall down dead"* (καταπεσόντων . . . νεκρόν). W. Michaelis, *TDNT* VI, 169f.

καταπλέω *katapleō* sail toward*

Luke 8:26: *travel* from the high sea to the coast "into the region of the Gerasenes."

καταπονέω *kataponeō* oppress, suppress*

In the NT only pres. pass. partc. ὁ καταπονούμενος, *the oppressed, mistreated:* Acts 7:24 (cf. Exod 2:12); 2 Pet 2:7, adj. of Lot, *who was harassed.*

καταποντίζομαι *katapontizomai* be drowned; sink*

In the NT only pass.; absolute *sink:* Matt 14:30; *"be drowned* in the depth of the sea": 18:6.

κατάρα, ας, ἡ *katara* malediction, curse*

Of unfruitful land, which brings forth thorns and thistles: κατάρας ἐγγύς, "it is near to being *cursed*" (Heb 6:8; cf. Gen 3:17); εὐλογία καὶ κατάρα should not come forth from the same mouth (Jas 3:10; cf. v. 9; Rom 12:14); κατάρας τέκνα, "children of the *curse*," "*accursed* ones" (2 Pet 2:14). In Paul of the *curse* of the law, which it expresses itself (Gal 3:10, 13a; cf. Deut 21:23; 27:26); according to Gal 3:13b "Christ has become a *curse* for us (γενόμενος . . . κατάρα)"; i.e., as the one who is hanged he has himself taken the curse (cf. v. 13c, ἐπικατάρατος): Christ, who is free of the curse, has borne the curse in order to liberate us (cf. also *Did.* 16:5). F. Büchsel, *TDNT* I, 449-51; *TWNT* X, 989 (bibliography); J. Becker, *Gal* (NTD) on 3:13.

καταράομαι *kataraomai* curse*

Used absolutely, *curse* (alongside εὐλογέω, Rom 12:14; cf. Philo *Her.* 177); with acc., *curse* (Luke 6:28; Matt 5:44 TR: εὐλογεῖτε τοὺς καταρωμένους ὑμᾶς; Jas 3:9: εὐλογοῦμεν . . . καταρώμεθα); of the *cursing* of a fig tree (Mark 11:21); pass. οἱ κατηραμένοι, "you *accursed*" (Matt 25:41). F. Büchsel, *TDNT* I, 448-51; *TWNT* X, 989f. (bibliography).

καταργέω *katargeō* destroy; render powerless; free (someone from something)*

1. Occurrences in the NT — 2. Meanings — 3. Paul

Lit.: K. W. CLARK, "The meaning of ἐνεργέω and καταργέω in the NT," *idem, The Gentile Bias and Other Essays* (1980) 183-91. — G. DELLING, *TDNT* I, 452-54. — H. HÜBNER, *Law in Paul's Thought* (1984) 137-44. — K. MÜLLER, *Anstoß und Gericht* (SANT 19, 1969) 116f. — H.-W. WILCKE, *Das Problem eines messianischen Zwischenreichs bei Paulus* (ATANT 51, 1967) 100-105.

1. Καταργέω appears 27 times in the NT, 22 times in Paul, 3 in the deutero-Paulines, and once each in Hebrews and Luke. It is noteworthy that Paul uses the vb. 15 times in the pass.

2. Καταργέω is, as a compound of ἀργέω, derived from ἀργός (ἀ-εργός), "ineffective, idle, inactive." In the NT it

includes the entire spectrum of meaning from the negative aspect *make ineffective, destroy, render powerless, annul, use up* (Luke 13:7) to the positive aspect of *liberate, set free.* Pass. means *perish, cease* (1 Cor 13:8, 10), *be separated, be cut off.*

3. A striking aspect of Paul's theological usage is that the grammatical or logical subj. of καταργέω is God or Christ (except in 1 Cor 13:11), while the topic is the actual destruction or rendering powerless (normally in an apocalyptic context): The Creator, from his powerful "Let there be," also speaks his "Let there cease" (καταργέω as the negative counterpart to → ποιέω, Heb. *bārā'*).

Not only will God *reduce* food and drink *to nothing* (1 Cor 6:13); through him also are hostile powers in particular *deprived of their power* (1 Cor 2:6; somewhat different H. Conzelmann, *1 Cor* [Hermeneia] 61n.46: "transient"; → ἄρχων 2.c: in 1 Cor 2:6, 8 ἄρχοντες is used of demonic powers). Clearer still is 1 Cor 15:24: As regent of the divine sovereignty (→ βασιλεία 4) Christ will *destroy* these powers, among them, last of all, death (v. 26; Conzelmann 271).

According to Rom 6:6 the "body of sin" is *deprived of power* "that we might no longer serve the power of sin" (καταργηθῇ here is almost a divine passive); according to E. Käsemann, *Rom* (Eng. tr., 1980) 159, καταργέω here means *destroyed* and (169) "has an eschatological sense"; see, however, Delling 453. Without actually describing the law as a power of destruction in a literal sense, 7:6 says that we *are freed* from it, just as in v. 2 the wife *is "free"* from her husband when he dies.

In continuity with this thought of Paul stand 2 Thess 2:8; 2 Tim 1:10; Eph 2:15; and Heb 2:14. Also, because no one can boast before God (the doctrine of justification!), God *destroys* the things that are (τὰ ὄντα, 1 Cor 1:28).

But in Gal 5:4 Paul uses καταργέω in a way opposite to the statements in Romans: not free from the law through Christ, but "free," i.e., *separated* from Christ, through the law.

If καταργέω as *annul, destroy* is a matter for God, neither humans nor angels are capable of this activity, esp. in view of the effectiveness of God's activity. Human unfaithfulness cannot *nullify* God's faithfulness (Rom 3:3); a law given by angels (Gal 3:19) cannot *annul* God's promise to Abraham (v. 17; cf. Rom 4:14); the "offense of the cross" could *be abolished* merely by the preaching of circumcision (Gal 5:11; so F. Mussner, *Gal* [HTKNT] 361f. *contra* Müller).

According to O. Michel, *Rom* [KEK] 157, the contrast νόμον καταργοῦμεν—νόμον ἱστάνομεν in Rom 3:31 is derived from Aram. *baṭṭel—qayyem.* His reference to *m. 'Abot* 4:9, however, is not capable of supporting the existence of such a rabbinic contrasting pair as a t.t. for "annul—uphold" in reference to the law or a stipulation of the law (Hübner 141); → καταλύω 3. Paul probably uses καταργέω in Rom 3:31 to take up an objection from his Judaizing opponents (who are reacting to Galatians) and to counter it with νόμον ἱστάνομεν: "We uphold the law"—namely as a "law of faith" (Rom 3:27; Hübner 140ff.).

In 2 Cor 3:7, 11, 13, 14 the transitory nature of the Mosaic dispensation is expressed with καταργέω. The subst. partc. τὸ καταργούμενον is the essence of this transitory and past epoch (on 2 Corinthians 3 see esp. R. Bultmann, *2 Cor* [Eng. tr., 1985] 78-96).

H. Hübner

καταριθμέω *katarithmeō* number (vb.), add*

Acts 1:17: Judas κατηριθμημένος ἦν ἐν ἡμῖν, "he *belonged* to our *number* [the Twelve]"; cf. Luke 22:3.

καταρτίζω *katartizō* put (again) into order, complete, prepare*

There are 13 occurrences in the NT. Mark 1:19 par. Matt 4:21: *mend* τὰ δίκτυα. Frequently in parenetic contexts: The Corinthians should *be equipped/complete* (κατηρτισμένοι ἐν τῷ αὐτῷ νοῒ καὶ ἐν τῇ αὐτῇ γνώμῃ, 1 Cor 1:10); Christians should *restore* those who have wandered away (Gal 6:1); pass. *be restored/mend your ways* (2 Cor 13:11); *complete* (τὰ ὑστερήματα τῆς πίστεως ὑμῶν, 1 Thess 3:10); similarly *equip* (ἐν παντὶ ἀγαθῷ, Heb 13:21; see O. Michel, *Heb* [KEK] ad loc.); *prepare, complete* (with στηρίζω, σθενόω, θεμελιόω, 1 Pet 5:10); the disciples should be "totally *equipped/complete*" (κατηρτισμένος δὲ πᾶς, Luke 6:40; see W. Grundmann, *Luke* [THKNT] ad loc.); *produce, prepare* ("you have *brought* praise" [mid.], Matt 21:16, citing Ps 8:3 LXX; "*made* for destruction," Rom 9:22; Heb 10:5 [mid.; cf. Ps 39:7 LXX]; Heb 11:3: κατηρτίσθαι τοὺς αἰῶνας ῥήματι θεοῦ). G. Delling, *TDNT* I, 476; Spicq, *Notes* I, 253-55, 416-19.

κατάρτισις, εως, ἡ *katartisis* improvement, completion*

2 Cor 13:9: τοῦτο καὶ εὐχόμεθα, τὴν ὑμῶν κατάρτισιν, "for your *improvement*/that you might be restored"; see R. Bultmann, *2 Cor* (Eng. tr., 1985) ad loc.; G. Delling, *TDNT* I, 475.

καταρτισμός, οῦ, ὁ *katartismos* equipping, preparation*

Eph 4:12: "the *equipping* of the saints for the work of ministry." G. Delling, *TDNT* I, 476; J. Gnilka, *Eph* (HTKNT) ad loc.

κατασείω *kataseiō* shake, wave, give a sign*

With dat. τῇ χειρί in Acts 12:17: "he *gestured* to them to be silent"; 13:16; 21:40; with acc. τὴν χεῖρα in 19:33: "he *waved* with his hand."

κατασκάπτω *kataskaptō* demolish, destroy*

Acts 15:16: τὰ κατεσκαμμένα αὐτῆς, "what has been *destroyed*/the ruins [of the dwelling of David]" (citing Amos 9:11 LXX); Rom 11:3: "*tear down* altars" (citing 3 Kgdms 19:10).

κατασκευάζω *kataskeuazō* prepare; build (up); install*

There are 11 occurrences in the NT, of which 6 are in Hebrews. Mark 1:2 par. Matt 11:10/Luke 7:27: "*prepare* the way" (cf. Exod 23:20; Mal 3:1 LXX); Luke 1:17: λαὸς κατεσκευασμένος, "a people *prepared/equipped*"; Heb 3:3, 4a: *build* a house; 11:7: *build* an ark (cf. 1 Pet 3:20); Heb 9:2, 6: the *furnishing* of the two tents of the sanctuary, the outer tent (the "holy place," v. 2) and the entire sanctuary (v. 6, τούτων δὲ οὕτως κατεσκευασμένων, "in accordance with this *arrangement*"); 3:4b: *create* (ὁ δὲ πάντα κατασκευάσας θεός).

κατασκηνόω *kataskenoō* (cause to) dwell; nest*

Mark 4:32 par. Matt 13:32/Luke 13:19, of the birds of the mustard bush which *nest* in its branches (cf. Ps 103:12 LXX; Dan 4:21 Theodotion; Ezek 31:6), according to Mark, in its shadow (cf. Ezek 17:23); Acts 2:26: ἡ σάρξ μου κατασκηνώσει ἐπ' ἐλπίδι, "my flesh *will dwell* [= *rest*] in hope" (citing Ps 15:9 LXX). W. Michaelis, *TDNT* VII, 387-89.

κατασκήνωσις, εως, ἡ *kataskēnōsis* home; nest*

Matt 8:20 par. Luke 9:58: The birds of the heaven have *nests*.

κατασκιάζω *kataskiazō* cover, overshadow*

According to Heb 9:5 the cherubim of glory *overshadow* the mercy seat (κατασκιάζοντα τὸ ἱλαστήριον; cf. Exod 25:19).

κατασκοπέω *kataskopeō* spy out*

Gal 2:4: κατασκοπῆσαι τὴν ἐλευθερίαν ἡμῶν, "in order to *spy out* our freedom." E. Fuchs, *TDNT* VII, 416f.

κατάσκοπος, ου, ὁ *kataskopos* spy, scout*

Heb 11:31, of the *spies* whom Rahab received in peace; cf. Josh 2:1ff. E. Fuchs, *TDNT* VII, 417.

κατασοφίζομαι *katasophizomai* dupe, treat deceitfully*

Acts 7:19, of the fate of Israel in Egypt after the death of Joseph; cf. Exod 1:8ff.

καταστέλλω *katastellō* sooth, calm*

Acts 19:35: καταστείλας . . . τὸν ὄχλον, "he *calmed* the crowd"; 19:36: κατεσταλμένος, *quiet*. K. H. Rengstorf, *TDNT* VII, 595f.

κατάστημα, ατος, τό *katastēma* disposition, behavior*

Titus 2:3: ἐν καταστήματι ἱεροπρεπεῖς, "honorable in *conduct.*"

καταστολή, ῆς, ἡ *katastolē* demeanor, bearing; appearance*

According to 1 Tim 2:9 women are to appear in a "respectable/worthy *demeanor*" (ἐν καταστολῇ κοσμίῳ) in worship. The parallel statement in v. 8 suggests that their total demeanor, which can be expressed in clothing, is in view (cf. Josephus *B.J.* ii.126; Isa 61:3; Tacitus *Hist.* iii.73.3). As v. 9 mentions particular aspects of outward appearance, including ἱματισμὸς πολυτελής, καταστολή apparently refers to demeanor. K. H. Rengstorf, *TDNT* VII, 596.

καταστρέφω *katastrephō* overturn, overthrow*

Mark 11:15 par. Matt 21:12: Jesus *overturned* (κατέστρεψεν) the tables of the money changers and the seats of the pigeon sellers in the temple; Acts 15:16 v.l.: τὰ κατεστραμμένα in place of τὰ κατεσκαμμένα. G. Bertram, *TDNT* VII, 715f.

καταστρηνιάω *katastrēniaō* become wanton against, pursue sensual impulses against*

1 Tim 5:11, in connection with the prohibition of younger widows entering the "office of widow": ὅταν γὰρ καταστρηνιάσωσιν τοῦ Χριστοῦ, γαμεῖν θέλουσιν, "when they pursue their passions in opposition to Christ"; cf. BDF §181; C. Schneider, *TDNT* III, 631.

καταστροφή, ῆς, ἡ *katastrophē* destruction, downfall*

2 Pet 2:6, of God: καταστροφῇ κατέκρινεν, "he condemned Sodom and Gomorrah to *destruction*"; fig. in 2 Tim 2:14: ἐπὶ καταστροφῇ τῶν ἀκουόντων, to the *destruction/confusion* of the hearers; cf. *Herm. Man.* v.2.1; *1 Clem.* 6:4; G. Bertram, *TDNT* VII, 716n.6.

καταστρώννυμι *katastrōnnymi* cut down, kill*

1 Cor 10:5, of the Israelites who were *killed* (κατεστρώθησαν) in the wilderness (cf. Num 14:16).

κατασύρω *katasyrō* drag away (forcibly), drag along*

Luke 12:58: "*drag* before the judge" (πρὸς τὸν κριτήν).

κατασφάζω, κατασφάττω *katasphazō, katasphattō* cut down, slay, slaughter*

Luke 19:27: κατασφάξατε αὐτούς, "*slay* them [my enemies] before my eyes"; cf. BDF §71.

κατασφραγίζω *katasphragizō* seal (vb.)*

Rev 5:1, of a scroll *sealed* with seven seals (βιβλίον . . . κατεσφραγισμένον); → βιβλίον 3, → ἑπτά. G. Fitzer, *TDNT* VII, 950f.

κατάσχεσις, εως, ἡ *kataschesis* taking possession; possession*

Acts 7:5: δοῦναι . . . εἰς κατάσχεσιν, "give [a land] as a *possession*" (cf. Gen 17:8; 48:4); 7:45: ἐν τῇ κατασχέσει τῶν ἐθνῶν, "at the *seizure* [of the land] of the Gentiles [by Israel]" = "when they took possession" (see also E. Haenchen, *Acts* [Eng. tr., 1971] ad loc. with n. 1); 20:16 v.l.

κατατίθημι *katatithēmi* lay/put down; mid.: grant*

Acts 24:27: χάριτα καταθέσθαι; 25:9: χάριν καταθέσθαι, "*do* a favor"; act. in Mark 15:46 v.l. of the burial of Jesus (in place of ἔθηκεν).

κατατομή, ῆς, ἡ *katatomē* cutting away, mutilation*

In Phil 3:2 Paul makes a charge against his (Jewish Christian) opponents in an ironic wordplay (paronomasia) that circumcision (περιτομή), which they hold in high regard, is in reality a *mutilation* (βλέπετε τοὺς κύνας . . . βλέπετε τὴν κατατομήν); cf. the corresponding polemic in Gal 5:11f. (περιτομή . . . ἀποκόπτω). Perhaps the expression reflects the OT prohibition of ritual mutilation (cf. κατατέμνω in 3 Kgdms 18:28; Hos 7:14). Similar wordplay is in Rom 12:3; 2 Thess 3:11. G. Barth, *Phil* (ZBK) ad loc.; H. Koester, *TDNT* VIII, 109 (bibliography); E. Lohmeyer, *Phil* (KEK) ad loc.

κατατοξεύω *katatoxeuō* shoot down

Heb 12:20 v.l.: ἢ βολίδι ("with a missile") κατατοξευθήσεται.

κατατρέχω *katatrechō* rush down*

Acts 21:32: κατέδραμεν ἐπ' αὐτούς, "he *hurried down* to them."

καταφέρω *katapherō* bring down; bring forward; pass.: sink*

Only in Acts: 25:7: καταφέροντες αἰτιώματα, "*bring forth* accusations"; 26:10: κατήνεγκα ψῆφον, "*cast* his vote [against someone]"; pass. in 20:9 (bis): καταφερόμενος/κατενεχθεὶς ὕπνῳ, "*overcome* by sleep."

καταφεύγω *katapheugō* flee; take refuge*

Literal in Acts 14:6: κατέφυγον εἰς τὰς πόλεις; fig. in Heb 6:18: οἱ καταφυγόντες κρατῆσαι . . . , "we who *have taken refuge* to seize the hope that lies before us." Spicq, *Notes* I, 420-22.

καταφθείρω *kataphtheirō* destroy, annihilate; pass.: be destroyed, be ruined*

Pass. in 2 Tim 3:8: κατεφθαρμένοι τὸν νοῦν, "with a *corrupted* mind"; 2 Pet 2:12 v.l.: *perish;* see also G. Harder, *TDNT* IX, 93-106; Spicq, *Notes* I, 423f.

καταφιλέω *kataphileō* kiss*

Intensive form of φιλέω, used esp. after Xenophon; cf. G. Stählin, *TDNT* IX, 113-44, esp. 118, 123f., 140 with n. 240. Mark 14:45 par. Matt 26:49, of Judas: καὶ κατεφίλησεν αὐτόν (cf. Luke 22:47: φιλῆσαι αὐτόν, the simple form with no difference in meaning, also in Mark 14:44 par. Matt 26:48); Luke 7:38, 45, of the sinful woman: κατεφίλει/κατεφιλοῦσα τοὺς πόδας, "*kiss* the feet" (as a sign of special devotion); 15:20: "embrace" and *kiss* someone as sign of greeting; Acts 20:37: upon departure.

καταφρονέω *kataphroneō* despise; treat scornfully, show contempt*

There are 9 occurrences in the NT: *Despise, scorn:* Matt 6:24 par. Luke 16:13, proverbial (cf. Billerbeck I, 433): *despise* one of two masters (opposite to ἀντέχομαι); 1 Cor 11:22: τῆς ἐκκλησίας τοῦ θεοῦ by unworthy conduct at the Lord's Supper; 2 Pet 2:10: κυριότητος καταφρονοῦντες, "those who *despise* the Lordship [of Christ]/ tolerate no Lord over them" (cf. Jude 8: κυριότητα δὲ ἀθετοῦσιν; see also *Herm. Sim.* v.6.1; *Did.* 4:1). *Treat scornfully/contemptuously:* Matt 18:10: ἑνὸς τῶν μικρῶν τούτων; 1 Tim 4:12: . . . σου τῆς νεότητος, ". . . you [Timothy] because of your youth." *Think scornfully, regard as nothing:* Rom 2:4: τοῦ πλούτου . . . ; absolute in 1 Tim 6:2, in an admonition to slaves with believing masters: μὴ καταφρονείτωσαν (αὐτῶν); Heb 12:2, of

Christ: αἰσχύνης καταφρονήσας, "as he *despised* the shame." C. Schneider, *TDNT* III, 631f.

καταφρονητής, οῦ, ὁ *kataphronētēs* one who despises*

Acts 13:41: οἱ καταφρονηταί, citing Hab 1:5 LXX in reference to Jews and proselytes (cf. v. 26). C. Schneider, *TDNT* III, 632f.

καταχέω *katacheō* pour out*

Of *pouring* ointment on the head of Jesus: Mark 14:3 (τῆς κεφαλῆς, see BDF §181) par. Matt 26:7 (ἐπὶ τῆς κεφαλῆς).

καταχθόνιος, 2 *katachthonios* subterranean*

Subst. in Phil 2:10 with ἐπουράνιοι and ἐπίγειοι in the hymnic naming of all existing beings and powers; cf. Rev 5:13; Ign. *Trall.* 9:1. H. Sasse, *TDNT* III, 633.

καταχράομαι, καταχρῆομαι *katachraomai, katachrēomai* use, utilize fully*

The compound is more intensive than the simple form. Absolute in 1 Cor 7:31: οἱ χρώμενοι . . . ὡς μὴ καταχρώμενοι, "making use [of the world] as those who *have no use for it*"; 9:18: εἰς τὸ μὴ καταχρήσασθαι τῇ ἐξουσίᾳ, "so that I *make no use* of my right." BAGD s.v.; H. Conzelmann, *1 Cor* (Hermeneia) on 7:31.

καταψύχω *katapsychō* cool (trans. vb.), refresh*

Luke 16:24: ἵνα καταψύξῃ, "so that he may *cool* [my tongue]."

κατείδωλος, 2 *kateidōlos* full of idols*

According to Acts 17:16 Paul saw the entire city of Athens *full of idols* (κατείδωλον οὖσαν τὴν πόλιν; Vg.: *idololatriae deditam*). E. Haenchen, *Acts* (Eng. tr., 1971) ad loc.; F. Büchsel, *TDNT* II, 379; R. E. Wycherley, "St. Paul at Athens," *JTS* 19 (1968) 619-21.

κατέναντι *katenanti* opposite*

There are 8 occurrences in the NT. Adv. in Luke 19:30: εἰς τὴν κατέναντι κώμην. Improper prep. with gen. in Mark 11:2 par. Matt 21:2: κατέναντι ὑμῶν, "the village *lying opposite/before* you"; Mark 12:41: κατέναντι τοῦ γαζοφυλακίου; 13:3: κατέναντι τοῦ ἱεροῦ; Matt 27:24 v.l.: κατέναντι τοῦ ὄχλου, "*in the presence of* the people"; in Paul always in reference to God: Rom 4:17: κατέναντι οὗ ἐπίστευσεν θεοῦ (attraction for κατέναντι τοῦ θεοῦ ᾧ ἐπίστευσεν); 2 Cor 2:17; 12:19: κατέναντι θεοῦ ἐν Χριστῷ λαλοῦμεν, "*before* God." BDF §214.4.

κατενώπιον *katenōpion* in the presence of, before*

An adv. used as improper prep. In reference to God: "(holy and) blameless *before* God" (Eph 1:4; Col 1:22; Jude 24), κατενώπιον θεοῦ ἐν Χριστῷ (2 Cor 2:17 v.l.; 12:19 v.l.); → ἐνώπιον 1. BAGD s.v. (bibliography).

κατεξουσιάζω *katexousiazō* use one's power against*

Mark 10:42 par. Matt 20:25, of rulers who *misuse their power against* the peoples (with κατακυριεύω). W. Foerster, *TDNT* II, 575.

κατεργάζομαι *katergazomai* complete, accomplish, bring about*

There are 22 occurrences in the NT, of which 11 are in Romans and 6 are in Rom 7:7, 15, 17, 18, 20.

Of that which is *accomplished* by one's activity: Rom 7:8, 13: sin *brings about* desires and *has brought about* death; 1:27: ἀσχημοσύνην κατεργαζόμενοι, *committing* shamelessness/*promoting* shame"; 2:9: τὸ κακόν; 15:18: ὧν οὐ κατειργάσατο δι' ἐμοῦ, "what Christ *has not accomplished* through me"; 1 Cor 5:3: οὕτως τοῦτο; 1 Pet 4:3: τὸ βούλημα τῶν ἐθνῶν; pass. in 2 Cor 12:12: τὰ μὲν σημεῖα τοῦ ἀποστόλου κατειργάσθη.

In Eph 6:13 ἅπαντα κατεργασάμενοι could mean "after you *have performed* everything," i.e., have become armed with the armor of God (cf. vv. 11, 13a, 14ff.), or "after you *have overcome* everything" (cf. vv. 12f.; 3 Ezra 4:4). The change from ἀντιστῆναι (v. 13b) to στῆναι (v. 13c; cf. στῆτε in v. 14a) suggests the first tr. *Produce, create:* Rom 4:15: ὁ γὰρ νόμος ὀργὴν κατεργάζεται; 5:3: θλῖψις . . . ὑπομονήν (cf. Jas 1:3; 2 Cor 4:17: αἰώνιον βάρος δόξης); Rom 7:10: θάνατον; v. 11: σπουδήν. *Effect:* Rom 9:11: εὐχαριστίαν τῷ θεῷ; Phil 2:12: τὴν ἑαυτῶν σωτηρίαν (see S. Pedersen, *ST* 32 [1978] 1-31). *Prepare:* 2 Cor 5:5: ἡμᾶς εἰς αὐτὸ τοῦτο, "for this very thing." G. Bertram, *TDNT* III, 634f.

κατέρχομαι *katerchomai* come down; arrive at*

There are 16 occurrences in the NT: 2 in Luke, 13 in Acts, 1 in James. Fig. in Jas 3:15: "*coming down* from above [ἄνωθεν, i.e., from God]." Elsewhere commonly with εἰς (Luke 4:31; Acts 8:5; 13:4; 15:30; 19:1) or πρός (9:32): *arrive at* a harbor from the high sea (Acts 18:22; 21:3; 27:5). With reference to the point of origin, with ἀπό (Luke 9:37; Acts 15:1; 18:5; 21:10). With reference to both origin and destination: ἀπὸ . . . εἰς (11:27; 12:19).

κατεσθίω, κατέσθω *katesthiō, katesthō* consume, devour, gulp down*

There are 15 occurrences in the NT. Literal in Mark 4:4 par. Matt 13:4/Luke 8:5, of birds that *devour* the seed; Rev 10:9, 10, of the seer who *consumes* the book (→ βιβλαρίδιον; cf. Ezek 2:8f.; 3:1-3); 12:4, of the dragon that tries to *devour* the child immediately after his birth. Elsewhere fig.: Mark 12:40 par. Luke 20:47/(Matt 23:14 v.l.): κατεσθίουσιν τὰς οἰκίας τῶν χηρῶν, of Pharisees who "*devour/seize* widows' houses" (cf. J. D. M. Derrett, "'Eating Up the Houses of Widows': Jesus's Comment on Lawyers?" *NovT* 14 [1972] 1-9); Luke 15:30: τὸν βίον, "*waste* his living"; John 2:17: *consume* (Ps 68:10 LXX); Gal 5:15: *eat up* in the sense of *tear to pieces* (with δάκνω); absolute in 2 Cor 11:20: *eat up* in the sense of *exploit* (cf. Ps 13:4 LXX); Rev 11:5; 20:9, of fire: *devour, consume.*

κατευθύνω *kateuthynō* make straight, guide, lead*

Luke 1:79: τοὺς πόδας ἡμῶν εἰς ὁδὸν εἰρήνης, "to *guide* our feet in the way of peace"; 1 Thess 3:11: τὴν ὁδὸν ἡμῶν πρὸς ὑμᾶς; 2 Thess 3:5: τὰς καρδίας εἰς τὴν ἀγάπην τοῦ θεοῦ (cf. 1 Chr 29:18 LXX).

κατευλογέω *kateulogeō* bless*

Mark 10:16 (not in par. Matthew/Luke): Jesus "embraced them [the children], placed his hands on them, and *blessed* them" (cf. Tob 10:14; 11:17 B A).

κατέφαγον *katephagon* eat up, consume 2nd aor. of → κατεσθίω, κατέσθω.

κατεφίσταμαι *katephistamai* rise up against*

Acts 18:12: κατεπέστησαν . . . οἱ Ἰουδαῖοι τῷ Παύλῳ. → Γαλλίων 3.

κατέχω *katechō* hold firm, hold back*

1. Occurrences in the NT — 2. Meaning — 3. Usage — 4. 2 Thess 2:6f.

Lit.: R. D. Aus, "God's Plan and God's Power: Isaiah 66 and the Restraining Factors of 2 Thess 2:6-7," *JBL* 96 (1977) 537-53. — E. Best, *1–2 Thess* (BNTC, ²1977) 295-301. — J. Coppens, "*Le katechon et le katechôn:* derniers obstacles à la parousie du Seigneur Jésus," *L'Apocalypse johannique et l'Apocalyptique dans le NT* (ed. J. Lambrecht, 1980) 345-48. — O. Cullmann, *Vorträge und Aufsätze 1925-1962* (1966) 305-66. — H. Hanse, *TDNT* II, 829f. — B. Rigaux, *1–2 Thess* (ÉBib, 1956) 259-80, 662-71. — Spicq, *Notes* Suppl. 379-85. — A. Strobel, *Untersuchungen zum eschatologischen Verzögerungsproblem* (NovTSup 2, 1961). — W. Trilling, *Untersuchungen zum zweiten Thessalonicherbrief* (ETSt 27, 1972). — *idem, 2 Thess* (EKKNT, 1980) 81-105 (bibliography). — C. A. Wanamaker, *1–2 Thess* (NIGTC, 1990) 249-57.

1. This vb. appears 17 times in the NT (excluding

John 5:4 v.l.). Its use is limited to a few writings (or groups of writings): there are 3 occurrences in Luke, 1 in Acts, 8 in the authentic letters of Paul, 2 in 2 Thessalonians, and 3 in Hebrews.

2. a) Used trans. κατέχω meant *restrain, hold fast, hold back* and had a wide sphere of usage (see Pape, *Wörterbuch* I, s.v.; LSJ s.v.). In the NT only one aspect is represented. b) Intrans. use appears once in the NT, in Acts 27:40, as a t.t. of nautical language: *proceed toward, head for* (the shore), or *come to land* (texts in BAGD s.v. 2; for bibliography on ancient nautical terms see E. Haenchen, *Acts* [Eng. tr., 1971] 708).

3. a) Κατέχω is used in the physical sense to mean: 1) *hold fast*, in the attempt (impf.) of the people to prevent Jesus from leaving (Luke 4:42), *keep, retain*, of Onesimus (Phlm 13), 2) *have, possess* (1 Cor 7:30; 2 Cor 6:10), *take* one's place (Luke 14:9 [L]).

b) The vb. is more frequently used figuratively: 1) negatively, of those who "*suppress* the truth in unrighteousness" (Rom 1:18), of the power of the law "by which we were *held* [captive]" (7:6; cf. Gal 3:23; H. Schlier, *Rom* [HTKNT] ad loc.); → 4 on 2 Thess 2:6f.; and 2) positively in the parenetic direction to *hold fast* "the word" (Luke 8:15; not in par. Mark/Matthew), "the traditions" (1 Cor 11:2), "the gospel" (15:2), "that which is good" (1 Thess 5:21), or the confidence and hope of the confession (Heb 3:6, 14 [meaning uncertain]; 10:23).

4. The meaning of κατέχω in 2 Thess 2:6, 7 has been disputed since antiquity. The distinction between neut. (τὸ κατέχον, v. 6) and masc. (ὁ κατέχων, v. 7) subst. participles cannot be explained with certainty either by grammatical or semiotic means. The immediate context, however, demands a tr. congruent with that which proceeds from linguistic analysis of vv. 5-7 (as an "excursus" between vv. 3b-4 and 8-10a) and from the function of this power (Trilling, *Untersuchungen* 77-92). The result will probably be that the κατέχων(-ον) has a positive function and is a factor in the postponement of the end of the world/history within a fixed tradition of a "delay" effected by God himself ("delay," "restrain"; cf. Hab 2:3f.; Cullmann; Strobel *passim*). Within the framework of this tradition the "restraining power" is best understood as a literary figure for the postponement of the appearance of the "person of sin" (v. 3b, i.e., the "Antichrist"; cf. ὁ ἄνομος, v. 8); this is a "theocentric interpretation").

All other interpretations (a hostile power: cf. C. H. Giblin, *The Threat to Faith* [1967] 167-242; Best 301; mythic: the "binding" of the "evil one": M. Dibelius, *1-2 Thess* [HNT] ad loc., etc.) are less probable or entirely misguided. Interpretations in terms of world history and eschatological history (since Hippolytus and Tertullian, esp. of the Roman Empire) and in terms of events

contemporary with the NT (the proclamation of the gospel, Claudius, Vespasian, etc.) have been discarded. The assumption that 2 Thessalonians is a pseudepigraphon provides the impulse for disregarding these interpretations (see Trilling, *Untersuchungen; idem, 2 Thess*, ad loc.).

W. Trilling

κατηγορέω *katēgoreō* accuse, bring charges*

There are 23 occurrences in the NT, in 22 of which it is a juridical t.t.; the vb. has a fig. meaning with no legal connotation only in Rom 2:15, where it refers to the thoughts of the Gentiles, which "*accuse/reproach* or defend" them (κατηγορούντων ἢ καὶ ἀπολογουμένων).

In the Synoptics the vb. is used in reference to Jesus: Mark 3:2 par. Matt 12:10/Luke 6:7, of his opponents' intention to *accuse* him; cf. John 8:6; Luke 11:54 TR; Luke 23:2: *bring charges;* Mark 15:3, 4: *accuse* (with acc. of the obj.); Luke 23:10, 14 (αἴτιον ὤν here probably by attraction); pass. in Matt 27:12. John 5:45a: *accuse* before God; v. 45b: ὁ κατηγορῶν, "the *accuser*"; Rev 12:10: Satan is ὁ κατήγωρ . . . ὁ κατηγορῶν (αὐτούς); cf. also Job 1:6ff.; Zech 3:1; *1 Enoch* 40:7. The occurrences in Acts appear in connection with Paul's trial: *bring charges:* 22:30; 24:2, 19; 25:5, 11: εἰ δὲ οὐδέν ἐστιν ὧν, "but if there proves to be nothing in the charges . . ."; 25:16: ὁ κατηγορούμενος, "the *accused*"; *accuse* (in the course of a trial): 24:8, 13; of the relationship of Paul to his people: 28:19: οὐχ ὡς . . . ἔχων τι κατηγορεῖν, "not as if I had *charges* to bring." F. Büchsel, *TDNT* III, 636f.

κατηγορία, ας, ἡ *katēgoria* accusation, charge*

John 18:29: κατηγορίαν φέρω, "bring an *accusation*"; Luke 6:7 TR; *complaint, charge* (with κατά): 1 Tim 5:19; with gen. ("because of") in Titus 1:6: ἐν κατηγορίᾳ ἀσωτίας. F. Büchsel, *TDNT* III, 637.

κατήγορος, ου, ὁ *katēgoros* accuser*

Only in Acts: 23:30, 35; 25:16, 18; 24:7f. v.l., of Paul's *accusers*; also John 8:10 TR; Rev 12:10 v.l. in place of κατήγωρ.

κατήγωρ, ορος, ὁ *katēgōr* accuser*

Rev 12:10 (only in A; 𝔭⁴⁷ ℵ C 051 Koine read κατήγορος; cf. *TCGNT* ad loc.): Satan is the *accuser* of people before God (with pres. partc. of → κατηγορέω), he who was thrown down from heaven (cf. Luke 10:18; Billerbeck I, 141-44). Κατήγωρ could be a vernacular form based on the gen. pl. κατηγόρων (so BAGD s.v.; BDF §52) or a Semitism based on the loanword (from κατήγορος) qātēgôr in rabbinic literature (see F. Büchsel, *TDNT* III, 636n.2; Billerbeck I, 141f.). The idea that such a Semitism might be preserved only in A (despite the vernacular κατήγωρ in Pap. London I, 124, 25) supports the difficult text-critical decision in this passage.

κατῆλθον *katēlthon* have come down
2nd aor. of → κατέρχομαι.

κατήνεγκα *katēnenka* have brought down
1st aor. of → καταφέρω.

κατήφεια, ας, ἡ *katēpheia* dejection, sadness*

Jas 4:9: μεταστραπήτω . . . ἡ χαρὰ εἰς κατήφειαν, "let joy be turned into *sorrow*" as a sign of turning to God; cf. 4:6; 5:1; Luke 6:25.

κατηχέω *katēcheō* impart, instruct, teach; pass.: learn*

1. Occurrences — 2. General meaning — 3. In reference to Christian teaching

Lit.: H. W. BEYER, *TDNT* III, 638-40. — A. GARCIA DEL MORAL, " 'Catequizar' según Pablo y Lucas," *Studium* 24 (1984) 57-110. — A. KNAUBER, "Zur Grundbedeutung der Wortgruppe κατηχέω-catechizo," *Oberrheinisches Pastoralblatt* 68 (1967) 291-304. — SPICQ, *Notes* I, 425-27. — K. WEGENAST, *DNTT* III, 771f. — R. B. ZUCK, "Greek Words for Teach," *BSac* 122 (165) 158-68. — For further bibliography see *TWNT* X, 1135.

1. The vb. κατηχέω appears in the NT 8 times, 4 times in the authentic Pauline letters (Rom 2:18; 1 Cor 14:19; Gal 6:6a, b), and 4 times in the Lukan literature (Luke 1:4; Acts 18:25; 21:21, 24). It is a late word that does not appear, e.g., in the LXX and appears only rarely in Josephus (act. in *Vita* 366) and Philo (pass. in *Leg. Gai.* 198).

The second-century occurrences in *2 Clem.* 17:1 and Lucian *JTr.* 39 are significant. *2 Clement* recalls a commandment "to draw people away from idols and *instruct* them" (ἀποσπᾶν καὶ κατηχεῖν)." It is doubtful whether κατηχέω is to be understood here already "in the specif. sense of catechetical instruction by the church" (despite BAGD s.v. 2b; cf. Knauber 301). Moreover, the frequent interpretation of the prefix κατα- based on appeal to the Lucian passage ("sound from above"; so, e.g., Beyer 638) is incorrect (Knauber 293f., 298-301). The Suidas *Lexicon* (III, 77 in the Adler edition), however, renders κατηχέω with προτρέπομαι and παραινέω.

2. In Acts 21:21, 24 the vb. appears (as in Josephus and Philo: → 1) with the general meaning *inform, report*. According to 21:21 the numerous Jewish Christians (v. 20) "*have learned* (κατηχήθησαν) about you [Paul], that you teach the Jews who live among Gentiles apostasy from Moses." Consequently (v. 24) it is recommended that Paul assume the costs associated with a vow. Thus the suspicious Jewish Christians can be reassured when they learn "that what *was reported* (κατήχηνται) about you [Paul] is nothing."

3. The other occurrences of κατηχέω in the Lukan literature (Luke 1:4; Acts 18:25) indicate that the vb. begins to take on a technical meaning in reference to religious instruction (see H. Schürmann, *Luke* [HTKNT] I, 15), which is likely also for Paul (BAGD s.v. 2). In Paul the reference is more precisely, except in Rom 2:18, to Christian instruction. In Luke 1:4 the pass. is used, as in Acts 21:21, 24, with περί (περὶ ὧν κατηχήθης λόγων). In two other instances what is taught is in the acc.: Acts 18:25: ἦν κατηχημένος τὴν ὁδὸν τοῦ κυρίου; Gal 6:6a: ὁ κατηχούμενος τὸν λόγον.

The pass. partc. designates those who are *instructed* (the Jews in Rom 2:18: κατηχούμενος ἐκ τοῦ νόμου, "*instructed* from the law"), and the act. partc. (ὁ κατηχῶν) is used of the one who *instructs*: Gal 6:6b: the one who is instructed should have fellowship with the one who instructs ἐν πᾶσιν ἀγαθοῖς. Since it is not certain that the reference is to the claim to financial support (H. Schlier, *Gal* [KEK] 275f.), we cannot call this "the earliest evidence we have for a 'full-time' teaching office in the early church" (Wegenast 771; cf. Beyer 639).

In 1 Cor 14:9 Paul says with respect to glossolalia that he would prefer to speak five words with his understanding in the assembly "so that I may *instruct* (ἵνα . . . κατηχήσω), than countless words ἐν γλώσσῃ."

The thesis that "Paul uses not only the common διδάσκειν but also this much rarer word, hardly known at all in the religious vocabulary of Judaism, as a technical term for Christian instruction," and thus emphasizes "the particular nature of instruction on the basis of the Gospel" (Beyer 639), cannot be demonstrated.   G. Schneider

κατιόομαι *katioomai* rust*

Jas 5:3: the gold and silver of the rich *has rusted* (i.e., will have been rusted at the time of the coming judgment); cf. Ep Jer 10:23; Sir 29:10; Matt 6:19f. What is supposedly permanent is thus not permanent; wealth will become a witness against those who have accumulated it (5:3b). O. Michel, *TDNT* III, 335; W. Schrage, *Jas* (NTD) ad loc.

κατισχύω *katischyō* be strong, succeed in, prevail*

Matt 16:18, with gen. οὐ κατισχύσουσιν αὐτῆς (= τῆς ἐκκλησίας): "*they will* not *prevail* against it"; with inf. *be capable of, be able* in Luke 21:36; absolute *get the upper hand, be strong* in 23:23. W. Grundmann, *TDNT* III, 398.

κατοικέω *katoikeō* dwell, inhabit*

1. Occurrences in the NT — 2. Meaning and usage — 3. Fig. usage

Lit.: BAGD s.v. — N. KEHL, *Der Christushymnus im Kolosserbrief* (1967) 110-25. — A. S. LAWHEAD, *A Study of the Theological Significance of 'yāšab' in the Masoretic Text, with*

Attention to Its Translation in the Septuagint (Diss. Boston University, 1975). — O. MICHEL, *TDNT* V, 153-55.

1. Κατοικέω appears 44 times in the NT, most frequently in Acts (20 occurrences) and Revelation (13 occurrences + 12:12; 14:6 v.l.), 6 times in the Gospels (all in Matthew and Luke), and 5 times in the Epistles (+ Jas 5:4 v.l.).

2. It is used in the NT both trans. (κατοικέω τι: *inhabit* something) and intrans. (*dwell, live,* usually with an adv. indicating place; absolute only in Acts 22:12). It appears seldom as a finite vb. and most often as the pl. pres. act. partc. (οἱ κατοικοῦντες = those *dwelling,* the *inhabitants*). Κατοικέω is usually used literally (34 times of the dwelling of people) and only 10 times in a fig. sense (→ 3).

In Acts the trans. (Acts 1:19; 2:9, 14; 4:16; 9:32, 35; 19:10, 17; cf. also Luke 13:4) and the intrans. with ἐν (Acts 1:20; 7:2, 4a, 48; 9:22; 11:29; 13:27; 17:24; so also Heb 11:9) are predominant. Use with εἰς (Acts 2:5; 7:4b; so also Matt 2:23; 4:13) is less common. Acts 22:12, "by all Jews *dwelling*" (Bauer supplies ἐκεῖ: "there"), is formulated in an unusual way, as is Acts 17:26, "*dwell* on (ἐπί) the face of the earth," probably with the intention of strengthening the expression (Michel 156).

In Revelation οἱ κατοικοῦντες ἐπὶ τῆς γῆς, "those who *dwell* on the earth," is a fixed expression (Rev 3:10; 6:10; 8:13; 11:10 bis; 13:8, 14 bis; 14:6 v.l.; 17:8); only Rev 13:12 and 17:2 are formulated differently.

3. Κατοικέω is used fig. of a persisting dwelling of spiritual or religious phenomena, including unclean spirits (Matt 12:45 par. Luke 11:26), God (Matt 23:21; Acts 7:48; 17:24), Christ (Eph 3:17), the (divine) "fullness" (Col 1:19; 2:9), righteousness (2 Pet 3:13), or Satan (Rev 2:13b). If Matt 23:21 speaks straightforwardly of God's dwelling in the temple, then the temple polemic of Acts 7:48 conflicts with it ("The most high does not *dwell* in the works of human hands"), as does, indeed, the OT (cf. 1 Kgs 8:27, 29). Acts 17:24 takes up this thought: the Creator "*dwells* not ἐν χειροποιήτοις ναοῖς."

In the petition of Eph 3:17 that "Christ *dwell* in your hearts through faith" the duration designated by κατοικέω is bound up with the continual renewal of faith (J. Gnilka, *Eph* [HTKNT] 184). In the hymn in Col 1:15-20 it is said of Christ "that it pleased the divine fulness *to dwell* in him" (Col 1:19; cf. 2:9). In a phrase shaped by the OT (cf. the combination of εὐδοκέω and κατοικέω in Ps 67:17 LXX) the reference is to the function of Christ as mediator of the presence of God in the cosmos (Kehl 123).

H. Fendrich

κατοίκησις, εως, ἡ *katoikēsis* dwelling*

Mark 5:3, of the Gerasene demoniac who had his *dwelling/shelter* in the tombs.

κατοικητήριον, ου, τό *katoikētērion* dwelling*

According to Eph 2:22 the Gentile Christians (together with the saints, the apostles, and the prophets and with Christ as the cornerstone, 2:11-21) "are built for a *house* of God in the Spirit" (εἰς κατοικητήριον τοῦ θεοῦ ἐν πνεύματι); Rev 18:2, of Babylon (= Rome), which became a *dwelling* of demons (cf. Isa 13:21; 21:9; Jer 9:10; 50:39; Bar 4:35). O. Michel, *TDNT* V, 156.

κατοικία, ας, ἡ *katoikia* dwelling, home*

Acts 17:26, of the "boundaries of *dwelling/habitation* (ὁροθεσίαι τῆς κατοικίας)" of the peoples; cf. Ps 73:17 LXX.

κατοικίζω *katoikizō* cause to dwell, give a dwelling place*

Jas 4:5 of the Spirit, to which God "*has given a dwelling place* in us"; cf. *Herm. Man.* iii.1; *Sim.* v.6.5. O. Michel, *TDNT* V, 156f.

κατοπτρίζομαι *katoptrizomai* look at (in a mirror)*

Lit.: R. BULTMANN, *2 Cor* (Eng. tr., 1985) 90-96. — J. DUPONT, "Le Chrétien, miroir de la gloire divine d'après 2 Cor. III,18," *RB* (1949) 392-411. — N. HUGEDÉ, *La métaphore du miroir dans les épîtres de S. Paul aux Corinthiens* (1957) 20-36. — G. KITTEL, *TDNT* II, 696f. — J. KREMER, "Christliche Schriftauslegung. Eine bibeltheologische Erwägung zu 2Kor 3,18," *Bibel und Liturgie* 52 (1979) 18-21. — J. LAMBRECHT, "Transformation in 2 Cor 3,18," *Bib* 64 (1983) 243-54. — K. PRÜMM, *Diakonia Pneumatos* I (1967) 166-202. — E. SCHWEIZER, "2 Korinther 3,12-18," *GPM* 60 (1971) 89-93. — W. C. VAN UNNIK, "'With Unveiled Face.' An Exegesis of 2 Corinthians III,12-18," *NovT* 6 (1963) 163-69.

Κατοπτρίζω (cf. κάτοπτρον, "mirror, mirror image"; → ἔσοπτρον) has the basic meaning *show in a mirror, reflect.* For the mid. κατοπτρίζομαι, besides the meaning *look at oneself in the mirror,* the meaning *look at something in the mirror* is attested twice (Philo *All.* iii.101; Gregory Thaumaturgus [see Hugedé]). The ancient versions and oldest commentators understood 2 Cor 3:18 in this simple sense: *behold.*

On the basis of the immediately preceding context ("unveiled face" [→ καλύπτω, → πρόσωπον] and "the glory" [→ δόξα]) a reference to the face of Moses in 3:7, 13 must be considered. Inasmuch as Moses' face reflects God's glory, the meaning "reflect" (Theodoret, Dupont, Prümm, van Unnik) in 3:18 becomes possible. This view would be particularly the case if 2 Cor 3:18 refers only to Paul (Schweizer; cf. p[46]: κατοπτριζόμεθα with omission of πάντες) and if the idea of a present transformation through the beholding of God's glory were un-Pauline (Dupont).

Paul, however, does not speak in 2 Cor 3:18 directly of his ministry, but rather of the benefit to all Christians (πάντες). The contrast is not with Moses, but with the Jews, who are mentioned in the immediate context (vv. 14f.). "Unveiled face" is thus to be understood in the sense of "unveiled heart" (Bultmann), as is indicated by the typological interpretation that Paul himself makes in 3:14f. of Exod 34:33, 36. Without being hindered by a "veil" (cf. 4:3f.), but rather being liberated by the Spirit of the Lord (v. 17b; cf. 4:6), they are now able to behold the glory of the Lord. That κατοπτρίζομαι is not to be understood in the refined sense of *behold* (= ἀτενίσαι, vv. 7, 13; so Bultmann) is required by the phrase τὴν αὐτὴν εἰκόνα: beholding Yahweh's glory in the mirror/image (cf. Wis 7:26) of Christ (cf. 4:4, 6) stands in the service (partc.) of the transformation produced by the Spirit (→ μεταμορφόομαι, → πνεῦμα) "into the same image" (cf. Rom 8:29; Phil 3:21; that the future transformation has already begun according to Paul is indicated by Gal 2:20; 4:19).   J. Kremer

κατόρθωμα, ατος, τό *katorthōma* ordered relationships, wholesome situation

Acts 24:2 TR: κατορθωμάτων γινομένων (in place of διορθωμάτων).

κάτω *katō* below (adv.), downward*

There are 9 occurrences in the NT (on the meanings see BDF §103): *below:* Mark 14:66: κάτω ἐν τῇ αὐλῇ; Acts 2:19: ἐν τῷ οὐρανῷ ἄνω . . . ἐπὶ τῆς γῆς κάτω; subst. in John 8:23: ἐκ τῶν κάτω . . . ἐκ τῶν ἄνω, "from *below* . . . from above"; *downward:* Matt 4:6 par. Luke 4:9; Mark 15:38 par. Matt 27:51: ἀπ' ἄνωθεν ἕως κάτω, "from top to *bottom;* John 8:6: κάτω κύπτω; 8:8 v.l.; Acts 20:9: πίπτω κάτω. Büchsel, *TDNT* III, 640f.; *TWNT* X, 1135f. (bibliography).

κατώτερος, 3 *katōteros* lower, further below*

Comparative (can also have superlative sense) of κάτω (see BDF §62). In Eph 4:9 (κατέβη εἰς τὰ κατώτερα μέρη τῆς γῆς; cf. Pss 62:10; 138:15 LXX) τῆς γῆς can be understood as gen. of apposition ("into the *lower* part, namely the earth"), obj. gen. ("into the *low ground* of the earth"), or partitive gen. ("into the *lowest* parts of the earth"; on the discussion cf. BAGD s.v.; BDF §167; F. Büchsel, *TDNT* III, 641; J. Gnilka, *Eph* [HTKNT] ad loc.). In connection with 4:7f. (cf. Ps 68:19) v. 9 most likely refers to the incarnation of Christ. Thus in agreement with the cosmology of Ephesians the earth is itself the *lower* part of the universe, in contrast to heaven (cf. M. Dibelius and H. Greeven, *Eph* [HNT] ad loc.; → κάτω).

κατωτέρω *katōterō* below (adv.), further below, downwards*

Matt 2:16: ἀπὸ διετοῦς καὶ κατωτέρω, "of two years and *below*"; cf. 1 Chr 27:23; → ἀπό 4.c.

Καῦδα *Kauda* Cauda*

Acts 27:16: the name of a small island (νησίον) *ca.* 40 km. south of the southwest coast of Crete, whose lee was useful for ships; v.l. Κλαῦδα ℵ* Aᵛⁱᵈ 33, etc. L. Bürchner, PW VII, 861; IX, 57; C. von Gablenz, *BHH* 961.

καῦμα, ατος, τό *kauma* burning, heat*

Rev 7:16: οὐδὲ . . . ὁ ἥλιος οὐδὲ πᾶν καῦμα, "neither . . . the sun nor any *scorching heat*" (cf. Ps 120:6 LXX); 16:9: ἐκαυματίσθησαν . . . καῦμα μέγα, "they were scorched with great *heat.*" J. Schneider, *TDNT* III, 643.

καυματίζω *kaumatizō* burn*

Rev 16:8: καυματίσαι ἐν πυρί; pass. in 16:9: ἐκαυματίσθησαν οἱ ἄνθρωποι (an effect of the fourth "bowl of wrath"); Mark 4:6 par. Matt 13:6: the seed fell on rocky ground and quickly sprang up, but just as quickly was *scorched* by the sun (with ἐξηράνθη). J. Schneider, *TDNT* III, 643.

καῦσις, εως, ἡ *kausis* burning*

According to Heb 6:8 the unproductive earth is near destruction, which will end with its *burning* (ἧς τὸ τέλος εἰς καῦσιν), a parable for the fate of apostate Christians (cf. 6:1ff.). J. Schneider, *TDNT* III, 643.

καυσόω *kausoō* burn*

Pass. in 2 Pet 3:10, 12: the world elements "will be destroyed" (v. 10) or "melted" (v. 12) "*in the fervent heat*" (στοιχεῖα καυσούμενα λυθήσεται/τήκεται). J. Schneider, *TDNT* III, 644.

καυστηριάζω *kaustēriazō* brand*

Pass. and fig. in 1 Tim 4:2, of false teachers "who *are branded* in their own consciences" (κεκαυστηριασμένων τὴν ἰδίαν συνείδησιν), apparently a reference to the scar from a brand placed on slaves; i.e., they are in bondage to sin (cf. J. Schneider, *TDNT* III, 644f.; J. Jeremias, *1–2 Tim, Titus* [NTD] ad loc.); cf. also 6:3ff.

καύσων, ωνος, ὁ *kausōn* heat (of the sun)*

Of the *heat* of the day, Matt 20:12; *heat brought by*

the south wind, Luke 12:55; *heat* of the sun (not "hot wind"), Jas 1:11. J. Schneider, *TDNT* III, 644.

καυτηριάζω *kautēriazō* brand*

1 Tim 4:2 TR in place of καυστηριάζω.

καυχάομαι *kauchaomai* boast (vb.)*
καύχημα, ατος, τό *kauchēma* pride, arrogance; object of boasting*
καύχησις, εως, ἡ *kauchēsis* boasting*

1. Occurrences and meanings — 2. Usage and semantic relationships — a) The vb. — b) The nouns — 3. The Pauline theology of boasting

Lit.: S. C. AGOURIDIS, "Ἡ καύχησις τοῦ ᾽ Ἀπ. Παύλου πρὸ τῆς ἐπιστροφῆς αὐτοῦ καὶ μετὰ ταύτην," idem, *Biblike Meletēmata 1* (1966) 87-109. — R. ASTING, *Kauchesis* (1925). — K. BERGER, *Exegese des NT* (UTB 658, 1977) 144-56. — R. BULTMANN, *TDNT* III, 645-54. — idem, *Theology* I, 242. — idem, "Christ the End of the Law," idem, *Essays Philosophical and Theological* (1955) 36-66. — M. CARREZ, "La confiance en l'homme et la confiance en soi selon l'apôtre Paul," *RHPR* 44 (1964) 191-99. — G. DAUTZENBERG, "Der Verzicht auf das apostolische Unterhaltsrecht," *Bib* 50 (1969) 212-32. — B. A. DOWDY, *The Meaning of kauchasthai in the NT* (Diss., 1978). — J. K. ELLIOTT, "In Favour of καυθήσομαι at 1 Corinthians 13,3," *ZNW* 62 (1971) 297f. — T. FAHY, "St. Paul's 'Boasting' and 'Weakness,' " *ITQ* 31 (1964) 214-27. — A. FRIDRICHSEN, "Zum Stil des paulinisches Peristasenkatalogs 2 Cor. 11,23ff.," *SO* 7 (1928) 25-29. — idem, "Peristasenkatalog und Res gestae," *SO* 8 (1929) 78-82. — P. GENTHS, "Der Begriff des καύχημα bei Paulus," *NKZ* 38 (1927) 501-21. — H. C. HAHN, *DNTT* I, 227-29. — M. JOIN-LAMBERT and X. LÉON-DUFOUR, *WBB* 624ff. — O. KUSS, *Der Römerbrief* I (1957) 219-24. — F. PACK, "Boasting in the Lord," *Restoration Quarterly* 19 (1976) 65-71. — J. H. PETZER, "Contextual Evidence in Favour of καυχήσωμαι in 1 Cor 13,3," *NTS* 35 (1989) 229-53. — K. PRÜMM, *Diakonia Pneumatos* II/2 (1962) 78ff., 340-55. — F. RAURELL, "Exégesis y teología del 'kauchēma,' " *EstFr* 72 (1971) 337-47. — J. SÁNCHEZ BOSCH, *"Gloriarse" según San Pablo. Sentido y teologia de καυχάομαι* (AnBib 40, 1970). — H. SCHLIER, *Rom* (HTKNT, 1977) 143f. — J. SCHREINER, "Jeremia 9,22.23 als Hintergrund des paulinischen 'Sich-Rühmens,' " FS Schnackenburg 530-42. — SPICQ, *Notes* Suppl. 386-94. — S. H. TRAVIS, "Paul's Boasting in 2. Corinthians 10–12," *SE* VI (1973) 527-32. — J. ZMIJEWSKI, *Der Stil der paulinischen "Narrenrede"* (BBB 52, 1978). — For further bibliography see *TWNT* X, 1136.

1. These 3 words appear in the NT a total of almost 60 times. Of these occurrences, 53 or 54 (depending on the disputed text-critical question of 1 Cor 13:3) are in the authentic Pauline letters. Καυχάομαι is also found in Eph 2:9; Jas 1:9; 4:16 (there with καύχησις) and καύχημα in Heb 3:6.

The vb. is most often intrans. and means *boast,* the context indicating whether *taking pride* in a positive sense or boasting in the negative sense of *bragging* is in

mind (cf. Berger 144: "A negative meaning of 'boasting' is determined only by the object"). Where the vb. is trans. (with acc. obj.: 2 Cor 7:14; 9:2; 10:8; 11:12, 16, 30b), it can be translated *boast about* ("*mention in order to boast of* [something]," BAGD s.v.).

A certain difference in meaning, based on the forms of the words, exists between the two nouns. Καύχημα expresses *what is said in boasting* (cf. 2 Cor 9:3), *the reason for boasting* (e.g., Gal 6:4), and *the basis for boasting* or *that which makes it possible* (so most often in Paul: Rom 4:2; 1 Cor 9:16; 2 Cor 1:14; Phil 2:16, etc.). Καύχησις designates more often *the action of boasting as such* (so 2 Cor 7:14; 8:24). Paul does not maintain this distinction consistently. Thus καύχημα can mean *the act of boasting* (2 Cor 5:12), and καύχησις can represent *that which makes boasting possible* (Rom 3:27), the *reason* (Rom 15:17), or the *object* of boasting (2 Cor 1:12).

2. a) Only rarely is the intrans. vb. used in an absolute sense (1 Cor 4:7 [13:3]; 2 Cor 11:18b, 30a; 12:1, 6; Eph 2:9; cf. also the subst. partc. ὁ καυχώμενος in 1 Cor 1:31a; 2 Cor 10:17a [otherwise Phil 3:3]). The vb. is most often defined more precisely, normally with a prep. phrase, most frequently (in about half of the occurrences) ἐν with the dat. ᾽Εν with the dative, ἐπί with the dat. (Rom 5:2: καυχώμεθα ἐπ᾽ ἐλπίδι, "let us boast *because of* our hope"), and εἰς with the acc. (2 Cor 10:16: εἰς τὰ ἕτοιμα καυχήσασθαι, "boast *with respect to* what has already been completed"; cf., however, the different sense of εἰς in 2 Cor 10:13, 15: εἰς τὰ ἄμετρα καυχᾶσθαι, "boast without measure") all give the object or basis of boasting (BDF §196: dat. of cause!). Objects of these preps. are God (ἐν θεῷ, Rom 2:17; 5:11), the Lord (ἐν κυρίῳ, 1 Cor 1:31; 2 Cor 10:17), Christ (ἐν Χριστῷ, Phil 3:3), the law (ἐν νόμῳ, Rom 2:23), the flesh (ἐν σαρκί, Gal 6:13), the cross (ἐν τῷ σταυρῷ, Gal 6:14), weaknesses (ἐν ἀσθενείαις, 2 Cor 12:9), tribulations (ἐν ταῖς θλίψεσιν, Rom 5:3), labors (ἐν κόποις, 2 Cor 10:15), etc. (cf. 1 Cor 3:21; 2 Cor 5:12; Jas 1:9f.). ᾽Ενώπιον with the gen. defines the one *before whom* boasting is done (1 Cor 1:29: ἐνώπιον τοῦ θεοῦ). Ὑπέρ with the gen. indicates *for whom* (i.e., *in whose interest* or *for whose recommendation* [cf. BDF §231.1]) one boasts (so twice in 2 Cor 12:5; cf. 7:14; 9:2, where acc. objects designate the object of boasting). Περί with the gen. designates the subject of boasting (cf. 2 Cor 10:8: περὶ τῆς ἐξουσίας). Κατά with the acc. designates the *measure* (*norm* or *manner*) of boasting (cf. 2 Cor 11:18: κατὰ σάρκα καυχῶνται, opposite of κατὰ κύριον λαλεῖν, v. 17).

The vb. appears significantly often in imperatives and prohibitions (e.g., [μὴ] καυχάσθω, "let him [not] boast": 1 Cor 1:31; 3:21; 2 Cor 10:17; Jas 1:9; μὴ γένοιτο καυχᾶσθαι: "far be it from me to boast": Gal 6:14; cf. μὴ κατακαυχᾶσθε, "do not boast": Jas 3:14). It appears similarly frequently in final or consecutive constructions (e.g., in ἵνα clauses: 1 Cor 1:31 [13:3]; 2 Cor 5:12; 11:16; Gal 6:13; Eph 2:9 [καύχημα in such clauses: 2 Cor 9:3; Phil 1:26]; or with ὅπως: 1 Cor 1:29). In the same way the vb. appears in typical recurring constructions that express certain semantic relationships; thus it is almost always found in contrasts ([οὐ] . . . ἀλλά/δέ, e.g., 2 Cor 5:12; 10:12f., 16f.; cf. also Phil 3:3 [. . . καὶ οὐκ]; also Eph 2:8f.; Jas 1:9f.), in relationships of correspondence (with καί, 2 Cor 1:14; 11:16, 18; cf. 8:24), in expressions of limitation (with εἰ μή, 2 Cor 12:5; Gal 6:14), or in expressions of surpassing quality (οὐ μόνον . . . ἀλλὰ καί, Rom 5:3, 11).

More important semantically than the forms previously mentioned are the numerous synonyms and antonyms of καυχᾶσθαι; they contribute decisively to clarifying the sense of the word. This is particularly the case where synonymous or similar expressions occur in the immediate context with "boast" (particularly in Paul).

Thus in 2 Cor 10:12f. ἑαυτὸν συνιστάναι appears with καυχᾶσθαι; the boasting mentioned here is thus characterized as "boasting of oneself" in the sense of "recommending oneself" (cf. the opposite in v. 18: "one who boasts in the Lord," "whom the Lord recommends"; cf. 5:12). In 10:15 Paul emphasizes that he boasts (in contrast to his opponents) not without measure in the labors of others, but expresses his hope for a (later) μεγαλυνθῆναι among the Corinthians. Thus he interprets *true* boasting as "being magnified by another." In 12:9 he says that he boasts in his weaknesses, and means the same thing as in v. 10, where he emphasizes that he "rejoices" (εὐδοκῶ) in his weaknesses.

In Phil 3:3 Paul says: "We *boast* in Christ Jesus and trust not in the flesh" (οὐκ ἐν σαρκὶ πεποιθότες), and thus portrays boasting as "the manner in which trust takes shape" (Schlier 143; on the parallel καυχᾶσθαι/πεποιθέναι cf. 2 Cor 10:7f.). When Rom 2:17 says that the Jew "relies on the law" (ἐπαναπαύομαι, literally "rest, find support" [BAGD s.v.]) and "boasts of God," here likewise the boasting is understood as trust (in specific privileges; cf. πέποιθας, v. 19).

Other synonyms with καυχᾶσθαι in Paul are: ἐπαίρομαι ("elevate oneself"; cf. 2 Cor 11:20 with 11:18), φυσιόομαι ("be puffed up"; cf. 1 Cor 4:6 with 4:7 and 3:21), τολμάω ("be bold, presumptuous"; cf. 2 Cor 11:21; also Rom 15:18 with 15:17). Antonyms are such vbs. as (κατ)αισχύνω ("shame, frustrate"; cf. Rom 5:5 with 5:2; 1 Cor 1:27 with 1:29, 31; 2 Cor 7:14; 9:4 with 9:2f.; 10:8; also Phil 1:20 with 1:26) and ἀτιμάζω ("dishonor," Rom 2:23).

b) The nouns also appear with other words that define their usage more precisely (except καύχησις in Rom 3:27), typically: the demonstrative pron. αὕτη (2 Cor 1:12; 11:10; cf. also the phrase "with this object of boasting," 11:17), the correlative pron. τοιαύτη (Jas 4:16) and,

esp. often in Paul, the possessive pron. of the first and second persons (μου, 1 Cor 9:15; ἡμῶν, 2 Cor 1:12, 14; 8:24; 9:3; ὑμῶν, 1 Cor 5:6; 2 Cor 1:14; Phil 1:26; cf. also the adj. ὑμετέρα, 1 Cor 15:31). Pred. adjs. such as καλός (1 Cor 5:6: "your boasting [is] not good") or πονηρός (Jas 4:6: "all such boasting is evil") give a value to boasting.

The nouns appear most often in connection with vbs. such as ἔχω ("have": Rom 4:2; 15:17; 1 Cor 15:31; cf. Gal 6:4, where ἔχω means "keep"), κατέχω ("preserve": Heb 3:6), εἰμί ("be": 2 Cor 1:12, 14; Jas 4:16; cf. 1 Cor 5:6; 2 Cor 7:4; and 1 Thess 2:19, where ἐστίν is to be supplied; also εἰμί with the dat. of the person [in the sense of ἔχω]: 1 Cor 9:16), κενόω ("deplete, destroy"; 1 Cor 9:15; 2 Cor 9:3), or περισσεύω ("abound, overflow": Phil 1:26; cf. μεγαλυνθῆναι εἰς περισσείαν, 2 Cor 10:15). Vbs. connected with καύχημα or καύχησις also have with them, though not so frequently as with καυχάομαι itself, prep. phrases that complete the thought, e.g., ἐν with the dat. (Rom 15:17; 1 Cor 15:31; Phil 1:26; according to Bultmann [*TDNT* III, 648f.n.35], ἐν in these three cases does not give the reason or the object, but rather "the sphere in which the self-glorying moves"), εἰς with the acc. (so Gal 6:4, where τὸ καύχημα εἰς ἑαυτὸν μόνον means "boasting with a few to oneself alone," so F. Mussner, *Gal* [HTKNT] 400; cf. also 2 Cor 11:10; Phil 2:16), πρός with the acc. (*with whom* one has a boast; cf. πρὸς [τὸν] θεόν, Rom 4:2; 15:17), ὑπέρ with the gen. (*on what basis* the boasting consists or *for whose benefit* it takes place: 2 Cor 5:12; 7:4; 8:24; 9:3).

Of special semantic significance are synonymous, parallel, and antonymous expressions (sometimes occurring in direct connection with καύχημα or καύχησις). Synonyms include the noun πεποίθησις ("confidence, trust"), which appears once each with καύχημα (2 Cor 1:14f.), καύχησις (8:22, 24), and καυχᾶσθαι (Phil 3:3f.) and παρρησία ("frankness, courage to speak"), in both of which the motif of confidence or trust is resonant. Thus Paul says in 2 Cor 7:4 to the Corinthians: "My *confidence* in you is great, my *pride* in you is great." He thus demonstrates that his καύχησις, i.e., what he says in boasting (to others) about the congregation, is an expression of that confident trust which binds him to the Corinthians. Heb 3:6 speaks of holding fast both to the παρρησία and to the καύχημα τῆς ἐλπίδος; the combination of "boldness" and "pride of hope" thus appears as an almost synonymous rendering of the phrase in 4:16 (portraying a traditional judgment motif), "to be permitted to approach the throne [of the judge] with boldness" (cf. Berger 147). (That Paul also knew and appropriated this combination of motifs is to be seen in Rom 5:2 in the juxtaposition of "obtaining access to grace" and "boasting of the hope of the glory of God").

Ἀγάπη in 2 Cor 8:24 is not a direct synonym but a parallel expression intended to elaborate on καύχησις.

Paul challenges the Corinthians to complete the Jerusalem collection with the words: "Give proof of your love and of our boasting about you before the [other] churches," thus demonstrating the inseparable connection between their conduct and his. Their ἀγάπη is the subject of his καύχησις; their proof of the authenticity of their love, which they give in the completion of the collection before the eyes of others, is thus also the justification of what he has proclaimed everywhere in boasting of them.

Καύχησις is also elaborated by a parallel expression in 2 Cor 1:12, where the concern is not with the church's reputation but with that of the apostle himself: "For this is our boast, the testimony of our conscience, that we have conducted ourselves in the world, and especially toward you, in holiness and godly sincerity, not in fleshly wisdom, but in the grace of God." Here Paul describes the sincerity of his conduct as the subject of his boasting; when he appeals to "the testimony of [his] conscience," he thus calls attention to "the agreement of his outward conduct with his mind and his intentions" (H. Windisch, *2 Cor* [KEK] 53), guaranteeing the truth of the καύχησις.

Other parallel expressions are in 1 Thess 2:19f.: "Who is our hope or joy or our crown of boasting—are you not —before our Lord Jesus Christ at his coming? Yes, you are our honor and joy." The connection of boasting with (thankful) joy, which exists already in the OT, is emphasized more clearly here than elsewhere. Ἐλπίς ("hope"), δόξα ("honor"), and the στέφανος καυχήσεως (the "crown of boasting") are parallel to χαρά and underline the eschatological dimension of this boasting. Indeed, the concern here is the καύχησις that Paul anticipates at the parousia.

In the Pauline "fool's speech" (2 Cor 11–12) the two antonyms ἀτιμία ("shame") and ἀφροσύνη ("foolishness") are found with καύχησις (cf. 11:17a with v. 17b and v. 17b with v. 21a, b).

3. As is the case already in the LXX (cf., e.g., Ps 48:7) the motif of trust is inherent in Paul's use of the term "boast." In boasting the individual declares what he relies on and what is his support in life, i.e., what his life is built on. Thus for Paul there are two alternative and mutually exclusive ways of boasting (cf. esp. Phil 3:3). The Christian rejects any kind of boasting by which one is supported by the flesh, outward existence, other people, or himself (1 Cor 1:29; 3:21; Gal 6:13, etc.).

This rejection is rooted in the theology of justification, as it is developed by Paul esp. in Romans. According to Rom 3:21-26 justification is based only on redemption in Christ alone; it occurs "as a gift" (δωρεάν, v. 24) and is granted to the individual only through faith. Consequently, every attempt to affirm oneself before God (i.e., by boasting of one's own achievements) is an unjustifiable and ungodly form of behavior. Paul addresses

this type of boasting when he asks (immediately after the exposition of the theme of justification) in 3:27: "Where [is] the καύχησις [= that which makes self-praise possible]?" and then immediately gives the terse answer: "It is excluded" (ἐξεκλείσθη is a pass. circumlocution for the act of God). As the context indicates (cf., e.g., χωρὶς [ἔργων] νόμου, 3:21, 28), Paul thinks here primarily, though not exclusively, of the Jew, of whom sinful trust in oneself that boasts before God of its own advantages and achievements is characteristic. The questionableness of such conduct is indicated in 2:17-24: indeed, the Jew "relies" "on the law," "boasts of his relation to God" (v. 17), and has privileges not available to Gentiles (cf. vv. 18-20); but his καύχησις is only a vain boasting, for he does not do what he teaches others (vv. 21f.), but rather "dishonors God" by his transgression of the law of which he "boasts" (v. 23). Thus he contributes to the blaspheming of God's name among the Gentiles (v. 24) and proves that he cannot be justified by works of the law (which he is not able to keep) and that the only way (according to 3:27, excluding any possibility of boasting of oneself) to justification is through faith alone. This is the case—so ch. 4—for Abraham, who according to Jewish tradition was perfectly just, having fulfilled all God's commandments (texts in Billerbeck III, 186f.). "If he were [as Jewish tradition affirmed] justified by works, then he would have [ἔχει contrary to fact?] grounds for boasting (καύχημα), but [he did] not before God" (4:2), for indeed he was not justified by works, but, as the Scripture (Gen 15:6) says, from faith (4:3).

The rejection of personal boasting stands in contrast to the "boasting" spoken of in 5:1-11, which is present for the Christian on the basis of faith alone, the "boasting of God through our Lord Jesus Christ" (v. 11). This refers to a threefold reality: 1) the condition (cf. v. 2a; on the connection of the motifs of "boasting" and "have access to grace" → 2.b) *attained already* by faith; 2) the *anticipated completion* by the δόξα of God (v. 2b); and 3) the *present* θλίψεις (v. 3a); for Paul the authenticity of Christian boasting is indicated in the seemingly paradoxical καυχώμεθα mentioned here. "The all-encompassing trust is demonstrated and the hope is confirmed" (Schlier 146).

Consistent with the way in which Paul argues against Jewish boasting in Romans in order to contrast it with Christian boasting, in 1 Corinthians he rejects the self-consciousness of the Hellenist, who boasts of his wisdom and despises the "foolishness of God" in the cross, which is "wiser than humans" (1 Cor 1:25). He emphasizes that God has himself decided for the weak and the foolish (cf. vv. 27f.) "so that no flesh may boast before God" (v. 29). He intensifies the argument to the Corinthians with a citation from the OT (Jer 9:22f.), understood now in view of the Christ-event, which provides the basic rule for any Christian boasting: "Let him who boasts, boast of the

Lord" (1 Cor 1:31). Paul quotes this rule specifically with a view to the dispute in Corinth, which involved a deviation from the basic principle, "Let no one boast of human beings" (3:21) and a φυσιοῦσθαι ("being puffed up," 4:6). In response Paul, in penetrating rhetorical questions, recalls what is fundamental for Christians: "Who gives you the advantage? What do you have which you have not received? If then you received it, why do you boast as if it were not a gift?" (4:7).

In Galatians Paul warns the Christians of Galatia against the danger of boasting: "When one imagines that he is something when he is nothing, he deceives himself. Let each one test his own work and then he will keep the subject of his boasting (καύχημα) for himself alone and not for others" (6:3). He specifically associates the boasting with the Judaizers who demand circumcision, who want "to boast of your flesh" (6:13). In contrast Paul says of himself: "Far be it from me to boast other than in the cross of our Lord Jesus Christ . . ." (v. 14).

Similarly Paul describes the Corinthian false teachers in 2 Corinthians as "those who boast of what is outward [ἐν προσώπῳ, literally "of the face"] and not of the heart" (2 Cor 5:12), "who recommend themselves," and "measure themselves" (10:12), who "boast beyond limit in other people's labors" (10:15), and who "boast according to the flesh" (11:18). He himself, however, maintains the principle (from Jer 9:22f.): "Let him who boasts, boast in the Lord. For the one who is accepted is not the one who recommends himself, but the one whom the Lord recommends" (10:17f.).

2 Corinthians provides good examples of Paul's strict following of this principle in his own "boasting." He speaks in 10:8 of boasting with regard to his ἐξουσία ("authority"), but this boasting is essentially a "boasting of the Lord," for the Lord has "given" (cf. also Rom 15:17) him the authority; in 2 Cor 10:13 Paul boasts of his mission work in the church ("to reach even to you"), but this is only a boasting "according to the measure of the principle which God has granted"; cf. the passages in which Paul describes himself as the boast (or pride) of the church or describes them as his own (1:14; 7:4, 14; 8:24; 9:2; also 1 Cor 15:31; Phil 1:26; 2:16; 1 Thess 2:19, etc.); such passages do not contradict the principle of 2 Cor 10:17, inasmuch as it refers either to the boasting in the Christian life that has been produced by grace or the boasting that anticipates the parousia. In 2 Cor 11:7-11 Paul speaks of the boasting that is due to him because of his refusal of the right of financial support (cf. 1 Cor 9:16f.), but this boasting is likewise a καυχᾶσθαι ἐν κυρίῳ, insofar as Paul "shares in the servant nature of Christ and in the gospel that has been formed by the cross" through this refusal (Dautzenberg 230f.).

The most striking example of Paul's adherence to the principle of "boasting [only] in the Lord" is his "fool's speech" (11:1–12:10). Not only does Paul characterize his boasting as mere "foolishness" (cf. 11:16f., 21, 23; 12:11), which he elsewhere concedes has been forced upon him, but that he boasts here "in the Lord" is also seen in the manner in which he proceeds "in this subject of boasting" (11:17). Indeed, he begins the principal section of the speech by reclaiming the honorific title of his opponents for himself (vv. 22, 23a)—in a form of fleshly boasting—but in the ensuring catalog of sufferings (from v. 23b) he drops the comparison with the others (corresponding to his intention in 11:30; 12:5, 9) and proceeds to a paradoxical boasting of his weaknesses and sufferings (11:23b-29, 32). Here he continues the dominant theme, proceeding to the subject of "visions and revelations" (12:1), which in the eyes of the opponents was the basis of καύχημα. Thus he reports of his ecstatic "ascent," not only in the third person (12:2-4), thus distancing himself, but even breaking off this one example immediately and describing how the Lord disciplined him with a mysterious illness, from which he asked in vain to be free, in order to preserve him from "arrogance" (ὑπεραίρεσθαι, 12:7f.). The Lord himself told Paul the meaning of his suffering: "My grace is sufficient for you, for my power is perfected in weakness" (12:9a). Paul will therefore "boast even more of [his] weaknesses" (12:9b), and he does so in the form of a small catalog of sufferings (12:10a), so that the paradoxical law of "power in weakness" (which is already visible in the cross of Christ [cf. 13:4]) may be fulfilled in him (12:10b). Thus the paradoxical "boasting in weaknesses" is described by the apostle as the most perfect way of καυχᾶσθαι ἐν κυρίῳ, insofar as "the power of the God who sends his message is demonstrated in the weakness of the messenger" (Kuss 220).

                                                                    J. Zmijewski

καύχημα, ατος, τό *kauchēma* pride, arrogance; object of boasting*
→ καυχάομαι.

καύχησις, εως, ἡ *kauchēsis* boasting
→ καυχάομαι.

Καφαρναούμ *Kapharnaoum* Capernaum*

Lit.: BAGD s.v. — BL 924f. — J. A. COMBER, "The Composition and Literary Characteristics of Matt 11:20-24," *CBQ* 39 (1977) 497-504. — V. C. CORBO, "Cafarnao," *Antonianum* 58 (1983) 102-11. — KOPP, *Places* 169-79. — A. LANCELLOTTI, "La casa di Pietro a Cafarnao nei Vangeli sinottici," *Antonianum* 58 (1983) 48-69. — S. LOFFREDA, *Cafarnao. La città di Gesù* (1976). — W. NAUCK, *BHH* 931. — B. SAPIR and D. NE'EMANN, *Capernaum* (1967). — For further bibliography see BAGD s.v.

This city, important in the ministry of Jesus and the home of the brothers Simon and Andrew (Mark 1:29; cf. Matt 8:14; Luke 4:38), is mentioned 16 times in the NT. The city was located on the northwest shore of Lake

Gennesaret, about 4 km. west of the mouth of the Jordan (at present Tell Ḥûm). It was on the border between the territories of Philip, which included Bethsaida, and Herod Antipas, which included Chorazin, and had a toll station (Matt 9:9) and a military garrison (to defend the border to the north) under the control of a non-Jewish centurion (ἑκατόνταρχος, Matt 8:5 par. Luke 7:1f.; cf. John 4:46), who built the Jewish synagogue (Luke 7:5). The city is not mentioned in the OT (Heb. *kᵉpar naḥûm*), but is mentioned by Josephus (*Vita* 72; *B.J.* iii.519). On the spelling, see BDF §39.2.

Jesus left Nazareth and went to Capernaum (Matt 4:13), which came to be his home (ἡ ἰδία πόλις, 9:1). He taught there in the synagogues (Mark 1:21 par. Luke 4:31; John 6:59), came and went "into the house" there (Mark 1:29; 2:1; 9:33; Matt 17:24f.; cf. also John 2:12; 6:17, 24), did great deeds there (Luke 4:23; cf. Matt 11:20), and nevertheless cursed the city because of its unbelief (Matt 11:23 par. Luke 10:15).

Κεγχρεαί, ῶν Kenchreai Cenchreae*

Lit.: BL 934. — P. BRATSIOTIS, *BHH* 940. — J. G. HAWTHORNE, "Cenchreae, Port of Corinth," *Archaeology* 18 (1965) 191-200. — W. MICHAELIS, "Kenchreä (Zur Frage des Abfassungsortes des Rm)," *ZNW* 25 (1926) 144-54. — R. SCRANTON, et al., *Kenchreai: Results of Investigations* I (1978).

A harbor of Corinth on the east side of the isthmus on the Saronic Gulf (cf. Philo *Flacc.* 155). According to Acts 18:18 Paul traveled from Cenchreae with Priscilla and Aquila to Syria after he had cut his hair because of an oath (→ εὔχομαι 3). In Rom 16:1 Phoebe is mentioned as διάκονος of the church of Cenchreae.

κέδρος, ου, ἡ kedros cedar

John 18:1: τοῦ κέδρου in ℵ* D W it, τῶν κέδρων in ℵ² B C Koine, etc., in place of τοῦ Κεδρών.

Κεδρών Kedrōn Kidron*

John 18:1: πέραν τοῦ χειμάρρου τοῦ Κεδρών, "[Jesus went] to the other side of the [seasonal] brook of Kidron," which ran southward in a deep valley east of Jerusalem; cf. Mark 14:26. *BL* 942f.; H. Kosmala, *BHH* 946f.; R. Schnackenburg, *John* III (Eng. tr., 1982) ad loc. with n. 4.

κεῖμαι keimai lie; find oneself; be destined

Lit.: BAGD s.v. — F. BÜCHSEL, *TDNT* III, 654. — M. SILVA, "New Lexical Semitisms?" *ZNW* 69 (1978) 253-57, esp. 255f.

Κεῖμαι appears 24 times in the NT, of which 3 are in Matthew, 6 in Luke, 7 in John, 4 in Paul, and 1 each in 1 Timothy, 1 John, and Revelation. Its basic mean-

ing is *lie* (of persons and things), *be laid,* then less definitely *find oneself, exist, appear.* Of theological relevance is the meaning *be destined for* (by God), which is seen in Luke 2:34 (Jesus "*is set* for the fall and rise of many in Israel"); Phil 1:16 (Paul was "*put in place* for the defense of the gospel"); and 1 Thess 3:3 (the Church *is destined* for the eschatological afflictions). Likewise in an apocalyptic text it is used in the words of the Baptist in Matt 3:10 par. Luke 3:9: "the axe *is* already *laid* at the root of the trees." On 1 Cor 3:11 → θεμέλιον 3.   H. Hübner

κειρία, ας, ἡ keiria bandage*

John 11:44, of the raised Lazarus: ἐξῆλθεν . . . δεδεμένος . . . κειρίαις, "his feet and hands wrapped with *bandages.*"

κείρω keirō shear*

Acts 8:32: ὁ κείρων, "the [sheep-]*shearer*" (citing Isa 53:7 LXX; cf. also *1 Clem.* 16:7; *Barn.* 5:2); mid. in 18:18: "have the head *shorn*" (cf. BDF §317); absolute in 1 Cor 11:6a, b (with ξυρᾶσθαι).

Κείς Keis Kish*

Alternative form of the name → Κίς.

κέλευσμα, ατος, τό keleusma cry of command*

1 Thess 4:16, of the eschatological events: αὐτὸς ὁ κύριος ἐν κελεύσματι . . . καταβήσεται ἀπ' οὐρανοῦ, "The Lord himself will descend from heaven with a *cry of command*" (with ἐν φωνῇ ἀρχαγγέλου καὶ ἐν σάλπιγγι θεοῦ), probably a signal for the resurrection of the dead; see also 1 Cor 15:52. L. Schmid, *TDNT* III, 656-59; G. Friedrich, *1 Thess* (NTD) ad loc.

κελεύω keleuō demand, command, bid*

There are 25 occurrences in the NT, of which 7 are in Matthew, 1 in Luke, and 17 in Acts. Except in Acts 25:23 (absolute: κελεύσαντος τοῦ Φήστου, "*at the command* of Festus") the vb. is always followed by an inf. With the name of the one commanded in acc.: Matt 14:19, 28 ("*bid* me to come to you"); 18:25; Acts 4:15; 22:30; 23:10. Without the one commanded named and with acc. + aor. pass. inf.: Matt 27:64; Luke 18:40; Acts 12:19; 25:6, 17. With acc. + aor. act. inf.: 8:38. With acc. + pres. pass. inf.: 21:34; 22:24; 23:3, 35; 25:21 (act. in 27:43). With inf. alone: Matt 8:18; 14:9; 27:58; Acts 5:34; 21:33 (aor. inf.); 16:22 (pres. inf.). With dat. + inf.: Matt 15:35 v.l.

κενοδοξία, ας, ἡ *kenodoxia* vain boasting, bragging*

Phil 2:3: μηδὲν κατ' ἐριθείαν μηδὲ κατὰ κενοδοξίαν; cf. Ign. *Phld.* 1:1; *1 Clem.* 35:5. A. Oepke, *TDNT* III, 662.

κενόδοξος, 2 *kenodoxos* boastful, full of empty boasting*

Gal 5:26: μὴ γινώμεθα κενόδοξοι; cf. *Did.* 3:5. A. Oepke, *TDNT* III, 662.

κενός, 3 *kenos* empty, vain*

1. Breadth of meaning and NT occurrences — 2. LXX citations and the Synoptics — 3. Κενός and εἰς κενόν in Paul — 4. Col 2:8; Eph 5:6. — 5. Κενός and κενῶς in James

Lit.: O. BAUERNFEIND, *TDNT* IV, 519-24. — G. BERTRAM, *TDNT* IV, 832-47. — C. J. BJERKELUND, " 'Vergeblich' als Missionsergebnis bei Paulus," FS Dahl 175-91. — A. OEPKE, *TDNT* III, 659-62. — SPICQ, *Notes* Suppl., 395-400. — A. SUHL, *Paulus und seine Briefe* (1975). — E. TIEDTKE, H.-G. LINK, and COLIN BROWN, *DNTT* I, 546-52. — For further bibliography see *TWNT* X, 1136f.

1. The adj. κενός is used not only in its literal and concrete sense (*empty* in reference to any possible content), but is also frequently used figuratively. The breadth of fig. usage, seen mainly in Paul, demands for a nuanced tr. an exact observation of the particular contexts and their emphases. Along with the 18 certain NT occurrences of κενός, more than half of them in Paul, the adv. κενῶς appears in Jas 4:5. A noteworthy feature is the occurrence of the word in fixed phrases and, esp. in Paul, in related thematic connections.

2. LXX language in more or less word-for-word citations dictates the use of κενός in a majority of the NT occurrences. Among these is Luke 1:53 (the Magnificat); that God sends the rich away *empty*, i.e., *without possessions* in the broadest sense, belongs to the anticipated eschatological reversal of relationships in regard to political power and possessions. In the parable of the evil vineyard workers (ἐξ)αποστέλλω τινα κενόν (Mark 12:3 par. Luke 20:10, 11) means send away *empty-handed* (BAGD s.v.). Κενός here refers to failure to receive an object; its use is on the boundary between literal and fig. In a prayer filled with LXX citations in Acts 4:25f., Ps 2:1 is cited word-for-word; in v. 25 φρυάσσω ("breathe vengeance") stands parallel to μελετάω κενά, which means something like "devise *nothingness*." The influence of the LXX (Isa 49:4; 65:23) is seen also in Paul in Phil 2:16 (εἰς κενὸν ἐκοπίασα). Yet one must not trace εἰς κενόν, which appears in Paul 4 times and is translated *in vain*, directly to the LXX.

3. It was an early concern (BDF §370) of Paul that his missionary work (κόπος) not be εἰς κενόν (1 Thess 3:5). However, he is certain that neither his visit among the Thessalonians (1 Thess 2:1) nor the work (κόπος) of the Corinthians (1 Cor 15:58) is κενός. He can admonish the Corinthians not to receive God's gracious deed εἰς κενόν (2 Cor 6:1; expressed positively, that they draw from God's acceptance the consequences for life). In the same way Paul also knows dialectically that he himself is unworthy and the least of the apostles, though the power of grace was not κενή in him, that he had labored (ἐκοπίασα) as had no one else (1 Cor 15:10). In these occurrences κενός or εἰς κενόν (cf. BDF §207.3) means *in vain* in the sense of *unsuccessful, ineffectual,* or *powerless.*

It is clear that in Gal 2:2 and Phil 2:16 the use of εἰς κενόν with the vb. τρέχω is related to the verb's origin in the language of disputation and use in the fig. language of diatribe. But the philological and theological understanding of these passages remain unclear. Is Gal 2:2b an expression of apprehension (BDF §370) or an indirect question (BAGD 1028 s.v. μήπως 2)? What Phil 2:16 more precisely calls καύχημα in the congregational paraklesis of vv. 14-16, which is shaped by the OT allusions, becomes clearer with → κενόω (3); here the eschatological direction is apparent. One must understand the double expression ὅτι οὐκ εἰς κενὸν ἔδραμον οὐδὲ εἰς κενὸν ἐκοπίασα, derived from the LXX (→ 2), as a synthetic, if not even synonymous, parallelism. It would be *vain* apostolic effort if the Church did not hold on to "the word of life," as the gospel is called only here by Paul.

Paul uses κενός also—synonymously with → μάταιος (v. 17)—in a basic, if also extremely difficult and disputed, discussion of the resurrection in 1 Corinthians 15. If the eschatological salvific event of the resurrection of Jesus Christ is denied, the kerygma and the faith are *empty of content* (v. 14b, c; cf. Rom 4:14 and 1 Cor 1:17 with → κενόω), i.e., *unfounded, meaningless,* and *void.*

4. The warning in Col 2:8, which takes up the admonition in v. 4 and is concretized in 2:16-23, makes clear the threatening and imprisoning danger that exists in "philosophy and [epexegetical καί?] *empty* deceit," which correspond not to Christ, but to "human tradition" and "the elements of the world." The warning in Eph 5:6 employs Col 2:4, 8 formally and verbally in the parenetic part of Ephesians. Like the threat of 5:5, it argues against misleading deception accomplished through *empty* words (κενοῖς λόγοις; also in 1 Cor 3:18 D).

5. In Jas 4:5 a rhetorical question appears prior to an unidentifiable "citation" with the affirmation that Scripture does not speak *in vain* (κενῶς). The "unconditional validity" (F. Mussner, *Jas* [HTKNT] ad loc.) of Scripture as a whole is not affirmed here. Instead the passage in-

dicates that use of a "Scripture citation" in a parenetic argument is not *without reason*.

In the appeal in Jas 2:20 in connection with the discussion of the relationship of faith and works, *empty* means something like *foolish* (μωρός). Perhaps κενέ brought about the v.l. represented by p[74] (in place of ἀργή or νεκρά). If on the one hand the textual variants are interesting for the breadth of meaning of κενός, on the other hand a comparison with 1 Cor 15:14 (→ 3) indicates the deep chasm between the understanding of faith in Paul and James.   M. Lattke

κενοφωνία, ας, ἡ *kenophōnia* empty talk, babble*

1 Tim 6:20; 2 Tim 2:16, in a warning to Timothy to have nothing to do with "destructive *empty talk/babble*" (αἱ βέβηλοι κενοφωνίαι).

κενόω *kenoō* make empty, destroy*

1. Meaning — 2. Phil 2:7 — 3. Paul's "boasting" (1 Cor 9:15; 2 Cor 9:3) — 4. The danger of making faith "null" (Rom 4:14; 1 Cor 1:17)

Lit.: → κενός. See also: K. E. BAILEY, "Recovering the Poetic Structure of 1 Cor 1,17–2,2," *NovT* 17 (1975) 265-96. — R. BAUMANN, *Mitte und Norm des Christlichen* (1968) 46-66. — G. BORNKAMM, "On Understanding the Christ Hymn (Phil. 2:6-11)," *Early Christian Experience* (1969) 112-22. — R. DEICH-GRÄBER, *Gotteshymnus und Christushymnus* (1967) 123f. — G. DELLING, *RGG* III, 1243f. — G. EICHHOLZ, *Die Theologie des Paulus* (1972) 132-54. — E. E. ELLIS, " 'Wisdom' and 'Knowledge' in I Corinthians," *idem, Prophecy and Hermeneutic in Early Christianity* (WUNT 18, 1978) 45-62. — J. GEWIESS, *LTK* VI, 115f. — O. HOFIUS, *Der Christushymnus Phil 2,6-11* (1976), esp. 56-74. — C.-H. HUNZINGER, "Zur Struktur der Christus-Hymnen in Phil 2 und 1. Petr 3," FS Jeremias (1970) 142-56. — J. JEREMIAS, "Zu Phil 2,7: ἑαυτὸν ἐκένωσεν," *NovT* 6 (1963) 182-88. — E. KÄSEMANN, "The Faith of Abraham in Romans 4," *idem, Perspectives on Paul* (1971) 79-101. — *idem,* "A Pauline Version of 'Amor Fati,' " *idem, NT Questions of Today* (1969) 217-35. — E. LARSSON, *Christus als Vorbild* (1962) 230-75. — E. LOHMEYER, *Kyrios Jesus* (²1961 = SHAW 1927/28). — W. PRATSCHER, "Der Verzicht des Paulus auf finanziellen Unterhalt durch seine Gemeinden," *NTS* 25 (1978/79) 284-98. — J. T. SANDERS, *The NT Christological Hymns* (1971), esp. 58-74. — E. SCHWEIZER, *Lordship and Discipleship* (SBT 28, 1960), 61-68. — M. SEILS, *HWP* IV, 813-15. — P. STUHLMACHER, "Eighteen Theses on Paul's Theology of the Cross," *idem, Reconciliation, Law, and Righteousness* (1986) 155-68. — U. WILCKENS, *Weisheit und Torheit* (1959) 11-21. — For further bibliography see *TWNT* X, 1136f.

1. The vb. κενόω, which appears in the NT only in Paul, means literally *make empty* and is the antonym of πληρόω. Like κενός, it is often used in a fig. sense and for the emptying, depriving, or destruction of various spatial or spiritual-psychic entities.

2. The meaning of ἑαυτὸν ἐκένωσεν (Phil 2:7) in the pre-Pauline hymn in Philippians is disputed; the clause

is not otherwise attested in Greek. The passage had considerable influence on the later dogmatic kenosis discussion. (Κένωσις, frequently used in the period of the Fathers [cf. *PGL* 744-46], is not found in the NT.) The thesis that ἑαυτὸν ἐκένωσεν is a philologically exact tr. of *he‿râ lam(m)āwet̲ napʰšô* (Isa 53:12) and "thus a reference not to the incarnation but to the death on the cross" (Jeremias 184) is generally recognized neither in purely linguistic terms nor as a matter of such sharply drawn alternatives. The immediate context of the hymn and 2 Cor 8:9 (where ἐπτώχευσεν πλούσιος ὤν is a paradoxical description of the incarnation) indicate that the clause speaks of the *self-giving* humility and *self-denying* impoverishment of the divine manner of being. That the death has not been obscured in the whole drama, but is the obedient consequence of the incarnation, is indicated in the radical realism of the salvation event proclaimed already before Paul.

3. As in Phil 2:16 (→ κενός 3) Paul defends his apostolic boasting when writing to the Corinthians. In the discussion of apostolic freedom in 1 Corinthians 9, v. 15 forms an anacoluthon within the excursus in vv. 15-18 (Käsemann, "Version" 218), in which Paul provocatively asserts that "no one will deprive [him] of his ground for boasting." In 2 Cor 9:3 as well καύχημα (in connection with the collection for Jerusalem) is viewed in a positive way; Paul does not want his boasting about the Corinthians to *be made vain*. Insofar as in these and the occurrences to be discussed an actual content is suggested, the literal meaning "make empty" strongly resonates along with the fig. usage.

4. Pass. κεκένωται (Rom 4:14) is almost synonymous with the parallel κατήργηται (cf., e.g., Gal 3:17 or Rom 3:3). Whereas the concern in 1 Cor 15:14, 17 (→ κενός) is with the premise of the resurrection, here, in a passage that is critical of the law, the concern is with the correct understanding of the promise to Abraham (vv. 13-16), because of the same danger, namely the *destruction* of faith. In 1 Cor 1:10-17, which in vv. 14-16 gives some information about Paul's baptismal practices, v. 17a concludes with the statement of Paul's specific commission, which was to proclaim the gospel. V. 17b, which serves as a transition to Paul's discussion of wisdom and foolishness in 1:18–2:16, excludes any part for wisdom of speech in the proclamation and then in a final negative clause warns against the *destruction* of the cross of Jesus, i.e., the *emptying* of the gospel of its basic and essential content.   M. Lattke

κέντρον, ου, τό *kentron* sting; goad*

Rev 9:10, in the fifth vision of the trumpets: the beasts like "locusts" (cf. Exod 10:1ff.; Joel 2:1ff.)

"have tails like scorpions and *stings*," i.e., poisonous stinging tails, with which they hurt people; fig. in 1 Cor 15:55: the *sting* of death, which is sin; v. 56 (citing Hos 13:14 LXX): *sting* can be an image for both violent rule *(goad)* and torture (poisonous stings as instrument of torture: Herodotus iii.130, with μάστιγες): with Christ's victory over sin death's power has been broken (see L. Schmid, *TDNT* III, 667f.; H. Conzelmann, *1 Cor* [Hermeneia] ad loc.); in a proverbial expression in Acts 26:14 (cf. 9:5 TR): πρὸς κέντρα λακτίζειν, "strike against the *stings* [of the goad]," of the struggle of a riding animal or beast of burden, fig. of resistance against a superior power. Cf. Pindar *P.* 2.94ff.; Aeschylus *A.* 1624; Euripides *Ba.* 794f., etc.; not attested in Jewish literature. The old discussion of a direct literary citation is today out-of-date (cf. Haenchen, *Acts* [Eng. tr., 1971] ad loc. [bibliography]; BAGD s.v; L. Schmid, *TDNT* III, 663-68.

κεντυρίων, ωνος, ὁ *kentyriōn* centurion*

Used only in Mark 15:39, 44, 45 (ἑκατόνταρχος/ἑκατοντάρχης in Matthew and Luke) of the Roman officer who stood before the crucified Jesus (v. 39) and confirmed that he was dead to Pilate (vv. 44f., only in Mark). Κεντυρίων represents Lat. *centurio,* "leader of a *centuria* (a group of one hundred, the smallest military unit)," and appears as a loanword also in rabbinic texts. C. Schneider, "Der Hauptmann am Kreuz," *ZNW* 33 (1934) 1-17; H.-E. Wilhelm, *BHH* 657f.; J. R. Michaels, "The Centurion's Confession and the Spear Thrust," *CBQ* 29 (1967) 102-9; *BL* 670; J. Gnilka, *Mark* (EKKNT) ad loc.

Κεγχρεαί, ῶν *Kenchreai* Cenchreae
Alternative form of → Κεγχρεαί.

κενῶς *kenōs* in an empty manner, without cause, to no purpose*

Jas 4:5 (possibly a question): κενῶς ἡ γραφὴ λέγει(;), "(is it that) the Scripture speaks *only with empty words/ to no purpose* (?)"; → κενός 1, 5.

κεραία, ας, ἡ *keraia* small hook or stroke
→ ἰῶτα (2).

κεραμεύς, έως, ὁ *kerameus* potter*

Rom 9:21, of the power of the *potter* over the clay (cf. Isa 29:16; 45:9; Jer 18:6; Wis 15:7), a figure of the authority of God over Israel; Matt 27:7, 10 (M): ἀγρὸς τοῦ κεραμέως, probably a potter's field in the valley of Hinnom (cf. Jer 19:2f.), which was purchased as a burial place for strangers with the money paid to Judas (v. 8, *contra* Acts 1:18); cf. also Jer 18:2ff.; 32:6ff.; Zech

11:12f.; E. Schweizer, *Matt* (Eng. tr., 1975) ad loc.; W. Grundmann, *Matt* (THKNT) ad loc. (bibliography). Kopp, *Places* 361-65; W. Schmauch, *BHH* 260; H. P. Rüger, *BHH* 2007f.; *BL* 253.

κεραμικός, 3 *keramikos* earthen, clay (adj.)*

Rev 2:27: σκεύη . . . κεραμικά, "*clay* vessels"; cf. BDF §113.2.

κεράμιον, ου, τό *keramion* pitcher, jar*

Mark 14:13 par. Luke 22:10: κεράμιον ὕδατος, "*jar* of water."

κέραμος, ου, ὁ *keramos* clay (noun), roof tile*

Luke 5:19: the lame man is let down "through the *roof tiles*" (διὰ τῶν κεράμων) into the house, i.e., "they uncovered the *roof tiles*." The author assumes a Western type of house. The description in Mark 2:4b, on the other hand, assumes the Palestinian house with a thatched roof. BAGD s.v. (bibliography); F. W. Deichmann and A. Hermann, *RAC* III, 517-57, esp. 524-29; *BL* 303.

κεράννυμι *kerannymi* mix; pour (mixed wine)*

Rev 14:10, fig.: "the wine of God's wrath, which *is poured out* (κεκερασμένου ἀκράτου)" unmixed, i.e., undiluted (cf. Jer 25:25 [LXX 32:15f.]; the same meaning also in Isa 19:14; Wis 8:14); Rev 18:6 (bis), in the instruction to the punishing angel concerning the double recompense for Babylon's evil deeds: "*Mix* for her double in the cup she *mixed* [ἐκέρασεν . . . κεράσατε, perhaps "pour"]." Cf. also H. Seesemann, *TDNT* V, 166.

κέρας, ατος, τό *keras* horn*

In the literal sense in the description of apocalyptic beasts: Rev 5:6; 12:3; 13:1 (bis), 11; 17:3, 7, 12, 16. The pl. refers in 9:13 to the four *corners* of the altar (cf. Exod 27:2; 29:12, etc.). Fig. for power and strength in Luke 1:69 (the Messiah as κέρας σωτηρίας; cf. Pss 88:18; 131:17 LXX, etc.). W. Foerster, *TDNT* III, 669-71; H.-G. Link and J. Schattenmann, *DNTT* III, 714-16.

κεράτιον, ου, τό *keration* pod*

Pl. in Luke 15:16 in reference to the fruits of the carob tree. AV and Luther: "husks." Spicq, *Notes* I, 428f.

κερδαίνω *kerdainō* win, gain*

Literal in Mark 8:36 par. Matt 16:26/Luke 9:25 ("the whole world"); Matt 25:16, 17, 20, 22 (earnings from the "talents"); Jas 4:13 (absolute). Fig. (missionary language?):

win (for the kingdom of God) in Matt 18:15; 1 Cor 9:19, 20 (bis), 21, 22; 1 Pet 3:1. Ἵνα Χριστὸν κερδήσω, Phil 3:8. The meaning *spare oneself, avoid* something (ὕβριν, ζημίαν) is seen in Acts 27:21 (cf. Josephus *Ant.* ii.31; x.39). H. Schlier, *TDNT* III, 672f.; D. Daube, "Κερδαίνω as a Missionary Term," *HTR* 40 (1947) 109-20; B. Siede, *DNTT* III, 136-38; Spicq, *Notes* I, 341f.

κέρδος, ους, τό *kerdos* gain*

Titus 1:11: "for the sake of shameful *gain*"; Phil 1:21: κέρδος is that which produces gain: "for me . . . death is *gain*"; likewise pl. in 3:7: ἅτινα ἦν μοι κέρδη. H. Schlier, *TDNT* III, 672f.; *TWNT* X, 1137 (bibliography); Spicq, *Notes* I, 341f.

κέρμα, ατος, τό *kerma* piece of money, coin*

In John 2:15 B Origen have the pl., while ℵ Koine Θ nave the (collective) sg.: Jesus "emptied out the *money* of the money changers."

κερματιστής, οῦ, ὁ *kermatistēs* money changer*

John 2:14, of the *money changers* in the outer temple court; cf. Schürer, *History* II, 67n.210 (from p. 66), 272n.54; Spicq, *Notes* I, 430-35.

κεφάλαιον, ου, τό *kephalaion* main point; capital*

Heb 8:1: κεφάλαιον ἐπὶ τοῖς λεγομένοις, "the *main point* in what has been said"; Acts 22:28: the (money) *capital*: The officer acquired Roman citizenship πολλοῦ κεφαλαίου.

κεφαλαιόω *kephalaioō* hit on the head

Alternative form (Mark 12:4) of → κεφαλιόω.

κεφαλή, ης, ἡ *kephalē* head; ruler*

1. Frequency, distribution, and breadth of meaning in the NT — 2. Κεφαλὴ γωνίας. — 3. Paul — a) The wisdom saying in Rom 12:20 (Prov 25:21 LXX) — b) The hierarchy of God–Christ–man–woman (1 Cor 11:3) — c) The head covering (1 Cor 11:4-10) — d) The head as a part of the body (1 Cor 12:21) — 4. The Gospels and Acts — a) Swearing by the head (Matt 5:36) — b) The curse formula in Acts 18:6 — c) The beheading of the Baptist — d) Shaking one's head — e) Anointing the head — f) Hair of the head — g) Cutting the hair in the Nazirite vow — h) Jesus' head in the Passion narrative — i) Κεφαλὴν κλίνω — j) Other occurrences — 5. Christ as κεφαλή — a) Colossians — b) Ephesians — 6. The many "heads" in Revelation

Lit.: M. ADINOLFI, "Il velo della donna e la rilettura paolina di 1 Cor 11,2-16," *RivB* 23 (1975) 147-73. — E. BAMMEL, "Versuch zu Col 1,15-20," *ZNW* 52 (1961) 88-95. — R. A. BATEY, "Jewish Gnosticism and the 'Hieros Gamos' of Eph. V.21-33," *NTS* 10 (1963/64) 121-27. — *idem,* "The μία σάρξ Union of Christ and the Church," *NTS* 13 (1966/67) 270-81. — P. BENOIT, "Corps, tête et plérôme dans les épîtres de la captivité," in Benoit, *Exégèse* II, 107-53. — W. BUJARD, *Stilanalytische Untersuchungen zum Kolosserbrief* (1973). — C. BURGER, *Schöpfung und Versöhnung* (1975). — C. COLPE, "Zur Leib-Christi-Vorstellung im Eph," FS Jeremias (1960; [2]1964) 172-87. — *idem, TDNT* VIII, 400-477. — R. W. CRABB, *The κεφαλή Concept in the Pauline Tradition with Special Emphasis on Col* (Diss. San Francisco Theological Seminary, 1966). — P. DACQUINO, "Cristo capo del corpo che è la Chiesa (Col 1,18)," *Atti della settimana biblica* 23 (1974, ed. 1976) 131-75. — J. ERNST, *Pleroma und Pleroma Christi* (1970). — A. FEUILLET, "L'homme 'gloire de Dieu' et la femme 'gloire de l'homme' (1 Cor. XI, 7b)," *RB* 81 (1974) 161-82. — *idem,* "Les deux onctions faites sur Jésus, et Marie-Madeleine," *Revue Thomiste* 75 (1975) 357-94. — K. M. FISCHER, *Tendenz und Absicht des Epheserbriefs* (1973). — J. A. FITZMYER, "A Feature of Qumran Angelology and the Angels of 1 Cor 11:10," *NTS* 4 (1957/58) 48-58 (= *Paul and Qumran,* ed. J. Murphy-O'Connor [1968, [2]1990 as *Paul and the Dead Sea Scrolls*] 31-47, with additions). — *idem,* "Another Look at κεφαλή in 1 Cor. 11,3," *NTS* 35 (1989) 503-11. — W. FOERSTER, *TDNT* III, 560-75. — H. J. Gabathuler, *Jesus Christus Haupt der Kirche, Haupt der Welt* (1965). — H. HEGERMANN, *Die Vorstellung vom Schöpfungsmittler im hellenistischen Judentum und Urchristentum* (1961). — M. D. HOOKER, "Authority on Her Head: An Examination of 1 Cor XI.10," *NTS* 10 (1963/64) 410-16. — F. HORST, *TDNT* IV, 555-68. — G. HOWARD, "The Head/Body Metaphors of Eph," *NTS* 20 (1973-74) 350-56. — J. B. HURLEY, "Did Paul Require Veils or the Silence of Women? A Consideration of 1 Cor 11:2-16 and 1 Cor 14:33b-36," *WTJ* 35 (1972/73) 190-220. — A. JAUBERT, "La voile des femmes (1 Cor XI.2-16)," *NTS* (1971/72) 419-39. — J. JERVELL, *Imago Dei* (1960). — H. KRAFT, *Rev* (HNT, 1974). — J. KÜRZINGER, "Frau und Mann nach 1 Kor 11,11f.," *BZ* 22 (1978) 270-75. — E. LOHSE, "Christusherrschaft und Kirche im Kol," *NTS* 11 (1964/65) 203-16. — J. P. MEIER, *Law and Gospel in Matthew* (1976). — *idem,* "On the Veiling of Hermeneutics (1 Cor 11:2-16)," *CBQ* 40 (1978) 212-26. — K. MUNZER and C. BROWN, *DNTT* II, 156-63. — J. MURPHY-O'CONNOR, "The Non-Pauline Character of 1 Corinthians 11:2-16?" *JBL* 95 (1976) 615-21. — A. P. O'HAGAN, "The Wife According to Eph 5:22-33," *Australasian Catholic Record* 53 (1976) 17-26. — I. J. DU PLESSIS, *Christus as Hoof van Kerk en Kosmos* (1962). — W. PÖHLMANN, "Die hymnischen All-Prädikationen in Kol 1,15-20," *ZNW* 64 (1973) 53-74. — P. POKORNÝ, *Der Epheserbrief und die Gnosis* (1965). — I. DE LA POTTERIE, "Le Christ, plérôme de l'église (Ep 1,22-23)," *Bib* 58 (1977) 500-524. — J. P. SAMPLEY, *"And the Two Shall Become One Flesh" (Eph 5:21-33)* (1971). — H.-M. SCHENKE, *Der Gott "Mensch" in der Gnosis* (1962). — *idem,* "Der Widerstreit gnostischer und kirchlicher Christologie im Spiegel des Kol," *ZTK* 61 (1964) 391-403. — H. SCHLIER, *TDNT* III, 673-82. — *idem, RAC* III, 437-53. — R. SCHNACKENBURG, "Die Aufnahme des Christushymnus durch den Verfasser des Kol.," *EKKNT* (V) I (1969) 33-50. — H. G. SCHÜTZ, S. WIBBING, and H. C. HAHN, *DNTT* I, 229-38. — E. SCHWEIZER, *TDNT* VII, 1024-94. — *idem,* "Die Kirche als

Leib Christi," *TLZ* 86 (1961) 161-74 (Paul), 241-56 (the deutero-Pauline letters). — *idem,* "Kol 1,15-20," EKKNT (V) I (1969) 7-31. — E. STAUFFER, *TDNT* II, 434-42. — F.-J. STEINMETZ, *Protologische Heilszuversicht* (1969). — G. STRECKER, "Die Antithesen der Bergpredigt (Mt 5,21-48 par.)," *ZNW* 69 (1978) 36-72. — G. THEISSEN, *The Social Setting of Pauline Christianity: Essays on Corinth* (1982) 69-119. — W. O. WALKER, JR., "1 Cor 11:2-16 and Paul's Views Regarding Women," *JBL* 94 (1975) 94-110. — N. WEEKS, "Of Silence and Head Covering," *WTJ* 35 (1972/73) 21-27. — For further bibliography see Kraft; Strecker; *TWNT* X, 1137f.; → γωνία.

1. If one includes the 5 occurrences of κεφαλὴ γωνίας, κεφαλή occurs 75 times in the NT, most often in the sg. (of the 17 pl. forms, 14 are in Rev; elsewhere → 4.d, j) with the literal meaning of the "principal" part of the human body (heads of animals only in Revelation, → 6): τὸ ἡγεμονικὸν τοῦ σώματος. Most of the occurrences are in the narratives in the Gospels, in the visions in Revelation, and in 1 Cor 11:4-10. The few theologically significant occurrences are concentrated, however, in Paul's letters (esp. 1 Cor 11:3) and the deutero-Pauline letters Colossians and Ephesians. NT usage does not reflect the entire breadth of meaning for κεφαλή (cf., e.g., LSJ 945; *PGL* 749; *ThGL* V, 1495-99). Yet certain word combinations, expressions, conceptual associations, and specific sayings of some NT writings require a very differentiated classification of meanings.

2. Κεφαλὴ γωνίας, a tr. of *rō'š pinnâ*, appears in Matt 21:42 par. Mark 12:10/Luke 20:17 and 1 Pet 2:7 in word-for-word citation of Ps 117:22 LXX, which is incorporated in a variant form in Peter's speech in Acts 4:11. Whether the OT image refers to the keystone or, more probably, to the cornerstone, in both Heb. and Gk. *rō'š*/κεφαλή is used of that which is extraordinary (cf. H.-J. Kraus, *Psalms 60-150* [Eng. tr., 1989] 399f.). On the expression and its NT occurrences → γωνία 3.

3. a) In the exhortation in Romans 12ff., which consists of individual admonitions, Paul cites in 12:20 Prov 25:21f. LXX. The figure of burning coals on the head of the enemy, which even in NT times was scarcely intelligible (on the origin, diffusion, and literature, cf. G. von Rad, *Wisdom in Israel* [Eng. tr., 1972] 133f.n.25; O. Michel, *Rom* [KEK] ad loc.; → ἄνθραξ), has in view repentance under the impression made by aggressive love.

b) The meaning of κεφαλή as *leader, chief, master,* which is attested for the Hebrew and Aramaic equivalents (see also *KQT* 197f.) and mediated through Hellenistic Judaism (LXX, Philo, *T. 12 Patr.*), allows Paul in 1 Cor 11:3 to combine the sociological fact of ancient patriarchalism (Theissen 107f.) with the theological idea of origin and rule. However, in the direct context, in accordance with the Pauline idea of freedom, the distinction

between men and women ἐν κυρίῳ (v. 11) is leveled, i.e., eschatologically relatized. The suggestion of a substantial idea of emanation in v. 7 (see H. Conzelmann, *1 Cor* [Hermeneia] 187f.) is dispelled by Paul's emphasis on *creatio ex nihilo*.

c) Along with further arguments from Scripture, nature, and custom (εἰκών in v. 7, πρέπω in v. 13, φύσις in v. 14, συνήθεια in v. 16), what follows 1 Cor 11:3 forms the basis for the discussion of the problem of the head covering in the Corinthian worship in vv. 4ff. The "block" (Conzelmann 182) consisting of vv. 2-16, the authenticity and integrity of which is disputed (Walker 97-108, whose view is challenged by Murphy-O'Connor), is full of exegetical difficulties. Paul's intention is clear: Women must cover their heads, but men are not to wear head coverings. What is unclear is, e.g., what kind of head covering is under consideration or whose (concrete?) protest is in view. Unless one assumes that there is a play on words in the meaning and statement of v. 3 (Hooker 410; cf. H. Lietzmann and W. G. Kümmel, *1-2 Cor* [HNT] ad loc.), κεφαλή in vv. 4b and 5b takes on the good Greek sense of "person, life." V. 10 remains a crux interpretum (→ ἄγγελος, → ἐξουσία; cf. with Hooker 413 the controversy between Fitzmyer and Braun [*Qumran* I, 193f.]).

d) Within the figure of the members of the body in 1 Cor 12:12ff., κεφαλή in v. 21 is to be understood only in the literal sense (cf. *1 Clem.* 37:5). Of greatest importance is the fact that Paul never speaks of Christ as *head* in connection with → σῶμα or → μέλος.

4. a) The fourth antithesis in Matt 5:34-36 (on the redaction of 5:17-48 cf. Meier, *Law*) argues against the ancient practice of swearing "by the *head.*" The reason given in v. 36b (→ 4.f) reflects on the actual head, while in v. 36a the meaning of κεφαλή is rhetorically expanded *(pars pro toto)* to human life (cf. Strecker 62).

b) Acts 18:6 is only one form of an ancient and widespread imprecation (Greek parallels in BAGD s.v.; LSJ 945). The most important NT parallel, Matt 27:25, where the liability is expressed without κεφαλή, indicates that κεφαλή here stands for the whole person (cf. Munzer 159). The curse is also by no means limited to → αἷμα (cf. from the LXX 2 Kgdms 1:16; 3 Kgdms 2:32ff.; Ezek 33:4 with 3 Kgdms 2:44; Neh 4:4; Jdt 8:22; 9:9; Ps 7:16; Sir 17:23; Joel 3:4, 7; Obad 15; Ezek 11:21; 17:19; 22:31; cf. also *Odes Sol.* 5:7).

c) In the legend in Mark 6:17-29 par. Matt 14:3-12 (see R. Pesch, *Mark* [HTKNT] I, 337-44; on Luke 9:9 → ἀποκεφαλίζω) the Baptist's head on the tray is the proof that he has been killed. Historical examples of such a horrible custom are to be found—not only in the Orient —up to the modern era; literary references are found in the OT (e.g., 2 Sam 4:7f.; 2 Kgs 10:6ff.; 1 Chr 10:9f.; Jdt 14:1ff.; 1 Macc 7:47; 2 Macc 15:30ff.).

d) The motif of the shaking of the head (κεφαλὴν κινέω, Mark 15:29 par. Matt 27:39) has an OT origin (cf.

Ps 21:8 LXX, etc.) and is "an apotropaic gesture of rejection" (Pesch ad loc.).

e) The anointing (cf. P. Welten, *BRL* 260-64) of Jesus' head (Mark 14:3 par. Matt 26:7; unlike Luke 7:38; cf. John 12:3) is a special act of esteem (so Luke 7:46) and is interpreted as an anticipatory anointing of the dead— not as a (messianic) royal anointing (Mark 14:8 par.). Over against Jewish exhibitionism, Matt 6:17 instructs in the practice of normal care of the body (washing, anointing, etc.).

f) The expression "hair(s) of the head (→ θρίξ)" appears in Matt 10:30 par. Luke 12:7; Luke 7:38 (cf. 7:46 and John 12:3); Luke 21:18, similarly Acts 27:34. On Rev 1:14 (κεφαλή καὶ αἱ τρίχες) → 6.

g) Also, in Acts 18:18 (→ κείρω mid.); 21:24 (→ ξυράω mid.) κεφαλή refers, of course, to the hair of the head.

h) The beating of Jesus on the head (Matt 27:30 par. Mark 15:19) indicates not only bodily torture, but also personal humiliation. The crown of thorns placed on his head (Matt 27:29 par. John 19:2; on στέφανος cf. BAGD s.v.) is, besides a painful torture, the mockery of a king (as in Philo *Flacc.* 37: an insane man mocked as a king with a papyrus crown). In reference to the inscription on Jesus' cross (Matt 27:37) κεφαλή refers simply to the location.

i) Κεφαλὴν κλίνω can mean "sleep, rest" (Matt 8:20 par. Luke 9:58). But just as "sleep" (καθεύδω, κοιμάομαι) can mean "die," it is possible that κεφαλὴν κλίνω in John 19:30 is a euphemism for the death of Jesus (W. Bauer, *John* [HNT] ad loc.).

j) The imv. ἐπάρατε τὰς κεφαλὰς ὑμῶν (Luke 21:28) calls for watchful readiness at the coming of the Son of Man. Along with feet and hands John 13:9 mentions κεφαλή as part of the body. John 20:7 speaks of the napkin (σουδάριον) on the head of a corpse. In John 20:12 πρὸς τῇ κεφαλῇ and πρὸς τοῖς ποσίν refer simply to the contrast above/below (cf. the Greek phrase εἰς πόδας ἐκ κεφαλῆς [LSJ 945] and the image in *Odes Sol.* 23:16; 42:13).

5. a) The tradition shaped in Jewish Hellenistic circles (cf. E. Lohse, *Col* [Hermeneia] 41-61) praises Christ in a hymn in Col 1:18 as κεφαλή τοῦ σώματος, i.e., the life principle and sovereign ruler of the cosmos. Equally comprehensive (→ πλήρωμα) is 2:10, according to which Christ Jesus is ἡ κεφαλὴ πάσης ἀρχῆς καὶ ἐξουσίας; only here is the OT and Pauline view of the "authority" of the Kyrios emphasized (E. Schweizer, *Col* [1982] ad loc.). With the addition of τῆς ἐκκλησίας in 1:18 the author has replaced the idea of the cosmic body with the Christian community. Paul's divergent understanding of Christ as head of the Church is developed further in 2:19 in two respects: The opponents do not hold fast to the *head* (D* and sy[h] add "Christ"); but the growth (→ αὐξάνω κτλ.) depends on the body, which is illustrated with the

physiological comparison. On the head-body schema cf. the similar head-members figure in *Odes Sol.* 17:15f.; Ign. *Trall.* 11:2.

b) Both the independence of Ephesians and its dependence on Paul and Colossians are seen in the three κεφαλή passages, in literary terms most clearly in Eph 4:15 (→ 5.a on Col 2:19). The (pre-)Pauline motif of the subjection of the cosmos (→ πᾶς) and of Christ's exaltation over everything determines the cosmic-ecclesiological κεφαλή Christology of Eph 1:22 (cf. Steinmetz 86-89). In 5:23 also, where the dominance of the husband over the wife (cf. 1 Cor 11:3, → 3.b) finds its analogy (ὡς) in the relationship of Christ to the Church; κεφαλή is intended to express sovereignty (cf. Howard 355f.). An association with the idea of the unity of Christ the head and his ecclesiastical body is made by means of the appearance of σῶμα in the immediate context (on the similarity of "the conception of the God of all as macroanthropos" see Fischer 76-78).

6. In the visions in Revelation heads play a significant role in numerical terms. With the "one like a son of man" in the vision at the seer's calling, in accordance with the OT background (Dan 7:9), allusion is made with κεφαλή αὐτοῦ καὶ αἱ τρίχες in 1:14 to the white hair on the head (→ 4.f). The mourning of the seafaring people at the destruction of the great city in 18:19 is expressed with Ezek 27:30; it is an oriental custom in mourning to scatter earth, dust, or ashes on one's head (cf. W. Zimmerli, *Ezek* [Hermeneia] ad loc.).

Stereotyped even in its linguistic expression is the concept of the (golden) crowns (→ διάδημα, → στέφανος) on heads: The twenty-four elders at the heavenly throne (4:4), the woman in heaven (12:1), the "one like a son of man" (14:14), the heavenly victor (19:12), the horses (9:7), and the seven-headed dragon (12:3) are all adorned with crowns. Indeed, the image of the crown of stars (12:1) is meant literally (on the crowning of the head, cf. Josephus *B.J.* i.671, etc.; on the fig. sense as in Rev 2:10, cf. Prov 4:9, etc. in the LXX, or *Odes Sol.* 1:1; 5:12; 9:8). The rainbow on the head of the angel (Rev 10:1; cf. on → ἶρις, 4:3) is like a crown.

The horses, lions, and "snake" heads of the fifth and sixth trumpet (9:7, 17, 19) appear especially ominous by their sheer numbers. The significance of the number seven (common in Revelation) has led to a series of seven-headed (and, at the same time, ten-horned) monsters, including the dragon in heaven in 12:3 (cf. Ps 73:13 LXX; *Odes Sol.* 22:5; *T. Ash.* 7:3), the beast from the sea with the blasphemies on his heads in 13:1, 3, and the beast similar to it in 17:3, whose seven heads the angel interprets in 17:7, 9 as seven mountains or as seven kings (on the relationship to Rome, cf. Kraft 221f.); → ἑπτά 2.

M. Lattke

κεφαλιόω *kephalioō* strike on the head*

Mark 12:4 (‭א‬ B L): ἐκεφαλίωσαν with ἠτίμασαν (τὸν δοῦλον). The meaning "kill" (Björck), or "behead," is likewise possible. G. Björck, in *Arbeiten und Mitteilungen aus dem neutestamentlichen Seminar zu Uppsala* II (ConNT 1, ed. A. Fridrichsen, 1936) 1-4; BDF §108.1.

κεφαλίς, ίδος, ἡ *kephalis* (little head)*

Heb 10:7, in the citation of Ps 39:8 LXX: κεφαλίς βιβλίου, "roll of the book." Κεφαλίς is actually the *end* of a scroll, but then came to designate the scroll itself; cf. Ezek 2:9; 3:1-3 LXX. O. Michel, *Heb* [KEK] ad loc.

κημόω *kēmoō* muzzle*

1 Cor 9:9, with acc. obj.: the ox that is threshing.

κῆνσος, ου, ὁ *kēnsos* tax, tribute, head-tax*

Lit.: BILLERBECK I, 770f., 884f. — J. GNILKA, *Mark* (EKKNT) II (1979) 150-55. — L. GOPPELT, "Die Freiheit zur Kaisersteurer (zu Mark 12:17 und Röm 13:1-7)," *Ecclesia und res publica* (FS K. D. Schmidt, 1961) 40-50. — W. KUBITSCHEK, PW III (1899) 1914-24. — G. PETZKE, "Der historische Jesus in der sozialethischen Diskussion," FS Conzelmann 223-35. — W. SCHRAGE, *Die Christen und der Staat nach dem NT* (1971) 29-40. — E. STAUFFER, *Die Botschaft Jesu—damals und heute* (1959) 95-118. — F. X. STEINMETZER, *RAC* II, 969-72. — W. STENGER, *"Gebt dem Kaiser, was des Kaisers ist . . . !" Eine sozialgeschichtliche Untersuchung zur Besteuerung Palästinas in neutestamentlicher Zeit* (1988). — H.-F. WEISS and B. REICKE, *BHH* 1868f. — K. WEISS, *TDNT* IX, 78-84, esp. 80f.

1. Κῆνσος appears 4 times in the NT; 3 of these occurrences are in the "story of the tribute money" in the phrase δοῦναι κῆνσον [Lat. *census*] Καίσαρι in the question posed by the Pharisees and Herodians to trap Jesus in Mark 12:14 (v.l. δοῦναι ἐπικεφάλαιον [*tributum capitis*] in D Θ 565 k) par. Matt 22:17 (par. Luke 20:22 has φόρον [*tributum*]). It also appears in the answer of Jesus in Matt 22:19 in reference to the money for the tax (τὸ νόμισμα τοῦ κήνσου; par. Mark 12:15/Luke 20:24 have δηνάριον). Also Matt 17:25 (M) has λαμβάνειν τέλη ἢ κῆνσον. Luke avoids the loanword κῆνσος (Lat. *census*) and uses other terms from taxation such as φόρος for the Roman *census* (cf. Luke 20:22 and 23:2); for the collection and listing of property to be taxed (cf. Kubitschek; Steinmetzer 969f.) he uses → ἀπογραφή (2:2; Acts 5:37; the vb. in Luke 2:1, 3, 5). Rabbinic texts know the loanword *q^enās* (e.g., *b. Ketub.* 35b) in the sense of "fine, penalty."

2. Κῆνσος is a t.t. of Roman taxation and, like φόρος, designates the tribute associated with the direct rule of the emperor. It was introduced into Palestine after Pompey (cf. Josephus *B.J.* i.154). It is to be distinguished from the τέλη, the "tolls" (user taxes or taxes on commerce). The *census* was exacted from landowners as a tax on the yield of the land (*tributum agri*); with

the rest of the population (with the exception of children and the aged) it was a tax on personal property (*tributum capitis*). After the first authenticated provincial census of Judea (with Samaria and Idumea) in A.D. 6 under the Syrian governor P. Sulpicius Quirinius, the Roman procurators were responsible for the census. They were assisted by local Jewish authorities who were authorized to collect taxes (cf. Josephus *B.J.* ii.403ff.). An embittered resistance rose up simultaneously with the tax, which was led by Judas the Galilean (cf. Acts 5:37; Josephus *Ant.* xviii.1ff.; *B.J.* ii.118). The fact that the emperor was the foreign master of the land and people was associated with the taxation, and this brought about lasting conflict with faith in God as the only master (cf. Josephus *Ant.* xviii.23; *B.J.* ii.433).

Throughout the Empire the coin for taxation in the time of Jesus was the silver dinar (→ δηνάριον, another loanword from Latin: Mark 12:15 par. Luke 20:2; cf. also *b. B. Qam.* 113a), which bore the emperor's likeness and inscription (Tiberius's in the NT texts; see Stauffer 100ff.). Thus the coin itself was a sign of sovereignty. Though it was used by many in daily commerce without thought to its meaning, others rejected it, e.g., the Essenes (Hippolytus *Haer.* ix.26).

Jesus answered the trap question of Mark 12:14 par. Matt 22:17/Luke 20:22 neither in the manner of Sadducean loyalty to Rome nor by the accommodation characteristic of Pharisaic circles nor with the opposition to Rome characteristic of the Zealot and Essene groups. According to Mark 12:17 he expanded the religious discussion about the census, which had taken place within the boundaries of the practical ("the dinar belongs to the Caesar and thus the census does also"), and confronted Caesar's demand with God's permanently valid claim. The purpose of this scene may thus be, on the one hand, to demonstrate the insincerity of the questioner and, on the other hand, to relativize the religiously based claim of the Roman power (cf. Schrage 36-40).

In Jesus' conversation with Peter in Matt 17:25 κῆνσος designates the *tribute* that the kings of the earth take from foreigners (λαμβάνουσιν), but not from their sons. Thus the obligation to pay the temple tax (δίδραχμον, v. 24; → δραχμή 2, 4) is fundamentally rejected, but at the same time the freedom (and the dispensation of God) for compromise is emphasized (ἵνα δὲ μὴ σκανδαλίσωμεν αὐτούς, v. 27).

H. Balz

κῆπος, ου, ὁ *kēpos* garden*

Luke 13:19: the grain of mustard seed (cf. par. Mark/Matthew) is sown in the *garden;* John 18:1, 26: the *garden* in which Jesus was arrested; 19:41 (bis): the grave of Jesus was in a *garden.*

κηπουρός, οῦ, ὁ *kēpouros* gardener*

John 20:15: Mary Magdalene thought the resurrected one was the *gardener;* cf. 19:41, → κῆπος. N. Wyatt, " 'Supposing Him to Be the Gardener' (John 20,15): A Study of the Paradise Motif in John," *ZNW* 81 (1990) 21-38.

κηρίον, ου, τό *kērion* wax; honeycomb

Luke 24:42 TR: Someone offered Jesus ἀπὸ μελισσίου κηρίου (κηρίον in E* Θ al), "some of a honey*comb.*"

κήρυγμα, ατος, τό *kērygma* proclamation
→ κηρύσσω.

κῆρυξ, υκος, ὁ *kēryx* herald, proclaimer
→ κηρύσσω.

κηρύσσω *kēryssō* proclaim*
κήρυγμα, ατος, τό *kērygma* proclamation*
κῆρυξ, υκος, ὁ *kēryx* herald, proclaimer*

1. Occurrences in the NT — 2. Paul — 3. The Synoptics and Acts — 4. Later NT literature — 5. Summary

Lit.: W. BAIRD, "What Is the Kerygma? A Study of 1 Cor 15,3-8 and Gal 1:11-17," *JBL* 76 (1957) 181-91. — BULTMANN, *Theology* I, 87-91. — P. BORMANN, *Die Heilswirksamkeit der Verkündigung nach dem Apostel Paulus* (KKTS 14, 1965). — C. BURCHARD, "Formen der Vermittlung christlichen Glaubens im NT. Beobachtungen anhand von κήρυγμα, μαρτυρία und verwandten Wörtern," *EvT* 38 (1978) 313-40. — L. COENEN, *DNTT* III, 48-57. — G. DELLING, *Wort Gottes und Verkündigung im NT* (SBS 53, 1971), esp. 106-20. — W. EGGER, *Frohbotschaft und Lehre. Die Sammelberichte des Wirkens Jesu im Markusevangelium* (FTS 19, 1976). — E. J. EPP, *The Theological Tendency of Codex Bezae Cantabrigiensis in Acts* (SNTSMS 3, 1966). — H. FLENDER, "Lehren und Verkündigung in den synoptischen Evangelien," *EvT* 25 (1965) 701-14. — G. FRIEDRICH, *TDNT* III, 683-718. — K. GOLDAMMER, "Der KERYGMA-Begriff in der ältesten christlichen Literatur," *ZNW* 48 (1957) 77-101. — F. W. GROSHEIDE, "The Pauline Epistles as Kerygma," FS de Zwaan 139-45. — M. H. GRUMM, "Translating *kērussō* and Related Verbs," *BT* 21 (1970) 176-79. — F. HAHN, *Mission in the NT* (1965). — *idem*, "Der Sendungsauftrag des Auferstandenen. Mt 28,16-20," *Fides pro mundi vita* (FS H.-W. Gensichen, 1980) 28-43. — I. HERMANN, "Kerygma und Kirche," FS Schmid (1963) 110-14. — K. KERTELGE, "Verkündigung und Amt im NT," *BibLeb* 10 (1969) 189-98. — X. LÉON-DUFOUR, *Dictionary of the NT* (1980) 258f., 331f. — E. LERLE, *Die Predigt im NT* (1956). — H. VON LIPS, *Glaube—Gemeinde—Amt. Zum Verständnis der Ordination in den Pastoralbriefen* (FRLANT 122, 1979). — W. MARXSEN, *Mark the Evangelist* (1969), esp. 121ff. — J. I. McDONALD, *Kerygma and Didache. The Articulation and Structure of the Earliest Christian Message* (SNTSMS 37, 1980). — E. NELLESSEN, *Zeugnis für Jesus und das Wort. Exegetische Untersuchungen zum lukanischen Zeugnisbegriff* (BBB 43, 1976). — F.-J. ORTKEMPER, *Das Kreuz in der Verkündigung des Apostels Paulus. Dargestellt an den Texten seiner Hauptbriefe* (SBS 24, 1968). — J. M. ROBINSON, "Kerygma and History in the NT," J. M. Robinson and H. Koester, *Trajectories through Early Christianity* (1971) 20-70. — J. ROLOFF, *Apostolat—Verkündigung—Kirche. Ursprung, Inhalt und Funktion des kirchlichen Apostelamtes nach Paulus, Lukas und den Pastoralbriefen* (1965). — H. SCHLIER, "Kerygma und Sophia. Zur neutestamentlichen Grundlegung des Dogmas," Schlier I, 206-32. — *idem*, "Die Ordnung der Kirche nach den Pastoralbriefen," *ibid.* 129-

47. — H. SCHÜRMANN, *Aufbau und Struktur der neutestamentlichen Verkündigung* (1949). — F. STAUDINGER, " 'Verkündigen' im lukanischen Geschichtswerk," *TPQ* 120 (1972) 211-18. — P. STUHLMACHER, *Das paulinische Evangelium* I: *Vorgeschichte* (1968). — H. G. WOOD, "Didache, Kerygma und Evangelium," *NT Essays: Studies in Memory of T. W. Manson* (1959) 306-14. — For further bibliography see *DNTT* III, 67f.; *TWNT* X, 1138f.

1. The occurrences are unequally distributed in the NT and do not correspond to the extent of words translatable "proclaim/proclamation." Κηρύσσω appears 61 times: 9 times in Matthew, 14 in Mark, 9 in Luke, 8 in Acts (+ the textual variants in 1:2; 16:4; 17:15; 19:15; see Epp 65f., 113, 116, 119), 17 in the Pauline epistles including Colossians, twice in the Pastorals, in 1 Pet 3:19; Rev 5:2, and not at all in the Johannine literature). Κήρυγμα appears in Matt 12:41 par. Luke 11:32; Mark 16:8 v.l. (the shorter Markan ending); 4 times in Paul (including Rom 16:25), twice in the Pastorals. Κῆρυξ appears in 1 Tim 2:7; 2 Tim 1:11; 2 Pet 2:5.

The word group is conceptually rooted in Greek-Hellenistic thought and is not grammatically aligned with biblical Greek (BDF §§206.4; 392.1d; 405.2). It does have equivalents among OT and post-OT terms (Friedrich 683ff., 694ff.; Coenen 50ff.; McDonald *passim*). The formation of the early Christian language of proclamation occurred in connection with these related terms, but added new content to them. Κηρύσσω and κήρυγμα are relevant in the beginnings of the Christian mission in connection with corresponding expressions (e.g., εὐαγγελίζω, εὐαγγέλιον; Bultmann 88f.; Egger 47ff.). They belong to the pre-Pauline tradition and are taken up by Paul; in the NT they are first comprehensible in his letters. The language was then developed in the wider early Christian tradition and associated with Jesus' own message (Mark, Matthew, esp. Luke). Κῆρυξ stands in Greek at the origin of the linguistic development of the word group (Friedrich 683ff.) and came to be filled with conceptual significance only at the late period of early Christianity.

2. For Paul the theological significance lies reciprocally in the relatively infrequent use of the special terminology: *Proclaiming* the gospel (1 Thess 2:9; Gal 2:2) is equivalent to *proclaiming* Christ (1 Cor 1:23; 2 Cor 1:19; 4:5; 11:4 bis; Phil 1:15); there the resurrected one is identical with the crucified one through God's act. Thus the proclamation is "the word of faith, which we *proclaim*" (Rom 10:8), which is nothing other than the fundamental *proclamation* of the Easter message (1 Cor 15:11, 12, 14), which is manifest in *proclaiming* the crucified one (1 Cor 1:21, 23; 2:2, 4). This proclamation does not take place without a commission and authorization (Rom 10:15; Gal 2:2). The authorization draws the life of the proclaimer into the proclamation (1 Cor 9:27; cf. 1 Thess 2:1-10; Phil 4:8) because the proclamation from God aims toward the hearer and his salvation (Rom 10:14; 1 Cor 1:21) and thus toward the explication of the faith that has been made possible through the proclamation (Rom 10:8ff.; 1 Cor 1:21).

Thus the basic determination is made: Proclaiming cannot be exhausted in the enumeration of commandments (Rom 2:21); this important fact can be seen in "the discrepancy between claim and performance," which can now be seen by "the Jew" in the judgment that has fallen on all (Rom 1:18–3:20; see E. Käsemann, *Rom* [Eng. tr., 1980] 69 [bibliography]). To proclaim circumcision as well (Gal 5:11) is therefore the de facto rejection of freedom (Gal 5:1; cf. 2:2) that is based on the Christ-event, explicit in justification (Gal 2:16ff.; 3:1–5:12), and proclaimed in the gospel. This freedom is at stake in the debate with "the Judaizers" in the Galatian churches.

Although 2 Cor 11:4 alone does not demonstrate the point, Paul's critical-polemical debate against Corinthian opponents who also claimed to proclaim Jesus demonstrates that the term κηρύσσω was of major importance in the struggles in early Christianity (see J. Zmijewski, *Der Stil der paulinischen "Narrenrede"* [1978] 92-100, 105f., 112f.). Gal 5:11; 2 Cor 11:4 appear to give at least a hypothetical basis for the view that Paul uses κηρύσσω in the debate with opponents of Jewish background.

According to Paul, "proclaiming" is an activity actively involving both proclaimer and hearer, and this activity is spoken of, as is the case widely in early Christianity, with the vb. κηρύσσω. Proclamation thus corresponds to the faith that excludes achievement (Bultmann 314ff.), in which the believer, who has been affected by the word that addresses him, becomes enlisted in the liberating service on the basis of the proclamation. In the coordination of "kerygma" and "didache" (Stuhlmacher; McDonald *passim*) the total aspect of Christian existence becomes visible in the unity of obedient faith, confession, and the concrete conduct of life. The associated word group thus becomes appropriately embedded in the wide current of the terminology of proclamation, which—apparently with the predominant use of κηρύσσω—then takes a special place in the terminology of missions.

Col 1:23, with its reference to the worldwide *proclamation* of the gospel, points to this missionary association of the terminology. Here, perhaps in the context of existing formulations and in transition to the post-Pauline view of missions, the horizon of the understanding of missions inaugurated by Paul is staked out (on the discussion see Hahn, *Mission* 144ff.; E. Lohse, *Col* [Hermeneia] ad loc.; E. Schweizer, *Col* [Eng. tr., 1982] 95f.; Kümmel, *Introduction* 335ff. [bibliography]).

In the post-Pauline doxology in Rom 16:25-27 κήρυγμα Ἰησοῦ Χριστοῦ designates the *proclamation* of (obj. gen.) Jesus Christ, according to which "the specific Pauline gospel" is seen joined to "every genuine message of Christ" and thus to the early Christian expansion of the witness to Christ (Käsemann, *Rom* 424f. [bibliography]; H. Schlier, *Rom* [HTKNT] 453, *contra* Goldammer 81; on the discussion see Friedrich 716n.16; E. Kamlah, *Traditionsgeschichtliche Untersuchungen zur Schlußdoxologie des Römerbriefs* [Diss. Tübingen, 1955] esp. 61ff.; Roloff 93n.173).

3. a) Except for the occurrences in Q (τὸ κήρυγμα Ἰωνᾶ, Matt 12:41 par. Luke 11:32, the only occurrences of the noun in the Synoptics]; Matt 10:27 par. Luke 12:3) all other Synoptic parallels depend on Mark (→ c.1).

b) The Q pericope containing the noun is preserved in its earliest form in Luke 11:29-32 (par. Matt 12:38-42). An apparently authentic saying of Jesus (v. 29; cf. also Mark 8:11f.) is interpreted by Q (v. 30): In "the sign of Jonah" is the reflection of Jesus' own work in the midst of an evil generation that demands signs. Jesus appears in a situation like that of Jonah, and everything depends on response to his message. In the early Christian reference to the Son of Man (here) emphasis is given to the parallel between the situation of the post-Easter Church and that in v. 29. This comparable situation is to be seen in two (apparently) early Christian sayings in the Q composition in vv. 31f.: The Gentiles themselves and the wisdom of Solomon will judge Israel in the final judgment. Unlike the people of Nineveh, who drew the consequences of Jonah's proclamation, the Jews have not drawn the consequences of the work of Jesus. Thus the time of decision offered to them at the time of the earthly Jesus, like the present situation of proclamation and mission, was to no avail (as it is said in evident dependence on LXX formulations: cf. Jonah 3:5 [οἱ ἄνδρες Νινευη]; 1:2; 3:2, 4 [κηρύσσω]; 3:2 [κήρυγμα]). Also to be considered is the saying: "Behold, something greater than Solomon is here" (Luke 11:31), "Behold, something greater than Jonah is here" (v. 32).

On the discussion see cf. A. Vögtle in *Das Evangelium und die Evangelien* (ed. Vögtle; 1971) 103-36; D. Lührmann, *Die Redaktion der Logienquelle* (1969) 36-43; R. A. Edwards, *The Sign of Jonah in the Theology of the Evangelists and Q* (1971); P. Hoffmann, *Studien zur Theologie der Logienquelle* (1972) 64, 113, 158, 181, etc.; *idem, BZ* 19 (1975) 111; Schulz, *Q* 250-57. A. Polag has shown that Q does not know "an explicit demand for repentance" and that there "Jesus is not seen as a preacher of repentance"; in such references there is rather "the demand for total orientation toward God" (see A. Polag, *Die Christologie der Logienquelle* (1977) 74 and n. 236; cf. 174.

That κήρυγμα takes on significance in connection with early Christian interpretation is confirmed by the more original saying transmitted in Luke 12:3 (par. Matt 10:27). In connection with a Q composition (Luke 12:2-9 par. Matt 10:26-33) in the context of the confession of the Son of Man and in connection with a saying shaped by the wisdom tradition (Luke 12:2 par. Matt 10:26-33), emphasis is given to the "public" nature (and the necessity) of proclamation by the disciples (in the transmission of the word of Jesus) as a post-Easter "eschatological event" (Hoffmann 275 and n. 125, cf. 132, 156; Lührmann 49f.; Schulz, *Q* 461ff.).

c) In Mark three lines of tradition, miraculous secret, messianic secret, and missionary proclamation, are brought together in redactional sayings, with the result that the author uses κηρύσσω of proclamation by John the Baptist (1:4, 7), Jesus (1:14, 38, 39), and the disciples (3:14; 6:12) as well as the worldwide missionary work of the Church (13:10; 14:9). In addition, the works of Jesus liberate individuals who have been healed for proclamation, including missionary activity (1:45; 5:20; 7:36). Not until the post-Easter period was the proclamation joined with the activity and message of Jesus in this comprehensive sense. It includes "the time of salvation prophesied in the OT" (E. Schweizer, *Neotestamentica* [1963] 94) in the form of the Baptist. In it the orientation toward worldwide proclamation corresponds to the Markan understanding of the "gospel."

Against the background of this "referring of the proclamation of the Church" (G. Strecker, *Eschaton und Historie* [1979] 217) to the earthly Jesus, which was done in light of the death and resurrection of Jesus, the foundation is given for the shaping of the Jesus tradition in the Gospel narratives. In addition, the theological perspective is demonstrated—under missionary considerations—in the relationship of proclamation and teaching in Mark (E. Schweizer, *Beiträge zur Theologie des NT* [1970] 24ff.; Egger; Hahn, *Mission* 111ff.; J. Gnilka, *Mark* [EKKNT] I, 64ff., 206f.; II, 190f., etc.; *contra* R. Pesch *passim,* who traces the passages cited to pre-Markan tradition [*Mark* (HTKNT) I, 100ff., etc.]).

c) 2) Of the two secondary endings of Mark (see G. W. Trompf, *Australian Biblical Review* 21 [1973] 15-26; J. Hug, *La finale de l'évangile de Marc [Mc 16,9-20]* [ÉBib, 1978]), the shorter (noncanonical) Markan ending employs the language of the 2nd cent. (cf. Ign. *Magn.* 6:2), τὸ ἱερὸν καὶ ἄφθαρτον κήρυγμα τῆς αἰωνίου σωτηρίας, to describe the central meaning of the kerygma "from the east to the west," thus expressing its missionary-universal nature (on individual features see Pesch, *Mark* II, 557ff.).

In the canonical Markan ending (Mark 16:9-20), κηρύσσω is used in 16:15 to describe the proclamation as a worldwide mission within the horizon of the creation (cf. Col 1:23) under the mandate of the resurrected and exalted one. It is characterized as "gospel" with no more precise indication of its content. Thus a tradition independent of the Markan understanding of the gospel is seen here, which can serve in the 2nd cent. with no further Christian language of proclamation and, when united with concepts from Judaism (cf. Jdt 9:12; 3 Macc 2:2, 7; 6:2), can continue on in the Apostolic Fathers (e.g., *1 Clem.* 19:3; 53:3): "Gospel" is the proclamation of the "sovereign authority" of the resurrected one "over creation" (evidence in Gnilka, *Mark* II, 352ff. [quote from 356]). Bearers of the proclamation may be "charismatics and missionaries," for in 16:20 "missionary commission and charisma" are united in a remarkable way (G. Kretschmar, *Kirchengeschichte als Missionsgeschichte* I: *Die Alte Kirche* [ed. H. Frohnes and U. W. Knorr; 1974] 94ff., esp. 96f. [quoted]).

d) Matthew uses κηρύσσω in a manner parallel to Markan usage (cf. 3:1 par. Mark 1:4; 4:17 par. Mark 1:14; 4:23 par. Mark 1:39; 24:14 par. Mark 13:10; 26:13 par. Mark 14:9), but omits the proclamation by the healed man (Mark 1:45; 5:20; 7:36), probably in consideration of the stronger christological concentration of Matthean miracle stories in comparison to Mark and the lack of regard for the Markan idea of the "messianic secret." In 9:35 par. Mark 6:6b Matthew brings into play the *proclamation* by Jesus, while in 10:7 the discourse associated with the limited commission, formed from Mark and Q, accents the mandate for *proclamation* by the disciples. In each instance κηρύσσω is used. But just as the juxtaposition of "teach" and *proclaim* in 11:1 points to Matthew's essential concern (cf. 28:19; teaching in chs. 5–7 [cf. 5:1; 7:28f.], deeds in chs. 8–9, both in 4:23; 9:35; see also G. Strecker, *Der Weg der Gerechtigkeit* [1971] 126ff.), with the reception of Q (→ b), Matthew also recognizes the post-Easter situation as it relates to proclamation, and in the redactional shaping of 10:7 (Luke 10:9b) the κηρύσσειν of the disciples is assimilated to that of John the Baptist and Jesus (3:1; 4:17; cf. 9:35; see Hoffmann 275; Schulz, *Q* 406n.22). The apparent orientation of κηρύσσω toward John the Baptist, Jesus, and the disciples (who are not just "the Twelve") indicates the author's conception of this vb. in relation to the Church (which does not, however, lose the horizon of the world; see Burchard 333ff.; Hahn, "Sendungsauftrag," 28ff., 35, 37ff.).

e) Luke takes up κηρύσσω with his own theological conception more sharply focused. Along with the simple adoption of the vb. (Luke 3:3 par. Mark 1:14; 4:44 par. Mark 1:39; 8:39 par. Mark 5:20; 9:2 par. Mark 6:12) there is also: 1) the equation of κηρύσσω with εὐαγγελίζομαι (4:43 differs from Mark 1:38; cf. Stuhlmacher 230n.5.a), which was obvious for him; 2) the emphasis on κηρύσσειν in Jesus' inaugural sermon (4:16-30), which refers to the OT, while 4:15, unlike Mark 1:14, does not mention "proclaiming"; 3) the fact that the expression βασιλεία τοῦ θεοῦ, which is connected with an expression of proclaiming in Luke alone, includes κηρύσσω, as the juxtaposition of διώδευεν . . . κηρύσσων with καὶ εὐαγγελιζόμενος τὴν βασιλείαν τοῦ θεοῦ in 8:1 and 9:2; Acts 20:25; 28:31 demonstrates.

In the "today" of salvation in the time of Jesus (Luke 4:16-20; cf. v. 21) prophetic announcement (v. 18) is placed in the context of salvation history and interpreted christologically. It is brought within the horizon of the proclamation (cf. U. Busse, *Das Nazareth-Manifest Jesu* [SBS 91, 1977]). John the Baptist is characterized as the proclaimer in the turning of the ages (cf. 16:16). Κηρύσσειν (in part traditional usage) is considered as a mandate (Luke 3:3; Acts 10:37). The summary of Luke-Acts in Acts 10:36-43 (cf. U. Wilckens, *Die Missionsreden der Apostelgeschichte* [WMANT 5, 1974] 63-70), beginning with the proclamation of John the Baptist (v. 37), aims

—God himself commanded that they preach (v. 42) to the people (the Jews)—at the present proclamation and is itself a sermon. The Jerusalem kergyma becomes the word that is attested: The κύριος (v. 36) is the Jesus attested in the gospel, the one designated by God judge of the living and the dead (v. 43; cf. Nellessen 183ff., etc.).

The proclamation event is, for Luke, with the numerous terms with which it is characterized, of great significance: Thus κηρύσσειν is anchored in God's plan of salvation, initiated by the resurrected one himself (Luke 24:47), and yet anticipated in Jesus' inaugural sermon (4:18). It proceeds "from Jerusalem" as a missionary mandate (24:48). The spread of the message beyond Jerusalem is characterized by κηρύσσειν. The vb. appears in Acts for the first time in the missionary activity of the "Hellenist" Philip (Acts 8:5, perhaps an old tradition that knows the connection between mission and κηρύσσειν). For Luke κηρύσσειν is also connected with Paul, the authoritative and decisive witness (Acts 9:20; 19:13; 20:25 [beyond the death of Paul]; 28:31). It is the proclamation of Christ (Acts 8:5; 9:20; the sermon in 10:36-43; 19:13; 20:25; 28:31) and thus attains a part in the hermeneutically noteworthy process, to bear witness in proclamation to the abiding presence of Jesus for the "time of the Church" (cf. O. Merk, FS Kümmel 201-20).

It is doubtful whether Acts 15:21 can be cited in this connection. V. 21 is equally doubtful as a basis for the apostolic decree since it is a difficult basis for the preceding citation from Amos 9:11f. LXX. If the latter were intended, it would provide a daring basis in salvation history for signifying a reference to the preaching of Christ (G. Stählin, *Acts* [NTD] 206), and the association with Christ's preaching in the synagogue—even outside Palestine—would be expounded. More likely the reference is to 15:20, to the proclamation of the law in every city. "Therefore the Gentile Christians must observe the four prohibitions, which are also required of Gentiles in general" (Haenchen, *Acts* [Eng. tr., 1971] 450, with discussion). Acts 15:21; Gal 5:11; 2 Cor 11:4 demonstrate that topics from Judaism or of probable Jewish origin are associated with κηρύσσω.

4. a) Among the later NT writings the word group is seen most clearly in the Pastorals. In the Christ hymn (1 Tim 3:16) "presentation in heaven" and "proclamation on earth" are connected, thus making the "worldwide" proclamation of "the universal sovereignty of Jesus Christ" the decisive task of mission (R. Deichgräber, *Gotteshymnus und Christushymnus in der frühen Christenheit* [1967] 133ff., 135 [quoted]; Schweizer, *Neotestamentica* 94), which has as its function the task of inculcating faith (N. Brox, *Pastoralbriefe* [RNT] 160f.).

2 Tim 4:17 and Titus 1:3 bring together the activity of proclaiming and the content of proclamation in the use of κήρυγμα (cf. von Lips 41ff.); proclaiming the word (also on the characterization of Timothy [2 Tim

4:2; cf. von Lips 41, 275]) is bound up with the total understanding of faith and gospel in the Pastorals, and the κῆρυξ (not commonly used until the late period of early Christianity, but for the first time in Christian usage) "Paul" (1 Tim 2:7; 2 Tim 1:11) remains ἀπόστολος in an exclusive "relationship to the gospel" (Roloff 239). The abiding presence of the gospel as a task of proclamation yet to be accomplished in a Church that is still being consolidated at the end of the 1st cent., and that has not yet surrendered the missionary accent while preserving tradition, can be seen in the numerous other terms for proclamation and teaching (Schlier, *Ordnung;* cf. Roloff 239-44; Brox 129, 233f., 263, etc.; O. Merk, *ZNW* 66 [1975] 91-102; von Lips 40-45, 132, 273, 275).

b) The interpretation of the statement about proclamation in 1 Pet 3:19 is encumbered by the context (vv. 19-22) and the uncertainty in determining the mythological assumptions in the history of religions behind the passage. It must be congruent with 4:6 (N. Brox, *1 Pet* [EKKNT] 196; L. Goppelt, *1 Pet* [KEK] 250). Despite the view of, e.g., H.-J. Vogels (*Christi Abstieg ins Totenreich und das Läuterungsgericht an den Toten* [FTS 102, 1976]) and L. Goppelt (249 etc., but cf. 250n.54), who regard the verse as following early Christian ideas of the cause of the Genesis flood, the indirect reference to the book of Enoch (or its traditions; comprehensive summary in Brox 172) can be concentrated in such a way as to result in traditional "associations of themes . . . , a typical construct of Jewish Christian theology." When these themes are found in Christian writings, they produce, on the one hand, christological overtones and, on the other hand, clear lines of separation from Christian usage. "Christ is not and will not be Enoch" (Brox 173). Christ cannot be interpreted as "proclaimer of destruction" (like Enoch), not even among the πνεύματα. "Either the clause in the Christian context . . . says that the 'angels' in prison were preached to, in which case it remains open whether it was for the purpose of repentance or judgment; or Christ proclaimed his victory to the most distant places of the cosmic scene, even (καί) to the 'Spirits' " (Brox 175; cf. 182ff.; on the state of the discussion, 163-89; Goppelt 242ff.; Vogels 88-141).

c) In the context of examples of divine punishment, 2 Pet 2:5 refers to Noah as κῆρυξ of righteousness. The reference has associations with the image of Noah at the end of the 1st cent. (*1 Clem.* 7:6; 9:4). The statement itself has its roots in characterizations of Noah that go beyond the Genesis account, primarily in Hellenistic Judaism (Josephus *Ant.* i.72ff.; esp. developed in *Jub.* 7:20-39; *Sib. Or.* i.128f., 150-98) and alluded to in rabbinic thought (*Gen. Rab.* 30 [18b]: "A herald came forth for God in the flood. It was Noah"; cf. W. Grundmann, *Jud, 2 Pet* [THKNT] 39).

d) In Rev 5:2 "The decisive key word of the entire vision" (5:1-14; E. Lohse, *Rev* [NTD] 38; cf. W. Bousset, *Rev* [KEK] 254ff.) is connected with the proclaiming by the "strong angel."

5. From the beginning of the Christian Church the word group is employed in the post-Easter situation and is thoroughly developed with its own theological understanding, as the message of Christ is transformed into a (missionary) preaching concerning existence. However, the meaning of the concept is disclosed as a whole only in the context of the variety of the language of proclamation in the 1st cent. On the post-NT impact, cf. the texts in Goldammer 85ff.   O. Merk

κῆτος, ους, τό *kētos* sea monster*

Matt 12:40 (cf. par. Mark/Luke), referring to Jonah 2:1: Jonah was three days and three nights ἐν τῇ κοιλίᾳ τοῦ κήτους. In *Herm. Vis.* iv.1.6, 9 κῆτος is used of an apocalyptic beast.

Κηφᾶς, ᾶ *Kēphas* Cephas*

1. Occurrences in the NT — 2. Origin and meaning — 3. John 1:42 — 4. 1 Cor 15:5 — 5. Paul (1 Corinthians, Galatians)

Lit.: C. K. BARRETT, "Cephas and Corinth," *idem, Essays on Paul* (1982) 28-39. — R. E. BROWN, K. P. DONFRIED, and J. REUMANN, ed., *Peter in the NT* (1973). — O. CULLMANN, *Peter: Disciple–Apostle–Martyr* (²1962). — *idem, TDNT* 95-112. — J. A. FITZMYER, "Aramaic *Kepha'* and Peter's Name," FS Black (1979) 121-32. — P. LAMPE, "Das Spiel mit dem Petrusnamen–Matt. XVI.18," *NTS* 25 (1978/79) 227-45. — R. PESCH, *Simon-Petrus. Geschichte und geschichtliche Bedeutung des ersten Jüngers Jesu Christi* (1980). — For further bibliography → πέτρα, → Πέτρος, see Brown, et al., 169-77; *TWNT* X, 1230-32.

1. Κηφᾶς is an epithet given to Simon (Peter), the disciple and apostle of Jesus, the first among the Twelve. The designation came to be regarded as a proper name. Κηφᾶς, which is the Greek transliteration of Aram. *kêpā'*, was used along with the tr., → Πέτρος, which came to be preferred in Greek-speaking Christianity. Κηφᾶς appears in the NT 9 times, in connection with Jesus' renaming of Simon (John 1:42), in the list of original resurrection appearances (1 Cor 15:5), and in connection with the Cephas group in Corinth (1 Cor 1:22; 3:22), Cephas's missionary journeys (1 Cor 9:5), Paul's first visit to Jerusalem (Gal 1:18), the Jerusalem conference and council of "pillars" (Gal 2:9), and the episode in Antioch (Gal 2:11, 14).

2. *Kêpā'* is a term for an object and is not attested as a name or epithet in the pre-Christian era (except possibly in the Elephantine texts from 416 B.C.). The predominant Aramaic meaning, which is reflected in the Greek tr. Πέτρος, is "stone" (also: "bundle," "lump," etc.). The meaning *rock* in Matt 16:18

(Πέτρος–πέτρα) plays only a subordinate role in the semantics of *kêpā'* in the Aramaic language of the Targums, where the word is so used only of the secure rock foundation, and that not frequently (tr. of Heb. *sela'*). Simon's receiving the epithet "stone" (Mark 3:16) has its setting in the significance in NT tradition history of the granting of names by Jesus (so also with the sons of Zebedee, v. 17). The original symbolism of the name, in view of its "success," was probably "precious stone" = significant person (Peter as "first" in the circle of the Twelve). Along with being an epithet or surname (preserved in the double name "Simon Peter"), Cephas very early became a proper name, as the old Church creed in 1 Cor 15:3ff. attests, and gradually supplanted the name Simon (most often in the Greek tr. Πέτρος). It is uncertain when the transformation from "stone" to "rock" attested in Matt 16:18 took place. However, one can safely assume that it was related to the early Christian ecclesiological position and function of Cephas, in which use is made of the epithet (Matt 16:18) and the proper name in connection with Easter traditions legitimizing Simon.

3. The bestowal of the name in John 1:42 (cf. analogies in Gen 17:45; 35:10; *Jub.* 15:7; 32:17; *Bib. Ant.* 8:3; *Jos. As.* 15:7; *T. Job* 2:1f.), in the context of the "call" of Simon, presupposes the ecclesiological meaning of *Kêpā'* in Matt 16:18.

4. In the pre-Pauline tradition of 1 Cor 15:5 Cephas is mentioned (with the Twelve, James, and the other apostles, v. 7), deliberately with his ecclesiological official name, as a witness of the appearance of the resurrected Christ and as a guarantor of the early Christian kerygma.

5. Paul attests that the ecclesiological relevance of the name associated with its bearer was widespread in Jewish Christian mission areas (1 Cor 1:12; 3:22; 9:5). 1 Cor 9:5 reflects the significance of Cephas as a missionary; 1:12 and 3:22 seem to presuppose that the Petrine claim to authority (as it is made in Matt 16:16-18) was asserted in Corinth, whether Cephas was ever in Corinth or not. Gal 1:18 confirms the leading position of Cephas in the early period of the Jerusalem church. It also confirms that later he, James, and John were considered the "pillars" (2:9) of the Messiah's eschatological temple. In the conflict at Antioch, which Paul describes from his own perspective, Cephas may have encountered a dilemma involving his theological insight (the possibility of a Gentile mission free of the law) and his loyalty to James and his previous interpretation of the result of the Jerusalem conference (the separation of the Jewish and Gentile missions and the binding of Jewish Christians to the law). An illuminating explanation for the change from Cephas (Gal 1:18; 2:9, 11, 14) to Πέτρος (2:7, 8) has not yet been found.

R. Pesch

κιβωτός, οῦ, ἡ *kibōtos* ark, box*

Matt 24:38 par. Luke 17:27: Noah's *ark* (Gen 7:7); likewise Heb 11:7; 1 Pet 3:20. Heb 9:4: ἡ κιβωτὸς τῆς διαθήκης, "the *ark* of the covenant" (cf. Exod 39:14 LXX, etc.); one is also present in the heavenly temple: Rev 11:19.

κιθάρα, ας, ἡ *kithara* zither, lyre*

1 Cor 14:7: κιθάρα appears with αὐλός (flute); Rev 5:8; 14:2; 15:2.

κιθαρίζω *kitharizō* play the lyre*

1 Cor 14:7; Rev 14:2 (κιθαρίζω ἐν κιθάρᾳ).

κιθαρῳδός, οῦ, ὁ *kitharōdos* one who sings with the lyre*

In distinction from the κιθαριστής, who only plays the lyre (Philo *Agr.* 35), κιθαρῳδός in Rev 14:2; 18:22 refers to one who sings (see 14:3).

Κιλικία, ας *Kilikia* Cilicia*

A region or Roman province in the southeastern part of Asia Minor whose capital was Tarsus. According to Gal 1:21, after Paul's (first) visit to Jerusalem (vv. 18f.), he went "into the regions of Syria and Cilicia." Tarsus in Cilicia was the home city of Paul (Acts 21:39; 22:3), and thus Cilicia was his home province (23:34). In Acts 6:9, among the Jews who disputed with Stephen, some "from Cilicia and Asia" are mentioned. The document from the "Apostolic Council" was addressed to the Gentile Christians "in Antioch, Syria and Cilicia" (15:23, 30, 41). 27:5 tells of a sea journey "along the coast of Cilicia and Pamphylia" toward Myra. G. E. Bean, *OCD* 239f.; R. Fellmann, *LAW* 1523; O. Volk, *LTK* VI, 144-46; *BL* 1930; *KP* III, 208f.

κινδυνεύω *kindyneuō* be in danger, run a risk*

1 Cor 15:30: "Why *are* we [emphatic ἡμεῖς] *in danger* every hour?"; Luke 8:23 (different from par. Mark); Acts 19:27, 40.

κίνδυνος, ου, ὁ *kindynos* danger*

Sg. only in Rom 8:35 in the enumeration that follows the question: "Who can separate us from the love of Christ?": θλῖψις . . . ἢ γυμνότης ἢ κίνδυνος ἢ μάχαιρα. Dat. pl. 8 times in 2 Cor 11:26 in the catalog of sufferings that enumerates various dangers. J. Zmijewski, *Der Stil der paulinischen "Narrenrede"* (1978) 254-59, 317-19.

κινέω *kineō* remove, take away; incite; pass.: move

With the simple meaning *remove:* Matt 23:4; Rev 2:5; 6:14 (pass.). *Shake* the head: Mark 15:29 par. Matt 27:39. Acts 21:30: "the whole city *was set into an*

uproar." The fig. meaning *incite* is present in Acts 24:5. Pass. κινούμεθα, we *move/have movement,* is seen in 17:28 between ζῶμεν and ἐσμέν. cf. E. Norden, *Agnostos Theos* (1913) 19-24; M. Pohlenz, *ZNW* 42 (1949) 69-104; H. Hommel, *ZNW* 48 (1957) 193-200; P. Colacides, *VC* 27 (1973) 161-64; J. Schneider, *TDNT* III, 718f.

κίνησις, εως, ἡ *kinēsis* movement

John 5:4 TR: ἡ τοῦ ὕδατος κίνησις, "the *movement* of the water."

κιννάμωμον, ου, τό *kinnamōmon* cinnamon*

Rev 18:13, in an enumeration of valuable items: κιννάμωμον καὶ ἄμωμον (amomum) καὶ θυμιάματα (incense).

Κίς *Kis* Kish*

Indeclinable Greek transliteration of Heb. *Qîš,* mentioned in Acts 13:21 as the name of King Saul's father (1 Kgdms 9:1, etc.).

κίχρημι *kichrēmi* lend*

Luke 11:5: χρῆσόν (aor. imv.) μοι τρεῖς ἄρτους.

κλάδος, ου, ὁ *klados* branch*

Mark 4:32: ποιέω κλάδους, "put forth *branches*"; 13:28 par. Matt 24:32; Matt 13:32 par. Luke 13:19: "in its *branches*"; Matt 21:8: "others cut *branches* from the trees." Paul speaks fig. of the root and *branches* of the olive tree in Rom 11:16, 17, 18, 19, 21. J. Schneider, *TDNT* III, 720-22.

κλαίω *klaiō* weep, bewail, lament*

1. NT occurrences and usage — 2. Human mourning — 3. Fig. and theological usage

Lit.: F. C. GRANT (with C.-M. EDSMAN), *RGG* IV, 195. — E. OSSWALD, *BHH* 2151. — L. RADERMACHER, *Weinen und Lachen* (1947). — K. H. RENGSTORF, *TDNT* II, 722-25. — L. SCHOTTROFF and W. STEGEMANN, *Jesus von Nazareth, Hoffnung der Armen* (1978) 32. — H. SCHÜRMANN, *Luke* (HTKNT) I (1969) 325-41. — F. STOLZ, *THAT* I, 313-16. — For further bibliography see *TWNT* X, 1138.

1. Of the 40 occurrences of κλαίω in the NT most are in Luke (11 occurrences), John (8), and Revelation (6). The vb. is used of strong emotions: for mourning and wailing over a death (16 times), something lost (6 times), or the pain of separation (Acts 21:13) and for the emotional response to one's own lost condition or the inaccessibility of another (3 times). It can also be used

figuratively of fear (John 16:20), remorse (5 times), or of generally unfulfilled and unhappy existence (6 times). Frequently κλαίω is found with other words for wailing or mourning such as πενθέω (6 times), θρηνέω (3 times), ἀλαλάζω (Mark 5:38), ὀλυλύζω (Jas 5:1), θορυβέω (Mark 5:38), κόπτομαι (3 times), συντρίβω (Acts 21:13), ταλαιπορέω (and πενθέω) (Jas 4:9). It is contrasted with γελάω (Luke 6:21, 25; cf. Jas 4:9) and χαίρω (John 16:20; Rom 12:15; 1 Cor 7:30; cf. also Rev 18:19f.). Κλαίω is trans. only in Matt 2:18; Rev 18:9 TR. It appears with ἐπί in Luke 19:41; 23:28 (bis); Rev 18:9, 11.

2. Κλαίω is most frequently used of human mourning. People *weep* in the presence of death (Matt 2:18 [of Rachel, cf. Jer 31:15]). Wailing at death (cf. Gen 23:2; Jer 22:10, but also Sir 22:11) often took place with a loud noise and confusion (Mark 5:38, 39 par. Luke 8:52 bis; cf. 7:13, 32; 23:28a; John 11:31, 33 bis; Acts 9:39; Mark 16:10: the disciples' mourning; John 20:11 bis, 13, 15: Mary Magdalene's mourning before the revelation of the resurrected one). Mourning in the face of death is terminated by Jesus (Luke 7:13: μὴ κλαῖε; cf. also Rev 5:5; Luke 8:52: μὴ κλαίετε; cf. also 23:28a; cf. John 20:13, 15: τί κλαίεις;).

The encounter with Jesus, however, does not lead only to the end of mourning, but can rather bring about the experience of one's own weakness and sinfulness. Thus Luke 7:38 of the sinful woman who wet Jesus' feet with her tears; Mark 14:72 (→ ἐπιβάλλω) par. Matt 26:75/Luke 22:62 (with πικρῶς) of Peter, who *wept* after his third denial of the Lord. According to Luke 23:28 Jesus rejects the weeping of the women of Jerusalem over his journey toward death, for in the lamenting over him there is only the ignorance and the lost condition of the mourners, who are apparently filled with emotion over their own future and that of their children (cf. 19:41[-44] of the weeping of Jesus over Jerusalem; see also Jer 13:17). Similarly the pain of Paul over the enemies of the cross of Christ (Phil 3:18: κλαίων with tears; see also 2 Cor 2:4; cf. Rev 5:4f.). In the NT weeping is never an expression of great joy (cf., however, e.g., Gen 46:29).

3. Κλαίω has stronger theological significance where, most often in the immediate context of expressions of joy (→ 1), it is an image for life in distress, need, or powerlessness. Thus according to the makarisms in the Lukan Sermon on the Plain the disciples of Jesus are the poor, those who hunger and who *weep* (οἱ κλαίοντες, Luke 6:21; cf. πενθοῦντες, Matt 6:4); to them the future "laughter" is promised (v. 21; cf. Rev 7:17; 21:4). But those who now laugh will in the future wail and *weep* (πενθήσετε καὶ κλαύσετε, v. 25; cf. Matt 8:12; also Jas 5:1; *1 Enoch* 94:8ff.; Rev 18:9, 11, 15, 19: the lament of the kings of the earth at the eschatological fall of Babylon

[following the model of the prophetic lament over the fall of Tyre, Ezek 26f.; see also Isa 32:11ff.]).

The experience of powerlessness from Jewish piety is taken up in the image of weeping; associated with this is the apocalyptic view of this world as a godless realm in which "laughing" characterizes worldliness and false presumption over against God and "weeping" characterizes those in the world who belong to God (cf. Isa 25:8; 35:10; 65:17-25; Job 16:16; 30:25; Pss 126:1ff.; 137:1ff.; Sir 35:20; 4 Ezra 4:27; 9:38ff.; see also K. H. Rengstorf, *TDNT* I, 658-62; Stolz 316; Schürmann 327; Schottroff and Stegemann; see above on Jas 4:9). Weeping is in this context a sign of reliance on God (cf. Rengstorf, *TDNT* III, 723), but not an attitude of remorse or contrition. This idea is also associated with the believer's anxiety in the world according to John 16:20 (κλαύσετε καὶ θρηνήσετε ὑμεῖς, ὁ δὲ κόσμος χαρήσεται) and the Pauline use of the vb. in 1 Cor 7:30 (οἱ κλαίοντες ὡς μὴ κλαίοντες), where *weeping* is an image for "the suffering of the world and over the world" (W. Schrage, *ZTK* 61 [1964] 151 with n. 82). Rom 12:15, on the other hand (χαίρειν μετὰ χαιρόντων, κλαίειν μετὰ κλαιόντων), is more strongly shaped by the wisdom tradition (cf. Sir 7:34; Eccl 3:4) and the idea of brotherly fellowship between the high and the low, the fortunate and the unfortunate.

In the parenesis in James sorrow and weeping are, in keeping with a widespread OT and Jewish tradition, required of the "friends of the world" and "enemies of God" (4:4) as a sign of insight into their own misery and repentance toward God (4:9; cf. Jer 4:8; Joel 2:12; Mic 1:8; Ps 6:9; 1 Macc 7:36; 4 Ezra 5:20), if not a prophetic announcement of future weeping and lamenting (cf. M. Dibelius, *Jas* [KEK] ad loc.), as is the case in 5:1 for the unjust rich (cf. Luke 6:24f.; Isa 13:6; Joel 1:8ff.; Ezek 22:24ff.; *1 Enoch* 94:8ff.; also Rev 18:9ff.).   H. Balz

κλάσις, εως, ἡ *klasis* breaking
→ κλάω.

κλάσμα, ατος, τό *klasma* fragment, scraps*

In the Gospels of scraps from a meal (Mark 6:43 par. Matt 14:20/Luke 9:17/John 6:12, 13; Mark 8:8 par. Matt 15:37; Mark 8:19, 20). J. Behm, *TDNT* III, 727ff.

Κλαύδη *Klaudē* Clauda

Name of the island → Καῦδα according to Acts 27:16 TR. ℵ and A read Κλαῦδα. *TCGNT* 498.

Κλαυδία, ας *Klaudia* Claudia*

A Christian woman who in 2 Tim 4:21, together with three men (named first), sends greetings.

Κλαύδιος, ου   *Klaudios*   Claudius*

Lit.: BAGD s.v. — F. F. Bruce, "Christianity under Claudius," *BJRL* 44 (1962) 309-26. — K. Gross, *LTK* II, 1219. — R. Hanslik, *KP* I, 1215-18. — Reicke, *NT Era* 238-40. — V. M. Scramuzza, *The Emperor Claudius* (Harvard Historical Studies 44, 1940).

On the famine of Acts 11:28: J. Dupont, "La famine sous Claude. Actes XI,28," *RB* 62 (1955) 52-55. — R. W. Funk, "The Enigma of the Famine Visit," *JBL* 75 (1956) 130-36. — K. S. Gapp, "The Universal Famine under Claudius," *HTR* 28 (1935) 258-65. — E. Haenchen, *Acts* (Eng. tr., 1971) 61-64. — J. Jeremias, "Sabbathjahr und neutestamentliche Chronologie," *ZNW* 27 (1928) 98-103. — K. Lake, "The Famine in the Time of Claudius," *Beginnings* V, 452-55.

On the edict of Acts 18:2: Wikenhauser, *Geschichtswert* 323f. — Schürer, *History* III, 77f.

1. Tiberius Claudius Drusus Nero Germanicus was emperor of Rome in the years A.D. 41-54. Acts 11:28 reports that a famine occurred under Claudius that was prophesied by the prophet Agabus and involved the whole Empire. Such a worldwide famine is not attested by the secular historians, but there were a number of partial famines during the reign of Claudius. Josephus *Ant.* xx.51, 101 mentions a famine in Jerusalem under the governor Tiberius Alexander (A.D. 46-48) and in iii.320 one in the entire land.

According to Acts 18:2 Paul encountered the couple Aquila and Priscilla in Corinth after they left Rome as a result of an order of expulsion by Claudius against the Jews of Rome (cf. Suetonius *Claudius* 25; Dio Cassius lx.6). Orosius *Historiae contra Paganos* vii.6.15f. dates the expulsion to A.D. 49.

2. Κλαύδιος Λυσίας is the name of the commander of the Roman garrison in Jerusalem who, according to Acts 23:26, sent Paul to Caesarea in protective custody.

A. Weiser

κλαυθμός, οῦ, ὁ   *klauthmos*   weeping*

Matt 2:18: κλαυθμὸς καὶ ὀδυρμὸς (wailing) πολύς (Jer 38:15 LXX); Acts 20:37: ἱκανὸς δὲ κλαυθμὸς ἐγένετο πάντων; elsewhere in the concluding statement derived from Q (Matt 8:12 par. Luke 13:28): "There will be *weeping* and gnashing of teeth (βρυγμὸς τῶν ὀδόντων)" (also in Matt 13:42, 50; 22:13; 24:51; 25:30). K. H. Rengstorf, *TDNT* III, 725f.; B. Schwank, *BZ* 16 (1972) 121f.

κλάω   *klaō*   break*
κλάσις, εως, ἡ   *klasis*   breaking*

1. Occurrences — 2. The (Jewish) meal practice of "breaking of bread" — 3. "Breaking of bread" in Acts

Lit.: J. Behm, *TDNT* III, 726-43. — J. Betz, *Eucharistie. In der Schrift und Patristik* (Handbuch der Dogmengeschichte IV/4a, 1979). — Billerbeck IV, 620f. — F. Cabrol, *DACL* V,

2103-16. — O. Cullmann, *Early Christian Worship* (SBT, 1953) 14-20. — idem, "The Meaning of the Lord's Supper in Primitive Christianity," O. Cullmann and F. J. Leenhardt, *Essays on the Lord's Supper* (Ecumenical Studies in Worship 1, 1958) 505-23. — G. Dalman, *Jesus-Jeschua* (1929) 122-34. — G. Delling, *TRE* I, 47-58. — W. A. Dowd, "Breaking Bread (Acts 2,46)," *CBQ* I (1939) 358-62. — M. Fraeyman, "Fractio panis in communitate primitiva," *CBG* 1 (1955) 370-73. — J. Gewiess, *LTK* II, 706f. — J. Jeremias, "Das Brotbrechen beim Passahmahl und Mk 14,22," *ZNW* 33 (1934) 203f. — idem, *The Eucharistic Words of Jesus* (1966). — P.-H. Menoud, "Les Actes des Apôtres et l'Eucharistie," *RHPR* 33 (1953) 21-36. — B. Reicke, *Diakonie, Festfreude und Zelos in Verbindung mit der altchristlichen Agapenfeier* (1951). — T. Schermann, "Das 'Brotbrechen' im Urchristentum," *BZ* 8 (1910) 33-52, 162-83. — H. Schürmann, *LTK* III, 1159-62. — idem, "Die Gestalt der urchristlichen Eucharistiefeier" (1955), Schürmann II, 77-99. — E. von Severus, *RAC* II, 620-26. — A. B. du Toit, *Der Aspekt der Freude im urchristlichen Abendmahl* (1965). — B. Trémel, "La fraction du pain dans les Actes des Apôtres," *Lumière et Vie* 94 (1969) 76-90. — A. Vööbus, "Kritische Beobachtungen über die lukanische Darstellung des Herrenmahls," *ZNW* 61 (1970) 102-10. — J. Wanke, *Beobachtungen zum Eucharistieverständnis des Lukas auf Grund der lukanischen Mahlberichte* (ETS 8, 1973). — For further bibliography see *TWNT* X, 1138-43.

1. The vb. κλάω is found in the NT only in connection with the rite of breaking bread at a meal (14 occurrences; cf. also 1 Cor 11:24 v.l.). Κατακλάω is used similarly (only in Mark 6:41; Luke 9:16). One may compare also ἐκκλάω, "break off" (branches: Rom 11:17, 19f.). Κλάσις (τοῦ ἄρτου) appears in the NT only in Luke 24:35 and Acts 2:42. Neither κλάω τὸν ἄρτον nor κλάσις τοῦ ἄρτου appears in secular Greek (or in Philo and Josephus); cf., however, Jer 16:7 LXX; Lam 4:4 LXX (διακλάω), in both of which the Hebrew original is *pāras leḥem;* cf. the different reading in Isa 58:7 LXX (διαθρύπτω; cf. 1 Cor 11:24 D* θρυπτόμενον). Lat. *panem frangere* is found in a few Roman authors and only as a poetic phrase with no religious connotation (von Severus 621).

2. "Breaking of bread" refers to a firmly fixed rite at the opening of the Jewish meal (Dalman 125f.; Billerbeck 621).

At the beginning of the meal the head of the household would rise, take a flat loaf of bread (soft and in the shape of a plate) and say a blessing, perhaps, "Blessed are you, Lord, our God, King of the world, who has brought forth bread from the earth." The participants in the meal would then answer with "Amen." The head of the household would then break off a piece of the loaf for each person, which would be passed to those sitting at some distance. Then he would break off a piece for himself and eat it, a sign for all that the meal was beginning. The piece of bread offered to each person was meant less to provide a portion in the table prayer (*contra* Dalman 125f.), which was indicated in the ratifying "Amen," than to represent a salvific mediation of the blessing (Schürmann, "Gestalt" 81n.31).

The phrase κλάσις τοῦ ἄρτου, "*breaking* of bread," is

derived from this ritual of breaking the loaf, but also had a wider significance, including the blessing (cf. Luke 24:35?) and the distribution of the bread (cf. Mark 8:19; 1 Cor 11:24). The phrase was unknown to Gentiles with this specific meaning (Schermann 39f.) and was used only of the beginning of the meal, not of the entire meal (cf. Exod 18:12; Mark 3:20; 7:2, 5: "eat bread").

The Gospels place Jesus in the role of the Jewish head of the household when he breaks bread at the feeding of the crowd (Mark 6:41; 8:6; Matt 14:19; 15:36; Luke 9:16) and at the Last Supper (Mark 14:22; Matt 26:26; Luke 22:19; cf. 1 Cor 11:24). It is possible that he gave his own version of the blessing over the bread, but it would not be one like the fourth petition of the Lord's Prayer, since the latter does not ask for the eschatological bread (*contra* Dalman 124; Jeremias, *Eucharistic Words* 109). At the Last Supper Jesus used the common ritual of breaking bread as a foundation for the new interpretation of his offering of the bread, which he—in contrast to the Jewish custom (cf. Dalman 127)—accompanied with words of interpretation.

3. In Christian usage "breaking of bread" took on the specific sense of "eucharistic" breaking of bread, so that the expression was able to remain in use after the shift of the action over the bread to the action over the cup at the end of the meal. The expression then came to involve the latter as well as the former (Schürmann I, 182-84; *contra* Jeremias, *Eucharistic Words* 115, who argues for a celebration *sub una*).

According to Acts 20:7 κλάσαι ἄρτον refers to the purpose for the assembling of the church at Troas. Thus κλάσας τὸν ἄρτον in 20:11 probably refers to the twofold eucharistic act. In 2:46 κλῶντες κατ᾽ οἶκον ἄρτον, "they *broke* bread at home" (Haenchen, *Acts* [Eng. tr., 1971] 192), or "in homes" (L. Goppelt, *Apostolic and Post-Apostolic Times* [1970] 45), is distinguished from the full meal (μεταλαμβάνειν τροφῆς). Thus κλάσις τοῦ ἄρτου in the summary in 2:42, in accordance with the Lukan intention, refers to this particular aspect of the community meals without the four terms mentioned (teaching, → κοινωνία = [table?] fellowship, breaking of bread, prayers) being understood as elements in a service of worship (against Jeremias, *Eucharistic Words* 118f.; with H. Zimmermann, *BZ* 5 [1961] 75f.; Haenchen, *Acts* 191). Luke shows that these meals were associated with eschatological joy (Acts 2:46, ἀγαλλίασις; cf. du Toit; → ἀγαλλιάω) and with reciprocal service (2:44f.; 6:1; cf. Reicke). According to Acts 27:35 Paul acted in accordance with Jewish table customs (→ 2). For Luke, however, an allusion to the nearness of the Lord experienced in the eucharist is not to be excluded (Wanke 25-30).

1 Cor 10:16 provides a reminder of the origin of the Christian term "breaking of bread" in the phrase "the bread that we *break*," which emphasizes the action itself.

"Breaking of bread" disappeared as a term for the eucharistic celebration (cf. *Did.* 14:1; Ign. *Eph.* 20:2; also κλάσμα, *Did.* 9:3f.). Used in its place was → εὐχαριστία, which is not attested in the NT (cf. *Did.* 9:5; Ign. *Phld.* 4:1; *Smyrn.* 7:1; 8:1; *Eph.* 13:1; Justin *Apol.* i.66.1; cf. H. Conzelmann, *TDNT* IX, 407-15; Betz 26-29).

J. Wanke

κλείς, δός, ἡ *kleis* key*
κλείω *kleiō* shut, close; lock (vb.)*

1. Occurrences in the NT — 2. Κλείς — 3. Κλείω

Lit.: BAGD s.v. — BDF §47.3. — E. LOHSE, *Rev* (NTD, 1960). — G. MINESTRINA, "Κλεὶς Δαυίδ," *BeO* 20 (1978) 182. — E. SCHWEIZER, *Matt* (Eng. tr., 1975).

1. Κλείς appears 6 times in the NT, all in fig. uses: "give the *keys* of the kingdom" (Matt 16:19); "take away the *key* of knowledge" (Luke 11:52); "have the *keys* of death and of the underworld [Hades]" (Rev 1:18); "have the *key* of David" (3:7a); "the *key* of the shaft of the bottomless pit was given" (9:1); "hold the *key* of the bottomless pit" (20:1). The acc. sg. and pl. are declined in different ways: κλεῖδα/κλεῖν or κλεῖδας/κλεῖς. Κλείω appears 16 times, of which 7 are literal (Matt 6:6; 25:10; Luke 11:7; John 20:19, 26; Acts 5:23; 21:30) and 9 are fig. (Matt 23:13; Luke 4:25; 1 John 3:17; Rev 3:7b, c, 8; 11:6; 20:3; 21:25; *contra* BAGD s.v. 1, which gives a literal sense in Rev 3:7b, c; 20:3; 21:25).

2. In biblical and early Jewish usage handing over of keys signified "authorization," and possession of keys signified "authority" (Jeremias 750). The exalted Christ has authority over the powers of death and the underworld, which have been defeated at his descent into the underworld. He, and not they, has "the *keys* of death and of Hades" (Rev 1:18; gen. of possession). Authority to raise the dead, which in Jewish tradition is reserved for God alone, has been handed over to the "resurrected" and "living" one. He is "the true one, who has the *key* of David, the one who opens so that no one can *close,* who *closes* so that no one can open" (3:7). The exalted one has the power of the coming world.

Besides Christ, Peter (Matt 16:19), the teachers of the law (Luke 11:52), and "the angel of the bottomless pit" are mentioned as holders of keys. In Matt 16:19 "I will give to you the *keys* of the kingdom of heaven" signifies that judicial authority has been handed over to the apostolic leader with regard to the kingdom of God. He is invested with authority to bind and loose (cf. Matt 18:18 for the apostolic role), i.e., to promise the grace of the kingdom of God or to deny it. According to Luke 11:52 Jesus accuses the scribes of not doing justice to the "power of the keys" that they claim: "You have taken away the *key* of knowledge [probably obj. gen.]," which may be understood from v. 52b as "the *key* to the kingdom of God." The teachers of the law misuse the authority to open salvation to people, which they claim. That the Jewish understanding of the law was a means of entry into the kingdom of God is thus indirectly rejected (cf. Matt 23:13).

According to the ancient understanding of things, both heaven and the underworld are locked with gates. According to Rev 9:1 "the *key* to the shaft leading to the bottomless pit was given to the star that had fallen from heaven." In v. 11 this "star" is identified with "the angel of the bottomless pit." Authority is handed over to this angel by God (divine pass., "from heaven")—authority to open the abyss (cf. 20:1). The consequence is that "the powers of the deep come up to be used as instruments of God's judgment. But at the end judgment will be extended also to them" (Lohse 53; cf. Rev 20:1-3).

3. Used literally κλείω means *close* (a door, Matt 6:6; 25:10; Luke 11:7; John 20:19, 26; Acts 21:30) or *lock* (a building, Acts 5:23). This usage appears to be present in Rev 3:7b, c; 3:8; 20:3; and 21:25. The citation of Isa 22:22 in 3:7b, c refers to the "shutting" of the house of David, the king's palace in Jerusalem. According to the messianic interpretation of this passage, however, Christ opens or "locks" access "to the eschatological palace of God" (Jeremias 748; cf. v. 8). The phrase "close the bottomless pit" in Rev 20:3 refers to the angel who possesses "the *key* to the bottomless pit" (v. 1) and has authority to open or close it. The statement that the gates of the new heavenly Jerusalem will never again "be shut" (21:25) could describe that time of fulfillment in which the exercise of "the power of the keys" is abolished.

The vb. has an unambiguously fig. meaning in Matt 23:13; Luke 4:25; 1 John 3:17. Jesus' woe on the Pharisees and scribes, that they *shut* the kingdom of heaven "from people" (Matt 23:13), can be explained from the figure of the "keys of the kingdom of heaven" in 16:19. Thus "closing" refers to inability to make the kingdom of God accessible to others (Schweizer 440).

In accordance with the Jewish view, the phrase "heaven was closed" (Luke 4:25; cf. Jeremias 745) refers to a period of time without rain; that it is pass. means that it is God who possesses the key of rain: He denies rain as a sign of judgment, just as he hands over the power of the keys to the emissaries of the eschaton as a sign of their prophecy (Rev 11:6).

The phrase *"close* one's heart against a brother" (1 John 3:17) has OT antecedents (cf. Jer 31:20b; Gen 43:30; Prov 12:10; Sir 30:7) and refers to refusal to have inner sympathy toward one's neighbor.

F. G. Untergassmair

κλείω *kleiō* shut, close; lock
→ κλείς.

κλέμμα, ατος, τό *klemma* stealing, theft*

Rev 9:21: μετανόησαν ἐκ τῶν κλεμμάτων, "repent of the *thefts*"; in a vice catalog, Mark 7:22 D; *Herm. Man.* viii.5.

Κλεοπᾶς, ᾶ *Kleopas* Cleopas*

Shortened form of the name Κλεόπατρος, which was used in place of the Semitic name → Κλωπᾶς. Luke 24:18: the name of a disciple of Jesus in Jerusalem who is not mentioned elsewhere.

κλέος, ους, τό *kleos* fame, glory*

1 Pet 2:20: ποῖον κλέος, followed by εἰ: "what *credit* is it if . . ."; cf. also *1 Clem.* 5:6; 54:3.

κλέπτης, ου, ὁ *kleptēs* thief*

Matt 6:19, 20 par. Luke 12:33, of treasures; Matt 24:43 par. Luke 12:39: "If the master had known at what watch [Luke: hour] of the night the *thief* would come . . ."; John 10:1, 8, 10, in contrast to "shepherd" (so also Homer *Il.* iii.11; 1 Pet 4:15); John 12:6: Judas was a *thief*; 1 Cor 6:10: *thieves* cannot inherit the kingdom of God; 1 Thess 5:2, 4; 2 Pet 3:10; Rev 3:3; 16:15: the thief breaking in (at night), as a figure for the sudden coming of the parousia (cf. above Matt 24:43 par.; W. Harnisch, *Eschatologische Existenz* [1973] 84-116). H. Preisker, *TDNT* III, 754-56; *TWNT* X, 1143f. (bibliography).

κλέπτω *kleptō* steal*

Mark 10:19 par. Matt 19:18/Luke 18:20; Rom 13:9, in the commandment of the Decalogue: "Do not *steal*"; Matt 6:19, 20, in Jesus' saying regarding gathering treasures (→ κλέπτης); 27:64; 28:13, of the alleged theft of the body of Jesus by the disciples; John 10:10a: "The thief comes only *to steal*, to slaughter, and to destroy" (→ κλέπτης); Rom 2:21: "You who preach that one should not *steal*, do you *steal*?"; Eph 4:28: "Let the *thief* (ὁ κλέπτων) *steal* no more. . . ." H. Preisker, *TDNT* III, 754-56; *TWNT* X, 1143f. (bibliography).

κλῆμα, ατος, τό *klēma* shoot, branch*

In the discourse about the vine in John 15: vv. 2, 4, 6 of the *branch/shoot* of the vine; v. 5 pl. J. Behm, *TDNT* III, 757; R. Borig, *Der wahre Weinstock* (1967).

Κλήμης, εντος *Klēmēs* Clement*

Greek form of the Latin name *Clement*. Clement is called a "coworker" of Paul (Phil 4:3; a Clement is attested in inscriptions from Philippi: *CIL* III, 633). A member of the Roman church later bore the name (*Herm. Vis.* ii.4.3; the author of *1 Clem.* is intended).

κληρονομέω *klēronomeō* inherit, receive as a possession*

κληρονομία, ας, ἡ *klēronomia* inheritance, possession*

κληρονόμος, ου, ὁ *klēronomos* heir*

1. Occurrences in the NT — 2. Literal usage — 3. Double meaning — 4. The inheritance promised to Israel in the OT — 5. The promise of inheritance in the NT — 6. The eschatological promise of inheritance of the land

Lit.: J. EICHLER, *DNTT* II, 295-303. — W. FOERSTER and R. HERRMANN, *TDNT* III, 758-85. — P. L. HAMMER, "A Comparison of Klēronomia in Paul and Ephesians," *JBL* 79 (1960) 267-72. — J. D. HESTER, "The Heir—and Heilsgeschichte. Study of Gal 4,1ff.," FS Cullmann (1967) 118-25. — *idem, Paul's Concept of Inheritance* (1968). — A. KERRIGAN, "Echoes of Themes from the Servant Songs in Pauline Theology," *Studiorum Paulinorum Congressus Internationalis Catholicus* (1963) II, 222-25. — H. W. KUHN, *Enderwartung und gegenwärtiges Heil* (1966) 72-75. — H. LANGKAMMER, " 'Den er zum Erben von allem eingesetzt hat' (Heb 1,2)," *BZ* 10 (1966) 273-80. — *idem,* "Die Verheißung vom Erbe," *BibLeb* 8 (1967) 157-65. — W. PESCH, *SacVb* 394-98. — G. VON RAD, *The Problem of the Hexateuch* (1966) 79-93. — G. WANKE, *THAT* II, 55-59. — For further bibliography see *TWNT* X, 1144f.

1. Κληρονομέω appears 18 times in the NT, κληρονομία 14 times, and κληρονόμος 15 times. These 47 occurrences are found in the following literary groupings: 14 in the Pauline Epistles, 15 in the Gospels and Acts, 9 in Hebrews, 8 in the other letters, and 1 in Revelation. The word group does not appear in the Johannine writings (Gospel and letters).

2. A word from this group appears without any suggestion of fig. use in only one passage of the NT: κληρονομία in Luke 12:13, in the request for Jesus to give an authoritative statement in response to a dispute over an inheritance. In secular Greek the procedure for inheritance was designated by κληρονομέω κτλ. So also the LXX uses the word group to render Heb. *naḥ^alâ,* which was used in the OT laws of inheritance (cf. Num 27:8-11).

3. A transition from literal to fig. usage is seen in Mark 12:7 par. Matt 21:38/Luke 20:14. Here κληρονόμος/ κληρονομία is used concretely in the parable, but the fig. sense resonates alongside the literal meaning. The promised inheritance (only in Matt 21:43 is it identified as "the kingdom of God") is to be taken away from Israel and given to the Gentiles (Mark 12:9). Gal 4:1, 30; Heb 12:17 are also to be understood as primarily literal: the allusion to the promised inheritance is in the background.

4. The reference to the promised inheritance was well known to every Jewish hearer. However, in the OT *naḥ^alâ* referred to the possession of the land that God gave to Israel as a permanent possession (cf. Exod 32:13; Num 26:52-56, etc.). The promise of possession of the land originated with the patriarchs, esp. Abraham (cf. Deut 6:10). The continued memory of this promise is to be seen in NT references to it, which occur esp. in Paul (Gal 3:18; 4:1, 7, 30; Rom 4:13f.), Hebrews (6:17; 11:8), and Acts (7:5). There were two aspects of the covenant with Abraham (cf. Acts 7:5): the promise of descendants (Gen 15:4; cf. 12:2; 17:5; in connection with *naḥ^alâ* first in Exod 32:13; cf. Gal 3:18, 29; 4:1, 7, 30; Heb 6:12ff., 17) and the promise of possession of the land by Abraham and his heirs (Gen 15:7; cf. 12:1; 15:18; 17:8; Rom 4:13f.; Heb 11:8; *naḥ^alâ* thus designates "permanent possession," which the LXX correctly renders with κληρονομέω/ κληρονομία). These promises were expanded already in the OT and in early Judaism in an eschatological direction.

This expansion began during the Exile (cf. Ezek 47:14), when the hope arose for a new inheritance, i.e., a retaking of possession of the land (cf. Deut 30:5). The land, according to this hope, would never be taken away from Israel again, but would be kept forever (Isa 60:21). The expansion of this concept reaches its end point in the ideas that this inheritance will be given "at the end of days" (cf. Dan 12:13 LXX, → κλῆρος [3]) and that only the righteous will possess it (Ps 37:9, 11, etc.; cf. also *1 Enoch* 39:8; 71:16) and in the conception of this inheritance in spiritualized terms (so already in Deut 10:9; cf. Lam 3:24; Ps 16:5; *1 Enoch* 40:9).

Hand in hand with this development is the universalistic expansion of the idea. This aspect became esp. prominent during the Exile (cf. Ezek 47:21-23). It was associated with the idea of a political empire of Israel (cf. Ps 2:8 from before the Exile). In this period the person of the inheritance, the Messiah who will bring this final empire, is closely associated with this motif (cf. Ps 2:2; Langkammer, "Verheißung" 164).

The NT takes up this universalistic expansion in a totally depoliticized way, associating it with the Jewish concepts of the "future aeon," the "kingdom of God," etc.

5. For Paul the idea of "inheritance" is esp. important: The promise was given once to Abraham and his descendants and is now realized in Christ (Gal 3:16; cf. Mark 12:7 par.), who is also heir of the promise given to Abraham (Gal 3:18). Christ mediates this promise to his people (Gal 3:29; 4:1, 7). Thus they are also "joint heirs" (συγκληρονόμοι) of the promise (Eph 3:18; Rom 8:17). In addition, the idea that the faithful are sons or children of God suggests their characterization as *heirs,* at least in the Greek and Jewish environment (Rom 8:17 bis; Gal 4:7; see Foerster 768f.). The Church thus receives the promise, not on the basis of law (Gal 4:30; Rom 4:13f.), but on the basis of faith (Rom 4:13f.; cf. Heb 11:7f.; 6:12; Titus 3:7—*contra* Jas 2:5: on the basis of love for God). The designation of Christ as the heir is found in the NT, however, without direct reference to Abraham (Heb 1:2),

whether because the subject is the Messiah who brings universal sovereignty or because the title *heir* for Jesus suggests the concept of the "Son of God" (cf. Heb 1:4; Rev 21:7; Mark 12:7).

6. The promise of the land that Abraham and his descendants are to receive plays a greater role as this idea is eschatologically extended. This extended meaning is found already in the oldest strata of the Gospels (Matt 5:5: τὴν γῆν; cf. 25:34: τὴν . . . βασιλείαν). In 1 Cor 15:50 "*inherit* the kingdom" is intended in an explicitly eschatological way, as in this passage it is a synonym for "rise from the dead." The expression is found in three other Pauline passages, as in Matt 25:34, in connection with the idea of the judgment: One who conducts himself rightly will *inherit* the kingdom of God (Matt 25:34; Jas 2:5). The unrighteous (1 Cor 6:9) or those who commit any type of vice (1 Cor 6:10; Gal 5:21; cf. Eph 5:5) will not *inherit* the kingdom of God. The phrase "*inherit* eternal life" belongs in the same eschatological frame of reference, and positive reward at the judgment is also intended (cf. Mark 10:17 par. Luke 18:18; 10:25; Matt 19:29; Titus 3:7; Col 3:24; Rev 21:7; probably also 1 Pet 3:9; cf. v. 7: "joint heirs" of life).

The word group is used in an eschatological sense in a special way in Hebrews. As in Paul it is established that the promised inheritance (Heb 6:12; eternal inheritance, 9:15; salvation as inheritance, 1:14), which could not be attained by the law of the old covenant, is attainable only through the sacrificial mediation of the new covenant (9:15) or on the basis of faith (11:7-9; 6:12; cf. 1 Pet 1:4). The juxtaposition of the "not yet" and the "already" is to be noticed already in the use of κληρονομία.

According to Ephesians 1 the Church has already received the earnest of the promised *inheritance* (vv. 14, 18; cf. v. 11: κληρόω; Acts 20:32; Hammer 269 sees of course in Ephesians its emphasis on the future, in contrast to Paul's emphasis on the present); the inheritance does not lie only in the future (so probably also earlier in Gal 3:15ff.; 4:1ff.).

J. H. Friedrich

κληρονομία, ας, ἡ *klēronomia* inheritance, possession
→ κληρονομέω.

κληρονόμος, ου, ὁ *klēronomos* heir
→ κληρονομέω.

κλῆρος, ου, ὁ *klēros* lot, share, portion*

1. Occurrences and basic meaning — 2. Casting lots — 3. Eschatological inheritance or portion — 4. Fig. for apostolic service

Lit.: → κληρονομέω. See also: J. BLINZLER, *Der Prozeß Jesu* (1969) 368f. — N. BROX, *1 Pet* (EKKNT, 1979) 232. — V. EHRENBERG, PW XI, 810-13. — W. NAUCK, "Probleme des früh-

christlichen Amtsverständnisses (1 Pt 5,2f.)," *ZNW* 48 (1957) 200-220. — F. NÖTSCHER, *Zur theologischen Terminologie der Qumran-Texte* (1956) 169-73. — H. H. SCHMID, *THAT* I, 412-15.

1. Κλῆρος appears 11 times in the NT, once in each of the Gospels, 5 times in Acts, and once each in Colossians and 1 Peter. Its range of meaning in these few occurrences is similar to that of Eng. *lot*. Originally the word referred in Greek, as in Hebrew thought, to the decree of the deity, independent of human influence, which can be received as an oracle for the selection of a person, for the legitimation of the distribution of the land, or in legal disputes. This explains the variety of meanings —*lot, casting of lots, momentous sign, portion, portion of land assigned by lot, inheritance*—that κλῆρος has in secular Greek. In Israel the only oracle permitted was the oracle by lot (Urim and Thummim, Deut 18:9-14; Num 27:21, etc.).

2. The occurrences in the Passion narratives (Mark 15:24 par. Matt 27:35/Luke 23:24; John 19:24) is dependent on Ps 22:19, which is cited here as a proof from Scripture. According to Roman law the executioner was permitted to seize the property of the one who was executed (cf. Blinzler 368f. with n. 47). In what is apparently the oldest part of the Passion narrative there is a description of the soldiers dividing the clothes of Jesus (presumably the outer garment and inner garments, belt, sandals, and headband). Since they did not want to cut the seamless inner garment, which was woven from one piece, into four pieces, they cast lots for it.

The description of casting of lots for clothes in Psalm 22, as in the Passion narrative, characterizes the total defeat of the one who is making the lament, i.e., Jesus, which is seen also in the cry: "My God, my God, why have you forsaken me?" (Mark 15:34). Even while the victim was alive his clothes were divided as if he were already dead. The scorn of the enemies could scarcely have been greater.

Acts 1:26 (bis) describes an actual procedure of casting lots (on the procedure, see G. Lohfink, *BZ* 19 [1975] 247-49). Matthias is chosen by lot as Judas's successor and thus, according to v. 17, he received "the *lot (share)* of this ministry" (κλῆρος τῆς διακονίας). In the procedure of casting lots God is given the responsibility for the result of the selection, since it is his plan (→ 1).

3. Κλῆρος in Col 1:12; Acts 26:18 is closely related to κληρονομία.

Just as in secular Greek κλῆρος can designate the *portion* determined by lot and the resulting possession of land and of the *inherited portion*, so also in the LXX it can be used with the more frequent κληρονομία (on the precise differentiation of the two words see W. Foerster, *TDNT* III, 759), not only as the tr. of "lot" (e.g., Lev 16:9: *gôrāl*), but also with the meanings "possession" (e.g., Num 33:53: *yāraš*), "(portion of) the possession of the land" (e.g., Num 16:14: *naḥᵃlâ*), and "inherited possession" (e.g., Num 18:21: *naḥ*ᵃ*lâ*) and then as a term for the *eternal inheritance* and eschatological destiny (cf. Isa 57:6; esp. Dan 12:13; also 1QS 2:17; *1 Enoch* 37:4; 39:8; Wis 3:14, etc.).

Over against the exclusivity of Judaism, in Acts 26:18 the astonishingly new fact is that the Gentiles also receive this *"hereditary right* among the saints." Similarly Col 1:12, where the Gentile Christian Church again is said to have a portion in the *"inheritance* of the saints in light," which stands in opposition to the "power of darkness" (v. 13), as at Qumran (cf. 1 QM 1:11). In both Acts and Colossians it is not entirely certain whether "the saints" is a designation for the Church or for the angels. Col 1:15 speaks of an event that has already taken place, and thus probably indicates that the Church already has a portion in the heavenly inheritance (cf. Eph 1:14, 18 and the use of → κληρόω in Eph 1:11). Perhaps Acts 8:21 belongs here also: Simon is denied a *"portion* in this word"— probably an early formula of excommunication.

4. In 4 occurrences a use of κλῆρος is to be noted in which it has a close relationship with the later designation of the ecclesiastical hierarchy as "clergy" (etymologically: "portion in spiritual service"). In Acts 1:25 a well-attested v.l. inserts κλῆρος (which is used twice in v. 26 for the procedure of casting lots for the apostolic replacement) in place of τόπος. The variant is probably to be regarded as an assimilation to 1:17, 26.

This use of κλῆρος for apostolic service is related to the selection procedure. We find in the NT, however, only four other passages that point to this: Acts 1:17: Judas's selection for the apostolic ministry; v. 26: Matthias's selection for the apostolic ministry; 8:21, where Peter says to Simon: "You have no part and *portion* in this word" (an apparent reference to the "ministry of the word," 6:4). Qumran also designates office with κλῆρος (cf. 1QS 2:23). Perhaps this conception has been influenced by the view that the Levites' only possession is God (Deut 10:9 LXX: μέρις καὶ κλῆρος, likewise Acts 8:21; cf. Deut 14:29; 18:1f.).

The meaning of κλῆρος in 1 Pet 5:3 is disputed. Nauck (210) enumerates six suggestions that have been made: "spiritual things, plots of land, individual communities, contributions, a portion of the believers, or the elder in the messianic kingdom." He himself opts for "offices and positions" that the elder cannot distribute arbitrarily (210f.). Brox (232 with n. 734), however, sees in κλῆρος the designation of the bishopric, "the provincial church over which the elders have respectively been appointed." Whatever aspect of the term the author of 1 Peter seeks to emphasize, one most appropriately renders κλῆρος in a comprehensive manner: "Tend the flock . . . not as those who rule violently over their *realm* [or *portion*]." Here the use of κλῆρος could indicate that God stands behind the conduct of the officebearer, having called him into office (→ 1).   J. H. Friedrich

κληρόω *klēroō* determine by lot; pass.: be chosen by lot*

In the NT only in Eph 1:11: ἐν ᾧ καὶ ἐκληρώθημεν, "in whom [Christ, v. 10] *our lot is cast.* . . ." W. Foerster, *TDNT* III, 765; J. Eichler, *DNTT* II, 295-303.

κλῆσις, εως, ἡ *klēsis* call (noun), summons
→ καλέω.

κλητός, 3 *klētos* called
→ καλέω

κλίβανος, ου, ὁ *klibanos* oven*

Matt 6:30 par. Luke 12:28, of grass, which tomorrow "is thrown into the *oven.*" According to *2 Clem.* 16:3 the day of judgment is ὡς κλίβανος καιόμενος (Hos 7:4 LXX).

κλίμα, ατος, τό *klima* region*

In the NT only in Paul and always pl.: 2 Cor 11:10: τὰ κλίματα τῆς Ἀχαΐας; similarly Gal 1:21: "the *regions* of Syria and Galatia"; Rom 15:23: "in these *regions.*"

κλινάριον, ου, τό *klinarion* bed*

Diminutive of κλίνη: Acts 5:15, in a summary with κράβαττος, pallet.

κλίνη, ης, ἡ *klinē* bed, pallet, stretcher*

The κλίνη is the bed for one who is resting, suffering, or even eating (Xenophanes 18:2; Ezek 23:41 LXX); in the NT, Mark 4:21; 7:4, 30; Luke 8:16; 17:34. It is also the *stretcher* on which a sick person is carried: Matt 9:2, 6; Luke 5:18. Thus also the phrase βάλλω (τινὰ) εἰς κλίνην, "throw (someone) on a *sickbed,*" i.e., strike (someone) with illness: Rev 2:22.

κλινίδιον, ου, τό *klinidion* stretcher, bier*

Diminutive of κλίνη. In the NT only in Luke 5:19, 24. Par. Mark 2:4, 11 has κράβαττος (pallet); cf. Luke 5:18: ἐπὶ κλίνης.

κλίνω *klinō* incline (vb.); bend; put away; intrans.: incline, slant*

Matt 8:20 par. Luke 9:58 and John 19:30: κλίνω τὴν κεφαλήν; Luke 24:5: κλίνω τὸ πρόσωπον εἰς τὴν γῆν. Intrans.: ἡ ἡμέρα κλίνει, "the day *is spent*" (Luke 9:12; 24:29); Heb 11:34: κλίνω παρεμβολὰς ἀλλοτρίων, "*bring about the downfall* of [foreign] armies."

κλισία, ας, ἡ *klisia* table fellowship*

Luke 9:14: κατακλίνω αὐτοὺς κλισίας, "have them recline *in groups* [to eat]." The word is known from the time of Homer, also in Judaism: 3 Macc 6:31; *Ep. Arist.* 183; Josephus *Ant.* xii.96.

κλοπή, ῆς, ἡ *klopē* theft*

Pl. in vice catalogs: Mark 7:21 par. Matt 15:19; *Did.* 3:5; 5:1.

κλύδων, ωνος, ὁ *klydōn* billowing, surge (of waves)*

Luke 8:24: κλύδων τοῦ ὕδατος (cf. par. Mark: θάλασσα); Jas 1:6: κλύδων θαλάσσης, *"breakers* of the sea."

κλυδωνίζομαι *klydōnizomai* be tossed to and fro by waves*

Fig. in Eph 4:14: παντὶ ἀνέμῳ τῆς διδασκαλίας, "by every wind of teaching."

Κλωπᾶς, ᾶ *Klōpas* Clopas*

John 19:25: Μαρία ἡ τοῦ Κλωπᾶ stood with Mary Magdalene at the cross of Jesus. What is meant is "the wife of Clopas." The name Κλωπᾶς is probably of Semitic origin, but cannot be interpreted with certainty. Hegesippus (in Eusebius *HE* iii.11; 32.1-4, 6; iv.22.4) mentions a Clopas, brother of Joseph.

κνήθω *knēthō* cause an itch; pass.: feel an itch*

2 Tim 4:3: κνηθόμενοι τὴν ἀκοήν (dependent on: "they will accumulate for themselves teachers according to their own desires"). The participial phrase probably means "in order to have their ears *tickled.*"

Κνίδος, ου *Knidos* Cnidus*

A peninsula (and city) on the coast of Caria. Paul's ship touched on it after the journey to Crete (Acts 27:7). *KP* III, 260.

κοδράντης, ου, ὁ *kodrantēs* quadrans, penny*

Mark 12:42: a κοδράντης has the value of approximately two pennies. Κοδράντης represents the smallest coin in the phrase "the last *penny*" (Matt 5:26 par. Luke 12:59 D it sy). → λεπτόν.

κοιλία, ας, ἡ *koilia* belly, abdominal cavity, womb*

Lit.: J. BEHM, *TDNT* III, 786-89. — BILLERBECK II, 492. — O. MICHEL, *Rom* (KEK, [4]1966). — R. SCHNACKENBURG, *John* II (Eng. tr., 1979) on 7:38.

1. Κοιλία appears 22 times in the NT, of which 1 is pl. (Luke 23:29). The basic meaning is *belly, abdominal cavity.* In the saying of Jesus in Mark 7:19 par. Matt 15:17

("Do you not understand that everything that enters through the mouth goes into the *stomach/belly* and then is eliminated?") κοιλία refers to the belly as a part of the digestive apparatus. This meaning for κοιλία is also present in 1 Cor 6:13 ("foods are for the *belly* and the *belly* for foods"); Matt 12:40 (Jonah in the *belly* of the fish); Luke 15:16 (fill his *stomach* with the husks = allay his hunger"); and Rev 10:9, 10 (cf. Ezek 3:1-3; Jer 15:16).

2. Paul uses κοιλία in his polemic against heretics. Rom 16:18 warns against false teachers who serve not Christian teaching but "their *belly.*" Κοιλία stands in the negative sense for "imprisonment to the particular nature and constraint of bodily existence in this world" (Michel 383f.). Κοιλία appears in a corresponding way in Phil 3:19 alongside "earthly"; the two words belong together over against the idea of "relationship to Christ."

In most NT occurrences κοιλία designates the *womb,* and is used absolutely (cf. Luke 2:21; 11:27; 23:29) or is followed by gen. μητρός (Matt 19:12; Luke 1:15; John 3:4; Acts 3:2; 14:8; Gal 1:15; cf. Luke 1:41, 42, 44). Ἐκ κοιλίας μητρός indicates a temporal beginning: "from earliest childhood," "from birth" (Matt 19:12; Luke 1:15; Acts 3:2; 14:8; Gal 1:15). Thus God elected Paul "from [his] mother's *womb*" (Gal 1:15). Κοιλία = "womb" as *pars pro toto* designates a woman as "mother" (Luke 11:27: "blessed is the *womb* that bore you . . ."; 23:29).

The use of κοιλία in John 7:38 is derived from the basic meaning of *abdominal cavity:* "Whoever believes in me, from that person's *innermost being* there will flow, as Scripture says, streams of living water." Κοιλία here is not to be associated with καρδία ("heart"), which has been proposed as an explanation since the time of the fathers. It is probably based on Aram. *gûp(ā'),* "cavity," which could be used of a person or in place of a personal pron. (Billerbeck II, 492). Ἐκ τῆς κοιλίας αὐτοῦ can thus be rendered with "from that person," "from that person's inner being." John 19:34, which speaks of blood and water coming from Jesus' side, is anticipated by 7:38.

F. G. Untergassmair

κοιμάομαι *koimaomai* sleep; fall asleep*

1. Occurrences and usage in the NT — 2. Pauline usage — 3. John 11

Lit.: J. W. BAILEY, "Is 'Sleep' the Proper Biblical Term for the Intermediate State?" *ZNW* 155 (1964) 161-67. — G. BARTH, "Erwägungen zu 1 Kor 15,20-28," *EvT* 30 (1970) 515-27. — J. BAUMGARTEN, *Paulus und die Apokalyptik* (WMANT 44, 1975) 111-30. — W. HARNISCH, *Eschatologische Existenz. Ein exegetischer Beitrag zum Sachanliegen von 1 Thess 4,13–5,11* (FRLANT 110, 1973) 19-51. — P. HOFFMANN, *Die Toten in Christus* (NTAbh N.F. 2, 1966) 186-206. — U. LUZ, *Das Geschichtsverständnis des Paulus* (BEvT 49, 1968) 318-86. — H. A. WILCKE, *Das Problem eines messianischen Zwischenreiches bei Paulus* (ATANT 51, 1967) 51-150.

1. Κοιμάομαι appears 18 times in the NT and, like καθεύδω, refers first of all to "sleep" in the natural sense (Matt 28:13; Luke 22:45; Acts 12:6), but is used predominantly in Paul as a term for death. It can be used both of the process of dying (Acts 7:60; 13:36; 1 Cor 7:39; 11:30; 15:6, 51; 2 Pet 3:4) and the state of death (Matt 27:52; 1 Cor 15:20; 1 Thess 4:13, 14, 15; see also 1 Cor 15:18), even if this distinction can be difficult and disputed in particular instances. The demarcation of the circle of those for whom κοιμάομαι is used is illuminating: It is in all instances, including 1 Cor 7:39, used consistently of Church members, David (Acts 13:36), or the ἅγιοι (Matt 27:52).

2. For the understanding of Pauline usage it is esp. noteworthy that κοιμάομαι is used primarily in connection with questions about the fate of Church members who die before the parousia (1 Thess 4:13ff.) or before the resurrection (1 Cor 15:12ff.). Here one cannot avoid the controversial question of the extent to which Paul is already articulating the hope for the resurrection by using κοιμάομαι, or whether he was only using traditional language (cf. Hoffmann 186ff.). Indeed, the Pauline occurrences are not sufficient to justify the long-held view that expectation of the resurrection was inherent in κοιμάομαι. Nevertheless one may affirm that κοιμάομαι, like οἱ νεκροὶ ἐν Χριστῷ (1 Thess 4:16), is a term directly relevant to death and the associated Christian hope (1 Thess 4:13b; 1 Cor 15:19; cf. 1 Cor 15:18: οἱ κοιμηθέντες ἐν Χριστῷ). Thus κοιμάομαι not only emphasizes the fact of death and is also not merely used in the customary ancient euphemistic sense. Instead the ambiguity of the term makes possible an affirmation of both the fact of death and the Christian hope.

3. The ambiguity of κοιμάομαι is also relevant in John 11:11f. The author uses the misunderstanding of the disciples (11:12) to describe an experience necessary for the disciples (11:4, 15, 25) in the face of the Jewish decree of death (11:45ff.) and the resulting beginning of the Passion of Jesus.
M. Völkel

κοίμησις, εως, ἡ *koimēsis* sleep, slumber*

John 11:13: ἡ κοίμησις τοῦ ὕπνου, "the *slumber* of sleep" (epexegetical gen.); → κοιμάομαι 3.

κοινός, 3 *koinos* common; impure*
κοινόω *koinoō* make common, defile, desecrate*

1. Occurrences in the NT — 2. "Common" — 3. Cultic impurity — 4. Κοινόω

Lit.: BAGD s.v. — F. HAUCK, *TDNT* III, 789-810. — M. HUFTIER, "Le corps, la pureté et la morale [dans la Bible]," *L'ami du clergé* 77 (1967) 582-87. — O. MICHEL, *Rom* (KEK,

[4]1966). — W. PASCHEN, *Rein und Unrein. Untersuchung zur biblischen Wortgeschichte* (SANT 24, 1970).

1. The adj. κοινός appears in the NT 4 times with its basic meaning *common/shared* (Acts 2:44; 4:32; Titus 1:4; Jude 3) and 10 times with the derived meaning *common/ordinary/profane/impure* (Mark 7:2, 5; Acts 10:14, 28; 11:8; Rom 14:14a, b, c; Heb 10:29; Rev 21:27). The vb. κοινόω is used in all 14 occurrences in the sense of *pollute/profane/desecrate* (→ 4).

2. In the summaries characterizing the early Church (Acts 2:43-47; 4:32-37) κοινός is used in reference to property (2:44; 4:32: "they had all things *in common*") and refers to the "community of goods" in the early Church. The idea of such a sharing can be explained against the background of the fraternal community life of Jesus and his disciples (cf. Luke 8:3; John 12:4-6; 13:29). Nevertheless at no time was there a "planned communistic economy, nor is it legal in the sense of a constitutional socialisation of property" (Hauck 796; cf., however, Acts 5:1-11; 4:36; 1 Cor 16:1-4; 2 Cor 8:9; Rom 15:26). Instead "community of goods" was the expression of a voluntary sense of brotherhood initiated by the Spirit (cf. Acts 5:3). With the formula "have all things *common*," which is unusual in biblical literature but common in Hellenistic literature (Hauck 796), Luke portrays the early Church as an ideal of community life. The reference to the "*common* faith" (Titus 1:4) or to the "*common* salvation" (Jude 3), promised in the OT to all Israel, and according to the NT opened through Christ to the whole world (cf. K. H. Schelkle, *Jude* [HTKNT] 149), corresponds to the community of Jesus.

3. Κοινός in the sense of *impure* is intelligible against the background of levitical purity law. "Eat with *unclean* hands" (Mark 7:2, 5) is elucidated with ἄνιπτος ("unwashed"), derived from Lev 15:11 (τὰς χεῖρας οὐ νένιπται). In accordance with Jesus' teaching (cf. Mark 7:1-23), Paul says that "nothing is *unclean* of itself" (Rom 14:14a). According to the NT there is no objective cultic impurity, but there is a subjective impurity: "it is *impure* only for one who views it as *impure*." Out of consideration for the brother Paul bows before this subjective judgment. Paul stands completely on the side of Jesus who, over against Judaism, introduced a new understanding of "pure" and "impure" (Michel 344). The reception of Jesus' teaching is illustrated in Acts by the example of Peter, who at first resisted eating "anything *unclean*" (Acts 10:14; cf. 11:8), then made "God's judgment" his own: "God has shown [me] that I may not call any person *unclean* or common" (10:28; cf. v. 15).

As a contrasting term to ἅγιος, κοινός designates one who has no access to that which is "holy" ("nothing *impure* will find entry" into the new Jerusalem, Rev

21:27) and no sense for the "holy" (Heb 10:29 speaks of one who considers the holy "blood of the covenant" as *ordinary* blood).

4. In the conflict story regarding "clean" and "unclean" (Mark 7:1-23 par. Matt 15:1-20) **κοινόω** appears with the adj. (→ 3). The saying of Jesus in Mark 7:15 ("Nothing that comes into a person from outside can *make him unclean,* but only what comes out of a person *makes him unclean*"; cf. 7:18; 7:20 par. Matt 15:18; 7:23 par. Matt 15:20a; Matt 15:20b) indicates, as does Acts 10:15 ("What God has declared clean, *do not call unclean*"; cf. Acts 11:9), the NT doctrine of "the common religious purity of all that God has created" (Hauck 797). Accordingly the charge that Paul "*desecrated* this holy place in taking Greeks [i.e., Gentiles] into the temple" (21:28) missed the mark. Heb 9:14 refers to the sacrificial blood of Christ; it alone is the means of God's grace (cf. 10:29) and the means of purification that surpasses everything anticipated in the levitical purity laws ("the blood of goats and bulls and the ashes of a heifer" sanctifies *the unclean:* 9:13; cf. Lev 16:3, 14f.; Num 19:9, 17).

F. G. Untergassmair

κοινόω *koinoō* make common, defile, desecrate*
→ κοινός 1, 4.

κοινωνέω *koinōneō* have a share; give a share; take a share; have fellowship
→ κοινωνία.

κοινωνία, ας, ἡ *koinōnia* community; fellowship; participation*
κοινωνέω *koinoneō* have a share; give a share; take a share; have fellowship*
κοινωνός, οῦ, ὁ *koinōnos* companion, partner*

1. Occurrences in the NT — 2. General meanings and constructions — 3. Special use, esp. in Paul — 4. Individual references

Lit.: P. C. BORI, *KOINΩNIA. L'idea della comunione nell' ecclesiologia recente e nel Nuovo Testamento* (1972). — T. Y. CAMPBELL, "Κοινωνία and its Cognates in the NT," *JBL* 51 (1932) 352-80. — P. J. T. ENDENBURG, *Koinonia, En Gemeenschap van zaken bij de Grieken in den klassieken tijd* (1937). — J. HAINZ, "Gemeinschaft (κοινωνία) zwischen Paulus und Jerusalem (Gal 2,9f)," FS Mussner 30-42. — idem, *Koinonia. "Kirche" als Gemeinschaft bei Paulus* (1982). — F. HAUCK, *TDNT* III, 789-810. — G. JOURDAN, "KOINΩNIA in 1 Corinthians 10,16," *JBL* 67 (1948) 111-24. — M. MANZANERA, "Koinonía en Hch 2,42," *EE* 52 (1977) 307-29. — J. M. McDERMOTT, "The Biblical Doctrine of KOINΩNIA," *BZ* 19 (1975) 64-77, 219-33.— G. PANIKULAM, *Koinonia in the NT* (1979). — P. PERKINS, "*Koinonía* in 1 John 1,3-7," *CBQ* 45 (1983) 631-41. — R. SCHNACKENBURG, "Die Einheit der Kirche unter dem Koinonia-Gedanken," F. Hahn, K. Kertelge, and R. Schnackenburg, *Einheit der Kirche* (1979) 52-93. — H. SEESEMANN, *Der Begriff KOINΩNIA im NT* (1933). — A. WEISER, "Basis und Führung in kirchlicher communio," *BK* 45 (1990) 66-71.

1. The word group represented by κοινωνία appears in the NT predominantly in Paul, in the epistolary literature influenced by Paul (Ephesians, 1 Timothy, and 1–2 Peter), Hebrews, and 1–2 John. Κοινωνός is found once each in Matthew (23:30), Luke (5:10), and Acts (2:42). Only the usage in Paul and writings influenced by Paul has a specific character (→ 3), while the rest of NT usage corresponds to general Greek usage (→ 2).

2. Adj. use of κοινωνός can be rendered *common* or *participating in;* subst. use can be rendered *partner, associate.* In the NT adj. use appears in 2 Pet 1:4: "*partakers* of the divine nature." Subst. use is most often pl. It is absolute in 2 Cor 8:23 and Phlm 17 *(partner).* The person with whom one is a partner or associate (Luke 5:10: "who were *partners* with Simon") is given in the dat. The obj. gen. indicates that in which one shares or how or whose partner one is (1 Cor 10:18, 20; 2 Cor 1:7; 1 Pet 5:1; Heb 10:33: "*partners* of those who so conducted themselves"). Of the prep. phrase modifiers appearing in nonbiblical Greek (ἐν εἰς, περί, ἐπί) only ἐν appears in the NT (Matt 23:30: "*partners,* i.e., those who shared the guilt for the blood of the prophets").

Κοινωνέω, the vb. derived from κοινωνός, means *have/take a share* in something where it appears with a gen. or dat. obj. (Rom 12:13; 15:27; 1 Tim 5:22; 1 Pet 4:13; Heb 2:14: "as now the children *share* flesh and blood . . ."; 2 John 11: "One who greets [a false teacher], *takes part* in his evil works"). It means *give a share, communicate, have fellowship* with someone, with the dat. of the person (Gal 6:6; Phil 4:15). That in which one gives a portion or the manner in which one holds fellowship is indicated with ἐν (Gal 6:6) or εἰς (Phil 4:15).

Κοινωνία, the related abstract form, is translated *fellowship, partnership* and also with *participation, sharing.* Absolute use suggests esp. the idea of *fellowship* (Gal 2:9; Acts 2:42: "They continued in the teaching of the apostles and in *fellowship*"; Heb 13:16: "Do not forget charity and *fellowship*"; 1 John 1:3: "so that you have *fellowship* with us; but our *fellowship* is also with the Father and with his Son, Jesus Christ"; similarly vv. 6, 7: κοινωνίαν ἔχομεν). Along with the normal gen. of the object in which one participates (1 Cor 10:16; 2 Cor 8:4; 13:13; Phil 2:1; 3:10; Phlm 6) Paul in one instance (1 Cor 1:9) also employs the gen. of the person, which is unusual elsewhere in Greek. Also unusual is the construction with the dat. of the object in 2 Cor 6:14 ("what *fellowship* has light with darkness?"). More frequently, however, one finds in the NT prep. designations of κοινωνία with εἰς (2 Cor 9:13; Phil 1:5), ἐν (Phlm 6), πρός (2 Cor 6:14), and μετά (1 John 1:3, 6, 7). Paul also uses κοινωνία specifically for the collection for the church in Jerusalem (Rom 15:26); this is to be explained against the background of the specific Pauline use of the word group (→ 3).

3. The special character of Pauline usage is always emphasized in the exegetical literature and its religious character is always emphasized. However, the neutral rendering, "participant," "participate," "participation," is overwhelmingly preferred. This takes place esp. out of aversion to the term "fellowship." In English the ideas of association, alliance, and unity, as well as similar ideas, easily enter in—conceptions that are misleading in regard to Pauline use of κοινωνία. Moreover, the lexicons indicate that the word group represented by κοινωνία is distinguished from synonyms by the idea of fellowship, of inner relationship. "Κοινωνία expresses a mutual relationship. . . . As with κοινωνέω either the giving or the receiving side of the relationship can stand in the foreground" (Hauck 798; cf. Moulton/Milligan 351). Indeed, in actual usage either one motif or the other is expressed. But the total Pauline usage has a unified structure for the word group as such, which can be seen in the interpretation of individual texts; fellowship/partnership (with someone) through (common) participation (in something).

Κοινωνία is in Paul a designation for various community relationships that come into being through (common) participation and are seen in reciprocal giving and taking of a portion. Where the community relationship (common participation in something) is mediated through someone (e.g., Jerusalem, apostles, teachers) an obligation comes into being that obligates the receiver to a response of giving a portion. Κοινωνοί are persons who stand in a relationship of community because they have a common share in something. In κοινωνέω the act of giving and receiving a portion itself is expressed, the experience of having fellowship with someone in something. The meaning *have fellowship, give a portion, impart* has occasionally been disputed for Paul; it emerges unambiguously, however, from Gal 6:6 and Phil 4:15 and is attested both in Greek (Endenburg) and early Christian literature (*Barn.* 19:8; *Did.* 4:8; Justin *Apol.* i.15.10). Because the word group represented by κοινωνία includes these various implications in content, a precise summary of these aspects is possible only by referring to particular contexts (→ 4).

4. The reciprocity of community relationships designated with the word group represented by κοινωνία is emphasized by Paul esp. in his description of the relationships of his churches to the mother church in Jerusalem and to him, the founding apostle. Rom 15:27 makes clear that these relationships are fundamentally relationships of obligation: "for if the Gentiles *receive a share* (ἐκοινώνησαν) in their [the Jerusalem Christians'] spiritual blessings [gospel, faith, salvation], they are obliged to provide them a ministry in bodily [material] matters." Thus benefits that are very different in nature are exchanged. But in the exchange κοινωνία, the recognition of the relationship in community in which having a share

obligates one to give a share, comes into existence (cf. Gal 6:6: "Let him who is taught *share* in all good things with him who teaches").

On this Paul bases his right—in principle—to receive material and personal support from the churches that came to faith through him; support, even if he de facto —out of fear of misinterpretation—made only sparing use of this right. Thus he reminds the Philippians that no church except them (Phil 4:15) "*entered into partnership* in giving and receiving." The gifts of the Philippians were an expression of gratitude, which they owed their founding apostle, and of partnership, which they wished to have with him and could have only in this form. In a general way this demand for reciprocal partnership and care is found also in Rom 12:13: "*Share* in the needs of the saints." Thus the relationship in community, which has come into existence between the believers, obliges them to give reciprocal assistance. Less Pauline is 1 Tim 5:22: "*Do* not *take part* in another person's sins." On 1 Pet 4:13 see below.

As with κοινωνέω Paul uses κοινωνία also for various common relationships of Christians with each other. Thus he thanks the Philippians for their "*partnership* in the gospel" (Phil 1:5). This partnership is based on the mediation of the gospel by the apostle and in the common participation in the gospel and is expressed in common service for the gospel (or for Paul as its mediator).

Such partnership exists between the apostle and all who came to faith through his proclamation, as with Philemon. Thus Paul hopes that the relationship that came into existence through "the *partnership* in faith (Phlm 6) will be effective in the fulfillment of his request. In connection with Phlm 17 ("If you thus consider me your *partner*," i.e., if you stand with me in this relationship of partnership), the word group represented by κοινωνία can be seen as the key to the total understanding of the letter to Philemon; i.e., the letter is a concrete demonstration of what Paul understands by κοινωνία.

A similar relationship in partnership exists between those who share together in the proclamation of the gospel. Thus Titus in 2 Cor 8:23 is described by Paul as "[with respect to the proclamation of the gospel] my *partner* and with respect to you [the foundation and strengthening of the Church] [God's and] my 'coworker.' "

The Pauline understanding of κοινωνία takes on its greatest significance in connection with statements about Christ and the Spirit. 1 Cor 1:9 speaks of the call through God "to *fellowship* with Jesus Christ [an unusual gen. of the person]," indicating neither how this fellowship comes into existence nor in what it consists. The relationships become clear, however, in 10:16ff., especially in contrast to μετέχω, which in Greek can be synonymous with κοινωνέω, but which in Paul expresses only the concrete receiving of a share, but not the most decisive aspect, which is the "partnership" in the body of Christ effected at the Lord's Supper through "participation in" the body of the exalted Christ, the Church, i.e., the partnership with the other partakers in the meal. The explication of 10:16 in 10:17 and the larger context, in which the concern is the various relationships between those who partake at the table of the Lord and those who partake at the altar, i.e., at the table of demons (10:18: "Do not those who eat the sacrifices stand in partnership through the common participation at the altar?") does not allude directly to the relationship of the one who eats at the altar to God (the OT nowhere ventures this idea, which is found first in Philo [*Vit. Mos.* i.158; *Spec. Leg.* i.221]), but to the partnership that they enter by eating. Thus also in reference to those who worship demons (cf. 10:20f., which one can translate: "I do not want you to to enter into partnership with those who are partners in sacrificing to idols and thus stand in relationship to demons"). One enters into partnership with the powers to which the sacrifices are dedicated and with those who share in the offerings. According to Paul, what takes place at the Lord's Supper is not fundamentally different from what takes place in Jewish and Gentile sacrifices.

Christ establishes partnership by offering not only participation in his body (and blood), but also "*partnership* in his sufferings" (Phil 3:10), i.e., partnership with him by partnership in his sufferings (cf. 1 Pet 4:13: "rejoice that you *share* in the sufferings of Christ"). Thus the hope for future partnership with Christ through participation in his glory (cf. 1 Pet 5:1: "as well as *partakers* of his glory") corresponds to participation in his sufferings. Thus the apostle is certain that the sufferings of Christ, which have come over him in abundance, but which are also the encouragement that he has richly experienced through Christ (on 2 Cor 1:5-7; cf. 1 Cor 15:31; 2 Cor 4:10f.; Col 1:24), are also shared by the Church (2 Cor 1:7: "*partakers* in the sufferings as well as the encouragement").

What binds all Christians, finally, is "the *partnership* [through common participation] of the Spirit" (2 Cor 13:13; Phil 2:1). This permits the apostle to postulate sympathy and mercy as demonstrations of this partnership (Phil 2:1).

The Pauline understanding of κοινωνία has special meaning in connection with the collection for Jerusalem. According to Gal 2:9 Paul and those who were considered authorities in the Jerusalem church extended "the hand of *fellowship*." The handshake was meant to confirm the partnership by a sign and express the willingness for partnership. The partnership thus sealed had its basis in the shared proclamation of the one gospel—at least in principle. And it was meant to have its visible expression in the collection (cf. Gal 2:10).

According to 2 Corinthians 8–9 the collection was a contribution to the solidarity of the churches with each other (cf. καὶ εἰς πάντας, 9:13), particularly with Jerusalem. It was a ministry to the mother church, in which the Macedonians requested that they might participate (8:4), for which (as a demonstration of the will for fellowship) the Christians of Jerusalem will praise God (9:13: because of the generosity of this "demonstration of partnership" with them). The collection is thus a concrete demonstration of the existing relationship of partnership and obligation in which the Gentile Christian churches stand in relationship to the mother church in Jerusalem. That this understanding demands fundamentally unlimited κοινωνία is indicated in Rom 15:25-31 (cf. also Gal 6:6); yet a partial manifestation suffices (Rom 15:26: the churches of Macedonia and Achaia decided to make κοινωνίαν τινὰ ποιήσασθαι, i.e., "some demonstration of partnership").

                                J. Hainz

κοινωνικός, 3 *koinōnikos* sharing, beneficial to the community*

1 Tim 6:18, in an admonition to the rich to be generous. F. Hauck, *TDNT* III, 809.

κοινωνός, οῦ, ὁ *koinōnos* companion, partner
→ κοινωνία.

κοίτη, ης, ἡ *koitē* bed; sexual intercourse*

Luke 11:7: εἰς τὴν κοίτην εἶναι, "be in *bed*"; Heb 13:4: ἡ κοίτη ἀμίαντος, "let the *marriage bed* be undefiled." Κοίτη stands euphemistically for *sexual intercourse* in Rom 9:10; 13:13. M. Silva, "New Lexical Semitisms?" *ZNW* 69 (1978) 255.

κοιτών, ῶνος, ὁ *koitōn* bedroom*

Acts 12:20, in the title ὁ ἐπὶ τοῦ κοιτῶνος, "the chamberlain"; cf. Epictetus *Diss.* iv.7.1.

κόκκινος, 3 *kokkinos* scarlet, red*

Matt 27:28: the *red* robe worn by the Roman soldiers; Heb 9:19: "*red* wool (ἔριον)"; Rev 17:3: the color of an apocalyptic beast; 17:4 (cf. 18:12, 16): "the woman was attired with purple and *scarlet*. . . ." O. Michel, *TDNT* III, 812-14.

κόκκος, ου, ὁ *kokkos* grain*

Mark 4:31 par. Matt 13:31/Luke 13:19; Matt 17:20 par. Luke 17:6: mustard *seed* (faith like a mustard seed); John 12:24; 1 Cor 15:37: *grain* of wheat. O. Michel, *TDNT* III, 810-12; *TWNT* X, 1146 (bibliography).

κολάζω *kolazō* punish, chastise*

Mid. with acc. in Acts 4:21; pass. in 2 Pet 2:9: The unrighteous will be kept *for punishment* (κολαζομένους) at the day of judgment. J. Schneider, *TDNT* III, 814-16.

κολακ(ε)ία, ας, ἡ *kolak(e)ia* flattery*

This noun is derived from κολακεύω, "entice by flattery." 1 Thess 2:5: λόγος κολακείας, "words of *flattery*." J. Schneider, *TDNT* III, 817f.; Spicq, *Notes* I, 436-39.

κόλασις, εως, ἡ *kolasis* punishment, chastisement*

Derived from → κολάζω. Matt 25:46: ἀπέρχομαι εἰς κόλασιν αἰώνιον, "come into eternal *punishment*"; 1 John 4:18: ὁ φόβος κόλασιν ἔχει, "fear has to do with *punishment*." J. Schneider, *TDNT* III, 816f.

κολαφίζω *kolaphizō* hit with the fist, box a person's ears, mistreat*

Mark 14:65 par. Matt 26:67: the mistreatment of Jesus in the Sanhedrin (cf. K. L. Schmidt, FS Goguel 218-27); 1 Cor 4:11: πεινῶμεν . . . καὶ κολαφιζόμεθα καὶ ἀστατοῦμεν, "we suffer hunger . . . and *are beaten* and have no permanent home"; 2 Cor 12:7: blows with the fist from an "angel of Satan" (on its interpretation as epilepsy, hysteria, depression, headaches, malaria, or stammering see BAGD s.v. 2); 1 Pet 2:20: "when you must endure *mistreatment* (κολαφιζόμενοι ὑπομενεῖτε)." K. L. Schmidt, *TDNT* III, 818-21; *TWNT* X, 1146 (bibliography).

κολλάω *kollaō* join together; pass.: cling (to)*

In the NT only pass.: Luke 10:11, of dust that *clings;* Rev 18:5, of sins that *have touched* heaven (= reach to heaven); Acts 8:29: "*follow* this chariot *closely*"; Matt 19:5: *join oneself* to a woman; 1 Cor 6:16: to a harlot; 6:17: to the Lord; similarly with the meaning *seek intimate contact* (Acts 5:13; 9:26; 10:28); Acts 17:34: *become* someone's *disciple;* Luke 15:15: *press oneself on* someone; Rom 12:9: κολλώμενοι τῷ ἀγαθῷ, "*attached* to what is good." K. L. Schmidt, *TDNT* III, 822f.; *TWNT* X, 1146 (bibliography).

κολλούριον, ου, τό *kollourion* eye salve*

Rev 3:18: ἀγοράσαι κολλούριον for "anointing your eyes." P.-R. Berger, "Kollyrium für die blinden Augen, Apk 3,18," *NovT* 27 (1985) 174-95.

κολλυβιστής, οῦ, ὁ *kollybistēs* money changer*

Mark 11:15 par. Matt 21:12: "he overturned the tables of the *money changers*"; John 2:15: "he poured out the coins of the *money changers* and overturned their tables." Spicq, *Notes* I, 430-35.

κολλύριον, ου, τό *kollyrion* eye salve

Alternative form of → κολλούριον in ℵ B C.

κολοβόω *koloboō* mutilate, maim*

Mark 13:20 (bis) par. Matt 24:22 (bis), act. in Mark (ἐκολόβωσεν) with acc. obj. τὰς ἡμέρας, pass. in Matthew (ἐκολοβώθησαν, κολοβωθήσονται) with subj. αἱ ἡμέραι ἐκεῖναι. The vb. refers to God's *shortening* of the time of tribulation. G. Delling, *TDNT* III, 823f.

Κολοσσαί, ῶν *Kolossai* Colossae*

In the salutation of Colossians (1:2): "Paul . . . and Timothy to the saints ἐν Κολοσσαῖς." The inscription of the letter has the noun (ὁ) Κολοσσαεύς in the pl.: "To the Colossians." Colossae on the upper Lycus in Phrygia had previously been a flourishing city (Herodotus vii.30; Xenophon *An.* i.2.6). It later lost significance (Strabo xii.8.13: πόλισμα), probably because of the growing importance of Laodicea, 15 km. away. The Colossian church was probably founded by Epaphras (Col 1:7; 4:2). M. Dibelius and H. Greeven, *Col* [HNT] 4; *BL* 967f.; E. Lohse, *Col and Phlm* [Hermeneia] 8f.; E. Schweizer, *Col* [Eng. tr., 1982] 13-15.

κόλπος, ου, ὁ *kolpos* bosom, breast; roll (of a garment); bay*

John 13:23 (ἐν τῷ κόλπῳ) and Luke 16:23 (ἐν τοῖς κόλποις): "lie at (someone's) *breast*" (a place of honor); cf. Luke 16:22: "brought to the *bosom* of Abraham." The pl. (Luke 16:23) can also be translated *lap* (BAGD s.v.). John 1:18, of the Son-logos: ὁ ὢν εἰς τὸν κόλπον τοῦ πατρός, "who rests at the *breast* of the Father." Of the *roll* of a garment, used as a purse, Luke 6:38. Of a *bay,* Acts 27:39. R. Meyer, *TDNT* III, 824-26; O. Hofius, " 'Der in des Vaters Schoß ist,' Joh 1,18," *ZNW* 80 (1989) 163-71.

κολυμβάω *kolymbaō* swim*

In the NT only in Acts 27:43. *Barn.* 10:5, with the meaning "submerge and rise to the surface."

κολυμβήθρα, ας, ἡ *kolymbēthra* pool*

John 5:2, 4, 7: the "*pool* of Bethesda" (→ Βηθζαθά); 9:7, 11: the "*pool* of Siloam" (→ Σιλωάμ). In 5:4 and 9:11 κολυμβήθρα appears only as a v.l.

κολωνία, ας, ἡ *kolōnia* colony*

A loanword from Latin *(colonia);* cf. Josephus *Ant.* xix.291. Acts 16:12, in reference to Philippi, which was changed by Augustus into a military colony.

κομάω *komaō* wear long hair*

1 Cor 11:14: For the man long hair (ἐὰν κομᾷ) is a shame, but according to 11:15 it is an honor for the woman (δόξα αὐτῇ ἐστιν). A. Jaubert, *NTS* 18 (1971/72) 419-30; J. P. Meier, *CBQ* 40 (1978) 212-26. → κεφαλή 3.c.

κόμη, ης, ἡ *komē* hair*

1 Cor 11:15b: "For [long] hair is given to her in place of a veil"; → κομάω.

κομίζω *komizō* bring; mid.: attain, obtain*

Act. *bring* appears in the NT in Luke 7:37. All other NT occurrences are mid. Objects of κομίζομαι are: the crown of glory (1 Pet 5:4), (unjust) recompense (2 Pet 2:13 v.l.), the ἐπαγγελία (i.e., the promised blessings, Heb 10:36; 11:13 v.l., 39: "as the goal of faith the salvation of their souls"; 1 Pet 1:9). In the Pauline corpus κομίζομαι is used of receiving the appropriate recompense (2 Cor 5:10; Col 3:25; Eph 6:8). The meaning *receive back* is seen in Matt 25:27 ("my money with interest"), similarly Heb 11:19 of Abraham, who *received* his son *again* (ἐκομίσατο).

κομψότερον *kompsoteron* better (adv.)*

John 4:52, of a sick person: κομψότερον ἔχω, "feel *on the way to improvement.*"

κονιάω *koniaō* whitewash (vb.), whiten*

The vb. is derived from κονία, "(chalk) dust." Matt 23:27, in the "woe" over the scribes: "You are like *whitewashed* tombs"; Acts 23:3 (Paul to the high priest): τοῖχε κεκονιαμένε, "you *whitewashed* wall!" (cf. Ezek 13:10). J. Schneider, *TDNT* III, 827.

κονιορτός, οῦ, ὁ *koniortos* dust*

"Shake the *dust* from (one's) feet": Matt 10:14 with ἐκτινάσσω, Acts 13:51 with ἐκτινάσσομαι (mid.), Luke 9:5 with ἀποτινάσσω, 10:11 with ἀπομάσσομαι (mid.: wipe oneself clean). Acts 22:23, of a raging crowd, which threw *dust* into the air (βάλλω εἰς τὸν ἀέρα).

κοπάζω *kopazō* subside, abate*

Mark 4:39; 6:51 par. Matt 14:32: ἐκόπασεν ὁ ἄνεμος, "the storm *ceased*" (so also Herodotus vii.191).

κοπετός, οῦ, ὁ *kopetos* lamentation*

Acts 8:2, at the end of the story of Stephen: "They made (ἐποίησαν) great *lamentation* over him"; cf. Mic 1:8; Zech 12:10 LXX. G. Stählin, *TDNT* III, 830-52; *TWNT* X, 1146 (bibliography).

κοπή, ῆς, ἡ *kopē* cut to pieces; thrash soundly; cut down, slay*

Heb 7:1 (Gen 14:17): Abraham "returned from the *slaughter* of the kings."

κοπιάω *kopiaō* become tired; labor, trouble oneself*

John 4:6 and Rev 2:3: *become tired;* Matt 11:28: οἱ κοπιῶντες, perhaps: *those who are exhausted* (see below). All other NT occurrences have the sense *toil, labor, trouble oneself* (Matt 6:28 par. Luke 12:27; Matt 11:28: οἱ κοπιῶντες καὶ πεφορτισμένοι; Luke 5:5; John 4:38 bis; Acts 20:35; Rom 16:6, 12 bis; 1 Cor 4:12; 15:10; 16:16; Gal 4:11; Phil 2:16: οὐδὲ εἰς κενὸν ἐκοπίασα [cf. Isa 65:23 LXX]; 1 Thess 5:12; Col 1:29; Eph 4:28; 1 Tim 4:10; 5:17; 2 Tim 2:6). F. Hauck, *TDNT* III, 827-30.

κόπος, ου, ὁ *kopos* work, trouble*

Lit.: A. VON HARNACK, "Κόπος (Κοπιᾶν, Οἱ Κοπιῶντες) im frühchristlichen Sprachgebrauch," *ZNW* 27 (1928) 1-10. — F. HAUCK, *TDNT* III, 827-30. — K. H. SCHELKLE, *TRE* III, 622-24. — M. SEITZ and H.-G. LINK, *DNTT* I, 262f. — For further bibliography see Schelkle.

1. Κόπος appears 18 times in the NT, predominantly in the Pauline corpus (11 times). 5 occurrences are in the Gospels (Matt 26:10; Mark 14:6; Luke 11:7; 18:5; John 4:38) and 2 are in Revelation (2:2; 14:13). Also Heb 6:10 Koine, where (as in 1 Thess 1:3) the expression τοῦ κόπου τῆς ἀγάπης appears.

2. Κόπος (originally "slap," from κόπτω), like the corresponding vb. → κοπιάω, designates exacting, "shattering" *work, hardship.* In the Synoptics (and Gal 6:17) κόπους (κόπον) παρέχω, *make trouble, bother,* appears: Mark 14:6 par. Matt 26:10: "Why do you *trouble* this woman?"

Paul gives a more specific meaning, using κόπος of the difficult work with his hands that he does in order not to be a burden to the churches (1 Thess 2:9; 2 Thess 3:8) and of the numerous struggles he experiences (2 Cor 6:5; 11:23, 27). Since such experiences commend him (6:4; 11:23: Paul uses κόπος frequently in defense of himself and his work) as a true servant of God or Christ, κόπος becomes a term for missionary labor (1 Cor 3:8; 2 Cor 10:15; 1 Thess 3:5) and for activity in the Christian community as a whole (1 Cor 15:58; 1 Thess 1:3). Eschatological fulfillment is always in view: "Everyone will receive his own reward according to his *effort*" (1 Cor 3:8); such work is not in vain (15:58) because of Christ's resurrection (cf. v. 14).

The other NT occurrences of κόπος are related to Pauline usage: John 4:38: missionary labor; Rev 2:2: works, *toil*, and patient endurance characterize the good church, as in 1 Thess 1:3; Rev 14:13: release from *toil* through the eschatological fulfillment.   H. Fendrich

κοπρία, ας, ἡ *kopria* dung heap*

Luke 14:35 (cf. Matt 5:13), in the metaphor regarding salt: οὔτε εἰς κοπρίαν εὔθετόν ἐστιν, "neither is it suitable for the *dung heap*"; 13:8 TR: βάλω κοπρίαν (→ κόπριον).

κόπριον, ου, τό *koprion* manure*

Luke 13:8: ἕως ὅτου ... βάλω κόπρια, "until I put on *manure*/until I have fertilized."

κόπτω *koptō* cut off; mid.: beat (one's breast), mourn greatly*

The act. basic meaning *cut off* (from something) is present in Mark 11:8 par. Matt 21:8. Mid. *hit oneself* (on the breast as a sign of mourning)/*mourn greatly* (e.g., Aeschylus *Pers.* 683; Plato *Phd.* 60b; LXX; Josephus *Ant.* vii.41) is seen in Matt 11:17; 24:30; Luke 8:52; 23:27; Rev 1:7; 18:9. Luke 8:52; 23:27 mention the person over whom one mourns in the acc.; Rev 1:7; 18:9 have ἐπί with the acc. G. Stählin, *TDNT* III, 830-52; F. Stolz, *THAT* I, 27-31.

κόραξ, ακος, ὁ *korax* raven*

Luke 12:24: One should observe the *ravens* (Matt 6:26, "the birds of heaven"), who neither sow nor harvest, yet God takes care of them. Perhaps Matthew has omitted the reference to the ravens because ravens were forbidden for food in Judaism (Lev 11:15; Deut 14:14). E. Fuchs, Ristow/Matthiae 385-88; Schulz, *Q* 149f.

κοράσιον, ου, τό *korasion* girl*

Diminutive of κόρη. Mark 5:41: τὸ κοράσιον (voc.: BDF §147); 5:42 par. Matt 9:25; Mark 6:22; 6:28a par. Matt 14:11; Mark 6:28b; Matt 9:24 (cf. Mark 5:39). C. Spicq, *RB* 85 (1978) 216-18.

κορβᾶν *korban* gift, offering*

The transliteration of Heb. *qorbān* is indeclinable and is explained in Mark 7:11 with ὅ ἐστιν δῶρον (cf. Lev 2:1, 4, 12, 13 LXX). It represents a *gift* that one devotes to God. Billerbeck I, 711-17; K. H. Rengstorf, *TDNT* III, 860-66; *TWNT* X, 1146f. (bibliography); J. D. M. Der-

rett, *Studies in the NT* (1977) 112-17; H. P. Rüger, *TRE* III, 607; H.-J. Fabry, *TWAT* VII, 165-71.

κορβανᾶς, ᾶ, ὁ *korbanas* temple treasury*

Transliteration of Aram. *qorbānā'*, a term for the *temple treasury* (Josephus *B.J.* ii.175). Matt 27:6 (M): "place (βάλλω) in the *temple treasury*." K. H. Rengstorf, *TDNT* III, 860-66; *TWNT* X, 1146f. (bibliography); H. P. Rüger, *TRE* III, 607.

Κόρε *Kore* Korah*

Indeclinable name of an Israelite who led a rebellion against Moses (Num 16:1-40; Sir 45:18): Jude 11.

κορέννυμι *korennymi* fill, satisfy; pass.: be filled, become full*

In the NT only pass.: Acts 27:38: κορεσθέντες δὲ τροφῆς, "as they had eaten enough"; fig. and ironic in 1 Cor 4:8: "you are already *full* (κεκορεσμένοι)."

Κορίνθιος, ου, ὁ *Korinthios* Corinthian*

An inhabitant of → Κόρινθος. Pl. in Acts 18:8 and 2 Cor 6:11; also in Acts 18:27 D; *1 Clem.* 47:6; inscriptions of 1 Corinthians and 2 Corinthians.

Κόρινθος, ου *Korinthos* Corinth*

Lit.: H. BYVANCK and T. LENSCHAU, PW Suppl. IV, 991-1036. — W. ELLIGER, *Paulus in Griechenland* (1978) 200-251. — E. MEYER, *LAW* 1598f. — J. MURPHY-O'CONNOR, *St. Paul's Corinth* (1983). — N. PAPAHATZIS, *Ancient Corinth* (1978). — J. SCHMID, *LTK* VI, 553f. — C. L. THOMPSON, *IDBSup* 179f. — *BL* 976-78. — *KP* III, 301-5.

The city of Corinth was from 27 B.C. capital of the province of Achaia (→ Ἀχαΐα, from 44 A.D. a senatorial province) and residence of the proconsul. Thus it developed, after its total destruction in 146 B.C. by the Romans, again into one of the most distinguished cities of Greece. The population was greatly mixed because of immigration from the Orient. The city had a reputation for serious moral decay. The harbor of Cenchreae (→ Κεγχρεαί on the Saronic Gulf) belonged to Corinth. The Church of Corinth goes back to Paul (Acts 18:1). According to Acts 18:12-17 Paul stood before the court of the Roman proconsul Gallio (→ Γαλλίων). Apollos (→ Ἀπολλῶς) was also active in Corinth (19:1). Paul addressed two letters (1 Cor 1:2; 2 Cor 1:1) to the ἐκκλησία τοῦ θεοῦ (τῇ οὔσῃ) ἐν Κορίνθῳ. In 2 Cor 1:23 Paul says that in order to spare (φειδόμενος) the recipients of the letter he "did not come to *Corinth*." In 2 Tim 4:20a it is said that "Erastus (→ Ἔραστος) has remained in *Corinth*."

Κορνήλιος, ου *Kornēlios* Cornelius*

A personal name, the transliteration of Lat. *Cornelius*. The NT mentions a Roman centurion in Caesarea (ἑκατοντάρχης) named Cornelius (Acts 10:1, 3, 17, 22, 24, 25, 30, 31; 10:7, 21 [v.l.]). On the narrative of Cornelius's baptism (Acts 10:1–11:18) see M. Dibelius, *Studies in the Acts of the Apostles* (1956) 109-22; F. Bovon, *TZ* 26 (1970) 22-45; E. Haulotte, *RSR* 58 (1970) 63-100; K. Löning, *BZ* 18 (1974) 1-19; K. Haacker, *BZ* 24 (1980) 234-51.

κόρος, ου, ὁ *koros* cor, measure*

Luke 16:7: A man owes ἑκατὸν κόρους σίτου, "a hundred cor [Luther: corn-measures]." Κόρος is a Semitic loanword *(kor)* and designates a measure of capacity for grain, flour, etc. (from Josephus *Ant.* xv.314 one can calculate that 1 cor = *ca.* 400 liters).

κοσμέω *kosmeō* put in order; decorate, adorn*

This vb. appears 10 times in the NT (not in Mark, John, or Paul). Its basic meanings are derived from those of the noun → κόσμος, "order, decoration." It has the meaning *set in order, prepare* (cf. Hesiod *Op.* 306; Sir 29:26) only in Matt 25:7: ἐκόσμησαν τὰς λαμπάδας ἑαυτῶν, "They *prepared* their lamps" (cf. Jeremias, *Parables* 175: "They snuff the lamps, removing the burnt wick, and fill them with oil, so that they may burn brightly again"; cf. → λαμπάς 3).

In Matt 12:44 par. Luke 11:25, because of the climax in εὑρίσκει [οἶκον] σχολάζοντα (in Luke only as v.l.) σεσαρωμένον καὶ κεκοσμημένον ("empty, cleaned, and *put in good order*"), the motif of adornment frequently associated with κοσμέω may be dominant. According to Luke 21:5 the temple is *"adorned"* (κεκόσμηται) with beautiful stones and offerings (cf. 2 Chr 3:6; 2 Macc 9:16; cf. par. Mark/Matthew: οἰκοδομαί); however, it is more important to know about the end than to know about the radiance of the temple; cf. also Rev 21:19 (pass.): the foundations of the wall of the heavenly Jerusalem are *adorned* with precious stones. With κοσμεῖτε τὰ μνημεῖα τῶν δικαίων (with οἰκοδομεῖτε τοὺς τάφους τῶν προφητῶν) in Matt 23:29 Jesus criticizes the Pharisees and scribes, who set up and adorn tombs for the prophets and the righteous who suffered martyrdom under "the fathers," in order to set themselves apart (in vain) from the fathers, who engaged in persecution (cf. also Josephus *Ant.* xiv.284; J. Jeremias, *Heiligengräber in Jesu Umwelt* [1958], index under Matt 23:29). "The bride *adorned* (νύμφη κεκοσμημένη τῷ ἀνδρὶ αὐτῆς)," Rev 21:2, is an image for the direct relationship of the heavenly Jerusalem (in contrast to "the harlot of Babylon," 18:1ff.) to God and to Christ (cf. 19:7f.; 21:9; also Isa 61:10; Ezek 16:11).

Κοσμέω is used of adornment of women only in a transferred sense, probably in critical allusion to widespread Greek traditions (see also N. Brox, *Die Pastoralbriefe* [RNT] ad loc.; cf. Jer 4:30 LXX; Jdt 12:15): "Wives . . . should *adorn* themselves (κοσμεῖν ἑαυτάς)" modestly and sensibly, not with artistic braiding of hair, gold, pearls, and costly attire (1 Tim 2:9; cf. also 1 Pet 3:5: ἐκόσμουν ἑαυτάς). The writer calls for inner adornment; outer adornment in the assembly leads only to envy and disorder (see also G. Holtz, *Pastoralbriefe* [THKNT] 65-68). According to Titus 2:10 slaves should, through their conduct and their faith, *adorn* "the doctrine . . . in everything [i.e., *give honor* to it, ἵνα τὴν διδασκαλίαν . . . κοσμῶσιν ἐν πᾶσιν]." BAGD s.v.; LSJ s.v.; H. Sasse, *TDNT* III, 867; J. Guhrt, *DNTT* I, 521-26, esp. 521, 524.
H. Balz

κοσμικός, 3 *kosmikos* earthly, worldly*

Heb 9:1: τὸ ἅγιον κοσμικόν, "the *earthly* sanctuary" (in contrast to the heavenly one); Titus 2:12: *worldly* desires." H. Sasse, *TDNT* III, 897f.

κόσμιος, 2 (3) *kosmios* respectable, honorable*

1 Tim 2:9: ἐν καταστολῇ κοσμίῳ, "in a *respectable* manner" (of women); 3:2, of the ἐπίσκοπος, who (among others) should be κόσμιος. The related adv. κοσμίως appears in 1 Tim 2:9 D* G H 33 pc. H. Sasse, *TDNT* III, 896; Spicq, *Notes* 440-45.

κοσμοκράτωρ, ορος, ὁ *kosmokratōr* world ruler*

In extrabiblical literature of gods who rule the world (Helios, Zeus, Hermes), also in general of "cosmic" spiritual beings (planets). Eph 6:12: κοσμοκράτορες τοῦ σκότους τούτου, "*world rulers* of this darkness," i.e., of this sinful world; cf. *T. Sol.* 8:2; 18:2: κοσμοκράτορες τοῦ σκότους, probably influenced by Eph 6:12. W. Michaelis, *TDNT* III, 913f.; J. Gnilka, *Eph* (HTKNT) ad loc.

κόσμος, ου, ὁ *kosmos* world, universe; ornament; totality

1. Occurrences in the NT — 2. Meanings in the NT and its environment — 3. Usage in the NT in general — 4. Paul and the deutero-Pauline writings — 5. The Johannine literature

Lit.: W. ANDERSEN, "Jesus Christus und der Kosmos," *EvT* 23 (1963) 471-93. — A. AUER, *LTK* X, 1021-27. — G. BAUMBACH, "Gemeinde und Welt im Johannesevangelium," *Kairos* 14 (1972) 121-36. — J. BAUR, "Wie nimmt der Glaube die Welt wahr? Einsichten und Folgen des christlichen Weltverständnisses," *EvT* 30 (1970) 582-93. — J. BLINZLER, "Lexikalisches zu dem Terminus τὰ στοιχεῖα τοῦ κόσμου bei Paulus," *SPCIC* II (1963) 429-43. — O. BÖCHER, *Der johanneische Dualismus* im Zusammenhang des nach-biblischen Judentums (1965) 23-33. — G. BORNKAMM, "Christ and World in the Early Christian Message," idem, Early Christian Experience (1969) 14-28. — R. G. BRATCHER, "The Meaning of kosmos, 'World,' in the NT," BT 31 (1980) 430-34. — R. BULTMANN, "Das Verständnis von Welt und Mensch im NT und im Griechentum," idem, Glauben II, 59-78. — N. H. CASSEM, "A Grammatical and Contextual Inventory of the Use of κόσμος in the Johannine Corpus with Some Implications for a Johannine Cosmic Theology," NTS 19 (1972/73) 81-91. — A. W. CRAMER, Stoicheia tou kosmou. Interpretatie van een nieuwtestamentische term (1961). — J. A. DVOŘÁČEK, "Zum evangelischen Weltverständnis," ZEE 15 (1971) 285-98. — H. FLENDER, "Das Verständnis der Welt bei Paulus, Markus und Lukas," KD 14 (1968) 1-27. — D. J. FURLEY, LAW 1602-8. — J. GUHRT, DNTT V, 521-26. — H. W. HUPPENBAUER, Der Mensch zwischen zwei Welten. Der Dualismus der Texte von Qumran (Höhle I) und der Damaskusfragmente (1959). — Y. IBUKI, "Über den johanneischen Kosmosbegriff," Bulletin of Seikei University 18/3 (1981) 27-55. — G. JOHNSTON, "Οἰχουμένη and κόσμος in the NT," NTS 10 (1963/64) 352-60. — E. JÜNGEL, "Die Welt als Möglichkeit und Wirklichkeit," EvT 29 (1969) 417-42. — A. LESKY, Kosmos (1963). — K. LÜTHI, "Säkulare Welt als Objekt der Liebe Gottes," EvT 26 (1966) 113-29. — C. F. D. MOULE, Man and Nature in the NT. Some Reflections on Biblical Ecology (1964). — F. MUSSNER, LTK VI, 575-77. — A. P. ORBÁN, Les dénominations du monde chez les premiers auteurs chrétiens (Graecitas Christianorum primaeva 4, 1970). — H. SASSE, TDNT III, 867-98. — H. SCHLIER, Principalities and Powers in the NT (1961). — L. SCHOTTROFF, Der Glaubende und die feindliche Welt (WMANT 37, 1970) 228-96. — W. SCHRAGE, "Die Stellung zur Welt bei Paulus, Epiktet und in der Apokalyptik," ZTK 61 (1964) 125-54. — A. VÖGTLE, Das NT und die Zukunft des Kosmos (KBANT, 1970). — H.-F. WEISS, Untersuchung zur Kosmologie des hellenistischen und palästinischen Judentums (TU 97, 1966). — H. ZIMMERMANN, BL 1883-86. — For further bibliography see TWNT X, 1147f.

1. Κόσμος appears 186 times in the NT with clear emphasis in the Johannine literature (78 occurrences in John, 23 in 1 John, also 2 John 7) and in Paul (37 occurrences, of which 9 are in Romans, 21 in 1 Corinthians, 3 in 2 Corinthians, 3 in Galatians, and 1 in Phil 2:15). In addition the Synoptics have 15 occurrences (of which 9 are in Matthew); 5 each are in Hebrews, James, and 2 Peter; Colossians has 4; Ephesians, 1 Timothy, 1 Peter, and Revelation each have 3; also Acts 17:24.

2. The basic meanings "arrangement" and "order," which are fundamental to the meaning of κόσμος in Greek usage and which are used of specific arrangements (e.g., Homer Od. viii.492; xiii.77; of the Spartan system of government in Herodotus i.76), for all interhuman regulations (e.g., εὖ κατὰ κόσμον, Homer Il. x.472), and of all possible forms of "adornment" (e.g., of adornment of women, Plato R. 373c), are not prominent in the NT. Κόσμος in reference to (superficial and objectionable) adornment of women is found only in 1 Pet 3:3 (cf. elsewhere → κοσμέω, κόσμιος).

The case is different with the meanings "world/universe," which κόσμος took on from the time of Plato as a central term of Greek philosophy. According to Diogenes Laertius vii.1.24 and Plutarch De Placitis Philosophorum ii.1, Pythagoras (6th

cent. B.C.) was the first to designate the "total world" as κόσμος because of the order inherent in it. From the time of the Ionic natural philosophy of the 6th cent. B.C., κόσμος assumes an order or standard by which the things of the world are held together (Anaximander frag. 9). Consequently the total world, when considered in spatial terms as world, is called κόσμος in the sense of "universe" "inasmuch as in it all individual things and creatures, heaven and earth, gods and men, are brought into unity by a universal order" (Sasse 871; cf. Plato Grg. 507e-508a; Ti. 92c: ζῷον . . . ὁρατὸν . . . , εἰκὼν τοῦ νοητοῦ θεὸς αἰσθητός . . .). The idea of a world being or a world soul soon gives way to a scientific view in which the κόσμος embraces everything that exists in time and space, as distinguished from transcendent existence, which is present beyond time and space in immutability and impassibility (cf. Aristotle Cael. i.9.279a; on the further philosophical and scientific development, see Sasse 869ff.; Furley).

In the NT neither the philosophical discussion of the unity and order of the κόσμος nor the Greek cosmology play a significant role (Bultmann 68ff.). However, contacts with the developing dualistic view of the world, esp. that of Neoplatonism, can be seen (including the Neoplatonic view of the two worlds, the κόσμος ἐκεῖνος or νοητός as the true and original world, which is contrasted with the κόσμος οὗτος or αἰσθητός, the empirical world. The Greek concept of κόσμος was mediated to early Christianity by Hellenistic Judaism, as is indicated esp. in the late and originally Greek writings of the LXX (cf. Wis 7:17; 9:3; 4 Macc 16:18, etc.) and in Philo. Philo, in accordance with the Platonic tradition, is able to distinguish between a visible world and the world of ideas, and at the same time to affirm the OT idea of the creation, as he regards the divine logos, which God causes to be the "father" and "savior" of this world, the copy of the true one, as the mediator between God and the world (Spec. Leg. i.81).

Here one finds anticipated the linguistic forms that are significant also in the NT, i.e., κόσμος as the whole world created by God (created "out of formless matter," Wis 11:17, or οὐκ ἐξ ὄντων, 2 Macc 7:28; cf. Ep. Arist. 254), as the "earth" inhabited by humankind (Wis 2:24; 4 Macc 16:18), and finally as the "human world" in itself (Wis 6:24; 4 Macc 17:14). The Greek terminology that has been adopted replaces the earlier Hebrew expression "heaven and earth" (Gen 1:1), sometimes also "the totality" (Ps 8:7); however, it introduces a further development of the ideas of κόσμος, one that gives a vocabulary to wisdom-apocalyptic dualism also within the realm of the terminology of the world and creation. It also provides a language for describing the autonomy of the "world" in relation to its creator as a consequence of the sin and disobedience of humankind as well as the separation between "this" and "that (true) world" (cf. 4 Ezra 4:26ff.; 1 Enoch 48:7; Jub. 10:1ff.).

3. Except in 1 Pet 3:3 (→ 2), κόσμος normally means world in both the NT and Hellenistic Judaism; the fig. meaning totality/epitome is present in the apocalyptic phrase ὁ κόσμος τῆς ἀδικίας (in reference to the tongue) in Jas 3:6 (cf. Prov 17:6a LXX and esp. 1 Enoch 48:7: "unrighteous world"). Κόσμος thus refers to the world, understood in differing ways:

a) In the first instance, κόσμος is the totality of everything created by God, thus including all that is created and transitory. A characteristic separation between the creation itself (→ κτίζω 2, 3) and the existing world, which is alienated from God, is evident in the language in Hellenistic contexts of God as ὁ ποιήσας τὸν κόσμον (Acts 17:24), but not as "Lord and king" of the κόσμος (as, e.g., in 2 Macc 7:9; 12:15; also *Barn.* 21:5; *1 Clem.* 19:2; otherwise, however, πατήρ, κύριος τοῦ οὐρανοῦ καὶ τῆς γῆς, Matt 11:25 par. Luke 10:21; cf. also Rev 11:15). Κόσμος connotes the (immeasurable) realm of the created order (John 21:25; cf. 1 Cor 8:4: ἐν κόσμῳ, parallel to ἐν οὐρανῷ . . . ἐπὶ γῆς, v. 5), perhaps also the universe (Phil 2:15: ὡς φωστῆρες ἐν κόσμῳ; cf. also Matt 5:14; John 9:5), and the fullness of the created order, that which belongs to believers (1 Cor 3:22).

The κόσμος has a beginning that has been established by God: πρὸ (ἀπὸ) καταβολῆς (τοῦ) κόσμου (Matt 13:35 v.l.; 25:34; Luke 11:50; John 17:24; Eph 1:4; Heb 4:3; 9:26; 1 Pet 1:20; Rev 13:8; 17:8; cf. also ἀπ᾽ ἀρχῆς κόσμου: Matt 24:21 [cf. Mark 13:19: ἀπ ἀρχῆς κτίσεως]; πρὸ τοῦ τὸν κόσμον εἶναι, John 17:5; ἀπὸ κτίσεως κόσμου, Rom 1:20). Correspondingly, some texts speak of the end of the κόσμος: ὁ κόσμος παράγεται (1 John 2:17; cf. 1 Cor 7:31; also συντέλεια τοῦ αἰῶνος, Matt 13:40), as it is also the place of φθορά (2 Pet 1:4).

"This *world*" is portrayed as the place of transitoriness and sin, characterized by the absence of salvation and knowledge of God: ὁ κόσμος οὗτος (John 8:23 bis; 9:39; 12:25, 31 bis; 13:1; 14:30; 16:11; 18:36 bis; 1 Cor 3:19; 5:10; 7:31; Eph 2:2: κατὰ τὸν αἰῶνα τοῦ κόσμου τούτου; 1 John 4:17; of the people before the blood, cf. ἀρχαῖος κόσμος, 2 Pet 2:5; ὁ τότε κόσμος, 3:6). In John this κόσμος is ruled by the ἄρχων τοῦ κόσμου (τούτου) (12:31; 14:30; 16:11; see also 1 John 4:4); cf. in Paul ἄρχοντες τοῦ αἰῶνος τούτου (1 Cor 2:6, 8; cf. also Rom 8:38; 16:20; 1 Cor 5:5; 15:24, 26; 2 Cor 2:11; 4:4). Ὁ αἰὼν οὗτος is also "this world" and "this world-age" (Luke 16:8; 20:34; Rom 12:2; 1 Cor 1:20; 3:18; 2 Cor 4:4; Eph 1:21; cf. Gal 1:4), that which stands in contrast to the future world-age (Matt 12:32; Mark 10:30; Luke 18:30; 20:35; never formulated with κόσμος, totally absent in Paul).

Simple κόσμος in this sense—esp. in John—refers to the present world, which was created by God through the Logos, but which is now alienated from him (1:10 ter; 3:16f.; 7:7; 13:1; 14:17; 15:18, 19 [5 occurrences]; 16:33; 17:25; cf. also Matt 18:7; Rom 3:6; 5:12f.; 1 Cor 1:20a, 21; 2:12 [τὸ πνεῦμα τοῦ κόσμου]; 2 Cor 5:19; 7:10; Gal 4:3 [τὰ στοιχεῖα τοῦ κόσμου, cf. Col 2:8, 20]; 6:14 bis; Jas 1:27; 2:5; 4:4; 1 John 2:15-17 [6 occurrences]; 3:17; 5:19, etc.). Here the various aspects of the world as the totality of creation and as globe and "human world" are closely related (→ b), even if κόσμος and the human world cannot be identified as a matter of course (cf. Bultmann, *Theology* I, 254ff.). The judgment of the world is the task of God or Christ (John 9:39; 12:31; 16:8, 11;

Rom 3:6, 19; 1 Cor 11:32; see also 6:2a [οἱ ἅγιοι τὸν κόσμον κρινοῦσιν], 2b), and the final βασιλεία τοῦ κόσμου will belong to God and to his Christ (Rev 11:15).

The NT does not have direct interest in a cosmological doctrine. Indeed, the different perspectives on the origin and structure of the κόσμος cannot be reduced to a common view. Cosmological speculations of Gnosticism are argued against, esp. in the later early Christian writings (cf. 1 Tim 1:4; 4:7; 2 Pet 1:16ff., etc.).

b) In a number of passages κόσμος has the special meaning of *world* as the dwelling place of humankind and as the totality of humanity or of human interrelationships. In Luke 4:5 πάσας τὰς βασιλείας τοῦ κόσμου (Matt 4:8) can be equated with the gen. τῆς οἰκουμένης; similarly the focus on the "world mission" in Mark 14:9 (εἰς ὅλον τὸν κόσμον) par. Matt 26:13 (ἐν ὅλῳ τῷ κόσμῳ) and on the "great commission" in Mark 16:14 (εἰς τὸν κόσμον ἅπαντα, with πάσῃ τῇ κτίσει); cf. also Matt 5:14; 13:38; Luke 12:30 (τὰ ἔθνη τοῦ κόσμου; cf. Matt 6:32: τὰ ἔθνη); Rom 1:8; 3:19; 4:13 (cf. Gen 18:18; 22:17f.); 1 Cor 4:13; 2 Cor 1:12; Col 1:6; 1 Tim 3:16; 1 Pet 5:9; 2 Pet 3:6; 1 John 2:2 (περὶ ὅλου τοῦ κόσμου); 3:1, 13, with special reference to the Gentiles (in contrast to the Jews), Rom 11:12, 15; esp. apparent in John: 1:10, 29 (ἁμαρτία τοῦ κόσμου); 6:33, 51; 12:19; 14:17, 19; 16:20; 17:21, etc. In a similar way, reference is made to earthly possessions and values and to the joy and suffering of the world (Mark 8:36 par. Matt 16:26/Luke 9:25 [with κερδαίνω τὸν κόσμον ὅλον]; cf. 1 Cor 1:20f., 27 bis, 28; 7:31 [χρώμενοι τὸν κόσμον], 33f. [τὰ τοῦ κόσμου]; Jas 4:4; 1 John 2:15f.; 4:5.

In his salvific acts God stands opposite the world; his emissary or his gifts come "into the *world*" ([εἰσ]έρχομαι / ἀποστέλλω εἰς τὸν κόσμον, etc.), i.e., the light (John 1:9; 3:19; 12:46), the Son (3:17a; 9:39; 10:36; 11:27; 16:28; 17:18a; 18:37), the prophet (6:14), Jesus (1 Tim 1:15), the Christ (Heb 10:5). But sin and death also came "into the world" (Rom 5:12f.; cf. Wis 2:24), as did false prophets (1 John 4:1; cf. v. 3), and the tempter (2 John 7). The Christ who departs from the world (John 13:1a; 16:28b; 17:11a) leaves behind those who are his (13:16; 17:11b; cf. 1 Cor 5:10b; 1 John 4:17), where they conduct their lives in constant conflict with the nature of the κόσμος (2 Cor 1:12; Jas 1:27; 4:4 bis; 2 Pet 1:4; 1 John 2:17; 5:4 bis).

A developed theological view of the κόσμος is to be seen esp. in the Pauline and Johannine traditions, where κόσμος is the (human) world, which has fallen into conflict with God, and for which God has acted to bring redemption and reconciliation.

4. Where Paul uses κόσμος in theological statements, the word refers to the world of humankind. Πᾶς ὁ κόσμος (Rom 3:19) refers to the same thing as πᾶσα σάρξ (v. 20), i.e., all of humankind in its lost condition before God.

Σοφία τοῦ κόσμου (1 Cor 1:20) is identical with wisdom κατὰ σάρκα (v. 26). Here κόσμος designates "the sphere of all that humans think, plan, and desire" (Bultmann, "Verständnis" 68). The sin of the individual has affected the condition of the κόσμος (Rom 5:12; cf. 8:19-22), but humanity does not have power over sin, but, as κόσμος, is ruled by it and brought thereby into full opposition to God (1 Cor 1:20f., 27f.; 3:19; 2 Cor 7:10; Gal 4:3). The κόσμος cannot perceive this opposition in and of itself. It is subject to futility and transience and finally to the judgment of God (1 Cor 7:31; Rom 3:6; 1 Cor 11:32), just as the ἄρχοντες τοῦ αἰῶνος τούτου made themselves the judge of Christ (1 Cor 2:6, 8).

The reconciliation of the κόσμος was initiated by God himself (Rom 11:15, cf. v. 12; 2 Cor 5:19: θεὸς ἦν ἐν Χριστῷ κόσμον καταλλάσσων ἑαυτῷ). Believers remain in the κόσμος (1 Cor 5:10), but live there as those who no longer are the κόσμος (2 Cor 1:12; Gal 4:3), who no longer must use the κόσμος as κόσμος (1 Cor 7:31), and who in freedom have the κόσμος at their disposal (1 Cor 3:22; cf. Col 2:20). Therefore they do not, as it might be assumed, have their life by means of a new and changed κόσμος, but rather as a renewed creation (καινὴ κτίσις, 2 Cor 5:17; Gal 6:15). Through the cross of Christ they have become alienated from this κόσμος and hence from the old carnal existence (Gal 6:14). Indeed, they are despised by the κόσμος (cf. 1 Cor 3:19; 4:9, 13), but nevertheless stand above it and will be its future judge (6:2); now they are the light illuminating the world's night (Phil 2:15).

Colossians goes beyond Paul's statements, probably in defense against gnosticizing speculations, when it regards the victory of Christ over the ἀρχαὶ καὶ ἐξουσίαι as an indication that life ἐν κόσμῳ is finished insofar as it involves any kind of subjection to the elements of the universe (2:8, 20; cf. Jas 1:27: ἄσπιλον ἑαυτὸν τηρεῖν ἀπὸ τοῦ κόσμου).

In Paul's understanding of the κόσμος, therefore, one finds a critical relationship with the world as both creation and hostile realm, a critical distancing of believers, and the possibility of a "cosmic-sarkic" existence, in which believers find their essential nature in the καινὴ κτίσις. The decisive fact is not that they are strangers in the world, but that the world is reconciled; that this reconciliation has already occurred through God is apparent in the disclosure and eschatological recovery of its essential nature as a creation of God.

5. In the Johannine theology one finds again the basic elements of the Pauline understanding of κόσμος in the extreme and intensified radicality of the estrangement and ungodliness of the κόσμος, which has been created by the Logos, and of the love of God for the κόσμος (cf. Bultmann, *Theology* II, 15ff.). In the term κόσμος (on the statistical evidence see esp. Cassem), there is both the totality of all that is created (→ 3.a) and the particular aspect of humankind as it represents the created order in its separation from God, without the two being distinguished from each other. The relationship of God to the κόσμος corresponds to the relationship of light to darkness; the created order does not recognize the creator, the darkness refuses the light (John 1:5, 9f.) and the truth (cf. 17:17; 18:37).

Thus redemption is portrayed as a dramatic event in which the love of the creator is fulfilled in the sending of the Son into the κόσμος (3:16f.; 10:36; 11:27; 12:46f.; 18:37; 1 John 4:9, 14). The one who "is not from this world" (John 8:21-23; cf. 18:36) comes as "the light" (1:9; 3:19; 8:12; 9:5; 12:46) and as "the savior" (4:42; 1 John 4:14) into the world in order to bring true life (John 6:33, 51) and to bear the sin of the κόσμος (1:29; 1 John 2:2); he finds there those who are in the κόσμος (John 17:6), but are not determined by the κόσμος (15:19; 17:14, 16), and who thus have to bear the hatred of the world (15:18f.; 17:14; 1 John 3:13; cf. 3:1; John 16:33), just as the Son himself has had to bear it (on hatred from the Jews, see 5:17f.; 8:37-47; 10:31, etc.); the Son demonstrates to his own the true love of the Father (13:1; 17:21-24) and with his departure from the κόσμος he leaves them in the κόσμος (17:11, 15; 1 John 4:17) as the fellowship of the Spirit (14:17) and of the love command (13:34f.; 15:9ff.). Indeed, he sends them into the κόσμος, just as the Father has sent him (17:18ff.).

The coming of the Son for the salvation of the κόσμος (John 3:17; 12:47) becomes judgment for the one who refuses salvation (3:19; 12:31: νῦν ὁ ἄρχων τοῦ κόσμου τούτου ἐκβληθήσεται ἔξω; 16:18ff.). Believers are, however, the representatives of the revelation of the Son and of the love of God for the κόσμος (17:21, 23) in the midst of the κόσμος. Thus the κόσμος itself is not rejected, but is overcome (16:33; 1 John 5:4f.). Believers can no longer love the κόσμος (1 John 2:15-17), for they have the one who is greater than the κόσμος (4:4).

In the statements regarding the κόσμος in Johannine theology the concern is with the nature of the world that has fallen away from God and is ruled by the evil one (apocalyptic phrases such as αἰὼν οὗτος or μέλλων/ἐρχόμενος do not appear). Apocalyptic dualism is esp. visible in regard to christology: The mystery of humankind's, esp. the Jews', refusal to accept the sending and the message of the Son is to be explained by the fact that humankind does not itself have the capacity to grasp life and truth. Those who reject the λόγος τῆς ζωῆς (1 John 1:1) demonstrate that they are determined by the κόσμος. Only through hearing, perception, and faith can people be freed from this power of the κόσμος. Correspondingly, the saving way of the Son has cosmic dimensions: The powers of the κόσμος are overcome permanently in the Spirit, in faith, and in brotherly love, and the darkness is illuminated by the true light of God. With this understanding, Johannine theology proceeds increasingly in the direction of early Christian and heretical Gnosticism, which the readers must, however (esp. in 1 John), resist (see J. Becker, *John* [ÖTK] I, 51-55, 147-51 [bibliography]).

H. Balz

Κούαρτος, ου *Kouartos* Quartus*

A Christian (ὁ ἀδελφός) mentioned in Rom 16:23 as one who sends greetings.

κουμ *koum* stand up (imv.)*

Mark 5:41 in the imv. ταλιθα κουμ, where the tr. is given: "Girl, I say to you, *stand up.*" Against A D (κουμι) the form in ℵ B C (κουμ) is to be preferred. Κουμ is the transliteration of the Mesopotamian form of the imv. *qum* (*qumi* is the corresponding form in Palestinian Aramaic). H. P. Rüger, *TRE* III, 609.

κουστωδία, ας, ἡ *koustōdia* guard*

This Latin loanword (*custodia*) appears in Matt 27:65 (ἔχω κουστωδίαν, "have a *guard*"), 66; 28:11 in reference to the guards at the tomb of Jesus. W. L. Craig, "The Guard at the Tomb," *NTS* 30 (1984) 273-81.

κουφίζω *kouphizō* lighten*

Acts 27:38: κουφίζω τὸ πλοῖον, "*lighten* the ship" by throwing cargo overboard; cf. Jonah 1:5 LXX; Polybius ii.5.11).

κόφινος, ου, ὁ *kophinos* basket*

Mark 6:43 par. Matt 14:20/Luke 9:17/John 6:13: a basket for carrying things ("twelve *baskets*"); Mark 8:19 par. Matt 16:9: πόσους κοφίνους; Luke 13:8 D: κόφινος κοπρίων, "a *basket* of manure."

κράβαττος, ου, ὁ *krabbatos* bed, pallet*

The origin of this loanword (found also in rabbinic literature) is uncertain. The form varies (κράββατος, κράβατος, κράβακτος; cf. BDF §42.4). In the NT κράβαττος appears only in Mark, John, and Acts. Mark 2:4; 6:55: a bed for a small man or a means of transport for the sick; Mark 2:9, 11, 12 and John 5:8, 9, 10, 11: αἶρω τὸν κράβαττον; Acts 5:15: κράβαττος with κλινάριον; 9:33: man who was lame for eight years "and was bedridden (ἐπὶ κραβάττου)."

κράζω *krazō* cry, call, call out

1. Occurrences in the NT — 2. Meaning — 3. The "cry" of Rom 8:15; Gal 4:6

Lit.: D. A. CARSON, *DNTT* I, 408-10. — W. GRUNDMANN, *TDNT* III, 898-903. — P. VON DER OSTEN-SACKEN, *Römer 8 als Beispiel paulinischer Soteriologie* (1975) 129-31. — C. RO-MANIUK, "Spiritus clamans," *VD* 40 (1962) 190-98. — H. SCHLIER, *Gal* (KEK, [5]1971) 198f. — For further bibliography see *TWNT* X, 1148.

1. Κράζω appears 56 times in the NT, most often in Matthew (12 occurrences), Acts and Revelation (11 occurrences each), and Mark (10 occurrences). Luke and John have 4 occurrences each, while Paul has 3 (Rom 8:15; 9:27; Gal 4:6) and James one (5:4).

2. The vb. is often found in a pleonastic combination with [ἐν] φωνῇ μεγάλῃ (Matt 27:50; Mark 5:7; Acts 7:57, 60; Rev 10:3, etc.) and occasionally designates an unintelligible *crying*: Jesus' cry at death (Matt 27:50; cf. Mark 15:39 v.l.), the disciples' cry of fear (Matt 14:26), the cry of a demon-possessed man (Mark 5:5; 9:26; Luke 9:39), the cries of one giving birth (Rev 12:2), the cry of an angel announcing the judgment (Rev 10:3; cf. Amos 1:2; Joel 4:16), and the cry of hate by the people against Stephen (Acts 7:57). Jesus speaks in a fig. sense in Luke 19:40 of the stones *crying out* should the disciples be hindered from giving a witness of his kingdom (see v. 38). According to Jas 5:4 wages withheld from workers *cries out* (to heaven, cf. Gen 4:10).

Elsewhere κράζω introduces discourse. In the Synoptics it is the special nature of the person of Jesus that is most often indicated: The demons who cry out recognize him as the Son of God (Mark 5:7 par. Matt 8:29, cf. par. Luke; Mark 3:11 par. Luke 4:41); blind men call to him for help as son of David (Mark 10:47 par. Matt 20:30, cf. par. Luke; Mark 10:48 par. Matt 20:31/Luke 18:39; Matt 9:27), as does the Canaanite woman (Matt 15:22). Also among the witnesses to Jesus are those who give the acclamatory cry of jubilation in Jerusalem (Mark 11:9 par. Matt 21:9; cf. par. Luke; cf., however, John 12:13 v.l. and Matt 21:15 [M]). Κράζω is also used of the fanatical *cry* of the crowd (Mark 15:13, 14 par. Matt 27:23; Acts 19:28, 32, 34; 21:28, 36) and of a loud *shout* to gain the attention of a crowd (Acts 14:14; 23:6; 24:21).

In contrast to the Synoptics, in John the vb. introduces Jesus' testimony to himself (John 7:28, 37; 12:44) or a word of the Baptist about Jesus (1:15). This *cry* is to be understood as a prophetic-authoritative proclamation (cf. 7:40f.). Κράζω appears as a t.t. for prophetic speech elsewhere in the NT only in Rom 9:27 (cf. Josephus *Ant.* x.117).

3. Rom 8:15 and Gal 4:6 both say that the Spirit of sonship (of the son) brings believers to *cry* "Abba, Father" (→ ἀββά). Paul apparently alludes to a worship situation (E. Käsemann, *Rom* [Eng. tr., 1980] 227). The Church's cry of Abba is inspired (cf. the rabbinic parallels to the cry of the Spirit [Romaniuk 193-96], which con-

sistently introduce citations of Scripture, i.e., inspired texts). The Spirit makes possible the relationship of sonship and at the same time attests it by impelling the faithful toward confession. Even though the cry is initiated by the Spirit, it is not to be understood as a reference to glossolalia (F. Mussner, *Gal* [HTKNT] 275) or to an ecstatic cry (O. Kuss, *Rom* 550f., 603f.). Similarly, a cry comparable to the uncontrolled cry of the demons (so von der Osten-Sacken 130) is scarcely in view. There is no reason to believe that human self-awareness is lost (Grundmann 903). For comparison one may note the passages where κράζω has a public-proclamatory (Schlier) or acclamatory character (→ 2).   H. Fendrich

κραιπάλη, ης, ἡ *kraipalē* intoxication, dizziness, staggering*

Luke 21:34: ἐν κραιπάλῃ καὶ μέθῃ, "with *dissipation and drunkenness.*"

κρανίον, ου, τό *kranion* skull
→ Γολγοθᾶ.

κράσπεδον, ου, τό *kraspedon* hem, border, tassel*

Mark 6:56 par. Matt 14:36; Matt 9:20 par. Luke 8:44 (cf. par. Mark): the *hem* of Jesus' garment; Matt 23:5: the *tassels* on the garments of the Pharisees (cf. Billerbeck IV, 276-92). J. Schneider, *TDNT* III, 904; M. Hutter, "Ein altorientalischer Bittgestus in Mt 9,20-22," *ZNW* 75 (1984) 133-35.

κραταιόομαι *krataioomai* become strong, strengthen*

Pass. of κραταιόω: Luke 1:80; 2:40, with αὐξάνω, of the child Jesus (τὸ παιδίον); 1:80, with dat. of relation πνεύματι; Eph 3:16, with dat. δυνάμει; 1 Cor 16:13: στήκετε . . . , ἀνδρίζεσθε, κραταιοῦσθε, "stand fast . . . , be courageous, *be strong.*" W. Michaelis, *TDNT* III, 912f.

κραταιός, 3 *krataios* strong, powerful*

1 Pet 5:6: the "*strong* hand of God," which exalts the humble. W. Michaelis, *TDNT* III, 912.

κρατέω *krateō* seize, grasp, take hold of; hold fast, keep*

1. Occurrences and meaning in the NT — 2. With gen. — 3. With acc.

Lit.: BAGD s.v. — G. BORNKAMM, "Das Bekenntnis im Hebräerbrief," idem, *Aufsätze* II, 188-213. — E. GRÄSSER, *Der Glaube im Hebräerbrief* (1965) 32. — W. MICHAELIS, *TDNT* III, 910-12.

1. Κρατέω appears 47 times in the NT. It is used both

literally and fig. of the act of *grasping* or what follows, the act of *holding firm.*

2. Κρατέω with the gen. consistently expresses an act done without violence. Jesus *grasps* the hand of a person while healing (only in Mark 1:31; 9:27) or raising the person from the dead (Mark 5:41 par. Matt 9:25/Luke 8:45). The travelers at sea in Acts 27:13 hope to be able to *carry out* their plan (κρατέω τῆς προθέσεως). The author of Hebrews exhorts the troubled church to *grasp* the baptismal confession (4:14; Bornkamm) or the hope that lies before them (6:18; less probable—as in *Herm. Vis.* iii.8.8—"hold firm"; against Grässer 32, see esp. the dynamic quality in καταφυγόντες . . . , 6:18 as well as κατέχειν, 3:6, 14; 10:23 on the designation of "holding fast").

3. a) Κρατέω with the acc. designates a more or less *forcible seizing:* The family of Jesus seek to *take him in custody* (Mark 3:21). Herod has John the Baptist *arrested* (Mark 6:17 par. Matt 14:3; with reference to Jesus: Mark 12:12 par. Matt 21:46; Mark 14:1, 44, 46, 49 par. Matt 26:4, 48, 50, 55; Matt 26:57; with reference to Paul: Acts 24:6). The unmerciful servant *seizes* his fellow servant (Matt 18:28); the guests who refused the invitation *seize* the servants of the king (22:6); the guards *seize* the young man who is fleeing (Mark 14:51); the lamb seizes the dragon (Rev 20:2). The women *cling to* (Matt 28:9) the feet of the resurrected one; the owner *seizes* the sheep (12:11) who has fallen into the ditch (12:11)—even here the idea of "force" is present: The action takes place in each case independently of the one who is affected.

b) Κρατέω with the acc. has the sense of *hold, hold firm* with various nuances: The resurrected one *holds firm* the seven stars in his hand as a sign of the preservation of his churches (Rev 2:1); the lame man who was healed *holds* Peter and John (Acts 3:11); the four angels *hold back* the four winds (Rev 7:1). Similarly, the pass. is used in the statement that the eyes of the Emmaus disciples were *kept,* as if *confined* (Luke 24:16; similarly Acts 2:24). Just as the departure of the apostles or the rushing of the winds is hindered, so here recognition of the resurrected is kept from these two disciples at the beginning of their encounter with him. Jesus grants to the disciples the authority to *retain* sins (John 20:23; Michaelis 912). The four witnesses at the transfiguration *keep* what is said by the heavenly voice among themselves, as they seek to understand it (Mark 9:10).

This phrase in Mark 9:10 leads to a larger, relatively homogeneous group of texts. With the expression "*keep* the traditions of the fathers" (cf. also 7:4, 8) Mark 7:3 describes the Pharisees' fidelity to the oral tradition. Similar usage is to be seen in 2 Thess 2:15, where Christians are challenged to "*hold fast* the traditions." The description of the heretic in Col 2:19 as one "who does not *hold firm* to the head" suggests such christological traditions as one finds in 1:15-20. Such traditions determine the relationship between the true and the untrue to the "head" (cf. also 2:8, 18). A final context for this use of κρατέω is to be found in the letters to the churches in Revelation. The attestation of the church in Pergamum (2:13) that it *holds firm* to the name of Jesus and the admonitions to the churches of Thyatira (2:25) and Philadelphia (3:11) to *hold fast* to their possession are, as the respective contexts indicate (cf. 2:13, 24; 3:8), given in reference to the christological confessions and doctrinal traditions that have been preserved (verified, confessed) in the churches. The corresponding designation of the heretics in 2:14f. as those who *hold firm* the doctrine of Balaam or of the Nicolaitans is thus to be understood as an allusion to the orientation to other traditions.

Common to these uses in Mark, 2 Thessalonians, Colossians, and Revelation of κρατέω with a term for tradition in the acc. (cf. similarly κατέχειν with acc. in Luke 8:15; 1 Cor 11:2; 15:2; Heb 3:6, 14; 10:23) is that they appear in polemical contexts. This usage goes back to the postexilic period with its religio-political debates (cf. the hiphil of *ḥāzaq* in Isa 56:2, 4, 6; 1QS 5:1, 3, etc.). It appears esp. theologically significant that the NT admonishes the very thing that Mark 7 passionately criticizes: the κρατεῖν of the traditions (the new "ancients").

                                P. von der Osten-Sacken

κράτιστος, 3 *kratistos* most revered, most excellent*

Lit.: BAGD s.v. — BDF §§5.3a; 60.2; 146.1a. — G. KLEIN, "Lukas 1,1-4 als theologisches Programm," *idem, Rekonstruktion und Interpretation* (BEvT 50, 1969) 237-61, esp. 255-57. — O. SEECK, PW V, 2006f. — A. VÖGTLE, "Was hatte die Widmung des lukanischen Doppelwerkes an Theophilus zu bedeuten?" *idem, Das Evangelium und die Evangelien* (1971) 31-42.

1. Κράτιστος is the superlative of κρατύς and is used as the official rendering of the title *vir egregius* and an honorific address to persons of high official position. Josephus *Ant.* xx.12 uses it of Vitellius, the governor of Syria. Felix, the governor of Judea, is addressed in Acts 23:26 with this title in the prescript of a letter, and in 24:3 at the beginning of a judicial proceeding involving Paul. In 26:25 Paul addresses the governor Festus in this way. The composition of the scenes and the style are both Lukan.

2. Κράτιστος can also be a polite address with no official character. As such κράτιστος appears in dedications of literary works, e.g., Josephus *Ap.* i.1; *Diog.* 1:1; Galenus 10.78. Luke uses the expression of Theophilus, to whom he dedicates his Gospel in Luke 1:3 and to whom Acts was later dedicated. The literary form of the

proemium, which seeks to satisfy certain paedagogic expectations, and the address κράτιστε lead to the assumption that the person to whom the work was addressed was a person of high position.

                                            A. Weiser

κράτος, ους, τό *kratos* power (of a ruler), authority, dominion*

1. Occurrences and usage in the NT — 2. The *power* of God — 3. Acts 19:20; Heb 2:14

Lit.: BAGD s.v. — W. GRUNDMANN, *Der Begriff der Kraft in der neutestamentlichen Gedankenwelt* (1932) (older bibliography). — W. MICHAELIS, *TDNT* III, 905-10. — E. PERCY, *Die Probleme der Kolosser- und Epheserbriefe* (1946) 195f. — E. PETERSON, *ΕΙΣ ΘΕΟΣ* (1926) 168f.— P. WINTER, "Some Observations on the Language in the Birth and Infancy Stories of the Third Gospel," *NTS* 1 (1954/55) 111-21. — For further bibliography see *TWNT* X, 1148.

1. Κράτος appears 12 times in the NT, predominantly in liturgically influenced passages in the later epistolary literature. Half of the occurrences are in doxologies, and three others are in prayers or hymns. While the frequency of the statements about God's power, might, and strength in prayers and hymns reflects the biblical-Jewish tradition (cf. Grundmann 109n.2; Percy; E. Lohse, *Col* [Hermeneia] on 1:11), the influence of the Roman ruler cult may be present in the doxologies (cf. Peterson; *contra* Michaelis 905). In accordance with this primary usage of the word the NT never speaks of the κράτος of persons (cf. Michaelis 907). In relation to the other terms for power, κράτος refers to "effective, superior power" (H. Schlier, *Eph* [1957] on 1:19). Special emphasis is given to the power of God as that of a powerful, if not warlike, ruler. One may even speak of a consistently militant aspect possessed by the term.

2. a) According to the Magnificat, God *shows* his *might* with his arm (cf. Pss 117:16; 88:11 LXX; cf. Winter 116; also 1QM 6:6; 11:5, etc.), while he scatters the proud (like or even as enemies in a struggle, Luke 1:51). In the request for strength in Col 1:11 (in the struggle of faith, cf. v. 29) κράτος might refer to the battle mentioned in v. 13. Similarly, according to the request of Eph 1:19, it is "the working of his (God's) great *might*," which Jesus Christ caused to be victorious over all other powers. In this sense Eph 6:10 does not admonish "in a very general sense" (J. Gnilka, *Eph* [HTKNT] ad loc.), but specifically and deliberately places the instruction to be strong in the "strong *might* (power for battle)" of the Lord (cf. 1QM 10:5; 1QH 7:17, 19; 12:35) before the advice to put on the armor for battle.

b) In the doxology in 1 Tim 6:16 the reference to αἰώνιον κράτος ("eternal *might*") alongside τιμή takes up the preceding predication of God as the immortal "Ruler, King of kings, and Lord of lords." In the doxologies to

Christ in 1 Pet 4:11; Rev 1:6; 5:13 and the doxologies to God in 1 Pet 5:1; Rev 5:13 the use of κράτος with δόξα (and other terms in Rev 5:13) is to be explained from the persecution facing the churches. In the praise of the sovereign power of God these predications express the certainty of the divine victory over the powers that now confront the churches. The motifs of the struggle of faith (Jude 3) and of judgment (vv. 5ff.) could account for the use of κράτος (power) along with ἐξουσία, etc., in the doxology to God in Jude 25. On κράτος in doxologies see also *1 Clem.* 64; 65:2; *Mart. Pol.* 20:2.

3. Contrary to the common view (BAGD; E. Haenchen, *Acts* [Eng. tr., 1971] ad loc.; H. Conzelmann, *Acts* [Hermeneia] ad loc.), Acts 19:20 is not an example of absolute use of κατὰ κράτος = "mightily." It belongs instead with what follows, τοῦ κυρίου, which therefore is not to be understood as a gen. modifying ὁ λόγος. In the first place the absence of the art. after κατά has an analogy in, e.g., Acts 22:3; in the second place ὁ λόγος never (!) appears as a *nomen regens* in Acts after its modifier; in the third place the summary statement that the word grew "according to" or "through the *power* of the Lord" has the best sense after the report about Paul's mighty deeds (19:11, 12ff.).

Heb 2:14 takes up a fixed expression with κράτος ἔχειν τινός ("have *power* over [something]"). With the atoning death of Jesus Christ the devil, the one who brings death by sin, is, as the ruler over death, overcome (cf. 1 Cor 15:24ff.; there also explicitly the motif of battle).

                    P. von der Osten-Sacken

κραυγάζω *kraugazō* cry out, bellow, howl (vb.)*

Of people in the sense of *scream, howl* in Matt 12:19; Acts 22:23. In the same sense, yet followed by direct speech in John 19:15, thus with λέγοντες in John 18:40; 19:6, 12. Luke 4:41 A D E W al of demons being driven out (in place of κράζω as in B ℵ C al). Loud calling in John 11:43 (Jesus' calling) and 12:13 (the cry of Hosanna from the crowd). W. Grundmann, *TDNT* III, 898-903.

κραυγή, ῆς, ἡ *kraugē* loud cry, shouting*

Of loud *shouting* or *clamor* in Acts 23:9; Eph 4:31; a cry of fear in Rev 21:4. A clearly articulated shout is meant in Matt 25:6; Luke 1:42; Heb 5:7. W. Grundmann, *TDNT* III, 898-903.

κρέας, κρέως (κρέατος), τό *kreas* meat*

Besides gen. κρέως there is the (later) form κρέατος. In the NT κρέας appears only in φάγω κρέα ("eat *meat*") in Rom 14:21; 1 Cor 8:13 (cf. *T. Jud.* 15:4). H. Seebass, *DNTT* I, 671-78.

κρείσσων/κρείττων, 2 *kreissōn/kreittōn* more prominent, more advantageous; adv.: better*

The precise form varies in the tradition (σσ or ττ; see BDF §34.1). Κρείσσων is used in the NT as the comparative of ἀγαθός. It describes the excellent qualities of persons (Heb 1:4; 7:7) and things (7:19, 22; 8:6 bis; 9:23; 10:34; 11:16, 35). 1 Cor 11:31a TR, of the *higher* things. Heb 11:40: κρεῖττόν τι, "something *greater*." The sense *more advantageous* is present in 1 Cor 7:9; 11:17 (εἰς τὸ κρεῖσσον συνέρχομαι); Phil 1:23; Heb 6:9; 1 Pet 3:17; 2 Pet 2:21. Only in 1 Cor 7:38 (κρεῖσσον ποιήσει) and Heb 12:24 (κρεῖττον λαλοῦντι) is κρείσσων/κρείττων used as an adv.

κρεμάννυμι *kremannymi* hang*

1. Occurrences in early Christian literature — 2. With reference to crucifixion — 3. Other literal usage — 4. Fig. usage

Lit.: BAGD s.v. — J. M. BAUMGARTEN, "Does *tlh* in the Temple Scroll Refer to Crucifixion?" *idem, Studies in Qumran Law* (1977) 172-82. — K. BERGER, *Die Gesetzesauslegung Jesu* I (1972) 56-257, esp. 227-32. — G. BERTRAM, *TDNT* III, 915-21. — BILLERBECK I, 775-78, 907f. — C. BURCHARD, "Das doppelte Liebesgebot in der frühen christlichen Überlieferung," FS Jeremias (1970) 39-62, esp. 55-57, 60f. — J. A. FITZMYER, "Crucifixion in Ancient Palestine, Qumran Literature, and the NT," *CBQ* 40 (1978) 493-513, esp. 498ff. — A. J. HULTGREN, "The Double Commandment of Love in Mt 22:34-40. Its Sources and Composition," *CBQ* 36 (1974) 373-78. — H.-W. KUHN, "Jesus als Gekreuzigter in der frühchristlichen Verkündigung bis zur Mitte des 2. Jahrhunderts," *ZTK* 72 (1975) 1-46, esp. 20, 33-36. — A. NISSEN, *Gott und der Nächste im antiken Judentum. Untersuchungen zum Doppelgebot der Liebe* (1974), esp. 498-502.

1. This vb. appears 7 times in the NT, 4 times in Luke-Acts, twice in Matthew, and once in Paul. In other early Christian literature (according to the delineation of BAGD vii) κρεμάννυμι is found 3 times (*Herm. Sim.* 2:3f.; *Apoc. Pet.* 7:22). The compound ἐκκρεμάννυμι ("hang on") appears in Luke 19:48; *1 Clem.* 12:7. In 4 instances, all in the NT, the simple form refers to the punishment of crucifixion.

2. The vb. is used in a citation of Deut 21:23 in Gal 3:13 for the execution of Jesus: While in the OT *tālâ ʿal/* κρεμάννυμι ἐπί refers to hanging the body of a person after execution, Paul applies the passage (as already in 4QpNah frags. 3-4 1:7f. and undoubtedly [*contra* Baumgarten] the Temple Scroll [11QT] 64:6-13; also the application of Deut 21:22 v.l. to the crucifixion of Jesus in Justin *Dial.* 89f.) to the punishment of crucifixion. In addition κρεμάσαντες ἐπὶ ξύλου in Acts 5:30 and 10:39 suggests an allusion to Deut 21:22f. Luke also uses κρεμάννυμι in the Gospel for the execution of the two

crucified with Jesus (21:39 cf. par. Mark/Matthew; cf. Luke 23:33, where σταυρόω is used instead). In addition, in non-Christian literature of the time κρεμάννυμι could have the simple meaning "crucify" as execution (e.g., Plutarch *Caes.* 2.2 [cf. 2.4, where ἀνασταυρόω is used in place of κρεμάννυμι]). → ξύλον 3.a.

3. The literal sense appears twice in the NT: as trans. with περί and acc. ("around") in Matt 18:6, "that a millstone *be hung* around his neck" (cf. par. Mark/Luke), and as intrans. with ἐκ ("on") in Acts 28:4, of a snake that had bitten Paul on the hand.

4. The vb. is used fig. in the sense of *be dependent* in Matt 22:40 (cf. par. Mark/Luke) of "the entire law and the prophets," which *hangs* "in (ἐν)" the double commandment of love (also par. Mark/Luke; from Deut 6:45 and Lev 19:18), which comprises the "embodiment" (so, e.g., also Burchard 57) of the divine will (cf. Matt 22:38). The closest linguistic parallels are are in *b. Ber.* 63a (also related in subject matter); *Sifre Deut.* 41 on 11:13; cf. also *m. Ḥag.* 1:8 (*tālâ* with *bᵉ*). The background for laying out a twofold love command, however, lies in Hellenistic Judaism: A distant parallel to κρεμάννυμι is seen in Philo *Spec. Leg.* ii.63: piety and love for people are the two fundamental teachings (δύο τὰ ἀνωτάτω κεφάλεια; on the special character of the content cf. Nissen 500f.). In the NT one finds pertinent parallels in content in Gal 5:14 (→ πληρόω) and Rom 13:8-10 (→ πληρόω; → ἀνακεφαλαιόω 2; → πλήρωμα); cf. Jas 2:8 (→ βασιλεύς 6)—but all three are only of love for the neighbor. See also, in addition to the par. in Mark 12:31, Matt 7:12 and 23:23. → ἀγάπη (3.a; bibliography).

H.-W. Kuhn

κρημνός, οῦ, ὁ   *krēmnos*   steep incline, slope*

Mark 5:13 par. Matt 8:32/Luke 8:33: κατὰ τοῦ κρημνοῦ, "down the *steep incline*" (of the fall of the herd of pigs into the sea).

Κρής, ητός, ὁ   *Krēs*   Cretan (noun)*

An inhabitant of the island of Crete. In the NT only pl. Κρῆτες appears: Acts 2:11: "*Cretans* and Arabians" (see O. Eissfeldt, *TLZ* 72 [1947] 207-12; B. M. Metzger, FS Bruce 123-33); Titus 1:12, in a negative characterization: "*Cretans* are always liars . . ." (following Epimenides; see N. Brox, *Die Pastoralbriefe* [RNT] ad loc.).

Κρήσκης, εντος   *Krēskēs*   Crescens*

Greek form of the Latin name *Crescens*. Crescens was, according to 2 Tim 4:10, a companion of Paul.

Κρήτη, ης   *Krētē*   Crete*

The name of the largest Greek island appears in Acts 27:7, 12, 13, 21 in the narrative of Paul's sea journey (the Cretan cities of Fair Havens and Lasea [v. 8] and Phoenix

[v. 12] are mentioned) and in Titus 1:5 (Paul left Titus on Crete). E. Kirsten, *Antike* 14 (1938) 295-346; K. Prümm and F. Dölger, *LTK* VI, 602-4; A. Heubeck, *LAW* 1614-16; *BL* 989f.; *KP* III, 338-42; N. Platon, *Kreta* (²1978).

κριθή, ῆς, ἡ   *krithē*   barley*

Rev 6:6: "three measures of *barley*"; cf. Dalman, *Arbeit* II, 251-56; III, 300-302.

κρίθινος, 3   *krithinos*   made from barley flour*

John 6:9, 13: "five *barley* loaves" (at the feeding miracle). Cf. → κριθή.

κρίμα, ατος, τό   *krima*   judgment*

1. Occurrences and meaning — 2. The Gospels and Acts — 3. Paul — 4. Other NT writings

Lit.: → κρίνω.

1. Κρίμα appears 27 times in the NT, of which 10 occurrences are in the Pauline letters. It commonly denotes the result of an action: the judge's *verdict*. However, it can also take on the meanings of κρίσις: the action of *judging, dividing,* or *accusing*. It is used once in the OT sense of *dominion* (Rev 20:4), once (pl.) in the sense of *legal dispute* (1 Cor 6:7), and once in the sense of God's *acts of judgment* in history (Rom 11:33).

2. Κρίμα appears in Mark only once. Jesus' warnings against the scribes threaten them, on the basis of their misconduct in their social obligations, with "a greater *condemnation*" (Mark 12:40 par. Luke 20:47; cf. the addition in a few mss. in Matt 23:14).

Jesus' statement on *judging* (Q: Matt 7:1 par. Luke 6:37) is based on the concise statement that "with what *judgment* you judge, you will also be judged." The measure (cf. μέτρον, 7:2) of God's eschatological judgment is our judgment upon our fellow human being.

In the Lukan writings κρίμα is normally the outcome of a judicial decision: Luke 23:40: *sentence* of crucifixion; 24:20: *sentence* of death; Acts 24:25: the future *judgment by God*.

John uses the word only once—in the sense of the *dividing* of humankind that takes place through the presence of Jesus on the basis of each person's attitude toward him. The consequence is that each either "sees" or is "blind" (9:39; → κρίνω 5).

3. In Paul the word is found only in Romans, 1 Corinthians, and Galatians. It refers to divine *condemnation* in Rom 2:2, 3 (→ κρίνω 3); 3:8 (in 13:2 either God's judgment or that of the state); Gal 5:10. Rom 5:16 emphasizes the superior power of grace in relation to the divine

sentence for the sin of Adam, which leads to the condemnation of the sinful world, which is connected with the sin of Adam. The power of grace exceeds the transgression and leads to justification in the Christ-event. The word also refers to "divine *condemnation*"—with reference to the present—in 1 Cor 11:29, 34, where Paul speaks of the circumstances at the Lord's Supper (v. 20) that threaten the unity of the church. Eating and drinking the Lord's Supper, which should be a proclamation of the saving death of the Lord (v. 26), can become a judgment: μὴ διακρίνων τὸ σῶμα (v. 29: when "the body" is not "discerned, correctly understood, or distinguished" (see F. Büchsel, *TDNT* III, 946). "The body" is often used in reference to the bread of the Lord's Supper (see Synofzik 50f.), but refers here to the body (of Christ), the Church (see G. Bornkamm, *Early Christian Experience* 149f.), which should be "saved" through the divine judgments (v. 32); → κρίνω.

4. According to 1 Tim 3:6 no "newly converted person" should become a bishop because the danger exists of such a person becoming arrogant, resulting in his being led into the κρίμα τοῦ διαβόλου, i.e., into the devil's *accusation* (cf. 5:12) before God's judgment (cf. Rev 12:10).

Heb 6:2 includes in Christian elementary instruction the doctrine of κρίμα αἰώνιον. Vv. 1f. refer to three pairs of correlated acts (in each case connected by "and"), in which the first has temporal precedence to the second. Thus "the resurrection of the dead" comes before the *judgment* of God. Αἰώνιος does not describe the judgment as lasting eternally, but rather—as often in the NT on the basis of the doctrine of the two aeons—as the final judgment that takes place in the future aeon.

Jas 3:1 expects an especially harsh *judgment* for teachers.

1 Pet 4:17 interprets the community's suffering under persecutions as *the administration of judgment,* which indicates "what the end will be for those who do not obey the gospel."

Κρίμα is used of divine *condemnation* in 2 Pet 2:3; Jude 4; Rev 17:1; 18:20, *dominion* in Rev 20:4 (cf. Dan 7:22, where κρίμα is a parallel to βασίλειον [LXX] or βασιλεία [Θ]).   M. Rissi

κρίνον, ου, τό *krinon* lily*

Matt 6:28 par. Luke 12:27 mentions τὰ κρίνα (Matthew: τοῦ ἀγροῦ), "the *lilies* (of the field)," as examples of beautiful flowers. Dalman, *Arbeit* I/2, 357-66; BAGD (bibliography); Schulz, *Q* 149-57, esp. 151.

κρίνω *krinō* judge (vb.)
κρίσις, εως, ἡ *krisis* judgment

1. Occurrences and meaning — 2. Q, the Synoptics, and Acts — 3. Paul — 4. Other NT writings — 5. Characteristic features of Johannine usage — 6. Compounds

Lit.: J. BLANK, *Krisis* (1964). — G. BORNKAMM, "The Revelation of God's Wrath (Rom 1-3)," *idem, Early Christian Experience* 47-70. — *idem,* "Lord's Supper and Church in Paul," *Early Christian Experience* 123-60. — E. BRANDENBURGER, *TRE* XII, 469-83. — H. BRAUN, *Gerichtsgedanke und Rechtfertigungslehre bei Paulus* (1930). — F. BÜCHSEL and V. HERNTRICH, *TDNT* III, 921-54. — H. CONZELMANN, *RGG* II, 1419-21. — A. CORELL, *Consummatum est: Eschatology and Church in the Gospel of St. John* (1958). — E. DINKLER, "Rechtsnahme und Rechtsverzicht (1 Kor 6,1-10)," *idem, Signum Crucis* (1967) 204-40. — K. P. DONFRIED, "Justification and Last Judgement in Paul," *ZNW* 67 (1976) 90-110. — F. V. FILSON, *St. Paul's Conception of Recompense* (1931). — G. FRIEDRICH, "Vom Richten im NT," *Das Richteramt* (ed. T. Heckel; 1958) 7-23. — K. KARNER, *BHH* 549f. — L. MATTERN, *Das Verständnis des Gerichts bei Paulus* (1966). — C. F. D. MOULE, "The Judgement Theme in the Sacraments," *FS Dodd* 464-81. — S. MOWINCKEL, *He That Cometh* (1956). — T. PREISS, "La justification dans la pensée johannique," *La vie en Christ* (ed. Preiss; 1951) 46-64. — C. R. ROETZEL, *Judgment in the Community* (1972). — S. SCHULZ, "Die Anklage in Röm 1,18-32," *TZ* 14 (1958) 161-73. — H. SCHUSTER, "Rechtfertigung und Gericht bei Paulus," *Stat crux dum volvitur orbis* (FS H. Lilje, 1959) 57-67. — E. SYNOFZIK, *Die Gerichts- und Vergeltungsaussage bei Paulus* (1977). — L. VISCHER, *Die Auslegungsgeschichte von 1 Kor 6,1-11* (1955). — R. WALKER, "Die Heiden und das Gericht," *EvT* 20 (1960) 302-14. — For further bibliography see *TWNT* X, 1148f.

1. The vb. appears 114 times in the NT (of which one-third are in the Pauline letters) with various nuances: *judge, distinguish, determine, make a legal judgment, punish* (pass.: *stand before the court* or *dispute*), in Matt 19:28 par. Luke 22:30 in the OT sense of *rule* (= *šāpaṭ,* Judg 3:10, etc.). Κρίσις occurs 47 times in the NT, of which 12 are in Matthew and 11 are in John, and normally connotes the *decision of the judge* or its result, in the OT sense of *justice;* in Matt 5:21 it designates a local court. Statements regarding judgment in the NT are not limited to the juristic terms. The NT generally shares OT and Jewish terms for the final judgment, although the understanding of the Christ-event in the NT introduces some basic differences.

2. In Q the vb. appears in Jesus' warning against human *judging* (in the sense of *condemning*) in Matt 7:1, 2 par. Luke 6:37. God, to whom alone judgment is given (divine passive), will judge the one who judges by the same standard (→ κρίμα 2). Only here does the vb. appear in the Synoptic tradition to refer to the eschatological judgment of God. Jesus' statements regarding those who refuse his message of salvation speak of the eschatological *judgment* ("the day of *judgment*"). Such people have a greater responsibility than the prototypical places of sin and Gentile cities (Sodom, etc.) and than the queen of the

South (Matt 10:15; 11:22 par. Luke 10:14; Matt 11:24; 12:41, 42 par. Luke 11:31, 32). The saying of Jesus about the future of Israel is also derived from Q: When God creates the world anew (Matt 19:28, → παλιγγενεσία), the disciples will sit on twelve thrones in order to *judge* the tribes of Israel, i.e., to *rule* them (Matt 19:28 par. Luke 22:30).

The thrones belong to the eschatological judgment scene from Dan 7:9f. Although Jewish tradition knows of the participation of the angels, the righteous, and the great ones of Israel in the judgment of the nations (see Volz, *Eschatologie* 275-76; cf. 1 Cor 6:2; Rev 20:4), Jesus speaks here rather of the dominion over the people comprised of the twelve tribes.

Jesus' saying anticipates a special future for the old people of God, not in the present age, but in the new creation (cf. Matt 23:39).

The first antithesis of the Sermon on the Mount (Matt 5:21f.) sharpens the prohibition against killing and gives the warning: Whoever is angry at his brother is liable to the *judgment;* i.e., in view of the intensification in v. 22b, he deserves to be handed over to the local *judicial authority.* Anger is equated with murder. This is the only passage in the NT in which κρίσις designates a judicial council. In Matt 5:40 the pass. of the vb. is used in the sense of *bring a lawsuit* (cf. 1 Cor 6:1; Rom 3:4) in Jesus' hyperbolic call to nonresistance toward evil: To one who *brings a lawsuit* for the sake of the shirtlike undergarment, the outer garment should be given as well (Luke 6:29 assumes a robbery and thus mentions the outer garment first). Matt 12:36 emphasizes the extent of the responsibility of the community of salvation: At the day of judgment an account must be given by everyone for every unsuitable word (Jewish parallels in Billerbeck I, 639f.). In Matt 23:33 the eschatological judgment is called "the judgment of Gehenna" (condemnation to Gehenna). The image is from Jewish tradition (see Billerbeck IV, 1036ff.) and gives no further or more precise information about the form of the punishment.

Luke often uses the vb. for human *judging* and *deciding* (Luke 7:43; Acts 4:19, etc.), for judicial *judging* (Acts 3:13, etc.), and for God's judgment within history (7:7) and once for the eschatological judging by God (17:31), which will take place in righteousnss through Jesus, who has been raised from the dead. In the citation of Isa 53:8 LXX in Acts 8:33 the death of Jesus is understood as κρίσις, i.e., as *judgment:* In his humiliation the judgment on Jesus was abolished. Although the text is not interpreted, the humiliation can only mean the crucifixion, and the abolition of his judgment can only be the resurrection (cf. 2:24).

3. In Paul judgment never becomes an independent topic (see Synofzik 105). It can even be absent from eschatological contexts such as 1 Corinthians 15 and 1 Thessalonians 4. Κρίσις appears only in 2 Thess 1:5:

The *final judgment* is anticipated in the sufferings of persecution; it will bring the kingdom of God to one who is oppressed; to the oppressor it will bring affliction. The vb. in Paul carries almost the entire range of its meanings. It is theologically significant for Paul that all judging remains the sole prerogative of God. With the OT and Jewish and early Christian tradition Paul knows of judgment and punishment by God within history. Thus the disregard of the Church as the body of Christ in the celebration of the Lord's Supper has resulted in sickness and death (1 Cor 11:29; → κρίμα 3). Yet divine judgment is intended not for the destruction but for the salvation of the Church: "*When we are punished* by the Lord, we are chastened so that we will not be condemned with the world" (11:32). God's administration of judgment is a call to repentance. Thus those who believe should "judge" themselves, i.e., test themselves, so that God's judgment not fall on them (11:31).

In connection with his demonstration of the lost condition of the Jews and Gentiles in Rom 1:18–3:20 Paul warns against human judging or condemnation of others: The condemnatory judgment of others falls on the one who judges, for all people are sinners (2:1f.; 3:10-18; 1 Cor 4:5; 10:29). God alone can perform righteous judgment, for God *judges* "the hidden things," i.e., the true nature of humankind (Rom 2:16). Inasmuch as salvation is offered to all people in Christ alone, God *will judge* "on the basis of the gospel," the saving message of Jesus, and "through Christ Jesus." Thus Paul can mention God or Christ as judge, making no distinction (Rom 14:10; 2 Cor 5:10).

There is also no contradiction in Paul when he connects the final judgment with "works" (Rom 2:6; 1 Cor 3:13ff.; 2 Cor 5:10), although no one can be "justified by works of the law" (Rom 3:20, 28, etc.). This is apparent in Rom 2:6, where Paul contrasts those who are "patient in good works" with those who are factious and disobedient against the truth. The antithetical parallelism of the terms indicates that disobedience against the truth is rebellion against the revelation of God in Christ, but that the good work of obedience toward God, who alone reveals himself, is what is good. The good work of obedience is the realization of life that God himself creates through the Spirit in the believer (Rom 14:23; Gal 5:22; Phil 1:6; 1 Thess 1:3; 2 Thess 1:11; 1 Cor 15:58; 2 Cor 9:8). The individual in his zeal, however, is not capable of justifying himself before God. Therefore the Gentile in whom Jer 31:33 has been fulfilled, in whom the will of God is "written on the heart," and who thus has become a doer of the law in faith, will *condemn* the Jew in the final judgment (Rom 2:27).

The divine final judgment, according to Paul, includes all humanity, even those who believe (Rom 2:16; 3:6; 14:10; 2 Cor 5:10). Those who believe, however, are free from condemnation (Rom 8:1). For the believer the final judgment becomes the confirmation of salvation (cf. Rom 8:11; 2 Cor 4:14). The language of judgment according to the deeds of the believer emphasizes, however, that grace does not abolish the individual's responsibility for his deeds.

The vb. appears also in Rom 3:1-8 (vv. 4, 6, 7) in connection with the problem of the fidelity of God to the covenant promises to Israel. Despite Israel's unfaithfulness God keeps his word. If one "disputes" with God, God will be victorious, i.e., his truthfulness will be revealed. This is the case not only of the word of promise to Israel: Every person will be unmasked as a liar in the dispute with God, and God's judgment will be revealed as justified. Otherwise God could not "judge the world" (3:6). The fidelity of God toward Israel is only a "special instance of his faithfulness to all creation" (E. Käsemann, *Rom* [Eng. tr., 1980] 82). God's victory is the reconciliation of the ungodly world through Christ (2 Cor 5:19; Rom 5:6, 10).

Thus the objection against the Pauline doctrine of reconciliation is raised in 3:8. However, the reconciliation must be appropriated in faith and then one is "justified." Thus Paul can only speak of the justification (but not of the reconciliation) through faith.

In his argument against taking lawsuits before pagan judges in 1 Cor 6:2 Paul takes up a Jewish apocalyptic expectation: "The saints *will judge* the world" (see Dan 7:22; Wis 3:8; 1QHab 5:4f.; Volz, *Eschatologie* 275; Billerbeck III, 363), even the angels (6:3). The Church must therefore be capable of settling the disputes in its midst.

Because judging is God's right alone, human judging is forbidden (Rom 2:1-3; 14:4, 10, 13; 1 Cor 4:5). One who *condemns* others condemns himself, inasmuch as all people do the same things (Rom 2:3; see above) and can live only on the basis of the reconciliation in Christ. Thus the freedom of decision should not be made dependent on the conscience of another (Rom 14:10, 13; 1 Cor 10:29). On the other hand, freedom must not lead to disobedience. Thus the blessing is pronounced on the one who "has no reason to *condemn* himself in what he approves" (Rom 14:22). However, the prohibition of condemning is not to lead to a view that is uncritical or undiscriminating within the congregation. "Those who are inside" should stand under the vigilant judgment of the Church (1 Cor 5:12). Even the apostle himself stands under their judgment (10:15).

4. In the literature dependent on Paul κρίσις is used only in the sense of *final judgment* (1 Tim 5:24). The vb. appears only in 2 Tim 4:1 in the confessional formula of judgment over the living and the dead; in Titus 3:12 it appears in the sense of human *decision-making;* in Col 2:16 it means *pass judgment on a matter, criticize* (cf. Jas 4:11f.).

In Heb 10:30; 13:4 the vb. is used of God's eschatological judgment. In 9:27 the once-for-all death of each person as the way to judgment is coordinated with the once-for-all sacrifice of Christ. Nothing is said here about the time of God's action as judge. However, such passages as 12:26-29 indicate clearly that the author thinks in terms of the final judgment. This "judgment" of God awaits those who resist him (10:27, cf. v. 29).

Jas 2:12 admonishes the reader to live in such a way as to be "*judged* by the law of liberty." This law is to be understood either in Hellenistic Jewish terms as the law that liberates from sin the one who keeps it, or, more probably, as the concrete expression of God's will, to which one should conform in freedom (according to v. 13, esp. mercy, according to 5:9, truthfulness).

1 Peter uses only the vb. and employs it for God's activity of judging. According to 1:17 the Father *performs judgment* without regard for the person and according to the work of each. For the Christian this will mean the fulfillment of the life given to him through the resurrection of Christ and the word of proclamation (1:3, 23f.). Judgment according to one's work is thus understood in a way similar to Paul's view. In the table of duties in 2:18-20 slaves are referred to the model of Christ (cf. the Christ-hymn from Isaiah 53 in 2:21ff.), who did not exercise vengeance, but instead left judgment to "*the one who judges* justly" (2:23). The seriousness of the Christian's responsibility is emphasized in 4:5 with a view toward the final judgment of the living and the dead. In 4:6 the reason is added that even a possibility of decision is offered also even to the dead through the proclamation of the gospel (cf. 3:19). Thus they *will be judged* "in the flesh" (i.e., their death is a divine judgment, as with all humanity); but through the gospel, with which they will be confronted after their death, they will be graciously granted a new life of salvation according to the will of God, which will be given through the Spirit.

According to 2 Peter and Jude the *judgment* befalls the disobedient angels and people (2 Pet 2:4, 9; Jude 6, 9, 15). In 2 Pet 2:11 κρίσις is a reviling *judgment*. In 1 John only the noun is found, in the sense of the final judgment: Love gives the Christian confidence in "the day of *judgment*" (4:17).

In Revelation the negative meaning of the vb. and noun are predominant. 16:5, 7 refers to *judgment* within history; the other occurrences speak of the eschatological acts of God. The martyrs under the altar of heaven cry aloud in 6:10 for the revelation of the divine righteousness, i.e., the punishment of the persecutors (cf. Deut 32:43; Ps 79:5, 10; *1 Enoch* 47:2). The hour of the world's judgment (11:18; 18:8, 20; 19:2) will be the judgment "for you," i.e., for the persecuted Church (18:20). God or the returning Christ (19:11) is the judge (6:10, etc.). The vision of judgment in 20:11-15 refers only to the lost (similarly *2 Bar.* 24:1), who will be judged on the basis of the books, i.e., their own ungodly deeds; for those who are saved are at this time already raised (20:6).

5. The idea of judgment takes on its own distinctive perspective in John, where it is entirely shaped by the special christology of the Evangelist. The Johannine Jesus is sent not to *judge* the world, but rather to save it (3:17f.; cf. 8:15; 12:47). Salvation occurs through the lamb of God, who takes away the sin of the world (1:29, 36), through the redeemer of the world (4:42), who gives to the world the life that the Father has given to the Son (5:26). The hour of the world's judgment is thus the hour in which the Son himself is executed, as he goes home to the Father through his death and resurrection (12:23ff.). This judgment consists in the fact that the prince of the world is cast out, i.e., driven from his position as lord of the cosmos.

The devil is not seen in John as a conquering power (thus there are no references to demoniacs; on how John follows the understanding of cosmic powers known in the wisdom literature see G. von Rad, *Wisdom in Israel* [1972] 308). Instead the devil is the prototype of unbelief (8:44) and the prince of the world of unbelief, over which he rules. This dominion is snatched away from him in the judgment that takes place in Jesus' death (12:31; 14:30; 16:11; cf. Col 2:15).

Thus the world has become free to be drawn to its Savior (12:32). Now everything is determined by one's relationship to him. One who believes in him does not await condemnation and has already gone over from the realm of death to the realm of life (5:24). Consequently the revelation of salvation has become the *separation* of humanity (3:19; 8:11f.). The rejection of the revelation discloses the evil of the works of humankind; for the good work is faith in Jesus (6:29). Through unbelief the revelation of salvation becomes condemnation. Thus there is no contradiction when Jesus speaks, on the one hand, of being sent for the sake of salvation and, on the other hand, of the true and valid *judgment* that will be performed by him and his Father (5:22, 24, 30; 8:16, 26, 50).

The statement in 5:27-29 does not fit within this theology of judgment and thus is a secondary insertion. Only in this passage is the authority of judgment by Jesus associated with the title of Son of Man in characteristic Jewish apocalyptic fashion (the art. is absent only here with the title, cf. Dan 7:13). In John Jesus is the judge in his role as Son. Only in this passage is the judgment separated from the present encounter with Jesus, and only here does the text speak of a double resurrection, either to life or to judgment. For John, on the other hand, "resurrection" refers to entry into redeemed life in fellowship with Jesus (5:24), for Jesus himself is "the resurrection" (11:25; cf. 5:26; 6:39f., 44, 54; 20:9).

Judgment in the present does not exclude belief in a future final judgment. When Jesus promises the believer that he will not "come into judgment" (5:24), what he says presupposes a future judgment.

6. Ἀνακρίνω* commonly means *interrogate, make a judicial investigation* (Luke 23:14; Acts 4:9; 12:19; 24:8; 28:18; 1 Cor 9:3); in Acts 17:11 it means *examine (the Scriptures) thoroughly.* According to 1 Cor 2:14 the matters of the Spirit of God must be *examined/tested* under the influence of the Spirit. Therefore the pneumatic *judges* all things, but can *be judged* by no one (2:15). A stranger can therefore *be examined* or *convicted* by a congregation under the influence of the Spirit, 14:24. Ἀνακρίνω is used in 1 Cor 4:3, 4 in the sense of κρίνω, *judge*: Paul is independent of the Church's judgment, knowing that he is "judged" only by the Lord. Ἀνάκρισις, *hearing, investigation,** is used in the NT only in Acts 25:26, there of a judicial *inquiry.*   M. Rissi

κρίσις, εως, ἡ *krisis* judgment
→ κρίνω.

Κρίσπος, ου *Krispos* Crispus*

Transliteration of the Latin name *Crispus* (see BDF §41.3). 1 Cor 1:14: "I baptized none of you except Crispus and Gaius"; Acts 18:8: Crispus, the head of the synagogue who, with his entire household, became believers. Both passages refer to the same person (E. Haenchen, *Acts* [Eng. tr., 1971] ad loc.).

κριτήριον, ου, τό *kritērion* lawsuit, trial*

Lit.: F. BÜCHSEL, *TDNT* III, 943.

1. This neut. subst. form of the adj., itself derived from the personal noun κριτής, is never used in its 3 NT occurrences (4 or 6 occurrences in the LXX) in the sense of *criterion, standard* and is used only in Jas 2:6 (in an apparently current phrase with ἕλκω εἰς; cf. BAGD s.v.) for the institution of the court (this meaning since Plato *Lg.* vi.767b; cf. Judg 5:10 B; 3 Kgdms 7:7; Sus 49 Theodotion), here as that to which the powerful haul the powerless. The noun is also not used in the NT with God as subj. (as in Exod 21:6; Dan 7:10, 26 Theodotion; the earliest Christian use of the noun with God as subj. is the citation of Dan 7:10 in Justin *Dial.* 31:2).

2. For 1 Cor 6:2, 4 (synonymous with κρίνεσθαι, v. 1, and → κρίμα, v. 7) one does not need to consider the formal meaning "insignificant courts" or "those [courts] that have jurisdiction over the petty details of everyday life" (so BAGD s.v. 1), since the meaning *trial* is adequately attested in inscriptional evidence (Cyrene Inscription 21 [ed. J. J. E. Hodius, *Suppl. Epigr. Graecum* IX, 1938]) and in Diodorus Siculus (i.72.4; xxxvi.3.3; see BAGD; Büchsel 943n.5): In view of their eschatological calling, it is beneath the dignity of Christians to take legal disputes involving everyday affairs before non-Christians.   W. Schenk

κριτής, οῦ, ὁ *kritēs* judge*

Lit.: F. Büchsel, *TDNT* III, 942. — G. Liedke, *THAT* II, 999-1009. — For further bibliography see *TWNT* X, 1148f.

1. The 19 occurrences in the NT (over 70 occurrences in the LXX, most often as tr. of Heb. *šôpēṭ* as one who restores the disturbed order of the community when the cause of the disturbance is removed) are concentrated in Luke-Acts (6 occurrences in the Gospel, 4 in Acts) and James (4 occurrences) and refer to a person.

2. The earliest Christian usage is in the juridical image about the timely settlement with one's accuser, which advises on the importance of reconciliation before one is brought before the judge (Luke 12:58 bis [Q] par. Matt 5:25 bis). In Luke 11:19 (Q) par. Matt 12:27, where the activity of the rabbinic students, which is like that of Jesus, condemns their teachers with the very charge that is directed against Jesus, the verbal construction means the same as → κατακρίνω (Luke 11:31f. [Q]) and may be derived from the analogous form of the Q redaction. In the dialogue that introduces the narrative of the rich fool and which shows the signs of Luke's redactional work in 12:14, Jesus, in a hendiadys, rejects the idea of appearing as "mediator in matters of inheritance." The surprising conduct in the story of the unfaithful *judge* (Luke 18:2, 6; v. 6 Semitizing gen. of quality, cf. 16:9 with 16:11; v. 11 has the antonym → πιστός) serves in the *a minore* conclusion to motivate unceasing prayer.

In Acts 24:10 the Roman procurator takes the function of an *attorney* who mediates a legal dispute and is addressed accordingly in Paul's defense speech. In 18:15 the proconsul, in a corresponding situation, declines to "decide" ("empty vb." construction) concerning an accusation because he is not appropriately qualified. In 13:20 the word designates the corresponding OT leaders from Judg 2:16-18 LXX (both *titulus* and *subscriptio;* cf. Josephus *Ant.* vi.85; xi.112), who exercised the ruling functions prior to the period of the Israelite state.

In the two occurrences in James an intensifying empty vb. construction appears after the respective vbs.: 2:4: "and become *judges* with evil thoughts" (gen. of quality, in which the partiality mentioned in vv. 1, 9 is meant); 4:11: "*one who lifts himself* above the law" (cf. νομοθέτης καὶ κριτής, v. 12).

Neither in Paul nor in the Synoptic tradition is either God or Christ called *judge.* This designation is first given in Jas 4:12, where it refers to God (also Heb 12:23, where it is a pred. used with a positive accent: God as *attorney* for the oppressed, who assists them in their final moment in court), while in Jas 5:9 (cf. vv. 7, 8: παρουσία) Christ may have, as also in 2 Tim 4:8 (cf. v. 1), a positive accent; likewise Acts 10:42 (cf.

17:31), parallel with "Lord of all" (10:36), of Christ, who grants forgiveness (v. 43, par. v. 36, "peace through Jesus Christ").   W. Schenk

κριτικός, 3 *kritikos* able to judge*

Heb 4:12: the word of God *decides/judges* (κριτικός with obj. gen.) the thoughts and intention of the heart. F. Büchsel, *TDNT* III, 943.

κρούω *krouō* knock*

In the NT always of knocking on a door, absolute in Matt 7:7, 8 par. Luke 11:9, 10; Luke 12:36; Acts 12:16; Rev 3:20; with acc. τὴν θύραν in Luke 13:25; Acts 12:13. G. Bertram, *TDNT* III, 954-57.

κρύπτη, ης, ἡ *kryptē* dark passage, hidden nook*

Luke 11:33: No one who lights a lamp (→ λύχνος 3.a) places it εἰς κρύπτην ("in a *cellar*"). A. Oepke, *TDNT* III, 960, 974.

κρυπτός, 3 *kryptos* hidden, secret
→ κρύπτω.

κρύπτω *kryptō* hide; bury; mix in*

1. Occurrences — 2. Meaning and usage — 3. Κρυπτός

Lit.: W. Mundle, *DNTT* II, 214-20. — A. Oepke and R. Meyer, *TDNT* III, 957-1000. — For further bibliography see *TWNT* X, 1149.

1. Κρύπτω appears 18 times in the NT. The largest number of occurrences are in Matthew (7), Luke (2), John (3), and Revelation (3). Κρύπτω also appears in Col 3:3; 1 Tim 5:25; and Heb 11:23 and as v.l. in Luke 13:21.

2. The mashal about the city on a hill, which cannot *be hidden* (Matt 5:14b), stands in connection with the statement about the disciples in v. 14a ("the light of the world"). More than likely this statement is dependent on Isa 2:2-5, where the image of the city on a hill (= Zion) stands in association with light, which is an allusion to Jerusalem and Zion. The interpretation in terms of the disciples defines them as the new Jerusalem (W. Grundmann, *Matt* [THKNT] 139), which allows Matthew to take the image of the new city of God from apocalyptic (cf. E. Lohse, *TDNT* VII, 324f.) and make the claim for the Church in its debates with Judaism.

In Jesus' prayer of thanksgiving in Matt 11:25 (on the form and function cf. Dibelius, *Tradition* 279-86) the aor. partc. presupposes Jesus' dialogue with God, "the Father and Lord of heaven and earth," who *has hidden* the revelation that has taken place in Jesus from the σοφοί and συνετοί and revealed it to the νήπιοι (cf. 1 Cor 1:18-29;

John 1:10f.). Thus the idea of "the contingent and paradoxical nature" of the revelation is expressed (H. Conzelmann, *TDNT* VI, 893). There is no direct precedent for the idea of the preference for the νήπιοι as the elect recipients of the revelation (in Isa 29:14 the blinding of the wise is a judgment motif; on Jewish wisdom and apocalyptic cf. Schulz, *Q* 219 n.295; the Qumran literature also has parallels [1QH 5:20f., etc.], but presupposes an esoteric wisdom possessed by the members of the community).

The allusion to Ps 77:2 LXX in Matt 13:35 gives the basis for Jesus' parables. The parable form is to be taken here, not as an instrument of the motif of hardening (cf. 13:10-15 par.), but as a type of prophetic revelatory discourse that makes known that which was "*hidden* from the foundation of the world." The expression aims at the saving will of the creator, which has manifested itself in Christ.

Matt 13:44 (bis) tells of a treasure *hidden* in a field and was *buried* again by the one who found it so that he might purchase the whole field from the sale of his possessions. The perspective of the parable does not take account of the questionable legality of the act of the one who discovered the treasure, but instead emphasizes the total involvement of the person in taking possession of the treasure (cf. Jeremias, *Parables* 198-200). Jesus demands the same resoluteness with respect to the βασιλεία.

In the parable of the talents (Matt 25:14-30) the servant who has *buried* his money (vv. 18, 25) must give an account of himself to the master who returns (on the interpretation, cf. D. O. Via, *Parables* 113-22; Jeremias, *Parables* 58-63).

In Luke 13:21 (B K L al) the kingdom of God is compared to leaven *mixed* with flour. The point is seen in the result that a small amount of leaven has on the large quantity of dough: The arrival of the kingdom has a similar impact on its surroundings.

In connection with the third Passion prediction, Luke 18:34 (redactional) emphasizes the disciples' lack of understanding, for whom "this word" was *hidden* (κρύπτω with οὐδὲν . . . συνῆκαν and οὐκ ἐγίνωσκον). According to the conception of Luke the disciples come to a complete understanding of the way of salvation only after they are instructed by the resurrected one (24:25, 27, 44-49).

Κρύπτω also appears in Luke in connection with Jesus' sorrow over Jerusalem to refer to the blindness for which the people themselves are responsible (19:42). The prophetic oracle of doom, expressed here in the style of a lament, is to be taken as a *vaticinium ex eventu* of the fate of the Jewish nationalist movement in A.D. 70.

In John 8:59 Jesus *hides* himself (withdraws) from the outraged Jews who regarded his self-designation as "Son" of the heavenly Father (vv. 35f.) and the reference to their origin as "sons of the devil" (v. 44) as blasphemy

and wanted to stone him (cf. Billerbeck I, 1013-19). The futility of the plot indicates "that the Revealer is beyond the reach of the world" (R. Bultmann, *John* [Eng. tr., 1971] 328). In John 12:36 κρύπτω marks the conclusion of the public activity of Jesus: He *withdraws* because he has found no faith, despite all the "signs" he has done. As a pred. nom. modifying μαθητὴς τοῦ Ἰησοῦ, κρύπτω in 19:38 refers to the *secret* discipleship of Joseph of Arimathea (cf. 12:42).

Over against a Gnostic understanding of ζωή as the reality of salvation already present in this life for the believer, Col 3:3 represents the view that the "life" of the believer "is *hidden* with God in Christ" (v. 4) and is to be revealed only at the parousia. The basis for the paranesis lies therefore in "eschatological mysticism" (Oepke 977; cf. M. Dibelius, *Col* [HNT] 40). 1 Tim 5:25 connects the comment that "good works" are visible to some but *hidden* to others with the admonition not to be hasty in ordaining (v. 22) someone to church office. In connection with the OT list of witnesses to faith in Hebrews 11, v. 23 says (with reference to Exod 2:2) that Moses was kept *hidden* three months after his birth by his parents.

In Rev 6:15f. those who *hide* themselves in the ravines of the mountains in order to escape "the wrath of the lamb" do not belong to the people of God—the full range of social positions is listed to represent all the world's population. The mountainous terrain as the place of refuge from the judgment of God is derived from OT conceptions (cf. Isa 2:10, 19; Jer 4:29, etc.). In taking up the apocalyptic expectation of a second eschatological miracle of manna (*2 Bar.* 29:8) Rev 2:17 promises the *hidden,* i.e., heavenly manna as a reward to "the one who overcomes" (i.e., martyrs).

3. **Κρυπτός**, *hidden**, occurs in the NT 17 times. The adj. remains within the same frame of reference as the vb.

In Matt 6:4 (bis) Jesus objects to the practice of charity by the pious intended for public recognition and demands of his disciples good deeds done anonymously. The promise corresponds to the postulate that God "who sees in *secret*" (cf. Sir 17:15; 23:19; 39:19) will reward these deeds. Within the context of this saying stands the commandment in Matt 6:6 (bis) to pray to God in *secret.* As a rejection of rabbinic custom in prayer, in which the address to God was intended as a demonstrative proof of one's piety (v. 5), prayer is here thought of as an intimate event in which the person who prays in *secret* and the God who sees in *secret* meet (cf. 14:23 par.; Luke 5:16; 6:12, etc.). The associated promise of reward is thus not meant to assume that prayer is a religious achievement; rather, it refers to the relationship to God that is attested in prayer.

The saying in Matt 10:26 par. Luke 12:2, which ap- ·

pears in synonymous parallelism and according to which nothing is *hidden* that will not be revealed, appears in this context as a challenge to fearless confession. On the other hand the saying in Mark 4:22 par. Luke 8:17 is found in connection with the parable of the sower, so that here the accent lies on the commission to proclaim, which gives the disciple the mandate not to *conceal* the word entrusted to him, but to become fruitful.

In John 7:4 Jesus is urged by his brothers to go to Judea and there make himself known by his works as the Revealer. The reason given for his going assumes for Jesus a corresponding ambition (v. 4). Jesus explicitly rejects the suggestion (v. 8), but nevertheless follows his brothers *secretly* to the feast in Jerusalem (v. 10). The contradiction that emerges is avoided here in view of John's intention, which is to show that Jesus does not go to the city to be honored in the sense suggested by his brothers. Instead, he goes in the consciousness of his fundamental opposition to "the world," whose hatred he evokes (v. 7). The Passover feast to which he goes marks his own fate (cf. R. Schnackenburg, *John* II [Eng. tr., 1979] ad loc.).

From this perspective Jesus' answer to the high priest's question about his followers and his teaching (18:19) takes on a deeper meaning. When Jesus indicates that he has always spoken (v. 20) in all openness, and that he did nothing in *secret,* he fends off the charge of conspiracy in only a superficial way. Indeed, the essential cause of the conflict lies here in the encounter of the Revealer with "the world."

Rom 2:16, which has been burdened with many hypotheses (cf. E. Käsemann, *Rom* [Eng. tr., 1980] ad loc.), may mean in its context that God's judgment, which uncovers what is *hidden* in humankind, judges Jews and Gentiles according to the measure of the divine demand. In this case Paul would be coordinating "law" with → συνείδησις (v. 15), which is derived from Hellenistic Judaism. In this parallel the law has, instead of the Jewish understanding of an objective salvific norm, the value of an inner claim on the person. Whether that claim is fulfilled, like the regard for the conscience, cannot be ascertained and thus comes to light only in the judgment. Rom 2:29 lies within the line of this argument, as Paul here contrasts a *hidden* Judaism, i.e., one based on the Spirit, with one that rests only on the covenantal sign of circumcision.

Perhaps it is with reference to the reservations of the Corinthian church toward his person that Paul admonishes the church members in 1 Cor 4:5 not to judge prematurely, but rather to await the parousia, when "the purposes of the heart" will be disclosed. Paul assumes here that the thoughts and intentions of each person will be evident only at the parousia. Thus, according to 14:25, this unveiling takes place in the church through the gift of the Spirit of prophecy (cf. H. Conzelmann, *1 Cor* [Hermeneia] ad loc.).

In 2 Cor 4:2 Paul defends himself against the charge of his opponents, who accuse him of "cowardly *secret* action" (R. Bultmann, *2 Cor* [Eng. tr., 1985] 100).

1 Pet 3:4 speaks of differing social backgrounds (against L. Goppelt, *1 Pet* [KEK] 216). The parenesis refers to women who wear expensive jewelry and who are contrasted with "the *hidden* person of the heart"; behind this expression is not the formula referring to "inner values," but rather the view that the whole person as a believer is determined by the Spirit (cf. Goppelt 216f.).

H.-J. Ritz

κρυσταλλίζω *krystallizō* shine like crystal*

Rev 21:11, of the light (φωστήρ) in the heavenly Jerusalem: "like a *bright crystal* jasper."

κρύσταλλος, ου, ὁ *krystallos* rock crystal*

In Revelation in comparisons: 4:6: "as it were a sea of glass, like *crystal* (ὁμοία κρυστάλλῳ)"; 22:1, of the stream of living water: "clear as *crystal* (ὡς κρύσταλλος)." Cf. → κρυσταλλίζω (21:11).

κρυφαῖος, 3 *kryphaios* hidden*

Matt 6:18a, b: ἐν τῷ κρυφαίῳ, "in *secret*." A. Oepke, *TDNT* III, 960, 974.

κρυφῇ *kryphē* secretly*

Eph 5:12: τὰ κρυφῇ γινόμενα ὑπ' αὐτῶν, "their deeds done *in secret*." A. Oepke, *TDNT* III, 960, 976; BDF §26.

κτάομαι *ktaomai* obtain, acquire, win*

Of a material gain or earnings of a person, Matt 10:9; Luke 18:12; Acts 1:18; 8:20; of the acquisition of the Roman right of citizenship, Acts 22:28; in reference to a wife, 1 Thess 4:4: κτᾶσθαι ἐν ἁγιασμῷ καὶ τιμῇ, "*obtain* her in holiness and honor"; of the obtaining of life through endurance, Luke 21:19: ἐν τῇ ὑπομονῇ κτήσασθε. . . .

κτῆμα, ατος, τό *ktēma* possession, property*

Pl. *possessions* with ὑπάρξεις, Acts 2:45; of the rich young man, Mark 10:22 par. Matt 19:22: "he had many *possessions*"; sg. in Acts 5:1: a concrete possession, namely, a *plot of land* (cf. v. 3: χωρίον). F. Selter, *DNTT* II, 845-47.

κτῆνος, ους, τό *ktēnos* domesticated animal: pet; animal belonging to a herd*

324

1 Cor 15:39: σάρξ κτηνῶν, *animal belonging to a herd;* Rev 18:13: κτήνη καὶ πρόβατα, *cattle;* Luke 10:34; Acts 23:24: an *animal for riding,* with ἐπιβιβάζω.

κτήτωρ, ορος, ὁ *ktētōr* owner*

Acts 4:34, in a summary statement: ὅσοι γὰρ κτήτορες χωρίων ἢ οἰκιῶν ὑπῆρχον, *"owners* of land and houses" sold them and brought the proceeds to the apostles.

κτίζω *ktizō* create, establish*
κτίσις, εως, ἡ *ktisis* creation, creature, that which is created*
κτίσμα, ατος, τό *ktisma* creature, that which is created*
κτίστης, ου, ὁ *ktistēs* creator*

1. Occurrences and forms — 2. The concept of the creation — 3. Use of the word group

Lit.: G. BAUMBACH, "Die Schöpfung in der Theologie des Paulus," *Kairos* 21 (1979) 196-205. — P. BONNARD, "Création et nouvelle création selon le NT," *idem, Anamnesis* (1980) 71-80. — R. BULTMANN, "Faith in God the Creator," *idem, Existence and Faith* (1960) 171-82. — M. ELIADE, "Vorwort: Gefüge und Funktion der Schöpfungsmythen," *Schöpfungsmythen* (ed. E. Klein et al.; 1980) 9-34. — H.-H. ESSER, *DNTT* I, 378-87. — W. FOERSTER, *TDNT* III, 1000-1035. — G. W. H. LAMPE, "Die neutestamentliche Lehre von der Ktisis," *KD* 11 (1965) 21-32. — G. LINDESKOG, *Studien zum neutestamentlichen Schöpfungsgedanken* (1952). — U. MELL, *Neue Schöpfung* (BZNW 56, 1989). — G. SCHNEIDER, *Neuschöpfung oder Wiederkehr?* (1961). — H. Schwantes, *Schöpfung und Endzeit. Ein Beitrag zum Verständnis der Auferweckung bei Paulus* (1963). — P. STUHLMACHER, "Erwägungen zum ontologischen Charakter der καινὴ κτίσις bei Paulus," *EvT* 27 (1967) 1-35. — C. WESTERMANN, "Neue Arbeiten zur Schöpfung," *VF* 14/1 (1969) 11-28. — For further bibliography see *TWNT* X, 1150-52.

1. Κτίζω appears 15 times in the NT, of which 2 are in Paul (Rom 1:25; 1 Cor 11:9) and 8 are in the deutero-Pauline letters (4 in Ephesians, 3 in Colossians, and 1 in 1 Timothy). The remaining occurrences are in Matt 19:4; Mark 13:19; and Revelation (3 occurrences). The 19 occurrences of κτίσις are similarly distributed: Here also the majority are found in the letters: 9 in Paul (7 in Romans, 1 each in 2 Corinthians and Galatians), 6 in the remaining Epistles (2 in Colossians, 2 in Hebrews, 1 each in 1 and 2 Peter), and additional occurrences in Mark (3) and Rev 3:14. Κτίσμα appears only in 1 Tim 4:4; Jas 1:18; Rev 5:13; 8:9. Κτίστης is a hapax legomenon in 1 Pet 4:19. As a whole the emphasis of the word group lies in Paul and in literature influenced by him.

All the words of the group refer to God as Creator or to his creation and creatures. The NT follows the LXX and postbiblical Judaism conceptually when it avoids, e.g., δημιουργός, which was common in the surrounding world, for the Creator. The LXX originally uses (esp. in

Genesis 1) ποιέω along with κτίζω. Κτίσις and κτίστης are likewise attested in the LXX for creation or creature, while κτίσμα is attested only in the Apocrypha (cf. Foerster 1023-28). The expressions used are all attested in the secular Greek of pre-NT times; the basic meaning is "establish, found" or "establishment/what has been established." In contrast to the association of δημιουργός with the work of the hands, κτίζω κτλ. connote the act of the will or decision (cf. Foerster 1025).

2. The idea that God created the world, which is assumed everywhere in the NT, is based on the OT conception. Thus just as God in the OT is the God of history and then also the Creator God, so also in the NT the conception of God as the Creator does not stand in the foreground, but recedes behind the idea of God's saving acts. The belief in creation was also not the distinctive feature of the Christian faith; the idea that the world was created by a deity or by the gods was widespread. Of course it was and is important for Christians that their God, the Father of Jesus, is believed to be the Creator of the world.

The NT does not explicitly describe how the creation of the world took place. Its concrete descriptions remain within the understanding provided by the OT creation narratives. The only direct reference is found in Gen 1:26 (Mark 10:6 par. Matt 19:4); it is to be assumed that the priestly narrative of Genesis 1–2 was regarded as the determining account.

The OT creation narratives are most intelligible within the framework of ancient Near Eastern views; each motif has parallels. Knowledge still stands "at its beginning in the investigation of the language of Creator and creation" (Westermann 13). It is increasingly being recognized that the function of the conception of the creation lies not so much in an (intellectual) explanation of the beginning of the world as in the interest in the continued existence of the world and of persons or in the concern of the person about his existence (cf. Eliade 11-34; Westermann 17). Thus the process of creation is consistly conceived of as a battle of the powers of order ("cosmos") against chaos (cf. Foerster 1001-5). Faith in the Creator God is thus faith in the reliability of the course of things and trust in the future; the idea of the person as creature expresses the experience of dependence on powers beyond human control. In OT and NT monotheism all powers except the *one* God become radically devalued. The new idea in the NT, in contrast to the OT view, is that of Christ as mediator in creation.

3. The word group is used in the NT in speaking of (a) the Creator, (b) the creation, (c) the new creation, and (d) the individual creature (being). These four areas of usage cannot always be sharply demarcated from each other.

(a) The belief that God created the world is assumed everywhere and is thus not especially emphasized. Thus, e.g., the reference in Mark 13:19 is to be understood in this way when the *creation* is characterized more precisely as *created* by God. According to Rom 1:25 the idolaters worship the *creation* in place of the *Creator,* and thus stand under the wrath of God. The reference to God the Creator can be used as the basis for a teaching: In Matt 19:4 (God *created* man and woman) and 1 Cor 11:9 (man was not *created* for the sake of woman) marriage, the relationship of man and woman, are characterized with reference to the "order of creation," as it can be formulated in modern terms. In a similar way 1 Tim 4:3 rejects asceticism: God *has created* food to be received with thanksgiving. God is sometimes characterized, explicitly in doxologies, as the one who *created* everything (Eph 3:9; Rev 4:11 bis; cf. 10:6: "heaven and that which is in it"). According to 1 Pet 4:19 the *Creator* is "faithful": The one who created the world can be trusted even today and in the future.

Independent of the generally attested creative activity of God, a role of mediator in creation is ascribed to Jesus Christ when it is said in Col 1:16 (bis) that everything "*has been created* in him . . . , through him, and to him." Some mss. have inserted a similar conception into Eph 3:9 ("through Jesus Christ").

In Col 3:10 (the new being is to be put on according to the image of the Creator) the transition is made to the idea of the new creation; the corresponding passages (cf. also Eph 2:10, 15; 4:24) are treated below (→ c).

b) In the reference to the creation in Mark 13:19, the temporal aspect stands in the foreground: such affliction has not been (will not be) since the beginning of the *creation,* which God *created.* In a similar way Paul refers in Rom 1:20 to the act of the *creation* of the world: Since then God's power and deity are apparent in the things that have been made. This temporal reference is used in Mark 10:6 as the basis of an argument: From the beginning of the *creation* God created male and female. In the mouth of the scoffers the observation that from the beginning of the *creation* everything remains the same becomes an argument against the promise of the parousia (2 Pet 3:4).

It is to the whole *creation* that the proclamation of the gospel is directed in Col 1:23 and in the secondary Markan ending (16:15). Christ is the firstborn or the beginning of the *creation* (Col 1:15; Rev 3:14); thus Christ, to whom the role of mediator in creation is attributed, is, as it were, distinguished from the creation. In a similar way a distinction is made explicitly between *Creator* and *creation* (Rom 1:25). The creation has a clear negative ring in Heb 9:11: The tabernacle through which Christ goes into the sanctuary is not made by hands and is thus not of this *creation.*

The term "creation" in Rom 8:19-22 (4 occurrences) is disputed: Does it refer to the whole creation, including (redeemed) humanity, or does it refer only to the rest of creation (nature)? It is clear from the context that the children of God (Christians) are contrasted to the cre-

ation; they are the promise for the (unredeemed) creation, which evidently includes the nonhuman creation. Fall (cf. v. 20) and redemption thus have not only an anthropological significance, but also a cosmological dimension (cf. Stuhlmacher 9f.; E. Käsemann, *Rom* [Eng. tr., 1980] ad loc.). This passage is a commentary on the concept of the new creation (Stuhlmacher).

c) Only in Paul and the deutero-Pauline literature is this word group used of the new creation. "New *creature*" is used of one who is "in Christ" (2 Cor 5:17); in the new creation the distinctions, e.g., between circumcision and uncircumcision, are abolished (Gal 6:15). Of course this new creation is most closely connected with Christ; cf. Eph 2:10 ("*created* in Christ"); 2:15 (Christ is the one who brings the new creation into being). The new being is "*created* according to God" (4:24) or is continually renewed in knowledge according to the image of its Creator (cf. Col 1:15: according to Christ). It is evident that this concept characterizes the existence of the Christian after baptism.

The concept of the new creation is derived from the OT (deutero- and trito-Isaiah) and is present in postbiblical Judaism (cf. Stuhlmacher 10ff.). Paul is to be interpreted within the context of the apocalyptic tradition; i.e., the conception is to be interpreted within both the cosmological horizon and the perspective of the history of election (with Stuhlmacher): The individual is born anew in baptism and is thus a new creation; the cosmological framework defines the gift as a task, inasmuch as the newly created individual is the sign of the promise to the (yet unredeemed) creation.

d) Jas 1:18 comes close in subject matter to the idea of the new creation; here κτίσμα, however, designates all *creatures;* likewise 1 Tim 4:4 ("every *creature* is good"); Rev 5:13 ("all *creatures* praise . . ."). In Rev 8:9 the *creatures* of the sea are named. Κτίσις can also be used of an individual creature: Rom 8:39 ("no *creature* can separate us . . ."); Heb 4:13 ("no *creature* is invisible to God"; possibly a circumlocution here for "person"). The tr. of 1 Pet 2:13 is disputed: "authority," "governing body," or "(human) creature"? The sense is to be derived from the following text: It concerns obedience to the established persons (the emperor and the governor); the use of κτίσις for governing body or authority is not demonstrable.

G. Petzke

κτίσις, εως, ἡ *ktisis* creation, creature, that which is created
→ κτίζω.

κτίσμα, ατος, τό *ktisma* creature, that which is created
→ κτίζω.

κτίστης, ου, ὁ *ktistēs* creator
→ κτίζω.

κυβεία, ας, ἡ *kybeia* game of dice*

Eph 4:14: ἐν τῇ κυβείᾳ τῶν ἀνθρώπων, "by the [deceitful] *dice game* of people."

κυβέρνησις, εως, ἡ *kybernēsis* guidance, leadership*

Pl. in 1 Cor 12:28 in the enumeration of ecclesiastical offices or ministries (with ἀντιλήμψεις and γένη γλωσσῶν). What is intended are demonstrations of capacity for leadership in the church. H. W. Beyer, *TDNT* III, 1035-37.

κυβερνήτης, ου, ὁ *kybernētēs* helmsman, captain*

Acts 27:11: the centurion believed the *captain* more than he believed the words of Paul; Rev 18:17: πᾶς κυβερνήτης καὶ πᾶς ὁ ἐπὶ τόπον πλέων, "all the *shipmasters* and all who travel on the sea."

κυκλεύω *kykleuō* surround, encircle*

Rev 20:9: the enemies of God "*surrounded* the camp of the saints."

κυκλόθεν *kyklothen* all around*

In the NT only in Revelation: 4:3, 4, as (improper) prep. with gen.: "*all around* the throne" (so also 5:11 v.l.); 4:8, as adv. with ἔσωθεν ("full of eyes *all around* and within").

κυκλόω *kykloō* surround, encircle*

Κυκλόω τινά, "*surround* someone," in John 10:24; Acts 14:20. Of the encirclement of Jerusalem, Luke 21:20 (cf. Rev 20:9 v.l.); pass. of the circling of the walls of Jericho, Heb 11:30.

κύκλῳ *kyklō* in a circle, all around*

Κύκλῳ is a fixed dat. of place: Mark 3:34; 6:6; 6:36 par. Luke 9:12. In Rom 15:19 the meaning is probably *beginning from Jerusalem and traveling around (describing a circle)* rather than *(beginning) from Jerusalem and its environs;* see BAGD s.v. 1.a. Κύκλῳ appears as prep. (with gen.) in Rev 4:6; 5:11; 7:11: κύκλῳ τοῦ θρόνου, "*around* the throne."

κυλίομαι *kyliomai* roll (vb.)*

Mark 9:20 of the epileptic: "he fell on the ground and rolled (ἐκυλίετο) foaming." Act. (*roll* a stone") appears in Luke 23:53 D.

κυλισμός, οῦ, ὁ *kylismos* rolling (noun)*

2 Pet 2:22: a pig is washed and then returns εἰς κυλισμὸν βορβόρου ("to *rolling* in the mire").

κυλλός, 3 *kyllos* crippled, maimed*

Mark 9:43 par. Matt 18:8: "better to enter into life *maimed.*" Matt 15:30, 31 mentions the *maimed* along with the lame and the dumb.

κῦμα, ατος, τό *kyma* wave*

In the NT only pl. τὰ κύματα: Mark 4:37 par. Matt 8:24; Matt 14:24; Acts 27:41. In the metaphorical characterization of the false teachers in Jude 13: κύματα ἄγρια θαλάσσης, "wild *waves* of the sea" (cf. Wis 14:1).

κύμβαλον, ου, τό *kymbalon* cymbal; wash basin*

1 Cor 13:1: ". . . I am a sounding brass or a clanging *cymbal* (κύμβαλον ἀλαλάζον)." K. L. Schmidt, *TDNT* III, 1037-39; H. Riesenfeld, "Note supplémentaire sur I Cor. XMI," ConNT 12 (1948) 50-53.

κύμινον, ου, τό *kyminon* cummin*

Matt 23:23: "You tithe mint, anise, and *cummin.*" Billerbeck I, 933.

κυνάριον, ου, τό *kynarion* little dog*

Diminutive of κύων: Mark 7:27, 28 par. Matt 15:26, 27. O. Michel, *TDNT* III, 1104; R. Pesch, *Mark* (HTKNT) I, 389f.

Κύπριος, ου, ὁ *Kyprios* Cypriot*

A resident of the island of Cyprus. Acts 4:36, of Barnabas: Κύπριος τῷ γένει, "a *Cypriot* by birth." According to 11:20 there were among the Christian "Hellenists" some *from Cyprus* and Cyrene (ἄνδρες Κύπριοι καὶ Κυρηναῖοι)"; they began the Gentile mission in Antioch. 21:16 mentions "Mnason *of Cyprus.*"

Κύπρος, ου *Kypros* Cyprus*

An island in the eastern Mediterranean, a senatorial province from 22 B.C. (Acts 13:7 mentions the proconsul Sergius Paulus). The Christian message came to Cyprus through the "Hellenists" prior to Paul (Acts 11:19). Acts 13:4-12 reports the work of Paul (and Barnabas) on Cyprus. Cyprus is mentioned further in 15:39 (Barnabas goes there with Mark); 21:3 (Cyprus comes into view); and 27:4 ("we sailed under the protection of Cyprus").

E. Oberhummer, PW XII, 59-117; *DBSup* II, 1-23; *BL* 301f.; *KP* III, 404-8.

κύπτω *kyptō* bend down*

Aor. partc. κύψας in Mark 1:7 and John 8:6; cf. John 8:8 v.l. (in place of κατακύψας).

Κυρηναῖος, ου, ὁ *Kyrēnaios* Cyrenian*

A person from → Κυρήνη. Acts 13:1, with the art.: "Lucius the *Cyrenian*"; elsewhere without the art.: Mark 15:21 par. Matt 27:32/Luke 23:26: Simon the Cyrenian; Acts 6:9: "the synagogue . . . of the *Cyrenians*"; 11:20: ἄνδρες Κύπριοι καὶ Κυρηναῖοι. Κυρηναῖος is used as an adj. in Matt 27:32 and Acts 11:20.

Κυρήνη, ης *Kyrēnē* Cyrene*

A north African city, the capital of the coastal district (from 27 B.C. connected with Crete as a senatorial province) of Cyrenaica (Pentapolis). The city had a large Jewish population (Schürer, *History* III/1, 60-62, 94f.). Acts 2:10 mentions inhabitants "of Egypt and the region of Libya belonging to Cyrene." H. C. Broholm, PW XII, 156-69; A. Wikenhauser and W. N. Schumacher, *LTK* VI, 702f.; *KP* III, 410f.; S. Applebaum, *Jews and Greeks in Ancient Cyrene* (1979).

Κυρήνιος, ου *Kyrēnios* Quirinius*

The Roman governor in Syria under whom, according to Luke 2:2, an enrollment for taxation purposes (according to v. 1 involving "the whole world") was undertaken (→ ἀπογραφή 3). *P. Sulpicius Quirinius* and a census under his administration are mentioned also in Josephus *Ant.* xvii.355; xviii.1-5; however, this census did not take place until A.D. 6-7. G. Schneider, *Luke* (ÖTK) I, 64 (bibliography) 68f.; *DBSup* IX, 693-720.

κυρία, ας, ἡ *kyria* lady*

In the NT only in 2 John 1, 5 as a fig. designation of a church: in v. 1 in the address "to the elect *lady* and her children," in v. 5 as a voc. address to the recipient church. W. Foerster, *TDNT* III, 1095; BAGD s.v.; R. Schnackenburg, *1–3 John* (HTKNT) 306f.; H.-J. Klauck, "Κυρία ἐκκλησία in Bauers Wörterbuch und die Exegese des zweiten Johannesbriefes," *ZNW* 81 (1990) 135-38.

κυριακός *kyriakos* belonging to the Lord → κύριος (12).

κυριεύω *kyrieuō* be lord, command, possess*

That over which one is *lord* is named in the gen.: Luke

22:25; 2 Cor 1:24; Acts 19:16 D Ψ. Rom 14:9 speaks of *being Lord* over the dead and the living. God is "Lord *of lords*" in 1 Tim 6:15. But in Paul other entities can be the subj. of κυριεύειν: death (Rom 6:9), sin (6:14), or the law (7:1). W. Foerster, *TDNT* III, 1097; K. W. Clark, "The Meaning of (KATA)KYPIEYEIN," FS Kilpatrick, 100-105.

κύριος, ου, ὁ *kyrios* owner, master, lord; Lord
κυριακός, 3 *kyriakos* belonging to the Lord*

1. Occurrences in the NT — 2. Meaning — 3. Secular usage — 4. Voc. κύριε used of Jesus — 5. Yahweh/God as κύριος in fixed expressions — 6. Other expressions (OT citations, etc.) — 7. The origin of the NT use of κύριος for God — 8. Use of κύριος for Jesus of Nazareth — 9. (Ὁ) Κύριος in the Gospels and Acts — 10. Other NT writings — 11. The significance of the use of κύριος for Jesus — 12. Κυριακός

Lit.: K. BERGER, "Zum traditionsgeschichtlichen Hintergrund christologischer Hoheitstitel," *NTS* 17 (1970/71) 413-22. — G. BORNKAMM, "Christ and the World in the Early Christian Message," *idem, Early Christian Experience* (1969) 14-28. — W. BOUSSET, *Kyrios Christos* (Eng. tr., 1970). — F. F. BRUCE, "Jesus is Lord," *Soli Deo Gloria* (FS W. C. Robinson, 1968), 23-36. — BULTMANN, *Theology* 121-33. — L. CERFAUX, *DBSup* V, 200-228. — *idem*, "Le titre 'Kyrios' et la dignité royale de Jésus," *RSPT* 11 (1922) 40-71 (= *Recueil L. Cerfaux* [1954] I, 3-63). — CONZELMANN, *Theology* 82-84. — O. CULLMANN, *The Christology of the NT* (NTL, ²1963) 195-237. — J. A. FITZMYER, *A Wandering Aramean* (SBLMS 25, 1979) 115-42. — W. FOERSTER, *Herr ist Jesus* (1924). — W. FOERSTER and G. QUELL, *TDNT* III, 1039-98. — HAHN, *Titles* 68-128. — I. HERMANN, *Kyrios und Pneuma* (1961). — G. HOWARD, "The Tetragram and the NT," *JBL* 96 (1977) 63-83. — L. W. HURTADO, "NT Christology: A Critique of Bousset's Influence," *TS* 40 (1979) 306-17. — W. KRAMER, *Christos, Kyrios, Gottessohn* (1963) 61-103, 149-81. — W. G. KÜMMEL, *Theology of the NT* (1973) 111-15, 157-60. — I. DE LA POTTERIE, "Le titre κύριος appliqué à Jésus dans l'évangile de Luc," FS Rigaux 117-46. — H. SCHLIER, "Über die Herrschaft Christi," *idem* III, 52-66. — G. SCHNEIDER, "Gott und Christus als ΚΥΡΙΟΣ nach der Apostelgeschichte," FS Zimmermann 161-74. — S. SCHULZ, "Maranatha und Kyrios Jesus," *ZNW* 53 (1962) 125-44. — E. SCHWEIZER, "Der Glaube an Jesus den 'Herrn,'" *EvT* 17 (1957) 7-21. — P. VIELHAUER, "Ein Weg zur neutestamentlichen Christologie?" *idem, Aufsätze zum NT* (1965) 141-98.

OT and LXX: W. W. GRAF BAUDISSIN, *Kyrios als Gottesname im Judentum . . .* (1926-29). — L. CERFAUX, "Le nom divin 'Kyrios' dans la Bible grecque: *RSPT* 20 (1931) 27-51 (= *Recueil L. Cerfaux* [1954] I, 113-26). — O. EISSFELDT, *TDOT* I, 59-72. — P. E. KAHLE, *The Cairo Geniza* (²1959) 218-28. — A. MURTONEN, *Philological and Literary Treatise on the OT Divine Names* (1952).

Hellenistic Usage: L. CERFAUX and J. TONDRIAU, *Le culte des souverains dans la civilisation gréco-romaine* (1957). — DEISSMANN, *Light* 349-59. — W. FAUTH, *KP* III, 413-17. — H. LIETZMANN, *Rom* (HNT, ⁵1971) 97-101. — HENGEL, *Judaism* I, 266f.; II, 177. — E. WILLIGER, PW XII/1 (1924) 176-83.

For further bibliography see P.-É. Langevin, *Bibliographie biblique* (1972, 1978) I, 542f., 809f.; II, 1012f.; *TWNT* X, 1152f.

1. Κύϱιος occurs 719 times in the NT, in every book except Titus and 1–3 John (but see Titus 1:4; 2 John 3 in TR). Luke makes the greatest use of κύϱιος: There are 104 occurrences in the Gospel and 107 in Acts. The noun appears 189 times in the seven undisputed letters of Paul, 64 times in Colossians, Ephesians, and 2 Thessalonians, and 22 times in 1–2 Timothy. Mark uses it 18 times, John 53, Matthew 80, Hebrews 16, James 14, 1 Peter 8, 2 Peter 14, Jude 7, and Revelation 23. The adj. κυϱιακός occurs twice (1 Cor 11:20; Acts 1:10).

2. Κύϱιος refers to a "master, owner, or lord," a person who has control or mastery over someone or something, with the power to dispose. It is used in a secular sense (literally and fig.) and in a religious sense—in the contemporary Greek world of gods (of Zeus [Pindar *I.* 5.53; Diodorus Siculus iii.61.6], of Isis [*CIG* 4897a]).

3. In secular usage, κύϱιος is often found in the NT in the literal sense of the "master/owner" of a house (Mark 13:35; cf. Luke 13:25), a vineyard (Matt 20:8; 21:40; Mark 12:9; Luke 20:13, 15), a harvest (Matt 9:38; Luke 10:2), servants, stewards, or slaves (Matt 10:24, 25; 13:27; 18:25-34; 24:45-50; 25:18-26; Luke 12:36f., 42b-47; 13:8; 14:21-23; 16:3, 5, 8; 19:16-25; John 13:16; 15:15, 20; Acts 16:16, 19; Rom 14:4a; Col 3:22a; 4:1a; Eph 6:5), animals (Matt 15:27; Luke 19:33), or a patrimony (Gal 4:1). In some instances such persons are addressed with voc. κύϱιε, which carries the connotation merely of "sir" and is used of a person regarded as being in authority. In this manner a son speaks to his father (Matt 21:29f.), Sarah refers to Abraham (1 Pet 3:6), female attendants address a bridegroom (Matt 25:11), and Greeks address Philip (John 12:21). This extended usage is also seen in the application of κύϱιος, "lord," "sir," to the Roman emperor (Acts 25:26), to worldly rulers (1 Cor 8:5; Acts 17:14b; 19:16b), to Pilate (Matt 27:63), to a king on David's throne (Matt 22:44b; Mark 12:36b; Luke 20:42b; Acts 2:34b), and even to an elder of the heavenly court (Rev 7:14). In a still more extended usage κύϱιος appears in the sayings about serving "two masters" (Matt 6:24; Luke 16:13) and about "the Lord of the sabbath" (Matt 12:8; Mark 2:28; Luke 6:5).

4. Voc. κύϱιε is often addressed to Jesus in the Gospels and Acts. Does it mean "sir" or "Lord"? On the lips of nondisciples or non-Jews, it might mean "sir": Thus the Syro-Phoenician woman (Mark 7:28; Matt 15:22, 25, 27), the (Roman) centurion (Luke 7:6), Zacchaeus (Luke 19:8b), the father of an epileptic boy (Matt 17:15), a group of blind men (Matt 9:28; 20:30, 31, 33; Luke 18:41), a leper (Matt 8:2; Luke 5:2), a Samaritan woman (John 4:11, 15, 19), a royal official (John 4:49), a cripple

at Bethesda (John 5:7), an adulteress (John 8:11), a man born blind (John 9:36), Mary Magdalene (John 20:15), and Saul on the road to Damascus (Acts 9:5a; 22:8, 10a; 26:15a).

But in many instances κύϱιε is also used of Jesus by disciples or followers: Thus would-be followers (Luke 9:57, 59, 61; Matt 8:21), disciples (Matt 8:25; 26:22; Luke 10:17; 11:1; 17:37; 22:38, 49; John 6:34; 11:12), righteous people (Matt 25:37), unrighteous people (Matt 25:44), an unnamed person (Luke 13:23), the cured blind man (John 9:38), the beloved disciple (John 13:25; 21:20), Peter (Matt 14:28, 30; 16:22; 17:4; 18:21; Luke 5:8; 12:41; 22:33; John 6:68; 13:6, 9, 36, 37; 21:15, 16, 17, 21), James and John (Luke 9:54), Martha and Mary of Bethany (Martha: Luke 10:40; John 11:21, 27, 39; Mary: John 11:32; both: John 11:3, 34), Thomas (John 14:5; 20:28 [ὁ κύϱιός μου]), Philip (John 14:8), and Jude (John 14:22). When κύϱιε is addressed to the *risen* Jesus (Acts 1:6; 7:59, 60; 9:10b, 13; 22:19) it clearly carries the nuance of "Lord." But in passages in the Gospels the meaning is often problematic. Some commentators would maintain that Jesus came to be acknowledged during his ministry not only as "sir" (i.e., a person of authority; cf. "teacher" [διδάσκαλε, Mark 4:38; 12:19], "rabbi" [ϱαβ-β(ουν)ί, Mark 10:51; 11:21]), but also as "Lord." If so, this would scarcely have connoted all that is meant by κύϱιος used of his risen status. But perhaps one should distinguish stages of the gospel tradition. Whereas κύϱιε may have meant only "sir" in stage I (Jesus' earthly ministry), it came to mean "Lord" in stage II (the apostolic preaching) or stage III (the period of the composition of the Gospels). Thus secular κύϱιε took on a religious nuance. A special problem is created by the double κύϱιε, κύϱιε in Jesus' saying in Matt 7:21-22; Luke 6:46. This saying, however, most likely stems from the early Christian community and its attempt to curb charismatics.

5. (Ὁ) Κύϱιος is often used in the NT of Yahweh/God. Though this usage is absent from Galatians, Ephesians, Philippians, Colossians, 1 Timothy, Titus, Philemon, and 1–3 John, it occurs abundantly elsewhere, not only in quotations from the OT (marked *in → 6, below), but in allusions to OT usage, e.g., "the angel of the Lord" (Matt 1:20, 24; 2:13, 19; 28:2; Luke 1:11; 2:9; Acts 5:19; 8:26; 12:7, 23), "the way of the Lord" (Acts 18:25; cf. 13:10), "the word of the Lord" (Acts 8:25; 12:24; 13:48-49; 15:35, 36; 19:10, 20; 1 Thess 4:15; 2 Thess 3:1), "the day of the Lord" (1 Cor 5:5; 1 Thess 5:2; 2 Thess 2:2; 2 Pet 3:10), "the name of the Lord" (Jas 5:10), and "the hand of the Lord" (Acts 11:21). In some of these instances the sense of κύϱιος may pass from OT Yahweh to NT Jesus.

6. Κύϱιος is otherwise used of Yahweh in the following NT passages (? indicates that κύϱιος may refer to

Jesus): Matt 1:20, 22; 3:3*; 4:7*, 10*; 5:33*; 11:25; 21:9*, 42; 22:37*, 44a*; 23:39*; 24:42(?); 27:10*; Mark 1:3*; 5:19(?); 11:9*, 10; 12:11*, 29a, b*, 30*, 36a*; 13:20; Luke 1:6, 9, 15, 16, 17, 25, 28, 32, 38, 45, 46, 58, 66, 68, 76(?); 2:9b, 15, 22, 23a, b*, 24, 26, 39; 3:4*; 4:8*, 12*, 18*, 19*; 5:17; 10:21, 27*; 13:35*; 19:38*; 20:37, 42a*; John 1:23*; 5:4; 12:13*, 38a, b*; Acts 1:24; 2:20*, 21*, 25*, 34a*, 39, 47; 3:20, 22; 4:26, 29; 5:9; 7:31, 33, 49*; 8:22, 24, 39; 10:4, 14(?), 33; 11:8, 16(?), 21a, 23(?); 12:11, 17; 13:2, 11, 12, 44, 47; 15:17a, b, 40; 16:14, 15, 30, 32(?); 17:24; 18:8, 9(?); 20:19(?), 28, 32; 21:14; Rom 4:8*; 9:28, 29*; 10:12, 13*, 16*; 11:3*, 34*; 12:19*; 14:4b, 6a, b, c, 11*; 15:11*; 1 Cor 1:31*; 2:16*; 3:5, 20*; 4:19; 7:17; 10:26*; 14:21*; 2 Cor 5:11(?); 6:17*, 18*; 8:19, 21; 10:17, 18; 2 Tim 2:14(?), 19a*, b*, 22(?), 24(?); Heb 1:10*; 7:21*; 8:2(?), 8*, 9*, 10*, 11*; 10:16*, 30a*, b*; 12:5*, 6*; 13:6*; Jas 3:9; 4:10, 15; 5:4, 11a, b; 1 Pet 1:25*; 2:3*, 13(?); 3:12a*, b*; 2 Pet 2:9, 11(?); 3:8, 9, 15; Jude 5(?):9, 14; Rev 1:8; 4:8, 11; 11:4, 15, 17; 15:3, 4; 16:5, 7; 18:8; 19:6; 21:22; 22:5, 6.

7. Whence did NT writers derive this Greek appellation for Yahweh? Use of absolute (ὁ) Κύϱιος for Yahweh has been thought to be derived from the LXX, in the great parchment codices of which Heb. *Yhwh* is translated by κύϱιος (so Cullmann, Hahn, et al.). But this tr. is found only in fourth- and fifth-century Christian copies of the LXX, not in those prepared for Greek-speaking Jews in pre-Christian times (e.g., Pap. Fuad 266 [from Egypt] and 8ḤevXII gr [from Palestine]). In these versions of the OT *Yhwh* is inserted in Hebrew or palaeo-Hebrew characters into the Greek text, and both Origen and Jerome knew of such copies in their days. Moreover, at least since W. Bousset it has been maintained that it was "unthinkable" that a Palestinian Jew would call God absolutely "the Lord" (see Bultmann, *Theology* I, 51f.).

Yet there was clearly a custom beginning among Palestinian Jews of the last two centuries B.C. of referring to God as "(the) Lord," in Aramaic as *mārêh* (indefinite, 11QtgJob 24:6-7; 1QapGen 20:12-13) or *māryā'* (definite, 4QEn[b] 1, iv.5), in Hebrew as *'ādôn* (even without the controversial suffix -*āy*, Ps 114:7; 11QPs[a] 28:7-8), and in Greek as κύϱιος (Josephus *Ant.* xx.4.90; xiii.68 [quoting Isa 19:19]; *T. Levi* 18:2 [κύϱιος]; *1 Enoch* [Greek] 10:9 [ὁ κύϱιος]). Even though none of these examples indicates that *Yhwh* was translated by κύϱιος, they at least show that it was not "unthinkable" for Palestinian Jews to call "God" (*'ēl*) or "the Almighty" (*šadday*) "Lord." The direct line has not yet been traced from this pre-Christian Jewish custom to the NT writers, but its influence on these writers is not unimaginable.

8. In a religious sense κύϱιος is also used in the NT of Jesus of Nazareth. It occurs as a title for him in all books except Titus and 1–3 John (→ 1). Normally it is used of

the *risen* Christ. It may have been applied to him originally as a title most apt for his coming at the parousia, as the Greek form of Aram. *māranā ṯā'* (1 Cor 16:22) suggests (see also 11:26, where the title is retrojected from the parousia to his death). Used absolutely, it forms the climax to the pre-Pauline (probably Jewish) Christian hymn to Christ in Phil 2:6-11, where it is "the name that is above every name," is applied to the exalted Jesus, and gives the reason that he is entitled to the same adoration that Isa 45:23 accords to Yahweh himself.

This pre-Pauline usage, echoed in the early confession "Jesus is Lord" (1 Cor 12:3; Rom 10:9), relates this title to the primitive Palestinian Jewish Christian kerygma, formulated in Aramaic by the "Hebrews" of the Jerusalem community (*dî mārêh Qĕšûa' mᵉ šîḥîḥā'*) or in Greek by the "Hellenists" (ὅτι Κύϱιος Ἰησοῦς Χϱιστός). The origin of this title for Jesus is not to be traced to Hellenistic soil, but rather to the use of *mārêh, 'ādôn,* or κύϱιος for Yahweh in pre-Christian Palestinian Judaism (→ 7). The title implies that the exalted Jesus is on a par with Yahweh, yet is not identified with him—he is not *'abbā'*! Κύϱιος does not immediately mean θεός.

This pre-Pauline usage developed into a widespread use of the title by the first NT writer. Paul mainly uses (ὁ) κύϱιος of Jesus in three ways: He uses it (a) absolutely, of the risen "Lord" (Rom 10:9; 14:8a, b; 1 Cor 2:8 [followed by τῆς δόξης]; 4:4, 5; 6:13a, b, 14, 17; 7:10, 12, 22, 25a, b, 32a, b, 34, 35; 9:1b, 5, 14; 10:9, 21a, b, 22; 11:23a, 26, 27a, b, 29, 32; 12:3, 5; 14:37; 15:58; 16:7; 2 Cor 3:16, 17a, b, 18a, b; 4:14; 5:6, 8, 11[?]; 8:5; 10:8; 11:17; 12:1, 8; 13:10; Gal 1:19; 6:17; Eph 4:5; 5:10, 17, 19, 22, 29; 6:4, 7, 8, 9; Phil 2:11; 4:5; Col 1:10; 3:13, 16, 22b, 23, 24; 4:1b; 1 Thess 1:6; 3:12; 4:6, 15b, 16, 17a, b; 5:27; 2 Thess 1:9; 2:13; 3:3, 5, 16a [τῆς εἰϱήνης], b). (b) It also appears in the prep. phrase ἐν κυϱίῳ (Rom 16:2, 8, 11, 12a, b, 13, 22; 1 Cor 4:17; 7:22, 39; 9:2; 11:11; 16:19; 2 Cor 2:12; Gal 5:10; Eph 2:21; 4:1, 17; 5:8; 6:1, 10, 21; Phil 1:14; 2:19, 24, 29; 3:1; 4:1, 2, 4, 10; Col 3:18, 20; 4:7, 17; 1 Thess 3:8; 4:1; 5:12; 2 Thess 3:4; Phlm 16:20a, b), often in exhortations and greetings or to express the union of the Christian with Christ. (c) Paul often also joins to the title the names Jesus and/or Christ: Κύϱιος Ἰησοῦς/Χϱιστός (Rom 1:4, 7; 4:24; 5:1, 11, 21; 6:11, 23; 7:25; 8:39; 12:11; 14:14; 15:6, 30; 16:18, 20, 24; 1 Cor 1:2, 3, 7, 8, 9, 10; 5:4a, b, 5; 6:11; 8:6; 9:1a; 11:23b; 15:31, 57; 16:23; 2 Cor 1:2, 3, 14; 4:5, 10; 8:9; 11:31; 13:13; Gal 1:3; 6:14, 18; Eph 1:2, 3, 15, 17; 3:11, 14; 5:20; 6:23, 24; Phil 1:2; 3:8, 20; 4:23; Col 1:2, 3; 2:6; 3:17, 24; 1 Thess 1:1a, b, 3; 2:15, 19; 3:11, 13; 4:2; 5:9, 23, 28; 2 Thess 1:1, 2, 7, 8, 12a, b; 2:1, 8, 14, 16; 3:6, 12, 18; Phlm 3, 5, 25), esp. at the beginnings of letters.

9. Apart from the voc. usage noted above (→ 4), (ὁ)

κύριος is also found in the Gospels and Acts where one detects the influence of the pre-Pauline tradition. (a) In Mark it occurs only twice in 11:3 ("the Lord"; cf. also the longer ending: 16:19, 20). (b) In Matthew it is found in the parallels to the Markan passages (21:3; 22:43, 45).

(c) In Luke (ὁ) κύριος is used not only of the risen Jesus (24:3, 34 [a primitive testimony here!), but even during his ministry (7:13, 19; 10:1, 39, 41; 11:39; 12:42a; 13:15; 17:5, 6; 18:6; 19:8a, 31, 34; 22:61a, b), at his birth (2:11), and before his birth (1:43). Apart from the parallel to the David passage (20:44), Luke's use of "the Lord" reflects the custom of his day, when the postresurrection title had become almost a name for Jesus among early Christians.

(d) In Acts Luke uses ὁ κύριος of Jesus' earthly ministry (1:21; 20:35) and of his risen status (2:36; 4:33; 9:27). But a series of typically Lukan phrases using (ὁ) κύριος occurs time and again: The (risen) Lord (Jesus) appeared and did or said something (9:10a, 11, 15, 17; 22:10b; 23:11; 26:15); Christians believe in, turn to, or are added to "the Lord" (5:14; 9:35, 42; 11:17, 21b, 24; 14:23; 16:31; 20:21); disciples "of the Lord" (9:1) preach him (11:20; 14:3; 28:31), or extol, preach, and baptize in his name (8:16; 9:28; 19:5, 13, 17; 21:3). There are also isolated phrases, such as "the way of the Lord" (18:25), "the fear of the Lord" (9:31), "the grace of the Lord" (15:11; cf. 20:24), "for the sake of the Lord" (15:26), and "the Lord of all" (10:36). Here one sees how "the Lord" has become the object of the Christian proclamation.

(e) In John ὁ κύριος is used in only a few passages. In 4:1; 6:23; 11:2 it resembles the usage in Lukan narrative sections of Jesus' ministry. But it is also found on the lips of Mary Magdalene, reporting that "the Lord" has been taken from the tomb (20:2), referring to him as "my Lord" (20:13), or announcing that she has seen "the Lord" (20:18). Other disciples, too, recognize him as such (20:20, 25; 21:7a, b, 12). The Johannine Gospel has simply repeated this usage of the earlier tradition.

10. The same must be said of occurrences of κύριος in other NT writings (1 Tim 1:2, 12, 14; 5:5 v.1; 6:3, 14, 15; 2 Tim. 1:2, 8, 16, 18a, b; 2:7; 4:1, 8, 14, 17, 18, 22; Heb 2:3; 7:14; 12:14; 13:20; Jas 1:1, 7; 2:1; 5:7, 8, 14, 15; 1 Pet 1:3; 3:15; 2 Pet 1:2, 8, 11, 14, 16; 2:20; 3:2, 18; Jude 4:17, 21, 25; Rev 11:8; 14:13; 17:14a; 19:16a; 22:20, 21).

11. In giving Jesus the title κύριος early Christians acknowledged his victory over a humiliating death, his exaltation to a transcendent status of glory, and his regal dominion over the lives of those who come to share their faith. In the face of widespread belief in Roman emperors as κύριοι (e.g., Augustus [ÄgU 1197, I, 15]) Christians proclaimed, as Paul echoes, "for us there is one Lord, Jesus Christ, through whom are all things and through

whom we exist" (1 Cor 8:6). Jesus was for them more than a Davidic Messiah (Mark 12:35-37 par.). The primitive kerygmatic proclamation about Jesus of Nazareth as the crucified and resurrected agent of God included his lordship and messiahship (Acts 2:36), his exaltation (2:33), and the recognition that there was no other name under heaven by which people were to be saved (4:12). He was exalted as Lord so that he might pour forth the Spirit as the vivifier of Christian life (2:33). That is why Paul could even say earlier, "the Lord is the Spirit" (2 Cor 3:17), a *crux interpretum,* but one which must certainly be explained in terms of 1 Cor 15:45 ("the last Adam became a life-giving spirit") as speaking of the resurrection and Rom 1:4 ("designated Son of God in power according to a spirit of holiness by the resurrection from the dead") in contrast to what he was "according to the flesh." In these verses Paul does not distinguish κύριος and πνεῦμα as carefully as he does in 2 Cor 13:13 or as the trinitarian teaching of later centuries would.

12. The adj. κυριακός, having no Semitic equivalent, was taken over from Hellenistic usage and acquired the religious sense of "belonging to the Lord," i.e., to Jesus as the risen Lord. Κυριακὸν δεῖπνον, "the Lord's supper" (1 Cor 11:20), is related to ποτήριον and τράπεζα κυρίου, "the Lord's cup" and "table" (10:12), illustrating the influence of the noun on the adj. It refers to the supper of eucharistic *anamnesis* at which Christians partake of "the body and blood of the Lord" (11:27) and proclaim his death until he comes (11:26). Ἡ κυριακὴ ἡμέρα (Rev 1:10), though possibly reminiscent of the OT "day of the Lord" (Joel 2:31 LXX), reveals by its adj. form that it refers to a day celebrated by Christians in honor of their risen Lord, probably "the first day of the week" (1 Cor 16:2; cf. John 20:1, 19; *Did.* 14:1).

J. A. Fitzmyer

κυριότης, ητος, ἡ *kyriotēs* position as lord, authority to rule*

Lit.: H. BIETENHARD, *Die himmlische Welt im Urchristentum und Spätjudentum* (WUNT 2, 1951) 50-65. — BILLERBECK III, 583f. — W. FOERSTER, *TDNT* III, 1096f. — G. H. C. MACGREGOR, "Principalities and Powers," *NTS* 1 (1954/55) 17-28. — B. NOACK, *Satanas und Soteria. Untersuchungen zur neutestamentlichen Dämonologie* (1948) 104-8. — H. RINGGREN, *RGG* II, 1301-3. — H. SCHLIER, *Principalities and Powers in the NT* (1961). — K. L. SCHMIDT, "Die Natur- und Geisteskräfte im paulinischen Erkennen und Glauben," *ErJb* 14 (1947) 87-143.

1. Κυριότης appears 4 times in the NT, once each in Colossians, Ephesians, 2 Peter, and Jude. Two NT usages are to be distinguished:

2. a) The basic meaning of κυριότης is *rule of the (a) lord.* It is not God, but rather Jesus Christ, of whom it is believed and to whom witness is given that he is the exalted → κύριος (2 Pet 2:10; Jude 8). This term, derived

from the political realm, implies (in contrast to δεσπότης) the claim of the legitimate and true lordship, which is considered the only and universal one.

b) Eph 1:21 and Col 1:16 include other powers and forces (which are subordinated to the κυριότης of Jesus Christ) as possessing κυριότης. Here the reference is primarily to Jewish apocalyptic interest in a fixed angelology, i.e., angels, demons, and spirit world, which originated in the Babylonian-Iranian cultural realm and then became intermingled with the degrading of ancient Canaanite deities (cf. Philo *Conf.* 171; *Mut.* 59; *Mart. Pol.* 14:1; 1QS 3:13ff.; *2 Enoch* 20:1; *1 Enoch* 61:10). This conception represented the attempt of people, made up to our own time, to comprehend from their own variegated experience of powerlessness the forces and powers that rule over humankind. Christianity, however, confesses that all power lies in God.   F. Schröger

κυρόω *kyroō* strengthen; make legally binding, validate*

Gal 3:15: "No one abrogates a *legally binding* testament (κεκυρωμένην διαθήκην)"; 2 Cor 2:8, with the meaning *resolve/decide (for);* Paul admonishes: κυρῶσαι εἰς αὐτὸν ἀγάπην, "*resolve* [to exercise] love toward him." J. Behm, *TDNT* III, 1098f.

κύων, κυνός, ὁ *kyōn* dog*

Lit.: BILLERBECK I, 447, 722-26; III, 621f., 773. — O. BÖCHER, *Dämonenfurcht und Dämonenabwehr* (BWANT 90, 1970) 86-88. — K. GALLING, *BRL* 149f. — J. JEREMIAS, "Matthäus 7,6a," FS Michel 271-75. — H. VON LIPS, "Schweine füttert man, Hunde nicht—ein Versuch das Rätsel von Mt 7,6 zu lösen," *ZNW* 79 (1988) 165-86. — O. MICHEL, *TDNT* III, 1101-4. — F. PERLES, "Zur Erklärung von Mt 7,6," *ZNW* 25 (1926) 163f. — W. RICHTER, *KP* II, 1245-49. — W. SCHMITHALS, *Paul and the Gnostics* (1972) 65-122. — G. SCHWARZ, "Matthäus VII 6a," *NovT* 14 (1972) 18-25. — For further bibliography see *TWNT* X, 1154.

1. With a few exceptions (Judg 7:5: neutral; Job 30:1: sheep dogs; Isa 56:10; Tob 11:4: watchdogs), the Bible regards dogs as despicable animals (along with hyenas [Sir 13:18], vultures [1 Kgs 14:11; 16:4; 21:24; Jer 15:3], and pigs [Matt 7:6; 2 Pet 2:22; cf. Horace *Ep.* i.2.23ff.; *Gos. Thom.* 93; Pap. Oxy. V, 840; *b. Ber.* 83a]). They are described as always hungrily prowling around (Isa 56:11), eating whatever is thrown out as garbage (Exod 22:31; cf. *Jos. As.* 10:13; 13:8), and attacking whatever is defenseless because it is weak, sick, or alone. The stubborn endurance of the dog can nevertheless be understood in a positive way, even with reference to Israel (*Exod. Rab.* 42:9 par.).

Accordingly, in the OT dogs represent both the extremity of baseness (Eccl 9:4; 1 Sam 17:43; 24:15; 2 Sam 9:8; 16:9; 2 Kgs 8:13; also 1 Kgs 21:19, 23; 2 Kgs 9:10; cf. Josephus *Ant.* xv.289; *B.J.* iv.324) and grave, possibly life-threatening, danger (Pss 22:17, 21; 59:7, 15f.; also Exod 11:7; Jdt 11:19).

2. The generally negative connotation is present also in the NT. Luke 16:21 emphasizes the misery of Lazarus by noting that he cannot even keep away the dogs prowling around outside. In Rev 22:15 it is said of the eschatological city that "outside are the dogs. . ." (ἔξω οἱ κύνες): Among the others who are "excluded" are Gentiles and false teachers (= everyone who loves and practices lies). In 2 Peter 2 κύων is a designation for heretics in the description of the lying teachers (ψευδοδιδάσκαλοι, v. 1) who infiltrate the community, thus bringing themselves and their followers into the final destruction (vv. 1, 3; also v. 12; cf. Prov 7:22 LXX). In their renunciation of the "holy commandment" (v. 1) entrusted to them, they are to be compared with dogs and pigs (v. 22, citing Prov 26:11; cf. also Ign. *Eph.* 7:2).

After the commandment in Matt 7:1-5 not to sit in judgment over others, a warning is given in v. 6 (M) particularly concerning those who, in trampling "what is holy" (= the gospel; cf. *Did.* 9:5: the Lord's Supper) under foot, are exposed as false Christians and thus pose a "destructive" danger to the Church (cf. the "abominable" wolves in Matt 7:15; Acts 20:29f.; see also Titus 3:9-11).

In Phil 3:2 the three reciprocally interpreting terms, "dogs, evil workers, mutilators," confirm that κύων in the NT is a term for heretics; here it refers concretely to Judaizing missionaries (probably of Jewish origin; cf. 2 Cor 11:13: ψευδαπόστολοι), who demand, among other things, circumcision (cf. the paronomasia in vv. 2-3; see also Phil 3:18f.; perhaps also Matt 7:6b).   S. Pedersen

κῶλον, ου, τό *kōlon* corpse*

Used esp. of unburied corpses. Heb 3:17: "whose *bodies* fell in the wilderness" (cf. Num 14:29, 32 LXX).

κωλύω *kōlyō* hinder, impede, forbid

Lit.: K. ALAND, *Did the Early Church Baptize Infants?* (Library of History and Doctrine, 1963) 96. — A. ARGYLE, "O. Cullmann's Theory Concerning κωλύειν," *ExpTim* 67 (1955) 17. — G. R. BEASLEY-MURRAY, *Baptism in the NT* (1963) 324f. — O. CULLMANN, *Baptism in the NT* (SBT 1, 1950) 71-80. — J. DUPONT, *Béatitudes* II, 151-61. — J. JEREMIAS, *Infant Baptism in the First Four Centuries* (1960) 53f. — S. LÉGASSE, *Jésus et l'enfant* (1969) 36-43, 187-95, 210-14, 326-33.

1. The vb. κωλύω appears 23 times in the NT. Its meaning in most cases is *hinder,* occasionally with the nuance *oppose (someone)* or *place an obstacle in the way* (of someone; Acts 11:17; 27:43) or *forbid* (1 Tim 4:3) and *refuse* (Luke 6:29; Acts 10:47). The compound διακωλύω (Matt 3:14; → 2.c) strengthens the meaning of the simple vb.

2. Neither in the LXX nor in the NT does κωλύω have in itself theological significance. Such significance is

seen only in particular contexts. The NT employs κωλύω —except for where its usage is neutral—in three different associations:

a) In relation to charismata: Mark 9:38, 39 par. Luke 9:49, 50 echoes Num 11:28 (κώλυσον αὐτούς) and is concerned with the freedom accorded to theurgic practitioners, non-Christians who use the name of Jesus. In 1 Cor 14:39 Paul recommends, in the context of the precedence given to prophecy, that the Christians not *hinder* the gift of tongues, as long as the proper order is maintained. In Acts 16:6 κωλύω is used of the activity of the Holy Spirit in directing the way that guides the apostles on their path.

b) Κωλύω appears in Acts 8:36; 10:47; 11:17 in connection with baptism. What is spoken of is the absence of any hindrance in the way of the baptism of the Gentiles, particularly in consideration of the wonderful guarantee that the gift of the Spirit brought forth. No proof exists (*contra Gos. Eb.* apud Epiphanius *Haer.* xxx.13.8; cf. Matt 3:14; *Ps.-Clem. Hom.* xiii.5.1; the Syriac version of the Irene legend) that κωλύω in these passages in Acts is derived from a baptismal formula (*contra* Jeremias); κωλύω is not used in a sense specific enough to demonstrate its use in a baptismal formula. Thus the "sacramental" connections, which have also been suggested for other passages, are without a sufficient basis.

c) Κωλύω takes on its greatest theological significance where it designates human resistance to the saving plan of God. Thus John wants to dissuade Jesus from being baptized (Matt 3:14: διεκώλυσεν αὐτόν); thus he resisted the plan of God set forth in the Scriptures (3:15). The same sense is present in the scene in which children are brought to Jesus (Mark 10:14 par. Matt 19:14/Luke 18:16): If the text offers only an indirect basis for the practice of infant baptism, it nevertheless demonstrates a characteristic attitude of Jesus, who censures anyone who —like the disciples with the children—wants to hinder the insignificant and the disenfranchised from being accepted. According to 1 Thess 2:14-16 the Jews opposed the apostolic mission: Paul stigmatizes those who stand on the side of the ungodly of the eschaton insofar as they *hinder* (v. 16) the apostles in the proclamation of the gospel. Jesus directs an analogous charge to the experts in the law: Through their false teaching they have *hindered* others from attaining the saving knowledge, while this knowledge was denied to them (Luke 11:52; cf. Matt 23:13).   S. Légasse

κώμη, ης, ἡ *kōmē* small town, village

In the NT only in the Evangelists: 7 times in Mark, 4 in Matthew, 12 in Luke-Acts (1 of those in Acts), and 3 in John. Κώμη appears in contrast to πόλις in Matt 9:35; 10:11; Mark 6:56; Luke 8:1; 13:22 and with ἀγρός in Mark 6:36; Luke 9:12. The pl. appears with the gen. of a greater area for the villages in a district in Mark 8:27 (Caesarea Philippi). Places called κῶμαι are Bethany (John 11:1, 30), Bethsaida (Mark 8:23, 26), Bethlehem (John 7:42), and Emmaus (Luke 24:13, 28). In Acts 8:25 κώμη is used of *inhabitants of a village.*

κωμόπολις, εως, ἡ *kōmopolis* market town*

Mark 1:38: "Let us go into the nearby *market towns.*"

κῶμος, ου, ὁ *kōmos* feasting*

Κῶμος originally designated the festal procession in honor of Dionysus, then the joyous meal, the feast. It appears in the NT only in a negative sense and in the pl.: Rom 13:13 and Gal 5:21, with μέθαι; 1 Pet 4:3, with πότοι. Spicq, *Notes* I, 449f.

κώνωψ, ωπος, ὁ *kōnōps* gnat*

Matt 23:24, in an accusation against the scribes and Pharisees: "You blind guides, who strain out (→ διϋλίζω) a *gnat* but swallow a camel!"

Κώς, Κῶ *Kōs* Cos*

An island in the Aegean Sea, the second largest of the Doric islands off the southwest coast of Asia Minor. From the 4th cent. B.C. a famous sanctuary of Asclepius existed southwest of the city by the same name on the island. Acts 21:1: ". . . we came by a straight course into Cos (εἰς τὴν Κῶ), on the following day to Rhodes, and from there to Patara." L. Bürchner, PW XI, 1467-80; E. Meyer, *LAW* 1601; *KP* III, 312-15.

Κωσάμ *Kōsam* Cosam*

A personal name in Jesus' genealogy in Luke 3:28.

κωφός, 3 *kōphos* mute; deaf*

The adj. originally meant *blunted, dulled;* it could refer to the organs of either speech or hearing and could thus mean *mute* as well as *deaf.* Most NT uses refer to muteness (Matt 9:32, 33; Matt 12:22 bis par. Luke 11:14 bis; Matt 15:30, 31 [cf. par. Mark]; Luke 1:22). The word is used of deafness in Mark 7:32, 37; 9:25; Matt 11:5 par. Luke 7:22.

Λ λ

λαγχάνω *lanchanō* attain, be selected by lot; cast lots*

Of the attainment of the apostolic office, Acts 1:17; of faith, 2 Pet 1:1. Zechariah "was *ordained by lot* to burn incense (ἔλαχε τοῦ θυμιᾶσαι)," Luke 1:9. Λαγχάνω has the meaning *cast lots* in John 19:24 (λάχωμεν περὶ αὐτοῦ τίνος ἔσται). H. Hanse, *TDNT* IV, 1f.; Spicq, *Notes* I, 451-53.

λάζαρος, ου *Lazaros* Lazarus*

A personal name corresponding to *l'zr*, a rabbinic abbreviation of *'el'āzār*. In John (11:1, 2, 5, 11, 14, 43; 12:1, 2, 9, 10, 17) it is the name of Mary and Martha's brother (11:2, 5). Lazarus and his sisters lived in Bethany (11:1). He was a friend of Jesus (11:5, 11), who raised him from the dead (11:17-44; 12:17). In Luke the beggar in the parable in 16:19-31 bears the same name (16:20, 23, 24, 25). J. Kremer, *Lazarus. Die Geschichte einer Auferstehung. Text, Wirkungsgeschichte und Botschaft von Johannes 11,1-46* (1985); A. Marchadour, *Lazare. Histoire d'un récit. Récits d'une histoire* (LD 132, 1988).

λάθρᾳ *lathrạ* secretly*

Matt 1:19, with ἀπολύω; 2:7, with καλέω; John 11:28, with φωνέω; Acts 16:37, with ἐκβάλλω. Spicq, *Notes* I, 454-57.

λαῖλαψ, απος, ἡ *lailaps* whirlwind*

Mark 4:37 par. Luke 8:23: λαῖλαψ ἀνέμου (so also *T. Naph.* 6:4), "a windstorm"; 2 Pet 2:17, fig. of false teachers: "mists driven by the *storm.*"

λακάω *lakaō* burst, split*

Acts 1:18, of Judas: ἐλάκησεν μέσος, "he *burst* in the middle."

λακτίζω *laktizō* kick, lash out*

Of draught animals kicking with their hoofs. Acts 26:14 (and 9:5 TR), fig.: πρὸς κέντρα λακτίζω, "*kick* against the goad [of the driver]." H. Hanse, *TDNT* IV, 3; Spicq, *Notes* I, 458f. → κέντρον.

λαλέω *laleō* speak, talk

1. Occurrences in the NT — 2. Meanings — 3. Idiomatic usages

Lit.: A. DEBRUNNER, et al., *TDNT* IV, 69-139, esp. 75f., 110f. — H. JASCHKE, " 'λαλεῖν' bei Lukas," *BZ* 15 (1971) 109-14. — H. W. KUHN, *Ältere Sammlungen im Markusevangelium* (SUNT 8, 1971) 133f. — H. RÄISÄNEN, *Die Parabeltheorie im Markusevangelium* (Schriften der Finnischen Exegetischen Gesellschaft 26, 1978) 48-64. — For further bibliography → γλῶσσα, λέγω, λόγος; see Räisänen; *TWNT* X, 1157f.

1. Λαλέω appears very frequently in the NT: 269 times (eleventh in frequency among vbs.), of which 196 are in the Gospels and Acts (esp. in John and Acts with 59 occurrences each). Of the 52 occurrences in Paul 34 are in 1 Corinthians. Hebrews has 16 occurrences and Revelation has 12.

2. The original meaning of λαλέω was *babble, stammer;* it was onomatopoeic for the unassisted expression of small children. Then, transferred to adult usage, it came to mean *chatter, prattle,* in deliberate contrast to reasonable speech (→ λέγω). However, already in classical Greek λαλέω, like λέγω, meant *speak, talk* (Debrunner 75f.; Frisk, *Wörterbuch* II, 76). In the NT λαλέω is found only with the meaning *speak, talk,* in which the nuance *be able to speak* is characteristic in many passages; e.g., ἐλάλησεν ὁ κωφός, "the dumb man *could speak again*" (Matt 9:33 par. Luke 11:14; cf. Mark 7:37; Matt 12:22; 15:31); ἐλάλει ὀρθῶς, "he *could again speak* correctly" (Mark 7:35).

Like λέγω, λαλέω can be trans., e.g., τὴν ἀλήθειαν . . . λελάληκα, "I have *spoken* the truth" (John 8:40; cf. the synonymous τὴν ἀλήθειαν λέγω in v. 45). The person addressed is most often dat. (always so in Matthew), also often expressed with πρός τινα (frequently in Luke-Acts), sometimes, as in Eng. *speak* with someone (about something), μετά τινος (John 4:27; 14:30). Λαλέω is distinguished from λέγω in that it only rarely means *say that* ... or is followed by indirect discourse (e.g., ἐλάλησεν μετ' ἐμοῦ λέγων, he *said to me:* ..., Rev 17:1; 21:9; see also Matt 28:18; John 8:12; Acts 8:26 [→ λέγω 2]; ἐλάλησεν ... λέγων is, however, very common in the LXX, esp. in the Pentatech and the historical literature). Use of the partc., e.g., ἡ ... λαλουμένη διδαχή, "the teaching that you *are presenting;* ὁ δι' ἀγγέλων λαληθεὶς λόγος, "the word *proclaimed* by angels" (Heb 2:2).

3. An idiomatic expression in the Johannine farewell discourse is ταῦτα λελάληκα ὑμῖν, "I *have said* this to you" (John 14:25; 15:11; 16:1, 4, 6, 25, 33). A more frequent idiomatic phrase is λαλέω τὸν λόγον (→ λόγος), used of preaching and proclamation (regarded by Kuhn 133 as a phrase from early Christian proclamation, by Räisänen 54 as the terminology of the Gospels; Mark 2:2; 4:33; 8:32 [among the Synoptic Gospels only in Mark, but see Luke 24:44]; Acts 11:19; 14:25; 16:6; Phil 1:14 [cf. John 12:48; Heb 2:2]; with attributive gen. σου in Acts 4:29, τοῦ θεοῦ in Acts 4:31; 13:46; Heb 13:7, τοῦ κυρίου in Acts 8:25; 16:32. The obj. of λαλέω is often ῥήμα(τα), though this is not a fixed idiomatic phrase, as the distinction in content demonstrates (cf., e.g., Acts 5:20 with 6:11, 13).

Only Mark (4:33f.) and Matthew (13:3, 10, 13, 33f.) have (ἐν) παραβολαῖς λαλεῖν, "*speak* in parables," and χωρὶς παραβολῆς λαλεῖν, "*speak* without a parable/*speak* plainly"; on the tension between Mark 4:34 and 4:33 see Räisänen 48-64; R. Pesch, *Mark* (HTKNT) I, 264-76; J. Gnilka, *Mark* (EKKNT) I, 190f.

On γλώσσαις (or γλώσσῃ) λαλέω, "*speak* in tongues" (Acts 19:6; 1 Cor 12:30; 13:1; 14:2, 4, 5, 6; 14:13, 18, 23, 27; 14:39) → γλῶσσα 6.   H. Hübner

λαλιά, ᾶς, ἡ *lalia* speech, manner of speaking*

John 4:42: "It is no longer for the sake of your *word* that we believe; for we ourselves have heard ..."; 8:43: "Why do you not understand my *word* [manner of speaking]?"; Matt 26:73 (par. Mark 14:70 Koine A, etc.): "Your *manner of speaking* betrays you."

λαμα *lama* why?

Mark 15:34 B Θ D par. Matt 27:46 D* have, instead of λεμα (from Aram. *lᵉmā'*), λαμα, from Heb. *lāmmâ*. → ελωι.

λαμβάνω *lambanō* grasp, seize, take hold of, take; attain; take up; receive

1. Occurrences in the NT — 2. Secular Greek basis and OT roots — 3. NT usage — 4. Compounds

Lit.: BAGD s.v. — G. DELLING, *TDNT* IV, 5-7. — H. H. SCHMIDT, *THAT* I, 875-79.

1. Λαμβάνω is used 260 times in the NT with the preponderance in Matthew (54 occurrences), followed by Luke-Acts (51) and John 46. It is strikingly frequent in two of the late NT documents, Hebrews (17 occurrences) and Revelation (23). However, in none of those documents can λαμβάνω be considered a predominant word. The noun λῆμψις, "receiving/taking," appears only in Phil 4:15.

2. a) The vb. λαμβάνω is attested in Greek literature from the time of Hesiod and Homer, in inscriptions (BAGD), and in papyri. It signifies the range of meaning, "grasp, take, seize," either peacefully or violently. It is used fig. of mental states and illnesses (e.g., seized by anger, fever: Herodotus, Hippocrates) as well as for mental grasping and conceiving (Pindar, Plato). In the latter case the semantic idea of "accept, take up, receive, undergo" appears, as it does in both poetry (Homer) and prose (Xenophon), and is used with reference to both the material realm (possessions) and the human realm (wives). In these texts a wide field is evident, in which λαμβάνω signifies both the active as well as receptive (understood as passive) meaning. This field is significant for the consideration of biblical texts.

b) In the LXX λαμβάνω most often renders Heb. *lqh* (qal of the vb.); in addition δέχομαι, as a translation of *lqh*, belongs to the word field "accept, receive." Two emphases emerge from this wide spectrum of meaning and from the unspecific usage: The motif of movement and tension is expressed in "take, take away," while the less active side is expressed in "accept, take up." In both instances points of departure for the NT usage can be seen.

3. a) The active meaning *take, grasp* is characteristic in the Synoptic Gospels of feeding and meal terminology (Mark 6:41; 8:1 par.; cf. also 7:27; supplemented in Matthew in 16:7, 9f.) and receives a eucharistic stamp through the celebration in the early Church (Mark 14:22f. par.; cf. 1 Cor 11:23f.; Luke 24:30, 43; John 21:13). Also to be noted are the narrative style of the parable of the vinedressers (Mark 12:3, 8 par. Matthew: in the violent sense) and the conflict story about the resurrection (Mark 12:19f., 21f. par. Luke: with reference to a wife as both person and possession).

b) The receptive meaning *accept, receive* is more frequently encountered and more theologically significant in the NT. It appears at the central place in the NT kerygma and can be used for the reciprocal relationship of asking and receiving (Mark 11:24 par. Matthew; Luke 11:10 par. Matt 7:10, probably from Q; John 16:24 and Jas 1:7; 4:3), which is characteristic of request parenesis in connection with the demand for faith (Mark 11:24). The origin and direction of the receiving can be strengthened and made more precise with a prep.: ἐκ (Gal 3:2; John 1:16; 16:14f.; Heb 5:1), ἀπό (Mark 12:2, παρά (Acts 17:9; 20:24; John 5:34, 41, and often in John), or διά (Rom 1:5; 5:11). This prep. connection and intensification is attested also in the papyri (examples in Mayser, *Grammatik* II/2, 609). The character of something as a gift of grace is seen where the giver is either God (2 John 4; 2 Pet 1:17; Rev 2:28) or Jesus Christ (Rom 1:5; 5:11).

What is given can take on a variety of forms: the πνεῦμα esp. is "received" (Rom 8:15; 1 Cor 2:12; Acts 1:8; 8:15, 17, 19, in connection with prayer and the laying on of hands; John 7:39; 20:22); also grace (Rom 1:5; 5:17), reconciliation (5:11), righteousness (5:17), forgiveness of sins (Acts 10:43; 26:18), the promised inheritance (Heb 9:15), knowledge of the truth (Heb 10:26), indeed, all the gifts that make Christian existence possible and determine it. "What have you, which you *have* not *received*" (1 Cor 4:7): "The thought of grace finds radical expression . . . as opposed to the Corinthian exaltation Christology, in which the moment of receipt is left behind" (H. Conzelmann, *1 Cor* [Hermeneia] 87). In this context λαμβάνω has an eschatological orientation *(acquire, attain)*, which is also seen in the saying about discipleship and reward in Mark 10:30 par. and is even intensified (cf. also 1 Cor 3:8, 14) in Matt 19:29 by the fut. and the divine pass.

The receptive sense can be extended by fixed phrases, which appear without special redactional emphases, e.g., λαμβάνω δύναμιν, "*receive* power" (Acts 1:8; Heb 11:11; Rev 4:11), "*attain* the power" (Rev 5:12; 11:17), λαμβάνω ἐξουσίαν, "*receive* power" (Acts 26:10; Rev 2:28; 17:12), but also λαμβάνω κρίμα, "*receive* punishment," in reference to the scribes (Mark 12:40 par. Luke 20:47), to Christians, who resist the legal power of the state (Rom 13:2), and to the false, unconscientious teachers (Jas 3:1). Similar instances, some from the Epistles, demonstrate a definite spectrum of meaning for this passively oriented sense of λαμβάνω *(get, receive, accept)* through such phrases as λαμβάνω ἀφορμήν (Rom 7:8, 11: impulse), λαμβάνω ὑπόμνησιν (2 Tim 1:5: remembrance), μισθαποδοσίαν (Heb 2:2: recompense), ἀρχήν (Heb 2:3: beginning), and λήθην (2 Pet 1:9: forgetfulness).

In addition, one finds the active significance of λαμβάνω in a similar manner, as in Heb 11:29, 36 (πεῖραν λαμβάνω, "*undertake* an attempt") and Jas 5:10 (ὑπόδειγμα λαμβάνω, "*take* as an example").

c) In addition to and in contrast to these general meanings of λαμβάνω under 3.a, b, individual redactional emphases are worthy of note:

A noteworthy example is Mark 14:65: ῥαπίσμασιν . . . ἔλαβον, "they [the servants] *received* him [Jesus] with blows" (R. Pesch, *Mark* [HTKNT] II, 442.

Matthew also exhibits noteworthy examples: 10:8: reception (of the gospel) as a gift impels one likewise to transmit it further; 10:38: acceptance of the cross in the course of one's discipleship; 10:41: the obligation to serve in love in contrast to the prophets and righteous people, with the corresponding promise of reward (cf.

here also 20:7, 9-11, the parable of the workers in the vineyard). A special Matthean phrase, συμβούλιον λαμβάνω ("*pass* a resolution," 12:14; 22:15; 27:1, 7; 28:12), is always used in reference to Jewish leaders. The partc. λαβών, often pleonastic (13:31 par. Luke 13:19; Matt 17:27; esp. Matt 25, etc.), might be a Semitism (BDF §419.1, 2), but is found also in secular Greek literature (Homer, Sophocles) and is thus rendered simply as "with." Λαμβάνω belongs to the terminology of taxation and finance in Matt 17:24f., 27 (cf. also 27:9 and 28:15 in a similar context), and is to be translated *collect, raise.*

In the Lukan tradition there is particular emphasis on the affective sense, which comes from secular Greek: People can be *seized* by confusion and fear (5:26; 7:16); they can be *held captive* by demonic sicknesses (9:39); or they can *take* courage (Acts 28:15). In Luke 19:12, 15 what is spoken of is taking by a ruler; in 5:5 it is an occupational taking (fishing). 20:21 reflects the OT background: πρόσωπον λαμβάνω (cf. Sir 4:22; Mal 1:8), "*accept* someone's face, look at someone, be partial" (cf. Gal 2:6). In Acts, along with reception of the Spirit (→ b), there is acceptance of offices (or ministries; 1:20, 25; 20:24); also, in a similar sense, *receive* a commission (17:15) or *obtain* authority (26:10). Heb 5:1 and 7:5 (acceptance of the high priesthood granted as a gift) may fit here thematically.

One might also point to Pauline texts already mentioned: 1 Cor 10:13: a description of the struggle facing the Christian (temptation comes over the individual); 14:5, in an ecclesiological context (οἰκοδομὴν λάβῃ: the Church is built up); Phil 2:7, in a christological statement (*accept* the form of a slave); 3:12, in an eschatological statement (*attain* the final goal).

Μαρτυρίαν λαμβάνω ("*receive* a witness"—or not receive it) contributes an important component to Johannine theology, both in reference to the sovereignty of the Johannine Christ (5:34) and in reference to the individual faced with decision (3:11, 32f.; 1 John 5:9). This decision comes as a result of one's accepting Christ himself (1:12; 13:20) and his word (17:8) or rejecting it (5:43; 12:48). In the Passion narrative John uses λαμβάνω to characterize the machinations of those responsible for the condemnation of Jesus (18:31; 19:1, 6, 23). However, it is also used of the loving acceptance of the mother (19:27) and the concern for the body of Jesus (19:40).

In Revelation the association of λαμβάνω with χάραγμα are noteworthy as theologically significant occurrences of the word: to *accept* the seal, i.e., the stamp (of idolatry) and to be judged (14:9, 11; 19:20) or to refuse it with saving consequences (20:4) and to *receive* the water of life as a thirsting person (22:17).

In conclusion it may be affirmed that the variety of NT attestations of λαμβάνω are indications of the vb.'s breadth of meaning. They are, however, concentrated with a significant theological emphasis: The meaning *accept, receive* "is predominant, esp. in theologically significant verses." From this it is apparent "how strongly the NT . . . views the relation of man to God as that of recipient and Giver . . ." (Delling 6).

4. The following compounds are formed with λαμβάνω and appear in the NT (number of occurrences in parentheses): ἀναλαμβάνω (13), ἐπιλαμβάνω (19), καταλαμβάνω (15), μεταλαμβάνω (7), παραλαμβάνω (50), προλαμβάνω (3), προσλαμβάνω (12), συλλαμβάνω (16), and ὑπολαμβάνω (5); also the double compounds συμπαραλαμβάνω (4), συμπεριλαμβάνω (1), and συναντιλαμβάνομαι (2).

A. Kretzer

Λάμεχ *Lamech* Lamech*

Indeclinable name of the father of Noah in the genealogy in Luke 3:36 (cf. Gen 5:28f.; 1 Chr 1:3).

λαμμᾶ *lamma* why?
Alternative form of → λαμα.

λαμπάς, άδος, ἡ *lampas* torch; lamp*

1. Occurrences in the NT — 2. General meaning — 3. Matthew 25: "torches" or "lamps"? — 4. Revelation

Lit.: G. FOHRER, *BHH* 462f. — J. GAGÉ, *RAC* VII, 154-217. — H. C. HAHN, *DNTT* II, 484-86. — J. JEREMIAS, "ΛΑΜΠΑΔΕΣ Mt 25,1, 3f, 7f," *ZNW* 56 (1965) 196-201. — A. MAU, *PW* VI/2, 1945-53. — C. MUGLER, *Dictionnaire historique de la terminologie optique des Grecs* (1964) s.v. — A. OEPKE, *TDNT* IV, 16-28. — E. SCHWEIZER, *Matt* (Eng. tr., 1975) 464-68. — F. ZORELL, "De lampadibus decem virginum," *VD* 10 (1930) 176-82.

1. The noun λαμπάς appears 9 times in the NT. 5 of these, all pl., are in the parable of the ten virgins (Matt 25:1, 3, 4, 7, 8). The pl. form λαμπάδες also appears in John 18:3; Acts 20:8; Rev 4:5. Only Rev 8:10 has the sg.

2. From the apparently oldest reference in Aeschylus *A.* 8 on λαμπάς designated a *torch* (normally of resinous pine or dry twigs covered with pitch; see Mau). Λαμπάδες were used in nocturnal activities, primarily out of doors (John 18:3; cf. Judg 7:16, 20). In the Hellenistic age an extension of the meaning can be observed. Occasionally (Jdt 10:22; Dan 5:5 Theodotion; Pap. Oxy. XII, 1449, 19) *lamps* are also called λαμπάδες (BAGD s.v. 2; Michaelis 17). Jeremias [197] interprets these passages as references to "lampstands," i.e., stands bearing oil lamps). In the NT Acts 20:8 has the same meaning ("There were many λαμπάδες in the upper chamber where we were assembled"). Here "lampstands" could be meant; however, the context suggests *lamps:* Despite the light of many

lamps the young man Eutychus fell asleep (v. 9); see H. Conzelmann, *Acts* (Hermeneia) 169. In Matt 25:1-8 the pl. of λαμπάς designates *lamps* (Oepke 17:39f.; BAGD) or (a special kind of) *torches* (Jeremias 197f.); → 3.

3. In Matt 25:1-2 in the parable of the ten virgins (cf. I. Maisch, *BibLeb* 11 [1970] 247-59; K. P. Donfried, *JBL* 93 [1974] 415-28) the λαμπάδες (vv. 1, 3, 4, 7, 8) are usually understood as oil *lamps,* esp. in view of the mention of oil as fuel. Zorell has suggested, however, that what is spoken of are *faces nuptiales* (wedding torches; cf. Gagé 160f.). Jeremias (197f.) interprets the λαμπάδες here—because of Palestinian wedding customs of around the end of the 19th cent.—as *torches* of which the upper end was rags saturated with olive oil (similarly Trench, *Synonyms* 165): At the call for a sudden response the young maidens in the parable prepare their torches (v. 7: ἐκόσμησαν), which, according to Jeremias (200), means: "they add oil to the rags already saturated with oil, so that they will flare up brightly, and then they ignite them." If one interprets the text in this way, the fear of the foolish maids (v. 8: αἱ λαμπάδες ἡμῶν σβέννυνται) is that their torches would "go out soon/easily/too quickly" (cf. Schweizer 465f.). But both the additional saturation of an oil cloth (cf. Jeremias, *Parables* 175: the maidens "wait with burning lamps") and the conclusion of the action in the parable—under the assumption that torches are in view—are scarcely conceivable (see Schweizer).

The text assumes (in the present context) *lamps* (which threaten to go out because the bridegroom is unexpectedly late, v. 8). However, one must take into account that a "hypothetical" story cannot definitely be concretized in all of its particulars. Furthermore, a type of compromise solution between torches and lamps is possible (Rashi, on *m. Kelim* 2:8 [Billerbeck I, 969], speaks of lamps of saturated cloth rags placed in copper vessels attached to long poles); cf. Schweizer. The λαμπάδες are at any rate to be distinguished from lanterns (→ φανός), as John 18:3 indicates (λαμπάδες with φανοί also in Pap. London 1159, 59).

4. In Revelation, λαμπάς is used primarily in the description of the throne of God. From him issue flashes of lightning, voices, and thunder; before him "burn seven *torches* of fire (λαμπάδες πυρός), which signify the seven spirits of God" (4:5). "The mode of expression is OT" (Oepke 26; cf. esp. Ezek 1:13). Original to Revelation are the number of the torches (but cf. the lampstand with seven arms in the temple) and its interpretation in terms of "the spirits of God" (cf. Ps 103:4 LXX: πνεύματα of God in parallelism with πῦρ φλέγον); on the exegesis see H. Kraft, *Rev* (HNT) 97, who sees "the torches as manifestations understood as the Holy Spirit." In 8:10 a "great star" (named Ἄψινθος, "wormwood," v. 11),

which falls from heaven at the sound of the trumpet of the third angel, is characterized as καιόμενος ὡς λαμπάς. The star bursts into flames when it falls and sprays sparks like a falling *torch* (or makes a trail); it makes a third of all rivers and springs on earth useless (v. 11).

G. Schneider

λαμπρός, 3 *lampros* radiating, shining*

This adj. refers in the NT to the morning star (Rev 22:16), to *(clear)* water (v. 1), esp. to *(radiant/glistening)* clothes (Luke 23:11; Acts 10:30; Jas 2:2, 3; Rev 15:6; 19:8). Subst. τὰ λαμπρά, *the glistening things* (so also Philo *Flacc.* 165; *Leg. Gai.* 327), appears in Rev 18:14. A. Oepke, *TDNT* IV, 16-28; Spicq, *Notes* I, 460-65.

λαμπρότης, ητος, ἡ *lamprotēs* radiance*

Acts 26:13: "brighter than the *radiance* of the sun." Spicq, *Notes* I, 460-65.

λαμπρῶς *lamprōs* sumptuously, radiantly*

Luke 16:19, of the rich man who "gratified himself *magnificently* (εὐφραινόμενος . . . λαμπρῶς)." Spicq, *Notes* I, 460-65.

λάμπω *lampō* give light, shine*

Matt 5:15, of a lamp; Luke 17:24, of lightning; Acts 12:7, of light. As a lamp should shine (Matt 5:15), so should Jesus' disciples shine before others (λαμψάτω τὸ φῶς ὑμῶν, 5:16). The face of the transfigured Jesus "*shone/radiated* like the sun" (Matt 17:2). 2 Cor 4:6a speaks of the shining forth of the light on the morning of creation at God's command (ἐκ σκότους φῶς λάμψει); 4:6b, of God, "who *shone forth* in our hearts" or trans. "who *has light shine/ who has let it be light*" (so R. Bultmann, *2 Cor* [Eng. tr., 1985] 108. A. Oepke, *TDNT* IV, 16-28.

λανθάνω *lanthanō* be hidden*

Mark 7:24: "he could not *remain hidden*"; Luke 8:47: the woman saw "that she did not *remain hidden* [i.e., could not remain hidden]"; Acts 26:26: λανθάνειν . . . αὐτόν τι τούτων οὐ πείθομαι οὐθέν, "I am not convinced that any of these matters *could have escaped him*"; Heb 13:2: ἔλαθον . . . ξενίσαντες ἀγγέλους, "they entertained angels *without being aware* of it." What remains hidden can also be expressed in a ὅτι clause: 2 Pet 3:5: "*it eludes them* that . . ."; 3:8: "*it should not be hidden* from you that. . . ." Spicq, *Notes* I, 466f.

λαξευτός, 3 *laxeutos* hewn in the rock*

Of the tomb of Jesus, Luke 23:53: μνῆμα λαξευτόν, "a *rock-hewn* tomb."

Λαοδίκεια, ας *Laodikeia* Laodicea*

A Phrygian city on the Lycus River in which many Jews lived (Josephus *Ant.* xiv.241-43; Schürer, *History* III/1, 27). There is evidence for a Christian church in Laodicea in Colossians (2:1; 4:13, 15, 16) and Revelation (1:11; 3:14). According to Col 4:16 Paul wrote a letter to the church of Laodicea (cf. the apocryphal Epistle to the Laodiceans). W. Ruge, *PW* XII, 722-24; B. Kötting, *LTK* VI, 793f.; *BL* 1015f.; *KP* III, 483f.; D. Boyd, *IDBSup* 526f.

Λαοδικεύς, έως, ὁ *Laodikeus* Laodicean*

An inhabitant of the city of → Λαοδίκεια. Col 4:16: "See that it [the letter to the Colossians] is read also in the church of the *Laodiceans*." Rev 3:14 TR reads (instead of "the church in Laodicea") ἐκκλησία Λαοδικέων. Marcion has as the superscription to Ephesians "To the Laodiceans."

λαός, οῦ, ὁ *laos* people; crowd of people; people of God

1. Occurrences in the NT — 2. Meanings (usage, context, early history) — 3. Theological usage — a) Paul — b) The oldest Synoptic traditions — c) Luke-Acts — d) Matthew — e) Other writings — 4. Theological problems

Lit.: M. BARTH, *The People of God (JSNT* Supplement Series 5, 1983). — H. BIETENHARD, *DNTT* II, 795-800. — L. CERFAUX, *The Church in the Theology of St. Paul* (1959) 49-82. — N. A. DAHL, "The People of God," *Ecumenical Review* 9 (1956/57) 154-61. — idem, *Das Volk Gottes. Eine Untersuchung zum Kirchenbewußtsein des Urchristentums* (²1963). — J. DUPONT, "ΛΑΟΣ ΈΞ ΈΘΝΩΝ (Ac 15,14)," idem, *Études sur les Actes des Apôtres* (1967) 361-65. — G. EICHHOLZ, "Der Begriff 'Volk' im NT," idem, *Tradition und Interpretation* (1965) 78-84. — H. FRANKEMÖLLE, *Jahwebund und Kirche Christi* (1974) 193-220 (on Matthew). — J. GNILKA, *Die Verstockung Israels. Isaias 6,9-10 in der Theologie der Synoptiker* (1961). — H. GOLDSTEIN, *Paulinische Gemeinde im Ersten Petrusbrief* (1975). — E. GRÄSSER, *Der Glaube im Hebräerbrief* (1965) 216-18. — H. F. HAMILTON, *The People of God* I-II (1912). — G. HARDER, "Kontinuität und Diskontinuität des Volkes Gottes," *Das gespaltene Gottesvolk* (ed. H. Gollwitzer and E. Sterling; 1966) 266-82. — R. HUMMEL, *Die Auseinandersetzung zwischen Kirche und Judentum im Matthäusevangelium* (²1966) 143-61. — J. JERVELL, *Luke and the People of God* (1972) 41-74. — E. KÄSEMANN, *The Wandering People of God* (1984) 48-63. — J. KODELL, "Luke's Use of *Laos*, 'People,' Especially in the Jerusalem Narrative," *CBQ* 31 (1969) 327-43. — T. C. DE KRUIJF, "Das Volk Gottes im NT," *Judentum und Kirche: Volk Gottes* (Theologische Berichte III, ed. J. Pfammatter and F. Furger; 1974) 119-33. — G. LOHFINK, *Die Sammlung Israels. Eine Untersuchung zur lukanischen Ekklesiologie* (1975) 33-61. — U. LUZ, *Das Geschichtsverständnis des Paulus* (1968) 269-79. — C. M. MARTINI, "L'esclusione della comunità del popolo di Dio e il nuovo Israele secondo Atti 3,23," *Bib* 50 (1969) 1-14.

— P. S. MINEAR, *Images of the Church in the NT* (1960) 66-104. — C. MÜLLER, *Gottes Gerechtigkeit und Gottes Volk. Eine Untersuchung zu Röm 9–11* (1964) 90-113. — F. MUSSNER, " 'Volk Gottes' im NT," idem, *Praesentia Salutis* (1967) 244-52. — F. B. NORRIS, *God's Own People* (1962). — A. OEPKE, *Das neue Gottesvolk in Schrifttum, Schauspiel, bildender Kunst und Weltgestaltung* (1950) 57-84, 198-230 (on Paul, Hebrews, and Revelation). — J. O'ROURKE, "The Church as People of God in the NT," *Divinitas* 13 (1969) 655-68. — R. POELMAN, "Peuple de Dieu," *Lumen Vitae* 20 (1965) 455-80. — S. PANCARO, " 'People of God' in St John's Gospel?" *NTS* 16 (1969/70) 114-29. — G. RAU, "Das Volk in der lukanischen Passionsgeschichte. Eine Konjektur zu Lk 23,13," *ZNW* 56 (1965) 41-51. — H. SCHLIER, "Ekklesiologie des NT," *Mysterium Salutis* IV/1 (1972) 101-221. — R. SCHNACKENBURG, *The Church in the NT* (1966) 149-57. — R. SCHNACKENBURG and J. DUPONT, "The Church as the People of God," *Dogma* (Concilium 1, 1965) 117-29. — H. STRATHMANN and R. MEYER, *TDNT* IV, 29-57. — W. TRILLING, *Das wahre Israel. Studien zur Theologie des Matthäus* (³1964). — H. F. WEISS, " 'Volk Gottes' und 'Leib Christi.' Überlegungen zur paulinischen Ekklesiologie," *TLZ* 102 (1977) 411-20. — D. ZELLER, *Juden und Heiden in der Mission des Paulus. Studien zum Römerbrief* (²1976), esp. 116-22. — For further bibliography see *TWNT* X, 1155f.

1. Considerable differences are seen in the use of λαός among the individual theologians of the NT; this is the case for the occurrences in general as well as for the specific content. Of the 142 occurrences in the NT, of which only 9 are pl., 12 are in the Pauline corpus, but only in Romans (8 occurrences), 1 Corinthians (2), 2 Corinthians (1), and Titus (1); 3 are in Mark, 14 in Matthew, 84 in the Lukan literature (36 in Luke, 48 in Acts), 3 in John, 13 in Hebrews, 3 in 1 Peter, 1 in 2 Peter, 1 in Jude, and 9 in Revelation. Λαός is, therefore, a favorite word of Luke. Noteworthy is the absence of λαός from Q (the common sayings tradition of Matthew and Luke), which correlates to its absence also from the *Gospel of Thomas*. The statistics of usage signifies nothing about the theological weight of the term with respect to the biblical concept of the people of God. The term is ambiguous and capable of a variety of meanings that can be established only in actual usage.

2. The sense of the word in semantically concrete usage is determined esp. by three factors: context, the word field in the respective writing, and the prior history of λαός in Jewish literature. The impact of the latter becomes understandable in the numerous citations from the LXX.

The spectrum of meaning for λαός in the NT extends from a) *tribe, race, population, people, crowd of people, mob*—without any national nuance—to b) λαός as a t.t. for Israel as people of God—in dependence on the usage of the LXX, with ἔθνος (Gentiles) as the opposite term —to c) λαός as a designation of the Christian church(es) —with the termination of the opposition to ἔθνος.

a) The sense of the word that has no theological significance is found in the sg. twice in Mark (11:32; 14:2) and three times in Matthew (4:23; 26:5 par. Mark; Matt 27:64). In Luke what should be included here is disputed, as the transition to theologically significant usage is fluid. Luke generally intensifies the motif of the crowd numerically where he introduces λαός into the tradition (Luke 7:1, 29; 8:47; 9:13; 18:43; 20:1, 9, 26; 21:38; 23:27, 35), in the same way that he introduces the undoubtedly untheological terms δῆμος (people as inhabitants of a city; in the NT only 4 occurrences, all in Acts), πλῆθος ("crowd": Luke 1:10; 2:13; 5:6; 6:17; 19:37; 23:1, 27, etc.), and ὄχλος (the crowd, the mass of people—in contrast to the upper class: 4:42; 5:15; 6:19; 9:11; 11:29; 12:1, 54; 13:17; 14:25; 19:39; 23:4, 48). A motivation for the linguistic change has not been determined (cf. ὄχλος in 13:17; 22:6). Is λαός, because of its prior history in the LXX, already stamped such that it is generally understood "in terms of salvation history" (Lohfink 35), or is a "vernacular meaning" present in theologically less important passages, which for Luke is even "entirely customary" (Strathmann 51; cf. Bietenhard 799)? The context and the Lukan conception (→ 3.c) may be decisive.

The general meaning is apparent where λαός follows and extends ὄχλος (7:29; 8:47; 9:13; Acts 5:37, etc.). Luke replaces a Markan ὄχλος with his archaizing LXX style without its being suggested by the subject matter (Luke 19:48; 20:6, 19, 45) and plerophorically speaks of "the whole λαός" in the sense of "everyone, all" (3:21; 7:29; 18:43; Acts 21:36). "The (whole/entire) crowd τοῦ λαοῦ" (Luke 1:10; 6:17; Acts 21:36) is to be understood in this sense. In passages, however, where the λαός is contrasted to the leading circles, which reject Jesus (Luke 22:2; 23:5; Acts 6:12; 10:41; 13:15), or where λαός is integrated into the front that rejects Jesus (Luke 23:15), what is decisive is not only the usage of the LXX (→ 2.b), but also the Lukan conception, which is based on the LXX (λαός = believing Israel as the people of God, the Gentile church as λαός).

Pl. λαοί is parallel to ἔθνη (peoples) in Rom 15:11; Rev 7:9; 10:11; 11:9; 21:3; Luke 2:30f.; Acts 4:25, 27; likewise sg. λαός is parallel to ἔθνος (John 11:50; 18:14; Rev 5:9; 13:7; 14:6; 17:15): What is intended is all, the numerical totality, all of humanity. The context and the terms used in it determine the meaning of λαός in all of these passages without any fixed association with salvation history. This sense may also be present in most of the 22 occurrences in Acts 1–6, even if λαός is limited there to Jewish crowds, e.g., listeners (cf. also 10:2; 12:4; 21:30, 36, etc.). Lukan usage is not consistent. Often the imitative LXX style is decisive. Perhaps the theologically determined λαός passages have had an impact on the semantically insignificant passages (as in Matthew).

b) Belief in Israel as the elect people of God (λαὸς

τοῦ θεοῦ) is unquestioned. This corresponds to the usage of the LXX, where λαός occurs *ca.* 2000 times, predominantly as a religious t.t. In the NT this significance of the prior history is assured esp. by OT citations (Matt 2:6; 4:16; 13:15; 15:8; Acts 3:23; 28:26, etc.; in Paul citations are present in every occurrence of the word! → 3.a), by explanatory additions (Acts 4:10; 13:17, 24: the λαός of Israel; 12:11: the λαός of the Jews; Matt 2:4; 21:23; 26:3, 47; 27:1; Luke 19:47; Acts 4:8: high priests and scribes [elders of the λαός]), by the contextually opposite term "Gentiles" (Luke 2:32; Acts 10:2; 26:17, 23; 28:27f.; Rom 15:10), or by terms for "Israel" that are theologically significant in context, such as temple, law, God of Israel, customs of the fathers, etc. (Luke 1:68, 77; 7:16; 24:19; Acts 21:28; 28:17). Λαός can also stand in isolation without such direct contextual explanatory comments (Luke 2:10; Acts 13:15; Rom 11:1; 1 Cor 10:7; 2 Pet 2:1; Jude 5) where the intention of the saying is certain.

c) The Christian churches understand themselves as λαὸς τοῦ θεοῦ in continuity with use of λαός as an honorary title, but at the same time deny that title to that part of Israel which rejects Jesus. That is to say, the continuity is christologically based: God (!) chose a λαός from the ἔθνη (Acts 15:14, in dependence on Zech 2:15 and Amos 9:11; cf. de Kruijf 127f.). Decisive for this election is one's attitude toward Jesus: "Everyone that does not listen to that prophet shall be destroyed from the people" (Acts 3:23, citing Lev 23:29). As the citations show, Acts 15:14 is not "an astounding and even a revolutionary saying" (Strathmann 54; cf. Müller 52, 94 on Paul), for already in Deuteronomy, moreover in all the prophets, the national-religious idea of λαός has become dispersed and the Gentile peoples included (on the OT literature see Frankemölle 198). Also in the OT Israel as λαός always stands in crisis. An end to λαός = all Israel is also found in the "remnant idea" at the time of Jesus, esp. in the elitist consciousness of election in Qumran (cf. Gnilka 155-85).

The NT did not go the direction taken at Qumran. In the NT, as well as in Jewish literature, it is evident that λαός in the entire Jewish realm was from the beginning a dynamic concept (so that this did not originate in the NT) that was open to change, standing in opposition to every security of salvation. Matthew and Hebrews esp. develop this aspect.

3. a) In Paul it is noteworthy that λαός appears exclusively in OT citations; where Paul himself speaks, he —unlike Luke (→ 3.c)—avoids the term (Cerfaux 12; Weiss 415, 418). Moreover, it is only Romans 9–11 (9:25, 26; 10:21; 11:1, 2) that he uses the citations within the context of the theme of the people of God; in the other occurrences (Rom 15:10, 11; 1 Cor 10:7; 14:21; 2 Cor

6:16; Titus 2:14) the citations are brought in for their traditional theological weight only insofar as subordinate, typologically based functions appear in the parenetic context. In the enumeration of honorific titles for Israel in Rom 9:3-5 λαός does not appear. The reasons for this is that "Not all who are descended from Israel belong to Israel" (9:6b), for as λαός it is "contrary and disobedient" (10:21). The true λαός, according to 9:25, is called from Jews (Ἰουδαίων) and Gentiles (ἐθνῶν); the not-my-people (Hos 2:25) becomes Yahweh's λαός on the basis of faith in the gospel. Nevertheless, "God has not rejected his λαός" (11:2); the promises remain valid for the true λαός. Even if the concrete Israel (9:27; 11:7), except for a "remnant," is hardened, all Israel will be saved (11:25ff.).

Even in Romans 9–11 Paul does not by means of λαός outline a people-of-God theology. Instead, from the blocks of material emerge the concepts of promise, faithfulness of God, law, gospel, righteousness; from the dialectical concept of Israel emerge points of departure that employ traditional universalistic λαός terminology and theology as a basis for addressing the problem of Israel and the Church. Like θεός (God, Yahweh) λαός is in Paul an "ideal" term, which, like θεός, is taken over from the Jewish tradition without alteration.

The earthly-theological manner of existence of this λαός is described by Paul in reference to both Israel and the Church alongside a variety of other terms; on the Church cf. ἐκκλησία (C/church), σῶμα (body of Christ), ναὸς θεοῦ (temple of God), etc. Only the total salvation-historical *and* christological semantic field sets free the Pauline ecclesiology, according to which λαός is the theo-centric component: "I will be their God and they will be my people" (2 Cor 6:16). Just as this promise was and is valid for Israel, so it is also according to Paul for the Church from the Gentiles. However, it is valid for Gentile Christians only on the basis of their conduct. Titus 2:14 also refers in a result clause to the creation of a "pure λαός" (cf. Deut 14:2) through the death of Jesus.

b) In the oldest Synoptic tradition λαός appears in Mark 7:6, citing Isa 29:13, but in Mark is not used of all Israel, but only of the hypocritical Pharisees and scribes. In Mark λαός does not take up the OT theologoumenon of the people of God. In Q λαός is not used.

c) Luke has consciously and intentionally inserted λαός into his double work. (It is noteworthy, however, that it does not appear in the travel narrative of the Gospel or in the "we" passages of Acts.) The *people*, designated by λαός, are mentioned where they have an extremely positive relationship to Jesus (in the Gospel) and to the apostles (in Acts 1–6). Thus they stand in great tension with the leading circles (including the Pharisees in the Passion narrative and in Acts); a deep rift separates the latter from the λαός (→ 2.a; see Luke 7:29f.; 19:47f.; 20:1, 6, 19, 26, 45-47; 22:2; 23:35; 24:19f.). The positive attitude (against Strathmann 51) of all Israel (cf. the frequent plerophoric πᾶς with λαός, 2:10, 31; 7:29; 8:47; 9:13; 18:43; 20:45; 21:38; 24:19; cf. 1:10; 3:21; 19:48; 20:6; Acts 3:9, 11; 4:10; 5:34; cf. 2:47) as people of God takes a critical turn in Luke with the threefold call for crucifixion by the λαός (against the conjecture of Rau: "leaders of the people"); in Acts the movement of gathering the λαός in its totality is ended with the death of Stephen (6:8ff.). Here also (6:12) the λαός can be integrated into the group that rejects the Christian message. It is therefore accused corporately and repudiated for its guilt in the death of Jesus.

From this point on, according to Luke, there are only a few believers from Israel; the entirety of the Ἰουδαῖοι (frequently, if not consistently: Acts 9:23; 10:22; 12:3, 11; 21:11, 20, etc.) is hardened (28:26f.). This historical-theological basis in the composition of Acts (cf. Gnilka 143-46; Lohfink 47-62) opens the way for the true people of God, the Christian Church composed of Jews (decreasing in numerical strength) and Gentiles (growing in numerical strength).

This literary construction guarantees the unity of the Lukan two-volume work. In Acts 3:11, the entire λαός can appropriately be charged with responsibility for the death of Jesus and called to repentance, in keeping with Luke 23:13. But it remains λαός, even after they call for Jesus' crucifixion (Luke 23:27, 35; 24:19; Matthew and John are entirely different: → 3.d). The Lukan schema has been established already in the early narrative; cf. the prophecy of Simeon in Luke 2:34: "He [Jesus] is set for the fall and rising of many in Israel." If this statement is taken to refer to the stereotypically emphasized cleft between the λαός and its leaders, then other texts place this cleft in the midst of the "people," who are *never* called λαός in other texts (cf. esp. the programmatic Nazareth pericope in 4:16-30 as well as 6:22f.; 7:9, 31f.; 8:10; 9:41; 10:13-15; 11:29-32, 49-51; 12:54-56; 13:26-29, 34f.; 20:16; cf. also 3:8f.).

Thus in Luke λαός consistently stands in opposition not only to the leaders who reject Jesus, but also in opposition to the unbelieving and hardened portion of Israel; this constitutes the Lukan redaction. (Only an investigation of the semantic field is able to establish this conception.) Correspondingly, the ethnically determined λαός concept is consistently extended: Luke 1:16f.: John the Baptist "will turn many of the sons of Israel, . . . to the Lord [from Israel], to make ready for the Lord a λαός prepared"; 2:30-32: Jesus is "the salvation that you prepared before the face of all peoples (πάντων τῶν λαῶν), a light of revelation for the Gentiles (ἐθνῶν) and for the glorification of your λαός Israel" (on the Gentile-Christian Lukan understanding, cf. the parallels in Acts 13:47).

In the historico-theological conception of Luke Jesus does indeed turn to the λαός in its entirety, which had been stamped in terms of salvation history by the LXX. It did not, however, actually exist in identity with Israel. The universal extension is—as in the OT (→ 2.c)—consistently included in λαός. In Luke there is the unproblematic continuity of the Christian Church (ἐκκλησία) with λαός. It nevertheless remains—entirely in contrast to Paul (→ 3.a)—to indicate that for Luke ἐκκλησία is only structured in a theocentric way in the Miletus speech of Acts 20:28: Elsewhere in Luke the term remains redactionally unspecified (= assembly of the people, t.t. for the Christian communities). The theological significance of λαός is not extended to ἐκκλησία. As a rule (except in Acts 20:28) it can be understood as the "profane" appearance and assembly of the λαός. The sharpest emphasis on ecclesiology in Luke is not associated with ἐκκλησία, but with λαός.

In addition, whether one belongs to λαός is determined by faith in the preaching of Jesus and the apostles (Acts 3:23). This corresponds to the fact that for Luke there is only *one* λαός: that composed of Jews and Gentiles who believe in Christ (Acts 3:22f.; 15:13-18; 18:10 *contra* Jervell's thesis, according to which only the Jewish Christian Church is λαός, in whose promises the Gentiles are merely participants).

The gathering of the λαός is—as in the OT—entirely the work of God (Luke 1:68; 2:28-32; 15:14; cf. also 1:72; Acts 5:35-39; 13:40f.; 15:14-18). A soteriology, except in Acts 20:28 ("the Church [ἐκκλησία] of God, which he purchased by his own [the Son's] blood"), does not come in view. The Lukan christology is very theocentric. The earthly Jesus has a function for the proclamation of the activity of God among the λαός (on the basis of the gathering of the twelve apostles): he leads the people into the crisis, but his gathering begins only in Acts 1–6 among Jews and in Acts 7–28 among Gentiles. Thus "the *people* among the peoples" (λαὸς ἐξ ἐθνῶν) that God has chosen according to Acts 15:14 comes into view in the threats of Luke on Israel (3:8f.; 10:13-15; 11:31f., 50; 13:26-28; 20:16), in the promises for the "others" (3:8; 13:29; 20:16), and in the acceptance of the Gentiles (7:1-10; 14:15-24). On this point also the salvation history carried forward by God is not only stamped by continuity in the entire Lukan work, but it stands also as a whole in continuity with the preceding Jewish salvation history. Last of all, this continuity is maintained by means of λαός.

d) Matthew, as the OT citations in 2:6; 4:16; 13:15; and 15:8 indicate, follows the usage of the LXX. Thus λαός is to be understood dialectically: There is the λαός that is hardened (13:15), but also Yahweh's (2:6) and Jesus' λαός (1:21), the λαός from "Galilee of the Gentiles" (4:15f.). In contrast to Luke, Matthew connects the λαός in the first sense with its representatives (2:4; 21:23; 26:3, 47; 27:1)—up to and including the cultic-legal didactic self-condemnation of 27:25, which is based on the Shechemite dodecalogue in Deut 27:15-16: "And all the people answered: His blood be on us and on our children!" Israel as λαός exists no longer; there are only— as in all of John, but differently in Luke—"the Jews to this day" (28:15).

The true λαός of the disciples of Jesus from all the peoples (28:19) is inaugurated through Jesus' sacrifice "for the forgiveness of sins" (1:21; 26:28: redactional; deleted in the narrative of John the Baptist taken from Mark 1:4), as Jesus is Immanuel (= God with us). As the λαός of Jesus it is the λαός of God. The redactional context in Matthew 1–2, the parallel terms ἐκκλησία μου (my Church) in 16:18 and βασιλεία σου (your kingdom) in 13:41; 16:28; 20:21, and the associated ecclesiological words (disciples, sons, brothers, etc.) strengthen this understanding.

In order to maintain the Church's own identity as λαός (with a strong emphasis on the lack of security for its own salvation) Matthew more than any other NT theologian denies this designation to Israel. This is the foundation of his "deuteronomically"-stamped historico-theological structure in the Gospel.

e) The remaining NT writings (1 Peter, Hebrews, and Revelation) explicitly attest (without polemicizing against Israel as λαός) the Christian self-understanding, in continuity with the OT, of being the true λαός. Cf. esp. the piling on of honorific titles in 1 Pet 2:9 (according to Isa 43:20; Exod 19:6; Mal 3:17) for a church of the diaspora among Gentiles (1:1; 2:12). The λαός from the Jews and Gentiles is—in contrast to Paul—not in view; only the self-understanding of the Gentile Christians is present.

The 13 occurrences in Hebrews are similarly clear. Λαός refers either to the Jewish λαός, which, however (as also the high priests, the cult, the tabernacle), refers typologically to the Church, or directly to the Church (2:17: Jesus makes expiation for the sins of the λαός; 13:12: through his death he sanctifies the λαός; 8:8, 10: Jesus is the mediator of a new covenant [Jer 31:33] with the house of Israel [!], and thus it becomes the λαός). The idea of the people of God, which was formulated in the OT and early Christianity (there is no contrast between Jew and Gentile) proves to be the key to the understanding of the letter (Oepke 57-74; Grässer 216). Just as the OT cult, etc., was preliminary, so also was the covenant and the λαός. The true λαός is the Church of Jesus, bound to the Christian ethos. In addition the judgment stands before this λαός. It is still the wandering people of God (3:7–4:13).

Revelation also emphasizes (in the context of the battle against "the synagogue of Satan": 2:9; 3:9) the λαός before and after Christ as a unified entity, as the transfer of OT λαός passages in 18:4 (Jer 51:45) and 21:3 (Zech 2:14; Ezek 37:27) indicates. It encompasses the world and its peoples (5:9; 7:9; 10:11; 11:9; 13:7; 14:6f.; 17:15; the pl. in 21:3 is consistent; cf. also ch. 7: Israel and the peoples). Elsewhere λαός is not a significant theological term. It is ecclesiologically relevant only in continuity with the ecclesiology of the OT (cf. esp. 7:1-17; 21:12-14).

4. The NT λαός sayings are not unified and do not have a single focus shared by all the NT writings. Where the word is used, it reflects the self-understanding of the writer and his church as λαὸς θεοῦ, implying a definite understanding of Israel as λαὸς θεοῦ. The NT never speaks of a "new λαός." Only in Heb 8:8-13, in connection with Jer 31:31-34, are λαός and "new covenant" contextually associated with Israel (καινὴ διαθήκη), but neither there nor elsewhere in Hebrews is the idea developed further. Thus there also—as in the other NT διαθήκη passages—the idea of a "new" λαὸς θεοῦ is not present. Λαός in the NT (developing the LXX theme) is a theocentric term, guaranteeing the continuity of the history of God with Israel and the peoples. Just as there is one θεός, so also there is only one λαὸς θεοῦ.

Therefore, neither Ἰσραήλ in the OT nor ἐκκλησία in the NT can represent exactly the same thing as λαός, inasmuch as they point to the historical existence of the Jewish and Christian "peoples." As in the LXX, Ἰσραήλ in the NT is dialectically understood (cf. the Pauline Ἰσραὴλ κατὰ σάρκα). What is decisive in the NT is faith in Jesus Christ. Only in the affirmation of this faith is Israel λαὸς θεοῦ; this is the case also for "the Church from all peoples." This dialectical understanding of λαός with regard to "Israel" and "Church" is Jewish, and is merely taken up by the NT from the Jewish background.

The relationship of Israel as λαὸς θεοῦ and Church as λαὸς θεοῦ is interpreted in various ways in the NT. Matthew, who represents a substitutional or displacement theory, is the most radical: All Israel is hardened (27:25); it has lost the preeminence that God granted it (21:43 within chs. 21–25). Yahweh's promises and faithfulness (Frankemölle 108-43, 257-307) are granted to the Church from all the peoples (including Jews, although Matthew never says this). This thesis, which appears radical to us, can only be understood in the context of the Matthean situation and the Jewish manner of thinking, which had its predecessor in Judaism.

According to Luke the one λαός is constituted by the fact that believing Gentiles come into believing Israel. The continuing salvation history that has been planned by God is thus demonstrated in this event.

According to Paul "Israel" remains λαὸς θεοῦ. It has not been rejected by God (Rom 11:1f.; 9:4f.). Through the hardening of a part of Israel "salvation came to the Gentiles in order to make them jealous" (11:11). When the Gentiles as a whole believe, "then all Israel will be saved" (11:26). For Paul as well there is only one λαὸς θεοῦ.

With respect to the idea of λαός in the NT (for Matthew as for the other writers), Christianity remains permanently bound to Judaism as it is bound to the Church in the *one* λαὸς θεοῦ. Both stand under the eschatological reservation.

                                       H. Frankemölle

λάρυγξ, υγγος, ὁ *larynx* throat, gullet*

Rom 3:13, citing Ps 5:10 (LXX): "their *throat* is an open grave." H. Hanse, *TDNT* IV, 57f.

Λασαία, ας *Lasaia* Lasea*

A city on the south coast of Crete. Acts 27:8 places the city of Lasea near Fair Havens. E. Haenchen, *Acts* (Eng. tr., 1971) 699n.4.

λατομέω *latomeō* hew out of rock*

Mark 15:46 par. Matt 27:60, of the tomb (μνημεῖον) of Jesus. Mark: ὃ ἦν λελατομημένον ἐκ πέτρας. Matthew: ὃ ἐλατόμησεν ἐν τῇ πέτρα.

λατρεία, ας, ἡ *latreia* worship, cult
→ λατρεύω.

λατρεύω *latreuō* serve (God), worship (vb.)*
λατρεία, ας, ἡ *latreia* worship (noun), cult*

1. Occurrences in the NT — 2. Usage in the LXX and meaning in the NT — 3. Hebrews — 4. Paul

Lit.: J. BLANK, "Zum Begriff des Opfers nach Röm 12,1-2," *Funktion und Struktur christlicher Gemeinde* (Festgabe für H. Fleckenstein, 1971) 35-51. — O. CASEL, "Die λογικὴ λατρεία der antiken Mystik in christlich-liturgischer Umdeutung," *Jahrbuch für Liturgiewissenschaft* 4 (1924) 37-47. — J. P. FLOSS, *Jahwe dienen—Göttern dienen* (BBB 45, 1975). — F. HAHN, *Worship of the Early Church* (1973) 36f., 62f. — K. HESS, *DNTT* III, 549-51. — E. KÄSEMANN, "Worship in Everyday Life," idem, *NT Questions of Today* (1969) 188-95. — H.-J. KRAUS, *Gottesdienst im alten und neuen Bund," EvT* 25 (1965) 171-206, esp. 176-79. — S. LYONNET, " 'Deus cui servio in spiritu meo' (Rom 1,9)," *VD* 41 (1963) 52-59. — J. M. NIELEN, *Gebet und Gottesdienst im NT* (²1963) 113-15, 121f. — H. STRATHMANN, *TDNT* IV, 58-65. — H. WENSCHKEWITZ, "Die Spiritualisierung der Kultusbegriffe Tempel, Priester und Opfer im NT," *Angelos* IV (1932) 70-230, esp. 189ff., 195ff. — C. WESTERMANN, *THAT* II, 182-200. — For further bibliography see *TWNT* X, 1156f.

1. Λατρεύω occurs 21 times in the NT; λατρεία occurs 5 times. The vb. is used esp. in Luke-Acts (8 occurrences) and Hebrews (6 occurrences); it appears twice each in Romans and Revelation and in Phil 3:3; 2 Tim 1:3. The noun appears twice each in Romans and Hebrews and in John 16:2.

2. The vb. λατρεύω appears only rarely in Greek literature and appears in the LXX almost exclusively in the religious and cultic sense of Israel's worship of God. It renders Heb. *'āḇaḏ* (thus clearly distinguished from its Greek synonym δουλεύω, which is more comprehensive in meaning; cf. also the distinction between the two vbs. in Acts 7:7; otherwise in 20:7) in, e.g., Exod 4:23; Deut 10:12. Λατρεία renders the cultic t.t. *'ăḇoḏâ* in, e.g., Josh 22:27; 1 Macc 2:19. Only in Deut 28:48 does the vb. have the basic Greek meaning of "render services" (e.g., Xenophon *Cyr.* iii.1.36 of slavery; in reference to the gods, however, e.g., Euripides *Ion* 152; Plato *Phdr.* 244e); the noun has the corresponding meaning only in 3 Macc 4:14. Biblical usage of λατρεύω and λατρεία are thus focused on the cultic sense of the words, while the the predominant cultic and religious term in Greek literature, θεραπεύειν, recedes into the background in biblical usage.

The NT retains the emphasis on the words derived from the LXX, although the motif of the cultic is maintained only in OT citations and references. Λατρεύω always alludes to worship, often where the place of God is occupied by other entities, thus where true worship is perverted and misguided (Acts 7:42: τῇ στρατιᾷ τοῦ οὐρανοῦ [cf. Jer 7:18 LXX; but also 16:13 LXX]; Rom 1:25, with σέβομαι: τῇ κτίσει παρὰ τὸν κτίσαντα; Heb 8:5: ὑποδείγματι καὶ σκιᾷ . . . τῶν ἐπουρανίων, namely the "tabernacle"; cf. 13:10: τῇ σκηνῇ).

A dat. obj. can be absent where λατρεύω is used in an extended or fig. sense for the life oriented toward God or for the perpetual "worship": Luke 2:37, of Hannah: νηστείαις καὶ δεήσεσιν λατρεύουσα νύκτα καὶ ἡμέραν (cf. Jdt 11:17); similarly Acts 26:7, of Israel's *serving* day and night (= "prayer/supplication"; cf. Ps 88:2; 2 Macc 13:10); see also Heb 9:9; 10:2. In Phil 3:3 (οἱ πνεύματι θεοῦ [v.l. θεῷ] λατρεύοντες) the concern is the contrast between, on the one hand, "the true circumcision" with its spiritual worship and, on the other hand, trust "in the flesh," "the mutilation" (cf. also λατρεύω ἐν τῷ πνεύματί μου, Rom 1:9; ἔχωμεν χάριν, δι' ἧς λατρεύωμεν, Heb 12:28). However, Rom 9:4 indicates that Paul cannot deny the validity of Israel's λατρεία (named among others of God's gifts; cf. also 11:29), but he does reject its misuse in relation to Christ (see also John 16:2: λατρείαν προσφέρειν τῷ θεῷ, of false *worship* in the sense of offering a sacrifice). God's Spirit, who directs the entire life of believers, alone leads to the true worship, which is bound neither to a specific people nor to a specific place (cf. also E. Lohmeyer, *Phil* [KEK] ad loc.; Wenschkewitz 175ff. on Paul).

References to the OT indicate that Luke in particular can see the essence of the new worship already established in the old covenant. Thus λατρεύω has the sense of *worship/reverence (cultically)*: Luke 1:74, of Abraham; 2:37, in connection with the temple; 4:8 par. Matt 4:10, with προσκυνέω (cf. Deut 6:13); Acts 7:7 (cf. Exod 3:12); 24:14, of Paul: λατρεύω τῷ πατρῴῳ θεῷ; 26:7, of the twelve tribes; see also Rev 7:15; 22:3 of the worship of the martyrs continuing day and night (cf. 1 Chr 9:33) before the heavenly throne and in the heavenly temple of God; 2 Tim 1:3.

The noun λατρεία continues in the NT to refer to sacrificial worship; cf. Heb 9:1 in addition to John 16:2 and Rom 9:4 (δικαιώματα λατρείας, "regulations for *worship*"); 9:6 (τὰς λατρείας ἐπιτελοῦντες, of the discharge of the cultic *ministries* by the priests; cf. Num 18:3f.: πάσας τὰς λειτουργίας τῆς σκηνῆς [v. 4] → 3); fig. in Rom 12:1 (→ 4).

3. In Hebrews the reference to the OT cult is especially accented (8:5; 9:1, 6, 9; 10:2; 13:10). Both vb. and noun encompass (against the LXX, → 2) the priestly sacrificial worship (→ λειτουργία [2]). This ministry is considered preliminary and limited to the earthly sanctuary (9:1, 9f., 11f.). It is surpassed and removed by the true worship, which is based on Christ's once-for-all self-sacrifice and the related purification of the Church of "dead" and earthly sacrifices. Consequently believers can now *serve* (λατρεύειν θεῷ ζῶντι, 9:14; λατρεύωμεν εὐαρέστως τῷ θεῷ, μετὰ εὐλαβείας καὶ δέους, 12:28) the living God with a purified conscience (cf. 2 Tim 1:3). This sense of λατρεύω indicates both the connection of Christian worship with the old worship of the priests and the discontinuity of the worship, in that the new ministry encompasses the entire life of the believer. It is based on gratitude for the gift of the unshakable kingdom and encounters the abiding, consuming claim of God (12:29) with the freedom of the redeemed who do not need a priestly mediator for their worship.

4. For Paul this new worship occurs in his ministry "in the gospel of his Son" (Rom 1:9—ἐν τῷ πνεύματί μου, in connection with the appeal to God as witness [v. 9a], the total commitment of Paul to his mission, which only God can test; see also E. Käsemann, *Rom* [Eng. tr., 1980] ad loc.). Phil 3:3, however, is determined by the contrast πνεῦμα—σάρξ and refers to the whole of Christian existence: The sign of relationship to God (περιτομή) is life and activity in the Spirit of God, not carnal trust in traditional assurances of "worship." Rom 12:1 indicates, however, that what is said does not involve a "spiritualization" of the traditional terminology of worship (cf. Wenschkewitz 189-95). The λογικὴ λατρεία consists of the offering (παριστάνω is Hellenistic sacrificial terminology; cf. Xenophon *An.* vi.1.22; also Josephus *Ant.* iv.113, in the LXX, however, in the sense of service and placing oneself at the disposal of another) of the whole life (τὰ σώματα) of the believer as a sacrifice to God. The use of the cultic expression represents clearly the shift that has taken place (Käsemann 192) over against a ritual understanding of worship (cf. also Deut 10:12ff.; Josh 22:5; Mic 6:6-8; see also Blank 41ff.; Kraus 177f.). The connection with → λογικός emphasizes that the Spirit of God itself enables believers

to carry out this worship in everyday life (cf. also *T. Levi* 3:6; John 4:23; 1 Pet 2:2, 5).

H. Balz

λάχανον, ου, τό *lachanon* edible garden herb, vegetable*

Mark 4:32 par. Matt 13:32: The mustard seed grows and becomes "greater than every [Matthew: "the"] *garden herb*"; Luke 11:42: "You tithe . . . every *herb* (πᾶν λάχανον)"; Rom 14:2: "the weak person eats [only] *vegetables* (λάχανα)." G. Bornkamm, *TDNT* IV, 65-67.

Λεββαῖος, ου *Lebbaios* Lebbaeus

The personal name Λεββαῖος appears as a v.l. in the lists of apostles in Mark 3:18 D it and Matt 10:3 D k Origen[lat] in place of name → Θαδδαῖος. Koine, etc., have in Matt 10:3: "Lebbaeus with the surname Thaddaeus." Dalman, *Worte* 40; B. Lindars, *NTS* 4 (1957/58) 220-22.

λεγιών, ῶνος, ἡ *legiōn* legion*

Lit.: A. R. NEUMANN, *KP* III, 538-46. — H. M. D. PARKER and G. R. WATSON, *OCD* 591-93. — H. PREISKER, *TDNT* IV, 68f. — E. RITTERLING, *PW* XII, 1186-1837.

1. Λεγιών, in many mss. written also λεγεών, is a loanword from Latin *(legio)* and designates the largest Roman unit of troops. In the 1st cent. twenty-five legions formed the core of the standing army. A legion consisted of 5600 men, divided into 10 *cohortes,* each with five or six *centuriae.* In addition there were 120 *equites* and *auxilia* (special troops). The commander of a legion was a *legatus legionis,* who was assisted by six *tribuni militum* and sixty *centuriones.* The individual legions were numbered and also bore a name. In Palestine of the 1st cent. the *Legio X Fretensis* played the greatest role. Its seal and standard was the boar.

2. Λεγιών occurs only four times in the NT. In Mark 5:9, 15 par. Luke 8:30 it appears as the name of demons. The name is explicitly based on the great number of the demons that dwell in the demoniac (cf. the two thousand pigs in Mark 5:13). In addition the name indicates the violent, organized power of the world of the demons. Hatred and fear toward the Roman occupation power is evident.

Λεγιών is used of angelic powers in Matt 26:53 ("more than twelve *legions* of angels"). The idea of the angels as military forces and their eschatological battle against the powers of evil is attested in Jewish literature of the time (cf. esp. 1QM). In addition the designation λεγιών expresses the great number and organized power of the spirits that serve God.

Λεγιών is used in the NT only for spiritual powers, and never for the military unit of the Roman army. In all instances it underscores directly the power of these (good or evil) spirits and indirectly indicates the power of Jesus, who has them at his disposal.

F. Annen

λέγω *legō* say, name, call

1. Frequency in the NT — 2. Meaning; syntactical and idiomatic usage — 3. Idioms of theological relevance

Lit.: W. BACHER, *Die exegetische Terminologie der jüdischen Traditionsliteratur* (1899 = 1965) I, 5-7. — J. BERGMANN, H. LUTZMANN, and H. W. SCHMIDT, *TDOT* III, 84-125. — H. BRAUN, *Spätjüdisch-häretischer und frühchristlicher Radikalismus* II (BHT 24, [2]1969) 9. — R. BULTMANN, *Der Stil der paulinischen Predigt und die kynisch-stoische Diatribe* (FRLANT 13, 1910) 10-19, 64-68. — *idem, History* 134-36, 147-49. — D. DAUBE, *The NT and Rabbinic Judaism* (1956) 50-62. — A. DEBRUNNER, G. KITTEL, et al., *TDNT* IV, 69-143. — E. E. ELLIS, *Paul's Use of the OT* (1957) 48f., 107-13, 155-85. — *idem,* "Λέγει κύριος Quotations in the NT," *idem, Prophecy and Hermeneutic in Early Christianity* (1978) 182-87. — G. GERLEMANN, *THAT* I, 433-43. — GOPPELT, *Theology* I, 98ff. — H. HÜBNER, *Das Gesetz in der synoptischen Tradition* (1973) 230-36. — JEREMIAS, *Theology* 35f., 250-55. — E. KÄSEMANN, "The Problem of the Historical Jesus," *idem, Essays on NT Themes* (1964) 15-47. — W. G. KÜMMEL, "Jesus und der jüdische Traditionsgedanke," *idem,* I, 15-35. — E. LOHSE, " 'Ich aber sage euch,'" *idem, Die Einheit des NT* ([2]1976) 73-87. — W. ROTHFUCHS, *Die Erfüllungszitate des Matthäusevangeliums* (BWANT 8, 1969). — H. H. SCHMID, *THAT* I, 211-16. — S. WAGNER, *TDOT* I, 328-45. — For further bibliography → γραφή, λόγος, νόμος, πληρόω; see *TWNT* X, 1157-60.

1. When considered with → εἶπον (2nd aor.), which is not under consideration here, λέγω is the most frequently occurring vb. in the NT after εἰμί.

2. From the basic meanings of λέγω (Debrunner 71-73; Frisk, *Wörterbuch* II, 94): *pick up, gather* (in Attic prose and in the NT only in συλλέγω), then *count, enumerate, narrate,* then in post-Homeric Greek *speak, say, tell,* in the NT *say* is dominant.

Λέγω is a trans. vb., e.g., ἀλήθειαν λέγω, "I *speak* the truth" (Rom 9:1). Occasionally it is found with an acc. with inf., e.g., τίνα με λέγουσιν οἱ ἄνθρωποι εἶναι; "who do people *consider* me to be?" (Mark 8:27). Normally direct discourse or ὅτι with an exact representation of direct discourse comes after λέγω in the NT, as with folk narrators before and outside the NT, for whom indirect speech is uncommon. Thus ὅτι *recitativum* assumes the place of quotation marks (BDF §470.1; on the shift from indirect to direct speech see §470.2). The person to whom something is said is most often in the dat., but also expressed with πρός τινα. Other prep. phrases are seen in τὶ περί τινος λέγω, "*say* something about someone"; τινὶ περί τινος λέγω with direct speech: "*say* to someone with reference to one . . ."; εἴς τινα λέγω, "*speak* against someone"; and ὑπέρ τινος λέγω, "*speak* on behalf of someone."

Alongside the meaning *say* is the meaning *believe, think* (frequently idiomatic in Plato: πῶς λέγεις; "what

did you *mean?*"), e.g., τοῦτο δὲ λέγω, "but I *mean* this" (Gal 3:17). Λέγω can also be used to mean *say* in the sense of *ask, answer, command,* and *affirm.* It appears with a double acc. in the sense of *call,* e.g., Δαυὶδ λέγει αὐτὸν κύριον, "David *calls* him Lord" (Mark 12:37).

The partc. λέγων after a finite vb. of saying is a Hebraism, a tr. of Heb. *lē'mōr.* As an LXX idiom, this construction is characteristic also of the Gospels and Acts (elsewhere only rarely in the NT, e.g., Heb 2:6; Jude 14; Rev 21:9; nowhere in Paul). The references in BDF §420 to Herodotus, e.g., ἔφη λέγων in iii.156; v.36, do not call into question this designation of the NT occurrences as Hebraistic. The Synoptic and Johannine ἀπεκρίθη λέγων occurs rarely. BDF is probably correct in tracing the more frequent Synoptic ἀποκριθεὶς εἶπεν to OT *wayyaʿan wayyōʾmer.* In any case ἔγραψεν λέγων in Luke 1:63 corresponds to *yiktōb lēʾmōr* (cf. 2 Kgdms 11:15: καὶ ἔγραψεν ἐν τῷ βιβλίῳ λέγων, etc.; so also BAGD s.v. 8b; BDF §420.3).

More frequent is the partc. λεγόμενος, sometimes with the meaning *so-called,* e.g., λεγόμενοι θεοί (1 Cor 8:5), occasionally with the meaning *with the name,* etc., e.g., ἄνθρωπον . . . Μαθθαῖον λεγόμενον, "a man *by the name* of Matthew" (Matt 9:9). This partc. can also be an indication of a tr., e.g., τόπον λεγόμενον Γολγοθᾶ, ὅ ἐστιν Κρανίου Τόπος λεγόμενος, "a place *called* Golgotha, *which is called* place of the skull" (Matt 27:33).

3. It is noteworthy and significant that the pres. first person sg. λέγω appears almost exclusively in words of Jesus in the Synoptic Gospels and John (126 [with Matt 25:12, 40, 45] of 128 occurrences). Jesus' consciousness of his mission, already indicated, is articulated esp. in the evidently authentic formula of authority and asseveration, "Amen, *I say* to you" with its introductory nonresponsive Amen (see also → ἀμήν), and in the words that are fundamental to the antitheses of the Sermon on the Mount, "but *I say* to you" (Matt 5:22, 28, 32, 34, 39, 44, regarded as authentic in the first, second, and fourth antitheses [e.g., Kümmel, Käsemann, Lohse], the first, second, fourth, and fifth [Hübner], or all six [Jeremias, *Theology* 250ff.]; for a critical view of "but *I say* to you" as an expression of messianic consciousness cf. Lohse 81 with n. 29; on the relationship of this phrase to rabbinic *weʾanî ʾomer,* see Daube 55-62; Lohse 78-84; Hübner 231-33, 235 n. 206). Jesus does not use the prophetic messenger formula *kōh ʾāmar JHWH,* "thus says Yahweh." The phrase (ἠκούσατε ὅτι) ἐρρέθη (τοῖς ἀρχαίοις), "(you have heard that) it *was said* (to those of old)," which is in each instance contrasted to "but *I say* to you," corresponds to rabbinic *šeneʾᵉmar* (Bacher I, 6: "the most frequent form for citation of biblical passages") only formally, inasmuch as Jesus does not appeal to scriptural passages as proof for his statements (Levy I, 100: *šeneʾᵉmar* means

that this or that precept is proven from the cited passage; → νόμος).

In Paul also pres. first person λέγω is an expression of the consciousness of his mission or, more precisely, of his consciousness of an apostolic calling. Typical for Paul is the manner in which citations of Scripture are introduced, not with the more usual καθὼς γέγραπται, etc., which he himself also uses (→ γραφή 3), but with "the Scripture *says*" (e.g., Rom 4:3; 9:17; 10:11; see also John 7:42; 19:37; 1 Tim 5:18; Jas 2:23), "the law *says*" (Rom 7:7), "David/Isaiah *says*" (e.g., Rom 4:6; 10:16), and also "the Scripture *says* in [in its report about] Elijah" (Rom 11:2). In each instance the concern is with the divine authority of the Scripture in which the basic OT idea, that God speaks and the individual hears, is indicated specifically in the Scripture (as already in Judaism). Thus in Rom 9:17 "Scripture" speaks to Pharaoh what God speaks to him, while directly preceding that reference in v. 15, because of the first person sg., ὁ θεός is most easily supplied. BDF §130.3 is correct: In the citation formula λέγει the subj. is ὁ θεός, ἡ γραφή, etc. In Gal 3:16 ἐρρέθησαν is divine pass.: "God has spoken the promises to Abraham." This sense is given by Paul in Rom 12:19f. in the citation of Deut 32:35, which is introduced with γέγραπται γάρ (see also 1 Cor 14:21).

With regard to λέγει κύριος: In the mixed citation in 2 Cor 6:16ff. this clause is introduced with the striking καθὼς εἶπεν ὁ θεός and appears in 6:14–7:1, which is scarcely Pauline (cf. Kümmel, *Introduction* 291f.; P. Vielhauer, *Geschichte der urchristlichen Literatur* [1975] 153). In Rom 14:11 it is an original part of the citation introduced with γέγραπται γάρ. In Hebrews all occurrences of λέγει κύριος are part of the respective OT citations (8:8, 9, 10; 10:16).

Typical for Paul is the question τί οὖν ἐροῦμεν; "what then shall we *say*?" which is derived from diatribe style (Bultmann, *Stil* 64-68). However, only in Romans (7 times, e.g., 6:1; 7:1; see also 9:19; 11:19: ἐρεῖς [μοι] οὖν, *"you will reply"*; see also 1 Cor 15:35). However, such a borrowing does not necessarily imply that the opposing conversation partner is a fiction (*contra* Bultmann 67).

The theology of Matthew is reflected clearly in its fulfillment citations (*Reflexionszitate*, called *Erfüllungszitate* by Rothfuchs; cf. R. E. Brown, *The Birth of the Messiah* [1977] 96f. n. 1), which are most often introduced by ἵνα (or ὅπως) πληρωθῇ τὸ ῥηθὲν (ὑπὸ κυρίου) διὰ τοῦ προφήτου λέγοντος, "so that what was spoken [by the Lord] through the prophets is fulfilled," etc. (1:22; 2:15; 4:14; 8:17; 12:17; 13:35; 21:4; twice τότε ἐπληρώθη τὸ ῥηθὲν διὰ Ἰερεμίου τοῦ προφήτου [λέγοντος]: 2:17; 27:9; → πληρόω). In setting forth God's authoritative speech through the OT prophets, Matthew thinks ultimately, of course, of the fulfillment in Christ.

Deserving of special emphasis in Acts are ἤκουσα φωνὴν

λέγουσαν (μοι), "I heard a voice, which *said* [to me]" (9:4; 11:7; 22:7; 26:14; see also Rev 12:10, etc.), and τάδε λέγει τὸ πνεῦμα τὸ ἅγιον, "thus the Holy Spirit *says*" (21:11; cf. 20:33; elsewhere in the NT πνεῦμα is rarely the subj. of λέγω: 1 Tim 4:1; Heb 3:7; on Revelation see below).

In the circular letters of Revelation the exalted Christ speaks to the seven churches of Asia Minor, referring to himself in each case with the OT prophetic messenger formula τάδε λέγει κύριος (most often a tr. of *kōh 'āmar JHWH*), always replacing κύριος with some other title (2:1, 8, 12, 18; 3:1, 7, 14). The letters all conclude with the same call to awaken (E. Lohse, *Rev* [NTD] 23): "He who has an ear, hear what the Spirit *says* to the churches (τί τὸ πνεῦμα λέγει)" (2:7, 11, 17; 3:6, 13, 22) with which an additional specific message is introduced. "The exalted Lord speaks through the Spirit" (Lohse 23).

H. Hübner

λεῖμμα, ατος, τό *leimma* remnant, remainder*

Rom 11:5: λεῖμμα κατ' ἐκλογὴν χάριτος, "a *remnant* chosen by grace." G. Schrenk and V. Herntrich, *TDNT* IV, 194-214; *TWNT* X, 1161f. (bibliography).

λεῖος, 3 *leios* smooth, level*

Luke 3:5: καὶ αἱ τραχεῖαι εἰς ὁδοὺς λείας, "and the rough ways shall become *smooth*" (citing [?] Isa 40:4 v.l.). G. Bornkamm, *TDNT* IV, 193.

λείπω *leipō* leave behind; mid.-pass.: be left behind, fall short of; intrans.-act.: lack*

The basic trans. meaning appears in the NT only in the mid.-pass. and only in James: 1:4: λείπομαι ἐν μηδενί, "*be lacking* in nothing"; 1:5: σοφίας, "*lack* wisdom"; 2:15: τῆς τροφῆς, "*lacking* food." Λείπω is used intrans. in Luke 18:22 ("you *lack* one thing [σοι λείπει]") and Titus 3:13 ("so that you *lack* nothing"). Τὰ λείποντα in Titus 1:5 is *what is still lacking/the rest*. Spicq, *Notes* I, 472-74.

λειτουργέω *leitourgeō* serve, administer an office, provide a service
→ λειτουργία.

λειτουργία, ας, ἡ *leitourgia* service, worship (noun)*
λειτουργέω *leitourgeō* serve, administer an office, provide a service*
λειτουργικός, 3 *leitourgikos* serving, concerning the service, subservient*
λειτουργός, οῦ, ὁ *leitourgos* servant, one commissioned for service*

1. Occurrences in the NT — 2. Greek usage and the LXX — 3. Luke and Hebrews — 4. Paul — 5. Acts 13:2

Lit.: R. M. COOPER, "Leitourgos Christou Iesou; Toward a Theology of Christian Prayer," *ATR* 47 (1965) 263-75. — A.-M. DENIS, "La fonction apostolique et la liturgie nouvelle en esprit," *RSPT* 42 (1958) 401-36, 617-56. — P. FERNÁNDEZ RODRÍGUEZ, "El término liturgia. Su etimologia y su uso," *Ciencia tomista* 97 (1970) 43-163. — G. FRIEDRICH, "Geist und Amt," *WuD* 3 (1952) 81-85, esp. 71f. — F. HAHN, *Worship of the Early Church* (1973) 37. — K. HESS, *DNTT* III, 551-53. — H.-J. KRAUS, "Gottesdienst im alten und im neuen Bund," *EvT* 25 (1965) 171-206, esp. 179. — E. J. LENGELING, *HTG* II, 75-97, esp. 75f., 78f. — N. LEWIS, "Leitourgia and Related Terms," *Greek, Roman and Byzantine Studies* 3 (1960) 175-84; 6 (1965) 229f. — J. M. NIELEN, *Gebet und Gottesdienst im NT* (²1963) 114f., 121f. — E. PETERSON, "La λειτουργία des prophètes et des didascales à Antioche," *RSR* 36 (1949) 577-79. — A. ROMEO, "Il termine ΛΕΙΤΟΥΡΓΙΑ nella grecità biblica," *Miscellanea Liturgica* II (FS L. C. Mohlberg, 1949) 467-519. — K. H. SCHELKLE, *Discipleship and Priesthood* (1965) 108-37. — H. SCHLIER, "Die 'Liturgie' des apostolischen Evangeliums (Röm 15,14-21)," *idem* III, 169-83. — SPICQ, *Notes* I, 475-81. — H. STRATHMANN and R. MEYER, *TDNT* IV, 215-31. — K. WEISS, "Paulus— Priester der christlichen Kultgemeinde," *TLZ* 79 (1954) 355-64. — For further bibliography see *TWNT* X, 1162.

1. Λειτουργία appears 6 times in the NT, λειτουργέω 3 times, λειτουργός 5 times, and λειτουργικός only in Heb 1:14. The word group appears with special frequency in Hebrews (6 occurrences), in the Gospels only in Luke 1:23, and not at all in the deutero-Pauline letters, the Catholic Epistles, or Revelation.

2. The word group is most commonly used in Greek literature for service rendered for the people as a political entity (corresponding to the etymological formation from Ionic λήϊτος, "concerning the people," and ἔργον, "work, service"). Along with its usage in a predominantly public sense in reference to taxes and general obligations of service, it is used frequently in the Hellenistic period, esp. in inscriptions, also in a cultic connection (examples in Strathmann 218f.).

In the LXX the word group is used in a fixed cultic sense, particularly to distinguish it from → λατρεύω (2) as a t.t. for the temple service of priests and Levites. Most often it renders Heb. *šērēṯ* or *ʿăḇōḏâ* where these terms are used in a priestly and cultic sense (e.g., Exod 28:35; Num 8:22; in a later period also fig. for prayer: Wis 18:21; in some instances for pagan cults: Ezek 44:12; 2 Chr 15:16). It may include the original meaning of an orderly and public service in the interest of the entire people (Strathmann 224).

3. In the NT the word group refers in three instances to the priestly ministry in the temple: Luke 1:23: αἱ ἡμέραι τῆς λειτουργίας, of the conclusion of the priestly service of Zechariah; Heb 9:21: πάντα τὰ σκεύη τῆς λειτουργίας, of the cultic vessels in the "tent"; 10:11: καθ' ἡμέραν λειτουργῶν (with προσφέρων θυσίας), of the daily temple ministry.

In Heb 8:2, 6 this terminology is used of the true temple ministry in "the [heavenly] sanctuary and true tent" (τῶν ἁγίων λειτουργὸς καὶ τῆς σκηνῆς τῆς ἀληθινῆς, v. 2). Consistent with the "new covenant," it represents "superior *worship* (διαφορωτέρα λειτουργία)" (v. 6). With the use of cultic and priestly terminology the author of Hebrews is able to interpret the saving event in Christ esp. as the overcoming of the previously futile worship. The previously ineffective service rendered by humans now stands in contrast to the once-for-all effective deed of God in Christ.

Noncultic use appears in Hebrews only in the introductory statement concerning the subordination of angels to the Son as heavenly *ministers* (λειτουργοί, 1:7, citing Ps 103:4 LXX) and "*ministering* spirits" (λειτουργικὰ πνεύματα, 1:14).

4. Paul makes use of the cultic sense of the word group when in Rom 15:16 he portrays his ministry in the gospel with the image of priestly service (ἱερουργῶν) and thus understands himself as λειτουργὸς Χριστοῦ Ἰησοῦ εἰς τὰ ἔθνη (cf. also the sacrificial terminology that follows: προσφορὰ . . . εὐπρόσδεκτος, ἡγιασμένη). One can note from the context that Paul's concern is not with a new cultic dimension of the gospel or even with a sacral function of the apostle as priest. Instead, the image of the final προσφορά, which consists of the Gentile world, refers to the eschatological fulfillment, which had previously been associated with the cult, in the world mission of Paul (Schlier; Cooper; on the discussion, see E. Käsemann, *Rom* [Eng. tr., 1980] ad loc.). A ritual understanding of worship is denied. At the same time Paul knows the authority, given by grace, that is associated with his commission, which enables him to conduct the true "priestly ministry."

Similarly the formulation ἐπὶ τῇ θυσίᾳ καὶ λειτουργίᾳ τῆς πίστεως ὑμῶν (Phil 2:17) is to be understood in a fig. sense (cf. Rom 12:1). Paul wants to accept his approaching martyrdom joyfully as a "drink offering" (σπένδομαι), which "is poured out over" "the sacrificial *ministry* for the faith" (obj. gen.) of the Philippians, which he has already offered. (In view of v. 16 and Rom 15:16 the idea of the Church's "sacrificial ministry" [understanding τῆς πίστεως as epexegetical gen.], to which Paul is added as a drink offering, though also grammatically possible, is less probable; cf. esp. E. Lohmeyer, *Phil* [KEK] ad loc.).

The word group appears also in a fig. sense in the wider context of Philippians where reference is made to the financial contribution and support for the apostle while he was in need. This support can be called "a pleasing sacrifice" to God as well as a λειτουργία (2:30). Epaphroditus, the deliverer of the contribution, is described as an ἀπόστολος of the church and λειτουργὸς τῆς χρείας μου (2:25). Inasmuch as Paul can emphasize the character of the support as both the church's gift and its obligation in relation to its founder (4:10ff.), and inasmuch as this gift is seen in an eschatological light in

4:18f., one is to recognize here not so much the general Greek background of "service rendered" as the fulfillment of the true Christian "worship" and the church's offering of "sacrifices" pleasing to God. This is the case also for the "fruit" that the apostle rightfully seeks from his church in God's name (4:17).

The use of λειτουργέω in Rom 15:27 and the use of διακονία τῆς λειτουργίας in 2 Cor 9:12 in reference to the collection of the Greek churches for the Jerusalem church is to be understood in a similar way, for according to Rom 15:25f., 28 this is a "fruit" of the Greek churches (according to 2 Cor 9:11-15 also a sign of the obedience of faith and of the grace of God, of thanksgiving and a desire for fellowship) and a sign of reciprocal service and of common participation in the gift of God (cf. D. Georgi, *Die Geschichte der Kollekte des Paulus für Jerusalem* [1965] 86; on the discussion, Käsemann, *Rom* ad loc.). Any correspondence to the idea of "the eschatological sacrificial ministry of the peoples" or to the Jewish temple tax is remote.

In Rom 13:6 Paul describes the Roman tax officials as λειτουργοὶ . . . θεοῦ (similarly θεοῦ . . . διάκονος, v. 4), i.e., as representatives or instruments commissioned by God for service. In accordance with the administrative and legal language of the context, the reference is not to a sacral function of the officeholders (cf. A. Strobel, *ZNW* 47 [1956] 86f.). Rather, the gen. θεοῦ qualifies their work as a contribution to the function that the imperium and its administrators have of providing order and authority, which is granted to them by God.

5. In Acts 13:2 the vb. λειτουργέω is used in a way unique in the NT (also for the LXX), when it is used in a special sense in reference to worship. The five prophets and teachers of the Antiochian church mentioned in v. 1 perform this activity in the midst of fasting (cf. also 13:3; 14:23; Luke 2:37). Luke takes up the ceremonious priestly terminology of the LXX (cf. 2 Chr 13:10; Ezek 40:46; Dan 7:10 Θ) in λειτουργούντων δὲ αὐτῶν τῷ κυρίῳ and refers—anticipating later Christian terminology (cf. *Did.* 15:1f.; Strathmann 235f.; Lengeling 76)—to the "worship" activity of individual officebearers in the church, who are deemed worthy of receiving the instruction of the Spirit.

H. Balz

λειτουργικός, 3 *leitourgikos* serving, concerning the service, subservient
→ λειτουργία.

λειτουργός, οῦ, ὁ *leitourgos* servant, one commissioned for service
→ λειτουργία.

λεμα *lema* why?
→ ελωι.

λέντιον, ου, τό *lention* linen cloth*

A loanword (from Lat. *linteum*). John 13:4: Jesus "took a *linen cloth* and girded himself." After the washing of feet he dried the feet of the disciples with it (τῷ λεντίῳ, v. 5).

λεπίς, ίδος, ἡ *lepis* scale*

Acts 9:18: "It fell from his [Paul's] eyes like *scales* and he could see again." W. Michaelis, *TDNT* IV, 233f.; Spicq, *Notes* I, 482f.

λέπρα, ας, ἡ *lepra* leprosy*

Mark 1:42 par. Matt 8:3/Luke 5:12, 13, in the pericope of the healing of the leper (→ λεπρός). According to Mark and Luke the leprosy left him; according to Matthew "the *leprosy* was cleansed." Billerbeck IV, 745-63; W. Michaelis, *TDNT* IV, 233; *TWNT* X, 1162f. (bibliography); *BL* 142; R. Pesch, *Jesu ureigene Taten?* (1970); W. Bruners, *Die Reinigung der zehn Aussätzigen und die Heilung des Samaritaners Lk 17,11-19* (1977).

λεπρός, 3 *lepros* leprous; subst.: leper*

The adj., like → λέπρα, occurs in the NT only in the Synoptic Gospels: in a healing story (Mark 1:40 par. Matt 8:2), with the mention of "Simon the *leper*" (Mark 14:3 par. Matt 26:6), in Jesus' commission ("make *lepers* clean," Matt 10:8), and in the report, "*lepers* are cleansed" (Matt 11:5 par. Luke 7:22). Luke 4:27 refers to "the many *lepers*" in the time of Elisha; 17:12 introduces the story of the ten *lepers*. For bibliography → λέπρα.

λεπτόν, οῦ, τό *lepton* lepton, farthing, small coin*

Lit.: H. CHANTRAINE, *KP* III, 582. — A. KINDLER, *Coins of the Land of Israel* (1974).

1. The adj. λεπτός means "thin, fine, delicate." It is used in phrases such as "thin texture," "fine dust," and "thin metal." When λεπτόν is used for coins, it can be used in connection with νόμισμα, κέρμα, χαλκός, ἀργύριον, and δραχμή (coin, copper, silver, drachma). It simply designates small change or distinguishes between lighter and heavier coins of the same name. Λεπτόν is also used subst. outside the NT for specific types of money.

2. Only Mark 12:42 offers the explanation of the two *lepta* cast into the treasury: "that is, a quadrans." Luke 21:2 omits the value, as does the only other NT occurrence, Luke 12:59. Inasmuch as the value of the Roman quadrans is known (one-fourth of an as), one can say that the two λεπτά of Mark 12:42 together had a value of one sixty-fourth of a denarius (1 denarius = 16 asses). In contemporary numismatic works these tiny copper coins appear as a "half-perutah" (or half-pruta, Heb. pl. half-

prutot). The diameter was *ca.* 11 mm., weight *ca.* 0.9 g., fixed under John Hyrcanus II and Herod I (63-4 B.C.).

B. Schwank

Λευί(ς) *Leui(s)* Levi*

1. The son of Jacob — 2. In the genealogy of Jesus — 3. The tax collector

Lit.: HENNECKE/SCHNEEMELCHER II, 64. — G. KUHN, "Die Geschlechtsregister Jesu bei Lukas und Matthäus, nach ihrer Herkunft untersucht," *ZNW* 22 (1923) 207-10, 223-28. — R. PESCH, "Levi-Matthäus (Mc 2,14/Mt 9,9; 10,3), ein Beitrag zur Lösung eines alten Problems," *ZNW* 59 (1968) 40-56. — H. STRATHMANN, *TDNT* IV, 234-39.

1. Of the 8 occurrences of the name Λευί or Λευίς (rendering of Heb. *lēwî;* Λευί indeclinable, Λευίς declinable) in the NT, 3 refer to to the third son of Jacob by Leah. Rev 7:7 mentions the tribe of Levi in a list of the twelve tribes of Israel. The other two occurrences are in Heb 7:5, 9, where Levi is introduced as the ancestor and representative of the OT or Israelite priesthood. This is related to Jewish speculation about Levi, as, e.g., in *Jubilees* and *T. 12 Patr.*

2. Luke includes the name Levi twice in his rendering of the genealogy of Jesus: the great grandfather of Joseph (3:24) and another ancestor of Jesus (3:29). It is possible that the lists of names from Joshua to Matthat (vv. 29-31) and from Jesus to Mattathias (vv. 23-26) were originally identical and that the redactor of the Gospel has erred in his arrangement of the sources, making Jesus and the other names in the list from postexilic times in vv. 29-31 into preexilic persons. Moreover, the names of the twelve tribal ancestors appear first in the postexilic Hellenistic period.

3. In Mark 2:14; Luke 5:27, 29 a tax collector named Levi ("son of Alphaeus," Mark 2:14) is called by Jesus to be one of his disciples (see also *Gos. Pet.* 60; *Gos. Mary* 18:6; 19:1; *Didascalia* v.14). In the parallel passage in Matt 9:9 "Matthew" is substituted for Levi.

H. W. Hollander

Λευίτης, ου, ὁ *Leuitēs* Levite*

The designation of a man from the tribe of Levi (→ Λευί), esp. one who, while not belonging to the family of Aaron, performs lower services in the cult. The parable of the Samaritan mentions a *Levite* (Luke 10:32, after the "priest," v. 31). John 1:19 speaks of "priests and *Levites*" sent from Jerusalem to John the Baptist. Acts 4:36 says of Barnabas that he was a *Levite* from Cyprus. R. Meyer, *TDNT* IV, 239-41; *TWNT* X, 1163 (bibliography).

Λευιτικός, 3 *Leuitikos* levitical*

Heb 7:11: There is no perfection (τελείωσις) through "the *levitical* priesthood (ἡ Λευιτικὴ ἱερωσύνη)."

λευκαίνω *leukainō* make white*

Literally, of garments, which the fuller *makes white,* in Mark 9:3; fig. in Rev 7:14 of martyrs, who have *made* their garments *white* in [through] the blood of the lamb." W. Michaelis, *TDNT* IV, 242, 250.

λευκός, 3 *leukos* white, radiant*

Lit.: H. BALTENSWEILER, *Die Verklärung Jesu* (ATANT 33, 1959) 62-69. — A. BRENNER, *Colour Terms in the OT* (*JSOT* Supplement Series 21, 1982). — F. H. DANIEL, *The Transfiguration (Mark 9:2-13 and parallels)* (Diss. Vanderbilt University, 1977) 47-51. — W. GERBER, "Die Metamorphose Jesu, Mark 9,2f. par.," *TZ* 23 (1967) 385-95. — R. GRADWOHL, *Die Farben im AT* (BZAW 83, 1963) 34-50. — E. HAULOTTE, *Symbolique du vêtement selon la Bible* (Théologie 65, 1966) 201-3, 207-16, 324-31. — H. W. HERTZBERG, *BHH* 463f. — J. JERVELL, *Imago Dei. Gen 1,26f. im Spätjudentum, in der Gnosis und in den paulinischen Briefen* (FRLANT 76, 1960) 44-46, 268-71. — J. MAIER, "Das Gefährdungsmotiv bei der Himmelsreise in der jüdischen Apokalyptik und 'Gnosis,'" *Kairos* 5 (1963) 18-40, esp. 30-33. — idem, *Vom Kultus zur Gnosis. Studien zur Vor- und Frühgeschichte der "jüdischen Gnosis"* (1964), esp. 96, 125-28. — W. MICHAELIS, *TDNT* IV, 241-50. — J. M. NÜTZEL, *Die Verklärungsgeschichte im Markusevangelium* (FzB 6, 1973), esp. 96-102. — R. PESCH, *Mark* (HTKNT) II (1977) 72-74. — H. RIESENFELD, *Jésus transfiguré. L'arrière-plan du récit évangélique de la transfiguration de Notre-Seigneur* (ASNU 16, 1947), esp. 115-29. — A. SCHLATTER, *Der Evangelist Matthäus* (1929) 527. — SCHÜRER, *History* II, 276. — For further bibliography see *TWNT* X, 1163.

1. Λευκός appears most frequently in Revelation (15 occurrences); there it is a sign of heavenly purity, glory, and victory. The significance of λευκός as *pure/light* (in the heavenly-eschatological sense) in the transfiguration narrative (Mark 9:3 par. Matt 17:2/Luke 9:29) corresponds to this usage. The reports of appearances by angels in Mark 16:5 par. Matt 28:3 (cf. John 20:12; Acts 1:10) are also to be understood in this way.

Only Matt 5:36 and John 4:35 deviate from this usage. To make the hair *white* or black (Matt 5:36) refers to the futile human attempt to change one's age: The individual stands in the order of creation and is incapable of binding himself to an oath on his own power. In John 4:35 λευκός is used of the ripe *bright golden* ears of wheat (on the range of colors covered by λευκός cf. Michaelis 241; Gradwohl 48-50).

2. Λευκός, *radiant white,* as a color of heavenly glory derives its vividness and significance from Jewish cult apocalyptic. White is the color of purity and thus the only appropriate color for the priestly clothing. The high priest, as a theocratic ruler in the postexilic period dressed in splendid clothing (cf. Exod 28:4-

43; 39:1-31), put on a white linen garment on the great Day of Atonement in order to be suitable for the extraordinary holiness and purity of the holy of holies, which was considered an earthly-heavenly place (cf. Lev 16:4; *m. Yoma* 3:6f.; 7:4; Josephus *B.J.* v.236).

Jewish cult apocalyptic developed on this foundation (cf. the basic details in Maier) with its portrayal of the heavenly world. It depicted the heavenly throne of God and the heavenly sanctuary as a place of perfect purity and holiness (cf. Dan 7:9); the angels who stand before God's throne (cf. Ezek 9:2f., 11; 10:2; Dan 10:5; 12:6f.) and the righteous who also participate in the heavenly worship are, or will be at the resurrection—cult apocalyptic has a strong present eschatology and knows of the transfiguration of the righteous at the hour of death—clothed in heavenly-white garments (cf. *2 Bar.* 51:5; *1 Enoch* 38:4; 50:1; 104:2; see earlier Dan 12:3).

It is originally the role of the high priest as an earthly-heavenly figure to enter into this heavenly glory and thus to be clothed with the radiant white garments of heavenly purity (cf. Lev 16:17 in Philo's interpretation, *Her.* 84; *Som.* ii.189, 231; cf. earlier Zech 3:3ff.: the high priest Joshua before the angel of the Lord, his heavenly-cultic new apparel). To be conformed to that heavenly purity is then the experience of the mystic who is temporarily transported to heaven (the Enoch tradition; cf. *2 Enoch* 22:8-10) and a sign of the heavenly transfiguration of the righteous (cf. *2 Bar.* 51:5, 12; *1 Enoch* 62:15f.; *Apoc. Abr.* 13:15).

The NT assumes these associations. In Mark 9:3 par. Jesus, in the presence of his disciples, is clothed in the heavenly glory in which he will then enter upon the way of the Son of Man: The visionary experience anticipates the human transfiguration and the heavenly exaltation; the combination of visionary experience and human rapture as a final entry into the heavenly glory corresponds to the basic details of the way of Moses and Elijah.

The portrayals of the one like a son of man in Rev 1:12ff. (v. 14 bis) are derived from the cult apocalyptic of Ezekiel and Daniel: The *white* hair of the figure on the throne in Daniel is here given to the one like a son of man; also, according to Rev 20:11 God's throne is *radiant white*. In Rev 14:14 the one like a son of man comes on a *white* cloud (cf. Ezek 30:3; Dan 7:13); as λόγος τοῦ θεοῦ (19:13) he sits on a *white* horse (19:11). Here white is the color of the glorious victor (cf. 6:2): Supported by pure angels on *white* horses and in *white* garments, the λόγος, according to Rev 19:14 (bis), destroys the impure enemy on earth through the heavenly purity brought about by the lamb. His victory signifies an eschatological climax, the reversal of the earthly relationships of aggressive impurity and cultically restricted purity. The righteous, who have not defiled their garments, i.e., have kept them *white* (= have kept themselves pure), receive the promise that they will put on the heavenly *white* garment of perfected purity and thus be permitted to be with Christ (3:4, 5; cf. v. 18). According to 4:4 the twenty-four elders (πρεσβύτεροι, "ministers/martyrs"? Cf. H. Kraft, *Rev* [HNT] 96f.; O. H. Steck, *Israel und das gewaltsame*

Geschick der Propheten (1967) 214f., 229 n. 5) are also furnished with *white* garments of heavenly purity: They share in the purifying power of the blood of the lamb (cf. 6:11; 7:9, 13f.).

The *white* stone on which the new heavenly name of the righteous is inscribed, according to Rev 2:17, is, as the imagery indicates, derived from the stone "permit" qualifying one to enter a cult fellowship (cf. Kraft, 66f.). As a sign of transfiguration and heavenly exaltation those who overcome (i.e., unyielding martyrs) receive a new name.

J.-A. Bühner

λέων, οντος, ὁ *leōn* lion*

Except in Heb 11:33 ("they stopped the mouths of lions") λέων occurs in the NT only as a metaphor (of the devil: "as a roaring *lion*," 1 Pet 5:8; other comparisons in Rev 4:7; 9:8, 17; 10:3; 13:2) or in a fig. sense (2 Tim 4:17; Rev 5:5). W. Michaelis, *TDNT* IV, 251-53; *TWNT* X, 1163 (bibliography).

λήθη, ης, ἡ *lēthē* forgetfulness*

2 Pet 1:9: λήθην λαμβάνω τινός, "forget something."

λῆμψις, εως, ἡ *lēmpsis* receiving, income*

Phil 4:15: εἰς λόγον δόσεως καὶ λήμψεως, "account of giving and *receiving*," i.e. (fig.), in reciprocal "settlement of accounts."

ληνός, οῦ, ἡ *lēnos* wine press*

Matt 21:33 (cf. Mark 12:1): "and dug a *wine press* in it [the vineyard]." Revelation uses ληνός metaphorically: 14:19, 20 (bis) of "the *wine press* of God's wrath," which is trodden outside the city and from which blood flows; 19:15: Christ "treads the *wine press* of the wine of God's wrath." G. Bornkamm, *TDNT* IV, 254-57.

λῆρος, ου, ὁ *lēros* chatter, idle talk*

Luke 24:11: The report of the women appeared to the apostles to be *empty chatter* (ὡσεὶ λῆρος), and they did not believe them. Spicq, *Notes* I, 484f.

λῃστής, οῦ, ὁ *lēstēs* robber, bandit*

Mark 11:17 par. Matt 21:13/Luke 19:46: "You have made it [my house] a den of *robbers*" (in which one is plundered, robbed; cf. Jer 7:11 LXX); Mark 14:48 par. Matt 26:55/Luke 22:52: "Have you come out as against a *robber . . . ?*" Of the two robbers, who were crucified with Jesus, Mark 15:27 par. Matt 27:38; Matt 27:44. In the parable of the Samaritan mention is made of the man who "fell among *robbers*," Luke 10:30, 36. In John 10:1, 8 λῃστής stands with κλέπτης (thief) and both are contrasted to ποιμήν (shepherd). John 18:40 emphasizes that Barabbas was a *robber*. In 2 Cor 11:26 Paul mentions "dangers from robbers." K. H. Rengstorf, *TDNT* IV, 257-62; *TWNT* X, 1163f. (bibliography); Spicq, *Notes* I, 486-92.

λίαν *lian* very much; entirely*

In the NT λίαν appears in connection with vbs. (Matt 2:16; 27:14; Mark 6:51; Luke 23:8; 2 Tim 4:15; 2 John 4:3; 3 John 3) and with adjs. (Matt 4:8; 8:28; Mark 1:35; 9:3; 16:2; also TR in 2 Cor 11:5 and 12:11 [ὑπὲρ λίαν]). BDF §474.

λίβανος, ου, ὁ *libanos* incense*

Matt 2:11, as a gift of the magi; Rev 18:13, with other valuable items. W. Michaelis, *TDNT* IV, 263f.; W. W. Müller, *Glotta* 52 (1974) 53-59.

λιβανωτός, οῦ, ὁ *libanōtos* incense; incense censer*

Λιβανωτός can, like → λίβανος, refer to *incense* (e.g., *Mart. Pol.* 15:2). In the NT it occurs only in Rev 8:3, 5 and refers to the *censer* on which the incense was burned. For bibliography → λίβανος.

Λιβερτῖνος, ου, ὁ *Libertinos* Libertine*

A loanword from Latin (*libertinus*, "freedman"). Acts 6:9, pl.: *freedmen* are mentioned with Cyrenians and Alexandrians. The three groups, as Greek-speaking Jews, had a synagogue in Jerusalem. W. Schrage, *TDNT* VII, 837f.; H. Strathmann, *TDNT* IV, 265f.; *KP* III, 624f.

Λιβύη, ης *Libyē* Libya*

A north African region between Egypt and Cyrene. Acts 2:10: "inhabitants . . . of Egypt and the areas of *Libya* belonging to Cyrene [thus, the western part of Libya]." *KP* III, 628-32.

λιθάζω *lithazō* stone (vb.)*

In Israel and in Judaism stoning was the death penalty for specific crimes (*m. Sanh.* 6:1-7:10). It was the punishment for adultery (John 8:5) and for blasphemy (10:31, 32, 33; 11:8). The vb. appears also in Acts 5:26; 14:19; 2 Cor 11:25 and is mentioned with other types of death in Heb 11:37. R. Hirzel, *Die Strafe der Steinigung* (1909 = 1967); Billerbeck II, 685f.; W. Michaelis, *TDNT* IV, 267f.

λίθινος, 3 *lithinos* made of stone*

Of idols, Rev 9:20; of water jars, John 2:6; of tablets of the law, 2 Cor 3:3 (Exod 31:18; *Barn.* 4:7). J. Jeremias, *TDNT* IV, 268f.

λιθοβολέω *lithoboleō* throw a stone; stone (vb.)*

The vb. in a general sense means *throw a stone* (Matt 21:35 par. Mark 12:4 TR; Acts 14:5). It has the meaning *stone* (i.e., kill by throwing stones) in Matt 23:37 par. Luke 13:34 and—in relation to Stephen—Acts 7:58, 59. It also appears in John 8:5 TR (in place of → λιθάζω). Of the killing of an animal: Heb 12:20 (cf. Exod 19:13). W. Michaelis, *TDNT* IV, 267f.

λίθος, ου, ὁ *lithos* stone*

1. Basic meaning — 2. Fig. usage

Lit.: O. BÖCHER, "Zur Bedeutung der Edelsteine in Offb 21," *Kirche und Bibel* (FS E. Schick, 1979) 19-32. — J. JEREMIAS, *TDNT* IV, 268-80. — H.-G. LINK, E. TIEDTKE, and C. BROWN, *DNTT* III, 390-94. — W. W. READER, "The Twelve Jewels of Revelation 21,19-20," *JBL* 100 (1981). — For further bibliography → πέτρα, γωνία, and θεμέλιον.

1. The Evangelists use λίθος in its basic meaning without any wider meaning.

a) Unhewn stones lying nearby and useful as objects for demonstration—one must consider the landscape of Palestine—are what is in view in Matt 3:9 par. Luke 3:8; Matt 4:3 par. Luke 4:3; Matt 4:6 par. Luke 4:11. In John 8:7, 59; 10:31 (ff.) the practice of stoning is mentioned (cf. Deut 17:7). In Mark 5:5 a stone is used for self-destruction. Luke 22:41 uses "a stone's throw" to indicate distance. The inedible character of stones provides the contrast to "bread" in Matt 7:9 par. Luke 11:11; Matt 4:3 par. Luke 4:3 (here understood as presumption of the divine power). Their lifeless character is the basis for the contrast (living) deity vs. (artificial, hand-hewn) idol in Acts 17:29 (in the Areopagus speech!). Matt 3:9 par. Luke 3:8 (in dependence on Isa 51:1f.) includes theological implications: The saying denies a dogmatic understanding of Jewish prerogatives on the basis of mere descent. God can awaken "living children" out of the dead matter (probably in reference to Gentiles; cf. Mark 7:24-30 par. Matt 15:21-28; Matt 8:10-12), if Abraham's children do not attain salvation (on the early Jewish understanding of Isa 51:1f. cf. Jeremias 272f.).

b) A hewn millstone is significant because of its weight in Luke 17:2; Rev 18:21, where it serves as a symbol of destruction, in Revelation of Babylon-Rome; likewise "the sea" may symbolize the place of damnation in both passages (less clearly in Luke). Luke 20:18 also accentuates the destructive power of a stone (in Matt 21:44 parallel influences are apparently present); of course, with the parallelism with the preceding verse, a personified understanding is present.

c) 2 Cor 3:7 alludes to the Mosaic law carved in stone. Here the ministry of the law written with letters is surpassed by the new ministry of the Spirit of Christ.

d) Most often a boulder serves as a seal for a tomb made from a cave or rock (Mark 15:46; 16:3, 4; Matt 27:60; 28:2; Luke 24:2; John 20:1: the tomb of Jesus; John 11:38-41: the tomb of Lazarus). In the Synoptic accounts of the tomb λίθος has a semantic function; it is used, e.g., in connection with the literary form "miracle of deliverance and of opening a door" (cf. also Charito *De Chaerea et Callirhoe* iii.3): The "large stone" refers to the secure sealing and the miraculous opening of the door of the tomb (which does not enter into the narrative) and points finally to the deliverance of Jesus from the tomb and death (cf. R. Kratz, *Rettungswunder, Motiv-, traditions- und formkritische Aufarbeitung einer biblischen Gattung* [1979] 500-541).

e) Rev 4:3; 17:4; 18:12, 16; 21, 11, 19 speaks of precious stones and jasper stones (often in connection with gold, silver, pearls, and other gems) in the description of the glory of God, of the heavenly Jerusalem, of the woman, and of the goods of the city of "Babylon."

f) The stones that cry out in Luke 19:40 are reminiscent of OT motifs in theophanies: Nature hails the appearance of Yahweh. If the disciples had remained silent in the presence of the messianic entry of Jerusalem, the lifeless stones would have voiced the cry of jubilation—this meant hyperbolically.

g) The reference to the huge building stones of the Herodian temple is taken as an occasion for the prophecy of its destruction (Mark 13:1f. par. Matt 24:2/Luke 21:5f.). This prophecy is undoubtedly a vaticinium ex eventu that looks back on the destruction of the temple in A.D. 70. Here, with its apocalyptic tone, the prophecy introduces the eschatological discourse. The reference in Mark 12:10 par. Matt 21:42/Luke 20:17; Acts 4:11; 1 Pet 2:7 is to a building stone; here, of course, the transition is made to a fig. symbolic understanding.

2. The messianic interpretation of "the stone" is attested in early Judaism in connection with such OT passages as Ps 118:22; Isa 8:14 (28:16); Dan 2:34f., 44f., etc. These passages are used in reference to Jesus as the cornerstone, keystone, and foundation stone.

a) The citation of Ps 118:22, which the early Church —not Jesus himself—attached as a scriptural proof to the parable of the evil vineyard workers in Mark 12:10, describes the fate of God's last messenger, who according to prophetic tradition is rejected. It indicates in addition, however, the coming of salvation in the resurrection of the Son of God who has become the cornerstone (cf. Mark 12:5f.). Jesus' rejection confirms the fate of the murderers of the prophets in Jerusalem, the old master builders, and initiates the building of the new community of salvation (in Peter's speech in Acts 4:11 the allocation of roles is indicated concretely: "this . . . , you . . .": cf. also 1 Pet 2:7).

b) In 1 Cor 3:12 precious stones and other "materials" are images for the various works that each individual "builds on," according to his ability, to Christ, "the foundation" (→ θεμέλιον). The image of the Church as "temple of God" corresponds to Eph 2:20-22 (cf. also Matt 16:18).

c) The comparison of the congregation with the house of God is most fully developed in 1 Pet 2:4-8; the various conceptions are brought together with a fig. meaning (OT background: Isa 8:14f.; 28:16; Ps 118:22). Christ is the living stone, rejected by people, but chosen by God as precious. The spirits divide over this "cornerstone": for believers he is the foundation, but for unbelievers he is "the stone of stumbling" (→ πέτρα).

d) As 1 Pet 2:8 indicates, the (messianic-christological) understanding of "the stone" is ambivalent. In Rom 9:32f. as well faith is the decisive criterion; membership in the community of salvation is not based on one's origin, neither in Judaism nor in paganism. One is not justified by works, but by faith. For unbelieving Israel Christ is "a *stone* of stumbling and a rock of offense" (v. 33: mixed citation from Isa 8:14; 28:16). Luke 20:18 also belongs within this context (cf. Dan 2:34f.).

R. Kratz

λιθόστρωτος, 2 *lithostrōtos* paved with stone or marble slabs*
Γαββαθά *Gabbatha* Gabbatha*

According to John 19:13 Pilate took Jesus to the judgment seat (→ βῆμα), to the place "that was called λιθόστρωτος, but in Hebrew *Gabbatha*." Here λιθόστρωτος (τόπος) or τὸ λιθόστρωτον (subst.) appears as a "name" (thus it is capitalized) of the place ("Marble Floor"). It refers to the platform in front of the praetorium of the governor (cf. 18:28) and was paved with stone slabs. The Aramaic designation *Gabbatha* has not yet been interpreted with certainty (Billerbeck II, 572; R. Schnackenburg, *John* III [Eng. tr., 1982] 454, n. 96). Spicq, *Notes* I, 496f. On the localization within Jerusalem, cf. → πραιτώριον 2.

λικμάω *likmaō* crush, grind*

Matt 21:44 par. Luke 20:18: The stone will *crush* the person upon whom it falls. The Matthean passage has an uncertain textual basis; cf. *TCGNT* 58. G. Bornkamm, *TDNT* IV, 280f.; Spicq, *Notes* I, 498f.

λιμήν, ένος, ὁ *limēn* harbor*

Acts 27:12a, b, referring to two different harbors; 27:8 in the place name → Καλοὶ λιμένες.

λίμμα, ατος, τό *limma* remnant, remainder

Alternative form of → λεῖμμα.

λίμνη, ης, ἡ *limnē* lake, pond; pool*

Of the Lake of Gennesaret in Luke 5:1, 2; 8:22, 23, 33 (cf. par. Mark in each case). In Revelation λίμνη is used of the *pool* of fire (20:14a, b, 15) or the *pool* of fire and brimstone (19:20; 20:10; 21:8) in which the enemies of God find their end. G. Theissen, " 'Meer' und 'See' in den Evangelien," *SNTU* 10 (1985) 5-25.

λιμός, οῦ, ὁ (ἡ) *limos* hunger; famine*

Luke 15:17; Rom 8:35; 2 Cor 11:27: *hunger.* Luke 4:25 (4 Kgdms 6:25); 15:14; Acts 7:11; 11:28; Rev 6:8; 18:8: *famine.* Λιμοί are among the tribulations of the eschaton: Mark 13:8 par. Matt 24:7/Luke 21:11. In Luke 15:14; Acts 11:28 λιμός is fem.

λίνον, ου, τό *linon* flax; linen garment*

Matt 12:20: lamp *wick* (cf. Isa 42:3); Rev 15:6: the *linen* garments of the seven angels.

Λίνος, ου *Linos* Linus*

An otherwise unknown Christian mentioned in 2 Tim 4:21. In later tradition (Irenaeus *Haer.* iii.3.3) Linus becomes the first bishop of Rome and is said to have received his office from "the apostles."

λῖος, 3 *lios* smooth, level

Alternative form of → λεῖος.

λιπαρός, 3 *liparos* bright, costly*

Rev 18:14: pl. subst. τὰ λιπαρά, the *valuables.*

λίτρα, ας, ἡ *litra* pound*

Designation for a Roman pound (= 327 g.). In the NT only in John 12:3 (oil of nard) and 19:39 (aloes).

λίψ, λιβός, ὁ *lips* southwest*

Acts 27:12: The harbor was open to the *southwest* (βλέπω κατὰ λίβα).

λογεία, ας, ἡ *logeia* collection*

1 Cor 16:1: the *collection* for "the saints"; v. 2: "*collections* will be organized." G. Kittel, *TDNT* IV, 282f.; D. Georgi, *Die Geschichte der Kollekte des Paulus für Jerusalem* (1965), esp. 40f.

λογίζομαι *logizomai* reckon, appraise, consider

1. Occurrences in the NT — 2. Non-NT usage — 3. Paul and the deutero-Pauline literature

Lit.: → λογισμός.

1. Of 40 NT occurrences of the vb., about half are in direct citations of the LXX or formulations influenced by OT citations. This is the case esp. in the Pauline Epistles, from which Mark 15:28 v.l. par. Luke 22:37 (citing Isa 53:12) stands out in relief, insofar as only here *mānâ* (niphal: "be numbered with") forms the foundation in the Hebrew text. The only other use of λογίζομαι for *mānâ* in the LXX is 2 Chr 5:6. The other NT occurrences of λογίζομαι outside the Pauline Epistles are in John 11:50; Acts 19:27; Heb 11:19: *consider, be of the opinion;* 1 Pet 5:12; Jas 2:23: *believe.* Jas 2:23 refers to Abraham's "work of faith," citing Gen 15:6, which is also decisive for Paul in Rom 4:3ff.

2. For the Pauline letters secular Greek usage must be taken into account along with the LXX. In secular usage λογίζομαι refers, on the one hand, to objective "reckoning/account" of value and debit in commerce; on the other hand in classical philosophy it is used of objective "affirmation" of matters by the philosophers (cf. Plato *Phd.* 65c; see H. W. Heidland, *TDNT* IV, 284-86). In political contexts the vb. could also take on a political significance.

In the LXX λογίζομαι involves greater subjectivity and is used of personal opinion (e.g., Gen 31:15; 1 Kgdms 1:13). The underlying Hebrew word is, with few exceptions (2 Kgdms 19:44; Deut 3:13; 2 Chr 5:6; Isa 53:12 [→ 1]; 44:19), *ḥāšab,* which always has a subjective meaning—on the one hand as a judgment of value (43 of the instances), e.g., "consider" (1 Kgdms 1:13; Isa 53:4; the LXX can also translate it with ἡγεῖσθαι: Job 13:24; 19:15), "credit something as" (Gen 15:6; 2 Kgdms 19:20), pass. "be reckoned with" (Lev 25:31; Josh 13:3)—on the other hand with the meanings "think, reflect" (Isa 10:7; Zech 8:17), "devise [something] evil" (Ps 140:3), and "intend/plan [to do something]" (1 Kgdms 18:25; Ps 140:5). The meaning "reckon, consider as," taken from the language of commerce, has become less important (Gen 31:15; Lev 25:31). The LXX often makes the vb. more precise through the use of compounds: with συν- in Lev 25:27, with ἐκ in 4 Kgdms 12:16, and with προς- in Lev 27:18.

In the religious realm the vb. is used of both the plan of God (Jer 18:8, 11; 27:45 LXX, etc.) and his judgment (Gen 15:6; Ps 105:31 LXX; negatively in 31:2 LXX). The meaning "credit, reckon," which resonates here already, appears in the cultic realm in Lev 7:18; 17:4 (cf. G. von Rad, *TZ* 76 [1951] 129-32).

In rabbinic literature other vbs. besides *ḥāšab* are used to mean "reckon something as." Thus the idea in Gen 15:6 and the controversial passage Lev 17:4 is extended, so that the unrighteousness that is committed is reckoned as credit after the repentance of the perpetrator (cf. Billerbeck III, 121-23).

3. Paul uses λογίζομαι in close connection with the LXX (→ 1). In the Abraham midrash in Romans 4, he cites Gen 15:6 three times (vv. 3, 9, 22; likewise Gal 3:6). In Rom 4:4 the usage derived from commerce plays a role, for a distinction is made between λογίζεσθαι κατὰ ὀφείλημα and κατὰ χάριν. Ὀφείλημα is (as in Deut 24:10 LXX) the sum of what is owed to a "worker." Thus

λογίζομαι is understood as *enter into the books*. The citation of Ps 31:2 LXX ("Blessed is the one to whom the Lord does not *reckon* sin") in Rom 4:8 interprets the statement, however, by employing the language of commerce of the God-human relationship, in which faith is not a substitute for works, but instead demonstrates openness to God's activity.

There is a disputed parallel in 4 Ezra 8:32f.: "For if you have desired to have pity on us, who have no works of righteousness, then you will be called merciful. For the righteous, who have many works laid up with you, shall receive their reward in consequence of their deeds." However, CD 1:19 argues against the idea: "They declare the ungodly righteous, but declare the righteous ungodly" (cf. E. Käsemann, *Rom* [Eng. tr., 1980] 111).

Not only in Romans 4 is λογίζομαι to be understood in this context, but in 2:26 as well: "Uncircumcision *is reckoned* as circumcision"; it is also to be seen in 9:8: "The children of the promise *are reckoned* as descendants [of Abraham]." This usage corresponds also to 2 Cor 5:19: "He did not *reckon* their transgressions to them"; cf. 2 Tim 4:16: "May this [their abandonment of Paul at his trial] not *be charged* to them." In 1 Cor 13:5 the vb. is used fig. of love: "It does not *calculate* the evil."

On the usage in Rom 8:36 (citing Ps 43:23 LXX): "We *are regarded* as sheep for the slaughter," cf. 1 Cor 4:1: "Thus one should *regard* us as servants of Christ"; negatively, 2 Cor 10:2: "*regard* us as walking in a fleshly manner." Here a clarifying ὡς is added, while in 2 Cor 12:6; Acts 19:27 εἰς is used with the same meaning as in Gen 15:6.

The vb. is used in dependence on LXX usage where it is followed by the acc. with the inf. in Rom 3:28: "For we *are of the opinion* (= *believe*) that the person is justified"; correspondingly Rom 6:11; 14:14; Phil 3:13. The vb. has the same meaning with a connecting ὅτι in Rom 8:18; Heb 11:19, where it is equivalent to πιστεύω: "[Abraham] *believed* that God can also raise the dead."

While in these passages the sense *suppose, think* is present, the vb. is used absolutely with the meaning *think* (something) only in 2 Cor 3:5. In 2 Cor 10:7, 11; Phil 4:8 *thinking* as a reasoning process comes more clearly into focus. This plays a role, without any reference to faith, in Rom 2:3: "Do you *suppose* this, that when you judge. . . ." Paul's self-evaluation in 2 Cor 11:5 is also to be understood in this way, as is the neutral usage of 1 Cor 13:11.

The meaning "*intend* to do something" (corresponding to Ps 139:5 LXX) is found only in 2 Cor 10:2a.

H.-W. Bartsch

λογικός, 3 *logikos* rational, spiritual*

Lit.: BAGD s.v. — O. CASEL, "Die λογικὴ θυσία der antiken Mystik in christlicher-liturgischer Umdeutung," *Jahrbuch für Liturgiewissenschaft* 4 (1924) 37-47. — E. KÄSEMANN, "Worship in Everyday Life: A Note on Romans 12," *idem, NT Questions of Today* (1969) 188-95. — G. KITTEL, *TDNT* IV, 142f. (older bibliography). — H. LIETZMANN, *Rom* (HNT, ⁴1933) 108f. — O. MICHEL, *Rom* (KEK, ⁵1977) 369-71. — R. REITZENSTEIN, *Hellenistic Mystery Religions* (1978) 415-21. — H. SCHLIER, *TDNT* I, 645-47. — idem, "Vom Wesen der apostolischen Ermahnung nach Röm 12,1-2," *idem* I, 74-89. — P. SEIDENSTICKER, *Lebendiges Opfer* (NTAbh 20, 1/3, 1954), esp. 17-43, 256-67. — H. WENSCHKEWITZ, *Die Spiritualisierung der Kultusbegriffe Tempel, Priester und Opfer im NT* (Angelos IV, 1932). For further bibliography → λατρεύω.

This adj. is esp. favored by classical philosophers (Epictetus *Diss.* ii.9.2: the human being is a ζῷον λογικόν), but not found in the LXX, though it is used by Philo and the postbiblical synagogue (cf. *Apostolic Constitutions* vii.34.6; 35.10; viii.9.8, etc.: prayers traced back to Jewish roots; cf. also *T. Levi* 3:6).

In the NT λογικός appears only twice. In λογικὴ λατρεία (Rom 12:1) λογική is translated in various ways: From "spiritual" (A. Nygren) to "rational" (T. Zahn) to "appropriate" (K. Barth) to "reasonable" (P. Althaus), all possibilities are exhausted. Michel (369f.) sees in Paul an influence extending from Greek usage to that of the Hermetica (cf. *Corp. Herm.* i.31: [of the holy God] δέξαι λογικὰς θυσίας ἁγνὰς ἀπὸ ψυχῆς καὶ καρδίας) and Hellenistic mysticism; his tr. is "worship in conformity with the word." In distinction to its origin, the word does not have, however, the sense of worship in song and prayer in the place of sacrifices. Instead, it refers to daily life determined by faith as the true worship. The term thus does not signify a spiritualization.

Τὸ λογικὸν ἄδολον γάλα (1 Pet 2:2) takes a phrase from the piety of the mysteries, which had been prepared in Gnosticism (cf. *Odes Sol.* 8:16: ". . . [I have given you] my holy milk to drink]"). The origin of this milk can be called "the twelve rational springs" (in an "Unbekanntes altgnostisches Werk" in C. Schmidt and W. Till, *Koptisch-gnostische Schriften* I [GCS 45, ³1962] 5, 16f.), which are filled with eternal life. The sacramental character of the term, which in Gnosticism is given cultically through the mystery, is determined in the NT by the gospel, the logos, and not cultically in the mystery. Instead, it is experienced in hearing the word. This significance is emphasized by the addition of ἄδολος, "unadulterated." The Gnostic term could thus be used in a defense against Gnostic mysteries.

H.-W. Bartsch

λόγιον, ου, τό *logion* word, saying*

In the NT and other early Christian literature always pl.: Acts 7:38, in reference to the law of God given by Moses: ὃς ἐδέξατο λόγια ζῶντα, "has received the *words* of life [at Sinai]" (cf. Deut 32:47); similarly Rom 3:2, where the granting of the *words* of promise is mentioned as the first of the advantages of Israel: ἐπιστεύθησαν τὰ λόγια τοῦ θεοῦ; Heb 5:12: τὰ στοιχεῖα τῆς ἀρχῆς τῶν λογίων τοῦ θεοῦ, "the first principles of the *words* of God," i.e., elementary Christian knowledge (cf. 6:1) of divine "teaching" (cf. also *1 Clem.* 62:3). Whereas these passages refer to the word of God that promises, reveals, and establishes the community, 1 Pet 4:11 (εἴ τις λαλεῖ, ὡς λόγια θεοῦ) refers to the speaking of Christian charismatics in the Christian worship: ". . . let him speak *words of God,*" i.e., words given by God through the Spirit (cf. the extrabiblical usage of λόγιον in the sense of "oracular/ prophetic speech," Herodotus vii.60.3; Philo *Gig.* 49).

In early Christian usage, λόγιον takes on a wider meaning, in which (τὰ) λόγια τοῦ Κυρίου is not used only for "sayings of the Lord," but also for the whole tradition of the Lord, i.e., the gospel (cf. Pol. *Phil.* 7:1; Papias apud Eusebius *HE* iii.39.1, 15f.). G. Kittel, *TDNT* IV, 142f.

H. Balz

λόγιος, 3 *logios* eloquent; learned*

According to Acts 18:24 Apollos was an ἀνὴρ λόγιος. In Lucian *Apol.* 2; Philo *Mut.* 220 the adj. means *fluent,* but in Aristotle *Pol.* ii.8.1267b; *Ep. Arist.* 6; Philo and Josephus *passim* it means *learned, educated.* One should not too hastily make judgments from Acts 18:25 (ζέων τῷ πνεύματι ἐλάλει) about the eloquence of Apollos. G. Kittel, *TDNT* IV, 136f.; LSJ s.v.; Spicq, *Notes* I, 500-502; → ᾿Απολλῶς (bibliography).

λογισμός, οῦ, ὁ *logismos* thought, consideration; wisdom*

Lit.: K. BERGER, "Abraham in den paulinischen Hauptbriefen," *MTZ* 17 (1966) 47-89, esp. 63-66. — BILLERBECK III, 121-23. — BULTMANN, *Theology* I, 211-20. — *idem,* "Glossen im Römerbrief," *TLZ* 72 (1947) 197-202. — F. HAHN, "Genesis 15,6 im NT," *Probleme biblischer Theologie* (FS G. von Rad, 1971) 90-107. — H.-W. HEIDLAND, *Die Anrechnung des Glaubens zur Gerechtigkeit* (BWANT IV, 18, 1936). — *idem, TDNT* IV, 284-92. — E. KÄSEMANN, "The Faith of Abraham in Romans 4," *idem, Perspectives on Paul* (1971) 79-101. — K. KERTELGE, *Rechtfertigung bei Paulus* (1967), esp. 185-95. — D. LÜHRMANN, "Pistis im Judentum," *ZNW* 64 (1973) 19-38. — G. VON RAD, "Die Anrechnung des Glaubens zur Gerechtigkeit," *TLZ* 76 (1951) 129-32. — For further bibliography see *TWNT* X, 1164.

Of the many tr. possibilities in classical Greek literature, only *thought, consideration, deliberation* come into view in the two NT occurrences. Of 121 occurrences in the LXX only 26 have a Hebrew basis in a noun of the root *ḥāšab.* This is an indication of the Hellenistic origin of the concept, which is demonstrated in the sparing use by Paul.

In Rom 2:15 Paul interprets the previously mentioned συνείδησις with "*thoughts* that accuse or excuse," thus demonstrating again the work of the νόμος written on the heart of the Gentiles. Hence one must determine in what connection the conflict of the thoughts is to be understood. It is not a dispute of the Gentiles among themselves (against Heidland, *TDNT* IV, 287), for the context calls for the

participles to be understood as an interpretation of "conscience." It is noteworthy that this conflict is not based on the law itself, but on the works of the law. Thus the passage does not offer any basis for assuming a natural revelation. Bultmann ("Glossen," 200) has convincingly excluded v. 16 as a gloss, for Paul is describing a present activity.

In 2 Cor 10:4 the word is used metaphorically and with a negative judgment for *thoughts* that are a barrier in the way of faith. Demolishing these thoughts is seen as the imprisonment of the νόημα in obedience to Christ. Paul's use of → λογίζομαι (3) indicates that he does not condemn reasonable thinking.

H.-W. Bartsch

λογομαχέω *logomacheō* dispute (vb.) about words*

2 Tim 2:14: μὴ λογομαχεῖν, a warning against clever speech that contradicts the word of truth (cf. vv. 15, 16; 1 Tim 6:4).

λογομαχία, ας, ἡ *logomachia* conflict, dispute (noun) about words*

1 Tim 6:4: νοσῶν περὶ ζητήσεις καὶ λογομαχίας, "unhealthy interest in controversies and *disputes about words*"; also in Titus 3:6 G (in place of γενεαλογίαι).

λόγος, ου, ὁ *logos* word, speech, account, sermon, logos

1. Occurrences in the NT — 2. Meaning — 3. In Jesus' preaching — 4. Paul — 5. The Johannine tradition — 6. The Johannine logos — 7. Particular passages (Revelation, Hebrews, Acts, the Pastorals, technical meanings)

Lit.: N. S. F. ALLDRIT, "The Logos Outside St John," *SE* VII (1982) 1-4. — P. BORGEN, "Der Logos war das wahre Licht," *Theologie aus dem Norden* (ed. A. Fuchs; 1976) 99-117. — G. BORNKAMM, "Gotteswort und Menschenwort im NT," *Kirche in der Zeit* 12 (1957) 301-5. — R. BULTMANN, "The Concept of the Word of God in the NT," *idem, Faith and Understanding* (1969) 286-312. — *idem, Theology* I, 306-14; II, 59-69. — A. DEBRUNNER, *TDNT* IV, 69-77. — G. DELLING, " '. . . als er uns die Schrift aufschloß,' " FS Friedrich 75-84. — *idem,* " 'Nahe ist dir das Wort.' Wort-Geist-Glaube bei Paulus," *TLZ* 99 (1974) 401-12. — E. FUCHS, *RGG* IV, 434-40. — HAENCHEN I, 114-43. — P. HOFRICHTER, *Im Anfang war der 'Johannesprolog.' Das urchristliche Logosbekenntnis—die Basis neutestamentlicher und gnostischer Theologie* (1986). — B. JENDORFF, *Der Logosbegriff. Seine philosophische Grundlegung bei Heraklit von Ephesos und seine theologische Indienstnahme durch Johannes den Evangelisten* (1976). — J. JEREMIAS, "Zum Logos-Problem," *ZNW* 59 (1968) 82-85. — E. KÄSEMANN, "The Structure and Purpose of the Prologue to John's Gospel," *idem, NT Questions of Today* (1969) 138-67. — W. KELBER, *Die Logoslehre von Heraklit bis Origenes* (1958). — G. KITTEL, *TDNT* IV, 100-141. — H. KUHN and R. SCHNACKENBURG, *LTK* VI, 1119-25. — E. LOHSE, "Wort und Sakrament in der paulinischen Theologie," *Zu Karl Barths Lehre von der Taufe* (1971) 44-59.

— B. L. MACK, *Logos und Sophia* (1973). — K. MÜLLER, *Anstoß und Gericht* (1969). — F. PORSCH, *Pneuma und Wort* (1974). — I. DE LA POTTERIE, *La vérité dans s. Jean* I-II (1977). — H. RITT, *Gebet zum Vater* (1979). — K. H. SCHELKLE, "Das Wort Gottes in der Kirche," *TQ* 133 (1953) 278-93. — SCHLIER I, 274-87. — H. SCHLIER, *Wort Gottes* (1958). — R. SCHNACKENBURG, "Logos-Hymnus und johanneischer Prolog," *BZ* 1 (1957) 69-109. — idem, *John* I (Eng. tr., 1968) 224-81. — G. STRECKER, "Das Evangelium Jesu Christi," FS Conzelmann 503-48. — P. STUHLMACHER, *Das Paulinische Evangelium* (1968). — J. SWETNAM, "Jesus as Λόγος in Hebr 4,12-13," *Bib* 62 (1981) 214-24. — H. WEDER, "Der Mythos vom Logos (Joh 1)," *Mythos und Rationalität* (ed. H. H. Schmid; 1988) 44-75. — D. ZELLER, "Jesu Wort und Jesus als Wort," *Freude am Gottesdienst* (FS J. G. Plöger, 1983) 145-54. — H. ZIMMERMANN, "Christushymnus und johanneischer Prolog," FS Schnackenburg 249-65.

1. The 330 occurrences of λόγος in the NT are relatively balanced in their distribution among the individual writings: 129 in the Gospels (Matthew has 33, Mark 24, Luke 32, John 40), an above average number in Acts (65), 48 occurrences in the undisputed Pauline letters, and the remaining occurrences distributed among Colossians (7), Ephesians (4), 2 Thessalonians (5), Hebrews (12), the Pastorals (20), Revelation (18), James (5), 1 and 3 John (7), and 1-2 Peter (10). Only in Philemon, 2 John, and Jude does λόγος not appear. Use of absolute λόγος of the historical appearance of Jesus, the eternal and divine giver of life on earth, in the Johannine prologue (John 1:1, 14) and in the introduction to 1 John (1:1) stands out sharply from all the other occurrences.

2. The great variety of meanings for λόγος — *word, speech, language, narrative, statement, pronouncement, question, report, account, sermon, teaching, call, sense* — can be accounted for esp.: a) on philological grounds and b) on theological grounds.

a) The root λεγ- represents a comprehensive and overarching unity of meaning: gather, collect, select, report, speak. The influence that the term λόγος exercised on philosophical interpretation (the essential abiding law of the world, thought, and custom) beginning with Heraclitus of Ephesus (550-480 B.C.) until Hegel and Nietzsche has little significance for NT exegesis. The basic principle is that the meaning of the word is always to be found from the *biblical* context.

b) The theological background arises from tr. of Heb. *dābār* ("word, report, command"; also "thing, matter, affair") by λόγος (most often in the Pentateuch) and by ῥῆμα (most often in the prophets). The "word of God theology" that proceeds from the creation story and the prophetic revelatory event leads further to the wisdom literature.

The breadth of possible meanings for λόγος in the NT extends from everyday usage (e.g., 2 Pet 2:3: "with lying *words*"; Eph 5:6: "with empty *words*") to the deepest christological terminology in the Johannine prologue. Even clauses that are almost untranslatable must be considered, e.g., Col 2:23, λόγον ἔχειν σοφίας (an approximate tr. is "considered as wisdom").

3. In Jesus' preaching the message of "the kingdom of God" stands at the thematic center: ἤγγικεν ἡ βασιλεία τοῦ θεοῦ (Mark 1:14f.; Luke 10:9 par. Matt 10:7). Hearing (→ ἀκούω) this word of the final salvation of humankind and the world is not sufficient; the human response to God's saving call is faith, which gives an altogether new motivation to human activity. In the survey of Jesus' teaching of his disciples in the logia source (Q) the emphasis is given in what is the final parable of the Sermon on the Mount (Matt 7:24 par. Luke 6:47): "Everyone who hears and does my *words* is like a wise man who builds his house on the rock." The early Church affirmed the unbreakable validity of Jesus' teaching authority: "Heaven and earth will pass away, but my *words* will not pass away" (Mark 13:31 par. Matt 24:35; Luke 21:33).

a) The approaching rule of God is connected not only with Jesus' proclamation as spoken word, but also equally with his person and work: "What kind of *saying* is this (τίς ὁ λόγος οὗτος)? With authority he commands the unclean spirits!" (Luke 4:36; cf. Mark 1:27; in reference to διδαχή); Matt 8:16: "And he cast out the spirits with his *word* and healed all illnesses"; Matt 8:8 par. Luke 7:7: "Only say a *word* (εἰπὲ λόγῳ), and my child will be healed." Early Christian missionary language consistently expressed the unity of word and deed in the Jesus' healing activity (cf. Luke 24:19; Acts 4:29-31; 8:25; 11:19; 13:46; 14:25; 16:6, 32).

With the statement that Jesus "spoke the *word* to them" the Markan redaction (Mark 2:2; 4:33) connects miracle (deed) and parable (word) traditions and as a single logion—in unveiled speech—the Passion prediction (8:32). The Matthean sayings material is connected with a systematically arranged tradition of deeds by means of the redactional framework provided by the words, "when Jesus had finished these *words*" (Matt 7:28; 19:1; 26:1). The extent to which the theological program of Luke gives priority to hearing the word and to the resulting action can be seen in redactional comments in Luke 5:1 (the introduction to the call of the disciples); 8:21 ("my mother and my brothers are those who hear the *word* of God and follow it"); 10:39 (vv. 38-42: hearing Jesus' word); 11:28 (a macarism). In the miracle stories also the motif of the circulation of the account is expressed with the term λόγος (5:15: ὁ λόγος περὶ αὐτοῦ, "the *report* concerning him"; otherwise Mark 1:45; Luke 7:17; cf. Matt 28:15 [M]).

b) The reaction of the hearers to Jesus' preaching is described in various ways: The rich man was exasperated at the *word* (Mark 10:22: ἐπὶ τῷ λόγῳ) of Jesus because wealth was his greatest obstacle to following Jesus (→ ἀκολουθέω); the disciples are amazed (Mark 10:24), the Pharisees take offense (Matt 15:12) or want to "catch him in his *talk*" (Mark 12:13; Luke 20:20). On the other hand, there must be astonishment at his teaching, for "his *word* went forth with [divine] authority" (Luke 4:32; cf. Mark

1:22). In the conflict story about Jesus' status as son of David he remains the nonviolent victor, for "no one could answer him a *word*" (Matt 22:46); this phrase is esp. interesting because λόγος can also mean *question* (Mark 11:29 par. Matt 21:24; Luke 20:3).

c) The parable of the different soils (of the sower: Mark 4:1-9; Matt 13:1-9; Luke 8:4-8) is followed by an allegorical interpretation (similar to what is seen in apocalyptic literature) already in the pre-Markan collection of parables (Mark 4:13-20; Matt 13:18-23; Luke 8:11-15). Here—the only occurrence of λόγος in the mouth of Jesus—the *word* is the missionary proclamation. The fate of the gospel is portrayed here with parenetic intent. Thus there is a description of both its failure and its missionary success in terms of qualitatively different soils (those who hear). Thus the parable is intended to give encouragement in the presence of failure and to make an appeal to have faith. In early Christian missionary terminology ὁ λόγος became a t.t. for missionary proclamation (e.g., 1 Thess 1:6: "You received the *word* with joy despite much tribulation; Col 4:3: to open a door for the *word;* Jas 1:21: the *word* is implanted, etc.).

d) The saying regarding denial of Jesus in the Q tradition (Luke 12:8f.) receives a Markan redaction as a doublet of Luke 9:26. In the post-Easter situation it emphasizes the eschatological role of Jesus as judge and (without the positive demand for confession seen in the Q tradition) says: "Whoever is ashamed of me and my *words* . . . , of that person the Son of Man will be ashamed . . ." (Mark 8:38). Here the entire message of Jesus is intended, which in the mission in Palestine has demanded a full commitment to confession.

4. For Paul the creative "*word* of God" (ὁ λόγος τοῦ θεοῦ), which was originally directed to Israel, "has not failed" (Rom 9:6); this would not be at all possible, for God himself is the source of this *word* (1 Cor 14:36; 2 Cor 4:2), the gospel (→ εὐαγγέλιον), which is clearly distinguishable from any "human *word*" (λόγος ἀνθρώπων, 1 Thess 2:13; 1:5; 2:5). Paul says of his preaching: "We do it not like so many, who make a business of the *word* of God. We proclaim it from a pure attitude and in Christ, from God and in God's presence (. . . ἀλλ᾽ ὡς ἐκ θεοῦ κατέναντι θεοῦ ἐν Χριστῷ λαλοῦμεν," 2 Cor 2:17).

a) In the repeated denial of self-seeking and "words of flattery" (1 Thess 2:5) Paul expresses the unity between the integrity of the proclaimer and the content of preaching that comes from God (cf. 2 Cor 1:12). Thus he rejects the charge of falsifying the word of God (2 Cor 4:2). He also denies that he attempts to support the word of God "with a word of wisdom" (1 Cor 1:17) or "in speech or wisdom" (2:1): "My *word* and my proclamation (ὁ λόγος μου καὶ τὸ κήρυγμά μου) did not consist in persuasive *words* of wisdom, but in demonstration of the

Spirit and of power, so that your faith might not rest on human wisdom, but on God's power" (1 Cor 2:4-5; cf. 1 Thess 1:5). 1 Cor 2:13 (polemical contrast!) and 2 Cor 11:6 (Paul defends himself as unskilled "in *speaking*") are worthy of special consideration.

b) "The *word* of the cross" (1 Cor 1:18: ὁ λόγος τοῦ σταυροῦ), which is the central content of the Pauline kerygma (Gal 3:1), stands in sharp contrast to "the wisdom of this world." The Church must be formed (Gal 4:19) by the publicly proclaimed preaching of the cross. Χριστὸς ἐσταυρωμένος (1 Cor 1:23; Gal 5:11; the pf. pass. partc. indicates the present actuality of the salvation) is the criterion of the Pauline proclamation; God's decision in favor of the world and the separation of humankind for salvation and condemnation have taken place in the cross. This cosmic deed of reconciliation (as a historical act) becomes a present experience in "the *word* of reconciliation" (2 Cor 5:19: ὁ λόγος τῆς καταλλαγῆς); apostolic ministry consists in communication of "the *word* of truth" (2 Cor 6:7: ἐν λόγῳ ἀληθείας). The fundamental demand for the Church in this world is to hold on to "the *word* of life" (Phil 2:16: λόγον ζωῆς ἐπέχοντες), which characterizes the gospel.

c) Use of λόγος elevates OT citations to a "*word* of promise" (Rom 9:9: ὁ λόγος ἐπαγγελίας): God's covenant faithfulness (3:4), the word of election to Isaac (9:9), God's call to the "remnant" of Israel (9:28), the fulfillment of the law in the one *word* of love (13:9; Gal 5:14: ἐν ἑνὶ λόγῳ), the last victory over the destructive powers of death and sin (1 Cor 15:54). A citation can, however, appeal not to the OT but to the authority of a "*word* of the Lord" (1 Thess 4:15: ἐν λόγῳ κυρίου; cf. 1 Cor 7:10) or can be a more precise description of the gospel (1 Cor 15:2: τίνι λόγῳ εὐηγγελισάμην ὑμῖν, introduction to the traditional formula of faith in vv. 3-5).

5. Without entering into questions of authorship of the writings that hand on the Johannine tradition, one can say the following about the use of λόγος in them:

a) Jesus' preaching is consistently attributed to the Father in a way consistent with John's strictly theocentric perspective: In the synonymous use of ῥήματα (John 3:34; 14:10; 17:8) and λόγος (John 5:38; 8:55; 14:24; 17:6, 14; 1 John 2:5, 14; cf. 1:10) the proclamation of the "word" is ascribed to the Father and his will. This "word" is the power of God that is at work in believers and that gives life to them. The missionary proclamation (John 17:20) creates a relationship between the disciples (believers) and the Father *through Jesus* (cf. 1 John 1:1-4: fellowship with God through Jesus Christ the mediator). In the rich rhetorical style the unique Johannine expression "keep my *word*" (τηρεῖν τὸν λόγον μου, John 8:51f.; 14:23; 15:20) becomes the way of describing the fellowship of life and love with God the Father.

b) The *word* of Jesus demands a clear decision by the hearers. It involves either acceptance of this word, i.e., in faith, or rejection, i.e., in judgment (John 5:24; 12:48; cf. 4:41, 50). "This is a hard *saying* (σκληρός ἐστιν ὁ λόγος οὗτος). Who can hear it?" (6:60): This is the reaction, and the discordant impression that Jesus' revelatory speech provokes is most clearly indicated in 10:19: "Again a division arose between the Jews because of these *words* (διὰ τοὺς λόγους τούτους)" (cf. 7:43), so that a theological echo is expressed in antithetical form at the end of the first part of John (12:47f.: ῥήματα). The essential challenge (especially for John's Jewish Christian audience) of "abiding in his *word*" (8:31; cf. 5:38; also 15:7 [ῥήματα]) is that of true discipleship (cf. 8:43, 47; 9:27); the word of God is the bearer and mediator of the truth (17:17: ὁ λόγος ὁ σὸς ἀλήθειά ἐστιν).

6. The rhythmically structured prologue of John (John 1:1-18) is an early Christian hymn that identifies Christ himself—in absolute word usage—with the personal λόγος. The diverse attempts at reconstructing this "logos hymn" converge when they reach the statements concerning Christ's way of redemption, which can be derived from the text itself: In his eternal preexistence (v. 1a) and personal relationship with God (vv. 1b, 2) the logos has an all-encompassing function in creation (v. 3) and a saving function (mediating "light" and "life") for the world (v. 4). This historical coming of the logos to the human world in the incarnation is discussed beginning in v. 5.

The clear redactional work (the insertions concerning John the Baptist in vv. 6-8, 15 are undoubtedly redactional; cf. the differences just in the attempts at reconstruction by Schnackenburg and Zimmermann) adds that the logos in his divine glory (v. 14b) takes on the full reality of historical palpability and human transience (v. 14a: καὶ ὁ λόγος σὰρξ ἐγένετο expresses the event of the full incarnation in its earthly-transient frailty). These statements about the incarnation point to a Christian origin for the "hymn"—as it stands—though it probably came from the world of Hellenistic Judaism. This is suggested by the theological background of wisdom speculation: One may note not only wisdom's role in creation and salvation (cf. Job 28:12-28; Prov 3:19; 8:22-36; Wis 7:12, 25-30; 8:4; 9:1f.: ὁ ποιήσας τὰ πάντα ἐν λόγῳ σου; *2 Enoch* 33:4; Sir 1:1-10, 15-20; 24:3-12), but also—and esp.—the tension between acceptance and rejection (on rejection cf. Sir 24:3-12; *1 Enoch* 42:1ff.).

The spiritual and literary relationship of the Johannine prologue to the proemium in 1 John 1:1-4 lies not only in the numerous textual connections (e.g., what is said about ἀρχή and ζωή), but esp. in the central position of the logos as λόγος τῆς ζωῆς (1 John 1:2), which unveils its nature to the eyes of faith in the historical hour (ἀκηκόαμεν, ἑωράκαμεν, ἐθεασάμεθα, ἐψηλάφησαν).

7. Of the numerous special instances in which λόγος appears the following can be mentioned:

a) In Rev 19:13 ("and his name means: The *word* of God") the image is taken from Wis 18:15. The victorious and returning Christ is identified with Jesus of Nazareth (cf. 1:2, 3, 9; 6:9; 20:4).

b) Hebrews, which is itself understood as a "*word* of exhortation" (13:22: λόγος τῆς παρακλήσεως), summons its readers to receive "the *word* of God" (13:7), which was made certain "in the *word* of the oath" (7:28) as God's guaranteed word of promise at the installation of Jesus as high priest; cf. 6:1 ("the beginning *word* about Christ").

c) In the Christian missionary terminology of Acts "the *word* of God"—used absolutely (4:31; 6:2, 7; 8:14; 11:1; 13:5, 7, 44, 46; 16:32; 17:13; 18:11)—is the term for the apostolic proclamation of the message of Jesus Christ; cf. also "the *word* of the Lord" (8:25; 13:44, 48, 49; 15:35, 36; 16:32; 19:10, 20). The messengers are qualified to preach "the *word* of this salvation" (13:26), i.e., for "the ministry of the *word*" (6:4; cf. Luke 1:2).

d) The characteristic formula of the Pastorals, "faithful is the *word*" (1 Tim 1:15; 3:1; 4:9; 2 Tim 2:11; Titus 3:8) refers to the kerygmatic, liturgical, and institutional faith tradition of the Christ-event.

e) Numerous technical usages of λόγος are intelligible only within their contexts, e.g., the commercial terminology of "settling accounts" (Phil 4:15, 16). These are derived both from Semitic usage (Matt 5:32) and from secular Greek (Acts 10:29; 18:14). "To give an *account*" (1 Pet 3:15; 4:5; Rom 14:12, etc.) is particularly worthy of mention.

H. Ritt

λόγχη, ης, ἡ *lonchē* lance*

According to John 19:34 "one of the soldiers pierced [Jesus'] side with a *lance*" (λόγχη . . . τὴν πλευρὰν ἔνυξεν); cf. Matt 27:49 v.l. (λαβὼν λόγχην ἔνυξεν).

λοιδορέω *loidoreō* abuse, revile*

The NT uses the word group represented by λοιδορέω more in the general Greek sense of "abuse/reviling" than in the sense of "disputing/quarreling," which the LXX (esp. in the rendering of Heb. *rîḇ*) knows. John 9:28: The Pharisees *reviled* the blind man who had been healed; Acts 23:4: Paul (unintentionally) *reviled* the high priest, thus coming near to blasphemy; in accordance with the Passion narrative, 1 Pet 2:23: Jesus is for reviled Christians the model to be imitated (cf. Mark 14:65 par.; 15:17ff. par.; 15:29ff. par.), ὃς λοιδορούμενος οὐκ ἀντελοιδόρει (cf. Josephus *Ant.* ii.60; *B.J.* vi.307, but also John 18:23); likewise Paul replies to *reviling* with blessing (λοιδορούμενοι εὐλογοῦμεν, 1 Cor 4:12; cf. also Matt 5:44; Luke 6:27f.; Rom 12:14, 20; 1 Pet 3:9; *Diog.* 5:15; Ps 108:28 LXX). H. Hanse, *TDNT* IV, 293f. Spicq, *Notes* I, 503-5.

λοιδορία, ας, ἡ *loidoria* abuse, reviling*

1 Pet 3:9 (bis), picking up on the command to love one's enemy (Luke 6:27f.): μὴ ἀποδιδόντες . . . λοιδορίαν ἀντὶ λοιδορίας, τοὐναντίον δὲ εὐλογοῦντες (cf. Pol. *Phil.* 2:2; Philo *Agr.* 110; Prov 24:29; → λοιδορέω). In 1 Tim 5:14 λοιδορίας χάριν means either "because of *abuse* [from opponents]" or, more likely (dependent on ἀφορμή), "for *abuse/vile gossip.*" H. Hanse, *TDNT* IV, 293f.; Spicq, *Notes* I, 503-5.

λοίδορος, ου, ὁ *loidoros* blasphemer, abuser*

Twice in the NT in vice catalogues, 1 Cor 5:11; 6:10, both times with μέθυσος and ἅρπαξ or εἰδωλολάτρης; cf. also *T. Benj.* 5:4 (antonym: ὁ ὅσιος).

λοιμός, 3 *loimos* diseased, pernicious, destructive*

Acts 24:5, fig. of Paul, who is, according to Tertullus's prosecutorial speech, a *pernicious* person who *infects* everything (cf. 1 Kgdms 25:25; 30:22: πᾶς ἀνὴρ λοιμὸς καὶ πονηρός).

λοιμός, οῦ, ὁ *loimos* pestilence; pl.: diseases, illnesses*

Luke 21:11 (par. Matt 24:7 v.l.), in a description of eschatological horrors: κατὰ τόπους λιμοὶ καὶ λοιμοί (cf. the wordplay in Hesiod *Op.* 243).

λοιπός, 3 *loipos* remaining

1. Occurrences — 2. Pl. usage — 3. — Adv. usage

Lit.: BAGD s.v. — BLACK, *Approach* 176. — BDF §160. — A. CAVALLIN, "(τὸ) λοιπόν. Eine bedeutungsgeschichtliche Untersuchung," *Eranos. Acta philologica Suecana* 39 (1941) 121-44. — H. CONZELMANN, *1 Cor* (Hermeneia, 1975) 83. — W. GÜNTHER and H. KRIENKE, *DNTT* III, 247-54. — H. G. MEECHAM, "The Meaning of (τὸ) λοιπόν in the NT," *ExpTim* 48 (1936/37) 331f. — THRALL, *Particles* 25-30.

1. The 55 occurrences of λοιπός (including Mark 16:13) are distributed throughout the NT. The word is not emphasized by any writer in a noteworthy way. It does not appear in John or in 1–3 John. The pl. usage *the remaining ones/the others* is predominant (40 occurrences). The adv. acc. (τὸ) λοιπόν is used 13 times; the adv. gen. τοῦ λοιποῦ is used twice.

2. Specific theological usage of λοιπός in the sense of the OT-prophetic idea of the remnant, which is taken up by Paul in Romans 9–11, but with λεῖμμα and ὑπόλειμμα, is barely present in the NT. Echoes of this theological association can be seen only later in Rev 2:24; 3:2 ("strengthen *what remains*" [τὰ λοιπά]; H. Kraft, *Rev* [HNT] 76, supplies πρόβατα, referring back to the parallel in Ezek 34:4f.); 11:13; 12:17.

At times, indeed, οἱ λοιποί has the opposite sense, representing those who stand outside the kingdom of God. In the parable of the royal wedding in Matt 22:1-14 it is used of those who kill the servants delivering the invitation (v. 6). In the parable of the ten maidens (Matt 25:1-13) it is used of the foolish maidens who were not permitted entry (v. 11). Λοιπός also has a negative nuance in Luke 8:10; Rom 11:7 (the hardened); Mark 16:13 (unbelievers); Acts 5:13 (non-Christians); Gal 2:13 (hypocrites); and Rev 9:20 (the unrepentant). In 1 Thess 4:13; 5:6; Eph 2:3 οἱ λοιποί is practically synonymous (so Black) with τὰ ἔθνη (→ ἔθνος 3.c).

3. The adv. acc. (τὸ) λοιπόν has various meanings. The NT occurrences cannot be organized in a uniform pattern. In Mark 14:41 par. Matt 26:45 ("You are *still* sleeping") and Heb 10:13 (Christ waits *henceforth* . . .) it certainly has the classical, purely temporal sense (so also τοῦ λοιποῦ, *in the future,* Gal 6:17). Frequently the formula is used to designate the last member in a series (Cavallin 132), to introduce a conclusion: *at last* (Acts 27:20), *beyond that* (1 Cor 1:16), *finally* (2 Cor 13:11; Phil 3:1; 4:8; 1 Thess 4:1; 2 Thess 3:1, regularly associated with the address ἀδελφοί [μου]). Τοῦ λοιποῦ in Eph 6:10 probably has the meaning *finally* (cf. J. Gnilka, *Eph* [HTKNT] 304 n. 1).

In 1 Cor 4:2 ὧδε λοιπόν is used to take up a preceding image (the steward) and develop it further ("*Now* one requires of stewards . . ."). Τὸ λοιπόν probably has the logical sense of *now, thus, therefore* also in 1 Cor 7:29; 2 Tim 4:8; the temporal meaning *for the future* (so BAGD) is, however, not to be fully ruled out.

H. Fendrich

Λουκᾶς, ᾶ *Loukas* Luke*

Lit.: BAGD s.v. — H. J. CADBURY, *Beginnings* II, 209-64. — J. ERNST, *Luke* (RNT, 1977) 30-32. — R. GLOVER, " 'Luke the Antiochene' and Acts," *NTS* 11 (1964/65) 97-106. — E. HAENCHEN, "Das 'Wir' in der Apg und das Itinerar," *idem* I, 227-64. — B. HEMELSOET and W. BAIER, *BL* 1065. — KÜMMEL, *Introduction* 147-50. — W. MARXSEN, *RGG* IV, 473. — R. PESCH, "Die Zuschreibung der Evangelien an apostolische Verfasser," *ZKT* 97 (1975) 56-71. — E. PLÜMACHER, *TRE* III, 483-528. — J. REGUL, *Die antimarcionitischen Evangelienprologe* (1969) 197-265. — J. SCHMID, *LTK* VI, 1203f. — G. SCHNEIDER, *Luke* (ÖTK) I (1977) 32f. — M. A. SIOTIS, "Luke the Evangelist as St. Paul's Collaborator," FS Cullmann (1972) 105-11. — A. STROBEL, "Lukas der Antiochener," *ZNW* 49 (1958) 131-34. — WIKENHAUSER/SCHMID 247-72, 344-79, esp. 252-56.

Λουκᾶς, a Gentile name attested in inscriptional evidence, is a shortened form of Λούκιος/*Lucius.* Luke is mentioned at the end of three NT writings: "Luke, the beloved physician, greets you" (Col 4:14); "Only Luke is with me" (2 Tim 4:11); "Demas and Luke, my coworkers, greet you . . ." (Phlm 24). He is to be distinguished from the → Λούκιος in Acts 13:1; Rom 16:21. Since the 2nd cent. the Pauline companion and physician Luke has been regarded as the author of Luke-Acts (cf. the superscription of Luke, the Muratorian Canon, Irenaeus *Haer.* iii.1.1). The internal evidence of Luke-Acts indicates otherwise. The tradition of the early Church can be attributed to the efforts to trace the NT writings to "apostles," in which their image of Luke is derived from the combination of information from the Pauline letters and the "we" reports of Acts. One can only say with certainty that the author of Luke-Acts was a Gentile Christian well-versed in the LXX, who perhaps was named Luke.

A. Weiser

Λούκιος, ου *Loukios* Lucius*

Acts 13:1: Λούκιος ὁ Κυρηναῖος, a prophet and teacher in Antioch mentioned with Barnabas, Simeon, Manaen, and Saul (see Haenchen, *Acts* [Eng. tr., 1971] ad loc.); Rom 16:21: a Corinthian Jewish Christian who, with other συγγενεῖς of Paul, sends greetings to the Roman church (since Origen often identified with → Λουκᾶς).

λουτρόν, οῦ, τό *loutron* bath, washing*

Used in the NT in reference to baptism. Greek and Jewish usage also resonates with the sense of purificatory washings (see A. Oepke, *TDNT* IV, 302-7). Eph 5:26, of the Church, which Christ has saved and purified "through the *bath* of water in the word" (τῷ λουτρῷ τοῦ ὕδατος ἐν ῥήματι), in order that he might present it to himself in splendor (v. 27). Baptism (in connection with the word) is understood here as the purificatory bath of a bride, who is then presented to her husband (cf. also 2 Cor 11:2; H. Schlier, *Eph* [1963] ad loc.). According to Titus 3:5 baptism is effective as a λουτρὸν παλιγγενεσίας καὶ ἀνακαινώσεως πνεύματος ἁγίου, a salvation given by God, for rebirth and new life come from the forgiveness of sins (not from one's own righteousness). A. Oepke, *TDNT* IV, 300-307; D. L. Norbie, *EvQ* 34 (1962) 36-38; G. R. Beasley-Murray, *DNTT* I, 150-53; Spicq, *Notes* I, 506-10; → λούω 2.

λούω *louō* wash, bathe*

1. Occurrences and meaning in the NT — 2. Baptism — 3. John 13:10

Lit.: M. É. Boismard, "Le lavement des pieds (Joh 13,1-17)," *RB* 71 (1964) 5-24. — G. Bornkamm, "Das Bekenntnis im Hebräerbrief," idem, *Aufsätze* II, 188-208. — J. D. G. Dunn, "The Washing of the Disciples' Feet in John 13,1-20," *ZNW* 61 (1970) 247-52. — H. Klos, *Die Sakramente im Johannesevangelium* (1970). — J. Michl, "Der Sinn der Fußwaschung," *Bib* 40 (1959) 697-708. — G. Richter, *Die Fußwaschung im Johan-*

nesevangelium. Geschichte ihrer Deutung (BU 1, 1967). — idem, "Die Fußwaschung Joh 13,1-20," *Studien zum Johannesevangelium* (ed. J. Hainz; 1977) 42-57. — J. A. T. Robinson, "The Significance of the Footwashing," FS Cullmann (1962) 144-57. — H. Thyen, "Joh 13 und die 'kirchliche Redaktion' des vierten Evangelium," FS Kuhn 343-56.

1. This vb. occurs 5 times in the NT (also Rev 1:5 v.l.). It primarily designates a total purification, so also in the NT, including Acts 16:33. Λούω means both *wash* in the literal sense (of the normal washing of the dead, Acts 9:37; cleansing of wounds, 16:33; the watering place of an animal [proverbially], 2 Pet 2:22) and *cleanse* in a metaphorical sense (John 13:10: the footwashing itself is described with νίπτω [13:5]; Heb 10:22).

2. Heb 10:22 alludes to baptism. The reader is summoned to hold fast and not to endanger (6:4-6; 10:26ff.) the access to the forgiveness of sins that has been granted once for all through Jesus' sacrificial death (10:2, etc.) and through baptism and the baptismal confession (10:22f.). 2 Pet 2:22 has a similar thought in a negative formulation, but without reference to baptism: The Gnostic false teachers (2:1) are like an animal "that returns to the mire after it has been *washed.*"

3. Λούω appears in one instance in the Johannine literature, in John 13:10, which is burdened by difficulties. Text-critically, it is disputed whether εἰ μὴ τοὺς πόδας (μόνον) belongs to the original text (so the majority of modern editions) or represents a later addition (so most exegetes). The mss. give no conclusive information. However, an addition in connection with the literal footwashing of Jesus is more easily explicable than a later deletion. Thus 13:10 is to be read: "He who has bathed (ὁ λελουμένος) does not need to wash, but is entirely clean" (Richter, "Fußwaschung" 45). Furthermore, the present wording of the pericope includes two differing interpretations: 13:12-17 interprets Jesus' footwashing as a model for the disciples' conduct in serving, while 13:10 formulates the concluding thought of the first interpretation, which is included in Jesus' conversation with Peter (13:6-10). Thus λελουμένος has always given occasion for seeing in the footwashing an allusion to the significance of baptism. Such an interpretation cannot be excluded. However, as the incident is placed at the beginning of the Passion account (cf. esp. 13:1) and since the emphasis is placed on the footwashing as an action that Jesus must perform (13:8), the christological-soteriological interpretation is preferable to the sacramental interpretation. The symbolic action of footwashing, the meaning of which the disciples understand (13:7) only "afterward," i.e., in the work of the Spirit, refers to the necessity of Jesus' death on the cross and thus requires no other interpretation (13:10).

M. Völkel

Λύδδα, ας   *Lydda*   Lod (Lydda)*

A city *ca.* 13 km. southeast of Joppa on the road to Jerusalem (Heb. *lôd;* today the site of Israel's main airport). According to Acts 9:32, 35, 38 Peter visited the Christian community at Lod and healed the lame man Aeneas; see also 1 Macc 11:34; Josephus *B.J.* ii.244; Pliny *HN* v.14.70. M. S. Enslin, *BHH* 1101; *BL* 1070.

Λυδία, ας   *Lydia*   Lydia*

A seller of purple fabric from Thyatira in Asia Minor who had become a member of the Jewish community in Philippi as a "godfearer." According to Acts 16:14 (15) she and her household were baptized by Paul as the first converts in Europe and provided hospitality to him (v. 40). W. Bieder, *BHH* 1115; E. Haenchen, *Acts* (Eng. tr., 1971) on 16:14.

Λυκαονία, ας   *Lykaonia*   Lycaonia*

A mountainous area in south central Asia Minor, after 25 B.C. part of the province of Galatia. Paul and Barnabas, according to Acts 14:6, fled from (Phrygian; cf. Xenophon *An.* i.2.19) Iconium (the capital of Lycaonia in the Roman period) to the Lycaonian cities of Lystra and Derbe (cf. also 13:51ff.; 16:1ff.). Luke probably did not regard Iconium as belonging to Lycaonia (cf. Pliny *HN* v.245). W. Ruge, *PW* XIII, 2253-65; G. Mayeda, *BHH* 1115f.; H. Conzelmann, *Acts* (Hermeneia) 108; R. Fellmann, *LAW* 1791; *KP* II, 1360; III, 807f.

Λυκαονιστί   *Lykaonisti*   in the Lycaonian language*

According to Acts 14:11(ff.) the crowd extolled Paul and Barnabas *in the Lycaonian language* as Hermes and Zeus, but the apostles did not at first understand them. Luke alludes thus to the Phrygian dialect; on the languages still in existence in Galatia alongside Greek cf. F. Müller, *Hermes* 4 (1939) 66-91; E. Haenchen, *Acts* (Eng. tr., 1971) ad loc.

Λυκία, ας   *Lykia*   Lycia*

A peninsula in southwest Asia Minor between Caria and Pamphylia, location of the harbor city Myra, which Paul came to on his journey to Rome coming from Sidon: Acts 27:5; cf. also 21:1 (Patara in Lycia). G. Mayeda, *BHH* 1118.

λύκος, ου, ὁ   *lykos*   wolf*

The NT speaks of the *wolf* always as a wild beast of prey in contrast to defenseless sheep: According to Matt 10:16 par. Luke 10:3 Jesus sends the disciples "as sheep ἐν μέσῳ λύκων," i.e., into a situation of persecution. The word is likewise metaphorical in John 10:12 (bis) of the threats against the flock (the Church), which has its protection and salvation only through Christ as the true shepherd. Images of the messianic kingdom of peace like those in Isa 11:6; 65:25 do not appear often in the NT. Fig. of false teachers: εἰσελεύσονται . . . λύκοι βαρεῖς (Acts 20:29), of false prophets who appear as "ravenous wolves (ἔσωθεν . . . λύκοι ἅρπαγες) in sheep's clothing" (Matt 7:15; cf. also Ezek 22:27f.; Zeph 3:3f.; *Did.* 11:6, 12; on the haircloth worn by prophets cf. 2 Kgs 1:8; Zech 13:4); see O. Böcher, *TZ* 24 (1968) 405-26. G. Bornkamm, *TDNT* IV, 308-11; Spicq, *Notes* I, 511f.

λυμαίνομαι   *lymainomai*   destroy, ruin*

Mid. in Acts 8:3: Σαῦλος δὲ ἐλυμαίνετο (impf.!) τὴν ἐκκλησίαν, "Saul *attempted to destroy* the Church."

λυπέω   *lypeō*   cause pain, give offense to; pass.: feel pain, be sad
→ λύπη.

λύπη, ης, ἡ   *lypē*   hurt, pain, sadness*
λυπέω   *lypeō*   cause pain, give offense to; pass.: feel pain, be sad*

1. Occurrences in the NT; related expressions — 2. Meanings; OT and Greek usage — 3. General use in the NT — 4. John 16 — 5. 2 Corinthians

Lit.: R. BULTMANN, *TDNT* IV, 313-24. — *idem, 2 Cor* (Eng. tr., 1985) 47-50. — C. DIETZFELBINGER, "Die eschatologische Freude der Gemeinde in der Angst der Welt," *EvT* 40 (1980) 420-36. — G. GERSTENBERGER and W. SCHRAGE, *Leiden* (Biblische Konfrontationen 1004, 1977). — H. HAARBECK and H.-G. LINK, *DNTT* 419-21. — J. H. H. INDEMANS, "Das Lukasevangelium XXII,45," *SO* 32 (1956) 81-83. — C. S. LEWIS, *The Problem of Pain* (1940). — E. OSSWALD, *BHH* 2021-23. — J. SCHARBERT, *Der Schmerz im AT* (1955). — *idem, HTG* II, 37-44. — SPICQ, *Notes* I, 513-19. — For further bibliography see *TWNT* X, 1164.

1. The noun appears 16 times in the NT, of which 9 are in Paul (5 in 2 Corinthians, 2 in Philippians, 1 in Romans), 4 are in John, and the rest in Luke 22:45; Heb 12:11; and 1 Pet 2:19. The noun does not occur in Mark, Matthew, or (as is the case with the vb.) Revelation. Of the total of 26 occurrences of the vb. (21 are pass., 5 are act., all in 2 Corinthians and Eph 4:30), 6 are in Matthew, 2 each in Mark and John, 14 in the Pauline corpus (12 in 2 Corinthians, the others in Rom 14:15; 1 Thess 4:13), and the rest in Eph 4:30; 1 Pet 1:6. This is to be compared with use of → κλαίω (40 occurrences, esp. in Luke, John, and Revelation), → πενθέω (10 occurrences, of which 3 are in Revelation), πένθος (5 occurrences, of which 4 are in Revelation), and esp. → χαίρω (74 occurrences, esp. in Luke, John, and Paul) and → χαρά (59 occurrences,

esp. in Matthew, Luke, John, and Paul). Also related are θλῖψις and ταραχή, and as antonyms also εὐφραίνω and ἀγαλλιάω.

2. Λύπη and λυπέω are used of bodily as well as emotional *pain, grief, sorrow,* and *trouble.* The vb. also can bear the meaning of *irritate, anger.*

Both noun and vb. have a wide range of meaning in the LXX (a total of 20 Hebrew equivalents). Pain and grief as a fundamental experience of humankind come into view, esp. in the wisdom literature. Pain and suffering are not to be abolished in this life, and even intermingle with joy (Prov 14:13 MT, otherwise LXX; Tob 2:5f.; Sir 12:9; 26:28; cf. also Eccl 3:4; 7:2f.). Nevertheless one must struggle against them (Prov 15:13; 25:20; Sir 3:12; 4:2; 14:1; 30:21, 23). They are usually the consequence of evil deeds (Prov 10:1, 10; Sir 18:15; Ezek 16:43) and esp. the result of hostility against the pious (Ps 54:3 LXX; Isa 15:2; Jer 15:18; Lam 1:22). Just as the fundamental theological reflection regards pain as decreed by God to humankind in this world (Gen 3:16f.: ἐν λύπαις, of woman's pain in childbearing and of man's troublesome work; cf. also 5:29: relief from the λῦπαι that have been present since Adam through Noah, the wine-grower; see also Prov 31:6), the devout one knows, nonetheless, that God adds no pain (Prov 20:22; Mic 6:3; otherwise with the evil, Isa 19:10). Pain is thus a means of education and chastisement (Isa 32:11; 57:17; Tob 13:16). The pious may, therefore, hope for the termination of suffering and pain by God (Isa 40:29; Tob 3:6; 7:17; Wis 8:9: wisdom as the encourager in time of suffering; as a hope for the future and end-time hope, Isa 35:10; 51:11; 4 Ezra 7:13; *T. Jud.* 25:4: οἱ ἐν λύπῃ τελευτήσαντες ἀναστήσονται ἐν χαρᾷ; cf. also Ps 125:5 LXX). Even if there is no life without λύπη, pain stands nevertheless in contradiction to the purposes of God with his creation.

Greek poets and thinkers know similarly that joy and pain are often connected and that any excess of joy most often leads to pain (Sophocles *OC* 1211ff.; Plato *Phd.* 60b, c). The Stoics advised, therefore, that one seek the true good and the true joy and avoid λύπη as a destructive πάθος (along with φόβος, ἐπιθυμία, and ἡδονή: Epictetus *Diss.* i.9.7; iii.11.2).

3. In the Gospels the concern is primarily with the individual's pain in response to an evil deed that cannot be avoided (Matt 19:9 [M], of Herod: λυπηθείς, *full of sorrow*) or that has happened (18:31 [M]: ἐλυπήθησαν σφόδρα), to Jesus' unanswered call to discipleship ("the rich young man," Mark 10:22 par. Matt 19:22: ἀπῆλθεν λυπούμενος), or to Jesus' announcement of betrayal and suffering (the disciples, Mark 14:19: ἤρξαντο λυπεῖσθαι; par. Matt 26:22: λυπούμενοι σφόδρα; Matt 17:23: ἐλυπήθησαν σφόδρα; cf. Mark 9:32/Luke 9:45: ἠγνόουν τὸ ῥῆμα . . . καὶ ἐφοβοῦντο . . . [ἐπ]ερωτῆσαι; cf. also John 21:17: ἐλυπήθη ὁ Πέτρος). According to Luke 22:45 Jesus finds the disciples sleeping on the Mount of Olives (overcome by *pain,* εὗρεν κοιμωμένους αὐτοὺς ἀπὸ τῆς λύπης). Jesus himself is overcome by pain in the presence of his own impending death (Matt 26:37: ἤρξατο λυπεῖσθαι καὶ ἀδημονεῖν, "he fell into *sorrow* and fear"; cf. περίλυπος, v. 38 [see Ps 41:6 LXX; Heb 5:7]).

Paul also speaks in a general way of pain and sorrow: Rom 9:2: "great *sorrow* and unending pain" burden his heart (λύπη μεγάλη . . . καὶ ἀδιάλειπτος ὀδύνη τῇ καρδίᾳ μου) for the sake of "Israel," to which he himself belongs; 14:15: εἰ . . . ὁ ἀδελφός . . . λυπεῖται, "when your brother *is injured/deeply troubled*" (cf. vv. 13, 15b); Phil 2:27: ἵνα μὴ λύπην ἐπὶ λύπην σχῶ, "so that I will not have *sorrow upon sorrow*"; 2 Cor 9:7: μὴ ἐκ λύπης ἢ ἐξ ἀνάγκης, "not *reluctantly* or under compulsion" (in the gathering of the "collection," but rather a free and cheerful decision in the heart [ἱλαρός; cf. Prov 22:8a LXX]); 1 Thess 4:13: those who do not know the hope for the resurrection of the dead regard pain over death as an unconquerable power (ἵνα μὴ λυπῆσθε καθὼς καὶ οἱ λοιποί).

1 Peter can describe the believer's suffering in the present time (of persecution) as a temporary misery that must be borne, as that which is connected with the eschatological testing of the people of God (1:6: ὀλίγον ἄρτι εἰ δέον [ἐστὶν] λυπηθέντες). It is an essential sign of the election of the faithful in a godless world, since God's grace is at work in it, so that one can "bear *sorrows/ blows*" for God's sake if one suffers unjustly (2:19: εἰ . . . ὑποφέρει τις λύπας πάσχων ἀδίκως). If the thought of chastisement and education by God play a role in 1 Peter (→ 2), it appears clearly—formulated in general terms —in Heb 12:11: Just as chastisement at the moment is never pleasant, but involves *suffering* (πᾶσα δὲ παιδεία . . . οὐ δοκεῖ χαρᾶς εἶναι ἀλλὰ λύπης), so also is the present way of God with his people through suffering (cf. v. 7; also Jas 1:2).

Eph 4:30 (μὴ λυπεῖτε τὸ πνεῦμα τὸ ἅγιον τοῦ θεοῦ, "Do not *grieve* the Holy Spirit of God") refers to the Spirit of God that dwells within the believer and in the whole Church, to whom "heavy blows are inflicted" (cf. Isa 63:10; *Herm. Man.* iii.4; x.2.2, 4f.) through inappropriate speech and conduct. The concrete reference is to the acts and attitudes listed in v. 31 ("bitterness, anger, wrath, clamor, slander"), which resist the Spirit given in baptism and thus destroy the believer's seal for future redemption.

4. According to John 16:6, 20-22 Jesus' departure to the Father causes sorrow and pain for the disciples "for a short time" (v. 6: ἡ λύπη πεπλήρωκεν ὑμῶν τὴν καρδίαν; v. 20: θρηνήσετε ὑμεῖς . . . ὑμεῖς λυπηθήσετε; v. 22: ὑμεῖς οὖν νῦν μὲν λύπην ἔχετε [v.l. ἕξετε]), while the κόσμος "will rejoice" (χαρήσεται, v. 20a) at its apparent victory. Because the disciples no longer have a home in the world (cf. 15:18f.), the pain of separation will be especially difficult for them. In the immediate future, they must first come through in the conflict with the world (cf. 13:33; 17:11). This announcement of Jesus affects not only the situation of the departure, but also exposes a fundamental structure of faith: As a woman in childbirth attains joy

only by going through the experience of fear, and then forgets the earlier fear in her joy over the birth (16:21; cf. Isa 66:7ff.; 4 Ezra 4:42f.; 1QH 3:7ff.), so in the world believers are not spared from experiencing in the midst of abandonment and suffering the presence of the Lord, in order that they might know the true joy later (v. 22), which has nothing to do with this world (cf. 16:33). What is referred to is the time of the Spirit and of certainty of faith, which begins at Easter (vv. 23ff.), in which all agonizing uncertainty comes to an end for the believer (see Dietzfelbinger 423-26).

5. In the debate in 2 Corinthians pain and grief play a major role. The context in 2:1-7 (λύπη, vv. 1, 3, 7; λυπέω, vv. 2 bis, 4, 5) is shaped by the contrast between "joy" (χαρά, 1:24; 2:3; χαίρω, 2:3; εὐφραίνω, 2:2) and "sorrow" (cf. also πολλὴ θλῖψις καὶ συνοχή, διὰ πολλῶν δακρύων, 2:4; παρακαλέω, 2:7). Just as the apostle is bound to the church in joy (1:4; cf. 2:3), so he is also bound to them in suffering. If he has found it necessary to be harsh with them in his earlier visit, he has now indicated through an additional letter—"with many tears" (2:3f.)—and not through a renewed visit, that he wants no more grief. His apparent severity was an expression of his love (2:4). The one in the church who *insulted* him (2:5; cf. 7:12) has affected the whole church, but as a member of the church he also deserves forgiveness and encouragement after the "rebuke," as a sign of the love that shapes the church (2:7). The testing and obedience of the church demonstrate this. Thus the purpose of the critical encounter with one another can only be the ultimate joy.

If severity and temporary sorrow (because of the letter) were painful for both the apostle and the church (7:8f.), they were not the intended result, but only an initial step toward joy (7:9), for the sorrow led to "repentance," which occurred "according to God's will" (ἐλυπήθητε εἰς μετάνοιαν· ἐλυπήθητε γὰρ κατὰ θεόν, v. 9). "*Pain* for God's sake" (ἡ κατὰ θεὸν λύπη, v. 10a) thus brings about "repentance unto salvation" (cf. *T. Gad* 5:7; → 2), while "worldly grief" (ἡ τοῦ κόσμου λύπη) produces death (v. 10b), because it originates for the sake of the world and is bound to concern for the world. Thus for the believer (and only for the believer), one may say: ὡς λυπούμενοι ἀεὶ δὲ χαίροντες (6:10), in human terms *grieved,* but still full of joy because this pain separates the believer from the world (cf. 4:8f.; 6:7ff.; 11:23ff.) and thus brings one near the cross of Christ and the fellowship of his resurrection (cf. Phil 2:27; Gal 6:14; → 4).

H. Balz

Λυσανίας, ου *Lysanias* Lysanias*

According to Luke 3:1 tetrarch of Abilene in the fifteenth year of Emperor Tiberius (A.D. 28). His tetrarchy,

according to Josephus *Ant.* xviii.237 (cf. 275), was given to Herod Agrippa I by Emperor Caligula (cf. also *CIG* 4521, 4523). BAGD s.v.; R. Hanhart, *BHH* 1116; *BL* 1070; *KP* III, 831.

Λυσίας, ου *Lysias* Lysias*

Acts 23:26; 24:22 (and 24:7 TR) mention the name of → Κλαύδιος Λυσίας, the chiliarch of the Roman garrison in Jerusalem, who as the military tribune took Paul into (protective) custody (21:31ff.; 22:24ff.; 23:10). According to 23:12ff., esp. vv. 23ff., he transferred Paul to Caesarea with an accompanying letter, in order that Paul might appear before Felix, the governor. According to 22:28 he purchased his Roman citizenship. Λυσίας is his (Greek) name. J. Müller-Bardoff, *BHH* 1116f.; E. Haenchen, *Acts* (Eng. tr., 1971) on 21:31.

λύσις, εως, ἡ *lysis* release, separation*

1 Cor 7:27: μὴ ζήτει λύσιν (i.e., "if you are bound to a wife"). According to the context, what is given here is either a fundamental prohibition of divorce, which would be an unnecessary repetition of 7:10f., or a specific recommendation that men not dissolve existing betrothals. G. Delling, *TDNT* V, 836; H. Conzelmann, *1 Cor* (Hermeneia) ad loc.

λυσιτελέω *lysiteleō* utilize, make use of*

Luke 17:2, impersonal: λυσιτελεῖ αὐτῷ, "it is more *useful* for him/*it is better* for him, if . . . , than"; on the comparative rendering see BDF §245.3.

Λύστρα, ων *Lystra* Lystra*

A city in the region of Lycaonia, southwest of Iconium; on the declension -α, -ων, -οις, -αν see BDF §57. Paul visited Lystra on the "first" (with Barnabas, Acts 14:6, 8, 21; stoning of Paul, 14:19; cf. 2 Tim 3:11) and "second" (without Barnabas, Acts 16:1, 2) missionary journeys. There he was joined by Timothy, a resident of Lystra. W. Ruge, *PW* XIV/1, 71f.; W. M. Ramsay, *The Cities of St. Paul* (1908) 407-19; A. Wikenhauser, *LTK* VI, 1254; BAGD s.v. (bibliography); T. Lohmann, *BHH* 1117f.; *KP* III, 846.

λύτρον, ου, τό *lytron* ransom (noun), redemption*

1. Occurrences in the NT — 2. Basic meaning — 3. Mark 10:45 par. — 4. Ἀντίλυτρον — 5. Λυτρόομαι, λύτρωσις — 6. Λυτρωτής

Lit.: C. K. BARRETT, "Mark 10,45: A Ransom for Many," idem, *NT Essays* (1972) 20-26. — M. CARREZ, *DBSup* IX, 1055-64. — P. FIEDLER, *Jesus und die Sünder* (1976). — J. GNILKA, *Mark* (EKKNT) II (1979) 98-107. — W. GRIMM, *Weil ich Dich*

liebe. Die Verkündigung Jesu und Deuterojesaja (1976). —
B. JANOWSKI, "Auslösung des verwirkten Lebens. Zur Geschichte und Struktur der biblischen Lösegeldvorstellung," ZTK
79 (1982) 25-59. — J. JEREMIAS, "Das Lösegeld für Viele (Mk.
10,45)," idem, Abba (1966) 216-29. — K. KERTELGE, "Der
dienende Menschensohn (Mk 10,45)," FS Vögtle 225-39. —
E. LOHSE. Märtyrer und Gottesknecht (FRLANT 64, ²1963). —
W. J. MOULDER, "The OT Background and the Interpretation of
Mark X.45," NTS 24 (1977/78) 120-27. — H. PATSCH, Abend-
mahl und historischer Jesus (1972). — O. PROCKSCH and
F. BÜCHSEL, TDNT IV, 328-56, esp. 330-35, 340-51. — J. RO-
LOFF, "Anfänge der soteriologischen Deutung des Todes Jesu
(Mk X.45 und Lk XXII.27)," NTS 19 (1972/73) 38-64. —
W. SCHMITHALS, Mark (ÖTK, 1979) 469-71. — SPICQ, Notes
Suppl., 429-35. — P. STUHLMACHER, "Vicariously Giving His
Life for Many, Mark 10:45 (Matt. 20:28)," idem, Reconciliation,
Law and Righteousness (1986) 16-29. — H. THYEN, Studien zur
Sündenvergebung im NT und seinen alttestamentlichen und jü-
dischen Voraussetzungen (FRLANT 96, 1970). — For further
bibliography → ἀπολύτρωσις; see TWNT X, 1165f.

1. Λύτρον appears in the NT only in Mark 10:45 par.
Matt 20:28. This important passage, which is significant
for understanding the Markan (and Matthean) and early
Christian tradition about the death of Jesus, raises several
problems for scholarship. The λύτρον saying in Mark
10:45 has a "Grecized variant" in 1 Tim 2:6 (with the
synonymous term ἀντίλυτρον, → 4), to which Titus 2:14
(ἵνα λυτρώσεται ἡμᾶς . . .) corresponds. Besides λυτρόομαι (Luke 24:21; 1 Pet 1:18), other derivatives are
λύτρωσις (Luke 1:68; Heb 9:12), λυτρωτής (Acts 7:35),
and → ἀπολύτρωσις. Similar in subject matter is
ἀντάλλαγμα (Mark 8:37 par. Matt 16:26).

2. Λύτρον is a noun derived from → λύω that designates
(with the ending -τρον) the "means" of release, i.e., the ransom.
"Ransom" is spoken of (frequently in the pl.) in Greek texts of
antiquity including the LXX, Philo, and Josephus, predominantly
in reference to prisoners of war, slaves, and debtors. Λύτρον is
thus the "price of release" for the liberation of a prisoner or
debtor, in which the extent of the price of redemption and the
manner of its payment follows certain conventions, but is commonly determined by the "right of the sovereign." OT and rabbinic texts (Exod 21:30; 30:12; Num 35:31; b. B. Qam. 40a, 41b;
b. Mak. 2b) indicate the connection between "ransom" and
"atonement." A ransom is paid for the expiation of a life that
has fallen into debt. This relationship to the OT and Jewish idea
of atonement is basic for NT use of λύτρον and ἀντίλυτρον.

3. The λύτρον saying in Mark 10:45, which Matthew
transmits almost unchanged, is to be explained on the one
hand from the early Christian tradition of the vicarious
atoning death of Jesus (Lohse 111-92) and on the other
hand from Markan or pre-Markan tradition. With a clear
echo of Isa 53:10-12 Jesus' sacrifice of his life is interpreted as a vicarious deed "for many." Of course λύτρον
does not appear in Isaiah 53 LXX. It appears possible to
interpret λύτρον as "a free rendering of 'āšām" (Isa 53:10
[so Jeremias 227]). It may be sufficient, however, to

recognize in the λύτρον saying an allusion to the OT text,
which points to the universal saving effect of the death
of Jesus.

The language used and the concept of atonement
characteristic of early Judaism do not give sufficient basis
for the derivation of the λύτρον saying from an original
Semitic form. The use of the concept of atonement in
similar formulations (of course without the universal reference) in Hellenistic Jewish literature (2 Macc 7:37f.;
4 Macc 6:27-29; 17:21f.: ἀντίψυχον) suggests instead
that Mark 10:45 originated in Greek-speaking Christianity. The close relationship between Mark 10:45 and Mark
14:24 suggests that the Lord's Supper tradition has the
same background. The further question of Jesus' own
understanding of his death as vicarious atonement may
be raised against this background (Patsch, Roloff).

In tradition-historical terms, the λύτρον saying is probably to be explained as a secondary expansion of the
statement about the ministry of the Son of Man (v. 45a)
with an "independent traditional fragment" (Gnilka 100).
The convergence of the two motifs of Jesus' manner of
existence as "one who serves" and of the atoning sacrifice
could have led to the present form of v. 45 as a concluding
instruction to the disciples about service.

Even if the interpretation of the λύτρον saying cannot
on methodological grounds be derived directly from
Isaiah 53 (Büchsel 343), the undeniable echoes of the OT
text indicate, nevertheless, the importance of Isaiah 53
for understanding the saying. The death of Jesus has
meaning for others, more precisely: ἀντὶ πολλῶν, "for
many." Thus there is an indication of both the universal
intention and the intercession of Jesus in the place of (→
ἀντί 2.d) individual sinners. The latter is expressed
particularly by λύτρον. Thus there is the idea that the "many,"
i.e., those imprisoned by sin, need an initiative coming
from outside in order to be freed from sin. Thus Jesus
appears in the unmistakable role of the one who stands
in relationship to all others. His "solidarity" with sinners
(cf. Mark 2:14-17) is effective as the essential redemption
of the "many" from their imprisonment. Jesus expresses
his solidarity when he appears in the place of the "many."
Unlike Isaiah 53, Mark 10:45 emphasizes the initiative
of Jesus, his sacrifice. However, in its accent on the
saving will of God, the passage corresponds in subject
matter to Isaiah 53.

In the self-sacrifice of Jesus, God is logically the object and
the many are the beneficiaries. However, here one notices the
limit of ransom as a depiction of what occcurs. According to the
general biblical view it is God himself who makes possible and
effects atonement for the sins of humankind. In this respect the
thought of the vicarious atonement in the death of Jesus is
associated in theme to the idea of the sending of the Son by God
(Rom 8:2-4). Jesus' death liberates because it is the deepest
expression of his obedience as God's Son and his identification
with God and his saving will.

Here one sees also the tension between the loving Father and the God who judges, between the forgiveness of sins by Jesus and the "condition" of his death. The redeemer is also the judge, and Jesus demonstrates in his story the dialectic between God's activity as judge and his unconditional forgiveness.

Grimm suggests a connection between Mark 10:45 and the Jewish idea of the "ransom in the final judgment" (231-77). In responding to the question of the possibility of Israel's salvation in the final judgment, the rabbinic literature refers back to the idea of ransom in Isa 43:4f. (!). A ransom is offered for the salvation of Israel: "The Gentiles are thrown into hell in the final judgment in Israel's place . . ." (246). Here reference is made to Ps 49:8, where it is attested that there can be, for sinners and Gentiles, no ransom with which they might redeem the life they have forfeited (*Tg. Ps.* 49:8; *Sifre Deut.* 329 (on 32:39); *Mek. Exod.* 21:30; cf. *1 Enoch* 98:10). The Jesus logion of Mark 10:45 would have been in debate with this idea. Thus the transformation of the concept of ransom would have taken place directly under the influence of Isa 43:22-25 (God becomes the servant of humankind) and only indirectly from Isaiah 53. Mark 10:45, however, does not offer adequate support for this interpretation. The Jesus logion is hardly derived from direct debate with the rabbis. Instead, it is derived from the reflection of Jesus and the post-Easter Church on his mission in salvation history. Thus not only the theological content of Isaiah 53 but also the figure of the suffering servant may have exercised an influence on the saying.

4. The idea of substitution is accented with the prefix ἀντι- in the compound **ἀντίλυτρον**, *ransom**. 1 Tim 2:6 repeats the logion of Jesus with this noun and other evident of echoes of Mark 10:45 in a strongly Grecized form. "The man Christ Jesus" demonstrated that he is "mediator between God and humankind" when "he gave himself as a *ransom* for all." The sacrifice of Jesus is understood as a means of redemption, through which he might "redeem us from all unlawlessness and purify a people for his own possession" (Titus 2:14). The concept of ransom is not developed here, but is determined from the previously established concept of the universally effective redemptive death of Jesus.

5. The vb. **λυτρόομαι*** (from λυτρόω, "set free for ransom") appears in the NT only in the mid. *(purchase freedom with a ransom)* and the pass. *(be purchased with a ransom)*. It occurs a few times only in late NT writings. Not only in Titus 2:14 (→ 4), but also in 1 Pet 1:18f. the image of the payment of ransom presupposes early Christian interpretation of the death of Jesus. The latter passage also mentions the price with which "you *were ransomed* from the futile ways inherited from your fathers": "by the precious blood of Christ as of a lamb without blemish or spot." Isa 52:3 is apparent in the background. The sacrificial death of Jesus is understood not only as a "valuable" form of ransom, but as an expression of that vicarious service of Jesus Christ, who brings to bear the "free-of-charge" character of the redemption by God in history. Luke 24:21 uses the inf. λυτροῦσθαι in connection

with the general expectation of Israel's "redemption," which was expected to take place through the Messiah. The concept of ransom plays no role here. Just as Luke 24:21 expresses in verbal form the anticipated redemption with the coming of the messianic era, so 1:68 and 2:38 employ the noun **λύτρωσις**, *redemption**. God is the one who—with an apparent echo of Ps 110:9 LXX—has prepared for his people the anticipated eschatological redemption. The immediate context of Luke 1:68 (esp. v. 71) can be understood within the context of Jewish expectations as a political event in salvation history. The fact that such expectations were to be corrected in the story of Jesus the Messiah can be seen in 2:38 and 24:21 as well as the totality of Luke-Acts.

Heb 9:12 speaks of the work of Jesus Christ with respect to its once-for-all nature as an "eternal *redemption*," thus indicating that it was a saving event that surpassed everything prior to it. It involved "redemption (ἀπολύτρωσις) from the transgressions committed under the first covenant" (v. 15).

6. **Λυτρωτής**, *redeemer**, is a *nomen agentis* for λυτρόω and appears only rarely: In Pss 18:15; 77:35 LXX it is used of God as redeemer of his people. In Acts 7:35 Moses is called ἄρχων καὶ λυτρωτής with reference to his mission to Israel. This designation contains a typological suggestion of the eschatological Moses and his work.

K. Kertelge

λυτρόομαι *lytroomai* liberate, redeem, ransom
→ λύτρον 5.

λύτρωσις, εως, ἡ *lytrōsis* redemption
→ λύτρον 5.

λυτρωτής, οῦ, ὁ *lytrōtēs* redeemer
→ λύτρον 6.

λυχνία, ας, ἡ *lychnia* lampstand*

1. Occurrences and meaning — 2. The Synoptics and Heb 9:2 — 3. Revelation

Lit.: H. C. HAHN, *DNTT* II, 486f. — W. MICHAELIS, *TDNT* IV, 324-27. — For further bibliography → λύχνος.

1. The noun λυχνία appears 12 times in the NT, primarily in Revelation (7 occurrences; → 3). The remaining occurrences are limited to the Synoptic image of the lamp (→ λύχνος 3.a), which belongs on the *lampstand* (Mark 4:21 par. Luke 8:16; Matt 5:15 par. Luke 11:33), and Heb 9:2. The λυχνία is a stand on which lamps (→ λύχνος 2) were hung or placed (BAGD s.v.).

2. In the Synoptic image of the lamp the alternative is between placing the lamp on the *lampstand* (τίθημι ἐπὶ

τὴν λυχνίαν, Mark 4:21 par. Matt 5:15/Luke 11:33 or τίθημι ἐπὶ λυχνίας, Luke 8:16) or under a basket (→ μόδιος, so Mark and Matthew). Only on the lampstand does the lamp carry out its function of giving light.

Heb 9:2 mentions the seven-armed lampstand in the earthly holy place (Exod 25:31-38; Josephus *Ant.* xiv.72). It is conspicuously mentioned before table of the showbread (unlike Exod 25:23-38; 37:10-24), perhaps in dependence on Hellenistic tradition (see O. Michel, *Heb* [KEK] 299).

3. In Revelation λυχνία is used of the seven churches of Asia Minor (1:12, 13, 20a, b; 2:1, 5). The idea of the lampstand with seven lamps (cf. Zech 4:2) is not the background for the "seven golden *lampstands*" (1:12, 20; 2:1); for in the midst of the lampstands there is "one like a son of man" (1:13; 2:1). According to Michaelis (327) the image of Matt 5:14 or Phil 2:15 has some influence. Yet there is possibly a conceptual analogy here. When the two witnesses of 11:4 are called "the two olive trees and the two *lampstands*," the imagery is occasioned by Zech 4:2f., 11 (cf. D. Haugg, *Die zwei Zeugen* [1936]). Also within the conceptual associations here is Rev 21:23, where "the lamb" is called the → λύχνος of the heavenly Jerusalem.

G. Schneider

λύχνος, ου, ὁ *lychnos* lamp*

1. Occurrences — 2. Meaning — 3. In the words of Jesus — a) The image of the lamp — b) The eye as λύχνος — c) Other references — 4. Revelation

Lit.: P.-E. BONNARD, "Poterie palestinienne," *DBSup* VIII, 136-240, esp. 231, 237. — A. VAN DEN BORN and W. BAIER, *BL* 1013-15. — DALMAN, *Arbeit* VII, index s.v. Lampe (Lampenständer). — J. DUPONT, "La lampe sur le lampadaire dans l'évangile de saint Luc (VIII,16; XI,33)," *Au service de la parole de Dieu* (FS A.-M. Charue, 1969) 43-59. — C. EDLUND, *Das Auge der Einfalt. Eine Untersuchung zu Mt 6,22-23 und Lk 11,34-35* (1952). — K. GALLING, "Die Beleuchtungsgeräte im israelitisch-jüdischen Kulturgebiet," *ZDPV* 46 (1923) 1-50. — W. H. GROSS, *KP* III, 469-71. — F. HAHN, "Die Worte vom Licht Lk 11,33-36," FS Schmid (1973) 107-38. — H. C. HAHN, *DNTT* II, 486f. — J. JEREMIAS, "Die Lampe unter dem Scheffel," *ZNW* 39 (1940) 237-40. — *idem, Parables* 120f. — W. MICHAELIS, *TDNT* IV, 324-27. — C. MUGLER, *Dictionnaire historique de la terminologie optique des Grecs* (1964) s.v. — M. PHILONENKO, "La parabole sur la lampe (Luc 11,33-36) et les horoscopes qoumrâniens," *ZNW* 79 (1988) 145-51. — G. SCHNEIDER, "Das Bildwort von der Lampe," *ZNW* 61 (1970) 183-209. — R. H. SMITH, "The Household Lamps of Palestine in NT Times," *BA* 29 (1966) 2-27. — H. WEIPPERT, *BRL* 198-201.

1. This noun appears 14 times in the NT, predominantly in the Third Gospel (6 occurrences) and in the other Gospels (twice in Matthew, once in Mark, once in John). The Synoptic Gospels have the various forms of the image of the lamp (Mark 4:21 par. Luke 8:16; Matt

5:15 par. Luke 11:33; in all 4 passages there is reference also to lampstands [→ λυχνία]) and the saying about the eye as the λύχνος τοῦ σώματος (Matt 6:22 par. Luke 11:34). Outside the Gospels λύχνος appears only in Revelation (18:23; 21:23; 22:5) and 2 Pet 1:19.

2. *Lamps* made of clay or metal, having a wick, and fueled with oil were designated λύχνοι (since Homer, also in the LXX and in nonliterary texts). A lamp could be placed on a lampstand (→ λυχνία; Philo *Spec. Leg.* i.296: καίεσθαι λύχνους ἐπὶ τῆς . . . λυχνίας; cf. Josephus *B.J.* vii.429; *Ant.* iii.182, 199). In the NT λύχνος is sometimes used literally (in the image of the lamp in the Synoptics; also Luke 11:36; 15:8; Rev 18:23; 22:5); in other instances it is used fig. (Matt 6:22 par. Luke 11:34, of the eye as the *lamp/light* of the body; Rev 21:23, of the "lamb" as the λύχνος of the new Jerusalem). Literal usage is also seen in imagery, as in Luke 12:35 ("your *lamps* should be burning"); John 5:35 (John the Baptist as ὁ λύχνος ὁ καιόμενος καὶ φαίνων); and 2 Pet 1:9 (the prophetic word [cf. Ps 118:105 LXX] is like a *lamp* shining [φαίνων] in a dark place).

The most frequently occurring usages are of lighting a lamp (Luke 8:16; 11:33; 15:8), of a lamp burning (Matt 5:15; Luke 12:35; John 5:35), of the light of a lamp (φῶς λύχνου, Rev 18:23; 22:5; cf. Luke 11:36, φωτίζω), and of a lamp shining (φαίνω, John 5:35; 2 Pet 1:19). The expression of the "coming" of the lamp (Mark 4:21) is evidently not a Semitism (Schneider 188; *contra* Jeremias, "Lampe" 238).

3. a) Jesus' imagery of the lamp has been transmitted in two basic forms: Matt 5:15 par. Luke 11:33 (Q) and Mark 4:21 par. Luke 8:16. The two basic variants of tradition can be traced back only with difficulty to a single original form. The authors of the Gospels have each shaped the imagery in a new way. The comparison with the lamp is used by Mark esp. with reference to the message of Jesus, while in Luke it is used of the gospel (8:16) and of Jesus himself (11:33, in dependence on Q). In Matt 5:15, although the (relatively) oldest form may be present, the imagery is, esp. by means of its position in the context (cf. 5:14), referred to the community of Jesus' disciples. Matt 5:15 moves within the framework of simple Palestinian household relationships: The house has only one room (v. 15b). Luke, with a ἵνα clause, has in mind an urban house with a vestibule and refers to the character of the message of Jesus as proclamation to others (this additional clause is omitted in 8:16 in 𝔓[75] and B; cf. G. Schneider, *Luke* [ÖTK] 186f., 271-73). The variant of the imagery in *Gos. Thom.* 33 is dependent on Luke.

b) The saying concerning the eye as "the *lamp* of the body" (Luke 11:34-36 par. Matt 6:22f.) is another λύχνος saying of Jesus derived from Q. The Q form was essentially equivalent to Luke 11:34, 35, 36a (F. Hahn 116). The wisdom saying (v. 34) takes on a parenetic shape in v. 35, while in v. 36 the basic idea is clearly stated. In referring to the eye as "the *lamp* of the body" (v. 34) the saying involves "the reception of light and the giving of light for the entire human body," while the reference to the light of the lamp (v. 33, → 3) involves "the saving reality that confronts humankind" (F. Hahn 130). The relationship of v. 33 to the concluding v. 36 (which is connected to v. 33: "as when the *lamp* with its rays gives you light") can—when one considers the motif of lightning in Luke 17:24 (par. Matthew)—be understood in such a way that "the person who is affected by the light and grasped in his whole existence is uncovered, confirmed, and recognized by the blazing ray of light in the last judgment" (F. Hahn 131).

c) Luke 12:35 is reminiscent thematically of the parable of the ten maidens (Matt 25:1-12), because Jesus demands that one keep the *lamps* burning. But there is hardly a literary relationship between the two texts. V. 35 is, in any case, secondary in relation to the following parable of the watchful servants (12:36-38). Perhaps it is a Lukan redaction. In the parable of the lost drachma (15:8-10) the woman lights a *lamp* in order to look for the drachma (v. 8).

According to John 5:35 Jesus says about the Baptist: "He was the burning and shining *lamp*," in whose light they were willing to rejoice. The statement refers to the "witness" that John gave (v. 33). The Evangelist avoids calling John φῶς ("light") because he reserves that symbolic word for Jesus (1:7f.; see Michaelis 327; R. Schnackenburg, *John* II [Eng. tr., 1979] ad loc.).

4. Besides 2 Pet 1:19 (→ 2), λύχνος appears outside the Gospels only in Revelation. At the destruction of "Babylon" (Rev 18:1-24) "the light of the *lamp* will no longer shine" in the city (v. 23), while in the new Jerusalem there will be no need for "the light of *lamps* or for sunshine" because there is no night there (22:5). The radiance of God illuminates the new Jerusalem and its *lamp* is "the lamb" (21:23).   G. Schneider

λύω *lyō* loose, untie; set free; dissolve, destroy*

Lit.: BAGD s.v. — G. BORNKAMM, "Die Binde- und Lösegewalt in der Kirche des Matthäus," FS Schlier 93-107. — F. BÜCHSEL, *TDNT* IV, 335f. — J. D. M. DERRETT, "Binding and Loosing (Matt 16,19; 18,18; John 20,23)," *JBL* 102 (1983) 112-17. — R. H. HIERS, " 'Binding' and 'Loosing': The Matthean Authorizations," *JBL* 104 (1985) 233-50. — K. KERTELGE, "Sündenvergebung an Stelle Gottes," *Dienst der Versöhnung* (TTS 31, 1974) 27-44. — O. MICHEL, *RAC* II, 374-80. — H. THYEN, *Studien zur Sündenvergebung im NT und seinen alttestamentlichen und jüdischen Voraussetzungen* (FRLANT 96, 1970) 218-59. — A. VÖGTLE, *LTK* II, 480-82.

1. Λύω appears 42 times in the NT, predominantly in the Gospels, Acts, and Revelation. Of the compounds with ἀνα-, ἀπο-, ἐκ-, ἐπι-, κατα-, and παρα-, ἀπολύω and καταλύω are used relatively frequently (67 and 17 occurrences).

a) Λύω appears with the basic meaning *loose* (opposite of → δέω, "bind") with an appropriate obj. in Mark 1:7; Luke 3:16; John 1:27 (sandal thong); Rev 5:2 (seal of a book); Mark 7:35 (ligament of the tongue).

b) Acts 22:30; Rev 9:14, 15; 20:3; John 11:44 speak of the *setting free* of a prisoner. Mark 11:2, 4, 5 par. Matt 21:2; Luke 19:30, 31, 33a, b; Luke 13:15 speak of the *unbinding* of an animal. Fig. language is used for the *liberation* of a sick woman "from the shackle" with which Satan had bound her. According to Rev 20:7 Satan is *loosed* from his prison after the millennium. Acts 7:33 and 13:25 speak of the *loosing* of the sandals of the feet (gen.). In 1 Cor 7:27 pf. λέλυσαι appears with the meaning *be free* (of the marital bond to a wife) without an indication of the previous marital bond. The usage in Rev 1:5 is unique in the NT: "To him who loves us and *has redeemed* us from our sins through his blood . . ." (if λούσαντι is not to be read here instead of λύσαντι, as some witnesses do). Only here can one observe a connection in meaning with λύτρον/λυτρόομαι.

c) Λύω appears in the temple saying in John 2:19 with the meaning *destroy* (Mark 14:58 has καταλύω in the fut.). One finds a similar meaning in Eph 2:14 ("he *tore down* the dividing wall"). The same meaning is found in Acts 27:41 (the stern of the ship); 13:43 (an assembly); 2 Pet 3:10, 11, 12 (the cosmic elements in the apocalyptic fiery judgment of fire). 1 John 3:8 speaks of the *destruction* of the works of the devil. In Acts 2:24 λύω refers to the conclusion of the woes of death and of the *destruction* of the "cords of death" (2 Sam 22:6; Pss 17:5; 114:3 MT), which, because of the LXX tr., were identified with the "birthpangs of death" (cf. E. Haenchen, *Acts* [Eng. tr., 1971] 180). 1 John 4:3 v.l. speaks of a "loosing" of Jesus rather than the refusal to confess Jesus. Thus: "Everyone who *disregards* Jesus (who does away with Jesus as the object of the Christian confession) is not from God." Λύω appears in a legal-theological sense in Matt 5:19; John 5:18; 7:23; 10:35 as an expression for the *repeal* of the law or of the sabbath commandment and the Scripture.

d) Binding and *loosing* are spoken of in Matt 16:19 (bis) and 18:18 (bis) as a fig. designation for authoritative ecclesiastical action. Here one may assume the presence of Jewish rabbinic usage (Billerbeck I, 738-42; IV, 304-21). 'Āsar and hittîr in Hebrew and 'asar and šerā' Aramaic are used, in regard to discipline, for the imposition and repeal of the synagogue ban and, in regard to the teaching office, for binding interpretation of the law —"forbid and *permit*." Cf. CD 13:10: "And he [the overseer] shall loose all their fetters"; Josephus *B.J.* i.111: The

Pharisees attained the "capacity . . . to *loose* and to bind (λύειν τε καὶ δεσμεῖν)."

2. Theologically significant usage is present esp. in the meanings indicated in → 1.c and 1.d. Matt 5:19 and John 5:18; 7:23; 10:35 reflect the dispute in early Christianity over the validity of the OT law. According to Matt 5:17, 19 Jesus has not come to *destroy* the law. Instead, he has come in order that what is commanded by the law might be fulfilled. Inasmuch as Jesus uncovers and fulfills the will of God within "the letter of the law," his action becomes the norm for the fulfillment of the law.

The authority to bind and to *loose* is granted to Peter, according to Matt 16:19, while according to 18:18 it is granted to the community of disciples. This authority is an expression of the abiding relationship of the post-Easter ἐκκλησία to the Lord, whose authority the apostle and the community claim. "Binding" and "loosing" in the postapostolic period have progressively taken on more significance in Church law. In the Jewish Christian tradition before and at the time of Matthew the presuppositions for an understanding of binding and loosing were present already as a teaching and disciplinary authority.

Matt 16:19 is more often understood as a reference to "teaching authority," while 18:18 refers more to "disciplinary authority" (Bornkamm 95f.). In any case the term involves the binding application of the standards that Jesus has established for the fulfillment of his mission. The NT tradition (cf. esp. John 20:23 and Matt 18:15-18, 21-35) uses the motif of loosing esp. to underscore the commission that Jesus has given to the Church *to forgive sins* in discipleship and in agreement with him.

K. Kertelge

Λωΐς, ΐδος *Lōïs* Lois*

Timothy's grandmother (from Lystra), who, along with his mother → Εὐνίκη, is mentioned in 2 Tim 1:5 because of her exemplary faith. F. Rehkopf, *BHH* 1103; C. Spicq, *RB* 84 (1977) 362-64.

Λώτ *Lōt* Lot*

The son of Haran and nephew of Abraham (Heb. *lôṭ*, Gen 19:1ff.). Luke 17:28, 29 (L) alludes to Lot's departure from Sodom. Lot's wife (Gen 19:26) is mentioned in Luke 17:32 (L). In 2 Pet 2:7 Lot is a type of those who suffer under the unrighteousness of the surrounding world. M. A. Beek, *BHH* 1105f.; *BL* 1062f.

M μ

Μάαθ *Maath* Maath*

A name in the genealogy of Jesus, Luke 3:26; cf. 1 Chr 6:20; 2 Chr 29:12 (son of Amasai); 31:13. According to Luke, however, Maath was son of Mattithiah (1 Chr 9:31).

Μαγαδάν *Magadan* Magadan*

Matt 15:39: the name of an otherwise unknown place on the Sea of Gennesaret in a region Jesus arrived at in a ship after the feeding of the four thousand. The Koine text reads → Μάγδαλα. In the parallel in Mark 8:10 the place is called → Δαλμανουθά (v.l. Μάγδαλα, Μαγεδά, Μελεγαδά, etc.). M. S. Enslin, *BHH* 1121; *BL* 1074 (bibliography).

Μάγδαλα *Magdala* Magdala

Matt 15:39 v.l. for → Μαγαδάν. Magdala lies on the northwest shore of the Sea of Gennesaret. E. W. Saunders, *BHH* 1121; → Μαγδαληνή.

Μαγδαληνή, ῆς, ἡ *Magdalēnē* (woman) of Magdala*

Μαγδαληνή is a fem. noun derived from the adj. Μαγδαληνός. It appears in the NT, in all four Gospels, only in reference to "Mary *Magdalene*" (→ Μαρία 3). The designation Magdalene probably refers to Magdala on the west side of the Sea of Gennesaret (Kopp, *Places* 190-96; L. Grollenberg, *LTK* VI, 1269; V. Corbo, *SBFLA* 24 [1974] 5-37; 28 [1978] 232-42; *BL* 1074; J. F. Strange, *IDBSup* 561; S. Loffreda, *BeO* 18 [1976] 133-35; F. Manns, S. Loffreda, and V. Corbo, *Studia Hierosolymitana in onore del B. Bagatti* I [1976] 307-78). The form most commonly used is Μαρία (Μαριάμ) ἡ Μαγδαληνή (Mark 15:40, 47 par. Matt 27:56, 61/John 19:25; Mark 16:1 par. Matt 28:1; John 20:1, 18 par. Mark 16:9). Luke 8:2 has Μαρία ἡ καλουμένη Μαγδαληνή; 24:10 has ἡ Μαγδαληνὴ Μαρία. G. Schneider

Μαγεδών *Magedōn* Magedon
Rev 16:16 v.l. for → Ἁρμαγεδών.

μαγεία, ας, ἡ *mageia* magic*

According to Acts 8:11 Simon the magician had amazed the population of Samaria for a long time with his *magic* (ταῖς μαγείαις ἐξεστακέναι αὐτούς); → Σίμων 10. G. Delling, *TDNT* IV, 359.

μαγεύω *mageuō* perform magic*

Acts 8:9, of Simon the magician: μαγεύων καὶ ἐξιστάνων τὸ ἔθνος τῆς Σαμαρείας; → Σίμων 10. G. Delling, *TDNT* IV, 359.

μαγία, ας, ἡ *magia* magic
Alternative form of → μαγεία.

μάγος, ου, ὁ *magos* magician, soothsayer*

There are 6 occurrences in the NT. According to the infancy narrative of Matthew (2:1, 7, 16 bis) "*magi/wise men* from the East (μάγοι ἀπὸ ἀνατολῶν)" (v. 1) came to Jerusalem to worship the newborn child (v. 2).

The term μάγος is derived from the name of a Median tribe that served as priests in the Persian religion (Herodotus i.101) and were involved in astrology and astronomy. Consequently in antiquity astrologers, interpreters of dreams, and soothsayers from the East were called magi (cf. Herodotus vii.37; Porphyry *De Abstinentia* iv.16; also Isa 47:13; Dan 2:2; Josephus *Ant.* xx.142), with emphasis on their secret knowledge and their capacity for magic. Jewish texts recognize the knowledge of the magi (Philo *Spec. Leg.* iii.100), while in the rabbinic literature the magi are known predominantly as deceivers and charlatans (*b. Šabb.* 75a; cf. Deut 18:9ff.; 2 Kgs 9:22).

Matthew understands the μάγοι as learned men (probably from Babylon) who understand the stars, who as Gentiles recognize the signs of the birth of Christ and consequently come to understand the Scripture (2:5f.).

The negative accent of the word comes into focus in Acts 13:6, 8, where the Jewish ψευδοπροφήτης Bar-Jesus (v. 6), also known as Elymas (v. 8), in Paphos on Cyprus is likewise called a μάγος. Paul overcomes his dangerous power through the Holy Spirit (vv. 9-11; → Βαριησοῦ, Ἐλύμας; cf. also 8:9, 11).

See BAGD s.v. (bibliography); G. Delling, *TDNT* IV, 356-59; *TWNT* X, 1166f. (bibliography); G. Fohrer, *BHH* 2204f.; W. Grundmann, *Matt* (THKNT) on 2:1ff.; *BL* 1075; P. Gaechter, *ZKT* 90 (1968) 257-95; M. Hengel and H. Merkel, *FS* Schmid (1973) 139-69; *KP* V, 1460-72; for further bibliography → ἀστήρ.   H. Balz

Μαγώγ *Magōg* Magog
→ Γώγ.

Μαδιάμ *Madiam* Midian*

Acts 7:29: γῆ Μαδιάμ, the "land of Midian" (Heb. *midyān,* Gen 25:2; Exod 2:15), in which Moses lived as an "alien" (πάροικος) according to Exod 2:15ff., after his flight from Egypt. The Midianites were a nomadic band of tribes which probably had its grazing places esp. in the region east of the Gulf of Aqaba. H. St. J. Philby, *The Land of Midian* (1957); R. Bach, *BHH* 1214; *BL* 1152.

μαθητεύω *mathēteuō* make a disciple; pass.: become a disciple
→ μαθητής.

μαθητής, ου, ὁ *mathētēs* pupil, disciple
μαθητεύω *mathēteuō* make a disciple, pass.: become a disciple*

1. Occurrences in the NT — 2. In relation to other words — 3. The disciples of John — 4. The disciples of Jesus — a) The extent of the group — b) Their call — c) The nature of discipleship — d) The disciples' lack of insight — e) Disciples in Acts

Lit.: E. BEST, *Following Jesus: Discipleship in the Gospel of Mark* (*JSNT* Supplement Series 4, 1981). — idem, "The Role of the Disciples in Mark," *NTS* 23 (1976/77) 377-401. — H. D. BETZ, *Nachfolge und Nachahmung Jesu Christi im NT* (BHT 37, 1967). — CONZELMANN, *Theology* 33f., 90, 147f. — J. D. M. DERRETT, "ἮΣΑΝ ΓΑΡ ᾿ΑΛΕΕΙΣ (Mk. I 16). Jesus's Fishermen and the Parable of the Net," *NovT* 22 (1980) 108-37. — J. K. ELLIOTT, "Mathētēs with a Possessive in the NT," *TZ* 35 (1979) 300-304. — B. GERHARDSSON, "Die Boten Gottes und die Apostel Christi," *SEÅ* 27 (1962) 89-131. — F. HAHN, *Mission in the NT* (1965) 40-46, 111-36. — M. HENGEL, *The Charismatic Leader and His Followers* (1981). — J. D. KINGSBURY, "The Figure of Peter in Matthew's Gospel as a Theological Problem," *JBL* 98 (1979) 67-83. — J. A. KIRK, "Apostleship Since Rengstorf," *NTS* 21 (1974/75) 249-64. — H.-J. KLAUCK, "Die erzählerische Rolle der Jünger im Markusevangelium," *NovT* 24 (1982) 1-26. — G. KLEIN, *Die zwölf Apostel* (FRLANT 77, 1961) 65-113, 202-16. — H. MERKLEIN, "Der Jüngerkreis Jesu," *Die Aktion Jesu und die Reaktion der Kirche* (ed. K. Müller; 1972) 65-100. — D. MÜLLER, *DNTT* I, 483-90. — M. PESCE, "Discepo-

lato gesuano e discepolato rabinico," *ANRW* II/25/1 (1982) 251-89. — H. RÄISÄNEN, *Die Parabeltheorie im Markusevangelium* (1973) 20ff. — K. H. RENGSTORF, *TDNT* IV, 390-461. — B. RIGAUX, "Die 'Zwölf' in Geschichte und Kerygma," *Das kirchliche Amt im NT* (ed. K. Kertelge; 1977) 279-304. — J. ROLOFF, *Apostolat —Verkündigung —Kirche* (1965) 138-235. — G. SCHMAHL, *Die Zwölf im Markusevangelium* (1974). — W. SCHMITHALS, *The Office of Apostle in the Early Church* (1969) 67-88. — R. SCHNACKENBURG, *John* III (Eng. tr., 1982) 203-17, 375-88. — A. SCHULZ, *Nachfolgen und Nachahmen* (1962) 117-33. — F. F. SEGOVIA, ed., *Discipleship in the NT* (1985). — G. THEISSEN, *The Social Setting of Pauline Christianity* (1982) 27-67. — idem, " 'Wir haben alles verlassen' (Mc X,28). Nachfolge und soziale Entwurzelung in der jüdisch-palästinischen Gesellschaft des 1. Jh. n. Chr.," *NovT* 19 (1977) 161-96 (= idem, *Studien zur Soziologie des Urchristentums* [1979] 106-41).

1. The noun μαθητής appears 261 times in the NT. It is found only in the Gospels and Acts (Matthew has 72 occurrences, Mark has 46, Luke has 37, John has 78, and Acts has 28). The vb. μαθητεύω appears 4 times (Matt 13:52; 27:57; 28:19; Acts 14:21).

2. The contrast between μαθητής and διδάσκαλος in the proverbial expression in Matt 10:24f. par. and the relationship between μαθητής and the vb. μανθάνω indicate that μαθητής is understood as a term for someone who stands in relation to another as pupil and is instructed by that person. Such a relationship was known in the NT era. The scribes were also teachers and had pupils *(talmîdîm),* whom they instructed in the Scripture and in the traditions of the fathers. Jesus as well was called rabbi or rabbuni (Matt 26:25, 49 par., etc.) and διδάσκαλος (Matt 8:19; 12:38, etc.) and taught (Matt 4:23; 26:55 par.). However, Jesus had an authority that was previously unknown (Matt 7:28f.; Mark 1:22, 27; Luke 4:32; John 7:46). Thus μαθητής in the context of his ministry took on a meaning that cannot be deduced from the word itself (cf. Rengstorf 390f.).

3. Even before Jesus appeared publicly and had disciples a group of disciples of John the Baptist existed. John's movement was perhaps not as strong as Mark 1:5 indicates, but nevertheless it was sufficient to cause concern on the part of Herod Antipas (Matt 14:3ff. par.; cf. Josephus *Ant.* xviii.116-19). Matt 11:2 par. indicates that John had people whom he could send, and according to Matt 14:12 par. there was a group of disciples who took the responsibility of burying him (see also Hengel 35-37). Those who followed John were baptized for repentance and subjected themselves to new ascetic ethical demands, e.g., fasting and cleansing (Mark 2:18 par.; John 3:25). The Baptist taught them to pray (Luke 11:1). The Fourth Gospel emphasizes that the Baptist—in his own view— was not the Messiah (John 1:6-8, 20; 3:28) and that he bore witness to Jesus as the expected Messiah (John 1:8,

19-36; 3:22-36). However, the emphasis with which the Gospel sets this forth betrays the fact that the Baptist was regarded by some as Messiah, and one has reason to assume that the transition from being a disciple of John to being a disciple of Jesus did not always take place in the harmonious way described in John 1:35-39. This is indicated also by the fact that, according to Acts 18:25; 19:1-6, there were disciples of the Baptist years later in Ephesus who had not even heard of the Holy Spirit.

4. a) Those who followed Jesus can—as is indicated in Mark 3:7-12—be divided into two main groups: the narrowly limited circle and the great multitude. This distribution is also indicated where Jesus is described as withdrawing from the crowds with his disciples alone (e.g., Matt 13:36; 14:22 par. Mark). Μαθητής is seldom used for the wider circle of followers/listeners. It is, however, so used in Luke 6:13, 17, where a distinction is made between three groups: a large mass of people, a great crowd of Jesus' disciples, and finally the Twelve selected from the group of disciples (v. 13; cf. Mark 4:10). Μαθητής is a term for people of the larger circle of followers also in Luke 19:37, 39; John 6:60, 66; 7:3; 8:31; 19:38.

But usually μαθητής is reserved for the narrower circle around Jesus, a group presumably of modest size, one that could gather in a boat (e.g., Matt 14:22 par.; John 6:17) or a house (e.g., Mark 7:17; 9:28). From the tradition one can ascertain that the small circle around Jesus consisted of "the Twelve" (see Rigaux 299ff.; Klein 202ff.; Schmithals 67ff.; Roloff 138ff.). Where Mark 6:35 reports that the *disciples* of Jesus came to him, the par. Luke 9:12 indicates that it was the Twelve who came; Mark 6:7 also says that it was the Twelve. The μαθητής whom Jesus commanded to prepare the Passover meal, according to Matt 26:17-19 par., were the Twelve, with whom he later celebrated the meal (Matt 26:20ff. par.). The names of the Twelve, whom Jesus selected at an early point in his public ministry as his special coworkers, are —except for small differences—given in Mark 3:13-19 par. There is no doubt that the number twelve had a symbolic meaning (→ δώδεκα; see also Jeremias, *Theology* 233f.). But this does not justify denying the pre-Easter existence of this group or of speaking of a predating of it. Even the traitor belonged to this narrow circle (Matt 26:14 par.; 26:47 par.; John 6:71). The designation "the Twelve" disappeared very quickly (Gerhardsson 125ff.). Except in 1 Cor 15:6 Paul does not use it (see also Kirk 249ff.; Klein 65ff.; Merklein 98).

It is possible that before the selection of the Twelve an even smaller group existed around Jesus. This could be the reason that Peter (Kingsbury 67ff.), James, and John appear to have stood esp. close to their Lord (Mark 5:37 par.; Matt 17:1 par.; 14:27 par.; Mark 1:29; Matt

20:20 par. Mark; Mark 13:3; see also Schmahl 128ff.). Matt 4:18-22 par. reports also that these were the first to be called (Derrett 108ff.); cf. John 1:35ff., where, however, along with Peter and Andrew the disciple who first came to Jesus with Andrew remains unnamed. It is also unclear whether "the disciple whom Jesus loved" (John 13:23; 19:26; 20:2; 21:7, 20) is John or even belonged to the group of Twelve (see R. E. Brown, *John* [AB] xciiff.; Schnackenburg 375-88). John mentions this group only once (6:67), and he has no list of apostles; he has thus placed no special weight on the number twelve.

b) Although there are instances in which a person comes to Jesus and asks permission to follow him and thus become a μαθητής, Jesus nevertheless presumably took the initiative in most cases and called people to follow him (Matt 4:18-22; Matt 9:9 par.; cf. also John 6:70; 15:16), just as God had chosen prophets in the OT.

c) A long series of sayings indicates how discipleship was understood. In the majority of these sayings it is the narrow circle of disciples that is addressed. But this does not exclude the possibility that these sayings had validity in a wider sense (Best 400f.). The special relationship that existed between Jesus and his disciples is attested, e.g., in that the mysteries of the kingdom of God were revealed to them and not to the masses (Matt 13:1 par.; cf. 16:15-17 par.; 16:21 par.; 17:22-23 par.; 20:17-19 par.). According to Matt 12:49 disciples are called Jesus' mother and brothers (cf. Mark 3:34 par.), and Jesus taught them to pray (Matt 6:9; cf. Luke 11:2). Disciples had to break with their previous manner of existence, e.g., give up their occupations (Matt 4:18-22 par.; 9:9 par.). They were called upon to abandon their families (Luke 14:26 par.; 9:61f.) and leave to others such elementary duties as burying one's own father (Matt 8:21f.; see also Hengel 3-15). In a certain sense the conditions for disciples were comparable to those for slaves. When, e.g., Jesus wished to go on his way to Jerusalem through Samaria, they were expected to find lodging (Luke 9:51f.). They had to prepare his entry also (Matt 21:2 par.) as well as the Passover meal that he wished to have (Matt 26:17f. par.). To be μαθητής and thus to follow Jesus meant radical self-denial. The μαθητής had to "take up his cross" (Matt 16:24-25 par.; cf. Matt 10:38 par.), and thus a fellowship of destiny with Jesus existed, consisting of persecution, suffering, and death (Matt 10:24-25; John 15:20; Matt 10:17-22 par.; 20:20ff. par.; 24:9 par.; John 16:2).

This very radical practice in living conditions distinguished the disciples in several points from the customs of the time (Rengstorf 444f.). But promises are associated with endurance of the sufferings that accompany discipleship (Matt 19:27-30 par.; 10:22; 24:13 par.; see also Schulz 117ff.; Theissen, "Nachfolge" 161ff.), while on the other hand denying the master brought with it forfeiture of salvation (Mark 8:38 par.; Matt 10:33 par.).

According to Mark 3:13-15 Jesus chose the Twelve so that they might be with him, but also—in contrast to the usual relationship of disciples—that he might send them out (6:7-13 par.; see also Conzelmann 290ff.). Luke 10:1ff. reports that Jesus, in addition to those who are mentioned, sent out seventy (or seventy-two) others—of whom the term μαθητής is of course not used. Luke has perhaps wished to indicate that the message was intended not only for the Jews, but that it had universal significance (cf. Gen 10:1ff.). Just as the master receives power from above, as Luke 4:14ff. (cf. Acts 10:37ff.) indicates, the disciples were empowered with ἐξουσία (Mark 3:14f. par.). They performed mighty works in the name of Jesus (Luke 10:17; cf. Acts 3:6, 12-16). Of greatest importance, they proclaimed the imminence of the kingdom of God (Matt 10:7f.) and, like Jesus himself, healed the sick and demoniacs (Matt 4:23 par.). There is no reason to doubt that Jesus initiated this mission. The basic structure of the missionary commission is evidently present in Luke 10:2-12 (see Hahn 40f.). Both Mark (6:30) and Luke (9:10; 10:17)—but not Matthew—report that the disciples returned to Jesus. This mission was limited to Israel (Matt 10:5f.) and was characterized by the disciples as a time in which nothing was lacking for them (Luke 22:35; cf. Theissen, *Social Setting* 27ff.).

An entirely different situation is present when disciples are sent out after the death and resurrection of Jesus (Matt 28:18-20 par.; cf. John 20:21-23). Now they are commanded to make disciples of all people as they proclaim the gospel everywhere, preach repentance for forgiveness, and baptize.

In their service the disciples are representatives of their Lord. Thus one could say that anyone who receives a μαθητής receives the one who sent the μαθητής (Matt 10:40 par.; cf. John 13:20). A disciple of Jesus can thus never appear as one who has surpassed the role of disciple and begins his own school.

d) A characteristic element of Jesus' disciples is their deficient understanding, e.g., of what Jesus said and did (Mark 6:52 par.; Matt 16:4-12 par.; 15:15-20 par.; Mark 4:13), esp. in relation to the Passion predictions and the question of who the master really was (Matt 16:21-23 par.; Mark 9:31-32 par.; Luke 18:34; Mark 4:40-41 par.). This tradition can—together with the frequently occurring command to silence—be determined by a secondary (Markan) conception (on the messianic secret see Räisänen 20f.; Best 377ff.). Of course one must consider that the disciples were not able to grasp the radical newness that came with Jesus, e.g., that the kingdom of God belongs to children (Matt 19:13-15 par.) and that customary conceptions have been reversed in this kingdom. However, it belongs to the NT image of the μαθητής that even those who were lacking in understanding and thus worked against Jesus (Matt 19:13-15 par.) and finally

abandoned their master (26:57-75 par.) were reconfirmed in their relationship to Jesus as disciples after the resurrection.

e) In Acts the designation μαθητής is used for all who belonged to the Church, whether in Jerusalem (6:1, 2, 7; 9:26), Damascus (9:10, 19), Antioch—where the term "Christian" was first used for the disciples (11:26, 29; 13:52)—or Ephesus (19:2; 20:1, 30). The term *disciple* here is not dependent on direct knowledge of Jesus, but expresses a relationship of fidelity to him (cf. John 9:28; Matt 22:16 concerning the disciples of Moses or of the Pharisees [see also Betz 27ff.]; also Acts 9:25, where the reference is to disciples of Paul).

P. Nepper-Christensen

μαθήτρια, ας, ἡ   *mathētria*   (female) disciple*

In Acts 9:36 Tabitha from Joppa is called a μαθήτρια (μαθήτρια ὀνόματι Ταβιθά); cf. → μαθητής 4.e.

Μαθθάθ   *Maththath*   Matthat
Variant of the name → Μαθθάτ in Luke 3:24, 29 ℵ.

Ματθαῖος, ου   *Maththaios*   Matthew*

Lit.: BAGD s.v. — BILLERBECK I, 536. — G. DALMAN, *Grammatik des jüdisch-palästinischen Aramäisch* (²1905 = 1960) 178 with n. 5. — W. GRUNDMANN, *Matt* (THKNT, ³1972) 269f. — *idem, Mark* (THKNT, ⁷1977) 104-7. — E. HAENCHEN, *Der Weg Jesu* (1966) 135-38. — B. HEMELSOET, *BL* 1109. — H. LJUNGMANN, *BHH* 1171. — P. NEPPER-CHRISTENSEN, *Das Matthäusevangelium—ein judenchristliches Evangelium?* (1958). — R. PESCH, "Levi-Matthäus (Mc 2,14/Mt 9,9; 10,3)," *ZNW* 59 (1968) 40-56. — G. SCHILLE, *Die urchristliche Kollegialmission* (ATANT 48, 1967) 131-44. — For further bibliography see Hemelsoet.

1. Matthew is mentioned in the four lists of apostles (Matt 10:3, where he is identified as ὁ τελώνης; Mark 3:18; Luke 6:15; Acts 1:13) in the seventh (Mark and Luke) or eighth (Matthew and Acts) position. The name is possibly derived from rabbinic *mattay*, "gift of God" (see Billerbeck, Dalman).

Matt 9:9 tells of an occasion when Jesus, as he passed the toll office, called to Matthew: "follow me," and that Matthew got up and followed Jesus. In the parallel reports (Mark 2:14; Luke 5:27) the tax collector is not called Matthew, but Levi. The reason for this difference could be that Matthew, like the others (there are no less than seven epithets in the lists of apostles—perhaps to avoid confusion), had an epithet, in which case he would have had, contrary to custom, two Hebrew/Aramaic names, even if one of them possessed a Greek ending. Matthew could have received the epithet from Jesus, and the old name might have been displaced, as with Peter (B. Weiss, *Matt* [KEK] 1f.). Pesch (56) represents the view that the

Matthean redactor first identified Levi the tax collector with Matthew.

Matthew is mentioned also in *b. Sanh.* 43a as *Mattay* and is first in the list of five disciples of Jesus who are named there. This indicates that in certain circles some wanted to push Matthew into the foreground. E. Klostermann is perhaps correct in saying (*Matt* [HNT] 81) that Matthew was placed "in the position of this man who was no longer of interest" (i.e., Levi). This would esp. be the case if Grundmann's assumption is correct that the tax collector Matthew was "the one who was significant for the tradition upon which the Gospel was based" (270). In any case only in the Gospel of Matthew is the Matthew of the list of disciples a tax collector (Matt 10:3). Finally, that the name of Levi is not mentioned in Matthew's Gospel may also reflect the fact that the name change has already taken place (E. Schweizer, *Matt* [Eng. tr., 1975] 225).

2. Except in Matt 9:9 the NT reports nothing about Matthew. According to Clement of Alexandria he was an ascetic and ate no meat (*Paed.* ii.16.1). According to Apollonius he, like other apostles, remained in Jerusalem at Jesus' command for twelve years after the resurrection (apud Eusebius *HE* v.18.12). Then he turned to the non-Hebrews (iii.24.6). Clement of Alexandria also reports, with Heracleon as his source (*Strom.* iv.71.3), that Matthew died a natural death. Nevertheless, his death by martyrdom is celebrated in the West on September 21 and in the East on November 16.

Papias reports that Matthew compiled the sayings (τὰ λόγια) in Hebrew (Ἐβραΐδι διαλέκτῳ) and that each one translated as well as he could (Eusebius *HE* iii.39.16; also iii.24.6; v.8.2; 10.3; vi.25.4; on Matthew traditions in the writings of Jerome see Nepper-Christensen 64ff., 211 [37ff. on Matthew traditions in general).

Of course Matthew is hardly the author of the Gospel of Matthew, as is demonstrated by the many double traditions in the Gospel, its combining of sayings of Jesus in long speeches, its groupings of miracle stories, and the fact that Matthew was written in Greek and is not a tr., as indicated by the plays on words and the use of the gen. absolute, although Semitisms are demonstrable in the text. Finally, the "ecclesiastical" theology of the Gospel attests that the author/redactor did not belong to the first generation of Christians (on this point see the reference to ἐκκλησία in Matt 16:18; 18:17 and the sayings in 16:19; 18:18).

P. Nepper-Christensen

Ματθάν *Maththan* Matthan

Variant of the name Ματθάν in Matt 1:15 (bis) in Codex B.

Ματθάτ *Maththat* Matthat*

The name of two people in the genealogy of Jesus: Luke 3:24: the son of Levi, father of Eli, and grandfather of Joseph; 3:29: the son of (another) Levi and father of Jorim.

Ματθίας, ου *Maththias* Matthias*

Lit.: A. van den Born, *BL* 1114. — W. Foerster, *RGG* IV, 810f. — R. H. Fuller, "The Choice of Matthias," *SE* VI (1973) 140-46. — P. Gaechter, "Petrus und seine Zeit: Neutestamentliche Studien (1958) 31-66. — E. Grässer, "Acta-Forschung seit 1960 (III)," *TRu* 42 (1977) 1-68, esp. 6-9. — C. Masson, "La reconstitution du collège des Douze d'après Actes 1,15-26," *RTP* 3/5 (1955) 193-201. — P.-H. Menoud, "Les additions au groupe des douze apôtres, d'après le livre des Actes," *RHPR* 37 (1957) 71-80. — F. Mussner, *LTK* VII, 179f. — E. Nellessen, *Zeugnis für Jesus und das Wort* (1976) 128-78. — K.-H. Rengstorf, "Die Zuwahl des Matthias (Apg 1,15ff.)," *ST* 15 (1961) 35-67. — J. Renié, "L'élection de Mathias (Act., I,15-26)," *RB* 55 (1948) 43-53. — A. Weiser, "Die Nachwahl des Mattias (Apg 1,15-26)," *Zur Geschichte des Urchristentums* (QD 87 = FS R. Schnackenburg, ed. K. Müller and H. Merklein; 1979) 97-110.

Matthias is an abbreviated form of the Jewish name Mattathias. In the NT the name appears only in Acts 1:23, 26, where the report is given of the selection of an apostle to replace Judas. The successful candidate in this selection process, which included a speech by Peter and the prayer of those who were present prior to the casting of lots, is Matthias. The name indicates that he was a Jew. This fact corresponds to the contact with the earthly Jesus assumed in Acts 1:21f. Nothing else is reported about him in the NT. Eusebius *HE* i.12; ii.1 counts him among the 70 disciples of Jesus. The *Gospel according to Matthias* and the *Traditions of Matthias* as well as the *Acts of Andrew and Matthias* (Hennecke/Schneemelcher I, 308-13; II, 576) offer further, but historically unverifiable, information.

A. Weiser

Ματθουσαλά *Mathousala* Methuselah*

A name (Heb. *mᵉtûšelaḥ,* Gen 5:21ff.) in the genealogy of Jesus in Luke 3:37, son of Enoch, father of Lamech, and grandfather of Noah. *BL* 1149; H. Schmid, *BHH* 1208.

Μαϊνάν *Maïnan* Menna

Alternative form of → Μεννά in Luke 3:31 TR.

μαίνομαι *mainomai* be out of one's mind, be possessed, rage*

The 5 occurrences in the NT always express a negative judgment about people who appear with special authority or who report about experiences with the power of God: John 10:20, a Jewish charge against Jesus: δαιμόνιον ἔχει καὶ μαίνεται; Acts 26:24, the governor Festus criticizes Paul after Paul has made his defense speech: μαίνῃ, Παῦλε, to which Paul said in response: οὐ μαίνομαι, . . . ἀλλὰ ἀληθείας καὶ σωφροσύνης ῥήματα ἀποφθέγγομαι (v. 25; cf. Plato *Phd.* 244a); 12:15, of the servant girl

Rhoda, who notifies Mary (mother of John Mark) in the house that Peter, who had been taken prisoner, is at the door. While in these passages people attempt, by means of resistance, to evade the works of God that have not been given a favorable hearing (cf. also the judgment of the members of the Athenian assembly, Diogenes Laertius i.49), Paul criticizes the Corinthian tongue speakers in 1 Cor 14:23 for not considering the effect of their conduct on outsiders: οὐκ ἐροῦσιν ὅτι μαίνεσθε; The idea of religious (Dionysiac) rapture (cf. Herodotus iv.79: ὑπὸ τοῦ θεοῦ μαίνεται) is not positively treated in the NT. H. Preisker, *TDNT* IV, 360f.; BAGD s.v.; Spicq, *Notes* II, 529.

H. Balz

μακαρίζω *makarizō* pronounce a blessing, bless*

Luke 1:48, of Mary: ἀπὸ τοῦ νῦν μακαριοῦσίν με πᾶσαι αἱ γενεαί; Jas 5:11: μακαρίζομεν τοὺς ὑπομείναντας (". . . those who endure patiently"; cf. Dan 12:12); → μακάριος.

μακάριος, 3 *makarios* happy, blessed*

1. Occurrences in the NT — 2. Meaning — 3. Background in the history of religions — 4. The Synoptics — a) The Sermon on the Mount/Sermon on the Plain — b) Other Q traditions — c) Other Synoptic traditions — 5. John — 6. Paul — 7. The Catholic Epistles — 8. Revelation

Lit.: S. AGOURIDES, "La tradition des Béatitudes chez Mattieu et Luc," FS Rigaux 9-27. — H. D. BETZ, *Essays on the Sermon on the Mount* (1985) 17-36. — I. BROER, *Die Seligpreisungen der Bergpredigt. Studien zu ihrer Überlieferung und Interpretation* (BBB 61, 1986). — DUPONT, *Béatitudes*. — H. FRANKEMÖLLE, "Die Makarismen (Mt 5,1-12; Lk 6,20-23). Motive und Umfang der redaktionellen Komposition," *BZ* 15 (1971) 52-75. — R. A. GUELICH, "The Matthean Beatitudes: 'Entrance-Requirements' or Eschatological Blessings?" *JBL* 95 (1976) 415-34. — F. HAUCK and G. BERTRAM, *TDNT* IV, 362-70. — C. KÄHLER, *Biblische Makarismen. Studien zur Form- und Traditionsgeschichte der biblischen Makarismen* (Diss. Jena, 1974). — K. KOCH, *The Growth of the Biblical Tradition* (1969) 6-8, 39-44, 59-62. — C. MICHAELIS, "Die Π-Alliteration der Subjektsworte der ersten vier Seligpreisungen in Mt V.3-6 und ihre Bedeutung für den Aufbau der Seligpreisungen bei Matt, Luke und Q," *NovT* 10 (1968) 148-61. — G. STRECKER, "Die Makarismen der Bergpredigt," *NTS* 17 (1970/71) 255-75. — N. WALTER, "Die Bearbeitung der Seligpreisungen durch Matthäus," *SE* IV (TU 102, 1968) 246-58. — H. WINDISCH, *Der Sinn der Bergpredigt* (UNT 16, ²1937). — W. ZIMMERLI, "Die Seligpreisungen der Bergpredigt und das AT," FS Daube 8-26. — For further bibliography see *TWNT* X, 1167.

1. Of the 50 references the overwhelming portion (28) are in the Synoptics (13 in Matthew, 9 of which are in the Sermon on the Mount; 15 in Luke). Outside the Gospels, Revelation is the only NT document that uses

μακάριος frequently (7 times). The remaining passages are distributed among Paul (4), the Pastorals (3), the Catholic Epistles (4), and John and Acts (2 each).

2. In the NT μακάριος can have the general meaning *happy* or *good;* thus it is used in a variety of grammatical contexts and with a variety of meanings. In the personal sense, Paul considers himself *fortunate* that he can defend himself before King Agrippa (Acts 26:2); an impersonal use occurs in the maxim attributed to Jesus, "It is *more blessed* to give than to receive" (20:35), which was handed on in Greek literature in this or another form (cf. E. Haenchen, *Acts* [Eng. tr., 1971] ad loc.). Paul uses the comparative expressed by (μακάριόν ἐστιν) μᾶλλον . . . ἢ to make an ethical value judgment: A woman no longer bound to her husband is *better off* (μακαριωτέρα . . . ἐστιν) if she remains unmarried (1 Cor 7:40). A theological meaning is present with μακάριος alongside ἐλπίς in Titus 2:13, which describes the content of Christian hope (i.e., the future epiphany of the glory of God and of Jesus Christ). This usage corresponds to that in the Pastorals, where μαράριος is employed as an adj. designation for God (1 Tim 1:11; 6:15).

In the overwhelming majority of passages μακάριος is used in reference to people. Thus in the typical NT makarism, to which the following discussion is limited, μακάριος is often placed first in a phrase that omits ἐστίν (etc.). It appears with the second or third person and expresses (in some cases implicitly; also with a rel. clause or a final clause) a "condition" (e.g., Matt 5:3ff.) and is set out in the schema of deed-result (Kähler 232). In addition to this primarily parenetic orientation, elements of consolation also appear (→ 4). Because of their eschatological motivation the NT makarisms appear consistently as prophetic-apocalyptic address or instruction. In such contexts, *Hail!* or the archaic *blessed* is more appropriate than "fortunate." Μακάριος has the same meaning in reference to parts of the human body when the person so designated is portrayed as esp. blessed (Matt 13:16 par. Luke 10:23; Luke 11:27).

3. Occurring from the time of Pindar in the Greek poetic literature, μακάριος designates the (supra-earthly) condition of the gods and of people who rejoice in extraordinary good fortune. In the time of Aristophanes the word describes, among others, the rich who are elevated above normal cares because of their wealth. Εὐδαίμων can appear with μακάριος as a synonym. The fixed form of the makarism (e.g., μακάριος ὅστις) is found in the early Greek tradition (Menander *Fragmenta* 114; Pindar *P.* v.46, etc.). As a word expressing praise, it refers to inner and outer values and can have a genuine religious sense (cf. BAGD s.v.). As a term for God (→ 2) μακάριος is known in Greek literature (Plutarch *De Defectu Oraculorum* 420e; cf. idem, *Is.* 358e, etc.). The t.t. for the deceased, οἱ μακάριοι ("the blessed"; so Plato *Lg.* xii.947d; also papyri; cf. Deissmann, *Light* 176f.), is not yet attested in the NT; it is found in post-Constantinian Christian tomb inscriptions (G. Bertram, *TDNT* IV, 367).

In the LXX μακάριος translates esp. *'ašrê*, which is also placed first in predicate constructions. OT makarisms offer praise of a secular happiness, referring to earthly goods (Gen 30:13; 3 Kgdms 10:8; Ps 126:5 LXX; 4 Macc 18:9). These seldom point beyond the present situation; only rarely does one find a reference to a future, messianic event (so perhaps in the messianic interpretation of Isa 31:9; cf. also the vb. in Ps 71:17 LXX and Num 24:17). Numerous texts in OT and Jewish wisdom literature have a parenetic function (e.g., Prov 3:13; Sir 14:1; 25:8; 26:1; cf. Ps 40:2 LXX). The hortatory character is also not to be overlooked in the praise of piety and fear of God (Pss 1:1; 40:2 LXX; Prov 8:34; 28:14, etc.). The promise included in the makarism is strengthened through the paradoxical reference to the suffering of pious individuals (Job 5:17; Dan 12:12; Tob 13:16; 4 Macc 7:22, etc.); it is not cancelled by martyrdom, but is instead fulfilled (4 Macc 7:15; 10:15, etc.). In some instances there is the expression of a hope for eternal bliss (4 Macc 17:18; 18:19 A). It is clearly expressed in the makarisms of Jewish apocalyptic literature (e.g., *Pss. Sol.* 17:15; *1 Enoch* 58:2: "Blessed are you righteous and elect ones; for glorious will be your lot").

The NT makarism can be derived unambiguously from neither the Greco-Hellenistic nor from the OT-Jewish realm. Instead its style (→ 2) is attested both in the OT-Jewish and the Greco-Hellenistic literature. Its content is influenced through elements of both the wisdom or ethical tradition and the apocalyptic tradition. It receives its unique nature through its connection with the Christ-event; this relationship was prepared for in Jesus' preaching and was then developed by early Christian prophets and the NT authors.

4. a) In addition to the concluding beatitude about the persecuted ones (Luke 6:22f. par. Matt 5:11f.), the undisputed Q material in the Matthean Sermon on the Mount or the Lukan Sermon on the Plain comprises three makarisms (Luke 6:20 par. Matt 5:3; Luke 6:21a par. Matt 5:6; Luke 6:21b par. Matt 5:4). The differences in the parallel texts can be traced back in part to differing Q traditions (Q-Matthew or Q-Luke), hence the difference between the third person (Matthew; exception: vv. 11f.) and the second person (Luke; cf. Strecker 256). In the first three parts of the series of Q makarisms, Jesus, in dependence on the OT-Jewish tradition of piety and poverty (cf. *Pss. Sol.* 5:2; 10:6), pronounces the kingdom of God on the poor, the hungry, and the mourners (those who weep), and thus he announces a turn from their distress. While these three makarisms brought together with the Π alliteration and pithy manner of expression constitute a unit, the beatitude concerning the persecuted is much more detailed, inasmuch as it gives concrete expression to the situation of duress (persecution by the Jewish synagogue). All of these makarisms are motivated eschatologically (ὅτι final clause); they have an orientation primarily to consolation. This corresponds with the Q portrayal of Jesus as the "friend of tax collectors and sinners" (Matt 11:19).

A second group of three is transmitted in the beatitudes concerning the merciful, the pure, and the peacemakers (Matt 5:7-9). Apparently already present in Q-Matthew, it possesses a parenetic function. Corresponding in content is the beatitude concerning the meek (Matt 5:5 = Ps 36:11 LXX), which likewise might have been present in Q-Matthew to fill out the pre-Matthean number seven (vv. 3-9). Matthew has intensified this ethical accent of the tradition by the insertion of "in spirit" (v. 3: τῷ πνεύματι), so that a beatitude about the poor has become one about the humble. He has also intensified the ethical aspect with the following: the addition of "(thirsting) after righteousness" (v. 6: διψῶντες τὴν δικαιοσύνην); the redactional shaping of the makarism about those "who have been persecuted for righteousness' sake" (v. 10; cf. v. 3b and the Matthean concept of righteousness in 5:6, 20; 6:1, 33; also 3:15; 21:32); and adapting to the situation of the Church (5:11f.; redactional διώκω as t.t. for persecution, 5:10-12, 44; 10:23). According to the Matthean understanding the makarisms as the prelude to the Sermon on the Mount indicate "the entrance requirements for the kingdom of God" (Windisch 45).

Luke handles his tradition in a more conservative way. The address in the second person and the woes about the rich and those who are filled (Luke 6:24-26) are provided by the tradition. Luke affirms the social-material understanding; he actualizes it through the addition of "now" (νῦν, v. 25 bis) and thus increases not only the consoling but also the parenetic understanding (cf. Luke 6:27ff.).

b) The makarism of Matt 11:6 (third person sg.) is transmitted in literal agreement in Luke 7:23 also. With Matt 11:5 par. it already stood in a larger literary context in Q (Matt 11:2ff. par.; Bultmann, *History* 23, 126, 128). In dependence on OT texts (Isa 35:5f.; 61:1), the time of salvation is described and its expectation and fulfillment are connected with recognition of the eschatological significance of Jesus, the prophet of the end time. If the makarism refers to the situation of hearing and seeing the words and deeds of Jesus, it is at the same time oriented in a futuristic-eschatological way: The future salvation is granted to those who do not reject the claim of Jesus.

The makarism about the witness of the eyes and ears (Matt 13:16 par. Luke 10:23), as an address in the second person pl., underlines the eschatological character of the time of Jesus as the fulfillment of the prophetic expectation. While Luke (thus standing closer to the Q tradition) emphasizes the object of seeing and thus takes up the preceding revelatory saying about the authority of Jesus, Matthew, in connection with the parallel teaching of Jesus, refers to the understanding of the disciples (v. 13), whose authority for the later generations is based on this text (G. Strecker, *Der Weg der Gerechtigkeit* [³1971] 197f.).

In Matt 24:46 par. Luke 12:43 one finds the promise addressed to the faithful and clever servant rather than his counterpart. In the presence of the delay of the parousia the Church is challenged to endure in keeping the commandments. The same situation is presupposed in the double chiastic makarism of Luke 12:37f. (Q?); the implicit admonition is based on the promise that the Lord who comes will prepare the festive meal for the watchful servants. Thus the imminent and distant apocalyptic expectation forms the theological framework of the Q makarisms. Here, in accordance with the predominantly parenetic character of the logia collection, the eschatological promise of salvation and ethical admonition are closely related in view of the coming kingdom of God, which is already present in Jesus.

c) Independent of the Q tradition in the Synoptic Gospels, μακάριος is also attested in special and redactional material (cf. → 4.a). Of theological-historical significance is the makarism that Jesus expresses in response to the confession of Peter at Caesarea Philippi, in which Peter is described as the bearer of revelation (Matt 16:17). It is also disputed whether the related Semitic-sounding saying about the rock and key (vv. 18-19) was originally connected here or whether it can be traced back to Jesus (cf. Strecker, *Weg* 201f.; Kähler 236-55). Nevertheless, the makarism reflects the dominant position of Peter in the beginning period of the Christian Church.

If the "story of Jesus" narrated here provides the substantive background, this is also the case for the makarism of Luke's special material: In the Lukan prologue Mary is praised because of her faith and is assured the fulfillment of what had been promised (Luke 1:45). Luke's special material also has the (indirect) praise of the mother of Jesus, which is taken up and corrected (11:27f.) with the (originally independent) makarism about those "who hear and keep the word of God"; likewise 14:14, where the admonition of Jesus to his host is brought to an end positively-antithetically, and the promise is made to the one who gives without hope of return of repayment "at the resurrection of the dead." In contrast, 14:15 ("*Blessed is the one who* eats bread in the kingdom of God") is not handed on as a saying of Jesus and a (redactional) introduction to the parable of the great supper (for which the decisive saying is given). The beatitude about the childless (23:29) is not to be understood literally, but as describing the inevitability of the future punishment.

5. The two passages in John raise the question of a prophetic-apocalyptic movement within the Johannine circle. It is certain that both eschatological promises have a future character: 13:17, in connection with the exemplary act of the revealer at the footwashing, calls for the understanding of the disciples in putting into practice

the deed of love; such a deed is the promised eschatological salvation (cf. R. Bultmann, *John* [Eng. tr., 1971] 476n.5: ἐάν = "when in the future"). The same promise is included in 20:29, where (in the Johannine revision of the praise of the eyewitnesses in Luke 10:23 par. Matt 13:16?), in anticipation of the coming generations, faith is fundamentally contrasted to seeing.

6. With the exception of the nontheological use in 1 Cor 7:40 (→ 2), μακάριος appears in Paul only in Romans: in 4:7, 8 (bis) the scriptural proof for the thesis that Abraham was justified by faith, not by works, is derived from Ps 31:1f. LXX. Whereas the OT makarism referred to the person who had experienced forgiveness insofar as sin was not reckoned, Paul infers, contrary to the literal wording, the "reckoning" of righteousness "without works." 14:22 contrasts with v. 23a: Whereas the one who is "judged" is one who eats meat contrary to his conscience, the cry of salvation is for the one who acts without scruple in conformity with the freedom of faith (E. Käsemann, *Rom* [Eng. tr., 1980] 378f.).

7. In accordance with the character of James as a wisdom-ethical tractate, the two references are both parenetic: 1:12 takes up the LXX formula to praise (μακάριος ἀνήρ; cf. Pss 1:1; 31:2 LXX; Isa 56:2; Prov 8:34, etc.) the patient endurance of temptation (cf. vv. 2-4) and places before the one who is tested the "crown of life" (almost proverbial for the future salvation; cf. Rev 2:10). Presumably futuristic-eschatological also (instead of a logical fut.), 1:25 indicates the necessity of doing, in contrast to merely hearing, for salvation (cf. vv. 21ff.).

More concretely, 1 Pet 3:14 refers to the situation of the church that has to reckon with hostility (opt. vb. form indicates the openness of the situation). This passage, which is not fully independent of Matt 5:10 (possibly mediated by oral tradition), like the latter, connects the promise of salvation with the condition that it take place διὰ δικαιοσύνην. Thus it agrees with the (indirect) admonition in the context to make the effort to do the good and to lay aside the fear of humankind (citing Isa 8:12; cf. also Dupont III, 345ff.). The Synoptic tradition (Matt 5:11f. par. Luke 6:12f.) is also presupposed in 1 Pet 4:14: if those who are "reproached for the name of Christ" suffer persecution as Christians (v. 16), they have reason to rejoice (v. 13) in the fellowship with the suffering of Christ; through the gift of the Spirit of God they already have a portion in the eschatological salvation (v. 14b).

8. The beatitudes of Revelation all appear in the third person; they address the Church indirectly as hearers of the message of the apocalyptist: 1:3 and 22:7 present a framework in which, through the makarism, the authority of the author is confirmed for that person who "keeps the words of the prophecy of this book." The situation of the

persecuted Church is assumed. The participation in the "first resurrection" and thus the final victory over death is promised (20:6) to the martyrs. To them, along with the confessors who are "the dead, who die in the Lord," "rest from their labors" is promised (14:13; cf. v. 12). They are those who "are invited to the marriage feast of the lamb" (19:9). In contrast to the murderers and idolaters, "they wash their garments" (image for martyrdom: 7:14) and will "enter through the gates into the city" (22:14; cf. v. 15; possibly in adopting and in contrast to the formula of anathema in the Lord's Supper liturgy; so U. B. Müller, *Prophetie und Predigt im NT* [1975] 204). In these martyrological texts the motif of comfort stands in the foreground. In contrast, 16:15 gives a call for vigilance based on the imminence of the unexpected coming of the Lord (cf. 3:3; 1 Thess 5:1ff.; Matt 24:43; 2 Pet 3:10). Comfort and admonition are thus combined in the makarisms of Revelation. They stand within the literary tradition of Jewish apocalyptic, but they have been interpreted christologically in connection with the imminent expectation of Christian apocalyptic.   G. Strecker

μακαρισμός, οῦ, ὁ *makarismos* blessing, beatitude*

In the NT only in Paul: Rom 4:6, 9, in reference to the *blessing* of Ps 31:1f. LXX (cf. *1 Clem.* 50:7); Gal 4:15: ποῦ οὖν ὁ μακαρισμὸς ὑμῶν; "Where then is the *blessing*?" (i.e., "your satisfaction" in the presence of the apostle).

Μακεδονία, ας *Makedonia* Macedonia*
Μακεδών, όνος, ὁ *Makedōn* Macedonian*

Lit.: BAGD s.v. — A. VAN DEN BORN, *BL* 1115. — A. BRUNOT, "L'Évangile passe en Europe," *BTS* 138 (1972) 6-16. — P. E. DAVIES, "The Macedonian Scene of Paul's Journeys," *BA* 26 (1963) 91-106. — C. EDSON, "Macedonia," *HSCP* 51 (1940) 125-36. — W. ELLIGER, *Paulus in Griechenland* (1978), index s.v. — F. GEYER and O. HOFFMANN, PW XIV, 638-771. — O. GLOMBITZA, "Der Schritt nach Europa. Erwägungen zu Act 16,9-15," *ZNW* 53 (1962) 77-82. — U. KAHRSTEDT, "Städte in Makedonien," *Hermes* 81 (1953) 85-111. — D. KANATSOULIS, *History of Macedonia* (1964, in modern Greek). — P. LEMERLE, *Philippes et la Macédoine Orientale à l'époque chrétienne et byzantine* (Bibliothèque des écoles françaises d'Athènes et de Rome 158, 1945). — E. MEYER, I. SEIBERT, and H. SCHMOLL, *LAW* 1815-19. — G. NEUMANN and H. VOLKMANN, *KP* III, 910-19. — O. VOLK, *LTK* VI, 1314. — A. WIKENHAUSER, "Religionsgeschichtliche Parallelen zu Apg 16,9," *BZ* 23 (1935) 180-86.

1. An area of northern Greece between the mountainous border region on Illyria and the Nestos River, an important area for commercial traffic. In the seventh century B.C. the Macedonian state was formed under the leadership of kings who resided first in Edessa and then in Pella. During the Argead dynasty (which lasted until 300 B.C.) Macedonia continued to develop, and under Philip II of Macedonia (359-336 B.C.) it

became the leading power of Greece. After 293 B.C. the Antigonids were in control. Their last king, Perseus, was defeated at Pydna in 168 B.C. and taken into Roman captivity. Macedonia was divided into four independent parts. After 148 B.C. it was a Roman province. In A.D. 15-44 it was administered by the imperial legates in Moesia, and after that it became a senatorial province. Roman colonies were established in Dyrrachium, Pella, and Philippi.

2. In the NT Μακεδονία appears as a term for the Roman province 22 times (8 in Acts; 14 in the Pauline corpus). Μακεδών is used as a term for an inhabitant of this province 3 times in Acts, 2 times in 2 Corinthians. Acts 16:9f., 12 describe how a Macedonian appeared in a vision to Paul in Troas on his second missionary journey and requested that he come over. The narrative of Paul's journey and arrival in Philippi, a "city in the first region of Macedonia, a colony," is then given. Luke emphasizes the significance of this important step in missionary history with an esp. graphic description.

In Corinth Paul awaits his coworkers Silas and Timothy, who had traveled from Macedonia to meet him (Acts 18:5). From here Paul also wrote the first letter to the church in Thessalonica, in which he emphasizes that the church was a model for all churches in Macedonia (1 Thess 1:7). From them the gospel (1:8) and brotherly love (4:10) spread in Macedonia. The effectiveness of Paul's work in Macedonia during the third missionary journey is indicated in Acts 20:1-3; 2 Cor 2:13; 1 Tim 1:3; according to 2 Cor 7:5 he had to go through "fighting without and fears within." Paul's travel plans, to go again from Ephesus to Macedonia, are mentioned in Acts 19:21; 1 Cor 16:5; and 2 Cor 1:6; Acts 19:22 report that he sent his coworkers Timothy and Erastus ahead to Macedonia. Acts 19:29 mentions the Macedonians Gaius and Aristarchus among the travel companions of Paul, and according to 27:2 the Macedonian Aristarchus accompanies Paul on the trip to Rome.

Paul says in Rom 15:26 that Macedonia and Achaia have their contributions for Jerusalem ready, and he offers Macedonia's readiness to help as an example for the Corinthians. He wants not to be humiliated when he comes to them accompanied by Macedonians, but rather he wants to praise them more than the Macedonians (9:2). Paul himself accepted personal support only from the Macedonian Christians (2 Cor 11:9; Phil 4:15).   A. Weiser

Μακεδών, όνος, ὁ *Makedōn* Macedonian
→ Μακεδονία.

μάκελλον, ου, τό *makellon* market, food market*

1 Cor 10:25: πᾶν τὸ ἐν μακέλλῳ πωλούμενον ἐσθίετε. Apparently derived from a Semitic root, μάκελλον is attested in Latin inscriptions (*macellum;* see PW XIV/1,

129ff.) and appears as a rabbinic loanword (Billerbeck III, 420). It referred originally to an enclosed place and then, as with, e.g., the *macellum* in Pompeii, a covered arcade with shops along the side, a chapel for the imperial cult, and a dining hall (cf. the outline in H. Lietzmann and W. G. Kümmel, *1 Cor* [HNT] ad loc.). A Latin inscription found in Corinth mentions the *macellum* of which Paul speaks (see H. J. Cadbury, "The Macellum of Corinth," *JBL* 53 [1934] 134-41). J. Schneider, *TDNT* IV, 370-72; BAGD s.v.; H. Conzelmann, *1 Cor* (Hermeneia) ad loc. with n. 13 (bibliography); G. D. Fee, *1 Cor* (NICNT) ad loc.; → εἴδωλον 4.b.

μακράν *makran* far (away)*

Originally an acc. (ellipsis of ὁδόν; cf. BDF §161.1), μακράν is used 10 times in the NT as an adv. (only Luke 7:6 v.l. as improper prep.); 5 times in the combination μακρὰν ἀπό; of these, it is used in a spatial sense in Matt 8:30; Luke 7:6; John 21:8; Acts 17:27 of the "nearness" of God (cf. Josephus *Ant.* viii.108; Seneca *Ep.* 41:1; 120:14); with a fig. meaning, Mark 12:34 (οὐ μακρὰν εἶ ἀπὸ τῆς βασιλείας τοῦ θεοῦ); elsewhere, spatially in Luke 15:20 (μακρὰν ἀπέχω); Acts 22:21 (εἰς ἔθνη μακράν, "to the Gentiles *far away*"); correspondingly also 2:39 (ὑμῖν . . . καὶ πᾶσιν τοῖς εἰς μακράν); fig. for the Gentiles who were once *far* removed from salvation, Eph 2:13 (οἵ ποτε ὄντες μακράν, followed by ἐγενήθητε ἐγγύς); 2:17 (cf. Isa 57:19 LXX).

μακρόθεν *makrothen* from far away*

Of the 14 occurrences in the NT, 12 are connected with ἀπό, since the suffix -θεν lost its force (see BAGD s.v.; BDF §104.2f.): Matt 26:58; 27:55; Mark 5:6; 8:3; 11:13; 14:54; 15:40; Luke 16:23; 23:49; Rev 18:10, 15, 17; without prep. only Luke 18:13; 22:54; cf. Matt 26:58 v.l.; Mark 8:3 v.l.; 11:13 v.l. It occurs in clauses with ἀκολουθέω, "follow *from afar*" (Mark 14:54 par. Matt 26:58/Luke 22:54), θεωρέω, "see *from afar*" (Mark 15:40 par. Matt 27:55), ὁράω (Mark 5:6; 11:13; Luke 16:23), ἥκω (Mark 8:3, v.l. εἶναι), and ἵστημι (Luke 18:13; 23:49 [cf. Ps 37:12 LXX]; Rev 18:10, 15, 17).

μακροθυμέω *makrothymeō* have forbearance, be patient
→ μακροθυμία.

μακροθυμία, ας, ἡ *makrothymia* patience, forbearance*

μακροθυμέω *makrothymeō* have forbearance, be patient*

μακροθύμως *makrothymōs* patiently*

1. Occurrences in the NT — 2. Meaning — 3. NT usage — 4. Luke 18:7

Lit.: U. FALKENROTH, W. MUNDLE, and C. BROWN, *DNTT* II, 764-76. — J. HORST, *TDNT* IV, 374-87. — H. LJUNGVIK, "Zur Erklärung einer Lk-Stelle (Luk. XVIII.7)," *NTS* 10 (1963/64) 289-94. — F. MUSSNER, *Jas* (HTKNT, 1964) 199-207. — W. OTT, *Gebet und Heil* (SANT 12, 1965) 44-59. — H. RIESENFELD, "Zu μακροθυμεῖν (Lk 18,7)," FS Schmid (1963) 214-17. — H. SAHLIN, *Zwei Lukas-Stellen* (SBU 4, 1945) 9-20, esp. 14-18. — A. STROBEL, *Untersuchungen zum eschatologischen Verzögerungsproblem* (NovTSup 2, 1961) 90-92, 129, 254-64. — A. WIFSTRAND, "Lukas XVIII.7," *NTS* 11 (1964/65) 72-74. — For further bibliography see *TWNT* X, 1168.

1. The vb. appears in the NT 10 times, the noun 14 times, and the adv. once. It is noteworthy that only the vb. is found in the Gospels (Matt 18:26, 29; Luke 18:7), that neither word appears in the Johannine literature, and that the adj. μακρόθυμος, which appears relatively frequently in the LXX, is not used in the NT.

2. In (secular) Greek literature μακροθυμία κτλ., unlike other compounds of → θυμός, is attested late and is rare. The noun means *patience, expectation, endurance, perseverance,* and the vb. means *have patience, persevere.* It always involves a human character trait but is not directed toward another human being.

In the LXX μακροθυμία κτλ. appears relatively often. The Hebrew expression that stands behind it in most instances is *'erek 'appayim,* "the delay of [the outbreak of] wrath." It is esp. a characteristic of God, closely associated with his mercy (ἔλεος, etc.). Μακροθυμία κτλ. designates esp. the *forbearance* of God with humankind, particularly toward sinners, on whom he does not pour his wrath but instead forgives and saves them, though only if they repent. In the wisdom literature μακροθυμία κτλ. also refers to one's relationship to others: the good and the wise do not quickly let their wrath come forth. Here the secular meaning *patience, perseverance* also appears.

In early Judaism this variety of meanings is also found. It is noteworthy that μακροθυμία κτλ. does not appear in Philo; Josephus uses it only in its secular meaning.

3. In the NT μακροθυμία κτλ. is both an attribute of God (and Jesus) and a characteristic of the Christian. Here there is a dependence in part on the OT and early Jewish use of this word. God's μακροθυμία refers also here to his *forbearance.* However, it is esp. the characteristic of an interim period in which God holds back his wrath in order to give people the opportunity to repent, to avoid the wrath of God, and to receive salvation. This motif is derived from early Judaism, of which traces are found already in the LXX (see Sir 5:4; 4 Ezra 7:74; *2 Bar.* 21:20; 59:6; cf. *Ep. Arist.* 188). In this sense it is found in Rom 2:4: *forbearance* is parallel to the "kindness" (χρηστότης) and the "patience" (ἀνοχή) of God (see also, e.g., Wis 15:1; Clement of Alexandria *Strom.* iii.3). Rom 9:22 is similar, though here the motif of repentance does not appear. According to 1 Pet 3:20 God waited patiently before the flood (cf. *1 Enoch* 66; *m. 'Abot* 5:2; cf.

Irenaeus *Haer.* i.10.3); according to 2 Pet 3:9, 15 God's judgment is delayed because God is forbearing and wants people to repent and be without sin and thus be saved (cf. Ign. *Eph.* 11:1; Hippolytus *Commentarius in Dan.* iv.22.1f.). The original OT meaning of μακροθυμία (thus connected with God's mercy: forgiveness and salvation after repentance) is present in 1 Tim 1:16 (cf. ἠλεήθην), but here Jesus Christ is the subject of the forbearance.

The person as subj. of μακροθυμία κτλ. is present in the parable of the unmerciful servant: Because the debtors can not repay their debts, they ask their creditors for *patience*, i.e., they ask them not to punish them immediately, but to extend to them time in order that they may repay it (Matt 18:26, 29; cf. *T. Job* 11:10).

Μακροθυμία is a typical attribute of the Christian: the control of the wrath that easily boils over. Thus the word is found (often with χρηστότης, πραΰτης, and ἀγάπη, and sometimes ὑπομονή) in the catalogs of virtues and in other series of Christian virtues (2 Cor 6:6; Gal 5:22; Eph 4:2; Col 1:11; 3:12; 1 Thess 5:14; 2 Tim 3:10). In addition, the proclamation of the gospel must occur "in *forbearance* and patience" (2 Tim 4:2). In the epigrammatic poem about the value of love, forbearance is not omitted (1 Cor 13:4; see also *1 Clem.* 49:5).

Μακροθυμία κτλ. is found with a secular meaning in Heb 6:12, 15; Jas 5:7 (bis), 8, 10. According to Hebrews the faithful should be patient in awaiting the future promises of God, just as Abraham was. Jas 5:7 refers to the imminent parousia and admonishes the brethren to wait, as the farmer does (cf. Origen *De Principiis* iii.1.14), to be always patient, and to have endurance, just as once Job (cf. ὑπομονή, v. 11) and the prophets persevered (for μακροθυμία—κακοπαθία, see also Josephus *B.J.* vi.37; cf. 2 Tim 4:2, 5).

The secular meaning (μακροθύμως, *patiently*) is present also in Acts 26:3 (cf. *Ps.-Clem. Hom.* iv.8.6).

4. Luke 18:7 (cf. *Ps.-Clem. Hom.* xvii.5.4) thus must, in all likelihood, be rendered as follows: "Will God not vindicate his elect, who cry to him day and night, as he *endures* [in reference to them; thus: remains immovable]?" Like the unjust judge, God will, as a consequence of the persistent entreaties of his elect, no longer remain unmoved, and he will vindicate them (and, indeed, "quickly," ἐν τάχει, v. 8; τάχος stands here in contrast to μακροθυμεῖν; see also Sir 5:11). For a similar meaning of μακροθυμία, "patience of God," cf. Sir 35:19; Chrysostom *Hom. in Matt.* 28:1.

                                        H. W. Hollander

μακροθύμως *makrothymōs* patiently
→ μακροθυμία.

μακρός, 3 *makros* distant, far, long*

Adj. in the expression εἰς χώραν μακράν (Luke 15:13; 19:12); neut. pl. as adv. in μακρὰ προσευχόμενοι, "praying *for a long time*, in a long-winded way" (Mark 12:40 par. Luke 20:47/Matt 23:14 TR).

μακροχρόνιος, 2 *makrochronios* long-lived*

Eph 6:3 (citing Exod 10:12; Deut 5:16 LXX): "so that you may *live long* on the earth."

μαλακία, ας, ἡ *malakia* feebleness, weakness, malady*

Only in Matthew in the expression πᾶσαν νόσον καὶ πᾶσαν μαλακίαν, "every sickness and every *infirmity*" (4:23; 9:35; 10:1; cf. Deut 7:15; 28:61; ÄgU 954, 12).

μαλακός *malakos* soft, gentle*

Of the 4 occurrences in the NT, 3 refer to people of high station "who are clothed in *soft* clothing": ἐν μαλακοῖς (ἱματίοις: Luke) ἠμφιεσμένον (Matt 11:8a par. Luke 7:25); οἱ τὰ μαλακὰ φοροῦντες (Matt 11:8b; cf. *Gos. Thom.* 78). According to the saying of Jesus, John the Baptist is distinguished from such people, for he is clothed as an ascetic prophet of the desert (cf. also Mark 1:6 par. Matt 3:4; Heb 11:37; Rev 11:3; see O. Böcher, *Christus Exorcista* [BWANT 96, 1972] 109f.; G. Schneider, *Luke* [ÖTK] ad loc. [bibliography]). The vice catalog of 1 Cor 6:9 mentions the μαλακοί, *soft people/weaklings*, as reprehensible examples of passive homosexuality (cf. Rom 1:27; Lev 20:13; *Ep. Arist.* 152; *Sib. Or.* 3:184ff., 584ff.; see Billerbeck III, 70; H. Conzelmann, *1 Cor* [Hermeneia] ad loc. [bibliography]).

Μαλελεήλ *Maleleēl* Mahalalel*

The name of the son of Kenan (Heb. *maḥalal'ēl*, Gen 5:12) in the genealogy of Jesus (Luke 3:37).

μάλιστα *malista* most of all, mostly, especially, above all*

There are 12 occurrences in the NT (none in the Gospels): Acts 20:38; 25:26; 26:3; Gal 6:10; Phil 4:22; 1 Tim 4:10; 5:8, 17; 2 Tim 4:13; Titus 1:10; Phlm 16 (μάλιστα . . . , πόσῳ δὲ μᾶλλον; → μᾶλλον 3.a); 2 Pet 2:10; see BDF §60.3.

μᾶλλον *mallon* (even) more, rather, more than ever

1. Occurrences in the NT — 2. Meaning — 3. Μᾶλλον in argumentation and stylistic images

Lit.: BAGD s.v. — L. RYDBECK, *Fachprosa, vermeintliche Volkssprache und NT* (1967) 80-85. — M. WOLTER, *Rechtfertigung und zukünftiges Heil* (BZNW 43, 1978) 177-80 (bibliography).

1. Μᾶλλον is the comparative of the adv. μάλα (which

does not appear in the NT), and it occurs 81 times in the NT. The meaning is determined by its semantic location.

2. a) In direct comparison (with ἤ or gen. of comparison): *more than:* Matt 18:13; Acts 4:19; 5:29 ("one must obey God *rather than* man"; both Acts passages reflect Plato *Ap.* 29d; cf. also Appian *Rom. Hist.* xxvi.101); 27:11. Whether μᾶλλον here or in John 3:19; 12:43; Acts 20:35 (→ c); 1 Tim 1:4; 2 Tim 3:4; Heb 11:25 has an exclusive or only a comparative meaning (cf. BDF §246) is determined not by μᾶλλον but by the respective antitheses (cf. 4 Macc 15:3 with 16:24).

b) Absolute (in indirect comparison): *even more* (than before, than others): Mark 10:48 par. Luke 18:39; Luke 5:15; John 5:18; 19:8; Acts 5:14; 9:22; 2 Cor 7:7; Phil 1:12; 2:12; 3:4; Heb 10:25; 2 Pet 1:10; Phil 1:9 (μᾶλλον καὶ μᾶλλον, *more and more*); 1 Thess 4:1, 10 in connection with → περισσεύω (4) (cf. also Mark 7:36; Rom 5:15, 17; 2 Cor 3:9; 7:13); also 1 Cor 9:12 (rhetorical question).

c) In connection with an adj. it marks the comparative: καλὸν . . . μᾶλλον, *better* (Mark 9:42; 1 Cor 9:15; also Acts 20:35: μακάριόν ἐστιν μᾶλλον διδόναι ἢ λαμβάνειν; cf. Thucydides ii.97.4; see E. Haenchen, *Acts* [Eng. tr., 1971] 594n.5; BDF §245a); *more necessary* (1 Cor 12:22); *more numerous* (Gal 4:27). As a strengthening of the comparative (Rydbeck) it means *many* (Phil 1:23; Mark 7:36; 2 Cor 7:13; see also Matt 6:26; → διαφέρω [3.a]).

d) In correspondence with a previously mentioned or only implied negation it can mean *rather* (Matt 27:24; Mark 5:26 [cf. Job 30:26 LXX]; 15:11; 2 Cor 5:8; 12:9; Phlm 9); → 3.c.

3. a) Πολλῷ (πόσῳ) μᾶλλον is the distinguishing sign of the conclusion of the argument *a maiori (minori) ad minus (maius)*, as it was called in ancient rhetoric. The rabbis call it *qal wāḥōmer* ("light and heavy"; Billerbeck III, 223ff.; C. G. Wilke, *Die neutestamentliche Rhetorik* [1843] 315; H. Lausberg, *Handbuch der literarischen Rhetorik* [²1973] §§396f.; Wolter). It involves a two-part a fortiori argument: from a difficult (improbable) premise, normally in the form of a real conditional clause (εἰ), a lighter and thus more probable conclusion is drawn from a higher level of evidence: if . . . , *how much more, more than ever* (Matt 6:30 par.; 7:11; 10:25; Luke 12:24; Phlm 16; Heb 9:14; 12:9 [in question form], 25); → πολύς 3.a.

This argumentation has theological relevance for Paul, who uses it in a salvation-history/typological framework (Rom 5:15, 17; 2 Cor 3:7f., 9, 11) in reference to God's activity in election (Rom 11:12, 24) and salvation (Rom 5:9f.).

b) Μᾶλλον δέ is used as a corrective, to make a saying more precise (*or rather*): Rom 8:34; 1 Cor 14:1, 5; Gal 4:9 (cf. Lausberg §§784-86).

c) Antithetically structured statements are related: The conduct that is advised is emphasized by μᾶλλον (*rather, instead of,* with imv.) in contrast to that which is rejected (Matt 10:6, 28; 25:9; Rom 14:13; Eph 4:28; 5:4, 11; 1 Tim 6:2; Heb 12:13; also 2 Cor 2:7, intensification of τοὐναντίον). A stylistic alteration is the form of the antithesis with the help of a negating (οὐ[χὶ] μᾶλλον) and thus affirming question ("not *rather?*"): 1 Cor 5:2; 6:7; Heb 12:9.

d) 1 Cor 7:21 is problematic (cf. P. Trummer, "Die Chance der Freiheit," *Bib* 56 [1975] 344-68): either "*rather* make use of it" (of the possibility of freedom; μᾶλλον then corresponds to μή σοι μελέτω), or "*rather* remain in it" (in slavery; μᾶλλον then reflects on ἀλλ' εἰ καὶ δύνασαι ἐλεύθερος γενέσθαι; → χράομαι).

M. Wolter

Μάλχος, ου *Malchos* Malchus*

The name (Greek/Latin form of Heb. *meleḵ*, frequent name of non-Jews in Nabatean inscriptions and in Josephus) of a slave of the high priest, whose right ear Simon Peter cut off (John 18:10; cf. without the name Mark 14:47 par.). BAGD s.v. (bibliography); *BL* 1087; R. Schnackenburg, *John* III (Eng. tr., 1982) ad loc.

μάμμη, ης, ἡ *mammē* grandmother*

In 2 Tim 1:5 Lois, the *grandmother* of Timothy, is mentioned along with Eunice, his mother, because of her unhypocritical faith; → Εὐνίκη.

μαμωνᾶς, ᾶ, ὁ *mamōnas* possession, wealth, property*

Lit.: BILLERBECK I, 434f. — *BL* 1088. — F. HAUCK, *TDNT* IV, 388-90. — W. NAUCK, *BHH* 1135. — H. P. RÜGER, *ZNW* 64 (1973) 127-31. — *idem*, *TRE* III, 607. — G. SCHNEIDER, *Luke* (ÖTK) ad loc. — For further bibliography see BAGD s.v.; *TWNT* X, 1168.

In the NT only in the words of Jesus: Matt 6:24 par. Luke 16:13 (οὐ δύνασθε θεῷ δουλεύειν καὶ μαμωνᾷ); Luke 16:9 (μαμωνᾶς τῆς ἀδικίας); 16:11 (ὁ ἄδικος μαμωνᾶς; cf. also 2 Clem. 6:1; Aram. *māmôn/māmônā'*; TR μαμμωνᾶς). The origin of the word is uncertain. Perhaps a connection exists with Heb. *'āman*, "be reliable," which does not appear in the Hebrew canon, but does occur in Sir 31:8; CD 14:20; 1QS 6:2 (probably also to be assumed in *1 Enoch* 63:10) and frequently in the Mishnah, Talmud, and Targums (cf. *m. 'Abot* 2:12; *m. Sanh.* 1:1; *b. Qidd.* 70a). *Māmôn* is frequently associated with dishonest acquisition and deceitful gain and is thus condemned (*māmôn dišqar*, etc., = μαμωνᾶς ἄδικος or τῆς ἀδικίας; cf. also Billerbeck II, 220; Jastrow, *Dictionary* II, 794; F. Hauck, *TDNT* IV, 388-90; see also Sir 5:8; 26:29–27:3).

Ὁ μαμωνᾶς appears in Q (Matt 6:24/Luke 16:13) personified as a power that comes into competition with God's claim on humankind. Along with the Jewish (apocalyptic) piety associated with poverty, Jesus rejects securing one's life through possessions and property, inasmuch as it would be an attempt to secure one's life by submitting to a false lord. Luke has probably brought together the Q logion with the two additional sayings in 16:9, 11 (apparently likewise present in the tradition) as an interpretation of the parable of the unjust steward (16:1-8). Thus v. 9 (perhaps in direct association with the parable) aims at making God one's "friend" in heaven through the "unrighteous mammon" in one's own life (through voluntary distribution of one's own wealth), while v. 11 calls literally for reliability itself in the realm of "unrighteous *possessions.*" In the present context, however, it warns disciples against failure in demonstrating the necessary eschatological insight (of the voluntary distribution of one's own possessions). One may scarcely regard ἐκ τοῦ μαμωνᾶ as a rendering of Aram. *mimmā-mônā'* ("make for yourselves friends rather than unrighteous mammon"; *contra* P. Colella, *ZNW* 64 [1973] 124-26).

H. Balz

Μαναήν *Manaēn* Manaen*

Acts 13:1: The name of a prophet and teacher (cf. Heb. *mᵉnaḥem;* cf. also 4 Kgdms 15:14; Josephus *Ant.* xv.373ff.) of the church at Antioch, who is described more precisely as σύντροφος ("confidant," often used of boys raised as companions of princes) of Herod the Tetrarch, thus educated with the monarch and perhaps provided a special position at the court; the honorific title remained with the adult. On the connection with Josephus *Ant.* xv.373ff., see E. Haenchen, *Acts* (Eng. tr., 1971) ad loc. A connection with John 4:46ff. cannot be proven. *BL* 1088; W. Bieder, *BHH* 1136.

Μαννασσῆς, ἡ *Manassēs* Manasseh*

The name (Heb. *mᵉnaššeh*) of: (a) the firstborn son of Joseph (Gen 41:51) and ancestor of one of the twelve tribes of Israel (Rev 7:6), (b) the son of King Hezekiah ('Εζεκίας; cf. 4 Kgdms 18:1) and father of Amos ('Αμώς, Matt 1:10; cf., however, 'Αμών, 4 Kgdms 21:18) in the genealogy of Jesus (Matt 1:10 bis; cf. Luke 3:23ff. D). *BL* 1090; J. A. Soggin, *BHH* 1136f.

μανθάνω *manthanō* learn

1. Occurrences in the NT — 2. Meaning — 3. Usage — 4. Theological significance

Lit.: E. JENNI, *THAT* I, 872-75. — E. KÄSEMANN, "Ministry and Community in the NT," *idem, Essays on NT Themes* (1968) 63-94. — H.-W. KUHN, "Nachfolge nach Ostern," FS Bornkamm 105-32. — E. LOHSE, *RGG* III, 1179. — U. LUZ, "Erwägungen zur Entstehung des 'Frühkatholizismus,'" *ZNW* 65 (1974) 88-111. — D. MÜLLER, *DNTT* I, 480-94. — K. H. RENGSTORF, *TDNT* IV, 390-461. — A. SEEBERG, *Der Katechismus der Urchristenheit* (1903 = 1966), esp. 211ff. — G. THEISSEN, *Sociology of Early Palestinian Christianity* (1978) 7ff. — For further bibliography see *TWNT* X, 1168.

1. Μανθάνω appears 25 times in the NT, 6 of which are in the Gospels, once in Acts, 7 in the Pauline Epistles, 9 in the deutero-Pauline letters (including Colossians, Ephesians), once in Hebrews, and once in Revelation. The distribution of μανθάνω in the NT is very different from μαθητεύω and μαθητής.

2. Μανθάνω (attested since the time of Homer; cf. Indo-European *mendh-,* "become acquainted, come to know"; see Frisk II, 170f.) means *learn.* Thus it is good to survey the NT passages, including the problematic ones (it means *come to know, discover* only in Acts 23:27).

3. Special syntactic relationships: Expression of origin or source with ἀπό, ἐν, παρά; expression of obj. with dir. (acc.) obj., ὅτι clause, inf. construction, participial construction (1 Tim 5:13: partc. in nom. as already in classical Greek, ἀργαί predicative with μανθάνω, second part of the verse constructed analogously), indirect question (Matt 9:13); absolute use or indirect or (partially) implied obj. (e.g., 1 Cor 14:31; Matt 9:13; 11:29). Examples of related ideas or words used in close connection: ἀκολουθέω (Matt 9:13), ἀκούω, γινώσκω κτλ., διδάσκω/διδαχή, οἶδα, ἐπερωτάω, παραλαμβάνω.

4. a) While a general secular use (on the ancient world, see Rengstorf) has no special significance (but see Acts 23:27), μανθάνω is important for the life of the Christian: an ethical and consoling use (1 Cor 14:31) is to be noted. All the usages have a significant basis in soteriology. According to Heb 5:8 even Christ *learns.*

b) Heb 5:8f. refers to Christ for consolation as an example and soteriologically as savior on the basis of his obedience. The passage compresses the consoling-eschatological perspective of Hebrews. Paul refers to the doctrine of justification only in Gal 3:2. Of course, Paul here raises the question in an ironical and critical way in order that the Galatians might *learn* (not "come to know") the Christian life. Elsewhere Paul's characteristic soteriology is expressed more indirectly (Rom 16:17; Phil 4:9). In Rev 14:3 the reference is to the song of the 144,000 who have been sealed (cf. on the content 19:1ff.), which only they can *learn* (i.e., probably "learn to sing," not "hear, understand," etc.). The sealing is documented in their ability to learn to sing. According to 2 Tim 3:7 there is a *learning* that never can come to a knowledge of the truth.

c) In the Jesus tradition of the four Gospels we encounter a similar structure in John 6:45 (Johannine interpretation of Isa 54:13). The connection between hearing and learning is to be seen in the contrast that faith has to seeing. In Matt 9:13 μανθάνω appears to be redactional. Like Hos 6:6, the reference is probably not to a divine but to a human mercy (cf. Matt 12:7; 23:23). Thus Matthew could (despite soteriological tensions in the context) give his church instruction with a view toward fulfilling the law (cf. the "better righteousness," 5:20). Thus μανθάνω appears (cf. Billerbeck I, 499) to refer back to a catechetical tradition of Matthew. In Matt 11:29 we again encounter Matthew's special material (cf. Kuhn 114n.53) or the Q tradition. This is the entire framework of 11:28-30 (cf. *Gos. Thom.* 90), a saying addressed by Jesus to those who are exhausted and burdened. The soteriological function of Jesus and the conduct that follows it are again thematic—cf. (possibly transparent) relationships to some of the beatitudes (Q), the Passion and cross of Jesus (Matt 10:38 Q; Mark 8:34 par.), the resurrection of Jesus (cf. also Mark 13:13 par.), the burden of the way of righteousness (Bultmann, *History* 159f., 163). Of course, Jesus indeed turned to "those who labored and were burdened"; he indicated his consciousness of (eschatological) suffering, and he gave instruction (in part, as teacher)—but did he do so in the dimensions expressed by this saying? Mark 13:28 par. Matt 24:32 (Luke without μανθάνω perhaps makes a narrower catechetical distinction) is perhaps redactional. However, earlier traditional material may be present in the parable (from the mouth of Jesus? Bultmann, *History* 123, 173, is critical; Jeremias, *Parables* 119-20, is favorable).

Here, in the use of μανθάνω in the Gospels, the post-Easter perspective predominates, at least in part with a possible basis in the teaching of Jesus, and brings the idea of discipleship into view (cf. the problems: is Jesus' call to individuals, in analogy to the rabbinate, charismatic-eschatological?; on the limits of μανθάνω in relation to ἀκολουθέω see Rengstorf 406). Thus, as Kuhn shows, new perspectives result here in understanding the problem of discontinuity and continuity, in view of Theissen's thesis about the wandering charismatics.

d) Religio-sociological usage becomes esp. important in the catechetical practice of early Christianity (for the Qumran community, cf. 1QS 3:13; 9:13). Here we find a *learning,* in a catechetical sense, upon entry into Christianity, commonly in reference to specific teachers (1 Cor 4:6; 2 Tim 3:7) or teaching derived from them. Arcane disciplines and ideas of revelation are not esp. emphasized. Particularly significant is *learning* on the part of women (Paul and the Pastorals), which distinguishes Gentile from Jewish Christianity (Titus 3:14; cf. Gal 3:2).

After earlier scholarship had emphasized a unified early Christian catechism (Seeberg), the development toward an "early Catholicism" entered the discussion (cf. Käsemann 85f.; Luz). Development of Church order and teaching had undoubtedly become important (Bultmann, *Theology* II, 95ff.). It is noteworthy, then, that on the one hand μανθάνω outside the Gospels refers esp. to the catechetical dimension and reflects developments that were taking place and, on the other hand, that the vb. does not appear at all in the Catholic Epistles, that it was maintained in the Jesus tradition, and that still in the Pastoral Epistles it is not narrowed down to a teaching system.

e) In hermeneutical terms, μανθάνω consistently has an intellectual focus in the various sources and themes: e.g., instruction about a doctrine (Rom 16:17), a parable (Mark 13:28), reference to Scripture (cf. 1 Cor 4:6), prophecy in the congregation (1 Cor 14:31). The *learning,* however, includes also the conduct of one's life (Matt 11:29; Phil 4:9, 11).

G. Nebe

μανία, ας, ἡ *mania* frenzy, madness*

The common expression εἰς μανίαν περιτρέπει (Acts 26:24, parallel to the twofold μαίνομαι, vv. 24f.; cf. Lucian *Abd.* 30) is scarcely to be interpreted in the sense of prophetic rapture (cf. LSJ s.v.), but is to be understood in a negative sense: "drive one out of one's senses" (contrasted with ἀλήθεια, σωφροσύνη, v. 25; cf. also Hos 8:7f.; Ps 39:5 LXX; *Sib. Or.* 1:171f.). The Roman (in contrast to the Jew Agrippa II) had no point of access to the truth of the Pauline message; → μαίνομαι.

μάννα, τό *manna* manna*

Μάννα (Heb. *mān,* Arabic *mann,* LXX μάν, Exod 16:35, elsewhere μάννα) appears in the NT 4 times: John 6:31, 49, of the manna in the wilderness for the fathers (cf. Exod 16:4ff.; described as "bread from heaven," v. 31; see Ps 77:24 LXX), as an antitype to "the true bread from heaven" (John 6:32f., 41, 50f., 58; cf. also vv. 35, 48; 1 Cor 10:3; Billerbeck II, 481f.); Heb 9:4, of the manna preserved in a golden urn (see Exod 16:32ff.; *t. Yoma* 3:7; cf. 1 Kgs 8:9); Rev 2:17: τὸ μάννα τὸ κεκρυμμένον as eschatological (heavenly) food of God for "those who overcome" (cf. *2 Bar.* 29:8; analogous to "the water of life," Rev 7:17; 21:6; 22:1, 17; probably in connection with the Jewish tradition of the saving and preservation [on the earth] of the objects of the most holy place from the destruction of Jerusalem until the eschaton; cf. 2 Macc 2:4ff.; *2 Bar.* 6:6ff.; see also Billerbeck III, 793f.).

Manna is a sweet secretion of the manna tamarisk, which is produced by scale insects and then falls to the ground in small bright balls and which is still gathered in the Sinai region. See *BL* 1090f.; F. S. Bodenheimer, *BA* 10 (1947) 2-6; P. Borgen, *Bread from Heaven* (NovTSup 10, 1965); E. Jenni, *BHH* 1141-43; R. Meyer, *TDNT* IV, 462-66; BAGD s.v. (bibliography); *TWNT* X, 1169 (bibliography).

μαντεύομαι *manteuomai* predict, foretell*

Acts 16:16, of a Gentile slave girl (μαντευομένη) who is possessed by a demon (πνεῦμα πύθων, v. 16a, a ventriloquist?); cf. 1 Kgdms 28:8; Josephus *Ap.* i.306.

μαραίνομαι *marainomai* (pass.) be extinguished, wither, wilt*

Jas 1:11 of the rich, who (like flowers of the meadow) *fade away* in their pursuits (μαρανθήσεται); cf. Job 15:30; Josephus *Ant.* xi.56. Spicq, *Notes* II, 531.

μαρανα θα *marana tha* Our Lord, come!*

Lit.: M. BLACK, "The Maranatha Invocation and Jude 14, 15 (1 Enoch 1:9)," FS Moule 189-96. — G. BORNKAMM, "The Anathema in the Early Christian Lord's Supper Liturgy," *idem, Early Christian Experience* (1969) 169-76, 178f. — H. CONZELMANN, *1 Cor* (Hermeneia) 300f. — O. CULLMANN, *The Christology of the NT* (²1963) 208-15. — HAHN, *Titles* 93-99. — G. KLEIN, *RGG* IV, 732f. — K. G. KUHN, *TDNT* IV, 466-74. — P.-É. LANGEVIN, *Jésus Seigneur et l'eschatologie* (1967) 168-298. — C. F. D. MOULE, "A Reconsideration of the Context of *maranatha*," *NTS* 6 (1959/60) 307-10. — J. A. T. ROBINSON, "Traces of a Liturgical Sequence in 1 Cor. 16,20-24," *JTS* 4 (1953) 38-41. — H. P. RÜGER, "Zum Problem der Sprache Jesu," *ZNW* 59 (1968) 113-22, esp. 120f. — *idem, TRE* III, 607. — B. SANDVIK, *Das Kommen des Herrn beim Abendmahl im NT* (1970) 13-36. — J. SCHMID, *LTK* VI, 1370. — For further bibliography see *TWNT* X, 1169.

1. The transliterated form μαρανα θα or μαρὰν ἀθά (thus D² L al lat) is found in the NT only in 1 Cor 16:22, within the context of the conclusion of the letter: "If anyone does not love the Lord, let him be accursed (ἤτω → ἀνάθεμα), *marana tha*." Then follows the wish: "the grace of the Lord Jesus be with you!" (v. 23). Μαρανα θα appears also in *Did.* 10:6 in the eucharistic prayer: "Let grace come and may this world pass away! Hosanna to the God [v.l. son] of David! If anyone is holy, let him come; if not, let him repent! μαρὰν ἀθά [or μαραναθά]. Amen."

The basis of μαρανα θα is either Aram. *māran(a') 'ᵃtā'*, "our Lord has come," or *māran(a') ('ᵉ)tā'*, "our Lord, come!" Both *māran* and *māranā'* are attested (Rüger, *TRE*). The decision between the two possibilities is difficult. Like the imv. *'ᵉtā'*, "come!" (also *tā'*), the pf. *'ᵃtā'*, "he has come," is attested. Inasmuch as one may see in the "(amen) come, Lord Jesus!" in Rev 22:20b the "translation" of the Aramaic cry, the imperatival reading of μαρανα θα (Our Lord, come!) is preferable.

2. The interpretation of the prayer must be based on the assumption that it involves a cry (in worship?) for the coming of the Lord at the parousia (so, e.g., Hahn 109; Langevin 206-8; C. K. Barrett, *1 Cor* [HNTC] 397f.); cf. Rev 22:20b; 1 Cor 11:26 (as allusion to the cry, → κύριος

8; see Hahn 97); 1 Thess 1:10. *Did.* 10:6 appears to intend to say (as a warning to those who are not holy): The Lord has come (or: is coming). The interpretation of the cry in terms of an invitation of the Lord to the meal (cf. Cullmann 212: "The people call upon the risen Christ to appear again at the table as he did on Easter Sunday, and thus to ensure his early final return"; similarly Sandvik) is less probable for 1 Cor 16:22 and Rev 22:20b. That μαρανα θα can be understood "in its tradition history as a continuation of the request in Matt 10:6a," which appears "to know already the delay of the parousia" (Klein), is a conclusion for which there is not sufficient evidence.

G. Schneider

μαργαρίτης, ου, ὁ *margarítēs* pearl*

Lit.: E. BURROWS, "The Pearl in the Apocalypse," *JTS* 43 (1942) 177-79. — J. DUPONT, "Les Paraboles du Trésor et de la Perle," *NTS* 14 (1967/68) 408-18. — O. GLOMBITZA, "Der Perlenkaufmann," *NTS* 7 (1960/61) 153-61. — F. HAUCK, *TDNT* IV, 472-73. — W. KRENKEL, *KP* III, 1020f. — H. KAHANE and R. KAHANE, "Pearls Before Swine? A Reinterpretation of Mt 7,6," *Traditio* 13 (1957) 421-24. — H. ROMMEL, PW XIV, 1682-1702. — R. SCHIPPERS, "The Mashal-Character of the Parable of the Pearl," *SE* II (1964) 236-41. — For further bibliography see Rommel; *TWNT* X, 1169.

1. Highly treasured in India, Mesopotamia, and Persia from earliest times, the pearl became known to the region of the Mediterranean through the conquests of Alexander the Great; see Rommel 1685ff. (Ancient Egypt and the OT know nothing of it, and Greek possesses no term for it: τὸ μάργαρον or ὁ μαργαρίτης [λίθος] is derived directly or indirectly from the ancient Indic; cf. J. B. Hofmann, *Etymologisches Wörterbuch des Griechischen* [reprint, 1950] 190.) Then, however, it quickly became for the Hellenistic-Roman world the epitome of what is valuable: *principium ergo columenque omnium rerum pretii margaritae tenent* (Pliny *HN* ix.106). Some texts refer to wasteful luxury with respect to pearls—esp. in adornment of the body or apparel; stories were widespread about the enormous value of single pearls (Suetonius *Caes.* i.50; Pliny *HN* ix.117, 119ff.; Seneca *De Beneficiis* vii.9.4).

2. In the NT pearls are mentioned 9 times: 3 times in Matthew, once in 1 Timothy, and 5 times in Revelation. The NT also describes them as extremely valuable. In Rev 18:12f. they appear in a catalog of choice merchandise (this passage is dependent on Ezek 27). *Pearls* are mentioned among the expensive jewelry of the "harlot" (idolater) Babylon (Rome) in Rev 17:4; 18:16 (cf. the OT statements against those who are so adorned in Isa 3; Ezek 28) and among things that Christian women at worship should reject because they are only an outward affectation (so 1 Tim 2:9; probably in the source: in general, see M. Dibelius and H. Conzelmann, *Pastoral Epistles* [Hermeneia] 45-46). The extraordinary splendor of the heavenly Jerusalem described in Revelation 21 is to be seen, e.g., in the twelve gates, each of which consists

of a giant *pearl* (not merely mother of pearl: see Burrows; v. 21 bis).

Wherever the point lies in the parable of the pearl (Matt 13:45f.; cf. *Gos. Thom.* 76)—in the joy of the discoverer (Jeremias, *Parables* 198f.) or in the decisive use of the unique opportunity (E. Linnemann, *Jesus of the Parables* [1966] 99ff.; cf. Dupont 413ff.)—for the parable (Schippers: a riddle like 2 Sam 12:1ff., based on a context corresponding to Mark 10:17ff.) the conviction of the preciousness of the pearl is as central here as is the difficult expression in 7:6 (perhaps based on a Parthian proverb; see G. Widengren, *Iranisch-semitische Kulturbegegnung* [1960] 36f.). *Did.* 9:5 interprets the pearl as the eucharist (cf. Kahane); E. Klostermann, *Matt*[3] (HNT) 66f., interprets it as the gospel; similarly, W. Grundmann, *Matt* (THKNT) 222.

                         E. Plümacher

Μάρθα, ας   *Martha*   Martha*

Lit.: J. A. BAILEY, *The Traditions Common to the Gospels of Luke and John* (NovTSup 7, 1963) 1-8. — BDF §53.3. — J. BRUTSCHECK, *Die Maria-Marta-Erzählung. Eine redaktionskritische Untersuchung zu Lk 10,38-42* (BBB 64, 1986). — E. LALAND, "Die Martha-Maria-Perikope Lukas 10,38-42," *ST* 13 (1949) 70-85. — W. MAGASS, "Maria und Martha," *LingBibl* 27/28 (1973) 2-5. — J. MICHL, *LTK* VII, 111. — G. RINALDI, "Marta," *BeO* 5 (1963) 123-26. — H. P. RÜGER, *TRE* III, 608. — G. SCHNEIDER, *Luke* (ÖTK, 1977) 251-53.

The fem. personal name Μάρθα is a transliteration of Aram. *mār^e̲tā'*, "lady, mistress" (ÄgU IV, 1153, i.3; 1155, 4; *CIJ* II, 1219, 1311; further references in Rüger). In the NT Martha is the name of the sister of Mary (→ Μαρία 6) and (according to John) of Lazarus in Bethany. Luke 10:38, 40f. characterizes her as an industrious, anxious mistress of the house (*she* receives Jesus in her house: v. 39), who serves Jesus when he visits (v. 40; so also John 12:2). She criticizes Mary, who sits at Jesus' feet listening to him (vv. 39f.). However, Jesus emphasizes the precedence given to hearing "his word": "Martha, Martha, you are anxious about many things. But only one thing is necessary. Mary has chosen the good portion; it shall not be taken from her" (vv. 41f.).

In the story of Lazarus Martha is mentioned as frequently as Mary (John 11:1, 5, 19; 12:2f.); though Mary is in the foreground in 11:1, Martha is named first (perhaps as the oldest) in 11:5, 19; 12:2f. She is the one who goes to meet Jesus, while Mary remains in the house (11:20; also v. 30). Prior to her sister, she says: "Lord, if you had been here, my brother would not have died" (v. 21; Mary makes the same charge in v. 32); yet she trusts in a favorable response to a prayer of Jesus (v. 22) and makes a christological confession (v. 27). She objects to the intent of taking away the stone from the grave (v. 39). John 12:2 is a parallel to Luke 10:40: While Martha is involved in serving when Jesus visits, Mary

anoints his feet (v. 3). Here one finds either the use of a shared tradition or a use of Luke by the Fourth Evangelist (Bailey 5f.).

                       G. Schneider

Μαρία, ας/Μαριάμ   *Maria/Mariam*   Mary*

1. Forms of the name; occurrences in the NT — 2. The mother of Jesus — a) In Mark — b) In Matthew — c) In Luke/Acts — d) In John — 3. Mary Magdalene — 4. The mother of James — 5. "Mary, the wife of Clopas" (John 19:25) — 6. The sister of Martha — 7. The mother of John Mark (Acts 12:12) — 8. A Mary not mentioned elsewhere (Rom 16:6)

Lit.: On 1: O. BARDENHEWER, *Der Name Maria* (1895). — M. GÖRG, "Mirjam—ein weiterer Versuch," *BZ* 23 (1979) 285-89. — E. KÖNIG, "Woher stammt der Name 'Maria,' " *ZNW* 17 (1916) 257-63. — F. ZORELL, "Was bedeutet der Name Maria?" *ZTK* 30 (1906) 356-60.

On 2: W. BAUER, *Das Leben Jesu im Zeitalter der neutestamentlichen Apokryphen* (1909) 8-21, also index s.v. (on NT apocrypha). — S. BEN-CHORIN, *Mutter Mirjam. Maria in jüdischer Sicht* (1971). — idem, "A Jewish View on the Mother of Jesus," Concilium 168 (1983) 12-16. — F.-M. BRAUN, *La mère des fidèles* ([2]1954) (on John). — R. E. BROWN, *The Birth of the Messiah* (1977). — idem, "The 'Mother of Jesus' in the Fourth Gospel," *L'Évangile de Jean* (BETL 44, 1977) 307-10. — R. E. BROWN, K. P. DONFRIED, et al., *Mary in the NT* (1978). — J. CANTINAT, *Marie dans la Bible* (1964). — W. DELIUS, *Geschichte der Marienverehrung*, (1963) esp. 9-34. — A. FEUILLET, *Jésus et sa mère* (1974) (on Luke 1–2 and John). — P. GAECHTER, *Maria im Erdenleben* (1953, [3]1955). — J. GALOT, *Marie dans l'Évangile* (1958). — A. GEORGE, "La mère de Jésus," idem, *Études sur l'oeuvre de Luc* (1978) 429-64 (on Luke-Acts). — idem, *Maria dans le NT* (1981). — J. A. GRASSI, "The Role of Jesus' Mother in John's Gospel," *CBQ* 48 (1986) 67-80. — P. GRELOT, *DSp* X, 409-23. — K. KERTELGE, "Maria, die Mutter Jesu in der Heiligen Schrift," *Catholica* 40 (1986) 253-69. — R. LAURENTIN, "Bulletin sur la Vierge Marie," *RSPT* 69 (1985) 611-43; 70 (1986) 101-50. — idem, *Struktur und Theologie der lukanischen Kindheitsgeschichte* (1967). — L. LEGRAND, *L'annonce à Marie (Lc 1,26-38). Une apocalypse aux origines de l'Évangile* (LD 106, 1981). — J. McHUGH, *The Mother of Jesus in the NT* (1975). — J. McKENZIE, "The Mother of Jesus in the NT," Concilium 168 (1983) 3-11. — R. MAHONEY, "Die Mutter Jesu im NT," *Die Frau im Urchristentum* (ed. G. Dautzenberg, et al.; 1983) 92-116. — J. MICHL, *LTK* VII, 25-27. — idem, *SacVb* 556-66. — E. NELLESSEN, *Das Kind und seine Mutter* (1969) (on Matt 2). — W. PRATSCHER, "Das neutestamentliche Bild Marias als Grundlage der Mariologie," *KD* 35 (1989) 189-211. — H. RÄISÄNEN, *Die Mutter Jesu im NT* (1969). — K. H. SCHELKLE, *Die Mutter des Erlösers* (1958, [2]1963). — H. SCHÜRMANN, *Luke* I (HTKNT, 1969), index s.v. (585). — A. SMITMANS, *BL* 1094-98. — O. DA SPINOTELI, *Maria nella Bibbia* (1988). — G. STÄHLIN, *RGG* IV, 747-49. — M. THURIAN, *Maria* (1965). — J. ZMIJEWSKI, *Die Mutter des Messias* (1989).

On 3: T. BERNARD and L. VESCO, *Marie de Magdala* (1981). — P. BENOIT, "Marie-Madeleine et les Disciples au Tombeau selon Joh 20,1-18," FS Jeremias (1960) 141-52. — F. BOVON, "Le privilège Pascal de Marie-Madeleine," *NTS* 30 (1984) 50-62. — R. L. BRUCKBERGER, *Maria Magdalena* (1954). —

G. GHIBERTI, *I, racconti pasquali del cap. 20 di Giovanni confrontati con le altre tradizioni neotestamentarie* (1972). — P. M. GUILLAUME, *DSp* X, 559-75. — M. HENGEL, "Maria Magdalena und die Frauen als Zeugen," *FS* Michel 243-56. — P. KETTER, *Die Magdalenenfrage* (1929). — J. MICHL, *LTK* VII, 39f. — E. PARVEZ, "Mary Magdalene: Sinner or Saint?" *The Bible Today* 23 (1985) 122-24. — V. SAXER, *Le culte de Marie Madeleine en Occident des origines à la fin du Moyen Age* (1959). — L. SCHOTTROFF, "Maria Magdalena und die Frauen am Grabe Jesu," *EvT* 42 (1982) 3-25. — A. SMITMANS, *BL* 1098f.

On 6: → Μάρθα.

1. The name Mary appears in the NT in two forms: Μαρία and Μαριάμ. The latter form is a transliteration (LXX) of the Hebrew name *miryām* (the name of Moses' sister, Exod 15:20f., etc.), targumic *maryām*. Josephus *Ant.* iii.54 writes: Μαριά[μ]μη (ης). Whether Μαρία (cf. also Moulton/Milligan s.v.) is a Hellenized form of this name cannot be determined with certainty, as the name *mryh* is also attested in inscriptions (cf. E. Y. Kutscher, *Scripta Hierosolymitana* IV [²1965] 23f.n.118; J. P. Kane, *JSS* 23 [1978] 270). In reference to the mother of Jesus Matt 13:55 and Luke 1:27, 30, 34, 38f., 46, 56; 2:5, 16, 19, 34 have the form of the name with -αμ; in the nom. only Luke 2:19 ℵ* D Θ pc have the shorter form Μαρία. Among the others in the NT with this name the text tradition shifts regularly between Μαριάμ and Μαρία. The gen. is always Μαρίας; Matt 1:20 and Rom 16:6 have the acc. Μαρίαν. Cf. BDF §53.3. In the NT seven different women have the name Mary (→ 2-8).

2. The name of Mary the mother of Jesus occurs 19 times in the NT (Matt 1:16, 18, 20; 2:11; 13:55; Mark 6:3; Luke 1:27, 30, 34, 38f., 41, 46, 56; 2:5, 16, 19, 34; Acts 1:14), 13 of which appear in Luke-Acts (12 in Luke 1–2 alone). Other passages refer to Mary but not by name (esp. in John, where Mary is never mentioned by name, although three other Marys are mentioned): References to the "mother of Jesus" (John 2:1, 3) or to "his mother" (Matt 2:13f., 20f.; 12:46; Mark 3:31; Luke 2:33, 48, 51; 8:19; John 2:5, 12; 19:25; cf. John 6:42; 19:26, "the mother"), without mentioning her name (cf. "your mother," Mark 3:32 par. Matt 12:47/Luke 8:20; "the mother of my Lord," Luke 1:43; → μήτηρ), are frequent.

"The woman clothed with the sun . . ." in Rev 12:1-17 is, however, not a reference to Mary; see H. Gollinger, *Das "große Zeichen" von Apk 12* (1971) esp. 27-48; A. Vögtle, *FS* Kuhn 396n.5.

a) While Mary is not mentioned in the logia source, two passages in the oldest Gospel do refer to the mother of Jesus: in the Nazareth pericope, Mark 6:3 (par. Matt 13:55/John 6:42) mentions her name, and in the apothegm of the true relatives of Jesus, Mark 3:31f. (par. Matt 12:46f./Luke 8:19f.; cf. also Mark 3:21) does not mention her name. In the first pericope the critics of Jesus ask: "Is this not the τέκτων, the son *of Mary* and brother

of James and Joses and Judas and Simon, and are not his sisters [i.e., do they not live] here among us?" (Mark 6:3). The reference to Jesus' origin casts doubt on his messianic status; the critics refuse to have faith in Jesus. The metronymic designation for Jesus, "son *of Mary*," is best explained under the assumption that he was so named as son of a widow; see J. Blinzler, *Die Brüder und Schwestern Jesu* (1967) 71f.; R. Pesch, *Mark* (HTKNT) I, 319 (cf. E. Stauffer, "Jeschu ben Mirjam," *FS* Black [1969] 119-28, who suggested that Jesus was defamed as an illegitimate child). Mark 3:31-35 mentions Jesus' mother and brothers in the introduction of the traditional material (v. 31). The people say to Jesus: "Behold, your mother and your brothers and your sisters are outside seeking you" (v. 32). This scenic exposition provides the background for Jesus' statements about true relatives (vv. 33-35). Mark shows no special interest in Mary.

b) Matthew has incorporated both Markan passages (→ 2). In Matt 13:55, he has the question: "Is this not the son τοῦ τέκτονος, is not his mother called Mary and his brothers . . . ?" The occupation of his father and the name of his mother are known. But Jesus is not called "son of the τέκτονος *and* of Mary." According to 12:46 the mother and brothers seek Jesus "in order to speak with him." In the following verse (om B ℵ* al) it is not the people (in contrast to Mark 3:32), but rather an individual: "Behold, your mother and your brothers . . . !" Matt 1:16 calls Joseph "the husband of Mary, of whom Jesus was born." V. 18 makes clear that Joseph (→ Ἰωσήφ 4) was only the "legal" father of Jesus: "As his mother Mary was betrothed to Joseph, before they came together, she was found to be with child by the Holy Spirit." An angel of God informed Joseph about this and instructed him to take Mary to himself: παραλαβεῖν Μαρίαν τὴν γυναῖκά σου (v. 20). The reason is then given: "for that which is conceived in her is from the Holy Spirit." The christological statement of the virginal conception of Jesus is derived from (Christian-Hellenistic) tradition (cf. Luke 1:35; → παρθένος 3). In the entire complex of the story of the magi in 2:1-23 Mary is mentioned only in v. 11: "and they saw the child (παιδίον) with Mary, his mother." "The child and his mother" are emphasized in relation to Joseph and are set off from him (vv. 13f., 20f.). Nevertheless, Matthew shows no special interest in the person of Mary.

c) Mark 3:31f. has been taken over by Luke (Luke 8:19f.), but not Mark 6:3. According to Luke 8:19 the mother and brothers of Jesus could not reach him "because [of the pressure] of the crowd." They desire "to see" Jesus (v. 20). In the Nazareth pericope Jesus' critics merely ask: "Is this not the son of Joseph?" (4:22, while Mark 6:2b-3 has four separate questions). They know nothing of Jesus' true "origin" (Luke 1:26-28; cf. 3:23), which is, of course, known to the reader (Schürmann

235). Mary is mentioned by name also in 1:26-28 (4 times), 39-56 (4 times), 2:1-20 (3 times), 25-35 (once); cf. 2:41-52 (no reference to her name). Mary was a virgin, betrothed to Joseph (1:27), when the angel addressed her by name (v. 30) and announced that she would, as a virgin, conceive the Messiah (v. 31; cf. Isa 7:14; also Luke 2:5; → παρθένος 3). Mary's question serves as the introduction to the christological statement about the conception of Jesus through the work of the Holy Spirit (v. 35; cf. Matt 1:18, 20; → b), which is here the basis for the child's status as "Son of God" (cf. διὸ καί, v. 35c).

In Luke Mary is emphasized as a person (1:48) and as mother of the Messiah (1:42f.). This accent is esp. visible in the reference to her exemplary faith, which is understood as her reliance on the promise of God (1:45). The comments in 2:19, 51b are also to be understood in the sense of an exemplary attitude of faith (cf. 8:15). The prophecy of Simeon (2:34: "he spoke to Mary, his [Jesus'] mother") sees the fate of Mary as closely connected to that of Jesus (see also 2:48-50). Acts 1:14 reports that Mary belonged to the early Jerusalem church after the ascension of Jesus and was among the disciples of Jesus who awaited the gift of the Spirit.

d) It is noteworthy that the Gospel of John does not mention Mary by name. This fact is related to the type of "symbolically elevated" understanding of the mother of Jesus. According to 2:1-11 she is a representative of those who await the salvation brought by Jesus; she represents them in requesting the gift of the Spirit. The gift of wine points symbolically to the future. The scene at the cross with the mother of Jesus and the disciple whom Jesus loved (19:25-27) refers back to 2:1-11. The disciple whom Jesus loved (as interpreter of the revelation of Jesus for humankind) receives in Mary those who seek revelation. On this interpretation, see Schürmann II, 13-28; R. Schnackenburg, *John* III (Eng. tr., 1982) 277-82; J. Wanke, *TPQ* 129 (1981) 105-13.

The question of the "Jews" in John 6:42 ("is this not Jesus, the son of Joseph, whose father and mother we know?"; cf. Mark 6:3; → a) is meant to reduce Jesus' claim to "have come from heaven" to an absurdity. According to 2:12 Mary went (temporarily) with Jesus, his "brothers," and the "disciples" to Capernaum.

3. All four Gospels mention Μαρία (Μαριὰμ) ἡ → Μαγδαληνή, *Mary Magdalene* (only in John 20:11, 16 does the reference to her place of origin not appear): in the scene at Jesus' crucifixion (Mark 15:40 par. Matt 27:56/John 19:25, with other Galilean women disciples) and at the burial (Mark 15:47 par. Matt 27:61). In both scenes Luke omits the names of the women from Galilee (23:49, 55) because they were already mentioned in 8:2: "some women, who had been healed from evil spirits and

illnesses: Mary, called ἡ Μαγδαληνή, from whom seven demons had been cast out. . . ."

The comment that Jesus had liberated Mary from severe possession is taken up in Mark 16:9 (ἐκβεβλήκει ἑπτὰ δαιμόνια). Christian tradition saw in this information a reference to an earlier life of wickedness by Mary, and identified her with the sinful woman of Luke 7:36-50 and (perhaps because of John 11:2) with Mary, the sister of Martha (→ Μάρθα; → 6). This was also done in the Latin liturgy and in pictorial art. Since Luke 8:2f. mentions Mary along with Joanna, the wife of Chuza, and reports that the Galilean women supported the disciples from their means, Mary was probably a wealthy woman. In Mark 16:1 par. Matt 28:1/Luke 24:10, Mary appears first among the three (Matthew: two; Luke: three "and the others with them") women who came to the tomb of Jesus on Easter morning. According to John 20:1 Mary went alone to the grave; she told Peter and the beloved disciple that someone had taken away the Lord (v. 2). Mary stood in front of the tomb (20:11) after the two disciples had inspected it (vv. 3-10). She saw the two angels (vv. 12f.) and finally Jesus himself, whom she thought to be the gardener (vv. 14-16). She received from him the charge to proclaim to the disciples his return to the Father (vv. 17f.). The secondary Markan ending (Mark 16:9f., dependent on John 20) also affirms that the resurrected one appeared first to Mary Magdalene.

4. Mark 15:40 mentions among the Galilean women disciples at the cross of Jesus, in addition to Mary Magdalene, "Mary, the mother of James the less and of Joses" (par. Matt 27:56: and of Joseph). According to Mark 15:47 (par. Matt 27:61: "the other Mary") she was at the burial of Jesus, and in Mark 16:1 par. Matt 28:1 ("the other Mary")/Luke 24:10 she is mentioned among those who went to the tomb at Easter. It cannot be ruled out that she is identical with the Mary of John 19:25 (cf. Mark 15:40; → 5).

5. Only John 19:25 (cf. par. Mark 15:40) mentions after the mother of Jesus and before Mary Magdalene "Mary, the [wife] of Clopas" at the cross of Jesus. The immediately preceding "and the sister of his mother" may refer to this Mary. She would then be a relative rather than an actual sister of the mother of Jesus; cf. R. Schnackenburg, *John* III (Eng. tr., 1982) 276f., who argues against equating the wife of Clopas with Mary mother of James (→ 4).

6. Luke and John know the sisters Mary and → Μάρθα. According to John 11:1f., 19f., 28, 31f., 45; 12:3, Mary is also the sister of Lazarus (11:2, 19) in Bethany. Mary anointed Jesus with ointment and dried his feet with her hair (11:2, in anticipation of 12:3). According to 11:32 she said to Jesus (after the death of Lazarus): "Lord, if

you had been here, my brother would not have died." In Luke 10:39, 42, Mary, in contrast to Martha, is an example: "she sat at the feet of the Lord and listened to his word" (v. 39), while Martha was concerned about serving. Jesus said: "Mary has chosen the good portion, which cannot be taken away from her" (v. 42).

7. According to Acts 12:12 many members of the Jerusalem church were gathered in prayer "in the house of *Mary*, the mother of John surnamed Mark," during the time of the persecution under Herod Agrippa I. On the tradition concerning the presumed place of Jesus' Last Supper, see Kopp, *Places* 323-33.

8. In Rom 16:6, a Christian woman to whom Paul sends greetings: "Greet Mary, who has worked hard among you."

G. Schneider

Μᾶρχος, ου   *Markos* Mark*

Lit.: E. BARNIKOL. "Personenprobleme der Apostelgeschichte. Johannes Markos, Silas und Titus," *Forschungen zur Entstehung des Urchristentums, des NT und der Kirche* 3 (1931) 1-32. — BAGD s.v. — J. BLINZLER, *LTK* VII, 12f. — N. BROX, *1 Pet* (EKKNT, 1979) 247f. (on 1 Pet 5:13). — J. C. FENTON. "Paul and Mark," *Studies in the Gospels: Essays in Memory of R. H. Lightfoot* (1955) 89-112. — J. GNILKA, *Mark* I (EKKNT, 1978) 32f. — B. HEMELSOET and W. BAIER, *BL* 1100. — B. T. HOLMES. "Luke's Description of John Mark," *JBL* 54 (1935) 63-72. — J. F. KELLY, "The Patristic Biography of Mark," *The Bible Today* 21 (1983) 39-44. — U. H. J. KÖRTNER, "Markus der Mitarbeiter des Petrus," *ZNW* 71 (1980) 160-73. — KÜMMEL, *Introduction* 95-97. — J. KÜRZINGER, "Die Aussage des Papias von Hierapolis zur literarischen Form des Markusevangeliums," *BZ* 212 (1977) 245-64. — W. MARXSEN, *RGG* IV, 772f. — K. NIEDERWIMMER, "Johannes Markus und die Frage nach dem Verfasser des zweiten Evangeliums," *ZNW* 58 (1967) 172-88. — R. PESCH. "Die Zuschreibung der Evangelien an apostolische Verfasser," *ZKT* 97 (1975) 56-71, esp. 61f. — *idem, Mark* I (HTKNT, 1976) 3-12. — E. STAUFFER, "Der Methurgeman des Petrus," *FS Schmid* (1963) 283-93. — WIKENHAUSER/SCHMID 210-16.

1. Mark is a frequently occurring proper name, attested in inscriptions, papyri, and literature (e.g., Philo, Josephus). In Acts 12:12 Mark is the surname of John, whose mother Mary owned a house in Jerusalem, to which Peter went after his liberation and where he found many Christians assembled. John Mark went with Paul and Barnabas to Antioch (12:25), participated in the first missionary journey as far as Pamphylia, but separated from them there (15:37f.; cf. 13:5, 13). For this reason Paul refused, against the wish of Barnabas, to take John Mark on the second missionary journey (15:37). After a dispute Barnabas and John Mark separated from Paul and went to Cyprus (15:39). Greetings from Mark are sent in Phlm 24; Col 4:10 (from Mark, the cousin of Barnabas); 1 Pet 5:13 (from Mark, "my son"); and according to 2 Tim 4:11 Paul asks the reader to bring Mark as a helper.

2. Early Church tradition, of which the earliest witness is Papias (in Eusebius *HE* iii.39.14f.), upon whom all other witnesses depend, identified the John Mark mentioned in Acts with the Mark mentioned in the Epistles and ascribed to him, as interpreter of Peter, the authorship of the Second Gospel (= Mark). The strongly apologetic tendency of the reference in Papias diminishes the value of the historical statement. Papias intended to ensure the authority of the Second Gospel by connecting its origin indirectly with Peter, perhaps by ascribing an anonymous gospel to Mark, the companion of Peter, or by equating someone already known as the author of the Second Gospel (but otherwise unknown) with the one mentioned in the NT; or perhaps John Mark from Jerusalem really was the author of the Second Gospel and Papias equated him with the figure of 1 Pet 5:13. The last hypothesis encounters the difficulty that the author of Mark had only uncertain knowledge of the region of Palestine and adopted various traditions that, at least in part, presuppose a long process of tradition.

A. Weiser

μάρμαρος, ου, ὁ   *marmaros* marble*

Rev 18:12: πᾶν σκεῦος ἐκ . . . μαρμάρου as an example of the luxurious cargo of "Babylon"; cf. Ep Jer 71.

μαρτυρέω   *martyreō* bear witness, attest*
διαμαρτύρομαι   *diamartyromai* swear, attest, testify*
μαρτύρομαι   *martyromai* swear, attest, testify*

1. Occurrences of μαρτυρέω in the NT — 2. Meanings — 3. Usage outside the Johannine literature — 4. "Witnessing" in the Johannine literature — 5. Μαρτύρομαι and διαμαρτύρομαι

Lit.: BAGD s.v. — J. BLANK, *Krisis* (1964). — J. M. BOICE, *Witness and Revelation in the Gospel of John* (1970). — J. C. HINDLEY, "Witness in the Fourth Gospel," *SJT* 18 (1965) 319-37. — J. NOLLAND, "Impressed Unbelievers as Witnesses to Christ (Luke 4:22a)," *JBL* 98 (1979) 219-29. — H. STRATHMANN, *TDNT* IV, 474-514. — M. C. TENNEY, "The Meaning of 'Witness' in John," *BSac* 132 (1975) 229-41. — For further bibliography see L. Coenen and A. A. Trites, *DNTT* III, 1038-51; → μάρτυς.

1. The vb. μαρτυρέω appears 76 times in the NT, 63 times in the act. and 13 times in the pass. It occurs most often in John (33 times) and 1–3 John (10 times). Acts has 11 occurrences, Hebrews 8, Paul 5, Revelation 4, the Pastorals 2, Matthew, Luke, and Colossians 1 each. In the pass. the most occurrences are in Hebrews (6) and Acts (4).

2. In the absolute sense μαρτυρέω means *bear witness* (1 John 5:6) or *swear (to)* (John 12:17; 13:21). With the acc. of the thing it means *attest, testify,* likewise with ὅτι (John 4:44, etc.). With the dat. of the person and ὅτι, μαρτυρέω means *"testify something to someone"* (John 3:28, etc.). The dat. can also be a dat. of disadvantage, "against someone" (→ 3, on Matt 23:31). Where the vb. stands with the true dat. of the person (Luke 4:22), it means *applaud a person;* where it stands with the dat. of

the thing, it means *"bear witness* for something" (only in John, 3 John, Acts 14:3). The pass. can be used in a neutral sense, to say that something is "witnessed, testified," always in reference to Scripture (Rom 3:21; Heb 7:8, 17; 11:4f., in the last two instances with the nom. and inf.), or it can be used in an evaluative sense, to say that someone "has received a good witness" (in the remaining passages).

3. In Matthew μαρτυρέω has a legal significance: The scribes witness against themselves that they are the sons of those who murdered the prophets (Matt 23:31; cf. par. Luke; → μάρτυς 2). Luke prefers a fig. meaning of the word (on Luke 4:22 → 2). The frequent pass. in Acts means that someone "has received a good witness" or "has a good reputation" (Acts 6:3, the seven; 10:22, Cornelius; 16:2, Timothy; 22:12, Ananias). The saying is also fig. that God "spoke to David testifying" (13:22), that "all the prophets bore witness" of Jesus (10:43), and that God "bore witness for the word of his grace with signs and wonders" (14:3, with uncertain ἐπί; cf. Heb 11:4). On the subject cf. here Heb 2:4 and John 5:36; 10:25 (→ 4). Acts 15:8 speaks of a witness of God for the Gentiles.

A stronger forensic use is found in Paul's defense speeches: All Jews know his conduct and can bear witness to it (Acts 26:5); he persecuted the Christian "way," as the high priest and the high council can attest (22:5): here the acc. of the thing is to be restored. A forensic sense is also possible in 23:11: "As you have testified of me (διεμαρτύρω), at Jerusalem, so you must also *testify* in Rome" (again, perhaps with an acc. of the thing to be supplied; cf. διεμαρτύρω τὰ περὶ ἐμοῦ; → 5). Here is an allusion to Paul's task and role according to Acts (→ μάρτυς 4).

Paul can use the absolute μαρτυρέω simply for an assertion (2 Cor 8:3) or with the dat. in the sense of "witness something to someone" (Rom 10:2; Gal 4:15; cf. Col 4:13). He also knows a scriptural "witness" for the eschatological way of salvation: the righteousness of God is *"witnessed* by the law and the prophets" (Rom 3:21). Paul comes closest to Lukan usage in 1 Cor 15:15, where he (and his fellow apostles) are described as "false witnesses of God," who *"testify* against God that he raised Christ," if the dead are not raised (→ ψευδόμαρτυς).

According to 1 Tim 6:13 the "good confession" that Jesus *"testified* before Pontius Pilate" (on ἐπί cf. BAGD s.v.) serves as an example and stimulus for the apostolic pupil. Cf. the similar expression in v. 12 (→ μάρτυς 3). The reference to the widows of 5:10 who "are *highly regarded* because of their good works" is reminiscent of the pass. usage of Luke in Acts (see above).

Hebrews speaks in various ways of a divine "attestation" or "confirmation." It normally involves words of Scripture, in which μαρτυρέω is constructed in the pass.

either in a personal (e.g., 7:8) or impersonal way (e.g., 7:17). In 10:15 the author refers to himself in the dat. and attributes the witness of Scripture to the Spirit. In ch. 11 the "witness" that the forefathers and the faithful people of Israel received (v. 2; cf. v. 39 with concessive partc.) is explicitly described as a witness of God (v. 4): The acceptable sacrifice of Abel (cf. Gen 4:4) was a "witness" that he was just (Heb 11:4, nom. with inf.). Enoch *"received the witness* [from Scripture] that he was pleasing to God" (v. 5, same construction).

4. Of the 33 instances of μαρτυρέω in John, the construction μαρτυρέω περί τινος (19 occurrences, used elsewhere in the NT only in 1 John) is found in most instances, and most commonly in reference to Jesus. The dispute with the "Jews" or "Judeans" who resist his message has the features of a judicial proceeding, as the other judicial expressions indicate (→ ἐλέγχω, κρίνω, κρίσις, παράκλητος, etc.). This has been known since W. Wrede (1903) and the commentary on John by W. Heitmüller (³1918; see Beutler 26).

Jesus appears before the bar of judgment and calls for "witnesses" who will vindicate his claim as revealer before the forum of the "world" and of the "Jews." According to the prologue John the Baptist is the one who *testified* (John 1:7f.) "of the light," i.e., of Jesus as the incarnate Logos, and who continues to testify of him (1:15, Johannine addition of a hymnic fragment). In 1:19-34 the content of the witness of the Baptist is expanded (cf. the *inclusio* with μαρτυρία in v. 19 and the vb. in vv. 32 and 34): The content is not the baptism of Jesus itself but his abiding gift of the Spirit and what is said by the heavenly voice (pf. in v. 34) that has permanent significance. After a brief reference in 3:26 (here with dat. of advantage: "to whom") the Baptist appears once more in 5:31-40: here as "witness for the truth" (5:33), i.e., the divine reality of revelation in Christ (see below on 18:37). However, it is not the Baptist but the Father who is the ἄλλος μαρτυρῶν of v. 32, with regard to whom Jesus rejects the charge of v. 31 of "witnessing to himself" (→ μαρτυρία 4). He bears witness to Jesus through the "works" (not simply "signs," but rather the "works" of giving life and judging, vv. 19-23) granted for Jesus to accomplish. Cf. 10:25. If the Father who has sent Jesus is himself directly called a witness for Jesus in 5:37, what is meant is not so much an inner witness of the Spirit of God (Trites, *Concept* 102, with Hindley, et al.) as the word of God about his Son in the old covenant (Beutler 260f.), which is once again to be distinguished from what is said in the Scriptures of the old covenant (v. 39).

In 8:12-20 the "Pharisees" also proceed from the charge against Jesus that he witnesses to himself, and thus they conclude that his testimony is not "credible" (v. 13; → μαρτυρία 4). Jesus rejects the charge (contrast 5:31), however, and applies to himself the OT-Jewish principle of Deut 19:15, according to which any matter may be established on the basis of the statement of two or three witnesses (vv. 14-18; cf. μάρτυς 3 and Van Vliet on the free citation in v. 17).

In what may be a post-Johannine saying in John 15:26f. the divine witness for Jesus continues in the witness of the Paraclete. The closest parallels for God and signs of confirmation as witnesses, besides Acts (14:3) and Hebrews (2:4; 11:4), are found in Hellenistic Jewish texts, esp. of the Exodus tradition (cf. Philo *Vit. Mos.* ii[iii].263f., 281; *All.* ii.55; Josephus *Ap.* ii.53; Beutler 152).

A stronger apocalyptic tone is found in the idea of Jesus as the witness of heavenly things, which occurs in John 3:11 (where perhaps only a literary pl. in allusion to v. 2 is present) and 3:32 (cf. below on Revelation and the reference to *Jubilees,* the Qumran texts, and *2 Enoch,* Proem; see Beutler 328f.). Related to it is the witness of Jesus (and of the Baptist) for the "truth" in John 18:37 (cf. 5:33). The divine revelation of reality is the subject (see I. de la Potterie in E. Castelli, ed., *Le Témoignage* [1972] 317-29). That eyewitness testimony is relied upon is indicated in the account of the piercing of Jesus' side (19:35); the acc. of the thing is to be supplied in this statement, which is probably post-Johannine; such a witness is also referred to with περί and the gen. of the thing in the identification of the beloved disciple with the Evangelist (21:24; cf. the same construction in 18:28; in reference to persons also in 2:25; 7:7; 4:39: Jesus).

This actual witness is also referred to in 1 John, where the reference is to Jesus as the "Logos of life" who has entered history (1:2). In 4:14 the witness more clearly involves a reality of faith, Jesus as "savior of the world." The threefold witness of spirit, water, and blood (5:6-10) is commonly understood in antidocetic terms, and is interpreted as a reference to baptism and the death of Jesus as salvific events, which witness to his coming. Perhaps the witness of God to his Son in v. 9 is also to be understood historically (cf. above on John 5:37); according to v. 10 it is appropriated only in faith (see the pf.; cf. Beutler 278-80). 3 John takes up the formulation of John 5:33; 18:37 (see above), but employs it differently—for the testimony of personal Christian conduct (vv. 3 and 6). In v. 12 the roles are exchanged: Truth has given its testimony concerning Demetrius.

Revelation refers to an apocalyptic "witnessing" (as in John 3:11, 32; see above): The seer bears witness to "what he has seen," namely, "the word of God and the testimony of Jesus," i.e., that which comes from Jesus (1:2; → μαρτυρία 5). The angels *bear witness* to the content of the book (22:16), i.e., so that it finally bears witness to Jesus (v. 20). Only in these three passages, in addition to John 3:11, 32; 1 Tim 6:13, is μαρτυρέω found

with the acc. of the thing. In a "formula of canonization" (Bousset/Gressmann 148), it is "witnessed" to everyone who adds or takes away from Scripture that they will receive God's punishment (22:18).

5. The related vb. μαρτύρομαι (mid., only pres.) appears in the NT only 5 times. The meaning *testify, attest* is present in three passages where the vb. is constructed with the dat. of the person: Paul *testifies* to everyone who is circumcised that he is bound to keep the whole law (Gal 5:3). Luke uses the same construction in relation to the elders of Ephesus in Acts 20:26. In Acts 26:22 the expression may be colored by v. 16: Paul, called to be a "witness," must *bear witness* before great and small. Μαρτύρομαι with the acc. and inf. in Eph 4:17 and 1 Thess 2:12 (εἰς τό) means *swear.*

Διαμαρτύρομαι (aor. mid. διεμαρτυράμην) is found 15 times in the NT, 9 of which are in Acts (26 times in LXX). The meaning corresponds to that of μαρτύρομαι: *swear, testify.* Against E. Günther (*ΜΑΡΤΥΣ* [1941]), one may not assume a special "apocalyptic usage." Paul uses the vb. in 1 Thess 4:6 with the dat. of the person, in reference to the content of earlier proclamation: the judgment. In Heb 2:6 διαμαρτύρομαι appears at the author's introduction of the Scripture citation, without the reference actually serving as a "proof from Scripture." In the Pastorals one may see a transition to a more formulaic Christian usage: Reference is made to a "swearing before (ἐνώπιον)" God, Jesus Christ, the angels (1 Tim 5:21, with ἵνα; 2 Tim 2:14; 4:1, here associated additionally with an acc. of the thing: "*at* his coming . . .").

Luke uses the vb. with the dat. of the person in the sense of urgent persuasion in Luke 16:28. In Acts (except for 2:40, where it parallels παρακαλέω and is related to its meaning in Luke 16:28), it becomes a t.t. for the proclamation of the apostles and of Paul. The contents include (with various addressees): the word of the Lord (8:25), repentance and faith in the Lord Jesus Christ (20:21), the gospel of God's grace (20:24), the kingdom of God (28:23), that Jesus is the Christ (with acc. and inf., 18:15), "the message about me" (Jesus, 23:11, parallel to μαρτυρῆσαι, here of Paul as → μάρτυς [4]). In 10:42 the content stands within a ὅτι clause (Jesus as judge) and the vb. is parallel to κηρύξαι, which confirms the interpretation that is given. Only in 20:23 is the Holy Spirit the subj. of the "witness": he promises to Paul his imminent suffering.

J. Beutler

μαρτυρία, ας, ἡ *martyria* testimony, evidence*

1. Frequency — 2. Meaning — 3. Usage — 4. The testimony of Jesus and testimony about Jesus in John and 1 John — 5. The witness of Jesus in Revelation — 6. Μαρτύριον

Lit.: → μάρτυς.

1. Μαρτυρία appears 37 times in the NT, the majority of which are in the Johannine literature (14 in John, 9 in Revelation, 6 in 1 John, and once in 3 John). The remainder of the occurrences are distributed among Mark with 3, Luke and Acts with one each, and the Pastorals with 2.

2. With BAGD s.v. one can distinguish between an act. and a pass. usage. The act. usage is found in John 1:7; Rev 11:7, where the word refers to "bearing witness": "he came in order to bear *witness*" (John 1:7); "and when they have completed their *testimony*" (Rev 11:7). In the remaining passages the word refers to "testimony" given before a court or a general "testimony" in the fig. sense. The "testimony" before a court is meant in Mark 14:55f., 59; Luke 22:71 (cf. par. Mark 14:63: μαρτύρων. Because Luke has not mentioned the two false witnesses before, he has the high priest say only now: "What need do we have of *testimony*?"). The fig. sense is used in Titus 1:13, when what is said by a pagan "prophet" (i.e., poet) is called a *testimony* about the Cretans. According to 1 Tim 3:7 the bishop must have a "good *testimony*," i.e., "a good reputation" among outsiders. The religious usage is found in Acts 22:18: The people of Jerusalem will not accept the *testimony* of Paul about Jesus (on the use of περί, in reference to Jesus, → μαρτυρέω 4). On the meaning and usage of the word in the other passages in Johannine literature → 4 and 5.

3. Μαρτυρία is sg. in the NT, except in Mark 14:56. Preceding it may be διά with the acc. as a prep. indicating cause, "because of the testimony" (to Jesus; → 5), Rev 1:9; 6:9; 20:4; εἰς with acc. in John 1:7 (→ 2); and εἰς indicating obj. after πιστεύω in 1 John 5:10: "believe in the testimony."

The noun is connected either with the attributive gen. or with the attributive adj. The gen. of the person bearing witness appears in Mark 14:59; Acts 22:18; 3 John 12, etc. On the usage in the Johannine literature → 4 and 5. The only attributive adj. to occur is καλήν (μαρτυρίαν) in 1 Tim 3:7; → 2. The μείζω (= μείζονα) in John 5:36 is used in a predicative manner: "I have a *testimony* greater than that which comes from John." In nom. clauses one finds the pred. adjs. μείζων (1 John 5:9a), ἀληθής, ἀληθινή, and ἴση/ἴσαι (Mark 14:59, 56: "agree"). While ἀληθής with μαρτυρία means "true" in Titus 1:13; John 5:32; 21:24; 3 John 12, in John 5:31; 8:13f., 17 it is understood in a more formal way and means much the same as "credible." Ἀληθινός in John 19:35 means the same as ἀληθής, "true" (cf. the continuation: "and he knows that he speaks the truth"). On the verbal associations → 4 and 5.

4. As was indicated under → μαρτυρέω (4), the Evan-gelist John has two characteristic uses of the idea of witness/testimony: According to John 3:11, 31f. Jesus is the witness of heavenly things, "but you do not accept our *testimony*" (v. 11), or "no one accepts his *testimony*" (v. 32). Here Jewish apocalyptic language and ideas may stand in the background (→ μαρτυρέω 4).

In 5:31-40 and 8:12-20, the concern is with witnesses who should legitimate Jesus' claim of divine revelation in the context of a juridical dispute with the Jews (→ μαρτυρέω 4). In 5:31 Jesus, the speaker, concedes that his testimony is not "credible" if he bears witness to himself, and thus he points to the Father as the ἄλλος μαρτυρῶν, whose witness is "true" (v. 32; cf. Beutler 257). In principle Jesus does not receive the testimony (confirming him) from people (v. 34), even if he can claim the testimony of the Baptist as an ad hominem argument for himself (v. 33, verbal; 1:7, 17). Jesus has "a *testimony* greater than John's" (5:36), namely, the testimony of the works that the Father granted for him to accomplish. In 8:12-20 Jesus absolutely rejects the charge that his testimony is "not credible" (v. 14) because it is testimony on his own behalf (v. 13), and he appeals to the (unformulated) rule of Deut 19:15 par. in v. 17, according to which "the *testimony* of two people is credible" (→ μάρτυς 3).

In 19:35 and 21:24 the μαρτυρία extends—perhaps post-Johannine—to facts about Jesus, not only to his person: one refers to his side that is opened, and the other refers to the report of the beloved disciple.

1 John takes up once more the total testimony about Jesus: in 5:9, as in John 5:34, 36, the divine testimony is the "greater" one that is contrasted with human testimony. The former could refer back to John 5:37: it has already taken place in the past (note the pf. vb.). Despite v. 10 ("anyone who believes in the Son of God has the *testimony* in himself"), the subject is not an inner witness of the Holy Spirit (against earlier authors), but rather God's testimony to himself in Scripture and in the work of Jesus (John 5:36-39) and in the disclosure of the life of Jesus (1 John 5:11f.), insofar as this μαρτυρία has found acceptance in faith among humankind.

5. In Revelation alone the expression "the *testimony* of Jesus" occurs 6 times (1:2, 9; 12:17; 19:10 bis; 20:4). Against earlier authors (e.g., H. von Campenhausen, *Die Idee des Martyriums in der alten Kirche* [1936]), this is not to be interpreted as a testimony about Jesus, but as one that comes from Jesus; thus the gen. is to be understood as a subj. gen., not an obj. gen. (with Brox, Trites, et al.). Thus one may note the parallelism with the "word of God" in 1:2, 9, and 20:4 and with the "commands of God" in 12:17. God's word and the *testimony* of Jesus are taken up by the seer and brought into play over against the accusing enemy. "Those who are slain . . . hold it firmly" (6:9); likewise the prophets of 19:10 and those

who were beheaded in 20:4. The two (prophetic) witnesses of 11:7 "finish" it after they have expressed it in word (λόγον), and then they are killed (cf. also 12:11).

Here, with the sequence of witness of the word and death, one may not yet speak of a martyrological use of μαρτυρία (so also Lohse, Brox, Trites; → μάρτυς 2, 5). This usage is first found in *Mart. Pol.* 1:1; 2:1; 18:2; 19:1; cf. BAGD s.v. 3, and Brox 227. An anticipation of this martyrological use can be found already in 4 Macc 12:16 A (cf. 16:16, διαμαρτυρία).

6. The related substantivized adj. **μαρτύριον**, *testimony, proof* (cf. Schwyzer, *Grammatik* I, 470), appears 19 times in the NT. The Synoptics each use it 3 times, Paul also 3 times, Acts and the Pastorals 2 times, and Hebrews, James, and Revelation once each.

The meaning is almost always *testimony, evidence, proof;* thus the word can become a t.t. for the language of proclamation (see below on Paul, Pastorals, and Acts). Ἡ σκηνὴ τοῦ μαρτυρίου (Acts 7:44; Rev 15:5), derived from the LXX, rests on a mistranslation of the LXX for Heb. '*ōhel mô'ēḏ;* the LXX translator incorrectly derived *mô'ēḏ* from the root '*d,* "witness," instead of *y'd,* "meet."

In the Synoptic tradition only εἰς μαρτύριον, "for the *testimony,*" occurs. According to Mark 1:44 par. Matt 8:4/ Luke 5:14 the leper who has been cleansed must show himself to the priest and offer the prescribed sacrifices "for a *testimony* to them." The reference is probably to the role of the priesthood in examining the healing. The clause is largely taken over by Matthew and Luke, including even the unusual word order. This is not the case in the two other passages in the Markan tradition. Matthew (10:14) removes the largely unintelligible εἰς μαρτύριον αὐτοῖς of Mark 6:11: "shake the dust from your feet for a *testimony* to [against?] them"; Luke (9:5) clarifies: εἰς μαρτύριον ἐπ' αὐτούς, i.e., unambiguously "against them."

According to Mark 13:9 the disciples will be brought before Jewish and Gentile courts "for *testimony* before them." Here one is to think of the confession of Christ by the persecuted ones. Matthew clarifies this thought and extends it: εἰς μαρτύριον αὐτοῖς καὶ τοῖς ἔθνεσιν (10:18); with the "governors and kings" he is apparently referring to Gentile court officers. Matt 24:14 uses the formula independently: the gospel of the kingdom must be proclaimed in the entire inhabited world "as a *testimony* to all the Gentiles." According to Luke (21:13) the situation becomes "a *testimony*" not to the judges but to the accused themselves.

Εἰς μαρτύριον appears twice more in the Epistles. According to Jas 5:3 the rust on the gold of the rich will become "a *testimony* against them" at the final judgment (dat., as in Mark 6:11). According to Heb 3:5, the faithfulness of Moses proves to be "a *testimony* of the future revelations," i.e., of the revelation to come in Christ (v. 6).

In Acts μαρτύριον becomes a t.t. for apostolic proclamation as a *testimony* of the resurrection of Jesus (→ μάρτυς 4). "The apostles gave [the] *testimony* of the resurrection of the Lord Jesus" (4:33). If with Luke μαρτύριον is more closely connected with the event of the resurrection in history, this element recedes in Paul. When 1 Cor 1:6 says, "the *testimony* of Christ has been confirmed among you," the emphasis is on neither the juridical nor the historical components. Correspondingly, 2 Thess 1:10 says that "you had faith in *our testimony.*" It must remain an open question to what extent Paul (or "Paul") consciously thinks of his role as a witness of the resurrection, in accordance with 1 Cor 15:8. The role of the apostle as witness to the resurrection, which was so central to Luke, has at least terminologically not yet disappeared. A v.l. to 1 Cor 2:1 regards μαρτύριον τοῦ θεοῦ simply as the subj. of the Pauline proclamation, synonymous with τὸ μυστήριον. Outside this usage Paul speaks in a parenthetical phrase of the "*testimony* of our conscience" (2 Cor 1:12).

The Pastorals, like Paul and Acts, regard μαρτύριον as an expression for the proclamation. Timothy is encouraged: "Do not be ashamed of the *witness* of our Lord" (2 Tim 1:8). In 1 Tim 2:6 the difficult τὸ μαρτύριον καιροῖς ἰδίοις refers either to the redemptive death of Jesus as the *testimony* of God or to the formula of faith and proclamation already mentioned in v. 5 (so Brox 35; against BAGD s.v. 1.a: Beutler 199).   J. Beutler

μαρτύριον, ου, τό *martyrion* testimony, proof → μαρτυρία 6.

μαρτύρομαι *martyromai* swear, attest, testify → μαρτυρέω (5).

μάρτυς, υρος, ὁ *martys* witness*

1. Occurrences — 2. Meaning — 3. Usage — 4. Witnesses for Jesus in Acts — 5. The witness of Jesus and Jesus as witness according to Revelation

Lit.: E. ALBRECHT, *Zeugnis durch Wort und Verhalten* (Diss. Basel, 1977). — T. BAUMEISTER, *Die Anfänge der Theologie des Martyriums* (Münsterische Beiträge zur Theologie 45, 1980). — J. BEUTLER, *Martyria* (FTS 10, 1972). — N. BROX, *Zeuge und Märtyrer* (SANT 5, 1961). — C. BURCHARD. *Der dreizehnte Zeuge* (FRLANT 105, 1970). — E. CASTELLI, ed., *Le Témoignage* (1972). — G. KLEIN, *Die zwölf Apostel* (FRLANT 77, 1961). — N. LASH, "What might martyrdom mean?" *Suffering and Martyrdom in the NT* (FS G. M. Styler, 1981) 183-98. — E. LOHSE, *Rev* (NTD, 1962). — P.-H. MENOUD, "Jésus et ses témoins," *Église et théologie* 23 (1960) 7-20 (= idem, *Jésus-Christ et la foi* [1975] 100-110). — E. NELLESSEN, *Zeugnis für Jesus und das Wort* (BBB 43, 1976). — G. SCHNEIDER, "Die zwölf Apostel als 'Zeugen,'" *Christuszeugnis der Kirche* (ed. P. W. Scheele and G. Schneider; 1970) 39-65. — H. STRATHMANN, *TDNT* IV, 474-515. — A. A. TRITES, "Μάρτυς and Martyrdom in the Apocalypse: A Semantic Study," *NovT* 15 (1973) 72-80. — *idem, The NT Concept of Witness* (SNTSMS 31, 1977). — H. VAN VLIET, *No Single Testimony* (1958).

1. Μάρτυς, which appears in the Synoptics only in isolated instances (Matthew twice, Mark once, Luke twice), appears most frequently in Acts (13 times); Paul (without the Pastorals) has 6 and Revelation has 5. The remainder of the 36 references are distributed among the Pastorals with 3, Hebrews with 2, and 1 Peter with one. A noteworthy fact is the absence of the word in John and 1–3 John (→ μαρτυρέω, → μαρτυρία), even though the subject is not absent.

2. The basic meaning *witness* is maintained in all NT passages. Frisk (*Wörterbuch* II, 179) connects both it and → μέριμνα with the ancient Indian *smárati* and sees the constitutive element in the "memory." The concrete datum (μάρτυς, μάρτυρ, also μάρτυρος) would then have developed from the abstraction (*μαρ-τυ-, "testimony").

The NT speaks several times of a "witness" before a court in alluding to a legal principle from the OT that "every fact must be affirmed from the mouth of two or three *witnesses*" (Deut 19:15, used in Matt 18:16; 2 Cor 13:1; 1 Tim 5:19) or that the evildoer must "die on the basis of two or three *witnesses*" (Deut 17:6; loose citation in Heb 10:28); → 3. Reference is made to witnessing in the juridical sense also in the trial of Jesus (Mark 14:63 par. Matt 26:65: "what need do we have of *witnesses*?" [cf. par. Luke 22:71: μαρτυρίας]) and in the trial of Stephen (Acts 6:13 [→ 3]; 7:58). In a wider sense the scribes at the time of Jesus are "witnesses" of the murders of the prophets committed by their forefathers, i.e., they "confirm" their deed when they build their tombs (Luke 11:48 [cf. par. Matt 23:31: μαρτυρεῖτε ἑαυτοῖς], Q tradition). The witnesses of the baptismal instruction of Timothy in 2 Tim 2:2 are understood in a similar forensic sense.

Luke develops a usage according to which the apostles are "witnesses" not only to the outward events of Jesus' life, death, and resurrection, but also to their salvific meaning according to Scripture (→ 4). Thus he distinguishes terminologically between μάρτυρες, *witnesses,* and αὐτόπται, "eyewitnesses" (Luke 1:2; see Menoud 4f. with reference to the same distinction in Josephus *Ap.* i.55 against i.4; both terms in *B.J.* vi.134). Μάρτυς, unlike αὐτόπτης, expresses not only the element of valuation but also that of personal engagement. However, the view represented by BAGD s.v. and numerous ancient (see BAGD) and modern authors (cf. E. Haenchen, *Acts* [Eng. tr., 1971], and H. Conzelmann, *Acts* [Hermeneia] on 22:20), that Luke and thus the NT already know (at least by way of suggestion) the "blood witness," who becomes a witness through the shedding of his blood, is hardly attested sufficiently. Apparently Stephen becomes a *witness* through his proclamation of the word, for which he

is responsible, and not through his death (cf. Brox 61-66; Beutler 188, 196).

Personal presence, interpretation, and engagement for what has been witnessed are combined also in 1 Pet 5:1, where "Peter" describes himself as *"witness* of the suffering of Christ." The engagement in a message appears also to be constitutive for the concept of *witness* in Revelation (→ 5).

Paul frequently calls on God as *witness* to his thoughts, intentions, and prayers (Rom 1:9; Phil 1:8; 2 Cor 1:23; 1 Thess 2:5) or for a deed that is brought about from a specific inner thought (1 Thess 2:10). In Israel there was a great fear of calling on God as witness because of the second commandment. It took on greater frequency in the LXX (Beutler 118), however, and is familiar in the Hellenistic world (see Philo's definition of the oath as μαρτυρία θεοῦ περὶ πράγματος ἀμφισβητουμένου [*Sacr.* 91, etc.]; cf. Beutler 147f., 151f.).

It is difficult to interpret the reference to the fathers in the faith as *witnesses* in Heb 12:1 (cf., however, 11:39: μαρτυρηθέντες). The general distinction between "witnesses to facts" and "witnesses of conviction" (so Strathmann) may be too simple; it may not do justice to the relationship between history and salvation in Luke.

3. Within the verbal associations of μάρτυς, the great frequency of numerical adjectives is striking. According to the OT principle that excludes the testimony of one person, "every [relevant criminal] case must be determined through the mouth [i.e., the statement] of two or three witnesses." Thus Deut 19:15 is cited in abbreviated form in Matt 18:16; 2 Cor 13:1; 1 Tim 5:19. On the causal διά with the gen., see BAGD s.v.; on ἐπί with the dat. ("he must die on the basis of two or three witnesses" in Heb 10:28 according to Deut 17:6), see BAGD s.v.; on the subject matter, cf. Van Vliet. Timothy made his confession of faith (at baptism or ordination, 1 Tim 6:12) "before (ἐνώπιον) many *witnesses*"; "he received the Christian message by means of [i.e., in the presence of] many *witnesses* (διὰ πολλῶν μαρτύρων)" (2 Tim 2:2). On the use of διά see BAGD s.v. with references; cf. Num 35:30 LXX. Two *witnesses* are mentioned in Rev 11:3 (→ 5); "one of these," according to Acts 1:22, becomes a witness "with us" (→ 4).

In addition to the attributive adjs. that refer to the number, the NT also has adjs. that characterize the credibility of the witnesses: they set up "false [i.e., lying] *witnesses*" (Acts 6:13); Jesus is "the true/reliable [i.e., truthful] *witness*" (Rev 1:5; 3:14; cf. 2:13, Antipas, where the gen. is required). The attributive gen. (μου) appears, in addition to 2:13, also in 11:3; 17:6 ('Ιησοῦ); and in Rom 1:9 and Phil 1:8 ("God is my *witness,* how I . . ."). The gen. in Luke-Acts may be without exception obj. gen.: The apostles and Paul are witnesses *to* the life, death, and resurrection of Jesus as saving deeds and *to*

Jesus himself (→ 4). The gen. of the thing is to be taken in the same sense in 1 Pet 5:1. In Acts 22:15 μάρτυς is connected with the dat. of advantage: *"witness* for him."

4. Luke has esp. developed a characteristic concept of *witness* in Acts that is of fundamental significance. One may begin, as Burchard correctly notes in his excursus (130-35), with Luke 24:48: The apostles (now eleven) are *"witnesses* of these things," i.e., of the suffering of Jesus (which has taken place according to Scripture), of his resurrection, and of the message of forgiveness that is to be proclaimed. The commission by the resurrected One is primarily that of "witnessing." It appears to correspond to the element of the commission, which is found in the parallel tradition of John 20:19-23. The bestowal of the Spirit there corresponds to the promise of the Spirit in Luke (as in Acts 1:8; Burchard 130f.). Luke thus appears to reserve the title of witness essentially for the Twelve, as Acts 1:21f. indicates (with Schneider *contra* Nellessen). Thus the presence at the life, death, and resurrection is only the prerequisite for the office of witness: The one who assumes the position of Judas must first, on the basis of the election by the resurrected One, *"become a witness* of his resurrection." Μάρτυς is thus more than "eyewitness" (→ 2). The subject of this apostolic witness is, according to the missionary sermons of the first half of Acts, esp. the resurrection of Jesus, which is intended in the neut. rel. pron. οὗ ("of this, for which") in Acts 2:32; 3:15, and to which reference is also made in 10:41 and 13:31. According to 5:32 the Spirit appears along with the apostles as a witness to the message of the death and resurrection of Jesus and to the message of forgiveness (cf. John 15:26f.; → μαρτυρέω 4). Only in Acts 10:39, in addition to 1:21f., is the earthly life of Jesus included. Yet Luke intentionally has the Twelve in their full number present at the proclamation of Jesus (cf. Luke 6:12-19) in order to ensure the continuity of the message that is proclaimed.

Paul was, of course, not a witness of the earthly life of Jesus, but of the resurrection, on the basis of the vision at his call or the appearance of Jesus in the temple in Acts 22:15 (with vv. 17-21; cf. Burchard 108, 111f., 135f.) and 26:16. The με in 26:16 could be the more difficult reading and thus be original.

In the *witnessing* by Stephen in Acts 22:20 the element of commissioning is not present. It is possible that he bears the title of witness on the basis of his vision of the Son of Man before his death (7:55f.; Nellessen 249f.), or on the basis of his proclamation of the word corresponding to that of the apostles and Paul (Brox 61-66; Beutler 188, 196; → 2). According to others he may be a witness on the basis of the end he suffered (Burchard 130n.291; cf. H. Conzelmann, *Acts* [Hermeneia] 188).

5. The author of Revelation uses the entire word field

of μαρτυ-, as does Luke. Here one may not assume that a martyrological use of μάρτυς is present in Revelation (with Brox and Trites against previous authors). The two *witnesses* of Jesus (Rev 11:3) "prophesy" first and then are killed after they have made their "witness" (11:7). Antipas, Jesus' "faithful *witness*" (2:13), is killed only after he has given his witness before the court. On the basis of the association with the use of the word group elsewhere, it is probable that the *"witnesses* of Jesus" in 17:6 are not to be understood as such only because of the shedding of their blood. Likewise, in 1:5 and 3:14 Jesus is called "the faithful (and true) *witness*" on the basis of his fearless proclamation before a hostile forum. Cf. the ὁ ἀμήν and the ἀληθινός in 3:14. On the linguistic formulation, cf. Ps 88:38 LXX: ὁ μάρτυς ἐν οὐρανῷ πιστός; cf. Prov 14:5, 25; Isa 8:2.

J. Beutler

μασάομαι *masaomai* bite*

Rev 16:10: ἐμασῶντο τὰς γλώσσας αὐτῶν, "they [those belonging to the "beast"] *bit* their tongues"; cf. *Apoc. Pet.* 28f. (Akhmimic text; 9, 11 in the Ethiopic text). C. Schneider, *TDNT* IV, 514f.

μασθός, οῦ, ὁ *masthos* nipple, breast
Alternative form of → μαστός.

μασσάομαι *massaomai* bite
Alternative form (TR) of → μασάομαι.

μαστιγόω *mastigoō* whip (vb.), scourge, chastise*

Μαστιγόω appears 7 times in the NT: In Jesus' (third) Passion prediction (Mark 10:34 par. Matt 20:19/Luke 18:33); twice in Matthew (in Jesus' commissioning speech, 10:17; also 23:34; cf. par. Luke 18:33); in John 19:1, also in connection with the Passion story; in Heb 12:6, fig. with the usage common in wisdom literature of *punish/chastise* (citing Prov 3:12; cf. also *Pss. Sol.* 10:2; 13:6ff.; Philo *Congr.* 177; Seneca *Prov.* 16; *1 Clem.* 56:4).

The flogging of Jesus in John 19:1; Mark 10:34 par. corresponds to the Roman punishment of scourging *(verberatio)*, which was done as chastisement or torture (not to Roman citizens; cf. Acts 16:37; 22:24ff.), esp. as a punishment accompanying other humiliating punishments and the sentence of death—above all, crucifixion, which it almost always preceded (cf. Josephus *B.J.* ii.306ff.; Livy x.9.4f.). As the number of blows was not limited, the scourging very often effected the death of the condemned person. In John 19:1 a separate flogging may be in view, perhaps in the sense of a torturing, in order to coerce a confession (cf. vv. 4f.; see also Luke 23:16: παιδεύσας; cf. par. Mark 15:15/Matt 27:26: φραγελλώσας [. . .] ἵνα σταυρωθῇ; cf. Mark 10:34 par.: μαστιγόω καὶ ἀποκτείνω/σταυρόω).

According to Matt 10:17 (ἐν ταῖς συναγωγαῖς αὐτῶν μαστιγώσουσιν; cf. par. Mark 13:9: δαρήσεσθε/Luke 21:12); 23:23, those whom Jesus sent out will be threatened with scourging, which is to be understood against the background of the Jewish punishment of thirty-nine stripes (cf. Deut 25:2f.; 22:18; Acts 5:40; 22:19; 2 Cor 11:24; more detailed in *m. Mak.* 3:1ff., 10ff.; Josephus *Ant.* iv.238, 248). This punishment was given by the servants of the synagogue to, among others, those who were guilty of bodily injury, offenses against the prohibition of incest and against the impurity and food laws (*m. Mak.* 3:12; specifics in Billerbeck III, 527ff.). Matt 10:17 (like Mark 13:9; cf. par. Luke 21:12) presupposes the trial and the condemnation in the synagogue (cf. *m. Sanh.* 1:2, 4, 6), which already existed alongside the Sanhedrin in Jerusalem. *BL* 533f.; B. Reicke, *BHH* 534; C. Schneider, *TDNT* IV, 515-19; Spicq, *Notes* II, 539-42; *TWNT* X, 1172 (bibliography); W. Waldstein, *RAC* IX, 469-90.

H. Balz

μαστίζω *mastizō* whip (vb.), scourge*

Acts 22:25, in reference to the Roman punishment of *verberatio* (→ μαστιγόω), which Paul avoids by referring to his right as a Roman citizen. Of decisive importance here is the *Lex Porcia* and the *Lex Julia; see esp. Beginnings* V, 297-338; E. Haenchen, *Acts* (Eng. tr., 1971) ad loc.

μάστιξ, ιγος, ἡ *mastix* lash, torture; pl.: stripes, lashes*

The pl. appears with the literal meaning *lashes* in the trial of Paul under torture (Acts 22:24: μάστιξιν ἀνετάζεσθαι αὐτόν; → μαστιγόω) and in Heb 11:36 (with ἐμπαιγμοί). Fig. of bodily *suffering* in Mark 3:10; 5:29, 34; Luke 7:21 (with νόσοι and πνεύματα πονηρά); cf. Job 21:9; Ps 38:11 LXX; 2 Macc 7:37. *TDNT* IV, 518f.

μαστός, οῦ, ὁ *mastos* nipple, breast*

Pl. of the mother's *breast* in Luke 11:27; 23:29; according to Rev 1:13 the "one like a son of man" wears the golden girdle (of a king) "around the *breast*" (πρὸς τοῖς μαστοῖς); cf. 1 Macc 10:89; Dan 10:5; Ezek 9:2, 11 LXX.

ματαιολογία, ας, ἡ *mataiologia* futile talk, loose chatter*

1 Tim 1:6, in connection with ἐκτρέπεσθαι εἰς, "turn to . . ." (namely, by turning away from ἀγάπη); cf. Pol. *Phil.* 2:1.

ματαιολόγος, 2 *mataiologos* talking idly, empty talker*

Titus 1:10, pl. subst. with ἀνυπότακτοι and φρεναπάται.

μάταιος, 3 *mataios* vain, futile, idle*

There are 6 occurrences in the NT (none in the Gospels). While in the related adj. → κενός the meaning "empty/meaningless" stands in the foreground, μάταιος also has (as already in the Greek linguistic realm), esp. from its biblical tradition, the meaning *vain/futile/deceitful* and refers to a senseless understanding of reality in contrast to the only valid reality of God or to skeptical resignation in the face of God's distance from this world (cf. the Hebrew synonyms 'āwen, "sin," hebel, "breath of wind, nothingness," kāzāb, "illusion," šāwᵉ, "futility, lies," etc.). In the LXX the lying words of the prophets not authorized by God (Zech 10:2; Ezek 13:6ff.) and everything else connected with the pagan gods and their images was considered μάταιος (Hos 5:11; Isa 2:20; Jer 2:5; 2 Chr 11:15). The pious can despair in the presence of the vanity of their activity and their state on earth (Jer 2:30; Pss 61:10; 88:48 [adv.]; 93:11; Wis 13:1; cf. esp. the noun ματαιότης, which appears more than 35 times in Ecclesiastes: 1:2, 14; 7:1; 9:9, etc.).

In the NT the μάταια include every false worship directed toward the veneration of humankind rather than the true, living God (Acts 14:15: ἀπὸ τούτων τῶν ματαίων ἐπιστρέφειν ἐπὶ θεὸν ζῶντα; cf. Jer 2:5; 1 Pet 1:18 [see below]). In addition the presumptuous thoughts of the wise people of this world (with Ps 93:11 LXX) are considered as *nothing* (1 Cor 3:20: διαλογισμοὶ . . . μάταιοι); the same judgment is made of Gnostic and nomistic speculations (cf. 1 Tim 1:3ff.; Titus 1:10ff.)—they are "unprofitable and *futile*" (Titus 3:9: ἀνωφελεῖς καὶ μάταιοι). Just as believers have been purchased from their *vain* earlier conduct that was "according to the tradition of the fathers" (1 Pet 1:18: ματαία ἀναστροφὴ πατροπαράδοτος), i.e., from their ἄγνοια and ἐπιθυμία (1:14f.; see L. Goppelt, *1 Pet* [KEK] ad loc.), so also is worship *vain* that corresponds to the word only in an outward way and is betrayed by the tongue (Jas 1:26: τούτου μάταιος ἡ θρησκεία); so also the faith of the Corinthians is *vain* when they do not trust God, the one who raises the dead (1 Cor 15:17: ματαία ἡ πίστις ὑμῶν). O. Bauernfeind, *TDNT* IV, 519-24; *TWNT* X, 1172 (bibliography); H. Balz, *Heilsvertrauen und Welterfahrung* (BEvT 59, 1971) 39-51; E. Tiedtke, H.-G. Link, and C. Brown, *DNTT* I, 549-53.

H. Balz

ματαιότης, ητος, ἡ *mataiotēs* vanity, nothingness, transitoriness*

The noun refers in Eph 4:17 to the *nothingness* of the purpose of the lives of the Gentiles (ἐν ματαιότητι τοῦ νοὸς αὐτῶν) and in 2 Pet 2:18 to the presumptuousness of false teachers "who speak pretentious words *without sense*" (ὑπέρογκα γὰρ ματαιότητος φθεγγόμενοι). According to Rom 8:20 the creation has been subjected by God to *nothingness/transitoriness* (τῇ . . . ματαιότητι . . . ὑπετάγη) because of the sin of humankind. Paul's hope is that this situation of transitoriness, with its (historical) beginning, will also have an (historical) end in the liberation of creation to the freedom awaited by the children of God; cf. also 4 Ezra 7:11f.; *2 Bar.* 15:32f.; → μάταιος (bibliography).

ματιόω *mataioō* give over to futility; pass.: become subject to futility*

In the NT only in Rom 1:21 (pass.) of the people who, rather than praise God as creator, *"have fallen into futility in their thoughts"* (ἐματαιώθησαν); cf. Jer 2:5 LXX; Acts 14:15; 1 Cor 3:20; → μάταιος.

μάτην *matēn* in vain, to no purpose, for nothing*

Mark 7:7 par. Matt 15:9, citing Isa 29:13 LXX: μάτην δὲ σέβονταί με, *"in vain do they worship me."*

Ματθαῖος, ου *Matthaios* Matthew
Alternative form (TR) of → Μαθθαῖος.

Ματθάν *Matthan* Matthan*

The name (Heb. *mattān;* cf. 2 Kgs 11:18; 2 Chr 23:17) of Joseph's grandfather in the genealogy of Jesus (Matt 1:15 bis; cf. Luke 3:23ff. D).

Ματθάτ *Matthat* Matthat
Alternative form (TR) of → Μαθθάτ.

Ματθίας, ου *Matthias* Matthias
Alternative form (TR) of → Μαθθίας.

Ματταθά *Mattatha* Mattatha*

The name (Heb. *mattatâ;* cf. Ezra 10:33) of the son of Nathan and grandson of David in the genealogy of Jesus (Luke 3:31).

Ματταθίας *Mattathias* Mattathias*

A name (Heb. *mattityâ;* cf. 1 Chr 9:31) of two men in the genealogy of Jesus: the son of Amos (Luke 3:25) and the son of Semein (v. 26).

μάχαιρα, ης, ἡ *machaira* sword*

1. Occurrences in the NT; meaning — 2. Literal usage — 3. Fig. and metaphorical usage

Lit.: H.-W. BARTSCH, "Jesu Schwertwort, Lk 22,35-38," *NTS* 20 (1973/74) 190-203. — BAGD s.v. — M. BLACK, "The Violent Word," *ExpTim* 81 (1969/70) 115-18. — J. FRIEDRICH,

W. PÖHLMANN, and P. STUHLMACHER, "Zur historischen Situation und Intention von Röm 13,1-7," *ZTK* 73 (1976) 131-66, esp. 140-45. — LSJ s.v. — W. MICHAELIS, *TDNT* IV, 524-27. — P. S. MINEAR, "A Note on Luke 22,36," *NovT* 7 (1964/65) 128-34. — A. SCHLATTER, *Die beiden Schwerter* (BFCT 20/6, 1916). — For further bibliography see *TWNT* X, 1172.

1. Μάχαιρα appears 29 times in the NT (13 times in the story of the arrest of Jesus in Mark 14:43-52 par.; cf. John 18:10f.) and always has the general meaning *sword*. Nowhere—including the more descriptive use of μάχαιρα as "two-edged" (δίστομος in Heb 4:12; cf. 11:34 and O. Hofius, *ZNW* 62 [1971] 129f.)—is precise information given concerning which of the various swords or pointed weapons then in use is referred to. The "cutting edge of the *sword*" is— probably in dependence on OT usage (Gen 34:26; Num 21:24, etc.)— μαχαίρης στόμα (Luke 21:24; Heb 11:34), the "sheath" is θήκη (John 18:11), and the "wound" is πληγὴ τῆς μαχαίρης (Rev 13:14).

Μάχαιρα (not derived from μάχομαι; see Chantraine, *Dictionnaire* s.v.) originally meant "knife" (so, e.g., in Homer); as a term for a weapon it first appears in Herodotus and most often refers to the small (short) sword or the dagger (occasionally the saber), while ῥομφαία is used of the literal (long) sword, and ξίφος refers to the rapier (cf. LSJ s.v.). In the Hellenistic age the specific meanings of the individual terms cannot be sharply distinguished. Thus these could be used, e.g., in the LXX, which translates Heb. *hereb* equally by μάχαιρα and ῥομφαία, and occasionally by ξίφος. Revelation (cf. 6:4; 19:21) and John use μάχαιρα and ῥομφαία alongside each other apparently without distinction.

2. As with the weapons necessary for the apprehension of robbers, *swords* are found along with clubs in the hands of those who arrest Jesus (Mark 14:43 par. Matt 26:47; Mark 14:48 par. Matt 26:55/Luke 22:52). The *sword* also belongs to the equipment of prison guards (Acts 16:27). One serves (John 18:10, for Peter) in the defense of Jesus (Mark 14:47 par. Matt 26:51; cf. Luke 22:49) at his arrest. The Passion story of Matthew includes a saying of the Lord (or citing *Tg. Isa* 50:11; see H. Kosmala, *NovT* 4 [1960] 3-5) in which this use of force is rejected in accordance with Matt 5:39 par.: Whoever takes the sword will die by it (26:52 bis; on the saying about the sword in Rev 13:10b as a threat against the persecutors cf. H. Kraft, *Rev* [HNT] 178, and *1 Enoch* 91:12). In the midst of persecution, death by the sword is an ever-present reality, which can be the fate of any Christian (Rev 13:10b; cf. Matt 10:34, 38f.) and which has already threatened or even struck the OT witnesses of faith (Heb 11:34, 37). The *executioner's sword* has already killed James (Acts 12:2) and is also mentioned in the catalog of sufferings in Rom 8:35 (E. Käsemann, *Rom* [Eng. tr., 1980] 249). In the Lukan form of the Synoptic apocalypse (Mark 13:5-37 par.), a prophecy of the Jewish war, the sword functions

as a murderous weapon of war (Luke 21:24) in the same way that it frequently does in such apocalyptic texts as *1 Enoch* 88:2; 90:19; *Jub.* 9:15; 1QH 6:29; and Rev 6:4 (here in the hands of the second apocalyptic horseman; cf. 19:21).

Apocalyptic (scarcely Zealot, but cf. Black 116f.) ideas are the basis for the core of the problem-laden saying about buying swords in Luke 22:35. In the background is the idea that one must be equipped for the messianic tribulations of the end time (v. 36). In the association of v. 36 with v. 35 the saying anticipates that Christian missionaries will confront hostility, for which they must be prepared. However, v. 36 does not involve a sympathetic understanding for the use of weapons by those who are brought to desperation (here, Jewish Christians in the Jewish rebellion against Rome; see Bartsch 201-3). V. 38 is a redactional construction (apparently with the use of pre-Lukan material: H. Schürmann, *Jesu Abschiedsrede* [1957] 131f.; cf. the two swords—interpreted allegorically in the Middle Ages as worldly and spiritual authority) and is meant to prepare for Luke 22:49-51. Thus Jesus' reaction to the disciples' possession of swords (v. 38) must here remain overshadowed by the answer (v. 51) to their question about the use of the sword (v. 49; see G. Schneider, *Luke* [ÖTK] 456).

3. Matt 10:34 is also to be understood against the background of apocalyptic ideas regarding the tribulations that accompany the appearance of the Messiah (cf. CD 19:10-14; 4QpIs^b 2:1; Billerbeck IV, 977-86), but scarcely as a threat by Jesus against the ungodly (analogous to 1QH 6:29ff.; see O. Betz, *NovT* 2 [1958] 129) and certainly not as Jesus' Zealot program (S. G. F. Brandon, *Jesus and the Zealots* [1967]). Like the contrast to εἰρήνη in Rev 6:4, μάχαιρα here in fig. speech refers to oppressive *violence* (not the division that extends into the families, against Michaelis 526). In persecution (Matt 10:38f.) the Church sees the fulfillment of Jesus' saying (Bultmann, *History* 155).

In a manner similar to 2 Cor 10:4, Eph 6:11-17 outlines the image of spiritual armor of Christians (for similar imagery in early Judaism and Christianity see Wis 5:18-21; 1QM 6:2-16; Ign. *Pol.* 6:2). The *sword* (of the Spirit, Eph. 6:17) appears alongside the breastplate (of righteousness), the shield (of faith), and other weaponry common to the hoplites. The *sword* is the only weapon more precisely defined: it is the Word of God (v. 17b). In Heb 4:12 the same association of word and sword appears, but used differently: the λόγος τοῦ θεοῦ, sharper (τομώτερος) than a *sword,* can both divide and—laying bare—judge. In the latter passage not only is the widespread metaphor of word as sword used (see, e.g., Ps 56:5 LXX; Pseudo-Phocylides 124; Diogenes Laertius v.82; *Tg. Cant.* 3:8 [here: the Torah as sword]), but the idea of

the apocalyptic sword of judgment or the Word of God as such has been adapted, as it also appears in 1QH 6:29; 1QM 19:11; cf. Isa 49:2; Wis 18:15; Rev 1:16; 19:15, 21; Philo *Cher.* 28; *Her.* 130f.—here hellenized into the λόγος τομεύς.

In Rom 13:4 μάχαιρα is understood as the identifying sign of the power to punish that has been granted to the state. It is questionable here whether μάχαιραν φορέω refers to the outward consequence, capital punishment (so, e.g., O. Michel, *Rom* [KEK] 401f.), or whether it can be interpreted on the basis of papyrus documents (e.g., Pap. Tebt. 391.20; Pap. Mich. 577, 7f.), which use μαχαιροφόροι for policemen who support the authorities as they carry out their duties, as is the case with tax collection. The latter interpretation would make μάχαιρα a reference to the state's power in punishment and police activity in general (Friedrich, et al., 144).

E. Plümacher

μάχη, ης, ἡ *machē* battle, dispute, dissension*

All 4 occurrences in the NT are pl. and have the nonliteral meaning *dispute with words* or something similar. Such disputes are esp. rejected in the Pastorals (cf. also *T. Reu.* 3:4; *T. Jud.* 16:3; *T. Benj.* 6:4). In 2 Cor 7:5 it occurs in connection with φόβος (ἔξωθεν μάχαι, ἔσωθεν φόβοι); according to 2 Tim 2:23 there are stupid controversies (ζητήσεις), which lead only "to quarrels" (ὅτι γεννῶσιν μάχας); similarly, Titus 3:9: μάχαι νομικαί, "disputes" over questions of the law"; Jas 4:1, with πόλεμοι. O. Bauernfeind, *TDNT* IV, 527f.

μάχομαι *machomai* battle (vb.), dispute, wrangle*

There are 4 occurrences in the NT, with a meaning similar to the noun → μάχη: John 6:52; Acts 7:26 (here in the sense of hand-to-hand combat; cf. Exod 2:13); 2 Tim 2:24 (opposite ἤπιον εἶναι πρὸς πάντας; cf. v. 23); Jas 4:2: μάχεσθε καὶ πολεμεῖτε (cf. v. 1). O. Bauernfeind, *TDNT* IV, 527f.

με *me* me
Acc. of → ἐγώ.

μεγαλαυχέω *megalaucheō* be proud, boast of (greater things)

Jas 3:5 TR instead of μεγάλα αὐχέω.

μεγαλεῖος, 3 *megaleios* grand, glorious, exalted*

In the NT only as neut. pl. subst.: τὰ μεγαλεῖα τοῦ θεοῦ, "the *mighty works* of God" (Acts 2:11; cf. Luke 1:49 v.l. instead of μεγάλα; cf. Ps 70:19 LXX absolute; Deut 11:2; 3 Macc 7:22 and often with gen.). W. Grundmann, *TDNT* IV, 541; Spicq, *Notes* II, 543.

μεγαλειότης, ητος, ἡ *megaleiotēs* grandeur, majesty*

With gen. θεοῦ, Luke 9:43; τοῦ κυρίου ἡμῶν . . . ἐκείνου μεγαλειότητος, 2 Pet 1:16; in reference to the worship of Artemis, Acts 19:27 (cf. μεγάλη θεά, v. 27a). W. Grundmann, *TDNT* IV, 541; Spicq, *Notes* II, 543.

μεγαλοπρεπής, 2 *megaloprepēs* majestic, exalted*

2 Pet 1:17: ἡ μεγαλοπρεπὴς δόξα, "the *majestic* glory," as a designation for God (cf. Ps 144:5, 12 LXX; *T. Lev.* 3:4; *1 Enoch* 14:20; 102:3; *Asc. Isa.* 11:32); see (also on general usage) Spicq, *Notes* II, 544f.; W. Grundmann, *TDNT* IV, 542f.

μεγαλύνω *megalynō* magnify, extol, praise; pass.: become great, grow*

There are 8 occurrences in the NT: In the literal sense, Matt 23:5: μεγαλύνουσιν τὰ κράσπεδα, "*make the tassels* [of their clothes] *longer/larger* [so that they may be seen]" (according to *b. Menaḥ.* 41b; *Sipre Num* 15:38, etc., only a minimal length is established); Luke 1:58, of God: ἐμεγάλυνεν τὸ ἔλεος αὐτοῦ, "*bestow* his mercy *richly*"; pass.: 2 Cor 10:15: μεγαλυνθῆναι . . . εἰς περισσείαν, "*grow* even more/reach the culminating point [granted to us]" (→ κανών 3). Elsewhere always fig., *praise/exalt:* τὸν κύριον, Luke 1:46; τὸν θεόν, Acts 10:46; pass.: *be glorified:* τὸ ὄνομα τοῦ κυρίου Ἰησοῦ, 19:17; Χριστός, Phil 1:20; act. in reference to the apostles, Acts 5:13. W. Grundmann, *TDNT* IV, 541f.; *TWNT* X, 1172 (bibliography); F. Thiele, *DNTT* II, 424-27; Spicq, *Notes* II, 545f.

μεγάλως *megalōs* greatly, extraordinarily*

The adv. of μέγας appears in the NT only in Phil 4:10 (ἐχάρην . . . μεγάλως; cf. *Ep. Arist.* 42, 312f.).

μεγαλωσύνη, ης, ἡ *megalōsynē* eminence, majesty*

As in the LXX (Deut 32:3; Ps 78:11; Wis 18:24), μεγαλωσύνη always appears in the NT in reference to God: in the doxology of Jude 25 with δόξα, κράτος, and ἐξουσία (cf. 1 Chr 29:11); as a periphrasis for the name of God, Heb 1:3 (ἐν δεξιᾷ τῆς μεγαλωσύνης ἐν ὑψηλοῖς); similarly 8:1. Cf. also *1 Enoch* 14:16; *1 Clem.* 20:12; 58:1. W. Grundmann, *TDNT* IV, 544; *TWNT* X, 1172 (bibliography); F. Thiele, *DNTT* II, 424-27; Spicq, *Notes* II, 546.

μέγας, μεγάλη, μέγα *megas, megalē, mega* great, loud, significant*

1. Occurrences in the NT — 2. The Gospels and Acts — 3. The Epistles — 4. Revelation

Lit.: O. BETZ, *TDNT* IX, 278-309. — H. CONZELMANN, *Acts* (Hermeneia). — W. GRIMM, *Weil ich Dich liebe* (1976) 231ff. — W. GRUNDMANN, *TDNT* IV, 529-41. — E. LOHMEYER, *Rev* (HNT, [2]1953). — For further bibliography see *TWNT* X, 1172.

1. The adj. μέγας appears in the NT about 194 times (not including → μείζων). It appears esp. in the "historical" books of the NT (Gospels 66 times, Acts 31 times; Matthew 20, Mark 15, Luke 26), less often in the Epistles, and frequently (80 occurrences) in Revelation. Its range of meaning corresponds largely to that of Heb. *gāḏôl*, in both literal and nonliteral usages; the latter predominates and stands often in the service of the eschatological revelation.

2. a) In the Gospels and Acts μέγας is used of that which is obviously *surpassing* or *expansive,* as with the branches of the mustard seed bush (Mark 4:32), the gulf separating the realm of the dead (Luke 16:26), the buildings of the temple (Mark 13:2), the upper room for the Last Supper (Mark 14:15 par. Luke 22:12), the stone in front of the tomb of Jesus (Mark 16:4 par. Matt 27:60), the fish at the miraculous catch (John 21:11), and the sheet coming down from heaven (Acts 11:5). In addition, *numerical and material extent* is called *great,* as with the herd of swine at Gadara (Mark 5:11), the meal with the tax collectors (Luke 5:29), and the meal signifying the invitation to the kingdom of God (14:16). Finally, there is also the *acoustic impression,* the speaking, praying, crying "with a *loud* voice," etc. (Mark 15:34 par. Matt 27:46; Luke 1:42; 17:15; 19:37; 23:46; cf. Acts 7:60, also 7:57; 23:9; 26:24).

The loud outcry of the demons indicates superhuman power, whether in an attack on Jesus (Mark 5:7 par. Luke 8:28) or in an exorcism (Mark 1:26 par. Luke 4:33; Acts 8:7), or Jesus' outcry at a raising from the dead (John 11:43), his cry at his death (Mark 15:37 par. Matt 27:50), and the trumpet's sound at the parousia (Matt 24:31).

b) Μέγας also designates the *unusual,* commonly the threatening *extent* of an event in nature: the earthquake in Philippi (Acts 16:26), the cosmic shaking at the end time (Luke 21:11), the epiphanic tremor at the resurrection of Jesus (Matt 28:2). The great tremor at the storm at sea (Matt 8:24), including the strong wind (Mark 4:37; John 6:18), is caused by the power of chaos, while "the *great* [i.e., full] stilling of the wind" indicates the victory of Jesus (Mark 4:39 par. Matt 8:26); the high fever of the mother-in-law of Peter (Luke 4:38) is also produced by demonic power.

c) The extent of acts that cause astonishment, whether of saving or destructive significance, can be called *great,* as with the miracles of false prophets (Matt 24:24), of Stephen (Acts 6:8), or of the apostles (8:13), the signs that announce the end (Luke 21:11), the light of salvation over Galilee (Matt 4:16, citing Isa 9:1 LXX), the fall of the house that signifies a state of eschatological existence (Matt 7:27 par. Luke 6:49), hunger (Luke 4:25; Acts 7:11; 11:28), tribulation (7:11), the persecution of Christians (8:1), eschatological woes (Luke 21:23), the "day of the Lord" (Acts 2:20, citing Joel 3:4 LXX), or feast days (John 7:37; 19:31). Μεγάλα appears in the absolute sense for "great [deeds] of God" (Luke 1:49).

d) Matt 22:36, 38 discuss the *great commandment* (Mark 12:28; cf. "the first commandment," Matt 22:38) on which the whole law and prophets hang (22:40), i.e., that which includes the sense and summation of the will of God. Corresponding to it is not the linguistic equivalent *miṣwâ gᵉḏôlâ*, the more important commandment in comparison with the lesser one (cf. Matt 5:19), but rather the "great principle *(kᵉlal gāḏôl)* in the Torah," which Rabbi Akiba saw handed down in Lev 19:18 (*y. Ned.* 9:41c).

e) Corresponding to the OT, μέγας designates the *strength* of human emotion, i.e., joy (Acts 15:3), esp. over the saving acts of God (Matt 2:10; Luke 2:10; 24:52; Acts 4:33), or fear in the presence of an event of epiphany (Mark 4:41; 5:42; Luke 2:9; 8:37; Acts 2:43; 5:5, 11), and the power of faith (Matt 15:28), of the witness to Christ (Acts 4:33), or of the mourning over death (8:2).

f) Finally, μέγας refers to the *extraordinary* person in world history or salvation history: thus in reference to God himself as the "*great* [i.e., highest] king" (μέγας as a superlative, Matt 5:35), in whose kingdom there will be lesser (Luke 7:28) as well as great (highly regarded) people (Matt 5:19; cf. 1QS 6:2; *m. Sanh.* 4:2). Jesus is called a "*great* prophet" (Luke 7:16); the order established for the disciples stands in contrast to the striving of the worldly "great ones" and rulers, who misuse their power (Mark 10:42): Whoever within the circle of disciples wants to be *great* (i.e., prominent) must be the servant of all (10:43); the Son of Man who came to serve is a model (10:45, citing Isa 43:3f., 23-26). Indeed, John the Baptist, who can be called *great* (i.e., significant in salvation history; Luke 1:15, 32), proclaims a "mightier one" who is coming (Mark 1:7), and he himself is surpassed by the smallest one in the kingdom of God (Luke 7:28). Therefore it is presumptuous when Simon Magus proclaims to be "a *great*" (Acts 8:9) or "the *great* power [of God]" (8:10), i.e., when he claims through the I-am sayings to be the representative of God (cf. Mark 14:62: δύναμις/gᵉbura as a term for God). *Great* appears in a cry of acclamation as an attribute of the Ephesian Artemis (Acts 19:27f., 34f.; cf. Xenophon Ephesius i.11.5; cf. Conzelmann 165). The phrase for totality, "from the small to the great" (superlative "young and old") in Acts 8:10, similarly 26:22 (cf. Heb 8:11, citing Jer 31:34), is based on the OT; the similar phrase in Acts 26:29 ("short or long") has a temporal significance.

3. In the Epistles the fig. meaning is predominant; thus on the one hand in the "*deep* grief" of Paul over the rejection by Israel (Rom 9:2); on the other hand with the "*great* and effective door" (1 Cor 16:9), which refers fig. to the mission among the Gentiles. The question "Is it *too much* [i.e., something extraordinary] when . . . ," which is answered negatively in 2 Cor 11:15, belongs to Paul's style of argument. In the deutero-Pauline literature, except for 2 Tim 2:20 (*large* house), μέγας accents the meaning of the reality of Christ that is now being revealed. The clause "*great* is the mystery," which perhaps takes up a cultic cry of acclamation, is applied to marriage in Eph 5:32, where the true meaning is disclosed in Christ and the Church. In 1 Tim 3:16 it is used for the Christian religion, which is founded on the saving plan of God that has now become a reality in Christ; thus godliness is a great (i.e., saving) gain (1 Tim 6:6). According to Titus 2:13 the glory "of the *great* God" will illuminate the returning Christ. The designation "*great* high priest" (Heb 4:14) is unusual, for the title "high priest" in the OT and Heb 10:20 can also read "*great* priest"; in reference to Christ it means the "author of eternal salvation" (5:9), who is also called "*great* shepherd of the sheep" (13:20). Thus confidence also has "a *great* [i.e., saving] reward" (10:35). In 11:24 μέγας γενόμενος means *grow*. The little tongue boasts of "*great* things" (Jas 3:5); Jude 6 mentions the "*great* day" of judgment.

4. a) In Revelation μέγας designates impressive heavenly and earthly phenomena of either a divine or a demonic type that occur during the end time and are perceived through vision and audition, including a mountain falling from heaven (8:8), a star (8:10), a millstone (18:20), an eagle (12:14), the throne of God (20:11) and the feast of God (19:17), a sword (6:4), a furnace (9:2), a wine press (14:19), a chain (20:1), a wall (21:12), a mountain (21:10). In describing entities such as the Euphrates River (9:14; 16:12) or the city (Jerusalem? 11:8) μέγας often refers to the political-economic and demonic concentration of power, esp. in the "*great* Babylon" (14:8; 16:19; 17:5; 18:2. 10, 21), the "*great* city" (16:19; 18:16, 18f.) and the "*great* harlot" (17:1; 19:2), and the "*great* dragon" (12:3, 9) in its diabolical power. In such stereotypical designations a cry of acclamation may be used ironically.

b) The frequently observed speaking and crying "with a *loud* voice" and the resounding "*loud* voice" refer esp. to angels who praise God and pass on his commandments to others (1:10; 5:2, 12; 7:2, 10; 8:13; 10:3; 11:12, 15; 12:10; 14:7, 9, 15, 18; 19:17); God himself calls with a "*loud* voice" from the heavenly temple (16:1, 17) or from the throne (21:3). In 6:10 and 19:1 the reference is to the loud crying of people. Great natural phenomena have the character of devastating punishment, including earthquakes (6:12; 11:13; 16:18 bis), wind (6:13), fire (16:19), and hail (16:21); cf. the *"great* plague" (16:21) and the *"great* tribulation" (2:22). They are accompanying manifestations of the *"great* day" of judgment (6:17; 16:14), of "God's *great* feast" (19:17).

c) In 15:3 the works of God are celebrated as *"great* and wonderful." A *"great* sign" (12:1; 15:1) signifies the beginning of a new vision, though *"great* signs and wonders" is also used of false prophets (13:13; cf. Deut 13:2). The power of God (11:17), the authority of an angel (18:1), and the power given to the beast of the dragon (13:2) are *great* (i.e., extensive); this beast speaks *"great* [i.e., insolent] words and blasphemies" (13:5; cf. Dan 7:8, 11, 20).

d) The intensive meaning of μέγας appears with fear (11:11), wrath (12:12), astonishment (17:6), in "small and *great*," etc. (11:18; 13:16; 19:5, 18; 20:12).   O. Betz

μέγεθος, ους, τό *megethos* greatness, power*

In the NT only fig. of God: τὸ ὑπερβάλλον μέγεθος τῆς δυνάμεως αὐτοῦ, "the surpassing *greatness* of his power," Eph 1:19; cf. Philo *Op.* 23; Exod 15:16; Wis 13:5. W. Grundmann, *TDNT* IV, 544.

μεγιστάν, ᾶνος, ὁ *megistan* nobleman, eminent person*

In the NT only pl. μεγιστᾶνες: of the courtiers of Herod Antipas (with χιλίαρχοι, Mark 6:21); generally: οἱ βασιλεῖς τῆς γῆς καὶ οἱ μεγιστᾶνες καὶ οἱ χιλίαρχοι (Rev 6:15; cf. also Ps 2:2; Isa 24:21; 34:12); of the merchants of "Babylon" as the μεγιστᾶνες τῆς γῆς (18:23; cf. Isa 23:8; Jer 25:18 LXX; 27:35 LXX; see also H. Kraft, *Rev* [HNT] ad loc.).

μέγιστος, 3 *megistos* very large, enormous*

Superlative of → μέγας; in the NT only 2 Pet 1:4 with the elative meaning: μέγιστα ἐπαγγέλματα, *"extraordinary* promise" (see BDF §60.2).

μεθερμηνεύω *methermēneuō* translate*

There are 8 occurrences in the NT, regularly pass. and, with the exception of Acts 13:8 (μεθερμηνεύεται), in the formula ὅ ἐστιν μεθερμηνευόμενον, "what *is translated"* (Matt 1:23; Mark 5:41; 15:22, 34; John 1:41; Acts 4:36; not in Luke and Paul), or ὃ λέγεται μεθερμηνευόμενον (John 1:38); → ἑρμηνεύω 2.

μέθη, ης, ἡ *methē* drunkenness*

In the NT only in vice catalogs: with κραιπάλη ("debauchery") and μέριμναι βιωτικαί ("daily cares"), Luke

21:34; pl. with κῶμοι ("carousing"), etc., Rom 13:13; Gal 5:21 (cf. also Philo *Ebr.* xv.154f., etc.; *Sobr.* 2). H. Preisker, *TDNT* IV, 545-48.

μεθίστημι (alternative form of **μεθιστάνω**) *methistēmi* (*methistanō*) remove, transplant; put down; lead astray*

There are 5 occurrences in the NT: In the spatial sense, 1 Cor 13:2 uses a common image for making possible what has been impossible (ὄρη μεθιστάναι; cf. Mark 11:23 par. Matt 21:21; Matt 17:20; cf. par. Luke 17:6; *b. Sanh.* 24a; Billerbeck I, 759); in another sphere, *transfer,* Col 1:13 (εἰς τὴν βασιλείαν . . . ; cf. also Josephus *Ant.* ix.235); *alienate from, divert,* Acts 19:26 (ἱκανὸν ὄχλον); *put down* (from the throne)/*separate* (from power), in reference to Saul, 13:22 (cf. 1 Sam 15:23; Dan 2:21; not "dispossess" [4 Kgdms 17:23] or "separate from life" [3 Macc 3:28]). Pass. Luke 16:4: *"be removed* from office" (ὅταν μετασταθῶ ἐκ τῆς οἰκονομίας; cf. also *Vita Aesopi* i.9).

μεθοδεία, ας, ἡ *methodeia* cunning, deceit; pl.: schemes*

Both NT occurrences are in Ephesians; it is not previously attested. The noun can be, like μέθοδος and μεθοδεύω, also understood in the neutral sense of "technique, method" (cf. Suidas s.v.; τέχνας ἢ δόλους), but in the NT it has only a negative meaning: Eph 4:14: "in malice, which leads to the *cunning* of error (μεθοδεία τῆς πλάνης)"; pl., 6:11, of the *"schemes* of the devil." W. Michaelis, *TDNT* V, 102-3; LSJ s.v.; Spicq, *Notes* II, 548.

μεθόριον, ου, τό *methorion* border, border area

Mark 7:24 TR: εἰς τὰ μεθόρια Τύρου instead of ὅρια.

μεθύσκω *methyskō* make drunk; pass.: get drunk*

All 5 occurrences are in the pass.: Luke 12:45 (with ἐσθίειν and πίνειν); John 2:10: ὅταν μεθυσθῶσιν, "when they *are drunk"*; Eph 5:18 (οἴνῳ); 1 Thess 5:7 (with νυκτὸς μεθύουσιν); Rev 17:2 (ἐκ τοῦ οἴνου τῆς πορνείας; cf. Jer 28:7 LXX; Nah 3:4). H. Preisker, *TDNT* IV, 545-48.

μέθυσος, ου, ὁ *methysos* drinker, drunkard*

In the NT only in vice catalogs: 1 Cor 5:11; 6:10, with λοίδορος (cf. Pap. Oxy. XV, 1828,3; *T. Jud.* 14:1, 8). H. Preisker, *TDNT* IV, 545-48.

μεθύω *methyō* be drunk, be intoxicated*

There are 5 occurrences in the NT: Matt 24:49 (οἱ μεθύοντες, "those *who are drunk"*); Acts 2:15; 1 Cor 11:21

(ὃς μὲν πεινᾷ, ὃς δὲ μεθύει, not to be understood against the background of the cult of Dionysus [contra H. Preisker, TDNT IV, 547], but as a critique challenging the ἴδιον δεῖπνον, v. 21a); 1 Thess 5:7 (νυκτὸς μεθύω with νυκτὸς καθεύδω as images for the existence that is not appropriate for the υἱοὶ φωτὸς . . . καὶ . . . ἡμέρας [v. 5]); fig. drunk, Rev 17:6. H. Preisker, TDNT IV, 545-48.

μείγνυμι, μειγνύω meignymi, meignyō mix, mingle*

There are 4 occurrences in the NT; on the orthography, cf. BDF §23. Matt 27:34: οἶνον μετὰ χολῆς μεμιγμένον, "wine mixed with gall" (cf. Ps 68:22 LXX); Luke 13:1, of Galileans: ὧν τὸ αἷμα Πιλᾶτος ἔμιξεν μετὰ τῶν θυσιῶν αὐτῶν, "whose blood Pilate mixed with their sacrifices [i.e., whom he had slain while they were sacrificing]"; Rev 8:7: μεμιγμένα αἵματι, "mixed with blood"; 15:2: μεμιγμένην πυρί, "mixed with fire" (of the "sea of glass"; apparently, as in 4:5, the reference is to the flashes of lightning; cf. also 2 Enoch 29:2).

μεῖζον meizon (even) more plentifully, (even) more (adv.)*

This adv. is formed from the comparative → μείζων (cf. BDF §102.1): Matt 20:31: μεῖζον ἔκραξαν, "they cried out even more."

μειζότερος, 3 meizoteros greater*

The comparative μειζότερος (with → μείζων as a "popular new formation": BDF §61.2) appears only in 3 John 4 (μειζοτέρα χαρά).

μείζων, 2 meizōn greater*

Lit.: H. CONZELMANN, 1 Cor (Hermeneia) 215f. — W. GRUNDMANN, TDNT IV, 529-44. — S. LÉGASSE, Jésus et l'enfant (1969) 23-36, 72-75, 215-31. — W. WINK, John the Baptist in the Gospel Tradition (1968) 24f.

1. Μείζων is the comparative of → μέγας, "great." In the NT it sometimes takes on the (Hellenistic) sense of the rel. superlative. The adv. μεῖζον appears in the NT only in Matt 20:31. Except for three cases (Rom 9:12, citing Gen 25:23; Mark 4:32 par. Matt 13:32; Luke 12:18) the adj. has a fig. meaning. The usage varies (Matt 23:17, 19; John 13:16; 15:20; 19:11; Heb 6:13, 16; 9:11; 11:26; Jas 4:6; 2 Pet 2:11; 1 John 3:20; 4:4; 3 John 4 [μειζότερος]).

2. A few types of usage deserve mention. a) The second part of the logion Luke 7:28 par. Matt 11:11 is a Christian "rectification"; it is not intended to contrast Jesus, as the one who comes later, with John the Baptist (who stands in contrast to the clarifying phrase "in the kingdom of God"), but instead demonstrates the essential

difference in level of importance, in which the least among the Christians is greater than the one who is "more than a prophet" (Luke 7:26 par. Matt 11:9). The dialogue about the one who is "the greatest" (μείζων) in Mark 9:33-35 (cf. 10:43f.) or Luke 22:24-27 corrects the (possible) ambition among community leaders when it indicates that true greatness consists in humility and service. In Matt 23:11 the same instruction is directed to the teachers. Luke 9:46-48 probably expresses an appeal to receive the poor person because (v. 48b: γάρ) of a dignity that makes him—paradoxically (cf. Jas 2:5)—"the greatest." Matt 18:1-4 discusses the true greatness "in the kingdom of heaven," i.e., greatness with respect to salvation and moral conduct: Only the lowly (cf. 5:3f.), depicted by the symbol of a child, will share in the eschatological bliss. The supplemental argumentation in Matt 12:5-7 justifying the freedom that Jesus claims with respect to the sabbath expresses an idea that is fundamentally less personal (v. 6 has the neut.: μεῖζόν ἐστιν ὧδε; cf. 12:41f.: πλεῖον).

b) In John μείζων corresponds in part to the "hierarchical" structure of theology: the Father, who "is greater than all things" (10:29; v.l. "all"), is "greater than" Jesus (14:28) and gives to him a power that he may give life to the dead (5:20f.). In this connection, Jesus is placed even above Jacob (4:12) and Abraham (8:53). He has a "greater witness" than John through the works that he does (5:36; 1 John 5:9; cf. John 1:50), i.e., the testimony of God himself, which is "greater" than that of humankind (1 John 5:9). However, the one who believes in Jesus will do works that "are greater" than those of Jesus (John 14:12), because he extends his revealing activity into the world (cf. 17:20; 20:21, 29).

c) John defines the "greater love" within the ethical order. It consists in the giving of one's own life for one's friends, as Jesus himself did (John 15:13). Love is itself the highest in the scale of values. When prophecy takes first place (1 Cor 12:31; 14:5) among the higher gifts, love—the subject of the greatest commandment (Mark 12:31)—surpasses faith and hope (1 Cor 13:13), probably not because it abides eternally but because the other virtues remain incomplete without it (Gal 5:6; cf. 1 Thess 1:3; 2 Thess 1:11).

d) Finally, the typology of Hebrews (9:11) underscores the transcendence of the heavenly sanctuary, which Jesus has passed through, corresponding to the superiority of the new worship over the old.

S. Légasse

μέλαν, ανος, τό melan ink*

The neut. of the adj. → μέλας is used 3 times as a subst. in the NT as a t.t. for the (black) ink most often made of soot (known from the time of Plato Phdr. 276c;

frequent in the papyri; see Preisigke, *Wörterbuch* s.v.; Moulton/Milligan s.v.; cf. also Jer 36:18 MT/43:18 LXX only in a few mss.; loanword in rabbinic literature): fig. ἐπιστολὴ . . . ἐγγεγραμμένη οὐ μέλανι, 2 Cor 3:3; διὰ χάρτου καὶ μέλανος, "with paper (papyrus) and *ink*," 2 John 12; διὰ μέλανος καὶ καλάμου, "with *ink* and pen," 3 John 13. *BL* 1758; G. Herzog-Hauser, PW Suppl. VII, 1574-79; H. Hunger, et al., *Die Textüberlieferung der antiken Literatur und der Bibel* (1961) 27-43; *KP* V, 856; W. Michaelis, *TDNT* IV, 549-51; L. Rost, *BHH* 1991.

μέλας, αινα, αν *melas* black*

Used of "*black* hair" in contrast to white (θρὶξ λευκὴ/ μέλαινα), probably as a sign of youth and age (Matt 5:36); ἵππος μέλας, as the color of the third of four (apocalyptic) horses (Rev 6:5; see also Zech 6:2, 6; *Herm. Vis.* iv.3.2); μέλας ὡς σάκκος τρίχινος, of the darkening of the sun "*black* as sackcloth [mourning garment]" (Rev 6:12; cf. Isa 50:3; also Ezek 32:7f.). In *Barn.* 4:9 the devil is called ὁ μέλας. BAGD s.v. (bibliography); W. Michaelis, *TDNT* IV, 549-51.

Μελεά *Melea* Melea*

The name (Heb. probably *m^ele'â*) of the son of Menna in the genealogy of Jesus (Luke 3:31).

μέλει (μοι) *melei (moi)* it concerns me, I am concerned about*

The third person sg. of μέλω appears 10 times in the NT (with one exception [Acts 18:17] in impersonal constructions): with the gen. only in 1 Cor 9:9 (cf. Deut 25:4; *Ep. Arist.* 144; Philo *Spec. Leg.* i.260; *b. B. Meṣ.* 88b); with περί and gen. in Mark 12:14 par. Matt 22:16 ("you care for no one"); John 10:13; 12:6; 1 Pet 5:7; with ὅτι in Mark 4:38; Luke 10:40; with subj. οὐδὲν τούτων ("nothing about") in Acts 18:17; absolute μή σοι μελέτω, "do not *let it trouble you*/you *should not be concerned*" in 1 Cor 7:21.

Μελελεήλ *Meleleēl* Mahalalel

Alternate form (Luke 3:37 ℵ² A N, etc.) of → Μαλελεήλ.

μελετάω *meletaō* be concerned about, worry, take great pains with, scheme, plan*

Acts 4:25: ἐμελέτησαν κενά, "*plan* vain things" (citing Ps 2:1 LXX); 1 Tim 4:15: ταῦτα μελέτα, "*take great pains with* that"; Mark 13:11 TR absolute: μηδὲ μελετᾶτε.

μέλι, ιτος, τό *meli* honey*

There are 4 occurrences in the NT: Of the food of John the Baptist, ἀκρίδες καὶ μέλι ἄγριον (Mark 1:6 par. Matt 3:4; cf. *Gos. Eb.* 2), probably honey from wild bees, which (like most types of locusts) belonged among the clean foods (cf. also W. Michaelis, *TDNT* IV, 552-54; Billerbeck I, 98-101); as "drink for those fasting," for ascetics, cf. O. Böcher, *Christus Exorcista* (1972) 120f.; *idem, NTS* 18 [1971/72] 90-92); "sweet as *honey*," Rev 10:9f. (cf. Ezek 3:3; Ps 118:103 LXX). *BL* 759f.; L. H. Silberman, *BHH* 747; *TWNT* X, 1173 (bibliography).

μελίσσιος, 2 *melissios* belonging to a bee

Luke 24:42 TR: ἀπὸ μελισσίου κηρίου, "from a honeycomb."

Μελίτη, ης *Melitē* Malta*

Lit.: W. BIEDER, *BHH* 1132f. — *BL* 1087f. — N. HEUTGER, " 'Paulus auf Malta' im Lichte der maltesischen Topographie," *BZ* 28 (1984) 86-88. — *KP* III, 1179. — H. WARNECKE, *Die tatsächliche Romfahrt des Apostels Paulus* (SBS 127, 1987). — J. WEHNERT, "Gestrandet. Zu einer neuen These über den Schiffbruch des Apostels Paulus auf dem Wege nach Rom (Apg 27-28)," *ZTK* 87 (1990) 67-99. — T. ZAHN, *Rev* (KNT) II, 441-44.

An island south of Sicily (Strabo vi.2.11), which, because of its many harbors, was a base for east-west commerce in the Mediterranean Sea and was used widely for spending the winter. According to Acts 27:39ff., after a shipwreck Paul was driven to Μελίτη (28:1), which had been under Roman rule from 218 B.C. The inhabitants spoke primarily Punic (28:2: βάρβαροι). Paul remained on the island for three months (28:11), hence a deep bay came to be called Paul's Bay.

μέλλω *mellō* intend, be about to, will (as auxiliary vb. for the fut.), be destined to; consider, hesitate, delay

1. Occurrences — 2. Meaning and constructions — 3. Usage

Lit.: BAGD s.v. — BDF §§66; 338; 350; 356. — KÜHNER, *Grammatik* II/1, 177-79. — A. J. MATTILL, JR., *Luke and the Last Things* (1979) 43-49, 53. — MAYSER, *Grammatik* II/1, 166, 226. — W. SCHNEIDER, *DNTT* I, 325-27.

1. Μέλλω appears in the NT 109 times. Luke's preference for it is to be seen in the 29 instances in Acts 16–28 alone (on Luke, cf. H. Schürmann, *Jesu Abschiedsrede. Lk 22,21-38* [²1977] 13). A partc. form of μέλλω appears 53 times. The augment can be either ἐ- or ἠ-: John and Revelation alternate; Luke, however— likewise Heb 11:8—prefers ἠ- (Luke 7:2; 9:31; 10:1; 19:4; Acts 12:6; 16:27; 27:33; otherwise only 21:27); it does not appear elsewhere.

2. a) In most instances μέλλω is connected with a following inf., though rarely with the fut. inf. (which regularly appears in classical literature): only in Acts

11:28; 24:15; 27:10; properly also in 3:3 and 20:7 (cf. BDF §350). Scarcely more frequent is the occurrence of the aor. inf., which is also rare in classical literature: Acts 12:6; Rom 8:18; Gal 3:23; Rev 3:2, 16; 12:4. In most instances it occurs with the pres. inf., which is often found in classical literature, belonging to the papyri of the common language.

The transformation of the basic meaning "I think" (Kühner 178) takes place throughout the various inf. constructions. Μέλλω has (1) the meaning *be about to, be present,* even *begin;* thus Luke 7:2: "he was *near* death/ *at the point* of dying"; Acts 16:27; Rev 10:4: "I *wanted to begin* to write"; 10:7: "he *began* to blow the trumpet/ he *sounded* the trumpet." (2) Μέλλω is often used periphrastically for the simple fut., esp. the disappearing inf. and partc. forms: the inf. only in Acts 28:6 and 19:27 (cf. BDF §356), while the partc. is frequent, as in 2 Tim 4:1 ("Christ Jesus, who *will* judge/the *future* judge" or—as a substitute for the fut. pass. partc.—Rom 8:18 ("the glory that *will* be [is intended to be] revealed"); likewise Gal 3:23; 1 Pet 5:1; cf. 1:5 (with ἕτοιμος). An exemplary case for the periphrasis of the fut. ind. is offered by *Herm. Man.* iv.4.3: ὅσα λαλῶ ἢ καὶ μέλλω λαλεῖν, "what I say or also *will* say." In Acts μέλλω contains no suggestion of a *near* future (against Mattill). (3) Μέλλω also designates the intended action, as in Matt 2:13: "*he intended* to search for the child"; Acts 20:3, 7, 13, with reference to the travel *plans* of Paul. (4) Finally, μέλλω can express the necessity of an event that is based on the divine will and thus is certain to occur, e.g., Matt 17:12: "he *must* suffer" (cf. Matt 16:21 par. Luke 9:22 with δεῖ); John 12:4: "Judas . . . , who *was later* to betray him" (or "who *intended* to betray him"—then the passage is to be arranged under 3; cf. BAGD s.v.). The latter example indicates clearly that μέλλω does not always have a fixed meaning.

b) Besides the combination with an inf., μέλλω appears in the NT 18 times as an absolute partc. (1) Used as an adj., it appears always in the attributive position and means *coming, future* (Matt 3:7 par. Luke 3:7; Matt 12:32; Acts 24:25; Rom 5:14; Eph 1:21; 1 Tim 4:8; Heb 2:5; 6:5; 10:1; 13:14). (2) As a substantive it designates *the future* (τὸ μέλλον, 1 Tim 6:19), once *the coming year* (εἰς τὸ μέλλον, Luke 13:9; so BAGD s.v. with reference to Pap. London 123.4), or *that which is to come* (τὰ μέλλοντα, Col 2:17; 1 Tim 1:16; Heb 11:20; with ἐνεστῶτα, the present situation, Rom 8:38; 1 Cor 3:22).

c) Μέλλω appears as an independent vb. only in Acts 22:16: "What is *still delaying* you?"

3. Except for Acts, most of the passages with μέλλω can be arranged under two categories. While Acts (except for the eschatological sayings in 17:31; 24:15, 25, and the announcement of impending death in 20:38) uses

μέλλω in less theological contexts, the other books give it essentially two reference points: suffering and the eschaton. The two passages in Mark reflect the Gospels in general: 12:32 points to the Passion of Jesus (cf. Matt 17:12, 22; 20:22; Luke 9:31, 44; 22:23; John 6:71; 7:35b, c; 11:51; 12:4, 33; 18:32), and Mark 13:4 refers to the event of the end (cf. Matt 3:7; 11:14; 12:32; 16:27; 24:6; Luke 3:7; 19:11; 21:7, 36; 24:21; John 7:39; 14:22). In the NT letters μέλλω is used with reference to the suffering (of Christians; 1 Thess 3:4) and for the anticipated future, the judgment, the new aeon, the future life, and other "blessings" that are objects of hope (Rom 4:24; 5:14; 8:13, 18; Eph 1:21; Col 2:17; 1 Tim 4:8; 6:19; 2 Tim 4:1; Jas 2:12; 1 Pet 5:1; Heb 1:14; 2:5; 6:5; 10:1, 27; 13:14, with the wordplay μένουσαν [πόλιν]— μέλλουσαν). In Revelation the two categories overlap: in 2:10a, b; 3:10; 6:11 martyrdom is connected with the end. One may compare also 1:9; 8:13; 10:7; 12:4f.; 17:8.

W. Radl

μέλος, ους, τό *melos* member of a body, member*

1. Occurrences in the NT; meaning — 2. Matt 5:29f. — 3. Paul — 4. Jas 3:1ff.

Lit.: U. BROCKHAUS, *Charisma und Amt. Die paulinische Charismenlehre auf dem Hintergrund der frühchristlichen Gemeindefunktionen* (1972) 164-75. — E. FUCHS, "Existentiale Interpretation von Röm 7,1-12 und 21-23," idem, *Aufsätze* III, 364-401. — J. HAINZ, *Ekklesia. Strukturen paulinischer Gemeinde-Theologie und Gemeinde-Ordnung* (1972) 73-88. — F. HORST, *TDNT* IV, 555-68. — E. KÄSEMANN, *Leib und Leib Christi. Eine Untersuchung zur paulinischen Begrifflichkeit* (1933). — E. SCHWEIZER, "Die Kirche als Leib Christi in den paulinischen Homologumena," idem, *Neotestamentica* (1963) 272-92. — idem, "Die Sünde in den Gliedern," FS Michel 437-39.

1. Μέλος appears in the NT 34 times, with its primary emphasis in the Pauline letters (Romans, 1 Corinthians, Ephesians, Colossians; in Eph 4:16 read μέρος); elsewhere only in Matt 5:29f.; Jas 3:5; 4:1. Μέλος designates (originally pl.) the *members of the body.* The meaning "song" (see Horst 560n.3) is not found in the NT. It is widely used within the framework of the image of the unity of the body and the multiplicity of the members in their various potential tasks.

2. In the Synoptic tradition μέλος appears only in the second antithesis of the Sermon on the Mount (Matt 5:29f., a statement derived from the sayings source), where it is used in contrast to σῶμα. The antithesis of Matt 5:28 is ethicized and radicalized with the addition of vv. 29f.; the demand is to turn away from a situation that causes danger.

3. The use of the term in Paul underlines esp. a central conviction of his anthropology: the situation of humankind in service to the power either of sin or of God

(as in the baptismal parenesis in Rom 6:13 bis, 19 bis; cf. 1 Cor 6:15 ter; Col 3:5), but then also one's imprisonment as one cries for redemption in the context of the division between two laws (Rom 7:5, 23 bis). Corresponding to this is not the empirical-moral difference between human volition and activity, but rather a division in the person, the deadly triumph (7:24) of the law of sin over the good law of God that dwells within (7:22). In this context μέλος designates in an emphatic way the person (not only one's deeds), insofar as the person does not have control of himself.

Paul takes up the image of the unity of the body and of the variety of functions of the members in Rom 12:4ff. and 1 Cor 12:11-27 within the context of the question about the gifts of grace. Though the statement of the problem is given in the variety of the functions of the members, the idea of the unity of the body is not derived from the clarity of the image; rather, the identification of "body" with "body of Christ," which extends beyond the image, is an anticipation of instruction on the cooperation between members (Rom 12:5; 1 Cor 12:12, 27). Accordingly, the discussion of the body of Christ does not take place within the context of soteriology, but in the parenesis (Schweizer, *Kirche*). The members *are* members of a body; they do not constitute its unity (cf. 1 Cor 12:18).

Similarly, in Eph 4:25; 5:30 the figure serves as a basis for parenesis. Thus in 4:25, with the isolated reference to the members alone, a clear hint is given that here the body takes precedence over the cooperation of the members.

4. In Jas 3:1-12 the image of the body and the members (3:2, 5f.), together with several other images and allusions, lies in the background. In the foreground is the warning (3:10) against the devastating effects of the smallest member, the tongue (cf. Sir 28:13-26), which is regarded from a thoroughly pessimistic perspective.

M. Völkel

Μελχί *Melchi* Melchi*

The name (Heb. *malkî*) of two men in the genealogy of Jesus: Luke 3:24: the son of Jannai; 3:28: the son of Addi.

Μελχισέδεκ *Melchisedek* Melchizedek*

Lit.: BILLERBECK IV, 252f., 452-65. — J. BONSIRVEN, "Le Sacerdoce et le sacrifice de Jésus Christ d'après l'Épître aux Hébreux," *NRT* 66 (1939) 641-60, 769-86. — J. CARMIGNAC, "Le document de Qumran sur Melkisédek," *RevQ* 7 (1970) 343-78. — J. A. FITZMYER, "Further Light on Melchizedek from Qumran Cave 11," *JBL* 86 (1967) 25-41. — M. FRIEDLÄNDER, "La Secte de Melchisédec et l'épître aux Hébreux," *REJ* 5 (1882) 1-26, 188-98; 6 (1883) 187-99. — W. HERTZBERG, "Die Melchisedeq-Traditionen," *JPOS* 8 (1928) 169-79. — F. L. HORTON,

The Melchizedek Tradition (1976). — M. DE JONGE and A. S. VAN DER WOUDE, "11QMelchizedek and the NT," *NTS* 12 (1965/66) 301-26. — E. KUTSCH, *RGG* IV, 843ff. — O. MICHEL, *TDNT* IV, 568-70. — J. J. PETUCHOWSKI, "The Controversial Figure of Melchizedek," *HUCA* 28 (1957) 127-36. — J. J. PETUCHOWSKI, et al., *Melchisedech—Urgestalt der Ökumene* (1979). — H. STORCK, *Die sogenannten Melchisedekianer mit Untersuchung ihrer Quellen auf Gedankengehalt und dogmengeschichtliche Entwicklung* (1928). — A. S. VAN DER WOUDE, "Melchisedech als himmlische Erlösergestalt in den neugefundenen eschatologischen Midraschim aus Qumran-Höhle XI," *OTS* 14 (1965) 354-73. — G. WUTTKE, *Melchisedech, der Priesterkönig von Salem* (1927). — W. ZIMMERLI, "Abraham und Melchisedek," FS L. Rost (BZAW 105, 1967) 255-64. — For further bibliography see *TWNT* X, 1173-75.

1. Melchizedek (the name means "my king is [called] righteousness") is a figure belonging to a very ancient tradition. The priest-king, who probably lived in the northern part of Canaan (Hertzberg 179), becomes in Jewish tradition king of (Jeru)-Salem and a contemporary of Abraham (Gen 14:18ff.). Through the act of blessing Melchizedek becomes for Israel a significant person of the past. From his role as "priest of the most high God" (Gen 14:18) he becomes the priestly-royal representative and predecessor of the Jerusalem priesthood.

2. Even as a mysterious outsider, who as ἀπάτωρ and ἀμήτωρ cannot be included among those with a human origin (Heb 7:3), Melchizedek remains an established figure of Israelite faith. And through the obscure path that can be seen in the apocalyptic literature of Qumran (see the literature on 11QMelch) and in Philo (cf. Michel 569), Melchizedek finds entry into the NT literature. As an interpretive model (F. Mussner in Petuchowski, *Melchisedech* 42), the subject of Melchizedek attains its relevance and incomparable position for christology and salvation history in Hebrews (5:6, 10; 6:20; 7:1, 10f., 15, 17). As king of peace and of righteousness (midrash typology) the original Melchizedek is merely an anticipatory figure.

The actual type to whom he is compared is Jesus Christ, the Messiah and Son of God. Jesus is the actual priest and king, the only high priest through whom peace and righteousness become reality (cf. Ps 110:4). Just as God has already established the sign of the eternal and immortal king-priest in the original Melchizedek—the death of Melchizedek is never mentioned—the expression "the order of Melchizedek" (Heb 5:6, 10; 6:20; 7:11, 17; 7:21 v.l.) is the eschatological guarantee: eternal priest. The Jewish priesthood is thus greatly transcended, even though Jesus came from the tribe of Judah, a non-priestly tribe, since he finally created direct access to God for all. The Melchizedek-Christ comprises primal history and eschaton at the same time and implies the completion of all things in the divine salvific plan. He is the mediator of salvation—and salvation itself, for which the anticipatory figure Melchizedek was only a hint.

F. Schröger

μεμβράνα, ης, ἡ *membrana* parchment*

2 Tim 4:13, pl. with τὰ βιβλία: "especially the *parchments*/parchment scrolls (?)." BAGD s.v.; → βιβλίον 1.

μέμφομαι *memphomai* blame, find fault (with)*

Rom 9:19: τί οὖν ἔτι μέμφεται, "how *can* he [God] still *find fault?*"; Heb 8:8: μεμφόμενος γὰρ αὐτοὺς λέγει, "for he *finds fault* with the following words"; Mark 7:2 TR. W. Grundmann, *TDNT* IV, 571-74.

μεμψίμοιρος, 2 *mempsimoiros* dissatisfied, struggling with his fate*

Jude 16: γογγυσταὶ μεμψίμοιροι, "murmuring *without any satisfaction.*" W. Grundmann, *TDNT* IV, 574.

μέν *men* indeed

1. Occurrences in the NT — 2. With correlative particles — 3. Formulaic phrases — 4. Without correlative particles

Lit.: BAGD s.v. — BDF §447. — KÜHNER, *Grammatik* II, 264-72. — MAYSER, *Grammatik* II/3, 125-31. — SCHWYZER, *Grammatik* II, 569f. — G. STRECKER, *1-3 John* (KEK) 99-101, 164f. — VKGNT II, s.v.

1. Μέν was widely used in classical Greek, less frequently in the popular Koine, and not at all in modern Greek. In the NT it occurs 180 times, of which 48 are in Acts, 20 in Matthew, 20 in 1 Corinthians, 20 in Hebrews, and 18 in Romans; elsewhere it appears less than 10 times. In proportion to the size of the book, μέν appears most frequently in Hebrews. Μέν does not appear in several NT writings (2 Thessalonians, 1 Timothy, Titus, 2 Peter, 1-3 John, Revelation), and in others it appears only once (Eph 4:11; Col 2:23; 1 Thess 2:18; Jas 3:17).

2. The intensifying particle μέν, originally a prepositive but used normally as a postpositive, has the function in the NT and its world—as also predominantly in classical Greek—of setting the stage for a strong or weak contrast (most often with δέ), and thus it contributes toward linking individual words or clauses. The correlation of μέν and δέ corresponds to English "*certainly*—but"; however, the particles often play a role through emphatic position or oral accentuation so that μέν but not δέ remains untranslated (e.g., Matt 10:13: ἐὰν μὲν . . . ἐὰν δὲ μή, "if—but if not").

A contrast begun by μέν can also be strengthened or weakened by other particles: strengthened as in μέν—ἀλλά (Mark 9:12f.; Acts 4:16f.; Rom 14:20), μέν—πλήν (Luke 22:22), μέν—μέντοι (John 7:12f.); weakened as in μέν—καί (Acts 1:18f.; 27:21; Rom 7:12; 10:1; 1 Thess 2:18).

3. In the Gospels free use of μέν—δέ predominates by a ratio of 3 to 2, while in the other literature the following three uses are predominant:

a) The most frequent formula by far is "the one—the other"; here the use of ὁ μέν—ὁ δέ seldom occurs (definite use only in Rom 2:7f.; 1 Cor 7:7; Gal 4:23; Eph 4:11; Phil 3:13; Heb 7:5, 23; 12:10); ὅς μέν—ὅς δέ is frequent and often varied, while in place of ὅς δέ one finds also καὶ ἄλλος (δέ), καὶ ἕτερος, or ἀλλ' ὁ ἕτερος—also in the Gospels.

Under these circumstances the NT editions are not justified, whenever the nom. masc. pl. of this formula appears, in preferring the art. (οἱ μέν—οἱ δέ) to the rel. pron. (οἳ μέν—οἳ δέ). The following passages are affected: Acts 14:4; 17:32; 28:24; Phil 1:16; see Matt 16:14 and John 7:12 with οἳ μέν—ἄλλοι δέ.

b) The formula μὲν οὖν occurs 32 times in the NT, 26 of which are in Acts. Without δέ following, μέν has an intensifying effect in this phrase (e.g., Rom 11:13; 1 Cor, 6:4, 7 [→ 4]; Heb 7:11); as a rule (cf. → 2), however, it points ahead to another clause, inasmuch as it corresponds to a following δέ (Acts 1:6f.; Phil 2:23; Heb 9:1, etc.) or καί (e.g., Acts 1:18).

c) Only in Heb 7:2; Jas 3:17 does πρῶτον μέν, *first/in the first place*, correspond to the anticipated ἔπειτα (δέ), "then/in the second place"; cf. the variant τότε μέν . . . ἔπειτα in John 11:6. In three other instances (Rom 1:8; 3:2; 1 Cor 11:18) πρῶτον μέν stands alone, meaning *above all.*

4. In addition to the instances already mentioned (→ 3), μέν appears in a few passages (apparently) without correlative particles/conjunctions. Several times, as also in classical Greek, other means are used to signify the contrast: Acts 3:13: ἐκείνου; 1 Cor 12:28: ἔπειτα; 5:3 (see v. 6); Col 2:23: οὐ (as in Heb 12:9, provided δέ is not to be supplied); in 2 Cor 9:1-3 and 11:4-6 the correlation of μέν and δέ is separated only by transitional phrases introduced by γάρ. A claim in 2 Cor 12:12 has no verbal correlation in the following statement; in 1 Cor 6:7, with the omission of οὖν, μέν takes on the preclassical sense and thus intensifies ἤδη: "*indeed already*"; in Acts 28:22 the correlative idea is omitted because it is anticipated at the beginning of the verse; in both 1:1 and 3:21 the initial idea appears not to be pursued to completion because the potential contrasting idea is introduced with temporal ἄχρι.

K.-H. Pridik

Μεννά *Menna* Menna*

The name of the son of Mattatha in the genealogy of Jesus (Luke 3:31; TR Μαϊνάν).

μενοῦν *menoun* rather, to the contrary, truly*

A particle used to emphasize or correct: Luke 11:28, at the beginning of the sentence (contrary to Greek usage elsewhere; cf. BDF §§448.6; 450.4); cf. also Rom 9:20 v.l.; Phil 3:8 v.l.

μενοῦνγε *menounge* rather, of course*

The particle → μενοῦν, intensified by -γε: Rom 9:20: "who are you, *then?*"; 10:18: *"of course, indeed!";* Phil 3:8: ἀλλὰ μενοῦνγε, *"indeed"* (→ ἀλλά 2); Luke 11:28 v.l.

μέντοι *mentoi* really, actually, nevertheless*

There are 8 occurrences in the NT, consistently with an adversative meaning: *of course/to be sure/nevertheless* (John 4:27; 7:13; 20:5; 21:4; 2 Tim 2:19); ὅμως μέντοι, "nevertheless, *however*" (John 12:42); εἰ μέντοι, "but if *truly/really*" (Jas 2:8); weakened in ὁμοίως μέντοι καί, *"(but)/truly in the same way"* (Jude 8, cf. vv. 5-7). See also BDF §450.1.

μένω *menō* remain, stay; await

1. Occurrences in the NT — 2. Meaning — 3. Immanence formulas in the Johannine literature

Lit.: F. HAUCK, *TDNT* IV, 574-79. — J. HEISE, *Bleiben. Menein in den johanneischen Schriften* (HUT 8, 1967). — B. LAMMERS, *Die MENEIN- Formeln der Johannesbriefe. Eine Studie zur johanneischen Anschauung der Gottesgemeinschaft* (Diss. Gregorian University, Rome, 1954). — E. MALATESTA, *Interiority and Covenant. An Exegetical Study of the εἶναι ἐν and μένειν ἐν Expressions in 1 John* (AnBib 69, 1976). — K. MUNZER, *DNTT* III, 223-26. — R. SCHNACKENBURG, *1-3 John* (HTKNT, ⁴1970) 105-10. — For further bibliography see *TWNT* X, 1175.

1. Μένω appears 118 times in the NT, esp. in the Johannine literature (the Gospel has 40 occurrences, 1 John has 24, 2 John has 3). Other occurrences are in the Lukan literature (20, including 13 in Acts), 1 Corinthians (8), Hebrews (6), then 3 occurrences each in Matthew, 2 Corinthians, and 2 Timothy, 2 each in Mark and 1 Peter, and 1 each in Romans, Philippians, 1 Timothy, and Revelation.

2. The basic meaning of μένω as an intrans. vb. is *remain, continue, stand firm;* as a trans. vb. it is *wait on, expect* (Frisk, *Wörterbuch* II, 209). In the NT one finds also the derivative meanings *dwell* (John 1:38f.), *remain alive* (21:22f.), *continue to live* (1 Cor 15:6), *be permanent* (3:14), *remain in a situation* (7:8, 11, 20, 24, 40).

According to R. Bultmann (*1-3 John* [Hermeneia] 26n.9) μένειν always involves a negation: *not to give way.* It does not, he says, respond to the question "where?" but rather to the question "how long?" In the earliest Greek usage it concerned *continuing* at an objectively fixed place for an objectively determined time, and then later it involved continuation in a personal bond (so in John and 1 John).

When, however, Bultmann plays off μένειν as a response to

the question "how long?" against the question "where?" he overstates the case, esp. when one observes the metaphorical use of the vb. with ἐν. One may note the correspondence between Plato's usage (e.g., μένε ἐν τοῖς ἤθεσιν, *Ep.* 10.358c; μείνειν ἐν τῇ δικαιοσύνῃ, *R.* 360b; cf. Heise 3) and NT usage (ὁ μένων ἐν τῇ διδαχῇ, 2 John 9; ἐὰν μείνωσιν ἐν πίστει καὶ ἀγάπῃ, 1 Tim 2:15; see also 2 Tim 3:14). The usual translation into German (*bleiben bei* . . .) obscures the fundamentally local meaning in Greek. This is even more the case for the Johannine immanence formulas (→ 3): *"abide in"* (ἐν) God or Christ (Heise 172).

Prep. phrases with μένω other than μένω ἐν include μένω μετά τινος/σύν τινι/παρά τινι, *"remain with someone."* When God is the subj. of μένω in significant passages, the linguistic prehistory of this usage is in the LXX, where μένειν εἰς τὸν αἰῶνα is characteristic of God or God's plan, righteousness, or word, esp. in the Psalms. "As distinct from the mutability and transitoriness of everything earthly and human, God is characterized by the fact that he endures" (Hauck 575). However, the significance is not primarily the idea of a suprahistorical nature of God, but rather that one can rely on him within history. Thus in the NT μένει εἰς τὸν αἰῶνα is cited from Ps 111:9 LXX (2 Cor 9:9) and Isa 40:8 (1 Pet 1:25): God's righteousness or word *"has unshakable permanence* into eternity"; see also 1 John 2:14. The Messiah also *abides* eternally (John 12:34; cf. Ps 109:4 LXX; see also Heb 7:23f.). God's foreordination, which occurs through election, *remains in effect* (Rom 9:11).

Furthermore, what is given to humankind on the basis of the saving event of Christ *remains.* This includes the ministry of righteousness "in glory" (2 Cor 3:11); faith, hope, and love *remain* (1 Cor 13:13); "whoever does the will of God *abides* eternally" (1 John 2:17). Of course "God's wrath *remains* on anyone" who is disobedient to the Son of God (John 3:36): Μένω is thus not only used to speak of salvation.

3. Of particular theological relevance is the use of μένω in the immanence formulas of the Johannine literature. Jesus challenges his followers to *abide* in him (John 15:4-7), as he also *abides* in them (v. 5, reciprocal immanence formulas; cf. also 6:56 [Church redaction]). In 1 John the immanence formulas (2:6, 24, 27f.; 3:6, 24; 4:12f., 15f.: sometimes reciprocal) refer to one's *abiding* in God or in Christ, sometimes in the ind. and sometimes in the imv. (cf. also 3:9: "his seed *abides* in him"; 3:17: "the love of God *abides* in him"). This involves an abiding as in a realm or a sphere, but is not to be understood in a mystical sense. One may note a partial correspondence between the reciprocal formulas and Paul's alternation between ἐν Χριστῷ and Χριστὸς ἐν ἡμῖν (Schnackenburg 107f.).

Heise (172f.) correctly demonstrates that in John and 1 John μένω is used in everyday speech to express an essential element of the saving event. Μένω ἐν in its local meaning (→ 2) is not used for a realm as a measurable, three-dimensional expanse.

"The new existence is a new realm and a new time, through which the existence of the individual is defined anew. . . . It is a change of locale resulting from the event of God's presence in Jesus Christ" (Heise 173).

R. Bultmann (*John* [Eng. tr., 1971] 535n.1) correctly emphasizes two aspects of μένω ἐν: In reference to humankind "*abide* in" designates "loyalty"; in reference to the revealer or God it designates "the eternal validity of the divine act of salvation for the believer."

H. Hübner

μερίζω *merizō* divide, apportion*

Lit.: → μέρος.

1. Μερίζω occurs 14 times in the NT: 8 times in the Synoptics, 5 times in Paul, once in Hebrews. It has the same root as μέρος and has the same factitive-instrumental sense as other vbs. in -ίζω. In 1 Cor 1:13; 7:34 it is mid. or pass., in Luke 12:13 clearly mid., in Mark 3:24ff. par. pass. (perhaps with a mid. sense: "divide into parties"). The meaning *divide* is found in Mark 6:41; *impart/ apportion* in Heb 7:2.

2. Usage is analogous to that of → μέρος. Thus the vb. is employed in an ecclesiological context in Rom 12:3 with the motif of the body of Christ: God *has distributed* to each a measure of faith (cf. the charismata, vv. 6ff.). 1 Cor 7:17 emphasizes conduct corresponding to what the Lord *has apportioned* to each one (cf. the rule in v. 20). In 2 Cor 10:13 Paul argues on the basis of the κανών of mission that he has received from God.

Μερίζω is, however, also used in a negative way. Here it becomes clear that Christian salvation includes unity, consistency, completeness, and exclusiveness (1 Cor 1:13; 7:34). In Mark 3:24-26 par.; Matt 12:24-26 (Q), the subject is the kingdom of Satan. Jesus attempts to protect himself, using fig. language, against the charge that he drives out demons by means of their own ruler. Within the context of eschatological dualism it becomes clear that even the rule of Satan requires unity and completeness: The saying involves an either-or, totally and entirely, for Jesus himself (however the historical question of the passage is answered) in the understanding of the "kingdom of God."

G. Nebe

μέριμνα, ης, ἡ *merimna* worry, care (noun)*
μεριμνάω *merimnaō* worry (vb.), be concerned

1. Occurrences in the NT — 2. Basic meaning and usage in the ancient world — 3. Usage in the NT

Lit.: R. BULTMANN, *TDNT* IV, 589-93. — H. RIESENFELD, "Vom Schätzesammeln und Sorgen—ein Thema urchristlicher Paränese," FS Cullmann (1962) 47-58. — SCHULZ, *Q* 149, 157, 442-44. — D. ZELLER, *Die weisheitlichen Mahnsprüche bei den Synoptikern* (1977) 82-94.

1. In the words of Jesus in the Synoptics and in the Epistles the noun occurs 6 times and the vb. 19 times (omitted in Luke 10:41 by D it syr[s]).

2. The widely attested root μεριμνα- refers to that which is existentially important, that which monopolizes the heart's concerns. The vb. appears in the NT with the acc. or gen. (sometimes with περί) or with indirect questions. The noun appears with the obj. gen.

The LXX uses μέριμνα (-άω) for various Hebrew roots. In Sirach it corresponds esp. to d'g, which has a variety of related meanings in the wisdom literature (Zeller 87f.). The Stoics, Philo, and Josephus use φροντίς and φροντίζω (in the NT only in Titus 3:8) instead of μέριμνα (-άω).

3. a) Pareneses from Jesus and the early Church warn against worry, which—except in a word of encouragement in Q (Matt 10:19f. par. Luke 12:11f.)—concerns the securing of one's material existence. In the sayings composition from Q in Matt 6:25-33 par. Luke 12:22-31, to which Matthew adds v. 34 (M), various arguments from the wisdom tradition are given (parallels in Zeller) against worry, along with the summons to seek first the kingdom (ζητέω, so also Luke v. 29 in place of μεριμνάω). Greek-speaking Christianity also knows that worldly *cares* (μέριμναι) can choke the word of God (interpretation of a parable in Mark 4:19 par. Matt 13:22/Luke 8:14) and thus Luke 10:38-42 (L) criticizes the busyness of Martha (μεριμνάω with θορυβάζομαι and περισπάομαι). The *worries* of life (μέριμναι βιωτικαί, according to Luke the dissipated life) hinder the Church's vigilance in prayer (Luke 21:34-36, probably redactional; cf. G. Schneider, *Luke* [ÖTK] II, 431ff.). But the expectation of repentance and prayer to God makes possible the freedom from worry that Paul demands in Phil 4:6. 1 Pet 5:7 recommends (with Ps 54:23 LXX): "Cast *everything that causes worry* on God" (cf. *Herm. Vis.* iii.11.3; iv.2.4f.)

b) In 1 Cor 7:32-34 Paul bases his advice for ascetic existence (vv. 25ff.) on the wish that the Corinthians might be without worry (ἀμέριμνος, v. 32), not "*concerned* with the things of the world" (v. 33), i.e., in this context, not preoccupied with seeking to please one's spouse (on the worries of married people, cf. Sophocles *Tr.* 147ff.; H. Beckby, *Anthologia Graeca* [1957, 1958] III, 220). The unmarried, on the other hand, can "*devote* themselves to the things of the Lord" in an undivided manner (vv. 32, 34; cf. Niederwimmer, *Askese und Mysterium* [1975] 111-16).

c) Μέριμνα (-άω) is, however, given a positive value when Paul (2 Cor 11:28) or his coworkers (Phil 2:20; cf. v. 21: τὰ ἑαυτῶν in contrast to τὰ Ἰησοῦ Χριστοῦ ζητεῖν) are concerned about the churches or when church members are told to "*care* mutually for one another" (1 Cor 12:25: τὸ αὐτὸ ὑπὲρ ἀλλήλων μεριμνᾶν, elsewhere φρονεῖν).

D. Zeller

μεριμνάω *merimnaō* worry (vb.), be concerned
→ μέριμνα.

μερίς, ίδος, ἡ *meris* part, portion, sphere, region*

There are 5 occurrences in the NT of this noun, which is basically synonymous with → μέρος: Luke 10:42: τὴν ἀγαθὴν μερίδα ἐξελέξατο, "she has chosen the good [better] *portion*" (cf. Ps 16:5f.); Acts 8:21: οὐκ . . . μερὶς οὐδὲ κλῆρος, "no *part* and no entitlement" (a "formula of excommunication"; cf. Deut 12:12; 14:27; → μέρος 3.e); cf. Col 1:12: ἡ μερὶς τοῦ κλήρου (→ κλῆρος 3; cf. also 1QS 11:7); 2 Cor 6:15: τίς μερὶς πιστῷ μετὰ ἀπίστου, "what *part* does the believer have with the unbeliever [what do they have in common]?" (a Hebraizing manner of expression; cf. Ps 49:18 LXX; Matt 24:51; John 13:8; see BDF §227.3).

In Acts 16:12 Philippi is called the πρώτη (p⁷⁴ ℵ A, etc. πρώτη τῆς, conjecture: πρώτης) μερίδος τῆς Μακεδονίας πόλις (on the text-critical problems, see *TCGNT* ad loc.). Since Philippi was the capital neither of Macedonia nor of one of its four subdivisions, a suggested tr. based on conjectured text is: "Philippi, a city of the first *district* of Macedonia." Likewise possible would be the rendering of πρώτη πόλις with "a leading city" (cf. the v.l. of p⁷⁴ ℵ A, etc.) or, with a temporal understanding, "the first city," in which a decisive event would take place. Cf. also BAGD s.v. (bibliography); E. Haenchen, *Acts* (Eng. tr., 1971) ad loc.   H. Balz

μερισμός, οῦ, ὁ *merismos* division, apportionment, separation*

Heb 2:4: πνεύματος ἁγίου μερισμοί, "*apportionment* of the Holy Spirit," in reference to the various gifts of the Spirit; 4:12: μερισμὸς ψυχῆς καὶ πνεύματος . . . , "*separation* of soul and Spirit, joints and marrow" as a figure for the effect of the word of God as it enters the innermost part of the person. It is used of the *separation* of heretics in Ign. *Phld.* 2:1; *Smyrn.* 7:2.

μεριστής, οῦ, ὁ *meristēs* divider, one who apportions an inheritance*

Luke 12:14: κριτὴς ἢ μεριστής, "judge or *arbitrator*" (cf. Exod 2:14; Acts 7:27, 35).

μέρος, ους, τό *meros* part, portion

1. Occurrences in the NT — 2. Meaning — 3. Theological usage

Lit.: J. HERRMANN and W. FOERSTER, *TDNT* III, 758-85. — W. MUNDLE, *DNTT* II, 303-4. — H. H. SCHMID, *THAT* I, 576-79. — J. SCHNEIDER, *TDNT* IV, 594-98. — For further bibliography see *TWNT* X, 1175.

1. Of 42 occurrences in the NT, 13 are in the Gospels, 7 in Acts, 14 in Paul, 2 in Ephesians, 1 each in Colossians and Hebrews, and 4 in Revelation (apart from phrases in which μέρος is understood, such as τὰ δεξιὰ [μέρη], τὸ τρίτον [μέρος]).

2. Μέρος, meaning "part, portion," has roots in Indo-European *(s)mer-*, "remember, recall, worry about" (cf. Frisk, *Wörterbuch* II, 212). This meaning developed in Greek literature in various ways, and this is also the case in the NT. Here μέρος is, first of all, quantitatively and concretely *part/portion, piece* of a possession, an inheritance, fish, clothing, etc. (e.g., Luke 15:12; 24:42). Then it comes to mean in a derived way *part/portion/ place* (Matt 24:51; John 13:8), *side* (John 21:6), *member* (? Eph 4:16), *party* (Acts 23:9), *branch* of a business (Acts 19:27), *matter/concern/relationship* (2 Cor 3:10; 9:3). In prep. phrases or used adverbially it has the quantitative meaning *partly* (Rom 15:15; 1 Cor 11:18, subst. in 1 Cor 13:10) or *individually* (1 Cor 12:27). It can signify something gradual: *in part* (Rom 15:24) or *to a certain extent* (2 Cor 2:5). It can be used in a numerical sense: *each in turn* (1 Cor 14:27), can differentiate: *in detail* (Heb 9:5), and can mean *because/concerning* (Col 2:16).

3. a) Μέρος can be used in a geographic-cosmological sense for parts of the earth, thus Eph 4:9 in reference to the *descensus ad inferos* of Christ (this interpretation is disputed). In the Gospels and Acts it is used of journeys. Worldview and geography come together in this usage.

b) In religio-sociological terms μέρος is used to mean *party* in Acts 23:6 ("part?"); in 23:9 it refers to Jewish groups. The Sanhedrin is not divided here into the commonly known three groups (chief priests, scribes, and elders), but in terms of theological positions into Sadducees (esp. priests and lay aristocracy) and Pharisees (the majority of the scribes).

c) In ecclesiological terms μέρος is used in 1 Cor 12:27; Eph 4:16 in connection with the idea of the body and its members (v.l. μέλος could be a synonym for μέρος). This motif is well known in antiquity (H. Lietzmann, *1–2 Cor* [HNT] 53). The relationship between the part and the whole in view here is, however, an element of a theological problem. Thus the Church as the body of Christ is a unity. Nevertheless each person has his or her significance and function. Correspondingly, Paul in 1 Cor 12:27 designates the Corinthians as the body of Christ; as *parts* of it (ἐκ μέρους) they are members of this body. Eph 4:16 (cf. Col 2:19) is further developed and differentiated in christological and ecclesiological terms: the readers are σῶμα Χριστοῦ (v. 12), and Christ is at the same time head of the body (vv. 15f.). Here one notes a shift in which christology and ecclesiology move in the direction of a cosmological-hierarchical framework (cf. v. 13).

d) The relationship of part and whole plays an anthropological role in Luke 11:36 in the images of light and eye (Q; cf. *Gos. Thom.* 33). The difficult v. 36 (perhaps a secondary expansion in the tradition attempting to explain v. 34, or a redactional reference to v. 33) again is concerned with darkness in the body and brings into play for Luke the self-examination and thorough illumination of the person and his standing in the light.

e) Explicit soteriological use is found in Matt 24:51 par. Luke 12:46 (Q); John 13:8; Rev 20:6; 21:8; 22:19. Μέρος is associated with a *part/portion/place* in particular eschatological ideas. Cf. phrases such as OT and Jewish *(hāyâ) heleq bᵉ/lᵉ/ʿim* (LXX μέρις, κλῆρος; Acts 8:21; Col 1:12; 1QS 11:7f.), NT λαμβάνω κλῆρον ἐν, cf. κοινωνίαν ἔχω μετά, εἰμὶ ἐν. The tradition history of the concept is rooted Israel's "portion of land" and the spiritualization and eschatologizing of that idea in the OT and Judaism.

f) In regard to eschatology and history the following Pauline passages are noteworthy: In 1 Cor 13:9 (bis), 10, 12 ἐκ μέρους, *in part,* contrasts past and present and so expresses an eschatological distinction. While 2 Cor 3:7ff. uses the argument *a minori ad maius* to contrast the ministry of death and the ministry of the Spirit, v. 10 makes a clear differentiation: "In this *relationship/in this case* what has been glorious [the ministry of Moses] is not glorious because of the overwhelming δόξα [of the Christian διακονία]." Rom 11:25 is concerned with the hardening of Israel, which Paul sees in terms of salvation history as a way toward the salvation of the Gentiles: It has only happened *in part,* until the full number of the Gentiles come to salvation.   G. Nebe

μεσημβρία, ας, ἡ   *mesēmbria*   midday; south*

Of *noontime* in Acts 22:6 (περὶ μεσημβρίαν; cf. 26:13; Deut 28:28f.); Acts 8:26, in the sense of the compass direction: "to the *south*" (κατὰ μεσημβρίαν, cf. also Dan 8:4, 9 LXX; see BDF §253.5; E. Haenchen, *Acts* (Eng. tr., 1971) ad loc.). G. B. Bruzzone, "*Mesēmbria* nella Bibbia," *BeO* 26 (1984) 115-17.

μεσιτεύω   *mesiteuō*   guarantee (vb.)
→ μεσίτης.

μεσίτης, ου, ὁ   *mesitēs*   mediator; guarantor*
μεσιτεύω   *mesiteuō*   guarantee (vb.)*

1. Occurrences in the NT — 2. Μεσίτης — 3. Μεσιτεύω

Lit.: O. BECKER, *DNTT* I, 372-76. — J. BEHM, *Der Begriff ΔΙΑΘΗΚΗ im NT* (1912) 77-97. — R. BRING, "Der Mittler und das Gesetz. Eine Studie zu Gal 3,20," *KD* 12 (1966) 292-309. — H. HEGERMANN, *Die Vorstellung vom Schöpfungsmittler im hellenistischen Judentum und Urchristentum* (TU 82, 1961). — H. W. HUPPENBAUER, *BHH* 1227f. — O. MICHEL, *Heb* (KEK,

[7]1975) esp. 292. — M. P. NILSSON, "The High God and the Mediator," *HTR* 56 (1963) 101-20. — A. OEPKE, *TDNT* IV, 598-624. — K. H. RENGSTORF, *RGG* IV, 1064f. — K. T. SCHÄFER, *LTK* VII, 498f. — J. SCHARBERT, *Heilsmittler im AT und im Alten Orient* (QD 23/24, 1964) 82-92, 242-44. — F. J. SCHIERSE, *HTG* II, 169-72. — SPICQ, *Notes* II, 549-52. — A. STEGMANN, "Ὁ δὲ μεσίτης ἑνὸς οὐκ ἔστιν, Gal 3,20," *BZ* 22 (1934) 30-42. — For further bibliography see *TWNT* X, 1175f.

1. The noun μεσίτης appears in the NT only 6 times (Gal 3:19, 20; 1 Tim 2:5; Heb 8:6; 9:15; 12:24), whereas the vb. derived from the noun is a NT hapax legomenon in Heb 6:17.

2. a) Corresponding to the breadth of meaning in English translations, the noun μεσίτης cannot be reduced to one simple meaning.

The term is attested in secular Greek since Polybius and is esp. common in the papyri (see BAGD s.v.; Behm 78f.). Its use is derived from Hellenistic legal terminology and refers to a) the "impartial" person who mediates in a dispute between two parties (Polybius xxviii.17.8; on the subject, cf. Homer *Il.* xxiii.574; Xenophon *An.* iii.1.21), b) the "mediating person" *(sequester)* in whose hands disputing parties place the object of dispute (cf. Pap. London III, 208, no. 1173), and c) the *witness* and *guarantor* in a legal matter (Diodorus Siculus iv.54.7; Pap. London II, 251, no. 370). While in secular Greek the technical use is predominant, in Hellenistic and Jewish usage μεσίτης is often used in a fig. sense for the "negotiator" and "mediator" among humans and between God and humankind (Josephus *Ant.* vii.193; Philo *Vit. Mos.* ii.166 [cf. *Her.* 205f.]; *Som.* i.142; *T. Mos.* 1:14; 3:12; cf. also Job 9:33 LXX) or the "intercessor" or advocate (*T. Dan* 6:2 [cf. *T. Levi* 5:6]; cf. Philo *Som.* i.143). In connection with the OT (Exod 19:3ff.; 20:19; Num 21:7; Deut 5:5, 27, etc.), both in rabbinic Judaism, which has the t.t. *sarsôr* ("negotiator, broker") for the function of a μεσίτης—and with both a secular and theological meaning (cf. Oepke, 602f.)—and in Hellenistic Judaism, Moses is the μεσίτης par excellence. God has given Israel the Torah through him (*y. Meg.* 4:74d.9; *Exod. Rab.* 3 [69b]; *Deut. Rab.* 3 [201a], etc.). In rabbinic literature, as in Hellenistic Judaism, Moses has soteriological significance because of his function. On the idea of a μεσίτης in Qumran, cf. 1QH 6:13f.

b) According to Gal 3:19 the law (νόμος) given to the people at Sinai was "ordained by angels through the hand of a *mediator.*" As the context indicates, this μεσίτης is Moses. What is involved is a double mediation of the νόμος: on the one hand through angels (cf. Josephus *Ant.* xv.136; Acts 7:38, 53; Heb 2:2), and on the other hand through Moses. Moses appears as representative and advocate of the angels between them and Israel. V. 20 indicates why Moses is necessary as μεσίτης: "But the mediator is not [the mediator] of one, but God is one." The most probable explanation of this statement is: The angels cannot come directly into association with Israel, the addressee of the νόμος, because they are many (ἀγγέλων, v. 19c). Thus they need someone to represent them. Moses is that person. But because God is one (εἷς), he does not need a *mediator.* Thus it follows that the νόμος cannot come directly from God (cf. here the commentaries ad loc.). The point of Paul's argument is to demonstrate the inferiority of the νόμος: It is not superior to the promises (ἐπαγγελία, cf. vv. 16-18), but is subordinate to them because God himself gave them to Abraham, and indeed without a μεσίτης. To see a negative view of μεσίτης here (so Huppenbauer 1228; Becker 163) is doubtful, inasmuch as Gal 3:19f. is not primarily concerned with the function of Moses, but rather with the relationship between the divine promise and the νόμος.

c) In 1 Tim 2:5, which has been liturgically shaped, the use of μεσίτης is in line with that which one finds in Hellenistic Judaism, as *T. Dan* 6:2 esp. indicates (οὗτός [the interceding angel] ἐστι μεσίτης θεοῦ καὶ ἀνθρώπων): "For there is one God, and there is one *mediator* between God and mankind, the man Christ Jesus." He is the one who represents God to mankind and mankind to God (Oepke 619). The close dependence on the Hellenistic Jewish understanding and language suggests that one should understand μεσίτης as *mediator of the covenant*, even if the corresponding t.t. → διαθήκη (covenant/testament) does not appear.

d) Half of the NT occurrences are in Hebrews, all with διαθήκη as a dependent gen. Hebrews sees the mediating role of Christ as a function of his true high-priestly activity (5:6, 10; 6:20; 7:17, 21, 26; 8:1, etc.). He is "the *mediator* of a better covenant" (8:6) and "the *mediator* of a new covenant" (διαθήκης καινῆς μεσίτης, 9:15; διαθήκης νέας μεσίτης, 12:24). The corresponding phrase in 7:22—Jesus as "surety (ἔγγυος) of a better covenant"— suggests that μεσίτης should be understood there and that a juridical sense should be given.

Jesus Christ is the *surety* of the better covenant and of the better promise (argument *a minori ad maius*) that God gave to his people according to Jer 31:31-34 (cf. Heb 8:8-12). Whereas the better covenant guaranteed through Jesus in Heb 8:6 is based on the promise of Jer 31:31-34, in 9:15, by contrast, the new covenant established by the death of Jesus is the prerequisite for the reception of the promise (cf. 6:12, 15; 10:36; 11:13, 33, 39) of the eternal inheritance. 9:15 thus recalls 8:6. "Christ is not only the priest and sacrifice, but also mediator of a new covenant" (Michel 316). 12:24 stands in close relationship to 12:18-24 in an antithetical construction. The images of the covenant ceremony at Sinai (cf. Exod 19:12, 16-21; Deut 4:11f.; 5:22f.; 9:19) are taken up eschatologically in the description of the gifts of the new covenant, whose *guarantor* is Jesus Christ (v. 24). The blood poured out through his death speaks to God (cf. 7:25) more loudly—for forgiveness—than the blood of Abel, which called out for vengeance (11:4; cf. *Jub.* 4:3; *1 Enoch* 22:5-7). Thus Jesus as the μεσίτης is the *guarantor* and pledge of the final divine promise.

3. In Heb 6:17 the vb. has the same basic significance as the noun: "[God] *guaranteed* the irrevocability of his will with an oath" (cf. 7:21; Ps 110:4; H. Köster, *Studien zur Theologie der alttestamentlichen Überlieferungen* [FS G. von Rad, 1961] 105ff.) and through the promises that he made to Abraham (Gen 22:16f.) and that he gave to the Church through Christ, who himself is the eschatological promise of God (1:2).

D. Sänger

μέσον (ου, τό) *meson* middle; amid
→ μέσος.

μεσονύκτιον, ου, τό *mesonyktion* midnight*

Mark 13:35: μεσονύκτιον, *about midnight* (acc. of time; cf. Ps 118:62 LXX); Luke 11:5: μεσονυκτίου (gen. of time; cf. μέσης νυκτός, Matt 25:6; BDF §186.2); Acts 16:25: κατὰ τὸ μεσονύκτιον, "about *midnight*"; 20:7: μέχρι μεσονυκτίου, "until *midnight*" (on the absence of the art. see BDF §255.3).

Μεσοποταμία, ας, ἡ *Mesopotamia* Mesopotamia*

Lit. the "land (χώρα) between the rivers," Heb. *'aram naharayim* (Gen 24:10), *paddan 'aram* (25:20), LXX in each case: Μεσοποταμία. In the Hellenistic age the name was used for a region between the middle Euphrates and Tigris, but in the NT it is used in reference to the entire region of the two rivers: Acts 2:9: οἱ κατοικοῦντες τὴν Μεσοποταμίαν, "the inhabitants of *Mesopotamia*," probably in reference to the great portion of the Jewish population that had been deported to "Babylon." Cf. Josephus *Ant.* i.154; *Gen. Rab.* 39 on 12:1; Billerbeck II, 608f., 666f.; and esp. Acts 7:2, according to which Abraham before his time in Haran experienced the appearance of God (cf. Gen 12:7) in *Mesopotamia* (ὄντι ἐν τῇ Μεσοποταμίᾳ; cf. the "Ur of the Chaldeans" on the lower Euphrates mentioned in Gen 11:31). Thus "Mesopotamia" is used in the wider sense for "Babylon" (Luke, contrary to the OT in Gen 12:1, 7, refers to the first departure of Abraham from Ur/Mesopotamia instead of the second departure, that from Haran (see also E. Haenchen, *Acts* [Eng. tr., 1971] ad loc.). F. Schachermeyr, PW XV, 1105-63; BAGD s.v.; B. Reicke, *BHH* 1197; *BL* 1138 (bibliography); *KP* III, 1237-41.

H. Balz

μέσος, 3 *mesos* in the middle, amid, in the midst, between

Lit.: BAGD s.v. — O. Becker, *DNTT* I, 372f. — BDF §§204; 215.3. — R. R. Brewer, "Revelation 4,6 and the Translations Thereof," *JBL* 71 (1952) 227-31. — U. Holzmeister, "Vox 'medium' et phrasis 'in medio' in S. Scriptura," *VD* 18 (1938)

279-84. — JOHANNESSOHN, *Präpositionen*, index s.v. — E. LOHMEYER, *Diatheke* (1913) 85f. — MAYSER, *Grammatik*, index s.v. — A. OEPKE, *TDNT* IV, 598-624. — O. SCHULTHESS, PW XV, 1097-99.

1. Μέσος occurs as an adj. (sometimes subst.), adv., or improper prep. 58 times in the NT. It appears esp. frequently in Luke-Acts (24 times), while it appears only 5 times in Paul's letters (1–2 Corinthians, Philippians, and 1 Thessalonians). The remaining occurrences are distributed among the other Gospels and Colossians, 2 Thessalonians, Hebrews, and Revelation.

2. a) The basic meaning is, in accordance with the original usage (cf. Homer *Il.* xviii.507; Xenophon *An.* iii.1.21; Aristotle *EN* v.4.1132a.22f): *in the middle, amid, in the midst of* (Matt 10:16; 14:6; 18:2; Mark 3:3; Luke 8:7; 10:3; John 8:3, 9; Acts 1:15; 4:7; Phil 2:15; 1 Thess 2:7; Heb 2:12; Rev 1:13; 4:6, etc.). Thus the adv. phrase ἐν (τῷ) μέσῳ or εἰς τὸ μέσον can appear as an improper prep. in the place of classical ἐν or εἰς (Matt 10:16; Mark 3:3, etc.). Μέσος can also function alone as a subst. adj. (John 1:26: μέσος ὑμῶν, "*in your midst*"; see BDF §215.3), or as an adv. (Phil 2:15: "*in the midst* of a crooked and perverse generation"). Ἐκ μέσου (cf. Heb. *mittôk*) in Matt 13:49; Acts 17:33; 23:10; 1 Cor 5:2 (a Latinism? cf. BDF §5.3b); 2 Thess 2:7 has a very similar usage, appearing in these passages in place of classical ἐκ and strengthening the preposition, designating the place from which a thing or a person stands out (*from the midst*, most often followed by the gen.). In addition one finds ἀνὰ μέσον (followed by the gen.) with the meaning *between* (Matt 13:25; Mark 7:31; Luke 17:11 v.l.; 1 Cor 6:5; Rev 7:17); κατὰ μέσον τῆς νυκτός in Acts 27:27 (so also 16:25 D for κατὰ δὲ τὸ μεσονύκτιον) is to be understood in a temporal sense: "*in the middle* of the night."

b) Mark and Luke in particular connect μέσος with a definite theological intention that goes beyond the merely local meaning in use elsewhere. In Mark 3:3 Jesus places the man with the withered hand *in the midst* of the Pharisees (v. 6). When Jesus places the sick man in this "exposed position" (R. Pesch, *Mark* [HTKNT] I, 191; cf. 9:36; 14:60), Mark emphasizes that Jesus, in a manner customary in legal disputes (cf. John 7:53–8:11; Acts 4:7), as the true object of dispute, places the person in his helplessness *in the midst* of the opponents in the proceedings. Thus he demonstrates fundamentally that the sabbath commandment loses its binding validity when it is no longer oriented toward humankind.

The frequency of μέσος in Luke-Acts is noteworthy. It serves esp., as it does elsewhere in the NT, to underscore something remarkable, esp. in scenes shaped by the Evangelist: At the age of twelve, Jesus sits *in the midst* of the teachers in the temple (Luke 2:46). Jesus,

the teacher, takes on the role of a servant *in the midst of* the disciples (22:27). While Luke is the only one to emphasize that Peter follows the imprisoned Jesus and even warm himself in the *middle* of the court of the high priest *among* the soldiers (22:55 bis), he does not go on to justify the denial that follows. The ἐν μέσῳ of Acts 1:5 in Peter's speech (1:15-22), which has been shaped by Peter, is, like that in Luke 24:36, etc., biblicizing Greek (ἐν μέσῳ in the LXX is the tr. of the Heb. *b^etôk*; see Hatch/Redpath I, 461-67; cf. also 1QS 6:22). Like the other biblicisms in this section (cf. E. Haenchen, *Acts* [Eng. tr., 1971] 160f.), this emphasizes that the selection of Matthias to the circle of the Twelve was based on Scripture.

The phrase διὰ μέσον in Luke 17:11 (Jesus comes "*through the middle* of Samaria and Galilee"), like διὰ with the acc., has a spatial meaning, "through the middle"; see, however, 4:30. Whether διὰ μέσον in 17:11 is original or not remains uncertain (cf. the v.l. ad loc. and H. Conzelmann, *The Theology of St. Luke* [1960] 69).

D. Sänger

μεσότοιχον, ου, τό *mesotoichon* dividing wall*

Eph 2:14: τὸ μεσότοιχον τοῦ φραγμοῦ, "the *dividing wall* formed by the barrier" of the law, which separated Jews and Gentiles before Christ (*contra* C. Schneider, *TDNT* IV, 625).

μεσουράνημα, ατος, τό *mesouranēma* middle of the sky, zenith*

Lit., of the highest point reached by the sun in the sky, and on that basis more generally *high above in heaven*: of an eagle (Rev 8:13), an angel (14:6), birds (19:17), in all three instances with a partc. of πέτομαι, "fly."

μεσόω *mesoō* be in the middle, reach the middle*

John 7:14: ἤδη δὲ τῆς ἑορτῆς μεσούσης, "as the *middle* of the feast *had passed*."

Μεσσίας, ου *Messias* Messiah*

The Greek form of Aram. *m^ešîḥâ'*, Heb. *māšîaḥ*, appears only in John: 1:41: εὑρήκαμεν τὸν Μεσσίαν, spoken by Andrew; 4:25: οἶδα ὅτι Μεσσίας ἔρχεται (on the absence of the art., cf. R. Schnackenburg, *John* I [Eng. tr., 1968] ad loc.: possibly a reference to the messianic figure expected by the Samaritans, the *Ta'eb*), spoken by the Samaritan woman; in both passages supplied with the tr. χριστός (→ Ἰησοῦς 4.a, → Χριστός). Thus ὁ λεγόμενος χριστός in 4:25 is certainly to be understood as explanatory: "which means/whose name is"). Cf. also 9:11; 11:16, 54; 19:13; 20:16. See also *Glotta* 36 (1957/58) 171; *TWNT* IX, 566-70.

μεστός, 3 *mestos* full, filled*

There are 9 occurrences of this adj. in the NT, all with the gen.: Literal in John 19:29a: "a bowl *full* of vinegar"; 21:11: "nets *full* of large fish." Fig., of persons in Matt 23:28: "*full* of hypocrisy and lawlessness"; Rom 1:29: "*full* of envy . . ."; 15:14: "*full* of goodness"; Jas 3:17: "*full* of mercy"; in reference to the eyes in 2 Pet 2:14: "*full* of [i.e., hankering after] adultery"; of the tongue in Jas 3:8: "*full* of deadly poison."

μεστόω *mestoō* fill*

In the NT only pass.: γλεύκους μεμεστωμένοι εἰσίν, "they are *full* of sweet wine" (Acts 2:13); → γλεῦκος.

μετά *meta* with gen.: with; with acc.: after, behind

1. Occurrences — 2. Meaning — a) With gen. — b) With acc. — 3. Theological usage

Lit.: On preps. in general → ἀνά. — BAGD s.v. — BDF §§198.3f.; 226f.; 402.3; 459.3. — H. FRANKEMÖLLE, *Jahwebund und Kirche Christi* (1974) 7-158. — W. GRUNDMANN, *TDNT* VII, 766-97. — JOHANNESSOHN, *Präpositionen* 202-16. — KÜHNER, *Grammatik* II/1, 505-9. — LSJ s.v. — MAYSER, *Grammatik* II/2, 440-45. — H. D. PREUSS, ". . . ich will mit dir sein!" *ZAW* 80 (1968) 139-73. — SCHWYZER, *Grammatik* II, 481-87. — W. C. VAN UNNIK, "Dominus vobiscum: The Background of a Liturgical Formula," *NT Essays: Studies in Memory of T. W. Manson* (1959) 270-305. — D. VETTER, *Jahwes Mit-Sein—ein Ausdruck des Segens* (1971).

1. The NT uses μετά 473 times, none of which is with the dat. It appears with the acc. about 100 times, relatively frequently only in Acts (29 occurrences among 65 [+ 24:7 v.l.]) and Hebrews (9 occurrences among 23). Μετά with the gen. appears in the NT much more often than the (largely synonymous) prep. σύν; the latter is not used at all in the Pastorals, Hebrews, 1 Peter, 1–3 John, or Revelation. It appears only a few times in Matthew, Mark, and John, while in Acts it becomes predominant (50 occurrences of σύν to 36 of μετά with gen.).

2. a) The basic meaning with the gen., *with*, varies in several ways (cf. BAGD s.v. A):
1) In the local sense it means *in the midst of, among, with*: Mark 1:13: "*among* the wild beasts."
2) Most often μετά expresses a form of (usually personal) relationship. First, it designates the person in whose fellowship or accompaniment something takes place. This includes going or coming *with* and remaining *with* someone: Matt 20:20: "they came *with* their sons to him"; in Rev 6:8 and 14:13 almost tautological with ἀκολουθέω: follow someone *as companion*. In addition, it refers to bringing or taking someone or something along: Matt 12:45: "he takes *along as a companion with* himself"; Acts 1:26: "he was reckoned *among* the apos-

tles." Finally, it is used of existence with someone, whether in the literal sense of a relationship, as in Mark 3:14; John 13:33 of Jesus and his disciples and Matt 5:25; John 3:26 of others, or in the fig. sense of the support that God (Matt 1:23), Christ (28:20), the Spirit (John 14:16), or the fellowship of these three (2 Cor 13:13) provide.—On the "Hebraizing" manner of speech (BDF §227.3) of Luke 1:72; 10:37; Acts 2:28; 14:27; 15:4; cf. BAGD s.v. A.II.1.c.γ. On the description of the two alternatives in Matt 12:30 par. Luke 11:23 see BAGD s.v. A.II.1.c.δ.

Second, μετά designates a common activity or experience, e.g., at a meal (Luke 7:36); third, it designates the joint activity of two parties, whether it is hostile (Rev 2:16) or peaceful (Rom 12:18). Finally, it refers to any other association of persons (Matt 2:11) or groups (22:16), of any two things (27:34) or spiritual beings (Eph 6:23).

3) Μετά can also designate the accompanying circumstances *within* which something takes place. Here belong esp. spiritual and bodily conditions as well as expressions, e.g., joy (Phil 2:29), fear and trembling (2 Cor 7:15), or (cries and) tears (Heb 5:7; 12:17), but also other accompanying situations such as persecutions (Mark 10:30), tumult (Acts 24:18), or a trumpet call (Matt 24:31), even weapons for defense such as lanterns and weapons (John 18:3).

b) Μετά with the acc. in the NT has 1) a local meaning in Heb 9:3 (cf. BDF §226). In all other passages μετά is temporal and designates either 2) the time *after* something occurs or 3) the time that elapses *after* a specific point until a specific event. Μετά appears often in the first of these temporal senses (33 times) in the phrase μετὰ ταῦτα (τοῦτο), *afterward*, which is limited to Luke-Acts, John, Hebrews, and Revelation. More often a subst. inf., always aor., is connected with μετά: Mark 1:14: "*after* the imprisonment of John the Baptist." The second temporal sense appears in "*after* three days" (Matt 27:63; Mark 8:31; 10:34; Luke 2:46).

3. Paul formulates the idea of being "with Christ" (cf. Col 2:13, 20; 3:3, 4) with → σύν (unlike Luke 23:43; John 15:27; 17:24); the existence of Christ and God among people he indicates, however, as do the other NT authors, with μετά. The wish for the divine presence is regularly a component of the concluding formula of blessing in the Pauline corpus and in Hebrews (cf. 1 John 1:3; 2 John 3); in Pauline usage μετά corresponds to the OT formulas of Yahweh's presence with his people (cf. 3 Kgdms 8:57; Ps 22:4 LXX).

Matthew is shaped at both the beginning (1:23; cf. Isa 7:14 and 8:8, 10 LXX) and the end (28:20) and thus in its entirely by the μετά promise of God (cf. Isa 41:10; Zech 8:28). According to Luke-Acts God's special presence (cf. Gen 28:15; Exod 3:12; Jer 1:8, 17, 19) is experienced by Jesus (Acts 10:38), John (Luke 1:66), Mary (1:28), Paul (and Barnabas: Acts 18:10; 14:27; 15:4), and elsewhere (7:9; 11:21). John emphasizes that God is *with* Jesus and that he is *with* his disciples (3:2; 8:29; 13:33; 14:9, 16; 16:4, 32; 17:12). Μετά is used—3 times!—of the future life of fellowship of God with humankind in Rev 21:3.

W. Radl

μεταβαίνω *metabainō* go to another place, go away; walk across; move*

There are 12 occurrences in the NT, most often with the literal meaning *go away from a place (to another)*: Matt 8:34 (ἀπό); 11:1; 12:9; 15:29; Acts 18:7 (ἐκεῖθεν); Matt 17:20, fig. of a mountain (μετάβα ἔνθεν ἐκεῖ, *"lift yourself* from here to there," καὶ μεταβήσεται); Luke 10:7 (ἐξ . . . εἰς, *"do* not *move* from one house to another"); John 7:3 (ἐντεῦθεν); 13:1 (ἐκ τοῦ κόσμου τούτου πρὸς τὸν πατέρα); fig. in John 5:24; 1 John 3:14: *cross over* (in both instances: ἐκ τοῦ θανάτου εἰς τὴν ζωήν). J. Schneider, *TDNT* I, 523.

μεταβάλλομαι *metaballomai* turn, change one's opinion*

Acts 28:6: μεταβαλόμενοι ἔλεγον, "they [suddenly] *changed their minds* and said."

μετάγω *metagō* guide in another direction; pass.: change course*

Jas 3:3, of the bridle (as a small instrument in the mouth of a horse), which *guides* the whole animal; 3:4, of the rudder of a ship (tiny in relation to the entire ship), in both instances as a figure for the great effects of the tongue.

μεταδίδωμι *metadidōmi* give a portion, impart, give away*

There are 5 occurrences in the NT: Luke 3:11: *give* one of the two undergarments; Eph 4:28: something from the goods that have been earned; *impart* in Rom 1:11; 1 Thess 2:8; absolute ὁ μεταδιδούς, "one who *distributes* [to others]," Rom 12:8.

μετάθεσις, εως, ἡ *metathesis* transformation, change; transfer, removal, translation*

Heb 7:12: νόμου μετάθεσις, *"change* of the law"; 12:27: τῶν σαλευομένων μετάθεσις ὡς πεποιημένων, *"transformation* of that which cannot be shaken" (cf. v. 26, citing Hag 2:6 LXX); Heb 11:5, of the *translation* of Enoch (cf. Gen 5:25; Sir 44:16; Wis 4:10, μετατίθημι [Heb. *lāqaḥ*]). C. Maurer, *TDNT* VIII, 161.

μεταίρω *metairō* go away, depart*

Matt 13:53: μετῆρεν ἐκεῖθεν; 19:1: ἀπὸ τῆς Γαλιλαίας, said of Jesus.

μετακαλέομαι *metakaleomai* call to oneself, summon*

In the NT only mid. and only in Acts: 7:14: Ἰακώβ; 10:32: Σίμωνα; 20:17: τοὺς πρεσβυτέρους; 24:25: σέ (in reference to Paul).

μετακινέω *metakineō* shift, remove*

Pass. in Col 1:23: τεθεμελιωμένοι . . . ἑδραῖοι . . . μὴ μετακινούμενοι, "founded . . . firm . . . not *being dissuaded"*—possibly mid.: "not *turning aside."* J. Schneider, *TDNT* III, 720.

μεταλαμβάνω *metalambanō* have a portion, share; obtain*

There are 7 occurrences in the NT. With acc. only in Acts 24:25: καιρὸν μεταλαβών, *"when I find* an appropriate/convenient time"; elsewhere with gen.: μεταλαμβάνω τροφῆς, *"take* food" (Acts 2:46; 27:33, 34); τῶν καρπῶν μεταλαμβάνειν, *"receive his portion* of the fruits" (2 Tim 2:6); *share* (Heb 6:7, εὐλογίας; 12:10, τῆς ἁγιότητος). G. Delling, *TDNT* IV, 10f.

μετάλημψις, εως, ἡ *metalēmpsis* sharing, accepting, receiving (noun)*

1 Tim 4:3, of food, which God (in contrast to food regulations then being promulgated) created "for *receiving/for enjoyment* with thanksgiving" (εἰς μετάλημψιν μετὰ εὐχαριστίας). G. Delling, *TDNT* IV, 10-11.

μεταλλάσσω *metallassō* exchange*

Rom 1:25: μετήλλαξαν τὴν ἀλήθειαν . . . ἐν τῷ ψεύδει, "they [the Gentiles] *exchanged* God's truth for lies" (cf. ἤλλαξαν, v. 23); 1:26: μετήλλαξαν τὴν φυσικὴν χρῆσιν εἰς . . . , *"change* the natural relations into the unnatural" (εἰς/ἐν corresponding to Heb. *bᵉ*, cf. LXX; cf. also *T. Naph.* 3:4). F. Büchsel, *TDNT* I, 259; Spicq, *Notes* II, 553f.; → ἀλλάσσω.

μεταμέλομαι *metamelomai* feel remorse, repent*

Μεταμέλομαι appears as a pass. deponent 6 times in the NT and expresses—in comparison to μετανοέω—a change not so much in consciousness as in one's feelings in relation to a thing or a deed (see O. Michel, *TDNT* IV, 626): Matt 21:29: ὕστερον δὲ μεταμεληθείς, "but later he *felt remorse/was sorry"* (cf. also v. 30 v.l.); similarly 27:3 of Judas; 21:32: μετεμελήθητε ὕστερον, "afterward [after not believing earlier] *repent/feel remorse*"; 2 Cor 7:8a, b, pres. and impf.: "I do not *regret* . . . ; if I also [earlier] *did regret*"; Heb 7:21: "The Lord has sworn and he *will not change his mind*" (citing Ps 109:4 LXX). O. Michel, *TDNT* IV, 626-29; F. Laubach, *DNTT* I, 353-55.

μεταμορφόω *metamorphoō* transform, change completely*

1. Occurrences — 2. Meanings — 3. Theological usage

Lit.: J. BEHM, *TDNT* IV, 755-59. — R. HERMANN, "Über den Sinn des Μορφοῦσθαι Χριστὸν ἐν ὑμῖν in Gal. 4,19," *TLZ* 80 (1955) 713-26. — E. LARSSON, *Christus als Vorbild* (1962) 179-82. — J. M. NÜTZEL, *Die Verklärungserzählung im Markusevangelium* (1973). — K. PRÜMM, *Diakonia Pneumatos* I. *Theologische Auslegung des 2 Korintherbriefs* (1967) 179-82. — For further bibliography see Nützel 317-24.

1. The vb. μεταμορφόω occurs 4 times in the NT: Mark 9:2 par. Matt 17:2; Rom 12:2; 2 Cor 3:18. In all four instances the pass. μεταμορφόομαι is used.

2. The basic meaning of μεταμορφόω is: *change the* → μορφή:

a) An outwardly visible transformation is described in Mark 9:2 par. Matt 17:2. Here a change in the nature of Jesus is not in view; the true nature of Jesus is made visible to the three disciples who witness the transfiguration. The pass. points to an action of God.

b) As a contrast to accommodation (→ συσχηματίζω) to this world (→ αἰών 4.c) Rom 12:2 calls for a change through the renewing of the mind. The goal of the change is that the Christian be consciously committed (→ δοκιμάζω 3.b) to the will of God, the good, the noble, and the perfect. The pass. indicates that Paul thinks not of what is achieved by the person but of God's persuasive power transforming human understanding. Imv. μεταμορφοῦσθε, of course, requires human readiness and cooperation. Inasmuch as Paul directs his demand to Christians, he cannot have in mind a once-for-all new orientation (perhaps with the acceptance of faith and in its confirmation in baptism); he apparently thinks of a lasting and continuing change of the inner being. That the inner transformation has outward effects is evident in this passage.

c) The transforming power of the κύριος or of the πνεῦμα is expressed clearly in 2 Cor 3:18. The goal of this work is transformation into the image (→ εἰκών 7.c) of the glory of the exalted Christ. The "unveiled seeing" of the glory (→ δόξα 4) of the Lord "in the mirror" (→ κατοπτρίζομαι), which is God himself (cf. H. Lietzmann, *1-2 Cor* [HNT] ad loc.) given through the Spirit of the Lord in faith, leads to one's becoming like what is seen. "From glory to glory" indicates that a continuing process is spoken of. Thus the idea can be either that of a growing of the δόξα in Christians (cf. *2 Bar.* 51:10) or of a con-

tinual overflowing of the δόξα of the Lord on Christians, who by this means are transformed into his image.

3. Μεταμορφόω is, therefore, used of:

a) a revelation of the glory of the earthly Jesus produced by God, thus also continuation in the knowledge of Jesus on the part of the disciples (and, through the narration, also on the part of the reader),

b) the continuing transformation produced in the Christian through the knowledge (made possible by faith) of the glory of the exalted Lord. The one who is known shapes the one who knows. The knowledge leads to the Christian's becoming like the image of Jesus Christ and thus to a free, conscious devotion to God's will.

J. M. Nützel

μετανοέω *metanoeō* turn around, change one's mind, repent
→ μετάνοια.

μετάνοια, ας, ἡ *metanoia* change of direction, conversion, repentance*
μετανοέω *metanoeō* turn around, change one's mind, repent*

1. Occurrences in the NT — 2. Meaning outside the NT — 3. John the Baptist — 4. Jesus — 5. The sayings source — 6. Mark — 7. Matthew — 8. Luke-Acts — 9. The Epistles — 10. Revelation

Lit.: P. AUBIN, *Le problème de la "conversion"* (1963). — J. BECKER, *TRE* VII, 446-51. — J. BEHM, "Metanoia—ein Grundbegriff der neutestamentlichen Verkündigung," *DTh* 7 (1940) 75-86. — J. BEHM and E. WÜRTHWEIN, *TDNT* IV, 975-1008. — H. BRAUN, " 'Umkehr' in spätjüdisch-häretischer und frühchristlicher Sicht," *ZTK* 50 (1953) 243-58. — C. E. CARLSTON, "Eschatology and Repentance in the Epistle to the Hebrews," *JBL* 79 (1959) 296-302. — E. K. DIETRICH, *Die Umkehr (Bekehrung und Buße) im AT und im Judentum* (1936). — A. H. DIRKSEN, *The NT Concept of Metanoia* (1932). — J. DUPONT, "Repentir et conversion d'après les Actes des Apôtres," *ScEc* 12 (1960) 137-73 (cf. *idem, The Salvation of the Gentiles* [1979] 61-84). — J. EMONDS and B. POSCHMANN, *RAC* II, 802-14. — H.-J. FABRY, "Umkehr und Metanoia als monastisches Ideal in der 'Mönchsgemeinde' von Qumran," *EuA* 53 (1977) 163-80. — *idem, Die Wurzel ŠÛB in der Qumran-Literatur* (1975). — A. FEUILLET, *SM* IV, 16-23. — J. FICHTNER, K. H. RENGSTORF, and G. FRIEDRICH, *RGG* I, 976-80. — P. FIEDLER, *Jesus und die Sünder* (1976). — G. FOHRER, "Umkehr und Erlösung beim Propheten Hosea," *idem, Studien zur alttestamentlichen Prophetie* (BZAW 99, 1967) 222-41. — H. A. FREI, "Metanoia im 'Hirten' des Hermas," *IKZ* 64 (1974) 118-39, 189-202; 65 (1975) 120-28, 176-204. — J. GIBLET and M. DENIS, *DBSup* VII, 628-87. — J. GOETZMANN, *DNTT* I, 357-59. — H. GROSS, "Umkehr im AT," *Zeichen des Glaubens* (FS B. Fischer, ed. H.-J. auf der Maur and B. Kleinheyer; 1972) 19-28. — J. GUILLET, *DSp* X, 1093-99. — E. HAAG, "Umkehr und Versöhnung im Zeugnis der Propheten," *Dienst der Versöhnung* (TTS 31, 1974) 9-25. — P. HAUDEBERT, "La *métanoia*, des Septante à Saint Luc," *La vie de la parole* (FS P. Grelot, 1987) 355-66. — M. HOFFER, *Metanoia (Bekehrung und Buße) im NT* (1947). — P. HOFFMANN, *HTG* II, 719-24. — W. L. HOLLADAY, *The Root šûb in the OT* (1958). — H. KARPP, *Die Buße* (1969). — R. KOCH, "Die religiös-sittliche Umkehr (Metanoia) nach den drei ältesten Evangelien und der Apostelgeschichte," *Anima* 14 (1959) 296-307. — M. LIMBECK, "Jesu Verkündigung und der Ruf zur Umkehr," *Das Evangelium auf dem Weg zum Menschen* (FS H. Kahlefeld, 1973) 35-42. — D. LÜHRMANN, "Henoch und die Metanoia," *ZNW* 66 (1975) 103-16. — H. MERKLEIN, *Die Gottesherrschaft als Handlungsprinzip* (1978). — idem, "Die Umkehrpredigt bei Johannes dem Täufer und Jesus von Nazaret," *BZ* 25 (1981) 29-46. — O. MICHEL, "Die Umkehr nach der Verkündigung Jesu," *EvT* 5 (1938) 403-13. — R. MICHIELS, "La conception lucanienne de la conversion," *ETL* 41 (1965) 42-78. — C. G. MONTEFIORE, *Rabbinic Literature and Gospel Teachings* (1930) 390-422. — MOORE, *Judaism* 1, 507-34. — E. NEUHÄUSLER, *Anspruch und Antwort Gottes* (1962) 125-40. — A. NISSEN, *Gott und der Nächste im antiken Judentum* (1974) 130-49. — A. D. NOCK, *RAC* II, 105-18. — W. PESCH, *Der Ruf zur Entscheidung* (1964). — J. J. PETUCHOWSKI, "The Concept of 'Teshuvah,' " *Judaism* 17 (1968) 175-85. — B. POSCHMANN, *Paenitentia secunda* (1940). — T. M. RAITT, "The Prophetic Summons to Repentance," *ZAW* 83 (1971) 30-49. — H. SAHLIN, "Die Früchte der Umkehr," *ST* 1 (1947) 54-68. — E. P. SANDERS, *Paul and Palestinian Judaism* (1977), index s.v. atonement. — G. SAUER, "Die Umkehrforderung in der Verkündigung Jesajas," *Wort—Gebot—Glaube* (FS W. Eichrodt, ed. H. J. Stoebe et al.; 1970) 277-95. — SCHELKLE, *Theology* III, 73-82. — SCHNACKENBURG I, 33-66. — SCHNACKENBURG, *Botschaft* 11-18. — R. SCHNACKENBURG, *LTK* VIII, 356-59. — J. SCHNIEWIND, *Die Freude der Buße* ([2]1960). — J. G. SCHÖNFELD, *Metanoia* (1970). — R. SCHÜTZ, *Johannes der Täufer* (1967) 32-57. — R. SCHULTE, "Die Umkehr (Metanoia) als Anfang und Form christlichen Lebens," *MySal* V, 117-35. — E. SJÖBERG, *Gott und die Sünder* (1938). — J. A. SOGGIN, *THAT* II, 884-91. — SPICQ, *Notes* Suppl., 452-58. — A. TOSATO, "Per una revisione degli studi sulla metanoia neotestamentaria," *RivB* 23 (1975) 3-45. — W. TRILLING, "Metanoia als Grundforderung der neutestamentlichen Lebenslehre," *Einübung des Glaubens* (FS K. Tillmann, 1965) 178-90. — J. WENDLING, "L'appel de Jésus à la conversion," *Hokhma* 27 (1984) 5-38. — U. WILCKENS, *Die Missionsreden der Apostelgeschichte* ([3]1974) 178-86. — H. W. WOLFF, "Das Kerygma des deuteronomistischen Geschichtswerks," *ZAW* 73 (1961) 171-86. — idem, "Das Thema 'Umkehr' in der alttestamentlichen Prophetie," *ZTK* 48 (1951) 129-48.

1. Μετάνοια and μετανοέω are found primarily in the Synoptic Gospels (they appear once and twice, respectively, in Mark; twice and 5 times in Matthew), esp. in Luke (5 times and 9 times; in Acts they appear 6 times and 5 times). The words are infrequent in the epistolary literature (Paul uses them 3 times and once [plus one use of ἀμετανόητος]; elsewhere we have only μετάνοια: once in the Pastorals, 3 times in Hebrews, and once in 2 Peter). Neither appears in the Johannine Epistles. The vb. μετανοέω is found frequently in Revelation (11 times).

2. In Greek, the distinguishing semantic characteristic of μετάνοια or μετανοέω is that of *change (of mind)*, in both good and bad senses. In the case of a moral change, the word is related to a particular rather than a comprehensive change of attitude affecting one's entire existence (cf. *TDNT* IV, 976-80). Decisive for the NT understanding of the word is OT *šûb* ("turning around," in the sense of a turning away from present things and returning to the point of departure; cf. Holladay 53). The LXX translates *šûb* almost without exception as → ἐπι(ἀπο-)στρέφω (-ομαι) and employs μετανοέω as the equivalent of *niḥam* ("be sorry [for something]").

Instances in which μετανοέω appears as the equivalent of *šûb* (Sir 48:15) or as a synonym of ἐπιστρέφω (Sir 17:24f., 29) appear for the first time in the wisdom literature (cf. Sir 44:16; Wis 11:23; 12:10, 19). This usage was reinforced in Hellenistic Jewish literature and in later Greek translations of the OT (esp. Symmachus; *TDNT* IV, 989-95). *Šûb* gained a specifically religious significance in the Prophets. It points to "the return to the original relation with Yahweh" (Wolff, "Umkehr" 134) and includes also the idea of "a totally new beginning" (Fohrer 225n.7). Esp. in Amos, Hosea, and Isaiah, *repentance* is strictly personally oriented (in the sense of one's return to Yahweh) and represents an act that relates to one's entire existence. In Jeremiah and then esp. in Ezekiel the idea of *turning away from (individual) sins* comes to the fore.

In early Judaism repentance was overwhelmingly understood as a *return to the law* and was often regarded as a prerequisite for holiness. Nevertheless, neither this understanding nor the stronger individualistic and, in part, casuistic orientation of the concept of repentance warrants the suspicion that it entails legalism (M. Limbeck, *Die Ordnung des Heils* [1971]; Fiedler); rather, the parenetic objective should be kept in view. Moreover, early Judaism shows at least in principle that both the law and *repentance* were gifts of God's grace (Wis 11:23; 12:10, 19; Pr Man 8; the fifth of the Eighteen Benedictions). The concept of repentance acquired a special significance in the Qumran sect, whose members designated themselves the *repentant ones* of Israel (on this subject see Fabry).

3. Of the 8 Synoptic occurrences of μετάνοια, 5 are related to John the Baptist (as is 1 instance of μετανοέω: Matt 3:2), for whose preaching the word was essential. Matt 3:7-12 (Q) may reproduce authentic material (J. Becker, *Johannes der Täufer und Jesus von Nazareth* [1972] 109n.21; Merklein 142f.).

Repentance is first of all a turning away from sin (Mark 1:4f.). The character of repentance, which in principle made its demand on all Israel, arose from the immediate proximity of the judgment (Matt 3:10 par.). For John, this judgment appeared to be the only certainty (Matt 3:7b par.) and nullified every attempt by Israel to rely upon the former promises of salvation (Matt 3:9 par.). John's conclusion was: "Therefore, produce fruit worthy of *repentance*" (Matt 3:8 par.).

Moreover, that John does not make "the fruit of *repentance*" more specific by inculcation of the demands of the Torah cannot be attributed to the precarious state of the sources (Luke 3:10-14 being secondary, according to P. Hoffmann, *Studien zur Theologie der Logienquelle* [1972] 15f., *contra* Sahlin). Even the claim that for John the Torah was a means of salvation falls, by way of analogy, under the verdict of Matt 3:9. "The fruit of repentance" might well be John's water baptism, which is set over against the baptism by fire (= judgment) by "the coming one" (Matt 3:11 par.; see Hoffmann, *Studien* 18-25, 28-31; cf. Becker, *Johannes* 34-37).

Repentance furthermore refers to a radical acknowledgment of God, who stands over against Israel in his wrath, as well as a radical confession of a sinful fallenness that is so total that recourse to the former means of salvation appears hopeless. Repentance is made concrete in the "baptism of *repentance*" (Mark 1:4 par. Luke 3:3), which precisely through the surrender of all certainty of salvation offers a final chance for it. Even the hints of salvation (Matt 3:10b, 12c par.) do not become promises of it.

4. Leaving aside those passages that are probably the work of the Lukan redactor (Luke 5:32; 15:7, 10; 16:30?; 17:3f.?; 24:47; see further Mark 6:12; Matt 11:20; → 6, 7), there remains astonishingly little evidence that Jesus preached *repentance*. Whether the connection between the proclamation of the kingdom and the demand for repentance is authentic remains doubtful (cf. by way of contrast Luke 10:9 par.). At best, Luke 10:13; 11:32 par., and esp. Luke 13:3, 5 could go back to Jesus himself (cf., however, Limbeck 36f.). In any case, use of μετάνοια was not typical for Jesus, as it was for John the Baptist (cf. Trilling 188).

If one takes the last passage mentioned as the point of departure, then Jesus, like John, demanded repentance of all, without exception; all who did not repent were calling down judgment upon themselves (Luke 13:3, 5), which Jesus no longer preached apodictically, but conditionally (Merklein 146-49). Positively, *repentance* required committing oneself to the words and deeds of Jesus (Luke 10:13; 11:32 par.). Repentance must therefore be seen in the context of the proclamation of the kingdom. While already with John repentance was no longer a return to former things (it is indeed a return to Yahweh, but Yahweh who desires to be feared for his future acts of judgment), with Jesus it meant to live in the light of the announced and already present salvation of the kingdom of God, which absolves all former guilt. As a result, the idea that God himself grants repentance is not only an exaggeration but even a distortion, when repentance is made the result of an a priori forgiveness (Merklein 204f.). The traditional concept of repentance, which semantically has been defined completely differently, thus plays a limited role with Jesus.

5. The sayings source (Q) adopts John the Baptist's preaching of judgment and repentance (Luke 3:8 par. Matt 3:8); it acquires a different emphasis, however, in that it identifies the "the one who is to come" with Jesus (Hoffmann, *Studien* 28-33). *Repentance* is, therefore,

both a turning away from former things (as with John the Baptist) and an acknowledgment of the message and mission of Jesus (A. Polag, *Die Christologie der Logienquelle* [1977] 74, 90), who, as the coming Son of Man, sanctions Q's proclamation of the renewed kingdom. When Q, bearing this message, encountered open rejection in Israel, it sharpened the preaching of judgment. Into this context the sayings of Luke 10:13 par. Matt 11:21 and Luke 11:32 par. Matt 12:41 were inserted (on this subject, D. Lührmann, *Die Redaktion der Logienquelle* [1969] 37-40, 63f.).

6. Mark 1:15 demands *repentance* in response to the announcement of the reign of God and thus properly represents the structural uniqueness of Jesus' concept of repentance. New is the connection between faith and the gospel. Repentance therefore acquires the sense of the beginning of a turning toward Christian faith (cf. Mark 6:12, redactional). Correspondingly, Mark eliminates the concept of judgment from the preaching of *repentance* by John (the "one who prepares the way"). The "baptism of *repentance* for the forgiveness of sins" in Mark 1:4 is understood primarily as preparation and cleansing for Jesus' message of salvation.

7. The water baptism of John is expressly oriented toward *repentance,* according to Matt 3:11 (redactional); it possesses, however, no power to forgive sins (*contra* Mark 1:4), which Matthew ascribes instead to the death of Jesus (26:28). In other respects, Matthew draws the forerunner even closer to Jesus; they both proclaim the same call (3:2; 4:17). The points at which Matthew diverges from Mark allow us to presume that Matthew is more concerned with (eschatologically motivated) responsible human conduct (G. Strecker, *Der Weg der Gerechtigkeit* [³1971] 226-28). The demand for fruit worthy of repentance in Matt 3:8—directed here toward the Pharisees and Sadducees—can also be understood in this sense. Inadequate repentance manifests itself in the Pharisees' demand for a sign in Matt 12:38-42 (v. 41) and in the rejection of the miracles of Jesus as messianic deeds (Matt 11:20 [redactional], 21; cf. 11:2, 19).

8. Characteristic of the Lukan understanding of *repentance* is its connection with the forgiveness of sins (Acts 2:38; 3:19; 5:31; 8:22; 26:18, 20; cf. Luke 3:3; 24:47) or with baptism and the reception of salvation (or the Spirit; Acts 2:38; 11:18). The relation can be defined as follows: repentance is the precondition for forgiveness, which in turn is the prerequisite for receiving salvation (Acts 2:38; 3:19; cf. 8:22). This usage of μετανοέω, supplemented occasionally by → ἐπιστρέφω (3:19; 26:20; cf. Luke 17:4), shows that Luke understood repentance differently (H. Conzelmann, *The Theology of St. Luke* [1961] 99-101, 227-30). Influenced by Greek usage, Luke under-

stands the term as the change of attitude that leads to *conversion,* which must be followed, however, by corresponding deeds (Acts 26:20; cf. Luke 3:7). Nevertheless, Luke remains true to the traditional biblical heritage in that he views repentance as a once-and-for-all act (the only exception being the anthropological tendency of Luke 17:3f.). Viewed as a whole, the Lukan concept of repentance has a strongly ethicizing bent (Michiels 76), although the eschatological orientation has not been entirely lost (Acts 3:19; 17:30f.).

As a result of this narrowing of the term, Luke does not adopt Jesus' call to *repentance* in Mark 1:15 (likewise Mark 6:12) as an all-encompassing demand. This ethicizing manifests itself in the redactional pl. "fruits *of repentance*" (Luke 3:8, *contra* Q), which is then made concrete in John's reply to his questioners (Luke 3:10-14), as well as in the fact that Jesus calls tax collectors and sinners (Pesch 49: "the morally fallen") to *repentance* (Luke 5:32; contrast Mark 15:7, 10; contrast Q [cf. Merklein 186-88]). Such people, however, merely illustrate the general condition of sinfulness (Luke 13:3, 5). In opposition to the rabbinic axiom "If to the sinner, how much more to the righteous" (cf. Sjöberg 66f. and *passim*), Luke has a higher estimate of the repentant sinner than of the unrepentant righteous (Luke 15:7; cf. v. 10).

The embedding of the ethical understanding in the Lukan redemptive-historical perspective is worth consideration: Turning from a sinful way of life is required in light of the forgiveness of sins and salvation, which have come in Jesus (Luke 4:16-21; 5:23; 7:47f.). The "baptism *of repentance* for the forgiveness of sins" (Luke 3:3) proclaimed by John, to which Luke hardly intended to ascribe any independent power to wipe away sin, can also be related to this ethical emphasis (cf. Acts 13:2; 19:4; H. Schürmann, *Luke* [HTKNT] I, 159f.). As a result of the salvation that has appeared in Jesus, whoever does not repent falls under judgment (Luke 10:13; 11:32). A characteristic coupling of these ethical and redemptive-historical aspects can be found in Luke 16:30, if one perceives there a reflection of the resurrection of Jesus.

For the age of the Church, however, a new possibility of *repentance* for the forgiveness of sins has arisen out of the death and resurrection of the Messiah, which now —beginning in Jerusalem—is to be proclaimed to all peoples (Luke 24:47; cf. Acts 5:31). The apostolic preaching of repentance is directed first toward Israel (Acts 2:38; 3:19) and then, inspired by the insight that God grants even the Gentiles the opportunity for repentance (thus was the traditional formulation in Acts 11:18 [cf. 5:31] to be interpreted, according to the Lukan understanding), to the Gentiles themselves (cf. Acts 17:30; 20:21; 26:20). The redemptive-historical aspect comes prominently to the fore in Acts (thus Wilckens): Repentance is negatively a turning away from former ignorance

(ἄγνοια) on the basis of the confirming act of God toward Jesus (Acts 3:17, 19; 23:30); positively it is a turning toward God, which manifests itself concretely in belief in the Lord Jesus (Acts 20:21; 26:18, 20; cf. 19:4).

A unique connection of ethical and salvation-historical aspects is seen in Luke 16:30f., provided that one can see there an allusion to Jesus' resurrection.

9. a) Following Jewish tradition (cf. Wis 11:23), the goodness and patience of God are intended to lead to *repentance,* according to Rom 2:4. Conversely, the unrepentant heart (ἀμετανόητος καρδία) draws upon itself the wrath of God (v. 5). The weakened sense of *repentance,* i.e., *change of mind* (in the midst of the Christian life), is present in 2 Cor 7:9f.; 12:21. The infrequent occurrence of μετάνοια in Paul can be explained by the fact that the event intended has been subsumed under the concept of → πίστις.

b) In 2 Tim 2:25 μετάνοια refers to the return (of false teachers) to true teaching and practice. On the understanding of the traditional Jewish expression "God grants *repentance*" (cf. Wis 12:10, 19; *Sib. Or.* iv.168f.) → 8, on Acts 5:31; 11:18 (cf. Pol. *Phil.* 11:4).

c) In Heb 6:1 "*repentance* from dead works" (= works that lead to death; cf. *Did.* 5) together with belief in God (Lührmann, "Henoch") form the foundation of Christian existence (cf. 9:14). It is considered impossible in 6:6 for a convert who has fallen away to be brought back to repentance (6:1; cf. *Herm. Sim.* ix.26.6; *Man.* iv.3.1). Yet this statement, which has had serious repercussions for the history of penance (e.g., see Montanism, Novatianism; cf. Poschmann) in that it lays radical stress on the eschatologically definitive character of salvation and the gift character of repentance, is hardly to be taken as a dogmatic declaration on God's power (to forgive). Rather, it arises from the pastoral experience of the author or is intended to address a parenetic need (cf. 6:9-12). Heb 12:17 clearly stands in a parenetic context, one that warns against losing the grace of God through irreversible delay: Esau found no possibility (τόπος) of *repentance* (i.e., of reversing the past), although he sought it with tears.

d. In 2 Pet 3:2, like Rom 2:4, the motif appears of the patience of the Lord, which is intended to lead to μετάνοια. What is meant by this, in addition to the *repentance* of the blasphemer (3:3f.), is generally the realization of the required life of piety (3:11f., 14f.).

10. In Revelation, μετανοέω belongs to the fixed vocabulary of the circular letter to the seven churches, inasmuch as these churches are presented with the threat of judgment (2:5 bis, 16, 21f.; 3:3, 19). The call to *repentance* appears to make up part of a fixed penance exhortation (U. B. Müller, *Prophetie und Predigt im NT* [1975] 57-92). Unlike its predominant meaning elsewhere in the NT, the word here does not refer to *repentance* but to the return of Christians to their original deeds (2:4f.; cf. 3:15f.;

for the connection with ἔργα, cf. further 2:22f.; 3:2f.; 9:20; 16:11), which correspond with the received teaching that was to be preserved (3:3; cf. 2:10, 25; 3:8, 10f.). Explicitly mentioned is the tolerance of some churches for the Nicolaitans (2:14-16, 20) and their followers, to whom, however, a chance of repentance is still extended (2:21-23). Striking is the ecclesiological connection, which no longer accepts repentance outside the Church (9:20f.; 16:9, 11). Repentance is understood as a final possibility, realized once and for all (cf. 2:5, 16; 3:3b) before the approaching end. The threat of judgment in the circular letter is accordingly conditional (2:5b, 16, 22; 3:3) and always flows over into the promise of salvation (cf. the statements about "the one who overcomes").

H. Merklein

μεταξύ *metaxy* in the middle, between; afterward, next*

There are 9 occurrences in the NT; as adv. (in temporal sense) only in John 4:31 (ἐν τῷ μεταξύ, *meanwhile, in the meantime*) and Acts 13:42 (εἰς τὸ μεταξὺ σάββατον, "on the *following* sabbath"; cf. also *Barn.* 13:5). Elsewhere μεταξύ is used as an improper prep.: Matt 18:15 (μεταξὺ σοῦ καὶ αὐτοῦ μόνου, "just *between* you and him"); Acts 15:9 (μεταξὺ ἡμῶν τε καὶ αὐτῶν, "*between* us and them"); Rom 2:15 (μεταξὺ ἀλλήλων, "*between* each other/*mutually*"). In Matt 23:35; Luke 11:51; 16:26; Acts 12:6 it has a local meaning.

μεταπέμπομαι *metapempomai* send for, summon; have brought back*

Μεταπέμπομαι occurs 9 times in the NT, all in mid. and pass. and only in Acts: 10:5, *bring back;* cf. 10:22, 29a (pass. μεταπεμφθείς, "*when I was sent for*"); 10:29b (τίνι λόγῳ μετεπέμψασθέ με; "for what reason *did you send for* me?"); 11:13; 20:1; 24:24, 26; 25:3 (ὅπως μεταπέμψηται αὐτὸν εἰς Ἰερουσαλήμ, "that *he have* him *brought back* to Jerusalem").

μεταστρέφω *metastrephō* turn, turn into, change*

Acts 2:20: ὁ ἥλιος μεταστραφήσεται εἰς σκότος καὶ ἡ σελήνη εἰς αἷμα, "the sun shall *be turned* into darkness and the moon into blood" (cf. Joel 3:4; elsewhere of changing into the opposite: Ps. 77:44 LXX; Sir 11:31; Jas 4:9 v.l.: "laughter to mourning"); in Gal 1:7 the obj. is τὸ εὐαγγέλιον τοῦ Χριστοῦ: "*change* (JB)/*pervert* (RSV) the gospel of Christ." G. Bertram, *TDNT* VII, 729.

μετασχηματίζω *metaschēmatizō* transform*

Lit.: J. KÜRZINGER, "Συμμόρφους τῆς εἰκόνος τοῦ υἱοῦ αὐτοῦ (Röm. 8:29)," *BZ* 2 (1958) 294-99, esp. 298. — J. SCHNEIDER, *TDNT* VII, 957f.

1. Μετασχηματίζω is found 5 times in the NT, exclu-

sively in the Pauline Epistles. Its basic meaning is *change the form of* (→ σχῆμα). Phil 3:21 speaks of the *transformation* of our lowly body by Jesus Christ at his future revelation, the parousia. There the transformation of the outer form corresponds to the inner transformation that the Lord will bring about in Christians so that they may share in the glory of his body (→ σύμμορφος). In 2 Cor 11:13, 14, 15, μετασχηματίζω has the negative sense of *pretend to be someone/hypocritically act as someone/ masquerade as someone,* with the assumed role indicated by εἰς or ὡς. Paul describes his opponents in Corinth as "false apostles," as "dishonest workers," who wrongly *pretend to be* apostles of Christ. He calls them "Satan's henchmen," who *act* as "servants of righteousness," just as Satan himself *masquerades* as an "angel of light." In 1 Cor 4:6, the meaning of μετασχηματίζω is difficult to discern precisely. The meaning assumed by many authors, "say something figuratively," does not commend itself, since no figure of speech appears in the preceding context. Perhaps Paul wanted to express that he had formulated what he had said "in an unusual way" because he had used himself and Apollos as examples.

2. a) The *transformation* into the glory of the Lord of which Phil 3:21 speaks must be taken in connection with 3:10. For Christians, communion with Christ in this life means adopting the form of their suffering, afflicted Lord. From this unity Paul derives the hope that on the last day they will also participate in the resurrection (Rom 6:5) and in the glory of Jesus Christ, i.e., in the form then of their exalted Lord (cf. also → μεταμορφόω 2.b, c; 3.b).

b) The idea that one's appearance or form is shaped by that of one's lord can also be found in 2 Cor 11:13-15. Whoever is "a servant of Satan" will, like Satan, behave hypocritically and presumptuously, according to Paul, in order to lead others astray. Those who belong to Christ, however, are conformed to their Lord and are therefore truly "servants of righteousness."

J. M. Nützel

μετατίθημι *metatithēmi* bring to another place, move, transport, change; mid.: turn away; pass.: be done away with, fall away*

The vb. μετατίθημι appears 6 times in the NT. In 3 of its uses, the meaning is literal: Acts 7:16 (pass. μετετέθησαν εἰς Συχέμ, "they [the bodies of Jacob and the fathers] *were transported* to Shechem"); Heb 11:5a (pass.) and 5b (act.), of the translation of Enoch (→ μετάθεσις). In the other 3 occurrences, the meaning is fig.: Gal 1:6 (pass. or mid.: ὅτι οὕτως ταχέως μετατίθεσθε, "that *you* so quickly *fall away/ turn away*"); Heb 7:12 (pass.: μετατιθεμένης . . . τῆς ἱερωσύνης, "*when* the priesthood *is changed/undergoes a change*"); Jude 4 (act.: τὴν . . . χάριτα μετατιθέντες, "*changing* the grace"). C. Maurer, *TDNT* VIII, 161f.

μετατρέπω *metatrepō* turn around; pass.: be changed, change*

Jas 4:9: ὁ γέλως ὑμῶν εἰς πένθος μετατραπήτω (v.l. μεταστραφήτω), "let your laughter *be turned* to mourning"; → μεταστρέφω.

μετέπειτα *metepeita* afterward*

Heb 12:17, of Esau: καὶ μετέπειτα θέλων κληρονομῆσαι τὴν εὐλογίαν . . . , "and *afterward,* when he wanted to inherit the blessing. . . ."

μετέχω *metechō* have a share in, share, partake of; gain; enjoy*

Μετέχω appears in the NT only in 1 Corinthians (5 times) and Hebrews (3 times). The element shared or partaken of appears as an obj. gen., except in 1 Cor 10:17, where it follows ἐκ. The occurrences are 1 Cor 9:10: ἐπ' ἐλπίδι τοῦ μετέχειν, "in the hope of *sharing* [in the fruits of plowing or threshing]"; 9:12: τῆς ὑμῶν ἐξουσίας μετέχουσιν, "*enjoy* the rights of possession over you"; 10:17: ἐκ τοῦ ἑνὸς ἄρτου μετέχομεν, "we *partake* of the one bread"; 10:21: τραπέζης κυρίου μετέχειν, "*have a share in* the table of the Lord"; 10:30: χάριτι μετέχω [sc. τῆς τροφῆς], "*enjoy* [the food] with thanks"; Heb 2:14: μετέσχεν τῶν αὐτῶν, "*he* [the son] *shared in* the same things [flesh and blood]/*took upon himself* the same condition"; 5:13: μετέχων γάλακτος, "*partaking of* milk"; and 7:13: φυλῆς ἑτέρας μετέσχηκεν, "*he belonged to* another tribe." H. Hanse, *TDNT* II, 830-32; Spicq, *Notes* II, 555-59.

μετεωρίζομαι *meteōrizomai* be anxious, worry*

In the NT only in Luke 12:29 (pass.). The LXX understands the vb. and its derivatives in the sense of "raise on high" or "be arrogant" (Ps 130:1; 2 Macc 7:34). The meaning "be anxious; worry" is seldom found (Pap. Oxy. no. 1679, ll. 16f.; Josephus *Ant.* xvi.135). The context of Luke 12:29, however, makes it clear that μὴ μετεωρίζεσθε here should be translated "*do not worry.*" (Cf. Old Latin *nolite solliciti esse;* d: *non abalienatis vos, contra* Vg.: *nolite in sublime tolli.* For further possible translations, cf. Thucydides viii.16.2; Josephus *Ant.* xviii.218; *B.J.* iv.118; Pap. Mich. 484, 5f.). BAGD s.v.; K. Deissner, *TDNT* IV, 630-31; J. Molitor, "Zur Übersetzung von μετεωρίζεσθε Lk 12,29," *BZ* 10 (1966) 107f.; Spicq, *Notes* II, 560-62.

μετοικεσία, ας, ἡ *metoikesia* migration; deportation, exile*

In the NT μετοικεσία appears only in the genealogy of Jesus recorded in Matthew 1. There ἡ μετοικεσία Βαβυλῶνος, "the Babylonian *captivity*" (vv. 11, 12, 17

bis), is a structural device, helping to divide the chronology into three parts: from Abraham to David, from David to the Babylonian *captivity,* and from the Babylonian *captivity* to Christ. Cf. 2 Kgs 24:16; 1 Chr 5:22.

μετοικίζω *metoikizō* resettle, remove, transplant*

In the 2 occurrences of μετοικίζω in the NT, God is the subj. Acts 7:4: μετῴκισεν αὐτὸν εἰς τὴν γῆν ταύτην, "he *settled* him [Abraham of Haran] in this land"; and 7:43: μετοικιῶ ὑμᾶς, "*I will transplant* you [beyond Babylon]" (cf. Amos 5:27 LXX, which specifies ἐπέκεινα Δαμασκοῦ).

μετοχή, ῆς, ἡ *metochē* participation; community*

2 Cor 6:14: τίς γὰρ μετοχὴ δικαιοσύνῃ καὶ ἀνομίᾳ; "What *common element* do righteousness and lawlessness have?" (cf. 6:15). H. Hanse, *TDNT* II, 830-32; Spicq, *Notes* II, 555-59.

μέτοχος, 2 *metochos* participating in; subst.: participant; companion*

There are 6 occurrences in the NT—in Luke 5:7 and 5 times in Hebrews. Μέτοχος is a (subst.) adj. in Heb 3:1 (κλήσεως ἐπουρανίου μέτοχοι), 6:4 (μετόχους . . . πνεύματος ἁγίου), and 12:8 (παιδείας . . . μέτοχοι). It is a subst. in Luke 5:7, Heb 1:9 (παρὰ τοὺς μετόχους σου, "above your *companions,*" citing Ps 44:8 LXX), and 3:14 (μέτοχοι γὰρ τοῦ Χριστοῦ γεγόναμεν, "for we have become *partners* of Christ," i.e., through participation in the heavenly calling; cf. 3:12 and 2:11f.; hardly "participants in Christ," as A. Stobel, *Heb* [NTD], and O. Michel, *Heb* [KEK]). On the "companions of the Messiah," cf. further 4 Ezra 7:28; 14:9; see also John 15:14f. and the literature in Michel. H. Hanse, *TDNT* II, 830-32; Spicq, *Notes* II, 555-59.

μετρέω *metreō* measure, measure out, apportion*

Μετρέω occurs 11 times in the NT; only in Revelation does it retain its original sense of *measure (out):* 11:1 (the temple, etc.); 11:2 (not the outer court); 21:15, 16 (the city, etc.); 21:17 (the walls); cf. Ezek 40:3ff.; Zech 2:1ff. It has a fig. meaning in Mark 4:24 (bis) par. Matt 7:2 (bis)/Luke 6:38: ἐν (Luke without ἐν) ᾧ μέτρῳ μετρεῖτε μετρηθήσεται (Luke ἀντιμετρηθήσεται) ὑμῖν, "the amount *you measure out* is the amount *you will be given*" (JB), a proverbial play on words. Μετρέω also has the meaning *apportion* (cf. Philo *Her.* 229; *1 Clem.* 13:2; Pol. *Phil.* 2:3; *m. Soṭa* 1:7); see 2 Cor 10:12: αὐτοὶ ἐν ἑαυτοῖς ἑαυτοὺς μετροῦντες, "when they *measure* themselves by themselves" (thus the reading of 𝔭⁴⁶ ℵ¹ B Hᵛⁱᵈ 33 etc.; cf. *TCGNT* ad loc.; the context also suggests, however, that the αὐτοί may refer to Paul himself, thus the reading of vv. 12f. in D* G it etc.; cf. also R. Bultmann, *2 Cor* [KEK] ad loc.). K. Deissner, *TDNT* IV, 632-34; → μέτρον.

μετρητής, οῦ, ὁ *metrētēs* measure (noun)*

Μετρητής is a liquid measure, used esp. in Attica (*ca.* 39 liters); it is mentioned in the NT only in John 2:6: ἀνὰ μετρητὰς δύο ἢ τρεῖς, "two or three *measures* each." BAGD s.v.; A. Strobel, *BHH* 1165f.; R. Schnackenburg, *John* I (1968) ad loc.

μετριοπαθέω *metriopatheō* moderate one's passions; be understanding*

This vb. meant originally "balance one's passions (πάθη)" (cf. Diogenes Laertius v.31; not found in LXX); in the NT only in Heb 5:2, of the high priest: μετριοπαθεῖν δυνάμενος, "as one who is able *to have compassion* on the ignorant and those going astray." He can have understanding for their situation, "since he himself is subject to weakness" (cf., regarding Christ, δυνάμενος συμπαθῆσαι in 4:15). In this context it is not a question of the Stoic middle way between passion and apathy, nor could it be concerned with the philosophical idea that μετριοπάθεια comes to one who has advanced but ἀπάθεια comes to the one who has been perfected (on this subject see esp. Spicq, *Notes* II, 563-65; O. Michel, *Heb* [KEK] ad loc.; cf. Plutarch *Cons. ad Apoll.* iii.22; Philo *Virt.* 195; *All.* iii.129ff.; *Abr.* 257). Rather, the wording is intended to emphasize the true humanity of Christ, who in the end was appointed high priest by God. E. Gräßer, *Heb* (EKKNT, 1990) I, 275f.; W. Michaelis, *TDNT* V, 938.

μετρίως *metriōs* moderately, slightly*

Acts 20:12: "They took the lad away alive, and were not *a little* comforted (παρεκλήθησαν οὐ μετρίως)."

μέτρον, ου, τό *metron* measure (noun)*

1. Occurrences in the NT — 2. The Jesus tradition — 3. Pauline texts — 4. Rev 21:15, 17

Lit.: BAGD s.v. — K. BERGER, "Zu den sogenannten Sätzen heiligen Rechts," *NTS* 17 (1970/71) 10-40, esp. 19. — B. COUROYER, "De la mesure dont vous mesurez il vous sera mesuré," *RB* 77 (1970) 366-70. — K. DEISSNER, *TDNT* IV, 632-34. — E. NEUHÄUSLER, "Mit welchem Maßstab mißt Gott die Menschen? Deutung zweier Jesussprüche," *BibLeb* 11 (1970) 104-13. — R. PESCH, *Mark* (HTKNT) I (1976) 251-54. — H. P. RÜGER, "Mit welchem Maß ihr meßt, wird euch gemessen werden," *ZNW* 60 (1969) 174-82. — R. B. Y. SCOTT, "Weights and Measures of the Bible," *BA* 22 (1959) 22-40.

1. The word group μέτρον/μετρέω is used in the NT primarily to describe the process of measuring (Matt 7:2;

23:32; Mark 4:24; Luke 6:38; Rev. 11:1f.; 21:15-17) or to give the size of a container (John 2:6; 3:34). Other important instances are found in related texts within the Jesus tradition (Mark 4:24 par.; Luke 6:38 par.), in Paul (Rom 12:3; 2 Cor 10:12-15; cf. Eph 4:7, 13, 16), and in Revelation (11:1f.; 21:15-17).

2. Jesus adopted from Jewish tradition the principle of "measure for measure" to set in sharp relief God's acts of judgment in the final judgment (Matt 7:2): God judges by the measure of justice when a person rejects the measure of love (18:23-35; 25:14-30). Moreover, Jesus says, the love of God is the only proper measure (Matt 7:2; Luke 6:38) of human action; he thereby rejects any keeping of accounts or calculations. Mark, however, placed 4:24 in a new context, that of the mission sayings, as an apocalyptic word of judgment, thereby emphasizing the responsibility of his hearers and the seriousness of the obligation to proclaim. Luke, by way of contrast, summons to unrestrained generosity, while stressing the reward motif: God will abundantly give to those who love magnanimously.

3. Paul designates the mission field entrusted to him as the *measure* given him by God (2 Cor 10:13-15); thus he puts his opponents, who boast "without measure," in their place (10:12; cf. v. 16). The idea that God destines a person to a particular measure (i.e., to a particular gift of grace) is expressed in the post-Pauline formula of Eph 4:7, 16 in a way consistent with the Pauline tradition (cf. Rom 12:3; 1 Cor. 12); the Church has an ideal, perfect *measure,* which it is necessary to achieve. Those who have been baptized should "reach unity in the faith and in the knowlege of the Son of God, and become mature, attaining to the whole *measure* of the fullness of Christ" (Eph 4:13).

4. The two occurrences in Rev 11:1f. and 21:15, 17 are related to one another: in 11:1 the prophet receives the command to "measure" the temple, and in 21:15-12 the measurement is carried out; in 11:1 the measuring is tantamount to a preservation of the temple. The passage to which this account refers is Ezek 40:3 and 40:5-41:4. Although the measurements in Revelation are round and harmonious, they are also greatly exaggerated; in them are reflected the paradisiacal and apocalyptic measurements of the new Jerusalem, the dwelling of God among mankind.

W. Pesch

μέτωπον, ου, τό *metōpon* forehead*

Μέτωπον appears 8 times in the NT, only in Revelation, where it always refers to a sign on (ἐπί) the forehead: the seal of God, in 7:3; 9:4; the name of God, in 14:1; 22:4; the evil sign of the "beast," in 13:16; 14:9; 20:4; and the name of Babylon on the forehead of the woman, in 17:5. The image of the seal could have been drawn from the sign of ownership on the foreheads of slaves (cf. οἱ δοῦλοι τοῦ θεοῦ in 7:3) and from the protective mark of Ezek 9:4, 6 (cf. further Exod 28:36; also Isa 44:5). The mark of the beast indicates the opposing relation of ownership (hardly the Tephillin [prayer bands]: contra C. Schneider, TDNT IV, 636), as does the name of the woman (if the latter is not an example of a distinctive headdress). Schneider, 635-37; E. Dinkler, Signum Crucis (1967), esp. 1-25, 26-54; E. Lohse, Rev (NTD) on 7:3; H. Kraft, Rev (HNT) on 7:3; 13:16; 17:5; → σφραγίζω, σφραγίς.

μέχρι, μέχρις *mechri, mechris* until, as far as*

The prep. μέχρι occurs 17 times in the NT (the form μέχρις appears only before vowels, in Mark 13:30; Gal 4:19; Heb 12:4). It functions 3 times as a conj. (twice in the combination μέχρις οὗ, in Mark 13:30 and Gal 4:19; once alone, in Eph 4:13) and 14 times as a prep.: of space (Rom 15:19), of time (Matt 11:23; 28:15; Luke 16:16; Acts 10:30; 20:7; Rom 5:14; 1 Tim 6:14; Heb 3:14; 9:10), and expressing degree of suffering—*unto* death (μέχρι θανάτου, Phil 2:8, 30), bondage as a criminal (μέχρι δεσμῶν, 2 Tim 2:9), or shedding blood (μέχρις αἵματος, Heb 12:4). BAGD s.v.; BDF index s.v.

μή *mē* (negative particle, interrogative particle, conj.)

1. Basic meaning — 2. In main clauses — 3. In subordinate clauses — 4. With participles and infinitives — 5. Οὐ μή

Lit.: BAGD s.v. — BDF index s.v. — J. CARMIGNAC, "Fais que nous n'entrions pas dans la tentation," *RB* 72 (1965) 218-26. — MOULTON, *Grammar* III, 281-87; IV, 33, 69, 92, *passim*. — J. W. ROBERTS, "The Independent Subjunctive," *Restoration Quarterly* 6 (1962) 98-101 (on οὐ μή). — THRALL, *Particles, passim* (εἰ δὲ μή, etc.). — ZERWICK, *Biblical Greek* §§440-42, 444, 468-71.

1. Μή is used to negate sentences that represent not reality but the conception of the speaker, involving something desired, demanded, considered, feared, etc. Conditional sentences are also, in the same sense, subjective statements that do not make any claim concerning the reality of their contents. In koine Greek, the range of possible uses for μή is expanded, so that (esp. with the partc. and the inf.) μή often replaces οὐ. As a general rule, οὐ negates the ind., μή the remaining moods, such as inf. and partc. Μή . . . μηδείς ("no one"), etc., are pleonastic.

2. In main clauses:
a) With the opt. without ἄν, as in classical Greek, μή expresses a fulfillable wish (2 Tim 4:16). The more refined μὴ γένοιτο appears in Luke 20:16 and 13 times in Paul.

b) Μή appears with the pres. imv. (Luke 6:30; John 20:17; Gal 5:13 [sc. ἔχετε]), occasionally also with the aor. imv. (Matt 24:17f. etc.). It is used elliptically in John 18:40.

c) With the subjunc., 1) μή appears in prohibitions; the 2nd and 3rd person aor. subjuncs. are used as negative aor. imvs. (Matt 24:23; 1 Cor 16:11); 2) μή negates the hortative: "let us *not* . . ." (Gal 6:9; Rom 3:8 [sc. possibly ποιήσωμεν]); 3) μή negates the vb. in deliberative questions (Mark 12:14: "should we or should we *not* pay?").

d) With the ind. in independent clauses μή presents a suggestive question: *surely not?* (→ μήτι). The expected answer is no (1 Cor 9:8; Matt 9:15). If a verb-negating οὐ is added (μή . . . οὐ, *surely?*), then an affirmative answer is expected (Rom 10:18f.; 1 Cor 9:4f.; 11:22).

3. In subordinate clauses:
a) Conditional clauses are almost always negated with μή. Only in indefinite (wrongly called "real") conditions is the classical μή replaced by οὐ. Εἰ (ἄν) μή after a negation means *except, unless* (Mark 4:22; 6:5; 10:18; Matt 5:13); occasionally, εἰ μή replaces ἀλλά with the meaning *but rather* (Matt 12:4; Gal 2:16). The Hellenistic ἐκτὸς εἰ μή means *except, unless* (1 Cor 14:5); εἰ δὲ μή (γε), *otherwise* (Luke 5:36).

b) Conditional rel. clauses with the ind. are only seldom negated with the classical μή in the NT (2 Pet 1:9; 1 John 4:3; cf. Titus 1:11). However, μή is used with the subjunc. with ἄν (final and iterative): ὃς ἄν, ὅστις ἄν, etc. = ἐάν τις (Matt 19:9; Luke 9:5; Acts 3:23).

c) A causal clause in John 3:18 has μή with the ind. (ὅτι μὴ πεπίστευκεν), unlike classical usage.

d) Final clauses introduced by ἵνα and ὅπως are negated by μή (Matt 7:1; Acts 20:16). Μή, however, can also become a conj.: *lest* (Acts 27:42 etc.).

e) As a conj. μή *(so that; οὐ μή, lest)* introduces obj. clauses that are subordinate to vbs. of fearing. It generally is used with the subjunc. when the concern regards the future (Acts 23:10; 2 Cor 8:20). The ind. appears when the concern is directed toward something that may have already happened (Gal 4:11). On Gal 2:2; 1 Thess 3:5, etc. → μήποτε 5.b. Originally, the μή clause after φοβοῦμαι μή was an asyndetic volitive clause: e.g., "I am afraid. May he not die." Through coupling of the two parts, μή faded to a simple *that:* "I am afraid that he may die."

f) Also as a conj., μή *(that not)* introduces obj. clauses following trans. vbs. of caution (e.g., "be careful, beware"). It is used with the fut. (Col 2:8) or the subjunc. (Heb 12:25; Gal 5:15). The majority of these μή clauses should rather be designated independent clauses expressing a prohibition (→ 2.c.1), which appear asyndetically with the imv. ὁρᾶτε/βλέπετε: "Beware; you shall not . . ." (Matt 18:10; 1 Thess 5:15; in Rev 19:10 and 22:9 [sc. ποιήσῃς]). The ind. expresses that which has already occurred: "Be careful *that* the light in you not be darkness" (Luke 11:35).

4. a) The partc. is usually negated by μή in koine Greek, even when classical Greek would prefer οὐ (Rom 4:17; 1 Cor 1:28; Heb 12:27).

b) The inf. is almost always negated with μή in koine Greek, unlike classical Greek, even after vbs. of asserting and maintaining (Mark 12:18). After negative vbs. ("hinder, dispute, shrink back," etc.) μή remains untranslated (Luke 22:34; Acts 20:27). The substantivized inf. in the gen. (τοῦ μή + inf.) often has a final (*in order that not*, Heb 11:5) or consecutive (*with the result that not*, Rom 7:3; Acts 10:47) sense. The dat. construction τῷ μή + inf. represents a causal clause (2 Cor 2:13).

5. Οὐ μή (probably from οὐ φόβος ἐστὶν μή) with the aor. subjunc. or the fut. is a strong, emphatic negation of the future. It occurs most frequently in the sayings of Jesus and in quotations from the LXX. It is translated as a future: "will *certainly not . . .*" (Luke 22:67f.; John 10:5; Acts 13:41). Pleonastic constructions such as οὐδ' οὐ μή and οὐκέτι οὐ μή are not classical: Matt 24:21, *and certainly not;* Mark 14:25, *certainly never;* Luke 10:19, *certainly nothing.* In questions that intend to suggest a positive answer, οὐ μή means *surely not?/certainly not?* (Luke 18:7; Rev 15:4; John 18:11). P. Lampe

μήγε *mēge* not

Alternate reading, occurring only in the expression εἰ δὲ μήγε instead of εἰ δὲ μή γε, "otherwise": Matt 6:1; 9:17; Luke 5:36f.; 10:6; 13:9; 14:32; 2 Cor 11:16.

μηδαμῶς *mēdamōs* in no way, absolutely not; no (as response)*

In the NT μηδαμῶς (μηθαμῶς only outside the NT, *1 Clem.* 33:1; 45:7; cf. BDF §33) appears only in Acts 10:14; 11:8 (μηδαμῶς, κύριε), both times in the refusal of Peter to eat anything unclean.

μηδέ *mēde* also not, and not, not even

There are 56 occurrences in the NT, esp. in Matthew (11 times), Mark (6 times), Luke (7 times), and 1 Corinthians (6 times), but lacking, e.g., in Galatians, 1 Thessalonians, James, and Revelation.

Μηδέ, *and not/also not,* continues an expressed negation; e.g., μὴ κτήσησθε in Matt 10:9a is followed twice in the same verse with μηδέ (where the same vb. is assumed), then with μὴ πήραν in v. 10a, and finally three more times with μηδέ; similarly Luke 14:12; cf. further 1 Cor 5:8; 1 John 2:15. Μηδέ may appear after ὃς ἄν with a different vb. and means *and not* (Matt 10:14; Mark 6:11); after ἵνα μή (Matt 24:20; John 4:15); after ὅπως μή

(Luke 16:26). Μηδέ is repeated several times with separate vbs. after μή (Rom 14:21; 1 Cor 10:7-10; Col 2:21) and with an inf. after μή + inf. (Acts 4:18; 21:21; 2 Thess 2:2; 1 Tim 1:4); likewise it appears with partcs. (Matt 22:29; Rom 9:11; 2 Cor 4:2; Phil 2:3; 1 Pet 5:2f.) and at the beginning of a result clause after a conditional clause with εἰ οὐ (2 Thess 3:10: "then he will *also not* eat"). It has the meaning *also not/not even* after ὥστε μηκέτι (Mark 2:2), after ὥστε μή (Mark 3:20), and after μή (1 Cor 5:8). Μηδέ appears without a preceding negation, which nevertheless is implied by the context, in Mark 8:26: "He sent him directly to his house and said, 'Do *not even* go into the village' "; Eph 5:3, *not even/by no means;* cf. also BDF §445.2f.

μηδείς, μηδεμία, μηδέν *mēdeis, mēdemia, mēden* none, not any; no one; in no way

This word appears 89 times in the NT, esp. in Acts (21 times; on Acts 27:33, → μηθείς). Μηδείς is not often used as an adj. (but see Acts 10:28; 13:28; 19:40; Heb 10:2); after a negation, it means "not . . . *anything*" (1 Cor 1:7; 2 Thess 2:3; 1 Pet 3:6). It is mostly a subst. (e.g., Matt 8:4; 17:9; Luke 10:4; Rom 12:17; 2 Cor 6:3; Eph 5:6; Jas 1:13) and appears after ἵνα (Matt 16:20; Mark 8:30), with an inf. (Luke 8:56; Acts 23:22), with a partc. (Acts 9:7), and after a negation (Acts 4:17). It is often the neut. *nothing* (Mark 6:8; Acts 8:24; 1 Cor 10:25, 27) or, after a negation, *something, anything,* esp. in Paul (Rom 13:8: μηδενὶ μηδέν, "*no one anything*"; 2 Cor 6:3: μηδεμίαν ἐν μηδενὶ . . . προσκοπήν, "in *no way* [gave] offense to *anyone*"; cf. Phil 1:28). Μηδείς can appear as acc. of internal obj., meaning *in no way/not at all* (Mark 5:26: μηδὲν ὠφεληθεῖσα, "but it did *not* help *at all*"; Luke 4:35: μηδὲν βλάψαν αὐτόν, "*without* harming him *in any way*"; cf. Acts 4:21; 10:20). Similarly, we have ἐν μηδενί, "in *nothing*" (2 Cor 6:3 [see above]; 7:9; Jas 1:4), and μηδὲν ὤν, "although there is *nothing*" (Gal 6:3).

μηδέποτε *mēdepote* never, never again*

2 Tim 3:7: μηδέποτε . . . δυνάμενα, "who are *never* able" (opposite of πάντοτε, "always"); cf. *Mart. Pol.* 2:3.

μηδέπω *mēdepō* not yet*

Heb 11:7: μηδέπω βλεπόμενα, "[events] that were *not yet* seen."

Μῆδος, ου, ὁ *Mēdos* Mede*

In Acts 2:9 the *Medes* are mentioned along with the Parthians and the Elamites as peoples of the East among whom a considerable number of Jews lived (see Billerbeck II, 606-8; cf. 2 Kgs 17:6; 18:11). In the age of early Christianity, however, the nations of the Medes and the

Elamites had long since disappeared. W. Hinz, *BHH* 1180; *BL* 1116f.; E. Haenchen, *Acts* (1971) ad loc.

μηθείς, μηθεμία, μηθέν *mētheis, mēthemia, mēthen* nothing, no one*

In the NT only in Acts 27:33: μηθὲν προσλαβόμενοι, "keeping *nothing* for yourselves." BDF §33.

μηκέτι *mēketi* no more, no longer*

There are 22 occurrences in the NT; μηκέτι appears in independent clauses with imv. (Luke 8:49; John 5:14; 8:11; Eph 4:28; 1 Tim 5:23), with subjunc. (Matt 21:19; Mark 9:25; hortatory in Rom 14:13), and with opt. (Mark 11:14: μηκέτι εἰς τὸν αἰῶνα . . . μηδείς, "no one *ever* again . . ."). Μηκέτι appears in subordinate clauses with double negation (Mark 2:2; Acts 4:17; 25:24), with ἵνα (2 Cor 5:15; Eph 4:14), with ὥστε (Mark 1:45; 2:2; cf. 1 Pet 4:2: εἰς τὸ μηκέτι with inf.), with partc. (Acts 13:34; Rom 15:23; 1 Thess 3:1, 5), and with inf. (Rom 6:6; Eph 4:17; see above Mark 2:2; Acts 4:17; 25:24).

μῆκος, ους, τό *mēkos* length*

Eph 3:18, in the naming of the incomprehensible four dimensions of the Holy God (τὸ πλάτος καὶ μῆκος καὶ ὕψος καὶ βάθος [→ βάθος 3], "the breadth and *length* and height and depth"); Rev 21:16 (bis), of the *length*, width, and height (in each case 12,000 stadia, about 1,500 miles!) of the heavenly city; cf. E. Lohse, *Rev* (NTD) ad loc.

μηκύνομαι *mēkynomai* become long, grow in length*

In the NT only in Mark 4:27 (mid.), of the grain that sprouts and *grows*.

μηλωτή, ῆς, ἡ *mēlōtē* sheepskin*

Heb 11:37, in a passage on the righteous and upright of Israel (which certainly includes the prophets—specifically Elijah, who, according to 1 Kgs 19:13, 19; 2 Kgs 2:8, 13f., was clothed in a sheepskin): περιῆλθον ἐν μηλωταῖς, ἐν αἰγείοις δέρμασιν, "they went about in *skins of sheep* and goats"). Μηλωτή thus signifies a prophet's clothing (cf. Zech 13:4; also Mark 1:6 par.; Josephus *Vita* 2) and is a sign of his critiquing civilization and consciously enduring privation. O. Michel, *TDNT* IV, 637f.; *TWNT* X, 1176 (bibliography); A. Strobel, *Heb* (NTD) ad loc.

μήν *mēn* truly, indeed*

Heb 6:14, in the oath formula εἰ μήν, *surely;* → εἰ μήν.

μήν, νός, ὁ *mēn* month; new moon*

The subst. μήν appears 18 times in the NT: 5 times in Luke (4 times in the infancy narratives), 5 in Acts, 6 in Revelation, and otherwise only in Gal 4:10 and Jas 5:17. The distribution is instructive for the narrative style of Luke in comparison with that of the other Gospel traditions. References to time in months in Luke 1:24, 26, 36, 56 make possible the linking of the history of John with that of Jesus. Both Luke 4:25 and Jas 5:17 mention "three years and six *months*" (cf. 1 Kgs 18:1: "in the third year") as a time of drought and famine (the length of apocalyptic times of woe; cf. Dan 7:25; 12:7; see below). Μήν appears in Acts 7:20 (cf. Exod 2:2) and esp. in the Pauline narratives in Acts: 18:11 (a year and six months in Corinth); 19:8 (three months in the synagogue of Ephesus; cf. v. 10); 20:3 (three months in Greece); 28:11 (three months on Malta).

Months are also mentioned in Rev 9:5, 10 (unbelievers are tormented by "locusts" for five months [the time of the destruction of the crops by locusts in Joel 1?]); 9:15: εἰς τὴν . . . μῆνα, "[prepared] for . . . the *month*"; 11:2 (the destruction of Jerusalem by the Gentiles lasts forty-two *months;* cf. the period of three and a half years in Dan 7:25; 12:7, or "2,300 evenings and mornings" in 8:14; see further Rev 11:3; 12:6, 14; 13:5 (cf. 11:2); 22:2, of the Tree of Life, which bears fruit κατὰ μῆνα), "every *month*," all twelve months (cf. Ezek 47:12). Gal 4:10 ("you are observing special days, *months/new moons*, seasons, and years"), like Col 2:16 (νεομηνία), is dealing with the celebration of the new moon (cf. Num 10:10; 28:11; Ezek 46:3; Ps 80:4 LXX; *1 Enoch* 75:3; 1QS 10:1-5; see further G. Delling, *TDNT* IV, 641-42) in connection with the observance of a Jewish calendar, which for the Galatians was at the same time a sign of backsliding into legalism and pagan idolatry. G. Delling, *TDNT* IV, 638-42; *TWNT* X, 1176f. (bibliography); A. Strobel, *BHH* 1232-35; *BL* 1164f.; D. Lührmann, *Gal* (ZBK) on 4:8f.   H. Balz

μηνύω *mēnyō* report, reveal*

In its proper sense, *make a report,* in John 11:57 and Acts 23:30 (pass.); according to Luke 20:37, Moses had already *revealed/announced* (ἐμήνυσεν) the resurrection of the dead at the burning bush (cf. Exod 3:6, 15). In 1 Cor 10:28 a non-Christian is ὁ μηνύσας, "the man *who had made known/revealed*" that the meat had been offered to idols; see H. Conzelmann, *1 Cor* (Hermeneia, 1975) ad loc.

μήποτε *mēpote* (negative particle; interrogative particle, conj.)

Lit.: BDF index s.v. — MOULTON, *Grammar* III, 98f.; IV, 13, 151, *passim.* — RADERMACHER, *Grammatik* 171f., 178, 195, 203f., *passim.*

1. Μήποτε with the ind. in an independent question means *perhaps?* (John 7:26; → μή 2.d).

2. Μήποτε with the ind. in a causal clause is Hellenistic (Heb 9:17; cf. John 3:18; → μή 3.c).

3. Μήποτε follows a final ἵνα (only Luke 14:29) or introduces a final clause as an independent conj. (esp. in Matthew, with 7 of the 8 instances). It is used with the subjunc. (Matt 4:6) and, unlike classical Greek, with the fut. (Matt 7:6).

4. Μήποτε follows vbs. of caution: "Beware/be careful *that not*..." (Luke 21:34; Heb 3:12; cf. 4:1). On this construction, → μή 3.f.

5. a) Φοβέομαι μήποτε is found only seldom in the NT (Acts 23:24 v.l.; 2 Cor 11:3 v.l.; Heb 4:1). In Matt 25:9 v.l., οὐκ is added as an amplification of μήποτε: "[we fear] *that* it will *not* be enough" = "it will probably not be enough"; μήποτε οὐ μή: "[we fear] *that* it will definitely *not* be enough" = "it definitely is not enough" (→ μή 5).

b) In most cases, the vb. of fearing is absent in koine Greek; the μήποτε clause is loosely dependent on an implied vb. that expresses fear, concern, or caution regarding something supposed: "[out of fear] *that*..." (Acts 5:39; Luke 14:8, which can also be translated as a final clause).

c) The prohibitive element of fear and caution can fade in koine Greek, with the result that μήποτε simply introduces a dubious question or assumption. The object of the assumption is no longer something feared but rather something hoped for; so Luke 3:15: "wondered *whether perhaps* he was not the Christ"; 2 Tim 2:25: "correct them [with the thought and anxious question] *whether perhaps* God might grant repentance"; perhaps also Mark 4:12: "[with the thought and anxious question] *whether* they *perhaps* might turn and it be forgiven them" (→ ἵνα 3). The last two examples are so closely related to the foregoing (→ b) that they can also be used as the main clause: "*Perhaps they will....*"

                                          P. Lampe

μήπου *mēpou*   lest somewhere/somehow*

Textual variant in Acts 27:29, instead of μή που.

μήπω *mēpō*   not yet*

Rom 9:11: μήπω γὰρ γεννηθέντων, "though they [Esau and Jacob] were *not yet* born" (cf. Gen 25:22-34); Heb 9:8: μήπω πεφανερῶσθαι, "that it had *not yet* been revealed."

μήπως *mēpōs*   that not, that perhaps, whether perhaps

In the NT only as a v.l. of earlier text additions: Acts 27:29; Rom 11:21; 1 Cor 8:9; 9:27; 2 Cor 2:7; 9:4; 11:3; 12:20 (bis); Gal 2:2; 4:11; 1 Thess 3:5; → μή, → πῶς.

μηρός, οῦ, ὁ *mēros*   thigh, hip*

According to Rev 19:13, 16, the apocalyptic horseman with the name ὁ λόγος τοῦ θεοῦ, "the Word of God," also bears written on his mantle and his thigh (hip?) a name of dominion (cf. Deut 10:17; Dan 2:47; 2 Macc 13:4; see also Rev 17:14). By way of comparison, note that names were inscribed on the thighs of statues in antiquity (Cicero *Verr.* iv.43); a reference to Isa 11:5 is also conceivable (on both, see H. Kraft, *Rev* [HNT] ad loc.).

μήτε *mēte*   and not, (not)... and not, neither... nor*

This word appears 34 times in the NT, in meaning sometimes close to → μηδέ (see BDF §445.2). Μήτε is always used with a negative and commonly is repeated: it appears once after μή, "not... *and not*" (Luke 7:33b); twice after μή, "not... *and not*... *and not*" (Acts 23:8; 1 Tim 1:7; Rev 7:1, 3); 3 times after μή (Jas 5:12) and after μή/μηδέ (2 Thess 2:2); 4 times after μή (Matt 5:34-36); and 5 times after μηδέν (Luke 9:3). In all of these chain constructions, the ramifications of the statement negated by μή/μηδέ/μηδέν are elaborated; see esp. Matt 5:34-36 and Jas 5:12, where the introductory μή (ὅλως) gives the general prohibition, for which a few examples are subsequently given ("not... *[in particular] also not*... *and not*," therefore in the sense of μηδέ; cf. also Rev 9:21; Billerbeck I, 328). The correlative μήτε... μήτε, *neither... nor*, appears in Matt 11:18; Acts 23:12, 21; 27:20; Heb 7:3.

μήτηρ, τρός, ἡ *mētēr*   mother

1. Occurrences in the NT — 2. Literal uses of μήτηρ — 3. The mother of Jesus — 4. Fig. uses of μήτηρ — 5. Ἐκ κοιλίας μητρός

Lit.: E. BEYREUTHER, *DNTT* III, 1068-71. — R. E. BROWN, *The Birth of the Messiah* (1977) 341-46, 471-95. — W. MICHAELIS, *TDNT* IV, 642-44. — E. NELLESSEN, *Das Kind und seine Mutter* (SBS 39, 1969) 94-97. — I. DE LA POTTERIE, "Das Wort 'Siehe, deine Mutter' und die Annahme der Mutter durch den Jünger (Joh 19, 27b)," FS Schnackenburg 191-219. — H. SCHÜRMANN, "Jesu letzte Weisung Jo 19,26-27a," Schürmann II, 13-28.

1. Μήτηρ is found 83 times in the NT, of which 71 occurrences are in the Gospels, 4 in Acts, 7 in the Epistles, and 1 in Revelation. It appears in both literal and fig. senses.

2. In its basic sense, μήτηρ refers to mothers of persons, e.g., the mother of the sons of Zebedee (Matt 20:20), of James and Joseph (27:56), of John Mark (Acts 12:12). One's mother deserves special honor, as inculcated by the command to honor one's parents (Exod 20:12; 21:17; Deut 5:16) in Mark 7:10 par. Matt 15:4/Luke 18:20 (cf. Mark 10:19; Eph 6:2). Thus 1 Tim 5:2 can exhort the leader to honor old women "as *mothers*." Paul honors the mother of

Rufus as his own (Rom 16:13). One cannot be released from the command to love one's parents by dedicating a gift to the temple (Matt 15:5f. par. Mark 7:11f.). Nevertheless, the marital bond takes precedence over the bond to parents (Matt 19:5 par. Mark 10:7f.; cf. Eph 5:31; Gen 2:24). One must leave one's parents for Jesus (Matt 19:29) and his gospel (Mark 10:29f.), or for the kingdom of God (Luke 18:29; cf. Matt 10:37 par. Luke 14:26).

3. The *mother of Jesus* plays a special role in the prehistories in the Gospels of Matthew and Luke. Luke regards her motherhood as more than physical; rather, she has true kinship with Jesus (Luke 1:38) inasmuch as she does the will of God (cf. Mark 3:31-35 par. Matt 12:46-50) or hears and does God's word (Luke 8:19-21). Thus he corrects the woman from the crowd who praises the physical motherhood of Mary by invoking a blessing rather on those who hear and keep God's word (11:27f.). For that reason also Elizabeth, after her song of praise for Mary's physical motherhood, blesses Mary for having believed (1:45). By greeting Mary as the mother of her Lord (1:43), Elizabeth acknowledges Jesus as Messiah (cf. 20:41-44; Acts 2:34). The reproachful question of his mother (Luke 2:48b) gives the twelve-year-old Jesus the opportunity to emphasize his relation to the Father, with whom he "must be," since he must proclaim the message of the kingdom of God (4:43) and suffer many things (9:22; 17:25; cf. 24:7, 26, 44). Jesus' mother reflects in her heart on this incomprehensible response (2:51c; cf. vv. 33f.). She is likewise open to the reception of the Spirit after Easter with the disciples (Acts 1:14).

The primary position of "child" in the expression "the child and his *mother*" (Matt 2:11, 13f., 20f.) apparently intends to make explicit that the mother gains her significance entirely from the child. In this way the Evangelist follows up directly on Matthew 1, where the origin of the child is primarily dealt with.

At the feast in Cana (John 2:1-11), Jesus distances himself from his mother, since it is the Father who determines his "hour" (2:4; cf. 13:1 among others). Through her attitude, she is probably showing herself to be the representative of those who expect salvation from Jesus, which already at that time was symbolically granted in the wine (Schürmann), with the result that the disciples come to faith in Jesus (2:11). Likewise, the mother of Jesus gains significance in the scene at the foot of the cross (19:25-27), since she and the beloved disciple, as the witnesses of the tradition of Jesus, are entrusted to one another. Whoever accepts this witness finds faith (cf. 19:35; 20:29, 31). It is unlikely that the mother of Jesus is here identified with Jewish Christians and the beloved disciple with Gentile Christians (*contra* R. Bultmann, *John* [Eng. tr., 1971] 673). For further possibilities, see R. Schnackenburg, *John* III (1982) 277-82.

4. When Gal 4:26 calls the Jerusalem above "our *mother*," it is referring to the realm of the resurrected, out of which proceeds eschatological salvation for those who believe. In Rev 17:5 the great whore of Babylon (Rome) is called "the *mother* of whores and of the abominations of the earth," by which she is designated the source of all evil. In Revelation 12 the woman (γυνή) represents the people of God. As such, she is the mother of the Messiah (v. 5) and of Christians (v. 17).

5. The biblical expression ἐκ κοιλίας μητρός (LXX Judg 16:17; Ps 70:6; Isa 49:1, among others) means "from the very beginning." It is found in Matt 19:12; Luke 1:15; Acts 3:2; 14:8; Gal 1:15.

                                       H. Giesen

μήτι *mēti* certainly not; perhaps*

Μήτι is found 18 times in the NT as an interrogative particle, usually in questions expecting a negative answer, but sometimes also in questions whose answer is uncertain (cf. BDF §427.2f.). In questions expecting a negative answer μήτι can be translated *surely not:* Matt 7:16; 26:22, 25 (contrast the negative answer Judas expected with Jesus' affirmative response); Mark 4:21; 14:19 (bis; see on Matt 26:22, 25 above); Luke 6:39 (where the expected affirmative answer to the subsequent question, by way of contrast, requires οὐχί); John 8:22; 18:35; Acts 10:47; 2 Cor 12:18; Jas 3:11. In questions without an expected negative answer, μήτι means *perhaps:* Matt 12:23 ("Is this *perhaps* the son of David *after all?*"); John 4:29. Μήτι also appears with other particles: εἰ μήτι, *unless/if perhaps not* (Luke 9:13; 1 Cor 7:5; 2 Cor 13:5); μήτι γε, *not to mention/how much more* (1 Cor 6:3; see BDF §427.3); μήτι ἄρα, (*consequently*) *perhaps then* (2 Cor 1:17; see BDF §440.2).

μήτιγε *mētige* not to mention

Textual variant in 1 Cor 6:3, for μήτι γε.

μήτις *mētis* no, no one

Textual variant in Rev 13:17, for μή τις.

μήτρα, ας, ἡ *mētra* womb*

Luke 2:23: διανοίγω μήτραν, "open the *womb*," of the firstborn (cf. Exod 13:2, 12); Rom 4:19: "the deadness of the *womb* of Sarah" (cf. Gen 17:17).

μητρολῷας, ου, ὁ *mētrolōas* matricide*

On the morphology of the word, cf. BAGD s.v.; BDF §§26, 35.2; it appears in 1 Tim 1:9 in a vice list along with πατρολῷας (perhaps with reference to the failure to fulfill the obligation to care for one's parents; see J. Jeremias, *1–2 Tim, Titus* [NTD] ad loc.).

μιαίνω *miainō* stain, defile*

This vb. occurs 5 times in the NT, always in a fig. sense; John 18:28, of the fear of ceremonial impurity (ἵνα μὴ μιανθῶσιν, "so that they might not *be defiled*") by entering the Roman praetorium before the Passover; Titus 1:15a, in reference to one's way of life (οἱ μεμιαμμένοι, "the *impure*"; with ἄπιστοι, "the unbelieving," and its antonym οἱ καθαροί, "the pure"); 1:15b (μεμίανται . . . ὁ νοῦς καὶ ἡ συνείδησις, "the mind and the conscience *corrupted*"; cf. further v. 16); Heb 12:15, in a warning against the defilement of the entire congregation (μὴ . . . μιανθῶσιν οἱ πολλοί, "lest the many *become defiled*") by those who have fallen from grace and therefore act like a poisonous root in the congregation (cf. Deut 29:17); Jude 8, with reference to general sexual libertinism (σάρκα . . . μιαίνουσιν, "*they defile* the flesh"). F. Hauck, *TDNT* IV, 644-47; *TWNT* X, 1177 (bibliography).

μίασμα, ατος, τό *miasma* stain, defilement*

2 Pet 2:20: τὰ μιάσματα τοῦ κόσμου, "the *defilements* emanating from the world," or "*defilement* by the world" (cf. Jdt 13:16, with μίασμα parallel with αἰσχύνη). F. Hauck, *TDNT* IV, 646f.

μιασμός, οῦ, ὁ *miasmos* stain, defilement*

2 Pet 2:10: ὀπίσω σαρκὸς ἐν ἐπιθυμίᾳ μιασμοῦ πορευόμενοι, "who behind the flesh are full of lust for *defilement*"; cf. *Herm. Sim.* v.7.2. F. Hauck, *TDNT* IV, 647.

μίγμα, ατος, τό *migma* mixture*

John 19:39, referring to perfume, not to salve: μίγμα σμύρνης καὶ ἀλόης, "a *mixture* of myrrh and aloes"; see R. Schnackenburg, *John* III (1982) ad loc.

μίγνυμι, μιγνύω *mignymi, mignyō* mix (vb.)

Alternate form of → μείγνυμι, μειγνύω.

μικρόν *mikron* acc. adv.: a little; a little while, a moment*

Μικρόν is found in 16 places in the NT as an acc. adv., with various meanings and in various constructions: *a short distance* (Matt 26:39; Mark 14:35); *a short time* (John 16:16 bis, 17 bis, 18 [τὸ μικρόν, "the [expression]: '*a short time*'"], 19 bis); μετὰ μικρόν, "after *a little while*" (Matt 26:73; Mark 14:70); ἔτι μικρόν, "yet *a little while*" (John 13:33; 14:19); ἔτι γὰρ μικρὸν ὅσον ὅσον, "for yet *a short while*, how short, how short!" or "only a very *short while* yet" (Heb 10:37, citing Isa 26:20 LXX; cf. *1 Clem.* 50:4; see also BDF §304); sarcastically μικρόν τι, a *little* (2 Cor 11:1, 16); → μικρός 4.

μικρός, 3 *mikros* small, little, short

1. In contrasts — 2. "These little ones" — 3. Luke 12:32 — 4. Referring to time

Lit.: H.-J. DEGENHARDT, *Lukas, Evangelist der Armen* (1965) 85-88. — S. LÉGASSE, *Jésus et l'enfant* (1969) 51-119. — O. MICHEL, " 'Diese Kleinen'—eine Jüngerbezeichnung Jesu," *TSK* 108 (1937/38) 401-15. — idem, *TDNT* IV, 648-59. — W. PESCH, "Zur Formgeschichte und Exegese von Lk 12:32," *Bib* 41 (1960) 26-31. — W. TRILLING, *Hausordnung Gottes: Eine Auslegung von Mt 18* (1960) 30-42. — For further bibliography see *TWNT* X, 1177.

1. Μικρός has theological ramifications in the NT primarily insofar as it appears in a series of contrasts. Small and great stand in contrast to one another in the kingdom of God and in the Church (Matt 11:11 par. Luke 7:28; Luke 9:48; in both passages ὁ μικρότερος, "he who is *least*," in the superlative sense; → μείζων 2.a). The mustard seed, "the *smallest* of all the seeds," illustrates the improbable beginnings of the proclamation of Jesus in contrast to the worldwide triumph of the coming kingdom (Mark 4:31f. par. Matt 13:31f.). The "*little* [amount of] yeast" (μικρὰ ζύμη) appears in a proverb that Paul employs to characterize the destruction caused by his Judaizing opponents (Gal 5:9; a closer connection with the context would be difficult to discern) or the evil consequences that toleration of immorality brings to the community (1 Cor 5:6).

2. In the Synoptic Gospels, the expression "these *little ones*" refers generally to Christians (Mark 9:42 par. Matt 18:6/Luke 17:2; Matt 10:42; 18:10; → ἐλάχιστος 2.a). They are often distinguished as a class from non-Christians; the latter have not repented and so have a more limited love of neighbor than the former. This difference, however, fosters an attitude of goodwill toward Christianity, like that of the strange exorcists, who in their practice used the name of Jesus (Mark 9:38-40). For that reason, an eschatological reward is assured (9:41). The same is true of the acts of kindness shown toward the poor messengers of the gospel (thus Matt 10:42). Another passage, reporting on the inner life of the community, refers to "these *little ones*," thereby designating Christians who believe but whose belief is still threatened and who are still prone to err (cf. "the weak" in 1 Cor 8 and Rom 14:1–15:1). In light of the mediation of the "angels" of these persons, who are God's charges, they have the right to the attention and care of the community with respect to their salvation (Matt 18:6, 10-14). The origination of this designation lies in Jesus' characteristic mode of speaking, as he used "these little ones" to refer not to children but to the outcasts of his nation, who were despised and scorned by the leading religious groups.

3. The eschatological comfort that Jesus gives to his

"*little* flock" of disciples in Luke 12:32 closes a section (12:22-31) that stands in contrast to the foregoing (12:13-21). While the rich are called to readiness and are exhorted to give alms as a precaution against the temptation of riches, Jesus tells the poor (the congregation) that they should not worry, for God will care for them.

4. In reference to time, μιχρός is found in Rev 6:11; 20:3 as a sign of the end times, but also in John 7:33; 12:35, where the expression "yet a *little* while" indicates an imminent moment when the heavenly Christ departs this world (cf. 16:28). The neut. (τὸ) μιχρόν, *(the) little*, is used in John 14:19 as an adv. (ἔτι μιχρόν; cf. LXX Isa 10:25; 29:17; Jer 28:33; Hos 1:4) and has an eschatological connotation: the return of Jesus on Easter, which initiated a new situation for the disciples. In John 13:33, by way of contrast, the same expression announces the departure of Jesus at his death, while in 16:16, 17, 19 a double μιχρόν—beyond the short absence that the death of Jesus represents—points to a new present, whose infinite duration is assured by the Paraclete (14:16; 16:7-15).

S. Légasse

μιχρότερος, 3 *mikroteros* smaller*

The comparative of μιχρός is found 5 times in the NT (only in the Synoptic Gospels) and can in all instances be translated as a comparative or (better) a superlative— the *smallest, least* (cf. BDF §§60f.): Matt 11:11 par. Luke 7:28; Mark 4:31 par. Matt 13:32; Luke 9:48; → μιχρός 1.

Μίλητος, ου *Milētos* Miletus*

A city with a Jewish community that blossomed during Roman times on the western coast of Asia Minor. It was situated on the Latmic Bay, on the southern bank of the mouth of the Maeander. According to Acts 20:15, Paul stopped at Miletus on his last journey from Greece to Jerusalem, coming directly from Samos. In v. 17 he has the elders from Ephesus brought to Miletus (in order not to lose too much time on the detour to Ephesus, v. 16) and takes leave of them with a speech (vv. 18-35). According to 2 Tim 4:20, Trophimus remained behind ill in Miletus, which cannot be reconciled with the other details of 2 Timothy or of Acts. BAGD s.v.; T. Lohmann, *BHH* 1216f. (map); *BL* 1155; W. Zschietzschmann, *KP* III, 1295-98; D. Boyd, *IDBSup* 597f.

μίλιον, ου, τό *milion* mile*

Matt 5:41: μίλιον ἕν . . . δύο (M), "one *mile;* [go with him] two." A Roman measure, literally one thousand paces (*mille;* also a rabbinic loanword), somewhat more than 1,500 m. (5,000 feet), divided into 7.5 stades.

μιμέομαι *mimeomai* imitate*
μιμητής, οῦ, ὁ *mimētēs* imitator*

1. Occurrences in the NT — 2. Meaning — 3. The objects of imitation — 4. Usage in the NT

Lit.: A.-M. ARTOLA, "L'Apôtre-ouvrier se donne en modèle, 2 Thess 3:7-12," *AsSeign* 64 (1969) 71-76. — P. VAN DEN BERGHE, " 'Oui, cherchez à imiter Dieu!' Ep 4,30–5,2," *AsSeign* 50 (1974) 37-41. — H. D. BETZ, *Nachfolge und Nachahmung Jesu Christi im NT* (BHT 37, 1967). — W. P. DE BOER, *The Imitation of Paul* (1962). — M. BUBER, "Nachahmung Gottes," idem, *Werke* II (1964) 1053-65. — E. EIDEM, "Imitatio Pauli," *Teologiska Studier tillägnade E. Stave* (1922) 67-85. — B. GERHARDSSON, *Memory and Manuscript* (ASNU 22, [2]1964) 288-323. — N. HYLDAHL, "Jesus og jøderne infolge 1 Thess 2,14-16," *SEÅ* 37/38 (1972/73) 238-54. — J. JERVELL, *Luke and the People of God* (1972). — H. KOSMALA, "Nachfolge und Nachahmung Gottes," *ASTI* 2 (1963) 38-85; 3 (1964) 65-110. — E. LARSSON, *Christus als Vorbild* (1962). — W. MICHAELIS, *TDNT* IV, 659-74. — L. NIEDER, *Die Motive der religiössittlichen Paränese in den paulinischen Gemeindebriefen* (MTS I/12, 1956), index s.v. Nachahmung. — B. A. PEARSON, "1 Thess 2:13-16: A Deutero-Pauline Interpolation," *HTR* 64 (1971) 74-94. — H. M. SCHENKE, "Determination und Ethik im ersten Johannesbrief," *ZTK* 60 (1963) 203-15. — R. SCHIPPERS, "The Pre-Synoptic Tradition in I Thess II 13-16," *NovT* 8 (1966) 223-34. — W. SCHRAGE, *Die konkreten Einzelgebote in der paulinischen Paränese* (1961), index s.v. μιμεῖσθαι. — A. SCHULZ, *Nachfolgen und Nachahmen* (SANT 6, 1962). — D. M. STANLEY, "Become Imitators of Me," *Bib* 40 (1959) 859-77. — idem, "Imitation in Paul's Letters: Its Significance for His Relationship to Jesus and to His Own Christian Foundations," *From Jesus to Paul* (FS F. W. Beare, 1984) 127-42. — E. J. TINSLEY, *The Imitation of God in Christ* (1960). — B. TRÉMEL, "La voie de la perfection chrétienne: Ph 3,17–4,1," *AsSeign* 15 (1973) 37-42. — H. C. WAETJEN, "Is the 'Imitation of Christ' Biblical?" *Dialogue* 2 (1963) 118-25. — For further bibliography see *TWNT* X, 1177f.

1. This word group appears only 11 times in the NT, 8 of these in the Pauline corpus (1 Thess 1:6; 2:14; 1 Cor 4:16; 11:1; Phil 3:17; 2 Thess 3:7, 9; Eph 5:1). The vb. also occurs in Heb 13:7 and 3 John 11, the noun in Heb 6:12.

2. The vb. means *imitate, emulate, follow after,* with the acc. of the person or thing; i.e., it represents the imitation of an example. The subst. refers to the *imitator.* In the NT the subst. is always used with εἰμί or γίνομαι and with the gen. The word group is used unambiguously in a positive sense in the NT, which is not always the case in classical Greek.

3. The terms belonging to this word group have various kinds of objects. In the non-Pauline passages we are to imitate "the good" (3 John 11), "the faith of the leaders" (Heb 13:7), "those who through faith and patience inherit the promise" (Heb 6:12). With Paul, the *imitatio Pauli* is predominant, as the apostle sets himself

up as an example for his own congregations (not those of others) to imitate. Furthermore, God, Christ, congregations, or groups within a congregation can—directly or indirectly—serve as examples. The Pauline statements contain a certain tendency to build *imitatio* into a hierarchical system (ranging downward from God to Christ, Paul, the congregation, and other congregations). The *imitation* can refer to a characteristic quality or act of the person referred to (e.g., 2 Thess 3:7, 9) or can mention the example's entire way of life (1 Cor 4:16f.; cf. Phil 3:17). To the *imitation* of God, Christ, the apostle, and other examples belongs the important aspect of obedience toward these authorities. We cannot, however, simply translate μιμέομαι as "be obedient" in the Pauline passages (*contra* Michaelis).

4. Exhortations to *imitate* the apostle are present in 2 Thess 3:6-9. Those addressed are called upon to imitate the work of the apostle in their own lives. He had gone without the support of the congregation in order to be able to provide an example (τύπος) for the Thessalonians (v. 9). This exemplary posture was supplemented by oral instruction (v. 6). The exhortation to imitation served the purpose of combating the tendency toward eschatological confusion, which expressed itself, among other ways, in the disdain of daily labor (v. 11). The *imitatio Pauli* appears also in 1 Thess 1:6. The exemplary nature of Paul lies not in his powerful actions (v. 5) but rather in his attitude toward suffering, which is expressed indirectly in v. 6 and is stated explicitly in 2:2 (cf. Acts 16:20-25; 17:5-10). The acceptance of the word of God by the Thessalonians had brought them into a community of suffering with Paul. It had also brought them into a relationship of suffering with Christ. They have in this way become imitators of Christ. Their joyful reception of the message of the Christ and the suffering associated with it had also made them an example for other congregations.

One's attitude during suffering is also in the foreground in 1 Thess 2:14-16. The Thessalonians had become μιμηταί of the congregations in Judea: they were persecuted by their fellow countrymen in the same way that Christians in Judea were persecuted by the Jews. This is not a simple comparison (*contra* Michaelis). Because of their knowledge of the attitude of Palestinian Christians (Jervell 19-39), those addressed could *imitate* their struggle. In so doing, however, they are placed in relation to the suffering of Jesus, the prophets, and the apostles (vv. 15f.), a community of suffering that entails a certain imitation on the part of the Thessalonians.

In 1 Cor 11:1 Paul calls for an *imitation* of himself, which indirectly constitutes an *imitatio Christi*. His attitude toward Christian freedom is exemplary (10:23–11:1): they should not become an offense to their brothers

(v. 29). Rather, they must advance the glory of God (v. 31), which Paul expresses as not striving after one's own good, but rather that of the many (v. 33, cf. v. 24). This attitude is worthy of imitation, also because it is a reflection of the life of Christ; see esp. Rom 15:3, 7; cf. 2 Cor 8:9; Phil 2:5-11.

In 1 Cor 4:16 there is a call to the Corinthians to become *imitators* of the apostle. The οὖν connects the exhortation closely to the preceding section (4:14f.; cf. vv. 8-13), where Paul designated himself the father of the readers. As τέκνα of the apostle (v. 14), they should *imitate* his humble way of life. The imitation refers here not only to the humility of the apostle but rather—as the description in 1 Cor 4:8-13 implies—to his entire life (which is, to be sure, characterized by humility). The "ways" of the apostle (v. 17) are the prescriptions for the Christian life, which he had given in his instruction (cf. 7:17; 14:33) and which are organically connected with his exemplary disposition (διὰ τοῦτο αὐτό connects v. 17 with v. 16). We may probably view the *imitatio Pauli* in 1 Cor 4:16f. as an imitation of Christ, insofar as the description of 4:9-13 points beyond Paul to the Lord as example (cf. 11:1; 1 Thess 1:6).

Eph 5:1 issues a call to the *imitatio Dei* (in form, unique in the NT). This verse is closely related to 4:32 but also serves as a transition to the following section (5:2-7). The meaning of this *imitation* is found primarily in 4:32. The forgiveness of God in Christ is the example for imitation. As μιμηταὶ τοῦ θεοῦ, the Ephesians should be kind and compassionate toward one another and should forgive one another (cf. Col 3:13f.). This *imitatio* of the τέκνα ἀγαπητά ("beloved children") of God is all the more natural, since they themselves have experienced the forgiveness of God (Eph 4:32). The act of God is therefore both example and motive (καθώς is comparison and justification). The imitation of God is further explained in 5:2. The forgiving attitude of the Ephesians, which is considered a reflection of the forgiveness of God, is identical with walking in love. As model for this life in ἀγάπη is the self-sacrifice of Christ. The imitation of God therefore consists of walking in love, with Christ as example.

The non-Pauline passages do not contribute much to the understanding of the word group. The author of Hebrews hopes that the readers will be *imitators* of those who through faith and patience inherited the promise (6:12). Faith is defined and elucidated by patience (O. Michel, *Heb* [KEK] ad loc.). The Hebrews should *imitate* this unwavering faith of the forefathers, esp. Abraham (v. 13; cf. ch. 11). Heb 13:7 also deals with an *imitation* of faith. The πίστις of the leaders is exemplary —in this case, however, not so much the content of faith as the attitude of faith (perhaps in martyrdom). The general exhortation to Gaius in 3 John 11 to *imitate* the good, not the evil, apparently refers to the actions of Demetrius (v. 12) or to those of Diotrephes (v. 9). The imitation therefore consists also here of the imitation of a person.   E. Larsson

μιμητής, οῦ, ὁ *mimētēs* imitator
→ μιμέομαι.

μιμνήσκομαι *mimnēskomai* remember, recall*

1. Occurrences and usage in the NT — 2. God as subj. — 3. Humans as subj.

Lit.: R. H. BARTELS and C. BROWN, *DNTT* III, 230-47. — N. A. DAHL, "Anamnesis," *ST* 1 (1947) 69-94. — G. HENTON DAVIES, *IDB* III, 344-46. — B. GERHARDSSON, *Memory and Manuscript* (ASNU 22, ²1964). — H. HAAG, *BL* 524-26. — O. HAGGENMÜLLER, "Erinnern und Vergessen Gottes und der Menschen," *BibLeb* 3 (1962) 1-15, 75-89, 193-201. — J. JEREMIAS, "Mc 14,9," *ZNW* 44 (1952/53) 103-7. — O. MICHEL, *TDNT* IV, 675-83. — G. SCHMIDT, "ΜΝΗΣΘΗΤΙ," *FS* H. Meiser (1951) 259-64. — O. SCHILLING, " 'Gedenken' und 'Gedächtnis' in der Sprache der Bibel," *LebZeug* 3 (1965) 30-37. — W. THEILER, *RAC* VI, 43-54. — For further bibliography → ἀνάμνησις; see *TWNT* X, 1178f.

1. Μιμνήσκομαι is found 23 times in the NT, including 6 times in Luke, 2 in Acts, and 4 in Hebrews; in Paul, it appears only in 1 Cor 11:2. The vb. is used only in the pass. (with reflexive meaning; in compounds also in act.); usually the simple and compound forms are used without distinction. Μνημονεύω and constructions with μνεία, μνήμη, μνημόσυνον, and ἀνάμνησις are used as synonyms.

2. While the *remembering* of God plays an important role in the OT, it is seldom spoken of in the NT, and even then usually represents an LXX idiom: μνησθῆναι ἐλέους ("*to remember* [God's] mercies") in Luke 1:54 derives from Ps 97:3 LXX (ἐμνήσθη τοῦ ἐλέους αὐτοῦ τῷ Ἰακωβ). The syntactic connection here is loose. The meaning could be: "He *remembers* the mercy that he had previously shown his people," or (preferably) "He *intends* to show mercy as he had promised to the fathers" (cf. Exod 32:13; Deut 9:27). In fact, Luke 1:72 amounts to the same thing: "to show mercy to our fathers and to *remember* his holy covenant." That God *remembers* his covenant with the fathers means that he will fulfill his promise. The reverse is also true: he will *remember* the evil deeds of the Gentiles (cf. Rev 16:19: Βαβυλὼν ἡ μεγάλη ἐμνήσθη ἐνώπιον τοῦ θεοῦ, "God *remembered* great Babylon").

Acts 10:31 displays a similar Semitism: "Your prayer has been heard and your acts of mercy *have been remembered* before God" (ἐμνήσθησαν ἐνώπιον τοῦ θεοῦ). The expression suggests that the angels literally bring the prayers before God and *remind* him of the deeds of human beings (Rev 8:3-5). Acts 10:4 corresponds even more

closely to the Greek of the LXX (μνημόσυνον). The remaining passages are quotations. Heb 8:12 and 10:17 are drawn from Jer 31:34. The forgiveness of sins is here emphasized by the fact that God no longer *remembers* sin. In summary, the righteousness and faithfulness to covenant are expressed by the "remembering" of God.

Only once does Jesus appear as the subj., and then as the divinely authorized Messiah. The repentant thief prays: "Jesus, *remember* me when you come into your kingdom" (Luke 23:42). The form μνήσθητι is common in Jewish prayers (Judg 16:28; Job 7:7; Ps 88:51 LXX).

3. The lack of distinction between the use of simple and compound forms is demonstrated by Mark 14:72 par. Luke 22:61/Matt 26:75: "Peter *remembered* [Matthew ἐμνήσθη, Mark ἀν-, Luke ὑπ-] what Jesus had said." This remembering the words of Jesus has a saving effect (cf. also Luke 24:6, 8). That it can also refer to a hostile memory is evident from Matt 27:63: "*We remember* that this deceiver said. . . ." Often "memory" indicates a reflection and a deeper understanding (cf. Luke 16:25). A somewhat different setting occurs in Matt 5:23, which involves not a systematic reconsideration but an incidental recollection.

Since the Church is bound to history and tradition, memory is fundamental. The deeds and fate of Jesus can be understood only by *reflection* on the prophetic words of Scripture (John 2:17; 12:16). *Recollection* of the words of Jesus has decisive importance for faith and life (John 2:22). Scripture, history, and the words of Jesus interpret one another (cf. the "reminding" of the Holy Spirit in John 14:26; 16:12-15). This motif is esp. prominent in John, although it is used generally. Acts 11:16 gives a concrete example: When the Spirit fell upon Cornelius, Peter *remembered* what the Lord had said: "John baptized with water, but you will be baptized with the Holy Spirit" (cf. 10:44-48).

The entire gospel tradition can be viewed from this perspective: it is the memory of a historical revelation that is fundamental for the Church. Also the Epistles (like Acts) are intended for this purpose of remembering. They are written to arouse "your sincere mind by way of *reminder* [ἐν ὑπομνήσει]; that you should *remember* [μνησθῆναι] the predictions of the holy prophets and the commandment of the Lord and Savior through your apostles" (2 Pet 3:1-2 RSV). The words of the apostles are the obj. of *remembering*, in part because they were also understood as prophecies that could elucidate the present and the future (e.g., Jude 17), primarily, however, because their moral and edifying exhortations possessed continuing significance (2 Pet 1:12f.). This formula applies esp. to late writings; its beginnings, however, are already present in Paul, who *reminds* (ἀναμιμνήσκω) the Corinthians of his "ways in Christ" (1 Cor 4:16f.), which embrace both his teaching and his exemplary way of life.

1 Cor 11:2 can also be understood in this way: "You *remember* me in all things and maintain the teachings as I gave them to you." By itself, πάντα μου μέμνησθε is ambiguous. Μιμνήσκω with a personal obj. often has another meaning: either "fondly remember/do not forget" (2 Tim 1:4: "I long to see you, *especially when I remember* your tears"; cf. 2 Cor 7:15) or "remember out of concern, with prayers and assistance" (Heb 13:3: "*Remember* those in prison . . ."). In 3 John 10 the compound ὑπομιμνήσκω is used reproachfully.

R. Leivestad

μισέω *miseō* hate, despise; disregard*

1. Occurrences and meaning — 2. The Jesus tradition in the Synoptics — 3. John and 1 John — 4. The rest of the NT

Lit.: H. BRAUN, *Spätjüdisch-häretischer und frühchristlicher Radikalismus* II (1969) 57-59 and n.1. — J. BRIÈRE, *DBT²*, 198-200. — A. DIHLE, *Die Goldene Regel* (1962) 114-16. — O. MICHEL, *TDNT* IV, 683-94. — H. SEEBASS, *DNTT* I, 555-57. — L. K. STACHOWIAK, *SacVb* I, 351-55. — E. F. SUTCLIFFE, "Hatred at Qumran," *RevQ* 2 (1959/60) 345-56. — For further bibliography see *TWNT* X, 1179.

1. There are 40 occurrences of μισέω in the NT, of which 13 are in the Synoptic Gospels, 12 in John, and 5 in 1 John. The remaining passages are divided between the Epistles and Revelation. Like its OT equivalent *śānē'*, μισέω runs the entire spectrum from *little love* to *disregard* to *hate*.

2. a) Matt 5:43f. par. Luke 6:27 demand the unreserved love of neighbor, including one's enemy, a duty that, according to Matt 5:45, is grounded in the unmerited love of the heavenly Father. The command to *hate* one's enemy (5:43), rejected by Jesus, cannot be found in the OT. One might attribute it to a popular maxim (thus Billerbeck I, 353) or to the command of the Qumran sect to *hate* the sons of darkness (1QS 1:9f. and elsewhere; thus Dihle). In the saying on serving two masters (Matt 6:24 par. Luke 16:13), μισέω is understood as "despise, show contempt for" and ἀγαπάω as "be loyal to." The conclusion is that service of God and mammon are mutually exclusive.

b) To *be hated* for Jesus' sake (Mark 13:13 par. Matt 24:9f. [10:22]/Luke 21:17; Luke 6:22) means to participate in the fate of Jesus. To *hate* is the fundamental disposition of the enemies of the people of God (Luke 1:71; already in Isa 66:5).

c) Jesus' commands to *hate* one's family and oneself for his sake (Luke 14:26) and not to love one's family more than him (Matt 10:37) amount to the same thing: the decisive factor for discipleship with Jesus is to *disregard* all else (cf. also Luke 9:59f.). Whoever *hates* Jesus and rejects his kingdom (Luke 19:14) is threatened with destruction (v. 27).

3. a) All those who *hate* Jesus, the Light, because they do evil (John 3:20), because they love darkness more than light, fall under judgment (v. 19). The unbelieving "brothers of Jesus" (7:5) do not have to fear the *hatred* of the world (which is at enmity with God), according to v. 7a. The world, however, *hates* Jesus because he testifies that their deeds are evil (v. 7b-d). The same fate befalls the disciples of Jesus. (In ch. 15, μισέω appears in vv. 18 bis, 19, 23 bis, 24, 25; cf. 17:14; 1 John 3:13.) Since the *hatred* is grounded in unbelief, it has no basis (John 15:25, quoting Pss 35:19; 69:4). John 12:25 gives a variation of a Synoptic saying of Jesus (Mark 8:35; Matt 10:39). Jesus places before the disciples the paradox that life can mean death, and death can mean life. Those who *hate* their life, and so set themselves apart for Christ, bear fruit (John 12:24).

b) In 1 John 2:9-11 brotherly love, as the one command (vv. 7f.), is placed over against *hatred* of one's brother. Whoever *hates* a brother is already in darkness (vv. 9, 11), i.e., without direction. Christians must not be surprised by the *hatred* of the world (3:13); they will fare as Abel did, whose righteous works provoked Cain to murder (v. 12). This comparison makes brotherly love appear to be the cause of the hatred. It is also evidence that Christians "have passed over from death to life" (v. 14). In contrast, the one who does not love, remains in death (v. 14d). Those who *hate* are murderers, inasmuch as they put to death true life, which comes through brotherly love (v. 15). All who claim to love God but *hate* their brother expose themselves as liars (4:20), for they prove that they have not received the prior love of God (v. 19). It is not possible to love God and also to exclude one's brother (vv. 20d, 21).

4. a) Rom 7:15, which speaks of unredeemed persons who do what they *hate,* thus confirming that the law is good (v. 16), expresses the absolute need of redemption. With the citation of Mal 1:2f., Rom 9:13 establishes the free, undeserved election of Israel by God. If only a portion of physical Israel belongs to the new Israel (9:6), it has a prototype in the election of Jacob and the rejection of Esau. In Eph 5:29, the deep communion of husband and wife in marriage is described thus: "For no one ever *hated* his own body, but he feeds and cares for it, as Christ does the Church." According to Titus 3:3, pre-Christian existence is characterized by, among other things, the fact that people *hated* each other. Against this background, 3:4-7 goes on to describe the greatness of Christ's act of redemption. Heb 1:9 says of Jesus, the Son of God, that he loved righteousness and *hated* evil (citing Ps. 44:8 LXX). The aor. vbs. point to the crucifixion. Jude 23 warns believers against maintaining fellowship with false teachers; believers are to "*hate* even the clothing stained by the flesh."

b) In Rev 2:6 the exalted Christ praises the church at Ephesus because they *"hate the practices of the Nicolaitans,"* which he also *hates.* According to 17:16 the powers that oppose God, acting upon God's orders, destroy the whore of Babylon, whom they *hate,* and carry out on her the eschatological judgment. Rev 18:2 speaks of the *detestable* bird that inhabits fallen Babylon (Rome) with the demons and unclean spirits (cf. Isa 21:9; Jer 51:8; Rev 14:8).   H. Giesen

μισθαποδοσία, ας, ἡ *misthapodosia* payment, reward; retribution*

Found only in Christian literature; in the NT, only in Hebrews—in 2:2: ἔνδικος μισθαποδοσίαν, "just *reward*" (in the sense of punishment for offenses and disobedience); 10:35: μεγάλη μισθαποδοσία, "great *reward*"; 11:26: ἀπέβλεπεν γὰρ εἰς τὴν μισθαποδοσίαν, "for he looked ahead to the *retribution* [the humiliation by God]."

μισθαποδότης, ου, ὁ *misthapodotēs* rewarder, one who repays*

Heb 11:6, of God: τοῖς ἐκζητοῦσιν αὐτὸν μισθαποδότης γίνεται, "he proves himself a *rewarder* of those who seek him" (cf. Wis 10:17); → μισθαποδοσία.

μίσθιος, ου, ὁ *misthios* day laborer, hired hand*

Actually an adj. used as a subst. in the NT, with occurrences only in Luke 15:17, 19, 21 v.l. Day laborers had more freedom than slaves but had accordingly less security as well. G. Wallis, *BHH* 1103.

μισθόομαι *misthoomai* hire, recruit*

The 2 occurrences in the NT are both in Matthew 20 and both in the mid. voice: v. 1: μισθώσασθαι ἐργάτας εἰς, "*recruit* workers for [the vineyard]"; v. 7: οὐδεὶς ἡμᾶς ἐμισθώσατο, "no one *has hired* us."

μισθός, οῦ, ὁ *misthos* pay, reward (noun)

1. Occurrences in the NT — 2. In the words of Jesus — 3. In Paul

Lit.: G. BORNKAMM, "Der Lohngedanke im NT," idem, *Aufsätze* II, 69-92. — G. DIDIER, *Désintéressement du chrétien. La rétribution dans la morale de S. Paul* (1955). — J. DUPONT, "Le logion des douze trônes (Mt 19,28; Lk 22,28-30)," *Bib* 45 (1964) 355-92. — J. I. H. MCDONALD, "The Concept of Reward in the Teaching of Jesus," *ExpTim* 89 (1977/78) 269-73. — W. PESCH, *Der Lohngedanke in der Lehre Jesu* (1955). — idem, "Der Sonderlohn für die Verkündiger des Evangeliums," FS Schmid (1963) 199-206. — idem, *SacVb* II, 775. — H. PREISKER and E. WÜRTHWEIN, *TDNT* IV, 695-728. — B. REICKE, "The NT Conception of Reward," FS Goguel 195-206. — K. H. RENGSTORF, "Die Frage des gerechten Lohnes in der Verkündigung Jesu," FS

K. Arnold (1955), 141-55. — H. GRAF REVENTLOW, "Sein Blut komme über sein Haupt," *VT* 10 (1960) 311-27. — SCHNACKENBURG, *Botschaft* 116-23, 224-26. — SPICQ, *Notes* Suppl. 473-86. — E. WILL, "Notes sur μισθός," FS C. Préaux (1975) 426-38. — For further bibliography see *TWNT* X, 1179.

1. The subst. μισθός occurs 29 times in the NT, including 10 in Matthew, 5 in Paul, and 4 in Luke-Acts. In addition we find μισθαποδοσία ("reward," 3 times in Hebrews), μισθαποδότης ("rewarder," Heb 11:6), μίσθιος ("day laborer," Luke 15:17, 19), μισθόομαι ("hire," Matt 20:1, 7), μίσθωμα (Acts 28:30), and μισθωτός (Mark 1:20; John 10:12f.), as well as ἀντιμισθία (Rom 1:27; 2 Cor 6:13). Of these 43 total occurrences of the words in this word group, 16 (all outside the Pauline Epistles) have no immediate theological significance. Of the rest, 12 appear in the words of Jesus in the Synoptics, and 7 in Paul.

Μισθός as *pay* in the literal sense refers primarily to the *wages* of a day laborer or a hired hand (Matt 20:8; cf. Luke 15:15-21; John 10:12f.); this corresponds to the usage in the LXX for the *wage* of a soldier (Ezek 29:18), for the *portion* of the Levites (Num 18:31) and of the priests (Mic 3:11), and for a worker's *pay* (Exod 2:9; Deut 15:18). It was a fundamental principle that every worker (Mark 1:20) deserved his *wage* (Luke 10:7; 1 Tim 5:18). The NT also strongly condemns exploiters who held back the *wages* of a worker (Jas 5:4f.). Jude 11 (cf. 2 Pet 2:13, 15) speaks of the *"reward* of unrighteousness," which is to be understood as "goods acquired through sin" (cf. Luke 16:9 and Acts 1:18), i.e., it refers to the material rewards of false teaching (cf. 2 Pet 2:3; Titus 1:11).

John 4:36 uses *reward* in a fig. sense to describe the results of mission work. A similar fig. use is found in Paul (1 Cor 9:18; → 3). According to Heb 10:35f., things that are promised are given as a *reward;* thus the image of the hope of individual reward is stressed in the Christian disposition of faith: the reward belongs to the benefits of salvation in Christ. The communion with God that is freely granted is the *reward* of faith, "which is a passionate yearning, a warm orientation to the world of God's radiant promise and its fulfillment" (Preisker and Würthwein 702).

2. The μισθός sayings of the Jesus tradition are embedded in Jesus' teaching on retribution and are derived from the formulas of the OT and Judaism. Μισθός is found in Mark 9:41 par. Matt 10:42; Matt 5:12 par. Luke 6:23; Matt 5:46; 6:1f., 5, 16; 10:41a, b, 42; 20:8; Luke 6:35; 10:7. Jesus fuses temporal and eschatological *retribution,* a feature of both the beatitudes and the woes (Luke 6:20-26 par.), of the promise of *reward* to the disciples (Mark 10:29f. and elsewhere), of the assurance of inner peace (Matt 11:28-30), and of the statements on judgment (Matt 23:37-39). Jesus occasionally acknowledges a "reward" in an earthly event (Mark 2:5; Luke

13:1-5; 19:31-44), although it supersedes all comprehension (Luke 17:20f.) and proceeds entirely from the love of God (Matt 20:1-15).

The *reward* of God exceeds all human concepts of space and quality; it knows no heavenly place and transcends all earthly time (Mark 13:31; Luke 12:20f.; Matt 25:13). Therefore, the Jesus tradition knows no petty calculation of reward, no counting of good works (and bad), no correspondence between achievement and reward. Jesus also, according to the Synoptics, understands the *reward* as a gift of grace that the Father gives out of love (Matt 20:1-15; Luke 15:11-32). Actually, the kingdom of God is the *reward* (Matt 5:3, 10; 25:34)—i.e., God himself is the reward for humans who, for all their striving, remain worthless (Luke 17:7-10) sinners (Luke 18:10-14). To make such a reward a motive for action is eminently theological.

3. The word group has no specific theological significance in Paul. The expressions are conditioned by the images of work and reciprocation present in the context. The apostle's opposition to the contemporary teaching of reward for merit is so intense that he expressly rejects any idea that justification is a reward, like that known in Judaism (Rom 4:4), and avoids the word μισθός and like terms in his positive description of justification (cf. Rom 6:23). Μισθός is also lacking in all Paul's explicit teaching on God's general judgment of human works (e.g., 2 Cor 5:10); nowhere is it used as an indication of eternal life, as it is in the teaching of Jesus. The teaching of judgment on the basis of works obviously is part of the teaching of the apostle, yet it plays an extremely subordinate role.

Not only is μισθός lacking in references to the gift of eternal life, but also the concept "treasure in heaven." This entire complex of ideas appears only when the polemic against the views of his (primarily Jewish) opponents provides occasion for it, or when the context presents a relevant image or expression. The meaning of the occurrences in 1 Cor 3:8, 14f. (dealing with a special eternal *reward* for the preacher) is unique among the Pauline μισθός passages. We may say, then, that Paul did use the image of a μισθός with varying content but held no specific doctrine of reward. There is no mention of being entitled to anything before God. The content is more precisely defined by Paul in the teaching that the faithful congregation itself will be the preacher's reward. It will always differ on the basis of the work of the individual, since the congregations also differ; and the more completely and perfectly the congregation conforms to the proclamation, the more glorious the *reward* (1 Cor 3:14; 1 Thess 2:19; Phil 4:1). Since such conformity is the gift of God, however, all that the preachers and the teachers of God's Word have coming to them remains an unmerited gift of grace.   W. Pesch

μίσθωμα, ατος, τό *misthōma* rent; that which is rented, rented dwelling*

According to Acts 28:30 Paul stayed "two full years in his own *rented dwelling*" (ἐν ἰδίῳ μισθώματι). This translation of the expression, which is not elsewhere attested, is also suggested by v. 16 (καθ' ἑαυτόν, "by himself") and v. 23 (ἦλθον πρὸς αὐτὸν εἰς τὴν ξενίαν, "they came to him at his lodging"). In v. 30 the translation "at his own *expense*" would also, in principle, be possible (thus *Beginnings* IV, 348; H. J. Cadbury, "Lexical Notes on Luke-Acts III. Luke's Interest in Lodging," *JBL* 45 [1926] 319-22; E. Hansack, "Er lebte . . . von seinem eigenen Einkommen," *BZ* 19 [1975] 249-53), although then the vb. ἐμμένω ("live") and the expression ἀπεδέχετο πάντας τοὺς εἰσπορευομένους πρὸς αὐτόν ("he welcomed all who came to him") in v. 30 would be difficult to understand. Spicq, *Notes* II, 566f.

μισθωτός, οῦ, ὁ *misthōtos* day laborer, hired hand*

Actually an adj. but in the NT always used as a subst.: Mark 1:20 (*hired hands* on Zebedee's boat); John 10:12f., used negatively of the *hired shepherd/hired hand* who cares nothing for the sheep; see Billerbeck II, 537f.

Μιτυλήνη, ης *Mitylēnē* Mitylene*

Capital city of the island of Lesbos, at which Paul arrived on the ship from Assos, according to Acts 20:14. C. Meister, *BHH* 1228.

Μιχαήλ *Michaēl* Michael*

Lit.: BAGD s.v. — BILLERBECK III, 786f., 813. — BL 1152. — BOUSSET/GRESSMANN 327f. — J. MICHL, *RAC* V, 243-51. — W. SCHRAGE, *Jas, 1-2 Pet, 1-3 John, Jude* (NTD) ad loc. — T. C. VRIEZEN, *BHH* 1212f. — H. WINDISCH and H. PREISKER, *Jude* (HNT) ad loc.

The theophoric name (Heb. *mîkā'ēl*, "who is like God?") of an archangel who, according to Jewish tradition, was the commander or great prince of the angels and the protector of Israel (cf. Dan 10:13, 21; 12:1), is among the angels before God's throne (cf. *1 Enoch* 20:1ff.), and leads the battle of the heavenly hosts against Satan (1QM 9:15f.; 17:5-9). According to Rev 12:7, ὁ Μιχαήλ καὶ οἱ ἄγγελοι αὐτοῦ ("*Michael* and his angels") wage war against Satan and his angels (cf. *Asc. Isa.* 7:9-12; *2 Enoch* 7:1; Luke 10:18). Jude 9 (ὁ δὲ Μιχαήλ ὁ ἀρχάγγελος, "the archangel *Michael*") mentions (probably with reference to a text of the *Ascension of Isaiah* that is no longer preserved) a struggle between Michael and the devil over the burial of the body of Moses (cf. Zech 3:2). In this contest even Michael refrains from blaspheming the devil and leaves it completely to the judgment of God, in contrast to the false teachers, of whom it is said that they "revile the glorious ones" (v. 8).

H. Balz

μνᾶ, ᾶς, ἡ *mna* mina*

A Semitic loanword for a Greek unit of weight (*ca.* 570 g.; cf. Deut 22:19; Ezek 45:12) and a coin (e.g., in 1 Macc 14:24). It appears in the NT only in Luke 19: vv. 13, 16 (bis), 18 (bis), 20, 24 (bis), 25. One *mina* was equal to about one-sixtieth of a talent, or one hundred drachmas; one drachma was about equal to one denarius (in Matt 20:2, a day's wage for a laborer). BAGD s.v.; A. Strobel, *BHH* 1159-69, esp. 1167; B. Kanael, *BHH* 1249-56; *BL* 1954.

Μνάσων, ωνος *Mnasōn* Mnason*

In the NT, Mnason (a common Greek name) was a Christian from Cyprus who, according to Acts 21:16, hospitably received Paul in Jerusalem (codex D: in a village along the way between Caesarea and Jerusalem). Mnason is described as ἀρχαῖος μαθητής, "an early disciple," perhaps one of the "Hellenists" from the early years of the congregation in Jerusalem. BAGD s.v.; E. Haenchen, *Acts* (1971) ad loc.

μνεία, ας, ἡ *mneia* remembrance*

Lit.: → μιμνῄσκομαι.

The word is found only in the Pauline corpus (7 instances, including Eph 1:16; 2 Tim 1:3), usually at the beginning of an epistle, in the expression μνείαν ποιέομαι, "I *mention*"; see Rom 1:9; Eph 1:16; 1 Thess 1:2; Phlm 4 (cf. μνήμην ποιέομαι in 2 Pet 1:15). The context clearly refers to the favorable *mention* of someone in prayer (ἐπὶ τῶν προσευχῶν). The expression bears the technical meaning "to pray for someone" and is in fact modeled after the δέησιν ποιέομαι construction (Phil 1:4). The expression μνείαν ἔχω in 2 Tim 1:3 has the same meaning, although it more strongly emphasizes the continuity of the action ("without fail—day and night"). The same expression appears to have a more comprehensive meaning in 1 Thess 3:6: ἔχετε μνείαν ἡμῶν ἀγαθὴν πάντοτε means that the congregation continually *remembers* the apostle and his fellow workers with joy and gratitude, not only in their prayers.

Phil 1:3, εὐχαριστῶ τῷ θεῷ μου ἐπὶ πάσῃ τῇ μνείᾳ ὑμῶν, is frequently rendered as "I thank my God whenever I *remember* you." Such a translation is linguistically possible but exegetically doubtful. First, ἐπί with the gen. is the more common construction (cf. Rom 1:10; Eph 1:16; 1 Thess 1:2; Phlm 4). Second, the thought of this verse is clearly expressed in v. 4 with other words—"I always pray for you in all my prayers with joy." Third,

v. 5 shows that ἐπί with the dat. is used to give the reason for thanks (ἐπὶ τῇ κοινωνίᾳ ὑμῶν, "for your partnership"; cf. 1 Cor 1:4; 2 Cor 9:5; 1 Thess 3:9). These factors indicate that the expression of thanks in Phil 1:3 actually has the meaning: "I thank my God for those indications of your *remembrance* [of me]," one that in this case consisted of concrete, material support (4:10).

In Rom 12:13 the textual variant μνείαις for χρείαις, attested by D, G, it, does not necessarily change the meaning of the sentence, since μνεία can also mean "care." Nevertheless, the meaning "commemoration" (of the martyrs) is to be preferred (see also O. Michel, *Rom* [KEK] ad loc.).

R. Leivestad

μνῆμα, ατος, τό *mnēma* grave, tomb*

In its 8 occurrences in the NT, μνῆμα is used of Jesus' *tomb:* Luke 23:53 (ἔθηκεν αὐτὸν ἐν μνήματι λαξευτῷ, "he laid him in a *tomb* hewn in the rock") and 24:1 (cf. Mark 15:46; 16:2 v.l.); of David's *tomb:* Acts 2:29; of the *grave* of the patriarchs in Shechem: Acts 7:16 (with τίθημι ἐν, to "lay in"); of the "witnesses" in Rev 11:9, whose bodies are not placed in (εἰς) a *tomb* but remain without burial in Jerusalem for three and a half days; and of the *graves/tombs* (pl.) that are the dwelling and habitation of a demoniac: Mark 5:3, 5; Luke 8:27. O. Michel, *TDNT* IV, 679f.; → μνημεῖον.

μνημεῖον, ου, τό *mnēmeion* memorial, grave

1. Occurrences in the NT — 2. General usage — 3. Jesus' grave

Lit.: J. BLINZLER, "Die Grablegung Jesu in historischer Sicht," *Resurrexit* (ed. E. Dhanis; 1974) 108-31. — I. BROER, *Die Urgemeinde und das Grab Jesu* (SANT 31, 1972) 138-200. — H. VON CAMPENHAUSEN, *Der Ablauf der Osterereignisse und das leere Grab* (1966). — W. L. CRAIG, "The Historicity of the Empty Tomb of Jesus," *NTS* 31 (1985) 39-67. — H. GRASS, *Ostergeschehen und Osterberichte* (1964) 138-86. — J. JEREMIAS, *Golgotha* (1926). — O. MICHEL, *TDNT* IV, 675-83, esp. 680f. — F. NEIRYNCK, "John and the Synoptics: The Empty Tomb Stories," *NTS* 30 (1984) 161-87. — R. PESCH, *Mark* (HTKNT) II (1977), index s.v. μνῆμα, μνημεῖον.

1. All 39 NT instances (except Acts 13:29) are found in the Gospels; outside of the Passion accounts, cf. esp. Matt 23:29; Luke 11:44, 47 (48 v.l.); John 11:17, 31, 38. In addition to μνημεῖον, Mark and Luke also use μνῆμα (see Pesch), and Matthew, like Josephus, τάφος. It is noteworthy, however, how closely the text tradition exhibits parallel influence. Μνημεῖον can always be translated as *grave* in the NT; it perhaps retains something of the original meaning *memorial* in Matt 23:29 and Luke 11:47.

2. Luke 11:44 plays on the Pharisaic problem of pollution through unmarked graves (cf. Matt 23:27), while

Luke 11:47 could appropriately be interpreted in line with Matt 23:29: it refers to the practice, not uncontested among the Jews, of adorning the monuments that were sometimes rebuilt on the graves of kings and prophets. Luke refers to this practice sarcastically in his paradox of killing and building (Luke 11:48); Matthew views it as a sign of absolute death (Matt 23:32). In John 11, the threefold mention of the grave of Lazarus not only serves to assure the reader of Lazarus's death (v. 39) but also points ahead from this concrete situation to Jesus' own path (vv. 4, 8, 41f.).

3. According to Mark 15:42-47, Jesus was placed in a burial chamber hewn into the rock (on a bench or in a trough) while it was still the day of preparation for the sabbath, after Joseph of Arimathea had acquired the release of the body. The grave could be closed with a rolling stone and could be entered (16:4). In spite of the alleged knowledge that the women had of the location of Jesus' grave (Mark 15:47, made literarily necessary by 16:1-8), these rather general details, the complete lack of more specific location (with the exception of the late and vague description of John 19:42), as well as a series of independent witnesses to the burial tradition do not permit us to draw any historically tenable conclusions regarding the actual location of the grave. These problems have also plagued the tradition behind the location of the tomb in the Church of the Holy Sepulcher from the very beginning.

It is also clear, however, that the burial of Jesus described in Mark 15:42-47 should be understood as a completely honorable burial (though not under the influence of Isa 53:9). The emphasis on the risks taken by Joseph of Arimathea to acquire the release of the body of a condemned man for the purpose of a proper burial serves to demonstrate this, as does the later description of the grave as unused (Luke 23:53) and intended for Joseph himself (Matt 27:60; cf. John 19:41). The attempt is therefore evident to change Jesus' "unjust fate into a noble act through his honorable burial" (Pesch)—an essential step beyond the simple ἐτάφη ("he was buried") of the older kerygmas (1 Cor 15:4).   M. Völkel

μνήμη, ης, ἡ *mnēmē* remembrance, memorial*

2 Pet 1:15: μνήμην ποιεῖσθαι, "hold in *remembrance*," or simply *"remember"* (with gen.; cf. Pap. Fayûm 19:10); cf. also *Mart. Pol.* 18:2. O. Michel, *TDNT* IV, 679.

μνημονεύω *mnēmoneuō* remember*

Lit.: → μιμνῄσκομαι.

1. Μνημονεύω appears 21 times in the NT. The vb. in most cases has the simple meaning *remember/recall*, where the thing remembered is in the gen. (usually) or the acc. (without difference in meaning). With a personal obj., it can have the sense of *remember with care or concern*. The usage in Heb 11:15, 22 is unique (→ 2.c).

2. a) The word per se has no religious connotations. Only in Rev 18:5 is God the subj.: ἐμνημόνευσεν ὁ θεὸς τὰ ἀδικήματα αὐτῆς, i.e., God will show no more leniency but will carry out the just punishment on "Babylon." In all other cases, people serve as the subj. Things, experiences, words, deeds, or persons appear as obj.; nowhere, however, does God or his nature or gracious acts appear as obj. (unlike the LXX: 1 Chr 16:12; Pss 6:6; 62:7). Christ is only once the obj., in 2 Tim 2:8: μνημόνευε Ἰησοῦν Χριστὸν ἐγηγερμένον ἐκ νεκρῶν, ἐκ σπέρματος Δαυίδ, κατὰ τὸ εὐαγγέλιόν μου, "*remember* Jesus Christ, risen from the dead, descended from David, as preached in my gospel" (RSV). This can hardly be the citation of a creedal formula; the elements would then have to stand in the opposite sequence. The meaning *"remember* that Jesus Christ has risen" is excluded by the second element. The exhortation must mean that one should *keep in mind* the proclamation of Jesus Christ in order to draw strength and comfort from it under persecution.

b) It is the exception for the thing *remembered* to be something secular or common, as in John 16:21. Typically it refers to the memory of something significant for faith and understanding—in particular, remembering the words (and deeds) of Jesus. Acts 20:35, where an otherwise unknown logion is quoted, shows that it was the custom in the congregations to learn the words of Jesus by heart in order to use them as guidelines (cf. 1 Cor 7:10). In the farewell discourse in John the necessity of *remembering* the words of Jesus is repeatedly emphasized (15:20; 16:4; cf. 14:26; 15:26). In these cases esp. it refers to the fact that the future events (the fate of Jesus, the suffering of the Church) can be properly understood only through the words of Jesus. *Remembering* the words of the apostles functions in a similar way (2 Thess 2:5). According to Mark 8:18; Matt 16:9, *remembering* the miracle of the loaves should have brought the disciples to deeper insight. In several places one is exhorted to *recall* one's pagan past (Eph 2:11), the first encounter with the gospel (Rev 3:3), and the joy of the early era (Rev 2:5) in order to renew and strengthen faith.

Remembering persons from redemptive history can have a similar function (e.g., Lot's wife in Luke 17:32; cf. the examples in Heb 11). Likewise *remembering* the courage and blamelessness of the apostles (Acts 20:31; 1 Thess 2:9) or the works of faith, hope, and love in the congregation (1 Thess 1:3) becomes a continual source of strength. Μνημονεύω can sometimes refer to *keeping someone in mind* out of concern or love, which expresses itself in prayer or assistance. The Colossians are urged to *remember* the imprisoned Paul (Col 4:18). At the apostolic council it was agreed that the apostle to the Gentiles should *remember* the poor in Jerusalem, i.e., that he should collect money in his congregations for them (Gal 2:10). One could also understand the exhortation in Heb 13:7 analogously: "*Remember* your leaders, who have announced to you the word of God." It is clear, however, from the following sentence that the author is thinking particularly of those who had died, whom the congregation should hold up as examples of faith. Only the context can decide whether μνημονεύω means aid or a grateful and inspiring memory.

c) A unique use of the word is found in Heb 11:15, 22. In the former passage μνημονεύω must be translated as *think*, and in the latter as *speak of something*. Remembering is excluded here, since Joseph is speaking prophetically of a future event.

R. Leivestad

μνημόσυνον, ου, τό *mnēmosynon* memory; memorial*

Mark 14:9 par. Matt 26:13: εἰς μνημόσυνον αὐτῆς (obj. gen.), "in her *memory*," or "in *memory* of her"; Acts 10:4: ἀνέβησαν εἰς μνημόσυνον ἔμπροσθεν τοῦ θεοῦ, "prayers and alms have ascended as a *memorial* before God." Here μνημόσυνον could be understood as a *memorial offering*, as in Lev 2:2, 9, 16 (the portion of the grain offering that was burned before God on the altar), which would then be spoken of in a fig. way. In its favor would be the ascent motif; cf. Exod 2:23 LXX and the parallel statement in Acts 10:31 (ἐμνήσθησαν ἐνώπιον τοῦ θεοῦ, "[your alms] *have been remembered* before God"), which also suggests a preference for the meaning *memorial/remembrance* in 10:4. BAGD s.v.; E. Haenchen, *Acts* (1971) ad loc.

μνηστεύομαι *mnēsteuomai* become engaged, be betrothed

In the NT only in the pass. and always in reference to Mary as the *betrothed* of Joseph: Matt 1:18 (μνηστευθείσης . . . Μαρίας τῷ Ἰωσήφ, "when . . . Mary *had been betrothed* to Joseph"); Luke 1:27 (παρθένος ἐμνηστευμένη ἀνδρί, "a virgin *betrothed* to a man"); 2:5 (σὺν Μαριὰμ τῇ ἐμνηστευμένῃ αὐτῷ, "with Mary, his *betrothed*"; cf. Matt 1:16 v.l.). An engagement legally established a marriage. C. M. Henze, *TPQ* 101 (1953) 308-13; → Μαρία 2.b.

μογιλάλος, 2 *mogilalos* mute; speaking with difficulty, hardly able to speak*

Mark 7:32: κωφὸς καὶ μογιλάλος, either "deaf and *mute*" or "deaf and *hardly able to speak*." Vv. 33-35 provide support for the first, more comprehensive meaning; ὀρθῶς conveys the amazement that a *mute* immediately after the healing was able to speak "correctly/normally." BAGD s.v. (bibliography).

μόγις *mogis* hardly, with difficulty*

Luke 9:39: μόγις ἀποχωρεῖ (v.l. → μόλις); cf. also Acts 14:18 D and Rom 5:7 v.l. (in each case instead of μόλις). J. Schneider, *TDNT* IV, 735f.

μόδιος, ίου, ὁ *modios* bushel*

A loanword from the Latin (*modius*), originally a measure of grain (*ca.* 8.7 liters). In the NT it is used only of the placing ὑπὸ τὸν μόδιον of a lamp, which no one "puts under a *bushel*" (since the light is soon extinguished and thus seen by no one): Mark 4:21 par. Matt 5:15/Luke 11:33 (*NTG*[26]). The thought is therefore of the vessel pertaining to the measure; cf. Judg 7:16; Josephus *Ant.* v.223; *m. Šabb.* 3:6; 16:7; BAGD s.v.; → λύχνος 3.a.

μοι *moi* to me, for me

Dat. of → ἐγώ (enclitic form).

μοιχαλίς, ίδος, (ἡ) *moichalis* adulterous; subst.: adulteress
→ μοιχεύω.

μοιχάομαι *moichaomai* be led into adultery; be an adulterer (adulteress), commit adultery
→ μοιχεύω.

μοιχεία, ας, ἡ *moicheia* adultery
→ μοιχεύω.

μοιχεύω *moicheuō* commit adultery*
μοιχαλίς, ίδος, (ἡ) *moichalis* adulterous; subst.: adulteress*
μοιχάομαι *moichaomai* be led into adultery; be an adulterer (adulteress), commit adultery*
μοιχεία, ας, ἡ *moicheia* adultery*
μοιχός, οῦ, ὁ *moichos* adulterer*

1. Occurrences in the NT — 2. Usage of μοιχεύω/μοιχάομαι — 3. Adultery in the world of the NT — 4. Usage of the word group in the NT — a) Citation and interpretation of the Decalogue — b) In vice lists and pronouncements of judgment — c) In connection with the prohibition of divorce — d) Fig. use

Lit.: BAGD 526. — H. BALTENSWEILER, "Die Ehebruchsklauseln bei Mt.," *TZ* 15 (1959) 340-56. — K. BERGER, *Die Gesetzesauslegung Jesu* I (WMANT 40, 1972) 307-26, 508-75. — J. BLINZLER, "Die Strafe für Ehebruch in Bibel und Halacha," *NTS* 4 (1957/58) 32-47. — G. DELLING, "Das Logion Mk 10,11 (und seine Abwandlungen) im NT," *NovT* 1 (1956) 263-74. — *idem*, *RAC* IV, 666-77. — K. HAACKER, "Der Rechtssatz Jesu zum Thema Ehebruch," *BZ* 21 (1977) 113-16. — F. HAUCK, *TDNT* IV, 729-35. — E. LÖVESTAM, "Die funktionale Bedeutung der synoptischen Jesusworte über Ehescheidung und Wieder-

heirat," *Theologie aus dem Norden* (ed. A. Fuchs; 1977) 19-28.
— B. SCHALLER, "Die Sprüche über Ehescheidung und Wiederheirat in der synoptischen Überlieferung," FS Jeremias (1970) 226-46. — R. SCHNACKENBURG, *John* II (Eng. tr., 1980) 162-71. — G. SCHNEIDER, "Jesu Wort über die Ehescheidung in der Überlieferung des NT," *TTZ* 80 (1970) 65-87. — G. STRECKER, "Die Antithesen der Bergpredigt," *ZNW* 69 (1978) 36-72, esp. 51-56. — For further bibliography see Schneider; Hauck; *TWNT* X, 1180.

1. Derivatives of the stem μοιχ- are found 35 times in the NT (of which 3 times in v.l.: Matt 19:9; Gal 5:19; Jas 4:4). The vb. forms appear most frequently: μοιχεύω, 15 times, and μοιχάομαι, 4 times. Μοιχαλίς appears 7 times, μοιχός and μοιχεία, 3 times each. Over half of all occurrences (18) are found in the Synoptics, 6 in Paul, 3 in James, 2 in John, and 1 each in Hebrews, 2 Peter, and Revelation.

Wherever this word group, which originally belonged to the secular sphere (Chantraine, *Dictionnaire* III, 709), is found in the NT, it appears in forms derived from Ionian-Attic usage, of which only μοιχαλίς is initially attested in Hellenistic texts (BAGD s.v.). Only Matthew and Mark use the Doric form μοιχάομαι (cf. Xenophon *HG* i.6.15). All derivatives of μοιχ- appearing in the NT are also found in the LXX (as equivalents of *nā'ap* and its derivatives), and the majority of them are in Philo, Josephus, and other Hellenistic-Jewish texts (such as *T. 12 Patr.*).

2. When in classical Greek the vbs. μοιχεύω/μοιχάομαι are found in the act. (used absolutely or with acc. obj.), they take only the male as subj.; the obj. is usually only the married woman. The pass. and mid. mean "to be led into adultery, to allow oneself to be seduced" and (of the woman!) "to commit adultery." The gender-specific use of this verbal group was later blurred, however, so that in the use of pass. and mid. forms in the LXX and the NT, including NT quotations of Exod 20:13 LXX/Deut 5:17, both genders are understood as the subj. (see Matt 5:32; 19:9; Schwyzer, *Grammatik* II, 235; BAGD 526).

3. In accordance with ancient oriental legal traditions, the OT considers adultery among the most severe of offenses; if it is committed with an Israelite woman and it violates the marriage of another (only this is considered adultery), it is considered worthy of death, since it is at the same time a rupture of the covenant with Yahweh (Lev. 20:10; Deut 22:22), a view that still prevails in *Jubilees* (30:8; 39:6) and in essence even for the rabbis (*Sipra Lev.* on 20:10; *m. Sanh.* 11:1; John 8:5), although admittedly softened with a series of provisos (Billerbeck I, 295f.). In Roman times, however, the death penalty could hardly be applied any more (cf. *b. Sanh.* 41a) and was replaced with the dismissal of the adulterous woman, with loss of the divorce settlement and prohibition of marriage for the adulterer (*m. Soṭa* 4:3e; 5:1b; cf. Jer 3:8).

The ancient Orient and the Greco-Roman world specified the death penalty for an unfaithful husband. In Rome this provision was first included in the legal code of Caesar Augustus. In Greece, however, an adulterer could be absolved simply by paying a fine (thus in the city charter of Gortyna; see also, however, Prov 5:9f.; 6:32-35). As in early Judaism, however (*Soṭa* 5:1b), a husband in Athens and in Rome had to separate

himself under all circumstances from a wife taken in adultery. The usual punishments for adultery in Roman law during the era of the Caesars were exile and loss of property.

Absolute marital fidelity was expected only of the wife in the ancient world. Only rarely did a husband's sexual relations with slaves or maids legally affect his marriage (Plutarch *Alc.* 8.4f.), and it had to be accepted by his wife (Plutarch *Praec. Con.* 16). Only philosophers—Plato, Aristotle, and esp. the Stoics (Musonius, Epictetus)—and the Hellenistic romances viewed such a relationship as improper or at least dishonorable. The romance in particular celebrated the absolute fidelity of both partners so programmatically that it later became the literary model for apocryphal Christian Acts (E. Plümacher, "Apokryphe Apostelakten," PW Suppl. XV, 63).

4. a) The continuing validity in the NT of the OT prohibition of adultery is self-evident: 6 times is Exod 20:13/Deut 5:17 cited (Matt 5:27; Mark 10:19 [par. Matt 19:18; Luke 18:20]; Rom 13:9; Jas 2:11). Except for Matt 5:27, in each case the command is mentioned with other commands from the Decalogue. The prohibition of adultery always stands as an unconditional component of ethical obligation: thus in the Synoptic account of the rich man's question concerning the conditions for achieving eternal life (Mark 10:17-22 par.); thus also in the Jewish-Christian catechetical tradition adopted by Paul in Rom 13:9f. (E. Käsemann, *Rom* [1980] 360f.; on the rabbinic background, see Billerbeck I, 357-64), which deals with the love command of Lev 19:18 as the common denominator of all individual commands; thus also in the diatribe of Jas 2:1-13, where vv. 10f., likewise formulated with dependence on corresponding rabbinic thought (cf. M. Dibelius, *James* [Hermeneia, 1976] 144-46), stress the conviction that the (moral) laws are indivisible and therefore require observance of all the commands.

In addition, a reference to the sixth commandment (although not explicitly quoted) appears in Rom 2:17-24, where Paul accuses the Jews who take pride in the law of greater violation of the law (vv. 21f.; the combination of adultery, theft, and temple robbing also in Philo *Conf.* 163; cf. CD 4:12-19). Luke 18:11 offers a contrasting image to this: the Pharisee who lauds himself for his uprightness also points precisely to his refraining from theft and adultery. Finally, in Rom 7:1-6 the power of the law, which comes to an end only in death, is illustrated by means of the bond between a woman and her husband, which, on the strength of the OT prohibition of divorce, excludes other relations as adulterous (vv. 2f.).

The prohibition of adultery in Matt 5:27f. is radically stated as an eschatologicallly grounded demand for "a perfect ethical disposition, which unifies outer act and inner orientation of the will" (Strecker 51f.). Once again, it accepts early Jewish concepts, which in some aspects were already shaped in the OT (cf. *Lev. Rab.* 23 [122b]; *Ḥal.* 1; Billerbeck I, 298-301). The concepts here are hardly of Hellenistic origin (*contra* H. Hommel, "Herrenworte im Lichte sokratischer Überlieferung," *ZNW* 57 [1966] 4-23). They are here brought into connection with the prohibition of covetousness (ἐπιθυμῆσαι) expressed in Exod 20:17/Deut 5:21, with the result that the act of adultery is already committed when the desire to violate the command, manifested in the covetous glance (or provocative look: Haacker), exists. In the polemic against heretics in 2 Peter, such a desire is attributed to the heretics: they have ὀφθαλμοὶ μεστοὶ μοιχαλίδος, "eyes full of *adultery*" (2:14).

The pericope on the γυνὴ ἐπὶ μοιχείᾳ κατειλημμένη, found in John 7:53–8:11 (on the terminology of 8:3f., cf. Aelian *NA* xi.15!), was very early misunderstood as a liberalizing of the harsh NT disposition toward adultery —in spite of 8:11b (cf. Augustine *Con. Adult.* ii.6). In no way, however, does it intend to address the problem of adultery. The secondary tradition between John 7:52 and 8:12 (U. Becker, *Jesus und die Ehebrecherin* [1963]; K. Aland, *Studien zur Überlieferung des NT und seines Textes* [1967] 39-46), in spite of the late witness (first in Eusebius *HE* iii.39.17), is definitely old and reflects a more Synoptic form and style (a biographical story: Schnackenburg, *John* II [1980] 169). As elsewhere in the NT (e.g., Mark 12:13-17), this pericope focuses much rather on Jesus' clever avoidance of a provocative question intended to trap him into taking a stand for the Torah and against mercy toward the sinner.

b) Adultery is also included among lists of the most severe vices. Along with the primary virtues, NT parenesis collected such vices into lists, in imitation of Hellenistic Judaism, which was in turn influenced by popular Stoic philosophy (see H. Conzelmann, *1 Cor* [Hermeneia, 1975] 108-10 [bibliography]). Μοιχεῖαι appears in the list of Mark 7:21f. par Matt 15:19 (cf. Gal 5:19 v.l.), and the clearly traditional list (see Gal 5:19-21) that Paul offers in 1 Cor 6:9f. places adulterers (μοιχοί) among those who will have no share in the kingdom of God. This condemnation is also traditional; it is present, e.g., in the list of Gal 5:19-21 and again in the admonitions of Heb 13:1-21, where v. 4 speaks of the judgment of God on πόρνοι and μοιχοί (H. Schlier, *Gal* [KEK] 255).

c) Both Mark (10:11f. par. Matt 19:9) and Q (Matt 5:31f. par. Luke 16:18) pass on a saying of Jesus, initially handed down as an independent tradition, that rejects divorce and the remarriage of a divorced person as μοιχεύειν or μοιχᾶσθαι.

The problem of the form of the saying—whether a legal saying (Bultmann, *History* 132; Schneider 73-75), "a precisely formulated statement of principle" (Delling, "Das Logion" 263), or parenesis in the form of wisdom literature (K. Berger, "Zu den sogenannten Sätzen heiligen Rechts," *NTS* 17 [1970/71] 28-30)—is as contested as the question concerning its earliest composition (was Q the earliest? see Schneider 70-72; Matt 5:32? see Berger, *Gesetzesauslegung* 569f.; Luke 16:18? see

J. Gnilka, *Mark* [EKKNT] II, 75; Mark 10:11? see Delling, "Das Logion" 265, and Schaller 237). An Aramaism preserved by Mark, the construction μοιχάομαι with ἐπί instead of with τινά with the same meaning ("*commit adultery* with someone") probably speaks here in favor of Mark 10:11 (Schaller 237-45).

The contradiction of the Jewish practice of divorce, which accorded the husband the right of divorce (→ ἀπολύω; ἀποστάσιον), is considered constitutive for the saying. Matt 5:32 is closest to Jewish norms, which, while not quite absolutely committed to monogamy, nonetheless prevented a man from breaking up his own marriage (cf. Billerbeck I, 297; Blinzler 43n.1). A divorced woman who remarries causes her new husband to violate the first marriage, which was viewed as still in existence, with regard to which Matt 5:32 consequently, however, also imputes blame to the first husband as the one who made this adultery possible (ποιεῖ αὐτὴν μοιχευθῆναι, "he makes her an *adulteress*"; cf Delling, "Das Logion" 266f.; Schneider 7). More radically (and different from the re-Judaizing of Matthew), Mark 10:11 and Luke 16:18a also indict a man who remarries after a divorce for the violation of his (first) marriage.

Since divorce and remarriage appear in a closer relationship (if not a unity) in the passages in Mark and Luke, it is conceivable that the logion (originating in Syria as a local catechism?) does not intend a prohibition of divorce, but rather of second marriages, with the result that "the act of divorce was accepted *de facto,* while *de jure* marriage was held to be an indissoluble entity." Jesus' absolute prohibition of divorce (Mark 10:2-9; 1 Cor 7:10f.) could thus still be satisfied, yet in a less formal way (Schaller 243f.).

Later adaptations of the tradition to actual demands are no doubt present in Mark 10:12, which takes into account the possibility of divorce and remarriage that existed for a wife under Greco-Roman law and which condemns a wife's divorcing and remarrying as adultery. Equally secondary are the adultery exception clauses (reflecting the views of Rabbi Shammai? cf. Billerbeck I, 313-15) in Matt 5:32 (παρεκτὸς λόγου πορνείας, "except on the ground of unchastity") and 19:9, which permit the husband to divorce his wife if she commits adultery (or if it turns out that she is too close a blood relative [Baltensweiler?] or if she engages in outright prostitution [A. Sand, *MTZ* 20 (1969) 128]?). See Lövestam; Strecker 54f.; J. B. Bauer, "Bemerkungen zu den matthäischen Unzuchtsklauseln (Mt 5,32; 19,9)," FS Zimmerman 23-31 (bibliography); → πορνεία 3.

d) The fig. use of μοιχεύω κτλ. in the NT is completely oriented to the OT, where the covenant made between Yahweh and Israel is understood as a marriage, and Israel's lapse into foreign cults as adultery (Hos 2:21f.; 4:12f.; Jer 3:8f. 13:26f.; Ezek 16:23; Hauck 738f.). Correspondingly, Israel, which rejected Jesus and his missionaries, can then be called γενεὰ μοιχαλίς, "*adulterous generation*" (Mark 8:38; R. Pesch, *Mark* [HTKNT] II, 64); Israel is also referred to as such in Matthew (12:39 = 16:4) when, represented by the Pharisees and scribes

(Sadducees), it demands a sign of confirmation but refuses to believe the sign of Jonah—the resurrection of Jesus (12:38-42; 16:1-4; R. Walker, *Die Heilsgeschichte im ersten Evangelium* [1967] 35-38).

Falling away from true belief into false teaching is likewise adultery (Rev 2:22). This passage may have arisen not simply from a desire to borrow OT metaphors but from the author's interest in attacking a heretical group in which a libertine prophetess who allegedly propagated πορνεία (and the consumption of meat offered to idols) played an important role (H. Kraft, *Rev* [HNT] 69f.; on the relation between heresy and adultery, cf. also 2 Pet 2:14).

The rigorist "conventicle-ethic" of James (M. Dibelius, *James* [Hermeneia] 49) has in view a withdrawal from the world; compromising oneself with the world is at the same time enmity with God (ἔχθρα τοῦ θεοῦ). For James, it is natural to characterize those who follow after φιλία τοῦ κόσμου as *adulterous* (4:4).   E. Plümacher

μοιχός, οῦ, ὁ *moichos* adulterer
→ μοιχεύω.

μόλις *molis* hardly, with difficulty, not easily*

Μόλις appears 6 times in the NT, with the meanings *(only) with difficulty* (Acts 14:18; 27:7, 8, 16); *hardly/ not easily* (Rom 5:7); *with difficulty* (1 Pet 4:18); cf. Luke 9:39 v.l. (→ μόγις). J. Schneider, *TDNT* IV, 735f.

Μόλοχ *Moloch* Moloch*

Μόλοχ is the name the LXX uses for a god worshiped by the northeastern and eastern Semites since at least the third millennium B.C. (Heb. *mlk*, vocalized by the Masoretes—probably with reference to *bōšet,* "shame"—as *mōlek*). The cult of Moloch gained significance in Israel in the eighth century B.C. under Assyrian influence. Child sacrifices are said to have been made to him, esp. in the Valley of Hinnom to the south of Jerusalem (2 Kgs 16:3; 23:10; Jer 32:35; prohibited in Lev 18:21; 20:2-5).

Acts 7:43 quotes Amos 5:26 LXX: ἀνελάβετε τὴν σκηνὴν τοῦ Μόλοχ, "you brought along the tent of *Moloch*," which suggests that already during the time of the sojourn in the wilderness the Israelites had worshiped Moloch. (The Hebrew text of Amos 5:26, by way of contrast, has *nᵉśā'tem 'ēt sikkût malkᵉkem,* "you shall take up Sikkuth, your king.") BAGD s.v. (bibliography); K.-H. Bernhardt, *BHH* 1232; *BL* 1163f. (bibliography).

μολύνω *molynō* soil, stain, defile*

In Rev 3:4, the *staining* of one's garments (μολύνω τὰ ἱμάτια) is a metaphor for an unclean and unrepentant life. In 14:4, μολύνω is applied fig. to the entire people (the

144,000), "who have not *defiled* themselves with women" (οἱ μετὰ γυναικῶν οὐκ ἐμολύνθησαν), i.e., as a metaphor for the faithful of the community who had not given in to adultery (or idolatry; cf. Hos 2:14-23; Jer 2:2–3:25; also 2 Cor 11:2). Also fig. is 1 Cor 8:7, on the conscience of the weak, which *is defiled* (ἡ συνείδησις αὐτῶν ἀσθενὴς οὖσα μολύνεται) by eating meat that has been offered to idols. F. Hauck, *TDNT* IV, 736f.

μολυσμός, οῦ, ὁ *molysmos* defilement*

In 2 Cor 7:1 μολυσμός is used fig. in urging a cleansing "from every *defilement* of body and spirit" (ἀπὸ παντὸς μολυσμοῦ σαρκὸς καὶ πνεύματος), at the close of a typically Jewish parenesis. (On 6:14–7:1, see R. Bultmann, *2 Cor* [Eng. tr., 1985] ad loc., and bibliography on pp. 264f. of the German ed. [KEK].)

μομφή, ῆς, ἡ *momphē* accusation, complaint*

Col 3:13: πρός τινα . . . μομφή, "a *complaint* against someone." W. Grundmann, *TDNT* IV, 573.

μονή, ῆς, ἡ *monē* dwelling, lodging; stay*

John 14:2: μοναὶ πολλαί, of many heavenly *dwellings* in the house of the Father, in which Jesus would prepare for the disciples "a place to stay" (cf. *1 Enoch* 39:4f.; 41:2; 71:16; Philo *Som.* i.256; see also Billerbeck II, 560; R. Schnackenburg, *John* III [1982] ad loc. [bibliography]; R. H. Gundry, " 'In My Father's House Are Many Μοναί' (John 14:2)," *ZNW* 58 [1967] 68-72; G. Fischer, *Die himmlischen Wohnungen* [1975]). John 14:23: μονὴν ποιέομαι, "prepare a *dwelling* for oneself" or "*dwell*/take up *residence*"—for the continuing dwelling of Christ and of the Father in those who love Jesus and keep his word (on the dwelling of God with his people, cf. Exod 25:8; Ezek 37:26f.; Zech 2:14; also Rev 21:3). F. Hauck, *TDNT* IV, 579-81; → μένω 3.

μονογενής, 2 *monogenēs* only (one of its kind), unique*

1. Occurrences in the NT — 2. Meaning — 3. In Luke — 4. Heb 11:17 (Isaac) — 5. Jesus Christ as μονογενής

Lit.: K.-H. BARTELS, *DNTT* II, 723-25, esp. 725. — F. BÜCHSEL, *TDNT* IV, 737-41. — H.-J. FABRY, *TDOT* VI, 40-48. — F. C. GRANT. " 'Only Begotten': A Footnote to the New Revision," *ATR* 36 (1954) 284-87. — F. HAHN, "Beobachtungen zu Joh 1:18, 34," FS Kilpatrick, 239-45. — D. MOODY, "God's Only Son," *JBL* 72 (1953) 213-19. — idem, *IDB* III, 604. — F. M. WARDEN. "God's Only Son," *Review and Expositor* 50 (1953) 216-23. — P. WINTER. "Μονογενὴς παρὰ πατρός," *ZRGG* 5 (1953) 335-65.

1. The adj. μονογενής appears 9 times in the NT: 3 times in Luke (7:12 and 9:38 of a son, 8:42 of a daughter),

4 times in John as a designation of Jesus' relationship to God (1:14, 18; 3:16, 18), in 1 John 4:9 (with the same meaning as the Gospel of John), and in Heb 11:17 (of Isaac).

2. Μονογενής means *only, one of a kind, unique* (derived from μόνος and γένος). This basic meaning is found in Plato *Ti.* 92c (of the heaven: εἰς οὐρανὸς ὅδε μονογενής); Wis 7:22 (of the Spirit of Wisdom); Cornutus *Theologia Graeca* 27 [49:13] (of this one and only world: εἰς καὶ μονογενὴς ὁ κόσμος; likewise Plutarch *Moralia* 423a); *1 Clem.* 25:2 (of the phoenix).

Although the noun γένος is related to the vb. γί(γ)νεσθαι, the root γενεσ- lost its originally sexual connotation and soon meant simply "become," without any reference to "birth." Nevertheless, μονογενής is often used to mean "only child," son or daughter, born to parents: e.g., Hesiod *Op.* 376 (μονογενὴς παῖς) and *Th.* 426 (of Hekate, μονογενὴς θεά); Herodotus vii.221; Eusebius *PE* i.10.33 (τὸν ἑαυτοῦ μονογενῆ υἱόν); Plutarch *Lyc.* 31:4; Diodorus Siculus iv.73.2. The same use is found in the LXX (Judg 11:34; Tob 3:15; 6:10, 14; 8:17; possibly also Pss 21:21 and 34:17). In these cases, μονογενής can have the nuance "only begotten." In some instances, the LXX translates Heb. *yāḥîd*, "only" (related to 'ʾeḥād, "one," which contains no connotation of "birth"). Many times μονογενής even has the Hebrew nuance of "lonely" (Bar 4:16; Ps 24:16; possibly also Pss 21:21; 34:17 LXX).

3. Μονογενής means *only* in all the Lukan passages. In 7:12 (L) it is used of the son born to the widow of Nain. The Gospel writer has inserted μονογενής in 8:42 in the account of the healing of Jairus's daughter (cf. Mark 5:23: τὸ θυγάτριόν μου) and in 9:38 in the pericope on the epileptic boy (cf. Mark 9:17: τὸν υἱόν μου). In these passages μονογενής intensifies the significance of Jesus' miracles.

4. That *unique* is the actual meaning of μονογενής can be seen in Heb 11:17, where it is used of Isaac, whom Abraham was ready to sacrifice, even though God had promised Abraham abundant descendants. The word here means *only* (son) *of his kind*, i.e., the only son of the promise (Gen 21:12). Abraham in fact had already begotten Ishmael through Hagar (Gen 16:3f.; 17:22-25) and later had six other sons by Keturah (Gen 25:1). Μονογενής here reflects Heb. *yāḥîd* of Gen 22:2, 12, 16, which the LXX prefers to translate as ἀγαπητός, "beloved" (Aquila uses μονογενής in Gen 22:2, as Symmachus does at Gen 22:12). Likewise, Josephus uses μονογενής in *Ant.* i.222 in the sense of *unique;* he expresses the idea "born" with a separate partc. (ὑπερηγάπα μονογενῆ ὄντα καὶ ἐπὶ γήρως οὐδῷ κατὰ δωρεὰν αὐτῷ τοῦ θεοῦ γενόμενον).

5. "The/his *only* son" is the clear meaning of the phrase with μονογενής in John 3:16, 18 and 1 John 4:9. The expression indicates Jesus' unique personality, relation to the Father, and mission. According to John 1:14,

18, the Logos is the "Only One" from the Father and therefore in his nature is the only revealer of the Father.

The Johannine use of μονογενής has been questioned because of John 1:14 (δόξαν ὡς μονογενοῦς παρὰ πατρός) and 1:18. In the last passage, the best reading (p[66, 75] א*, c B C* L et al.) is (ὁ) μονογενὴς θεός, "the *only* God" (cf. Θ Koine Vg.: ὁ μονογενὴς υἱός, "the *only* son"). Even if one places a comma after the adj. ([ὁ] μονογενής, θεός), the absence of υἱός leads one to question the meaning of μονογενής. BAGD (527) suggests the meaning "only-begotten," or "begotten of the Only One" (cf. v. 13, ἐκ θεοῦ γεννᾶσθαι). In this way, μονογενής would equal μονογέννητος.

Yet this meaning cannot be correct, since ἐκ θεοῦ γεννᾶσθαι in 1:13 refers to Christian believers (οἱ . . . ἐγεννήθησαν, according to all Greek mss.; *contra* JB et al.). Old Latin (ms. a) translates μονογενής as *unicus;* yet Jerome (Vg.) changes this to *unigenitus* in John 1:14, 18; 1 John 4:9; Heb 11:17 (he retains *unicus* in the three Lukan passages; → 3). With the change, the text apparently seeks to exclude an Arian interpretation. It should be noted, however, that the second article of the Apostles' Creed, as found in Epiphanius *Anc.* 119:4, uses *two* words in order to express "only-begotten": γεννηθέντα ἐκ θεοῦ πατρὸς μονογενῆ. Thus the possible meaning "only-born" contains a further, later nuance: "only-begotten"—a nuance that the original Greek text of John hardly permits.

J. A. Fitzmyer

μόνον *monon* only, alone
→ μόνος 5.

μονόομαι *monoomai* be isolated, be left alone*

The pf. pass. partc. is found in 1 Tim 5:5 in reference to "the one who is really a widow and *is left alone*" (ἡ δὲ ὄντως χήρα καὶ μεμονωμένη).

μόνος, 3 *monos* only, unique; alone*

1. Occurrences in the NT — 2. Meaning — 3. Use as adj. — 4. Κατὰ μόνας — 5. Μόνον as adv.

Lit.: K.-H. BARTELS, *DNTT* II, 723-25. — BEYER, *Syntax* 126-29. — E. F. F. BISHOP, "Some NT Occurrences of *Monos* with *Theos*," *Muslim World* 51 (1961) 123-27. — G. DELLING, "Μόνος Θεός," *TLZ* 77 (1952) 469-76. — J. DUPONT, "Μόνῳ σοφῷ Θεῷ (Rom. XVI,27)," *ETL* 22 (1946) 362-75. — P.-É. LANGEVIN, *Bibliographie biblique* (1970-78) I, 722f.; II, 1236f. — N. LOHFINK and J. BERGMAN, *TDOT* I, 193-201. — MOULTON/ MILLIGAN s.v. — E. NORDEN, *Agnostos Theos* (⁴1956) 245-56.

1. Μόνος appears in the NT 47 times as a pronominal adj. and 66 times in the neut. as an adv. The adj. appears in every NT book except Acts, 2 Corinthians, Ephesians, 2 Thessalonians, Titus, Philemon, James, 1–2 Peter, and 3 John; the adv. occurs in all books except Colossians, Titus, Philemon, 2 Peter, 2–3 John, Jude, and Revelation. John 8:9 and Acts 15:34 TR can also be added to the 113 total instances of μόνος. In four passages (Acts 11:19; Rom 3:29; 1 John 2:2; 5:6), the preferred reading has the adv., although some mss. attest the adj.

2. In the NT μόνος expresses the uniqueness, isolation, or exclusivity of persons, things, or actions. The word can also connote spatial isolation or seclusion, loneliness, or uniqueness. Both the adv. and the adj. contain these nuances, although occasionally the meaning of the adv. can be distinguished from that of the predicate use of the adj. Thus σὺ μόνος παροικεῖς Ἰερουσαλήμ . . . ; means "Are you the *only* visitor to Jerusalem who . . . ?" (Luke 24:18), while σὺ μόνον παροικεῖς Ἰερουσαλήμ; would mean "Are you *only* a visitor to Jerusalem?" (see LSJ s.v.). Cf. 1 Cor 9:6; 14:36; Acts 26:14 (ms. 614).

3. a) The adj. is used attributively with a noun or pron. to express uniqueness, e.g., τὸν μόνον δεσπότην καὶ κύριον ἡμῶν Ἰησοῦν Χριστὸν ἀρνούμενοι, "denying our *only* master and lord, Jesus Christ" (Jude 4). The author warns his readers about persons in their midst who wanted to contest the singular lordship of Christ (see K. H. Rengstorf, *TDNT* II, 48f.). In the context of ὁ μόνος ἔχων ἀθανασίαν, "[God,] the *only one* possessing immortality" (1 Tim 6:16), Timothy is urged to fight the good fight of faith until the Lord appears, who will be made manifest by the *unique* ruler (v. 15: μόνος δυνάστης)—God, the *sole* possessor of immortality.

b) 1) More frequently, however, μόνος is used as a predicate to express uniqueness, exclusivity, or isolation. Thus καὶ αὐτὸς μόνος ἐπὶ τῆς γῆς, "and he was *alone* on the land" (Mark 6:47), i.e., without companion, since the disciples were crossing the sea by boat. Or, in Jesus' answer to Satan, αὐτῷ μόνῳ λατρεύσεις, "him *alone* shall you serve" (Matt 4:10 par. Luke 4:8, which add μόνῳ to Deut 6:13). Similarly Matt 18:15 (*alone; privately*); Mark 9:2 (*alone*, i.e., apart from the other disciples); Luke 24:12 ("the strips of linen *only/alone*," but not Jesus); John 6:15, 22; 1 Cor 14:36; Gal 3:2 (BAGD s.v. 2b, however, includes this passage under the adv. use); 6:4; Col 4:11; Heb 9:7; Rev 15:4 (addressed to God, the "*only* Holy One"); Acts 15:34 TR.

This predicate use can also be found in conjunction with vbs. Thus with εἶναι: μόνος ἦν ἐκεῖ, "he was there *alone*" (Matt 14:23, of Jesus praying on the mountain while the disciples were crossing the sea); μόνος οὐκ εἰμί, "I am not *alone*" (John 8:16), since Jesus is bound to the one who sent him (cf. 10:30). Likewise John 16:32b; 2 Tim 4:11. Thus also with other vbs.: μόνην με κατέλειπεν διακονεῖν, "she has left me *alone* to serve" (Luke 10:40: when Mary failed to help her sister Martha); οὐκ ἀφῆκέν με μόνον, "he has not left me *alone*"—i.e., on my own (John 8:29: since Jesus always spoke what the Father had taught him). Likewise Luke 9:36 (*alone*, i.e., without Moses and Elijah); 24:18 (→ 2); John 12:24 (*alone* the kernel produces no fruit); 16:32a (*alone*, i.e., abandoned); Rom 11:3 (= 1 Kgs 19:10); 1 Cor 9:6; 1 Thess 3:1 (*alone*, i.e., without companion); John 8:9 TR.

2) A pleonastic use of μόνος is found after negatives with εἰ μή, which intensifies the uniqueness or isolation. Thus it is said of David: ὃ οὐκ ἐξὸν ἦν αὐτῷ φαγεῖν . . . εἰ μὴ τοῖς ἱερεῦσιν μόνοις, "which it was not lawful for him to eat . . . but *only* for the priests" (Matt 12:4; cf. Luke 6:4); οὐδένα εἶδον εἰ μὴ τὸν Ἰησοῦν μόνον, "they saw no one except Jesus *only*" (Mark 9:8; cf. Matt 17:8). Thus also Matt 24:36; Phil 4:15. On Luke 5:21 → c.

3) Predicate μόνος is also connected with a preceding negative and constructed with a correlative ἀλλά (καί), "not *only* . . . but (also, even)." This construction negates the uniqueness or isolation and emphasizes an alternative: οὐκ ἐπ' ἄρτῳ μόνῳ . . . ἀλλ' ἐπὶ παντὶ ῥήματι, "not by bread *alone* . . . but by every word" (Matt 4:4 par. Luke 4:4 [Deut 8:3]). Likewise Rom 16:4; Phil 2:27 (BAGD s.v. 2c views μόνῳ here as an adv.); 2 John 1.

c) A more obviously theological use of μόνος is in reference to God, which occurs frequently in doxologies and credal statements. In the NT this usage can be traced back to monotheistic statements from the OT and inter-testamental Jewish authors (e.g., Deut 6:13; Isa 44:24 LXX; 2 Macc 7:37; *Sib. Or.* frag. 1.16f. [GCS 8, 228]; Josephus *Ant.* viii.335).

1) The adj. is used predicatively in εἰ μὴ μόνος ὁ θεός; "[who can forgive sins] except God *alone*?" (Luke 5:21; Luke himself has inserted μόνος here, in contrast to the source material in Mark 2:7, which has εἷς). If the NT thus suggests the idea that Jesus somehow stands on a level with Yahweh, it nevertheless makes it clear that the latter is "the *only* God," and it places in the mouth of Jesus the affirmation that to God alone worship is due (Matt 4:10 par. Luke 4:8, → 3.b.1), thus acknowledging its indebtedness to the monotheistic heritage of the OT and Judaism. See further Rev 15:4.

2) Often, however, μόνος is used attributively to indicate "the *only* God": τὴν δόξαν τὴν παρὰ τοῦ μόνου θεοῦ οὐ ζητεῖτε, "you do not seek the glory [that comes] from the *only* God" (John 5:44), i.e., from the one and only God; Jesus criticizes the Jews for seeking glory from one another. In this passage, p[66, 75] B W omit θεοῦ; if this reading is preferred, μόνος must be taken as a subst.: "from the *Only One*." In John 17:3 the Gospel writer interprets "eternal life" by having Jesus say, ἵνα γινώσκωσιν σὲ τὸν μόνον ἀληθινὸν θεόν, "that they may know you, the *only* true God." Here Yahweh is implicitly contrasted with other deities. Likewise 1 Tim 1:17 (in a doxology that praises "the *only* God"); Jude 25 ("to the *only* God, our Savior," also a doxology); Rom 16:27 ("the *only* wise God" is praised for bringing about "the obedience of faith" in accordance with Paul's gospel; God is thus the only one who deserves the attribute σοφός). Cf. 1 Tim 6:15 (with δυνάστης, "ruler," instead of θεός).

4. In two passages we find the elliptic expression κατὰ

μόνας, which is used as an adv. meaning *alone:* καὶ ὅτε ἐγένετο κατὰ μόνας, "and when he was *alone*" (Mark 4:10), i.e., apart from the crowd, yet with the Twelve; ἐν τῷ εἶναι αὐτὸν προσευχόμενον κατὰ μόνας, "while he was praying *alone*" (Luke 9:18). In this expression, κατά governs an unexpressed acc. fem. pl. (χώρας?). In the NT passages mentioned, the phrase has a spatial connotation, as it does in Jer 15:17 LXX and Josephus *Ant.* xvii.336. Yet it does not always have this connotation (see Gen 32:17 and Ps 4:9 LXX). This enigmatic expression is attested in both classical and Hellenistic Greek and in the LXX.

5. a) The neut. μόνον often functions as an adv. and indicates the same uniqueness, isolation, or exclusivity. It is used to modify vbs., nouns/prons., advs., prep. phrases, clauses, and negatives, limiting their action, scope, or condition.

1) With vbs.: ἀλλὰ μόνον εἰπὲ λόγῳ, "but *just* say a word" (Matt 8:8); ἐὰν μόνον ἅψωμαι τοῦ ἱματίου αὐτοῦ, "if *only* I touch his garment" (Matt 9:21; cf. 14:36). Likewise Mark 5:36; Luke 8:50; Acts 8:16 (misplaced, since it qualifies the prep. phrase; cf. 18:25); 1 Cor 15:19 (misplaced?); Gal 1:23; 5:13 (the vb. must be supplied).

2) With nouns/prons.: ἐὰν ἀσπάσησθε τοὺς ἀδελφοὺς ὑμῶν μόνον, "if you greet *only* your brothers" (Matt 5:47), i.e., and not all people; ὃς ἐὰν ποτίσῃ ἕνα τῶν μικρῶν τούτων ποτήριον ψυχροῦ μόνον εἰς ὄνομα μαθητοῦ, "whoever gives *only* a cup of cool water to one of these little ones because he is a disciple" (or perhaps, if μόνον modifies the prep. phrase, ". . . a cup of cool water . . . *simply* because he is a disciple") (Matt 10:42; D E*, however, omit the adv.). Similarly Acts 18:25 (although here perhaps μόνον is the neut. adj.); Rom 3:29 (but D reads μόνος and B μόνων); Gal 2:10; 2 Thess 2:7; Jas 1:22.

3) With advs., prep. phrases, or clauses: μόνον ἐν κυρίῳ, "*only* in the Lord" (1 Cor 7:39), i.e., marry a Christian (referring to a widow who was permitted to remarry after the death of her husband); καὶ μὴ μόνον ἐν τῷ παρεῖναί με πρὸς ὑμᾶς, "and not *only* when I am present with you" (Gal 4:18). Likewise Gal 6:12; Phil 1:27; Heb 9:10; Jas 2:24 ("not by faith *alone*," apart from works).

b) The adv. μόνον is also used pleonastically with εἰ μή: οὐδὲν εὗρεν ἐν αὐτῇ εἰ μὴ φύλλα μόνον, "he found nothing on it [sc. the fig tree] except leaves *only*" (Matt 21:19); ἵνα μηδὲν αἴρωσιν εἰς ὁδὸν εἰ μὴ ῥάβδον μόνον, "that they should take nothing with them for the journey but a staff *only*" (Mark 6:8; here μόνον could possibly be understood as an adj.: "except a staff *alone*"; both Matt 10:9 and Luke 9:3 omit the pleonasm); μηδενὶ λαλοῦντες τὸν λόγον εἰ μὴ μόνον Ἰουδαίοις, "preaching the word of God to no one except *only* Jews" (Acts 11:19; D 614 read μόνοις instead of the adv.).

c) The correlative use of the adv. is also found after a negative: οὐ μόνον ἔλυεν τὸ σάββατον, ἀλλὰ καὶ πατέρα ἴδιον ἔλεγεν τὸν θεόν, "he was not *only* breaking the sabbath but even calling God his own father" (John 5:18); μὴ τοὺς πόδας μου μόνον ἀλλὰ καὶ τὰς χεῖρας καὶ τὴν κεφαλήν, "not *only* my feet but also my hands and head" (John 13:9). Likewise Matt 21:21; John 11:52; 12:9; 17:20; Acts 19:26f.; 21:23; 26:29; 27:10; Rom 1:32; 4:12, 16, 23 (μόνον here could be a masc. acc. sg. adj.); 9:24; 13:4; 2 Cor 7:7; 8:10, 21; 9:12; Eph 2:23; Phil 1:29; 1 Thess 1:5, 8; 2:8; 1 Tim 5:13; 2 Tim 2:20; 4:8; Heb 12:26 (added to Hag 2:6 LXX); 1 Pet 2:18; 1 John 2:2 (B reads μόνων); 5:6 (B has μόνῳ). In most of these passages, the construction is simply "not *only* . . . but also."

In Phil 2:12, however, one finds a fuller form: μὴ ὡς ἐν τῇ παρουσίᾳ μου μόνον ἀλλὰ νῦν πολλῷ μᾶλλον ἐν τῇ ἀπουσίᾳ μου, "not *only* as in my presence but now much more in my absence." An elliptic form of the correlative appears in a few Pauline passages. After speaking of the grace that is obtained through Christ and of the Christian's hope of sharing God's glory, Paul continues: οὐ μόνον δέ, ἀλλὰ καὶ καυχώμεθα ἐν ταῖς θλίψεσιν, "not *only* [this], but we also rejoice in afflictions" (Rom 5:3; D adds τοῦτο after δέ). Similarly Rom 5:11 (D G add τοῦτο); 8:23; 9:10; 2 Cor 8:19. In all of these passages the ellipsis points to something that immediately precedes.

J. A. Fitzmyer

μονόφθαλμος, 2 *monophthalmos* one-eyed*

Mark 9:47 par. Matt 18:9, in a series of sayings of Jesus in which hearers are called to leave everything that might cause them to fall: μονόφθαλμον εἰσελθεῖν, "to enter [the kingdom] *with only one eye.*"

μορφή, ῆς, ἡ *morphē* form, visible appearance*

1. Occurrences in the NT — 2. Usage and meaning — 3. Μορφή in the spurious ending of Mark — 4. Μορφή in Phil 2:6f. — 5. Related terms

Lit.: J. BEHM, *TDNT* IV, 742-59. — CREMER/KÖGEL 736-39. — P. GRELOT, "Deux expressions difficiles de Phil 2,6-7," *Bib* 53 (1972) 495-507. — J. HÉRING, *Le royaume de Dieu et sa venue* (²1959) 159-70. — O. HOFIUS, *Der Christushymnus Phil 2,6-11* (WUNT 17, 1976) 56-74. — J. JERVELL, *Imago Dei. Gen 1:26f. im Spätjudentum, in der Gnosis, und in den paulinischen Briefen* (FRLANT 76, 1960) 197-231. — E. KÄSEMANN, "Kritische Analyse von Phil. 2:5-11," idem, *Versuche* I, 51-95. — E. LARSSON, *Christus als Vorbild. Eine Untersuchung zu den paulinischen Tauf- und Eikontexten* (ASNU 23, 1962) 230-75. — E. LOHMEYER, *Kyrios Jesus. Eine Untersuchung zu Phil 2:5-11* (²1961), esp. 17-20. — R. P. MARTIN, *Carmen Christi: Philippians II.5-11 in Recent Interpretation and in the Setting of Early Christian Worship* (SNTSMS 4, 1967), index s.v. μορφή. — PGL 884f. — E. SCHWEIZER, *Lordship and Discipleship* (SBT

28, 1960) 61-67. — C. Spicq, "Note sur ΜΟΡΦΗ dans les papyrus et quelques inscriptions," *RB* 80 (1973) 37-45. — *idem, Notes* II, 568-73. — D. H. Wallace, "A Note on *morphē,*" *TZ* 22 (1966) 19-25. — For further bibliography see *TWNT* X, 1181.

1. Μορφή appears only 3 times in the NT (Mark 16:12; Phil 2:6, 7), which is infrequent, considering the broad significance of the term in Greek. Even if one includes all of the noun and vb. constructions derived from the root μορφ- (μεταμορφόομαι, μορφόω, μόρφωσις, συμμορφίζομαι, σύμμορφος), the occurrences remain confined to the Synoptic Gospels (3 times), the Pauline Epistles (9 times), and the deutero-Pauline Epistles (2 Tim 3:5).

2. The NT contains only a small sample of the wide range of meanings for μορφή in classical and Hellenistic Greek ("shape, something known by the senses, esp. physical appearance, form, beauty, loveliness, outward form of appearance, appearance"). Its usage is limited to two areas. In Mark 16:12, the risen Lord appears "in another *form*" and therefore can not be recognized by his familiar physical form of appearance. The assumption here is that supernatural forms were capable of changing their μορφή. In Phil 2:6f., however, we should not relate the twofold μορφή of Christ to the concept of metamorphosis (*contra* Spicq). The antithetical description of the preexistent and earthly Christ does not derive from the idea of the adaptability of a divine being. Μορφὴ θεοῦ and μορφὴ δούλου are metaphoric expressions (Hofius 58) that should be interpreted as poetic approaches to the state of Christ before and during his work on earth.

3. The appearance of the risen Lord "in another *form*" (ἐν ἑτέρᾳ μορφῇ) to two disciples in what is known as the spurious ending of Mark (Mark 16:12) refers to Luke 24:13-35 (R. Pesch, *Mark* [HTKNT, 1977] II, 545, 551f.); the idea of change, however, is not found in the Lukan account. Μορφή here means the form—the unique physical appearance—by which a person is recognized and is distinguished from others. According to Greek and Hellenistic views, the μορφή of figures on the periphery of the human race (gods, heroes, the dying, ecstatics) is mutable (e.g., Sophocles *Tr.* 10: ὅς μ' ἐν τρισὶν μορφαῖσιν ἐξήτει; *PGM* 13:69-71, 73 [ἵνα μοι φανῆς ἀγαθῇ μορφῇ], 271f., 582f.; *Acts Pet. and Andr.* 2; *Acts Phil.* 144, 148; *Acts Thom.* 8 [ἔβλεπον τὸ εἶδος αὐτοῦ ἐνηλλαγμένον ἐν ἑτέρᾳ μορφῇ]; cf. further 34, 43, 45]; → μεταμορφόομαι).

4. The antithetical use of μορφὴ θεοῦ and μορφὴ δούλου in Phil 2:6f. is crucial for understanding the hymn as a whole. In contrast to the traditional Lutheran interpretation, which relates both expressions to the λόγος ἔνσαρκος, it is generally accepted today that 2:6 refers to the preexistent Son of God, and 2:7 to the Son of God become a man. Any additional interpretation of the pair must be based on the parallelism of 2:6 and 7. The change

from μορφὴ θεοῦ to μορφὴ δούλου is neither a simple change of appearance, leaving the nature unchanged (*contra* J. Schneider, *TDNT* V, 197: "The earthly μορφή is also the husk which encloses His unchanging essential existence"), nor a change of the Son's nature (Käsemann 72: "The heavenly nature was laid aside; the earthly was put on"). To contrast "appearance" and "substance" ignores the wording of the hymn itself (Schweizer; Hofius 57), which we cannot characterize as a reflection on substance, nor does it anticipate the doctrine of the two natures or deal with a change of "mode of existence" (M. Dibelius, *Phil* [HNT] 60; Käsemann 67; J. Gnilka, *Phil* [HTKNT] 114; G. Barth, *Phil* [ZBK] 40).

Μορφή rarely refers to the external appearance as opposed to the essence (thus, e.g., in tomb inscriptions in the antithesis between μορφή and ψυχή: Preisigke, *Sammelbuch* V, 8071.10, 15). The understanding of μορφή as essential being (Käsemann 65ff.) possibly points to Gnosticism, where μορφή and εἰκών are synonyms (Jervell 228). But Gnosticism had as little influence on Phil 2:6-11 (*contra* Jervell 229) as did the Greek magical papyri. Μορφή in Phil 2:6f. refers not to any changeable form but to the specific form on which identity and status depend. Μορφὴ δούλου is thus to be understood with Cremer/Kögel 736 as "the form proper to a slave, as an expression of his state," and μορφὴ θεοῦ likewise as "the expression of the divine state." Basic to the understanding of μορφή in Phil 2:6-11, therefore, is not mutability but precisely the immutability of μορφὴ θεοῦ and μορφὴ δούλου.

5. In spite of all attempts to identify μορφή with other Greek terms, μορφή retains its own meaning in Hellenistic Greek ("form") and—apart from Gnostic usage—is not interchangeable with εἰκών (with Wallace 22f.; Spicq, "Note" 44; *idem, Notes* II, 570f.; *contra* Héring 159ff.; Martin 106-20). The equation of μορφή and οὐσία is first attested in patristic exegesis (*PGL* 884f.).

W. Pöhlmann

μορφόω *morphoō* form, shape; build*

1. Occurrence and meaning in the NT — 2. Μορφόω in Gal 4:19 — 3. Μόρφωσις

Lit.: BAGD 528. — J. Behm, *TDNT* IV, 742-59, esp. 752-54. — Cremer/Kögel 703. — R. Hermann, "Über den Sinn des Μορφοῦσθαι Χριστὸν ἐν ὑμῖν in Gal. 4,19," *TLZ* 80 (1955) 713-26. — E. Lesky, *Die Zeugungs- und Vererbungslehren der Antike und ihr Nachwirken* (AAWLM.G 19, 1950) 1358-63. — F. Mussner, *Gal* (HTKNT, 1976) 312f. — *PGL* 885f. — For further bibliography see *TWNT* X, 1181.

1. The vb. μορφόω appears only in μέχρις οὗ μορφωθῇ Χριστὸς ἐν ὑμῖν, "until Christ *is formed* in you" (Gal 4:19).

The NT thus does not use μορφόω for the creative acts of God (Philo *Plant.* 3; *Fug.* 12, 69; *Som.* i.210; ii.45; *Abr.* 118; *Spec. Leg.* i.171; *Aet.* 41) or for the work of artisans, who form idols out of stone or metal (Isa 44:13 A; Philo *Decal.* 7, 21, 66, 72; *Spec. Leg.* ii.255; Josephus *Ant.* xv.329; Justin *Apol.* i.9.1).

2. In Gal 4:19 Paul describes his relationship to the Galatians using the metaphor of conception and birth. We must understand his image against the background of the ancient conception of reproduction, according to which men had the active role in reproduction and women the passive. The woman provides the material (ὕλη), which receives its form through the man (λαμβάνον τὴν μορφήν: Aristotle *GA* i.21.729b; Lesky 1359). The pass. of μορφόω is used in this connection for the formation of the embryo in the mother's womb (Behm 753). The Pauline metaphor in Gal 4:19 combines both functions: the apostle is both the father and the mother of the community. He has begotten it (cf. 1 Cor 4:15) and has molded it in the form of Christ through his preaching. Through his apostolic labor (ὠδίνω, Gal 4:19) he brought the commuity to life. His work is threatened by the Galatians' turning to false teaching, but Paul is prepared to repeat the process of conception and birth. The Pauline expression is therefore not to be understood in the sense of a Christ-mysticism (with Hermann, *contra* Behm 754), but as a forced metaphor. The apostle desires to begin again the proclamation of the gospel and the formation of the community so that an authentic community of Christ may arise.

3. The use of **μόρφωσις**, *appearance, formation, education**, in Rom 2:20b could mean that the Jew who is faithful to the law possesses "the *embodiment* of knowledge and truth in the book of the law" (BAGD); A. Schlatter's interpretation is also worthy of mention: through the law the Jew has received the "molding" that mediates to him knowledge and truth (*Gottes Gerechtigkeit* [³1959] 103). The expression in Rom 2:20b is often regarded as a citation from a tradition out of Diaspora Judaism (most recently, U. Wilckens, *Rom* [EKKNT] I, 149), a view, however, that lacks concrete support (see O. Kuss, *Rom* [1957] I, 85).

In 2 Tim 3:5 it is said that in the last days some will have the μόρφωσις of godliness but will deny its power. The word here should be understood in terms of one's *training* in the faith (with Schlatter, *Gerechtigkeit* 104), and not so much in terms of a contrast between essence and appearance (thus BAGD et al.). W. Pöhlmann

μόρφωσις, εως, ἡ *morphōsis* appearance; formation; education
→ μορφόω 3.

μοσχοποιέω *moschopoieō* make a calf*

Acts 7:41: ἐμοσχοποίησαν, *they made a calf.* This verse incorporates Exod 32:4 (said of Aaron): ἐποίησεν αὐτὰ [the gold rings] μόσχον χωνευτόν. The vb. is found only in Christian texts; cf., however, εἰδωλοποιέω (since Plato; e.g., Diodorus Siculus xxxi.25.2).

μόσχος, ου, ὁ *moschos* calf, (young) bull or ox*

Μόσχος appears 6 times in the NT: Luke 15:23, 27, 30 deal with the slaughter of a "fatted *calf*" (ὁ σιτευτὸς μόσχος; cf. Judg 6:25 A; Jer 21:26 LXX); in Heb 9:12 the blood of "goats and *calves*" is mentioned as the conventional offering on the Day of Atonement (otherwise in 9:13: "blood of goats and bulls and the ashes of a heifer," cf. 10:4; see also Lev 16:2-28). Μόσχος can also have a pejorative sense, as it does in Heb 9:19, where the blood of "*calves* and goats" (cf. Exod 24:3-8) is mentioned as the blood offering of the first sealing of the covenant (see A. Strobel, *Heb* [NTD] ad loc.). According to Rev 4:7, the second of the four figures around the throne of God is "like an ox" (ὅμοιον μόσχῳ; cf. Ezek 1:5, 10 [πρόσωπον μόσχου]), which deviates from the sequence and description of the four living creatures of Ezekiel 1 and the Babylonian animal ring on which it is certainly based. They are, according to Rev 4:8, viewed as angelic beings (in accordance with Isa 6:1-3); cf. further *1 Clem.* 52:2; *Barn.* 8:2. O. Michel, *TDNT* IV, 760-62; *TWNT* X, 1181 (bibliography); K.-H. Bernhardt, *BHH* 920f.; *BL* 1481; Spicq, *Notes* II, 574f.

μου *mou* of me; my

Gen. of → ἐγώ (enclitic form).

μουσικός, 3 *mousikos* musical; subst.: musician*

In the NT μουσικός appears only as a subst.: in Rev 18:22 φωνὴ . . . μουσικῶν, along with harpists, flutists, and trumpeters, will no longer be heard in "Babylon" (cf. also Isa 24:8; Jer 25:10). In the context it probably refers to singers, since the κιθαρῳδός sings as he plays (cf. Ezek 26:13).

μόχθος, ου, ὁ *mochthos* effort; difficulty, hardship*

In the NT in the pair κόπος καὶ μόχθος, "labor and *difficulty/hardship*": 2 Cor 11:27; 1 Thess 2:9; 2 Thess 3:8.

μυελός, οῦ, ὁ *myelos* (bone) marrow*

Heb 4:12: μερισμὸς . . . ἁρμῶν τε καὶ μυελῶν, "division of joints and *marrow*," as a metaphor for the effects of the word of God, which reaches the innermost being.

μυέω *myeō* initiate; pass.: be initiated*

A t.t. in the mystery religions, used by extension in

Phil 4:12 to describe the power of Christ operative in the apostle: ἐν παντὶ καὶ ἐν πᾶσιν μεμύημαι, "in each and every [circumstance] *I am an initiate*" (i.e., *I have learned the secret*—to be in abundance and in want, to be well fed and to be hungry). Precisely for this reason, the apostle is "content" (v. 11); cf. also 3 Macc 2:30; Wis 8:4.

μῦθος, ου, ὁ *mythos* poetic narrative; myth, fable*

There are 5 occurrences in the NT (all pl.), consistently (as often in Jewish [cf. Philo *Exsec.* 162; Josephus *Ant.* i.122] and always in the early Christian tradition) in a negative and pejorative sense for contrived tales void of truth, or speculations derived from (Jewish or Gnostic) false teachings. Consistent with such a nuance, the word appears only late in the NT (only in the Pastorals and 2 Peter; cf. Ign. *Magn.* 8:1; also as a critique of the Christian message in *2 Clem.* 13:37).

The Pastorals present a consistent view of μῦθοι. According to 1 Tim 1:4 μῦθοι καὶ γενεαλογίαι ἀπέραντοι, "*myths* and endless genealogies" (→ γενεαλογία), which certainly do not make up the whole of the "false teachings" (v. 3), nevertheless lead the community into idle speculation rather than insight into God's plan of salvation, which can be perceived only through faith (v. 4b; cf. ματαιολογία, νομοδιδάσκαλοι, vv. 6f.); likewise 4:7: βέβηλοι καὶ γραώδεις μῦθοι, "godless, old wives' *tales.*" In 2 Tim 4:4 οἱ μῦθοι is the opposite of ἀλήθεια (v. 4a); they come from false teaching, which was pleasant to hear and spread by teachers the group selected, over against the ὑγιαίνουσα διδασκαλία (v. 3); Titus 1:14 also places it in opposition to ἀλήθεια and speaks directly of Ἰουδαϊκοὶ μῦθοι καὶ ἐντολαὶ ἀνθρώπων (cf. also 3:9). According to 2 Pet 1:16, the "apostolic" message of the power and presence (both past and future) of Christ is based not on "clever *myths*" (οὐ γὰρ σεσοφισμένοις μύθοις ἐξακολουθήσαντες) but on an eyewitness account of his majesty (cf. Mark 9:2-8 par.).

The references to μῦθοι perhaps all point to cosmological, genealogical, and angelological speculations of a Hellenistic-Jewish Gnosticism, which is somewhat comparable to the so-called Colossian heresy (cf. Col 2:8-23) and which was found to be an increasing threat to the Church esp. in the postapostolic era. Also pointing in the direction of Gnosticism is information provided by Irenaeus (*Haer.* i.1) and Tertullian (*Praescr. Haer.* vii.33, et al.), while other Church fathers (Theodore of Mopsuestia, Theodoret, Augustine; see G. Stählin, *TDNT* IV, 783) prefer to view them as Jewish haggadah (cf. Ambrosiaster on 1 Tim 1:4: "fabulae, quas narrare consueti sunt Judaei de generatione suarum originum"). G. Stählin, *TDNT* IV, 762-95; *TWNT* X, 1181f. (bibliography); M. Dibelius and H. Conzelmann, *1-2 Tim, Titus* (Hermeneia) at 1 Tim 1:4 (bibliography); Spicq, *Notes* II, 576-81. H. Balz

μυκάομαι *mykaomai* roar (vb.)*

Rev 10:3, of the call of an angel: ὥσπερ λέων μυκᾶται, "*roared* like a lion" (cf. Hos 11:10; Amos 3:8).

μυκτηρίζω *myktērizō* mock, jeer*

Gal 6:7, in the pass.: θεὸς οὐ μυκτηρίζεται, "God *is not mocked*" (literal meaning: "turn up the nose"). H. Preisker, *TDNT* IV, 796; Spicq, *Notes* II, 582f.

μυλικός, 3 *mylikos* pertaining to a mill*

Luke 17:2; Mark 9:42 TR: λίθος μυλικός, millstone (the upper stone of a hand mill, with a hole in the middle; the image is used proverbially, cf. *b. Qidd.* 29b). Billerbeck I, 775-78; J. Rogge, *BHH* 1246f.

μύλινος, 3 *mylinos* pertaining to a mill*

Rev 18:21: λίθος ὡς μύλινος μέγας, "a stone as large as a *millstone*" (v.l. ὡς μύλος).

μύλος, ου, ὁ *mylos* mill; millstone*

This word is used for a *millstone* in Mark 9:42 par. Matt 18:6/Luke 17:2 TR: μύλος ὀνικός, "a *millstone* powered by a donkey," referring to the larger mills (worked by mules), in contrast to the hand mill. Ὀνικός could, as in Jewish texts, refer to the lower part of the mill (Billerbeck I, 775, 777) or, as in Greek texts, to the upper stone (BAGD 529). The image here is that of an especially heavy (bored) millstone. Matt 24:41: ἀλήθέω ἐν τῷ μύλῳ, "grind with a *mill*" (as the work of women; cf. also Billerbeck II, 966f.); Rev 18:22: φωνὴ μύλου, "[dull, grinding] sound of the [turning] *mill*," which was an everyday occurrence (cf. Jer 25:10); 18:21 v.l.; J. Rogge, *BHH* 1246f.; *BL* 1180; BDF §50.

μυλών, ῶνος, ὁ *mylōn* millhouse*

Matt 24:41 TR for → μύλος.

Μύρα, ων *Myra* Myra*

Μύρα is the name (neut. pl.) of a city (modern Dembre) on the southern coast of Lycia, situated on the Myros. It was an important grain harbor. According to Acts 27:5, Paul stopped in Μύρα on his journey to Rome, where he was put on a ship from Alexandria for the continuation of his voyage (v. 6; probably a grain ship). W. Bieder, *BHH* 1263; *BL* 1189; G. Neumann, *KP* III, 1518f.

μυριάς, άδος, ἡ *myrias* myriad, host; ten thousand*

Μυριάς appears 8 times in the NT: in the literal sense, Acts 19:19 (ἀργυρίου μυριάδες πέντε, "fifty thousand pieces of silver"); in the sense of *myriads/thousands/tens of thousands* (without further specification of the exact number), Luke 12:1; Acts 21:20; Heb 12:22 (μυριάδες ἀγγέλων); likewise Jude 14 (ἐν ἁγίαις μυριάσιν, cf. *1 Enoch* 1:9); Rev 5:11 (μυριάδες μυριάδων, *countless tens of thousands/myriads upon myriads,* along with χιλιάδες χιλιάδων, cf. *1 Enoch* 14:22; the partitive gen. is a Semitism [cf. Gen 24:60, but also Dan 7:10]; see BDF §164.1); 9:16 (δισμυριάδες μυριάδων, "two myriads *upon myriads,*" as the number of troops on horseback [TR δύο μυριάδες]).

μυρίζω *myrizō* anoint*

Mark 14:8: "she *has anointed* my body in preparation for burial"; → μύρον.

μύριοι, 3 *myrioi* ten thousand*

Matt 18:24: ὀφειλέτης μυρίων ταλάντων, "one who owed *ten thousand* talents."

μυρίος, 3 *myrios* innumerable, countless*

1 Cor 4:15: μυρίοι παιδαγωγοί, "*countless* guides"; 14:19: μυρίοι λόγοι, "*countless* words"; also possible is a translation in the sense of → μύριοι, "ten thousand."

μύρον, ου, τό *myron* ointment*

With the exception of Rev 18:13, this Semitic loan-word is found only in the Gospels, where it appears primarily in connection with the anointings of Jesus: Mark 14:3, 4, 5 par. Matt 26:7, 12; Luke 7:37, 38, 46; John 11:2; 12:3a, b, 5. Luke 23:56 reports that on Good Friday the women disciples who had accompanied Jesus from Galilee prepared μύρα as well as ἀρώματα (par. Mark 16:1) to anoint the body of Jesus. Rev 18:13 mentions μύρον along with other commodities. W. Michaelis, *TDNT* IV, 800f.

Μύρρα *Myrra* Myra

Acts 27:5 v.l., scribal error for → Μύρα.

Μυσία, ας *Mysia* Mysia*

Μυσία is the name of a province in northwest Asia Minor. Acts 16:7, 8 reports that Paul passed by or through Μυσία on his way to Troas on his "second missionary journey." W. P. Bowers, "Paul's Route through Mysia: A Note on Acts xvi.8," *JTS* 30 (1979) 507-11.

μυστήριον, ου, τό *mystērion* mystery, secret*

1. Secular Greek usage — a) Cultic — b) Metaphoric — 2. Judaism — a) LXX — b) Apocalyptic, Qumran — c)

Philo — d) Josephus — 3. NT — a) Gospels — b) Paul (1 Corinthians, Rom 11:25) — c) Colossians, Ephesians, Rom 16:25 — d) 1 Timothy — e) 2 Thessalonians — f) Revelation — g) Conclusion

Lit.: R. BAUMANN, *Mitte und Norm des Christlichen (1 Kor 1,1–3,4)* (NTAbh N.F. 5, 1968) 152f., 174-99, 215-18. — G. BORNKAMM, *TDNT* IV, 802-28. — R. E. BROWN, "The Semitic Background of the NT *mystêrion,*" *Bib* 39 (1958) 426-48; 40 (1959) 70-87. — C. CARAGOUNIS, *The Ephesian Mysterion* (CB.NT 8, 1977). — H. CONZELMANN, *1 Cor* (Hermeneia, 1975) 58-83, 290. — G. FINKENRATH, *DNTT* III, 501-6. — O. GIGON. *Die antike Kultur und das Christentum* (1966) 86-103. — J. GNILKA, *LTK* VII, 727-29. — idem, *Mark* (EKKNT, 1978) I, 162-72. — K. HAACKER, "Erwägungen zu Mc IV,11," *NovT* 14 (1972) 219-25. — JEREMIAS, *Parables* 11-19. — E. KÄSEMANN, *Rom* (Eng. tr., 1980) 308-10. — H. KRÄFT, *Rev* (HNT, 1974) 148f., 215. — H. KRÄMER, "Zur Wortbedeutung 'Mysteria,'" *WuD* 6 (1959) 121-25. — P. LAMPE, "Die markinische Deutung des Gleichnisses von Sämann, Mk 4,10-12," *ZNW* 65 (1974) 140-50. — A. LINDEMANN, *Die Aufhebung der Zeit* (SNT 12, 1975) 74-80, 91-95, 221-30. — E. LOHSE, *Col, Phlm* (Hermeneia, 1971) 73-75, 164-66. — D. LÜHRMANN, *Das Offenbarungsverständnis bei Paulus und in paulinischen Gemeinden* (WMANT 16, 1965) 98-140. — H. MERKLEIN, *Das kirchliche Amt nach dem Epheserbrief* (SANT 33, 1973) 202-4, 210-19. — W. F. OTTO, "The Meaning of the Eleusinian Mysteries," *The Mysteries* (Papers from the Eranos Yearbooks 2, 1955) 14-31. — H. SCHLIER, *Der Brief an die Epheser* ([2]1958) 59-66, 148-58, 262f. — E. VOGT, "'Mysteria' in textibus Qumrān," *Bib* 37 (1956) 247-57. — H. WEDER, *Die Gleichnisse Jesu als Metaphern* (FRLANT 120, 1978) 99-116. — For further bibliography see Baumann; Bornkamm; Lührmann; Weder; *TWNT* X, 1182-84.

1. a) Μυστήρια (in classical Greek used primarily in the pl.) is composed of the suffix -τηρια, denoting the place where an action occurs, plus the onomatopoeic verbal root μυ-, "make an inarticulate sound with closed lips; keep one's mouth shut." It refers to the content of the cultic ceremony, which is ineffable because it is inaccessible to discursive reason. The initiate does not participate in the sacred event on a rational-cognitive level (μαθεῖν) but rather is taken to a deeper level of experience (παθεῖν; Aristotle *Fr.* 15 [Rose]). The concept of the indissoluble bond between life and death can be inferred as the central content of the mysteries; life in the literal and the more abstract senses cries out from the depths of death (demonstrable as early as the 2nd cent. A.D. in Apuleius *Met.* xi.23.7). The mystery gods thus have aspects of both life and death, either divided between an older, originally life-bestowing fertility goddess and a younger, suffering deity (the Eleusis and Attis mysteries), or unified in a single deity (Dionysius); Isis, as goddess of power, also possesses both aspects. Since initiates are united with these divine beings in the celebration of the cult (e.g., in Eleusis through ἐποπτεία, "viewing"), they obtain for themselves personal salvation (σωτηρία) in the confidence that they will be kept safe in this life and the next through the protection of the god.

In distinction from the state cult, the mysteries focus on the individual, who voluntarily (in the Isis cult, after being called by the goddess) undergoes the initiation rites. Distinctions in social class and gender are subsequently of no account, but the distinction between the initiated and uninitiated becomes all the more important. This esoteric character of the mysteries necessitated the command of absolute silence regarding the content of the mystery. The common English translation "secret" reflects this aspect (μυστήριον = "that which is kept silent"), which is only part of the entire range of meaning of μυστήριον.

b) The metaphoric use of μυστήριον begins with Plato. On the one hand, the way of knowledge that leads to perceiving the truth of being is described as the path through the levels of Eleusinian initiation, which leads to ἐποπτεία (Smp. 209e-12a). On the other hand, the teaching of a fellow philosopher is somewhat sarcastically described as μυστήριον because its hidden truth (ἀλήθειαν ἀποκεκρυμμένην) has to be sought out (Tht. 155d-56a). Understanding a matter more deeply by talking about it is compared to a μυστήριον (Grg. 497c; Men. 76e). Through this metaphoric use, the connotation of μυστήριον came to mean something more casual and arbitrary until it became purely secular. While, e.g., the Gnome Menand Sententiae 784 (ὕπνος τὰ μικρὰ τοῦ θανάτου μυστήρια) still clearly refers to the Eleusinian mysteries and their predecessor in Agrai (W. Fauth, KP III, 1535), an expression from the imperial era, μυστήριόν σου μήποτ᾽ εἴπῃς τῷ φίλῳ, in Comparatio Menandri et Philistionis (ed. Jaekel, 1964) i.45 (cf. ii.89), refers only to a private secret that one should keep to oneself.

2. a) In the LXX, μυστήριον appears only in texts from the Hellenistic era. While in Wis 14:15, 23 it is a t.t. for pagan cultic acts, which are to be avoided, purely secular "secrets" that should be kept are intended in Jdt 2:2; Tob 12:7, 11 (political); Sir 22:22; 27:16f., 21 (private); and 2 Macc 13:21 (military). In contrast, the theologically understood μυστήρια in Wis 2:22; 6:22, which ultimately designate the creative activity of God, are not private matters but should be recognized and proclaimed by the godly. In Daniel, μυστήριον is the translation of the Persian loanword rāz. In 2:18f., 27, it indicates the content of the dream of Nebuchadnezzar, a veiled disclosure of the future events intended by God (2:28-30). Only God can divulge the hidden meaning (2:28, 47), and he does so to the one inspired by him (4:9 Theodotion). Here for the first time, μυστήριον is understood as eschatological secret.

b) In apocalyptic literature, the profound and innumerable mysteries of God (1 Enoch 63:3) are viewed as existing in heaven (106:9); they are the hidden, transcendent basis for all that is and occurs, esp. of that which will be revealed at the end of time (103:2f.; 38:3; 83:7). To certain men in OT history these mysteries were made known through rapture (52:1f.), dreams (4 Ezra 10:59), or visions (1 Enoch 13:8; 93:2); they require interpretation and should be imparted only to the wise among the people (4 Ezra 12:36-39; 14:5f., 45f.).

In the Qumran texts one generally finds rāz (mostly in the pl.), and occasionally sōd (usually sg.), with the sense of "mystery" (cf. 1QH 4:27f.). The marvelous mysteries of God (1QH 4:27f.; 1QpHab 7:8; 1QM 14:14, etc.), frequently qualified as mysteries of wisdom (1QH 9:23), of insight (13:13), of knowledge (1QS 4:6), of truth (9:18), etc., refer to the created order (3:15-25, including the mystery of the stars: 1QH 1:11, 13), the preservation of Israel in the community of Qumran (through the forgiveness of sins, CD 3:18f.; in its purification, 1QM 17:9; in its faithfulness to the covenant of God, 14:9f.), as well as the last days (see below).

Only God himself knows the full depth of his mysteries (1QS 11:18f.), which are hidden to human beings (11:6); but he has made known all the mysteries of the words of the prophets to

the "Teacher of Righteousness" (1QpHab 7:4f.), who must in turn teach them to the members of the community (1QS 9:17-21). Understanding of the mysteries is thus given to the godly (1QH 7:27; 11:10; 12:13) that they may become interpreters of this knowledge (2:13). They must be silent on this subject with those who are outside of the community (1QS 4:6; cf. 1QH 5:25). The plans and works of the power opposed to God (Belial) are also called "mysteries" (of hostility, 1QM 14:9; of sin, 1QH 5:36). That this opposition is given a limited power is among the mysteries of God (1QS 3:21-25), as is its ultimate overthrow and destruction on the last day (1QS 4:18; 1QM 3:9; 16:11).

c) In 9 of 14 instances, Philo uses μυστήριον metaphorically for the "mysteries" of God (θεοῦ μυστήρια, All. iii.3; τοῦ κυρίου μυστήρια, iii.71), which primarily have as their content his authorship of the universe and his effective power and virtues. God considers the souls of the godly worthy of the knowledge of these μυστήρια (iii.27). In addition to this mediate knowledge of God through his works, the higher level of the immediate vision of God is, under Platonic influence, "initiation into the great mysteries" (iii.100f.), which nevertheless can be only partially achieved as a gift of grace. It has as its biblical model the calling of Moses on the mountain of God (iii.100f.); as a result, Moses becomes a mystagogue (Cher. 49).

d) Josephus uses μυστήριον 7 times, 6 of which are in the cultic sense. In B.J. i.470 he refers metaphorically to the life of the scheming Antipatros as κακίας μυστήριον, "an unspeakable, hidden [and therefore ritual] consummation of evil."

3. In the 28 NT passages in which μυστήριον is found it has neither a cultic nor a purely secular meaning. In order to understand the term properly, the full range of meanings that developed up to the time of the NT must be taken into account. From the Greek concept of μυστήριον comes a strictly esoteric sense of an experience that is inaccessible to human reason, as well as the theme of life from death. Out of the Jewish tradition comes a less stringently esoteric and the transcendent, humanly inaccessible mystery of God, which is historically set in action by God himself in his acts of salvation and judgment in the past, present, and future, which already now has been made evident to the one who is called and will be made evident to all on the last day. In terms of content, μυστήριον refers primarily to the saving acts of God in Christ.

a) In the Gospels μυστήριον is found only in Mark 4:11 par. in the expression "the mystery of the kingdom of God" (→ βασιλεία 3.b). The saying uses μυστήριον to describe the experience of the breaking in of God's rule in the words and works of Jesus. It is basically still hidden, to be revealed in all its glory only in the end times, but is made accessible (pass. δέδοται) already now to Jesus' disciples and can be experienced and comprehended by them in faith, while to those who stand on the outside it remains a puzzle (→ παραβολή) and therefore hidden. This difficult logion came to stand between the parable and its interpretation, since one finds the same distinction expressed in the parable and in the logion between belief and unbelief with respect to the word of Jesus. The parallels in Matt 13:11 and Luke 8:10 (γνῶναι τὰ μυστήρια for τὸ μυστήριον) focus not so much on the fact of the breaking in (sg. μυστήριον) as they do on the presence of the kingdom of God in the comprehensive sense, the proclamation of which is understood by the disciples/the Church (cf. also συνίημι, found 6 times in Matt 13).

b) In 1 Cor 2:1 Paul designates his proclamation of the crucified Christ (1:23; 2:2) the μυστήριον τοῦ θεοῦ (the v.l. μαρτύριον derives from 1:6). This saving event is inaccessible to human reason because it appears to the reason to be foolishness (1:23-31); furthermore, since the one who was crucified is also the one who rose, the Greek idea of life from death may have influenced Paul's choice of μυστήριον. In 4:1 Paul has in mind the content of this proclamation of Christ when he refers to himself as the servant of Christ, i.e. (epexegetical καί), one entrusted (cf. 9:17f.) with the *mysteries* of God. In 2:7, the placement of ἐν μυστηρίῳ between σοφίαν and the attributive partc. τὴν ἀποκεκρυμμένην clearly indicates that the prep. is attributive to σοφίαν and therefore defines σοφία as a power: "the hidden wisdom of God, which is working itself out in a *mystery*" (i.e., is being realized in history). Also here the κύριος τῆς δόξης (2:8) is included in the reference of μυστήριον. At the same time this μυστήριον of the wisdom of God is apocalyptically described as an element of salvation, hidden by God in heaven before the ages, kept ready for our (eschatological) glory, and now revealed through his Spirit (2:7, 10). We have here the full scope of God's revelatory plan (→ 3.c).

In 14:2 the μυστήρια are *mysteries* (sc. of God) that are expressed through ecstatic speaking in tongues that are humanly incomprehensible; in the interest of the edification of the church, they must be translated into a language understandable to all. In 13:2, the knowledge of all μυστήρια refers in the widest sense to the spiritual gift of prophecy. In 15:51f., Paul uses μυστήριον in connection with the death/life theme (cf. 15:36) for the content of a statement about the transformation (→ ἀλλάσσω 2) of Christians who are still living at the time of the parousia.

In Rom 11:25f., μυστήριον (cf. also the adj. "impenetrable, indiscernible" in v. 33) refers to God's saving activity toward Israel: the traditional apocalyptic expectation of the restoration of Israel is altered in that the partial hardening of Israel creates room for the conversion of the Gentiles. All Israel will be saved at the parousia, after the acceptance of the Gentiles.

c) In Colossians, Ephesians, and Rom. 16:25f., the fully developed plan of revelation, which was once hidden but now has been revealed, is made known in the distinction between the two ages (→ αἰών 4-6). In Col 1:26 τὸ μυστήριον stands in the context of the whole saving activity of God directed toward the entire world, "hidden for eons and generations" as the plan of salvation, but now revealed to Christians (τοῖς ἁγίοις) and realized through their proclamation of Christ among the nations (Gentiles). The μυστήριον is therefore the Christ proclaimed among the nations (ἐν ὑμῖν = ἐν τοῖς ἔθνεσιν, 1:27; cf. 2 Cor 1:19), which is the ground and content of the present hope that the glory that is being revealed will be perfected (3:4). The *mystery* of Christ in 2:2 and 4:3 should also be understood in this way.

In Ephesians, μυστήριον lacks the eschatological element: it refers to that which God has already accomplished, therefore to a present reality. The plan of revelation has in view less the temporal succession of two ages than the distinction between cosmic realms that correspond to the knowledge or ignorance of the μυστήριον. In 1:9 the μυστήριον is the realization of God's creative and saving will on a cosmic scale in the bringing together (→ ἀνακεφαλαιόω 3) of all things in Christ, which is then elaborated in ch. 3. In 3:3f. the insight, granted by God, into the *mystery* of Christ (ἐν = Heb. *bᵉ*; cf. 1QH 2:13; 12:13), as in Col 1:26f., refers to the incorporation of Gentiles into the body of Christ, the Church (Eph 3:6). This μυστήριον has been revealed in the Spirit (3:5) to the apostles and the (Christian) prophets (a further narrowing of τοῖς ἁγίοις in Col 1:26), given for proclamation (Eph 3:8), and is made known (vv. 9f.) through the Church (as cosmic entity) to the cosmic powers and authorities (→ ἀρχή 3.c; ἐξουσία 2.d) as the saving plan of the wisdom of God. In 6:19 the "μυστήριον of the gospel" also refers in succinct but comprehensive fashion to the proclamation of the *mystery* of Christ (as the borrowing of παρρησία from 3:12 also shows). In 5:32 μυστήριον means the deeper, not immediately evident meaning of Gen 2:24, quoted in this passage. The author explains the *mystery* ecclesiologically, referring to the bond between Christ and the Church.

The secondary closing doxology of Rom 16:25-27 (2nd cent.) stands in the same tradition as Colossians and Ephesians. The revelation of the μυστήριον develops over time: it was "kept silent" (an intensification of "hidden"), and its revelation to all nations is carried out "by means of prophetic [sc. early Christian] writings" (cf. Lührmann 123).

d) In 1 Timothy, the formal, somewhat ceremonial use of μυστήριον should be understood in the sense of "ineffable ultimate ground (root, basis)" of a particular mode of conduct. In 3:9 the phrase "hold on to the μυστήριον of the faith" (sc. τῆς ἐν Χριστῷ Ἰησοῦ; cf. 3:13) actually refers to the teaching that has been handed down (cf. the "sound teaching" in 1:10)—in general, therefore, orthodoxy. In 3:16f. the "μυστήριον of a holy life" (W. Foerster, *TDNT* VII, 182) is the Christ-event, as it is described in the following hymn (part of the tradition available to the author) from the cosmic perspective of the incarnation and exaltation and its proclamation.

e) In 2 Thess 2:7 the present work of the antichrist ("man of lawlessness," 2:3) is referred to as μυστήριον τῆς ἀνομίας (→ ἀνομία 5). The expression has a verbal parallel in Josephus *B.J.* i.470 (→ 2.d) and a verbal and conceptual parallel in 1QM 14:9; 1QH 5:36 (→ 2.b). In the apocalyptic view, the antichrist who is now still working in secret, being allowed to do so by God (2:11), will be permitted to appear openly (ἀποκαλυφθήσεται, 2:8) before the parousia and then will be destroyed by Christ.

f) Rev 10:7 speaks of the eschatological realization of the "μυστήριον of God" (the subjunc. with ἄν in a subordinate clause renders the aor. ἐτελέσθη a fut.); God has announced it to the (early Christian) prophets (cf. Amos 3:7, although εὐαγγελίζω replaces ἀποκαλύπτω). Lying behind the content (the sealing of the scroll and the oath of the angel in 10:4-6) is Dan 12:1-7, with the result that the μυστήριον can be related to the resurrection of the dead (Kraft 149). In 1:20, μυστήριον refers to the hidden meaning of the seven stars and seven lamps, which are immediately identified as the seven angels of the churches and the churches themselves. In 17:5, "Babylon" is a name for Rome. The "μυστήριον of the woman and the beast" in 17:7 is not so much a veiled reference to Rome (17:9, 18) as it is a reference to the eschatological event alluded to in 17:8, in which it is said that the beast (in direct contrast to what is predicated of God in 1:4, 8) "once was, now is not, and is coming again."

g) Fundamental to the use of μυστήριον in the NT is the basic meaning of the Greek word: "that which is unspeakable," i.e., inaccessible to natural reason (but accessible to faith). As a result, the term is ambiguous; assertions regarding its specific content must be made on the basis of the respective context. The conceptual tradition of Jewish apocalyptic (the hidden and then revealed *mystery*) plays a prominent role here. The Greek elements that the word bears also must be considered, for they are retained even when the word is a translation for Hebrew terms.

H. Krämer

Μυτιλήνη *Mytilēnē* Mitylene

An older form of → Μιτυλήνη. BDF §42.3.

μυωπάζω *myōpazō* be nearsighted*

2 Pet 1:9, in a fig. sense: "One is blind (sees nothing) *because one is nearsighted* (μυωπάζων)."

μώλωψ, ωπος, ὁ *mōlōps* wound, welt*

1 Pet 2:24: *"by his wounds you have been healed"* (Isa 53:5 LXX). C. Schneider, *TDNT* IV, 829.

μωμάομαι *mōmaomai* mock, deride, blaspheme*

2 Cor 8:20: "lest anyone *mock* us"; 6:3, in pass. sense: "lest the ministry *be mocked.*"

μῶμος, ου, ὁ *mōmos* defect, blemish*

In 2 Pet 2:13 false teachers are referred to as σπίλοι καὶ μῶμοι ("blots and *blemishes*"). F. Hauck, *TDNT* IV, 829-31.

μωραίνω *mōrainō* make foolish, show to be a fool; pass.: become tasteless
→ μωρία.

μωρία, ας, ἡ *mōria* stupidity, foolishness*
μωραίνω *mōrainō* make foolish, show to be a fool; pass.: become tasteless*
μωρός, 3 *mōros* stupid, foolish; subst.: fool, foolishness*

1. Occurrences in the NT — 2. Meaning — 3. Usage in Matthew — 4. Usage in Paul

Lit.: R. BAUMANN, *Mitte und Norm des Christlichen (1 Kor 1,1–3,4)* (NTAbh N.F. 5, 1968). — G. BERTRAM, *TDNT* IV, 832-47. — W. D. DAVIES, *The Setting of the Sermon on the Mount* (1964) 235-39. — J. GOETZMANN, *DNTT* III, 1023-26. — M. HENGEL, *Crucifixion: In the Ancient World and the Folly of the Message of the Cross* (1977). — A. KRETZER, *Die Herrschaft der Himmel und die Söhne des Reiches* (1971) 113-15, 191-206. — I. MAISCH, "Das Gleichnis von den klugen und törichten Jungfrauen," *BibLeb* 11 (1970) 247-59. — U. WILCKENS, *Weisheit und Torheit (1 Kor 1/2)* (BHT 26, 1959). — For further bibliography, in addition to the commentaries, see the bibliographies under synonyms and antonyms such as → ἀφροσύνη, → νήπιος, → σοφία.

1. In contrast to the preference for ἀφρ- in the LXX, in the NT μωρ- predominates. The vb. is found 4 times (of which 2 times in Paul, both, following the example of the LXX, used transitively), the subst. 5 times (only in 1 Cor 1–3). The adj. appears 12 times (in some cases substantivized): in 1 Corinthians 1–4 (4 times), Matthew (6 times), and the Pastorals (2 times). We also have → μωρολογία in Eph 5:4.

2. In the Bible the basic concept of a thing or person that is deficient has a religious nuance. The secular meaning, which was adopted by wisdom literature, can no longer be discerned in Matthew and Paul. The use of the term in Eph 5:4 (which rejects "foolish gossip"; on its correlation with αἰσχρότης and εὐτραπελία, cf. 1QS 10:21-23), as well as in 2 Tim 2:23 (with ἀπαίδευτοι) and in Titus 3:9 (the warning to keep away from foolish controversies with heretics, i.e., controversies that amount to nothing), makes the "Christian" understanding unambiguous.

The same applies to the use of the vb. in the salt metaphor, where it represents a natural reduction in value (derived from Q) found in Matt 5:13 par. Luke 14:34f. The loss of flavor by salt (corresponding to "becoming saltless" in the parallel saying in Mark 9:50) is probably meant to be an absurdity (cf. *b. Bek.* 8b). Some, however, make reference either to salt blocks used in baking, which were always discarded as worthless after some fifteen years of use, or (if we are dealing here with salt as a spice) to the inedible contamination of the salts mined in the land of Palestine (Jeremias, *Parables* 125f.). The distinction between Q (μωρανθῇ) and Mark (ἄναλον γένηται) results from a difference in translation (J. Lightfoot, *A Commentary on the NT from the Talmud and Hebraica* [1859 ed.] II, 426). Yet, this reconstruction remains as hypothetical as the interpretation that views the clearly subordinate clause as "a kind of parable of the kingdom" spoken by Jesus, the point being the impossibility of the loss of potency (Bertram 838f.). In light of the preceding context, in any case, it is unambiguously applied to discipleship and its risks, which Luke makes concrete in terms of the Christian's relation to possessions (14:33).

3. In Matthew 5:13, as an introduction to the instructions of the Sermon on the Mount, a warning to the disciples against *becoming fools* is added to the admonition expressed in the closing double parable to be like the ἀνὴρ φρόνιμος (and not like the fool: v. 26), i.e., to hear and do the words of Jesus (7:24-27). To this usage corresponds the message of the highly allegorical parable in 25:1-13, which is oriented to the parousia. The constant readiness of the five virgins, which Matthew characterizes as "vigilance," stands in contrast to the others, who were foolish (μωραί, vv. 2f., 8), which is manifest in their failure to acquire the "oil" of good deeds; the punishment that threatens this foolishness at the judgment is exclusion from the eschatological banquet.

The same "crisis" is present in another form in the warning against verbal outbursts of anger in 5:22b, in connection with the first "antithesis." The sharp distinction commonly made between Aram. ῥακά ("empty head"; cf. κενέ in Jas 2:20) and μωρέ (godless "fool" in the sense of Ps 14:1 etc.) places too much weight on these apparently popular curse words; moreover, it would run against the intention of Matt 5:22a. Rather, both these examples of Jesus should be interpreted as warnings against anger—analogous to Jewish parallels such as 1QS 6:24-7:18 or *b. B. Meṣ.* 58b (cf. also Matt 12:36). As a result, one can easily recognize the tension created when the invective against the scribes and Pharisees as μωροὶ καὶ τυφλοί is attributed to Jesus (23:17). It arises from the early Christian polemic against the leaders of Israel, who were considered *not* σοφοὶ καὶ συνετοί (cf. 11:25).

4. In Paul the word group is also applied to a conflict situation—in this case among Christians. In 1 Corinthians 1-4 Paul attacks the factions in Corinth by placing the message of the cross against the background of divine wisdom as the measure and judgment of human wisdom and folly. "Normal" human wisdom is thus now made foolish by God and so is judged (this idea, which is picked up in Rom 1:22 from 1 Cor 1:20b [cf. on this esp. Isa 44:25; Jer 10:14], is elaborated in Rom 1:18-3:31). Because of the current view of the practice of crucifixion, the non-Christian considered the foolishness of the "word of the cross" (1 Cor 1:18), and therefore of the Pauline kerygma (vv. 21, 23), completely obvious (cf. Hengel). Since, however, its content—the crucified Christ—represents the power and wisdom of God, its contradiction by self-proclaimed human wisdom was inconsequential (v. 25). The subst. use of the adj. (τὸ μωρόν) in the bold paradox of the *"foolishness* [and weakness] of God" is here preferred to the subst. not only for the sake of variation but also with a view toward the parallel in v. 27, where the paradox is applied to the structure of the Corinthian church. There Paul, out of consideration for those he is addressing (*contra* Wilckens 41), uses the neut. pl. (τὰ μωρά replacing the masc.).

The word of the cross in 2:14, characterized as revelation of the Spirit of God (Baumann 254), exposes and condemns as foolishness not only the wisdom of the world in general but also the factions that lead to human boasting among the Corinthian Christians in particular, as 3:19 emphasizes. This sentence is the basis of the preceding admonition (v. 18) to make themselves fools for the sake of the gospel by actually renouncing the wisdom of the world, thus making themselves wise before God. Finally, Paul also suggests that the Corinthian Christians renounce factions when he describes for them (the "wise in Christ"—the echo of 1:26ff., clearly recognizable though adapted, lends a certain degree of irony) all the heralds of the faith named by the various factions as "fools for Christ's sake" (4:10), thus calling the disputing parties to their senses.

P. Fiedler

μωρολογία, ας, ἡ *mōrologia* foolish gossip*

In Eph 5:4, along with αἰσχρότης and εὐτραπελία. G. Bertram, *TDNT* IV, 844f.; → μωρία 1, 2.

μωρός, 3 *mōros* stupid, foolish; subst.: fool, foolishness
→ μωρία.

Μωϋσῆς, έως *Mōysēs* Moses

1. Occurrences in the NT — 2. Moses the lawgiver — 3. Moses the prophet — 4. Moses as type — 5. Moses

criticized — 6. Legendary accounts — 7. Theological significance

Lit.: E. AUERBACH, Moses (1953). — A. BENTZEN, Messias, Moses redivivus, Menschensohn (ATANT 17, 1948). — E. BOCK, Mose und sein Zeitalter (1961). — M. BUBER, Moses (Eng. tr., 1947). — H. CAZELLES et al., Moïse, l'homme de l'alliance (1955 = Mose in Schrift und Überlieferung [1963]). — D. DAICHES, Moses, Man in the Wilderness (1975). — S. FREUD, Moses and Monotheism (1939). — J. G. GAGER, Moses in Greco-Roman Paganism (SBLMS 16, 1972). — E. GILLABERT, Moïse et le phénomène judéo-chrétien (1976). — E. GRÄSSER, "Mose und Jesus. Zur Auslegung von Hebr 3:1-6," ZNW 75 (1984) 2-23. — HAHN, Titles 372-88. — S. HERRMANN, A History of Israel in OT Times (1981) 56-85. — idem, Israels Aufenthalt in Ägypten (SBS 40, 1970). — idem, "Mose," EvT 28 (1968) 301-28. — J. JEREMIAS, TDNT IV, 848-73. — K. KOCH, "Der Tod des Religionsstifters," KD 8 (1962) 100-123. — W. A. MEEKS, "Moses in the NT," IDBSup 605-7. — idem, The Prophet-King: Moses Traditions and the Johannine Christology (NovTSup 14, 1967). — E. OSSWALD, Das Bild des Mose in der kritischen alttestamentlichen Wissenschaft seit J. Wellhausen (Theologische Arbeiten 18, 1962). — T. SAITO, Die Mosevorstellungen im NT (EHS 23/100, 1977). — H. SEEBASS and C. BROWN, DNTT II, 635-43. — R. SMEND, Das Mosebild von H. Ewald bis M. Noth (1959). — H. ULONSKA, "Die Doxa des Moses," EvT 26 (1966) 378-88. — For further bibliography see Cazelles (BL); TWNT X, 1184f.

1. Moses is mentioned 80 times in the NT (vs. Elijah 40 times, David 59). This figure itself demonstrates that early Christianity viewed Moses as an integral part of its history—indeed, as the predominant figure in the history of God with the people of Israel. This was the tradition received from Judaism. "Moses is for later Judaism the most important figure in salvation history thus far" (Jeremias 854). The same is true also for Jesus and the authors of the NT scriptures. While in the OT Moses was the immediate recipient of the teaching of God, the Torah, in the NT the giving of the law is often depicted as having been mediated through angels (Gal 3:19: "put into effect by angels, through the hand of a mediator"). Nevertheless, Moses is the one who speaks with God. According to John 9:28f. the Jews say, "We are Moses' disciples. We know that God spoke with Moses, but as for this fellow [Jesus], we do not even know where he comes from." This is based on Exod 33:11: "The Lord spoke with Moses face to face, as a man speaks with his friend." Paul quotes Exod 33:19 with the formula, "For he said to Moses" (Rom 9:15).

2. Moses functions in many passages as a lawgiver who mediated the definitive word of God, including the ceremonial law, and brought it to mankind. Thus Jesus commands the healed leper, "Bring the gift that Moses commanded to them as a testimony" (Mark 1:44 par. Matt 8:4/Luke 5:14). Without any hesitation whatsoever, the ceremonial law ascribed to Moses remains valid: "when the days of their purification according to the law of Moses were completed (κατὰ τὸν νόμον Μωϋσέως)" (Luke 2:22). In the question about divorce, appeal is made to the permission granted by Moses in Deut 24:1, which Jesus clarifies by adding, "Moses permitted you to divorce because of the hardness of your heart" (Mark 10:3f. par. Matt 19:7). In the question regarding the resurrection the Sadducees cite the command concerning the levirate ("Moses has written," Mark 12:19 par. Matt 22:24/Luke 20:28; cf. Deut 25:5-10). Jesus replied with another saying of Moses: "Have you not read in the book of Moses at the burning bush how God said to him . . . ?" (Mark 12:26 par. Luke 20:37; contrast Matt 22:31). The closing sentence, "God is not a God of the dead but of the living" (Mark 12:27 par.), does not appear in "the book of Moses." According to Matt 23:2f. Jesus says, "The scribes and Pharisees sit on the seat of Moses; do all that they tell you and keep it (τηρεῖτε); but do not do what they do." The word of Moses and the word of God are considered one and the same in Mark 7:10 ("for Moses said, 'Honor your father and mother' ") and Matt 15:4 ("for God said"); thus also Mark 12:26; cf. Matt 22:31.

According to John, Jesus asks the Jews: "Did Moses not give you the law? Yet none of you does the law" (7:19); cf. 7:22a: "Therefore Moses gave you circumcision," and the added correction of the Gospel writer in v. 22b: "Not that it is from Moses, but from the patriarchs." In the late addition of the account of the woman taken in adultery it is said, "In the law Moses forbade us . . ." (8:5). It is succinctly stated in the prologue that "the law was given through Moses, grace and truth through Jesus Christ" (1:17).

As in the prologue of John, Moses and faith in Christ are also set over against one another in Paul: "For Moses writes concerning the righteousness from the law that anyone who does these things will live by them; but the righteousness from faith says . . ." (Rom 10:5f.). Moses is the lawgiver: "Death reigned from Adam to Moses" (Rom 5:14). The author of Hebrews, in saying, "without the shedding of blood, there is no forgiveness" (9:22b), points to Moses: "For, after the command was spoken according to the law given by Moses, he took the blood of calves and goats . . ." (9:19).

This Moses is living and is currently present; he "has had since ancient times those who preach in every city, because he is read in the synagogues every sabbath" (Acts 15:21). In Stephen's speech, the entire history of Moses from his birth on, with all its miracles, is reviewed up to the appearance in the burning bush, and it closes with the assertion that this man was not recognized by his people, although God had sent him to them as leader and redeemer (ἄρχοντα καὶ λυτρωτήν; see Acts 7:20-44, where Moses occurs 9 times). In entirely the same way, the author of Hebrews views Moses as an important witness to faith (11:23f.; 12:21); 10:28 also deals with the law of *Moses,* as does 8:5. Finally, salvation can also be found through the lawgiver: "They have *Moses* and the prophets; let them hear them" (Luke 16:29).

3. At the beginning of the work of Jesus, John records that Philip says to Nathanael, "We have found the one concerning whom *Moses* wrote in the law and the prophets, Jesus, the son of Joseph of Nazareth" (1:45). The risen Jesus chides the two disciples on the way to Emmaus for their slowness of heart, and then "he began to explain, from *Moses* and all the prophets on, what was said concerning him in all the scriptures" (Luke 24:27); cf. further v. 44: "Everything must be fulfilled that was written about me in the law of *Moses* and the prophets and the Psalms." Luke has Paul say something similar in his speech before Agrippa II (Acts 26:22f.); cf. also his proclamation in Rome (28:23). In Heb 7:14 an argument is made from silence: *Moses* said nothing about priests from the tribe of Judah, from which Jesus came.

4. Acts 3:22 views Moses as a type, quoting Deut 18:15: "*Moses* said, 'The Lord your God will raise up for you a prophet like me from among your people; you shall listen to everything he tells you' " (thus also 7:37). According to Hahn (373f.) the speech of Stephen (→ 2) offers a Moses typology with Deut 18:15 as its central point. Moses is, moreover, both example and type: "If you believed *Moses,* you would also believe me" (John 5:46). The raising up of the serpent in the desert becomes a type of the raising up of the Son of Man (3:14). Paul creates a sacramental metaphor: "All were baptized into *Moses* in the cloud and the sea" (1 Cor 10:2). The faithfulness of the apostles and Jesus the high priest is compared with that of "*Moses* in his whole house" (Heb 3:2f.). Christ is placed higher than Moses, however, since he is the son, while Moses was but a servant (θεράπων, 3:5). Also in the transfiguration account, *Moses* and Elijah are to be seen as types, with whom Jesus enters into conversation (Mark 9:4f. par. Matt 17:3f./Luke 9:30, 33).

5. A certain distancing from Moses is present in the comparisons made in John 6:32f. and 7:22f., as it is when Paul speaks disparagingly about "the veil over the face of *Moses*" and "the veil over their hearts" (2 Cor 3:13-15). Opposition to Moses is prominent among the accusations raised against Stephen: "We have heard him speak blasphemous words against *Moses* and against God" (Acts 6:11; cf. v. 14). The accusation was also raised

against Paul that he taught people to turn away from Moses and was against circumcision (21:21). Paul articulated his basic disposition toward the law in Romans (cf. 2:20; 3:25; 7:12; 10:4). Acts echoes Pauline theology in having Paul say that the forgiveness of sins comes through Jesus: "Even for everything for which you were not able to be justified by the law of *Moses,* there is justification through Jesus for everyone who believes" (13:38f.). Galatians and Acts testify to the sharpness of the contrast made between the law and circumcision.

6. As in Josephus *Ant.* ii.201–iv.331 and Philo *Vit. Mos.,* legendary accretions surrounding the figure of Moses are also present in the NT. In John 5:45 Moses is called the accuser. Jude 9 mentions that the archangel Michael disputed with the devil over the body of Moses (H. Windisch and H. Preisker, *Jude* [HNT] ad loc.; → Μιχαήλ). Jannes and Jambres play a legendary role as opponents of Moses in 2 Tim 3:8 (Billerbeck III, 660). When those who gained the victory over "the beast" sing "the song of *Moses,* the servant of God" (Rev 15:3), the reference is not to the song of Exod 15:1.

7. Although the figure of Moses is reflected in the NT in rich and variegated measure, something is at the same time assumed that does not come to direct expression in the NT. Since for Moses, "the God of the patriarchs"— the God of Abraham, Isaac, and Jacob—was identical with Yahweh, who was active in the history of the people, history was assumed to be divine history. "It is the God of Israel who appeared to the patriarchs, and who would also now guarantee the Exodus event. Whatever the name of this God might be, he is the one who is active in the past and the present" (Herrmann, *Aufenthalt* 78). Even when the eschatological moment played a definite role in the NT, it cannot be denied that the history signaled by Moses was assumed by Jesus and the early Christian community. With John the Baptist, Jesus has become the turning point in history, which is directed to all peoples (Matt 28:19) and therefore has become the history of the people of God, as it is theologically articulated by Paul in Romans 9–11. The "song of *Moses,* the servant of God" and the "song of the lamb" are identical: "Great and marvelous are your deeds, Lord God Almighty; just and true are your ways, King of the nations. Who will not fear you, O Lord, and praise your name? For you alone are holy, so that all the nations will come and worship you; for your righteous acts have been revealed" (Rev 15:3f.). Thus the history of *Moses* is embraced and receives a universal character. G. Fitzer

N ν

Ναασσών *Naassōn* Nahshon*

Indeclinable personal name in Matt 1:4a, b; Luke 3:32 (cf. Ruth 4:20 LXX).

Ναγγαί *Naggai* Naggai*

Indeclinable personal name in Luke 3:25.

Ναζαρά *Nazara* Nazareth

Alternate form of the place name → Ναζαρέτ. According to *NTG*[26] and *UBSGNT*, Ναζαρά appears in Matt 4:13 and Luke 4:16.

Ναζαρέθ *Nazareth* Nazareth

Orthographic variant of → Ναζαρέτ. *NTG*[26] and *UBSGNT* have the form ending in -θ in Matt 21:11; Luke 1:26; 2:4, 39, 51; Acts 10:38.

Ναζαρέτ (Ναζαρά, Ναζαρέθ) *Nazaret (-a, -eth)* Nazareth*

1. Occurrences — 2. Forms and etymology — 3. Historical and geographic considerations — 4. Nazareth in the NT

Lit.: ABEL. *Géographie* II, 395. — W. F. ALBRIGHT, "The Names 'Nazareth' and 'Nazoraean,'" *JBL* 65 (1946) 397-401. — A. ALT, "Die Stätten des Wirkens Jesu in Galiläa," *idem, Kleine Schriften zur Geschichte des Volkes Israel* II (1953) 441-45. — B. BAGATTI, *DBSup* VI, 318-33. — *idem, EAEHL* III, 919-22. — D. BALDI, *Enchiridion locorum sanctorum* ([2]1955) 1-42. — J. BLINZLER, "Die Heimat Jesu. Zu einer neuen Hypothese," *BK* 25 (1970) 14-20. — G. DALMAN, *Orte und Wege Jesu* (BFCT II/1, 1924) 61-88. — J. FINEGAN, *The Archeology of the NT* (1969) 27-33. — H. GUTHE, *Palästina* (Monographien zur Erdkunde 21, [2]1927) 149ff. — *idem, RE* XIII, 676-79. — C. KOPP, *LTK* VII, 851-53. — *idem, Places* 49-86. — E. LOHSE, *RGG* IV, 1388. — D. C. PELLETT, *IDB* III, 524-26. — H. P. RÜGER. "ΝΑΖΑΡΕΘ / ΝΑΖΑΡΑ ΝΑΖΑΡΗΝΟΣ/ΝΑΖΩ-ΡΑΙΟΣ," *ZNW* 72 (1981) 257-63. — E. W. SAUNDERS, *BHH* 1291f. — B. SCHALLER, *KP* IV, 27. — W. SCHMAUCH, *Orte der Offenbarung und der Offenbarungsort im NT* (1956) 20-26. —

E. TESTA, *Nazaret giudeo-cristiana* (1969). — P. WINTER, " 'Nazareth' and 'Jerusalem' in Luke chs. I and II," *NTS* 3 (1956/57) 136-42. — For further bibliography → Ναζαρηνός; see Bagatti *(DBSup);* Dalman; Guthe *(RE);* B. M. Metzger, *Index to Periodical Literature on Christ and the Gospels* (NTTS 6, 1966) 198; commentaries, esp. at Matt 2:23; Mark 1:9; Luke 4:16.

1. Before the 3rd cent. A.D. the indeclinable place name Ναζαρέτ is attested only in the NT, where, with the exception of Acts 10:38, it appears only in the Gospels: Mark once (1:9); Matthew 3 times (2:23; 4:13 [Ναζαρά]; 21:11); Luke 5 times (1:26 [omitted in D]; 2:4, 39, 51; 4:16 [Ναζαρά]); John 2 times (1:45, 46). Thematic points of concentration are the infancy narratives of Matthew and Luke (5 times) and the accounts of the beginning of Jesus' activity (5 times).

2. The form is extremely inconsistent and varies—often in one and the same passage—between the spelling Ναζαρέτ (e.g., Luke 1:26 [א B]) and Ναζαρέθ (e.g., Matt 21:11 [א B C D]), infrequently also Ναζαρέδ (Luke 4:16 D). In addition we have the form Ναζαρά, an Aramaic variant (cf. G. Dalman, *Grammatik des jüdisch-palästinischen Aramäisch* [[2]1905] 152) that is not fully Grecized (*contra* A. Schlatter, *Matt* [[6]1963] 113). With *NTG*[26] and *UBSGNT*, Ναζαρά is to be preferred in two passages to the variants Ναζαρέθ/τ/δ as the lectio difficilior: Matt 4:13 (v.l. -εθ א* [C] D Θ pm lat/ -ετ L al) and Luke 4:16 (v.l. -εδ D).

The forms of the place name Nazareth that are passed on in the Greek NT, like its Arabic equivalent *en nāṣira*, permit the reconstruction of a geographic reference (Aram. *nāṣᵉrā/nāṣᵉraṯ* [cf. *Onomasticon* 285]; the vocalization of the corresponding Heb. form is contested: *nᵉṣeret* [F. Delitzsch, *NT Hebraice* (1877 [= 1960)])] or *nōṣeret* [Dalman, *Grammatik* 152]). The form is based on the root *nṣr* ("protect, guard"). The name refers to its exposed position above the Plain of Jezreel, perhaps also to a military function (as a border outpost?).

3. In view of the traditional character of Palestinian place names (of the 219 Galilean villages mentioned by Josephus [*Vita* 235], only a portion are known by name; cf. C. Möller and G. Schmitt, *Siedlungen Palästinas nach Flavius Josephus* [Beihefte zum Tübinger Atlas des vorderen Orients B 14, 1976]), the lack of attestation in non-Christian literature is not of particular importance. Ναζαρέτ is cited in both literature (Eusebius *HE* i.7.6-12) and inscriptions (*IEJ* 12 [1962] 137ff.), and archaeo-

logical discoveries have confirmed a continuous habitation of the site since *ca.* 900 B.C. The ancient settlement, which was situated somewhat above the current site (343 m. above sea level), is completely insignificant, lacking even all the characteristics of an ancient Palestinian city. (The NT, however, always designates Nazareth as a → πόλις [Matt 2:23; Luke 1:26; 2:4, 39; see Alt 441-45].)

4. a) Nazareth appears in the NT only in connection with Jesus and his family. It refers, by means of an apposition (ὁ ἀπὸ Ναζαρέθ, "the [one] from *Nazareth*"), to Jesus' hometown (Matt 21:11; John 1:45; Acts 10:38), thereby and in accordance with ancient custom making more precise his identity; also it gives the destination (Matt 2:23; Luke 2:29, 51; 4:16) or the point of departure (Matt 4:13; Mark 1:9; Luke 2:4; John 1:46) of Jesus or his parents.

While for Luke the family of Jesus comes from Nazareth and his birth in Bethlehem results from a trip by his parents to the city of David (Luke 2:4-7), Matthew assumes that Bethlehem is the original residence and was abandoned only upon the flight of Joseph and Mary to Egypt (Matt 2:14), who then settled in Nazareth upon their return from exile (Matt 2:23). Matt 2:23 relates this change of location to a prophetic quotation of uncertain origin that makes a connection, perhaps by folk etymology, between the place name Nazareth and the name → Ναζωραῖος. (Most commentators take Isa 11:1 as the source; W. F. Albright and C. S. Mann, *Matt* [AB] 21; and E. Zolli, "Nazarenus vocabitur," *ZNW* 49 [1958] 136, assume Jer 31:6.)

In Mark 1:9 Nazareth marks Jesus' point of departure (ἀπὸ Ναζαρέτ clearly modifies the vb.) on his way to be baptized, which is less a historical reminiscence than a conscious parallel drawn between the coming of Jesus and the "going out" of "all Judea" (v. 5; cf. E. Lohmeyer, *Mark* [KEK] 21). The redactional character of the notice in Matt 4:13 (Bultmann, *History* 65, 352) in the seam between the Baptist cycle and the beginning of Jesus' own activity makes more difficult any historical evaluation of the statement about Jesus' change of location (again based on a significant prophetic quotation, 4:14-16) from Nazareth (here Ναζαρά) to Capernaum (*contra* Grundmann, *Matt* [THKNT] 108). In place of the nameless hometown (→ πατρίς) of Jesus (Mark 6:1), Luke 4:16 expressly identifies "*Nazara*, where he grew up," as the place where his compatriots rejected him. Nathanael's ridicule of Jesus' geographic origin (John 1:46) does not reflect any bad reputation of the inhabitants of Nazareth (*contra* T. Zahn, *John* [KNT] 140) but rather derives from the insignificance of the place.

b) The relatively loose connection between the place name Nazareth and the Jesus tradition and the still unresolved issue of its relationship to Ναζωραῖος give good grounds for doubting the historical reliability of accounts

of Nazareth as Jesus' home. Thus H. Stegemann (cf. on this Blinzler 14ff.) and W. Schmithals (*Mark* [ÖTK] 83) consider the possibility that Jesus first became "Jesus of Nazareth" because the name Ναζωραῖος or its variant form Ναζαρηνός was no longer understood, while the historical home of Jesus could better be sought in Capernaum.

H. Kuhli

Ναζαρηνός, 3 *Nazarēnos* from/of Nazareth; subst.: Nazarene*
Ναζωραῖος, ου, ὁ *Nazōraios* one who is from/of Nazareth, Nazorean*

1. Occurrences in the NT — 2. Ναζαρηνός — 3. Ναζωραῖος — a) Individual passages — b) The linguistic problem

Lit.: L. Abramowski, "Jesus, der Naziräer," *ZTK* 81 (1984) 441-46. — W. F. Albright, "The Names 'Nazareth' and 'Nazorean,'" *JBL* 65 (1946) 397-401. — G. Allan, "He Shall Be Called—a Nazirite?" *ExpTim* 95 (1983/84) 81f. — BAGD s.v. — W. Caspari, "Ναζωραῖος. Mt 2,23 nach alttestamentlichen Voraussetzungen," *ZNW* 21 (1922) 122-27. — G. Delling, *BHH* 1291. — A. Díez Macho, "Jesús 'Ho Nazoraios,'" *Quaere Paulum* (FS L. Turrado, 1981) 9-26. — B. Gärtner, *Die rätselhaften Termini Nazoräer und Iskariot* (Horae Soederblomianae 4, 1957). — J. S. Kennard, Jr., "Nazorean and Nazareth," *JBL* 66 (1947) 79-81. — M. Lidzbarski, *Mandäische Liturgien* (1920) xvi-xix. — S. Lyonnet, "Quoniam Nazaraeus vocabitur," *Bib* 25 (1944) 196-206. — E. Meyer, *Ursprung und Anfänge des Christentums* II (1963) 408f., 423-25. — G. F. Moore, "Nazarene and Nazareth," *Beginnings* I, 426-32. — B. Reicke, *BHH* 1293. — J. A. Sanders, "Ναζωραῖος in Matthew 2,23," *JBL* 84 (1965) 169-72. — H. H. Schaeder, *TDNT* IV, 874-79. — G. Schille, *EKL* II, 538. — W. Schmauch, *Orte der Offenbarung und der Offenbarungsort im NT* (1956) 20-26. — J. Schmid, *LTK* VII, 854f. — E. Schweizer, "'Er wird Nazoräer heißen.' Zu Mk 1,24; Mt 2,23," *idem*, *Neotestamentica* (1963) 51-55. — S. M. Shires, "The Meaning of the Term 'Nazarene,'" *ATR* 29 (1947) 19-27. — H. Smith, "Ναζωραῖος," *JTS* 28 (1926/27) 60. — W. B. Tatum, "Mt 2,23—Wordplay and Misleading Translations," *BT* 27 (1976) 135-38. — D. B. Taylor, "Jesus—of Nazareth?" *ExpTim* 92 (1980/81) 336f. — H. Thyen, *RGG* IV, 1385. — H. Zimmern, "Nazoräer (Nazarener)," *ZDMG* 74 (1920) 429-38. — E. Zolli, "Nazarenus vocabitur," *ZNW* 49 (1958) 135f. — E. Zuckschwerdt, "Nazōraios in Mt 2,23," *TZ* 31 (1975) 65-77. — See also commentaries on Matt 2:23. — For further bibliography see BAGD; Schaeder; Zuckschwerdt; *TWNT* X, 1185.

1. Ναζαρηνός (6 total occurrences in the NT) and Ναζωραῖος (13 occurrences) appear only in the Gospels and Acts in the NT writings. While Mark uses only the form Ναζαρηνός (4 times: 1:24; 10:47 [v.l. Ναζωραῖος ℵ C Koine pm]; 14:67; 16:6 [omitted in ℵ* D]), Matthew, John, and Acts consistently confine themselves to using the form Ναζωραῖος (Matthew 2 times: 2:23; 26:71; John 3 times: 18:5 [v.l. Ναζαρηνόν D lat], 7; 19:19; Acts 7 times: 2:22; 3:6; 4:10; 6:14; 22:8; 24:5 [pl.]; 26:9). In

contrast, Luke uses both terms interchangeably, following his sources in the use of Ναζαρηνός (Luke 4:34 [= Mark 1:24] and also 24:19 [v.l. Ναζωραίου Koine D Θ pm]), while his redactional usage, as in Acts, prefers the form Ναζωραῖος (Luke 18:37 [v.l. Ναζαρηνός D λ pc]).

2. The adj. form Ναζαρηνός (on the morphology cf. Moulton, *Grammar* II, 150) appears only as a subst. in the NT and also only in apposition to the name of Jesus, whose identity is indicated, in accordance with common ancient custom (cf. H. Rix, *KP* IV, 658), by his place of origin: Jesus *from* or *of Nazareth*. The adj./subst., whose correspondence to the place name Ναζαρέτ was not doubted by the users of the NT, appears to mean the same as the adverbial designation ὁ ἀπὸ Ναζαρέτ, which also appears several times with the personal name of Jesus (Matt 21:11; Acts 10:38; John 1:45). Mark 10:47; 14:67; 16:6; and Luke 24:19 thus simply provide "the identification of the bearer of the common name of Jesus in terms of his origin" (R. Pesch, *Mark* [HTKNT] II, 171). We may explain the inclusion of this otherwise superfluous detail in the demon's address in Mark 1:24 as an attempt by the demon to gain some protection against Jesus (W. Schmithals, *Mark* [ÖTK] I, 124), on the theory that a more exact designation of one's object affords greater magical control over that one (O. Bauernfeind, *Die Worte der Dämonen im Markusevangelium* [1927] 13ff.).

3. a) Ναζωραῖος and Ναζαρηνός are clearly simply two morphologically variant forms of the same word with the same meaning. Thus the use of Ναζωραῖος corresponds syntactically and semantically to that of Ναζαρηνός, in that as a governing subst. (exceptions: Matt 2:23; Acts 24:5) in appositional construction it delimits the identity of Jesus with respect to bearers of the same name: Jesus *of* or *from Nazareth* (Matt 26:71; Luke 18:37; John 18:5, 7, etc.). The appositive ὁ Ναζωραῖος with the name of Jesus in the Johannine version of the written accusation on the cross can be explained in terms of John's efforts to attribute to the title the character of an official document (cf. A. Dauer, *Die Passionsgeschichte im Johannesevangelium* [1972] 176f.).

The synonymity of the two terms for Matthew is also confirmed by his substitution of the form Ναζωραῖος in Matt 26:71 for the form Ναζαρηνός in Mark 14:67 and by his explicit discussion of the connection between the designation Ναζωραῖος and the place name Nazareth in the quotation in Matt 2:23: "He settled in a city called Nazareth, so that what was said by the prophet might be fulfilled: 'He will be called a *Nazorean.'*" The origin of this alleged quotation is unknown. Some have argued that this verse refers to a specific OT saying (Isa 11:1: J. Schniewind, *Matt* [NTD] 20; H. J. Holtzmann, *Die Synoptischen Evangelien*[3] [HKNT] 194 and *passim;* Jer

31:6: W. F. Albright and C. S. Mann, *Matt* [AB] 21; Zolli 136 and *passim;* Judg 13:5, 7 [16:17]: Schweizer 53-55; Zuckschwerdt 69-71 et al.). More probably, it reflects an unspecified combination of several prophetic passages (E. Klostermann, *Matt* [HNT] 19; A. Schlatter, *Matt* [6][1963] 49; W. Rothfuchs, *Die Erfüllungszitate des Matthäusevangeliums* [1969] 66; G. Strecker, *Der Weg der Gerechtigkeit* [2][1966] 62; et al.).

In the same way the synonymity of Ναζωραῖος and Ναζαρηνός in Luke can be deduced from the alternating use of the two references and the similarity of their usage. Luke takes over the form Ναζαρηνός from his sources (4:34 par. Mark 1:24; Luke 24:19) but prefers the form Ναζωραῖος in his own compositions (18:37). Of the 7 occurrences in Acts, its mention in the formal self-designation of the exalted Christ to Paul (22:8) and its use in the oath formula "in the name of Jesus Christ the *Nazorean*" (3:6) or the report of the healing after it had been realized (4:10) are worthy of special mention.

The only instance of the pl. form is found in the accusation of Tertullus against Paul that he was "a leader of the sect of the *Nazoreans*" (Acts 24:5). Jesus' epithet, transferred to his followers, corresponds both in function and meaning to the alternate reference Χριστιανοί (Acts 11:26), which is derived from the title "Christ."

b) The once hotly debated question whether Ναζωραῖος was to be derived from the place name Nazareth or originally had an entirely different meaning has been largely decided since Schaeder (875-79, following Moore 426-28 et al.) furnished proof that in spite of the recognized difficulties (primarily the change of vowel from *a* to *ō* in the second syllable and the transcription of the Aramaic consonant *ṣ* as ζ rather than σ), its derivation from the place name *nāṣᵉraṯ* was in principle possible. Nevertheless, it remains to be said that these and other irregularities (e.g., the loss of the final consonant *ṯ;* cf. Schweizer 56; Kennard 80), esp. when taken cumulatively, make this assumption more difficult (cf. K. Rudolph, *Die Mandäer* I [1960] 113ff.). In addition the problem remains "whether the matter is decided with this linguistic possibility" (F. Hahn, *Christologische Hoheitstitel* [4][1974] 237n.4).

Therefore, in spite of the thoroughly plausible explanation of Ναζωραῖος as a derivative of "Nazareth," the alternative possibility—that the word in question originally had a different meaning and was connected with "Nazareth" only via a popular etymology—cannot be summarily dismissed. In spite of the objections of Schaeder (876f.) and C. Colpe ("Die rätselhaften Termini Nazoräer und Iskariot," *TLZ* 86 [1961] 31-34), the statement in Epiphanius *Haer.* xxix.6 on the pre-Christian Jewish sect of the Νασαραῖοι and the Mandean self-designation as *nāṣᵒrāyā*, as well as the deviant use of this term in two NT passages that could reflect a more primitive stage of its use and meaning (Matt 2:23; Acts 24:5), all speak for this possibility, even though the contexts in which we now find them intend to express nothing other than a connection with the place name "Nazareth."

As a result, in addition to the predominant interpretation of Ναζωραῖος as a Gentilizing of the place name *nāṣᵉraṯ* (Albright, Meyer, Moore, Sanders, Schmauch, Schmid, et al.), the following derivations are suggested: 1) Ναζιραῖος (Heb. *nāzîr;*

Schweizer 51-55; Zuckschwerdt 71-77; Hahn, loc. cit.; et al.); 2) an Aramaic subst. derived from the stem *nṣr*, whose pl. *nāṣōrāyā* would refer to a group or a personal association of "watchers" or "keepers" (in the sense of "observers" of [baptismal] rites; see Lidzbarski; Kennard 81; Gärtner; Thyen, et al.).

H. Kuhli

Ναζωραῖος, ου, ὁ *Nazōraios* one who is from/of Nazareth, Nazorean*
→ Ναζαρηνός.

Ναθάμ *Natham* Nathan*

Ναθάμ is an indeclinable personal name in Luke 3:31. Nathan was a son of David (2 Kgs 5:14; there, as in Luke 3:31 Koine A Θ al lat, the form is Ναθαν).

Ναθαναήλ *Nathanaēl* Nathanael*

Ναθαναήλ is the indeclinable personal name of a disciple of Jesus, which is found only in John: 1:45, 46, 47, 48, 49, and 21:2. According to 21:2, he originated from Cana in Galilee. U. Holzmeister, "Nathanael fuitne idem ac S. Bartholomaeus apostolus?" *Bib* 21 (1940) 28-39; E. Leidig, "Natanael, ein Sohn des Tholomäus," *TZ* 36 (1980) 374f.; R. Schnackenburg, *John* (1968) I, 313-18.

ναί *nai* yes, certainly*

The particle ναί is used for affirmation, assent, or confirmation.
1. Ναί provides an answer to questions of others (*yes*: Matt 9:28; 13:51; 17:25; 21:16; John 11:27; 21:15, 16; Acts 5:8; 22:27) or to questions that speakers themselves have posed (*certainly/surely*: Matt 11:9 par. Luke 7:26; with a negative question, *of course*: Rom 3:29).
2. Ναί also represents agreement with the statement of another (*certainly, surely, to be sure*: Matt 15:27; here, too, Rev 14:13; 16:7; 22:20b TR should be reckoned) or an emphatic repetition of one's own statement (*yes, indeed*: Matt 11:26 par. Luke 10:21; Luke 11:51; 12:5; Phlm 20; after a prior request, Phil 4:3).
3. Ναί may appear in a solemn declaration: Rev 1:7: ναί, ἀμήν, "*yes*, it will surely be"; 22:20a: "*yes*, I am coming soon."
4. In plays on words ναί is used with οὔ. According to Jas 5:12: "Let your '*yes*' be *yes* and your 'no' be no"; i.e., the truthfulness of one's statements should make a sworn affirmation unnecessary. In Matt 5:37 the same instruction reads, "Let your word be '*yes, yes*' and 'no, no'"; i.e., no (sworn) asseveration should be needed beyond a clear and unambiguous yes or no; see P. Minear, "Yes or No: The Demand for Honesty in the Early Church," *NovT* 13 (1971) 1-13 (E. Klostermann, *Matt* [HNT] ad loc., among others, however, interprets this passage in the same sense as Jas 5:12). Paul denies that he is so muddled in his decisions "that my *yes yes* is at the same time no no" (2 Cor 1:17); his word is not (both) "*yes and no*" (v. 18). In the gospel "*yes and no*" are not preached together (v. 19). Jesus Christ is the *yes* to all God's promises (v. 20); he has shown them to be trustworthy. See F. Hahn, "Das Ja des Paulus und das Ja Gottes. Bemerkungen zu 2 Kor 1,12–2,1," FS Braun 229-39; *idem*, "Ist das textkritische Problem von 2 Kor 1,17 lösbar?" FS Greeven 158-65; R. Bultmann, *2 Cor* (Eng. tr., 1985) 39-41.

Ναιμάν *Naiman* Naaman*

Ναιμάν is the indeclinable personal name of a Syrian whom Elisha healed from leprosy (2 Kgs 5:1-27). Luke 4:27 alludes to 2 Kings 5. The Greek form of the name Ναιμάν corresponds to the form in the LXX; for other forms see BDF §37.

Ναΐν *Nain* Nain*

Ναΐν is the indeclinable name of a Galilean village in Luke 7:11 (Kopp, *Places* 236-41). The place name is derived from Heb. *nāʿîm* ("pleasant, lovely," a Talmudic name).

ναός, οῦ, ὁ *naos* temple*

1. Occurrences and usage — 2. The edifice — 3. The temple as God's possession and holy place — 4. The temple as God's dwelling — 5. The temple in Jerusalem — 6. The temple sayings of Jesus

Lit.: BAGD s.v. — X. LÉON-DUFOUR, *Dictionary of the NT* (1980) 396f., index s.v. — O. MICHEL, *TDNT* IV, 880-90. — MOULTON/MILLIGAN s.v. — PREISIGKE, *Wörterbuch* II, 124; III, 381.

For general lit. on "temple": F. AMIOT, *WBB* 650-55. — M. BACHMANN, *Jerusalem und der Tempel* (BWANT 109, 1979). — W. BAIER, *BL* 1720-29. — M. BEN-DOV, *IDBSup* 870-72. — G. CORNFELD and G. J. BOTTERWECK, *Die Bibel und ihre Welt* II (1969) 1411-21. — K. GALLING, *RGG* VI, 681-86. — B. GÄRTNER, *The Temple and the Community in Qumran and the NT* (1965). — L. GASTON, *No Stone on Another* (1970). — A. R. S. KENNEDY and N. H. SNAITH, *HDB* (rev. ed., 1963) 961-68. — KOPP, *Places* 283-304. — A. KUSCHKE, *BRL* 333-42. — D. LÜHRMANN, "Mk 14,55-64: Christologie und Zerstörung des Tempels im Markusevangelium," *NTS* 27 (1980/81) 457-74. — J. MAIER, "Tempel und Tempelkult," Maier/Schreiner 371-90. — W. VON MEDING, *DNTT* III, 781-85. — F. MUSSNER, "Jesus und 'das Haus des Vaters'—Jesus als 'Tempel,'" *Freude am Gottesdienst* (FS J. G. Plöger, 1983) 267-75. — J. QUELLETTE, *IDBSup* 872-74. — B. REICKE and H. P. RÜGER, *BHH* 1940-47. — W. H. SCHMIDT and G. DELLING, *Wörterbuch zur Bibel* (1971) 562-66. — W. F. STINESPRING, *IDB* IV, 534-60. — R. DE VAUX, *LTK* IX, 1350-58. — C. WESTERMANN, *EKL* III, 1324-28. — For further bibliography see *TWNT* X, 1114-18, 1185f.

1. The 45 occurrences of ναός in the NT are divided among the historical books (3 times in Mark, 9 in Matthew, 4 in Luke, 2 in Acts, and 3 in John), Pauline literature (4 times in 1 Corinthians, twice in 2 Corinthians, and once in Ephesians and 2 Thessalonians), and Revelation (16 times). Only two passages, both referring to paganism, use the pl.: "[God] does not live in *temples* made by hand" (Acts 17:24, a point made generally in the NT; → 4.a.b), and Demetrius made silver *shrines* of Artemis (Acts 19:24). There are frequent references to the temple in Jerusalem (20 instances). John and Paul use ναός primarily in a fig. sense for people or for a body (9 instances) and often draw on the actual design of the temple (1 Cor 3:17a, b; 2 Cor 6:16a, b; Eph 2:21; cf. John 2:19, 21). The majority of the passages in Revelation deal with God's temple in heaven (11 instances). Rev 3:12 is intended to depict the relationship of the community with God. In the new Jerusalem, no temple will be needed, for God and the lamb are the temple (21:22a, b).

2. While → ἱερόν 1 designates the holy area of the temple as a whole, ναός refers to the edifice (see Michel 887). The *temple* is a building; Eph 2:20f. mentions its foundation and its cornerstone (fig.; see J. Gnilka, *Eph* [HTKNT] 132, 159f.). It can be expanded and demolished (Mark 14:58 par. Matt 26:61/John 2:19f.; cf. Acts 6:14; Mark 15:29 par. Matt 27:40). The temple is made by hands (Mark 14:58; Acts 17:24 [pl.]). It has pillars (Rev 3:12; fig. and sg.) and can be measured (11:1f.). Noteworthy is the exception of the temple of Artemis in Ephesus: the holy place of the goddess is called τὸ ἱερόν (Acts 19:27); the silver replicas of the building are, however, ναοί (v. 24; see G. Schrenk, *TDNT* III, 232).

3. a) A temple bears the name of its god: "the *shrines* of Artemis" (Acts 19:24); "the *temple* of God" (Matt 26:61; 1 Cor 3:16, 17a, b; 2 Cor 6:16a; 2 Thess 2:4; Rev 11:1, 19a), or "of the living God" (2 Cor 6:16b). It is his temple (Rev 7:15; 11:19b); the temple of "my God" (3:12; i.e., the temple of the God of Christ; see H. Kraft, *Rev* [HNT] 79, 83) or of the Lord (i.e., of God; Luke 1:9). The body of Christians is a temple of the Holy Spirit, which stems from God; therefore it does not belong to oneself (1 Cor 6:19).

b) The temple of God is holy; whoever destroys it will be destroyed (1 Cor 3:17). The edifice of the Church grows into the temple in the Lord (i.e., in Christ, Eph 2:21; see Gnilka, *Eph* 159). The gold in the temple is made holy by the temple (Matt 23:17; → 5.b).

4. a) An image of the god is placed in the pagan temple; it is therefore considered the dwelling place of the god (see Michel 880). In contrast, God dwells above heaven and earth, "not in *temples* made with hands" (Acts 17:24, → 1).

b) The temple in Jerusalem contained no image; cf. 2 Cor 6:16: "What agreement does the *temple* of God have with idols?" regarding which see H. Windisch, *2 Cor* (KEK) 215. The temple is, however, inhabited (by God or by the name of God, Matt 23:21; see A. R. Hulst, *THAT* II, 904-9). In the last days, the "man of lawlessness" will set himself up in the temple, according to 2 Thess 2:4, and will thus assume the place of God (fig., of the temple in Jerusalem; see E. von Dobschütz, *1-2 Thess* [KEK] 276f., *contra* G. Friedrich, *1-2 Thess* [NTD] 264). Stephen aroused the fury of the Jews when, with respect to the temple of Solomon, he said that the "Most High" did not dwell in buildings made by hands (Acts 7:47f.; → a; see O. Michel, *TDNT* V, 124, 154; E. Haenchen, *Acts* [Eng. tr., 1971] 285f.).

c) Christians are a temple of (the living) God, since God dwells in them (2 Cor 6:16, a loose quotation of Ezek 37:27 LXX) and since the Spirit of God dwells in them (1 Cor 3:16). Their body is a temple of the Holy Spirit, who is given by God and is in them (6:19). In a parallel passage, the whole Church is called a "holy temple in the Lord" and is described as the dwelling of God in the Spirit (Eph 2:21f.; → 3.b).

d) God lives in the temple (of God) in heaven (Rev 11:19; 14:17) or in the temple of the tent of witness (the tabernacle) in heaven (15:5). He reveals his presence through the ark of the covenant (11:19), through smoke (15:8), and through the loud voice (of God or an angel, 16:1, 17; see Kraft, *Rev* 204, 210f.). Angels go out from the temple and command or act (14:15, 17; 15:6). The redeemed (see Kraft, *Rev* 130) serve God in the temple before his throne (7:15).

e) In the new Jerusalem that descends from heaven (Rev 21:10), God and the Lamb are everywhere present: they are themselves the temple, so that a separate temple is superfluous (21:22). The concept of the presence of God in the temple of the earthly Jerusalem is here assumed (see Michel, *TDNT* IV, 889).

5. a) The building efforts of Herod I began in 20/19 B.C. with the renovation of the temple in Jerusalem. Approximately ten years were needed for the temple building itself. The construction of the entire temple complex lasted longer; the official opening was not made until 63 A.D. The forty-six years of construction in John 2:20 render the date A.D. 27/28 and fit well with the chronology of Jesus (cf. Luke 3:1; see R. Schnackenburg, *John* I, 351f.). The temple building itself was surrounded by courts; non-Jews were permitted to enter only the outermost court (see Rev 11:2; → ἱερόν 3.h, taken over in a spiritual sense from the Herodian temple; see Kraft, *Rev* 152). The betrayer Judas threw the pieces of silver "in the *temple*" (Matt 27:5), perhaps in the temple treasury, for he would have had no access to the temple itself (see E. Klostermann, *Matt* [HNT] 217).

b) In front of the temple itself stood the altar of burnt sacrifice (cf. Matt 23:16-21; Rev 11:1). "Between the *temple* and the altar," where refuge was sometimes taken, the murder of Zechariah took place (Matt 23:35; see Klostermann, *Matt* 185; Michel, *TDNT* IV, 883). Zechariah entered "the *temple* of the Lord" ("the holy place") in order to burn incense there (Luke 1:9f.). An angel appeared to him next to the altar of incense (v. 11). Those praying outside wondered about the delay and his failure to speak the blessing (vv. 21f.; see H. Schürmann, *Luke* [HTKNT] I, 37f.). The temple had two veils: the outer veil hung between the inner court and the holy place; the inner veil covered the entrance to the holy of holies. Immediately after (Luke: before) the death of Jesus, the veil (probably the inner veil; see Schrenk, *TDNT* III, 237; C. Schneider, *TDNT* III, 629f.) was torn in two (Mark 15:38 par. Matt 27:51/Luke 23:45; → καταπέτασμα 1), symbolizing the displacement of the dispensation of the temple by "the new saving community of the crucified" (L. Schenke, *Der gekreuzigte Christus* [1974] 100; contra R. Pesch, *Mark* [HTKNT] II, 499; → 6.a).

6. a) False witnesses attributed to Jesus the statement that he would destroy the "man-made *temple*" and would build another in three days not made by human hands (Mark 14:57-59; cf. 15:29). Whether the author views the accusation as pure fabrication or as a misinterpretation is an open question; the "three days" suggests, however, a link with the Easter event (G. Delling, *TDNT* VIII, 220; contra Pesch 433f.). "(Not) made by human hands" is certainly a Hellenistic expression. One could further ask whether an authentic logion of Jesus lies behind it, or whether it deals with polemical influence from Judaism (Pesch) or with a saying from Hellenistic Jewish-Christian circles that proclaimed the death and resurrection of Jesus as the transition from the Jewish temple to the new, spiritual temple of the messianic community (see Schenke 34f.; → 5.b).

b) The Matthean version of the logion has been altered in several ways (see G. Schneider, *Die Passion Jesu nach den drei älteren Evangelien* [1973] 65f.): "I can destroy the *temple* of God and in three days build it up again" (26:61; cf. 27:40). Jesus is charged with making a blasphemous statement against the temple. The author views it as either a groundless slander or a messianic claim of Jesus with the threat of an eschatological judgment on the temple (E. Lohmeyer and W. Schmauch, *Matt* [KEK] 368f.).

c) Luke-Acts takes up only the first part of the logion, which is rendered as an accusation against Stephen (Acts 6:14; see W. Wiater, *Komposition als Mittel der Interpretation im lukanischen Doppelwerk* [1972] 216; → τόπος).

d) In the Fourth Gospel, Jesus himself makes an ob-

scure, symbolic statement about the temple of his body, which the Jews mistakenly relate to the temple in Jerusalem (John 2:18-22; see H. Leroy, *Rätsel und Mißverständnis* [1968] 137-47; → 5.a).

U. Borse

Ναούμ *Naoum* Nahum*

Indeclinable personal name in Luke 3:25 (cf. Nah 1:1 LXX, for Heb. *naḥûm*).

νάρδος, ου, ἡ *nardos* nard oil*

The subst. originally designated the plant *nard* (thus, e.g., *1 Enoch* [Greek] 32:1; *Apoc. Pet.* 3:10). In the two passages in which it occurs in the NT, νάρδος appears in the phrase μύρον νάρδου, "*nard* ointment" (Mark 14:3 par. John 12:3; the oil is obtained from compressing the roots of the nard plant); → πιστικός. K. Ziegler, *KP* III, 1572.

Νάρκισσος, ου *Narkissos* Narcissus*

In Rom 16:11 Paul greets τοὺς ἐκ τῶν Ναρκίσσου, "the Narcissus-people," i.e., the members of the house of Narcissus, since they are Christians. H. Schlier, *Rom* (HTKNT) 445. In *Acts Pet.*, the man *Narcissus* is a presbyter (48:7; 49:15; 53:13; 61:8, 27).

ναυαγέω *nauageō* be shipwrecked*

This vb. is used in a literal sense in 2 Cor 11:25 ("three times *I have suffered shipwreck*") and in a fig. sense in 1 Tim 1:19 ("certain persons *have made shipwreck* of their faith [περὶ τὴν πίστιν]"). H. Preisker, *TDNT* IV, 891.

ναύκληρος, ου, ὁ *nauklēros* ship owner; captain of a ship*

Acts 27:11 mentions the ναύκληρος after the κυβερνήτης ("captain"). H. Conzelmann, *Acts* (Hermeneia) 216f., and Moulton/Milligan s.v. defend the meaning "captain."

ναῦς, acc. ναῦν, ἡ *naus* ship*

In the NT only in Acts 27:41: "They ran the *ship* aground."

ναύτης, ου, ὁ *nautēs* seaman, sailor*

In the NT always pl.: Acts 27:27, 30; Rev 18:17.

Ναχώρ *Nachōr* Nahor*

Indeclinable personal name in Luke 3:34 (see Gen 11:22-26).

νεανίας, ου, ὁ *neanias* youth, young man*

In the NT only in Acts: 7:58, of Saul; 20:9, of Eutychus; 23:17 (23:18, 22 v.l.), of Paul's nephew, who was to give a report to the χιλίαρχος; → νεανίσκος.

νεανίσκος, ου, ὁ *neaniskos* youth, young man*

The subst., like νεανίας, designates a young man until about the age of forty years. The sing. is used for "the rich *young man*" in Matt 19:20, 22 (contrast Mark), the young man who fled naked in Mark 14:51, the angel at the grave in Mark 16:5, the young man of Nain in Luke 7:14, as well as the nephew of Paul in Acts 23:18, 22. The pl. is found in Acts 2:17 (citing Joel 3:1 LXX) and 5:10 (where it can hardly mean "the servant"; *contra* BAGD s.v. 2), as well as 1 John 2:13, 14 (as address: *"young men"*). E. L. Schellbächer, "Das Rätsel des νεανίσκος bei Markus," *ZNW* 73 (1982) 127-35.

Νέα πόλις *Nea polis* Neapolis ("New City")*

Acts 16:11 (also Ign. *Pol.* 8:1) uses this name to designate the harbor of Philippi in Macedonia, where Paul reached the European continent on his "second missionary journey" (modern Kavalla). During the battle of Philippi in 42 B.C., Neapolis was the naval base of Brutus and Cassius. C. Danoff, *KP* IV, 29f. (bibliography); → νέος 2.a.

Νεάπολις *Neapolis* Neapolis

Variant form of → Νέα πόλις.

Νεεμάν *Neeman* Naaman

Variant form of → Ναιμάν.

νεκρός, 3 *nekros* dead

1. Occurrences in the NT and meaning — 2. Literal νεκρός — 3. Jesus as savior, judge, and firstborn from the dead — 4. Metaphoric νεκρός

Lit.: A. BERTHOLET et al., *RGG* VI, 908-14. — J. BLANK, *Krisis. Untersuchungen zur johanneischen Christologie und Eschatologie* (1964) 143-58, 172-82. — R. BULTMANN, *TDNT* IV, 892-95. — L. COENEN, *DNTT* I, 443-46. — A. FEUILLET, "Mort du Christ et mort du chrétien d'après les épîtres pauliniennes," *RB* 66 (1959) 481-513. — A. GRILLMEIER, *Der Gottessohn im Totenreich: Mit ihm und in ihm* (²1978) 76-174. — E. GÜTT-GEMANNS, *Der leidende Apostel und sein Herr* (FRLANT 90, 1966) 94-126. — P. HOFFMANN, *Die Toten in Christus* (NTAbh N.F. 2, ²1969) 26-57, 66-73, 180-85, 236-38. — idem, *HTG* II, 661-70. — J. JEREMIAS, "Zwischen Karfreitag und Ostern," idem, *Abba* (1966) 323-31. — E. JÜNGEL, *Death: The Riddle and Mystery* (1975). — C. KEARNS, "The Interpretation of Romans 6:7," *SPCIC 1961* I (1963) 301-7. — E. KLAAR, "'Ο γὰρ ἀποθανὼν δεδικαίωται ἀπὸ τῆς ἁμαρτίας," *ZNW* 59 (1968) 131-34. —

J. KREMER, *Die Osterevangelien—Geschichten um Geschichte* (1977). — F. NEUGEBAUER, *In Christus* (1961) 110-12. — R. SCHNACKENBURG, "Zur Aussage: 'Jesus ist von den Toten auferstanden,' " *BZ* 13 (1969) 1-17. — E. SCHÜSSLER FIORENZA, "Die tausendjährige Herrschaft der Auferstandenen (Apk 20,4-6)," *BibLeb* 13 (1972) 107-24. — E. SCHWEIZER, "Die Mystik des Sterbens und Auferstehens mit Christus bei Paulus," idem, *Beiträge zur Theologie* (1970) 183-203. — R. SCROGGS, "Romans VI,7," *NTS* 10 (1963/64) 104-8. — R. C. TANNEHILL, *Dying and Rising with Christ* (BZNW 32, 1967). — H.-J. VOGELS, *Christi Abstieg ins Totenreich und das Läuterungsgericht an den Toten* (FTS 102, 1976). — U. WILCKENS, *Resurrection* (1978) 1-44, 71-132. — For further bibliography see *TWNT* X, 1100-1103.

1. Νεκρός is used in the NT, as it frequently is in the ancient world, both as adj. (15 times sg. and 7 times pl.) and as subst. (twice sing. and 104 times pl.). As adj. the word means *dead,* in the sense of "no longer living." It characterizes people as well as things, in both the literal and fig. senses. The subst. designates a *dead person* or *the dead* in contrast to the living as "no longer alive." The pl. subst. is primarily used in the NT in statements related to the resurrection (*ca.* 86 times). It includes (usually without the art.) "all the dead, all those who are in the underworld" (BAGD 535) and—used with a prep.— the realm of the dead in general (→ ἀνάστασις; → ἐγείρω). The subst. is also used metaphorically.

2. Acts 5:10 reports concerning Sapphira that after she told the lie, she collapsed and died; "young men found her *dead* and . . . buried her." Likewise, Eutychus, who fell from the third floor, was considered *dead* (20:9). The natives of Malta expected that Paul would fall over *dead* after being bitten by the snake (28:6). Also, Jesus was *dead* before God raised him (Rev 1:18). After the appearance of the angel of the Lord to the Roman guards, "they were as *dead men*" (Matt 28:4). This expression intensifies their fear as much as possible and at the same time describes their reaction in a way that corresponds to the divine epiphany (cf. Dan 8:19; 10:9; *Apoc. Abr.* 10:2).

The extremely varied conceptions of the abode of the dead extant in the NT era can be recognized in the NT as well. Thus, in Mark 16:5f. it is the "grave" (cf. John 5:28); in Rom 10:7-9 it is Sheol (→ ἄβυσσος 2); in Luke 16:22-26 very different destinations in the afterlife (→ ᾅδης; → γέεννα; cf. *1 Enoch* 22; see Billerbeck IV, 1016-1165; Hoffmann, *Toten* 26-57). "The *dead* ἐν Χριστῷ," who according to 1 Thess 4:16 will "rise first," are those who died as Christians. Even in death they remain bound to the one whose death and resurrection has determined their life. "The *dead* who die in the Lord from now on" in Rev 14:13, by way of contrast, should probably be understood as martyrs. On the vicarious baptism "for the *dead,*" attested in 1 Cor 15:29, see H. Conzelmann, *1 Cor* (Hermeneia) ad loc., and → βαπτίζω 7.

3. Jesus appears as a savior from death in Mark 9:26 with the healing of the epileptic boy. He was "as one *dead,* so that many said, 'He has died.'" Even more pointedly, Luke 7:11-17 portrays Jesus as lord over death when he calls back to life with but a word the young man who was lying on the burial bier. The dramatic resuscitation of Lazarus, "whom Jesus had raised from the *dead*" (John 12:1, 9, 17), could hardly have been more emphatic, for he had been dead for four days and already stank (11:39). Deeds such as these laid the groundwork for the summary of Matt 11:5 par.: νεχροὶ ἐγείρονται. Before Jesus could ultimately be considered the savior from death, he himself had to die—according to God's will—and actually to be *dead* (Rev 1:18; 2:8). The fact that Christ not only belonged to the living but even for a time belonged to the dead intensifies the Christian hope of resurrection. God, "who makes the *dead* alive" (2 Cor 1:9; cf. John 5:21; Rom 8:11), raised him up. He is the πρωτότοχος ἐχ (τῶν) νεχρῶν.

Moreover, since Christ can be called not only the "firstfruits of those who sleep" (1 Cor 15:20) but also the "first to rise from the *dead*" (Acts 26:23), his resurrection opens the possibility that others might follow him. It is the beginning and cause of all other resurrections, including the resurrection of the *dead* on the last day. In this sense, the hymnic predication "firstborn from the *dead*" (Col 1:18; cf. Rev 1:5) accentuates not only his temporal priority but also his unique cosmic superiority, since in the verses immediately preceding he is praised as the firstborn of all creation.

Corresponding to this position of power is the fact that the living and the *dead*—therefore all people— belong to the realm of his kingdom. God has destined him to be χριτὴς ζώντων χαὶ νεχρῶν (Acts 10:42; cf. 17:31; 2 Tim 4:1). In 1 Pet 4:5, however, as also in Rom 2:16; 3:6; 14:10, God appears as judge of the living and the *dead,* i.e., over *all the dead.*

1 Pet 4:6 decisively establishes the universality of the judgment over all people, without exception, including the "Gentiles" who were threatening the Church (4:1-4): "For that is why the gospel was also preached to the *dead,* so that they might be judged as [all] people. . . ." Since, according to 4:17, all people will ultimately be judged according to their disposition toward the gospel, through this proclamation the *dead,* like the living, are confronted with the decision and can be judged along with all others. It remains an open question, however, when, how, and where the message of salvation is proclaimed to them, or how it gets through to them. "To infer Christ's descent into hell (which is first known only in post-NT literature) is an obvious possibility" (N. Brox, *1 Pet* [EKKNT] 198). Since, however, in this case the *dead* in 4:5f. would not be identical with the spirits in 3:19, and the two passages would therefore not be interpreted as contem-

poraneous, 4:6 refers to *all the dead,* and 3:19 probably has in mind the "sons of God" from Gen 6:2 (cf. Brox 174, *contra,* e.g., Vogels 142f.).

Revelation 20 describes in more detail the judgment of the *dead:* some of them, the martyrs, are raised in "the first resurrection." They already participate, therefore, in the age of salvation, and "the second death," the lake of fire, has no more power over them (20:4-6). All the remaining *dead* are revived only at the last judgment, in order to be judged for their deeds.

4. The fig. sense of νεχρός, in the NT as in general usage in antiquity, has a very wide range. The Stoics, for example, characterize people and their status in life as *dead* when their orientation is not to the world of philosophy (cf. further Bultmann 892; Coenen 1232). In the NT, the meaning is to be determined by the context.

Already in the OT the very ill were numbered among the *dead* (Pss 30:2-4; 86:13). The rabbis also call the godless "dead" because they have no part in the benefits of salvation and no relation to God. The righteous, in contrast, can be called "living," even in death (Billerbeck I, 489; III, 652). It is in this context that we should interpret Jesus' statement to a follower about discipleship: "Follow me and let the *dead* bury their own *dead*" (Matt 8:22; cf. Luke 9:60). Apparently, the first νεχρούς refers to those who do not follow Jesus and do not wish to enter into a relationship with him. Luke 15:24 calls the lost son, who showed no signs of life and was separated from the life of the family circle, *dead.* "The *dead,* who hear the voice of God's Son," are not those who have "actually died," or "inhabitants of the realm of the dead" (Vogels 53, 56), but all those who because of their unbelief have no relationship with the Logos or the ζωή mediated through him. They live in their sins in darkness, in the cosmos. The *dead* in John 5:25 are "all those who find themselves 'in death' because of their lack of salvation" (Blank 142).

In Rom 6:11, Paul encourages Christians to draw out the consequences of their baptism: "In the same way consider yourselves *dead* to sin but alive to God in Jesus Christ." This liberation from the power of sin and from its claims takes place through participation in the fate of Christ, in his death and life, for he has vicariously given to sin what it demanded of mankind. By dying, Christ has finally removed its claims, in accordance with the sentence based on rabbinic law (6:7): "Whoever has died is [legally] free from sin." The life of all people *leads to death,* "whereas the life possessed by Jesus Christ is a life that *emerges from death.* To the extent that Jesus *shares* his life with those who wish to belong to him, they also are set free from death, even though they must yet die" (Jüngel 84). This deliverance from the kingdom of sin and death must be maintained in daily discipleship:

"Place yourselves at God's disposal as those who have been raised from *the dead*" (6:13). In similar words the baptismal song of Eph 5:14 exhorts them to lift themselves out of death caused by sin and to receive Christ, the light: "Rise from the *dead*."

In Rom 7:8 Paul makes a theological statement: "Without law, sin is *dead*." Here he uses νεκρά in the sense of "ineffective, powerless, dormant." Without the law, sin had no occasion to attack human beings and to lead them astray. As long as sin is *dead*, we live. As soon as sin could make use of the law, however, it came to life (v. 10: ἀνέζησεν); it obtained the power of life (1 Cor 15:16: "The power of sin is the law"). It awakened desire in human beings, tempting them to transgress the commandment and disposing them against God. In this way it made them guilty and, as a consequence of their conduct, delivered them over to death (cf. Rom 6:21-23).

The disputed statement in Rom 8:10 (τὸ μὲν σῶμα νεκρὸν διὰ ἁμαρτίαν) should probably not be interpreted in connection with v. 11, but rather in connection with the contrast between "body of sin" (6:6) and "body of death" (7:24). In baptism, the sinful body is put to death (6:2-4). Therefore the body is *dead* with respect to sin; i.e., sin has no more claim to or power over the body. Above all, however, it has lost its death-producing power, since Christ vicariously took death upon himself. His Spirit now lives in the baptized and defines their lives (8:10).

In Rom 11:15 Paul attempts to clarify for the Gentile Christians the fullness of blessing that the restitution of Israel will bring for them and for the entire world. Using the form of argument that concludes with the *qal-wāḥômer* (→ μᾶλλον 3.a), he argues that if the rejection of Israel has led to God's reconciliation with the world, what can the acceptance of Gentiles mean, other than ζωὴ ἐκ νεκρῶν? What is here meant, as in v. 12 (καταλλαγὴ κόσμου), is an event, likewise mediated through Israel, that will unimaginably supersede the present salvation. E. Käsemann (*Rom* [Eng. tr., 1980] ad loc.) understands ἀνάστασις νεκρῶν, and C. E. B. Cranfield (*Rom* [ICC] II, ad loc.) suggests "the final resurrection."

In Col 2:13, Gentile Christians are addressed, in accordance with rabbinic usage, with reference to the time before their baptism as those who "were *dead* in your sins and the uncircumcision of your flesh." The deathlike character of this life before and without baptism is conditioned and determined by their sins as well as through their uncircumcision. Then, because they had no Torah or covenant, their life was characterized by blasphemy, which produced death. Only forgiveness in communion with Christ (vv. 13f.) and the removal of ἀκροβυστία through the περιτομὴ ἀχειροποίητος (2:11) liberates from this state of death and makes alive. Eph 2:1, 5 describes in similar fashion the preconversion state of the entire

Church (cf. 2:3, 5) as *dead* and thus consistently connects the unsaved state of death not with uncircumcision but rather with trespasses and sins, lusts, and selfishness.

In Heb 6:1; 9:14, "*dead* works" must certainly not be understood as the efforts of natural man to please God. Rather, what seems to be in view here is preconversion conduct, which was carried out without trust in or relationship with God or Jesus Christ. These works, in accord with their nature, only hide death within themselves and therefore lead to death. Perhaps we should similarly understand "deeds of death," or blasphemy, in 4 Ezra 7:119; cf. also "the way of death" in *Did.* 5:1.

In Jas 2:17-26, the parallel expression to *dead* is ἀργή (v. 20, "useless, unfruitful"), which provides the key to interpretation. According to v. 26, faith without works is as *dead* as a body without the spirit that animates it and that makes life possible (→ πνεῦμα). A faith that does not manifest itself as faith through acts of love is *dead* (v. 17); i.e., it is worthless and ineffective for salvation, or does not save in the final judgment (v. 14). When it says, concerning Sardis in Rev 3:1, "that you have a reputation for being alive, but you are *dead*," νεκρός means that the church has fallen prey to temptation and fallen away from God. They have let themselves be led astray and polluted by idol worship.

R. Dabelstein

νεκρόω *nekroō* kill, put to death; pass.: die*
νέκρωσις, εως, ἡ *nekrōsis* deadness, dying; putting to death*

Lit.: → νεκρός.

1. The vb. is found three times in the NT (Rom 4:19; Col 3:5; Heb 11:12), the subst. 2 times (Rom 4:19; 2 Cor 4:10). The words are not found in the LXX but were in use already in the Hellenistic era. They refer in medical terms primarily to the process of dying or the state of death of the body or some part of the body. The Stoics also used them in a fig. sense (cf. Bultmann 894f.; Coenen 1232).

2. In Rom 4:19, Paul uses the vb. to refer to the impotence of the aged Abraham, and the subst. to refer to Sarah's inability to become a mother (cf. Gen 17:17; 18:11f.): "And he [sc. Abraham] was not weak in faith when he considered *that* his body *had died* (νενεκρωμένον)—he was nearly one hundred years old—and the womb of Sarah [also was] *dead* (τὴν νέκρωσιν τῆς μήτρας Σάρρας)." Nevertheless, against all human expectations, God fulfilled his promise to them. Heb 11:12 (pass.) mentions the same with similar wording.

In Col 3:5 members of the church are exhorted to live out the consequences of their baptism and to struggle against the vice that had penetrated: "*Mortify* (νεκρώσατε) therefore your members that are upon the earth: fornication, uncleanness. . . ." This identification of body parts and vices derives from the Jewish conception, in which sin acts upon individual parts of the body (cf. Rom 7:5, 23; Jas 4:1; *2 Bar.* 49:3). The vices have dominion over the body parts and keep them "on the earth," while the Church or believer already lives "above" in his or her true self. Here we may assume that the cosmological concepts are Hellenistic (E. Schweizer, *Col* [Eng. tr., 1982] 141; J. Gnilka, *Col* [HTKNT] 179f., finds "Iranian" influence). Vice must therefore be "put off" (v. 9) and made harmless, "put to death" (v. 5), in order in this way to free the body part under attack from its grasp and deadly effects.

In 2 Cor 4:10, Paul uses the subst. to interpret his apostolic suffering Christologically: "Always bearing about in the body the *dying* of the Lord Jesus (νέϰϱωσιν τοῦ ᾽Ιησοῦ), that the life of Jesus might also be made manifest in our body." Güttgemanns rightly has rejected interpretations that invoke "mystical" categories (e.g., H. Lietzmann and W. G. Kümmel, *1–2 Cor* [HNT] ad loc.) or that view νέϰϱωσις as a process (e.g., C. F. G. Heinrici, *2 Cor* [KEK] ad loc.). Rather, as in Rom 4:19 (cf. Mark 3:5 v.l.; *Herm. Sim.* 9.16.2f.), Paul uses the expression to refer to a *state of death,* or more specifically, the *death* of Jesus. Paul may have had Jesus' crucifixion in mind. The vb. περιφέρω also implies a state. In vv. 10f., Paul construes the suffering inflicted upon him by humans (cf. vv. 8f., 11a) in terms of the ultimate goal of the christological epiphany. Since for Paul the crucified Christ is identical with the risen Kyrios, he can also link his own death and life in paradoxical unity and can even regard his own mortal body as the place and object in which and through which Jesus reveals his ζωή—in the present, however, through the paradoxical fact that the apostle carries about and makes evident this dying in his body.

R. Dabelstein

νέϰϱωσις, εως, ἡ *nekrōsis* deadness, dying; putting to death
→ νεϰϱόω.

νεομηνία, ας, ἡ *neomēnia* new moon*

The *new moon,* which was celebrated by the Jews and also often by Gentiles, is mentioned only in Col 2:16 in the NT (see, however, also *Barn.* 2:5; 15:8 [cf. Isa 1:13]; *Diog.* 4:1): the series "religious festivals, *new moons,* or sabbaths" corresponds directly to the LXX (Hos 2:13; Ezek 45:17). Col 2:16-19 contends against religious-cultic regulations. G. Delling, *TDNT* IV, 638-42; T. C. G. Thornton, "Jewish New Moon Festivals (Gal 4,3-11 and Col 2,16)," *JTS* 40 (1989) 97-100; E. Schweizer, *Col* (Eng. tr., 1982) ad loc.

νέος, 3 *neos* new, fresh, young*
ἀνανεόω *ananeoō* renew*
νεότης, ητος, ἡ *neotēs* youth*

1. Occurrences in the NT — 2. Literal usage — a) Of things — b) Of persons — 3. Fig. and theological usage — a) Mark 2:22 par. — b) 1 Cor 5:7 — c) Colossians and Ephesians

Lit.: J. BEHM, *TDNT* IV, 896-901. — P. BENOIT, "L'horizon Paulinien de l'Épître aux Éphésiens," idem, *Exégèse* II, 53-96. — R. BULTMANN, *Der alte und der neue Mensch in der Theologie des Paulus* (1964). — H. HAARBECK, *DNTT* 674-76. — F. HAHN, "Die Bildworte vom neuen Flicken und vom jungen Wein (Mk. 2:21f. parr)," *EvT* 31 (1971) 357-75. — W. MATTHIAS, "Der alte und der neue Mensch in der Anthropologie des Paulus," *EvT* 17 (1957) 385-97. — R. NORTH, *TDOT* IV, 225-44. — R. SCHNACKENBURG, "Der neue Mensch—Mitte christlichen Weltverständnisses. Kol 3,9-11," idem, *Schriften zum NT* (1971) 392-413. — G. SCHNEIDER, "Die Idee der Neuschöpfung beim Apostel Paulus und ihr religionsgeschichtlicher Hintergrund," *TTZ* 68 (1959) 257-70. — idem, *Neuschöpfung oder Wiederkehr?* (1961), esp. 65-90. — idem, *BL* 422, 1228f. — TRENCH, *Synonyms* 219-25. — C. WESTERMANN, *THAT* I, 524-30. — For further bibliography → ϰαινός; see *TWNT* X, 1186.

1. In this word group, the adj. is the most frequent in the NT (24 times), while the vb. is found only once. The abstract subst. νεότης appears in 4 passages. Νέος, like → ϰαινός, means *new.* In contrast to the latter, νέος designates not so much the quality of being new as (in a temporal sense) being fresh or not yet old. It is often used in the sense of *young* (→ 2.b). In corresponding fashion, νεότης means *youth* (cf. ϰαινότης in Rom 6:4; 7:6). The vb. ἀνανεόω means (in the act. trans.) *renew* (e.g., *Herm. Sim.* ix.14.3) and intrans. "become young again" (*Herm. Vis.* iii.11.3). In Eph 4:23 ἀνανεοῦσθαι . . . τῷ πνεύματι should be understood not as a reflexive mid. *(renew oneself)* but as a pass.: *"be renewed* in the Spirit" (or "let yourselves *be renewed* . . ."; see Behm 900f.; BAGD s.v. 1). The prep. compound with ἀνα- does not refer to a prior state that is then regained.

2. a) Νέος, when used literally to refer to things, means *new, fresh:* "new" wine, which has not yet fully fermented (Mark 2:22a, c par. Matt 9:17a, c/Luke 5:37a, b, 38; Luke 5:39); "new lump (φύραμα)," to which no yeast has yet been added (1 Cor 5:7). Heb 12:24 speaks of the "new [i.e., having just been put into effect] declaration of God's will (διαθήϰη)"; see O. Michel, *Heb* (KEK) 468n.3. The city name → Νέα πόλις, "New City," which in the NT appears only in Acts 16:11, is connected with the harbor of Philippi in Macedonia (thus also Ign. *Pol.* 8:1).

b) In references to persons, the adj. means *young.* The comparative νεώτερος is most common; e.g., Luke 15:13: "the *younger* son" (as opposed to the πρεσβύτερος, v. 25); cf. 15:12: ὁ νεώτερος αὐτῶν. The comparative meaning is elsewhere hardly discernible; e.g., 1 Tim 5:11: "the *young* widows" (cf. v. 14: νεώτεραι); John 21:18: ὅτε ἧς νεώτερος, "when you were *young*" (cf. Ps 36:25 LXX). Νέος/νεώτερος is also used as a subst.: αἱ νέαι, the *young women* (Titus 2:4; likewise the νεώτεραι in 1 Tim 5:2); (οἱ) νεώτεροι, the *young men* (Acts 5:6; 1 Tim 5:1; Titus 2:6; 1 Pet 5:5).

Whether νεώτεροι is used as a t.t. in the NT, as it is elsewhere in the Hellenistic world (Schürer, *History* III, 103; Behm 897), is doubtful; in 1 Pet 5:5 and 1 Tim 5:1 νεώτεροι stand as a kind of class within the church over against the πρεσβύτεροι or the πρεσβύτερος. Along with ὁ μείζων in Luke 22:26, ὁ νεώτερος has a superlative meaning: the *youngest* (cf. Gen 42:20). Here we must understand that normally the youngest is required to carry out the most menial duties. Νεότης is primarily found in the fixed expression ἐκ νεότητος, "from *youth* on" (Homer *Il.* xiv.86; also throughout the LXX): Mark 10:20 par Matt 19:20 (C D Koine W etc.); Luke 18:21; Acts 26:4. The subst. has independent meaning only in 1 Tim 4:12 in the exhortation: "Let no one look down on your *youth* (σου τῆς νεότητος καταφρονείτω)."

3. a) The proverbial statements in Mark 2:21f. are analogically structured and connected with καί. Both sayings go back to Jesus himself (Hahn 369), who through them addresses the coming of the kingdom of God and its incompatibility with the old: "And no one pours *new* wine into old wineskins; otherwise the wine will burst the wineskins, and the wine and the wineskins will be ruined. Rather, *new* wine [is poured] into new wineskins (εἰς ἀσκοὺς καινούς)" (v. 22). In the context of the message of Jesus the saying means, "The eschatological new can in no way be contained within the standards, limitations, and possibilities of the old; whoever attempts to do such loses both" (Hahn 372). Jesus' disposition toward the past is that of a superior detachment. The Synoptic Gospels (→ 2.a) place the two sayings after the question on fasting and thus interpret them as referring to the new way and the new forms of godliness. In Luke 5:39 another proverb is added that at first glance corresponds to the saying on new wine (v. 39 is therefore deleted by Marcion, Irenaeus, D it): old wine is preferred to *new* wine. The Gospel writer uses this general statement to illustrate the fact that many people find the old more palatable and thus are closed to the new of Christianity (cf. G. Schneider, *Luke* [ÖTK] I, 141).

b) 1 Cor 5:7 exhorts: "Clean out the old leaven that you may be a *new* lump (νέον φύραμα), even as you already are (in fact) unleavened (ἄζυμοι). For Christ, our Passover lamb, has already been sacrificed." Unleavened bread, which was prepared at the moment, becomes here the image of the Church, which must keep itself pure from sin (imv. ἐκκαθάρατε) in order that it may be what

it in essence already is: ἄζυμοι. The "old lump" refers to leavened bread, which had to be removed from the house during the celebration of the Passover (Exod 12:15); here it is used as an image of that which makes impure.

c) Col 3:9f. stands within the Pauline tradition (cf. Rom 6:4, 6) and states that Christians have put off the "old man" along with its evil deeds (v. 9) and have put on "the *new* [man] (τὸν νέον)." Behind this image lies the baptismal event (cf. Gal 3:27). That which has been brought about in a person in baptism must be realized in living (Col 3:8, 12). The "*new* man" is characterized by τὸν ἀνακαινούμενον εἰς ἐπίγνωσιν κατ᾽ εἰκόνα τοῦ κτίσαντος αὐτόν (v. 10). In baptism, a *new* creation is brought about, in accordance with which conduct is also renewed.

Eph 4:23 stands in a parenetic context, with v. 22 calling for putting off the "old man." The inf. phrase ἀνανεοῦσθαι δὲ τῷ πνεύματι τοῦ νοὸς ὑμῶν (v. 23), like ἐνδύσασθαι τὸν καινὸν ἄνθρωπον (v. 24), is governed by ἐδιδάχθητε in v. 21. The infs. are reminiscent of baptismal parenesis. It is necessary to give up "the former walk" (v. 22) and consequently to live in accordance with "the *new* man" in righteousness and holiness (v. 24); see H. Schlier, *Eph* (1957) 216-22.							G. Schneider

νεοσσός, οῦ, ὁ *neossos* the young (of a bird)

Variant form of → νοσσός.

νεότης, ητος, ἡ *neotēs* youth
→ νέος.

νεόφυτος, 2 *neophytos* newly planted; newly converted*

In 1 Tim 3:6, in fig. sense: the overseer should not be *newly converted,* "lest he become conceited and fall into the judgment of the devil." The meaning of νεόφυτος is, "newly planted in the Christian church" (BAGD s.v.). M. Dibelius and H. Conzelmann, *1-2 Tim, Titus* (Hermeneia) ad loc.

νεύω *neuō* nod*

John 13:24: Peter *nodded to* the beloved disciple (thus signaling him); Acts 24:10: the governor *motioned to* Paul that he should begin speaking.

νεφέλη, ης, ἡ *nephelē* cloud*

Luke 12:54 speaks of the cloud that comes from the West and brings rain; Jude 12 (cf. 2 Pet 2:17 v.l.) of "waterless *clouds*" (that produce no rain). The cloud motif has theological implications in the remaining NT passages. In 1 Thess 4:17 Paul speaks of the clouds into which "we" will be taken up to the risen Kyrios with those who have risen at the parousia. Clouds also represent vehicles between heaven and earth in Mark 13:26 par. Matt 24:30/Luke 21:27 as well as Mark 14:26 par. Matt 26:64 (at the coming of the Son of Man). Here, too, belong the passages in which the Book of Revelation refers to the clouds (1:7) or the cloud (10:1; 11:12; 14:14 bis, 15, 16). In Luke, νεφέλη stands in the sg., both in Acts 1:9 (ascension) and in Luke 21:27 (parousia), and thus is no longer an eschatological motif. Mark 9:7a, b par. Matt 17:5a, b/Luke 9:34a, b, 35 contain the idea of the cloud of revelation, or the theophany motif, in the account of the transfiguration. The motif of the cloud in the desert is found only in 1 Cor 10:1, 2, in connection with the passage of deliverance through the sea. A. Oepke, *TDNT* IV, 902-10; *TWNT* X, 1186 (bibliography); S. Luzarraga, *Las tradiciones de la nube en la Biblia y en el Judaísmo primitivo* (1973); L. Sabourin, "The Biblical Cloud: Terminology and Traditions," *BTB* 4 (1974) 290-311.

Νεφθαλίμ *Nephthalim* Naphtali*

Naphtali was one of the sons of the patriarch Jacob (Gen 30:7f.; a child of Bilhah, 49:21). In the NT the name applies to the tribe of Naphtali (Rev 7:6) or to the tribal area west of the sea of Gennesaret named after it (Matt 4:13, 15). L. Grollenberg, *LTK* VII, 788.

νέφος, ους, τό *nephos* cloud*

Heb 12:1, in fig. sense, for a large, tightly packed crowd (cf. Homer *Il.* iv.127; Diodorus Siculus iii.29.2): "Since we have such a *cloud* of witnesses around us." A. Oepke, *TDNT* IV, 902f.

νεφρός, οῦ, ὁ *nephros* kidney*

In Rev 2:23, in a description of God, who examines (or tests) "*kidneys* and hearts," i.e., who knows the innermost parts of human beings (cf. LXX Ps 7:10; Jer 11:20; 17:10; 20:12). H. Preisker, *TDNT* IV, 911; G. Lanczkowski, *RGG* IV, 1474.

νεωκόρος, ου, ὁ *neōkoros* temple keeper*

In Acts 19:35, the city clerk begins his speech with the statement that Ephesus is "*temple keeper* of the great Artemis." This title is also attested for the city in *CIG* 2966, 2972. BAGD s.v.

νεωτερικός, 3 *neōterikos* youthful*

In 2 Tim 2:22 νεωτερικός is connected with ἐπιθυμίαι: "Flee the passions *of youth*."

νή *nē* truly, indeed*

This particle of strong affirmation governs the acc. of the person or thing. In the NT only in 1 Cor 15:31: "*truly, by my pride in you.*"

νήθω *nēthō* spin (vb.)*

In Matt 6:28 par. Luke 12:27, of the "lilies of the field," which "do not *spin*" and yet are beautifully clothed. Schulz, *Q* 149-57.

νηπιάζω *nēpiazō* be a child; be naive*

1 Cor 14:20: "Do not be children in your thinking (ταῖς φρεσίν), but *be naive* in evil (τῇ κακίᾳ νηπιάζετε)." → νήπιος.

νήπιος, 3 *nēpios* childlike, naive*

Lit.: G. BERTRAM, *TDNT* IV, 913-25. — J. DUPONT, *Les Béatitudes* II (1969) 149-51, 181-97. — idem, "Les 'simples' (*petâyim*) dans la Bible et à Qumrân. A propos des νήπιοι de Mt 11,25," *Studi sull'Oriente e la Bibbia offerti a P. G. Rinaldi* (1967) 329-36. — W. GRUNDMANN, "Die νήπιοι in der urchristlichen Paränese," *NTS* 5 (1958/59) 188-205. — S. LÉGASSE, *Jésus et l'enfant* (1969) 353, index s.v. — For further bibliography see *TWNT* X, 1186f.

1. Not counting 1 Thess 2:7 and 2 Tim 2:24, where νήπιος contrasts with → ἤπιος, νήπιος is found 14 times in the NT. In the Gospels, besides Matt 11:25 par. Luke 10:21, this adj. is found only in Matt 21:16 (quoting Ps 8:3 LXX). In addition to 1 Thess 2:7, the genuine Pauline letters contain 9 occurrences, 5 of which are found in 1 Cor 13:11 (the rest in Rom 2:20; 1 Cor 3:1; Gal 4:1, 3). Further instances are in Eph 4:14 and Heb 5:13. The adj. designates a child of a young age, a minor, or an infant; it is used literally (→ 2) and fig. (→ 3).

2. In the literal sense νήπιος refers to a child only to illustrate a situation or certain behavior. In general, the comparison is negative. In Gal 4:1, 3, Paul compares humanity before and without Christ, standing under the law and the "powers," to a child under tutelage. In 1 Cor 3:1; Eph 4:14; Heb 5:13, νήπιος is used as an image of a Christian who is still immature with respect to faith and conduct: the immature is still sustained by milk, or is highly impressionable. The spiritual immaturity of the νήπιος in comparison with the adult (ἀνήρ) is transferred in 1 Cor 13:11 to the "lowly" level of the present existence of the Christian in comparison to the perfection of the eschaton (vv. 10, 12). In contrast, children are given a positive role in Matt 21:15f. (cf. → νηπιάζω): the children, who hail Jesus as the Messiah and are related to Ps 8:3 LXX, embody the perceptive faith of the uninstructed, in contrast to the unbelief of the religious leaders of Judaism.

3. In its fig. use, the adj. refers not directly to one who is a child but to one who is *ignorant*. This nuance has its roots in the LXX (Prov 1:32; Pss 18:8; 114:6; 118:130 LXX), although it has less of a pietistic stamp in the NT than it does in the OT. In this vein Paul points out in Rom 2:20 the presumptuousness of a Judaism that would instruct those who do not know the true wisdom. In the thanksgiving in Matt 11:25f. par. Luke 10:21, Jesus praises the revelation of the mystery of salvation to those who at that time made up the "little flock" (→ μικρός 3) of his disciples. They had no academic qualifications, in contrast to those who possessed knowledge of the law. Christians can be identified as νήπιοι when they realize that all human knowledge is vain in comparison with the salvation offered in Jesus Christ and the power of the divine εὐδοκία that requires of a person no conditions—except faith—for receiving true wisdom (cf. 1 Cor 1:17–2:16; Matt 13:11-17 par.).			S. Légasse

Νηρεί *Nērei* Neri

Variant of → Νηρί.

Νηρεύς, έως *Nēreus* Nereus*

In Rom 16:15 Paul sends greetings to "*Nereus* and his sister."

Νηρί *Nēri* Neri*

Indeclinable personal name in the genealogy of Jesus in Luke 3:27.

νησίον, ου, τό *nēsion* small island*

Diminutive of → νῆσος; in Acts 27:16, of the island of → Καῦδα.

νῆσος, ου, ἡ *nēsos* island*

In Acts 27:26, of an unnamed island; in 13:6, of Cyprus; in 28:1, of Malta (also 28:7, 9, 11); in Rev 1:9, of Patmos. In the last days, Rev 6:14 and 16:20 prophesy the dislocation of *islands* (and mountains).

νηστεία, ας, ἡ *nēsteia* fast (noun)
→ νηστεύω.

νηστεύω *nēsteuō* fast (vb.)*
νηστεία, ας, ἡ *nēsteia* fast (noun)*

1. a) Occurrences in the NT — b) Usage — c) Meaning — 2. Fasting in the NT — a) Duration and occasion — b) Motivation — 3. Attitude of Jesus and the early Church toward fasting — a) Mark 2:18-22 — b) Matt 6:16-18

Lit.: R. ARBESMANN, *RAC* VII, 447-93. — F. BAMMEL and F. SCHMIDT-CLAUSING, *RGG* II, 881-85. — J. BEHM, *TDNT* IV, 924-35. — F. G. CREMER, *Die Fastenansage Jesu* (BBB 23, 1965). — J. GAMBERONI, *SacVb* I, 257-60. — H. MANTEL, S. G. HALL, and J. H. CREHAN, *TRE* XI, 45-59. — B. REICKE, "Die Fastenfrage nach Luk. 5,33-39," *TZ* 30 (1974) 321-28. — W. C. ROBINSON, *BHH* 465f. — F. S. ROTHENBERG, *DNTT* I, 611-13. — K. T. SCHÄFER, " '. . . und dann werden sie fasten an jenem Tage' (Mk 2,20 und Par.)," *FS Wikenhauser* 124-47. — M. WAIBEL, "Die Auseinandersetzung mit der Fasten- und Sabbatpraxis Jesu in urchristlichen Gemeinden," *Zur Geschichte des Urchristentums* (QD 87, 1979) 63-80. — J. W. WIMMER, *The Meaning and Motivation of Fasting according to the Synoptic Gospels* (Diss. Gregorian University, Rome, 1979). — For further bibliography see *TWNT* X, 1187.

1. a) The vb. appears 20 times in the NT, but only in the Synoptic Gospels (Matt 4:2; 6:16 bis, 17, 18; 9:14 bis, 15; Mark 2:18 ter, 19 bis, 20; Luke 5:33, 34, 35; 18:12) and Acts (13:2, 3). The subst. is found in 5 passages (3 in Luke-Acts: Luke 2:37; Acts 14:23; 27:9; and 2 in Paul: 2 Cor 6:5; 11:27).

b) The vb. and subst. in the NT almost always mean *fast*, in the special religious (ritual or ascetic) sense. Open to question, however, is whether with the pl. expression ἐν νηστείαις in 2 Cor 6:5 Paul is referring to the fasts he frequently underwent voluntarily for religious-ascetic reasons or to the hunger he endured as a result of dire circumstances. In favor of the latter interpretation is the expression "in hunger and in thirst" (11:27), as well as the fact that the phrase stands in both cases in a list of circumstances of suffering and hardship "that befell the apostle, against which he could not defend himself, that he simply had to endure" (J. Zmijewski, *Der Stil der paulinischen "Narrenrede"* [1978] 263).

c) In all instances a physical fasting is intended. Synonymous expressions are "not eat" (Luke 4:2; cf. par. Matt 4:2 with νηστεύσας) and "hunger and thirst" (2 Cor 11:27, instead of *fast*); an antonym is "eat and drink" (Luke 5:33; the par. Mark 2:19 and Matt 9:14 have the phrase "not fast"). A fig. understanding of "fast" can nowhere be unambiguously discerned (cf., however, Schäfer 140f.; Gamberoni 379, in whose view the vb. in the saying of Jesus recorded in Mark 2:20, because of the image of the bridegroom, should be given the fig. meaning *mournfully do without*).

2. The NT clearly reflects the forms and motivation of the Jewish and early Christian practice of fasting.

a) In Judaism, fasting was required by the law only on the Day of Atonement (cf. Lev 16:29-34; 23:27-32; Num 29:7); Acts 27:9 refers to this required fast ("since it was already after the *fast*"). There were in addition the voluntary fasts of individuals and groups. These, too, are attested in the NT, which usually mentions the duration or occasion for the fast: Jesus fasted forty days in the wilderness (Matt 4:2 par. Luke 4:2; contrast Mark 1:13); the prophetess Anna fasted "day and night" (Luke 2:37);

the Pharisees and the disciples of John fasted regularly (Mark 2:18: ἦσαν . . . νηστεύοντες; Luke 18:12: "twice a week"); the five prophets and teachers of the church in Antioch fasted on the occasion of sending out Barnabas and Paul as missionaries (Acts 13:2f.); Paul and Barnabas fasted upon the appointment of presbyters (Acts 14:23).

b) The religious motivation for fasting is clearest when the term *fast* appears in conjunction with other religious terms. "Fast" most frequently stands in parallel with "pray" (Luke 2:37; 5:33; Acts 13:3; 14:23; cf. also the variant reading at Mark 9:29 par. Matt 17:21; 1 Cor 7:5; Acts 10:30). Both are signs of the worship of God (cf. λατρεύουσα in Luke 2:27 and λειτουργούντων in Acts 13:2). The idea that the effectiveness of prayer can be enhanced through fasting can be found already in the OT (Jer 14:11f.; Neh 1:4; and elsewhere). For the Jews (esp. the Pharisees) fasting was included along with prayer and almsgiving among the most important works of godliness (cf. on this combination Matt 6:2-6, 16-18 [note the key word δικαιοσύνη in v. 1]; also Luke 18:9-14 [the Pharisee who prayed in the temple refers to his fasting twice a week and to his tithing]). From the earliest reference to fasting, it possessed an essentially vicarious, expiatory character. Fasting was for the pious an expression of repentance and sorrow for the sins of the nation against God's law (cf. the equation of fasting and mourning in Matt 9:15).

3. The attitude of Jesus and the early Church toward fasting is esp. evident in Mark 2:18-22 (par. Matt 9:14-17/Luke 5:33-39) and Matt 6:16-18.

a) The conflict saying in Mark 2:18-22 appears to have had a long tradition history, which we may deduce from the several inconsistencies, repetitions, etc. in the current Markan text. Note, e.g., the repeated mention of the opponents in v. 18a, b, where the disciples of John—both times named first—are paired first with the "Pharisees" and then with the "disciples of the Pharisees"; the juxtaposition of the two time indications ἐν ᾧ ("while") and ὅσον χρόνον ("so long as") in v. 19a, b; the discrepancy between the expression "the days will come" (pl.) and "on that day" (sg.) in v. 20; and the addition of the two metaphoric sayings (inconsistent with a conflict saying in terms of both form and content) on the patch and the new wine in vv. 21f. We can reconstruct the process of transmission as follows.

The original conflict saying spoken by Jesus, which apparently addressed the fasting of John's disciples (not the disciples of the Pharisees as yet) or the lack of fasting by Jesus' disciples, probably contained only the comment that people came and asked Jesus a question (v. 18b; the general statement in v. 18a was probably first constructed by the Markan redactor). The question corresponded to the metaphoric saying (in the form of a rhetorical question) about the wedding guests who could not fast while the bridegroom was with them (v. 19a), which was construed as Jesus' answer. The disciples of John understood

their fasting as in essence "a preparation for the Messiah and his kingdom" (P. Gächter, *Matt* [1963] I, 296).

By making use of the wedding metaphor, which already served as an image for messianic-eschatological salvation in Judaism (see references in Billerbeck I, 517f.), Jesus was making clear that such fasting was no longer an issue for his disciples, since the era of salvation had already dawned (in him) and a new situation now existed. Since the two metaphoric sayings in vv. 21f. already dealt with the "old-new" question, it was possible to join them to the conflict saying at this earliest level. (According to J. Gnilka, *Mark* [EKKNT] ad loc., however, the phrase "but new wine in new skins" [v. 22] breaks the parallelism and is a later addition [following the second layer of tradition], while the insertion "the new from the old" in v. 21 is from the Gospel writer, who intended thereby to emphasize the concept of "new teaching" [1:27].)

The second level of the tradition saw not only the introduction of the disciples of the Pharisees in v. 18b but also the expansion of the rhetorical question in v. 19a into the statements in vv. 19b, 20: "So long as the bridegroom is with them, they cannot *fast*; the days will come, however, when the bridegroom will be taken from them, and then they will *fast*." Through the addition of these statements, which clearly have a christological orientation (cf. the double reference to "the bridegroom"), the meaning of the pericope shifts. It no longer gives a theological-eschatological justification for the fact that Jesus' disciples could not fast, since the era of salvation has dawned; rather, the situation of the Church after the death of Jesus is now contrasted with the time when Jesus was still on earth, and the pericope seeks to explain the (new) practice of fasting to Christians (who are now represented by the disciples of Jesus) within the framework of the early church's "crucifixion-and-death christology" (Waibel 79). It thus seeks to justify the new Christian practice of fasting in contrast to that of Judaism (as whose representatives the disciples of the Pharisees now appear alongside the disciples of John), which possessed an essentially different motivation.

At the final level of tradition the statement in v. 20 was expanded by adding "on that day." As a result it deals not with a general justification of the early Church's practice of fasting and its genuine Christian motivation but with a special justification for the times of fasting: "that day" could mean specifically the day of Jesus' death (Friday); the pericope would then become a defense of the Christian practice of fasting on Friday (on this see *Did.* 8:1) over against the Jewish practice on Mondays and Thursdays.

If the early Church did indeed use this pericope to establish and justify their practice of fasting, that does not imply a falsification of the original message of Jesus. As we have just seen, Jesus apparently did not universally reject fasting (cf. Reicke 325) but simply declared superfluous the type of fasting that was understood as an expression of repentance and sorrow and was thought to serve as a preparation for salvation, such as the fasting (regularly) practiced by the disciples of John.

b) The statements about fasting in Matt 6:16-18 (which can be regarded, at least in essence, as an authentic saying of Jesus) can also be understood in this way. Here, too, Jesus does not reject fasting per se; on the contrary, he lends it (along with prayer and almsgiving) great religious significance. He does, however, oppose hypocritical fasting, which is done simply to be seen and praised by others (cf. v. 16a). In its place he calls for fasting in which the orientation is completely toward God (as is the case with every true act of piety [cf. Schnackenburg, *Botschaft* 118]). Fasting should therefore take place "in private" (v. 18: ἐν τῷ ϰρυφαίῳ) and be marked by "joy," which "corresponds strikingly well with the wedding motif in the saying on fasting" (Reicke 325).

J. Zmijewski

νῆστις, ιος (ιδος) [ὁ (ἡ)] *nēstis* hungry*

The adj. is found in Mark 8:3 par. Matt 15:32: Jesus did not want to dismiss the people *hungry* (acc. pl.: νήστεις), i.e., without feeding them. BDF §47.3; J. Behm, *TDNT* IV, 924-35.

νηφάλιος, 3 *nēphalios* sober*

This adj. appears in the NT only in the Pastorals: 1 Tim 3:2, among the exhortations for the bishop; 3:11, among those for the wives of deacons (see also 3:8); Titus 2:2, in the instruction for older men (cf. 2:3 with reference to women). The absolute use of the adj. refers in these passages to the moderate use of wine. (The TR has the spelling νηφάλεος.) O. Bauernfeind, *TDNT* IV, 939-41.

νήφω *nēphō* be sober*

The vb. is found in the NT only in the fig. sense, always in exhortations. It is used with γρηγορέω in 1 Thess 5:6 and 1 Pet 5:8; with σωφρονέω in 1 Pet 4:7; and in the sense of sober watchfulness in 1 Thess 5:8 and 1 Pet 1:13. 2 Tim 4:5 reads: σὺ δὲ νῆφε ἐν πᾶσιν, "you, however, *show sound judgment* in all things." O. Bauernfeind, *TDNT* IV, 936-39; E. Lövestam, "Über die neutestamentliche Aufforderung zur Nüchternheit," *ST* 12 (1958) 80-109.

Νίγερ *Niger* Niger*

Νίγερ, a Latin loanword, is a personal name. According to Acts 13:1 it was the surname òf the Christian Simeon (→ Συμεών) from Antioch, who is mentioned immediately after Barnabas. E. Haenchen, *Acts* (Eng. tr., 1971) 394n.4.

Νιϰάνωρ, ορος *Nikanōr* Nikanor*

A common Greek personal name (Thucydides 1, 2; 4 Maccabees; Aristotle; Josephus; *CIJ* 1256; also in rabbinic literature), Νιϰάνωρ in Acts 6:5 is the name of one of the group of seven headed up by Stephen.

νιϰάω *nikaō* conquer, gain victory*
νίϰη, ης, ἡ *nikē* victory*

1. Occurrences in the NT — 2. Non-Johannine passages — 3. John and 1 John — 4. Revelation

Lit.: O. BAUERNFEIND, *TDNT* IV, 942-45. — W. GÜNTHER, *DNTT* I, 650-52. — F. HAHN, "Die Sendschreiben der Johannesapokalypse," FS Kuhn 357-94, esp. 382-86. — T. HOLTZ, *Die Christologie der Apokalypse des Johannes* (TU 85, 1971), esp. 36-39. — A. POLAG, *Die Christologie der Logienquelle* (WMANT 45, 1977) 42f. — For further bibliography see *TWNT* X, 1187f.

1. Aside from the 17 occurrences of νιϰάω in Revelation and the 6 in 1 John, the vb. is found only in Luke 11:22; Rom 3:4; 12:21 (bis); and John 16:33; and the subst. only in 1 John 5:4.

2. The form of the parable of the strong man who is *overcome* by one stronger (Luke 11:21f.) is that of the Q tradition. The parable itself qualifies the use of νιϰάω. The citation from the LXX in Rom 3:4 refers to a legal victory, which is in terms of διϰαιοῦσθαι (v. 5). Yet the statement that God *prevails* over his opponent in the legal battle is important for Paul. The summarizing instruction of 12:21 is characteristic (cf. *T. Benj.* 4:2f.; the normal use of νιϰάω can also be assumed in Pseudo-Phocylides 80; cf. P. W. van der Horst, *The Sentences of Pseudo-Phocylides* [1978] 168f.). The spiritual battle that is here conceived of (cf. *T. Gad* 5:4) is also carried on through one's actions. The situation of the addressees as well as the neuter τὸ ϰαϰόν suggests an eschatological accent.

3. John 16:33 summarizes the result of the process through which Jesus *shows himself to be superior* to the world. In 16:11 victory is declared with reference to the "prince of this world," and 12:31f. shows that such "victory" takes place through the "lifting up" on the cross.

In 1 John νιϰάω (and νίϰη) are applied to believers. The use in 1 John 5:4f. is pregnant and comprehensive: the one who is born of God *overcomes* the cosmos. This *victory* is faith directed toward Jesus as the Son of God. Being born of God is made manifest in faith, which has a basis in reality (i.e., is true) only when it confesses Jesus as the Son of God. With this faith believers participate in the reality of Jesus and have therefore overcome the world as power over their life. Νιϰάω in 1 John 4:4 refers to the *victory* of those who are from God and to the defeat of the false teachers; 2:13f. addresses the group of young men with the assertion that they *have overcome* the evil one. The statement in v. 14 varies from that of v. 13; the context makes turning toward one's brother and turning away from the world and its dangers (v. 16) a sign of this *victory*.

4. In Rev 11:7; 13:7; 17:14 a victory in battle is in mind, or this idea is at least in the background, as the

presence of πολεμ- in the immediate context shows. A direct result of the battle is the *victory*—initially only that of the "beast" in 11:7 and 13:7—in accordance with which 17:14 consciously mentions only the warring of the ten kings in conjunction with the *victory* of the lamb. The hymn in 12:10 interprets the destruction of the dragon in the battle with the angels as the triumph of members of the community but has in mind a legal process, as κατήγωρ/-εῖν in v. 10 shows. In 15:2, with the transfigured forms of those who have gained the victory over (ἐκ) the beast, we come very close to the absolute use of the subst. partc. ὁ νικῶν for the *victor*.

The absolute is found in the victor sayings in the letters to the churches (2:7, 11, 17, 26; 3:5, 12, 21) as well as 21:7. Elsewhere the absolute form of νικάω is found only in 3:21 and 5:5 of Christ and 6:2 (bis) of the archer mounted on the white horse, representing the inevitable violence of war. The absolute use of νικάω did not arise from a shortened form of the longer statement. The attempt to interpret all passages within the parameters of the theology of suffering (Hahn) is not convincing. Nor does it derive from the Jewish (apocalyptic) use of the word (*1 Enoch* 46:3, of the Son of Man; 50:2, of the righteous, in each instance in legal battle; 4 Ezra 7:115, 127, of the righteous, first in legal battle, then in war; according to 1QM 4:13, upon return from battle the banners read [among other things], *nṣḥ 'l*, "victory of God"). Rev 5:5 refers to battle (cf. 17:14). Since the victory of Christ in 3:21 is placed in parallel with the victory of the recipient of the promise, ὁ νικῶν cannot have the primary meaning of victor in a legal battle. Nevertheless, 4 Ezra 7:115, 127f. and Rev 12:7-11 show how closely related the ideas of victory in battle and victory in court actually are.

The absolute use of νικάω represents the eschatological trial through which participation in salvation and exaltation are achieved. At its base lies the concept of the world as the theater of the battle waged by the antigod against God, in which the historical actions of the individual can either support or oppose the antigod.

T. Holtz

νικέω *nikeō* conquer, gain victory

Variant of → νικάω. BDF §90.

νίκη, ης, ἡ *nikē* victory
→ νικάω.

Νικόδημος, ου *Nikodēmos* Nicodemus*

Nicodemus is the name of a Pharisee and "ruler of the Jews" (John 3:1) who sought Jesus at night (3:4, 9); 7:50 and 19:39 refer to that nocturnal conversation. According to 19:39 Nicodemus brought "a mixture of myrrh and aloes, about seventy-five pounds," for the burial of Jesus. On John

3 see J. Becker, "J 3,1-21 als Reflex johanneischer Schuldiskussion," FS Friedrich 85-96; G. Gaeta, *Il dialogo con Nicodemo* (1974); H. Zimmermann, "Die christliche Taufe nach Joh. 3. Ein Beitrag zur Logoschristologie des Vierten Evangeliums," *Catholica* 30 (1976) 81-93.

Νικολαΐτης, ου, ὁ *Nikolaitēs* Nicolaitan*

In the pl. it designates the followers of a certain Nicolaus (not further known) who is regarded as the founder of a sect in Rev 2:6, 15. He is probably not directly related to the → Νικόλαος mentioned in Acts 6:5 (*contra* T. Zahn, *Acts* [KNT] at 6:5), since the name Nicolaus was very common. The self-designation of the sect was perhaps intended to draw on the well-known Hellenist "Nicolaus" (as proof of "apostolic" origin) without the sect's actually having been founded by him (N. Brox, "Nikolaos und Nikolaiten," *VC* 19 [1965] 23-30). See also M. Goguel, "Les Nicolaïtes," *RHR* 115 (1965) 23-30.

Νικόλαος, ου *Nikolaos* Nicolaus*

The name of a proselyte from Antioch who belonged to the group of seven headed up by Stephen (Acts 6:5; → Νικολαΐτης).

Νικόπολις, εως *Nikopolis* Nicopolis*

Of the many cities bearing this name, Titus 3:12 (and the subscription in 1 Timothy and Titus) probably has in mind Nicopolis in Epirus (according to C. Danoff, *KP* IV, 124f., Nicopolis since the time of Nero was the capital city of the province of Epirus): " . . . then come quickly to me in *Nicopolis,* for I plan to spend the winter there." M. Dibelius and H. Conzelmann, *1–2 Tim, Titus* (Hermeneia) 152-54.

νῖκος, ους, τό *nikos* victory*

1. Occurrences in the NT — 2. 1 Cor 15:54, 55, 57 — 3. Matt 12:20.

Lit.: G. BARTH, in G. Bornkamm, G. Barth, and H. J. Held, *Tradition and Interpretation in Matthew* (NTL, 1963) 137-53. — O. BAUERNFEIND, *TDNT* IV, 941-45. — R. H. GUNDRY, *The Use of the OT in St. Matthew's Gospel* (NovTSup 18, 1967) 110-16. — R. A. KRAFT, "ΕΙΣ ΝΙΚΟΣ = Permanently, Successfully: 1 Cor 15:54, Matt 12:20," *Septuagintal Lexicography* (SBLSCS 1, ed. R. A. Kraft; 1972) 153-56. — W. ROTHFUCHS, *Die Erfüllungszitate des Matthäusevangeliums* (BWANT V/8, 1969) 72-77. — K. STENDAHL, *The School of St. Matthew* (ASNU 20, 1954) 107-15. — G. STRECKER, *Der Weg der Gerechtigkeit* (FRLANT 82, 1971) 67-70.

1. The 4 instances of νῖκος are concentrated in two passages: Matt 12:20 and 1 Cor 15:54, 55, 57. In both passages the word is apparently taken over from the OT tradition in the form εἰς νῖκος. The word has no independent meaning in NT usage.

2. The quotation in 1 Cor 15:54f. combines Isa 25:8 with Hos 13:14. The text of Isa 25:8 corresponds to Theodotion (εἰς νῖκος also in A) and led to the substitution of νῖκος for δίκη in Hos 13:14. The combined passage had probably already been constructed in this form before its inclusion by Paul. The brief thanksgiving in 1 Cor 15:57, which presents the foregoing thought by way of application, picks up on νῖκος once again. The repeated inclusion of the word shows that it is understood in the sense of *victory, complete conquest* (although in Isa 25:8 [Theodotion A] εἰς νῖκος, as the tr. of Heb. *lānesaḥ*, could mean "permanently"; see Kraft, but also G. B. Caird, "Towards a Lexicon of the Septuagint," *ibid.* 136). The quotation proclaims, at the end of Paul's statements on the reality of resurrection, the eschatological victory over death (cf. 1 Cor 15:26), and the final thanksgiving proclaims the victory over the eschatological power of death as the present gift of God through Christ (cf. Rom 8:37).

3. In Matt 12:20 νῖκος appears in a quotation from Isa 42:1-4, although it is not drawn directly from any known form of the OT text tradition. Apparently, Isa 42:3b and 4a are compressed together in Matt 12:20c (Strecker). Matthew could have taken over the quotation in this form, which is supported not only by 12:21 but also by the fact that νῖκος appears even though Matthew nowhere else uses words of the νικ- stem. The reflective quotation develops the saving acts of Jesus contained in the summary of Matt 12:15f. (par. Mark 3:7-12). Matt 12:20c gives the eschatological goal toward which the merciful deliverance of the servant is directed. Εἰς νῖκος here also means "to *salvation*/to *unlimited validity*," where the aspect of duration is also in mind. In adding v. 21, Matthew also includes Gentiles in the hope for achieving the eschatological realization of justice, i.e., righteousness.

T. Holtz

Νινευί *Nineui* Nineveh

Νινευί is the indeclinable place name found in Luke 11:32 TR for the former capital of the Assyrian empire; cf. BDF §39.1. Luke 11:32 draws on the biblical account of Jonah, according to which the inhabitants of Nineveh willingly performed acts of penance (Jonah 3:5 LXX).

Νινευίτης, ου, ὁ *Nineuitēs* Ninevite*

This noun designates the inhabitants of Nineveh (→ Νινευί) in the Q logion of Matt 12:41 par. Luke 11:32: "The people *of Nineveh* will rise up in judgment with this generation" and will put to shame the unrepentant present generation. Luke 11:30, in which Jonah became a sign τοῖς Νινευίταις, also probably stems from Q. Schulz, *Q* 250-57.

νιπτήρ, ῆρος, ὁ *niptēr* washbasin*

According to John 13:5, Jesus poured "water in the *basin* and began to wash (→ νίπτω) the feet of the disciples."

νίπτω *niptō* wash; mid.: wash oneself*

Νίπτω is one of the words preferred by John (13 occurrences; of which 8 are found in the account of the footwashing, 5 in the healing of the blind man in John 9; the rest of the NT contains just 4). The act. vb. is found in the account of the footwashing by Jesus (John 13:5, 6, 8 bis, 12, 14 bis) and in 1 Tim 5:10 (footwashing as an act of love toward others). The mid. *wash oneself* is found in John 9:7 (bis), 11 (bis), 15. The mid. meaning *I wash for myself* with an acc. obj. is also found: Matt 6:17 (the face); Mark 7:3 par. Matt 15:2 (ritual washing of the hands); John 13:10 (the feet). F. Hauck, *TDNT* IV, 946-48; G. R. Beasley-Murray, *DNTT* I, 153f.

νοέω *noeō* know, understand*

1. Occurrences and meaning — 2. Νοέω with entire texts — 3. Νοέω and morality — 4. Νοέω and heresy — 5. Νοέω and faith

Lit.: J. BEHM, *TDNT* IV, 948-60. — G. BORNKAMM, "Faith and Reason in Paul," *idem, Early Christian Experience* (1969) 29-46. — BULTMANN, *Theology* I, 211-13. — CONZELMANN, *Theology* 180f. — R. JEWETT, *Paul's Anthropological Terms* (1971) 358-90. — For further bibliography see *TWNT* X, 1188f.

1. The vb., which refers to the proper understanding of a matter, is found 14 times and is synonymous with (ἐπι-)γινώσκω and συνίημι (3 occurrences in Mark, 4 in Matthew with a doublet, twice in Ephesians, and once in John, Romans, 1 Timothy, 2 Timothy, and Hebrews; it is altogether lacking in Luke-Acts; cf. νόημα: 6 times in Paul; νοῦς: 24 times in the NT, of which 14 are in Paul). If → νοῦς indicates the faculty (organ) for the proper understanding of matters (not only thinking, but also knowledge), then, roughly speaking, νοέω means the corresponding act, and νόημα the result.

2. In a striking usage, νοέω refers to insight into the overall aim of a writing. Readers are addressed directly and urged to *understand* (not just contemplate or consider) the entire work (Mark 13:14 par. Matt 24:15). In contrast, the narrative audience fails to *understand* (noted earlier in Mark 7:18 par. Matt 15:17 and Mark 8:17 par. Matt 16:9, 11). In the same way the reader of Eph 3:4 should *perceptively understand* the insight of the author into the plan of salvation therein recorded (v. 6). In 2 Tim 2:7 such an exhortation marks the main part of the letter in 2:8-13 (cf. also 2 Thess 2:2; Luke 24:25; Rev 13:18; 17:9). John 12:40 could also ironically, by way of negation, have such a function for the entire book (→ 5).

3. In passages dealing with ethics νοέω itself never refers to one's disposition as a fundamental moral attitude. In Rom 1:20 the structures of ordered reality are universally apparent (i.e., the structures of reality are related, as creation revelation, to the structures of thought and language), since they can be *intellectually perceived* (pass. partc.). Their equally apparent universal rejection has resulted, however, in human intellect becoming permanently useless and dysfunctional (1:28, cf. v. 21; not however, a reprehensible or reprobate disposition). The renewal of the faculty of judgment takes place in such a way that reconciliation with God (Phil 4:7) pervades and controls one's mind—including its particular thoughts. Only after the literary incorporation of Eph 3:20 and the transformation of this prayer into a doxology did the inclusive component of Paul become one that more sharply differentiates a transcendence of the *understanding*.

4. In the post-Pauline polemic against false teachers in 1 Tim 1:7 the false teachers do not *understand* what they are saying and therefore are regarded as having a "corrupt mind" (1 Tim 6:5; cf. 2 Tim 3:8; Titus 1:15; Col 2:18).

5. In the statement on faith in Heb 11:3, where the definition of faith is ethical (= trust, piety) rather than specifically Christian, knowing (as a cognitive faculty of faith) is subordinated to faith. In a sharper statement of such an epistemological dualism, John 12:40 (quoting Isa 6:10, with the insertion, however, of the vb. from Mark 8:17), a reflection on the entire work of the Johannine Jesus, states that in accordance with the will of God it would not *be understood*.   W. Schenk

νόημα, ατος, τό *noēma* thought, mind; intention*

This noun is found in the NT only in the Pauline letters, 5 times in 2 Corinthians and in Phil 4:7, all pl. except once sg. in a pl. sense (2 Cor 10:5). Except in Phil 4:7, νόημα is used in a negative sense. It designates the result of thinking (νοέω). 2 Cor 3:14; 4:4; 11:3; and—without negative connotations—Phil 4:7 speak of human thoughts. Evil *intentions/schemes* are in mind in 2 Cor 2:11 (cf. Eph 6:11; 1 Pet 5:8). The figure in 2 Cor 10:5, αἰχμαλωτίζοντες πᾶν νόημα εἰς τὴν ὑπακοὴν τοῦ Χριστοῦ, should be interpreted as follows: the warrior Paul takes all human schemes against Christ captive and forces them into subjection. J. Behm, *TDNT* IV, 960f.

νόθος, 3 *nothos* illegitimate*

Fig. in Heb 12:8 of those who do not experience God's discipline and therefore (according to Prov 3:11f.) cannot be true sons: "then you are *illegitimate* (νόθοι), and not true sons."

νομή, ῆς, ἡ *nomē* pasture; fodder*

John 10:9: "He will go in and out and will find *pasture*"; 2 Tim 2:17 fig.: the false teaching "will eat away (νομὴν ἕξει) like a cancer."

νομίζω *nomizō* think, believe, assume*

1. Occurrences, meaning, and usage — 2. Luke-Acts — 3. Matthew

1. Of the 15 NT occurrences, 9 are Lukan (2 in the Gospel, 7 in Acts), 3 are Matthean (independent of Luke), and the others are in 1 Cor 7:26, 36 (here in the positive sense of *have a grounded conviction*; cf. vv. 25, 37) and 1 Tim 6:5 (an accusation against the false teachers, who *imagine*, cf. Acts 8:20). The vb. is synonymous with the trans. use of δοκέω. The 15 LXX occurrences are all in the deuterocanonical portions. Except in Matthew, the vb. generally is followed by acc. + inf. (or, as in Luke 3:23 [pass.], by nom. + partc.; in Acts 8:20 only the inf.; in 21:29 acc. with ὅτι).

2. Except in Acts 16:13, where a positive narrative character makes a correct assumption, νομίζω in Luke-Acts always is used of a false assumption, which in some instances is criticized in direct discourse by the opponent (Acts 8:20; 17:29; in 7:25 by the narrative opponent) and is elsewhere related as an *erroneous assumption* (Luke 2:44; 3:23, a redactional addition intended to balance the genealogy of Joseph with the virgin birth; Acts 14:19; 16:27; 21:29). All the Lukan occurrences are the result of redaction.

3. The three Matthean occurrences are also redactional, since in contrast to all other NT instances they are constructed with ὅτι instead of acc. + inf. In Matt 5:17; 10:34 prohibitions are used (as frequently in 2 and 4 Maccabees) to introduce some form of ἦλθον for the purpose of dispelling a christological misunderstanding. Since, however, the positive inverse immediately follows, the clauses could simply represent rhetorical heightening in typically Matthean antithetical constructions. On the basis of these two passages, it is also clear to the reader of Matt 20:10 that, as previously, an erroneous assumption is intended.   W. Schenk

νομικός, 3 *nomikos* legal, pertaining to the law; subst.: lawyer, teacher of the law*
νομοδιδάσκαλος, ου, ὁ *nomodidaskalos* teacher of the law*

Lit.: W. GUTBROD, *TDNT* IV, 1088. — K. H. RENGSTORF, *TDNT* II, 159. — For further bibliography → γραμματεύς.

1. (Ὁ) νομικός is found 9 times in the NT, of which 6 are in Luke. In classical Gk. νομικός was always adjec-

tival—"pertaining to the law/corresponding to the law" —but is so in the NT only in Titus 3:9: μάχας νομικάς, "controversies *over the law.*" In later Greek ὁ νομικός used substantivally gained the meaning "lawyer/notary"; it probably has this sense in the NT only in Titus 3:13 (M. Dibelius and H. Conzelmann, *The Pastoral Epistles* [Hermeneia] 152; Gutbrod 1088). In all other NT occurrences ὁ νομικός refers to the Jewish *experts in the law/ teachers of the law.* The occurrences of νομικός in Luke are with great probability either redactional (7:30 [par. Matt 21:31?]; 11:45f., 52; 14:3), or they rest on traditions handed down to him (10:25—although par. Matt 22:35: εἷς ἐξ αὐτῶν [sc. the Pharisees, mentioned in v. 34] νομικός; contrast Mark 12:28: εἷς τῶν γραμματέων). A clear distinction between νομικός in this specific sense and → γραμματεύς does not exist.

2. Νομοδιδάσκαλος, which is not found in secular Greek, is found only 3 times in the NT: in Luke 5:17 (a redactional addition to Φαρισαῖοι); in Acts 5:34 for Gamaliel I (→ Γαμαλιήλ; see H. Hübner, "Gal 3,10 und die Herkunft des Paulus," *KD* 19 [1973] 228f.); and in 1 Tim 1:7 "to denote the legalism of the errorists opposed by the author, but in an ironical sense," for they "do not really know what the νόμος is all about" (Rengstorf).

H. Hübner

νομίμως *nomimōs* in accordance with the law, according to the rule*

Only the adv. form of the adj. νόμιμος is found in the NT. In 2 Tim 2:5 it does not mean "according to the OT law," but, in accordance with the metaphor of competition, *according to the rule.* In 1 Tim 1:8 the decision is more difficult; the Torah may also be in mind here. W. Gutbrod, *TDNT* IV, 1088f.

νόμισμα, ατος, τό *nomisma* coin*

Matt 22:19a: "show me the *coin* for the tax (τὸ νόμισμα τοῦ κήνσου)." The par. in Mark 12:15 has → δηνάριον.

νομοδιδάσκαλος, ου, ὁ *nomodidaskalos* teacher of the law
→ νομικός.

νομοθεσία, ας, ἡ *nomothesia* lawgiving; law*

Νομοθεσία is found in Rom 9:4 in the enumeration of the prerogatives of the Israelites: ὧν . . . αἱ διαθῆκαι καὶ ἡ νομοθεσία καὶ ἡ λατρεία. Here the result of the lawgiving (the Torah) is intended. W. Gutbrod, *TDNT* IV, 1089.

νομοθετέω *nomotheteō* be a lawgiver*

This vb. is found only twice in the NT, both times

pass. and both in Hebrews. 7:11: "the people *received the law*" 8:6: the better διαθήκη "*was established* on better promises." W. Gutbrod, *TDNT* IV, 1090.

νομοθέτης *nomothetēs* lawgiver*

Of God in James 4:12: "One is *lawgiver* and judge." W. Gutbrod, *TDNT* IV, 1089.

νόμος, ου, ὁ *nomos* law

1. Occurrences in the NT — 2. Meaning — a) In classical and Hellenistic Greek — b) In the LXX — c) In the NT — 3. Syntactical usage — 4. a) Jesus and the Synoptics, Acts — b) Paul and Pauline influence — c) John

Lit.: A. J. BANDSTRA, *The Law and the Elements of the World* (1964). — R. BANKS, *Jesus and the Law in the Synoptic Tradition* (1975). — G. BARTH, "Matthew's Understanding of the Law," G. Bornkamm, G. Barth, and H. J. Held, *Tradition and Interpretation in Matthew* (1963) 58-164. — M. BARTH, "Die Stellung des Paulus zu Gesetz und Ordnung," *EvT* 33 (1973) 496-526. — K. BERGER, *Die Gesetzesauslegung Jesu.* I: *Markus und Parallelen* (1972). — H. D. BETZ, "Geist, Freiheit und Gesetz," *ZTK* 71 (1974) 78-93. — P. BLÄSER, *Das Gesetz bei Paulus* (1941). — G. BORNKMAMM, *Jesus of Nazareth* (1960) 88-92. — idem, "Wandlungen im alt- und neutestamentlichen Gesetzesverständnis," idem, *Aufsätze* IV, 73-119. — F. BOVON, "L'homme nouveau et la loi chez l'apôtre Paul," *Die Mitte des NT* (FS E. Schweizer, 1983) 22-33. — H. BRAUN, *Spätjüdisch-häretischer und frühchristlicher Radikalismus* I/II (1969). — R. BRING, *Christus und das Gesetz* (1969). — F. F. BRUCE, "Paul and the Law of Moses," *BJRL* 57 (1975) 259-79. — I. BROER, *Freiheit vom Gesetz und Radikalisierung des Gesetzes. Ein Beitrag zur Theologie des Evangelisten Mattthäus* (SBS 98, 1980). — BULTMANN, *Theology* 259-69. — idem, "Christus des Gesetzes Ende," idem, *Glauben* II, 32-68. — C. E. B. CRANFIELD, *Rom* (ICC) II (1979) 845-62. — W. D. DAVIES, *Paul and Rabbinic Judaism* (⁴1980) 147-76. — idem, *Torah in the Messianic Age and/or the Age to Come* (1952). — idem, *The Setting of the Sermon on the Mount* (1966), index s.v. Torah. — J. W. DRANE, *Paul: Libertine or Legalist?* (1975). — A. VAN DÜLMEN, *Die Theologie des Gesetzes bei Paulus* (1968) — J. D. G. DUNN, "Mark 2,1–3,6: A Bridge between Jesus and Paul in the Question of the Law," *NTS* 30 (1984) 395-415 (= idem, *Jesus, Paul, and the Law* [1990] 10-31 [with "Additional Note," 32-36]). — E. L. EHRLICH, "Tora im Judentum," *EvT* 37 (1977) 536-49. — H.-H. ESSER, *DNTT* II, 438-51. — A. FEUILLET, "Loi de Dieu, loi du Christ et loi de l'Esprit d'après les épîtres pauliniennes," *NovT* 22 (1980) 29-65. — P. FIEDLER, *Jesus und die Sünder* (1976) 37-95. — G. FRIEDRICH, "Das Gesetz des Glaubens," idem, *Auf das Wort kommt es an* (1978) 107-22. — idem, "' Ἁμαρτία οὐκ ἐλλογεῖται Röm 5,13," ibid, 123-31. — V. P. FURNISH, *Theology and Ethics in Paul* (1968) 135-62, 191-94. — H. GESE, "The Law," idem, *Essays on Biblical Theology* (1981) 60-92. — E. GRÄSSER, *Das Problem der Parusieverzögerung in den synoptischen Evangelien und in der Apostelgeschichte* (BZNW 22, ³1977) 180-83. — idem, "Die antijüdische Polemik im Johannesevangelium," idem, *Text und Situation* (1973) 50-69. — F. HAHN, "Das Gesetzesverständnis im Römer und Galaterbrief,"

ZNW 67 (1976) 29-63. — M. HENGEL, "Jesus und die Tora," *TBeitr* 9 (1978) 152-72. — F. HEINIMANN, *Nomos und Physis* ([2]1945 = 1972). — O. HOFIUS, "Das Gesetz des Mose und das Gesetz Christi," *ZTK* 80 (1983) 262-86. — G. HOWARD, *Paul: Crisis in Galatia* (1979) 66-82. — K. HRUBY, "Gesetz und Gnade in der rabbinischen Überlieferung," *Judaica* 25 (1969) 30-63. — M. HUBAUT, "Jésus et la Loi de Moïse," *RTL* 7 (1976) 401-25. — H. HÜBNER, "Das ganze und das eine Gesetz. Zum Problemkreis Paulus und die Stoa," *KD* 21 (1975) 239-56. — idem, "Das Gesetz als elementares Thema einer Biblischen Theologie?" *KD* 22 (1976) 250-76. — idem, *Das Gesetz in der synoptischen Tradition* (1973). — idem, *Law in Paul's Thought* (1984). — idem, "Mk 7,15 und das 'jüdisch-hellenistische' Gesetzesverständnis," *NTS* 22 (1975/76) 319-45. — idem, "Pauli theologiae proprium," *NTS* 26 (1979/80) 445-73. — idem, Was heißt bei Paulus 'Werke des Gesetzes'? *Glaube und Eschatologie* (FS W. G. Kümmel, 1985) 123-33. — J. JERVELL, "Der unbekannte Paulus," *Die paulinische Literatur und Theologie* (ed. S. Pedersen, 1980) 29-49. — E. JÜNGEL, "Das Gesetz zwischen Adam und Christus. Eine theologische Studie zu Röm 5:12-21," *ZTK* 60 (1963) 42-74. — M. KALUSCHE, " 'Das Gesetz als Thema biblischer Theologie'?" *ZNW* 77 (1986) 194-205. — R. KAMPLING, "Zur Diskussion um das Verständnis des Gesetzes im NT," *TRev* 83 (1987) 441-48. — K. KERTELGE, ed., *Das Gesetz im NT* (1986). — idem, "Gesetz und Freiheit im Galaterbrief," *NTS* 30 (1984) 382-94. — H. KLEINKNECHT and W. GUTBROD, *TDNT* IV, 1022-91. — K. KOCH, J. AMIR, et al., *TRE* XIII, 40-126. — H.-J. KRAUS, "Freude an Gottes Gesetz," *EvT* 8 (1950/51) 337-51. — idem, "Zum Gesetzesverständnis der nachexilischen Zeit," idem, *Biblisch-theologische Aufsätze* (1972) 179-94. — W. G. KÜMMEL, "Jesus und der jüdische Traditionsgedanke," idem I, 15-35. — O. KUSS, "Nomos bei Paulus," *MTZ* 17 (1966) 173-227. — J. LAMBRECHT, "Jesus and the Law. An Investigation of Mark 7,1-23," *ETL* 53 (1977) 24-82. — F. LANG, "Gesetz und Bund bei Paulus," FS Käsemann 305-20. — E. LARSSON, "Paul: Law and Salvation," *NTS* 31 (1985) 425-36. — G. LIEDKE and C. PETERSEN, *THAT* II, 1032-43. — J. N. LIGHTSTONE, "Torah is *nomos*—Except When It Is Not. Prolegomena to the Study of the Law in Late Antique Judaism," *SR* 13 (1984) 29-37. — M. LIMBECK, *Die Ordnung des Heils. Untersuchungen zum Gesetzesverständnis des Frühjudentums* (1971). — idem, *Von der Ohnmacht des Rechts. Zur Gesetzeskritik des NT* (1972). — H. LJUNGMAN, *Das Gesetz erfüllen. Mt 5,17ff und 3,15 untersucht* (1954). — E. LOHSE, "ὁ νόμος τοῦ πνεύματος τῆς ζωῆς," FS Braun 279-87. — U. LUZ, *Das Geschichtsverständnis des Paulus* (1968) 136-226. — J. MARBÖCK, "Gesetz und Weisheit. Zum Verständnis des Gesetzes bei Jesus Ben Sira," *BZ* 20 (1976) 1-21. — W. MARXSEN, "Der ἕτερος νόμος Röm 13:8," *TZ* 11 (1955) 230-37. — C. MAURER, *Die Gesetzeslehre des Paulus nach ihrem Ursprung und ihrer Entfaltung dargelegt* (1941). — R. S. MCCONNELL, *Law and Prophecy in Matthew's Gospel* (1969). — J. P. MEIER, *Law and History in Matthew's Gospel* (1976). — J. MERKLEIN, *Die Gottesherrschaft als Handlungsprinzip* (1978) 72-107. — G. MIEGGE, *Il sermone sul monte* (1970) 83-161. — L. MONSENGWO PASINYA, *La notion de nomos dans le Pentateuque grec* (1973). — U. B. MÜLLER, "Zur Rezeption gesetzeskritischer Jesusüberlieferung im frühen Christentum," *NTS* (1980/81) 158-85. — F. MUSSNER, *Gal* (HTKNT, [3]1977) 277-90. — J. NEUSNER, *The Rabbinic Tradition about the Pharisees before 70* III (1975) 5-43. — K. NIEDERWIMMER, *Der Begriff "Freiheit" im NT* (1966) 192-212. — M. NOTH, "The

Laws in the Pentateuch," idem, *The Laws in the Pentateuch and Other Studies* (1984) 1-107. — idem, " 'For All Who Rely on Works of the Law Are Under a Curse,' " ibid., 118-31. — P. VON DER OSTEN-SACKEN, "Das paulinische Verständnis des Gesetzes im Spannungsfeld von Eschatologie und Geschichte," *EvT* 37 (1977) 549-87. — idem, *Römer 8 als Beispiel paulinischer Soteriologie* (1975) 245-60. — E. H. PAGELS, *The Gnostic Paul* (1975). — S. PANCARO, *The Law in the Fourth Gospel* (1975). — H. RÄISÄNEN, *Paul and the Law* (WUNT 29, 1983). — idem, *The Torah and Christ* (Publications of the Finnish Exegetical Society 45, 1986). — P. L. REDDITT, "The Concept of *Nomos* in Fourth Maccabees," *CBQ* 45 (1983) 249-70. — A. SAND, *Das Gesetz und die Propheten* (1974). — E. P. SANDERS, *Paul and Palestinian Judaism* (1977) 474-523. — idem, *Paul, the Law, and the Jewish People* (1983). — J. A. SANDERS, "Torah and Paul," FS Dahl 132-40. — idem, "Torah and Christ," *Int* 29 (1975) 372-90. — P. SCHÄFER, "Die Torah in messianischer Zeit," *ZNW* 65 (1974) 27-42. — J. SCHARBERT, J. SCHMID, and P. BLÄSER, *LTK* IV, 815-22. — H. SCHLIER, *Gal* (KEK, [5]1971) 176-88. — idem, *Grundzüge einer paulinischen Theologie* (1978) 77-97. — H. SCHMID, "Gesetz und Gnade im AT," *Judaica* 25 (1969) 1-29. — E. J. SCHNABEL, *Law and Wisdom from Ben Sira to Paul* (WUNT II/16, 1985). — N. SCHNEIDER, *Die rhetorische Eigenart der paulinischen Antithese* (1970) 95-100, 125. — H.-J. SCHOEPS, *Paul: The Theology of the Apostle in the Light of Jewish Religious History* (1961) 168-218. — idem, "Jesus und das jüdische Gesetz," idem, *Aus frühchristlicher Zeit* (1950) 212-20. — W. SCHRAGE, *Die konkreten Einzelgebote in der paulinischen Paränese* (1961) 109, 228-38. — SCHULZ, Q 94-141. — H. SCHÜRMANN, " 'Das Gesetz des Christus' Gal 6,2," FS Schnackenburg 282-300.—G. SCHUNACK, *Das hermeneutische Problem des Todes* (1967) 101-233.—A. F. SEGAL, "Torah and *nomos* in Recent Scholarly Discussion," *SR* 13 (1984) 19-27. — H. SIMONSEN, "Die Auffassung vom Gesetz im Matthäusevangelium," *SNTU* 2 (1977) 44-67. — R. SMEND and U. LUZ, *Gesetz* (Kohlhammer Taschenbücher 1015, Biblische Konfrontationen, 1981). — G. STRECKER, "Befreiung und Rechtfertigung," FS Käsemann 479-508. — idem, *Der Weg der Gerechtigkeit* ([3]1971) 130-47. — P. STUHLMACHER, *Gerechtigkeit Gottes bei Paulus* ([2]1966) 91-101. — idem, " 'The End of the Law.' On the Origin and Beginnings of Pauline Theology," idem, *Reconciliation, Law, and Righteousness* (1986) 134-154. — idem, "The Law as a Topic of Biblical Theology," ibid., 110-33. — P. VIELHAUER, "Gesetzesdienst und Stoicheiadienst im Gal," FS Käsemann 543-55. — H. WEDER, "Gesetz und Sünde. Gedanken zu einem qualitiven Sprung im Denken des Paulus," *NTS* 31 (1985) 357-76. — S. WESTERHOLM, *Israel's Law and the Church's Faith: Paul and His Recent Interpreters* (1988). — idem, *Jesus and Scribal Authority* (1978). — D. E. H. WHITELEY, *The Theology of St. Paul* ([2]1974) 76-86, 295-303. — U. WILCKENS, "Zur Entwicklung des paulinischen Gesetzesverständnisses," *NTS* 28 (1982) 154-90. — E. WÜRTHWEIN, E. LOHSE, and O. BAUERNFEIND, *RGG* II, 1513-19. — For further bibliography see *TDNT* X, 1190-95.

1. Νόμος occurs 195 times in the NT. Of that number 118 are in Paul (27 in Romans, 32 in Galatians, the rest in 1 Corinthians and Philippians), 8 in Matthew, 27 in the Lukan writings (9 + 18), 15 in John, 1 in Ephesians, 2 in 1 Timothy, 14 in Hebrews, and 10 in James. Al-

though Mark contains discussion of several weighty matters pertaining to the law, νόμος is not found there.

2. a) Etymologically, νόμος derives from νέμω "assign." Νόμος was therefore originally that which has been "assigned." In Hesiod *Op.* 276ff. νόμος is "the order assigned to a group of creatures and in force among them . . . , something objective, therefore, which stands over them" (Heinimann 62). As a life order, therefore, νόμος was also understood as existing mores. Greek civilization, which understood itself in terms of the polis, saw the polis as secured by its own νόμος, the *law* of the city-state, especially since all laws were thought to receive their essence from the one divine law (Heraclitus *fragment* 114: . . . ἰσχυρίζεσθαι χρὴ . . . νόμῳ πόλις . . . τρέφονται γὰρ πάντες οἱ ἀνθρώποι νόμοι ὑπὸ ἑνὸς τοῦ θείου). In the 5th cent. B.C. νόμος became the written law of the polis in the developing Greek democracy; it is probably the case that "even the written νόμος was cosidered in the polis to be an expression of the will of the deity which ruled over the city" (Kleinknecht 1018).

Therefore, use of νόμος developed in two distinct directions: The Greek Sophists analyzed the νόμοι and saw in them the expression of the mostly false opinions of the majority. In contrast, the νόμος was increasingly regarded as the universal law, esp. by the Stoics. While the Greek enlightenment separated φύσις and νόμος, the Stoics were saying: φύσει εἶναι τὸν νόμον (von Arnim, *Stoicorum Veterum Fragmenta* III (1905) 76, no. 308); ὁ νόμος πάντων ἐστὶ βασιλεὺς θείων τε καὶ ἀνθρωπίνων πραγμάτων (*ibid.*, 77, no. 314).

Philo, too, in the Stoic tradition, understood νόμος as the one universal law: . . . ὅδε ὁ κόσμος . . . μιᾷ χρῆται πολιτείᾳ καὶ νόμῳ ἑνί. λόγος δέ ἐστι φύσεως προστακτικός (*Jos.* ii.46; see also ὁ τῆς φύσεως νόμος, *Abr.* 135). Philo is primarily concerned with the agreement of the OT law (→ b) and the world order (Gutbrod 1053; Monsengwo Pasinya 193).

In Hellenistic writings the ruler was viewed as the epiphany of God and therefore as the νόμος ἔμψυχος of the eternal universal law (e.g., Musonius Rufus p37.2ff.). At the time of the NT, the meaning of νόμος was generally restricted to "law."

b) In translating νόμος in the NT one should not resort immediately to the OT understanding of *tôrâ*. Rather, that a shift in meaning has occurred from *tôrâ* to νόμος should be taken into account (of the approximately 220 OT occurrences of *tôrâ* the LXX translates approximately 200 with νόμος; altogether νόμος is found approximately 430 times in the LXX).

One should also take into account that *tôrâ* in the OT displays a wide spectrum of meaning: 1) instruction of priests on individual questions, usually with regard to clean and unclean, 2) individual commandments of the covenantal law given on Sinai, esp. cultic commandments in the priestly document, 3) the covenantal law as a whole (though only for the first time in Deuteronomy). The Torah in the sense of the entire law must be understood, from the self-identity of Israel, as the demand of the God who freed his people from slavery in Egypt and sealed his covenant (→ διαθήκη 2) with them: The Torah is, therefore, the "law" or "instruction" of Israel found already in the covenant. It was in no way the case that salvation was initially achieved through keeping the commandments of the Torah. From the very beginning the Torah was not understood "legally." Therefore the translation "law" (instead of "teaching") does not necessarily imply a "legal" understanding.

It is open to question whether in the course of the postexilic era the first traces of a legal understanding of the Torah are evident (thus, e.g., Noth 85-103, esp. 86: " 'The Law' became an *absolute entity,* valid without respect to precedent, time, or history"; cf. 91; in contrast, more cautiously, Von Rad, *Old Testament Theology* II (1965) 405-7; more energetically, Kraus, "Freude,"; *idem,* "Gesetzesverständnis"; Hübner, "Gesetz als elementares Thema," 261-64 is critical of Kraus).

Did the Alexandrian translators of the OT understand the Torah "legally" when they chose νόμος to translate *tôrâ?* According to Gutbrod, the use of νόμος in the LXX means that the nuance of "law" that was predominant later in the Torah "triumphs and achieves domination" (1047). The statement of J. Schmid is even more pointed: The choice of νόμος is evidence of a change in the meaning of *tôrâ*: it is restricted to that part of the revelation containing God's commands to humankind (*LTK* IV, 818). Monsengwo Pasinya strongly contests this view: " . . . nomos does not signify 'Law' in the legal and juridical sense of classical Greek, but rather 'Instruction, Teaching, Doctrine,' in accordance with the original sense of the corresponding Hebrew term *tôrâ* . . . " (138, referring to Deuteronomy). Monsengwo Pasinya, however, stretches the interpretation of, e.g., νομοθετέω in Deut 17:10 with the help of the (undoubtedly) later tr. of the Psalms, to mean "instruct, teach" (131ff.). According to Monsengwo Pasinya, νόμος in the LXX should be translated as "instruction/teaching," indeed, as "revelation" (203). If such were the case, however, the LXX translator would have been detaching himself completely from the contemporary meaning of νόμος.

Νόμος in the LXX should for most part, therefore, be translated as "law." Yet it remains an open question whether and in what sense the LXX gives evidence of "legal" thinking. It is in any case striking that the LXX translates pl. *tôrôt* almost exclusively with sg. νόμος; pl. νόμοι is found only infrequently, e.g., in 2 Esdr 19:13 for the law given at Sinai. In contrast, the pl. in Prov 1:8 (א A; παιδείαν in B) represents *mûsār*, i.e., the "teaching" of the fathers; in 6:20 it represents pl. *miswôt*. Most LXX occurrences of νόμοι are in 2 Maccabees, which was composed in Greek (C. Habicht, *JSHRZ* I, 193). Nevertheless, sg. νόμος is found in the letters contained in 2 Maccabees (e.g., 1:4; 2:2f.), which have Hebrew or Aramaic originals (Habicht 199ff.). Noteworthy is the tr. of sg. *tôratî* (Jer 31:33) by νόμους μου (Jer 38:33 LXX; pl. νόμοι in LXX Jeremiah only in 38:36, where οἱ νόμοι stands for *haḥuqqîm*; sg. νόμος occurs in LXX Jeremiah 8 times). Is it perhaps the case that the νόμοι of the new covenant are distinguished here from the old Torah?

c) In the NT—primarily due to LXX influence—νόμος should be translated *law.* Usually the Mosaic law as a whole is intended, frequently in its commands and therefore its role of determining judgment (e.g., Rom 2:12ff.). Νόμος is not used in the NT for the instruction of the priests or the patriarchs, nor for individual commandments of the Torah (in Rom 7:7 νόμος refers to the entire Torah; the individual command is called → ἐντολή). The concept, esp. typical of Qumran, of an inherent connection between the cosmic order and the Mosaic law (Limbeck, *Ordnung* 134-82, esp. 181; see also Hengel, Judaism 231-41) plays no role in the NT.

The couplet (ὁ) νόμος καὶ (οἱ) προφῆται is used as a

synonym for → γραφή (Rom 3:21; Luke 24:44 [+ καὶ ψαλμοῖς]; Acts 24:14; 28:23 [13:15, however, refers to a preassigned reading from the Torah and the Prophets]; John 1:45); ἐν τῷ νόμῳ is a synonym for "in Scripture" (Rom 3:19; 1 Cor 14:21; John 10:34; 15:25; cf. 12:34). "The Law and the Prophets" in Luke 16:16 refers to the era up to the time of John the Baptist (Matt 11:13 reformulates; see further → 4.a). In Matthew this idiom usually carries the nuance "the *Law* together with its interpretation through the prophets" (Matt 5:17; 7:12; 22:40). The designations "the Law," "the Law and the Prophets," and the threefold designation in Luke 24:44 for the entire OT are also found in Jewish usage (2 Macc 15:9; cf. *T. Lev.* 16:2).

It is a matter of contention, however, whether Paul in certain passages uses νόμος in the sense of "principle/ order of salvation" or the like (→ 4.b).

3. In the NT νόμος is found in nearly every possible syntactical construction. Over half of all occurrences are found in prep. phrases, if one includes those instances where (τοῦ) νόμου is found as an attributive gen. in prep. phrases. Here LXX influence is clear. Κατὰ (τὸν) νόμον (Μωϋσέως/τοῦ κυρίου) is found esp. in Luke (Luke 2:22, 39; see also 2:24, 27; Acts 22:12; 23:3; 24:14) and Hebrews (7:5, 16; 8:4; 9:19, 22; 10:8); it occurs in the LXX (e.g., Num 9:3; Deut 17:11; 24:8; κατὰ πάντα τὸν νόμον). Ἐν (τῷ) νόμῳ (Μωϋσέως) (γέγραπται) is found in Matthew, Luke-Acts, John, and Paul (e.g., Matt 12:5; Luke 2:23; 10:26; John 8:17; 1 Cor 9:9). Ἐξ ἔργων νόμου is a uniquely Pauline polemical formula (only found in Gal 2:16; 3:2, 5, 10; Rom 3:20, 27f.; 9:32) with no LXX parallels.

A number of vbs., found in both the LXX and the NT, also have νόμον as their acc. obj., e.g., νόμον φυλάσσω (4 Kgdms 17:13; Ps 118:55, 57, 136 LXX; Wis 6:4, etc.; Gal 6:13; Acts 7:53; 21:24; cf. Rom 2:26) and ποιέω τὸν νόμον (1 Chr 22:12; 2 Chr 14:4; 2 Esdr 19:34; cf. the typically Deuteronomic ποιέω πάντας τοὺς λόγους [πάντα τὰ ῥήματα] τοῦ νόμου τούτου, Deut 29:29; 31:12; 32:46; see also Num 5:30; 9:3; Esth 1:13; John 7:19; Gal 5:3; Rom 2:14). Πληρόω τὸν νόμον (Matt 5:17; Gal 5:14 [cf. 6:2]; Rom 13:8) is not found in the LXX, although the LXX does have πληρωθῆναι λόγον κυρίου (2 Chr 36:21; cf. 3 Kgdms 1:14) and πληρωθῆναι (τό) ῥῆμα κυρίου (3 Kgdms 2:27; 2 Chr 36:22; cf. 3 Esdr 1:54).

Νόμος is found as a subj. in the NT twice as often (ca. 30 times) as in the LXX. While in the LXX this syntactical construction possesses no theological relevance (except on Isa 2:3/Mic 4:2; Bar 4:1), in the NT, esp. for Paul, νόμος has a distinctive meaning when the pred. has a verbal sense: "The *law* brings about [God's] wrath" (Rom 4:15); it "snuck in" (5:20); it "rules (κυριεύει) over humankind" (7:1); "the law of the spirit of life has set

you free (ἠλευθέρωσεν)" (8:2). That the law "speaks" (→ λέγω 3), an expression found in Rom 3:19; 7:7; 1 Cor 14:34, is also found in the LXX (4 Macc 2:5; 2:6 as parallel to Rom 7:7), although it is not a fixed expression there.

4. a) With the exception of the conflict saying in Luke 16:16 par. Matt 11:12f., the original wording of which is difficult to reconstruct, we possess no authentic saying of Jesus in which the word νόμος appears. In all probability, the closed epoch of the Law and the Prophets could be in view in the conflict saying (W. G. Kümmel, *Promise and Fulfillment* [SBT 23, 1957] 121-24; E. Käsemann, "The Problem of the Historical Jesus," idem, *Essays on NT Themes* [1964] 42f.). For precisely that reason, however, its authenticity is contested (Schulz 261-67; authentic according to Kümmel; Käsemann; Hübner, *Synoptische Tradition* 62, 227; probably authentic according to Merklein 90); nevertheless, the grounds against authenticity would not be valid if it is contended that Jesus was aware of the implications of his abrogation of the Torah.

Sayings that express such an abrogation do not contain the word νόμος, e.g., Mark 7:15, which is authentic according to Hübner (*Synoptische Tradition* 157-75; against Berger's arguments against authenticity [461ff.] see Hübner, "Mk 7,15"); R. Pesch *Mark* [HTKNT] I, 377-84, and Westerholm, *Jesus* 82, however, do not understand the saying as an explicit abrogation of Leviticus 11. Nevertheless, when Jesus saw the will of God expressed in the demands of the Torah, esp. in statements on the Decalogue (Mark 7:9-13 [authentic according to Kümmel; Hübner, *Synoptische Tradition* 146-55; Pesch, *Mark* I, 368-77]; Matt 5:21ff., 27f.), he intensified and radicalized these demands. This abrogation and intensification of the Torah cannot be classified as "nonessential" (contra Braun II, 5n.2, 7ff.). One must maintain, with Merklein (105), that the kingdom of God (→ βασιλεία 3), and not the Torah, is the decisive prinicple of action for Jesus.

To be sure, Jesus' understanding of God is evident in his interpretation of the Torah (Hübner, *Synoptische Tradition* 152-54: Jesus' struggle against the casuistry of the Pharisees, which was certainly not *the* distinguishing feature of Judaism at that time, but nevertheless was undeniably practiced). As Bornkamm points out, the close connection between Jesus' interpretation of the law and his critique of the law is emphasized by his message of the nearness of the kingdom of God ("Wandlungen" 102).

With regard to Mark, in 7:15 we find the nullification of Leviticus 11, without, however, explicit mention of the theme of law (see also Mark 10:2-12: Deut 24:1 is no longer valid). The Matthean and Lukan writings deal with the theme of the law in very different ways, however.

How the issue of the law stands in the theological thought of Matthew is not yet settled, although agreement has been reached on important points: 1) That the law is very important for Matthew is evident already from the appearance of νόμος only in the compositions of the redactor (5:17 [partially?]; 12:5; 22:40) and in verses reformulated or expanded by the redactor (5:18; 11:13; 22:36; 23:23). 2) Matt 5:17-20 is "the most important programmatic statement on the Law in Matthew" (Meier 164). 3) There is, at least at first glance, a tension between the invalidation of the contents of the Torah in the antitheses in the Sermon on the Mount (at least in 5:33ff. and 5:38ff.) and 5:18.

One should, like Strecker (Weg 146f.), view this modification and therefore critique of the wording of the OT law as a realization of fulfillment of the law (and the prophets who interpreted the law) mentioned in Matt 5:17 (→ 2; → πληρόω). One cannot, however, conclude from this that Matthew was a Gentile Christian (contra Strecker, Meier). Matt 5:43-48 (the love of enemies, which supersedes love of neighbor, as the fulfillment of the law) is not in any case consistent with 22:34-40 (love of God and neighbor as the central points of the law).

The problem is, moreover, up to what point in time, according to Matt 5:18d (ἕως ἂν πάντα γένηται), no jot or tittle will pass away from the law. The view of Davies, e.g., is "only until the death of Jesus inaugurates finally the New Covenant" (Setting 334: taken as authentic words of Jesus). Meier's solution initially appears attractive: "until all things prophesied come to pass" (164). Matthew has, according to Meier, adapted an originally harsh saying on the eternal validity of the Torah to his "economy" of salvation history (65). Accordingly, the norm for the disciples would be 28:19: that which Jesus commanded them in his words (65, 164f.). In spite of his extensive analysis of 24:34 Meier lends too little significance to the fact that 24:34c has in mind the apocalyptic end events (Hübner, Synoptische Tradition 18f.). Thus Meier overemphasizes Matt 28:16-20: after the resurrection of Jesus "the exalted Son of Man comes in proleptic parousia to proclaim a universal mission" (165). Merklein regards 5:18 as the eschatologically or "Jesuanically" interpreted Torah (94). Whether a fully convincing interpretation of 5:18 can be found that is consistent with the invalidation of the demands of the Torah found in the antitheses is difficult to say. In any case, 5:17, as the work of the redactor, interprets v. 18, which at least in terms of substance shows itself to be traditional (Q). Once again Banks defends the authenticity of 5:17 (204-13). At most, however, he can only show that 5:17 could possibly contain elements of tradition.

In Luke, the law is seen from two perspectives:

1) That which must be fulfilled is written in the Law, as well as in the Psalms and the Prophets: the death and resurrection of Jesus (Luke 24:44ff.; cf. v. 27; see also Acts 24:14; 28:23). 2) The life of Jesus was a life under the law. Just as already in Luke 1:6 the parents of John the Baptist walked blamelessly in all the commandments and regulations of the Lord, so also the very beginning of the life of Jesus is carried out κατὰ τὸν νόμον (2:22f., 27, 39). The saying on violence from Q recorded in 16:16 is reformulated in such a way that up to the time of John the Baptist there was "only" the Law and the Prophets; from that time on, however, there is also the preaching of the kingdom (H. Conzelmann, The Theology of St Luke [1960] 20; → also 4.a). Corresponding to this is the fact that Luke in 16:15 consciously avoids including Mark 7:1-23 with its invalidation of Leviticus 11.

The abrogation of the contents of the Torah is rather transferred to the time of the Church and for that reason recorded instead in Acts. Thus, the nullification of the cultic food laws takes place in Acts 10–11: God has declared unclean food clean (10:15: ἐκαθάρισεν, aor.!), without, however, using the word νόμος (Hübner, Synoptische Tradition 189-91). At the synod on the Gentile mission in Acts 15 Gentile Christians were released from the requirement of circumcision "in accordance with the custom" of Moses (15:1: τῷ ἔθει τῷ Μωϋσέως; ἔθος here is nearly synonymous with νόμος; cf. v. 5); the regulations of the "apostolic decree" (15:20f., 28f.), however, remain in effect, i.e., the prohibitions of eating meat offered to idols, blood, and strangled animals and of adultery (→ πορνεία). The entire composition is clearly Lukan and describes a gradual and only partial lifting of the Torah after Pentecost. Along with the fundamental retention of the validity of the law, a partial release was conceded in order to remove unbearable burdens (v. 10). Consequently, the at least partial abrogation of the Torah was more Church-political pragmatism than theological reflection.

b) A presentation of Paul's statements on the law cannot be separated from the biographical aspects of Paul's life. Therefore, the theme "Paul and the law" must be dealt with on two levels: that of his biography, which ought to be reconstructed primarily from his letters, and that of νόμος statements in his letters, esp. Galatians and Romans. These two levels may not be separated when giving an account.

Before his call to become apostle to the Gentiles, Paul was "a Pharisee regarding the law . . . , blameless regarding righteousness in the law" (Phil 3:5f.), "exceedingly zealous for the traditions of the fathers" (Gal 1:14), i.e., for the written Law and the oral Pharisaic interpretation of it. When as a result he persecuted the Church (Gal 1:13; 1 Cor 15:9; Phil 3:6), it can be assumed that he persecuted them—more specifically, the Hellenistic-

Jewish Christian community in (and around?) Damascus —for their damnable (in the eyes of Jews) freedom from the law. That the group in Jerusalem surrounding Stephen (Acts 6) practiced some form of criticism of and freedom from the law (E. Haenchen, *Acts* [Eng. tr., 1971] 259-72; G. Schneider, *Acts* [HTKNT] I, 406-40 [bibliography]; M. Hengel, *Between Jesus and Paul* [1983] 1-29, 48-64) —these Hellenists more boldly advanced the line of Jesus than did the Twelve (see H. Conzelmann, *Acts* [Hermeneia] 45; *contra* Conzelmann see Müller 167)—is evident from the accusation against Stephen that he spoke against the temple and the law (κατὰ τοῦ νόμου, Acts 6:13) and from Stephen's speech itself (the temple critique in 7:2-52). "The criticism of law and temple is connected with the eschatological 'enthusiasm' of the Hellenists" (Hengel, *Between Jesus and Paul* 23).

The call of Paul to be apostle to the Gentiles entailed the surrender of his former Torah rigorism and a conscious affirmation of the freedom from the law practiced by these Hellenists (cf., however, Strecker, "Befreiung," 480f.: Paul pondered the meaning of the law and justification for the first time in Galatians, since 1 Thessalonians does not yet address the issue of the law; on this see Hübner, "Pauli theologiae proprium," 454-60).

At the synod on the Gentile mission Paul gained the release of converted Gentiles from the requirement of circumcision and even from Jewish dietary laws (Gal 2:1-13). As can be seen from the argumentation in Galatians, Paul understood this exemption as, in principle, freedom from the law (Hübner, *Law* 20-24, 60-65), since he condemns circumcision as an obligation to keep the entire law (ὅλον τὸν νόμον ποιῆσαι, 5:3), which necessarily leads to separation from Christ and a fall from grace, since no one can keep the entire law (Gal 3:10, quoting Deut 27:26 LXX). The function of the law, which was given by an angel (a demonic being: God is removed from the act of lawgiving) and was temporally limited, was to provoke sinful deeds so that all would be placed "under the power of sin" (ὑπὸ ἁμαρτίαν, 3:22). Therefore Paul places ὑπὸ νόμον (3:23; 4:4f.) in parallel with ὑπὸ ἁμαρτίαν (3:22), ὑπὸ παιδαγωγόν (3:25), ὑπὸ ἐπιστρόπους καὶ οἰκονόμους (4:2), and ὑπὸ τὰ στοιχεῖα τοῦ κόσμου (4:3).

The objection that there is no religious-historical parallel for interpreting the angel (→ ἄγγελος 2) as an ill-willed demonic lawgiver (F. T. Fallon, review of the German original of Hübner, *Law, CBQ* 41 [1979] 652), with the exception of the Gnostics (Pagels 107), says little since neither is there any parallel for the indisputable (demonstrable from Gal 3:19f.) exclusion of God from the process of lawgiving either. Therefore the triad "law through an angel—absence of God—inferiority of the law" requires an explanation on the basis of the flow of the argument of Galatians. For an angel at the giving of the law in a positive sense, see Deut 33:2 LXX (*contra* MT); on the rabbinic idea see Billerbeck III, 554-56.

The tr. of ὁ πᾶς νόμος (Gal 5:14) must take into account its difference in content from ὅλον τὸν νόμον ποιῆσαι (5:3); the latter deals with the fact that it is not possible to do the whole law, in the former the law is fulfilled in the one love command and therefore should be done. Therefore, ὁ πᾶς νόμος cannot be identical with ὅλος ὁ νόμος. 5:14 could be an ironic and critical comment, esp. since πᾶς generally denotes the opposite of many but here indicates the opposite to one command alone: ἐν ἑνὶ λόγῳ (Hübner, "Das ganze und das eine Gesetz"; *Law* 36f.). The whole law for the Christian is in this way contrasted with the whole law of Moses; see also 6:2: νόμος τοῦ Χριστοῦ.

The polemic of Galatians against the Mosaic law with its decisive theological statement that there is no justification ἐξ ἔργων νόμου (2:16) corresponds to the positive statements on justification through faith and on love, which gains its "energy" from faith, as the fruit of the Spirit (5:6, 22).

Paul makes his fundamental theological statement that justification comes not through works of the law but through faith alone in Romans as well as Galatians (Rom 3:20-22, 28). Only when one considers that he does so does the importance of the (now, in Romans, altered) νόμος concept become clear. The constant between Galatians and Romans is the teaching of justification; the variable is the concept of the law. In Romans we find statements that would have been impossible in the flow of the argument in Galatians: the law is holy, its commandment is holy, righteous, and good (7:12). It is spiritual (πνευματικός, 7:14) and therefore is allied with God. Even circumcision is no longer viewed as purely negative (2:25-27; 3:1f.; 4:10-12). There is no longer mention of the law being given through an angel or its being intended to provoke evil deeds; the function of the law is now to make sin conscious (3:20; 7:7). That the commandment of the law, originally ἡ ἐντολὴ ἡ εἰς ζωήν, now works death (7:10), is only the fault of the power of sin. The argument regarding the "whole law" is also lacking; in 13:8-10 love is the fulfillment of the (now, finally) Mosaic law; every commandment is fulfilled in the love command.

The interpretation of the phrase νόμος πίστεως in Rom 3:27 is debated. Does it mean in the literal sense "norm" (Bultmann, *Theology* I, 259), a "new order" that stands in contrast to the order of the Torah (E. Käsemann, *Rom* [Eng. tr., 1980] 102f.), or the "Torah" itself, only seen from a different perspective (Friedrich, "Gesetz," 120: the law that attests to the righteousness of faith [Rom 3:21]; so also Lohse 281)? In favor of understanding νόμος πίστεως as "Torah" is that "the law of works" (3:27) could be referring to that view of the Torah which does not exclude boasting (Hübner, *Law* 116). In that case νόμος πίστεως would express the opposite view of the law, and νόμος ἱστάνομεν (3:31) would refer to the law as the law itself wants to be and as it testifies concerning itself in the proof from Scripture in ch. 4: It is a law of faith, not of works. Ὁ νόμος τοῦ πνεύματος τῆς ζωῆς (8:2) should be interpreted analogously. While for the Galatians it could be said "Christ is the absolute end of the law," τέλος νόμου Χριστός in Rom 10:4 means that Christ is the end of the fleshly misuse of the law.

Hebrews modifies the Pauline concept of the end of the law in a unique way. Νόμος appears only in chs. 7–10, and even there almost exclusively as the law regulating the OT priesthood (except in 10:28). That which is κατὰ (τὸν) νόμον (7:5, 16; 8:4; 9:19, 22; 10:8) is no longer valid; for Christ, the eternal high priest, is the end of the OT priestly law. Hebrews speaks explicitly of the ἀθέτησις ("abolition") of the former command, which occurred because the command was weak and useless (7:18; cf. 10:9). The law is weak because the sacrifices required by it did nothing more than cleanse the flesh. The blood of Christ, on the other hand, cleanses our conscience from dead works (9:11-14; 10:4). The new covenant definitively supersedes the old (→ διαθήκη 4.c), for in it, according to Jer 38:33 LXX, God places his laws in the heart (Heb 8:10; 10:16). These laws are, then, not identical with the cultic law of the old covenant. The extent to which they might overlap in terms of content with the moral commandments of the Mosaic law is not pondered. The positive aspect of the OT law is seen in the fact that it was the law of God and always possessed a shadow of the coming good (10:1). By using the cultic concepts of the OT priesthood to depict Christ Hebrews has, in fact, radically broken with cultic categories.

James, too, should be placed under the historical influence of Paul. In his polemic against a misunderstood Paulinism, however (2:14-26), he conspicuously does not use the word νόμος. He does refer to the νόμον τέλειον τὸν τῆς ἐλευθερίας (1:25; cf. 2:12), which certainly cannot simply be identified with the OT law (Gutbrod [1081] consciously distinguishes it from the OT law). Nevertheless, as the νόμος βασιλικός it is grounded in Scripture (κατὰ τὴν γραφήν), i.e., in the love command of Lev 11:18 (cf. Gal 5:14; Rom 13:8-10), and as such must be fulfilled (τελεῖτε, 2:8; F. Mussner, Jas [HTKNT] 107: neither just the OT law nor just the "gospel," but the will of God: "The gospel is for him 'law'"; it is questionable, however, whether James would have understood gospel in this way). Jas 2:10 is reminiscent of Gal 3:10; 5:3: "Whoever keeps the whole law (ὅλον τὸν νόμον), but stumbles on a single point, has become guilty of all"— but this does not draw the consequences pointed out by Paul. James expects the entire law to be kept. Jas 2:9 is reminiscent of Rom 2:23-27 (see also 4:11), but only in its terminology, not in its form of theological argumentation.

c) John, too, employs νόμος in his own unique dialectical way. The word implies both continuity and discontinuity. John speaks in the same way about the fulfillment of Scripture (→ γραφή 4.d) as he does of the words recorded in the law (15:25), where he is obviously referring to a saying from the Psalms. Νόμος can, therefore, refer to the entire OT (see also 10:34; 12:34). Shortly after the Johannine Jesus admonishes the Jews to study the Scriptures, since the Scriptures bear witness to him (5:39), he says that Moses accuses the unbelieving Jews, for Moses wrote about Jesus (5:45f.). Moses, however, stands for the Law in the narrower sense (7:23). In spite of this almost completely identical function of Scripture and Law as witness to Jesus, Jesus still says to the Jews: "your law" (8:17; 10:34; see also 15:26: "their law"), as if it were not the law of Jesus or those who believed in him. Here one must take into account the typically Johannine use of misunderstanding: the Jews, as unbelievers and therefore blinded, do not understand their own law. Consequently, the law is ultimately for them the means by which to put to death the one who is life (11:25; 14:6). The law therefore becomes their judgment—a concept found in Paul. Nevertheless, "John . . . is not interested in the Law as an ethical norm which leads man to confide in his own strength and merits" (Pancaro 528). 1:17 is antithetical parallelism: the law was given through Moses; in contrast, grace and truth have become reality only through Jesus Christ (R. Bultmann, John [Eng. tr., 1971] 78f.; Grässer, "Antijüdische Polemik" 54ff.; Pancaro 534ff.). For only through faith in Jesus, who is the Truth, is truth revealed. " 'Truth' is not to be found in the Law . . . The function of the Law . . . is reduced to that of leading men to recognize the 'truth' in Jesus—it has a purely prophetic or pedagogical function" (Pancaro 539).

H. Hübner

νοσέω noseō be ill*

Fig. in 1 Tim 6:4, with περί + acc. (be ill from something): "he is sick for nothing but controversies and arguments." A. Oepke, TDNT IV, 1091-98; H.-G. Link, DNTT III, 996-98.

νόσημα, ατος, τό nosēma illness

John 5:4 (v.l.): "would be healed of whatever illness he had." A. Oepke, TDNT IV, 1091-98.

νόσος, ου, ἡ nosos illness*

The NT speaks (usually in summary statements) of illness(es) only in the literal sense, primarily in reference to Jesus' healing of them (→ θεραπεύω): Mark 1:34; Matt 4:23, 24; 8:17; 9:35; Luke 4:40; 6:18; 7:21. Jesus also imparted authority to heal to the disciples: Matt 10:1 par.

Luke 9:1 (the Twelve); Acts 19:12 (Paul). A. Oepke, *TDNT* IV, 1091-98; H.-G. Link, *DNTT* III, 996-98. For further bibliography see *TWNT* X, 1195.

νοσσιά, ᾶς, ἡ *nossia* nest; brood*

Luke 13:34, in Jesus' words to Jerusalem: "How often I have wished to gather your children like a bird gathers her *brood* under her wings"; cf. par. Matt 23:37 (with pl. of → νοσσίον).

νοσσίον, ου, τό *nossion* (the) young (of a bird)*

Matt 23:37: "like a bird gathers her *young* (τὰ νοσσία αὐτῆς) under her wings"; cf. Luke 13:34 (→ νοσσιά).

νοσσός, οῦ, ὁ *nossos* (the) young (of a bird)*

Luke 2:24: δύο νοσσοὺς περιστερῶν, "two *young* pigeons"; cf. Lev 12:8; 14:22.

νοσφίζομαι *nosphizomai* set aside for oneself, embezzle*

Of Ananias, who *set aside for himself* part of the proceeds from the sale of a piece of property (Acts 5:2, 3). In the admonition to slaves in Titus 2:10: μὴ νοσφιζομένους. Spicq, *Notes* II, 584.

νότος, ου, ὁ *notos* south(west) wind; south*

In Acts 27:13 and 28:13 the southwest wind is intended, as it no doubt is in Luke 12:55 (the wind that brings scorching heat). Luke 13:29 refers to the direction south ("from north and *south*") as does Rev 21:13 ("in the south"). A nation in the south (= southern kingdom) is referred to in Matt 12:42 par. Luke 11:31.

νουθεσία, ας, ἡ *nouthesia* admonition, warning*

1 Cor 10:11: "It was written as a *warning* for us"; Eph 6:4, with παιδεία (as in Philo *Imm.* 54); Titus 3:10, of the admonition of heretics. J. Behm, *TDNT* IV, 1019-22; Spicq, *Notes* II, 585-88.

νουθετέω *noutheteō* admonish*

In the NT, except in Acts 20:31 (Paul's speech), the vb. is found only in the Pauline corpus: 1 Cor 4:14: like a father admonishes his children; Rom 15:14: ἀλλήλους; 1 Thess 5:12, 14; Col 1:28: everyone; 3:16: ἑαυτούς; 2 Thess 3:15: ὡς ἀδελφόν. J. Behm, *TDNT* IV, 1013-16; Spicq, *Notes* II, 585-88.

νουμηνία, ας, ἡ *noumēnia* new moon

A variant of → νεομηνία.

νουνεχῶς *nounechōs* prudently*

The adv. related to νουνεχής is found in the NT only in Mark 12:34: Jesus saw that the teacher of the law "had answered *prudently.*"

νοῦς, νοός, ὁ *nous* mind, understanding, intellect*

1. Occurrences and meaning — 2. Usage — 3. Paul — 4. The deutero-Pauline literature — 5. Further occurrences

Lit.: J. BEHM, *TDNT* IV, 958f. — P. BONNARD, "L'intelligence chez saint Paul," *idem, Anamnesis* (1980). — G. BORNKAMM, "Glaube und Vernunft bei Paulus," *idem, Aufsätze* II, 119-37. — G. HARDER, *DNTT* III, 122-30. — R. JEWETT, *Paul's Anthropological Terms* (1971) 358-90. — W. G. KÜMMEL, *Man in the NT* (1963) 38-71. — G. MENESTRINA, "νοῦς," *BeO* 20 (1978) 134. — W. D. STACEY, *The Pauline View of Man* (1956) 198-205. — For further bibliography see *TWNT* X, 1188.

1. Except in Luke 24:45; Rev 13:18; 17:9 the NT occurrences of νοῦς are in Paul (14 occurrences) and in the deutero-Pauline writings (7 occurrences). While νοῦς played a central role in Greek thought (in an anthropologically dualistic sense in Plato and Aristotle and in a metaphysically dualistic sense in the *Corp. Herm.*; cf. Harder 122), its usage in the LXX is greatly diminished; the Hebrew language knew of no adequate equivalent to Gk. νοῦς. Consequently, the noun also plays no special role in the NT; it appears only 24 times. The meaning is not univocal. Νοῦς can indicate the *understanding* of a matter, the individual *capacity to judge,* and human *views* and *convictions.* At times, νοῦς approximates → σοφία or is a designation for the proper disposition—in contrast to earthly-human, therefore false, conduct.

2. Three times the νοῦς of the κύριος or of the Χριστός is mentioned, whereby the superiority of God or of Christ is emphasized (Rom 11:34; 1 Cor 2:16 bis). In Rom 7:23, 25, the human νοῦς stands in contrast to the divine law. Νοῦς stands in contrast to πνεῦμα 4 times, whereby both conflict (1 Cor 14:14) and agreement (14:15 bis) can be expressed. Eph 4:23 speaks of the renewal of the νοῦς in the Spirit. Also unusual is the usage of Col 2:18, which refers to the νοῦς of the flesh.

3. Rom 1:28 speaks of the rejection of those who have forced God out of their consciousness; as a result, God hands them over to a *mind* that is ἀδόκιμος ("useless, nonexistent"). According to 7:23 the law struggles in the members against the law of the *intellect;* this law of the *intellect* is attributed to God as the ἔσω ἄνθρωπος (v. 22; → ἔσω 6) and stands in opposition to "the law in my members," which is identical with "the law of sin" (v. 23). Νοῦς is the inner judicial court that is able to distinguish good and evil (cf. 1:20). 7:25b (the verse is intrusive in this position; cf. the commentaries ad loc.

and the literature on → ἄνθρωπος) is a sort of summary of vv. 22f.: with the *intellect* the person serves the law of God and with the flesh the law of sin (the opposition here between νοῦς and σάρξ is not Pauline).

In Rom 11:34, Paul quotes Isa 40:13 LXX (and Job 41:3). The νοῦς κυρίου should be understood as the *Spirit* of God, which eludes all human comprehension. In Rom 12:2 and 14:5, νοῦς takes on a parenetic character; the transformation called for in 12:2 is to take place through "the renewal of the *mind/thinking*," so that a person can discern God's will. In 14:5 Paul asks that each person be convinced in his or her own *judgment*, i.e., self-assurance. Isa 40:13 is also quoted in 1 Cor 2:16, where Paul elaborates the thought: the νοῦς of the κύριος (of God) is interpreted as the νοῦς Χριστοῦ (thus the majority of mss.). The νοῦς is then the *Spirit* of Christ who made the Corinthians spiritual people (cf. vv. 14f.).

The phrase αὐτὸς νοῦς in 1 Cor 1:10 states: unity must replace factionalism. This would be represented by one *point of view;* point of view and conviction (γνώμη) are synonyms (cf. Bultmann, *Theology* 205f.) and are interpreted reciprocally (unlike the Church Fathers; cf. H. Conzelmann, *1 Cor* [Hermeneia] 32n.14).

In the discussion of speaking in tongues νοῦς is found 4 times (1 Cor 14:14, 15 bis, 19). The νοῦς, as critical authority, determines clear *thinking:* according to v. 14, the πνεῦμα is subject to the control of the *understanding.* V. 15 ranks intelligible prayer on a par with prayer in the Spirit; otherwise, the νοῦς becomes useless (ἄκαρπός ἐστιν); in v. 19 νοῦς refers to clear understanding, which is able to instruct wisely the members of the congregation.

Phil 4:7 distinguishes between νοῦς, νοήματα, and → καρδία. Greek-Hellenistic influence has made itself felt here rather than OT anthropology: νοῦς is the intellectual-rational understanding—with a pejorative accent.

4. In 2 Thess 2:2 νοῦς is used of reasonableness, the calm reflection in which the Thessalonians should not let themselves be quickly confused. Eph 4:17 is reminiscent of Rom 1:28: The νοῦς of the Gentiles is referred to negatively; what is meant is the understanding that as the instrument of knowledge tends toward vanity and causes the Gentiles to be darkened in their understanding (διάνοια, v. 18). Νοῦς, διάνοια, and καρδία (v. 18) have somewhat the same meaning. V. 23, by way of contrast, speaks of νοῦς in a positive way: Christians are to renew themselves in *mind* in the spirit, i.e., in a *mind* filled with the Spirit. In Col 2:18 νοῦς τῆς σαρκός designates literally the *mind* or *habits* of the flesh, which is negatively defined as a false disposition determined by the world. The expression describes the person whose *spirit* is determined only by fleshly existence (cf. Rom 8:7: φρόνημα τῆς σαρκός). In the vice list in 1 Tim 6:4b-5, v. 5 con-

demns those whose *understanding* is corrupted, who no longer think clearly. The same expression is found in 2 Tim 3:8 (with καταφθείρω in place of διαφθείρω). Titus 1:15 has a similar meaning, but with the addition of συνείδησις the *understanding* of the unbeliever is characterized as without conscience.

5. Luke 24:45 uses νοῦς in the sense of *understanding, comprehension:* The resurrected Christ opens for the disciples, who do not yet understand, correct and complete understanding (cf. G. Schneider, *Luke* [ÖTK] II, 502). Also in Rev 13:18 and 17:9 νοῦς designates the cognitive aspect of the understanding: Whoever has *understanding* can calculate the number of the beast (13:18), and this *understanding,* when properly employed, possesses wisdom (17:19; the connection between νοῦς and σοφία also already in 13:18).

A. Sand

Νύμφα *Nympha* Nympha*

Col 4:15 has acc. Νύμφαν, which can be constructed from a masc. name ending in -ας or a fem. name ending in -α. Since in the same verse αὐτῆς (B) is better attested than αὐτῶν (א A C) or αὐτοῦ (Koine D G), a fem. personal name is probably intended. *TCGNT* 627; E. Lohse, *Col, Phlm* (Hermeneia) ad loc.

νύμφη, ης, ἡ *nymphē* bride; daughter-in-law*

Matt 10:35 par. Luke 12:53 (bis): the division between *daughter-in-law* and mother-in-law (Gen 11:31; Ruth 1:6). Elsewhere *bride* is intended: John 3:29; Rev 18:23; 21:2. Rev 21:9; 22:17 speak of the *bride* of the lamb. J. Jeremias, *TDNT* IV, 1099-1106; *TWNT* X, 1196 (bibliography).

νυμφίος, ου, ὁ *nymphios* bridegroom*

John 2:9 and Rev 18:23 speak of the bridegroom in the general sense. The remaining occurrences are christological. According to Mark 2:19 (bis) par. Matt 9:15a/Luke 5:34, the sons of the wedding party cannot fast (→ νηστεύω) as long as the *bridegroom* is with them. When, however, the *bridegroom* is taken from them, they will fast (Mark 2:20 par. Matt 9:15b/Luke 5:35). In Matt 25:1, 5, 6, 10, νυμφίος is used of Jesus (the "delayed" Christ of the parousia). In the saying of John the Baptist in John 3:29 νυμφίος appears 3 times: "he who has the bride is the *bridegroom;* the friend of the *bridegroom,* however, who stands near him and hears him, rejoices exceedingly that he hears the voice of the *bridegroom.*" J. Jeremias, *TDNT* IV, 1099-1106; *TWNT* X, 1196 (bibliography).

νυμφών, ῶνος, ὁ *nymphōn* wedding chamber; wedding party*

Matt 22:10 v.l.: the room where the wedding is celebrated. The expression "sons of the *wedding party*" (Mark 2:19 par. Matt 9:15/Luke 5:24: they "cannot fast as long as the bridegroom is with them") is a Hebraism referring to the invited friends of the bridegroom or the banquet guests at the celebration of the wedding. Billerbeck I, 500-518.

νῦν *nyn* now, at this time

1. Occurrences — 2. Usage — 3. Meaning — 4. Different understandings of "now"

Lit.: BAGD s.v. — H.-C. HAHN. *DNTT* III, 833-39. — KÜHNER, *Grammatik* II/2, 116-19. — A. LAURENTIN, *"We'attah—Kai nun.* Formule caractéristique des textes juridiques et liturgiques (à propos de Jean 17,5)," *Bib* 45 (1964) 168-97, 413-32. — U. LUZ, *Das Geschichtsverständinis des Paulus* (BEvT 49, 1968) 87f., 125, 168f., 297f. — E. NEUHÄUSLER, *LTK* V, 969f. — *idem,* "Der entscheidende Augenblick im Zeugnis des NT ('Jetzt,' 'Heute')," *BibLeb* 13 (1972) 1-16. — SCHWYZER, *Grammatik* II, 570f. — G. STÄHLIN, *TDNT* IV, 1106-23. — P. TACHAU, *"Einst" und "Jetzt" im NT* (FRLANT 105, 1972). — THRALL, *Particles* 30-34. — For further bibliography see *TWNT* X, 1196.

1. The particle νῦν appears 148 times in the *UBSGNT* text. On the uncertain reading of Acts 13:31 and Rom 11:31b, see *TCGNT* (in the latter Luz [297] regards νῦν as *lectio difficilior*). It is often difficult to distinguish between νῦν and νυνί; cf. Heb 8:6: νυν(ί). Νῦν is found in all the writings of the NT except Philemon, 3 John, and Revelation, with particular frequency in John (29), Acts (25), and the primary Pauline letters (Romans–Galatians: 33 instances).

2. Νῦν is usually used adverbially, but also occasionally as a subst. or adj. As a subst., νῦν appears in conjunction with a prep. in ἀπὸ τοῦ νῦν (e.g., Luke 1:48), ἄχρι τοῦ νῦν (Rom 8:22), or ἕως τοῦ νῦν (Mark 13:19) and as an acc. in τὰ νῦν (Acts 4:29; adv. in 24:25). Νῦν functions as an attributive adj. in ὁ νῦν αἰών (e.g., 1 Tim 6:17f.) and ὁ νῦν καιρός (Rom 3:26); cf. Gal 4:25; 1 Tim 4:8; 2 Pet 3:7.

3. Νῦν is related to Lat. *nu(m)* (in *etiamnum, nunc,* and *nuper*) and Germ. *nun* (cf. *Nu* and *neu*). It usually indicates the present (in John 8:52; 21:10 also the time immediately preceding the present). In addition to this use with the meaning *now* (or *just now*) νῦν is also used nontemporally, or in a continuous sense, or as an expression of logical contradiction.

a) Esp. in the Lukan and Johannine writings νῦν functions as a justifying or logical continuation with an imv. or ind.: 1) The true imv. appears in Matt 27:42 (par. Mark 15:32), 43; in John 2:8 a temporal νῦν may also be present, not, however, in the interjection in Jas 4:13; 5:1: ἄγε νῦν, *now!* In Acts 13:11; 20:22, 25, with ἰδού, νῦν functions in a similar way: *"Now look,"* as in 7:34 (= Exod

3:10 LXX) with δεῦρο: *"Now* come." Καὶ νῦν (Heb. *wᵉ'attâ*) can introduce an imv. or a similar construction (John 17:5 [cf. Luke 2:29]; Acts 10:5; 22:16; 1 John 2:28; 2 John 5); likewise καὶ τὰ νῦν, *and now* (Acts 4:29; 5:38; 20:32; 27:22) and νῦν οὖν, *now therefore* (10:33; 15:10; 16:36; 23:15). 2) With the ind. νῦν, *now,* is used simply as a conj. in Luke 11:39 and the interjection καὶ νῦν, *now then,* in John 14:29; Acts 3:17; and perhaps 2 Thess 2:6 (cf. BDF §§442.15; 474.5c; 475.1). Consequently, νῦν refers to a new understanding in John 8:52; 16:30; 17:7; Acts 12:11 and καὶ νῦν to a new situation in 23:21.

b) A contradiction of what has already been said is indicated by νῦν in John 6:42 (". . . how can he *now* say . . . ?") and καὶ νῦν in Acts 16:37; 26:6. Since it is here a question of (irreconcilable) actions, νῦν δέ means *now however, but instead of this,* indicating the opposite of an assumed circumstance that is described, in John 8:39; 9:41; 15:22, 24; 18:36; 1 Cor 5:11; 7:14; 12:18, 20; Heb 11:16; in Jas 4:16 with an unreal condition and in 1 Cor 14:6 with ἐκτὸς εἰ μή.

c) John 11:22 is text-critically ambiguous. Καὶ νῦν οἶδα means either (without ἀλλά) the consequence of a new understanding *(and now)* or (with ἀλλά) the continuation of a previous understanding *(but even so).*

4. The sense of νῦν, used temporally, varies:

a) In the genuine Pauline letters two important points are clear: 1) Νῦν designates "the time of salvation begun through Christ" (Luz 88), therefore the eschatological situation which has "already now" begun, since it is evident to all in the revelation of Christ (Rom 3:26; 5:9, 11; 8:1; 11:5, 30, 31a [b]; 2 Cor 6:2 bis; Gal 4:29) and to the individual in baptism (Rom 6:19, 21; Gal 2:20; cf. 1:23). Paul contrasts present and past with νῦν (see Tachau 12, 81) in Rom 6:21; 11:30; Gal 1:23. 2) Νῦν refers to the situation of the apostle: He is in prison (Phil 1:20, 30; 2:12; 3:18; cf. Col 1:24) and absent (2 Cor 13:2) and is concerned about his churches (7:9; 1 Thess 3:8; cf. 1 Cor 3:2; Gal 3:3; 4:9). The personal letter to the Philippians knows only this "apostolic" νῦν while the more doctrinal Romans (also 8:18 and 13:11?) knows only the eschatological νῦν.

b) The post-Pauline letters present the "once–now" contrast in a very formal way (Eph 5:8; 1 Pet 2:10a, b, 25; 3:21; cf. Rom 16:26). Here νῦν can also designate the contrast of present and future, in which case it has the sense of "yet now" (Eph 2:2; 1 Tim 4:8; 6:17; 2 Tim 4:10; Titus 2:12; Heb 2:8); this is not represented in Paul, with his explicit eschatological parenesis, except in Rom 8:18.

c) In the blessings and woes of Luke (Luke 6:21 bis, 25 bis) νῦν indicates the present world. In the sayings on struggle and witness (Luke 22:36; Acts 13:31; 17:30) it indicates the time of the Church.

d) John deals with the "hour" of the work of salvation

that has come and of its fulfillment in Jesus (4:23; 5:25; 12:27, 31a, b; 13:36; 16:5, 22, 29; 17:13).

W. Radl

νυνί *nyni* now, at this time*

Lit.: → νῦν.

1. Νυνί appears 20 times in the *UBSGNT* text, 6 times in Romans alone. Apart from Acts 22:1; 24:13; Heb 8:6; 9:26, νυνί is found only in the Pauline corpus and, except in Acts, always with δέ. Only in Acts 22:1 is νυνί used as an adj.

2. Νυνί has the same meaning as νῦν. The demonstrative suffix ι (cf. Lat. *nunc* from *num ce*) simply gives it greater emphasis. That is true of both the adv. and the conj. νυνί. When accompanied by δέ, νυνί designates a clear contrast. This is many times stated in terms of content, but usually has a temporal element as well. Νυνὶ δέ can designate actual reality in contrast to an assumption—without or almost always without temporal significance—in the sense of *for, however* (Rom 7:17), *now however* (1 Cor 13:13) or, after an unreal condition, with εἰ (ἐπεί), *but then* (1 Cor 12:18; 15:20; Heb 8:6; 9:26).

Temporal νυνὶ δέ, however, indicates present reality in contrast to a past (or future: Rom 15:25) reality. In the eschatological context of Rom 3:21 it is used of the present situation created by the Christ-event in contrast to the past under the law (cf. 7:6). The aeon has been realized (6:22; Eph 2:13; Col 1:22) and is to be put into effect (Col 3:8) in baptism. With reference to the ministry of the apostle, νυνί signals a change in the circumstances of Paul (Rom 15:23, 25; Phlm 9), his fellow workers (2 Cor 8:22; Phlm 11), or a congregation (2 Cor 8:11).

W. Radl

νύξ, νυκτός, ἡ *nyx* night*

1. Occurrences in the NT — 2. Simple chronological usage — 3. As the locus of God's saving work — 4. As the sphere of the eschatological judgment — 5. As the place of the decision of faith — 6. As God's fullness of time: "day and night" as an intensifying formula

Lit.: S. AALEN, *Die Begriffe "Licht" und "Finsternis" im AT, im Spätjudentum und im Rabbinismus* (SNVAO II/1, 1951) 15-20, 67-69, 104-7, 308-12. — R. BULTMANN, "Zur Geschichte der Lichtsymbolik im Altertum," *idem, Exegetica* (1967) 323-55. — O. CULLMANN, *Christ and Time* (1964). — D. DAUBE, "The Night of Death," *HTR* 61 (1968) 629-32. — G. DELLING, *TDNT* IV, 1123-26. — *idem, Das Zeitverständnis im NT* (1940). — H. C. HAHN, *DNTT* I, 420f. — A. GRABNER-HAIDER, *Paraklese und Eschatologie bei Paulus* (1967). — F. N. KLEIN, *Die Lichtterminologie bei Philon von Alexandrien und in den hermetischen Schriften* (1962). — E. LÖVESTAM, *Spiritual Wakefulness in the NT* (1963). — M. MEINERTZ, "Die 'Nacht' im Johannes-Evangelium," *TQ* 133 (1953) 400-407. — F. MUSSNER, *LTK* VII, 771f. — F. NÖTSCHER, *Zur Terminologie der Qumran-texte* (1956) 76f.

— C. RAMNOUX, *La nuit et les enfants de la nuit dans la tradition grecque* (1959). — E. T. REIMBOLD, *Die Nacht im Mythos, Kultus, Volksglauben und in der transpersonalen Erfahrung* (1970). — H. SCHÄR, *Erlösungsvorstellungen und ihre psychologischen Aspekte* (1950). — R. STAATS, "Die Sonntagnachtgottesdienste der christlichen Frühzeit," *ZNW* 66 (1975) 242-63. — A. STROBEL, "In dieser Nacht (Lk 17,34)," *ZTK* 58 (1961) 16-29.

1. Νύξ appears in the NT 61 times, 20 times in the Synoptics, 16 in Acts, 11 in the Pauline corpus, 6 in John, and 8 in Revelation. In the LXX it appears *ca.* 200 times, usually for Heb. *laylâ*.

Influence of OT religious usage is seen in the NT. According to Gen 1:5 God's creative word penetrates the darkness of chaos and turns it into *night,* a sphere of Yahweh. As a result, *night* now proclaims God's glory (Ps 19:3; Dan 3:71), allows mankind to perceive God's will (Gen 20:3; 26:24; 31:24; 2 Chr 7:12; Pss 16:7; 77:7; Dan 7:1; Zech 1:8), calls to prayer (Pss 4:5; 42:9; 63:7; 77:3; 88:2; 119:55; Job 35:10), and brings wonderful deliverance from God (Exod 11:4; 13:21; 14:21-28; Judg 7:9-22; Isa 17:14; 37:36f.). On the other hand, *night* is also the realm of activity of the anti-Yahweh, of evil powers and forces, of fear and evil acts, of Sheol (Ps 91:5; Wis 17:13f.: Hell; Gen 19:33: drunkenness; Jer 49:9: theft; Judg 19:25: rape; Neh 6:10: murder; 1 Sam 28:8: occultism). According to Zech 14:7, there will be no more *night* in the eschatological time of salvation (cf. *2 Enoch* 65:9).

2. Νύξ appears least in the NT in the neutral chronological sense; it usually has a theological symbolic function (see 3-6).

According to Jewish time designations, *night* was divided into three watches, according to Greco-Roman designations into four. Matt 14:25 par. Mark 6:48 speaks of the fourth watch of the night, Luke 12:38 of the second or third watch (φυλακή; cf. G. Bertram, *TDNT* IX, 2241-44). "Nightwatch," however, has already become a parabolic reference to the eschaton in many passages in the NT, as the parables of the watchful owner of the house (Matt 24:43), of the watchful doorkeeper (Mark 13:33-37), and of the praise of the watchful servant (Luke 12:38) and the account of Jesus walking on the sea (Mark 6:48 par.) make clear (cf. A. Strobel, *Untersuchungen zum eschatologischen Verzögerungsproblem* [1961] 209). The *night* could also be divided into twelve hours (ὥρα) of varying length (cf. Acts 23:23: "Have two hundred soldiers ready from the third hour of the *night* on"; v. 31: "the soldiers brought Paul to Antipatris by *night*").

A simple time designation appears to be present in Matt 28:13 in the lie spoken by the high priests and the elders: "His disciples have come at *night* and stolen it [the body of Jesus]." Luke 21:37: Jesus spends the night on the Mount of Olives, after he taught in the temple during the day; Acts 17:10: the congregation sent Paul and Silas to Berea while it was still *night*; 23:31: the soldiers brought Paul to Antipatris at *night*; 27:27: "During the fourteenth *night* that we were drifting on the

Adriatic, in the middle of the *night*, the sailors noticed that land was approaching them" (Malta); yet even with this use of *night* it is not clear whether *night* and the intervention of God belong together as motifs, as is clearly the case with the following examples.

3. The *night* can in NT usage be the preferred locus of the eschatological activity of God, so that it is precisely at *night* that God's saving intervention through Jesus can be experienced. In the account of Jesus walking on the sea, which no doubt has an eschatological-ecclesiological dimension, Jesus comes during the fourth watch of the *night* to the disciples on the sea (Matt 14:25 par. Mark 6:48; cf. John 6:15-21; Luke 24:37). In the parable of the ten virgins the cry goes up in the middle of the *night* because the bridegroom is coming (Matt 25:6). In the parable of the self-growing seed, "day and *night*" (Mark 4:27) similarly designates the realm of the eschatological process of growth of the kingdom of God, which grows without human effort or understanding. Likewise, the proclamation of God in Luke 2:8 takes place at *night*: the shepherds were keeping watch over their flocks at *night*, when the angel of the Lord appeared to them and the glory of the Lord shown all around them. *Night* has an obvious eschatological focus in the context of the calling of the disciples at the miraculous catch of fish in Luke 5:5: "Master, we have worked the entire *night* and have caught nothing"; cf. the appearance of the resurrected Christ by the sea in John 21:3: during the *night* they catch nothing; when it is morning, Jesus stands on the shore.

For Luke in Acts *night* is a typical stylistic device for the saving intervention of God: Acts 5:19: an angel of God opens the prison doors during the *night* and leads the apostles out; 9:24: at the flight of Paul from Damascus, the city gates are watched day and *night*; 9:25: his disciples let him down from the city wall during the *night* in a basket; 12:6: in the *night* before Herod was to have Peter put to death, Peter slept between two soldiers; 27:27: the deliverance at Malta took place in the middle of the *night*. Related to this is the Lukan motif of visions from God experienced at *night*: Acts 16:9: Paul has a vision in Troas in which a Macedonian stands and begs him to come; 18:9: the Lord spoke to Paul during the *night* in a vision; 27:23: "for during this *night* an angel of the Lord came to me" (Paul at Malta).

4. *Night* is also the sphere of eschatological judgment: Luke 12:20: "Then God said: 'You fool! In this *night* your soul will be required of you'"; 17:34: "I tell you, in that *night* two people will be in one bed; one will be taken and the other left" (at the coming of the Son of Man); John 9:4: "A *night* is coming in which no one will be able to do anything anymore" (the healing of the blind man). The poignant mention of *night* at the betrayal of Judas (John 13:30) must also be understood as a judgment

scene, since Judas's betrayal is divulged as an action of the anti-Yahweh, as a symptom of separation from God, enmity with God, and the *night* of the world.

The eschatological *night* symbol is familiar to Paul as well: Rom 13:12: "the *night* is nearly over, the day is near," with clear adoption of the OT motif of "the day of Yahweh." The rhetorical antithesis "*night*–day" is used to portray the passing away of the old and the in-breaking of the new eschatological aeon, the new age of salvation that has dawned in Christ. Paul also understands the recollection of the Passion—"in the *night* on which the Lord Jesus was betrayed" (1 Cor 11:23)—as a statement of judgment (cf. R. Pesch, *Das Abendmahl und Jesu Todesverständnis* [1978] 53ff.). The same circumstance prevails in 1 Thess 5:2: "I am certain that the day of the Lord will come like a thief in the *night*."

In the language of Revelation the *night* metaphor bears a fundamental judgment trait: 8:12: as a result of the third trumpet, the sky became a third darker; 12:10: the accuser of the brethren, who accuses before God day and *night*, is destroyed; 14:11: those who worship idols will have no rest day or *night*; 20:10: the devil, the beast, and the false prophet are tormented day and *night*; 21:25 (like 22:5) picks up on Zech 14:7: in the culmination of the eschaton there will be no more *night*.

5. *Night* is also the realm of the decision of faith: Matt 2:14: Joseph decides to flee and takes the child and his mother; 26:31, on the Mount of Olives: "You will all fall away because of me in this *night*"; 26:34 par. Mark 14:30: "In this *night*, before the cock crows, you will deny me three times"; John 3:2: Nicodemus seeks out Jesus at *night* (cf. 19:39); in 11:10 also a decision is demanded: "If anyone walks about at *night*, he stumbles, because the light is not in him" (at the death of Lazarus); Acts 16:33: the jailkeeper takes Paul and Silas aside and has himself and his family baptized. 1 Thess 5:5, 7 also falls within the circle of decision parenesis: "You are all children of light and children of the day. We do not belong to the *night* and the darkness. . . . Whoever sleeps, sleeps at *night*; whoever gets drunk, gets drunk at *night*."

6. *Night* can also represent the divine fullness of time: Matt 4:2: Jesus fasted forty days and forty *nights*; 12:40: "just as Jonah was in the belly of the whale three days and three *nights*, so the Son of Man will also be in the heart of the earth three days and three *nights*"; see also 20:19; 27:63 (cf. K. Lehmann, *Auferweckt am dritten Tag nach der Schrift* [QD 38, 1968]). To this group also belongs the combination "day and *night*," which in many cases designates the time willed by God and expresses intensity: Luke 2:37: the prophetess Anna served God day and *night* with fasting and prayer; 18:7: the elect, who cry to God day and *night*; Mark 5:5: the demoniac from Gerasa screamed day and *night* among the graves;

1 Thess 2:9 par. 2 Thess 3:8: "working day and *night* so as not to become a burden to any of you"; 1 Thess 3:10: pray day and *night;* 1 Tim 5:5: a "real" widow prays day and *night;* 2 Tim 1:3: "I thank God day and *night*"; Acts 9:24; 20:31, Paul in Miletus: "Remember that for three years I did not stop warning each of you *night* and day with tears"; 26:7: Israel serves God day and *night;* Rev 4:8: the four living creatures cry out "holy" day and *night;* 7:15: the martyrs serve before God's throne day and *night;* 12:10: the accuser accuses before God's throne day and *night;* 14:11: those who worship idols will have no rest day or *night* (final judgment); 20:10: Satan, the beast, and the false prophet will be tormented day and *night* forever.

The term "night" thus is used overwhelmingly in the NT as a symbolic metaphor in which the eschatological symbolic function has special importance in the context of parenesis.   P. G. Müller

νύσσω *nyssō* nudge; pierce*

John 19:34: "One of the soldiers pierced him with a spear in the side." Matt 27:49 TR has ἔνυξεν αὐτοῦ τὴν πλευράν, in dependence on John 19:34.

νυστάζω *nystazō* nod; sleep*

Matt 25:5: "When the bridegroom delayed, however, all *became drowsy* and fell asleep"; fig. in 2 Pet 2:3 with subj. ἀπώλεια: "their destruction *is* not *sleepy*" (i.e., it is at hand).

νυχθήμερον, ου, τό *nychthēmeron* night and day, twenty-four-hour time period*

2 Cor 11:25: "I spent *a night and a day* [drifting] on the open sea." BDF §121.

Νῶε *Nōe* Noah*

This indeclinable personal name (Gen 5:29, etc.) is found in the genealogy in Luke 3:36. 2 Pet 2:5 calls Noah "a preacher of righteousness"; Heb 11:7 praises his faith. The expression ἐν (ταῖς) ἡμέραις Νῶε recalls the generation of the flood (Luke 17:26; 1 Pet 3:20; cf. Matt 24:37: "the days of Noah"). "The day of the Son of Man" (the parousia) is compared to the sudden arrival of the flood in the time of Noah (Luke 17:26, 27 par. Matt 24:37, 38; see D. Lührmann, *ZNW* 63 [1972] 130-32; J. Schlosser, *RB* 80 [1973] 13-36). J. P. Lewis, *A Study of the Interpretation of Noah and the Flood in Jewish and Christian Literature* (1968).

νωθρός, 3 *nōthros* sluggish, lazy*

Heb 6:12: ἵνα μὴ νωθροὶ γένησθε, in the exhortation to persevere in the faith; 5:11: νωθροὶ γεγόνατε ταῖς ἀκοαῖς, "you have become hard of hearing" (literally: "*sluggish* with respect to the ears"). H. Preisker, *TDNT* IV, 1126; Spicq, *Notes* II, 589-91.

νῶτος, ου, ὁ *nōtos* back*

Rom 11:10 (citing Ps 68:24 LXX): "May their *backs* be bent forever."

Ξ ξ

ξενία, ας, ἡ *xenia* hospitality, kindness toward strangers; lodging*

Phlm 22: "At the same time, prepare *lodging* [?] for me"; Acts 28:23: Roman Jews came to Paul "at his *lodging*." G. Stählin, *TDNT* V, 20-23; Spicq, *Notes* II, 596f.; J. Schreiner, *TTZ* 89 (1980) 50-60.

ξενίζω *xenizō* receive as a guest, provide lodging, entertain; be a stranger, appear strange to*

1. Occurrences — 2. Concrete meaning — 3. Hospitality in the Bible — 4. Abstract meaning

Lit.: H. BIETENHARD, *DNTT* I, 687-90. — DALMAN, *Arbeit* 129-48. — J. FRIEDRICH, *Gott im Bruder?* (CTM 7, 1977). — R. GYLLENBERG and B. REICKE, *BHH* 498f. — J. B. MATHEWS, *Hospitality and the NT Church* (Diss. Princeton, 1964). — H. RUSCHE, "Gastfreundschaft im AT, im Spätjudentum und in den Evangelien," *ZM* 41 (1957) 170-88. — *idem*, "Gastfreundschaft und Mission in der Apostelgeschichte und in den Apostelbriefen," *ZM* 41 (1957) 250-68. — *idem, Gastfreundschaft in der Verkündigung des NT und ihr Verhältnis zur Mission* (1958). — Spicq, *Notes* II, 592-97. — G. STÄHLIN, *TDNT* V, 1-36. — For further bibliography see *TWNT* X, 1196f.

1. The vb. appears in the NT 10 times, of which 7 are in Acts, 2 in 1 Peter, and 1 in Hebrews. As with → ξένος, the word is used in two very different senses. The meaning *receive as a guest* is numerically predominant (7 of the occurrences, 6 of those in Acts).

2. The frequency of occurrences in Acts (10:6, 18, 23, 32; 21:16; 28:7) in and of itself demonstrates the importance of hospitality for the work of the early Christian mission. Hospitality is for that reason mentioned as a virtue in Heb 13:2; the OT example of hospitality is also in mind:

3. Heb 13:2 refers to Genesis 18-19: the reception of God in the form of his messengers by Abraham (18:1f.) and Lot (19:1, 18, 21). *Hospitality* was a highly regarded virtue in antiquity. Its basis was the anxiety felt in a strange environment and the consequent dependence on hospitality, which gave rise to the "culture-historical sequence" (Stählin 3): the foreigner is first the enemy who is to be fought. Soon, however, it became evident that hospitality offered another way to cope with hostile foreigners. Consequently, the outlaw was made the ward by religion.

Thus also the OT clearly depicts both the vulnerability of the foreigner (Gen 9:4-6) and the obligation of hospitality (Gen 19; Deut 14:29). This obligation is mentioned in the OT only a few times, however, as, e.g., in Isa 58:7, where it stands in series with a number of other "acts of kindness." "Feed the hungry" and "give the thirsty drink" are aspects of hospitality mentioned more frequently than the overriding principle. Hospitality in some form or another is, however, found in almost every list of acts of kindness we know from Israel and its surrounding world (see extensively on this subject Friedrich 164-72).

The high regard for hospitality in the early Christian community (cf. also Rom 12:13) could therefore have a broader background: a) the general regard for this virtue in Israel and in the OT; b) the fact that not only the early Christian missionary, but also already Jesus himself was dependent on this hospitality (cf. Luke 10:38; Mark 2:15; 14:3, etc.); and c) the proclamation of Jesus in parables and sayings (e.g., Matt 22:1-14; Luke 14:7-14, esp. v. 12; and most clearly Matt 25:31-46, where the demand for hospitality toward strangers is explicitly given in a list of acts of kindness).

4. Already in secular Greek the vb. had the second, more abstract, meaning *be a stranger,* which is derived from the double meaning of → ξένος (1, 3) as "guest" and "stranger" (cf. BAGD s.v.). Christians are strangers in this world since they belong to God (Eph 2:19; → ξένος 2); therefore their nonworldly attitude *appears strange* to the world (1 Pet 4:4), which persecutes them; this persecution is a logical result of the alienation between the world and the Christian, which can at the same time be equated with animosity. For this reason, it should not *appear strange* to Christians when they are persecuted (1 Pet 4:12); cf. ξενίζοντα, *strange* (Acts 17:20).

J. H. Friedrich

ξενοδοχέω *xenodocheō* show hospitality*

1 Tim 5:10, of the good works recommended for widows: "if she *has shown hospitality* to strangers (ἐξ-

ενοδόχησεν)." G. Stählin, *TDNT* V, 19-23; Spicq, *Notes* II, 596; J. Schreiner, *TTZ* 89 (1980) 50-60; T. Hirunuma, *"xenodocheō," Shinyaku Kenkyū* 149 (Osaka, 1979) 1239f.

ξένος, 3 *xenos* foreign; out of place; unusual; subst.: foreigner; guest; host*

1. Occurrences — 2. "Foreign" — 3. "Guest"

Lit.: → ξενίζω.

1. Ξένος occurs 14 times in the NT, 5 times in Matthew, twice in Acts, Ephesians, and Hebrews, and once in 1 Peter, 3 John, and Romans. The word represents two distinct meanings; in the NT the meaning *foreign* predominates (11 times), once it means *host* (Rom 16:23), and twice it is used in conjunction with a synonym for "foreign" and can there mean *foreigner* as well as *guest* (Eph 2:19; Heb 11:13). The meaning found in secular Gk., *"friendly guest,"* is not found in the NT. The word appears in the NT as both an adj. (5 times) and a subst. (9 times).

2. Antiquity initially held a hostile posture toward foreigners ("barbarians"), which was gradually displaced by the developing rights of foreigners and strangers. For Israel, foreign peoples were regarded as enemies, a disposition based on historical experiences (cf. Deut 20:14-18, etc.), and pagans, since they practiced foreign religions that all too quickly led astray (cf. Jer 5:19). Nevertheless, from very early foreign individuals and travelers were shown hospitality (→ ξενίζω 3), from which a form of rights for foreigners developed.

"Foreign" is also a category applied to God's relationship to the world. While according to the Greek view the soul is a foreigner in this world and seeks its heavenly home, according to the biblical view God and mankind are foreign to one another (cf. Isa 28:21; Ps 39:13; 1 Chr 29:15), even though mankind and the world, as God's creation, actually belong to him. Yet the godly know that they cannot attain this goal here on earth (cf. 1 Chr 29:15; Heb 11:13).

These different perspectives can also be found in NT use of ξένος. In Matthew 25, in the discourse on the great final judgment, hospitality toward strangers (vv. 35, 38, 43f.) is among the acts of kindness (→ ξενίζω 3) that make up the criteria for judgment. Fear of foreign religions is also visible in the NT, however. Foreigners are Gentiles and unclean; therefore they are buried in unclean places (Matt 27:7; cf. extensively on this Stählin 14f.). Separation from all foreigners is not, however, found only in the OT; it was in fact essential to every religion (cf. Acts 17:18 [also v. 20]: the Greeks; perhaps, however, ξένος is not intended to be an accusation here, but rather simply indicates the interest of the people of Athens). One must be warned about strangers (Heb 13:9: directed toward the Jewish alienation of Christianity). In contrast to the people of Israel, whose covenantal relationship with God was valid only for them and therefore erected

a wall between themselves and foreign nations and abandoned foreigners to separation from God (Eph 2:12), now no one is excluded from the Christian community because of being a foreigner (2:19). In the Church there are only new people, who together have right of domicile in God's house and are "God's house guests." The promise that the separation between God and mankind would be removed, which believers did not achieve before Christ (Heb 11:13), has now been fulfilled (11:15f.). The world, however, remains foreign to Christians (cf. 1 Pet 4:12; → ξενίζω 4). Ξένος in Acts 17:21, by way of contrast, is to be understood neutrally: "the *foreigners* staying there."

3. The noteworthy tension in the root has already been mentioned (→ 1, → ξενίζω 4). It is also evident in two passages mentioned above, Eph 2:19 and Heb 11:13, where ξένος occurs in conjunction with synonyms for "foreign" (πάροικος and παρεπίδημος) and therefore could better be translated as *guest,* where in each case a "foreign guest" is in mind (cf the similar context of Gen 23:4, etc.).

Ξένος in the sense of "friend" is found only in Rom 16:23, where only "host" can be meant: Gaius apparently took in not only Paul, but also other traveling Christians from the universal Church, a virtue without which the early Christian mission would not have been possible (cf. 3 John, esp. v. 5; Friedrich 272-76). For that reason it is less probable that v. 23 means that the church gathering was held in the house of Gaius.   J. H. Friedrich

ξέστης, ου, ὁ *xestēs* vessel, jug*

A liquid measure, about one-half liter, generally referred to with no connotation of measure. Mark 7:4 (7:8 v.l.), with ποτήριον and χαλκίον.

ξηραίνω *xērainō* dry up; pass.: become dry/parched*

The active meaning is found in the NT only in Jas 1:11. The pass. is used literally of trees (Mark 11:20, 21), of plants (without roots: Mark 4:6 par. Matt 13:6/Luke 8:6; 1 Pet 1:24; Rev 14:15), of a pruned branch (John 15:6), of the drying up of waters (Rev 16:12: the Euphrates), and of a flow of blood that dried up (Mark 5:29). In Mark 9:18 the vb. is used of a demoniac who *became stiff* when possessed and in 3:1 of a withered hand.

ξηρός, 3 *xēros* dry, parched*

Literally: of wood in Luke 23:31; of the earth in Heb 11:29 ("the dry land"); of *dry land* (Gen 1:9) in contrast to θάλασσα in Matt 23:15. Fig., of diseases: of a hand in Mark 3:3 par. Matt 12:10/Luke 6:6, 8; absolute ξηροί: *the sick* in John 5:3.

ξύλινος, 3 *xylinos* wooden, made of wood*

Rev 9:20: τὰ εἴδωλα τὰ ξύλινα, *wooden* idols; 2 Tim 2:20: *wooden* vessels/tools (σκεύη).

ξύλον, ου, τό *xylon* wood*

1. Occurrences in the NT — 2. In its earthly nature and in the eschatological paradise — a) As "wood" — b) As "tree" — 3. In conjunction with violence — a) As "cross" — b) As "club" — c) As "stocks"

Lit.: BAGD s.v. — BOUSSET/GRESSMANN 284 (the "tree of life"). — K. ERDMANN, et al., *RAC* II, 1-34. — E. O. JAMES, *The Tree of Life* (SHR 11, 1966). — A. G. LEVIN, *The Tree of Life: Genesis 2:9 and 3:22-24 in Jewish, Gnostic and Early Christian Texts* (Dissertation Harvard, summarized in *HTR* 59 [1966] 449f.). — G. Q. REIJNERS, *The Terminology of the Holy Cross in Early Christian Literature* (1965). — S. J. RENO, *The Sacred Tree as an Early Christian Literary Symbol: A Phenomenological Study* (FARG 4, 1978). — J. SCHNEIDER (K. G. KUHN), *TDNT* V, 37-41. — J. A. SOGGIN, *THAT* II, 356-59. — T. C. G. THORNTON, "Trees, Gibbets, and Crosses," *JTS* 23 (1972) 130f. — J. VERGOTE, *RAC* VIII, 112-41, esp. 117. — P. VOLZ, *Die Eschatologie der jüdischen Gemeinde im neutestamentlichen Zeitalter* (1934), index s.v. "Lebensbaum." — M. WILCOX, "'Upon the Tree'—Deut 21:22-23 in the NT," *JBL* 96 (1977) 85-99. — For further bibliography on the "tree of life" see Soggin 358; on ξύλον in the sense of *cross* → κρεμάννυμι (2), → σταυρός.

1. Ξύλον appears in four different senses in the NT, two of which are in fixed expressions. It appears 5 times in the Synoptics in connection with the arrest of Jesus in the expression μετὰ μαχαιρῶν καὶ ξύλων, 5 times as a designation for the cross of Jesus, 4 times in Revelation in (τὸ) ξύλον (τῆς) ζωῆς, and 3 (possibly 4) times simply as *wood*.

2. Ξύλον appears in its original sense as a term for *wood* in its earthly nature and in a derived eschatological sense in connection with Paradise.

a) *Wood* as a construction material is mentioned in 1 Cor 3:12; ξύλον τιμιώτατον, costly *wood*, is mentioned in Rev 18:12b and, more specifically, citron *wood* in v. 12a. See also Luke 23:31 → b.

b) A *tree* as "green" or as "dry" (as, e.g., in Ezek 17:24) or simply *wood* as "green" or "dry" is mentioned in Luke 23:31 in a metaphorical and proverbial saying of Jesus (cf. for a verbal parallel *Seder Eliahu Rabba* 14 [65] and for a material parallel *Gen. Rab.* 27:27 [Kuhn, 38n.7]). Revelation refers several times in an eschatological sense to the ξύλον (τῆς) ζωῆς (for the same expression see LXX Gen 2:9, etc.; for ξύλον τῆς ζωῆς also in the eschatological sense in Paradise see *Pss. Sol.* 14:3 [pl.]; *T. Levi* 18:11; *Apoc. Mos.* 28): 2:7: "give to eat of the *tree* of life, which is in God's Paradise"; 22:2a: "trees of life on each side of the river bearing fruit twelve times a year" (the construction is ambiguous); 22:2b: "the leaves of the *trees* are [used] for the healing of the Gentiles"; (the sg. in both cases is collective [*contra*, e.g., Schmidtke

in Erdmann, et al., 23]; see for the subject matter esp. Ezek 47:12; "tree of life" by the water, 1QH 8:5f.; cf. also 4 Esdr 7:123); 22:14: the godly "have the right to the *tree* of life" (cf. *1 Enoch* [Greek] 25:4); 22:19, in the warning at the end of the book as a threat of punishment: a "share in the *tree* of life." A play on the cross of Christ is not yet evident in these passages in Revelation (*contra*, recently, H. Kraft, *Rev* [HNT] 59).

3. Ξύλον also appears in connection with the use of wood for human violence: *cross, club,* or *stocks* for the feet.

a) In Gal 3:13 Paul quotes Deut 21:23 in reference to the crucifixion of Jesus (in a text form agreeing with neither the LXX nor the MT): *ʿēs*/ξύλου refers to a "pole" on which a person's body was hanged after execution (on the use of this passage in early Judaism in relation to crucifixion → κρεμάννυμι 2; cf. also, e.g., *tālâ ʿal ʿēs*/κρεμαννύναι ἐπὶ ξύλου in Gen 40:19, which was also interpreted in Josephus *Ant.* ii.73, 77 and Philo *Som.* ii.213 as referring to Roman crucifixion). It is also clear from the expression κρεμάσαντες ἐπὶ ξύλου that Deut 21:22(f.) stands behind the mention of the execution of Jesus in Acts 5:30; 10:39. Acts 13:29 employs ξύλον in reference to the act of taking Jesus down from the *cross* (likewise dependent on OT sources [cf. Wilcox 92f.]). In the context of a play on Isa 53:4, 12 LXX, *wood,* in the sense of the cross, is the place where Jesus "bore our sins in his body" (cf. Deut 21:23aα [Wilcox 93]) according to 1 Pet 2:24 (= Pol. *Phil.* 8:1); it does not have "himself" or "his body" as obj. (as in Heb 7:27), and to that extent there is actually no sacrificial terminology present here (correctly so L. Goppelt, *1 Pet* [KEK] ad loc.; otherwise BAGD s.v. ἀναφέρω 2; J. Kremer in the present work → ἀναφέρω 3; an echo of the scapegoat of Lev 16:21f. is not verifiable).

In Jewish and secular texts as well ξύλον could possibly (!) refer to the cross as a means of execution (e.g., Philo *Som.* ii.213, in a play on Gen 40:19 [see above]; Artemidorus Onirocriticus iv.33 [with σταυρός and ξύλον as "piece of wood"]). In the NT, use of ξύλον in all the passages mentioned in the preceding paragraph could be dependent on Deut 21:22f.

b) In the account of the arrest of Jesus we find the expression "with swords and *clubs*" (Mark 14:43 par. Matt 26:47; Mark 14:48 par. Matt 26:55/Luke 22:52).

c) Acts 16:24 uses ξύλον for *stocks* for the feet of prisoners in prison (cf. Vergote), in this case Paul and Silas in Philippi (ξύλον for both feet also in Job 33:11; Plutarch *De Genio Socrates* [*Moralia* 598B]; cf. esp. also Herodotus ix.37; Lysias x.16; *OGIS* II, 438, 181).

H.-W. Kuhn

ξυράω (**ξυρέω, ξύρω**) *xyraō (xyreō, xyrō)* shave*

Acts 21:24: fut. mid. ξυρήσονται τὴν κεφαλήν, they *will have themselves shaved* (bald); 1 Cor 11:5: pf. pass. partc. ἐξυρημένη: absolute *a shaved* (head); 11:6 pres. mid. inf. ξυρᾶσθαι, used absolutely.

O o

ὁ, ἡ, τό *ho, hē, to* the (art.)

1. Original demonstrative pron. — 2. Individualizing and generic usage — 3. Substantivizing function — 4. Attributive and pred. positions — 5. With pred. nouns — 6. With proper nouns — 7. Nonuse of the art.

Lit.: BAGD, s.v. — BDF §§249-76; 398-404. — F. EAKIN, "The Greek Article in First and Second Century Papyri," *American Journal of Philology* 37 (1916) 333-40. — R. W. Funk, *The Syntax of the Greek Article* (Diss. Vanderbilt, 1953). — KÜHNER, *Grammatik* II/1, 575-640. — LSJ s.v. — MAYSER, *Grammatik* II/1, 56-62; 2, 1-50. — MOULTON, *Grammar* I, 80-84; III, 36f., 140-46, 150-53, 165-84, 197-201. — RADERMACHER, *Grammatik* 112-18. — I. W. ROBERTS, "Exegetical Helps: The Greek Noun with and without the Article," *Restoration Quarterly* 14 (1971) 28-44. — H. M. TEEPLE, "The Greek Article with Personal Names in the Synoptic Gospels," *NTS* 19 (1972/73) 302-17. — For further bibliography see Roberts 28nn.1, 2.

The use of the art. in the NT essentially agrees with classical usage; Heb. influence is seldom demonstrable.

1. The use of the art. with a substantive to specify that a specific member or group of members of a class is meant arises from its original demonstrative meaning, which can still be found in the NT in formulaic fragments: ὁ μὲν—ὁ δέ, "this one—that one"; ὁ δέ, "he, however"; οἱ δέ, "they, however." Ὁ (οἱ) μὲν οὖν, "now he (they)," is found only in Acts.

2. a) The individualizing use of the art. specifies that a particular previously mentioned ("anaphoric" use) or generally known ("definitional" use) person or thing is meant. Anaphoric use is seen in *"the* Magi" (Matt 2:7— introduced in v. 1 without art.); *"the* five loaves" (Luke 9:16—after "five loaves" in v. 13); *"the* beast" (following "a beast" in Rev 13:1); cf. Luke 4:17b (with v. 17a); John 4:43 (with v. 40); Acts 9:17 (with v. 11), etc. Definitional use is seen in ὁ προφήτης, "the [expected] prophet" (John 1:21); ἡ ἡμέρα, *"the* day [of judgment]" (1 Cor 3:13); μοι τῷ ἁμαρτωλῷ, "to me, *the* sinner" (Luke 18:13); ἐν τῇ ἐπιστολῇ, "in *the* letter [that is known to you]" (1 Cor 5:9).

b) The generic use of the art. designates the class rather than the individual: *"the* good person [in general]" (Matt 12:35; cf. 15:11); ἐν τῷ ἀνθρώπῳ, "in [every] person" (John 2:25; cf. individualizing use in 4:50: ὁ ἄνθρωπος, *"the* person," here the official at Capernaum). It is accordingly found frequently in the parables: *"(the)* foxes and *(the)* birds" (Luke 9:58); *"the* worker" = every worker (10:7); *"the* owner of the house" and *"the* thief" (Matt 24:43); *"the* heir" (Gal 4:1).

c) The distributive use (a form of the generic use) specifies "every individual": τοῦ ἐνιαυτοῦ, "yearly" (Heb 9:7); τῆς ἡμέρας, "daily" (Luke 17:4).

3. The art. can be used to substantivize any word, clause, or part of a clause:

a) Adj.: ὁ πονηρός, "the evil one" = the devil (Matt 13:19; John 17:15); τὸ ἀγαθόν σου, "your good deed" (Phlm 14: individualizing); τὸ ἀγαθόν, *"the* good" (Gal 6:10: generic).

b) Adv. and prep. phrases ("elliptic" use): ἡ αὔριον (supply ἡμέρα), *"the* following day" (Jas 4:14); τὸ ἐντός— τὸ ἐκτός *"the* inside—*the* outside" (Matt 23:26; cf. John 8:23; Phil 3:13, etc.); οἱ ἐκεῖ, *"the people* there" (Matt 26:71); ἀπὸ τοῦ νῦν, "from now on" (Luke 1:48); τὸ ἐξ ὑμῶν, *"as far it depends* on you" (Rom 12:18: adverbial acc.); τὸ κατὰ σάρκα, *"as far as* the body *is concerned"* (9:5). Similarly the art. with a following gen.: *"the sons* (οἱ) of Zebedee" (John 21:2); *"those belonging* to Christ" (1 Cor 15:23); τὰ Καίσαρος, *"that which belongs* to Caesar" (Luke 20:25); *"that which leads* to peace" (Rom 14:19); *"the* contents (τό) of the proverb" (2 Pet 2:22).

c) Participles: ὁ βαπτίζων, *"the* baptizer" (Matt 6:14); ὁ κλέπτων, *"the* thief" (Eph 4:28); τὰ ὑπάρχοντα, "the possessions" (Luke 12:33, 44); τὰ γινόμενα, "the events" (9:7); πρὸς τὸ παρόν, "for *the* moment" (Heb 12:11); frequently ὁ λεγόμενος (καλούμενος) followed by a proper name, *"the* one called/named . . ."; thus also "Saul, *the* one also (ὁ καί) called Paul" (Acts 13:9); occasionally in place of an expected rel. clause: "to some *who* (πρός τινας τούς) trusted in themselves" (Luke 18:9; cf. Acts 4:12; 11:21; Mark 15:41).

d) Infinitives: the substantival inf. is much more widely used in the NT, as in all koine Greek, than in classical Greek, esp. in Luke, Paul, and Hebrews and seldom in John. The art. in such constructions functions more to indicate case than to make definite (it usually remains untranslated): "the hope of sharing" (τοῦ μετέχειν, 1 Cor 9:10); "the faith to be healed" (τοῦ σωθῆναι, Acts 14:9); "keep from sacrificing" (τοῦ μὴ θύειν, v. 18). An acc. can appear with a substantival inf.: "the time for her to give birth" (τοῦ τεκεῖν αὐτήν, Luke 1:57; cf. 2:6); "the hope that we will be saved" (τοῦ σῴζεσθαι ἡμᾶς, Acts 27:20). Substantival infs. also appear frequently with preps.: εἰς τὸ σταυρῶσαι, "in order to crucify" (Matt 27:31); ἐν τῷ πορεύεσθαι, "on *the* journey" (Acts 9:3); ἕως τοῦ ἐλθεῖν αὐτόν, "until he came" (8:40). A gen. substantival inf. often indicates a final or consecutive relationship: "*in order to* sow" (Matt 13:3 par.); "*in order to* be baptized" (3:13); τοῦ πιστεῦσαι αὐτῷ, "*and* believe him" (21:32).

e) Quotations: τὸ ἀνέβη, "*the* [statement that] 'he went up' " (Eph 4:9; cf. Matt 19:18; Rom 13:9). The art. is also used by Luke with indirect questions (Luke 1:62; Acts 4:21, etc.).

4. With some prons. pred. and attributive uses of the art. can be distinguished (possessive and demonstrative pronouns, however, generally take the art.):

a) Αὐτός: *the* Spirit *itself* (Rom 8:26: predicate), but "*the same* spirit" (2 Cor 4:13: attributive).

b) Πᾶς: πᾶσαν τὴν ἀλήθειαν, "the *whole* truth" (Matt 5:33; πᾶς without the art. would mean "each"), but ὁ πᾶς νόμος, "the law *as a whole*" (Gal 5:14: attributive, emphasizing integral unity); "twelve men *altogether*" (Acts 19:7).

5. Unlike classical Greek, which does not use the art. in such instances, NT use of the art. with a pred. noun appears to depend on word order: after the vb. it has the art., before the vb. it does not (cf. E. C. Colwell, "A Definite Rule for the Use of the Article in the Greek NT," *JBL* 52 [1933] 12-21): John 10:36: "I am *the* Son of God" (as in Matt 14:33; cf. John 9:5); but then also Matt 27:54: θεοῦ υἱὸς ἦν, "he was *the* son of (a) G(g)od." There are, nevertheless, many exceptions to this rule.

6. No binding rule can be discerned for use of the art. with proper nouns. In most cases the following applies:

a) Names of persons have the art. when the person has already been named (without the art.; → 2.a): "Mary" (Luke 2:19, after v. 5); "Stephen" (Acts 6:9, after v. 8); "Pilate" (Matt 27:13, 17, 22, 24, after v. 2); "Jesus" and "Christ" (actually an appellative: "*the* anointed") in the Gospels almost always have the art. (→ Ἰησοῦς 4.a [col. A in the chart]). Hebrew names (indeclinable in Greek) take the art. as a rule to identify their case.

b) Names of countries, which were originally adjectival, take the art.: ἡ Ἰουδαία (γῆ or χώρα), "Judea"; ἡ Γαλιλαία, "Galilee"; also, e.g., ἡ Εὐρώπη, "Europe"; ἡ Ἀσία, "Asia."

c) Names of peoples do not necessarily need the art.; Paul has Ἰουδαῖοι, "*the* Jews," and Ἕλληνες, "*the* Greeks"; the Gospels, however, usually have the art. with such names.

7. There are several situations in which the art. is typically lacking:

a) In lists (e.g., Rom 8:35, 38f.; 1 Cor 13:12; vice lists), definitions (Rom 1:16f.), at the beginnings of letters, in greetings, etc. (Matt 1:1; 1 Cor 1:1, 3; Eph 6:23).

b) With designations of class and relation that are synonymous with personal names (cf. classical Gk. βασιλεύς = "*the* king of the Persians"): Καῖσαρ, "*the* emperor" (with the art. only in John 19:12); θεὸς πατήρ, "God *the* Father"; σατανᾶς "(*the*) Satan" (usually, however, with the art., as also θεός, "God," and κύριος, "Lord," when the Jewish and Christian God is intended); also natural phenomena such as sun, moon, earth, sea (on Luke 21:25 cf. Plato *Cra.* 397d), heaven, death, etc.

c) With abstract concepts (in Paul): ἁμαρτία, "sin"; σάρξ, "flesh"; σωτηρία, "salvation," etc.

d) With indications of place and time (because of their adverbial character): ἀπ' ἀγροῦ, "from *the* field"; ἐν ἀγορᾷ, "at *the* market"; ἕως ἑσπέρας, "until *that* evening"; κατὰ καιρόν, "at *the* right time"; therefore also in Luke 8:27: better "at home" than "in a house."

e) The lack of an art. can also signify a nuanced meaning: the essence of a person or thing is emphasized, rather than its individuality: Heb 5:8: καίπερ ὢν υἱός, "in spite of his sonship"; John 1:18: "no one has seen God (θεόν)" (invisibility belongs to the divine essence); cf. Gal 2:6. Consequently a distinction should be made between πνεῦμα, "spirit," as "substance" (e.g., Mark 1:8, corresponding to anarthrous ὕδατι, "with water"), and τὸ πνεῦμα, "*the* (Holy) Spirit" as a personal being (v. 12), and between νόμος, "law," as a principle (Gal 4:21a: all forms of law), and ὁ νόμος, "*the* [Jewish] law" (v. 21b).

W. Elliger

ὀγδοήκοντα *ogdoēkonta* eighty*

Luke 16:7: "Take your bill and write *eighty*"; 2:37: Anna had been a widow ἕως (v.l. ὡς) ἐτῶν ὀγδοήκοντα τεσσάρων, "for *eighty*-four years."

ὄγδοος, 3 *ogdoos* eighth (ordinal)*

Luke 1:59; Acts 7:8: circumcision (of Jesus and Isaac) "on the *eighth* day" (Gen 21:4); 2 Pet 2:5: God preserved the life of Noah as the eighth, i.e., along with seven others (see BAGD s.v.); Rev 17:11: the "beast" is the *eighth* (head; referring to Nero, see W. Bousset, *Rev* [KEK] 407f.); 21:20: the *eighth* stone, which is beryl.

ὄγκος, ου, ὁ *onkos* load, burden*

Heb 12:1: "Let us lay aside every hindering *burden*" (the parallel term is ἁμαρτία). H. Seesemann, *TDNT* V, 41; Spicq, *Notes* II, 598-600.

ὅδε, ἥδε, τόδε *hode, hēde, tode* this*

Of the 10 occurrences of this demonstrative pron. in the NT 7 are in Revelation, all in introductory formulas (as also in the edicts of the Persian kings and in the OT in prophetic discourse): τάδε λέγει ὁ . . . (2:1, 8, 12, 18; 3:1, 7, 14). Acts 21:11 is similar: τάδε λέγει τὸ πνεῦμα τὸ ἅγιον. The pron. is also used to refer back to what has been mentioned: Luke 10:39: τῇδε ἦν ἀδελφή, "*she* had a sister"; Jas 4:13: "we will travel to *this* city."

ὁδεύω *hodeuō* go, journey, travel*

Luke 10:33, of the Samaritan: ὁδεύων ἦλθεν, "he came *while he was on a journey.*"

ὁδηγέω *hodēgeō* lead, guide; instruct*

Matt 15:14 par. Luke 6:39, in the saying on the blind man who *leads* the blind; John 16:13: "the Spirit of Truth" "will *instruct* you in all truth"; Acts 8:31, of instruction in the (Christian) understanding of the Scriptures; Rev 7:17: the "lamb" will *lead* the martyrs to springs of the water of life. W. Michaelis, *TDNT* V, 97-102; G. Ebel, *DNTT* III, 942f.

ὁδηγός, οῦ, ὁ *hodēgos* leader*

Matt 15:14; 23:16, 24, of blind *leaders* of the blind (→ ὁδηγέω); Acts 1:16: Judas was the *leader* of the arrest party (cf. Luke 22:47); Rom 2:19, of the (blind) *guide* that the Jew considers himself to be. W. Michaelis, *TDNT* V, 97-102; G. Ebel, *DNTT* III, 942f.

ὁδοιπορέω *hodoiporeō* travel, journey*

Acts 10:9: ὁδοιπορούντων ἐκείνων, "while they were *on the way.*"

ὁδοιπορία, ας, ἡ *hodoiporia* trip, journey*

John 4:6: Jesus was "tired from the *journey*" and rested at Jacob's well; 2 Cor 11:26, in a list of hardships: "often traveling."

ὁδοποιέω *hodopoieō* make a path

Mark 2:23 B, etc., of the disciples of Jesus: "they

began to *make a path,*" i.e., by plucking grain. R. Pesch, *Mark* (HTKNT) I ad loc. (180n.5).

ὁδός, οῦ, ἡ *hodos* way, road; journey

1. General overview — 2. The Synoptics — 3. John's Gospel — 4. Acts — 5. Hebrews

Lit.: C. COLPE, "Die 'Himmelsreise der Seele' außerhalb und innerhalb der Gnosis," *The Origins of Gnosticism* (ed. U. Bianchi; 1967) 429-47. — F. C. FENSHAM, "I Am the Way, the Truth and the Life," *Neot* 2 (1968) 81-88. — O. HOFIUS, "Das 'erste' und das 'zweite' Zelt. Ein Beitrag zur Auslegung von Hebr 9,1-10," *ZNW* 61 (1970) 271-77. — idem, "Inkarnation und Opfertod Jesu nach Hebr 10,19f.," FS Jeremias (1970) 132-41. — idem, *Katapausis. Die Vorstellung vom endzeitlichen Ruheort im Hebräerbrief* (WUNT 11, 1970) 127-31, 146-51. — W. G. JOHNSSON, "The Pilgrimage Motif in the Book of Hebrews," *JBL* 97 (1978) 239-51. — E. KÄSEMANN, *The Wandering People of God* (1984). — E. MANICARDI, *Il cammino di Gesù nel Vangelo di Marco* (AnBib 96, 1981). — S. V. McCASLAND, "The Way," *JBL* 77 (1958) 222-30. — W. MICHAELIS, *TDNT* V, 42-96. — F. NÖTSCHER, *Gotteswege und Menschenwege in der Bibel und in Qumran* (BBB 15, 1958). — I. DE LA POTTERIE, " 'Je suis la Voie, la Vérité et la Vie' (Jn 14,6)," *NRT* 88 (1966) 907-42. — E. REPO, *Der Weg als Selbstbezeichnung des Urchristentums* (1964). — W. C. ROBINSON, *Der Weg des Herrn. Studien zur Geschichte und Eschatologie im Lukasevangelium* (TF 36, 1964). — R. SCHNACKENBURG, "Das Anliegen der Abschiedsrede Jesu in Joh 14," FS Schelkle 89-104. — G. THEISSEN, "Wanderradikalismus. Literatur-soziologische Aspekte der Überlieferung von Worten Jesu im Urchristentum," *ZTK* 70 (1973) 245-71. — G. WINGREN, "Weg, Wanderung und verwandte Begriffe," *ST* 3 (1949) 111-23. — For further bibliography see *TWNT* X, 1197f.

1. Ὁδός is found 101 times in the NT with obvious importance in the narrative writings, especially in Luke-Acts, which contains nearly one-third of all occurrences. John uses the term only in 14:4, 5, 6 (leaving aside the citation in 1:23). In the Pauline corpus there are isolated occurrences in Romans, 1 Corinthians, and 1 Thessalonians. Further occurrences in the NT are confined to Hebrews, James, 2 Peter, Jude, and Revelation.

The word displays an extemely varied range of meanings. In its basic senses, it refers to a *path, road,* or *street* or *walking* or a *journey* as an action. The difference can in some cases be difficult to discern (cf. ἡμέρας ὁδόν, "a day's *journey,*" Luke 2:44; σαββάτου ὁδόν, "the *walking distance* permitted on the sabbath," Acts 1:12, etc.).

Likewise it is often difficult to separate literal from fig. use. The metaphorical uses of the word are the common property of the culture. This is esp. true of the widespread concept of the "two ways" (cf. Matt 7:13f.; Michaelis 42-65). In the NT ὁδός primarily refers to the *way of life,* the *manner of life* demanded by God (Acts 14:6; Rom 3:16f.; Jas 1:8; 5:20; 2 Pet 2:15, 21, etc.; 2 Pet 2:2, however, probably refers to Christianity as the true teaching). 1 Cor 4:17 connects the way of life demonstrated by the person of the apostle with his proclamation. The ὁδὸς καθ' ὑπερβολήν mentioned in 1 Cor 12:31 should not be related to receiving the gift of grace, but refers to the most excellent way of conducting one's life. The term is also used with prep. phrases: ἐν τῇ ὁδῷ, *on the way* (Matt 15:32; Mark 8:3, 27; 9:33f.; Acts 9:27, etc.), thus also κατὰ τὴν ὁδόν (Acts 26:13, etc.; see further BAGD s.v.; BDF §161.1 on Matt 4:15; for gen. of direction with ὁδός see BDF §166 on Matt 10:5).

2. According to the statistical analysis, ὁδός is found in its basic sense of *way/journey* primarily in the Synoptic Gospels. Particular roads are mentioned in Luke 10:31 (Jerusalem to Jericho) and Acts 8:26 (Jerusalem to Gaza).

ὁδός is found with an indication of direction only in Mark 10:32. Mark picks up on the indication of situation ἐν τῇ ὁδῷ of both the announcement of suffering (8:27) and the discussion of the disciples (9:33f.) and makes it more precise by adding an indication of destination that indicates the significance of the "way" in light of the Jerusalem event. In the interests of the redacted arrangement of the individual elements of tradition, therefore, the indication ἐν τῇ ὁδῷ goes beyond its function as a simple topographical notice. The concluding notice of Jesus' journey to Jerusalem concerning the healed blind man who followed Jesus (10:52) should also be understood in this way, as a paradigm for the way of discipleship. The negative counterexample is passed on in Mark 10:17. The notice ἐκπορευομένου εἰς ὁδόν, stricken from Matt 19:16/Luke 18:18, is superfluous, if not meaningless, in terms of the need for a simple statement of context. The emphasis on the journeying situation of Jesus in Mark, insofar as it is articulated by means of the word ὁδός, should therefore be viewed as having some material relation to the content of the passages introduced by ἐν τῇ ὁδῷ (εἰς ὁδόν). Luke 9:57 is materially similar. The relation of the indication of context (πορευομένων ἐν τῇ ὁδῷ) to the content of the following saying on discipleship (vv. 57-62) is clear, as is the reference of v. 57 back to the direction of the journey of Jesus toward Jerusalem in v. 51.

Jesus' traveling instructions to the Twelve (Mark 6:8; Matt 10:10; Luke 9:3; cf. Luke 22:35f.) appear to be related to the early Christian context of mission as a traveling mission, possibly also to early Christian "Wanderradikalismus" (travel-radicalism).

The frequently cited double metaphor of the narrow and wide door or the narrow and broad path (Matt 7:13f.) ought not to be pressed too much. Decisive for the understanding of this double metaphor is the conclusion, inherent in the metaphor itself and expressed in the opposition of πολλοί and ὀλίγοι. What is illustrated is not the difficulty of following Jesus. Rather, the metaphor calls for caution in following, since the criterion of dis-

cipleship is not large numbers (cf. 7:21 and the πολλοί taken up again in 7:22), but rather doing the words of Jesus (7:16-20, 24, 26).

3. The revelation formula ἐγώ εἰμι, which introduces Jesus self-designation as the *way* (John 14:6), is unique to the NT and more specifically to John's Gospel. The classification of the three expressions "the *way*, the truth, and the life" raises difficulties (on the relation of these expressions in Gnostic texts see R. Bultmann, *John* [Eng. tr., 1971] 603n.4), as does the question of the religious-historical proximity of the metaphors used by Jesus to Gnostic, in particular Mandean concepts. Older exegetes typically attempted to distinguish the *way* from the destination (reached by the way) given in the two following terms. But the leading term *way* is, rather, explained in terms of "truth and life." To paraphrase: there is only one true approach to the Father that leads to life. If one takes into account the identification of Jesus with the Father (14:9, 11), then 14:6 should be understood in the strictest sense as a revelatory saying. The strictly personal reference of the metaphor of the way stresses the historical nature of the revelation. Precisely this is what ultimately distinguishes John 14:6 from all parallels in the history of religions.

4. Equally unique to the NT is the use of ὁδός, found only in Acts, for the Christian teaching as a whole (19:23; 22:4; 24:22) or for Christians as a group (9:2; 24:14). Reference to the Essene writings does not explain this usage (cf. 1QS 9:17, 19; 10:20f.; CD 1:13; 2:6, etc.), since the use there lacks the succinctness that the expression has in Acts: ὁδός with the general meaning of a way of life (corresponding to the Essene interpretation of the law) can never be excluded in the Qumran passages; consequently, a direct relation or even dependence is not demonstrable. In Acts ὁδός implies not so much the definition of Christianity as the true teaching as distinct from other teachings, even in 24:14. Ὁδός is used, rather, as part of the attempt to avoid the impression that Christianity is a deviant Jewish αἵρεσις. This, too, distinguishes the usage of Acts from the entire context of the Essene writings. To that extent the contention that ὁδός is the self-designation of Christians should be handled with care. The term more probably owes its origin to the fact that Christianity as a whole, continually finding itself in situations of conflict and strife, felt the need to conceptually define itself.

5. In Heb 3:10 ὁδός is found in the long quotation from Ps 95:7-11. Two changes in the quotation are decisive for understanding ὁδός: First, the temporal indication τεσσεράκοντα ἔτη is connected with τὰ ἔργα μου, and second, διό is accordingly moved. These changes can be satisfactorily explained by the assumption of two dif-

ferent time periods of forty years each (Heb 3:10, 17; cf. Hofius, *Katapausis* 128f.). As a result, the ways of God mentioned in 3:10 are identical with the forty-year period of God's acts (of grace). 9:8 and 10:20 speak of *access* to the holy of holies, which up to the time of Christ had not been revealed (9:8), but now through his death has been opened (cf. BDF §163), not of a "way of the saints" in the "heavenly holy of holies" (with Hofius, *Katapausis* 149, contra Käsemann 36f.). In both passages the motif of the journey cannot be excluded. Ὁδός in 9:8, as in the rel. clause in 10:20 (qualifying 10:19), has the sense of εἴσοδος (access); a difference in meaning between ὁδός and εἴσοδος is not probable (cf. further on 10:19f., which is difficult, Hofius, "Inkarnation").   M. Völkel

ὀδούς, ὀδόντος, ὁ *odous* tooth

Matt 5:38: "eye for eye, tooth for tooth"; ὁ βρυγμὸς τῶν ὀδόντων, "gnashing of teeth" (Matt 8:12; 13:42, 50; 22:13; 24:51; 25:30; Luke 13:28). To the latter correspond Acts 7:54: βρύχω τοὺς ὀδόντας (ἐπί τινα); and Mark 9:18: τρίζω τοὺς ὀδόντας, "gnash the *teeth*." Rev 9:8: "*their teeth* were like those of lions."

ὀδυνάομαι *odynaomai* (pass.) experience pain*

Only in Luke-Acts in the NT: Luke 2:48: "we have looked *anxiously* for you"; 16:24, 25, of the torment of the rich man in hell; Acts 20:38: ὀδυνώμενοι μάλιστα, of a painful farewell, esp. because of the announcement of Paul (v. 25) that they would not see him again. F. Hauck, *TDNT* V, 115.

ὀδύνη, ης, ἡ *odynē* pain, anguish*

Rom 9:2: ἀδιάλειπτος ὀδύνη, "unceasing anguish" with λύπη μεγάλη; 1 Tim 6:10, for the pangs of conscience: those who have fallen into greed "have caused themselves many *pains*." F. Hauck, *TDNT* V, 115.

ὀδυρμός, οῦ, ὁ *odyrmos* mourning

Matt 2:18: κλαυθμὸς καὶ ὀδυρμὸς πολύς, "wailing and much mourning" (citing Jer 38:15 LXX); 2 Cor 7:7, with ἐπιπόθησις and ζῆλος. F. Hauck, *TDNT* V, 116.

Ὀζίας, ου *Ozias* Uzziah*

Matt 1:8, 9, in the genealogy of Jesus (the son of Joram).

ὄζω *ozō* produce an odor, smell*

In a bad sense in John 11:39: ἤδη ὄζει, of the body of Lazarus.

ὅθεν *hothen* from where, whence; therefore*

This adv. appears in the NT only in Matthew (4 times), in Luke-Acts (4 times), in Hebrews (6 times), and 1 John 2:18. It occurs in the local sense in Matt 12:44 par. Luke 11:24; Acts 14:26; 28:13 and in the expression ἐκεῖθεν ὅπου, "there, where" (Matt 25:24, 26). At the beginnings of sentences, however, it takes the meaning *therefore* (Matt 14:7; Acts 26:19; Heb 2:17; 3:1; 7:25; 8:3; 9:18; 11:19). In 1 John 2:18 it means *from this fact* (cf. Josephus *Ant.* ii.36).

ὀθόνη, ης, ἡ *othonē* sheet*

Acts 10:11; 11:5: σκεῦός τι ὡς ὀθόνην μεγάλην, "a container like a large *sheet*."

ὀθόνιον, ου, τό *othonion* linen strip, linen cloth*

In the NT only pl. (ὀθόνια) for the wrapping around the body of Jesus (Luke 24:12; John 19:40; 20:5, 6, 7). In contrast, Mark 15:46 par. Matt 27:59/Luke 23:53, where Jesus is wrapped in a burial cloth (sg. σινδών). J. Blinzler, *Philologus* 99 (1955) 158-66; R. Schnackenburg, *John* III (Eng. tr., 1982) 350; Spicq, *Notes* II, 601-5.

οἶδα *oida* know, understand

1. Occurrences in the NT — 2. Meaning — 3. Usage

Lit.: BAGD s.v. — BDF index s.v. εἰδέναι. — D. W. BURDICK, "Οἶδα and γινώσκω in the Pauline Epistles," *New Dimensions in NT Studies* (ed. R. N. Longenecker and M. C. Tenney; 1974) 344-56. — E. HEITSCH, "Das Wissen des Xenophanes," *RMP* 109 (1966) 193-35, 207-16. — HELBING, *Grammatik* 108. — KÜHNER, *Grammatik* II/2, 351f. — M. LEUMANN, "Griech. hom. εἰδώς, ἰδυῖα und . . . ," *idem, Kleine Schriften* (1959) 251-58, esp. 251f. — LSJ s.v. εἴδω B. — MAYSER, *Grammatik* I/2, 130, 149. — I. DE LA POTTERIE, "Οἶδα et γινώσκω. Les deux modes de la connaissance dans le quatrième Évangile," *Bib* 40 (1959) 709-25. — SCHMIDT, *Synonymik* I, 282-309, esp. 289-95. — SCHWYZER, *Grammatik* II, 395. — H. SEESEMANN, *TDNT* V, 116-19. — B. SNELL, *Der Weg zum Denken und zur Wahrheit* (Hypomnemata 57, 1978), esp. 21-43 (= *JHS* 93 [1973] 172-84). — ThGL s.v. εἰδέω. — W. VEITCH, *Greek Verbs Irregular and Defective. Their Forms, Meaning and Quantity* (1887, 1967). — ZORELL, *Lexicon* s.v.

1. This vb., the nonreduplicated pf. with present force of → εἶδον, "perceive" (ablaut stages are ϝοιδ-, ϝειδ- and ϝιδ-; cf. Leumann 251), is known from Homer (*Iliad*) on, and is found in the NT 318 times, esp. in John (84 occurrences) and in the Pauline corpus (103 occurrences), less frequently in the Synoptic Gospels (24 occurrences in Matthew, 21 in Mark, 25 in Luke) and Acts (19 occurrences). It is lacking only in 2 John.

As a v.l. οἶδα replaces γινώσκω in John 14:7 (*NTG*[25] in the text); 1 Cor 8:2; Phil 2:22 and εἶδον in Matt 9:4 (*NTG*[25] in the text); Mark 12:28 (*NTG*[25] in the text); John 8:56; Acts 28:26;

Jas 5:11; 1 Pet 1:8. The reverse is also the case: v.l. γινώσκω in Luke 6:8; John 21:4; Acts 20:22; Rom 15:29; Rev 2:17 [not noted in the apparatus of *NTG*[26]); v.l. εἶδον in Matt 12:25; Mark 12:15; Luke 13:27; John 19:28; 1 Cor 2:2, 12; and both in Luke 9:47.

In contrast to classical usage (for references see Veitch 218-20; cf. also *ThGL; LSJ*) the following forms do not appear in the NT: οἶδας, οἴδαμεν (except in place of subjunc. in 1 John 5:15; → ἐάν 2), οἴδατε (ἴστε in Eph 5:5; Heb 12:17; Jas 1:19; on the mood cf. F. Mussner, *Gal* [HTKNT] at 4:13), οἴδασι(ν) (ἴσασι in Acts 26:4), ἤδειτε, ἤδεισαν, εἰδήσουσιν (except in Heb 8:11 [citing Jer 38:34 LXX]). On frequency and other forms see *VKGNT* II s.v.; on the LXX see Helbing, *Grammatik* 108; on the papyri see Mayser, *Grammatik* I/2, 130, 149.

2. → Γινώσκω was originally an inceptive vb. (as indicated by the stem in -σκ-) representing the acquisition of knowledge ("come to know"); → ἐπίσταμαι is resultative and points more to the practical faculty of knowing. Οἶδα, on the other hand (originally *have seen* [with the mind's eye]; cf., e.g, Snell 26; LSJ s.v.) in classical Greek denotes the theoretical possession of knowledge (*know, be acquainted with*; see Schmidt 285-89; all three vbs. together in Thucydides i.69.3 as cited in Schmidt 295). This knowledge, based on observation (cf. Herodotus iv.31.1, cited in Snell 58n.18), was able already in Homer to take on a very abstract form (Heitsch 207-16). It is a purely mental discernment apart from experience per se (Schmidt 289).

This classical distinction between οἶδα and γινώσκω is generally preserved in the NT. There is to date, however, no comprehensive investigation of the Synoptic Gospels (isolated comments in Seesemann 117f., who defends synonymous usage). In John, οἶδα, in contrast to γινώσκω, always designates an intuitive or certain knowledge, which de la Potterie demonstrates where the subj. is Jesus (715-17) or the disciples (722-24). Burdick concludes that of the 103 occurrences of οἶδα in the Pauline corpus 90 have the classical meaning, only 5 are synonymous with γινώσκω (Rom 8:26; 13:11; 2 Cor 5:11; 9:2; 2 Tim 1:15), and 8 have the classical sense of γινώσκω (Rom 7:7, 18; 1 Cor 2:12; 11:3; Eph 1:18; 6:21; Col 2:1; 1 Thess 5:12).

3. The subj. of οἶδα is almost always a person (e.g., ὁ Ἰησοῦς in John 6:64; ὁ θεός in 2 Cor 11:11; ὁ πατήρ in Matt 6:32 par. Luke 12:30; both together in 2 Cor 11:31; κύριος in 2 Pet 2:9; ὁ διάβολος in Rev 12:12) or groups of persons (e.g., the disciples in John 21:4; the Gentiles in Gal 4:8; 1 Thess 4:5; τὰ δαιμόνια in Mark 1:34 par. Luke 4:41; the exception is τὰ πρόβατα in John 10:4, 5).

The complement can be any of the following (see *VKGNT* I s.v.):

a) The acc. of a person (e.g., Ἰησοῦν in 1 Cor 2:2; τὸν θεόν in 1 Thess 4:5; τὸν πατέρα in John 8:19) with 1) a partc. (2 Cor 12:2; BDF §416.2; to be supplied in Mark

6:20; also classical: Schwyzer, *Grammatik* II, 395); 2) an inf. (Luke 4:41; BDF §397.1; to be supplied in Mark 1:34); or 3) (proleptically) with direct or indirect discourse following ὅτι (2 Cor 12:3; cf., e.g., Plato *Men.* 94b) or an indirect question (e.g., Mark 1:24 par. Luke 4:34).

b) The acc. of an abstract noun or a thing (e.g., πάντα, John 16:30; 21:17; Jude 5; cf. Homer *Il.* ii.458; *Od.* xii.189 and on these Snell 27, 37) with 1) the acc. of a person (Acts 10:37f.; 1 Cor 2:2); 2) an inf. (1 Pet 5:9; v.l. has a ὅτι clause); or 3) direct or indirect discourse introduced by ὅτι (e.g., after ἕν in John 9:25; cf. Ps.-Democritus B 304 [= Diels, *Fragmente* II, 223, l. 26]; after τοῦτο in Eph 5:5; 1 Tim 1:9; 2 Tim 1:15) or indirect question (Eph 6:21).

c) Περί with the gen. of an abstract noun or a thing (cf. Plato *Criti.* 107b; Matt 24:36 par. Mark 13:32; with ὅτι following: 1 Cor 8:1, 4).

d) Direct or indirect discourse with ὅτι as a fixed phrase (more than 130 times; cf. F. Mussner, *Gal* [HTKNT] at 2:16): οἴδαμεν ὅτι, οὐκ οἴδατε ὅτι (passages in BAGD s.v. 1.e), εἰδώς (εἰδότες) ὅτι (passages in Zorell 4).

e) A rel. clause (e.g., Mark 5:33; similarly [substantival partc.] Acts 5:7).

f) An indirect question introduced by 1) an interrogative pron. (usually τίς; ποῖος in Matt 24:42; 24:43 par. Luke 12:39; οἷος in 1 Thess 1:5; ἡλίκος in Col 2:1); 2) an interrogative adv. (πόθεν, πότε, ποῦ, πῶς: passages in BAGD s.v. 1.f; ὡς in Acts 10:37f.; 1 Thess 2:11; see BDF §396); 3) εἰ (→ εἰ 2.c); or 4) εἴτε-εἴτε (2 Cor 12:2, 3);

g) An inf. (*know how to*, e.g., Matt 7:11 par. Luke 11:13), occasionally accompanied by an adv. (ἀκριβῶς in 1 Thess 5:2; see also BAGD s.v.), sometimes comparative (Acts 24:22; cf. 23:15; Ps.-Plato *Ax.* 369a), ἀληθῶς (Acts 12:11; cf. Plato *Men.* 71c; with γινώσκω in John 7:26; 17:8). The common classical advs. εὖ (see LSJ s.v.) and σαφῶς (e.g., Sophocles *El.* 660; see also BAGD s.v.) are not found with οἶδα.

Absolute use is found in responses (Matt 21:27 par. Mark 11:33; John 9:12), in insertions with ὡς (Matt 27:65; Mark 4:27). With καθώς (Acts 2:22; 1 Thess 2:2, 5; 3:4). The complement must be supplied in Luke 11:44; John 2:9b; 2 Pet 1:12; 1 John 2:20 (v.l. πάντα for πάντες); Rev 7:14. A main clause follows in Jas 1:19 (cf. Kühner, *Grammatik* II/2, 351f.).

                                                            A. Horstmann

οἰκεῖος, 2 (3) *oikeios* belonging to the house; subst.: members of the household*

With ἴδιοι, of family members, 1 Tim 5:8; fig. οἰκεῖοι τοῦ θεοῦ, of the Christian as "a *member of the household of God*" in Eph 2:19; of the "*members of the household of faith*" in Gal 6:10. O. Michel, *TDNT* V, 134f.; J. Goetzmann, *DNTT* II, 251.

οἰκετεία, ας, ἡ *oiketeia* household servant*

Matt 24:45, of the δοῦλος whom the master "placed over his *household*"; par. Luke 12:42 replaces οἰκετεία with θεραπεία.

οἰκέτης, ου, ὁ *oiketēs* (household) slave*

The antonyms are δεσπότης in 1 Pet 2:18 and κύριος in Luke 16:13. The expression ἀλλότριος οἰκέτης in Rom 14:4 refers to the *slave* of someone else. According to Acts 10:7 Cornelius "called two of his slaves and a devout soldier" to send them to Joppa. C. Spicq, "Le vocabulaire de l'esclavage dans le NT," *RB* 85 (1978) 218-20.

οἰκέω *oikeō* live, dwell; trans.: inhabit*

Intrans. of the cohabitation of marriage, 1 Cor 7:12, 13; of the Spirit of God, who *lives* in a person, Rom 8:9, 11, 20. Trans. in 1 Tim 6:16, of God, who "*dwells in unapproachable light.*" O. Michel, *TDNT* V, 135f.

οἴκημα, ατος, τό *oikēma* living quarters, room*

As a euphemism for prison, Acts 12:7 (cf. Thucydides iv.47.3; 48.1; Lucian *Tox.* 29; Plutarch *Agis* 19.5, 8, 9).

οἰκητήριον, ου, τό *oikētērion* habitation, dwelling*

2 Cor 5:2, fig. for the body of transfigured Christians; Jude 6, literal for the angels who abandoned "their own *dwelling.*" O. Michel, *TDNT* V, 155.

οἰκία, ας, ἡ *oikia* house, household, family

1. Occurrences and meaning — 2. Meanings not dealt with under → οἶκος — a) "My Father's house" — b) House as metaphor for body — c) "Caesar's household"

Lit.: → οἶκος. — See also G. FISCHER, *Die himmlischen Wohnungen* (1975). — O. MICHEL, *TDNT* V, 131-34.

1. The word is attested from the time of Herodotus, but is lacking in the Greek tragedians. In frequency and range of meanings it is surpassed by → οἶκος, which is essentially a synonym. In the LXX, οἰκία and οἶκος translate primarily *bayit.* As such, οἶκος is found approximately 8 times more often than οἰκία. In the NT, οἰκία is found 94 times: 26 in Matthew, 18 in Mark, 24 in Luke, 5 in John, 12 in Acts, 2 in 1–2 Corinthians, 1 in Philippians, 1 in 1 Timothy, 2 in 2 Timothy, and 1 in 2 John. It means a) *house/dwelling place,* b) *household, family.* These meanings coincide with → οἶκος and will be dealt with under that entry. From these two basic meanings, all other meanings are derived.

2. a) Fig. use of οἰκία in the revelation saying in John

14:2—"in my Father's *house*" (thus also *1 Enoch* 45:3; *Acts of Peter and Paul* 82)—is reminiscent of the contemporary conception of heavenly dwellings (cf. Luke 16:9), which is seen primarily in Gnostic texts (cf. R. Schnackenburg, *John* III [Eng. tr., 1982] ad loc.). This revelation saying emphasizes the glory of the Father as the ultimate goal.

b) The equally fig. use of οἰκία in 2 Cor 5:1 designates the body. Here Paul contrasts the earthly body as a mortal, "earthly tent-*dwelling*" with the transfigured body, "an eternal *house* in heaven, not built by human hands." The image of the body as a house is widespread (cf. Job 4:19; Philo *Praem.* 120; → οἶκος 3.f), but was first elaborated by the Gnostics, especially the Mandeans (on the image of the body as a tent cf. Isa 38:12; Wis 9:15; *Corp. Herm.* 13.12, 15).

c) Derived from the meaning *household* is the expression "those of the *household* of Caesar" (οἱ ἐκ τῆς Καίσαρος οἰκίας) in Phil 4:22. Intended are those who serve in the court of the emperor, both slave and free and hailing from many parts of the Roman Empire (see also J. Gnilka, *Phil* [HTKNT] ad loc.).   P. Weigandt

οἰκιακός, οῦ, ὁ *oikiakos* member of a household*

Matt 10:25, in contrast to οἰκοδεσπότης; 10:36: "a person's enemies will be the *members of his or her own household* (= family)."

οἰκοδεσποτέω *oikodespoteō* manage a household*

In the regulations for widows in 1 Tim 5:14: "I want younger [widows] to marry, to have children, to *manage the household*"; cf. → δεσπότης 5.

οἰκοδεσπότης, ου, ὁ *oikodespotēs* master of the house*

Mark 14:14 par. Luke 22:11, of the master of the house where Jesus wanted to celebrate the Passover; Matt 24:43 par. Luke 12:39, of the οἰκοδεσπότης who did not know the time of the break-in; with ἄνθρωπος in Matt 13:52; 20:1; 21:33. In parables and metaphors for God: Matt 13:27; 20:1, 11; 21:33; Luke 14:21; applied by Jesus to himself: Matt 10:25; Luke 13:25. Cf. → δεσπότης 5.

οἰκοδομέω *oikodomeō* build, erect
→ οἰκοδομή.

οἰκοδομή, ῆς, ἡ *oikodomē* building, edifice; building up, edification*
οἰκοδομέω *oikodomeō* build, erect*

1. Occurrences in the NT — 2. Meaning — 3. Οἰκοδομή — a) As *nomen rei actae:* Sacred structures in the literal

and fig. sense — b) As *nomen actionis:* Building up, edification — c) Edification of the body — d) Anthropological: "Tent dwelling" — e) Οἰκοδομή τῆς χρείας — 4. Οἰκοδομέω — a) Theological significance: Building up the ἐκκλησία — b) The builders in Ps. 118:22 — c) Special nuances in secular usage — d) Secular usage — e) Οἰκοδομέω = εὐαγγελίζομαι — f) In the conflicts in Corinth and Galatia — g) Jesus' edification of the eschatological-messianic temple — 5. Compound forms

Lit.: J. M. CASCIARO, *El vocabulario técnico de Qumrân en relación con el concepto de comunidad* (Scripta Theologica 1, 1969) 7-54, 243-313. — B. GÄRTNER, *The Temple and the Community in Qumran and the NT* (1965). — G. KLINZING, *Die Umdeutung des Kultus in der Qumrangemeinde und im NT* (1971). — G. J. LOPEZ, "Sentido Misional del 'edificar' la Iglesia en S. Pablo," *Misiones Extranjeras* 16 (1968) 478-90. — R. J. MCKELVEY, *The New Temple: The Church in the NT* (1969). — O. MICHEL, *TDNT* V, 136-48. — F. MUSSNER, *Christus, das All und die Kirche* (1968). — H. MUSZYNSKI, *Fundament, Bild und Metapher in den Handschriften von Qumran* (1975). — J. PFAMMATTER, *Die Kirche als Bau. Eine exegetisch-theologische Studie zur Ekklesiologie der Paulusbriefe* (1960). — J. SZLAGA, "Chrystus i Apostolowie jako fundament Kosciola," *Roczniki Teologiczno-Kanoniczne* 18 (1971) 113-30. — idem, " 'Zbudowani na fundamencie Apostolów i Proroków.' Problemy egzegetyczne Ef 2,19-22," *Collectanea Theologica* 46 (1976) 45-64, 65. — A. VANHOYE, "La Chiesa come casa spirituale secondo la prima lettera di S. Pietro," *Sinodo Documentazione* 6 (1975) 89-104. — P. VIELHAUER, *Oikodome. Das Bild vom Bau in der christlichen Literatur vom NT bis Clemens Alexandrinus* (1940) (= idem, *Oikodome* [1979] 1-168). — H. WENSCHKEWITZ, *Die Spiritualisierung der Kultusbegriffe Tempel, Priester und Opfer im NT* (Angelos Beihefte 4, 1932) 70-230.

1. The noun οἰκοδομή appears 3 times in the Synoptics (Matt 24:1 par. Mark 13:1, 2, referring to the temple complex) and 15 times in the Pauline corpus, always metaphorically. The vb. (40 occurrences) is common in the NT (24 occurrences in the Synoptics, 1 in John, 4 in Acts, 9 in Paul, 2 in 1 Peter). The Synoptics often use the vb. in its original sense of a human-made structure, in part, however, already with an ecclesiological nuance (Mark 12:10 par.; 14:58 par.; Matt 16:18; cf. John 2:19f.). Of the 4 occurrences in Acts, 7:47, 49 refer to the temple building and 9:31 and 20:32 are related to Pauline ecclesiological usage. The 11 occurrences in the NT Epistles (Rom 15:20; 1 Cor 8:1, 10; 10:23; 14:4a, b, 17; Gal 2:18; 1 Thess 5:11; 1 Pet 2:5, 7) are all in ecclesiological contexts, from which the word receives its content.

2. The root οἰκοδομ- designates the activity of building in the broad sense. In the NT that which is built can be structures of all kinds (houses, cities, towers, monuments, barns). When used fig., that which is built can be the ἐκκλησία as a whole or its individual members, and in Acts 15:16 (→ 5.b) the house of David. When used absolutely (e.g., Luke 17:28; 1 Cor 8:1; Rom 15:2; 1 Cor

14:3) the meaning of both noun and vb. is indicated by the context. In those instances where the term has theological relevance, the one who builds is God (Acts 20:32), Jesus (Matt 16:18), or a person acting with the authority of God or Jesus (1 Cor 14:4; 2 Cor 10:8; 13:10), but also every believer (1 Thess 5:11). In the NT the word group is used basically of God's saving acts. Moreover, fig. use characterizes the soteriological service of person for person as leading into the Church, the sacrament of salvation. For the NT interpretation of οἰκοδομοῦντες in Ps 118:22 → 4.b.

3. a) οἰκοδομή in Mark 13:1, 2 par. Matt 24:1 (in all three cases pl.) is used of the sacred buildings of the temple in Jerusalem.

According to 1 Cor 3:9, the members of the congregation addressed in the letter are θεοῦ οἰκοδομή, "God's *building*," and θεοῦ γεώργιον, "God's planted field." Human builders are at best God's fellow workers (3:9), but never owners (or even masters, cf. 2 Cor 1:24) of the Church. In Eph 2:21, οἰκοδομή represents a sacred building; those who come to believe make up its parts. Πᾶσα οἰκοδομή should be understood (in spite of the lack of an art.) as "the whole *building*," which grows toward the goal of becoming "a holy temple in the Lord" or "the dwelling of God in the Spirit" (vv. 21f.).

Through the use of the partc. συναρμολογουμένη the image of the building approaches that of the body (elsewhere in the NT συναρμολογέω is found only in Eph 4:16; there the body of Christ, here the οἰκοδομή, is "joined together"). The images of building and body (intermingled in 4:12, 16) illustrate the fact that the Church *is* and always *will be*—"The Church *exists* even as it grows" (H. Schlier, *Eph* [1957] 144)—where the growth, however (αὔξει, 2:21; cf. 4:16), is not externally verifiable or quantitative, but "the overall movement of the Church toward holiness in and of itself" *(ibid.).*

b) When the Pauline Epistles use οἰκοδομή as a *nomen actionis* (the action or process of building or edification: Rom 14:19; 15:2; 1 Cor 14:3, 5, 12, 26; 2 Cor 12:19), what is built is never a building but always the ἐκκλησία. The characteristic meaning of the theologically significant use of οἰκοδομή is present in all these passages, as in also 2 Cor. 10:8 and 13:10: the apostolic authority bestowed by God serves the *edification*, not the destruction, of the Church.

c) The phrase οἰκοδομή τοῦ σώματος τοῦ Χριστοῦ (Eph 4:12) is unique (as is εἰς οἰκοδομὴν θεοῦ [sc. τοῦ σώματος] in 4:16). Certain persons are "given" to the Church of God as builders (4:11). Ultimately, however, the inner dynamic of the body itself is that in and through Christ the head brings about the body's growth. Consideration should be given to Schlier's suggestion (209) that πᾶν τὸ σῶμα (v. 16a) refers to the Church as well as to the body of Christ, but that τὴν αὔξησιν τοῦ σώματος (v. 16b) no longer refers to the Church, but to the world-body. We would then have an expression of the fact that the body of the Church, "in its self-edification in the body," accomplishes at the same time the growth of the world-body into Christ.

d) The single occurrence of οἰκοδομή with an anthropological meaning (2 Cor 5:1) combines in its own way the building metaphor with that of the human body as a garment: It is a "tent dwelling," which is destroyed at death, while an eternal dwelling not built by human hands has been prepared in heaven as a new garment. Although 5:1f. can best be explained "in terms of the Mandean concepts of the earthly and heavenly body as a house/ building or garment," it remains difficult to discern a single trajectory from Paul to the Mandeans, esp. since building and house "did not become anthropological terms in Judaism," and since only those Iranian building concepts were adopted "that were capable of giving figurative expression to the concepts of the apocalyptic temple and Jerusalem, the holy city, in which the pious had their individual 'dwelling' or 'eternal tents'" (Vielhauer 108). Paul is moving here in a realm that he himself has configured. Noteworthy, in any case, not only in terms of terminology, is the proximity of 2 Cor 5:1 and Mark 14:58.

e) The gen. construction οἰκοδομή τῆς χρείας in Eph 4:29 is unusual and very early attracted elucidating corrections (D* F G it vg^cl read τῆς πίστεως). This is almost certainly not an obj. gen., but a qualitative gen.; χρεία could be taken over from v. 28 through a link with the cue word. The parenesis of v. 29 then would again have as its content "edification" in the Pauline sense: "wherever there is need," or "according to need."

4. The theologically relevant uses of the vb. οἰκοδομέω and its compounds (→ 5) are generally in accordance with the already discussed ecclesiological use of the noun *(building up, edification)*.

a) Statistically and in terms of content the main focus of the theologically relevant occurrences of οἰκοδομέω is the meaning *build up, edify*. The objects of this vb., explicit and implicit, are always the ἐκκλησία (Matt 16:18; 1 Cor 14:4b) or an individual member of the ἐκκλησία (Acts 20:32; 1 Cor 8:1; 10:23; 14:4a, 17; 1 Thess 5:11; cf. 1 Pet 2:5). Even the use of the building metaphor (Matt 16:18; Paul *passim*) follows as a rule from ecclesiological considerations. The congregation (and "the whole Church," Eph 2:21f.) is a holy temple of God (1 Cor 3:16ff.) but at the same time is also a construction site, where work is continually in process, since new building blocks may always be added (Eph 2:22; 1 Pet 2:5). To make explicit what is implicit in this image: The local church and "the whole Church" possess a static

element where their building plans are concerned, but a dynamic element where their growth is concerned.

In Acts 20:32 "God and his word" are the acting subjects of οἰκοδομῆσαι, which here indicates "progress in the personal realization of the gospel" (J. Dupont, *Paulus an die Seelsorger* [1966] 184). According to Acts 9:31 God leads the building of the Church. As in Matt 16:18 and Acts 20:32, therefore, no human is the actual builder, and the Church as a whole is in view.

b) According to the witness of the Synoptics (Mark 12:10 par. Matt 21:42/Luke 20:17) Jesus viewed his contemporaries, or more specifically the Jerusalem authorities who rejected (killed) him, the Son (there may be a wordplay here: stone = 'bn, son = hbn), as the οἰκοδομοῦντες of Ps 118:22. Their actions give rise to a new community that understands itself as the building and Jesus as the cornerstone (cf. R. Pesch, *Mark* [HTKNT] II, ad loc.). In Acts 4:11 οἰκοδόμοι (instead of οἰκοδομοῦντες) is a NT hapax legomenon, although there is a LXX tradition that underlies it. Ps 118:22 functions (as in Mark 12:10) as a resurrection testimony. 1 Pet 2:7f. uses Ps 118:22 with Isa 8:14 and thus gives to the Psalm passage a new interpretation: The crucified (rejected) one becomes, through his resurrection, for those who do not believe (the word) a stone of stumbling and a rock of offense.

c) In certain passages the context lends the secular use of οἰκοδομέω a theological nuance; thus, e.g., Acts 7:47 (in light of the structure of Stephen's speech, the temple of Solomon points ahead to the building of the new eschatological community); Luke 11:47, 48 (Jesus' "woe" saying is directed against the builders of the monuments [in Matt 23:29 the graves] of the murdered prophets, since they build them for the wrong reasons); in the discourse on the conditions of discipleship (Luke 14:28, 30) and in the closing parable of the Sermon on the Mount (Matt 7:24, 26 par. Luke 6:48a, b, 49) the image (construction of a tower or house) and the issue (becoming a disciple of Jesus) are certainly not juxtaposed without any relation to each other (*contra* Vielhauer 59).

d) Passages with no particular theological relevance for the word group are Luke 4:29; 7:5; 17:28; Mark 12:1 par. Matt 21:33. In Luke 12:16-20, the building metaphor (v. 18) represents the possibilities and limitations of striving for security with and without God.

e) In Rom 15:20 οἰκοδομέω with no obj. has the same meaning as εὐαγγελίζομαι; it "describes here the participation of those who proclaim the gospel in the edification of the community of God" (O. Michel, *Rom* [KEK] ad loc.).

f) Οἰκοδομέω with no obj. in 1 Cor 8:1, 10; 10:23 gains its specific content from the question of meat offered to idols dealt with in chs. 8–10. In 8:1 it is qualified by being placed in contrast to φυσιόω: gnosis "puffs up" (gives only the appearance of growth and strength), love *builds up* (gives true growth and strength). In 10:23 οἰκοδομέω relativizes the key phrase πάντα ἔξεστιν by recalling the principal necessity of the edification of the community as a check on unbridled ἐξουσία. The process of building is thus accomplished through the "ethical attitude, in practical life" (Vielhauer 96). The reckless attitude of the "strong" (8:10) is edification perverted into its opposite: "The weak is destroyed by your [immoderately practiced] knowledge" (v. 11). Gal 2:18 likewise uses the vb. in a nonspecific way and thus allows its typical meaning to come more clearly to the fore: Οἰκοδομέω refers here to redeclaring as valid as a way of salvation the nullified law.

g) Mark 14:58 par. Matt 26:61 and Mark 15:29 par. Matt 27:40 pass on a logion according to which Jesus granted himself the authority to destroy the Jerusalem temple and to build in its stead the messianic temple. John 2:19, which is clearly a variant of this saying, sees the messianic temple in one and the same line with the body of the resurected (and perhaps with the ἐκκλησία). This assumption is further supported by the fact that the unambiguous οἰκοδομέω is replaced by the ambiguous ἐγείρω. In Mark 16:18, which should be viewed as a variant of this logion, "the future building of the messianic temple coincides with that of the future ekklesia. . . . Thus it becomes clear that the building is accomplished by exercising the power of teaching and suffering passed on by Jesus" (H. Schlier, *LTK* III, 960).

5. The compound ἐποικοδομέω occurs 7 (or 8) times in the NT, ἀνοικοδομέω 2 times, and συνοικοδομέω once.

a) Ἐποικοδομέω, *build, build upon, build up**: All 4 occurrences in 1 Corinthians (3:10a, b, 12, 14) are found in the metaphor of laying a foundation and building upon it, which determines the content of the word here. Eph 2:20 lies closest to this sense: the believer, viewed as a building block, is built onto (or into) the foundation of the apostles and (NT) prophets (1 Cor 3:11: on the foundation of Jesus Christ). In Col 2:7, the strength of the metaphor ἐποικοδομούμενοι is greatly reduced in connection with ἐρριζωμένοι (cf., however, its closeness to 1 Cor 3:9!) and esp. with the imv. περιπατεῖτε (v. 6). The reader should allow himself to remain rooted (pf. partc.) in the soil and bedrock, Jesus Christ, and to be continually (pres. partc.) built up. Jude 20, by way of contrast, calls upon the reader to *build* himself *up*; the foundation here (unique in the NT) is "the holy faith." The original reading of 1 Pet 2:5 (οἰκοδομέω or ἐποικοδομέω) can not be text-critically discerned with certainty; in both readings the meaning corresponds to Eph 2:20; 1 Cor 3:10.

b) Ἀνοικοδομέω, *build upon (again)**, is found only in Acts 15:16a, b, in a loose quotation of Amos 9:11f. LXX. By reworking his LXX source Luke further inten-

sifies the basic meaning of the prefix ἀν- (build *again*). According to the speech of James (Acts 15:13-21) the eschatological rebuilding of the people of God is *already* under way: the name of the Lord was to be spoken first over Israel, and then over all the nations (15:17).

c) Συνοικοδομέω, *build together** (in the LXX only in 3 Esdr 5:65 [act.]), appears in the NT only in Eph 2:22 (pass.), where it entails not only the process of being incorporated, but also community with others, i.e., with believers in general (J. Gnilka, *Eph* [HTKNT] ad loc.; likewise Schlier, *Eph* ad loc.), with Christ, with the apostles and prophets, as well as with other Christians (Michel 151).

                                                          J. Pfammatter

οἰκοδόμος, ου, ὁ *oikodomos* builder*

Acts 4:11: "This [i.e., Jesus] is the stone that was despised by you, the *builders*" (cf. Ps 117:22: οἰκοδομοῦντες). Perhaps Luke has chosen the noun οἰκοδόμος because of the ἄρχοντες τοῦ λαοῦ (v. 8: the members of the Sanhedrin) who are here accused. O. Michel, *TDNT* V, 136.

οἰκονομέω *oikonomeō* administer, act as administrator
→ οἰκονομία

οἰκονομία, ας, ἡ *oikonomia* office of administrator, administration*
οἰκονομέω *oikonomeō* administer, act as administrator*
οἰκονόμος, ου, ὁ *oikonomos* administrator (of a household), steward*

1. Occurrences in the NT — 2. Meaning and usage — 3. Οἰκονόμος and οἰκονομέω — a) Literal usage — b) Nonliteral usage — 4. Οἰκονομία — a) Literal usage — b) Nonliteral usage

Lit.: BAGD s.v. — B. Botte, "Oikonomia," FS E. Dekkers (1975) I, 3-9. — H. Brattgård, *Im Haushalt Gottes. Eine theologische Studie über Grundgedanke und Praxis der Stewardship* (1964) — H. J. Cadbury, "Erastus of Corinth," *JBL* 50 (1931) 42-58. — K. Duchatelez, "La notion d'économie et ses richesses théologiques," *NRT* 102 (1970) 267-92. — J. Goetzmann, *DNTT* II, 253-56. — H.-J. Horn, "Κατ' οἰκονομίαν τοῦ κυρίου. Stoische Voraussetzungen der Vorstellung vom Heilsplan Gottes," *Vivarium* (FS T. Klauser, 1984) 188-93. — P. Landvogt, *Epigraphische Untersuchungen über den οἰκονόμος* (Diss. Strasbourg, 1908). — LSJ s.v. — O. Lillie, *Das patristische Wort οἰκονομία, seine Grundlage und seine Geschichte bis auf Origenes* (Diss. Erlangen, 1955) — O. Michel, *TDNT* V, 149-53. — J. Reumann, "Οἰκονομία as 'Ethical Accommodation' in the Fathers and its Pagan Background," *Studia Patristica* III (TU 78, ed. F. R. Cross; 1961) 370-79. — idem, "Οἰκονομία = Covenant. Terms for Heilsgeschichte in Early Christian Usage," *NovT* 3 (1959) 282-99. — idem, "Οἰκονομία-Terms in Paul in

Comparison with Lucan Heilsgeschichte," *NTS* 13 (1966/67) 147-67. —*idem,* " 'Stewards of God.' Pre-Christian Religious Application of οἰκονόμος in Greek," *JBL* 77 (1958) 339-49. — *idem,* "The Use of *Oikonomia* and Related Terms in Greek Sources to about A.D. 100," *Ekklesiastikos Pharos* 60 (Addis Ababa, 1978) 482-579. — *idem, The Use of οἰκονομία and Related Terms in Greek Sources to about A.D. 100 as a Background for Patristic Applications* (Diss. University of Pennsylvania, 1957). — SPICQ, *Notes* II, 606-13. — W. TOOLEY, "Stewards of God. An Examination of the Terms οἰκονόμος and οἰκονομία in the NT," *SJT* 19 (1966) 74-86. — D. WEBSTER, "Primary Stewardship," *ExpTim* 72 (1960/61) 274-76. — For further bibliography see *TWNT* X, 1198f.

1. In the Synoptics both the vb. and the noun οἰκονομία are confined to the parable of the "dishonest steward" (the noun in Luke 16:2, 3, 4; the vb. in 16:2), while reference to the position of steward also appears in Luke 12:42; 16:1, 3, 8. Οἰκονομία occurs in the Pauline corpus 6 times (1 Cor 9:17; Eph 1:10; 3:2, 9; Col 1:25; 1 Tim 1:4), οἰκονόμος 5 times (Rom 16:23; 1 Cor 4:1, 2; Gal 4:2; Titus 1:7). The only other NT occurrence of these words is in 1 Pet 4:10 (οἰκονόμος).

2. The meaning of the 3 words is characteristically nonspecific and diffuse and can be decided only case by case on the basis of context. The NT range of meanings, which extends from reference to the steward and his position or activity in the literal sense (Luke 12:42; 16:1-9) to metaphorical usage for ecclesiastical offices and functions (1 Cor 4:1; 9:17; Col 1:25, etc.) and to a circumlocution for God's plan of salvation (Ephesians), lacks the semantic structure that was already extant in secular Greek (cf. LSJ s.v.), although the basic meaning *(managerial activity in connection with certain [entrusted] affairs)* is still recognizable, whether the accent falls on the aspect of management (e.g., Eph 1:10) or on that of stewardship (e.g., 1 Cor 4:1f.; 9:17).

3. a) Stewards were responsible for personal oversight of all labor, including its (natural) product (references in Sqicq 607n.5). Luke's insertion of οἰκονόμος in place of δοῦλος in the Q parable of the faithful servant (12:42) takes this relation into account, but is also no doubt influenced by the fact that Christian officebearers were called οἰκονόμοι of God (→ b; see A. Weiser, *Die Knechtsgleichnisse der synoptischen Evangelien* [SANT 29, 1971] 220). While in Luke 12:42 οἰκονόμος refers to a slave who has been given responsibility over a limited area and who will be rewarded for managing it properly by being entrusted with the management of all the possessions of the master (12:44), Luke 16:1-9 presupposes that the one designated οἰκονόμος already holds this position and is legally authorized to act, whether to his master's good or detriment. He fulfills the function of steward not only with regard to internal matters, but also

with regard to things external (16:5-8). Through misuse of this trusted position he is then no longer able to *exercise the office of steward* (οἰκονομέω, v. 2), having been exposed as unfaithful (v. 8).

In Gal 4:2 Paul refers to the "guardians and *stewards,*" the overseers of the underage heir and stewards of his possessions (cf. H. Schlier, *Gal* [KEK] 189). Paul's reference to Erastus (cf. Cadbury) as οἰκονόμος τῆς πόλεως (Rom 16:23) deals with the abundantly attested (see Preisigke, *Wörterbuch* III, s.v.; Spicq 611) title of civil officials with a relatively unspecific task (see also G. Theissen, *The Social Setting of Pauline Christianity: Essays on Corinth* [1982] 73-83).

b) The obligations placed on the οἰκονόμος as manager of outside assets made his trustworthiness and honesty essential qualifications (→ a). Consequently, relating the Christian imagery of building to office-bearers provided a metaphor for proper conduct in the office of apostle (1 Cor 4:2). Thus Paul wants to be "servant of Christ and *steward* of the mystery of God" (v. 1). The suggestion that this language was derived from the mystery cults (thus Reumann, "Stewards of God" 345ff., referring to use of οἰκονόμος for a cultic functionary in the Serapis and Hermes Trismegistos cult), is questionable. 1 Cor 4:1 offers no evidence for such a technical use of the word, and the religious connection lies not in the term οἰκονόμος itself, but only in the thing to be managed, the μυστήρια θεοῦ (H. Conzelmann, *1 Cor* [Hermeneia] 83).

Titus 1:7 applies the image of the *steward* to the "bishop" (→ ἐπίσκοπος), and 1 Pet 4:10 to all Christians.

4. a) In classical Greek οἰκονομία most commonly referred to "the craft (τέχνη) of maintaining a household (both production and consumption)" and the practical application of that craft: "household management" (Plato *Ap.* 36b; *R.* 498a; Xenophon *Oec.* i.1). This sense of the word has not been taken over in the NT, although when used in connection with the person of the οἰκονόμος it expresses itself both as a designation of the *office of steward* (Luke 16:3f.; cf. Pap. Tebt. 24.62) and of the activity of the person holding the office, *stewardship* (Luke 16:2 [*nomen actionis*]).

b) Like οἰκονόμος, which is the term for the office holder (→ 3.b), the noun οἰκονομία becomes in context of Christian building imagery a metaphor for the office of apostle (1 Cor 9:17). Col 1:25 places the task of the apostle with respect to God's word in relation to the οἰκονομία τοῦ θεοῦ, but it is doubtful that God's plan of salvation is here intended (*contra* E. Lohmeyer, *Col* [KEK] 80). What is in view is, rather, the divine office handed down to Paul (Michel 152; E. Lohse, *Col* [Hermeneia] 72f.; E. Schweizer, *Col* [Eng. tr., 1982] 106).

Eph 1:10 discloses the content of the mystery of

God (→ μυστήριον, v. 9) as "the bringing together of all things in Christ." "The fullness of times" (→ πλήρωμα) marks "that point in time . . . at which the supra-historical decision and its infra-historical fulfillment intersect, and the 'economy' of the fullness of times emphatically underscores the aspect of completeness" (J. Gnilka, *Eph* [HTKNT] 79). This usage is determined by use of οἰκονομία in official language, where it designates the activity of arranging (see Preisigke, *Wörterbuch* II, s.v.) or executing, and therefore also in Eph 1:10 should be understood as an *ordering, arranging,* or *implementing.* Therefore, since it is related to the implementation of the decision made by God, it approaches the meaning seen in the common second-century use as a t.t. for "the plan of salvation" (cf. Ign. *Eph.* 18:2; 20:1; Goppelt, *Theology* II, 60), but is not yet identical with it (U. Luz, *Das Geschichtsverständnis des Paulus* [BEvT 49] 1968, 14n.11, *contra* Reumann, *Covenant* 283, among others).

As in Col 1:25, the majority of interpreters assume for οἰκονομία in Eph 3:2 the meaning "office," "administration" (BAGD 559; Michel 152; M. Dibelius, *Eph* [HNT] 73, among others). This does not, however, give adequate consideration to the fact that, unlike Col 1:25, the partc. δοθεῖσα modifies not οἰκονομία but → χάρις. Consequently, the author is concerned less with Paul's office of apostle than with "God's plan of salvation . . . and the position of the office of apostle within the divine plan" (H. Merklein, *Das kirchliche Amt nach dem Epheserbrief* [SANT 33, 1973] 174). Formal identification of οἰκονομία with God's plan of salvation, however, is not yet complete here (*contra* Lohmeyer, *Col* 80, among others). Instead, as in Eph 3:9, only the connection of the term with the ordering and implementation of this plan of salvation, conceived as mystery, is here established (cf. Gnilka, *Eph* 163).

In 1 Tim 1:4 οἰκονομία θεοῦ (the v.l. οἰκοδομή in D* lat sy[p, hmg] Irenaeus[lat] is an insignificant gloss) appears in contrast to ἐκζήτησις, so that it is more profitable to assume here the transition to the sense of "instruction in the faith" attested in patristic literature (Clement of Alexandria *Paed.* i.8.64.3; 70.1; cf. e.g., BAGD 560; Michel 153; M. Dibelius and H. Conzelmann, *The Pastoral Epistles* [Hermeneia] 17f.; G. Holtz, *Die Pastoralbriefe* [THKNT] 36) than to posit the rather unsatisfying tr. "order of salvation" (e.g., N. Brox, *Die Pastoralbriefe* [RNT] 103) or "authority" or "administration" (A. Schlatter, *Die Kirche der Griechen im Urteil des Paulus* [1958] 37f.; C. Spicq, *Épîtres Pastorales* [ÉBib] I, 323f.; *idem, Notes* 612n.4).   H. Kuhli

οἰκονόμος, ου, ὁ *oikonomos* administrator (of a household), steward
→ οἰκονομία (3).

οἶκος, ου, ὁ *oikos* house; household, family; possessions

1. Occurrences and meaning — 2. Interchangeability with → οἰκία — 3. House, building, dwelling — a) Overview — b) Mark — c) Luke-Acts — d) "House of God" — e) "House of God" as metaphor for the Church — f) Dwelling as metaphor for the body — 4. Household/family — a) Overview — b) ". . . and his house," "The house of . . ." — c) Descendants/lineage — d) The household church — 5. "House" as a comprehensive term for building and family — a) Overview — b) Father's house — c) Community, city — 6. Possessions

Lit.: K. ALAND, *Did the Early Church Baptize Infants?* (Library of History and Doctrine, 1963) 87-94. — *idem, Die Stellung der Kinder in den frühen christlichen Gemeinden—und ihre Taufe* [TEH 138, 1967] 30-33. — G. R. BEASLEY-MURRAY, *Baptism in the NT* (1972) 312-20. — G. DELLING, "Zur Taufe von 'Häusern' im Urchristentum," *NovT* 7 (1964/65) 285-311. — M. GIELEN, "Zur Interpretation der paulinischen Formel ἡ κατ' οἶκον ἐκκλησία," *ZNW* 77 (1986) 109-25. — J. GOETZMANN, *DNTT* II, 636-45. — H. A. HOFFNER, *TDOT* II, 107-16. — E. JENNI, *THAT* I, 308-13. — J. JEREMIAS, *Infant Baptism in the First Four Centuries* (1960) 19-24 — *idem, The Origins of Infant Baptism* (1963). — H.-J. KLAUCK, "Die Hausgemeinde als Lebensform im Urchristentum," *MTZ* 32 (1981) 1-15. — *idem, Hausgemeinde und Hauskirche im frühen Christentum* (SBS 103, 1981). — D. LÜHRMANN, "Neutestamentliche Haustafeln und antike Ökonomie," *NTS* 27 (1980/81) 83-97. — O. MICHEL, *TDNT* V, 119-31. — L. SCHENKE, "Zur sogenannten 'Oikosformel' im NT," *Kairos* 13 (1971) 226-43. — E. STAUFFER, "Zur Kindertaufe in der Urkirche," *Deutsches Pfarrerblatt* 49 (1949) 152-54. — A. STROBEL, "Der Begriff des 'Hauses' im griechischen und römischen Privatrecht," *ZNW* 56 (1965) 91-100. — P. STUHLMACHER, *Der Brief an Philemon* (EKKNT, 1975) 70-75. — W. VOGLER, "Die Bedeutung der urchristlichen Hausgemeinden für die Ausbreitung des Evangeliums," *TLZ* 107 (1982) 785-94. — P. WEIGANDT, "Zur sogenannten 'Oikosformel,'" *NovT* 6 (1963) 49-74. — For further bibliography see Michel; *TWNT* X, 1198f.

1. Οἶκος is already attested in the Mycenean Linear B tablets. From the time of Homer, the following primary meanings were current, all of them derived from the basic meaning *house:* a) *house/building* of any of a number of kinds/*dwelling;* b) *household/family,* those who live in the house; and therefore c) *possessions/belongings,* that which is found in the house, in part also including the house itself. There are also a few other meanings derived from these, some of which are proper to the NT.

Οἶκος is more common in the NT (115 occurrences including the v.l. of Acts 16:33) than → οἰκία and occurs 10 times in Matthew, 13 times in Mark, 33 times in Luke, 5 times in John, 26 times in Acts, once in Romans, 4 times in 1 Corinthians, once in Philemon, once in Colossians, 5 times in 1 Timothy, twice in 2 Timothy, once in Titus, 11 times in Hebrews, and twice in 1 Peter. In Luke-Acts and the Pastorals οἶκος is more common than οἰκία, while οἰκία is predominant in Mark and esp. in Matthew. Hebrews knows only οἶκος. In John the two terms are completely interchangeable and in Paul almost so. In the remaining books the terms are too infrequent to render an evaluation.

2. Originally, οἶκος and οἰκία had distinct meanings; Οἶκος was more comprehensive and could represent all one's possessions, while οἰκία designated only one's dwelling (cf. Xenophon *Oec.* i.5). In most NT passages in which both appear, they are interchangeable and are, indeed, interchanged. Thus, οἰκία will also be dealt with below where its meaning coincides with that of οἶκος.

Luke especially, in several instances, uses the two terms for *house* alongside each another with no distinction between them (Luke 15:6, 8; also 1 Cor 11:22, 34), usually in reference to a single house (Luke 7:6, 10; 7:36, 37, 44; 8:27, 39; 8:41, 51; 10:5a, b, 7a; also John 11:20, 31; Acts 16:32, 34). In similar fashion, both words are used in 1 Cor 1:16; 16:15 with the meaning *family* (of Stephanas). But in Acts 10:1–11:18 Luke distinguishes between two different houses with the aid of οἶκος and οἰκία: The house of Simon the tanner he calls consistently an οἰκία (10:6, 17, 32; 11:11) and that of the Roman centurion Cornelius is consistently an οἶκος (10:22, 30; 11:12f.).

In Luke-Acts οἶκος can occasionally be found in the same passage alternating between the meanings *house* and *family* (Luke 19:5 over against v. 9 [of Zacchaeus]; Acts 10:22, 30; 11:12f. over against 10:2; 11:14 [of Cornelius; see above]; 16:15b over against v. 15a [of Lydia]).

In parallel passages in the Synoptics, the word appearing in the source is not always adopted in the parallel: Occasionally οἶκος replaces οἰκία or vice versa. Thus Mark 5:38 has οἶκος while Matt 9:23 and Luke 8:51 have οἰκία. In Mark 3:25 and Matt 12:25 we find οἰκία in contrast to οἶκος in Luke 11:17; and Matt 24:43 has οἰκία and Luke 12:39 οἶκος.

3. a) By far most frequent for οἶκος and οἰκία is the basic meaning *house/building/dwelling* (οἶκος 46 times, οἰκία 71 times). In NT documents in which both words appear frequently with this meaning the distribution is varied: Matthew has οἰκία 21 times and οἶκος only 3 times while Mark, Luke, and Acts present only a slight numerical edge for οἰκία and John for οἶκος. With the exception of Matt 11:8 (a king's palace) and John 2:16 (a marketplace), the buildings mentioned are private homes, whose owner either is mentioned (Matt 8:14; 9:23; 26:6; Mark 1:29; 5:38; 14:3; Luke 1:40; 4:38; 5:29; 7:36, 37; 9:61; 14:1; 22:54; Acts 9:11; 10:6, 17, 32; 17:5; 18:7; 21:8) or can be inferred from the context (Luke 19:5; John 11:31; 12:3; Acts 9:17; 10:22, 30; 11:11, 12f.; 16:15, 32). We also see expressions such as "at *home*" (ἐν τῷ οἴκῳ [τινός]: Mark 2:1; John 11:20; 1 Cor 11:34;

14:35; ἐν (τῇ) οἰκίᾳ [τινός]: Matt 8:6; 9:10; Mark 2:15; 9:33; Luke 8:27; εἰς τὴν οἰκίαν: Mark 10:10) and "(toward) *home*" (εἰς [τὸν] οἶκόν [τινός]: Matt 8:6f.; Mark 2:11; 3:20; 5:19; 7:17, 30; 8:3, 26; 9:28; Luke 1:23, 56; 56:24f.; 7:10; 8:39; 15:6; 18:14; John 7:53; Acts 16:34; εἰς τὴν οἰκίαν: Matt 9:28; 13:36; 17:25). *House* is used metaphorically in 2 Tim 2:20 of the Church.

b) Mark on various occasions has Jesus or Jesus and his disciples seek out a house in order to separate themselves from the crowd, i.e., from the public (7:17, 24; 9:28, 33; 10:10). These occurrences all appear in the Evangelist's redacted additions and are lacking in Matthew and Luke. Mark also speaks of the separation of Jesus or Jesus and his disciples with expressions such as κατὰ μόνας, "alone" (4:10), or κατ' ἰδίαν, "privately" (4:34; in 9:2 with μόνους; in 9:28 with εἰς οἶκον; 13:3). This separation is employed by Mark as a means of expressing his idea of the messianic secret: Opportunity is given only to the disciples to recognize the messiahship of Jesus. To the public, the people, it remains hidden. Nevertheless, even the disciples do not come to proper recognition of it before Easter.

It is striking that of the 24 occurrences of οἰκία or οἶκος meaning *house* in Markan passages paralleled by Matthew and Luke, the word is taken up by Matthew only 11 times and by Luke only 9 times. In all the other instances the word is lacking for various reasons (stylistic changes, contraction, theological considerations).

c) Acts reports that Christians met early in the morning in private homes. Οἶκος/οἰκία designates the gathering place of the Christian community (→ 4.d). Whereas Acts 12:12 mentions that the members of the church gathered at the οἰκία of Mary, the mother of John, to pray, in 2:46 and 5:42 Luke uses the expression κατ' οἶκον and in 8:3; 20:20 κατ' (ἀ τοὺς) οἴκους as a t.t. to indicate that the Christians met "in *houses*," i.e., in particular private homes. Common meals, prayer, proclamation, and teaching provided the occasion. Thus they could also be found there when someone wanted to find them (8:3).

d) The Gospels and Acts sometimes use οἶκος (sometimes without the attributive gen. θεοῦ) of the "*house* (of God)"/*temple* (→ ναός), but only in OT quotations (Mark 11:17a par.: "my *house*"; 11:17b par.: "*house* of prayer"; John 2:16: "the *house* of my Father"; Acts 7:49) or allusions (Mark 2:26 par.; Luke 11:51; Acts 7:47) or their context (John 2:17: "your *house*"; → 4.d). Οἰκία is seen with this meaning nowhere else, while οἶκος is so used outside the NT only in Euripides *Ph.* 1372; Herodotus viii.143, as well as frequently in the LXX.

e) Certain non-Pauline letters of the NT call οἶκος the Church as God's *house* (1 Tim 3:15; Heb 3:2, 5, 6; 10:21; 1 Pet 2:5; 4:17). There is present here a concept known also in the Qumran community (1QS 5:6; 8:5, 9; 9:6; CD 3:19; cf. also 1QH 7:8f.) and closely related to the idea of the Church as the temple of God (1 Cor 3:16f.; 6:19; 2 Cor 6:16; cf. also Eph 2:19-22, as well as the idea of the "*house* of Yahweh" in Hos 8:1; 9:8, 15; Jer 12:7; Zech 9:8).

f) In Matt 12:44 par. a person's body is fig. called the *dwelling/habitation* of a demon. This corresponds to the not uncommon notions of late antiquity and of Judaism (Philo *Det.* 33; Seneca *Ep.* xx.3.14; b. *Ḥul.* 105b; b. *Giṭ.* 52a); → οἰκία 2.b.

4. a) Οἶκος with the meaning *family/household* is definitely attested since Hesiod, perhaps since Homer, and οἰκία with that meaning at least since Herodotus. In Attic law οἰκία is defined in this sense: Οἰκία δὲ τέλειος ἐκ δούλων καὶ ἐλευθέρων, "A complete house consists of both slaves and free," and is therefore more specifically defined as consisting of husband, wife, children, and slaves (Aristotle *Pol.* 1253b.4-7; cf. also the household codes in Eph 5:22–6:9; Col 3:18–4:1). This is also consistent with the usage of οἰκία and οἶκος in the LXX (Stuhlmacher 72f.; Weigandt 52-55) and in the NT. The group of persons included in such a *house* can, however, be expanded. Thus dependent relatives can belong to it as well as other dependents. The circle can be extended even further where οἶκος refers to the extended family or even a nation (→ 4.c). A narrower circumference for οἶκος or οἰκία in the sense of *family/household* can only be derived from the context, which provides such information.

In 1 Tim 3:5, 12, where bishops and deacons are required to be able to manage their own *households* before they manage the church (the greater size of God's *house* is the issue), οἶκος could possibly extend to the economic realm (cf. Lührmann 95).

Οἶκος/οἰκία in the sense of *household/family* is relatively uncommon in the NT (18 + occurrences: Mark 3:25 par.; 6:4 par.; Luke 19:9; John 4:53; 8:35; Acts 10:2; 11:14; 16:15a, 31, 33 v.l.; 18:8; 1 Cor 1:16; 16:15; 1 Tim 3:4f., 12; 5:4; 2 Tim 1:16; 3:6; 4:19; Titus 1:11; Heb 11:7). Matthew, Mark, and John use only οἰκία in this sense, Luke, Acts, and Hebrews only οἶκος, Paul both, and the Pastorals (with the exception of 2 Tim 3:6) only οἶκος.

b) In John 4:53 and in the passages in Acts mentioned above (→ a) we find the expression " . . . and his (whole) *house*" or something similar. In 1 Cor 1:16; 16:15; 2 Tim 1:16; 4:19; Heb 11:7 we find the expression "the *house* of . . ." and the like. Both expressions are attested in secular Greek and in the LXX (Delling 290-93; Jeremias, *Origins*). In 1 Tim 3:12 children (τέκνα) are mentioned in addition to the οἶκος. Such usage is also common (cf. Pap. Hamburg [ed. P. M. Meyer; 1911-24] 54, II, 13f.; Pap. Geneva [ed. J. Nicole; 1896-1909] I, 54.29; Ign. *Smyrn.* 13:1; *Pol.* 8:2; *Herm. Man.* xii.3.6; *Sim.* v.3.9;

7.6). In none of these uses of the expression ". . . and his *house*" is it possible to deduce specifically which persons are intended. In any case, however, the context restricts us to the conclusion that infants and small children are not included. This is also true for the report that "the *house* of . . ." has been baptized (Acts 16:15a, 33 v.l.; 1 Cor 1:16) or saved (Acts 11:14; 16:31) or has believed (Acts 18:8). Neither expression can tell us whether the Christian Church in the NT baptized infants or small children. It is, however, possible that Luke made use of expressions such as ". . . and his (whole) *house*" (with the exception of John 4:53, found only in Acts) to allude to the resulting establishment of churches.

c) The meaning *descendants/lineage* is derived from the meaning *family;* thus the aggregate of those who trace their origin to a common ancestor.

The expression "the *house* of David" (οἶκος Δαυίδ) appears only in Luke 1:27, 69; 2:4 (hendiadys: "house and descendants"). *House* here indicates blood relatives descended through the paternal line from the founder of the lineage (cf. the genealogy in Luke 3:23-31). All three occurrences of the expression have christological significance, since for Luke that Jesus is a son of David is one of the proofs of his messiahship. The passages focus on Jesus' birth in Bethlehem and elucidate the close connection seen by Luke between Jesus as son of David and Jesus as Son of God (cf. 1:32-35; 3:23-38).

We find the word expanded to include all descendants of the founder of a lineage in the phrase "*house* of Israel" (οἶκος Ἰσραήλ, Matt 10:6; 15:24 [both M]; Acts 2:36; 7:42, a quotation of Amos 5:27 LXX). Every NT occurrence of this phrase refers to the people of Israel, the people of God, in Acts 7:42 during the long past wilderness era, elsewhere in the present. Synonymous with "*house* of Israel" is "*house* of Jacob" (οἶκος Ἰακώβ), which appears only in Luke (Luke 1:33; Acts 7:46), but the sense of which is already present in Isa 9:7; 10:20; 14:1; and elsewhere. Deviating from the other uses of "*house* of Israel" is that of Heb 8:8, 10, where it refers only to the northern kingdom; "*house* of Judah" (οἶκος Ἰούδα) is used in 8:8 of the southern kingdom. Hebrews follows here the content of Jer 31:31-34 word for word.

d) Acts reports the regular gatherings of the first Christians (→ 3.c). This is reflected in the expression "the *house* church of . . ." (ἡ κατ᾽ οἶκόν τινος ἐκκλησία) found in the introductory and closing greetings of NT letters (Rom 16:5; 1 Cor 16:19; Phlm 2; Col 4:15). The house church is named after the owner of the house that serves as its gathering place. The composition of such house churches must be decided from the context, where such information is available.

5. a) In some instances it is difficult to decide whether οἶκος/οἰκία should be understood as *house* or as *family*.

BAGD (s.v. οἰκία 3) suggests for οἰκία in Matt 10:12f. a "middle position" between the two meanings. That would also then be true for Matt 10:14; Mark 6:10; Luke 9:4; 10:5a, 7 and for οἶκος in Luke 10:5b; 12:52. We are more probably dealing here, however, with a meaning that includes *both the house and those living in the house*, which was best represented simply by *house*. That this inclusive meaning of οἰκία is intended is underscored in Mark 6:10 par.; Matt 10:12f. with the expression "shake the dust from the feet" in Mark 6:11 par.; Matt 10:14: Leaving the place is the portrayal of breaking fellowship with its inhabitants.

Οἰκία in Mark 10:29f. par. can also be understood as a comprehensive term that includes both family relationships and property.

b) That which was said under → a is also applicable to the expression "(my) father's *house*" in Luke 16:27; Acts 7:20. The context of Luke 16:27 makes it clear that the Evangelist was thinking not only of the building. In Acts 7:20 the allusion to Exod 2:1-3, where we are also dealing with more than simply a building, should not be overlooked.

c) In Matt 23:38 par. οἶκος refers to a *city, a large community*, i.e., Jerusalem. Here, too, both the buildings and their inhabitants are intended. Οἶκος is found in this sense already in Jer. 12:7; 22:5 (cf. also *1 Enoch* 89 *passim; T. Levi* 10:4).

6. From the time of Homer οἶκος was used with the meaning *possessions/belongings*. In the NT it appears thus only in Acts 7:10, based on Gen 45:8.

P. Weigandt

οἰκουμένη, ης, ἡ *oikoumenē* inhabited earth, world, mankind*

1. NT occurrences and usage — 2. General Greek and LXX usage — 3. Luke — 4. Remaining NT passages

Lit.: W. BIEDER, "Die missionarische Bedeutung der 'Oikumene' und die ihr drohende 'Verkirchlichung,' " *EvT* 22 (1962) 180-94. — E. FASCHER, "Ökumenisch und katholisch. Zur Geschichte zweier, heute viel gebrauchter Begriffe," *TLZ* 85 (1960) 7-20. — O. FLENDER, *DNTT* I, 518f. — F. GISINGER, *PW* XVII/2, 2123-74. — G. JOHNSTON, "Οἰκουμένη and κόσμος in the NT," *NTS* 10 (1963/64) 352-60. — J. KAERST, *Die antike Idee der Oikumene in ihrer politischen und kulturellen Bedeutung* (1903). — F. LASSERRE, *LAW* 1221. — idem, *KP* IV, 254-56. — O. MICHEL, *TDNT* V, 157-59. — M. PAESLACK, "Die 'Oikumene' im NT," *TViat* 2 (1950) 33-47. — A. VANHOYE, "L'οἰκουμένη dans l'épître aux Hébreux," *Bib* 45 (1964) 248-53. — J. VOGT, *Orbis Romanus. Zur Terminologie des römischen Imperialismus* (1929). — W. A. VISSER 'T HOOFT, *Der Sinn des Wortes "ökumenisch"* (1954).

1. Οἰκουμένη is a pres. pass. partc. of → οἰκέω ("dwell") used from classical times primarily as a subst., originally supplemented by γῆ. With but 15 occurrences,

it is not common in the NT and is in fact a preferred word only in Luke-Acts (3 times in the Gospel, 5 times in Acts); it is found elsewhere 3 times in Revelation, twice in Hebrews, and once each in Matthew (24:14) and Paul (Rom 10:18, quoting Ps 18:5 LXX).

This distribution is in striking contrast to the use, e.g., of κόσμος as a comprehensive term for "world/this world": 102 occurrences in the Johannine literature, 37 in Paul, from which οἰκουμένη is completely (John, 1–3 John) or almost completely (Paul) absent. In Luke, by way of contrast, use of κόσμος is greatly curtailed (3 occurrences in Luke, of which 12:30 [πάντα τὰ ἔθνη τοῦ κόσμου] refers to the inhabited world; in Acts only 17:24). Οἰκουμένη is not used in the "commission" sayings: Matt 28:19 has πάντα τὰ ἔθνη (see, however, 24:14), Mark 16:5 has κόσμος ἅπας/πᾶσα ἡ κτίσις, Luke 24:47 has πάντα τὰ ἔθνη, and Acts 1:8 has ἕως ἐσχάτου τῆς γῆς (see further Johnston; Paeslack 33-37). This is probably best explained by the fact that in Roman times οἰκουμένη increasingly gained a political meaning in connection with the widespread "imperial" formulas (Michel 157; Paeslack 34; → 2), which distanced the word ever more from the original theological sense that it has in the LXX (→ 2). Furthermore, in late antiquity → κόσμος (2) was becoming a theological term in Hellenistic Judaism and therefore also in early Christianity.

In the NT we also find attributives that manifest the extent and meaning of οἰκουμένη: ὅλος (Matt 24:14; Acts 11:28; Rev 3:10; 12:9; 16:14; cf. also Acts 19:27), πᾶς (Luke 2:1; cf. also 4:5; Acts 24:5), also εἰς τὰ πέρατα τῆς οἰκουμένης (Rom 10:18). Also mentioned are the kingdoms (Luke 4:5; Rev 16:14) and nations of the οἰκουμένη (Matt 24:14; cf. Acts 19:27 [οἰκουμένη with ὅλη ἡ ᾿Ασία]; 24:5 [πάντες οἱ ᾿Ιουδαῖοι]). Οἰκουμένη is found in judgment sayings in Luke 21:26 and Acts 17:31; cf. also Heb 1:6; 2:5 (ἡ οἰκουμένη ἡ μέλλουσα).

2. The LXX uses οἰκουμένη approximately 40 times (ca. 17 times in the Psalms, where → κόσμος [2] is lacking [→ 1]; ca. 14 times in Isaiah), usually as a tr. of 'ereṣ ("earth") or tēbēl ("firm ground"). In all instances it refers to the earth as a whole, its inhabitants, and its "kingdoms," which God has created, leads, punishes, and will ultimately judge (cf. esp. Pss 9:9 [likewise 95:31; 97:9; quoted in Acts 17:31]; 18:5 [quoted in Rom 10:18]; 49:12; 88:12; Isa 10:14; 37:16; 62:4; see also Visser 't Hooft 10-12).

In secular Greek οἰκουμένη was originally a geographical term (attested since Xenophanes 21.A.41a [Diels, *Fragmente* I, 125, l. 7]; Herodotus iii.114; iv.110) for the inhabited and inhabitable parts of the earth in distinction from uninhabited places (desert areas, etc.). Already in the classical but then esp. in the Hellenistic era οἰκουμένη was used of the Greek cultural world in contrast to the barbarian peoples living on its periphery (see further Gisinger, Larresse, Kaerst, Fascher). In the Roman era (esp. since Sulla), particularly under the influence of Stoic cosmopolitanism and eastern imperialism (cf. the decree of Cyrus in 3 Esdr 2:2), οἰκουμένη increasingly became a hyperbolic term for the centrally governed and ordered world of the Roman Empire, the *orbis terrae (terrarum)* whose rule was in Roman hands (cf. Cicero *Pro Murena* 22; Virgil *Aen.* vi.850; Josephus *Ant.* xi.3; see further Vogt 12ff.). In this connection, e.g., Josephus (*B.J.* i.633) could call the Roman emperor "the leader of the οἰκουμένη" (ὁ τῆς οἰκουμένης προστάτης Καῖσαρ); Nero could also thus be called ἀγαθὸς δαίμων τῆς οἰκουμένης (Pap. Oxy. 1021, ll. 5ff.; cf. *OGIS* 666, 5; likewise of Marcus Aurelius, see Preisigke, *Sammelbuch* 176, 2; cf. further *OGIS* 669, 10; *SIG* 906A, 3f.; Philo *Leg. Gai.* 16; Josephus *B.J.* iv.656; see also Michel 157f.; Visser 't Hooft 8-10).

3. Luke values the word οἰκουμένη because it enables him to bring to the fore the worldwide dimensions of the Christ-event, its proclamation, and its effect on the entire Empire. In so doing he does not shy away from echoes of imperial language; thus Luke 2:1 (L), with reference to the imperial census of the entire Empire (hyperbolic and therefore not historically accurate): ἀπογράφεσθαι πᾶσαν τὴν οἰκουμένην (→ ἀπογραφή); Acts 17:6, referring to the (Jewish) accusation that the Pauline mission was causing public unrest: οἱ τὴν οἰκουμένην ἀναστατώσαντες (although Paul had only gone as far as Thessolonica by then); cf. 24:5: στάσεις πᾶσιν τοῖς Ἰουδαίοις τοῖς κατὰ τὴν οἰκουμένην; probably also 11:28: λιμὸν μεγάλην . . . ἐφ' ὅλην τὴν οἰκουμένην, but historically only verifiable for Palestine (see E. Haenchen, *Acts* [Eng. tr., 1971] ad loc.); cf. also 19:27, where the entire οἰκουμένη is claimed for the Artemis cult of the Ephesians (probably with reason; see Haenchen ad loc.). Luke 4:5 (redactional) probably also belongs here (ἔδειξεν αὐτῷ πάσας τὰς βασιλείας τῆς οἰκουμένης; contrast Matt 4:8: . . . τοῦ κόσμου).

In no way can it be concluded that Luke gives vent to a "negative judgment of the political world" (Paeslack 37-39). On the contrary, Luke precisely avoids criticism of the Roman οἰκουμένη and posits instead that any possible or actual conflict with Rome does not stem from the Christian message itself (see also Luke 4:5; Acts 17:6; 24:5). Therefore the statements in Luke's writings containing οἰκουμένη can be viewed better as constituting a plerophoric reference that intends to make the Christian message the hidden nucleus of the Roman world. Furthermore, Luke is so deeply influenced by the usage of the LXX that his οἰκουμένη statements almost always entail a reference to all humanity as created and judged by God (Luke 21:16 [L]: τὰ ἐπερχόμενα τῇ οἰκουμένῃ, of the eschatological woes; Acts 17:31). Nevertheless, οἰκουμένη can also for Luke be so loaded with imperial Roman self-understanding that he avoids it in the programmatic formula in Acts 1:8 and instead uses the idiom of the LXX (ἕως ἐσχάτου τῆς γῆς; cf. Isa 49:6 LXX).

4. Matt 24:14 expands the expression εἰς πάντα τὰ ἔθνη . . . δεῖ κηρυχθῆναι τὸ εὐαγγέλιον (Mark 13:10) into a formula unique in the NT: κηρυχθήσεται τοῦτο τὸ εὐαγγέλιον . . . ἐν ὅλῃ τῇ οἰκουμένῃ εἰς μαρτύριον πᾶσιν

τοῖς ἔθνεσιν. The concluding reference to the imminent end (vv. 15ff.) and the final judgment (25:31) make it clear that for Matthew the entire world must still be confronted with the gospel, since the gospel will be the standard for the judge (cf. 25:32).

In Rom 10:18 Paul relates the praise given God by his creation (Ps 18:5 LXX) to the eschatological reality of the preaching of the gospel throughout the entire world (εἰς τὰ πέρατα τῆς οἰκουμένης). We should not think that he is somehow immoderately exaggerating the gains of the Christian mission. Rather, he is speaking of God's comprehensive eschatological work of salvation, which the Israel of the Creator God certainly cannot ignore.

Heb 1:6 (like its entire context) is also determined by the idiom of the LXX. It picks up on the motif of the judgment of the world (εἰς τὴν οἰκουμένην; cf. Matt 24:14; Acts 17:31; → 2) in connection with the parousia of the Son. The statement of 1:6 is related to statements on the (first) coming of the Son into the world (εἰς τὸν κόσμον, 10:5; cf. 2:7-9), yet at the same time marks an advance in "salvation history." It is no longer only the κόσμος (cf. 9:1; 11:7; also 11:3) that the Son will encounter as judge, but also the οἰκουμένη, which again speaks of the purpose of the creation through Christian believers (cf. 12:18-29; also LXX of Pss 92:1; 23:1; 88:12; 97:7; Isa 62:4; see also Vanhoye; erroneously Paeslack; we can hardly assume here a Hebraism *[hēḇî' lᵉʿôlām]* for an "entrance into the world to come" [*contra* Michel, *Heb* (KEK) ad loc.]). To this statement corresponds the expression οἰκουμένη ἡ μέλλουσα in Heb 2:5, where 1:6 is explicitly taken up again (περὶ ἧς λαλοῦμεν). In light of the interpretation of Psalm 110 by the author (1:13) it becomes clear that he is thinking of "the coming οἰκουμένη" as the reign of Christ during the time of the defeat of all the enemies of God (cf. 2:7f.; 6:5; 12:26-29).

Revelation, by way of contrast, focusses on the negative side of the οἰκουμένη: It is exclusively unbelievers and enemies of God who make up the οἰκουμένη. According to 3:10, the πειρασμός of the last times will be applied to all the inhabitants of the earth (ἐπὶ τῆς οἰκουμένης ὅλος), i.e., esp. to sinners (cf. 6:10; 8:13)—believers will be protected from that hour. According to 12:9 ἡ οἰκουμένη ὅλη is led astray by God's adversary, who will be destroyed at the end. 16:14 also refers to the world and its kings as the enemies of God at the eschaton (οἱ βασιλεῖς τῆς οἰκουμένης ὅλης), who will fall down before him. Since the οἰκουμένη consists only of unbelievers and enemies of God, it does not refer to the Roman Empire in particular (*contra* Paeslack 39f.), but to unbelieving inhabitants of all the earth (cf. the frequent expression οἱ κατοικοῦντες [ἐπὶ] τῆς γῆς, 3:10; 6:10; 8:13; 13:8, 12; 17:2, etc.), those who represent—also in the form of antidivine Roman imperialism—the eschatological struggle of this world against the God's salvation.

H. Balz

οἰκουργός, 2 *oikourgos* domestic*

Οἰκουργός is found (in place of classical οἰκουρός) in Titus 2:5 with reference to women.

οἰκουρός, 2 *oikouros* domestic, economic

TR in Titus 2:5 for → οἰκουργός.

οἰκτείρω *oikteirō* have compassion

A variant of → οἰκτίρω.

οἰκτιρμός, οῦ, ὁ *oiktirmos* compassion, mercy*

Col 3:12: σπλάγχνα οἰκτιρμοῦ, "heartfelt *compassion*"; sometimes pl. (from Heb. *raḥᵃmîm*?): of human compassion (Phil 2:1); of God's mercy (Rom 12:1; 2 Cor 1:3) with no subj. (Heb 10:28: χωρὶς οἰκτιρμῶν, "without *mercy*"). R. Bultmann, *TDNT* V, 159-61; *TWNT* X, 1199f. (bibliography); H.-H. Esser, *DNTT* II, 598.

οἰκτίρμων, 2 *oiktirmōn* compassionate, merciful*

Of God (in combination with πολύσπλαγχνος): Jas 5:11; of people and God: Luke 6:36 (bis): "be *merciful* even as your Father is *merciful*." R. Bultmann, *TDNT* V, 159-61; *TWNT* X, 1199f. (bibliography); H.-H. Esser, *DNTT* II, 598.

οἰκτίρω *oiktirō* have compassion*

Rom 9:15 (bis) in the quotation of Exod 33:19 LXX (God's address to Moses): "I will have mercy (ἐλεήσω) on whom I have mercy, and I *will have compassion* (οἰκτιρήσω) on whom I *have compassion* (οἰκτίρω)." R. Bultmann, *TDNT* V, 159-61; *TWNT* X, 1199f. (bibliography); H.-H. Esser, *DNTT* II, 598.

οἶμαι *oimai* think, suppose
Contracted form of → οἴομαι (John 21:25).

οἰνοπότης, ου, ὁ *oinopotēs* drinker of wine, drunkard*

In Matt 11:19 par. Luke 7:34 οἰνοπότης is found in an accusation against Jesus, "the Son of Man," who "eats and drinks," i.e., does not live as an ascetic: "Look, a glutton and a *boozer*, a friend of tax collectors and sinners!"

οἶνος, ου, ὁ *oinos* wine*

Most of the 34 occurrences of οἶνος in the NT are literal (John 2:3a, b, 9, 10a, b; 4:46; see H. Windisch, *ZNW* 14 [1913] 248-57 on John 2). According to Matt 27:34 Jesus was given "*wine* mixed with gall" on Gol-

gotha (cf. Mark 15:23: ἐσμυρνισμένον οἶνον). In Luke 10:34 wine and oil are mentioned together as a treatment for wounds; Rev 18:13 mentions *wine* together with oil and other natural products. John the Baptist drank no *wine* (Luke 1:15; 7:33). The "weak" practice abstinence from meat and wine (Rom 14:21). A metaphor used by Jesus speaks of "new *wine* in old wineskins" (Mark 2:22 par. Matt 9:17/Luke 5:37, 38; see F. Hahn, "Die Bildworte vom neuen Flicken und vom junger Wein (Mk 2,21 parr)," *EvT* 31 [1971] 357-75). Eph 5:18; 1 Tim 3:8; and Titus 2:3 warn against excessive use of *wine*. In contrast, 1 Tim 5:23 recommends moderate use of wine as a medication for the stomach: οἴνῳ ὀλίγῳ χρῶ διὰ τὸν στόμαχον (→ νηφάλιος).

Revelation uses οἶνος to portray the punishment that God gives to the godless to drink like wine ("the wine of God's wrath," 14:10; 16:19; 19:15; cf. Pss 60:5; 75:8f.; Isa 51:17, 22; Jer 25:15) and in speaking of "the *wine* [of the wrath] of the adultery" of Babylon (14:8; 17:2; 18:3; → θυμός 3). In Rev 6:6 οἶνος is found (effect for cause) for *vineyard/vine*. J. Döller, "Der Wein in Bibel und Talmud," *Bib* 4 (1923) 143-67, 267-99; Dalman, *Arbeit* IV, 291-413; H. Seesemann, *TDNT* V, 162-66; *TWNT* X, 1200 (bibliography); C. Seltmann, *Wine in the Ancient World* (1957); W. Dommershausen, *TTZ* 84 (1975) 253-60; *BRL* 362f.

οἰνοφλυγία, ας, ἡ *oinophlygia* drunkenness*

In 1 Pet 4:3 the pl. is used of isolated outbreaks of excessive drinking (cf. Philo *Vit. Mos.* ii.185; *Spec. Leg.* iv.91).

οἴομαι *oiomai* think, suppose*

With acc. + inf. in John 21:25, with inf. in Phil 1:17, and with a ὅτι clause in Jas 1:7.

οἷος, 3 *hoios* of which sort, such as (rel. pron.)*

With the correlative τοιοῦτος this pron. means "as ... so" in 1 Cor 15:48a, b; 2 Cor 10:11. Likewise in Phil 1:30: τὸν αὐτὸν ἀγῶνα ... οἷον, "the same struggle ... *as* [you saw in me]." In other instances the correlation derives from the context (Matt 24:21; Mark 9:3; 2 Cor 12:20a, b; 2 Tim 3:11a; Rev 16:18). In Mark 13:19 οἷος is pleonastic: θλῖψις, οἵα οὐ γέγονεν τοιαύτη. It is found in indirect questions in 1 Thess 1:5 and Luke 9:55 TR and in an exclamation in 2 Tim 3:11b. In Rom 9:6 οὐχ οἷον ὅτι is a combination of οὐχ οἷον and οὐχ ὅτι (BDF §§304; 480.5). Οἱοσδηποτοῦν in John 5:4 v.l. means "*of whatever* illness he had (οἵῳ δή ποτ' οὖν ...)."

ὀκνέω *okneō* hesitate, delay*

Acts 9:38: "do not *hesitate* to come to us." Spicq, *Notes* II, 614.

ὀκνηρός, 3 oknēros lazy, idle*

Matt 25:26, in what is spoken to the servant: πονηρὲ δοῦλε καὶ ὀκνηρέ; Rom 12:11: "not *lazy* in zeal"; Phil 3:1: "I am not *reluctant* to write the same things to you (ἐμοὶ οὐκ ὀκνηρόν)"; cf. Sophocles *OT* 834. F. Hauck, *TDNT* V, 166f.; Spicq, *Notes* II, 614f.

ὀκταήμερος, 2 oktaēmeros eighth-day (adj.)*

Phil 3:5: περιτομῇ ὀκταήμερος, "with respect to circumcision, *eighth-day*" (i.e., circumcised on the eighth day).

ὀκτώ oktō eight*

Luke 2:21, of the *eight* days before circumcision; also of the eighth day: 9:28; John 20:26; Acts 25:6. Acts 9:33: ἐξ ἐτῶν ὀκτώ, "for *eight* years"; 1 Pet 3:20: ὀκτὼ ψυχαί, "*eight* persons" entered the ark and were saved. Cf. δεκαοκτώ, Luke 13:4, 11 (v. 16: δέκα καὶ ὀκτὼ ἔτη); τριάκοντα [καὶ] οκτὼ ἔτη, John 5:5

ὀλεθρευτής, οῦ, ὁ olethreutēs destroyer

Variant of → ὀλοθρευτής.

ὀλεθρεύω olethreuō destroy, annihilate

Variant of → ὀλοθρεύω.

ὀλέθριος, 2 olethrios causing destruction

2 Thess 1:9 (A 33 pc): δίκην ὀλέθριον, "punishment *that brings destruction*"; → ὄλεθρος.

ὄλεθρος, ου, ὁ olethros destruction, ruin*

1 Thess 5:3: the "sudden *destruction*" associated with the in-breaking of the parousia; 2 Thess 1:9: ὄλεθρος αἰώνιος, "eternal *destruction*," i.e., death (cf. *T. Reu.* 6:3); 1 Cor 5:5: "let the one involved be handed over to Satan for the *destruction* of the flesh," i.e., to death (see H. Conzelmann, *1 Cor* [Hermeneia] 97); 1 Tim 6:9: βυθίζω τινὰ εἰς ὄλεθρον, "plunge [them] into *destruction*." J. Schneider, *TDNT* V, 168f.; H.-C. Hahn and C. Brown, *DNTT* I, 465-67.

ὀλιγοπιστία, ας, ἡ oligopistia smallness of faith*
ὀλιγόπιστος, 2 oligopistos of little faith*

Lit.: G. Barth, "Glaube und Zweifel in den synoptischen Evangelien," *ZTK* 72 (1975) 269-92. — G. Bornkamm. G. Barth, and H. J. Held, *Tradition and Intepretation in Matthew* (NTL, 1963) 99-108 (Barth), 288-96 (Held). — D. Lührmann, *RAC* XI, 48-122, esp. 72.

1. Ὀλιγοπιστία and ὀλιγόπιστος are found only in Christian literature, e.g., in the sixth of the *Sentences of Sextus:* ὀλιγόπιστος ἐν πίστει ἄπιστος (*ca.* 200; cf. H. Chadwick, *The Sentences*

of *Sextus* [1959]), and in Leontius of Neapolis (*Leben des heiligen Johannes des Barmherzigen* [ed. H. Gelzer, 1893] 14, ll. 18 and 21, 15, l. 5 [7th cent.]), but has a parallel in rabbinic usage: qᵉṭannê ʾᵃmānâ or mᵉ ḥûssrê ʾᵃmānâ (Billerbeck I, 438f.).

2. In the NT ὀλιγοπιστία and ὀλιγόπιστος are found only in Matthew (the noun once, the adj. 4 times) and Luke (the adj. once), primarily in the saying against worry in Matt 6:30 par. Luke 12:28: "But if that is how God clothes the grass, how much more you, O you *of little faith.*" Concern about life's necessities shows need of faith, *little faith.* One can assume from the agreement of Matt 6:30 and Luke 12:28 that the expression was found already in Q and was therefore current in Palestinian Jewish Christianity.

Matthew adopted the word group and gave it his own nuance within his ecclesiological framework. He (unlike *Sextus* 6) places ὀλιγόπιστος (8:26; 14:31; 16:8) and ὀλιγοπιστία (17:20) in clear contrast to ἄπιστος (17:17) and ἀπιστία (13:58), since he confines the accusation of smallness of faith to the disciples, and designates the masses as ἄπιστος: "Understanding" (→ συνίημι; cf. 13:11-15, 19, 23, 51, etc.) has been given to the disciples, who broadly represent the Christian community, but not to the people. "Smallness of faith" therefore takes on the specific form in which the disciple who knows and has accepted the message of salvation and has responded to the call to discipleship stumbles as a believer. Therefore it is always in the situations of trial in which the followers of Jesus find themselves that *smallness of faith* is mentioned: their fearful disposition in danger (8:26; 14:31), with concerns about food (6:30; 16:8). Their failures to heal the sick are also criticized as smallness of faith. Accordingly, in 14:31 ὀλιγόπιστος is parallel to διστάζω ("doubt"). Not a fundamental refusal of faith, but lack of trust, of perseverance in faith, is indicated by ὀλιγοπιστία and ὀλιγόπιστος.

G. Barth

ὀλιγόπιστος, 2 oligopistos of little faith
→ ὀλιγοπιστία.

ὀλίγος, 3 oligos little, slight, small, short; a little*

1. NT occurrences and usage — 2. Pl. — 3. Sg. and adv. usage — 4. Acts

Lit.: BAGD s.v. — E. F. F. Bishop, "*Oligoi* in 1 Pet 3:20," *CBQ* 13 (1951) 44f. — BDF §405.1. — E. Boissard, "Note sur l'interpretation du texte 'Multi sunt vocati, pauci vero electi,'" *Revue Thomiste* 52 (1952) 569-85. — N. Brox, *1 Pet* (EKKNT, 1979) 171-77. — E. Haenchen, *Acts* (Eng. tr., 1971) 689n.2. — Preisigke, *Wörterbuch* II, 167f. — H. Seesemann, *TDNT* V, 171-73. — F. Thiele, *DNTT* II, 427-29. — G. H. Whitaker, "The Words of Agrippa to St Paul," *JTS* 15 (1914) 82f.

1. Ὀλίγος appears 40 times in the NT, of which 16 are in the Synoptic Gospels, 10 in Acts, 4 in 1 Peter, 4

in Revelation, 2 in 1 Timothy, and 1 each in Ephesians (3:3), Hebrews (12:10), James (4:14), and Paul (2 Cor 8:15); it is lacking in John (see, however, → μικρός [4]). In the Synoptics, the pl. is predominant (11 occurrences [→ 2]; adv. sg. neut. in the other 5 occurrences [→ 3]). Acts shows a preference for οὐκ ὀλίγος with the same meaning as πολύς (8 occurrences [→ 4], not found elsewhere in the NT; as litotes in 12:18; 15:2; 19:23, 24; 27:20; otherwise in 14:28; 17:4, 12, probably an indication of elevated style; see also BDF §495.2) and also has the prep. phrase ἐν ὀλίγῳ (26:28, 29 [→ 4], elsewhere only in Eph 3:3). In the rest of the NT the sg. appears 8 times (→ 3; 1 Tim 4:8; Jas 4:14 in a prep. phrase with πρός) and the pl. 5 times (→ 2).

NT usage corresponds for the most part with that of the LXX (103 occurrences) and classical Greek. In the pl. ὀλίγος means *few,* in the sg. *little, small, slight* or in adv. use *a little* (quantitatively or temporally). The opposite of ὀλίγος is πολύς (Matt 7:14; 9:37 par.; 22:14; 25:21, 23; Luke 7:47 bis; 10:42 v.l.; 12:48; 13:28; 2 Cor 8:15), οὐδεμία δύναμις (Mark 6:5), and πάντα (1 Tim 4:8).

2. The pl. is used to designate a limited number of things or persons—often in contrast to a prior request or expectation. With a noun: Matt 9:37 par. Luke 10:2: "the workers are *[but] few"* (in contrast to the great harvest); Matt 15:34 par. Mark 8:7: *"a few/a couple* (small) fish (ὀλίγα ἰχθύδια)," even with the seven or five loaves, too little to feed the hungry crowd; Mark 6:5: *"a few* sick people"; Rev 3:4: *"(but) a few* names/people (ὀνόματα)" from the entire congregation at Sardis; Heb 12:10: πρὸς ὀλίγας ἡμέρας, "for *a few* days/for only a little while," referring to the relatively limited period of "discipline" by earthly fathers in comparison to the discipline of God, which occurs throughout life (cf. Jas 4:14: πρὸς ὀλίγον). Used absolutely in the sayings of Jesus of the limited number of those who, in contrast to the many, have a share in salvation: Matt 7:14; 22:14: πολλοὶ . . . κλητοί, ὀλίγοι δέ ("but *only a few")* ἐκλεκτοί, certainly a "contrast saying" that cannot be mitigated by a comparative rendering of πολλοί/ὀλίγοι as a simple difference in number between those called and those chosen (*contra* Boissard); cf. also Luke 13:23. In 1 Pet 3:20 the deliverance of *a few* (ὀλίγοι, τοῦτ᾽ ἔστιν ὀκτὼ ψυχαί, διεσώθησαν) through the midst of the flood (in accordance with Gen 7:7, 13: Noah, his wife, his three sons, and their wives; cf. also 2 Pet 2:5) is an antitype for the deliverance of the small, threatened Church through baptism (cf. also Brox 176f.; Bishop).

Neut. pl.: Matt 25:21, 23: ἐπὶ ὀλίγα, "over *a few (things)/a little"* (cf. Luke 16:10; 19:17: ἐν ἐλαχίστῳ); 1 Pet 5:12: δι᾽ ὀλίγων ἔγραψα, "I have *briefly* written" (cf. Heb 13:22; *Ep. Arist.* 128); Rev 2:14: ἔχω κατὰ σοῦ ὀλίγα, "I have *a few things/something* against you" (after

praise). In Luke 12:48 (δαρήσεται ὀλίγας, "he will receive *few* [blows]") πληγάς must be supplied.

3. Sg. as an adj.: 1 Tim 5:23: οἶνος ὀλίγος, *"a little* wine"; Rev 12:12: ὀλίγος καιρός, *"a short* time." Subst.: 2 Cor 8:15 (quoting Exod 16:18): ὁ τὸ πολὺ . . . , ὁ τὸ ὀλίγον, "the one who had much had no surplus, and the one who had *little* did not lack."

In the majority of sg. occurrences neut. sg. ὀλίγον is used adv.: of a short distance, Mark 1:19; Luke 5:3; of a short time, Mark 6:31; 1 Pet 1:6; 5:10 (contrasted with αἰώνιος δόξα); Rev 17:10; likewise πρὸς ὀλίγον, Jas 4:14; quantitatively with reference to a style of speaking or writing: ἐν ὀλίγῳ, *briefly,* Eph 3:3 (cf. 1 Pet 5:12); more generally: πρὸς ὀλίγον ὠφέλιμος, "useful for *(only) a few things,"* 1 Tim 4:8. According to Luke 7:47b the degree of love that a person is capable of shows the degree of forgiveness that person has experienced (ᾧ δὲ ὀλίγον ἀφίεται, ὀλίγον ἀγαπᾷ [omitted in D]). When the "sinful woman" (in contrast to Simon) shows unlimited love for Jesus, Jesus then, for precisely that reason, no longer deals with her as a sinner; the forgiveness for her sinful life, which has already been granted her before God, can be extended to her by Jesus. The Church was to learn from this saying to regard the conversion of sinners as the surprising work of God's love toward them, and in so doing become open to the experience of the love of God themselves.

4. In Acts οὐκ ὀλίγοι (→ 1) indicates a large number from a large crowd (partitive gen.: 17:4, with πλῆθος πολύς; 17:12, with πολλοί). Οὐκ ὀλίγος is temporal in 14:28 (*"some* time/quite a while"). As litotes οὐκ ὀλίγος can also mean *not a little/considerable* (of "confusion," 12:18; 19:23; of a "disagreement," 15:2; of a "storm," 27:20; quantitatively, of a *"considerable* income," 19:24).

In Acts 26:29 καὶ ἐν ὀλίγῳ καὶ ἐν μεγάλῳ is periphrastic instrumental dat. with ἐν (see BDF §195), "whether by *short* or by long." Ἐν ὀλίγῳ in the statement of Agrippa II to Paul (v. 28), however, is probably not instrumental but an indication of time: *"in a little while/ soon* you will persuade me to become a Christian"; an instrumental sense is, however, also conceivable: *"with little effort/almost.* . . ." See also Whitaker, who paraphrases: "Regard winning me for a Christian a matter of little moment," which requires, however, a conjectural emendation of πείθεις to πείθειν; otherwise A. Fridrichsen, ConNT 3 [1939] 13-16; see further BAGD s.v. 3.b (bibliography); s.v. πείθω 1.b (bibliography), 3.a; BDF §405.1; Haenchen; H. Conzelmann, *Acts* [Hermeneia] 212.   H. Balz

ὀλιγόψυχος, 2 *oligopsychos* timid*

1 Thess 5:14: "Comfort *the timid,* accept the weak." A. Dihle, *TDNT* IX, 665f.

ὀλιγωρέω *oligōreō* disregard*

Heb 12:5: "My son, do not think lightly of the discipline (παιδεία) of the Lord" (quoting Prov 3:11a LXX).

ὀλίγως *oligōs* hardly*

2 Pet 2:18: The false teachers lure with high-sounding words "those who have *barely* escaped from those who walk in error (τοὺς ὀλίγως ἀποφεύγοντας)."

ὀλοθρευτής, οῦ, ὁ *olothreutēs* destroyer*

1 Cor 10:10 of the "angel of death" (Exod 12:23: ὁ ὀλεθρεύων) or Satan (BAGD s.v.). J. Schneider, *TDNT* V, 169f.

ὀλοθρεύω *olothreuō* destroy, annihilate*

On the form ὀλεθρεύω see BDF §32.1. Heb 11:28 plays on Exod 12:23: the "angel of death" (ὀλοθρεύων) would not touch the firstborn. J. Schneider, *TDNT* V, 167f.

ὁλοκαύτωμα, ατος, τό *holokautōma* burnt offering*

In the burnt offering, the sacrificial animal was completely burned (R. de Vaux, *Ancient Israel* [1961] II, 415-17, 426-29). Ὁλοκαύτωμα is found in the LXX but is lacking in secular Gk. It is found in the literal sense in Mark 12:33 (with θυσία); Heb 10:6, 8 (with περὶ ἁμαρτίας, "sin offering," Ps 39:7 LXX). Mark 12:33 ranks love of neighbor, and Heb 10:6f. obedience to God, above all sacrifice.

ὁλοκληρία, ας, ἡ *holoklēria* wholeness, completeness*

Acts 3:16: Faith gave the lame man τὴν ὁλοκληρίαν ταύτην ("this *complete health*"). W. Foerster, *TDNT* III, 767f.; Spicq, *Notes* II, 616f.

ὁλόκληρος, 2 *holoklēros* whole, complete*

1 Thess 5:23: "May your spirit be *whole* . . . at the coming of our Lord Jesus Christ"; Jas 1:4: "so that you might be perfect (τέλειοι) and *whole* (ὁλόκληροι)." W. Foerster, *TDNT* III, 766f.; Spicq, *Notes* II, 616f.

ὀλολύζω *ololyzō* cry loudly*

Jas 5:1, in the prophetic saying to the rich: κλαύσατε ὀλολύζοντες, "weep, *crying loudly* [over the coming suffering]." H. W. Heiland, *TDNT* V, 173f.

ὅλος, 3 *holos* whole, complete

1. Usage in the NT — 2. Meaning — 3. The whole and the part

Lit.: BAGD s.v. — LSJ s.v. — MOULTON, *Grammar* III, 199. — H. SEESEMANN, *TDNT* V, 174f.

1. Unlike the similar word → πᾶς there is with ὅλος no semantic difference between anarthrous and arthrous use (cf. ὅλους οἴκους, "*entire* families," Titus 1:11; ἡ οἰκία αὐτοῦ ὅλη, "his *entire* family," John 4:53). When accompanied by the art., ὅλος is almost always used predicatively; whether before or after the subst., the meaning is the same (cf. ὅλη ἡ πόλις, Mark 1:33; ἡ πόλις ὅλη, Acts 21:30: "the *entire* city").

2. Ὅλος functions as an indication of totality in the following expressions:

a) Esp. with measures of time or space: "the *entire* night" (Luke 5:5), "the *entire* day" (Matt 20:6; Rom 8:36; 10:21), "an *entire* year" (Acts 11:26; likewise 28:30), καθ' ὅλης τῆς . . . , "in *all* . . ." (common in Luke-Acts: e.g., "Judea," Luke 23:5; Acts 9:31; cf. 9:42; Luke 4:14; 8:39), ἡ οἰκουμένη ὅλη, "the *entire* [inhabited] world" (Rev 3:10; 12:9; 16:14), ὅλος ὁ κόσμος, "the *whole* world" (Rom 1:8; 1 John 2:2; 5:19; as a comprehensive term for all worldly goods in Matt 16:26 par.).

b) With groups of people, corporate bodies, and the like: "the *entire* Sanhedrin" (Matt 26:59), "the *whole* church" (Rom 16:23), "the *entire* nation" (John 11:50), thus also "*all* Jerusalem" (Acts 21:31), "the *entire* city" (Mark 1:33, etc., where the thought is less of spatial extension than of the inhabitants).

c) Less frequently of things: "the *whole* lump" (1 Cor 5:6), "the *whole* law" (Matt 22:40; Gal 5:3).

d) In Matthew in the formula "*all* this happened so that . . . ," as a summary of an event in which an OT saying is fulfilled (1:22; 26:56).

3. Theologically significant is the use of ὅλος in the imagery of part and whole found in various connections. In Matt 5:29f. it is antithetical: It is better to lose an eye or hand than to have "the *whole* body" cast into Gehenna (ἓν τῶν μελῶν—ὅλον τὸ σῶμα). Paul gives it a different accent in 1 Cor 12:12-27: The eye can never be "the *whole* body" (ὅλον τὸ σῶμα, v. 17), since then the organism ("many members—one body") would be destroyed. A similar relation is found in Matt 6:22f. and Luke 11:34-36: The healthy eye illuminates "the *whole* body," while the sick eye relegates it to darkness.

James uses the formula ὅλον τὸ σῶμα in the sense found in popular Hellenistic philosophy with a strong ethical slant: Whoever does not stumble in what he says is capable of controlling the *whole* body (3:2f.); conversely the tongue, "a small member" by itself, can defile "the *whole* body" (3:5f.).

Only in John is anarthrous ὅλος used predicately: One who has bathed is καθαρὸς ὅλος, "clean *as a whole*," i.e., *"completely"* (John 13:10). The opposite is expressed in 9:34: *"completely"* (ὅλος) born in sin. Jesus heals "the *whole* person" (7:23: ὅλον ἄνθρωπον, in contrast to the partial treatment of circumcision). The idea of complete unity is also expressed in 19:23 in regard to Jesus' garment: ὑφαντὸς δι' ὅλου, "woven *in one piece*."

Finally, in Matt 12:30 par., in agreement with the idiom of the LXX, ὅλος is used of total devotion to God: You shall love the Lord your God "with *all* your heart, *all* your soul . . . ," etc. (the closest parallel for the formula, which is repeatedly adapted in the OT, is Deut 6:5: a series with anaphoric ἐξ ὅλης). W. Elliger

ὀλοτελής, 2 *holotelēs* completely whole, entirely undamaged*

1 Thess 5:23: "May the God of peace sanctify you *through and through*." Cf. → ὁλόκληρος. H. Seesemann, *TDNT* V, 175f.

Ὀλυμπᾶς, ᾶ *Olympas* Olympas*

Abbreviated form of a longer personal name beginning with Ὀλυμπ-; in Rom 16:15 for the recipient of a greeting.

ὄλυνθος, ου, ὁ *olynthos* late fig*

Ὄλυνθος designates the immature late fig. Rev 6:13, in connection with the opening of the sixth seal: "The stars of the heavens fell to the earth as when a fig tree (συκῆ) shaken by a strong wind drops its *winter figs*." C.-H. Hunzinger, *TDNT* VII, 751f., 757.

ὅλως *holōs* at all, actually*

Matt 5:34: "But I say to you that you should not swear *at all*"; 1 Cor 5:1: ὅλως ἀκούεται, "one *actually* hears"; 6:7: ἤδη οὖν ὅλως, "now *at all*"; 15:29: "if the dead are not *actually* raised."

ὄμβρος, ου, ὁ *ombros* rain shower*

Luke 12:54: "When you see a cloud rise in the west [from the Mediterranean Sea] you say: 'There is a *rain shower* coming'; and it happens."

ὀμείρομαι *homeiromai* yearn*

1 Thess 2:8, with τινός ("for someone"); here, however, the meaning "harbor loving affection [for someone]" is also possible. H. W. Heiland, *TDNT* V, 176; N. Baumert, "Ὁμειρόμενοι in 1Thess 2,8," *Bib* 68 (1987) 552-63.

ὁμιλέω *homileō* converse; speak (to)*
ὁμιλία, ας, ἡ *homilia* company, social intercourse, association*

1. General features of NT occurrences — 2. Usage and meaning of ὁμιλέω in Luke-Acts — 3. Ὁμιλία in the Menander quotation in 1 Cor 15:33

Lit.: A. BONHOEFFER, *Epiktet und das NT* (1911). — W. GÖRLER, *ΜΕΝΑΝΔΡΟΥ ΓΝΩΜΑΙ* (Diss. Berlin, 1963). — E. NORDEN, *Die antike Kunstprosa* (1909). — E. PLÜMACHER, *Lukas als hellenistischer Schriftsteller* (1972). — W. POPKES, *RAC* IX, 1100-1145. — R. REITZENSTEIN, *The Hellenistic Mystery Religions* (1978). — T. B. L. WEBSTER, *An Introduction to Menander* (1974).

1. From the word group that includes ὅμιλος (Frisk, *Wörterbuch* II, 386f.) only the vb. ὁμιλέω belongs to NT usage, and that only in the Lukan writings (twice each in Luke and Acts). The noun ὁμιλία in 1 Cor 15:33 is a quotation from an outside writing (cf. Bonhöffer 122). Corresponding to the imbalance and infrequency of NT usage is the narrowness of the NT spectrum of meanings (cf. BAGD 565 with LSJ 1222; *PGL* 951; Passow II/1, 458f.). As a result, when dealing with the vb. ὁμιλέω, the strong impression given by contextual synonyms that it has primarily to do with speaking (→ λέγω) is misleading. Rather, the aspect of community, of social interaction, should always be kept in mind (on the connection between συνεῖναι and ὁμιλέω see Schmidt, *Synonymik* III, 234): *Verbal* communication is only one component of its meaning. There is no trace in the NT of the nearly technical usage of the term for sexual relations (cf. esp. Philo, who uses, however, μῖξις and συνουσία as parallels) nor of use of it for the union of the initiate with God in the mystery religions (e.g., *Corp. Herm.* xii.19; cf. Reitzenstein, index s.v. [567]; Bonhöffer 122).

2. a) In the Emmaus pericope (24:13-35, L) the Passion and resurrection events form the content of the ὁμιλεῖν πρὸς ἀλλήλους referred to in v. 14 with περὶ κτλ. (cf. the summary in vv. 19-24). If what follows in v. 14 (like what follows εἶπαν in v. 17, modified by D to πρὸς ἑαυτούς) emphasizes communication, then the synonyms ἀντιβάλλω πρὸς ἀλλήλους in v. 17 and esp. συζητέω in v. 15 (cf. in terms of material Mark 9:10 or Luke 22:23) suggest a lively dispute.

b) In the context of Acts 24:26, ὡμίλει αὐτῷ ("he *spoke* with him") is found in conjunction with διαλέγομαι (v. 25). The synonymity of the two expressions is underscored by the v.l. διελέγετο for ὡμίλει. The brief scene relating the discussion between Felix and Paul belongs to those "passages in which Luke depicts the representatives of Christianity . . . as representatives . . . of Hellenistic education" (Plümacher 22).

c) The section of the "we"-source in Acts 20:7-12 has the same juxtaposition of διαλέγομαι (v. 7) and ὁμιλέω

(v. 11) that is unique to the literary style of Luke. If "break bread" is here a t.t. for the Lord's Supper (→ ἄρτος 3), then ὁμιλέω could also already have the meaning "preach" that established itself in the patristic era from the time of Ign. *Pol.* 5:1 (ὁμιλίαν ποιεῖσθαι) in connection with the classical and Hellenistic philosophical "address" (cf. *PGL* 951; Bonhöffer 122; Norden II, 541; see also the articles on "Homiletik" and "Predigt" in *EKL, LTK,* and *RGG*) .

3. The noun ὁμιλία does not yet, in the NT, belong to the vocabulary of proclamation and explanation of Scripture. In 1 Cor 15:33 Paul quotes a well-known monostichic gnomic proverb from Menander (ΘΑΙΣ frag. 218; cf. Diodorus Siculus xvi.54.4; *Ep. Arist.* 130; on the ancient "collections of sayings from the comedies of Menander" see Görler 6). Here ὁμιλίαι (pl. in congruence with pl. of ἦθος) has the general meaning of χρεία πρὸς ἕτερον (Iamblichus *VP* 180) and therefore refers to social intercourse in the broadest sense (cf. Webster 189: "bad company"; → κακός). As is demonstrated by *Acts Thom.* 139 (cf. *Acts of John* 46), ὁμιλία can in this sense almost be a substitute for → κοινωνία (see Popkes *passim*).

M. Lattke

ὁμιλία, ας, ἡ *homilia* company, social intercourse, association
→ ὁμιλέω (3).

ὅμιλος, ου, ὁ *homilos* crowd

Rev 18:17 TR: "the entire *throng* [of those who travel] on ships."

ὁμίχλη, ης, ἡ *homichlē* fog*

2 Pet 2:17: pl. with ὁ → ζόφος τοῦ σκότους.

ὄμμα, ατος, τό *omma* eye*

Literal in Mark 8:23 of the eyes of a blind man and in Matt 20:34 of the eyes of the blind men of Jericho that Jesus touched.

ὀμνύω, ὄμνυμι *omnyō, omnymi* swear, swear to, vow, make an oath*

1. NT occurrences and origin — 2. Usage and semantic field — 3. Oath-taking in the world of the Bible — 4. The individual NT passages

Lit.: BAGD s.v. — BDF, index s.v. (292). — G. DAUTZENBERG, "Ist das Schwurverbot Mt 5,33-37; Jak 5,12 ein Beispiel für die Torakritik Jesu?" *BZ* 25 (1981) 47-66. — *idem, TRE* IX, 379-82. — C. A. KELLER, *THAT* II, 855-63. — H.-G. LINK, *DNTT* III, 737-43. — MAYSER, *Grammatik* II/2, 303f. — F. MUSSNER, *Jas* (HTKNT, 1975) on 5:12. — J. SCHNEIDER, *TDNT* V, 176-85, 458-67. — For further bibliography see *DNTT* III, 743; *TWNT* X, 1200.

1. Ὀμνύω, a Hellenistic variant of classical Attic ὄμνυμι (cf. BDF §92), appears 26 times in the NT, of which only Mark 14:71 contains the form ὄμνυμι. The vb. is preferred in the more strongly early Jewish-Christian writings: Matthew has 13 occurrences and Hebrews 7. In these writings the vb. derives its reflexive perspective (to/for oneself) and its basic reciprocal character (with each other) from the Heb. root *šbʿ* ("swear") in the niphal (translated by the LXX *ca.* 100 times as ὀμνύω).

2. The grammatical usage is characterized by a variety of constructions. The person or thing by which someone swears can be specified in the acc. (Jas 5:12) or dat. (Heb 3:18) or with a prep. such as πρός (Luke 1:73); κατά (Heb 6:13, 16); ἐν, or εἰς (Matt 5:34, 36, probably under the influence of Heb. *bᵉ*). A following main or subordinate clause conveys the content or consequences of the oath (Heb 3:11; 4:3; 7:21; Mark 14:71 par. Matt 26:74).

Belonging to the same semantic field as ὀμνύω and also based on Heb. *šbʿ* are ἐξομολογέομαι (Isa 45:23; cf. Luke 22:6 [act.]), ὁρκίζω and ἐξορκίζω in the causative sense "make [someone] swear" (Gen 50:5f.; 24:3), and the noun ὅρκος, used with ὁρκίζω (Exod 13:19) and ὀμνύω (Num 30:3; Luke 1:73; Acts 2:30; Jas 5:12), ὁμολογέω (Matt 14:7), and ἀρνέομαι (Matt 26:72). The negative counterpart ἐπιορκέω, "swear falsely" (Matt 5:33), can also be mentioned here. The difficulty in defining the meaning of the word, which was a factor already in the biblical world, is here manifest.

3. An oath, as a religio-historical phenomenon, is an assurance, expressed in a solemn form, that a statement corresponds to the truth or that a promise will be fulfilled (so already in Hesiod, Homer, and the divine and royal oaths of the papyri). Oath-taking is frequently mentioned in the OT as a formulaic promise directed to God (Num 30:3; Ps 132:2) or accompanied by an appeal to God as the guarantor and witness of its truth (Josh 2:12f.; 1 Sam 20:42), frequently reinforced with corresponding gestures (e.g., raising of the hand, Deut 32:40). Since an oath constitutes "an irrevocable statement of will that places one under obligation" (Keller 858), false oaths are urgently warned against (Lev 19:12) and flippant oaths are likewise condemned (Sir 23:9-11).

The intensification of oath formulas (abundant material in the papyri; Preisgke, *Wörterbuch* II, s.v.) reveals the waning effectiveness of oaths in the time of the Bible. From this also resulted the circumspect application or complete prohibition of oaths among the Pythagoreans and Stoics. Corresponding to this in part is the disposition of Judaism, as can be gathered from Philo (esp. *Spec. Leg.* ii.2-38), Josephus (esp. *B.J.* ii.135: the Essenes), and the rabbinic writings (see Billerbeck I, 328-30). Along with that comes the circumlocution of the divine name, derived from Exod 20:7, which is extended with a critical stress in the NT (cf. Matthew and James), as is the pledge of Yahweh himself to mankind (cf. Gen 22:16 and Ps 110:4 in Luke and Hebrews).

4. In Paul there are no explicit oath formulas. In terms of content, however, his oathlike asseverations, which

appeal to God as witness to the truth, may be classified here. Thus, e.g., in Gal 1:20 we read, "God knows that I am not lying!" and in Rom 9:1, "I speak the truth in Jesus Christ. . . . "

The question and problem of oaths is dealt with most extensively in Matthew. In the fourth antithesis (Matt 5:33-37) the author emphatically (note the solemn long form of introduction in v. 33, cf. 5:21) reinforces the OT prohibition of false oaths (Lev 19:12) and the related commandment to keep one's vows (Num 30:3). He then contrasts this with Jesus' instruction not to swear at all —not by a circumlocution for the name of God (vv. 34f.), because of the insincerity of such hair-splitting casuistry, nor by one's own life (v. 36), since it, too, belongs to God. "In the order of life ruled by the kingdom of God there is no further place for the oath. It makes sense only when there is reason to question the veracity of men" (Schneider 178). In v. 37 it is claimed that all else is from the evil one.

This antithesis, portrayed as a saying of Jesus, although probably redacted and given catechetical form by Matthew, points to a shorter parallel in Jas 5:12. At their base lies a common tradition that issues from the time of Jesus in its absolute demand for speaking the truth: "In sense there is agreement between the saying of Jesus in Mt. and the saying of James" (Schneider 182). The demand for absolute truthfulness in speaking makes oaths superfluous (Mussner 212).

The harsh polemic against the "blind" Jewish leaders in Matt 23:16-22 (ὀμνύω occurs 10 times here) should be classified with that against the casuistry of the teachers of the law. The temple and the gold in the temple, the altar and the sacrifice, belong together and are therefore equally consecrated to God: that which human pettiness seeks to divide belongs together by God's will.

In contrast to this critical disposition toward swearing, the author of Hebrews adopts a different approach, reflecting completely that of early Judaism. He speaks equally without inhibition of Yahweh swearing in his wrath (according to Ps 95:11) against his unfaithful people (Heb 3:11, 18; 4:3) as he does of his sworn promise to Abraham (6:13, 16f.). Heb 7:20-22 argues in the same way, and concludes (in accord with Ps 110:4) from the sworn statement of Yahweh that the priesthood of Jesus supersedes that of the Levites since the latter is not established by oath. The author thereby seeks to demonstrate that "the divine oath is the guarantee which rules out all doubt and gives faith assurance of the promise" (Schneider 184).

Rev 10:6, in line with Dan 12:7, presents the figure of the swearing angel, according to whom the mystery of God will be fulfilled and the hour of salvation will arrive without delay.

Finally, when in the Gospels an oath is made as a

promise (Herod: Mark 6:23) or as a self-imprecation (Peter: Mark 14:71 par. Matt 26:74), the contemporary Jewish disposition toward this question is manifest. "It is expected of the Christian, however, that his word will be unconditionally rivetted to the truth. Hence his Yes and No are enough" (Schneider 182).

                            A. Kretzer

ὁμοθυμαδόν *homothymadon* unanimously, with one mind*

This adv. is preferred in Acts (10 occurrences), appearing elsewhere in the NT only in Rom 15:6. In Acts it appears primarily in summaries (1:14; 2:46; 4:42; 5:12) but also elsewhere (15:25), designating the exemplary harmony of Christians, as well as that of those who hear the Christian message (8:6). Other occurrences refer to the crowds who are *unanimously* hostile toward Christians (7:57; 18:12; 19:29; cf. 12:20). It also appears in Rom 15:6 in the prayer of Paul for the Roman Christian community: "that they may praise God *with one mind and one mouth*." H. W. Heiland, *TDNT* V, 185f.; E. D. Schmitz, *DNTT* III, 908f.; Spicq, *Notes* II, 618-20.

ὁμοιάζω *homoiazō* be similar/like

In Mark 14:70 Koine A al: ἡ λαλιά σου ὁμοιάζει, "your speech is like [that of a Galilean]" (cf. Matt 26:73); Matt 23:27 B λ: ὁμοιάζετε (in place of παρομοιάζετε).

ὁμοιοπαθής, 2 *homoiopathēs* of the same kind*

With τινί, in Acts 14:15; Jas 5:17: "We are human *like you*"; "Elijah was a man *like us*." W. Michaelis, *TDNT* V, 938f.; E. Beyreuther and G. Finkenrath, *DNTT* II, 500-503.

ὅμοιος, 3 *homoios* like, similar*

1. Occurrences and usage — 2. The Synoptics — 3. Revelation — 4. Other occurrences

Lit.: E. BEYREUTHER and G. FINKENRATH, *DNTT* II, 500-503. — BILLERBECK II, 7-9. — D. A. CARSON, "The ὅμοιος Word-Group as Introduction to Some Matthean Parables," *NTS* 31 (1985) 277-82. — JEREMIAS, *Parables*, 77-80. — J. SCHNEIDER, *TDNT* V, 186-88. — For further bibliography → παραβολή; see *TWNT* X, 1200f.

1. There are 45 occurrences in the NT, of which 18 are in the Synoptics, 21 in Revelation, 3 in the Johannine writings, and 1 each in Acts, Galatians, and Jude. That which the subj. is compared to is in the dat. But in Rev 1:13; 14:14 solecism leads to assimilation: ὅμοιον υἱὸν ἀνθρώπου (cf. BDF §182.4). The Synoptics have ὅμοιος with εἶναι: "*be alike/resemble*" (so also Acts 17:29; John 8:55; 1 John 3:2). Only in Matt 22:39 does the meaning shift to "*be of equal value/equal rank*" (so also Rev 13:4;

18:18; John 9:9: "to be *similar*"). In the remaining occurrences Revelation uses ὅμοιος as a comparative particle with the same meaning as ὡς. In Gal 5:21, the subst. pl. of ὅμοιος is placed at the end of a series: *and the like;* in Jude 7 the sg. is used adv.: *likewise.*

2. Synoptic uses of ὅμοιος are almost all in parable pericopes—in questions (Luke 7:31; 13:18) and statements (6:47) introducing parables, as well as in first lines of parables (Luke 6:48f.; 7:32 par.; Matt 13:31, 33, 44, 45, 47; 20:1). What is compared is the kingdom of God/ heaven (Luke 13:18, 19, 21; Matt 13:31, 33, 44, 45, 47; 20:1), this generation (Luke 7:31 par.), or the one who does or does not do the word of Jesus (Luke 6:47-49). Like the vb. ὁμοιόω, the adj. ὅμοιος, in correspondence with rabbinic usage (shortened dat. construction with *lᵉ* or a more developed dat. introduction), indicates not equivalence but comparison with the entire event that is related: "It is the case with the kingdom of God as it is with. . . ."

Outside the parables ὅμοιος is also found in metaphorical sayings regarding the righteous scribe (Matt 13:52) and the disciples (Luke 12:36). In Matt 22:39 the command to love one's neighbor is made *of equal value* or *equal importance* with the command to love God.

3. Revelation uses ὅμοιος predominantly in fig. comparisons that explain the beings and leading figures, either as independent statements (1:15; 2:18; 4:3b, 7; 9:7a, 19; 13:2; 21:11) or as explanations dependent on a preceding statement (4:3a, 6; 9:7b, 10; 11:1; 13:11; 21:18). Several times OT idiom functions as a model. Two questions focus rhetorically on the incomparability of the beast from the sea (13:4) and the city of Babylon (18:18) as representatives of evil. In dependence on Dan 7:13 the exalted Jesus is designated as ὅμοιον υἱὸν ἀνθρώπου in 1:13 and 14:14 and thus interpreted as the Messiah.

4. In Gal 5:21 Paul uses καὶ τὰ ὅμοια τούτοις to break off the list of works of the flesh, which exclude one from the kingdom of God. Acts 17:29 apologetically emphasizes that God is not like gold or silver or stone, or indeed like any product of human skill or imagination. In John 8:55 Jesus declares to the Jews that he would be "*like* them" if he were to deny that he, unlike them, possessed true knowledge of God. In 1 John 3:2 the author assures his readers that the perfection of the children of God is still to come: Only the eschatological revelation of Christ will lead to likeness with his nature. In John 9:9 ὅμοιος is used of just personal physical resemblance. The warning in Jude 7 points out that Sodom and Gomorrah *likewise* (in the same way as the angels) committed sexual immorality and (like the angels) will fall victim to the eternal fire.

G. Haufe

ὁμοιότης, ητος, ἡ *homoiotēs* similarity, agreement*

Heb 4:15: καθ᾽ ὁμοιότητα, "in the *same way*"; 7:15: κατὰ τὴν ὁμοιότητα Μελχισέδεκ, "in the *same way* as Melchizedek." J. Schneider, *TDNT* V, 189f.; E. Beyreuther and G. Finkenrath, *DNTT* II, 502, 505.

ὁμοιόω *homoioō* make like; compare*

1. Occurrences and meaning — 2. In the parables — 3. Other occurrences

Lit.: → ὅμοιος. — See also J. Schneider, *TDNT* V, 188f.

1. The NT contains 15 occurrences of ὁμοιόω, of which 12 are in the Synoptics and 1 each in Romans, Acts, and Hebrews. In 11 instances the vb. is employed in the introductions to parables with the meaning *compare.* In 4 instances the pass. is used of the adaptation of people: *become like.*

2. The usage in the parables takes two forms: (1) The first person fut. act. is used in questions that introduce a parable, sometimes in the sg. (Matt 11:16 par. Luke 7:31; Luke 13:18, 20) and sometimes in the pl. (Mark 4:30). These questions usually refer to the kingdom of God, but also once to "this present generation" (Matt 11:16 par.). Behind this construction lies rabbinic usage; materially it expresses the difficulty of finding adequate language. (2) The passive is unique to the Matthean parables and is always found in the first sentence of the parable, sometimes in the fut. (Matt 7:24, 26; 25:1) and sometimes in the aor. (13:24; 18:23; 22:2). What is compared is usually the kingdom of heaven, but also twice (Matt 7:24, 26) the one who does or does not do the words of Jesus. Like the first form, this second form does not indicate equivalence, but rather a comparison with the event mentioned; → ὅμοιος 2.

3. The remaining uses are in the pass. and speak of conformity viewed negatively or positively. Paul in Rom 9:29 bases God's free election on Isa 1:9 LXX: ". . . and we *would have become like* Gomorrah" (aor. ind.). The observers of Paul's healing of a lame man in Lystra declare: "The gods *have become like* humans [aor. partc.] and have descended to us" (Acts 14:11). The Hellenistically formulated kenosis christology teaches (in Heb 2:17): "Therefore he had to *become like* his brothers in all things" (aor. inf.). Jesus speaks against the way Gentiles pray (Matt 6:8): "Do not *be like* them" (aor. subjunc.).

G. Haufe

ὁμοίωμα, ατος, τό *homoiōma* image, likeness*
ὁμοίωσις, εως, ἡ *homoiōsis* likeness, correspondence*

1. Occurrences — 2. Ὁμοίωσις — 3. Ὁμοίωμα in Paul — a) Occurrences determined by tradition — b) Rom 6:5 and 5:14 — 4. Rev 9:7

Lit.: H.-W. Bartsch, "Die theologische Bedeutung des Begriffes OMOIΩMA im NT," *idem, Entmythologisierende Auslegung* (TF 26, 1962) 156-69. — G. Bornkamm, "Baptism and New Life in Paul (Romans 6)," *idem, Early Christian Experience* (1969) 71-86. — N. Gäumann, *Taufe und Ethik* (BEvT 47, 1967) 50-52. — E. Jenni, *THAT* I, 452. — O. Kuss, "Zu Röm 6,5a," Kuss I, 151-61. — F. Mussner, *James* (HTKNT, ³1975) 167f. — H. D. Preuss, *TDOT* III, 257-60. — J. Schneider, *TDNT* V, 190-98. — P. Siber, *Mit Christus leben* (ATANT 61, 1971) 218-21. — U. Vanni, "Ὁμοίωμα in Paolo," *Gregorianum* 58 (1977) 321-45, 431-70. — J. Weiss, *Earliest Christianity (A.D. 30-150)* (1937) 488-91. — For further bibliography see *TWNT* X, 1200f.

1. The verbal substs. based on ὁμοιόω and already attested in classical Greek and the LXX see only limited use in the NT. Ὁμοίωσις is found only in Jas 3:9 and ὁμοίωμα in Rev 9:7 and 5 times in Paul.

2. In Jas 3:9, which is determined by Judaism both in form and content, ὁμοίωσις is derived from Gen 1:26 LXX. The nature of the tongue is made clear by means of a sharp antithesis: With it we praise God and curse humans made in *correspondence* to God (constructions with -σις are abstracts; see BDF §109.4; it cannot be coincidence that James does not use κατ᾽ εἰκόνα from Gen 1:26). Jewish parenesis in similar cases likewise refers to human similarity to God (*Mek. Exod.* on 20:26; *Gen. Rab.* 24:8; *2 Enoch* 44:1).

3. a) Ὁμοίωμα in Rom 1:23 is likewise influenced by Gen 1:26f. More directly, however, the sentence is determined by Ps 105:20 LXX and Deut 4:15-20; 5:8. In these passages ὁμοίωμα is the "form," the "image" (Heb. *t᷊emûnâ, tabnît*). In the gen. construction ὁμοίωμα εἰκόνος, which has a remarkable parallel in rabbinic literature (cf. J. Jervell, *Imago Dei* [FRLANT 76, 1960] 97f.), ὁμοίωμα is paralleled by δόξα: in this way, in spite of the sharp polemic, too narrow an identification of the essence of God with idols is avoided. Gentile religion perverts the glory of God into an image of the likeness (on → εἰκών [7.b, c] cf. Rom 8:29; 2 Cor 3:18) of the creature. It is not improbable that the formulation of the sentence, including the addition ἐν ὁμοιώτατι εἰκόνος, is derived from Jewish tradition.

Ὁμοίωμα in Phil 2:7 has with great probability been taken over by Paul as part of a Christ-hymn. The origin of the entire hymn and of the parallel expressions in the hymn suggests an understanding of ὁμοίωμα that corresponds with the LXX, i.e., as a *concrete form or image*. The phrase ἐν ὁμοιώματι ἀνθρώπων identifies the "incarnate one" with the human form of appearance, but remains open to a difference in this identity. In substance

the use of ὁμοίωμα in Rom 8:3 is close to that of Phil 2:7. A tradition-historical connection cannot be ruled out. In any case, ἁμαρτίας is more likely possessive gen. than gen. of quality. The problem of the sinlessness of the Son is therefore not directly addressed by the statement. Nevertheless, ὁμοίωμα emphasizes that the one whom God has sent in the historical form of humans who have fallen into sin is the Son, in spite of his identification with the world.

b) Ὁμοίωμα in Rom 6:5 can also be understood in terms of the usage observed above. A prior stage of tradition history is not discernible here. The connection of this saying with the process of baptism is widely made today, and with good reason. In baptism we are united to the *form* of the death of Christ. It is the death of Christ with which the one who is baptized is united and which has a liberating effect with respect to sin—not the historically unique death on Golgotha, but rather that which took place in this death. Thus, this saying also points to both identification and difference.

Finally, that is the case with Rom 5:14 as well. The contrast of Adam and Christ in vv. 12-21 is dependent on the demonstration of sin's universality from the time of Adam. Paul demonstrates this indirectly for the era between Adam and Moses, the era without "law," on the basis of its effects. Death also ruled over these generations, although they did not commit the *same kind* of trespass as Adam did. Since they had no law, there was for them no "trespass" (Rom 4:15). And yet they must have acted against God, since they, too, suffered the consequences of sin. Underlying the difference signalled primarily by ὁμοίωμα is an identity, even when that identity eludes closer definition.

4. The direct meaning of ὁμοίωμα, *manner of appearance/form*, which is also attested in the LXX (Deut 4:12; Josh 22:28; cf. also Ezek 1:26; → 3.a on Rom 1:23), is found in Rev 9:7: The locusts' *manner of appearance* was like that of armed war horses.

                                          T. Holtz

ὁμοίως *homoiōs* similarly, likewise*

The adv. of → ὅμοιος is used in the NT primarily in Luke (11 of 30 total occurrences). The only Synoptic parallels are Mark 15:31 and Matt 27:41. Further occurrences in the Gospels are: Matt 22:26 (cf. par. Mark); Matt 26:35 (cf. par. Mark); John 5:19; 6:11; 21:13. In Luke (Acts has no occurrences) it is found in 5:33 (cf. par. Mark); 6:31 (cf. par. Matthew); and in Lukan special material in 3:11; 5:10; 10:32, 37; 13:3; 16:25; 17:28, 31; 22:36 (see H. Schürmann, *Jesu Abschiedsrede* [1957] 122). Ὁμοίως δὲ καί is found in Luke 5:10 and 10:32 as well as 1 Cor 7:3, 4 and Jas 2:25; cf. ὁμοίως τε καί in Rom 1:27. In Jude 8 we find ὁμοίως μέντοι καί, "*in the same way* now also." Ὁμοίως also joins sequences *(likewise)* in 1 Pet 3:1, 7; 5:5. The remaining occurrences are in 1 Cor 7:22; Heb 9:21; and, with ὁμοίως occupying a final position, Rev 2:15; 8:12.

ὁμοίωσις, εως, ἡ *homoiōsis* likeness, correspondence
→ ὁμοίωμα (2).

ὁμολογέω *homologeō* confess, praise*
ὁμολογία, ας, ἡ *homologia* confession*

1. Occurrences in the NT — 2. Meaning outside the NT — 3. Usage in the NT — 4. Matt 10:32f. par. Luke 12:8f. — 5. Confession of Christ — 6. Ὁμολογουμένως

Lit.: G. BORNKAMM, "Das Bekenntnis im Hebräerbrief," *idem, Aufsätze* II, 188-203. — *idem,* "Das Wort Jesu vom Bekennen," *ibid.,* III, 122-39. — *idem,* "Homologia," *ibid,* III, 140-56. — H. VON CAMPENHAUSEN, "Das Bekenntnis im Urchristentum," *ZNW* 63 (1972) 210-53 (see also 66 [1975] 127-29). — J. CASTELVECCHI, "La homologia en la carta a los Hebreos," *Ciencia y Fe* 19 (1963) 329-69. — H. CONZELMANN, "Was glaubte die frühe Christenheit?" *idem, Theologie als Schriftauslegung* (1974) 106-19. — O. CULLMANN, *The Earliest Christian Confessions* (1949). — R. DEICHGRÄBER, *Gotteshymnus und Christushymnus in der frühen Christenheit* (1967) 114f., 117f. — G. DELLING, *Der Gottesdienst im NT* (1952) 77-88. — D. FÜRST, *DNTT* I, 344-48. — E. KÄSEMANN, *The Wandering People of God* (1984) 167-74. — *idem,* "Das Formular einer neutestamentlichen Ordinationsparänese," *idem, Versuche* I, 101-8. — W. KRAMER, *Christos Kyrios Gottessohn* (1963) 61-71. — W. G. KÜMMEL, "Das Verhalten Jesus gegenüber und das Verhalten des Menschensohns," *FS* Vögtle 210-24. — H. LÖWE, "Bekenntnis, Apostelamt und Kirche im Kolosserbrief," *FS* Bornkamm 299-314. — O. MICHEL, *TDNT* V, 199-220. — V. H. NEUFELD, *The Earliest Christian Confessions* (1963). — R. PESCH, "Über die Autorität Jesu. Eine Rückfrage anhand des Bekenner- und Verleugnerspruchs Lk 12,8f par.," *FS* Schürmann 22-25. — H. SCHLIER, "Die Anfänge des christologischen Credo," *Zur Frühgeschichte der Christologie* (ed. B. Welte; 1970) 13-58. — A. SEEBERG, *Der Katechismus der Urchristenheit* (1903 = TBü 26, 1966). — SPICQ, *Notes* II, 621f. — D. G. VAN VREUMINGEN, "De betekenis van ὁμολογεῖν in het NT," *Theologie en Praktijk* 21 (1961) 121-32. — H. ZIMMERMANN, *Das Bekenntnis der Hoffnung* (1977) esp. 44-52. — For further bibliography see Kümmel; Michel; Pesch; *TWNT* X, 1201f.

1. Of the 26 NT occurrences of the vb. 11 are in the Johannine corpus (4 in the Gospel, 5 in 1 John, 1 each in 2 John and Revelation), 4 in Matthew, 3 in Acts, and 2 each in Luke, Romans, the Pastorals (1 Timothy and Titus), and Hebrews. The noun occurs 6 times (3 in Hebrews, 2 in 1 Timothy, 1 in 2 Corinthians).

2. In secular Gk. ὁμολογέω displays a wide range of meanings, particularly "agree," "approve/consent," "concede," "admit/acknowledge, confess/profess," "accept/affirm," "(openly) declare /maintain," "give assent to/promise," "agree/commit oneself to /make a treaty." The same breadth of meaning is evident for the noun ὁμολογία. Hellenistic Jewish literature uses both vb. and noun predominantly in the common Greek sense. Occasionally,

however, we find another usage shaped by the Hebrew vb. *hôḏâ,* which in the MT and the Qumran texts has the religious meanings "praise (God)" and "confess sin" (cf. ἐξομολογέω 1). In rabbinic literature *hôḏâ* takes on the meanings of ὁμολογέω: "agree," "approve/consent," "concede," "admit/acknowledge," "confess/profess," "accept/affirm."

The vb. → ἀρνέομαι forms a clear antonym to ὁμολογέω. The contrasting pair ὁμολογέω/ἀρνέομαι can bring various nuances to expression: "confess/deny" (Thucydides vi.60.3); "admit/dispute" (Aristotle *Rh.* ii.3.5 p1380a, 16-18; Pap. Zenon Col. ii.83.13f.; Josephus *Ant.* vi.151; *T. Gad* 6:3; Aelian *NA* ii.43; cf. Philo *Ebr.* 192). In rabbinic literature one frequently encounters the contrasting pair *hôḏâ bᵉ/kāpar bᵉ,* esp. with the meaning "profess (someone or something)/deny (someone or something)" or "accept (someone or something)/reject (someone or something)" (e.g., *Mek. Exod.* on 15:11; *Sifra Lev.* on 11:45; 26:14; *Sifre Num.* 111 on 15:22f.; *Sifre Deut.* 54 on 11:28; *y. Ber.* 9:1; *Exod. Rab.* 32:5 on 23:22; *Deut. Rab.* 2:5 on 3:24).

3. a) The vb. ὁμολογέω is used in the same sense as in secular Gk. in 7 of its occurrences in the NT with the following nuances in meaning: 1) *speak frankly/confess* (Acts 24:14; cf. *T. Dan* 1:4), 2) *affirm/acknowledge* (Acts 23:8: "The Sadducees say that there is no resurrection from the dead, and neither angel nor spirit; the Pharisees, however, *acknowledge/affirm* both"), 3) *openly declare* (Matt 7:23; cf. Josephus *Ant.* x.166), *explicitly state* (Heb 11:13, as in Philo *Op.* 25 with reference to a saying from the OT [Gen 23:4; 47:9 in Heb 11:13]), *assert* (Titus 1:16, as in Xenophon *Mem.* ii.3.9), and 4) *promise* (Matt 14:7, as in Xenophon *An.* vii.4.22; Lysias 12.9; Josephus *Ant.* iv.76, 136), *bind oneself to with a promise* (Acts 7:17, of God's promise to Abraham, as in Philo *Abr.* 275; cf. *Det.* 60; *Ebr.* 39).

In 2 Cor 9:13 ὁμολογία could have the general sense of *assent, acknowledgment, obligation:* With reference to the money gathered from the Gentile Christians the church in Jerusalem will praise God "for the obedience *with which you profess* the gospel of Christ," i.e., your obedience by which you testify that you acknowledge the claims of the gospel as obligatory for you." The gen. τῆς ὁμολογίας ὑμῶν explains ὑποταγή, and the attributive prep. εἰς τὸ εὐαγγέλιον modifies ὁμολογία.

b) The non-Greek construction ὁμολογεῖν ἐν, *confess to (someone)* in Matt 10:32 par. Luke 12:8 (→ 4) is a Semitism corresponding to Heb. *hôḏâ bᵉ* (→ 2; see also *Midr. Ps.* 100 §1 on v. 1; *Gen. Rab.* 53:12 on 21:12) and Aram. *'ôḏî bᵉ* (*y. Šabb.* 7:10c; *y. Yebam.* 1:2c; *Tg. Onq. Gen.* 49:8; *Tg. Isa.* 26:13; cf. also Syriac *'awdî bᵉ* in the tr. of Acts 23:8; Rev 3:5).

c) Specifically Christian religious usage is present in the NT where either the vb. or the noun is used of confession of Christ (→ 5). This sense of "confess" or "confession" combines the characteristic Greek aspects of "affirmation" and "acknowledgment" with those of "open and binding declaration."

'Ομολογέω, *confess*, is constructed with the acc. of the person (1 John 2:23; 4:3) or thing (1 Tim 6:12), with the double acc. (John 9:22; Rom 10:9; 1 John 4:2 [3 v.l.]; 2 John 7), with acc. + inf. (John 9:22 v.l.; 1 John 4:2 v.l.), or with a ὅτι-clause (1 John 4:15; cf. BAGD s.v. 4; BDF §§157.2; 397; 416.3). A definite connection can be discerned between Christian religious usage and the characteristic formulations of Hellenistic Jewish literature; see, e.g., Philo *Post.* 175; *Cher.* 107; *Ebr.* 117; *Abr.* 203 (ὁμολογίαν ὁμολογέω, "make a confession," as in 1 Tim 6:12); further 2 Macc 7:37; Josephus *B.J.* vii.418 (Καίσαρα δεσπότην ὁμολογέω, "acknowledge the emperor as lord" [cf. 419]).

d) Like the compound ἐξομολογέομαι, which occurs several times in the NT, the simple form is used in 1 John 1:9 of *confession of sins* (ὁμολογέω τὰς ἁμαρτίας; cf. Sir 4:26; Philo *Praem.* 163; *Vit. Proph.* 4:13[15]; Prov 28:13 A Theodotion). The intention is not only an inner admission, but also an open confession of sins before God. The author of 1 John shares with ancient Judaism both the conviction that confession of sins is the precondition for God's forgiveness and the certainty that God responds to confession of sin with the comfort of forgiveness (cf. Philo *Praem.* 163; *Tanḥuma* [ed. S. Buber] *Gen. wyšb* §11 [182]; *Pesiq. Rab. Kah.* 24:8; *Sifra Lev.* on 26:40; on the OT background see, e.g., Ps 32:5; Prov 28:13).

In secular Gk. texts as well open admission of guilt or error is represented by ὁμολογέω (Euripides *Fr.* 265; Arrian *An.* [ed. A. G. Roos] vii.29.2; Appian *Romanae Historiae* viii.79; Aelian *NA* xi.17; also Philo *All.* iii.66; Josephus *Ant.* vi.151; *T. Gad* 2:1; 6:3). These texts, however, do not deal with confession of sin in a specifically religious sense.

e) The use of ὁμολογέω found in Heb 13:15 is completely foreign to secular Greek usage. Here the vb. is used with the dat. obj. τῷ ὀνόματι αὐτοῦ (= τοῦ θεοῦ) and has the meaning *praise/glorify*, not "confess" ("confess the name" would have to be ὁμολογέω τὸ ὄνομα; see Justin *Apol.* i.45.5; *Dial.* 39.6). Hebrews does not have in mind a hymnic confession of Christ, but, "generally, a song of praise that the Church offers to God through the mediation of its heavenly high priest, Jesus" (Deichgräber 118; cf. *1 Clem.* 61:3; *Mart. Pol.* 14:3).

Parallels to the unusual usage of Heb 13:15 can be found in 1 Esdr 4:60; 5:58(= 61); Ps 99:3 Symmachus (cf. also Philo *All.* i.82). As in the case of the synonymous expressions ἀνθομολογέομαι with the dat. (Luke 2:38; Ps 78:13 LXX; Dan 4:37 LXX; *T. Jud.* 1:3) and → ἐξομολογέομαι with the dat., this usage is derived from Heb. *hôḏâ l^e* (cf. 1 Esdr 5:58[= 61] with Ezra 3:11 MT). 'Ομολογέω τῷ ὀνόματι (τοῦ θεοῦ) also has its own parallel in Heb. *hôḏâ l^ešēm* (Pss 106:47; 122:4; 140:14; 1 Chr 16:35; 1Q34 1:6) and in Aram. *'ôḏî (hôḏî) lišmā'* (Tg. 1 Kgs 8:33, 35; Tg. Pss 122:4; 140:14) or *'ôḏî l^ešûm* (Tg. 1 Chr 16:35).

4. The double saying derived from Q on confessing and denying in Matt 10:32f. par. Luke 12:8f., the original form of which is probably most nearly preserved in Luke, clearly betrays its Semitic origin.

The structure (a double saying in antithetical parallelism, conditional correspondence), which is also found in 1 John 2:23; 4:2f., has analogies in rabbinic sayings: "Whoever confesses idolatry, denies [thereby] the entire Torah; and whoever denies idolatry, confesses [thereby] the entire Torah" (*Sifre Deut.* 54 on 11:28); "Whoever confesses two worlds [i.e. the resurrection of the dead], will be called your [Abraham's] seed; and whoever does not confess two worlds will not be called your seed" (*Gen. Rab.* 53:16 on 21:12). On ὁμολογέω ἐν → 3.b. The closest parallel to the contrasting pair ὁμολογέω/ἀρνέομαι is provided by *y. Ber.* 9:1: "Someone has a relative: If the relative is rich, then that person confesses him [i.e., openly acknowledges that he is a relative, *môdeh bô*], but if he is poor, that person denies him [i.e., does not want to know him [*kôper bô*]"; cf. also *Exod. Rab.* 32:5 on 23:22 and the Peter scene in Mark 14:66-72, which also provides a material parallel.

The authenticity of the Q saying, which is directed to the circle of disciples, ought not be contested. It is an expression of Jesus' unique claims to sovereignty and authority: Jesus identifies himself in this saying with the coming Son of Man, to whom God has entrusted the governance of the world (cf. *1 Enoch* 45:3; 49:4; 61:8f.; 69:27); and he makes clear, through promises and warnings, that the decision regarding eternal salvation or destruction is determined by one's disposition toward him. The saying has in view the enmity that Jesus experienced, an enmity also encountered by the disciples because of him. Whoever openly acknowledges before the human forum his relation with Jesus under these circumstances will be acknowledged by Jesus as belonging to him in the final judgment before the heavenly court. On the other hand, whoever distances himself or herself from Jesus or renounces him will in the final judgment hear from Jesus' own mouth the word of rejection that will separate him or her from Jesus and salvation forever (cf. Matt 7:23; 25:12).

Matthew and Luke—fully preserving the original intent—relate the double saying to the situation of the post-Easter Church (note the context). Matthew connects ὁμολογέω with public confession of Jesus Christ by his messengers in the context of their missionary activities. Luke has in mind open confession by Christians in situations of persecution to give an account of their faith before hostile tribunals.

The promise of Rev 3:5 picks up on this saying on confession: Christ will in the final judgment confess those who have remained faithful to him. This confession entails preservation in judgment and the reward of eternal life.

5. 'Ομολογέω is used of *confession of Christ* in John 1:20 (bis); 9:22; 12:42; Rom 10:9f.; 1 Tim 6:12; 1 John 2:23; 4:2f., 15; 2 John 7; ὁμολογία is so used in 1 Tim 6:12f.; Heb 3:1; 4:14; 10:23. In all of these passages these terms refer exclusively to the person of Jesus himself. The confession does not consist of a recounting of chris-

tological statements of faith describing the saving work
of Jesus, but rather of "the short yet unambiguous
reference to the one divine being, whose affirmation
makes the individual Christian a Christian and distinguishes him or her from every non-Christian" (von Campenhausen 211). Affirmation and acknowledgment of
Jesus is expressed in the simple confession of title, which,
like the OT confession YHWH hû' hā-ᵉ lôhîm (Deut 4:35,
39; 1 Kgs 8:60; 18:39; Ps 100:3), combines in a concise
nominal clause the name of Jesus (as subj.) with an
honorific title (as pred. noun): "Jesus is Lord," "Jesus is
the Messiah," "Jesus is the Son of God." The accent here
lies on the honorific titles, which bring to expression
Jesus' unique dignity and therefore, at the same time, his
nature.

a) In Romans 10 Paul designates the cry of adoration
κύριος Ἰησοῦς (v. 9; 1 Cor 12:3) as the fundamental confession to which eschatological salvation is connected
(Rom 10:9f.; cf. vv. 12f.). This confession manifests a
faith that acknowledges the one who was crucified as the
Lord whom God raised from the dead and exalted to the
position of ruler of this world, and which submits to his
kingdom and confesses him in praise and worship (cf.
Phil 2:9-11). Like faith itself, the confession is the result
of the "nearby word" (Rom 10:8a), i.e., the preached
gospel (vv. 8b, 14-20), which, because it is the word of
Christ (v. 17), proves to be the δύναμις θεοῦ εἰς σωτηρίαν
(1:16). According to 1 Cor 12:3 the confession κύριος
Ἰησοῦς can only be uttered "in the Holy Spirit"; in this
connection it should be remembered that the believer
receives the Spirit ἐξ ἀκοῆς πίστεως, "from the preaching
that works faith" (Gal 3:2, 5).

b) In Hebrews, ὁμολογέω in 3:1; 4:14; and 10:23 refers, in an objective sense, to the confession of the
Church, which the individual makes his own in the act
of personal confession. As can be discerned from 4:14,
the transmitted confession is "Jesus is the Son of God."
This refers (according to the interpretation of the author
of Hebrews) to the Son of God as the true and eternal
high priest who by his self-sacrifice has gained for the
people of God the high-priestly right to enter the heavenly
holy of holies on the day of salvation (6:20; 9:11-28;
10:19-25). The εἴσοδος (10:19; 3:7-19) is the content and
goal of the "heavenly calling" (3:1) and is therefore the
eschatological salvation promised to the Church and to
be expected with confident hope (6:18). For that reason
confession of Jesus can be characterized as ὁμολογία τῆς
ἐλπίδος (10:23). The author calls the Church, which was
threatened by flagging faith, to hold unshakably to this
confession and hope (4:14; 10:23; 3:6; 6:11). Whether
ὁμολογία refers to baptismal confession (thus esp. Bornkamm) or to a confession used in worship (thus, e.g.,
Zimmermann) cannot be discerned with certainty.

c) In John the confession "Jesus is the Son of God"

is heard more frequently (esp. 1:34, 49; 11:27). The three
passages in which ὁμολογέω appears (1:20; 9:22; 12:42)
have in mind the confession "Jesus is the Messiah" (the
Χριστός). In 12:42 the vb., used absolutely, not only has
the general meaning "admit" (in contrast to "conceal"),
but also refers here, as in 9:22, to the open and public
confession by which true faith in the messianic character
of Jesus is (according to John, must be) made manifest
(cf. 1:49; 11:27). The three passages make it clear that
the Evangelist is making a polemical reference to the
attitude of his time (the end of the first century A.D.).
When 9:22 and 12:42 mention the decision of "the Jews"
to put out of the synagogue everyone confessing Jesus as
the Messiah (cf. 16:2f.), they presuppose the definitive
separation of Jewish Christians from the Jewish community and the sharp opposition between the two that ensued
around A.D. 90 (for details see R. Schnackenburg, John
II [Eng. tr., 1980] 250, 417f.). The Evangelist wants the
open declaration of John the Baptist, "I am not the Messiah" (1:20), to be understood as an indirect confession
of Jesus as Messiah. In so doing he must have turned
against the followers of John the Baptist, who saw in him
the messianic bringer of salvation and who, unlike John
the Baptist himself (οὐκ ἠρνήσατο!), contested the designation of Jesus as Messiah (cf. the entire context, 1:19-34
and 1:6-8, 15; 5:36).

d) For the author of the Johannine Epistles the confessions "Jesus is the Messiah" (1 John 2:22; 5:1) and
"Jesus is the Son of God" (4:15; 5:5) serve as means of
identifying the false Christian teaching that denied the
reality of the incarnation and thus also the true humanity
and death (5:6) of the Christ, the Son of God. In the
struggle with docetic Christianity the accent is moved
from the pred. to the subj. of the confessional formula:
Jesus, the true man Jesus from Nazareth, is the Messiah,
the Son of God. The confession that has been handed
down acknowledges, as the author in his interpretation
formulates, that "Jesus Christ has come in the flesh"
(1 John 4:2f.; 2 John 7; cf. John 1:14). The Spirit of God
leads the believer to this true confession (1 John 2:20,
27; 4:2, 13-15), and the spirit of falsehood leads the false
teacher to contest it (4:3, 6) and so to deny not only the
Son, but also God the Father (2:22f.).

e) In the Pastorals 1 Tim 6:12f. speaks of the "good,"
i.e., orthodox, confession of Jesus as the Son of God.
"Timothy" made this confession at his baptism (other
possibilities are at his ordination or before pagan authorities) "before many witnesses" (v. 12) and thereby took
up precisely that ὁμολογία that Jesus himself had expressed in his trial before Pilate (v. 13).

6. The adv. ὁμολογουμένως* is found in 1 Tim 3:16a
in a clause introducing the quotation of a christological
hymn in v. 16b. Two translations are possible: a) obvious-

ly/incontestably/without a doubt (cf. 4 Macc 6:31; 7:16; 16:1; Philo Det. 18; Imm. 71) and b) according to general knowledge/according to all (cf. Thucydides vi.90.3; Xenophon An. ii.6.1; Josephus Ant. i.180; ii.229; Athenaeus iv.239b; Diog. 5:4). The latter should be given preference (cf. Spicq): "Indeed—on this all [Christians] are in agreement—the mystery of the truth of faith [as attested in the Church] is great." That the adv. might have the simple sense of "truly" or "indeed" (thus Seeberg 113) cannot be established. O. Hofius

ὁμολογία, ας, ἡ homologia confession
→ ὁμολογέω.

ὁμολογουμένως homologoumenōs according to all, unanimously, generally known
→ ὁμολογία 6.

ὁμόσε homose at the same place, together

Acts 20:18 p⁷⁴ D lat: ὁμόσε ὄντων αὐτῶν, regarding Paul and the elders from Ephesus.

ὁμότεχνος, 2 homotechnos practicing the same trade*

Acts 18:3: "because they [Aquila and Priscilla, v. 2] were "of the same trade" as Paul, i.e., all three were "tentmakers" (σκηνοποιοί). R. Silva, EstBib 24 (1965) 123-34; R. F. Hock, "Paul's Tentmaking and the Problem of His Social class," JBL 97 (1978) 555-64; idem, The Social Context of Paul's Ministry: Tentmaking and Apostleship (1980).

ὁμοῦ homou together, at the same time*

John 21:2: ἦσαν ὁμοῦ, "they were together" (in the same place); Acts 2:1: "they were all together in the same place (ἐπὶ τὸ αὐτό)"; John 20:4: "the two were walking together"; 4:36: "so that the sower and the reaper rejoice together."

ὁμόφρων, 2 homophrōn like-minded, harmonious*

1 Pet 3:8, at the beginning of the general parenesis: πάντες ὁμόφρονες, "all [of you be] like-minded. . . ." Spicq, Notes II, 618-20.

ὅμως homōs nevertheless, yet*

In John 12:42 intensified by μέντοι. Paul's usage is unique: In 1 Cor 14:7 and Gal 3:15, ὅμως is frequently translated nevertheless. Since, however, a comparison is introduced in both passages, one should (with BDF §450.2) consider it a reflection of the old ὁμῶς, "equally"; it would then mean "likewise" (BAGD s.v.). H. Schlier,

Gal (KEK) 143n.4; J. Jeremias, ZNW 52 (1961) 127f.; R. Keydell, ZNW 54 (1963) 145f.

ὄναρ, τό (nom. and acc. sg. only) onar dream*

Lit.: J. BERGMANN, G. J. BOTTERWECK, and M. OTTOSSON, TDOT IV, 421-32. — E. L. EHRLICH, Der Traum im AT (1953). — idem, "Der Traum im Talmud," ZNW 47 (1956) 133-45. — A. OEPKE, TDNT V, 220-38. — W. RICHTER, "Traum und Traumdeutung im AT. Ihre Form und Verwendung," BZ 7 (1963) 202-20. — B. STEMBERGER, "Der Traum in der rabbinischen Literatur," Kairos 18 (1976) 1-42. — A. WIKENHAUSER, "Doppelträume," Bib 29 (1948) 100-111. — For further bibliography see TWNT X, 1202.

Ὄναρ appears in the NT only in Matthew, and there only in the relatively late idiom κατ' ὄναρ, "in a dream": 1:20: Joseph's dream before the birth of Jesus; 2:12: the directions to the wise men not to return to Herod; 2:13, 19, 22: the instructions to Joseph in connection with the flight into Egypt; 27:19: the wife of Pilate "suffered much in a dream" because of Jesus. The reserve of the NT with respect to dreams (see also, however, Acts 16:9f.; 18:9; 23:11; 27:23f.) can be attributed to a position critical of dreams. Interpretation of dreams is completely lacking in the NT.

ὀνάριον, ου, τό onarion (small) donkey*

John 12:14: "Jesus found a young donkey and sat on it" (v. 15 refers to Zech 9:9 LXX, where πῶλος is used). O. Michel, TDNT V, 283-87.

ὀνειδίζω oneidizō grumble, complain; revile, reproach*
ὀνειδισμός, οῦ, ὁ oneidismos reviling, reproach, insult (noun)*
ὄνειδος, ους, τό oneidos insult, shame, reproach (noun)*

1. Occurrences, derivation, and usage in the NT — 2. Barrenness as shame — 3. The Psalm quotations in Rom 15:3-4 — 4. Ὀνειδίζω and ὀνειδισμός in connection with the Passion and persecution — 5. Reproach by Jesus — 6. "God gives and does not grumble"

Lit.: E. GRÄSSER, "Der historische Jesus im Hebräerbrief," ZNW 56 (1965) 63-91. — H. KÖSTER, "'Outside the Camp': Hebrews 13,9-14," HTR 55 (1962) 299-315. — H.-J. KRAUS, Theology of the Psalms (1986) 177-203. — E. KUTSCH, TDOT V, 211-15. — H. MILLAUER, Leiden als Gnade (1976). — K. H. SCHELKLE, Die Passion Jesu (1949). — J. SCHNEIDER, TDNT V, 238-42. — SPICQ, Notes II, 623-25. — O. H. STECK, Israel und das gewaltsame Geschick der Propheten (WMANT 23, 1967). — H. WÄHRISCH and C. BROWN, DNTT III, 340-45.

1. The vb., including the three variant readings in Mark 15:34 (a weakening of ἐγκαταλείπω); Heb 10:33 (for θεατρίζω); and 1 Tim 4:10 (an "amplification" of

ἀγωνίζομαι; see Schelkle 109), appears 12 times in the NT (in the LXX *ca.* 30 times for the piel of *hārap̄*, "be ashamed"; KBL³ 341). The late form ὀνειδισμός (BDF §109; this verbal subst. is not yet found, e.g., in Philo, and is found in Josephus only in *Ant.* xix.319) occurs 5 times in the NT. The more frequent noun ὄνειδος is a NT hapax legomenon (→ 3). Although already in the LXX the boundaries between the two nouns are fluid (*ca.* 50 occurrences of ὀνειδισμός and *ca.* 25 of ὄνειδος, translating *herpâ*, "reproach, scorn"; KBL³ 342), the textual tradition of *T. Lev.* 10:4; 15:2 shows their complete interchangeability.

Many of the NT occurrences are shaped by the idiom of the LXX or are even taken over word for word from the LXX. The NT range of meanings corresponds to the general usage (cf. Spicq 623). The synonyms are deserving of special attention (cf. Schmidt, *Synonymik* I, 136-49; III, 536-43), and the nuances derived from the approximately 50 instances in Philo are very informative.

2. In Luke 1:25 ὄνειδος is used in reference to the *shame* of barrenness (cf. Gen 30:23).

3. As scriptural proof that Christ did not live to please himself (→ ἀρέσκω) Paul quotes Ps 68:10b LXX (Rom 15:3). Psalm 69 (68) is also sometimes (John 2:17; Rom 11:9f.) viewed as prophetic (cf. H.-J. Kraus, *Pss* II [Eng. tr., 1989] 65).

4. Along with the messianic Psalm 69 (68), Ps 88:51f. LXX has influenced the use of the Passion-theological "words of proclamation" and the early Christian "martyrs' language" (Schelkle 108f.; cf. later Eusebius *HE* v.1.60). Jesus had to "endure blasphemies, mockery, and insults" (R. Pesch, *Mark* [HTKNT] II, 483; → βλασφημέω, → ἐμπαίζω) on the cross according to Mark 15:32 par. Matt 27:44 (cf. Luke 23:39 and the respective contexts). The beatitude in Matt 5:11 par. Luke 6:22 (see Schulz, *Q* 452-57) links "the suffering of the righteous" with the OT persecution of the prophets (Steck 20-27, 257-60), in connection with which *revile* is one of the "Geschickverben," i.e., one of the vbs. used to describe the fate of the prophets (Steck 258). The beatitude of 1 Pet 4:14 stands in striking parallel to such reproach categories (→ ὄνομα). In vv. 12-19 *be reproached* is an expression of suffering (N. Brox, *1 Pet* [EKKNT] ad loc.; Millauer §39 *passim;* → πάσχω). In Hebrews, where ὀνειδισμός plays the primary role, "the *reproach* of Christ" (11:26) is the exegetical point of departure (cf. O. Michel, *Heb* [KEK] ad loc.). Here the author speaks paradoxically when he states that Moses acted not because of the reproach, but "because of the reward" (O. Kuss, *Heb* [RNT] ad loc.). The expression "his *reproach*" (13:13) refers to the crucifixion, which is also sometimes designated as → αἰσχύνη (12:2). The connection between, on the one hand, affliction (→ θλῖψις) and

insults in 10:33, which are not further specified, and, on the other hand, the reproach of the historical Jesus (see Grässer!) must be maintained. The negative final clause in 1 Tim 3:7 seems odd against the background of such a *theologia crucis,* even if one assumes that it reflects a different situation for the Church and a change in the understanding of office.

5. The harshness of the denunciation of the unrepentant cities in Matt 11:20 (on the following "woe" see Schulz, *Q* 360-66) fits well with the familiar image of the authority of Jesus (see Schneider 240). Direct influence on the composition of the longer ending of Mark is possible, even when Jesus, according to Mark 16:14, *rebukes* the unbelief of his own disciples.

6. The single saying about God in Jas 1:5 should be viewed as a counterpoint to such wisdom sayings as that found in Sir 20:14f. (etc.; cf. F. Mussner, *Jas* [HTKNT] ad loc.). The author is leveling an indirect polemic against *grumbling* as "an abuse with regard to giving" (M. Dibelius, *Jas* [Hermeneia] ad loc., with other material).

                                      M. Lattke

ὀνειδισμός, οῦ, ὁ *oneidismos* reviling, reproach, insult (noun)
→ ὀνειδίζω.

ὄνειδος, ους, τό *oneidos* insult, shame, reproach
→ ὀνειδίζω (2).

Ὀνήσιμος, ου *Onēsimos* Onesimus*

Onesimus means "the useful one" and is a frequently attested slave name. In Phlm 10 Paul writes: "I appeal to you for my child, whom I bore in [my] chains, *Onesimus.*" Intended is a slave, Onesimus, who had run away from Philemon and become a Christian through Paul; there is also a wordplay on the name in v. 11. According to Col 4:9, Paul sent Onesimus back to Colossae together with Tychicus. P. Stuhlmacher, *Phlm* (EKKNT) 21-24, 38f.; P. Lampe, "Keine 'Sklavenflucht' des Onesimus," *ZNW* 76 (1985) 135-37.

Ὀνησίφορος, ου *Onēsiphoros* Onesiphorus*

A personal name found in 2 Tim 1:16: "May the Lord show mercy toward the house of Onesiphorus; for he has often refreshed me and was not ashamed of my chains." According to v. 17 Onesiphorus had "sought hard" for Paul in Rome. In 4:19 greetings are sent to "the house of Onesiphorus" as well as to Aquila and Priscilla.

ὀνικός, 3 *onikos* pertaining to a donkey*

Mark 9:42 par. Matt 18:6, with → μύλος: "donkey's

millstone." A donkey-driven millstone was significantly heavier than that of a hand mill.

ὀνίμαμαι *onimamai* mid.: rejoice, be happy*

The 2nd aor. opt. ὀναίμην is used formulaically ("I *would like to rejoice*") with the gen. of that for which one rejoices. In Phlm 20 it is found with σοῦ and ἐν κυρίῳ, "I would like to rejoice over you in the Lord."

ὄνομα, ατος, τό *onoma* name

1. Occurrences and usage in the NT — 2. Names and name bearers generally — 3. The name of God — 4. The name of Jesus — 5. Ὄνομα in formulaic combination with ἐν, ἐπί, and εἰς

Lit.: R. ABBA, *IDB* III, 500-508. — K. BALTZER, *RGG* IV, 1302-4. — H. BIETENHARD, *TDNT* V, 242-83. — *idem, DNTT* II, 648-55. — S. H. BLANK, "Some Observations Concerning Biblical Prayer," *HUCA* 32 (1961) 75-90. — A. J. H. W. BRANDT, "Onoma en de Doopsformule in het NT," *TT* 25 (1891) 565-610. — R. G. BRATCHER, " 'The Name' in Prepositional Phrases in the NT," *BT* 14 (1963) 72-80. — H. A. BRONGERS, "*bᵉšēm JHWH,*" *NedTTs* 11 (1956/57) 401-16. — *idem,* "Die Wendung *bᵉšēm jhwh* im AT," *ZAW* 77 (1965) 1-20. — H. VON CAMPENHAUSEN, "Taufen auf den Namen Jesu?" *VC* 25 (1971) 1-16. — N. A. DAHL, " 'A People for His Name' (Acts XV.14)," *NTS* 4 (1957/58) 319-27. — G. DELLING, *Die Zueignung des Heils in der Taufe. Eine Untersuchung zum neutestamentlichen "taufen auf den Namen"* (1961). — J. DUPONT, *DBSup* VI, 514-41. — L. HARTMAN, " 'Into the Name of Jesus': A Suggestion concerning the Earliest Meaning of the Phrase," *NTS* 20 (1973/74) 432-40. — W. HEITMÜLLER, *"Im Namen Jesu"* (FRLANT 2, 1903). — H. B. HUFFMON, *IDBSup* 619-21. — H. KOSMALA, "In My Name," *ASTI* 5 (1967) 87-109. — G. VAN DER LEEUW, *Phänomenologie der Religion* (²1956), esp. §17. — G. LOHFINK, " 'Meinen Namen zu tragen . . . ' (Apg 9,15)," *BZ* 10 (1966) 108-15. — W. PHILIPP, *RGG* IV, 1298-1300. — L. POZNANSKI, "À propos de la collation du nom dans le monde antique," *RHR* 194 (1978) 113-27. — B. REICKE, *RGG* IV, 1304-6. — D. TABACHOVITZ, " 'Heißen' und 'Sein' im Griechischen," *Eranos* 58 (1960) 9-11. — F. G. UNTERGASSMAIR, *Im Namen Jesu. Der Namensbegriff im Johannesevangelium* (1974). — M. WILCOX, *The Semitisms of Acts* (1965). — L. YAURE, "Elymas—Nehelamite—Pethor," *JBL* 70 (1960) 297-314. — J. YSEBAERT, *Greek Baptismal Terminology* (1962).

1. Ὄνομα occurs 230 times in the NT and is esp. frequent in the writings of Luke (34 occurrences in Luke, 60 in Acts) and Revelation (38 occurrences). It is also found in Matthew (22 occurrences), Mark (15), and John (25), as well as 15 times in Paul. NT usage of ὄνομα only partially corresponds to general Greek usage. The reason for this is a religious technical usage that is primarily attested in the LXX. Nevertheless, the expression, e.g., "he gave them the name Boanerges" (Mark 3:17) reflects common Greek. The meaning "reputation" (Mark 6:14; Rev 3:1) is likewise common Greek; ὄνομα = "person" (Acts 1:15; 18:15?; Rev 3:4; 11:13) is also found in

nonbiblical texts. Also corresponding to widespread usage is the meaning "person" or perhaps "terms" (in contrast to "actualities") in Acts 18:15.

2. There is nothing unusual about many NT references to the name of a person or place (esp. in Luke-Acts). Often lying behind the NT texts, however, is the widely held belief that the name communicates something essential or characteristic about the bearer of the name. Jesus' name is explicitly interpreted in this way in Matthew (1:21, 25; cf. Sir 46:1). That the name was given to him on divine command (thus also Luke 1:31; 2:21) indicates that the bearer has been specially chosen by God. The same is true of John the Baptist: His person is determined not so much by his family ties as by his divine task (Luke 1:13, 59, 61, 63). The names "Peter" and "Sons of Thunder" express something essential about their bearers (Mark 3:16f.), as does the name "Legion" (Mark 5:9 par. Luke 8:30), that of the magician Elymas (Acts 13:8), and the names of various figures in Revelation (6:8; 8:11; 9:11; 17:5; 19:12f., 16), including the blasphemous names of the beast, which imply that the beast claims for himself names and honors due only to God (14:11; 15:2; 17:3; 13:1, 17 [ἀριθμὸς τοῦ ὀνόματος]). In Rev 3:1 this belief about names is reversed: The name ("reputation") says nothing true about the person.

The close connection between the name and the person/essence entails that whoever knows the name can also control the person (Mark 5:9 par. Luke 8:30). When Jesus gives someone a new name, he thereby grants that person a new identity (Mark 3:16f.; Rev 2:17; cf. John 10:3). Therefore something about the entire person is expressed when the name of a person is written in heaven or in the book of life. God has written the name there and in so doing has provided and promised life to the person (Luke 10:20; Phil 4:3; Rev 3:5; 13:8; 17:8).

When "the one who overcomes" is marked with God's name, the name of the city of God, and the new name of Christ (Rev 3:12; 14:1; 22:4), a new relation comes into existence between the name and its bearer: The saved now belong to the personal realm of God and Christ, are their personal possession, are protected by them, and have rights of citizenship in the city of God. Conversely, those who are marked with the name of the beast are correspondingly shaped by its nature (13:17; 14:11). Moreover, that the twelve towers of the holy city bear the names of the twelve tribes of Israel (21:12; cf. Ezek 48:30-35) probably means that the dispersed members of God's people will enter the city as its citizens from all directions. This is the new people of God, since the foundation stones bear the names of the twelve apostles (21:14): They are the patriarchs, the foundation laid by Christ himself.

The connection of name and person is also seen in

Mark 6:14, where the reputation of a person is intended. This connection is also present in Luke 6:22, although the specific meaning there is unclear; that a bad reputation is referred to is reasonably obvious, although the ideas of excommunication and slander could also possibly be present. One could also then perhaps paraphrase Eph 1:21 thus: ". . . over every rule and authority and power and dominion and whatever *classification* that one might find for such powers" (i.e., ὄνομα = *classification* of heavenly beings; the name says something about its nature and power: → ὀνομάζω 2).

3. Expressions like "the name of God" are found primarily in OT quotations and in expressions influenced by the OT. Here, too, a close connection exists between the name and its bearer. Whoever knows God's name, knows God—or as much of God as he has revealed. This revelation is made primarily in the person of Jesus Christ and is proclaimed through apostolic preaching (Rom 9:17 [quoting Exod 9:16]; cf. Heb 2:12). Whoever praises or calls upon God's name turns to the God who first turned toward mankind (Rom 10:13 [quoting Joel 3:5]; 15:9 [quoting Ps 18:50]; Heb 13:15; Rev 15:4 [cf. Ps 86:9]). To blaspheme God's name is to blaspheme God (Rom 2:24 [quoting Isa 52:5]; 1 Tim 6:1; Rev 13:6; 16:9). Such blasphemy can be committed when those who belong to God do not live in a way worthy of his holiness (Rom 2:24; 1 Tim 6:1). The following expressions are also derived from the OT: According to Acts 15:14 (quoting Amos 9:12 LXX) God will make the Gentiles a people of his *name* (λαὸν τῷ ὀνόματι αὐτοῦ; cf., e.g., 1 Kgs 8:17), i.e., he has chosen them as the people of his possession; Acts 15:17 (quoting Amos 9:11 LXX) speaks of the Gentiles over whom God's name has been spoken, i.e., those who have been consecrated to him. In Heb 6:10 the expression "love for his name" is equivalent to "love for him" (cf. Pss 5:12; 69:37; for the use of εἰς with ἐνδείχνυμι cf. Gen 50:15 v.l.).

Q contains in the Lord's Prayer the petition for the consecration of the name of the Father. The one who consecrates is ultimately God himself. Since ὄνομα here represents, as it were, the God who has turned toward mankind, and since holiness is God's essence (cf. Luke 1:49; → ἅγιος 4), the petition also asks that God cause mankind to acknowledge him as God and be molded by him. Such a prayer also entails the petition for openness toward God and his kingdom (cf Ezek 36:23).

John's Gospel assumes the OT idea that knowledge of God's name is knowledge of God himself: Through the person and work of the Son, the Father reveals himself to mankind. Thus the Johannine Jesus can say that he has revealed the Father's name (17:6, 26) and that through his work the Father's name is "glorified" (12:28)

4. Except in the prep. constructions dealt with below (→ 5) the expression "the *name* of Jesus" is found primarily in Acts and the Johannine literature. In Acts the usage of ὄνομα expressions seems to serve the author's efforts to mediate to the reader a sense of the biblical style. The OT expression "call on the name of God" is applied to Jesus (Acts 2:21 [quoting Joel 3:5]; 9:14, 21; 22:16; cf. 19:17). As in Jewish writings it expresses the proper relation to God—only now expressed as one's relation to Christ. "The *name* of Jesus" is often interchangeable with simply "Jesus": by faith in the name of Jesus or in Jesus, his ὄνομα healed the lame man (3:16; see also 4:30); nevertheless, one senses that the name represents the proclaimed (8:12) Lord, who is active in the Church—through this name alone is there salvation and healing (4:12; cf. 19:13; on this → ὀνομάζω 2); through it forgiveness of sins is possible (10:43), Paul fought this name (26:9), but later bore it as an apostle (9:15); "in" it he fearlessly appeared (9:27f.), and for its sake Paul and Barnabas "laid down their lives" (15:26; see also 9:16; 21:13), just as other disciples would have to suffer "for the sake of the *name*" (5:41).

Applying to Jesus ὄνομα constructions that were applied to God in the OT belongs to the style of other NT writers as well. In 1 Cor 1:2 persons are mentioned "who call on the name of Jesus Christ" (cf., e.g., Isa 64:6 and Acts, cited above); according to 2 Thess 1:12 the name of Christ is glorified by the lives of those who are addressed (cf., e.g., Ps 86:9, 12), i.e., the same Jesus Christ who has been proclaimed to them, in whom they believe, and whose parousia they await (vv. 10f.). In Jas 2:7, too, we find OT terminology: The good name that has been spoken over Christians (cf., e.g., Amos 9:12 LXX and Acts 15:17; → 3) is here the name of Jesus, whose own possession they (in baptism) had become (cf. 2 Tim 2:19; → ὀνομάζω 2). On Matt 7:22, → 5. An expression reminiscent of OT usage is found in Rom 1:5 and 3 John 7: "for the sake of (ὑπέρ with gen.) his [or the] name" Paul has become an apostle or missionaries have gone out, so that Jesus may be known and acknowledged (cf., e.g., Ps 102:16; Mal 1:11).

John and 1 John contain a typically Johannine construction: πιστεύω εἰς τὸ ὄνομα (John 1:12; 2:23; 3:18; 1 John 5:13), which means the same as πιστεύω εἰς with the acc. of the person and is found 31 times in reference to Jesus. This construction implies complete surrender of the person to the divine revelation in Christ. The expression πιστεύω τῷ ὀνόματι (1 John 3:23) is equivalent to πιστεύω with the dat. of the person (e.g., John 5:46; 1 John 5:3). In contrast to the εἰς construction, this latter expression points more to acknowledgment of what a person says. The same identification of name and person is found in John 15:21 (persecution "for the sake of Jesus' *name*") and 1 John 2:12 (forgiveness of sins "for his *name's* sake"; cf. 1 John 1:7). In both passages the person of Jesus is linked with his work as the revealer of God.

In certain other passages as well, expressions like "the name of Jesus" are used interchangeably with "Jesus." There is reference to hatred and persecution "for his name's sake" (διά with acc., Mark 13:13 par. Matt 10:22; 24:9; Luke 21:17; ἔνεκεν, Matt 19:29; Luke 21:12, where Mark in both instances has only ἐμοῦ; see also Rev 2:3) and to exhortations "in the name" (διά with gen.) of the Lord Jesus (1 Cor 1:10; cf. Rom 15:30), i.e., supported by and with the authority of the Lord. The statement in Rev 2:13; 3:8 must be understood differently: It is there a question of confessional faithfulness of the readers to the invisible yet real Lord (see also 3:5b).

Two NT texts speak of the name of the exalted Christ: Phil 2:9 and Heb 1:4 (cf. also Rev 3:12). According to Phil 2:9 God gives to "the exalted one" "the *name* that is above every other *name,*" i.e., the name Kyrios (→ κύριος 7, 8): The name represents his divine essence. Heb 1:4 refers to a similar enthronement: Christ has inherited a name that is more excellent than that of the angels, i.e., God had given him the name and therefore also the nature and position of "Son."

5. Prep. constructions with ὄνομα are for the most part non-Greek and should be considered direct or indirect Semitisms or biblicisms. Here we will deal only with expressions with ἐν (on Acts 9:27f.; → 4), ἐπί, and εἰς, singling out those expressions which are related to baptism (see further → 4).

a) Expressions with ἐν are the most common and display a variety of meaning and usage. This rather undefined range of connotations corresponds to the LXX. Relatively common are the meanings "by the commission of," "with reference to (the authority of)," and "with appeal to." Mark 11:9 (par. Matt 21:9; Luke 19:38) and Q (Matt 23:39 par. Luke 13:35) quote Ps 118:26 in this way. In Mark 11:9 Jesus is hailed in the Triumphal Entry as the humble Messiah sent by God; in the Lukan parallel, Jesus appears, by the addition "the King," to be depicted as King by divine commission. Q deals with a coming with divine authority as the representative of God at the parousia.

Mark and Luke-Acts also use the expression "in (ἐν) the *name*" with exorcisms and healings: With (explicit) appeal to Jesus, whose name stands for the power of his person as present through the Holy Spirit, the disciples were able to drive out demons (Mark 9:38 par. Luke 9:49; Luke 10:17; Acts 16:18) and heal diseases (Acts 3:6; 4:7, 10; cf. 9:34). In 2 Thess 3:6 appeals are made "in the *name*" of Jesus Christ, i.e., by his commission, and in a similar sense it is said of the prophets in Jas 5:10 that they "spoke in the *name* of the Lord." According to v. 14 anointing of the sick should be carried out "in the *name* of the Lord," i.e., probably, on the summons of and with appeal to the Christ who heals the sick (cf. v. 15b). In

1 Cor 5:4 "in the *name* of the Lord" could be connected with "I have already judged," "hand him over to Satan," or "assemble." With the first two constructions the meaning would be: "by the commission of/with reference to the authority of"; with the third: "calling upon."

The LXX attests the use of "in (ἐν) the *name* of the Lord" with vbs. that represent cultic acts: One lifts up one's hands (Ps 62:5), praises (Ps 104:3), or blesses (Ps 128:6) "in the *name* of the Lord." The formula also names the one called on; the context also, however, justifies viewing the expression "in the name" as a reference to the basis, presuppositions, and conditions of the cultus, namely, the work and revelation of God for his people and his presence with them. The formulas in Acts 2:38 (v.l.); 10:48; Eph 5:20; Phil 2:10; and Col 3:17 appear to serve the same function as does 1 Cor 6:11, although there "the Lord" is Christ.

John uses "in (ἐν) the *name*" in the way just described, but with the nuances explained above (→ 3). Thus, John 12:13 also cites Ps 118:26, but "the King who comes by commission of the Lord," comes as one who reveals God by being lifted up. In 17:11f., too, God's name is referred to in the sense of the revelation of God in the Son, since there the disciples will be kept "in the *name*" of the Father. In 5:43 and 10:25 as well as in 20:31, the same connotation of revelation of God is present, although in 20:31 the name could also be understood to be interchangeable with the person. The "cultic" use is found in the statements on prayer "in the *name*" of Jesus (14:13f.; 15:16; 16:24, 26): Jesus' revelation of God forms the foundation, prerequisite, and condition of prayer. The same could be said for those passages according to which the Paraclete is sent "in the *name*" of Jesus (14:26; 16:23).

1 Pet 4:14 (reproach "in the *name* of Christ"; cf. Matt 5:11f.) should be compared with Mark 9:41 (ἐν ὀνόματι, ὅτι). The expression should be translated "on account of /because of."

b) In the LXX, ἐπὶ τῷ ὀνόματι is used interchangeably with ἐν τῷ ὀνόματι with the same meaning, esp. with "by commission of/on the authority of." This sense is found in Mark 13:6 (par. Matt 24:5/Luke 21:8) and 9:39. Matthew uses the simple dat. in the same sense (3 times in 7:22; cf., e.g., Jer 33:9 LXX). When the reference is to speaking "in the name of/by commission of," Luke-Acts consistently uses ἐπί (Luke 24:47; Acts 4:17, 18; 5:28, 40). The expression in Mark 9:37 (par. Matt 18:5/Luke 9:48) has a similar meaning, but without the aspect of authority: A child should be received "in the *name*" of Jesus, i.e., with a view toward Jesus. A "cultic" usage (cf., e.g., Deut 21:5 LXX) may lie behind Acts 2:38: Baptism is done with appeal to and with a view toward Jesus; the nuance of ὄνομα touched on above (→ 4) could also be present here in Acts.

c) Other than in the baptismal formula, εἰς τὸ ὄνομα

appears only in Matthew (on Heb 6:10 → 3; on Johannine πιστεύω εἰς τὸ ὄνομα → 4). The expression "in the *name* of [a prophet/righteous person/disciple]" (Matt 10:41f.) is a literal rendering of a Semitic idiom attested in rabbinic literature which describes the type or motive of an act (Heitmüller 112; Hartman). Thus one should receive a prophet because he is a prophet, etc. Matt 18:20 can be understood in the same way: two or three are gathered "in my *name*," i.e., Jesus is the fundamental condition determining the gathering (cf. *m. 'Abot* 4:11: "Every gathering that takes place in the name of heaven . . . ," i.e., is of such a nature that God fundamentally determines it).

d) The baptismal formula "baptize in (εἰς) the *name*" appears to be the latest of the formulas used (on Acts 10:48 [ἐν] and 2:38 [ἐπί] → a, b).

It is Heitmüller's opinion that behind the formula (which is not attested in the LXX) lies the language of money transfers from the Hellenistic era, so that the formula fig. expresses that the one baptized is "transferred" to the Lord's account and so becomes his possession. In contrast, Brandt and Bietenhard (among others) want to trace the baptismal formula to the above-mentioned rabbinic usage. The meaning would then be comparable to reception of a sacrifice, i.e., it would accordingly refer to dedication. Delling, in turn, thinks that ὄνομα represents the event of salvation through Christ: "Baptism 'into (in) the Name . . .' introduces the event of salvation that is bound up with the name [of Jesus]" (97).

The Hebrew and Aramaic expression *lešēm*, an expression not uncommon in cultic contexts, appears to stand behind this formula (Hartman; Matt 18:20 [→ c] is also actually "cultic"). The expression gave the type, the basis, the purpose, and even the basic reference of a ritual. Thus, this formula would present baptism as a rite that is fundamentally determined by the person and work of Jesus (cf., e.g., *t. 'Abod. Zar.* 3:13: "A Samaritan circumcises in the name of Mt. Gerizim," i.e., the rite is fundamentally determined by the Samaritan cult on Mt. Gerizim). The formula would, then, characterize the baptismal rite as one that does not represent Johannine baptism, nor any other such ritual bath, but is fundamentally determined by Jesus and the events concerning Jesus. It is, moreover, completely conceivable that the name of Jesus was spoken at baptism. This could stand behind Jas 2:7 (cf. also → 4).

This held true from the time of the early Church to the time of our oldest texts and must necessarily rest on assumptions. One should also take into account here that the formula could later be reinterpreted. Paul did not explicitly use it, but he shows in 1 Cor 1:13, 15 that he is familiar with it. The context could give evidence of a Pauline view of the formula, in which baptism is related to Christ alone (v. 13: μεμέρισται), and indeed, to his decisive saving act, his death on the cross (see also Rom 6:3; Gal 3:27; cf. 1 Cor 10:2—in each case simply εἰς).

In Acts 19:5 baptism into the name of the Lord Jesus is contrasted with the baptism of John. The fomula as such does not in this case appear to have any other purpose than to designate typical Christian baptism, which

in contrast to the baptism of John bestows the Holy Spirit in connection with the laying on of hands (8:16; 19:6; see also → 4).

The traditional formula "in the *name* of the Father and the Son and the Holy Spirit" is found in Matt 28:19. In view of the "rabbinic" usage attested elsewhere in Matthew (→ c) 28:18 could also be understood in the "cultic" sense represented there. Baptism is fundamentally related to the Father, the Son, and the Holy Spirit (in light of passages like 3:11, 16; 10:20, 40; 11:27).   L. Hartman

ὀνομάζω *onomazō* call, name (vb.)*

Lit.: H. BIETENHARD, *TDNT* V, 282.

1. Ὀνομάζω occurs 9 times in the NT—twice in Luke, once in Acts, twice in Paul, 3 times in Ephesians, and once in 2 Timothy.

2. Ὀνομάζω generally has the same connotations as → ὄνομα. Thus, e.g., that certain disciples, including Peter, were named by Jesus says something about their character and person (Luke 6:13f.; Mark 3:14 v.l.): They are what they are called. Conversely, according to 1 Cor 5:11, the life of "a *so-called* brother" does not correspond to that which the name ἀδελφός should express. The difficult expression in Eph 3:15 could also be seen from this perspective: All lineages (πατριά) in heaven and on earth acquire their *names* from the Father, the creator (3:9; cf. 1:21; 3:10; Ps 147:4), i.e., he is the origin of their identity.

The name can be a representation of the person. Thus, e.g., in Acts 19:13 certain people seek to use the name of Jesus for exorcisms; to be able to use the name of Jesus, however, one must be a follower of Jesus. To name "the name of the Lord" (2 Tim 2:19) can also mean that one submits to his lordship and in this way calls upon him (cf. Isa 26:13). Eph 1:21 could also be understood in this way; cf., however, also → ὄνομα 2. In light of Rom 1:5, it is not only said in 15:20 that Christ's reputation was spreading (cf. 1 Macc 39), but also that he was known and *acknowledged* (as Lord).

In Eph 5:3 ὀνομάζω can be understood as "mentioning" as opposed to "committing" (adultery): It "should not even *be mentioned*."   L. Hartman

ὄνος, ου, ὁ (ἡ) *onos* donkey*

With βοῦς in Luke 13:15, quoting Isa 1:3; John 12:15: πῶλος ὄνου, the foal of a *donkey;* Matt 21:2, 5, 7 refers to two animals, the ὄνος and the πῶλος (αὐτῆς), probably in conformity with Zech 9:9 LXX. O. Michel, *TDNT* V, 283-87; *TWNT* X, 1203 (bibliography).

ὄντως *ontōs* actually, really*

Ὄντως is found as a true adv. in Mark 11:32; Luke

23:47; 24:34; John 8:36; 1 Cor 14:25; Gal 3:21. On the other hand, it is used attributively in 1 Tim 5:3, 5, 16: "the *true* widow," in contrast to the widow with relatives or still capable of marriage or married more than once; 6:19: "the *true* life"; cf. also 2 Pet 2:18 TR.

ὄξος, ους, τό *oxos* bitter wine, wine vinegar*

Ὄξος appears in the NT only in the Gospels, more specifically in the Passion narratives: Mark 15:36 par. Matt 27:48/John 19:29a, b, 30 speak of a sponge soaked in ὄξος (Blinzler: "wine vinegar diluted with water, a common refreshment for field hands and soldiers") that was given to the crucified one. Luke 23:36 has simply ὄξος προσφέροντες αὐτῷ (as a form of mockery). H. J. Heiland, *TDNT* V, 288f.; *TWNT* X, 1203 (bibliography); J. Blinzler, *Der Prozeß Jesu* (⁴1969) 369f.

ὀξύς, 3 *oxys* sharp; quick*

Of a *sharp* sword (Ezek 5:1): Rev 1:16; 2:12; 19:15; of a sickle: 14:14, 17, 18 (bis). With the meaning *fast* (so also LXX; Philo; Josephus *Ant.* v.261) with aor. inf.: Rom 3:15: "*quick* to shed blood" (Ps 13:3 LXX).

ὀπή, ῆς, ἡ *opē* hole, crevice, hollow*

Heb 11:38: ὀπὴ τῆς γῆς, as a place to flee to; absolute in Jas 3:11: the *crevice* from which a spring flows.

ὄπισθεν *opisthen* from behind; behind*

Adv. use in the sense *from behind* is found in Mark 5:27 par. Matt 9:20/Luke 8:44; in the sense *behind* in Rev 4:6; 5:1. The word is also used as an improper prep. with gen. ("*behind* [someone]") in Matt 15:23; Luke 23:26; Rev 1:10 v.l. H. Seesemann, *TDNT* V, 289-92; W. Bauder, *DNTT* I, 492f.

ὀπίσω *opisō* as adv.: behind, back; as improper prep.: behind, after*

1. Occurrences in the NT — 2. Usage — 3. In discipleship terminology

Lit.: W. BAUDER, *DNTT* I, 492f. — BLACK, *Approach* 218. — BDF §215.1. — RADERMACHER, *Grammatik* 144f. — H. SEESEMANN, *TDNT* V, 289-92.

1. Ὀπίσω occurs 35 times in the NT, esp. frequently in the Gospels (6 times in Matthew, 6 in Mark, 7 in Luke, and 7 in John). The remaining occurrences are in Acts 5:37; 20:30; Phil 3:13; 1 Tim 5:15; 2 Pet 2:10; Jude 7; Rev 1:10; 12:15; 13:3. The Synoptic parallels are Mark 1:7 par. Matt 3:11 (of "the greater one" who comes ὀπίσω μου); Mark 1:17 par. Matt 4:19 (δεῦτε ὀπίσω μου); Mark 8:33 par. Matt 16:23 (ὕπαγε ὀπίσω μου, σατανᾶ, " . . . get *behind* me, Satan," i.e., "out of my sight"; cf. Black); Mark 8:34 par.

Matt 16:24/Luke 9:23 (ὀπίσω μου); Mark 13:16 par. Matt 24:18/Luke 17:31 (ἐπιστρεψάτω [Mark/Luke: εἰς τὰ] ὀπίσω); and Matt 10:38 par. Luke 14:27 (ὀπίσω μου). It is evident that Matthew uses ὀπίσω only in dependence on his sources. Lukan occurrences dependent neither on Mark nor on Q are 7:38; 9:62; 19:14; and 21:8 (redactional). The occurrences in John 1:15, 27, 30 are probably influenced by the Synoptic tradition (cf. Mark 1:7).

2. Ὀπίσω is used in the NT both as an adv. and as an improper prep. (with gen.). Prep. usage is alien to secular authors, but is frequent in the LXX (translating '*aḥᵃrê*, "behind"). This usage (in the local sense) appears in the majority of NT occurrences (Matt 4:19; 10:38; 16:23, 24; Mark 1:17, 20; 8:33, 34; Luke 9:23; 14:27; 19:14; 21:8; John 12:19; Acts 5:37; 20:30; 1 Tim 5:15; 2 Pet 2:10; Jude 7; Rev 1:10; 12:15; 13:3). Ὀπίσω is used as an improper prep. with a temporal sense (= *afterwards, after*) in Mark 1:7 par. Matt 3:11/John 1:15, 27, 30.

As an adv., ὀπίσω answers the question "where?" (= *behind*: Phil 3:13; John 6:66; 18:6; 20:14; also Mark 13:16 par. Luke 17:31; Luke 9:62) or the question "to where?" (= *backwards, back*: Matt 24:18; Luke 7:38). The construction εἰς τὰ ὀπίσω is found in Mark 13:16; Luke 9:62; 17:31; John 6:66; 18:6; 20:14.

3. As a prep. ὀπίσω is found in the local sense in the expression ἔρχομαι ὀπίσω, probably as an older alternative to → ἀκολουθέω (3, 4) patterned on Heb. *hālak ʾaḥᵃrê*. In Mark 1:17 par. Matt 4:19 Jesus calls to Simon and Andrew: δεῦτε ὀπίσω μου, "come *after* me" (cf. 2 Kgs 6:19 LXX); the declaration that he would make the two brothers "fishers of people" follows immediately. Mark 1:20 picks up this expression again where it reports: ἀπῆλθον ὀπίσω αὐτοῦ, while Matt 4:22 reads ἠκολού-θησαν αὐτῷ. In the saying on bearing the cross Mark 8:34 has εἴ τις θέλει ὀπίσω μου ἀκολουθεῖν, while Matt 16:24 has ὀπίσω μου ἐλθεῖν and Luke 9:23 has ὀπίσω μου ἔρχεσθαι. Using Q's composition of these words Matt 10:38 has καὶ ἀκολουθεῖ ὀπίσω μου, and Luke 14:27 reads καὶ ἔρχεται ὀπίσω μου. According to John 12:19 the Pharisees exclaim with resignation "See, the [whole] world has gone *after* him (ὀπίσω αὐτοῦ ἀπῆλθεν)!"

Discipleship terminology is also reflected in Luke 21:8 (cf. par. Mark), where Jesus warns against false messiahs who declare that the καιρός has come: μὴ πορευ-θῆτε ὀπίσω αὐτῶν. Acts 5:37 reports of the Galilean rebel leader Judas: ἀπέστησεν λαὸν ὀπίσω αὐτοῦ, i.e., he caused a group of people to rebel while at the same time causing them to follow *after* him. In Acts 20:30 Paul warns against false teachers "who speak distortions in order to draw disciples *after* them (ἀποσπᾶν . . . ὀπίσω αὐτῶν)." 1 Tim 5:15 complains: "Some have already turned away *after* Satan (ὀπίσω τοῦ σατανᾶ)." See also Rev 13:3.

G. Schneider

ὁπλίζομαι *hoplizomai* mid.: arm oneself, prepare oneself*

Fig. in 1 Pet 4:1: "Now since Christ has suffered in the flesh, you too *equip yourselves* with the same insight." A. Oepke, *TDNT* V, 294f.

ὅπλον, ου, τό *hoplon* tool; weapon*

John 18:3: the arms of those who arrested Jesus. Otherwise, only fig. in Paul: Rom 6:13: ὅπλα, "*tools* of . . ." ἀδικίας in 13a, δικαιοσύνης in 13b; fig. of the struggle of the Christian life: Rom 13:12: "let us put on the *weapons* of light"; 2 Cor 6:7: "*weapons* of righteousness"; 10:4: "the *weapons* of our battle (στρατεία)." A. Oepke, *TDNT* V, 292-94; *TWNT* X, 1203 (bibliography).

ὁποῖος, 3 *hopoios* of what sort, what kind of*

As correlative pron. in Acts 26:29; Gal 2:6; as interrogative pron. in indirect questions in 1 Cor 3:13; 1 Thess 1:9; Jas 1:24.

ὁπότε *hopote* when, since

This temporal particle is used with the ind. to refer to specific past events: Luke 6:3 A R Θ al; *Barn.* 12:9. BDF §455.1.

ὅπου *hopou* where, to where

Lit.: BAGD s.v. — BDF §§293; 300; 456. — C. Fabricius, *Zu den Jugendschriften des Johannes Chrysostomos* (Diss. Lund, 1962) 74-79. — LSJ s.v. — Mayser, *Grammatik* II/1, 76; II/3, 52. — Moulton, *Grammar* III, 116. — Moulton / Milligan s.v. — Pape, *Wörterbuch* s.v. — L. Rydbeck, *Fachprosa, vermeintliche Volksprache und NT* (SGU 5, 1967) 119-44, esp. 132-37. — Zerwick, *Biblical Greek* §217. — Zorell, *Lexicon* s.v.

1. The (in)definite rel. adv. of place (synonym of → οὗ, which appears in John 6:62; 10:40; and Acts 20:6 as a v.l. [contrast Zerwick §217]; correlative with → ποῦ; cf. Apollonius Dyscolus *Adv.* 172.10; known from the time of Herodotus) is found 82 times in the NT (excluding the secondary repetition of Mark 9:44, 46), esp. in John (30 occurrences) and the Synoptic Gospels (13 occurrences in Matthew, 15 in Mark, and 15 in Luke—in Matthew and Mark only in parallel passages, elsewhere οὗ; cf. BDF §293); but infrequently in the Pauline corpus (only Rom 15:20; 1 Cor 3:3; Col 3:11). It is lacking in the Pastoral Epistles, 1 Peter, 1–3 John, and Jude.

Its use as an interrogative pron. (only in indirect questions; known from the time of Homer *Od.*) cannot be substantiated in the NT (*contra* Moulton III, 116; Zorell s.v. 1.b; cf. generally BDF §300.1; only one example from papyri in Mayser II/3, 52; on this → ποῦ, e.g., John 14:4f.).

2. Ὅπου is used a) literally and b) figuratively.

a) 1) When used literally, it occurs with the ind. and means *where.* It is frequently found after a reference to place (BAGD s.v. 1.a.α), instead of the (prep. with) rel. pron. (e.g., Mark 6:10: ὅπου . . . εἰς . . . , par. Matt 10:11/ Luke 9:4: εἰς ἥν . . .), esp. after τόπος (cf. Dan 2:38 Theodotion): Matt 28:6 par. Mark 16:6; John 4:20; 6:23; 10:40; 11:30; 19:18, 20, 41; Rev 12:14 (in the last passage and in 12:6 with the pleonastic ἐκεῖ [cf., e.g., Ruth 3:4; likewise Rev 17:9: ὅπου . . . ἐπ᾽ αὐτῶν; see BAGD s.v.]). The correlative ἐκεῖ (cf. scholium C in Dionysius Thrax [ed. A. Hilgard, *Grammatici Graeci* I/3 (1901)] 27.16f.: ἐπιφέρεται . . . τὸ ἐκεῖ) follows ὅπου in Matt 6:21 par. Luke 12:34; Luke 17:37; John 12:26 (BAGD s.v.; after οὗ in Matt 18:20; v.l. ὅπου omitted in *NTG*[26]). It can also be delimited by the context (*there* or *to there;* 11 and 7 instances, respectively, in BAGD s.v.). Ὅπου plus ἄν with the impf. serves to give the past iterative *(wherever)* in Mark 6:56 (BAGD s.v. 1.a.β; cf. Xenophon *Ages.* ii.24).

It is found with the aor. subjunc. in Mark 14:14b = Luke 22:11 (final rel. clause; see BAGD s.v. 1.a.γ) and the conjoining ἐάν (pres. or fut. iterative; examples since the 4th cent. B.C. in Rydbeck 132n.3, 135-37; see also BAGD s.v. 1.a.δ; Mayser II/1, 76; Moulton/Milligan s.v.) in Matt 26:13 par. Mark 14:9; Mark 9:18; 14:14a (v.l. ἄν omitted in *NTG*[26]; likewise Luke 22:10: εἰς ἥν, v.l. οὗ [ἄν, ἐάν]). The correlative ἐκεῖ (see above) follows in Mark 6:10 and Matt 24:28 (ὅπου ἐάν with the pres. subjunc.; omitted in Luke 17:37). The partitive gen. is not found with ὅπου in the NT (cf., e.g., Pape s.v.).

2) Ὅπου with the ind. after a reference to place, meaning *to where* (ὅποι is lacking in the NT; cf. generally Fabricius), does not appear in the NT (fig. in Heb 6:20; but cf. BAGD s.v. οὗ 2), except with the amplifying ἐκεῖ *(to there;* 7 references in BAGD s.v. 1.b.α).

Ὅπου with the pres. subjunc. and ἄν *(to wherever;* with the aor. subjunc., e.g., Plato *Euthphr.* 11.b, c) is found in Rev 14:4, and with ἐάν (→ a.1; instead of ἄν: both v.l. Jas 3:4; cf. Moulton/Milligan s.v.) in Matt 8:19 par. Luke 9:57 (cf. οὗ ἐάν, 1 Cor 16:6).

b) In the fig. sense, ὅπου indicates 1) (temporal) circumstance or condition *(when;* cf. Zorell s.v. 2.a; LSJ s.v. II.1) in Col 3:11; Heb 9:16; 10:18; and with the correlative ἐκεῖ (→ a.1) in Jas 3:16; or 2) causal *(inasmuch as, since;* cf. BAGD s.v. 2.b; ὅπου γε [see LSJ s.v. II.2; BAGD s.v. 2.b] is not found in the NT) in 1 Cor 3:3. The interpretation of 1 Pet 2:11 varies *(where* [i.e., in the situation in which], BAGD s.v. 2.a; *while,* Moulton/Milligan s.v.; *since,* BDF §456.3).   A. Horstmann

ὀπτάνομαι *optanomai* appear*

In Acts 1:3 for the risen Jesus: δι᾽ ἡμερῶν τεσσεράκοντα ὀπτανόμενος αὐτοῖς, "*when he appeared* to them [the disciples] over a period of forty days." W. Michaelis, *TDNT* V, 344.

ὀπτασία, ας, ἡ *optasia* vision, appearance*

2 Cor 12:1: "but I want to go on to *visions* and revelations (ἀποκαλύψεις) of the Lord"; cf. H. Saake, *Bib* 53 (1972) 404-10; *idem, NovT* 15 (1973) 153-60; K. H. Schelkle, *TQ* 158 (1978) 285-93; A. T. Lincoln, "Paul the Visionary," *NTS* 25 (1978/79) 204-20. In Acts 26:19 the Lukan Paul speaks of the "heavenly *vision*," i.e., the Christophany on the way to Damascus, to which he "was not disobedient." The two occurrences in Luke refer to the appearing of an angel: 1:22 to the angel appearing to Zacharias in the temple, and 24:23 to the two angels appearing to the women at the grave of Jesus. W. Michaelis, *TDNT* V, 372f.; K. Dahn, *DNTT* III, 515.

ὀπτός, 3 *optos* broiled, fried*

Luke 24:42: the *"broiled* fish" that the disciples gave to the risen Jesus. The fact that the risen Jesus ate "before their very eyes" (v. 43) underscores the corporeal nature of the resurrection (cf. the misgivings in vv. 37f.).

ὀπώρα, ας, ἡ *opōra* fruit*

Rev 18:14: ἡ ὀπώρα σου τῆς ἐπιθυμίας τῆς ψυχῆς, "the *fruit* that your [Babylon] soul desired."

ὅπως *hopōs* how, in which way; that, in order that

1. Occurrences in the NT — 2. Usage and meaning — 3. Theological emphases

Lit.: BAGD s.v. — BDF §§369; 392.1.c. — LSJ s.v. — MAYSER, *Grammatik* II/1, 254-57.

1. Ὅπως occurs 53 times in the NT, predominantly in Matthew (17 occurrences) and Luke-Acts (21 occurrences). By contrast, in the Epistles it is found 8 times in Paul (including 2 Thess 1:12), twice in Hebrews, and twice in the Catholic Epistles (Jas 5:16; 1 Pet 2:9). It also occurs in Mark 3:6 and John 11:57.

2. Ὅπως, which in classical Greek is a frequently used, multifaceted particle (esp. from the time of Thucydides and Xenophon; cf. LSJ s.v.), is sometimes found in the NT in adv. but primarily in subjunc. constructions, as it already was in the approximately 500 LXX occurrences. As an adv. *(how, in which way)* ὅπως is used to introduce indirect questions (Luke 24:20), and as a conj. *(that, so that)* it is used with the subjunc. to indicate purpose, goal, or objective (Matt 2:8; 5:16), and is strengthened with ἄν (Luke 2:35; Acts 3:20) and negated with μή (Luke 16:26; 1 Cor 1:29). In final clauses ὅπως can be used interchangeably and with the same

meaning as ἵνα, as is frequently attested in the papyri (Mayser), and in conjunction with ἄν as was characteristic of official documents and the legal language of the Ptolemaic era; in the NT, e.g., in Paul (1 Cor 1:28f.; 2 Cor 8:14) and Luke (16:24, 26-28). Ὅπως can also pick up and continue a preceding ἵνα clause, as it does in 2 Thess 1:11f. Noteworthy is its use after verbs of asking (Matt 9:38; Luke 10:2) and deciding (Matt 12:14; 22:15; cf. Mark 3:6) instead of the inf. (cf. BDF §392.1.c).

3. Theological emphases are evident in conjunction with the OT quotations introduced by Matthew, the fulfillment character of which is designated by ὅπως ("so that it might be fulfilled"; "in this way was fulfilled"), thus proclaiming the will of God revealed in the Scriptures in connection with a specific event (Matt 2:23; 8:17; 13:35). Ὅπως is also characteristically used after verbs of asking in a precatory style that combines trusting knowledge (imv.) and obedient submission (subjunc.: Matt 9:38 par. Luke 10:2; Acts 8:15, 24; Jas 5:16). While vbs. of decision always combine ὅπως with a negative obj. and reveal the evil of the Jewish leaders (Mark 3:6; Matt 12:14; 22:15), the christological statements of Hebrews (2:9 and 9:15: the saving significance of the death of Jesus) and the ecclesiologically important passage 1 Pet 2:9 (duty of proclamation of the people of God based on their calling) have an unambiguously positive sense.   A. Kretzer

ὅραμα, ατος, τό *horama* that which is seen, appearance, vision*

1. Occurrences in the NT — 2. Relation to the appearances of the resurrected Jesus — 3. Meaning in the LXX — 4. "Appearance" in Acts

Lit.: H.-W. BARTSCH, "Inhalt und Funktion des urchristlichen Osterglaubens," *NTS* 26 (1979/80) 180-96. — BAGD s.v. — M. BUBER, *Ecstatic Confessions* (1985). — K. Dahn, *DNTT* III, 511-18. — F. G. DOWNING, *Has Christianity a Revelation?* (1964). — J. S. HANSON, "Dreams and Visions in the Graeco-Roman World and Early Christianity," *ANRW* II/23/2 (1980) 1395-1427. — W. Michaelis, *TDNT* V, 371f. — For further bibliography see *TWNT* X, 1204f.

1. Ὅραμα occurs 12 times in the NT, all in Acts, except for Matt 17:9, where it is a redaction of ἃ εἶδον in Mark 9:9. It is lacking in primitive Christian literature and in the Apostolic Fathers. Ὅραμα occurs 43 times in the LXX. Of the 7 occurrences in Isaiah, 6 have ῥῆμα as v.l. In Daniel it often interchanges with → ὅρασις. In both OT and NT apocalyptic the same interchangeability can be observed. In the Pseudo-Clementine homilies, the ὁράματα to which Simon (= Paul) appeals are discounted, specifically the appearance of Jesus in xvii.19.1.

2. Ὅραμα is never used to describe the appearance of Christ. The early Christian tradition in 1 Cor 15:5-7,

Χριστὸς . . . ὤφθη Κηφᾷ (cf. Luke 24:34), is not included among the prophetic visions. This accounts for the disuse of the term in early Christian tradition. Nevertheless, in Acts 7:30f. Luke posits a link between the exclusive use of ὤφθη (→ ὁράω 4, 5) and ὅραμα in the quotation of Exod 3:3f., and furthermore combines ὤφθη with ὅραμα in Acts 16:9: ὅραμα διὰ τῆς νυκτὸς Παύλῳ ὤφθη (cf. v. 10). He thus reveals the exclusive character of ὤφθη and places the appearance of Christ, for all intents and purposes, in line with the OT visions.

3. In Gen 15:1 and 46:2 ἐν ὁράματι refers functionally to the coming of the word to Abraham and Jacob, even as it does in Num 12:6 and in Daniel. The same expression can also, however, indicate the mighty deeds of the Lord in Deut 4:34; 26:8; 28:34, 67; here ὅραμα is found along with βραχίων κυρίου, τέρατα, and σημεῖα.

The variants in Isaiah (→ 1) show that the appearances are verbal revelations. That is also true of the occurrences in Daniel and later apocalyptic. Thus the great visions in the Greek portion of *1 Enoch* are always individually called ὅραμα, as they are also generally labeled in 83:1. In the Christian era the title ἀποκάλυψις is subsequently given to such visions in Rev 1:1, *5 Esdras, Apocalypse of Sedrach, Apocalypse of John, Apocalypse of Paul,* etc.

4. Ἐν ὁράματι in Acts 9:10, 12, the Lord's instruction to Ananias to go to Paul, has a functional sense. The instruction to Cornelius in 10:3 is introduced with the same expression. In 18:9 the instruction of the Lord goes out to Paul: ἐν νυκτὶ δι' ὁράματος. The designation of the vision of Peter in 10:17, 19 as ὅραμα, on the other hand, corresponds to the usage in the apocalyses (→ 3). This is underscored in 11:5 in Peter's report: καὶ εἶδον ἐν ἐκστάσει ὅραμα.

Although this usage of ὅραμα is generally determined by the LXX, Acts 12:9 refers to the liberating angel: [Πέτρος] ἐδόκει δὲ ὅραμα βλέπειν. The use of ὅραμα as opposed to reality is nowhere else attested.

H.-W. Bartsch

ὅρασις, εως, ἡ *horasis* appearance, seeing, vision, spectacle*

Lit.: BAGD s.v. — W. Michaelis, *TDNT* V, 370f. — For further bibliography → ὅραμα, → ὁράω; see *TWNT* X, 1204f.

1. Ὅρασις occurs 4 times in the NT: it means *vision/apparition* in Acts 2:17 (quoting Joel 3:1) and in Rev 9:17; it means *appearance* in Rev 4:3 (bis). In *2 Clem.* 1:6 it refers to seeing as "eyesight/sight," and in 7:6 and 17:5 it is found in the quotation of Isa 66:24. In continuity with OT apocalyptic, ὅρασις also has an established role in NT apocalyptic.

2. In the LXX, ὅρασις occurs more than 110 times with a wide variety of meanings. It often has → ὅραμα (1, 3) as a variant. The range of meanings extends from the beautiful "appearance" of the tree in Gen 2:8 to the name of the springs in

24:62 and 25:11 (τὸ φρέαρ τῆς ὁράσεως, meaning uncertain, perhaps a cultic etiology) to the meaning "vision" found in (though predating) Daniel and Ezekiel. In Ezek 1:1 the seer calls the content of his book: εἶδον ὁράσεις θεοῦ. This designation is also found in Num 24:4, 16; Ezek 8:3; 40:2. In terms of content, however, it applies to all visions.

One can infer from Rev 9:17 that early Christian apocalyptic took on ὅρασις as a t.t. The author of *Hermas Visions* uses ὅρασις as the title for three of the visions as well as employing the term 10 other times. Later apocalypses written under the name of Daniel have the title in Codex Parisiensis 947: ἐσχάτη ὅρασις τοῦ Δανιήλ (K. von Tischendorf, *Apocalypses Apocryphae* [1866 = 1966] XXX). Likewise, the *Apocalypse of Paul* refers to the τρίτη ὅρασις of an angel (von Tischendorf 35). With time, however, this designation, too, gives way to the imposing term ἀποκάλυψις (→ ὅραμα 3).

H.-W. Bartsch

ὁρατός, 3 *horatos* visible
→ ὁράω 1, 6.

ὁράω *horaō* see
ἀόρατος, 2 *aoratos* invisible*
ὁρατός, 3 *horatos* visible*

1. Occurrences and basic meaning — 2. Usage — 3. Seeing and believing — 4. Prophetic/apocalyptic (visionary) seeing — 5. Appearances of the resurrected Jesus — 6. (Not) seeing God

Lit.: H.-W. BARTSCH, "Inhalt und Funktion des urchristlichen Osterglaubens," *NTS* 26 (1979/80) 180-96. — H. F. FUHS, *Sehen und Schauen. Die Wurzel ḥzh im Alten Orient und im AT* (FzB 32, 1978). — H. GESE, "The Question of a World View," *idem, Essays on Biblical Theology* (1981) 223-46. — F. HAHN, "Sehen und Glauben im Johannesevangelium," FS Cullmann (1972) 125-41. — P. HOFFMANN, *TRE* IV, 478-513. — J. KREMER, *Die Osterevangelien—Geschichten um Geschichte* (1977). — F. LENTZEN-DEIS, *Die Taufe Jesu nach den Synoptikern* (FTS 4, 1970). — J. LINDBLOM, *Gesichte und Offenbarungen* (1968) 85-89. — W. MARXSEN, *The Resurrection of Jesus of Nazareth* (1970). — W. MICHAELIS, *TDNT* V, 315-70. — F. MUSSNER, *Die johanneische Sehweise und die Frage nach dem historischen Jesus* (QD 28, 1965). — A. PELLETIER, "Les apparitions du Ressuscité en termes de la Septante," *Bib* 51 (1970) 76-79. — R. PESCH, "Zur Entstehung des Glaubens an die Auferstehung Jesu," *TQ* 153 (1973) 201-28, 270-83. — H. SCHLIER, *Über die Auferstehung Jesu Christi* (1968). — D. VETTER, *THAT* I, 533-37; II, 692-701. — A. VÖGTLE and R. PESCH, *Wie kam es zum Osterglauben?* (1975). — H. WENZ, "Sehen und Glauben bei Johannes," *TZ* 17 (1961) 17-25. — U. WILCKENS, "Der Ursprung der Überlieferung der Erscheinungen des Auferstandenen," *Dogma und Denkstrukturen* (ed. W. Joest and W. Pannenberg; 1963) 56-95 (cf. *idem, Resurrection* [1978]). — For further bibliography see *TWNT* X, 1204f.

1. The vb. ὁράω appears 449 times in the NT (including those forms built from other stems [esp. εἶδον, *ca.*

350 occurrences], but excluding ἴδε, ἰδού); other vbs. that express seeing are less frequent in the NT. The verbal adj. ὁρατός is found only in Col 1:16, and ἀόρατος occurs 6 times (→ 6). Because of its durative meaning ("to be seeing"), only the pres., imf., and pf. are attested for the ὁρ- stem. The aor. pass. ὤφθην (and the fut. pass. ὀφθή-σομαι) as well as the fut. ὄψομαι (and ὄψησθε in Luke 13:28 v.l.) are built from the ὀπ- stem, and the aor. εἶδον from the ἰδ- stem (cf. οἶδα). The vb. can be trans. (with an acc. object or a subordinate clause [ὅτι]) or intrans. (without an obj., with a prep. [εἰς, πρός], or with an acc. of reference).

The basic meaning of ὁράω is *see* (with the eyes). The act. forms refer to the activity implicit in the act of seeing, and the mid. fut. forms to the subjective aspect. When used fig., ὁράω means *perceive, recognize, experience, visit, consider*. As in the LXX (equivalent of *r'h* and *ḥzh;* cf. Michaelis 324ff.), ὁράω in the NT is often used as a synonym for → βλέπω, → θεωρέω, → θεάομαι.

When interpreting the word one must keep in mind that in antiquity the photographic model of seeing (exclusion of the mental aspect), the positive correspondence between reality and perception, and the categories of contemporary psychology (subjective and objective) were unknown (cf. Gese 228).

2. The subject of ὁράω in the NT is always a person (or the πνεῦμα [Mark 9:20] or δράκων [Rev 12:13] conceived as persons). Ὁράω is never used in the NT in references to aesthetic qualities, and only occasionally in connection with everyday objects (e.g., the coin for paying taxes in Mark 12:15; boats in Luke 5:2; → βλέπω is used more frequently for this). Usually, ὁράω refers to people, e.g., Jesus, the disciples, the sick, the Pharisees, or the crowd. The one who *sees* is able to perceive particular persons in their individuality (cf. "*see* the face" in Acts 20:25; Col 2:1), often in their individual mode of being or conduct (e.g., Matt 11:8; Mark 1:16). Very often ὁράω refers to supernatural acts (→ 3). Natural occurrences, e.g., the cloud in Luke 12:54, are usually objects of ὁράω only when they bear some symbolic significance, e.g., stars (Matt 2:2, 10), earthquake (27:54). In addition, to the *seeing* of people, ὁράω can refer to supernatural beings (→ 4), the resurrected Christ (→ 5), or even God (→ 6).

This primarily anthropocentric usage also comes into play when the basic meaning of *see* has all but lost its significance and ὁράω has a fig. sense. Thus, ὁράω often means *recognize* (e.g., "their faith" in Matt 9:2; "that he [Jesus] was condemned," 27:3; "that they are not walking according to the truth of the gospel," Gal 2:14). In Acts 15:6, ὁράω means *test/examine* (cf. Luke 2:15). On more than one occasion ὁράω means *find/discover* (e.g., Matt 2:11), *find/meet* (e.g., Matt 11:8f. par.; Rom 1:11; also John 12:21), or *visit* (1 Cor 16:7; Heb 13:23). Under the influence of the OT, ὁράω often means *experience* (e.g.,

"*see* the realization of" in Acts 2:27, 31; Heb 11:5), "*see* the kingdom of God" (John 3:3). In the imv., ὁράω often has an intrans. meaning: "*be careful*" (Matt 16:6), "*see to it*" (27:24; cf. 27:4; Acts 18:15), and with a following μή plus aor. subjunc.: "*make sure not . . .*" (e.g., Mark 1:44). Here also belongs the elliptical expression ὅρα μή (ποιήσῃς): "*Make sure not* (to do it)" (Rev 19:10; 22:9).

3. In the Gospels, ὁράω (and → βλέπω, etc.) often refers to the deeds of Jesus, which earlier generations were not able to *see* (i.e., experience; Luke 10:24 par.). Different reactions (e.g., consternation in Matt 9:8; praise in Mark 2:12 par.; Luke 18:43; 19:37; rejection in Matt 21:15) are based on different ways of seeing: whether out of pure curiosity (Luke 23:8), or sign-demanding unbelief (Matt 12:38; Mark 15:32; John 4:48; 6:30; 20:25), or faith as indicated in John (prior [9:37; 20:8, 29; cf. 11:45]; or subsequent [11:40]; cf. Hahn 136f.). In John, ὁράω many times indicates a seeing that does not comprehend the full dimension of that which is seen and therefore does not lead to faith (cf. 6:36; 12:40; 15:24); furthermore, ὁράω often indicates a faith-related perception of Jesus' glory in his "signs" (1 John 1:3f.; cf. John 1:14). Such believing sight is promised to the disciples in 1:39, 50f. and is granted to Thomas in 20:27ff. (cf. Wenz 19f.; Kremer 192f.); it even causes one to see the Father in Jesus (14:7, 9; → 6). As a result of this "Johannine mode of seeing" (Mussner 18-24) the disciples and John the Baptist (1:34) are qualified to be witnesses of Jesus and his work (3:11; 19:35; 1 John 1:2), just as Jesus can give witness of the Father (John 3:32; cf. 6:46). As a result of the witness of the disciples, later generations are enabled to believe without *seeing* (20:29; cf. 1 Pet 1:8).

4. Many of the occurrences of ὁράω in the NT must be interpreted in the light of the prophetic and apocalyptic texts of the OT and Judaism (cf. Michaelis 328-40; Vetter I, 537; II, 701; Fuhs [bibliography]); thus, e.g., the "signifying vision" (Lentzen-Dies) at the baptism (Mark 1:10) and the *seeing* of the appearance (ὤφθη) at the transfiguration (Mark 9:4, 9), but also the statements on *seeing* the Son of Man (Mark 13:26; 14:62). The individual authors rarely use ὁράω in this sense in the same way.

Thus Luke is heavily dependent on the LXX for his use of ὁράω and εἶδον (cf. Acts 7:2, 30, 35, 44) and writes more frequently of the appearances of angels (Luke 1:11; 22:43; Acts 11:13), which he generally characterizes as ὀπτασία (Luke 1:22; 24:23), and relatively frequently (cf. Acts 2:17 [Joel 3:3]) of visions (Acts 7:55; 10:3, 17; 11:5, 6; 16:9). He includes among them the appearance of Christ on Saul's way to Damascus (9:17; 22:14f.; 26:16) and in the temple (22:18), which he distinguishes from the appearance at the ascension (13:31; cf. 1:3; → 5). The visionary experiences, including those that are more specifically described as "in a vision" (10:3, 17), "in a dream" (16:9), or "in a trance" (11:5; 22:18), are in Luke's opinion in no way simply inner psychological phenomena (cf. Luke 24:22 with 24:6; and Acts 26:16 with 26:13f.); they are depicted in a way that is related to the Hellenistic epiphany reports (Lindblom 75-77).

According to John, Abraham and Isaiah already *saw* in a prophetic way the day and the glory of Christ (8:57; 12:41), and John the Baptist *saw* at the baptism who Jesus was (1:33-34). The disciples were promised that they would *see* the glory of the Son of Man (1:51; cf. 1:39, 50): following Gen 28:12, the early Church sayings on the eschatological seeing of the Son of Man (Mark 14:62) are related to the (interpretive) *seeing* of the glory of Christ in the life of Jesus that is derived from faith (→ 3). Apocalyptic language is present in the farewell speech in the form of present eschatology: "and again a little while and *you will see* me" (John 16:16-19; cf. R. Bultmann, *John* [Eng. tr., 1971] 576f.). The wordplay "but *I will see* [visit] you again" (16:22) demonstrates that ὁράω here means the new communion of life with Christ (17:3).

In Revelation, εἶδον frequently (e.g., in 1:9-20) refers to the visionary experiences of the seer in a trance (1:10; 4:2). The style of the many only apparently related "visions" and their literary dependence on the OT and Jewish models (on this see esp. H. Kraft, *Rev* [HNT] 38) forces us to conclude that εἶδον here, as in other apocalypses, is often used in a rather formulaic sense. The author considers that which he has received or himself prophesied as "inspiration" and lends it authority with this formula (Lindblom 237).

5. The appearances of the risen Christ were in the oldest texts indicated exclusively by ὁράω. In 1 Cor 15:5-8 and Luke 24:34 (cf. Acts 13:31) ὤφθη can be translated as an aor. mid., *appeared/let himself be seen*, in accordance with LXX usage. Interpreting this phrase as a theological pass., "God caused him to be visible," founders on the fact that Christ is the subj. Only occasionally is ὤφθη found in general contexts, e.g., Acts 7:26; in the LXX it is a t.t. for theophanies and angelophanies (Pelletier 76f.; Bartsch 184ff.; cf. also Acts 7:2, 30, 35), thus also frequently in the NT (e.g., Luke 1:22; 22:43; Mark 9:4 par.). Therefore, one ought not to deny ὤφθη any visual element, as though it were simply a formulaic term for revelation (Michaelis 358-61; *contra* Vögtle and Pesch 42ff., and Hoffmann 492f.). It is not used here simply as a legitimation formula (in order to establish the authority of Cephas et al.) without reference to the appearance (Wilckens 75; Marxsen 98ff.; Busse 101ff.; Pesch 213ff.; *contra* esp. Vögtle and Pesch 44ff.); ὤφθη is used for such a purpose neither in the prophets nor elsewhere in the NT, and clearly not in 1 Cor 15:6 ("to more than 500 brothers") or 1 Tim 3:16 ("to the angels");

standing as it does at the end of the sequence "died . . . buried . . . raised . . . ," ὤφθη can be understood as nothing other than a statement about an event and a confirmation of the assertion "raised"; ὤφθη assumes here a heavenly dwelling and the power of the crucified Christ to act, which made the appearances possible (Vögtle and Pesch 58). The choice of this t.t. can signify that the power characteristic of Yahweh and the angels to appear visibly is ascribed to the resurrected Christ (Bartsch 196 even sees in this the transference of κύριος titles to Jesus). In any case, ὤφθη in 1 Cor 15:5-8 and Luke 24:34 implies that the crucified Jesus allowed himself to be recognized in a personal way by several persons he knew by name (thus not simply an "event" [Marxsen 115f.] without an "encounter" [Schlier 38]).

In 1 Cor 15:8, Paul includes himself among the Easter witnesses of the resurrected Christ (unlike Acts 9:17; 26:16 in comparison with 13:31). He uses ἑώρακα, *I have seen*, in 1 Cor 9:1 analogously with Isa 6:1, 5 (εἶδον τὸν κύριον) to underscore his authority (cf. Vögtle and Pesch 65f.), but at the same time to express his personal "*seeing*" of the appearances (1 Cor 15:8) or "revelation" (Gal 1:12, 15f.). Due to the mode of existence of that which was perceived (cf. 1 Cor 15:44), this was not a routine "seeing," but rather a perception that leads to recognition (cf. Phil 3:10); according to 2 Cor 4:6 and 1 Cor 12:3 it was not possible without → πνεῦμα. Since Paul does not assume that the Corinthians have experienced the same thing in 1 Cor 9:1, this *seeing* should be distinguished from any other "coming to faith" (Marxsen 104ff., 149ff.). Paul does not include it among his ecstatic experiences in 2 Cor 12:1ff.

In Mark 16:7 a *seeing* of the resurrected one in the near future is announced (ὄψεσθε, *you will see*). This does not refer to the parousia (as again recently was assumed by Bartsch 191n.15). The vivid portraits of John 20:18, 20, 25, 27, 29 clearly state that in order to see Jesus a call (v. 16), self-disclosure (v. 20), and faith (v. 27) were required (cf. Kremer 171f., 186f., 192f.).

In the Lukan writings, the appearances before the ascension are depicted as a materialization (ὁράω is completely lacking). The increasingly material conceptions of the Easter gospel correspond to the choice of θεάομαι in Mark 16:11; θεωρέω in Luke 24:37, 39; John 20:14; φανερόω in John 21:1, 14; Mark 16:12, 14; *Barn.* 15:9; φαίνω in Mark 16:9; Justin *Apol.* i.67.7; *Dial.* 138.1; ἐμφανῆ γενέσθαι in Acts 10:40; and ὀπτάνομαι in Acts 1:3.

6. God himself is characterized in Col 1:15; 1 Tim 1:17; Heb 11:27 (in accordance with Jewish-Hellenistic usage) as ἀόρατος, *the invisible one*, not least in distinction from the pagan concept of the visible presence of the gods in cultic images. In Col 1:16 τὰ ἀόρατα, *the invisible things*, refers to the powers listed there in contrast to τὰ

ὀρατά, *the visible things* (the perceivable world). In Rom 1:20 τὰ ἀόρατα αὐτοῦ, *the invisible things* (of God), refers to those things that are "perceived" by the intellect in the works of creation (→ καθοράω), the omnipotence and sovereignty of God that are hidden from the human senses and are often denied by humans (H. Schlier, *Rom* [HTKNT] ad loc.; cf. U. Wilckens, *Rom* I [EKKNT] 116-21).

1 John 4:20 and 1 Tim 6:16 express the conviction found in Hellenistic Judaism that no one can *see* God. John 1:18; 5:37; and 6:46 mention this in order to accentuate the uniqueness of Jesus, who *has seen* the Father (John 6:46); in him the believer is able to *see* the Father: "Whoever *sees* me *sees* the Father" (John 14:9; ἑωρακώς and ἑώρακεν have here a present meaning; cf. John 12:45). 3 John 11 should also be understood in this way: "Whoever does evil *has* not *seen* God," i.e., has not recognized God in Christ (cf. 1 John 3:6).

From this must be distinguished the few promises of the eschatological vision of God: in Matt 5:8 as the granting of the vision (i.e., experience, sought after in the temple) of the face of God for those who are "pure in heart" (not just cultically clean); 1 John 3:2 and Rev 22:4 as fulfillment of the hope of the revelation and vision of God or his glory (cf. Isa 40:5; 62:2f.; 66:18; Ps 84:8, etc.).   J. Kremer

ὀργή, ῆς, ἡ *orgē* wrath*

1. Occurrences and meaning — 2. Human wrath — 3. "Wrath" in the words and deeds of Jesus — 4. God's wrath in NT theologies

. *Lit.:* G. BORNKAMM, "The Revelation of God's Wrath," idem, *Early Christian Experience* (1969) 47-70. — BULTMANN, *Theology* I, 288f. — H. CONZELMANN, *RGG* VI, 1931f. — H.-J. ECKSTEIN, " 'Denn Gottes Zorn wird vom Himmel her offenbar werden.' Exegetische Erwägungen zur Röm 1,18," *ZNW* 78 (1987) 74-89. — A. T. HANSON, *The Wrath of the Lamb* (1957). — G. HEROLD, *Zorn und Gerechtigkeit Gottes bei Paulus. Eine Untersuchung zu Röm 1,16-18* (EHS 23/14, 1973). — G. H. C. MacGREGOR, "The Concept of the Wrath of God in the NT," *NTS* 7 (1960/61) 101-9. — H. RINGGREN, "Einige Schilderungen des göttlichen Zorns," *Tradition und Situation* (FS A. Weiser, 1963) 107-13. — C. SCHOONHOVEN, *The Wrath of Heaven* (1966). — G. SCHRENK, *Unser Glaube an den Zorn Gottes nach dem Römerbrief* (1944). — G. STÄHLIN, *TDNT* V, 419-48. — P. STUHLMACHER, *Gerechtigkeit Gottes bei Paulus* (FRLANT 87, 1966). — R. V. G. TASKER, *The Biblical Doctrine of the Wrath of God* (1951). — U. WILCKENS, *Rom* (EKKNT) I (1978) 101f. — For further bibliography see *TWNT* X, 1205.

1. Ὀργή referred originally to "the impulsive nature," but gained already in classical Greek a connection with tragedy ("demonic excess of the will") and with theology ("the righteous wrath of God"). In the LXX, ὀργή is found not infrequently with → θυμός with precisely the same meaning. This usage is also typical of the NT, where,

however, ὀργή is preferred for the wrath of God, probably because it had fewer connotations of emotion and excess. Ὀργή is found 36 times in the NT, of which 12 fall in Romans alone. Revelation has 6 occurrences, then follow 1 Thessalonians and Ephesians with 3 each. The wrathful indignation that leads to bitterness, called παροργισμός in Eph 4:26 (and only there; cf. Eph 6:4), exceeds the bounds of ὀργή; → ὀργίζομαι.

2. In addition, ὀργή in the NT refers to *wrath* as a human emotion. With this meaning the term stands along with → πικρία and → θυμός. The key passage for evaluating the NT usage is Jas 1:20: humans do in wrath that which is not right before God (cf. 1:19). According to Rev 11:18 the wrath of the nations is the same as the wrath of the dragon over the saving work of God (cf. 12:17). These fundamental theological dispositions are also found in the ethical judgments of the deutero-Pauline letters. While Paul still spoke of the renunciation of revenge, making room for the wrath of God (Rom 12:19), the deutero-Pauline letters speak of wrath as an inferior human trait, and usually as a sin of the tongue (Col 3:8; Eph 4:31). One must be especially on one's guard for this sin; one should not provoke the wrath of others (Eph 6:4: μὴ παροργίζετε). Only in this way will one be pure for worship (1 Tim 2:8; cf. Tit 1:7). Here and in later writings (e.g., Ign. *Phld.* 1:2; 8:1) Stoic influence cannot be ruled out. Yet the warning against human wrath in the NT is taken in a fundamentally religious sense: "wrath does not contribute to the righteousness that matters before God" (Stählin 442).

3. Ὀργή also appears in passages dealing with the words and deeds of Jesus (Mark 3:5). Jesus displays wrath toward Satan (Matt 4:10; 16:23) and the demons (Mark 1:25; 9:25; Luke 4:41), and he is wrathful toward diabolical people (John 8:44; cf. Matt 23:33). His wrath meets every form of unbelief (John 11:33) and lack of understanding (11:38). His full wrath (that which most deeply saddens him) is directed toward the Pharisees (Mark 3:5), since he is not able to overcome their lack of repentance. In the parables of Jesus such wrath is occasionally explicitly mentioned (Luke 14:21; Matt 18:34). In these passages the wrath of Jesus approaches ever more closely the wrath of the eschatological judge: he judges the unrepentant cities (Matt 11:20-24) and the traders in the temple (21:12-13); he casts them into the valley of fire (11:23; cf. 13:42; 25:41; 22:7). In Revelation it is proclaimed concerning Jesus Christ that he wades in the blood of his enemies and tramples the winepress of the wine of God's wrath (19:15; → θυμός). The wrath of the Lamb (6:16) is the wrath of the exalted Lord toward the enemies of God.

4. In the NT ὀργή usually expresses the judgment of God (Rom 3:5f.), in part using traditional formulas (Rom

2:8 together with θυμός) and older conceptions (2:5: "day of *wrath*"). As the proclamation goes, Christians are saved from "the judgment of the *wrath* of God" through Jesus Christ (1 Thess 1:9f.; Rom 5:9). John the Baptist already preached → μετάνοια (3) for deliverance from the wrath (Matt 3:7f. par. Luke 3:7f.). Among the sayings of Jesus, ὀργή occurs in the message concerning the destruction of the holy city (Luke 21:23). The several occurrences in Revelation expand this further when they speak of the coming wrath of God (11:18; 19:15), of the cup of the wine of God's wrath (14:8-10; 16:19), of the great day of wrath (6:17), and of a day of the wrath of the Lamb (6:16; for details → θυμός). In the images of the fire (→ πῦρ), of the chaotic waters (Matt 24:38f.; → κατακλυσμός), and of the poison cup (→ βασανίζω), as well as those of the scales of wrath, the winepress of wrath, and the "reserves" of wrath (Rom 2:5), we are dealing with the eschatological wrath of God. Johannine theology, moreover, emphasizes the presence of this eschatological wrath here and now, albeit only once (John 3:36): the saving mission of Jesus becomes a judgment for the one who does not believe in Jesus; the unbeliever is already in the realm of the dead. Behind this lies for John the demand that the individual person accept the witness of the Son (3:31-36).

According to Paul, the wrath of God will be borne out in the final judgment (Rom 2:5, 8; 3:5; 5:9; 9:22a, b; 1 Thess 1:10; 5:9); the Pauline school also retained this concept (Col 3:6; Eph 5:6; cf. 2:3). In Romans, however, Paul also speaks explicitly of the present activity of God, of the saving and judging function of the gospel (1:17f.), which ultimately confronts both Jew and Gentile, i.e., all humanity, with decision. In his theology of the ὀργή of God, Paul takes a twofold position: on the one hand he holds to the future character of the eschatological wrath and to the expectation of the judgment of God "according to works" (2:5ff.); on the other hand he can speak of the present revelation of wrath, which is contrasted with the revelation of δικαιοσύνη. Beyond faith in the gospel, there is only ὀργή (cf. 3:9ff., 23). The double revelation of the wrath and righteousness of God (4:15; 13:4f.; 1 Thess 2:16) does not take place in the same way or at the same time; "it is not *a proclamation* of both wrath *and* righteousness, but rather righteousness as salvation from the wrath that already prevails" (Conzelmann 1932). The decisive question for Paul is therefore not preparing and leading people to faith ("the preaching of wrath in the service of the preaching of faith"), but rather God's plan of salvation for the world: the theological (in the literal sense) foundation and its christological presupposition are prior to any anthropology in Paul's teaching on the wrath of God as well. As in his conception of the righteousness of God (→ δικαιοσύνη 4), so also in his conception of the wrath of God the cross of Jesus and the

salvation effected by the resurrection remain the keys to understanding. Thus, ἐν αὐτῷ in Rom 1:18 is to be supplemented by 1:17. In the same gospel, the same people meet wrath and salvation. This does not occur in such a way that wrath affects only the sinner and salvation only the righteous; on the contrary, all are sinners (3:23), and the removal of wrath in the cross of Jesus applies to all (3:24). According to Romans, the gospel proclaims the wrath of God as being other and more important than simply an apocalyptic threat; inasmuch as it confronts humans with the present wrath of God, it summons them: you are saved (3:21-26) through baptism and confession (3:9f.). Therefore, according to Paul the wrath of God is not a divine property, but the judgment of God on sin that humans now recognize through Jesus Christ, when they encounter the crucified one in the kerygma; humans are now saved from this wrath through faith (Rom 5:9; cf. 10:4). Heb 3:11 and 4:3 quote Ps 94:11 LXX ("as I have sworn in my *wrath:* you shall not enter my rest").   W. Pesch

ὀργίζομαι *orgizomai* be (become) angry*

Lit.: → ὀργή.

Ὀργίζομαι appears 8 times in the NT. In Matt 18:34 and 22:7 (par. Luke 14:21) ὀργίζομαι is a metaphor for the wrath of God (→ ὀργή); otherwise the word is used only for human anger. In two passages ὀργίζομαι derives from quotations of the OT Psalms (Eph 4:26; Rev 11:18). The anger of the older brother in Luke 15:28 reveals his lack of compassion and hardheartedness and contrasts with the image of the love of the father, i.e., the angry brother stands opposite the loving Jesus. The thought already evident here is advanced in Revelation: the wrath of the nations against God is pure folly and self-condemnation (Rev 11:18), and the statement that the dragon wrathfully persecutes the heavenly woman demonstrates how this anger intersects God's plan of salvation; in Rev 12:17, ὀργίζομαι is described as the typical disposition of the devil. When Matt 5:22 uses ὀργίζομαι as a designation of the sinful disposition of one person toward another, it emphasizes that ὀργίζομαι perverts a person. Not only the act (more specifically, murder: 5:21), but even the thought and the word place humans under God's judgment and destruction.   W. Pesch

ὀργίλος, 3 *orgilos* angry, quick-tempered*

In Titus 1:7 ὀργίλος appears among the instructions to the ἐπίσκοπος: "not overbearing, not *quick-tempered,* not a drunkard, not violent." G. Stählin, *TDNT* V, 420f.

ὀργυιά, ᾶς, ἡ *orgyia* fathom*

A measure of length (*ca.* 6 feet or 1.85 m.); used as

a t.t. in nautical language as a measure for water depths (Diodorus Siculus iii.40.3): Acts 27:28a, b.

ὀρέγομαι *oregomai* (mid.) stretch oneself, reach, try, strive*

1 Tim 3:1: ἐπισκοπῆς ὀρέγομαι, "*strive* for the office of bishop"; Heb 11:16: κρείττονος ὀρέγομαι, "*strive* for a better [i.e., heavenly home]"; 1 Tim 6:10: *striving* after φιλαργυρία (improperly for ἀργύριον). H. W. Heiland, *TDNT* V, 447f.; J. Guhrt, *DNTT* I, 460f.; Spicq, *Notes* II, 626f.

ὀρεινός, 3 *oreinos* hilly, mountainous*

The fem. subst. ἡ ὀρεινή means *hill country, mountainous region* (LXX, Philo, Josephus). In Luke 1:39, Mary traveled εἰς τὴν ὀρεινήν, and 1:65 refers to ἡ ὀρεινὴ τῆς Ἰουδαίας, "the *hill country* of Judea."

ὄρεξις, εως, ἡ *orexis* desire (noun), longing*

In Rom 1:27 for men who (instead of natural relations with a woman) "burn with their *desire* (ἐν τῇ ὀρέξει αὐτῶν) for each other." H. W. Heiland, *TDNT* V, 447f.; J. Guhrt, *DNTT* I, 460f.; Spicq, *Notes* II, 626f.

ὀρθοποδέω *orthopodeō* walk straight, upright*

Gal 2:14 says of Cephas and the Jewish Christians: They "*do not walk straight* (ὀρθοποδοῦσιν) according to the gospel" (since they had abandoned table fellowhip with the Gentile Christians in Antioch). On the image used here, cf. Prov 4:26 LXX; Heb 12:13 (→ ὀρθός). On the prep. phrase πρὸς τὴν ἀλήθειαν τοῦ εὐαγγελίου see BAGD s.v. πρός III.5.d (cf. Luke 12:47; 2 Cor 5:10; Eph 3:4). H. Preisker, *TDNT* V, 451; G. D. Kilpatrick, FS Bultmann (1954) 269-74; F. Mussner, *Gal* (HTKNT) ad loc.; Spicq, *Notes* II, 628f.

ὀρθός, 3 *orthos* straight, upright, correct*

Acts 14:10, in Paul's words to the lame man: "Stand *straight* on your feet"; on the adv. use of the adj. see BDF §243; Heb 12:13 (Prov 4:26 LXX): "Make *straight* paths for your feet." H. Preisker, *TDNT* V, 449f.; *TWNT* X, 1205 (bibliography); R. Klöber, *DNTT* III, 351f.

ὀρθοτομέω *orthotomeō* cut in the right direction, divide correctly

2 Tim 2:15, in the instruction to Timothy, who should show himself to be a zealous workman "who *correctly administers* the word of truth." In accordance with its original meaning, ὀρθοτομέω can also mean here: "follow the right way," or "proclaim [the word] forthrightly," i.e.,

without unprofitable disputes (Brox). H. Köster, *TDNT* VIII, 111f.; N. Brox, *Die Pastoralbriefe* (RNT) 247f.; Spicq, *Notes* II, 630.

ὀρθρίζω *orthrizō* get up early in the morning*

Luke 21:38: The people (λαός) *got up early each morning* (ὤρθριζεν) in order to hear Jesus in the temple. It also occurs in the LXX (Exod 24:4; 4 Kgdms 6:15, etc.).

ὀρθρινός, 3 *orthrinos* early morning*

Luke 24:22: The women from among the group of Jesus' disciples were at the grave of Jesus "already in the *early morning*" (γενόμεναι ὀρθριναί).

ὄρθριος, 3 *orthrios* early morning

This adj. is found in Luke 24:22 TR, probably a shortened form of an original → ὀρθρινός.

ὄρθρος, ου, ὁ *orthros* dawn, daybreak*

Luke 24:1: ὄρθρου βαθέως, "*at first light*"; John 8:2 v.l.: ὄρθρου, *early in the morning*; Acts 5:21: ὑπὸ τὸν ὄρθρον, "around *daybreak*."

ὀρθῶς *orthōs* rightly, correctly*

Mark 7:35: λαλέω ὀρθῶς, "speak *correctly*," for the healed deaf mute, who before had been μογιλάλος (v. 32). The Lukan occurrences combine the adv. with κρίνω (Luke 7:43), ἀποκρίνομαι (10:28), and (referring to Jesus) λέγω καὶ διδάσκω (20:21).

ὅρια, ων, τά *horia* borders, region*

In the NT τὸ ὅριον appears only in the pl., meaning *region*. It appears both without mention of the name of the region (Mark 5:17 par. Matt 8:34; Matt 2:16; Acts 13:50) and with mention of the name (Mark 7:24, 31a: τὰ ὅρια Τύρου [cf. Matt 15:22]; Mark 7:31b: Δεκαπόλεως; 10:1: τῆς Ἰουδαίας [par. Matt 19:1]; Matt 4:13: Ζαβουλὼν καὶ Νεφθαλίμ; 15:39: Μαγαδάν).

ὀρίζω *horizō* determine, set, explain*

1. Occurrences in the NT — 2. Designation/appointment of persons (Christ) — a) Rom 1:4 — b) Acts — 3. Designation/arrangement of objects

Lit.: L. C. ALLEN, "The OT Background of (προ)ὁρίζειν in the NT," *NTS* 17 (1970/71) 104-8. — M.-É. BOISMARD, "Constitué Fils de Dieu (Rom., I,4)," *RB* 60 (1953) 5-17. — H. CONZELMANN, *The Theology of St. Luke* (1960) 151f., 158. — M. DIBELIUS, *Studies in the Acts of the Apostles* (1956) 27-34 (on Acts 17:26). — G. DULON, *DNTT* I, 472-74. — J. D. G.

DUNN, "Jesus—Flesh and Spirit: An Exposition of Romans I,3-4," *JTS* 24 (1973) 40-68. — V. GATTI, *Il senso dell'espressione* ὁϱίσας προστεταγμένους ϰαιρούς (Act. 17,26b) (Diss. Gregorian University, Rome, 1977). — É. DES PLACES, "Actes 17,30-31," *Bib* 52 (1971) 526-34. — H. SCHLIER, "Zu Röm 1,3f," FS Cullmann (1972) 207-18. — K. L. SCHMIDT, *TDNT* V, 452-56. — For further bibliography see *TWNT* X, 1205f.

1. Ὁϱίζω occurs mostly in the Lukan writings (6 occurrences: Luke 22:22 [contrast Mark]; Acts 2:23; 10:42; 11:29; 17:26, 31); it is found in the rest of the NT only twice (Rom 1:4; Heb 4:7). With the exception of Acts 11:29 God is always the subj. of the vb. (so also with → προορίζω); it refers primarily, esp. in the Lukan writings, to God's plan of salvation; see Conzelmann 151f.

2. a) Rom 1:4 uses a pre-Pauline christological formula to say that the one descended "from the seed of David" was *appointed to be* Son of God (τοῦ ὁρισθέντος υἱοῦ θεοῦ), and also ἐξ ἀναστάσεως νεκρῶν ("because of the resurrection from the dead"). Since the point in time from which the sonship dates is given, here ὁϱίζω must mean *install*, even though elsewhere it means *determined, declared, decreed*. The pre-Pauline formula (which probably lacked the ἐν δυνάμει of v. 4) states "that Jesus, by his earthly origins a descendant of David, was the earthly messiah, whom God declared the Son of God in connection with his resurrection from the dead, and thus enthroned him as messianic king" (Schlier 215).

b) According to Acts 17:31 (the end of Paul's Areopagus speech) God will judge the world ἐν ἀνδρὶ ᾧ ὥρισεν, "through the man whom *he has appointed* [for the task]." According to Acts 10:42, Peter spoke to Cornelius of Jesus Christ as the "judge *appointed* by God." An older christological formula could lie behind both of the passages in Acts 9 (→ a).

3. Other passages speak of the arrangements of God, i.e., his plan of salvation, in which the matter referred to forms the acc. obj. of ὁϱίζω (only in Acts 11:29 is the decision [here a human decision] expressed by means of an inf.: ὥρισαν . . . πέμψαι): according to Heb 4:7 God has *appointed* a day; according to Acts 17:26 he has "*determined* the times" (for a discussion of whether seasons or historical epochs, etc., are in mind here, see Dibelius, Gatti; → ϰαιρός). The pass. can also be used in corresponding fashion: ἡ ὡρισμένη βουλή, "the *determined* plan," Acts 2:23; or also the subst.: ϰατὰ τὸ ὡρισμένον, "according to the *determined* [by God] *plan*" the Son of Man "goes his way," Luke 22:22 (Mark 14:21 par. Matt 26:24 has ϰαθὼς γέγραπται περὶ αὐτοῦ).

G. Schneider

ὀϱινός, 3 *orinos* hilly, mountainous
Variant of → ὀϱεινός.

ὁϱϰίζω *horkizō* swear an oath, implore
→ ὅϱϰος.

ὅϱϰος, ου, ὁ *horkos* oath*
ὁϱϰίζω *horkizō* swear an oath, implore*

1. Occurrences in the NT — 2. Meaning — 3. Usage

Lit.: E. BERNEKER, *KP* II, 209f. — BILLERBECK II, 321-37. — R. HIERSCHE, "Note additionnelle relative à l'étymologie d'ὅϱϰος et d'ὀμνύναι," *Revue des Études grecques* 71 (1958) 35-41. — H.-G. LINK, *DNTT* III, 737-43. — J. SCHNEIDER, *TDNT* V, 457-67. — E. ZIEBARTH, *PW* V, 2075-83. — For further bibliography see *TWNT* X, 1206.

1. With the exception of ὅϱϰος (10 occurrences) and → ὁϱϰωμοσία (4 occurrences), the words built on the ὁϱϰ-root are found only occasionally in the NT. The occurrences are concentrated in Matthew (ὅϱϰος 4 occurrences, plus ἐξορϰίζω in 26:63, ἐπιορϰέω in 5:33, and 13 occurrences of → ὀμνύω) and in Hebrews (ὅϱϰος twice, ὁϱϰωμοσία 4 occurrences, plus 7 occurrences of → ὀμνύω).

2. Ὅϱϰος originally designated the staff that was held when swearing an oath. In the NT ὅϱϰος means *oath* (in Matt 5:33 perhaps with the sense of "vow"), i.e., the reinforcement of a person's word by calling on God as witness to the truth (cf. the "definition" in Heb 6:16). The following expressions are found in the NT: ὀμνύω ὅϱϰον (Luke 1:73; Jas 5:12) or ὅϱϰῳ (Acts 2:30: swear an *oath);* μεσιτεύω ὅϱϰῳ (Heb 6:17: confirm *with an oath);* ὁμολογέω μεθ' ὅϱϰου (Matt 14:7: promise *with an oath);* ἀρνέομαι μεθ' ὅϱϰου (26:72: deny *with an oath);* ἀποδίδωμι τοὺς ὅϱϰους (5:33: keep the *oaths).* No difference in meaning is apparent between ὅϱϰος and → ὁϱϰωμοσία in the NT. Likewise, ὁϱϰίζω and the compounds ἐνορϰίζω and ἐξορϰίζω mean *cause to swear, implore,* with no discernible difference in meaning (Mark 5:7; Acts 19:13; 1 Thess 5:27; perhaps Matt 26:63).

3. In most instances in the NT, ὅϱϰος is used in the usual way, i.e., to designate the reinforcement of one person's word to another person. Thus the addition of μετὰ ὅϱϰου to the two denials of Peter in Matt 26:72 is an intensification. The oath heightens the binding nature of a promise; Herod dares not breach such a promise (Matt 14:7, 9; Mark 6:26). Going beyond the OT, which condemns false oaths (Matt 5:33; cf. Lev 19:12; Num 30:3; Deut 23:22-24; Ps 50:14; Eccl 5:3-4 LXX), Matt 5:34-37 and Jas 5:12 forbid swearing altogether, regardless of the way in which the oath is expressed. According to the NT, God himself uses an oath as a reinforcement of his word (with ὅϱϰος in Luke 1:73; Acts 2:30; Heb 6:17; with ὁϱϰωμοσία in Heb 7:20f., 28). Each of these passages refers to the OT (covenant with Abraham, Luke 1:73; Heb 6:17; covenant with David, Acts 2:30; Melchizedek, Heb 7:20f., 28). The oath in these cases em-

phasizes the binding character and eternal validity of the divine promise. According to Heb 7:20f., 28, the superiority of the priesthood of Christ lies in the fact that it is based on God's oath, while the priests of the OT owe their office to the law.

The vbs. ὀρκίζω, ἐνορκίζω, and ἐξορκίζω display a different usage. They always appear in the NT in direct discourse, in the form of an oath formula: ὀρκίζω (or one of its compounds), followed by the acc. of the person implored and the acc. (or κατά with the gen.) of the authority appealed to (in the NT, God or Jesus). This was a first-century Hellenistic formula for exorcizing demons found frequently in the magical papyri. According to Acts 19:13, this formula is used by the Jewish ἐξορκισταί who made use of the name of Jesus. In Mark 5:7 the demon-possessed man turns the tables and uses the oath formula against Jesus. It is found in 1 Thess 5:27 (ἐνορκίζω) in a weakened sense, to express an "imploring" request. Also, Matt 26:63 (ἐξορκίζω) should probably be understood not so much as the demand to swear an oath as the coercive demand to answer the question.   F. Annen

ὀρκωμοσία, ας, ἡ *horkōmosia* sworn affirmation*

Heb 7:20a, b, 21, 28 speak of the "introduction of a better hope," which "was not without an ὀρκωμοσία" (v. 20a); for Christ became priest μετὰ ὀρκωμοσίας (v. 21; see Ps 110:4; cf. Heb 7:28), while the former priesthood was χωρὶς ὀρκωμοσίας (v. 20b). J. Schneider, *TDNT* V, 463f.; → ὅρκος.

ὁρμάω *hormaō* attack (vb.), rush headlong, rage*

The herd of swine "*rushed headlong* down the cliff into the sea" (Mark 5:13 par. Matt 8:32/Luke 8:33). In Acts 7:57 the members of the Sanhedrin (6:15) "all *rushed at* him [Stephen]," dragged him out of the city, and stoned him. In Acts 19:29 the crowd in Ephesus "all *rushed into* the theater." J. Bertram, *TDNT* V, 467-72.

ὁρμή, ῆς, ἡ *hormē* eagerness, desire*

Acts 14:5: ἐγένετο ὁρμὴ τῶν ἐθνῶν τε καὶ Ἰουδαίων, in reference to the attack against Paul and Barnabas in Iconium; Jas 3:4, for the pilot whose ὁρμή steers the ship. G. Bertram, *TDNT* V, 467-72.

ὅρμημα, ατος, τό *hormēma* violent rush, impulsiveness*

Rev 18:21: "In this way the great city of Babylon will be overthrown *with sudden violence* (ὁρμήματι)." G. Bertram, *TDNT* V, 470f.

ὄρνεον, ου, τό *orneon* bird*

Rev 18:2: Babylon as the "hideout of all unclean and detestable *birds*"; and 19:17: an angel cries "to all the *birds* that fly in mid-heaven," that they should come to the "great supper of God"; cf. 19:21: "and all the *birds* filled themselves with their flesh."

ὄρνιξ, ἡ *ornix* mother bird, hen

Luke 13:34 ℵ D W instead of → ὄρνις.

ὄρνις, ιθος, ὁ (ἡ) *ornis* bird, rooster (hen)*

The activity of a bird or more specifically the mother bird (ἡ ὄρνις) functions as an image of protective care (cf. Deut 32:11; Isa 31:5; Ps 36:7): Matt 23:37 par. Luke 13:34. Schulz, *Q* 346-56.

ὁροθεσία, ας, ἡ *horothesia* drawing up of borders, established borders*

Acts 17:26, in the Areopagus speech: God has established (ὁρίζω) τὰς ὁροθεσίας τῆς κατοικίας αὐτῶν (τῶν ἀνθρώπων), i.e., "the *established borders* of their abode." According to M. Dibelius (*Studies in the Acts of the Apostles* [1956] 37) delimited zones for human habitation are intended here. According to W. Eltester (FS Bultmann [1954], 202-27) ὁροθεσίαι refers to rivers and mountains (212n.14) or to the boundaries to which God banished the primeval waters (214-19). One should probably, however, assume "borders between nations" here; on this see M. Pohlenz, *ZNW* 42 (1949) 69-104, esp. 86; H. J. Cadbury, *The Book of Acts in History* (1955) 36f.; Spicq, *Notes* II, 631.

ὄρος, ους, τό *oros* mountain*

1. Occurrences in the NT — 2. Ὄρος in the life of Jesus — 3. Apocalyptic-eschatological traditions and contexts — 4. Mount Sinai

Lit.: R. L. COHN, "The Sacred Mountain in Ancient Israel" (Diss. Stanford University, 1974). — T. L. DONALDSON, *Jesus on the Mountain. A Study in Matthean Theology* (*JSNT* Supplement Series 8, 1985). — W. FOERSTER, *TDNT* V, 475-87. — H. HAAG, *BL* 193. — J. LANGE, *Das Erscheinen des Auferstandenen im Evangelium nach Matthäus* (FzB 11, 1973) 392-446. — X. LÉON-DUFOUR, *DBT* 372-74. — W. SCHMAUCH, *Orte der Offenbarung und der Offenbarungsort im NT* (1956) 48-80. — E. STOMMEL (and M. KLOEPPEL), *RAC* II, 136-38. — A. STROBEL, "Der Berg der Offenbarung (Mt 28,16; Apg 1,12)," FS Stählin 133-46.

1. Of the 63 occurrences in the NT, ὄρος is found 44 times in the Gospels: a) in narrative material: 11 times in Matthew, 9 in Mark, 9 in Luke, and 2 in John; b) in discourse material: 5 times in Matthew, 2 in Mark, 3 in Luke, and 2 in John. The remaining occurrences are found in Revelation (8 occurrences), Hebrews (4), Acts (3), as well as 1 Cor 13:2; Gal 4:24f.; 2 Pet 1:18. Mentioned by

name are the Mount of Olives (12 times), Mount Zion (twice), and Mount Sinai (4 times). John 4:20f. has in mind Mount Gerizim, and Heb 8:5 and 12:20 Mount Sinai, without mentioning them by name.

2. a) In the narrative material of the Gospels, ὄρος is used as an indication of place or situation. The use of final προσεύξασθαι (Mark 6:46 par. Matt 14:23; Luke 6:12; 9:28) as well as the fact that the *mountain* is often the locus of extraordinary events can also function, however, to single out the mountain as the place of special proximity to God (see also the emphasis on the highness of the mountain: Mark 9:2 par. Matt 17:1). In Mark the mountain is the place of revelatory events that are hidden from the people: the mountain of the selection of the Twelve (Mark 3:13 par. Luke 6:12), the mount of transfiguration (Mark 9:2, 9 par. Matt 17:1, 9/Luke 9:28, 37; cf. 2 Pet 1:18), the apocalyptic discourse on the Mount of Olives (Mark 13:3 par. Matt 24:3). The ὄρος is a place of prayer in Mark 6:46 par. Matt 14:23. Jesus' words on the Mount of Olives before entering Jerusalem (Mark 11:1 par. Matt 21:1/Luke 19:29; Luke 19:37) and his departure for the Mount of Olives after the Last Supper (Mark 14:26 par. Matt 26:30/Luke 22:39) should be considered a simple indication of place or situation. The ὄρος is mentioned as a place of pasture for a herd of swine in Mark 5:11 par. Luke 8:32, and the mountains and graves that formed the place of abode for the demon-possessed man in Mark 5:5 characterize him as an unclean man living in isolation.

In five passages Matthew takes over ὄρος from Mark. Above and beyond that, however, the mountain is also a place of revelation for the people according to Matthew: in the Sermon on the *Mount* (5:1; 8:1) Jesus gives his people the new law ("over against" the giving of the law at Sinai), and he heals many sick on the mountain (15:29). After having withstood on the mountain (4:8) the devil's offer to place in his possession all the kingdoms of the world, Jesus revealed himself on a mountain in Galilee (28:16) as the one who had been given all authority.

Of the 9 occurrences of ὄρος in Luke, 6 have been taken over from Mark. Nevertheless, the mountain in Luke has more the character of a place of prayer (cf. 6:12; 9:28; 22:39ff.). The Mount of Olives is the place of Jesus' nightly abode (21:37; cf. 22:39: κατὰ τὸ ἔθος). Jesus was supposed to have been cast down from the precipice of the mount on which Nazareth was built (4:29). The implicit statement in Acts 1:12, that Jesus ascended into heaven from the Mount of Olives, functions as part of the Lukan Jerusalem motif.

In John 6:3, ὄρος designates the solitary place where Jesus fed the five thousand. According to 6:15, Jesus withdrew from the people on the mountain, and 8:1 recounts that Jesus in the evening went to the Mount of Olives.

b) Several of the occurrences of ὄρος in the discourse material in the Synoptic Gospels are found in apocalyptic-eschatological contexts (→ 3). The saying on "mountain-moving faith" is found in Mark 11:23 par. Matt 21:21; Matt 17:20; 1 Cor 13:2. According to Matt 5:14, the height of the mountain guarantees the security of the city. In Matt 18:12 τὰ ὄρη designates a dangerous place for the shepherd. According to John 4:20f., Jesus removed any special significance assigned to the mountain (here Gerizim) and Jerusalem as places of prayer and worship.

3. Mountains are mentioned as places of flight and refuge in the tribulations of the last days: Mark 13:14 par. Matt 24:16/Luke 21:21; Rev 6:15f. (cf. Hos 10:8 LXX); cf. also Heb 11:38. According to Luke 23:30 (cf. Hos 10:8 LXX) the people would call on the mountains to fall on them so that they might escape the divine wrath. In Rev 6:14 the uprooting of the mountains and islands demonstrates the severity of the earthquake, and in 16:20 the disappearance of the mountains indicates the beginning of the eschaton. In connection with John the Baptist's preaching of repentance, the "leveling" of the mountains (Luke 3:5; cf. Isa 40:4 LXX), which would prepare the way for the Messiah, should be understood as conversion. In Rev 8:8 the mountain characterizes the size of a star that falls into the sea. The seven mountains of 17:9 refer to the seven hills of Rome. In 21:10, the mountain is mentioned as a special place for viewing. In 14:1 Zion is the place of safety where the NT people of God are gathered. In Heb 12:22 Ζιὼν ὄρος is a designation of the new covenant.

4. Sinai is mentioned in Acts 7:30, 38 and Heb 8:5 for its significance as an OT place of revelation. For Paul, Sinai is a symbol of the old, enslaving law (Gal 4:24f.). In Hebrews as well, Sinai (12:20) is opposed to Zion (12:22) as the symbol of the new covenant.

H. Kleine

ὀρύσσω *oryssō* dig, dig up, bury*

There are 3 occurrences in the NT: Matt 25:18: ὤρυξεν γῆν, "*he dug up* the ground," in order to hide the money entrusted to him (see Billerbeck I, 971f.); Mark 12:1 par. Matt 21:33: ὤρυξεν ὑπολήνιον/ληνόν, "*he dug* a pit."

ὀρφανός, 3 *orphanos* orphaned, without parents; subst.: orphan*

2 occurrences in the NT: John 14:18, used fig. in the Farewell Discourse of Jesus, who will not leave his followers *orphaned/alone* (on the interpretation of this passage, see R. Bultmann, *John* (Eng. tr., 1971) 618n.1; R. Schnackenburg, *John* III (Eng. tr., 1982) 77n.97; cf.

also in terms of the teacher-student relationship Plato *Phdr.* 116a); Jas 1:27, subst. in a parenetic context: ἐπισκέπτεσθαι ὀρφανοὺς καὶ χήρας, "visit the *orphans* and widows" (on the special need of widows and orphans for protection see Exod 22:21; Ezek 22:7; 2 Macc 3:10; Ign. *Smyrn.* 6:2; *Herm. Man.* viii.10; *Sim.* ix.26.2; Mark 12:40 v.l.). BAGD s.v.; Billerbeck IV, 536ff., 559ff.; H. Seesemann, *TDNT* V, 486-88; V. Hasler, *BHH* 2133; P. Sandevoir, *DBT* 652f.

ὀρχέομαι *orcheomai* dance*

4 occurrences in the NT: Mark 6:22 par. Matt 14:6: Salome, who *danced* for Herod; Matt 11:17 par. Luke 7:32: "We played for you and you *did* not *dance*" (οὐκ ὠρχήσασθε). *WBB* 425; W. Grundmann, *Luke* (THKNT) 167.

ὅς, ἥ, ὅ *hos, hē, ho* (rel. pron.) who, which, what, that

1. Usage in the NT — 2. Agreement with antecedent — 3. Constructio ad sensum — 4. With preps.

Lit.: BAGD s.v. — BDF §§293-97; 377-80. — KÜHNER, *Grammatik* II/1, 587f.; II/2, 406-21, 434-39. — LSJ s.v. — MAYSER, *Grammatik* II/1, 76-78; II/3, 98-108. — MOULTON, *Grammar* I, 91-94; III, 47-50. — RADERMACHER, *Grammatik* 62f. — V. SPOTTORNO, "The Relative Pronoun in the NT," *NTS* 28 (1982) 132-41.

1. The NT usage of the rel. pron. is more liberal than that of classical Greek.

a) A sharp distinction is no longer made between the individual ὅς, *who*, and the general → ὅστις, "whoever"; cf. βασιλεῖ ὅς in Matt 18:23 and βασιλεῖ ὅστις in 22:2: "a king, *who.*" Luke even uses ὅστις with personal names (Luke 2:4; Acts 8:14f.); in contrast, Paul uses the terms correctly.

b) Occasionally, as in classical Greek, the rel. pron. is found after vbs. of knowing instead of the (indirect) interrogative pron.: "not knowing *what* (ὅ) he was saying," Luke 9:33; cf. John 13:7; 18:21; both prons. interchangeably, 1 Tim 1:7.

c) The personal pron. of the third person can sometimes appear pleonastically with the rel. pron. due to Semitic influence: "the woman *whose* daughter" (ἧς . . . αὐτῆς), Mark 7:25; cf. 1:7; Matt 3:12; Luke 3:16f.

d) The rel. pron. is used as a demonstrative in the same instances in which the art. is used demonstratively (→ ὁ 1): frequently ὃς μέν . . . ὃς δέ, "*this* one . . . *that* one"; ὃς δέ, "but he (this person)," Mark 15:23.

e) Occasionally a rel. clause has a final or consecutive sense (vb. in the fut. or subjunc.), in which cases the rel. can or must be translated with the corresponding conj.: 1) final: "my messenger, *who* will prepare" (παρα- σκευάσει), Mark 1:2 par.; 2) consecutive: "*so that he* (ὅς) could teach him," 1 Cor 2:16; "he is worthy *that* this should be granted *him*" (ἄξιος ᾧ), Luke 7:4.

f) At times a rel. clause functions independently even though by its construction it is subordinate to the main clause ("relative connective": "You, too, guard yourself against *him* [ὅν]," 2 Tim 4:15).

2. Frequently the rel. pron. (although almost exclusively when it should properly be an acc.) takes on the case of its antecedent ("attraction" or "assimilation").

a) ἐν ὥρᾳ ᾗ (= ἥν) οὐ γινώσκει, "at an hour *which* he does not know," Matt 24:50; ἐπὶ πᾶσιν οἷς (= ἅ) ἤκουσαν, "because of all *that* they had heard," Luke 2:20; τῶν ἰχθύων ὧν (= οὓς) συνέλαβον, "the fish *that* they had caught," 5:9; cf. 3:19; 1 Cor 6:19; ἕως τῆς ἡμέρας ἧς (= ᾗ), "until the day *when,*" Acts 1:22; cf. 2 Cor 1:4. There is no attraction in cases like Acts 1:21: ἐν χρόνῳ ᾧ, "in the time *in which,*" where the prep. is simply not repeated before the rel. (cf. 13:2, 38, etc.).

b) Where the antecedent is included in the rel. clause: περὶ πασῶν ὧν εἶδον δυνάμεων, "on account of all the mighty acts *that* they had seen," Luke 19:37; cf. 1:4; Rom 6:17; 2 Cor 10:13.

c) The demonstrative pron. that the rel. pron. modifies is often implied: "[He] *who* (ὅς) does not take up his cross," Matt 10:38; ὃ λέγω, "[that] *which* I say," 10:27; "blessed [are those] *whose* sins are forgiven," Rom 4:7; likewise 15:21; Luke 7:43; 2 Tim 1:12; ἐν ᾧ, "in [that] *which,*" Rom 14:21. Under these circumstances, the rel. pron. will sometimes take on the case of the lacking demonstrative (attraction): οὐδὲν ὧν ἑώρακαν = οὐδὲν τούτων ἃ ἑώρακαν, "nothing *of* [that] *which* they had seen," Luke 9:36 (cf. 23:14; Acts 8:24); ἄξια ὧν ἐπράξαμεν, "worthy [of those things] *which* we have done," Luke 23:41; τι λαλεῖν ὧν, "to say something [of that] *which,*" Rom 15:18; περὶ ὧν, "for [those] *who,*" John 17:9.

3. Occasionally the rel. will differ from its antecedent in gender or in number (constructio ad sensum).

a) Gender (the natural gender of the antecedent rather than its grammatical gender emerges): παιδάριον ὅς, "a child *who,*" John 6:9; ἔθνη ἐφ᾽ οὕς, "Gentiles over *whom,*" Acts 15:17; cf. 26:17; Gal 4:19; Col 2:19.

b) Number (where the sense suggests a pl.): πλῆθος πολὺ οἵ, "a large crowd *who,*" Luke 6:17f.; πόλιν πᾶσαν ἐν αἷς, "every city in *which,*" Acts 15:36; δευτέραν ἐπιστολὴν ἐν αἷς, "the second letter in *which,*" 2 Pet 3:1. Infrequently the sg. replaces the pl.: Phil 3:20; Acts 24:11.

c) The expression ὅ ἐστιν, "*that* is," is a fixed formula with explanations, translations, etc.: Heb 7:2; Mark 3:17, etc.

4. Formulaic expressions with a conj. sense are created when the rel. is combined with certain preps.: ἀνθ᾽ ὧν, "since, because," Luke 1:20, etc.; ἀφ᾽ οὗ, "since" (temporal), 24:21, etc.; ἄχρι (ἕως, μέχρι) οὗ, "until," Acts 7:18; ἐν ᾧ, ἐν οἷς, "while," Mark 2:19, etc.; ἐφ᾽ ᾧ, "therefore, since," Rom 5:12; 2 Cor 5:4; Phil 3:12.

W. Elliger

ὀσάκις *hosakis* as often as, every time that (adv.)*

3 occurrences in the NT, always in the combination ὀσάκις ἐάν: 1 Cor 11:25f., in connection with the Lord's Supper; Rev 11:6: ὀσάκις ἐὰν θελήσωσιν, *"whenever* they wanted."

ὅσιος, 3 *hosios* holy, godly, pleasing to God*
ὁσιότης, ητος, ἡ *hosiotēs* holiness, godliness*

1. Occurrences and usage — a) In the NT — b) In the LXX and general Greek usage — 2. Of God and Christ — 3. Of believers

Lit.: BAGD s.v. — J. C. BOLKESTEIN, Ὅσιος en Εὐσεβής (Diss. Utrecht, 1936). — M. DIBELIUS and H. CONZELMANN, *The Pastoral Epistles* (Hermeneia) 44f. — B. HÄRING, *Das Heilige und das Gute* (1950). — F. HAUCK, *TDNT* V, 489-92. — H. SEEBASS, *DNTT* II, 236-38. — M. VAN DER VALK, "Zum Worte ὅσιος," *Mnemosyne* 10 (1941/42) 113-40. — For further bibliography → ἅγιος; see also Hauck; *TWNT* X, 1207.

1. a) With 8 occurrences (5 in OT quotations), ὅσιος is relatively infrequent in the NT (not found in the Gospels, 3 occurrences in Acts, 2 in the Pastorals [1 Tim 2:8; Titus 1:8] and in Revelation [15:4; 16:5], and 1 in Heb 7:26) compared to ἅγιος. The subst. ὁσιότης is found only in Luke 1:75 and Eph 4:24 (always in combination with δικαιοσύνη).
b) In the LXX, ὅσιος refers primarily to the "godly" and for the most part translates Heb. *ḥāsîd* (in the majority of the passages in the pl. for the congregation of the godly that lives in covenant relation with God; cf. Pss 29:5; 36:28; 49:5; in the absolute, Pss 11:2; 17:26; 85:2; ἐκκλησία ὁσίων, Ps 149:1), but not *qāḏôš* or *ṣaddîq*; it can also be used generally for the trust and hope of the godly in God (Pss 85:2; 96:10; Wis 4:15 [with ἐκλεκτοί]) and as an expression of purity or that which is pleasing to God (Prov 22:11 [with ἄμωμοι]; 10:15). The *ḥasîdîm-ʾAsidaîoi* are found as a distinctly defined group only beginning with the time of the Maccabees (1 Macc 2:42; 7:13; 2 Macc 14:6; cf. Philo *Omn. Prob. Lib.* 91), though the reference is lacking at Qumran. Ὅσιος is found (with δίκαιος) in Deut 32:4 and Ps 144:17 with reference to the faithfulness and righteousness of God; the pl. τὰ ὅσια is found in Isa 55:3 (→ 2), in the sense of divine possessions, for God's promises to David; see also B. Lifshitz, *ZDPV* 78 (1962) 64-88, esp. 73.
Unlike the LXX usage, in the NT ὅσιος has not become a t.t. and has been displaced as a designation of the believer esp. by → ἐκλεκτός and → ἅγιος. It was, however, able to gain a specific meaning in the more markedly Hellenistic writings in the general Greek sense

of "clean/godly/bound to the obligations (established by the gods)" (cf. Plato *Euthphr.* 6e, 12d, 15b [see Hauck 489n.10]; *Grg.* 507b; τὰ δίκαια καὶ τὰ ὅσια, *Plt.* 301d; τὰ πρὸς τοὺς ἀνθρώπους δίκαια καὶ τὰ πρὸς τοὺς θεοὺς ὅσια, Polybius xxii.10.8; also Josephus *Ant.* x.83).

2. When used in connection with God, ὅσιος is found in hymns of praise closely related to OT expressions (Rev 15:4: ὅτι μόνος ὅσιος; 16:5: δίκαιος εἶ, ὁ ὢν καὶ ὁ ἦν, ὁ ὅσιος; cf. on this Deut 32:4; Ps 144:17 LXX). Both passages in Revelation deal, in connection with the final redemption and judgment, with the holiness of God, whose justice does not conform to human standards but rather lays out for the first time the standards of eternal justice. Acts 13:34 picks up on Isa 55:3 LXX and thus relates the "trustworthy manifestations of grace" (τὰ ὅσια Δαυὶδ τὰ πιστά) originally bestowed on David to Christ (fut. δώσω). The statement must be interpreted in connection with v. 35 (likewise fut.: οὐ δώσεις τὸν ὅσιόν σου ἰδεῖν διαφθοράν, identical to 2:27; both a quotation of Ps 15:10 LXX), according to which the saving promises of God, intended as they were for eternity, could not possibly have been exhausted by David, who was bound by mortality, but necessarily found their fulfillment for the first time when Jesus was raised (cf. Acts 13:36f.). The point of this Lukan interpretation of the OT is the lasting validity of the saving promises, which in accordance with the self-authenticating holiness of God can only find fulfillment in definitive, eternal salvation, not temporary, historical circumstances. In Heb 7:26 ὅσιος is transferred as an originally divine predicate to Christ as the true, heavenly high priest: he is ὅσιος ἄκακος ἀμίαντος, and as the one who is free from all sin has through his death offered the true and eternally valid sin offering (v. 27; on ἔπρεπεν cf. v. 26 and 2:10). Therefore, Christ is *holy* in his perfect reflection of God, which is manifest in his distance from all defilement and evil (cf. O. Michel, *Heb* [KEK] ad loc.).

3. Ὅσιος is applied to the believer in the Pastoral Epistles: according to 1 Tim 2:8 men should lift up *"holy/godly* hands" to God in prayer (referring to the usual posture of prayer with raised hands: ἐπαίροντας ὁσίους χεῖρας), which then is explained: "without anger or disputing." Ὅσιος is thus taken over as an original expression of cultic purity (cf. "puras ad caelum manus tollere," Seneca *QN* iii.praefatio.14; see also Josephus *B.J.* v.380; 1QS 9:15; *1 Clem.* 29:1; see also Dibelius and Conzelmann) and is applied to one's entire way of life and disposition. There can hardly be any direct influence from the language of the mystery religions here, even though the mystics could sometimes be designated ὅσιοι (Plato *R.* 363c; Aristophanes *Ra.* 327, 336; see BAGD s.v. 1.a). In Titus 1:8, ὅσιος, *godly, pleasing to God,* is found along with ἀνέγκλητος, σώφρων, δίκαιος ἐγκρατής, and other

virtues in a list of the responsibilities of the πρεσβύτερος or ἐπίσκοπος (cf. also 1 Tim 3:1-7).

The subst. ὁσιότης means *godliness/holiness* in Luke 1:75 generally for the life of the godly in the salvation of God (ἐν ὁσιότητι καὶ δικαιοσύνῃ; cf. Wis 9:3; Philo *Abr.* 208; Josephus *Ant.* xix.300; *1 Clem.* 48:4); and in Eph 4:24 (ἐν δικαιοσύνῃ καὶ ὁσιότητι ἀληθείας) for the nature of the new person, created after the image of God: "in righteousness and true *holiness*," i.e., in full conformity to God in terms of one's own actions and being (cf. also Col 3:10).   H. Balz

ὁσιότης, ητος, ἡ *hosiotēs* godliness, holiness
→ ὅσιος.

ὁσίως *hosiōs* in a godly, holy, God-pleasing way*

In 1 Thess 2:10 with δικαίως and ἀμέμπτως for Paul's God-pleasing, conscientious, and irreproachable relation to the Church (cf. also Titus 1:8; Heb 7:26; *1 Enoch* [Greek] 104:12; *1 Clem.* 45:7; *2 Clem.* 15:3; → ὅσιος).

ὀσμή, ῆς, ἡ *osmē* fragrance, aroma
→ εὐωδία.

ὅσος, 3 *hosos* as large, as wide, as long, as much

Ὅσος is a correlative pron. attested from the time of Homer; it appears in the NT 110 times (excluding several v.l.). Noteworthy is the concentration in Phil 4:8 (there alone 6 of the 7 occurrences in Philippians). The pron. is found almost exclusively in the nom. and acc. (BDF §293), the exceptions being Luke 11:8 (δώσει αὐτῷ ὅσων χρῄζει); Heb 8:6 (ὅσῳ, *to the extent that/insofar as*), and the expression τοσούτῳ . . . ὅσῳ, *as much . . . as,* Heb 1:4; 10:25. Ὅσος can designate an extension of space (Rev 21:16) or time (ἐφ' ὅσον χρόνον, Rom 7:1; ἐφ' ὅσον, Matt 9:15; ὅσον χρόνον, Mark 2:19). With numbers and statements of quantity ὅσος can mean *as much/as much as* (John 6:11), or in the pl. in connection with πάντες (or ἅπαντες), "all *who*" (Luke 4:40; John 10:8; Acts 3:24, etc.; in the same sense but without πάντες, 9:34; 10:45, etc.). In comparisons, ὅσος gives the proportions of the things compared; cf. Mark 7:36 (ὅσον . . . , μᾶλλον περισσότερον, "the more . . . the more"); Heb 3:3 (πλείων . . . , καθ' ὅσον πλείων, "as much more . . . as than"); 10:25 (τοσούτῳ μᾶλλον ὅσῳ, "all the more *as*"), etc. Among the special expressions are the exclamatory ἔτι μικρὸν ὅσον ὅσον in Heb 10:37 (quoting Isa 26:20 LXX), "only a little, *how little, how little!*" = "only a very little while yet" (→ μικρόν; BDF §304); likewise, Luke 5:3 D: ὅσον ὅσον, "very little" (instead of ὀλίγον).

ὅσπερ, 3 *hosper* just the one who, which indeed

Mark 15:6 TR: ὅσπερ ᾐτοῦντο (instead of ὃν παρῃτοῦντο).

ὀστέον, ου (ὀστοῦν, οῦ), τό *osteon (ostoun)* bones, skeleton*

In the NT used only in the pl. without the art., with the exception of John 19:36, where the contracted form ὀστοῦν is used in an LXX quotation (Exod 12:10, 46; cf. BDF §45). The resurrected Jesus demonstrates his corporeality in Luke 24:39 with reference to flesh and *bones*. According to Matt 23:27 the Pharisees are like graves filled with the *bones* of the dead (cf. E. Haenchen, *Gott und Mensch* 29-54, esp. 50). Heb 11:22 refers to the *bones* of Joseph (cf. Gen 50:24); see also Eph 5:30 v.l. (quoting Gen 2:23 LXX).

ὅστις, ἥτις, ὅ τι *hostis, hētis, ho ti* whoever/whichever; (the one) who/which; who/which (rel. pron.)

Lit.: BAGD s.v. — BDF §§293; 300. — H. J. CADBURY, "The Relative Pronouns in Acts and Elsewhere," *JBL* 42 (1923) 150-57. — RADERMACHER, *Grammatik* 75. — V. SPOTTORNO, "The Relative Pronoun in the NT," *NTS* 28 (1982) 132-41. — ZERWICK, *Biblical Greek* §§215-20.

1. The pron. is found in the text of *UBSGNT* 148 times (see *VKGNT* II, 202f.), and is rather evenly distributed with the exception of Mark (only 5 occurrences), John (6), and the Catholic Epistles (5); but aside from the acc. ὅ τι (Acts 9:6, *everything that;* with ἐάν, Mark 6:23; 1 Cor 16:2; Col 3:17; and with ἄν, Luke 10:35; John 2:5; 14:13; 15:16, *whatever/everything that*) and the fixed formula ἕως ὅτου (instead of ἕως οὗ [Matt 1:25, etc.]), *so long as/until* (Matt 5:25; Luke 12:50; 13:8; 15:8; 22:16, 18; John 9:18), it is found only in the nom. sg. and pl. It is usually mixed with the simple rel. as follows: in the sg., ὅς, ἥτις, ὅ; οὗ, ἧς, οὗ, etc.; in the pl., οἵτινες, αἵτινες, ἅ; ὧν, etc. The form οἵτινες (60 occurrences in the NT) is found with particular frequency in Acts (18 of the 24 passages in Acts in which some form of ὅστις occurs).

2. Ὅστις has various functions. a) It can be used for generalization, e.g., in Matt 7:24, here even—pleonastically—with πᾶς (as in 10:32; 19:29), *everyone who* (with πᾶς and ἐάν, Col 3:17). b) It can have a qualitative sense, e.g., in Matt 7:15: "Guard yourselves against false prophets *(namely, the type who/that is, those)* who come to you in sheep's clothing." In corresponding fashion, Rom 16:3-7 uses both ὅς and ὅστις; cf. BAGD s.v. and Zerwick. c) ὅστις can—particularly in koine—replace ὅς; cf. Matt 18:23 with 22:2, where the same introductory sentence ὡμοιώθη . . . βασιλεῖ is continued in the one case with ὅς and in the other with ὅστις; likewise cf. Rom 4:16 with Gal 4:26; also Heb 9:2, 9; 13:7. On ὅστις as an interrogative pron. see BDF §300.   W. Radl

ὀστοῦν, οῦ, τό *ostoun* bones, skeleton
→ ὀστέον.

ὀστράκινος, 3 *ostrakinos* earthen, clay (adj.)*

In the NT found only in the combination σκεύη ὀστράκινα, "clay/fragile vessel" (cf. Lev 11:33; also Dan 2:34, 42 LXX; Lam 4:2; Artemidorus *Onirocriticus* v.25): 2 Cor 4:7, fig. for the weak and *fragile* body of the apostle as a "vessel" of the new ministry of glory (ἐν ὀστρακινοῖς σκεύεσιν; cf. further R. Bultmann, 2 Cor [Eng. tr., 1985] 111-12); 2 Tim 2:20, fig. for the false teachers who are σκεύη ξύλινα καὶ ὀστράκινα (in contrast to χρυσᾶ καὶ ἀργυρᾶ).

ὄσφρησις, εως, ἡ *osphrēsis* sense of smell, nose*

1 Cor 12:17, as a bodily function or part of the body with ὀφθαλμός and ἀκοή, most likely the faculty of smell.

ὀσφῦς, ύος, ἡ *osphys* waist, loin*

8 occurrences in the NT: according to Mark 1:6 par. Matt 3:4 John the Baptist wore "a leather belt around his *waist*" (cf. 4 Kgdms 1:8 of Elijah). The exhortation to gird up the *loins* is tantamount to a call to readiness for departure and action, since the garment was worn un-girded in the house (cf. Dalman, *Arbeit* II, 151f.; V, 232f.; Exod 12:11; Jer 1:17; Ezek 9:11; Isa 11:5 messianically): Luke 12:35; Eph 6:14 (ἐν ἀληθείᾳ; cf. Isa 11:5); 1 Pet 1:13 (τὰς ὀσφύας τῆς διανοίας ὑμῶν). Fig., "(fruit) of the *loins*" in reference to physical descent: Acts 2:30 (cf. Ps 131:11 LXX); Heb 7:5, 10 (cf. Gen 35:11; 2 Cor 6:9). H. Seesemann, *TDNT* V, 496f.; G. Fohrer, *BHH* 1074; R. Feuillet, *DBT* 320; E. Levine, "The Wrestling-belt Legacy in the NT," *NTS* 28 (1982) 560-64.

ὅταν *hotan* then, when, whenever

The 123 occurrences are concentrated in the Gospels (Matthew has 19 occurrences, Mark 21, Luke 29 [Acts only in 23:35 and 24:22], John 17); elsewhere less frequently, e.g., 1 Corinthians has 12 occurrences (9 in chs. 15–16) and Revelation 9 occurrences.

The temporal particle ὅταν (on its iterative meaning cf. BDF §367) is found as a rule with the subjunc., where its meaning approaches that of ἐάν (see Kühner, *Grammatik* II/2, 447f.; BDF §382.3f.; cf. esp. 1 John 2:28, where the majority of mss. read ὅταν instead of ἐάν): with the pres. usually with an iterative sense: *whenever/as often as,* Matt 6:2, 5f., 16; noniterative with following τότε, "*when* . . . then," 1 Thess 5:3; the expression ἕως τῆς ἡμέρας ἐκείνης ὅταν . . . πίνω (Mark 14:25 par. Matt 26:29) paraphrases the classical πρὶν ἄν, "until the day *when* . . . /before"; frequently with the aor. when an action is indicated which precedes that of the main clause (often with a following τότε): Matt 5:11; 9:15; Mark 4:15f., 29, 31f.; 8:38; Luke 6:22 (bis); Rom 2:14; 2 Cor 13:9, etc.

Less frequently ὅταν is also found (postclassical, see BDF §382.4) with the fut. and pres. ind. to express an expectation: Mark 11:25: *whenever;* Luke 13:28 v.l.; Rev 4:9 (see also BDF §382.4); with the aor. in Mark 11:19 (iterative); Rev 8:1 (with the sense of the v.l. ὅτε, "when"); with the impf. in Mark 3:11 (iterative).

ὅτε *hote* when, then, after

Ὅτε appears 103 times in the NT (excluding several v.l.), including 12 times in each of the Synoptic Gospels, 21 times in John, 10 times in Acts, and 13 times in Revelation.

As a conj. (with ind.) ὅτε indicates the point in time when an event occurs, esp. in combination with the aor. (BDF §382.1): ὅτε ἐπιστεύσαμεν, "*at the time when* we began to believe," Rom 13:11; in Matthew frequently as a transitional formula, καὶ ἐγένετο ὅτε, "and it happened *when,*" 7:28; 13:53, etc.; cf. further Matt 11:1; Luke 22:14; Gal 2:11, etc.; with impf.: *so long as,* Mark 14:12; 15:41; Rom 6:20; 1 Cor 12:2; with the pf.: *after,* 1 Cor 13:11b; with pres.: *when,* Mark 11:1 (historical pres.; cf. D impf.); *as long as,* Heb 9:17.

Ὅτε after a subst. indicating time can also take the place of a rel. pron.: ἔρχεται ὥρα (. . .) ὅτε, John 4:21, 23; 5:25; ἔρχεται νὺξ ὅτε, 9:4; ἔσται γὰρ καιρὸς ὅτε, 2 Tim 4:3; cf. further Luke 17:22; John 16:25. In Luke 13:35, ἕως ἥξει ὅτε εἴπητε, καιρός should probably be supplied from ὅτε (only here subjunc.; cf. v.l. ἕως ἄν), "*until the point in time* comes *when* he says" (BDF §382.2).

ὅτι *hoti* that, because

1. Occurrences and usage — 2. Ὅτι = *that* — 3. Recitative ὅτι — 4. Causal ὅτι

Lit.: BAGD s.v. — BDF §§388; 394; 408; 456.1f.; 470.1. — Kühner, *Grammatik* II/2 (index s.v.). — Mayser, *Grammatik* II/1, 310-16; II/3, 46f., 204. — Moulton, *Grammar* II, 453f.; III, 49f., 136f., 318. — Radermacher, *Grammatik* 78, 179, 184, 192f., 195-97, 208f.

1. The 1,297 total occurrences of the conj. ὅτι (origi-nally neut. of → ὅστις) are relatively evenly distributed throughout the NT writings, although one can discern a concentration of usage in the Johannine writings (John, 1 John). The use of ὅτι in the NT corresponds essentially to that of classical Greek. In contrast to classical usage, however, ὅτι more frequently takes the place of what would elsewhere usually be a construction with the inf. or partc. Having the same meaning as ὅτι, *that,* is the more subjectively nuanced ὡς or πῶς.

2. Ὅτι, *that,* indicates content or obj. after vbs. of mental or sensual perception (Matt 2:22; 24:33, etc.), of believing, thinking, judging, hoping (Matt 5:17; 6:7; John 11:50, etc.), and of saying and announcing (Luke 22:70;

Rom 10:2; 1 Cor 15:50, etc.). The subj. of the ὅτι clause is frequently supplied by the obj. of the main clause (e.g., Acts 4:13c; 1 Cor 16:15b). In the Johannine writings, ὅτι is also used where one would expect an epexegetical inf. (John 3:19; 1 John 4:9, 13, etc.).

Ὅτι is found in direct and indirect questions as an interrogative pron.: *what?/why?* (Mark 2:16c; 9:11; John 8:25 v.l.; Acts 9:6 v.l., etc.). Ὅτι also has a consecutive sense: *that/so that* (Matt 8:27 par.; Heb 2:6, etc.).

3. The recitative ὅτι functions much like quotation marks to introduce direct speech (Matt 7:23; Mark 1:37; John 10:36; 2 Thess 3:10, etc.). Scripture quotations are also introduced in this way (Matt 21:16; Mark 12:19; Luke 2:23; John 10:34, etc.).

4. Ὅτι also introduces subordinate causal clauses: *since/because* (Mark 1:34; John 8:47; 20:29; Rom 9:32, etc.). The subordination is often so loose that it demands the translation *for* (Matt 7:13; Luke 9:12; 13:31; 2 Cor 4:6, etc.). H. Kleine

ὅτου *hotou* of everyone who/everything which; after prep.: then, when*

The gen. ὅτου of the pron. ὅστις is found 5 times in the NT in the fixed prep. expression ἕως ὅτου, *until (up to the time when)*, with the ind., John 9:18; with the subjunc., Luke 12:50; 13:8; 15:8 v.l.; 22:16, 18 v.l.; with the meaning *while/so long as* (with the ind.), Matt 5:25 (cf. BDF §455.3; → ὅς 4).

οὗ *hou* where, wherever (adv.)

The locative adv., which derives from the gen. of → ὅς, is found 24 times in the NT, esp. in the Lukan writings (Luke has 5 occurrences [only in passages original to Luke, elsewhere → ὅπου] and in 22:10 v.l.; Acts has 8 occurrences and 20:6 v.l.; see BDF §293). Elsewhere, Matthew and Romans each have 3 occurrences, and 1–2 Corinthians, Colossians, Hebrews, and Revelation all have 1; οὗ does not appear in Mark or in the Johannine writings (with the exception of John 11:41 v.l.).

Οὗ can also replace a rel. pron. where it usually stands after a subst. indicating a place: *where*, Luke 4:16f.; 23:53; Acts 1:13; 7:29, etc.; also ἐπάνω οὗ, "the place *where*," Matt 2:9; οὗ . . . ἐκεῖ, "*where* . . . there," Matt 18:20 (both literal and fig. senses are possible); in fig. sense in Rom 4:15: οὗ δὲ οὐκ ἔστιν νόμος, "*where* there is no law," as a reference to the condition under which something applies; cf. 5:20; 2 Cor 3:17.

In the literal sense *where*, 1 Cor 16:6: οὗ ἐὰν πορεύωμαι, "*wherever* I go"; εἰς . . . τόπον οὗ, "to every place *where*," Luke 10:1; εἰς τὸ ὄρος οὗ, Matt 28:16; εἰς τὴν κώμην οὗ, Luke 24:28.

οὔ *ou* no, not*

In the NT, οὔ (with accent) is found 17 times; in John 1:21 and 21:5 independently as the negative response *no* (also in Matt 13:29; John 7:12); in the wordplay ναὶ καὶ οὔ in 2 Cor 1:18f.; doubled: ναὶ ναί, ου οὔ in Matt 5:37, substantivized: τὸ ναὶ ναὶ καὶ τὸ ου οὔ in Jas 5:12; 2 Cor 1:17 (→ ναί 3). Also at the end of a clause with the same meaning as οὐ: Mark 12:14 par. Matt 22:17/Luke 20:22; Luke 14:3; Rom 7:18. BDF §§432.1; 493; → οὐ 1.3.

οὐ (οὐκ, οὐχ) *ou (ouk, ouch)* not
οὔ *ou* no, not

1. Occurrences in the NT — 2. Stylistic function in theological rhetoric — 3. The decisive "no"

Lit.: BAGD s.v. — BDF index s.v.

1. Οὐ appears 1,612 times in the NT. It is lacking only in Philemon. The accented form οὔ is found 17 times.

The negative particle is used as an obj. negation *(not)* and as an exclamation *(no);* before unaspirated vowels it becomes οὐκ and before aspirated vowels οὐχ. With an accent (οὔ) it is used as a negative answer: *no*, e.g., Matt 13:29; John 1:21; 7:12; 21:5. Esp. in quotations from the LXX, οὐ translates Heb. *lō'*, frequently in combination with a partc. or in the form of the fut. prohibition, "you shall (will) *not*," Matt 5:21; 19:18; Rom 7:7; 13:9; dependent on the Decalogue, Exod 20:13-17; Deut 5:17-21. In rhetorical questions that expect an affirmative answer, it may or may not be used: Matt 6:26; 17:24; 27:13; Mark 6:3; 7:18; 12:24; Luke 11:40; John 4:35; 6:70; 7:25; Acts 9:21; cf. Mark 4:38, in the account of the storm at sea: "Master, does it *not* bother you that we are perishing?"

In questions in which the vb. is already negated by οὐ, the negation can be nullified by the interrogative particle μή, which itself demands a negative answer, with the result that a positive affirmation ensues; cf. Rom 10:18: μὴ οὐκ ἤκουσαν; "Surely you have heard?"; 1 Cor 9:4: μὴ οὐκ ἔχομεν ἐξουσίαν; "Do we *not* have the right?"; 1 Cor 11:22: μὴ οἰκίας οὐκ ἔχετε; "Do you *not* have houses [in which to eat and drink]?" The rhetorical configurations οὐ . . . δέ (Acts 12:9, 14; Heb 4:13, 15), οὐ μόνον, ἀλλὰ (καί), and οὐ . . . εἰ μή are very common, esp. in Paul.

2. The negative particle plays an important rhetorical role in apologetic argumentation, since it can be used emphatically to delimit and distinguish between points of view and practices, thus making it possible to achieve a high degree of contrast; cf., e.g., Matt 6:24: "You are *not* able to serve God and mammon." In Gal 4:8f.: τότε οὐκ . . . νῦν δέ ("At that time, of course, when you did *not* know God, you served gods who in reality are no gods"). Or 2 Cor 4:8: θλιβόμενοι ἀλλ' οὐ στενοχωρούμενοι ("We

are hard pressed on every side, but *not* crushed; perplexed, but *not* in despair"). These apologetic undertones are also present in Rom 9:25: τὸν οὐ λαόν μου ("I will call them 'my people' who are *not* my people"; cf. Hos 2:25 LXX; 1 Pet 2:10); likewise, in Rom 10:19: οὐκ ἔθνος ("those who are *not* a nation," Deut 32:21). The actual negation of nonbeing can be turned into being through the election of the almighty creator God (cf. Rom 4:17: "God, who makes the dead alive, and calls things that are *not* as though they were").

3. The NT emphasizes repeatedly the decisive nature of "no" (οὐ) as a point of conviction and a clear expression of faith. In Matt 5:37: "Let your 'Yes' be 'Yes,' and your 'No' be 'No'; anything beyond this comes from the evil one." Likewise in Jas 5:12: "Rather let your 'Yes' be yes, and your 'No,' no, so that you do not fall under judgment." The demand for absolute truthfulness and trustworthiness should make all swearing and oaths superfluous; cf. *1 Enoch* 49:1; Billerbeck I, 337. Paul is also familiar with this ethic of honesty and candor: 2 Cor 1:17: "Or do I make my plans in a worldly manner, so that in the same breath I say 'Yes, yes' and 'No, no'?" The Son of God "was not 'Yes' and 'No,' but in him it has always been 'Yes'" (v. 19). Paul gives this decisiveness a dogmatic foundation in the fact that Jesus Christ incarnates God's comprehensive "Yes" to the world, history, and humanity; in the incarnation of the Son, God has, in principle, said "Yes" to the world and to each individual person. From this conviction also results the decisive "No," the trustworthiness and confidence that demands from the congregation recognition of apostolic authority.

P.-G. Müller

οὐά *oua* Well! So!*

In Mark 15:29, the interjection of astonishment οὐά introduces the mocking calls of those who passed by the cross.

οὐαί *ouai* Woe!; subst.: woe*

1. Οὐαί is a NT Semitism (cf. Heb. *hôy, 'ôy*), but also a Latinism (cf. Lat. *vae*); it is used as an interjection expressing pain, lament, and esp. a threat in 41 passages in the NT, and with the exception of 1 Cor 9:16 (subst.) and Jude 11, primarily in Revelation (9 texts: 8:13 [threefold cry of woe]; 18:10, 16, 19 [each time a twofold cry of woe]; 12:12; substantivized [indeclinable], 9:12 [bis]; 11:14 [bis] of the three woes) and in the Synoptic Gospels (Matthew has 13 occurrences, Mark 2, and Luke 15), where the series of woes spoken by Jesus figures prominently (Matt 11:21; 18:7 [bis]; 23:13, 15f., 23, 25, 27, 29; Luke 6:24-26 [4 occurrences]; 10:13 [bis]; and 11:42-44 [ter], 46f.). Usually οὐαί is combined with the

dat. (30 times, including Luke 17:1 [οὐαί δι' οὗ = οὐαί τούτῳ δι' οὗ]), with the nom. (as voc.), Luke 6:25b (cf. also, however, 6:25a); Rev 18:10, 16, 19; with the acc., Rev 8:13; 12:12; with following ὅταν (without indication of person), Luke 6:26; with following ὅτι, Luke 6:24f.; 11:42-44, 46 (οὐαί placed after), 47, 52; Jude 11; with following ἐάν, 1 Cor 9:16; see also BDF §§190.2; 412.5.

2. In the OT, the cry of woe as lament or esp. as threat is found primarily in prophetic usage (Hos 7:13; Isa 1:4; 10:5; Jer 23:1; Ezek 24:6; Isa 5:8-22 sixfold woe; with blessings, Isa 3:9-11; Eccl 10:16f.; Tob 13:12, 14; see also *2 Bar.* 10:6f.); *1 Enoch* 94-100 has several series of woes: 94:6ff.; 95:5ff. threefold; 96:4ff. fivefold; 97:7f. twofold; 98:9–99:2 eightfold; 99:11ff. fivefold; 100:7f. twofold; in 99:10 a contrasting blessing is found.

The NT cries of woe link up with this prophetic usage. Esp. in the Jesus tradition they convey the threat of judgment and exclusion from eschatological salvation: "Jesus'" cries of woe are also applied to cities (Matt 11:21 bis par. Luke 10:13 bis), the cosmos (Matt 18:7a), individuals (18:7b par. Luke 17:1), the Pharisees and the scribes (Matt 23:13ff.; cf. Luke 11:42ff.; on this see Bultmann, *History* 113f.; W. Grundmann, *Luke* [THKNT] 244ff.). The apocalyptic cries of lament (Mark 13:17 par. Matt 24:19/Luke 21:23) and the cry of woe against the betrayer of Jesus (Mark 14:21 par. Matt 26:24/Luke 22:22) originate with Mark. Luke contrasts the four blessings (→ μακάριος 4.a) of the Sermon on the Plain with four analogously constructed, antithetical cries of woe (6:24-26; redacted: J. Dupont, *Les Béatitudes* I, 299ff.; C. Michaelis, *NovT* 10 [1968] 148-61; P. Klein, *ZNW* 17 [1980] 150-59, et al.; from Q: Bultmann, *History* 111f.; H. Schürmann, Luke I [HTKNT] ad loc.; G. Schneider, *Luke* [ÖTK] ad loc., et al.).

In Revelation, the threefold apocalyptic cry of woe (8:13) announces the horrors of the end times for unbelieving humanity (cf. the loose connection with the "fifth trumpet" in 9:12, and also 11:14; 12:12). The subst. ἡ οὐαί is treated as a fem. in 9:12 and 11:14 (cf. ἡ θλῖψις and the like; BDF §58). In 18:10, 16, 19 a cry of lament, repeated three times, goes up from those who observe the fall of Babylon from a distance (for the doubling of οὐαί cf. Amos 5:16; Mic 7:4; on Babylon Jer 28:2 LXX; also Ezekiel 26–27). E. Höhne, *BHH* 2147f. (bibliography); *BL* 1873 (bibliography); P. Klein, "Die lukanischen Weh"rufe Lk 6,24-26," *ZNW* 71 (1980) 150-59; A. D. Lowe, *Hermes, Zeitschrift für klassische Philologie* 105 (1967) 34-39; J. C. Margot, "The Translation of οὐαί," *BT* 19 (1968) 26f.

H. Balz

οὐδαμῶς *oudamōs* in no way, absolutely not*

In Matt 2:6 Bethlehem is designated as οὐδαμῶς ἐλαχίστη . . . ἐν τοῖς ἡγεμόσιν (contrast Mic 5:1 LXX: ὀλιγοστός . . . ἐν χιλιάσιν Ιουδα).

οὐδέ *oude* and not, also not, not (nor) even

Οὐδέ appears in the NT 143 times, esp. in the Synoptic Gospels (Matthew has 27 occurrences, Mark 10, Luke 21), John (17), Acts (12), Revelation (11), 1 Corinthians (10), and Galatians (9).

As a negative conj., οὐδέ connects negative clauses or partial clauses and is found primarily after οὐ: *and not/ nor* (Matt 6:20, 28; Mark 4:22; John 6:24, etc.); after οὐδείς in Matt 9:17 and Rev 5:3 (οὐδείς . . . οὐδέ . . . οὐδέ, "no one . . . *and* . . . *and*"); οὐδὲ γάρ, "for *not*," John 5:22; 8:42; with the meaning *also not* (Matt 6:15; 21:27; 25:45; Rom 4:15; 1 Cor 15:13, etc.); οὐδὲ γάρ, "for *also not*" (Gal 1:12).

Οὐδέ can also, however, be used to emphasize an extraordinary fact: "*Not even* Solomon was dressed as one of these," Matt 6:29; cf. also Mark 5:3; 12:10; Luke 7:9; 12:26; 23:15; 1 Cor 3:2; 5:1, etc.; οὐδείς . . . οὐδὲ . . . οὐδέ, Mark 13:32 par. Matt 24:36 ("no one . . . *not even . . . nor even*"); οὐδὲ εἷς, "*and not* one," Matt 27:14; Acts 4:32; Rom 3:10 (cf. BDF §445.2); οὐδέ can also intensify a preceding οὐ: Luke 18:13 (οὐκ ἤθελεν οὐδέ, "he did *not even* want"); Acts 7:5; cf. also Rom 3:10. BAGD s.v. (bibliography).

οὐδείς, οὐδεμία, οὐδέν *oudeis, oudemia, ouden* no, no one, nothing
οὐθείς *outheis* no, no one, nothing

1. Occurrences in the NT — 2. Function in theological argumentation — 3. In descriptions of christological exclusivity

Lit.: BAGD s.v. — BDF index s.v.

1. Οὐδείς occurs 227 times in the NT (Matthew has 19 occurrences, Mark 26, Luke 33, John 53, Acts 25, the Pauline corpus 49, Revelation 12), and the grammatical forms are distributed as follows: οὐδείς (98 occurrences), οὐδεμία (3), οὐδεμίαν (8), οὐδέν (85), οὐδένα (16), οὐδενί (9), and οὐδενός (8). In addition, the orthographic variant οὐθείς is found in the form οὐθέν 5 times, and οὐθενός twice. As an adj. negation (οὐδεὶς προφήτης, "*no* prophet," Luke 4:24) or as a negative subst., "no one" (Matt 6:24; 8:10; 9:16; Mark 2:21; 5:4; 7:24; Luke 5:36, 39; John 1:18; Rom 14:7; 1 Cor 2:11; 3:11), sometimes with partitive gen. (οὐδεὶς ἀνθρώπων, "*no man*," Mark 11:2), sometimes with ἐκ (John 7:19; 16:5; οὐδὲν ἐκτὸς ὤν, "*nothing* beyond that which," Acts 26:22), it designates the exclusivity of a matter or group of persons. In conditional negation it is found in the combination οὐδείς . . . εἰ μή, "*no one . . . except*" (Matt 11:27; 17:8; Mark 10:18; Luke 10:22; 18:19; John 14:6; 17:12; 1 Cor 1:14; 8:4; Rev 2:17; 14:3; 19:12); in the combination οὐδείς . . . ἐὰν μή (John 3:2; 6:44, 65); in pleonastic construction: οὐ . . . οὐδείς, "*not . . . anyone*" (Matt 22:16; Mark 3:27;

5:37; 12:14; Luke 8:43; John 8:15; 18:31; Acts 4:12; 1 Cor 6:5), οὐκέτι . . οὐδείς (Mark 9:8; 12:34), οὐδεὶς οὔπω, "*no one* ever" (Luke 23:53; Mark 11:2), οὐδέπω οὐδείς, "*no one* ever" (John 19:41), "not yet . . . *anyone*" (Acts 8:16), οὐδὲ . . . οὐκέτι οὐδείς, "*no one* [had yet been able to bind him]" (Mark 5:3), οὐδενὶ οὐδέν, "[and they said] *nothing to anyone*" (Mark 16:8).

In a fig. sense the word indicates a meaningless, invalid, useless, senseless matter: "Whoever swears by the temple, [this oath] is *invalid*" (Matt 23:16; cf. John 8:54; 1 Cor 7:19); εἰ καὶ οὐδέν εἰμι, "even though I am [in your eyes] *nothing*" (2 Cor 12:11; Acts 21:24; 25:11). The acc. οὐδέν, "not in any respect, in no connection, in no way": οὐδὲν διαφέρει, "he does not distinguish himself *in any respect*" (Gal 4:1); οὐθὲν διέκρινεν, "[and made] *no* distinction [between us and them]" (Acts 15:9); Ἰουδαίους οὐδὲν ἠδίκησα, "I have not *in any way* done an injustice to the Jews" (Acts 25:10); οὐδέν μοι διαφέρει, "it is all the same to me" (Gal 2:6).

2. Οὐδεὶς κτλ. display their semantic relevance esp. in apologetic argumentation for the restrictive exclusivity of the kingdom of God, of faith in Jesus Christ, and of the Church as the community of Christ into which "no one enters who. . . ." The excommunicative delimitation is, esp. in Paul and John, carried over to membership in the community, to which no one belongs who does not meet certain confessional, ethical, and legal requirements: "*No one* can say 'Lord Jesus'" (1 Cor 12:3); "Without holiness, *no one* will see God" (Heb 12:14). Conversely, the word designates the universality of the kingdom of God and of salvation in Jesus Christ, which cannot be confined by anyone or any human limitation or restriction (Gal 4:1; Acts 15:9). By emphasizing the exclusion of all human authorities and powers, the authority of God is given its full validity. Through the rhetorical accentuation of "nothing, no one, no," the radical decisiveness and the general validity of the statements, esp. in proverbs and aphorisms, is underscored: "*No one* can serve two masters" (Matt 6:24; Luke 16:13); "I have found such faith in *no one* in Israel" (Matt 8:10); "*No one* is good, except God" (Matt 19:17 C Koine W; Mark 10:18; Luke 18:19); "*No one* pours new wine in old wineskins" (Mark 2:22; Luke 5:37); "*Nothing* that enters the man from outside can make him unclean, but that which comes out of the man makes the man unclean" (Mark 7:15); "*No* prophet is welcome in his own country" (Luke 4:24); "*None* of us lives for himself alone" (Rom 14:7). Paul employs this rhetoric of decisiveness esp. in controversies over the law: "through the law *no one* is righteous before God" (Gal 3:11).

3. Finally, the terms of negation are used to delimit the christological exclusivity of the Son, Jesus Christ. "*No one* knows the Son, except the Father" (Matt 11:27;

Luke 10:22) emphasizes the unity of Jesus' relation with God, i.e., the Sonship of the Christ. Likewise, the account of the transfiguration emphasizes the uniqueness of Jesus: "They raised their eyes and saw *no one* except Jesus alone" (Matt 17:8). There are differing traditions for the Synoptic saying: "Of that day and hour *no one* knows, not even the angels in heaven (not even the Son), but only the Father" (Matt 24:36; Mark 12:32; cf. on this B. M. F. van Iersel, *Der "Sohn" in den synoptischen Jesusworten* [1964] 77-88). As a weakening of the exclusivity of Jesus, Luke 7:28 reads: "*No one* born of woman is greater than John the Baptist."

Esp. in John, the exclusivity of the Son is formulated with the contrasting construction with "no one": "*No one* can do these signs" (3:2); "*No one* has ascended into heaven" (3:13); "The Son can do *nothing* by himself" (5:19; cf. 8:28; 9:33); "*No one* can come to me" (6:44, 65); "When the Messiah comes, *no one* will know where he is from" (7:27); only the Son knows: "You know *nothing*" (11:49); "*No one* comes to the Father except through me" (14:6); "Without me you are able to do *nothing*" (15:5); "*No one* has seen God" (1:18; 1 John 4:12). Acts 4:12 also stresses this exclusivity: "In *no one* else is there salvation"; likewise 1 Cor 3:11: "*No one* can lay any other foundation"; where the uniqueness of the Son is grounded in the uniqueness of the Father: there is but *one* God (1 Cor 8:4: οὐδεὶς θεὸς εἰ μὴ εἷς). The word group "no, no one, nothing" in the repertoire of theological language in the NT therefore plays a significant role in delimiting, rejecting, and finally also christologically defining.   P.-G. Müller

οὐδέποτε *oudepote* not ever, never*

16 occurrences in the NT, the majority with the aor.: Matt 7:23; 9:33; 21:16, 42; Mark 2:12, 25; Luke 15:29 (bis); John 7:46; Acts 10:14; 11:8; 14:8; with the pres.: 1 Cor 13:8; Heb 10:1, 11; with the fut.: Matt 26:33; in questions: Matt 21:16, 42; Mark 2:25 (οὐδέποτε ἀνέγνωτε; "Have you *never* read?"). Οὐδέποτε serves esp. to designate something unique, previously unknown: Matt 9:33; Mark 2:12; John 7:46; Acts 10:14; 11:8; 14:8; or to stress the conclusiveness of a statement: Matt 7:23; 1 Cor 13:8; Heb 10:1, 11.

οὐδέπω *oudepō* not yet, not ever*

4 occurrences in the NT, 3 in John (plus Luke 23:53 v.l.; 1 Cor 8:2 v.l., each time for → οὔπω): John 7:39 (picking up on οὔπω); 20:9; 19:41: οὐδέπω οὐδείς, "*not ever* anyone"; cf. Acts 8:16.

οὐθείς, οὐθέν *outheis, outhen* no one, no; neut.: nothing
→ οὐδείς.

οὐκ *ouk* not
→ οὐ.

οὐκέτι *ouketi* no more, no longer

47 occurrences in the NT, including 12 in John, 7 each in Mark and Romans, 4 in Galatians; noteworthy is the absence of οὐκέτι in 1–3 John.

Οὐκέτι is usually found in the literal temporal sense (Matt 19:6; Mark 10:8; Luke 15:19; John 11:54; Acts 20:38; Rom 6:9; 2 Cor 1:23; 5:16; Acts 10:6, etc.); in John occasionally with a following pres. with a fut. sense (14:19; 16:10, 16; 17:11); in connection with another negative, "[and] not . . . any more," and the like (Matt 22:46; Mark 5:3); οὐκέτι οὐδέν, "nothing *any more*" (Mark 7:12; 15:5); οὐδεὶς οὐκέτι (Mark 12:34); οὐκέτι οὐ μή, "*not* ever *again*" (Mark 14:25; Rev 18:14).

In Paul, along with the temporal sense, οὐκέτι often has a logical significance: *no longer* (Rom 7:17; 11:6b; Gal 3:25), esp. in the apodosis of conditional sentences: *then no longer/then not anymore* (Rom 7:20; 11:6a; 14:15; Gal 3:18).

οὐκοῦν *oukoun* therefore; so, then (?)*

In the NT it is only used as an interrogative conj., when the question arises from the immediate context: *then (?)/so (?)* (John 18:37; cf. v. 36); see BDF §451.1; cf. *Barn.* 5:2.

οὖν *oun* therefore, then, consequently, accordingly

Of the 500 occurrences in the NT, approximately 200 are found in John (in contrast to 1–3 John, where there is but one instance); Matthew has 56 occurrences, Luke 33, Acts 63, Romans 48, and Mark only 6.

Οὖν functions as an inferential and connective conj. except in statements (e.g., Matt 1:17; 13:40; Luke 3:7; Rom 5:1; 3 John 8, etc.) and commands (Matt 3:8; 10:31; Mark 13:35; Luke 3:8; Acts 2:36; 16:36; Rom 6:12; Gal 5:1, etc.; John only 8:38), also esp. in questions (Matt 13:28; 21:25; Luke 22:70; John 9:10; 18:8; Acts 19:3; Rom 2:21), in rhetorical questions (Matt 12:12, 26; Luke 7:31; Rom 11:1), and (esp. in Paul) in formulaic, abbreviated questions: τί οὖν; *why then?/what then?* (John 1:21; Rom 3:9; 6:15; 11:7); τί οὖν ἐροῦμεν; "what should we *then* say?" (4:1; 7:7; 8:31; 9:14, 30); τί οὖν ἐστιν; "How *then* do things stand?/what *then?*" (Acts 21:22; 1 Cor 3:5: "what *then* is . . ."; 14:15, 26); τί οὖν φημι (1 Cor 10:19). Also, οὖν resumes the previous train of thought after a parenthetical remark: *therefore/as was said* (Luke 3:7; 19:12; John 4:6; Acts 8:25; 1 Cor 8:4), or introduces something new: *since* (esp. frequent in John; see also BDF §462.1); on combinations with other particles see BDF §451.1. H. Reynen, *Glotta* 36 (1957)

1-47; W. Nauck, *ZNW* 49 (1958) 134f.; D. C. Parker, "The Translation of οὖν in the Old Latin Gospels," *NTS* 31 (1985) 252-76.

οὔπω *oupō* not yet*

26 occurrences in the NT, of which 11 are in John, 5 in Mark.

The temporal adv. οὔπω has in all passages the meaning *not yet:* Matt 16:9; 24:6; Mark 4:40; 8:17, 21; 11:2; 13:7; Luke 23:53; John 2:4 (cf. 7:6, 30; 8:20); 3:24; 6:17; 7:8, 39; 8:57; 11:30; 20:17; 1 Cor 3:2; 8:2; Heb 2:8; 12:4; 1 John 3:2; Rev 17:10, 12 (four times in questions); as an introduction to a parenthetical statement, John 3:24 (οὔπω γάρ); οὐδεὶς οὔπω, "no one *yet*" (Mark 11:2); οὐκ . . . οὐδεὶς οὔπω, "no one *ever*" (Luke 23:53).

οὐρά, ᾶς, ἡ *oura* tail*

5 occurrences in the NT, all in Revelation: pl. 9:10 (bis), in the description of the locust; 9:19 (bis), of the horses that belong to the punishment of the fifth or sixth trumpet; sg. 12:4, of the dragon, which threatened the woman and her child. The threatening violence of the apocalyptic beings always resides in their tails, which are compared to scorpions (9:10) and snakes (9:19).

οὐράνιος, 2 *ouranios* heavenly, pertaining to heaven, deriving from heaven
→ οὐρανός 5.

οὐρανόθεν *ouranothen* from heaven*

A locative adv. responding to the question "from where?": Acts 14:17, of God's heavenly acts of kindness toward the Gentiles (rain and fruitful seasons; → καιρός 6; οὐρανόθεν most likely refers here to God's right to dispense his gifts as he will; cf. also Luke 4:25; Rev 11:6); 23:13, in the account of the call of Paul (a light shone on him *from heaven;* cf. ἐκ τοῦ οὐρανοῦ, 9:3; 22:6). H. Traub, *TDNT* V, 542f.; K. Stendahl, *BHH* 719f.; H. Bietenhard, *DNTT* II, 188, 193; → οὐρανός (3).

οὐρανός, οῦ, ὁ *ouranos* heaven

1. Occurrences and basic meaning — 2. Hermeneutical presuppositions — 3. Field of application — 4. Exemplaric contexts — 5. Οὐράνιος

Lit.: J. BECKER, *John* (ÖTK) esp. 147ff. — H. D. BETZ, *Der Apostel Paulus und die sokratische Tradition* (1972) 84-92. — H. BIETENHARD, *Die himmlische Welt im Urchristentum und Spätjudentum* (WUNT 2, 1954). — idem, *DNTT* II, 188-96. — A. CODY, "God and Heaven: The NT," *Concilium* 123 (1979) 34-42. — E. HAENCHEN, *Acts* (Eng. tr., 1971) esp. 148ff. — F. LENTZEN-DEIS, "Das Motiv der 'Himmelsöffnung' in verschiedenen Gattungen der Umweltliteratur des NT," *Bib* 50

(1969) 301-27. — G. LOHFINK, *Die Himmelfahrt Jesu* (SANT 26, 1971). — C. F. RUSSEL, *A Historical and Exegetical Study of οὐρανός and παραδεῖσος* (Diss. Southern Baptist Theological Seminary, 1951). — H. SCHLIER, *Eph* (1962). — E. SCHWEIZER, *Col* (Eng. tr., 1982) esp. 51f., 79ff., 171ff. — H. TRAUB and G. VON RAD, *TDNT* V, 497-543. — H. WINDISCH, *2 Cor* (KEK, 1924 = 1970) 369ff. — For further bibliography see *TWNT* X, 1207.

1. It is no wonder that οὐρανός is among the frequently used words in the NT. A preference for it in the narrative writings is discernible (Matthew has 82 occurrences, Luke 35, Acts 26, Mark 19, John 18, Acts 52), while usage in the discursive epistolary literature is less prominent (the authentic Pauline letters have 11 occurrences, Ephesians and Colossians 9, Hebrews 10, 2 Peter 6). Among the 274 occurrences, 91 are found in the pl., which was unknown to secular Greek writers; it may have entered NT usage via the LXX. The reasons for this may have been the translation of Heb. *šāmayim*, the plerophory of hymnic and doxological style, or simply oriental influence. An unambiguous rule cannot be discerned. Worthy of mention are the unique expressions used by Matthew: πατὴρ ἡμῶν ὁ ἐν τοῖς οὐρανοῖς (15 occurrences) and βασιλεία τῶν οὐρανῶν (32 occurrences).

Οὐρανός combines physical and metaphysical components. It designates everything that is actually or fig. located over the earth and above humanity: "the firmament, the vault of heaven, the expanse, the divine." From these global differentiations ensue different aspects of meaning, which correspond to contemporary first-century life-situations. Moreover, the nuances that the word displays when combined with preps., or the range produced when οὐρανός is used as an alternative term, are also significant for the description of its content.

2. Among the conditions for understanding οὐρανός are the sociocultural factors of the ancient worldview, in which the NT Scriptures are steeped. That which had power over humans and lay beyond their control was heaven, the heavenly, or in heaven. "Below" and the things that are "below" were defined in contradistinction to "above." Thus the world can become the counterpart or opposite of heaven. A prefigured primal image or antitype to heaven is reflected in earthly events.

To spatial categories can be added those that emphasize temporal priority and thereby secure the primacy of heaven to all that exists. In myth, the empirical is combined with the speculative in a statement on the unity of the world. In addition to variegated Greek thought and Gnostic speculation, it was esp. the OT and apocalyptic (cf. J. A. Soggin, *THAT* II, 965ff.) that gave οὐρανός concrete, historical contours. Encounters with foreign cultures and experiences of suffering and persecution brought in their wake an expansion in linguistic content (visionary heavenly journeys and ecstatic experiences, the construction of a royal, heavenly court; the soteriological functions of the heavenly beyond; remythologization, but also skepticism). Heaven became a substitute term for God (already on the periphery of the canon: Ps 73:9; Job 20:27; Dan 4:23) and provided local correspondence for a future transcendence. Those who reflected on heaven or the heavenly understood themselves as challenged by this realm of power. Whether through acknowledgment or criticism, they objectified their self-understanding. Therefore one ought to recognize in οὐρανός not so much speculative elements of a worldview but rather statements expressed in theological reflection on humanity, the world, and their relation to the One on whom everything depends.

3. Like the worldview of antiquity, the NT combines elements of cosmology with the idea of God. This reciprocity is superseded, however, in that definiteness is brought to bear from the side of the kerygma. The Christ-event lends to this religious word a shift in accent, a transference, and a deprivation of its force.

a) God and heaven belong together. Since God is defined as ὁ θεὸς τοῦ οὐρανοῦ (Matt 11:25; 23:22; Luke 10:21; Acts 7:49; Col 4:1; Rev 11:13; 16:11), heaven shares in the inherent power of God. This absolute status becomes evident through the projection of immanent elements of dominion, e.g., "throne" (cf. Matt 5:34; Mark 14:62; Acts 2:34; Heb 8:1) or "sitting on the right hand" (cf. Eph 1:20; Col 3:1; Heb 1:3, 13; 10:12; Rev 4:9, 10; 5:1, 7, etc.), into heaven. Decisive for the understanding of the scope of the matter is that God himself is determinative of what is predicated to heaven.

The expression πατὴρ ἡμῶν ὁ ἐν τοῖς οὐρανοῖς (Matt 5:16, 45, 48; 6:1, 9; 7:11, 21; 10:32, etc.) displays an analogous relation. The existence of God in space is not at stake here. On the contrary, ἐν τοῖς οὐρανοῖς demonstrates that God is not bound to any geographical location. Heaven thus becomes a "dynamic point of departure" (Traub 521, 532). This is esp. evident in the Sermon on the Mount, which calls that which comes from God perfectly just and good. Since "heaven" is a substitute designation for God, these attributes can be transferred to it. Esp. in Matthew (3:2; 4:17; 11:25; 13:1ff.; 18:1ff., etc.) heaven represents the sovereignty of God. Here the substitute character of this metaphor should be kept in mind. The dynamic of the expression βασιλεία τῶν οὐρανῶν demonstrates, however, that heaven is more and different than an embellishing adj. It refers to the βασιλεία τοῦ θεοῦ, which comes to expression "as a parable within a parable" (Matt 20:1ff., etc.); E. Jüngel, *Paulus und Jesus* [1972] 135). A new reality breaks in in the words and deeds of Jesus. It formulates its principles (Matt 5:3ff.) in opposition to a world that seeks its own autonomy, i.e., confuses itself with God and heaven (cf. Matt 23:13). On the day of the Son of Man (Matt 24:30; 26:64; Mark 13:27; 14:62) the currently disputed metaphor (cf. Matt 19:12; 20:23) will be brought out into the open (cf. 10:33).

b) God has created heaven and earth through his word (Acts 4:24; 14:15; 17:24; Heb 1:10; 2 Pet 3:5; Rev 10:6; 14:7). Quotations and allusions maintain continuity with the OT topos. Οὐρανός is viewed as the highest part of the universe, which is usually described as οὐρανὸς καὶ γῆ καὶ θάλασσα. When the reference is to τὰ πάντα (cf. 1 Cor 15:27ff.; Phil 3:21; Col 1:16; Eph 1:10; 3:15; Heb 1:3; Rev 4:11), the totality of creation, including οὐρανός, is intended. Linked to the created nature of heaven is the knowledge of its transitoriness (Mark 13:31; Heb 1:11f.; 12:26; 2 Pet 3:7, 10; Rev 21:1). It was apocalyptic thought that thematized its historical limitations and expressed its subordination (Matt 5:18f.; 5:34f.; Mark 13:31; Luke 16:17; 21:33). For at the same time that God created the heavens, he also created an "alternative heaven" (cf. Rev 21:1; 2 Pet 3:13), which already exists in perfection and which the visionary can see already (Rev 3:12; 11:19; 20:11; 21:2, 10).

To this sphere also belong those words which compare heaven to a depository, from which the righteous receive their reward (Matt 5:12, 20; 6:20; 8:11; 19:21; Mark 10:21; Luke 10:20; 12:21, 33; 18:22; 1 Pet 1:4; Col 1:5). The righteous are, among others, the martyrs, whose future lies in heaven (Rev 7:15; 11:12; 13:6; 18:20; 19:1), since it is withheld from them on earth. Picking up on an existing tradition, Paul can say that Christians have their home in *the heavens* (Phil 3:20; 2 Cor 5:1f.), without meaning thereby a specific geographical location. The reality of the created heaven remains paradoxical and hidden.

c) In all the literary circles of the NT, heaven is identified as an empirical point of reference (cf. Matt 11:23; Rev 18:5), which is perceived through observation (Luke 17:24). The one who prays looks to heaven (Matt 14:19 par.), the one who makes an oath appeals to heaven as guarantee (Matt 23:22; Jas 5:12; Rev 10:5). It changes colors (Matt 16:2; Luke 12:56). It is the firmament high above the earth (Mark 6:41; 7:34; Luke 18:13; John 17:1; Heb 11:12). It serves as an abode for the birds (Matt 6:26; 8:20; Mark 4:32; Luke 8:5; 9:58; 13:19; Acts 10:12; 11:6). In it amazing phenomena (Acts 2:2, 19; 10:16; 11:10) or signs (Matt 16:1; Luke 11:16; 12:56; Acts 26:13; Rev 15:1) are visible, requiring interpretation.

The local empirical meaning has theological implications as soon as the discussion turns to humanity. For to be human means to live on earth: ὑπὸ τὸν οὐρανόν (Acts 2:5; 4:12; Col 1:23). "Man is under heaven; in principle, then, he can be only a passive recipient. Heaven here denotes the action of God which embraces the whole world and which controls all men" (Traub 531). From this it follows that even as God's preserving and sustaining power is displayed from heaven (Acts 14:17; 1 Pet 1:12), so also his wrath is made manifest from there (Luke 9:54; 17:29; Rom 1:18; 2 Thess 1:7f.; Heb 12:25; Rev 16:21; 20:9). The gesture of the publican (Luke 18:13) is all too understandable. His spatial point of reference at the same time makes his religious structure apparent. In the tradition one uncovers traces that heaven is considered the place of the angels (cf. Matt 22:30 par.; 28:2; Mark 13:32; Luke 2:15; 22:43; Gal 1:8; Rev 10:1, etc.) or the region in which demons exist (1 Cor 8:5f.; 15:24; Col 1:16; 2:10, 15; Eph 1:21; 3:10; 6:12; Acts 7:42; Rev 13:13). The battle is declared against these powers. In heaven a war takes place that brings about the ultimate destruction of their power (cf. Rev 12:7ff.). With the coming of Jesus Christ, the βασιλεία τῶν οὐρανῶν was realized, visibly manifest in the casting down of Satan from heaven (Luke 10:18). Where apocalyptic thought dominates, this war is described as the eschatological end and collapse of the heavenly vault. It is preceded by dramatic events and signs in heaven that announce its arrival (cf. Mark 13:25 par.; Luke 21:11, 26, 33; Rev 6:13f.; 8:10; 9:1; 12:4).

d) Behind the plerophoric phrase ἐν οὐρανῷ/ἐπὶ γῆς (often θάλασσα is mentioned as well; cf. Acts 4:24; 14:15; Rev 10:6; 14:7; 21:1) stands the need to extend the premises of faith to the unity of the world (τὰ πάντα). This composition can be found in the liturgical and hymnic materials (1 Cor 8:5; Col 1:16, 20; Eph 1:10). The point of departure for these expressions is the experience that heaven and earth are at odds with one another. Demonic powers are present in heaven to usurp power for themselves. In the spheres of earthly order humans undergo the basic shaking of the transcendental horizon. They hope for peace and reconciliation through "a return to unity" (Schweizer 80). Christ overcomes division and distress (Col 1:20), in that he casts down the powers arrayed against God, simultaneously initiating a new creation. His ascent to power brings about a change in power, which definitively makes clear what is and is not in heaven (Phil 2:9ff.; 1 Cor 8:6; Eph 3:15; 1 Pet 3:22; Rev 5:3, 13). But the sovereignty of Christ also prevails on earth and summons us to responsible service (cf. the parenesis in Colossians and Ephesians).

The summarizing close of Matthew (28:18ff.) is significant. Even as God and humanity have entered a new relationship as a result of the saving events, so also heaven and earth have entered a new relationship. Heaven is no longer elevated above the earth, as something alien. Rather, it is moved by and concerned with what takes place on earth (Luke 15:7, 18, 21). Heaven becomes a reality when people comply with the will of God (cf. Matt 6:10; 7:21; 12:50; 16:19; 18:18f.). This convergence is made concrete in the "idea of an eschatological taking up of earth into heaven, or descent of heaven to earth" (Traub 519). The prerogative of heaven, however, remains in effect insofar as God in his Word (Matt 5:18; Mark 13:31) remains prior to the whole.

4. The Christ-event expanded the semantic dimensions of οὐρανός.

a) The baptism of Jesus is a key passage (Mark 1:9-11; Matt 3:16f.; Luke 3:21f.; cf. John 1:32). Heaven opens above Jesus and God bears witness to him. This event contradicts the apocalyptic sense of the world, which suffered under a closed heaven and a silent God (cf. Luke 4:25; Jas 5:18; Rev 11:6). Here the ancient expectations were realized (Mark refers to Isa 63:19, Matthew and Luke to Ezek 1:1). For in Jesus of Nazareth eschatological blessing is set in motion. He is not only the door to heaven (cf. John 10:7, 9), but wherever he is, heaven becomes a reality (cf. John 1:51 and Gen 28:12). The voice sounding from heaven (Mark 1:11 par.; cf. 2 Pet 1:18) defines authoritatively the beginning of the eschatological era. That which is from heaven (cf. Mark 11:30f. par.; John 12:28; Acts 11:9; 2 Pet 1:18 in conjunction with Mark 9:7 par.; see further Rev 10:4, 8; 11:12; 14:2, 13, etc.) is distinguished by a contingent and unmistakable claim. In the baptismal account, Mark employs the vb. σχίζω, which surfaces again in the Passion accounts (cf. 1:10 with 15:38), i.e., the cross verifies the history begun in the baptism: God stands by this man from Nazareth. For that reason, visions and experiences from heaven (cf. Acts 7:55ff.; 9:3; 10:11, 16; 11:5; 22:6; Rev 4:1; 8:1; 12:1, 3; 15:5, etc.) are possible here on earth.

b) A second problem area links heaven with the resurrection, exaltation, and return of Jesus Christ. The statements converge in a paradox. On the one hand the Christ-event was revelation, the breakdown of all barriers. On the other hand, this reality remains hidden and withdrawn.

According to an old kerygmatic formula, the return of Christ from heaven is awaited on the basis of his resurrection. At that time, this corrupted cosmos will dissolve in judgment (1 Thess 1:10; cf. 4:16). The resurrected Christ has all power in heaven and on earth. He has been exalted to heaven (Acts 2:33; 3:21) and sits at the right hand of God (cf. Rom 8:34 with 10:6; cf. also Ps 110:1, which is frequently cited in this context). From this "in some sense localizing of the initiative of the divine sovereignty" (Traub 523) one arrives at the resurrection of all the dead. The correspondence in 1 Cor 15:20ff. of ἐκ τῶν νεκρῶν and ἐκ τῶν οὐρανῶν is significant. Paul is not yet familiar with the ascension topos. He conceives of the resurrected Christ as the ἀπαρχή of ἄνθρωπος οὐράνιος, i.e., the resurrected Christ realizes the goal established by God for humanity: he lives ἐκ/ἀπ' οὐρανοῦ. What and who is the ἄνθρωπος ἐκ οὐρανοῦ (15:47) is conveyed in the context by πρῶτος ἄνθρωπος —δεύτερος ἄνθρωπος, πρῶτος Ἀδάμ—ἔσχατος Ἀδάμ. There is no doubt that Paul is here playing on Gen 2:7 LXX and is arguing against speculative logic. The victory of the resurrected one over death introduces the new aeon and classifies the present as the eschaton. He is awaited from heaven as an incarnate contradiction to the scheme of this world. All the affirmations that he has already come from heaven are grounded in this hope.

As long as the hope is unassailed, "he has risen" means the same as "he is coming from heaven" (cf. Mark 14:62 par., picking up on Dan 7:13 and Ps 110:1), without the effect of a naive ontology. With the waning expectation of the parousia, however, this ontology pushed itself to the fore. Daily life demanded compromises and rationalized the enthusiastic hope. It developed into the spheres concept (cf. Col 4:1; Eph 6:9, or the convergence of "above" and "from"), which replaced the lack of theological precision. Resurrection, exaltation, and parousia were torn from each other. One result of this process was the introduction of the "ascension." Yet the concept of exaltation as such did not first result from the experience of the delay of the parousia.

c) Luke 24:51; Acts 1:10f.; and 2:32ff. broach the topic of heaven as the firmament and the limit of the earthly. In Luke 24:50f., after the statement διέστη ἀπ' αὐτῶν follows the clause καὶ ἀνεφέρετο εἰς τὸν οὐρανόν. In some textual witnesses (א* D it) this clause is lacking. Apart from the better attestation of the longer text (𝔭75 A B C) one must consider that the omission of the portion of the verse relating to the ascension can better be explained by a later insertion. In this way a contradiction with Acts 1:9 can be avoided (cf., in contrast, the tradition of Acts 1:2). One could read the Lukan account as though the resurrected Christ had returned to earthly life. In the composition as a whole, the ascension marks the close of the appearances of the resurrected Christ and constructs in legendary form the bridge between the resurrection and the awaited parousia (cf. Bultmann, *History* 286f.). To the one who ascended into heaven (cf. the kerygmatic language in Mark 16:19; 1 Pet 3:22 and the christologically interpreted Ps 110:1) definitively belongs God's sphere of power, a fact that the extension of time cannot diminish (Acts 2:32f.).

At the core of the history in Acts 1:9f. (Haenchen 151: "unsentimental, almost uncannily austere") stand the concrete fact of the ascension (4 occurrences of οὐρανός) and a critical commentary on the attitude of the disciples. The confidence in the parousia, which may have been doubted, is supposed to be strengthened. The author has replaced the imminent expectation with a new form of hope, in that he renounces such dating and depicts the coming one as the one who is. Since the resurrected one is among Christians, the Church gains new worth and direction. This real presence is accordingly lived when the ascension and the parousia of the Lord are distinguished.

d) The ascension of the soul mentioned in 2 Cor 12:2ff. is a unique occurrence and has nothing to do with the complex just described. It deals neither with a Gnostic process of redemption nor with an extraordinary source of knowledge nor with an actual fact. In Gnostic circles this topos was certainly well known (cf. the references in

Windisch 371ff.). But one must begin with its literary usage in the context in order to understand the Pauline intention. As Betz has demonstrated (84ff.), Paul parodies a report of an ascension. In his conversation with the congregation, the apostle slips into the role of the fool (cf. 11:16ff.; 12:11), in order to be able to argue in a rhetorically convincing way against the attacks of his opponent.

e) Eph 4:8ff. also speaks of a journey into heaven (ἀναβὰς εἰς ὕψος; cf. Rom 10:6f.). In contrast to the widespread three-tiered model, Ephesians plays on a conception in which the world is a plane surrounded by spheres (i.e., heavens). From the earth, existence extends into the heavenly realms. There is no underworld, since the realm of the demons and the devil are found "above" the earth in the lower spheres of heaven (cf. 2:2; 3:10; 6:12). These powers destroy the unity of the universe and obstruct humanity's relation to God. With reference to Christ (2:14), who has removed the enslaving obstacles and the isolation, the author composes his parenetic call to unity (4:1ff.). He quotes Ps 68:19 LXX, albeit with modifications, so that the reference to Christ is clear, as it is in the parenesis in vv. 9f. Ascent and descent refer to the same person. The descended redeemer breaks through the realms of heaven that isolate humans. They become realms of transit. The ascent into heaven that follows the descent realizes the liberation of the oppressed and the subjection of the oppressor. By virtue of the ascension a path is completed on which the incarnate and exalted one lays claim to the universe (1:10, 22; 4:15). As triumphant warrior (cf. Rom 9:5) he is the peace of all those who were both far and near, in heaven and on earth.

Ephesians develops its ecclesiology from the cosmic Christ-event. The Church, as the body or πλήρωμα (1:23) of Christ, extends from "above," where Christ reigns, down to earth. Those who are incorporated into this Church still live in the world and are embroiled in the battle with the powers. As those who have been baptized, however, they belong to the side of the victor. Thus Christians experience who they are by being told where they are. With such affirmative tendencies the author of Ephesians comes very close to a Gnostic redemption consciousness (cf. 2:5f.). Moreover, the preference for spatial categories leads easily to ideological misunderstanding. When the Church "represents something as remarkable as heaven on earth" (Schweizer 51; cf. Col 1:12ff.), the desire to exercise lordship and claims to exclusivity grow.

f) To the question "Who can attain to the heavenly world?" John gives the answer "Only the one who has come from the heavenly world" (3:13; cf. also the supplementary textual variants). Ὁ ἐκ τοῦ οὐρανοῦ ἐρχόμενος gains almost titular power (cf. 6:14), for οὐρανός identifies that which is ἐπάνω πάντων (3:31). There is a striking concentration of οὐρανός in chs. 3 and 6, where it appears only in the sg. Apparently an anti-Gnostic tendency is here being expressed. The power opposed to God is not located in heaven, but is the κόσμος or ὁ ἄρχων τοῦ κόσμου (cf. 12:31). Heaven and the one coming from heaven stand in opposition to all that occurs in the world (3:31). When it is said that heaven opened above Jesus at his baptism, the antithesis to the human world is thereby made concrete. The eternal communion with the Father did not come to an end in the incarnation. In him and through him the cosmos was first revealed for what it was (1:14). The debate is over whether humanity belongs to the cosmos or to heaven. The brusque argumentation of ch. 6 ascribes to the heavenly world truth and life (6:31ff.; cf. 5:26). Death falls to the part of the cosmos. By sharing in the bread from heaven (6:38, 41f., 50f., 58) the believer has life. By means of the bread discourse, the author highlights the incarnation, which was under dispute in the Church.

g) An independent variant of the "ascension" theme is found in Hebrews, which creates a new basic tenet of faith by making Good Friday and Ascension Day coincide (O. Michel, *Heb*[7] [KEK] 292f.). The affirmation that Christ was exalted to the right hand of God ἐν τοῖς οὐρανοῖς (8:1) is limited by the conviction that he passed through the heavens. As a result, he attained to the temple beyond, above all the heavens (7:26). In 9:23ff., the author elevates this true heaven above the created and therefore also transitory heaven (cf. 1:10-12; 12:26). It is the dwelling, temple, and throne of God (cf. Rev 4:1; 11:19; 14:17; 15:5; 16:17; 19:11), even though it is referred to simply as σκηνή (9:10ff.). In it one stands in all clarity before the face of God. "In Hb., then, God is high above the heavens, and yet He is in the heavens" (Traub 528). On the basis of an OT-oriented, sacrificial theology spatial conceptualization is combined with theological content. Hebrews knows no ontological dualism. The historic way of the believer is consistently described as the way of hope (3:7ff.). For "in *heaven*" the promised inheritance awaits (9:15), the righteous are inscribed (12:23), and the "enduring city" stands prepared (13:14). In the confession of Jesus, the author and perfecter of this way, one finds the criterion for distinguishing specialized theological language about οὐρανός from ideological speculation. Heaven is wherever Jesus finds a follower and gathers him or her into the grace of the righteous God. Christology therefore provides the critique of religious language and calls forth praxis that reflects the unity of heaven and earth.

5. The adj. **οὐράνιος**, *heavenly/pertaining to heaven/ deriving from heaven**, shares the above-mentioned nuances. In Luke 2:13 and Acts 26:19 it is intended to emphasize divine origin. It appears 7 times in Matthew (5:48; 6:14, 26, 32; 23:9; 15:13; 18:35). The formulaic expression ὁ πατὴρ ὁ οὐράνιος corresponds to ὁ πατὴρ μοῦ/ὑμῶν ὁ ἐν τοῖς οὐρανοῖς. The NT prefers, however, → ἐπουράνιος and similar alterations. Whether extrabiblical usage of οὐράνιος led to this remains an open question.

U. Schoenborn

Οὐρβανός, οῦ *Ourbanos* Urbanus*

In Rom 16:9 Urbanus receives a greeting (along with other members of the congregation); he is called a → συνεργὸς ἡμῶν ἐν Χριστῷ. Urbanus is a Latin name (from *urbs*) frequently found among slaves and freed members of the imperial court. F. F. Bruce, *BHH* 2060.

Οὐρίας, ου *Ourias* Uriah*

Οὐρίας (Heb. *'ûrîyâ*) is found in Matt 1:6 in the genealogy of Jesus as the name of the husband of Bathsheba (ἐκ τῆς τοῦ Οὐρίου), through whom David begat Solomon (cf. 2 Sam 11:3ff.; 12:24).

οὖς, ὠτός, τό *ous* ear

1. Occurrences and usage in the NT — 2. The attention formula — 3. Refusal to hear — 4. Luke 10:23/Matt 10:16

Lit.: M. DIBELIUS, "Wer Ohren hat, zu hören, der höre," *TSK* 83 (1910) 461-71. — J. GNILKA, *Die Verstockung Israels* (SANT 3, 1961). — F. HAHN, "Die Sendschreiben der Johannesapokalypse," FS Kuhn 357-94. — F. HORST, *TDNT* V, 543-59. — K. LAMMERS, *Hören, Sehen und Glauben im NT* (SBS 11, 1966). — For further bibliography see *TWNT* X, 1207f.; → ἀκούω.

1. Οὖς is found 36 times in the NT: 18 times in the Synoptic Gospels, 5 in Acts, and the rest in Romans, 1 Corinthians, James, 1 Peter, and Revelation. There are two clear groupings of usage: in the attention formulas, εἴ τις ἔχει ὦτα ἀκούειν ἀκουέτω and the like (Matt 11:15; 13:9, 43; Mark 4:9, 23; Luke 8:8; 14:35; Rev 2:7, 11, 17, 29; 3:6, 13, 22; 13:9; and as v.l. in Matt 25:29; Luke 12:21; 21:4; Mark 7:16; cf. also the related warning in Mark 13:14; Matt 24:15), and in the frequent OT quotations and allusions, esp. in the statements on hardening (Matt 13:14f.; Acts 28:26f. [cf. Acts 7:51]; Rom 11:8; of the ears of God, 1 Pet 3:12; Jas 5:4).

Οὖς always means the natural ear in the NT, esp. insofar as it entails the capacity of hearing. It is rarely described with the term for the process of hearing (Luke 1:44; 4:21; Acts 11:22). In Luke 9:44 the phrase θέσθε εἰς τὰ ὦτα simply refers to the understanding of the one who hears. On the whole, one cannot speak of a predominance of the ear among the sense organs in the NT.

2. It is difficult to determine the origin and nature of

the attention formula. It may stem "from the apocalyptic tradition, which [links] the proclamation of eschatological mysteries with proper hearing and understanding" (Hahn 380). Nevertheless, the textual basis is rather thin. The formula in Mark 4:3-9 par. Matthew/Luke and in the letter to the churches in Revelation appears to be clearly appended. The basis for the exhortation to special hearing arose in the first instance from the early beginnings of the allegorization of the parables (Mark 4:14-20), and in the second from the affiliation of the formula with the saying on overcoming (cf. Dibelius 469f.). In Mark 4:23 and Matt 13:43, however, the formula is apparently a redacted addition (Bultmann, *History* 326, even considers this possibility for Mark 4:9!). In the texts that parallel Matt 11:15 and Luke 14:35, there is no apparent reason for its omission by the other Evangelists, meaning that here, too, we may assume a redacted insertion. The text-critical findings with respect to Matt 25:29; Mark 7:16; Luke 12:21; 21:4 finally require the recognition that the formula displays at least the tendency toward a wider and less specific usage or toward becoming an added gloss, although it certainly did not owe its origin to this. Outside the NT cf. *Gos. Thom.* 8:21, 63, 65, 96; the *Gospel of Thomas* only strengthens this suspicion.

3. This discrepancy between the ability to hear and the actual refusal to hear determines true hearing in Matt 13:14f. (similarly Acts 28:26f., quoting Isa 6:9f.) and Rom 11:8 (composite quotation of Deut 29:3 and Isa 29:10). This discrepancy is intensified in the contradiction between Israel's election and its attitude toward the Christian message. Rom 11:8 crassly formulates this contradiction: "Ears, so that they may not hear" (see BDF §393.6; 400.2)—the direct opposite of the formual ὦτα ἀκούειν. In contrast to Mark 4:12, Matt 13:13f. contains an anti-Israel focus as a result of the full quotation of the passage from Isaiah and should probably not be related only to the specific parable in Matt 13:3-8 (cf. John 12:38f.).

4. Jesus' blessing of the eye- (Luke 10:23) and ear-witnesses (Matt 13:16) is preserved in its original form in Luke. In its current form, Matt 13:16 blesses Christians who (or because they) hear, in contrast to Israel. But Luke 10:23 emphasizes more strongly the object of seeing, the presence of Jesus, as the fulfillment of OT expectations.

M. Völkel

οὐσία, ας, ἡ *ousia* wealth, possessions*

In Luke 15:12f. along with → βίος (2). The younger son asks his father for the share of the *wealth* that he had coming to him (τὸ ἐπιβάλλον μέρος τῆς οὐσίας, v. 12), and then wastes it (διεσκόρπισεν τὴν οὐσίαν αὐτοῦ, v. 13; cf. also Tob 8:21 B A with 14:13 B A; 3 Macc 3:28). On

the legal questions surrounding the division of an inheritance see Billerbeck II, 212; III, 545-53; L. Schottroff, *ZTK* 68 (1971) 27-52, esp. 39ff.; W. Pöhlmann, *ZNW* 70 (1979) 194-213, esp. 208ff.

οὔτε *oute* and not

There are 87 occurrences in the NT, including 9 in Luke, 14 in John, 10 in Acts, 13 in Romans, and 15 in Revelation. Οὔτε functions as a copulative conj., continuing a previous negation ("not . . . *and not/neither . . . nor*"); cf. → μήτε. It is often found as a v.l. to → οὐδέ (Mark 5:3; Luke 12:26f., 33; John 1:25, etc.), just as οὔτε is often found for οὐδέ in the mss. (John 4:11; Gal 1:12; Jas 3:12; see BDF §445.1). Οὐδείς . . . οὔτε, "no one . . . *and no one/nor anyone*" (Rev 5:3f.); οὐ . . . οὔτε (Matt 12:32); μή (!) . . . οὔτε (Jas 3:12; 3 John 10); οὐ . . . οὐδὲ . . . οὔτε, "not . . . and not . . . *nor*" (Gal 1:12); most frequently in the series οὔτε . . . οὔτε . . . (οὔτε), *neither . . . nor . . . (nor);* twofold οὔτε in Matt 6:20; 12:32; Mark 12:25; 14:68 (BDF §445.2); John 4:21; 1 Cor 3:7, etc.; threefold οὔτε in Acts 24:12 (v. 13 continues with οὐδέ, "nor even"); 25:8; 1 Thess 2:5-6a (continued with a double οὔτε in v. 6b); Rev 9:20; 9:21 (after οὐ); 21:4 (continued with οὐ), esp. in the Pauline lists: Rom 8:38f. (tenfold οὔτε) of that which cannot separate Christians from the love of God; 1 Cor 6:9f. (vice list with sevenfold οὔτε continued with a threefold οὐ), of those who have no share in the kingdom of God. In John 4:11 and 3 John 10 in the infrequent correlative construction with a positive member: οὔτε . . . καί, "*on the one hand . . . on the other*" (see BDF §445.3; cf. also Matt 10:38; Luke 14:27).

οὗτος, αὕτη, τοῦτο *houtos, hautē, touto* this

1. Occurrences — 2. Meaning — 3. Usage

Lit.: BDF §§290; 292. — KÜHNER, *Grammatik* §467 (II/1, 641-51).

1. The demonstrative pron., with its 1,391 occurrences, occupies twelfth position on the list of most frequently used words in the NT. It has almost completely replaced ὅδε (only 10 occurrences, 8 of which are in the formula τάδε λέγει). It is found with relative frequency in John and 1–3 John (20.6% of NT occurrences of οὗτος are found in a block of literature that comprises 13.1% of all NT words) and Luke-Acts (33.5% of all occurrences of οὗτος in a block of literature that comprises 27.5% of all NT words); in contrast, the relative occurrences in Revelation are strikingly limited (3.5% of all occurrences in 7.1% of NT words). The position after the subst. preferred by the NT reflects Semitic influence (cf. Radermacher, *Grammatik* 28; BDF §292).

2. Οὗτος designates that which the one speaking or writing sees before him or her. In contrast, (the much less

frequent) → ἐκεῖνος points to that which is further away; cf. Jas 4:15; Luke 18:14; John 5:38; Luke 20:34f.; and —noteworthy—John 1:7f.

3. a) In what follows, it is possible to touch on only some of the more salient features of usage. Since οὗτος has also generally taken over the function of ὅδε (on the original distinction see Kühner 641), the word designates an immediate fact. Thus the αἰὼν οὗτος is the *"presently existing* world" (Matt 12:32; Luke 16:8; 1 Cor 1:20; 2:6, etc.; → αἰών 4), the καιρὸς οὗτος is the *"present age"* (Mark 10:30 par. Luke 18:30), and the γενεὰ αὕτη is the "generation *now living"* (e.g., Matt 12:41f., 45; 24:34; Mark 8:38; Luke 17:25; Heb 3:10). This intensified usage underlies the apocalyptic opposition of past/present, in which the present is viewed negatively. That is especially evident in the last phrase cited.

b) Likewise, τοῦτο in the interpretive statement in Mark 14:22, 24 par. and in 1 Cor 11:24 refers to that which is immediately at hand. However, the form of the statement may also be influenced by the identification formula οὗτός ἐστιν, and the like, found in the interpretation of parables (Mark 4:15f., 18 [differently, v. 20]; Matt 13:38); it introduces exegetical equations and is apparently adopted from the interpretation of visions and dreams (cf. H.-J. Klauck, *Allegorie und Allegorese in synoptischen Gleichnistexten* [NTAbh N.F. 13, 1978] 88 [n.273 for references], 100). To be distinguished from this is the formulaic expression τοῦτ᾽ ἔστιν, *"that is,"* which can almost be considered a single word (τουτέστι[ν]; BDF §§12.3; 132.2; cf., however, Rom 1:12).

c) A trace of the original, slightly derogatory sense has perhaps been preserved in the contemptuous use of the pron. (cf. Kühner 644) in 1 Cor 6:11: καὶ ταῦτά τινες ἦτε, *"that sort of people";* cf. further Luke 14:30; 15:30; 18:11; Acts 17:18 (see BDF §290.6).

d) It is frequently combined with preps. (διά, εἰς, ἐκ, ἐν, ἐπί, μετά, also τούτου χάριν). Καὶ ταῦτα in Heb 11:12, as in classical usage, emphasizes a circumstance that lends particular significance to that which has been said, and takes on the sense of "although" (cf. LSJ s.v. C.VIII.2.a).

e) The predicate use of the pron., esp. frequent with terms expressing quantity, is sometimes more difficult to grasp. In Acts 1:5, οὐ μετὰ πολλὰς ταύτας ἡμέρας, "after not many days/*from these (days) on"*; 24:21, ἢ περὶ μιᾶς ταύτης φωνῆς, "except concerning *this* one thing which I said." In the last instance ταύτης points ahead to the following statement of what was said, a frequent usage. It is also present, e.g., in 1 Thess 4:15, where τοῦτο points to the words of Jesus quoted in v. 15b; cf. Gal 3:17; 1 Cor 15:50; and 1 Cor 1:12.

                                            T. Holtz

οὕτω, οὕτως *houtō, houtōs* thus, in this way

The adv. of → οὗτος is found 208 times in the NT (Matthew has 32 occurrences, Mark 10, Luke 21, John 14, Acts 27, Romans 17, 1 Corinthians 31, Hebrews 9, 2 Corinthians and James 7 each, elsewhere it is less frequent). The form without -ς (on movable -ς see BDF §21) is attested in the NT with certainty only in Acts 23:11; Phil 3:17; Heb 12:21; and Rev 16:18.

Οὕτως can refer to the foregoing, usually in a correlative construction (in Rom 12:4f., etc., with → καθάπερ; in Luke 11:30, etc., with → καθώς; in Acts 8:32, etc., with → ὡς; in Matt 12:40, etc., with → ὥσπερ; in Heb 9:27f. with καθ᾽ ὅσον; in 2 Tim 3:8 with ὃν τρόπον), which can be translated "as . . . so also"; when used absolutely οὕτως means (with reference to the foregoing): *thus/in this way,* or *accordingly/therefore* (Matt 6:9, 30; Mark 10:43; Luke 14:33; Rom 1:15; 11:5; 1 Cor 7:26, 40; 14:25, etc.; elliptically in Luke 22:26: ὑμεῖς δὲ οὐχ οὕτως, "but you [should] not [be] *like this";* cf. also 1 Cor 7:7: οὕτως . . . οὕτως, *in this way . . . in that way).* Οὕτως can also summarize a participial construction (only Acts 20:11; 27:17; see BDF §425.6).

Οὕτως is found as a reference to what follows in Luke 24:24; John 21:1; Acts 1:11, etc., and has then the meaning *as follows,* esp. in references to Scripture: οὕτως γέγραπται in Matt 2:5; οὕτως λέγει in Rom 10:6; οὕτως . . . καθὼς γέγραπται in 11:26; cf. further Acts 7:6; 13:34; Matt 6:9 as a reference to the wording of the Lord's Prayer (οὕτως οὖν προσεύχεσθε ὑμεῖς).

Before adjs. and advs. οὕτως means *so* (with reference to the extent or degree; Gal 3:3; Heb 12:21; Rev 16:18); before a vb. *so much* (John 3:16; 1 John 4:11). In John 4:6 ἐκαθέζετο οὕτως means "he sat down *as he was* (or *just like that/simply).* An adj. use is found in Matt 1:18; 19:10; Rom 4:18; Rev 9:17, and a subst. use *(such a one)* in Matt 9:33; Mark 2:12; Luke 1:25; 2:48.

οὐχ *ouch* not
→ οὐ.

οὐχί *ouchi* not, no, in no way

Intensified form of → οὐ, occurring 54 times in the NT, concentrated in Matthew (9 occurrences), Luke (18), and 1 Corinthians (12); infrequent in Mark, the Pastoral and Catholic Epistles, and Revelation.

As simple negation (John 13:11; Luke 18:30, etc.); as interrogative particle in questions to which an affirmative response is expected (Matt 5:46; Rom 3:29, etc., but esp. in 1 Corinthians: 1:20; 3:3; 5:12; 6:1, etc.); οὐχὶ μᾶλλον, *"not* much more?" (5:2; 6:7 bis), which arises from the discussion style of the letter; cf. R. Pesch, Concilium 7 (1971) 166-71; πῶς οὐχί, "how then *not?"* (Rom 8:32; cf. 2 Cor 3:8).

ὀφειλέτης, ου, ὁ *opheiletēs* debtor, sinner*
ὀφείλημα, ατος, τό *opheilēma* debt, sin*

1. Occurrences in the NT — 2. Matthew and Luke — 3. Paul

Lit.: DALMAN, *Worte* 334-44. — F. HAUCK, *TDNT* V, 565f. — LEVY II, 19-21, 43f. — E. LOHMEYER, *"Our Father"* (1965) 160-90. — P. S. MINEAR, "Gratitude and Mission in the Epistle to the Romans," *Basileia* (FS W. Freytag, ed. J. Hermelink and H. J. Margull; 1959) 42-48.

1. Ὀφειλέτης is found 7 times in the NT, and ὀφείλημα twice. The occurrences are limited to Matthew/Luke and Paul, although the respective range of meanings of these two groups differs significantly from each other.

2. a) In Matt 18:24 ὀφειλέτης is used in the technical financial sense: *debtor* (cf. Plato *Leg.* v.736d; *T. Job* 11:12). The acc. obj. of → ὀφείλω (2) becomes the gen. of the amount of the sum (see Jülicher II, 305): ὀφειλέτης μυρίων ταλάντων, "the one who owed [him] 10,000 talents." Ὀφείλημα ("debts") is not found with this sense in the NT, even though it is in the LXX (Deut 24:10; 1 Esdr 3:20; 1 Macc 15:8 [see *OGIS* i.149; Polybius xxv.3.3]) and in secular Greek (Plato *Leg.* iv.717b; Pap. Hibeh i.42.10, etc.).

b) In Matt 6:12 (fifth petition of the Lord's Prayer), ὀφείλημα corresponds to Aram. *ḥôḇâ* ("debt"), which, as a derivation of *ḥôḇ* ("money debt"), became in rabbinic literature the standard expression for indebtedness to God or to other humans and was used with the sense of "sin" (cf. Black, *Approach* 140; Dalman; Jastrow, *Dictionary* s.v.; Levy). The targums, e.g., frequently render the Hebrew term for sin as *ḥôḇâ* and the like (cf., e.g., *Tg. Onq.* on Gen 13:33; 42:21; Exod 10:17; further references in Jastrow; Dalman). As a result of the transference of the image of financial debt to that of the debt of sin, and the transference of the debtor/creditor relationship to the person's relationship to God, ὀφείλημα becomes the equivalent of and interchangeable with → ἁμαρτία. This can be seen, e.g., in the fact that Luke replaces ὀφείλημα with ἁμαρτία in the fifth petition of the Lord's Prayer (11:4). This interchangeability is also evident in the fact that → ἀφίημι can be used with both ὀφείλημα and ἁμαρτία (→ ὀφείλω 2; also Matt 6:12/Luke 11:4). The ὀφειλέτης (Matt 6:12; *Did.* 8:2; Luke 13:4; Aram. *ḥayyāḇ*) is accordingly *the one liable* (for a sin)/*the sinner*, and therefore has the same meaning as ἁμαρτωλός (cf. Luke 13:2 with 13:4; *1 Enoch* 6:3; Pol. *Phil.* 6:1: ὀφειλέτης ἁμαρτίας).

3. Paul uses ὀφειλέτης first in Rom 15:27 with the gen. as *debtor* (→ 2.a) in the fig. sense: The congregations in Macedonia and Achaia shared in the πνευματικά of the congregation in Jerusalem and so were obligated to reciprocate through the collection. In Paul, ὀφειλέτης always appears with εἰμί as a pred. nom., "be *obligated*," and thus corresponds to → ὀφείλω (3.b). In Gal 5:3 Paul polemicizes (as he does in the par. passage in Rom 2:25) against the idea that circumcision has a unique saving effect, as his Galatian opponents had contended: Circumcision entails the obligation to fulfill the whole law. Such an attempt, however, has already been ruled out as a means of salvation and leads to separation from Christ and to the loss of the state of grace (Gal 5:4; cf. also Jas 2:10 [and M. Dibelius, *Jas* (Hermeneia) 144-46]). It is also found with the inf. in Rom 8:12 (cf. Sophocles *Aj.* 590), where the obligation no longer to allow our lives to be determined by the regulations of the σάρξ arises from the fact that the πνεῦμα lives in us (v. 11). Ὀφειλέτης is used in Rom 1:14 with the dat. of the person to whom the obligation is due: In the light of his apostolic commission, Paul regards himself as indebted to the entire Gentile world, to preach the gospel to it.

Ὀφείλημα is found in Paul only in Rom 4:4 as a term of contrast with χάρις (also in Thucydides ii.40.4). It is worked into the antithesis of faith and works (law), which determines the flow of the argument, and is placed on the side of → ἔργον (5): Although completed work receives a reward as owed compensation, δικαιοσύνη, as the "reward of faith," can be received only κατὰ χάριν.

M. Wolter

ὀφειλή, ῆς, ἡ *opheilē* debt, guilt, obligation*

Lit.: F. HAUCK, *TDNT* V, 564.

First found in Matt 18:32 as a monetary *debt* (→ ὀφειλέτης 2.a; → ὀφείλω 2; esp. in the papyri: ÄgU i.112.11; iv.1158.18; Pap. Oxy. no. 286, l. 18, etc.) and in *Did.* 8:2 as a person's debt (sin) to God (→ ὀφειλέτης 2.b). In Rom 13:7, αἱ ὀφειλαί are the taxes owed to the state (φόρος and τέλος, v. 7b; cf. 1 Macc 15:8; *OGIS* I, 149; Polybius xxv.3.3, where they are designated ὀφείλημα βασιλικόν) or the proper attitude toward authorities (φόβος and τιμή, v. 7c), which Paul admonishes the congregation in Rome to pay (→ ἀποδίδωμι 2; → ὀφείλω 2; see also A. Strobel, *ZNW* 47 [1956] 88n.114). In 1 Cor 7:3, the sexual relation in marriage is described as the ὀφειλή, *obligation*, that a husband and wife owe (again → ἀποδίδωμι [2]) to each other for the purpose of avoiding → πορνεία (see v. 2). In Judaism as well, the marital relation was considered an obligatory command (cf. Billerbeck III, 368ff.) and was frequently described in corresponding fashion (cf., e.g., *b. ʿErub.* 100b: *miṣwâ*; on this see Hauck 564).

M. Wolter

ὀφείλημα, ατος, τό *opheilēma* debt, sin
→ ὀφειλέτης.

ὀφείλω *opheilō* owe, have to, be obligated*

1. Occurrences in the NT — 2. Technical financial meaning — 3. Necessity and obligation

Lit.: R. D. Aus, "The Liturgical Background of the Necessity and Propriety of Giving Thanks according to 2 Thes 1,3," *JBL* 92 (1973) 432-38. — A. Fridrichsen, "Exegetisches zu den Paulusbriefen," *TSK* 102 (1930) 291-301. — F. Hauck, *TDNT* V, 559-64. — For further bibliography → ὀφειλέτης.

1. Ὀφείλω is found 35 times in the NT. The occurrences are distributed throughout almost all the NT writings and groups of writings (with the exception of Mark, Colossians, the Pastorals, the majority of Catholic Epistles, and Revelation). As with → ὀφειλέτης, the usage of Matthew/Luke is to be distinguished, with a few limited exceptions, from that of the rest of the writings.

2. Ὀφείλω is found with the acc. obj. in certain parables of M and L with the meaning *"owe something"* (money: Matt 18:28, 30; Luke 7:41; natural materials: Luke 16:5, 7). It is very frequently found with this meaning in the papyri, esp. in references to private accounts (cf. Moulton/Milligan s.v.; Preisigke, *Wörterbuch* s.v.; Preisigke, *Sammelbuch* s.v.; Hauck 559). The neut. pass. partc. τὸ ὀφειλόμενον (Matt 18:30, 34) refers, accordingly, to *the (amount of) debt* (→ ὀφειλή). Standing in direct relation with ὀφείλω are → ἀποδίδωμι for the payment (Matt 18:28, 30, 34; Luke 7:42; outside the NT: Ezek 18:7; Aristotle *EN* 1165a.3; idem, *Pol.* 1304b.29; Preisigke, *Sammelbuch* 6753, 5f.; Josephus *Ant.* ix.50, etc.) and → ἀφίημι for the forgiveness of debts (Matt 18:27, 32; outside the NT: Deut 15:2; 1 Macc 13:39). In Phlm 18, ὀφείλω refers to a material loss, which Philemon had suffered as a result of the flight of his slave (or due to a concomitant theft), and for which Paul makes himself legally responsible (cf. Pap. Strassburg [ed. F. Preisigke] i.32.9f.; E. Lohse, *Col/Phlm* [Hermeneia] 204nn.69-73; → ἀποτίνω; → ἐλλογέω).

In the two parables in Matt 18:23-35 and Luke 7:41-43 the remission of a debt functions as a metaphor for the forgiveness of sins (cf. Matt 18:21f., 35; Luke 7:47; the bridge between the metaphorical and the actual is in each instance ἀφίημι); this idea also finds expression in this literary form in rabbinic parables (cf. Tanḥuma ʾᵃmôr 178a; *Exod. Rab.* 31 [Billerbeck I, 798f., 800f.]; see also A. Weiser, *Die Knechtsgleichnisse der synoptischen Evangelien* [SANT 24, 1971] 76). Ὀφείλω is here influenced by Aram. ḥûḇ (ḥayyāḇ; see Levy II, s.v.), which is also reflected in Luke 11:4: ἀφίομεν παντὶ ὀφείλοντι ἡμῖν, "we forgive everyone *who has become indebted to us.*" Here Ὀφείλω τινί assumes the meaning of ἁμαρτάνω εἴς τινα (cf. *Inscriptiones Graecae* [1873-1939] iii.74.15: ἁμαρτίαν ὀφιλέτω Μηνὶ Τυράννῳ; for details → ὀφειλέτης [2.b]).

3. In the remaining writings of the NT, ὀφείλω is almost without exception followed by an inf. construction.

a) With the sense of *have to,* it usually describes general *necessity* (1 Cor 5:10; 7:36; 9:10; 2 Cor 12:11, 14; Heb 2:17; 5:12; in 1 Cor 5:10 and 2 Cor 12:11 the imv. with ἄν expresses, as it does in classical Greek, the nonreality of the necessity: *would have to;* cf. BDF §358.1), with negation (οὐκ ὀφείλω), *ought not* (Acts 17:29; 1 Cor 11:7). Ὀφείλω can also, then, express a legal or cultic regulation (LSJ s.v.: "as a legal term"). Thus, e.g., with reference to the punishment demanded by the law for a specific trespass (John 19:7: κατὰ τὸν νόμον ὀφείλει ἀποθανεῖν, *according to the law he ought to die* [see also Tob 6:13 B A; Wis 12:20; 4 Macc 11:15; *T. Jos.* 14:6; reversed in Philo *Spec. Leg.* iii.59: the innocent woman leads a pure life καὶ ζῆν ὀφείλει]), or in reference to certain cultic requirements (1 Cor 11:10; Heb 5:3), or prohibitions (1 Cor 11:7). The necessity expressed by ὀφείλω is always explicitly grounded in these instances (ὅτι clause; διά phrase; gen. construction).

b) Above and beyond this, ὀφείλω expresses the obligation to act in a specific way: *be obligated.* This is true primarily of the statements of thanksgiving in 2 Thess 1:3; 2:13, which are distinguished from the thanksgivings in other NT epistolary introductions (→ εὐχαριστέω [2]) by the addition of ὀφείλω (cf. P. Schubert, *Form and Function of the Pauline Thanksgivings* [BZNW 20, 1939] 54; P. T. O'Brien, *Introductory Thanksgivings in the Letters of Paul* [NovTSup 49, 1977] 167ff.). In the background lie expressions borrowed esp. from the *debt* of thanks (χάριν ὀφείλω) in secular Greek (e.g., Sophocles *Ant.* 331; Theocritus II, 130; Plato *Plt.* 257a; Preisigke, *Sammelbuch* 6789, 4; Pap. Ryl. 77.39); parallels can also be drawn, however, from the Jewish-Christian tradition (cf. Aus) which point to a cultic-liturgical context (Philo *Spec. Leg.* i.224; *Apostolic Constitutions* vii.39.2; *Pesiq.* 10:5; *b. Taʿan.* 64b; *1 Clem.* 38:4; *Barn.* 5:3; 7:1; cf. also *Apostolic Constitutions* vii.35.4; *Herm. Sim.* ix.28.5; *1 Clem.* 40:1f.). While here the obligation to give thanks is supplied by the ὅτι clause that constitutes part of the form (see Schubert), in "exemplary parenesis" (see A. Schulz, *Nachfolgen und Nachahmen* [SANT 6, 1962] 302ff.) the ethical obligation is grounded, esp. in Johannine literature, in the corresponding example of the conduct of Christ or God (John 13:14; 1 John 2:6; 3:16; 4:11; also Rom 15:1[-3]; Eph 5:[25,] 28 [on this see G. Bouwman, "Eph. v 28—Versuch einer Übersetzung," *Miscellanea Neotestamentica* (NovTSup 48/2, 1978) 179-90]). Ὀφείλω is in this respect an element of a causal connection and almost takes on the function of an imv. (cf. the overview in Schulz 303ff.), although it lends an argumentative character. By way of analogy this also applies to the obligations in Rom 15:27 and 3 John 8. In Rom 15:27, as in John 13:14 and 1 John 4:11, ὀφείλω is dependent on a conditional clause that should be understood causally (BDF §372.1); in 3 John 8 it derives its importance from the accompanying final clause (cf. also Luke 17:10: correspondence with → διατάσσω [2.b]).

c) Ὀφείλω in Matt 23:16, 18 is elliptical and, as part of a rabbinic oath formula, a translation of Aram. *ḥayyāḇ* (see *m. Ned.* 2:3): *he is obligated* (to fulfill his oath).

d) In Rom 13:8 (cf. Fridrichsen), by picking up again on → ὀφειλή (v. 7), Paul emphasizes mutual love as the highest and most comprehensive obligation, which supersedes all other obligations—even those mentioned in v. 7 (cf. v. 8b): "*Be obligated* to no one for anything, except (that you are obligated) to love one another." In this way Paul formulates the dialectic of radical freedom from all people in every respect, and of the radical bond to one another in mutual love.   M. Wolter

ὄφελον *ophelon* (partc.) O that, if only*

Ὄφελον (mss. ὤφελον) occurs 4 times in the NT. It is a partc. with which ἐστίν was originally to be supplied (see BDF §67.2); as a particle used to express unattainable (1 Cor 4:8; Gal 5:12; Rev 3:15), but also attainable, wishes (2 Cor 11:1, where the impf. ἀνείχεσθε could have replaced an opt.; cf. BDF §§384; 448.6; see also R. Bultmann, *2 Cor* [Eng. tr., 1985] ad loc.; contrast BAGD s.v.; BDF §359.1); cf. Ign. *Smyrn.* 12:1. E. Tiedtke and H.-G. Link, *DNTT* II, 668.

ὄφελος, ους, τό *ophelos* profit*

3 occurrences in the NT, always in the question: τί (μοι) τὸ ὄφελος; "what does it *profit* (me)?"; in 1 Cor 15:32 regarding the martyrdom of Paul, which would have no meaning without the hope of the resurrection from the dead; Jas 2:14, 16 regarding faith, which is useless without works (v. 16: practical example; cf. Sir 4:3; 1 John 3:17; *Did.* 4:8); cf. *2 Clem.* 6:2; *Herm. Vis.* iii.3.1.

ὀφθαλμοδουλία, ας, ἡ *ophthalmodoulia* eye service*

In the domestic code of Col 3:22 and Eph 6:6 the exhortation is made to Christian slaves not to give their masters only *eye service* (ἐν ὀφθαλμοδουλίᾳ [v.l.: pl.]/κατ' ὀφθαλμοδουλίαν, always with ὡς ἀνθρωπάρεσκοι), i.e., only "for the sake of appearances" (without inner obligation). K. H. Rengstorf, *TDNT* II, 283.

ὀφθαλμός, οῦ, ὁ *ophthalmos* eye

1. Occurrences in the NT and overview — 2. Jesus' healing of the blind — 3. Gal 3:1

Lit.: E. BEST, "Discipleship in Mark: Mark 8,22–10,52," *SJT* 23 (1970) 323-37. — H. D. BETZ, "Matthew VI.22f and Ancient Greek Theories of Vision," FS Black (1979) 43-56. — G. BORNKAMM, "Die Heilung des Blindgeborenen," idem, *Aufsätze* IV, 65-72. — H. CONZELMANN, "Was von Anfang war," FS Bultmann (1954) 194-201. — H. J. HELD, "Matthew as Interpreter of the Miracle Stories," G. Bornkamm, G. Barth, and H. J. Held, *Tradition and Interpretation in Matthew* (1963) 165-299. — K. KERTELGE, *Die Wunder Jesu im Markus-Evangelium* (1970). — W. MICHAELIS, *TDNT* V, 315-81. — K. WENGST, *1-3 John* (ÖTK, 1978) 95f.

1. With its approximately 100 occurrences in the NT, the eye statistically plays the leading role among parts of the body in general and sense organs in particular, although this fact does not correspond completely to the significance of the meaning of the eye as compared, e.g., to the ear. Far and away the majority of passages with ὀφθαλμός have in mind more than the eye as a physical organ or the faculty of sense perception. Perception in the sense of recognizing or understanding, characteristic of most of the vbs. of seeing in the NT, is present in ὀφθαλμός as well (cf., however, Mark 12:11 par. Matt 21:42; Luke 24:31; Acts 26:18; Eph 1:18; and the negative examples in Luke 19:42; 24:16). The sayings on hardening, which are based on Isa 6:9f., rest on this distinction between the natural faculty of sight and the lack of understanding (Matt 13:14f.; Acts 28:26f.; John 12:40), as does Mark 8:18 (concerning the disciples!) and Rom 11:8, 10. A special significance is attributed to the sense of sight in that it can be the conveyor of definite impressions and therefore can be representative of the entire person. To this category belongs ὀφθαλμὸς πονηρός: In Matt 20:15 and Mark 7:22 the expression stands for envy (cf. Matt 6:22f. par. Luke 11:34). Since the eye is the λύχνος τοῦ σώματος, it reflects the appearance of the entire person. Ἁπλοῦς and πονηρός should not be understood in the sense of a single moral quality, but rather should be translated respectively as "pure, sincere" and "bad." The unique NT expression ἐπιθυμία τῶν ὀφθαλμῶν should not be read as desire in the sexual sense, but rather as an expression of "envy, greed." The eye is nevertheless clearly conceived of as the vehicle of sexual temptation in Matt 5:29; 2 Pet 2:14. The group of sayings on offense (Mark 9:43-47; Matt 18:8f.; cf. Matt 5:29) does not mention the eye, along with the hand and foot, in order to express thereby any special threat of temptation by these parts of the body. Rather, the group positively expresses the admonition to radical and absolute obedience.

Jesus' blessing of those who had witnessed with their eyes and ears, as reported in the differing accounts of Luke (10:23) and Matthew (13:16), does not contain any special value or preference for seeing and hearing. In its present form, the saying in the Lukan context emphasizes the object of seeing, namely, the presence of Jesus, as the fulfillment of OT expectations, while Matthew blesses Christians who (or because they) "see" (= understand) and hear in faith. Finally, the emphasis on the fact that the editorial "we" had seen with the eyes and heard with the ears in the prologue to 1 John (1:1) already anticipates the Epistle's central theological themes: The sense perception of the witnesses corresponds to the revelation of God in Jesus, since it emphasizes and confirms the confession of Jesus ἐν σαρκὶ ἐληλυθότα (4:2; cf. 5:6, etc.).

2. Worthy of special attention are Jesus' healings of the blind (Mark 8:22-26; 10:46-52 par. Matt 20:29-34 [9:27-31]/Luke 18:35-43; John 9:1-41). These healings, taken as a group, do not deal only with the restoration of the natural faculty of sight. That is evident already in Mark from the prominent arrangement of the two healings in the flow of his Gospel. Mark 8:22-26 immediately precedes the confession of Peter and the first announcement of the Passion (8:27-33). In the background of 8:18 lies the blind man as a metaphor for the disciples, who like him needed to have their eyes opened. 10:46-52 brings to a close the public activity of Jesus before his journey toward Jerusalem. The healed blind man becomes a type of the follower of Jesus. In Luke, the healing of the blind man follows the statement on the disciples' lack of understanding, closing Jesus' third announcement of his Passion (18:34). It functions as a paradigm of believing "sight," which leads to the recognition of Jesus as κύριος (18:41) and son of David (18:38f.). Matthew has reworked and condensed the two miracle stories in his own way into an ideal scene that "illustrates the faith to which a miracle has been granted" (Held 225). Finally, in John 9:1-7 there is more at issue than the healing of this individual and the response to the central question of 9:2, as the discussion following the healing (9:8-38) and esp. the conflict saying (9:39-41) already show. In reality the question is: Who will remain "blind" toward Jesus' mission and who will begin to "see" (9:41)?

3. Gal 3:1 also deserves special mention. Not only is the expression προγράφω as a description of the proclamation unusual for Paul and the NT, but also the combination of the vb. with ὀφθαλμός is unique, as is the use of βασκαίνω for the activity of the opponents. The phrase προγράφω κατ' ὀφθαλμούς is therefore difficult to define precisely. It means either the public character (προγράφω; cf. προτίθεμαι in Rom 3:25) of Paul's preaching of the cross in contrast to the secret bewitching of the Galatians by the opponents of Paul, or it describes—in the sense of 1 Cor 1:23—the special intensity and urgency of the preaching of Christ as the preaching of the one who had been crucified. The latter possibility corresponds better with the combination of προγράφω and ὀφθαλμός as well as the emphatic form of address and the position of ἐσταυρωμένος at the end of the clause.   M. Völkel

ὄφις, εως, ὁ *ophis* snake*

Lit.: O. Böcher, *Dämonenfurcht und Dämonenabwehr* (1970) 92-95 and index s.v. — J. Ernst, *Die eschatologischen Gegenspieler in den Schriften des NT* (1967) 241-50 and index

s.v. — W. Foerster, *TDNT* V, 566-82. — M.-L. Henry, *BHH* 1699-1701. — R. Merkelbach, *RAC* IV, 226-50. — For further bibliography see *TWNT* X, 1208; *DNTT* I, 511.

There are 14 occurrences of ὄφις in the NT, 5 of which are in Revelation. The NT does not attribute any special value to snakes, as was the case— in addition to negative evaluations—in antiquity (see PW II/1, 506-21); the exception is, however, John 3:14, where, with a view toward Num 21:4-9, the raising up of the "brass serpent" by Moses is presented as a type of the raising up of Jesus (cf. R. Schnackenburg, *John* I [Eng. tr., 1968] 395f.). Elsewhere, however, the snake is regarded, without symbolic significance, as a dangerous animal that a man does not give his son (Matt 7:10 par. Luke 11:11; here the snake functions as an image for Jesus' Pharisaic opponents, on account of its poisonous bite (Matt 23:33: pl. with γεννήματα ἐχιδνῶν), which can do no harm to believers (Mark 16:18; Luke 10:19; cf. also Acts 28:3ff.: ἔχιδνα), but can harm those who test the Lord (1 Cor 10:9; cf. Num 21:5ff.). One can, however, learn astuteness from the serpent (Matt 10:16: pl. opposite αἱ περιστεραί). On the negative side the snake is also assigned a symbolic-mythical position (Rev 9:19) and can designate the devil as the original and eschatological opponent (→ δράκων 3; see Rev 12:9; 20:2 [ὁ ὄφις ὁ ἀρχαῖος]; 12:14f.; 2 Cor 11:3 [ὡς ὁ ὄφις ἐξηπάτησεν Εὕαν]); cf. *Barn.* 12:5-7; Ign. *Pol.* 2:2.

ὀφρῦς, ύος, ἡ *ophrys* slope, cliff*

According to Luke 4:29, an attempt was made in Nazareth to throw Jesus down the slope of the mountain on which, according to Luke, "their city was built": ἤγαγον αὐτὸν ἕως ὀφρύος τοῦ ὄρους. G. Dalman, *Orte und Wege Jesu* (1924) 83f.; G. Schneider, *Luke* (ÖTK) ad loc.

ὀχλέομαι *ochleomai* be tormented*

In the NT only in the pass.: Acts 5:16: ὀχλούμενοι ὑπὸ πνευμάτων ἀκαθάρτων, "tormented by unclean spirits" (with ἀσθενεῖς); cf. also Luke 6:18; *Acts Thom.* 12.

ὀχλοποιέω *ochlopoieō* form a mob*

Acts 17:5: Jews who out of envy *formed a mob* (ὀχλοποιήσαντες) together with others.

ὄχλος, ου, ὁ *ochlos* people, crowd, (large) masses, throng

Lit.: H. Bietenhard, *DNTT* II, 800f. — B. Citron, "The Multitudes in the Synoptic Gospels," *SJT* 7 (1954) 408-18. — P. Joüon, *RSR* 27 (1937) 618f. — R. Meyer, *TDNT* V, 582-90. — H. Graf Reventlow, *BHH* 2112. — P. Zingg, *Das Wachsen der Kirche* (1974) 61-63. — For further bibliography see *TWNT* X, 1208.

There are 175 occurrences in the NT, all in the Gospels (Matthew has 50 occurrences, Mark 38, Luke 41, John 20), Acts (22), and Revelation (4).

The widespread use of the word in the Jesus tradition shows that the appearance of Jesus did not take place, nor was it understood, privately, but (as already with John the Baptist: Luke 3:7, 10) always took place before the crowd (cf. on this U. Hedinger, *TZ* 32 [1976] 201-6). According to Matt 4:25, a *large crowd* (ὄχλοι πολλοί) followed Jesus from Galilee (contrast Mark 3:7 [πολὺ πλῆθος]/Luke 6:17 [ὄχλος πολὺς μαθητῶν αὐτοῦ, καὶ πλῆθος πολὺ τοῦ λαοῦ]; cf. v. 19 [πᾶς ὁ ὄχλος]) and was therefore witness to the Sermon on the Mount when it was addressed to the disciples (Matt 5:1: ἰδὼν δὲ τοὺς ὄχλους; cf. 7:28: ἐξεπλήσσοντο οἱ ὄχλοι; contrast Luke 6:20). According to Mark 6:34 par. Matt 9:36 Jesus was "seized by compassion (→ σπλαγχνίζομαι) when he saw the *people*/the *crowd* [although ὄχλος is elsewhere the equivalent of ὄχλοι, the pl. is found in Mark only in 10:1 and in John only in 7:12a] as sheep without a shepherd" (likewise Matt 14:13f., 19; 15:32 par. Mark 8:1). The leaders and teachers of the people, like the crowd itself, thought that Jesus was leading the people astray (John 7:12b [πλανᾷ τὸν ὄχλον], 20, 32, 43, 49 [ὁ ὄχλος οὗτος, "this *mob*"]). Usually, however, the ὄχλος is the "anonymous background to Jesus' ministry" (R. Meyer, *TDNT* V, 586), e.g., in Matt 13:2; 14:23; 15:10; Mark 3:20; 9:25; Luke 5:1; John 11:42, etc. The Gospels are also conscious of the double-mindedness of the crowds: On the one hand they provide for Jesus a triumphal entry into Jerusalem (Matt 21:1-11, esp. vv. 8f., 11; contrast Mark 11:1-11; Luke 19:28-38 without ὄχλος); on the other hand, they are incited to demand his crucifixion (Matt 27:15, 20, 24; Mark 15:8, 11, 15; Luke 23:4). Luke 23:48 (L) reports at the close of the death of Jesus the mourning of the ὄχλοι. In Matt 14:5; 21:26; Mark 12:12, etc., the crowd also stands in opposition to its leaders.

Acts carries on the nonexclusive offer of the gospel (1:15; 6:7; 8:6; 11:24; 13:45); but here, too, the crowd proves to be double-minded and easily led astray (14:19; 16:22; 17:8; 19:26, etc.).

Individual expressions: ὄχλος, *"a large group"* (Mark 14:43; cf. Matt 26:47; Luke 22:47); ὁ πλεῖστος ὄχλος, "a very large *crowd*" (Matt 21:8); ὄχλος ἱκανός, "a rather large/considerable *crowd*" (Mark 10:46; Luke 7:12); αἱ μυριάδες τοῦ ὄχλου, "thousands (upon thousands) of *people*" (Luke 12:1); ὄχλος . . . τελωνῶν, "a *crowd* . . . of tax collectors" (Luke 5:29; cf. further 6:17 [see above]; Acts 6:7); ὄχλος ὀνομάτων . . . ὡσεὶ ἑκατὸν εἴκοσι, "a *throng* of about 120 people" (1:15). In Rev 7:9 and 19:1, 6 ὄχλος is used for the *throng* of the redeemed; in 17:15 the pl. *throngs* (with λαοί, ἔθνη, and γλῶσσαι) is found.   H. Balz

᾿Οχοζίας, ου   *Ochozias*   Ahaziah

Name in the genealogy of Jesus in Matt 1:8 syᶜ; Luke 3:23ff. D (cf. 4 Kgdms 8:24; 2 Chr 22:1).

ὀχύρωμα, ατος, τό   *ochyrōma*   stronghold, fortress*

According to 2 Cor 10:4, Paul's spiritual weapons are "powerful . . . to demolish *strongholds* [of the opponent]" (cf. Prov 21:22; Philo *Conf.* 129f.), namely, the λογισμοί, etc., of those who rise up against the γνῶσις τοῦ θεοῦ. H. W. Heiland, *TDNT* V, 590f.

ὀψάριον, ου, τό   *opsarion*   fish*

There are 5 occurrences in the NT: in conjunction with the miraculous feeding of the 5,000, only in John 6:9, 11 (v. 9: πέντε ἄρτους . . . καὶ δύο ὀψάρια; v. 11: ὁμοίως καὶ ἐκ τῶν ὀψαρίων, instead of the Synoptic: δύο ἰχθύες, Mark 6:38, 41 par.); according to John 21:9, 13 the resurrected Jesus offers his disciples "bread and (a) *fish*" to eat; in v. 10 the *fish* caught in the net are called ὀψάρια (as well as ἰχθύες in v. 11). In each case the fish is viewed as food and a complement to bread (ὀψάριον is a diminutive of τὸ ὄψον, "cooked food"). BAGD s.v. (bibliography); → ἰχθύς (3, 4).

ὀψέ   *opse*   late (in the day), in the evening, after (adv.)*

The gen. combination ὀψὲ σαββάτων (Matt 28:1) should be translated as *"after* the sabbath" (not "late on the sabbath"); cf. BDF §164.4; BAGD s.v. 3 (bibliography); in this case ὀψέ is used as an improper prep. Mark 11:19: ὅταν ὀψὲ ἐγένετο, "when it was *late/evening*"; 13:35, in an admonition to watchfulness: The master of the house can return "*late/in the evening*, or in the middle of the night, or early in the morning." S. Zeitlin, *JQR* 43 (1952/53) 197f.

ὀψία, ας, ἡ   *opsia*   evening*

There are 14 occurrences in the NT, all in Matthew, Mark, and John, in the combination ὀψίας (δὲ) γενομένης (John 6:16: ὡς δὲ ὀψία ἐγένετο; 20:19: οὔσης οὖν ὀψίας τῇ ἡμέρᾳ ἐκείνῃ): "when it was *evening*/in the *evening*" (Matt 8:16; 14:15, 23; 16:2; 20:8; 26:20; 27:57; Mark 1:32; 4:35; 6:47; 14:17; 15:42; also Mark 1:32 with ὅτε ἔδυ ὁ ἥλιος. ᾿Οψία was originally an adj.; as a result of the ellipsis of the accompanying subst. (ὥρα) it has taken on a subst. meaning; cf. BDF §241.3.

ὄψιμος, 2   *opsimos*   late; subst.: that which is late, late fruit, late rain*

In Jas 5:7 the subst. occurs in the admonition to be patient, even as the farmer who waits for the fruit of the land, "the early and the *late*" (πρόϊμον καὶ ὄψιμον). The mss. add καρπός (ℵ et al.) or ὑετός (A P Ψ Koine). More probably the thought is of early rain (in the fall) and late rain (in the spring; cf. ἕως λάβῃ, also 5:18). H. W. Hertzberg, *BHH* 1568-71.

ὄψιος, 3 *opsios* late*

Mark 11:11: ὀψίας ἤδη οὔσης τῆς ὥρας, "since the hour was already *late*/it was already *late* in the evening"; v.l. → ὀψέ ℵ C L etc.

ὄψις, εως, ἡ *opsis* face, countenance, appearance*

With the meaning *face*/*countenance* in John 11:44 in reference to the resurrected Lazarus; in Acts 1:16 of Christ as the "Son of Man" whose "*face* shone like the sun in all its strength" (cf. Judg 5:31). John 7:24: μὴ κρίνετε κατ᾽ ὄψιν, "do not judge by *appearance*" (cf. also 1 Kgs 16:7).

ὀψώνιον, ου τό *opsōnion* pay, wages, compensation*

Ὀψώνιον appears 4 times in the NT: In Luke 3:14 in John the Baptist's reply to the question regarding the *wages* (pl.) of the soldiers (στρατευόμενοι, probably soldiers of Herod Antipas): ἀρκεῖσθε τοῖς ὀψωνίοις ὑμῶν (as a military t.t. also in 1 Macc 3:28; 4:32); a standard amount is in mind (pl.) which provided for only a minimal subsistence and was often the reason for attack; in the same sense in 1 Cor 9:7 as a metaphor for the care (actually) owed to the apostle by the congregation (cf. Matt 10:10), which he accepted not from the Corinthians but from the other congregations (in Macedonia), to the detriment of the Corinthians: λαβὼν ὀψώνιον πρὸς τὴν ὑμῶν διακονίαν, "by letting myself be reimbursed for my ministry to you" (2 Cor 11:8; on the weakening of its meaning see BDF §126.2). In Rom 6:23 fig. for the *pay*/*reimbursement* that sin has prepared for the services rendered it, i.e., death: τὰ γὰρ ὀψώνια τῆς ἁμαρτίας θάνατος (in contrast with χάρισμα τοῦ θεοῦ ζωὴ αἰώνιος). Metaphorically of the believer as a soldier of Christ receiving pay from him, Ign. *Pol.* 6:2. H. W. Heiland, *TDNT* V, 591f.; BAGD s.v.; C. C. Caragounis, "Ὀψώνιον: A Reconsideration of its Meaning," *NovT* 16 (1974) 35-57; O. Becker, *DNTT* III, 144f.; Spicq, *Notes* II, 635-38.

CPSIA information can be obtained
at www.ICGtesting.com
Printed in the USA
LVOW09s1420020517
532995LV00009B/78/P